Checkpoint®

3 Simple Ways **Checkpoint®** Helps You Make Sense of All Those Taxes.

- Find what you are looking for quickly and easily online with Checkpoint®.
- A comprehensive collection of primary tax law, cases, and rulings, along with analytical insight you simply can't find anywhere else.
- Checkpoint® has built-in productivity tools such as calculators to make researc more efficient – a resource more tax pros use than any other.

Titles that include Checkpoint® Student Edition

- **Hoffman/Smith,** *South-Western Federal Taxation: Individual Income Taxes, 2012 Edition*
- **Hoffman/Raabe/Smith/Maloney,** *South-Western Federal Taxation: Corporations, Partnerships, Estates & Trusts, 2012 Edition*
- **Hoffman/Maloney/Raabe/Young,** *South-Western Federal Taxation: Comprehensive Volume, 2012 Edition*
- **Smith/Raabe/Maloney,** *South-Western Federal Taxation: Taxation of Business Entities, 2012 Edition*
- **Murphy/Higgins,** *Concepts in Federal Taxation, 2012 Edition*

IMPORTANT INFORMATION

The purchase of this textbook includes access to Checkpoint® Student Edition from Thomson Reuters for a 6-month duration.

To log in visit **http://checkpoint.thomsonreuters.com**
You will be asked to supply a User ID and Password. Please use the following:

USER ID: [redacted]

PASSWORD:

PLEASE NOTE:** ***If you have purchased a used copy of this text, *the User ID and Password may have already been used. A new User ID and Password may be obtained by purchasing a* ***new copy*** *of this text.*

THOMSON REUTERS

ISBN-13: 978-1-111-95684-4 • ISBN-10: 1-111-95684-7

"★★★★★"
CPA Technology Advisor 2004, 2005, 2006, 2007, 2008, 2009, 2010

For technical support please visit
www.cengage.com/support

CPAexcel™
CPA Exam Review

With your purchase of this new **Cengage Learning** Taxation textbook, you have 12-month access to select **CPAexcel** content, *the best CPA review course for busy students!* With CPA exam content matched to your taxation course, you will have access to:

- Online exam preparation activities that may be accessed anytime and anywhere.
- Over 800 past exam questions and proficiency questions.
- Exam-identical simulations and comprehensive diagnostics.

To register, visit **www.cengage.com/login**

Please register with the following access code:

Access Code:

By purchasing this New Edition, you qualify to receive 20% off the purchase price of CPAexcel review courses!

Don't Throw This Away!

CPAexcel™
CPA Exam Review

For technical support, please visit **www.cengage.com/support**

SOUTH-WESTERN
CENGAGE Learning™

Tax Formula for Individuals

Income (broadly conceived)	$xx,xxx
Less: Exclusions	(x,xxx)
Gross income	$xx,xxx
Less: Deductions *for* adjusted gross income	(x,xxx)
Adjusted gross income	$xx,xxx
Less: The greater of— Total itemized deductions *or* standard deduction	(x,xxx)
Less: Personal and dependency exemptions	(x,xxx)
Taxable income	$xx,xxx
Tax on taxable income	$ x,xxx
Less: Tax credits (including Federal income tax withheld and other prepayments of Federal income taxes)	(xxx)
Tax due (or refund)	$ xxx

Basic Standard Deduction Amounts

	Standard Deduction Amount	
Filing Status	**2010**	**2011**
Single	$ 5,700	$ 5,800
Married, filing jointly	11,400	11,600
Surviving spouse	11,400	11,600
Head of household	8,400	8,500
Married, filing separately	5,700	5,800

Amount of Each Additional Standard Deduction

Filing Status	2010	2011
Single	$1,400	$1,450
Married, filing jointly	1,100	1,150
Surviving spouse	1,100	1,150
Head of household	1,400	1,450
Married, filing separately	1,100	1,150

Personal and Dependency Exemption

2010	2011
$3,650	$3,700

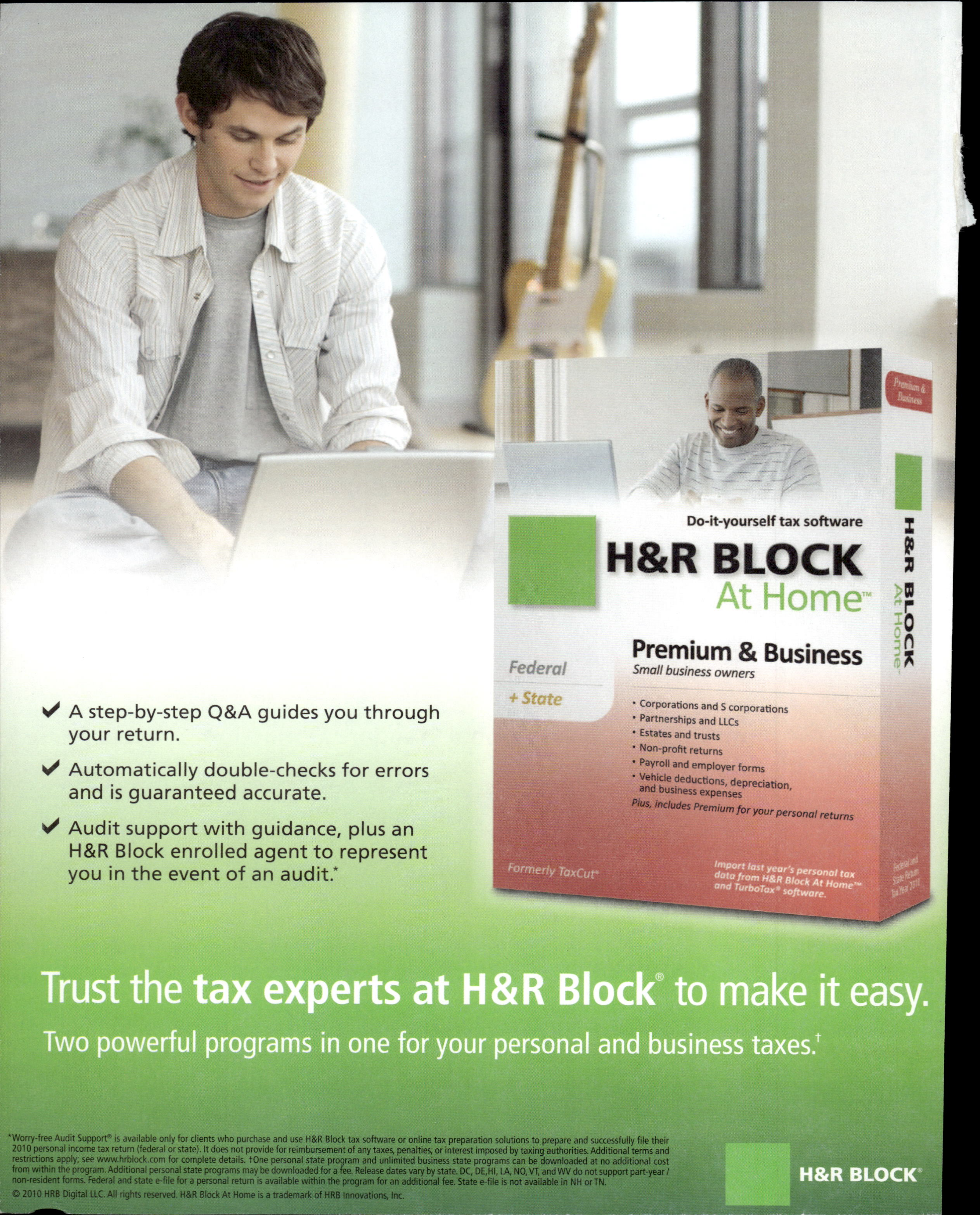
Do-it-yourself tax software
H&R BLOCK
At Home™
Premium & Business
Small business owners
Federal
+ State
• Corporations and S corporations
• Partnerships and LLCs
• Estates and trusts
• Non-profit returns
• Payroll and employer forms
• Vehicle deductions, depreciation, and business expenses
Plus, includes Premium for your personal returns
Formerly TaxCut®
Import last year's personal tax data from H&R Block At Home™ and TurboTax® software.
H&R BLOCK
At Home™
✔ A step-by-step Q&A guides you through your return.
✔ Automatically double-checks for errors and is guaranteed accurate.
✔ Audit support with guidance, plus an H&R Block enrolled agent to represent you in the event of an audit.*
Trust the tax experts at H&R Block® to make it easy.
Two powerful programs in one for your personal and business taxes.†
*Worry-free Audit Support® is available only for clients who purchase and use H&R Block tax software or online tax preparation solutions to prepare and successfully file their 2010 personal income tax return (federal or state). It does not provide for reimbursement of any taxes, penalties, or interest imposed by taxing authorities. Additional terms and restrictions apply; see www.hrblock.com for complete details. †One personal state program and unlimited business state programs can be downloaded at no additional cost from within the program. Additional personal state programs may be downloaded for a fee. Release dates vary by state. DC, DE, HI, LA, NO, VT, and WV do not support part-year / non-resident forms. Federal and state e-file for a personal return is available within the program for an additional fee. State e-file is not available in NH or TN.
© 2010 HRB Digital LLC. All rights reserved. H&R Block At Home is a trademark of HRB Innovations, Inc.
H&R BLOCK®

South-Western Federal Taxation

Comprehensive Volume

2012 Edition

GENERAL EDITORS

William H. Hoffman, Jr.
J.D., Ph.D., CPA

David M. Maloney
Ph.D., CPA

William A. Raabe
Ph.D., CPA

James C. Young
Ph.D., CPA

CONTRIBUTING AUTHORS

James H. Boyd
Ph.D., CPA
Arizona State University

D. Larry Crumbley
Ph.D., CPA
Louisiana State University

Jon S. Davis
Ph.D., CPA
University of Wisconsin–Madison

Steven C. Dilley
J.D., Ph.D., CPA
Michigan State University

William H. Hoffman, Jr.
J.D., Ph.D., CPA
University of Houston

David M. Maloney
Ph.D., CPA
University of Virginia

Gary A. McGill
Ph.D., CPA
University of Florida

Mark B. Persellin
Ph.D., CPA, CFP®
St. Mary's University

William A. Raabe
Ph.D., CPA
The Ohio State University

Boyd C. Randall
J.D., Ph.D.
Brigham Young University

Debra L. Sanders
Ph.D., CPA
Washington State University, Vancouver

W. Eugene Seago
J.D., Ph.D., CPA
Virginia Polytechnic
Institute and State University

James E. Smith
Ph.D., CPA
College of William and Mary

James C. Young
Ph.D., CPA
Northern Illinois University

SOUTH-WESTERN
CENGAGE Learning™

Australia • Brazil • Japan • Korea • Mexico • Singapore • Spain • United Kingdom • United States

SOUTH-WESTERN
CENGAGE Learning™

South-Western Federal Taxation: Comprehensive Volume, 2012 Edition

William H. Hoffman, Jr., David M. Maloney, William A. Raabe, James C. Young

Vice President of Editorial, Business: Jack W. Calhoun

Editor-in-Chief: Rob Dewey

Senior Acquisitions Editor: Mike Schenk

Senior Developmental Editor: Craig Avery

Editorial Assistant: Ann Mazzaro

Marketing Manager: Natalie Livingston

Senior Content Project Manager: Colleen A. Farmer

Media Editor: Chris Valentine

Senior Frontlist Buyer, Manufacturing: Doug Wilke

Marketing Communications Manager: Libby Shipp

Production Service: Cadmus Communications

Senior Art Director: Michelle Kunkler

Internal and Cover Designer: Chris Miller

Cover Image: ©iolo72/Shutterstock

Rights Acquisitions Specialist – Text: John Hill

For product information and technology assistance, contact us at **Cengage Learning Customer & Sales Support, 1-800-354-9706**

For permission to use material from this text or product, submit all requests online at **www.cengage.com/permissions**
Further permissions questions can be emailed to **permissionrequest@cengage.com**

Student Edition ISBN 13: 978-1-111-22171-3
Student Edition ISBN 10: 1-111-22171-5
Student Edition with CD ISBN 13: 978-1-111-22170-6
Student Edition with CD ISBN 10: 1-111-22170-7

ISSN: 0741-5184
2012 Annual Edition

South-Western
5191 Natorp Boulevard
Mason, OH 45040
USA

Cengage Learning products are represented in Canada by Nelson Education, Ltd.

For your course and learning solutions, visit **www.cengage.com**
Purchase any of our products at your local college store or at our preferred online store **www.cengagebrain.com**

Printed in the United States of America
1 2 3 4 5 6 7 15 14 13 12 11

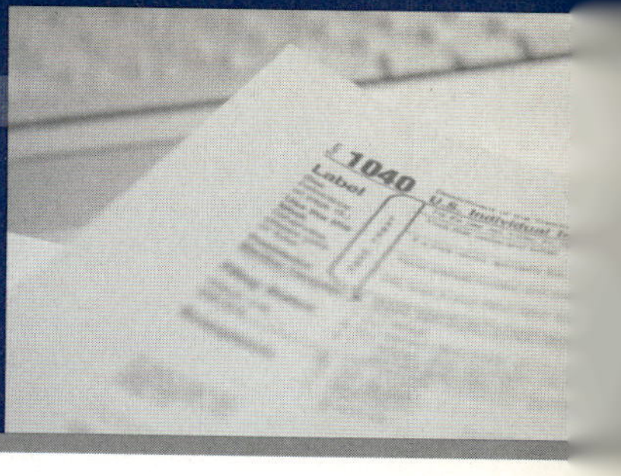

Preface

To The Student

SOUTH-WESTERN
CENGAGE Learning™

THE LEADERSHIP YOU TRUST.
THE INNOVATION YOU EXPECT.
THE SERVICE YOU DESERVE.

South-Western Federal Taxation is the most trusted and best-selling series in college taxation. We are focused exclusively on providing the most useful, comprehensive, and up-to-date tax texts, online study aids, tax preparation tools, and printed study guides to help you succeed in your tax courses and beyond.

Studying Is Easier with the Right Tools. ***Comprehensive Volume, 2012 Edition*** provides a dynamic learning experience inside and outside of the classroom. Built with resources and tools that students have identified as the most important, our complete study system provides options for the way you learn.

Here's how ***Comprehensive Volume, 2012 Edition*** is designed to help you learn!

PRACTICAL TAX SCENARIOS AT THE START OF EVERY CHAPTER. . .

The Big Picture: Tax Solutions for the Real World. Taxation comes alive at the start of each chapter. **The Big Picture** is a glimpse into the lives, families, careers, and tax situations of typical individual and business taxpayers. Each **Big Picture** case asks you to apply what you will learn in the upcoming chapter to develop the best tax solution to these real-life dilemmas.

THE BIG PICTURE **Tax Solutions for the Real World**

EDUCATION TAX CREDITS

Tom and Jennifer Snyder have two children in college. Lora is a freshman, and her tuition and required fees in 2011 total $14,000. Lora has a partial scholarship amounting to $6,500, and the Snyders paid the balance of her tuition ($7,500), plus room and board of $8,500. Sam is a junior, and the Snyders paid $8,100 for his tuition, plus $7,200 for his room and board. Both students qualify as Tom and Jennifer's dependents.

The Snyders have AGI of $158,000. They would like to know what tax options are available to them related to these education expenses. They have heard about various education-related deductions and credits, but they believe that their income is too high for them to get any benefit. Are they correct? **Read the chapter and formulate your response.**

. . . BIG PICTURE EXAMPLES TO HELP YOU FOLLOW CLIENTS THROUGH THE CHAPTER. . .

Among the many examples in every chapter are an average of almost four examples per chapter based on the Big Picture tax situation that opens the text. That means less confusion understanding new topics, a more consistent application of data for you to learn, and practical tax stories that span the whole chapter.

EXAMPLE 33
THE BIG PICTURE

Return to the facts of *The Big Picture* on p.12–2. Assume that Tom and Jennifer's modified AGI is $172,000, instead of $158,000. The Snyders are eligible to claim a $2,000 American Opportunity credit. Their available credit is reduced because AGI exceeds the $160,000 limit for married taxpayers. The percentage reduction is computed as the amount by which modified AGI exceeds the limit, expressed as a percentage of the phaseout range, or [($172,000 − $160,000)/$20,000)], resulting in a 60% reduction. Therefore, the maximum available credit is $2,000 ($5,000 × 40% allowable portion). ■

. . .AND PRACTICAL CONCLUSIONS TO THOSE TAX SCENARIOS

Refocus on the Big Picture. Returning to the client situations introduced in the chapter-opening **Big Picture**, these end-of-chapter summaries and tax planning scenarios apply concepts and topics from the chapter in a reasonable and professional solution. A **What If?** section then demonstrates how tax treatments might change as a result of potential changes in the filer's situation—making **What If?** a valuable consideration in tax planning.

REFOCUS ON THE BIG PICTURE

EDUCATION TAX CREDITS

Lora and Sam qualify for the American Opportunity credit as they are both in their first four years of postsecondary education. Lora and Sam both qualify for a $2,500 credit (100 percent of the first $2,000 and 25 percent of the next $2,000 of qualified expenses).

These credits phase out over an income range of $20,000 once married taxpayers' AGI exceeds $160,000. The total education credits available to the Snyders amount to $5,240, and they may claim this amount as a credit on their Form 1040. Further, the education credits may be used to offset any AMT liability, and a portion of the credits is refundable to the Snyders.

What If?

What if the Snyders's AGI is $188,000? In that case, the Snyders would not qualify for any education credits (their income exceeds the limits for both the American Opportunity and the lifetime learning credits). Although a deduction *for* AGI is allowed for qualified tuition and related expenses involving higher education, the taxpayers' AGI exceeds the $160,000 maximum allowed for a deduction (see Chapter 9 for additional details).

What If? adds realistic options that will spur you to think about how changes in taxpayers' situations affect how they would file their returns.

NEW FINANCIAL DISCLOSURE INSIGHTS

Increasingly, tax professionals need to understand how taxes affect the income statement and balance sheet. These features, appearing throughout the text, use current data about existing taxpayers to highlight book-tax reporting differences, effective tax rates, and trends in reporting conventions. **Financial Disclosure Insights** help you integrate financial knowledge with state and Federal tax law. **SWFT's coverage of the role of tax data on the financial statements far exceeds that of any other tax text.**

FINANCIAL DISCLOSURE *Insights*

TAX AND BOOK DEPRECIATION

A common book-tax difference relates to the depreciation amounts that are reported for GAAP and Federal income tax purposes. Typically, tax depreciation deductions are accelerated; that is, they are claimed in earlier reporting periods than is the case for financial accounting purposes. Almost every tax law change since 1980 has included depreciation provisions that accelerate the related deductions relative to the expenses allowed under GAAP. Accelerated cost recovery deductions represent a means by which the taxing jurisdiction infuses the business with cash flow created by the reduction in the year's tax liabilities.

For instance, recently about one-quarter of General Electric's deferred tax liabilities related to depreciation differences. For Toyota's and Ford's depreciation differences, that amount was about one-third. And for the trucking firm Ryder Systems, depreciation differences accounted for all but 1 percent of the deferred tax liabilities.

ORGANIZED AROUND KEY TAX CONCEPTS, LEARNING OBJECTIVES, AND EXAMPLES

Fitting It All Together: The Income Tax Formula for Individuals. This study feature introduced in Chapter 3 demonstrates how topics within the Individual Taxation chapters of the text are aligned, using the Income Tax Formula for Individuals as the framework.

Chapter-Opening Tax Formula Framework Using Form 1040. Framework 1040, the Tax Formula Framework for Individuals, helps you organize your understanding of key topics within each Individual Taxation chapter in terms of the basic tax formula and then identifies where these items are reported on the individual tax Form 1040. **Framework 1040** is a **handy navigation tool** that helps explain how tax concepts are organized.

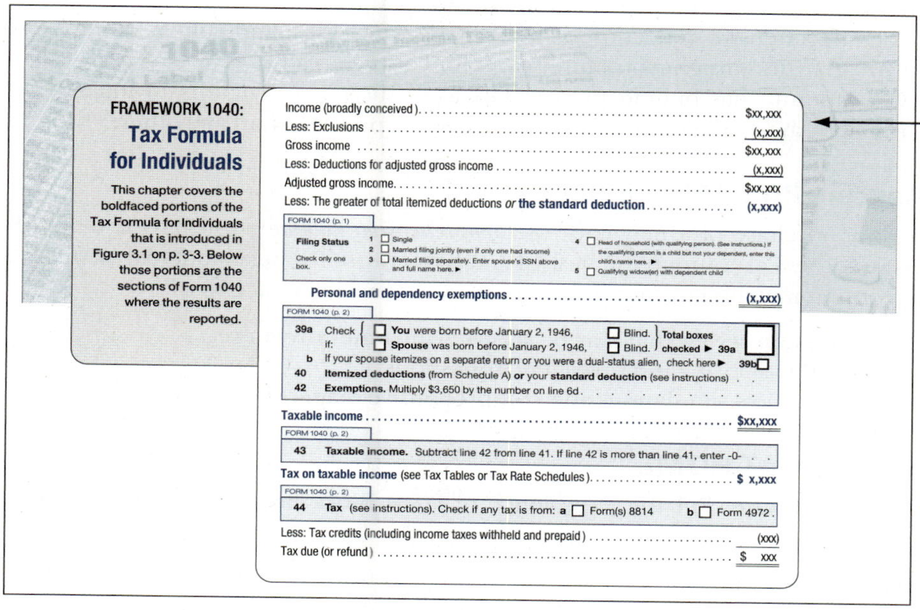

Use this chapter-opening **Framework 1040**, which shows the topics as they appear in the individual tax formula, to understand where on Form 1040 these chapter topics would appear.

Examples You'll Use in Every Chapter. An **average of over 40 examples in each chapter** use realistic situations to illustrate the complexities of the tax law and demonstrate concepts.

EXAMPLE 16

Jennifer, age 17, lives in the same household with her parents during the entire year. If her parents file separate returns, the one with the higher AGI has priority as to the dependency exemption. ■

Homework Linked to Chapter Learning Objectives. Students tell us that for maximum learning value, homework assignments should refer back to specific chapter topics and sections. Each end-of-chapter Question and Problem is labeled with the Learning Objective(s) that appear beside key topics in the text margins. **Now it is easier to go back to the section of the text where the concept in the homework item is covered—saving you time, better organizing your study, and increasing your confidence in earning a better grade.**

49. **LO.1, 3, 6, 7** Ava, age 18, is claimed as a dependent on her parents' 2011 return, on which they report taxable income of $100,000 (no qualified dividends or capital gains). Ava earned $2,900 pet sitting and $3,000 in interest on a savings account. What are Ava's taxable income and tax liability?

aplia™ Engage. Prepare. Educate.

ONLINE RESOURCES AND STUDY TOOLS

Aplia™ is an online interactive homework solution that improves learning by increasing student effort and engagement. Aplia for tax ensures that you stay on top of your coursework with regularly scheduled homework assignments. The Aplia assignments are derived from select end-of-chapter problems from the textbook, allowing you to apply what you learn. To explore the benefits Aplia offers, ask your instructor or visit **www.aplia.com/tax**.

THOMSON REUTERS Checkpoint® Student Edition

CHECKPOINT® STUDENT EDITION

Checkpoint® Student Edition from Thomson Reuters comes with every NEW copy of this textbook to help you succeed in the tax research portion of your studies.*

3 Simple Ways Checkpoint® Helps You Make Sense of All Those Taxes:

- Intuitive web-based design makes it fast and simple to find what you need.
- A comprehensive collection of primary tax law, cases, and rulings along with analytical insight you simply can't find anywhere else.
- Checkpoint® has built-in productivity tools such as calculators to make research more efficient—a resource more tax pros use than any other.

CPAexcel CPA Exam Review

CPAexcel CPA EXAM REVIEW

With your purchase of a new copy of ***Comprehensive Volume****, you have a 6-month access to CPAexcel content, the best CPA review course for busy students! With CPA exam content matched to your taxation course, you will have access to:

- Online exam review that may be accessed anytime, anywhere.
- Over 800 past exam and proficiency questions.
- Exam-identical simulations and comprehensive diagnostics.

H&R BLOCK At Home™

H&R BLOCK AT HOME™

More than software: Put the experience of H&R Block tax professionals on your side.

- A step-by-step interview guides you through a customized process.
- Accurate calculations and 100% satisfaction—guaranteed.
- Worry-free Audit Support™ and tax advice from an H&R Block tax professional.

H&R Block At Home™ is offered with each NEW copy of **South-Western Federal Taxation**—at no additional cost to students!

CENGAGEbrain.com

ONLINE STUDENT RESOURCES

Go to **www.cengagebrain.com** for free resources to help you study as well as the opportunity to purchase additional study aids. These valuable free study resources will help you earn a better grade:

- **Interactive quizzes** are short and auto-graded to help you brush up on important chapter topics.
- **Flashcards** use chapter terms and definitions to aid you in learning tax terminology for each chapter.
- **Online glossary** for each chapter provides terms and definitions from the text in alphabetical order for easy reference.
- **Learning objectives** can be downloaded for each chapter to help keep you on track.

*Not available with the Professional Editions of *South-Western Federal Taxation.*

- **Tax Tips for the Recent Graduate** introduce the college graduate to some common tax considerations that could be beneficial in reducing the dreaded "tax bite."
- **Tax Updates** provide the most recent tax information and major changes to the tax law.
- **Tax tables** used in the textbook are downloadable for reference.

ADDITIONAL STUDENT RESOURCES

Study Guide, ISBN 1-111-82480-0
Do you need more help studying for your taxation class? Order the study guide to receive:

- **Study Highlights**—an outline of key topics for each chapter.
- **Key Terms** used in the chapter.
- **Self-Quizzing** with helpful, annotated answers that are keyed to pages in the 2012 Edition.

Check with your bookstore or order on **CengageBrain.com**.

Individual Practice Sets, ISBN 1-111-82452-5
Corporations, S Corporations, and Partnerships Practice Sets, ISBN 1-111-82475-4
Ask your instructor about assigning these practice sets.

Written specifically for the ***South-Western Federal Taxation*** Series, these practice sets are comprehensive and designed to be completed near the end of the course using tax preparation software such as H&R Block at Home™.

Check with your instructor before ordering practice sets. **Solutions are available to instructors only.**

For over 35 years, the **South-Western Federal Taxation** Series has guided more than 1.5 million students through the ever-changing field of Federal taxation.

With our promise of leadership, innovation, and service, we are committed to your success both now and in the future.

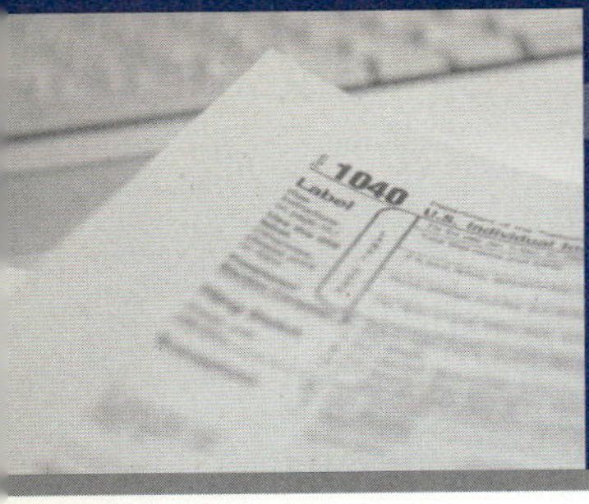

About the Editors

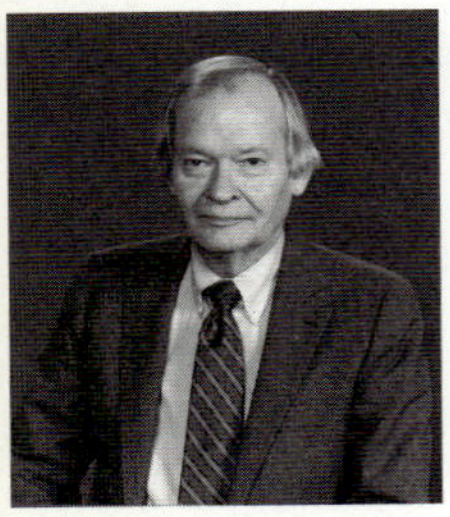

WILLIAM H. HOFFMAN JR. earned B.A. and J.D. degrees from the University of Michigan and M.B.A. and Ph.D. degrees from The University of Texas. He is a licensed CPA and attorney in Texas. His teaching experience includes The University of Texas (1957–1961), Louisiana State University (1961–1967), and the University of Houston (1967–1999). Professor Hoffman has addressed many tax institutes and conferences and has published extensively in academic and professional journals. His articles appear in *The Journal of Taxation, The Tax Adviser, Taxes—The Tax Magazine, The Journal of Accountancy, The Accounting Review,* and *Taxation for Accountants.*

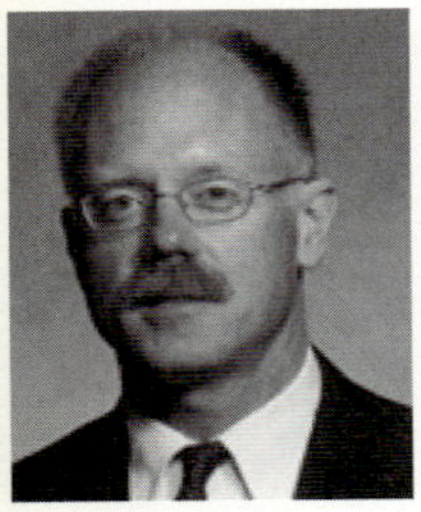

DAVID M. MALONEY Ph.D., CPA, is the Carman G. Blough Professor of Accounting at the University of Virginia's McIntire School of Commerce. He completed his undergraduate work at the University of Richmond and his graduate work at the University of Illinois at Urbana-Champaign. Since joining the Virginia faculty in January 1984, Professor Maloney has taught Federal taxation in the graduate and undergraduate programs and has received major research grants from the Ernst & Young and KPMG Foundations. In addition, his work has been published in numerous professional journals, including *Journal of Taxation, The Tax Adviser, Tax Notes, Corporate Taxation, Accounting Horizons, Journal of Taxation of Investments,* and *Journal of Accountancy.* He is a member of several professional organizations, including the American Accounting Association and the American Taxation Association.

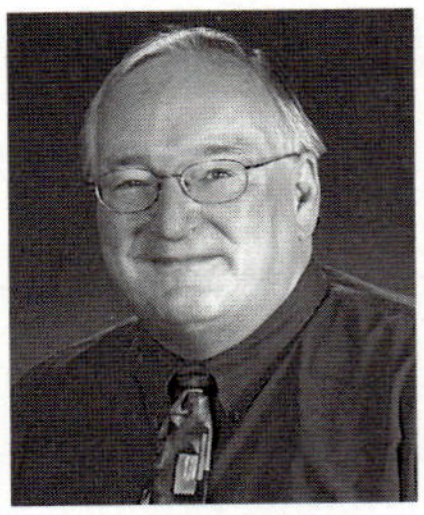

WILLIAM A. RAABE teaches tax courses in the Fisher College of Business at The Ohio State University. A graduate of Carroll University (Wisconsin) and the University of Illinois, Dr. Raabe's teaching and research interests include international and multistate taxation, technology in tax education, personal financial planning, and the economic impact of sports teams and fine arts groups. Professor Raabe also writes *Federal Tax Research* and the PricewaterhouseCoopers Tax Case Studies. He has written extensively about book-tax differences in financial reporting, including a book about the corporate Schedule M–3 and articles and cases addressing FIN 48 issues. Dr. Raabe has been a visiting tax faculty member for a number of public accounting firms, bar associations, and CPA societies. He has received numerous teaching awards, including the Accounting Educator of the Year award from the Wisconsin Institute of CPAs. He has been the faculty adviser for student teams in the Deloitte Tax Case Competition (national finalists at three different schools) and the PricewaterhouseCoopers Extreme Tax policy competition (national finalist). For more information about Dr. Raabe, visit http://fisher.osu.edu/~raabe_12/.

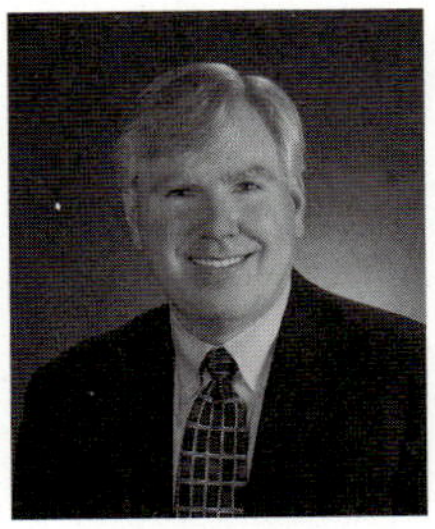

JAMES C. YOUNG is the Crowe Horwath Professor of Accountancy at Northern Illinois University. A graduate of Ferris State University (B.S.) and Michigan State University (M.B.A. and Ph.D.), Professor Young's research focuses on taxpayer responses to the income tax using archival data. His dissertation received the PricewaterhouseCoopers/American Taxation Association Dissertation Award, and his subsequent research has received funding from a number of organizations, including the Ernst & Young Foundation Tax Research Grant Program. His work has been published in a variety of academic and professional journals including the *National Tax Journal, The Journal of the American Taxation Association,* and *Tax Notes.* He was named a Northern Illinois University Presidential Teaching Professor in 2007 and has received outstanding teaching awards from George Mason University and Michigan State University.

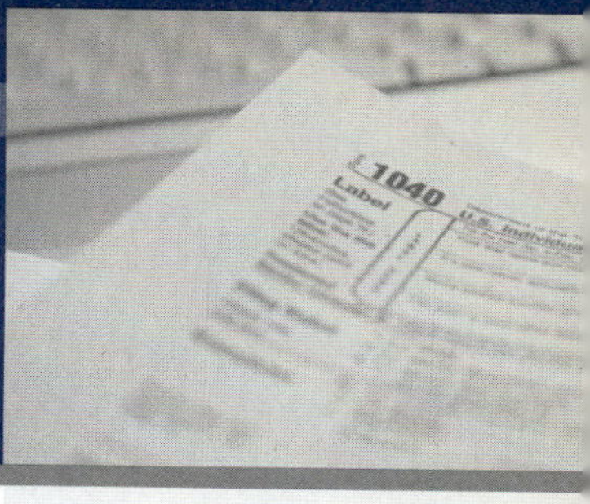

Brief Contents

PART 5: SPECIAL TAX COMPUTATIONS AND ACCOUNTING PERIODS AND METHODS

PART 6: CORPORATIONS

PART 7: FLOW-THROUGH ENTITIES

PART 8: ADVANCED TAX PRACTICE CONSIDERATIONS

PART 9: FAMILY TAX PLANNING

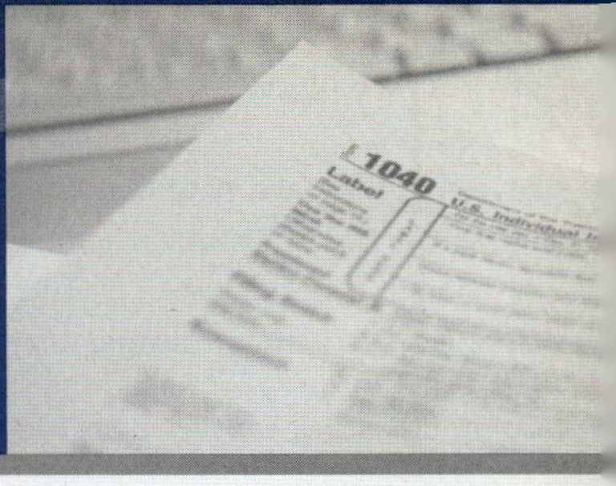

Contents

PART 9: Family Tax Planning

APPENDIXES

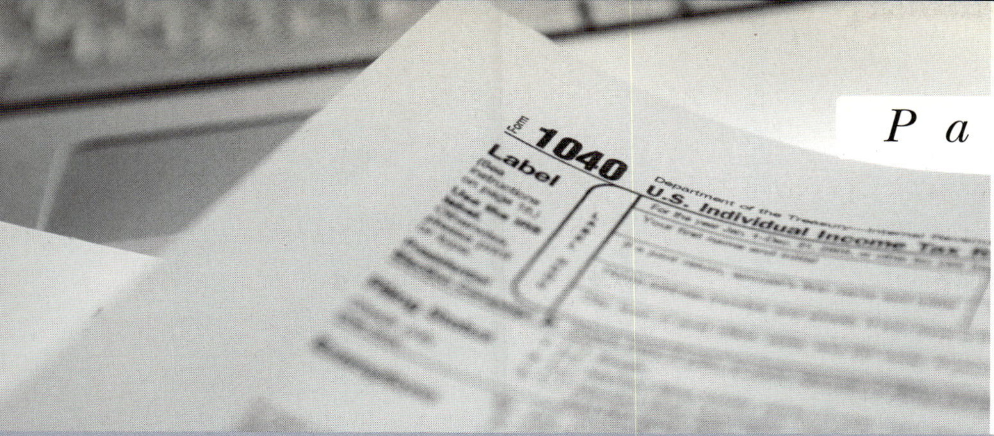

Part 1

Introduction and Basic Tax Model

Part 1 provides an introduction to taxation in the United States. Although the primary orientation of this text is income taxation, other types of taxes are also discussed briefly. The purposes of the Federal tax law are examined, and the legislative, administrative, and judicial sources of Federal tax law, including their application to the tax research process, are analyzed. Part 1 concludes with the introduction of the basic tax model for the individual taxpayer.

An Introduction to Taxation and Understanding the Federal Tax Law

CHAPTER 1

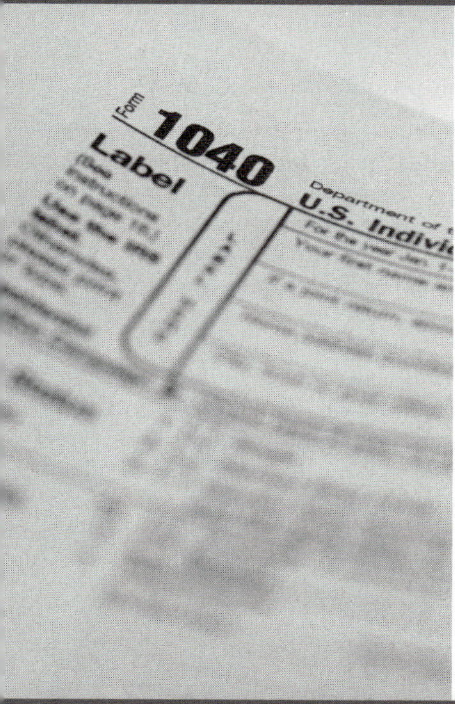

LEARNING OBJECTIVES

After completing Chapter 1, you should be able to:

LO.1
Appreciate why taxation is important.

LO.2
Describe some of the history and trends of the Federal income tax.

LO.3
Assess some of the criteria for selecting a tax structure; understand the components of a tax structure.

LO.4
Identify the different taxes imposed in the United States at the Federal, state, and local levels.

LO.5
Explain the administration of the tax law, including the audit process utilized by the IRS.

LO.6
Evaluate some of the ethical guidelines involved in tax practice.

LO.7
Recognize the economic, social, equity, and political considerations that justify various aspects of the tax law.

LO.8
Describe the role played by the IRS and the courts in the evolution of the Federal tax system.

OUTLINE

For the latest in changes to tax legislation, visit **www.cengage.com/taxation/swft.**

THE BIG PICTURE **Tax Solutions for the Real World**

FAMILY AND TAXES— A TYPICAL YEAR

Travis and Betty Carter are married and live in a state that imposes both a sales tax and an income tax. They have two children, April (age 17) and Martin (age 18). Travis is a mining engineer who specializes in land reclamation. After several years with a mining corporation, Travis established a consulting practice that involves a considerable amount of travel. Betty is a registered nurse who, until recently, was a homemaker. In November of this year, she decided to reenter the job market and accepted a position with a medical clinic. The Carters live only a few blocks from Ernest and Mary Walker, Betty Carter's parents. The Walkers are retired and live on interest, dividends, and Social Security benefits.

Various developments occurring during the year with possible tax ramifications are summarized below.

- The ad valorem property taxes on the Carters' residence are increased, while those on the Walkers' residence are lowered.
- When Travis registers an automobile purchased last year in another state, he is forced to pay a sales tax to his home state.
- As an anniversary present, the Carters gave the Walkers a recreational vehicle (RV).
- When Travis made a consulting trip to Chicago, the client withheld Illinois state income tax from the payment made to Travis for his services.
- Travis employs his children to draft blueprints and prepare scale models for use in his work. Both April and Martin have had training in drafting and topography.
- Early in the year the Carters are audited by the state on an income tax return filed several years ago. Later in the year, they are audited by the IRS on a Form 1040 they filed for the same year. In each case, a tax deficiency and interest were assessed.
- The Walkers are audited by the IRS. Unlike the Carters, they did not have to deal with an agent but settled the matter by mail.

Explain these developments and resolve the issues raised. **Read the chapter and formulate your response.**

The primary objective of this chapter is to provide an overview of the Federal tax system. Among the topics discussed are the following:

- The importance and relevance of taxation.
- The history of the Federal income tax in brief.
- The types of taxes imposed at the Federal, state, and local levels.
- Some highlights of tax law administration.
- Tax concepts that help explain the reasons for various tax provisions.
- The influence that the Internal Revenue Service (IRS) and the courts have had in the evolution of current tax law.

1.1 Learning and Coping with Taxation

LO.1

Appreciate why taxation is important.

The study of taxation is important because taxes permeate our society. Even the simplest of decisions can carry tax implications. Does it matter, for example, which son or daughter pays the medical bills when all of four adult children contribute to the support of their widowed mother? Or if you use your automobile in a business, is it worth your time and effort to use the actual cost method of calculating the expenses rather than the simpler automatic mileage method?

Effectively coping with taxes often involves making decisions based on timing considerations. Does the employee who is trying to decide between a traditional Individual Retirement Account (IRA) and a Roth IRA want the tax benefit up front (i.e., traditional) or at retirement (i.e., Roth)? Timing considerations are paramount when it is deemed desirable to accelerate (or defer) income or accelerate (or defer) deductions for any one year.

The study of taxation teaches us not to overlook the less obvious taxes that can block our intended objective. A grandson inherits his grandmother's personal residence. He has heard that rental property can generate significant income tax benefits. But does he realize that a change of ownership may unlock an appraised-value freeze on the property? Or that conversion from residential to income-producing use will cause an increase in ad valorem taxes on realty? Thus, an attractive income tax result could be materially diminished by adverse property tax consequences.

It is essential in working with taxation to maintain a balanced perspective. A corporation that is deciding where to locate a new factory does not automatically select the city or state that offers the most generous tax benefits. Nor does the person who is retiring to a warmer climate pick Belize over Arizona because the former has no income tax while the latter does. Tax considerations should not control, but they remain one of many factors to be considered.

The study of taxation involves reviewing a multitude of rules and exceptions and, when possible, trying to understand the justification for them. But the desired goal of this learning process is the ability to recognize issues that carry tax implications. Suppose, for example, that you come upon a situation that involves a discharge of indebtedness. If you know that forgiveness of debt results in income but there are exceptions to this rule, the battle is won! The issue has been identified, and the outcome (i.e., when an exception applies) can easily be resolved by additional research.

1.2 History of U.S. Taxation

EARLY PERIODS

LO.2

Describe some of the history and trends of the Federal income tax.

The concept of an income tax can hardly be regarded as a newcomer to the Western Hemisphere. An income tax was first enacted in 1634 by the English colonists in the Massachusetts Bay Colony, but the Federal government did not adopt this form of taxation until 1861. In fact, both the Federal Union and the Confederate States of America used the income tax to raise funds to finance the Civil War. Although modest in its reach and characterized by broad exemptions and low rates, the income tax generated $376 million of revenue for the Federal government during the Civil War.

When the Civil War ended, the need for additional revenue disappeared, and the income tax was repealed. Once again the Federal government was able to finance its operations almost exclusively from customs duties (tariffs). It is interesting to note that the courts held that the Civil War income tax was not contrary to the Constitution.

When a new Federal income tax on individuals was enacted in 1894, its opponents were prepared and were able to successfully challenge its constitutionality. The U.S. Constitution provided that "No Capitation, or other direct, Tax shall be laid, unless in Proportion to the Census or Enumeration herein before directed to be taken." In *Pollock v. Farmers' Loan and Trust Co.*, the U.S. Supreme Court found that taxes on the income of real and personal property were the legal equivalent of a tax on the property involved and, therefore, required apportionment.[1]

A Federal corporate income tax, enacted by Congress in 1909, fared better in the judicial system. The U.S. Supreme Court found this tax to be constitutional because it was treated as an excise tax.[2] In essence, it was a tax on the right to do business in the

[1] 3 AFTR 2602, 15 S.Ct. 912 (USSC, 1895). See Chapter 2 for an explanation of the citations of judicial decisions.

[2] *Flint v. Stone Tracy Co.*, 3 AFTR 2834, 31 S.Ct. 342 (USSC, 1911).

FIGURE 1.1 Federal Budget Receipts—2011

Individual income taxes	44%
Corporation income taxes	12
Social insurance taxes and contributions	36
Excise taxes	4
Other	4
	100%

corporate form. As such, it was likened to a form of the franchise tax.[3] The corporate form of doing business had been developed in the late nineteenth century and was an unfamiliar concept to the framers of the U.S. Constitution. Since a corporation is an entity created under law, jurisdictions possess the right to tax its creation and operation. Using this rationale, many states still impose franchise taxes on corporations.

The ratification of the Sixteenth Amendment to the U.S. Constitution in 1913 sanctioned both the Federal individual and corporate income taxes and, as a consequence, neutralized the continuing effect of the *Pollock* decision.

REVENUE ACTS

Following ratification of the Sixteenth Amendment, Congress enacted the Revenue Act of 1913. Under this Act, the first Form 1040 was due on March 1, 1914. The law allowed various deductions and personal exemptions of $3,000 for a single individual and $4,000 for married taxpayers. Rates ranged from a low of 2 percent to a high of 6 percent. The 6 percent rate applied only to taxable income in excess of $500,000![4]

Various revenue acts were passed between 1913 and 1939. In 1939, all of these revenue laws were codified into the Internal Revenue Code of 1939. In 1954, a similar codification of the revenue law took place. The current law is entitled the Internal Revenue Code of 1986, which largely carries over the provisions of the 1954 Code. To date, the Code has been amended numerous times since 1986. This matter is discussed further in Chapter 2 under Origin of the Internal Revenue Code.

HISTORICAL TRENDS

The income tax has proved to be a major source of revenue for the Federal government. Figure 1.1, which contains a breakdown of the major revenue sources,[5] demonstrates the importance of the income tax. *Estimated* income tax collections from individuals and corporations amount to 56 percent of the total receipts.

The need for revenues to finance the war effort during World War II converted the income tax into a *mass tax*. For example, in 1939, less than 6 percent of the U.S. population was subject to the Federal income tax. In 1945, more than 74 percent of the population was subject to the Federal income tax.[6]

Certain changes in the income tax law are of particular significance in understanding the Federal income tax. In 1943, Congress passed the Current Tax Payment Act, which provided for the first pay-as-you-go tax system. A pay-as-you-go income tax system requires employers to withhold for taxes a specified portion of an employee's wages. Persons with income from other than wages may have to make quarterly payments to the IRS for estimated taxes due for the year.

One trend that has caused considerable concern is the increasing complexity of the Federal income tax laws. In the name of tax reform, Congress has added to this

[3]See the discussion of state franchise taxes later in the chapter.

[4]This should be contrasted with the highest 2011 tax rate of 35%, which applies once taxable income exceeds $379,150.

[5]The Budget of the United States Government for Fiscal Year 2011, Office of Management and Budget (Washington, D.C.: U.S. Government Printing Office, 2010).

[6]Richard Goode, *The Individual Income Tax* (Washington, D.C.: The Brookings Institution, 1964), pp. 2–4.

TAX *in* *the NEWS*

Adam Smith Stopped Too Soon

The American Institute of Certified Public Accountants (AICPA) has issued suggestions for Federal tax policy. Titled *Guiding Principles of Good Tax Policy: A Framework for Evaluating Tax Proposals*, the monograph sets forth 10 tax principles that are commonly used as indicators of desirable tax policy.

The first four principles are adapted from Adam Smith's *The Wealth of Nations*. The other six are summarized below:

- The tax system should be simple.
- The tax should be neutral in terms of its effect on business decisions.
- The tax system should not reduce economic growth and efficiency.
- The tax should be clear and readily understood so that taxpayers know about it and when it applies.
- The tax should be structured so as to minimize noncompliance.
- The tax system should enable the IRS to predict the amount and timing of revenue production.

Source: Adapted from a Tax Policy Concept Statement issued by the Tax Division of the AICPA.

complexity by frequently changing the tax laws. Most recent legislation continues this trend. Increasingly, this complexity forces many taxpayers to seek assistance. According to recent estimates, about 64 percent of all taxpayers who file a return pay a preparer, and slightly more than 20 percent purchase tax software. At this time, therefore, substantial support exists for tax law simplification.

1.3 Criteria Used in the Selection of a Tax Structure

LO.3

Assess some of the criteria for selecting a tax structure; understand the components of a tax structure.

In the eighteenth century, Adam Smith identified the following *canons of taxation*, which are still considered when evaluating a particular tax structure:[7]

- *Equality*. Each taxpayer enjoys fair or equitable treatment by paying taxes in proportion to his or her income level. Ability to pay a tax is the measure of how equitably a tax is distributed among taxpayers.
- *Convenience*. Administrative simplicity has long been valued in formulating tax policy. If a tax is easily assessed and collected and its administrative costs are low, it should be favored. An advantage of the withholding (pay-as-you-go) system is its convenience for taxpayers.
- *Certainty*. A tax structure is *good* if the taxpayer can readily predict when, where, and how a tax will be levied. Individuals and businesses need to know the likely tax consequences of a particular type of transaction.
- *Economy*. A *good* tax system involves only nominal collection costs by the government and minimal compliance costs on the part of the taxpayer. Although the government's cost of collecting Federal taxes amounts to less than one-half of 1 percent of the revenue collected, the complexity of our current tax structure imposes substantial taxpayer compliance costs.

By these canons, the Federal income tax is a contentious product. *Equality* is present as long as one accepts ability to pay as an ingredient of this component. *Convenience* exists due to a heavy reliance on pay-as-you-go procedures. *Certainty* probably generates the greatest controversy. In one sense, certainty is present since a mass of administrative and judicial guidelines exists to aid in interpreting the tax law. In another sense, however, certainty does not exist since many questions remain unanswered and frequent changes in the tax law by Congress lessen stability. Particularly troublesome in this regard are tax provisions that are given a limited life (e.g., 2010).

[7] *The Wealth of Nations* Part II (New York: Dutton, 1910), Book V, Chapter II.

If not extended by Congress, the provisions expire. All too often, Congress does not give the necessary approval in time, and the extension has to be applied retroactively. *Economy* is present if only the collection procedure of the IRS is considered. Economy is not present, however, if one focuses instead on taxpayer compliance efforts and costs.

1.4 The Tax Structure

TAX BASE

A tax base is the amount to which the tax rate is applied. In the case of the Federal income tax, the tax base is *taxable income.* As noted later in the chapter (Figure 1.2), taxable income is gross income reduced by certain deductions (both business and personal).

TAX RATES

Tax rates are applied to the tax base to determine a taxpayer's liability. The tax rates may be proportional or progressive. A tax is *proportional* if the rate of tax remains constant for any given income level. Examples of proportional taxes include most excise taxes, general sales taxes, and employment taxes (FICA, FUTA).

EXAMPLE 1

Bill has $10,000 of taxable income and pays a tax of $3,000, or 30%. Bob's taxable income is $50,000, and the tax on this amount is $15,000, or 30%. If this constant rate is applied throughout the rate structure, the tax is proportional. ■

A tax is *progressive* if a higher rate of tax applies as the tax base increases. The Federal income tax, Federal gift and estate taxes, and most state income tax rate structures are progressive.

EXAMPLE 2

If Cora, a married individual filing jointly, has taxable income of $10,000, her tax for 2011 is $1,000 for an average tax rate of 10%. If, however, Cora's taxable income is $50,000, her tax will be $6,650 for an average tax rate of 13.3%. The tax is progressive since higher rates are applied to greater amounts of taxable income. ■

INCIDENCE OF TAXATION

The degree to which various segments of society share the total tax burden is difficult to assess. Assumptions must be made concerning who absorbs the burden of paying the tax. For example, since dividend payments to shareholders are not deductible by a corporation and are generally taxable to shareholders, the same income is subject to a form of double taxation. Concern over double taxation is valid to the extent that corporations are *not* able to shift the corporate tax to the consumer through higher commodity prices. Many research studies have shown a high degree of shifting of the corporate income tax, converting it into a consumption tax that is borne by the ultimate purchasers of goods.

The progressiveness of the Federal income tax rate structure for individuals has varied over the years. As late as 1986, for example, there were 15 rates, ranging from 0 to 50 percent. These later were reduced to two rates of 15 and 28 percent. Currently, there are six rates ranging from 10 to 35 percent.

LO.4

Identify the different taxes imposed in the United States at the Federal, state, and local levels.

1.5 Major Types of Taxes

Why does a text devoted primarily to the Federal income tax discuss state and local taxes? A simple illustration shows the importance of non-Federal taxes.

EXAMPLE 3

Rick is employed by Flamingo Corporation in San Antonio, Texas, at a salary of $74,000. Rick's employer offers him a chance to transfer to its New York City office at a salary of $94,000. A quick computation indicates that the additional taxes (Federal, state, and local) involve approximately $12,000. ■

Although Rick must consider many nontax factors before he decides on a job change, he should also evaluate the tax climate. How do state and local taxes compare? For example, neither Texas nor San Antonio imposes an income tax, but New York State and New York City both do. Consequently, what appears to be a $20,000 pay increase is only $8,000 when the additional taxes of $12,000 are taken into account.

PROPERTY TAXES

Correctly referred to as **ad valorem taxes** because they are based on value, property taxes are a tax on wealth, or capital. In this regard, they have much in common with estate taxes and gift taxes discussed later in the chapter. Although property taxes do not tax income, the income actually derived (or the potential for any income) may be relevant insofar as it affects the value of the property being taxed.

Property taxes fall into *two* categories: those imposed on realty and those imposed on personalty, or assets other than land and buildings. Both have added importance since they usually generate a deduction for Federal income tax purposes (see Chapter 10).

Ad Valorem Taxes on Realty

Property taxes on realty are used exclusively by states and their local political subdivisions, such as cities, counties, and school districts. They represent a major source of revenue for *local* governments, but their importance at the *state* level has waned over the past few years. Some states, for example, have imposed freezes on upward revaluations of residential housing.

How realty is defined can have an important bearing on which assets are subject to tax. This is especially true in jurisdictions that do not impose ad valorem taxes on personalty. Primarily a question of state property law, **realty** generally includes real estate and any capital improvements that are classified as fixtures. Simply stated, a *fixture* is something so permanently attached to the real estate that its removal will cause irreparable damage. A built-in bookcase might well be a fixture, whereas a movable bookcase would not be a fixture. Certain items such as electrical wiring and plumbing cease to be personalty when installed in a building and become realty.

The following are some of the characteristics of ad valorem taxes on realty:

- Property owned by the Federal government is exempt from tax. Similar immunity usually is extended to property owned by state and local governments and by certain charitable organizations.
- Some states provide for lower valuations on property dedicated to agricultural use or other special uses (e.g., wildlife sanctuaries). Reductions in appraised valuations may also be available when the property is subject to a conservation easement (e.g., a limitation on further development).
- Some states partially exempt the homestead, or personal residence, portion of property from taxation. Additionally, modern homestead laws normally protect some or all of a personal residence (including a farm or ranch) from the actions of creditors pursuing claims against the owner.
- Lower taxes may apply to a residence owned by a taxpayer age 65 or older.

EXAMPLE 4
THE BIG PICTURE

Return to the facts of *The Big Picture* on p. 1-2. Why did the Walkers' taxes decrease while those of the Carters increase? A likely explanation is that one (or both) of the Walkers achieved senior citizen status. In the case of the Carters, the assessed value of their property was probably increased (see below). Perhaps they made significant home improvements (e.g., kitchen/bathroom renovation, addition of a sundeck). ■

TAX *in* the NEWS

The Backdoor Tax Increase

Can a landowner's property taxes increase even though the tax rate has not changed? Yes, if the assessed value of the property is increased! Known as a "backdoor tax increase," this procedure allows the taxing authority to generate additional revenue without having to secure voter approval for an increase in the tax rate. Even more aggravating for the property owner is an increase in assessed value that is based on past market values and does not reflect the true current value. This kind of increase often occurs during periods of economic downturn, when real estate prices decline. Under these conditions, increases in assessed value are likely to cause considerable taxpayer dissatisfaction and lead to proposals for legislative relief, such as a freeze on upward property assessments.

Source: Adapted from Jennifer Levitz, "Calls Grow to Cap Property Taxes," *Wall Street Journal*, January 5, 2009, p. A3.

- When non-income-producing property (e.g., a personal residence) is converted to income-producing property (e.g., a rental house), typically the appraised value increases.
- Some jurisdictions extend immunity from tax for a specified period of time (a *tax holiday*) to new or relocated businesses. A tax holiday can backfire, however, and cause more harm than good. If it is too generous, it can damage the local infrastructure (e.g., less funding for public works and education).

Unlike the ad valorem tax on personalty (see below), the tax on realty is difficult to avoid. Since real estate is impossible to hide, a high degree of taxpayer compliance is not surprising. The only avoidance possibility that is generally available is associated with the assessed value of the property. For this reason, the assessed value of the property—particularly, a value that is reassessed upward—may be subject to controversy and litigation.

The history of the ad valorem tax on realty has been marked by inconsistent application due to a lack of competent tax administration and definitive guidelines for assessment procedures. In recent years, however, some significant improvements have occurred. Some jurisdictions, for example, have computerized their reassessment procedures so that they will immediately affect all property located within the jurisdiction.

Several jurisdictions provide homeowners with a measure of protection from increased property taxes by "freezing" existing assessments and limiting future upward adjustments. Such restrictions on reassessments, however, do not carry over to the new owner when the property is sold. Thus, such measures tend to lock in ownership and restrict the mobility of those who might otherwise change residences.

Ad Valorem Taxes on Personalty

Personalty can be defined as all assets that are not realty. It may be helpful to distinguish between the *classification* of an asset (realty or personalty) and the *use* to which it is put. Both realty and personalty can be either business use or personal use property. Examples include a residence (realty that is personal use), an office building (realty that is business use), surgical instruments (personalty that is business use), and regular wearing apparel (personalty that is personal use).[8]

Personalty can also be classified as tangible property or intangible property. For ad valorem tax purposes, intangible personalty includes stocks, bonds, and various other securities (e.g., bank shares).

[8]The distinction, important for ad valorem and for Federal income tax purposes, often becomes confused when personalty is referred to as "personal" property to distinguish it from "real" property. This designation does not give a complete picture of what is involved. The description "personal" residence, however, is clearer, since a residence can be identified as being realty. What is meant, in this case, is realty that is personal use property.

TAX *in* the NEWS

More Excise Taxes from the Federal Government—Good or Bad?

The recent increase in the Federal excise tax on tobacco (from $0.39 to $1.01 per package of cigarettes) has met with a mixed reaction. On the positive side, the increase will fund a good cause—SCHIP (State Children's Health Insurance Program). Likewise, no one can take issue with a sin tax that purports to reduce smoking.

As for the negative aspects, most heavy smokers are lower-income taxpayers. Thus, this tax increase will largely fall on the poor. Furthermore, various states have increased their tobacco taxes as well. Faced with a substantially higher cost for cigarettes, smokers who cannot kick the habit may see the cheaper price provided by an illegal market (i.e., smuggling) as an attractive alternative. Tax increases that foster criminal activity are not a good way to raise revenue.

More importantly, does this foray into tobacco taxes portend a new trend on the part of Congress to find new sources of revenue? Note that the cigarette tax increase has recently been followed by a new excise tax on tanning salons. Will other new excise taxes be imposed (e.g., a tax on soft drinks) or existing excise taxes increased (e.g., more taxes on alcoholic beverages)?

The following generalizations may be made concerning the ad valorem taxes on personalty:

- Particularly with personalty devoted to personal use (e.g., jewelry, household furnishings), taxpayer compliance ranges from poor to zero. Some jurisdictions do not even attempt to enforce the tax on these items. For automobiles devoted to personal use, many jurisdictions have converted from value as the tax base to arbitrary license fees based on the weight of the vehicle. Some jurisdictions also consider the vehicle's age (e.g., automobiles six years or older are not subject to the ad valorem tax because they are presumed to have little, if any, value).
- For personalty devoted to business use (e.g., inventories, trucks, machinery, equipment), taxpayer compliance and enforcement procedures are measurably better.
- Which jurisdiction possesses the authority to tax movable personalty (e.g., railroad rolling stock) always has been and continues to be a troublesome issue.
- A few states levy an ad valorem tax on intangibles such as stocks and bonds. Taxpayer compliance may be negligible if the state lacks a means of verifying security transactions and ownership.

TRANSACTION TAXES

Transaction taxes, which characteristically are imposed at the manufacturer's, wholesaler's, or retailer's level, cover a wide range of transfers. Like many other types of taxes (e.g., income taxes, estate taxes, and gift taxes), transaction taxes usually are not within the exclusive province of any level of taxing authority (Federal, state, local government). As the description implies, these levies place a tax on transfers of property and normally are determined by multiplying the value involved by a percentage rate.

Federal Excise Taxes

Long one of the mainstays of the Federal tax system, Federal **excise taxes** had declined in relative importance until recently. In recent years, Congress substantially increased the Federal excise taxes on such items as tobacco products, fuel and gasoline sales, and air travel. Other Federal excise taxes include the following:

- Manufacturers' excise taxes on trucks, trailers, tires, firearms, sporting equipment, and coal and the gas guzzler tax on automobiles.[9]

[9]The gas guzzler tax is imposed on the manufacturers of automobiles (both domestic and foreign) and increases in amount as the mileage ratings per gallon of gas decrease. For example, a Maserati Gran Turismo manages 19 miles per gallon in combined city/highway driving and starts at $121,100, which includes a $2,100 gas guzzler tax.

TAX in the NEWS

TEXAS'S "POLE TAX"—"SIN TAX" OR TAX ON FREE SPEECH?

A 2007 Texas law imposes a $5-per-visit excise tax on patrons who visit one of the state's roughly 170 strip clubs. The tax is being challenged in the courts as a discriminatory way to raise revenue and a measure that squelches freedom of speech. Arguably, "pole dancing" involves a form of emotional expression that is protected by the First Amendment to the U.S. Constitution. Supporters of the pole tax disagree and maintain that its purpose is to combat sexual assault by discouraging the "combustible combination" of drinking and nude dancing. The state of Utah has imposed a similar tax that has been sustained by the state supreme court but probably will be appealed to the U.S. Supreme Court.

Depending on what happens to these taxes in the courts, other states seeking new sources of revenue are likely to respond accordingly.

Source: Adapted from Leslie Eaton, "'Sin Tax' Called Naked Money Grab," *Wall Street Journal*, March 26, 2010, p. A3.

- Alcohol taxes.
- Miscellaneous taxes (e.g., the tax on wagering).

The list of transactions covered, although seemingly impressive, has diminished over the years. At one time, for example, there was a Federal excise tax on admission to amusement facilities (e.g., theaters) and on the sale of such items as leather goods, jewelry, furs, and cosmetics.

When reviewing the list of both Federal and state excise taxes, one should recognize the possibility that the tax laws may be trying to influence social behavior. For example, the gas guzzler tax is intended as an incentive for the automobile companies to build fuel-efficient cars.

State and Local Excise Taxes

Many state and local excise taxes parallel the Federal version. Thus, all states tax the sale of gasoline, liquor, and tobacco products; however, unlike the Federal version, the rates vary significantly. For gasoline products, for example, compare the 37.5 cents per gallon imposed by the state of Washington with the 7.5 cents per gallon levied by the state of Georgia. For tobacco sales, contrast the 17 cents per pack of 20 cigarettes in effect in Missouri with the $4.35 per pack applicable in the state of New York. Given the latter situation, is it surprising that the smuggling of cigarettes for resale elsewhere is so widespread?

Other excise taxes found at some state and local levels include those on admission to amusement facilities, on the sale of playing cards, and on prepared foods. Most states impose a transaction tax on the transfer of property that requires the recording of documents (e.g., real estate sales).[10] Some extend the tax to the transfer of stocks and other securities.

Over the last few years, two types of excise taxes imposed at the local level have become increasingly popular: the hotel occupancy tax and the rental car "surcharge." Since they tax the visitor who cannot vote, they are a political windfall and are often used to finance special projects that generate civic pride (e.g., convention centers, state-of-the-art sports arenas). These levies can be significant, as demonstrated by Houston's hotel tax of 17 percent and the car rental tax and fees of 35 percent at the Kansas City, Missouri airport.

General Sales Taxes

The distinction between an excise tax and a general **sales tax** is easy to make. One is restricted to a particular transaction (e.g., the 18.4 cents per gallon Federal excise

[10] This type of tax has much in common with the stamp tax levied by Great Britain on the American colonies during the pre-Revolutionary War period in U.S. history.

tax on the sale of gasoline), while the other covers a multitude of transactions (e.g., a 5 percent tax on *all* retail sales). In actual practice, however, the distinction is not always that clear. Some state statutes exempt certain transactions from the application of the general sales taxes (e.g., sales of food to be consumed off the premises, sales of certain medicines and drugs). Also, it is not uncommon to find that rates vary depending on the commodity involved. Many states, for example, allow preferential rates for the sale of agricultural equipment or apply different rates (either higher or lower than the general rate) to the sale of automobiles. With many of these special exceptions and classifications of rates, a general sales tax can take on the appearance of a collection of individual excise taxes.

A **use tax** is an ad valorem tax, usually at the same rate as the sales tax, on the use, consumption, or storage of tangible property purchased outside the state but used within the state. The purpose of a use tax is to prevent the avoidance of a sales tax. Every state that imposes a general sales tax levied on the consumer also has a use tax. Alaska, Delaware, Montana, New Hampshire, and Oregon have neither tax. There is no Federal general sales or use tax.

EXAMPLE 5
THE BIG PICTURE

Return to the facts of *The Big Picture* on p.1-2. The payment Travis made when he registered the car is probably a use tax. When the car was purchased in another state, likely no (or a lesser) sales tax was levied. The current payment makes up for the amount of sales tax he would have paid had the car been purchased in his home state. ■

The use tax is difficult to enforce for many purchases and therefore the purchaser often does not pay it. In some cases, for example, it may be worthwhile to make purchases through an out-of-state mail-order business or the websites of local vendors. In spite of shipping costs, the avoidance of the local sales tax that otherwise might be incurred can lower the cost of such products as computer components. Some states are taking steps to curtail this loss of revenue. For items such as automobiles (refer to Example 5), the use tax probably will be collected when the purchaser registers the item in his or her home state.

ETHICS & *Equity*

Making Good Use of Out-of-State Relatives

Marcus, a resident of Texas, has found the ideal gift for his wife in celebration of their upcoming wedding anniversary—a $22,000 diamond tennis bracelet. However, Marcus is appalled at the prospect of paying the state and local sales tax of $1,815 (combined rate of 8.25 percent). He, therefore, asks his aunt, a resident of Montana, to purchase the bracelet. The jewelry store lists the aunt as the buyer and ships the bracelet to her. Prior to the anniversary, Marcus receives the bracelet from his aunt. Is Marcus able to save $1,815 on the present for his wife? What can go wrong?

Local general sales taxes, over and above those levied by the state, are common. It is not unusual to find taxpayers living in the same state but paying different general sales taxes due to the location of their residence.

EXAMPLE 6

Pete and Sam both live in a state that has a general sales tax of 3%. Sam, however, resides in a city that imposes an additional general sales tax of 2%. Even though Pete and Sam live in the same state, one is subject to a rate of 3%, while the other pays a tax of 5%. ■

For various reasons, some jurisdictions will suspend the application of a general sales tax. New York City does so to stimulate shopping. Illinois has permanently suspended the tax on construction materials used to build power-generating plants. Texas and numerous other states do so annually on clothing right before the beginning of the school year. Such suspensions are similar to the tax holidays granted for ad valorem tax purposes. As state revenues have declined in recent years, many states have had misgivings about the advisability of scheduling further sales tax holidays. Turning off the spigot could have political consequences, however. These holidays are extremely popular with both merchants and shoppers, so their termination could cause voter backlash at the polls.

Severance Taxes

Severance taxes are transaction taxes that are based on the notion that the state has an interest in its natural resources (e.g., oil, gas, iron ore, coal). Therefore, a tax is imposed when the natural resources are extracted.

For some states, severance taxes can be a significant source of revenue. Due to the severance tax on oil production, Alaska has been able to avoid both a state income tax and a state general sales tax.

TAXES ON TRANSFERS AT DEATH

The right to transfer property or to receive property upon the death of the owner may be subject to estate and/or inheritance taxes. Consequently, such taxes fall into the category of excise taxes. If the tax is imposed on the right to pass property at death, it is classified as an **estate tax**. If it taxes the right to receive property from a decedent, it is termed an **inheritance tax**. As is typical of other types of excise taxes, the value of the property transferred provides the base for determining the amount of the tax.

The Federal government imposes only an estate tax. State governments, however, may levy inheritance taxes, estate taxes, or both. Some states (e.g., Florida, Texas) levy neither tax.

EXAMPLE 7

At the time of her death, Wilma lived in a state that imposes an inheritance tax but not an estate tax. Mary, one of Wilma's heirs, lives in the same state. Wilma's estate is subject to the Federal estate tax, and Mary is subject to the state inheritance tax. ■

The Federal Estate Tax

The Revenue Act of 1916 incorporated the estate tax into the tax law. The tax was originally intended to prevent large concentrations of wealth from being kept within a family for many generations. Whether this objective has been accomplished is debatable. Like the income tax, estate taxes can be reduced through various planning procedures.

The gross estate includes property the decedent owned at the time of death. It also includes property interests, such as life insurance proceeds paid to the estate or to a beneficiary other than the estate if the deceased-insured had any ownership rights in the policy. Quite simply, the gross estate represents property interests subject to Federal estate taxation.[11] All property included in the gross estate is valued as of the date of death or, if the alternate valuation date is elected, six months later.[12]

Deductions from the gross estate in arriving at the taxable estate include funeral and administration expenses, certain taxes, debts of the decedent, casualty losses[13] incurred during the administration of the estate, transfers to charitable organizations, and, in some cases, the marital deduction. The *marital deduction* is available for amounts actually passing to a surviving spouse (a widow or widower).

Once the taxable estate has been determined and certain taxable gifts made by the decedent during life have been added to it, the estate tax can be computed. From the amount derived from the appropriate tax rate schedules, various credits should be subtracted to arrive at the tax, if any, that is due.[14] Although many other credits are also available, probably the most significant is the *unified transfer tax credit.*

[11] For further information on these matters, see Chapter 27.

[12] See the discussion of the alternate valuation date in Chapter 13.

[13] For a definition of "casualty losses," see the Glossary in Appendix C.

[14] For tax purposes, it is always crucial to appreciate the difference between a deduction and a credit. A *credit* is a dollar-for-dollar reduction of tax liability. A *deduction*, however, benefits the taxpayer only to the extent of his or her tax bracket. A taxpayer in a 50% tax bracket, for example, would need $2 of deductions to prevent $1 of tax liability. In contrast, $1 of credit neutralizes $1 of tax liability.

The main reason for this credit is to eliminate or reduce the estate tax liability for modest estates. For 2011, the amount of the credit is $1,730,800. Based on the estate tax rates, the credit exempts a tax base of up to $5 million.

EXAMPLE 8

Ned made no taxable gifts before his death in 2011. If Ned's taxable estate amounts to $5 million or less, no Federal estate tax is due because of the application of the unified transfer tax credit. Under the tax law, the estate tax on a taxable estate of $5 million is $1,730,800. ■

State Taxes on Transfers at Death

As noted earlier, states may levy an inheritance tax, an estate tax, or both. The two forms of taxes on transfers at death differ according to whether the tax is imposed on the heirs or on the estate.

Characteristically, an inheritance tax divides the heirs into classes based on their relationship to the decedent. The more closely related the heir, the lower the rates imposed and the greater the exemption allowed. Some states completely exempt from taxation amounts passing to a surviving spouse.

GIFT TAXES

Like taxes on transfers at death, a **gift tax** is an excise tax levied on the right to transfer property. In this case, however, the tax is imposed on transfers made during the owner's life and not at death. A gift tax applies only to transfers that are not offset by full and adequate consideration.

EXAMPLE 9

Carl sells property worth $50,000 to his daughter for $1,000. Although property worth $50,000 has been transferred, only $49,000 represents a gift, since this is the portion not supported by full and adequate consideration. ■

The Federal Gift Tax

First enacted in 1932, the Federal gift tax was intended to complement the estate tax. If lifetime transfers by gift were not taxed, it would be possible to avoid the estate tax and escape taxation entirely.

Only taxable gifts are subject to the gift tax. For this purpose, a taxable gift is measured by the fair market value of the property on the date of transfer less the *annual exclusion per donee* and, in some cases, less the *marital deduction,* which allows tax-free transfers between spouses. Each donor is allowed an annual exclusion of $13,000 in 2011 for each donee.[15]

EXAMPLE 10

On December 31, 2010, Louise (a widow) gives $13,000 to each of her four married children, their spouses, and her eight grandchildren. On January 2, 2011, she repeats the procedure, giving $13,000 to each recipient. Due to the annual exclusion, Louise has not made a taxable gift, although she transferred $208,000 [$13,000 (annual exclusion) × 16 (donees)] in 2010 and $208,000 [$13,000 (annual exclusion) × 16 (donees)] in 2011, for a total of $416,000 ($208,000 + $208,000). ■

A special election applicable to married persons allows one-half of the gift made by the donor-spouse to be treated as being made by the nondonor-spouse (*gift splitting*). This election to split the gifts of property made to third persons has the effect of increasing the number of annual exclusions available. Also, it allows

[15] The purpose of the annual exclusion is to avoid the need to report and pay a tax on *modest* gifts. Without the exclusion, the IRS could face a real problem of taxpayer noncompliance. The annual exclusion is indexed as the level of inflation warrants. The exclusion was $12,000 from 2006 through 2008.

the use of the nondonor-spouse's unified transfer tax credit and may lower the tax rates that will apply.

EXAMPLE 11
THE BIG PICTURE

Return to the facts of *The Big Picture* on p. 1-2. Although the value of the RV is not stated, it is highly likely to exceed the annual exclusion allowed—$52,000 for two donees (the Walkers) from two donors (the Carters). Thus, a taxable gift results, and a Form 709 (Gift Tax Return) must be filed. Whether any gift tax is due depends on the past taxable gifts the Carters have made and how much of their unified transfer tax credit (see below) is still available. ■

The gift tax rate schedule is the same as that applicable to the estate tax. The schedule is commonly referred to as the *unified transfer tax schedule.*

The Federal gift tax is *cumulative* in effect. What this means is that the tax base for current taxable gifts includes past taxable gifts. Although a credit is allowed for prior gift taxes, the result of adding past taxable gifts to current taxable gifts could be to force the donor into a higher tax bracket.[16] Like the Federal estate tax rates, the Federal gift tax rates are progressive (see Example 2 earlier in this chapter).

The unified transfer tax credit is available for all taxable gifts; the amount of this credit for 2011 is $1,730,800. There is, however, only one unified transfer tax credit, and it applies both to taxable gifts and to the Federal estate tax. In a manner of speaking, therefore, once the unified transfer tax credit has been exhausted for Federal gift tax purposes, it is no longer available to insulate a decedent's transfers from the Federal estate tax, except to the extent of the excess of the credit amount for estate tax purposes over that for gift tax purposes.

Even though a unified transfer tax credit of $1,730,800 in 2011 is available for transfers by death, lifetime gifts continue to be attractive. If income-producing property is involved (e.g., marketable securities, rental real estate), a gift may reduce income taxes for the family unit by shifting subsequent income to lower-bracket donees. If the gift involves property that is expected to appreciate in value (e.g., life insurance policies, real estate, artworks), future increases in value will be assigned to the donee and will not be included in the donor's estate. Also important is that due to the annual exclusion ($13,000 per donee in 2011), some of the gift is not subject to any gift tax. Recall that the gift-splitting election enables married donors to double up on the annual exclusion.

INCOME TAXES

Income taxes are levied by the Federal government, most states, and some local governments. The trend in recent years has been to place greater reliance on this method of taxation. This trend is not consistent with what is happening in other countries, and in this sense, our system of taxation is somewhat different.

Income taxes generally are imposed on individuals, corporations, and certain fiduciaries (estates and trusts). Most jurisdictions attempt to assure the collection of income taxes by requiring pay-as-you-go procedures, including withholding requirements for employees and estimated tax prepayments for all taxpayers.

Federal Income Taxes

The Federal income tax that is imposed on individuals follows the formula set forth in Figure 1.2. The formula for the individual income tax establishes the framework followed in the text. Beginning with Chapter 3, each component of the formula is illustrated and explained. In large part, the text coverage of individual taxpayers follows the same order as the components in the formula.

Like its individual counterpart, the Federal corporate income tax is progressive in nature. But its application does not require the computation of adjusted gross

[16]For further information on the Federal gift tax, see Chapter 27.

FIGURE 1.2 **Formula for Federal Income Tax on Individuals**

Income (broadly conceived)	$xx,xxx
Less: Exclusions (income that is not subject to tax)	(x,xxx)
Gross income (income that is subject to tax)	$xx,xxx
Less: Certain deductions (usually referred to as deductions *for* adjusted gross income)	(x,xxx)
Adjusted gross income	$xx,xxx
Less: The greater of certain personal and employee deductions (usually referred to as *itemized deductions*) *or* The standard deduction (including any additional standard deduction)	(x,xxx)
and	
Less: Personal and dependency exemptions	(x,xxx)
Taxable income	$xx,xxx
Tax on taxable income (see the Tax Tables and Tax Rate Schedules in Appendix A)	$ x,xxx
Less: Tax credits (including Federal income tax withheld and other prepayments of Federal income taxes)	(xxx)
Tax due (or refund)	$ xxx

income (AGI) and does not provide for the standard deduction and personal and dependency exemptions. All allowable deductions of a corporation fall into the business-expense category. In effect, therefore, the taxable income of a corporation is the difference between gross income (net of exclusions) and deductions. Chapter 17 summarizes the rules relating to the determination of taxable income of corporations.

State Income Taxes

All but the following states impose an income tax on individuals: Alaska, Florida, Nevada, South Dakota, Texas, Washington, and Wyoming. New Hampshire and Tennessee impose an individual income tax only on interest and dividends.

Some of the characteristics of state income taxes are summarized as follows:

- With few exceptions, all states require some form of withholding procedures.
- Most states use as the tax base the income determination made for Federal income tax purposes.
- A minority of states go even further and impose a flat rate upon AGI as computed for Federal income tax purposes. Several apply a rate to the Federal income tax liability. This is often referred to as the piggyback approach to state income taxation. Although the term *piggyback* does not lend itself to precise definition, in this context, it means making use, for state income tax purposes, of what was done for Federal income tax purposes.
- Some states are somewhat eroding the piggyback approach by "decoupling" from selected recent tax reductions passed by Congress. The purpose of the decoupling is to retain state revenue that would otherwise be lost. In other words, the state cannot afford to allow its taxpayers the same deductions for state purposes that are allowed for Federal purposes.
- Because of the tie-ins to the Federal return, a state may be notified of any changes made by the IRS upon audit of a Federal return. In recent years, the exchange of information between the IRS and state taxing authorities has increased. Lately, some states (e.g., California) are playing a major role in revealing tax shelter abuses to the IRS.
- Most states allow a deduction for personal and dependency exemptions. Some states substitute a tax credit for a deduction.

FINANCIAL DISCLOSURE *Insights*

WHAT DO YOU MEAN BY "INCOME" ANYWAY?

Most business taxpayers keep at least "two sets of books," in that they report one amount of "income" for financial accounting purposes and another amount of "taxable income" as required by various taxing jurisdictions—the definition that will be used throughout this book. In fact, "income" might be defined in many different ways, as required by the recipients of the income reports of the enterprise. For instance, a business entity might prepare markedly different income reports for lenders, employee unions, managers in operating divisions, and international agencies.

Financial accounting income guidance is provided for U.S. businesses by the **Financial Accounting Standards Board (FASB)**, using the accumulated **Generally Accepted Accounting Principles (GAAP)** for the reporting period. When an entity conducts business outside the United States, the **International Financial Reporting Standards (IFRS)** of the **International Accounting Standards Board (IASB)** also may apply.

Throughout this book, we will point out some of the effects that Federal income tax provisions can have on the taxpayer's financial accounting results for the tax year. The vast majority of an entity's business transactions receive identical treatment under GAAP, IFRS, and the Federal tax law. But when the applicable provisions differ, "income" can be reported as different amounts—accounting professionals often refer to these as "book-tax differences." A tax professional must be able to identify and explain the various constructs of "income" so that the

- A diminishing minority of states allow a deduction for Federal income taxes.
- Virtually all state income tax returns provide checkoff boxes for donations to various causes. Many are dedicated to medical research and wildlife programs, but special projects are not uncommon. For example, Oklahoma has one to retire the debt incurred for its new capitol dome, while Wisconsin tries to finance part of the renovation of Lambeau Field (home of the Green Bay Packers). These checkoff boxes have been criticized as adding complexity to the returns (e.g., one state has 24 boxes) and misleading taxpayers.[17]
- Most states allow their residents some form of tax credit for income taxes paid to other states.

EXAMPLE 12
THE BIG PICTURE

Return to the facts of *The Big Picture* on p. 1-2. Because the income earned by Travis on his Chicago trip will be subject to tax by his home state, he probably will be able to claim an offsetting credit. Whether this negates the double taxation of the same income depends on the amount of credit allowed. ■

- The objective of most states is to tax the income of residents and those who regularly conduct business within the state (e.g., nonresidents who commute to work). These states also purport to tax the income of nonresidents who earn income within the state on an itinerant basis. Usually, however, the visitors actually taxed are highly paid athletes and entertainers. This so-called *jock tax* has been much criticized as being discriminatory due to its selective imposition.
- The due date for filing generally is the same as for the Federal income tax (the fifteenth day of the fourth month following the close of the tax year).
- Some states have occasionally instituted amnesty programs that allow taxpayers to pay back taxes (and interest) on unreported income with no (or

[17] Many taxpayers do not realize that they are paying for the checkoff donation (usually with some of their income tax refund). Unlike the presidential election campaign fund available for Federal income tax purposes ($3 in this case), the contribution is *not made* by the government.

reduced) penalty. In many cases, the tax amnesty has generated enough revenue to warrant the authorization of follow-up programs covering future years—one state has had four amnesty periods, and seven states have had at least three.[18] Amnesties usually include other taxes as well (e.g., sales, franchise, severance). One major advantage of amnesty programs is that they uncover taxpayers that were previously unknown to the taxing authority.

- Because many consumers do not pay state and local sales taxes on out-of-state purchases, state income tax returns often contain a separate line for the reporting of the use tax that is due. The instructions to the form may provide tables of suggested amounts based on income levels for those who lack records on the purchases not previously taxed. Thus, the income tax return serves as a means of collecting delinquent sales taxes.

Nearly all states have an income tax applicable to corporations. It is difficult to determine those that do not because a state franchise tax (discussed later in the chapter) sometimes is based in part on the income earned by the corporation.

Local Income Taxes

Cities imposing an income tax include, but are not limited to, Baltimore, Cincinnati, Cleveland, Detroit, Kansas City (Missouri), New York, Philadelphia, and St. Louis. The application of a city income tax is not limited to local residents.

EMPLOYMENT TAXES

Classification as an employee usually leads to the imposition of **employment taxes** and to the requirement that the employer withhold specified amounts for income taxes. The material that follows concentrates on the two major employment taxes: FICA (Federal Insurance Contributions Act—commonly referred to as the Social Security tax) and FUTA (Federal Unemployment Tax Act). Both taxes can be justified by social and public welfare considerations: FICA offers some measure of retirement security, and FUTA provides a modest source of income in the event of loss of employment.

Employment taxes come into play only if two conditions are satisfied. First, is the individual involved an *employee* (as opposed to *self-employed*)? The differences between an employee and a self-employed person are discussed in Chapter 9. Second, if the individual involved is an employee, is he or she covered under FICA or FUTA or both? Detailed coverage of both of these taxes is included in *Employer's Tax Guide,* an IRS publication.

FICA Taxes

The **FICA tax** rates and wage base have increased steadily over the years. It is difficult to imagine that the initial rate in 1937 was only 1 percent of the first $3,000 of covered wages. Thus, the maximum tax due was only $30!

Currently, the FICA tax has two components: Social Security tax (old age, survivors, and disability insurance) *and* Medicare tax (hospital insurance). The Social Security tax rate is 6.2 percent for 2010 and 4.2 percent for 2011, and the Medicare tax rate is 1.45 percent for these years. The base amount for Social Security is $106,800 for 2010 and 2011.[19] There is no limit on the base amount for the Medicare tax. The employer must match the employee's portion for both the Social Security tax and the Medicare tax. Note that for 2011, the Social Security tax matching for the employer is at the 6.2 percent rate.

[18] Although the suggestion has been made, no comparable amnesty program has been offered for the Federal income tax.

[19] The base amount is subject to adjustment annually.

TAX *in the NEWS*

WAS LEBRON JAMES AWARE OF THE TAX SAVINGS INVOLVED WHEN HE CHOSE THE MIAMI HEAT?

As a free agent, basketball star LeBron James had narrowed his choices to the Cavaliers (Ohio), the Knicks (New York), the Nets (New Jersey), and the Heat (Florida). In terms of state (and local) income taxes, was he aware that the maximum rates involved were quite varied—7+ percent, 12.85 percent, 9 percent, and 0 percent, respectively? Projecting a salary of $100 million over five years, what is the saving between a tax of 12.85 percent (Knicks) and 0 percent (Heat)? Although some of the salary will be subject to the jock tax (when an away game is played in a state that imposes an income tax), what about the considerable income from endorsements? This will be assigned to LeBron's place of residence, Florida, which imposes no income tax.

Undoubtedly, LeBron chose to sign with the Heat for basketball reasons. For tax purposes, though, the choice has probably saved him millions of dollars currently and over the next few years.

Source: Adapted from "LeBron's Tax Holiday," *Wall Street Journal*, July 10–11, 2010, p. A12.

A spouse employed by another spouse is subject to FICA. However, children under the age of 18 who are employed in a parent's unincorporated trade or business are exempted.

EXAMPLE 13
THE BIG PICTURE

Return to the facts of *The Big Picture* on p. 1-2. Presuming April and Martin perform meaningful services for Travis (which the facts seem to imply), they are legitimate employees. April is not subject to Social Security tax because she is under age 18. However, Martin is age 18 and needs to be covered. Furthermore, recall that Betty Carter is now working and will likewise be subject to Social Security tax. Travis, as an independent contractor, is subject to self-employment tax. ■

Taxpayers who are not employees (e.g., sole proprietors, independent contractors) may also be subject to Social Security taxes. Known as the self-employment tax, the rates are 12.4 percent (10.4 percent in 2011) for Social Security and 2.9 percent for Medicare, or twice that applicable to an employee. The tax is imposed on net self-employment income up to a base amount of $106,800 for 2010 and 2011. See Chapter 12 for additional coverage of the self-employment tax.

FUTA Taxes

The purpose of the **FUTA tax** is to provide funds that the states can use to administer unemployment benefits. This leads to the somewhat unusual situation of one tax being handled by both Federal and state governments. The end result of such joint administration is to compel the employer to observe two sets of rules. Thus, state and Federal returns must be filed and payments made to both governmental units.

In 2011, FUTA is 6.2 percent (6.0 percent plus a 0.2 percent surtax) on the first $7,000 of covered wages paid during the year to each employee. The Federal government allows a credit for FUTA paid (or allowed under a merit rating system) to the state. The credit cannot exceed 5.4 percent of the covered wages. Thus, the amount required to be paid to the IRS could be as low as 0.8 percent (6.2% − 5.4%).

States follow a policy of reducing the unemployment tax on employers who experience stable employment. Thus, an employer with little or no employee turnover might find that the state rate drops to as low as 0.1 percent or, in some states, even to zero. The reason for the merit rating credit is that the state has to pay fewer unemployment benefits when employment is steady.

FUTA differs from FICA in the sense that the incidence of taxation falls entirely upon the employer. A few states, however, levy a special tax on employees to provide either disability benefits or supplemental unemployment compensation, or both.

OTHER U.S. TAXES

To complete the overview of the U.S. tax system, some missing links need to be covered that do not fit into the classifications discussed elsewhere in this chapter.

Federal Customs Duties

One tax that has not yet been mentioned is the tariff on certain imported goods.[20] Generally referred to as customs duties or levies, this tax, together with selective excise taxes, provided most of the revenues needed by the Federal government during the nineteenth century. In view of present times, it is remarkable to note that tariffs and excise taxes alone paid off the national debt in 1835 and enabled the U.S. Treasury to pay a surplus of $28 million to the states.

In recent years, tariffs have served the nation more as an instrument for carrying out protectionist policies than as a means of generating revenue. Thus, a particular U.S. industry might be saved from economic disaster, so the argument goes, by imposing customs duties on the importation of foreign goods that can be sold at lower prices. Protectionists contend that the tariff thereby neutralizes the competitive edge held by the producer of the foreign goods.[21]

Protectionist policies seem more appropriate for less-developed countries whose industrial capacity has not yet matured. In a world where a developed country should have everything to gain by encouraging international free trade, such policies may be of dubious value. History shows that tariffs often lead to retaliatory action on the part of the nation or nations affected.

Miscellaneous State and Local Taxes

Most states impose a franchise tax on corporations. Basically, a **franchise tax** is levied on the right to do business in the state. The base used for the determination of the tax varies from state to state. Although corporate income considerations may come into play, this tax most often is based on the capitalization of the corporation (either with or without certain long-term indebtedness).

Closely akin to the franchise tax are **occupational fees** applicable to various trades or businesses, such as a liquor store license, a taxicab permit, or a fee to practice a profession such as law, medicine, or accounting. Most of these are not significant revenue producers and fall more into the category of licenses than taxes. The revenue derived is used to defray the cost incurred by the jurisdiction in regulating the business or profession in the interest of the public good.

EXAMPLE 14
THE BIG PICTURE

Return to the facts of *The Big Picture* on p. 1-2. Although the facts do not mention the matter, both Travis and Betty will almost certainly pay occupational fees—Travis for engineering and Betty for nursing. ■

PROPOSED U.S. TAXES

Considerable dissatisfaction with the U.S. Federal income tax has led to several recent proposals that, to say the least, are rather drastic in nature. One proposal would retain the income tax but with substantial change. Two other proposals would replace the Federal income tax with an entirely different system of taxation.

[20] Less-developed countries that rely principally on one or more major commodities (e.g., oil, coffee) are prone to favor *export* duties as well.

[21] The North American Free Trade Agreement (NAFTA), enacted in 1993, substantially reduced the tariffs on trade between Canada, Mexico, and the United States. The General Agreement on Tariffs and Trade (GATT) legislation enacted in 1994 also reduced tariffs on selected commodities among 124 signatory nations.

The Flat Tax

One proposal is for a **flat tax** that would replace the current graduated income tax with a single rate of 17 percent. Large personal exemptions (e.g., approximately $30,000 for a family of four) would allow many low- and middle-income taxpayers to pay no tax. All other deductions would be eliminated, and no tax would be imposed on income from investments.

Various other versions of the flat tax have been suggested that would retain selected deductions (e.g., interest on home mortgages and charitable contributions) and not exclude all investment income from taxation.

The major advantage of the flat tax is its simplicity. Everyone agrees that the current Federal income tax is inappropriately complex. Consequently, compliance costs are disproportionately high. Proponents of the flat tax further believe that simplifying the income tax will significantly reduce the current "tax gap" (i.e., the difference between the amount of taxes that *should be paid* and what is *actually paid*).

Political considerations are a major obstacle to the enactment of a flat tax in its pure form. Special interest groups, such as charitable organizations and mortgage companies, are not apt to be complacent over the elimination of a tax deduction that benefits their industry. In addition, there is uncertainty as to the economic effects of the tax.

It is interesting to note that Russia's attempt at a progressive income tax was quite disastrous. Not only did high rates drive capital out of the country but also failure to report income was rampant. In early 2000, the income tax was repealed and replaced with a 13 percent flat tax. To date, the flat tax has worked quite well. Several Baltic states (Estonia, Latvia, and Lithuania) have followed Russia's example. Albania, Romania, Slovakia, Georgia, Ukraine, and Serbia have also adopted a flat tax.

Value Added Tax

The **value added tax (VAT)** is one of two proposals that would replace the Federal income tax. Under the VAT, a business would pay the tax (approximately 17 percent) on all of the materials and services required to manufacture its product. In effect, the VAT taxes the increment in value as goods move through production and manufacturing stages to the marketplace. Moreover, the VAT paid by the producer will be reflected in the selling price of the goods. Thus, the VAT is a tax on consumption.

The United States is the only country in the OECD (Organization for Economic Cooperation and Development) that does not have a VAT. Approximately 136 countries around the world use a VAT, ranging from 5 percent in Japan to 25 percent in Denmark. Instead, the United States relies heavily on income taxes.

The VAT is an effective generator of revenue. Many view this trait as a major disadvantage. With additional revenue available, the government may be tempted to expand the entitlements available to the general public in the future.

Sales Tax

A **national sales tax** differs from a VAT in that it would be collected on the final sale of goods and services. Consequently, it is collected from the consumer and not from businesses that add value to the product. Like the VAT, the national sales tax is intended to replace the Federal income tax.

A current proposal for a national sales tax, called the "Fair Tax," would tax almost all purchases, including food and medicine, at approximately 23 percent. Exempt items include business expenses, used goods, and the costs of education. The "Fair Tax" would replace not only the income tax (both individual and corporate) but also payroll taxes (including the self-employment tax) and the gift and estate taxes. Current sponsors of this proposal, which is reintroduced in each new Congress, include Saxby Chambliss (R–Ga.) in the Senate and John Linder (R–Ga.) in the House.

Critics contend that both forms of consumption taxes, a VAT and a national sales tax, are regressive. They impose more of a burden on low-income taxpayers who must spend larger proportions of their incomes on essential purchases. The proposals attempt to remedy this inequity by granting some sort of credit, rebate, or exemption to low-income taxpayers.

In terms of taxpayer compliance, a VAT is preferable to a national sales tax. Without significant collection efforts, a national sales tax could easily be circumvented by resorting to a barter system of doing business. Its high rate would also encourage smuggling and black market activities.

1.6 Tax Administration

LO.5

Explain the administration of the tax law, including the audit process utilized by the IRS.

INTERNAL REVENUE SERVICE

The responsibility for administering the Federal tax laws rests with the Treasury Department. Administratively, the IRS is part of the Department of the Treasury and is responsible for enforcing the tax laws. The Commissioner of Internal Revenue is appointed by the President and is responsible for establishing policy and supervising the activities of the IRS. See Chapter 26 for more in-depth coverage of the IRS and tax administration issues.

THE AUDIT PROCESS

Selection of Returns for Audit

Due to budgetary limitations, only a small minority of tax returns are audited. For the fiscal year ended September 30, 2009, the IRS audited only 1 percent of all individual income tax returns filed.

The IRS utilizes mathematical formulas and statistical sampling techniques to select tax returns that are most likely to contain errors and to yield substantial amounts of additional tax revenues upon audit. The mathematical formula yields what is called a Discriminant Information Function (DIF) score. It is the DIF score given to a particular return that may lead to its selection for audit.

To update the DIF components, the IRS selects a cross section of returns, which are subject to various degrees of inspection (i.e., information return verification, correspondence, and face-to-face audits with filers). The results of these audits highlight areas of taxpayer noncompliance and enable the IRS to use its auditors more productively. In recent years, IRS audits have resulted in an increasing number of "no change" results. This indicates that the IRS is not always choosing the right returns to audit (i.e., the ones with errors).

Though the IRS does not openly disclose all of its audit selection techniques, the following observations may be made concerning the probability of selection for audit:

- Certain groups of taxpayers are subject to audit much more frequently than others. These groups include individuals with large amounts of gross income, self-employed individuals with substantial business income and deductions, and taxpayers with prior tax deficiencies. Also vulnerable are businesses that receive a large proportion of their receipts in cash (e.g., cafés and small service businesses) and thus have a high potential for tax avoidance.

EXAMPLE 15

Jack owns and operates a liquor store on a cash-and-carry basis. Since all of Jack's sales are for cash, he might well be a prime candidate for an audit by the IRS. Cash transactions are easier to conceal than those made on credit. ■

- If information returns (e.g., Form 1099, Form W–2) are not in substantial agreement with reported income, an audit can be anticipated.
- If an individual's itemized deductions are in excess of norms established for various income levels, the probability of an audit is increased.
- Filing of a refund claim by the taxpayer may prompt an audit of the return.

- Information obtained from other sources (e.g., informants, news items) may lead to an audit. Recently, for example, the IRS advised its agents to be on the alert for newspaper accounts of large civil court judgments. The advice was based on the assumption that many successful plaintiffs were not reporting as income the taxable punitive damages portion of awards.

The tax law permits the IRS to pay rewards to persons who provide information that leads to the detection and punishment of those who violate the tax laws. The rewards may not exceed 30 percent of the taxes, fines, and penalties recovered as a result of such information.

EXAMPLE 16

After 15 years of service, Rita is discharged by her employer, Dr. Smith. Shortly thereafter, the IRS receives an anonymous letter stating that Dr. Smith keeps two separate sets of books and that the one used for tax reporting substantially understates his cash receipts. ■

EXAMPLE 17

During a divorce proceeding, it is revealed that Leo, a public official, kept large amounts of cash in a shoe box at home. This information is widely disseminated by the news media and comes to the attention of the IRS. Needless to say, the IRS is interested in knowing whether these funds originated from a taxable source and, if so, whether they were reported on Leo's income tax returns. ■

Types of Audits

Once a return is selected for audit, the taxpayer is notified. If the issue involved is minor, the matter often can be resolved simply by correspondence (a **correspondence audit**) between the IRS and the taxpayer.

EXAMPLE 18

During 2009, Janet received dividend income from Green Corporation. In early 2010, Green Corporation reported the payment on Form 1099–DIV (an information return for reporting dividend payments), the original being sent to the IRS and a copy to Janet. When preparing her income tax return for 2009, Janet apparently overlooked this particular Form 1099–DIV and failed to include the dividend on Schedule B, Interest and Dividend Income, of Form 1040. In 2011, the IRS sends a notice to Janet calling her attention to the omission and requesting a remittance for additional tax, interest, and penalty. Janet promptly mails a check to the IRS for the requested amount, and the matter is closed. ■

Other examinations are generally classified as either office audits or field audits. An **office audit** usually is restricted in scope and is conducted in the facilities of the IRS. In contrast, a **field audit** involves an examination of numerous items reported on the return and is conducted on the premises of the taxpayer or the taxpayer's representative.

EXAMPLE 19
THE BIG PICTURE

Return to the facts of *The Big Picture* on p. 1-2. The audit of the Walkers by the IRS obviously was a correspondence type. The reason for the audit was probably a minor oversight, such as the omission of some interest or dividend income (see Example 18). The audit of the Carters, however, was more serious—probably a field or office type. Since the Federal audit followed a state audit that was productive (i.e., led to the assessment of a deficiency), there may have been an exchange of information between the two taxing authorities—see p. 16 in this chapter. ■

Upon the conclusion of the audit, the examining agent issues a Revenue Agent's Report (RAR) that summarizes the findings. The RAR will result in a refund (the tax was overpaid), a deficiency (the tax was underpaid), or a *no change* (the tax was correct) finding. If, during the course of an audit, a special agent accompanies (or takes over from) the regular auditor, this means the IRS suspects fraud. If the matter has progressed to an investigation for fraud, the taxpayer should retain competent counsel.

TAX *in the NEWS* **PAY OR SHAME!**

An increasing number of states and local jurisdictions are learning that the threat of public humiliation can be rewarding. When someone owes taxes but does not pay, the prospect of having one's name listed on a public website may make a difference. Often payment is made in order to avoid the cybershame that comes from being exposed as a tax deadbeat. Some taxing jurisdictions have found the shaming procedure so productive that they maintain separate lists for different types of taxes (e.g., sales taxes, income taxes) or different types of delinquents (e.g., personal, business). As of yet, the IRS has not considered this approach for Federal tax scofflaws. Perhaps the length of the list would be too overwhelming!

Source: Adapted from Amy Merrick, "Cash-Starved States Put Tax Scofflaws in Crosshairs," *Wall Street Journal*, March 12, 2010, p. A3.

Settlement Procedures

If an audit results in an assessment of additional tax and no settlement is reached with the IRS agent, the taxpayer may attempt to negotiate a settlement with a higher level of the IRS. If an appeal is desired, an appropriate request must be made to the Appeals Division of the IRS. The Appeals Division is authorized to settle all disputes based on the *hazard of litigation* (the probability of favorable resolution of the disputed issue or issues if litigated). In some cases, a taxpayer may be able to obtain a percentage settlement or a favorable settlement of one or more disputed issues.

If a satisfactory settlement is not reached within the administrative appeal process, the taxpayer can litigate the case in the Tax Court, a Federal District Court, or the Court of Federal Claims. However, litigation is recommended only as a last resort because of the legal costs involved and the uncertainty of the final outcome. Tax litigation considerations are discussed more fully in Chapter 2.

STATUTE OF LIMITATIONS

A **statute of limitations** is a provision in the law that offers a party a defense against a suit brought by another party after the expiration of a specified period of time. The purpose of a statute of limitations is to preclude parties from prosecuting stale claims. The passage of time makes the defense of such claims difficult since witnesses may no longer be available or evidence may have been lost or destroyed. Found at the state and Federal levels, such statutes cover a multitude of suits, both civil and criminal.

For our purposes, the relevant statutes deal with the Federal income tax. The two categories involved cover both the period of limitations applicable to the assessment of additional tax deficiencies by the IRS and the period applicable to claims for refunds by taxpayers.

Assessment by the IRS

Under the general rule, the IRS may assess an additional tax liability against a taxpayer within *three years* of the filing of the income tax return. If the return is filed early, the three-year period begins to run from the due date of the return (usually April 15 for a calendar year individual taxpayer). If the taxpayer files the return late (i.e., beyond the due date), the three-year period begins to run on the date filed.

If a taxpayer omits an amount of gross income in excess of 25 percent of the gross income reported on the return, the statute of limitations is increased to six years.

EXAMPLE 20

For 2011, Mark, a calendar year taxpayer, reported gross income of $400,000 on a timely filed income tax return. If Mark omitted more than $100,000 (25% × $400,000), the six-year statute of limitations would apply to the 2011 tax year. ■

The six-year provision on assessments by the IRS applies only to the omission of income and does not cover other factors that might lead to an understatement of tax liability, such as overstatement of deductions and credits.

There is *no* statute of limitations on assessments of tax if *no return* is filed or if a *fraudulent* return is filed.

Limitations on Refunds

If a taxpayer believes that an overpayment of Federal income tax was made, a claim for refund should be filed with the IRS. A *claim for refund,* therefore, is a request to the IRS that it return to the taxpayer the excessive income taxes paid.[22]

A claim for refund generally must be filed within *three years* from the date the return was filed *or* within *two years* from the date the tax was paid, whichever is later. Income tax returns that are filed early are deemed to have been filed on the date the return was due.

INTEREST AND PENALTIES

Interest rates are determined quarterly by the IRS based on the existing Federal short-term rate. Currently, the rates for tax refunds (overpayments) for individual taxpayers are the same as those applicable to assessments (underpayments). For the first quarter (January 1–March 31) of 2011, the rates are 3 percent for refunds and assessments.[23]

For assessments of additional taxes, the interest begins running on the unextended due date of the return. With refunds, however, no interest is allowed if the overpayment is refunded to the taxpayer within 45 days of the date the return is filed. For this purpose, returns filed early are deemed to have been filed on the due date.

In addition to interest, the tax law provides various penalties for lack of compliance by taxpayers. Some of these penalties are summarized as follows:

- For a *failure to file* a tax return by the due date (including extension), a penalty of 5 percent per month up to a maximum of 25 percent is imposed on the amount of tax shown as due on the return. Any fraction of a month counts as a full month.
- A penalty for a *failure to pay* the tax due as shown on the return is imposed in the amount of 0.5 percent per month up to a maximum of 25 percent. Again, any fraction of a month counts as a full month. During any month in which both the failure to file penalty and the failure to pay penalty apply, the failure to file penalty is reduced by the amount of the failure to pay penalty.

EXAMPLE 21

Adam files his tax return 18 days after the due date of the return. Along with the return, he remits a check for $1,000, which is the balance of the tax he owed. Disregarding the interest element, Adam's total penalties are as follows:

Failure to pay penalty (0.5% × $1,000)		$ 5
Plus:		
Failure to file penalty (5% × $1,000)	$50	
Less failure to pay penalty for the same period	(5)	
Failure to file penalty		45
Total penalties		$50

Note that the penalties for one full month are imposed even though Adam was delinquent by only 18 days. Unlike the method used to compute interest, any part of a month is treated as a whole month. ■

[22]Generally, an individual filing a claim for refund should use Form 1040X.

[23]The rates applicable after March 31, 2011, were not available when this text went to press.

- A *negligence* penalty of 20 percent is imposed if any of the underpayment was for intentional disregard of rules and regulations without intent to defraud. The penalty applies to just that portion attributable to the negligence.

EXAMPLE 22

Cindy underpaid her taxes for 2010 in the amount of $20,000, of which $15,000 is attributable to negligence. Cindy's negligence penalty is $3,000 (20% × $15,000). ■

- Various penalties may be imposed in the case of *fraud.* Fraud involves specific intent on the part of the taxpayer to evade a tax. In the case of *civil* fraud, the penalty is 75 percent of the underpayment attributable to fraud. In the case of *criminal* fraud, the penalties can include large fines as well as prison sentences. The difference between civil and criminal fraud is one of degree. Criminal fraud involves the presence of willfulness on the part of the taxpayer. Also, the burden of proof, which is on the IRS in both situations, is more stringent for criminal fraud than for civil fraud. The negligence penalty is not imposed when the fraud penalty applies. For possible fraud situations, refer to Examples 16 and 17.

TAX PRACTICE

If a practitioner is a member of a profession, such as law or public accounting, he or she must abide by certain ethical standards. Furthermore, the Internal Revenue Code imposes penalties upon the preparers of Federal tax returns who violate proscribed acts and procedures.

Ethical Guidelines

LO.6

Evaluate some of the ethical guidelines involved in tax practice.

The American Institute of CPAs has issued numerous pronouncements dealing with CPAs engaged in tax practice. Originally called "Statements on Responsibilities in Tax Practice," these pronouncements were intended to be only *guides* to action. In 2000, however, the AICPA redesignated the pronouncements as "Statements on Standards for Tax Services" and made them *enforceable* as part of its Code of Professional Conduct. They include the provisions summarized below.

- Do not take questionable positions on a client's tax return in the hope that the return will not be selected for audit by the IRS. Any positions taken should be supported by a good-faith belief that they have a realistic possibility of being sustained if challenged. The client should be fully advised of the risks involved and of the penalties that will result if the position taken is not successful.
- A practitioner can use a client's estimates if they are reasonable under the circumstances. If the tax law requires receipts or other verification, the client should be so advised. In no event should an estimate be given the appearance of greater accuracy than is the case. For example, an estimate of $1,000 should not be deducted on a return as $999.
- Every effort should be made to answer questions appearing on tax returns. A question need not be answered if the information requested is not readily available, the answer is voluminous, or the question's meaning is uncertain. The failure to answer a question on a return cannot be justified on the grounds that the answer could prove disadvantageous to the taxpayer.
- Upon learning of an error on a past tax return, advise the client to correct it. Do not, however, inform the IRS of the error. If the error is material and the client refuses to correct it, consider withdrawing from the engagement. This will be necessary if the error has a carryover effect and prevents the current year's tax liability from being determined correctly.

ETHICS & Equity

Let Bygones Be Bygones

Arturo is a new client who wants you to prepare his Federal income tax return for 2011. In the past, he has prepared his own returns but has become overwhelmed by the time and effort involved. In your first meeting with Arturo, you learn that he inherited some foreign rental property several years ago. As of yet, however, he has not reported any transactions regarding the property on his tax returns. He is not averse to including the rent income on his 2011 return but wishes to avoid the hassle of filing amended returns. He prefers to "let bygones be bygones."

Under these circumstances, do you accept the engagement? Why or why not?

Statutory Penalties Imposed on Tax Return Preparers

In addition to ethical constraints, a tax return preparer may be subject to certain statutorily sanctioned penalties, including the following:

- Various penalties involving procedural matters. Examples include failing to furnish the taxpayer with a copy of the return; endorsing a taxpayer's refund check; failing to sign the return as a preparer; failing to furnish one's identification number; and failing to keep copies of returns or maintain a client list.
- Penalty for understatement of a tax liability based on a position that lacks any realistic possibility of being sustained. If the position is not frivolous, the penalty can be avoided by disclosing it on the return.
- Penalty for any willful attempt to understate taxes. This usually results when a preparer disregards or makes no effort to obtain pertinent information from a client.
- Penalty for failure to exercise due diligence in determining eligibility for, or the amount of, an earned income tax credit.

1.7 Understanding the Federal Tax Law

LO.7

Recognize the economic, social, equity, and political considerations that justify various aspects of the tax law.

The Federal tax law is a mosaic of statutory provisions, administrative pronouncements, and court decisions. Anyone who has attempted to work with this body of knowledge would have to admit to its complexity. For the person who has to trudge through a mass of rules to find the solution to a tax problem, it may be of some consolation to know that the law's complexity can generally be explained. Whether sound or not, there is a reason for the formulation of every rule. Knowing these reasons, therefore, is a considerable step toward understanding the Federal tax law.

The Federal tax law has as its *major objective* the raising of revenue. But although the fiscal needs of the government are important, other considerations explain certain portions of the law. Economic, social, equity, and political factors also play a significant role. Added to these factors is the marked impact the IRS and the courts have had and will continue to have on the evolution of Federal tax law. These matters are treated in the remainder of the chapter, and, wherever appropriate, the discussion is referenced to subjects covered later in the text.

REVENUE NEEDS

The foundation of any tax system has to be the raising of revenue to cover the cost of government operations. Ideally, annual outlays should not exceed anticipated revenues, thereby leading to a balanced budget with no resulting deficit.

When enacting tax legislation, a deficit-conscious Congress often has been guided by the concept of **revenue neutrality**. Also referred to as "pay-as-you-go" ("paygo"), the concept means that every new tax law that lowers taxes must include a revenue offset

GLOBAL Tax Issues

Outsourcing of Tax Return Preparation

The use of foreign nationals to carry out certain job assignments for U.S. businesses is an increasingly popular practice. Outsourcing such activities as telemarketing to India, for example, usually produces the same satisfactory result as having the work done in the United States but at a much lower cost.

Outsourcing is also being applied to the preparation of tax returns. Not only can this practice be expected to continue, but it probably will increase in volume. Outsourcing tax return preparation does not violate Federal law and is compatible with accounting ethical guidelines as long as three safeguards are followed: First, the practitioner must make sure that client confidentiality is maintained. Second, the practitioner must verify the accuracy of the work that has been outsourced. Third, the practitioner must inform clients, preferably in writing, when any third-party contractor is used to provide professional services.

Practitioners justify outsourcing as a means of conserving time and effort that can be applied toward more meaningful tax planning on behalf of their clients.

Source: AICPA Ethics Ruling No. 1 (under Rule 301), see **www.aicpa.org/Research/standards/CodeofConduct/Pages/et_391.aspx**.

that makes up for the loss. Revenue neutrality does not mean that any one taxpayer's tax liability will remain the same. Since the circumstances involved will differ, one taxpayer's increased tax liability could be another's tax savings. Although revenue-neutral tax reform does not reduce deficits, at least it does not aggravate the problem.

In addition to making changes in the tax law revenue neutral, several other procedures can be taken to mitigate any revenue loss. When tax reductions are involved, the full impact of the legislation can be phased in over a period of years.[24] Or, as an alternative, the tax reduction can be limited to a period of years. When the period expires, the prior law is reinstated through a **sunset provision**. Most of the major tax bills recently passed by Congress have contained numerous sunset provisions. They provide some semblance of revenue neutrality as some of the bills include tax cuts that were not offset by new sources of revenue. It remains to be seen, however, whether Congress will allow the sunset provisions to take effect and, thereby, kill the tax cuts that were enacted.

Does the recent passage of the American Recovery and Reinvestment Tax Act of 2009 (ARRTA), which contains almost $300 billion in tax relief and negligible revenue offsets, foretell the abandonment of the paygo approach? Probably not. ARRTA represents a drastic attempt to use the tax system as a means of coping with the current economic downturn. As an emergency measure, it should be regarded as an exception to the norm.

ECONOMIC CONSIDERATIONS

Using the tax system in an effort to accomplish economic objectives has become increasingly popular in recent years. Generally, proponents of this goal use tax legislation to amend the Internal Revenue Code in ways designed to help control the economy or encourage certain activities and businesses.

Control of the Economy

Congress has used depreciation write-offs as a means of controlling the economy. Theoretically, shorter asset lives and accelerated methods should encourage additional investment in depreciable property acquired for business use. Conversely,

[24] The same approach can be taken with tax increases. The phaseout and phase-in of limitations on the deductibility of personal exemptions and itemized deductions for certain high-bracket taxpayers (see Chapters 3 and 10) are examples of both of these approaches.

longer asset lives and the required use of the straight-line method of depreciation dampen the tax incentive for capital outlays.

Another approach that utilizes depreciation as a means of controlling capital investment is the amount of write-off allowed upon the acquisition of assets. This is the approach followed by the § 179 election to expense assets (see Chapter 8).

A change in the tax rate structure has a more immediate impact on the economy. With lower tax rates, taxpayers are able to retain additional spendable funds. If lower tax rates are accompanied by the elimination of certain deductions, exclusions, and credits, however, the overall result may not be lower tax liabilities.

Encouragement of Certain Activities

Without passing judgment on the wisdom of any such choices, it is quite clear that the tax law encourages certain types of economic activity or segments of the economy. For example, the favorable treatment allowed research and development expenditures can be explained by the desire to foster technological progress. Under the tax law, such expenditures can be either deducted in the year incurred or capitalized and amortized over a period of 60 months or more. In terms of the timing of the tax savings, these options usually are preferable to capitalizing the cost with a write-off over the estimated useful life of the asset created. If the asset developed has an indefinite useful life, no write-off would be available without the two options allowed by the tax law.

Part of the tax law addresses the energy crisis—in terms of both our reliance on foreign oil and the need to ease the problem of global warming. For example, a tax credit is allowed for electricity produced from renewable sources, such as biomass, solar, and wind. In addition, tax credits are available to those who purchase motor vehicles that operate on alternative (i.e., nonfossil) fuels. Residential energy credits are allowed for home improvements that conserve energy or make its use more efficient (e.g., solar hot water, geothermal heat pumps). Ecological considerations justify a tax provision that permits a more rapid expensing of the costs of installing pollution control facilities. Measures such as these that aid in maintaining a clean air environment and conserving energy resources can also be justified under social considerations.

Is it wise to stimulate U.S. exports of services? Along this line, Congress has deemed it advisable to establish incentives for U.S. citizens who accept employment overseas. Such persons receive generous tax breaks through special treatment of their foreign-source income.

Is saving desirable for the economy? Saving leads to capital formation and thereby makes funds available to finance home construction and industrial expansion. The tax law encourages saving by according preferential treatment to private retirement plans. Not only are contributions to Keogh (H.R. 10) plans and certain IRAs deductible, but income from the contributions accumulates free of tax. As noted below, the encouragement of private-sector pension plans can also be justified under social considerations.

Encouragement of Certain Industries

No one can question the proposition that a sound agricultural base is necessary for a well-balanced national economy. Undoubtedly, this can explain why farmers are accorded special treatment under the Federal tax system. Among the benefits are the election to expense rather than capitalize certain soil and water conservation expenditures and fertilizers and the election to defer the recognition of gain on the receipt of crop insurance proceeds.

To stimulate the manufacturing industry, Congress enacted a domestic production activities deduction. The provision provides a tax benefit in the form of a deduction for profits derived from manufacturing activities conducted within the United States. By restricting the deduction to manufacturing income attributable to wages reportable to the IRS, new U.S. jobs will result, and the outsourcing of labor is discouraged. Thus, the tax system is used to encourage both domestic manufacturing and job growth.

Encouragement of Small Business

At least in the United States, a consensus exists that what is good for small business is good for the economy as a whole. Whether valid or not, this assumption has led to a definite bias in the tax law favoring small business.

In the corporate tax area, several provisions can be explained by the desire to benefit small business. One provision permits the shareholders of a small business corporation to make a special election that generally will avoid the imposition of the corporate income tax.[25] Furthermore, such an election enables the corporation to pass through its operating losses to its shareholders.

SOCIAL CONSIDERATIONS

Some provisions of the Federal tax law, particularly those dealing with the income tax of individuals, can be explained by social considerations. Some notable examples and their rationales include the following:

- Certain benefits provided to employees through accident and health plans financed by employers are nontaxable to employees. Encouraging such plans is considered socially desirable since they provide medical benefits in the event of an employee's illness or injury.
- Most premiums paid by an employer for group term insurance covering the life of the employee are nontaxable to the employee. These arrangements can be justified on social grounds in that they provide funds for the family unit to help it adjust to the loss of wages caused by the employee's death.
- A contribution made by an employer to a qualified pension or profit sharing plan for an employee may receive special treatment. The contribution and any income it generates are not taxed to the employee until the funds are distributed. Such an arrangement also benefits the employer by allowing a tax deduction when the contribution is made to the qualified plan. Private retirement plans are encouraged to supplement the subsistence income level the employee otherwise would have under the Social Security system.[26]
- A deduction is allowed for contributions to qualified charitable organizations. The deduction attempts to shift some of the financial and administrative burden of socially desirable programs from the public (the government) to the private (the citizens) sector.
- A tax credit is allowed for amounts spent to furnish care for certain minor or disabled dependents to enable the taxpayer to seek or maintain gainful employment. Who could deny the social desirability of encouraging taxpayers to provide care for their children while they work?
- Various tax credits, deductions, and exclusions are designed to encourage taxpayers to obtain additional education.[27]
- A tax deduction is not allowed for certain expenditures deemed to be contrary to public policy. This disallowance extends to such items as fines, penalties, illegal kickbacks, bribes to government officials, and gambling losses in excess of gains. Social considerations dictate that the tax law should not encourage these activities by permitting a deduction.

Many other examples could be cited, but the conclusion would be unchanged. Social considerations do explain a significant part of the Federal tax law.

EQUITY CONSIDERATIONS

The concept of equity is relative. Reasonable persons can, and often do, disagree about what is fair or unfair. In the tax area, moreover, equity is most often tied to a particular taxpayer's personal situation. To illustrate, compare the tax positions of

[25]Known as the S election, it is discussed in Chapter 22.

[26]The same rationale explains the availability of similar arrangements for self-employed persons (the H.R. 10, or Keogh, plan).

[27]These provisions can also be justified under the category of economic considerations. No one can take issue with the conclusion that a better educated workforce carries a positive economic impact.

those who rent their personal residences with those who own their homes. Renters receive no Federal income tax benefit from the rent they pay. For homeowners, however, a large portion of the house payments they make may qualify for the Federal interest and property tax deductions. Although renters may have difficulty understanding this difference in tax treatment, the encouragement of home ownership can be justified on both economic and social grounds.

In the same vein, compare the tax treatment of a corporation with that of a partnership. Although the two businesses may be of equal size, similarly situated, and competitors in the production of goods or services, they are not treated comparably under the tax law. The corporation is subject to a separate Federal income tax; the partnership is not. Whether the differences in tax treatment can be justified logically in terms of equity is beside the point. The point is that the tax law can and does make a distinction between these business forms.

Equity, then, is not what appears fair or unfair to any one taxpayer or group of taxpayers. Some recognition of equity does exist, however, and explains part of the law. The concept of equity appears in tax provisions that alleviate the effect of multiple taxation and postpone the recognition of gain when the taxpayer lacks the ability or wherewithal to pay the tax. Provisions that mitigate the effect of the application of the annual accounting period concept and help taxpayers cope with the eroding results of inflation also reflect equity considerations.

Alleviating the Effect of Multiple Taxation

The income earned by a taxpayer may be subject to taxes imposed by different taxing authorities. If, for example, the taxpayer is a resident of New York City, income might generate Federal, state of New York, and city of New York income taxes. To compensate for this apparent inequity, the Federal tax law allows a taxpayer to claim a deduction for state and local income taxes. The deduction does not, however, neutralize the effect of multiple taxation, since the benefit derived depends on the taxpayer's Federal income tax rate. Only a tax credit, rather than a deduction, would eliminate the effects of multiple taxation on the same income.

Equity considerations can explain the Federal tax treatment of certain income from foreign sources. Since double taxation results when the same income is subject to both foreign and U.S. income taxes, the tax law permits the taxpayer to choose between a credit and a deduction for the foreign taxes paid.

ETHICS & Equity

TREATING EVERYONE THE SAME

As noted in the text, a Federal income tax deduction for state and local income taxes paid is allowed to mitigate the effect of having the same income taxed more than once. But what if a state does not impose an income tax and, instead, derives comparable amounts of revenue from a general sales tax? Is it fair to deny a deduction to residents of this state just because the state imposes a tax on sales rather than on income?

Recent legislation resolved this purported inequity by allowing a Federal income tax deduction for state and local general sales taxes. However, a taxpayer who is subject to both state income and sales taxes must make a choice. One or the other, but not both, can be claimed as a deduction. Should the taxpayer have to choose?

The Wherewithal to Pay Concept

The **wherewithal to pay** concept recognizes the inequity of taxing a transaction when the taxpayer lacks the means with which to pay the tax. It is particularly suited to situations in which the taxpayer's economic position has not changed significantly as a result of the transaction.

An illustration of the wherewithal to pay concept is the provision of the tax law dealing with the treatment of gain resulting from an involuntary conversion.

An involuntary conversion occurs when property is destroyed by a casualty or taken by a public authority through condemnation. If gain results from the conversion, it need not be recognized if the taxpayer replaces the property within a specified period of time. The replacement property must be similar or related in service or use to that involuntarily converted.

EXAMPLE 23

Some of the pasture land belonging to Ron, a rancher, is condemned by the state for use as a game preserve. The condemned pasture land cost Ron $120,000, but the state pays him $150,000 (its fair market value). Shortly thereafter, Ron buys more pasture land for $150,000. ■

In Example 23, Ron has a realized gain of $30,000 [$150,000 (condemnation award) – $120,000 (cost of land)]. It would be inequitable to force Ron to pay a tax on this gain for two reasons. First, without disposing of the property acquired (the new land), Ron would be hard-pressed to pay the tax. Second, his economic position has not changed.

A warning is in order regarding the application of the wherewithal to pay concept. If the taxpayer's economic position changes in any way, tax consequences may result.

EXAMPLE 24

Assume the same facts as in Example 23, except that Ron reinvests only $140,000 of the award in new pasture land. Now, Ron has a taxable gain of $10,000. Instead of ending up with only replacement property, Ron now has $10,000 in cash. ■

Mitigating the Effect of the Annual Accounting Period Concept

For purposes of effective administration of the tax law, all taxpayers must report to and settle with the Federal government at periodic intervals. Otherwise, taxpayers would remain uncertain as to their tax liabilities, and the government would have difficulty judging revenues and budgeting expenditures. The period selected for final settlement of most tax liabilities, in any event an arbitrary determination, is one year. At the close of each year, therefore, a taxpayer's position becomes complete for that particular year. Referred to as the annual accounting period concept, its effect is to divide each taxpayer's life, for tax purposes, into equal annual intervals.

The finality of the annual accounting period concept could lead to dissimilar tax treatment for taxpayers who are, from a long-range standpoint, in the same economic position.

EXAMPLE 25

José and Alicia, both sole proprietors, have experienced the following results during the past three years:

	Profit (or Loss)	
Year	**José**	**Alicia**
2009	$50,000	$150,000
2010	60,000	60,000
2011	60,000	(40,000)

Although José and Alicia have the same profit of $170,000 over the period from 2009 to 2011, the finality of the annual accounting period concept places Alicia at a definite disadvantage for tax purposes. The net operating loss procedure offers Alicia some relief by allowing her to apply some or all of her 2011 loss to the earlier profitable years (in this case, 2009). Thus, with a net operating loss carryback, Alicia is in a position to obtain a refund for some of the taxes she paid on the $150,000 profit reported for 2009. ■

The same reasoning used to support the deduction of net operating losses can explain the special treatment the tax law accords to excess capital losses and excess charitable contributions.[28] Carryback and carryover procedures help mitigate the effect of limiting a loss or a deduction to the accounting period in which it was realized. With such procedures, a taxpayer may be able to salvage a loss or a deduction that might otherwise be wasted.

The installment method of recognizing gain on the sale of property allows a taxpayer to spread tax consequences over the payout period.[29] The harsh effect of taxing all the gain in the year of sale is thereby avoided. The installment method can also be explained by the wherewithal to pay concept since recognition of gain is tied to the collection of the installment notes received from the sale of the property. Tax consequences, then, tend to correspond to the seller's ability to pay the tax.

Coping with Inflation

Because of the progressive nature of the income tax, a wage adjustment to compensate for inflation can increase the income tax bracket of the recipient. Known as *bracket creep,* its overall impact is an erosion of purchasing power. Congress recognized this problem and began to adjust various income tax components, such as tax brackets, standard deduction amounts, and personal and dependency exemptions, through an indexation procedure. Indexation is based upon the rise in the consumer price index over the prior year.

POLITICAL CONSIDERATIONS

A large segment of the Federal tax law is made up of statutory provisions. Since these statutes are enacted by Congress, is it any surprise that political considerations influence tax law? For purposes of discussion, the effect of political considerations on the tax law is divided into the following topics: special interest legislation, political expediency situations, and state and local government influences.

Special Interest Legislation

There is no doubt that certain provisions of the tax law can largely be explained by the political influence some pressure groups have had on Congress. Is there any other realistic reason that, for example, prepaid subscription and dues income is not taxed until earned while prepaid rents are taxed to the landlord in the year received?

The American Jobs Creation Act of 2004 included several good examples of special interest legislation. One provision, sponsored by former Senator Zell Miller (D–Ga.), suspended the import duties on ceiling fans. The nation's largest seller of ceiling fans is Home Depot, which is based in Atlanta, Georgia. Another provision, sponsored by then House Speaker Dennis Hastert (R–Ill.), reduced the excise taxes on fishing tackle boxes. Representative Hastert's district includes Plano Molding, a major manufacturer of tackle boxes. The justification for this change was that it placed tackle boxes on a more level playing field with toolboxes (which are not subject to tax). Allegedly, fishermen had been buying and converting toolboxes to avoid the excise tax!

Special interest legislation is not necessarily to be condemned if it can be justified on economic, social, or some other utilitarian grounds. In most cases, however, it is objectionable in that it adds further complexity to an already cluttered tax law. At any rate, it is an inevitable product of our political system.

---

[28]The tax treatment of these items is discussed in Chapters 7, 10, and 14.

[29]Under the installment method, each payment received by the seller represents both a recovery of capital (the nontaxable portion) and profit from the sale (the taxable portion). The tax rules governing the installment method are discussed in Chapter 16.

Political Expediency Situations

Various tax reform proposals rise and fall in favor with the shifting moods of the American public. That Congress is sensitive to popular feeling is an accepted fact. Therefore, certain provisions of the tax law can be explained by the political climate at the time they were enacted.

Measures that deter more affluent taxpayers from obtaining so-called preferential tax treatment have always had popular appeal and, consequently, the support of Congress. A direct approach bars the benefit completely and explains such provisions as the imputed interest rules and the limitations on the deductibility of interest on investment indebtedness. More subtle are provisions that phase out tax breaks as income rises. Because taxpayers may be unaware of what is causing the shift to higher marginal tax rates, these phaseouts are often called "stealth taxes." The tax law contains several dozen such phaseout provisions. Examples include the earned income credit, child tax credit, lifetime learning credit, and the credit for first-time home purchases. At least for the immediate future, the use of these stealth taxes can be expected to increase.

Other changes explained at least partially by political expediency include the lowering of individual income tax rates, the increase in the personal and dependency exemptions, and the increase in the amount of the earned income credit.

State and Local Government Influences

Political considerations have played a major role in the nontaxability of interest received on state and local obligations. In view of the furor that has been raised by state and local political figures every time any modification of this tax provision has been proposed, one might well regard it as next to sacred.

Somewhat less apparent has been the influence state law has had in shaping our present Federal tax law. Such was the case with community property systems. The nine states with community property systems are Louisiana, Texas, New Mexico, Arizona, California, Washington, Idaho, Nevada, and Wisconsin. The rest of the states are classified as common law jurisdictions.[30] The difference between common law and community property systems centers around the property rights possessed by married persons. In a common law system, each spouse owns whatever he or she earns. Under a community property system, one-half of the earnings of each spouse is considered owned by the other spouse.

EXAMPLE 26

Al and Fran are husband and wife, and their only income is the $80,000 annual salary Al receives. If they live in New Jersey (a common law state), the $80,000 salary belongs to Al. If, however, they live in Arizona (a community property state), the $80,000 is divided equally, in terms of ownership, between Al and Fran. ■

At one time, the tax position of the residents of community property states was so advantageous that many common law states adopted community property systems. Needless to say, the political pressure placed on Congress to correct the disparity in tax treatment was considerable. To a large extent this was accomplished in the Revenue Act of 1948, which extended many of the community property tax advantages to residents of common law jurisdictions.

The major advantage extended was the provision allowing married taxpayers to file joint returns and compute their tax liability as if the income had been earned one-half by each spouse. This result is automatic in a community property state, since half of the income earned by one spouse belongs to the other spouse. The

[30] In Alaska, spouses can choose to have the community property rules apply. Otherwise, property rights are determined under common law rules.

income-splitting benefits of a joint return are now incorporated as part of the tax rates applicable to married taxpayers. See Chapter 3.

LO.8

Describe the role played by the IRS and the courts in the evolution of the Federal tax system.

INFLUENCE OF THE INTERNAL REVENUE SERVICE

The influence of the IRS is apparent in many areas beyond its role in issuing the administrative pronouncements that make up a considerable portion of our tax law. In its capacity as the protector of the national revenue, the IRS has been instrumental in securing the passage of much legislation designed to curtail the most flagrant tax avoidance practices (to close *tax loopholes*). As the administrator of the tax law, the IRS has sought and obtained legislation to make its job easier (to attain administrative feasibility).

The IRS as Protector of the Revenue

Innumerable examples can be given of provisions in the tax law that stem from the direct influence of the IRS. Usually, such provisions are intended to prevent a loophole from being used to avoid the tax consequences intended by Congress. Working within the letter of existing law, ingenious taxpayers and their advisers devise techniques that accomplish indirectly what cannot be accomplished directly. As a consequence, legislation is enacted to close the loopholes that taxpayers have located and exploited. Some tax law can be explained in this fashion and is discussed in the chapters to follow.

In addition, the IRS has secured from Congress legislation of a more general nature that enables it to make adjustments based on the substance, rather than the formal construction, of what a taxpayer has done. For example, one such provision permits the IRS to make adjustments to a taxpayer's method of accounting when the method used by the taxpayer does not clearly reflect income.[31]

EXAMPLE 27

Tina, a cash basis taxpayer, owns and operates a pharmacy. All drugs and other items acquired for resale, such as cosmetics, are charged to the purchases account and written off (deducted) for tax purposes in the year of acquisition. As this procedure does not clearly reflect income, it would be appropriate for the IRS to require that Tina establish and maintain an ending inventory account. ■

Administrative Feasibility

Some tax law is justified on the grounds that it simplifies the task of the IRS in collecting the revenue and administering the law. With regard to collecting the revenue, the IRS long ago realized the importance of placing taxpayers on a pay-as-you-go basis. Elaborate withholding procedures apply to wages, while the tax on other types of income may be paid at periodic intervals throughout the year. The IRS has been instrumental in convincing the courts that accrual basis taxpayers should in most cases pay taxes on prepaid income in the year received and not when earned. The approach may be contrary to generally accepted accounting principles, but it is consistent with the wherewithal to pay concept.

Of considerable aid to the IRS in collecting revenue are the numerous provisions that impose interest and penalties on taxpayers for noncompliance with the tax law. Provisions such as the penalties for failure to pay a tax or to file a return that is due, the negligence penalty for intentional disregard of rules and regulations, and various penalties for civil and criminal fraud serve as deterrents to taxpayer noncompliance.

One of the keys to an effective administration of our tax system is the audit process conducted by the IRS. To carry out this function, the IRS is aided by provisions that reduce the chance of taxpayer error or manipulation and therefore simplify the audit effort that is necessary. An increase in the amount of the standard deduction, for example, reduces the number of individual taxpayers who will choose

[31]See Chapter 16.

the alternative of itemizing their personal deductions.[32] With fewer deductions to check, the audit function is simplified.[33]

INFLUENCE OF THE COURTS

In addition to interpreting statutory provisions and the administrative pronouncements issued by the IRS, the Federal courts have influenced tax law in two other respects.[34] First, the courts have formulated certain judicial concepts that serve as guides in the application of various tax provisions. Second, certain key decisions have led to changes in the Internal Revenue Code.

Judicial Concepts Relating to Tax

A leading tax concept developed by the courts deals with the interpretation of statutory tax provisions that operate to benefit taxpayers. The courts have established the rule that these relief provisions are to be narrowly construed against taxpayers if there is any doubt about their application.

Important in this area is the *arm's length* concept. Particularly in dealings between related parties, transactions may be tested by looking to whether the taxpayers acted in an arm's length manner. The question to be asked is: Would unrelated parties have handled the transaction in the same way?

EXAMPLE 28

Rex, the sole shareholder of Silver Corporation, leases property to the corporation for a yearly rent of $60,000. To test whether the corporation should be allowed a rent deduction for this amount, the IRS and the courts will apply the arm's length concept. Would Silver Corporation have paid $60,000 a year in rent if it had leased the same property from an unrelated party (rather than from Rex)? Suppose it is determined that an unrelated third party would have paid an annual rent for the property of only $50,000. Under these circumstances, Silver Corporation will be allowed a deduction of only $50,000. The other $10,000 it paid for the use of the property represents a nondeductible dividend. Accordingly, Rex will be treated as having received rent income of $50,000 and dividend income of $10,000. ■

Judicial Influence on Statutory Provisions

Some court decisions have been of such consequence that Congress has incorporated them into statutory tax law. For example, many years ago the courts found that stock dividends distributed to the shareholders of a corporation were not taxable as income. This result was largely accepted by Congress, and a provision in the tax statutes now covers the issue.

On occasion, however, Congress has reacted negatively to judicial interpretations of the tax law.

EXAMPLE 29

Nora leases unimproved real estate to Wade for 20 years. At a cost of $400,000, Wade erects a building on the land. The building is worth $150,000 when the lease terminates and Nora takes possession of the property. Does Nora have any income either when the improvements are made or when the lease terminates? In a landmark decision, a court held that Nora must recognize income of $150,000 upon the termination of the lease. ■

Congress felt that the result reached in Example 29 was inequitable in that it was not consistent with the wherewithal to pay concept. Consequently, the tax law was amended to provide that a landlord does not recognize any income either when the improvements are made (unless made in lieu of rent) or when the lease terminates.

---

[32] For a discussion of the standard deduction, see Chapter 3.

[33] The same justification was given by the IRS when it proposed to Congress the $100 limitation on personal casualty and theft losses. Imposition of the limitation eliminated many casualty and theft loss deductions and, as a consequence, saved the IRS considerable audit time. Later legislation, in addition to retaining the $100 feature, limits deductible losses to those in excess of 10% of a taxpayer's adjusted gross income. See Chapter 7.

[34] A great deal of case law is devoted to ascertaining congressional intent. The courts, in effect, ask: What did Congress have in mind when it enacted a particular tax provision?

1.8 Summary

In addition to its necessary revenue-raising objective, the Federal tax law has developed in response to several other factors:

- *Economic considerations.* The emphasis here is on tax provisions that help regulate the economy and encourage certain activities and types of businesses.
- *Social considerations.* Some tax provisions are designed to encourage (or discourage) certain socially desirable (or undesirable) practices.
- *Equity considerations.* Of principal concern in this area are tax provisions that alleviate the effect of multiple taxation, recognize the wherewithal to pay concept, mitigate the effect of the annual accounting period concept, and recognize the eroding effect of inflation.
- *Political considerations.* Of significance in this regard are tax provisions that represent special interest legislation, reflect political expediency, and exhibit the effect of state and local law.
- *Influence of the IRS.* Many tax provisions are intended to aid the IRS in the collection of revenue and the administration of the tax law.
- *Influence of the courts.* Court decisions have established a body of judicial concepts relating to tax law and have, on occasion, led Congress to enact statutory provisions to either clarify or negate their effect.

These factors explain various tax provisions and thereby help in understanding why the tax law developed to its present state. The next step involves learning to work with the tax law, which is the subject of Chapter 2.

REFOCUS ON THE BIG PICTURE

FAMILY AND TAXES—A TYPICAL YEAR

The explanation given for the difference in the ad valorem taxes—the Carters' increase and the Walkers' decrease—seems reasonable (see Example 4). It is not likely that the Carters' increase was due to a *general* upward assessment in valuation, as the Walkers' taxes on their residence (located nearby) dropped. More business use of the Carters' residence (presuming Travis conducts his consulting practice from his home) might be responsible for the increase, but capital improvements appear to be a more likely cause.

The imposition of the use tax when Travis registered the new automobile illustrates one of the means by which a state can preclude the avoidance of its sales tax (see Example 5).

When gifts between family members are material in amount (e.g., an RV) and exceed the annual exclusion, a gift tax return needs to be filed (see Example 11). Even though no gift tax may be due because of the availability of the unified transfer tax credit, the filing of a return starts the running of the statute of limitations.

The imposition of the "jock tax" on nonathletes is unusual but not improper. The Carters must recognize that some of their income is subject to income taxes in two states and take advantage of whatever relief is available to mitigate the result (see Example 12).

Employment within and by the family group (e.g., children, other relatives, domestics) has become a priority item in the enforcement of Social Security tax and income tax withholdings. Thus, the Carters need to be aware of the need to cover their son, Martin (see Example 13).

Because of the double audit (i.e., both state and Federal) and the deficiency assessed, the Carters need to make sure that future returns do not contain similar errors (see Example 19). As the text suggests, taxpayers with prior deficiencies are among those whose returns may be selected for audit.

KEY TERMS

Ad valorem taxes, 1–7
Correspondence audit, 1–22
Employment taxes, 1–17
Estate tax, 1–12
Excise taxes, 1–9
FICA tax, 1–17
Field audit, 1–22
Financial Accounting Standards Board (FASB), 1–16
Flat tax, 1–20
Franchise tax, 1–19
FUTA tax, 1–18
Generally Accepted Accounting Principles (GAAP), 1–16
Gift tax, 1–13
Inheritance tax, 1–12
International Accounting Standards Board (IASB), 1–16
International Financial Reporting Standards (IFRS), 1–16
National sales tax, 1–20
Occupational fees, 1–19
Office audit, 1–22
Personalty, 1–8
Realty, 1–7
Revenue neutrality, 1–26
Sales tax, 1–10
Severance taxes, 1–12
Statute of limitations, 1–23
Sunset provision, 1–27
Use tax, 1–11
Value added tax (VAT), 1–20
Wherewithal to pay, 1–30

DISCUSSION QUESTIONS

1. **LO.1** Marvin is the executor and sole heir of his aunt's estate. The estate includes her furnished home, which Marvin is considering converting to rental property to generate additional cash flow. What are some of the tax problems that Marvin may confront? **ISSUE ID**

2. **LO.2** The effect of the Sixteenth Amendment to the U.S. Constitution was to validate the Federal income tax imposed on individuals. Do you agree?

3. **LO.2** World War II converted the Federal income tax into a *mass tax*. Explain.

4. **LO.2** How does the pay-as-you-go procedure apply to wage earners? To persons who have income from other than wages?

5. **LO.3** In terms of Adam Smith's canon of *economy*, how does the Federal income tax fare?

6. **LO.3** Using Adam Smith's canon of *certainty*, evaluate the Federal income tax.

7. **LO.3** Distinguish between taxes that are *proportional* and those that are *progressive*.

8. **LO.4** Several years ago, Ethan purchased the former parsonage of St. James Church to use as a personal residence. To date, Ethan has not received any ad valorem property tax bills from either the city or the county tax authorities. **ISSUE ID**
   a. What is a reasonable explanation for this oversight?
   b. What should Ethan do?

9. **LO.4** The Adams Independent School District wants to sell a parcel of unimproved land that it does not need. Its three best offers are as follows: from the State Department of Public Safety (DPS), $2.3 million; from the Second Baptist Church, $2.2 million; and from Baker Motors, $2.1 million. DPS would use the property for a new state highway patrol barracks; Second Baptist would start a church school; and Baker would open a car dealership. If you are the financial adviser for the school district, which offer would you prefer? Why? **ISSUE ID**

10. **LO.4** The commissioners for Colby County are actively negotiating with Eagle Industries regarding the location of a new manufacturing facility in the county. As Eagle is considering several other sites, a "generous tax holiday" may be needed to influence its choice. The local school district is opposed to any "generous tax holiday."
    a. In terms of a "generous tax holiday," what might the proposal entail?
    b. Why should the school district be opposed?

11. **LO.4** The Williams family made significant improvements to their personal residence and then converted it to a bed and breakfast facility. They were surprised when the property taxes on the residence were raised twice. Explain what probably happened.

12. **LO.4** Franklin County is in dire financial straits and is considering a number of sources for additional revenue. Evaluate the following possibilities in terms of anticipated taxpayer compliance:
    a. A property tax on business inventories.
    b. A tax on intangibles (i.e., stocks and bonds) held as investments.
    c. A property tax on boats used for recreational purposes.

13. **LO.4** Many excise taxes are imposed by *both* the Federal and state governments. Give several examples of this practice.

14. **LO.4** After his first business trip to a major city, Herman is alarmed when he reviews his credit card receipts. Both the hotel bill and the car rental charge are in excess of the price he was quoted. Was Herman overcharged, or is there an explanation for the excess amounts?

15. **LO.4** What is the difference between an excise tax and a general sales tax?
    a. Do all states impose a general sales tax?
    b. Does the Federal government impose a general sales tax?

16. **LO.4** Eileen, a resident of Wyoming, goes to Montana to purchase her new automobile. She does this because Wyoming imposes a sales tax while Montana does not. Has Eileen successfully avoided the Wyoming sales tax? Explain.

ISSUE ID

17. **LO.4** Velma lives in Wilson County, which is adjacent to Grimes County. Although the retail stores in both counties are comparable, Velma drives an extra 10 miles to do all of her shopping in Grimes County. Why might she do this?

ISSUE ID

18. **LO.4** During a social event, Muriel and Earl are discussing the home computer each recently purchased. Although the computers are identical makes and models, Muriel is surprised to learn that she paid a sales tax, while Earl did not. Comment as to why this could happen.

19. **LO.4** Distinguish between an estate tax and an inheritance tax.
    a. Do some states impose both? Neither?
    b. Which, if either, does the Federal government impose?

ISSUE ID

20. **LO.4** Jake (age 72) and Jessica (age 28) were recently married. To avoid any transfer taxes, Jake has promised to leave Jessica all of his wealth when he dies. Is Jake under some misconception about the operation of the Federal gift and estate taxes? Explain.

21. **LO.4** Address the following issues:
    a. What is the purpose of the unified transfer tax credit?
    b. Is the same amount available for both the Federal gift tax and the estate tax? Explain.
    c. Does the use of the credit for a gift affect the amount of credit available for the estate tax? Explain.

22. **LO.4** Miles and Trudy are husband and wife and have six married children and ten minor grandchildren. For tax year 2011, what is the maximum amount they can give to the family (including the sons- and daughters-in-law) without using any of their unified transfer tax credit?

23. **LO.4** In arriving at taxable income, how does the Federal income tax imposed on corporations differ from that imposed on individuals?

24. **LO.4** With reference to state income taxes, what is meant by the "piggyback" approach? "Decoupling" from this approach?

ISSUE ID

25. **LO.4** Mike Barr was an outstanding football player in college and expects to be drafted by the NFL in the first few rounds. Mike has let it be known that he would prefer to sign with a club located in Florida, Texas, or Washington. Mike sees no reason why he should have to pay state income tax on his player's salary! Is Mike under any delusions? Explain.

ISSUE ID

26. **LO.4, 5** A question on a state income tax return asks the taxpayer if he or she made any out-of-state Internet or mail-order catalog purchases during the year. The question requires a yes or no answer, and if the taxpayer answers yes, the amount of such purchases is to be listed.
    a. Does such an inquiry have any relevance to the state income tax? If not, why is it being asked?

b. Your client, Harriet, wants to leave the question unanswered. As the preparer of her return, how do you respond?

27. **LO.4** As to those states that impose an income tax on individuals, comment on the following:
    a. Use of withholding procedures.
    b. Treatment of Federal income taxes paid.
    c. Due date for filing.
    d. Credit for income taxes paid to other states.

28. **LO.4** Many state income tax returns contain checkoff boxes that allow taxpayers to make donations to a multitude of local charitable causes. On what grounds has this procedure been criticized?

29. **LO.4** Many states have occasionally adopted amnesty programs that allow taxpayers to pay back taxes with reduced penalties.
    a. Besides the revenue generated, how are these programs advantageous?
    b. Could an amnesty program be used by a state that does not levy an income tax?
    c. Does the IRS utilize this approach?

30. **LO.4** Contrast FICA and FUTA as to the following:
    a. Purpose of the tax.
    b. Upon whom imposed.
    c. Governmental administration of the tax.
    d. Reduction of tax based on a merit rating system.

31. **LO.4** One of the tax advantages of hiring family members to work in your business is that FICA taxes are avoided. Do you agree with this statement? Explain.

32. **LO.4** Describe the nature and purpose of the following taxes:
    a. Severance taxes.
    b. Franchise taxes.
    c. Occupational fees.

33. **LO.4** Regarding the value added tax (VAT), comment on the following:
    a. Popularity of this type of tax.
    b. Nature of the tax.

34. **LO.4** Both a value added tax (VAT) and a national sales tax have been criticized as being *regressive* in their effect.
    a. Explain.
    b. How could this shortcoming be remedied in the case of a national sales tax?

35. **LO.4, 5** Serena operates a lawn maintenance service in Southern California. As most of her employees are itinerant, they are paid on a day-to-day basis. Because of cash-flow problems, Serena requires her customers to pay cash for the services she provides. **ISSUE ID**
    a. What are some of the tax problems Serena might have?
    b. Assess Serena's chances of audit by the IRS.

36. **LO.5** Assess the probability of an audit in each of the following independent situations:
    a. As a result of a jury trial, Linda was awarded $3.5 million because of job discrimination. The award included $3 million for punitive damages.
    b. Mel operates a combination check-cashing service and pawnshop.
    c. Cindy has annual AGI in excess of $500,000.
    d. Pierre is the maître d' at a five-star restaurant and also manages the valet parking concession.
    e. Giselle is a cocktail waitress at an upscale night club. She has been audited several times in past years.
    f. Marcus was recently assessed a large *state* income tax deficiency by the state of California for his utilization of an abusive tax shelter.
    g. Guy, a professional gambler, recently broke up with his companion of 10 years and married her teenage daughter.
    h. Rick's only source of income is the wages he earns working on the assembly line of a lawn mower manufacturer.

37. **LO.5** With regard to the IRS audit process, comment on the following:
    a. Availability of an "informant's fee."

b. DIF score.
c. The audit is resolved by mail.
d. The audit is conducted at the office of the IRS.
e. A "no change" RAR results.
f. Special agent joins the audit team.

38. **LO.5** Aldo has just been audited by the IRS. He does not agree with the agent's findings but feels he has only two choices: pay the proposed deficiency or resort to the courts. Do you agree with Aldo's conclusion? Why or why not?

39. **LO.5** What purpose is served by a statute of limitations? How is it relevant in the case of tax controversies?

40. **LO.5** Regarding the statute of limitations on additional assessments of tax by the IRS, determine the applicable period in each of the following situations. Assume a calendar year individual with no fraud or substantial omission involved.
    a. The income tax return for 2010 was filed on February 23, 2011.
    b. The income tax return for 2010 was filed on June 24, 2011.
    c. The income tax return for 2010 was prepared on April 7, 2011, but was never filed. Through some misunderstanding between the preparer and the taxpayer, each expected the other to file the return.
    d. The income tax return for 2010 was never filed because the taxpayer thought no additional tax was due.

41. **LO.5** Brianna, a calendar year taxpayer, files her income tax return for 2010 on February 4, 2011. Although she makes repeated inquiries, she does not receive her refund from the IRS until May 27, 2011. Is Brianna entitled to interest on the refund? Explain.

42. **LO.5, 6** On a Federal income tax return filed five years ago, Andy inadvertently omitted a large amount of gross income.
    a. Andy seeks your advice as to whether the IRS is barred from assessing additional income tax in the event he is audited. What is your advice?
    b. Would your advice differ if you are the person who prepared the return in question? Explain.
    c. Suppose Andy asks you to prepare his current year's return. Would you do so? Explain.

43. **LO.5** Lori files her income tax return 45 days after the due date of the return without obtaining an extension from the IRS. Along with the return, she remits a check for $40,000, which is the balance of the tax she owes. Disregarding the interest element, what are Irene's penalties for failure to file and for failure to pay?

ISSUE ID

44. **LO.5** For tax year 2008, the IRS assesses a deficiency against Rhett for $500,000. Disregarding the interest component, what is Rhett's penalty if the deficiency is attributable to:
    a. Negligence?
    b. Fraud?

45. **LO.5, 6** In March 2011, Jim asks you to prepare his Federal income tax returns for tax years 2008, 2009, and 2010. In discussing this matter with him, you discover that he also has not filed for tax year 2007. When you mention this fact, Jim tells you that the statute of limitations precludes the IRS from taking any action as to this year.
    a. Is Jim correct about the application of the statute of limitations? Why?
    b. If Jim refuses to file for 2007, should you prepare returns for 2008 through 2010?

46. **LO.5, 6** The Benson CPA firm is considering utilizing an offshore service provider to prepare many of its tax returns. In this regard, what are the ethical considerations that must be taken into account?

47. **LO.7** In terms of tax reform policy, what do the following mean?
    a. Revenue neutrality.
    b. Pay-as-you-go or "paygo."
    c. Sunset provision.

48. **LO.7** Some tax rules can be justified on multiple grounds (e.g., economic, social, etc.). In this connection, comment on the possible justification for the rules governing the following:

a. Energy conservation and pollution control.
b. Pension plans.
c. Education.
d. Home ownership.

49. **LO.7** Discuss the probable justification for each of the following provisions of the tax law:
   a. The § 179 election to expense certain business assets upon their acquisition.
   b. Favorable treatment accorded to research and development expenditures.
   c. A deduction allowed for income resulting from U.S. production (manufacturing) activities.
   d. The deduction allowed for contributions to qualified charitable organizations.
   e. An election that allows certain corporations to avoid the corporate income tax and pass losses through to their shareholders.
   f. A tax credit for amounts spent to furnish care for minor children while the parent works.

50. **LO.7** The state highway department condemns some of Chad's grazing land. The land cost Chad $20,000, and the condemnation award is the land's fair market value of $100,000. Shortly after the condemnation, Chad buys replacement grazing land. What is his recognized gain if the replacement land costs:
   a. $70,000?
   b. $110,000?
   c. $20,000?
   d. What, if any, is the justification for deferring the recognition of gain on an involuntary conversion?

51. **LO.7, 8** Discuss the probable justification for each of the following aspects of the tax law:
   a. Net operating losses of a current year can be carried back to profitable years.
   b. A taxpayer that sells property on an installment basis can recognize gain on the sale over the period the payments are received.
   c. Every year the tax brackets and the amounts of the standard deduction and dependency exemptions are adjusted by the IRS.
   d. Certain preferential tax treatment is phased out for more affluent taxpayers.
   e. The exclusion from Federal tax of certain interest income from state and local bonds.
   f. Prepaid income is taxed to the recipient in the year received and not in the year it is earned.
   g. The deduction for personal casualty losses is subject to dollar and percentage limitations.

52. **LO.8** A mother sells a valuable collection of antiques to her daughter for $1,000. What judicial concept might the IRS invoke to question this transaction?

53. **LO.8** Edward leases real estate to Janet for a period of 20 years. Janet makes capital improvements to the property. When the lease expires, Edward reclaims the property, including the improvements made by Janet.
   a. Under current law, at what point does Edward recognize income as a result of Janet's improvements?
   b. Has the law in part (a) always been the rule?
   c. What is the justification, if any, for the current rule?

CHAPTER 2

Working with the Tax Law

LEARNING OBJECTIVES

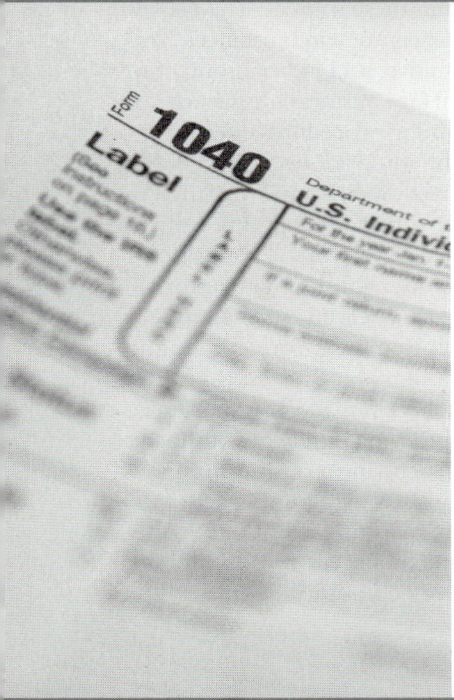

After completing Chapter 2, you should be able to:

LO.1 Distinguish between the statutory, administrative, and judicial sources of the tax law and understand the purpose of each source.

LO.2 Locate and work with the appropriate tax law sources.

LO.3 Have an awareness of tax research tools.

LO.4 Understand the tax research process.

LO.5 Communicate the results of the tax research process in a client letter and a tax file memorandum.

LO.6 Apply tax research techniques and planning procedures.

LO.7 Be aware of taxation on the CPA examination.

OUTLINE

For the latest in changes to tax legislation, visit **www.cengage.com/taxation/swft.**

2.1 Tax Sources

LO.1

Distinguish between the statutory, administrative, and judicial sources of the tax law and understand the purpose of each source.

Understanding taxation requires a mastery of the sources of the *rules of tax law*. These sources include not only legislative provisions in the form of the Internal Revenue Code, but also congressional Committee Reports, Treasury Department Regulations, other Treasury Department pronouncements, and court decisions. Thus, the *primary sources* of tax information include pronouncements from all three branches of government: legislative, executive, and judicial.

In addition to being able to locate and interpret the sources of the tax law, a tax professional must understand the relative weight of authority within these sources. The tax law is of little significance, however, until it is applied to a set of facts and circumstances. This chapter, therefore, both introduces the statutory, administrative, and judicial sources of the tax law *and* explains how the law is applied to individual and business transactions. It also explains how to apply research techniques and use planning procedures effectively.

A large part of tax research focuses on determining the intent of Congress. While Congress often claims simplicity as one of its goals, a cursory examination of the tax law indicates that it has not been very successful. Faced with a 48-page tax return, author James Michener said, "It is unimaginable in that I graduated from one of America's better colleges, yet I am totally incapable of understanding tax returns." David Brinkley, the former television news commentator, observed that "settling a dispute is difficult when our tax regulations are all written in a foreign tongue whose language flows like damp sludge leaking from a sanitary landfill."

Frequently, uncertainty in the tax law causes disputes between the Internal Revenue Service (IRS) and taxpayers. Due to these *gray areas* and the complexity of the tax law, a taxpayer may have more than one alternative for structuring a business transaction. In structuring business transactions and engaging in other tax planning activities, the tax adviser must be cognizant that the objective of tax planning is not necessarily to minimize the tax liability. Instead a taxpayer should maximize his or her after-tax return, which may include maximizing nontax as well as noneconomic benefits.

STATUTORY SOURCES OF THE TAX LAW

Origin of the Internal Revenue Code

Before 1939, the statutory provisions relating to taxation were contained in the individual revenue acts enacted by Congress. The inconvenience and confusion that resulted from dealing with many separate acts led Congress to codify all of the Federal tax laws. Known as the Internal Revenue Code of 1939, the codification arranged all Federal tax provisions in a logical sequence and placed them in a separate part of the Federal statutes. A further rearrangement took place in 1954 and resulted in the Internal Revenue Code of 1954, which continued in effect until it was replaced by the Internal Revenue Code of 1986.

The following observations help clarify the codification procedure:

- Neither the 1939, the 1954, nor the 1986 Code changed all of the tax law existing on the date of enactment. Much of the 1939 Code, for example, was incorporated into the 1954 Code. The same can be said for the transition from the 1954 to the 1986 Code. This point is important in assessing judicial and administrative decisions interpreting provisions under prior codes. For example, a decision interpreting § 121 of the Internal Revenue Code of 1954 will have continuing validity since this provision carried over unchanged to the Internal Revenue Code of 1986.
- Statutory amendments to the tax law are integrated into the existing Code. Thus, subsequent tax legislation, such as the Economic Stimulus Act of 2008, the Housing Assistance Tax Act of 2008, the American Recovery and Reinvestment Tax Act of 2009, the Worker, Homeownership, and Business Assistance Act of 2009, the Hiring Incentives to Restore Employment Act of 2010, the Patient Protection and Affordable Care Act of 2010, and the Health Care and Education Reconciliation Act of 2010, has all become part of the Internal

TAX *in the NEWS*

Tax Freedom Day?

In income tax history, 1913 was an important year. In that year, the Sixteenth Amendment to the Constitution was ratified:

> The Congress shall have power to tax and collect taxes on incomes, from whatever source derived, without apportionment among the several States, and without regard to any census or enumeration.

The first income tax legislation that definitely was constitutional was passed that same year.

According to the Tax Foundation, in 2010 Tax Freedom Day fell on April 9, one day later than in 2009, but one week earlier than in 2008. Tax Freedom Day is the date on which an average taxpayer through working has paid off his or her taxes for the year. Nevertheless, Americans still paid more in taxes in 2010 than they spent on food, clothing, and shelter combined. Of course, if you lived in Connecticut with the heaviest total tax burden, Tax Freedom Day fell on April 27. Alaska and Louisiana celebrated Tax Freedom Day the earliest—on March 26, the 85th day of the year.

Source: Tax Foundation, "America Celebrates Tax Freedom Day," **www.taxfoundation.org/taxfreedomday.html.**

Revenue Code of 1986. In view of the frequency with which tax legislation has been enacted in recent years, it appears that the tax law will continue to be amended frequently.

The Legislative Process

Federal tax legislation generally originates in the House of Representatives, where it is first considered by the House Ways and Means Committee. Tax bills originate in the Senate when they are attached as riders to other legislative proposals.[1] If acceptable to the committee, the proposed bill is referred to the entire House of Representatives for approval or disapproval. Approved bills are sent to the Senate, where they initially are considered by the Senate Finance Committee.

The next step is referral from the Senate Finance Committee to the entire Senate. Assuming no disagreement between the House and Senate, passage by the Senate means referral to the President for approval or veto. If the bill is approved or if the President's veto is overridden, the bill becomes law and part of the Internal Revenue Code of 1986.

Both the House and the Senate passed the Food, Conservation, and Energy Act of 2008 on May 15, 2008. On May 21, 2008, President George Bush vetoed the bill, but both houses of Congress overwhelmingly voted on May 22, 2008, to override the President's veto. Thus, the tax provisions contained in this 2008 Act became part of the Internal Revenue Code of 1986.

House and Senate versions of major tax bills frequently differ. One reason bills are often changed in the Senate is that each individual senator has considerable latitude to make amendments when the Senate as a whole is voting on a bill referred to it by the Senate Finance Committee. In contrast, the entire House of Representatives either accepts or rejects what is proposed by the House Ways and Means Committee, and changes from the floor are rare. When the Senate version of the bill differs from that passed by the House, the Joint Conference Committee, which includes members of both the House Ways and Means Committee and the Senate Finance Committee, is called upon to resolve the differences. The deliberations of the Joint Conference Committee usually produce a compromise between the two versions, which is then voted on by both the House and the Senate. If both bodies accept the bill, it is referred to the President for approval or veto. Former Senator Daniel Patrick Moynihan observed that in the last hours of Congress, the White House and lawmakers often agree on a "1,200-page monster, we vote for it; nobody knows what is in it." Figure 2.1 summarizes the typical legislative process for tax bills.

The role of the Joint Conference Committee indicates the importance of compromise in the legislative process. As an example of the practical effect of the

[1]The Tax Equity and Fiscal Responsibility Act of 1982 originated in the Senate, and its constitutionality was unsuccessfully challenged in the courts. The Senate version of the Deficit Reduction Act of 1984 was attached as an amendment to the Federal Boat Safety Act.

FIGURE 2.1 Legislative Process for Tax Bills

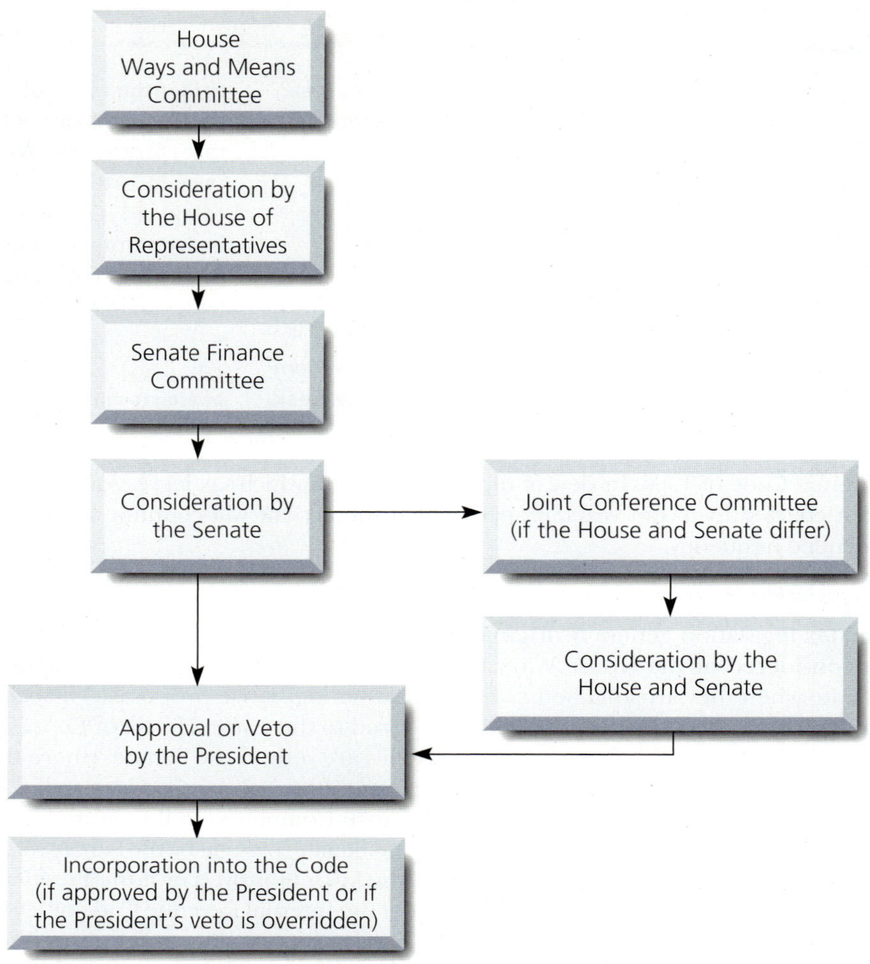

compromise process, consider Figure 2.2, which shows what happened with amendments to the first-time homebuyer credit in the American Recovery and Reinvestment Tax Act (ARRTA) of 2009.

Referrals from the House Ways and Means Committee, the Senate Finance Committee, and the Joint Conference Committee are usually accompanied by Committee Reports. These Committee Reports often explain the provisions of the proposed legislation and are therefore a valuable source for ascertaining the *intent of Congress.* What Congress had in mind when it considered and enacted tax legislation is the key to interpreting the legislation. Since Regulations normally are not issued immediately after a statute is enacted, taxpayers and the courts look to Committee Reports to determine congressional intent.

Arrangement of the Code

The Internal Revenue Code of 1986 is found in Title 26 of the U.S. Code. In working with the Code, it helps to understand the format. Note the following partial table of contents:

Subtitle A. Income Taxes
  Chapter 1. Normal Taxes and Surtaxes
    Subchapter A. Determination of Tax Liability
      Part I. Tax on Individuals
        Sections 1–5
      Part II. Tax on Corporations
        Sections 11–12

* * *

FIGURE 2.2 Example of Compromise in the Joint Conference Committee

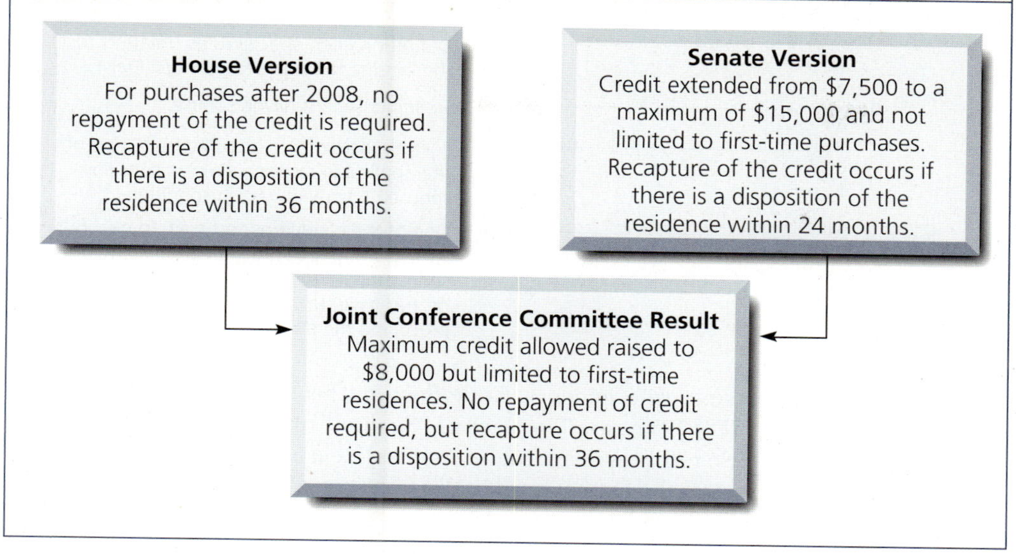

In referring to a provision of the Code, the key is usually the Section number. In citing Section 2(a) (dealing with the status of a surviving spouse), for example, it is unnecessary to include Subtitle A, Chapter 1, Subchapter A, Part I. Merely mentioning Section 2(a) will suffice, since the Section numbers run consecutively and do not begin again with each new Subtitle, Chapter, Subchapter, or Part. Not all Code Section numbers are used, however. Note that Part I ends with Section 5 and Part II starts with Section 11 (at present there are no Sections 6, 7, 8, 9, and 10).[2]

Tax practitioners commonly refer to a specific area of income tax law by Subchapter designation. Some of the more common Subchapter designations include Subchapter C ("Corporate Distributions and Adjustments"), Subchapter K ("Partners and Partnerships"), and Subchapter S ("Tax Treatment of S Corporations and Their Shareholders"). Particularly in the last situation, it is much more convenient to describe the effect of the applicable Code provisions (Sections 1361–1379) as "S corporation status" than as the "Tax Treatment of S Corporations and Their Shareholders."

Citing the Code

Code Sections are often broken down into subparts.[3] Section 2(a)(1)(A) serves as an example.

[2]When the Code was drafted, Section numbers were intentionally omitted so that later changes could be incorporated into the Code without disrupting its organization. When Congress does not leave enough space, subsequent Code Sections are given A, B, C, etc., designations. A good example is the treatment of Sections 280A through 280H.

[3]Some Code Sections do not have subparts. See, for example, §§ 211 and 241.

[4]Some Code Sections omit the subsection designation and use, instead, the paragraph designation as the first subpart. See, for example, §§ 212(1) and 1222(1).

Broken down by content, Section 2(a)(1)(A) appears as follows:

§ 2 →	Definitions and special rules (relating to the income tax imposed on individuals).
(a) →	Definition of a survivng spouse.
(1) →	For purposes of § 1 (the determination of the applicable rate schedule), a surviving spouse must meet certain conditions.
(A) →	One of the conditions necessary to qualify as a surviving spouse is that the taxpayer's spouse must have died during either of his or her two taxable years immediately preceding the present taxable year.

Throughout the text, references to Code Sections are in the form given above. The symbols "§" and "§§" are used in place of "Section" and "Sections." Unless otherwise stated, all Code references are to the Internal Revenue Code of 1986. The following table summarizes the format used in the text:

Complete Reference	Text Reference
Section 2(a)(1)(A) of the Internal Revenue Code of 1986	§ 2(a)(1)(A)
Sections 1 and 2 of the Internal Revenue Code of 1986	§§ 1 and 2
Section 2 of the Internal Revenue Code of 1954	§ 2 of the Internal Revenue Code of 1954
Section 12(d) of the Internal Revenue Code of 1939[5]	§ 12(d) of the Internal Revenue Code of 1939

ADMINISTRATIVE SOURCES OF THE TAX LAW

The administrative sources of the Federal tax law can be grouped as follows: Treasury Department Regulations, Revenue Rulings and Revenue Procedures, and various other administrative pronouncements (see Exhibit 2.1). All are issued by either the U.S. Treasury Department or the IRS.

ETHICS & *Equity*

Is It Ethical to Report a Tax Cheat?

The IRS makes it worthwhile to turn in someone who cheats on income taxes. The person who reports a cheater can receive up to 15 to 30 percent of any underpayment, up to a maximum of $10 million. The IRS's tip line is 1-800-829-0433, and the appropriate form to report a cheat is Form 3949A (Information Referral). The IRS estimates that taxpayers underpay their taxes by $345 billion each year. Is it ethical to report a tax cheat?

[5] Section 12(d) of the Internal Revenue Code of 1939 is the predecessor to § 2 of the Internal Revenue Code of 1954 and the Internal Revenue Code of 1986.

EXHIBIT 2.1 Administrative Sources

Source	Location	Authority**
Regulations	*Federal Register**	Force and effect of law.
Temporary Regulations	*Federal Register** *Internal Revenue Bulletin* *Cumulative Bulletin*	May be cited as a precedent.
Proposed Regulations	*Federal Register** *Internal Revenue Bulletin* *Cumulative Bulletin*	Preview of final Regulations.
Revenue Rulings Revenue Procedures Treasury Decisions Actions on Decisions	*Internal Revenue Bulletin* *Cumulative Bulletin*	Do not have the force and effect of law.
General Counsel Memoranda Technical Advice Memoranda	Tax Analysts' *Tax Notes* RIA's *Internal Memoranda of the IRS* CCH's *IRS Position Reporter*	May not be cited as a precedent.
Letter Rulings	Research Institute of America and Commerce Clearing House tax services	Applicable only to taxpayer addressed. No precedential force.

*Finalized, Temporary, and Proposed Regulations are published in soft-cover form by several publishers.
**Each of these sources may be substantial authority for purposes of the accuracy-related penalty in § 6662. Notice 90–20, 1990–1 C.B. 328.

Treasury Department Regulations

Regulations are issued by the U.S. Treasury Department under authority granted by Congress.[6] Interpretive by nature, they provide taxpayers with considerable guidance on the meaning and application of the Code. Regulations carry considerable authority as the official interpretation of tax statutes. They are an important factor to consider in complying with the tax law.

Since Regulations interpret the Code, they are arranged in the same sequence as the Code. A number is added at the beginning, however, to indicate the type of tax or administrative, procedural, or definitional matter to which they relate. For example, the prefix 1 designates the Regulations under the income tax law. Thus, the Regulations under Code § 2 would be cited as Reg. § 1.2, with subparts added for further identification. The numbering patterns of these subparts often have no correlation with the Code subsections. The prefix 20 designates estate tax Regulations, 25 covers gift tax Regulations, 31 relates to employment taxes, and 301 refers to procedure and administration. This list is not all-inclusive.

New Regulations and changes in existing Regulations are usually issued in proposed form before they are finalized. The interval between the proposal of a Regulation and its finalization permits taxpayers and other interested parties to comment on the propriety of the proposal. **Proposed Regulations** under Code § 2, for example, are cited as Prop.Reg. § 1.2. The Tax Court indicates that Proposed Regulations carry little weight—no more than a position advanced in a written brief prepared by a litigating party before the Tax Court. **Finalized Regulations** have the force and effect of law.[7]

Sometimes the Treasury Department issues **Temporary Regulations** relating to matters where immediate guidance is important. These Regulations are issued without the comment period required for Proposed Regulations. Temporary Regulations

[6]§ 7805.

[7]*F. W. Woolworth Co.*, 54 T.C. 1233 (1970); *Harris M. Miller*, 70 T.C. 448 (1978); and *James O. Tomerlin Trust*, 87 T.C. 876 (1986).

have the same authoritative value as final Regulations and may be cited as precedents. Temporary Regulations must also be issued as Proposed Regulations and automatically expire within three years after the date of issuance.[8]

Proposed, Temporary, and final Regulations are published in the *Federal Register*, in the *Internal Revenue Bulletin* (I.R.B.), and by major tax services. Final Regulations are issued as Treasury Decisions (TDs).

Regulations may also be classified as *legislative, interpretive,* or *procedural.* This classification scheme is discussed under Assessing the Validity of a Treasury Regulation later in the chapter.

Revenue Rulings and Revenue Procedures

Revenue Rulings are official pronouncements of the National Office of the IRS.[9] They typically provide one or more examples of how the IRS would apply a law to specific fact situations. Like Regulations, Revenue Rulings are designed to provide interpretation of the tax law. However, they do not carry the same legal force and effect as Regulations and usually deal with more restricted problems. Regulations are approved by the Secretary of the Treasury, whereas Revenue Rulings generally are not.

A Revenue Ruling often results from a specific taxpayer's request for a letter ruling. If the IRS believes that a taxpayer's request for a letter ruling deserves official publication due to its widespread impact, the letter ruling will be converted into a Revenue Ruling and issued for the information and guidance of taxpayers, tax practitioners, and IRS personnel. Names, identifying descriptions, and money amounts are changed to conceal the identity of the requesting taxpayer. Revenue Rulings also arise from technical advice to District Offices of the IRS, court decisions, suggestions from tax practitioner groups, and various tax publications.

Revenue Procedures are issued in the same manner as Revenue Rulings, but deal with the internal management practices and procedures of the IRS. Familiarity with these procedures increases taxpayer compliance and helps make the administration of the tax laws more efficient. The failure of a taxpayer to follow a Revenue Procedure can result in unnecessary delay or, in a discretionary situation, can cause the IRS to decline to act on behalf of the taxpayer.

Both Revenue Rulings and Revenue Procedures serve an important function in that they provide *guidance* to IRS personnel and taxpayers in handling routine tax matters. Revenue Rulings and Revenue Procedures generally apply retroactively and may be revoked or modified by subsequent rulings or procedures, Regulations, legislation, or court decisions.

Revenue Rulings and Revenue Procedures are published weekly by the U.S. Government in the *Internal Revenue Bulletin* (I.R.B.). Semiannually, the *Internal Revenue Bulletins* for a six-month period are gathered together and published in a bound volume called the *Cumulative Bulletin* (C.B.).[10]

The proper form for citing Rulings and Procedures depends on whether the item has been published in the *Cumulative Bulletin* or is available only in I.R.B. form. Consider, for example, the following transition:

Temporary Citation	Rev.Rul. 2010–19, I.R.B. No. 31, 174. *Explanation:* Revenue Ruling Number 19, appearing on page 174 of the 31st weekly issue of the *Internal Revenue Bulletin* for 2010.
Permanent Citation	Rev.Rul. 2010–19, 2010–2 C.B. 174. *Explanation:* Revenue Ruling Number 19, appearing on page 174 of Volume 2 of the *Cumulative Bulletin* for 2010.

[8]§ 7805(e).

[9]§ 7805(a).

[10]Usually, only two volumes of the *Cumulative Bulletin* are published each year. However, in the past, when Congress has enacted major tax legislation, other volumes have been published containing the Congressional Committee Reports supporting the Revenue Act. See, for example, the two extra volumes for 1984 dealing with the Deficit Reduction Act of 1984. The 1984–3 *Cumulative Bulletin,* Volume 1, contains the text of the law itself; 1984–3, Volume 2, contains the Committee Reports. There are a total of four volumes of the *Cumulative Bulletin* for 1984: 1984–1; 1984–2; 1984–3, Volume 1; and 1984–3, Volume 2.

Note that the page reference of 174 is the same for both the I.R.B. (temporary) and C.B. (permanent) versions of the ruling. The IRS numbers the pages of the I.R.B.'s consecutively for each six-month period so as to facilitate their conversion to C.B. form. Revenue Rulings and other tax resources may be found on Tax Almanac, a free online resource from Intuit at **www.taxalmanac.org**.

Revenue Procedures are cited in the same manner, except that "Rev.Proc." is substituted for "Rev.Rul." Some recent Revenue Procedures dealt with the following matters:

- Where and how to mail forms or returns that seek a prompt refund.
- Guidance on the U.S. and area medium gross income figures needed by issuers of qualified mortgage bonds and mortgage credit certificates.
- The 2011 inflation-adjusted amounts for Health Savings Accounts.

Letter Rulings

Letter rulings are issued for a fee upon a taxpayer's request and describe how the IRS will treat a *proposed* transaction for tax purposes. They apply only to the taxpayer who asks for and obtains the ruling, but post-1984 letter rulings may be substantial authority for purposes of the accuracy-related penalty.[11] Letter rulings can be useful to taxpayers who wish to be certain of how a transaction will be taxed before proceeding with it. Letter rulings also allow taxpayers to avoid unexpected tax costs. Although the procedure for requesting a ruling can be quite cumbersome, sometimes requesting a ruling is the most effective way to carry out tax planning. Nevertheless, the IRS limits the issuance of individual rulings to restricted, preannounced areas of taxation. The main reason the IRS will not rule in certain areas is that they involve fact-oriented situations. Thus, a ruling may not be obtained on many of the problems that are particularly troublesome to taxpayers.[12] The IRS issues more than 2,000 letter rulings each year.

Although letter rulings once were private and not available to the public, the law now requires the IRS to make such rulings available for public inspection after identifying details are deleted.[13] Published digests of private letter rulings can be found in RIA's *Private Letter Rulings*, BNA's *Daily Tax Reports*, and Tax Analysts' *Tax Notes*. In addition, computerized databases of letter rulings are available through several private publishers.

Letter rulings are issued multidigit file numbers, which indicate the year and week of issuance as well as the number of the ruling during that week. Consider, for example, Ltr.Rul. 201008049, which provides the tax consequences of the disposition of the assets of two Individual Retirement Accounts (IRAs) previously held by a decedent.

2010	08	049
Year 2010	8th week of issuance	49th ruling issued during the 8th week

Other Administrative Pronouncements

Treasury Decisions (TDs) are issued by the Treasury Department to promulgate new Regulations, amend or otherwise change existing Regulations, or announce the

[11]Notice 90–20, 1990–1 C.B. 328. In this regard, letter rulings differ from Revenue Rulings, which are applicable to *all* taxpayers. A letter ruling may later lead to the issuance of a Revenue Ruling if the holding affects many taxpayers. In its Agents' Manual, the IRS indicates that letter rulings may be used as a guide with other research materials in formulating a District Office position on an issue. The IRS is required to charge a taxpayer a fee for letter rulings, determination letters, etc.

[12]Rev.Proc. 2011–1, I.R.B. No. 1, 1 contains a list of areas in which the IRS will not issue advance rulings. From time to time, subsequent Revenue Procedures are issued that modify or amplify Rev.Proc. 2011–1.

[13]§ 6110.

position of the Government on selected court decisions. Like Revenue Rulings and Revenue Procedures, TDs are published initially in the *Internal Revenue Bulletin* and subsequently transferred to the *Cumulative Bulletin.*

The IRS also publishes other administrative communications in the *Internal Revenue Bulletin,* such as Announcements, Notices, IRs (News Releases), Legal Memoranda (ILMs), Chief Counsel Notices (CC), and Prohibited Transaction Exemptions.

Like letter rulings, **determination letters** are issued at the request of taxpayers and provide guidance on the application of the tax law. They differ from letter rulings in that the issuing source is an Area Director rather than the National Office of the IRS. Also, determination letters usually involve *completed* (as opposed to proposed) transactions. Determination letters are not published and are made known only to the party making the request.

EXAMPLE 1

The shareholders of Red Corporation and Green Corporation want assurance that the consolidation of the corporations into Blue Corporation will be a nontaxable reorganization. The proper approach is to ask that the National Office of the IRS issue a letter ruling concerning the income tax effect of the proposed transaction. ■

EXAMPLE 2

Chris operates a barber shop in which he employs eight barbers. To comply with the rules governing income tax and payroll tax withholdings, Chris wants to know whether the barbers working for him are employees or independent contractors. The proper procedure is to request a determination letter on their status from the appropriate Area Director. ■

The law now requires that several internal memoranda that constitute the working law of the IRS be released. These General Counsel Memoranda (GCMs), Technical Advice Memoranda (TAMs), and Field Service Advices (FSAs) are not officially published, and the IRS indicates that they may not be cited as precedents by taxpayers.[14] However, these working documents do explain the IRS's position on various issues.

The National Office of the IRS releases **Technical Advice Memoranda (TAMs)** weekly. TAMs resemble letter rulings in that they give the IRS's determination of an issue. Letter rulings, however, are responses to requests by taxpayers, whereas TAMs are issued by the National Office of the IRS in response to questions raised by IRS field personnel during audits. TAMs deal with completed rather than proposed transactions and are often requested for questions relating to exempt organizations and employee plans. TAMs are not officially published and may not be cited or used as precedent.[15]

The Office of Chief Counsel prepares Field Service Advices (FSAs) to help IRS employees. They are issued in response to requests for advice, guidance, and analysis on difficult or significant tax issues. FSAs are not binding on either the taxpayer to whom they pertain or on the IRS.

Field Service Advices are being replaced by a new form of field guidance called Technical Expedited Advice Memoranda (TEAMs). The purpose of TEAMs is to expedite legal guidance to field agents as disputes are developing. FSAs are reverting to their original purpose of case-specific development of facts.

A TEAM guidance differs from a TAM in several ways, including a mandatory presubmission conference involving the taxpayer. In the event of a tentatively adverse conclusion for the taxpayer or the field agent, a conference of right is offered to the taxpayer and to the field agent; once the conference of right is held, no further conferences are offered.

---

[14] These are unofficially published by the publishers listed in Exhibit 2.1. Such internal memoranda may be substantial authority for purposes of the accuracy-related penalty for post-1984 transactions. Notice 90–20, 1990–1 C.B. 328.

[15] § 6110(j)(3).

FIGURE 2.3 Federal Judicial System

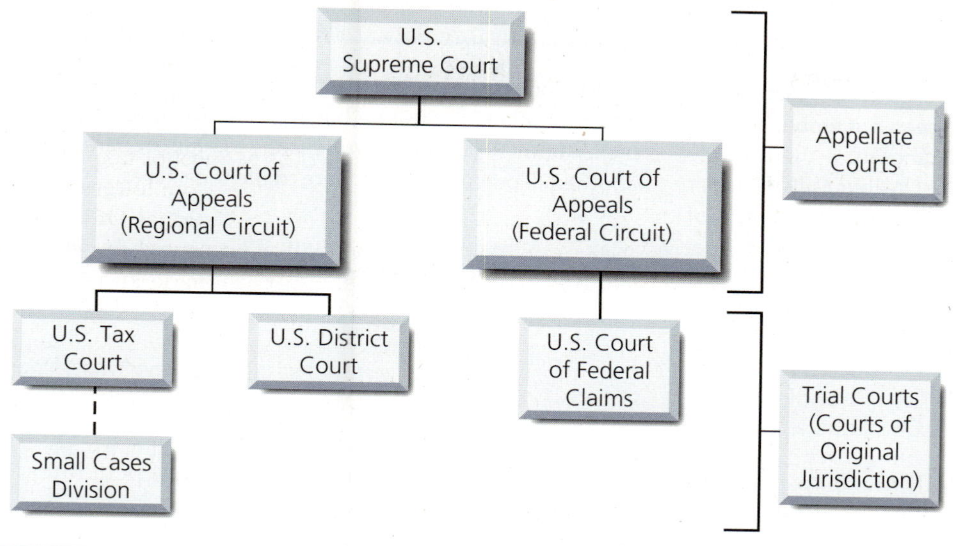

JUDICIAL SOURCES OF THE TAX LAW

The Judicial Process in General

After a taxpayer has exhausted some or all of the remedies available within the IRS (i.e., no satisfactory settlement has been reached at the agent level or at the Appeals Division level), the dispute can be taken to the Federal courts. The dispute is first considered by a **court of original jurisdiction** (known as a trial court), with any appeal (either by the taxpayer or the IRS) taken to the appropriate appellate court. In most situations, the taxpayer has a choice of any of four trial courts: a **Federal District Court**, the **U.S. Court of Federal Claims**, the **U.S. Tax Court**, or the **Small Cases Division** of the U.S. Tax Court. The trial and *appellate court* system for Federal tax litigation is illustrated in Figure 2.3.

The broken line between the U.S. Tax Court and the Small Cases Division indicates that there is no appeal from the Small Cases Division. The jurisdiction of the Small Cases Division is limited to cases involving amounts of $50,000 or less, and some of its decisions can now be found on the U.S. Tax Court website.

American law, following English law, is frequently "made" by judicial decisions. Under the doctrine of *stare decisis*, each case (except in the Small Cases Division) has precedential value for future cases with the same controlling set of facts. Most Federal and state appellate court decisions and some decisions of trial courts are published. Published court decisions are organized by jurisdiction (Federal or state) and level of court (trial or appellate).

A decision of a particular court is called its *holding*. Sometimes a decision includes dicta or incidental opinions beyond the current facts. Such passing remarks, illustrations, or analogies are not essential to the current holding. Although the holding has precedential value under *stare decisis*, dicta are not binding on a future court.

Knowledge of several terms is important in understanding court decisions. The term *plaintiff* refers to the party requesting action in a court, and the *defendant* is the party against whom the suit is brought. Sometimes a court uses the terms *petitioner* and *respondent*. In general, "petitioner" is a synonym for "plaintiff," and "respondent" is a synonym for "defendant." At the trial court level, a taxpayer is normally the plaintiff (or petitioner), and the Government is the defendant (or respondent).

TAX in the NEWS

The Code Is Too Complex!

Is the tax law too complicated? Tax attorney Sanford J. Schlesinger says that "there hasn't been a member of Congress with a comprehensive understanding of the tax laws since Wilbur Mills, and I'm not a fan of Wilbur Mills." Former Senator Sam Nunn described the tax code as "thousands of pages of pet rocks that have nothing to do with the national interest."

IRS Commissioner Douglas Shulman has used a tax preparer for years because he believes the tax code is so complex. About 60 percent of Americans use tax preparers, and another 20 percent use software to file their taxes.

Source: Adapted from Bob Cusack, "IRS Commissioner Doesn't File His Own Taxes," The Hill's Blog Briefing Room, January 10, 2010.

If the taxpayer wins and the Government appeals as the new petitioner (or appellee), the taxpayer becomes the new respondent.

Trial Courts

The differences among the various trial courts (courts of original jurisdiction) can be summarized as follows:

- *Number of courts.* There is only one U.S. Court of Federal Claims and only one Tax Court, but there are many Federal District Courts. The taxpayer does not select the District Court that will hear the dispute but must sue in the one that has jurisdiction where the taxpayer resides.
- *Number of judges.* District Courts have various numbers of judges, but only one judge hears a case. The Court of Federal Claims has 16 judges, and the Tax Court has 19 regular judges. The entire Tax Court, however, reviews a case (the case is sent to court conference) only when important or novel tax issues are involved. Most cases are heard and decided by 1 of the 19 judges.
- *Location.* The Court of Federal Claims meets most often in Washington, D.C., while a District Court meets at a prescribed seat for the particular district. Each state has at least one District Court, and many of the populous states have more than one. Choosing the District Court usually minimizes the inconvenience and expense of traveling for the taxpayer and his or her counsel. The Tax Court is officially based in Washington, D.C., but the various judges travel to different parts of the country and hear cases at predetermined locations and dates. This procedure eases the distance problem for the taxpayer, but it can mean a delay before the case comes to trial and is decided.
- *Jurisdiction of the Court of Federal Claims.* The Court of Federal Claims has jurisdiction over any claim against the United States that is based upon the Constitution, any Act of Congress, or any Regulation of an executive department. Thus, the Court of Federal Claims hears nontax litigation as well as tax cases. This forum appears to be more favorable for issues having an equitable or pro-business orientation (as opposed to purely technical issues) and those requiring extensive discovery.
- *Jurisdiction of the Tax Court and District Courts.* The Tax Court hears only tax cases and is the most popular forum. The District Courts hear a wide variety of nontax cases, including drug crimes and other Federal violations, as well as tax cases. Some Tax Court judges have been appointed from IRS or Treasury Department positions. For this reason, some people suggest that the Tax Court has more expertise in tax matters.

CONCEPT SUMMARY 2.1

Federal Judicial System: Trial Courts

Issue	U.S. Tax Court	U.S. District Court	U.S. Court of Federal Claims
Number of judges per court	19*	Varies	16
Payment of deficiency before trial	No	Yes	Yes
Jury trial available	No	Yes	No
Types of disputes	Tax cases only	Most criminal and civil issues	Claims against the United States
Jurisdiction	Nationwide	Location of taxpayer	Nationwide
IRS acquiescence policy	Yes	Yes	Yes
Appeal route	U.S. Court of Appeals	U.S. Court of Appeals	U.S. Court of Appeals for the Federal Circuit

*There are also 14 special trial judges and 9 senior judges.

- *Jury trial.* The only court in which a taxpayer can obtain a jury trial is a District Court. Juries can decide only questions of fact and not questions of law. Therefore, taxpayers who choose the District Court route often do not request a jury trial. If a jury trial is not elected, the judge will decide all issues. Note that a District Court decision is controlling only in the district in which the court has jurisdiction.
- *Payment of deficiency.* Before the Court of Federal Claims or a District Court can have jurisdiction, the taxpayer must pay the tax deficiency assessed by the IRS and then sue for a refund. If the taxpayer wins (assuming no successful appeal by the Government), the tax paid plus appropriate interest will be recovered. Jurisdiction in the Tax Court, however, is usually obtained without first paying the assessed tax deficiency. In the event the taxpayer loses in the Tax Court (and no appeal is taken or an appeal is unsuccessful), the deficiency must be paid with accrued interest. With the elimination of the deduction for personal (consumer) interest, the Tax Court route of delaying payment of the deficiency can become expensive. For example, to earn 7 percent after tax, a taxpayer with a 35 percent marginal tax rate will have to earn 10.77 percent. By paying the tax, a taxpayer limits underpayment interest and penalties on the underpayment.
- *Termination of running of interest.* A taxpayer who selects the Tax Court may deposit a cash bond to stop the running of interest. The taxpayer must deposit both the amount of the tax and any accrued interest. If the taxpayer wins and the deposited amount is returned, the Government does not pay interest on the deposit.
- *Appeals.* Appeals from a District Court or a Tax Court decision are to the U.S. Court of Appeals for the circuit in which the taxpayer resides. Appeals from the Court of Federal Claims go to the Court of Appeals for the Federal Circuit. Few Tax Court cases are appealed, and when appeals are made, most are filed by the taxpayer rather than the IRS.
- *Bankruptcy.* When a taxpayer files a bankruptcy petition, the IRS, like other creditors, is prevented from taking action against the taxpayer. Sometimes a bankruptcy court may settle a tax claim.

For a summary of the Federal trial courts, see Concept Summary 2.1.

FIGURE 2.4 The Federal Circuit Courts of Appeals

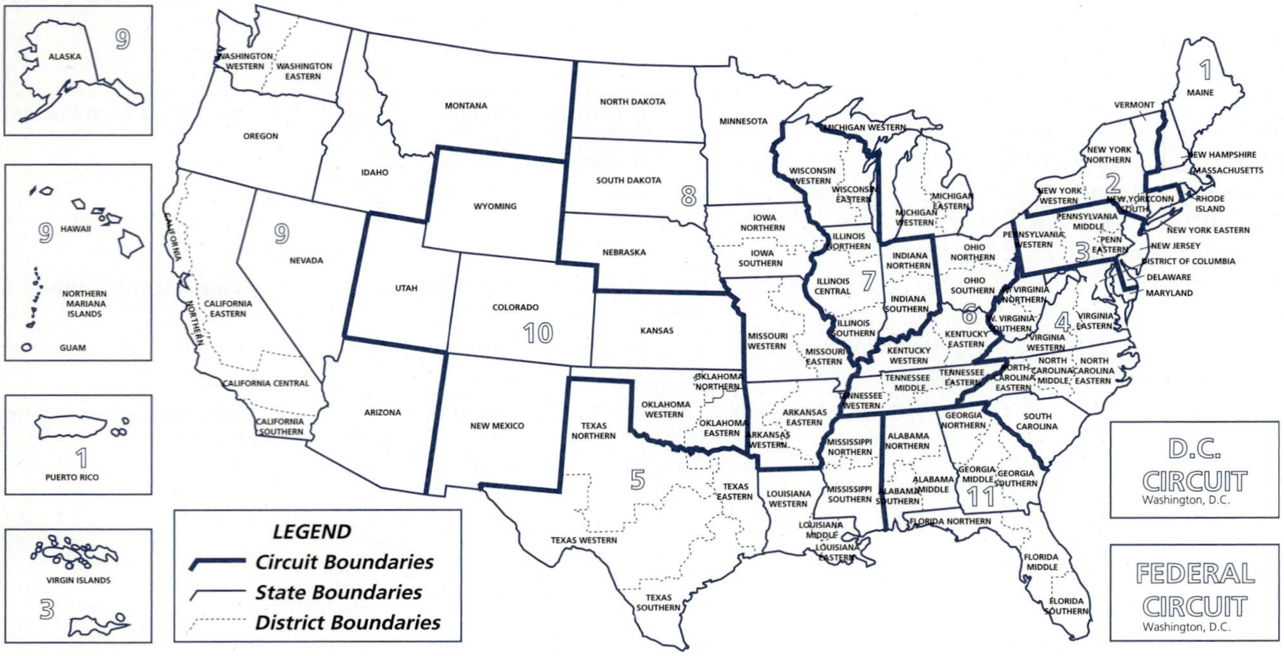

ADMINISTRATIVE OFFICE OF THE UNITED STATES SUPREME COURT
APRIL 1988

Appellate Courts

The losing party can appeal a trial court decision to a **Circuit Court of Appeals**. The 11 geographic circuits, the circuit for the District of Columbia, and the Federal Circuit[16] are shown in Figure 2.4. The appropriate circuit for an appeal depends on where the litigation originated. For example, an appeal from New York goes to the Second Circuit.

If the Government loses at the trial court level (District Court, Tax Court, or Court of Federal Claims), it need not (and frequently does not) appeal. The fact that an appeal is not made, however, does not indicate that the IRS agrees with the result and will not litigate similar issues in the future. The IRS may decide not to appeal for a number of reasons. First, if the current litigation load is heavy, the IRS may decide that available personnel should be assigned to other, more important cases. Second, the IRS may determine that this case is not a good one to appeal. For example, the taxpayer may be in a sympathetic position, or the facts may be particularly strong in his or her favor. In that event, the IRS may wait to test the legal issues involved with a taxpayer who has a much weaker case. Third, if the appeal is from a District Court or the Tax Court, the Court of Appeals of jurisdiction could have some bearing on whether the IRS decides to pursue an appeal. Based on past experience and precedent, the IRS may conclude that the chance for success on a particular issue might be more promising in another Court of Appeals. If so, the IRS will wait for a similar case to arise in a different jurisdiction.

The Federal Circuit at the appellate level provides a taxpayer with an alternative forum to the Court of Appeals of his or her home circuit for the appeal. Appeals from both the Tax Court and the District Court go to a taxpayer's home circuit. When a particular circuit has issued an adverse decision, the taxpayer may prefer the Court of Federal Claims route since any appeal will be to the Federal Circuit.

[16]The Court of Appeals for the Federal Circuit was created, effective October 1, 1982, by P.L. 97–164 (4/2/82) to hear decisions appealed from the Claims Court (now the Court of Federal Claims).

The Appellate Process The *role* of the appellate courts is limited to a review of the record of trial compiled by the trial courts. Thus, the appellate process usually involves a determination of whether the trial court applied the proper law in arriving at its decision. Usually, an appellate court will not dispute a lower court's fact-finding determination.

An appeal can have any of a number of possible outcomes. The appellate court may approve (affirm) or disapprove (reverse) the lower court's finding, or it may send the case back for further consideration (remand). When many issues are involved, a mixed result is not unusual. Thus, the lower court may be affirmed (*aff'd.*) on Issue A and reversed (*rev'd.*) on Issue B, while Issue C is remanded (*rem'd.*) for additional fact finding.

When more than one judge is involved in the decision-making process, disagreements are not uncommon. In addition to the majority view, one or more judges may concur (agree with the result reached but not with some or all of the reasoning) or dissent (disagree with the result). In any one case, the majority view controls. But concurring and dissenting views can have influence on other courts or, at some subsequent date when the composition of the court has changed, even on the same court.

Appellate Precedents and the Tax Court District Courts, the Tax Court, and the Court of Federal Claims must abide by the **precedents** set by the Court of Appeals of jurisdiction. A particular Court of Appeals need not follow the decisions of another Court of Appeals. All courts, however, must follow the decisions of the **U.S. Supreme Court**.

This pattern of appellate precedents raises an issue for the Tax Court. Because the Tax Court is a national court, it decides cases from all parts of the country. For many years, the Tax Court followed a policy of deciding cases based on what it thought the result should be, even when its decision might be appealed to a Court of Appeals that had previously decided a similar case differently. A number of years ago this policy was changed in the *Golsen*[17] decision. Now the Tax Court will decide a case as it feels the law should be applied *only* if the Court of Appeals of appropriate jurisdiction has not yet passed on the issue or has previously decided a similar case in accord with the Tax Court's decision. If the Court of Appeals of appropriate jurisdiction has previously held otherwise, the Tax Court will conform even though it disagrees with the holding. This policy is known as the *Golsen* rule.

EXAMPLE 3

Emily lives in Texas and sues in the Tax Court on Issue A. The Fifth Circuit Court of Appeals is the appellate court of appropriate jurisdiction. It has already decided, in a case involving similar facts but a different taxpayer, that Issue A should be resolved against the Government. Although the Tax Court feels that the Fifth Circuit Court of Appeals is wrong, under its *Golsen* policy it will render judgment for Emily. Shortly thereafter, Rashad, a resident of New York, in a comparable case, sues in the Tax Court on Issue A. Assume that the Second Circuit Court of Appeals, the appellate court of appropriate jurisdiction, has never expressed itself on Issue A. Presuming the Tax Court has not reconsidered its position on Issue A, it will decide against Rashad. Thus, it is entirely possible for two taxpayers suing in the same court to end up with opposite results merely because they live in different parts of the country. ■

Appeal to the U.S. Supreme Court Appeal to the U.S. Supreme Court is by **Writ of Certiorari**. If the Court agrees to hear the case, it will grant the Writ (*Cert. granted*). Most often, it will deny jurisdiction (*Cert. denied*). For whatever reason or reasons, the Supreme Court rarely hears tax cases. The Court usually grants certiorari to resolve a conflict among the Courts of Appeals (e.g., two or more appellate courts have assumed opposing positions on a particular issue) or where the tax issue is extremely

[17] *Jack E. Golsen*, 54 T.C. 742 (1970).

important. The granting of a *Writ of Certiorari* indicates that at least four members of the Supreme Court believe that the issue is of sufficient importance to be heard by the full Court.

LO.2

Locate and work with the appropriate tax law sources.

Judicial Citations

Having briefly described the judicial process, it is appropriate to consider the more practical problem of the relationship of case law to tax research. As previously noted, court decisions are an important source of tax law. The ability to locate a case and to cite it is therefore a must in working with the tax law. Judicial citations usually follow a standard pattern: case name, volume number, reporter series, page or paragraph number, court (where necessary), and the year of decision. Specific citation formats for each court are presented in the following sections.

Judicial Citations—The U.S. Tax Court A good starting point is the U.S. Tax Court (formerly the Board of Tax Appeals). The Tax Court issues two types of decisions: Regular and Memorandum. The Chief Judge decides whether the opinion is issued as a Regular or Memorandum decision. The distinction between the two involves both substance and form. In terms of substance, *Memorandum* decisions deal with situations necessitating only the application of already established principles of law. *Regular* decisions involve novel issues not previously resolved by the court. In actual practice, however, this distinction is not always preserved. Not infrequently, Memorandum decisions will be encountered that appear to warrant Regular status, and vice versa. At any rate, do not conclude that Memorandum decisions possess no value as precedents. Both represent the position of the Tax Court and, as such, can be relied on.

The Regular and Memorandum decisions issued by the Tax Court also differ in form. Memorandum decisions are made available but are not published by the government. Regular decisions are published by the U.S. Government in a series called *Tax Court of the United States Reports* (T.C.). Each volume of these *Reports* covers a six-month period (January 1 through June 30 and July 1 through December 31) and is given a succeeding volume number. But there is usually a time lag between the date a decision is rendered and the date it appears in bound form. A temporary citation may be necessary to help the researcher locate a recent Regular decision. Consider, for example, the temporary and permanent citations for *Larry G. Mitchell*, a decision filed on December 15, 2008:

Temporary Citation	*Larry G. Mitchell*, 131 T.C. ___, No. 15 (2008). *Explanation:* Page number left blank because not yet known.
Permanent Citation	*Larry G. Mitchell*, 131 T.C. 215 (2008). *Explanation:* Page number now available.

Both citations tell us that the case will ultimately appear in Volume 131 of the *Tax Court of the United States Reports.* Until this volume is bound and made available to the general public, however, the page number must be left blank. Instead, the temporary citation identifies the case as being the 15th Regular decision issued by the Tax Court since Volume 130 ended. With this information, the decision can easily be located in either of the special Tax Court services published by Commerce Clearing House and Research Institute of America (formerly by Prentice-Hall). Once Volume 131 is released, the permanent citation can be substituted and the number of the case dropped. Starting in 1999, both Regular decisions and Memorandum decisions are published on the U.S. Tax Court website (**www.ustaxcourt.gov**).

Before 1943, the Tax Court was called the Board of Tax Appeals, and its decisions were published as the *United States Board of Tax Appeals Reports* (B.T.A.). These 47 volumes cover the period from 1924 to 1942. For example, the citation *Karl Pauli,* 11 B.T.A. 784 (1928) refers to the 11th volume of the *Board of Tax Appeals Reports,* page 784, issued in 1928.

If the IRS loses in a decision, it may indicate whether it agrees or disagrees with the results reached by the court by publishing an **acquiescence** ("A" or "*Acq.*") or

nonacquiescence ("NA" or "*Nonacq.*"), respectively. Until 1991, acquiescences and nonacquiescences were published only for certain Regular decisions of the Tax Court, but the IRS has expanded its acquiescence program to include other civil tax cases where guidance is helpful. The acquiescence or nonacquiescence is published in the *Internal Revenue Bulletin* and the *Cumulative Bulletin* as an *Action on Decision.* The IRS can retroactively revoke an acquiescence.

Although Memorandum decisions were not published by the U.S. Government until recently (they are now published on the U.S. Tax Court website), they were—and continue to be—published by Commerce Clearing House (CCH) and Research Institute of America (RIA [formerly by Prentice-Hall]). Consider, for example, the three different ways that *Nick R. Hughes* can be cited:

> *Nick R. Hughes*, T.C.Memo. 2009–94
> The 94th Memorandum decision issued by the Tax Court in 2009.
> *Nick R. Hughes*, 97 TCM 1488
> Page 1488 of Vol. 97 of the CCH *Tax Court Memorandum Decisions.*
> *Nick R. Hughes*, 2009 RIA T.C.Memo. ¶2009,094
> Paragraph 2009,094 of the RIA *T.C. Memorandum Decisions.*

Note that the third citation contains the same information as the first. Thus, ¶2009,094 indicates the following information about the case: year 2009, 94th T.C.Memo. decision. Before the Prentice-Hall Information Services division was incorporated into Research Institute of America, "P-H" was used instead of "RIA" for the third citation.[18]

U.S. Tax Court Summary Opinions relate to decisions of the Tax Court's Small Cases Division. These opinions are published commercially, and on the U.S. Tax Court website, with the warning that they may not be treated as precedent for any other case. For example, *Howard Slater*, filed on January 11, 2010, is cited as follows:

> *Howard Slater*, T.C. Summary Opinion 2010–1.

In 2005, the U.S. Supreme Court held that decisions of the Small Cases Division must be made public.

Judicial Citations—The U.S. District Courts, Court of Federal Claims, and Courts of Appeals

District Court, Court of Federal Claims, Court of Appeals, and Supreme Court decisions dealing with Federal tax matters are reported in both the CCH *U.S. Tax Cases* (USTC) and the RIA *American Federal Tax Reports* (AFTR) series.

Federal District Court decisions, dealing with *both* tax and nontax issues, are also published by West (owned by Thomson Reuters) in its *Federal Supplement Series* (F.Supp.). Volume 999, published in 1998, is the last volume of the *Federal Supplement Series.* It is followed by the *Federal Supplement Second Series* (F.Supp.2d). A District Court case can be cited in three different forms as the following examples illustrate:

> *Turner v. U.S.*, 2004–1 USTC ¶60,478 (D.Ct. Tex., 2004).
> *Explanation:* Reported in the first volume of the *U.S. Tax Cases* published by Commerce Clearing House for calendar year 2004 (2004–1) and located at paragraph 60,478 (¶60,478).

> *Turner v. U.S.*, 93 AFTR 2d 2004–686 (D.Ct. Tex., 2004).
> *Explanation:* Reported in the 93rd volume of the second series of the *American Federal Tax Reports* (AFTR 2d) published by RIA and beginning on page 686.

> *Turner v. U.S.*, 306 F.Supp.2d 668 (D.Ct. Tex., 2004).
> *Explanation:* Reported in the 306th volume of the *Federal Supplement Second Series* (F.Supp.2d) published by West and beginning on page 668.

---

[18]In this text, this Memorandum decision of the U.S. Tax Court would be cited as *Nick R. Hughes*, 97 TCM 1488, T.C.Memo. 2009–94.

In all of the preceding citations, note that the name of the case is the same (Turner being the taxpayer), as are the references to the Federal District Court of Texas (D.Ct. Tex.) and the year the decision was rendered (2004).[19]

Decisions of the Court of Federal Claims[20] and the Courts of Appeals are published in the USTCs, AFTRs, and a West reporter called the *Federal Second Series* (F.2d). Volume 999, published in 1993, is the last volume of the *Federal Second Series.* It is followed by the *Federal Third Series* (F.3d). Beginning with October 1982, decisions of the Court of Federal Claims are published in another West reporter entitled the *Claims Court Reporter* (abbreviated as Cls. Ct.). Beginning with Volume 27 on October 30, 1992, the name of the reporter changed to the *Federal Claims Reporter* (abbreviated as Fed.Cl.). The following examples illustrate the different forms:

Estate of Gribauskas v. Comm. (CA–2, 2003)

2003–2 USTC ¶60,466 (CCH citation)
92 AFTR 2d 2003–5914 (RIA citation)
342 F.3d 85 (West citation)

Apollo Computer, Inc. v. U.S. (Fed.Cl., 1994)

95–1 USTC ¶50,015 (CCH citation)
74 AFTR 2d 94–7172 (RIA citation)
32 Fed.Cl. 334 (West citation)

Note that *Estate of Gribauskas v. Comm.* is a decision rendered by the Second Circuit Court of Appeals in 2003 (CA–2, 2003), while *Apollo Computer, Inc.* was issued by the Court of Federal Claims in 1994 (Fed.Cl., 1994).

Judicial Citations—The U.S. Supreme Court Like all other Federal tax decisions (except those rendered by the U.S. Tax Court), Supreme Court decisions are published by Commerce Clearing House in the USTCs and by RIA in the AFTRs. The U.S. Government Printing Office also publishes these decisions in the *United States Supreme Court Reports* (U.S.), as do West in its *Supreme Court Reporter* (S.Ct.) and the Lawyer's Co-operative Publishing Company in its *United States Reports, Lawyer's Edition* (L.Ed.). The following illustrates the different ways the same decision can be cited:

U.S. v. The Donruss Co. (USSC, 1969)

69–1 USTC ¶9167 (CCH citation)
23 AFTR 2d 69–418 (RIA citation)
89 S.Ct. 501 (West citation)
393 U.S. 297 (U.S. Government Printing Office citation)
21 L.Ed.2d 495 (Lawyer's Co-operative Publishing Co. citation)

The parenthetical reference (USSC, 1969) identifies the decision as having been rendered by the U.S. Supreme Court in 1969. In this text, the citations of Supreme Court decisions are limited to the CCH (USTC), RIA (AFTR), and West (S.Ct.) versions. See Concept Summary 2.2.

[19] In this text, the case would be cited in the following form: *Turner v. U.S.*, 2004–1 USTC ¶60,478, 93 AFTR 2d 2004–686, 306 F.Supp.2d 668 (D.Ct. Tex., 2004). Prentice-Hall Information Services is now owned by Research Institute of America. Although recent volumes contain the RIA imprint, many of the older volumes continue to have the P-H imprint.

[20] Before October 29, 1992, the Court of Federal Claims was called the Claims Court. Before October 1, 1982, the Court of Federal Claims was called the Court of Claims.

CONCEPT SUMMARY 2.2

Judicial Sources

Court	Location	Authority
U.S. Supreme Court	S.Ct. Series (West) U.S. Series (U.S. Gov't.) L.Ed.2d (Lawyer's Co-op.) AFTR (RIA) USTC (CCH)	Highest authority
U.S. Courts of Appeal	Federal 3d (West) AFTR (RIA) USTC (CCH)	Next highest appellate court
Tax Court (Regular decisions)	U.S. Gov't. Printing Office RIA/CCH separate services	Highest trial court*
Tax Court (Memorandum decisions)	RIA T.C.Memo. (RIA) TCM (CCH)	Less authority than Regular T.C. decision
U.S. Court of Federal Claims**	Federal Claims Reporter (West) AFTR (RIA) USTC (CCH)	Similar authority as Tax Court
U.S. District Courts	F.Supp.2d Series (West) AFTR (RIA) USTC (CCH)	Lowest trial court
Small Cases Division of Tax Court	U.S. Tax Court website***	No precedent value

*Theoretically, the Tax Court, Court of Federal Claims, and District Courts are on the same level of authority. But some people believe that since the Tax Court hears and decides tax cases from all parts of the country (i.e., it is a national court), its decisions may be more authoritative than a Court of Federal Claims or District Court decision.
**Before October 29, 1992, the U.S. Claims Court.
***Starting in 2001.

OTHER SOURCES OF THE TAX LAW

Other sources of tax information that a tax practitioner may need to consult include tax treaties and tax periodicals.

Tax Treaties

The United States signs certain tax treaties (sometimes called tax conventions) with foreign countries to render mutual assistance in tax enforcement and to avoid double taxation. Neither a tax law nor a tax treaty automatically takes precedence. When there is a direct conflict, the most recent item will take precedence. A taxpayer must disclose on the tax return any position where a treaty overrides a tax law.[21] There is a $1,000 per *failure to disclose* penalty for individuals and a $10,000 per failure to disclose penalty for corporations.[22]

Tax Periodicals

The use of tax periodicals can often shorten the research time needed to resolve a tax issue. If the article is relevant to the issue at hand, it may provide the references needed to locate the primary sources of the tax law that apply (e.g., citations to judicial decisions, Regulations, and other IRS pronouncements). Thus, the researcher obtains a "running start" in arriving at a solution to the problem.

[21] § 7852(d).

[22] Reg. §§ 301.6114–1, 301.6712–1, and 301.7701(b)(7).

GLOBAL
Tax Issues

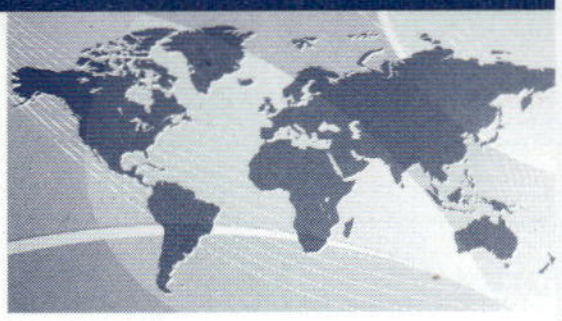

Tax Treaties

The United States has entered into treaties with most of the major countries of the world in order to eliminate possible double taxation. For example, nonresident alien students wishing to claim exemption from taxation are required to provide an information statement as set forth in several Revenue Procedures. The withholding agent must also certify the form.

Chinese students are required to prepare a four-part statement. Part 3 of the student's statement is as follows:

> I will receive compensation for personal services performed in the United States. This compensation qualifies for exemption from withholding of Federal income tax under the tax treaty between the United States and the People's Republic of China in an amount not in excess of $5,000 for any taxable year.

Among the many indexes available for locating tax articles on a particular tax problem is Commerce Clearing House's *Federal Tax Articles.* This multivolume service includes a subject index, a Code Section number index, and an author's index.

Another is the *Index to Federal Tax Articles* (published by Warren, Gorham, and Lamont). Both of these indexes are updated periodically, but are available only in print form.

The following are some of the more useful tax periodicals:

Journal of Taxation
Journal of International Taxation
Practical Tax Strategies
Estate Planning
Corporate Taxation
Business Entities
ria.thomsonreuters.com/Journals

The Tax Executive
www.tei.org

The Tax Adviser
aicpa.org/pubs/taxadv

Tax Law Review
www.law.nyu.edu/llmjsd/tax/taxlawreview/ECM_DLV_005627

Journal of the American Taxation Association
aaahq.org/ata/_ATAMenu/ATAPubJATA.html

The ATA Journal of Legal Tax Research
aaahq.org/ata/_ATAMenu/ATAPubJLTR.html

Oil, Gas & Energy Quarterly
www.bus.lsu.edu/accounting/faculty/lcrumbley/oilgas.html

Trusts and Estates
trustsandestates.com

Journal of Passthrough Entities
TAXES—The Tax Magazine
tax.cchgroup.com/Books

Tax Notes
taxanalysts.com

2.2 Working with the Tax Law—Tax Research Tools

LO.3

Have an awareness of tax research tools.

Tax law consists of a body of legislative (e.g., Code Sections, tax treaties), administrative (e.g., Regulations, Rulings), and judicial (e.g., court cases) pronouncements. Working with the tax law requires being able to effectively locate and use these sources. A key consideration is the time required to carry out this research and finding activity.

Unless the problem is simple (e.g., the Code Section is known, and there is a Regulation on point), the research process should begin with a tax service.

COMMERCIAL TAX SERVICES

Due to various changes, categorizing tax services has become an almost impossible task. Previously, services could be classified as *annotated* (i.e., organized by Internal Revenue Code) or *topical* (i.e., organized by major topics), but this classification system is no longer appropriate for many tax services as their format has been modified. Often the change is due to the acquisition of what was a competing tax service. For example, the *United States Tax Reporter* (annotated) now has a version that contains the *Federal Tax Coordinator 2d* (topical).

Tax services also can no longer be distinguished based on whether they are available only in hard copy or online versions. Previously, for example, *Tax Management Portfolios* was solely a print publication. Now, like most other tax services, it is also accessible online.

In addition, the list of publishers producing the tax services is not the same. Not only have there been ownership changes (e.g., Research Institute of America [RIA] now owns Prentice-Hall [P-H]), but also new players have arrived. LexisNexis for example, through *Tax Center*, offers primary tax services such as the Code and Regulations as well as material obtained from the Matthew Bender and Kleinrock services. Westlaw, due to its common ownership by Thomson, offers the RIA products and also the Mertens service.

Many new tax services have become like automobiles with a version to fit every practitioner's needs and financial resources. At one extreme, an abbreviated version of the regular ("Standard") service (e.g., CCH and its two-volume *Federal Tax Guide*) is designed for those with minimal tax research needs. For others, the basic product can include "extras" (e.g., CCH and its *Federal Excise Tax Reporter*).

A partial list of the available commercial tax services includes:

- *Standard Federal Tax Reporter*, Commerce Clearing House.
- *CCH IntelliConnect*, Commerce Clearing House Internet service.
- *United States Tax Reporter*, Research Institute of America.
- RIA *Checkpoint*, Research Institute of America. The online version of *United States Tax Reporter* also can include the *Federal Tax Coordinator 2d.*
- ATX/Kleinrock *Tax Expert*, CCH/Wolters Kluwer Business services.
- *Tax Management Portfolios*, Bureau of National Affairs.
- *Mertens Law of Federal Income Taxation*, West Group.
- Westlaw services—compilations include access to *Tax Management Portfolios*, *Federal Tax Coordinator 2d*, and *Mertens.*
- *TaxCenter*, LexisNexis compilation of primary sources and various materials taken from CCH, Matthew Bender, Kleinrock, and Bureau of National Affairs.
- *Federal Research Library*, Tax Analysts (a nonprofit organization) databases dealing with explanations and commentaries on primary source materials.

USING ONLINE TAX SERVICES

Instructions on how to use a tax service are not particularly worthwhile unless a specific service is involved. Even here, instructions need to be followed by hands-on experience to be effective. For online versions of a tax service, however, following certain procedures can simplify the research process. Since a practitioner's time is valuable and several research services base usage charges on time spent, time is of the essence.

When the principal emphasis is on time, every shortcut helps. The following suggestions (most of which are familiar to any user of the Internet) may be helpful.[23]

[23]For a more complete discussion of the use of RIA *Checkpoint* and CCH *Tax Research NetWork* and Internet research in taxation, see Raabe, Whittenburg, Sanders, and Sawyers, *South-Western's Federal Tax Research*, 9th ed. (Cengage Learning South-Western, 2011), Chapters 6 and 7.

- Choose keywords for the search carefully. Words with a broad usage, such as *income*, are worthless when standing alone. If the researcher is interested in qualified dividend income, even *dividend income* is too broad because it will call up stock dividends, constructive dividends, liquidating dividends, and more. By using *qualified dividend income* at the outset, the search is considerably narrowed. In RIA *Checkpoint*, for example, these two modifications narrowed the search from over 10,000 items to 3,824 and finally to 884. Obviously, further contraction will be needed, but at least the researcher is starting with a considerably smaller number of potential items.
- Take advantage of *connectors* to place parameters on the search and further restrict the output. Although each service has its own set of connectors, many are used by several services. Thus, quotation marks around a phrase mean *exact phrase* in both RIA *Checkpoint* and CCH *NetWork* (e.g., "personal service corporation").
- Be selective in choosing a database. For example, if the research project does not involve case law, there is no point in including the judicial decision component in the search database. Doing so just adds to the output items and will necessitate further screening through a search modification.
- Use a table of contents, index, or citation approach when appropriate. Although the keyword approach is most frequently used, databases can be searched in other ways. Using the table of contents or index is the usual approach with print versions of a tax service. With the citation route, access may be through a statutory (e.g., Code Section), administrative (e.g., Rev.Rul.), or judicial citation (e.g., Tax Court), depending on the tax service. When a judicial citation is involved and only the taxpayer's last name is known, though, problems can arise. For example, how many responses would a taxpayer named Smith yield? Likewise, before a Code Section is used, consider its scope. How many items would § 162 retrieve? Nevertheless, the use of a table of contents, index, or citation approach can be a valuable time-saver under the right circumstances.

NONCOMMERCIAL ONLINE SERVICES

The Internet provides a wealth of tax information in several popular forms, sometimes at no direct cost to the researcher. Using so-called browser software that often is distributed with new computer systems and their communication devices, the tax professional can access information provided around the world that can aid the research process.

- *Home pages (sites) on the Web* are provided by accounting and consulting firms, publishers, tax academics and libraries, and governmental bodies as a means of making information widely available or of soliciting subscriptions or consulting engagements. The best sites offer links to other sites and direct contact to the site providers. One of the best sites available to the tax practitioner is the Internal Revenue Service's home page, illustrated in Exhibit 2.2. This site offers downloadable forms and instructions, "plain English" versions of Regulations, and news update items. Exhibit 2.3 lists some of the websites that may be most useful to tax researchers and their Internet addresses as of press date. Particularly useful is the directory at **taxsites.com**, which provides links to accounting and tax sources (including international as well as payroll).
- *Newsgroups* provide a means by which information related to the tax law can be exchanged among taxpayers, tax professionals, and others who subscribe to the group's services. Newsgroup members can read the exchanges among other members and offer replies and suggestions to inquiries as desired. Discussions address the interpretation and application of existing law, analysis of proposals and new pronouncements, and reviews of tax software.

GLOBAL *Tax Issues*

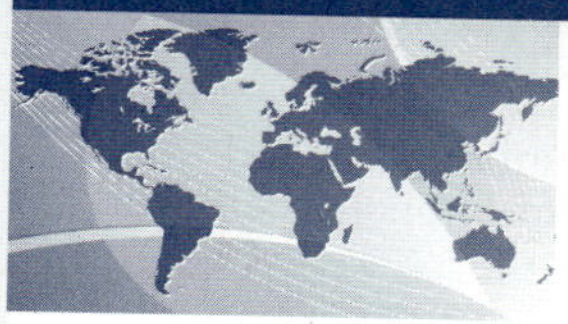

Data Warehousing Reduces Global Taxes

Many global companies are using data warehouses to collect data, which can be analyzed and used to minimize their global tax liabilities. "You take all of your tax data and dump it into a data warehouse," says Michael S. Burke of KPMG's e-tax solutions. "Next, it's applying a tool to define user requirements—compliance, real time analysis, etc." The company can then manipulate all of this information to reduce compliance costs, facilitate planning for value added taxes, and minimize time spent dealing with international tax problems.

For example, a company wishes to implement an e-procurement technique that would save it $100 million in expenses and increase taxable income. That could mean that about $40 million in additional taxes would go to the U.S. Treasury and state treasuries. By looking at the tax laws worldwide, the company may decide to base the operation in Bermuda, Ireland, or the Philippines where the tax will be only $20 million. That's a savings of $20 million, which is not taxable.

Source: Adapted from Jay Weinstein, "Internet Tax Solutions Proliferate," *Global Finance,* January 2001, pp. 74–75.

EXHIBIT 2.2 **The IRS's Home Page**

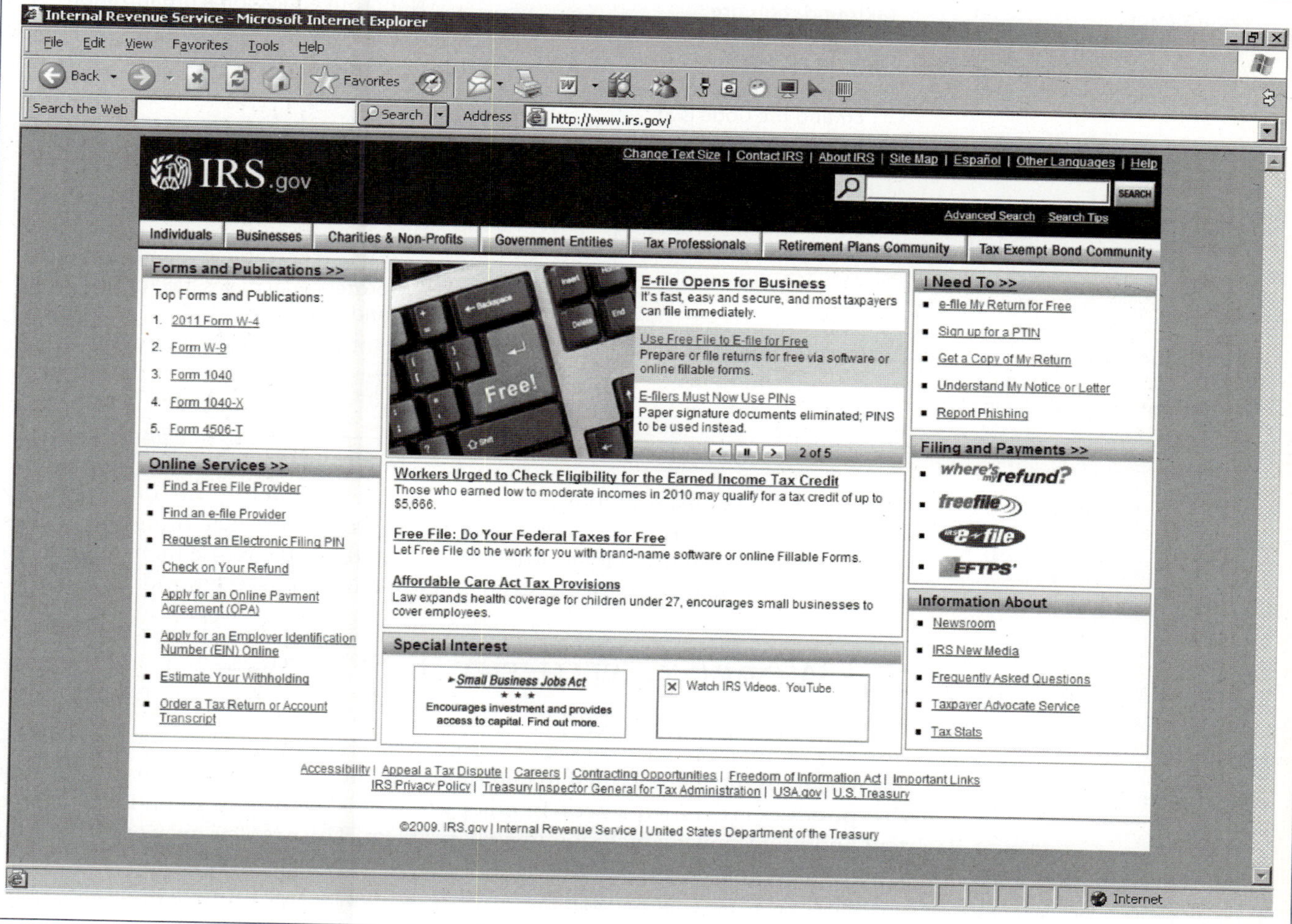

EXHIBIT 2.3 Tax-Related Websites

Website	Web Address at Press Date (usually preceded by http://www.)	Description
Accounting firms and professional organizations	For instance, the AICPA's page is at **aicpa.org**, Ernst and Young is at **ey.com**, and KPMG is at **kpmg.com**	Tax planning newsletters, descriptions of services offered and career opportunities, and exchange of data with clients and subscribers
Cengage Learning South-Western	**cengage.com/taxation/swft**	Informational updates, newsletters, support materials for students and adopters, and continuing education
Commercial tax publishers	For instance, **tax.com** and **cch.com**	Information about products and services available for subscription and newsletter excerpts
Court opinions	The site at **lexisone.com/lx1/caselaw/freecaselaw** covers some state, Federal circuit (last 10 years), and Supreme Court (all years) decisions but not the Tax Court	Provides a synopsis of result reached by the court
Internal Revenue Service	**irs.gov**	News releases, downloadable forms and instructions, tables, Circular 230, and e-mail
Tax Almanac	**taxalmanac.org**	Smorgasbord of tax research resources
Tax Analysts	**taxanalysts.com**	Policy-oriented readings on the tax law and proposals to change it, moderated bulletins on various tax subjects
Tax Foundation	**taxfoundation.org**	Nonprofit educational organization that promotes sound tax policy and measures tax burdens
Tax laws online	Regulations are at **law.cornell.edu/cfr** and the Code is at **uscode.house.gov/search/criteria.shtml** and **www4.law.cornell.edu/uscode**	
Tax Sites Directory	**taxsites.com**	References and links to tax sites on the Internet, including state and Federal tax sites, academic and professional pages, tax forms, and software
U.S. Tax Court decisions	**ustaxcourt.gov**	Recent U.S. Tax Court decisions

NOTE: Caution: addresses change frequently.

In many situations, solutions to research problems benefit from, or require, the use of various electronic tax research tools. A competent tax professional must become familiar and proficient with these tools and be able to use them to meet the expectations of clients and the necessities of work in the modern world.[24]

2.3 Working with the Tax Law—Tax Research

LO.4

Understand the tax research process.

Tax research is the method used to determine the best available solution to a situation that possesses tax consequences. In other words, it is the process of finding a competent and professional conclusion to a tax problem. The problem may originate from

[24]For a more detailed discussion of the use of electronic tax research in the modern tax practice, see Raabe, Whittenburg, Sanders, and Sawyers, *South-Western's Federal Tax Research*, 9th ed. (Cengage Learning South-Western, 2011).

FIGURE 2.5 Tax Research Process

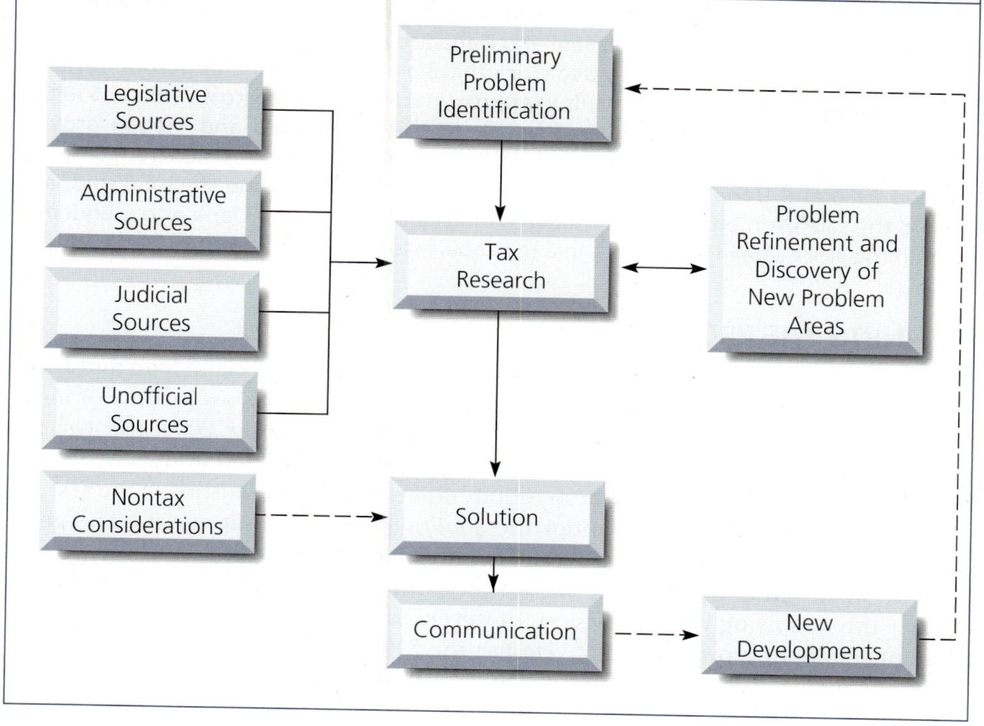

completed or proposed transactions. In the case of a completed transaction, the objective of the research is to determine the tax result of what has already taken place. For example, is the expenditure incurred by the taxpayer deductible or not deductible for tax purposes? When dealing with proposed transactions, the tax research process is concerned with the determination of possible alternative tax consequences. To the extent that tax research leads to a choice of alternatives or otherwise influences the future actions of the taxpayer, it becomes the key to effective tax planning.

Tax research involves the following procedures:

- Identifying and refining the problem.
- Locating the appropriate tax law sources.
- Assessing the validity of the tax law sources.
- Arriving at the solution or at alternative solutions while giving due consideration to nontax factors.
- Effectively communicating the solution to the taxpayer or the taxpayer's representative.
- Following up on the solution (where appropriate) in light of new developments.

This process is depicted schematically in Figure 2.5. The broken lines indicate steps of particular interest when tax research is directed toward proposed, rather than completed, transactions.

IDENTIFYING THE PROBLEM

Problem identification starts with a compilation of the relevant facts involved. In this regard, *all* of the facts that may have a bearing on the problem must be gathered, as any omission could modify the solution reached. To illustrate, consider what appears to be a very simple problem.

EXAMPLE 4

Early in December 2011, Fred and Megan review their financial and tax situation with their son, Sam, and daughter-in-law, Dana, who live with them. Fred and Megan are in the 28% tax bracket in 2011. Both Sam and Dana are age 21. Sam, a student at a nearby university, owns some publicly traded stock that he inherited from his grandmother. A current sale of the stock would result in approximately $8,000 of gross income ($19,000 amount realized – $11,000 adjusted basis). At this point, Fred and Megan provide about 55% of Sam and Dana's support. Although neither is now employed, Sam has earned $960 and Dana has earned $900. The problem: Should the stock be sold, and would the sale prohibit Fred and Megan from claiming Sam and Dana as dependents? Would the stock sale in 2011 result in a tax liability for Sam and Dana? ■

REFINING THE PROBLEM

Initial reaction is that Fred and Megan in Example 4 could not claim Sam and Dana as dependents if the stock is sold, since Sam would then have gross income of more than the exemption amount under § 151(d).[25] However, after 2004, the test for whether a child qualifies for dependency status is first conducted under the *qualifying child* requirements. Only if these requirements cannot be satisfied is the test for dependency status conducted under the *qualifying relative* requirements. The gross income test is applicable only under the qualifying relative status.[26] Thus, Sam could sell the stock without penalizing the parents with respect to the gross income test. Under the qualifying child provision, however, Sam must not have provided more than one-half of his own support.[27] Hence, the $19,000 of proceeds from the sale of the stock might lead to the failure of the not self-supporting requirement, depending on how much Sam spends for his support.

Assume, however, that further fact gathering reveals the following additional information:

- Sam does not really need to spend the proceeds from the sale of the stock.
- Sam receives a sizable portion of his own support from a scholarship.

With these new facts, additional research leads to § 152(f)(5) and Regulation § 1.152–1(c), which indicate that a scholarship received by a student is not included for purposes of determining whether Sam is self-supporting under the qualifying child provisions. Further, if Sam does not spend the proceeds from the sale of the stock, the unexpended amount is not counted for purposes of the not self-supporting test. Thus, it appears that the parents would not be denied the dependency exemptions for Sam and Dana, as the qualifying child requirements appear to be satisfied for Sam and the qualifying relative requirements appear to be satisfied for Dana.

LOCATING THE APPROPRIATE TAX LAW SOURCES

Once the problem is clearly defined, what is the next step? Although the next step is a matter of individual judgment, most tax research begins with the index volume of a hard copy tax service or a keyword search on an online tax service as described earlier. If the problem is not complex, the researcher may bypass the tax service or online service and turn directly to the Internal Revenue Code and the Treasury Regulations. For the beginner, the latter procedure saves time and will solve many of the more basic problems. If the researcher does not have a personal copy of the Code or Regulations, resorting to the appropriate volume(s) of a tax service will be necessary.[28]

[25] See related discussion in Chapter 3.

[26] Compare § 152(c) for qualifying child with § 152(d) for qualifying relative.

[27] § 152(c)(1)(D).

[28] Several of the major tax services publish paperback editions of the Code and Treasury Regulations that can be purchased at modest prices. These editions are usually revised twice each year. For an annotated and abridged version of the Code and Regulations that is published annually, see James E. Smith, *South-Western Federal Taxation: Internal Revenue Code of 1986 and Treasury Regulations: Annotated and Selected* (Cengage Learning South-Western, 2012).

ASSESSING THE VALIDITY OF THE TAX LAW SOURCES

Once a source has been located, the next step is to assess it in light of the problem at hand. Proper assessment involves careful interpretation of the tax law and consideration of its relevance and validity.

Interpreting the Internal Revenue Code

The language of the Code often is difficult to comprehend fully. Contrary to many people's suspicions, the Code is not written deliberately to confuse. Unfortunately, though, it often has that effect. The Code is intended to apply to more than 200 million taxpayers, many of whom are willing to exploit any linguistic imprecision to their benefit—to find a "loophole" in popular parlance. Many of the Code's provisions are limitations or restrictions involving two or more variables. Expressing such concepts algebraically would be more direct; using words to accomplish this task instead is often quite cumbersome. Among the worst such attempts was former § 341(e) relating to so-called collapsible corporations. One sentence had more than 450 words (twice as many as in Abraham Lincoln's Gettysburg Address). Within this same subsection was another sentence of 300 words.

Assessing the Validity of a Treasury Regulation

Treasury Regulations are the official interpretation of the Code and are entitled to great deference. Occasionally, however, a court will invalidate a Regulation or a portion thereof on the grounds that the Regulation is contrary to the intent of Congress. Usually, the courts do not question the validity of Regulations because of the belief that "the first administrative interpretation of a provision as it appears in a new act often expresses the general understanding of the times or the actual understanding of those who played an important part when the statute was drafted."[29]

Keep in mind the following observations when assessing the validity of a Regulation:

- IRS agents must give the Code and the Regulations issued thereunder equal weight when dealing with taxpayers and their representatives.
- Proposed Regulations provide a preview of future final Regulations, but they are not binding on the IRS or taxpayers.
- In a challenge, the burden of proof is on the taxpayer to show that a Regulation varies from the language of the statute and has no support in the Committee Reports.
- If the taxpayer loses the challenge, the negligence penalty may be imposed.[30] This accuracy-related penalty applies to any failure to make a reasonable attempt to comply with the tax law and to any disregard of rules and Regulations.[31]
- Final Regulations can be classified as procedural, interpretive, or legislative. **Procedural Regulations** neither establish tax laws nor attempt to explain tax laws. Procedural Regulations are *housekeeping-type* instructions, indicating information that taxpayers should provide the IRS, as well as information about the internal management and conduct of the IRS itself.
- Some **interpretive Regulations** rephrase and elaborate what Congress stated in the Committee Reports that were issued when the tax legislation was enacted. Such Regulations are *hard and solid* and almost impossible to overturn because they clearly reflect the intent of Congress.
- In some Code Sections, Congress has given the *Secretary or his delegate* the authority to prescribe Regulations to carry out the details of administration or to otherwise complete the operating rules. Under such circumstances, Congress effectively is delegating its legislative powers to the Treasury Department. Regulations issued pursuant to this type of authority possess

[29] *Augustus v. Comm.*, 41–1 USTC ¶9255, 26 AFTR 612, 118 F.2d 38 (CA–6, 1941).

[30] §§ 6662(a) and (b)(1).

[31] § 6662(c).

the force and effect of law and are often called **legislative Regulations** (e.g., consolidated return Regulations).

Assessing the Validity of Other Administrative Sources of the Tax Law

Revenue Rulings issued by the IRS carry less weight than Treasury Department Regulations. Revenue Rulings are important, however, in that they reflect the position of the IRS on tax matters. In any dispute with the IRS on the interpretation of tax law, taxpayers should expect agents to follow the results reached in any applicable Revenue Rulings.

Actions on Decisions further tell the taxpayer the IRS's reaction to certain court decisions. Recall that the IRS follows a practice of either acquiescing (agreeing) or nonacquiescing (not agreeing) with selected judicial decisions. A nonacquiescence does not mean that a particular court decision is of no value, but it does indicate that the IRS may continue to litigate the issue involved.

Assessing the Validity of Judicial Sources of the Tax Law

The judicial process as it relates to the formulation of tax law has been described. How much reliance can be placed on a particular decision depends upon the following variables:

- The higher the level of the court that issued a decision, the greater the weight accorded to that decision. A decision rendered by a trial court (e.g., a Federal District Court) carries less weight than one issued by an appellate court (e.g., the Fifth Circuit Court of Appeals). Unless Congress changes the Code, decisions by the U.S. Supreme Court represent the last word on any tax issue.
- More reliance is placed on decisions of courts that have jurisdiction in the area where the taxpayer's legal residence is located. If, for example, a taxpayer lives in Texas, a decision of the Fifth Circuit Court of Appeals means more than one rendered by the Second Circuit Court of Appeals. This is the case because any appeal from a District Court or the Tax Court would be to the Fifth Circuit Court of Appeals and not to the Second Circuit Court of Appeals.[32]
- A Tax Court Regular decision carries more weight than a Memorandum decision because the Tax Court does not consider Memorandum decisions to be binding precedents.[33] Furthermore, a Tax Court *reviewed* decision carries even more weight. All of the Tax Court judges participate in a reviewed decision.
- A Circuit Court decision where certiorari has been requested and denied by the Supreme Court carries more weight than a Circuit Court decision that was not appealed. A Circuit Court decision heard *en banc* (all the judges participate) carries more weight than a normal Circuit Court case.
- A decision that is supported by cases from other courts carries more weight than a decision that is not supported by other cases.
- The weight of a decision also can be affected by its status on appeal. For example, was the decision affirmed or overruled?

In connection with the last two variables, a citator is helpful to tax research.[34] A **citator** provides the history of a case, including the authority relied on (e.g., other judicial decisions) in reaching the result. Reviewing the references listed in the citator discloses whether the decision was appealed and, if so, with what result (e.g., affirmed, reversed, remanded). It also reveals other cases with the same or similar issues and how they were decided. Thus, a citator reflects on the validity of a case and may lead to other relevant judicial material.[35] If one intends to rely on a judicial decision to any significant degree, "running" the case through a citator is imperative.

[32]Before October 1, 1982, an appeal from the then-named U.S. Court of Claims (the other trial court) was directly to the U.S. Supreme Court.

[33]*Severino R. Nico, Jr.*, 67 T.C. 647 (1977).

[34]The major citators are published by Commerce Clearing House, RIA, Westlaw, and Shepard's Citations, Inc.

[35]The CCH version is available online through the CCH *NetWork* service; for RIA, use *Checkpoint*. Shepard's Internet version is part of LexisNexis.

TAX *in the NEWS*

THE AFTERMATH OF HEALTH CARE REFORM

In the recently passed health care reform legislation, Congress gave the IRS vast new powers and duties, but no extra money and personnel. For example, one new provision will affect 30 million sole proprietors and S corporations, 2 million farms, and 1 million charities. National Taxpayer Advocate Nina Olson says "the agency is now responsible for the most extensive social benefit program the IRS has been asked to implement in recent history." She indicates that without "sufficient funding" the IRS will not be able to discharge its new duties. This situation provides a reminder of attorney Jonathan Blattmachr's comment that "the U.S. Code is the most political law in the world."

Source: Adapted from "Lost in Taxation," Review and Outlook, *Wall Street Journal*, July 17, 2010.

Assessing the Validity of Other Sources

Primary sources of tax law include the Constitution, legislative history materials, statutes, treaties, Treasury Regulations, IRS pronouncements, and judicial decisions. In general, the IRS regards only primary sources as substantial authority. However, reference to *secondary materials* such as legal periodicals, treatises, legal opinions, General Counsel Memoranda, and written determinations may be useful. In general, secondary sources are not authority.

Although the statement that the IRS regards only primary sources as substantial authority is generally true, there is one exception. In Notice 90–20,[36] the IRS expanded the list of substantial authority *for purposes of* the accuracy-related penalty in § 6662 to include a number of secondary materials (e.g., letter rulings, General Counsel Memoranda, the Bluebook). "Authority" does not include conclusions reached in treatises, legal periodicals, and opinions rendered by tax professionals.

A letter ruling or determination letter is substantial authority *only* for the taxpayer to whom it is issued, except as noted above with respect to the accuracy-related penalty.

Upon the completion of major tax legislation, the staff of the Joint Committee on Taxation (in consultation with the staffs of the House Ways and Means and Senate Finance Committees) often will prepare a General Explanation of the Act, commonly known as the Bluebook because of the color of its cover. The IRS will not accept this detailed explanation as having legal effect. The Bluebook does, however, provide valuable guidance to tax advisers and taxpayers until Regulations are issued. Some letter rulings and General Counsel Memoranda of the IRS cite Bluebook explanations.

ARRIVING AT THE SOLUTION OR AT ALTERNATIVE SOLUTIONS

Example 4 raised the question of whether a taxpayer would be denied dependency exemptions for a son and a daughter-in-law if the son sold some stock near the end of the year. A refinement of the problem supplies the following additional information:

- Sam and Dana anticipate filing a joint return.

Section 152(b)(2) indicates that a taxpayer is not permitted a dependency exemption for a married dependent if the married individual files a joint return. Initial reaction is that a joint return by Sam and Dana would be disastrous to the parents. However, more research uncovers two Revenue Rulings that provide an exception if neither the dependent nor the dependent's spouse is required to file a return but does so solely to claim a refund of tax withheld. The IRS asserts that each spouse must have gross income of less than the exemption amount.[37] Therefore, if Sam sells the stock and he and Dana file a joint return, the parents would lose the dependency exemption for both Sam and Dana.

[36] 1990–1 C.B. 328; see also Reg. § 1.6661–3(b)(2).

[37] Rev.Rul. 54–567, 1954–2 C.B. 108; Rev.Rul. 65–34, 1965–1 C.B. 86.

FINANCIAL DISCLOSURE *Insights*

Where Does GAAP Come From?

As this chapter has described, the tax law is developed by many entities including Congress and the legislators of other countries, the courts, and the IRS. Accounting principles also have many sources. Consequently, in reconciling the tax and financial accounting reporting of a transaction, the tax professional will need to know the hierarchy of authority of accounting principles, and in particular, the level of importance to assign to a specific GAAP document. The diagram below presents the sources of GAAP, arranged in a general order of authority, from highest to lowest.

Professional research is conducted to find and analyze the sources of accounting reporting standards, in much the same way that a tax professional conducts research into an open tax question. In fact, many of the publishers that provide tax research materials also can be used to find GAAP and International Financial Reporting Standards (IFRS) documents. These include the Research Institute of America (RIA) and Commerce Clearing House (CCH). The Financial Standards Accounting Board (FASB) also makes its standards and interpretations available by subscription.

Highest Authority

- Financial Accounting Standards and Interpretations of the FASB.
- Pronouncements of bodies that preceded the FASB, such as the Accounting Principles Board (APB).

- FASB Technical Bulletins.
- Audit and Accounting Guides, prepared by the American Institute of CPAs (AICPA) and cleared by the FASB.
- Practice Bulletins, prepared by the American Institute of CPAs (AICPA) and cleared by the FASB.

- Interpretation Guides of the FASB Staff.
- Accounting Interpretations of the AICPA.
- IASB Accounting Standards.
- FASB Concepts Statements.
- Widely accepted accounting practices, professional journals, accounting textbooks, and treatises.

If the stock is not sold until January 2012, both dependency exemptions are available to the parents in 2011 even if Sam and Dana file a joint return. However, under § 151(d)(2), a personal exemption is not available to a taxpayer who can be claimed as a dependent by another taxpayer (whether actually claimed or not). Thus, if the parents can claim Sam and Dana as dependents, Sam and Dana would lose their personal exemptions on their tax return.

LO.5

Communicate the results of the tax research process in a client letter and a tax file memorandum.

COMMUNICATING TAX RESEARCH

Once the problem has been researched adequately, a memo, letter, or oral presentation setting forth the result may need to be prepared. The form such a communication takes could depend on a number of considerations. For example, does the employer or instructor recommend a particular procedure or format for tax research memos? Is the memo to be given directly to the client, or will it first go to the preparer's employer? Who is the audience for the oral presentation? How long should you talk?[38] Whatever form it takes, a good tax research communication should contain the following elements.

[38] For more on crafting oral presentations, see W. A. Raabe and G. E. Whittenburg, "Talking Tax: How to Make a Tax Presentation," *The Tax Adviser*, March 1997, pp. 179–182.

- A clear statement of the issue.
- In more complex situations, a short review of the fact pattern that raises the issue.
- A review of the pertinent tax law sources (e.g., Code, Regulations, Revenue Rulings, judicial authority).
- Any assumptions made in arriving at the solution.
- The solution recommended and the logic or reasoning supporting it.
- The references consulted in the research process.

Illustrations of the memos for the tax file and the client letter associated with Example 4 appear in Figures 2.6, 2.7, and 2.8.

2.4 Working with the Tax Law—Tax Planning

LO.6

Apply tax research techniques and planning procedures.

Tax research and tax planning are inseparable. The *primary* purpose of effective tax planning is to maximize the taxpayer's after-tax wealth. This statement does not mean that the course of action selected must produce the lowest possible tax under the circumstances. The minimization of tax liability must be considered in the context of the legitimate business goals of the taxpayer.

A *secondary* objective of effective tax planning is to reduce or defer the tax in the current tax year. Specifically, this objective aims to accomplish one or more results. Some possibilities are eradicating the tax entirely, eliminating the tax in the current year, deferring the receipt of income, proliferating taxpayers (i.e., forming partnerships and corporations or making lifetime gifts to family members), eluding double taxation, avoiding ordinary income, or creating, increasing, or accelerating deductions. However, this second objective should be approached with considerable reservation and moderation. For example, a tax election in one year may accomplish a current reduction in taxes, but it could saddle future years with a disadvantageous tax position.

NONTAX CONSIDERATIONS

There is a danger that tax motivations may take on a significance that does not conform to the true values involved. In other words, tax considerations can operate to impair the exercise of sound business judgment. Thus, the tax planning process can lead to ends that are socially and economically objectionable. Unfortunately, a tendency exists for planning to go toward the opposing extremes of either not enough or too much emphasis on tax considerations. The happy medium is a balance that recognizes the significance of taxes, but not beyond the point at which planning detracts from the exercise of good business judgment.

The remark is often made that a good rule is to refrain from pursuing any course of action that would not be followed were it not for certain tax considerations. This statement is not entirely correct, but it does illustrate the desirability of preventing business logic from being *sacrificed at the altar of tax planning*.

COMPONENTS OF TAX PLANNING

The popular perception of tax planning often is restricted to the adage "defer income and accelerate deductions." Although this timing approach does hold true and is important, meaningful tax planning involves considerably more.

Preferable to deferring income is complete *avoidance*. Consider, for example, the corporate employee who chooses nontaxable fringe benefits (e.g., group term life insurance, health insurance) over a fully taxable future pay increase.[39] Complete

[39]See Examples 19, 20, and 23 in Chapter 5.

FIGURE 2.6 Tax File Memorandum

August 16, 2011

TAX FILE MEMORANDUM

FROM: John J. Jones
SUBJECT: Fred and Megan Taxpayer
Engagement: Issues

Today I talked to Fred Taxpayer with respect to his August 12, 2011 letter requesting tax assistance. He wishes to know if his son, Sam, can sell stock worth $19,000 (basis = $11,000) without the parents losing the dependency exemptions for Sam and Sam's wife, Dana. Fred would also like to know the effect on Sam and Dana's tax liability in 2011 if the stock is sold.

Fred Taxpayer is married to Megan, and Sam is a full-time student at a local university. Sam inherited the stock from his grandmother about five years ago. If he sells the stock, he will save the proceeds from the sale. Sam does not need to spend the proceeds if he sells the stock because he receives a $5,500 scholarship that he uses for his own support (i.e., to pay for tuition, books, and fees). Although neither Sam nor Dana is currently employed, Sam has earned income of $960, and Dana has earned income of $900. Fred and Megan are in the 28% tax bracket and furnish approximately 55% of Sam and Dana's support.

ISSUES: If the stock is sold, would the sale prohibit Fred and Megan from claiming Sam and Dana as dependents? What is the effect on Sam and Dana's tax liability if the stock is sold in 2011? I told Fred that we would have an answer for him within two weeks.

avoidance of gain recognition also occurs when the owner of appreciated property transfers it by death. Presuming a step-up in basis occurs, the built-in appreciation escapes the income tax forever.[40]

If the recognition of income cannot be avoided, its deferral will postpone income tax consequences. *Deferral* of income can take many forms. Besides like-kind exchanges and involuntary conversions, most retirement plans put off income tax consequences until the payout period. Deferral of gain recognition also can occur when appreciated property is transferred to a newly formed corporation or partnership.[41]

A corollary to the deferral of income is the acceleration of deductions. For example, an accrual basis, calendar year corporation desires an additional charitable deduction for 2011 but has a cash-flow problem. If the corporation authorizes the contribution in 2011 and pays it on or before March 15, 2012, the deduction can be claimed for 2011.[42] Taxes can be saved by *shifting* income to lower-bracket taxpayers. Gifts of appreciated property to lower-bracket family members can reduce the applicable capital gain rate on a later sale by 15 percentage points (from 15 percent to 0 percent).[43]

If income cannot be avoided, deferred, or shifted, the nature of the gain can be *converted*. By changing the classification of property, income taxes can be reduced.[44] Thus, a taxpayer who transfers appreciated inventory to a controlled corporation has converted ordinary income property to a capital asset. When the taxpayer's stock is later sold, preferential capital gain rates apply.

The conversion approach also can work in tax planning for losses. Properly structured, a loan to a corporation that becomes worthless can be an ordinary loss rather than the less desirable capital loss. Likewise, planning with § 1244 permits an investor in qualified small business stock to convert what would be a capital loss into an ordinary loss.[45]

40 See Examples 25 and 27 in Chapter 13.

41 See Example 1 in Chapter 18, Examples 8 and 9 in Chapter 21, and Section 4.6 in Chapter 4.

42 See Example 15 in Chapter 17.

43 See Section 13.9 in Chapter 13.

44 See Example 53 in Chapter 4.

45 See Example 8 in Chapter 7.

FIGURE 2.7 Tax File Memorandum

August 26, 2011

TAX FILE MEMORANDUM

FROM: John J. Jones
SUBJECT: Fred and Megan Taxpayer
Engagement: Conclusions

See the Tax File Memorandum dated August 16, 2011, which contains the facts and identifies the tax issues.

Section 152(a) provides that in order for a taxpayer to take a dependency exemption, the potential dependent must satisfy either the qualifying child requirements or the qualifying relative requirements (see Chapter 3). Fred and Megan provide about 55% of the support of their son, Sam, and their daughter-in-law, Dana. If Sam should sell the stock in 2011, he would not need to spend the proceeds for support purposes (i.e., he would save the proceeds). Thus, the stock sale would not affect his qualifying as not self-supporting under § 152(c)(1)(D). In calculating the percentage of support provided by Fred and Megan, a $5,500 scholarship received by Sam is not counted in determining the amount of support Sam provides for himself [see § 152(f)(5) and Reg. § 1.152–1(c)]. Note, however, that if the $5,500 had been provided by student loans, it would have been included in calculating support [*Philip J. McCauley*, 56 T.C. 48 (1971)].

Section 152(d)(1)(B) provides that in order to qualify for a dependency exemption as a qualifying relative, the potential dependent's gross income must be less than the exemption amount (i.e., $3,700 in 2011). Without the stock sale, the gross income of both Sam ($960) and Dana ($900) will be below the exemption amount in 2011. The $5,500 Sam receives as a scholarship is excluded from his gross income under § 117(a) because he uses the entire amount to pay for his tuition, books, and fees at a local university.

Although the gross income test is not applicable to Sam (as a qualifying child), it is applicable to Dana, the daughter-in-law (a qualifying relative). [See Concept Summary 3.1.] A key issue is whether the stock sale that will produce $8,000 of recognized gain for Sam and Dana will cause the gross income test to be violated for Dana. Since the $8,000 recognized gain is from the sale of Sam's separately owned asset and they do not live in a community property state, Dana should qualify as a dependent because her gross income would be only $900.

Sam must not be self-supporting under the qualifying child requirements. So, if the stock is sold, he must limit his spending of the sales proceeds such that he continues to be supported by his parents. Since he plans on not spending any of the sales proceeds, this should not be an issue.

The stock sale would result in the parents' loss of the dependency exemptions for Sam and Dana if they file a joint return for 2011 [see § 152(b)(2)]. The joint return requirement does not apply, however, if the dependent files a joint return solely to claim a refund and neither spouse had a tax liability on a separate return (Rev.Rul. 65–34, 1965–1 C.B. 86). However, sale of the stock would keep this exception from applying.

From a tax planning perspective, Sam can choose to sell the stock in 2011. However, if this choice is made, Sam and Dana need to file separate returns so as not to violate the absence of a joint return provision. Under these circumstances, the sale will not interfere with Fred and Megan's ability to claim dependency exemptions for Sam and Dana on their 2011 return. Note, however, that neither Sam nor Dana will be permitted to take a personal exemption deduction on their 2011 tax return since they are claimed as dependents on someone else's return [see § 151(d)(2)]. This disallowance of the personal exemption deduction will not produce any significant negative tax consequences for Dana since her tax liability would be $0. However, Sam's tax liability would now be $915 (see the kiddie tax in Chapter 3). Alternatively, Sam could delay the sale of the stock until 2012. In this case, Sam and Dana's tax liability in 2011 would be $0. The disallowance of the personal exemption deductions by Sam and Dana will not produce any negative tax consequences since both Sam and Dana's tax liability would be $0.

Effective tax planning requires that careful consideration be given to the *choice of entity* used for conducting a business. The corporate form results in double taxation but permits shareholder-employees to be covered by fringe benefit programs. Partnerships and S corporations allow a pass-through of losses and other tax attributes, but transferring ownership interests as gifts to family members may be difficult.[46]

Although the substance of a transaction, rather than its form, generally controls, this rule is not always the case with tax planning. *Preserving formalities* often is crucial to the result. Is an advance to a corporation a loan or a contribution to capital? The answer may well depend on the existence of a note. Along with preserving formalities, the taxpayer should keep records that support a transaction. Returning to the

[46]See Chapters 21 and 22.

FIGURE 2.8 **Client Letter**

Hoffman, Maloney, Raabe, and Young CPAs
5191 Natorp Boulevard
Mason, Ohio 45040

August 30, 2011

Mr. and Ms. Fred Taxpayer
111 Boulevard
Williamsburg, Virginia 23185

Dear Mr. and Ms. Taxpayer:

This letter is in response to your request for us to review your family's financial and tax situation. Our conclusions are based upon the facts as outlined in your August 12th letter. Any change in the facts may affect our conclusions.

You provide over 50% of the support for your son, Sam, and his wife, Dana. The scholarship Sam receives is not included in determining support. If the stock is not sold, you will qualify for a dependency exemption for both Sam and Dana.

If the stock is sold, a gain of approximately $8,000 will result. If Sam and Dana then file a joint return, you would lose the dependency exemption for Sam as a qualifying child and would lose the dependency exemption for Dana as a qualifying relative. You can avoid the loss of these two dependency exemptions if Sam and Dana file separate returns. This would result in a tax liability of $0 for Dana and $915 for Sam.

From a family tax planning and tax avoidance perspective, Sam should not sell the stock in 2011. Delaying the stock sale will enable you to claim dependency exemptions for both Sam and Dana and will enable Sam and Dana to have a $0 tax liability for 2011.

Should you need more information or need to clarify our conclusions, do not hesitate to contact me.

Sincerely yours,

John J. Jones, CPA
Partner

issue of loan versus contribution to capital, how is the advance listed on the books of the borrower? What do the corporate minutes say about the advance?

Lastly, effective tax planning requires *consistency* on the part of taxpayers. A shareholder who treats a corporate distribution as a return of capital cannot later avoid a stock basis adjustment by contending that the distribution was really a dividend.

In summary, the key components of tax planning include the following:

- *Avoid* the recognition of income (usually by resorting to a nontaxable source or nontaxable event).
- *Defer* the recognition of income (or accelerate deductions).
- *Convert* the classification of income (or deductions) to a more advantageous form (e.g., ordinary income into capital gain).
- *Choose* the business *entity* with the desired tax attributes.
- Preserve *formalities* by generating and maintaining supporting documentation.
- Act in a manner *consistent* with the intended objective.

TAX EVASION AND TAX AVOIDANCE

A fine line exists between legal tax planning and illegal tax planning—tax avoidance versus tax evasion. **Tax avoidance** is merely tax minimization through legal techniques. In this sense, tax avoidance is the proper objective of all tax planning. Though eliminating or reducing taxes is also a goal of tax evasion, the term implies the use of subterfuge and fraud as a means to this end. Perhaps because common goals are involved, popular usage has blurred the distinction between the two concepts. Consequently, the association of tax avoidance with tax evasion has kept some taxpayers from properly taking advantage of planning possibilities. The now classic words of Judge Learned Hand in *Commissioner v. Newman* reflect the true values a taxpayer should have:

> Over and over again courts have said that there is nothing sinister in so arranging one's affairs as to keep taxes as low as possible. Everybody does so, rich or poor; and all do right, for nobody owes any public duty to pay more than the law demands: taxes are enforced extractions, not voluntary contributions. To demand more in the name of morals is mere cant.[47]

As Denis Healy, a former British Chancellor, once said, "The difference between tax avoidance and tax evasion is the thickness of a prison wall."

ETHICS & Equity

WHO DID NOT PAY HIS INCOME TAXES PROPERLY?

Representative Charles P. Rangel had to write six checks for a total of approximately $10,800 in back (Federal and state) taxes due on his 2005, 2006, and 2007 tax returns. Among other items, he overlooked paying income taxes on rent income on a beach house he owns in the Dominican Republic. Rangel was chairman of the tax writing committee—the House Ways and Means Committee. Apparently, penalties and interest were not included in the amount paid. What are your thoughts?

Source: Adapted from "Morality and Charles Rangel's Taxes," *Wall Street Journal* online, July 27, 2009.

The Government Accountability Office estimates that U.S. taxpayers spend at least $107 billion each year on tax compliance costs. The Treasury Department estimates that individuals spend at least 6.4 billion hours preparing Federal income tax returns. Small businesses, self-employed persons, and taxpayers with the highest marginal tax rates have the highest levels of tax evasion.[48]

FOLLOW-UP PROCEDURES

Because tax planning usually involves a proposed (as opposed to a completed) transaction, it is predicated upon the continuing validity of the advice based upon the tax research. A change in the tax law (either legislative, administrative, or judicial) could alter the original conclusion. Additional research may be necessary to test the solution in light of current developments (refer to the broken lines at the right in Figure 2.5).

TAX PLANNING—A PRACTICAL APPLICATION

Returning to the facts of Example 4, what could be done to protect the dependency exemptions for the parents? If Sam and Dana refrain from filing a joint return, both could be claimed by the parents.

An obvious tax planning tool is the installment method. Could the securities be sold using the installment method under § 453 so that most of the gain is deferred into the next year? Under the installment method, certain gains may be postponed and recognized as the cash proceeds are received. The problem is that the installment method is not available for stock traded on an established securities market.[49]

A little more research, however, indicates that Sam may be able to sell the stock and postpone the recognition of gain until the following year by selling short an equal number of substantially identical shares and covering the short sale in the subsequent year with the shares originally held. Selling short means that Sam sells borrowed stock (substantially identical) and repays the lender with the stock held on the date of the short sale. This *short against the box* technique would allow Sam to protect his $8,000 profit and defer the closing of the sale until the following year.[50]

[47] *Comm. v. Newman,* 47–1 USTC ¶9175, 35 AFTR 857, 159 F.2d 848 (CA–2, 1947).

[48] Adapted from J. A. Tackett, Joe Antenucci, and Fran Wolf, "A Criminological Perspective of Tax Evasion," *Tax Notes,* February 6, 2006, pp. 654–658; L. E. Burman, "Tax Evasion, IRS Priorities, and the EITC," *Statement before the United States House of Representatives Committee on the Budget; On Waste, Fraud, and Abuse in Federal Mandatory Programs,* July 9, 2003.

[49] See Chapter 16 for a discussion of installment sales.

[50] §§ 1233(a) and 1233(b)(2). See Chapter 14 for a discussion of short sales.

TAX *in* *the NEWS*

The Disappearing Taxpayers

Should income taxes be increased, or not decreased, especially on the bottom 50 percent of taxpayers? Should the tax base be expanded? Recent tax data lend credence to such unpopular opinions.

In 2007, the top 50 percent of taxpayers paid 97.11 percent of Federal income taxes, and the bottom 50 percent paid only 2.89 percent. The top 10 percent paid 71.33 percent of Federal income taxes. For 2009, almost 47 percent of potential taxpayers paid no taxes, either because their income was too low or because they qualified for enough credits, exclusions, and deductions to eliminate their Federal income tax liability. More disturbing is the fact that the bottom 40 percent made a profit from the Federal income tax—our government sent them a payment. It would appear that these people are getting something for nothing.

President Obama's making work pay credit and the expanded child tax credit and earned income tax credit have shifted the tax burden even further onto the top earners. Shifting the tax burden onto a smaller and smaller segment of high-income earners could be economically dangerous.

Another problem is that the Internet is helping taxpayers to disappear. In a *New Yorker* magazine cartoon, two dogs are sitting in front of a computer screen: one tells the other, "On the Internet, nobody knows that you are a dog." Similarly, in order to collect a tax, the government must know who is liable to pay the tax. Taxpayers are becoming increasingly more difficult to identify as anonymous electronic money and uncrackable encryption techniques are developed.

Sources: Adapted from Curtis S. Dubay, "The Rich Pay More Taxes: Top 20 Percent Pay Record Share of Income Taxes," The Heritage Foundation, **www.heritage.org/research/taxes/wm2420.cfm**; Stephen Ohlmacher, "Nearly Half of U.S. Households Escape Fed Income Tax," Yahoo! News, April 7, 2010.

However, additional research indicates that 1997 tax legislation provides that the short against the box technique will no longer produce the desired postponement of recognized gain. That is, at the time of the short sale, Sam will have a recognized gain of $8,000 from a constructive sale. Note the critical role of obtaining the correct facts in attempting to resolve the proper strategy for the taxpayers.

Throughout this text, most chapters include observations on Tax Planning. Such observations are not all-inclusive but are intended to illustrate some of the ways in which the material covered can be effectively utilized to minimize taxes.

2.5 Taxation on the CPA Examination

LO.7

Be aware of taxation on the CPA examination.

The CPA examination has changed from a paper-and-pencil exam to a computer-based exam with increased emphasis on information technology and general business knowledge. The 14-hour exam has four sections, and taxation is included in the 3-hour Regulations section.

The CPA examination is not curved to produce a designated pass rate. In theory, if all candidates are well prepared, they will all pass. Of course, if all are unprepared, all could fail. The likelihood of passing at least one section is greater for candidates who take more than one CPA examination section in a testing window.

As of January 1, 2011, the CPA examination has been reorganized so that all written communication tasks are concentrated in the Business Environment & Concepts section. Shorter simulations have replaced the longer simulations.

Each exam section includes both multiple-choice questions and two other sections that will have short task-based simulation (TBS) questions. The Regulations section is 60 percent Taxation and 40 percent Law & Professional Responsibilities (all areas other than Business Structure). The three-hour Regulations section has a new format. It now contains:

- Three multiple-choice question (MCQ) testlets consisting of 72 questions.
- One testlet (i.e., a group of questions prepared to appear together) containing six short task-based simulations with the research question in a new format.

A candidate may review and change answers within each testlet but cannot go back after exiting a testlet. Candidates take different, but equivalent exams.

Simulations are small case studies designed to test a candidate's tax knowledge and skills using real-life work-related situations. Simulations include a four-function pop-up calculator, a blank spreadsheet with some elementary functionality, and authoritative literature appropriate to the subject matter. The taxation database includes authoritative excerpts (e.g., Internal Revenue Code, Regulations, IRS publications, and Federal tax forms) that are necessary to complete the tax case study simulations. Examples of such simulations follow.

EXAMPLE 5

The *tax citation type* simulation requires the candidate to research the Internal Revenue Code and enter a Code Section and subsection. For example, Amber Company is considering using the simplified dollar-value method of pricing its inventory for purposes of the LIFO method that is available to certain small businesses. What Internal Revenue Code Section is the relevant authority to which you should turn to determine whether the taxpayer is eligible to use this method? To be successful, the candidate needs to find § 474. ■

EXAMPLE 6

A *tax form completion* simulation requires the candidate to fill out a portion of a tax form. For example, Red Company is a limited liability company (LLC) for tax purposes. Complete the income section of the IRS Form 1065 for Red Company using the values found and calculated on previous tabs along with the following data:

Ordinary income from other partnerships	$ 5,200
Net gain (loss) from Form 4797	2,400
Management fee income	12,000

The candidate is provided with page 1 of Form 1065 on which to record the appropriate amounts.

Any field that requires an entry is a shaded rectangular cell. Some white rectangular cells will automatically calculate based on the entries in the shaded cell. ■

Candidates can learn more about the CPA examination at **www.cpa-exam.org**. This online tutorial site's topics include:

- Common tools.
- Navigation.
- Forms completion.
- Numeric entry.
- Research questions.
- Authoritative literature search.
- Written communication.

The common tools are a calculator, spreadsheet, reminder flags, and examination clock. A 30- to 60-minute sample exam will familiarize a candidate with the types of questions on the examination.

KEY TERMS

Acquiescence, 2–16
Circuit Court of Appeals, 2–14
Citator, 2–28
Court of original jurisdiction, 2–11
Determination letters, 2–10
Federal District Court, 2–11
Finalized Regulations, 2–7
Interpretive Regulations, 2–27
Legislative Regulations, 2–28
Letter rulings, 2–9
Nonacquiescence, 2–17
Precedents, 2–15
Procedural Regulations, 2–27
Proposed Regulations, 2–7
Revenue Rulings, 2–8
Revenue Procedures, 2–8
Small Cases Division, 2–11
Tax avoidance, 2–34
Tax research, 2–24
Technical Advice Memoranda (TAMs), 2–10
Temporary Regulations, 2–7
U.S. Court of Federal Claims, 2–11
U.S. Supreme Court, 2–15
U.S. Tax Court, 2–11
Writ of Certiorari, 2–15

DISCUSSION QUESTIONS

1. **LO.1** What are the primary sources of tax information?
2. **LO.1** Taxpayers should always minimize their tax liability. Discuss this statement.
3. **LO.1** When did Congress first codify all of the Federal tax laws?
4. **LO.1** What happens when the House and Senate versions of major tax bills differ?
5. **LO.1** Why may Committee Reports be valuable to tax practitioners and taxpayers?

COMMUNICATIONS

6. **LO.2, 5** Butch Bishop operates a small international firm named Tile, Inc. A new treaty between the United States and France conflicts with a Section of the Internal Revenue Code. Butch asks you for advice. If he follows the treaty position, does he need to disclose this on his tax return? If he is required to disclose, are there any penalties for failure to disclose? Prepare a letter in which you respond to Butch. Tile's address is 100 International Drive, Tampa, FL 33620.
7. **LO.1, 2** Interpret this Regulation citation: Reg. § 1.162–5(a)(1).
8. **LO.1, 2** Explain how Regulations are arranged. How would the following Regulations be cited?
   a. Finalized Regulations under § 351.
   b. Proposed Regulations under § 2036.
   c. Temporary Regulations under § 482.
   d. Legislative Regulations under § 1504.
9. **LO.1, 4** Distinguish between legislative, interpretive, and procedural Regulations.
10. **LO.1** In the citation Rev.Rul. 76–175, 1976–1 C.B. 92, to what do the 175 and the 92 refer?
11. **LO.1, 4** Rank the following items from the lowest authority to the highest in the Federal tax law system:
    a. Interpretive Regulation.
    b. Legislative Regulation.
    c. Letter ruling.
    d. Revenue Ruling.
    e. Internal Revenue Code.
    f. Proposed Regulation.
12. **LO.1** Interpret each of the following citations:
    a. Prop.Reg. § 1.1001–3(h)(2).
    b. Rev.Proc. 2002–38, 2002–1 C.B. 1037.
    c. Ltr.Rul. 9015014.

ISSUE ID

13. **LO.1** Dwain receives a 90-day letter after his discussion with an appeals officer. He is not satisfied with the $92,000 settlement offer. Identify the relevant tax research issues facing Dwain.
14. **LO.1** Which of the following would be considered advantages of the Small Cases Division of the Tax Court?
    a. Appeal to the U.S. Tax Court is possible.
    b. A hearing of a deficiency of $65,000 is considered on a timely basis.
    c. Taxpayer can handle the litigation without using a lawyer or certified public accountant.
    d. Taxpayer can use Small Cases Division decisions for precedential value.
    e. The actual hearing is conducted informally.
    f. Travel time will probably be reduced.
15. **LO.1** List an advantage and a disadvantage of using the U.S. District Court as the trial court for Federal tax litigation.

COMMUNICATIONS

16. **LO.1, 5** Caleb Toombs is considering litigating a tax deficiency of approximately $323,000 in the court system. He asks you to provide him with a short description of his alternatives indicating the advantages and disadvantages of each. Prepare your response to Caleb in the form of a letter. His address is 200 Mesa Drive, Tucson, AZ 85714.

17. **LO.1** List an advantage and a disadvantage of using the U.S. Tax Court as the trial court for Federal tax litigation.

18. **LO.1** A taxpayer lives in Michigan. In a controversy with the IRS, the taxpayer loses at the trial court level. Describe the appeal procedure for each of the following trial courts:
    a. Small Cases Division of the U.S. Tax Court.
    b. U.S. Tax Court.
    c. U.S. District Court.
    d. U.S. Court of Federal Claims.

19. **LO.1** What is meant by *petitioner*?

20. **LO.1** An appellate court will often become involved in fact-finding determination. Discuss the validity of this statement.

21. **LO.1** In which of the following states could a taxpayer appeal the decision of a U.S. District Court to the Ninth Circuit Court of Appeals?
    a. Alaska.
    b. Arkansas.
    c. Florida.
    d. New York.
    e. Kansas.

22. **LO.1** What determines the appropriate Circuit Court of Appeals for a particular taxpayer?

23. **LO.1, 4** In assessing the validity of a prior court decision, discuss the significance of the following on the taxpayer's issue:
    a. The decision was rendered by the U.S. District Court of Wyoming. Taxpayer lives in Wyoming.
    b. The decision was rendered by the U.S. Court of Federal Claims. Taxpayer lives in Wyoming.
    c. The decision was rendered by the Second Circuit Court of Appeals. Taxpayer lives in California.
    d. The decision was rendered by the U.S. Supreme Court.
    e. The decision was rendered by the U.S. Tax Court. The IRS has acquiesced in the result.
    f. Same as (e), except that the IRS has nonacquiesced in the result.

24. **LO.2** Is there an automatic right to appeal to the U.S. Supreme Court? What is the process?

25. **LO.2** Interpret each of the following citations:
    a. 81 T.C. 782 (1983).
    b. 125 F.3d 120 (CA–3, 1997).
    c. 2005–2 USTC ¶50,575 (CA–2, 2005).
    d. 96 AFTR 2d 2005–6344 (CA–2, 2005).
    e. 330 F.Supp.2d 122 (D.Ct. Conn., 2004).

26. **LO.1, 2** Explain the following abbreviations:
    a. CA–2.
    b. Fed.Cl.
    c. *aff'd.*
    d. *rev'd.*
    e. *rem'd.*
    f. *Cert. denied.*
    g. *acq.*
    h. B.T.A.
    i. USTC.
    j. AFTR.
    k. F.3d.
    l. F.Supp.
    m. USSC.
    n. S.Ct.
    o. D.Ct.

27. **LO.2** Give the Commerce Clearing House citation for each of the following courts:
    a. Small Cases Division of the Tax Court.
    b. Federal District Court.
    c. U.S. Supreme Court.
    d. U.S. Court of Federal Claims.
    e. Tax Court Memorandum decision.

28. **LO.2** Where can you locate a published decision of the U.S. Court of Federal Claims?

29. **LO.1, 2** Which of the following items can probably be found in the *Cumulative Bulletin*?
    a. Action on Decision.
    b. Small Cases Division of the U.S. Tax Court decision.
    c. Letter ruling.

d. Revenue Procedure.
e. Finalized Regulation.
f. U.S. Court of Federal Claims decision.
g. Senate Finance Committee Report.
h. Acquiescences to Tax Court decisions.
i. U.S. Circuit Court of Appeals decision.

ISSUE ID

30. **LO.3** Yvonne has to prepare a research paper discussing the tax aspects of alimony payments for her tax class. Explain to Yvonne how she can research this topic using hard copy.

31. **LO.6** What is the difference between tax avoidance and tax evasion?

PROBLEMS

32. **LO.1** In which Subchapter of the Internal Revenue Code would one find information about partnership taxation?
 a. Subchapter S.
 b. Subchapter C.
 c. Subchapter P.
 d. Subchapter K.
 e. Subchapter M.

33. **LO.1** In order to locate an IRS Revenue Procedure that was issued during the past week, which source would you consult?
 a. *Cumulative Bulletin.*
 b. *Federal Register.*
 c. *Internal Revenue Bulletin.*
 d. Internal Revenue Code.
 e. Some other source.

34. **LO.1, 4** Rank the items below from the most reliable to the least reliable:
 a. Letter Ruling.
 b. Legislative Regulation.
 c. Code Section.
 d. Revenue Ruling.
 e. Proposed Regulation.
 f. Interpretive Regulation.
 g. Recent Temporary Regulation.

35. **LO.1, 2** Using the legend provided, classify each of the following citations as to publisher:

Legend		
RIA	=	Research Institute of America
CCH	=	Commerce Clearing House
W	=	West
U.S.	=	U.S. Government
O	=	Others

 a. 24 T.C. 818.
 b. 64 TCM 1594.
 c. 563 F.Supp. 379.
 d. 45 AFTR 2d 80–1487.
 e. 54–2 USTC ¶9714.
 f. RIA T.C.Memo. Dec. ¶92726.
 g. Announcement 2006–30, 2006–1 C.B. 879.
 h. Rev.Rul. 71–381, 1971–2 C.B. 126.
 i. 104 S.Ct 1495.
 j. 348 U.S. 426.

36. **LO.6** Using the legend provided, classify each of the following statements:

Legend		
A	=	Tax avoidance
E	=	Tax evasion
N	=	Neither

a. Monica writes a $1,000 check for a charitable contribution on December 28, 2011, but does not mail the check to the charitable organization until January 10, 2012. She takes a deduction in 2011.
b. Robert decides not to report interest income from a bank because the amount is only $11.75.
c. Jim pays property taxes on his home in December 2011 rather than waiting until February 2012.
d. Jane switches her investments from taxable corporate bonds to tax-exempt municipal bonds.
e. Ted encourages his mother to save most of her Social Security benefits so that he will be able to claim her as a dependent.

RESEARCH PROBLEMS

Note: Solutions to Research Problems can be prepared by using the **Checkpoint® Student Edition** online research product, which is available to accompany this text. It is also possible to prepare solutions to the Research Problems by using tax research materials found in a standard tax library.

THOMSON REUTERS
Checkpoint® Student Edition

Research Problem 1. Determine the missing data in these court decisions and rulings:

a. *Deputy v. DuPont*, 308 U.S. 488 (______).
b. *Katz v. U.S.*, 67 AFTR 2d 91–733 (Cl.Ct., ______).
c. *General Electric Co. v. U.S.*, 83–2 USTC ¶9532 (______, 1983).
d. *U.S. v. Scott*, 167 F.2d ______ (CA–8, 1948).
e. *Ralph R. Garrow*, 43 T.C. 890 (______).
f. *Estate of Clint M. Smith*, 36 TCM ______ (1977).
g. Rev.Rul. 69–______, 1969–1 C.B. 100.
h. Rev.Rul. 60–226, 1960–1 C.B. ______.

Research Problem 2. Most major airlines offer frequent-flyer programs that allow passengers to accumulate miles for each flight. Individuals may also earn frequent-flyer miles or other promotional benefits in other ways, such as through rental cars or hotels. These promotional benefits may generally be exchanged for upgraded seating, free travel, discounted travel, travel-related services, or other services or benefits. Are frequent-flyer miles taxable?

Use the tax resources of the Internet to address the following question. Do not restrict your search to the Web, but include a review of newsgroups and general reference materials, practitioner sites and resources, primary sources of the tax law, chat rooms and discussion groups, and other opportunities.

INTERNET *activity*

Research Problem 3. Go to **www.taxalmanac.org** and **www.Legalbitstream.com** on the Internet and find the following:

a. Letter Rulings.
b. Actions on Decisions.
c. IRS Notices.
d. General Counsel Memoranda.
e. Technical Advice Memoranda.
f. Treasury Decisions.
g. Revenue Rulings.
h. Revenue Procedures.
i. IRS Announcements.
j. U.S. Tax Court Summary Decisions.
k. U.S. Tax Court Memorandum Decisions.

CHAPTER 3

Computing the Tax

LEARNING OBJECTIVES

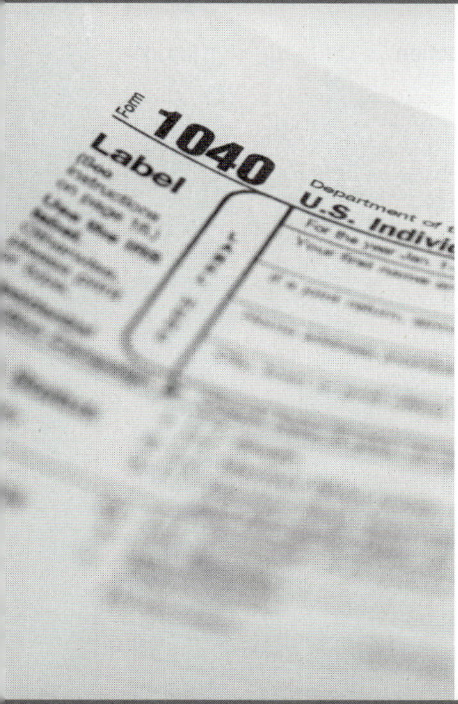

After completing Chapter 3, you should be able to:

LO.1 Recognize and apply the components of the Federal income tax formula.

LO.2 Explain the use of the standard deduction in computing taxable income.

LO.3 Apply the rules for arriving at personal exemptions.

LO.4 Apply the rules for determining dependency exemptions.

LO.5 List the filing requirements and choose the proper filing status.

LO.6 Use the proper method for determining the tax liability.

LO.7 Identify and work with kiddie tax situations.

LO.8 Describe the tax treatment of property transactions.

LO.9 Identify tax planning opportunities associated with the individual tax formula.

OUTLINE

For the latest in changes to tax legislation, visit **www.cengage.com/taxation/swft.**

FRAMEWORK 1040: Tax Formula for Individuals

This chapter covers the boldfaced portions of the Tax Formula for Individuals that is introduced in Figure 3.1 on p. 3-3. Below those portions are the sections of Form 1040 where the results are reported.

Income (broadly conceived)	$xx,xxx
Less: Exclusions	(x,xxx)
Gross income	$xx,xxx
Less: Deductions for adjusted gross income	(x,xxx)
Adjusted gross income	$xx,xxx
Less: The greater of total itemized deductions *or* **the standard deduction**	**(x,xxx)**

FORM 1040 (p. 1)

Filing Status

Check only one box.

1 ☐ Single
2 ☐ Married filing jointly (even if only one had income)
3 ☐ Married filing separately. Enter spouse's SSN above and full name here. ▶
4 ☐ Head of household (with qualifying person). (See instructions.) If the qualifying person is a child but not your dependent, enter this child's name here. ▶
5 ☐ Qualifying widow(er) with dependent child

Personal and dependency exemptions	**(x,xxx)**

FORM 1040 (p. 2)

39a Check if: ☐ **You** were born before January 2, 1946, ☐ Blind. ☐ **Spouse** was born before January 2, 1946, ☐ Blind. **Total boxes checked ▶ 39a** ☐

b If your spouse itemizes on a separate return or you were a dual-status alien, check here ▶ **39b** ☐

40 **Itemized deductions** (from Schedule A) **or** your **standard deduction** (see instructions)

42 **Exemptions.** Multiply $3,650 by the number on line 6d

Taxable income	**$xx,xxx**

FORM 1040 (p. 2)

43 **Taxable income.** Subtract line 42 from line 41. If line 42 is more than line 41, enter -0-

Tax on taxable income (see Tax Tables or Tax Rate Schedules)	**$ x,xxx**

FORM 1040 (p. 2)

44 **Tax** (see instructions). Check if any tax is from: **a** ☐ Form(s) 8814 **b** ☐ Form 4972

Less: Tax credits (including income taxes withheld and prepaid)	(xxx)
Tax due (or refund)	$ xxx

THE BIG PICTURE Tax Solutions for the Real World

A DIVIDED HOUSEHOLD

Polly maintains a household in which she lives with her unemployed husband (Nick), stepdaughter (Paige), and a family friend (Maude). Polly provides more than one-half of the support of both Paige and Maude. Maude was fatally injured in an automobile accident in February, and Polly paid for Maude's hospitalization and funeral expenses. Paige, an accomplished gymnast, graduated from high school last year. Paige has a part-time job but spends most of her time training and looking for an athletic scholarship to the "right" college. In March, Nick left for parts unknown and has not been seen or heard from since. Polly was more surprised than distressed over Nick's unexpected departure. One reaction, however, was to sell her wedding rings to a cousin who was getting married. The rings cost $15,000 and were sold for their approximate value of $8,000.

Based on these facts, what are Polly's income tax concerns for the current year? **Read the chapter and formulate your response.**

The framework for the application of the Federal income tax to individuals is the tax formula. As Chapter 1 mentioned, the tax formula is an integral part of our U.S. tax system (i.e., local, state, and Federal), and Chapter 3 provides a summary of its components. In addition, several of its key components—the

FIGURE 3.1 Tax Formula for Individuals

		Text Discussion
Income (broadly conceived)	$xx,xxx	Chs. 3, 4
Less: **Exclusions**	(x,xxx)	Ch. 5
Gross income	$xx,xxx	Chs. 4, 13, 14
Less: **Deductions** *for* adjusted gross income	(x,xxx)	Chs. 6–11, 13, 14
Adjusted gross income	$xx,xxx	
Less: The greater of—		
Total **itemized deductions** *or* **standard deduction**	(x,xxx)	Chs. 6, 9, 10, 11 Ch. 3
Less: **Personal** and **dependency exemptions**	(x,xxx)	Ch. 3
Taxable income	$xx,xxx	Chs. 3, 12, 15
Tax on taxable income	$ x,xxx	Chs. 3, 12, 15
Less: **Tax credits**	(xxx)	Ch. 12
Tax due (or refund)	$ xxx	Chs. 3, 12

standard deduction, personal and dependency exemptions, and tax determination—are discussed at length in Chapter 3.

By introducing the tax formula, therefore, Chapter 3 establishes the framework for almost all of the rest of the individual tax materials in the text.[1] The formula and its impact on the chapters to follow are reflected in Figure 3.1.

3.1 Tax Formula

Before illustrating the application of the Figure 3.1 tax formula, a brief discussion of its components is helpful.

LO.1

Recognize and apply the components of the Federal income tax formula.

COMPONENTS OF THE TAX FORMULA

Income (Broadly Conceived)

In the tax formula, "income" is broadly conceived and includes all the taxpayer's income, both taxable and nontaxable. Although it is essentially equivalent to gross receipts, it does not include a return of capital or receipt of borrowed funds.

EXAMPLE 1

Dan decides to quit renting and move into a new house. Consequently, the owner of the apartment building returns to Dan the $600 damage deposit that Dan previously made. To make a down payment on the house, Dan sells stock for $20,000 (original cost of $8,000) and borrows $50,000 from a bank. Only the $12,000 gain from the sale of the stock is income to Dan. The $600 damage deposit and the $8,000 cost of the stock are a return of capital. The $50,000 bank loan is not income as Dan has an obligation to repay that amount. ■

Exclusions

For various reasons, Congress has chosen to exclude certain types of income from the income tax base. The principal income exclusions are discussed in Chapter 5. A partial list of these exclusions is shown in Exhibit 3.1.

Gross Income

The Internal Revenue Code defines gross income broadly as "except as otherwise provided . . . , all income from whatever source derived."[2] The "except as otherwise provided" refers to exclusions. Gross income includes, but is not limited to, the items in the partial list in Exhibit 3.2. It does not include unrealized gains. Gross income is discussed in Chapters 4, 13, and 14.

[1] Variations of the framework apply to other taxpayers, e.g., corporations and trusts.

[2] § 61(a).

EXHIBIT 3.1 **Partial List of Exclusions from Gross Income**

- Accident insurance proceeds
- Annuities (cost element)
- Bequests
- Child support payments
- Cost-of-living allowance (for military)
- Damages for personal injury or sickness
- Gifts received
- Group term life insurance, premium paid by employer (for coverage up to $50,000)
- Inheritances
- Interest from state and local (i.e., municipal) bonds
- Life insurance paid on death
- Meals and lodging (if furnished for employer's convenience)
- Military allowances
- Minister's dwelling rental value allowance
- Railroad retirement benefits (to a limited extent)
- Scholarship grants (to a limited extent)
- Social Security benefits (to a limited extent)
- Unemployment compensation (to a limited extent)
- Veterans' benefits
- Welfare payments
- Workers' compensation benefits

EXHIBIT 3.2 **Partial List of Gross Income Items**

- Alimony
- Annuities (income element)
- Awards
- Back pay
- Bargain purchase from employer
- Bonuses
- Breach of contract damages
- Business income
- Clergy fees
- Commissions
- Compensation for services
- Death benefits
- Director's fees
- Dividends
- Embezzled funds
- Employee awards (in certain cases)
- Employee benefits (except certain fringe benefits)
- Estate and trust income
- Farm income
- Fees
- Gains from illegal activities
- Gains from sale of property
- Gambling winnings
- Group term life insurance, premium paid by employer (for coverage over $50,000)
- Hobby income
- Interest
- Jury duty fees
- Living quarters, meals (unless furnished for employer's convenience)
- Mileage allowance
- Military pay (unless combat pay)
- Partnership income
- Pensions
- Prizes
- Professional fees
- Punitive damages
- Rents
- Rewards
- Royalties
- Salaries
- Severance pay
- Strike and lockout benefits
- Supplemental unemployment benefits
- Tips and gratuities
- Travel allowance (in certain cases)
- Treasure trove (found property)
- Wages

GLOBAL
Tax Issues

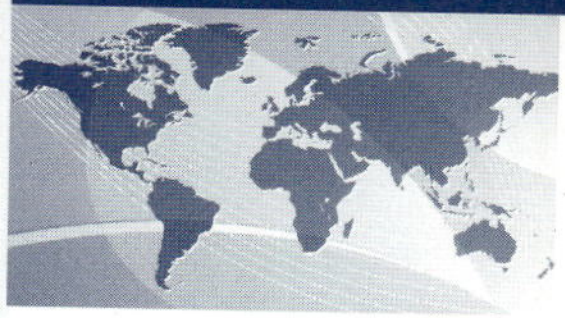

Citizenship Is Not Tax-Free

Gross income from "whatever source derived" includes income from both U.S. and foreign sources. This approach to taxation, where the government taxes its citizens and residents on their worldwide income regardless of where earned, is referred to as a *global system*. Income earned by U.S. citizens outside the United States can be subject to additional taxes, however, because all countries maintain the right to tax income earned within their borders. Consequently, the U.S. tax law includes various mechanisms to alleviate the double taxation that arises when income is subject to tax in multiple jurisdictions. These mechanisms include the foreign tax deduction, the foreign tax credit, the foreign earned income exclusion for U.S. citizens and residents working abroad, and various tax treaty provisions.

Most industrialized countries use variants of the global system. An alternative approach is the *territorial system*, where a government taxes only the income earned within its borders. Hong Kong and France, for example, use a territorial approach.

EXAMPLE 2

Beth received the following amounts during the year.

Salary	$30,000
Interest on savings account	900
Gift from her aunt	10,000
Prize won in state lottery	1,000
Alimony from ex-husband	12,000
Child support from ex-husband	6,000
Damages for injury in auto accident	25,000
Ten $50 bills in an unmarked envelope found in an airport lounge (airport authorities could not locate anyone who claimed ownership)	500
Federal income tax refund for last year's tax overpayment	120
Increase in the value of stock held for investment	5,000 ■

Review Exhibits 3.1 and 3.2 to determine the amount Beth must include in the computation of taxable income and the amount she may exclude.[3]

Deductions for Adjusted Gross Income

Individual taxpayers have two categories of deductions: (1) deductions *for* adjusted gross income (deductions to arrive at adjusted gross income) and (2) deductions *from* adjusted gross income.

Deductions *for* adjusted gross income (AGI) are sometimes known as *above-the-line* deductions because on the tax return they are taken before the "line" designating AGI. They are also referred to as *page 1 deductions* since they are claimed, either directly or indirectly (i.e., through supporting schedules), on page 1 of Form 1040. Deductions *for* AGI include, but are not limited to, the following.[4] Many of these items are subject to computational limitations.

- Expenses incurred in a trade or business.
- One-half of self-employment tax paid.
- Unreimbursed moving expenses.
- Contributions to traditional Individual Retirement Accounts (IRAs) and certain other retirement plans.

[3]Beth includes $44,400 in computing taxable income ($30,000 salary + $900 interest + $1,000 lottery prize + $12,000 alimony + $500 found property). She excludes $41,000 ($10,000 gift from aunt + $6,000 child support + $25,000 damages). The $120 Federal income tax refund is excluded because it represents a refund of a nondeductible expenditure made in the previous year. The unrealized gain on the stock held for investment is not included in gross income. Such gain is included in gross income only when it is realized upon disposition of the stock.

[4]§ 62.

- Fees for college tuition and related expenses.
- Contributions to Health Savings Accounts (HSAs).
- Penalty for early withdrawal from savings.
- Interest on student loans.
- Excess capital losses.
- Alimony payments.

The principal deductions *for* AGI are discussed in Chapters 6 through 11, 13, and 14.

Adjusted Gross Income (AGI)

AGI is an important subtotal that is the basis for computing percentage limitations on certain itemized deductions, such as medical expenses, charitable contributions, and certain casualty losses. For example, medical expenses are deductible only to the extent they exceed 7.5 percent of AGI, and charitable contribution deductions may not exceed 50 percent of AGI. These limitations might be described as a 7.5 percent *floor* under the medical expense deduction and a 50 percent *ceiling* on the charitable contribution deduction.

EXAMPLE 3

Keith earned a salary of $68,000 this year. He contributed $5,000 to his traditional Individual Retirement Account (IRA) and paid $3,000 alimony to his ex-wife. His AGI is computed as follows.

Gross income		
Salary		$68,000
Less: Deductions *for* AGI		
IRA contribution	$5,000	
Alimony payment	3,000	(8,000)
AGI		$60,000

■

EXAMPLE 4

Assume the same facts as in Example 3, and that Keith also incurred medical expenses of $5,800. Medical expenses are included in itemized deductions to the extent they exceed 7.5% of AGI. In computing his itemized deductions, Keith includes medical expenses of $1,300 [$5,800 medical expenses − $4,500 (7.5% × $60,000 AGI)]. ■

Personal and Dependency Exemptions

Exemptions are allowed for the taxpayer, for the taxpayer's spouse, and for each dependent of the taxpayer. The exemption amount is $3,700, up from is $3,650 for 2010.

Itemized Deductions

As a general rule, personal expenditures are disallowed as deductions in arriving at taxable income. However, Congress allows specified personal expenses as **itemized deductions**. Such expenditures include medical expenses, certain taxes and interest, and charitable contributions.

In addition to these personal expenses, taxpayers are allowed itemized deductions for expenses related to (1) the production or collection of income and (2) the management of property held for the production of income.[5] These expenses, sometimes referred to as *nonbusiness expenses*, differ from trade or business expenses. Trade or business expenses, which are deductions *for* AGI, are incurred in connection with a trade or business. Nonbusiness expenses, on the other hand, are expenses incurred in connection with an income-producing activity that does not qualify as a trade or business.

EXAMPLE 5

Leo is the owner and operator of a video game arcade. All allowable expenses he incurs in connection with the arcade business are deductions *for* AGI. In addition, Leo has an extensive portfolio of stocks and bonds. Leo's investment activity is not treated as a

[5] § 212.

EXHIBIT 3.3 **Partial List of Itemized Deductions**

- Medical expenses in excess of 7.5% of AGI
- State and local income or sales taxes
- Real estate taxes
- Personal property taxes
- Interest on home mortgage
- Investment interest (to a limited extent)
- Charitable contributions (within specified percentage limitations)
- Casualty and theft losses in excess of 10% of AGI
- Miscellaneous expenses (to the extent the total exceeds 2% of AGI)
  - Union dues
  - Professional dues and subscriptions
  - Certain educational expenses
  - Tax return preparation fee
  - Investment counsel fees
  - Unreimbursed employee business expenses (after a percentage reduction for meals and entertainment)

trade or business. All allowable expenses that Leo incurs in connection with these investments are itemized deductions. ■

Itemized deductions include, but are not limited to, the expenses listed in Exhibit 3.3. See Chapter 10 for a detailed discussion of itemized deductions.

Nondeductible Expenditures

Many expenditures are not deductible and, therefore, provide no tax benefit. Examples include, but are not limited to, the following.

- Personal living expenses, including any losses on the sale of personal use property.
- Hobby losses.
- Life insurance premiums.
- Expenses incident to jury duty.
- Gambling losses (in excess of gains).
- Child support payments.
- Fines and penalties.
- Political contributions.
- Certain passive losses.
- Funeral expenses.
- Expenses paid on another's behalf.
- Capital expenditures.

Most of the nondeductible items in this list are discussed further in Chapter 6. Passive loss limitations, however, are treated in Chapter 11.

STANDARD DEDUCTION

LO.2

Explain the use of the standard deduction in computing taxable income.

The **standard deduction** is specified by Congress and depends on the filing status of the taxpayer. The effect of the standard deduction is to exempt a taxpayer's income, up to the specified amount, from Federal income tax liability. In the past, Congress has attempted to set the tax-free amount represented by the standard deduction approximately equal to an estimated poverty level,[6] but it has not always been consistent in doing so.

[6]S.Rep. No. 92–437, 92nd Cong., 1st Sess., 1971, p. 54. Another purpose of the standard deduction was discussed in Chapter 1 under Influence of the Internal Revenue Service—Administrative Feasibility. The size of the standard deduction has a direct bearing on the number of taxpayers who can itemize deductions. Reducing the number of taxpayers who can itemize also reduces the audit effort required from the IRS.

TABLE 3.1 Basic Standard Deduction Amounts

Filing Status	Standard Deduction Amount 2010	2011
Single	$ 5,700	$ 5,800
Married, filing jointly	11,400	11,600
Surviving spouse	11,400	11,600
Head of household	8,400	8,500
Married, filing separately	5,700	5,800

Basic and Additional Standard Deduction

The standard deduction is the sum of two components: the *basic* standard deduction and the *additional* standard deduction.[7] Table 3.1 lists the basic standard deduction allowed for taxpayers in each filing status. All taxpayers allowed a *full* standard deduction are entitled to the applicable amount listed in Table 3.1. The standard deduction amounts are subject to adjustment for inflation each year.

Federal tax law does not recognize same-sex marriages. By virtue of the Defense of Marriage Act, a marriage means a legal union only between a man and a woman as husband and wife.

Certain taxpayers are not allowed to claim *any* standard deduction, and the standard deduction is *limited* for others. These provisions are discussed later in the chapter.

A taxpayer who is age 65 or over *or* blind qualifies for an *additional standard deduction* of $1,150 or $1,450, depending on filing status (see amounts in Table 3.2). Two additional standard deductions are allowed for a taxpayer who is age 65 or over *and* blind. The additional standard deduction provisions also apply for a qualifying spouse who is age 65 or over or blind, but a taxpayer may not claim an additional standard deduction for a dependent.

To determine whether it is best to itemize, the taxpayer compares the *total* standard deduction (the sum of the basic standard deduction and any additional standard deductions) with total itemized deductions. Taxpayers can deduct the *greater* of itemized deductions or the standard deduction. Approximately 65 percent of individual tax returns employ the standard deduction.

The taxpayer chooses whether to itemize or claim the standard deduction. This is an annual election; the default choice is to use the standard deduction. A taxpayer is not bound by what was done on returns filed for past years. For example, many taxpayers who previously have claimed the standard deduction switch to itemizing after purchasing a home (because of the mortgage interest and property tax deductions). In other circumstances, a taxpayer may switch from itemizing to the standard deduction.

EXAMPLE 6

Prior to 2011, Sara, who is single, always had chosen to itemize. In 2011, however, she reaches age 65. Her itemized deductions for 2011 are $6,500, but her total standard deduction is $7,250 [$5,800 (basic standard deduction) + $1,450 (additional standard deduction)]. Sara should compute her taxable income for 2011 using the standard deduction, since it exceeds her itemized deductions. ■

Individuals Not Eligible for the Standard Deduction

The following individual taxpayers cannot use the standard deduction and therefore must itemize.[8]

[7] § 63(c)(1).

[8] § 63(c)(6).

TABLE 3.2 Amount of Each Additional Standard Deduction

Filing Status	2010	2011
Single	$1,400	$1,450
Married, filing jointly	1,100	1,150
Surviving spouse	1,100	1,150
Head of household	1,400	1,450
Married, filing separately	1,100	1,150

- A married individual filing a separate return where either spouse itemizes deductions.
- A nonresident alien.
- An individual filing a return for a period of less than 12 months because of a change in the annual accounting period.

The death of an individual does not eliminate the standard deduction for the year of death, nor is the deduction allocated to the pre-death portion of the year. If, for example, Sandy (age 80 and single) died on January 14, 2011, his executor could claim a standard deduction of $7,250 [$5,800 (basic standard deduction) + $1,450 (additional standard deduction for age)] on his final income tax return (covering the period from January 1 to January 14, 2011).

Limitations on the Standard Deduction for Individuals Who Can Be Claimed as Dependents

Special rules apply to the standard deduction and personal exemption of an individual who can be claimed as a dependent on another person's tax return.

When filing his or her own tax return, a *dependent's* basic standard deduction for 2011 is limited to the greater of $950 or the sum of the individual's earned income for the year plus $300.[9] However, if the sum of the individual's earned income plus $300 exceeds the standard deduction, the standard deduction is limited to the appropriate amount shown in Table 3.1. These limitations apply only to the basic standard deduction. A dependent who is 65 or over or blind or both also is allowed the additional standard deduction amount on his or her own return (refer to Table 3.2).

EXAMPLE 7

Susan, who is 17 years old and single, is claimed as a dependent on her parents' tax return. During 2011, she received $1,200 interest (unearned income) on a savings account. She also earned $400 from a part-time job. When Susan files her own tax return, her standard deduction is $950 [the greater of $950 or the sum of earned income plus $300 ($400 + $300 = $700)]. ■

EXAMPLE 8

Assume the same facts as in Example 7, except that Susan is 67 years old and is claimed as a dependent on her son's tax return. In this case, when Susan files her own tax return, her standard deduction is $2,400 [$950 (the greater of $950 or the $700 sum of earned income plus $300) + $1,450 (the additional standard deduction allowed because Susan is age 65 or over)]. ■

[9] § 63(c)(5). Both the $950 amount and the $300 amount are subject to adjustment for inflation each year.

EXAMPLE 9

Peggy, who is 16 years old and single, earned $700 from a summer job and had no unearned income during 2011. She is claimed as a dependent on her parents' tax return. Her standard deduction is $1,000 (the greater of $950 or the sum of $700 earned income plus $300). ■

EXAMPLE 10

Jack, who is a 20-year-old, single, full-time college student, is claimed as a dependent on his parents' tax return. He worked as a musician during the summer of 2011, earning $5,900. Jack's standard deduction is $5,800 (the greater of $950 or the sum of $5,900 earned income plus $300, but limited to the $5,800 standard deduction for a single taxpayer). ■

APPLICATION OF THE TAX FORMULA

The structure of the individual income tax return (Form 1040, 1040A, or 1040EZ) parallels the tax formula in Figure 3.1. Like the formula, the tax return places major emphasis on the adjusted gross income (AGI) and taxable income (TI) subtotals. In arriving at AGI, however, most exclusions are not reported on the tax return.

EXAMPLE 11

Grace, age 25, is single. She lives with her disabled and dependent mother. Grace is a high school teacher and earned a $60,000 salary in 2011. Her other income consisted of $1,000 interest from a bank account and $500 interest on municipal bonds that she previously had received as a graduation gift. During 2011, she sustained a deductible capital loss of $1,000. Her itemized deductions are $8,800. Grace's taxable income is computed as follows.

Salary	$60,000
Interest from bank account	1,000
Interest on municipal bonds	500
Income (broadly conceived)	$61,500
Less: Exclusion—Interest on municipal bonds	(500)
Gross income	$61,000
Less: Deduction *for* adjusted gross income— Capital loss	(1,000)
Adjusted gross income	$60,000
Less: The greater of total itemized deductions ($8,800) *or* the standard deduction for a head of household ($8,500)	(8,800)
Personal and dependency exemptions (2 × $3,700)	(7,400)
Taxable income	$43,800

■

3.2 Personal Exemptions

LO.3

Apply the rules for arriving at personal exemptions.

The use of exemptions in the tax system is based in part on the idea that a taxpayer with a small amount of income should be exempt from Federal income taxation. An exemption frees a specified amount of income from tax ($3,700 for 2011 or $3,650 for 2010). The exemption amount is indexed (adjusted) annually for inflation.

Exemptions that are allowed for the taxpayer and spouse are designated as **personal exemptions**. Those exemptions allowed for the care and maintenance of other persons are called dependency exemptions. An individual cannot claim a personal exemption if he or she is claimed as a dependent by another.[10]

When a husband and wife file a joint return, they claim two personal exemptions. However, when separate returns are filed, a married taxpayer cannot claim an exemption for his or her spouse *unless* the spouse has no gross income and is not claimed as the dependent of another taxpayer.[11]

The determination of marital status generally is made at the end of the taxable year, except when a spouse dies during the year. Spouses who enter into a legal

[10]§ 151(d)(2).

[11]§ 151(b).

TABLE 3.3 Marital Status for Exemption Purposes

Taxpayers	Marital Status
• Walt is the widower of Helen, who died on January 3.	Walt and Helen are married.
• Bill and Jane entered into a divorce decree that is effective on December 31.	Bill and Jane are unmarried.

separation under a decree of divorce or separate maintenance before the end of the year are considered to be unmarried at the end of the taxable year. Table 3.3 illustrates the effect of death or divorce upon marital status.

The amount of the exemption is not reduced due to the taxpayer's death. For example, refer to the case of Helen in Table 3.3. Although she lived for only three days, a full personal exemption is allowed for the tax year. The same rule applies to dependency exemptions. As long as an individual qualified as a dependent at the time of death, the full amount of the exemption is claimed for the year.

3.3 Dependency Exemptions

LO.4

Apply the rules for determining dependency exemptions.

As is the case with personal exemptions, a taxpayer is permitted to claim an exemption of $3,700 for 2011 or $3,650 for 2010 for each person who qualifies as a dependent. A **dependency exemption** is available for either a *qualifying child* or a *qualifying relative.*

QUALIFYING CHILD

The term *qualifying child* is used in several Code provisions, including those relating to:

- Dependency exemption.
- Head-of-household filing status.
- Earned income tax credit.
- Child tax credit.
- Credit for child and dependent care expenses.

A **qualifying child** must meet the relationship, abode, age, and support tests.[12] For dependency exemption purposes, a qualifying child also must satisfy the joint return test and the citizenship or residency test, both discussed in a later section.

Relationship Test

The relationship test includes a taxpayer's child (son, daughter), adopted child, stepchild, eligible foster child, brother, sister, half brother, half sister, stepbrother, stepsister, or a *descendant* of any of these parties (e.g., grandchild, nephew, niece). Note that *ancestors* of any of these parties (e.g., uncles and aunts) and in-laws (e.g., son-in-law, brother-in-law) are not included.

An adopted child includes a child lawfully placed with the taxpayer for legal adoption even though the adoption is not final. An eligible foster child is one who is placed with the taxpayer by an authorized placement agency or by a judgment decree or other order of any court of competent jurisdiction.[13]

EXAMPLE 12

Maureen's household includes her mother, grandson, stepbrother, stepbrother's daughter, uncle, and sister. All meet the relationship test for a qualifying child except the mother and uncle. ■

[12] § 152(c).

[13] § 152(f)(1)(A)(ii).

Abode Test

A qualifying child must live with the taxpayer for more than half of the year. For this purpose, temporary absences (e.g., school, vacation, medical care, military service, detention in a juvenile facility) are disregarded. Special rules apply in the case of certain kidnapped children.[14]

Age Test

A qualifying child must be under age 19 or under age 24 in the case of a student. A student is a child who, during any part of five months of the year, is enrolled full time at a school or government-sponsored on-farm training course.[15] An individual cannot be older than the taxpayer claiming him or her as a qualifying child (e.g., a brother cannot claim his older sister as a qualifying child). The age test does not apply to a child who is disabled during any part of the year.

EXAMPLE 13
THE BIG PICTURE

Return to the facts of *The Big Picture* on p. 3-2. Does Paige meet the requirements of a qualifying child as to Polly? Paige satisfies the relationship and abode tests, but the application of the age test remains unclear. Since Paige is not a full-time student or disabled, she must be under 19 to meet the age test. Unfortunately, the facts given do not provide Paige's precise age. ■

Support Test

A qualifying child cannot be self-supporting (i.e., provide more than one-half of his or her own support). In the case of a child who is a full-time student, scholarships are not considered to be support.[16]

EXAMPLE 14

Shawn, age 23, is a full-time student and lives with his parents and an older cousin. Shawn receives his support from the following sources: 30% from a part-time job, 30% from a scholarship, 20% from his parents, and 20% from the cousin. Shawn is not self-supporting, so he can be claimed by his parents as a dependent. (Note: Shawn cannot be a qualifying child as to his cousin due to the relationship test.) ■

Tiebreaker Rules

In some situations, a child may be a qualifying child to more than one person. In this event, the tax law specifies which person has priority in claiming the dependency exemption.[17] Called "tiebreaker rules," these rules are summarized in Table 3.4 and are illustrated in the examples that follow.

EXAMPLE 15

Tim, age 15, lives in the same household with his mother and grandmother. As the parent (see Table 3.4), the mother has priority as to the dependency exemption. ■

EXAMPLE 16

Jennifer, age 17, lives in the same household with her parents during the entire year. If her parents file separate returns, the one with the higher AGI has priority as to the dependency exemption. ■

EXAMPLE 17

Carlos, age 12, lives in the same household with his two aunts. The aunt with the higher AGI has priority as to the dependency exemption. ■

[14] § 152(f)(6).
[15] § 152(f)(2).
[16] § 152(f)(5).
[17] § 152(c)(4).

TABLE 3.4 Tiebreaker Rules for Claiming a Qualifying Child

Persons Eligible to Claim Exemption	Person Prevailing
One of the persons is the parent.	Parent
Both persons are the parents, and the child lives with one parent for a longer period.	Parent with the longer period of residence
Both persons are the parents, and the child lives with each the same period of time.	Parent with the higher adjusted gross income (AGI)
None of the persons is the parent.	Person with highest AGI

ETHICS & Equity **WHOSE QUALIFYING CHILD IS HE?**

The Rands are successful professionals and have combined AGI of approximately $400,000. Their household includes two children: Henry (age 16) and Belinda (age 22). Belinda is not a student and has a job where she earns $15,000. After a short family meeting in early April, the parties decide that Belinda should claim Henry as her qualifying child. Under this result, Belinda deducts Henry's dependency exemption, and she claims a child tax credit and an earned income tax credit, for a total tax saving of more than $3,000. Had the Rands claimed Henry on their joint return, no child tax credit or earned income tax credit would have been available. As noted in Chapter 12, these amounts are phased out for higher-income taxpayers.

Has the Rand family acted properly?

QUALIFYING RELATIVE

A **qualifying relative** must meet the relationship, gross income, and support tests.[18] Qualifying relative status also requires that the joint return and nonresident alien tests be met (both are discussed below). One who does not satisfy the qualifying child definition still may be a qualifying relative.

EXAMPLE 18

Inez provides more than half of the support of her son Manuel, age 20, who is neither disabled nor a full-time student. Manuel is not a qualifying child due to the age test, but he is a qualifying relative if the gross income test is met. Consequently, Inez may claim a dependency exemption for Manuel. ■

Relationship Test

The relationship test for a qualifying relative is more expansive than for a qualifying child. Also included are:

- Lineal ascendants (e.g., parents, grandparents).
- Collateral ascendants (e.g., uncles, aunts).
- Certain in-laws (e.g., son-, daughter-, father-, mother-, brother-, and sister-in-law).[19]

The relationship test also includes unrelated parties who live with the taxpayer (i.e., they are members of the same household). Member-of-the-household status is not available for anyone whose relationship with the taxpayer violates an enforced

[18] § 152(d).

[19] Once established by marriage, in-law status continues to exist and survives divorce.

local law, or for anyone who was a spouse during any part of the year.[20] However, an ex-spouse can qualify as a member of the household in a year following that of the divorce.

As the relationship test indicates, the term *qualifying relative* is somewhat misleading. Persons other than relatives can qualify as dependents. Furthermore, not all relatives qualify—notice the absence of "cousin."

EXAMPLE 19
THE BIG PICTURE

Return to the facts of *The Big Picture* on p. 3-2. Although Maude is unrelated to Polly, she qualifies as Polly's dependent by being a member of the household. Since Maude is a dependent, Polly can claim the medical expenses she paid on Maude's behalf. The funeral expenses are not deductible. Although Maude lived for only two months this year, the full amount of the dependency exemption is allowed. ■

Gross Income Test

A qualifying relative's gross income must be *less* than the exemption amount—$3,700 for 2011 and $3,650 for 2010. Gross income is the amount that the tax law counts as taxable. In the case of scholarships, for example, include the taxable portion (e.g., amounts received for room and board) and exclude the nontaxable portion (e.g., amounts received for books and tuition). In contrast, the qualifying child rule does not contain a gross income test.

EXAMPLE 20

Elsie provides more than half of the support of her son, Tom, who does not live with her. Tom, age 26, is a full-time student in medical school, earns $2,000 from a part-time job, and receives a $42,000 scholarship covering his tuition. Elsie may claim Tom as a dependent since he is a qualifying relative, and his gross income is $2,000 (Note: Tom is not a qualifying child due to either the abode or the age test.) ■

EXAMPLE 21

Aaron provides more than half of the support of his widowed aunt, Myrtle, who does not live with him. Myrtle's income for the year is as follows: dividend income of $1,100, earnings from pet sitting of $1,200, Social Security benefits of $6,000, and $8,000 interest from City of Milwaukee bonds. Since Myrtle's gross income is only $2,300 ($1,100 + $1,200), she meets the gross income test and can be claimed as Aaron's dependent. ■

EXAMPLE 22
THE BIG PICTURE

Return to the facts of *The Big Picture* on p. 3-2. Assuming that Paige is not a qualifying child (see Example 13), can she be a qualifying relative for dependency exemption purposes? Paige meets the relationship and support tests, but what about the gross income test? If her income from her part-time job is less than $3,700, she does qualify and can be claimed by Polly as a dependent. ■

Support Test

Over one-half of the support of the qualifying relative must be furnished by the one claiming the exemption. Support includes food, shelter, clothing, toys, medical and dental care, education, and the like. However, a scholarship (both taxable and nontaxable portions) received by a student is not counted as support.

EXAMPLE 23

Hal contributed $3,400 (consisting of food, clothing, and medical care) toward the support of his nephew, Sam, who lives with him. Sam earned $1,500 from a part-time job and received a $10,000 scholarship to attend a local university. Assuming that the other dependency tests are met, Hal can claim Sam as a dependent since he has contributed

[20] §§ 152(d)(2)(H) and (f)(3).

more than half of Sam's support. The scholarship is not included as support for purposes of this test. ■

If the individual does not spend funds that have been received from any source, the unexpended amounts are not counted as support. An individual's own funds, however, are taken into account if they are applied toward support. In this regard, the source of the funds so used is immaterial.

EXAMPLE 24

Emily contributed $3,000 to her father Ernie's support during the year. In addition, Ernie received $2,400 in Social Security benefits, $200 of interest, and wages of $600. Ernie deposited the Social Security benefits, interest, and wages in his own savings account and did not use any of the funds for his support. Thus, the Social Security benefits, interest, and wages are not counted as support provided by Ernie. Emily may claim her father as a dependent if the other tests are met. ■

Capital expenditures for items such as furniture, appliances, and automobiles are included in total support if the item does, in fact, constitute support.

EXAMPLE 25

Norm purchased a television set costing $650 and gave it to his mother who lives with him. The television set was placed in the mother's bedroom and was used exclusively by her. Norm should include the cost of the television set in determining the support of his mother. ■

Multiple Support Agreements An exception to the support test involves a **multiple support agreement**. A multiple support agreement permits one of a group of taxpayers who furnish support for a qualifying relative to claim a dependency exemption for that individual, even if no one person provides more than 50 percent of the support.[21] The group together must provide more than 50 percent of the support. Any person who contributed *more than 10 percent* of the support is entitled to claim the exemption if each person in the group who contributed more than 10 percent agrees in a written consent. This provision frequently enables one of the children of aged dependent parents to claim an exemption when none of the children individually meets the 50 percent support test.

Each person who is a party to the multiple support agreement must meet all other tests (except the support requirement) for claiming the exemption. A person who does not meet the relationship or member-of-the-household requirement, for instance, cannot claim the dependency exemption, even under a multiple support agreement.

EXAMPLE 26

Wanda, who resides with her son, Adam, received $12,000 from various sources during the year. This constituted her entire support for the year.

	Support Received	Percentage of Total
Adam, a son	$ 5,760	48
Bob, a son	1,200	10
Carol, a daughter	3,600	30
Diane, a friend	1,440	12
	$12,000	100

If Adam and Carol file a multiple support agreement, either may claim the dependency exemption for Wanda. Bob may not claim Wanda because he did not contribute more than 10% of her support. Bob's consent is not required for Adam and Carol to file

[21]§ 152(d)(3).

a multiple support agreement. Diane does not meet the relationship or member-of-the-household test and cannot be a party to the agreement.

The decision as to who claims Wanda rests with Adam and Carol. If Adam agrees, Carol can claim Wanda, even though Adam furnished more of Wanda's support. ■

Each person who qualifies under the more-than-10 percent rule (except for the person claiming the exemption) must complete Form 2120 (Multiple Support Declaration) waiving the exemption. The person claiming the exemption attaches all Forms 2120 to his or her own return.

ETHICS & *Equity*

Discovering Lost Dependency Exemptions

For the six years prior to his death, Jesse lived with his daughter, Hannah. Because he had no source of income, Jesse was supported by equal contributions from Hannah and his two sons, Bill and Bob. At Jesse's funeral, his surviving children are amazed to discover that none of them has been claiming Jesse as a dependent. Upon the advice of the director of the funeral home, they decide to divide, among themselves, the dependency exemptions for the past six years. Multiple Forms 2120 are executed, and each of the three children files amended returns for different past years. As Jesse died late in the current year, none of the children plans to claim him for this tax year.

Comment on the tax expectations of the parties involved.

Children of Divorced or Separated Parents Another exception to the support test applies when parents with children are divorced or separated under a decree of separate maintenance. Generally, the parent having custody of the child (children) for the greater part of the year (i.e., the custodial parent) is entitled to the dependency exemption(s). A special rule applies if the now-unmarried parents live apart for the last six months of the year, and:[22]

- They would have been entitled to the dependency exemption(s) had they been married and filed a joint return.
- They have custody (either jointly or singly) of the child (or children) for more than half of the year.

The special rule grants the dependency exemption(s) to the noncustodial parent if the divorce (or separate maintenance) decree so specifies *or* the custodial parent issues a waiver on Form 8332.[23]

If the special rule does not apply (i.e., the divorce decree is silent or the custodial parent does not sign Form 8332), the dependency exemption(s) for the child (children) is awarded in accordance with the qualifying child or qualifying relative rules. When support of the child is determined, alimony received by the custodial parent does not count as support by the payor parent, but child support received probably does.[24]

OTHER RULES FOR DEPENDENCY EXEMPTIONS

In addition to fitting into either the qualifying child or the qualifying relative category, a dependent must meet the joint return and the citizenship or residency tests.

[22] § 152(e)(1).

[23] §§ 152(e)(2) and (5).

[24] § 152(d)(5)(A).

Joint Return Test

If a dependent is married, the supporting taxpayer (e.g., the parent of a married child) generally is not permitted a dependency exemption if the married individual files a joint return with his or her spouse.[25] The joint return rule does not apply, however, if the following conditions are met.

- The reason for filing is to claim a refund for tax withheld.
- No tax liability would exist for either spouse on separate returns.
- Neither spouse is required to file a return.

See Table 3.5 later in the chapter and the related discussion concerning income level requirements for filing a return.

EXAMPLE 27

Paul provides over half of the support of his son Quinn. He also provides over half of the support of Vera, who is Quinn's wife. During the year, both Quinn and Vera hold part-time jobs. To recover the taxes withheld, they file a joint return. If Quinn and Vera are not required to file a return, Paul can claim both as dependents. ■

Citizenship or Residency Test

To be a dependent, the individual must be either a U.S. citizen, a U.S. resident, or a resident of Canada or Mexico for some part of the calendar year in which the taxpayer's tax year begins.[26]

QUALIFYING FOR DEPENDENCY EXEMPTIONS

Concept Summary 3.1 sets forth the tests for the two categories of dependency exemptions. In contrasting the two categories, the following observations are in order.

- As to the relationship tests, the qualifying relative category is considerably more expansive. Besides including those prescribed under the qualifying child grouping, other relatives are added. Nonrelated persons who are members of the household are also included.

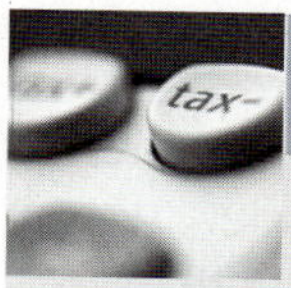

CONCEPT SUMMARY 3.1

Tests for Dependency Exemption

Category	
Qualifying Child[1]	**Qualifying Relative**
Relationship[2]	Support
Abode[3]	Relationship[4] or member of household[3]
Age	Gross income
Support	
Joint return[5]	Joint return[5]
Citizenship or residency[6]	Citizenship or residency[6]

[1] These tests are used as well by other tax rules.
[2] Children and their descendants, and siblings and stepsiblings and their descendants.
[3] The rules for abode are the same as for member of the household.
[4] Children and their descendants, siblings and their children, parents and their ascendants, uncles and aunts, stepparents and stepsiblings, and certain in-laws.
[5] The joint return rules are the same for each category.
[6] The citizenship or residency rules are the same for each category.

---

[25] § 152(b)(2).

[26] § 152(b)(3).

- The support tests are entirely different. In the case of a qualifying child, support is not necessary. What is required in that case is that the child not be self-supporting.
- The qualifying child category has no gross income limitation, whereas the qualifying relative category has no age restriction.

CHILD TAX CREDIT

In addition to providing a dependency exemption, a child of the taxpayer also may generate a tax credit. Called the **child tax credit**, the amount allowed is $1,000 for each dependent child (including stepchildren and eligible foster children) under the age of 17.[27] For a more complete discussion of the child tax credit, see Chapter 12.

3.4 Filing the Return

LO.5

List the filing requirements and choose the proper filing status.

FILING STATUS

The amount of tax varies considerably depending on which filing status[28] the taxpayer uses.

EXAMPLE 28

The following amounts of tax are computed using the 2011 Tax Rate Schedules for a taxpayer (or taxpayers in the case of a joint return) with $60,000 of taxable income (see Appendix A).

Filing Status	Amount of Tax
Single	$11,125
Married, filing joint return	8,150
Married, filing separate return	11,125
Head of household	9,768

■

Single Taxpayers

State law governs whether a taxpayer is considered married, divorced, or legally separated. A taxpayer who is unmarried or separated from his or her spouse by a decree of divorce or separate maintenance and does not qualify for another filing status must use the rates for single taxpayers. Marital status is determined as of the last day of the tax year, except when a spouse dies during the year. In that case, marital status is determined as of the date of death.

Under a special relief provision, however, married persons who live apart may be able to qualify as single. Married taxpayers who are considered single under the *abandoned spouse rules* are allowed to use the head-of-household rates. This filing status is discussed later in the chapter.

Married Individuals

The joint return was enacted in 1948 to establish equity between married taxpayers in community property states and those in common law states. Before the joint return was available, taxpayers in community property states were in an advantageous position relative to taxpayers in common law states because they could split their income. For instance, if one spouse earned $100,000 and the other spouse was not employed, each spouse could report $50,000 of income. Splitting the income in this manner caused the total income to be subject to lower marginal tax rates. Each spouse would start at the bottom of the rate structure.

[27] § 24(a).

[28] §§ 1 and 2.

Taxpayers in common law states did not have this income-splitting option, so their taxable income was subject to higher marginal rates. This inconsistency in treatment was remedied by the joint return provisions. The progressive rates in the joint return Tax Rate Schedule are constructed based on the assumption that income is earned equally by the two spouses.

If married individuals elect to file separate returns, each reports only his or her own income, exemptions, deductions, and credits, and each must use the Tax Rate Schedule for married taxpayers filing separately. It generally is advantageous for married individuals to file a joint return, since the combined amount of tax is lower. However, special circumstances (e.g., significant medical expenses incurred by one spouse subject to the 7.5 percent limitation) may warrant the election to file separate returns. It may be necessary to compute the tax under both assumptions to determine the most advantageous filing status.

The Code places some limitations on married persons who file separate returns. Some examples of these limitations are listed below. In such cases, being single would be preferable to being married and filing separately.

- If either spouse itemizes deductions, the other spouse must also itemize.
- The earned income credit and the credit for child and dependent care expenses cannot be claimed (see Chapter 12).
- No deduction is allowed for interest paid on qualified education loans (see Chapter 10).
- Only $1,500 of excess capital losses can be claimed each year (see Chapter 14).

EXAMPLE 29

Duke and Carla are in the process of divorcing. They qualify this year for a $4,000 earned income credit. If the taxpayers stay married but file separate returns this year, neither party can claim the credit. If instead a joint return is filed, the credit is available, presumably to be divided with the couple's other assets. If the divorce is finalized this year, both parties will file Forms 1040 using single filing status, and either of them can claim the credit. ■

Surviving Spouse

The joint return rates also apply for two years following the death of one spouse, if the surviving spouse maintains a household for a dependent child. The child must be a son, stepson, daughter, or stepdaughter who qualifies as a dependent of the taxpayer. This is referred to as **surviving spouse** status.[29]

EXAMPLE 30

Fred dies in 2009 leaving Ethel with a dependent child. For 2009, Ethel files a joint return with Fred (presuming the consent of Fred's executor is obtained). For the next two years (2010 and 2011), Ethel, filing as a surviving spouse, may use the joint return rates. In subsequent years, Ethel uses the head-of-household rates if she continues to maintain a household as her home that is the domicile of the child. ■

Head of Household

Unmarried individuals who maintain a household for one or more dependents may qualify to use the **head-of-household** rates.[30] The tax liability using the head-of-household rates falls between the liability using the joint return Tax Rate Schedule and the liability using the Tax Rate Schedule for single taxpayers.

To qualify for head-of-household rates, a taxpayer must pay more than half the cost of maintaining a household as his or her home. The household must also be the principal home of a dependent. Except for temporary absences (e.g., school, hospitalization), the dependent must live in the taxpayer's household for over half the

[29] § 2(a). The IRS label for surviving spouse status is "Qualifying Widow(er) with Dependent Child."

[30] § 2(b).

GLOBAL
Tax Issues

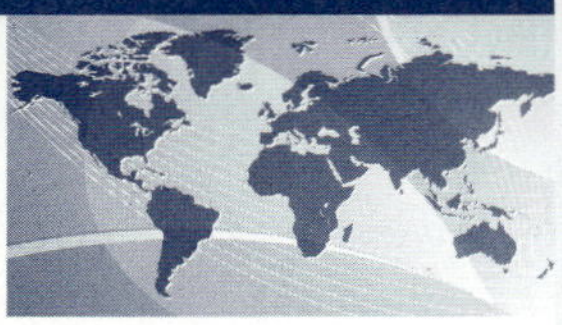

FILING A JOINT RETURN

John Garth is a U.S. citizen and resident, but he spends a lot of time in London where his employer sends him on frequent assignments. John is married to Victoria, a citizen and resident of the United Kingdom.

Can John and Victoria file a joint return for U.S. Federal income tax purposes? Although § 6013(a)(1) specifically precludes the filing of a joint return if one spouse is a nonresident alien, another Code provision permits an exception. Under § 6013 (g), the parties can elect to treat the nonqualifying spouse as a "resident" of the United States. This election would allow John and Victoria to file jointly.

But should John and Victoria make this election? If Victoria has considerable income of her own (from non-U.S. sources), the election could be ill-advised. As a nonresident alien, Victoria's non-U.S. source income *would not* be subject to the U.S. income tax. If she is treated as a U.S. resident, however, her non-U.S. source income *will be subject to U.S. tax.* Under the U.S. global approach to taxation, all income (regardless of where earned) of anyone who is a *resident* or *citizen* of the United States is subject to tax.

year. The dependent must be either a qualifying child or a qualifying relative who meets the relationship test.[31]

EXAMPLE 31
THE BIG PICTURE

Return to the facts of *The Big Picture* on p. 3-2. Assuming that Polly can be treated as single (i.e., not married), can Maude qualify Polly for head-of-household filing status? The answer is no. Even though Maude can be claimed as Polly's dependent (see Example 19), she does not meet the relationship test. ■

EXAMPLE 32

Emma, a widow, maintains a household in which she and her aunt live. If the aunt qualifies as a dependent, Emma may file as head of household. An aunt meets the relationship test. ■

EXAMPLE 33

Nancy maintains a household in which she and her daughter, Bernice, live. Bernice, age 27, is single and earns $9,000 from a part-time job. Nancy does not qualify for head-of-household filing status, as she cannot claim Bernice as a dependent (due to the gross income test).[32] ■

Head-of-household status still may be claimed if the taxpayer maintains a *separate home* for his or her *parent or parents,* if at least one parent qualifies as a dependent of the taxpayer.[33]

EXAMPLE 34

Rick, an unmarried individual, lives in New York City and maintains a household in Scottsdale for his dependent parents. Rick may use the head-of-household rates, even though his parents do not reside in his New York home. ■

---

[31] § 2(b)(3)(B). The member-of-the-household test cannot be used for this purpose.

[32] Can Bernice be a dependent under the qualifying child rules? Even though the gross income test is inapplicable for a qualifying child, Bernice does not meet the age test.

[33] § 2(b)(1)(B).

ETHICS & Equity

TEMPORARY OR PERMANENT ABSENCE?

For several years, Minerva, a widow, has maintained a household in which she and her uncle Luther live. Because Luther has no income, he is supported by Minerva and claimed by her as a dependent. In June 2011, Luther is admitted to a medical facility for treatment of a mental disability. In January 2012, Luther unexpectedly dies while still at the facility.

In completing her Federal income tax returns for 2011 and 2012, Minerva intends to file as head of household and claim Luther as her dependent. Comment on the propriety of what Minerva plans to do.

Abandoned Spouse Rules

When married persons file separate returns, several unfavorable tax consequences result. For example, the taxpayer likely must use the very expensive Tax Rate Schedule for married taxpayers filing separately. To mitigate such harsh treatment for some individuals, Congress enacted provisions commonly referred to as the **abandoned spouse** rules. These rules allow a married taxpayer to file as *not married,* and thus either as single or head of household, if all of the following conditions are satisfied.[34]

- The taxpayer does not file a joint return.
- The taxpayer paid more than one-half the cost of maintaining his or her home for the tax year.
- The taxpayer's spouse did not live in the home during the last six months of the tax year.
- The home was the principal residence of the taxpayer's son, daughter, stepson, stepdaughter, foster child, or adopted child for more than half the year, and the child can be claimed as a dependent.[35]

EXAMPLE 35
THE BIG PICTURE

Return to the facts of *The Big Picture* on p. 3-2. Can Polly qualify as an abandoned spouse? Yes, if she can claim Paige as a dependent—either as a qualifying child (see Example 13) or as a qualifying relative (see Example 22). If so, Polly can use head-of-household filing status. If not, her filing status is married person filing separately. ■

TAX in the NEWS

FILING STATUS DATA

For tax year 2008 Forms 1040, taxpayers used the following filing status categorizations.

Filing Status	Number of Returns (Millions)
Married, filing jointly	53.65
Married, filing separately	2.72
Head of household	21.10
Surviving spouse	0.08
Single	64.90
Total	142.45

[34] § 7703(b).

[35] § 152(f)(1). The dependency requirement does not apply, however, if the taxpayer could have claimed a dependency exemption except for the fact that the exemption was claimed by the noncustodial parent under a written agreement.

TABLE 3.5 Filing Levels

Filing Status	2010 Gross Income	2011 Gross Income
Single		
Under 65 and not blind	$ 9,350	$ 9,500
Under 65 and blind	9,350	9,500
65 or older	10,750	10,950
Married, filing joint return		
Both spouses under 65 and neither blind	$18,700	$19,000
Both spouses under 65 and one or both spouses blind	18,700	19,000
One spouse 65 or older	19,800	20,150
Both spouses 65 or older	20,900	21,300
Married, filing separate return		
All—whether 65 or older or blind	$ 3,650	$ 3,700
Head of household		
Under 65 and not blind	$12,050	$12,200
Under 65 and blind	12,050	12,200
65 or older	13,450	13,650
Qualifying widow(er)		
Under 65 and not blind	$15,050	$15,300
Under 65 and blind	15,050	15,300
65 or older	16,150	16,450

FILING REQUIREMENTS

General Rules

An individual must file a tax return if certain minimum amounts of *gross income* have been received. The general rule is that a tax return is required for every individual who has gross income that equals or exceeds the sum of the exemption amount plus the applicable standard deduction.[36] For example, a single taxpayer under age 65 must file a tax return in 2011 if gross income equals or exceeds $9,500 ($3,700 exemption plus $5,800 standard deduction). Table 3.5 lists the income levels[37] that require the filing of tax returns.

The additional standard deduction for those age 65 or older is considered in applying the gross income filing requirements. For example, note in Table 3.5 that the 2011 filing requirement for a single taxpayer age 65 or older is $10,950 ($5,800 basic standard deduction + $1,450 additional standard deduction + $3,700 exemption). The additional standard deduction for blindness is not taken into account for this purpose. The 2011 filing requirement for a single taxpayer under age 65 and blind is $9,500 ($5,800 basic standard deduction + $3,700 exemption).

A self-employed individual with net earnings of $400 or more from a business or profession must file a tax return regardless of the amount of gross income.

Even though an individual has gross income below the filing level amounts and therefore does not owe any tax, he or she must file a return to obtain a tax refund of amounts withheld. A return is also necessary to obtain the benefits of the earned income credit allowed to taxpayers with little or no tax liability. Chapter 12 discusses the earned income credit.

[36] The gross income amounts for determining whether a tax return must be filed are adjusted for inflation each year.

[37] § 6012(a)(1).

GLOBAL *Tax Issues*

Tracking Down Tax Dollars

Non-U.S. persons who earn income within the United States may need to file a Federal income tax return, but they may not have a Social Security number for filing purposes. If not, they can use a nine-digit Individual Tax Identification Number (ITIN) instead. The IRS issues ITINs upon the submission of an application and proof of identification (e.g., a driver's license). As the IRS does not require an applicant to show that he or she is in the United States legally, the ITINs are freely available to undocumented persons (i.e., illegal immigrants). The use of an ITIN also can enable the holder to carry out other financial transactions (e.g., establish a bank account, secure a credit card, obtain a loan).

The position of the IRS is that the current ITIN procedure brings in revenue that otherwise would not be forthcoming. Some undocumented workers want to comply with the law and pay the income taxes they owe. This practice should not be discouraged, as the tax law applies with equal force to legal and illegal residents of the United States.

Filing Requirements for Dependents

Computation of the gross income filing requirement for an individual who can be claimed as a dependent on another person's tax return is subject to more complex rules. Such an individual must file a return if he or she has *any* of the following.

- Earned income only and gross income that is more than the total standard deduction (including any additional standard deduction) that the individual is allowed for the year.
- Unearned income only and gross income of more than $950 plus any additional standard deduction that the individual is allowed for the year.
- Both earned and unearned income and gross income of more than the larger of $950 or the sum of earned income plus $300 (but limited to the applicable basic standard deduction), plus any additional standard deduction that the individual is allowed for the year.

Thus, the filing requirement for a dependent who has no unearned income is the total of the *basic* standard deduction plus any *additional* standard deduction, which includes both the additional deduction for blindness and the deduction for being age 65 or older. For example, the 2011 filing requirement for a single dependent who is under age 65 is $5,800, the amount of the basic standard deduction.

Selecting the Proper Form

The 2011 tax forms had not been released at the date of publication of this text. The following comments apply to the 2010 forms. It is possible that some provisions will change for the 2011 forms.

Although a variety of forms are available to individual taxpayers, the use of some of these forms is restricted. For example, Form 1040EZ cannot be used if the:

- Taxpayer claims any dependents;
- Taxpayer (or spouse) is 65 or older or blind; or
- Taxable income is $100,000 or more.

Taxpayers who desire to itemize deductions *from* AGI cannot use Form 1040A, but must file Form 1040 (the long form).

E-Filing

The **e-file** program is an increasingly popular alternative to traditional paper returns. Here, the required tax information is transmitted to the IRS electronically either

TAX *in* the NEWS

SPECIAL RULES FOR CERTAIN MILITARY PERSONNEL

Certain members of the military are granted more time to file their Federal income tax returns. If they are outside the United States and Puerto Rico *but not* in a combat zone, the filing date is extended to June 15. If additional taxes are due, however, interest still begins to accrue after April 15.

For those deployed in a designated combat zone, the filing date is postponed until 180 days after the last day of combat service. Furthermore, in such cases, interest *does not* accrue during the deferral period. These filing dates are equally applicable when the military person is married and files a joint return.

directly from the taxpayer (i.e., an "e-file online return") or indirectly through an electronic return originator (ERO). EROs are tax professionals who have been accepted into the electronic filing program by the IRS. Such parties hold themselves out to the general public as "authorized IRS e-file providers."

For direct e-filing, a taxpayer uses a personal computer and tax preparation software with the capability of conveying the information online to an electronic return transmitter.

A taxpayer then can use the free smartphone app "IRS2Go" to check the status of a refund.

Through an arrangement with the IRS, about 20 software providers offer free e-filing services. These services are available only to lower-income taxpayers. A list of these "Free-File" providers and their eligibility requirements can be obtained at **www.irs.gov**.

All e-filing taxpayers and tax return preparers must attest to the returns they file. For most taxpayers, this attesting can be done through an electronic return signature using a personal identification number.

The e-file approach has two major advantages. First, compliance with the format required by the IRS eliminates many math and clerical errors that would otherwise occur. Second, the time required for processing a refund usually is reduced to three weeks or less.

When and Where to File

Tax returns of individuals are due on or before the fifteenth day of the fourth month following the close of the tax year. For the calendar year taxpayer, the usual filing date is on or before April 15 of the following year.[38] When the due date falls on a Saturday, Sunday, or legal holiday, the last day for filing falls on the next business day. The return should be sent or delivered to an IRS Regional Service Center.[39]

If the return is mailed to the proper address with sufficient postage and is postmarked on or before the due date, it is deemed timely filed. The IRS has issued rules governing the filing of returns using various private delivery services (e.g., FedEx, UPS).[40]

If a taxpayer is unable to file the return by the specified due date, a six-month extension of time is obtained by filing Form 4868 (Application for Automatic Extension of Time to File U.S. Individual Income Tax Return).[41]

Although obtaining an extension excuses a taxpayer from a penalty for failure to file, it does not insulate against the penalty for failure to pay. If more tax is owed, the filing of Form 4868 should be accompanied by an additional remittance to cover the balance due. The failure to file and failure to pay penalties are discussed in Chapter 1.

If an individual taxpayer needs to file an amended return (e.g., because of a failure to report income or to claim an additional deduction or tax credit), Form 1040X is filed. The form generally is filed within three years of the filing date of the original return or within two years from the time the tax was paid, whichever is later.

[38]§ 6072(a).

[39]The Regional Service Centers and the geographic area each covers also are listed at **www.irs.gov/file**.

[40]§ 7502(f).

[41]Reg. § 1.6081–4.

TAX *in* the NEWS

"CHARGE IT"—CONVENIENT BUT NOT CHEAP!

When a consumer uses a credit card to buy goods, the merchant pays a fee to the credit card company. When a credit card is used to pay income taxes, however, Federal law prevents the IRS from paying any such fee. Instead, the credit card company charges the user a "convenience fee" of up to 2.5 percent of the tax paid. The fee must be paid even if the user pays the credit card bill in full when it arrives.

If, for example, John uses his Visa card to pay the $10,000 in taxes that he owes, he may be charged $250 (2.5% × $10,000) as a convenience fee. Furthermore, regular credit card interest is charged on extended time payments.

Mode of Payment

Usually, a Federal tax payment is made by check. In that event, the check should be made out to "United States Treasury." Payments by credit card or electronic fund transfer also are allowed.

3.5 Tax Determination—Computation Procedures

LO.6

Use the proper method for determining the tax liability.

The computation of income tax due (or refund) involves applying the proper set of tax rates to taxable income and then adjusting for available credits. In certain cases, however, the application of the kiddie tax will cause a modification of the means by which the tax is determined.

TAX RATES

The basic Federal income tax rate structure is progressive, with current rates ranging from 10 percent to 35 percent. By way of comparison, the lowest rate structure, which was in effect in 1913–1915, ranged from 1 to 7 percent, and the highest, in effect during 1944–1945, ranged from 23 to 94 percent.

TAX TABLE METHOD

The tax liability is computed using either the Tax Table method or the Tax Rate Schedule method. Most taxpayers compute their tax using the **Tax Table**. Eligible taxpayers compute taxable income (as shown in Figure 3.1) and *must* determine their tax by reference to the Tax Table. The following taxpayers, however, may not use the Tax Table method.

- An individual who files a short period return (see Chapter 16).
- Individuals whose taxable income exceeds the maximum (ceiling) amount in the Tax Table. The Tax Table addresses taxable incomes below $100,000 for Form 1040.
- An estate or trust.

The IRS does not release the Tax Tables until late in the year to which they apply. The Tax Rate Schedules, however, are released at the end of the year preceding their applicability.[42] For purposes of estimating tax liability and making quarterly prepayments, the Tax Rate Schedules usually are consulted. Based on its availability, the 2010 Tax Table will be used to illustrate the tax computation using the Tax Table method.

[42]The 2011 Tax Table was not available from the IRS at the date of publication of this text. The Tax Table for 2010 and the Tax Rate Schedules for 2010 and 2011 are reproduced in Appendix A. For quick reference, the Tax Rate Schedules also are reproduced inside the front cover of this text.

TABLE 3.6 2011 Tax Rate Schedule for Single Taxpayers

If Taxable Income Is Over	But Not Over	The Tax Is:	Of the Amount Over
$ –0–	$ 8,500	10%	$ –0–
8,500	34,500	$ 850 + 15%	8,500
34,500	83,600	4,750 + 25%	34,500
83,600	174,400	17,025 + 28%	83,600
174,400	379,150	42,449 + 33%	174,400
379,150		110,016.50 + 35%	379,150

Although the Tax Table is derived by using the Tax Rate Schedules (discussed below), the tax calculated using the two methods may vary slightly. This variation occurs because the tax for a particular income range in the Tax Table is based on the average tax for that range.

EXAMPLE 36

Linda is single and has taxable income of $30,000 for calendar year 2010. To determine Linda's tax using the Tax Table (see Appendix A), find the $30,000 to $30,050 income line. The tax of $4,085 actually is the tax that the Tax Rate Schedule would yield on taxable income of $30,025 (i.e., the average tax between $30,000 and $30,050). ■

TAX RATE SCHEDULE METHOD

The 2011 rate schedule for single taxpayers is reproduced in Table 3.6.[43]

EXAMPLE 37

Pat is single and had $5,870 of taxable income in 2011. His tax is $587 ($5,870 × 10%). ■

Several terms are used to describe tax rates. The rates in the Tax Rate Schedules often are referred to as *statutory* (or nominal) rates. The *marginal* rate is the highest rate that is applied in the tax computation for a particular taxpayer. In Example 37, the statutory rate and the marginal rate both are 10 percent.

EXAMPLE 38

Chris is single and had taxable income of $90,000 in 2011. Her tax is $18,817 [$17,025 + 28% ($90,000 – $83,600)]. ■

The *average* rate is equal to the tax liability divided by taxable income. In Example 38, Chris has statutory rates of 10 percent, 15 percent, 25 percent, and 28 percent, and a marginal rate of 28 percent. Chris's average rate is 21 percent ($18,817 tax liability ÷ $90,000 taxable income).

A special computation limits the effective tax rate on qualified dividends (see Chapter 4) and net long-term capital gain (see Chapter 14).

COMPUTATION OF NET TAXES PAYABLE OR REFUND DUE

The pay-as-you-go feature of the Federal income tax system requires payment of all or part of the taxpayer's income tax liability during the year. These payments take the form of Federal income tax withheld by employers or estimated tax paid by the taxpayer, or both.[44] The payments are applied against the tax from the Tax Table or

[43] § 1(i).

[44] § 3402 for withholding; § 6654 for estimated payments.

Tax Rate Schedules to determine whether the taxpayer will get a refund or pay additional tax.

Employers are required to withhold income tax on compensation paid to their employees and to pay this tax over to the government. The employer notifies the employee of the amount of income tax withheld on Form W–2 (Wage and Tax Statement). The employee should receive this form by January 31 after the year in which the income tax is withheld.

If taxpayers receive income that is not subject to withholding or income from which not enough tax is withheld, they may need to pay estimated tax. These individuals must file Form 1040–ES (Estimated Tax for Individuals) and pay in quarterly installments the income tax and self-employment tax estimated to be due.

The income tax from the Tax Table or the Tax Rate Schedules is reduced first by the individual's tax credits. There is an important distinction between tax credits and tax deductions. Tax credits reduce the tax liability dollar-for-dollar. Tax deductions reduce taxable income on which the tax liability is based.

EXAMPLE 39

Gail is a taxpayer in the 25% tax bracket. As a result of incurring $1,000 in child care expenses (see Chapter 12 for details), she is entitled to a $200 child care credit ($1,000 child care expenses × 20% credit rate). She also contributed $1,000 to the American Cancer Society and included this amount in her itemized deductions. The child care credit results in a $200 reduction of Gail's tax liability for the year. The contribution to the American Cancer Society reduces taxable income by $1,000 and results in a $250 reduction in Gail's tax liability ($1,000 reduction in taxable income × 25% tax rate). ■

Tax credits are discussed in Chapter 12. The following are several of the more commonly encountered credits.

- Earned income credit.
- Credit for child and dependent care expenses.
- Foreign tax credit.
- Child tax credit.

EXAMPLE 40

Return to the facts of Example 11. Grace's taxable income is $43,800. Now further assume that Grace reports the following: income tax withheld, $2,300; estimated tax payments, $3,600; and a credit for dependent care expenses, $200. Grace's net tax payable is computed as follows.

Income tax (from 2011 Tax Rate Schedule for Head of Household, Appendix A, rounded)		$ 5,963
Less: Tax credits and prepayments—		
Credit for dependent care expenses	$ 200	
Income tax withheld	2,300	
Estimated tax payments	3,600	(6,100)
Net taxes payable (or refund due if negative)		$ (137)

■

UNEARNED INCOME OF CHILDREN TAXED AT PARENTS' RATE

LO.7

Identify and work with kiddie tax situations.

At one time, a dependent child could claim an exemption on his or her own return even if claimed as a dependent by the parents. This enabled a parent to shift investment income (such as interest and dividends) to a child by transferring ownership of the assets producing the income. The child would pay no tax on the income to the extent that it was sheltered by the child's exemption and standard deduction amounts.

An additional tax motivation existed for shifting income from parents to children. Although a child's unearned income in excess of the exemption and standard deduction amounts was subject to tax, it was taxed at the child's rate, rather than the parents' rate.

To reduce the tax savings that result from shifting income from parents to children, the net **unearned income** (commonly called investment income) of certain children is taxed as if it were the parents' income. Unearned income includes such income as taxable interest, dividends, capital gains, rents, royalties, pension and annuity income, and income (other than earned income) received as the beneficiary of a trust. This provision, commonly referred to as the **kiddie tax**, applies to any child for any taxable year if the child has not reached age 19 by the close of the taxable year (age 24 if a full-time student) and has unearned income of more than $1,900.[45]

The kiddie tax does not apply if the child's earned income exceeds half of his or her support, or if both parents are deceased, or if the child is married and files a joint return.

Net Unearned Income

Net unearned income of a dependent child is computed as follows.[46]

Unearned income

Less: **$950**

Less: **The greater of**

- **$950 of the standard deduction** *or*
- **The amount of allowable itemized deductions directly connected with the production of the unearned income**

Equals: **Net unearned income**

If net unearned income is zero (or negative), the child's tax is computed without using the parents' rate. If the amount of net unearned income is positive, the net unearned income is taxed at the parents' rate, even if the parents did not transfer the income to the child.

Tax Determination

If a child is subject to the kiddie tax, there are two options for computing the tax on the income. A separate return may be filed for the child, or the parents may elect to report the child's income on their own return. If a separate return is filed for the child, the tax on net unearned income (referred to as the *allocable parental tax*) is computed on Form 8615 as though the income had been included on the parents' return.

EXAMPLE 41

Olaf and Olga have a child, Hans (age 10). In 2011, Hans received $3,000 of interest income and paid investment-related fees of $200. Olaf and Olga had $70,000 of taxable income, not including their child's investment income. The parents have no qualified dividends or capital gains. Olaf and Olga do not make the parental election.

1. Determine Hans's net unearned income	
Gross income (unearned)	$ 3,000
Less: $950	(950)
Less: The greater of • $950 or • Investment expense ($200)	(950)
Equals: Net unearned income	$ 1,100
2. Determine allocable parental tax	
Parents' taxable income	$70,000
Plus: Hans's net unearned income	1,100
Equals: Revised taxable income	$71,100
Tax on revised taxable income	$10,025
Less: Tax on parents' taxable income	(9,750)
Allocable parental tax	$ 275

[45]§ 1(g)(2).

[46]The $950 amounts in the formula are subject to adjustment for inflation each year.

3.	**Determine Hans's nonparental tax**	
	Hans's AGI	$ 3,000
	Less: Standard deduction	(950)
	Less: Personal exemption	(–0–)
	Equals: Taxable income	$ 2,050
	Less: Net unearned income	(1,100)
	Nonparental taxable income	$ 950
	Equals: Tax ($950 × 10% rate)	$ 95
4.	**Determine Hans's total tax liability**	
	Nonparental source tax (step 3)	$ 95
	Allocable parental tax (step 2)	275
	Total tax	$ 370

■

Election to Claim Certain Unearned Income on Parent's Return

If a child subject to the kiddie tax must file a tax return and meets all of the following requirements, the parent may elect to report the child's unearned income that exceeds $1,900 on the parent's own tax return.

- Gross income is from interest and dividends only.
- Gross income is more than $950 but less than $9,500.
- No estimated tax has been paid in the name and Social Security number of the child, and the child is not subject to backup withholding.

If the parental election is made, the child is treated as having no gross income and then is not required to file a tax return. The parental election is made by completing and filing Form 8814.

The parent(s) also must pay an additional tax equal to the smaller of $95 or 10 percent of the child's gross income over $950. Parents who have substantial itemized deductions based on AGI (see Chapter 10) may find that making the parental election increases total taxes for the family unit. Taxes should be calculated both with the parental election and without it to determine the appropriate choice.

Other Provisions

If parents have more than one child subject to the tax on net unearned income, the tax for the children is computed as shown in Example 41 and then allocated to the children based on their relative amounts of income. For children of divorced parents, the taxable income of the custodial parent is used to determine the allocable parental tax. This parent is the one who may elect to report the child's unearned income. For married individuals filing separate returns, the individual with the greater taxable income is the applicable parent.

3.6 Gains and Losses from Property Transactions—In General

LO.8

Describe the tax treatment of property transactions.

Gains and losses from property transactions are discussed in detail in Chapters 13 and 14. Because of their importance in the tax system, however, they are introduced briefly at this point.

When property is sold or otherwise disposed of, gain or loss may result. Such gain or loss has an effect on the income tax position of the party making the sale or other disposition when the *realized* gain or loss is *recognized* for tax purposes. Without realized gain or loss, there generally can be no recognized gain or loss.

Amount realized from the sale – **Adjusted basis of the property** = **Realized gain (or loss)**

The amount realized is the selling price of the property less any costs of disposition (e.g., brokerage commissions) incurred by the seller. The adjusted basis of the property is determined as follows.

Cost (or other original basis) at date of acquisition	
Add:	**Capital additions**
Subtract:	**Depreciation (if appropriate) and other capital recoveries (see Chapter 8)**
Equals:	**Adjusted basis at date of sale or other disposition**

All realized gains are recognized (taxable) unless some specific part of the tax law provides otherwise (see Chapter 13 dealing with certain nontaxable exchanges). Realized losses may or may not be recognized (deductible) for tax purposes, depending on the circumstances involved. Generally, losses realized from the disposition of personal use property (property neither held for investment nor used in a trade or business) are not recognized.

EXAMPLE 42

Ted sells his sailboat (adjusted basis of $4,000) for $5,500. Ted also sells one of his personal automobiles (adjusted basis of $8,000) for $5,000. Ted's realized gain of $1,500 from the sale of the sailboat is recognized. On the other hand, the $3,000 realized loss on the sale of the automobile is not recognized and will not provide Ted with any deductible tax benefit. ■

Once it has been determined that the disposition of property results in a recognized gain or loss, the next step is to classify the gain or loss as capital or ordinary. Although ordinary gain is fully taxable and ordinary loss is fully deductible, the same may not hold true for capital gains and capital losses.

3.7 Gains and Losses from Property Transactions—Capital Gains and Losses

Capital gains and losses can generate unique tax consequences. For in-depth treatment of property transactions (including capital gains and losses), refer to Chapters 13 and 14. For now, the overview appearing below should suffice.

CAPITAL ASSETS

Capital assets include any property held by the taxpayer *other than* property listed in § 1221. The list in § 1221 includes inventory, accounts receivable, and depreciable property or real estate used in a business. Thus, the sale or exchange of assets in these categories usually results in ordinary income or loss treatment (see Chapter 14).

The principal capital assets held by an individual taxpayer include assets held for personal (rather than business) use, such as a personal residence or an automobile, and assets held for investment purposes (e.g., corporate securities and land).

Capital assets include collectibles, which can be subject to unique tax treatment. **Collectibles** include art, antiques, gems, metals, stamps, some coins and bullion, and alcoholic beverages that are held as investments.

When an individual sells a capital asset, a capital gain or loss results. Capital gains are taxable, and capital losses are netted against them, resulting in a net capital gain or loss. Special tax rates apply to most capital asset sales, but an individual cannot deduct a capital loss that results from the sale of a personal use asset.

EXAMPLE 43

Kelly owns a pizza parlor. During the current year, she sells two automobiles. The first automobile, which had been used as a pizza delivery car for three years, was sold at a loss of $1,000. Because this automobile is an asset used in her business, Kelly claims an ordinary loss deduction of $1,000, rather than a capital loss deduction. The second automobile, which Kelly had owned for two years, was her personal use car. It was sold for a gain of $800. The personal use car is a capital asset. Therefore, Kelly recognizes a capital gain of $800. ■

TAXATION OF NET CAPITAL GAIN

Net capital gains are classified and taxed as follows.

Classification	Maximum Rate
Short-term gains (held for one year or less)	35%
Long-term gains (held for more than one year)—	
Collectibles	28%
Certain depreciable property used in a trade or business (known as unrecaptured § 1250 gain and discussed in Chapter 14)	25%
All other long-term capital gains	15% or 0%

The special tax rate applicable to long-term capital gains is called the alternative tax computation. It is used only if the taxpayer's regular tax rate *exceeds* the applicable alternative tax rate. The 0 percent rate, noted above, applies only if the taxpayer's regular tax bracket is 15 percent or less.[47]

EXAMPLE 44

Polly is in the 15% tax bracket and reports the following capital gains.

Robin Corporation stock (held for 6 months)	$1,000
Crow Corporation stock (held for 13 months)	1,000

Polly's tax on these transactions is $150 ($1,000 × 15%) as to Robin and $0 ($1,000 × 0%) as to Crow. ■

EXAMPLE 45

Assume the same facts as in Example 44, except that Polly's regular tax bracket for the year is 28% (not 15%). Polly's tax on these transactions becomes $280 ($1,000 × 28%) as to Robin and $150 ($1,000 × 15%) as to Crow. ■

DETERMINATION OF NET CAPITAL GAIN

To arrive at a *net* capital gain, capital losses are taken into account. The capital losses are aggregated by holding period (short term and long term) and applied against the gains in that category. If excess losses result, they then are shifted to the category carrying the *highest* tax rate. A *net capital gain* occurs if the net long-term capital gain (NLTCG) exceeds the net short-term capital loss (NSTCL).

EXAMPLE 46

Colin is in the 35% tax bracket and reports the following capital transactions.

Penguin Corporation stock (held for 8 months)	$ 1,000
Owl Corporation stock (held for 10 months)	(3,000)
Stamp collection (held for 5 years)	2,000
Land (held as an investment for 3 years)	4,000

47 § 1(h)(1).

The Penguin short-term capital gain (STCG) of $1,000 is offset by the Owl short-term capital loss (STCL) of $3,000. The remaining STCL of $2,000 then is applied against the collectible gain of $2,000. The end result is a net long-term capital gain of $4,000 from the land sale, taxed at a 15% rate. ■

TREATMENT OF NET CAPITAL LOSS

For individual taxpayers, net capital loss can be used to offset ordinary income of up to $3,000 ($1,500 for married persons filing separate returns). If a taxpayer reports both short- and long-term capital losses, the short-term category is used first to arrive at the $3,000. Any remaining net capital loss is carried over indefinitely until exhausted. When carried over, the excess capital loss retains its classification as short or long term.

EXAMPLE 47

In 2011, Tina has a short-term capital loss of $2,000, a long-term capital loss of $2,500, and no capital gains. She can deduct $3,000 ($2,000 short-term + $1,000 long-term) of this amount as an ordinary loss. The remaining $1,500 is carried over to 2012 as a long-term capital loss. ■

EXAMPLE 48
THE BIG PICTURE

Return to the facts of *The Big Picture* on p. 3-2. Polly's sale of her wedding rings resulted in a realized capital loss of $7,000 [$8,000 (selling price) – $15,000 (cost basis)]. However, because they were personal use property, Polly cannot deduct the loss. ■

TAX PLANNING:

3.8 Maximizing the Use of the Standard Deduction

LO.9

Identify tax planning opportunities associated with the individual tax formula.

In most cases, the choice between using the standard deduction and itemizing deductions *from* AGI is a simple matter—pick whichever yields the larger tax benefit. Families in the initial stages of home ownership, for example, will invariably make the itemization choice due to the substantial mortgage interest and property tax payments involved. Older taxpayers, however, may have paid for their homes or are enjoying senior citizen property tax exemptions. For them, the more attractive benefit is the additional standard deduction that can accompany the standard deduction choice.

In some cases, the difference between the standard deduction and itemizing may not be a significant amount. Here, taxes might be saved by alternating between the two options. The taxpayer does this by using the cash method to concentrate multiple years' deductions in a single year (e.g., paying off a five-year church pledge in one year). Then, the standard deduction is used in alternate years.

3.9 Dependency Exemptions

THE JOINT RETURN TEST

A married person can be claimed as a dependent only if that individual does not file a joint return with his or her spouse. If a joint return has been filed, the damage may be undone if separate returns are substituted on a timely basis (on or before the due date of the return). The latest-filed timely return prevails.[48]

[48] Reg. § 1.6013–1(a)(1).

Keep in mind that the filing of a joint return is not fatal to the dependency exemption if the parties are filing solely to recover all income tax withholdings, they are not required to file a return, and no tax liability would exist on separate returns.

SUPPORT CONSIDERATIONS

The support of a qualifying child becomes relevant only if the child is self-supporting. In cases where the child has an independent source of funds, planning could help prevent an undesirable result. When a qualifying relative is involved, meeting the support test is essential, as the dependency exemption is not otherwise available.

EXAMPLE 49

Imogene maintains a household that she shares with her son and mother. The son, Barry, is 23 years of age and a full-time student in law school. The mother, Gladys, is 68 years old, and she is active in charitable causes. Barry works part-time for a local law firm, while Gladys has income from investments. In resolving the support issue (or self-support in the case of Barry), compare Imogene's contribution with that made by Barry and Gladys.

In this connection, what Barry and Gladys do with their funds becomes crucial. The funds that are used for nonsupport purposes (e.g., purchase of investments) or not used at all (e.g., deposited in a bank) should not be considered. To the extent possible, the parties should control how much Barry and Gladys contribute to their own support. Records should be maintained showing the amount of support and its source. ■

Example 49 does not mention the possible application of the gross income test. Presuming Barry is a qualifying child, the amount he earns does not matter, as the gross income test does not apply. Gladys, however, comes under the qualifying relative category, where the gross income test applies. Therefore, for her to be claimed as a dependent, her income that is taxable will have to be less than $3,500.

COMMUNITY PROPERTY RAMIFICATIONS

In certain cases, state law can have an effect on the availability of a dependency exemption.

EXAMPLE 50

Mitch provides more than half of the support of his son, Ross, and daughter-in-law, Connie, who live with him. Ross, age 22, is a full-time student, while Connie earns $4,000 from a part-time job. Ross and Connie do not file a joint return. All parties live in New York, a common law state. Mitch can claim Ross as a dependent, as he is a qualifying child. Connie is not a dependent because she does not meet the gross income test under the qualifying relative category. ■

EXAMPLE 51

Assume the same facts as in Example 50, except that all parties live in Arizona, a community property state. Now, Connie also qualifies as a dependent. Since Connie's gross income is only $2,000 (one-half of the community income), she satisfies the gross income test. ■

RELATIONSHIP TO THE DEDUCTION FOR MEDICAL EXPENSES

Generally, medical expenses are deductible only if they are paid on behalf of the taxpayer, his or her spouse, and their dependents. Since deductibility may rest on dependency status, planning is important in arranging multiple support agreements.

EXAMPLE 52

Zelda will be supported next year by her two sons (Vern and Vito) and her daughter (Maria). Each will furnish approximately one-third of the required support. If the parties decide that the dependency exemption should be claimed by the daughter under a multiple support agreement, any medical expenses incurred by Zelda should be paid by Maria. ■

In planning a multiple support agreement, take into account which of the parties is most likely to exceed the 7.5 percent limitation on medical expense deductions (see Chapter 10). In Example 52, for instance, Maria might be a poor choice if she and her family do not expect to incur many medical and drug expenses of their own.

One exception permits the deduction of medical expenses paid on behalf of someone who is not a spouse or a dependent. If the person could be claimed as a dependent *except* for the gross income or joint return test, the medical expenses are, nevertheless, deductible. For additional discussion, see Chapter 10.

ETHICS & Equity

A Tax Benefit from Nondependents

Kristen provides more than half of the support of her parents who do not live with her. She cannot claim them as dependents, however, because they have too much gross income and file a joint return. She pays $20,000 for her mother's dental implants and $42,000 for her father's knee replacement. From a tax standpoint, has Kristen acted wisely?

3.10 Taking Advantage of Tax Rate Differentials

It is natural for taxpayers to be concerned about the tax rates they are paying. How does a tax practitioner communicate information about rates to clients? There are several possibilities.

The marginal tax rate (refer to Examples 37 and 38) provides information that can help a taxpayer evaluate a particular course of action or structure a transaction in the most advantageous manner. For example, a taxpayer who is in the 15 percent bracket this year and expects to be in the 28 percent bracket next year should, if possible, defer payment of deductible expenses until next year, to maximize the tax benefit of the deduction.

A note of caution is in order with respect to shifting income and expenses between years. Congress has recognized the tax planning possibilities of such shifting and has enacted many provisions to limit a taxpayer's ability to do so. The kiddie tax is one example. More of these limitations on the shifting of income are discussed in Chapters 4, 5, and 16. Limitations that affect a taxpayer's ability to shift deductions are discussed in Chapters 6 through 11 and in Chapter 16.

A taxpayer's *effective rate* can be an informative measure of the effectiveness of tax planning. The effective rate is computed by dividing the taxpayer's tax liability by the total amount of income. A low effective rate can be considered an indication of effective tax planning.

One way of lowering the effective rate is to exclude income from the tax base. For example, a taxpayer might consider investing in tax-free municipal bonds rather than taxable corporate bonds. Although pre-tax income from corporate bonds is usually higher, after-tax income may be higher if the taxpayer invests in tax-free municipal bonds.

Another way of lowering the effective rate is to make sure that the taxpayer's expenses and losses are deductible. For example, losses on investments in passive activities may not be deductible (see Chapter 11). Therefore, a taxpayer who plans to invest in an activity that will produce a loss in the early years should take steps to ensure that the business is treated as active rather than passive. Often, active losses are deductible while passive losses are not.

3.11 Unearned Income of Certain Children

Taxpayers can use several strategies to avoid or minimize the effect of the kiddie tax rules. Parents should consider giving a younger child assets that defer taxable income until the child is free of the kiddie tax. For example, U.S. government Series EE savings bonds can be used to defer income until the bonds are cashed in (see Chapter 4).

Growth stocks typically pay little in the way of dividends. However, the capital gain on an astute investment may more than offset the lack of dividends. The stock can be held and then sold only when the child's own tax rates apply.

Taxpayers in a position to do so can employ their children in their business and pay them a reasonable wage for the work they actually perform (e.g., light office help, such as filing). The child's earned income is sheltered by the standard deduction, and the parents' business is allowed a deduction for the wages. The kiddie tax rules have no effect on earned income, and the income could be sheltered further if it is contributed to a retirement plan.

REFOCUS ON THE BIG PICTURE

A DIVIDED HOUSEHOLD

Of major concern to Polly is her filing status. If she qualifies as an abandoned spouse, she is entitled to file as head of household. If not, she is considered to be a married person filing separately. Moreover, to be an abandoned spouse, Polly must be able to claim Paige as a dependent. To be a dependent, Paige must meet the requirements of a qualifying child *or* a qualifying relative.

For qualifying child purposes, Paige must meet either the age (i.e., under age 19) or the full-time student (under age 24) test. Because Paige currently is not a full-time student, is she under age 19? If so, she is a qualifying child. If Paige is not a qualifying child, is she a qualifying relative? Here, the answer depends on meeting the gross income test. How much did Paige earn from her part-time job? If her earnings are under $3,700, she satisfies the gross income test. Thus, if Paige can be claimed as a dependent as either a qualifying child or a qualifying relative, Polly is an abandoned spouse entitled to head-of-household filing status. If not, she is a married person filing separately.

Maude can be claimed as Polly's dependent because Maude is a member of the household. It does not matter that Maude died in February, and the dependency exemption amount is allowed in full. Because Maude is her dependent, Polly can claim the medical expenses she paid on Maude's behalf. The funeral expenses, however, are not deductible (see Example 19).

Does Maude qualify Polly for head-of-household filing status? Although Maude is Polly's dependent, Maude does not meet the relationship test (see Example 31).

The sale of the wedding rings results in a capital loss of $7,000 ($8,000 − $15,000). Because the loss is for personal use property, it cannot be deducted for tax purposes.

What If?

Assume that Nick left for parts unknown in August (not March). Now Polly cannot qualify as an abandoned spouse. Her husband lived in the home during part of the last six months of the year. Consequently, Polly is treated as married and cannot qualify for head-of-household filing status. She must file as a married person filing separately. When Nick left does not affect the dependency issue regarding Paige, however.

KEY TERMS

Abandoned spouse, 3–21
Child tax credit, 3–18
Collectibles, 3–30
Dependency exemption, 3–11
E-file, 3–23
Head of household, 3–19
Itemized deductions, 3–6
Kiddie tax, 3–28
Multiple support agreement, 3–15
Personal exemptions, 3–10
Qualifying child, 3–11
Qualifying relative, 3–13
Standard deduction, 3–7
Surviving spouse, 3–19
Tax Table, 3–25
Unearned income, 3–28

DISCUSSION QUESTIONS

1. **LO.1** Rearrange the following items to show the correct formula for arriving at *taxable income* of individuals under the Federal income tax.
   a. Deductions *for* AGI.
   b. Income (broadly conceived).
   c. Taxable income.
   d. Adjusted gross income.
   e. Personal and dependency exemptions.
   f. Gross income.
   g. Exclusions.
   h. The greater of the standard deduction or itemized deductions.

ISSUE ID

2. **LO.1, 5, 8, 9** During the year, Lucy is involved in the following transactions. What are the possible Federal income tax effects of these transactions?
   - Won money gambling on a trip to a casino.
   - Paid a traffic ticket received while double parking to attend a business meeting.
   - Contributed to the mayor's reelection campaign. The mayor had promised Lucy to rezone some of her land.
   - Borrowed money from a bank to make a down payment on a residence.
   - Sold a houseboat and a camper on eBay. Both were personal use items, and the gain from one offset the loss from the other.
   - Her dependent Aunt Katherine died on January 3 of the year.
   - Paid for Katherine's funeral expenses.
   - Paid premiums on her dependent son's life insurance policy.

3. **LO.1** Which of the following items can be *inclusions* in gross income?
   a. During the year, shares of stock that the taxpayer had purchased as an investment doubled in value.
   b. Amount an off-duty motorcycle police officer received for escorting a funeral procession.
   c. While his mother Shirley was in the hospital, the taxpayer sold Shirley's jewelry and gave the money to his girlfriend Serena.
   d. Child support payments received.
   e. A damage deposit the taxpayer recovered when he vacated the apartment he had rented.
   f. Interest received by the taxpayer on an investment in bonds issued by IBM.
   g. Amounts received by the taxpayer, a baseball "Hall of Famer," for autographing sports equipment (e.g., balls, gloves).
   h. Jury duty fees received.

4. **LO.1** Which of the following items can be *exclusions* from gross income?
   a. Alimony payments received.
   b. Award received by the taxpayer for punitive damages.
   c. A new golf cart won in a church raffle.
   d. Amount collected on a loan previously made to a college friend.
   e. Insurance proceeds paid to the taxpayer on the death of her uncle—she was the designated beneficiary under the policy.
   f. Interest income on City of Miami bonds.

g. Scholarship award that covers the taxpayer's college tuition.
h. Reward paid by the IRS for information provided that led to the conviction of the taxpayer's former employer for tax evasion.
i. A "store refund" of $200 that the taxpayer received when she discovered an overcharge on the purchase of home appliances.
j. Rare coins worth $8,000 found in an old trunk purchased by the taxpayer at a garage sale.

5. **LO.1** Harold, a U.S. citizen, accepts employment overseas. He was careful to choose a country that does not impose an income tax. Has Harold avoided an income tax completely? Explain.

6. **LO.1** One class of deductions is variously described as *deductions for AGI, above-the-line deductions,* and *page 1 deductions.* Explain the meaning of these designations.

7. **LO.1, 8, 9** In late 2011, the Polks come to you for tax advice. They are considering selling some stock investments for a loss and making a contribution to a traditional IRA. In reviewing their situation, you note that they have large medical expenses and a casualty loss, with neither being covered by insurance. What advice would you give to the Polks? **DECISION MAKING**

8. **LO.2** In choosing between the standard deduction and itemizing deductions *from* AGI, what effect, if any, does each of the following variables have? **ISSUE ID**
   a. The age of the taxpayer(s).
   b. Taxpayer's filing status (e.g., single; married, filing jointly).
   c. The taxpayers have paid off the mortgage on their personal residence.
   d. Because of a senior citizen exemption, the taxpayers paid $3,000 less in property taxes on their personal residence.
   e. Whether married taxpayers decide to file separate returns.
   f. The taxpayer's uninsured personal residence was recently destroyed by fire.
   g. The number of personal and dependency exemptions the taxpayer can claim.

9. **LO.2** In connection with the standard deduction alternative, comment on the following.
   a. Percentage of taxpayers who chose the standard deduction rather than itemize.
   b. Status of a taxpayer who dies before year-end.
   c. Types of standard deductions available.
   d. When not available.

10. **LO.2, 3, 5** Mel, age 76 and a widower, is being claimed as a dependent by his daughter. How does this situation affect the following?
    a. Mel's own individual filing requirement.
    b. Mel's personal exemption.
    c. The standard deduction allowed to Mel.
    d. The availability of any additional standard deduction.

11. **LO.2** Bernice and Drew are dependents of their parents, and each earns gross income of $2,000 for the year. Bernice's standard deduction for the year is $950, while Drew's is $2,300. As their income is the same, what causes the difference in the amount of the standard deduction? **ISSUE ID**

12. **LO.4** Kirby, age 18, lives with her parents in a household maintained by them. As an actress, she earns $600,000 during the year, which, after taxes, is placed in a trust for her. Can Kirby be claimed as a dependent by her parents?

13. **LO.4** Patsy maintains a household that includes her eldest son (age 30) and one of Patsy's cousins (age 28). She can claim the cousin as a dependent but not her son. Explain. **ISSUE ID**

14. **LO.4** Heather, age 12, lives in the same household with her mother, grandmother, and uncle.
    a. Who can claim Heather as a dependent on a Federal income tax return?
    b. Which of Heather's relatives takes precedence in claiming the exemption?

15. **LO.4** Under what circumstances, if any, can a taxpayer claim an ex-spouse as a dependent? What about claiming the ex-spouse's relatives as dependents?

16. **LO.4** Joshua and his two sisters provide more than half of the support of their mother, who has significant health problems. After comparing notes, Joshua tells his sisters to split the dependency exemption between them, as the deduction will result in a greater tax benefit. Do you see any flaw in Joshua's advice? **ISSUE ID**

17. **LO.4** Jerry and Arlene were divorced in 2009. In 2011, Arlene has custody of their children, but Jerry provides nearly all of their support. Who is entitled to claim the children as dependents?

ISSUE ID

18. **LO.4** Marcus maintains a household in which his 18-year-old daughter Joely and her husband Thom live. Although Marcus provides most of their support, he does not claim them as dependents because Joely and Thom file a joint return. Is Marcus correct?

ISSUE ID

19. **LO.4** Alberto, who is single, is a U.S. citizen and resident. He provides almost all of the support of his parents and two aunts, who are citizens and residents of Mexico. Alberto's parents and aunts are seriously considering moving to and becoming residents of El Salvador. Would such a move have any impact on Alberto? Why or why not?

ISSUE ID

20. **LO.5, 9** Jack and Joyce, who are married, reported 2011 itemized deductions of $7,500 and $500, respectively. Jack suggests that they file their Federal income tax returns separately—he will itemize his deductions *from* AGI, and she will claim the standard deduction.
    a. Evaluate Jack's suggestion.
    b. What should they do?

21. **LO.4, 5** Comment on the availability of head-of-household filing status in each of the following situations.
    a. Al lives alone but maintains the household of his parents. In July 2011, the parents use their savings to purchase a Lexus automobile for $51,000.
    b. Bree maintains a home in which she and her father live. The father then enters a nursing facility for treatment for a mental illness.
    c. Chloe a single parent, maintains a home in which she and Dean, Chloe's unmarried son, live. Dean, age 18, earns $4,000 from a part-time job.
    d. Assume the same facts as in (c) except that Dean is age 20, not 18.
    e. Evie lives alone but maintains the household where her dependent daughter Zoe lives.
    f. Frank maintains a household that includes Georgia, an unrelated friend who qualifies as his dependent.

ISSUE ID

22. **LO.5** Several years ago, after a particularly fierce argument, Fran's husband moved out and has not been heard from or seen since. Because Fran cannot locate her husband, she uses a "married, filing separate" income tax return. Comment on Fran's Federal filing status.

23. **LO.7** In connection with the kiddie tax, comment on each of the following.
    a. Justification for the tax.
    b. Earned income versus unearned income.
    c. Age exception.
    d. Effect of parental election.
    e. Parents file separate returns.
    f. Parents are divorced.

24. **LO.8** During the year, Hernando recorded the following transactions. How should Hernando treat these transactions for income tax purposes?

    - Gain on the sale of stock held as an investment for 10 months.
    - Gain on the sale of land held as an investment for 4 years.
    - Gain on the sale of a houseboat owned for 2 years and used for family vacations.
    - Loss on the sale of a reconditioned motorcycle owned for 3 years and used for recreational purposes.

ISSUE ID

25. **LO.8** Several years ago, Milton and Arlene inherited equal shares of their father's coin collection. When they sold the collection this year, Milton paid a tax based on 28% of his profit while Arlene's tax rate was only 25%. Presuming each had the same amount of gain, explain the difference in result.

26. **LO.8** During the year, Brandi recorded the following transactions: a long-term capital gain from the sale of land; a short-term capital loss from the sale of stock; and a long-term capital gain from the sale of a gun collection.
    a. How are these transactions treated for income tax purposes?
    b. Does this treatment favor the taxpayer or the IRS? Explain.

ISSUE ID

27. **LO.4, 5, 9** Marcie is divorced, and her married son, Jamie (age 25), and his wife, Audrey (age 18), live with her. During the year, Jamie earned $4,800 from a part-time job and

filed a joint return with Audrey to recover his withholdings. Audrey reports zero gross income.

Marcie can prove that she provided more than 50% of Jamie and Audrey's support. Marcie does not plan to claim Jamie as a dependent because Jamie earns too much gross income. She does not plan to claim Audrey as a dependent because Audrey signed the joint return with Jamie. In fact, Marcie plans to use single filing status, as none of the persons living in her household qualifies as her dependent.

Comment on Marcie's intentions based on the following assumptions.

a. All parties live in Indiana (a common law state).
b. All parties live in California (a community property state).

PROBLEMS

28. **LO.1** Compute taxable income in each of the following independent situations.
    a. Drew and Meg, ages 40 and 41, are married and file a joint return. In addition to four dependent children, they have AGI of $65,000 and itemized deductions of $12,000.
    b. Sybil, age 40, is single and supports her dependent parents who live with her and also supports her grandfather who lives in a nursing home. She has AGI of $80,000 and itemized deductions of $8,000.
    c. Scott, age 49, is an abandoned spouse. His household includes two unmarried stepsons who qualify as his dependents. He has AGI of $75,000 and itemized deductions of $9,500.
    d. Amelia, age 33, is a surviving spouse and maintains a household for her three dependent children. She has AGI of $58,000 and itemized deductions of $10,200.
    e. Dale, age 42, is divorced but maintains the home in which he and his daughter, Jill, live. Jill is single and qualifies as Dale's dependent. Dale has AGI of $64,000 and itemized deductions of $9,900.

Note: *Problems 29 and 30 can be solved by referring to Figure 3.1, Exhibits 3.1 through 3.3, Tables 3.1 and 3.2, and the discussion under Deductions for Adjusted Gross Income in this chapter.*

29. **LO.1, 8** Compute the taxable income for 2011 for Curtis on the basis of the following information. His filing status is single.

Salary	$80,000
Interest income from bonds issued by City of San Diego	3,000
Alimony payments made	3,600
Contribution to traditional IRA	5,000
Gift from grandparents	26,000
Capital loss from stock investment	3,000
Amount lost in football office pool (sports gambling is illegal where Curtis lives)	1,500
Number of potential dependents (two nephews, who live in another state)	?
Age	39

30. **LO.1** Compute the taxable income for 2011 for Mattie on the basis of the following information. Mattie is married but has not seen or heard from her husband since 2009.

Salary	$ 70,000
Interest on bonds issued by AT&T Corporation	3,000
Interest on CD issued by Wells Fargo Bank	2,000
Cash dividend received on Chevron common stock	2,200
Life insurance proceeds paid on death of aunt (Mattie was the designated beneficiary of the policy)	100,000
Inheritance received on death of aunt	200,000
Casey (a cousin) repaid a loan Mattie made to him in 2007 (no interest was provided for)	5,000
Itemized deductions (state income tax, property taxes on residence, interest on home mortgage, charitable contributions)	10,200
Number of dependents (children, ages 17 and 18; mother-in-law, age 60)	3
Age	40

31. **LO.2** Determine the amount of the standard deduction allowed for 2011 in the following independent situations. In each case, assume the taxpayer is claimed as another person's dependent.
    a. Edward, age 18, has income as follows: $600 interest from a certificate of deposit and $5,900 from repairing cars.
    b. Sarah, age 18, has income as follows: $400 cash dividends from a stock investment and $4,600 from handling a paper route.
    c. Colin, age 16, has income as follows: $900 interest on a bank savings account and $800 for painting a neighbor's fence.
    d. Kara, age 15, has income as follows: $300 cash dividends from a stock investment and $600 from grooming pets.
    e. Kay, age 67 and a widow, has income as follows: $1,200 from a bank savings account and $3,100 from baby-sitting.

32. **LO.4** Using the legend provided below, classify each statement as to the taxpayer for dependency exemption purposes.

Legend

QC	=	Could be a qualifying child
QR	=	Could be a qualifying relative
B	=	Could satisfy the definition of both a qualifying child and a qualifying relative
N	=	Could not satisfy the definition of *either* a qualifying child or a qualifying relative

    a. Taxpayer's son has gross income of $7,000.
    b. Taxpayer's niece has gross income of $3,000.
    c. Taxpayer's mother lives with him.
    d. Taxpayer's daughter is age 25 and disabled.
    e. Taxpayer's daughter is age 18 but does not live with him. Her gross income is $8,000.
    f. Taxpayer's cousin lives with her.
    g. Taxpayer's brother does not live with her.
    h. Taxpayer's sister lives with him. She is age 20 and has dropped out of school.
    i. Taxpayer's nephew is age 20 and a full-time student.
    j. Taxpayer's grandson does not live with her. His gross income is $7,000.

33. **LO.3, 4** Determine the number of personal and dependency exemptions in each of the following independent situations.
    a. Leo and Amanda (ages 48 and 46) are husband and wife and furnish more than 50% of the support of their two children, Elton (age 18) and Trista (age 24). During the year, Elton earns $4,500 providing transportation for elderly persons with disabilities, and Trista receives a $5,000 scholarship for tuition at the law school she attends.
    b. Audrey (age 65) is divorced and lives alone. She maintains a household in which she, her ex-husband, Clint, and his mother, Olive, live. Audrey furnishes more than 50% of the household's support. Olive is age 82 and blind.
    c. Crystal, age 45, furnishes more than 50% of the support of her married son, Andy (age 18), and his wife, Paige (age 19), who live with her. During the year, Andy earned $8,000 from a part-time job. All parties live in Arizona (a community property state).
    d. Assume the same facts as in (c), except that all parties live in New Mexico (a common law state).

34. **LO.3, 4** Determine the number of personal and dependency exemptions in each of the following independent situations.
    a. Reginald, a U.S. citizen and resident, contributes 100% of the support of his parents who are citizens of Canada and live there.
    b. Pablo, a U.S. citizen and resident, contributes 100% of the support of his parents who are citizens of Mexico. Pablo's father is a resident of Mexico, and his mother is a legal resident of the United States.
    c. Marlena, a U.S. citizen and resident, contributes 100% of the support of her parents who are also U.S. citizens but are residents of Germany.
    d. Elena is a U.S. citizen and a resident of Italy. Her household includes Mario, a four-year-old adopted son who is a citizen of Spain.

35. **LO.3, 4** Determine how many personal and dependency exemptions are available in each of the following independent situations. Specify whether any such exemptions would come under the qualifying child or the qualifying relative category.
    a. Andy maintains a household that includes a cousin (age 12), a niece (age 18), and a son (age 26). All are full-time students. Andy furnishes all of their support.
    b. Minerva provides all of the support of a family friend's son (age 20) who lives with her. She also furnishes most of the support of her stepmother who does not live with her.
    c. Raul, a U.S. citizen, lives in Costa Rica. Raul's household includes an adopted daughter, Helena, who is age 9 and a citizen of Costa Rica. Raul provides all of Helena's support.
    d. Karen maintains a household that includes her ex-husband, her mother-in-law, and her brother-in-law (age 23 and not a full-time student). Karen provides more than half of all of their support. Karen is single and was divorced in the current year.

36. **LO.4** Jenny, age 14, lives in a household with her father, uncle, and grandmother. The household is maintained by the uncle. The parties, all of whom file separate returns, have AGI as follows: father ($30,000), uncle ($50,000), and grandmother ($40,000).
    a. Who is eligible to claim Jenny as a dependent on a Federal income tax return?
    b. Which of Jenny's relatives takes precedence in claiming the exemption? Explain.

37. **LO.3, 4** Determine the number of personal and dependency exemptions for 2011 in each of the following independent situations.
    a. Marcus (age 68) and Alice (age 65 and blind) file a joint return. They furnish more than 50% of the support of a cousin, Ida, who lives with them. Ida (age 20) is a full-time student and earns $5,000 during the year tutoring special needs children.
    b. Penny (age 45) is single and maintains a household in which she and her nephew, Clint, live. Clint (age 18) earns $4,900 from doing yard work, but receives more than 50% of his support from Penny.
    c. Trent (age 38) is single and lives alone. He provides more than 50% of the support of his parents (ages 69 and 70) who are in a nursing home.
    d. Jack and Carol were divorced in 2007, and Carol has custody of their three children (ages 5, 7, and 9). Jack does not furnish more than half of their support, and the divorce decree is silent as to the dependency exemptions. Carol signs a Form 8332.

38. **LO.4, 9** Isaiah and Inez (ages 88 and 89) live in an assisted care facility and for years 2010 and 2011 received their support from the following sources.

	Percentage of Support
Social Security benefits	17%
Daughter	21
Nephew	30
Cousin	11
Sister	10
Family friend (not related)	11

    a. Who is eligible to claim the Federal income tax dependency exemptions under a multiple support agreement?
    b. Must Isaiah and Inez be claimed by the same person(s) for both 2010 and 2011?
    c. Who, if anyone, can claim an itemized deduction for paying Isaiah's and Inez's medical expenses?

39. **LO.5** In each of the following *independent* situations, determine Winston's filing status. Winston is not married.
    a. Winston lives alone, but he maintains a household in which his parents live. The mother qualifies as Winston's dependent, but the father does not.
    b. Winston lives alone, but he maintains a household in which his married daughter, Karin, lives. Both Karin and her husband (Winston's son-in-law) qualify as Winston's dependents.
    c. Winston maintains a household in which he and a family friend, Ward, live. Ward qualifies as Winston's dependent.

40. **LO.4, 5** Christopher died in 2009 and is survived by his wife, Chloe, and their 18-year-old son, Dylan. Chloe is the executor of Christopher's estate and maintains the household in which she and Dylan live. All of their support is furnished by Chloe. Dylan saves his earnings. Dylan reports the following information.

Year	Earnings	Student?
2009	$5,000	Yes
2010	7,000	No
2011	6,000	Yes

What is Chloe's Federal income tax filing status for:

a. 2009?
b. 2010?
c. 2011?

41. **LO.3, 4, 5** Nadia died in 2010 and is survived by her husband, Jerold (age 44), her married son, Travis (age 22), and her daughter-in-law, Macy (age 18). Jerold is the executor of his wife's estate. He maintains the household where he, Travis, and Macy live, and Jerold furnished all of their support. During 2010 and 2011, Travis is a full-time student, while Macy earns $7,000 each year from a part-time job. Travis and Macy do not file jointly during either year.

What is Jerold's Federal income tax filing status for 2010 and 2011 if all parties reside in:

a. Idaho (a community property state)?
b. Kansas (a common law state)?

ISSUE ID

DECISION MAKING

42. **LO.4, 9** Walter and Nancy provide 60% of the support of their daughter (age 18) and son-in-law (age 22). The son-in-law (John) is a full-time student at a local university, while the daughter (Irene) holds various part-time jobs from which she earns $11,000. Walter and Nancy engage you to prepare their tax return for 2011. During a meeting with them in late March 2012, you learn that John and Irene have filed a joint return. What tax advice would you give based on the following assumptions?

a. All parties live in Louisiana (a community property state).
b. All parties live in New Jersey (a common law state).

43. **LO.1, 2, 3, 4, 5, 6** Using the Tax Rate Schedules, compute the 2011 tax liability for Miles. Miles (age 42) is a surviving spouse and provides all of the support of his four minor children who live with him. He also maintains the household in which his parents live and furnished 60% of their support. Besides interest on City of Miami bonds in the amount of $1,500, Miles's father received $2,400 from a part-time job. Miles earns a $90,000 salary, a short-term capital loss of $4,000, and a cash prize of $2,000 at a church raffle. Miles reports itemized deductions of $9,500.

44. **LO.1, 2, 3, 4, 5, 6, 8** Morgan (age 45) is single and provides more than 50% of the support of Rosalyn (a family friend), Flo (a niece, age 18), and Jerold (a nephew, age 18). Both Rosalyn and Flo live with Morgan, but Jerold (a citizen of France) lives in Canada. Morgan earns a $95,000 salary, contributes $5,000 to a traditional IRA, and receives sales proceeds of $15,000 for an RV that cost $60,000 and was used only for vacations. She has $8,200 in itemized deductions. Use the Tax Rate Schedules to compute Morgan's 2011 tax liability.

45. **LO.5** Which of the following individuals are required to file a 2011 Federal income tax return? Should any of these individuals file a return even if filing is not required? Why?

a. Patricia, age 19, is a self-employed single individual with gross income of $4,500 from an unincorporated business. Business expenses amounted to $4,300.
b. Mike is single and is 67 years old. His gross income from wages was $10,800.
c. Ronald is a dependent child under age 19 who received $5,100 in wages from a part-time job.
d. Sam is married and files a joint return with his spouse, Lana. Both Sam and Lana are 67 years old. Their combined gross income was $21,400.

46. **LO.5** Which of the following taxpayers must file a 2011 Federal income tax return?

a. Ben, age 19, is a full-time college student. He is claimed as a dependent by his parents. He earned $5,000 wages during the year.

b. Anita, age 12, is claimed as a dependent by her parents. She earned interest income of $1,200 during the year.

c. Earl, age 16, is claimed as a dependent by his parents. He earned wages of $2,700 and interest of $1,100 during the year.

d. Ellen, age 17, is claimed as a dependent by her parents. She earned interest of $300 during the year. In addition, she earned $550 during the summer operating her own business at the beach, where she painted caricatures of her customers.

47. **LO.5, 6, 9** Corey and Addison are engaged and plan to get married. Corey is a full-time student and earns $8,000 from a part-time job. With this income, student loans, savings, and nontaxable scholarships, he is self-supporting. For the year, Addison is employed and reports $60,000 wages. How much 2011 Federal income tax, if any, can Addison save if she and Corey marry in 2011 and file a joint return?

DECISION MAKING

48. **LO.1, 3, 6, 7** Taylor, age 18, is claimed as a dependent by her parents. For 2011, she records the following income: $4,000 wages from a summer job; $1,900 interest from a money market account; and $1,000 interest from City of Boston bonds.
   a. What is Taylor's taxable income?
   b. What is Taylor's Federal income tax? Her parents file a joint return and report taxable income of $120,000 (no dividends or capital gains).

49. **LO.1, 3, 6, 7** Ava, age 18, is claimed as a dependent on her parents' 2011 return, on which they report taxable income of $100,000 (no qualified dividends or capital gains). Ava earned $2,900 pet sitting and $3,000 in interest on a savings account. What are Ava's taxable income and tax liability?

50. **LO.1, 3, 6, 7** Terri, age 16, is claimed as a dependent on her parents' 2011 return. During the year, Terri earned $5,000 in interest income and $3,000 from part-time jobs.
   a. What is Terri's taxable income?
   b. How much of Terri's income is taxed at her own tax rate? At her parents' rate?
   c. Can the parental election for the kiddie tax be made? Why or why not?

51. **LO.6, 8** During the year, Ophelia recorded the following transactions involving capital assets.

Gain on the sale of unimproved land (held as an investment for 3 years)	$ 3,000
Loss on the sale of a camper (purchased 2 years ago and used for family vacations)	(5,000)
Loss on the sale of ADM stock (purchased 9 months ago as an investment)	(1,000)
Gain on the sale of a fishing boat and trailer (acquired 11 months ago at an auction and used for recreational purposes)	2,000

   a. If Ophelia is in the 35% bracket, how much income tax results?
   b. If Ophelia is in the 15% bracket?

52. **LO.6, 8** During the year, Chester incurred the following transactions involving capital assets.

Gain on the sale of an arrowhead collection (acquired as an investment at different times but all pieces have been held for more than one year)	$ 6,000
Loss on the sale of IBM Corporation stock (purchased 11 months ago as an investment)	(4,000)
Gain on the sale of a city lot (acquired 5 years ago as an investment)	2,000

   a. If Chester is in the 33% bracket, how much income tax results?
   b. If Chester is in the 15% bracket?

53. **LO.9** Each year, the Hundleys normally have itemized deductions of $9,500, including a $3,600 pledge payment to their church. Upon the advice of a friend, they do the following: in early January 2011, they pay their pledge for 2010; during 2011, they pay the pledge for 2011; and in late December 2011, they prepay their pledge for 2012.
   a. Explain what the Hundleys are trying to accomplish.
   b. What will be the tax saving if their marginal tax bracket is 25% for all three years? (Assume the standard deduction amounts for 2011 and 2012 are the same.)

DECISION MAKING

CUMULATIVE PROBLEMS

TAX RETURN PROBLEM

H&R BLOCK At Home

54. Lance H. and Wanda B. Dean are married and live at 431 Yucca Drive, Santa Fe, NM 87501. Lance works for the convention bureau of the local Chamber of Commerce, while Wanda is employed part-time by a law firm as a paralegal.

During 2010, the Deans recorded the following receipts.

Salaries ($60,000 for Lance, $41,000 for Wanda)		$101,000
Interest income—		
City of Albuquerque general purpose bonds	$1,000	
Ford Motor Company bonds	1,100	
Ally Bank certificate of deposit	400	2,500
Child support payments from John Allen		7,200
Annual gifts from Lance's parents		26,000
Settlement from Roadrunner Touring Company		90,000
Lottery winnings		600
Federal income tax refund (for tax year 2009)		400

Wanda previously was married to John Allen. When they divorced several years ago, Wanda was awarded custody of their two children, Penny and Kyle. (Note: Wanda never issued a Form 8332 waiver.) Under the divorce decree, John was obligated to pay alimony and child support. The alimony payments terminate if Wanda remarries.

In July, while going to lunch in downtown Santa Fe, Wanda was injured by a tour bus. As the driver was clearly at fault, the owner of the bus, Roadrunner Touring Company, paid Wanda's medical expenses (including a one-week stay in a hospital). To avoid a lawsuit, Roadrunner also paid a $90,000 settlement award for the personal injuries she sustained.

The Deans keep track of their lottery winnings but have no idea what their losses are.

The Deans made the following expenditures for 2010.

Medical expenses (not covered by insurance)		$8,100
Taxes—		
Property taxes on personal residence	$3,600	
State of New Mexico income tax (includes amount withheld from wages during 2010)	4,200	7,800
Interest on home mortgage		6,000
Paid church pledge		3,600
Life insurance premiums (policy on Lance's life)		1,200
Contribution to traditional IRA (on Wanda's behalf)		5,000
Traffic fines		300
Contribution to the reelection campaign fund of the mayor of Santa Fe		300
Funeral expenses for Wayne Boyle		5,100

The life insurance policy was taken out by Lance several years ago and designates Wanda as the beneficiary. As a part-time employee, Wanda is excluded from coverage under her employer's pension plan. Consequently, Wanda provides for her own retirement with a traditional IRA obtained at a local trust company. Because the mayor is a member of the local Chamber of Commerce, Lance felt compelled to make the political contribution.

The Deans' household includes the following, for whom they provide more than half of the support.

	Social Security Number	Birth Date
Lance Dean (age 42)	123–45–6786	12/16/1968
Wanda Dean (age 40)	123–45–6787	08/08/1970
Penny Allen (age 19)	123–45–6788	10/09/1991
Kyle Allen (age 17)	123–45–6789	05/03/1993
Wayne Boyle (age 70)	123–45–6785	06/15/1940

Penny graduated from high school on May 9, 2010, and is undecided about whether she will attend college. During 2010, she earned $8,500 (placed in a savings account) playing the harp in the lobby of a local hotel. Wayne is Wanda's widower father who died on January 10, 2010. For the past few years, Wayne qualified as a dependent of the Deans.

Federal income tax withheld is $5,200 (Lance) and $3,100 (Wanda). The proper amount of Social Security and Medicare tax was withheld.

Determine the 2010 Federal income tax for the Deans on a joint return by completing the appropriate forms. The Deans do not contribute to the Presidential Election Campaign Fund. If an overpayment results, it is to be refunded to them. Suggested software: H&R BLOCK At Home.

55. Ellen M. Rand, age 48, is a widow whose husband, Clint, died on May 9, 2008. She lives at 384 Meadowlark Land, Overland Park, KS 66204. Ellen is employed as a business manager for a local medical clinic. During 2010, she reported the following receipts.

TAX RETURN PROBLEM

DECISION MAKING

COMMUNICATIONS

H&R BLOCK At Home

Salary		$ 85,000
Interest income—		
Money market account at Prosperity Bank	$ 240	
Savings account at Lawrence State Bank	1,900	
City of Wichita general purpose bonds	2,400	4,540
Inheritance from Aunt Mary		40,000
Life insurance proceeds		100,000
Amount from sale of a Kansas City plot of land		60,000
Proceeds from estate sale		18,000
Fees for jury duty service		400

Ellen inherited securities worth $40,000 from her aunt, Mary Wilcox, who died in 2010. Ellen also was the designated beneficiary of a $100,000 insurance policy on Mary's life.

The Kansas City land was purchased by Ellen and Clint on May 2, 2003, for $65,000 and held as an investment. As the neighborhood has deteriorated, Ellen decided to cut her losses and sold the lot on January 5, 2010, for $60,000.

The estate sale consisted largely of items belonging to Clint and Mary (e.g., camper, boat, furniture, fishing and hunting equipment). Ellen estimates that the sold property originally cost at least twice the $18,000 she received, but that the property values have declined or stayed the same since Clint and Mary died.

Ellen's expenditures for 2010 include the following.

Medical expenses (including $9,500 for dental costs)		$10,500
Taxes—		
State of Kansas income tax (includes withholdings during 2010)	$3,800	
Property taxes on personal residence	4,200	8,000
Interest on home mortgage		4,500
Contribution to church (paid pledges for 2010 *and* 2011)		4,800

Ellen and her dependents are covered by her employer's health insurance policy. However, Ellen is subject to a deductible, and dental care is not included. The $9,500 charge was for Herbert's dental implants. Herbert is Ellen's widowed father who lives with her (see below).

Ellen normally pledges $2,400 ($200 per month) each year to her church. On December 5, 2010, upon the advice of her pastor, she prepaid her pledge for 2011.

Ellen's household members, all of whom she supports, include the following.

	Social Security Number	Birth Date
Ellen Rand (age 48)	123–45–6787	08/30/1962
Herbert Martin (age 70)	123–45–6780	01/13/1940
Neil Rand (age 23)	123–45–6783	07/18/1987
Donna Rand (age 22)	123–45–6784	02/16/1988

Herbert Martin receives a modest Social Security benefit. Neil is a full-time student in dental school and earns $4,500 as a part-time dental assistant. Donna is not employed. She is engaged to be married.

Part 1—Tax Computation
Using the appropriate forms and schedules, compute Ellen's 2010 Federal income tax. In addition to Federal income tax of $6,200 withheld from her wages, Ellen applied her 2009 tax refund of $300 to her 2010 tax liability. Ellen wants any 2010 overpayment handled in the same way.

The proper amounts of Social Security and Medicare taxes were withheld. Ellen does not contribute to the Presidential Election Campaign Fund. Suggested software: H&R BLOCK At Home.

Part 2—Follow-up Advice
In early 2011, the following events occur.

- Herbert moves to Florida to live with one of his sons.
- Neil graduates from dental school and joins an existing practice in Kansas City.
- Donna marries, and she and her husband move in with his parents.
- Using the insurance proceeds she received on Aunt Mary's death, Ellen pays off the mortgage on her personal residence.

Ellen believes these events may have an effect on her tax position for 2011. Therefore, she requests your advice.

Write a letter to Ellen explaining in general terms the changes that will occur for 2011 for Federal income tax purposes. Assume that Ellen's salary and other factors not mentioned (e.g., property and state income taxes) remain the same. Use the Tax Rate Schedules in projecting Ellen's 2011 tax.

RESEARCH PROBLEMS

THOMSON REUTERS
Checkpoint® Student Edition

Note: Solutions to Research Problems can be prepared by using the **Checkpoint® Student Edition** online research product, which is available to accompany this text. It is also possible to prepare solutions to the Research Problems by using tax research materials found in a standard tax library.

COMMUNICATIONS

Research Problem 1. Don and Mary Dewey are successful professionals with a combined AGI of approximately $400,000. Their household includes two children: Debra (age 16) and Van (age 23). Van is not a student but works at a part-time job, where he earns $16,000. Don has heard that it might be beneficial if Van, rather than Don and Mary, claims Debra as a qualified child for income tax purposes. At a Chamber of Commerce meeting, Don asks you to advise him on this matter.

Prepare a letter to Don at 4321 Mount Vernon Road, Dover, DE 19901, advising him about the advantages of such a choice and whether it is feasible. In your letter, discuss the relevance of Code §§ 24, 32, 151, and 152.

Research Problem 2. Bernice and Nate were divorced on July 7, 2009. Under the divorce decree, Bernice received full custody of their three children, and Nate was awarded the dependency exemptions for them. After the trial was over, Nate had Bernice sign a release of her rights to the dependency exemptions for the next five years. In early April 2011, Bernice realizes the tax costs to her of losing the deduction for the dependency exemptions. Besides contacting Nate, who is already delinquent in his child support payments, does Bernice have any way to improve her Federal income tax position?

INTERNET *activity*

Use the tax resources of the Internet to address the following questions. Do not restrict your search to the Web, but include a review of newsgroups and general reference materials, practitioner sites and resources, primary sources of the tax law, chat rooms and discussion groups, and other opportunities.

COMMUNICATIONS

Research Problem 3. When taxpayers pay federal income taxes by means of a credit or debit card, they are charged "convenience fees" by the issuer of the card. Are these fees themselves deductible? (*Hint:* The IRS has issued a notice clarifying its position on this matter.) Summarize your findings in a memo to the tax research file.

Research Problem 4. Send to your instructor a table showing the amounts of the standard deduction and personal exemption for a single individual as they have changed over the last 10 years.

COMMUNICATIONS

Research Problem 5. Prepare a graph for your school's Accounting Club of the Federal income tax rates that apply at taxable income levels up to $200,000 for each filing status.

COMMUNICATIONS

Research Problem 6. Locate IRS Form 2120, which is used to register a multiple support declaration for a dependency exemption.

a. Who must sign the form?

b. Who must file the form?

c. Can the form be used for someone who is not related to the taxpayer?

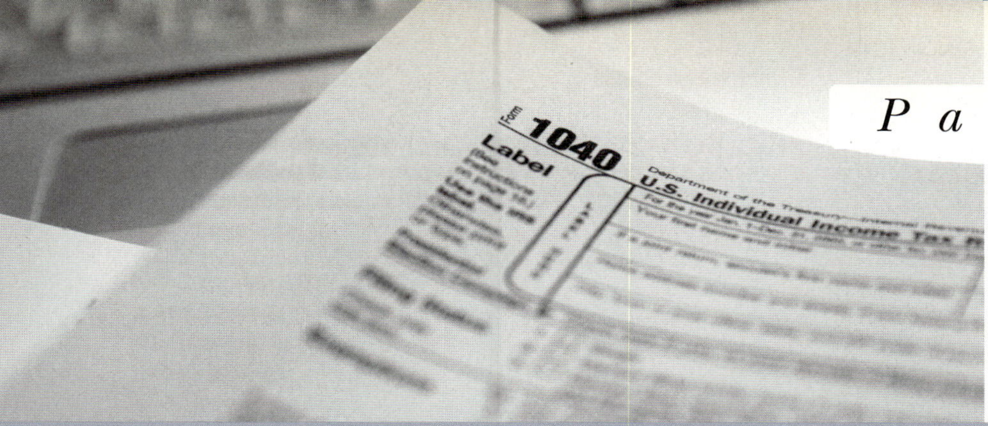

Part 2

Gross Income

Part 2 presents the income component of the basic tax model. Included in this presentation are the determination of what is income and the statutory exclusions that are permitted in calculating gross income. Because the taxpayer's accounting method and accounting period affect when income is reported, an introductory discussion of these topics is also included.

CHAPTER 4

Gross Income: Concepts and Inclusions

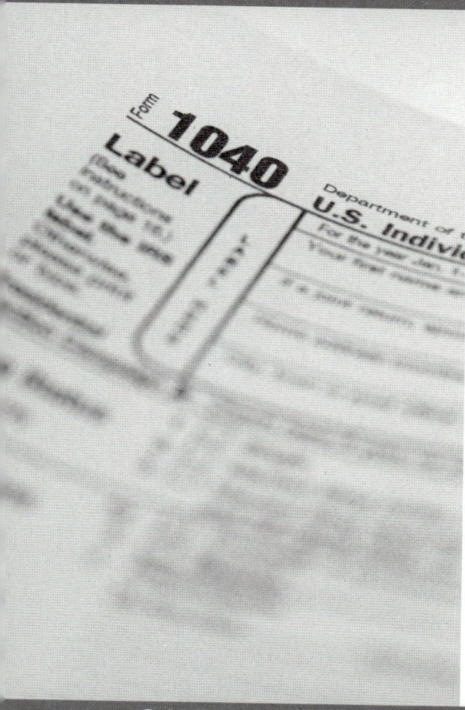

LEARNING OBJECTIVES

After completing Chapter 4, you should be able to:

LO.1

Explain the concepts of gross income and realization and distinguish between the economic, accounting, and tax concepts of gross income.

LO.2

Describe the cash and accrual methods of accounting and the related effects of the choice of taxable year.

LO.3

Identify who should pay the tax on a particular item of income in various situations.

LO.4

Apply the Internal Revenue Code provisions on alimony, loans made at below-market interest rates, annuities, prizes and awards, group term life insurance, unemployment compensation, and Social Security benefits.

LO.5

Identify tax planning strategies for minimizing gross income.

OUTLINE

For the latest in changes to tax legislation, visit **www.cengage.com/taxation/swft.**

FRAMEWORK 1040: Tax Formula for Individuals

This chapter covers the boldfaced portions of the Tax Formula for Individuals that was introduced in Figure 3.1 on p. 3-3. Below those portions are the sections of Form 1040 where the results are reported.

Income (broadly conceived)	**$xx,xxx**
Less: Exclusions	**(x,xxx)**
Gross income	**$xx,xxx**

FORM 1040 (p. 1)

7	Wages, salaries, tips, etc. Attach Form(s) W-2	
8a	**Taxable** interest. Attach Schedule B if required	
b	**Tax-exempt** interest. **Do not** include on line 8a	**8b**
9a	Ordinary dividends. Attach Schedule B if required	
b	Qualified dividends	**9b**
11	Alimony received	
12	Business income or (loss). Attach Schedule C or C-EZ	
20a	Social security benefits **20a**	**b** Taxable amount
21	Other income. List type and amount	

Less: Deductions for adjusted gross income	(x,xxx)
Adjusted gross income	$ xx,xxx
Less: The greater of total itemized deductions *or* the standard deduction	(x,xxx)
Personal and dependency exemptions	(x,xxx)
Taxable income	$ xx,xxx
Tax on taxable income (see Tax Tables or Tax Rate Schedules)	$ x,xxx
Less: Tax credits (including income taxes withheld and prepaid)	(xxx)
Tax due (or refund)	$ xxx

THE BIG PICTURE Tax Solutions for the Real World

CALCULATION OF GROSS INCOME

At the beginning of the year, Dr. Cliff Payne opened his dental practice as a sole proprietorship. He previously had worked at a large dental clinic where he was a salaried employee. For his new business, he selected a December 31 year-end. He also entered into a contract to have a building constructed for his medical practice. In addition, now that he has completed his medical education and repaid all of his education loans, he used $12,000 of extra money to purchase some stock.

Dr. Payne's financial reporting system provides him with the following information regarding the income from his dental practice for the first year of operation.

Revenues (amounts billed patients for dental services)	$385,000
Accounts receivable: January 1	–0–
Accounts receivable: December 31	52,000

The accounts receivable represent the amounts he has billed patients that will be paid by the patients, paid by insurance companies, or charged off as uncollectible bad debts.

During the year, Sam Jones, a contractor who owed Dr. Payne $4,000 for dental services, satisfied the account by installing solar panels on the roof of Dr. Payne's new medical building.

As an undergraduate student at State University, Cliff took an accounting course. He originally had planned to major in accounting and go to work for one of the Big 4 Accounting Firms, but decided that he liked science courses better than accounting and business courses. From his accounting course, he remembers that the accrual method of accounting provides a better measure of the income and expenses of a business. Using the information provided by his financial reporting system, he concludes that the gross income for Federal income tax purposes is the $385,000 that he billed his patients for the dental services rendered.

Has Dr. Payne correctly calculated the gross income of this dental practice? **Read the chapter and formulate your response.**

Mr. Zarin lost over $2.5 million of his own money gambling. The casino then allowed him to gamble on credit. After several months, his liability to the casino totaled more than $3.4 million. Following protracted negotiations, the casino agreed to settle its claim against Mr. Zarin for a mere $500,000. Although Mr. Zarin had paid for gambling losses of $3 million, the IRS had the audacity to ask him to pay tax on $2.9 million, that is, the amount the casino marked down his account.[1] Mr. Zarin undoubtedly had difficulty understanding how he could be deemed to have income in this situation.

Given an understanding of the income tax formula, though, one can see how the "free" gambling Mr. Zarin enjoyed could constitute income. The starting point in the formula is the determination of gross income rather than "net income." Once gross income is determined, the next step is to determine the allowable deductions. In Mr. Zarin's way of thinking, these steps were collapsed.

This chapter is concerned with the first step in the computation of taxable income—the determination of gross income. Questions that are addressed include the following:

- What: What is income?
- When: In which tax period is the income recognized?
- Who: Who must include the item of income in gross income?

The Code provides an all-inclusive definition of gross income in § 61. Chapter 5 presents items of income that are specifically excluded from gross income (exclusions).

4.1 Gross Income—What Is It?

DEFINITION

LO.1

Explain the concepts of gross income and realization and distinguish between the economic, accounting, and tax concepts of gross income.

Section 61(a) of the Internal Revenue Code defines the term **gross income** as follows:

> Except as otherwise provided in this subtitle, gross income means all income from whatever source derived.

This definition is derived from the language of the Sixteenth Amendment to the Constitution.

Supreme Court decisions have made it clear that all sources of income are subject to tax unless Congress specifically excludes the type of income received:

> The starting point in all cases dealing with the question of the scope of what is included in "gross income" begins with the basic premise that the purpose of Congress was to use the full measure of its taxing power.[2]

Although at this point we know that *income* is to be broadly construed, we still do not have a satisfactory definition of the term *income.* Congress left it to the judicial and administrative branches to thrash out the meaning of income.

[1] *Zarin v. Comm.*, 90–2 USTC ¶50,530, 66 AFTR 2d 90–5679, 916 F.2d 110 (CA–3, 1990).

[2] *James v. U.S.*, 61–1 USTC ¶9449, 7 AFTR 2d 1361, 81 S.Ct. 1052 (USSC, 1961).

GLOBAL *Tax Issues*

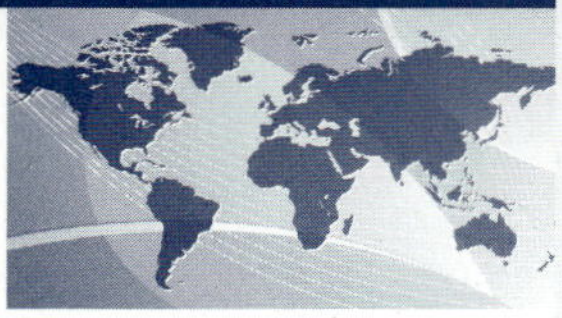

From "All Sources" Is a Broad Definition

When § 61 refers to "income from whatever source derived," the taxing authorities are reaching far beyond the borders of the United States. Although one interpretation of "source" in this context is type of income (wages, interest, etc.), a broader interpretation revolves around the place where the income is generated. In this context, citizens and residents of the United States are subject to taxation on income earned from sources both inside and outside the country. This "worldwide income" tax base can cause potential double taxation problems, with other countries also taxing income earned within their borders, but mechanisms such as the foreign tax credit can alleviate these tax burdens.

Recently, some U.S. corporations have relocated to other countries to avoid the higher U.S. tax rates on income earned abroad. Congress is considering ways of stopping this "flight of capital."

RECOVERY OF CAPITAL DOCTRINE

The Constitution grants Congress the power to tax income but does not define the term. Because the Constitution does not define income, it would seem that Congress could simply tax gross receipts. Although Congress does allow certain deductions, none are constitutionally required. However, the Supreme Court has held that there is no income subject to tax until the taxpayer has recovered the capital invested.[3] This concept is known as the **recovery of capital doctrine**.

In its simplest application, this doctrine means that sellers can reduce their gross receipts (selling price) by the adjusted basis of the property sold.[4] This net amount, in the language of the Code, is gross income.

EXAMPLE 1
THE BIG PICTURE

Return to the facts of *The Big Picture* on p. 4-2. Dr. Payne sells common stock for $15,000. He had purchased the stock for $12,000. Dr. Payne's gross receipts are $15,000. This amount consists of a $12,000 recovery of capital and $3,000 of gross income. ■

Collections on annuity contracts and installment payments received from sales of property must be allocated between recovery of capital and income. Annuities are discussed in this chapter, and installment sales are discussed in Chapter 16.

ECONOMIC AND ACCOUNTING CONCEPTS

The term **income** is used in the Code but is not separately defined. Thus, the courts were required to interpret "the commonly understood meaning of the term which must have been in the minds of the people when they adopted the Sixteenth Amendment to the Constitution."[5] Early in the development of the income tax law, a choice had to be made between two competing models: economic income and accounting income. In determining the definition of income, the Supreme Court rejected the economic concept of income.

Economists measure income (**economic income**) by first determining the fair market value of the individual's net assets (assets minus liabilities) at the beginning and end of the year (change in net worth). Then, to arrive at economic income, this change in net worth is added to the goods and services that person actually

[3] *Doyle v. Mitchell Bros. Co.*, 1 USTC ¶17, 3 AFTR 2979, 38 S.Ct. 467 (USSC, 1916).

[4] For a definition of "adjusted basis," see the Glossary in Appendix C.

[5] *Merchants Loan and Trust Co. v. Smietanka*, 1 USTC ¶42, 3 AFTR 3102, 41 S.Ct. 386 (USSC, 1921).

TAX *in* the NEWS

The General Welfare Exception

The broad concept of gross income and the government's role in promoting the general welfare sometimes are in conflict. For example, if the government makes payments to persons based on their need, it does not make sense for the government to extract a tax from those same individuals and thus reduce the relief it intended to confer. Therefore, the courts and the IRS have created the "general welfare exception," which excludes from gross income certain types of governmental payments that might otherwise be taxable under the broad gross income concept. To qualify for this exception, the payments must be:

- Made from a governmental welfare fund.
- Based on need.
- Not made as a payment for services.

The exception has been applied to a wide range of government payments including Federal grants to rebuild homes destroyed by Hurricane Katrina and to make mortgage payments for persons suffering severe hardship. It also applies to grants by state governments to motivate the purchase of appliances with an Energy Star rating.

Sources: Adapted from Robert W. Woods, "Updating General Welfare Exception Authorities," 123 *Tax Notes,* June 22, 2009, p. 1443; Rev.Rul. 2009–19, I.R.B. No. 28, 111.

consumed during the period. Economic income also includes imputed values for such items as the rental value of an owner-occupied home and the value of food a taxpayer might grow for personal consumption.[6]

EXAMPLE 2

Helen, who is Dr. Payne's aunt, has economic income as follows:

Fair market value of Helen's assets on December 31, 2011	$220,000	
Less liabilities on December 31, 2011	(40,000)	
Net worth on December 31, 2011		$ 180,000
Fair market value of Helen's assets on January 1, 2011	$200,000	
Less liabilities on January 1, 2011	(80,000)	
Net worth on January 1, 2011		(120,000)
Increase in net worth		$ 60,000
Consumption		
Food, clothing, and other personal expenditures		25,000
Imputed rental value of the home Helen owns and occupies		12,000
Economic income		$ 97,000

The need to value assets annually would make compliance with the tax law burdensome and would cause numerous controversies between the taxpayer and the IRS over valuation. In addition, using market values to determine income for tax purposes could result in liquidity problems. The taxpayer's assets may increase in value even though they are not readily convertible into the cash needed to pay the tax (e.g., commercial real estate). Thus, the IRS, Congress, and the courts have rejected the economic concept of income as impractical.

In contrast, the accounting concept of income is founded on the realization principle.[7] According to this principle, income (**accounting income**) is not recognized until it is realized. For realization to occur, (1) an exchange of goods or services must take place between the accounting entity and some independent, external group, and (2) in the exchange the accounting entity must receive assets that are capable of being objectively valued. Thus, income is recognized when an employee embezzles

[6]See Henry C. Simons, *Personal Income Taxation* (Chicago: University of Chicago Press, 1933), Chapters 2–3.

[7]See the American Accounting Association Committee Report on the "Realization Concept," *The Accounting Review* (April 1965): 312–322.

TAX *in the* NEWS

Is Your Cell Phone a Smart Phone When It Comes to Tax Benefits?

If your employer provides you with a cell phone or a smart phone and you use it for personal purposes, do you have income? Under the usual interpretation of § 61, which defines "gross income," the answer appears to be yes.

That was the conclusion reached by the IRS. To eliminate uncertainty, the IRS proposed a safe harbor that would permit up to 25 percent personal use. The reaction of the "rest of the world"—that is, taxpayers—was decidedly negative. As a result, the IRS has withdrawn the proposal and asked Congress to change the law so that personal use of employer-provided phones qualifies for exclusion treatment.

Source: Adapted from Laura Saunders, "A Few Quirky Tax Breaks That Aren't Going Away," *Wall Street Journal*, May 8, 2010, p. B9.

his employer's funds, when the income from an illegal business is realized, and when a person discovers buried treasure.[8] On the other hand, the appreciation in the market value of an asset owned is not realized and thus is not included in gross income until the asset is sold. Income is not realized when an individual creates assets for her own use (e.g., vegetables grown in a personal garden) because there is no exchange transaction with another party.

The Supreme Court expressed an inclination toward the accounting concept of income when it adopted the realization requirement in *Eisner v. Macomber*:

> Income may be defined as the gain derived from capital, from labor, or from both combined, provided it is understood to include profit gained through a sale or conversion of capital assets. . . . Here we have the essential matter: not a gain accruing to capital; not a *growth* or *increment* of value *in* investment; but a gain, a profit, something of exchangeable value, *proceeding from* the property, *severed from* the capital however invested or employed, and *coming in*, being "*derived*"—that is, *received* or *drawn by* the recipient for his separate use, benefit and disposal—*that is*, income derived from the property.[9]

In summary, *income* represents an increase in wealth recognized for tax purposes only upon realization.

COMPARISON OF THE ACCOUNTING AND TAX CONCEPTS OF INCOME

Although income tax rules frequently parallel financial accounting measurement concepts, differences do exist. Of major significance, for example, is the fact that unearned (prepaid) income received by an accrual basis taxpayer often is taxed in the year of receipt. For financial accounting purposes, such prepayments are not treated as income until earned.[10] Because of this and other differences, many corporations report financial accounting income that is substantially different from the amounts reported for tax purposes (see Reconciliation of Corporate Taxable Income and Accounting Income in Chapter 17).

The Supreme Court provided an explanation for some of the variations between accounting and taxable income in a decision involving inventory and bad debt adjustments:

> The primary goal of financial accounting is to provide useful information to management, shareholders, creditors, and others properly interested; the major responsibility of the accountant is to protect these parties from being misled. The primary goal of the income tax system, in contrast, is the equitable

[8]*Rutkin v. U.S.*, 52–1 USTC ¶9260, 41 AFTR 2d 596, 72 S.Ct. 571 (USSC, 1952); Rev.Rul. 61, 1953–1 C.B. 17.

[9]1 USTC ¶32, 3 AFTR 3020, 40 S.Ct. 189 (USSC, 1920).

[10]Similar differences exist in the deduction area.

TAX *in the NEWS*

Academy Awards Presenters Must "Walk the Line"

Movie stars and other film industry luminaries who make the presentations at the Academy Awards ceremony receive "gift baskets" for participating in the event. The gift baskets include expense-paid vacations, pearls, chocolates, clothing, and a variety of other items. The IRS has estimated that the value of some of the baskets has exceeded $100,000.

The Commissioner of the IRS has put Hollywood on notice that "movie stars face the same obligation as ordinary Americans." Thus, the presenters must include the value of the basket contents in their gross income.

collection of revenue . . . . Consistently with its goals and responsibilities, financial accounting has as its foundation the principle of conservatism, with its corollary that 'possible errors in measurement [should] be in the direction of understatement rather than overstatement of net income and net assets.' In view of the Treasury's markedly different goals and responsibilities, understatement of income is not destined to be its guiding light.

. . . Financial accounting, in short, is hospitable to estimates, probabilities, and reasonable certainties; the tax law, with its mandate to preserve the revenue, can give no quarter to uncertainty.[11]

FORM OF RECEIPT

Gross income is not limited to cash received. "It includes income realized in any form, whether in money, property, or services. Income may be realized [and recognized], therefore, in the form of services, meals, accommodations, stock or other property, as well as in cash."[12]

EXAMPLE 3

Ostrich Corporation allows Bill, an employee, to use a company car for his vacation. Bill realizes income equal to the rental value of the car for the time and mileage. ■

EXAMPLE 4

Terry owes $10,000 on a mortgage. The creditor accepts $8,000 in full satisfaction of the debt. Terry realizes income of $2,000 from retiring the debt.[13] ■

ETHICS *& Equity*

A Business Made Possible by eBay

Each Saturday morning Ted makes the rounds of the local yard sales. He has developed a keen eye for bargains, but he cannot use all the items he thinks are "real bargains." Ted has found a way to share the benefits of his talent with others. If Ted spots something priced at $40 that he knows is worth $100, for example, he will buy it and list it on eBay for $70. Ted does not include his gain in his gross income because he reasons that he is performing a valuable service for others (both the original sellers and the future buyers) and sacrificing profit he could receive. "Besides," according to Ted, "the IRS does not know about these transactions." Should Ted's ethical standards depend on his perception of his own generosity and the risk that his income-producing activities will be discovered by the IRS? Discuss.

[11] *Thor Power Tool Co. v. Comm.*, 79–1 USTC ¶9139, 43 AFTR 2d 79–362, 99 S.Ct. 773 (USSC, 1979).

[12] Reg. § 1.61–1(a).

[13] Reg. § 1.61–12. See *U.S. v. Kirby Lumber Co.*, 2 USTC ¶814, 10 AFTR 458, 52 S.Ct. 4 (USSC, 1931). Exceptions to this general rule are discussed in Chapter 5.

EXAMPLE 5
THE BIG PICTURE

Return to the facts of *The Big Picture* on p. 4-2. When Sam Jones performed the services in satisfaction of his $4,000 account, Dr. Payne realized income equal to the value of the services of $4,000. ■

4.2 Year of Inclusion

LO.2

Describe the cash and accrual methods of accounting and the related effects of the choice of taxable year.

TAXABLE YEAR

The annual accounting period or **taxable year** is a basic component of our tax system.[14] Generally, an entity must use the *calendar year* to report its income. However, a *fiscal year* (a period of 12 months ending on the last day of any month other than December) can be elected if the taxpayer maintains adequate books and records. This fiscal year option generally is not available to partnerships, S corporations, and personal service corporations, as discussed in Chapter 16.[15]

Determining the particular year in which the income will be taxed is important for determining when the tax must be paid and the present value of the tax. Assuming the tax rates do not change between years, the longer payment of the tax can be postponed, the lower the present value of the tax. The year each item of income is subject to tax can also affect the total tax liability over the entity's lifetime. This is true for the following reasons:

- With a progressive rate system, a taxpayer's marginal tax rate can change from year to year.
- Congress may change the tax rates.
- The relevant rates may change because of a change in the entity's status (e.g., a person may marry or a business may be incorporated).
- Several provisions in the Code are dependent on the taxpayer's gross income for the year (e.g., whether the person can be claimed as a dependent, as discussed in Chapter 3).

ACCOUNTING METHODS

The year an item of income is subject to tax often depends upon which acceptable **accounting method** the taxpayer regularly employs.[16] The three primary methods of accounting are (1) the cash receipts and disbursements method, (2) the accrual method, and (3) the hybrid method. Most individuals use the cash receipts and disbursements method of accounting, whereas most larger corporations use the accrual method. The Regulations require the accrual method for determining purchases and sales when inventory is an income-producing factor.[17] Some businesses employ a hybrid method that is a combination of the cash and accrual methods of accounting.

In addition to these overall accounting methods, a taxpayer may choose to spread the gain from an installment sale of property over the collection periods by using the *installment method* of income recognition. Contractors may either spread profits from contracts over the periods in which the work is done (the *percentage of completion method*) or defer all profit until the year in which the project is completed (the *completed contract method*, which can be used only in limited circumstances).[18]

[14] See Accounting Periods in Chapter 16.

[15] §§ 441(a) and (d).

[16] See Accounting Methods in Chapter 16.

[17] Reg. § 1.446–1(c)(2)(i). Other circumstances in which the accrual method must be used are presented in Chapter 16. For the small business exception to the inventory requirement, see Rev.Proc. 2002–28, 2002–1 C.B. 815.

[18] §§ 453 and 460. See Chapter 16 for limitations on the use of the installment method and the completed contract method.

The IRS has the power to prescribe the accounting method to be used by the taxpayer. Section 446(b) grants the IRS broad powers to determine if the accounting method used *clearly reflects income*:

> If no method of accounting has been regularly used by the taxpayer, or *if the method used does not clearly reflect income, the computation of taxable income shall be made under such method as, in the opinion of the Secretary . . . does clearly reflect income.*

A change in the method of accounting requires the consent of the IRS.[19]

Cash Receipts Method

Under the **cash receipts method**, property or services received are included in the taxpayer's gross income in the year of actual or constructive receipt by the taxpayer or agent, regardless of whether the income was earned in that year.[20] The income received need not be reduced to cash in the same year. All that is necessary for income recognition is that property or services received have a fair market value—a cash equivalent.[21] Thus, a cash basis taxpayer who receives a note in payment for services has income in the year of receipt equal to the fair market value of the note. However, a creditor's mere promise to pay (e.g., an account receivable), with no supporting note, usually is not considered to have a fair market value.[22] Thus, the cash basis taxpayer defers income recognition until the account receivable is collected.

EXAMPLE 6

Dana, an accountant, reports her income by the cash method. In 2011, she performed an audit for Orange Corporation and billed the client for $5,000, which was collected in 2012. In 2011, Dana also performed an audit for Blue Corporation. Because of Blue's precarious financial position, Dana required Blue to issue an $8,000 secured negotiable note in payment of the fee. The note had a fair market value of $6,000. Dana collected $8,000 on the note in 2012. Dana's gross income for the two years is as follows:

	2011	2012
Fair market value of note received from Blue	$6,000	
Cash received		
From Orange on account receivable		$ 5,000
From Blue on note receivable		8,000
Less: Recovery of capital		(6,000)
Total gross income	$6,000	$ 7,000

■

Generally, a check received is considered a cash equivalent. Thus, a cash basis taxpayer must recognize the income when the check is received. This is true even if the taxpayer receives the check after banking hours. An exception to this rule is that if the person paying with the check requests that the check not be cashed until a subsequent date, the cash basis income is deferred until the date the check can be cashed.[23]

Accrual Method

Under the **accrual method**, an item is generally included in the gross income for the year in which it is earned, regardless of when the income is collected. The income is earned when (1) all the events have occurred that fix the right to receive such income and (2) the amount to be received can be determined with reasonable accuracy.[24]

[19] § 446(e). See Chapter 16.
[20] *Julia A. Strauss*, 2 B.T.A. 598 (1925). See the Glossary in Appendix C for a discussion of the terms "cash equivalent doctrine" and "constructive receipt."
[21] Reg. §§ 1.446–1(a)(3) and (c)(1)(i).
[22] *Bedell v. Comm.*, 1 USTC ¶359, 7 AFTR 8469, 30 F.2d 622 (CA–2, 1929).
[23] *Charles F. Kahler*, 18 T.C. 31 (1952); *Bright v. U.S.*, 91–1 USTC ¶50,142, 67 AFTR 2d 91–673, 926 F.2d 383 (CA–5, 1991).
[24] Reg. § 1.451–1(a).

Generally, the taxpayer's rights to the income accrue when title to property passes to the buyer or the services are performed for the customer or client.[25] If the rights to the income have accrued but are subject to a potential refund claim (e.g., under a product warranty), the income is reported in the year of sale, and a deduction is allowed in subsequent years when actual claims accrue.[26]

Where the taxpayer's rights to the income are being contested (e.g., when a contractor fails to meet specifications), the year in which the income is subject to tax depends upon whether payment has been received. If payment has not been received, no income is recognized until the claim is settled. Only then is the right to the income established.[27] However, if the payment is received before the dispute is settled, the court-made **claim of right doctrine** requires the taxpayer to recognize the income in the year of receipt.[28]

EXAMPLE 7
THE BIG PICTURE

Return to the facts of *The Big Picture* on p. 4-2. On completing the construction of Dr. Payne's medical office building in 2011, the contractor submitted a bill. Dr. Payne refused to pay the bill, however, claiming that the contractor had not met specifications. The contractor did not reach a settlement with Dr. Payne until 2012. No income accrues to the contractor until 2012. If Dr. Payne had paid for the work and then filed suit for damages, the contractor could not defer the income (the income would be taxable in 2011). ■

The measure of accrual basis income is generally the amount the taxpayer has a right to receive. Unlike the cash basis, the fair market value of the customer's obligation is irrelevant in measuring accrual basis income.

EXAMPLE 8

Assume the same facts as in Example 6, except that Dana is an accrual basis taxpayer. Dana must recognize $13,000 ($8,000 + $5,000) gross income in 2011, the year her rights to the income accrued. ■

Hybrid Method

The **hybrid method** is a combination of the accrual method and the cash method. Generally, when the hybrid method is used, inventory is a material income-producing factor. Therefore, the Regulations require that the accrual method be used for determining sales and cost of goods sold. In this circumstance, to simplify record keeping, the taxpayer accounts for inventory using the accrual method and uses the cash method for all other income and expense items (e.g., dividend and interest income). The hybrid method is primarily used by small businesses.

EXCEPTIONS APPLICABLE TO CASH BASIS TAXPAYERS

Constructive Receipt

Income that has not actually been received by the taxpayer is taxed as though it had been received—the income is constructively received—under the following conditions:

- The amount is made readily available to the taxpayer.
- The taxpayer's actual receipt is not subject to substantial limitations or restrictions.[29]

[25] *Lucas v. North Texas Lumber Co.*, 2 USTC ¶484, 8 AFTR 10276, 50 S.Ct. 184 (USSC, 1930).

[26] *Brown v. Helvering*, 4 USTC ¶1222, 13 AFTR 851, 54 S.Ct. 356 (USSC, 1933).

[27] *Burnet v. Sanford and Brooks*, 2 USTC ¶636, 9 AFTR 603, 51 S.Ct. 150 (USSC, 1931).

[28] *North American Oil Consolidated Co. v. Burnet*, 3 USTC ¶943, 11 AFTR 16, 52 S.Ct. 613 (USSC, 1932).

[29] Reg. § 1.451–2(a).

The rationale for the **constructive receipt** doctrine is that if the income is available, the taxpayer should not be allowed to postpone the income recognition. For instance, a taxpayer is not permitted to defer income for December services by refusing to accept payment until January. However, determining whether the income is *readily available* and whether *substantial limitations or restrictions exist* necessitates a factual inquiry that leads to a judgment call.[30] The following are some examples of the application of the constructive receipt doctrine.

EXAMPLE 9

Ted is a member of a barter club. In 2011, Ted performed services for other club members and earned 1,000 points. Each point entitles him to $1 in goods and services sold by other members of the club; the points can be used at any time. In 2012, Ted exchanged his points for a new high-definition TV. Ted must recognize $1,000 gross income in 2011 when the 1,000 points were credited to his account.[31] ■

EXAMPLE 10
THE BIG PICTURE

Return to the facts of *The Big Picture* on p. 4-2. On December 31, Dr. Payne has $10,000 in patients'checks that have not been deposited. They include a check for $3,000 from a patient who asked Dr. Payne not to deposit the check until after January 4 of next year, because her account did not contain sufficient funds to pay the debt. Under the cash method, Dr. Payne must recognize $7,000 income from the $7,000 in checks on hand in the current year because the checks are a cash equivalent that is actually received. The income from the $3,000 check is neither actually nor constructively received in the current year because an insufficient account means that the funds are not available.[32] ■

EXAMPLE 11

Rick owns interest coupons that mature on December 31. The coupons can be converted to cash at any bank at maturity. Thus, the income is constructively received by Rick on December 31, even though Rick failed to cash in the coupons until the following year.[33] Dove Company mails a dividend check to Rick on December 31, 2011. Rick does not receive the check until January 2012. Rick does not realize gross income until 2012.[34] ■

The constructive receipt doctrine does not reach income that the taxpayer is not yet entitled to receive even though the taxpayer could have contracted to receive the income at an earlier date.

EXAMPLE 12
THE BIG PICTURE

Return to the facts of *The Big Picture* on p. 4-2. Assume that Dr. Payne elected to use the cash basis of accounting. If he allowed patients to pay by credit card, Dr. Payne would receive immediate credit in his bank account for 96% of the charge. The other 4% would be retained by the credit card issuer. To avoid the 4% charge, Dr. Payne chose not to accept credit card payments. Instead, he established a policy of requiring all bills to be paid within 30 days after the dental services were provided. He communicated this policy to patients before he performed the services. At the end of the year, several patients who owed a combined $2,000 offered to pay with credit cards, but his office rejected their offers.

The $2,000 was not constructively received at the end of the year. Although Dr. Payne could have received payment by credit card in the current year, he contracted to receive payment at a later date before the dental services were performed. Moreover, the 4% charge by the credit card company would be a "substantial limitation." [35] ■

[30] *Baxter v. Comm.*, 87–1 USTC ¶9315, 59 AFTR 2d 87–1068, 816 F.2d 493 (CA–9, 1987).

[31] Rev.Rul. 80–52, 1980–1 C.B. 100.

[32] *L. M. Fischer*, 14 T.C. 792 (1950).

[33] Reg. § 1.451–2(b).

[34] Reg. § 1.451–2(b).

[35] *Cowden v. Comm.*, 61–1 USTC ¶9382, 7 AFTR 2d 1160, 289 F.2d 20 (CA–5, 1961).

Income set apart or made available is not constructively received if its actual receipt is subject to *substantial restrictions.* The life insurance industry has used substantial restrictions as a cornerstone for designing life insurance contracts with favorable tax features. Ordinary life insurance policies provide (1) current protection—an amount payable in the event of death—and (2) a savings feature—a cash surrender value payable to the policyholder if the policy is terminated during the policyholder's life. The annual increase in cash surrender value is not taxable because the policyholder must cancel the policy to actually receive the increase in value. Because the cancellation requirement is a substantial restriction, the policyholder does not constructively receive the annual increase in cash surrender value.[36] Employees often receive from their employers property subject to substantial restrictions. Generally, no income is recognized until the restrictions lapse.[37]

EXAMPLE 13

Carlos is a key employee of Red, Inc. The corporation gives stock with a value of $10,000 to Carlos. The stock cannot be sold, however, for five years. Carlos is not required to recognize income until the restrictions lapse at the end of five years. ■

ETHICS & Equity

DISCOUNTS FOR CASH

Independent contractors are one source of the "tax gap." Sometimes, especially when working for an individual rather than a corporation, an independent contractor does not receive a W–2 or Form 1099 from the employer or customer. In these situations, some independent contractors will give a discount if paid in cash. The apparent reason for this discount is that the independent contractor does not intend to report the income and is concerned that with a check, the IRS is more likely to discover the unreported income. Evaluate the behavior of the independent contractor and that of the customer who pays in cash.

Original Issue Discount

Lenders frequently make loans that require a payment at maturity of more than the amount of the original loan. The difference between the amount due at maturity and the amount of the original loan is actually interest but is referred to as **original issue discount**. Under the general rules of tax accounting, the cash basis lender would not report the original issue discount as interest income until the year the amount is collected, although an accrual basis borrower would deduct the interest as it is earned. However, the Code puts the lender and borrower on parity by requiring that the original issue discount be reported when it is earned, regardless of the taxpayer's accounting method.[38] The interest "earned" is calculated by the effective interest rate method.

EXAMPLE 14

On January 1, 2011, Mark, a cash basis taxpayer, pays $82,645 for a 24-month certificate. The certificate is priced to yield 10% (the effective interest rate) with interest compounded annually. No interest is paid until maturity, when Mark receives $100,000. Thus, Mark's gross income from the certificate is $17,355 ($100,000 − $82,645). Mark's income earned each year is calculated as follows:

2011(.10 × $82,645) =	$ 8,264
2012 [.10 × ($82,645 + $8,264)] =	9,091
	$17,355

■

[36] *Theodore H. Cohen*, 39 T.C. 1055 (1963).
[37] § 83(a).
[38] §§ 1272(a)(3) and 1273(a).

Tax Credit Neutralizes Foreign Income Taxes

GLOBAL *Tax Issues*

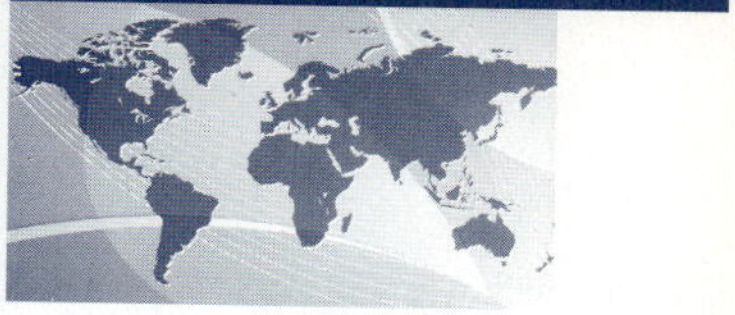

When a U.S. taxpayer invests in a foreign country, that investment income is subject to tax in the United States and may also be subject to tax in the foreign country. However, the taxpayer is allowed a credit on his or her U.S. Federal income tax return for income taxes paid to the foreign country. The credit system allows the taxpayer to treat the taxes paid to the foreign country as though they were paid to the United States. If the foreign taxes paid are less than the U.S. tax on the income, the foreign taxes have cost the taxpayer nothing. On the other hand, if the foreign taxes are greater than the U.S. tax on the income, the credit is limited to the amount of the U.S. tax on the income. In this case, the taxes paid by the taxpayer will exceed what they would have been if the income had been earned in the United States.

The original issue discount rules do not apply to U.S. savings bonds (discussed in the following paragraphs) or to obligations with a maturity date of one year or less from the date of issue.[39] See Chapter 14 for additional discussion of the tax treatment of original issue discount.

Series E and Series EE Bonds

Certain U.S. government savings bonds (Series E before 1980 and Series EE after 1979) are issued at a discount and are redeemable for fixed amounts that increase at stated intervals. No interest payments are actually made. The difference between the purchase price and the amount received on redemption is the bondholder's interest income from the investment.

The income from these savings bonds is generally deferred until the bonds are redeemed or mature. Furthermore, Series E bonds previously could be exchanged within one year of their maturity date for Series HH bonds, and the interest on the Series E bonds could be further deferred until maturity of the Series HH bonds.[40] Thus, U.S. savings bonds have attractive income deferral features not available with corporate bonds and certificates of deposit issued by financial institutions.

Of course, the deferral feature of government bonds issued at a discount is not an advantage if the investor has insufficient income to be subject to tax as the income accrues. In fact, the deferral may work to the investor's disadvantage if the investor has other income in the year the bonds mature or the bunching of the bond interest into one tax year creates a tax liability. Fortunately, U.S. government bonds have a provision for these investors. A cash basis taxpayer can elect to include in gross income the annual increment in redemption value.[41]

EXAMPLE 15

Kate purchases Series EE U.S. savings bonds for $500 (face value of $1,000) on January 2 of the current year. If the bonds are redeemed during the first six months, no interest is paid. At December 31, the redemption value is $519.60.

If Kate elects to report the interest income annually, she must report interest income of $19.60 for the current year. If she does not make the election, she will report no interest income for the current year. ■

When a taxpayer elects to report the income from the bonds on an annual basis, the election applies to all such bonds the taxpayer owns at the time of the election and to all such securities acquired subsequent to the election. A change in the method of reporting the income from the bonds requires permission from the IRS.

---

39 § 1272(a)(2).

40 Treas. Dept. Circulars No. 1–80 and No. 2–80, 1980–1 C.B. 714, 715. Note that interest is paid at semiannual intervals on the Series HH bonds and must be included in income as received. Refer to Chapter 5 for a discussion of the savings bond interest exclusion. This exchange opportunity applied through August 31, 2004.

41 § 454(a).

Amounts Received under an Obligation to Repay

The receipt of funds with an obligation to repay that amount in the future is the essence of borrowing. Because the taxpayer's assets and liabilities increase by the same amount, no income is realized when the borrowed funds are received. Because amounts paid to the taxpayer by mistake and customer deposits are often classified as borrowed funds, receipt of these funds is not a taxable event.

EXAMPLE 16

A landlord receives a damage deposit from a tenant. The landlord does not recognize income until the deposit is forfeited because the landlord has an obligation to repay the deposit if no damage occurs.[42] However, if the deposit is in fact a prepayment of rent, it is taxed in the year of receipt. ■

EXCEPTIONS APPLICABLE TO ACCRUAL BASIS TAXPAYERS

Prepaid Income

For financial reporting purposes, advance payments received from customers are reflected as prepaid income and as a liability of the seller. However, for tax purposes, the prepaid income often is taxed in the year of receipt.

EXAMPLE 17

In December 2011, a tenant pays his January 2012 rent of $1,000. The accrual basis landlord must include the $1,000 in her 2011 gross income for tax purposes, although the unearned rent income is reported as a liability on the landlord's December 31, 2011 financial accounting balance sheet. ■

Taxpayers have repeatedly argued that deferral of income until it is actually earned properly matches revenues and expenses. Moreover, a proper matching of income with the expenses of earning the income is necessary to clearly reflect income, as required by the Code. The IRS responds that § 446(b) grants it broad powers to determine whether an accounting method clearly reflects income. The IRS further argues that generally accepted financial accounting principles should not dictate tax accounting for prepaid income because of the practical problems of collecting Federal revenues. Collection of the tax is simplest in the year the taxpayer receives the cash from the customer or client.

After a number of years of continual disputes between the IRS and taxpayers, in 1971 the IRS relented and modified its rules on the prepaid income issue in some situations, as explained below.

Deferral of Advance Payments for Goods

Generally, a taxpayer can elect to defer recognition of income from *advance payments for goods* if the method of accounting for the sale is the same for tax and financial reporting purposes.[43]

EXAMPLE 18

Brown Company will ship goods only after payment for the goods has been received. In December 2011, Brown received $10,000 for goods that were not shipped until January 2012. Brown can elect to report the income for tax purposes in 2012, assuming the company reports the income in 2012 for financial reporting purposes. ■

[42] *John Mantell*, 17 T.C. 1143 (1952).

[43] Reg. § 1.451–5(b). See Reg. § 1.451–5(c) for exceptions to this deferral opportunity. The financial accounting conformity requirement is not applicable to contractors who use the completed contract method.

Deferral of Advance Payments for Services

Revenue Procedure 2004–34[44] permits an accrual basis taxpayer to defer recognition of income for *advance payments for services* to be performed after the end of the tax year of receipt. The portion of the advance payment that relates to services performed in the tax year of receipt is included in gross income in the tax year of receipt. The portion of the advance payment that relates to services to be performed after the tax year of receipt is included in gross income in the *tax year following the tax year of receipt* of the advance payment.

EXAMPLE 19

Yellow Corporation, an accrual basis calendar year taxpayer, sells its services under 12-month, 24-month, and 36-month contracts. The corporation provides services to each customer every month. On May 1, 2011, Yellow Corporation sold the following customer contracts:

Length of Contract	Total Proceeds
12 months	$3,000
24 months	4,800
36 months	7,200

Yellow may defer until 2012 all of the income that will be earned after 2011.

Length of Contract	Income Recorded in 2011	Income Recorded in 2012
12 months	$2,000 ($3,000 × 8/12)	$1,000 ($3,000 × 4/12)
24 months	1,600 ($4,800 × 8/24)	3,200 ($4,800 × 16/24)
36 months	1,600 ($7,200 × 8/36)	5,600 ($7,200 × 28/36)

■

Revenue Procedure 2004–34 does not apply to prepaid rent or prepaid interest. Advance payments for these items are always taxed in the year of receipt.

4.3 Income Sources

PERSONAL SERVICES

LO.3

Identify who should pay the tax on a particular item of income in various situations.

It is a well-established principle of taxation that income from personal services must be included in the gross income of the person who performs the services. This principle was first established in a Supreme Court decision, *Lucas v. Earl*.[45] Mr. Earl entered into a binding agreement with his wife under which Mrs. Earl was to receive one-half of Mr. Earl's salary. Justice Holmes used the celebrated **fruit and tree metaphor** to explain that the fruit (income) must be attributed to the tree from which it came (Mr. Earl's services). A mere **assignment of income** does not shift the liability for the tax.

Services of an Employee

Services performed by an employee for the employer's customers are considered performed by the employer. Thus, the employer is taxed on the income from the services provided to the customer, and the employee is taxed on any compensation received from the employer.[46]

EXAMPLE 20

Dr. Shontelle incorporates her medical practice and enters into a contract to work for the corporation for a salary. All patients contract to receive their services from the corporation, and those services are provided through the corporation's employee,

[44] 2004–1 C.B. 991.

[45] 2 USTC ¶496, 8 AFTR 10287, 50 S.Ct. 241 (USSC, 1930).

[46] *Sargent v. Comm.*, 91–1 USTC ¶50,168, 67 AFTR 2d 91–718, 929 F.2d 1252 (CA–8, 1991).

Dr. Shontelle. The corporation must include the patients' fees in its gross income. Dr. Shontelle must include her salary in her gross income. The corporation is allowed a deduction for the reasonable salary paid to Dr. Shontelle (see the discussion of unreasonable compensation in Chapters 6 and 19). ■

Services of a Child

In the case of a child, the Code specifically provides that amounts earned from personal services must be included in the child's gross income. This result applies even though the income is paid to other persons (e.g., the parents).[47]

INCOME FROM PROPERTY

Income from property (interest, dividends, rent) must be included in the gross income of the *owner* of the property. If a father clips interest coupons from bonds shortly before the interest payment date and gives the coupons to his son, the interest will still be taxed to the father. A father who assigns rents from rental property to his daughter will be taxed on the rent since he retains ownership of the property.[48]

Often income-producing property is transferred after income from the property has accrued, but before the income is recognized under the transferor's method of accounting. The IRS and the courts have developed rules to allocate the income between the transferor and the transferee.

Interest

According to the IRS, interest accrues daily. Therefore, the interest for the period that includes the date of the transfer is allocated between the transferor and transferee based on the number of days during the period that each owned the property.

EXAMPLE 21

Floyd, a cash basis taxpayer, gave his son, Seth, bonds with a face amount of $10,000 and an 8% stated annual interest rate. The gift was made on January 31, 2011, and the interest was paid on December 31, 2011. Floyd must recognize $68 in interest income (8% × $10,000 × $^{31}/_{365}$). Seth will recognize $732 in interest income ($800 − $68). ■

When the transferor must recognize the income from the property depends upon the method of accounting and the manner in which the property was transferred. In the case of a gift of income-producing property, the donor must recognize his or her share of the accrued income at the time it would have been recognized had the donor continued to own the property.[49] However, if the transfer is a sale, the transferor must recognize the accrued income at the time of the sale. This results because the accrued interest will be included in the sales proceeds.

EXAMPLE 22

Assume the same facts as in Example 21, except that the interest that was payable as of December 31 was not actually or constructively received by the bondholders until January 3, 2012. As a cash basis taxpayer, Floyd generally does not recognize interest income until it is received. If Floyd had continued to own the bonds, the interest would have been included in his 2012 gross income, the year it would have been received. Therefore, Floyd must include the $68 accrued income in his gross income as of January 3, 2012.

Further assume that Floyd sold identical bonds on the date of the gift. The bonds sold for $9,900, including accrued interest. On January 31, 2011, Floyd must recognize the accrued interest of $68 on the bonds sold. Thus, the selling price of the bonds is $9,832 ($9,900 − $68). ■

Dividends

A corporation is taxed on its earnings, and the shareholders are taxed on the dividends paid to them from the corporation's after-tax earnings. The dividend can take

[47] § 73. For circumstances in which the child's unearned income is taxed at the parents' rate, see Kiddie Tax—Unearned Income of Children Taxed at Parents' Rate in Chapter 3.

[48] *Galt v. Comm.*, 54–2 USTC ¶9457, 46 AFTR 633, 216 F.2d 41 (CA–7, 1954); *Helvering v. Horst*, 40–2 USTC ¶9787, 24 AFTR 1058, 61 S.Ct. 144 (USSC, 1940).

[49] Rev.Rul. 72–312, 1972–1 C.B. 22.

the form of an actual dividend or a constructive dividend (e.g., shareholder use of corporate assets).

Partial relief from the double taxation of dividends has been provided in the Jobs and Growth Tax Relief Reconciliation Act of 2003 and extended by the Tax Increase Prevention Act of 2005 (TIPRA). Generally, dividends received in taxable years beginning after 2002 are taxed at the same marginal rate that is applicable to a net capital gain.[50] Thus, individuals otherwise subject to the 10 or 15 percent marginal tax rate paid only a 5 percent tax on qualified dividends received in 2007, and in 2008–2012 such individuals are eligible for a 0 percent tax on qualified dividends received. Individuals subject to the 25, 28, 33, or 35 percent marginal tax rate pay a 15 percent tax on qualified dividends received. Thus, dividends receive favorable treatment as compared to interest income. Such favorable treatment of dividends is scheduled to expire for dividends received after December 31, 2012.

Note that qualified dividends are not treated as capital gains in the gains and losses netting process; thus, they are *not* reduced by capital losses. Qualified dividend income is merely taxed at the rates that would apply to the taxpayer if he or she had an excess of net long-term capital gain over net short-term capital loss.

Because the beneficial tax rate is intended to mitigate double taxation, only certain dividends are eligible for the beneficial treatment. Excluded are certain dividends from foreign corporations, dividends from tax-exempt entities, and dividends that do not satisfy the holding period requirement.

A dividend from a foreign corporation is eligible for qualified dividend status only if one of the following requirements is met: (1) the foreign corporation's stock is traded on an established U.S. securities market, or (2) the foreign corporation is eligible for the benefits of a comprehensive income tax treaty between its country of incorporation and the United States.

To satisfy the holding period requirement, the stock on which the dividend is paid must have been held for more than 60 days during the 121-day period beginning 60 days before the ex-dividend date.[51] The purpose of this requirement is to prevent the taxpayer from buying the stock shortly before the dividend is paid, receiving the dividend, and then selling the stock at a loss (a capital loss) after the stock goes ex-dividend. A stock's price often declines after the stock goes ex-dividend.

EXAMPLE 23

In June 2011, Green Corporation pays a dividend of $1.50 on each share of its common stock. Madison and Daniel, two unrelated shareholders, each own 1,000 shares of the stock. Consequently, each receives $1,500 (1,000 shares × $1.50). Assume Daniel satisfies the 60/121-day holding period rule, but Madison does not. The $1,500 Daniel receives is subject to preferential 15%/0% treatment in 2011. The $1,500 Madison receives, however, is not. Because Madison did not comply with the holding period rule, her dividend is not a *qualified dividend* and is taxed at ordinary income rates. ■

EXAMPLE 24

Assume that both Madison and Daniel in Example 23 are in the 35% tax bracket. Consequently, Madison pays a tax of $525 (35% × $1,500) on her dividend, while Daniel pays a tax of $225 (15% × $1,500) on his. The $300 saving that Daniel enjoys underscores the advantages of receiving a qualified dividend before January 1, 2013. ■

Unlike interest, dividends do not accrue on a daily basis because the declaration of a dividend is at the discretion of the corporation's board of directors. Generally, dividends are taxed to the person who is entitled to receive them—the shareholder of record as of the corporation's record date.[52] Thus, if a taxpayer sells stock after a dividend has been declared but before the record date, the dividend generally will be taxed to the purchaser.

[50] § 1(h)(11).

[51] The ex-dividend date is the date before the record date on which the corporation finalizes the list of shareholders who will receive the dividends.

[52] Reg. § 1.61–9(c). The record date is the cutoff for determining the shareholders who are entitled to receive the dividend.

If a donor makes a gift of stock to someone (e.g., a family member) after the declaration date but before the record date, the Tax Court has held that the donor does not shift the dividend income to the donee. The *fruit* has sufficiently ripened as of the declaration date to tax the dividend income to the donor of the stock.[53] In a similar set of facts, the Fifth Circuit Court of Appeals concluded that the dividend income should be included in the gross income of the donee (the owner at the record date). In this case, the taxpayer gave stock to a qualified charity (a charitable contribution) after the declaration date and before the record date.[54]

EXAMPLE 25

On June 20, the board of directors of Black Corporation declares a $10 per share dividend. The dividend is payable on June 30, to shareholders of record on June 25. As of June 20, Maria owned 200 shares of Black Corporation's stock. On June 21, Maria sold 100 of the shares to Norm for their fair market value and gave 100 of the shares to Sam (her son). Both Norm and Sam are shareholders of record as of June 25. Norm (the purchaser) will be taxed on $1,000 since he is entitled to receive the dividend. However, Maria (the donor) will be taxed on the $1,000 received by Sam (the donee) because the gift was made after the declaration date of the dividend. ■

ETHICS & Equity

Enhancing Lottery Winnings

Some family members have net losses from gambling, which can be used only to reduce gambling gains. Another family member has a substantial gain from winning the lottery. Suppose that the winner gives the winning ticket to the family members with gambling losses, thereby creating what is tantamount to tax-exempt income. Evaluate this proposal.

INCOME RECEIVED BY AN AGENT

Income received by the taxpayer's agent is considered to be received by the taxpayer. A cash basis principal must recognize the income at the time it is received by the agent.[55]

EXAMPLE 26

Jack, a cash basis taxpayer, delivered cattle to the auction barn in late December. The auctioneer, acting as the farmer's agent, sold the cattle and collected the proceeds in December. The auctioneer did not pay Jack until the following January. Jack must include the sales proceeds in his gross income for the year the auctioneer received the funds. ■

INCOME FROM PARTNERSHIPS, S CORPORATIONS, TRUSTS, AND ESTATES

A **partnership** is not a separate taxable entity. Rather, the partnership merely files an information return (Form 1065), which serves to provide the data necessary for determining the character and amount of each partner's distributive share of the partnership's income and deductions. Each partner must then report his or her distributive share of the partnership's income and deductions for the partnership's tax year ending within or with the partner's tax year. The income must be reported by each partner in the year it is earned, even if such amounts are not actually

[53] *M. G. Anton*, 34 T.C. 842 (1960).

[54] *Caruth Corp. v. U.S.*, 89–1 USTC ¶9172, 63 AFTR 2d 89–716, 865 F.2d 644 (CA–5, 1989).

[55] Rev.Rul. 79–379, 1979–2 C.B. 204.

TAX *in* the NEWS

THE ATTORNEY'S FEE WAS THE PLAINTIFF'S INCOME

Mr. Banks sued his employer for employment discrimination and received a settlement. Banks's attorney received approximately one-third of the settlement, and Banks reasoned that he should include only the remaining amount in his gross income.

The U.S. Supreme Court disagreed. The Court applied "assignment of income" and "principal-agent" reasoning to conclude that Banks was required to include the entire settlement amount in his gross income. The Court considered the lawsuit a property interest. Banks controlled the lawsuit and diverted some of the proceeds to the attorney; that is, Banks assigned a portion of his income to the attorney. The Court rejected Banks's argument that he and the attorney were partners pursuing the lawsuit. Instead, the Court concluded that Banks and his attorney maintained a "quintessential principal-agent relationship," with the attorney-agent pursuing the rights of his principal, Banks. Under well-settled principles of tax law, the amount received as a result of the agent's efforts nevertheless belonged to Banks, the principal. According to the Court, the tax treatment of the amount due the attorney would have to be addressed through the tax deduction rules. For Mr. Banks, this deduction was classified as a miscellaneous itemized deduction subject to the 2 percent floor under § 67. After the Supreme Court decision, Congress modified § 67 to allow the deduction as a deduction *for* AGI.

distributed to the partners. Because a partner pays tax on income as the partnership earns it, a distribution by the partnership to the partner is treated under the recovery of capital rules.[56]

EXAMPLE 27

Tara owns a one-half interest in the capital and profits of T & S Company (a calendar year partnership). For tax year 2011, the partnership earned revenue of $150,000 and had operating expenses of $80,000. During the year, Tara withdrew from her capital account $2,500 per month (for a total of $30,000). For 2011, Tara must report $35,000 as her share of the partnership's profits [½ × ($150,000 − $80,000)] even though she received distributions of only $30,000. ■

Contrary to the general provision that a corporation must pay tax on its income, a *small business corporation* may elect to be taxed similarly to a partnership. Thus, the shareholders, rather than the corporation, pay the tax on the corporation's income.[57] The electing corporation is referred to as an **S corporation**. Generally, the shareholders report their proportionate shares of the corporation's income and deductions for the year, whether or not the corporation actually makes any distributions to the shareholders.

The *beneficiaries of estates and trusts* generally are taxed on the income earned by the estates or trusts that is actually distributed or required to be distributed to them.[58] Any income not taxed to the beneficiaries is taxable to the estate or trust.

ETHICS & Equity

THE HONEST AND DISHONEST PARTNERS

Suppose that a partner in a professional practice collects a large fee from a client but does not tell the other partners. The partner subsequently loses the fee gambling. Later the IRS discovers the partner's diversion of the partnership's income. Because the fee was earned by the partnership, each of the partners was required to report a share of the diverted income, although the dishonest partner received all the benefit of the income. The other partners' legal remedy is to collect from their dishonest partner. If the efforts to collect are unsuccessful, the partners' tax remedy is a bad debt deduction when the receivable is determined to be worthless.

Is it fair that the honest partners must pay income tax on funds they unintentionally "loaned" to their dishonest colleague?

---

56 § 706(a) and Reg. § 1.706–1(a)(1). For further discussion, see Chapter 21.

57 §§ 1361(a) and 1366. For further discussion, see Chapter 22.

58 §§ 652(a) and 662(a). For further discussion of the taxation of income from partnerships, S corporations, trusts, and estates, see Chapters 21, 22, and 28.

INCOME IN COMMUNITY PROPERTY STATES

General

State law in Louisiana, Texas, New Mexico, Arizona, California, Washington, Idaho, Nevada, and Wisconsin is based upon a community property system. In Alaska, spouses can choose to have the community property rules apply. All other states have a common law property system. The basic difference between common law and community property systems centers around the property rights of married persons. Questions about community property income most frequently arise when the husband and wife file separate returns.

Under a **community property** system, all property is deemed either to be separately owned by the spouse or to belong to the marital community. Property may be held separately by a spouse if it was acquired before marriage or received by gift or inheritance following marriage. Otherwise, any property is deemed to be community property. For Federal tax purposes, each spouse is taxed on one-half of the income from property belonging to the community.

The laws of Texas, Louisiana, Wisconsin, and Idaho distinguish between separate property and the income it produces. In these states, the income from separate property belongs to the community. Accordingly, for Federal income tax purposes, each spouse is taxed on one-half of the income. In the remaining community property states, separate property produces separate income that the owner-spouse must report on his or her Federal income tax return.

What appears to be income, however, may really represent a recovery of capital. A recovery of capital and gain realized on separate property retain their identity as separate property. Items such as nontaxable stock dividends, royalties from mineral interests, and gains and losses from the sale of property take on the same classification as the assets to which they relate.

EXAMPLE 28

Bob and Jane are husband and wife and reside in California. Among other transactions during the year, the following occurred:

- Nontaxable stock dividend received by Jane on stock that was given to her after her marriage by her mother.
- Gain of $10,000 on the sale of unimproved land purchased by Bob before his marriage.
- Oil royalties of $15,000 from a lease Jane acquired after marriage with her separate funds.

Since the stock dividend was distributed on stock held by Jane as separate property, it also is her separate property. The same result occurs for the oil royalties Jane receives. All of the proceeds from the sale of the unimproved land (including the gain of $10,000) are Bob's separate property. ■

In all community property states, income from personal services (e.g., salaries, wages, income from a professional partnership) is generally treated as if one-half is earned by each spouse.

EXAMPLE 29

Fred and Wilma are married but file separate returns. Fred received $25,000 salary and $300 taxable interest on a savings account he established in his name. The deposits to the savings account were made from Fred's salary that he earned since the marriage. Wilma collected $2,000 taxable dividends on stock she inherited from her father. Wilma's gross income is computed as follows under three assumptions as to the state of residency of the couple:

	California	Texas	Common Law States
Dividends	$ 2,000	$ 1,000	$2,000
Salary	12,500	12,500	–0–
Interest	150	150	–0–
	$14,650	$13,650	$2,000

■

TAX *in* the NEWS

Tax Law and Marital Property

Before the joint return rules were enacted in 1948, married couples in community property states were treated more favorably than couples living in the other states. This result occurred because in the community property states the couple's income was taxed as though each spouse earned one-half of their combined income, whereas in the other states each spouse paid tax on only his or her own income. Thus, if one spouse earned most of the income, as was the case in most households, the income for the couple that did not live in a community property state would be subjected to higher marginal tax rates than the income of an identical couple living in a community property state. In effect, half the income in the community property states was shifted from the higher-income earner to the lower-income spouse.

Some states changed their marital property laws from a common law system to a community property system, primarily so that their residents could enjoy the Federal tax benefits of residents of community property states. In 1948, Congress enacted the joint return rules so that such state actions would be unnecessary.

Community Property Spouses Living Apart

The general rules for taxing the income from services performed by residents of community property states can create complications and even inequities for spouses who are living apart.

EXAMPLE 30

Cole and Debra were married but living apart for the first nine months of 2011 and were divorced as of October 1, 2011. In December 2011, Cole married Emily, who was married but living apart from Frank before their divorce in June 2011. Cole and Frank had no income from personal services in 2011.

Cole brought into his marriage to Emily a tax liability on one-half of Debra's earnings for the first nine months of the year. However, Emily left with Frank a tax liability on one-half of her earnings for the first six months of 2011. ■

Congress has developed a simple solution to the many tax problems of community property spouses living apart. A spouse (or former spouse) is taxed only on his or her actual earnings from personal services if the following conditions are met:[59]

- The individuals live apart for the entire year.
- They do not file a joint return with each other.
- No portion of the earned income is transferred between the individuals.

EXAMPLE 31

Jim and Lori reside in a community property state, and both are gainfully employed. On July 1, 2011, they separated, and on June 30, 2012, they were divorced. Assuming their only source of income is wages, one-half of such income for each year is earned by June 30, and they did not file a joint return for 2011, each should report the following gross income:

	Jim's Separate Return	Lori's Separate Return
2011	One-half of Jim's wages	One-half of Jim's wages
	One-half of Lori's wages	One-half of Lori's wages
2012	All of Jim's wages	All of Lori's wages

The results would be the same if Jim or Lori married another person in 2012, except that the newlyweds would probably file a joint return. ■

The IRS may absolve from liability an *innocent spouse* who does not live apart for the entire year and files a separate return but omits his or her share of the community income received by the other spouse. To qualify for the innocent spouse relief, the taxpayer must not know or must have no reason to know of the omitted

[59] § 66.

community income. Even if all of these requirements cannot be satisfied, the IRS has additional statutory authority to absolve the innocent spouse from tax liability. If, under the facts and circumstances, it is inequitable to hold the spouse liable for any unpaid tax, the IRS can absolve the spouse from tax liability.

4.4 Items Specifically Included in Gross Income

LO.4
Apply the Internal Revenue Code provisions on alimony, loans made at below-market interest rates, annuities, prizes and awards, group term life insurance, unemployment compensation, and Social Security benefits.

The general principles of gross income determination (discussed in the previous sections) as applied by the IRS and the courts have on occasion yielded results Congress found unacceptable. Consequently, Congress has provided more specific rules for determining the gross income from certain sources. Some of these special rules appear in §§ 71–90 of the Code.

ALIMONY AND SEPARATE MAINTENANCE PAYMENTS

When a married couple divorce or become legally separated, state law generally requires a division of the property accumulated during the marriage. In addition, one spouse may have a legal obligation to support the other spouse. The Code distinguishes between the support payments (alimony or separate maintenance) and the property division in terms of the tax consequences.

Alimony and separate maintenance payments are *deductible* by the party making the payments and are *includible* in the gross income of the party receiving the payments.[60] Thus, income is shifted from the income earner to the income beneficiary, who is better able to pay the tax on the amount received.

EXAMPLE 32

Pete and Tina are divorced, and Pete is required to pay Tina $15,000 of alimony each year. Pete earns $31,000 a year. The tax law presumes that because Tina receives the $15,000, she is better able than Pete to pay the tax on that amount. Therefore, Tina must include the $15,000 in her gross income, and Pete is allowed to deduct $15,000 from his gross income. ■

A transfer of property *other than cash* to a former spouse under a divorce decree or agreement is not a taxable event. The transferor is not entitled to a deduction and does not recognize gain or loss on the transfer. The transferee does not recognize income and has a cost basis equal to the transferor's basis.[61]

EXAMPLE 33

Paul transfers stock to Rosa as part of a 2011 divorce settlement. The cost of the stock to Paul is $12,000, and the stock's value at the time of the transfer is $15,000. Rosa later sells the stock for $16,000. Paul is not required to recognize gain from the transfer of the stock to Rosa, and Rosa has a realized and recognized gain of $4,000 ($16,000 − $12,000) when she sells the stock. ■

In the case of *cash payments*, however, it is often difficult to distinguish payments under a support obligation (alimony) and payments for the other spouse's property (property settlement). In 1984, Congress developed objective rules to classify the payments.

Post-1984 Agreements and Decrees

Payments made under post-1984 agreements and decrees are *classified as alimony* only if the following conditions are satisfied:

[60]§§ 71 and 215.

[61]§ 1041, added to the Code in 1984 to repeal the rule of *U.S. v. Davis*, 62–2 USTC ¶9509, 9 AFTR 2d 1625, 82 S.Ct. 1190 (USSC, 1962). Under the *Davis* rule, which applied to pre-1985 divorces, a property transfer incident to divorce was a taxable event.

TAX *in the NEWS*

A Voluntary Payment Is Not Alimony

When Mr. Benzin and his wife were divorced, the final agreement specified that neither party would be required to pay for the maintenance of the other party. Five years later Mr. Benzin retired and began receiving a pension. He was financially comfortable, but his former spouse was in need. He concluded that the "right thing to do" would be to share some of his wealth with his ex-wife. Therefore, he began sending her $475 a month and deducted it on his return as alimony paid. The Tax Court concluded that the payments were not alimony because they were not pursuant to the divorce agreement. Although this was bad news for Mr. Benzin, it was good news for his former spouse because she is not required to include the payments in her gross income as alimony.

Source: *Donald A. Benzin,* T.C. Summary Opinion 2009–198.

1. The payments are in cash.
2. The agreement or decree does not specify that the payments are not alimony.
3. The payor and payee are not members of the same household at the time the payments are made.
4. There is no liability to make the payments for any period after the death of the payee.[62]

Requirement 1 simplifies the law by clearly distinguishing alimony from a property division; that is, if the payment is not in cash, it must be a property division. Requirement 2 allows the parties to determine by agreement whether or not the payments will be alimony. The prohibition on cohabitation—requirement 3—is aimed at assuring the alimony payments are associated with duplicative living expenses (maintaining two households).[63] Requirement 4 is an attempt to prevent alimony treatment from being applied to what is, in fact, a payment for property rather than a support obligation. That is, a seller's estate generally will receive payments for property due after the seller's death. Such payments after the death of the payee could not be for the payee's support.

Front-Loading

As a further safeguard against a property settlement being disguised as alimony, special rules apply to post-1986 agreements if payments in the first or second year exceed $15,000. If the change in the amount of the payments exceeds statutory limits, **alimony recapture** results to the extent of the excess alimony payments. In the *third* year, the payor must include the excess alimony payments for the first and second years in gross income, and the payee is allowed a deduction for these excess alimony payments. The recaptured amount is computed as follows:[64]

$$R = D + E$$

$$D = B - (C + \$15{,}000)$$

$$E = A - \left(\frac{B - D + C}{2} + \$15{,}000\right)$$

R = amount recaptured in Year 3 tax return
D = recapture from Year 2
E = recapture from Year 1
A, B, C = payments in the first (A), second (B), and third (C) calendar years of the agreement or decree, where $D \geq 0$, $E \geq 0$

[62] § 71(b)(1). This set of alimony rules can also apply to pre-1985 agreements and decrees if both parties agree in writing. The rules applicable to pre-1985 agreements and decrees are not discussed in this text.

[63] *Alexander Washington,* 77 T.C. 601 (1981) at 604.

[64] § 71(f).

CONCEPT SUMMARY 4.1

Tax Treatment of Payments and Transfers Pursuant to Post-1984 Divorce Agreements and Decrees

	Payor	Recipient
Alimony	Deduction from gross income.	Included in gross income.
Alimony recapture	Included in gross income of the third year.	Deducted from gross income of the third year.
Child support	Not deductible.	Not includible in gross income.
Property settlement	No income or deduction.	No income or deduction; basis for the property is the same as the transferor's basis.

The recapture formula provides an objective technique for determining alimony recapture. Thus, at the time of the divorce, the taxpayers can ascertain the tax consequences. The general concept is that if the alimony payments decrease by more than $15,000 between years in the first three years, there will be alimony recapture with respect to the decrease in excess of $15,000 each year. This rule is applied for the change between Year 2 and Year 3 (D in the above formula). However, rather than making the same calculation for Year 2 payments versus Year 1 payments, the Code requires that the *average* of the payments in Years 2 and 3 be compared with the Year 1 payments (E in the preceding formula). For this purpose, revised alimony for Year 2 (alimony deducted for Year 2 minus the alimony recapture for Year 2) is used.

EXAMPLE 34

Wes and Rita are divorced in 2011. Under the agreement, Rita is to receive $50,000 in 2011, $20,000 in 2012, and nothing thereafter. The payments are to cease upon Rita's death or remarriage. In 2013, Wes must include an additional $32,500 in gross income for alimony recapture, and Rita is allowed a deduction for the same amount.

$$D = \$20{,}000 - (\$0 + \$15{,}000) = \$5{,}000$$

$$E = \$50{,}000 - \left(\frac{\$20{,}000 - \$5{,}000 + \$0}{2} + \$15{,}000\right) = \$27{,}500$$

$$R = \$5{,}000 + \$27{,}500 = \$32{,}500$$

Note that for 2011 Wes deducts alimony of $50,000, and Rita includes $50,000 in her gross income. For 2012, the amount of the alimony deduction for Wes is $20,000, and Rita's gross income from the alimony is $20,000.

If instead Wes paid $50,000 of alimony in 2011 and nothing for the following years, $35,000 would be recaptured in 2013.

$$D = \$0 - (\$0 + \$15{,}000) = -\$15{,}000, \text{ but D must be } \geq \$0$$

$$E = \$50{,}000 - \left(\frac{\$0 - \$0 + \$0}{2} + \$15{,}000\right) = \$35{,}000$$

$$R = \$0 + \$35{,}000 = \$35{,}000$$

■

Alimony recapture does not apply if the decrease in payments is due to the death of either spouse or the remarriage of the payee.[65] Recapture is not applicable because these events typically terminate alimony under state laws. In addition, the recapture rules do not apply to payments where the amount is contingent (e.g., a

[65] § 71(f)(5)(A).

percentage of income from certain property or a percentage of the payor spouse's compensation), the payments are to be made over a period of three years or longer (unless death, remarriage, or other contingency occurs), and the contingencies are beyond the payor's control.[66]

EXAMPLE 35

Under a 2011 divorce agreement, Ed is to receive an amount equal to one-half of Nina's income from certain rental properties for 2011–2014. Payments are to cease upon the death of Ed or Nina or upon the remarriage of Ed. Ed receives $50,000 in 2011 and $50,000 in 2012; in 2013, however, the property is vacant, and Ed receives nothing. Nina, who deducted alimony in 2011 and 2012, is not required to recapture any alimony in 2013 because the payments were contingent. ■

Child Support

A taxpayer does not realize income from the receipt of child support payments made by his or her former spouse. This result occurs because the money is received subject to the duty to use the money for the child's benefit. The payor is not allowed to deduct the child support payments because the payments are made to satisfy the payor's legal obligation to support the child.

In many cases, it is difficult to determine whether an amount received is alimony or child support. If the amount of the payments would be reduced upon the happening of a contingency related to a child (e.g., the child attains age 21 or dies), the amount of the future reduction in the payment is deemed child support.[67]

EXAMPLE 36

A divorce agreement provides that Matt is required to make periodic alimony payments of $500 per month to Grace. However, when Matt and Grace's child reaches age 21, marries, or dies (whichever occurs first), the payments will be reduced to $300 per month. Grace has custody of the child. Since the required contingency is the cause for the reduction in the payments, from $500 to $300, child support payments are $200 per month, and alimony is $300 per month. ■

IMPUTED INTEREST ON BELOW-MARKET LOANS

As discussed earlier in the chapter, generally no income is recognized unless it is realized. Realization generally occurs when the taxpayer performs services or sells goods and thus becomes entitled to a payment from the other party. It follows that no income is realized if the goods or services are provided at no charge. Under this interpretation of the realization requirement, before 1984, interest-free loans were used to shift income between taxpayers.

EXAMPLE 37

Veneia (daughter) is in the 20% (combined Federal and state rates) tax bracket and has no investment income. Kareem (father) is in the 50% (combined Federal and state rates) tax bracket and has $400,000 in a money market account earning 5% interest. Kareem would like Veneia to receive and pay tax on the income earned on the $400,000. Because Kareem would also like to have access to the $400,000 should he need the money, he does not want to make an outright gift of the money, nor does he want to commit the money to a trust.

Before 1984, Kareem could achieve his goals as follows. He could transfer the money market account to Veneia in exchange for her $400,000 non-interest-bearing note, payable on Kareem's demand. As a result, Veneia would receive the income, and the family's taxes would be decreased by $6,000.

[66] § 71(f)(5)(C).

[67] § 71(c)(2).

CONCEPT SUMMARY 4.2

Effect of Certain Below-Market Loans on the Lender and Borrower

Type of Loan		Lender	Borrower
Gift	Step 1	Interest income	Interest expense
	Step 2	Gift made	Gift received
Compensation-related	Step 1	Interest income	Interest expense
	Step 2	Compensation expense	Compensation income
Corporation to shareholder	Step 1	Interest income	Interest expense
	Step 2	Dividend paid	Dividend income

Decrease in Kareem's tax— (.05 × $400,000).50 =	($10,000)
Increase in Veneia's tax— (.05 × $400,000).20 =	4,000
Decrease in the family's taxes	($ 6,000)

■

Under the 1984 amendments to the Code, Kareem in Example 37 is required to recognize **imputed interest** income.[68] Veneia is deemed to have incurred interest expense equal to Kareem's imputed interest income. Veneia's interest may be deductible on her return as investment interest if she itemizes deductions (see Chapters 10 and 11). To complete the fictitious series of transactions, Kareem is then deemed to have given Veneia the amount of the imputed interest she did not pay. The gift received by Veneia is not subject to income tax (see Chapter 5), although Kareem may be subject to the gift tax (unified transfer tax) on the amount deemed given to Veneia (refer to Chapter 27).

Imputed interest is calculated using the rate the Federal government pays on new borrowings and is compounded semiannually. This Federal rate is adjusted monthly and is published by the IRS.[69] Actually, there are three Federal rates: short-term (not over three years and including demand loans), mid-term (over three years but not over nine years), and long-term (over nine years).[70]

EXAMPLE 38

Assume the Federal rate applicable to the loan in Example 37 is 3.5% through June 30 and 4% from July 1 through December 31. Kareem made the loan on January 1, and the loan is still outstanding on December 31. Kareem must recognize interest income of $15,140, and Veneia has interest expense of $15,140. Kareem is deemed to have made a gift of $15,140 to Veneia. The interest calculations are as follows:

January 1–June 30— .035 ($400,000) (½ year)	$ 7,000
July 1–December 31— .04 ($400,000 + $7,000) (½ year)	8,140
	$15,140

■

If interest is charged on the loan but is less than the Federal rate, the imputed interest is the difference between the amount that would have been charged at the Federal rate and the amount actually charged.

[68] § 7872(a)(1).

[69] §§ 7872(b)(2) and (f)(2).

[70] § 1274(d).

TAX in the NEWS

Loans to Executives Prohibited

Interest-free loans have become a popular form of compensation for executives. Several examples of multimillion-dollar loans have come to light as a result of recent bankruptcies by large corporations. The board of directors often justifies the loans as necessary to enable the executive to purchase a residence or to buy stock in the company.

Loans by publicly held corporations to their executives are now generally prohibited by Federal law. The Sarbanes-Oxley Act of 2002 (Public Law No. 107–294) places a general prohibition on loans by corporations to their executives. However, an exception permits corporate loans to finance the acquisition of a personal residence for an executive.

EXAMPLE 39

Assume the same facts as in Example 38, except that Kareem charged 3% interest, compounded annually.

Interest at the Federal rate	$ 15,140
Less interest charged (.03 × $400,000)	(12,000)
Imputed interest	$ 3,140

■

The imputed interest rules apply to the following *types* of below-market loans:[71]

1. Gift loans (made out of love, affection, or generosity, as in Example 37).
2. Compensation-related loans (employer loans to employees).
3. Corporation-shareholder loans (a corporation's loans to its shareholders).
4. Tax avoidance loans and other loans that significantly affect the borrower's or lender's Federal tax liability (discussed in the following paragraphs).

The effects of the first three types of loans on the borrower and lender are summarized in Concept Summary 4.2.

Tax Avoidance and Other Below-Market Loans

In addition to the three specific types of loans that are subject to the imputed interest rules, the Code includes a catchall provision for *tax avoidance loans* and other arrangements that have a significant effect on the tax liability of the borrower or lender. The Conference Report provides the following example of an arrangement that might be subject to the imputed interest rules.[72]

EXAMPLE 40

Annual dues for the Good Health Club are $400. In lieu of paying dues, a member can make a $4,000 deposit, refundable at the end of one year. The club can earn $400 interest on the deposit.

If interest were not imputed, an individual with $4,000 could, in effect, earn tax-exempt income on the deposit. That is, rather than invest the $4,000, earn $400 in interest, pay tax on the interest, and then pay $400 in dues, the individual could avoid tax on the interest by making the deposit. Thus, income and expenses are imputed as follows: interest income and nondeductible health club fees for the club member; income from fees and interest expense for the club. ■

Many commercially motivated transactions could be swept into this other below-market loans category. However, the Temporary Regulations have carved out a frequently encountered exception for customer prepayments. If the prepayments are included in the recipient's income under the recipient's method of accounting, the payments are not considered loans and, thus, are not subject to the imputed interest rules.[73]

---

[71] § 7872(c).

[72] H. Rep. No. 98–861, 98th Cong., 2d Sess., 1984, p. 1023.

[73] Prop.Reg. § 1.7872–2(b)(1)(i).

Exceptions and Limitations

No interest is imputed on total outstanding *gift loans* of $10,000 or less between individuals, unless the loan proceeds are used to purchase income-producing property.[74] This exemption eliminates from these complex provisions immaterial amounts that do not result in apparent shifts of income. However, if the proceeds of such a loan are used to purchase income-producing property, the limitations discussed in the following paragraphs apply instead.

On loans of $100,000 or less between individuals, the imputed interest cannot exceed the borrower's net investment income for the year (gross income from all investments less the related expenses).[75] As discussed previously, one of the purposes of the imputed interest rules is to prevent high-income taxpayers from shifting income to relatives in a lower marginal bracket. This shifting of investment income is considered to occur only to the extent the borrower has net investment income. Thus, the income imputed to the lender is limited to the borrower's net investment income. As a further limitation, or exemption, if the borrower's net investment income for the year does not exceed $1,000, no interest is imputed on loans of $100,000 or less. However, these limitations for loans of $100,000 or less do not apply if a principal purpose of a loan is tax avoidance. In such a case, interest is imputed, and the imputed interest is not limited to the borrower's net investment income.[76]

EXAMPLE 41

Vicki made interest-free gift loans as follows:

Borrower	Amount	Borrower's Net Investment Income	Purpose
Susan	$ 8,000	$ –0–	Education
Dan	9,000	500	Purchase of stock
Bonnie	25,000	–0–	Purchase of a business
Megan	90,000	15,000	Purchase of a residence
Olaf	120,000	–0–	Purchase of a residence

Assume that tax avoidance is not a principal purpose of any of the loans. The loan to Susan is not subject to the imputed interest rules because the $10,000 exception applies. The $10,000 exception does not apply to the loan to Dan because the proceeds were used to purchase income-producing assets. However, under the $100,000 exception, the imputed interest is limited to Dan's investment income ($500). Since the $1,000 exception also applies to this loan, no interest is imputed.

No interest is imputed on the loan to Bonnie because the $100,000 exception applies. Interest is imputed on the loan to Megan based on the lesser of (1) the borrower's $15,000 net investment income or (2) the interest as calculated by applying the Federal rate to the outstanding loan. None of the exceptions apply to the loan to Olaf because the loan was for more than $100,000.

Assume the relevant Federal rate is 10% and the loans were outstanding for the entire year. Vicki would recognize interest income, compounded semiannually, as follows:

Loan to Megan:	
First 6 months (.10 × $90,000 × ½ year)	$ 4,500
Second 6 months (.10 × $94,500 × ½ year)	4,725
	$ 9,225
Loan to Olaf:	
First 6 months (.10 × $120,000 × ½ year)	$ 6,000
Second 6 months (.10 × $126,000 × ½ year)	6,300
	$12,300
Total imputed interest ($9,225 + $12,300)	$21,525

■

[74] § 7872(c)(2).

[75] § 7872(d).

[76] *Deficit Reduction Tax Bill of 1984: Explanation of the Senate Finance Committee* (April 2, 1984), p. 484.

CONCEPT SUMMARY 4.3

Exceptions to the Imputed Interest Rules for Below-Market Loans

Exception	Eligible Loans	Ineligible Loans and Limitations
De minimis—aggregate loans of $10,000 or less	Gift loans	Proceeds used to purchase income-producing assets.
	Employer-employee	Principal purpose is tax avoidance.
	Corporation-shareholder	Principal purpose is tax avoidance.
Aggregate loans of $100,000 or less	Between individuals	Principal purpose is tax avoidance. For all other loans, interest is imputed to the extent of the borrower's net investment income if that income exceeds $1,000.

As with gift loans, there is a $10,000 exemption for *compensation-related loans* and *corporation-shareholder loans*. However, the $10,000 exception does not apply if tax avoidance is one of the principal purposes of a loan.[77] This vague tax avoidance standard makes practically all compensation-related and corporation-shareholder loans suspect. Nevertheless, the $10,000 exception should apply when an employee's borrowing was necessitated by personal needs (e.g., to meet unexpected expenses) rather than tax considerations.

These exceptions to the imputed interest rules are summarized in Concept Summary 4.3.

INCOME FROM ANNUITIES

Annuity contracts generally require the purchaser (the annuitant) to pay a fixed amount for the right to receive a future stream of payments. Typically, the issuer of the contract is an insurance company and will pay the annuitant a cash value if the annuitant cancels the contract. The insurance company invests the amounts received from the annuitant, and the income earned serves to increase the cash value of the annuity. No income is recognized by the annuitant at the time the cash value of the annuity increases because the taxpayer has not actually received any income. The income is not constructively received because, generally, the taxpayer must cancel the policy to receive the increase in value (the increase in value is subject to substantial restrictions).

EXAMPLE 42

Jean, age 50, pays $30,000 for an annuity contract that is to pay her $500 per month beginning when she reaches age 65 and continuing until her death. If Jean should cancel the policy after one year, she would receive $30,200. The $200 increase in value is not includible in Jean's gross income as long as she does not actually receive the $200. ■

The tax accounting problem associated with receiving payments under an annuity contract is one of apportioning the amounts received between recovery of capital and income.

EXAMPLE 43

In 2011, Tom purchased for $15,000 an annuity intended as a source of retirement income. In 2013, when the cash value of the annuity is $17,000, Tom collects $1,000 on the contract. Is the $1,000 gross income, recovery of capital, or a combination of recovery of capital and income? ■

[77] § 7872(c)(3).

The statutory solution to this problem depends upon whether the payments began before or after the annuity starting date and upon when the policy was acquired.

Collections before the Annuity Starting Date

Generally, an annuity contract specifies a date on which monthly or annual payments will begin—the annuity starting date. Often the contract will also allow the annuitant to collect a limited amount before the starting date. The amount collected may be characterized as either an actual withdrawal of the increase in cash value or a loan on the policy. In 1982, Congress changed the rules applicable to these withdrawals and loans.

Collections (including loans) equal to or less than the post–August 13, 1982 increases in cash value must be included in gross income. Amounts received in excess of post–August 13, 1982 increases in cash value are treated as a recovery of capital until the taxpayer's cost has been entirely recovered. Additional amounts are included in gross income.[78]

The taxpayer may also be subject to a penalty on early distributions of 10 percent of the income recognized. The penalty generally applies if the amount is received before the taxpayer reaches age 59½ or is disabled.[79] The early distribution penalty is deemed necessary to prevent taxpayers from using annuities as a way of avoiding the original issue discount rules. That is, the investment in the annuity earns a return that is not taxed until it is collected under the annuity rules, whereas the interest on a certificate of deposit is taxed each year as the income accrues. Thus, the annuity offers a tax advantage (deferral of income) that Congress does not want exploited.

EXAMPLE 44

Jack, age 50, purchased an annuity contract for $30,000 in 2009. In 2011, when the cash value of the contract has increased to $33,000, Jack withdraws $4,000. He must recognize $3,000 of income ($33,000 cash value − $30,000 cost) and must pay a penalty of $300 ($3,000 × 10%). The remaining $1,000 is a recovery of capital and reduces Jack's basis in the annuity contract to $29,000. ■

Collections on and after the Annuity Starting Date

The annuitant can exclude from income (as a recovery of capital) the proportion of each payment that the investment in the contract bears to the expected return under the contract. The *exclusion amount* is calculated as follows:

$$\frac{\text{Investment}}{\text{Expected return}} \times \text{Annuity payment} = \text{Exclusion amount}$$

The *expected return* is the annual amount to be paid to the annuitant multiplied by the number of years the payments will be received. The payment period may be fixed (a *term certain*) or for the life of one or more individuals. When payments are for life, the taxpayer generally must use the annuity table published by the IRS to determine the expected return (see Table 4.1). This is an actuarial table that contains life expectancies.[80] The expected return is calculated by multiplying the appropriate multiple (life expectancy) by the annual payment.

---

[78] § 72(e)(3); Reg. § 1.72–9.

[79] § 72(q).

[80] The life expectancies in Table 4.1 apply for annuity investments made on or after July 1, 1986. See *General Rules for Pensions and Annuities*, IRS Publication 939 (Rev. April 2003), p. 25. See also *Pension and Annuity Income*, IRS Publication 575 (Rev. 2009).

TABLE 4.1 Ordinary Life Annuities: One Life—Expected Return Multiples

Age	Multiple	Age	Multiple	Age	Multiple
5	76.6	42	40.6	79	10.0
6	75.6	43	39.6	80	9.5
7	74.7	44	38.7	81	8.9
8	73.7	45	37.7	82	8.4
9	72.7	46	36.8	83	7.9
10	71.7	47	35.9	84	7.4
11	70.7	48	34.9	85	6.9
12	69.7	49	34.0	86	6.5
13	68.8	50	33.1	87	6.1
14	67.8	51	32.2	88	5.7
15	66.8	52	31.3	89	5.3
16	65.8	53	30.4	90	5.0
17	64.8	54	29.5	91	4.7
18	63.9	55	28.6	92	4.4
19	62.9	56	27.7	93	4.1
20	61.9	57	26.8	94	3.9
21	60.9	58	25.9	95	3.7
22	59.9	59	25.0	96	3.4
23	59.0	60	24.2	97	3.2
24	58.0	61	23.3	98	3.0
25	57.0	62	22.5	99	2.8
26	56.0	63	21.6	100	2.7
27	55.1	64	20.8	101	2.5
28	54.1	65	20.0	102	2.3
29	53.1	66	19.2	103	2.1
30	52.2	67	18.4	104	1.9
31	51.2	68	17.6	105	1.8
32	50.2	69	16.8	106	1.6
33	49.3	70	16.0	107	1.4
34	48.3	71	15.3	108	1.3
35	47.3	72	14.6	109	1.1
36	46.4	73	13.9	110	1.0
37	45.4	74	13.2	111	.9
38	44.4	75	12.5	112	.8
39	43.5	76	11.9	113	.7
40	42.5	77	11.2	114	.6
41	41.5	78	10.6	115	.5

EXAMPLE 45

The taxpayer, age 60, purchases an annuity from an insurance company for $90,000. She is to receive $500 per month for life. Her life expectancy (from Table 4.1) is 24.2 years from the annuity starting date. Thus, her expected return is $500 × 12 × 24.2 = $145,200, and the exclusion amount is $3,719 [($90,000 investment/$145,200 expected return) × $6,000 annual payment]. The $3,719 is a nontaxable return of capital, and $2,281 is included in gross income. ■

The *exclusion ratio* (investment ÷ expected return) applies until the annuitant has recovered his or her investment in the contract. Once the investment is recovered, the entire amount of subsequent payments is taxable. If the annuitant dies before

TABLE 4.2 Number of Anticipated Monthly Annuity Payments under the Simplified Method

Age	Number of Anticipated Monthly Payments
55 and under	360
56–60	310
61–65	260
66–70	210
71 and over	160

recovering the investment, the unrecovered cost (adjusted basis) is deductible in the year the payments cease (usually the year of death).[81]

EXAMPLE 46

Assume the taxpayer in Example 45 receives annuity payments for 25.2 years (302 months). For the last 12 months [302 – (12 × 24.2) = 12], the taxpayer will include $500 each month in gross income. If instead the taxpayer dies after 36 months, she is eligible for a $78,843 deduction on her final tax return.

Cost of the contract	$ 90,000
Cost previously recovered [$90,000/$145,200 × 36 ($500)]	(11,157)
Deduction	$ 78,843

■

Simplified Method for Annuity Distributions from Qualified Retirement Plans

A simplified method is required for allocating basis to the annuity payments received under a qualified retirement plan. The portion of each annuity payment that is excluded as a return of capital is the employee's investment in the contract divided by the number of anticipated monthly payments determined in accordance with Table 4.2.[82]

EXAMPLE 47

Andrea, age 62, receives an annuity distribution of $500 per month for life from her qualified retirement plan beginning in January 2011. Her investment in the contract is $100,100. The excludible amount of each payment is $385 ($100,100 investment/260 monthly payments). Thus, $115 ($500 – $385) of each annuity payment is included in Andrea's gross income. ■

The rules for annuity payments received after the basis has been recovered by the annuitant and for the annuitant who dies before the basis is recovered are the same as under the exclusion ratio method discussed earlier.

PRIZES AND AWARDS

The fair market value of prizes and awards (other than scholarships exempted under § 117, to be discussed subsequently) must be included in gross income.[83] Therefore, TV giveaway prizes, magazine publisher prizes, door prizes, and awards from an employer to an employee in recognition of performance are fully taxable to the recipient.

A narrow exception permits a prize or award to be excluded from gross income if *all* of the following requirements are satisfied:

[81] § 72(b).
[82] § 72(d).
[83] § 74.

- The prize or award is received in recognition of religious, charitable, scientific, educational, artistic, literary, or civic achievement (e.g., Nobel Prize, Pulitzer Prize, faculty teaching award).
- The recipient transfers the prize or award to a qualified governmental unit or nonprofit organization.
- The recipient was selected without any action on his or her part to enter the contest or proceeding.
- The recipient is not required to render substantial future services as a condition for receiving the prize or award.[84]

Because the transfer of the property to a qualified governmental unit or nonprofit organization ordinarily would be a charitable contribution (an itemized deduction as presented in Chapter 10), the exclusion produces beneficial tax consequences in the following situations:

- The taxpayer does not itemize deductions and thus would receive no tax benefit from the charitable contribution.
- The taxpayer's charitable contributions exceed the annual statutory ceiling on the deduction.
- Including the prize or award in gross income would reduce the amount of deductions the taxpayer otherwise would qualify for because of gross income limitations (e.g., the gross income test for a dependency exemption, the adjusted gross income limitation in calculating the medical expense deduction).

The taxpayer can avoid including prizes and awards by refusing to accept the prize or award.

ETHICS *& Equity*

Tax Effects of a Donated Prize

The Allen family wins an expensive flat panel television at their church raffle. The TV retails for $4,200, but the church paid the wholesale price of $3,400 (one of its members owns an appliance store). Because the Allens already have enough TVs, they donate their prize to the church and claim a $4,200 charitable contribution deduction on their income tax return. Have the Allens acted properly? Wisely?

Another exception is provided for certain *employee achievement awards* in the form of tangible personal property (e.g., a gold watch). The awards must be made in recognition of length of service or safety achievement. Generally, the ceiling on the excludible amount for an employee is $400 per taxable year. However, if the award is a qualified plan award, the ceiling on the exclusion is $1,600 per taxable year.[85]

GROUP TERM LIFE INSURANCE

For many years, the IRS did not attempt to tax the value of life insurance protection provided to an employee by the employer. Some companies took undue advantage of the exclusion by providing large amounts of insurance protection for executives. Therefore, Congress enacted § 79, which created a limited exclusion for **group term life insurance**. The premiums on the first $50,000 of group term life insurance protection are excludible from the employee's gross income.

The benefits of this exclusion are available only to employees. Proprietors and partners are not considered employees. The Regulations generally require broad-scale coverage of employees to satisfy the *group* requirement (e.g., shareholder-employees would not constitute a qualified group). The exclusion applies only to term insurance (protection

[84] § 74(b).

[85] §§ 74(c) and 274(j).

TABLE 4.3 Uniform Premiums for $1,000 of Group Term Life Insurance Protection

Attained Age on Last Day of Employee's Tax Year	Cost per $1,000 of Protection for One-Month Period*
Under 25	$ .05
25–29	.06
30–34	.08
35–39	.09
40–44	.10
45–49	.15
50–54	.23
55–59	.43
60–64	.66
65–69	1.27
70 and above	2.06

*Reg. § 1.79–3, effective for coverage after June 30, 1999.

for a period of time but with no cash surrender value) and not to ordinary life insurance (lifetime protection plus a cash surrender value that can be drawn upon before death).

As mentioned, the exclusion applies to the first $50,000 of group term life insurance protection. For each $1,000 of coverage in excess of $50,000, the employee must include the amounts indicated in Table 4.3 in gross income.[86]

EXAMPLE 48

Finch Corporation has a group term life insurance policy with coverage equal to the employee's annual salary. Keith, age 52, is president of the corporation and receives an annual salary of $75,000. Keith must include $69 in gross income from the insurance protection for the year.

$$\frac{\$75,000 - \$50,000}{\$1,000} \times \$0.23 \times 12 \text{ months} = \$69$$

■

Generally, the amount that must be included in gross income, computed from Table 4.3, is much less than the price an individual would pay an insurance company for the same amount of protection. Thus, even the excess coverage provides some tax-favored income for employees when group term life insurance coverage in excess of $50,000 is desirable.

If the plan discriminates in favor of certain key employees (e.g., officers), the key employees are not eligible for the exclusion. In such a case, the key employees must include in gross income the *greater* of actual premiums paid by the employer or the amount calculated from the Uniform Premiums in Table 4.3. The other employees are still eligible for the $50,000 exclusion and continue to use the Uniform Premiums table to compute the income from excess insurance protection.[87]

UNEMPLOYMENT COMPENSATION

The unemployment compensation program is sponsored and operated by the states and Federal government to provide a source of income for people who have been employed and are temporarily (hopefully) out of work. In a series of rulings over a period of 40 years, the IRS exempted unemployment benefits from tax. These payments were considered social benefit programs for the promotion of the general welfare.

[86]Reg. § 1.79–3(d)(2).

[87]§ 79(d).

After experiencing dissatisfaction with the IRS's treatment of unemployment compensation, Congress amended the Code to provide that the benefits are taxable.[88]

In the American Recovery and Reinvestment Tax Act (ARRTA) of 2009, Congress provided that the first $2,400 of unemployment compensation in 2009 is excluded from gross income. Congress chose not to extend this exclusion relief in 2010 legislation.

SOCIAL SECURITY BENEFITS

If a taxpayer's income exceeds a specified base amount, as much as 85 percent of Social Security retirement benefits must be included in gross income. The taxable amount of benefits is determined through the application of one of two formulas that utilize a unique measure of income—*modified adjusted gross income* (*MAGI*).[89] MAGI is, generally, the taxpayer's adjusted gross income from all sources (other than Social Security) plus the foreign earned income exclusion and any tax-exempt interest income.

In the formulas, two sets of base amounts are established. The first set is as follows:

- $32,000 for married taxpayers who file a joint return.
- $0 for married taxpayers who do not live apart for the entire year but file separate returns.
- $25,000 for all other taxpayers.

The second set of base amounts is as follows:

- $44,000 for married taxpayers who file a joint return.
- $0 for married taxpayers who do not live apart for the entire year but file separate returns.
- $34,000 for all other taxpayers.

If MAGI plus one-half of Social Security benefits exceeds the first set of base amounts, but not the second set, the taxable amount of Social Security benefits is the *lesser* of the following:

- .50(Social Security benefits).
- .50[MAGI + .50(Social Security benefits) – first base amount].

EXAMPLE 49

A married couple with adjusted gross income of $30,000, no tax-exempt interest, and $11,000 of Social Security benefits who file jointly must include $1,750 of the benefits in gross income. This works out as the lesser of the following:

1. .50($11,000) = $5,500.
2. .50[$30,000 + .50($11,000) – $32,000] = .50($3,500) = $1,750.

If instead the couple had adjusted gross income of $15,000 and their Social Security benefits totaled $5,000, none of the benefits would be taxable, since .50[$15,000 + .50($5,000) – $32,000] is not a positive number. ■

If MAGI plus one-half of Social Security benefits exceeds the second set of base amounts, the taxable amount of Social Security benefits is the *lesser* of 1 or 2 below:

1. .85(Social Security benefits).
2. Sum of:
   a. .85[MAGI + .50(Social Security benefits) – second base amount], and
   b. Lesser of:
      - Amount included through application of the first formula.
      - $4,500 ($6,000 for married filing jointly).

EXAMPLE 50

A married couple who file jointly have adjusted gross income of $72,000, no tax-exempt interest, and $12,000 of Social Security benefits. Their includible Social Security benefits will be $10,200.

[88] § 85.

[89] § 86. The rationale for taxing 85% of the Social Security benefits is as follows: For the average Social Security recipient, 15% of the amount received is a recovery of amounts that the individual paid into the program, and the remainder of the benefits is financed by the employer's contribution and interest earned by the Social Security trust fund.

TAX *in* the NEWS

SOCIAL SECURITY BENEFITS AS A SOURCE OF FEDERAL REVENUE

Recipients' Social Security benefits are indexed for inflation, but the base amounts used in the formula to calculate the taxable portion of the benefits are not indexed. The $25,000 and $32,000 base amounts were established in 1984. If they were indexed for inflation, these nontaxable amounts would have doubled by 2010. Thus, as income and Social Security benefits rise with inflation, taxable income increases more than the related increase in "real" benefits.

Include the lesser of the following:

1. .85($12,000) = $10,200.
2. Sum of:
   a. .85[$72,000 + .50($12,000) – $44,000] = $28,900, and
   b. Lesser of:
      - Amount calculated by the first formula, which is the lesser of:
        - *.50($12,000) = $6,000.*
        - *.50[$72,000 + .50($12,000) – $32,000] = $23,000.*
      - $6,000.

The sum equals $34,900 ($28,900 + $6,000). Since 85% of the Social Security benefits received is less than this amount, $10,200 is included in the couple's gross income. ■

LO.5

Identify tax planning strategies for minimizing gross income.

TAX PLANNING:

The materials in this chapter have focused on the following questions:

- What is income?
- When is the income recognized?
- Who is the taxpayer?

Planning strategies suggested by these materials include the following:

- Maximize economic benefits that are not included in gross income.
- Defer the recognition of income.
- Shift income to taxpayers who are in a lower marginal tax bracket.

Some specific techniques for accomplishing these strategies are discussed in the following paragraphs.

4.5 Nontaxable Economic Benefits

Home ownership is a prime example of economic income from capital that is not subject to tax. If the taxpayer uses his or her capital to purchase investments, but pays rent on a personal residence, the taxpayer would pay the rent from after-tax income. However, if the taxpayer purchases a personal residence instead of the investments, he or she would give up gross income from the forgone investments in exchange for the rent savings. The savings in rent enjoyed as a result of owning the home are not subject to tax. Thus, the homeowner will have substituted nontaxable for taxable income.

4.6 Tax Deferral

GENERAL

Since deferred taxes are tantamount to interest-free loans from the government, the deferral of taxes is a worthy goal of the tax planner. However, the tax planner must also consider the tax rates for the years the income is shifted from and to. For example, a one-year deferral of income from a year in which the taxpayer's tax rate was 28 percent to a year in which the tax rate will be 35 percent would not be advisable if the taxpayer expects to earn less than a 7 percent after-tax return on the deferred tax dollars.

The taxpayer can often defer the recognition of income from appreciated property by postponing the event triggering realization (the final closing on a sale or exchange of property). If the taxpayer needs cash, obtaining a loan by using the appreciated property as collateral may be the least costly alternative. When the taxpayer anticipates reinvesting the proceeds, a sale may be inadvisable.

EXAMPLE 51

Ira owns 100 shares of Pigeon Company common stock with a cost of $20,000 and a fair market value of $50,000. Although the stock's value has increased substantially in the past three years, Ira thinks the growth days are over. If he sells the Pigeon stock, Ira will invest the proceeds from the sale in other common stock. Assuming Ira's marginal tax rate on the sale is 15%, he will have only $45,500 [$50,000 − .15($50,000 − $20,000)] to reinvest. The alternative investment must substantially outperform Pigeon in the future in order for the sale to be beneficial. ■

SELECTION OF INVESTMENTS

Because no tax is due until a gain has been recognized, the law favors investments that yield appreciation rather than annual income.

EXAMPLE 52

Vera can buy a corporate bond or an acre of land for $10,000. The bond pays $1,000 of interest (10%) each year, and Vera expects the land to increase in value 10% each year for the next 10 years. She is in the 40% (combined Federal and state) tax bracket for ordinary income and 26% for qualifying capital gains. Assuming the bond would mature or the land would be sold in 10 years and Vera would reinvest the interest at a 10% before-tax return, she would accumulate the following amount at the end of 10 years.

		Bond	Land
Original investment		$10,000	$10,000
Annual income	$1,000		
Less tax	(400)		
	$ 600		
Compound amount reinvested for 10 years at 6% after-tax	×13.18	7,908	
		$17,908	
Compound amount, 10 years at 10%			× 2.59
			$25,900
Less tax on sale:			
26%($25,900 − $10,000)			(4,134)
			$21,766

Therefore, the value of the deferral that results from investing in the land rather than in the bond is $3,858 ($21,766 − $17,908). ■

Series EE bonds can also be purchased for long-term deferrals of income. In situations where the taxpayer's goal is merely to shift income one year into the future, bank certificates of deposit are useful tools. If the maturity period is one year or less, all interest is reported in the year of maturity. Time certificates are especially useful for a taxpayer who realizes an unusually large gain from the sale of property in one year (and thus is in a high tax bracket) but expects his or her gross income to be less the following year.

CASH BASIS

The timing of income from services can often be controlled through the use of the cash method of accounting. Although taxpayers are somewhat constrained by the constructive receipt doctrine (they cannot turn their backs on income), seldom will customers and clients offer to pay before they are asked. The usual lag between billings and collections (e.g., December's billings collected in January) will result in a continuous deferring of some income until the last year of operations. A salaried individual approaching retirement may contract with the employer before the services are rendered to receive a portion of compensation in the lower tax bracket retirement years.

PREPAID INCOME

For the accrual basis taxpayer who receives advance payments from customers, the transactions should be structured to avoid payment of tax on income before the time the income is actually earned. Revenue Procedure 2004–34 provides the guidelines for deferring the tax on prepayments for services, and Regulation § 1.451–5 provides the guidelines for deferrals on sales of goods. In addition, both cash and accrual basis taxpayers can sometimes defer income by stipulating that the payments are deposits rather than prepaid income. For example, a landlord should require an equivalent damage deposit rather than prepayment of the last month's rent under the lease.

4.7 Shifting Income to Relatives

The tax liability of a family can be minimized by shifting income from higher- to lower-bracket family members. This can be accomplished through gifts of income-producing property. Furthermore, in many cases, income can be shifted with no negative effect on the family's investment plans.

EXAMPLE 53

Adam, who is in the 28% tax bracket, would like to save for his children's education. All of the children are under 19 years of age and are dependents of Adam. Adam could transfer income-producing properties to the children, and the children could each receive up to $950 of income each year (refer to Chapter 3) with no tax liability. The next $950 would be taxed at the child's tax rate. After a child has more than $1,900 of unearned income, there is no tax advantage to shifting more income to the child (because the income will be taxed at the parents' rate) until the child is 19 years old (or age 24 if a full-time student), when all income will be taxed according to the child's tax rate. ■

The Uniform Gifts to Minors Act, a model law adopted by all states (but with some variations among the states), facilitates income shifting. Under the Act, a gift of intangibles (e.g., bank accounts, stocks, bonds, life insurance contracts) can be made to a minor but with an adult serving as custodian. Usually, a parent who makes the gift is also named as custodian. The state laws allow the custodian to sell or redeem and reinvest the principal and to accumulate or distribute the income, practically at the custodian's discretion provided there is no commingling of the child's income with the parent's property. Thus, the parent can give appreciated securities to the child, and the donor custodian can then sell the securities and reinvest the proceeds, thereby shifting both the gain and the annual income to the child. Such planning is limited by the tax liability calculation provision for a child under the age of 19 (or age 24 if a full-time student) (refer to Chapter 3).

U.S. government bonds (Series EE) can be purchased by parents for their children. When this is done, the children generally should file a return and elect to report the income on the accrual basis.

EXAMPLE 54

Abby pays $7,500 for Series EE bonds in 2011 and immediately gives them to Wade (her son), who will enter college the year of original maturity of the bonds. The bonds have a maturity value of $10,000. Wade elects to report the annual increment in redemption value as income for each year the bonds are held. The first year the increase is $250, and Wade includes that amount in his gross income. If Wade has no other income, no tax will be due on the $250 bond interest, since such an amount will be more than offset by his available standard deduction. The following year, the increment is $260, and Wade includes this amount in income. Thus, over the life of the bonds, Wade will include $2,500 in income ($10,000 – $7,500), none of which will result in a tax liability, assuming he has no other income. However, if the election had not been made, Wade would be required to include $2,500 in income on the bonds in the year of original maturity, if they were redeemed as planned. This amount of income might result in a tax liability. ■

In some cases, it may be advantageous for the child not to make the accrual election. For example, a child under age 19 (or age 24 if a full-time student) with investment income of more than $1,900 each year and parents in the 25, 28, 33, or 35 percent tax bracket would probably benefit from deferring the tax on the savings bond interest. The child would also benefit from the use of the usually lower tax rate (rather than subjecting the income to the parents' tax rate) if the bonds mature after the child is age 19 or older (or age 24 or older if a full-time student).

4.8 Accounting for Community Property

The classification of income as community or separate property becomes important when either of two events occurs:

- Husband and wife, married taxpayers, file separate income tax returns for the year.
- Husband and wife obtain a divorce and therefore have to file separate returns for the year (refer to Chapter 3).

For planning purposes, it behooves married persons to keep track of the source of income (community or separate). To be in a position to do this effectively when income-producing assets are involved, it may be necessary to distinguish between separate and community property.[90]

4.9 Alimony

The person making the alimony payments favors a divorce settlement that includes a provision for deductible alimony payments. On the other hand, the recipient prefers that the payments do not qualify as alimony. If the payor is in a higher tax bracket than the recipient, both parties may benefit by increasing the payments and structuring them so that they qualify as alimony.

EXAMPLE 55

Carl and Polly are negotiating a divorce settlement. Carl has offered to pay Polly $10,000 each year for 10 years, but payments would cease upon Polly's death. Polly is willing to accept the offer if the agreement will specify that the cash payments are not alimony. Carl is in the 35% tax bracket, and Polly's marginal rate is 15%.

If Carl and Polly agree that Carl will pay Polly $12,000 of alimony each year, both will have improved after-tax cash flows.

	Annual Cash Flows	
	Carl	Polly
Nonalimony payments	($10,000)	$10,000
Alimony payments	($12,000)	$12,000
Tax effects		
.35($12,000)	4,200	
.15($12,000)		(1,800)
After-tax cash flows	($ 7,800)	$10,200
Benefit of alimony option	$ 2,200	$ 200

Both parties benefit at the government's expense if the $12,000 alimony option is used. ■

[90]Being able to distinguish between separate and community property is crucial to the determination of a property settlement incident to a divorce. It also is vital in the estate tax area (refer to Chapter 27) since the surviving wife's or husband's share of the community property is not included in the gross estate of the deceased spouse.

REFOCUS ON THE BIG PICTURE

CALCULATION OF GROSS INCOME

Using the accrual method of accounting, Dr. Cliff Payne has correctly calculated the gross income of his sole proprietorship. He will report the $385,000 amount on Schedule C of Form 1040.

What If?

From a tax planning perspective, what can Dr. Payne do to decrease his gross income from his first year of operating his dental practice and thereby produce better financial results for him?

Rather than electing to use the accrual method of accounting, Dr. Payne should elect the cash method of accounting since his dental practice is a service entity rather than a merchandising entity. His gross income for Federal income tax purposes under the cash method is calculated as follows:

Revenues	$385,000
Plus: Accounts receivable: January 1	–0–
Less: Accounts receivable: December 31	(52,000)
Gross income	$333,000

Electing to use the cash method of accounting enables Dr. Payne to defer paying Federal income taxes on the unpaid accounts receivable. Furthermore, each year that Dr. Payne has accounts receivable at the end of the tax year, that income is continuously deferred. Thus, if his accounts receivable remain at $52,000 at the end of each tax year, by using the cash method of accounting rather than the accrual method, he will defer that amount of income until he terminates his practice.

KEY TERMS

Accounting income, 4–5
Accounting method, 4–8
Accrual method, 4–9
Alimony and separate maintenance payments, 4–22
Alimony recapture, 4–23
Annuity, 4–29
Assignment of income, 4–15
Cash receipts method, 4–9
Claim of right doctrine, 4–10
Community property, 4–20
Constructive receipt, 4–11
Economic income, 4–4
Fruit and tree metaphor, 4–15
Gross income, 4–3
Group term life insurance, 4–33
Hybrid method, 4–10
Imputed interest, 4–26
Income, 4–4
Original issue discount, 4–12
Partnership, 4–18
Recovery of capital doctrine, 4–4
S corporation, 4–19
Taxable year, 4–8

DISCUSSION QUESTIONS

1. **LO.1** According to the Supreme Court, what are the goals of financial accounting and tax accounting in regard to measuring annual income?

2. **LO.1** Why do the tax laws employ the realization principle to measure income rather than the economists' concept of income?

ISSUE ID

3. **LO.1** Allen visits Reno, Nevada, once each year to gamble. This year his gambling loss was $25,000. He commented to you, "At least I didn't have to pay for my airfare and hotel room. The casino paid that because I am such a good customer. That was worth at least $3,000." What are the relevant tax issues for Allen?

4. **LO.1** Ben works full-time, and his hobby is gardening. He spent $1,400 on seeds and fertilizer to grow enough vegetables to last him the entire year. Should Ben be required to recognize income equal to the fair market value of the vegetables in excess of their cost?

5. **LO.1** Howard buys wrecked cars and stores them on his property. Recently, he purchased a 1990 Ford Taurus for $400. If he can sell all of the usable parts, his total proceeds from the Taurus would be over $2,500. As of the end of the year, he has sold only the radio for $75, and he does not know how many, if any, of the remaining parts will ever be sold. What are Howard's income recognition issues? **ISSUE ID**

6. **LO.2, 3** On December 31, 2011, an employee received a $6,000 check from her employer's client. The check was payable to the employer, but the employee did not receive it until after the bank had closed. The employee did not remit the funds to the employer until January 2, 2012. When is the cash basis employer required to include the $6,000 in gross income?

7. **LO.2** Why does the constructive receipt doctrine apply to cash basis taxpayers, but not to accrual basis taxpayers?

8. **LO.2** On December 31, 2011, Maurice received a $5,000 check from his employer's client. The check was payable to the employer, but Maurice did not receive the check until after the bank was closed. The bank would not reopen until January 2012. Maurice remitted the check to the employer late on December 31. Identify the cash basis employer's income recognition issues. **ISSUE ID**

9. **LO.2** In 2011, Sandra, a cash basis taxpayer, purchased a certificate of deposit for $943 that will be redeemed in 2013 for $1,000. Is Sandra required to recognize any income from the certificate in 2011 and 2012?

10. **LO.2** A Series EE U.S. government savings bond accrues 3.5% interest each year. The bond matures in three years, at which time the principal and interest will be paid. The bank will pay the taxpayer at a 3.5% interest rate each year if he agrees to leave money on deposit for three years. What tax advantage does the Series EE bond offer that is not available with the bank deposit?

11. **LO.2** Why is it often advantageous to the taxpayer to use the cash method of accounting rather than the accrual method?

12. **LO.3, 5** Wade paid $7,000 for an automobile that needed substantial repairs. He worked nights and weekends to restore the car and spent $2,400 on parts for it. He knows he can sell the car for $13,000. His daughter's college tuition is due in a few days. Would it matter, after taxes, whether Wade sells the car and pays the tuition, or whether he gives the car to his daughter and she sells it for $13,000 and pays her tuition?

13. **LO.3** Anita, a cash basis taxpayer, sued her former employer for wage discrimination. Her attorney agreed to pursue the case on a contingent fee basis—the attorney would receive one-third of any settlement or court award. The parties reached a settlement, and the attorney for Anita's former employer wrote a check payable to Anita for $320,000 and a check payable to her attorney for $160,000. Anita reasons that she and the attorney were partners in the lawsuit who shared profits two-thirds and one-third. Therefore, she includes $320,000 in her gross income. Is Anita's analysis correct? Explain.

14. **LO.3** Rex is a partner with a 40% interest in the partnership profits. In 2011, the partnership generated $400,000 of taxable income, and Rex withdrew $120,000. In 2012, the partnership had $500,000 of taxable income, and Rex was able to withdraw $200,000. What is Rex's gross income from the partnership in 2011 and 2012?

15. **LO.3, 5** Mike and Debbie were residents of Texas. In 2011, Debbie left Mike, and he has been unable to find her even though he hired a private investigator to do so. Mike and Debbie are still married at year-end. Both Debbie and Mike were employed, and each had substantial investments. They did not have any children. How will Debbie's absence complicate Mike's 2011 income tax return? **ISSUE ID**

16. **LO.4** What are the tax consequences if the alimony recapture rules apply to a cash payment to a former spouse?

17. **LO.4** Why is a married couple's cost of assets (adjusted basis) for appreciated assets relevant in negotiating their divorce agreement?

18. **LO.4, 5** William and Abigail, who live in San Francisco, have been experiencing problems with their marriage. They have a three-year-old daughter, April, who stays with William's parents during the day since both William and Abigail are employed. Abigail worked to **ISSUE ID**

support William while he attended medical school, and now she has been accepted by a medical school in Mexico. Abigail has decided to divorce William and attend medical school. April will stay in San Francisco because of her strong attachment to her grandparents and because they can provide her with excellent day care. Abigail knows that William will expect her to contribute to the cost of raising April. Abigail also feels that, to finance her education, she must receive cash for her share of the property they accumulated during their marriage. In addition, she feels she should receive some reimbursement for her contribution to William's support while he was in medical school. She expects the divorce proceedings will take several months. Identify the relevant tax issues for Abigail.

DECISION MAKING

19. **LO.4, 5** Patrick and Eva are planning to divorce. Patrick has offered to pay Eva $12,000 each year for 10 years, until their daughter reaches age 21, or to transfer to her common stock he owns with a fair market value of $100,000 in satisfaction of Eva's share of the marital property. What factors should Patrick and Eva consider in deciding between these two options?

20. **LO.4, 5** Brenda loaned her son Bart $250,000 to purchase a new home. Brenda did not charge interest on the loan. Brenda was required to recognize imputed interest income, and Bart had imputed home mortgage interest expense that he deducted as an itemized deduction. Would Brenda's and Bart's combined total income taxes likely increase or decrease as a result of the imputed interest?

21. **LO.4** The Rose Corporation made a $1 million interest-free loan to John Rose, the corporation's controlling shareholder. Mr. Rose is also the corporation's chief executive officer. Why would the corporation prefer to characterize the loan as a compensation-related loan rather than a corporation-shareholder loan?

ISSUE ID

22. **LO.2, 4** Brad is the president of the Yellow Corporation. He and other members of his family control the corporation. Brad has a temporary need for $50,000, and the corporation has excess cash. He could borrow the money from a bank at 9%, and Yellow is earning 6% on its temporary investments. Yellow has made loans to other employees on several occasions. Therefore, Brad is considering borrowing $50,000 from the corporation. He will repay the loan principal in two years plus interest at 5%. Identify the relevant tax issues for Brad and the Yellow Corporation.

23. **LO.4** On July 1, 1998, when Betty was 65 years old, she purchased an annuity contract for $108,000. The annuity was to pay Betty $9,000 on June 30 each year for the remainder of her life. Betty died on March 31, 2011. What are the effects of the annuity on Betty's gross income and taxable income for 2011?

24. **LO.4** An employer provides all of his employees with life insurance protection equal to twice the employee's annual salary. Melba, who is age 39, has an annual salary of $40,000. Is Melba required to recognize income even though she is still alive at the end of the year and thus nothing has been collected on the life insurance policy?

ISSUE ID

25. **LO.4** Eve is age 67 and unmarried. She receives $12,000 a year in Social Security benefits and $20,000 from a taxable pension. She is in the 15% marginal tax bracket on her Federal income tax return. She claims the standard deduction. She is considering selling stock she has held for more than one year. Her cost of the stock is $6,000, and its fair market value is $13,000. She has no other gains or losses for the year. She has asked you to estimate the tax consequences of selling the stock.

PROBLEMS

26. **LO.1** Determine the taxpayer's current-year (1) economic income and (2) gross income for tax purposes from the following events:
    a. Sue, a coach, was paid $950,000 to terminate her coaching contract.
    b. Elliot, a six-year-old child, was paid $10,000 for appearing in a television commercial. His parents put the funds into a savings account for the child's education.
    c. Valery's land increased in value by $100,000 when he was successful in having the zoning changed from residential to commercial.
    d. Winn purchased a lottery ticket for $5 and won $900,000.
    e. Larry spent $600 to raise vegetables that he and his family consumed. The cost of the vegetables in a store would have been $2,400.

27. **LO.1, 5** Andy recently completed medical school and is beginning his medical practice. Most of his patients are covered by health insurance with a co-pay requirement (e.g., the patient pays $10, and the insurance company is billed for the remainder). It takes approximately two months to collect from the health insurance plan. What advice can you provide Andy regarding the selection of a tax accounting method? **ISSUE ID**

28. **LO.1, 2, 5** A taxpayer is considering three alternative investments of $10,000. Assume the taxpayer is in the 28% marginal tax bracket for ordinary income and 15% for qualifying capital gains in all tax years. The selected investment will be liquidated at the end of five years. The alternatives are: **DECISION MAKING**

- A taxable corporate bond yielding 5% before tax, and the interest can be reinvested at 5% before tax.
- A Series EE bond that will have a maturity value of $12,200 (a 4% before-tax rate of return).
- Land that will increase in value.

The gain on the land will be classified and taxed as a long-term capital gain. The income from the bonds is taxed as ordinary income. How much must the land increase in value to yield a greater after-tax return than either of the bonds?

Given: Compound amount of $1 and compound value of annuity payments at the end of five years:

Interest Rate	$1 Compounded for 5 Years	$1 Annuity Compounded for 5 Years
5%	$1.28	$5.53
4%	1.22	5.42
3.6%	1.19	5.37

29. **LO.1** Determine the taxpayer's gross income for tax purposes in each of the following situations:
    a. Deb, a cash basis taxpayer, traded a corporate bond with accrued interest of $300 for corporate stock with a fair market value of $11,000 at the time of the exchange. Deb's cost of the bond was $10,000. The value of the stock had increased to $12,000 by the end of the year.
    b. Deb needed $10,000 to make a down payment on her house. She instructed her broker to sell some stock to raise the $10,000. Deb's cost of the stock was $3,000. Based on her broker's advice, instead of selling the stock, she borrowed the $10,000 using the stock as collateral for the debt.
    c. Deb's boss gave her two tickets to the Rabid Rabbits rock concert because she met her sales quota. At the time she received the tickets, they had a face price of $200 and were selling on eBay for $350 each. On the date of the concert, the tickets were selling for $400 each. Deb and her son attended the concert.

30. **LO.1, 2** Determine Amos Seagull's gross income in each of the following cases:
    a. In the current year, Seagull Corporation purchased an automobile for $25,000. The company was to receive a $1,500 rebate from the manufacturer. However, the corporation directed that the rebate be paid to Amos, the corporation's sole shareholder.
    b. Amos sold his corporation. In addition to the selling price of the stock, he received $50,000 for a covenant not to compete—an agreement that he will not compete with his former business for five years.
    c. Amos and his neighbor got into an argument over Amos's dog. The neighbor built a fence to keep the dog out of his yard. The fence cost $2,000 but added $3,000 to the value of Amos's property.

31. **LO.2, 5** Al is a medical doctor who conducts his practice as a sole proprietor. During 2011, he received cash of $280,000 for medical services. Of the amount collected, $40,000 was for services provided in 2010. At the end of 2011, Al had accounts receivable of $60,000, all for services rendered in 2011. In addition, at the end of the year, Al received **DECISION MAKING**

$12,000 as an advance payment from a health maintenance organization (HMO) for services to be rendered in 2012. Compute Al's gross income for 2011:

a. Using the cash basis of accounting.
b. Using the accrual basis of accounting.
c. Advise Al on which method of accounting he should use.

32. **LO.2** Selma operates a contractor's supply store. She maintains her books using the cash method. At the end of the year, her accountant computes her accrual basis income that is used on her tax return. For 2011, Selma had cash receipts of $1.5 million, which included $300,000 collected on accounts receivable from 2010 sales. It also included the proceeds of a $100,000 bank loan. At the end of 2011, she had $350,000 in accounts receivable from customers, all from 2011 sales.
    a. Compute Selma's accrual basis gross receipts for 2011.
    b. Selma paid cash for all of the purchases. The total amount paid for merchandise in 2011 was $1.2 million. At the end of 2010, she had merchandise on hand with a cost of $100,000. At the end of 2011, the cost of merchandise on hand was $300,000. Compute Selma's gross income from merchandise sales for 2011.

DECISION MAKING

COMMUNICATIONS

33. **LO.2, 3, 5** Your client is a new partnership, ARP Associates, which is an engineering consulting firm. Generally, ARP bills clients for services at the end of each month. Client billings are about $50,000 each month. On average, it takes 45 days to collect the receivables. ARP's expenses are primarily for salary and rent. Salaries are paid on the last day of each month, and rent is paid on the first day of each month. The partnership has a line of credit with a bank, which requires monthly financial statements. These must be prepared using the accrual method. ARP's managing partner, Amanda Sims, has suggested that the firm should also use the accrual method for tax purposes and thus reduce accounting fees by $600. Assume the partners are in the 35% (combined Federal and state) marginal tax bracket. Write a letter to your client explaining why you believe it would be worthwhile for ARP to file its tax return on the cash basis even though its financial statements are prepared on the accrual basis. ARP's address is 100 James Tower, Denver, CO 80208.

COMMUNICATIONS

34. **LO.2** Color Paint Shop, Inc. (459 Ellis Avenue, Harrisburg, PA 17111), is an accrual basis taxpayer that paints automobiles. During the year, the company painted Samuel's car and was to receive a $1,000 payment from his insurance company. Samuel was not satisfied with the work, however, and the insurance company refused to pay. In December 2011, Color and Samuel agreed that Color would receive $800 for the work, subject to final approval by the insurance company. In the past, Color had come to terms with customers only to have the insurance company negotiate an even lesser amount. In May 2012, the insurance company reviewed the claim and paid the $800 to Color. An IRS agent thinks that Color, as an accrual basis taxpayer, should report $1,000 of income in 2011, when the work was done, and then deduct a $200 loss in 2012. Prepare a memo to Susan Apple, a tax partner for whom you are working, with the recommended treatment for the disputed income.

35. **LO.2** Determine the effects of the following on a cash basis taxpayer's gross income for 2011 and 2012.
    a. On the morning of December 31, 2011, the taxpayer received a $1,500 check from a customer. The taxpayer did not cash the check until January 3, 2012.
    b. The same as part (a), except the customer asked the taxpayer not to cash the check until January 3, 2012, after the customer's salary check could be deposited.
    c. The same as part (a), except the check was not received until after the bank had closed on December 31, 2011.

36. **LO.2** Marlene, a cash basis taxpayer, invests in Series EE U.S. government savings bonds and bank certificates of deposit (CDs). Determine the tax consequences of the following on her 2011 gross income.
    a. On July 1, 2011, she purchased a CD for $10,000. The CD matures on June 30, 2013, and will pay $10,816, thus yielding a 4% annual return.
    b. On December 31, 2011, she cashed in a CD and received $11,025. She purchased the CD on January 1, 2010, and the yield to maturity was 5%.
    c. On September 30, 2011, she cashed in Series EE bonds for $10,000. She purchased the bonds in 2001 for $7,025. The yield to maturity on the bonds was 4.5%.

37. **LO.2** Drake Appliance Company, an accrual basis taxpayer, sells home appliances and service contracts. Determine the effect of each of the following transactions on the

company's 2011 gross income assuming that the company uses any available options to defer its taxes.

a. In December 2010, the company received a $1,200 advance payment from a customer for an appliance that Drake special ordered from the manufacturer. The appliance did not arrive from the manufacturer until January 2011, and Drake immediately delivered it to the customer. The sale was reported in 2011 for financial accounting purposes.

b. In October 2011, the company sold a 6-month service contract for $240. The company also sold a 36-month service contract for $1,260 in July 2011.

c. On December 31, 2011, the company sold an appliance for $1,200. The company received $500 cash and a note from the customer for $700 and $260 interest, to be paid at the rate of $40 a month for 24 months. Because of the customer's poor credit record, the fair market value of the note was only $600. The cost of the appliance was $750.

38. **LO.2, 5** Freda is a cash basis taxpayer. In 2011, she negotiated her salary for 2012. Her employer offered to pay her a total of $250,000 for the year. Freda countered that she would accept $10,000 each month for the 12 months in 2012 and the remaining $130,000 in January 2013. The employer accepted Freda's terms for 2012 and 2013.

a. Did Freda actually or constructively receive $250,000 in 2012?

b. What could explain Freda's willingness to spread her salary over a longer period of time?

39. **LO.2, 5** The Bluejay Apartments is a new development and is in the process of structuring its lease agreements. The company would like to set the damage deposits high enough that tenants will keep the apartments in good condition. The company is actually more concerned about damage than about tenants not paying their rent.

DECISION MAKING

a. Discuss the tax effects of the following alternatives:

- $1,000 damage deposit with no rent prepayment.
- $500 damage deposit and $500 rent for the final month of the lease.
- $1,000 rent for the final two months of the lease and no damage deposit.

b. Which option do you recommend?

40. **LO.3** Rusty has been experiencing serious financial problems. His annual salary was $100,000, but a creditor garnished his salary for $20,000, so the employer paid the creditor (rather than Rusty) the $20,000. To prevent creditors from attaching his investments, Rusty gave his investments to his 21-year-old daughter, Rebecca. Rebecca received $5,000 in dividends and interest from the investments during the year. Rusty transferred some cash to a Swiss bank account that paid him $6,000 interest during the year. Rusty did not withdraw the interest from the Swiss bank account. Rusty also hid some of his assets in his wholly owned corporation that received $150,000 rent income but had $160,000 in related expenses, including a $20,000 salary paid to Rusty. Rusty reasons that his gross income should be computed as follows:

Salary received	$ 80,000
Loss from rental property ($150,000 – $160,000)	(10,000)
Gross income	$ 70,000

Compute Rusty's correct gross income for the year, and explain any differences between your calculation and Rusty's.

41. **LO.2, 3** Troy, a cash basis taxpayer, is employed by Eagle Corporation, also a cash basis taxpayer. Troy is a full-time employee of the corporation and receives a salary of $60,000 per year. He also receives a bonus equal to 10% of all collections from clients he serviced during the year. Determine the tax consequences of the following events to the corporation and to Troy:

a. On December 31, 2011, Troy was visiting a customer. The customer gave Troy a $10,000 check payable to the corporation for appraisal services Troy performed during 2011. Troy did not deliver the check to the corporation until January 2012.

b. The facts are the same as in (a), except that the corporation is an accrual basis taxpayer and Troy deposited the check on December 31, but the bank did not add the deposit to the corporation's account until January 2012.

c. The facts are the same as in (a), except that the customer told Troy to hold the check until January 2012 when the customer could make a bank deposit that would cover the check.

42. **LO.3, 4** Fran, Gary, and Heidi each have a one-third interest in the capital and profits of the FGH Partnership. Each partner had a capital account of $50,000 at the beginning of the tax year. The partnership profits for the tax year were $240,000. Changes in their capital accounts during the tax year were as follows:

	Fran	Gary	Heidi	Total
Beginning balance	$ 50,000	$ 50,000	$ 50,000	$150,000
Withdrawals	(25,000)	(35,000)	(10,000)	(70,000)
Additional contributions	–0–	–0–	5,000	5,000
Allocation of profits	80,000	80,000	80,000	240,000
Ending balance	$105,000	$ 95,000	$125,000	$325,000

In arriving at the $240,000 of partnership profits, the partnership deducted $1,800 ($600 for each partner) in premiums paid for group term life insurance on the partners. Fran and Gary are 39 years old, and Heidi is 35 years old. Other employees are also eligible for group term life insurance equal to their annual salary. These premiums of $10,000 have been deducted in calculating the partnership profits of $240,000. Compute each partner's gross income from the partnership for the tax year.

43. **LO.3, 5** In 2011, Alva received dividends on her stocks as follows:

Amur Corporation (a French corporation whose stock is traded on an established U.S. securities market)	$55,000
Blaze, Inc., a Delaware corporation	25,000
Grape, Inc., a Virginia corporation	12,000

a. Alva purchased the Grape stock four years ago, and she purchased the Amur stock two years ago. She purchased the Blaze stock 15 days before it went ex-dividend and sold it 20 days later at a $22,000 loss. Alva had no other capital gains and losses for the year. She is in the 35% marginal tax bracket. Compute Alva's tax on her dividend income for 2011.

b. Alva's daughter, who is age 25 and who is not Alva's dependent, had taxable income of $6,000, which included $1,000 of dividends on Grape, Inc. stock. The daughter had purchased the stock two years ago. Compute the daughter's tax liability on the dividends.

c. Alva can earn 5% before-tax interest on a corporate bond or a 4% dividend on a preferred stock. Assuming the appreciation in value is the same, which investment produces the greater after-tax income?

d. The same as part (c), except Alva's daughter is to make the investment.

44. **LO.3** Liz and Doug were divorced on July 1 of the current year after 10 years of marriage. Their current year's income received before the divorce was as follows:

Doug's salary	$41,000
Liz's salary	55,000
Rent on apartments purchased by Liz 15 years ago	8,000
Dividends on stock Doug inherited from his mother 4 years ago	1,900
Interest on a savings account in Liz's name funded with her salary	2,400

Allocate the income to Liz and Doug assuming they live in:

a. California.

b. Texas.

45. **LO.4** Nell and Kirby are in the process of negotiating their divorce agreement. What should be the tax consequences to Nell and Kirby if the following, considered individually, became part of the agreement?

a. In consideration for her one-half interest in their personal residence, Kirby will transfer to Nell stock with a value of $200,000. Kirby's cost of the stock was $150,000, and the value of the personal residence is $400,000. They purchased the residence three years ago for $300,000.

b. Nell will receive $1,000 per month for the lesser of 120 months or the number of months she lives after the divorce becomes final.

c. Nell is to have custody of their 12-year-old son, Bobby. She is to receive $1,200 per month until Bobby (1) dies or (2) attains age 21 (whichever occurs first). After either of these events occurs, Nell will receive only $300 per month for the remainder of her life.

46. **LO.4** Karen and Al are in the process of negotiating a divorce. They have tentatively agreed on all the terms, and Karen is to pay Al $240,000 over a three-year period. Furthermore, the payments are to be spread over the three years in amounts that will qualify as alimony and minimize alimony recapture. Al desires to receive as much of the $240,000 as soon as possible because if he dies or remarries within the three years, the payments will cease. Which of the two following patterns of payments will result in the least alimony recapture in year 3?

Year	Option 1: Amount Paid	Option 2: Amount Paid
1	$100,000	$100,000
2	70,000	90,000
3	70,000	50,000
Total	$240,000	$240,000

47. **LO.4** Alicia and Rafel are in the process of negotiating a divorce agreement. They both worked during the marriage and contributed an equal amount to the marital assets. They own a home with a fair market value of $400,000 (cost of $300,000) that is subject to a mortgage for $250,000. They have lived in the home for 12 years. They also have investment assets with a cost of $160,000 and a fair market value of $410,000. Thus, the net worth of the couple is $560,000 ($400,000 − $250,000 + $410,000). The holding period for the investments is longer than one year. Alicia would like to continue to live in the house. Therefore, she has proposed that she receive the residence subject to the mortgage, a net value of $150,000. In addition, she would receive $17,600 each year for the next 10 years, which has a present value (at 6% interest) of $130,000. Rafel would receive the investment assets. If Rafel accepts this plan, he must sell one-half of the investments so that he can purchase a home. Assume that you are counseling Alicia. Explain to Alicia whether the proposed agreement would be "fair" on an after-tax basis.

DECISION MAKING

48. **LO.4, 5** Roy decides to buy a personal residence and goes to the bank for a $150,000 loan. The bank tells him he can borrow the funds at 7% if his father will guarantee the debt. Roy's father, Hal, owns CDs currently yielding 6%. The Federal rate is 5%. Hal is willing to do either of the following:

DECISION MAKING

- Cash in the CDs and lend Roy the funds at 6% interest.
- Guarantee the loan for Roy.

Hal will consider lending the funds to Roy at an even lower interest rate, depending on the tax consequences. Hal is in the 35% marginal tax bracket. Roy, whose only source of income is his salary, is in the 15% marginal tax bracket. The interest Roy pays on the mortgage will be deductible by him. Considering only the tax consequences, which option will maximize the family's after-tax wealth?

49. **LO.2, 4** On June 30, 2011, Ridge borrowed $62,000 from his employer. On July 1, 2011, Ridge used the money as follows:

Interest-free loan to Ridge's controlled corporation (operated by Ridge on a part-time basis)	$31,000
Interest-free loan to Tab (Ridge's son)	11,000
National Bank of Grundy 5% CD ($14,700 due at maturity, June 30, 2012)	14,000
National Bank of Grundy 5.5% CD ($6,678 due at maturity, June 30, 2013)	6,000
	$62,000

Ridge's employer did not charge him interest. The applicable Federal rate was 5% throughout the relevant period. Tab had investment income of $800 for the year, and he used the loan proceeds to pay medical school tuition. There were no other outstanding loans between Ridge and Tab. What are the effects of the preceding transactions on Ridge's taxable income for 2011?

50. **LO.4** Indicate whether the imputed interest rules should apply in the following situations. Assume all the loans were made at the beginning of the tax year unless otherwise indicated.
    a. Mike loaned his sister $90,000 to buy a new home. Mike did not charge interest on the loan. The Federal rate was 5%. Mike's sister had $900 of investment income for the year.
    b. Sam's employer maintains an emergency loan fund for its employees. During the year, Sam's wife was very ill, and he incurred unusually large medical expenses. He borrowed $8,500 from his employer's emergency loan fund for six months. The Federal rate was 5.5%. Sam and his wife had no investment income for the year.
    c. Jody borrowed $25,000 from her controlled corporation for six months. She used the funds to pay her daughter's college tuition. The corporation charged Jody 4% interest. The Federal rate was 5%. Jody had $3,500 of investment income for the year.
    d. Kait loaned her son, Jake, $60,000 for six months. Jake used the $60,000 to pay off college loans. The Federal rate was 5%, and Kait did not charge Jake any interest. Jake had dividend and interest income of $2,100 for the tax year.

51. **LO.4** Vito is the sole shareholder of Vito, Inc. He is also employed by the corporation. On June 30, 2011, Vito borrowed $8,000 from Vito, Inc., and on July 1, 2012, he borrowed an additional $4,000. Both loans were due on demand. No interest was charged on the loans, and the Federal rate was 8% for all relevant dates. Vito used the money to purchase a boat, and he had $1,100 of investment income. Determine the tax consequences to Vito and Vito, Inc. in each of the following situations:
    a. The loans are considered employer-employee loans.
    b. The loans are considered corporation-shareholder loans.

52. **LO.4** Tess retires after 30 years of service with her employer. She is 66 years old and has contributed $37,800 to her employer's qualified pension fund. She elects to receive her retirement benefits as an annuity of $3,000 per month for the remainder of her life.
    a. Assume that Tess retires in June 2011 and collects six annuity payments this year. What is her gross income from the annuity payments in the first year?
    b. Assume that Tess lives 30 years after retiring. What is her gross income from the annuity payments in the twenty-ninth year?
    c. Assume that Tess dies after collecting 180 payments. She collected six payments in the year of her death. What are Tess's gross income and deductions from the annuity contract in the year of her death?

53. **LO.4** For each of the following, determine the amount that should be included in gross income:
    a. Don was selected as the most valuable player in the World Series. In recognition of this, he was awarded a sports car worth $75,000 and $100,000 in cash.
    b. Wanda won the Mrs. America beauty contest. She received various prizes valued at $200,000. None of the $200,000 was for a scholarship or travel expenses.
    c. Jacob was awarded the Nobel Prize in Medicine. He donated the $1.4 million check he received to City University, his alma mater.

54. **LO.4** The LMN Partnership has a group term life insurance plan. Each partner has $150,000 protection, and each employee has protection equal to twice his or her annual salary. Employee Alice (age 36) has $85,000 of insurance under the plan, and partner Kay (age 54) has $150,000 of coverage. Because the plan is a "group plan," it is impossible to determine the cost of coverage for an individual employee or partner.
    a. Assuming the plan is nondiscriminatory, how much must Alice and Kay each include in gross income as a result of the partnership paying the insurance premiums?
    b. Assume that the partnership is incorporated. Kay becomes a shareholder and an employee who receives a $75,000 annual salary. The corporation provides Kay with $150,000 of group term life insurance coverage under a nondiscriminatory plan. What is Kay's gross income as a result of the corporation paying the insurance premiums?

55. **LO.2, 4** Herbert was employed for the first six months of 2011 and earned $90,000 in salary. During the next six months, he collected $8,800 of unemployment compensation, borrowed $12,000 (using his personal residence as collateral), and withdrew $2,000 from his savings account (including $60 interest). He received dividends of $550. His luck was not all bad, for in December he won $1,500 in the lottery on a $5 ticket. Calculate Herbert's gross income.

56. **LO.4, 5** Linda and Don are married and file a joint return. In 2011, they received $12,000 in Social Security benefits and $35,000 in taxable pension benefits and interest.

DECISION MAKING

   a. Compute the couple's adjusted gross income on a joint return.
   b. Don would like to know whether they should sell for $100,000 (at no gain or loss) a corporate bond that pays 8% in interest each year and use the proceeds to buy a $100,000 nontaxable State of Virginia bond that will pay $6,000 in interest each year.
   c. If Linda in (a) works part-time and earns $30,000, how much would Linda and Don's adjusted gross income increase?

57. **LO.4** Melissa, who is 70 years old, is unmarried and has no dependents. Her annual income consists of a taxable pension of $20,000, $12,000 in Social Security benefits, and $3,000 of dividend income. She does not itemize her deductions. She is in the 15% marginal income tax bracket. She is considering getting a part-time job that would pay her $10,000 a year.
   a. What would be Melissa's after-tax income from the part-time job, considering Social Security and Medicare tax (7.65%) as well as Federal income tax on the earnings of $10,000?
   b. What would be the effective tax rate (increase in tax/increase in income) on the additional income from the part-time job?
   c. Assume instead that Melissa's only income is a taxable pension of $18,000 and $12,000 in Social Security benefits. She is considering selling land for $10,000 that she purchased as an investment in 2007 for $3,000. Her marginal tax rate on ordinary income is 15%. What would be the effective tax rate on the gain from the sale of the land?

58. **LO.3, 4** Donna does not think she has an income tax problem but would like to discuss her situation with you just to make sure she will not get hit with an unexpected tax liability. Base your suggestions on the following relevant financial information:
   a. Donna's share of the SAT Partnership income is $150,000, but none of the income can be distributed because the partnership needs the cash for operations.
   b. Donna's Social Security benefits totaled $8,400, but Donna loaned the cash received to her nephew.
   c. Donna assigned to a creditor the right to collect $1,200 interest on some bonds she owned.
   d. Donna and her husband lived together in California until September, when they separated. Donna has heard rumors that her husband had substantial gambling winnings since they separated.

CUMULATIVE PROBLEMS

59. Daniel B. Butler and Freida C. Butler, husband and wife, file a joint return. The Butlers live at 625 Oak Street in Corbin, KY 27521. Dan's Social Security number is 111–11–1111, and Freida's is 123–45–6789. Dan was born on January 15, 1962, and Freida was born on August 20, 1962.

TAX RETURN PROBLEM

DECISION MAKING

COMMUNICATIONS

H&R BLOCK At Home

During 2010, Dan and Freida furnished over half of the total support of each of the following individuals, all of whom still live at home:
   a. Gina, their daughter, age 22, a full-time student, who married on December 21, 2010, has no income of her own, and for 2010 did not file a joint return with her husband, Casey, who earned $10,600 during 2010. Gina's Social Security number is 123–45–6788.
   b. Sam, their son, age 20, who had gross income of $6,300 in 2010, dropped out of college in October 2010. He had graduated from high school in May 2010. Sam's Social Security number is 123–45–6787.

c. Ben, their oldest son, age 26, is a full-time graduate student with gross income of $5,200. Ben's Social Security number is 123–45–6786.

Dan was employed as a manager by WJJJ, Inc. (employer identification number 11–1111111, 604 Franklin Street, Corbin, KY 27521), and Freida was employed as a salesperson for Corbin Realty, Inc. (employer identification number 98–7654321, 899 Central Street, Corbin, Ky 27521). Information from the W–2 Forms provided by the employers is presented below. Dan and Freida use the cash method.

Line	Description	Dan	Freida
1	Wages, tips, other compensation	$86,000	$65,000
2	Federal income tax withheld	$12,000	$11,400
3	Social Security wages	$86,000	$65,000
4	Social Security tax withheld	$5,332	$4,030
5	Medicare wages and tips	$86,000	$65,000
6	Medicare tax withheld	$1,247	$943
15	State	Kentucky	Kentucky
16	State wages, tips, etc.	$86,000	$65,000
17	State income tax withheld	$2,900	$2,700

Freida sold a house on December 30, 2010, and will be paid a commission of $3,100 (not included in the $65,000 reported on the W–2) on the January 10, 2011 closing date.

Other income (as reported on 1099 Forms) for 2010 consisted of the following:

Dividends on CSX stock (qualified)	$3,500
Interest on savings at Second Bank	1,600
Interest on City of Corbin bonds	900
Interest on First Bank CD	383

The $383 from First Bank was original issue discount. Dan and Freida collected $15,000 on the First Bank CD that matured on September 30, 2010. The CD was purchased on October 1, 2008, for $14,000, and the yield to maturity was 3.5%.

Dan received a Schedule K–1 from the Falcon Partnership, which showed his distributive share as $9,000. In addition to the above information, Dan and Freida's itemized deductions included the following:

Paid on 2009 Kentucky income tax	$ 400
Personal property tax paid	600
Real estate taxes paid	1,800
Interest on home mortgage (Corbin S&L)	4,900
Cash contributions to the Boy Scouts	975

Sales tax from the sales tax table is $1,860. Dan and Freida made Federal estimated tax payments of $8,000.

Part 1—Tax Computation

Compute Dan and Freida's 2010 Federal income tax payable (or refund due). If you use tax forms for your computations, you will need Form 1040 and Schedules A, B, and E. Suggested software: H&R BLOCK At Home.

Part 2—Tax Planning

Dan plans to reduce his work schedule and work only halftime for WJJJ in 2011. He has been writing songs for several years and wants to devote more time to developing a career as a songwriter. Because of the uncertainty in the music business, however, he would like you to make all computations assuming he will have no income from songwriting in 2011. To make up for the loss of income, Freida plans to increase the amount of time she spends selling real estate. She estimates she will be able to earn $70,000 in 2011. Assume all other income and expense items will be approximately the same as they were in 2010. Assume Sam will be enrolled in college as a full-time student for the summer and fall semesters. Will the Butlers have more or less disposable income (after Federal income tax) in 2011? Write a letter to the Butlers that contains your advice and prepare a memo for the tax files.

TAX COMPUTATION PROBLEM

60. Cecil C. Seymour is a 66-year-old widower. He had income for 2011 as follows:

Pension from former employer	$36,000
Interest income from Alto National Bank	5,500
Interest income on City of Alto bonds	4,500
Dividends received from IBM	2,000
Collections on annuity contract he purchased from Great Life Insurance	5,400
Social Security benefits	12,000
Rent income on townhouse	7,600

The cost of the annuity was $54,000, and Cecil was expected to receive a total of 240 monthly payments of $450. Cecil has received 22 payments through 2011.

Cecil's 40-year-old daughter, Sarah C. Seymour, borrowed $60,000 from Cecil on January 2, 2011. She used the money to start a new business. Cecil does not charge her interest because she could not afford to pay it, but he does expect to eventually collect the principal. Sarah is living with Cecil until the business becomes profitable. Except for housing, Sarah provides her own support from her business and $1,600 in dividends on stocks that she inherited from her mother.

Other relevant information is presented below:

- Cecil's Social Security number: 123–45–6785
- Address: 3840 Springfield Blvd., Alto, GA 30754
- Sarah's Social Security number: 123–45–6784
- Expenses on rental townhouse:

Utilities	$2,800
Maintenance	1,000
Depreciation	2,000
Real estate taxes	750
Insurance	700

- State income taxes paid: $3,500
- County personal property taxes paid: $2,100
- Payments on estimated 2011 Federal income tax: $5,900
- Charitable contributions of cash to Alto Baptist Church: $6,400
- Federal interest rate: 6%
- Sales taxes paid: $912

Compute Cecil's 2011 Federal income tax payable (or refund due).

RESEARCH PROBLEMS

Note: Solutions to Research Problems can be prepared by using the **Checkpoint® Student Edition** online research product, which is available to accompany this text. It is also possible to prepare solutions to the Research Problems by using tax research materials found in a standard tax library.

THOMSON REUTERS
Checkpoint® Student Edition

Research Problem 1. Your client was the beneficiary of an annuity contract purchased by her stepmother. When the stepmother died, the insurance company paid the client $400,000 and sent her a Form 1099 indicating that the taxable portion (i.e., the amount in excess of the investment in the contract) was $50,000. However, according to the client, her father fraudulently convinced her that he was the intended beneficiary. She gave her father a check equal to the amount she had received from the insurance company. She did not report any of the annuity proceeds in her income tax return. She later discovered the fraud and filed a lawsuit to collect from her father. The IRS has examined your client's return and has taken the position that she must include the $50,000 in her gross income.

Evaluate the IRS's position.

Research Problem 2. Clint, your client, is considering a job that would require him to live in Alaska for two years. He has heard that residents of Alaska receive a payment each year from the state's "permanent fund," which is funded from mineral royalties. He would like to know whether the amounts received from the permanent fund must be included in his Federal taxable income.

Partial list of research aids:
IRS Publication 17, *Your Federal Income Tax.*

INTERNET *activity*

Use the tax resources of the Internet to address the following question. Do not restrict your search to the Web, but include a review of newsgroups and general reference materials, practitioner sites and resources, primary sources of the tax law, chat rooms and discussion groups, and other opportunities.

Research Problem 3. Determine the applicable Federal rate for purposes of below-market loans. Use this figure to complete Problem 49 for this chapter.

CHAPTER 5

Gross Income: Exclusions

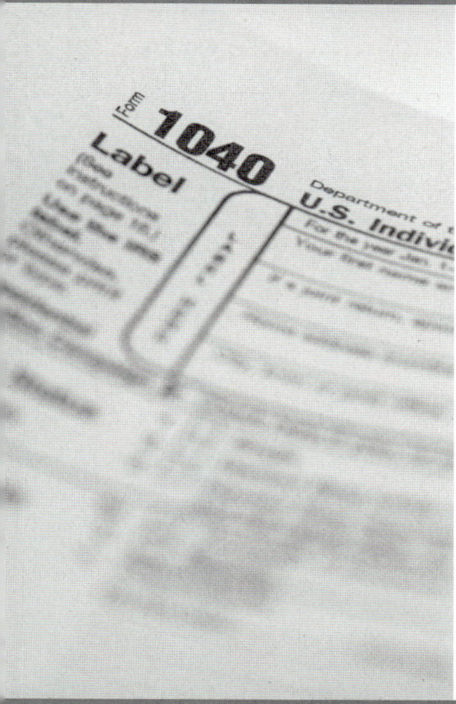

LEARNING OBJECTIVES

After completing Chapter 5, you should be able to:

LO.1

Understand that statutory authority is required to exclude an item from gross income.

LO.2

Identify the circumstances under which various items are excludible from gross income.

LO.3

Determine the extent to which receipts can be excluded under the tax benefit rule.

LO.4

Describe the circumstances under which income must be reported from the discharge of indebtedness.

LO.5

Identify tax planning strategies for obtaining the maximum benefit from allowable exclusions.

OUTLINE

For the latest in changes to tax legislation, visit **www.cengage.com/taxation/swft.**

FRAMEWORK 1040: Tax Formula for Individuals

This chapter covers the boldfaced portions of the Tax Formula for Individuals that was introduced in Figure 3.1 on p. 3-3. Below those portions are the sections of Form 1040 where the results are reported.

Income (broadly conceived)	**$xx,xxx**
Less: Exclusions	**(x,xxx)**

FORM 1040 (p. 1)

8b	**Tax-exempt** interest. **Do not** include on line 8a	8b

Gross income	**$xx,xxx**

FORM 1040 (p. 1)

10	Taxable refunds, credits, or offsets of state and local income taxes
19	Unemployment compensation
21	Other income. List type and amount

Less: Deductions for adjusted gross income	(x,xxx)
Adjusted gross income	$xx,xxx
Less: The greater of total itemized deductions *or* the standard deduction	(x,xxx)
Personal and dependency exemptions	(x,xxx)
Taxable income	$xx,xxx
Tax on taxable income (see Tax Tables or Tax Rate Schedules)	$ x,xxx
Less: Tax credits (including income taxes withheld and prepaid)	(xxx)
Tax due (or refund)	$ xxx

THE BIG PICTURE Tax Solutions for the Real World

EXCLUSIONS

Paul is a graduate student in the last semester of an accounting program at State University. This past summer he was an intern with a CPA firm, working in the compliance area. Paul was paid well enough for his work as an intern that he was able to pay for his meals and lodging and to save some for school. The CPA firm was so pleased with Paul's work that at the conclusion of his internship, he was given a bonus of $1,500 more than the firm had agreed to pay him. The extra amount was intended to help with his graduate school expenses. The CPA firm has offered him a full-time job after he completes his graduate program in December.

The university has awarded Paul a graduate assistantship that waives his tuition of $6,000 per semester and pays him $500 per month. Paul is required to teach a principles of accounting course each semester. Paul has used the $500 per month for books and for room and board.

In November, Paul was crossing a street in the pedestrian crosswalk when a delivery van struck him. The driver of the truck had a blood alcohol level of .12. Paul suffered a severe injury to his right arm that has delayed his starting date for work by three months. The delivery company's insurance company settled the case by paying damages, itemized as follows:

Compensatory damages:	
Medical expenses	$ 30,000
Injury to Paul's right arm	100,000
Pain and suffering	50,000
Loss of income	15,000
Legal fees	25,000
Punitive damages	160,000
	$380,000

Paul's mother was with him in the crosswalk. Fortunately, the van did not hit her, and she was not physically injured. But she did suffer emotional distress and received $25,000 in the settlement.

Besides being Paul's girlfriend, you also are a senior accounting major and have a keen interest in taxation. You tell Paul that you will look into the tax consequences of the settlement. **Read the chapter and formulate your response.**

5.1 Items Specifically Excluded from Gross Income

Chapter 4 discussed the concepts and judicial doctrines that affect the determination of gross income. If an income item is within the all-inclusive definition of gross income, the item can be excluded only if the taxpayer can locate specific authority for doing so. Chapter 5 focuses on the exclusions Congress has authorized. These exclusions are listed in Exhibit 5.1.

Tax advisers spend countless hours trying to develop techniques to achieve tax-exempt status for income. Employee benefits planning is greatly influenced by the availability of certain types of exclusions. Taxes play an important role in employee benefits, as well as in other situations, because attaining an exclusion is another means of enhancing after-tax income. For example, for a person whose combined Federal and state marginal tax rate is 40 percent, $1.00 of tax-exempt income is equivalent to $1.67 [$1 ÷ (1 − .4)] in income subject to taxation. The tax adviser's optimal strategy is to attach the right labels or provide the right wording to render income nontaxable without affecting the economics of the transaction.

Consider the case of an employee who is in the 28 percent marginal tax bracket and is paying $3,000 a year for health insurance. If the employer provided this protection in a manner that qualified for exclusion treatment but reduced the employee's salary by $3,000, the employee's after-tax and after-insurance income would increase at no additional cost to the employer.

Salary received to use to purchase health insurance	$ 3,000
Less: Taxes ($3,000 × 28%)	(840)
Cash available to purchase health insurance	$ 2,160
Less: Cost of health insurance	(3,000)
Excess of cost of health insurance over cash available	($ 840)

Thus, the employee in this case is $840 better off with a salary reduction of $3,000 and employer-provided health insurance. The employee may still decide that the $3,000 salary is preferable if, for example, the employee has access to health insurance through a spouse's employer. Understanding the tax influence, however, does enable the employee to make a more informed choice.

EXHIBIT 5.1 Summary of Principal Exclusions from Gross Income

1. Donative items
   Gifts, bequests, and inheritances (§ 102)
   Life insurance proceeds paid by reason of death (§ 101)
   Accelerated death benefits [§ 101(g)]
   Survivor benefits for public safety officer killed in the line of duty [§ 101(h)]
   Scholarships (§ 117)
2. Personal and welfare items
   Injury or sickness payments (§ 104)
   Public assistance payments (Rev.Rul. 71–425, 1971–2 C.B. 76)
   Amounts received under insurance contracts for certain living expenses (§ 123)
   Reimbursement for the costs of caring for a foster child (§ 131)
   Disaster relief payments (§ 139)
3. Wage and salary supplements
   a. Fringe benefits
      Accident and health benefits (§§ 105 and 106)
      Health Savings Accounts [§ 106(d)]
      Lodging and meals furnished for the convenience of the employer (§ 119)
      Rental value of parsonages (§ 107)
      Employee achievement awards [§ 74(c)]
      Employer contributions to employee group term life insurance (§ 79)
      Cafeteria plans (§ 125)
      Educational assistance payments (§ 127)
      Child or dependent care (§ 129)
      Services provided to employees at no additional cost to the employer (§ 132)
      Employee discounts (§ 132)
      Working condition and *de minimis* fringes (§ 132)
      Athletic facilities provided to employees (§ 132)
      Qualified transportation fringe (§ 132)
      Qualified moving expense reimbursement (§ 132)
      Qualified retirement planning services (§ 132)
      Tuition reductions granted to employees of educational institutions (§ 117)
      Child adoption expenses (§ 137)
      Long-term care insurance (§ 7702B)
   b. Military benefits
      Combat pay (§ 112)
      Housing, uniforms, and other benefits (§ 134)
   c. Foreign earned income (§ 911)
4. Investor items
   Interest on state and local government obligations (§ 103)
   Improvements by tenant to landlord's property (§ 109)
   Exclusion (50%, 75%, or 100%) for gain from sale of certain small business stock (§ 1202)
5. Benefits for the elderly
   Social Security benefits (except in the case of certain higher-income taxpayers)(§ 86)
6. Other benefits
   Income from discharge of indebtedness (§ 108)
   Recovery of a prior year's deduction that yielded no tax benefit (§ 111)
   Gain from the sale of personal residence (§ 121)
   Educational savings bonds (§ 135)
   Qualified tuition program (§ 529)
   Coverdell Education Savings Account (§ 530)
   Lessee construction allowances for short-term leases (§ 110)
   Conservation cost-sharing payments (§ 126)

TAX *in* the NEWS

Tough Economic Times Raise Tough Tax Issues

Individuals and businesses that were victims of the recent economic downturn received assistance in many different forms. The Federal government's "Cash for Clunkers" program benefited customers, automobile dealers, and automobile manufacturers. Various government programs assisted homeowners who could not meet their mortgage payments. Under one program, mortgage holders adjusted the terms of the loans so that homeowners could afford to make the mortgage payments and thereby avoid foreclosure. Clearly, under the broad concept of gross income, all of the beneficiaries of these programs experienced an increase in wealth. In many cases, however, assessing a tax seemed inappropriate under the circumstances; that is, the law and justice seemed to be at odds. Reconciliation could be achieved only by fitting the benefit received within one of the existing categories of tax-exempt income or by creating new exclusions.

In a recent ruling, the IRS found a nonstatutory basis for excluding payments received by homeowners to assist them in meeting their mortgage obligations. Under the Federal Homeowner Affordability and Stability Plan, homeowners who had a record of meeting their mortgage payments but were currently experiencing financial difficulties were given cash payments to be applied toward their mortgages. The IRS ruled that "payments under governmental social benefit programs for the promotion of the general welfare and not for services rendered . . . are not includible in the recipient's gross income."

Source: Rev.Rul. 2009–19, I.R.B. No. 28, 111 (June 23, 2009).

5.2 Statutory Authority

LO.1

Understand that statutory authority is required to exclude an item from gross income.

Sections 101 through 150 provide the authority for excluding specific items from gross income. In addition, other exclusions are scattered throughout the Code. Each exclusion has its own legislative history and reason for enactment. Certain exclusions are intended as a form of indirect welfare payments. Other exclusions prevent double taxation of income or provide incentives for socially desirable activities (e.g., nontaxable interest on certain U.S. government bonds where the owner uses the funds for educational expenses).

In some cases, Congress has enacted exclusions to rectify the effects of judicial decisions. For example, the Supreme Court held that the fair market value of improvements (not made in lieu of rent) made by a tenant to the landlord's property should be included in the landlord's gross income upon termination of the lease.[1] The landlord was required to include the value of the improvements in gross income even though the property had not been sold or otherwise disposed of. Congress provided relief in this situation by enacting § 109, which defers taxing the value of the improvements until the property is sold.[2]

At times Congress responds to specific events. For example, in 2001 Congress enacted § 139 to ensure that victims of a *qualified disaster* (disaster resulting from a terrorist attack, presidentially declared disaster, common carrier accident of a catastrophic nature) would not be required to include payments received for living expenses, funeral expenses, and property damage resulting from the disaster in gross income.

5.3 Gifts and Inheritances

GENERAL

LO.2

Identify the circumstances under which various items are excludible from gross income.

Beginning with the Income Tax Act of 1913 and continuing to the present, Congress has allowed the recipient of a gift to exclude the value of the property from gross income. The exclusion applies to gifts made during the life of the donor (*inter vivos* gifts) and transfers that take effect upon the death of the donor (bequests and inheritances).[3]

[1] *Helvering v. Bruun*, 40–1 USTC ¶9337, 24 AFTR 652, 60 S.Ct. 631 (USSC, 1940).

[2] If the tenant made the improvements in lieu of rent, the value of the improvements is not eligible for exclusion.

[3] § 102.

TAX in the NEWS

Begging as a Tax-Disfavored Occupation

In five recent decisions, the Tax Court ruled that amounts received from begging are nontaxable gifts. In a reversal of the normal roles, the beggars contended that the amounts received were earned income while the IRS argued that the taxpayers had merely received gifts. The beggars wanted the fruit of their efforts to be treated as earned income in order to qualify them for the earned income credit. See Chapter 12 for a discussion of the earned income credit.

However, as discussed in Chapter 4, the recipient of a gift of income-producing property is subject to tax on the income subsequently earned from the property. Also, as discussed in Chapters 1 and 27, the donor or the decedent's estate may be subject to gift or estate taxes on the transfer.

In numerous cases, gifts are made in a business setting. For example, a salesperson gives a purchasing agent free samples; an employee receives cash from his or her employer on retirement; a corporation makes payments to employees who were victims of a natural disaster; a corporation makes a cash payment to a deceased employee's spouse. In these and similar instances, it is frequently unclear whether the payment was a gift or represents compensation for past, present, or future services.

The courts have defined a **gift** as "a voluntary transfer of property by one to another without adequate [valuable] consideration or compensation therefrom."[4] If the payment is intended to be for services rendered, it is not a gift, even though the payment is made without legal or moral obligation and the payor receives no economic benefit from the transfer. To qualify as a gift, the payment must be made "out of affection, respect, admiration, charity or like impulses."[5] Thus, the cases on this issue have been decided on the basis of the donor's intent.

In a landmark case, *Comm. v. Duberstein*,[6] the taxpayer (Duberstein) received a Cadillac from a business acquaintance. Duberstein had supplied the businessman with the names of potential customers with no expectation of compensation. The Supreme Court concluded:

> ... despite the characterization of the transfer of the Cadillac by the parties [as a gift] and the absence of any obligation, even of a moral nature, to make it, it was at the bottom a recompense for Duberstein's past service, or an inducement for him to be of further service in the future.

Duberstein was therefore required to include the fair market value of the automobile in gross income.

GIFTS TO EMPLOYEES

In the case of cash or other property *received by an employee* from his or her employer, Congress has eliminated any ambiguity. Transfers from an employer to an employee cannot be excluded as a gift.[7] However, victims of a qualified disaster who are reimbursed by their employers for living expenses, funeral expenses, and property damage can exclude the payments from gross income under § 139, as previously discussed.

EMPLOYEE DEATH BENEFITS

Frequently, an employer makes payments (**death benefits**) to a deceased employee's surviving spouse, children, or other beneficiaries. If the decedent had a nonforfeitable right to the payments (e.g., the decedent's accrued salary), the amounts are generally taxable to the recipient just the same as if the employee had lived and collected the payments. But when the employer makes voluntary payments, the gift

[4] *Estate of D. R. Daly*, 3 B.T.A. 1042 (1926).

[5] *Robertson v. U.S.*, 52–1 USTC ¶9343, 41 AFTR 1053, 72 S.Ct. 994 (USSC, 1952).

[6] 60–2 USTC ¶9515, 5 AFTR 2d 1626, 80 S.Ct. 1190 (USSC, 1960).

[7] § 102(c).

TAX *in* the NEWS

Frequent-Flyer Miles Will Not Be Taxed

IRS officials believe that when a taxpayer receives frequent-flyer miles in connection with business travel, the taxpayer has received income. This is clearly true if the taxpayer has deducted the cost of the airline ticket. Under the tax benefit rule, the frequent-flyer miles should be included in gross income as a recovery of a prior deduction. If the employer pays for the business travel but the employee is awarded the frequent-flyer miles, the employee has obviously received additional compensation.

Nevertheless, the IRS has announced (Announcement 2002–18) that it will not attempt to tax frequent-flyer miles. The major consideration in creating this nonstatutory exemption was the complexity that would result from attempting to tax the miles. Distinguishing the miles awarded for personal travel (nontaxable reduction in the cost of ticket) from the business miles would be difficult. Furthermore, the valuation issues would be horrendous.

issue arises. Generally, the IRS considers such payments to be compensation for prior services rendered by the deceased employee.[8] However, some courts have held that payments to an employee's surviving spouse or other beneficiaries are gifts if the following are true:[9]

- The payments were made to the surviving spouse and children rather than to the employee's estate.
- The employer derived no benefit from the payments.
- The surviving spouse and children performed no services for the employer.
- The decedent had been fully compensated for services rendered.
- Payments were made pursuant to a board of directors' resolution that followed a general company policy of providing payments for families of deceased employees (but not exclusively for families of shareholder-employees).

When all of the above conditions are satisfied, the payment is presumed to have been made *as an act of affection or charity.* When one or more of these conditions is not satisfied, the surviving spouse and children may still be deemed the recipients of a gift if the payment is made in light of the survivors' financial needs.[10]

5.4 Life Insurance Proceeds

GENERAL RULE

Life insurance proceeds paid to the beneficiary because of the death of the insured are exempt from income tax.[11]

EXAMPLE 1

Mark purchases an insurance policy on his life and names his wife, Linda, as the beneficiary. Mark pays $45,000 in premiums. When he dies, Linda collects the insurance proceeds of $200,000. The $200,000 is exempt from Federal income tax. ■

Congress chose to exempt life insurance proceeds for the following reasons:

- For family members, life insurance proceeds serve much the same purpose as a nontaxable inheritance.
- In a business context (as well as in a family situation), life insurance proceeds replace an economic loss suffered by the beneficiary.

[8] Rev.Rul. 62–102, 1962–2 C.B. 37.

[9] *Estate of Sydney J. Carter v. Comm.*, 72–1 USTC ¶9129, 29 AFTR 2d 332, 453 F.2d 61 (CA–2, 1972), and the cases cited there.

[10] *Simpson v. U.S.*, 58–2 USTC ¶9923, 2 AFTR 2d 6036, 261 F.2d 497 (CA–7, 1958), *cert. denied* 79 S.Ct. 724 (USSC, 1958).

[11] § 101(a).

TAX in the NEWS

An Insurable Interest?

One of the tenets of insurance law is that the beneficiary of a life insurance policy must have an interest in the well-being of the person whose life is being insured that is substantial enough that insuring against the death of that person does not amount to a mere wager. In other words, the beneficiary must benefit in some way from the well-being of the insured and not merely be betting that the insured is going to die.

The principle of insurable interest is at the heart of a number of lawsuits involving "stranger-originated" life insurance policies that are now before the courts. Such policies typically come about when insurance agents and investors persuade an elderly person to take out a substantial life insurance policy. The insured person in turn sells the policy to the investors who then pay the premiums and collect the insurance when the person dies. Often there is little or no connection between the investors and the insured person.

In one case, both the beneficiary of the policy and the family of the decedent are suing American International Group (AIG) to collect on a $15 million life insurance policy on a 74-year-old woman who drowned in her bathtub. The beneficiary of the policy, who was also the last person to see the decedent alive, claims that he took out the policy because the decedent was a director of his media company and that the insurance was simply "key person" insurance. AIG has refused to pay out the insurance on the ground that the beneficiary lacked an insurable interest in the decedent's life. Meanwhile, the decedent's family has entered the suit. They agree that the beneficiary lacked an insurable interest, but say that since AIG accepted the premiums, it should pay out the insurance proceeds—but to the family, not the beneficiary on the policy.

Source: Adapted from Leslie Scism and Mark Maremont, "More Life Insurance Was Sought on Woman," *Wall Street Journal*, April 14, 2010, p. A3.

EXAMPLE 2

Gold Corporation purchases a life insurance policy to cover its key employee. If the proceeds were taxable, the corporation would require more insurance coverage to pay the tax as well as to cover the economic loss of the employee. ■

Thus, in general, Congress concluded that making life insurance proceeds exempt from income tax was a good policy.

ACCELERATED DEATH BENEFITS

Generally, if the owner of a life insurance policy cancels the policy and receives the cash surrender value, the taxpayer must recognize gain equal to the excess of the amount received over premiums paid on the policy (a loss is not deductible). The gain is recognized because the general exclusion provision for life insurance proceeds applies only to life insurance proceeds paid upon the death of the insured. If the taxpayer cancels the policy and receives the cash surrender value, the life insurance policy is treated as an investment by the insured.

In a limited circumstance, however, the insured is permitted to receive the benefits of the life insurance contract without having to include the gain in gross income. Under the **accelerated death benefits** provisions, exclusion treatment is available for insured taxpayers who are either terminally ill or chronically ill.[12] A terminally ill taxpayer can collect the cash surrender value of the policy from the insurance company or assign the policy proceeds to a qualified third party. The resultant gain, if any, is excluded from the insured's gross income. A *terminally ill* individual is one whom a medical doctor certifies as having an illness that is reasonably expected to cause death within 24 months.

In the case of a chronically ill patient, no gain is recognized if the proceeds of the policy are used for the long-term care of the insured. A person is *chronically ill* if he or she is certified as being unable to perform without assistance certain activities of daily living. These exclusions for the terminally ill and the chronically ill are available

[12] § 101(g).

only to the insured. Thus, a person who purchases a life insurance policy from the insured does not qualify.

EXAMPLE 3

Tom owned a term life insurance policy at the time he was diagnosed as having a terminal illness. After paying $5,200 in premiums, he sold the policy to Amber Benefits, Inc., a company that is authorized by the State of Virginia to purchase such policies. Amber paid Tom $50,000. When Tom died six months later, Amber collected the face amount of the policy, $75,000. Tom is not required to include the $44,800 gain ($50,000 – $5,200) on the sale of the policy in his gross income. Assume Amber pays additional premiums of $4,000 during the six-month period. When Amber collects the life insurance proceeds of $75,000, it must include the $21,000 gain [$75,000 proceeds – ($50,000 cost + $4,000 additional premiums paid)] in gross income. ■

ETHICS & *Equity*

SHOULD THE TERMINALLY ILL PAY SOCIAL SECURITY TAXES?

The rationale for excluding accelerated death benefits from the gross income of the terminally ill is that they often use the funds to pay medical expenses and other costs associated with dying and do not have the ability to pay tax on the gain from the accelerated receipt of the life insurance proceeds. Yet the wages of a terminally ill person who is employed (or profits of a self-employed person) are subject to Social Security taxes. The Social Security taxes are intended to pay for retirement benefits, but a terminally ill person is unlikely to collect any Social Security benefits.

Several bills have been introduced in Congress to exempt the terminally ill from the Social Security tax. Evaluate the equity of the current tax treatment versus that in the proposed legislation.

TRANSFER FOR VALUABLE CONSIDERATION

A life insurance policy (other than one associated with accelerated death benefits) may be transferred after it is issued by the insurance company. If the policy is *transferred for valuable consideration*, the insurance proceeds are includible in the gross income of the transferee to the extent the proceeds received exceed the amount paid for the policy by the transferee plus any subsequent premiums paid.

EXAMPLE 4

Adam pays premiums of $4,000 for an insurance policy in the face amount of $10,000 upon the life of Beth and subsequently transfers the policy to Carol for $6,000. On Beth's death, Carol receives the proceeds of $10,000. The amount that Carol can exclude from gross income is limited to $6,000 plus any premiums she paid subsequent to the transfer. ■

The Code, however, provides four exceptions to the rule illustrated in the preceding example. These exceptions permit exclusion treatment for transfers to the following:

1. A partner of the insured.
2. A partnership in which the insured is a partner.
3. A corporation in which the insured is an officer or shareholder.
4. A transferee whose basis in the policy is determined by reference to the transferor's basis.

The first three exceptions facilitate the use of insurance contracts to fund buy-sell agreements.

EXAMPLE 5

Rick and Sam are equal partners who have an agreement that allows either partner to purchase the interest of a deceased partner for $50,000. Neither partner has sufficient cash to actually buy the other partner's interest, but each has a life insurance policy on his own life in the amount of $50,000. Rick and Sam could exchange their policies (usually at little or no taxable gain), and upon the death of either partner, the surviving partner could collect tax-free insurance proceeds. The proceeds could then be used to purchase the decedent's interest in the partnership. ■

The fourth exception applies to policies that were transferred pursuant to a tax-free exchange or were received by gift.[13]

Investment earnings arising from the reinvestment of life insurance proceeds are generally subject to income tax. Often the beneficiary will elect to collect the insurance proceeds in installments. The annuity rules (discussed in Chapter 4) are used to apportion the installment payment between the principal element (excludible) and the interest element (includible).[14]

5.5 Scholarships

GENERAL INFORMATION

Payments or benefits received by a student at an educational institution may be (1) compensation for services, (2) a gift, or (3) a scholarship. If the payments or benefits are received as compensation for services (past or present), the fact that the recipient is a student generally does not render the amounts received nontaxable.[15]

EXAMPLE 6
THE BIG PICTURE

Return to the facts of *The Big Picture* on p. 5-2. State University waives tuition for all graduate teaching assistants. The tuition waived is intended as compensation for services and is therefore included in the graduate assistant's gross income. Therefore, the $6,000 Paul received in the form of a tuition waiver each semester is compensation for his services. The $500 he received each month also is compensation for services. The fact that he used the funds for educational expenses does not change the tax treatment of the compensation. ■

As discussed earlier, gifts are not includible in gross income.

The **scholarship** rules are intended to provide exclusion treatment for education-related benefits that cannot qualify as gifts but are not compensation for services. According to the Regulations, "a scholarship is an amount paid or allowed to, or for the benefit of, an individual to aid such individual in the pursuit of study or research."[16] The recipient must be a candidate for a degree at an educational institution.[17]

EXAMPLE 7

Terry enters a contest sponsored by a local newspaper. Each contestant is required to submit an essay on local environmental issues. The prize is one year's tuition at State University. Terry wins the contest. The newspaper has a legal obligation to Terry (as contest winner). Thus, the benefits are not a gift. However, since the tuition payment aids Terry in pursuing her studies, the payment is a scholarship. ■

A scholarship recipient may exclude from gross income the amount used for tuition and related expenses (fees, books, supplies, and equipment required for courses), provided the conditions of the grant do not require that the funds be used

[13]See the discussion of gifts in Chapter 13 and tax-free exchanges in Chapters 13, 18, and 21.

[14]Reg. §§ 1.72–7(c)(1) and 1.101–7T.

[15]Reg. § 1.117–2(a). See *C. P. Bhalla*, 35 T.C. 13 (1960), for a discussion of the distinction between a scholarship and compensation. See also *Bingler v. Johnson*, 69–1 USTC ¶9348, 23 AFTR 2d 1212, 89 S.Ct. 1439 (USSC, 1969). For potential exclusion treatment, see the subsequent discussion of qualified tuition reductions.

[16]Prop.Reg. § 1.117–6(c)(3)(i).

[17]§ 117(a).

for other purposes.[18] Amounts received for room and board are *not* excludible and are treated as earned income for purposes of calculating the standard deduction for a taxpayer who is another taxpayer's dependent.[19]

EXAMPLE 8

Kelly receives a scholarship of $9,500 from State University to be used to pursue a bachelor's degree. She spends $4,000 on tuition, $3,000 on books and supplies, and $2,500 for room and board. Kelly may exclude $7,000 ($4,000 + $3,000) from gross income. The $2,500 spent for room and board is includible in Kelly's gross income.

The scholarship is Kelly's only source of income. Her parents provide more than 50% of Kelly's support and claim her as a dependent. Kelly's standard deduction of $2,800 ($2,500 + $300) exceeds her $2,500 gross income. Thus, she has no taxable income. ■

TIMING ISSUES

Frequently, the scholarship recipient is a cash basis taxpayer who receives the money in one tax year but pays the educational expenses in a subsequent year. The amount eligible for exclusion may not be known at the time the money is received. In that case, the transaction is held *open* until the educational expenses are paid.[20]

EXAMPLE 9

In August 2011, Sanjay received $10,000 as a scholarship for the academic year 2011–2012. Sanjay's expenditures for tuition, books, and supplies were as follows:

August–December 2011	$3,000
January–May 2012	4,500
	$7,500

Sanjay's gross income for 2012 includes $2,500 ($10,000 – $7,500) that is not excludible as a scholarship. None of the scholarship is included in his gross income in 2011. ■

DISGUISED COMPENSATION

Some employers make scholarships available solely to the children of key employees. The tax objective of these plans is to provide a nontaxable fringe benefit to the executives by making the payment to the child in the form of an excludible scholarship. However, the IRS has ruled that the payments are generally includible in the gross income of the parent-employee.[21]

QUALIFIED TUITION REDUCTION PLANS

Employees (including retired and disabled former employees) of nonprofit educational institutions are allowed to exclude a tuition waiver from gross income if the waiver is pursuant to a **qualified tuition reduction plan.**[22] The plan may not discriminate in favor of highly compensated employees. The exclusion applies to the employee, the employee's spouse, and the employee's dependent children. The exclusion also extends to tuition reductions granted by any nonprofit educational institution to employees of any other nonprofit educational institution (reciprocal agreements).

EXAMPLE 10

ABC University allows the dependent children of XYZ University employees to attend ABC University with no tuition charge. XYZ University grants reciprocal benefits to the children of ABC University employees. The dependent children can also attend tuition-free the university where their parents are employed. Employees who take advantage of these benefits are not required to recognize gross income. ■

[18] § 117(b).
[19] Prop.Reg. § 1.117–6(h).
[20] Prop.Reg. § 1.117–6(b)(2).
[21] Rev.Rul. 75–448, 1975–2 C.B. 55; *Richard T. Armantrout*, 67 T.C. 996 (1977).
[22] § 117(d).

TAX in the NEWS

The Tax on a Whistleblower's Damages Award Declared Unconstitutional—But Only for a Short While

When an employer retaliated against a whistleblowing employee who had reported various alleged infractions, the employee was awarded compensatory damages for emotional distress and damage to her professional reputation. In *Murphy v. IRS*, the U.S. Court of Appeals for the D.C. Circuit recently held that the award was not includible in gross income, but rather was a recovery of capital. The court concluded that Congress exceeded the bounds of its constitutional authority when it enacted a statute that taxes as income damages received for nonphysical injury. Most commentators thought that the Supreme Court would reverse the decision because the taxpayer had no capital invested in the emotions that gave rise to the damages award.

Rather than filing a Writ of Certiorari with the Supreme Court, the government petitioned the Court of Appeals for the D.C. Circuit to rehear the case. In the rehearing, the court changed its mind. It rejected all of "Murphy's arguments in all aspects." So the full amount of the award Murphy received must be included in gross income.

Generally, the exclusion is limited to *undergraduate* tuition waivers. However, in the case of teaching or research assistants, graduate tuition waivers may also qualify for exclusion treatment. According to the Proposed Regulations, the exclusion is limited to the value of the benefit in excess of the employee's reasonable compensation.[23] Thus, a tuition reduction that is a substitute for cash compensation cannot be excluded.

EXAMPLE 11

Susan is a graduate research assistant. She receives a $5,000 salary for 500 hours of service over a nine-month period. This pay, $10 per hour, is reasonable compensation for Susan's services. In addition, Susan receives a waiver of $6,000 for tuition. Susan may exclude the tuition waiver from gross income. ■

5.6 Compensation for Injuries and Sickness

DAMAGES

A person who suffers harm caused by another is often entitled to **compensatory damages**. The tax consequences of the receipt of damages depend on the type of harm the taxpayer has experienced. The taxpayer may seek recovery for (1) a loss of income, (2) expenses incurred, (3) property destroyed, or (4) personal injury.

Generally, reimbursement for a loss of income is taxed the same as the income replaced (see the exception under Personal Injury below). The recovery of an expense is not income, unless the expense was deducted. Damages that are a recovery of the taxpayer's previously deducted expenses are generally taxable under the tax benefit rule, discussed later in this chapter.

A payment for damaged or destroyed property is treated as an amount received in a sale or exchange of the property. Thus, the taxpayer has a realized gain if the damages payments received exceed the property's basis. Damages for personal injuries receive special treatment under the Code.

Personal Injury

The legal theory of personal injury damages is that the amount received is intended "to make the plaintiff [the injured party] whole as before the injury."[24] It follows

[23] Prop.Reg. § 1.117–6(d).

[24] *C. A. Hawkins*, 6 B.T.A. 1023 (1928).

CONCEPT SUMMARY 5.1

Taxation of Damages

Type of Claim	Taxation of Award or Settlement
Breach of contract (generally loss of income)	Taxable.
Property damages	Recovery of cost; gain to the extent of the excess over basis. A loss is deductible for business property and investment property to the extent of basis over the amount realized. A loss may be deductible for personal use property (see discussion of casualty losses in Chapter 7).
Personal injury	
Physical	All compensatory amounts are excluded unless previously deducted (e.g., medical expenses). Amounts received as punitive damages are included in gross income.
Nonphysical	Compensatory damages and punitive damages are included in gross income.

that if the damages payments received were subject to tax, the after-tax amount received would be less than the actual damages incurred and the injured party would not be "whole as before the injury."

In terms of personal injury damages, a distinction is made between compensatory damages and punitive damages. Under specified circumstances, compensatory damages may be excluded from gross income. Under no circumstances may punitive damages be excluded from gross income.

Compensatory damages are intended to compensate the taxpayer for the damages incurred. Only those compensatory damages received on account of *physical personal injury or physical sickness* can be excluded from gross income.[25] Such exclusion treatment includes amounts received for loss of income associated with the physical personal injury or physical sickness. Compensatory damages awarded on account of emotional distress are not received on account of physical injury or physical sickness and thus cannot be excluded (except to the extent of any amount received for medical care) from gross income. Likewise, any amounts received for age discrimination or injury to one's reputation cannot be excluded.

Punitive damages are amounts the person who caused the harm must pay to the victim as punishment for outrageous conduct. Punitive damages are not intended to compensate the victim, but rather to punish the party who caused the harm. Thus, it follows that amounts received as punitive damages may actually place the victim in a better economic position than before the harm was experienced. Logically, punitive damages are thus included in gross income.

EXAMPLE 12
THE BIG PICTURE

Return to the facts of *The Big Picture* on p. 5-2. The damages Paul received were awarded as a result of a physical personal injury. Therefore, all of the compensatory damages can be excluded. Note that even the compensation for the loss of income of $15,000 can be excluded. The punitive damages Paul received, however, must be included in his gross income.

Paul's mother did not suffer a personal physical injury or sickness. Therefore, the $25,000 she received must be included in her gross income. ■

[25] § 104(a)(2).

ETHICS & Equity

TAX TREATMENT OF DAMAGES NOT RELATED TO PHYSICAL PERSONAL INJURY

An individual who prevails in a personal injury claim for something other than a physical injury or sickness must include the amount of the award or settlement in gross income. In contrast, an award or settlement for a physical personal injury or sickness can be excluded (except for punitive damages) from gross income. Should damages awarded for a physical personal injury or sickness be treated more favorably than damages awarded for emotional distress or other nonphysical personal injuries such as age and sex discrimination?

WORKERS' COMPENSATION

State workers' compensation laws require the employer to pay fixed amounts for specific job-related injuries. The state laws were enacted so that the employee will not have to go through the ordeal of a lawsuit (and possibly not collect damages because of some defense available to the employer) to recover the damages. Although the payments are intended, in part, to compensate for a loss of future income, Congress has specifically exempted workers' compensation benefits from inclusion in gross income.[26]

ACCIDENT AND HEALTH INSURANCE BENEFITS

The income tax treatment of accident and health insurance benefits depends on whether the policy providing the benefits was purchased by the taxpayer or the taxpayer's employer. Benefits collected under an accident and health insurance policy *purchased by the taxpayer* are excludible. In this case, benefits collected under the taxpayer's insurance policy are excluded even though the payments are a substitute for income.[27]

EXAMPLE 13

Bonnie purchases a medical and disability insurance policy. The insurance company pays Bonnie $1,000 per week to replace wages she loses while in the hospital. Although the payments serve as a substitute for income, the amounts received are tax-exempt benefits collected under Bonnie's insurance policy. ■

EXAMPLE 14

Joe's injury results in a partial paralysis of his left foot. He receives $20,000 for the injury from his accident insurance company under a policy he had purchased. The $20,000 accident insurance proceeds are tax-exempt. ■

A different set of rules applies if the accident and health insurance protection was *purchased by the individual's employer*, as discussed in the following section.

5.7 EMPLOYER-SPONSORED ACCIDENT AND HEALTH PLANS

Congress encourages employers to provide employees, retired former employees, and their dependents with **accident and health benefits**, disability insurance, and long-term care plans. The *premiums* are deductible by the employer and excluded from the employee's income.[28] Although § 105(a) provides the general rule that the employee has includible income when he or she collects the insurance *benefits*, two exceptions are provided.

Section 105(b) generally excludes payments received for medical care of the employee, spouse, and dependents. However, if the payments are for expenses that do

[26] § 104(a)(1).

[27] § 104(a)(3).

[28] § 106, Reg. § 1.106–1, and Rev.Rul. 82–196, 1982–1 C.B. 106.

GLOBAL *Tax Issues*

When Jobs Leave the Country, So Do the Health Insurance Benefits

Firms in the textile industry generally provided health insurance coverage for their employees. As textile mills in the United States close and production is moved to foreign countries, often the U.S. employees lose their health insurance as well as their jobs. If and when the former textile worker finds new employment, the new employer may not provide health insurance. In addition, the pay on the new job is often so low that the worker cannot afford to purchase health insurance, which may cost over $500 per month.

Among the factors contributing to increased foreign competition for the domestic textile industry are the North American Free Trade Agreement of 1993, the Caribbean Basin Initiative of 2000, and the opening up of trade with China.

not meet the Code's definition of medical care,[29] the amount received must be included in gross income. In addition, the taxpayer must include in gross income any amounts received for medical expenses that were deducted by the taxpayer on a prior return.

EXAMPLE 15

In 2011, Tab's employer-sponsored health insurance plan pays $4,000 for hair transplants that do not meet the Code's definition of medical care. Tab must include the $4,000 in his gross income for 2011. ■

Section 105(c) excludes payments for the permanent loss or the loss of the use of a member or function of the body or the permanent disfigurement of the employee, spouse, or a dependent. Payments that are a substitute for salary (e.g., related to the period of time absent) are includible.

EXAMPLE 16

Jill loses an eye in an automobile accident unrelated to her work. As a result of the accident, Jill incurs $2,000 of medical expenses, which she deducts on her return. She collects $10,000 from an accident insurance policy carried by her employer. The benefits are paid according to a schedule of amounts that vary with the part of the body injured (e.g., $10,000 for loss of an eye, $20,000 for loss of a hand). Because the payment is for loss of a *member or function of the body,* the $10,000 is excluded from gross income. Jill is absent from work for a week as a result of the accident. Her employer provides her with insurance for the loss of income due to illness or injury. Jill collects $500, which is includible in gross income. ■

ETHICS *& Equity*

The Health Care Exclusions Affect Progressivity of the Tax

Employer-provided health insurance and medical reimbursement plans are usually provided to employees in the middle- and higher-income classes. The lower-income groups frequently have jobs that do not provide health care benefits. Furthermore, those taxpayers in the higher tax brackets can benefit more in terms of absolute dollars of tax savings from the exclusions than can lower-income employees. To provide equity to the lower-income taxpayers who do receive health insurance benefits from their employers, should the health benefit exclusion be replaced with a tax credit?

[29] See the discussion of medical care in Chapter 10.

MEDICAL REIMBURSEMENT PLANS

In lieu of providing the employee with insurance coverage for hospital and medical expenses, the employer may agree to reimburse the employee for these expenses. The amounts received through the insurance coverage (insured plan benefits) are excluded from income under § 105 (as previously discussed). Unfortunately in terms of cost considerations, the insurance companies that issue this type of policy usually require a broad coverage of employees. An alternative is to have a plan that is not funded with insurance (a self-insured arrangement). The benefits received under a self-insured plan can be excluded from the employee's income if the plan does not discriminate in favor of highly compensated employees.[30]

There is also an alternative means of accomplishing a medical reimbursement plan. The employer can purchase a medical insurance plan with a high deductible (e.g., the employee is responsible for the first $2,400 of the family's medical expenses) and then make contributions to the employee's **Health Savings Account (HSA).**[31] The employer can make contributions each month up to the maximum contribution of 100 percent of the deductible amount. The monthly deductible amount is limited to one-twelfth of $3,050 under a high-deductible plan for self-only coverage. The monthly amount for an individual who has family coverage is limited to one-twelfth of $6,150 under a high-deductible plan. Withdrawals from the HSA must be used to reimburse the employee for the medical expenses paid by the employee that are not covered under the high-deductible plan. The employee is not taxed on the employer's contributions to the HSA, the earnings on the funds in the account, or the withdrawals made for medical expenses.[32]

LONG-TERM CARE INSURANCE BENEFITS

Generally, **long-term care insurance**, which covers expenses such as the cost of care in a nursing home, is treated the same as accident and health insurance benefits. Thus, the employee does not recognize income when the employer pays the premiums. This exclusion is subject to annual limits as follows:

Insured's Age before Close of Tax Year	2010	2011
40 or less	$ 330	$ 340
41 to 50	620	640
51 to 60	1,230	1,270
61 to 70	3,290	3,390
More than 70	4,110	4,240

When benefits are received from the policy, whether the employer or the individual purchased the policy, the exclusion from gross income is limited to the greater of the following amounts:

- $300 in 2011 (indexed amount for 2010 was $290) for each day the patient receives the long-term care.
- The actual cost of the care.

The above amount is reduced by any amounts received from other third parties (e.g., damages received).[33]

EXAMPLE 17

Hazel, who suffers from Alzheimer's disease, is a patient in a nursing home for the last 30 days of 2011. While in the nursing home, she incurs total costs of $7,600. Medicare pays $3,200 of the costs. Hazel receives $6,000 from her long-term care insurance policy (which pays $200 per day while she is in the facility).

[30] § 105(h).

[31] §§ 106(d) and 223. See additional coverage in Chapter 10.

[32] §§ 106(d), 223(b), and 223(d). The amounts for 2010 were $3,050 and $6,150.

[33] §§ 7702B and 213(d)(10).

The amount that Hazel may exclude is calculated as follows:

Greater of:		
Daily statutory amount of $300 ($300 × 30 days)	$9,000	
Actual cost of the care	7,600	$ 9,000
Less: Amount received from Medicare		(3,200)
Amount of exclusion		$ 5,800

Therefore, Hazel must include $200 ($6,000 − $5,800) of the long-term care benefits received in her gross income. ■

The exclusion for long-term care insurance is not available if it is provided as part of a cafeteria plan or a flexible spending plan.

5.8 Meals and Lodging

FURNISHED FOR THE CONVENIENCE OF THE EMPLOYER

As discussed in Chapter 4, income can take any form, including meals and lodging. However, § 119 excludes from income the value of meals and lodging provided to the employee and the employee's spouse and dependents under the following conditions:[34]

- The meals and/or lodging are *furnished* by the employer, on the employer's *business premises*, for the *convenience of the employer.*
- In the case of lodging, the *employee is required* to accept the lodging as a condition of employment.

The courts have construed both of these requirements strictly.

Furnished by the Employer

The following two questions have been raised with regard to the *furnished by the employer* requirement:

- Who is considered an *employee*?
- What is meant by *furnished*?

The IRS and some courts have reasoned that because a partner is not an employee, the exclusion does not apply to a partner. However, the Tax Court and the Fifth Circuit Court of Appeals have ruled in favor of the taxpayer on this issue.[35]

The Supreme Court held that a cash meal allowance was ineligible for the exclusion because the employer did not actually furnish the meals.[36] Similarly, one court denied the exclusion where the employer paid for the food and supplied the cooking facilities but the employee prepared the meal.[37]

On the Employer's Business Premises

The *on the employer's business premises* requirement, applicable to both meals and lodging, has resulted in much litigation. The Regulations define business premises as simply "the place of employment of the employee."[38] Thus, the Sixth Circuit Court of Appeals held that a residence, owned by the employer and occupied by an employee, two blocks from the motel that the employee managed was not part of the business premises.[39] However, the Tax Court considered an employer-owned house

[34] § 119(a). The meals and lodging are also excluded from FICA and FUTA tax. *Rowan Companies, Inc. v. U.S.*, 81–1 USTC ¶9479, 48 AFTR 2d 81–5115, 101 S.Ct. 2288 (USSC, 1981).

[35] Rev.Rul. 80, 1953–1 C.B. 62; *Comm. v. Doak*, 56–2 USTC ¶9708, 49 AFTR 1491, 234 F.2d 704 (CA–4, 1956); but see *G. A. Papineau*, 16 T.C. 130 (1951); *Armstrong v. Phinney*, 68–1 USTC ¶9355, 21 AFTR 2d 1260, 394 F.2d 661 (CA–5, 1968).

[36] *Comm. v. Kowalski*, 77–2 USTC ¶9748, 40 AFTR 2d 6128, 98 S.Ct. 315 (USSC, 1977).

[37] *Tougher v. Comm.*, 71–1 USTC ¶9398, 27 AFTR 2d 1301, 441 F.2d 1148 (CA–9, 1971).

[38] Reg. § 1.119–1(c)(1).

[39] *Comm. v. Anderson*, 67–1 USTC ¶9136, 19 AFTR 2d 318, 371 F.2d 59 (CA–6, 1966).

across the street from the hotel that was managed by the taxpayer to be on the business premises of the employer.[40] Apparently, the closer the lodging to the business operations, the more likely the convenience of the employer is served.

For the Convenience of the Employer

The *convenience of the employer* test is intended to focus on the employer's motivation for furnishing the meals and lodging rather than on the benefits received by the employee. If the employer furnishes the meals and lodging primarily to enable the employee to perform his or her duties properly, it does not matter that the employee considers these benefits to be a part of his or her compensation.

The Regulations give the following examples in which the tests for excluding meals are satisfied:[41]

- A restaurant requires its service staff to eat their meals on the premises during the busy lunch and breakfast hours.
- A bank furnishes meals on the premises for its tellers to limit the time the employees are away from their booths during the busy hours.
- A worker is employed at a construction site in a remote part of Alaska. The employer must furnish meals and lodging due to the inaccessibility of other facilities.

If more than half of the employees to whom meals are furnished receive their meals for the convenience of the employer, then all such employee meals are treated as provided for the convenience of the employer.[42] Thus, in this situation, all employees are treated the same (either all of the employees are allowed exclusion treatment, or none of the employees can exclude the meals from gross income).

EXAMPLE 18

Allison's Restaurant has a restaurant area and a bar. Nine employees work in the restaurant and three work in the bar. All of the employees are provided one meal per day. In the case of the restaurant workers, the meals are provided for the convenience of the employer. The meals provided to the bar employees do not satisfy the convenience of the employer requirement. Because more than half of the employees receive their meal for the convenience of the employer, all 12 employees qualify for exclusion treatment. ■

Required as a Condition of Employment

The *employee is required to accept* test applies only to lodging. If the employee's use of the housing would serve the convenience of the employer, but the employee is not required to use the housing, the exclusion is not available.

EXAMPLE 19

VEP, a utilities company, has all of its service personnel on 24-hour call for emergencies. The company encourages its employees to live near the plant so that the employees can respond quickly to emergency calls. Company-owned housing is available rent-free. Only 10 of the employees live in the company housing because it is not suitable for families.

Although the company-provided housing serves the convenience of the employer, it is not required. Therefore, the employees who live in the company housing cannot exclude its value from gross income. ■

In addition, if the employee has the *option* of cash or lodging, the *required* test is not satisfied.

EXAMPLE 20

Khalid is the manager of a large apartment complex. The employer gives Khalid the option of rent-free housing (value of $6,000 per year) or an additional $5,000 per year. Khalid selects the housing option. Therefore, he must include $6,000 in gross income. ■

[40] *J. B. Lindeman*, 60 T.C. 609 (1973).

[41] Reg. § 1.119–1(f).

[42] § 119(b)(4).

OTHER HOUSING EXCLUSIONS

Employees of Educational Institutions

An employee of an educational institution may be able to exclude the value of campus housing provided by the employer. Generally, the employee does not recognize income if he or she pays annual rents equal to or greater than 5 percent of the appraised value of the facility. If the rent payments are less than 5 percent of the value of the facility, the deficiency must be included in gross income.[43]

EXAMPLE 21

Swan University provides on-campus housing for its full-time faculty during the first three years of employment. The housing is not provided for the convenience of the employer. Professor Edith pays $3,000 annual rent for the use of a residence with an appraised value of $100,000 and an annual rental value of $12,000. Edith must recognize $2,000 of gross income [.05($100,000) – $3,000 = $2,000] for the value of the housing provided to her. ■

Ministers of the Gospel

Ministers of the gospel and other religious leaders can exclude (1) the rental value of a home furnished as compensation; (2) a rental allowance paid to them as compensation, to the extent the allowance is used to rent or provide a home; or (3) the rental value of a home owned by the minister.[44] The housing or housing allowance must be provided as compensation for the conduct of religious worship, the administration and maintenance of religious organizations, or the performance of teaching and administrative duties at theological seminaries.

EXAMPLE 22

Pastor Bill is allowed to live rent-free in a house owned by the congregation. The annual rental value of the house is $6,000 and is provided as part of the pastor's compensation for ministerial services. Assistant Pastor Olga is paid a $4,500 cash housing allowance. She uses the $4,500 to pay rent and utilities on a home she and her family occupy. Neither Pastor Bill nor Assistant Pastor Olga is required to recognize gross income associated with the housing or housing allowance. ■

Military Personnel

Military personnel are allowed housing exclusions under various circumstances. Authority for these exclusions generally is found in Federal laws that are not part of the Internal Revenue Code.[45]

5.9 Other Employee Fringe Benefits

SPECIFIC BENEFITS

Congress has enacted exclusions to encourage employers to (1) finance and make available child care facilities, (2) provide athletic facilities for employees, (3) finance certain employees' education, and (4) pay or reimburse child adoption expenses. These provisions are summarized as follows:

- The employee does not have to include in gross income the value of child and dependent care services paid for by the employer and incurred to enable the employee to work. The exclusion cannot exceed $5,000 per year ($2,500 if married and filing separately). For a married couple, the annual

[43] § 119(d).

[44] § 107 and Reg. § 1.107–1.

[45] H. Rep. No. 99–841, 99th Cong., 2d Sess., p. 548 (1986). See also § 134.

exclusion cannot exceed the earned income of the spouse who has the lesser amount of earned income. For an unmarried taxpayer, the exclusion cannot exceed the taxpayer's earned income.[46]

- The value of the use of a gymnasium or other athletic facilities by employees, their spouses, and their dependent children may be excluded from an employee's gross income. The facilities must be on the employer's premises, and substantially all of the use of the facilities must be by employees and their family members.[47]
- Qualified employer-provided educational assistance (tuition, fees, books, and supplies) at the undergraduate and graduate level is excludible from gross income. The exclusion does not cover meals, lodging, and transportation costs. In addition, it does not cover educational payments for courses involving sports, games, or hobbies. The exclusion is subject to an annual employee statutory ceiling of $5,250.[48]
- The employee can exclude from gross income up to $13,360 of expenses incurred to adopt a child where the adoption expenses are paid or reimbursed by the employer under a qualified adoption assistance program.[49] The limit on the exclusion is the same even if the child has special needs (is not physically or mentally capable of caring for himself or herself). However, for a child with special needs, the $13,360 exclusion from gross income applies even if the actual adoption expenses are less than that amount. The exclusion is phased out as adjusted gross income increases from $185,210 to $225,210.

CAFETERIA PLANS

Generally, if an employee is offered a choice between cash and some other form of compensation, the employee is deemed to have constructively received the cash even when the noncash option is elected. Thus, the employee has gross income regardless of the option chosen.

An exception to this constructive receipt treatment is provided under the **cafeteria plan** rules. Under such a plan, the employee is permitted to choose between cash and nontaxable benefits (e.g., group term life insurance, health and accident protection, and child care). If the employee chooses the otherwise nontaxable benefits, the cafeteria plan rules enable the benefits to remain nontaxable.[50] Cafeteria plans provide tremendous flexibility in tailoring the employee pay package to fit individual needs. Some employees (usually the younger group) prefer cash, while others (usually the older group) will opt for the fringe benefit program. However, Congress excluded long-term care insurance from the excludible benefits that can be provided under a cafeteria plan.[51] Thus, the employer must provide these benefits separate from the cafeteria plan.

EXAMPLE 23

Hawk Corporation offers its employees (on a nondiscriminatory basis) a choice of any one or all of the following benefits:

Benefit	Cost
Group term life insurance	$ 200
Hospitalization insurance for family members	2,400
Child care payments	1,800
	$4,400

[46] § 129. The exclusion applies to the same types of expenses that, if they were paid by the employee (and not reimbursed by the employer), would be eligible for the credit for child and dependent care expense discussed in Chapter 12.

[47] § 132(j)(4).

[48] § 127.

[49] § 137.

[50] § 125.

[51] § 125(f).

If a benefit is not selected, the employee receives cash equal to the cost of the benefit. Kay, an employee, has a spouse who works for another employer that provides hospitalization insurance but no child care payments. Kay elects to receive the group term life insurance, the child care payments, and $2,400 of cash. Only the $2,400 must be included in Kay's gross income. ■

FLEXIBLE SPENDING PLANS

Flexible spending plans (often referred to as flexible benefit plans) operate much like cafeteria plans. Under these plans, the employee accepts lower cash compensation in return for the employer agreeing to pay certain costs that the employer can pay without the employee recognizing gross income. For example, assume the employer's health insurance policy does not cover dental expenses. The employee could estimate his or her dental expenses for the upcoming year and agree to a salary reduction equal to the estimated dental expenses. The employer then pays or reimburses the employee for the actual dental expenses incurred, with a ceiling of the amount of the salary reduction. If the employee's actual dental expenses are less than the reduction in cash compensation, the employee cannot recover the difference. Hence, these plans are often referred to as *use or lose* plans. As is the case for cafeteria plans, flexible spending plans cannot be used to pay long-term care insurance premiums.

Under recently issued IRS rules for these *use or lose* plans, the taxpayer has until the fifteenth day of the third month after the end of the plan year to use the funds for qualified expenses (a two and one-half month grace period). Employers have generally amended their plans to provide that payments made during the grace period will be taken first from the balance in the flexible spending account at the beginning of the plan year.

GENERAL CLASSES OF EXCLUDED BENEFITS

An employer can confer numerous forms and types of economic benefits on employees. Under the all-inclusive concept of income, the benefits are taxable unless one of the provisions previously discussed specifically excludes the item from gross income. The amount of the income is the fair market value of the benefit. This reasoning can lead to results that Congress considers unacceptable, as illustrated in the following example.

EXAMPLE 24

Vern is employed in New York as a ticket clerk for Trans National Airlines. He has a sick mother in Miami, Florida, but has no money for plane tickets. Trans National has daily flights from New York to Miami that often leave with empty seats. The cost of a round-trip ticket is $400, and Vern is in the 25% tax bracket. If Trans National allows Vern to fly without charge to Miami, under the general gross income rules, Vern has income equal to the value of a ticket. Therefore, Vern must pay $100 tax (.25 × $400) on a trip to Miami. Because Vern does not have $100, he cannot visit his mother, and the airplane flies with another empty seat. ■

If Trans National in Example 24 will allow employees to use resources that would otherwise be wasted, why should the tax laws interfere with the employee's decision to take advantage of the available benefit? Thus, to avoid the undesirable results that occur in Example 24 and in similar situations, as well as to create uniform rules for fringe benefits, Congress established seven broad classes of nontaxable employee benefits:[52]

- No-additional-cost services.
- Qualified employee discounts.
- Working condition fringes.
- *De minimis* fringes.
- Qualified transportation fringes.
- Qualified moving expense reimbursements.
- Qualified retirement planning services.

[52]See, generally, § 132.

TAX in the NEWS

Patient Protection and Affordable Care Act of 2010 to Affect Flexible Spending Plans

Determining all of the tax ramifications of the 2010 health care law will take time. But already it is clear that companies will be modifying their flexible spending plans as a result of the legislation. Beginning in 2013, the annual income exclusion under flexible benefit plans will be limited to $2,500.

Also, in 2011 and subsequent years, with respect to medicines, only prescription drugs and insulin will be eligible for reimbursement.

Source: Internal Revenue Code §§ 125(i) and 106(f).

No-Additional-Cost Services

Example 24 illustrates the **no-additional-cost service** type of fringe benefit. The services will be nontaxable if all of the following conditions are satisfied:

- The employee receives services, as opposed to property.
- The employer does not incur substantial additional cost, including forgone revenue, in providing the services to the employee.
- The services are offered to customers in the ordinary course of the business in which the employee works.[53]

EXAMPLE 25

Assume that Vern in Example 24 can fly without charge only if the airline cannot fill the seats with paying customers. That is, Vern must fly on standby. Although the airplane may burn slightly more fuel because Vern is on the airplane and Vern may receive the same meal or snacks as paying customers, the additional costs would not be substantial. Thus, the trip could qualify as a no-additional-cost service.

On the other hand, assume that Vern is given a reserved seat on a flight that is frequently full. The employer would be forgoing revenue to allow Vern to fly. This forgone revenue would be a substantial additional cost, and thus the benefit would be taxable. ■

Note that if Vern were employed in a hotel owned by Trans National, the receipt of the airline ticket would be taxable because Vern did not work in that line of business. However, the Code allows the exclusion for reciprocal benefits offered by employers in the same line of business.

EXAMPLE 26

Grace is employed as a desk clerk for Plush Hotels, Inc. The company and Chain Hotels, Inc., have an agreement that allows any of their employees to stay without charge in either company's resort hotels during the off-season. If Grace takes advantage of the plan by staying in a Chain Hotel, she is not required to recognize income. ■

The no-additional-cost exclusion extends to the employee's spouse and dependent children and to retired and disabled former employees. In the Regulations, the IRS has conceded that partners who perform services for the partnership are employees for purposes of the exclusion.[54] (As discussed earlier in the chapter, the IRS's position is that partners are not employees for purposes of the § 119 meals and lodging exclusion.) However, the exclusion is not allowed to highly compensated employees unless the benefit is available on a nondiscriminatory basis.

Qualified Employee Discounts

When the employer sells goods or services (other than no-additional-cost benefits just discussed) to the employee for a price that is less than the price charged regular

[53] Reg. § 1.132–2.

[54] Reg. § 1.132–1(b).

customers, the employee realizes income equal to the discount. However, the discount, referred to as a **qualified employee discount**, can be excluded from the gross income of the employee, subject to the following conditions and limitations:

- The exclusion is not available for real property (e.g., a house) or for personal property of the type commonly held for investment (e.g., common stocks).
- The property or services must be from the same line of business in which the employee works.
- In the case of *property*, the exclusion is limited to the *gross profit component* of the price to customers.
- In the case of *services*, the exclusion is limited to 20 percent of the customer price.[55]

EXAMPLE 27

Silver Corporation, which operates a department store, sells a television set to a store employee for $300. The regular customer price is $500, and the gross profit rate is 25%. The corporation also sells the employee a service contract for $120. The regular customer price for the contract is $150. The employee must include $75 in gross income.

Customer price for property	$ 500
Less: Gross profit (25%)	(125)
	$ 375
Employee price	(300)
Income	$ 75
Customer price for service	$ 150
Less: 20 percent	(30)
	$ 120
Employee price	(120)
Income	$ -0-

■

EXAMPLE 28

Assume the same facts as in Example 27, except that the employee is a clerk in a hotel operated by Silver Corporation. Because the line of business requirement is not met, the employee must recognize $200 income ($500 – $300) from the purchase of the television and $30 income ($150 – $120) from the service contract. ■

As in the case of no-additional-cost benefits, the exclusion applies to employees (including service partners), employees' spouses and dependent children, and retired and disabled former employees. However, the exclusion does not apply to highly compensated individuals unless the discount is available on a nondiscriminatory basis.

Working Condition Fringes

Generally, an employee is not required to include in gross income the cost of property or services provided by the employer if the employee could deduct the cost of those items if he or she had actually paid for them.[56] These benefits are called **working condition fringes.**

EXAMPLE 29

Mitch is a CPA employed by an accounting firm. The employer pays Mitch's annual dues to professional organizations. Mitch is not required to include the payment of the dues in gross income because if he had paid the dues, he would have been allowed to deduct the amount as an employee business expense (as discussed in Chapter 9). ■

In many cases, this exclusion merely avoids reporting income and an offsetting deduction. However, in two specific situations, the working condition fringe benefit rules allow an exclusion where the expense would not be deductible if paid by the employee:

[55] § 132(c).

[56] § 132(d).

- Automobile salespeople are allowed to exclude the value of certain personal use of company demonstrators (e.g., commuting to and from work).[57]
- The employee business expense would be eliminated by the 2 percent floor on miscellaneous itemized deductions under § 67 (see Chapter 10).

Unlike the other fringe benefits discussed previously, working condition fringes can be made available on a discriminatory basis and still qualify for the exclusion.

De Minimis *Fringes*

As the term suggests, ***de minimis* fringe** benefits are so small that accounting for them is impractical.[58] The House Report contains the following examples of *de minimis* fringes:

- The typing of a personal letter by a company secretary, occasional personal use of a company copying machine, occasional company cocktail parties or picnics for employees, occasional supper money or taxi fare for employees because of overtime work, and certain holiday gifts of property with a low fair market value are excluded.
- Subsidized eating facilities (e.g., an employees' cafeteria) operated by the employer are excluded if located on or near the employer's business premises, if revenue equals or exceeds direct operating costs, and if nondiscrimination requirements are met.

When taxpayers venture beyond the specific examples contained in the House Report and the Regulations, there is obviously much room for disagreement as to what is *de minimis.* However, note that except in the case of subsidized eating facilities, the *de minimis* fringe benefits can be granted in a manner that favors highly compensated employees.

Qualified Transportation Fringes

The intent of the exclusion for **qualified transportation fringes** is to encourage the use of mass transit for commuting to and from work. Qualified transportation fringes encompass the following transportation benefits provided by the employer to the employee:[59]

1. Transportation in a commuter highway vehicle between the employee's residence and the place of employment.
2. A transit pass.
3. Qualified parking.
4. Qualified bicycle commuting reimbursement.

Statutory dollar limits are placed on the amount of the exclusion. Categories (1) and (2) above are combined for purposes of applying the limit. In this case, the limit on the exclusion for 2010 was $230 and for 2011 is $230. Category (3) has a separate limit. For qualified parking, the limit on the exclusion for 2011 is $230 per month ($230 in 2010). Both of these dollar limits are indexed annually for inflation.

A *commuter highway vehicle* is any highway vehicle with a seating capacity of at least six adults (excluding the driver). In addition, at least 80 percent of the vehicle's use must be for transporting employees between their residences and place of employment.

Qualified parking includes the following:

- Parking provided to an employee on or near the employer's business premises.
- Parking provided to an employee on or near a location from which the employee commutes to work via mass transit, in a commuter highway vehicle, or in a carpool.

[57] § 132(j)(3).

[58] § 132(e).

[59] § 132(f).

The *qualified bicycle commuting reimbursement* enables an employee to exclude up to $20 per month received from an employer as reimbursement for the cost of commuting by bicycle (i.e., bicycle purchase, improvement, repair, and storage).

Qualified transportation fringes may be provided directly by the employer or may be in the form of cash reimbursements.

EXAMPLE 30

Gray Corporation's offices are located in the center of a large city. The company pays for parking spaces to be used by the company officers. Steve, a vice president, receives $250 of such benefits each month. The parking space rental qualifies as a qualified transportation fringe. Of the $250 benefit received each month by Steve, $230 is excludible from gross income. The balance of $20 is included in his gross income. The same result would occur if Steve paid for the parking and was reimbursed by his employer. ■

Qualified Moving Expense Reimbursements

Qualified moving expenses that are reimbursed or paid by the employer are excludible from gross income. A qualified moving expense is one that would be deductible under § 217. See the discussion of moving expenses in Chapter 9.

Qualified Retirement Planning Services

Qualified retirement planning services include any retirement planning advice or information that an employer who maintains a qualified retirement plan provides to an employee or the employee's spouse.[60] Congress decided to exclude the value of such services from gross income because they are a key part of retirement income planning. Such an exclusion should motivate more employers to provide retirement planning services to their employees.

Nondiscrimination Provisions

For no-additional-cost services, qualified employee discounts, and qualified retirement planning services, if the plan is discriminatory in favor of highly compensated employees, these key employees are denied exclusion treatment. However, the non-highly compensated employees who receive benefits from the plan can still enjoy exclusion treatment for the no-additional-cost services, qualified employee discounts, and qualified retirement planning services.[61]

EXAMPLE 31

Dove Company's officers are allowed to purchase goods from the company at a 25% discount. Other employees are allowed only a 15% discount. The company's gross profit margin on these goods is 30%.

Peggy, an officer in the company, purchased goods from the company for $750 when the price charged to customers was $1,000. Peggy must include $250 in gross income because the plan is discriminatory.

Leo, an employee of the company who is not an officer, purchased goods for $850 when the customer price was $1,000. Leo is not required to recognize gross income because he received a qualified employee discount. ■

De minimis (except in the case of subsidized eating facilities) and working condition fringe benefits can be provided on a discriminatory basis. The *de minimis* benefits are not subject to tax because the accounting problems that would be created are out of proportion to the amount of additional tax that would result. A nondiscrimination test would simply add to the compliance problems. In the case of working condition fringes, the types of services required vary with the job. Therefore, a nondiscrimination test probably could not be satisfied, although usually there is no deliberate plan to benefit a chosen few. Likewise, the qualified transportation fringe and the qualified moving expense reimbursement can be provided on a discriminatory basis.

[60] §§ 132(a)(7) and (m).

[61] §§ 132(j)(1) and 132(m)(2).

TAXABLE FRINGE BENEFITS

If the fringe benefits cannot qualify for any of the specific exclusions or do not fit into any of the general classes of excluded benefits, the taxpayer must recognize gross income equal to the fair market value of the benefits. Obviously, problems are frequently encountered in determining values. The IRS has issued extensive Regulations addressing the valuation of personal use of an employer's automobiles and meals provided at an employer-operated eating facility.[62]

If a fringe benefit plan discriminates in favor of highly compensated employees, generally those employees are not allowed to exclude the benefits they receive that other employees do not enjoy. However, the highly compensated employees, as well as the other employees, are generally allowed to exclude the nondiscriminatory benefits.[63]

EXAMPLE 32

MED Company has a medical reimbursement plan that reimburses officers for 100% of their medical expenses, but reimburses all other employees for only 80% of their medical expenses. Cliff, the president of the company, was reimbursed $1,000 during the year for medical expenses. Cliff must include $200 in gross income [(1 – .80) × $1,000 = $200]. Mike, an employee who is not an officer, received $800 (80% of his actual medical expenses) under the medical reimbursement plan. None of the $800 is includible in his gross income. ■

5.10 Foreign Earned Income

A U.S. citizen is generally subject to U.S. tax on his or her income regardless of the income's geographic origin. The income may also be subject to tax in the foreign country, and thus the taxpayer must carry a double tax burden. Out of a sense of fairness and to encourage U.S. citizens to work abroad (so that exports might be increased), Congress has provided alternative forms of relief from taxes on foreign earned income. The taxpayer can elect *either* (1) to include the foreign income in his or her taxable income and then claim a credit for foreign taxes paid or (2) to exclude the foreign earnings from his or her U.S. gross income (the **foreign earned income exclusion**).[64] The foreign tax credit option is discussed in Chapter 12, but as is apparent from the following discussion, most taxpayers will choose the exclusion.

Foreign earned income consists of the earnings from the individual's personal services rendered in a foreign country (other than as an employee of the U.S. government). To qualify for the exclusion, the taxpayer must be either of the following:

- A bona fide resident of the foreign country (or countries).
- Present in a foreign country (or countries) for at least 330 days during any 12 consecutive months.[65]

EXAMPLE 33

Sandra's trips to and from a foreign country in connection with her work were as follows:

Arrived in Foreign Country	Arrived in United States
March 10, 2010	February 1, 2011
March 7, 2011	June 1, 2011

[62]Reg. § 1.61–21(d). Generally, the income from the personal use of the employer's automobile is based on the lease value of the automobile (what it would have cost the employee to lease the automobile). Meals are valued at 150% of the employer's direct costs (e.g., food and labor) of preparing the meals.

[63]§§ 79(d), 105(h), 127(b)(2), and 132(j)(1).

[64]§ 911(a).

[65]§ 911(d). For the definition of resident, see Reg. § 1.871–2(b). Under the Regulations, a taxpayer is not a resident if he or she is there for a definite period (e.g., until completion of a construction contract).

CONCEPT SUMMARY 5.2

General Classes of Excluded Benefits

Benefit	Description and Examples	Coverage Allowed	Effect of Discrimination
1. No-additional-cost services	The employee takes advantage of the employer's excess capacity (e.g., free passes for airline employees).	Current, retired, and disabled employees; their spouses and dependent children; spouses of deceased employees. Partners are treated as employees.	No exclusion for highly compensated employees.
2. Qualified discounts on goods	The employee is allowed to purchase the employer's merchandise at a price that is not less than the employer's cost.	Same as (1) above.	Same as (1) above.
3. Qualified discounts on services	The employee is allowed a discount (maximum of 20%) on services the employer offers to customers.	Same as (1) above.	Same as (1) above.
4. Working condition fringes	Expenses paid by the employer that would be deductible if paid by the employee (e.g., a mechanic's tools). Also, includes auto salesperson's use of a car held for sale.	Current employees, partners, directors, and independent contractors.	No effect.
5. *De minimis* items	Expenses so immaterial that accounting for them is not warranted (e.g., occasional supper money, personal use of the copy machine).	*Any recipient* of a fringe benefit.	No effect.
6. Qualified transportation fringes	Transportation benefits provided by the employer to employees including commuting in a commuter highway vehicle, a transit pass, qualified parking, and qualified bicycle commuting.	Current employees.	No effect.
7. Qualified moving expense reimbursements	Qualified moving expenses that are paid or reimbursed by the employer. A qualified moving expense is one that would be deductible under § 217.	Current employees.	No effect.
8. Qualified retirement planning services	Qualified retirement planning services that are provided by the employer.	Current employees and spouses.	Same as (1) above.

During the 12 consecutive months ending on March 10, 2011, Sandra was present in the foreign country for at least 330 days (365 days less 28 days in February and 7 days in March 2011). Therefore, all income earned in the foreign country through March 10, 2011, is eligible for the exclusion. The income earned from March 11, 2011, through May 31, 2011, is also eligible for the exclusion because Sandra was present in the foreign country for 330 days during the 12 consecutive months ending on May 31, 2011. ■

The exclusion is *limited* to an indexed amount of $92,900 for 2011 ($91,500 in 2010). For married persons, both of whom have foreign earned income, the

GLOBAL
Tax Issues

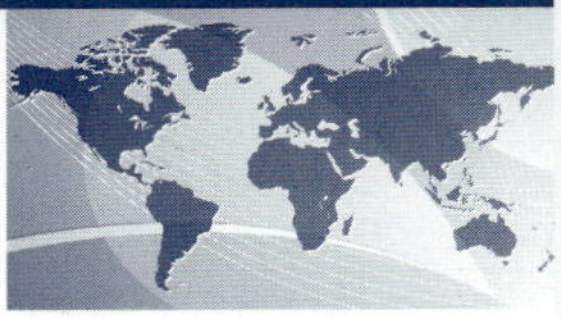

U.S. Taxpayers Abroad Are Gone but Not Forgotten

U.S. citizens and residents working and living abroad create unique compliance issues for the IRS. These individuals are potentially liable for U.S. taxes and must file U.S. tax returns, even if they earn less than the foreign earned income exclusion amount. However, in practical terms, many of these individuals are outside the enforcement net of the IRS. In recent years, the IRS has taken several steps to improve compliance, including taxpayer education, simplification of the filing burden, and increased enforcement efforts.

exclusion is computed separately for each spouse. Community property rules do not apply (the community property spouse is not deemed to have earned one-half of the other spouse's foreign earned income). If all the days in the tax year are not qualifying days, then the taxpayer must compute the maximum exclusion on a daily basis ($92,900 divided by the number of days in the entire year and multiplied by the number of qualifying days).

EXAMPLE 34

Keith qualifies for the foreign earned income exclusion. He was present in France for all of 2011. Keith's salary for 2011 is $100,000. Since all of the days in 2011 are qualifying days, Keith can exclude $92,900 of his $100,000 salary.

Assume instead that only 335 days were qualifying days. Then, Keith's exclusion is limited to $85,264, computed as follows:

$$\$92{,}900 \times \frac{\text{335 days in foreign country}}{\text{365 days in the year}} = \$85{,}264$$

■

Some tax policy experts believe that the nation's benefits from the foreign earned income exclusion are not worth the loss of revenues. Rather than eliminating the exclusion, Congress recently decreased its benefit by requiring a special tax computation. The tax on the taxable income after the foreign earned income exclusion is calculated using the tax rate that would apply if the excluded foreign earned income were included in gross income.

EXAMPLE 35

In 2011, Carol, who is not married, had taxable income of $89,450 after excluding $83,600 of foreign earned income. Without the benefit of the exclusion, Carol's taxable income would have been $173,050 ($83,600 + $89,450). The tax on the taxable income of $89,450 is calculated using the marginal rate applicable to income between $83,600 and $173,050, which is 28%. Therefore, Carol's tax liability is $25,046 (.28 × $89,450). ■

In addition to the exclusion for foreign earnings, the *reasonable housing costs* incurred by the taxpayer and the taxpayer's family in a foreign country in excess of a base amount may be excluded from gross income. The base amount is 16 percent of the statutory amount (indexed amount for 2011 is $92,900) assuming all of the days are qualifying days for the foreign earned income exclusion. The housing costs exclusion is limited to 30 percent of the statutory amount (as indexed) for the foreign earned income exclusion.[66]

As previously mentioned, the taxpayer may elect to include the foreign earned income in gross income and claim a credit (an offset against U.S. tax) for the foreign tax paid. The credit alternative may be advantageous if the individual's foreign earned income far exceeds the excludible amount so that the foreign taxes paid exceed the U.S. tax on the amount excluded. However, once an election is made, it applies to all subsequent years unless affirmatively revoked. A revocation is effective for the year of the change and the four subsequent years.

[66]§ 911(c).

TAX *in* the NEWS

To Qualify for the Foreign Earned Income Exclusion, You Must Work in a "Country"

Mr. Arnett found out that to qualify for the foreign earned income exclusion, it is not sufficient that where you work is "foreign"—you must also work in a country. Mr. Arnett worked in Antarctica for the requisite period of time, but the court concluded that the term "foreign country" means a territory under the sovereignty of a government other than that of the United States. Under various treaties, Antarctica is not under the sovereignty of any government. Therefore, Mr. Arnett did not qualify for the foreign earned income exclusion. Apparently, the exclusion would also be denied to a person working in outer space (i.e., at the International Space Station).

Source: *Arnett v. Comm.*, 99 AFTR 2d 2007–492, 473 F.3d 790 (CA–7, 2007).

5.11 Interest on Certain State and Local Government Obligations

At the time the Sixteenth Amendment was ratified by the states, there was some question as to whether the Federal government possessed the constitutional authority to tax interest on state and local government obligations. Taxing such interest was thought to violate the doctrine of intergovernmental immunity in that the tax would impair the state and local governments' ability to finance their operations.[67] Thus, interest on state and local government obligations was specifically exempted from Federal income taxation.[68] However, the Supreme Court has concluded that there is no constitutional prohibition against levying a nondiscriminatory Federal income tax on state and local government obligations.[69] Nevertheless, currently the statutory exclusion still exists.

Obviously, the exclusion of the interest reduces the cost of borrowing for state and local governments. A taxpayer in the 35 percent tax bracket requires only a 5.2 percent yield on a tax-exempt bond to obtain the same after-tax income as a taxable bond paying 8 percent interest [5.2% ÷ (1 − .35) = 8%].

The current exempt status applies solely to state and local government bonds. Thus, income received from the accrual of interest on a condemnation award or an overpayment of state income tax is fully taxable.[70] Nor does the exemption apply to gains on the sale of tax-exempt securities.

EXAMPLE 36

Megan purchases State of Virginia bonds for $10,000 on July 1, 2010. The bonds pay $400 interest each June 30th and December 31st. On March 31, 2011, Megan sells the bonds for $10,500 plus $200 accrued interest. Megan must recognize a $500 gain ($10,500 − $10,000), but the $200 accrued interest is exempt from taxation. ■

Although the Internal Revenue Code excludes from Federal gross income the interest on state and local government bonds, the interest on U.S. government bonds is not excluded from the Federal tax base. Congress has decided, however, that if the Federal government is not to tax state and local bond interest, the state and local governments are prohibited from taxing interest on U.S. government bonds.[71] While this parity between the Federal and state and local governments exists in regard to taxing each others' obligations, the states are free to tax one another's

[67] *Pollock v. Farmer's Loan & Trust Co.*, 3 AFTR 2602, 15 S.Ct. 912 (USSC, 1895).

[68] § 103(a).

[69] *South Carolina v. Baker III*, 88–1 USTC ¶9284, 61 AFTR 2d 88–995, 108 S.Ct. 1355 (USSC, 1988).

[70] *Kieselbach v. Comm.*, 43–1 USTC ¶9220, 30 AFTR 370, 63 S.Ct. 303 (USSC, 1943); *U.S. Trust Co. of New York v. Anderson*, 3 USTC ¶1125, 12 AFTR 836, 65 F.2d 575 (CA–2, 1933).

[71] 31 U.S.C.A. § 742.

TAX *in* the NEWS

U.S. Supreme Court Rules on State Taxation of Other States' Interest

Like many other states, Kentucky exempts from taxation interest earned on its own state bonds, but taxes its residents on interest income received from bonds issued by other states. A married couple residing in Kentucky challenged the law as unconstitutionally discriminating against interstate commerce by treating Kentucky bonds more favorably than the bonds issued by other states. The U.S. Supreme Court ruled in favor of Kentucky, thus permitting the state (and the 41 other states with similar laws) to tax the out-of-state bond interest while exempting Kentucky bond interest.

This is a very important case because many taxpayers invest in state and local bond funds. These funds often purchase bonds issued by several states. Although the interest from all of the state bonds is generally exempt from Federal income tax, the investor may owe state income tax to the state of residence on the interest received on the bonds of other states. Thus, the bond fund must inform the investor of the amount of interest income earned from the bonds issued by the various states.

Source: *Department of Revenue of Kentucky v. Davis,* 128 S.Ct. 1801 (USSC, 2008).

obligations. Thus, some states exempt the interest on the bonds they issue, but tax the interest on bonds issued by other states.[72]

EXAMPLE 37

Aaron is a resident of Virginia. He owns U.S. government bonds that paid him $800 interest during the current year. He also invests in American States Bond Fund, which reports to Aaron that his share of Virginia interest income is $300 and his share of interest income from other states is $600. Aaron must include the $800 in his Federal gross income. Virginia exempts from Virginia taxation the interest on the Virginia bonds, but taxes the interest on bonds issued by other states. Therefore, Aaron must include $600 of interest from other states in his Virginia gross income. ■

5.12 Dividends

GENERAL INFORMATION

A *dividend* is a payment to a shareholder with respect to his or her stock (see Chapters 4 and 19). Dividends to shareholders are taxable only to the extent the payments are made from *either* the corporation's *current earnings and profits* (similar to net income per books) or its *accumulated earnings and profits* (similar to retained earnings per books).[73] Distributions that exceed earnings and profits are treated as a nontaxable recovery of capital and reduce the shareholder's basis in the stock. Once the shareholder's basis is reduced to zero, any subsequent distributions are taxed as capital gains (see Chapter 13).[74]

Some payments are frequently referred to as dividends but are not considered dividends for tax purposes:

- Dividends received on deposits with savings and loan associations, credit unions, and banks are actually interest (a contractual rate paid for the use of money).
- Patronage dividends paid by cooperatives (e.g., for farmers) are rebates made to the users and are considered reductions in the cost of items purchased from the association. The rebates are usually made after year-end (after the cooperative has determined whether it has met its expenses) and are apportioned among members on the basis of their purchases.

[72]The practice of a state exempting interest on its bonds from tax but taxing the interest on bonds issued by other states was upheld by the Supreme Court in 2008. See the "Tax in the News" entitled "U.S. Supreme Court Rules on State Taxation of Other States' Interest."

[73]§ 316(a). Refer to the discussion of the beneficial tax rates for qualified dividends in Chapter 4.

[74]§ 301(c). See Chapter 19 for a detailed discussion of corporate distributions.

- Mutual insurance companies pay dividends on unmatured life insurance policies that are considered rebates of premiums.
- Shareholders in a mutual investment fund are allowed to report as capital gains their proportionate share of the fund's gains realized and distributed. The capital gain and ordinary income portions are reported on the Form 1099 that the fund supplies its shareholders each year.

STOCK DIVIDENDS

When a corporation issues a simple stock dividend (e.g., common stock issued to common shareholders), the shareholder has merely received additional shares that represent the same total investment. Thus, the shareholder does not realize income.[75] However, if the shareholder has the *option* of receiving either cash or stock in the corporation, the individual realizes gross income whether he or she receives stock or cash.[76] A taxpayer who elects to receive the stock could be deemed to be in constructive receipt of the cash he or she has rejected.[77] However, the amount of the income in this case is the value of the stock received, rather than the cash the shareholder has rejected. See Chapters 13 and 19 for a detailed discussion of stock dividends.

5.13 Educational Savings Bonds

The cost of a college education has risen dramatically during the past 15 years. According to U.S. Department of Education estimates, the cost of attending a publicly supported university for four years now commonly exceeds $60,000. For a private university, the cost often exceeds $200,000. Consequently, Congress has attempted to assist low- to middle-income parents in saving for their children's college education.

The assistance is in the form of an interest income exclusion on **educational savings bonds.**[78] The interest on Series EE U.S. government savings bonds may be excluded from gross income if the bond proceeds are used to pay qualified higher education expenses. The exclusion applies only if both of the following requirements are satisfied:

- The savings bonds are issued after December 31, 1989.
- The savings bonds are issued to an individual who is at least 24 years old at the time of issuance.

The exclusion is not available for a married couple who file separate returns.

The redemption proceeds must be used to pay qualified higher education expenses. *Qualified higher education expenses* consist of tuition and fees paid to an eligible educational institution for the taxpayer, spouse, or dependent. In calculating qualified higher education expenses, the tuition and fees paid are reduced by excludible scholarships and veterans' benefits received. If the redemption proceeds (both principal and interest) exceed the qualified higher education expenses, only a pro rata portion of the interest will qualify for exclusion treatment.

EXAMPLE 38

Tracy's redemption proceeds from qualified savings bonds during the taxable year are $6,000 (principal of $4,000 and interest of $2,000). Tracy's qualified higher education expenses are $5,000. Since the redemption proceeds exceed the qualified higher education expenses, only $1,667 [($5,000/$6,000) × $2,000] of the interest is excludible. ■

The exclusion is limited by the application of the wherewithal to pay concept. That is, once the modified adjusted gross income exceeds a threshold amount, the phaseout of the exclusion begins. *Modified adjusted gross income* (*MAGI*) is adjusted gross income prior to the § 911 foreign earned income exclusion and the

[75] *Eisner v. Macomber*, 1 USTC ¶32, 3 AFTR 3020, 40 S.Ct. 189 (USSC, 1920); § 305(a).

[76] § 305(b).

[77] Refer to the discussion of constructive receipt in Chapter 4.

[78] § 135.

educational savings bond exclusion. The threshold amounts are adjusted for inflation each year. For 2011, the phaseout begins at $71,100 ($106,650 on a joint return).[79] The phaseout is completed when MAGI exceeds the threshold amount by more than $15,000 ($30,000 on a joint return). The otherwise excludible interest is reduced by the amount calculated as follows:

$$\frac{\text{MAGI} - \$71{,}100}{\$15{,}000} \times \begin{array}{c}\text{Excludible interest}\\ \text{before phaseout}\end{array} = \begin{array}{c}\text{Reduction in}\\ \text{excludible interest}\end{array}$$

On a joint return, $106,650 is substituted for $71,100 (in 2011), and $30,000 is substituted for $15,000.

EXAMPLE 39

Assume the same facts as in Example 38, except that Tracy's MAGI for 2011 is $80,000. The phaseout results in Tracy's interest exclusion being reduced by $989 {[($80,000 – $71,100)/$15,000] × $1,667}. Therefore, Tracy's exclusion is $678 ($1,667 – $989). ■

5.14 Qualified Tuition Programs (§ 529 Plans)

Nearly all, if not all, states have created programs whereby parents can in effect prepay their child's college tuition. The prepayment serves as a hedge against future increases in tuition. Generally, if the child does not attend college, the parents are refunded their payments plus interest. Upon first impression, these prepaid tuition programs resemble the below-market loans discussed in Chapter 4. That is, assuming the tuition increases, the parent receives a reduction in the child's tuition in exchange for the use of the funds. However, Congress has created an exclusion provision for these programs.[80]

Under a **qualified tuition program (§ 529 plan)**, the amounts contributed must be used for qualified higher education expenses. These expenses include tuition, fees, books, supplies, room and board, and equipment required for enrollment or attendance at a college, university, or certain vocational schools. Under ARRTA of 2009, the allowable expenses are extended to computers and computer technology, including software that provides access to the Internet. Qualified higher education expenses also include the expenses for special needs services that are incurred in connection with the enrollment and attendance of special needs students.

The earnings of the contributed funds, including the discount on tuition charged to participants, are not included in Federal gross income provided that the contributions and earnings are used for qualified higher education expenses. Some states also exclude these educational benefits from state gross income.

EXAMPLE 40

Agnes paid $20,000 into a qualified tuition program to be used for her son's college tuition. When her son graduated from high school, the fund balance had increased to $30,000 as a result of interest credited to the account. The interest was not included in Agnes's gross income. During the current year, $7,500 of the balance in the fund was used to pay the son's tuition and fees. None of this amount is included in either Agnes's or the son's gross income. ■

If the parent receives a refund (e.g., child does not attend college), the excess of the amount refunded over the amount contributed by the parent is included in the parent's gross income.

Qualified tuition programs have been expanded to apply to private educational institutions as well as public educational institutions. Distributions made after December 31, 2003, from such a plan maintained by an entity other than the state for qualified higher education expenses are eligible for exclusion from gross income.

[79] The indexed amounts for 2010 were $70,100 and $105,100.

[80] § 529.

5.15 Tax Benefit Rule

LO.3

Determine the extent to which receipts can be excluded under the tax benefit rule.

Generally, if a taxpayer obtains a deduction for an item in one year and in a later year recovers all or a portion of the prior deduction, the recovery is included in gross income in the year received.[81]

EXAMPLE 41

A taxpayer deducted as a loss a $1,000 receivable from a customer when it appeared the amount would never be collected. The following year, the customer paid $800 on the receivable. The taxpayer must report the $800 as gross income in the year it is received. ■

However, the § 111 **tax benefit rule** provides that no income is recognized upon the recovery of a deduction, or the portion of a deduction, that did not yield a tax benefit in the year it was taken. If the taxpayer in Example 41 had no tax liability in the year of the deduction (e.g., itemized deductions and personal exemptions exceeded adjusted gross income), the recovery would be partially or totally excluded from gross income in the year of the recovery.[82]

EXAMPLE 42

Ali filed his 2010 income tax return as a single individual. His AGI for 2010 was $48,000. He had $6,200 in itemized deductions, including $1,200 in state income tax. His personal exemption was $3,650. In 2011, he received a $700 refund of the state income taxes that he paid in 2010. Because the standard deduction in 2010 was $5,700, the $1,200 of state income taxes Ali paid in 2010 yielded a tax benefit of only $500 ($6,200 itemized deduction − $5,700 standard deduction) in 2010. Under the tax benefit rule, only $500 of the state income tax refund is included in gross income in 2011. ■

5.16 Income from Discharge of Indebtedness

LO.4

Describe the circumstances under which income must be reported from the discharge of indebtedness.

A transfer of appreciated property (fair market value is greater than adjusted basis) in satisfaction of a debt is an event that triggers the realization of income. The transaction is treated as a sale of the appreciated property followed by payment of the debt.[83] Foreclosure by a creditor is also treated as a sale or exchange of the property.[84]

EXAMPLE 43

Juan owes State Bank $100,000 on an unsecured note. He satisfies the note by transferring to the bank common stock with a basis of $60,000 and a fair market value of $100,000. Juan must recognize a $40,000 gain on the transfer. Juan also owes the bank $50,000 on a note secured by land. When Juan's basis in the land is $20,000 and the land's fair market value is $50,000, the bank forecloses on the loan and takes title to the land. Juan must recognize a $30,000 gain on the foreclosure. ■

In some cases, creditors will not exercise their right of foreclosure and will even forgive a portion of the debt to assure the vitality of the debtor. In such cases, the debtor realizes income from discharge of indebtedness.

EXAMPLE 44

Brown Corporation is unable to meet the mortgage payments on its factory building. Both the corporation and the mortgage holder are aware of the depressed market for industrial property in the area. Foreclosure would only result in the creditor's obtaining unsalable property. To improve Brown Corporation's financial position and thus improve Brown's chances of obtaining the additional credit necessary for survival from other lenders, the creditor agrees to forgive all amounts past due and to reduce the principal amount of the mortgage. ■

[81] § 111(a).

[82] Itemized deductions are discussed in Chapter 10.

[83] Reg. § 1.1001–2(a).

[84] *Estate of Delman v. Comm.*, 73 T.C. 15 (1979).

TAX *in* the NEWS

One Way to Avoid Bankruptcy

Many businesses rely heavily on debt obligations (e.g., notes, bonds) to finance their operations. If these obligations come due when other credit sources are scarce and refinancing is not possible, the debtor's default could lead to bankruptcy. To avoid bankruptcy, the debtor may be able to purchase the obligation at a discount. Unfortunately, the discount component constitutes forgiveness of debt and generates income to the business debtor.

In ARRTA of 2009, Congress recognized the problem and provides some relief to the debtor. For repurchases of debt after December 31, 2008, and before January 1, 2011, the debtor may defer income recognition to 2014. Even better, such recognition can be spread over five years. Evidently, Congress is trying to provide the tax incentive that will encourage the repurchase option and discourage the bankruptcy approach.

Generally, the income realized by the debtor from the forgiveness of a debt is taxable.[85] A similar debt discharge (produced by a different creditor motivation) associated with personal use property is illustrated in Example 45.

EXAMPLE 45

In 2006, Joyce borrowed $60,000 from National Bank to purchase her personal residence. Joyce agreed to make monthly principal and interest payments for 15 years. The interest rate on the note was 7%. In 2011, when the balance on the note has been reduced through monthly payments to $48,000, the bank offers to accept $45,000 in full settlement of the note. The bank makes the offer because interest rates have increased to 11%. Joyce accepts the bank's offer. As a result, Joyce must recognize $3,000($48,000 − $45,000) of gross income.[86] ■

The following discharge of indebtedness situations are subject to special treatment:[87]

1. Creditors' gifts.
2. Discharges under Federal bankruptcy law.
3. Discharges that occur when the debtor is insolvent.
4. Discharge of the farm debt of a solvent taxpayer.
5. Discharge of **qualified real property business indebtedness**.
6. A seller's cancellation of the buyer's indebtedness.
7. A shareholder's cancellation of the corporation's indebtedness.
8. Forgiveness of certain loans to students.
9. Discharge of indebtedness on the taxpayer's principal residence that occurs between January 1, 2007, and January 1, 2013, and is the result of the financial condition of the debtor.

If the creditor reduces the debt as an act of *love, affection*, or *generosity*, the debtor has simply received a nontaxable gift (situation 1). Rarely will a gift be found to have occurred in a business context. A businessperson may settle a debt for less than the amount due, but as a matter of business expediency (e.g., high collection costs or disputes as to contract terms) rather than generosity.[88]

In situations 2, 3, 4, 5, and 9, the Code allows the debtor to reduce his or her basis in the assets by the realized gain from the discharge.[89] Thus, the realized gain is merely deferred until the assets are sold (or depreciated). Similarly, in situation 6 (a price reduction), the debtor reduces the basis in the specific assets financed by the seller.[90]

A shareholder's cancellation of the corporation's indebtedness to him or her (situation 7) usually is considered a tax-free contribution of capital to the corporation

[85] *U.S. v. Kirby Lumber Co.*, 2 USTC ¶814, 10 AFTR 458, 52 S.Ct. 4 (USSC, 1931), codified in § 61(a)(12).

[86] Rev.Rul. 82–202, 1982–1 C.B. 35.

[87] §§ 108 and 1017.

[88] *Comm. v. Jacobson*, 49–1 USTC ¶9133, 37 AFTR 516, 69 S.Ct. 358 (USSC, 1949).

[89] §§ 108(a), (c), (e), and (g). Note that § 108(b) provides that other tax attributes (e.g., net operating loss) will be reduced by the realized gain from the debt discharge prior to the basis adjustment unless the taxpayer elects to apply the basis adjustment first.

[90] § 108(e)(5).

TAX *in* the NEWS

Hope for Exclusion of Credit Card Debt Forgiveness

The airwaves are full of advertisements about how credit card debt can be reduced without actually paying the debt. Generally, the reduction in the debt creates income from discharge of indebtedness. But in a recent petition to the U.S. Supreme Court, the taxpayers unveiled a new theory for excluding the gain from income. The taxpayers argued that the interest portion of the debt forgiven was not taxable because it was an adjustment to the purchase price that the credit card issuer charged. Another theory that will undoubtedly be tested in the context of consumer debt adjustments is that the cancellation of the debt is not taxable income under the tax benefit rule. That is, because the expenditure that created the debt was not deductible, the recovery should not be taxable.

by the shareholder. Thus, the corporation's paid-in capital is increased, and its liabilities are decreased by the same amount.[91]

Many states make loans to students on the condition that the loan will be forgiven if the student practices a profession in the state upon completing his or her studies. The amount of the loan that is forgiven (situation 8) is excluded from gross income.[92]

TAX PLANNING:

The present law excludes certain types of economic gains from taxation. Therefore, taxpayers may find tax planning techniques helpful in obtaining the maximum benefits from the exclusion of such gains. Following are some of the tax planning opportunities made available by the exclusions described in this chapter.

LO.5

Identify tax planning strategies for obtaining the maximum benefit from allowable exclusions.

5.17 Life Insurance

Life insurance offers several favorable tax attributes. As discussed in Chapter 4, the annual increase in the cash surrender value of the policy is not taxable (because no income has been actually or constructively received). By borrowing on the policy's cash surrender value, the owner can actually receive the policy's increase in value in cash but without recognizing income.

5.18 Employee Benefits

Generally, employees view accident and health insurance, as well as life insurance, as necessities. Employees can obtain group coverage at much lower rates than individuals would have to pay for the same protection. Premiums paid by the employer can be excluded from the employees' gross income. Because of the exclusion, employees will have a greater after-tax and after-insurance income if the employer pays a lower salary but also pays the insurance premiums.

EXAMPLE 46

Pat receives a salary of $30,000. The company has group insurance benefits, but Pat is required to pay his own premiums as follows:

Hospitalization and medical insurance	$1,400
Term life insurance ($30,000 coverage)	200
Disability insurance	400
	$2,000

To simplify the analysis, assume Pat's tax rate on income is 25%. After paying taxes of $7,500 (.25 × $30,000) and $2,000 for insurance, Pat has $20,500 ($30,000 − $7,500 − $2,000) for his other living needs.

[91] § 108(e)(6).

[92] § 108(f).

TAX *in the NEWS*

Debt Forgiveness on a Principal Residence

The Federal government and state governments continue to push big banks to expand their debt forgiveness programs as a way to reduce foreclosures associated with the mortgage crisis. Not only does the government want interest forgiven (to make monthly payments more affordable), but it also wants some of the principal balance to be forgiven. The expectation is that forgiving principal will reduce the number of foreclosures because fewer homeowners will be "underwater" (mortgage exceeds the fair market value of the house).

Bank of America has announced a plan to reduce mortgage loan balances by as much as 30 percent. An estimated 45,000 customers will receive loan reductions of $60,000 on average. Other banks including Wells Fargo and Citigroup have announced similar programs.

From a Federal income tax perspective, the "under distress homeowner" can benefit by being able to exclude the debt forgiveness from gross income if the debt qualifies as qualified principal residence indebtedness. To be eligible, the following requirements must be satisfied:

- The house must be the taxpayer's principal residence.
- The mortgage must be acquisition indebtedness (used to purchase, build, or substantially improve the residence).
- The ceiling is the portion of the loan not exceeding $2 million ($1 million if married filing separately).

The taxpayer must reduce the basis of the principal residence by the excluded amount.

Source: Adapted from James Hagerty and Nick Timiraos, "Bank Launches Big Plan to Cut Mortgage Debt," *Wall Street Journal*, March 25, 2010, p. A1.

If Pat's employer reduced Pat's salary by $2,000 (to $28,000) but paid his insurance premiums, Pat's tax liability would be only $7,000 ($28,000 × .25). Thus, Pat would have $21,000 ($28,000 − $7,000) to meet his other living needs. The change in the compensation plan would save Pat $500 ($21,000 − $20,500). ■

Similarly, employees must often incur expenses for child care and parking. The employee can have more income for other uses if the employer pays these costs for the employee but reduces the employee's salary by the cost of the benefits.

The use of cafeteria plans has increased dramatically in recent years. These plans allow employees to tailor their benefits to meet their individual situations. Thus, where both spouses in a married couple are working, duplications of benefits can be avoided, and other needed benefits can often be added. If less than all of the employee's allowance is spent, the employee can receive cash.

The meals and lodging exclusion enables employees to receive from their employer what they ordinarily must purchase with after-tax dollars. Although the requirements that the employee live and take his or her meals on the employer's premises limit the tax planning opportunities, the exclusion is an important factor in the employee's compensation in certain situations (e.g., hotels, motels, restaurants, farms, and ranches).

The employees' discount provision is especially important for manufacturers and wholesalers. Employees of manufacturers can avoid tax on the manufacturer's, wholesaler's, and retailer's markups. The wholesaler's employees can avoid tax on an amount equal to the wholesale and retail markups.

It should be recognized that the exclusion of benefits is generally available only to employees. Proprietors and partners must pay tax on the same benefits their employees receive tax-free. By incorporating and becoming an employee of the corporation, the former proprietor or partner can also receive these tax-exempt benefits. Thus, the availability of employee benefits is a consideration in the decision to incorporate.

5.19 Investment Income

Tax-exempt state and local government bonds are almost irresistible investments for many high-income taxpayers. To realize the maximum benefit from the exemption, the investor can purchase zero-coupon bonds. Like Series EE U.S. government savings bonds, these investments pay interest only at maturity. The advantage of the zero-coupon feature for a tax-exempt bond is that the investor can earn tax-exempt interest on the accumulated principal and interest. If the investor purchases a bond that pays the interest each year, the interest received may be such a small amount that an additional tax-exempt investment cannot be made. In addition, reinvesting the interest may entail transaction costs (broker's fees). The zero-coupon feature avoids these problems.

Series EE U.S. government savings bonds can earn tax-exempt interest if the bond proceeds are used for qualified higher education expenses. Many taxpayers can foresee these expenditures being made for their children's educations. In deciding whether to invest in the bonds, however, the investor must take into account the income limitations for excluding the interest from gross income.

REFOCUS ON THE BIG PICTURE

EXCLUSIONS

You have looked into Paul's tax situation and have the following information for him:

- *Compensation.* The amount Paul was paid for his internship is compensation for services rendered and must be included in his gross income. This includes both his base pay and the $1,500 bonus.
- *Graduate assistantship.* The tuition waiver of $6,000 and the related payments of $500 per month are also intended as a form of compensation. So Paul must include both of these in his gross income.
- *Damages.* Damages awards that relate to personal physical injury or sickness can be excluded from gross income if the payments are for compensatory damages. So all of the compensatory damages of $220,000 can be excluded from gross income. The punitive damages of $160,000 must be included in Paul's gross income. Likewise, the compensatory damages of $25,000 received by Paul's mother must be included in her gross income since emotional distress does not qualify as personal physical injury or sickness.

What If?

From a tax planning perspective, can Paul do anything to reduce the amount of the punitive damages settlement that he must include in his gross income?

As things now stand (i.e., a completed settlement), Paul cannot reduce the $160,000 punitive damages amount he must include in gross income. However, proper tax planning might have enabled Paul to reduce the amount includible in gross income. Note that both the amount of the damages and the labels attached to the damages are negotiated. If a larger portion of the settlement had been assigned to compensatory damages rather than punitive damages, Paul could have reduced the amount he must include in his gross income.

KEY TERMS

DISCUSSION QUESTIONS

1. **LO.2** Uncle Tom promised John, "Come and take care of me and I will leave you the farm when I die." John took care of Uncle Tom for the five years preceding his death. When Uncle Tom died, in accordance with his will, John received the farm. Can John exclude the value of the farm from his gross income as a gift or inheritance, or has he received compensation income?

2. **LO.2** Albert was a flood victim and had to spend a considerable amount to restore his home after the flood. His church held a special collection and gave him $1,500. Also, his employer gave him $1,000 to help him in "his time of need." How much gross income must Albert recognize from the receipt of the $2,500?

3. **LO.1, 2** Twenty college fraternity brothers each placed $2,500 in a mutual fund account. They agreed that upon the death of a fraternity brother, his beneficiary would receive $20,000 that was to be paid from the mutual fund account. The beneficiary of the last remaining fraternity brother would receive the balance remaining in the account. The mutual fund did very well. Earl was the last to die, at age 92, and his beneficiary received $250,000. Can the $250,000 be excluded from the beneficiary's gross income?

4. **LO.2** Janice was a cash basis taxpayer. At the time of her death, she was owed $30,000 in accrued salary. She also owned several thousand shares of stock in her corporate employer. Her cost of the stock was $25,000. Her employer was required to purchase the stock on Janice's death for $150,000. To fund the agreement, the employer had purchased an insurance policy on Janice's life that cost $60,000. The insurance company paid the employer the life insurance proceeds of $150,000 on Janice's death. Wayne, as the sole beneficiary of Janice's estate, received the $180,000 from Janice's estate, which included Janice's $30,000 of accrued salary. What are the employer's and Wayne's gross income from these transactions?

5. **LO.2** Matt is a waiter in a restaurant. His usual tip is 20% of the price of the meal. A customer, whose meal cost $5, left a $100 bill as a tip. Matt is sure the customer thought he had left a $1 bill. Nevertheless, Matt believes he can exclude the entire amount (or at least $99) from his gross income because it was received as a gift rather than as compensation for services rendered. Is Matt correct?

6. **LO.2** Carey is a self-employed landscaper. He contracted to maintain Ted's lawn for $150 per month. Ted was very pleased with Carey's work and at the end of the year paid Carey an additional $500. Does the fact that Ted had no legal obligation to make the payment mean that Carey can exclude the $500 from gross income as a gift?

7. **LO.2** Lime Finance Company requires its customers to purchase a credit life insurance policy associated with the loans it makes. Lime is the beneficiary of the policy to the extent of the remaining balance on the loan at the time of the customer's death. In 2010, Lime wrote off as uncollectible a $5,000 account receivable from Wally, which included $1,500 of accrued interest. When Wally died in 2011, the life insurance policy was still in force, and Lime received $3,500. Is the $3,500 of life insurance proceeds received by Lime included in its gross income?

8. **LO.2** Sarah, who has a terminal illness, cashed in her life insurance policy (cost of $24,000 and proceeds of $50,000) to go on an around-the-world cruise. Ed paid $24,000 of life insurance premiums before cashing in his life insurance policy for the $50,000 cash surrender value. He decided he could invest the money and earn a higher rate of return. Tom's wife died, and Tom collected $50,000 as the beneficiary on a group term life insurance policy purchased by her employer. Determine the amounts that Sarah, Ed, and Tom should include in their gross income.

9. **LO.2** Joe is a graduate student who works as a resident adviser (RA) in the college dormitory. As compensation for serving as an RA, he is not charged the $2,200 other students pay for their dormitory rooms for the fall 2011 semester. As an RA, he is required to live in the dormitory. He is also paid $1,500 for being available to dormitory residents at all hours during the fall semester. Joe also has a scholarship that pays him $12,000 to be used for his tuition for the academic year. He uses the scholarship proceeds to pay $6,000 of tuition in August 2011. In January 2012, he pays $6,000 for his spring semester tuition. What is Joe's gross income for 2011?

10. **LO.2** Billy fell off a bar stool and hurt his back. As a result, he was unable to work for three months. He sued the bar owner and collected $100,000 for the physical injury and $50,000 for the loss of income. Billy also collected $15,000 from an income replacement insurance policy purchased by his employer. Amber was away from work for three months following heart bypass surgery. Amber collected $30,000 under an income replacement insurance policy she had purchased. Are the amounts received by Billy and Amber treated the same under the tax law?

11. **LO.2** Wes was a major league baseball pitcher before a career-ending injury caused by a negligent driver. Wes sued the driver and collected $15 million as compensation for lost estimated future income as a pitcher and $10 million as punitive damages. Sam was also a major league baseball pitcher and earned $25 million for pitching. Do the amounts that Wes and Sam received have the same effect on their gross income? Explain.

12. **LO.2** Holly was injured while working in a factory and received $12,000 as workers' compensation while she was unable to work because of the injury. Jill, who was self-employed, was also injured and unable to work. Jill collected $12,000 on an insurance policy she had purchased to replace her loss of income while she was unable to work. How much are Holly and Jill each required to include in their gross income?

13. **LO.2** Melba's employer provides a flexible spending plan for medical and dental expenses not covered by insurance. Melba contributed $1,500 during 2011, but by the end of December 2011, she still had $300 remaining in the account. Melba intended to get new eyeglasses, but was too busy during the holiday season. Is Melba required to forfeit the balance in her flexible spending account?

14. **LO.2, 5** Casey is in the 15% marginal tax bracket, and Jean is in the 35% marginal tax bracket. Their employer is experiencing financial difficulties and cannot continue to pay for the company's health insurance plan. The annual premiums are approximately $7,000 per employee. The employer has proposed to either (1) require the employee to pay the premiums or (2) reduce each employee's pay by $8,000 per year with the employer paying the premium. Which option is less objectionable to Casey, and which is less objectionable to Jean? **DECISION MAKING**

15. **LO.2** What is the difference between a "cafeteria plan" and an employee "flexible spending plan"?

16. **LO.2** Ted works for Sage Motors, an automobile dealership. All employees can buy a car at the company's cost plus 2%. The company does not charge employees the $175 transfer service fee that nonemployees must pay. Ted purchased an automobile for $24,480 ($24,000 + $480). The company's cost was $24,000. The price for a nonemployee would have been $27,775 ($27,600 + $175 transfer service fee). What is Ted's gross income from the purchase of the automobile?

17. **LO.2, 5** Ted has been offered a job where his salary would be $150,000 and he would also receive health insurance coverage. Another potential employer has offered to match the first offer but would not provide any health insurance coverage. Ted can purchase health insurance for $8,000 per year. Assume that Ted is in the 28% marginal tax bracket and does not itemize his deductions. How much salary must the second potential employer pay so that Ted's financial status will be the same under both offers?

18. **LO.2, 5** Eagle Life Insurance Company pays its employees $.30 per mile for driving their personal automobiles to and from work. The company reimburses each employee who rides the bus $100 a month for the cost of a pass. Tom collected $100 for his automobile mileage, and Ted received $100 as reimbursement for the cost of a bus pass.
    a. What are the effects of the above on Tom's and Ted's gross income?
    b. Assume that Tom and Ted are in the 28% marginal tax bracket and the actual before-tax cost for Tom to drive to and from work is $.30 per mile. What are Tom's and Ted's after-tax costs of commuting to and from work?

19. **LO.2** Several of Egret Company's employees have asked the company to create a hiking trail that employees could use during their lunch hours. The company owns vacant land that is being held for future expansion but would have to spend approximately $50,000 if it were to make a trail. Nonemployees would be allowed to use the facility as part of the company's effort to build strong community support. What are the relevant tax issues for the employees? **ISSUE ID**

20. **LO.2** The Azure Company has the opportunity to purchase a building located next to its office. Azure would use the building as a day care center for the children of its employees and an exercise facility for the employees. Occasionally, portions of the building could be used for employees' family events such as reunions, birthday parties, and anniversaries. The company would like to know if the planned uses of the building would fit into a beneficially taxed employee compensation plan.

21. **LO.2** For a U.S. citizen, what are the possible beneficial tax consequences of working in a foreign country in terms of the calculation of gross income?

DECISION MAKING

22. **LO.2, 5** Tammy, a resident of Virginia, is considering purchasing a corporate bond that yields 7% before tax. She is in the 35% Federal marginal tax bracket and the 5% marginal state tax bracket. She is aware that State of Virginia bonds of comparable risk are yielding 4.6% and State of North Carolina bonds are yielding 4.7%. Which of the three options will provide the greatest after-tax return to Tammy?

23. **LO.3** In 2011, Montgomery County experienced a budget surplus. The County is considering using a portion of the surplus to rebate part of the real estate taxes paid by county real estate owners. What would be the income tax consequences to the real estate owners of receiving the rebate in 2012?

24. **LO.2** Andrea entered into a § 529 qualified tuition program for the benefit of her daughter, Joanna. Andrea contributed $15,000 to the fund. The fund balance had accumulated to $25,000 by the time Joanna was ready to enter college. However, Joanna received a scholarship that paid for her tuition, fees, books, supplies, and room and board. Therefore, Andrea withdrew the funds from the § 529 plan and bought Joanna a new car.
    a. What are the tax consequences to Andrea of withdrawing the funds?
    b. Assume instead that Joanna's scholarship did not cover her room and board, which cost $7,500 per academic year. During the current year, $7,500 of the fund balance was used to pay for Joanna's room and board. The remaining amount was left in the § 529 plan to cover her room and board for future academic years. What are the tax consequences to Andrea and to Joanna of using the $7,500 to pay for the room and board?

25. **LO.3** Molly is a cash basis taxpayer. In 2011, she earned only $6,500, which was less than her standard deduction and personal exemption. In January 2012, Molly's employer determined that he had miscalculated her December 2011 bonus and that she should have received an additional $1,000 of compensation in 2011. The employer paid Molly the $1,000 in 2012. If Molly had received the $1,000 in 2011, it would not have resulted in any tax liability because her gross income would still have been less than her standard deduction and personal exemption. In 2012, Molly had over $30,000 in taxable income. Does the tax benefit rule apply to Molly's situation? Explain.

26. **LO.4** Harry was experiencing financial difficulties and could not make the mortgage payments on his home. The mortgage holder agreed to reduce the debt principal by $50,000 because the real estate market was depressed. Assuming that Harry is not bankrupt or insolvent, would the tax consequences differ under the following circumstances?
    - The mortgage is held by the person who sold him the property.
    - The mortgage is held by the financial institution that made the loan for the purchase of his residence.

ISSUE ID

27. **LO.4** Harry has experienced financial difficulties as a result of his struggling business. He has been behind on his mortgage payments for the last six months. The mortgage holder, who is a friend of Harry's, has offered to accept $80,000 in full payment of the $100,000 owed on the mortgage and payable over the next 10 years. The interest rate of the mortgage is 7%, and the market rate is now 8%. What tax issues are raised by the creditor's offer?

PROBLEMS

28. **LO.2** Ed, an employee of the Natural Color Company, suffered from a rare disease that was very expensive to treat. The local media ran several stories about Ed's problems, and the family received more than $10,000 in gifts from individuals to help pay the medical bills. Ed's employer provided hospital and medical insurance for its employees, but the policy did not cover Ed's illness. When it became apparent that Ed could not pay all of his

medical expenses, the hospital canceled the $25,000 Ed owed at the time of his death. After Ed's death, his former employer paid Ed's widow $12,000 in "her time of need." Ed's widow also collected $50,000 on a group term life insurance policy paid for by Ed's employer. What are Ed's and his widow's gross income?

29. **LO.2** Determine the gross income of the beneficiaries in the following cases:
    a. Justin lost his job when his employer moved the plant to China. His employer gave Justin $15,000 to help him in his transition to a new job, even though the employer was not legally obligated to make the payment.
    b. Trina was injured while working. She collected $1,200 in workers' compensation and $1,500 on a loss of income policy she had purchased.
    c. Coral Corporation collected $1 million on a key person life insurance policy when its chief executive died. The corporation had paid the premiums on the policy of $77,000.
    d. Juan collected $50,000 on a life insurance policy when his wife, Leona, died. The policy was provided by Leona's employer, and the premiums were excluded from Leona's gross income as group term life insurance.
    e. Juan in part (d) above collected Leona's accrued vacation pay of $6,000 from her employer.

30. **LO.2, 5** Laura was recently diagnosed with cancer and has begun chemotherapy treatments. A cancer specialist has stated that Laura has less than one year to live. She has incurred a lot of medical bills and other general living expenses and is in need of cash. Therefore, she is considering selling stock that cost $35,000 and has a fair market value of $50,000. This amount would be sufficient to pay her medical bills. However, she has read about a company (the Vital Benefits Company) that would purchase her life insurance policy for $50,000. She has paid $30,000 in premiums on the policy.

DECISION MAKING

    a. Considering only the tax effects, would selling the stock or selling the life insurance policy result in more beneficial tax treatment?
    b. Assume that Laura is a dependent child and that her mother owns the stock and the life insurance policy, which is on the mother's life. Which of the alternative means of raising the cash would result in more beneficial tax treatment?

31. **LO.2** What is the taxpayer's gross income in each of the following situations?
    a. Darrin received a salary of $50,000 in 2011 from his employer, Green Construction Associates, Inc. In July 2011, Green gave each employee $2,500 as a bonus for exceeding the monthly sales goals.
    b. Megan received $10,000 from her employer to help her pay the college expenses of her daughter.
    c. Blake received $15,000 from his deceased wife's employer in "recognition of her 30 years of faithful service to the company."
    d. Clint collected $50,000 as the beneficiary of a group term life insurance policy for which his deceased wife's employer had paid the premiums.

32. **LO.2** Donald was killed in an accident while he was on the job in 2011. His employer had provided Donald with group term life insurance of $160,000 (twice his annual salary), which was payable to his widow, Darlene. Premiums on this policy totaling $2,700 have been included in Donald's gross income under § 79. Darlene received the $160,000 as a lump sum in 2011. Darlene also received Donald's accrued bonus of $20,000. In addition, Donald had purchased a $100,000 life insurance policy (premiums totaled $70,000) that paid $200,000 in the event of accidental death. The proceeds were payable to Darlene, who elected to receive installment payments of $25,000 each year for a 20-year period. She received her first installment this year. What is Darlene's gross income from the above in 2011?

33. **LO.2** Ray and Carin are partners in an accounting firm. The partners have entered into an arm's length agreement requiring Ray to purchase Carin's partnership interest from Carin's estate if she dies before Ray. The price is set at 120% of the book value of Carin's partnership interest at the time of her death. Ray purchased an insurance policy on Carin's life to fund this agreement. After Ray had paid $45,000 in premiums, Carin was killed in an automobile accident, and Ray collected $800,000 of life insurance proceeds. Ray used the life insurance proceeds to purchase Carin's partnership interest.
    a. What amount should Ray include in his gross income from receiving the life insurance proceeds?
    b. The insurance company paid Ray $16,000 interest on the life insurance proceeds during the period Carin's estate was in administration. During this period, Ray had left the insurance proceeds with the insurance company. Is this interest taxable?

c. When Ray paid $800,000 for Carin's partnership interest, priced as specified in the agreement, the fair market value of Carin's interest was $1 million. How much should Ray include in his gross income from this bargain purchase?

34. **LO.2** Sally was an all-state soccer player during her junior and senior years in high school. She accepted an athletic scholarship from State University. The scholarship provided the following:

Tuition and fees	$15,000
Housing and meals	7,500
Books and supplies	2,000

a. Determine the effect of the scholarship on Sally's gross income.
b. Sally's brother, Willy, was not a gifted athlete, but he received $17,000 from their father's employer as a scholarship during the year. The employer grants the children of all executives a scholarship equal to annual tuition, fees, books, and supplies. Determine the effect of the scholarship on Willy's and his father's gross income.

35. **LO.2** Adrian was awarded an academic scholarship to State University for the 2011–2012 academic year. He received $6,000 in August and $7,000 in December 2011. Adrian had enough personal savings to pay all expenses as they came due. Adrian's expenditures for the relevant period were as follows:

Tuition, August 2011	$3,600
Tuition, January 2012	3,700
Room and board	
August–December 2011	3,000
January–May 2012	2,400
Books and educational supplies	
August–December 2011	1,100
January–May 2012	1,200

Determine the effect on Adrian's gross income for 2011 and 2012.

36. **LO.2** Leigh sued an overzealous bill collector and received the following settlement:

Damage to her automobile the collector attempted to repossess	$ 3,300
Physical damage to her arm caused by the collector	15,000
Loss of income while her arm was healing	6,000
Punitive damages	80,000

a. What effect does the settlement have on Leigh's gross income?
b. Assume Leigh also collected $25,000 of damages for slander to her personal reputation caused by the bill collector misrepresenting the facts to Leigh's employer and other creditors. Is this $25,000 included in Leigh's gross income?

37. **LO.2** Determine the effect on gross income in each of the following cases:
a. Eloise received $150,000 in settlement of a sex discrimination case against her former employer.
b. Nell received $10,000 for damages to her personal reputation. She also received $40,000 in punitive damages.
c. Orange Corporation, an accrual basis taxpayer, received $50,000 from a lawsuit filed against its auditor who overcharged for services rendered in a previous year.
d. Beth received $10,000 in compensatory damages and $30,000 in punitive damages in a lawsuit she filed against a tanning parlor for severe burns she received from using its tanning equipment.
e. Joanne received compensatory damages of $75,000 and punitive damages of $300,000 from a cosmetic surgeon who botched her nose job.

38. **LO.2** Rex, age 45, is an officer of Blue Company, which provides him with the following nondiscriminatory fringe benefits in 2011:

- Hospitalization insurance premiums for Rex and his dependents. The cost of the coverage for Rex is $2,700 per year, and the additional cost for his dependents is $3,600 per year. The plan has a $2,000 deductible, but his employer contributed $1,500 to Rex's Health Savings Account. Rex withdrew only $800 from the HSA, and the account earned $50 interest during the year.

- Long-term care insurance premiums for Rex, at a cost of $3,600 per year.
- Insurance premiums of $840 for salary continuation payments. Under the plan, Rex will receive his regular salary in the event he is unable to work due to illness. Rex collected $4,500 on the policy to replace lost wages while he was ill during the year.
- Rex is a part-time student working on his bachelor's degree in engineering. His employer reimbursed his $5,200 tuition under a plan available to all full-time employees.

Determine the amount Rex must include in gross income.

39. **LO.2** The UVW Union and HON Corporation are negotiating contract terms. Assume the union members are in the 28% marginal tax bracket and all benefits are provided on a nondiscriminatory basis. Write a letter to the UVW Union members explaining the tax consequences of the options discussed below. The union's address is 905 Spruce Street, Washington, D.C. 20227.

COMMUNICATIONS

   a. The company would impose a $100 deductible on medical insurance benefits. Most employees incur more than $100 each year in medical expenses.
   b. Employees would get an additional paid holiday with the same annual income (the same pay but less work).
   c. An employee who did not need health insurance (because the employee's spouse works and receives family coverage) would be allowed to receive the cash value of the coverage.

40. **LO.2, 5** Mauve Corporation has a group hospitalization insurance plan that has a $200 deductible amount for hospital visits and a $15 deductible for doctor visits and prescriptions. The deductible portion paid by employees who have children has become substantial for some employees. The company is considering adopting a medical reimbursement plan or a flexible benefits plan to cover the deductible amounts. Either of these plans can be tailored to meet the needs of the employees. What are the cost considerations to the employer that should be considered in choosing between these plans?

DECISION MAKING

41. **LO.2** Belinda spent the last 60 days of 2011 in a nursing home. The cost of the services provided to her was $15,000. Medicare paid $8,500 toward the cost of her stay. Belinda also received $10,500 of benefits under a long-term care insurance policy she purchased. What is the effect on Belinda's gross income?

42. **LO.2** Tim is the vice president of western operations for Maroon Oil Company and is stationed in San Francisco. He is required to live in an employer-owned home, which is three blocks from his company office. The company-provided home is equipped with high-speed Internet access and several telephone lines. Tim receives telephone calls and e-mails that require immediate attention any time of day or night because the company's business is spread all over the world. A full-time administrative assistant resides in the house to assist Tim with the urgent business matters. Tim often uses the home for entertaining customers, suppliers, and employees. The fair market value of comparable housing is $9,000 per month. Tim is also provided with free parking at his company's office. The value of the parking is $350 per month. Calculate the amount associated with the company-provided housing and free parking that Tim must include in his gross income.

43. **LO.2** Does the taxpayer recognize gross income in the following situations?
   a. Ava is a filing clerk at a large insurance company. She is permitted to leave the premises for her lunch, but she always eats in the company's cafeteria because doing so is much less expensive than purchasing a comparable meal at a nearby restaurant. On average, she pays $3 for a lunch that would cost $8 at a restaurant. However, if the prices in the cafeteria were not so low and the food was not so delicious, she would probably bring her lunch at a cost of $2 per day.
   b. Scott is a resident adviser (RA) in a college dormitory and is provided with lodging in the dormitory. He is not required to pay the $300 per month that a room costs other students. In addition, he is paid $100 per month.
   c. Ira recently moved to accept a job. For the first month on the new job, Ira was searching for a home to purchase or rent. During this time, his employer permitted Ira to

live in an apartment the company maintains for customers during the buying season. The month that Ira occupied the apartment was not during the buying season, however, and the apartment would not otherwise have been occupied.

DECISION MAKING

44. **LO.2, 5** Bertha is considering taking an early retirement offered by her employer. She would receive $2,600 per month, indexed for inflation. However, she would no longer be able to use the company's health facilities, and she would be required to pay her hospitalization insurance of $8,000 each year. Bertha and her husband will file a joint return and take the standard deduction. She currently receives a salary of $50,000 a year, and her employer pays for all of her hospitalization insurance. If she retires, Bertha would not be able to use her former employer's exercise facilities because of the commuting distance. She would like to continue to exercise, however, and will therefore join a health club at a cost of $50 per month. Also, if she retires, she will spend approximately $300 less each month for commuting and clothing. Bertha and her husband have other sources of income and are in and will remain in the 25% marginal tax bracket. She currently pays Social Security and Medicare taxes of 7.65% on her salary, but her retirement pay would not be subject to this tax. She will earn about $11,000 a year from a part-time job if she retires from the company. Bertha would like to know whether she should accept the early retirement offer.

COMMUNICATIONS

45. **LO.2, 5** Finch Construction Company provides the carpenters it employs with all of the required tools. However, the company believes that this practice has led to some employees not taking care of the tools and to the mysterious disappearance of some tools. The company is considering requiring all of its employees to provide their own tools. Each employee's salary would be increased by $1,500 to compensate for the additional cost. Write a letter to Finch's management explaining the tax consequences of this plan to the carpenters. Finch's address is 300 Harbor Drive, Vermillion, SD 57069.

46. **LO.2, 5** Bluebird, Inc., does not provide its employees with any tax-exempt fringe benefits. The company is considering adopting a hospital and medical benefits insurance plan that will cost approximately $7,500 per employee. In order to adopt this plan, the company may have to reduce salaries and/or lower future salary increases. Bluebird is in the 35% (combined Federal and state rates) bracket. Bluebird is also responsible for matching the Social Security and Medicare taxes withheld on employees' salaries. The benefits insurance plan will not be subject to the Social Security and Medicare taxes, and the company is not eligible for the small business credit for health insurance. The employees generally fall into three marginal tax rate groups:

Income Tax	Social Security and Medicare Tax	Total
.15	.0765	.2265
.25	.0765	.3265
.35	.0145	.3645

The company has asked you to assist in its financial planning for the benefits insurance plan by computing the following:

a. How much taxable compensation is the equivalent of $7,500 of exempt compensation for each of the three classes of employees?
b. What is the company's after-tax cost of the taxable compensation computed in (a) above?
c. What is the company's after-tax cost of the exempt compensation?
d. Briefly explain your conclusions from the above analysis.

DECISION MAKING

47. **LO.2, 5** Rosa's employer has instituted a flexible benefits program. Rosa will use the plan to pay for her daughter's dental expenses and other medical expenses that are not covered by health insurance. Rosa is in the 25% marginal tax bracket and estimates that the medical and dental expenses not covered by health insurance will be within the range of $3,000 to $5,000. Her employer's plan permits her to set aside as much as $5,000 in the flexible benefits account. Rosa does not itemize her deductions.

a. Rosa puts $3,000 into her flexible benefits account, and her actual expenses are $5,000. What is her cost of underestimating the expenses?

b. Rosa puts $5,000 into her flexible benefits account, and her actual expenses are only $3,000. What is her cost of overestimating her expenses?
c. What is Rosa's cost of underfunding as compared to the cost of overfunding the flexible benefits account?
d. Does your answer in part (c) suggest that Rosa should fund the account closer to the low end or to the high end of her estimates?

48. **LO.2** Sparrow Corporation would like you to review its employee fringe benefits program with regard to the tax consequences of the plan for the company's president (Polly), who is also the majority shareholder:
a. The company has a qualified retirement plan. The company pays the cost of employees attending a retirement planning seminar. The employee must be within 10 years of retirement, and the cost of the seminar is $1,500 per attendee.
b. The company owns a parking garage that is used by customers, employees, and the general public. Only the general public is required to pay for parking. The charge to the general public for Polly's parking for the year would have been $3,000 (a $250 monthly rate).
c. All employees are allowed to use the company's fixed charge long-distance telephone services, as long as the privilege is not abused. Although no one has kept track of the actual calls, Polly's use of the telephone had a value (what she would have paid on her personal telephone) of approximately $600.
d. The company owns a condominium at the beach, which it uses to entertain customers. Employees are allowed to use the facility without charge when the company has no scheduled events. Polly used the facility 10 days during the year. Her use had a rental value of $1,000.
e. The company is in the household moving business. Employees are allowed to ship goods without charge whenever there is excess space on a truck. Polly purchased a dining room suite for her daughter. Company trucks delivered the furniture to the daughter. Normal freight charges would have been $750.
f. The company has a storage facility for household goods. Officers are allowed a 20% discount on charges for storing their goods. All other employees are allowed a 10% discount. Polly's discounts for the year totaled $900.

49. **LO.2** George is a U.S. citizen who is employed by Hawk Enterprises, a global company. Beginning on June 1, 2011, George began working in London. He worked there until January 31, 2012, when he transferred to Paris. He worked in Paris the remainder of 2012. His salary for the first five months of 2011 was $100,000, and it was earned in the United States. His salary for the remainder of 2011 was $175,000, and it was earned in London. George's 2012 salary from Hawk was $300,000, with part being earned in London and part being earned in Paris. What is George's gross income in 2011 and 2012 (assume the 2012 indexed amount is the same as the 2011 indexed amount)?

50. **LO.2, 3** Determine Hazel's gross income from the following receipts for the year:

Gain on sale of Augusta County bonds	$800
Interest on U.S. government savings bonds	400
Interest on state income tax refund	200
Interest on Augusta County bonds	700
Patronage dividend from Potato Growers Cooperative	350

The patronage dividend was received in March of the current year for amounts paid for her garden and lawn supplies.

51. **LO.2** In January 2011, Ezra purchased 1,000 shares of Gold Utility Mutual Fund for $20,000. In June, Ezra received an additional 50 shares as a dividend, in lieu of receiving $600 in cash dividends. In December, the company declared a two-for-one stock dividend. Ezra received an additional 1,050 shares, but there was no option to receive cash. At the time of the stock dividend in December and at the end of the year, the fund shares were trading for $8 per share. Also, at the end of the year, the fund offered to buy outstanding shares for $9. Ezra did not sell any shares during the year.
a. What is Ezra's gross income from the 50 shares received in June?
b. What is Ezra's gross income from the receipt of the 1,050 shares as a two-for-one stock dividend?

c. Should Ezra be required to recognize gross income in 2011 even though the value of his investment at the end of the year was less than the fair market value at the beginning of the year?

DECISION MAKING

52. **LO.2** Tonya, who lives in Virginia, inherited a $10,000 State of Virginia bond in 2011. Her marginal Federal tax rate is 35%, and her marginal state tax rate is 5%. The Virginia bond pays 4% interest, which is not subject to Virginia income tax. She can purchase a corporate bond of comparable risk that will yield 6% or a U.S. government bond that pays 5.6% interest. Tonya does not itemize her deductions. Which investment will provide the greatest after-tax yield?

DECISION MAKING

COMMUNICATIONS

53. **LO.2** Lynn Swartz's husband died three years ago. Her parents have an income of over $200,000 a year and want to assure that funds will be available for the education of Lynn's 8-year-old son, Eric. Lynn is currently earning $45,000 a year. Lynn's parents have suggested that they start a savings account for Eric. They have calculated that if they invest $4,000 a year for the next 8 years, at the end of 10 years sufficient funds will be available for Eric's college expenses. Lynn realizes that the tax treatment of the investments could significantly affect the amount of funds available for Eric's education. She asked you to write a letter to her advising her about options available to her parents and to her for Eric's college education. Lynn's address is 100 Myrtle Cove, Fairfield, CT 06432.

54. **LO.2** Starting in 2002, Chuck and Luane have been purchasing Series EE bonds in their name to use for the higher education of their daughter (Susie, who currently is age 18). During the year, they cash in $12,000 of the bonds to use for freshman year tuition, fees, and room and board. Of this amount, $5,000 represents interest. Of the $12,000, $8,000 is used for tuition and fees, and $4,000 is used for room and board. Their AGI, before the educational savings bond exclusion, is $112,000.
   a. Determine the tax consequences for Chuck and Luane, who will file a joint return, and for Susie.
   b. Assume that Chuck and Luane purchased the bonds in Susie's name. Determine the tax consequences for Chuck and Luane and for Susie.
   c. How would your answer for (a) change if Chuck and Luane file separate returns?

55. **LO.2** Albert established a qualified tuition program for each of his twins, Kim and Jim. He started each fund with $20,000 when the children were five years old. Albert made no further contributions to his children's plans. Thirteen years later, both children have graduated from high school. Kim's fund has accumulated to $45,000 while Jim's has accumulated to $42,000. Kim decides to attend a state university, which will cost $60,000 for four years (tuition, fees, room and board, and books). Jim decides to go to work instead of going to college. During the current year, $7,500 is used from Kim's plan to pay the cost of her first semester in college. Since Jim is not going to go to college now or in the future, Albert withdraws the $42,000 plan balance and gives it to Jim to start his new life after high school.
   a. During the period since the plans were established, should Albert or the twins have been including the annual plan earnings in gross income?
   b. What are the tax consequences to Kim and Albert of the $7,500 being used for the first semester's higher education costs?
   c. Because of her participation in the qualified tuition program, Kim received a 10% reduction in tuition charges, so less than $7,500 was withdrawn from her account. Is either Albert or Kim required to include the value of this discount in gross income?
   d. What are the tax consequences to Albert and Jim of Jim's qualified tuition program being closed?

56. **LO.3** How does the tax benefit rule apply in the following cases?
   a. In 2009, the Orange Furniture Store, an accrual method taxpayer, sold furniture on credit for $1,000 to Sammy. The cost of the furniture was $600. In 2010, Orange took a bad debt deduction for the $1,000. Orange was in the 35% marginal tax bracket in 2010. In 2011, Sammy inherited some money and paid Orange the $1,000. Orange was in the 15% marginal tax bracket in 2011.
   b. In 2010, Marvin, a cash basis taxpayer, took a $2,000 itemized deduction for state income taxes paid. This increased his itemized deductions to a total that was $1,200 more than the standard deduction. In 2011, Marvin received a $2,100 refund when he filed his 2010 state income tax return. Marvin was in the 15% marginal tax bracket in 2010, but was in the 35% marginal tax bracket in 2011.

c. In 2010, Barb, a cash basis taxpayer, was in an accident and incurred $7,000 in medical expenses, which she claimed as an itemized deduction for medical expenses. Because of the 7.5%-of-AGI reduction, the expense reduced her taxable income by only $5,000. In 2011, Barb collected $15,000 from the person who caused the accident that resulted in her personal injury. Barb was in the 15% marginal tax bracket in both 2010 and 2011.

57. **LO.4, 5** Fran, who is in the 35% tax bracket, recently collected $100,000 on a life insurance policy she carried on her father. She currently owes $120,000 on her personal residence and $120,000 on business property. National Bank holds the mortgage on both pieces of property and has agreed to accept $100,000 in complete satisfaction of either mortgage. The interest rate on the mortgages is 8%, and both mortgages are payable over 10 years. What would be the tax consequences of each of the following alternatives, assuming Fran currently deducts the mortgage interest on her tax return?

DECISION MAKING

a. Retire the mortgage on the residence.
b. Retire the mortgage on the business property.

Which alternative should Fran select?

58. **LO.4** Vic, who was experiencing financial difficulties, was able to adjust his debts as follows:
a. His father agreed to cancel a $25,000 debt. Vic's father told him, "I am not going to treat you any better than I treat your brothers and sisters; therefore, the $25,000 is coming out of your inheritance from me."
b. The Land Company, which had sold land to Vic for $80,000, reduced the mortgage on the land by $12,000.
c. The Subprime Bank reduced the principal of the mortgage on his principal residence by $9,000.

Determine the tax consequences to Vic.

CUMULATIVE PROBLEMS

59. Alfred E. Old and Beulah A. Crane, each age 42, married on September 7, 2009. Alfred and Beulah will file a joint return for 2010. Alfred's Social Security number is 111–11–1111. Beulah's Social Security number is 123–45–6789, and she adopted "Old" as her married name. They live at 211 Brickstone Drive, Atlanta, GA 30304.

TAX RETURN PROBLEM

H&R BLOCK At Home

Alfred was divorced from Sarah Old in March 2008. Under the divorce agreement, Alfred is to pay Sarah $1,250 per month for the next 10 years or until Sarah's death, whichever occurs first. Alfred pays Sarah $20,000 in 2010. In addition, in January 2010, Alfred pays Sarah $50,000, which is designated as being for her share of the marital property. Also, Alfred is responsible for all prior years' income taxes. Sarah's Social Security number is 123–45–6788.

Alfred's salary for 2010 is $150,000, and his employer, Cherry, Inc. (Federal I.D. No. 98–7654321), provides him with group term life insurance equal to twice his annual salary. His employer withheld $24,900 for Federal income taxes and $8,000 for state income taxes. The following amounts were withheld for FICA taxes: $6,622 ($106,800 × 6.2%) for Social Security and $2,175 ($150,000 × 1.45%) for Medicare.

Beulah recently graduated from law school and is employed by Legal Aid Society, Inc. (Federal I.D. No. 11–1111111), as a public defender. She receives a salary of $40,000 in 2010. Her employer withheld $7,500 for Federal income taxes and $2,400 for state income taxes. The following amounts were withheld for FICA taxes: $2,480 ($40,000 × 6.2%) for Social Security and $580 ($40,000 × 1.45%) for Medicare.

Beulah has $3,000 in qualified dividends on Yellow Corporation stock she inherited. Alfred and Beulah receive a $1,600 refund on their 2009 state income taxes. They itemized deductions on their 2009 Federal income tax return (total = $15,000). Alfred and Beulah pay $4,500 interest and $1,450 property taxes on their personal residence in 2010. Their charitable contributions total $2,100 (all to their church). They paid sales taxes of $1,400 for which they maintain the receipts.

Compute the Olds' net tax payable (or refund due) for 2010. If you use tax forms for your solution, you will need Form 1040 and Schedules A and B. Suggested software: H&R BLOCK At Home.

TAX COMPUTATION PROBLEM

DECISION MAKING

COMMUNICATIONS

60. Martin S. Albert (Social Security number 111–11–1111) is 39 years old and is married to Michele R. Albert (Social Security number 123–45–6789). The Alberts live at 512 Ferry Road, Newport News, VA 23601. They file a joint return and have two dependent children (Charlene, age 17, and Jordan, age 18). Charlene's Social Security number is 123–45–6788, and Jordan's Social Security number is 123–45–6787. In 2011, Martin and Michele had the following transactions:
    a. Martin received $115,000 in salary from Red Steel Corporation, where he is a construction engineer. Withholding for Federal income tax was $10,750. The amounts withheld for FICA tax were as follows: $4,486 ($106,800 × 4.2%) for Social Security and $1,668 ($115,000 × 1.45%) for Medicare. Martin worked in Mexico from January 1, 2010, until February 15, 2011. His $115,000 salary for 2011 includes $16,000 he earned for January and one-half of February 2011 while working in Mexico.
    b. Martin and Michele received $800 in qualified dividends on Green, Inc. stock and $400 interest on Montgomery County (Virginia) school bonds.
    c. Martin received $2,300 interest from a Bahamian bank account.
    d. Michele received 50 shares of Applegate Corporation common stock as a stock dividend. The shares had a fair market value of $2,000 at the time Michele received them, and she did not have the option of receiving cash.
    e. Martin and Michele received a $900 refund on their 2010 Virginia income taxes. Their itemized deductions in 2010 totaled $12,500.
    f. Martin paid $6,000 alimony to his former wife, Rose T. Morgan (Social Security number 123–45–6786).
    g. Martin and Michele kept the receipts for their sales taxes paid of $1,100.
    h. Martin and Michele's itemized deductions were as follows:

        - State income tax paid and withheld totaled $5,100.
        - Real estate taxes on their principal residence were $3,400.
        - Mortgage interest on their principal residence was $2,500.
        - Cash contributions to the church totaled $2,800.

    Part 1—Tax Computation
    Compute the Alberts' net tax payable (or refund due) for 2011.

    Part 2—Tax Planning
    The Alberts are considering buying another house. Their house mortgage payments would increase by $500 (to $1,500) per month, which includes a $250 increase in interest and a $100 increase in property tax. The Alberts would like to know how much the mortgage payments would increase net of any change in their income tax. Write a letter to the Alberts that contains your advice.

RESEARCH PROBLEMS

THOMSON REUTERS
Checkpoint® Student Edition

Note: Solutions to Research Problems can be prepared by using the **Checkpoint® Student Edition** online research product, which is available to accompany this text. It is also possible to prepare solutions to the Research Problems by using tax research materials found in a standard tax library.

Research Problem 1. Murray reported to the Environmental Protection Agency that his employer was illegally dumping chemicals into a river. His charges were true, and Murray's employer was fined. In retaliation, Murray's employer fired him and made deliberate efforts to prevent Murray from obtaining other employment. Murray sued the employer claiming that his reputation had been damaged. Murray won his lawsuit and received an award for "damages to his personal and professional reputation and for his mental suffering." Now he would like to know whether the award is taxable. He argues that he was awarded damages as a recovery of his human capital and a recovery of capital is not income. Therefore, the Federal government does not have the power to tax the award.

Research Problem 2. The employees of the City of Greenville must make mandatory contributions to the City's postretirement health benefit plan. The employees' contributions are placed in a trust and are used exclusively for the employees' benefits. The employees believe that since they are required to make the contributions from their base salaries, the result should be the same as if the employer made the contribution and had reduced their salaries by the amount of the contributions. Therefore, the employees believe they should be permitted to exclude the payments from gross income. The employees have asked you to research the issue.

INTERNET *activity*

Use the tax resources of the Internet to address the following question. Do not restrict your search to the Web, but include a review of newsgroups and general reference materials, practitioner sites and resources, primary sources of the tax law, chat rooms and discussion groups, and other opportunities.

COMMUNICATIONS

Research Problem 3. Go to the IRS site on the Internet and download instructions and Regulations relative to educational savings bonds and qualified tuition programs. Summarize one of the key provisions in these materials in outline format.

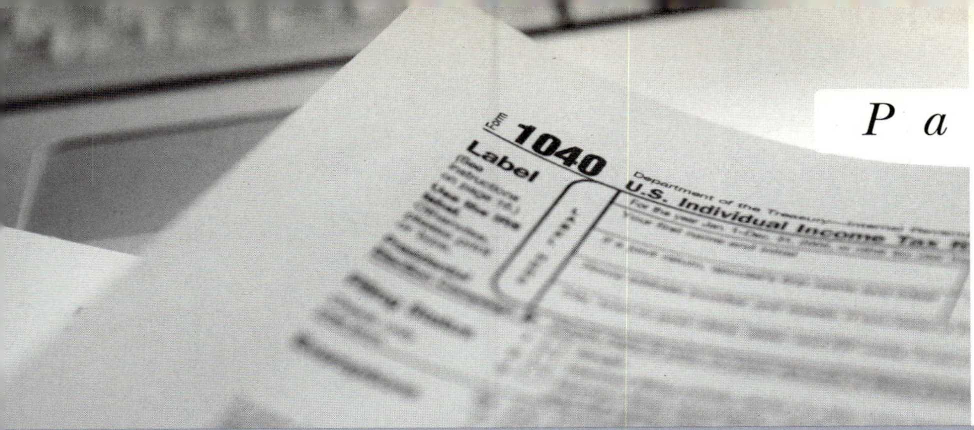

Part **3**

Deductions and Credits

Part 3 presents the deduction component of the basic tax model. Deductions are classified as business versus nonbusiness, "for" versus "from," employee versus employer, active versus passive, and reimbursed versus unreimbursed. The effect of each of these classifications is analyzed. The presentation includes not only the deductions that are permitted, but also limitations and disallowances associated with deductions. Because deductions can exceed gross income, the treatment of losses is also included. After deductions offset the income subject to tax in the basic tax model and the tax is computed, tax credits further reduce the amount of the calculated tax liability. The general procedures for the timing of the payment of the tax liability are also discussed.

CHAPTER

6

Deductions and Losses: In General

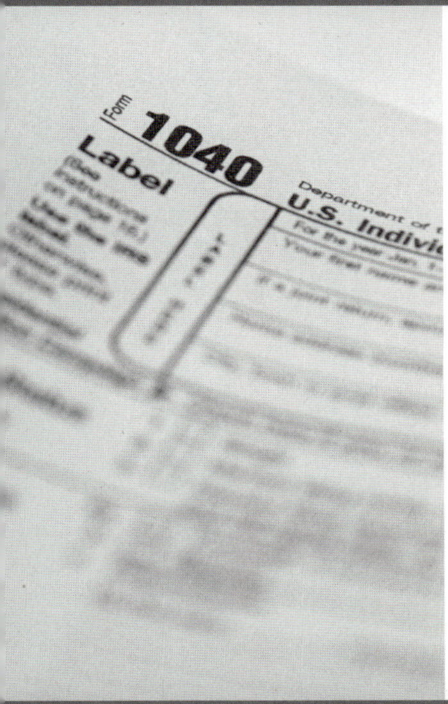

LEARNING OBJECTIVES

After completing Chapter 6, you should be able to:

LO.1

Differentiate between deductions *for* and *from* adjusted gross income and understand the relevance of the differentiation.

LO.2

Describe the cash and accrual methods of accounting.

LO.3

Apply the Internal Revenue Code deduction disallowance provisions associated with the following: public policy limitations, political activities, excessive executive compensation, investigation of business opportunities, hobby losses, vacation home rentals, payment of others' expenses, personal expenditures, capital expenditures, related-party transactions, and expenses related to tax-exempt income.

LO.4

Identify tax planning opportunities for maximizing deductions and minimizing the disallowance of deductions.

OUTLINE

For the latest in changes to tax legislation, visit **www.cengage.com/taxation/swft.**

FRAMEWORK 1040:
Tax Formula for Individuals

This chapter covers the boldfaced portions of the Tax Formula for Individuals that was introduced in Figure 3.1 on p. 3-3. Below those portions are the sections of Form 1040 where the results are reported.

Income (broadly conceived)	$xx,xxx
Less: Exclusions	(x,xxx)
Gross income	$xx,xxx
Less: Deductions for adjusted gross income	**(x,xxx)**

FORM 1040 (p. 1)

12 Business income or (loss). Attach Schedule C or C-EZ . . . .

Adjusted gross income	$xx,xxx
Less: The greater of total **itemized deductions** *or* the standard deduction	**(x,xxx)**

FORM 1040 (p. 2)

40 **Itemized deductions** (from Schedule A) **or** your **standard deduction** (see instructions) .

Personal and dependency exemptions	(x,xxx)
Taxable income	$xx,xxx
Tax on taxable income (see Tax Tables or Tax Rate Schedules)	$ x,xxx
Less: Tax credits (including income taxes withheld and prepaid)	(xxx)
Tax due (or refund)	$ xxx

THE BIG PICTURE **Tax Solutions for the Real World**

CALCULATION OF DEDUCTIBLE EXPENSES

Dr. Cliff Payne extracts the following information from his financial reporting system associated with his dental practice.

Salaries including FICA (unpaid at year-end of $5,000)	$120,000
Building rent	24,000
Depreciation of dental equipment and office furnishings and equipment	52,000
Insurance (malpractice and of dental equipment and office furnishings and equipment)	22,000
Dental supplies (ending inventory of $7,000)	16,000
Office supplies (ending inventory of $1,500)	3,000
Contribution to U.S. Senate campaign fund of Barbara Boxer	1,000
Contribution to U.S. Senate campaign fund of Carly Fiorina	1,000
Legal expenses associated with patient lawsuit (jury decision for defendant)	4,000
Draw by Dr. Payne for living expenses ($5,000 monthly)	60,000

Dr. Payne calculates the deductible expenses that he can report on Schedule C of Form 1040 as follows:

Salaries including FICA	$120,000
Building rent	24,000
Depreciation of dental equipment and office furnishings and equipment	52,000
Insurance (malpractice and of dental equipment and office furnishings and equipment)	22,000
Dental supplies ($16,000 – $7,000)	9,000
Office supplies ($3,000 – $1,500)	1,500
Contribution to U.S. Senate campaign fund of Barbara Boxer	-0-
Contribution to U.S. Senate campaign fund of Carly Fiorina	-0-
Legal expenses associated with patient lawsuit (jury decision for defendant)	4,000
Draw by Dr. Payne for living expenses ($5,000 monthly)	60,000
	$292,500

Dr. Payne's close relatives include the following:

Terry	mother
Jack	father
Camille	mother-in-law
Walter	father-in-law
Pauline	sister (age 15)
Neal	brother (age 16)

Has Dr. Payne correctly calculated the business expenses for his dental practice? **Read the chapter and formulate your response.**

6.1 Classification of Deductible Expenses

LO.1

Differentiate between deductions *for* and *from* adjusted gross income and understand the relevance of the differentiation.

The tax law has an all-inclusive definition of income; that is, income from whatever source derived is includible in gross income. Income cannot be excluded unless there is a specific statement to that effect in the Internal Revenue Code.

Similarly, deductions are disallowed unless a specific provision in the tax law permits them. The inclusive definition of income and the exclusive definition of deductions may not seem fair to taxpayers, but it is the structure of the tax law.

The courts have held that whether and to what extent deductions are allowed depends on legislative grace.[1] In other words, any exclusions from income and all deductions are gifts from Congress!

It is important to classify deductible expenses as **deductions for adjusted gross income** (AGI) or **deductions from adjusted gross income**. Deductions *for* AGI can be claimed whether or not the taxpayer itemizes. Deductions *from* AGI result in a tax benefit only if they exceed the taxpayer's standard deduction. If itemized deductions (*from* AGI) are less than the standard deduction, they provide no tax benefit.

[1] *New Colonial Ice Co. v. Helvering*, 4 USTC ¶1292, 13 AFTR 1180, 54 S.Ct. 788 (USSC, 1934).

EXAMPLE 1

Steve is a self-employed CPA. Ralph is one of Steve's employees. During the year, Steve and Ralph incur the following expenses:

	Steve	Ralph
Dues to American Institute of CPAs and State Society of CPAs	$ 400	$ 300
Subscriptions to professional journals	500	200
Registration fees for tax conferences	800	800
	$1,700	$1,300

Steve does not reimburse any of his employees for dues, subscriptions, or educational programs.

Steve's expenses are classified as a deduction *for* AGI. Therefore, he can deduct the $1,700 on his Federal income tax return. Ralph's expenses are classified as deductions *from* AGI. Ralph will be able to benefit from the $1,300 of expenses on his Federal income tax return only if he itemizes deductions. If he takes the standard deduction instead, the $1,300 of expenses will have no effect on the calculation of his taxable income. Even if Ralph does itemize deductions, he must reduce the $1,300 of expenses, which are classified as miscellaneous itemized deductions, by 2% of his AGI. As this example illustrates, whether a deduction is classified as *for* AGI or *from* AGI can affect the benefit the taxpayer receives from the deduction. ■

See Concept Summary 6.3 later in the chapter for the classification of deductions as deductions *for* AGI or as deductions *from* AGI.

Deductions *for* AGI are also important in determining the *amount* of itemized deductions because many itemized deductions are limited to amounts in excess of specified percentages of AGI. Examples of itemized deductions that are limited by AGI are medical expenses and personal casualty losses. Itemized deductions that are deductible only to the extent that they exceed a specified percentage of AGI are increased when AGI is decreased. Likewise, when AGI is increased, these itemized deductions are decreased.

EXAMPLE 2

Tina earns a salary of $20,000 and has no other income. She itemizes deductions during the current year. Medical expenses for the year are $1,800. Since medical expenses are deductible only to the extent they exceed 7.5% of AGI, Tina's medical expense deduction is $300 [$1,800 − (7.5% × $20,000)]. If Tina had a $2,000 deduction *for* AGI, her medical expense deduction would be $450 [$1,800 − (7.5% × $18,000)], or $150 more. If the $2,000 deduction was *from* AGI, her medical expense deduction would remain $300 since AGI is unchanged. ■

DEDUCTIONS FOR ADJUSTED GROSS INCOME

To understand how deductions of individual taxpayers are classified, it is necessary to examine the role of § 62. The purpose of § 62 is to classify various deductions as deductions *for* AGI. It does not provide the statutory authority for taking the deduction. For example, § 212 allows individuals to deduct expenses attributable to income-producing property. Section 212 expenses that are attributable to rents or royalties are classified as deductions *for* AGI. Likewise, a deduction for trade or business expenses is allowed by § 162. These expenses are classified as deductions *for* AGI.

If a deduction is not listed in § 62, it is an itemized deduction, not a deduction *for* AGI. Following is a *partial* list of the items classified as deductions *for* AGI by § 62:

- Expenses attributable to a trade or business carried on by the taxpayer. A trade or business does not include the performance of services by the taxpayer as an employee.
- Expenses incurred by a taxpayer in connection with the performance of services as an employee if the expenses are reimbursed and other conditions are satisfied.

- Deductions that result from losses on the sale or exchange of property by the taxpayer.
- Deductions attributable to property held for the production of rents and royalties.
- The deduction for payment of alimony.
- The deduction for one-half of the self-employment tax paid by a self-employed taxpayer.
- The deduction for the medical insurance premiums paid by a self-employed taxpayer for coverage of the taxpayer, spouse, and any dependents.
- Certain contributions to pension, profit sharing, and annuity plans of self-employed individuals.
- The deduction for certain retirement savings allowed by § 219 (e.g., traditional IRAs).
- The penalty imposed on premature withdrawal of funds from time savings accounts or deposits.
- The deduction for moving expenses.
- The deduction for interest paid on student loans.
- The deduction for qualified tuition and related expenses under § 222 (refer to Chapter 9).
- The deduction for up to $250 for teacher supplies for elementary and secondary school teachers (refer to Chapter 9).

These items are covered in detail in various chapters in the text.

ITEMIZED DEDUCTIONS

The Code defines itemized deductions as the deductions allowed other than "the deductions allowable in arriving at adjusted gross income."[2] Thus, if a deduction is not properly classified as a deduction *for* AGI, then it is classified as an itemized deduction.

Section 212 Expenses

Section 212 allows deductions for ordinary and necessary expenses paid or incurred by an individual for the following:

- The production or collection of income.
- The management, conservation, or maintenance of property held for the production of income.
- Expenses paid in connection with the determination, collection, or refund of any tax.

Section 212 expenses related to rent and royalty income are deductions *for* AGI. Expenses paid in connection with the determination, collection, or refund of taxes related to the income of sole proprietorships, rents and royalties, or farming operations are deductions *for* AGI. All other § 212 expenses are itemized deductions (deductions *from* AGI). For example, investment-related expenses (e.g., safe deposit box rentals) are deductible as itemized deductions attributable to the production of investment income.[3]

Deductible Personal Expenses

Taxpayers are allowed to deduct certain expenses that are primarily personal in nature. These expenses, which generally are not related to the production of income, are deductions *from* AGI (itemized deductions). Some of the more frequently encountered deductions in this category include the following:

- Contributions to qualified charitable organizations (not to exceed a specified percentage of AGI).
- Medical expenses (in excess of 7.5 percent of AGI).

---

[2] § 63(d).

[3] § 62(a)(4) and Reg. § 1.212–1(g).

- Certain state and local taxes (e.g., real estate taxes and state and local income or sales taxes).
- Personal casualty losses (in excess of an aggregate floor of 10 percent of AGI and a $100 floor per casualty).[4]
- Certain personal interest (e.g., mortgage interest on a personal residence).

Itemized deductions are discussed in detail in Chapter 10.

TRADE OR BUSINESS EXPENSES AND PRODUCTION OF INCOME EXPENSES

Section 162(a) permits a deduction for all ordinary and necessary expenses paid or incurred in carrying on a trade or business. These include reasonable salaries paid for services, expenses for the use of business property, and one-half of self-employment taxes paid. Such expenses are deducted *for* AGI.

It is sometimes difficult to determine whether an expenditure is deductible as a trade or business expense. The term "trade or business" is not defined in the Code or Regulations, and the courts have not provided a satisfactory definition. It is usually necessary to ask one or more of the following questions to determine whether an item qualifies as a trade or business expense:

- Was the use of the particular item related to a business activity? For example, if funds are borrowed for use in a business, the interest is deductible as a business expense.
- Was the expenditure incurred with the intent to realize a profit or to produce income? For example, expenses in excess of the income from raising horses are not deductible if the activity is classified as a personal hobby rather than a trade or business.
- Were the taxpayer's operation and management activities extensive enough to indicate the carrying on of a trade or business?

Section 162 *excludes* the following items from classification as trade or business expenses:

- Charitable contributions or gifts.
- Illegal bribes and kickbacks and certain treble damage payments.
- Fines and penalties.

A bribe paid to a domestic official is not deductible if it is illegal under the laws of the United States. Foreign bribes are deductible unless they are unlawful under the Foreign Corrupt Practices Act of 1977.[5]

Ordinary and Necessary Requirement

The terms **ordinary and necessary** are found in both §§ 162 and 212. To be deductible, any trade or business expense must be "ordinary and necessary." In addition, compensation for services must be "reasonable" in amount.

Many expenses that are necessary are *not* ordinary. Neither "ordinary" nor "necessary" is defined in the Code or Regulations. The courts have held that an expense is *necessary* if a prudent businessperson would incur the same expense and the expense is expected to be appropriate and helpful in the taxpayer's business.[6]

EXAMPLE 3

Pat purchased a manufacturing concern that had just been adjudged bankrupt. Because the business had a poor financial rating, Pat satisfied some of the obligations to employees and outside salespeople incurred by the former owners. Pat had no legal obligation to pay these debts, but felt this was the only way to keep salespeople and employees. The Second Circuit Court of Appeals found that the payments were

[4]For 2009 the $100 floor was increased to $500.

[5]§ 162(c)(1).

[6]*Welch v. Helvering*, 3 USTC ¶1164, 12 AFTR 1456, 54 S.Ct. 8 (USSC, 1933).

necessary in that they were both appropriate and helpful. However, the court held that the payments were *not* ordinary but were in the nature of capital expenditures to build a reputation.[7] Therefore, no deduction was allowed. ■

An expense is *ordinary* if it is normal, usual, or customary in the type of business conducted by the taxpayer and is not capital in nature.[8] However, an expense need not be recurring to be deductible as ordinary.

EXAMPLE 4

Albert engaged in a mail-order business. The post office judged that his advertisements were false and misleading. Under a fraud order, the post office stamped "fraudulent" on all letters addressed to Albert's business and returned them to the senders. Albert spent $30,000 on legal fees in an unsuccessful attempt to force the post office to stop. The legal fees (though not recurring) were ordinary business expenses because they were normal, usual, or customary in the circumstances.[9] ■

For § 212 deductions, the law requires that expenses bear a reasonable and proximate relationship to (1) the production or collection of income or to (2) the management, conservation, or maintenance of property held for the production of income.[10]

EXAMPLE 5
THE BIG PICTURE

Return to the facts of *The Big Picture* on p. 6-2. Dr. Payne owns a small portfolio of investments, including 10 shares of Hawk, Inc. common stock worth $1,000. He incurred $350 in travel expenses to attend the annual shareholders' meeting where he voted his 10 shares against the current management group. No deduction is permitted because a 10-share investment is insignificant in value in relation to the travel expenses incurred.[11] ■

Reasonableness Requirement

The Code refers to **reasonableness** solely with respect to salaries and other compensation for services.[12] But the courts have held that for any business expense to be ordinary and necessary, it must also be reasonable in amount.[13]

What constitutes reasonableness is a question of fact. If an expense is unreasonable, the excess amount is not allowed as a deduction. The question of reasonableness generally arises with respect to closely held corporations where there is no separation of ownership and management.

Transactions between the shareholders and the closely held company may result in the disallowance of deductions for excessive salaries and rent expense paid by the corporation to the shareholders. The courts will view an unusually large salary in light of all relevant circumstances and may find that the salary is reasonable despite its size.[14] If excessive payments for salaries and rents are closely related to the percentage of stock owned by the recipients, the payments are generally treated as dividends.[15] Since dividends are not deductible by the corporation, the disallowance results in an increase in the corporate taxable income. Deductions for reasonable salaries will not be disallowed *solely* because the corporation has paid insubstantial portions of its earnings as dividends to its shareholders.

[7] *Dunn and McCarthy, Inc. v. Comm.*, 43–2 USTC ¶9688, 31 AFTR 1043, 139 F.2d 242 (CA–2, 1943).

[8] *Deputy v. DuPont*, 40–1 USTC ¶9161, 23 AFTR 808, 60 S.Ct. 363 (USSC, 1940).

[9] *Comm. v. Heininger*, 44–1 USTC ¶9109, 31 AFTR 783, 64 S.Ct. 249 (USSC, 1943).

[10] Reg. § 1.212–1(d).

[11] *J. Raymond Dyer*, 36 T.C. 456 (1961).

[12] § 162(a)(1).

[13] *Comm. v. Lincoln Electric Co.*, 49–2 USTC ¶9388, 38 AFTR 411, 176 F.2d 815 (CA–6, 1949).

[14] *Kennedy, Jr. v. Comm.*, 82–1 USTC ¶9186, 49 AFTR 2d 82–628, 671 F.2d 167 (CA–6, 1982), *rev'g* 72 T.C. 793 (1979).

[15] Reg. § 1.162–8.

EXAMPLE 6

Sparrow Corporation, a closely held C corporation, is owned equally by Lupe, Carlos, and Ramon. The company has been highly profitable for several years and has not paid dividends. Lupe, Carlos, and Ramon are key officers of the company, and each receives a salary of $200,000. Salaries for similar positions in comparable companies average only $100,000. Amounts paid the owners in excess of $100,000 may be deemed unreasonable, and, if so, a total of $300,000 in salary deductions by Sparrow is disallowed. The disallowed amounts are treated as dividends rather than salary income to Lupe, Carlos, and Ramon because the payments are proportional to stock ownership. Salaries are deductible by the corporation, but dividends are not. ■

BUSINESS AND NONBUSINESS LOSSES

Section 165 provides for a deduction for losses not compensated for by insurance. As a general rule, deductible losses of individual taxpayers are limited to those incurred in a trade or business or in a transaction entered into for profit. Individuals are also allowed to deduct losses that are the result of a casualty. Casualty losses include, but are not limited to, those caused by fire, storm, shipwreck, and theft. See Chapter 7 for a further discussion of this topic. Deductible personal casualty losses are reduced by $100 per casualty, and the aggregate of all personal casualty losses is reduced by 10 percent of AGI. A personal casualty loss is an itemized deduction. See Concept Summary 6.3 near the end of the chapter for the classification of expenses.

REPORTING PROCEDURES

All deductions *for* and *from* AGI wind up on pages 1 and 2 of Form 1040. All deductions *for* AGI are reported on page 1. The last line on page 1 is adjusted gross income.

The first item on page 2 is also adjusted gross income. Itemized deductions are entered next, followed by the deduction for personal and dependency exemptions. The result is taxable income.

Most of the deductions *for* AGI on page 1 originate on supporting schedules. Examples include business expenses (Schedule C); rent, royalty, partnership, and fiduciary deductions (Schedule E); and farming expenses (Schedule F). Other deductions *for* AGI, such as traditional IRAs, Keogh retirement plans, and alimony, are entered directly on page 1 of Form 1040.

All itemized deductions on page 2 are carried over from Schedule A. Some Schedule A deductions originate on other forms. Examples include investment interest, noncash charitable contributions in excess of $500, casualty losses, and unreimbursed employee expenses.

Form 1040 becomes a summary of the detailed information entered on the other schedules and forms. See Figure 6.1.

See Concept Summary 6.3 later in the chapter for the classification of deductions as deductions *for* AGI or as deductions *from* AGI.

6.2 DEDUCTIONS AND LOSSES—TIMING OF EXPENSE RECOGNITION

LO.2

Describe the cash and accrual methods of accounting.

IMPORTANCE OF TAXPAYER'S METHOD OF ACCOUNTING

A taxpayer's **accounting method** is a major factor in determining taxable income. The method used determines when an item is includible in income and when an item is deductible on the tax return. Usually, the taxpayer's regular method of record keeping is used for income tax purposes.[16] The taxing authorities do not require uniformity among all taxpayers. They do require that the method used clearly reflect

[16] § 446(a).

FIGURE 6.1 **Format of Form 1040**

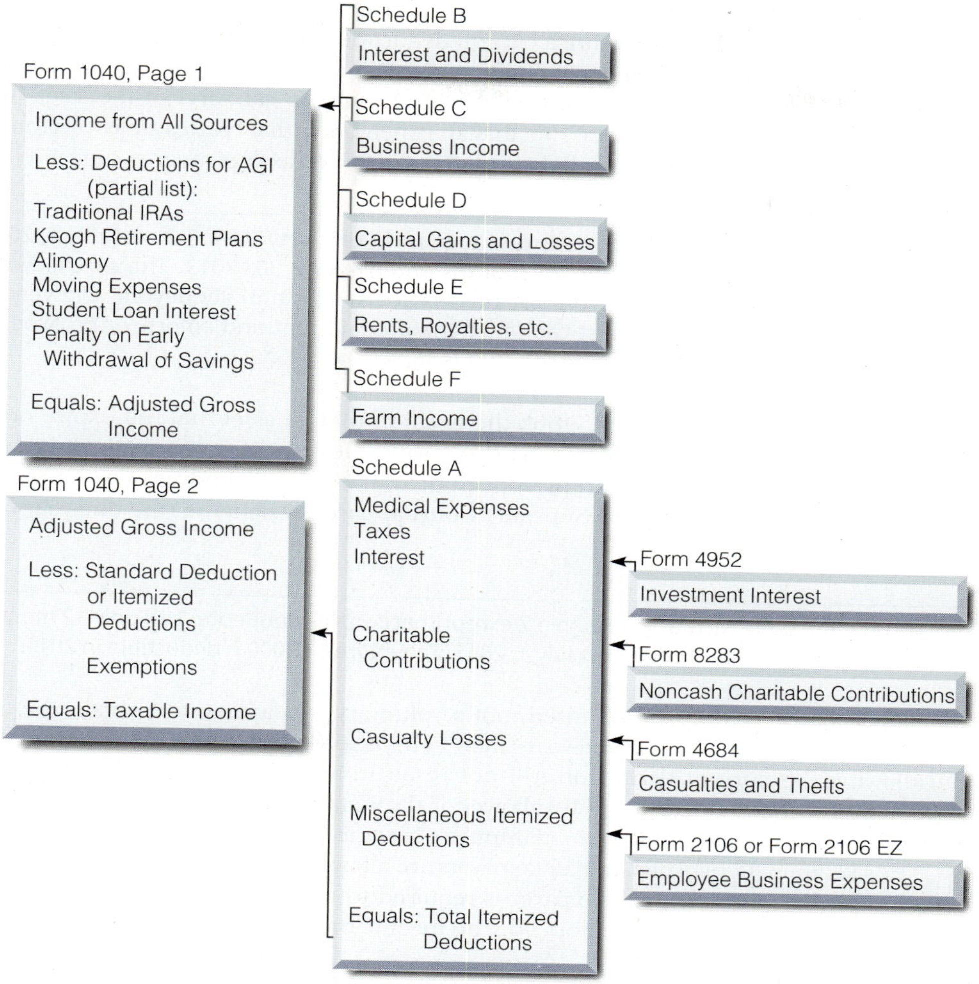

income and that items be handled consistently.[17] The most common methods of accounting are the cash method and the accrual method. If a taxpayer owns multiple businesses, it may be possible to use the cash method for some and the accrual method for others.

Throughout the portions of the Code dealing with deductions, the phrase "paid or incurred" is used. *Paid* refers to the cash basis taxpayer who gets a deduction only in the year of payment. *Incurred* concerns the accrual basis taxpayer who obtains the deduction in the year in which the liability for the expense becomes certain (refer to Chapter 4).

CASH METHOD REQUIREMENTS

The expenses of cash basis taxpayers are deductible only when they are actually paid with cash or other property. Promising to pay or issuing a note does not satisfy the actually paid requirement.[18] However, the payment can be made with borrowed funds. At the time taxpayers charge expenses on their credit cards, they are allowed

[17] §§ 446(b) and (e); Reg. § 1.446–1(a)(2).

[18] *Page v. Rhode Island Trust Co., Exr.*, 37–1 USTC ¶9138, 19 AFTR 105, 88 F.2d 192 (CA–1, 1937).

to claim the deduction. They are deemed to have simultaneously borrowed money from the credit card issuer and constructively paid the expenses.[19]

Although the cash basis taxpayer must have actually or constructively paid the expense, payment does not assure a current deduction. Cash basis and accrual basis taxpayers cannot take a current deduction for capital expenditures except through amortization, depletion, or depreciation over the life (actual or statutory) of the asset. The Regulations set forth the general rule that an expenditure that creates an asset having a useful life that extends substantially beyond the end of the tax year must be capitalized.[20]

EXAMPLE 7

John, a calendar year and cash basis taxpayer, rents property from Carl. On July 1, 2011, John pays $24,000 rent for the 24 months ending June 30, 2013. The prepaid rent extends 18 months after the close of the tax year—substantially beyond the year of payment. Therefore, John must capitalize the prepaid rent and amortize the expense on a monthly basis. His deduction for 2011 is $6,000. ■

The Tax Court and the IRS took the position that an asset that will expire or be consumed by the end of the tax year following the year of payment must be prorated. The Ninth Circuit Court of Appeals held that such expenditures are currently deductible, however, and the Supreme Court apparently concurs (the one-year rule for prepaid expenses).[21]

EXAMPLE 8

Assume the same facts as in Example 7 except that John is required to pay only 12 months' rent in 2011. He pays $12,000 on July 1, 2011. The entire $12,000 is deductible in 2011. ■

The payment must be required, not a voluntary prepayment, to obtain the current deduction under the one-year rule.[22] The taxpayer must also demonstrate that allowing the current deduction will not result in a material distortion of income. Generally, the deduction will be allowed if the item is recurring or was made for a business purpose rather than to manipulate income.[23]

As Chapter 16 explains, not all taxpayers are allowed to use the cash method.[24] For example, in most cases the taxpayer is required to use the accrual method for sales and cost of goods sold if inventories are an income-producing factor of the business.

ACCRUAL METHOD REQUIREMENTS

The period in which an accrual basis taxpayer can deduct an expense is determined by applying the *all events test* and the *economic performance test.* A deduction cannot be claimed until (1) all the events have occurred to create the taxpayer's liability and (2) the amount of the liability can be determined with reasonable accuracy. Once these requirements are satisfied, the deduction is permitted only if economic performance has occurred. The economic performance test is met only when the service, property, or use of property giving rise to the liability is actually performed for, provided to, or used by the taxpayer.[25]

EXAMPLE 9

On December 22, 2011, Chris's entertainment business sponsored a jazz festival in a rented auditorium at a local college. His business is responsible for cleaning up the auditorium after the festival and for reinstalling seats that were removed so more people could attend the festival. Since the college is closed over the Christmas holidays, the company hired by Chris to perform the work did not begin these activities until

[19]Rev.Rul. 78–39, 1978–1 C.B. 73. See also Rev.Rul. 80–335, 1980–2 C.B. 170, which applies to pay-by-phone arrangements.

[20]Reg. § 1.461–1(a).

[21]*Zaninovich v. Comm.*, 80–1 USTC ¶9342, 45 AFTR 2d 80–1442, 616 F.2d 429 (CA–9, 1980), *rev'g* 69 T.C. 605 (1978). Cited by the Supreme Court in *Hillsboro National Bank v. Comm.*, 83–1 USTC ¶9229, 51 AFTR 2d 83–874, 103 S.Ct. 1134 (USSC, 1983).

[22]*Bonaire Development Co. v. Comm.*, 82–2 USTC ¶9428, 50 AFTR 2d 82–5167, 679 F.2d 159 (CA–9, 1982).

[23]*Keller v. Comm.*, 84–1 USTC ¶9194, 53 AFTR 2d 84–663, 725 F.2d 1173 (CA–8, 1984), *aff'g* 79 T.C. 7 (1982).

[24]§ 448.

[25]§ 461(h).

January 2, 2012. The cost to Chris is $1,200. Chris cannot deduct the $1,200 until 2012, when the services are performed. ■

An exception to the economic performance requirements allows certain *recurring items* to be deducted if the following conditions are met:

- The item is recurring in nature and is treated consistently by the taxpayer.
- Either the accrued item is not material, or accruing it results in better matching of income and expenses.
- All the events have occurred that determine the fact of the liability, and the amount of the liability can be determined with reasonable accuracy.
- Economic performance occurs within a reasonable period (but not later than 8½ months after the close of the taxable year).[26]

EXAMPLE 10

Rick, an accrual basis, calendar year taxpayer, entered into a monthly maintenance contract during the year. He makes a monthly accrual at the end of every month for this service and pays the fee sometime between the first and fifteenth of the following month when services are performed. The amount involved is immaterial, and all the other tests are met. The December 2011 accrual is deductible in 2011 even though the service is performed on January 12, 2012. ■

EXAMPLE 11

Rita, an accrual basis, calendar year taxpayer, shipped merchandise sold on December 30, 2011, via Greyhound Van Lines on January 2, 2012, and paid the freight charges at that time. Since Rita reported the sale of the merchandise in 2011, the shipping charge should also be deductible in 2011. This procedure results in a better matching of income and expenses. ■

Reserves for estimated expenses (frequently employed for financial accounting purposes) generally are not allowed for tax purposes because the economic performance test cannot be satisfied.

EXAMPLE 12

Blackbird Airlines is required by Federal law to test its engines after 3,000 flying hours. Aircraft cannot return to flight until the tests have been conducted. An unrelated aircraft maintenance company does all of the company's tests for $1,500 per engine. For financial reporting purposes, the company accrues an expense based upon $.50 per hour of flight and credits an allowance account. The actual amounts paid for maintenance are offset against the allowance account. For tax purposes, the economic performance test is not satisfied until the work has been done. Therefore, the reserve method cannot be used for tax purposes. ■

6.3 Disallowance Possibilities

LO.3

Apply the Internal Revenue Code deduction disallowance provisions associated with the following: public policy limitations, political activities, excessive executive compensation, investigation of business opportunities, hobby losses, vacation home rentals, payment of others' expenses, personal expenditures, capital expenditures, related-party transactions, and expenses related to tax-exempt income.

The tax law provides for the disallowance of certain types of expenses. Without specific restrictions in the tax law, taxpayers might attempt to deduct certain items that in reality are personal expenditures. For example, specific tax rules are provided to determine whether an expenditure is for trade or business purposes or related to a personal hobby.

Certain disallowance provisions are a codification or extension of prior court decisions. After the courts denied deductions for payments considered to be in violation of public policy, the tax law was changed to provide specific authority for the disallowance of these deductions. Discussions of specific disallowance provisions in the tax law follow.

[26] § 461(h)(3)(A).

PUBLIC POLICY LIMITATION

Justification for Denying Deductions

The courts developed the principle that a payment that is in violation of public policy is not a necessary expense and is not deductible.[27] Although a bribe or fine may be appropriate and helpful, and even contribute to the profitability of an activity, the courts held that to allow such expenses would frustrate clearly defined public policy. A deduction would dilute the effect of the penalty since the government would be indirectly subsidizing a taxpayer's wrongdoing.

Accordingly, the IRS was free to restrict deductions if, in its view, the expenses were contrary to public policy. But since the law did not explain which actions violated public policy, taxpayers often had to go to court to determine whether their expense fell into this category.

Furthermore, the public policy doctrine could be arbitrarily applied in cases where no clear definition had emerged. To solve these problems, Congress enacted legislation that attempts to limit the use of the doctrine. Under the legislation, deductions are disallowed for certain specific types of expenditures that are considered contrary to public policy:

- Bribes and kickbacks including those associated with Medicare or Medicaid (in the case of foreign bribes and kickbacks, only if the payments violate the U.S. Foreign Corrupt Practices Act of 1977).
- Fines and penalties paid to a government for violation of law.

EXAMPLE 13

Brown Corporation, a moving company, consistently loads its trucks with weights in excess of the limits allowed by state law. The additional revenue more than offsets the fines levied. The fines are for a violation of public policy and are not deductible. ■

- Two-thirds of the treble damage payments made to claimants resulting from violation of the antitrust law.[28]

To be disallowed, the bribe or kickback must be illegal under either Federal or state law and must also subject the payor to a criminal penalty or the loss of a license or privilege to engage in a trade or business. For a bribe or kickback that is illegal under state law, a deduction is denied only if the state law is generally enforced.

EXAMPLE 14

During the year, Keith, an insurance salesman, paid $5,000 to Karen, a real estate broker. The payment represented 20% of the commissions Keith earned from customers referred by Karen. Under state law, the splitting of commissions by an insurance salesperson is an act of misconduct that could warrant a revocation of the salesperson's license. Keith's $5,000 payments to Karen are not deductible provided the state law is generally enforced. ■

Legal Expenses Incurred in Defense of Civil or Criminal Penalties

To deduct legal expenses, the taxpayer must be able to show that the origin and character of the claim are directly related to a trade or business, an income-producing activity, or the determination, collection, or refund of a tax. Personal legal expenses are not deductible. Thus, legal fees incurred in connection with a criminal defense are deductible only if the crime is associated with the taxpayer's trade or business or income-producing activity.[29]

EXAMPLE 15

Debra, a financial officer of Blue Corporation, incurs legal expenses in connection with her defense in a criminal indictment for evasion of Blue's income taxes. Debra may

[27] *Tank Truck Rentals, Inc. v. Comm.*, 58–1 USTC ¶9366, 1 AFTR 2d 1154, 78 S.Ct. 507 (USSC, 1958).

[28] §§ 162(c), (f), and (g).

[29] *Comm. v. Tellier*, 66–1 USTC ¶9319, 17 AFTR 2d 633, 86 S.Ct. 1118 (USSC, 1966).

GLOBAL
Tax Issues

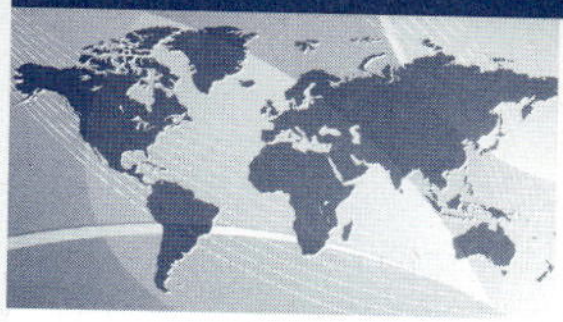

Bribes That Are Deductible?

Under the Foreign Corrupt Practices Act of 1977, a payment that is a common business practice in the country where it is made is legal and is not disallowed as a bribe.

According to a study published by the Brookings Institution, bribes, patronage, and other forms of public corruption are major sources of Greece's ballooning debt. Such costs deprive Greece of at least 8 percent of its GDP each year. In 2009, 13.5 percent of Greek households paid at least one bribe, amounting to 1,355 euros on average (about $1,900 in 2010 dollars). Ordinary citizens hand out "little envelopes" to get driver's licenses, doctor's appointments, and building permits. Such envelopes are also used to reduce taxes owed to the government. Some tax offices apparently operate under the "4-4-2" system, a name derived from a soccer tactic. For example, if an individual or company owes the government 10,000 euros, it is distributed as follows: pay 4,000 to the tax inspector, keep 4,000, and pay 2,000 to the government.

In this environment, bribes of government officials would probably be deductible under the provisions of the Foreign Corrupt Practices Act.

Source: Adapted from Marcus Walker, "Tragic Flaw: Graft Feeds Greek Crisis," *Wall Street Journal,* April 16, 2010, p. A1.

deduct her legal expenses because she is deemed to be in the trade or business of being an executive. The legal action impairs her ability to conduct this business activity.[30] ■

Deductible legal expenses associated with the following are deductible *for* AGI:

- Ordinary and necessary expenses incurred in connection with a trade or business.
- Ordinary and necessary expenses incurred in conjunction with rental or royalty property held for the production of income.

All other deductible legal expenses are deductible *from* AGI. For example, legal expenses generally are deductible *from* AGI if they are for fees for tax advice relative to the preparation of an individual's income tax return. Contrast this with the deduction *for* classification of legal fees for tax advice relative to the preparation of the portion of the tax return for a sole proprietor's trade or business (Schedule C) or an individual's rental or royalty income (Schedule E).

Expenses Relating to an Illegal Business

The usual expenses of operating an illegal business (e.g., a numbers racket) are deductible.[31] However, § 162 disallows a deduction for fines, bribes to public officials, illegal kickbacks, and other illegal payments.

EXAMPLE 16

Sam owns and operates an illegal gambling establishment. In connection with this activity, he has the following expenses during the year:

Rent	$ 60,000
Payoffs to the police	40,000
Depreciation on equipment	100,000
Wages	140,000
Interest	30,000
Criminal fines	50,000
Illegal kickbacks	10,000
Total	$430,000

30 Rev.Rul. 68–662, 1968–2 C.B. 69.

31 *Comm. v. Sullivan,* 58–1 USTC ¶9368, 1 AFTR 2d 1158, 78 S.Ct. 512 (USSC, 1958).

All of the usual expenses (rent, depreciation, wages, and interest) are deductible; payoffs, fines, and kickbacks are not deductible. Of the $430,000 spent, $330,000 is deductible and $100,000 is not. ■

An exception applies to expenses incurred in illegal trafficking in drugs.[32] *Drug dealers* are not allowed a deduction for ordinary and necessary business expenses incurred in their business. In arriving at gross income from the business, however, dealers may reduce total sales by the cost of goods sold.[33] In this regard, no distinction is made between legal and illegal businesses in calculating gross income. Treating cost of goods sold as a negative income item rather than as a deduction item produces the unseemly result that a drug dealer's taxable income is reduced by cost of goods sold.

ETHICS & Equity

Too Much of a Good Thing

Clark, a prospective new client, visits your office on March 12, 2011. He wants you to prepare a Form 1120S for 2010 for his washateria, Wash Clean, an S corporation. Clark owns at least six different businesses in your community and has a reputation of being a risk taker and an "operator." He provides you with the financial data prepared monthly for Wash Clean by a local bookkeeping service. He hopes to file the S corporation return by March 15 "to avoid any problems with the IRS." Clark also is the president of the Chamber of Commerce.

In preparing the Form 1120S, you note that the net income for Wash Clean far exceeds that of several other washateria clients. About a month ago, one of your golfing companions mentioned that he had heard that Wash Clean was laundering more than clothes.

You have all the data you need to complete the Form 1120S for Wash Clean. Should you do so?

POLITICAL CONTRIBUTIONS AND LOBBYING ACTIVITIES

Political Contributions

Generally, no business deduction is permitted for direct or indirect payments for political purposes.[34] Historically, the government has been reluctant to accord favorable tax treatment to business expenditures for political purposes. Allowing deductions might encourage abuses and enable businesses to have undue influence upon the political process.

Lobbying Expenditures

Lobbying expenses incurred in attempting to influence state or Federal legislation or the actions of certain high-ranking public officials (e.g., the President, Vice President, cabinet-level officials, and the two most senior officials in each agency of the executive branch) are not deductible.[35] The disallowance also applies to a pro rata portion of the membership dues of trade associations and other groups that are used for lobbying activities.

EXAMPLE 17

Egret Company pays a $10,000 annual membership fee to the Free Trade Group, a trade association for plumbing wholesalers. The trade association estimates that 70% of its dues are allocated to lobbying activities. Thus, Egret Company's deduction is limited to $3,000 ($10,000 × 30%). ■

[32] § 280E.

[33] Reg. § 1.61–3(a). Gross income is defined as sales minus cost of goods sold. Thus, while § 280E prohibits any deductions for drug dealers, it does not modify the normal definition of gross income.

[34] § 276.

[35] § 162(e).

TAX *in the NEWS*

RECENT INROADS ON THE DEDUCTIBILITY OF EXECUTIVE COMPENSATION

Under the Emergency Economic Stabilization Act of 2008, Congress established the Troubled Asset Relief Program (TARP) to help bail out ailing financial institutions. Under TARP, the government is authorized to make direct purchases or sponsored-auction purchases of troubled assets. For the participating companies, standards are set on the deductibility of executive compensation (e.g., for CEOs, CFOs, and other key officers). In direct purchase situations, the IRS is empowered to establish compensation parameters. In auction cases, however, a cap of $500,000 is imposed. Also affected are golden parachutes (i.e., severance bonuses paid to executives in change of ownership or control situations).

A last-minute amendment to the American Recovery and Reinvestment Tax Act of 2009 by Senator Christopher Dodd (D-Conn.) has imposed even more stringent restrictions on executive bonuses paid by firms receiving Federal aid. Under the provision, a bonus cannot exceed more than one-third of the executive's total annual compensation (e.g., a salary of $1 million would allow a bonus of not more than $500,000—one-third of the salary plus bonus). Also, a "clawback" feature would compel a repayment of excessive bonuses previously paid.

Nontax legislation has imposed other limits on compensation that can be paid by TARP recipients. These provisions are being administered by the so-called compensation czar, the Treasury Department's special master for TARP executive compensation. His powers include veto authority over the compensation paid by seven companies that received huge sums of Federal aid under TARP. He must approve or review the compensation paid to senior executive officers and the 100 highest-paid employees.

There are three exceptions to the disallowance of lobbying expenses. An exception is provided for influencing local legislation (e.g., city and county governments). Second, the disallowance provision does not apply to activities devoted solely to monitoring legislation. Third, a *de minimis* exception is provided for annual in-house expenditures (lobbying expenses other than those paid to professional lobbyists or any portion of dues used by associations for lobbying) if such expenditures do not exceed $2,000. If the in-house expenditures exceed $2,000, none of the in-house expenditures can be deducted.

EXCESSIVE EXECUTIVE COMPENSATION

Prior to tax legislation enacted in 2008, the deduction of executive compensation was subject to only two limitations. As discussed earlier in this chapter, the compensation of shareholder-employees of closely held corporations is subject to the reasonableness requirement. The second limitation, the so-called millionaires' provision, applies to publicly held corporations (a corporation that has at least one class of stock registered under the Securities Exchange Act of 1934).[36]

The millionaires' provision does not limit the amount of compensation that can be paid to an employee. Instead, it limits the amount the employer can deduct for the compensation of a covered executive to $1 million annually. Covered employees include the chief executive officer and the four other most highly compensated officers.

Employee compensation *excludes* the following:

- Commissions based on individual performance.
- Certain performance-based compensation based on company performance according to a formula approved by a board of directors compensation committee (composed solely of two or more outside directors) and by shareholder vote. The performance attainment must be certified by this compensation committee.
- Payments to tax-qualified retirement plans.
- Payments that are excludible from the employee's gross income (e.g., certain fringe benefits).

[36]§ 162(m).

GLOBAL
Tax Issues

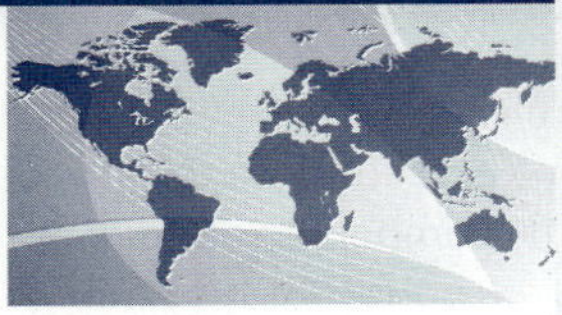

GERMANY'S EXECUTIVE PAY LIMITS

The pay of top executives of major U.S. corporations has become a controversial issue that is frequently discussed in the media and at shareholders' meetings. Nevertheless, all of this attention has had little success at reducing the compensation of top executives or narrowing the pay gap between those executives and the average worker.

In Germany, the government is getting involved in the executive pay controversy. The lower house of the German parliament, the Bundestag, has approved a law that will place restraints on executive pay. The goal is to encourage firms to focus on long-term, rather than short-term, performance.

The law extends the period that board members must hold their stock options before cashing them in from two years to four years. Compensation oversight boards will be subject to increased liability if they approve excessive executive compensation. Disclosure of executive compensation will be mandatory unless 75 percent of the shareholders vote against such disclosure.

Source: Adapted from Klaus Lauer, Dave Graham, and Victoria Main, "Germany Passes Law Imposing Limits on Executive Pay," *Reuters*, June 18, 2009.

The third limitation, which was added by 2008 tax legislation, applies only to covered executives of companies receiving Troubled Asset Relief Program (TARP) assistance. In this case, the deduction for compensation paid to a covered executive is limited to \$500,000. The exception to the statutory limit under the aforementioned millionaires' provision for performance-based compensation does not apply to the \$500,000 limit. Covered employees are somewhat similar to those under the millionaires' provision and include the chief executive officer, the chief financial officer, and the three other most highly compensated officers.

INVESTIGATION OF A BUSINESS

Investigation expenses are expenses paid or incurred to determine the feasibility of entering a new business or expanding an existing business. They include such costs as travel, engineering and architectural surveys, marketing reports, and various legal and accounting services. How such expenses are treated for tax purposes depends on a number of variables, including the following:

- The current business, if any, of the taxpayer.
- The nature of the business being investigated.
- The extent to which the investigation has proceeded.
- Whether or not the acquisition actually takes place.

If the taxpayer is in a business the *same as or similar to* that being investigated, all investigation expenses are deductible in the year paid or incurred. The tax result is the same whether or not the taxpayer acquires the business being investigated.[37]

EXAMPLE 18
THE BIG PICTURE

Return to the facts of *The Big Picture* on p. 6-2. Dr. Payne's mother, Terry, an accrual basis sole proprietor, owns and operates three motels in Georgia. In the current year, Terry incurs expenses of \$8,500 in investigating the possibility of acquiring several additional motels located in South Carolina. The \$8,500 is deductible in the current year whether or not Terry acquires the motels in South Carolina. ■

[37] § 195. *York v. Comm.*, 58–2 USTC ¶9952, 2 AFTR 2d 6178, 261 F.2d 421 (CA–4, 1958).

CONCEPT SUMMARY 6.1

Costs of Investigating a Business

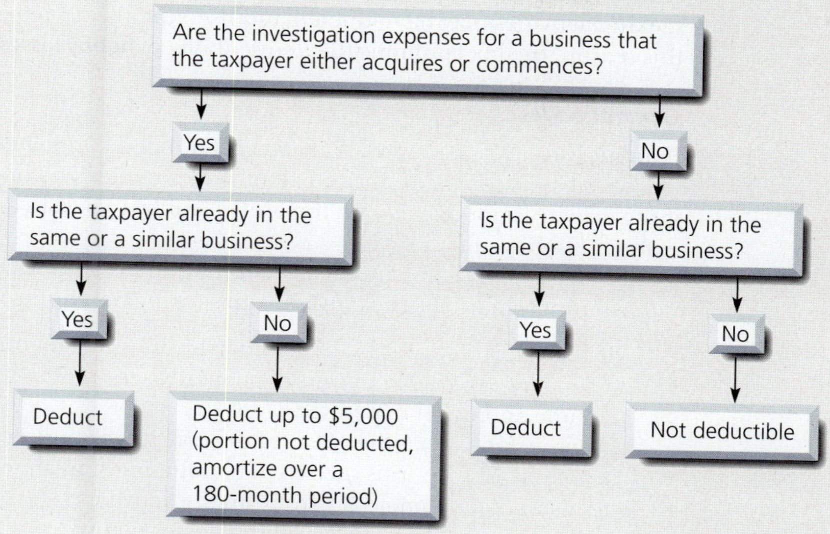

When the taxpayer is *not* in a business that is the same as or similar to the one being investigated, the tax result depends on whether the new business is acquired. If the business is not acquired, all investigation expenses generally are nondeductible.[38]

EXAMPLE 19

Lynn, a retired merchant, incurs expenses in traveling from Rochester, New York, to California to investigate the feasibility of acquiring several auto care centers. If no acquisition takes place, none of the expenses are deductible. ■

If the taxpayer is *not* in a business that is the same as or similar to the one being investigated and actually acquires the new business, the expenses must be capitalized as startup expenses. At the election of the taxpayer, the first $5,000 of the expenses can be immediately deducted. Any excess expenses can be amortized over a period of 180 months (15 years). In arriving at the $5,000 immediate deduction allowed, a dollar-for-dollar reduction must be made for those expenses in excess of $50,000.[39]

EXAMPLE 20

Tina owns and operates 10 restaurants located in various cities throughout the Southeast. She travels to Atlanta to discuss the acquisition of an auto dealership. In addition, she incurs legal and accounting costs associated with the potential acquisition. After incurring total investigation costs of $52,000, she acquires the auto dealership on October 1, 2011.

Tina may immediately deduct $3,000 [$5,000 − ($52,000 − $50,000)] and amortize the balance of $49,000 ($52,000 − $3,000) over a period of 180 months. For calendar year 2011, therefore, Tina can deduct $3,817 [$3,000 + ($49,000 × 3/180)]. ■

[38] Rev.Rul. 57–418, 1957–2 C.B. 143; *Morton Frank*, 20 T.C. 511 (1953); and *Dwight A. Ward*, 20 T.C. 332 (1953).

[39] § 195(b). For startup expenses incurred in 2010, up to $10,000 could be deducted immediately and the phaseout began at $60,000.

HOBBY LOSSES

Business or investment expenses are deductible only if the taxpayer can show that the activity was entered into for the purpose of making a profit. Certain activities may have either profit-seeking or personal attributes, depending upon individual circumstances. Examples include raising horses and operating a farm used as a weekend residence. While personal losses are not deductible, losses attributable to profit-seeking activities may be deducted and used to offset a taxpayer's other income. For this reason, the tax law limits the deductibility of **hobby losses**.

General Rules

If an individual can show that an activity has been conducted with the intent to earn a profit, losses from the activity are fully deductible. The hobby loss rules apply only if the activity is not engaged in for profit. Hobby expenses are deductible only to the extent of hobby income.[40]

The Regulations stipulate that the following nine factors should be considered in determining whether an activity is profit seeking or a hobby:[41]

- Whether the activity is conducted in a businesslike manner.
- The expertise of the taxpayers or their advisers.
- The time and effort expended.
- The expectation that the assets of the activity will appreciate in value.
- The taxpayer's previous success in conducting similar activities.
- The history of income or losses from the activity.
- The relationship of profits earned to losses incurred.
- The financial status of the taxpayer (e.g., if the taxpayer does not have substantial amounts of other income, this may indicate that the activity is engaged in for profit).
- Elements of personal pleasure or recreation in the activity.

The presence or absence of a factor is not by itself determinative of whether the activity is profit seeking or a hobby. Rather, the decision is a subjective one that is based on an analysis of the facts and circumstances.

ETHICS & Equity

When Is a Dairy Farm a Trade or Business?

Randolph has been an orthopedic surgeon in New Orleans for 15 years. He would like to devote less time to his medical practice, spend more time with his family, and pay less income tax. His net income from his medical practice has been about $500,000 per year for the past five years.

Randolph grew up on a dairy farm in southeastern Louisiana. He has many fond memories of his childhood and believes a farm would be an excellent environment for his three children.

Randolph purchases a dairy farm across Lake Pontchartrain from New Orleans. He hires two full-time employees to handle the milking operations and other part-time employees as needed. In addition, Randolph and his family participate in performing various activities on the farm.

Randolph commutes to New Orleans four days a week to continue his medical practice. Because he is devoting less time to the practice, his net income decreases to $400,000. Randolph has a loss of $75,000 for the dairy farm that he attributes to depressed milk prices and his inexperience at running the farm. He considers the medical practice and the dairy farm to be separate trades or businesses. Therefore, on the Federal income tax return, the $75,000 net loss is offset against the $400,000 net income. Assume that the net income and net loss from the medical practice and the dairy farm, respectively, remain approximately the same for the next four years.

Is the position adopted by Randolph defensible? Discuss.

[40] § 183(b)(2).

[41] Reg. §§ 1.183–2(b)(1) through (9).

TAX *in* the NEWS

IRS Doing Poorly in Policing Hobby Loss Deductions

The Treasury Inspector General for Tax Administration (TIGTA) has issued a report on the number of taxpayers who file Schedule C of Form 1040 showing losses over several consecutive years. Many of the returns examined reported substantial income from other sources, and the majority of the individuals involved had their tax returns prepared by tax practitioners. By claiming the Schedule C losses, approximately 1.2 million taxpayers were able to save $2.8 billion in taxes for tax year 2005.

Because of the subjective nature of the hobby loss rules (i.e., whether or not a profit motive exists), these Schedule C losses can be controlled only through thorough policing by the IRS. Unfortunately, the IRS has neither the time nor the resources to carry out the audit efforts required. The TIGTA report, therefore, suggests that § 183 be changed by legislation to establish a clear standard for determining whether an activity is a business or a hobby.

Source: "Significant Challenges Exist in Determining Whether Taxpayers with Schedule C Losses Are Engaged in Tax Abuse," *Treasury Inspector General for Tax Administration,* September 7, 2007 (Reference No. 2007-30-173).

Presumptive Rule of § 183

The Code provides a rebuttable presumption that an activity is profit seeking if the activity shows a profit in at least three of any five prior consecutive years.[42] If the activity involves horses, a profit in at least two of seven consecutive years meets the presumptive rule. If these profitability tests are met, the activity is presumed to be a trade or business rather than a personal hobby. In this situation, the IRS bears the burden of proving that the activity is personal rather than trade or business related.

EXAMPLE 21
THE BIG PICTURE

Return to the facts of *The Big Picture* on p. 6-2. Recall that Camille and Walter are Dr. Payne's mother- and father-in-law. Camille, who is an executive for a large corporation, is paid a salary of $800,000. Walter is a collector of antiques. Several years ago, he opened an antique shop in a local shopping center and spends most of his time buying and selling antiques. He occasionally earns a small profit from this activity but more frequently incurs substantial losses. If Walter's losses are business related, they are fully deductible against Camille's salary on a joint return. In resolving this issue, consider the following:

- Initially determine whether Walter's antique activity has met the three-out-of-five years profit test.
- If the presumption is not met, the activity may nevertheless qualify as a business if Walter can show that the intent is to engage in a profit-seeking activity. It is not necessary to show actual profits.
- Attempt to fit the operation within the nine criteria prescribed in the Regulations and listed previously. These criteria are the factors considered in trying to rebut the § 183 presumption. ■

Determining the Amount of the Deduction

If an activity is deemed to be a hobby, the expenses are deductible only to the extent of the gross income from the hobby. These expenses must be deducted in the following order:

- Amounts deductible under other Code sections without regard to the nature of the activity, such as property taxes and home mortgage interest.
- Amounts deductible under other Code sections if the activity had been engaged in for profit, but only if those amounts do not affect adjusted basis. Examples include maintenance, utilities, and supplies.

[42] § 183(d).

- Amounts that affect adjusted basis and would be deductible under other Code sections if the activity had been engaged in for profit.[43] Examples include depreciation, amortization, and depletion.

These deductions are deductible *from* AGI as itemized deductions to the extent they exceed 2 percent of AGI.[44] If the taxpayer uses the standard deduction rather than itemizing, all hobby loss deductions are wasted.

EXAMPLE 22

Jim, the vice president of an oil company, has AGI of $80,000. He decides to pursue painting in his spare time. He uses a home studio, comprising 10% of the home's square footage. During the current year, Jim incurs the following expenses:

Frames	$ 350
Art supplies	300
Fees paid to models	1,000
Home studio expenses:	
Total property taxes	900
Total home mortgage interest	10,000
Depreciation on 10% of home	500
Total home maintenance and utilities	3,600

During the year, Jim sold paintings for a total of $3,200. If the activity is held to be a hobby, Jim is allowed deductions as follows:

Gross income		$ 3,200
Deduct: Taxes and interest (10% of $10,900)		(1,090)
Remainder		$ 2,110
Deduct: Frames	$ 350	
Art supplies	300	
Models' fees	1,000	
Maintenance and utilities (10%)	360	(2,010)
Remainder		$ 100
Deduct: Depreciation ($500, but limited to $100)		(100)
Net income		$ –0–

Jim includes the $3,200 of income in AGI, making his AGI $83,200. The taxes and interest are itemized deductions, deductible in full. The remaining $2,110 of expenses are reduced by 2% of his AGI ($1,664), so the net deduction is $446. Since the property taxes and home mortgage interest are deductible anyway, the net effect is a $2,754 ($3,200 less $446) increase in taxable income. ■

EXAMPLE 23

Assume that Jim's activity in Example 22 is held to be a business. The business is located in a small office building he owns. Expenses are property taxes of $90, mortgage interest of $1,000, frames of $350, art supplies of $300, models' fees of $1,000, maintenance and utilities of $360, and depreciation of $500. Under these circumstances, Jim could deduct expenses totaling $3,600. All these expenses would be trade or business expenses deductible *for* AGI. His reduction in AGI would be as follows:

Gross income		$ 3,200
Less: Taxes and interest	$1,090	
Other business expenses	2,010	
Depreciation	500	(3,600)
Reduction in AGI		($ 400)

■

[43] Reg. § 1.183–1(b)(1).

[44] Reg. § 1.67–1T(a)(1)(iv) and Rev.Rul. 75–14, 1975–1 C.B. 90.

TAX *in* the NEWS

Tax-Free Rent Income

If a taxpayer's rental use of his or her vacation home or residence for the year is less than 15 days (see the discussion below), the rent income can be excluded from gross income. Why was this exclusion included in the tax law? Evidently, some members of Congress and/or lobbyists were golfers.

A prime example of the use of this exclusion occurs in Augusta, Georgia, when the Masters Tournament is held each April. A number of homeowners who live near the Augusta National Golf Club consider this a good time to escape the Georgia heat while earning tax-free income for two weeks. Some homes reportedly have rented for as much as $20,000 during the tournament.

Source: Adapted from Laura Saunders, "A Few Quirky Tax Breaks That Aren't Going Away," *Wall Street Journal*, May 8, 2010, p. B9.

RENTAL OF VACATION HOMES

Restrictions on the deductions allowed for part-year rentals of personal **vacation homes** were written into the law to prevent taxpayers from deducting essentially personal expenses as rental losses. Many taxpayers who owned vacation homes had formerly treated the homes as rental property and generated rental losses as deductions *for* AGI. For example, a summer cabin would be rented for 2 months per year, used for vacationing for 1 month, and left vacant the rest of the year. The taxpayer would then deduct 11 months' depreciation, utilities, maintenance, etc., as rental expenses, resulting in a rental loss. Section 280A eliminates this treatment by allowing deductions on residences used primarily for personal purposes only to the extent of the income generated. Only a break-even situation is allowed; no losses can be deducted.

There are three possible tax treatments for residences used for both personal and rental purposes. The treatment depends upon the *relative time* the residence is used for personal purposes versus rental use.

Primarily Personal Use

If the residence is *rented* for *fewer than 15 days* in a year, it is treated as a personal residence. The rent income is excluded from gross income, and mortgage interest and real estate taxes are allowed as itemized deductions, as with any personal residence.[45] No other expenses (e.g., depreciation, utilities, maintenance) are deductible. Although this provision exists primarily for administrative convenience, several bills have been introduced in Congress that would have repealed this exclusion from gross income.

EXAMPLE 24
THE BIG PICTURE

Return to the facts of *The Big Picture* on p. 6-2. Camille, Dr. Payne's mother-in-law, owns a vacation cottage on the lake. During the current year, she rented it for $1,600 for two weeks, lived in it two months, and left it vacant the remainder of the year. The year's expenses amounted to $6,000 mortgage interest expense, $500 property taxes, $1,500 utilities and maintenance, and $2,400 depreciation. Since the property was not rented for at least 15 days, the income is excluded, the mortgage interest and property tax expenses are itemized deductions, and the remaining expenses are nondeductible personal expenses. ■

Primarily Rental Use

If the residence is *rented* for 15 days or more in a year and is *not used* for personal purposes for more than the greater of (1) 14 days or (2) 10 percent of the total days

[45] § 280A(g).

rented, the residence is treated as rental property.[46] The expenses must be allocated between personal and rental days if there are any personal use days during the year. The deduction of the expenses allocated to rental days can exceed rent income and result in a rental loss. The loss may be deductible, subject to the at-risk and passive activity loss rules (discussed in Chapter 11).

EXAMPLE 25
THE BIG PICTURE

Return to the facts of *The Big Picture* on p. 6-2. Assume instead that Camille in Example 24 used the cottage for 12 days and rented it for 48 days for $4,800. Since she rented the cottage for 15 days or more but did not use it for more than 14 days, the cottage is treated as rental property. The expenses must be allocated between personal and rental days.

	Percentage of Use	
	Rental 80%	**Personal 20%**
Income	$ 4,800	$ -0-
Expenses		
Mortgage interest ($6,000)	($ 4,800)	($1,200)
Property taxes ($500)	(400)	(100)
Utilities and maintenance ($1,500)	(1,200)	(300)
Depreciation ($2,400)	(1,920)	(480)
Total expenses	($ 8,320)	($2,080)
Rental loss	($ 3,520)	$ -0-

Camille deducts the $3,520 rental loss *for* AGI (assuming she satisfies the at-risk and passive activity loss rules, discussed in Chapter 11). She also has an itemized deduction for property taxes of $100 associated with the personal use. The mortgage interest of $1,200 associated with the personal use is not deductible as an itemized deduction because the cottage is not a qualified residence (qualified residence interest) for this purpose (see Chapter 10). The portion of utilities and maintenance and depreciation attributable to personal use is not deductible. ■

EXAMPLE 26
THE BIG PICTURE

Return to the facts of *The Big Picture* on p. 6-2. Assume instead that Camille in Example 24 rented the cottage for 200 days and lived in it for 19 days. The cottage is primarily rental use since she rented it for 15 days or more and did not use it for personal purposes for more than 20 days (10% of the rental days). The expenses must be allocated between personal and rental days as illustrated in Example 25. ■

Personal/Rental Use

If the residence is rented for 15 days or more in a year *and* is used for personal purposes for more than the greater of (1) 14 days or (2) 10 percent of the total days rented, it is treated as a personal/rental use residence. The expenses must be allocated between personal days and rental days. Expenses are allowed only to the extent of rent income.

[46] § 280A(d) and Prop.Reg. § 1.280A–3(c).

EXAMPLE 27
THE BIG PICTURE

Return to the facts of *The Big Picture* on p. 6-2. Assume instead that Camille in Example 24 rented the property for 30 days and lived in it for 30 days. The residence is classified as personal/rental use property since she used it more than 14 days and rented it for 15 days or more. The expenses must be allocated between rental use and personal use, and the rental expenses are allowed only to the extent of rent income. ■

If a residence is classified as personal/rental use property, the expenses that are deductible anyway (e.g., real estate taxes and mortgage interest) must be deducted first. If a positive net income results, otherwise nondeductible expenses that do not affect adjusted basis (e.g., maintenance, utilities, insurance) are allowed next. Finally, if any positive balance remains, depreciation is allowed. Any disallowed expenses allocable to rental use are carried forward and used in future years subject to the same limitations.

Expenses must be allocated between personal and rental days before the limits are applied. The courts have held that real estate taxes and mortgage interest, which accrue ratably over the year, are allocated on the basis of 365 days.[47] The IRS, however, disagrees and allocates real estate taxes and mortgage interest on the basis of total days of use.[48] Other expenses (utilities, maintenance, depreciation, etc.) are allocated on the basis of total days used.

EXAMPLE 28

Jason rents his vacation home for 60 days and lives in the home for 30 days. The limitations on personal/rental use residences apply. Jason's gross rent income is $10,000. For the entire year (not a leap year), the real estate taxes are $2,190; his mortgage interest expense is $10,220; utilities and maintenance expense equals $2,400; and depreciation is $9,000. Using the IRS approach, these amounts are deductible in this specific order:

Gross income	$10,000
Deduct: Taxes and interest ($^{60}/_{90}$ × $12,410)	(8,273)
Remainder to apply to rental operating expenses and depreciation	$ 1,727
Deduct: Utilities and maintenance ($^{60}/_{90}$ × $2,400)	(1,600)
Balance	$ 127
Deduct: Depreciation ($^{60}/_{90}$ × $9,000 = $6,000 but limited to above balance)	(127)
Net rent income	$ –0–

The nonrental use portion of real estate taxes and mortgage interest ($4,137 in this case) is deductible if the taxpayer elects to itemize (see Chapter 10). The personal use portion of utilities, maintenance, and depreciation is not deductible in any case. Jason has a carryover of $5,873 ($6,000 – $127) of the unused depreciation. Also note that the basis of the property is not reduced by the $5,873 depreciation not allowed because of the above limitation. (See Chapter 13 for a discussion of the reduction in basis for depreciation allowed or allowable.) ■

EXAMPLE 29

Using the court's approach in allocating real estate taxes and mortgage interest, Jason, in Example 28, would have this result:

Gross income	$10,000
Deduct: Taxes and interest ($^{60}/_{365}$ × $12,410)	(2,040)
Remainder to apply to rental operating expenses and depreciation	$ 7,960
Deduct: Utilities and maintenance ($^{60}/_{90}$ × $2,400)	(1,600)
Balance	$ 6,360
Deduct: Depreciation ($^{60}/_{90}$ × $9,000)	(6,000)
Net rent income	$ 360

[47] *Bolton v. Comm.*, 82–2 USTC ¶9699, 51 AFTR 2d 83–305, 694 F.2d 556 (CA–9, 1982).

[48] Prop.Reg. § 1.280A–3(d)(4).

Jason can deduct $10,370 ($12,410 paid − $2,040 deducted as expense in computing net rent income) of personal use mortgage interest and real estate taxes as itemized deductions. ■

Note the contrasting results in Examples 28 and 29. The IRS's approach (Example 28) results in no rental gain or loss and an itemized deduction for real estate taxes and mortgage interest of $4,137. In Example 29, Jason has net rent income of $360 and $10,370 of itemized deductions. The court's approach decreases his taxable income by $10,010 ($10,370 itemized deductions less $360 net rent income). The IRS's approach reduces his taxable income by only $4,137.

EXAMPLE 30

Assume instead that Jason in Example 28 had not lived in the home at all during the year. The house is rental property. The rental loss is calculated as follows:

Gross income	$10,000
Expenses	
Taxes and interest	($12,410)
Utilities and maintenance	(2,400)
Depreciation	(9,000)
Total expenses	($23,810)
Rental loss	($13,810)

Whether any of the rental loss would be deductible depends upon whether Jason actively participated in the rental activity and met the other requirements for passive activity losses and the at-risk limitations (discussed in Chapter 11). ■

Conversion to Rental Property

A related issue is whether or not a taxpayer's *primary residence* is subject to the preceding rules if it is converted to rental property. If the vacation home rules apply, a taxpayer who converts a personal residence to rental property during the tax year, without any tax avoidance motive, could have the allowable deductions limited to the rent income. This would occur if the personal use exceeded the greater of 14 days or 10 percent of rental days test (a likely situation). The Code, however, provides that during a *qualified rental period*, any personal use days are not counted as personal use days in terms of classifying the use of the residence as *personal/rental use* rather than as *primarily rental use.*[49] In effect, the deduction for expenses of the property incurred during a qualified rental period is not subject to the personal use test of the vacation home rules. A qualified rental period is a consecutive period of 12 or more months. The period begins or ends in the taxable year in which the residence is rented or held for rental at a fair price. The residence must not be rented to a related party. If the property is sold before the 12-month period expires, the qualified rental period is the actual time rented.

EXAMPLE 31

Rhonda converts her residence to rental property on May 1 and rents it for the remainder of 2011 for $5,600 and for all of 2012 for $8,400. The house would be classified as personal/rental use property (personal use days during 2011 are greater than both 14 days and 10% of rental days) except that this is a qualified rental period. Therefore, Rhonda's deduction for rental expenses is not limited to the gross income of $5,600 in 2011. ■

See Concept Summary 6.2 for a summary of the vacation home rules.

EXPENDITURES INCURRED FOR TAXPAYER'S BENEFIT OR TAXPAYER'S OBLIGATION

To be deductible, an expense must be incurred for the taxpayer's benefit or arise from the taxpayer's obligation. An individual cannot claim a tax deduction for the payment of the expenses of another individual.

[49] § 280A(d).

CONCEPT SUMMARY 6.2

Vacation/Rental Home

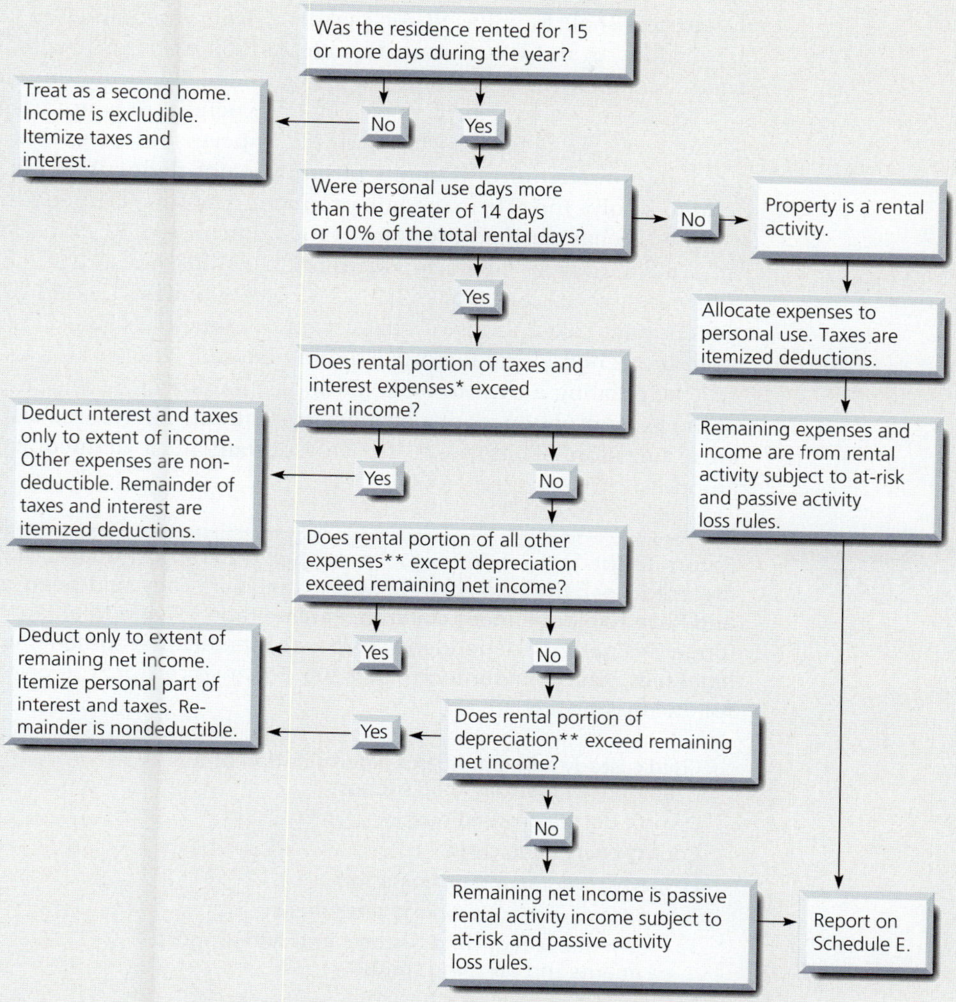

*Allocated on the basis of 365 (366 in a leap year) days (court) or total days of use (IRS).
**Allocated on the basis of total days of use.

EXAMPLE 32

During the current year, Fred pays the property taxes on his son Vern's home. Neither Fred nor Vern can take a deduction for the amount paid for Vern's property taxes. Fred is not entitled to a deduction because the property taxes are not his obligation. Vern cannot claim a deduction because he did not pay the property taxes. The tax result would have been more favorable had Fred made a cash gift to Vern and let him pay the property taxes. Then Vern could have deducted the property taxes. Fred likely would not be liable for any gift taxes depending upon the amount involved due to the annual exclusion (see Chapters 1 and 27). A deduction would have been created with no cash difference to the family. ■

One exception to this disallowance rule is the payment of medical expenses for a dependent. Such expenses are deductible by the payor subject to the normal rules that limit the deductibility of medical expenses (see Chapter 10).[50]

DISALLOWANCE OF PERSONAL EXPENDITURES

Section 262 states that "except as otherwise expressly provided in this chapter, no deduction shall be allowed for personal, living, or family expenses." To justify a deduction, an individual must be able to identify a particular section of the Code that sanctions the deduction (e.g., charitable contributions, medical expenses). Sometimes the character of a particular expenditure is not easily determined. For example, the legal fee associated with a property settlement that results in one party retaining ownership of a family business is not deductible. Likewise, the legal fee paid to resolve the title to income-producing property is not deductible.

The IRS has clarified the issue of the deduction of legal fees incurred in connection with a divorce.[51] To be deductible, an expense must relate solely to tax advice in a divorce proceeding. For example, legal fees attributable to the determination of dependency exemptions of children are deductible if the fees are distinguishable from the general legal fees incurred in obtaining a divorce. Other examples are the costs of creating a trust to make periodic alimony payments and the determination of the tax consequences of a property settlement. Therefore, it is advisable to request an itemization of attorney's fees to substantiate a deduction for the tax-related amounts.

EXAMPLE 33
THE BIG PICTURE

Return to the facts of *The Big Picture* on p. 6-2. Terry and Jack, Dr. Payne's parents, are divorced near the end of the current tax year. They had been married for 28 years and have two dependent children, Pauline (age 15) and Neal (age 16). (Dr. Payne is no longer his parents' dependent.) As part of the divorce agreement, Jack paid all of the legal fees, which amounted to $24,300. The invoice from the divorce lawyer listed the following charges:

Child custody agreement and determination of amount of monthly child support	$ 3,000
Divorce decree proceedings	10,000
County court filing costs	1,800
Property settlement determination	6,000
Tax consequences of property settlement	2,000
Tax consequences of child custody and child support payments and tax filing status	1,500

Only the $3,500 ($2,000 + $1,500) paid by Jack for the charges relating to tax advice is deductible. ■

DISALLOWANCE OF DEDUCTIONS FOR CAPITAL EXPENDITURES

The Code specifically disallows a deduction for "any amount paid out for new buildings or for permanent improvements or betterments made to increase the value of any property or estate."[52] The Regulations further define capital expenditures to include those expenditures that add to the value or prolong the life of property or adapt the property to a new or different use.[53] Incidental repairs and maintenance of the property are not capital expenditures and can be deducted as ordinary and necessary business expenses. Repairing a roof is a deductible expense, but replacing a roof is a capital expenditure subject to depreciation deductions over its recovery period.

[50] § 213(a).
[51] Rev.Rul. 72–545, 1972–2 C.B. 179.
[52] § 263(a)(1).
[53] Reg. § 1.263(a)–1(b).

The tune-up of a delivery truck is an expense; a complete overhaul probably is a capital expenditure.

Capitalization versus Expense

When an expenditure is capitalized rather than expensed, the deduction is at best deferred and at worst lost forever. Although an immediate tax benefit for a large cash expenditure is lost, the cost may be deductible in increments over a longer period of time.

If the expenditure is for a tangible asset that has an ascertainable life, it is capitalized and may be deducted as depreciation (or cost recovery) over the life of the asset (for depreciation) or over a statutory period (for cost recovery under either ACRS or MACRS).[54] Land is not subject to depreciation (or cost recovery) since it does not have an ascertainable life.

EXAMPLE 34

Stan purchased a prime piece of land located in an apartment-zoned area. Stan paid $500,000 for the property, which had an old but usable apartment building on it. He immediately had the building demolished at a cost of $100,000. The $500,000 purchase price and the $100,000 demolition costs must be capitalized, and the basis of the land is $600,000. Since land is a nondepreciable asset, no deduction is allowed. ■

If the expenditure is for an intangible asset (e.g., copyright, patent, covenant not to compete, goodwill), the capitalized expenditure can be amortized, regardless of whether or not the intangible asset has an ascertainable life. Intangible assets, referred to as § 197 intangibles, are amortized over a 15-year statutory period using the straight-line method. See Chapter 8 for additional discussion of the amortization of intangibles.

TRANSACTIONS BETWEEN RELATED PARTIES

The Code places restrictions on the recognition of gains and losses from **related-party transactions**. Without these restrictions, relationships created by birth, marriage, and business would provide endless possibilities for engaging in financial transactions that produce tax savings with no real economic substance or change. For example, to create an artificial loss, a wife could sell investment property to her husband at a loss and deduct the loss on their joint return. Her husband could then hold the asset indefinitely, and the family would sustain no real economic loss. A complex set of laws has been designed to eliminate such possibilities.

Losses

The Code provides for the disallowance of any "losses from sales or exchanges of property . . . directly or indirectly" between related parties.[55] When the property is subsequently sold to a nonrelated party, any gain recognized is reduced by the loss previously disallowed. Any disallowed loss not used by the related-party buyer to offset the recognized gain on a subsequent sale or exchange to an unrelated party is permanently lost.

EXAMPLE 35

Freida sells common stock with a basis of $10,000 to her son, Bill, for its fair market value of $8,000. Bill sells the stock several years later for $11,000. Freida's $2,000 loss is disallowed upon the sale to Bill, and only $1,000 of gain ($11,000 selling price – $8,000 basis – $2,000 disallowed loss) is taxable to him upon the subsequent sale. ■

---

[54] See Chapter 8 for the discussion of depreciation and cost recovery.

[55] § 267(a)(1).

EXAMPLE 36

George sells common stock with a basis of $10,500 to his son, Ray, for its fair market value of $8,000. Ray sells the stock eight months later to an unrelated party for $9,000. Ray's gain of $1,000 ($9,000 selling price – $8,000 basis) is not recognized because of George's previously disallowed loss of $2,500. Note that the offset may result in only partial tax benefit upon the subsequent sale (as in this case). If the property had not been transferred to Ray, George could have recognized a $1,500 loss upon the subsequent sale to the unrelated party ($10,500 basis – $9,000 selling price). ■

EXAMPLE 37

Pete sells common stock with a basis of $10,000 to an unrelated third party for its fair market value of $8,000. Pete's son repurchased the same stock in the market on the same day for $8,000. The $2,000 loss is not allowed because the transaction is an indirect sale between related parties.[56] ■

Unpaid Expenses and Interest

The law prevents related taxpayers from engaging in tax avoidance schemes where one related taxpayer uses the accrual method of accounting and the other uses the cash basis. An accrual basis, closely held corporation, for example, could borrow funds from a cash basis individual shareholder. At the end of the year, the corporation would accrue and deduct the interest, but the cash basis lender would not recognize interest income since no interest had been paid. Section 267 specifically defers the deduction of the accruing taxpayer until the recipient taxpayer must include it in income; that is, when it is actually paid to the cash basis taxpayer. This *matching* provision applies to interest as well as other expenses, such as salaries and bonuses.

This deduction deferral provision does not apply if both of the related taxpayers use the accrual method or both use the cash method. Likewise, it does not apply if the related party reporting income uses the accrual method and the related party taking the deduction uses the cash method.

Relationships and Constructive Ownership

Section 267 operates to disallow losses and defer deductions only between related parties. Losses or deductions generated by similar transactions with an unrelated party are allowed. *Related parties* include the following:

- Brothers and sisters (whether whole, half, or adopted), spouse, ancestors (parents, grandparents), and lineal descendants (children, grandchildren) of the taxpayer.
- A corporation owned more than 50 percent (directly or indirectly) by the taxpayer.
- Two corporations that are members of a controlled group.
- A series of other complex relationships between trusts, corporations, and individual taxpayers.

Constructive ownership provisions are applied to determine whether the taxpayers are related. Under these provisions, stock owned by certain relatives or related entities is *deemed* to be owned by the taxpayer for purposes of applying the loss and expense deduction disallowance provisions. A taxpayer is deemed to own not only his or her stock but also the stock owned by lineal descendants, ancestors, brothers and sisters or half-brothers and half-sisters, and spouse. The taxpayer is also deemed to own his or her proportionate share of stock owned by any partnership, corporation, estate, or trust of which the taxpayer is a member. An individual is deemed to own any stock owned, directly or indirectly, by his or her partner. However, constructive ownership

[56] *McWilliams v. Comm.*, 47–1 USTC ¶9289, 35 AFTR 1184, 67 S.Ct. 1477 (USSC, 1947).

by an individual of the partnership's and the other partner's shares does not extend to the individual's spouse or other relatives (no double attribution).

EXAMPLE 38

The stock of Sparrow Corporation is owned 20% by Ted, 30% by Ted's father, 30% by Ted's mother, and 20% by Ted's sister. On July 1 of the current year, Ted loaned $10,000 to Sparrow Corporation at 8% annual interest, principal and interest payable on demand. For tax purposes, Sparrow uses the accrual basis, and Ted uses the cash basis. Both are on a calendar year. Since Ted is deemed to own the 80% owned by his parents and sister, he directly and constructively owns 100% of Sparrow Corporation. If the corporation accrues the interest within the taxable year, no deduction can be taken until payment is made to Ted. ■

SUBSTANTIATION REQUIREMENTS

The tax law is built on a voluntary compliance system. Taxpayers file their tax returns, report income and take deductions to which they are entitled, and pay their taxes through withholding or estimated tax payments during the year. The taxpayer has the burden of proof for substantiating expenses deducted on the returns and must retain adequate records. Upon audit, the IRS will disallow any undocumented or unsubstantiated deductions. These requirements have resulted in numerous conflicts between taxpayers and the IRS.

In the case of charitable contributions, Congress has enacted stringent substantiation requirements. All cash contributions, for example, must be supported by receipts (e.g., canceled checks).[57] Single donations of $250 or more of both cash and property require an acknowledgment from the charity. Substantial donations of property (i.e., $500 or more) necessitate the filing of Form 8283 and may have to be supported by appraisals—see Chapter 10 for further details.

Specific and *more stringent* rules for deducting travel, entertainment, and gift expenses are discussed in Chapter 9. Certain mixed-use (both personal and business use) and listed property are also subject to the adequate records requirement (discussed in Chapter 8).

EXPENSES AND INTEREST RELATING TO TAX-EXEMPT INCOME

Certain income, such as interest on municipal bonds, is tax-exempt.[58] The law also allows the taxpayer to deduct expenses incurred for the production of income.[59] Deduction disallowance provisions, however, make it impossible to make money at the expense of the government by excluding interest income and deducting interest expense.[60]

EXAMPLE 39

Sandy, a taxpayer in the 35% bracket, purchased $100,000 of 6% municipal bonds. At the same time, she used the bonds as collateral on a bank loan of $100,000 at 8% interest. A positive cash flow would result from the tax benefit as follows:

Cash paid out on loan	($8,000)
Cash received from bonds	6,000
Tax savings from deducting interest expense (35% of $8,000 interest expense)	2,800
Net positive cash flow	$ 800

■

To eliminate the possibility illustrated in Example 39, the Code specifically disallows as a deduction the expenses of producing tax-exempt income. Interest on any

[57] Rev.Proc. 92–71, 1992–2 C.B. 437, addresses circumstances where checks are not returned by a financial institution or where electronic transfers are made.

[58] § 103.

[59] § 212.

[60] § 265.

indebtedness incurred or continued to purchase or carry tax-exempt obligations also is disallowed.

Judicial Interpretations

It is often difficult to show a direct relationship between borrowings and investment in tax-exempt securities. Suppose, for example, that a taxpayer borrows money, adds it to existing funds, buys inventory and stocks, then later sells the inventory and buys municipal bonds. A series of transactions such as these can completely obscure any connection between the loan and the tax-exempt investment. One solution would be to disallow interest on any debt to the extent that the taxpayer holds any tax-exempt securities. This approach would preclude individuals from deducting part of their home mortgage interest if they owned any municipal bonds. The law was not intended to go to such extremes. As a result, judicial interpretations have tried to be reasonable in disallowing interest deductions.

In one case, a company used municipal bonds as collateral on short-term loans to meet seasonal liquidity needs.[61] The court disallowed the interest deduction on the grounds that the company could predict its seasonal liquidity needs. The company could anticipate the need to borrow the money to continue to carry the tax-exempt securities. The same company *was* allowed an interest deduction on a building mortgage, even though tax-exempt securities it owned could have been sold to pay off the mortgage. The court reasoned that short-term liquidity needs would have been impaired if the tax-exempt securities were sold. Furthermore, the court ruled that carrying the tax-exempt securities bore no relationship to the long-term financing of a construction project.

EXAMPLE 40

In January of the current year, Alan borrowed $100,000 at 8% interest. He used the loan proceeds to purchase 5,000 shares of stock in White Corporation. In July, he sold the stock for $120,000 and reinvested the proceeds in City of Denver bonds, the income from which is tax-exempt. Assuming the $100,000 loan remained outstanding throughout the entire year, Alan cannot deduct the interest attributable to the period in which he held the bonds. ■

TAX PLANNING:
6.4 Time Value of Tax Deductions

LO.4

Identify tax planning opportunities for maximizing deductions and minimizing the disallowance of deductions.

Cash basis taxpayers often have the ability to make early payments for their expenses at the end of the tax year. This may permit the payments to be deducted currently instead of in the following tax year. In view of the time value of money, a tax deduction this year may be worth more than the same deduction next year. Before employing this strategy, the taxpayer must consider next year's expected income and tax rates and whether a cash-flow problem may develop from early payments. Thus, the time value of money as well as tax rate changes must be considered when an expense can be paid and deducted in either of two years.

EXAMPLE 41

Jena pledged $50,000 to her church's special building fund. She can make the contribution in December 2011 or January 2012. Jena is in the 35% tax bracket in 2011, and in the 28% bracket in 2012. She itemizes in both years. Assume Jena's discount rate is 8%. If she takes the deduction in 2011, she saves $4,536 ($17,500 − $12,964), due to the decrease in the tax rates and the time value of money.

[61] *The Wisconsin Cheeseman, Inc. v. U.S.*, 68–1 USTC ¶9145, 21 AFTR 2d 383, 388 F.2d 420 (CA–7, 1968).

	2011	2012
Contribution	$50,000	$50,000
Tax bracket	.35	.28
Tax savings	$17,500	$14,000
Discounted @ 8%	1.0	.926
Savings in present value	$17,500	$12,964

■

6.5 Unreasonable Compensation

In substantiating the reasonableness of a shareholder-employee's compensation, an internal comparison test is sometimes useful. If it can be shown that nonshareholder-employees and shareholder-employees in comparable positions receive comparable compensation, it is indicative that compensation is not unreasonable.

Another possibility is to demonstrate that the shareholder-employee has been underpaid in prior years. For example, the shareholder-employee may have agreed to take a less-than-adequate salary during the unprofitable formative years of the business. The expectation is that the "postponed" compensation would be paid in later, more profitable years. The agreement should be documented, if possible, in the corporate minutes.

Keep in mind that in testing for reasonableness, the *total* pay package must be considered. Look at all fringe benefits or perquisites, such as contributions by the corporation to a qualified pension plan. Even though those amounts are not immediately available to the covered shareholder-employee, they must be taken into account.

6.6 Excessive Executive Compensation

With the $1 million limit ($500,000 for TARP recipients) on the deduction of compensation of covered employees, many corporations and their executives must engage in additional tax planning. Previously, concerns over the deductibility of compensation related primarily to closely held corporations. The $1 million limit applies specifically to publicly held corporations. In many instances, it is now necessary for these corporations to restructure the compensation packages of their top executives in order to deduct payments in excess of $1 million. Opportunities include compensation payable on a commission basis, certain other performance-based compensation, payments to qualified retirement plans, and payments that are excludible fringe benefits.

6.7 Shifting Deductions

Taxpayers should manage their obligations to avoid the loss of a deduction. Deductions can be shifted among family members, depending upon which member makes the payment. For example, a father buys a condo for his daughter and puts the title in both names. The taxpayer who makes the payment gets the deduction for the property taxes. If the condo is owned by the daughter only and her father makes the payment, neither is entitled to a deduction. In this case, the father should make a cash gift to the daughter who then makes the payment to the taxing authority.

CONCEPT SUMMARY 6.3

Classification of Expenses

Expense Item	Deductible For AGI	Deductible From AGI	Not Deductible	Applicable Code §
Investment expenses				
Rent and royalty	X			§ 62(a)(4)
All other investments		X[4]		§ 212
Employee expenses				
Commuting expenses			X	§ 262
Travel and transportation[1]		X[4,5]		§ 162(a)(2)
Reimbursed expenses[1]	X			§ 62(a)(2)(A)
Moving expenses	X			§ 62(a)(15)
Entertainment[1]		X[4,5]		§ 162(a)
Teacher supplies	X[11]	X[4]		§ 62(a)(2)(D)
All other employee expenses[1]		X[4,5]		§ 162(a)
Certain expenses of performing artists	X			§ 62(a)(2)(B)
Trade or business expenses	X			§§ 162 and 62(a)(1)
Casualty losses				
Business	X			§ 165(c)(1)
Personal		X[6]		§ 165(c)(3)
Tax determination				
Collection or refund expenses	X[8]	X		§§ 212 and 62(a)(1) or (4)
Bad debts	X			§§ 166 and 62(a)(1) or (3)
Medical expenses		X[7]		§ 213
Charitable contributions		X		§ 170
Taxes				
Trade or business	X			§§ 162, 164, and 62(a)(1)
Personal taxes				
Real property		X		§ 164(a)(1)
Personal property		X		§ 164(a)(2)
State and local income *or* sales		X		§§ 164(a)(3) and (b)(5)
Investigation of a business[2]	X			§§ 162 and 62(a)(1)
Interest				
Business	X			§§ 162, 163, and 62(a)(1)
Personal	X[9]	X[3]	X[10]	§§ 163(a), (d), and (h)
Qualified tuition and related expenses	X			§§ 62(a)(18) and 222
All other personal expenses			X	§ 262

[1] Deduction *for* AGI if reimbursed, an adequate accounting is made, and employee is required to repay excess reimbursements.
[2] Provided certain criteria are met.
[3] Subject to the excess investment interest and the qualified residence interest provisions.
[4] Subject (in the aggregate) to a 2%-of-AGI floor imposed by § 67.
[5] Only 50% of meals and entertainment are deductible.
[6] Subject to a $100 floor per event and a 10%-of-AGI floor per tax year.
[7] Subject to a 7.5%-of-AGI floor.
[8] Only the portion relating to business, rental, or royalty income or losses.
[9] Only the portion relating to student loans.
[10] Other personal interest is disallowed.
[11] Subject to a statutory limit of $250.

6.8 Hobby Losses

To demonstrate that an activity has been entered into for the purpose of making a profit, a taxpayer should treat the activity as a business. The business should engage in advertising, use business letterhead stationery, and maintain a business phone.

If a taxpayer's activity earns a profit in three out of five consecutive years, the presumption is that the activity is engaged in for profit. It may be possible for a cash basis taxpayer to meet these requirements by timing the payment of expenses or the receipt of revenues. The payment of certain expenses incurred before the end of the year might be made in the following year. The billing of year-end sales might be delayed so that collections are received in the following year.

Keep in mind that the three-out-of-five-years rule under § 183 is not absolute. All it does is shift the presumption. If a profit is not made in three out of five years, the losses may still be allowed if the taxpayer can show that they are due to the nature of the business. For example, success in artistic or literary endeavors can take a long time. Also, depending on the state of the economy, even full-time farmers and ranchers are often unable to show a profit. How can one expect a part-time farmer or rancher to do so?

Merely satisfying the three-out-of-five-years rule does not guarantee that a taxpayer is automatically home free. If the three years of profits are insignificant relative to the losses of other years, or if the profits are not from the ordinary operation of the business, the taxpayer is vulnerable. The IRS may still be able to establish that the taxpayer is not engaged in an activity for profit.

EXAMPLE 42

Ashley had the following gains and losses in an artistic endeavor:

2007	($50,000)
2008	(65,000)
2009	400
2010	200
2011	125

Under these circumstances, the IRS might try to overcome the presumption. ■

If Ashley in Example 42 could show conformity with the factors enumerated in the Regulations or could show evidence of business hardships (e.g., injury, death, or illness), the government cannot override the presumption.[62]

6.9 Capital Expenditures

On the sale of a sole proprietorship where the sales price exceeds the fair market value of the tangible assets and stated intangible assets, a planning opportunity may exist for both the seller and the buyer. The seller's preference is for the excess amount to be allocated to goodwill. Goodwill is a capital asset, whereas a covenant not to compete produces ordinary income treatment (see Chapter 14).

Because both a covenant and goodwill are amortized over a statutory 15-year period, the tax results of a covenant and goodwill are the same for the buyer. However, the buyer should recognize that an allocation to goodwill rather than a covenant may provide a tax benefit to the seller. Therefore, the seller and buyer, in negotiating the sales price, should factor in the tax benefit to the seller of having the excess amount labeled goodwill rather than a covenant not to compete. Of course, if the noncompetition aspects of a covenant are important to the buyer, part of the excess amount can be assigned to a covenant.

[62] *Faulconer, Sr. v. Comm.*, 84–2 USTC ¶9955, 55 AFTR 2d 85–302, 748 F.2d 890 (CA–4, 1984), *rev'g* 45 TCM 1084, T.C.Memo. 1983–165.

REFOCUS ON THE BIG PICTURE

CALCULATION OF DEDUCTIBLE BUSINESS EXPENSES AND TAX PLANNING

Using the accrual method of accounting, Dr. Payne has correctly calculated the deductible business expenses of his dental practice except for the $60,000 deduction he shows for his monthly $5,000 draw for living expenses. Since the dental practice is operated as a sole proprietorship, Dr. Payne will report the net income (gross income − deductible business expenses) of the practice on his Form 1040. So a deduction for his monthly draw is not permitted. The $232,500 ($292,500 − $60,000) amount will be reported by Dr. Payne on Schedule C of Form 1040.

Several of the items included in Dr. Payne's calculation of deductible business expenses require clarification. Political contributions ($1,000 + $1,000) cannot be deducted. The dental supplies expense and the office supplies expense must be reduced by the amount of the ending inventory (i.e., $7,000 and $1,500, respectively) since Dr. Payne is using the accrual method of accounting.

What If?

From a tax planning perspective, should Dr. Payne calculate his deductible business expenses using the accrual method of accounting or the cash method?

In Chapter 4, we concluded that Dr. Payne could minimize his Federal income tax liability if he used the cash method of accounting. If the cash method is used for reporting the gross income of a Schedule C business, then the cash method must be used for reporting the deductible business expenses that will appear on Schedule C of Form 1040. So the correct amount of deductible business expenses for his dental practice using the cash method of accounting is calculated as follows:

Salaries including FICA ($120,000 – $5,000)	$115,000
Building rent	24,000
Depreciation of dental equipment and office furnishings and equipment	52,000
Insurance (malpractice and of dental equipment and office furnishings and equipment)	22,000
Dental supplies	16,000
Office supplies	3,000
Contribution to U.S. Senate campaign fund of Barbara Boxer	–0–
Contribution to U.S. Senate campaign fund of Carly Fiorina	–0–
Legal expenses associated with patient lawsuit (jury decision for defendant)	4,000
Draw by Dr. Payne for living expenses	–0–
	$236,000

KEY TERMS

Accounting method, 6–8

Deductions for adjusted gross income, 6–3

Deductions from adjusted gross income, 6–3

Hobby losses, 6–18

Ordinary and necessary, 6–6

Reasonableness, 6–7

Related-party transactions, 6–27

Vacation homes, 6–21

DISCUSSION QUESTIONS

1. **LO.1** "All income must be reported and all deductions are allowed unless specifically disallowed in the Code." Discuss.

2. **LO.1** Michael has AGI of $60,000 and deductions of $6,500. Does it matter to Michael whether the deductions are *for* or *from* AGI? Why or why not?

3. **LO.1** Billy earned $13,000 at the K-M Resort Golf Club during the summer prior to his senior year in college. He wants to make a contribution to a traditional IRA, but the amount is dependent on whether it reduces his taxable income. If Billy is going to claim the standard deduction, how much should he contribute to a traditional IRA?

4. **LO.1** Classify each of the following expenditures as a deduction *for* AGI, a deduction *from* AGI, or not deductible:
   a. Allison pays qualified moving expenses.
   b. Emalie gives cash to the Girl Scouts.
   c. Amos pays monthly alimony to his former spouse.
   d. Arnold pays real estate taxes levied by the county on his personal residence.
   e. April pays the premiums for insurance on her personal residence.
   f. Lonnie pays property taxes levied by the city on his SUV (used exclusively for business).

5. **LO.1** Classify each of the following expenditures as a deduction *for* AGI, a deduction *from* AGI, or not deductible:
   a. Amos contributes to his H.R. 10 plan (i.e., a retirement plan for a self-employed individual).
   b. Keith pays child support to his former wife, Renee, for the support of their son, Chris.
   c. Judy pays for professional dues that are reimbursed by her employer.
   d. Ted pays $500 as the monthly mortgage payment on his personal residence. Of this amount, $100 represents a payment on principal, and $400 represents an interest payment.
   e. Lynn pays a moving company for moving her household goods to Detroit where she is starting a new job. She is not reimbursed by her employer.
   f. Ralph pays property taxes on his personal residence.

6. **LO.1** Larry and Susan each invest $10,000 in separate investment activities. They each incur deductible expenses of $800 associated with their respective investments. Explain why Larry's expenses might be properly classified as deductions *from* AGI (itemized deductions) and Susan's expenses might be appropriately classified as deductions *for* AGI.

7. **LO.1** Nanette is a third-grade teacher. Potential deductions are charitable contributions of $520, personal property taxes on her car of $225, and various supplies purchased for use in her classroom of $225 (none reimbursed by her school). How will these items affect Nanette's Federal income tax return?

8. **LO.1** Mabel, a machinist employed by Silver Airlines, owns 100 shares of Silver Airlines stock. Silver has 900,000 shares of stock outstanding. Mabel spends $1,500 to travel to Denver for Silver's annual meeting. Her expenses would have been $750 more, but she was permitted to fly free on Silver. She attended both days of the shareholders' meeting and actively participated. What are the tax consequences of the trip for Mabel?

9. **LO.1** In the determination of whether a business expense is deductible, the reasonableness requirement applies only to salaries. Evaluate this statement.

10. **LO.1** Dave uses the second floor of a building for his residence and the first floor for his business. The uninsured building is destroyed by fire. Are the tax consequences the same for each part of the building?

11. **LO.1** Mary Kate owns a building that she leases to an individual who operates a grocery store. Rent income is $10,000 and rental expenses are $6,000. On what Form 1040 schedule or schedules are the income and expenses reported?

12. **LO.2** Under the cash method of accounting, the taxpayer can deduct expenses when they are paid. Evaluate this statement.

13. **LO.2** Aubry, a cash basis and calendar year taxpayer, decides to reduce his taxable income for 2011 by buying $65,000 worth of supplies for his business on December 27, 2011. The supplies will be used up in 2012.
    a. Can Aubry deduct the expenditure for 2011?
    b. Would your answer in part (a) change if Aubry bought the supplies because the seller was going out of business and offered a significant discount on the price?

14. **LO.2** What is the significance of the all events and economic performance tests?

15. **LO.2** Why is the reserve method not allowed to be used for Federal income tax purposes?

16. **LO.3** Are any bribes or kickbacks deductible?

ISSUE ID

17. **LO.3** Ted is an agent for an airline manufacturer and is negotiating a sale with a representative of the U.S. government and with a representative of a developing country. Ted's company has sufficient capacity to handle only one of the orders. Both orders will have the same contract price. Ted believes that if his employer will authorize a $500,000 payment to the representative of the foreign country, he can guarantee the sale. He is not sure that he can obtain the same result with the U.S. government. Identify the relevant tax issues for Ted.

18. **LO.3** Stuart, an insurance salesman, is arrested for allegedly robbing a convenience store. He hires an attorney who is successful in getting the charges dropped. Is the attorney's fee deductible?

19. **LO.3** Linda operates a drug-running operation. Which of the following expenses she incurs can reduce taxable income?
    a. Bribes paid to border guards.
    b. Salaries to employees.
    c. Price paid for drugs purchased for resale.
    d. Kickbacks to police.
    e. Rent on an office.
    f. Depreciation on office furniture and equipment.
    g. Tenant's casualty insurance.
    h. Utilities.

20. **LO.3** Gordon anticipates that being positively perceived by the individual who is elected mayor will be beneficial for his business. Therefore, he contributes to the campaigns of both the Democratic and the Republican candidates. The Republican candidate is elected mayor. Can Gordon deduct any of the political contributions he made?

21. **LO.3** Carmine, Inc., a tobacco manufacturer, incurs certain expenditures associated with political contributions and lobbying activities. Which of these expenditures can be deducted?

Payments to Washington, D.C. law firm to lobby members of Congress	$800,000
Payments to Washington, D.C. law firm to lobby the head of the FDA	25,000
Payments to Richmond law firm to lobby members of the state legislature	50,000
Payments to Lexington law firm to lobby members of the Lexington City Council	5,000
Political contribution to Committee to Reelect the Mayor of Lexington	6,000

22. **LO.3** Agnes, an executive of a large corporation, receives a salary of $1.5 million. Taylor, who is an executive of another large corporation, receives a salary of $1.3 million. Agnes's corporation is permitted to deduct all of her salary while Taylor's corporation is permitted to deduct only part of his. Neither corporation is a TARP recipient. Assuming both salaries are reasonable, explain the result.

23. **LO.3** What is the significance of a taxpayer's occupation in the deductibility of expenses incurred in investigating another business?

24. **LO.3** Al has been working for an advertising agency during the two years since he graduated from college with a double major in marketing and art. In his spare time, Al enjoys painting landscapes. He sold his first painting in February at an art festival and has sold three more since then through contacts made at the festival. What are the tax consequences of the sales income and the related expenses (e.g., art supplies, cost of travel to the art festival, advertising in the art festival program folder):
    a. If Al's art activity is classified as a hobby?
    b. If Al's art activity is classified as a trade or business?

25. **LO.3** Are there any circumstances under which taxpayers can rent their personal residence and not be required to report the rent income received? Does this have an effect on the deductions allowed?

26. **LO.3** Under what circumstances may a taxpayer deduct a rental loss associated with a vacation home?

27. **LO.3** Karen and Andy own a beach house. They have an agreement with a rental agent to rent it up to 200 days per year. For the past three years, the agent has been successful in renting it for 200 days. Karen and Andy use the beach house for one week during the summer and one week during Thanksgiving. Their daughter, Sarah, a college student, has asked if she and some friends can use the beach house for the week of spring break. Advise Karen and Andy how they should respond and identify any relevant tax issues. **ISSUE ID**

28. **LO.3** Hank was transferred from Phoenix to North Dakota on March 1 of the current year. He immediately put his home in Phoenix up for rent. The home was rented May 1 to November 30 and was vacant during the month of December. It was rented again on January 1 for six months. What expenses, if any, can Hank deduct on his return? Which deductions are *for* AGI and which ones are *from* AGI?

29. **LO.3** Ray loses his job as a result of a corporate downsizing. Consequently, he falls behind on the mortgage payments on his personal residence. His friend Ted would like to make the delinquent mortgage payments for him. **DECISION MAKING**
    a. Could the payments be structured so that Ray can deduct the mortgage interest?
    b. Could the payment arrangement deny both Ray and Ted a mortgage interest deduction?
    c. Could the payments be structured so that Ted could deduct the mortgage interest?

30. **LO.3** Edna incurs various legal fees in obtaining a divorce. Which types of expenses associated with the divorce are deductible by Edna, and which are not?

31. **LO.3** Ella owns 60% of the stock of Peach, Inc. The stock has declined in value since she purchased it five years ago. She is going to sell 5% of the stock to a relative. Ella is also going to make a gift of 10% of the stock to another relative. Identify the relevant tax issues for Ella. **ISSUE ID**

32. **LO.3** Jarret owns City of Savannah bonds with an adjusted basis of $150,000. During the year, he receives interest payments of $4,500. Jarret partially financed the purchase of the bonds by borrowing $100,000 at 5% interest. Jarret's interest payments on the loan this year are $4,800, and his principal payments are $1,400.
    a. Should Jarret report any interest income this year?
    b. Can Jarret deduct any interest expense this year?

PROBLEMS

33. **LO.1** Amber is a self-employed tax attorney. She and Jon, her employee, attend a conference in Dallas sponsored by the American Institute of CPAs. The following expenses are incurred during the trip:

	Amber	Jon
Conference registration	$500	$500
Airfare	900	600
Taxi fares	75	–0–
Lodging in Dallas	700	300

    a. Amber pays for all these expenses. Calculate the effect of these expenses on Amber's AGI.
    b. Would your answer to part (a) change if the American Bar Association had sponsored the conference?

DECISION MAKING

34. **LO.1** Daniel is single and has the following income and expenses in 2011:

Salary income	$60,000
Net rent income	6,000
Dividend income	3,500
Payment of alimony	12,000
Mortgage interest on residence	4,900
Property tax on residence	1,200
Contribution to traditional IRA	5,000
Contribution to United Church	2,100
Loss on the sale of real estate (held for investment)	2,000
Medical expenses	3,250
State income tax	300
Federal income tax	7,000

a. Calculate Daniel's AGI.
b. Should Daniel itemize his deductions *from* AGI or take the standard deduction?

35. **LO.1** Julie is a student and earns $9,000 working part-time at the college ice cream shop in 2011. She has no other income. Her medical expenses for the year totaled $2,700. During the year, she suffered a casualty loss of $3,500 when her apartment burned. Julie contributed $1,950 to her church. On the advice of her parents, Julie is trying to decide whether to contribute $1,000 to the traditional IRA her parents have set up for her. What effect would the IRA contribution have on Julie's itemized deductions?

36. **LO.1** Drew and his wife Cassie own all of the stock of Thrush. Cassie is the president and Drew is the vice president. Cassie and Drew are paid salaries of $400,000 and $300,000, respectively, each year. They consider the salaries to be reasonable based on a comparison with salaries paid for comparable positions in comparable companies. They project Thrush's taxable income for next year, before their salaries, to be $800,000. They decide to place their four teenage children on the payroll and to pay them total salaries of $100,000. The children will each work about five hours per week for Thrush.
a. What are Drew and Cassie trying to achieve by hiring the children?
b. Calculate the tax consequences of hiring the children on Thrush, and on Drew and Cassie's family.

37. **LO.1** This has not been a good year for Betsy. During the year, she had losses from the following sales:

Personal use sailboat	$ 6,000
Personal residence	30,000
Rental house	12,000
Orange, Inc. stock	4,000
City of James bonds	2,000

a. What is the amount of Betsy's deductible losses?
b. Classify the deductible losses as deductions *for* or *from* AGI.

38. **LO.2** The income statement for Monroe's business shows the following revenues and expenses for 2011, the initial year of operations:

Sales revenue (including $19,000 credit sales uncollected at year-end)	$106,000
Wage expenses (including $3,000 unpaid at year-end)	32,000
Office expenses (supplies, copying, etc.)	2,000
Bad debt expense (of the $4,000 reserve established, $500 was written off as being currently uncollectible)	4,000
Utilities and telephone expense*	6,400
Insurance expense*	3,500
Rent expense (January 1, 2011–January 31, 2012)	9,750

*Amount incurred is the same as the amount paid.

a. Calculate Monroe's AGI using the accrual method.
b. Calculate Monroe's AGI using the cash method.

39. **LO.2** Maud, a calendar year taxpayer, is the owner of a sole proprietorship that uses the cash method. On February 1, 2011, she leases an office building to use in her business for $120,000 for an 18-month period. In order to obtain this favorable lease rate, she pays the $120,000 at the inception of the lease. How much rent expense may Maud deduct on her 2011 tax return?

40. **LO.2** Duck, an accrual basis corporation, sponsored a rock concert on December 29, 2011. Gross receipts were $300,000. The following expenses were incurred and paid as indicated:

Expense		Payment Date
Rental of coliseum	$ 25,000	December 21, 2011
Cost of goods sold:		
Food	30,000	December 30, 2011
Souvenirs	60,000	December 30, 2011
Performers	100,000	January 5, 2012
Cleaning of coliseum	10,000	February 1, 2012

Since the coliseum was not scheduled to be used again until January 15, the company with which Duck had contracted did not actually perform the cleanup until January 8–10, 2012.

Calculate Duck's net income from the concert for tax purposes for 2011.

41. **LO.3** Doug incurred and paid the following expenses during the year:

- $50 for a ticket for running a red light while he was commuting to work.
- $100 for a ticket for parking in a handicapped parking space.
- $200 to an attorney to represent him in traffic court as to the two tickets.
- $500 to an attorney to draft an agreement with a tenant for a one-year lease on an apartment that Doug owns.
- $1,000 to an attorney to negotiate a reduction in his child support payments.
- $2,500 to an attorney to negotiate a reduction in his qualified alimony payments to a former spouse.

Calculate the amount of Doug's deductible expenses.

42. **LO.3** Trevor, a friend of yours from high school, works as a waiter at the ST Café. He asks you to help him prepare his Federal income tax return. When you inquire about why his bank deposits substantially exceed his tip income, he confides to you that on the side he is a "bookie." Trevor then provides you with the following documented income and expenses for the year:

Tip income	$16,000
Gambling income	52,000
Gambling expenses	
Payouts to winners	29,000
Employee compensation	8,000
Bribe to police officer who is aware of Trevor's bookie activity	7,500

a. How will these items affect Trevor's AGI?
b. His taxable income?
c. If Trevor's business was an illegal drug operation and the cost of the illegal drugs sold was $6,200, how would your answers to parts (a) and (b) differ?

43. **LO.3** You are a senior government major. Two of the five seats on city council are up for election. Friends, knowing your interest in local politics, encourage you to run for city council. You are elected by a two-to-one majority. You received campaign contributions from the following:

Your parents	$1,000
Government professor who is your faculty adviser	500
Friends who are classmates	750
Other friends	400

All of these funds were used for legitimate campaign purposes (e.g., signs, ads in local newspaper). How much of the campaign contributions can be deducted by the donors?

DECISION MAKING

COMMUNICATIONS

44. **LO.3, 4** Amber, a publicly held corporation (not a TARP recipient), currently pays its president an annual salary of $900,000. In addition, it contributes $20,000 annually to a defined contribution pension plan for him. As a means of increasing company profitability, the board of directors decides to increase the president's compensation. Two proposals are being considered. Under the first proposal, the salary and pension contribution for the president would be increased by 30%. Under the second proposal, Amber would implement a performance-based compensation program that is projected to provide about the same amount of additional compensation and pension contribution for the president.
    a. Evaluate the alternatives from the perspective of Amber, Inc.
    b. Prepare a letter to Amber's board of directors that contains your recommendations. Address the letter to the board chairperson, Agnes Riddle, whose address is 100 James Tower, Cleveland, OH 44106.

45. **LO.3** Vermillion, Inc., a publicly held corporation (not a TARP recipient), pays the following salaries to its executives:

	Salary	Bonus	Retirement Plan Contribution
CEO	$2,000,000	$100,000	$80,000
Executive vice president	1,800,000	90,000	72,000
Treasurer	1,600,000	–0–	64,000
Marketing vice president	1,500,000	75,000	60,000
Operations vice president	1,400,000	70,000	56,000
Distribution vice president	1,200,000	60,000	48,000
Research vice president	1,100,000	–0–	44,000
Controller	800,000	–0–	32,000

Vermillion normally does not pay bonuses, but after reviewing the results of operations for the year, the board of directors decided to pay a 5% bonus to selected executives. What is the amount of these payments that Vermillion may deduct?

46. **LO.3** Joan, the owner of a very successful restaurant chain in the Southeast, is exploring the possibility of expanding the chain into a city in the Northeast. She incurs $28,000 of expenses associated with this investigation. Based on the regulatory environment for restaurants in the city, she decides not to expand. During the year, she also investigates opening a hotel that will be part of a national hotel chain. Her expenses for this are $53,000. The hotel begins operations on July 1. Determine the amount that Joan can deduct in the current year for investigating these two businesses.

47. **LO.3** Terry traveled to a neighboring state to investigate the purchase of two hardware stores. His expenses included travel, legal, accounting, and miscellaneous expenses. The total was $52,000. He incurred the expenses in June and July 2011. Under the following circumstances, what can Terry deduct in 2011?
    a. Terry was in the hardware store business and did not acquire the two hardware stores.
    b. Terry was in the hardware store business and acquired the two hardware stores and began operating them on October 1, 2011.
    c. Terry did not acquire the two hardware stores and was not in the hardware store business.
    d. Terry acquired the two hardware stores, but was not in the hardware store business when he acquired them. Operations began on October 1, 2011.

48. **LO.3** Sonam makes pottery in her spare time. She sold $17,000 worth of pottery during the year and incurred expenses as follows:

Supplies	$14,000
Depreciation on business property	4,000
Advertising	2,000
Booth at arts and crafts fair	500

Her AGI, without considering the effect of the sales of the pottery, is $100,000. Calculate Sonam's AGI if the activity is:

a. A hobby.
b. A business.

49. **LO.3** Sandra, an orthodontist, is single and has net earnings of $90,000 from her practice. In addition, she collects antique books that she buys and sells at antique shows. She participates in six to eight weekend shows per year. Her income and expenses for the current year are as follows:

Revenue from sale of antique books	$22,000
Expenses	
Cost of goods sold	12,000
Show registration costs	3,000
Advertising	1,000
Dealer's license—annual fee	500
Insurance	900
Depreciation of display cases	1,200

Sandra has no other items that would affect her AGI. Itemized deductions consisting of taxes, interest, and charitable contributions are $19,000. Calculate Sandra's taxable income if the antique book activity is classified as:

a. A hobby.
b. A business.

50. **LO.3** Adelene, who lives in a winter resort area, rented her personal residence for 14 days while she was visiting Brussels. Rent income was $5,000. Related expenses for the year were as follows:

Real property taxes	$ 3,800
Mortgage interest	7,500
Utilities	3,700
Insurance	2,500
Repairs	2,100
Depreciation	15,000

Determine the effect on Adelene's AGI.

51. **LO.3** During the year (not a leap year), Anna rented her vacation home for 30 days, used it personally for 20 days, and left it vacant for 315 days. She had the following income and expenses:

Rent income	$ 7,000
Expenses	
Real estate taxes	2,500
Interest on mortgage	9,000
Utilities	2,400
Repairs	1,000
Roof replacement (a capital expenditure)	12,000
Depreciation	7,500

a. Compute Anna's net rent income or loss and the amounts she can itemize on her tax return, using the court's approach to allocating property taxes and interest.
b. How would your answer in part (a) differ using the IRS's method of allocating property taxes and interest?

52. **LO.3** How would your answer in Problem 51 differ if Anna had rented the house for 87 days and had used it personally for 13 days?

53. **LO.1, 3** Chee, single, age 40, had the following income and expenses during the year (not a leap year):

Income	
Salary	$43,000
Rental of vacation home (rented 60 days, used personally 60 days, vacant 245 days)	4,000
Municipal bond interest	2,000
Dividend from General Electric	400
Expenses	
Interest	
On home mortgage	8,400
On vacation home	4,758
On loan used to buy municipal bonds	3,100
Taxes	
Property tax on home	2,200
Property tax on vacation home	1,098
State income tax	3,300
State sales tax	900
Charitable contributions	1,100
Tax return preparation fee	300
Utilities and maintenance on vacation home	2,600
Depreciation on rental 50% of vacation home	3,500

Calculate Chee's taxable income for the year before personal exemptions.

DECISION MAKING

54. **LO.1, 3, 4** Velma and Clyde operate a retail sports memorabilia shop. For the current year, sales revenue is $50,000 and expenses are as follows:

Cost of goods sold	$19,000
Advertising	1,000
Utilities	2,000
Rent	4,000
Insurance	1,500
Wages to Boyd	7,000

Velma and Clyde pay $7,000 in wages to Boyd, a part-time employee. Since this amount is $1,000 below the minimum wage, Boyd threatens to file a complaint with the appropriate Federal agency. Although Velma and Clyde pay no attention to Boyd's threat, Chelsie (Velma's mother) gives Boyd a check for $1,000 for the disputed wages. Both Velma and Clyde ridicule Chelsie for wasting money when they learn what she has done. The retail shop is the only source of income for Velma and Clyde.

a. Calculate Velma and Clyde's AGI.
b. Can Chelsie deduct the $1,000 payment on her tax return?
c. How could the tax position of the parties be improved?

55. **LO.3** Max is purchasing a sole proprietorship business from Darlene. The amount being paid exceeds the fair market value of the identifiable assets of the business by $930,000. Advise Max on the tax consequences of the $930,000 being allocated to goodwill versus it being allocated to a nine-year covenant not to compete.

DECISION MAKING

56. **LO.3, 4** Jay's sole proprietorship has the following assets:

	Basis	Fair Market Value
Cash	$ 10,000	$ 10,000
Accounts receivable	18,000	18,000
Inventory	25,000	30,000
Patent	22,000	40,000
Land	50,000	75,000
	$125,000	$173,000

The building in which Jay's business is located is leased. The lease expires at the end of the year.

Jay is age 70 and would like to retire. He expects to be in the 35% tax bracket. Jay is negotiating the sale of the business with Lois, a key employee. They have agreed on the fair market value of the assets, as indicated above, and agree the total purchase price should be about $200,000.

a. Advise Jay regarding how the sale should be structured.
b. Advise Lois regarding how the purchase should be structured.
c. What might they do to achieve an acceptable compromise?

57. **LO.3** Eleanor Saxon sold stock (basis of $65,000) to her brother, Ridge, for $61,000, the fair market value.

DECISION MAKING

COMMUNICATIONS

a. What are the tax consequences to Eleanor?
b. What are the tax consequences to Ridge if he later sells the stock for $66,000? For $58,000? For $62,000?
c. Write a letter to Eleanor in which you inform her of the tax consequences if she sells the stock to Ridge for $61,000 and explain how a sales transaction could be structured that would produce better tax consequences for her. Eleanor's address is 32 Country Lane, Lawrence, KS 66045.

58. **LO.3** The Robin Corporation is owned as follows:

Isabelle	26%
Peter, Isabelle's husband	19%
Sonya, Isabelle's mother	15%
Reggie, Isabelle's father	25%
Quinn, an unrelated party	15%

Robin is on the accrual basis, and Isabelle and Peter are on the cash basis. Isabelle and Peter each loaned the Robin Corporation $40,000 out of their separate funds. On December 31, 2011, Robin accrued interest at 7% on both loans. The interest was paid on February 4, 2012. What is the tax treatment of this interest expense/income to Isabelle, Peter, and Robin?

59. **LO.3** For each of the following independent transactions, calculate the recognized gain or loss to the seller and the adjusted basis to the buyer.
a. Bonnie sells Parchment, Inc. stock (adjusted basis $17,000) to Phillip, her brother, for its fair market value of $12,000.
b. Amos sells land (adjusted basis $85,000) to his nephew, Boyd, for its fair market value of $70,000.
c. Susan sells a tax-exempt bond (adjusted basis $20,000) to her wholly owned corporation for its fair market value of $19,000.
d. Ron sells a business truck (adjusted basis $20,000) that he uses in his sole proprietorship to his cousin, Agnes, for its fair market value of $18,500.
e. Martha sells her partnership interest (adjusted basis $175,000) in Pearl Partnership to her adult daughter, Kim, for $220,000.

60. **LO.3** Chris has a brokerage account and buys on the margin, which resulted in an interest expense of $18,000 during the year. Income generated through the brokerage account was as follows:

Municipal interest	$20,000
Taxable dividends and interest	80,000

How much investment interest can Chris deduct?

61. **LO.1** Lee incurred the following expenses in the current tax year. Indicate, in the spaces provided, whether each expenditure is deductible *for* AGI, *from* AGI, or not deductible.

	Expense Item	Deductible For AGI	Deductible From AGI	Not Deductible
a.	Lee's personal medical expenses	_____	_____	_____
b.	Lee's dependent daughter's medical expenses	_____	_____	_____
c.	Real estate taxes on Lee's rental property	_____	_____	_____
d.	Real estate taxes on Lee's personal residence	_____	_____	_____
e.	Real estate taxes on daughter's personal residence	_____	_____	_____
f.	Lee's state income taxes	_____	_____	_____
g.	Interest on Lee's rental property mortgage	_____	_____	_____
h.	Interest on Lee's personal residence mortgage	_____	_____	_____
i.	Interest on daughter's personal residence mortgage	_____	_____	_____
j.	Interest on Lee's business loans	_____	_____	_____
k.	Lee's charitable contributions	_____	_____	_____
l.	Depreciation on Lee's rental property	_____	_____	_____
m.	Depreciation on auto used in Lee's business	_____	_____	_____
n.	Depreciation on Lee's personal use auto	_____	_____	_____
o.	Depreciation on daughter's personal use auto	_____	_____	_____

CUMULATIVE PROBLEMS

TAX RETURN PROBLEM

H&R BLOCK At Home

62. Roberta Santos, age 41, is single and lives at 120 Sanborne Avenue, Springfield, IL 60740. Her Social Security number is 123–45–6789. Roberta has been divorced from her former husband, Wayne, for three years. She has a son, Jason, who is age 17, and a daughter, June, who is age 18. Jason's Social Security number is 111–11–1111, and June's is 123–45–6788. Roberta does not wish to contribute $3 to the Presidential Election Campaign Fund.

Roberta, an advertising executive, earned a salary of $75,000 in 2010. Her employer withheld $8,500 in Federal income tax, $3,100 in state income tax, and the appropriate amount of FICA tax: $4,650 for Social Security tax and $1,087.50 for Medicare tax.

Roberta has legal custody of Jason and June. The divorce decree provides that Roberta is to receive the dependency deductions for the children. Jason lives with his father during summer vacation. Wayne indicates that his expenses for Jason are $10,500. Roberta can document that she spent $6,500 for Jason's support during 2010. In prior years, Roberta gave a signed Form 8332 to Wayne regarding Jason. For 2010, she has decided not to do so. Roberta provides all of June's support.

Roberta's mother died on January 7, 2010. Roberta inherited assets worth $625,000 from her mother. As the sole beneficiary of her mother's life insurance policy, Roberta received insurance proceeds of $300,000. Her mother's cost basis for the life insurance policy was $120,000. Roberta's favorite aunt gave her $13,000 for her birthday in October.

On November 8, 2010, Roberta sells for $20,000 Amber stock that she had purchased for $24,000 from her first cousin, Walt, on December 5, 2005. Walt's cost basis for the stock was $26,000, and the stock was worth $23,000 on December 5, 2005. On December 1, 2010, Roberta sold Falcon stock for $13,500. She had acquired the stock on July 2, 2007, for $7,000.

An examination of Roberta's records reveals that she received the following:

- Interest income of $2,000 from First Savings Bank.
- Groceries valued at $750 from a local grocery store for being the 100,000th customer.
- Qualified dividend income of $1,800 from Amber.
- Interest income of $3,750 on City of Springfield school bonds.
- Alimony of $15,000 from Wayne.
- Distribution of $4,800 from ST Partnership. Her distributive share of the partnership passive taxable income was $5,300.

From her checkbook records, she determines that she made the following payments during 2010:

- Charitable contributions of $3,500 to First Presbyterian Church and $1,500 to the American Red Cross (proper receipts obtained).
- Mortgage interest on her residence of $7,800.
- Property taxes of $3,100 on her residence and $1,100 on her car.
- Estimated Federal income taxes of $3,800 and estimated state income taxes of $1,000.
- Medical expenses of $5,000 for her and $800 for Jason. In December her medical insurance policy reimbursed $1,500 of her medical expenses.
- A $1,000 ticket for parking in a handicapped space.
- Attorney's fees of $500 associated with unsuccessfully contesting the parking ticket.
- Contribution of $250 to the campaign of a candidate for governor.
- Since she did not maintain records of the sales tax she paid, she calculates the amount from the sales tax table to be $994.

Calculate Roberta's net tax payable or refund due for 2010. If you use tax forms, you will need Form 1040 and Schedules A, B, D, and E. Suggested software: H&R BLOCK At Home.

TAX COMPUTATION PROBLEM

DECISION MAKING

COMMUNICATIONS

63. John and Mary Jane Sanders are married, filing jointly. Their address is 204 Shoe Lane, Blacksburg, VA 24061. They are expecting their first child in early 2012. John's salary in 2011 was $90,000, from which $20,200 of Federal income tax and $4,700 of state income tax were withheld. Mary Jane made $50,000 and had $3,000 of Federal income tax and $3,100 of state income tax withheld. The appropriate amount of FICA tax was withheld for John and for Mary Jane: for John, Social Security tax of $3,780 and Medicare tax of $1,305; for Mary Jane, Social Security tax of $2,100 and Medicare tax of $725. John's Social Security number is 111–11–1111, and Mary Jane's Social Security number is 123–45–6789.

John and Mary Jane are both covered by their employer's medical insurance policies with three-fourths of the premiums being paid by the employers. The total premiums were $6,000 for John and $4,200 for Mary Jane. Mary Jane received medical benefits of $6,200 under the plan. John was not ill during 2011.

John makes child support payments of $12,000 for his son, Rod, who lives with June, John's former spouse, except for two months in the summer when he visits John and Mary Jane. At the time of the divorce, John worked for a Fortune 500 company and received a salary of $250,000. As a result of corporate downsizing, he lost his job.

Mary Jane's father lived with them until his death in November. His only sources of income were salary of $1,900, unemployment compensation benefits of $3,500, and Social Security benefits of $3,200. Of this amount, he deposited $4,800 in a savings account. The remainder of his support of $9,000, which included funeral expenses of $5,100, was provided by John and Mary Jane.

Other income received by the Sanderses was as follows:

Interest on certificates of deposit	$3,500
Share of S corporation taxable income (distributions from the S corporation to Mary Jane were $600)	1,200
Award received by Mary Jane from employer for outstanding suggestion for cutting costs	1,500

John has always wanted to operate his own business. In October 2011, he incurred expenses of $10,000 in investigating the establishment of a retail computer franchise. With the birth of their child expected next year, however, he decides to forgo self-employment for at least a couple of years.

John and Mary Jane made charitable contributions of $4,000 during the year and paid an additional $1,200 in state income taxes in 2011 upon filing their 2010 state income tax return. Their deductible home mortgage interest was $7,500, and their property taxes came to $4,500. They paid sales taxes of $1,700 for which they have receipts.

Part 1—Tax Computation

Calculate John and Mary Jane's tax (or refund) due for 2011.

Part 2—Tax Planning

Assume that the Sanderses come to you for advice in December 2011. John has learned that he will receive a $30,000 bonus. He wants to know if he should take it in December 2011 or in January 2012. Mary Jane will quit work on December 31 to stay home with the baby. Their itemized deductions will decrease by $3,100 because Mary Jane will not have state income taxes withheld. Mary Jane will not receive the employee award in 2012. She expects the medical benefits received to be $9,000. The Sanderses expect all of their other income items to remain the same in 2012. Write a letter to John and Mary Jane that contains your advice and prepare a memo for the tax files.

RESEARCH PROBLEMS

THOMSON REUTERS
Checkpoint® Student Edition

Note: Solutions to Research Problems can be prepared by using the **Checkpoint® Student Edition** online research product, which is available to accompany this text. It is also possible to prepare solutions to the Research Problems by using tax research materials found in a standard tax library.

Research Problem 1. Robin, Inc., acquired all the assets of Sparrow, Inc. In addition, Robin assumed certain liabilities of Sparrow. Robin agreed that it would be legally responsible for any judgment in a patent infringement claim being litigated against Sparrow. Experts' opinions indicated that the likelihood that a contingent liability would result was remote (i.e., between 0% and 5%).

After a trial, a jury concluded that patent infringement had occurred and awarded a judgment of $5 million. Robin paid the $5 million and deducted it as an ordinary and necessary business expense. Upon audit, the IRS reclassified the $5 million payment and treated it as a capital expenditure under § 263. Evaluate the positions taken by Robin and by the IRS.

Research Problem 2. In early 2009, Walter Hodges began investigating the real estate market with the intention of acquiring real estate for investment or rental. He had not previously been involved in any real estate rental or investment ventures.

Walter started marketing his business via business cards, flyers, and word of mouth in spring 2009. At the same time, he completed a business plan for buying, remodeling, and renting property.

In October 2009, Walter paid $25,000 for training classes designed to provide real estate investment skills. He obtained a loan for his business of $45,000 from the U.S. Small Business Administration in November 2009. During the same month, he obtained an employer ID number from the IRS. In December 2009, he opened a checking account and obtained a credit card in the name of the business.

Walter attempted to purchase several properties during the last half of 2009, but was unsuccessful until he acquired property on December 30, 2009. He listed the property for rent in early January 2010 and was successful in renting it in March 2010.

On his Form 1040 for 2009, Walter prepared a Schedule C on which he showed a business loss of $29,000. He included the cost of the training classes, automobile expenses, meals and entertainment, computer and software expenses, and supplies.

The IRS has disallowed Walter's $29,000 deduction on the grounds that he was not yet in a trade or business during 2009. Evaluate the position taken by the IRS.

INTERNET *activity*

Use the tax resources of the Internet to address the following question. Do not restrict your search to the Web, but include a review of newsgroups and general reference materials, practitioner sites and resources, primary sources of the tax law, chat rooms and discussion groups, and other opportunities.

Research Problem 3. Locate and read a recent judicial or administrative ruling regarding the deductibility of hobby losses. Look for rulings that deal with horse breeding, professional sports teams, or art collecting activities. Which criteria did the ruling emphasize in upholding or reversing the taxpayer's deduction for such losses?

CHAPTER 7

Deductions and Losses: Certain Business Expenses and Losses

LEARNING OBJECTIVES

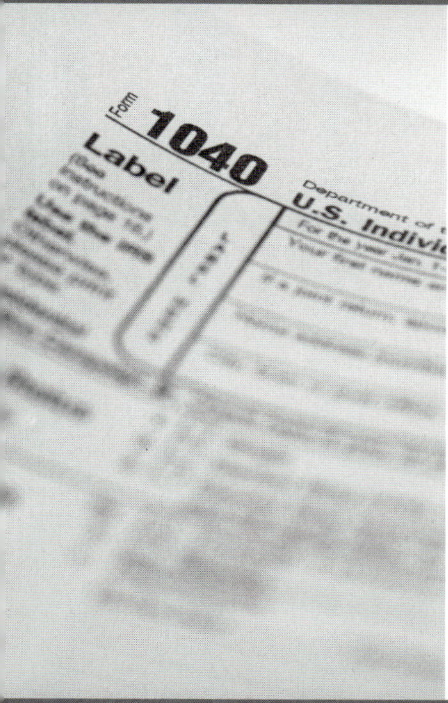

After completing Chapter 7, you should be able to:

LO.1

Determine the amount, classification, and timing of the bad debt deduction.

LO.2

Understand the tax treatment of worthless securities including §1244 stock.

LO.3

Distinguish between deductible and nondeductible losses of individuals.

LO.4

Identify a casualty and determine the amount, classification, and timing of casualty and theft losses.

LO.5

Recognize and apply the alternative tax treatments for research and experimental expenditures.

LO.6

Calculate the domestic production activities deduction.

LO.7

Understand the tax impact of a net operating loss and recognize the effect of the carryback and carryover provisions.

LO.8

Identify tax planning opportunities in deducting certain business expenses, business losses, and personal losses.

OUTLINE

For the latest in changes to tax legislation, visit **www.cengage.com/taxation/swft**

FRAMEWORK 1040: Tax Formula for Individuals

This chapter covers the boldfaced portions of the Tax Formula for Individuals that was introduced in Figure 3.1 on p. 3-3. Below those portions are the sections of Form 1040 where the results are reported.

Income (broadly conceived)	$ xx,xxx
Less: Exclusions	(x,xxx)
Gross income	$ xx,xxx
Less: Deductions for adjusted gross income	**(x,xxx)**

FORM 1040 (p. 1)

12 Business income or (loss). Attach Schedule C or C-EZ

35 Domestic production activities deduction. Attach Form 8903

Adjusted gross income	$ xx,xxx
Less: The greater of total **itemized deductions** *or* the standard deduction	**(x,xxx)**

FORM 1040 (p. 2)

40 **Itemized deductions** (from Schedule A) **or** your **standard deduction** (see instructions)

Personal and dependency exemptions	(x,xxx)
Taxable income	$ xx,xxx
Tax on taxable income (see Tax Tables or Tax Rate Schedules)	$ x,xxx
Less: Tax credits (including income taxes withheld and prepaid)	(xxx)
Tax due (or refund)	$ xxx

THE BIG PICTURE Tax Solutions for the Real World

LOSSES

Martha is nearing the end of a year that she would like to forget. Several years ago she loaned a friend $25,000 to enable him to start a business. The friend had made scheduled payments of $7,000 ($1,000 of this was interest) when he unexpectedly died in January. At the time of his death, he was insolvent. Martha's attempts to collect on the debt were fruitless.

Last October Martha invested $50,000 in the stock of a pharmaceutical company that previously had been profitable. However, as a result of losing a patent infringement suit, the company declared bankruptcy in May of this year. Martha is notified by the bankruptcy trustee that she can expect to receive nothing from the company.

Martha has owned and operated a bookstore as a sole proprietorship for the past 10 years. The bookstore previously has produced annual profits of about $75,000. Due to a chain bookstore opening down the street, Martha's bookstore sustained a net loss of $180,000 this year.

In September, a hurricane caused a large oak tree to blow over onto Martha's house. The cost of removing the tree and making repairs was $32,000. Martha received a check for $25,000 from her insurance company in final settlement of the claim. Her adjusted basis for the house was $280,000.

Can you help to relieve Martha's feeling of hopelessness by making her aware of beneficial loss provisions in the tax law? **Read the chapter and formulate your response.**

Working with the tax formula for individuals requires the proper classification of items that are deductible *for* adjusted gross income (AGI) and items that are deductions *from* AGI (itemized deductions). Business expenses and losses, discussed in this chapter, are reductions of gross income to arrive at the taxpayer's AGI. Expenses and losses incurred in connection with a transaction entered into for profit and attributable to rents and royalties are deducted *for* AGI. All other expenses and losses incurred in connection with a transaction entered into for profit are deducted *from* AGI.

The situation of Robert P. Groetzinger provides an interesting insight into the importance of the proper classification for the individual taxpayer. Groetzinger terminated his employment with a private company and devoted virtually all of his working time to pari-mutuel wagering on dog races. He had no other profession or employment, and his only sources of income, apart from his gambling winnings, were interest, dividends, and sales from investments. During the tax year in question, he went to the track six days a week and devoted 60 to 80 hours per week to preparing and making wagers on his own account.

The tax question that this case presents is whether Groetzinger's gambling activities constitute a trade or business. If the gambling is a trade or business, his gambling losses are deductions *for* AGI. If the gambling activity is not a trade or business, the losses are itemized deductions, and Groetzinger's taxes increase by $2,142.[1]

Deductible losses on personal use property are deducted as an itemized deduction. Itemized deductions are deductions *from* AGI. While the general coverage of itemized deductions is in Chapter 10, casualty and theft losses on personal use property are discussed in this chapter.

In determining the amount and timing of the deduction for bad debts, proper classification is again important. A business bad debt is classified as a deduction *for* AGI, and a nonbusiness bad debt is classified as a short-term capital loss.

Other topics discussed in Chapter 7 are research and experimental expenditures, the domestic production activities deduction, and the net operating loss deduction.

7.1 Bad Debts

LO.1

Determine the amount, classification, and timing of the bad debt deduction.

If a taxpayer sells goods or provides services on credit and the account receivable subsequently becomes worthless, a **bad debt** deduction is permitted only if income arising from the creation of the account receivable was previously included in income.[2] No deduction is allowed, for example, for a bad debt arising from the sale of a product or service when the taxpayer is on the cash basis because no income is reported until the cash has been collected. Permitting a bad debt deduction for a cash basis taxpayer would amount to a double deduction because the expenses of the product or service rendered are deducted when payments are made to suppliers and to employees, or at the time of the sale.

EXAMPLE 1

Tracy, an individual, is a sole proprietor. She operates a business named Executive Accounting and Tax Services. Last year, Pat hired Tracy to help him with the accounting for his small business. Tracy also prepared the S corporation income tax return for the business and Pat's personal income tax return. Tracy billed Pat $8,000 for the services she performed. Pat has never paid the bill, his business no longer exists, and his whereabouts are unknown.

If Tracy is an accrual basis taxpayer, she includes the $8,000 in income when the services are performed. When she determines that Pat's account will not be collected, she deducts the $8,000 as a bad debt expense.

[1] *Groetzinger v. Comm.*, 85–2 USTC ¶9622, 56 AFTR 2d 85–5683, 771 F.2d 269 (CA–7, 1985).

[2] Reg. § 1.166–1(e).

If Tracy is a cash basis taxpayer, she does not include the $8,000 in income until payment is received. When she determines that Pat's account will not be collected, she cannot deduct the $8,000 as a bad debt expense because it was never recognized as income. ■

A bad debt can also result from the nonrepayment of a loan made by the taxpayer or from purchased debt instruments.

SPECIFIC CHARGE-OFF METHOD

Taxpayers (other than certain financial institutions) may use only the **specific charge-off method** in accounting for bad debts. Certain financial institutions are allowed to use the **reserve method** for computing deductions for bad debts.

A taxpayer using the specific charge-off method may claim a deduction when a specific business debt becomes either partially or wholly worthless or when a specific nonbusiness debt becomes wholly worthless.[3] For the business debt, the taxpayer must satisfy the IRS that the debt is partially worthless and must demonstrate the amount of worthlessness.

If a business debt previously deducted as partially worthless becomes totally worthless in a future year, only the remainder not previously deducted can be deducted in the future year.

In the case of total worthlessness, a deduction is allowed for the entire amount in the year the debt becomes worthless. The amount of the deduction depends on the taxpayer's basis in the bad debt. If the debt arose from the sale of services or products and the face amount was previously included in income, that amount is deductible. If the taxpayer purchased the debt, the deduction is equal to the amount the taxpayer paid for the debt instrument.

One of the more difficult tasks is determining if and when a bad debt is worthless. The loss is deductible only in the year of partial or total worthlessness for business debts and only in the year of total worthlessness for nonbusiness debts. Legal proceedings need not be initiated against the debtor when the surrounding facts indicate that such action will not result in collection.

EXAMPLE 2

In 2009, Ross loaned $1,000 to Kay, who agreed to repay the loan in two years. In 2011, Kay disappeared after the note became delinquent. If a reasonable investigation by Ross indicates that he cannot find Kay or that a suit against Kay would not result in collection, Ross can deduct the $1,000 in 2011. ■

Bankruptcy is generally an indication of at least partial worthlessness of a debt. Bankruptcy may create worthlessness before the settlement date. If this is the case, the deduction may be taken in the year of worthlessness.

EXAMPLE 3

In Example 2, assume that Kay filed for personal bankruptcy in 2010 and that the debt is a business debt. At that time, Ross learned that unsecured creditors (including Ross) were ultimately expected to receive 20 cents on the dollar. In 2011, settlement is made and Ross receives only $150. He should deduct $800 ($1,000 loan − $200 expected settlement) in 2010 and $50 in 2011 ($200 balance − $150 proceeds). ■

If a receivable has been written off (deducted) as uncollectible during the current tax year and is subsequently collected during the current tax year, the write-off entry is reversed. If a receivable has been written off (deducted) as uncollectible, the collection of the receivable in a later tax year may result in income being recognized. Income will result if the deduction yielded a tax benefit in the year it was taken. See Examples 41 and 42 in Chapter 5.

[3] § 166(a) and Reg. § 1.166.

CONCEPT SUMMARY 7.1

Specific Charge-Off Method

Expense deduction and account write-off	The expense arises and the write-off takes place when a specific business account becomes either partially or wholly worthless or when a specific nonbusiness account becomes wholly worthless.
Recovery of accounts previously written off	If the account recovered was written off during the current taxable year, the write-off entry is reversed. If the account recovered was written off during a previous taxable year, income is created subject to the tax benefit rule.

BUSINESS VERSUS NONBUSINESS BAD DEBTS

A **nonbusiness bad debt** is a debt unrelated to the taxpayer's trade or business either when it was created or when it became worthless. The nature of a debt depends on whether the lender was engaged in the business of lending money or whether there is a proximate relationship between the creation of the debt and the lender's trade or business. The use to which the borrowed funds are put by the debtor is of no consequence. Loans to relatives or friends are the most common type of nonbusiness bad debt.

EXAMPLE 4
THE BIG PICTURE

Return to the facts of *The Big Picture* on p. 7-2. Martha loaned her friend, Jamil, $25,000. Jamil used the money to start a business, which subsequently failed. When Jamil died after having made payments of $7,000 on the loan, he was insolvent. Even though the proceeds of the loan were used in a business, the loan is a nonbusiness bad debt because the business was Jamil's, not Martha's. ■

The distinction between a business bad debt and a nonbusiness bad debt is important. A **business bad debt** is deductible as an ordinary loss in the year incurred, whereas a nonbusiness bad debt is always treated as a short-term capital loss. Thus, regardless of the age of a nonbusiness bad debt, the deduction may be of limited benefit due to the limitations on capital loss deductibility in any one year. The maximum amount of a net short-term capital loss that an individual can deduct against ordinary income in any one year is $3,000 (see Chapter 14 for a detailed discussion). Although no deduction is allowed when a nonbusiness bad debt is partially worthless, the taxpayer is entitled to deduct the net amount of the loss upon final settlement.

The following example is an illustration of business bad debts adapted from the Regulations.[4]

EXAMPLE 5

In 2010, Leif sold his business but retained a claim (note or account receivable) against Bob. The claim became worthless in 2011. Leif's loss is treated as a business bad debt because the debt was created in the conduct of his former trade or business. Leif is accorded business bad debt treatment even though he was holding the note as an investor and was no longer in a trade or business when the claim became worthless. ■

The nonbusiness bad debt provisions are *not* applicable to corporations. It is assumed that any loans made by a corporation are related to its trade or business. Therefore, any bad debts of a corporation are business bad debts.

LOANS BETWEEN RELATED PARTIES

Loans between related parties (especially family members) raise the issue of whether the transaction was a *bona fide* loan or a gift. The Regulations state that a bona fide

[4]Reg. § 1.166–5(d).

GLOBAL
Tax Issues

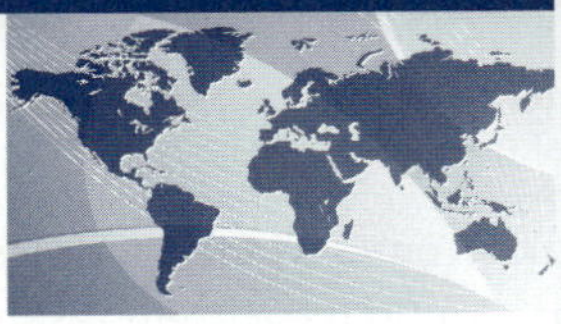

Writing Off Bad Debts

As a result of the recession, English banks and building societies were forced to write off £3.5 billion (about $5.5 billion) between April and June of 2010. This was equivalent to writing off around £40 million every day. The largest part of the bad debts—£2.1 billion—was the result of credit card debt.

Source: Adapted from Becky Barrow, "Banks Are Writing Off Pounds 40m a Day in Bad Debts," *Daily Mail London*, September 1, 2010, p. 4.

debt arises from a debtor-creditor relationship based on a valid and enforceable obligation to pay a fixed or determinable sum of money. Thus, individual circumstances must be examined to determine whether advances between related parties are gifts or loans. Some considerations are these:

- Was a note properly executed?
- Was there a reasonable rate of interest?
- Was collateral provided?
- What collection efforts were made?
- What was the intent of the parties?

EXAMPLE 6

Lana loans $2,000 to her widowed mother for an operation. Lana's mother owns no property and is not employed, and her only income consists of Social Security benefits. No note is issued for the loan, no provision for interest is made, and no repayment date is mentioned. In the current year, Lana's mother dies, leaving no estate. Assuming the loan is not repaid, Lana cannot take a deduction for a nonbusiness bad debt because the facts indicate that no debtor-creditor relationship existed. ■

7.2 Worthless Securities

LO.2

Understand the tax treatment of worthless securities including § 1244 stock.

A loss is allowed for securities that become *completely* worthless during the year (**worthless securities**).[5] Such securities are shares of stock, bonds, notes, or other evidence of indebtedness issued by a corporation or government. The losses generated are treated as capital losses deemed to have occurred on the *last day* of the taxable year. By treating the loss as having occurred on the last day of the taxable year, a loss that would otherwise have been classified as short term (if the date of worthlessness was used) may be classified as a long-term capital loss. Capital losses may be of limited benefit due to the $3,000 capital loss limitation.[6]

EXAMPLE 7
THE BIG PICTURE

Return to the facts of *The Big Picture* on p. 7-2. Assume that Martha is a calendar year taxpayer. She owned stock in Owl Corporation (a publicly held company). She acquired the stock as an investment on October 1, 2010, at a cost of $50,000. On May 31, 2011, the stock became worthless as the company declared bankruptcy. Since the stock is deemed to have become worthless as of December 31, 2011, Martha has a capital loss from an asset held for 15 months (a long-term capital loss). ■

SMALL BUSINESS STOCK

The general rule is that shareholders receive capital gain or loss treatment upon the sale or exchange of stock. However, it is possible to receive an ordinary loss deduction if the loss is sustained on **small business stock (§ 1244 stock)**. This loss could arise

5 § 165(g).

6 § 1211(b).

CONCEPT SUMMARY 7.2

Bad Debt Deductions

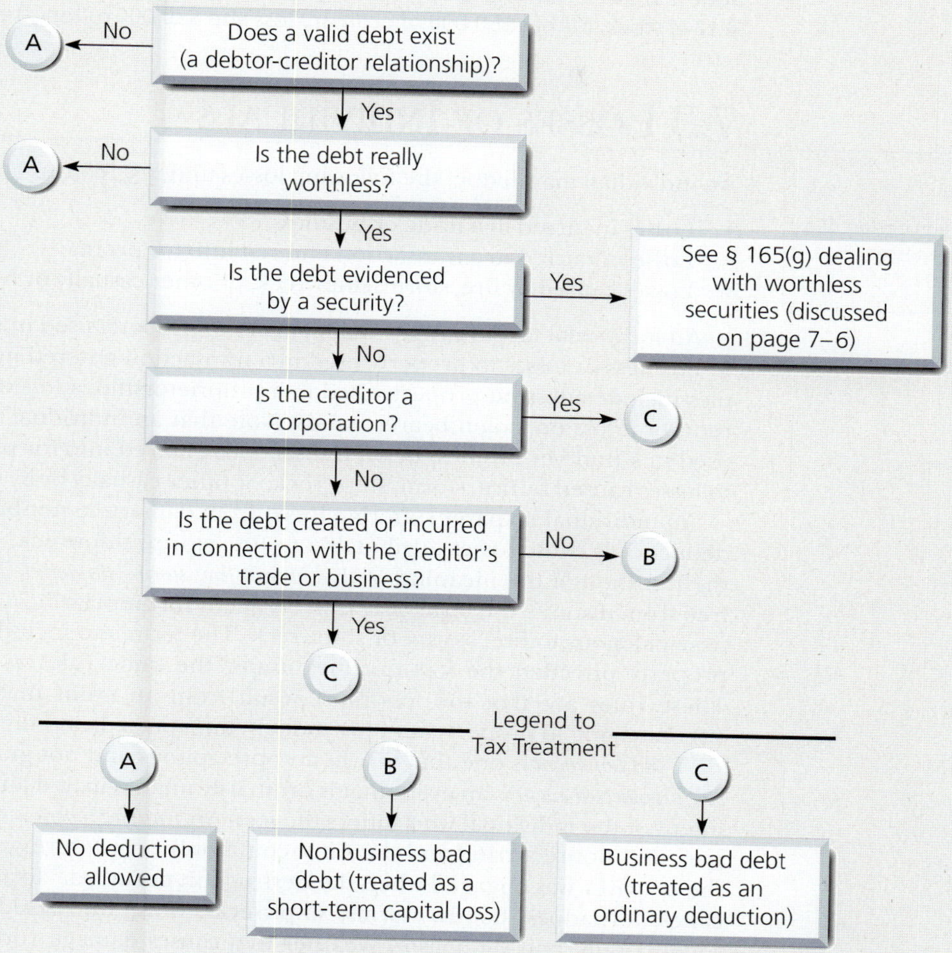

from a sale of the stock or from the stock becoming worthless. Only *individuals*[7] who acquired the stock *from* the corporation are eligible to receive ordinary loss treatment under § 1244. The ordinary loss treatment is limited to $50,000 ($100,000 for married individuals filing jointly) per year. Losses on § 1244 stock in excess of the statutory limits receive capital loss treatment.

The corporation must meet certain requirements for the loss on such stock to be treated as an *ordinary*—rather than a capital—loss. The major requirement is that the total amount of money and other property received by the corporation for stock as a contribution to capital (or paid-in surplus) does not exceed $1 million. The $1 million test is made at the time the stock is issued. Section 1244 stock can be common or preferred stock. Section 1244 applies only to losses. If § 1244 stock is sold at a gain, the Section is not applicable, and the gain is capital gain. See Chapter 18 for additional discussion of § 1244.

[7]The term "individuals" for this purpose includes a partnership but not a trust or an estate.

EXAMPLE 8

Iris, a single individual, was looking for an investment that would give some diversity to her stock portfolio. A friend suggested she acquire some stock in Eagle Corporation, a new start-up company. On July 1, 2009, Iris purchased 100 shares of Eagle Corporation for $100,000. At the time Iris acquired her stock from Eagle Corporation, the corporation had $700,000 of paid-in capital. Hence, the stock qualified as § 1244 stock. On June 20, 2011, Iris sold all of her Eagle stock for $20,000. Because the Eagle stock is § 1244 stock, Iris has $50,000 of ordinary loss and $30,000 of long-term capital loss. ■

7.3 Losses of Individuals

LO.3

Distinguish between deductible and nondeductible losses of individuals.

An individual may deduct the following losses under § 165(c):

- Losses incurred in a trade or business.
- Losses incurred in a transaction entered into for profit.
- Losses caused by fire, storm, shipwreck, or other casualty or by theft.

An individual taxpayer may deduct losses to property used in the taxpayer's trade or business or losses to property used in a transaction entered into for profit. Examples include a loss on property used in a proprietorship, a loss on property held for rent, or a loss on stolen bearer bonds. Note that an individual's losses on property used in a trade or business or on transactions entered into for profit are not limited to losses caused by fire, storm, shipwreck, or other casualty or by theft.

An individual taxpayer suffering losses from damage to nonbusiness property can deduct only those losses attributable to fire, storm, shipwreck, or other casualty or theft. Although the meaning of the terms *fire, storm, shipwreck,* and *theft* is relatively free from dispute, the term *other casualty* needs further clarification. It means casualties analogous to fire, storm, or shipwreck. The term also includes accidental loss of property provided the loss qualifies under the same rules as any other casualty. These rules are that the loss must result from an event that is (1) identifiable; (2) damaging to property; and (3) sudden, unexpected, and unusual in nature.

A *sudden event* is one that is swift and precipitous and not gradual or progressive. An *unexpected event* is an event that is ordinarily unanticipated and occurs without the intent of the individual who suffers the loss. An *unusual event* is one that is extraordinary and nonrecurring and does not commonly occur during the activity in which the taxpayer was engaged when the destruction occurred.[8] Examples include hurricanes, tornadoes, floods, storms, shipwrecks, fires, auto accidents, mine cave-ins, sonic booms, and vandalism. Weather that causes damage (drought, for example) must be unusual and severe for the particular region. Damage must be to the taxpayer's property to qualify as a **casualty loss**.

A taxpayer can take a deduction for a casualty loss from an automobile accident only if the damage was not caused by the taxpayer's willful act or willful negligence.

EXAMPLE 9

Ted parks his car on a hill and fails to set the brake properly and to curb the wheels. As a result of Ted's negligence, the car rolls down the hill and is damaged. The repairs to Ted's car should qualify for casualty loss treatment since Ted's act of negligence appears to be simple rather than willful. ■

LO.4

Identify a casualty and determine the amount, classification, and timing of casualty and theft losses.

EVENTS THAT ARE NOT CASUALTIES

Not all acts of God are treated as casualty losses for income tax purposes. Because a casualty must be sudden, unexpected, and unusual, progressive deterioration (such as erosion due to wind or rain) is not a casualty because it does not meet the suddenness test.

[8] Rev.Rul. 72–592, 1972–2 C.B. 101.

TAX in the NEWS

TAINTED CHINESE DRYWALL

A study published by the Consumer Product Safety Commission (CPSC) concluded that there was a strong association between tainted Chinese drywall and a gas smelling like rotten eggs, caused by high levels of sulfur in the drywall. As a consequence of the study, lawmakers and the CPSC asked the Internal Revenue Service to decide if taxpayers incurring this problem could claim a casualty loss deduction on their tax returns.

An IRS spokesperson indicated that the Service would consider granting a tax deduction if the homeowner could prove that the Chinese drywall caused sudden, unusual, and unexpected damage to the taxpayer's home. A key to claiming a deduction is expert documentation.

Source: Adapted from Isaac Wolf, "IRS: Tax Deduction May Go to Homeowners with Tainted Chinese Drywall," *Scripps Howard News Service,* December 3, 2009.

Examples of nonsudden events that generally do not qualify as casualties include disease and insect damage. When the damage was caused by termites over a period of several years, some courts have disallowed a casualty loss deduction.[9] On the other hand, some courts have held that termite damage over periods of up to 15 months after infestation constituted a sudden event and was, therefore, deductible as a casualty loss.[10] Despite the existence of some judicial support for the deductibility of termite damage as a casualty loss, the current position of the IRS is that termite damage is not deductible.[11]

Other examples of events that are not casualties are losses resulting from a decline in value rather than an actual loss of the property. No loss was allowed where the taxpayer's home declined in value as a result of a landslide that destroyed neighboring homes but did no actual damage to the taxpayer's home.[12] Similarly, a taxpayer was allowed a loss for the actual flood damage to his property but not for the decline in market value due to the property's being flood-prone.[13]

THEFT LOSSES

Theft includes, but is not necessarily limited to, larceny, embezzlement, and robbery.[14] Theft does not include misplaced items.[15]

Theft losses are computed like other casualty losses (discussed in the following section), but the *timing* for recognition of the loss differs. A theft loss is deducted in the year of discovery, not the year of the theft (unless, of course, the discovery occurs in the same year as the theft). If, in the year of the discovery, a claim exists (e.g., against an insurance company) and there is a reasonable expectation of recovering the adjusted basis of the asset from the insurance company, no deduction is permitted.[16] If, in the year of settlement, the recovery is less than the asset's adjusted basis, a partial deduction may be available. If the recovery is greater than the asset's adjusted basis, gain may be recognized.

EXAMPLE 10

Keith's new sailboat, which he uses for personal purposes, was stolen from the storage marina in December 2010. He discovered the loss on June 3, 2011, and filed a claim with his insurance company that was settled on January 30, 2012. Assuming there is a reasonable expectation of full recovery, no deduction is allowed in 2011. A partial deduction may be available in 2012 if the actual insurance proceeds are less than the lower of the fair market value or the adjusted basis of the asset. (Loss measurement rules are discussed later in this chapter.) ■

[9] *Fay v. Helvering,* 41–2 USTC ¶9494, 27 AFTR 432, 120 F.2d 253 (CA–2, 1941); *U.S. v. Rogers,* 41–1 USTC ¶9442, 27 AFTR 423, 120 F.2d 244 (CA–9, 1941).

[10] *Rosenberg v. Comm.,* 52–2 USTC ¶9377, 42 AFTR 303, 198 F.2d 46 (CA–8, 1952); *Shopmaker v. U.S.,* 54–1 USTC ¶9195, 45 AFTR 758, 119 F.Supp. 705 (D.Ct. Mo., 1953).

[11] Rev.Rul. 63–232, 1963–2 C.B. 97.

[12] *H. Pulvers v. Comm.,* 69–1 USTC ¶9222, 23 AFTR 2d 69–678, 407 F.2d 838 (CA–9, 1969).

[13] *S. L. Solomon,* 39 TCM 1282, T.C.Memo. 1980–87.

[14] Reg. § 1.165–8(d).

[15] *Mary Francis Allen,* 16 T.C. 163 (1951).

[16] Reg. §§ 1.165–1(d)(2) and 1.165–8(a)(2).

WHEN TO DEDUCT CASUALTY LOSSES

General Rule

Generally, a casualty loss is deducted in the year the loss occurs. However, no casualty loss is permitted if a reimbursement claim with a *reasonable prospect of full recovery* exists.[17] If the taxpayer has a partial claim, only part of the loss can be claimed in the year of the casualty, and the remainder is deducted in the year the claim is settled.

EXAMPLE 11

Brian's new sailboat was completely destroyed by fire in 2011. Its cost and fair market value were $10,000. Brian's only claim against the insurance company was on a $7,000 policy and was not settled by year-end. The following year, 2012, Brian settled with the insurance company for $6,000. He is entitled to a $3,000 deduction in 2011 and a $1,000 deduction in 2012. If Brian held the sailboat for personal use, the $3,000 deduction in 2011 is reduced first by $100 and then by 10% of his 2011 AGI. The $1,000 deduction in 2012 is reduced by 10% of his 2012 AGI (see the following discussion on the $100 and 10% floors). ■

If a taxpayer receives reimbursement for a casualty loss sustained and deducted in a previous year, an amended return is not filed for that year. Instead, the taxpayer must include the reimbursement in gross income on the return for the year in which it is received to the extent that the previous deduction resulted in a tax benefit.

EXAMPLE 12

Fran had a deductible casualty loss of $5,000 on her 2010 tax return. Fran's taxable income for 2010 was $60,000. In June 2011, Fran is reimbursed $3,000 for the prior year's casualty loss. Fran includes the entire $3,000 in gross income for 2011 because the deduction in 2010 produced a tax benefit. ■

Disaster Area Losses

An exception to the general rule for the time of deduction is allowed for **disaster area losses**, which are casualties sustained in an area designated as a disaster area by the President of the United States.[18] In such cases, the taxpayer may *elect* to treat the loss as having occurred in the taxable year immediately *preceding* the taxable year in which the disaster actually occurred. The rationale for this exception is to provide immediate relief to disaster victims in the form of accelerated tax benefits.

If the due date, plus extensions, for the prior year's return has not passed, a taxpayer makes the election to claim the disaster area loss on the prior year's tax return. If the disaster occurs after the prior year's return has been filed, it is necessary to file either an amended return or a refund claim. In any case, the taxpayer must show clearly that such an election is being made.

Disaster loss treatment also applies in the case of a personal residence that has been rendered unsafe for use as a residence because of a disaster. This provision applies when, within 120 days after the President designates the area as a disaster area, the state or local government where the residence is located orders the taxpayer to demolish or relocate the residence.[19]

EXAMPLE 13
THE BIG PICTURE

Return to the facts of *The Big Picture* on p. 7-2. On September 28, 2011, Martha's personal residence was damaged when a hurricane caused an oak tree to fall onto the house. The amount of her uninsured loss was $7,000. Because of the extent of the damage in the area, the President of the United States designated the area a disaster area. Because Martha's loss is a disaster area loss, she may elect to file an amended return for 2010 and take the loss in that year. If Martha elects this course of action, the amount of the loss will be reduced first by $100 (the materiality amount in 2010) and then by 10% of her 2010 AGI. If Martha forgoes the election, she may take the loss on her 2011 income tax return. The amount of the loss will be reduced first by $100 (the materiality amount in 2011) and then by 10% of her 2011 AGI. ■

[17] Reg. § 1.165–1(d)(2)(i).
[18] § 165(h).
[19] § 165(k).

GLOBAL *Tax Issues*

Notification of Casualty Losses

Tropical storm Ondoy and Typhoon Pepeng hit Manila on September 26 and October 2, 2009, respectively. These were two of the most devastating storms ever to hit the Philippines. In response to the anticipated losses caused by these storms, the Philippines Bureau of Internal Revenue issued a Revenue Memorandum Order that provided guidelines for reporting losses. The order gave affected taxpayers less than 45 days to file a Sworn Declaration of Loss and all the supporting documents. Unless they filed a Sworn Declaration of Loss, taxpayers could not claim a casualty loss on their tax returns.

Source: Adapted from José Jaffy Y. Azarraga, "Taxwise or Otherwise," *Business World Manila*, April 29, 2010.

MEASURING THE AMOUNT OF LOSS

Amount of Loss

The rules for determining the amount of a loss depend in part on whether business use, income-producing use, or personal use property was involved. Another factor that must be considered is whether the property was partially or completely destroyed.

If business property or property held for the production of income (e.g., rental property) is *completely destroyed*, the loss is equal to the adjusted basis of the property at the time of destruction.

EXAMPLE 14

Vicki's automobile, which was used only for business purposes, was destroyed by fire. Vicki had unintentionally allowed her insurance coverage to expire. The fair market value of the automobile was $9,000 at the time of the fire, and its adjusted basis was $10,000. Vicki is allowed a loss deduction of $10,000 (the basis of the automobile). The $10,000 loss is a deduction *for* AGI. ■

A different measurement rule applies for *partial destruction* of business property and income-producing property and for *partial* or *complete destruction* of personal use property. In these situations, the loss is the *lesser* of the following:

- The adjusted basis of the property.
- The difference between the fair market value of the property before the event and the fair market value immediately after the event.

EXAMPLE 15

Kelly's uninsured automobile, which was used only for business purposes, was damaged in an accident. At the date of the accident, the fair market value of the automobile was $12,000, and its adjusted basis was $9,000. After the accident, the automobile was appraised at $4,000. Kelly's loss deduction is $8,000 (the lesser of the adjusted basis or the decrease in fair market value). The $8,000 loss is a deduction *for* AGI. ■

The deduction for the loss of property that is part business and part personal must be computed separately for the business portion and the personal portion.

Any insurance recovery reduces the loss for business, production of income, and personal use losses. In fact, a taxpayer may realize a gain if the insurance proceeds exceed the amount of the loss. Chapter 14 discusses the treatment of net gains and losses on business property and income-producing property.

A taxpayer is not permitted to deduct a casualty loss for damage to insured personal use property unless a *timely insurance claim* is filed with respect to the damage to

TAX *in* *the NEWS*

A Proposal for Changing the Casualty Loss Limits

On July 24, 2008, Senate Finance Committee Chairman Max Baucus introduced legislation aimed at promoting American jobs, developing clean energy, and providing families with targeted tax relief and incentives. Under the proposal, the 10 percent-of-AGI rule for casualty losses would be waived, and the $100 floor would be permanently raised to $500. The bill would also allow nonitemizers to take the loss as an addition to the standard deduction. To date, this bill has not become law. Since Baucus chairs the Senate Finance Committee, it will be interesting to see if it is enacted.

Source: Adapted from U.S. Senate Documents.

the property. This rule applies to the extent that any insurance policy provides for full or partial reimbursement for the loss.[20]

Generally, an appraisal before and after the casualty is needed to measure the amount of the loss. However, the *cost of repairs* to the damaged property is acceptable as a method of establishing the loss in value provided the following criteria are met:

- The repairs are necessary to restore the property to its condition immediately before the casualty.
- The amount spent for such repairs is not excessive.
- The repairs do not extend beyond the damage suffered.
- The value of the property after the repairs does not, as a result of the repairs, exceed the value of the property immediately before the casualty.[21]

Reduction for $100 and 10 Percent-of-AGI Floors

The amount of the loss for personal use property must be further reduced by a $100 *per event* floor and a 10 percent-of-AGI *aggregate* floor.[22] The $100 floor applies separately to each casualty and applies to the entire loss from each casualty (e.g., if a storm damages both a taxpayer's residence and automobile, only $100 is subtracted from the total amount of the loss). The losses are then added together, and the total is reduced by 10 percent of the taxpayer's AGI. The resulting loss is the taxpayer's itemized deduction for casualty and theft losses.

EXAMPLE 16

Rocky, who had AGI of $30,000, was involved in a motorcycle accident in 2011. His motorcycle, which was used only for personal use and had a fair market value of $12,000 and an adjusted basis of $9,000, was completely destroyed. He received $5,000 from his insurance company. Rocky's casualty loss deduction is $900 [$9,000 basis − $5,000 insurance recovery − $100 floor − $3,000 (.10 × $30,000 AGI)]. The $900 casualty loss is an itemized deduction (*from* AGI). ■

When a nonbusiness casualty loss is spread between two taxable years because of the *reasonable prospect of recovery* doctrine, the loss in the second year is not reduced by the $100 floor. This result occurs because this floor is imposed per event and has already reduced the amount of the loss in the first year. However, the loss in the second year is still subject to the 10 percent floor based on the taxpayer's second-year AGI (refer to Example 11).

Taxpayers who suffer qualified disaster area losses can elect to deduct the losses in the year preceding the year of occurrence. The disaster loss is treated as having

[20] § 165(h)(5)(E).
[21] Reg. § 1.165–7(a)(2)(ii).
[22] § 165(c)(3).

occurred in the preceding taxable year. Hence, the 10 percent-of-AGI floor is determined by using the AGI of the year for which the deduction is claimed.[23]

Multiple Losses

The rules for computing loss deductions where multiple losses have occurred are explained in Examples 17 and 18.

EXAMPLE 17

During the year, Tim had the following casualty losses:

Asset	Adjusted Basis	Fair Market Value of Asset: Before the Casualty	Fair Market Value of Asset: After the Casualty	Insurance Recovery
A	$900	$600	$-0-	$400
B	300	800	250	100

Assets A and B were used in Tim's business at the time of the casualty. The following losses are allowed:

Asset A: $500. The complete destruction of a business asset results in a deduction of the adjusted basis of the property (reduced by any insurance recovery) regardless of the asset's fair market value.

Asset B: $200. The partial destruction of a business (or personal use) asset results in a deduction equal to the lesser of the adjusted basis ($300) or the decline in value ($550), reduced by any insurance recovery ($100).

Both the Asset A and Asset B losses are deductions *for* AGI. The $100 floor and the 10%-of-AGI floor do not apply because the assets are business assets. ■

EXAMPLE 18

In 2011, Emily had AGI of $20,000 and the following casualty losses:

Asset	Adjusted Basis	Fair Market Value of Asset: Before the Casualty	Fair Market Value of Asset: After the Casualty	Insurance Recovery
A	$1,900	$1,400	$ -0-	$200
B	2,500	4,000	1,000	-0-
C	800	400	100	250

Assets A, B, and C were held for personal use, and the losses to these three assets are from three different casualties. The loss for each asset is computed as follows:

Asset A: $1,100. The lesser of the adjusted basis of $1,900 or the $1,400 decline in value, reduced by the insurance recovery of $200, minus the $100 floor.

Asset B: $2,400. The lesser of the adjusted basis of $2,500 or the $3,000 decline in value, minus the $100 floor.

Asset C: $0. The lesser of the adjusted basis of $800 or the $300 decline in value, reduced by the insurance recovery of $250, minus the $100 floor.

Emily's itemized casualty loss deduction for the year is $1,500:

Asset A loss	$ 1,100
Asset B loss	2,400
Asset C loss	-0-
Total loss	$ 3,500
Less: 10% of AGI (10% × $20,000)	(2,000)
Itemized casualty loss deduction	$ 1,500

■

[23] § 165(i).

STATUTORY FRAMEWORK FOR DEDUCTING LOSSES OF INDIVIDUALS

Casualty and theft losses incurred by an individual in connection with a trade or business are deductible *for* AGI.[24] These losses are not subject to the $100 per event and the 10 percent-of-AGI limitations. Casualty and theft losses incurred by an employee in connection with a trade or business are deductible *for* AGI if the loss is reimbursed by the employer. If the loss is not reimbursed, the loss is deductible *from* AGI as a miscellaneous itemized deduction subject to the 2 percent-of-AGI floor. These losses are not subject to the $100 per event and the 10 percent-of-AGI limitations.

Casualty and theft losses incurred by an individual in a transaction entered into for profit are not subject to the $100 per event and the 10 percent-of-AGI limitations. If these losses are attributable to rents or royalties, the deduction is *for* AGI.[25] However, if these losses are not connected with property held for the production of rents and royalties, they are deductions *from* AGI. More specifically, these losses are classified as other miscellaneous itemized deductions. An example of this type of loss would be the theft of a security. However, theft losses of investment property are not subject to the 2 percent-of-AGI floor on certain miscellaneous itemized deductions (explained in Chapters 9 and 10).

Casualty and theft losses attributable to personal use property are subject to the $100 per event and the 10 percent-of-AGI limitations. These losses are itemized deductions, but they are not subject to the 2 percent-of-AGI floor.[26]

PERSONAL CASUALTY GAINS AND LOSSES

If a taxpayer has personal casualty and theft gains as well as losses, a special set of rules applies for determining the tax consequences. A **personal casualty gain** is the recognized gain from a casualty or theft of personal use property. A **personal casualty loss** for this purpose is a casualty or theft loss of personal use property after the application of the $100 floor. A taxpayer who has both gains and losses for the taxable year must first net (offset) the personal casualty gains and personal casualty losses. If the gains exceed the losses, the gains and losses are treated as gains and losses from the sale of capital assets. The capital gains and losses are short term or long term, depending on the period the taxpayer held each of the assets. In the netting process, personal casualty and theft gains and losses are not netted with the gains and losses on business and income-producing property.

EXAMPLE 19

During the year, Cliff had the following personal casualty gains and losses (after deducting the $100 floor):

Asset	Holding Period	Gain or (Loss)
A	Three months	($ 300)
B	Three years	(2,400)
C	Two years	3,200

Cliff computes the tax consequences as follows:

Personal casualty gain	$ 3,200
Personal casualty loss ($300 + $2,400)	(2,700)
Net personal casualty gain	$ 500

Cliff treats all of the gains and losses as capital gains and losses and has the following:

Short-term capital loss (Asset A)	$ 300
Long-term capital loss (Asset B)	2,400
Long-term capital gain (Asset C)	3,200

■

[24] § 62(a)(1).

[25] § 62(a)(4).

[26] § 67(b)(3).

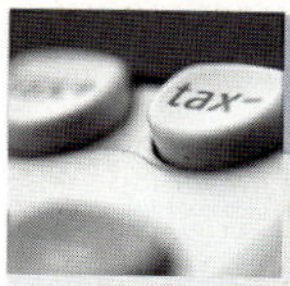

CONCEPT SUMMARY 7.3

Casualty Gains and Losses

	Business Use or Income-Producing Property	Personal Use Property
Event creating the loss	Any event.	Casualty or theft.
Amount	The lesser of the decline in fair market value or the adjusted basis, but always the adjusted basis if the property is totally destroyed.	The lesser of the decline in fair market value or the adjusted basis.
Insurance	Insurance proceeds received reduce the amount of the loss.	Insurance proceeds received (or for which there is an unfiled claim) reduce the amount of the loss.
$100 floor	Not applicable.	Applicable per event.
Gains and losses	Gains and losses are netted (see detailed discussion in Chapter 14).	Personal casualty and theft gains and losses are netted.
Gains exceeding losses		The gains and losses are treated as gains and losses from the sale of capital assets.
Losses exceeding gains		The gains—and the losses to the extent of gains—are treated as ordinary items in computing AGI. The losses in excess of gains, to the extent they exceed 10% of AGI, are itemized deductions.

If personal casualty losses exceed personal casualty gains, all gains and losses are treated as ordinary items. The gains—and the losses to the extent of gains—are treated as ordinary income and ordinary loss in computing AGI. Losses in excess of gains are deducted as itemized deductions to the extent the losses exceed 10 percent of AGI.[27]

EXAMPLE 20

During the year, Hazel had AGI of $20,000 and the following personal casualty gain and loss (after deducting the $100 floor):

Asset	Holding Period	Gain or (Loss)
A	Three years	($2,700)
B	Four months	200

Hazel computes the tax consequences as follows:

Personal casualty loss	($2,700)
Personal casualty gain	200
Net personal casualty loss	($2,500)

Hazel treats the gain and the loss as ordinary items. The $200 gain and $200 of the loss are included in computing AGI. Hazel's itemized deduction for casualty losses is computed as follows:

Casualty loss in excess of gain ($2,700 − $200)	$ 2,500
Less: 10% of AGI (10% × $20,000)	(2,000)
Itemized deduction	$ 500

■

[27] § 165(h).

ETHICS & Equity

The Amount of a Casualty Loss

In the case of a casualty loss to personal use property, the loss is allowed only to the extent that it exceeds $100 and the net casualty loss for the tax year exceeds 10 percent of AGI. The amount of the loss allowed is the lesser of (1) the decline in the fair market value of the property as a result of the casualty or (2) the adjusted basis of the property.

George and Mabel purchased their house 60 years ago for $100,000. Shortly after they moved in, they purchased an oak tree for $10 and planted it in front of their new home. Earlier this year, a severe windstorm passed through their neighborhood and uprooted the oak tree. No damage was done to their house. After the storm, George had the property appraised. The appraiser told George that the value of the property had declined by $10,000 because of the loss of the oak tree. George also contacted a nursery and was told that it would cost at least $20,000 to replace the oak with a tree much smaller than the one that was destroyed. George is considering claiming a loss deduction of at least $20,000 for the destroyed oak tree. Evaluate George's plan.

7.4 Research and Experimental Expenditures

LO.5

Recognize and apply the alternative tax treatments for research and experimental expenditures.

Section 174 covers the treatment of research and experimental expenditures. The Regulations define **research and experimental expenditures** as follows:

> all such costs incident to the development of an experimental or pilot model, a plant process, a product, a formula, an invention, or similar property, and the improvement of already existing property of the type mentioned. The term does not include expenditures such as those for the ordinary testing or inspection of materials or products for quality control or those for efficiency surveys, management studies, consumer surveys, advertising, or promotions.[28]

Expenses in connection with the acquisition or improvement of land or depreciable property are not research and experimental expenditures. Rather, they increase the basis of the land or depreciable property. However, depreciation on a building used for research may be a research and experimental expense. Only the depreciation that is a research and experimental expense (not the cost of the asset) is subject to the three alternatives discussed below.

The law permits the following *three alternatives* for the handling of research and experimental expenditures:

- Expensed in the year paid or incurred.
- Deferred and amortized.
- Capitalized.

If the costs are capitalized, a deduction is not available until the research project is abandoned or is deemed worthless. Since many products resulting from research projects do not have a definite and limited useful life, a taxpayer should ordinarily elect to write off the expenditures immediately or to defer and amortize them. It is generally preferable to elect an immediate write-off of the research expenditures because of the time value of the tax deduction.

The law also provides for a research activities credit. The credit amounts to 20 percent of certain research and experimental expenditures.[29] (The credit is discussed more fully in Chapter 12.)

EXPENSE METHOD

A taxpayer can elect to expense all of the research and experimental expenditures incurred in the current year and all subsequent years. The consent of the IRS is not

[28]Reg. § 1.174–2(a)(1).

[29]§ 41.

required if the method is adopted for the first taxable year in which such expenditures were paid or incurred. Once the election is made, the taxpayer must continue to expense all qualifying expenditures unless a request for a change is made to, and approved by, the IRS. In certain instances, a taxpayer may incur research and experimental expenditures before actually engaging in any trade or business activity. In such instances, the Supreme Court has applied a liberal standard of deductibility and permitted a deduction in the year of incurrence.[30]

DEFERRAL AND AMORTIZATION METHOD

Alternatively, research and experimental expenditures may be deferred and amortized if the taxpayer makes an election.[31] Under the election, research and experimental expenditures are amortized ratably over a period of not less than 60 months. A deduction is allowed beginning with the month in which the taxpayer first realizes benefits from the experimental expenditure. The election is binding, and a change requires permission from the IRS.

EXAMPLE 21

Gold Corporation decides to develop a new line of adhesives. The project begins in 2011. Gold incurs the following expenses in 2011 in connection with the project:

Salaries	$25,000
Materials	8,000
Depreciation on machinery	6,500

Gold incurs the following expenses in 2012 in connection with the project:

Salaries	$18,000
Materials	2,000
Depreciation on machinery	5,700

The benefits from the project will be realized starting in March 2013. If Gold Corporation elects a 60-month deferral and amortization period, there is no deduction prior to March 2013, the month benefits from the project begin to be realized. The deduction for 2013 is $10,867, computed as follows:

Salaries ($25,000 + $18,000)	$43,000
Materials ($8,000 + $2,000)	10,000
Depreciation ($6,500 + $5,700)	12,200
Total	$65,200
$65,200 × (10 months/60 months) =	$10,867

■

The option to treat research and experimental expenditures as deferred expense is usually employed when a company does not have sufficient income to offset the research and experimental expenses. Rather than create net operating loss carryovers that might not be utilized because of the 20-year limitation on such carryovers, the deferral and amortization method may be used. The deferral of research and experimental expenditures should also be considered if the taxpayer expects higher tax rates in the future.

7.5 Domestic Production Activities Deduction

LO.6

Calculate the domestic production activities deduction.

The American Jobs Creation Act of 2004 was enacted to replace certain tax provisions that our world trading partners regarded as allowing unfair advantage to U.S. exports. Among other changes, the Act created a deduction based on the income

[30] *Snow v. Comm.*, 74–1 USTC ¶9432, 33 AFTR 2d 74–1251, 94 S.Ct. 1876 (USSC, 1974).

[31] § 174(b)(2).

from manufacturing activities (designated as *production activities*).[32] The **domestic production activities deduction (DPAD)** is contained in § 199.

OPERATIONAL RULES

Calculation of the Domestic Production Activities Deduction

For tax years beginning in 2010 and thereafter, the DPAD is based on the following formula:[33]

9% × Lesser of
- Qualified production activities income (QPAI)
- Taxable (or modified adjusted gross) income or alternative minimum taxable income

For tax years beginning in 2005 or 2006, the 9 percent factor was 3 percent. For tax years beginning in 2007, 2008, and 2009, the 9 percent factor was 6 percent.

Taxable income is determined without regard to the DPAD. In the case of an individual (a sole proprietorship or an owner of a flow-through entity), **modified adjusted gross income** is substituted for taxable income.[34]

The taxable income limitation is determined after the application of any net operating loss (NOL) deduction for the tax year (NOLs are explained later in the chapter). Thus, a company with an NOL carryforward for a tax year is ineligible for the DPAD if the carryforward eliminates current taxable income. Further, a taxpayer that has an NOL carryback may lose part or all of the DPAD benefit for that year. As taxable income is reduced by the NOL carryback, there is a corresponding reduction in the DPAD. If qualified production activities income (QPAI) cannot be used in a particular year due to the taxable income limitation (see the above formula), it is lost forever. (The calculation of QPAI is explained in the next section.)

EXAMPLE 22

Opal, Inc., manufactures and sells costume jewelry. It also sells costume jewelry purchased from other manufacturers. During 2011, Opal had a *profit* of $200,000 (QPAI) from the sale of its own manufactured jewelry and a *loss* of $50,000 from the sale of the purchased jewelry. Based on this information, Opal's QPAI is $200,000, and its taxable income is $150,000 ($200,000 − $50,000). Opal's DPAD becomes $13,500 [9% of the lesser of $200,000 (QPAI) or $150,000 (taxable income)]. ■

EXAMPLE 23

Assume the same facts as in Example 22, except that Opal also has an NOL carryover from 2010 of $300,000. As taxable income for 2011 is zero ($200,000 − $50,000 − $300,000), there is no DPAD. ■

Another important limitation is that the amount of the DPAD cannot exceed 50 percent of certain **W–2 wages** paid by the taxpayer during the tax year.[35] The purpose of this limitation is to preserve U.S. manufacturing jobs and to discourage their outsourcing. An employer's W–2 wages include the sum of the aggregate amount of wages and elective deferrals required to be included on the W–2 wage statements for certain employees during the employer's taxable year. Elective deferrals include those amounts deferred under § 457 plans and Roth contributions. An employer previously included wages paid to all workers during a tax year and not just the wages of the employees engaged in qualified production activities. However, as a result of a recent statutory change, an employer is permitted to include only those W–2 wages paid to employees engaged in qualified production activities.

[32] Section 101 of the *American Jobs Creation Act of 2004*, Public Law No. 108-357 (October 22, 2004).

[33] § 199(a).

[34] § 199(d)(2). Generally, modified AGI is AGI prior to the effect of § 199.

[35] § 199(b).

TAX *in the NEWS*

Repeal of § 199 for Oil Producers

Senator Max Baucus has added an amendment to a small business lending bill that would repeal § 199 (the domestic production activities deduction) for the top five U.S. oil-producing firms. Baucus believes that these firms no longer need this incentive because they have been highly profitable in recent years. The American Petroleum Institute claims that its studies show that the repeal would result in lower oil production and the loss of thousands of jobs. It will be interesting to see if this repeal provision is enacted in this or subsequent legislation.

Source: Adapted from Mike Godfrey, "U.S. Oil Warns against Tax Hike," *Tax-News.com*, August 18, 2010.

EXAMPLE 24

In 2011, Red, Inc., a calendar year taxpayer, has QPAI of $2 million and taxable income of $2.1 million. Since Red outsources much of its work to independent contractors, its W–2 wage base, which for Red is related entirely to production activities, is $80,000. Although Red's DPAD normally would be $180,000 [9% of the lesser of $2 million (QPAI) or $2.1 million (taxable income)], it is limited to $40,000 [50% of $80,000 (W–2 wages)]. ■

EXAMPLE 25

Assume the same facts as in Example 24, except that Red also pays salaries of $50,000 related to its *nonproduction* activities. Because these wages are not paid to employees engaged in production activities, the wage limitation on the DPAD remains at $40,000 [50% of $80,000 ($80,000 + $0)]. ■

Calculation of Qualified Production Activities Income

Qualified production activities income (QPAI) is the excess of **domestic production gross receipts (DPGR)** over the sum of:

- The cost of goods sold allocated to such receipts.
- Other deductions, expenses, or losses directly allocated to such receipts.
- The ratable portion of deductions, expenses, and losses not directly allocable to such receipts or another class of income.[36]

QPAI is determined on an item-by-item basis—not on a division-by-division or a transaction-by-transaction basis. Because all items must be netted in the calculation, the final QPAI amount can be either positive or negative. The effect of the netting rule is to preclude taxpayers from selecting only profitable product lines or profitable transactions when calculating QPAI.

EXAMPLE 26

A taxpayer manufactures pants and shirts with the following QPAI results: $5 for one pair of pants and a negative $2 for one shirt. Because the two items are netted, the QPAI amount that controls is $3 ($5 – $2). ■

Five specific categories of DPGR qualify for the DPAD:[37]

- The lease, license, sale, exchange, or other disposition of qualified production property (QPP) that was manufactured, produced, grown, or extracted (MPGE) in the United States.
- Qualified films largely created in the United States.
- The production of electricity, natural gas, or potable water.
- Construction (but not self-construction) performed in the United States.
- Engineering and architectural services for domestic construction.

[36] § 199(c).

[37] § 199(c)(4).

FINANCIAL DISCLOSURE *Insights*

Tax Losses and the Deferred Tax Asset

To some people, a current-year net operating loss (NOL) represents a failure of an entity's business model, but others see it as an immediate tax refund. But when an NOL hits the balance sheet as a deferred tax asset, the story is not over. The NOL creates or increases a deferred tax asset that may or may not be used in future financial accounting reporting periods: the key question for a financial analyst is whether the entity will generate enough net revenue in future years that can be offset by the NOL carryover amount.

When a business entity holds a loss carryforward, for every reporting period its management must assess whether the loss is likely to be used to create cash flow in the future, as the loss carryforward offsets operating or other profits from future years. When it is more likely than not that a loss carryforward *will not be realized*, GAAP requires that a valuation allowance be created to reduce the deferred tax asset to a lower amount that is expected to be realized in the future. The valuation allowance is a contra-asset account (like accumulated depreciation on a fixed asset) against the deferred tax asset.

A valuation allowance against an NOL carryforward might be created when there is doubt as to the level of the entity's future net profits. The valuation allowance is reduced or eliminated, though, when it appears that the NOL will be fully realized due to any of the following:

- Future years' net income from operations or other activities.
- New product orders or contracts for the business.
- The reversal of other temporary book-tax differences.
- An effective use of tax planning strategies.

Evidence that a loss carryforward might not be realized in the future includes the following.

- A series of operating losses in previous years for the reporting entity.
- A history of the entity's tax losses expiring unused.
- Open transactions, such as lawsuits and regulatory challenges, that might reduce the business's future profits.

The current version of IFRS does not allow for a valuation allowance. Under IAS 12, a deferred tax asset is recorded only when it is "probable" (a higher standard than GAAP's "more likely than not") that the deferred tax amount will be realized, and then only to the extent of that probable amount. Thus, no offsetting valuation allowance is needed.

The sale of food and beverages prepared by a taxpayer at a retail establishment and the transmission or distribution of electricity, natural gas, or potable water are specifically excluded from the definition of DPGR.

ELIGIBLE TAXPAYERS

The deduction is available to a variety of taxpayers including individuals, partnerships, S corporations, C corporations, cooperatives, estates, and trusts. For a pass-through entity (e.g., partnerships, S corporations), the deduction flows through to the individual owners. In the case of a sole proprietor, a deduction *for* AGI results and is claimed on Form 1040, line 35 on page 1. A Form 8903 must be attached to support the deduction.

For additional information on the DPAD, see Chapters 17, 21, and 22.

7.6 Net Operating Losses

LO.7

Understand the tax impact of a net operating loss and recognize the effect of the carryback and carryover provisions.

The requirement that every taxpayer file an annual income tax return (whether on a calendar year or a fiscal year) may result in certain inequities for taxpayers who experience cyclical patterns of income or expense. Inequities result from the application of a progressive rate structure to taxable income determined on an annual basis. A **net operating loss (NOL)** in a particular tax year would produce no tax benefit if the Code did not provide for the carryback and carryforward of such losses to profitable years.

TAX *in* the NEWS

NOL Carryback Benefits Homebuilders

The Worker, Homeownership, and Business Assistance Act of 2009 changed the rules for net operating losses to allow companies to carry back 2008 or 2009 NOLs for five years. As a result, public company homebuilders have claimed millions of dollars in tax refunds. Pulte Homes, the housing industry's largest builder, reported that the change in the tax law resulted in an $800 million tax refund.

Source: Adapted from John Caulfield, "Builders Cash in on Tax Refunds," *Builder Magazine*, February 9, 2010.

EXAMPLE 27

Juanita has a business and realizes the following taxable income or loss over a five-year period: Year 1, $50,000; Year 2, ($30,000); Year 3, $100,000; Year 4, ($200,000); and Year 5, $380,000. She is married and files a joint return. Hubert also has a business and has a taxable income pattern of $60,000 every year. He, too, is married and files a joint return. Note that both Juanita and Hubert have total taxable income of $300,000 over the five-year period. Assume there is no provision for carryback or carryover of NOLs. Juanita and Hubert would have the following five-year tax bills:

Year	Juanita's Tax	Hubert's Tax
1	$ 6,650	$ 8,150
2	–0–	8,150
3	17,250	8,150
4	–0–	8,150
5	102,872	8,150
	$126,772	$40,750

The computation of tax is made without regard to any NOL benefit.
Rates applicable to 2011 are used to compute the tax.

Even though Juanita and Hubert realized the same total taxable income ($300,000) over the five-year period, Juanita had to pay taxes of $126,772, while Hubert paid taxes of only $40,750. ■

To provide partial relief from this inequitable tax treatment, a deduction is allowed for NOLs.[38] This provision permits NOLs for any one year to be offset against taxable income of other years. The NOL provision is intended as a form of relief for business income and losses. Thus, only losses from the operation of a trade or business (or profession), casualty and theft losses, or losses from the confiscation of a business by a foreign government can create an NOL. In other words, a salaried individual with itemized deductions and personal exemptions in excess of gross income is not permitted to deduct the excess amounts as an NOL. On the other hand, a personal casualty loss is treated as a business loss and can therefore create (or increase) an NOL for an individual.

CARRYBACK AND CARRYOVER PERIODS

General Rules

An NOL generally must be applied initially to the two taxable years preceding the year of the loss (unless an election is made not to carry the loss back at

[38] § 172.

all). It is carried first to the second prior year, and then to the immediately preceding tax year (or until used up). If the loss is not fully used in the carryback period, it must be carried forward to the first year after the loss year, and then forward to the second, third, etc., year after the loss year. The carryover period is 20 years. A loss sustained in 2011 is used in this order: 2009, 2010, 2012 through 2031.

A three-year carryback period is available for any portion of an individual's NOL resulting from a casualty or theft loss. The three-year carryback rule also applies to NOLs that are attributable to presidentially declared disasters that are incurred by a small business. A small business is one whose average annual gross receipts for a three-year period are $5 million or less.

A 5-year carryback period and a 20-year carryover period are allowed for a farming loss. A taxpayer may elect to waive the special five-year carryback period. If this election is made, the general two-year carryback period applies. A farming loss is the amount of the NOL for the taxable year if only income and deductions attributable to the farming business are taken into account. However, the amount of the farming loss cannot exceed the amount of the taxpayer's NOL for the taxable year. To determine the amount of the carryback and carryover, a farming loss for any taxable year is treated as a separate NOL for such year and applied after the remaining portion of the NOL for the year is taken into account.

EXAMPLE 28

For the year 2011, the taxpayer and spouse have an NOL of $50,000. The $50,000 NOL includes a $40,000 loss that is attributable to a farming business. Only the $40,000 loss attributable to the farming business can be carried back five years. The loss not attributable to the farming business can be carried back only two years. ■

If the loss is being carried to a preceding year, an amended return is filed on Form 1040X, or a quick refund claim is filed on Form 1045. In either case, a refund of taxes previously paid is requested. Form 1045 is an application for a tentative refund. The IRS normally will process Form 1045 and pay the refund within 90 days of the date it is filed. When the loss is carried forward, the current return shows an NOL deduction for the prior year's loss.

Sequence of Use of NOLs

When the taxpayer has NOLs in two or more years, the rule is always to use the earliest year's loss first until it is completely absorbed. The later years' losses can then be used until they also are absorbed or lost. Thus, one year's return could show NOL carryovers from two or more years. Each loss is computed and applied separately.

Election to Forgo Carryback

A taxpayer can *irrevocably elect* not to carry back an NOL to any of the prior years. In that case, the loss is available as a carryover for 20 years. The election is made if it is to the taxpayer's tax advantage. For example, a taxpayer might be in a low marginal tax bracket in the carryback years but expect to be in a high marginal tax bracket in future years. Therefore, it would be to the taxpayer's advantage to use the NOL to offset income in years when the tax rate is high rather than use it when the tax rate is relatively low.

EXAMPLE 29

For 2011, taxpayer and spouse have an NOL of $10,000. The NOL may be carried back and applied against taxable income first in 2009 and then in 2010. Any remaining NOL is carried forward to years 2012 through 2031. If, however, the taxpayer and spouse elect to forgo the carryback period, the NOL initially is carried to 2012 and then to years 2013 through 2031. ■

ETHICS & Equity **NOL CARRYOVER**

John timely filed his 2007 and 2008 Federal income tax returns, reporting AGI of $90,000 and $100,000, respectively. For the years 2009 and 2010, John had NOLs of $25,000 and $40,000, respectively. Because John had NOLs for 2009 and 2010, he did not file tax returns for those years. In 2011, John has taxable income, so he is considering using his NOLs from 2009 and 2010 to offset his income for 2011. Evaluate John's plan.

TAX PLANNING:

7.7 TAX CONSEQUENCES OF THE *GROETZINGER* CASE

LO.8

Identify tax planning opportunities in deducting certain business expenses, business losses, and personal losses.

In the *Groetzinger* case discussed earlier in the chapter, the court established that the appropriate tests for determining if gambling is a trade or business are whether an individual engages in gambling full-time in good faith, with regularity, and for the production of income as a livelihood, and not as a mere hobby. The court held that Robert Groetzinger satisfied the tests because of his constant and large-scale effort. Skill was required and was applied. He did what he did for a livelihood, though with less than successful results. His gambling was not a hobby, a passing fancy, or an occasional bet for amusement. Therefore, his gambling was a trade or business, and hence, he was able to deduct his gambling losses *for* AGI. If the court had ruled that Groetzinger's gambling was not a trade or business, his gambling losses would have been limited to his gambling winnings and would have been classified as itemized deductions.

7.8 DOCUMENTATION OF RELATED-TAXPAYER LOANS, CASUALTY LOSSES, AND THEFT LOSSES

Since non-bona fide loans between related taxpayers may be treated as gifts, adequate documentation is needed to substantiate a bad debt deduction if the loan subsequently becomes worthless. Documentation should include proper execution of the note (legal form) and the establishment of a bona fide purpose for the loan. In addition, it is desirable to stipulate a reasonable rate of interest and a fixed maturity date.

Since a theft loss is not permitted for misplaced items, a loss should be documented by a police report and evidence of the value of the property (e.g., appraisals, pictures of the property, newspaper clippings). Similar documentation of the value of property should be provided to support a casualty loss deduction because the amount of loss is measured, in part, by the decline in fair market value of the property. Casualty loss deductions must be reported on Form 4684.

7.9 WORTHLESS SECURITIES

To be deductible, a security must be completely worthless. To obtain the deduction, the taxpayer must prove that the security was not worthless in a prior year and that the security was worthless in the year claimed. Because of the subjectivity associated with this burden of proof, the only safe practice is to claim a loss for

TAX *in* the NEWS

When Is a Security Worthless?

Usually, losses that have not been documented by the marketplace cannot be deducted (i.e., unrealized losses). An exception exists for securities that are completely worthless. But proving complete worthlessness can sometimes be difficult. Just because a company declares bankruptcy does not necessarily prove that its stock is completely worthless because in some cases the stock can recover. Determining whether this can happen requires an analysis of the relevant facts and circumstances. Even though a stock may be selling for a fraction of a penny (i.e., it has some value), some tax advisers argue that if the stock's selling price would be less than the broker's commission for selling the stock, a deduction can be taken at that time.

the earliest year when it may possibly be allowed and to renew the claim in subsequent years if there is any reasonable chance that it will be applicable to the income for those years.[39] Fortunately, the statute of limitations for worthless securities is seven years.[40]

7.10 Small Business Stock

Because § 1244 limits the amount of loss classified as ordinary loss on a yearly basis, a taxpayer might maximize the benefits of § 1244 by selling the stock in more than one taxable year. The result could be that the losses in any one taxable year would not exceed the § 1244 limits on ordinary loss.

EXAMPLE 30

Mitch, a single individual, purchased small business stock in 2009 for $150,000 (150 shares at $1,000 per share). On December 20, 2011, the stock is worth $60,000 (150 shares at $400 per share). Mitch wants to sell the stock at this time. Mitch earns a salary of $80,000 a year, has no other capital transactions, and does not expect any in the future. If Mitch sells all of the small business stock in 2011, his recognized loss will be $90,000 ($60,000 − $150,000). The loss will be characterized as a $50,000 ordinary loss and a $40,000 long-term capital loss. In computing taxable income for 2011, Mitch could deduct the $50,000 ordinary loss but could deduct only $3,000 of the capital loss. The remainder of the capital loss could be carried over and used in future years subject to the $3,000 limitation if Mitch has no capital gains. If Mitch sells 82 shares in 2011, he will recognize an ordinary loss of $49,200 [82 × ($1,000 − $400)]. If Mitch then sells the remainder of the shares in 2012, he will recognize an ordinary loss of $40,800 [68 × ($1,000 − $400)]. Mitch could deduct the $49,200 ordinary loss in computing 2011 taxable income and the $40,800 ordinary loss in computing 2012 taxable income. ■

7.11 Casualty Losses

A special election is available for taxpayers who sustain casualty losses in an area designated by the President as a disaster area. This election affects only the timing, not the calculation, of the deduction. The deduction can be taken in the year before the year in which the loss occurred. Thus, for a loss occurring between January 1 and December 31, 2011, an individual can take the deduction on the 2010 return. The benefit, of course, is a faster refund (or reduction in tax). It will also be advantageous to carry the loss back if the taxpayer's tax rate in the carryback year is higher than the tax rate in the year of the loss.

[39] *Young v. Comm.*, 41–2 USTC ¶9744, 28 AFTR 365, 123 F.2d 597 (CA–2, 1941).

[40] § 6511(d)(1).

FINANCIAL DISCLOSURE *Insights*

VALUATION ALLOWANCES FOR NOLs

Financial analysts use the valuation allowance system to help them determine the entity's expected future cash flows. Some critics of the GAAP rules for valuation allowances maintain that they enable management to manipulate profits and earnings per share in an arbitrary fashion.

Only a few of the largest business entities, supported by going-concern assumptions and access to worldwide debt and equity capital, need to record sizable valuation allowances. But smaller entities and those in volatile industries are more likely to present questions as to their future profitability, so valuation allowances may be found in those financial reports somewhat more often.

In a recent reporting year, for instance, the following telecommunications businesses reported valuation allowances related to expectations that their NOLs (for Federal and/or state taxing jurisdictions) would expire unused.

	Deferred Tax Assets ($000)	Valuation Allowance ($000)
Verizon	$10,750	$2,700
Bell South	2,100	1,100
AT&T	11,400	1,050
SBC Communications	3,900	150

Establishing a valuation allowance does not affect the entity's internal cash balances, but it might have an effect on the stock price. Valuation allowances can be "released" by management when evidence develops that the carryforwards are likely to be used in the future, for example, if profitability has improved and appears to be sustainable. For instance, the homebuilder Toll Brothers created a large valuation allowance when the real estate market collapsed, but it will release the allowance when housing prices stabilize and increase. Several corporations estimated that the health care reform legislation would force them to create sizable valuation allowances because the mandated expenditures would reduce their future profitability.

	Estimated Reduction in Deferred Tax Assets Due to Health Care Reform ($ million)
AT&T	$1,000
John Deere	150
Caterpillar	100
3M	90
Norfolk Southern	27

To find out if an event qualifies as a disaster area loss, one can look in any of the major tax services, the Weekly Compilation of Presidential Documents, or the *Internal Revenue Bulletin.*

7.12 NET OPERATING LOSSES

In certain instances, it may be advisable for a taxpayer to elect not to carry back an NOL. For an individual, the benefits from the loss carryback could be scaled down or lost due to the economic adjustments that must be made to taxable income for the year to which the loss is carried. For example, a taxpayer should attempt to minimize the number of taxable years to which an NOL is carried. The more years to which the NOL is applied, the more benefits are lost from adjustments for items such as personal and dependency exemptions.

The election not to carry back the loss might also be advantageous if there is a disparity in marginal tax rates applicable to different tax years.

EXAMPLE 31

Abby sustained an NOL of $10,000 in Year 3. Her marginal tax bracket in Year 1 was 15%. In Year 4, however, she expects her bracket to be 35% due to a large profit she will make on a business deal. If Abby carries her loss back, her refund will be $1,500 (15% × $10,000). If she elects not to carry it back to Year 1 but chooses, instead, to carry it forward, her savings will be $3,500 (35% × $10,000). Even considering the time value of an immediate tax refund, Abby appears to be better off using the carryover approach. ■

REFOCUS ON THE BIG PICTURE

LOSSES

Martha can receive tax benefits associated with her unfortunate occurrences during the current tax year. Some of the losses, however, will provide a greater tax benefit than others as a result of different tax provisions governing the amount and the classification of the losses.

Bad Debt

Based on the facts provided, it appears that Martha's loan to her friend was a bona fide debt. Otherwise, nothing would be deductible. The amount of the deduction is the unpaid principal balance of $19,000 ($25,000 – $6,000). Unfortunately, since the bad debt is a nonbusiness bad debt, it is classified as a short-term capital loss (see Example 4).

Loss from Investment

The $50,000 loss is deductible. However, it appears that the loss should be classified as a long-term capital loss rather than as a short-term capital loss. Although the actual holding period was not greater than one year (October through May), the disposal date for the stock (qualifies as a worthless security) is deemed to be the last day of the tax year (October of last year through end of December of the current year). The loss does not appear to qualify for ordinary loss treatment under § 1244 (see Example 7).

Loss from Bookstore

The $180,000 loss from the bookstore is reported on Schedule C of Form 1040. It is an ordinary loss, and it qualifies for NOL treatment. Therefore, Martha can carry the $180,000 net loss back and offset it against the net income of the bookstore for the past two years. Any amount not offset (probably about $30,000) can be carried forward for the next 20 years. The carryback will produce a claim for a tax refund.

Casualty Loss

The loss on the damage to Martha's personal residence is classified as a personal casualty loss. Using the cost of repairs method, the amount of the casualty loss is $7,000 ($32,000 – $25,000). However, this amount must be reduced by the statutory materiality amounts of $100 and 10 percent of AGI.

If the President classified the area in which Martha's house is located as a disaster area, Martha has the option of deducting the casualty loss on the prior year's tax return (see Example 13).

KEY TERMS

Bad debt, 7–3
Business bad debt, 7–5
Casualty loss, 7–8
Disaster area losses, 7–10
Domestic production activities deduction (DPAD), 7–18
Domestic production gross receipts (DPGR), 7–19
Modified adjusted gross income, 7–18
Net operating loss (NOL), 7–20
Nonbusiness bad debt, 7–5
Personal casualty gain, 7–14
Personal casualty loss, 7–14
Qualified production activities income (QPAI), 7–19
Research and experimental expenditures, 7–16
Reserve method, 7–4
Small business stock (§ 1244 stock), 7–6
Specific charge-off method, 7–4
Theft losses, 7–9
W–2 wages, 7–18
Worthless securities, 7–6

DISCUSSION QUESTIONS

1. **LO.1** Explain how a purchased debt instrument can give rise to a bad debt deduction.
2. **LO.1** Ron sells his business accounts receivable of $100,000 to Mike for $70,000 (70% of the actual accounts receivable). Mike later determines that he will be able to collect only $6,000 of a $10,000 receivable. Discuss the amount and classification of Mike's bad debt deduction.
3. **LO.1** Discuss when a bad debt deduction can be taken for a nonbusiness debt.
4. **LO.1** During the past tax year, Jane identified $50,000 as a nonbusiness bad debt. In that tax year, Jane had $100,000 of taxable income, of which $5,000 consisted of short-term capital gains. During the current tax year, Jane collected $10,000 of the amount she had previously identified as a bad debt. Discuss Jane's tax treatment of the $10,000 received in the current tax year.
5. **LO.1** Bob owns a collection agency. He purchases uncollected accounts receivable from other businesses at 60% of their face value and then attempts to collect these accounts. Discuss the treatment of any account Bob is unable to collect.
6. **LO.1** Discuss the treatment of a business bad debt when the business also has long-term capital gains.
7. **LO.1** Many years ago, Jack purchased 400 shares of Canary stock. During the current year, the stock became worthless. It was determined that the company "went under" because several corporate officers embezzled a large amount of company funds. Identify the relevant tax issues for Jack. **ISSUE ID**
8. **LO.2** Sean is in the business of buying and selling stocks and bonds. He has a bond of Green Corporation for which he paid $200,000. The bond is currently worth only $50,000. Discuss whether Sean can take a $150,000 loss for a business bad debt or for a worthless security.
9. **LO.2** Discuss the tax treatment of the sale of § 1244 stock at a loss.
10. **LO.3, 4** Jim discovers that one of his business warehouses has extensive termite damage. Discuss whether he may take a deduction for the damage to the building.
11. **LO.3, 4** The value of Mary's personal residence has declined significantly because of a recent forest fire in the area where she lives. Mary's house suffered no actual damage during the fire, but because much of the surrounding area was destroyed, the value of all of the homes in the area declined substantially. Discuss whether Mary can take a casualty loss for the decline in value of her residence caused by the fire.
12. **LO.4** Discuss at what point in time a casualty loss generally is recognized.
13. **LO.4** Mary's diamond ring was stolen in 2010. She originally paid $8,000 for the ring, but it was worth considerably more at the time of the theft. Mary filed an insurance claim for the stolen ring, but the claim was denied. Because the insurance claim was denied, Mary took a casualty loss for the stolen ring on her 2010 tax return. In 2010, Mary had AGI of $40,000. In 2011, the insurance company had a "change of heart" and sent Mary a check for $5,000 for the stolen ring. Discuss the proper tax treatment of the $5,000 Mary received from the insurance company in 2011.
14. **LO.4** Discuss the measurement rule for partial or complete destruction of personal use property.
15. **LO.4** Discuss the tax consequences of not making an insurance claim when insured personal use property is subject to a loss.
16. **LO.4** Discuss the circumstances under which the cost of repairs to the damaged property can be used to measure the amount of a casualty loss.
17. **LO.4** Discuss the treatment of a loss on rental property under the following facts:

Basis	$700,000
FMV before the loss	900,000
FMV after the loss	–0–

18. **LO.4** Hazel sustained a loss on the theft of a painting. She had paid $50,000 for the painting, but it was worth $40,000 at the time of the theft. Evaluate the tax consequences of treating the painting as investment property or as personal use property.

19. **LO.4** When casualty losses exceed casualty gains, only the amount of the casualty loss in excess of casualty gains is subject to the 10%-of-AGI floor. Discuss the significance of netting losses against gains in this manner rather than having the entire casualty loss be subject to the 10%-of-AGI floor.

ISSUE ID

20. **LO.4** Kelly decided to invest in Lime, Inc. common stock after reviewing Lime's public disclosures, including recent financial statements and a number of press releases issued by Lime. On August 7, 2009, Kelly purchased 60,000 shares of Lime for $210,000. In May 2010, Lime entered into a joint venture with Cherry, Inc. In November 2010, the joint venture failed, and Lime's stock began to decline in value. In December 2010, Cherry filed a lawsuit against Lime for theft of corporate opportunity and breach of fiduciary responsibility. In February 2011, Lime filed a countersuit against Cherry for fraud and misappropriation of funds. At the end of December 2011, Kelly's stock in Lime was worth $15,000. Identify the relevant tax issues for Kelly.

ISSUE ID

21. **LO.3, 4** In 2008, John opened an investment account with Randy Hansen who held himself out to the public as an investment adviser and securities broker. John contributed $200,000 to the account in 2008. John provided Randy with a power of attorney to use the $200,000 to purchase and sell securities on John's behalf. John instructed Randy to reinvest any gains and income earned. In the years 2008, 2009, and 2010, John received statements of the amount of income earned by his account and included these amounts in his gross income for these years. In 2011, it was discovered that Randy's purported investment advisory and brokerage activity was in fact a fraudulent investment arrangement known as a "Ponzi" scheme. In reality, John's account balance was zero, the money having been used by Randy in his scheme. Identify the relevant tax issues for John.

22. **LO.5** Green Corporation made extensive modifications to a portion of a building so that it could be used to conduct product research. Discuss whether the modification costs would qualify as research and experimental expenditures.

23. **LO.5** Discuss under what circumstances a company would elect to amortize research and experimental expenditures rather than use the expense method.

ISSUE ID

24. **LO.6** Amos began a business, Silver, Inc., on July 1, 2008. The business extracts and processes silver ore. During 2011, Amos becomes aware of the domestic production activities deduction (DPAD) and would like to take advantage of this deduction. Identify the relevant tax issues for Silver, Inc.

25. **LO.6** The DPAD is unlike other deductions and is designed to provide a tax benefit in a somewhat unique manner. Explain this statement.

26. **LO.6** Discuss the impact of an NOL on the DPAD.

27. **LO.7** Discuss how the carryback period for a loss attributable to a farming business differs from the carryback period for a regular NOL.

PROBLEMS

COMMUNICATIONS

28. **LO.1** Several years ago John Johnson, who is not in the lending business, loaned Sara $30,000 to purchase an automobile to be used for personal purposes. In August of the current year, Sara filed for bankruptcy, and John was notified that he could not expect to receive more than $4,000. As of the end of the current year, John has received $1,000. John has contacted you about the possibility of taking a bad debt deduction for the current year.

    Write a letter to John that contains your advice as to whether he can claim a bad debt deduction for the current year. Also, prepare a memo for the tax files. John's address is 100 Tyler Lane, Erie, PA 16563.

29. **LO.1** Monty loaned his friend Ned $20,000 three years ago. Ned signed a note and made payments on the loan. Last year, when the remaining balance was $11,000, Ned filed for

bankruptcy and notified Monty that he would be unable to pay the balance on the loan. Monty treated the $11,000 as a nonbusiness bad debt. Last year Monty had no capital gains and taxable income of $12,000. During the current year, Ned paid Monty $5,000 in satisfaction of the debt. Determine Monty's tax treatment for the $5,000 received in the current year.

30. **LO.1** Sally is in the business of purchasing accounts receivable. Last year, Sally purchased an account receivable with a face value of $80,000 for $60,000. During the current year, Sally settled the account, receiving $55,000. Determine the maximum amount of the bad debt deduction for Sally for the current year.

31. **LO.1, 2** Mable and Jack file a joint return. For the current year, they had the following items:

Salaries	$ 90,000
Loss on sale of § 1244 stock acquired two years ago	105,000
Gain on sale of § 1244 stock acquired six months ago	20,000
Nonbusiness bad debt	19,000

Determine their AGI for the current year.

DECISION MAKING

32. **LO.2, 8** Mary, a single taxpayer, purchased 10,000 shares of § 1244 stock several years ago at a cost of $20 per share. In November of the current year, Mary received an offer to sell the stock for $12 per share. She has the option of either selling all of the stock now or selling half of the stock now and half of the stock in January of next year. Mary will receive a salary of $80,000 for the current year and $90,000 next year. Mary will have long-term capital gains of $8,000 for the current year and $10,000 next year. If Mary's goal is to minimize her AGI for the two years, determine whether she should sell all of her stock this year or half of her stock this year and half next year.

33. **LO.4** During 2011, someone broke into Jacob's personal residence and took the following items:

Asset	Adjusted Basis	FMV before	FMV after	Insurance Recovery
Business computer	$12,000	$10,000	$-0-	$7,000
Bearer bonds	30,000	32,000	-0-	-0-
Silverware	7,000	10,000	-0-	2,000
Cash	8,000	8,000	-0-	-0-

Jacob is an employee and used the computer 100% of the time in his employment. Although his homeowner's insurance policy paid Jacob $7,000 for the stolen computer, Jacob's employer did not reimburse Jacob for any of the remainder of his loss. Jacob's AGI for the year, before considering any of the above items, is $50,000. Determine the total deduction for the stolen items on Jacob's 2011 tax return.

DECISION MAKING

34. **LO.3, 4, 8** Olaf owns a 500-acre farm in Minnesota. A tornado hit the area and destroyed a farm building and some farm equipment and damaged a barn. Fortunately for Olaf, the tornado occurred after he had harvested his corn crop. Applicable information is as follows:

Item	Adjusted Basis	FMV before	FMV after	Insurance Proceeds
Building	$90,000	$ 70,000	$ -0-	$70,000
Equipment	40,000	50,000	-0-	25,000
Barn	90,000	120,000	70,000	25,000

Because of the extensive damage caused by the tornado, the President designated the area as a disaster area.

Olaf, who files a joint return with his wife, Anna, had $174,000 of taxable income last year. Their taxable income for the current year, excluding the loss from the tornado, is $250,000.

Determine the amount of Olaf and Anna's loss and the year in which they should take the loss.

35. **LO.3, 4** Heather owns a two-story building. The building is used 60% for business use and 40% for personal use. During 2011, a fire caused major damage to the building and its contents. Heather purchased the building for $800,000 and has taken depreciation of $150,000 on the business portion. At the time of the fire, the building had a fair market value of $900,000. Immediately after the fire, the fair market value was $200,000. The insurance recovery on the building was $600,000. The contents of the building were insured for any loss at fair market value. The business assets had an adjusted basis of $220,000 and a fair market value of $175,000. These assets were totally destroyed. The personal use assets had an adjusted basis of $50,000 and a fair market value of $65,000. These assets were also totally destroyed. If Heather's AGI is $100,000 before considering the effects of the fire, determine her itemized deduction as a result of the fire. Also determine Heather's AGI.

DECISION MAKING

COMMUNICATIONS

36. **LO.3, 4** On July 24 of the current year, Sam Smith was involved in an accident with his business use automobile. Sam had purchased the car for $30,000. The automobile had a fair market value of $20,000 before the accident and $8,000 immediately after the accident. Sam has taken $20,000 of depreciation on the car. The car is insured for the fair market value of any loss. Because of Sam's history, he is afraid that if he submits a claim, his policy will be canceled. Therefore, he is considering not filing a claim. Sam believes that the tax loss deduction will help mitigate the loss of the insurance reimbursement. Sam's current marginal tax rate is 35%.

Write a letter to Sam that contains your advice with respect to the tax and cash-flow consequences of filing versus not filing a claim for the insurance reimbursement for the damage to his car. Also, prepare a memo for the tax files. Sam's address is 450 Colonel's Way, Warrensburg, MO 64093.

37. **LO.5** Blue Corporation, a manufacturing company, decided to develop a new line of merchandise. The project began in 2011. Blue had the following expenses in connection with the project:

	2011	2012
Salaries	$500,000	$600,000
Materials	90,000	70,000
Insurance	8,000	11,000
Utilities	6,000	8,000
Cost of inspection of materials for quality control	7,000	6,000
Promotion expenses	11,000	18,000
Advertising	-0-	20,000
Equipment depreciation	15,000	14,000
Cost of market survey	8,000	-0-

The new product will be introduced for sale beginning in July 2013. Determine the amount of the deduction for research and experimental expenditures for 2011, 2012, and 2013 if:

a. Blue Corporation elects to expense the research and experimental expenditures.
b. Blue Corporation elects to amortize the research and experimental expenditures over 60 months.

38. **LO.6** Sarah Ham, operating as a sole proprietor, manufactures printers in the United States. For 2011, the proprietorship has QPAI of $300,000. Sarah's modified AGI was $350,000. The W–2 wages paid by the proprietorship to employees engaged in the qualified domestic production activity were $90,000. Calculate Sarah's DPAD for 2011.

39. **LO.6** Barbara, a calendar year taxpayer, owns and operates a company that manufactures toys. For 2011, she has modified AGI of $600,000 and QPAI of $550,000. Ignoring the W–2 wage limitation, calculate Barbara's DPAD.

40. **LO.6** Red Corporation manufactures hand tools in the United States. For the current year, the QPAI derived from the manufacture of hand tools was $1 million. Red's taxable income for the current year was $1.5 million. Last year, Red had an NOL of $800,000, which Red elected to carry forward. Calculate Red's DPAD for the current year.

41. **LO.6** Green Corporation manufactures skirts and blouses in the United States. The DPGR derived from the manufacture of one skirt is $12, and the DPGR from one blouse is $10. The cost of goods sold is $5 for one skirt and $6 for one blouse. Other allocated costs are $1 for one skirt and $5 for one blouse. What amount of QPAI is available to Green for calculating the DPAD?

42. **LO.6** In 2011, Rose, Inc., has QPAI of $4 million and taxable income of $3 million. Rose pays independent contractors $500,000. Rose's W–2 wages are $600,000, but only $400,000 of the wages are paid to employees engaged in qualified domestic production activities. **DECISION MAKING**
    a. Calculate the DPAD for Rose, Inc., for 2011.
    b. What suggestions could you make to enable Rose to increase its DPAD?

43. **LO.1, 3** Nell, single and age 38, had the following income and expense items in 2011:

Nonbusiness bad debt	$ 6,000
Business bad debt	2,000
Nonbusiness long-term capital gain	4,000
Nonbusiness short-term capital loss	3,000
Salary	50,000
Interest income	3,000

Determine Nell's AGI for 2011.

44. **LO.1, 4** Assume that in addition to the information in Problem 43, Nell had the following items in 2011:

Personal casualty gain on an asset held for four months	$10,000
Personal casualty loss on an asset held for two years	1,000

Determine Nell's AGI for 2011.

CUMULATIVE PROBLEMS

TAX RETURN PROBLEM

DECISION MAKING

COMMUNICATIONS

H&R BLOCK At Home

45. Jane Smith, age 40, is single and has no dependents. She is employed as a legal secretary by Legal Services, Inc. She owns and operates Typing Services located near the campus of Florida Atlantic University at 1986 Campus Drive. Jane is a material participant in the business. She is a cash basis taxpayer. Jane lives at 2020 Oakcrest Road, Boca Raton, FL 33431. Jane's Social Security number is 123–45–6789. Jane indicates that she wishes to designate $3 to the Presidential Election Campaign Fund. During 2010, Jane had the following income and expense items:
    a. $100,000 salary from Legal Services, Inc.
    b. $20,000 gross receipts from her typing services business.
    c. $700 interest income from Acme National Bank.
    d. $1,000 Christmas bonus from Legal Services, Inc.
    e. $60,000 life insurance proceeds on the death of her sister.
    f. $5,000 check given to her by her wealthy aunt.
    g. $100 won in a bingo game.
    h. Expenses connected with the typing service:

Office rent	$7,000
Supplies	4,400
Utilities and telephone	4,680
Wages to part-time typists	5,000
Payroll taxes	500
Equipment rentals	3,000

    i. $9,500 interest expense on a home mortgage (paid to San Jose Savings and Loan).
    j. $15,000 fair market value of silverware stolen from her home by a burglar on October 12, 2010. Jane had paid $14,000 for the silverware on July 1, 2001. She was reimbursed $1,500 by her insurance company.

k. Jane had loaned $2,100 to a friend, Joan Jensen, on June 3, 2007. Joan declared bankruptcy on August 14, 2010, and was unable to repay the loan. Assume the loan is a bona fide debt.

l. Legal Services, Inc., withheld Federal income tax of $18,000 and FICA tax of $7,376 {Social Security tax of $5,978 [($101,000 – $4,580) × 6.2%] + Medicare tax of $1,398 [($101,000 – $4,580) × 1.45%]}.

m. Alimony of $10,000 received from her former husband, Ted Smith.

n. Interest income of $800 on City of Boca Raton bonds.

o. Jane made estimated Federal tax payments of $1,000.

p. Sales taxes from the sales tax table of $964.

q. Charitable contributions of $2,500.

Part 1—Tax Computation

Compute Jane Smith's 2010 Federal income tax payable (or refund due). If you use tax forms for your computations, you will need Forms 1040 and 4684 and Schedules A, C, and D. Suggested software: H&R BLOCK At Home.

Part 2—Tax Planning

In 2011, Jane plans to continue her job with Legal Services, Inc. Therefore, items a, d, and l will recur in 2011. Jane plans to continue her typing services business (refer to item b) and expects gross receipts of $26,000. She projects that all business expenses (refer to item h) will increase by 10%, except for office rent, which, under the terms of her lease, will remain the same as in 2010. Items e, f, g, j, and k will not recur in 2011. Items c, i, m, n, p, and q will be approximately the same as in 2010.

Jane would like you to compute the minimum amount of estimated tax she will have to pay for 2011 so that she will not have to pay any additional tax upon filing her 2011 Federal income tax return. Write a letter to Jane that contains your advice and prepare a memo for the tax files.

TAX COMPUTATION PROBLEM

46. Alan Rice, age 45, and his wife, Ruth, live at 230 Wood Lane, Salt Lake City, UT 84201. Alan's Social Security number is 111–11–1111. Ruth's Social Security number is 123–45–6789. Alan and Ruth are cash basis taxpayers and had the following items for the year 2011:

- Salary of $95,000.
- Business bad debt of $28,000 from uncollected rent.
- Sale of § 1244 stock resulting in a loss of $25,000. The stock was acquired nine months earlier.
- Rental income of $52,000.
- Rental expenses of $28,000.
- Casualty loss on rental property of $12,000.
- Personal casualty loss (from one event) of $25,000.
- Other itemized deductions of $17,000.
- NOL carryover from 2010 of $18,000.
- Federal income tax withheld of $6,000.

Compute Alan and Ruth's 2011 Federal income tax payable (or refund due).

RESEARCH PROBLEMS

THOMSON REUTERS
Checkpoint® Student Edition

Note: Solutions to Research Problems can be prepared by using the **Checkpoint® Student Edition** online research product, which is available to accompany this text. It is also possible to prepare solutions to the Research Problems by using tax research materials found in a standard tax library.

Research Problem 1. During 2011, John was the chief executive officer and a shareholder of Maze, Inc. He owned 60% of the outstanding stock of Maze. In 2008, John and Maze, as co-borrowers, obtained a $100,000 loan from United National Bank. This loan was secured by John's personal residence. Though Maze was listed as a co-borrower, John repaid the loan in full in 2011. On Maze's Form 1120 tax returns, no loans from shareholders were reported. Discuss whether John is entitled to a bad debt deduction for the amount of the payment on the loan.

Partial list of research aids:
U.S. v. Generes, 405 U.S. 93 (1972).
Dale H. Sundby, T.C.Memo. 2003–204.
James M. Arrigoni, 73 T.C. 792 (1980).
Estate of Herbert M. Rapoport, T.C.Memo. 1982–584.
Clifford L. Brody and Barbara J. DeClerk, T.C. Summary Opinion, 2004–149.

Research Problem 2. In June of the current year, Bob attended a party at a friend's house. Because of the amount of alcohol Bob consumed at the party, he asked a friend to drive him home. Several hours after arriving home, Bob decided to drive to his parents' home. On the way there, he failed to negotiate a turn, and his car slid off the road and rolled. The car was extensively damaged from the rollover, but Bob was not severely injured. At the time of the accident, Bob's blood-alcohol level was slightly over the state legal limit. Hence, he was cited and arrested for driving under the influence of alcohol (DUI). Bob's automobile insurance carrier denied his loss claim in accordance with the terms of his policy because of his DUI citation and arrest. As a result of the accident, Bob's car suffered $35,000 of damages. Discuss whether Bob is entitled to a casualty loss deduction on his current year's tax return.

INTERNET *activity*

Use the tax resources of the Internet to address the following question. Do not restrict your search to the Web, but include a review of newsgroups and general reference materials, practitioner sites and resources, primary sources of the tax law, chat rooms and discussion groups, and other opportunities.

COMMUNICATIONS

Research Problem 3. Scan several publications that are read by owners of small businesses. Some of the articles in these publications address tax-related issues such as how to structure a new business. Do these articles do an adequate job of conveying the benefits of issuing § 1244 small business stock? Prepare a short memo explaining the use of § 1244 stock and post it to a newsgroup that is frequented by inventors, engineers, and others involved in startup corporations.

CHAPTER 8

Depreciation, Cost Recovery, Amortization, and Depletion

LEARNING OBJECTIVES

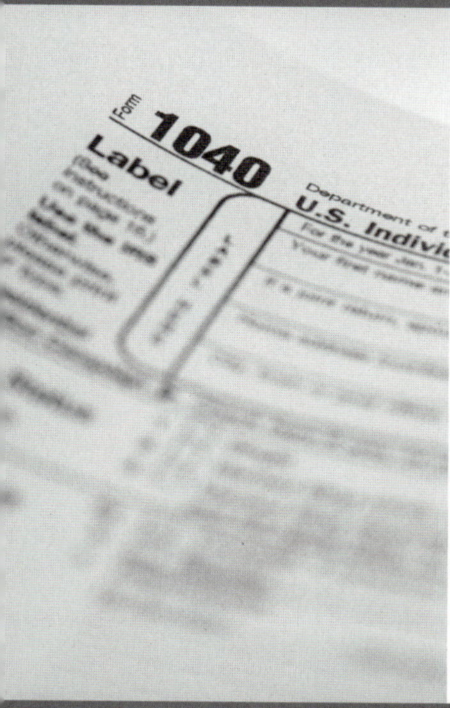

After completing Chapter 8, you should be able to:

LO.1

Understand the rationale for the cost consumption concept and identify the relevant time periods for depreciation, ACRS, and MACRS.

LO.2

Determine the amount of cost recovery under MACRS.

LO.3

Recognize when and how to make the § 179 expensing election, calculate the amount of the deduction, and apply the effect of the election in making the MACRS calculation.

LO.4

Identify listed property and apply the deduction limitations on listed property and on luxury automobiles.

LO.5

Determine when and how to use the alternative depreciation system (ADS).

LO.6

Be aware of the major characteristics of ACRS.

LO.7

Identify intangible assets that are eligible for amortization and calculate the amount of the deduction.

LO.8

Determine the amount of depletion expense including being able to apply the alternative tax treatments for intangible drilling and development costs.

LO.9

Identify tax planning opportunities for cost recovery, amortization, and depletion.

OUTLINE

For the latest in changes to tax legislation, visit **www.cengage.com/taxation/swft.**

FRAMEWORK 1040: Tax Formula for Individuals

This chapter covers the boldfaced portions of the Tax Formula for Individuals that was introduced in Figure 3.1 on p. 3-3. Below those portions are the sections of Form 1040 where the results are reported.

Income (broadly conceived)	$xx,xxx
Less: Exclusions	(x,xxx)
Gross income	$xx,xxx
Less: Deductions for adjusted gross income	**(x,xxx)**

FORM 1040 (P.1)

12	Business income or (loss). Attach Schedule C or C-EZ

Adjusted gross income	$xx,xxx
Less: The greater of total itemized deductions *or* the standard deduction	(x,xxx)
Personal and dependency exemptions	(x,xxx)
Taxable income	$xx,xxx
Tax on taxable income (see Tax Tables or Tax Rate Schedules)	$ x,xxx
Less: Tax credits (including income taxes withheld and prepaid)	(xxx)
Tax due (or refund)	$ xxx

THE BIG PICTURE Tax Solutions for the Real World

CALCULATION OF DEPRECIATION EXPENSE AND TAX PLANNING

Dr. Cliff Payne purchases and places in service in his dental practice the following fixed assets during the current year:

Office furniture and fixtures	$ 70,000
Computers and peripheral equipment	67,085
Dental equipment	475,000

Using his financial reporting system, he concludes that the depreciation expense on Schedule C of Form 1040 is $91,298.

Office furniture and fixtures ($70,000 × 14.29%)	$10,003
Computers and peripheral equipment ($67,085 × 20%)	13,417
Dental equipment ($475,000 × 14.29%)	67,878
	$91,298

In addition, during the current year, Dr. Payne purchased another personal residence for $300,000 and converted his original residence to rental property. He also purchased a condo for $170,000 near his office that he is going to rent.

Has Dr. Payne correctly calculated the depreciation expense for his dental practice? Will he be able to deduct any depreciation expense for his rental properties? **Read the chapter and formulate your response.**

8.1 Overview

GENERAL

LO.1

Understand the rationale for the cost consumption concept and identify the relevant time periods for depreciation, ACRS, and MACRS.

The Internal Revenue Code provides for a deduction for the consumption of the cost of an asset through depreciation, cost recovery, amortization, or depletion. These deductions are applications of the recovery of capital doctrine (discussed in Chapter 4). The concept of depreciation is based on the premise that the asset acquired (or improvement made) benefits more than one accounting period. Otherwise, the expenditure is deducted in the year incurred—see Chapter 6 and the discussion of capitalization versus expense.

Congress completely overhauled the **depreciation** rules in 1981 tax legislation by creating the accelerated **cost recovery** system (ACRS). Substantial modifications were made to ACRS in 1986 tax legislation (MACRS). These changes to the depreciation rules and the time frames involved are noted in Concept Summary 8.1. A knowledge of all of the depreciation and cost recovery rules may be needed as Example 1 illustrates for cost recovery.

EXAMPLE 1

The Brown Company owns a building purchased in 1986 that has a 19-year cost recovery life. In 2011, the business purchased a computer. To compute the cost recovery for 2011, Brown used the ACRS rules for the building and the MACRS rules for the computer. For 2011, there would be no additional cost recovery for the building because the basis of the building at the beginning of 2011 would be $0. ■

The statutory changes that have taken place since 1980 have widened the gap that exists between the accounting and tax versions of depreciation. The tax rules that existed prior to 1981 were much more compatible with generally accepted accounting principles.

This chapter initially focuses on the MACRS rules.[1] Because they cover more recent property acquisitions (i.e., after 1986), their use is more widespread. The ACRS rules, however, are reviewed in Concept Summary 8.5 and briefly discussed on p. 8–22. The chapter concludes with a discussion of the amortization of intangible property and startup expenditures and the depletion of natural resources.

Taxpayers may write off the cost of certain assets that are used in a trade or business or held for the production of income. A write-off may take the form of depreciation (or cost recovery), depletion, or amortization. Tangible assets, other than natural resources, are *depreciated.* Natural resources, such as oil, gas, coal, and timber, are *depleted.* Intangible assets, such as copyrights and patents, are *amortized.* Generally, no write-off is allowed for an asset that does not have a determinable useful life.

CONCEPTS RELATING TO DEPRECIATION

Nature of Property

Property includes both realty (real property) and personalty (personal property). Realty generally includes land and buildings permanently affixed to the land. Personalty is defined as any asset that is not realty.[2] Personalty includes furniture, machinery, equipment, and many other types of assets. Do not confuse personalty (or personal property) with *personal use* property. Personal use property is any property (realty or personalty) that is held for personal use rather than for use in a trade or business or an income-producing activity. Write-offs are not allowed for personal use assets.

In summary, both realty and personalty can be either business use/income-producing property or personal use property. Examples include a residence (realty that is personal use), an office building (realty that is business use), a dump truck

[1] § 168. The terms "depreciation" and "cost recovery" are used interchangeably in the text and in § 168.

[2] Refer to Chapter 1 for a further discussion.

CONCEPT SUMMARY 8.1

Depreciation and Cost Recovery: Relevant Time Periods

System	Date Property Is Placed in Service
Pre-1981 depreciation	Before January 1, 1981, and *certain* property placed in service after December 31, 1980.
Original accelerated cost recovery system (ACRS)	After December 31, 1980, and before January 1, 1987.
Modified accelerated cost recovery system (MACRS)	After December 31, 1986.

(personalty that is business use), and regular wearing apparel (personalty that is personal use). It is imperative that this distinction between the *classification* of an asset (realty or personalty) and the *use* to which the asset is put (business or personal) be understood.

Assets used in a trade or business or for the production of income are eligible for cost recovery if they are subject to wear and tear, decay or decline from natural causes, or obsolescence. Assets that do not decline in value on a predictable basis or that do not have a determinable useful life (e.g., land, stock, antiques) are not eligible for cost recovery.

Placed in Service Requirement

The key date for the commencement of depreciation is the date an asset is placed in service. This date, and not the purchase date of an asset, is the relevant date. This distinction is particularly important for an asset that is purchased near the end of the tax year, but not placed in service until after the beginning of the following tax year.

Cost Recovery Allowed or Allowable

The basis of cost recovery property must be reduced by the cost recovery allowed and by not less than the allowable amount. The *allowed* cost recovery is the cost recovery actually taken, whereas the *allowable* cost recovery is the amount that could have been taken under the applicable cost recovery method. If the taxpayer does not claim any cost recovery on property during a particular year, the basis of the property must still be reduced by the amount of cost recovery that should have been deducted (the allowable cost recovery).

EXAMPLE 2

On March 15, 2011, Jack purchased a copier, to use in his business, for $10,000. The copier is five-year property, and Jack elected to use the straight-line method of cost recovery. Jack made the election because the business was a new undertaking and Jack reasoned that in the first few years of the business, a large cost recovery deduction was not needed. Because the business was doing poorly, Jack did not even take any cost recovery deductions in years 3 and 4. In years 5 and 6, Jack took the proper amount of cost recovery. Therefore, the allowed cost recovery (cost recovery actually deducted) and the allowable cost recovery are as follows:

	Cost Recovery Allowed	Cost Recovery Allowable
Year 1	$1,000	$1,000
Year 2	2,000	2,000
Year 3	–0–	2,000
Year 4	–0–	2,000
Year 5	2,000	2,000
Year 6	1,000	1,000

GLOBAL *Tax Issues*

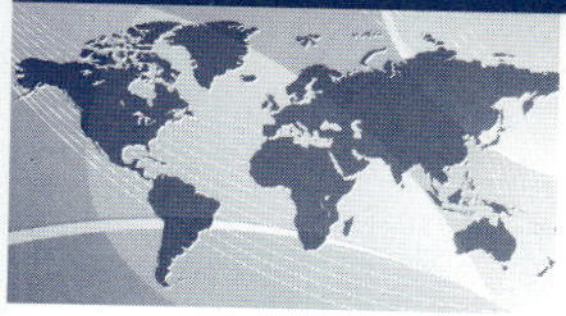

Depreciation Deductions Not Being Taken

Property investors in Townsville, Australia, are not taking $60 million to $90 million in tax depreciation benefits each year. These amounts are not being taken because taxpayers assume that depreciation can be taken only on new properties. The Australian Tax Office allows depreciation on older properties as well as on renovations or improvements completed after 1992.

Source: Adapted from Alexis Gillham, "Appreciate Value of Depreciation," *Townsville Bulletin,* June 16, 2010, p. 18.

If Jack sold the copier for $800 in year 7, he would recognize an $800 gain ($800 amount realized − $0 adjusted basis) because the adjusted basis of the copier is zero. ■

Cost Recovery Basis for Personal Use Assets Converted to Business or Income-Producing Use

If personal use assets are converted to business or income-producing use, the basis for cost recovery and for loss is the *lower* of the adjusted basis or the fair market value at the time the property was converted. As a result of this lower-of-basis rule, losses that occurred while the property was personal use property will not be recognized for tax purposes through the cost recovery of the property.

EXAMPLE 3
THE BIG PICTURE

Return to the facts of *The Big Picture* on p. 8-2. Five years ago Dr. Payne had purchased a personal residence for $250,000. In the current year, with the housing market down, Dr. Payne found a larger home that he acquired for his personal residence. Because of the downturn in the housing market; however, he was not able to sell his original residence and recover his purchase price of $250,000. The residence was appraised at $180,000. Instead of continuing to try to sell the original residence, Dr. Payne converted it to rental property. The basis for cost recovery of the rental property is $180,000 because the fair market value is less than the adjusted basis. The $70,000 decline in value is deemed to be personal (since it occurred while the property was held for personal use by Dr. Payne) and therefore nondeductible. ■

8.2 Modified Accelerated Cost Recovery System (MACRS)

LO.2
Determine the amount of cost recovery under MACRS.

Under the **modified accelerated cost recovery system (MACRS)**, the cost of an asset is recovered over a predetermined period that is generally shorter than the useful life of the asset or the period the asset is used to produce income. The MACRS rules were designed to encourage investment, improve productivity, and simplify the law and its administration.

MACRS provides separate cost recovery tables for realty (real property) and personalty (personal property). Write-offs are not available for land because it does not have a determinable useful life. Cost recovery allowances for real property, other than land, are based on recovery lives specified in the law. The IRS provides tables that specify cost recovery allowances for personalty and for realty.

PERSONALTY: RECOVERY PERIODS AND METHODS

Classification of Property

The general effect of TRA of 1986 was to lengthen asset lives compared with those used under ACRS. MACRS provides that the cost recovery basis of eligible personalty

EXHIBIT 8.1 **Cost Recovery Periods: MACRS Personalty**

Class of Property	Examples
3-year	Tractor units for use over-the-road.
	Any horse that is not a racehorse and is more than 12 years old at the time it is placed in service.
	Any racehorse that is more than 2 years old at the time it is placed in service.
	Breeding hogs.
	Special tools used in the manufacturing of motor vehicles such as dies, fixtures, molds, and patterns.
5-year	Automobiles and taxis.
	Light and heavy general-purpose trucks.
	Buses.
	Trailers and trailer-mounted containers.
	Typewriters, calculators, and copiers.
	Computers and peripheral equipment.
	Breeding and dairy cattle.
	Rental appliances, furniture, carpets, etc.
7-year	Office furniture, fixtures, and equipment.
	Breeding and work horses.
	Agricultural machinery and equipment.
	Railroad track.
10-year	Vessels, barges, tugs, and similar water transportation equipment.
	Assets used for petroleum refining or for the manufacture of grain and grain mill products, sugar and sugar products, or vegetable oils and vegetable oil products.
	Single-purpose agricultural or horticultural structures.
15-year	Land improvements.
	Assets used for industrial steam and electric generation and/or distribution systems.
	Assets used in the manufacture of cement.
	Assets used in pipeline transportation.
	Electric utility nuclear production plant.
	Municipal wastewater treatment plant.
20-year	Farm buildings except single-purpose agricultural and horticultural structures.
	Gas utility distribution facilities.
	Water utilities.
	Municipal sewer.

(and certain realty) is recovered over 3, 5, 7, 10, 15, or 20 years. Property is classified by recovery period under MACRS as follows (see Exhibit 8.1 for examples):[3]

3-year 200% class . . . . . . ADR midpoints of 4 years and less.[4] Excludes automobiles and light trucks. Includes racehorses more than 2 years old and other horses more than 12 years old.

[3]§ 168(e).

[4]Rev.Proc. 87–56, 1987–2 C.B. 674 is the source for the ADR midpoint lives.

ETHICS & Equity

CAPITALIZATION VERSUS EXPENSING

Joe Carter owns 15 apartment buildings. During the year, Joe replaced the carpeting in many of the apartments. Because the costs associated with replacing the carpeting are relatively small in comparison with the gross rents, Joe is considering expensing the costs as repairs and maintenance. Evaluate the appropriateness of Joe's plan.

5-year 200% class . . . . . . ADR midpoints of more than 4 years and less than 10 years, adding automobiles, light trucks, qualified technological equipment, renewable energy and biomass properties that are small power production facilities, research and experimentation property, semiconductor manufacturing equipment, and computer-based central office switching equipment.

7-year 200% class . . . . . . ADR midpoints of 10 years and more and less than 16 years, adding property with no ADR midpoint not classified elsewhere. Includes railroad track and office furniture, fixtures, and equipment.

10-year 200% class . . . . . ADR midpoints of 16 years and more and less than 20 years, adding single-purpose agricultural or horticultural structures, any tree or vine bearing fruits or nuts.

15-year 150% class . . . . . ADR midpoints of 20 years and more and less than 25 years, including sewage treatment plants, and telephone distribution plants and comparable equipment used for the two-way exchange of voice and data communications.

20-year 150% class . . . . . ADR midpoints of 25 years and more, other than real property with an ADR midpoint of 27.5 years and more, and including sewer pipes.

Accelerated depreciation is allowed for these six MACRS classes of property. Two hundred percent declining-balance is used for the 3-, 5-, 7-, and 10-year classes, with a switchover to straight-line depreciation when it yields a larger amount. One hundred and fifty percent declining-balance is allowed for the 15- and 20-year classes, with an appropriate straight-line switchover.[5] The appropriate computation methods and conventions are built into the tables, so it is not necessary to calculate the appropriate percentages. To determine the amount of the cost recovery allowances, simply identify the asset by class and go to the appropriate table for the percentage. The MACRS percentages for personalty appear in Table 8.1 *(all tables are located at the end of the chapter prior to the problem materials).*

Taxpayers may *elect* the straight-line method to compute cost recovery allowances for each of these classes of property. Certain property is not eligible for accelerated cost recovery and must be depreciated under an alternative depreciation system (ADS). Both the straight-line election and ADS are discussed later in the chapter.

MACRS views property as placed in service in the middle of the first year (the **half-year convention**).[6] Thus, for example, the statutory recovery period for three-year property begins in the middle of the year an asset is placed in service and ends three years later. In practical terms, this means that taxpayers must wait an extra year to recover the cost of depreciable assets. That is, the actual write-off periods are 4, 6, 8, 11, 16, and 21 years. MACRS also allows for a half-year of cost recovery in the year of disposition or retirement.

[5] § 168(b).

[6] § 168(d)(4)(A).

CONCEPT SUMMARY 8.2

Statutory Percentage Method under MACRS

	Personal Property	Real Property*
Convention	Half-year or mid-quarter	Mid-month
Cost recovery deduction in the year of disposition	Half-year for year of disposition or half-quarter for quarter of disposition	Half-month for month of disposition

*Straight-line method must be used.

EXAMPLE 4

Kareem acquires a five-year class asset on April 10, 2011, for $30,000. Kareem's cost recovery deduction for 2011 is $6,000, computed as follows:

MACRS cost recovery [$30,000 × .20 (Table 8.1)]	$6,000

■

EXAMPLE 5

Assume the same facts as in Example 4 and that Kareem disposes of the asset on March 5, 2013. Kareem's cost recovery deduction for 2013 is $2,880 [$30,000 × ½ × .192 (Table 8.1)]. ■

Additional First-Year Depreciation

The Economic Stimulus Act of 2008 provided for **additional first-year depreciation** on qualified property acquired after December 31, 2007, and before January 1, 2009, and placed in service before January 1, 2009. The American Recovery and Reinvestment Tax Act of 2009 extended additional first-year depreciation for an additional year (qualified property acquired and placed in service before January 1, 2010). The Small Business Jobs Act of 2010 extended additional first-year depreciation for one more year (qualified property acquired and placed in service before January 1, 2011). The provision allows for an additional 50 percent cost recovery in the year the asset is placed in service. The term *qualified property* includes most types of *new* property other than buildings. The term *new* means original or first use of the property. Property that is used but new to the taxpayer does not qualify.[7]

The Tax Relief Act of 2010 extends additional first-year depreciation for 2011 and increases the percentage from 50 percent to 100 percent. The act also extends additional first-year depreciation for 2012, but at the 50 percent rate. The effective date for 100 percent additional first-year depreciation is for qualified property placed in service after September 8, 2010, and before January 1, 2012. The effective date for 50 percent additional first-year depreciation is for qualified property placed in service after December 31, 2011, and before January 1, 2013.

The additional first-year depreciation is taken in the year in which the qualifying property is placed in service and may be claimed in addition to the otherwise available depreciation deduction. For property placed in service in 2011, the adjusted basis of the property after additional first-year depreciation is deducted is $0. So no standard cost recovery deduction under MACRS would be available. However, for property placed in service in 2012, after calculating the additional first-year depreciation, the standard cost recovery allowance under MACRS is calculated by multiplying the cost recovery basis (original cost recovery basis less additional first-year depreciation) by the percentage that reflects the applicable cost recovery method and the applicable cost recovery convention. A taxpayer may make an election to not take additional first-year depreciation.

Examples 6 and 7 reflect the tax treatment for 2011.

EXAMPLE 6

Morgan acquires and places in service a five-year class asset on March 20 for $50,000. Morgan's total cost recovery deduction depends on whether the asset was placed in service on March 20, 2011, or March 20, 2012, as indicated below.

[7] § 168(k).

TAX *in the NEWS*

EFFECTIVE CORPORATE TAX RATE: EFFECT OF BONUS DEPRECIATION

A study found that the effective combined U.S. Federal and state tax rate on new capital investment, taking into account all credits and deductions, is 35 percent. This rate is above the average rate of 28.8 percent in the G7 nations (Canada, France, Germany, Italy, Japan, the United Kingdom, and the United States). However, the study does not take into account bonus depreciation, which was available in 2009 and 2010. When bonus depreciation is taken into account, the effective tax rate drops to 17 percent, which is below the G7 average rate.

Source: Adapted from "America's Effective Corporate Tax Rate Is Competitive," *Wall Street Journal*, October. 1, 2010, p. A18.

March 20, 2011:

Under additional first-year depreciation, $50,000 is deducted. So the total cost recovery is $50,000 and the adjusted basis is $0.

March 20, 2012:

50% additional first-year depreciation ($50,000 × .50)	$25,000
MACRS cost recovery [($50,000 – $25,000) × .20 (Table 8.1)]	5,000
Total cost recovery	$30,000

■

EXAMPLE 7

Assume the same facts as in Example 6 and that Morgan disposes of the asset in October of the year following acquisition. Morgan's cost recovery deduction for the asset placed in service in 2011 (100% additional first-year depreciation was deducted in 2011) is $0. Morgan's cost recovery deduction for the asset placed in service in 2012 (50% additional first-year depreciation was deducted in 2011) is $2,400 [$25,000 × ½ × .192 (Table 8.1)]. ■

Mid-Quarter Convention

If more than 40 percent of the value of property other than eligible real estate (see Realty: Recovery Periods and Methods for a discussion of eligible real estate) is placed in service during the last quarter of the year, a **mid-quarter convention** applies.[8] Under this convention, property acquisitions are grouped by the quarter they were acquired for cost recovery purposes. Acquisitions during the first quarter are allowed 10.5 months (three and one-half quarters) of cost recovery; the second quarter, 7.5 months (two and one-half quarters); the third quarter, 4.5 months (one and one-half quarter); and the fourth quarter, 1.5 months (one-half quarter). The percentages are shown in Table 8.2.

EXAMPLE 8

Silver Corporation acquires the following five-year class property in 2011 and elects not to take additional first-year depreciation:

Property Acquisition Dates	Cost
February 15	$ 200,000
July 10	400,000
December 5	600,000
Total	$1,200,000

If Silver Corporation uses the statutory percentage method, the cost recovery allowances for the first two years are computed as indicated below. Since more than 40% ($600,000/$1,200,000 = 50%) of the acquisitions are in the last quarter, the mid-quarter convention applies.

[8] § 168(d)(3).

2011

	Mid-Quarter Convention Depreciation	Total Depreciation
February 15	\$200,000 × .35 (Table 8.2)	\$ 70,000
July 10	\$400,000 × .15	60,000
December 5	\$600,000 × .05	30,000
		\$160,000

2012

	Mid-Quarter Convention Depreciation	Total Depreciation
February 15	\$200,000 × .26 (Table 8.2)	\$ 52,000
July 10	\$400,000 × .34	136,000
December 5	\$600,000 × .38	228,000
		\$416,000

■

When property to which the mid-quarter convention applies is disposed of, the property is treated as though it were disposed of at the midpoint of the quarter. Hence, in the quarter of disposition, cost recovery is allowed for one-half of the quarter.

EXAMPLE 9

Assume the same facts as in Example 8, except that Silver Corporation sells the \$400,000 asset on November 30 of 2012. The cost recovery allowance for 2012 is computed as follows:

February 15	\$200,000 × .26 (Table 8.2)	\$ 52,000
July 10	\$400,000 × .34 × (3.5/4)	119,000
December 5	\$600,000 × .38	228,000
Total		\$399,000

■

REALTY: RECOVERY PERIODS AND METHODS

Under MACRS, the cost recovery period for residential rental real estate is 27.5 years, and the straight-line method is used for computing the cost recovery allowance. **Residential rental real estate** includes property where 80 percent or more of the gross rental revenues are from nontransient dwelling units (e.g., an apartment building). Hotels, motels, and similar establishments are not residential rental property. Low-income housing is classified as residential rental real estate. Nonresidential real estate has a recovery period of 39 years (31.5 years for such property placed in service before May 13, 1993) and is also depreciated using the straight-line method.[9]

Some items of real property are not treated as real estate for purposes of MACRS. For example, single-purpose agricultural structures are in the 10-year MACRS class. Land improvements are in the 15-year MACRS class.

All eligible real estate is depreciated using the **mid-month convention**.[10] Regardless of when during the month the property is placed in service, it is deemed to have been placed in service at the middle of the month. This allows for one-half month's cost recovery for the month the property is placed in service. If the property is disposed of before the end of the recovery period, one-half month's cost recovery is permitted for the month of disposition regardless of the specific date of disposition.

Cost recovery is computed by multiplying the applicable rate (Table 8.6) by the cost recovery basis.

[9] §§ 168(b), (c), and (e).

[10] § 168(d)(1).

EXAMPLE 10

Alec acquired a building on April 1, 1996, for $800,000. If the building is classified as residential rental real estate, the cost recovery deduction for 2011 is $29,088 (.03636 × $800,000). If the building is sold on October 7, 2011, the cost recovery deduction for 2011 is $23,028 [.03636 × (9.5/12) × $800,000]. (See Table 8.6 for percentage.) ■

EXAMPLE 11

Jane acquired a building on March 2, 1993, for $1 million. If the building is classified as nonresidential real estate, the cost recovery deduction for 2011 is $31,750 (.03175 × $1,000,000). If the building is sold on January 5, 2011, the cost recovery deduction for 2011 is $1,323 [.03175 × (.5/12) × $1,000,000]. (See Table 8.6 for percentage.) ■

EXAMPLE 12

Mark acquired a building on November 19, 2011, for $1.2 million. If the building is classified as nonresidential real estate, the cost recovery deduction for 2011 is $3,852 [.00321 × $1,200,000 (Table 8.6)]. The cost recovery deduction for 2012 is $30,768 [.02564 × $1,200,000 (Table 8.6)]. If the building is sold on May 21, 2012, the cost recovery deduction for 2012 is $11,538 [.02564 × (4.5/12) × $1,200,000 (Table 8.6)]. ■

STRAIGHT-LINE ELECTION

Although MACRS requires straight-line depreciation for all eligible real estate as previously discussed, the taxpayer may *elect* to use the straight-line method for personal property.[11] The property is depreciated using the class life (recovery period) of the asset with a half-year convention or a mid-quarter convention, whichever is applicable. The election is available on a class-by-class and year-by-year basis. The percentages for the straight-line election with a half-year convention appear in Table 8.3.

EXAMPLE 13

Terry acquires a new 10-year class asset on August 4, 2011, for $100,000. He elects the straight-line method of cost recovery. Terry's cost recovery deduction for 2011 is $5,000 ($100,000 × .050). His cost recovery deduction for 2012 is $10,000 ($100,000 × .100). (See Table 8.3 for percentages.) ■

EXAMPLE 14

Assume the same facts as in Example 13, except that Terry sells the asset on November 21, 2012. His cost recovery deduction for 2012 is $5,000 [$100,000 × .100 × (½) (Table 8.3)]. ■

FARM PROPERTY

When tangible personal property is used in a farming business, generally the cost of the asset is recovered under MACRS using the 150 percent declining-balance method.[12] However, the MACRS straight-line method is required for any tree or vine bearing fruits or nuts.[13] The cost of real property used in the farming business is recovered over the normal periods (27.5 years and 39 years) using the straight-line method. A farming business is defined as the trade or business of farming, which includes operating a nursery or sod farm and the raising or harvesting of trees bearing fruit, nuts, or other crops, or ornamental trees.[14] The applicable cost recovery method is also affected if the taxpayer elects to not have the uniform capitalization rules apply to the farming business.[15] Under the uniform capitalization rules, the costs of property produced or acquired for resale must be capitalized. When this election is made, the cost recovery method required is the alternative depreciation system (ADS) straight-line method (discussed further later in the chapter). This method must be applied to all assets placed in service in any taxable year during which the election is in effect. Even though this election is made and the straight-line method must be used, it does not prevent the taxpayer from electing to expense

[11] § 168(b)(5).
[12] § 168(b)(2)(B).
[13] §§ 168(b)(3)(E) and 168(e)(3)(D)(ii).
[14] § 263A(e)(4).
[15] § 263A(d)(3)(A).

EXHIBIT 8.2 **Cost Recovery Periods for Farming Assets**

Assets	Recovery Period in Years	
	MACRS	**ADS**
Agricultural structures (single purpose)	10	15
Cattle (dairy or breeding)	5	7
Farm buildings	20	25
Farm machinery and equipment	7	10
Fences (agricultural)	7	10
Horticultural structures (single purpose)	10	15
Trees or vines bearing fruit or nuts	10	20
Truck (heavy duty, unloaded weight 13,000 pounds or more)	5	6
Truck (actual weight less than 13,000 pounds)	5	5

personalty under § 179.[16] Exhibit 8.2 shows examples of cost recovery periods for farming assets.

EXAMPLE 15

James purchased new farm equipment on July 10, 2011, for $80,000. If James does not elect to expense any of the cost under § 179, his cost recovery deduction for 2011 is $8,568 [(.1071 × $80,000) (Table 8.4)]. ■

EXAMPLE 16

Assume the same facts as in Example 15, except that James has made an election to not have the uniform capitalization rules apply. His 2011 cost recovery deduction is $4,000 [(.05 × $80,000) (Table 8.5)]. ■

LEASEHOLD IMPROVEMENT PROPERTY

When the lessor is the owner of leasehold improvement property, the cost recovery period is the statutorily prescribed life. The recovery period for residential rental real estate is 27.5 years, and the recovery period for nonresidential real estate is 39 years. For these real property leasehold improvements, the straight-line method is used. If the improvement is tangible personal property, the shorter MACRS lives and accelerated methods are used.

When lessor-owned leasehold improvements are disposed of or abandoned by the lessor because of the termination of the lease, the property will be treated as disposed of by the lessor, and hence, a loss can be taken for the unrecovered basis.[17]

EXAMPLE 17

On April 7, 2011, Mary signed a 10-year lease with John on a building to be used for her business. The lease period begins on May 1, 2011, and ends on April 30, 2021. Prior to the signing of the lease, John paid $300,000 to have a unique storefront added to the building. John's cost recovery deduction for 2011 for the addition is $4,815 [(.01605 × $300,000) (Table 8.6)]. ■

EXAMPLE 18

Assume the same facts as in Example 17. John's cost recovery deduction for 2021 is $2,244 {[.02564 × (3.5/12) × $300,000] (Table 8.6)}. At the end of the lease, John has to remove the unique storefront, so he can lease the building to other tenants. John's loss as a result of the termination of the lease and the removal of the unique storefront is $223,713 computed as follows:

[16] Reg. § 1.263A–4(d)(4)(ii).

[17] § 163(i)(8)(B).

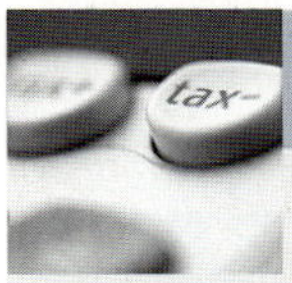

CONCEPT SUMMARY 8.3

Straight-Line Election under MACRS

	Personal Property	Real Property*
Convention	Half-year or mid-quarter	Mid-month
Cost recovery deduction in the year of disposition	Half-year for year of disposition or half-quarter for quarter of disposition	Half-month for month of disposition
Elective or mandatory	Elective	Mandatory
Breadth of election	Class by class	

*Straight-line method must be used.

Cost	$300,000
Less: Cost recovery	
2011 (Example 17)	(4,815)
2012–2020 (.02564 × $300,000 × 9 years)	(69,228)
2021	(2,244)
Loss (unrecovered cost)	$223,713

■

The costs of leasehold improvements made to leased property and owned by the lessee are recovered in accordance with the general cost recovery rules. This means that the cost recovery period is determined without regard to the lease term. Any unrecovered basis in the leasehold improvement property not retained by the lessee is deducted in the year the lease is terminated.

The Tax Relief Act of 2010 extends 15-year straight-line cost recovery for *qualified* leasehold improvement property. The Act also allows for 100 percent additional first-year depreciation for a qualified leasehold improvement to an interior portion of a building which is nonresidential real property. The improvement must be made under or pursuant to a lease by the lessee or lessor and placed in service more than 3 years after the date the building was first placed in service.

ELECTION TO EXPENSE ASSETS

LO.3

Recognize when and how to make the § 179 expensing election, calculate the amount of the deduction, and apply the effect of the election in making the MACRS calculation.

Section 179 (Election to Expense Certain Depreciable Business Assets) permits the taxpayer to elect to write off up to $500,000 in 2010 and 2011 of the acquisition cost of *tangible personal property* used in a trade or business. Amounts that are expensed under § 179 may not be capitalized and depreciated. The **§ 179 expensing** election is an annual election and applies to the acquisition cost of property placed in service that year. The immediate expense election is generally not available for real property or for property used for the production of income.[18]

In addition, any elected § 179 expense is taken *before* additional first-year depreciation is computed. The base for calculating the standard MACRS deduction is net of the § 179 expense and the additional first-year depreciation (100 percent for assets placed in service in 2011 and 50 percent for assets placed in service in 2012).

EXAMPLE 19

Kelly acquires machinery (five-year class asset) on February 1, 2011, at a cost of $525,000 and elects to expense $500,000 under § 179. Kelley takes the statutory percentage cost recovery (see Table 8.1 for percentage) for 2011. As a result, the total deduction for the year is calculated as follows:

[18]The § 179 amount allowed is per taxpayer, per year. On a joint return, the statutory amount applies to the couple. If the taxpayers are married and file separate returns, each spouse is eligible for 50% of the statutory amount.

TAX in the NEWS

Economics and the Utility of § 179

In February 2008, Congress passed an economic stimulus package that was intended to stimulate the economy. One provision increased the amount of certain fixed asset acquisition costs that could be expensed rather than depreciated. Given the faltering economy, however, many companies will not be able to take advantage of the increased amount because they cannot afford to purchase new assets. Companies are not going to purchase assets simply because they can save on taxes.

Source: Adapted from Joyce Rosenberg, "Deduction Dilemma Hits Companies," *Telegraph Herald* (Dubuque, Iowa), November 9, 2008, p. B2.

§ 179 expense	$500,000
100% additional first-year depreciation [($525,000 – $500,000) × 100%]	25,000
Standard MACRS calculation [($525,000 – $500,000 – $25,000) × .20]	–0–
	$525,000

■

Annual Limitations

Two additional limitations apply to the amount deductible under § 179. First, the ceiling amount on the deduction is reduced dollar-for-dollar when § 179 property placed in service during the taxable year exceeds $2 million in 2010 and 2011. Second, the amount expensed under § 179 cannot exceed the aggregate amount of taxable income derived from the conduct of any trade or business by the taxpayer. Taxable income of a trade or business is computed without regard to the amount expensed under § 179. Any § 179 expensed amount in excess of taxable income is carried forward to future taxable years and added to other amounts eligible for expensing. The § 179 amount eligible for expensing in a carryforward year is limited to the *lesser* of (1) the statutory dollar amount ($500,000 in 2011) reduced by the cost of § 179 property placed in service in excess of $2 million in the carryforward year or (2) the business income limitation in the carryforward year.

EXAMPLE 20

Jill owns a computer service and operates it as a sole proprietorship. In 2011, she will net $80,000 before considering any § 179 deduction. If Jill spends $2.3 million on new equipment, her § 179 expense deduction is computed as follows:

§ 179 deduction before adjustment	$500,000
Less: Dollar limitation reduction ($2,300,000 – $2,000,000)	(300,000)
Remaining § 179 deduction	$200,000
Business income limitation	$ 80,000
§ 179 deduction allowed	$ 80,000
§ 179 deduction carryforward ($200,000 – $80,000)	$120,000

■

The Small Business Jobs Act of 2010 expands the definition of property qualifying for § 179 to include certain real property[19]. The real property included is qualified leasehold improvement property, qualified restaurant property, and qualified retail improvement property. The maximum amount of qualified real property that may be expensed is $250,000. In addition, § 179 deductions in 2011 attributable to qualified real property that are disallowed under the trade or business income limitation may not be carried over to 2012. Any amounts that are not used in 2011 are treated

[19]Section 179 property includes qualified real property only if an election is made to treat the qualified real property as § 179 property.

FINANCIAL DISCLOSURE *Insights* — TAX AND BOOK DEPRECIATION

A common book-tax difference relates to the depreciation amounts that are reported for GAAP and Federal income tax purposes. Typically, tax depreciation deductions are accelerated; that is, they are claimed in earlier reporting periods than is the case for financial accounting purposes. Almost every tax law change since 1980 has included depreciation provisions that accelerate the related deductions relative to the expenses allowed under GAAP. Accelerated cost recovery deductions represent a means by which the taxing jurisdiction infuses the business with cash flow created by the reduction in the year's tax liabilities.

For instance, recently about one-quarter of General Electric's deferred tax liabilities related to depreciation differences. For Toyota's and Ford's depreciation differences, that amount was about one-third. And for the trucking firm Ryder Systems, depreciation differences accounted for all but 1 percent of the deferred tax liabilities.

as property placed in service in 2011 for purposes of computing cost recovery. If a taxpayer does not elect to include qualified real property as § 179 property, then it is excluded from the definition of § 179 property.

EXAMPLE 21

During 2011, Green Corporation purchased § 179 equipment costing $200,000 and qualifying leasehold improvement property costing $350,000. Green has no other asset purchases during 2011 and is not subject to the taxable income limitation. The maximum § 179 deduction Green can claim for 2011 is $450,000 ($200,000 with respect to the equipment and $250,000 with respect to the qualifying leasehold improvements). ■

EXAMPLE 22

During 2011, Red Corporation purchased and placed in service $1.9 million of § 179 equipment and $200,000 of qualifying leasehold improvement property. If Red elects to treat the qualified leasehold improvement property as § 179 property, the § 179 deduction is limited to $400,000 [$500,000 − ($2,100,000 − $2,000,000)]. If Red does not elect to treat the qualifying leasehold improvement property as § 179 property, the § 179 deduction will be $500,000. ■

Effect on Basis

The basis of the property for cost recovery purposes is reduced by the § 179 amount after it is adjusted for property placed in service in excess of $2 million. This adjusted amount does not reflect any business income limitation.

EXAMPLE 23

Assume the same facts as in Example 20 and that the new equipment is five-year class property. Jill elects not to take additional first-year depreciation. After considering the § 179 deduction, Jill's cost recovery deduction for 2011 (see Table 8.1 for percentage) is calculated as follows:

Standard MACRS calculation [($2,300,000 − $200,000) × .20]	$420,000

■

Conversion to Personal Use

Conversion of the expensed property to personal use at any time results in recapture income (see Chapter 14). A property is converted to personal use if it is not used predominantly in a trade or business. Regulations provide for the mechanics of the recapture.[20]

[20]Reg. § 1.179–1(e).

LO.4

Identify listed property and apply the deduction limitations on listed property and on luxury automobiles.

BUSINESS AND PERSONAL USE OF AUTOMOBILES AND OTHER LISTED PROPERTY

Limits exist on MACRS deductions for automobiles and other listed property that are used for both personal and business purposes.[21] If the listed property is *predominantly used* for business, the taxpayer is allowed to use the *statutory percentage method* to recover the cost. In cases where the property is *not predominantly used* for business, the cost is recovered using the *straight-line method.*

Listed property includes the following:

- Any passenger automobile.
- Any other property used as a means of transportation.
- Any property of a type generally used for purposes of entertainment, recreation, or amusement.
- Any computer or peripheral equipment, with the exception of equipment used exclusively at a regular business establishment, including a qualifying home office.
- Any other property specified in the Regulations.

Automobiles and Other Listed Property Used Predominantly in Business

For listed property to be considered as *predominantly used in business,* its *business usage* must exceed 50 percent.[22] The use of listed property for production of income does not qualify as business use for purposes of the more-than-50 percent test. However, both production of income and business use percentages are used to compute the cost recovery deduction.

EXAMPLE 24

On September 1, 2011, Emma places in service listed five-year recovery property. The property cost $10,000. She elects not to take additional first-year depreciation. If Emma uses the property 40% for business and 25% for the production of income, the property is not considered as predominantly used for business. The cost is recovered using straight-line cost recovery. Emma's cost recovery allowance for the year is $650 ($10,000 × 10% × 65%). If, however, Emma uses the property 60% for business and 25% for the production of income, the property is considered as used predominantly for business. Therefore, she may use the statutory percentage method. Emma's cost recovery allowance for the year is $1,700 ($10,000 × .200 × 85%). ■

The method for determining the percentage of business usage for listed property is specified in the Regulations. The Regulations provide that for automobiles a mileage-based percentage is to be used. Other listed property is to use the most appropriate unit of time (e.g., hours) the property is actually used (rather than available for use).[23]

Limits on Cost Recovery for Automobiles

The law places special limitations on the cost recovery deduction for passenger automobiles. These statutory dollar limits were imposed on passenger automobiles because of the belief that the tax system was being used to underwrite automobiles whose cost and luxury far exceeded what was needed for their business use.

A *passenger automobile* is any four-wheeled vehicle manufactured for use on public streets, roads, and highways with an unloaded gross vehicle weight (GVW) rating of 6,000 pounds or less.[24] This definition specifically excludes vehicles used directly in the business of transporting people or property for compensation such as taxicabs, ambulances, hearses, and trucks and vans as prescribed by the Regulations.

[21] § 280F.
[22] § 280F(b)(3).
[23] Reg. § 1.280F–6T(e).
[24] § 280F(d)(5).

The following limits apply to the cost recovery deductions for passenger automobiles for 2010:[25]

Year	Recovery Limitation*
1	$3,060
2	4,900
3	2,950
Succeeding years until the cost is recovered	1,775

*The indexed amounts for 2011 were not available at the time of this writing.

For an automobile placed in service in 2009, the limitation for subsequent years' cost recovery will be based on the limits for the year the automobile was placed in service. Hence, the limit for the third year's cost recovery for an automobile placed in service in 2009 is $2,850 and not a limit published in 2011.[26]

In the event that a passenger automobile used predominantly for business qualifies for additional first-year depreciation (i.e., new property), the first-year recovery limitation is increased by $8,000. Therefore, for acquisitions made in 2011, the initial-year cost recovery limitation increases from $3,060 to $11,060 ($3,060 + $8,000).

There are also separate cost recovery limitations for trucks and vans and for electric automobiles. Because these limitations are applied in the same manner as those imposed on passenger automobiles, these additional limitations are not discussed further in this chapter.

The limits are imposed before any percentage reduction for personal use. In addition, the limitation in the first year includes any amount the taxpayer elects to expense under § 179.[27] If the passenger automobile is used partly for personal use, the personal use percentage is ignored for the purpose of determining the unrecovered cost available for deduction in later years.

EXAMPLE 25

On July 1, 2011, Dan places in service a new automobile that cost $40,000. He does not elect § 179 expensing. The car is always used 80% for business and 20% for personal. Dan chooses the MACRS 200% declining-balance method of cost recovery (see the 5-year column in Table 8.1). The depreciation computation for 2011–2016 is summarized below if Dan elects not to take additional first-year depreciation.

Year	MACRS Amount	Recovery Limitation	Depreciation Allowed
2011	$6,400 ($40,000 × 20% × 80%)	$2,448 ($3,060 × 80%)	$2,448
2012	$10,240 ($40,000 × 32% × 80%)	$3,920 ($4,900 × 80%)	$3,920
2013	$6,144 ($40,000 × 19.2% × 80%)	$2,360 ($2,950 × 80%)	$2,360
2014	$3,686 ($40,000 × 11.52% × 80%)	$1,420 ($1,775 × 80%)	$1,420
2015	$3,686 ($40,000 × 11.52% × 80%)	$1,420 ($1,775 × 80%)	$1,420
2016	$1,843 ($40,000 × 5.76% × 80%)	$1,420 ($1,775 × 80%)	$1,420

The cost recovery allowed is the lesser of the MACRS amount or the recovery limitation. If Dan continues to use the car after 2016, his cost recovery is limited to the lesser of the

[25] § 280F(a)(1). Since the 2011 indexed amounts were not available at the time of this writing, the 2010 amounts are used in the Examples and in the Problem Materials.

[26] Cost recovery limitations for prior years can be found in IRS Publication 463.

[27] § 280F(d)(1).

recoverable basis or the recovery limitation (i.e., $1,775 × business use percentage). For this purpose, the recoverable basis is computed as if the full recovery limitation was allowed even if it was not. Thus, the recoverable basis as of January 1, 2017, is $23,765 ($40,000 – $3,060 – $4,900 – $2,950 – $1,775 – $1,775 – $1,775).

If Dan takes additional first-year depreciation, the calculated amount of additional first-year depreciation is $32,000 ($40,000 × 100% × 80%). However, the recovery limitation in 2011 would be $8,848 [($8,000 + $3,060) × 80%]. ■

The cost recovery limitations are maximum amounts. If the regular calculation produces a lesser amount of cost recovery, the lesser amount is used.

EXAMPLE 26

On April 2, 2011, Gail places in service a used automobile that cost $10,000. The car is always used 70% for business and 30% for personal use. Therefore, the cost recovery allowance for 2011 is $1,400 ($10,000 × 20% × 70%), which is less than $2,142 ($3,060 × 70%). ■

Note that the cost recovery limitations apply *only* to passenger automobiles and not to other listed property.

Special Limitation

The American Jobs Creation Act of 2004 (AJCA) placed a limit of $25,000 on the § 179 deduction for certain vehicles not subject to the statutory dollar limits on cost recovery deductions that are imposed on passenger automobiles. The limit applies to sport utility vehicles (SUVs) with an unloaded GVW rating of more than 6,000 pounds and not more than 14,000 pounds.[28]

EXAMPLE 27

During 2011, Jay acquires and places in service an SUV that cost $70,000 and has a GVW of 8,000 pounds. Jay uses the vehicle 100% of the time for business use. The total deduction for 2011 with respect to the SUV is $70,000, computed as follows:

§ 179 expense	$25,000
100% additional first-year depreciation [($70,000 – $25,000) × 100%]	45,000
Standard MACRS calculation [($70,000 – $25,000 – $45,000) × .20 (Table 8.1)]	–0–
	$70,000

■

Automobiles and Other Listed Property Not Used Predominantly in Business

The cost of listed property that does not pass the more-than-50 percent business usage test in the year the property is placed in service must be recovered using the straight-line method.[29] In addition, such property does not qualify for additional first-year depreciation. The straight-line method to be used is that required under the alternative depreciation system (explained later in the chapter). This system requires a straight-line recovery period of five years for automobiles. However, even though the straight-line method is used, the cost recovery allowance for passenger automobiles cannot exceed the dollar limitations.

EXAMPLE 28

On July 27, 2011, Fred places in service an automobile that cost $20,000. The auto is used 40% for business and 60% for personal use. The cost recovery allowance for 2011 is $800 [$20,000 × 10% (Table 8.5) × 40%]. ■

EXAMPLE 29

Assume the same facts as in Example 28, except that the automobile cost $50,000. The cost recovery allowance for 2011 is $1,224 [$50,000 × 10% (Table 8.5) = $5,000 (limited to $3,060) × 40%]. ■

[28] § 179(b)(6).

[29] § 280F(b)(1).

TAX *in* the NEWS

Leasing versus Buying a Car

Studies show that a new car, on average, loses a much larger portion of its value during the first five years through depreciation than it loses during later years. Depreciation accounts for about 35 percent of the ownership costs of a car during this five-year period. Leasing a car will not eliminate the problem because the monthly lease payments are determined, in part, by the value of the car at the end of the lease. Because a new car loses its value faster in the earlier years, the shorter the lease, the higher the cost of depreciation.

Source: Adapted from Peter Levy, "The Intellichoice Report/Depreciation; A Loss of Value Any Car Buyer Can Appreciate; Study Finds That Depreciation Accounts for 35% of Ownership Cost during First Five Years. Leasing Offers No Break," *Los Angeles Times*, June 25, 2008, p. 17.

If the listed property fails the more-than-50 percent business usage test, the straight-line method must be used for the remainder of the property's life. This applies even if at some later date the business usage of the property increases to more than 50 percent. Even though the straight-line method must continue to be used, however, the amount of cost recovery will reflect the increase in business usage.

EXAMPLE 30

Assume the same facts as in Example 28, except that in 2012, Fred uses the automobile 70% for business and 30% for personal use. Fred's cost recovery allowance for 2012 is $2,800 [$20,000 × 20% (Table 8.5) × 70%], which is less than 70% of the second-year limit. ■

Change from Predominantly Business Use

If the business use percentage of listed property falls to 50 percent or lower after the year the property is placed in service, the property is subject to *cost recovery recapture.* The amount required to be recaptured and included in the taxpayer's return as ordinary income is the excess cost recovery.

Excess cost recovery is the excess of the cost recovery deduction taken in prior years using the statutory percentage method over the amount that would have been allowed if the straight-line method had been used since the property was placed in service.[30]

EXAMPLE 31

Seth purchased a new car on January 22, 2011, at a cost of $20,000. Business usage was 80% in 2011, 70% in 2012, 40% in 2013, and 60% in 2014. Seth elects not to take additional first-year depreciation. Seth's excess cost recovery to be recaptured as ordinary income in 2013 is computed as follows:

2011	
MACRS [($20,000 × .20 × .80) limited to $3,060 × .80]	$ 2,448
Straight-line [($20,000 × .10 × .80) limited to $3,060 × .80]	(1,600)
Excess	$ 848
2012	
MACRS [($20,000 × .32 × .70) limited to $4,900 × .70]	$ 3,430
Straight-line [($20,000 × .20 × .70) limited to $4,900 × .70]	(2,800)
Excess	$ 630
2013	
2011 excess	$ 848
2012 excess	630
Ordinary income recapture	$ 1,478

■

[30] § 280F(b)(2).

After the business usage of the listed property drops below the more-than-50 percent level, the straight-line method must be used for the remaining life of the property.

EXAMPLE 32

Assume the same facts as in Example 31. Seth's cost recovery allowance for the years 2013 and 2014 would be $1,180 and $1,065, computed as follows:

2013—$1,180	[($20,000 × 20% × .40) limited to $2,950 × 40%]
2014—$1,065	[($20,000 × 20% × .60) limited to $1,775 × 60%]

■

Leased Automobiles

A taxpayer who leases a passenger automobile must report an *inclusion amount* in gross income. The inclusion amount is computed from an IRS table for each taxable year for which the taxpayer leases the automobile. The purpose of this provision is to prevent taxpayers from circumventing the cost recovery dollar limitations by leasing, instead of purchasing, an automobile.

The dollar amount of the inclusion is based on the fair market value of the automobile and is prorated for the number of days the auto is used during the taxable year. The prorated dollar amount is then multiplied by the business and income-producing usage percentage to determine the amount to be included in gross income.[31] The taxpayer deducts the lease payments, multiplied by the business and income-producing usage percentage. The net effect is that the annual deduction for the lease payment is reduced by the inclusion amount.

EXAMPLE 33

On April 1, 2011, Jim leases and places in service a passenger automobile worth $40,000. The lease is to be for a period of five years. During the taxable years 2011 and 2012, Jim uses the automobile 70% for business and 30% for personal use. Assuming the dollar amounts from the IRS table for 2011 and 2012 are $50 and $109, Jim must include $26 in gross income for 2011 and $76 for 2012, computed as follows:

2011	$50 × (275/365) × 70% = $26
2012	$109 × (366/366) × 70% = $76

In addition, Jim can deduct 70% of the lease payments each year because this is the business use percentage. ■

Substantiation Requirements

Listed property is now subject to the substantiation requirements of § 274. This means that the taxpayer must prove the business usage as to the amount of expense or use, the time and place of use, the business purpose for the use, and the business relationship to the taxpayer of persons using the property. Substantiation requires adequate records or sufficient evidence corroborating the taxpayer's statement. However, these substantiation requirements do not apply to vehicles that, by reason of their nature, are not likely to be used more than a *de minimis* amount for personal purposes.[32]

LO.5

Determine when and how to use the alternative depreciation system (ADS).

ALTERNATIVE DEPRECIATION SYSTEM (ADS)

The **alternative depreciation system (ADS)** must be used for the following:[33]

- To calculate the portion of depreciation treated as an alternative minimum tax (AMT) adjustment for purposes of the corporate and individual AMT (see Chapter 15).[34]
- To compute depreciation allowances for property for which any of the following is true:

[31] Reg. § 1.280F–7(a).

[32] §§ 274(d) and (i).

[33] § 168(g).

[34] This AMT adjustment applies for real and personal property placed in service before January 1, 1999. However, it will continue to apply for personal property placed in service after December 31, 1998, if the taxpayer uses the 200% declining-balance method for regular income tax purposes. See Chapter 15.

CONCEPT SUMMARY 8.4

Listed Property Cost Recovery

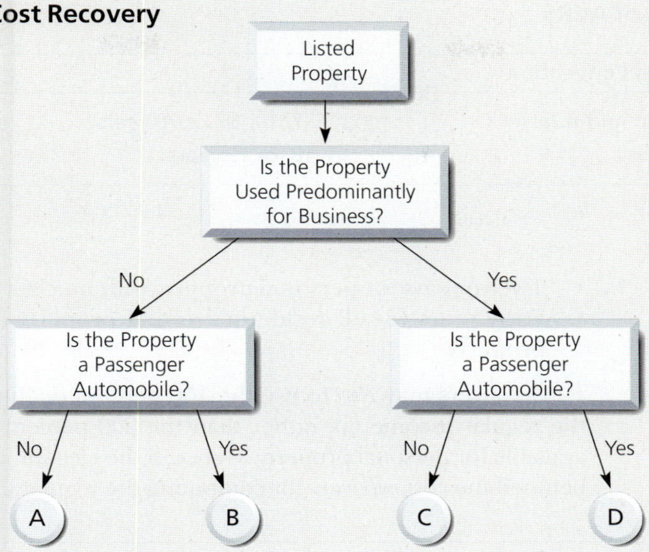

Legend to Tax Treatment

A Straight-line cost recovery reduced by the personal use percentage.
B Straight-line cost recovery subject to the recovery limitations ($3,060, $4,900, $2,950, $1,775) and reduced by the personal use percentage.
C Statutory percentage cost recovery reduced by the personal use percentage.
D Statutory percentage cost recovery subject to the recovery limitations ($3,060, $4,900, $2,950, $1,775) and reduced by the personal use percentage.

- *Used predominantly outside the United States.*
- *Leased or otherwise used by a tax-exempt entity.*
- *Financed with the proceeds of tax-exempt bonds.*
- *Imported from foreign countries that maintain discriminatory trade practices or otherwise engage in discriminatory acts.*

- To compute depreciation allowances for earnings and profits purposes (see Chapter 19).

In general, ADS depreciation is computed using straight-line recovery without regard to salvage value. However, for purposes of the AMT, depreciation of personal property is computed using the 150 percent declining-balance method with an appropriate switch to the straight-line method.

The taxpayer must use the half-year or the mid-quarter convention, whichever is applicable, for all property other than eligible real estate. The mid-month convention is used for eligible real estate. The applicable ADS rates are found in Tables 8.4, 8.5, and 8.7.

The recovery periods under ADS are as follows:[35]

- The ADR midpoint life for property that does not fall into any of the following listed categories.
- Five years for qualified technological equipment, automobiles, and light-duty trucks.

[35]The class life for certain properties described in § 168(e)(3) is specially determined under § 168(g)(3)(B).

CONCEPT SUMMARY 8.5

Characteristics of ACRS

Property	Accounting Convention	Life	Method
Personalty	Half-year or mid-quarter	3, 5, 7, 10, 15, or 20 years	Accelerated or straight-line
Realty	Mid-month	15, 18, or 19 years	Accelerated or straight-line

- Twelve years for personal property with no class life.
- Forty years for all residential rental property and all nonresidential real property.

Taxpayers may *elect* to use the 150 percent declining-balance method to compute the regular income tax rather than the 200 percent declining-balance method that is available for personal property. Hence, if the election is made, there will be no difference between the cost recovery for computing the regular income tax and the AMT.[36]

EXAMPLE 34

On March 1, 2011, Abby purchases computer-based telephone central office switching equipment for $80,000. Abby elects not to take additional first-year depreciation. If Abby uses statutory percentage cost recovery (assuming no § 179 election), the cost recovery allowance for 2011 is $16,000 [$80,000 × 20% (Table 8.1, five-year class property)]. If Abby elects to use ADS 150% declining-balance cost recovery for the regular income tax (assuming no § 179 election), the cost recovery allowance for 2011 is $12,000 [$80,000 × 15% (Table 8.4, five-year class property)]. ■

In lieu of depreciation under the regular MACRS method, taxpayers may *elect* straight-line under ADS for property that qualifies for the regular MACRS method. The election is available on a class-by-class and year-by-year basis for property other than eligible real estate. The election for eligible real estate is on a property-by-property basis. One reason for making this election is to avoid a difference between deductible depreciation and earnings and profits depreciation.

EXAMPLE 35

Polly acquires an apartment building on March 17, 2011, for $700,000. She takes the maximum cost recovery allowance for determining taxable income. Polly's cost recovery allowance for computing 2011 taxable income is $20,153 [$700,000 × .02879 (Table 8.6)]. However, Polly's cost recovery for computing her earnings and profits is only $13,853 [$700,000 × .01979 (Table 8.7)]. ■

8.3 Accelerated Cost Recovery System (ACRS)

LO.6

Be aware of the major characteristics of ACRS.

The major characteristics of the **accelerated cost recovery system (ACRS)** are listed in Concept Summary 8.5. Note that for personalty, except for 20-year property, the recovery period expired (all of the cost recovery basis has been recovered) prior to 2005. For 20-year property, the recovery period expired during 2005. For realty, the recovery period also expired during 2005.

[36] For personal property placed in service before January 1, 1999, taxpayers making the election are required to use the ADS recovery periods in computing cost recovery for the regular income tax. The ADS recovery periods generally are longer than the regular recovery periods under MACRS.

TAX *in the NEWS*

AMORTIZING A FRANCHISE

Tom Ricketts has made an offer to purchase the Chicago Cubs for $845 million from the Tribune Company. The deal makes sense for Ricketts because the tax breaks will enable him to save $100 million. Section 197 of the Internal Revenue Code allows the cost of a franchise to be amortized over 15 years. Dividing the $845 million purchase price by 15 years produces a $56.3 million deduction against income each year for the next 15 years. If the projected income for the Cubs is about $45 million a year, the $56 million would shelter all of the income and no tax would be due.

Source: Adapted from Josh Peter, "Buying Cubs Could Be a Steal for Ricketts," *Yahoo! Sports*, September 16, 2010.

8.4 AMORTIZATION

LO.7

Identify intangible assets that are eligible for amortization and calculate the amount of the deduction.

Taxpayers can claim an **amortization** deduction on intangible assets called "amortizable § 197 intangibles." The amount of the deduction is determined by amortizing the adjusted basis of such intangibles ratably over a 15-year period beginning in the month in which the intangible is acquired.[37]

An *amortizable § 197 intangible* is any § 197 intangible acquired after August 10, 1993, and held in connection with the conduct of a trade or business or for the production of income. Section 197 intangibles include goodwill and going-concern value, franchises, trademarks, and trade names. Covenants not to compete, copyrights, and patents are also included if they are acquired in connection with the acquisition of a business. Generally, self-created intangibles are not § 197 intangibles. The 15-year amortization period applies regardless of the actual useful life of an amortizable § 197 intangible. No other depreciation or amortization deduction is permitted with respect to any amortizable § 197 intangible except those permitted under the 15-year amortization rules.

EXAMPLE 36

On June 1, 2011, Neil purchased and began operating the Falcon Café. Of the purchase price, $90,000 is correctly allocated to goodwill. The deduction for amortization for 2011 is $3,500 [($90,000/15) × (7/12)]. ■

ETHICS *& Equity*

ALLOCATION OF PURCHASE PRICE TO COVENANT NOT TO COMPETE

Red Corporation and Bernie Jones, an officer of the corporation, signed an agreement that called for $400,000 to be paid to Bernie for the redemption of his stock in Red Corporation and for a covenant not to compete. When Bernie and the corporation negotiated the agreement, neither side called for the $400,000 to be allocated between the stock and the covenant not to compete. The agreement itself specifically stated that the amount to be paid was for the purchase of Bernie's stock. Nothing in the agreement allocated a portion of the payment to the covenant not to compete. Now that the transaction has been completed, Red Corporation is considering unilaterally allocating a portion of the payment to the covenant not to compete so that the allocated amount can be capitalized and amortized under § 197. Evaluate the appropriateness of Red Corporation's plan.

Startup expenditures are also partially amortizable under § 195. This treatment is available only by election.[38] A taxpayer must make this election no later than the time prescribed by law for filing the return for the taxable year in which the trade or business begins.[39] If no election is made, the startup expenditures must be capitalized.[40]

[37] § 197(a).
[38] § 195(b).
[39] § 195(d).
[40] § 195(a).

The elective treatment for startup expenditures allows the taxpayer to deduct the lesser of (1) the amount of startup expenditures with respect to the trade or business or (2) $5,000, reduced, but not below zero, by the amount by which the startup expenditures exceed $50,000. Any startup expenditures not deducted may be amortized ratably over a 180-month period beginning in the month in which the trade or business begins.[41]

EXAMPLE 37

Green Corporation begins business on August 1, 2011. The corporation has startup expenditures of $47,000. If Green Corporation elects § 195, the total amount of startup expenditures that Green Corporation may deduct in 2011 is $6,167, computed as follows:

Deductible amount	$5,000
Amortizable amount {[($47,000 – $5,000)/180] × 5 months}	1,167
Total deduction	$6,167

■

EXAMPLE 38

Assume the same facts as in Example 37, except that the startup expenditures are $53,000. The total deduction for the year 2011 is $3,417, computed as follows:

Deductible amount [$5,000 – ($53,000 – $50,000)]	$2,000
Amortizable amount {[($53,000 – $2,000)/180] × 5 months}	1,417
Total deduction	$3,417

■

Expenditures that are subject to capitalization and elective amortization under § 195 as startup expenditures generally must satisfy two requirements.[42] First, the expenditures must be paid or incurred in connection with any one of the following:

- The creation of an active trade or business.
- The investigation of the creation or acquisition of an active trade or business.
- Any activity engaged in for profit in anticipation of such activity becoming an active trade or business.

Second, such costs must be the kinds of costs that would be currently deductible if paid or incurred in connection with the operation of an existing trade or business in the same field as that entered into by the taxpayer.

The costs of creating a new active trade or business could include advertising; salaries and wages; travel and other expenses incurred in lining up prospective distributors, suppliers, or customers; and salaries and fees for executives, consultants, and professional services. Costs that relate to either created or acquired businesses could include expenses incurred for the analysis or survey of potential markets, products, labor supply, transportation facilities, and the like. Startup expenditures do not include any amount with respect to which a deduction is allowable under § 163(a) (interest), § 164 (taxes), and § 174 (research and experimental expenditures).[43]

Other assets that could be subject to amortization include research and experimental expenditures under § 174 (see Chapter 7) and organizational expenses under § 248.

ETHICS & Equity

Business Expense or Startup Expense?

Mark works as a writer for a local newspaper. Ten years ago he wrote a book about gardening. The book was a moderate success, and he ended up making about $15,000 from sales of the book. During the current year, Mark had $20,000 of expenses in connection with writing a book dealing with soccer. The expenses were for travel, meals, lodging, and research. Mark is considering expensing these items in the current year as trade and business expenses rather than capitalizing and amortizing them as startup expenses. Evaluate the appropriateness of Mark's plan.

[41] §§ 195(b)(1)(A) and (B). For 2010, the $5,000 was increased to $10,000, and the $50,000 was increased to $60,000.

[42] §§ 195(c)(1)(A) and (B).

[43] § 195(c).

TAX *in* the NEWS

DEPLETION OF LANDFILL SITES

Landfill operators are allowed a depletion allowance, which is a deduction in computing Federal taxable income. The depletion deduction is the value of the air space that is being filled up. The value of the air space is the product of some of the goodwill costs, some of the land costs, and all of the engineering, siting, and construction costs.

8.5 DEPLETION

LO.8

Determine the amount of depletion expense including being able to apply the alternative tax treatments for intangible drilling and development costs.

Natural resources (e.g., oil, gas, coal, gravel, timber) are subject to **depletion**, which is simply a form of depreciation applicable to natural resources. Land generally cannot be depleted.

The owner of an interest in the natural resource is entitled to deduct depletion. An owner is one who has an economic interest in the property.[44] An economic interest requires the acquisition of an interest in the resource in place and the receipt of income from the extraction or severance of that resource. Like depreciation, depletion is a deduction *for* adjusted gross income.

Although all natural resources are subject to depletion, oil and gas wells are used as an example in the following paragraphs to illustrate the related costs and issues.

In developing an oil or gas well, the producer must make four types of expenditures:

- Natural resource costs.
- Intangible drilling and development costs.
- Tangible asset costs.
- Operating costs.

Natural resources are physically limited, and the costs to acquire them (e.g., oil under the ground) are, therefore, recovered through depletion. Costs incurred in making the property ready for drilling such as the cost of labor in clearing the property, erecting derricks, and drilling the hole are **intangible drilling and development costs (IDC)**. These costs generally have no salvage value and are a lost cost if the well is dry. Costs for tangible assets such as tools, pipes, and engines are capital in nature. These costs must be capitalized and recovered through depreciation (cost recovery). Costs incurred after the well is producing are operating costs. These costs would include expenditures for such items as labor, fuel, and supplies. Operating costs are deductible when incurred (on the accrual basis) or when paid (on the cash basis).

The expenditures for depreciable assets and operating costs pose no unusual problems for producers of natural resources. The tax treatment of depletable costs and intangible drilling and development costs is quite a different matter.

INTANGIBLE DRILLING AND DEVELOPMENT COSTS (IDC)

Intangible drilling and development costs can be handled in one of two ways at the option of the taxpayer. They can be *either* charged off as an expense in the year in which they are incurred *or* capitalized and written off through depletion. The taxpayer makes the election in the first year such expenditures are incurred either by taking a deduction on the return or by adding them to the depletable basis. No formal statement of intent is required. Once made, the election is binding on both the taxpayer and the IRS for all such expenditures in the future. If the taxpayer fails to make the election to expense IDC on the original timely filed return the first year such expenditures are incurred, an automatic election to capitalize them has been made and is irrevocable.

[44] Reg. § 1.611–1(b).

As a general rule, it is more advantageous to expense IDC. The obvious benefit of an immediate write-off (as opposed to a deferred write-off through depletion) is not the only advantage. Since a taxpayer can use percentage depletion, which is calculated without reference to basis (see Example 42), the IDC may be completely lost as a deduction if they are capitalized.

DEPLETION METHODS

There are two methods of calculating depletion: cost and percentage. Cost depletion can be used on any wasting asset (and is the only method allowed for timber). Percentage depletion is subject to a number of limitations, particularly for oil and gas deposits. Depletion should be calculated both ways, and the method that results in the larger deduction should be used. The choice between cost depletion and percentage depletion is an annual election. Thus, the taxpayer can use cost depletion in one year and percentage depletion in the following year.

Cost Depletion

Cost depletion is determined by using the adjusted basis of the asset.[45] The basis is divided by the estimated recoverable units of the asset (e.g., barrels, tons) to arrive at the depletion per unit. The depletion per unit then is multiplied by the number of units sold (*not* the units produced) during the year to arrive at the cost depletion allowed. Cost depletion, therefore, resembles the units-of-production method of calculating depreciation.

EXAMPLE 39

On January 1, 2011, Pablo purchases the rights to a mineral interest for $1 million. At that time, the remaining recoverable units in the mineral interest are estimated to be 200,000. The depletion per unit is $5 [$1,000,000 (adjusted basis) ÷ 200,000 (estimated recoverable units)]. If during the year 60,000 units are mined and 25,000 are sold, the cost depletion is $125,000 [$5 (depletion per unit) × 25,000 (units sold)]. ■

If the taxpayer later discovers that the original estimate was incorrect, the depletion per unit for future calculations must be redetermined based on the revised estimate.[46]

EXAMPLE 40

Assume the same facts as in Example 39. In 2012, Pablo realizes that an incorrect estimate was made. The remaining recoverable units now are determined to be 400,000. Based on this new information, the revised depletion per unit is $2.1875 [$875,000 (adjusted basis) ÷ 400,000 (estimated recoverable units)]. Note that the adjusted basis is the original cost ($1,000,000) reduced by the depletion claimed in 2011 ($125,000). If 30,000 units are sold in 2012, the depletion for the year is $65,625 [$2.1875 (depletion per unit) × 30,000 (units sold)]. ■

Percentage Depletion

Percentage depletion (also referred to as statutory depletion) is a specified percentage provided for in the Code. The percentage varies according to the type of mineral interest involved. A sample of these percentages is shown in Exhibit 8.3. The rate is applied to the gross income from the property, but in no event may percentage depletion exceed 50 percent of the taxable income from the property before the allowance for depletion.[47]

[45] § 612.

[46] § 611(a).

[47] § 613(a). Special rules apply for certain oil and gas wells under § 613A (e.g., the 50% ceiling is replaced with a 100% ceiling, and the percentage depletion may not exceed 65% of the taxpayer's taxable income from all sources before the allowance for depletion).

GLOBAL *Tax Issues*

Is an Additional Natural Resource Tax Good for Australia?

How can the Australian Federal government reap billions of dollars of new revenue? It proposes to do so by imposing additional taxes on the natural resource industry. Under the proposal, taxes will be increased on wealthy mining companies while those on smaller companies will be reduced.

Imposing additional taxes would supposedly result in two benefits. First, additional revenue would be provided to the Federal government. Second, corporate taxes could be cut, enabling Australia to be more globally competitive.

Opponents such as Scott Driscoll, national president of the United Retail Foundation, believe that these supposed benefits will never materialize. Xstrata PLC, the Anglo-Swiss mining giant, has indicated its disappointment with the tax-overhaul plan. According to Xstrata CEO Mick Davis, under the plan Australia would have the highest taxes on the mineral sector of any country in the world when the 40 percent tax on profits is included.

Source: Adapted from Rachel Pannett, "Australia Plans New Resource Tax," *Wall Street Journal*, May 3, 2010, p. A15; and Neil Sands, "Xstrata Objects to Australian Tax," *Wall Street Journal*, May 3, 2010, p. B3.

EXHIBIT 8.3 **Sample of Percentage Depletion Rates**

22% Depletion	
Cobalt	Sulfur
Lead	Tin
Nickel	Uranium
Platinum	Zinc
15% Depletion	
Copper	Oil and gas
Gold	Oil shale
Iron	Silver
14% Depletion	
Borax	Magnesium carbonates
Calcium carbonates	Marble
Granite	Potash
Limestone	Slate
10% Depletion	
Coal	Perlite
Lignite	Sodium chloride
5% Depletion	
Gravel	Pumice
Peat	Sand

EXAMPLE 41

Assuming gross income of $100,000, a depletion rate of 22%, and other expenses relating to the property of $60,000, the depletion allowance is determined as follows:

Gross income	$100,000
Less: Other expenses	(60,000)
Taxable income before depletion	$ 40,000
Depletion allowance [the lesser of $22,000 (22% × $100,000) or $20,000 (50% × $40,000)]	(20,000)
Taxable income after depletion	$ 20,000

The adjusted basis of the property is reduced by $20,000, the depletion allowed. If the other expenses had been only $55,000, the full $22,000 could have been deducted, and the adjusted basis would have been reduced by $22,000. ■

Note that percentage depletion is based on a percentage of the gross income from the property and makes no reference to cost. Thus, when percentage depletion is used, it is possible to deduct more than the original cost of the property. If percentage depletion is used, however, the adjusted basis of the property (for computing cost depletion) must be reduced by the amount of percentage depletion taken until the adjusted basis reaches zero. See Example 45.

Effect of Intangible Drilling Costs on Depletion

The treatment of IDC has an effect on the depletion deduction in two ways. If the costs are capitalized, the basis for cost depletion is increased. As a consequence, the cost depletion is increased. If IDC are expensed, they reduce the taxable income from the property. This reduction may result in application of the provision that limits depletion to 50 percent (100 percent for certain oil and gas wells) of taxable income before deducting depletion.

EXAMPLE 42

Iris purchased the rights to an oil interest for $1 million. The recoverable barrels were estimated to be 200,000. During the year, 50,000 barrels were sold for $2 million. Regular expenses amounted to $800,000, and IDC were $650,000. If the IDC are capitalized, the depletion per unit is $8.25 ($1,000,000 + $650,000 ÷ 200,000 barrels), and the following taxable income results:

Gross income	$2,000,000
Less: Expenses	(800,000)
Taxable income before depletion	$1,200,000
Cost depletion ($8.25 × 50,000) = $412,500	
Percentage depletion (15% × $2,000,000) = $300,000	
Greater of cost or percentage depletion	(412,500)
Taxable income	$ 787,500

If the IDC are expensed, the taxable income is $250,000, calculated as follows:

Gross income	$ 2,000,000
Less: Expenses, including IDC	(1,450,000)
Taxable income before depletion	$ 550,000
Cost depletion [($1,000,000 ÷ 200,000 barrels) × 50,000 barrels] = $250,000	
Percentage depletion (15% of $2,000,000 = $300,000, limited to 100% of $550,000 taxable income before depletion) = $300,000	
Greater of cost or percentage depletion	(300,000)
Taxable income	$ 250,000

■

For further restrictions on the use or availability of the percentage depletion method, see § 613.

TAX PLANNING:

8.6 Cost Recovery

LO.9

Identify tax planning opportunities for cost recovery, amortization, and depletion.

Cost recovery schedules should be reviewed annually for possible retirements, abandonments, and obsolescence.

EXAMPLE 43

An examination of the cost recovery schedule of Eagle Company reveals the following:

- Asset A was abandoned when it was discovered that the cost of repairs would be in excess of the cost of replacement. Asset A had an adjusted basis of $3,000.
- Asset J became obsolete this year, at which point, its adjusted basis was $8,000.

Assets A and J should be written off for an additional expense of $11,000 ($3,000 + $8,000). ■

Because of the deductions for cost recovery, interest, and ad valorem property taxes, investments in real estate can be highly attractive. In figuring the economics of such investments, one should be sure to take into account any tax savings that result.

EXAMPLE 44

THE BIG PICTURE

Return to the facts of *The Big Picture* on p. 8-2. In early January 2010, Dr. Payne purchased residential rental property for $170,000 (of which $20,000 was allocated to the land and $150,000 to the building). He made a down payment of $25,000 and assumed the seller's mortgage for the balance. Under the mortgage agreement, monthly payments of $1,000 are required and are applied toward interest, taxes, insurance, and principal. Since the property was already occupied, Dr. Payne continued to receive rent of $1,200 per month from the tenant. He actively participates in this activity and hence comes under the special rule for a rental real estate activity with respect to the limitation on passive activity losses (refer to Chapter 11). He is in the 28% tax bracket.

During 2011, Dr. Payne's expenses were as follows:

Interest	$10,000
Taxes	800
Insurance	1,000
Repairs and maintenance	2,200
Depreciation ($150,000 × .03636)	5,454
Total	$19,454

The deductible loss from the rental property is computed as follows:

Rent income ($1,200 × 12 months)	$ 14,400
Less expenses (see above)	(19,454)
Net loss	($ 5,054)

But what is Dr. Payne's overall position for the year when the tax benefit of the loss is taken into account? Considering just the cash intake and outlay, it is summarized below:

Intake—		
Rent income	$14,400	
Tax savings [28% (income tax bracket) × $5,054 (loss from the property)]	1,415	$ 15,815
Outlay—		
Mortgage payments ($1,000 × 12 months)	$12,000	
Repairs and maintenance	2,200	(14,200)
Net cash benefit		$ 1,615

■

It should be noted, however, that should Dr. Payne cease being an active participant in the rental activity, the passive activity loss rules would apply, and Dr. Payne could lose the current period benefit of the loss.

Another consideration when making decisions with respect to cost recovery is whether fast or slow cost recovery will be more beneficial for the taxpayer. If the taxpayer's goal is to recover the cost of fixed assets as quickly as possible, the following strategies should be used:

- When constructing a facility, try to avoid "fixture" classification. Refer to the discussion in Chapter 1 on p. 1–7.
- When electing § 179 expensing, choose assets with longer lives.
- Choose accelerated cost recovery methods where available.

If a taxpayer has a new business with little income or a business with a net operating loss carryover, the taxpayer's goal may be to slow down cost recovery. In such a situation, the taxpayer should:

- Elect not to take additional first-year depreciation.
- Choose the straight-line cost recovery method.
- Make no election under § 179.
- Defer placing assets in service in the current tax year or postpone capital outlays until future tax years.

8.7 Amortization

When a business is purchased, goodwill and covenants not to compete are both subject to a statutory amortization period of 15 years. Therefore, the purchaser does not derive any tax benefits when part of the purchase price is assigned to a covenant rather than to goodwill.

Thus, from the purchaser's perspective, bargaining for a covenant should be based on legal rather than tax reasons. Note, however, that from the seller's perspective, goodwill is a capital asset and the covenant is an ordinary income asset.

Since the amortization period for both goodwill and a covenant is 15 years, the purchaser may want to attempt to minimize these amounts if the purchase price can be assigned to assets with shorter lives (e.g., inventory, receivables, and personalty). Conversely, the purchaser may want to attempt to maximize these amounts if part of the purchase price will otherwise be assigned to assets with longer recovery periods (e.g., realty) or to assets not eligible for cost recovery (e.g., land).

8.8 Depletion

While a basis remains in a depletable asset, cost depletion or percentage depletion, whichever method produces the larger deduction, will be used. When the basis of the asset is exhausted, percentage depletion can still be taken.

EXAMPLE 45

Assume the following facts for Melissa:

Remaining depletable basis	$ 11,000
Gross income (10,000 units)	100,000
Expenses (other than depletion)	30,000

Since cost depletion is limited to the basis of $11,000 and if the percentage depletion is $22,000 (assume a 22% rate), Melissa would choose the latter. Her basis is then reduced to zero. In future years, however, she can continue to take percentage depletion since percentage depletion is taken without reference to the remaining basis. ■

The election to expense intangible drilling and development costs is a one-time election. Once the election is made to either expense or capitalize the IDC, it is binding on all future expenditures. The permanent nature of the election makes it extremely important for the taxpayer to determine which treatment will provide the greater tax advantage. (Refer to Example 42 for an illustration of the effect of using the two different alternatives for a given set of facts.)

8.9 Cost Recovery Tables

Summary of Tables

Table 8.1	Modified ACRS statutory percentage table for personalty. Applicable depreciation methods: 200 or 150 percent declining-balance switching to straight-line. Applicable recovery periods: 3, 5, 7, 10, 15, 20 years. Applicable convention: half-year.
Table 8.2	Modified ACRS statutory percentage table for personalty. Applicable depreciation method: 200 percent declining-balance switching to straight-line. Applicable recovery periods: 3, 5, 7 years. Applicable convention: mid-quarter.
Table 8.3	Modified ACRS optional straight-line table for personalty. Applicable depreciation method: straight-line. Applicable recovery periods: 3, 5, 7, 10, 15, 20 years. Applicable convention: half-year.
Table 8.4	Alternative minimum tax declining-balance table for personalty. Applicable depreciation method: 150 percent declining-balance switching to straight-line. Applicable recovery periods: 3, 5, 7, 9.5, 10, 12 years. Applicable convention: half-year.
Table 8.5	Alternative depreciation system straight-line table for personalty. Applicable depreciation method: straight-line. Applicable recovery periods: 5, 10, 12 years. Applicable convention: half-year.
Table 8.6	Modified ACRS straight-line table for realty. Applicable depreciation method: straight-line. Applicable recovery periods: 27.5, 31.5, 39 years. Applicable convention: mid-month.
Table 8.7	Alternative depreciation system straight-line table for realty. Applicable depreciation method: straight-line. Applicable recovery period: 40 years. Applicable convention: mid-month.

TABLE 8.1 MACRS Accelerated Depreciation for Personal Property Assuming Half-Year Convention

For Property Placed in Service after December 31, 1986

Recovery Year	3-Year (200% DB)	5-Year (200% DB)	7-Year (200% DB)	10-Year (200% DB)	15-Year (150% DB)	20-Year (150% DB)
1	33.33	20.00	14.29	10.00	5.00	3.750
2	44.45	32.00	24.49	18.00	9.50	7.219
3	14.81*	19.20	17.49	14.40	8.55	6.677
4	7.41	11.52*	12.49	11.52	7.70	6.177
5		11.52	8.93*	9.22	6.93	5.713
6		5.76	8.92	7.37	6.23	5.285
7			8.93	6.55*	5.90*	4.888
8			4.46	6.55	5.90	4.522
9				6.56	5.91	4.462*
10				6.55	5.90	4.461
11				3.28	5.91	4.462
12					5.90	4.461
13					5.91	4.462
14					5.90	4.461
15					5.91	4.462
16					2.95	4.461
17						4.462
18						4.461
19						4.462
20						4.461
21						2.231

*Switchover to straight-line depreciation.

TABLE 8.2 MACRS Accelerated Depreciation for Personal Property Assuming Mid-Quarter Convention

For Property Placed in Service after December 31, 1986 (Partial Table*)

Recovery Year	First Quarter	*3-Year* Second Quarter	Third Quarter	Fourth Quarter
1	58.33	41.67	25.00	8.33
2	27.78	38.89	50.00	61.11
Recovery Year	**First Quarter**	***5-Year* Second Quarter**	**Third Quarter**	**Fourth Quarter**
1	35.00	25.00	15.00	5.00
2	26.00	30.00	34.00	38.00
Recovery Year	**First Quarter**	***7-Year* Second Quarter**	**Third Quarter**	**Fourth Quarter**
1	25.00	17.85	10.71	3.57
2	21.43	23.47	25.51	27.55

*The figures in this table are taken from the official tables that appear in Rev.Proc. 87–57, 1987–2 C.B. 687. Because of their length, the complete tables are not presented.

TABLE 8.3 **MACRS Straight-Line Depreciation for Personal Property Assuming Half-Year Convention***

For Property Placed in Service after December 31, 1986

MACRS Class	% First Recovery Year	Other Recovery Years		Last Recovery Year	
		Years	%	Year	%
3-year	16.67	2–3	33.33	4	16.67
5-year	10.00	2–5	20.00	6	10.00
7-year	7.14	2–7	14.29	8	7.14
10-year	5.00	2–10	10.00	11	5.00
15-year	3.33	2–15	6.67	16	3.33
20-year	2.50	2–20	5.00	21	2.50

*The official table contains a separate row for each year. For ease of presentation, certain years are grouped in this table. In some instances, this will produce a difference of .01 for the last digit when compared with the official table.

TABLE 8.4 **Alternative Minimum Tax: 150% Declining-Balance Assuming Half-Year Convention**

For Property Placed in Service after December 31, 1986 (Partial Table*)

Recovery Year	3-Year 150%	5-Year 150%	7-Year 150%	9.5-Year 150%	10-Year 150%	12-Year 150%
1	25.00	15.00	10.71	7.89	7.50	6.25
2	37.50	25.50	19.13	14.54	13.88	11.72
3	25.00**	17.85	15.03	12.25	11.79	10.25
4	12.50	16.66**	12.25**	10.31	10.02	8.97
5		16.66	12.25	9.17**	8.74**	7.85
6		8.33	12.25	9.17	8.74	7.33**
7			12.25	9.17	8.74	7.33
8			6.13	9.17	8.74	7.33
9				9.17	8.74	7.33
10				9.16	8.74	7.33
11					4.37	7.32
12						7.33
13						3.66

*The figures in this table are taken from the official table that appears in Rev.Proc. 87–57, 1987–2 C.B. 687. Because of its length, the complete table is not presented.
**Switchover to straight-line depreciation.

TABLE 8.5 ADS Straight-Line for Personal Property Assuming Half-Year Convention

For Property Placed in Service after December 31, 1986 (Partial Table)*

Recovery Year	5-Year Class	10-Year Class	12-Year Class
1	10.00	5.00	4.17
2	20.00	10.00	8.33
3	20.00	10.00	8.33
4	20.00	10.00	8.33
5	20.00	10.00	8.33
6	10.00	10.00	8.33
7		10.00	8.34
8		10.00	8.33
9		10.00	8.34
10		10.00	8.33
11		5.00	8.34
12			8.33
13			4.17

*The figures in this table are taken from the official table that appears in Rev.Proc. 87–57, 1987–2 C.B. 687. Because of its length, the complete table is not presented. The tables for the mid-quarter convention also appear in Rev.Proc. 87–57.

TABLE 8.6 MACRS Straight-Line Depreciation for Real Property Assuming Mid-Month Convention*

For Property Placed in Service after December 31, 1986: 27.5-Year Residential Real Property

Recovery Year(s)	The Applicable Percentage Is (Use the Column for the Month in the First Year the Property Is Placed in Service): 1	2	3	4	5	6	7	8	9	10	11	12
1	3.485	3.182	2.879	2.576	2.273	1.970	1.667	1.364	1.061	0.758	0.455	0.152
2–18	3.636	3.636	3.636	3.636	3.636	3.636	3.636	3.636	3.636	3.636	3.636	3.636
19–27	3.637	3.637	3.637	3.637	3.637	3.637	3.637	3.637	3.637	3.637	3.637	3.637
28	1.970	2.273	2.576	2.879	3.182	3.485	3.636	3.636	3.636	3.636	3.636	3.636
29	0.000	0.000	0.000	0.000	0.000	0.000	0.152	0.455	0.758	1.061	1.364	1.667

For Property Placed in Service after December 31, 1986, and before May 13, 1993: 31.5-Year Nonresidential Real Property

Recovery Year(s)	The Applicable Percentage Is (Use the Column for the Month in the First Year the Property Is Placed in Service): 1	2	3	4	5	6	7	8	9	10	11	12
1	3.042	2.778	2.513	2.249	1.984	1.720	1.455	1.190	0.926	0.661	0.397	0.132
2–19	3.175	3.175	3.175	3.175	3.175	3.175	3.175	3.175	3.175	3.175	3.175	3.175
20–31	3.174	3.174	3.174	3.174	3.174	3.174	3.174	3.174	3.174	3.174	3.174	3.174
32	1.720	1.984	2.249	2.513	2.778	3.042	3.175	3.175	3.175	3.175	3.175	3.175
33	0.000	0.000	0.000	0.000	0.000	0.000	0.132	0.397	0.661	0.926	1.190	1.455

For Property Placed in Service after May 12, 1993: 39-Year Nonresidential Real Property

Recovery Year(s)	The Applicable Percentage Is (Use the Column for the Month in the First Year the Property Is Placed in Service): 1	2	3	4	5	6	7	8	9	10	11	12
1	2.461	2.247	2.033	1.819	1.605	1.391	1.177	0.963	0.749	0.535	0.321	0.107
2–39	2.564	2.564	2.564	2.564	2.564	2.564	2.564	2.564	2.564	2.564	2.564	2.564
40	0.107	0.321	0.535	0.749	0.963	1.177	1.391	1.605	1.819	2.033	2.247	2.461

*The official tables contain a separate row for each year. For ease of presentation, certain years are grouped in these tables. In some instances, this will produce a difference of .001 for the last digit when compared with the official tables.

TABLE 8.7 ADS Straight-Line for Real Property Assuming Mid-Month Convention

For Property Placed in Service after December 31, 1986

Recovery Year	Month Placed in Service											
	1	2	3	4	5	6	7	8	9	10	11	12
1	2.396	2.188	1.979	1.771	1.563	1.354	1.146	0.938	0.729	0.521	0.313	0.104
2–40	2.500	2.500	2.500	2.500	2.500	2.500	2.500	2.500	2.500	2.500	2.500	2.500
41	0.104	0.312	0.521	0.729	0.937	1.146	1.354	1.562	1.771	1.979	2.187	2.396

REFOCUS ON THE BIG PICTURE

CALCULATION OF DEPRECIATION EXPENSE AND TAX PLANNING

Regardless of whether the accrual method or the cash method of accounting is used, MACRS must be used in calculating the depreciation expense for fixed assets for tax purposes. Evidently, Dr. Payne's financial reporting system uses MACRS because $91,298 is the correct amount of depreciation expense. The computers and peripheral equipment are five-year property. The office furniture and fixtures and the dental equipment are seven-year property. Based on the IRS cost recovery tables, the following percentages are used in calculating depreciation expense for the first year of each asset's life:

5-year property	20.00%
7-year property	14.29%

Dr. Payne will also be able to deduct depreciation on the house he converted from personal use to rental use and on the rental house that he purchased.

What If?

From a tax planning perspective, what can Dr. Payne do to increase the amount of depreciation expense associated with the purchase of these fixed assets and thereby reduce the amount of business net income reported on Schedule C of Form 1040 for his dental practice?

In addition to the standard MACRS deduction using the aforementioned percentages for 2011, § 179 provides for the limited expensing of fixed assets. This provision applies to personalty, but does not apply to realty (e.g., buildings). The maximum amount that can be deducted under this limited expensing provision is subject to several overall limits. First, the total amount deducted cannot exceed $500,000. Second, the $500,000 amount is reduced dollar-for-dollar for § 179 asset purchases placed in service during the tax year once such purchases exceed $2 million. Finally, the § 179 deduction for a tax year cannot exceed the taxable income from the trade or business.

If Dr. Payne elects § 179 treatment for some of the fixed asset purchases of his dental practice, he could reduce the Schedule C net income of his dental practice to $0. The remaining amount of the $612,085 purchases of § 179 assets not deducted in the current year would be eligible for MACRS depreciation in future years.

For future reference associated with similar fixed asset purchases for his business, the sequence of calculating the deduction is as follows:

- § 179 limited expensing.
- Additional first-year depreciation.
- Standard MACRS cost recovery.

KEY TERMS

Accelerated cost recovery system (ACRS), 8–22
Additional first-year depreciation, 8–8
Alternative depreciation system (ADS), 8–20
Amortization, 8–23
Cost depletion, 8–26
Cost recovery, 8–3
Depletion, 8–25
Depreciation, 8–3
Half-year convention, 8–7
Intangible drilling and development costs (IDC), 8–25
Listed property, 8–16
Mid-month convention, 8–10
Mid-quarter convention, 8–9
Modified accelerated cost recovery system (MACRS), 8–5
Percentage depletion, 8–26
Residential rental real estate, 8–10
Section 179 expensing, 8–13
Startup expenditures, 8–23

DISCUSSION QUESTIONS

1. **LO.1** Discuss whether property that is classified as personalty is subject to cost recovery.

2. **LO.1** If a taxpayer does not take any cost recovery on an asset during the year, what will be the impact on the basis of the asset?

3. **LO.1** Discuss whether land improvements are eligible for cost recovery.

ISSUE ID

4. **LO.2** At the beginning of the current year, Henry purchased a ski resort for $10 million. Henry does not own the land on which the resort is located. The Federal government owns the land, and Henry has the right to operate the resort on the land pursuant to Special Use Permits, which are terminable at will by the Federal government, and Term Special Use Permits, which allow the land to be used for a fixed number of years. In preparing the income tax return for the current year, Henry properly allocated $2 million of the purchase price to the costs of constructing mountain roads, slopes, and trails. Since the acquisition, Henry has spent an additional $1 million on maintaining the mountain roads, slopes, and trails. Identify the relevant tax issues for Henry.

5. **LO.2** Discuss whether the date an asset is purchased is important in determining whether the mid-quarter convention applies for personalty.

6. **LO.2** Discuss the actual recovery period for the cost of an asset if the half-year convention applies.

7. **LO.2** Discuss the computation of cost recovery in the year an asset is placed in service when the half-year convention is being used.

8. **LO.2** Discuss whether the acquisition of real property affects the 40% test to determine whether the mid-quarter convention must be used.

9. **LO.2** Discuss the computation of cost recovery in the year of sale of an asset when the mid-quarter convention is being used.

10. **LO.2** Discuss the mid-month convention.

11. **LO.2** Robert purchased and placed in service $100,000 of seven-year class assets on August 10 of the current year. He also purchased and placed in service $500,000 of five-year class assets on November 15 of the current year. He elects not to take additional first-year depreciation. If Robert elects to use the MACRS straight-line method of cost recovery on the seven-year class assets, discuss the calculation of cost recovery for the five-year class assets.

12. **LO.2** Discuss the general cost recovery method and period for new farm machinery placed in service in 2011.

13. **LO.2** Discuss the applicable convention for farming assets if an election is made to not have the uniform capitalization rules apply.

ISSUE ID

14. **LO.2** Jim owns a very large ranch. A large part of his business is the production and raising of breeding cattle. Jim understands that under MACRS he is entitled to cost recovery on breeding cattle. Identify the relevant tax issues for Jim with respect to taking cost recovery on his self-produced breeding cattle.

15. **LO.2** Discuss the cost recovery periods and methods to be used on leasehold improvement property owned by the lessor.

16. **LO.2** Discuss the cost recovery periods and methods to be used on qualified leasehold improvement property owned by the lessee.

17. **LO.2** Discuss the tax treatment for the unrecovered basis in leasehold property owned by the lessee when the lease terminates.

18. **LO.3** Discuss whether § 179 expensing may be taken on qualified leasehold improvement real property.

19. **LO.3** Explain how the § 179 limited expensing deduction affects the computation of MACRS cost recovery.

20. **LO.3** Discuss the treatment of a § 179 expensing carryforward.

21. **LO.3** Discuss the definition of *taxable income* as it is used in limiting the § 179 expensing amount.

22. **LO.2, 3** A professional consulting business sells professional tools and equipment and provides associated services, such as repair and maintenance, to its customer base. The company's employees include technicians, who are required to provide and maintain their own tools and equipment for performing the repairs and maintenance work. The company will reimburse a technician for amounts spent to purchase tools and equipment eligible for a § 179 deduction up to a set amount each year. Any costs for tools and equipment that exceed the set amount will not be reimbursed. John is a technician for the company. During the current year, he purchased equipment that qualifies for the § 179 deduction. John paid $50,000 for the equipment and was reimbursed the set amount of $40,000. Identify the relevant tax issues for John with respect to § 179 and the computation of his taxable income. **ISSUE ID**

23. **LO.3, 4** Discuss the implications of an automobile used in a trade or business having a gross vehicle weight (GVW) exceeding 6,000 pounds.

24. **LO.4** Discuss how the limits on cost recovery apply to listed property.

25. **LO.4** Discuss the purpose of the lease inclusion amount and explain how it is determined with respect to leased passenger automobiles.

26. **LO.7** Explain the amortization period of a § 197 intangible if the actual useful life is less than 15 years.

27. **LO.7** Harold and Bart own 75% of the stock of Orange Motors. The other 25% of the stock is owned by Jeb. Orange Motors entered into an agreement with Harold and Bart to acquire all of their stock in Orange Motors. In addition, Harold and Bart signed a noncompete agreement with Orange Motors. Under the terms of the noncompete agreement, Orange will pay Harold and Bart $15,000 each per year for four years. Identify the relevant tax issues for Orange Motors. **ISSUE ID**

28. **LO.7** Discuss the amortization of startup expenditures.

29. **LO.7** In May 2011, George began searching for a trade or business to acquire. In anticipation of finding a suitable aquisition, George hired an investment banker to evaluate three potential businesses. He also hired a law firm to begin drafting regulatory approval documents for a target company. Eventually, George decided to purchase all the assets of Blue Corporation. Blue Corporation and George entered into an acquisition agreement on December 1, 2011. Identify the relevant tax issues for George. **ISSUE ID**

30. **LO.8** Discuss how the cost of mineral rights enters into the calculation of percentage depletion.

PROBLEMS

31. **LO.1, 2** On November 4, 2009, Blue Company acquired an asset (27.5-year residential real property) for $200,000 for use in its business. In 2009 and 2010, respectively, Blue took $642 and $5,128 of cost recovery. These amounts were incorrect because Blue

applied the wrong percentages (i.e., those for 39-year rather than 27.5-year). Blue should have taken $910 and $7,272 cost recovery in 2009 and 2010. On January 1, 2011, the asset was sold for $180,000. Calculate the gain or loss on the sale of the asset in 2011.

32. **LO.1, 2** José purchased a house for $300,000 in 2008. He used the house as his personal residence. In March 2011, when the fair market value of the house was $250,000, he converted the house to rental property. What is José's cost recovery for 2011?

33. **LO.2** Orange Corporation acquired new office furniture on August 15, 2011, for $130,000. Orange did not elect immediate expensing under § 179. Orange elects not to take additional first-year depreciation. Determine Orange's cost recovery for 2011.

34. **LO.2** Weston acquires a used office machine (seven-year class asset) on November 2, 2011, for $75,000. This is the only asset acquired by Weston during the year. He does not elect immediate expensing under § 179. On September 15, 2012, Weston sells the machine.
    a. Determine Weston's cost recovery for 2011.
    b. Determine Weston's cost recovery for 2012.

35. **LO.2** Juan acquires a new five-year class asset on March 14, 2011, for $150,000. This is the only asset acquired by Juan during the year. He does not elect immediate expensing under § 179. He elects not to take additional first-year depreciation. On July 15, 2012, Juan sells the asset.
    a. Determine Juan's cost recovery for 2011.
    b. Determine Juan's cost recovery for 2012.

36. **LO.2** Debra acquired the following new assets during the current year:

Date	Asset	Cost
April 11	Furniture	$40,000
July 28	Trucks	40,000
November 3	Computers	70,000

Determine the cost recovery for the current year. Debra does not elect immediate expensing under § 179. She elects not to take additional first-year depreciation.

37. **LO.2** On August 2, 2011, Wendy purchased a new office building for $3.7 million. On October 1, 2011, she began to rent out office space in the building. On July 15, 2015, Wendy sold the office building.
    a. Determine Wendy's cost recovery for 2011.
    b. Determine Wendy's cost recovery for 2015.

38. **LO.2** On April 3, 2011, Terry purchased and placed in service a building. The building cost $2 million. An appraisal determined that 25% of the total cost was attributed to the value of the land. The bottom floor of the building is leased to a retail business for $32,000. The other floors of the building are rental apartments with an annual rent of $160,000. Determine Terry's cost recovery for 2011.

39. **LO.2** On May 5, 2011, Christy purchased and placed in service a hotel. The hotel cost $1.8 million. Calculate Christy's cost recovery for 2011. For 2021.

40. **LO.2** Janice acquired an apartment building on June 4, 2011, for $1.6 million. The value of the land is $300,000. Janice sold the apartment building on November 29, 2017.
    a. Determine Janice's cost recovery for 2011.
    b. Determine Janice's cost recovery for 2017.

41. **LO.2** On April 20, 2011, Ralph purchased new equipment to be used in his farming business. The cost of the equipment is $150,000. Ralph does not elect immediate expensing under § 179; nor does he elect to not have the uniform capitalization rules apply. Compute Ralph's cost recovery for 2011.

42. **LO.2** During the month of March 2011, Sam constructed agricultural fences on his farm. The cost of the fencing was $70,000. Sam does not elect immediate expensing under § 179, but an election to not have the uniform capitalization rules apply is in effect. Compute Sam's cost recovery for 2011.

43. **LO.2** As a condition of leasing a 10-year-old warehouse, Martha had to make capital improvements to the building to accommodate the lessee. These improvements cost Martha $300,000. The improvements were completed and the 10-year lease commenced on October 28, 2011. Martha elects not to deduct any amount under § 179 nor take additional first-year depreciation. Determine Martha's cost recovery for 2011 with respect to the leasehold improvement.

44. **LO.2** On January 1, 2004, Jim leased a building to be used in his business as an office building. The lease will terminate on December 31, 2011. On February 2, 2005, Jim made a capital improvement to the building. The cost of the leasehold improvement to Jim was $80,000. Jim has no legal rights in the capital improvement after the termination of the lease. Determine Jim's loss in 2011, if any, with respect to the leasehold improvement as a result of the termination of the lease.

45. **LO.2, 3, 9** Lori, who is single, purchased five-year class property for $150,000 and seven-year class property for $400,000 on May 20, 2011. Lori expects the taxable income derived from her business (without regard to the amount expensed under § 179) to be about $800,000. Lori wants to elect immediate § 179 expensing, but she doesn't know which asset she should expense under § 179. She elects not to take additional first-year depreciation.

DECISION MAKING

   a. Determine Lori's total deduction if the § 179 expense is first taken with respect to the five-year class asset.
   b. Determine Lori's total deduction if the § 179 expense is first taken with respect to the seven-year class asset.
   c. What is your advice to Lori?

46. **LO.2, 3** Olga is the proprietor of a small business. In 2011, the business income, before consideration of any cost recovery or § 179 deduction, is $750,000. Olga spends $2,050,000 on new seven-year class assets and elects to take the § 179 deduction on them. She elects not to take additional first-year depreciation. Olga's cost recovery deduction for 2011, except for the cost recovery with respect to the new seven-year assets, is $95,000. Determine Olga's total cost recovery for 2011 with respect to the seven-year assets and the amount of any § 179 carryforward.

47. **LO.2, 3, 9** On June 5, 2011, Dan purchased and placed in service a seven-year class asset costing $150,000. On July 10, Dan placed in service qualified leasehold improvement property on a commercial building that cost $350,000. Dan does not take additional first-year depreciation. Determine Dan's total cost recovery deduction with respect to these two assets.

48. **LO.3, 4** John Johnson is considering acquiring an automobile at the beginning of 2011 that he will use 100% of the time as a taxi. The purchase price of the automobile is $35,000. John has heard of cost recovery limits on automobiles and wants to know how much of the $35,000 he can deduct in the first year. Write a letter to John in which you present your calculations. Also, prepare a memo for the tax files. John's address is 100 Morningside, Clinton, MS 39058.

COMMUNICATIONS

49. **LO.2, 4** On October 15, 2011, Jon purchased and placed in service a used car. The purchase price was $25,000. This was the only business use asset Jon acquired in 2011. He used the car 80% of the time for business and 20% for personal use. Jon used the statutory percentage method of cost recovery. He elects not to take additional first-year depreciation. Calculate the total deduction Jon may take for 2011 with respect to the car.

50. **LO.4** On June 5, 2011, Leo purchased and placed in service a new car that cost $20,000. The business use percentage for the car is always 100%. He elects not to take additional first-year depreciation. Compute Leo's cost recovery deduction in 2011 and 2012.

51. **LO.2, 3, 4** On March 15, 2011, Helen purchased and placed in service a new Escalade. The purchase price was $62,000, and the vehicle had a rating of 6,500 GVW. The vehicle was used 100% for business.
   a. Calculate the maximum total deduction Helen may take with respect to the vehicle in 2011.
   b. How would your answer above change if Helen elected not to take additional first-year depreciation?

52. **LO.2, 4** On May 28, 2011, Mary purchased and placed in service a new $20,000 car. The car was used 60% for business, 20% for production of income, and 20% for personal use in 2011. In 2012, the usage changed to 40% for business, 30% for production of income, and

30% for personal use. Mary did not elect immediate expensing under § 179. She elects not to take additional first-year depreciation. Compute the cost recovery and any cost recovery recapture in 2012.

DECISION MAKING

53. **LO.2, 4, 9** Sally purchased a new computer (five-year property) on June 1, 2011, for $4,000. Sally could use the computer 100% of the time in her business, or she could allow her family to also use the computer. Sally estimates that if her family uses the computer, the business use will be 45% and the personal use will be 55%. Determine the tax cost to Sally, in the year of acquisition, of allowing her family to use the computer. Assume that Sally would not elect § 179 limited expensing and that her marginal tax rate is 28%. She elects not to take additional first-year depreciation.

DECISION MAKING

COMMUNICATIONS

54. **LO.2, 4, 9** Dennis Harding is considering acquiring a new automobile that he will use 100% for business. The purchase price of the automobile would be $35,000. If Dennis leased the car for five years, the lease payments would be $375 per month. Dennis will acquire the car on January 1, 2011. The inclusion dollar amounts from the IRS table for the next five years are $40, $87, $130, $156, and $179. Dennis desires to know the effect on his adjusted gross income of purchasing versus leasing the car for the next five years. He elects not to take additional first-year depreciation. Write a letter to Dennis and present your calculations. Also, prepare a memo for the tax files. His address is 150 Avenue I, Memphis, TN 38112.

55. **LO.2, 5** In 2011, Muhammad purchased a new computer for $16,000. The computer is used 100% for business. Muhammad did not make a § 179 election with respect to the computer. He elects not to take additional first-year depreciation. If Muhammad uses the statutory percentage method, determine his cost recovery deduction for 2011 for computing taxable income and for computing his alternative minimum tax.

DECISION MAKING

56. **LO.2, 5, 9** Jamie purchased $100,000 of new office furniture for her business in June of the current year. Jamie understands that if she elects to use ADS to compute her regular income tax, there will be no difference between the cost recovery for computing the regular income tax and the AMT. Jamie wants to know the *regular* income tax cost, after three years, of using ADS rather than MACRS. Assume that Jamie does not elect § 179 limited expensing and that her marginal tax rate is 28%. She elects not to take additional first-year depreciation.

DECISION MAKING

COMMUNICATIONS

57. **LO.2, 7, 9** Mike Saxon is negotiating the purchase of a business. The final purchase price has been agreed upon, but the allocation of the purchase price to the assets is still being discussed. Appraisals on a warehouse range from $1.2 million to $1.5 million. If a value of $1.2 million is used for the warehouse, the remainder of the purchase price, $800,000, will be allocated to goodwill. If $1.5 million is allocated to the warehouse, goodwill will be $500,000. Mike wants to know what effect each alternative will have on cost recovery and amortization during the first year. Under the agreement, Mike will take over the business on January 1 of next year. Write a letter to Mike in which you present your calculations and recommendation. Also, prepare a memo for the tax files. Mike's address is 200 Rolling Hills Drive, Shavertown, PA 18708.

58. **LO.7** Oleander Corporation, a calendar year entity, begins business on March 1, 2011. The corporation has startup expenditures of $54,000. If Oleander elects § 195 treatment, determine the total amount of startup expenditures that it may deduct in 2011.

59. **LO.7** Martha was considering starting a new business. During her preliminary investigations, she incurred the following expenditures:

Salaries	$20,000
Travel	18,000
Interest on short-term note	2,000
Professional fees	13,000

Martha begins the business on June 1 of the current year. If Martha elects § 195 treatment, determine her startup expenditure deduction for the current year.

60. **LO.8** Wes acquired a mineral interest during the year for $10 million. A geological survey estimated that 250,000 tons of the mineral remained in the deposit. During the year, 80,000 tons were mined, and 45,000 tons were sold for $12 million. Other expenses amounted to $5 million. Assuming the mineral depletion rate is 22%, calculate Wes's lowest taxable income.

61. **LO.8, 9** Chris purchased an oil interest for $2 million. Recoverable barrels were estimated to be 500,000. During the year, 120,000 barrels were sold for $3.84 million, regular expenses (including cost recovery) were $1.24 million, and IDC were $1 million. Calculate Chris's taxable income under the expensing and capitalization methods of handling IDC.

DECISION MAKING

CUMULATIVE PROBLEMS

62. Janice Morgan, age 32, is single and has no dependents. She is a freelance writer. In January 2010, Janice opened her own office located at 2751 Waldham Road, Pleasantville, NM 17196. She called her business Writers Anonymous. Janice is a cash basis taxpayer. She lives at 132 Stone Avenue, Pleasantville, NM 17196. Her Social Security number is 123–45–6789. Janice desires to contribute to the Presidential Election Campaign Fund.

TAX RETURN PROBLEM

H&R BLOCK At Home

During 2010, Janice had the following income and expense items connected with her business:

Income from sale of articles	$105,000
Rent	16,500
Utilities	7,900
Supplies	1,800
Insurance	5,000
Travel (including meals of $1,200)	3,500

Janice purchased and placed in service the following fixed assets for her business:

- Furniture and fixtures (new) costing $17,000 on January 10, 2010.
- Computer equipment (new) costing $40,000 on July 28, 2010.

Janice did not elect immediate expensing under § 179. She elected not to take additional first-year depreciation.

Janice's itemized deductions are as follows:

State income tax	$3,000
Home mortgage interest paid to First Bank	6,000
Property taxes on home	1,500
Charitable contributions	1,200

Janice did not keep a record of the sales tax she paid. The amount from the sales tax table is $437.

Janice has interest income of $5,000 on certificates of deposit at Second Bank. Janice makes estimated tax payments of $17,000 for 2010.

Compute Janice Morgan's 2010 Federal income tax payable (or refund due). If you use tax forms for your computations, you will need Form(s) 1040 and 4562 and Schedules A, B, C, and SE. Suggested software: H&R BLOCK At Home.

63. John Smith, age 31, is single and has no dependents. At the beginning of 2011, John started his own excavation business and named it Earth Movers. John lives at 1045 Center Street, Lindon, UT, and his business is located at 381 State Street, Lindon, UT. The zip code for both addresses is 84059. John's Social Security number is 111–11–1111, and the business identification number is 11–1111111. John is a cash basis taxpayer. During 2011, John had the following items in connection with his business:

TAX COMPUTATION PROBLEM

DECISION MAKING

COMMUNICATIONS

Fees for services	$912,000
Building rental expense	36,000
Office furniture and equipment rental expense	9,000
Office supplies	2,500
Utilities	4,000
Salary for secretary	34,000
Salary for equipment operators	42,000
Payroll taxes	7,000
Fuel and oil for the equipment	21,000
Purchase of three new front-end loaders on January 15, 2011, for $600,000. John made the election under § 179.	600,000
Purchase of a new dump truck on January 18, 2011	85,000

During 2011, John had the following additional items:

Interest income from First National Bank	$10,000
Dividends from ExxonMobil	9,500
Quarterly estimated tax payments	11,500

John elected not to take additional first-year depreciation.

On October 8, 2011, John inherited IBM stock from his Aunt Mildred. John had been her favorite nephew. According to the data provided by the executor of Aunt Mildred's estate, the stock was valued for estate tax purposes at $110,000. John is considering selling the IBM stock for $115,000 on December 29, 2011, and using $75,000 of the proceeds to purchase an Acura ZDX. He would use the car 100% for business. John wants to know what effect these transactions would have on his 2011 adjusted gross income.

Write a letter to John in which you present your calculations. Also, prepare a memo for the tax files.

RESEARCH PROBLEMS

THOMSON REUTERS
Checkpoint® Student Edition

Note: Solutions to Research Problems can be prepared by using the **Checkpoint® Student Edition** online research product, which is available to accompany this text. It is also possible to prepare solutions to the Research Problems by using tax research materials found in a standard tax library.

COMMUNICATIONS

Research Problem 1. Harry Pickart, one of your clients, operates a business that rents aircraft parts to motion picture studios for use in film production. Harry purchased most of the aircraft parts at auctions held throughout the United States. At those auctions, Harry usually acquired the parts in large quantities because he speculated that he would be able to use at least some of them in his rental business. After the conclusion of a film production, the movie studio returns the aircraft parts it rented from Harry. The parts are often returned in damaged condition or with pieces missing. Harry sometimes attempts to repair a damaged part so that it can be rented again. After being subjected to wear and tear from use, however, a part deteriorates over time, which varies depending on the particular part and its treatment by the studios during rental. Harry believes that all of the aircraft parts have a useful life of less than four years and, therefore, are entitled to be classed as three-year property. Write a letter to Harry that contains your advice on whether the aircraft parts can be depreciated over three years. Also, prepare a memo for the tax files. Harry's mailing address is P.O. Box 100, Sun River, OR 97600.

Research Problem 2. Blue Power and Light Corporation is an energy company. It produces electricity, sells wholesale and retail electricity, and delivers electricity to customers. Blue also provides street and highway lighting and area lighting for public and private entities. The equipment used to provide street and area lighting is called streetlights. Blue wants to know the appropriate asset class to determine the cost recovery deduction for the streetlights.

INTERNET *activity*

Use the tax resources of the Internet to address the following question. Do not restrict your search to the Web, but include a review of newsgroups and general reference materials, practitioner sites and resources, primary sources of the tax law, chat rooms and discussion groups, and other opportunities.

Research Problem 3. Changes to depreciation systems often are discussed by policy makers and observers of the tax system. Outline the terms and policy objectives of one of the changes currently proposed by the Treasury, a member of Congress, or a tax policy think tank.

CHAPTER 9

Deductions: Employee and Self-Employed-Related Expenses

LEARNING OBJECTIVES

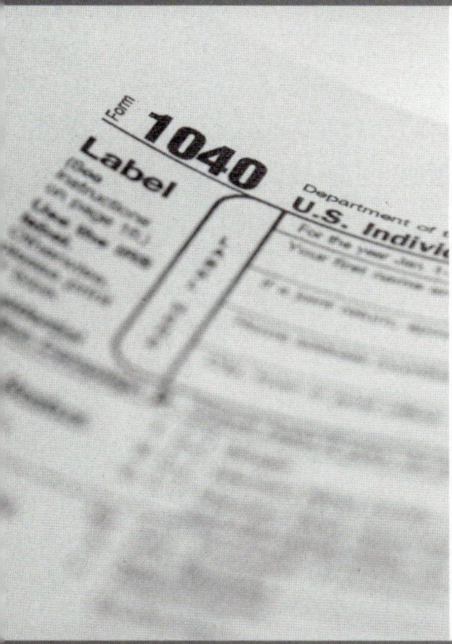

After completing Chapter 9, you should be able to:

LO.1 Distinguish between employee and self-employed status.

LO.2 Recognize deductible transportation expenses.

LO.3 Describe how travel expenses are treated.

LO.4 Determine the moving expense deduction.

LO.5 Differentiate between deductible and nondeductible education expenses.

LO.6 Explain how entertainment and meal expenses are treated.

LO.7 Identify other employee expenses.

LO.8 Compare various deductions for contributions to retirement accounts.

LO.9 Demonstrate the difference between accountable and nonaccountable employee plans.

LO.10 Apply the limitations on miscellaneous itemized deductions.

LO.11 Discuss tax planning ideas related to employee business expenses.

OUTLINE

For the latest in changes to tax legislation, visit **www.cengage.com/taxation/swft.**

FRAMEWORK 1040:

Tax Formula for Individuals

This chapter covers the boldfaced portions of the Tax Formula for Individuals that was introduced in Figure 3.1 on p. 3-3. Below those portions are the sections of Form 1040 where the results are reported.

Income (broadly conceived)	$xx,xxx
Less: Exclusions	(x,xxx)
Gross income	$xx,xxx
Less: Deductions for adjusted gross income	**(x,xxx)**

FORM 1040 (p. 1)

12	Business income or (loss). Attach Schedule C or C-EZ		
23	Educator expenses	**23**	
24	Certain business expenses of reservists, performing artists, and fee-basis government officials. Attach Form 2106 or 2106-EZ	**24**	
26	Moving expenses. Attach Form 3903	**26**	
32	IRA deduction	**32**	
34	Tuition and fees. Attach Form 8917	**34**	

Adjusted gross income	$xx,xxx
Less: The greater of total **itemized deductions** *or* the standard deduction	**(x,xxx)**

FORM 1040 (p. 2)

40 **Itemized deductions** (from Schedule A) **or** your **standard deduction** (see instructions)

Personal and dependency exemptions	(x,xxx)
Taxable income	$xx,xxx
Tax on taxable income (see Tax Tables or Tax Rate Schedules)	$ x,xxx
Less: Tax credits (including income taxes withheld and prepaid)	(xxx)
Tax due (or refund)	$ xxx

THE BIG PICTURE Tax Solutions for the Real World

THE FIRST JOB

After an extensive search, Morgan, a recent college graduate with a major in finance, has accepted a job with Kite Corporation. The job is in sales and will require travel and some entertainment (i.e., business lunches). She will be based in a major metropolitan area in another state. Kite has no available space in the locale, so she will have to maintain her own work facility. In addition to her salary, Morgan will receive a travel allowance. However, Kite has made it clear that the allowance *will not* cover all of her travel expenses.

Morgan is delighted with the new job since it will enable her to maintain a flexible work schedule. Furthermore, working out of her own apartment avoids a time-consuming and costly commute.

What are some of the income tax problems presented by this situation? **Read the chapter and formulate your response.**

Considering the large number of taxpayers affected, the tax treatment of job-related expenses is unusually complex. To resolve this matter in a systematic fashion, a number of key questions must be asked:

- Is the taxpayer an *employee* or *self-employed?*
- If an employee, what expenses *qualify* as deductions?
- How are the expenses that qualify *classified* for tax purposes?
- To the extent the expenses are classified as deductions *from* AGI, are they subject to any *limitation?*

Once these questions have been posed and answered, the chapter considers various planning procedures available to maximize the deductibility of employee and self-employed expenses.

9.1 Employee versus Self-Employed

LO.1

Distinguish between employee and self-employed status.

When one person performs services for another, the person performing the service is either an employee or self-employed (an **independent contractor**). Failure to recognize employee status can have serious consequences. Tax deficiencies as well as interest and penalties may result.

The problem is likely to intensify since businesses are increasingly relying on the services of self-employed persons for numerous reasons. Unlike employees, self-employed persons do not have to be included in various fringe benefit programs (e.g., group term life insurance) and retirement plans. Since they are not covered by FICA and FUTA (see Chapter 1), these payroll costs are avoided. The IRS is very much aware of the tendency of businesses to wrongly classify workers as self-employed rather than as employees.

In terms of tax consequences, employment status also makes a great deal of difference to the persons who perform the services. Expenses of self-employed taxpayers, to the extent allowable, are classified as deductions *for* AGI and are reported on Schedule C (Profit or Loss From Business) of Form 1040.[1] With the exception of reimbursement under an accountable plan (see later in the chapter), expenses of employees are deductions *from* AGI. They are reported on Form 2106 (Employee Business Expenses) and Schedule A (Itemized Deductions) of Form 1040.[2]

Most persons classified as employees are common law employees. The common law employee classification originated in judicial case law and is summarized in various IRS pronouncements.[3] Revenue Ruling 87–41, for example, lists 20 factors that can be used in determining whether a worker is a common law employee or an independent contractor (and, thus, self-employed).[4]

But when does a common law employee-employer relationship exist? Such a relationship exists when the employer has the right to specify the end result and the ways and means by which that result is to be attained.[5] An employee is subject to the will and control of the employer with respect not only to what shall be done but also to how it shall be done. If the individual is subject to the direction or control of another only to the extent of the end result but not as to the means of accomplishment, an employee-employer relationship does not exist.

Certain factors indicate an employee-employer relationship. These include the performance of the following by the employer:

- Furnishing of tools or equipment and a place to work.
- Providing support services including the hiring of assistants to help do the work.
- Making training available to provide needed job skills.

[1]Under certain conditions, a Schedule C–EZ can be substituted. Also, a Schedule SE (Self-Employment Tax) must be filed.

[2]In certain cases, a Form 2106–EZ (Unreimbursed Employee Business Expenses) can be substituted.

[3]See, for example, *Employer's Supplemental Tax Guide* (IRS Publication 15-A).

[4]1987–1 C.B. 296.

[5]Reg. § 31.3401(c)–(1)(b).

- Allowing participation in various workplace fringe benefits (e.g., accident and health plans, group life insurance, retirement plans).
- Paying for services based on time rather the task performed.

For their part, independent contractors are more likely than employees to have unreimbursed business expenses, a significant investment in tools and work facilities, and less permanency in their business relationships. Independent contractors, moreover, anticipate a profit from their work, make their services available to the relevant marketplace, and are paid a flat fee on a per job basis. Although the right to discharge may depend on any contractual arrangement between the parties, employees generally are easier to terminate than independent contractors.

In resolving employment status, each case must be tested on its own merits. Keep in mind, however, that the right to control the means and methods of accomplishment is the definitive test that leads to a common law employee result.

EXAMPLE 1

Arnold is a lawyer whose major client accounts for 60% of his billings. He does the routine legal work and income tax returns at the client's request. He is paid a monthly retainer in addition to amounts charged for extra work. Arnold is a self-employed individual. Even though most of his income comes from one client, he still has the right to determine how the end result of his work is attained. ■

EXAMPLE 2

Ellen is a lawyer hired by Arnold to assist him in the performance of services for the client mentioned in Example 1. Ellen is under Arnold's supervision; he reviews her work and pays her an hourly fee. Ellen is an employee of Arnold. ■

When one taxpayer holds multiple jobs, it is possible to have dual status as both an employee and an independent contractor (i.e., self-employed).

EXAMPLE 3

Dr. Davis, DDS, is a full-time employee at the Robin University Health Center. In the evenings and on weekends, he shares a practice with another dentist who works the Monday through Friday daytime shifts. Dr. Davis is both employed and self-employed. ■

Certain workers who *are not* common law employees are treated as employees for employment tax purposes. Known as **statutory employees**, this group includes certain drivers (e.g., nondairy beverage distributors, laundry and dry cleaning pickup service), life insurance sales agents, home workers, and other sales persons. These employees are allowed to claim their business-related expenses as deductions *for* AGI by using Schedule C. The wages or commissions paid to statutory employees are not subject to Federal income tax withholding but are subject to Social Security tax.[6]

If a taxpayer wants clarification as to whether employee or independent contractor status exists, a ruling from the IRS can be obtained by filing Form SS–8 (Determination of Worker Status for Purposes of Federal Employment Taxes and Income Tax Withholding). An adverse ruling is appealable to the U.S. Tax Court.[7]

9.2 Employee Expenses—In General

Once the employment relationship is established, employee expenses fall into one of the following categories:

- Transportation.
- Travel.
- Moving.

[6] § 3121(d)(3). See Circular E, *Employer's Tax Guide* (IRS Publication 15), for further discussion of statutory employees.

[7] § 7436.

- Education.
- Entertainment.
- Other.

These expenses are discussed below in the order presented.

Keep in mind, however, that these expenses are not necessarily limited to employees. A deduction for business transportation, for example, is equally available to taxpayers who are self-employed.

9.3 Transportation Expenses

QUALIFIED EXPENDITURES

LO.2
Recognize deductible transportation expenses.

An employee may deduct unreimbursed employment-related transportation expenses as an itemized deduction *from* AGI. **Transportation expenses** include only the cost of transporting the employee from one place to another in the course of employment when the employee is *not* away from home *in travel status.* Such costs include taxi fares, automobile expenses, tolls, and parking.

Commuting Expenses

Commuting between home and one's place of employment is a personal, nondeductible expense. The fact that one employee drives 30 miles to work and another employee walks six blocks is of no significance.

EXAMPLE 4

Geraldo is employed by Sparrow Corporation. He drives 22 miles each way to work. The 44 miles he drives each workday are nondeductible commuting expenses. ■

The rule that disallows a deduction for commuting expenses has several exceptions. An employee who uses an automobile to transport heavy tools to work and who otherwise would not drive to work is allowed a deduction, but only for the additional costs incurred to transport the work implements. Additional costs are those exceeding the cost of commuting by the same mode of transportation without the tools. For example, the rental of a trailer for transporting tools is deductible, but the expenses of operating the automobile generally are not deductible. The Supreme Court has held that a deduction is permitted only when the taxpayer can show that the automobile would not have been used without the necessity to transport tools or equipment.[8]

Another exception is provided for an employee who has a second job. The expenses of getting from one job to another are deductible. If the employee goes home between jobs, the deduction is based on the distance between jobs.

EXAMPLE 5

In the current year, Cynthia holds two jobs, a full-time job with Blue Corporation and a part-time job with Wren Corporation. During the 250 days that she works (adjusted for weekends, vacation, and holidays), Cynthia customarily leaves home at 7:30 A.M. and drives 30 miles to the Blue Corporation plant, where she works until 5:00 P.M. After dinner at a nearby café, Cynthia drives 20 miles to Wren Corporation and works from 7:00 to 11:00 P.M. The distance from the second job to Cynthia's home is 40 miles. Her deduction is based on 20 miles (the distance between jobs). ■

If the taxpayer is required to incur a transportation expense to travel between work stations, that expense is deductible.

[8]*Fausner v. Comm.*, 73–2 USTC ¶9515, 32 AFTR 2d 73–5202, 93 S.Ct. 2820 (USSC, 1973).

EXAMPLE 6

Norman is the local manager for a national chain of fast-food outlets. Each workday he drives from his home to his office to handle administrative matters. Most of his day, however, is then spent making the rounds of the retail outlets, after which he drives home. The costs incurred in driving to his office and driving home from the last outlet are nondeductible commuting expenses. The other transportation costs are deductible. ■

Likewise, the commuting costs from home to a temporary work station and from the temporary work station to home are deductible.

EXAMPLE 7

Vivian works for a firm in downtown Denver and commutes to work. She occasionally works in a customer's office. On one such occasion, Vivian drove directly to the customer's office, a round-trip distance from her home of 40 miles. She did not go into her office, which is a 52-mile round-trip. Her mileage for going to and from the temporary work station is deductible. ■

Also deductible is the reasonable travel cost between the general working area and a temporary work station outside that area.

EXAMPLE 8

Sam, a building inspector in Minneapolis, regularly inspects buildings for building code violations for his employer, a general contractor. During one busy season, the St. Paul inspector became ill, and Sam was required to inspect several buildings in St. Paul. The expenses for transportation for the trips to St. Paul are deductible. ■

What constitutes the general working area depends on the facts and circumstances of each situation. Furthermore, if an employee customarily works on several temporary assignments in a localized area, that localized area becomes the regular place of employment. Transportation from home to these locations becomes a personal, nondeductible commuting expense.

If a taxpayer has an office in the home that qualifies as a principal place of business, the transportation between home and various work locations is not a commuting expense.

EXAMPLE 9
THE BIG PICTURE

Return to the facts of *The Big Picture* on p. 9-2. Because Morgan will have an office in her home, the apartment will be her principal place of business. Thus, any transportation from her home to business sites *will not* be disallowed as a commuting expense. ■

COMPUTATION OF AUTOMOBILE EXPENSES

A taxpayer has two choices in determining automobile expenses: the automatic mileage method and the actual cost method. If a mixed-use automobile is involved, only the expenses attributable to the business use are deductible. The percentage of business use is usually arrived at by comparing the business mileage with total mileage—both business and personal.

Automatic Mileage Method

Also called the standard mileage method, the **automatic mileage method** is convenient in that it simplifies record keeping. The rate allowed per mile takes into account average operating expenses (such as gas and oil, repairs, and depreciation). Consequently, the taxpayer only has to multiply the automatic mileage rate by the miles driven to compute the deduction for business transportation.

For 2011, the deduction is based on 51 cents per mile for business miles.[9] For 2010, the business mileage rate was 50 cents. In some past years, however, the rate set did not remain the same for the entire year. Due to sizable fluctuations in fuel prices, a different rate was set for the last part of the year. The possibility of such a change makes

[9]Rev. Proc. 2010–51, I.R.B. No. 51, 883 and Notice 2010–88, I.R.B. No. 51, 882.

it important that the taxpayer be able to identify when the mileage took place. The automatic mileage rate for deductible education expenses is the same as for business; 19 cents per mile is allowed for moving (discussed later in this chapter) and medical purposes, and the rate for the charitable contribution deduction is 14 cents a mile (as to medical and charitable deductions, see Chapter 10). Parking fees and tolls are allowed in addition to expenses computed using the automatic mileage method.

Generally, a taxpayer may elect either method for any particular year. However, the following restrictions apply:

- The vehicle must be owned or leased by the taxpayer.
- The vehicle is not used for hire (e.g., taxicab).
- If five or more vehicles are in use (for business purposes) at the *same* time (not alternately), a taxpayer may not use the automatic mileage method.
- A basis adjustment is required if the taxpayer changes from the automatic mileage method to the actual operating cost method. Depreciation is considered allowed for the business miles in accordance with the following schedule for the most recent five years:

Year	Rate per Mile
2011	22 cents
2010	23 cents
2009	21 cents
2008	21 cents
2007	19 cents

EXAMPLE 10

Tim purchased his automobile in 2008 for $36,000. It is used 90% for business purposes. Tim drove the automobile for 10,000 business miles in 2010; 8,500 business miles in 2009; and 6,000 business miles in 2008. At the beginning of 2011, the basis of the business portion is $27,055.

Depreciable basis ($36,000 × 90%)	$32,400
Less depreciation:	
2010 (10,000 miles × 23 cents)	(2,300)
2009 (8,500 miles × 21 cents)	(1,785)
2008 (6,000 miles × 21 cents)	(1,260)
Adjusted business basis 1/1/2011	$27,055

■

- Use of the automatic mileage method in the first year the auto is placed in service is considered an election to exclude the auto from the MACRS method of depreciation (discussed in Chapter 8).
- A taxpayer may not switch to the automatic mileage method if the MACRS statutory percentage method or the election to expense under § 179 has been used.

Actual Cost Method

Under this method, the actual cost of operating the automobile is used to compute the deduction. Actual costs include the following expenses:

- Gas and oil, lubrication.
- Depreciation (or lease payments).
- Insurance.
- Dues to auto clubs.
- Repairs.
- Tires and other parts.
- Licenses and registration fees.
- Parking and tolls.

As noted in Chapter 8, the allowance for depreciation (or lease payments) is subject to limitations when mixed-use vehicles are involved (see Example 24 on p. 8–16). Interest on car loans is not deductible if the taxpayer is an employee, but it can qualify as a business expense if the taxpayer is self-employed.[10] Sales taxes paid on the purchase of a car are added to the cost of the car and recovered by means of the depreciation deduction. In mixed-use situations, the portion of the sales tax attributable to personal use may, in some cases, be claimed as a deduction *from* AGI (see Chapter 10 and the choice required between state and local income and sales taxes).

Except for parking and tolls, none of the expenses noted previously can be separately claimed under the automatic mileage method. A deduction for parking tickets and other traffic violations is not allowed under either method due to the public policy limitation (see Chapter 6).

EXAMPLE 11
THE BIG PICTURE

Return to the facts of *The Big Picture* on p. 9-2. During Morgan's senior year in college, her parents gave her one of the family cars—a 2008 Chevrolet Impala. Morgan has no idea as to the car's original cost or the odometer reading at the time the car was registered in her name. She has, however, kept track of the miles driven for business since she accepted her new job. Morgan should use the automatic mileage method in claiming business use of the car. ■

9.4 Travel Expenses

LO.3

Describe how travel expenses are treated.

DEFINITION OF TRAVEL EXPENSES

An itemized deduction is allowed for unreimbursed travel expenses related to a taxpayer's employment. **Travel expenses** are more broadly defined in the Code than are transportation expenses. Travel expenses include transportation expenses and meals and lodging while away from home in the pursuit of a trade or business. Meals cannot be lavish or extravagant under the circumstances. Transportation expenses (as previously discussed) are deductible even though the taxpayer is not away from home. A deduction for travel expenses is available only if the taxpayer is away from his or her tax home. Travel expenses also include reasonable laundry and incidental expenses.

AWAY-FROM-HOME REQUIREMENT

The crucial test for the deductibility of travel expenses is whether the employee is away from home overnight. "Overnight" need not be a 24-hour period, but it must be a period substantially longer than an ordinary day's work and must require rest, sleep, or a relief-from-work period.[11] A one-day business trip is not travel status, and meals and lodging for such a trip are not deductible.

Temporary Assignments

The employee must be away from home for a temporary period. If the taxpayer-employee is reassigned to a new post for an indefinite period of time, that new post becomes his or her tax home. *Temporary* indicates that the assignment's termination is expected within a reasonably short period of time. The position of the IRS is that the tax home is the business location, post, or station of the taxpayer. Thus, travel expenses are not deductible if a taxpayer is reassigned for an indefinite period and does not move his or her place of residence to the new location.

[10] An interest deduction could be available if the purchase of the auto was financed with a home equity loan. See the discussion of itemized deductions in Chapter 10.

[11] *U.S. v. Correll*, 68–1 USTC ¶9101, 20 AFTR 2d 5845, 88 S.Ct. 445 (USSC, 1967); Rev.Rul. 75–168, 1975–1 C.B. 58.

TAX *in the NEWS*

Turning a Saturday Leisure Day into a Business Day

The high cost of air travel together with the substantial discount allowed for a Saturday night stayover may offer travelers an opportunity to do some sightseeing or shopping on business trips. The extra meals and lodging expenses for the nonbusiness day are deductible if the cost is less than the additional cost of flying without a Saturday stay. For the employee, any reimbursement for such costs is nontaxable. Thus, the Saturday is treated as a business day even though no business activity takes place.

Source: Private Letter Ruling (Ltr.Rul.) 9237014.

EXAMPLE 12

Malcolm's employer opened a branch office in San Diego. Malcolm was assigned to the new office for three months to train a new manager and to assist in setting up the new office. He tried commuting from his home in Los Angeles for a week and decided that he could not continue driving several hours a day. He rented an apartment in San Diego, where he lived during the week. He spent weekends with his wife and children at their home in Los Angeles. Malcolm's rent, meals, laundry, incidentals, and automobile expenses in San Diego are deductible. To the extent that Malcolm's transportation expense related to his weekend trips home exceeds what his cost of meals and lodging would have been, the excess is personal and nondeductible. ■

EXAMPLE 13

Assume that Malcolm in Example 12 was transferred to the new location to become the new manager permanently. His wife and children continued to live in Los Angeles until the end of the school year. Malcolm is no longer "away from home" because the assignment is not temporary. His travel expenses are not deductible. ■

To curtail controversy in this area, the Code specifies that a taxpayer "*shall not* be treated as *temporarily* away from home during any period of employment if such period exceeds 1 year."[12]

Determining the Tax Home

Under ordinary circumstances, determining the location of a taxpayer's tax home does not present a problem. The tax home is the area in which the taxpayer derives his or her source of income.

It is possible for a taxpayer never to be away from his or her tax home. In other words, the tax home follows the taxpayer. Thus, all meals and lodging remain personal and are not deductible.

EXAMPLE 14

Jim is single and works full-time as a long-haul truck driver. He lists his mother's home as his address and stays there during holidays. However, he contributes nothing toward its maintenance. Since Jim has no regular place of duty or place where he regularly lives, his tax home is where he works (i.e., on the road). As an itinerant (transient), he is never away from home, and all of his meals and lodging while on the road are personal and not deductible. ■

The result reached in Example 14 is justified on the grounds that there is no duplication of living expenses in the case of itinerant taxpayers.[13]

When a taxpayer has more than one place of business or work, the main one is considered to be the tax home. This is determined by considering the time spent, the level of activity involved, and the income earned at each job.

---

[12] § 162(a).

[13] Rev.Rul. 73–539, 1973–2 C.B. 37 and *James O. Henderson*, 70 TCM 1407, T.C.Memo. 1995–559, *aff'd* by 98–1 USTC ¶50,375, 81 AFTR 2d 98–1748, 143 F.3d 497 (CA–9, 1998).

EXAMPLE 15

Art, a physical therapist, lives with his family in Lancaster (Pennsylvania). For seven months of each year, he is employed by the New Orleans Saints football team at a salary of $150,000. During this period, he rents an apartment in New Orleans. In the offseason, he works for the Lancaster YMCA at a salary of $15,000. Art's tax home is clearly New Orleans and not Lancaster. Consequently, his living expenses while in New Orleans (i.e., food, lodging) are not deductible. ■

RESTRICTIONS ON TRAVEL EXPENSES

The possibility always exists that taxpayers will attempt to treat vacation or pleasure travel as deductible business travel. To prevent such practices, the law contains restrictions on certain travel expenses.

Conventions

For travel expenses to be deductible, a convention must be directly related to the taxpayer's trade or business.[14]

EXAMPLE 16

Dr. Hill, a pathologist who works for a hospital in Ohio, travels to Las Vegas to attend a two-day session on recent developments in estate planning. No deduction is allowed for Dr. Hill's travel expenses. ■

EXAMPLE 17

Assume the same facts as in Example 16, except that the convention deals entirely with recent developments in pathology. Now, a travel deduction is allowed. ■

If the proceedings of the convention are videotaped, the taxpayer must attend convention sessions to view the videotaped materials along with other participants. This requirement does not disallow deductions for costs (other than travel, meals, and entertainment) of renting or using videotaped materials related to business.

EXAMPLE 18

A CPA is unable to attend a convention at which current developments in taxation are discussed. She pays $200 for videotapes of the lectures and views them at home later. The $200 is an itemized deduction if the CPA is an employee. If she is self-employed, the $200 is a deduction *for* AGI. ■

The Code places stringent restrictions on the deductibility of travel expenses of the taxpayer's spouse or dependent.[15] Generally, the accompaniment by the spouse or dependent must serve a bona fide business purpose, and the expenses must be otherwise deductible.

EXAMPLE 19

Assume the same facts as in Example 17 with the additional fact that Dr. Hill is accompanied by Mrs. Hill. Mrs. Hill is not employed, but possesses secretarial skills and takes notes during the proceedings. No deduction is allowed for Mrs. Hill's travel expenses. If, however, Mrs. Hill is a nurse trained in pathology and is employed by Dr. Hill as his assistant, her travel expenses become deductible. ■

Education

Travel as a form of education is not deductible.[16] If, however, the education qualifies as a deduction, the travel involved is allowed.

EXAMPLE 20

Greta, a German teacher, travels to Germany to maintain general familiarity with the language and culture. No travel expense deduction is allowed. ■

[14] § 274(h)(1).
[15] § 274(m)(3).
[16] § 274(m)(2).

EXAMPLE 21

Jean-Claude, a scholar of French literature, travels to Paris to do specific library research that cannot be done elsewhere and to take courses that are offered only at the Sorbonne. The travel costs are deductible, assuming that the other requirements for deducting education expenses (discussed later in the chapter) are met. ■

COMBINED BUSINESS AND PLEASURE TRAVEL

To be deductible, travel expenses need not be incurred in the performance of specific job functions. Travel expenses incurred in attending a professional convention are deductible by an employee if attendance is connected with services as an employee. For example, an employee of a law firm can deduct travel expenses incurred in attending a meeting of the American Bar Association.

Domestic Travel

Travel deductions have been used in the past by persons who claimed a tax deduction for what was essentially a personal vacation. As a result, several provisions have been enacted to govern deductions associated with combined business and pleasure trips. If the business/pleasure trip is from one point in the United States to another point in the United States, the transportation expenses are deductible only if the trip is *primarily for business.*[17] If the trip is primarily for pleasure, no transportation expenses qualify as a deduction. Meals, lodging, and other expenses are allocated between business and personal days.

EXAMPLE 22

In the current year, Hana travels from Seattle to New York primarily for business. She spends five days conducting business and three days sightseeing and attending shows. Her plane and taxi fare amounts to $1,160. Her meals amount to $200 per day, and lodging and incidental expenses are $350 per day. She can deduct the transportation charges of $1,160, since the trip is primarily for business (five days of business versus three days of sightseeing). Meals are limited to five days and are subject to the 50% cutback (discussed later in the chapter) for a total of $500 [5 days × ($200 × 50%)], and other expenses are limited to $1,750 (5 days × $350). If Hana is an employee, the unreimbursed travel expenses are miscellaneous itemized deductions. ■

EXAMPLE 23

Assume Hana goes to New York for a two-week vacation. While there, she spends several hours renewing acquaintances with people in her company's New York office. Her transportation expenses are not deductible. ■

Foreign Travel

When the trip is *outside the United States,* special rules apply. Transportation expenses must be allocated between business and personal unless (1) the taxpayer is away from home for seven days or less *or* (2) less than 25 percent of the time was for personal purposes. No allocation is required if the taxpayer has no substantial control over arrangements for the trip or the desire for a vacation is not a major factor in taking the trip. If the trip is primarily for pleasure, no transportation charges are deductible. Days devoted to travel are considered business days. Weekends, legal holidays, and intervening days are considered business days, provided that both the preceding and succeeding days were business days.[18]

EXAMPLE 24

In the current year, Robert takes a trip from New York to Japan primarily for business purposes. He is away from home from June 10 through June 19. He spends three days vacationing and seven days conducting business (including two travel days). His airfare is $4,000, his meals amount to $200 per day, and lodging and incidental expenses are

[17]Reg. § 1.162–2(b)(1).

[18]§ 274(c) and Reg. § 1.274–4. For purposes of the seven-days-or-less exception, the departure travel day is not counted.

$300 per day. Since Robert is away from home for more than seven days and more than 25% of his time is devoted to personal purposes, only 70% (7 days business/10 days total) of the transportation is deductible. His deductions are as follows:

Transportation (70% × $4,000)		$2,800
Lodging ($300 × 7)		2,100
Meals ($200 × 7)	$1,400	
Less: 50% cutback (discussed later)	(700)	700
Total		$5,600

■

EXAMPLE 25

Assume the same facts as in Example 24. Robert is gone the same period of time, but spends only two days (rather than three) vacationing. Now no allocation of transportation is required. Since the pleasure portion of the trip is less than 25% of the total, all of the airfare qualifies for the travel deduction. ■

9.5 Moving Expenses

LO.4

Determine the moving expense deduction.

Moving expenses are deductible for moves in connection with the commencement of work at a new principal place of work.[19] Both employees and self-employed individuals can deduct these expenses. To be eligible for a moving expense deduction, a taxpayer must meet two basic tests: distance and time.

DISTANCE TEST

To meet the distance test, the taxpayer's new job location must be at least 50 miles farther from the taxpayer's old residence than the old residence was from the former place of employment. In this regard, the location of the new residence is not relevant. This eliminates a moving deduction for taxpayers who purchase a new home in the same general area without changing their place of employment. Those who accept a new job in the same general area as the old job location are also eliminated.

EXAMPLE 26

Harry is permanently transferred to a new job location. The distance from Harry's former home to his new job (80 miles) exceeds the distance from his former home to his old job (30 miles) by at least 50 miles. Harry has met the distance test for a moving expense deduction. (See the following diagram.)

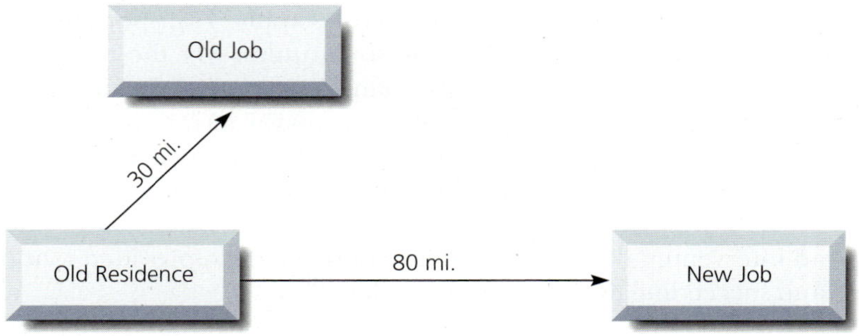

If Harry is not employed before the move, his new job must be at least 50 miles from his former residence. In this instance, Harry has met the distance test if he was not previously employed. ■

[19] § 217(a).

TIME TEST

To meet the time test, an employee must be employed on a full-time basis at the new location for 39 weeks in the 12-month period following the move. If the taxpayer is a self-employed individual, he or she must work in the new location for 78 weeks during the next two years. The first 39 weeks must be in the first 12 months. The time test is disregarded if the taxpayer dies, becomes disabled, or is discharged (other than for willful misconduct) or transferred by the new employer.

A taxpayer might not be able to meet the 39-week test by the due date of the tax return for the year of the move. For this reason, two alternatives are allowed. The taxpayer can take the deduction in the year the expenses are incurred, even though the 39-week test has not been met. If the taxpayer later fails to meet the test, either (1) the income of the following year is increased by an amount equal to the deduction previously claimed for moving expenses, or (2) an amended return is filed for the year of the move. The second alternative is to wait until the test is met and then file an amended tax return for the year of the move.

TREATMENT OF MOVING EXPENSES

What Is Included

"Qualified" moving expenses include *reasonable* expenses of:

- Moving household goods and personal effects.
- Traveling from the former residence to the new place of residence.

For this purpose, *traveling* includes lodging, but not meals, for the taxpayer and members of the household.[20] The taxpayer can elect to use actual auto expenses (no depreciation is allowed) or the automatic mileage method. In this case, moving expense mileage is limited in 2011 to 19 cents per mile for each car. The automatic mileage rate for 2010 was 16.5 cents per mile. These expenses are also limited by the reasonableness standard. For example, if one moves from Texas to Florida via Maine and takes six weeks to do so, the transportation and lodging must be allocated between personal and moving expenses.

EXAMPLE 27

Jill is transferred by her employer from the Atlanta office to the San Francisco office. In this connection, she spends the following amounts:

Cost of moving furniture	$4,800
Transportation	700
Meals	450
Lodging	600

Jill's total qualified moving expense is $6,100 ($4,800 + $700 + $600). ■

The moving expense deduction is allowed regardless of whether the employee is transferred by the existing employer or is employed by a new employer. It is allowed if the employee moves to a new area and obtains employment or switches from self-employed status to employee status (and vice versa). The moving expense deduction is also allowed if an individual is unemployed before obtaining employment in a new area.

What Is Not Included

In addition to meals while en route, the moving expense deduction does *not* include the following costs:

- New car tags and driver's licenses.
- Loss on the sale of a residence or penalty for breaking a lease.
- Forfeiture of security deposits and loss from disposing of club memberships.

[20] § 217(b).

GLOBAL
Tax Issues

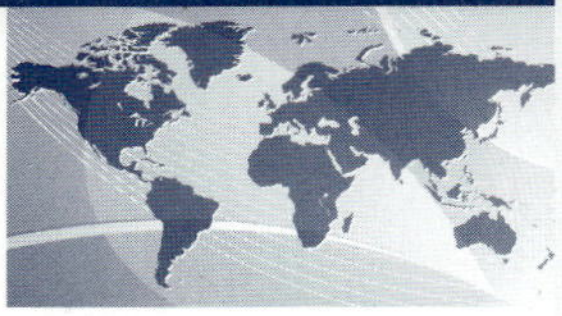

Expatriates and the Moving Expense Deduction

Expatriates, U.S. persons who accept work assignments overseas, enjoy several favorable tax advantages regarding foreign moves. First, the cost of storing household goods qualifies as a moving expense. This could lead to a major tax saving since expatriates do not ship most of their household effects to the foreign location. Furthermore, the cost of storage, particularly in a climate-controlled facility, is not insignificant.

The second advantage expatriates could enjoy is an exemption from the time test. Those who return to the United States to retire are absolved from the 39-week or 78-week work requirement. Thus, the return home expenses are treated as qualified moving expenses.

Source: Internal Revenue Code § 217(i).

- Pre-move house-hunting expenses.
- Temporary living expenses.

Also not deductible are the costs of moving servants and others who are not members of the household.

How Treated

Qualified moving expenses that are paid (or reimbursed) by the employer are not reported as part of the gross income of the employee.[21] Moving expenses that are paid (or reimbursed) by the employer and are not qualified moving expenses are included in the employee's gross income and are not deductible.

The employer is responsible for allocating the reimbursement between the qualified and nonqualified moving expenses. Reimbursed qualified moving expenses are separately stated on the Form W–2 given to the employee for the year involved. Qualified moving expenses that are not reimbursed and those of self-employed taxpayers are deductions *for* AGI.[22]

EXAMPLE 28
THE BIG PICTURE

Return to the facts of *The Big Picture* on p. 9-2. Even though this is her first job, Morgan will be entitled to a moving expense deduction. This presumes that she is not reimbursed by Kite Corporation for these expenses. She should not forget that the mileage on her auto (at the rate of 19 cents per mile) also is allowed. Her deduction is *for* AGI and can be claimed even if she chooses the standard deduction option. ■

Form 3903 is used to report the details of the moving expense deduction if the employee is not reimbursed or a self-employed person is involved.

9.6 Education Expenses

LO.5

Differentiate between deductible and nondeductible education expenses.

GENERAL REQUIREMENTS

An employee can deduct expenses incurred for education (**education expenses**) as ordinary and necessary business expenses provided the expenses are incurred for either of two reasons:

- To maintain or improve existing skills required in the present job.
- To meet the express requirements of the employer or the requirements imposed by law to retain his or her employment status.

[21]§§ 132(a)(6) and (g).

[22]§ 62(a)(15).

Education expenses are *not* deductible if the education is for either of the following purposes (except as discussed below under A Limited Deduction Approach):

- To meet the minimum educational standards for qualification in the taxpayer's existing job.
- To qualify the taxpayer for a new trade or business.[23]

Fees incurred for professional qualification exams (the bar exam, for example) and fees for review courses (such as a CPA review course) are not deductible.[24] If the education incidentally results in a promotion or raise, the deduction still can be taken as long as the education maintained and improved existing skills and did not qualify a person for a new trade or business. A change in duties is not always fatal to the deduction if the new duties involve the same general work. For example, the IRS has ruled that a practicing dentist's education expenses incurred to become an orthodontist are deductible.[25]

REQUIREMENTS IMPOSED BY LAW OR BY THE EMPLOYER FOR RETENTION OF EMPLOYMENT

Taxpayers are permitted to deduct education expenses if additional courses are required by the employer or are imposed by law. Many states require a minimum of a bachelor's degree and a specified number of additional courses to retain a teaching job. In addition, some public school systems have imposed a master's degree requirement and require teachers to make satisfactory progress toward a master's degree in order to keep their positions. If the required education is the minimum degree required for the job, no deduction is allowed.

A taxpayer classified as a staff accountant who went back to school to obtain a bachelor's degree in accounting was not allowed to deduct the expenses. Although some courses tended to maintain and improve his existing skills in his entry-level position, the degree was the minimum requirement for his job.[26]

Expenses incurred for education required by law for various professions will also qualify for deduction.

EXAMPLE 29

In order to satisfy the State Board of Public Accountancy rules for maintaining her CPA license, Nancy takes an auditing course sponsored by a local college. The cost of the education is deductible. ■

MAINTAINING OR IMPROVING EXISTING SKILLS

The "maintaining or improving existing skills" requirement in the Code has been difficult for both taxpayers and the courts to interpret. For example, a business executive may be permitted to deduct the costs of obtaining an MBA on the grounds that the advanced management education is undertaken to maintain and improve existing management skills. The executive is eligible to deduct the costs of specialized, nondegree management courses that are taken for continuing education or to maintain or improve existing skills. Expenses incurred by the executive to obtain a law degree are not deductible, however, because the education constitutes training for a new trade or business. The Regulations deny a self-employed accountant a deduction for expenses relating to law school.[27]

CLASSIFICATION OF SPECIFIC ITEMS

Education expenses include books, tuition, typing, and transportation (e.g., from the office to night school) and travel (e.g., meals and lodging while away from home at summer school).

[23]Reg. §§ 1.162–5(b)(2) and (3).

[24]Reg. § 1.212–1(f) and Rev.Rul. 69–292, 1969–1 C.B. 84.

[25]Rev.Rul. 74–78, 1974–1 C.B. 44.

[26]Reg. § 1.162–5(b)(2)(iii) (Example 2); *Collin J. Davidson*, 43 TCM 743, T.C.Memo. 1982–119. But see the subsequent discussion of § 222 (i.e., the deduction for higher education qualified tuition and related expenses).

[27]Reg. § 1.162–5(b)(3)(ii) (Example 1).

TAX *in the NEWS*

IS AN MBA DEGREE DEDUCTIBLE?

Education that maintains or improves existing skills is deductible, but education that qualifies a taxpayer for a new field is not. But how do these basic rules apply to a conventional (i.e., nonspecialized) MBA degree? Does being a manager or a consultant require an MBA degree? Generally, the answer has always been that it does not. In this regard, therefore, the education does not create a new skill, so its cost should be deductible.

Several recent holdings, however, have found that an MBA degree can lead to qualifying for a new trade or business. But these holdings involved situations where the education resulted in a job change and satisfied different minimum requirements set by the employer. In one case, for example, the taxpayer moved from the position of investment analyst to become an investment banker, and the latter position required an MBA degree. Under these circumstances, the cost of the education was held to be nondeductible.

But barring a change to a job where the degree is required, the cost of an MBA degree should be deductible as merely improving existing managerial skills.

Source: Daniel R. Allemeier, Jr., 90 TCM 197, T.C.Memo. 2005–207.

EXAMPLE 30

Bill, who holds a bachelor of education degree, is a secondary education teacher in the Charleston school system. The school board recently raised its minimum education requirement for new teachers from four years of college training to five. A grandfather clause allows teachers with only four years of college to continue to qualify if they show satisfactory progress toward a graduate degree. Bill enrolls at the University of South Carolina and takes two graduate courses. His unreimbursed expenses for this purpose are as follows:

Books and tuition	$3,600
Lodging while in travel status (June–August)	2,150
Meals while in travel status	1,100
Laundry while in travel status	220
Transportation	900

Bill has an itemized deduction as follows:

Books and tuition	$3,600
Lodging	2,150
Meals less 50% cutback (see below)	550
Laundry	220
Transportation	900
	$7,420

■

A LIMITED DEDUCTION APPROACH

One of the major shortcomings of the education deduction, previously discussed, is that it is unavailable for taxpayers obtaining a basic skill. Thus, a taxpayer working for an accounting firm cannot deduct the cost of earning a bachelor's degree in accounting. Under 2001 tax legislation, this shortcoming has been partly resolved with the **deduction for qualified tuition and related expenses.**

A deduction *for* AGI is allowed for qualified tuition and related expenses involving higher education (i.e., postsecondary). The deduction is the lesser of the qualifying amount spent or the maximum amount allowed by § 222. The maximum deductions allowed are shown in Table 9.1. Note that the limitations are based on the taxpayer's MAGI and filing status.[28] Although a phaseout is provided for, note its short and

[28]MAGI is modified adjusted gross income as defined in § 222(b)(2)(C). Examples of some of these modifications include the adding back to regular AGI of the foreign earned income exclusion and the domestic production activities deduction. See *Tax Benefits for Education* (IRS Publication 970).

TABLE 9.1 Limitations for Qualified Tuition Deduction

Filing Status	MAGI Limit	Maximum Deduction Allowed
Single	$ 65,000	$4,000
Married	130,000	
Single	65,001 to 80,000*	2,000
Married	130,001 to 160,000*	2,000

*No deduction at all is available if MAGI exceeds this amount.

drastic effect. Only two steps are involved ($65,000/$80,000 for single and $130,000/$160,000 for married), and the benefit of § 222 *disappears completely* after the second step. Thus, a married couple with MAGI of $160,000 would lose the entire deduction if they earned an additional $1. The § 222 limitations are not indexed for inflation.[29]

Various aspects of the higher education tuition deduction are summarized below:

- Qualified tuition and related expenses include whatever is required for enrollment at the institution. Usually, student activity fees, books, and room and board are not included.[30]
- The expense need not be employment related, although it can be.
- The deduction is available for a taxpayer's spouse or anyone who can be claimed as a dependent and is an eligible student.
- The deduction is not available for married persons who file separate returns.
- To avoid a "double benefit," the deduction must be coordinated with other education provisions (e.g., American Opportunity and lifetime learning credits). Along this same line, no deduction is allowed for a taxpayer who qualifies as another's dependent.[31]
- The deduction *for* AGI classification avoids the 2 percent-of-AGI floor on miscellaneous itemized deductions. As noted later in the chapter, this is the fate suffered by other education-related employee expenses.

EXAMPLE 31
THE BIG PICTURE

Return to the facts of *The Big Picture* on p. 9-2. After starting her new job, Morgan enrolls in the night program of a local law school and begins attending classes. Although Morgan does not plan to practice law, she feels that a law degree would advance her career. Except for the tuition she pays (see the discussion of § 222), none of her expenses relating to the education will be deductible.[32] ■

The deduction for qualified tuition and related expenses can be determined by completing Form 8917 (Tuition and Fees Deduction). The form should be attached to Form 1040 (or Form 1040–A).

[29]Section 222 expired at the end of 2009, but has been extended through 2011.

[30]Section 222(d) refers to § 25A(f), which deals with the American Opportunity and lifetime learning credits (see Chapter 12). Student activity fees and prescribed course-related books could be allowed if they are a condition for enrollment.

[31]§ 222(c).

[32]*Steven Galligan*, 83 TCM 1859, T.C.Memo. 2002–150.

ETHICS & Equity **MAXIMIZING THE TUITION DEDUCTION**

Blake maintains a household that includes his daughter Bianca who is 23 years old and a full-time student. Using funds from a savings account she inherited from her aunt, Bianca pays for her $5,000 college tuition. For the year, Blake properly claims Bianca as a dependent (under the qualifying child category) and, making use of § 222, deducts $4,000 of the tuition. On her own income tax return, Bianca also uses § 222 to deduct the $1,000 balance of the $5,000 tuition. What are the parties trying to accomplish? Have they acted properly? Explain.

OTHER PROVISIONS DEALING WITH EDUCATION

Although this chapter deals with employment-related expenses, mention should be made of various other tax provisions that deal with education. Because the encouragement of education is a desirable social goal, Congress has not been hesitant in enacting laws that provide tax incentives. The incentives come in the form of income exclusions, deductions (both *for* AGI and *from* AGI), and various credits. The paragraphs that follow summarize these benefits.

Similar to the § 222 deduction for qualified tuition and related expenses just discussed is a deduction for interest on student loans.[33] Also treated as a deduction *for* AGI, a maximum of up to $2,500 per year is allowed.

In the area of exclusions from gross income are Coverdell Education Savings Accounts (CESAs).[34] The maximum annual contribution to a CESA is $2,000. Although no deduction is allowed for contributions, earnings on these funds accumulate free of tax. Distributions also are nontaxable if used for tuition and related expenses.

Qualified tuition programs (commonly referred to as "§ 529 plans") have the same objective as CESAs—to help pay for a beneficiary's (usually a dependent family member's) education. The tax consequences are also similar, with no deduction allowed for any contribution to the plan and no tax imposed on income accumulations.[35] Since the plan must be sponsored by a state or a private university, the terms and conditions set forth in the plan will vary accordingly.

Another exclusion from gross income comes in the form of educational assistance programs.[36] Sponsored by employers, such programs cover up to $5,250 per year of an employee's education costs (e.g., tuition, fees, books, supplies), which can be at the undergraduate or graduate level.

Last but not least in the area of exclusions are certain scholarship awards.[37] Exclusion treatment is available for scholarships covering tuition and related expenses but not for those providing room and board.

In the area of tax credits, taxpayers benefit significantly from two provisions: the American Opportunity credit (formerly the HOPE scholarship) and the lifetime learning credit.[38] Both cover tuition and related expenses but not room and board costs. The American Opportunity credit allows no more than $2,500 per year for the first four years of college, while the lifetime learning credit permits up to $2,000 (20 percent of qualifying costs up to $10,000) per year with no time constraints. Concept Summary 9.1 reviews the tax consequences of the various provisions dealing with education and indicates where they are discussed in the text.

[33] § 221.

[34] § 530.

[35] The major advantage of one of the two types of § 529 plans is protection against increasing tuition cost. The plan freezes the tuition that will be charged to the current amount.

[36] § 127.

[37] § 117.

[38] § 25A.

CONCEPT SUMMARY 9.1

Tax Consequences of Provisions Dealing with Education

			Reference	
Provision	**Tax Effect**	**Income Phaseout**[a]	**Code**	**Text**
Educational savings bonds	*Exclusion* for interest on U.S. Series EE bonds used for qualified higher education	Yes	§ 135	Ch. 5, p. 5-31
Qualified tuition program	No deduction; *exclusion* for distributions	No	§ 529	Ch. 5, p. 5-32
Educational assistance plans	*Exclusion* of up to $5,250 for employer-provided assistance	No[b]	§ 127	Ch. 5, p. 5-20
Scholarships	*Exclusion* allowed for education costs (excluding room and board)	No	§ 117	Ch. 5, p. 5-10
Qualified tuition reduction plan	*Exclusion* as to tuition waivers for employees (and dependents) of nonprofit educational institutions	No	§ 117(d)	Ch. 5, p. 5-11
Coverdell Education Savings Account (CESA)	No deduction; *exclusion* for distributions	Yes	§ 530	Ch. 9, p. 9-18
Premature distributions from IRAs	If used for qualified higher education, income recognized but penalty waived	—	§ 72(t)	Ch. 9, p. 9-31
Qualified tuition and related expenses	*Deduction for* AGI; up to $4,000	Yes	§ 222	Ch. 9, p. 9-16
Educator expenses	*Deduction for* AGI; up to $250	No	§ 62(a)(2)(D)	Ch. 9, p. 9-26
Interest on student loans	*Deduction for* AGI; up to $2,500 per year	Yes	§ 221	Ch. 10, p. 10-14
Job-related education expenses	*Deduction from* AGI for an *employee* and subject to 2%-of-AGI floor; *deduction for* AGI for *self-employed*	No	§ 162	Ch. 9, p. 9-14
American Opportunity credit	Formerly the HOPE credit; extended to 4 years of postsecondary education; up to $2,500 per year	Yes	§ 25A(i)	Ch. 12, p. 12-22
Lifetime learning credit	20% of qualifying expenses (not to exceed $10,000 per year)	Yes	§ 25A(c)	Ch. 12, p. 12-22

[a] The phaseout of benefits occurs when income reaches a certain level. The phaseout amounts vary widely, depend on filing status (i.e., single, married filing jointly) and are based on MAGI (modified AGI).
[b] The availability of the benefit cannot be discriminatory (i.e., cannot favor higher-income taxpayers).

9.7 Entertainment and Meal Expenses

LO.6

Explain how entertainment and meal expenses are treated.

Many taxpayers attempt to deduct personal entertainment expenses as business expenses. For this reason, the tax law restricts the deductibility of entertainment expenses. The Code contains strict record-keeping requirements and provides restrictive tests for the deduction of certain types of **entertainment expenses**.

CUTBACK ADJUSTMENT

During the administration of Jimmy Carter, considerable controversy arose regarding the "three martini" business lunch. By virtue of allowing a tax deduction, should the tax law be subsidizing a practice that contained a significant element of personal pleasure? One possible remedy for the situation was to disallow any deduction for business entertainment, but this option was regarded as being too harsh. Instead the *cutback* rule was instituted. Rather than disallowing *all* of the deduction, allow only a certain percentage, and the rest of the expenditure would be cut back. Currently, only 50 percent of meal and entertainment expenses are allowed as a deduction.[39] The limitation applies in the context of both employment and self-employment status. Although the 50 percent cutback can apply to either the employer or the employee, it will not apply twice. The cutback applies to the one who really pays (economically) for the meals or entertainment.

EXAMPLE 32

Jane, an employee of Pato Corporation, entertains one of her clients. If Pato Corporation does not reimburse Jane, she is subject to the cutback adjustment. If, however, Pato Corporation reimburses Jane (or pays for the entertainment directly), Pato suffers the cutback. ■

In certain situations, however, a full 50 percent cutback seems unfair. If, for example, the hours of service are regulated (by the U.S. Department of Transportation) and away-from-home meals are frequent and necessary, the "three martini" business lunch type of abuse is unlikely. Consequently, the cutback rule is mitigated for the following types of employees:

- Certain air transportation employees, such as flight crews, dispatchers, mechanics, and control tower operators.
- Interstate truck and bus drivers.
- Certain railroad employees, such as train crews and dispatchers.
- Certain merchant mariners.

Effective for 2008 and thereafter, 80 percent of the cost of meals is allowed as a deduction.

What Is Covered

Transportation expenses are not affected by the cutback rule—only meals and entertainment. The cutback also applies to taxes and tips relating to meals and entertainment. Cover charges, parking fees at an entertainment location, and room rental fees for a meal or cocktail party are also subject to the 50 percent rule.

EXAMPLE 33

Joe pays a $40 cab fare to meet his client for dinner. The meal costs $150, and Joe leaves a $30 tip. His deduction is $130 [($150 + $30) × 50% + $40 cab fare]. ■

What Is Not Covered

The cutback rule has a number of exceptions. One exception covers the case where the full value of the meals or entertainment is included in the compensation of the employee (or independent contractor).

EXAMPLE 34

Myrtle wins an all-expense-paid trip to Europe for selling the most insurance for her company during the year. Her employer treats this trip as additional compensation to Myrtle. The cutback adjustment does not apply to the employer. ■

Another exception applies to meals and entertainment in a subsidized eating facility or where the *de minimis* fringe benefit rule is met (see Chapter 5).

EXAMPLE 35

General Hospital has an employee cafeteria on the premises for its doctors, nurses, and other employees. The cafeteria operates at cost. The cutback rule does not apply to General Hospital. ■

EXAMPLE 36

Canary Corporation gives a ham, a fruitcake, and a bottle of wine to each employee at year-end. Since the *de minimis* fringe benefit exclusion applies to business gifts of packaged foods and beverages, their *full* cost is deductible by Canary. ■

[39] § 274(n).

A similar exception applies to employer-paid recreational activities for employees (e.g., the annual Christmas party or spring picnic).[40]

CLASSIFICATION OF EXPENSES

Entertainment expenses are categorized as follows: those *directly related* to business and those *associated with* business.[41] Directly related expenses are related to an actual business meeting or discussion. These expenses are distinguished from entertainment expenses that are incurred to promote goodwill, such as maintaining existing customer relations. To obtain a deduction for directly related entertainment, it is not necessary to show that actual benefit resulted from the expenditure as long as there was a reasonable expectation of benefit. To qualify as directly related, the expense should be incurred in a clear business setting. If there is little possibility of engaging in the active conduct of a trade or business due to the nature of the social facility, it is difficult to qualify the expenditure as directly related to business.

Expenses associated with, rather than directly related to, business entertainment must serve a specific business purpose, such as obtaining new business or continuing existing business. These expenditures qualify only if the expenses directly precede or follow a bona fide business discussion. Entertainment occurring on the same day as the business discussion meets the test.

RESTRICTIONS UPON DEDUCTIBILITY

Business Meals

Any business meal is deductible only if the following are true:[42]

- The meal is directly related to or associated with the active conduct of a trade or business.
- The expense is not lavish or extravagant under the circumstances.
- The taxpayer (or an employee) is present at the meal.

A business meal with a business associate or customer is not deductible unless business is discussed before, during, or after the meal. This requirement is not intended to disallow the deduction for a meal consumed while away from home on business.

EXAMPLE 37

Lacy travels to San Francisco for a business convention. She pays for dinner with three colleagues and is not reimbursed by her employer. They do not discuss business. She can deduct 50% of the cost of her meal. However, she cannot deduct the cost of her colleagues' meals. ■

The taxpayer or an employee must be present at the business meal for the meal to be deductible. An independent contractor who renders significant services to the taxpayer is treated as an employee.

EXAMPLE 38

Lance, a party to a contract negotiation, buys dinner for other parties to the negotiation but does not attend the dinner. No deduction is allowed. ■

Club Dues

The Code provides: "No deduction shall be allowed . . . for amounts paid or incurred for membership in any club organized for business, pleasure, recreation, or other social purpose."[43] Although this prohibition seems quite broad, the IRS does allow a deduction for dues to clubs whose primary purpose is public service and community volunteerism (e.g., Kiwanis, Lions, Rotary).

Even though dues are not deductible, actual entertainment at a club may qualify.

[40] § 274(e)(4).

[41] § 274(a)(1)(A).

[42] § 274(k).

[43] § 274(a)(3).

EXAMPLE 39

During the current year, Vincent spent $1,400 on business lunches at the Lakeside Country Club. The annual membership fee was $6,000, and Vincent used the facility 60% of the time for business. Presuming the lunches meet the business meal test, Vincent may claim $700 (50% × $1,400) as a deduction. None of the club dues are deductible. ■

Ticket Purchases for Entertainment

A deduction for the cost of a ticket for an entertainment activity is limited to the face value of the ticket.[44] This limitation is applied before the 50 percent rule. The face value of a ticket includes any tax. Under this rule, the excess payment to a scalper for a ticket is not deductible. Similarly, the fee to a ticket agency for the purchase of a ticket is not deductible.

Expenditures for the rental or use of a luxury skybox at a sports arena in excess of the face value of regular tickets are disallowed as deductions. If a luxury skybox is used for entertainment that is directly related to or associated with business, the deduction is limited to the face value of nonluxury box seats. All seats in the luxury skybox are counted, even when some seats are unoccupied.

The taxpayer may also deduct stated charges for food and beverages under the general rules for business entertainment. The deduction for skybox seats, food, and beverages is limited to 50 percent of cost.

EXAMPLE 40

In the current year, Jay Company pays $12,000 to rent a 10-seat skybox at City Stadium for three football games. Nonluxury box seats at each event range in cost from $55 to $120 a seat. In September, a Jay representative and eight clients use the skybox for the first game. The entertainment follows a bona fide business discussion, and Jay spends $490 for food and beverages during the game. The deduction for the first sports event is as follows:

Food and beverages	$ 490
Deduction for seats ($120 × 10 seats)	1,200
Total entertainment expense	$1,690
50% limitation	× .50
Deduction	$ 845

■

Business Gifts

Business gifts are deductible to the extent of $25 per donee per year.[45] An exception is made for gifts costing $4 or less (e.g., pens with the employee's or company's name on them) or promotional materials. Such items are not treated as business gifts subject to the $25 limitation. In addition, incidental costs such as engraving of jewelry and nominal charges for gift-wrapping, mailing, and delivery are not included in the cost of the gift in applying the limitation. Gifts to superiors and employers are not deductible.

The $25 limitation on business gifts cannot be circumvented by having the donor's spouse join in the gift or by making multiple gifts that include the customer's family.

An activity that can be considered either a gift or entertainment generally will be classified as entertainment. However, packaged food or beverages intended for later consumption are treated as a gift. Tickets to a theater performance or sporting event can be treated as *either* entertainment or a gift if the taxpayer *does not* accompany the client. However, if the taxpayer also attends (see Example 40), the gift option is not available.

Records must be maintained to substantiate business gifts.

[44] § 274(l).

[45] § 274(b)(1).

9.8 Other Employee Expenses

OFFICE IN THE HOME

LO.7

Identify other employee expenses.

Employees and self-employed individuals are not allowed a deduction for **office in the home expenses** unless a portion of the residence is used *exclusively* on a *regular basis* as either of the following:

- The principal place of business for any trade or business of the taxpayer.
- A place of business used by clients, patients, or customers.

Employees must meet an additional test: The use must be for the *convenience of the employer* rather than merely being "appropriate and helpful."[46]

The precise meaning of "principal place of business" has been the subject of considerable controversy.[47] Congress ultimately resolved the issue by amending the Code.[48] The term "principal place of business" now includes a place of business that satisfies the following requirements:

- The office is used by the taxpayer to conduct administrative or management activities of a trade or business.
- There is no other fixed location of the trade or business where the taxpayer conducts these activities.

EXAMPLE 41

Dr. Smith is a self-employed anesthesiologist. During the year, he spends 30 to 35 hours per week administering anesthesia and postoperative care to patients in three hospitals, none of which provides him with an office. He also spends two or three hours per day in a room in his home that he uses exclusively as an office. He does not meet patients there, but he performs a variety of tasks related to his medical practice (e.g., contacting surgeons, bookkeeping, reading medical journals). A deduction will be allowed since Dr. Smith uses the office in the home to conduct administrative or management activities of his trade or business, and there is no other fixed location where these activities can be carried out. ■

The exclusive use requirement means that part of the home must be used solely for business purposes. An exception allows mixed use (both business and personal) of the home if a licensed day-care business is involved.

EXAMPLE 42

Troy is self-employed and maintains an office in his home for business purposes. The office is also used by his wife to pay the family bills and by his children to do homework assignments. Troy does not satisfy the exclusive use requirement, and no office in the home deduction is allowed. ■

EXAMPLE 43

Muriel operates a licensed day-care center in her home. The children use the living room as a play area during the day, and Muriel and her family use it for personal purposes in the evening and on weekends. The mixed use of the living room does not disqualify Muriel from an office in the home deduction. ■

In arriving at the office in the home deduction, relevant expenses are categorized as direct or indirect. Direct expenses benefit only the business part of the home (e.g., the office is repainted) and are deducted in full. Indirect expenses are for maintaining and operating the home. Since they benefit both business and personal use, an allocation between the two is necessary. The allocation is made based on the floor space involved—divide the business area by the total home area to arrive at the business percentage.

[46]§ 280A(c)(1).

[47]See the restrictive interpretation arrived at in *Comm. v. Soliman*, 93–1 USTC ¶50,014, 71 AFTR 2d 93–463, 113 S.Ct. 701 (USSC, 1993).

[48]§ 280A(c)(1) as modified by the Tax Reform Act of 1997.

The allowable home office expenses cannot exceed the gross income from the business less all other business expenses attributable to the activity. Furthermore, the home office expenses that are allowed as itemized deductions anyway (e.g., mortgage interest and real estate taxes) must be deducted first. All home office expenses of an employee are miscellaneous itemized deductions, except those (such as interest and taxes) that qualify as other personal itemized deductions. Home office expenses of a self-employed individual are trade or business expenses and are deductible *for* AGI.

ETHICS *& Equity*

Whose Office Is It?

Gene and Mary are married, and both work at home. Gene is self-employed, while Mary is employed. They have set aside 20 percent of the living area of their residence for an office that they both use. On a joint return for the year, the full office in the home expenses are deducted on Gene's Schedule C (Profit or Loss From Business), while Mary's Form 2106 (Employee Business Expenses) contains no such deduction. What are the parties trying to accomplish? Have they acted properly?

Any disallowed home office expenses are *carried forward* and used in future years subject to the same limitations.

EXAMPLE 44

Rick is a certified public accountant employed by a regional CPA firm as a tax manager. He operates a separate business in which he refinishes furniture in his home. For this business, he uses two rooms in the basement of his home exclusively and regularly. The floor space of the two rooms constitutes 10% of the floor space of his residence. Gross income from the business totals $8,000. Expenses of the business (other than home office expenses) are $6,500. Rick incurs the following home office expenses:

Real property taxes on residence	$ 4,000
Interest expense on residence	7,500
Operating expenses of residence	2,000
Depreciation on residence (based on 10% business use)	250

Rick's deductions are determined as follows:

Business income		$ 8,000
Less: Other business expenses		(6,500)
		$ 1,500
Less: Allocable taxes ($4,000 × 10%)	$400	
Allocable interest ($7,500 × 10%)	750	(1,150)
		$ 350
Allocable operating expenses of the residence ($2,000 × 10%)		(200)
		$ 150
Allocable depreciation ($250, limited to remaining income)		(150)
		$ –0–

Rick has a carryover of $100 (the unused excess depreciation). Because he is self-employed, the allocable taxes and interest ($1,150), the other deductible office expenses ($200 + $150), and $6,500 of other business expenses are deductible *for* AGI. ■

To claim the office in the home deduction, use Form 8829 (Expenses for Business Use of Your Home). For further information on the deduction, see the instructions for Form 8829 and *Business Use of Your Home* (Publication 587) issued by the IRS.

TAX *in the NEWS*

MORE WORKERS ARE USING AN OFFICE IN THE HOME

One bright spot in a depressed economy with a high rate of unemployment is the increasing number of those working at home. By the end of 2009, an estimated 11 million full-time workers, including employees, independent contractors, and freelancers, were working from their homes. The number of home-based workers is increasing at the rate of 200,000 per year. Home-based work offers benefits for both employers and workers. Employers find it cost-effective (e.g., savings on office space), and workers find it highly convenient. Not only do they avoid long commutes and the cost of day care, but the flexible work schedules also allow for the pursuit of other activities (e.g., volunteer work, obtaining college degrees).

Source: Adapted from Sue Shellenbarger, "Commuting in Five Seconds," *Wall Street Journal*, November 25, 2009, p. D1.

The office in the home deduction includes an allocable portion of the depreciation on the personal residence. To arrive at this depreciation, use the MACRS percentage for 39-year nonresidential real property. Except for the first and last years (i.e., 1 and 40), the applicable percentage is 2.564 percent—see Table 8.6 in Chapter 8. The furnishings of the office are handled separately and are either expensed under § 179 or depreciated in accordance with the rules set forth in Chapter 8—see Exhibit 8.1 and Table 8.1.

An office in the home deduction is also available to those who rent (rather than own) their home. If the taxpayer does not own the property, the applicable percentage of business use is applied to the rent being paid.

EXAMPLE 45
THE BIG PICTURE

Return to the facts of *The Big Picture* on p. 9-2. The portion of Morgan's rent, utilities, renters' insurance, and the like allocable to her office will qualify for the deduction. Because she will be working in an apartment where space is limited, she must be careful to meet the exclusive-use requirement for the area set aside. For the furnishings she acquires (e.g., desk, file cabinet), Morgan may prefer to forgo expensing (§ 179) and claim depreciation instead. This way the tax deduction is deferred to later, higher-income years. ■

MISCELLANEOUS EMPLOYEE EXPENSES

Miscellaneous employee expenses include those costs that are job related and are not otherwise covered elsewhere. As the focus here is on their deductibility, this discussion presumes that such expenses have not been reimbursed by the employer under an accountable plan arrangement (discussed later in the chapter).

Expenses related to maintaining job status make up a significant category of miscellaneous expenses. They include such costs as union dues, membership dues to professional organizations, subscriptions to trade publications and professional journals, and various license fees paid to government agencies and other regulatory bodies.

Special Clothing

To be deductible, special clothing must be both specifically required as a condition of employment and not adaptable for regular wear. For example, a police officer's uniform must be worn when "on duty" but is not suitable for "off-duty" activities. Its cost, therefore, is deductible. When special clothing qualifies for deductibility, so does the cost of its maintenance (i.e., alterations, laundry, dry cleaning).

Whether the out-of-pocket cost of military uniforms is deductible depends on the duty status of the taxpayer. If a member of the National Guard (or reserves) is not on active duty, then the cost of the uniform qualifies for deductibility. For those on active duty, the cost of regular uniforms does not qualify because the uniforms are suitable for ordinary street wear. Even for those on active duty, some apparel, such as ceremonial attire (dress blues) or combat gear, will qualify because it is not adaptable for regular wear.

The cost of clothing possessing *safety* features to prevent workplace injuries will qualify. This includes such items as safety glasses, shoes (e.g., "steel-toed"), special gloves, lab coats, and "hard hats." The tolerance of the IRS in the area of safety clothing is partially attributable to its lack of suitability for personal use.

Job Hunting

The expenses incurred in seeking employment can be deductible under certain conditions. The search must involve the same trade or business as the taxpayer's current position. No deduction is allowed for the cost of obtaining the first job. An unemployed person, however, can qualify for the deduction if there has not been a significant time lapse since the last job. In terms of deductibility, it does not matter whether the job search is successful. Nor does a change in jobs have to result. Costs that qualify include job counseling, compilation and distribution of biographical data (such as work history), and unreimbursed travel for job interviews.

EXAMPLE 46
THE BIG PICTURE

Return to the facts of *The Big Picture* on p. 9-2. Recall that Morgan conducted an extensive job search before obtaining her position with Kite Corporation. Because this is her first job, the expenses she incurred in the search are not deductible. ■

Educator Expenses

Many teachers purchase school supplies for classroom use and are not reimbursed by their employer. These out-of-pocket expenses can be deducted only if the teacher itemizes his or her deductions *from* AGI, and even then they are subject to the 2 percent-of-AGI floor (see later in this chapter). Thus, these restrictions can reduce or eliminate any tax benefit available to the teacher. Recent legislation provides *modest* relief for such out-of-pocket expenses by allowing elementary and secondary school teachers to claim up to $250 for school supplies as a deduction *for* AGI.[49] Eligible educators must work at least 900 hours during a school year as a teacher, instructor, counselor, principal, or aide at either public or private elementary and secondary schools. Covered costs include unreimbursed expenses for books, supplies, computer and other equipment, and supplementary materials used in the classroom.

EXAMPLE 47

Hortense is a full-time teacher at Hoover Elementary. During 2011, she spends $1,200 for school supplies for her fourth grade class. Under an accountable plan (see later in the chapter), Hoover reimburses her for $400 of these supplies. As to the $800 balance, Hortense may claim $250 as a deduction *for* AGI and $550 as a miscellaneous itemized deduction (subject to the 2%-of-AGI floor). ■

9.9 Contributions to Retirement Accounts

LO.8

Compare various deductions for contributions to retirement accounts.

Pension considerations are an essential feature of any compensation arrangement. As noted in Chapter 1, providing retirement security for employees can be justified on both economic and social grounds. Because the public sector (i.e., Social Security) will not provide sufficient retirement security for recipients, the private sector must fill the need. Congress has given the private sector the necessary incentive by enacting various measures that provide significant tax advantages for retirement plans.

[49] § 62(a)(2)(D). This provision expired at the end of 2007, but was extended through 2009 and now has been extended through 2011.

Although amounts that may be deferred under these plans are limited, the tax advantages are substantive and include (1) the deductibility of contributions (individuals are not taxed on these contributions until they are distributed), (2) income earned on the contributions is not subject to tax until distributed (thus growing at a tax-free rate of return), and (3) employer contributions to and benefits payable under qualified plans generally are not subject to FICA and FUTA taxes.

Although a wide variety of retirement plans exist, we will focus on some typical qualified retirement plans: (1) § 401(k) plans (a defined contribution plan[50] typically offered to employees); (2) Individual Retirement Accounts (available to any person who has earned income); and (3) plans available to self-employed individuals, including Keogh plans (also known as H.R. 10 plans), Solo § 401(k) plans, Saving Incentive Match for Employees (SIMPLE) plans, and Simplified Employee Pension (SEP) plans.

§ 401(K) PLANS

In General

A **§ 401(k) plan** allows participants to elect either to receive up to $16,500 (in 2011)[51] in cash (taxed currently) or to have a contribution made on their behalf to a profit sharing or stock bonus plan. The plan may also be in the form of a salary-reduction agreement between an eligible participant and an employer under which a contribution will be made only if the participant elects to reduce his or her compensation or to forgo an increase in compensation.

Any pretax amount elected by the employee as a plan contribution is not includible in gross income in the year of deferral and is 100 percent vested. Any employer contributions are tax deferred until distributed, as are earnings on contributions in the plan.

EXAMPLE 48

Sam participates in a § 401(k) plan of his employer. The plan permits the participants to choose between a full salary or a reduced salary where the reduction becomes a before-tax contribution to a retirement plan. Sam elects to contribute 10% of his annual compensation of $30,000 to the plan. Income taxes are paid on only $27,000. No income taxes are paid on the $3,000—or on any earnings—until it is distributed from the plan to Sam. The main benefit of a § 401(k) plan is that Sam can shift a portion of his income to a later taxable year. ■

Although the maximum annual elective contribution to a § 401(k) plan is $16,500 (in 2011), that amount is reduced dollar-for-dollar by other salary-reduction contributions to tax-sheltered annuities, simplified employee pension plans, and § 401(k) plans. Elective contributions in excess of the maximum limitation are taxable in the year of deferral. These amounts may be refunded from the plan tax-free before April 15 of the following year. Excess amounts not timely distributed will be double-taxed because they will be taxable in the year of distribution, even though they were included in income in the year of deferral. Annual elective contributions are also limited by complicated nondiscrimination requirements designed to encourage participation by non-highly compensated employees and by the general defined contribution plan limitations.

A person who has attained age 50 by the end of the tax year can make catch-up contributions of $1,000 for 2002, $2,000 for 2003, $3,000 for 2004, $4,000 for 2005, $5,000 for 2006 through 2008, and $5,500 for 2009, 2010, and 2011.[52]

[50]There are two types of qualified pension plans: defined benefit plans and defined contribution plans. A defined benefit plan includes a formula that defines the *benefits* employees are to receive. A defined contribution plan defines the amount of the *contribution* to the plan. The majority of employer pension plans today are defined contribution plans.

[51]§§ 402(g)(1) and (4). Starting in 2003, this amount was increased in $1,000 increments until it reached $15,000 in 2006. It is indexed in $500 increments in years after 2006. The amount was $12,000 for 2003; $13,000 for 2004; $14,000 for 2005; $15,000 for 2006; $15,500 for 2007 and 2008; and $16,500 for 2009 and 2010.

[52]The $5,000 amount is indexed in $500 increments in 2007 and thereafter. For 2007 and 2008, the amount remained at $5,000. For 2009, the amount increased to $5,500. For 2010, the amount remained at $5,500. For 2011, the amount remains at $5,500.

TABLE 9.2 Phaseout of IRA Deduction of an Active Participant in 2011

AGI Filing Status	Phaseout Begins*	Phaseout Ends
Single and head of household	$56,000	$66,000
Married, filing joint return	90,000	110,000
Married, filing separate return	–0–	10,000

*These amounts are indexed annually for inflation.

9.10 Individual Retirement Accounts (IRAs)

GENERAL RULES

Employees not covered by another qualified plan can establish their own tax-deductible **Individual Retirement Accounts (IRAs)**. For years 2005–2007, the contribution ceiling was the smaller of $4,000 (or $8,000 for spousal IRAs) or 100 percent of compensation. For 2008, 2009, 2010, and 2011, the contribution ceiling is the smaller of $5,000 (or $10,000 for spousal IRAs) or 100 percent of compensation.[53] The contribution ceiling applies to all types of IRAs (traditional deductible, traditional nondeductible, and Roth).

An individual who attains the age of 50 by the end of the tax year can make additional catch-up IRA contributions of $1,000 for years after 2005 ($500 for the period 2002 through 2005).

If the taxpayer is an *active participant* in a qualified plan, the traditional IRA deduction limitation is phased out *proportionately* between certain AGI ranges, as shown in Table 9.2.[54]

AGI is calculated taking into account any § 469 passive losses and § 86 taxable Social Security benefits and ignoring any § 911 foreign income exclusion, § 135 savings bonds interest exclusion, and the IRA deduction. There is a $200 floor on the IRA deduction limitation for individuals whose AGI is not above the phaseout range.

EXAMPLE 49

Dan, who is single, has compensation income of $62,000 in 2011. He is an active participant in his employer's qualified retirement plan. Dan contributes $5,000 to a traditional IRA. The deductible amount is reduced from $5,000 by $3,000 because of the phaseout mechanism:

$$\frac{\$6{,}000}{\$10{,}000} \times \$5{,}000 = \$3{,}000 \text{ reduction}$$

Therefore, of the $5,000 contribution, Dan can deduct only $2,000 ($5,000 − $3,000). ■

EXAMPLE 50

Ben, an unmarried individual, is an active participant in his employer's qualified retirement plan in 2011. With AGI of $65,800, he would normally have an IRA deduction limit of $100 {$5,000 − [($65,800 − $56,000)/$10,000 × $5,000]}. However, because of the special floor provision, Ben is allowed a $200 IRA deduction. ■

An individual is not considered an active participant in a qualified plan merely because the individual's spouse is an active participant in such a plan for any part of a plan year. Thus, most homemakers may take a full $5,000 deduction regardless of the participation status of their spouse, unless the couple has AGI above $169,000. If their AGI is above $169,000, the phaseout of the deduction begins at $169,000 and

[53] §§ 219(b)(1) and (c)(2). The ceiling was $3,000 for 2002–2004. After 2008, the limit is adjusted annually for inflation in $500 increments.

[54] § 219(g).

ends at $179,000 (phaseout over the $10,000 range) rather than beginning and ending at the phaseout amounts in Table 9.2.[55]

EXAMPLE 51

Nell is covered by a qualified employer retirement plan at work. Her husband, Nick, is not an active participant in a qualified plan. If Nell and Nick's combined AGI is $135,000, Nell cannot make a deductible IRA contribution because she exceeds the income threshold for an active participant in Table 9.2. However, since Nick is not an active participant, and their combined AGI does not exceed $169,000, he can make a deductible contribution of $5,000 to an IRA. ■

To the extent that an individual is ineligible to make a deductible contribution to an IRA, *nondeductible contributions* can be made to separate accounts.[56] The nondeductible contributions are subject to the same dollar limits as deductible contributions ($5,000 of earned income, $10,000 for a spousal IRA). Income in the account accumulates tax-free until distributed. Only the account earnings are taxed upon distribution because the account basis equals the contributions made by the taxpayer. A taxpayer may elect to treat deductible IRA contributions as nondeductible. If an individual has no taxable income for the year after taking into account other deductions, the election would be beneficial. The election is made on the individual's tax return for the taxable year to which the designation relates.

Starting in 2002, there is a nonrefundable credit for contributions to a traditional IRA or elective deferrals for a § 401(k) plan (see Chapter 12). Distributions to a traditional IRA holder must begin no later than April 1 of the calendar year *following* the year in which the IRA holder reaches 70½.[57]

Roth IRAs

Introduced by Congress to encourage individual savings, a **Roth IRA** is a *nondeductible* alternative to the traditional deductible IRA. Earnings inside a Roth IRA are not taxable, and all qualified distributions from a Roth IRA are tax-free.[58] The maximum allowable annual contribution to a Roth IRA for 2011 is the smaller of $5,000 ($10,000 for spousal IRAs) or 100 percent of the individual's compensation for the year. Contributions to a Roth IRA must be made by the due date (excluding extensions) of the taxpayer's tax return. Roth IRAs are not subject to the minimum distribution rules that apply to traditional IRAs. Contributions to a Roth IRA (unlike a traditional IRA) may continue beyond age 70½ so long as the person generates compensation income and is not barred by the AGI limits.

A taxpayer can make tax-free withdrawals from a Roth IRA after an initial five-year holding period if any of the following requirements is satisfied:

- The distribution is made on or after the date on which the participant attains age 59½.
- The distribution is made to a beneficiary (or the participant's estate) on or after the participant's death.
- The participant becomes disabled.
- The distribution is used to pay for qualified first-time homebuyer's expenses (statutory ceiling of $10,000).

EXAMPLE 52

Edith establishes a Roth IRA at age 42 and contributes $5,000 per year for 20 years. The account is now worth $149,400, consisting of $100,000 of nondeductible contributions and $49,400 in accumulated earnings that have not been taxed. Edith may withdraw

[55] § 219(g)(7). However, a special rule in § 219(g)(4) allows a married person filing a separate return to avoid the phaseout rules even though the spouse is an active participant. The individual must live apart from the spouse at all times during the taxable year and must not be an active participant in another qualified plan.

[56] § 408(o).

[57] § 401(a)(9).

[58] § 408A.

the $149,400 tax-free from the Roth IRA because she is over age 59½ and has met the five-year holding period requirement. ■

If the taxpayer receives a distribution from a Roth IRA and does not satisfy the aforementioned requirements, the distribution may be taxable. If the distribution represents a return of capital, it is not taxable. Conversely, if the distribution represents a payout of earnings, it is taxable. Under the ordering rules for Roth IRA distributions, distributions are treated as first made from contributions (return of capital).

EXAMPLE 53

Assume the same facts as in the previous example, except that Edith is only age 50 and receives a distribution of $55,000. Since her adjusted basis for the Roth IRA is $100,000 (contributions made), the distribution is tax-free, and her adjusted basis is reduced to $45,000 ($100,000 – $55,000). ■

Roth IRAs are subject to income limits. In 2011, the maximum annual contribution of $5,000 is phased out beginning at AGI of $107,000 for single taxpayers and $169,000 for married couples who file a joint return. The phaseout range is $10,000 for married filing jointly and $15,000 for single taxpayers. For a married taxpayer filing separately, the phaseout begins with AGI of $0 and is phased out over a $10,000 range.[59]

EXAMPLE 54

Bev, who is single, would like to contribute $5,000 to her Roth IRA. However, her AGI is $117,000, so her contribution is limited to $1,667 ($5,000 – $3,333) calculated as follows:

$$\frac{\$10{,}000}{\$15{,}000} \times \$5{,}000 = \$3{,}333 \text{ reduction}$$

■

Spousal IRA

If both spouses work, each can individually establish an IRA. Deductible IRA contributions of up to $5,000 may be made by each spouse if the combined compensation of both spouses is at least equal to the contributed amount. Thus, if each spouse has compensation of at least $5,000, they each may contribute a maximum of $5,000. Likewise, if only one spouse is employed, they each may contribute a maximum of $5,000 if the employed spouse has compensation of at least $10,000. Finally, if both spouses are employed, but one has compensation of less than $5,000, they each may contribute a maximum of $5,000 if their combined compensation is at least $10,000.

For the spousal IRA provision to apply, a joint return must be filed.[60] The spousal IRA deduction is also proportionately reduced for active participants whose AGI exceeds the above target ranges.

EXAMPLE 55

Tony, who is married, is eligible to establish an IRA. He received $30,000 in compensation in 2011, and his spouse does not work outside the home. Tony can contribute up to $10,000 to two IRAs, to be divided in any manner between the two spouses, except that no more than $5,000 can be allocated to either spouse. ■

EXAMPLE 56

Assume the same facts as in the previous example, except that Tony's wife has compensation income of $2,200. Without the spousal IRA provision, Tony could contribute $5,000 to his IRA, and his spouse could contribute only $2,200 to her IRA. With the spousal IRA provision, they both can contribute $5,000 to their IRAs. ■

Alimony is considered to be earned income for purposes of IRA contributions. Thus, a person whose only income is alimony can contribute to an IRA.

[59]The income limits for Roth IRA contributions are indexed for tax years after 2006.

[60]§ 219(c).

Timing of Contributions

Contributions (both deductible and nondeductible) can be made to an IRA anytime before the due date of the individual's tax return.[61] For example, an individual can establish and contribute to an IRA through April 16, 2012 (the return due date), and deduct this amount on his or her tax return for 2011. IRA contributions that are made during a tax return extension period do not satisfy the requirement of being made by the return due date.[62]

Taxation of Benefits

A participant has a zero basis in the *deductible* contributions of a traditional IRA because the contributions were deducted.[63] Therefore, all withdrawals from a deductible IRA are taxed as ordinary income in the year of receipt. They are not eligible for the 10-year averaging allowed for certain lump-sum distributions.

A participant has a basis equal to the contributions made for a *nondeductible* traditional IRA. Therefore, only the earnings component of withdrawals is included in gross income. Such amounts are taxed as ordinary income in the year of receipt and are not eligible for the 10-year averaging allowed for certain lump-sum distributions.

In addition to being included in gross income, payments from IRAs made to a participant before age 59½ are subject to a nondeductible 10 percent penalty tax on such actual, or constructive, payments.[64] However, an individual may make penalty-free withdrawals to pay for medical expenses in excess of 7.5 percent of AGI, to pay for qualified higher education expenses, and to pay for qualified, first-time homebuyer expenses (up to $10,000). Note that a qualified first-time homebuyer is defined as an individual (and spouse) who has not owned a principal residence in the two-year period preceding the date of acquisition of a principal residence. Further, an individual who has received unemployment compensation for at least 12 consecutive weeks may use IRA withdrawals to pay for health insurance for himself or herself, the spouse, and dependents without incurring the 10 percent penalty tax.[65]

Rollovers: General Provisions

An IRA may be the recipient of a rollover from another qualified plan, including another IRA. Such a distribution from a qualified plan is not included in gross income if it is transferred within 60 days of receipt to an IRA or another qualified plan. For a series of distributions that constitute a lump-sum distribution, the 60-day period does not begin until the last distribution. Amounts received from IRAs may be rolled over tax-free only once in a 12-month period. If a person has more than one IRA, the one-year waiting period applies separately to each IRA.[66]

EXAMPLE 57

Nonemployer stock worth $60,000 is distributed to an employee from a qualified retirement plan. Hubert, the employee, sells the stock within 60 days for $60,000 and transfers one-half of the proceeds to a traditional IRA. Hubert has $30,000 of ordinary income, which is not eligible for 10-year forward averaging or for capital gain treatment under the pre-1987 rules. One-half of the distribution, or $30,000, does escape taxation because of the rollover. ■

A rollover is different from a direct transfer of funds from a qualified plan to an IRA or another qualified plan by a trustee or issuer. A direct transfer is not subject to the one-year waiting period and the withholding rules.[67] Further, in many states, IRA amounts are subject to claims of creditors, which is not the case for some employer plans.

---

[61] § 219(f)(3).

[62] § 404(h)(1)(B).

[63] § 408(d)(1).

[64] § 72(t). There are limited exceptions to the penalty on early distributions.

[65] §§ 72(t)(2)(B), (D), (E), and (F). For purposes of the unemployment provision, a self-employed individual who otherwise would have been eligible for unemployment compensation will qualify.

[66] § 408(d)(3)(B) and Reg. § 1.408–4(b)(4).

[67] Reg. § 35.3405–1.

Rollovers and Conversions: Roth IRAs

A Roth IRA may be rolled over tax-free into another Roth IRA.[68]

A traditional IRA may be rolled over or converted to a Roth IRA. A conversion occurs when the taxpayer notifies the IRA trustee that the IRA is now a Roth IRA. A rollover or conversion of a traditional IRA to a Roth IRA can occur only if the following requirements are satisfied:[69]

- The participant's AGI does not exceed $100,000 (excluding the amount included in gross income resulting from the rollover or conversion).
- The participant is not married filing a separate return.
- The rollover occurs within 60 days of the IRA distribution.

The $100,000 AGI limitation for conversions and rollovers goes away in 2010 and 2011. Thus, contributions made to a traditional IRA could be converted to a Roth IRA in 2010. Taxes are due on the conversion amount in 2010, but these taxes can be spread over two years.[70] For 2011 conversions, this two-year option goes away (tax is currently due). Further, unlike a traditional IRA, which requires withdrawals at age 70½, there are no required withdrawals from a Roth IRA. Thus, money can be accumulated over the taxpayer's lifetime and then passed to heirs without tax penalties.

When a traditional IRA is rolled over or converted to a Roth IRA, the tax consequences depend on whether the traditional IRA was deductible or nondeductible. If deductible, then the basis for the IRA is zero. Thus, the entire amount of the rollover or conversion is included in gross income. If nondeductible, then the basis for the IRA is equal to the sum of the contributions. Thus, only the IRA earnings included in the rollover or conversion are included in gross income. The 10 percent penalty tax will not apply in either case.[71]

9.11 Retirement Plans for Self-Employed Individuals

A wide variety of retirement plans are available to self-employed individuals. In addition to Individual Retirement Accounts (discussed previously), self-employed individuals can establish a Keogh plan (also known as an H.R. 10 plan), a Solo § 401(k) plan, a Saving Incentive Match for Employees (SIMPLE) plan, or a Simplified Employee Pension plan (SEP).

KEOGH (H.R. 10) PLANS

Keogh plans are the self-employed equivalent of corporate pension plans. As Keogh plans are qualified retirement plans, these plans must be administered by an independent trustee. When an individual decides to make all investment decisions, a self-directed retirement plan is established. However, the individual may prefer to invest the funds with a financial institution such as a broker, a bank, or a savings and loan institution. A variety of funding vehicles can be used for Keogh investments, such as mutual funds, annuities, real estate shares, certificates of deposit, debt instruments, commodities, securities, and personal properties. Investment in most collectibles is not allowed in a self-directed plan.

Contribution Limitations

A self-employed individual may annually contribute the smaller of $49,000 (in 2011) or 100 percent of earned income to a *defined contribution* Keogh plan.[72] However, if

[68] § 408A(c)(3)(B).
[69] § 408A(c)(3)(B).
[70] § 408A(d)(3)(A).
[71] § 408A(d)(3)(A)(ii).
[72] § 415(c)(1).

the defined contribution plan is a profit sharing plan or stock bonus plan, a 25 percent deduction limit applies. Under a *defined benefit* Keogh plan, the annual benefit payable to an employee is limited to the smaller of $195,000 (in 2011) or 100 percent of the employee's average compensation for the three highest years of employment.[73] An employee includes a self-employed person.

Earned income refers to net earnings from self-employment as defined in § 1402(a).[74] Net earnings from self-employment means the gross income derived by an individual from any trade or business carried on by that individual, less appropriate deductions, plus the distributive share of income or loss from a partnership.[75] Earned income is reduced by contributions to a Keogh plan on the individual's behalf and by 50 percent of any self-employment tax.[76]

EXAMPLE 58

Pat, a sole proprietor, has earned income of $150,000 in 2011 (after the deduction for one-half of self-employment tax). The maximum contribution Pat may make to a defined contribution Keogh plan is $49,000, the lesser of $150,000 or $49,000. ■

Although a Keogh plan must be established before the end of the year in question, contributions may be made up to the normal filing date for that year. Self-employed individuals who hire employees may want to choose a different retirement plan for a simple reason—the plan must provide retirement benefits to all employees on a nondiscriminatory basis (i.e., the sole proprietor's employees must also be covered by the Keogh plan). This could be a substantial cost to the owner. Obviously, a sole proprietor with no employees is an ideal candidate for a Keogh plan.

SOLO § 401(K) PLANS

A Solo § 401(k) plan is designed for self-employed individuals and combines a regular § 401(k) plan with a profit sharing plan. As previously discussed, the maximum annual elective contribution to a § 401(k) plan is $16,500 (in 2011)—with an additional catch-up adjustment of $5,000 allowed to a self-employed individual who reaches age 50 by the end of the tax year. Under the profit sharing plan rules, the proprietor can contribute an additional 20 percent of net earnings from self-employment (computed in the same way as for a Keogh plan). The maximum deduction allowed is $49,000 (in 2011) or 100 percent of net earnings from self-employment.[77] Because the amount of compensation deferred as part of a § 401(k) plan does not count toward the 20 percent limit, the proprietor can defer the maximum amount of compensation under the § 401(k) plan and still contribute an additional 20 percent of self-employment income.[78]

EXAMPLE 59

Dan is 35 years old and is a sole proprietor. His net earnings from self-employment in 2011 are $100,000. Dan sets up a Solo § 401(k) plan for his retirement. Under current tax law, Dan's plan account can accept a profit sharing contribution of $20,000 (20% of $100,000), plus a § 401(k) elective deferral contribution of $16,500. As a result, Dan can make total plan contributions of $36,500 ($20,000 plus $16,500, which is less than the maximum allowed of $49,000). ■

SAVING INCENTIVE MATCH PLAN FOR EMPLOYEES (SIMPLE PLANS)

Employers with 100 or fewer employees who do not maintain another qualified retirement plan may establish a *savings incentive match plan for employees* (SIMPLE

[73] § 415(b)(1). This amount is indexed annually.

[74] § 401(c)(2).

[75] § 1402(a).

[76] §§ 401(c)(2)(A)(v) and 164(f).

[77] §§ 415(c) and (d).

[78] Prop.Reg. § 1.401(k)–1(a)(6)(ii).

plan).[79] The plan can be in the form of a § 401(k) plan or an IRA. A SIMPLE § 401(k) plan is not subject to the nondiscrimination rules that are normally applicable to § 401(k) plans.

All employees who received at least $5,000 in compensation from the employer during any two preceding years and who reasonably expect to receive at least $5,000 in compensation during the current year must be eligible to participate in the plan. The decision to participate is up to the employee. A self-employed individual may also participate in the plan.

The contributions made by the employee (a salary-reduction approach) must be expressed as a percentage of compensation rather than as a fixed dollar amount. The SIMPLE plan must not permit the SIMPLE elective employee contribution for the year to exceed $11,500 (in 2011).[80] The SIMPLE elective deferral limit is increased under the catch-up provision for employees age 50 and over. The catch-up amount is $2,500, and this amount is indexed for inflation in $500 increments beginning in 2007 (it remains at $2,500 for 2007, 2008, 2009, 2010, and 2011).

Generally, the employer must either match elective employee contributions up to 3 percent of the employee's compensation or provide nonmatching contributions of 2 percent of compensation for each eligible employee. Thus, the maximum amount that may be contributed to the plan for an employee under age 50 for 2011 is $18,850 [$11,500 employee contributions + $7,350 ($245,000 compensation ceiling × 3%) employer match].

No other contributions may be made to the plan other than the employee elective contribution and the required employer matching contribution (or nonmatching contribution under the 2 percent rule). All contributions are fully vested.

SIMPLIFIED EMPLOYEE PENSION PLANS (SEPs)

Simplified Employee Pensions—referred to as SEPs or SEP-IRAs—are generic retirement plans that allow the proprietor to deduct up to 20 percent of self-employment income.[81] As with Keogh and Solo § 401(k) plans, the maximum deduction allowed is $49,000 (in 2011). SEPs are much simpler to establish and administer than Keogh profit sharing and pension plans, and costs are minimal. The IRS provides a standardized plan that can be adopted (Form 5305-SEP), and no annual reporting to the IRS is required. Overall, SEPs are as easy to administer as deductible IRAs, but have a larger contribution limit.

9.12 Classification of Employee Expenses

LO.9

Demonstrate the difference between accountable and nonaccountable employee plans.

The classification of employee expenses depends on whether they are reimbursed by the employer under an accountable plan. If so, then they are not reported by the employee at all. In effect, therefore, this result is equivalent to treating the expenses as deductions *for* AGI. If the expenses are reimbursed under a nonaccountable plan or are not reimbursed at all, then they are classified as deductions *from* AGI and can be claimed only if the employee-taxpayer itemizes. An exception is made for moving expenses and the employment-related expenses of a qualified performing artist.[82] Here, deduction *for* AGI classification is allowed.

For classification purposes, therefore, the difference between accountable and nonaccountable plans is significant.

[79] § 408(p).

[80] For 2004, the limit was $9,000. The $10,000 amount for 2005 is indexed for inflation in $500 increments in 2006 and thereafter. For 2006, the amount remained at $10,000. For 2007 and 2008, it increased to $10,500. For 2009, it increased to $11,500 and remained at this amount in 2010. § 408(p)(2)(E)(i).

[81] § 408.

[82] As defined in § 62(b).

ACCOUNTABLE PLANS

In General

An **accountable plan** requires the employee to satisfy these two requirements:

- Adequately account for (substantiate) the expenses. An employee renders an *adequate accounting* by submitting a record, with receipts and other substantiation, to the employer.[83]
- Return any excess reimbursement or allowance. An "excess reimbursement or allowance" is any amount that the employee does not adequately account for as an ordinary and necessary business expense.

Substantiation

The law provides that no deduction is allowed for any travel, entertainment, business gift, or listed property (automobiles, computers) expenditure unless properly substantiated by adequate records. The records should contain the following information:[84]

- The amount of the expense.
- The time and place of travel or entertainment (or date of gift).
- The business purpose of the expense.
- The business relationship of the taxpayer to the person entertained (or receiving the gift).

This means the taxpayer must maintain an account book or diary in which the above information is recorded at the time of the expenditure. Documentary evidence, such as itemized receipts, is required to support any expenditure for lodging while traveling away from home and for any other expenditure of $75 or more. If a taxpayer fails to keep adequate records, each expense must be established by a written or oral statement of the exact details of the expense and by other corroborating evidence.[85]

EXAMPLE 60

Bertha has travel expenses substantiated only by canceled checks. The checks establish the date, place, and amount of the expenditure. Because neither the business relationship nor the business purpose is established, the deduction is disallowed.[86] ■

EXAMPLE 61

Dwight has travel and entertainment expenses substantiated by a diary showing the time, place, and amount of the expenditure. His oral testimony provides the business relationship and business purpose. However, since he has no receipts, any expenditures of $75 or more are disallowed.[87] ■

Deemed Substantiation

In lieu of reimbursing actual expenses for travel away from home, many employers reduce their paperwork by adopting a policy of reimbursing employees with a *per diem* allowance, a flat dollar amount per day of business travel. Of the substantiation requirements listed above, the *amount* of the expense is proved, or *deemed substantiated*, by using such a per diem allowance or reimbursement procedure. The amount of expenses that is deemed substantiated is equal to the lesser of the per diem allowance or the amount of the Federal per diem rate.

The regular Federal per diem rate is the highest amount that the Federal government will pay to its employees for lodging, meals, and incidental expenses[88] while in

---

[83]Reg. § 1.162–17(b)(4).

[84]§ 274(d).

[85]Reg. § 1.274–5T(c)(3).

[86]*William T. Whitaker*, 56 TCM 47, T.C.Memo. 1988–418.

[87]*W. David Tyler*, 43 TCM 927, T.C.Memo. 1982–160.

[88]Incidental expenses include tips and fees to porters, bellhops, hotel maids, etc. For travel away from home, the term does *not* include expenses for laundry and dry cleaning of clothing, lodging taxes, and telephone calls.

travel status away from home in a particular area. The rates are different for different locations.[89]

The use of the standard Federal per diem rates for meals and incidental expenses constitutes an adequate accounting. Employees and self-employed persons can use these standard allowances instead of deducting the actual cost of daily meals and incidental expenses, even if not reimbursed. There is no standard lodging allowance, however.

Only the amount of the expense is considered substantiated under the deemed substantiated method. The other substantiation requirements must be provided: place, date, business purpose of the expense, and the business relationship of the parties involved.

NONACCOUNTABLE PLANS

A **nonaccountable plan** is one in which an adequate accounting or return of excess amounts, or both, is not required. All reimbursements of expenses are reported in full as wages on the employee's Form W–2. Any allowable expenses are deductible in the same manner as are unreimbursed expenses.

Unreimbursed Employee Expenses

Unreimbursed employee expenses are treated in a straightforward manner. Meals and entertainment expenses are subject to the 50 percent limit. Total unreimbursed employee business expenses are usually reported as miscellaneous itemized deductions subject to the 2 percent-of-AGI floor (see below). If the employee could have received, but did not seek, reimbursement for whatever reason, none of the employment-related expenses are deductible.

Failure to Comply with Accountable Plan Requirements

An employer may have an accountable plan and require employees to return excess reimbursements or allowances, but an employee may fail to follow the rules of the plan. In that case, the expenses and reimbursements are subject to nonaccountable plan treatment.

REPORTING PROCEDURES

The reporting requirements range from no reporting at all (accountable plans when all requirements are met) to the use of some or all of the following forms: Form W–2 (Wage and Tax Statement), Form 2106 (Employee Business Expenses) or Form 2106–EZ (Unreimbursed Employee Business Expenses), and Schedule A (Itemized Deductions) for nonaccountable plans and unreimbursed employee expenses.

Reimbursed employee expenses that are adequately accounted for under an accountable plan are deductible *for* AGI on Form 2106. Allowed excess expenses, expenses reimbursed under a nonaccountable plan, and unreimbursed expenses are deductible *from* AGI on Schedule A, subject to the 2 percent-of-AGI floor.

When a reimbursement under an accountable plan is paid in separate amounts relating to designated expenses such as meals or entertainment, no problem arises. The reimbursements and expenses are reported as such on the appropriate forms. If the reimbursement is made in a single amount, an allocation must be made to determine the appropriate portion of the reimbursement that applies to meals and entertainment and to other employee expenses.

EXAMPLE 62

Elizabeth, who is employed by Green Company, had AGI of $42,000. During the year, she incurred $2,000 of transportation and lodging expense and $1,000 of meals and entertainment expense, all fully substantiated. Elizabeth received $1,800 reimbursement under an accountable plan. The reimbursement rate that applies to meals and entertainment is 33.33% ($1,000 meals and entertainment expense/$3,000 total

[89] *Per Diem Rates* (IRS Publication 1542) contains the list and amounts for the year. This publication is available only on the Internet at **www.irs.gov**. A print edition is no longer published. Links to per diem rates can also be found at **www.gsa.gov**.

expenses). Thus, $600 ($1,800 × 33.33%) of the reimbursement applies to meals and entertainment, and $1,200 ($1,800 – $600) applies to transportation and lodging. Elizabeth's itemized deduction consists of the $800 ($2,000 total – $1,200 reimbursement) of unreimbursed transportation and lodging expenses and $400 ($1,000 – $600) of unreimbursed meal and entertainment expenses as follows:

Transportation and lodging	$ 800
Meals and entertainment ($400 × 50%)	200
Total (reported on Form 2106)	$1,000
Less: 2% of $42,000 AGI (see limitation discussed below)	(840)
Deduction (reported on Schedule A)	$ 160

In summary, Elizabeth reports $3,000 of expenses and the $1,800 reimbursement on Form 2106 and $160 as a miscellaneous itemized deduction on Schedule A. ■

ETHICS & *Equity*

A SANITIZED EXPENSE ACCOUNT

Donald is a star traveling salesperson for Cardinal Supply, a nationwide wholesaler of sporting goods equipment. He also has a reputation with management of being very conservative in his use of company funds. Because of these traits—salesmanship and frugality—Donald has received frequent promotions and bonuses.

Unknown to the company, Donald is quite generous when entertaining customers. He feels that his high level of "wine and dine" is largely responsible for his outstanding sales record. In the expense account he submits to the company, Donald omits the excessive portion. He is not sure that the company would reimburse him for the extra costs, and he wants to maintain his reputation for frugality. On his own tax return, however, Donald deducts the portion of the expenses that were not included in his expense account.

What difficulties, if any, do you anticipate with what Donald is doing?

9.13 LIMITATIONS ON ITEMIZED DEDUCTIONS

LO.10

Apply the limitations on miscellaneous itemized deductions.

Many itemized deductions, such as medical expenses and charitable contributions, are subject to limitations expressed as a percentage of AGI. These limitations may be expressed as floors or ceilings and are discussed in Chapter 10.

MISCELLANEOUS ITEMIZED DEDUCTIONS SUBJECT TO THE 2 PERCENT FLOOR

Certain miscellaneous itemized deductions, including most *unreimbursed employee business expenses*, are aggregated and then reduced by 2 percent of AGI.[90] Expenses subject to the 2 percent floor include the following:

- All § 212 expenses, except expenses of producing rent and royalty income (refer to Chapter 6).
- All unreimbursed employee expenses (after the 50 percent reduction, if applicable) except moving.
- Professional dues and subscriptions.
- Union dues and work uniforms.
- Employment-related education expenses (except for § 222 qualified tuition and related expenses).
- Malpractice insurance premiums.
- Expenses of job hunting (including employment agency fees and résumé-writing expenses).

[90] § 67.

TAX *in* the NEWS

Relief for Members of the Armed Forces Reserves

In the Military Family Tax Relief Act of 2003, Congress provided various tax benefits for reservists, one of which deals with the classification of travel expenses. Members of the Reserves or National Guard who travel to drills and other service-related activities may claim the expenses as deductions *for* AGI. Previously, the expenses were not deductible unless the taxpayer itemized. (As miscellaneous itemized deductions, they were subject to the 2 percent-of-AGI floor.) To qualify for the deduction *for* AGI classification, the trip must be more than 100 miles from home and include an overnight stay. Any deduction is limited to the Federal per diem rates applicable to the area involved.

Source: *Armed Forces' Tax Guide* (IRS Publication 3), p. 5.

- Home office expenses of an employee or outside salesperson.
- Legal, accounting, and tax return preparation fees.
- Hobby expenses (up to hobby income).
- Investment expenses, including investment counsel fees, subscriptions, and safe deposit box rental.
- Custodial fees relating to income-producing property or a traditional IRA or a Keogh plan.
- Any fees paid to collect interest or dividends.
- Appraisal fees establishing a casualty loss or charitable contribution.

MISCELLANEOUS ITEMIZED DEDUCTIONS NOT SUBJECT TO THE 2 PERCENT FLOOR

Certain miscellaneous itemized deductions, including the following, are not subject to the 2 percent floor:

- Impairment-related work expenses of handicapped individuals.
- Gambling losses to the extent of gambling winnings.
- Certain terminated annuity payments.

EXAMPLE 63

Ted, who has AGI of $40,000, has the following miscellaneous itemized deductions:

Gambling losses (to extent of gains)	$2,200
Tax return preparation fees	500
Unreimbursed employee transportation	600
Professional dues and subscriptions	360
Safe deposit box rental	90

Ted's itemized deductions are as follows:

Deduction not subject to 2% floor (gambling losses)		$2,200
Deductions subject to 2% floor ($500 + $600 + $360 + $90)	$1,550	
Less 2% of AGI	(800)	750
Total miscellaneous itemized deductions		$2,950

If instead Ted's AGI is $80,000, the floor is $1,600 (2% of $80,000), and he cannot deduct any expenses subject to the 2% floor. ■

TAX *in* *the NEWS*

"Exotic Dancers"—Employees or Independent Contractors?

Many businesses are motivated to classify their workers as independent contractors rather than as employees. By doing so, the employers avoid having to pay unemployment insurance, workers' compensation, and Social Security taxes for the workers. In addition, independent contractors are not covered by minimum wage, overtime, and antidiscrimination laws. But these benefits to the business can be detrimental to the worker. As a result, more and more workers are bringing lawsuits claiming that they should be treated as employees.

Recently, several class-action suits were filed in Massachusetts by exotic dancers against the adult clubs where they worked. The dancers say that they have been denied the usual benefits available to employees by being classified as independent contractors. Considering the results reached in similar cases filed in other states, it appears that the dancers may succeed in their lawsuit.

Source: Adapted from Cari Tuna, "'Contractor' Label Provokes Legal Disputes," *Wall Street Journal*, November 19, 2009, p. B8.

TAX PLANNING:
9.14 Self-Employed Individuals

LO.11

Discuss tax planning ideas related to employee business expenses.

Some taxpayers have the flexibility to be classified as either employees or self-employed individuals. Examples include real estate agents and direct sellers. These taxpayers should carefully consider all factors and not automatically assume that self-employed status is preferable.

It is advantageous to deduct one's business expenses *for* AGI and avoid the 2 percent floor. However, a self-employed individual may have higher expenses, such as local gross receipts taxes, license fees, franchise fees, personal property taxes, and occupation taxes. In addition, the record-keeping and filing requirements can be quite burdensome.

One of the most expensive considerations is the Social Security tax versus the self-employment tax. For an employee in 2011, for example, the Social Security tax applies at a rate of 4.2 percent on a base amount of wages of $106,800, and the Medicare tax applies at a rate of 1.45 percent with no limit on the base amount. For self-employed persons, the rate, but not the base amount, for each tax doubles. Even though a deduction *for* AGI is allowed for part of the self-employment tax paid, an employee and a self-employed individual are not in the same tax position on equal amounts of earnings. For the applicability of these taxes to employees, see Chapter 1.

If a taxpayer misclassifies workers as self-employed, rather than employees, one of the penalties for being wrong is the liability for the employment taxes that should have been paid. But this penalty for misclassifying workers will be avoided if *all* three of the following requirements are met:

- The employer has a reasonable basis for *not* treating the workers as employees. Reasonable basis means reliance on any of the following—
  - *A judicial precedent, published ruling, or technical advice.*
  - *A past IRS audit that resulted in no employment tax assessment.*
  - *A longstanding practice of independent contractor status in the same industry.*
- The employer has consistently treated the workers as independent contractors.
- The employer has filed Form 1099 MISC (Miscellaneous Income) for each worker (when such filing was required).

Satisfaction of these requirements will help an employer avoid disputes with the IRS over workers' employment status.[91]

[91]This safe harbor for withholding purposes originated in § 530 of the Revenue Act of 1978. See IRS *Headliner* vol. 152 (March 27, 2006).

9.15 Shifting Deductions between Employer and Employee

An employee can avoid the 2 percent floor for employee business expenses. Typically, an employee incurs travel and entertainment expenses in the course of employment. The employer gets the deduction if it reimburses the employee, and the employee gets the deduction *for* AGI. An adequate accounting must be made, and excess reimbursements cannot be kept by the employee.

9.16 Transportation and Travel Expenses

Adequate detailed records of all transportation and travel expenses should be kept. Since the regular mileage allowance often is modest in amount, a new, expensive automobile used primarily for business may generate a higher expense based on actual cost. In using the actual cost method, include the business portion of depreciation, repairs and maintenance, automobile club dues, insurance, gasoline and oil, and other related costs. The cost of gasoline, when coupled with the poor mileage performance of some vehicles, can be a significant factor. If the taxpayer is located in a metropolitan area, automobile insurance is more expensive. For the self-employed taxpayer, the business portion of finance charges (i.e., interest on car loans) can be included.

Once a method is chosen, a later change may be possible. Conversion from the automatic mileage method to the actual cost method is allowed if a basis adjustment is made for depreciation deemed taken (see Example 10). Conversion from the actual cost method to the automatic mileage method is possible only if the taxpayer has not used the MACRS statutory percentage method or claimed § 179 limited expensing.

If a taxpayer wishes to sightsee or vacation on a business trip, it would be beneficial to schedule business on both a Friday and a Monday to turn the weekend into business days for allocation purposes. It is especially crucial to schedule appropriate business days when foreign travel is involved.

ETHICS *& Equity*

Walking to Soccer Practice

Mel Wilson is married and has three children, ages 9, 12, and 14. Mel works in the city, but the family lives in the suburbs. Mrs. Wilson does not work outside the home. The Wilsons own only one automobile and for tax purposes classify it as being used 95 percent for business use and 5 percent for personal use. Do you envision any problems with this allocation? Would it matter whether the Wilsons base their deduction on the actual cost method or the automatic mileage method?

9.17 Moving Expenses

Persons who retire and move to a new location incur personal nondeductible moving expenses. If the retired person accepts a full-time job in the new location, the moving expenses are deductible.

EXAMPLE 64

At the time of his retirement from the national office of a major accounting firm, Gordon had an annual salary of $420,000. He moves from New York City to Seattle to retire. To qualify for the moving expense deduction, Gordon accepts a full-time teaching position at a Seattle junior college at an annual salary of $15,000. If Gordon satisfies the 39-week test, his moving expenses are deductible. The disparity between the two salaries (previous and current) is of no consequence. ■

9.18 Education Expenses

Education expenses are treated as nondeductible personal items unless the individual is employed or is engaged in a trade or business. A temporary leave of absence for further education is one way to reasonably assure that the taxpayer is still qualified, even if a full-time student. An individual was permitted to deduct education expenses even though he resigned from his job, returned to school full-time for two years, and accepted another job in the same field upon graduation. The court held that the student had merely suspended active participation in his field.[92]

If the time out of the field is too long, educational expense deductions will be disallowed. For example, a teacher who left the field for four years to raise her child and curtailed her employment searches and writing activities was denied a deduction. She was not actively engaged in the trade or business of being an educator.[93]

To secure the deduction, an individual should arrange his or her work situation to preserve employee or business status.

The deduction for qualified tuition and related expenses provides some relief from the current restrictions on the deduction of education expenses by employees. First, the education expense does not have to be work related. Second, it is a deduction *for* (not *from*) AGI. Unfortunately, the deduction possesses severe shortcomings: not only is the annual amount allowed quite modest, but it may be unavailable to certain taxpayers. It is not available, for example, to those who exceed an AGI ceiling or to someone who can be claimed as a dependent of another.

Before selecting the § 222 deduction approach, however, consider the possible availability of the American Opportunity credit (formerly the HOPE credit) or the lifetime learning credit under § 25A.[94] As credits provide a dollar-for-dollar reduction of tax liability, these provisions could yield a greater tax benefit than deductions *for* AGI. But these credits may not be available to higher-income taxpayers.

9.19 Entertainment and Meal Expenses

Proper documentation of expenditures is essential because of the strict record-keeping requirements and the restrictive tests that must be met. For example, documentation that consists solely of credit card receipts and canceled checks may be inadequate to substantiate the business purpose and business relationship.[95] Taxpayers should maintain detailed records of amounts, time, place, business purpose, and business relationships. A credit card receipt details the place, date, and amount of the expense. A notation made on the receipt of the names of the person(s) attending, the business relationship, and the topic of discussion should constitute proper documentation.

Associated with or goodwill entertainment is not deductible unless a business discussion is conducted immediately before or after the entertainment. Furthermore, a business purpose must exist for the entertainment. Taxpayers should arrange for a business discussion before or after such entertainment. They must provide documentation of the business purpose, such as obtaining new business from a prospective customer.

Unreimbursed meals and entertainment are subject to the 50 percent cutback rule in addition to the 2 percent floor. Consequently, the procedure of negotiating a salary reduction, as discussed in the next section, is even more valuable to the taxpayer.

92 *Stephen G. Sherman*, 36 TCM 1191, T.C.Memo. 1977–301.

93 *Brian C. Mulherin*, 42 TCM 834, T.C.Memo. 1981–454; *George A. Baist*, 56 TCM 778, T.C.Memo. 1988–554.

94 These credits are briefly mentioned on page 18 in this chapter and are discussed at greater length in Chapter 12.

95 *Kenneth W. Guenther*, 54 TCM 382, T.C.Memo. 1987–440.

9.20 Unreimbursed Employee Business Expenses

The 2 percent floor for unreimbursed employee business expenses offers a tax planning opportunity for married couples. If one spouse has high miscellaneous expenses subject to the floor, it may be beneficial for the couple to file separate returns. If they file jointly, the 2 percent floor is based on the incomes of both. Filing separately lowers the reduction to 2 percent of only one spouse's income.

Other provisions of the law should be considered, however. For example, filing separately could cost a couple losses of up to $25,000 from self-managed rental units under the passive activity loss rules (discussed in Chapter 11).

Another possibility is to negotiate a salary reduction with one's employer in exchange for the 100 percent reimbursement of employee expenses. The employee is better off because the 2 percent floor does not apply. The employer is better off because certain expense reimbursements are not subject to Social Security and other payroll taxes.

REFOCUS ON THE BIG PICTURE

THE FIRST JOB

The first issue that might arise as a result of Morgan's new job is the dependency exemption possibility. If Morgan was living at home and accepted the job late in the year, she could qualify as a dependent of her parents. If so, they might also be able to claim the qualified tuition deduction (or the lifetime learning credit). If, however, her employment began early in the year, she could not be a qualifying child (due to the self-supporting limitation) or a qualifying relative (due to the gross income limitation)—see Chapter 3.

Although Morgan's "extensive search" for employment indicates that she may have incurred job hunting expenses, such expenses are not deductible in a *first job* setting (see Example 46). Her qualified moving expenses, however, are not so restricted. Moving expenses are deductions *for* AGI (see Example 28).

Under the circumstances, Morgan is justified in claiming an office in the home deduction. The deduction would include a portion of the rent paid for the apartment, depreciation on office equipment, and other operating expenses (e.g., utilities). She must be careful not to violate the "exclusive use" restriction (see Example 45).

As she is required to travel as part of her job, Morgan will use her car for business. Thus, she will need to make a choice between the automatic mileage method and the actual cost method (see Example 11). Since her tax home is in her apartment, she will have no nondeductible commuting expenses (see Example 9).

If she renders an adequate accounting (and has to return any excess) to Kite Corporation, then her allowance need not be reported on her Federal tax return. Nonreimbursed amounts, however, will have to be allocated between meals and entertainment (subject to the 50 percent cutback adjustment) and other employment-related expenses. The balance is an itemized deduction subject to the 2 percent-of-AGI floor.

If she does not render an adequate accounting, the full allowance is included in her gross income. All of the meals and entertainment expenses are subject to the 50 percent cutback adjustment, and the total of all employment-related expenses is an itemized deduction subject to the 2 percent-of-AGI floor.

If Morgan started the job with Kite Corporation late in the year, it is unlikely that she will be in a position to itemize her deductions *from* AGI. Instead, she will claim the standard deduction.

Morgan must maintain adequate substantiation regarding all of these employment-related transactions. Detailed records are particularly important in arriving at the office in the home deduction and the business use of an automobile (under the actual cost method). If Morgan does not render an accounting to Kite, records are crucial in supporting the travel and entertainment expenses.

KEY TERMS

Accountable plan, 9–35
Automatic mileage method, 9–6
Deduction for qualified tuition and related expenses, 9–16
Education expenses, 9–14
Entertainment expenses, 9–19
Independent contractor, 9–3
Individual Retirement Accounts (IRAs), 9–28
Keogh plans, 9–32
Moving expenses, 9–12
Nonaccountable plan, 9–36
Office in the home expenses, 9–23
Roth IRA, 9–29
Section 401(k) plan, 9–27
Statutory employees, 9–4
Transportation expenses, 9–5
Travel expenses, 9–8

DISCUSSION QUESTIONS

1. **LO.1, 9** Kirk and Yvette are married and file a joint return. Their return for 2010 included a Form 2106 for each of them. Their return for 2011, however, included a Form 2106 for Kirk and a Schedule C for Yvette. In terms of employment status, what probably occurred?

ISSUE ID

2. **LO.1, 9** Yolanda is employed but is not reimbursed by her employer for her job-related expenses. If Yolanda always claims the standard deduction, she can never deduct any of these expenses. Do you agree with this conclusion? Explain.

ISSUE ID

3. **LO.1** Milton performs services for Junco Company. In determining whether Milton is an employee or an independent contractor, discuss the relevance of each of the independent factors listed below:
   a. Milton acquired his job skills at Junco's training program.
   b. Milton sets his own work schedule.
   c. Milton uses the tools provided by Junco.
   d. Milton furnishes his own assistants.
   e. The services are performed at Milton's workplace.
   f. Junco issues a Form W–2 to Milton at year-end.
   g. Milton is paid on an hourly basis.
   h. Milton reports his unreimbursed expenses on a Form 2106.

4. **LO.1** Bernard operates a hair styling salon as a sole proprietor. Because his shop has several extra work stations that are not being used, he is considering renting these to other stylists, but he wants to avoid any employer-employee relationship with them. Advise Bernard on the type of working arrangement he should set up to ensure that any new stylists will be classified as independent contractors and not as employees.

DECISION MAKING

5. **LO.2, 11** Garth recently purchased a new automobile for which he plans mixed use (i.e., both business and personal). In the next few years, he intends to use the actual cost method to maximize the depreciation deduction on the car and, thereafter, to convert to the automatic mileage method. He expects that this approach will maximize his tax benefits from the business use of the car. Are there any flaws in Garth's plan?

ISSUE ID

6. **LO.2, 11** Kristen has just purchased a new automobile that she plans to use about 70% of the time for business. As to the difference between the actual cost method and the automatic mileage method, advise Kristen on the tax treatment of the following items:
   a. State and local sales tax on the purchase of the auto.
   b. Business parking.
   c. Interest on auto loan.
   d. Depreciation.
   e. Auto insurance and automobile club dues.
   f. Toll charges while on family vacation trip.
   g. Periodic oil changes and rotation of tires.
   h. Fines for traffic violations incurred during business use.

DECISION MAKING

7. **LO.2** In 2009, Emma purchased an automobile, which she uses for both business and personal purposes. Although Emma does not keep records as to operating expenses (e.g., gas, oil, repairs), she can prove the percentage of business use and the miles

ISSUE ID

driven each year. In March 2011, Emma seeks your advice as to what income tax benefit, if any, she can derive from the use of her automobile. What would you suggest?

8. **LO.2, 3** Explain the difference between *travel* expenses and *transportation* expenses.

9. **LO.3** Lance, who practices law in New York City, leaves his office on Tuesday at 4:00 A.M., flies to Los Angeles, makes a court appearance at 1:00 P.M., and flies back to New York that same day.
   a. Was Lance away from home for income tax purposes?
   b. What difference does it make?

ISSUE ID

10. **LO.3** Dr. Werner is a full-time professor of accounting at Pelican University. During the year, he teaches continuing education programs for CPA groups in several cities. He also serves as an expert witness in numerous lawsuits involving accounting fraud. Comment on the possible tax treatment of Dr. Werner's job-related expenses.

11. **LO.3** Bill and Jean Wilder attend a three-day seminar in Chicago on current developments in taxation. Bill is a partner in a law firm in Memphis specializing in tax practice, while his wife, Jean, is a paralegal with the same firm. Comment on the deductibility of the Wilders' expenses in attending the seminar.

DECISION MAKING

12. **LO.3** Rick is scheduled to go to London on business and would like to do some sightseeing while there. A colleague advises him that to maximize his deductible expenses he should plan the business and personal portions of the trip carefully and maximize the use of weekends and holidays. What is meant by this advice?

13. **LO.4** In order to qualify for the moving expense deduction, a taxpayer must satisfy a time test.
   a. What is the time test?
   b. When might the taxpayer be excused from satisfying the time test?

14. **LO.4** Provide some examples (at least three) of moving expenses that are not "qualified" and, therefore, not deductible.

15. **LO.5, 10** Jamie has an undergraduate degree in finance and is employed full-time by a bank. She is taking courses at a local university leading to an MBA degree.
   a. Is the cost of this education deductible to her?
   b. If so, are any limitations imposed on the deduction?

16. **LO.5, 10** In connection with § 222 (deduction for qualified tuition and related expenses), comment on the relevance of the following:
   a. A dentist enrolls in medical school.
   b. The standard deduction is claimed.
   c. Enrollment at a college requires the payment of a student activity fee.
   d. The lifetime learning credit is claimed.
   e. The taxpayer is married and has MAGI of $160,001.
   f. Miscellaneous itemized deductions exceed 2% of AGI.
   g. The tuition is paid by the taxpayer who qualifies as a dependent of his parents.
   h. The taxpayer is married and files a separate return.

17. **LO.5, 10** The Federal income tax contains many provisions that encourage education. In this regard, give examples of various benefits available in the form of:
   a. Exclusions from gross income.
   b. Deductions.
   c. Credits.

18. **LO.6** In each of the following situations, indicate whether there is a cutback adjustment.
   a. Each year the employer awards its top salesperson an expense-paid trip to Jamaica.
   b. The employer has a cafeteria for its employees where meals are furnished at cost.
   c. The employer sponsors an annual Labor Day picnic for its employees.
   d. Every Christmas, the employer gives each employee a fruit cake.
   e. The taxpayer, an airline pilot, pays for meals and lodging during a layover between flights.
   f. The taxpayer pays a cover charge to take key clients to a nightclub.
   g. The taxpayer gives business gifts to her clients at Christmas.
   h. The taxpayer purchases tickets in order to take clients to an athletic event.

19. **LO.6** At the last minute, a law firm purchases 10 tickets to the Super Bowl in order to entertain certain key clients. Comment on some possible tax ramifications of this situation.

ISSUE ID

20. **LO.7** In connection with the office in the home deduction, comment on the following:
    a. When justified if the taxpayer is an employee.
    b. The exclusive use requirement.
    c. The distinction between *direct* and *indirect* expenses.
    d. Taxpayer is self-employed and claims the standard deduction.
    e. The deduction is not available to taxpayers who do not own their home (e.g., live in rented apartments).
    f. The treatment of expenses that exceed the gross income from the business.
    g. The treatment of expenses that might otherwise be deductible (e.g., interest on home mortgage).

21. **LO.4, 7** Trent, a resident of Florida, attends Vanderbilt University. After graduation, he moves to Dallas where he begins a job search. Shortly thereafter, he accepts a position with a local radio station as an announcer. Trent's college degree is in management. Presuming no reimbursement, what employment-related expenses might Trent be eligible to deduct?

ISSUE ID

22. **LO.8** Regarding the tax implications of various retirement plans, comment on the following:
    a. The difference between Keogh (H.R. 10) and traditional deductible IRA plans.
    b. The difference between traditional IRA and Roth IRA plans.

23. **LO.8** Joey, who is single, is not covered by another qualified plan and earns $109,000 at his job in 2011. How much can he contribute to a traditional IRA or to a Roth IRA in 2011?

24. **LO.9** What tax return reporting procedures must be followed by an employee under the following circumstances?
    a. Expenses and reimbursements are equal under an accountable plan.
    b. Reimbursements at the appropriate Federal per diem rate exceed expenses, and an adequate accounting is made to the employer.
    c. Expenses exceed reimbursements under a nonaccountable plan.

25. **LO.3, 6, 9, 10, 11** Kim recently graduated from college and is interviewing for a position in marketing. Crane Corporation has offered her a job as a sales representative that will require extensive travel and entertainment but provide valuable experience. Under the offer, she has two options: a salary of $48,000 and she absorbs all expenses; a salary of $35,000 and Crane reimburses for all expenses. Crane assures Kim that the $13,000 difference in the two options will be adequate to cover the expenses incurred. What issues should have an impact on Kim's choice?

DECISION MAKING

26. **LO.4, 11** Ralph plans to retire and move to New Mexico. Discuss Ralph's deduction for moving expenses under the following circumstances:
    a. He is a self-employed physician living and practicing in York, Pennsylvania.
    b. He is a geologist for a major oil company living and working in Nigeria (Africa).
    c. What suggestions, if any, do you have that would improve Ralph's tax position under each assumption?

ISSUE ID

DECISION MAKING

27. **LO.10** Comment on the deductibility of each of the following items:
    a. Gambling losses that are less than gambling gains. Taxpayer is not a professional gambler.
    b. Expenses incurred in applying for the CFO (chief financial officer) position of a grocery chain. Taxpayer, an auditor with a CPA firm, did not get the job.
    c. Club dues for the Coronado Club. Taxpayer, a lawyer, uses the luncheon club exclusively for business.
    d. Cost of visual aids prepared by a college professor for use in a graduate seminar.
    e. Cost of dry cleaning uniforms (including alterations by a tailor). Taxpayer is the doorman at a New York City hotel.
    f. Cost of safety shoes. Taxpayer is a self-employed stone mason.
    g. Cost of noncredit CPA exam review program. Taxpayer just graduated from business school and is employed by an accounting firm.
    h. Expenses incurred by taxpayer, a member of the Vermont National Guard, to participate in a two-day training session conducted in Pennsylvania.

PROBLEMS

28. **LO.2, 3** During the year, Judith holds two jobs. After an eight-hour day at the first job, she works three hours at the second job. On Fridays of each week, she returns home for dinner before going to the second job. On the other days (Monday through Thursday), she goes directly from the first job to the second job, stopping along the way for a meal. The mileage involved is as follows:

Home to first job	20
First job to second job	18
Home to second job	29

 a. Assuming Judith works 48 weeks during the year, how much of her mileage is deductible?
 b. Can Judith deduct the dinners she purchased? Why or why not?

29. **LO.2, 5** Byron is employed by an accounting firm and uses his automobile in connection with his work. During the month of August 2011, he works at the office for 5 days and participates in the audit of a key client for 18 days. In the audit situation, Byron goes directly from his home to the client's office. On all other days, he drives to his employer's office. On four Saturdays in August, he drives from his home to a local university where he attends classes in a part-time MBA program. Relevant mileage is as follows:

Home to office	12
Office to audit client	13
Home to audit client	9
Home to university	16

 Using the automatic mileage method, what is Byron's deduction for the month?

30. **LO.2** Jeri is the regional sales manager for a fast-food chain. She starts her working day by driving from home to the regional office, works there for several hours, and then visits the three sales outlets in her region. Relevant mileage is as follows:

Home to regional office	10
Regional office to sales outlet #1	11
Sales outlet #1 to sales outlet #2	13
Sales outlet #2 to sales outlet #3	12
Sales outlet #3 to home	15

 If Jeri uses the automatic mileage method and works on 240 days in 2011, what is her deduction for the year?

31. **LO.2** On July 1, 2009, Rex purchases a new automobile for $40,000. He uses the car 80% for business and drives the car as follows: 8,000 miles in 2009; 19,000 miles in 2010; and 20,000 miles in 2011. Determine Rex's basis in the auto as of January 1, 2012, under the following assumptions.
 a. Rex uses the automatic mileage method.
 b. Rex uses the actual cost method. [Assume that no § 179 expensing is claimed and that 200% declining-balance cost recovery with the half-year convention is used—see Chapter 8. The recovery limitation for 2009 is as follows: $2,960 (first year), $4,800 (second year), $2,850 (third year).]

32. **LO.3** Carla, the regional manager for a national retail drug chain, is based in Atlanta. During March and April of this year, she has to replace temporarily the district manager in Jackson, Mississippi. During this period, Carla flies to Jackson on Sunday night, spends the week at the district office, and returns home to Atlanta on Friday afternoon. The cost of returning home is $650, while the cost of spending the weekend in Jackson would have been $500.
 a. Presuming no reimbursement by her employer, how much, if any, of these weekend expenses may Carla deduct?
 b. Would your answer in (a) change if the amounts involved are reversed (i.e., the trip home cost $500; staying in Jackson would have been $650)?

33. **LO.3, 6** In June of this year, Dr. and Mrs. Bret Spencer traveled to Denver to attend a three-day conference sponsored by the American Society of Implant Dentistry. Bret, a practicing

oral surgeon, participated in scheduled technical sessions dealing with the latest developments in surgical procedures. On two days, Mrs. Spencer attended group meetings where various aspects of family tax planning were discussed. On the other day, she went sightseeing. Mrs. Spencer does not work for her husband, but she does their tax returns and handles the family investments. Expenses incurred in connection with the conference are summarized below:

Airfare (two tickets)	$2,000
Lodging (single and double occupancy are the same rate—$250 each day)	750
Meals ($200 × 3 days)*	600
Conference registration fee (includes $120 for Family Tax Planning sessions)	620
Car rental	300

*Split equally between Dr. and Mrs. Spencer.

How much, if any, of these expenses can the Spencers deduct?

34. **LO.1, 3, 6** Louise works for a clothing manufacturer as a dress designer. She travels to New York City to attend three days of fashion shows and then spends three days sightseeing. Her expenses are as follows;

Airfare	$1,400
Lodging (6 nights)	1,800
Meals (6 days)	1,200
Airport transportation	120

[Assume lodging/meals are the same amount for the business and personal portion of the trip (e.g., $200 per day for meals).]

a. Presuming no reimbursement, how much can Louise deduct as to the trip?
b. Would the tax treatment of Louise's deduction differ if she was an independent contractor (rather than an employee)? Explain.

35. **LO.3** On Thursday, Justin flies from Baltimore (his home office) to Cadiz (Spain). He conducts business on Friday and Tuesday; vacations on Saturday, Sunday, and Monday (a legal holiday in Spain); and returns to Baltimore on Thursday. Justin was scheduled to return home on Wednesday, but all flights were canceled due to bad weather. Therefore, he spent Wednesday watching floor shows at a local casino.

a. For tax purposes, what portion of Justin's trip is regarded as being for business?
b. Suppose Monday had not been a legal holiday. Would this change your answer in (a)?
c. Under either (a) or (b), how much of Justin's airfare qualifies as a deductible business expense?

36. **LO.3** Monica travels from her office in Boston to Lisbon, Portugal, on business. Her absence of 13 days was spent as follows: **DECISION MAKING**

Thursday	Depart for and arrive at Lisbon
Friday	Business transacted
Saturday and Sunday	Vacationing
Monday through Friday	Business transacted
Saturday and Sunday	Vacationing
Monday	Business transacted
Tuesday	Depart Lisbon and return to office in Boston

a. For tax purposes, how many days has Monica spent on business?
b. What difference does it make?
c. Could Monica have spent more time than she did vacationing on the trip without loss of existing tax benefits? Explain.

37. **LO.4** Marlo, a financial planner, decides to quit his job with an investment bank in Columbia, South Carolina, and establish a private practice in Albuquerque, New Mexico. In connection with the move, he incurs the following expenses:

Moving van charge	$4,300
Lodging during move	520
Meals during move	360

Loss on sale of residence in Columbia	$4,000
Mileage for personal autos	3,400 miles

How much of these expenses, if any, can Marlo deduct?

38. **LO.4, 7** Upon losing his job as a plant manager in Quincy (Massachusetts), Anthony incurs $6,200 in job search expenses. Having no success in finding new employment in the same type of work, Anthony moves to Clearwater (Florida) and begins a charter boat business. His expenses in connection with the move are summarized below:

Penalty for breaking lease on Quincy rented residence	$2,800
Forfeiture of membership in Quincy Country Club	2,200
Packing and moving van charges	7,100
Lodging during move (3 nights)	380
Meals during move	360
Mileage (for two automobiles)	2,400 miles

How much of these expenses may Anthony deduct?

39. **LO.4** After being downsized by his former employer, in November 2010 Wayne moves from Minnesota to Alabama to accept a new job. When filing his Federal income tax return for 2010, Wayne deducts the $14,000 in moving expenses he incurred (none of which were reimbursed by either his former or new employer). On June 6, 2011, Wayne's employment terminates. What are the tax consequences if the termination occurred because:
   a. Wayne was killed by a drunk driver?
   b. Wayne was downsized by the new employer?
   c. Wayne was fired by the new employer because he assaulted a client?
   d. Wayne quit because he inherited a large amount of money and decided he did not want to work anymore?

40. **LO.5** Eric is employed as a full-time high school teacher. The school district where he works recently instituted a policy requiring all of its teachers to start working on a master's degree. Pursuant to this new rule, Eric spent most of the summer of 2011 taking graduate courses at an out-of-town university. His expenses are as follows:

Tuition	$6,300
Books and course materials	1,300
Lodging	1,500
Meals	2,200
Laundry and dry cleaning	280
Campus parking	250

In addition, Eric drove his personal automobile 1,900 miles in connection with the education. He uses the automatic mileage method.
   a. How much, if any, of these expenses might qualify as deductions *for* AGI?
   b. How much, if any, of these expenses might qualify as deductions *from* AGI?

41. **LO.5** In each of the following independent situations, determine how much, if any, qualifies as a deduction *for* AGI under § 222 (qualified tuition and related expenses):
   a. Sophia is single and is employed as an architect. During 2011, she spends $3,900 in tuition to attend law school at night. Her MAGI is $64,000.
   b. John is single and is employed as a pharmacist. During 2011, he spends $2,300 ($2,100 for tuition and $200 for books) to take a course in herbal supplements at a local university. His MAGI is $70,000.
   c. Hailey is married and is employed as a bookkeeper. She spends $5,200 for tuition and $900 for books and supplies pursuing a bachelor's degree in accounting. Her MAGI is $40,000 on the separate return she files.
   d. How much, if any, of the above amounts *not allowed under* § 222 might otherwise qualify as a deduction *from* AGI?

42. **LO.5** In each of the following independent situations, determine how much, if any, qualifies as a deduction *for* AGI under § 222 (qualified tuition and related expenses):
   a. Carmen is a divorced mother with MAGI of $66,000. She pays $4,800 to enroll her dependent son at a local college.

b. The Bells have MAGI of $80,000 and file a joint return. They spend $4,100 to enroll their dependent daughter at a state college. The $4,100 includes $3,800 for tuition and $300 for a student activity fee.

c. Charles is single and has MAGI of $100,000. He pays $5,000 in tuition for his dependent mother to attend graduate school.

d. Benjamin is single and is claimed as a dependent by his parents. He pays $3,000 from his savings for tuition at a junior college.

43. **LO.6, 9** Dexter is a licensed commercial pilot who works for Kite Charter Jet Service. Typically, Dexter, who lives near the airport, flies a charter out of Frankfort, Kentucky, to either Las Vegas or Reno, spends several nights there, and then returns home with the same group. Kite provides Dexter with a travel allowance of $1,700 per month but requires no accountability. For the current calendar year, Dexter had the following job-related expenses:

Meals	$ 8,000
Lodging	11,000
Transportation (taxis, limos)	600
Uniforms	1,100
Dry cleaning of uniforms	300
Annual physical exam	1,000

The uniforms are required to be worn on the job. The Federal Aviation Administration requires the annual physical exam for the maintenance of a commercial pilot's license. How may Dexter treat these expenses for Federal income tax purposes?

44. **LO.6** Snipe Associates paid $60,000 for a 20-seat skybox at Veterans Stadium for eight professional football games. Regular seats to these games range from $80 to $200 each. At one game, an employee of Snipe entertained 18 clients. Snipe furnished food and beverages for the event at a cost of $1,000. The game was preceded by a bona fide business discussion, and all expenses are adequately substantiated.

a. How much may Snipe deduct for this event?

b. What, if any, is the deduction if no representative from Snipe attended the game?

c. What if there was no bona fide business discussion either preceding or after the event?

45. **LO.6** During the current year, Paul, the vice president of a bank, made gifts in the following amounts:

To Sarah (Paul's personal assistant) at Christmas	$36
To Darryl (a key client)—$3 was for gift-wrapping	53
To Darryl's wife (a homemaker) on her birthday	20
To Veronica (Paul's boss) at Christmas	30

In addition, on professional assistants' day, Paul takes Sarah to lunch at a cost of $82. Presuming Paul has adequate substantiation and is not reimbursed, how much can he deduct?

46. **LO.7** Christine is employed full-time as an accountant for a national hardware chain. She also has a private consulting practice, which provides tax advice and financial planning to the general public. For this purpose, she maintains an office in her home. Expenses relating to her home are as follows:

Real property taxes	$3,900
Interest on home mortgage	4,000
Operating expenses of home	1,100
Depreciation allocated to 20% business use	1,600

Christine's income from consulting is $16,000, and the related expenses are $5,000.

a. What is Christine's office in the home deduction?

b. Suppose that Christine also spent $3,000 to repaint and replace the carpet in the office. How do these additional costs change the answer to part (a)?

c. Suppose that Christine's income from consulting is only $8,000 (not $16,000). How does this change the answer to part (a)?

47. **LO.7** Melanie is a full-time teacher of the fifth grade at Tern Academy. During the year, she spends $1,300 for classroom supplies. Upon the submission of adequate substantiation, Tern reimburses her for $600 of these expenses—the maximum amount

of reimbursement allowed for supplies under school policy. [The reimbursement is not shown as income (box 1) on the Form W–2 Tern sends to Melanie.] What are the income tax consequences of the $1,300 if Melanie:

a. Claims the standard deduction?

b. Chooses to itemize her deductions *from* AGI?

DECISION MAKING

48. **LO.8** Amber's employer, Lavender, Inc., has a § 401(k) plan that permits salary deferral elections by its employees. Amber's salary is $99,000, and her marginal tax rate is 33%.

a. What is the maximum amount Amber can elect for salary deferral treatment for 2011?

b. If Amber elects salary deferral treatment for the amount in (a), how much can she save in taxes?

c. What amount would you recommend that Amber elect for salary deferral treatment for 2011?

49. **LO.8** Sally, a single individual, participates in her employer's SIMPLE § 401(k) plan. The plan permits participants to contribute a percentage of their salary. Sally elects to contribute 5% of her annual salary of $111,000 to the plan. On what amount of her salary does Sally pay income taxes in 2011?

50. **LO.8** Harvey is a self-employed accountant with earned income from the business of $120,000 (after the deduction for one-half of his self-employment tax). He has a profit sharing plan (e.g., defined contribution Keogh plan). What is the maximum amount Harvey can contribute to his retirement plan in 2011?

51. **LO.8** Answer the following independent questions with respect to traditional IRA contributions for 2011:

a. Juan, age 41, earns a salary of $28,000 and is not an active participant in any other qualified plan. His wife, Agnes, has no earned income. What is the maximum total deductible contribution to their IRAs? Juan wishes to contribute as much as possible to his own IRA.

b. Abby, age 29, has earned income of $25,000, and her husband, Sam, has earned income of $2,600. They are not active participants in any other qualified plan. What is the maximum contribution to their IRAs?

c. Leo's employer makes a contribution of $3,500 to Leo's simplified employee pension plan. If Leo is single, has earned income of $32,000, and has AGI of $29,000, what amount, if any, can he contribute to an IRA?

52. **LO.8** Frank established a Roth IRA at age 25 and contributed a total of $131,244 to it over 38 years. The account is now worth $376,000. How much of these funds can Frank withdraw tax-free?

53. **LO.8** Beth, age 51, has a traditional deductible IRA with an account balance of $221,419, of which $160,400 represents contributions and $61,019 represents earnings. In 2011, she converts her traditional IRA into a Roth IRA. What amount, if any, must Beth include in her gross income in 2011?

54. **LO.3, 6, 9** Tim has AGI of $92,000 during the year and the following expenses related to his employment:

Lodging while in travel status	$4,000
Meals during travel	3,800
Business transportation	5,200
Entertainment of clients	3,600
Professional dues and subscriptions	1,000

Tim is reimbursed $13,000 under his employer's accountable plan. What are his deductions *for* and *from* AGI?

DECISION MAKING

55. **LO.3, 6, 9** During the year, Brenda has the following expenses related to her employment:

Airfare	$8,500
Meals	4,000
Lodging	4,900
Transportation while in travel status (taxis, limos)	940
Entertainment of clients	8,000

Although Brenda renders an adequate accounting to her employer, she is reimbursed for only $12,000 of the above expenses. What are Brenda's tax consequences based on the following assumptions?

a. The $12,000 reimbursement does not designate which expenses are covered.
b. The reimbursement specifically covers *only* the meals and entertainment expenses.
c. The reimbursement covers any of the expenses *other than* meals and entertainment.
d. If Brenda has a choice of reimbursement procedures [parts (a), (b), or (c) above], which should she select and why?

56. **LO.6, 9, 10** Audry, age 38 and single, earns a salary of $59,000. She has interest income of $1,600 and has a $2,000 long-term capital loss from the sale of a stock investment. Audry incurs the following employment-related expenses during the year:

Transportation	$5,500
Meals	2,800
Lodging	4,200
Entertaining clients	2,200
Professional dues and subscriptions	300

Under an accountable plan, Audry receives reimbursements of $4,500 from her employer. Calculate her AGI and itemized employee business expenses.

57. **LO.5, 7, 10** B. J. and Carolyn Grace are full-time employees. B. J. is an elementary school teacher, and Carolyn is a registered nurse at a hospital. During 2011, they incur the following employment-related expenses:

School supplies for use in the classroom	$1,400
Emergency room uniforms	800
Union dues (teachers association)	200
Job hunting expenses (Carolyn obtained another nursing position but decided not to change jobs)	1,300
Continuing education correspondence courses (required to maintain nursing license)	380
Professional dues and subscriptions	1,100

None of these expenses are reimbursed by the employers.

For the year, the Graces file a joint return reflecting salary income of $90,000. They also have gambling income of $6,000 and gambling losses of $7,000 (fully substantiated). They pay $400 to have their tax return prepared. They have other itemized deductions (i.e., interest on home mortgage, property taxes on personal residence, state income taxes, charitable contributions) of $14,500. Determine the total amount of itemized deductions allowed to the Graces for tax year 2011.

58. **LO.1, 2, 4, 5, 7, 10** Complete the following table by classifiying each of the independent expenditures (assume no reimbursement takes place).

	Expense Item	Deductible *for* AGI	Deductible *from* AGI	Not Deductible
a.	Moving expense of an employee	______	______	______
b.	Moving expense of a self-employed taxpayer	______	______	______
c.	Gambling losses in excess of gambling gains incurred by a retired taxpayer	______	______	______
d.	Cost of taking the bar exam	______	______	______
e.	Tax return preparation fee incurred by an employed plumber	______	______	______
f.	Safety glasses purchased by an employed pipefitter	______	______	______
g.	Club dues to Rotary Club paid by self-employed dentist	______	______	______
h.	Dues to auto club (e.g., AAA) for taxpayer who uses the automatic mileage method	______	______	______
i.	Nursing refresher course for taxpayer who retired from nursing five years ago	______	______	______

CUMULATIVE PROBLEMS

TAX RETURN PROBLEM

H&R BLOCK At Home

59. Kirk B. and Trudy N. Ward (ages 44 and 42) are husband and wife and live at 4321 Peak Avenue, Denver, CO 80202. Kirk is a regional sales manager for Eagle Industries, a national wholesaler of plumbing and heating supplies, while Trudy is a part-time dental hygienist for a chain of dental clinics.

- Kirk is classified by Eagle as a statutory employee with compensation for 2010 (based on commissions) of $92,000. He is expected to maintain his own office and pay for all business expenses from this amount. Eagle does not require him to render an accounting. It does not withhold for Federal and state income taxes but does withhold and account for the payroll taxes incurred (e.g., Social Security and Medicare). Kirk is covered by Eagle's noncontributory medical plan but has chosen not to participate in its § 401(k) retirement plan.

  Kirk's employment-related expenses for 2010 are summarized below:

Airfare	$7,700
Lodging	5,200
Meals (during travel status)	4,800
Entertainment	3,200
Ground transportation (e.g., limos, rental cars, taxis)	900
Business gifts	600
Office supplies (includes postage, overnight delivery, copying)	1,200

  The entertainment involved business meals for purchasing agents, store owners, and building contractors. The business gifts consisted of $50 gift certificates to a national steak house. These were sent by Kirk during the Christmas holidays to 12 of his major customers.

  In addition, Kirk drove his 2008 Ford Expedition 12,000 miles for business (3,000 for personal) during 2010. He purchased the Expedition on March 15, 2008, and has always used the automatic (standard) mileage method for tax purposes. Parking and tolls relating to business use total $280 for 2010. (Assume the mileage on the Ford took place evenly during the year.)

- When the Wards purchased their present residence in March 2008, they devoted 300 of the 3,000 square feet of living space to an office for Kirk. The property cost $340,000 ($40,000 of which is attributable to the land) and has since appreciated in value. Expenses during 2010 relating to the residence (see below for mortgage interest and property taxes) are as follows:

Insurance	$2,400
Repairs and maintenance	900
Utilities	4,500
Carpeting (office area only)	1,500

  In terms of depreciation, the Wards use the MACRS percentage tables applicable to 39-year nonresidential real property.

- Trudy works part-time as a substitute for whichever hygienist is ill or on vacation or when one of the clinics is particularly busy (e.g., prior to the beginning of the school year). Besides her transportation, she has to provide and maintain her own uniforms. Her expenses for 2010 appear below:

Uniforms (including laundry charges of $240)	$610
State and city occupational licenses	240
Professional journal and membership dues in the American Dental Hygiene Association	310
Correspondence study course (taken online) dealing with teeth whitening procedures	400

  In addition, Trudy drove the family Chevrolet Suburban 1,800 miles going from her home to and from work assignments.

  Her Form W–2 for the year shows earnings of $41,000 and income tax withholdings of $4,000 (Federal) and $1,000 (state) and the proper amount of payroll taxes (Social Security and Medicare). Since Trudy is a part-time employee, she is not included in her employer's medical or retirement plans.

- Besides the items already mentioned, the Wards had the following receipts during 2010:

Interest income—		
State of Idaho general-purpose bonds	$1,400	
Ford Motor Company bonds	600	
Wells Fargo Bank CD	900	$ 2,900
Federal income tax refund for tax year 2009		180
Life insurance proceeds paid by Falcon Assurance Corporation		100,000
Inheritance of savings account from Louise Ward		100,000
Sales proceeds from two ATVs		8,000

For several years, the Wards' household has included Kirk's divorced mother, Louise, who has been claimed as their dependent. In late November 2010, Louise unexpectedly died in her sleep of a coronary arrest. Unknown to them, Louise had a life insurance policy and a savings account (with Kirk as the designated beneficiary of each). In 2009, the Wards purchased two ATVs for $12,000. After several near mishaps, they decided the sport was too dangerous. In 2010, they sold the ATVs to their neighbor.

Additional expenditures for 2010 include:

Funeral expenses for Louise Ward		$ 6,500
Taxes—		
Real property taxes on personal residence	$5,200	
Colorado state income tax due (paid in April 2010 for tax year 2009)	310	5,510
Mortgage interest on personal residence		6,200
Paid church pledge		2,400
Contributions to traditional IRAs for Trudy and Kirk ($5,000 + $5,000)		10,000

In 2010, the Wards made quarterly estimated tax payments of $1,400 (Federal) and $500 (state) for a total of $5,600 (Federal) and $2,000 (state).

Compute the Wards' Federal income tax payable or refund due, assuming they file a joint income tax return for 2010. If they have overpaid, they want the amount refunded. They do not want to contribute to the Presidential Election Campaign Fund. Social Security numbers are as follows: 123–45–6787 (Louise); 123–45–6788 (Trudy); and 123–45–6789 (Kirk). Kirk's business code number is 421700. Suggested software: H&R BLOCK At Home.

60. Gloria L. Carson, age 35, is single and lives alone at 430 Poplar Street, Apartment 300, Memphis, TN 38101. Gloria is the regional manager for STAFIT, a national chain of weight control and physical fitness centers.

TAX COMPUTATION PROBLEM

- STAFIT pays Gloria an annual salary of $70,000 plus an expense allowance of $25,000. STAFIT requires no accounting as to the expense allowance and expects Gloria to use the funds as needed to absorb her employment-related expenses (including maintaining an office in her home). She participates in STAFIT's contributory health and § 401(k) plans. In 2011, she paid in $2,400 for the medical insurance and contributed $8,000 to the § 401(k) retirement plan.
- Gloria's employment-related expenses for 2011 include the following:

Airfare	$4,200
Lodging	3,900
Meals (while in travel status)	4,200
Entertainment	1,000
Business gifts	600
Ground transportation while in travel status (e.g., rental cars, limos, taxis)	300
Subscriptions to trade journals	120
Online correspondence course on Pilates exercises	280

The gifts consisted of fruit baskets [$25 (cost) + $2 (wrapping) + $3 (shipping)] that Gloria sent to 20 key managers at Christmas. Gloria took the correspondence course to help her evaluate the Pilates programs offered at the STAFIT centers.

- Of the 1,600 square feet of living space in Gloria's apartment, she has devoted 400 square feet for exclusive use as an office. Expenses in connection with her apartment during 2011 are as follows:

Insurance (renter's casualty and theft coverage)	$ 1,200
Rent	12,000
Utilities	3,600
Wallpapering (office area only)	1,800

- Gloria owns a Chrysler 300 that she purchased on June 29, 2009, for $32,000 (no trade-in involved). The car is used 80% for business and 20% for personal purposes. Depreciation has been claimed under the MACRS 200% declining-balance method, and no § 179 election was made in the year of purchase. (For depreciation information, see Chapter 8 in the text and the IRS Instructions to Form 4562, Part V.) During 2011, Gloria drove 14,000 miles. Expenses relating to the car are:

Gasoline	$1,950
Repairs and maintenance	310
Auto club dues	250
Insurance	3,000
Interest on car loan	1,200
Traffic fines (all during business use)	420
Parking and tolls (all during business use)	580

- Gloria provides more than half of the support of her parents, Doyle and Grace Carson, who live in their own house in Franklin, Tennessee. In addition to Social Security benefits, the parents have a small amount of interest from municipal bonds. Besides some medical expenses (see below), Gloria also pays the premiums of $1,800 on Doyle's life insurance policy.
- Gloria had the following additional receipts in 2011:

Proceeds from the sale of land	$15,000
Fees for serving on a jury	600
TV set won in a church raffle	1,500
Cash found in a parking lot	1,000

The land sale consisted of a city lot located in Nashville (Tennessee) purchased by Gloria as an investment on April 9, 2002. She paid $20,000 for the property in the hope of future appreciation. When she was offered $15,000 for the lot, Gloria accepted and transferred title on January 6, 2011. In connection with the jury duty, Gloria incurred unreimbursed expenses (e.g., parking) of $80. The TV set cost the church $1,500 but has a retail value of $2,200. Since Gloria already owns a TV, she declined to accept the prize. While shopping at a mall during the Christmas season, Gloria found an unmarked envelope in the parking lot containing 20 $50 bills. Gloria decided to keep the money as she saw no realistic way of locating the true owner.

- Other expenditures for 2011 are summarized below:

Medical and dental expenses not covered by insurance	$6,800
Net gambling loss	1,200
State and local general sales tax	3,300
Paid church pledges for 2010 and 2011	3,600
Fee paid for preparation of 2010 Federal income tax return	500
Contribution to the reelection campaign fund of the mayor of Memphis	100

The medical expenses include $5,000 paid for dental implants received by Grace. During 2011, Gloria had gambling winnings of $600 and losses of $1,800. The $1,200 represents the end result after offsetting gains against losses. Gloria keeps a record of all of her purchases and can, therefore, substantiate the $3,300 sales tax amount. Gloria pledges $1,800 a year to her church. On January 4, 2011, she paid the pledges for 2010 and 2011.

Relevant Social Security numbers are 123–45–6786 (Gloria); 123–45–6784 (Doyle); and 123–45–6785 (Grace). Gloria's employer withheld $4,600 for Federal income tax purposes, and she applied her $450 overpayment for 2010 toward the 2011 tax liability.

Compute Gloria's Federal income tax payable or refund for 2011.

RESEARCH PROBLEMS

Note: Solutions to Research Problems can be prepared by using the **Checkpoint® Student Edition** online research product, which is available to accompany this text. It is also possible to prepare solutions to the Research Problems by using tax research materials found in a standard tax library.

THOMSON REUTERS
Checkpoint® Student Edition

Research Problem 1. Aaron, a resident of Minnesota, has been a driver for Green Delivery Service for the past six years. For this purpose, he leases a truck from Green, and his compensation is based on a percentage of the income resulting from his pickup and delivery services. Green allows its drivers to choose their 10-hour shifts and does not exercise any control on how these services are carried out (e.g., the route to be taken or the order in which parcels are delivered or picked up). Under Green's operating agreement with its drivers, Green can terminate the arrangement after 30 days' notice. In practice, however, Green allows its truckers to quit immediately without giving advance notice. The agreement also labels the drivers as independent contractors. Green maintains no health or retirement plans for its drivers, and each year it reports their income by issuing Forms 1099–MISC (and not Forms W–2). Green requires its drivers to maintain a commercial driver's license and be in good standing with the state highway law enforcement division.

Citing the employment tax Regulations in §§ 31.3121(d)–1(c)(2) and 31.3306(i)–1(b), an IRS agent contends that Aaron is an independent contractor and, therefore, is subject to the self-employment tax. Based on *Peno Trucking, Inc.* (93 TCM 1027, T.C.Memo. 2007–66), Aaron disagrees and contends that he is an employee (i.e., not self-employed). Who is correct and why?

Research Problem 2. Richard Harding is the sheriff of Howard County, Indiana. In addition to the usual law enforcement duties, the sheriff has the responsibility of maintaining the detention facility (i.e., county jail). Further, he must furnish meals for all prisoners in accordance with certain nutritional standards prescribed by the state. Although the sheriff must absorb the cost of the meals, the county provides a personal allowance.

During the year, Sheriff Harding received a salary of $35,000 (as reported on a Form W–2 issued by Howard County). He spent $90,000 on prisoner meals and received meal allowances of $110,000. On his income tax return, he reported the salary as employee income, but listed the allowances and meals on a Schedule C. Thus, he treated himself as self-employed by claiming the cost of the meals as a deduction *for* AGI.

Upon audit, the IRS determined that the Schedule C treatment was improper. Harding was not in a separate trade or business of providing meals, but was merely carrying out his employment-related duties. The costs of the meals are employee business expenses deductible only as miscellaneous itemized deductions on Schedule A. As such, they are subject to the 2%-of-AGI floor.

Is Sheriff Harding or the IRS correct? Why?

Use the tax resources of the Internet to address the following question. Do not restrict your search to the Web, but include a review of newsgroups and general reference materials, practitioner sites and resources, primary sources of the tax law, chat rooms and discussion groups, and other opportunities.

INTERNET *activity*

Research Problem 3. What are the guidelines regarding the deductibility of luxury water travel (e.g., cruise ship) for business purposes? Refer to Chapter 1 of IRS Publication No. 463.

CHAPTER

10

Deductions and Losses: Certain Itemized Deductions

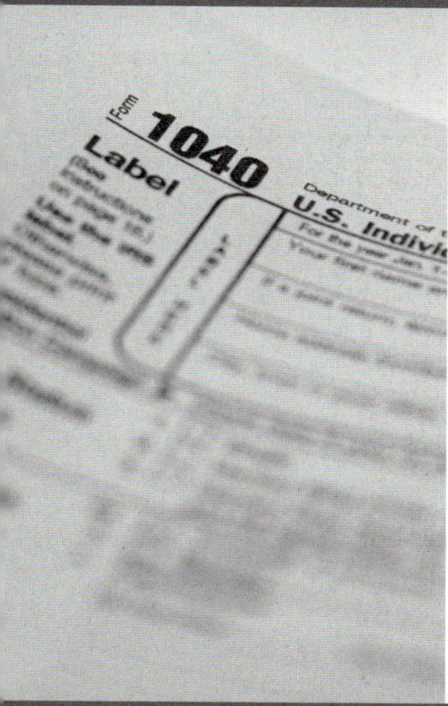

LEARNING OBJECTIVES

After completing Chapter 10, you should be able to:

LO.1

Distinguish between deductible and nondeductible personal expenses.

LO.2

Define medical expenses and compute the medical expense deduction.

LO.3

Contrast deductible taxes with nondeductible fees, licenses, and other charges.

LO.4

Understand the Federal income tax treatment of state and local income taxes and sales taxes.

LO.5

Distinguish between deductible and nondeductible interest and apply the appropriate limitations to deductible interest.

LO.6

Understand charitable contributions and their related measurement problems and percentage limitations.

LO.7

List the business and personal expenditures that are deductible either as miscellaneous itemized deductions or as other itemized deductions.

LO.8

Identify tax planning strategies that can maximize the benefit of itemized deductions.

OUTLINE

For the latest in changes to tax legislation, visit **www.cengage.com/taxation/swft.**

FRAMEWORK 1040: Tax Formula for Individuals

This chapter covers the boldfaced portions of the Tax Formula for Individuals that was introduced in Figure 3.1 on p. 3-3. Below those portions are the sections of Form 1040 where the results are reported.

Income (broadly conceived)	$xx,xxx
Less: Exclusions	(x,xxx)
Gross income	$xx,xxx
Less: Deductions for adjusted gross income	(x,xxx)
Adjusted gross income	$xx,xxx
Less: The greater of total **itemized deductions** *or* the standard deduction	**(x,xxx)**

FORM 1040 (p. 2)

40 **Itemized deductions** (from Schedule A) **or** your **standard deduction** (see instructions) . .

Personal and dependency exemptions	(x,xxx)
Taxable income	$xx,xxx
Tax on taxable income (see Tax Tables or Tax Rate Schedules)	$ x,xxx
Less: Tax credits (including income taxes withheld and prepaid)	(xxx)
Tax due (or refund)	$ xxx

THE BIG PICTURE Tax Solutions for the Real World

IMPACT OF ITEMIZED DEDUCTIONS ON MAJOR PURCHASES

John and Susan Williamson, a young professional couple, have been renting an apartment since they were married. Their income has grown as they've become more established in their careers, and they now feel that the time has come to purchase their own home. John and Susan's current monthly rent is $2,000, but they are willing to spend $2,500 per month on an after-tax basis if necessary for their first home.

After months of house hunting, they have found the perfect home, but they fear it may be too expensive. If they acquire a standard mortgage to finance the purchase of the home, the total cash outlay during the first year of ownership would be $42,000 ($2,000 principal payments, $37,000 interest payments, $3,000 real estate taxes). Alternatively, if they use their retirement and taxable investments to secure the home financing, they could qualify for a lower interest rate and thereby reduce the interest charge from $37,000 to $35,000. They expect their Federal taxable income to range between $160,000 and $185,000 for the year. John and Susan have not itemized their deductions in prior years because the amount of their qualifying personal expenditures has fallen just short of the standard deduction amount. The Williamsons live in a state that imposes an income tax at a flat rate of 6 percent.

Can John and Susan Williamson afford to pursue their dream of home ownership? **Read the chapter and formulate your response.**

10.1 General Classification of Expenses

LO.1

Distinguish between deductible and nondeductible personal expenses.

As a general rule, the deduction of personal expenditures is disallowed by § 262 of the Code. However, Congress has chosen to allow certain personal expenditures to be deducted as itemized deductions. Personal expenditures that are deductible as itemized deductions include medical expenses, certain taxes, mortgage interest, investment interest, and charitable contributions. These expenditures and other personal expenditures that are allowed as itemized deductions are covered in this chapter. Though certain exceptions exist (e.g., alimony and traditional IRA contributions are deductible *for* AGI), personal expenditures not specifically allowed as itemized deductions by the tax law are nondeductible.

Allowable itemized deductions are deductible *from* AGI in arriving at taxable income if the taxpayer elects to itemize. The election to itemize is appropriate when total itemized deductions exceed the standard deduction based on the taxpayer's filing status.[1]

EXAMPLE 1
THE BIG PICTURE

Return to the facts of *The Big Picture* on p. 10-2. John and Susan Williamson will discover that with the purchase of a home, they will be able to itemize their deductions for the first time instead of claiming the standard deduction. Assuming the home mortgage interest expense and real estate taxes meet the requirements discussed in this chapter, they will be deducted *from* AGI because their total would exceed the amount of the standard deduction for a married couple filing a joint return. Further, other qualifying expenditures, such as state income taxes or sales tax and charitable contributions, likewise will be deductible as itemized deductions, providing an explicit tax benefit to the Williamsons. ■

10.2 Medical Expenses

LO.2

Define medical expenses and compute the medical expense deduction.

GENERAL REQUIREMENTS

Medical expenses paid for the care of the taxpayer, spouse, and dependents are allowed as an itemized deduction to the extent the expenses are not reimbursed. The **medical expense** deduction is limited to the amount by which such expenses *exceed* 7.5 percent of the taxpayer's AGI. Beginning in 2013, the 7.5 percent threshold is scheduled to become 10 percent.

EXAMPLE 2

During the year, Iris had medical expenses of $4,800, of which $1,000 was reimbursed by her insurance company. If her AGI for the year is $40,000, the itemized deduction for medical expenses is limited to $800 [($4,800 − $1,000) − (7.5% × $40,000)]. ■

MEDICAL EXPENSES DEFINED

The term *medical care* includes expenditures incurred for the "diagnosis, cure, mitigation, treatment, or prevention of disease, or for the purpose of affecting any structure or function of the body."[2] A *partial* list of deductible and nondeductible medical items appears in Exhibit 10.1.

A medical expense does not have to relate to a particular ailment to be deductible. Since the definition of medical care is broad enough to cover preventive measures, the cost of periodic physical and dental exams qualifies even for a taxpayer in good health.

Amounts paid for unnecessary *cosmetic surgery* are not deductible medical expenses. However, if cosmetic surgery is deemed necessary, it is deductible as a medical expense. Cosmetic surgery is necessary when it ameliorates (1) a deformity arising from a congenital abnormality, (2) a personal injury, or (3) a disfiguring disease.

---

[1] See §§ 63(c) and (d), respectively, for the definitions of the terms "standard deduction" and "itemized deductions."

[2] § 213(d)(1)(A).

TAX *in* the NEWS

The President and Vice President Itemize

Approximately two-thirds of all individual taxpayers take the standard deduction each year rather than itemize. President Barack H. Obama and Vice President Joseph R. Biden are among the one-third who itemize. Both the President and the Vice President, who file joint returns with their wives, released their 2009 income tax returns to the public in 2010. Their itemized deductions, along with certain other information from their tax returns, are shown to the right.

	President Obama	Vice President Biden
Gross income	$5,623,690	$333,182
Adjusted gross income	$5,505,409	$333,182
Itemized deductions:		
Medical expenses	$ –0–	$ –0–
Taxes	186,910	31,038
Interest	52,195	30,349
Charitable contributions	329,100	4,820
Job expenses and other miscellaneous deductions	–0–	–0–
Total itemized deductions	$ 568,205	$ 66,207

EXAMPLE 3

Art, a calendar year taxpayer, paid $11,000 to a plastic surgeon for a face lift. Art, age 75, merely wanted to improve his appearance. The $11,000 does not qualify as a medical expense since the surgery was unnecessary. In contrast, Marge's face is disfigured as a result of a serious automobile accident. The cost of restorative cosmetic surgery is deductible as a medical expense. ■

The cost of care in a *nursing home or home for the aged,* including meals and lodging, can be included in deductible medical expenses if the primary reason for being in the home is to get medical care. If the primary reason for being there is personal,

EXHIBIT 10.1 **Examples of Deductible and Nondeductible Medical Expenses**

Deductible	Nondeductible
Medical (including dental, mental, and hospital) care	Funeral, burial, or cremation expenses
Prescription drugs and insulin	Nonprescription drugs (except insulin)
Special equipment	Bottled water
Wheelchairs	Toiletries, cosmetics
Crutches	Diaper service, maternity clothes
Artificial limbs	Programs for the *general* improvement of health
Eyeglasses (including contact lenses)	Weight reduction
Hearing aids	Health spas
Transportation for medical care	Social activities (e.g., dancing and swimming lessons)
Medical and hospital insurance premiums	Unnecessary cosmetic surgery
Long-term care insurance premiums (subject to limitations)	
Cost of alcohol and drug rehabilitation	
Certain costs to stop smoking	
Weight reduction programs related to obesity	

any costs for medical or nursing care can be included in deductible medical expenses, but the cost of meals and lodging must be excluded.[3]

EXAMPLE 4

Norman has a chronic heart ailment. In October, his family decides to place Norman in a nursing home equipped to provide medical and nursing care facilities. Total nursing home expenses amount to $15,000 during the year. Of this amount, $4,500 is directly attributable to medical and nursing care. Since Norman is in need of significant medical and nursing care and is placed in the facility primarily for this purpose, all $15,000 of the nursing home costs are deductible (subject to the 7.5% floor). ■

Tuition expenses of a dependent at a special school may be deductible as a medical expense. The cost of medical care can include the expenses of a special school for a mentally or physically handicapped individual. The deduction is allowed if a principal reason for sending the individual to the school is the school's special resources for alleviating the infirmities. In this case, the cost of meals and lodging, in addition to the tuition, is a proper medical expense deduction.[4]

EXAMPLE 5

Jason's daughter Marcia attended public school through the seventh grade. Because Marcia was a poor student, she was examined by a psychiatrist who diagnosed a problem that created a learning disability. Upon the recommendation of the psychiatrist, Marcia is enrolled in a private school so that she can receive individual attention. The school has no special program for students with learning disabilities and does not provide special medical treatment. The expense related to Marcia's attendance is not deductible as a medical expense. The cost of any psychiatric care, however, qualifies as a medical expense. ■

Example 5 shows that the recommendation of a physician does not automatically make the expenditure deductible.

CAPITAL EXPENDITURES FOR MEDICAL PURPOSES

Some examples of *capital expenditures* for medical purposes are swimming pools if the taxpayer does not have access to a neighborhood pool and air conditioners if they do not become permanent improvements (e.g., window units).[5] Other examples include dust elimination systems,[6] elevators,[7] and vans specially designed for wheelchair-bound taxpayers. These expenditures are medical in nature if they are incurred as a medical necessity upon the advice of a physician, the facility is used primarily by the patient alone, and the expense is reasonable.

Capital expenditures normally are adjustments to basis and are not deductible. However, both a capital expenditure for a permanent improvement and expenditures made for the operation or maintenance of the improvement may qualify as medical expenses. If a capital expenditure qualifies as a medical expense, the allowable cost is deductible in the year incurred. Although depreciation is required for most other capital expenditures, it is not required for capital expenditures for medical purposes.

A capital improvement that ordinarily would not have a medical purpose qualifies as a medical expense if it is directly related to prescribed medical care and is deductible to the extent that the expenditure *exceeds* the increase in value of the related property. Appraisal costs related to capital improvements are also deductible, but not as medical expenses. These costs are expenses incurred in the determination of the taxpayer's tax liability.[8]

EXAMPLE 6

Fred is afflicted with heart disease. His physician advises him to install an elevator in his residence so he will not be required to climb the stairs. The cost of installing the elevator is $3,000, and the increase in the value of the residence is determined to be only $1,700. Therefore, $1,300 ($3,000 − $1,700) is deductible as a medical expense. Additional

[3]Reg. § 1.213–1(e)(1)(v).

[4]*Donald R. Pfeifer*, 37 TCM 816, T.C.Memo. 1978–189. Also see Rev.Rul. 78–340, 1978–2 C.B. 124.

[5]Reg. § 1.213–1(e)(1)(iii).

[6]Ltr.Rul. 7948029.

[7]*Riach v. Frank*, 62–1 USTC ¶9419, 9 AFTR 2d 1263, 302 F.2d 374 (CA–9, 1962).

[8]§ 212(3).

utility costs to operate the elevator and maintenance costs are deductible as medical expenses as long as the medical reason for the capital expenditure continues to exist. ■

The full cost of certain home-related capital expenditures incurred to enable a *physically handicapped* individual to live independently and productively qualifies as a medical expense. Qualifying costs include expenditures for constructing entrance and exit ramps to the residence, widening hallways and doorways to accommodate wheelchairs, installing support bars and railings in bathrooms and other rooms, and adjusting electrical outlets and fixtures.[9] These expenditures are subject to the 7.5 percent floor only, and the increase in the home's value is deemed to be zero.

MEDICAL EXPENSES INCURRED FOR SPOUSE AND DEPENDENTS

In computing the medical expense deduction, a taxpayer may include medical expenses for a spouse and for a person who was a dependent at the time the expenses were paid or incurred. Of the requirements that normally apply in determining dependency status,[10] neither the gross income nor the joint return test applies in determining dependency status for medical expense deduction purposes.

EXAMPLE 7

Ernie (age 22) is married and a full-time student at a university. During the year, Ernie incurred medical expenses that were paid by Matilda (Ernie's mother). She provided more than half of Ernie's support for the year. Even if Ernie files a joint return with his wife, Matilda may claim the medical expenses she paid for him. Matilda would combine Ernie's expenses with her own before applying the 7.5% floor. ■

For *divorced persons* with children, a special rule applies to the noncustodial parent. The noncustodial parent may claim any medical expenses he or she pays even though the custodial parent claims the children as dependents.

EXAMPLE 8

Irv and Joan were divorced last year, and Joan was awarded custody of their child, Keith. During the current year, Irv pays $2,500 of Keith's medical bills. Together, Irv and Joan provide more than half of Keith's support. Even though Joan claims Keith as a dependent, Irv can combine the $2,500 of medical expenses that he pays for Keith with his own when calculating his medical expense deduction. ■

TRANSPORTATION, MEAL, AND LODGING EXPENSES FOR MEDICAL TREATMENT

Payments for transportation to and from a point of treatment for medical care are deductible as medical expenses (subject to the 7.5 percent floor). Transportation expenses for medical care include bus, taxi, train, or plane fare, charges for ambulance service, and out-of-pocket expenses for the use of an automobile. A mileage allowance of 19 cents per mile[11] for 2011 may be used instead of actual out-of-pocket automobile expenses. Whether the taxpayer chooses to claim out-of-pocket automobile expenses or the 19 cents per mile automatic mileage option, related parking fees and tolls can also be deducted. The cost of meals while en route to obtain medical care is not deductible.

A deduction is also allowed for the transportation expenses of a parent who must accompany a child who is receiving medical care or for a nurse or other person giving assistance to a person who is traveling to get medical care and cannot travel alone.

A deduction is allowed for lodging while away from home for medical care if the following requirements are met:[12]

[9] For a complete list of the items that qualify, see Rev.Rul. 87–106, 1987–2 C.B. 67.

[10] Refer to Chapter 3 for discussion of these requirements.

[11] This amount is adjusted periodically. The allowance was 16.5 cents for 2010.

[12] § 213(d)(2).

- The lodging is primarily for and essential to medical care.
- Medical care is provided by a doctor in a licensed hospital or a similar medical facility (e.g., a clinic).
- The lodging is not lavish or extravagant under the circumstances.
- There is no significant element of personal pleasure, recreation, or vacation in the travel away from home.

The deduction for lodging expenses included as medical expenses cannot exceed $50 *per* night for *each* person. The deduction is allowed not only for the patient but also for a person who must travel with the patient (e.g., a parent traveling with a child who is receiving medical care).

EXAMPLE 9

Herman, a resident of Winchester, Kentucky, is advised by his family physician that Martha, Herman's dependent and disabled mother, needs specialized treatment for her heart condition. Consequently, Herman and Martha fly to Cleveland, Ohio, where Martha receives the therapy at a heart clinic on an outpatient basis. Expenses in connection with the trip are as follows:

Round-trip airfare ($250 each)	$500
Lodging in Cleveland for two nights ($60 each per night)	240

Herman's medical expense deduction for transportation is $500, and his medical expense deduction for lodging is $200 ($50 per night per person). Because Martha is disabled, it is assumed that his accompanying her is justified. ■

No deduction is allowed for the cost of meals unless they are part of the medical care and are furnished at a medical facility. When allowable, such meals are not subject to the 50 percent limit applicable to business meals.

ETHICS & Equity

TRAVEL EXPENSES: MEDICAL OR PERSONAL?

Ron, who lives in Phoenix, has a chronic heart problem. He flies to Rochester, Minnesota, several times each year for checkups and treatment at the Mayo Clinic, which has one of the most highly rated heart treatment programs in the United States. On each trip, he visits his two children, who live in Rochester with his ex-wife. Is Ron justified in deducting the cost of his airline tickets and his lodging in Rochester as a medical expense?

AMOUNTS PAID FOR MEDICAL INSURANCE PREMIUMS

Medical insurance premiums are included with other medical expenses subject to the 7.5 percent floor. Premiums paid by the taxpayer under a group plan or an individual plan are included as medical expenses. If an employer pays all or part of the taxpayer's medical insurance premiums, the amount paid by the employer is not included in gross income by the employee. Likewise, the premium is not included in the employee's medical expenses.

If a taxpayer is *self-employed*, insurance premiums paid for medical coverage are deductible as a *business* expense (*for* AGI).[13] The deduction *for* AGI is allowed for premiums paid on behalf of the taxpayer, the taxpayer's spouse, and dependents of the taxpayer. The deduction is not allowed to any taxpayer who is eligible to participate in a subsidized health plan maintained by any employer of the taxpayer or of the taxpayer's spouse. Premiums paid for medical insurance coverage of *employees* are deductible as business expenses.

[13] § 162(l).

EXAMPLE 10

Ellen, a sole proprietor of a restaurant, has two dependent children. During the year, she paid health insurance premiums of $8,400 for her own coverage and $7,000 for coverage of her two children. Ellen can deduct $15,400 as a business deduction (*for* AGI) in computing her taxable income. ■

Taxpayers may also include premiums paid on qualified long-term care insurance contracts in medical expenses, subject to limitations based on the age of the insured. For 2011, the per-person limits range from $340 for taxpayers age 40 and under to $4,240 for taxpayers over age 70. See IRS Publication 502 for details relating to requirements for deducting costs of qualified long-term care insurance contracts.[14]

YEAR OF DEDUCTION

Regardless of a taxpayer's method of accounting, medical expenses are deductible only in the year *paid*. In effect, this places all individual taxpayers on a cash basis as far as the medical expense deduction is concerned. One exception, however, is allowed for deceased taxpayers. If the medical expenses are paid within one year from the day following the day of death, they can be treated as being paid at the time they were *incurred*. Thus, such expenses may be reported on the final income tax return of the decedent or on earlier returns if incurred before the year of death.

No current deduction is allowed for payment for medical care to be rendered in the future unless the taxpayer is under an obligation to make the payment. Whether an obligation to make the payment exists depends upon the policy of the physician or the institution furnishing the medical care.

EXAMPLE 11

Upon the recommendation of his regular dentist, in December 2011 Gary consults Dr. Smith, a prosthodontist, who specializes in crown and bridge work. Dr. Smith tells Gary that he can do the restorative work for $12,000 and that he requires all new patients to prepay 40% of the total cost of the procedure. Accordingly, Gary pays $4,800 in December 2011. The balance of $7,200 is paid when the work is completed in January 2012. Under these circumstances, the qualifying medical expense deductions are $4,800 for 2011 and $7,200 in 2012. The result would be the same even if Gary prepaid the full $12,000 in 2011. ■

REIMBURSEMENTS

If medical expenses are reimbursed in the same year as paid, no problem arises. The reimbursement merely reduces the amount that would otherwise qualify for the medical expense deduction. But what happens if the reimbursement occurs in a later year than the expenditure? In computing casualty losses, any reasonable prospect of recovery must be considered (refer to Chapter 7). For medical expenses, however, any expected reimbursement is disregarded in measuring the amount of the deduction. Instead, the reimbursement is accounted for separately in the year in which it occurs.

Under the *tax benefit rule*, a taxpayer who receives an insurance reimbursement for medical expenses deducted in a previous year might have to include the reimbursement in gross income in the year of receipt. However, a taxpayer who did not itemize deductions in the year the expenses were paid did not receive a tax benefit and is *not* required to include a reimbursement in gross income.

The tax benefit rule applies to reimbursements if the taxpayer itemized deductions in the previous year. In this case, the taxpayer may be required to report some or all of the medical expense reimbursement in income in the year the reimbursement is received. Under the tax benefit rule, the taxpayer must include the reimbursement in income up to the amount of the deductions that decreased taxable income in the earlier year.

[14]The amounts for 2010 were $330 for taxpayers age 40 and under and $4,110 for taxpayers over age 70.

EXAMPLE 12

Homer had AGI of $60,000 for 2011. He was injured in a car accident and paid $4,300 for hospital expenses and $700 for doctor bills. Homer also incurred medical expenses of $600 for his dependent child. In 2012, Homer was reimbursed $650 by his insurance company for the medical expenses attributable to the car accident. His deduction for medical expenses in 2011 is computed as follows:

Hospitalization	$ 4,300
Bills for doctor's services	700
Medical expenses for dependent	600
Total	$ 5,600
Less: 7.5% of $60,000	(4,500)
Medical expense deduction (assuming Homer itemizes his deductions)	$ 1,100

Assume that Homer would have elected to itemize his deductions even if he had no medical expenses in 2011. If the reimbursement for medical care had occurred in 2011, the medical expense deduction would have been only $450 [$5,600 (total medical expenses) – $650 (reimbursement) – $4,500 (floor)], and Homer would have paid more income tax.

Since the reimbursement was made in a subsequent year, Homer will include $650 in gross income for 2012. If Homer had not itemized in 2011, he would *not* include the $650 reimbursement in 2012 gross income because he would have received no tax benefit for the medical expenses in 2011. ■

HEALTH SAVINGS ACCOUNTS

Qualifying individuals may make deductible contributions to a **Health Savings Account (HSA)**. An HSA is a qualified trust or custodial account administered by a qualified HSA trustee, which can be a bank, insurance company, or other IRS-approved trustee. The HSA funds are used to pay for the individual's medical expenses in excess of the deductible amount under a high-deductible policy.[15]

A taxpayer can use an HSA in conjunction with a high-deductible medical insurance policy to help reduce the overall cost of medical coverage. Converting from a low-deductible to a high-deductible plan can generally save an individual 20 to 40 percent in premiums. The high-deductible policy provides coverage for extraordinary medical expenses (in excess of the deductible), and expenses not covered by the policy can be paid with funds withdrawn tax-free from the HSA.

EXAMPLE 13

Sanchez, who is married and has three dependent children, carries a high-deductible medical insurance policy with a deductible of $4,400. He establishes an HSA and contributes the maximum allowable amount to the HSA in 2011. During 2011, the Sanchez family incurs medical expenses of $7,000. The high-deductible policy covers $2,600 of the expenses ($7,000 expenses – $4,400 deductible). Sanchez may withdraw $4,400 from the HSA to pay the medical expenses not covered by the high-deductible policy. ■

High-Deductible Plans

High-deductible policies are less expensive than low-deductible policies, so taxpayers with low medical costs can benefit from the lower premiums and use funds from the HSA to pay costs not covered by the high-deductible policy. A plan must meet two requirements to qualify as a high-deductible plan.[16]

1. The annual deductible in 2011 is not less than $1,200 for self-only coverage ($2,400 for family coverage).
2. The annual limit in 2011 on total out-of-pocket costs (excluding premiums) under the plan does not exceed $5,950 for self-only coverage ($11,900 for family coverage).

[15] § 223.

[16] § 223(c)(2).

Tax Treatment of HSA Contributions and Distributions

To establish an HSA, a taxpayer contributes funds to a tax-exempt trust.[17] As illustrated in the preceding example, funds can be withdrawn from an HSA to pay medical expenses that are not covered by the high-deductible policy. The following general tax rules apply to HSAs:

1. Contributions made by the taxpayer to an HSA are deductible from gross income to arrive at AGI (deduction *for* AGI). Thus, the taxpayer does not need to itemize in order to take the deduction.
2. Earnings on HSAs are not subject to taxation unless distributed, in which case taxability depends on the way the funds are used.[18]
   - Distributions from HSAs are excluded from gross income if they are used to pay for medical expenses not covered by the high-deductible policy.
   - Distributions that are not used to pay for medical expenses are included in gross income and are subject to an additional 10 percent penalty if made before age 65, death, or disability. Such distributions made by reason of death or disability and distributions made after the HSA beneficiary becomes eligible for Medicare are taxed but not penalized.

HSAs have at least two other attractive features. First, an HSA is portable. Taxpayers who switch jobs can take their HSAs with them. Second, more people than ever before can qualify to set up an HSA. Generally, anyone under age 65 who has a high-deductible plan and is not covered by another policy that is not a high-deductible plan can establish an HSA.

Deductible Amount

The annual deduction for contributions to an HSA is limited to the sum of the monthly limitations. The monthly limitation is calculated for each month that the individual is an eligible individual. The monthly deduction is not allowed after the individual becomes eligible for Medicare coverage.

The amount of the monthly limitation for an individual who has self-only coverage in 2011 is one-twelfth of $3,050, while the monthly limitation for an individual who has family coverage in 2011 is one-twelfth of $6,150. These amounts are subject to annual cost-of-living adjustments.[19] An eligible taxpayer who has attained age 55 by the end of the tax year may make an additional annual contribution in 2011 of up to $1,000. This additional amount is referred to as a *catchup* contribution.

EXAMPLE 14

Liu, who is married and self-employed, carries a high-deductible medical insurance policy with family coverage and an annual deductible of $4,000. In addition, he has established an HSA. Liu's maximum annual contribution to the HSA in 2011 is $6,150. ■

EXAMPLE 15

During 2011, Adam, who is self-employed, made 12 monthly payments of $875 for an HSA contract that provides medical insurance coverage with a $3,600 deductible. The plan covers Adam, his wife, and two children. Of the $875 monthly fee, $400 was for the high-deductible policy and $475 was deposited into an HSA. The deductible monthly contribution to the HSA is calculated as follows:

Maximum annual deduction for family coverage	$ 6,150
Monthly limitation (1/12 of $6,150)	$512.50

[17] § 223(d).

[18] § 223(f).

[19] § 223(b)(2). The annual limits also were $3,050 and $6,150 in 2010. Section 223(b)(8) allows a taxpayer who is an eligible member of a high-deductible plan as of the first day of December (for a calendar year taxpayer) to be *treated* as an eligible member of the plan for the entire year. Therefore, for example, if a calendar year taxpayer enrolls in an HSA by December 2011, the limit on the contribution is $3,050 (or $6,150 in the event of family coverage) and not the sum of the monthly limits.

Because Adam is self-employed, he can deduct $4,800 of the amount paid for the high-deductible policy ($400 per month × 12 months) as a deduction *for* AGI (refer to Example 10). In addition, he can deduct the $5,700 ($475 × 12) paid to the HSA as a deduction *for* AGI. Note that the $5,700 HSA deduction does not exceed the $6,150 ceiling. ■

10.3 TAXES

LO.3

Contrast deductible taxes with nondeductible fees, licenses, and other charges.

A deduction is allowed for certain state and local taxes paid or accrued by a taxpayer.[20] The deduction was created to relieve the burden of multiple taxes upon the same source of revenue.

DEDUCTIBILITY AS A TAX

A distinction must be made between a tax and a fee, since fees are not deductible unless incurred as an ordinary and necessary business expense or as an expense in the production of income. The IRS has defined a tax as follows:

> A tax is an enforced contribution exacted pursuant to legislative authority in the exercise of taxing power, and imposed and collected for the purpose of raising revenue to be used for public or governmental purposes, and not as payment for some special privilege granted or service rendered. Taxes are, therefore, distinguished from various other contributions and charges imposed for particular purposes under particular powers or functions of the government. In view of such distinctions, the question whether a particular contribution or charge is to be regarded as a tax depends upon its real nature.[21]

Accordingly, fees for dog licenses, automobile inspections, automobile titles and registration, hunting and fishing licenses, bridge and highway tolls, drivers' licenses, parking meter deposits, and postage are not deductible if personal in nature. These items, however, could be deductible if incurred as a business expense or for the production of income. Deductible and nondeductible taxes are summarized in Exhibit 10.2.

EXHIBIT 10.2 **Deductible and Nondeductible Taxes**

Deductible	Nondeductible
State, local, and foreign real property taxes	Federal income taxes
State and local personal property taxes	FICA taxes imposed on employees
State and local income taxes *or* sales/use taxes*	Employer FICA taxes paid on domestic household workers
Foreign income taxes	Estate, inheritance, and gift taxes
	Federal, state, and local excise taxes (e.g., gasoline, tobacco, spirits)
	Foreign income taxes if the taxpayer chooses the foreign tax credit option
	Taxes on real property to the extent such taxes are to be apportioned and treated as imposed on another taxpayer

* Currently, the sales/use tax alternative is available through 2011.

[20] Most deductible taxes are listed in § 164, while nondeductible items are included in § 275.

[21] Rev.Rul. 57–345, 1957–2 C.B. 132, and Rev.Rul. 70–622, 1970–2 C.B. 41.

PROPERTY TAXES

State, local, and foreign taxes on real property are generally deductible only by the person upon whom the tax is imposed. Deductible personal property taxes must be *ad valorem* (assessed in relation to the value of the property). Therefore, a motor vehicle tax based on weight, model, year, and horsepower is not an ad valorem tax. However, a tax based on value and other criteria may qualify in part.

EXAMPLE 16
THE BIG PICTURE

Return to the facts of *The Big Picture* on p. 10-2. Assuming that the Williamsons proceed with the purchase of a home, the real estate taxes they pay will be deductible *from* AGI because they qualify to itemize their deductions. However, if they also pay a personal property tax on their automobile, the payment may be only partially deductible. In their state, the government imposes a motor vehicle registration tax on 4% of the value of the vehicle plus 40 cents per hundredweight. The Williamsons own a car having a value of $20,000 and weighing 3,000 pounds. They pay an annual registration fee of $812. Of this amount, $800 (4% of $20,000) is deductible as a personal property tax. The remaining $12, based on the weight of the car, is not deductible. ■

Assessments for Local Benefits

As a general rule, real property taxes do not include taxes assessed for local benefits because such assessments tend to increase the value of the property (e.g., special assessments for streets, sidewalks, curbing, and other similar improvements). A taxpayer was denied a deduction for the cost of a new sidewalk (relative to a personal residence), even though the construction was required by the city and the sidewalk may have provided an incidental benefit to the public welfare.[22] Such assessments are added to the adjusted basis of the taxpayer's property.

Apportionment of Real Property Taxes between Seller and Purchaser

Real estate taxes for the entire year are apportioned between the buyer and seller on the basis of the number of days the property was held by each during the real property tax year. This apportionment is required whether the tax is paid by the buyer or the seller or is prorated according to the purchase agreement. It is the apportionment that determines who is entitled to deduct the real estate taxes in the year of sale. The required apportionment prevents the shifting of the deduction for real estate taxes from the buyer to the seller, or vice versa. In making the apportionment, the assessment date and the lien date are disregarded.[23]

EXAMPLE 17

A county's real property tax year runs from January 1 to December 31. Susan, the owner on January 1 of real property located in the county, sells the real property to Bob on June 30 (assume this year is not a leap year). Bob owns the real property from June 30 through December 31. The tax for the real property tax year, January 1 through December 31, is $3,650. The portion of the real property tax treated as imposed upon Susan, the seller, is $1,800 [(180/365) × $3,650, January 1 through June 29], and $1,850 [(185/365) × $3,650, June 30 through December 31] of the tax is treated as imposed upon Bob, the purchaser. ■

If the actual real estate taxes are not prorated between the buyer and seller as part of the purchase agreement, adjustments are required. The adjustments are necessary to determine the amount realized by the seller and the adjusted basis of the property to the buyer. If the buyer pays the entire amount of the tax, he or she has, in effect, paid the seller's portion of the real estate tax and has therefore paid more for the property than the actual purchase price. Thus, the amount of real estate tax

[22] *Erie H. Rose*, 31 TCM 142, T.C.Memo. 1972–39; Reg. § 1.164–4(a).

[23] For most years, the apportionment is based on a 365-day year. However, in a leap year (i.e., a year that is evenly divisible by 4), the taxes are prorated over 366 days. In making the apportionment, the date of sale counts as a day the property is owned by the buyer.

GLOBAL
Tax Issues

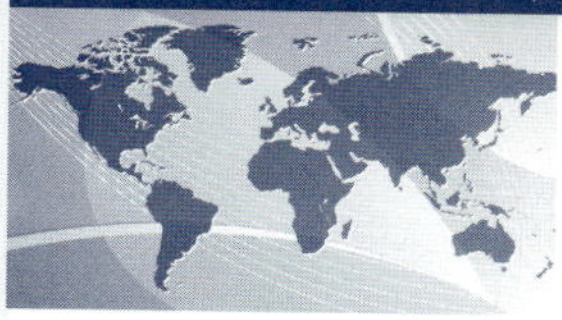

Deductibility of Foreign Taxes

Josef, a citizen of the United States who works primarily in New York, also works several months each year in Austria. He owns a residence in Austria and pays income taxes to Austria on the income he earns there. Both the property tax he pays on his Austrian residence and the income tax he pays on his Austrian income are deductible in computing U.S. taxable income. However, if Josef deducts the Austrian income tax, he may not claim the foreign tax credit with respect to this tax (see Chapters 12 and 25).

that is apportioned to the seller (for Federal income tax purposes) and paid by the buyer is added to the buyer's adjusted basis. The seller must increase the amount realized on the sale by the same amount.

EXAMPLE 18

Seth sells real estate on October 3 for $400,000. The buyer, Wilma, pays the real estate taxes of $3,650 for the calendar year, which is the real estate property tax year. Assuming this is not a leap year, $2,750 (for 275 days) of the real estate taxes is apportioned to and is deductible by the seller, Seth, and $900 (for 90 days) of the taxes is deductible by Wilma. The buyer has, in effect, paid Seth's real estate taxes of $2,750 and has therefore paid $402,750 for the property. Wilma's basis is increased to $402,750, and the amount realized by Seth from the sale is increased to $402,750. ■

The opposite result occurs if the seller (rather than the buyer) pays the real estate taxes. In this case, the seller reduces the amount realized from the sale by the amount that has been apportioned to the buyer. The buyer is required to reduce his or her adjusted basis by a corresponding amount.

EXAMPLE 19

Ruth sells real estate to Butch for $400,000 on October 3. While Ruth held the property, she paid the real estate taxes of $3,650 for the calendar year, which is the real estate property tax year. Although Ruth paid the entire $3,650 of real estate taxes, $900 of that amount is apportioned to Butch, based on the number of days he owned the property, and is therefore deductible by him. The effect is that the buyer, Butch, has paid only $399,100 ($400,000 − $900) for the property. The amount realized by Ruth, the seller, is reduced by $900, and Butch reduces his basis in the property to $399,100. ■

STATE AND LOCAL INCOME TAXES AND SALES TAXES

LO.4

Understand the Federal income tax treatment of state and local income taxes and sales taxes.

The position of the IRS is that state and local income taxes imposed upon an individual are deductible only as itemized deductions, even if the taxpayer's sole source of income is from a business, rents, or royalties.

Cash basis taxpayers are entitled to deduct state income taxes withheld by the employer in the year the taxes are withheld. In addition, estimated state income tax payments are deductible in the year the payment is made by cash basis taxpayers even if the payments relate to a prior or subsequent year.[24] If the taxpayer overpays state income taxes because of excessive withholdings or estimated tax payments, the refund received is included in gross income of the following year to the extent that the deduction reduced taxable income in the prior year.

EXAMPLE 20

Leona, a cash basis, unmarried taxpayer, had $800 of state income tax withheld during 2011. Additionally in 2011, Leona paid $100 that was due when she filed her 2010 state income tax return and made estimated payments of $300 on her 2011 state income tax.

[24]Rev.Rul. 71–190, 1971–1 C.B. 70. See also Rev.Rul. 82–208, 1982–2 C.B. 58, where a deduction is not allowed when the taxpayer cannot, in good faith, reasonably determine that there is additional state income tax liability.

When Leona files her 2011 Federal income tax return in April 2012, she elects to itemize deductions, which amount to $7,500, including the $1,200 of state income tax payments and withholdings, all of which reduce her taxable income.

As a result of overpaying her 2011 state income tax, Leona receives a refund of $200 early in 2012. She will include this amount in her 2012 gross income in computing her Federal income tax. It does not matter whether Leona received a check from the state for $200 or applied the $200 toward her 2012 state income tax. ■

Itemized Deduction for Sales Taxes Paid

Individuals can elect to deduct either their state and local income taxes *or* their sales/use taxes paid as an itemized deduction on Schedule A of Form 1040. The annual election can reflect actual sales/use tax payments *or* an amount from an IRS table (see Appendix A). The amount from the table may be increased by sales tax paid on the purchase of motor vehicles, boats, and other specified items. Most likely, the sales tax deduction will be elected by those living in states with no individual income tax. At the time of this writing, this deduction alternative is available through 2011.

10.4 Interest

LO.5

Distinguish between deductible and nondeductible interest and apply the appropriate limitations to deductible interest.

A deduction for interest has been allowed since the income tax law was enacted in 1913. Despite its long history of congressional acceptance, the interest deduction has been one of the most controversial areas in the tax law. The controversy centered around the propriety of allowing the deduction of interest charges for the purchase of consumer goods and services and interest on borrowings used to acquire investments (investment interest). Currently, personal (consumer) interest is not deductible. This includes credit card interest, interest on car loans, and any other interest that is not interest on qualified student loans, home mortgage interest, investment interest, or business interest. Interest on qualified student loans, **qualified residence** (home mortgage) **interest**, and investment interest continue to be deductible, subject to the limits discussed on the following pages.

ALLOWED AND DISALLOWED ITEMS

The Supreme Court has defined *interest* as compensation for the use or forbearance of money.[25] The general rule permits a deduction for interest paid or accrued within the taxable year on indebtedness.

Interest on Qualified Student Loans

Taxpayers who pay interest on a qualified student loan may be able to deduct the interest as a deduction *for* AGI. The deduction is allowable only to the extent that the proceeds of the loan are used to pay qualified education expenses. Such payments must be made to qualified educational institutions. See IRS Publication 970, *Tax Benefits for Education*, for details.

The maximum annual deduction for qualified student loan interest is $2,500. However, in 2011 the deduction is phased out for taxpayers with modified AGI (MAGI) between $60,000 and $75,000 ($120,000 and $150,000 on joint returns). The deduction is not allowed for taxpayers who are claimed as dependents or for married taxpayers filing separately.[26]

The numerator in the phaseout computation is equal to MAGI minus the floor of the phaseout range (i.e., $60,000 or $120,000, depending on filing status). The denominator is equal to the amount in the phaseout range (e.g., $150,000 − $120,000 = $30,000 for married taxpayers filing jointly).

[25] *Old Colony Railroad Co. v. Comm.*, 3 USTC ¶880, 10 AFTR 786, 52 S.Ct. 211 (USSC, 1932).

[26] § 221. See § 221(b)(2)(C) for the definition of MAGI. For 2010, the MAGI threshold amounts also were $60,000 and $75,000 ($120,000 and $150,000 on joint returns).

EXAMPLE 21

In 2011 Curt and Rita, who are married and file a joint return, paid $3,000 of interest on a qualified student loan. Their MAGI was $135,000. Their maximum potential deduction for qualified student loan interest is $2,500, but it must be reduced by $1,250 as a result of the phaseout rules.

$2,500 interest × ($135,000 MAGI − $120,000 phaseout floor)/
$30,000 phaseout range = $1,250 reduction

Curt and Rita would be allowed a student loan interest deduction of $1,250 ($2,500 maximum deduction − $1,250 reduction = $1,250 deduction *for* AGI). ■

Qualified Residence Interest

Qualified residence interest is interest paid or accrued during the taxable year on indebtedness (subject to limitations) *secured* by any property that is a qualified residence of the taxpayer. Qualified residence interest falls into two categories: (1) interest on acquisition indebtedness and (2) interest on home equity loans. Before discussing each of these categories, however, the term *qualified residence* must be defined.

A *qualified residence* includes the taxpayer's principal residence and one other residence of the taxpayer or spouse. The *principal residence* is one that meets the requirement for nonrecognition of gain upon sale under § 121 (see Chapter 13). The *one other residence,* or second residence, refers to one that is used as a residence if not rented or, if rented, meets the requirements for a personal residence under the rental of vacation home rules (refer to Chapter 6). A taxpayer who has more than one second residence can make the selection each year as to which one is the qualified second residence. A residence includes, in addition to a house in the ordinary sense, cooperative apartments, condominiums, and mobile homes and boats that have living quarters (sleeping accommodations and toilet and cooking facilities).

Although in most cases interest paid on a home mortgage is fully deductible, there are limitations.[27] Interest paid or accrued during the tax year on aggregate **acquisition indebtedness** of $1 million or less ($500,000 for married persons filing separate returns) is deductible as qualified residence interest. *Acquisition indebtedness* refers to amounts incurred in acquiring, constructing, or substantially improving a qualified residence of the taxpayer.

EXAMPLE 22
THE BIG PICTURE

Return to the facts of *The Big Picture* on p. 10-2. Because John and Susan Williamson will need to borrow at least a portion of the purchase price of a new home, a standard mortgage likely will qualify as acquisition indebtedness because the borrowed funds are used to acquire a principal residence. However, the interest on the acquisition indebtedness will be fully deductible only if the amount of the mortgage is $1 million or less (assuming John and Susan file a joint return) and the mortgage is secured by the home, which is the typical case. Recall that the Williamsons are also considering what appears to be a less expensive route of using their retirement and taxable investments to secure the debt. If they choose this alternative, the interest will not be deductible as qualified residence interest because the loan would not be acquisition indebtedness (i.e., the loan would not be secured by the home). ■

Qualified residence interest also includes interest on **home equity loans**. These loans utilize the personal residence of the taxpayer as security, typically in the form of a second mortgage. Because the funds from home equity loans can be used for personal purposes (e.g., auto purchases, medical expenses), what would otherwise have been nondeductible consumer interest becomes deductible qualified residence interest.

However, interest is deductible only on the portion of a home equity loan that does not exceed the *lesser of*:

[27] § 163(h)(3).

- The fair market value of the residence, reduced by the acquisition indebtedness, *or*
- $100,000 ($50,000 for married persons filing separate returns).

EXAMPLE 23

Larry owns a personal residence with a fair market value of $450,000 and an outstanding first mortgage of $420,000. Therefore, his equity in his home is $30,000 ($450,000 – $420,000). Larry issues a second mortgage on the residence and in return borrows $15,000 to purchase a new family automobile. All interest on the $435,000 of first and second mortgage debt is treated as qualified residence interest. ■

EXAMPLE 24

Leon and Pearl, married taxpayers, took out a mortgage on their home for $290,000 in 1994. In March of the current year, when the home has a fair market value of $400,000 and they owe $195,000 on the mortgage, Leon and Pearl take out a home equity loan for $120,000. They use the funds to purchase a boat to be used for recreational purposes. The boat, which does not have living quarters, does not qualify as a personal residence. On a joint return, Leon and Pearl can deduct all of the interest on the first mortgage since it is acquisition indebtedness. Of the $120,000 home equity loan, only the interest on the first $100,000 is deductible. The interest on the remaining $20,000 is not deductible because it exceeds the statutory ceiling of $100,000. ■

Interest Paid for Services

Mortgage loan companies commonly charge a fee, often called a loan origination fee, for finding, placing, or processing a mortgage loan. Loan origination fees are typically nondeductible amounts included in the basis of the acquired property. Other fees, sometimes called **points** and expressed as a percentage of the loan amount, are paid to reduce the interest rate charged over the term of the loan. Essentially, the payment of points is a prepayment of interest and is considered compensation to a lender solely for the use or forbearance of money. To be deductible, points must be in the nature of interest and cannot be a form of service charge or payment for specific services.[28]

Points must be capitalized and are amortized and deductible ratably over the life of the loan. A special exception, however, permits the purchaser of a principal residence to deduct qualifying points in the year of payment.[29] The exception also covers points paid to obtain funds for home improvements.

Points paid to *refinance* an existing home mortgage cannot be immediately deducted, but must be capitalized and amortized as an interest deduction over the life of the new loan.[30]

EXAMPLE 25

Sandra purchased her residence several years ago, obtaining a 30-year mortgage at an annual interest rate of 8%. In the current year, Sandra refinances the mortgage in order to reduce the interest rate to 5%. To obtain the refinancing, she has to pay points of $2,600. The $2,600 paid comes under the usual rule applicable to points. The $2,600 must be capitalized and amortized over the life of the mortgage. ■

Points paid by the seller for a buyer are, in effect, treated as an adjustment to the price of the residence, and the buyer is treated as having used cash to pay the points that were paid by the seller. A buyer may deduct seller-paid points in the tax year in which they are paid if several conditions are met. Refer to Revenue Procedure 94–27 for a complete list of these conditions.[31]

Mortgage Insurance Payments

Mortgage insurance is an additional cost that some taxpayers incur when purchasing a home. To protect their interests, mortgage lenders may require this coverage if the homebuyer cannot afford to make a down payment of at least 20 percent. The borrower pays the premiums on the policy, but the lender is the beneficiary who

[28] Rev.Rul. 69–188, 1969–1 C.B. 54.
[29] § 461(g)(2).
[30] Rev.Rul. 87–22, 1987–1 C.B. 146.
[31] Rev.Proc. 94–27, 1994–1 C.B. 613.

receives reimbursement in the event of foreclosure. Under currrent law, mortgage insurance premiums are deductible as interest if they relate to a qualified residence of the taxpayer. However, the deduction begins to phase out for taxpayers with AGI in excess of $100,000 ($50,000 for married taxpayers filing separately).[32]

Prepayment Penalty

When a mortgage or loan is paid off in full in a lump sum before its term (early), the lending institution may require an additional payment of a certain percentage applied to the unpaid amount at the time of prepayment. This is known as a prepayment penalty and is considered to be interest (e.g., personal, qualified residence, investment) in the year paid. The general rules for deductibility of interest also apply to prepayment penalties.

Investment Interest

Taxpayers frequently borrow funds that they use to acquire investment assets. Congress, however, has limited the deductibility of interest on funds borrowed for the purpose of purchasing or continuing to hold investment property. Under this limitation, the deduction for investment interest expense may not exceed the net investment income for the year. A complete discussion of investment interest occurs in Chapter 11 in the context of the limitations that taxpayers face when dealing with assets held for investment purposes.

Interest Paid to Related Parties

Nothing prevents the deduction of interest paid to a related party as long as the payment actually took place and the interest meets the requirements for deductibility. Recall from Chapter 6 that a special rule for related taxpayers applies when the debtor uses the accrual basis and the related creditor is on the cash basis. If this rule is applicable, interest that has been accrued but not paid at the end of the debtor's tax year is not deductible until payment is made and the income is reportable by the cash basis recipient.

Tax-Exempt Securities

The tax law provides that no deduction is allowed for interest on debt incurred to purchase or carry tax-exempt securities.[33] A major problem for the courts has been to determine what is meant by the words *to purchase or carry*. Refer to Chapter 6 for a detailed discussion of these issues.

RESTRICTIONS ON DEDUCTIBILITY AND TIMING CONSIDERATIONS

Taxpayer's Obligation

Allowed interest is deductible if the related debt represents a bona fide obligation for which the taxpayer is liable.[34] Thus, for interest to be deductible, both the debtor and the creditor must intend for the loan to be repaid. Intent of the parties can be especially crucial between related parties such as a shareholder and a closely held corporation. In addition, an individual may not deduct interest paid on behalf of another taxpayer. For example, a shareholder may not deduct interest paid by the corporation on his or her behalf.[35] Likewise, a husband may not deduct interest paid on his wife's property if he files a separate return, except in the case of qualified residence interest. If both husband and wife consent in writing, either the husband or the wife may deduct the allowed interest on the principal residence and one other residence.

[32] §§ 163(h)(3)(E)(i) and (ii). The deduction is fully phased out when AGI exceeds $109,000 ($54,500 for married taxpayers filing separately). The deduction thresholds are not subject to indexation for inflation. This provision is scheduled to expire after 2011.

[33] § 265(a)(2).

[34] *Arcade Realty Co.*, 35 T.C. 256 (1960).

[35] *Continental Trust Co.*, 7 B.T.A. 539 (1927).

CONCEPT SUMMARY 10.1

Deductibility of Personal, Student Loan, Mortgage, and Investment Interest

Type	Deductible	Comments
Personal (consumer) interest	No	Includes any interest that is not qualified residence interest, qualified student loan interest, investment interest, or business interest. Examples include interest on car loans and credit card debt.
Qualified student loan interest	Yes	Deduction *for* AGI; subject to limitations.
Qualified residence interest on acquisition indebtedness	Yes	Deductible as an itemized deduction; limited to indebtedness of $1 million.
Qualified residence interest on home equity indebtedness	Yes	Deductible as an itemized deduction; limited to indebtedness equal to lesser of $100,000 or FMV of residence minus acquisition indebtedness.
Investment interest (*not* related to rental or royalty property)	Yes	Itemized deduction; limited to net investment income for the year; disallowed interest can be carried over to future years. See Chapter 11 for a complete discussion of investment interest.
Investment interest (related to rental or royalty property)	Yes	Deduction *for* AGI; limited to net investment income for the year; disallowed interest can be carried over to future years. See Chapter 11 for a complete discussion of investment interest.

Time of Deduction

Generally, interest must be paid to secure a deduction unless the taxpayer uses the accrual method of accounting. Under the accrual method, interest is deductible ratably over the life of the loan.

EXAMPLE 26

On November 1, 2011, Ramon borrows $1,000 to purchase appliances for a rental house. The loan is payable in 90 days at 12% interest. On the due date in January 2012, Ramon pays the $1,000 note and interest amounting to $30. Ramon can deduct the accrued portion ($^2/_3 \times \$30 = \$20$) of the interest in 2011 only if he is an accrual basis taxpayer. Otherwise, the entire amount of interest ($30) is deductible in 2012. ■

Prepaid Interest

Accrual method reporting is imposed on cash basis taxpayers for interest prepayments that extend beyond the end of the taxable year.[36] Such payments must be allocated to the tax years to which the interest payments relate. These provisions are intended to prevent cash basis taxpayers from *manufacturing* tax deductions before the end of the year by prepaying interest.

CLASSIFICATION OF INTEREST EXPENSE

Whether interest is deductible *for* AGI or as an itemized deduction (*from* AGI) depends on whether the indebtedness has a business, investment, or personal purpose. If the indebtedness is incurred in relation to a business (other than performing services as an employee) or for the production of rent or royalty income, the interest is deductible *for* AGI. If the indebtedness is incurred for personal use, such as qualified residence interest, any deduction allowed is taken *from* AGI and is reported on Schedule A of Form 1040 if the taxpayer elects to itemize. Note, however, that interest on a student loan is a deduction *for* AGI. If the taxpayer is an employee who incurs debt in relation to his or her employment, the interest is

[36] § 461(g)(1).

considered to be personal, or consumer, interest. Business expenses appear on Schedule C of Form 1040, and expenses related to rents or royalties are reported on Schedule E.

If a taxpayer deposits money in a certificate of deposit (CD) that has a term of one year or less and the interest cannot be withdrawn without penalty, the full amount of the interest must still be included in income, even though part of the interest is forfeited due to an early withdrawal. However, the taxpayer will be allowed a deduction *for* AGI as to the forfeited amount.

10.5 Charitable Contributions

LO.6

Understand charitable contributions and their related measurement problems and percentage limitations.

Section 170 allows individuals and corporations to deduct contributions made to qualified *domestic* organizations. Contributions to qualified charitable organizations serve certain social welfare needs and thus relieve the government of the cost of providing these needed services to the community.

The **charitable contribution** provisions are among the most complex in the tax law. To determine the amount deductible as a charitable contribution, several important questions must be answered:

- What constitutes a charitable contribution?
- Was the contribution made to a qualified organization?
- When is the contribution deductible?
- What record-keeping and reporting requirements apply to charitable contributions?
- How is the value of donated property determined?
- What special rules apply to contributions of property that has increased in value?
- What percentage limitations apply to the charitable contribution deduction?
- What rules apply to amounts in excess of percentage limitations (carryovers)?

These questions are addressed in the sections that follow.

CRITERIA FOR A GIFT

A *charitable contribution* is defined as a gift made to a qualified organization.[37] The major elements needed to qualify a contribution as a gift are a donative intent, the absence of consideration, and acceptance by the donee. Consequently, the taxpayer has the burden of establishing that the transfer was made from motives of *disinterested generosity* as established by the courts.[38] This test is quite subjective and has led to problems of interpretation (refer to the discussion of gifts in Chapter 5).

Benefit Received Rule

When a donor derives a tangible benefit from a contribution, he or she cannot deduct the value of the benefit.

EXAMPLE 27

Ralph purchases a ticket at $100 for a special performance of the local symphony (a qualified charity). If the price of a ticket to a symphony concert is normally $35, Ralph is allowed only $65 as a charitable contribution. Even if Ralph does not attend the concert, the deduction is limited to $65. However, if Ralph does not accept the ticket from the symphony, he can deduct the full $100. ■

An exception to this benefit rule provides for the deduction of an automatic percentage of the amount paid for the right to purchase athletic tickets from colleges

[37] § 170(c).

[38] *Comm. v. Duberstein*, 60–2 USTC ¶9515, 5 AFTR 2d 1626, 80 S.Ct. 1190 (USSC, 1960).

TAX in the NEWS

PAYING FOR THE RIGHT TO SIT

Generally, the value of a charitable contribution is reduced by any benefits received by the taxpayer. An exception provides that 80 percent of the amount paid for rights to preferred seating at college and university athletic events can be deducted, even though a benefit is received in return.

UCLA's renovated basketball arena is scheduled to reopen in 2012. Interested individuals can purchase the right to a courtside seat for $500,000. To retain the right after the first year costs a mere $17,000.

Source: Adapted from "The Count," *Wall Street Journal*, July 2, 2009, p. D6.

and universities.[39] Under this exception, 80 percent of the amount paid to or for the benefit of the institution qualifies as a charitable contribution deduction.

EXAMPLE 28

Janet donates $500 to State University's athletic department. The payment guarantees that she will have preferred seating on the 50-yard line at football games. Subsequently, Janet buys four $35 game tickets. Under the exception to the benefit rule, she is allowed a $400 (80% of $500) charitable contribution deduction for the taxable year.

If, however, Janet's $500 donation includes four $35 tickets, that portion [$140 ($35 × 4)] and the remaining portion of $360 ($500 − $140) are treated as separate amounts. Thus, Janet is allowed a charitable contribution deduction of $288 (80% of $360). ■

Contribution of Services

No deduction is allowed for a contribution of one's services to a qualified charitable organization. However, unreimbursed expenses related to the services rendered may be deductible. For example, the cost of a uniform (without general utility) that is required to be worn while performing services may be deductible, as are certain out-of-pocket transportation costs incurred for the benefit of the charity. In lieu of these out-of-pocket costs for an automobile, a standard mileage rate of 14 cents per mile is allowed.[40] Deductions are permitted for transportation, reasonable expenses for lodging, and the cost of meals while away from home incurred in performing the donated services. The travel expenses are not deductible if the travel involves a significant element of personal pleasure, recreation, or vacation.[41]

EXAMPLE 29

Grace, a delegate representing her church in Miami, Florida, travels to a two-day national meeting in Denver, Colorado, in February. After the meeting, Grace spends two weeks at a nearby ski resort. Under these circumstances, none of the transportation, meals, or lodging is deductible because the travel involved a significant element of personal pleasure, recreation, or vacation. ■

Nondeductible Items

In addition to the benefit received rule and the restrictions placed on contributions of services, the following items may *not* be deducted as charitable contributions:

- Dues, fees, or bills paid to country clubs, lodges, fraternal orders, or similar groups.
- Cost of raffle, bingo, or lottery tickets.
- Cost of tuition.

[39] § 170(l).
[40] § 170(i).
[41] § 170(j).

TAX *in the NEWS*

A Charitable Contribution Deduction for Burning Down Your House?

Sometimes taxpayers purchase a less than desirable house, intending to tear it down and build a new home on the land. The demolition and removal costs, however, are not deductible. Instead, they must be capitalized as part of the cost of the new home.

An alternative is to donate the old house to the local police and fire departments for training purposes. First, the police SWAT team will practice beating down doors to "rescue" persons at risk. Then the fire department will intentionally set fire to the building to give the firefighters practice in putting out fires. Not only do members of the police and fire departments benefit from the training, but the homeowner avoids the cost of destroying and removing the house because it's been burned to ashes. This strategy seems like a "win-win" proposition.

Some clever taxpayers, however, have strived for even greater benefits. In some cases, they have sought to claim a charitable contribution for the gift of the house. Such deductions raise a number of questions, though. For example, what was the value of the house at the time of the gift, and was the benefit received by the taxpayer equal to or greater than the value transferred to the police and fire departments? An even more important issue is how the IRS will react to such a charitable contribution deduction. Thus far, the IRS has not been happy about such arrangements!

Source: Adapted from Meghan Barr, "Burning Down the House? IRS Nixes Tax Deductions," Associated Press, September 25, 2009.

- Value of blood given to a blood bank.
- Donations to homeowners associations.
- Gifts to individuals.
- Rental value of property used by a qualified charity.

QUALIFIED ORGANIZATIONS

To be deductible, a contribution must be made to one of the following organizations:[42]

- A state or possession of the United States or any subdivisions thereof.
- A corporation, trust, community chest, fund, or foundation that is situated in the United States and is organized and operated exclusively for religious, charitable, scientific, literary, or educational purposes or for the prevention of cruelty to children or animals.
- A veterans' organization.
- A fraternal organization operating under the lodge system.
- A cemetery company.

The IRS publishes a list of organizations that have applied for and received tax-exempt status under § 501 of the Code.[43] This publication is updated frequently and may be helpful in determining if a gift has been made to a qualifying charitable organization.

Because gifts made to needy individuals are not deductible, a deduction will not be permitted if a gift is received by a donee in an individual capacity rather than as a representative of a qualifying organization.

TIME OF DEDUCTION

A charitable contribution generally is deducted in the year the payment is made. This rule applies to both cash and accrual basis individuals. (An interesting exception to this rule arose following the devastating earthquake in Haiti in early 2010. To encourage Americans to assist the victims affected by the earthquake in Haiti,

[42] § 170(c).

[43] Although this *Cumulative List of Organizations*, IRS Publication 78, may be helpful, qualified organizations are not required to be listed. Not all organizations that qualify are listed in this publication. The list is available on the Web at **www.irs.gov**.

ETHICS & *Equity*

An Indirect Route to a Contribution Deduction

In July, a plane crashed into a residential community in Middleboro, destroying and damaging many homes. Tanya's church, a qualified charitable organization, initiated a fund-raising drive to help the Middleboro citizens whose homes had been affected. Tanya donated $50,000 to First Middleboro Church and suggested to the pastor that $25,000 of her contribution should be given to her sister, Tanesha, whose home had suffered extensive damage. The pastor appointed a committee to award funds to needy citizens. The committee solicited applications from the community and awarded Tanesha $15,000. Discuss whether Tanya is justified in deducting $50,000 as a charitable contribution.

Congress provided that an otherwise qualifying charitable contribution made after January 11, 2010, and before March 1, 2010, could be deducted on a taxpayer's 2009 income tax return rather than on the 2010 return.) A contribution is ordinarily deemed to have been made on the delivery of the property to the donee. For example, if a gift of securities (properly endorsed) is made to a qualified charitable organization, the gift is considered complete on the day of delivery or mailing. However, if the donor delivers the certificate to his or her bank or broker or to the issuing corporation, the gift is considered complete on the date the stock is transferred on the books of the corporation.

A contribution made by check is considered delivered on the date of mailing. Thus, a check mailed on December 31, 2011, is deductible on the taxpayer's 2011 tax return. If the contribution is charged on a credit card, the date the charge is made determines the year of deduction.

RECORD-KEEPING AND VALUATION REQUIREMENTS

Record-Keeping Requirements

No deduction is allowed for a charitable contribution made to a qualified organization unless the taxpayer gathers (and, in some cases, supplies to the IRS) the appropriate documentation and substantiation. The specific type of documentation required depends on the amount of the contribution and whether the contribution is made in cash or noncash property.[44] In addition, special rules may apply to gifts of certain types of property (e.g., used automobiles) where Congress has noted taxpayer abuse in the past. Further, for certain gifts of noncash property, Form 8283 (Noncash Charitable Contributions) must be attached to the taxpayer's return.

GLOBAL *Tax Issues*

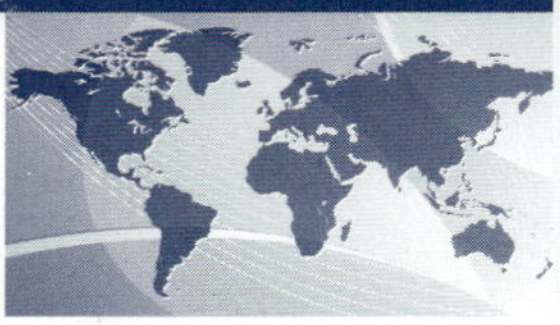

Choose the Charity Wisely

Ibrahim, a U.S. citizen of Turkish descent, was distressed by the damage caused by a major earthquake in Turkey. He donated $100,000 to the Earthquake Victims' Relief Fund, a Turkish charitable organization that was set up to help victims of the earthquake. Ahmed, also a U.S. citizen of Turkish descent, donated $100,000 to help with the relief effort. However, Ahmed's contribution went to his mosque, which sent the proceeds of a fund drive to the Earthquake Victims' Relief Fund in Turkey. Ibrahim's contribution is not deductible, but Ahmed's is. Why? Contributions to charitable organizations are not deductible unless the organization is a U.S. charity.

[44]The specific documentation thresholds and requirements are provided in § 170(f).

CONCEPT SUMMARY 10.2

Documentation and Substantiation Requirements for Charitable Contributions

Cash gifts	• A deduction is allowed only if the taxpayer has a proper receipt (e.g., bank record such as a canceled check, written statement from the charity) showing the name of the charitable organization and the date and amount of the contribution. • A written statement from the charity is required if a payment is for more than $75 and is partly a contribution and partly for goods or services. The statement must provide an estimate of the value of the goods and services received by the donor.
Noncash gifts (e.g., household items)	• A receipt from the charity must be kept for any gift of property other than money. Clothes or other household items are deductible if they are in "good used condition or better" at the time of the gift. • If the items are not in good used condition or better and their value is $500 or more, a deduction is allowed if a "qualified appraisal" is included with the return.
Used automobiles	• The deduction is generally limited to the amount the charity receives on the sale of the car. The taxpayer should obtain a statement from the charity documenting the sales price of the automobile. However, FMV may be deducted if it is $500 or less.
Cash or noncash gifts of $250 or more	• Written acknowledgment from the charity (or certain payroll records in the case of gifts made by payroll deductions) is required to deduct a single cash or property contribution of $250 or more. The acknowledgment must include the amount of money and a description of any other property contributed, whether the charity provided any goods or services in return for the contribution, and a description and estimated value of the goods or services provided.
Noncash gifts of more than $500	• Additional substantiation (e.g., how the property was acquired and its basis) is required on the tax return if donated noncash property is valued at more than $500. Qualified appraisals may be required if noncash contributions exceed $5,000 in value.
Antiques, paintings, jewelry, and other "tangible personal property"	• The deduction is equal to the property's appreciated FMV only if the charity puts the property to "a use related to its tax-exempt purpose." Otherwise, the deduction is limited to the property's cost. The taxpayer should obtain a statement from the charity documenting the property's use.

The required substantiation must be obtained before the earlier of (1) the due date (including extensions) of the return for the year the contribution is claimed or (2) the date the return is filed. Failure to comply with the reporting rules may result in disallowance of the charitable contribution deduction. Additionally, significant overvaluation exposes the taxpayer to stringent penalties.

Common documentation and substantiation requirements are summarized in Concept Summary 10.2.

Valuation Requirements

Property donated to a charity is generally valued at fair market value at the time the gift is made. The Code and Regulations give very little guidance on the measurement of the fair market value except to say, "The fair market value is the price at which the property would change hands between a willing buyer and a willing seller, neither being under any compulsion to buy or sell and both having reasonable knowledge of relevant facts."

Generally, charitable organizations do not attest to the fair market value of the donated property. Nevertheless, as noted in Concept Summary 10.2, the taxpayer must maintain reliable written evidence of the donation.

LIMITATIONS ON CHARITABLE CONTRIBUTION DEDUCTION

In General

The potential charitable contribution deduction is the total of all donations, both money and property, that qualify for the deduction. After this determination is made, the actual amount of the charitable contribution deduction that is allowed for individuals for the tax year is limited as follows:

- If the qualifying contributions for the year total 20 percent or less of AGI, they are fully deductible.
- If the qualifying contributions are more than 20 percent of AGI, the deductible amount may be limited to either 20 percent, 30 percent, or 50 percent of AGI, depending on the type of property given and the type of organization to which the donation is made.
- In any case, the maximum charitable contribution deduction may not exceed 50 percent of AGI for the tax year.

To understand the complex rules for computing the amount of a charitable contribution deduction, it is necessary to understand the distinction between capital gain property and ordinary income property. In addition, it is necessary to understand when the 50 percent, 30 percent, and 20 percent limitations apply. If a taxpayer's contributions for the year exceed the applicable percentage limitations, the excess contributions may be carried forward and deducted during a five-year carryover period. These topics are discussed in the sections that follow.

Ordinary Income Property

Ordinary income property is any property that, if sold, will result in the recognition of ordinary income. The term includes inventory for sale in the taxpayer's trade or business, a work of art created by the donor, and a manuscript prepared by the donor. It also includes, *for purposes of the charitable contribution calculation,* a capital asset held by the donor for less than the required holding period for long-term capital gain treatment (long term is a period longer than one year). To the extent that disposition of property results in the recognition of ordinary income due to the recapture of depreciation, it is ordinary income property.[45]

If ordinary income property is contributed, the deduction is equal to the fair market value of the property less the amount of ordinary income that would have been reported if the property were sold. In most instances, the deduction is limited to the adjusted basis of the property to the donor.

EXAMPLE 30

Tim donates stock in White Corporation to a university on May 1, 2011. Tim had purchased the stock for $2,500 on March 3, 2011, and the stock had a value of $3,600 when he made the donation. Since he had not held the property long enough to meet the long-term capital gain requirement, Tim would have recognized a short-term capital gain of $1,100 if he had sold the property. Since short-term capital gain property is treated as ordinary income property for charitable contribution purposes, Tim's charitable contribution deduction is limited to the property's adjusted basis of $2,500 ($3,600 – $1,100). ■

In Example 30, suppose the stock had a fair market value of $2,300 (rather than $3,600) when it was donated to charity. Because the fair market value now is less than the adjusted basis, the charitable contribution deduction is $2,300.

Capital Gain Property

Capital gain property is any property that would have resulted in the recognition of long-term capital gain or § 1231 gain if the property had been sold by the donor.[46]

[45] For a more complete discussion of the difference between ordinary income and capital gain property, see Chapter 14.

[46] See General Scheme of Taxation in Chapter 14 for a discussion of holding periods.

As a general rule, the deduction for a contribution of capital gain property is equal to the fair market value of the property.

Three major exceptions disallow the deductibility of the appreciation on capital gain property. One exception concerns certain private foundations. Private foundations are organizations that traditionally do not receive their funding from the general public (e.g., the Bill and Melinda Gates Foundation). Generally, foundations fall into two categories: operating and nonoperating. A private *operating* foundation is one that spends substantially all of its income in the active conduct of the charitable undertaking for which it was established. Other private foundations are *nonoperating* foundations. Often, only the private foundation knows its status (operating or nonoperating) for sure, and the status can change from year to year.

If capital gain property is contributed to a private nonoperating foundation, the taxpayer must reduce the contribution by the long-term capital gain that would have been recognized if the property had been sold at its fair market value. The effect of this provision is to limit the deduction to the property's adjusted basis.[47]

EXAMPLE 31

Walter purchased land for $8,000 on January 1, 1998, and has held it as an investment since then. This year, when the land is worth $20,000, he donates it to a private nonoperating foundation. Walter's charitable contribution is $8,000 ($20,000 – $12,000), the land's basis. ■

If, in Example 31, Walter had donated the land to either a public charity or a private operating foundation, his charitable contribution would be $20,000, the fair market value of the land.

A second exception applying to capital gain property relates to *tangible personalty.* Tangible personalty is all property that is not realty (land and buildings) and does not include intangible property such as stock or securities. If tangible personalty is contributed to a public charity such as a museum, church, or university, the charitable deduction may have to be reduced. The amount of the reduction is the long-term capital gain that would have been recognized if the property had been sold for its fair market value. In general, the reduction is required if the property is put to an *unrelated use.* The term *unrelated use* means a use that is unrelated to the exempt purpose or function of the charitable organization. For example, a piece of artwork donated to the American Red Cross is unlikely to be put to a related use. Instead, the Red Cross would likely sell the art to generate funds that would then be used to support its mission of providing assistance to individuals who have been struck by disasters.

This reduction generally will not apply if the property is, in fact, not put to an unrelated use or if, at the time of the contribution, it was reasonable to anticipate that the property would not be put to an unrelated use by the donee.[48]

EXAMPLE 32

Myrtle contributes a Picasso painting, for which she paid $20,000, to a local museum. She had owned the painting for four years. It had a value of $30,000 at the time of the donation. The museum displays the painting for five years and subsequently sells it for $50,000. The charitable contribution is $30,000. It is not reduced by the unrealized appreciation since the painting is not put to an unrelated use even though it is later sold by the museum. ■

A third exception applying to capital gain property disallows a deduction for the appreciation on several types of intellectual property. Patents, certain copyrights, trademarks, trade names, trade secrets, know-how, and some software are subject to this rule, which limits the contribution to the lesser of the taxpayer's basis in the property or the property's fair market value. As a consequence of this exception, if

[47] § 170(e)(1)(B)(ii). However, § 170(e)(5) provides that taxpayers who donate *qualified appreciated stock* to private nonoperating foundations may deduct the fair market value of the stock. Qualified appreciated stock is stock for which market quotations are readily available on an established securities market.

[48] § 170(e)(1)(B)(i) and Reg. § 1.170A–4(b)(3)(ii)(b). In certain situations, if the donee disposes of the property within three years of the contribution, the donor is required to recapture the appreciation element of the deduction unless the donee certifies that it put the property to a related use or intended to put the property to a related use.

CONCEPT SUMMARY 10.3

Determining the Deduction for Contributions of Appreciated Property by Individuals

If the Type of Property Contributed Is:	And the Property Is Contributed to:	The Contribution Is Measured by:	But the Deduction Is Limited to:
1. Capital gain property	A 50% organization	Fair market value of the property	30% of AGI
2. Ordinary income property	A 50% organization	The basis of the property*	50% of AGI
3. Capital gain property (and the property is tangible personal property put to an unrelated use by the donee)	A 50% organization	The basis of the property*	50% of AGI
4. Capital gain property (and the reduced deduction is elected)	A 50% organization	The basis of the property	50% of AGI
5. Capital gain property	A private nonoperating foundation that is not a 50% organization	The basis of the property*	The lesser of: 1. 20% of AGI 2. 50% of AGI minus other contributions to 50% organizations

*If the fair market value of the property is less than the adjusted basis (i.e., the property has declined in value instead of appreciating), the fair market value is used.

many of these types of intellectual property are donated by their creator, the charitable contribution deduction will be relatively small because the creator usually has a low basis for them.

Fifty Percent Ceiling

Contributions made to public charities may not exceed 50 percent of an individual's AGI for the year. Excess contributions may be carried over to the next five years. The 50 percent ceiling on contributions applies to public charities such as churches, schools, hospitals, and Federal, state or local governmental units. The 50 percent ceiling also applies to contributions to private operating foundations and certain private nonoperating foundations.

In the remaining discussion of charitable contributions, public charities and private foundations (both operating and nonoperating) that qualify for the 50 percent ceiling will be referred to as *50 percent organizations.*

Thirty Percent Ceiling

A 30 percent ceiling applies to contributions of cash and ordinary income property to private nonoperating foundations that are not 50 percent organizations. The 30 percent ceiling also applies to contributions of appreciated capital gain property to 50 percent organizations unless the taxpayer makes a special election (see below).

In the event the contributions for any one tax year involve both 50 percent and 30 percent property, the allowable deduction comes first from the 50 percent property.

EXAMPLE 33

During the year, Lisa makes the following donations to her church: cash of $2,000 and unimproved land worth $30,000. Lisa had purchased the land four years ago for

$22,000 and held it as an investment. Therefore, it is capital gain property. Lisa's AGI for the year is $60,000. Disregarding percentage limitations, Lisa's potential deduction is $32,000 [$2,000 (cash) + $30,000 (fair market value of land)].

In applying the percentage limitations, however, the *current* deduction for the land is limited to $18,000 [30% (limitation applicable to capital gain property) × $60,000 (AGI)]. Thus, the total current deduction is $20,000 ($2,000 cash + $18,000 land). Note that the total deduction does not exceed $30,000, which is 50% of Lisa's AGI. ■

Under a special election, a taxpayer may choose to forgo a deduction of the appreciation on capital gain property. Referred to as the *reduced deduction election,* this enables the taxpayer to move from the 30 percent limitation to the 50 percent limitation.

EXAMPLE 34

Assume the same facts as in Example 33, except that Lisa makes the reduced deduction election. Now the deduction becomes $24,000 [$2,000 (cash) + $22,000 (basis in land)] because both donations fall under the 50% limitation. Thus, by making the election, Lisa has increased her current charitable contribution deduction by $4,000 [$24,000 – $20,000 (Example 33)]. ■

Although the reduced deduction election appears attractive, it should be considered carefully. The election sacrifices a deduction for the appreciation on capital gain property that might eventually be allowed. Note that in Example 33, the potential deduction was $32,000, yet in Example 34 only $24,000 is allowed. The reason the potential deduction is decreased by $8,000 ($32,000 – $24,000) is that no carryover is allowed for the amount sacrificed by the election.

Twenty Percent Ceiling

A 20 percent ceiling applies to contributions of appreciated capital gain property to private nonoperating foundations that are not 50 percent organizations.

Contribution Carryovers

Contributions that exceed the percentage limitations for the current year can be carried over for five years. In the carryover process, such contributions do not lose their identity for limitation purposes. Thus, if the contribution originally involved 30 percent property, the carryover will continue to be classified as 30 percent property in the carryover year.

EXAMPLE 35

Assume the same facts as in Example 33. Because only $18,000 of the $30,000 value of the land is deducted in the current year, the balance of $12,000 may be carried over to the following year. But the carryover will still be treated as capital gain property and is subject to the 30%-of-AGI limitation. ■

In applying the percentage limitations, current charitable contributions must be claimed first before any carryovers can be considered. If carryovers involve more than one year, they are utilized in a first-in, first-out order.

10.6 Miscellaneous Itemized Deductions

LO.7

List the business and personal expenditures that are deductible either as miscellaneous itemized deductions or as other itemized deductions.

In general, no deduction is allowed for personal, living, or family expenses.[49] However, a taxpayer may incur a number of expenditures related to employment. If an employee or outside salesperson incurs unreimbursed business expenses or expenses that are reimbursed under a nonaccountable plan, including travel and

[49]§ 262.

transportation, the expenses are deductible as **miscellaneous itemized deductions.**[50] Certain other expenses also fall into the special category of miscellaneous itemized deductions. Some are deductible only if, in total, they exceed 2 percent of the taxpayer's AGI. These miscellaneous itemized deductions include (but are not limited to) the following:

- Professional dues to membership organizations.
- Uniforms or other clothing that cannot be used for normal wear.
- Fees incurred for the preparation of one's tax return or fees incurred for tax litigation before the IRS or the courts.
- Job-hunting costs.
- Fee paid for a safe deposit box used to store papers and documents relating to taxable income-producing investments.
- Investment expenses that are deductible under § 212 as discussed in Chapter 6.
- Appraisal fees to determine the amount of a casualty loss or the fair market value of donated property.
- Hobby losses up to the amount of hobby income (refer to Chapter 6).
- Unreimbursed employee expenses (refer to Chapter 9).

Certain employee business expenses that are reimbursed are not itemized deductions, but are deducted *for* AGI. Employee business expenses are discussed in depth in Chapter 9.

10.7 Other Miscellaneous Deductions

Certain expenses and losses do not fall into any category of itemized deductions already discussed but are nonetheless deductible. The following expenses and losses are deductible on line 28 of Schedule A as Other Miscellaneous Deductions.

- Gambling losses up to the amount of gambling winnings.
- Impairment-related work expenses of a handicapped person.
- Federal estate tax on income in respect of a decedent.
- Deduction for repayment of amounts under a claim of right if more than $3,000 (discussed in Chapter 16).
- The unrecovered investment in an annuity contract when the annuity ceases by reason of death, discussed in Chapter 4.

Unlike the expenses and losses discussed previously under Miscellaneous Itemized Deductions, the above expenses and losses are not subject to the 2 percent-of-AGI floor.

10.8 Comprehensive Example of Schedule A

Harry and Jean Brown, married filing jointly, had the following transactions for 2010:

Medicines that required a prescription	$ 430
Doctor and dentist bills paid and not reimbursed	2,120
Medical insurance premium payments	1,200
Contact lenses	170
Transportation for medical purposes on March 1, 2010 (321 miles × 16.5 cents/mile + $10.00 parking)	63
State income tax withheld (This amount exceeds the sales tax from the sales tax table.)	1,900
Real estate taxes	1,580

[50] Actors and performing artists who meet certain requirements are not subject to this rule. See § 62(a)(2)(B).

TAX *in* the NEWS

THE FIRST FAMILY AND ITEMIZED DEDUCTION PHASEOUTS

In 2010, President Barack H. and Michelle L. Obama itemized deductions on their 2009 tax return (refer to Tax in the News, p. 10-4). Because of their income level, their itemized deductions were reduced, as shown in the column to the right.

The top marginal rate of 35 percent applied to the Obamas' taxable income in 2009. Therefore, the phaseout of itemized deductions cost them $18,685 in additional Federal income tax ($53,386 reduction × 35% marginal tax rate).

While this phaseout provision expired after 2009 and is not currently part of the law (i.e., does not apply for 2011 and 2012), many commentators expect it could return sooner than 2013 once Congress begins to focus on ways to reduce the large budget deficit.

Itemized Deductions	
Medical expenses	$ –0–
Taxes	186,910
Interest	52,195
Charitable contributions	329,100
Job expenses and most other miscellaneous deductions	–0–
Total itemized deductions	$568,205
Reduction due to phaseout [($5,505,409 AGI – $166,800) × .03 × 1/3]	(53,386)
Itemized deductions allowed	$514,819

Interest paid on qualified residence mortgage	$2,340
Qualifying charitable contributions paid by check	860
Transportation in performing charitable services (800 miles × 14 cents/mile + $7.00 parking and tolls)	119
Unreimbursed employee expenses (from Form 2106)	870
Tax return preparation	150
Safe deposit box (used for keeping investment documents and tax records)	170

The Browns' AGI is $40,000. Their completed 2010 Schedule A on the following page reports itemized deductions totaling $8,172. Schedule A for 2010 is used for illustration purposes because the 2011 form was not available at the date of this printing.

10.9 OVERALL LIMITATION ON CERTAIN ITEMIZED DEDUCTIONS

Recall from the discussion in Chapter 3 that certain higher income taxpayers were subject to a phaseout of personal and dependency exemptions that is no longer in effect as of the beginning of 2010. A similar phaseout provision also formerly applied to certain itemized deductions where a limitation was placed on their full deductibility. Phaseouts of this type are sometimes referred to as "stealth taxes." The Tax in the News above illustrates the effect of the limitation on President and Mrs. Obamas' 2009 income tax return, which required them to pay $18,685 more in Federal income taxes than they would have paid had their itemized deductions been fully deductible. That limitation does not apply to individual taxpayers for tax years beginning after 2009, and now taxpayers may *fully* deduct any itemized deductions to which they are entitled.[51] Even though the phaseout provision currently is not scheduled to return until 2013, many tax commentators expect it could return sooner than then once Congress begins to focus on ways to reduce the large budget deficit.

[51] § 68. In 2009, before the provision's expiration, the limitation applied to taxpayers whose AGI exceeded $166,800 ($83,400 for married taxpayers filing separately). Section 68(g) provides for its termination for tax years beginning after December 31, 2009.

SCHEDULE A (Form 1040)

Department of the Treasury
Internal Revenue Service (99)

Itemized Deductions

▶ Attach to Form 1040. ▶ See Instructions for Schedule A (Form 1040).

OMB No. 1545-0074
2010
Attachment Sequence No. 07

Name(s) shown on Form 1040: *Harry and Jean Brown*

Your social security number: *111 11 1111*

Section	Line	Description	Box	Amount	Line	Amount
Medical and Dental Expenses		**Caution.** Do not include expenses reimbursed or paid by others.				
	1	Medical and dental expenses (see instructions)	1	*3,983*		
	2	Enter amount from Form 1040, line 38	2	*40,000*				
	3	Multiply line 2 by 7.5% (.075)	3	*3,000*		
	4	Subtract line 3 from line 1. If line 3 is more than line 1, enter -0-			4	*983*
Taxes You Paid	5	State and local **(check only one box):** a ☒ Income taxes, **or** b ☐ General sales taxes	5	*1,900*		
	6	Real estate taxes (see instructions)	6	*1,580*		
	7	New motor vehicle taxes from line 11 of the worksheet on back (for certain vehicles purchased in 2009). Skip this line if you checked box 5b	7			
	8	Other taxes. List type and amount ▶	8			
	9	Add lines 5 through 8			9	*3,480*
Interest You Paid	10	Home mortgage interest and points reported to you on Form 1098	10	*2,340*		
Note. Your mortgage interest deduction may be limited (see instructions).	11	Home mortgage interest not reported to you on Form 1098. If paid to the person from whom you bought the home, see instructions and show that person's name, identifying no., and address ▶	11			
	12	Points not reported to you on Form 1098. See instructions for special rules	12			
	13	Mortgage insurance premiums (see instructions)	13			
	14	Investment interest. Attach Form 4952 if required. (See instructions.)	14			
	15	Add lines 10 through 14			15	*2,340*
Gifts to Charity	16	Gifts by cash or check. If you made any gift of $250 or more, see instructions	16	*860*		
If you made a gift and got a benefit for it, see instructions.	17	Other than by cash or check. If any gift of $250 or more, see instructions. You **must** attach Form 8283 if over $500	17	*119*		
	18	Carryover from prior year	18			
	19	Add lines 16 through 18			19	*979*
Casualty and Theft Losses	20	Casualty or theft loss(es). Attach Form 4684. (See instructions.)			20	
Job Expenses and Certain Miscellaneous Deductions	21	Unreimbursed employee expenses—job travel, union dues, job education, etc. Attach Form 2106 or 2106-EZ if required. (See instructions.) ▶	21	*870*		
	22	Tax preparation fees	22	*150*		
	23	Other expenses—investment, safe deposit box, etc. List type and amount ▶ *Safe deposit box*	23	*170*		
	24	Add lines 21 through 23	24	*1,190*		
	25	Enter amount from Form 1040, line 38	25	*40,000*				
	26	Multiply line 25 by 2% (.02)	26	*800*		
	27	Subtract line 26 from line 24. If line 26 is more than line 24, enter -0-			27	*390*
Other Miscellaneous Deductions	28	Other—from list in instructions. List type and amount ▶			28	
Total Itemized Deductions	29	Add the amounts in the far right column for lines 4 through 28. Also, enter this amount on Form 1040, line 40			29	*8,172*
	30	If you elect to itemize deductions even though they are less than your standard deduction, check here ▶ ☐				

For Paperwork Reduction Act Notice, see Form 1040 instructions. Cat. No. 17145C **Schedule A (Form 1040) 2010**

ETHICS & Equity

BETWEEN A ROCK AND A HARD PLACE

Robert Ryan, a candidate for governor, has released his income tax return to the public. As Ryan's former tax adviser, you examine the return closely and realize that a considerable amount of his income was not reported on the return. You confide to a friend in the tabloid newspaper business that you are aware that a candidate for high public office has filed a fraudulent tax return. Your friend assures you that you will be able to sell your story for at least $25,000 to a tabloid and still remain anonymous. Another friend, a CPA, argues that you should inform Ryan and give him an opportunity to correct the problem. You tell your friend that you are concerned that Ryan will be very vindictive if you approach him about the issue. Which course of action will you choose?

TAX PLANNING:

10.10 EFFECTIVE UTILIZATION OF ITEMIZED DEDUCTIONS

LO.8

Identify tax planning strategies that can maximize the benefit of itemized deductions.

Since an individual may use the standard deduction in one year and itemize deductions in another year, it is frequently possible to obtain maximum benefit by shifting itemized deductions from one year to another. For example, if a taxpayer's itemized deductions and the standard deduction are approximately the same for each year of a two-year period, the taxpayer should use the standard deduction in one year and shift itemized deductions (to the extent permitted by law) to the other year. The individual could, for example, prepay a church pledge for a particular year to shift the deduction to the current year or avoid paying end-of-the-year medical expenses to shift the deduction to the following year.

10.11 UTILIZATION OF MEDICAL DEDUCTIONS

When a taxpayer anticipates that medical expenses will approximate the percentage floor, much might be done to generate a deductible excess. Any of the following procedures can help build a deduction by the end of the year:

- Incur the obligation for needed dental work or have needed work carried out.[52] Orthodontic treatment, for example, may have been recommended for a member of the taxpayer's family.
- Have elective remedial surgery that may have been postponed from prior years (e.g., tonsillectomies, vasectomies, correction of hernias, hysterectomies).
- Incur the obligation for capital improvements to the taxpayer's personal residence recommended by a physician (e.g., an air filtration system to alleviate a respiratory disorder).

As an aid to taxpayers who may experience temporary cash-flow problems at the end of the year, the use of credit cards is deemed to be payment for purposes of timing the deductibility of charitable and medical expenses.

EXAMPLE 36

On December 13, 2011, Marge (a calendar year taxpayer) purchases two pairs of prescription contact lenses and one pair of prescribed orthopedic shoes for a total of $450. These purchases are separately charged to Marge's credit card. On January 6, 2012, Marge receives her statement containing these charges and makes payment shortly

[52]Prepayment of medical expenses does not generate a current deduction unless the taxpayer is under an obligation to make the payment.

thereafter. The purchases are deductible as medical expenses in the year charged (2011) and not in the year the account is settled (2012). ■

Recognizing which expenditures qualify for the medical deduction also may be crucial to exceeding the percentage limitations.

EXAMPLE 37

Mortimer employs Lana (an unrelated party) to care for his incapacitated and dependent mother. Lana is not a trained nurse but spends approximately one-half of the time performing nursing duties (e.g., administering injections and providing physical therapy) and the rest of the time doing household chores. An allocable portion of Lana's wages that Mortimer pays (including the employer's portion of FICA taxes) qualifies as a medical expense. ■

10.12 Timing the Payment of Deductible Taxes

It is sometimes possible to defer or accelerate the payment of certain deductible taxes, such as state income tax, real property tax, and personal property tax. For instance, the final installment of estimated state income tax is generally due after the end of a given tax year. Accelerating the payment of the final installment could result in larger itemized deductions for the current year.

EXAMPLE 38

Jenny, who is single, expects to have itemized deductions of $5,500 in 2011 and $2,500 in 2012. She plans to pay $900 as the final installment on her 2011 estimated state income tax, which is due on January 15, 2012. The standard deduction for 2011 is $5,800 for single taxpayers. If Jenny does not pay the final installment until 2012, she will not itemize in either 2011 or 2012. However, if she pays the final installment in December 2011, her itemized deductions will be $6,400 ($5,500 + $900) in 2011, and she will benefit from itemizing. ■

10.13 Protecting the Interest Deduction

Although the deductibility of prepaid interest by a cash basis taxpayer has been severely restricted, a notable exception allows a deduction for points paid by the buyer to obtain financing for the purchase or improvement of a principal residence in the year of payment. However, such points must actually be paid by the taxpayer obtaining the loan and must represent a charge for the use of money. It has been held that points paid from the mortgage proceeds do not satisfy the payment requirement.[53] Also, the portion of the points attributable to service charges does not represent deductible interest.[54] Taxpayers financing home purchases or improvements usually should direct their planning toward avoiding these two hurdles to immediate deductibility.

In rare instances, a taxpayer may find it desirable to forgo the immediate expensing of points in the year paid. Instead, it could prove beneficial to capitalize the points and write them off as interest expense over the life of the mortgage.

EXAMPLE 39

Gerald purchases a home on December 15, 2011, for $380,000 with $120,000 cash and a 15-year mortgage of $260,000 financed by the Greater Metropolis National Bank. Gerald pays two points in addition to interest allocated to the period from December 15 until December 31, 2011, at an annual rate of 6%. Since Gerald does not have enough itemized deductions to exceed the standard deduction for 2011, he should elect to capitalize the points and amortize them over 15 years. In this instance, Gerald would

[53] *Alan A. Rubnitz*, 67 T.C. 621 (1977). Seller-paid points may also be deductible by the buyer under the provisions of Rev.Proc. 94–27, cited in footnote 31.

[54] *Donald L. Wilkerson*, 70 T.C. 240 (1978).

TAX in the NEWS

Getting the Biggest Bang for the Buck When Supporting Charity

Individuals are often motivated to support a charitable organization's goals for numerous reasons: they want to help by providing food and shelter to those in need, responding to natural disasters, or delivering other basic goods or services to the needy. But in a world of limited resources, donors also must choose *which* organization(s) to support from among many worthwhile causes because it is impossible to support all of them in a meaningful way. So what factors might be helpful to a prospective donor in deciding how to deploy limited charitable dollars?

- All other things being equal, a deductible gift is better than a nondeductible gift. Therefore, to ensure a charitable contribution deduction, the donor should be certain that the recipient is a qualified domestic organization. Check with the IRS to verify that a particular charity is qualified (**www.irs.gov**).
- The donor may want to know whether the charitable organization is efficient in using the resources at its disposal in meeting its objectives. To compare the relative efficiency of charities on a scale of 0 to 10, check with Charity Navigator (**www.charitynavigator.org**).
- Is the organization efficient in its fund-raising efforts, or does the charity typically incur a large amount of fund-raising expenditures relative to the resources it generates? This type of information is reflected in a grade assigned by the American Institute of Philanthropy (**www.charitywatch.org**).

deduct $346.67 for 2012, as part of his qualified residence interest expense [$5,200 (two points) divided by 15 years], if he elects to itemize that year. ■

Because personal (consumer) interest is not deductible, taxpayers should consider making use of home equity loans. Recall that these loans utilize the personal residence of the taxpayer as security. The funds from these loans can be used for personal purposes (e.g., auto loans, vacations). By making use of home equity loans, therefore, what would have been nondeductible consumer interest becomes deductible qualified residence interest.

10.14 Assuring the Charitable Contribution Deduction

For a charitable contribution deduction to be available, the recipient must be a qualified charitable organization. Sometimes the mechanics of how the contribution is carried out can determine whether a deduction results.

EXAMPLE 40

Fumiko wants to donate $5,000 to her church's mission in Kobe, Japan. In this regard, she considers three alternatives:

1. Send the money directly to the mission.
2. Give the money to her church with the understanding that it is to be passed on to the mission.
3. Give the money directly to the missionary in charge of the mission who is currently in the United States on a fund-raising trip.

If Fumiko wants to obtain a deduction for the contribution, she should choose alternative 2. A direct donation to the mission (alternative 1) is not deductible because the mission is a foreign charity. A direct gift to the missionary (alternative 3) does not comply since an individual cannot be a qualified charity for income tax purposes.[55] ■

[55] *Thomas E. Lesslie*, 36 TCM 495, T.C.Memo. 1977–111.

A clearly established rule provides that a donor may not claim a charitable contribution to the extent that a benefit is received in return. For example, if $100 is paid to attend a charity ball and a reasonable value of that privilege is $35, the charitable contribution is $65. However, consider the following circumstances.

EXAMPLE 41

In response to a solicitation from the University Medical Association, Rich and Lucile pay $200, which allows them to attend a fund-raising benefit event. The charity mails them a ticket and a statement indicating that for a contribution at the $200 level, $140 may be deducted because the value of the benefit provided to the donor equals $60. If Rich and Lucile accept the ticket, whether they attend the benefit or not, their deduction is $140. However, if they *return* the ticket to the charity for resale (e.g., they know their schedule will prevent them from attending), the charitable contribution deduction equals the entire amount paid for the ticket. ■

When making noncash donations, the type of property chosen can have decided implications in determining the amount, if any, of the deduction.

EXAMPLE 42

Sam wants to give $60,000 in value to his church in some form other than cash. In this connection, he considers four alternatives:

1. Stock held for two years as an investment with a basis of $100,000 and a fair market value of $60,000.
2. Stock held for five years as an investment with a basis of $10,000 and a fair market value of $60,000.
3. The rent-free use for a year of a building that normally leases for $5,000 a month.
4. A valuable stamp collection held as an investment and owned for 10 years with a basis of $10,000 and a fair market value of $60,000. The church plans to sell the collection if and when it is donated.

Alternative 1 is ill-advised as the subject of the gift. Even though Sam would obtain a deduction of $60,000, he would forgo the potential loss of $40,000 that would be recognized if the property were sold.[56] Alternative 2 makes good sense since the deduction still is $60,000 and none of the $50,000 of appreciation that has occurred must be recognized as income. Alternative 3 yields no deduction at all and is not a wise choice. Alternative 4 involves tangible personalty that the recipient does not plan to use. As a result, the amount of the deduction is limited to $10,000, the stamp collection's basis.[57] ■

For property transfers (particularly real estate), the ceiling limitations on the amount of the deduction allowed in any one year (50 percent, 30 percent, or 20 percent of AGI, as the case may be) could be a factor to take into account. With proper planning, donations can be controlled to stay within the limitations and therefore avoid the need for a carryover of unused charitable contributions.

EXAMPLE 43

Andrew wants to donate a tract of unimproved land held as an investment to Eastern University (a qualified charitable organization). The land has been held for six years and has a current fair market value of $300,000 and a basis to Andrew of $50,000. Andrew's AGI for the current year is estimated to be $200,000, and he expects much the same for the next few years. In the current year, he deeds (transfers) an undivided one-fifth interest in the real estate to the university. ■

What has Andrew in Example 43 accomplished for income tax purposes? In the current year, he will be allowed a charitable contribution deduction of $60,000 ($^1/_5$ × $300,000), which will be within the applicable limitation of AGI (30% × $200,000). Presuming no other charitable contributions for the year, Andrew has avoided the possibility of a carryover. In future years, Andrew can arrange donations of

[56] *LaVar M. Withers*, 69 T.C. 900 (1978).

[57] No reduction of appreciation is necessary in alternative 2 since stock is intangible property and not tangible personalty.

undivided interests in the real estate to stay within the bounds of the percentage limitations. The only difficulty with this approach is the need to revalue the real estate each year before the donation, since the amount of the deduction is based on the fair market value of the interest contributed at the time of the contribution.

EXAMPLE 44

Tiffany dies in October 2011. In completing her final income tax return for 2011, Tiffany's executor determines the following information: AGI of $104,000 and a donation by Tiffany to her church of stock worth $60,000. Tiffany had purchased the stock two years ago for $50,000 and held it as an investment. Tiffany's executor makes the reduced deduction election and, as a consequence, claims a charitable contribution deduction of $50,000. With the election, the potential charitable contribution deduction of $50,000 ($60,000 − $10,000) is less than the 50% ceiling of $52,000 ($104,000 × 50%). If the executor had not made the election, the potential charitable contribution deduction of $60,000 would have been reduced by the 30% ceiling to $31,200 ($104,000 × 30%). No carryover of the $28,800 ($60,000 − $31,200) would have been available because Tiffany's 2011 income tax return is her final return. ■

REFOCUS ON THE BIG PICTURE

ITEMIZED DEDUCTIONS CAN REDUCE THE AFTER-TAX COST OF MAJOR PURCHASES

Because the Federal tax law provides that qualified residence interest and real estate taxes are deductible by individual taxpayers, the after-tax cost of a home purchase will be reduced by the tax savings associated with these itemized tax deductions (see Example 1). Given the Williamsons' projected taxable income, they are in the 28 percent Federal tax bracket and the 6 percent state tax bracket (i.e., aggregate marginal tax bracket of 34 percent). As a result, the after-tax cost of financing the purchase of the home will be:

Nondeductible principal payments	$ 2,000
Deductible qualified residence interest and real estate taxes [($37,000 + $3,000) × (1 − .34)]	26,400
Total	$28,400
After-tax monthly cost ($28,400 ÷ 12)	$ 2,367

Because the Williamsons will be able to itemize their deductions if they purchase a new home and will be able to deduct most of their monthly house payment, the home purchase will be affordable (see Examples 16 and 22).

What If?

What if the Williamsons use the less expensive route to finance the purchase of their home by using their retirement and taxable portfolio as security for the loan? What may at first appear to be a cost-effective approach ends up being more costly when considering the impact of the tax law. With this approach, the interest expense is not deductible because it is not qualified residence interest (see Example 22); further, it is not deductible as investment interest (see Chapter 11). Therefore, the after-tax cost of financing the home using this approach makes the home unaffordable.

Nondeductible principal and interest payments	$37,000
Deductible real estate taxes [$3,000 × (1 − .34)]	1,980
Total	$38,980
After-tax monthly cost ($38,980 ÷ 12)	$ 3,248

KEY TERMS

Acquisition indebtedness, 10–15
Capital gain property, 10–24
Charitable contribution, 10–19
Health Savings Account (HSA), 10–9
Home equity loans, 10–15
Medical expense, 10–3
Miscellaneous itemized deductions, 10–28
Ordinary income property, 10–24
Points, 10–16
Qualified residence interest, 10-14

DISCUSSION QUESTIONS

1. **LO.1, 2** Erin, who prepared her own income tax return for the current year, failed to claim a deduction for her contribution to a traditional Individual Retirement Account (IRA). Her AGI, as reported on the incorrect return, was $100,000, and her medical expenses were $10,000.
   a. Will the correction of this omission affect the amount of medical expenses Erin can deduct? Explain.
   b. Will Erin's medical expense deduction increase or decrease when she corrects her return?

2. **LO.2** Roberta incurred the following expenditures during the year:

   - Medical insurance premiums.
   - Life insurance premiums.
   - Nonprescription calcium supplements to prevent osteoporosis.
   - Fees for an alcohol rehabilitation program.
   - Contact lenses.
   - Travel expenses to obtain treatment at the Mayo Clinic in Minnesota.

   Which of these expenses can Roberta include as medical expenses for purposes of computing her medical expense deduction?

3. **LO.2** Joe was in an accident and required cosmetic surgery for injuries to his nose. He also had the doctor do additional surgery to reshape his chin, which had not been injured. Will the cosmetic surgery to Joe's nose qualify as a medical expense? Will the cosmetic surgery to Joe's chin qualify as a medical expense? Explain.

DECISION MAKING

4. **LO.2, 8** Frank, a widower, had a serious stroke and is no longer capable of caring for himself. He has three sons, all of whom live in different states. Because they are unable to care for Frank in their homes, his sons have placed him in a nursing home equipped to provide medical and nursing care. Total nursing home expenses amount to $36,000 per year. Of this amount, $15,000 is directly attributable to medical and nursing care. Frank's Social Security benefits are used to pay for $10,000 of the nursing home charges. He has no other income. His sons plan to split the remaining medical expenses equally.
   a. What portion of the nursing home charges is potentially deductible as a medical expense?
   b. Can you provide Frank's sons with a tax planning idea for maximizing the deduction for his medical expenses?

5. **LO.2** Nathan, who is physically handicapped, paid $10,000 for the installation of wheelchair ramps, support bars, and railings in his personal residence. These improvements increased the value of his personal residence by $2,500. How much of Nathan's expenditure qualifies as a medical expense deduction (subject to the 7.5% floor)? Explain.

6. **LO.2** Bob and June were divorced in 2009. In July 2011, their daughter, Harriet, broke her leg while playing soccer. Harriet lives with June, and June claims her as a dependent. Bob pays for the medical expenses related to Harriet's injury. Can Bob claim the medical expenses he pays for Harriet on his tax return?

7. **LO.2** David, a sole proprietor of a bookstore, pays a $7,500 premium for medical insurance for himself and his family. Joan, an employee of a small firm that doesn't provide her with medical insurance, pays medical insurance premiums of $8,000 for herself. How does the tax treatment differ for David and Joan?

8. **LO.2** Arturo, a calendar year taxpayer, paid $16,000 in medical expenses and sustained a $20,000 casualty loss in 2011. He expects $12,000 of the medical expenses and $14,000 of the casualty loss to be reimbursed by insurance companies in 2012. Before considering any limitations on these deductions, how much can Arturo include in determining his itemized deductions for 2011?

9. **LO.2** Hubert, a self-employed taxpayer, is married and has two children. He has asked you to explain the tax and nontax advantages of creating a Health Savings Account (HSA) for himself and his family.

10. **LO.2** A local ophthalmologist's advertising campaign included a certificate for free LASIK eye surgery for the lucky winner of a drawing. Ahmad held the winning ticket, which was drawn in December 2010. Ahmad had no vision problems and was uncertain what he should do with the prize. In February 2011, Ahmad's daughter, who lives with his former wife, was diagnosed with a vision problem that could be treated with either prescription glasses or LASIK surgery. The divorce decree requires that Ahmad pay for all medical expenses incurred for his daughter. Identify the relevant tax issues for Ahmad. **ISSUE ID**

11. **LO.3** Diego sold his personal residence to Dinah on July 1, 2011. He had paid real property taxes on March 1, 2011, the due date for property taxes for 2011. **ISSUE ID**
    a. How will Diego's payment affect his deduction for property taxes in 2011?
    b. Will Diego's payment of the taxes have any effect on Dinah's itemized deductions for 2011?
    c. What other tax or financial effects will Diego's payment of the taxes have on either party?

12. **LO.5, 8** Julia owns a principal residence in California, a condo in New York City, and a houseboat in Florida. All of the properties have mortgages on which Julia pays interest. What are the limitations on Julia's mortgage interest deduction? What strategy should Julia consider to maximize her mortgage interest deduction? **DECISION MAKING**

13. **LO.5, 8** Mason Gregg's car was destroyed by a flood. Unfortunately, his insurance had lapsed two days before he incurred the loss. Mason uses his car for both business and personal use. Mason, who is self-employed, does not have adequate savings to replace the car and must borrow money to purchase a new car. He is considering taking out a home equity loan, at a 5% interest rate, to obtain funds for the purchase. Margaret, his wife, would prefer not to do so because they paid off their mortgage recently and she does not want to incur any obligations related to their home. She would prefer to sell some of their stock in Bluebird, Inc., to raise funds to purchase the new car. Mason does not want to sell the stock because it has declined in value since they purchased it and he is convinced that its price will increase within the next two years. Mason has suggested that they obtain conventional financing for the purchase from their bank, which charges 7% interest on car loans. Identify the tax issues related to each of the three alternatives Mason and Margaret are considering. **ISSUE ID**

14. **LO.5** Ed borrows $20,000 and purchases an automobile. Jack borrows $20,000 to purchase a diamond engagement ring for his fiancée. Ed qualifies for an interest deduction on the amount he borrowed, but Jack does not. Can you offer any explanation for the difference?

15. **LO.5** Thomas purchased a personal residence from Rachel. In order to sell the residence, Rachel agreed to pay $5,500 in points related to Thomas's mortgage. Discuss the deductibility of the points.

16. **LO.5** Ellen borrowed $50,000 from her parents for a down payment on the purchase of a new home. She paid interest of $3,200 in 2009, $0 in 2010, and $9,000 in 2011. The IRS disallowed the deduction. Can you offer any explanation for the disallowance?

17. **LO.6** To dissuade his pastor from resigning and taking a position with a larger church, Michael, an ardent leader of the congregation, gives the pastor a new car. Is the cost of the car deductible by Michael as a charitable contribution? Explain.

18. **LO.6** Paula contributed Orange Corporation common stock to the United Way, a qualified charitable organization. In addition, she contributed tables and chairs from her proprietorship's inventory to the high school in her city. Should Paula's charitable contribution deduction for these contributions be determined by the basis or fair market value of the contributed items?

ISSUE ID

19. **LO.6** Nancy, who is a professor at State University, does some of her writing and class preparation at home at night. Her department provides faculty members with a $1,500 allowance for a desktop computer for use at school, but does not ordinarily provide computers for use at home. In order to have a computer for use at school and at home, Nancy has asked the department to provide her with a notebook computer that costs $2,500. The head of her department is willing to provide the standard $1,500 allowance and will permit Nancy to purchase the $2,500 notebook computer if she makes a donation of $1,000 to the department. If she acquires the notebook computer, Nancy's home use of the computer will be approximately 60% for business and 40% for personal use not related to her job. Discuss the tax issues that Nancy should consider in deciding whether to acquire the notebook computer under these conditions.

20. **LO.6** Fran traveled to San Francisco during the year to do volunteer work for one week for the Salvation Army. She normally receives $1,500 salary per week at her job and is planning to deduct the $1,500 as a charitable contribution. In addition, Fran incurred the following costs in connection with the trip: $400 for transportation, $1,600 for lodging, and $550 for meals. What is Fran's deduction associated with this charitable activity?

ISSUE ID

21. **LO.6, 8** William, a high school teacher, earns about $50,000 each year. In December 2011, he won $1 million in the state lottery. William plans to donate $100,000 to his church. He has asked you, his tax adviser, whether he should donate the $100,000 in 2011 or 2012. Identify the tax issues related to William's decision.

ISSUE ID

22. **LO.6, 8** The "Top Four Games," which involves four of the top golfers on the PGA Tour, is held each year on the weekend after Thanksgiving. Total prize money amounts to $1 million, and the leading money winner also receives an automobile as a prize. Twenty percent of the money won by each player goes to charity. In addition, on the par three holes, the winner of the hole receives the keys to an automobile, which goes to the player's favorite charity. Identify the relevant tax issues for the players. Consider the following possibilities with respect to the car won by the leading money winner: (1) keep the car for personal use and sell his or her present car; (2) sell the new car; (3) give the car to a friend or relative; (4) donate the car to charity; or (5) give the car to his or her caddy.

DECISION MAKING

23. **LO.6, 8** Colin had AGI of $180,000 in 2011. He contributed stock in White, Inc. (a publicly traded corporation), to the United Way, a qualified charitable organization. The stock was worth $105,000 on the date it was contributed. Colin had acquired it as an investment two years ago at a cost of $84,000.
    a. What is the total amount that Colin can deduct as a charitable contribution, assuming he carries over any disallowed contribution from 2011 to future years?
    b. What is the maximum amount that Colin can deduct as a charitable contribution in 2011?
    c. What factors should Colin consider in deciding how to treat the contribution for Federal income tax purposes?
    d. Assume Colin dies in December 2011. What advice would you give the executor of his estate with regard to possible elections that can be made relative to the contribution?

PROBLEMS

24. **LO.2** Doug and Karen are married and together have AGI of $80,000 in 2011. They have two dependents and file a joint return. They pay $3,000 for a high-deductible health insurance policy and contribute $2,400 to a qualified Health Savings Account. During the year, they paid the following amounts for medical care: $7,500 in doctor and dentist bills and hospital expenses, and $1,700 for prescription drugs. In November 2011, they received an insurance reimbursement of $2,100 for hospitalization. They expect to receive an additional reimbursement of $1,000 in January 2012. Determine the maximum deduction allowable for medical expenses in 2011.

25. **LO.2** Andy had AGI of $80,000 for 2011. He was injured in a rock-climbing accident and paid $5,200 for hospital expenses and $2,800 for doctor bills. Andy also incurred medical expenses of $2,400 for his child, Jodi, who lives with his former wife, Pearl, and is claimed as a dependent by her. In 2012, Andy was reimbursed $2,600 by his insurance company for the medical expenses attributable to the rock-climbing accident.

a. Compute Andy's deduction for medical expenses in 2011.
b. Assume that Andy would have elected to itemize his deductions even if he had no medical expenses in 2011. How much, if any, of the $2,600 reimbursement must be included in gross income in 2012?
c. Assume that Andy's other itemized deductions in 2011 were $5,300 and that he filed as a head of household. How much of the $2,600 reimbursement must he include in gross income in 2012?

26. **LO.2** Jung suffers from heart problems and, upon the recommendation of a physician, has an elevator installed in his personal residence. In connection with the elevator, Jung incurs and pays the following amounts during the current year:

Elevator and cost of installation	$7,500
Increase in utility bills due to the elevator	400
Cost of certified appraisal	300

The system has an estimated useful life of 10 years. The appraisal was to determine the value of Jung's residence with and without the system. The appraisal states that the system increased the value of Jung's residence by $1,500. How much of these expenses qualifies for the medical expense deduction in the current year?

27. **LO.2** For calendar year 2011, Jean was a self-employed consultant with no employees. She had $80,000 net profit from consulting and paid $7,000 in medical insurance premiums on a policy covering 2011. How much of these premiums may Jean deduct as a deduction *for* AGI, and how much may she deduct as an itemized deduction (subject to the 7.5% floor)?

28. **LO.2** During the current year, Susan incurred and paid the following expenses for Beth (her daughter), Ed (her father), and herself:

Surgery for Beth	$4,500
Red River Academy charges for Beth:	
Tuition	5,100
Room, board, and other expenses	4,800
Psychiatric treatment	5,100
Doctor bills for Ed	2,200
Prescription drugs for Susan, Beth, and Ed	780
Insulin for Ed	540
Nonprescription drugs for Susan, Beth, and Ed	570
Charges at Heartland Nursing Home for Ed:	
Medical care	5,000
Lodging	2,700
Meals	2,650

Beth qualifies as Susan's dependent, and Ed would also qualify except that he receives $7,400 of taxable retirement benefits from his former employer. Beth's psychiatrist recommended Red River Academy because of its small classes and specialized psychiatric treatment program that is needed to treat Beth's illness. Ed, who is a paraplegic and diabetic, entered Heartland in October. Heartland offers the type of care that he requires.

Upon the recommendation of a physician, Susan has an air filtration system installed in her personal residence. She suffers from severe allergies. In connection with this equipment, Susan incurs and pays the following amounts during the year:

Filtration system and cost of installation	$6,500
Increase in utility bills due to the system	700
Cost of certified appraisal	360

The system has an estimated useful life of 10 years. The appraisal was to determine the value of Susan's residence with and without the system. The appraisal states that the system increased the value of Susan's residence by $2,200. Ignoring the 7.5% floor, what is the total of Susan's expenses that qualifies for the medical expense deduction?

ISSUE ID

29. **LO.2** In May, Rebecca's daughter, Susan, sustained a serious injury that made it impossible for her to continue living alone. Susan, who is a novelist, moved back into Rebecca's home after the accident. Susan has begun writing a new novel based on her recent experiences. To accommodate Susan, Rebecca incurred significant remodeling expenses (widening hallways, building a separate bedroom and bathroom, making kitchen appliances accessible to Susan). In addition, Rebecca had an indoor swimming pool constructed so Susan could do rehabilitation exercises prescribed by her physician.

    In September, Susan underwent major reconstructive surgery in Denver. The surgery was performed by Dr. Rama Patel, who specializes in treating injuries of the type sustained by Susan. Rebecca drove Susan from Champaign, Illinois, to Denver, a total of 1,100 miles, in Susan's specially equipped van. They left Champaign on Tuesday morning and arrived in Denver on Thursday afternoon. Rebecca incurred expenses for gasoline, highway tolls, meals, and lodging while traveling to Denver. Rebecca stayed in a motel near the clinic for eight days while Susan was hospitalized. Identify the relevant tax issues based on this information and prepare a list of questions that you would need to ask Rebecca and Susan in order to advise them as to the resolution of any issues you have identified.

30. **LO.2** During 2011, Felicia, who is self-employed, paid $500 per month for an HSA plan that provides medical insurance coverage with a $2,900 deductible. The plan covers Felicia, her husband, and three children. Of the $500 monthly payment, $200 was for the high-deductible policy and $300 was deposited into an HSA. How much of the amount paid for the high-deductible policy can Felicia deduct as a deduction *for* AGI?

COMMUNICATIONS

31. **LO.3** In 2004, Angela purchased a personal residence from Victor. She paid $300,000 for the residence. Victor paid real estate taxes of $9,125 for the real estate property tax year, of which $5,500 was allocable to the portion of the year that Angela owned the residence. Angela sold the residence to Earl for $350,000 on December 8, 2011. Earl paid real estate taxes of $10,220 for the real estate property tax year, of which $9,576 was allocable to the portion of the year that Angela owned the residence. Angela has provided you with the above information and asked that you determine her basis in the residence at the date of sale, the amount realized for the residence, her realized gain on the sale, and her property tax deduction for 2011. Write a letter to Angela Henson, who lives at 17250 Calistoga Drive, El Dorado, KS 67042, to communicate your answers.

32. **LO.4** Dylan is a self-employed, calendar year taxpayer. He reports on the cash basis. Dylan made the following estimated state income tax payments:

Date	Amount
January 18, 2011	$1,800 (4th payment for 2010)
April 15, 2011	2,250 (1st payment for 2011)
June 15, 2011	2,250 (2nd payment for 2011)
September 15, 2011	2,250 (3rd payment for 2011)
January 17, 2012	2,250 (4th payment for 2011)

    Dylan had a tax overpayment of $1,200 on his 2010 state income tax return and, rather than requesting a refund, had the overpayment applied to his 2011 state income taxes. What is the amount of Dylan's state income tax itemized deduction for his 2011 Federal income tax return?

33. **LO.5** In 2002, Roland, who is single, purchased a personal residence for $340,000 and took out a mortgage of $200,000 on the property. In May of the current year, when the residence had a fair market value of $440,000 and Roland owed $140,000 on the mortgage, he took out a home equity loan for $220,000. He used the funds to purchase a recreational vehicle, which he uses 100% for personal use. What is the maximum amount on which Roland can deduct home equity interest?

34. **LO.5** Ron and Tom are equal owners in Robin Corporation. On July 1, 2011, each lends the corporation $30,000 at an annual interest rate of 10%. Ron and Tom are brothers. Both shareholders are on the cash method of accounting, and Robin Corporation is on the accrual method. All parties use the calendar year for tax purposes. On June 30, 2012, Robin repays the loans of $60,000 together with the specified interest of $6,000.

a. How much of the interest can Robin Corporation deduct in 2011? In 2012?
b. When is the interest included in Ron and Tom's gross income?

35. **LO.6** Nadia donates $4,000 to Eastern University's athletic department. The payment guarantees that Nadia will have preferred seating near the 50-yard line.
    a. Assume Nadia subsequently buys four $100 game tickets. How much can she deduct as a charitable contribution to the university's athletic department?
    b. Assume that Nadia's $4,000 donation includes four $100 tickets. How much can she deduct as a charitable contribution to the university's athletic department?

36. **LO.6** Rachel had AGI of $100,000 in 2011. She donated Bronze Corporation stock with a basis of $9,000 to a qualified charitable organization on July 5, 2011.
    a. What is the amount of Rachel's deduction, assuming that she purchased the stock on December 3, 2010, and the stock had a fair market value of $16,000 when she made the donation?
    b. Assume the same facts as in (a), except that Rachel purchased the stock on July 1, 2008.
    c. Assume the same facts as in (a), except that the stock had a fair market value of $5,000 (rather than $16,000) when Rachel donated it to the charity.

37. **LO.6, 8** Pedro contributes a painting to an art museum in October of this year. He has owned the painting for 12 years, and it is worth $130,000 at the time of the donation. Pedro's adjusted basis for the painting is $90,000, and his AGI for the year is $250,000. Pedro has asked you whether he should make the reduced deduction election for this contribution. Write a letter to Pedro Valdez at 1289 Greenway Avenue, Foster City, CA 94404 and advise him on this matter.

DECISION MAKING

COMMUNICATIONS

38. **LO.6** During the year, Ricardo made the following contributions to a qualified public charity:

Cash	$220,000
Stock in Seagull, Inc. (a publicly traded corporation)	280,000

Ricardo acquired the stock in Seagull, Inc., as an investment five years ago at a cost of $120,000. Ricardo's AGI is $840,000.
    a. What is Ricardo's charitable contribution deduction?
    b. How are excess amounts, if any, treated?

39. **LO.8** Ramon had AGI of $180,000 in 2011. He contributed stock in Charlton, Inc. (a publicly traded corporation), to the American Heart Association, a qualified charitable organization. The stock was worth $105,000 on the date it was contributed. Ramon had acquired it as an investment two years ago at a cost of $84,000.
    a. Assuming that Ramon carries over any disallowed contribution from 2011 to future years, what is the total amount that he can deduct as a charitable contribution?
    b. What is the maximum amount that Ramon can deduct as a charitable contribution in 2011?
    c. What factors should Ramon consider in deciding how to treat the contribution for Federal income tax purposes?
    d. Assume Ramon dies in December 2011. What advice would you give the executor of his estate with regard to possible elections that can be made relative to the contribution?

DECISION MAKING

40. **LO.6** On December 30, 2011, Roberta purchased four tickets to a charity ball sponsored by the city of San Diego for the benefit of underprivileged children. Each ticket cost $200 and had a fair market value of $35. On the same day as the purchase, Roberta gave the tickets to the minister of her church for personal use by his family. At the time of the gift of the tickets, Roberta pledged $4,000 to the building fund of her church. The pledge was satisfied by a check dated December 31, 2011, but not mailed until January 3, 2012.
    a. Presuming Roberta is a cash basis and calendar year taxpayer, how much can she deduct as a charitable contribution for 2011?
    b. Would the amount of the deduction be any different if Roberta is an accrual basis taxpayer? Explain.

41. **LO.6, 8** In December each year, Eleanor Young contributes 10% of her gross income to the United Way (a 50% organization). Eleanor, who is in the 28% marginal tax bracket, is considering the following alternatives for satisfying the contribution.

DECISION MAKING

COMMUNICATIONS

	Fair Market Value
(1) Cash donation	$23,000
(2) Unimproved land held for six years ($3,000 basis)	23,000
(3) Blue Corporation stock held for eight months ($3,000 basis)	23,000
(4) Gold Corporation stock held for two years ($28,000 basis)	23,000

Eleanor has asked you to help her decide which of the potential contributions listed above will be most advantageous taxwise. Evaluate the four alternatives and write a letter to Eleanor to communicate your advice to her. Her address is 2622 Bayshore Drive, Berkeley, CA 94709.

DECISION MAKING

COMMUNICATIONS

42. **LO.2, 3, 4, 5, 7, 8** Manuel and Rosa Garcia, both age 47, are married and have no dependents. They have asked you to advise them whether they should file jointly or separately in 2011. They present you with the following information:

	Manuel	Rosa	Joint
Salary	$40,000		
Business net income		$100,000	
Interest income	1,500	2,300	$2,200
Deductions *for* AGI	3,000	14,000	
Medical expenses	10,000	600	
State income tax	800	2,000	
Real estate tax			3,400
Mortgage interest			5,200
Unreimbursed employee expenses	1,100		

If they file separately, Manuel and Rosa will split the real estate tax and mortgage interest deductions equally. Write Manuel and Rosa a letter in which you make and explain a recommendation on filing status for 2011. Manuel and Rosa reside at 2003 Highland Drive, Durham, NC 27707.

43. **LO.2, 3, 4, 5, 6, 7** Kelsey, who is a head of household with one dependent, had AGI of $315,000 for 2011. She incurred the following expenses and losses during the year:

Medical expenses before the 7.5%-of-AGI limitation	$25,000
State and local income taxes	4,300
State sales tax	1,205
Real estate taxes	3,705
Home mortgage interest	4,400
Credit card interest	820
Charitable contribution	3,800
Casualty loss before 10% limitation (after $100 floor)	38,000
Unreimbursed employee expenses subject to the 2%-of-AGI limitation	7,100

Calculate Kelsey's allowable itemized deductions for the year.

44. **LO.2, 3, 4, 5, 6, 7** For calendar year 2011, Stuart and Pamela Gibson file a joint return reflecting AGI of $264,000. Their itemized deductions are as follows:

Medical expenses	$25,300
Casualty loss after $100 floor (not covered by insurance)	28,600
Home mortgage interest	11,000
Credit card interest	800
Property taxes on home	14,300
Charitable contributions	18,700
State income tax	16,500
Tax return preparation fees	1,200

Calculate the amount of itemized deductions the Gibsons may claim for the year.

CUMULATIVE PROBLEMS

TAX RETURN PROBLEM

DECISION MAKING

H&R BLOCK At Home

45. Alice J. and Bruce M. Byrd are married taxpayers who file a joint return. Their Social Security numbers are 123–45–6789 and 111–11–1111, respectively. Alice's birthday is September 21, 1963, and Bruce's is June 27, 1962. They live at 473 Revere Avenue, Ames, MA 01850. Alice is the office manager for Ames Dental Clinic, 433 Broad Street, Ames, MA 01850 (employer identification number 98–7654321). Bruce is the manager of a Super Burgers fast-food outlet owned and operated by Plymouth Corporation, 1247 Central Avenue, Hauppauge, NY 11788 (employer identification number 11–1111111).

The following information is shown on their Wage and Tax Statements (Form W–2) for 2010.

Line	Description	Alice	Bruce
1	Wages, tips, other compensation	$52,600	$61,500
2	Federal income tax withheld	4,180	5,990
3	Social Security wages	52,600	61,500
4	Social Security tax withheld	3,261	3,813
5	Medicare wages and tips	52,600	61,500
6	Medicare tax withheld	763	892
15	State	Massachusetts	Massachusetts
16	State wages, tips, etc.	52,600	61,500
17	State income tax withheld	2,280	2,290

The Byrds provide over half of the support of their two children, Cynthia (born January 25, 1986, Social Security number 123–45–6788) and John (born February 7, 1990, Social Security number 123–45–6786). Both children are full-time students and live with the Byrds except when they are away at college. Cynthia earned $3,700 from a summer internship in 2010, and John earned $3,400 from a part-time job.

During 2010, the Byrds furnished 60% of the total support of Bruce's widower father, Sam Byrd (born March 6, 1934, Social Security number 123–45–6787). Sam lived alone and covered the rest of his support with his Social Security benefits. Sam died in November, and Bruce, the beneficiary of a policy on Sam's life, received life insurance proceeds of $600,000 on December 28.

The Byrds had the following expenses relating to their personal residence during 2010:

Property taxes	$4,720
Qualified interest on home mortgage	9,130
Repairs to roof	4,780
Utilities	3,810
Fire and theft insurance	2,290

The following facts relate to medical expenses for 2010:

Medical insurance premiums	$4,380
Doctor bill for Sam incurred in 2009 and not paid until 2010	7,760
Operation for Sam	7,310
Prescription medicines for Sam	860
Hospital expenses for Sam	2,850
Reimbursement from insurance company, received in 2010	3,000

The medical expenses for Sam represent most of the 60% Bruce contributed toward his father's support.

Other relevant information follows:

- When they filed their 2009 state return in 2010, the Byrds paid additional state income tax of $950.

- During 2010, Alice and Bruce attended a dinner dance sponsored by the Ames Police Disability Association (a qualified charitable organization). The Byrds paid $400 for the tickets. The cost of comparable entertainment would normally be $160.
- The Byrds contributed $4,800 to Ames Presbyterian Church and gave used clothing (cost of $1,100 and fair market value of $450) to the Salvation Army. All donations are supported by receipts and are in very good condition.
- In 2010, the Byrds received interest income of $2,695, which was reported on a Form 1099–INT from Second National Bank.
- Alice's employer requires that all employees wear uniforms to work. During 2010, Alice spent $482 on new uniforms and $211 on laundry charges.
- Bruce paid $320 for an annual subscription to the *Journal of Franchise Management.*
- Neither Alice's nor Bruce's employer reimburses for employee expenses.
- The Byrds do not keep the receipts for the sales taxes they paid and had no major purchases subject to sales tax.
- Alice and Bruce paid no estimated Federal income tax. Neither Alice nor Bruce wishes to designate $3 to the Presidential Election Campaign Fund.

Part 1—Tax Computation

Compute net tax payable or refund due for Alice and Bruce Byrd for 2010. If they have overpaid, they want the amount to be refunded to them. If you use tax forms for your computations, you will need Forms 1040 and 2106 and Schedules A, B, and M. Suggested software: H&R BLOCK At Home.

Part 2—Tax Planning

Alice and Bruce are planning some significant changes for 2011. They have provided you with the following information and asked you to project their taxable income and tax liability for 2011.

The Byrds will invest the $600,000 of life insurance proceeds in short-term certificates of deposit (CDs) and use the interest for living expenses during 2011. They expect to earn total interest of $21,000 on the CDs.

Bruce has been promoted to regional manager, and his salary for 2011 will be $85,000. He estimates that state income tax withheld will increase by $4,000 and the Social Security tax withheld will be $3,570.

Alice, who has been diagnosed with a serious illness, will take a leave of absence from work during 2011. The estimated cost for her medical treatment is $14,500, of which $5,500 will be reimbursed by their insurance company in 2011.

John will graduate from college in December 2010 and will take a job in New York City in January 2011. His starting salary will be $37,500.

Assume all the information reported in 2010 will be the same in 2011 unless other information has been presented above.

TAX COMPUTATION PROBLEM

46. Paul and Donna Decker are married taxpayers, ages 44 and 42, who file a joint return for 2011. The Deckers live at 1121 College Avenue, Carmel, IN 46032. Paul is an assistant manager at Carmel Motor Inn, and Donna is a teacher at Carmel Elementary School. They present you with W–2 forms that reflect the following information:

	Paul	Donna
Salary	$60,000	$61,000
Federal tax withheld	7,000	7,200
State income tax withheld	950	1,000
FICA (Social Security and Medicare) withheld	3,390	3,447
Social Security numbers	111–11–1111	123–45–6789

Donna is the custodial parent of two children from a previous marriage who reside with the Deckers through the school year. The children, Larry and Jane Parker, reside with their father, Bob, during the summer. Relevant information for the children follows:

	Larry	Jane
Age	17	18
Social Security numbers	123–45–6788	123–45–6787
Months spent with Deckers	9	9

Under the divorce decree, Bob pays child support of $200 per month per child during the nine months the children live with the Deckers. Bob says he spends $225 per month per child during the three summer months they reside with him. Donna and Paul can document that they provide $3,000 support per child per year. The divorce decree is silent as to which parent can claim the exemptions for the children.

In August, Paul and Donna added a suite to their home to provide more comfortable accommodations for Hannah Snyder (123–45–6786), Donna's mother, who had moved in with them in February 2010 after the death of Donna's father. Not wanting to borrow money for this addition, Paul sold 300 shares of Acme Corporation stock for $50 per share on May 3, 2011, and used the proceeds of $15,000 to cover construction costs. The Deckers had purchased the stock on April 29, 2006, for $30 per share. They received dividends of $800 on the jointly owned stock a month before the sale.

Hannah, who is 66 years old, received $7,500 in Social Security benefits during the year, of which she gave the Deckers $2,500 to use toward household expenses and deposited the remainder in her personal savings account. The Deckers determine that they have spent $3,000 of their own money for food, clothing, medical expenses, and other items for Hannah. They do not know what the rental value of Hannah's suite would be, but they estimate it would be at least $300 per month.

Interest paid during the year included the following:

Home mortgage interest (paid to Carmel Federal Savings & Loan)	$8,000
Interest on an automobile loan (paid to Carmel National Bank)	1,490
Interest on Citibank Visa card	870

In July, Paul hit a submerged rock while boating. Fortunately, he was thrown from the boat, landed in deep water, and was uninjured. However, the boat, which was uninsured, was destroyed. Paul had paid $25,000 for the boat in June 2010, and its value was appraised at $18,000 on the date of the accident.

The Deckers paid doctor and hospital bills of $9,000 and were reimbursed $2,100 by their insurance company. They spent $700 for prescription drugs and medicines and $2,810 for premiums on their health insurance policy. They have filed additional claims of $1,200 with their insurance company and have been told they will receive payment for that amount in January 2012. Included in the amounts paid for doctor and hospital bills were payments of $380 for Hannah and $850 for the children.

Additional information of potential tax consequence follows:

Real estate taxes paid	$3,700
Sales taxes paid (per table)	1,379
Contributions to church	4,500
Appraised value of books donated to public library	750
Paul's unreimbursed employee expenses to attend hotel management convention:	
Airfare	840
Hotel	270
Meals	125
Registration fee	340
Refund of state income tax for 2010 (the Deckers itemized on their 2010 Federal tax return)	1,600

Compute net tax payable or refund due for the Deckers for 2011. Ignore the child tax credit in your computations. If they have overpaid, the amount is to be credited toward their taxes for 2012.

RESEARCH PROBLEMS

THOMSON REUTERS
Checkpoint® Student Edition

Note: Solutions to Research Problems can be prepared by using the **Checkpoint® Student Edition** online research product, which is available to accompany this text. It is also possible to prepare solutions to the Research Problems by using tax research materials found in a standard tax library.

COMMUNICATIONS

Research Problem 1. After several years of a difficult marriage, Donald and Marla agreed to a divorce. As part of the property settlement, Marla transferred to Donald corporate stock, a commercial building, and a personal residence. Donald transferred other property to Marla, but the fair market value of the property was $600,000 less than the fair market value of the property Marla had transferred to him. To make the settlement equal, Donald agreed to pay Marla $600,000, payable over 10 years at 8% interest. For several years, Donald deducted the interest on his Federal income tax return as investment interest. Upon audit, the IRS disallowed the interest deduction, classifying it as nondeductible personal interest. Donald believes the interest is deductible and has asked you to find support for the deduction. Write a letter indicating your findings to Donald Jansen, 104 South Fourth Street, Dalton, GA 30720.

Partial list of research aids:
U.S. v. Gilmore, 63–1 USTC ¶9285, 11 AFTR 2d 758, 83 S.Ct. 623 (USSC, 1963).
John L. Seymour, 109 T.C. 279 (1997).

Research Problem 2. Tom and Mary Smith, whose son was found murdered in a parking garage, offered a $100,000 reward for the city police to use to obtain information leading to the arrest and conviction of the murderer. As a result of the reward, a person who had overheard the murderer telling a friend about the crime reported the conversation to the police. The murderer was arrested and convicted, and the Smiths contributed the money to the police department, which gave the reward to the informant. Can the Smiths treat the payment as an itemized deduction?

INTERNET *activity*

Use the tax resources of the Internet to address the following question. Do not restrict your search to the Web, but include a review of newsgroups and general reference materials, practitioner sites and resources, primary sources of the tax law, chat rooms and discussion groups, and other opportunities.

Research Problem 3. Search the Internet for stories about major charitable contributions by individuals, including Bill Gates, Warren Buffett, Steve Jobs, and at least one other individual. Briefly discuss any tax issues that are related to the contributions.

CHAPTER 11

Investor Losses

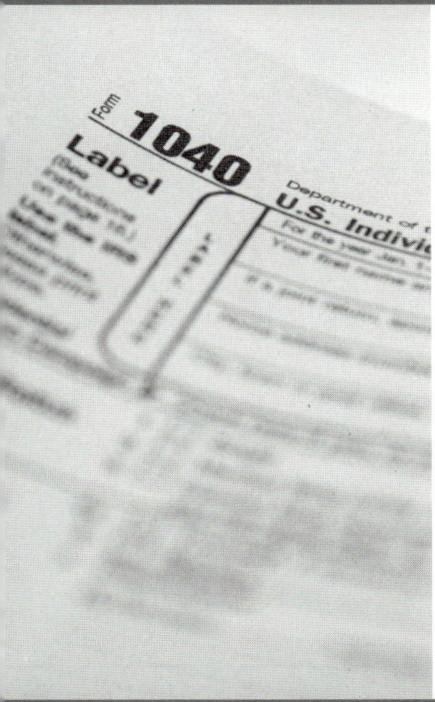

LEARNING OBJECTIVES

After completing Chapter 11, you should be able to:

LO.1

Discuss tax shelters and the reasons for at-risk and passive loss limitations.

LO.2

Explain the at-risk limitation.

LO.3

Describe how the passive loss rules limit deductions for losses, and identify the taxpayers subject to these restrictions.

LO.4

Discuss the definition of passive activities and the rules for identifying an activity.

LO.5

Analyze and apply the tests for material participation.

LO.6

Understand the nature of rental activities under the passive loss rules.

LO.7

Recognize the relationship between the at-risk and passive activity limitations.

LO.8

Discuss the special treatment available to real estate activities.

LO.9

Determine the proper tax treatment upon the disposition of a passive activity.

LO.10

Identify restrictions placed on the deductibility of other investor losses and deductions, including those that apply to investment interest.

LO.11

Suggest tax planning strategies to minimize the effect of the passive loss limitations.

OUTLINE

For the latest in changes to tax legislation, visit **www.cengage.com/taxation/swft.**

FRAMEWORK 1040: Tax Formula for Individuals

This chapter covers the boldfaced portions of the Tax "#Formula for Individuals that was introduced in Figure 3.1 on p. 3-3. Below those portions are the sections of Form 1040 where the results are reported.

Income (broadly conceived)	$xx,xxx
Less: Exclusions	(x,xxx)
Gross income	$xx,xxx
Less: Deductions for adjusted gross income	**(x,xxx)**

FORM 1040 (p. 1)

12	Business income or (loss). Attach Schedule C or C-EZ
13	Capital gain or (loss). Attach Schedule D if required. If not required, check here ▶ ☐
14	Other gains or (losses). Attach Form 4797
17	Rental real estate, royalties, partnerships, S corporations, trusts, etc. Attach Schedule E

Adjusted gross income	$xx,xxx
Less: The greater of total **itemized deductions** *or* the standard deduction	**(x,xxx)**

FORM 1040 (p. 2)

40	**Itemized deductions** (from Schedule A) **or** your **standard deduction** (see instructions)

Personal and dependency exemptions	(x,xxx)
Taxable income	$xx,xxx
Tax on taxable income (see Tax Tables or Tax Rate Schedules)	$ x,xxx
Less: Tax credits (including income taxes withheld and prepaid)	(xxx)
Tax due (or refund)	$ xxx

THE BIG PICTURE — Tax Solutions for the Real World

INVESTOR LOSS LIMITATIONS AFFECT THE VIABILITY OF CERTAIN INVESTMENT OPPORTUNITIES

Trudy and Jim Reswick are considering ways to enhance their financial security. In fact, they are willing to borrow a substantial sum so that they can make an appropriate investment.

Currently, Trudy and Jim's sole source of income is their salaries from full-time jobs, totaling $100,000. Their most significant asset is their personal residence (fair market value of $500,000 with a mortgage of $350,000). Their broker suggests that the Reswicks borrow $100,000 at 8 percent and use the proceeds to make *one* of the following investments:

- A high-growth, low-yield portfolio of marketable securities. The portfolio's value is expected to grow 10 percent each year.
- An interest in a limited partnership that owns and operates orange groves in Florida. The limited partnership interest is expected to generate tax losses of $25,000 in each of the next five years, after which profits are expected. The broker predicts that after taking into account the tax benefit from the losses, the Reswicks would average an annual 10 percent return over a 10-year period.
- An interest in a local limited partnership that owns and rents apartments to college students. This limited partnership interest also would generate losses of $25,000 per year for five years, after which profits would follow. These expected profits and losses would produce an average annual total return of 10 percent over a 10-year period.

Trudy and Jim want to choose the alternative that produces the best after-tax return over a 10-year planning horizon. They are aware, however, that tax restrictions may limit the advantages of some of these investment options. In this connection, evaluate each option. **Read the chapter and formulate your response.**

As discussed in Chapter 6, a tax deduction for an expense or a loss is not allowed unless specifically provided for by Congress. For example, losses can be recognized and deducted in the case of certain unprofitable investments only because the Code so provides. Such losses can arise from the operation of an activity or upon its ultimate disposition. For most individual taxpayers, deductible investor losses come within the scope of § 165(c)(2) relating to transactions entered into for profit.[1] In many situations, the tax law limits the *amount* or *timing* of a deduction or loss, or even changes its *nature* (i.e., ordinary rather than capital). Thus, for various reasons, Congress has imposed restrictions on the deductibility of investor losses. This, in turn, may affect the viability of the investment itself.

11.1 The Tax Shelter Problem

LO.1

Discuss tax shelters and the reasons for at-risk and passive loss limitations.

Before Congress enacted legislation to reduce their effectiveness, **tax shelters** provided a popular way to avoid or defer taxes, as they could generate deductions and other benefits to offset income from other sources. Because of the tax avoidance potential of many tax shelters, they were attractive to wealthy taxpayers in high income tax brackets. Many tax shelters merely provided an opportunity for "investors" to buy deductions and credits in ventures that were not expected to generate a profit, even in the long run.

Although it may seem odd that a taxpayer would intentionally invest in an activity that was designed to produce losses, there is a logical explanation. The typical tax shelter operated as a partnership and relied heavily on nonrecourse financing.[2] Accelerated depreciation and interest expense deductions generated large losses in the early years of the activity. At the very least, the tax shelter deductions deferred the recognition of any net income from the venture until the activity was sold. In the best of situations, the investor could realize additional tax savings by offsetting other income (e.g., salary, interest, and dividends) with deductions flowing from the tax shelter. Ultimately, the sale of the investment would result in capital gain. The following examples illustrate what was possible *before* Congress enacted legislation to curb tax shelter abuses.

EXAMPLE 1

Bob, who earned a salary of $400,000 as a business executive and dividend income of $15,000, invested $20,000 for a 10% interest in a cattle-breeding tax shelter. Through the use of $800,000 of nonrecourse financing and available cash of $200,000, the partnership acquired a herd of an exotic breed of cattle costing $1 million. Depreciation, interest, and other deductions related to the activity resulted in a loss of $400,000, of which Bob's share was $40,000. Bob was allowed to deduct the $40,000 loss, even though he had invested and stood to lose only $20,000 if the investment became worthless. The net effect of the $40,000 deduction from the partnership was that a portion of Bob's salary and dividend income was "sheltered," and as a result, he was required to calculate his tax liability on only $375,000 of income [$415,000 (salary and dividends) − $40,000 (deduction)] rather than $415,000. If this deduction were available under current law and if Bob was in a combined Federal and state income tax bracket of 40%, this deduction would generate a tax savings of $16,000 ($40,000 × 40%) in the first year alone! ■

A review of Example 1 shows that the taxpayer took a *two-for-one* write-off ($40,000 deduction, $20,000 investment). In the heyday of these types of tax shelters, promoters often promised *multiple* write-offs for the investor.

[1] If the losses are incurred in connection with a trade or business, § 165(c)(1) applies.

[2] Nonrecourse debt is an obligation for which the borrower is not personally liable. An example of nonrecourse debt is a liability on real estate acquired by a partnership without the partnership or any of the partners assuming any liability for the mortgage. The acquired property generally is pledged as collateral for the loan.

The first major provision aimed at tax shelters was the **at-risk limitation**. Its objective is to limit a taxpayer's deductions to the amount "at risk," which is the amount the taxpayer stands to lose if the investment becomes worthless.

EXAMPLE 2

Returning to the facts of Example 1, under the current at-risk rules Bob would be allowed to deduct $20,000 (i.e., the amount that he could lose if the business failed). This deduction would reduce his other income, and as a result, Bob would have to report only $395,000 of income ($415,000 – $20,000). The remaining nondeductible $20,000 loss and any future losses flowing from the partnership would be suspended under the at-risk rules and would be deductible in the future only as his at-risk amount increased. ■

The second major attack on tax shelters came with the passage of the passive activity loss rules. These rules are intended to halt an investor's ability to benefit from the mismatching of an entity's expenses and income that often occurs in the early years of the business. Congress observed that despite the at-risk limitations, investors could still deduct losses flowing from an entity and thereby defer their tax liability on other income. In effect, the passive activity rules have, to a great degree, limited the tax benefits arising from such investments. Now, ventures where investors are not involved in the day-to-day operations of the business are generally referred to as passive investments, or *passive activities*, rather than tax shelters.

The **passive loss** rules require the taxpayer to segregate all income and losses into three categories: active, passive, and portfolio. In general, the passive loss limits disallow the deduction of passive losses against active or portfolio income, even when the taxpayer is at risk to the extent of the loss. In general, passive losses can only offset passive income.

EXAMPLE 3

Returning to the facts of Example 1, the passive activity loss rules further restrict Bob's ability to claim the $20,000 tax deduction shown in Example 2. Because Bob is a passive investor and does not materially participate in any meaningful way in the activities of the cattle-breeding operation, the $20,000 loss allowed under the at-risk rules is disallowed under the passive loss rules. The passive loss is disallowed because Bob does not generate any passive income that could absorb his passive loss. Further, his salary (active income) and dividends (portfolio income) cannot be used to absorb any of the passive loss. Consequently, Bob's current-year taxable income must reflect his nonpassive income of $415,000, and he receives no current benefit from his share of the partnership loss. However, all is not lost because Bob's share of the entity's loss is *suspended*; it is carried forward and can be deducted in the future when he has passive income or sells his interest in the activity. ■

The nature of the at-risk limits and the passive activity loss rules and their impact on investors are discussed in the pages that follow. An interesting consequence of these rules is that now investors evaluating potential investments must consider mainly the economics of the venture instead of the tax benefits or tax avoidance possibilities that an investment may generate.

11.2 At-Risk Limits

LO.2

Explain the at-risk limitation.

The at-risk provisions limit the deductibility of losses from business and income-producing activities. These provisions, which apply to individuals and closely held corporations, are designed to prevent taxpayers from deducting losses in excess of their actual economic investment in an activity. In the case of an S corporation or a partnership, the at-risk limits apply at the owner level. Under the at-risk rules, a taxpayer's deductible loss from an activity for any taxable year is limited to the amount the taxpayer has at risk at the end of the taxable year (the amount the taxpayer could actually lose in the activity).

While the amount at risk generally vacillates over time, the initial amount considered at risk consists of the following:[3]

- The amount of cash and the adjusted basis of property contributed to the activity by the taxpayer.
- Amounts borrowed for use in the activity for which the taxpayer is personally liable or has pledged as security property not used in the activity.

This amount generally is increased each year by the taxpayer's share of income and is decreased by the taxpayer's share of losses and withdrawals from the activity. In addition, because general partners are jointly and severally liable for recourse debts of the partnership, their at-risk amounts are increased when the partnership increases its debt and are decreased when the partnership reduces its debt. However, a taxpayer generally is not considered at risk with respect to borrowed amounts if either of the following is true:

- The taxpayer is not personally liable for repayment of the debt (e.g., nonrecourse debt).
- The lender has an interest (other than as a creditor) in the activity.

An important exception provides that in the case of an activity involving the holding of real property, a taxpayer is considered at risk for his or her share of any *qualified nonrecourse financing* that is secured by real property used in the activity.[4]

Subject to the passive activity rules discussed later in the chapter, a taxpayer may deduct a loss as long as the at-risk amount is positive. However, once the at-risk amount is exhausted, any remaining loss cannot be deducted until a later year. Any losses disallowed for any given taxable year by the at-risk rules may be deducted in the first succeeding year in which the rules do not prevent the deduction—that is, when there is, and to the extent of, a positive at-risk amount.

EXAMPLE 4

In 2011, Sue invests $40,000 in an oil partnership that, by the use of nonrecourse loans, spends $60,000 on deductible intangible drilling costs applicable to her interest. Assume Sue's interest in the partnership is subject to the at-risk limits but is not subject to the passive loss limits. Since Sue has only $40,000 of capital at risk, she cannot deduct more than $40,000 against her other income and must reduce her at-risk amount to zero ($40,000 at-risk amount − $40,000 loss deducted). The nondeductible loss of $20,000 ($60,000 loss generated − $40,000 loss allowed) can be carried over to 2012. ■

EXAMPLE 5

In 2012, Sue has taxable income of $15,000 from the oil partnership and invests an additional $10,000 in the venture. Her at-risk amount is now $25,000 ($0 beginning balance + $15,000 taxable income + $10,000 additional investment). This enables Sue to deduct the carryover loss and requires her to reduce her at-risk amount to $5,000 ($25,000 at-risk amount − $20,000 carryover loss allowed). ■

An additional complicating factor is that previously allowed losses must be recaptured to the extent the at-risk amount is reduced below zero.[5] That is, previous losses that were allowed must be offset by the recognition of enough income to bring the at-risk amount up to zero. This rule applies in such situations as when the amount at risk is reduced below zero by distributions to the taxpayer or when the status of indebtedness changes from recourse to nonrecourse.

[3]§ 465(b)(1).

[4]Section 465(b)(6) defines qualified nonrecourse financing.

[5]§ 465(e).

CONCEPT SUMMARY 11.1

Calculation of At-Risk Amount

Increases to a taxpayer's at-risk amount:

- Cash and the adjusted basis of property contributed to the activity.
- Amounts borrowed for use in the activity for which the taxpayer is personally liable or has pledged as security property not used in the activity.
- Taxpayer's share of amounts borrowed for use in the activity that are qualified nonrecourse financing.
- Taxpayer's share of the activity's income.

Decreases to a taxpayer's at-risk amount:

- Withdrawals from the activity.
- Taxpayer's share of the activity's deductible loss.
- Taxpayer's share of any reductions of debt for which recourse against the taxpayer exists or reductions of qualified nonrecourse debt.

11.3 Passive Loss Limits

LO.3

Describe how the passive loss rules limit deductions for losses, and identify the taxpayers subject to these restrictions.

CLASSIFICATION AND IMPACT OF PASSIVE INCOME AND LOSSES

The passive loss rules operate by requiring taxpayers to classify their income and losses into various categories. Then the rules limit the extent to which losses in the passive category can be used to offset income in the other categories.

Classification

The passive loss rules require income and losses to be classified into one of three categories: active, passive, or portfolio. **Active income** includes the following:

- Wages, salary, commissions, bonuses, and other payments for services rendered by the taxpayer.
- Profit from a trade or business in which the taxpayer is a material participant.
- Gain on the sale or other disposition of assets used in an active trade or business.
- Income from intangible property if the taxpayer's personal efforts significantly contributed to the creation of the property.

Portfolio income includes the following:

- Interest, dividends, annuities, and royalties not derived in the ordinary course of a trade or business.
- Gain or loss from the disposition of property that produces portfolio income or is held for investment purposes.

Section 469 provides that income or loss from the following activities is treated as *passive*:

- Any trade or business or income-producing activity in which the taxpayer does not materially participate.
- Subject to certain exceptions, all rental activities, whether the taxpayer materially participates or not.

Although the Code defines rental activities as passive activities, several exceptions allow losses from certain real estate rental activities to offset nonpassive (active or portfolio) income. These exceptions are discussed under Special Passive Activity Rules for Real Estate Activities later in the chapter.

General Impact

Losses or expenses generated by passive activities can be deducted only to the extent of income from all of the taxpayer's passive activities. Any excess may not be used to offset income from active sources or portfolio income. Instead, any unused passive losses are suspended and carried forward to future years to offset passive income generated in those years. Otherwise, suspended losses may be used only when a taxpayer disposes of his or her entire interest in an activity. In that event, all current and suspended losses related to the activity may offset active and portfolio income.

EXAMPLE 6

Kim, a physician, earns $150,000 from her full-time practice. She also receives $10,000 in dividends and interest from various portfolio investments, and her share of loss from a passive investment not limited by the at-risk rules is $60,000. Because the loss is a passive loss, it is not deductible against her other income. The loss is suspended and is carried over to the future. If Kim has passive income from this investment or from other passive investments in the future, she can offset the suspended loss against that passive income. If she does not have passive income to offset this suspended loss in the future, she will be allowed to offset the loss against other types of income when she eventually disposes of the passive activity. ■

Impact of Suspended Losses

When a taxpayer disposes of his or her entire interest in a passive activity, the actual economic gain or loss from the investment, including any suspended losses, can finally be determined. As a result, under the passive loss rules, upon a fully taxable disposition, any overall loss realized from the activity by the taxpayer is recognized and can be offset against any income.

A fully taxable disposition generally involves a sale of the property to a third party at arm's length and thus, presumably, for a price equal to the property's fair market value. Gain recognized upon a transfer of an interest in a passive activity generally is treated as passive and is first offset by the suspended losses from that activity.

EXAMPLE 7

Rex sells an apartment building, a passive activity, with an adjusted basis of $100,000 for $180,000. In addition, he has suspended losses of $60,000 associated with the building. His total gain, $80,000, and his taxable gain, $20,000, are calculated as follows:

Net sales price	$ 180,000
Less: Adjusted basis	(100,000)
Total gain	$ 80,000
Less: Suspended losses	(60,000)
Taxable gain (passive)	$ 20,000

■

If current and suspended losses of the passive activity exceed the gain realized or if the sale results in a realized loss, the amount of

- any loss from the activity for the tax year (including losses suspended in the activity disposed of)

in excess of

- net income or gain for the tax year from all passive activities (without regard to the activity disposed of)

is treated as a loss that is not from a passive activity. In computing the loss from the activity for the year of disposition, any gain or loss recognized is included.

EXAMPLE 8

Dean sells an apartment building, a passive activity, with an adjusted basis of $100,000 for $150,000. In addition, he has current and suspended losses of $60,000 associated with the building and has no other passive activities. His total gain of $50,000 and his deductible loss of $10,000 are calculated as follows:

Net sales price	$ 150,000
Less: Adjusted basis	(100,000)
Total gain	$ 50,000
Less: Suspended losses	(60,000)
Deductible loss (not passive)	($ 10,000)

The $10,000 deductible loss is offset against Dean's active and portfolio income. ■

Carryovers of Suspended Losses

In the above examples, it was assumed that the taxpayer had an interest in only one passive activity, and as a result, the suspended loss was related exclusively to the activity that was disposed of. Taxpayers often own interests in more than one activity, however, and in that case, any suspended losses must be allocated among the activities in which the taxpayer has an interest. The allocation to an activity is made by multiplying the disallowed passive activity loss from all activities by the following fraction:

$$\frac{\text{Loss from activity}}{\text{Sum of losses for taxable year from all activities having losses}}$$

EXAMPLE 9

Diego has investments in three passive activities with the following income and losses for 2010:

Activity A	($ 30,000)
Activity B	(20,000)
Activity C	25,000
Net passive loss	($ 25,000)
Net passive loss allocated to:	
Activity A ($25,000 × $30,000/$50,000)	($ 15,000)
Activity B ($25,000 × $20,000/$50,000)	(10,000)
Total suspended losses	($ 25,000)

■

Suspended losses are carried over indefinitely and are offset in the future against any passive income from the activities to which they relate.[6]

EXAMPLE 10

Assume the same facts as in Example 9 and that Activity A produces $10,000 of income in 2011. Of the suspended loss of $15,000 from 2010 for Activity A, $10,000 is offset against the income from this activity. If Diego sells Activity A in early 2012, then the remaining $5,000 suspended loss is used in determining his taxable gain or loss. ■

Passive Credits

Credits arising from passive activities are limited in much the same way as passive losses. Passive credits can be utilized only against regular tax attributable to passive income,[7] which is calculated by comparing the tax on all income (including passive income) with the tax on income excluding passive income.

EXAMPLE 11

Sam owes $50,000 of tax, disregarding net passive income, and $80,000 of tax, considering both net passive and other taxable income (disregarding the credits in both cases). The amount of tax attributable to the passive income is $30,000. ■

Sam in the preceding example can claim a maximum of $30,000 of passive activity credits; the excess credits are carried over. These passive activity credits (such as the low-income housing credit and rehabilitation credit—discussed in Chapter 12) can be used only against the *regular* tax attributable to passive income. If a taxpayer has a net loss from passive activities during a given year, no credits can be used.

[6]§ 469(b).

[7]§ 469(d)(2).

Carryovers of Passive Credits

Tax credits attributable to passive activities can be carried forward indefinitely much like suspended passive losses. Unlike passive losses, however, passive credits are lost forever when the activity is disposed of in a taxable transaction where loss is recognized. Credits are allowed on dispositions only when there is sufficient tax on passive income to absorb them.

EXAMPLE 12

Alicia sells a passive activity for a gain of $10,000. The activity had suspended losses of $40,000 and suspended credits of $15,000. The $10,000 gain is offset by $10,000 of the suspended losses, and the remaining $30,000 of suspended losses is deductible against Alicia's active and portfolio income. The suspended credits are lost forever because the sale of the activity did not generate any tax. ■

EXAMPLE 13

If Alicia in Example 12 had realized a $100,000 gain on the sale of the passive activity, the suspended credits could have been used to the extent of the regular tax attributable to the net passive income.

Gain on sale	$100,000
Less: Suspended losses	(40,000)
Taxable gain	$ 60,000

If the tax attributable to the taxable gain of $60,000 is $15,000 or more, the entire $15,000 of suspended credits can be used. If the tax attributable to the gain is less than $15,000, the excess of the suspended credits over the tax attributable to the gain is lost forever. ■

When a taxpayer has sufficient regular tax liability from passive activities to trigger the use of suspended credits, the credits lose their character as passive credits. They are reclassified as regular tax credits and made subject to the same limits as other business credits (discussed in Chapter 12).

Passive Activity Changes to Active

If a formerly passive activity becomes an active one, suspended losses are allowed to the extent of income from the now active business.[8] If any of the suspended loss remains, it continues to be treated as a loss from a passive activity. The excess suspended loss can be deducted from passive income or carried over to the next tax year and deducted to the extent of income from the now active business in the succeeding year(s). The activity must continue to be the same activity.

TAXPAYERS SUBJECT TO THE PASSIVE LOSS RULES

The passive loss rules apply to individuals, estates, trusts, personal service corporations, and closely held C corporations.[9] Passive income or loss from investments in partnerships or S corporations (see Chapters 21 and 22) flows through to the owners, and the passive loss rules are applied at the owner level.

Personal Service Corporations

Application of the passive loss limitations to personal service corporations is intended to prevent taxpayers from sheltering personal service income by creating personal service corporations and acquiring passive activities at the corporate level.

[8] § 469(f).

[9] § 469(a).

TAX *in* the NEWS — If You Can't Trust Your Tax Preparer, Who Can You Trust?

Many taxpayers choose to remain ignorant of the tax law because they assume that by paying a "professional" to complete their returns, they have shifted all responsibility to someone else. But they do so at their own risk. Failure to have at least a general understanding of the tax rules that apply to one's return can be a big mistake and can lead to various tax penalties.

One such taxpayer invested in several partnerships that engaged in horse activities in California. Being fully employed in New York, he did not participate in the partnerships' activities and had no knowledge of their business operations. When he received the tax information from the partnerships about his investments, he simply turned over the statements to his tax preparer who included the information on the return filed. Essentially, the tax return reflected the taxpayer's losses from the horse activities, even though they are disallowed under the passive loss rules.

When the IRS discovered the error, the taxpayer pleaded ignorance and blamed the tax preparer. He claimed that he had been "duped by a charlatan" and pleaded for mercy. The Tax Court showed no compassion and held that the taxpayer owed additional taxes, interest, and penalties (*Ralph P. Cunningham,* 98 TCM 143, T.C.Memo. 2009–194). Perhaps the result would have been different if the taxpayer had had a better understanding of the tax law in general and the passive activity rules in particular. Reliance on a tax preparer is not an excuse for blindly signing a tax return without understanding its content.

EXAMPLE 14

Two tax accountants, who earn an aggregate of $200,000 a year in their individual practices, agree to work together in a newly formed personal service corporation. Shortly after its formation, the corporation invests in a passive activity that produces a $200,000 loss during the year. Because the passive loss rules apply to personal service corporations, the corporation may not deduct the $200,000 loss against the $200,000 of active income. ■

Determination of whether a corporation is a **personal service corporation** is based on rather broad definitions. A personal service corporation is a regular (or C) corporation that meets *both* of the following conditions:

- The principal activity is the performance of personal services.
- Such services are substantially performed by employee-owners.

Generally, personal service corporations include those in the fields of health, law, engineering, architecture, accounting, actuarial science, performing arts, and consulting.[10] A corporation is treated as a personal service corporation if more than 10 percent of the stock (by value) is held by employee-owners.[11] An employee is treated as an employee-owner if he or she owns stock on *any day* during the taxable year.[12] For these purposes, shareholder status and employee status do not have to occur on the same day.

Closely Held C Corporations

Application of the passive loss rules to closely held (non-personal service) C corporations is also intended to prevent individuals from incorporating to avoid the passive loss limitations. A corporation is classified as a **closely held corporation** if at any time during the taxable year more than 50 percent of the value of its outstanding stock is owned, directly or indirectly, by or for five or fewer individuals. Closely held C corporations (other than personal service corporations) may use passive losses to offset *active* income, but not portfolio income.

[10] § 448(d)(2)(A).

[11] § 469(j)(2).

[12] § 269A(b)(2).

EXAMPLE 15

Silver Corporation, a closely held (non-personal service) C corporation, has $500,000 of passive losses from a rental activity, $400,000 of active income, and $100,000 of portfolio income. The corporation may offset $400,000 of the $500,000 passive loss against the $400,000 of active business income, but may not offset the remainder against the $100,000 of portfolio income. Thus, $100,000 of the passive loss is suspended ($500,000 passive loss – $400,000 offset against active income). ■

Application of the passive loss limitations to closely held C corporations prevents taxpayers from transferring their portfolio investments to such corporations in order to offset passive losses against portfolio income.

PASSIVE ACTIVITIES DEFINED

LO.4

Discuss the definition of passive activities and the rules for identifying an activity.

Section 469 specifies that the following types of activities are to be treated as passive:

- Any trade or business or income-producing activity in which the taxpayer does not materially participate.
- Subject to certain exceptions, all rental activities.

To understand the meaning of the term *passive activity* and the impact of the rules, one must address the following issues, each of which is the subject of statutory or administrative guidance:

- What constitutes an activity?
- What is meant by material participation?
- When is an activity a rental activity?

Even though guidance is available to help the taxpayer deal with these issues, their resolution is anything but simple.

Identification of an Activity

Identifying what constitutes an activity is a necessary first step in applying the passive loss limitations. Taxpayers who are involved in complex business operations need to determine whether a given segment of their overall business operations constitutes a separate activity or is to be treated as part of a single activity. Proper treatment is necessary in order to determine whether income or loss from an activity is active or passive.

EXAMPLE 16

Ben owns a business with two separate departments. Department A generates net income of $120,000, and Department B generates a net loss of $95,000. Ben participates for 700 hours in the operations of Department A and for 100 hours in Department B. If Ben is allowed to treat the departments as components of a single activity, he can offset the $95,000 loss from Department B against the $120,000 of income from Department A. ■

EXAMPLE 17

Assume the same facts as in the previous example. If Ben is required to treat each department as a separate activity, the tax result is not as favorable. Because he is a material participant in Department A (having devoted 700 hours to it), the $120,000 profit is active income. However, he is not considered a material participant in Department B (100 hours), and the $95,000 loss is a passive loss. Therefore, Ben cannot offset the $95,000 passive loss from Department B against the $120,000 of active income from Department A. (A complete discussion of the material participation rules follows.) ■

Recall that on the disposition of a passive activity, a taxpayer is allowed to offset suspended losses from the activity against other types of income. Therefore, identifying what constitutes an activity is of crucial importance for this purpose too.

EXAMPLE 18

Linda owns a business with two departments. Department A has a net loss of $125,000 in the current year, and Department B has a $70,000 net loss. She disposes of Department B at the end of the year. Assuming Linda is allowed to treat the two departments as separate passive activities, she can offset the passive loss from Department B against other types of income in the following order: gain from disposition of the passive activity, other passive income, and nonpassive income. This treatment leaves her with a suspended loss of $125,000 from Department A. If Departments A and B are treated as components of the same activity, however, on the disposal of Department B, its $70,000 net loss would be suspended along with the other $125,000 of suspended loss of the activity. ■

The rules used to delineate what constitutes an activity for purposes of the passive loss limitations are provided in the Regulations.[13] These guidelines state that, in general, a taxpayer can treat one or more trade or business activities or rental activities as a single activity if those activities form an *appropriate economic unit* for measuring gain or loss. To determine what ventures form an appropriate economic unit, all of the relevant facts and circumstances must be considered. Taxpayers may use any reasonable method in applying the facts and circumstances. The following example, adapted from the Regulations, illustrates the application of the general rules for grouping activities.[14]

EXAMPLE 19

George owns a men's clothing store and an Internet café in Chicago. He also owns a men's clothing store and an Internet café in Milwaukee. Reasonable methods of applying the facts and circumstances test may result in any of the following groupings:

- All four activities may be grouped into a single activity because of common ownership and control.
- The clothing stores may be grouped into an activity, and the Internet cafés may be grouped into a separate activity.
- The Chicago activities may be grouped into an activity, and the Milwaukee activities may be grouped into a separate activity.
- Each of the four activities may be treated as a separate activity. ■

Regrouping of Activities Taxpayers should carefully consider all tax factors in deciding how to group their activities. Once activities have been grouped, they cannot be regrouped unless the original grouping was clearly inappropriate or there has been a material change in the facts and circumstances. The Regulations also grant the IRS the right to regroup activities when both of the following conditions exist:[15]

- The taxpayer's grouping fails to reflect one or more appropriate economic units.
- One of the primary purposes of the taxpayer's grouping is to avoid the passive loss limitations.

Special Grouping Rules for Rental Activities Two rules deal specifically with the grouping of rental activities. These provisions are designed to prevent taxpayers from grouping rental activities, which are generally passive, with other businesses in a way that would result in a tax advantage.

First, a rental activity may be grouped with a trade or business activity only if one activity is insubstantial in relation to the other. That is, the rental activity must be insubstantial in relation to the trade or business activity, or the trade or business activity must be insubstantial in relation to the rental activity. The Regulations provide no clear guidelines as to the meaning of "insubstantial."[16]

[13] Reg. § 1.469–4.

[14] Reg. § 1.469–4(c)(3).

[15] Reg. § 1.469–4(f).

[16] Reg. § 1.469–4(d).

EXAMPLE 20

Schemers, a firm of CPAs, owns a building in downtown Washington, D.C., in which they conduct their public accounting practice. The firm also rents space on the street level of the building to several retail establishments. Of the total revenue generated by the firm, 95% is associated with the public accounting practice, and 5% is related to the rental operation. It is likely that the rental activity would be considered insubstantial relative to the accounting practice and the two ventures could be grouped as one nonrental activity. This grouping could be advantageous to the firm, particularly if the rental operation generates a loss! Alternatively, treating the rental operation as a *separate* activity may be advantageous if this operation produces (passive) income. The passive income could then be used to absorb otherwise nondeductible passive losses. ■

Second, taxpayers generally may not treat an activity involving the rental of real property and an activity involving the rental of personal property as a single activity.

Material Participation

LO.5

Analyze and apply the tests for material participation.

If an individual taxpayer materially participates in a nonrental trade or business activity, any loss from that activity is treated as an active loss that can offset active or portfolio income. If a taxpayer does not materially participate, however, the loss is treated as a passive loss, which can only offset passive income. Therefore, controlling whether a particular activity is treated as active or passive is an important part of the tax strategy of a taxpayer who owns an interest in one or more businesses. Consider the following examples.

EXAMPLE 21

Dewayne, a corporate executive, earns a salary of $600,000 per year. In addition, he owns a separate business in which he participates. The business produces a loss of $100,000 during the year. If Dewayne materially participates in the business, the $100,000 loss is an active loss that may offset his active income from his corporate employer. If he does not materially participate, the loss is passive and is suspended. Dewayne may use the suspended loss in the future only when he has passive income or disposes of the activity. ■

EXAMPLE 22

Kay, an attorney, earns $350,000 a year in her law practice. She owns interests in two activities, A and B, in which she participates. Activity A, in which she does *not* materially participate, produces a loss of $50,000. Kay has not yet met the material participation standard for Activity B, which produces income of $80,000. However, she can meet the material participation standard if she spends an additional 50 hours in Activity B during the year. Should Kay attempt to meet the material participation standard for Activity B? If she continues working in Activity B and becomes a material participant, the $80,000 of income from the activity is *active*, and the $50,000 passive loss from Activity A must be suspended. A more favorable tax strategy is for Kay to *not meet* the material participation standard for Activity B, thus making the income from that activity passive. This enables her to offset the $50,000 passive loss from Activity A against the passive income from Activity B. ■

It is possible to devise numerous scenarios in which the taxpayer could control the tax outcome by increasing or decreasing his or her participation in different activities. Examples 21 and 22 demonstrate some of the possibilities. The conclusion reached in most analyses of this type is that taxpayers will benefit by having profitable activities classified as passive so that any passive losses can be used to offset that passive income. If the activity produces a loss, however, the taxpayer will benefit if it is classified as active so that the loss is not subject to the passive loss limitations.

As discussed previously, a nonrental trade or business in which a taxpayer owns an interest must be treated as a passive activity unless the taxpayer materially participates. As the Staff of the Joint Committee on Taxation explained, a material participant is one who has "a significant nontax economic profit motive" for taking on activities and selects them for their economic value. In contrast, a passive investor mainly seeks a return from a capital investment (including a possible reduction in taxes) as a supplement to an ongoing source of livelihood.[17] Even if the concept or the implication of being a material participant is clear, the precise meaning of the term **material participation** can be vague. As enacted, § 469 requires a taxpayer to participate on a *regular, continuous, and substantial* basis in order to be a material participant. In many situations, however, it is difficult or impossible to gain any assurance that this nebulous standard is met.

In response to this dilemma, Temporary Regulations[18] provide seven tests that are intended to help taxpayers cope with these issues. Material participation is achieved by meeting any *one* of the tests. These tests can be divided into three categories:

- Tests based on current participation.
- Tests based on prior participation.
- Test based on facts and circumstances.

Tests Based on Current Participation The first four tests are quantitative tests that require measurement, in hours, of the taxpayer's participation in the activity during the year.

1. *Does the individual participate in the activity for more than 500 hours during the year?*

The purpose of the 500-hour requirement is to restrict deductions from the types of trade or business activities Congress intended to treat as passive activities. The 500-hour standard for material participation was adopted for the following reasons:[19]

- Few investors in traditional tax shelters devote more than 500 hours a year to such an investment.
- The IRS believes that income from an activity in which the taxpayer participates for more than 500 hours a year should not be treated as passive.

2. *Does the individual's participation in the activity for the taxable year constitute substantially all of the participation in the activity of all individuals (including nonowner employees) for the year?*

EXAMPLE 23

Ned, a physician, operates a separate business in which he participates for 80 hours during the year. He is the only participant and has no employees in the separate business. Ned meets the material participation standard of Test 2. If he had employees, it could be difficult to apply Test 2, because the Temporary Regulations do not define the term *substantially all*. ■

3. *Does the individual participate in the activity for more than 100 hours during the year, and is the individual's participation in the activity for the year not less than the participation of any other individual (including nonowner employees) for the year?*

EXAMPLE 24

Adam, a college professor, owns a separate business in which he participates 110 hours during the year. He has an employee who works 90 hours during the year. Adam meets the material participation standard under Test 3, but probably does not meet it under Test 2 because his participation is only 55% of the total participation. It is unlikely that 55% would meet the *substantially all* requirement of Test 2. ■

Tests 2 and 3 are included because the IRS recognizes that the operation of some activities does not require more than 500 hours of participation during the year.

[17] *General Explanation of the Tax Reform Act of 1986* ("Blue Book"), prepared by The Staff of the Joint Committee on Taxation, May 4, 1987, H.R. 3838, 99th Cong., p. 212.

[18] Temp.Reg. § 1.469–5T(a). The Temporary Regulations are also Proposed Regulations. Temporary Regulations have the same effect as final Regulations. Refer to Chapter 2 for a discussion of the different categories of Regulations.

[19] T.D. 8175, 1988–1 C.B. 191.

4. *Is the activity a significant participation activity for the taxable year, and does the individual's aggregate participation in all significant participation activities during the year exceed 500 hours?*

A **significant participation activity** is a trade or business in which the individual's participation exceeds 100 hours during the year. This test treats taxpayers as material participants if their aggregate participation in several significant participation activities exceeds 500 hours. Test 4 thus accords the same treatment to an individual who devotes an aggregate of more than 500 hours to several significant participation activities as to an individual who devotes more than 500 hours to a single activity.

EXAMPLE 25

Mike owns five different businesses. He participates in each activity during the year as follows:

Activity	Hours of Participation
A	110
B	140
C	120
D	150
E	100

Activities A, B, C, and D are significant participation activities, and Mike's aggregate participation in those activities is 520 hours. Therefore, Activities A, B, C, and D are not treated as passive activities. Activity E is not a significant participation activity (not more than 100 hours), so it is not included in applying the 500-hour test. Activity E is treated as a passive activity, unless Mike meets one of the other material participation tests for that activity. ■

EXAMPLE 26

Assume the same facts as in the previous example, except that Activity A does not exist. All of the activities are now treated as passive under Test 4. Activity E is not counted in applying the more-than-500-hour test, so Mike's aggregate participation in significant participation activities is 410 hours (140 in Activity B + 120 in Activity C + 150 in Activity D). He could meet the significant participation test for Activity E by participating for one more hour in the activity. This would cause Activities B, C, D, and E to be treated as nonpassive activities. However, before deciding whether to participate for at least one more hour in Activity E, Mike should assess how the participation would affect his overall tax liability. ■

Tests Based on Prior Participation Tests 5 and 6 are based on material participation in prior years. Under these tests, a taxpayer who is no longer a participant in an activity can continue to be *classified* as a material participant. The IRS takes the position that material participation in a trade or business for a long period of time is likely to indicate that the activity represents the individual's principal livelihood, rather than a passive investment. Consequently, withdrawal from the activity, or reduction of participation to the point where it is not material, does not change the classification of the activity from active to passive.

5. *Did the individual materially participate in the activity for any 5 taxable years (whether consecutive or not) during the 10 taxable years that immediately precede the taxable year?*

EXAMPLE 27

Dawn, who owns a 50% interest in a restaurant, was a material participant in the operations of the restaurant from 2005 through 2009. She retired at the end of 2009 and is no longer involved in the restaurant except as an investor. Dawn will be treated as a material participant in the restaurant in 2010. Even if she does not become involved in the restaurant as a material participant again, she will continue to be treated as a material participant in 2011, 2012, 2013, and 2014. In 2015 and later years, Dawn's share of income or loss from the restaurant will be classified as passive unless she materially participates in those years. ■

6. *Is the activity a personal service activity, and did the individual materially participate in the activity for any three preceding taxable years (whether consecutive or not)?*

As indicated above, the material participation standards differ for personal service activities and other businesses. An individual who was a material participant in a personal service activity for *any three years* prior to the taxable year continues to be treated as a material participant after withdrawal from the activity.

EXAMPLE 28

Evan, a CPA, retires from the EFG Partnership after working full-time in the partnership for 30 years. As a retired partner, he will continue to receive a share of the profits of the firm for the next 10 years, even though he will not participate in the firm's operations. Evan also owns an interest in a passive activity that produces a loss for the year. Because he continues to be treated as a material participant in the EFG Partnership, his income from the partnership is active income. Therefore, he is not allowed to offset the loss from his passive investment against the income from the EFG Partnership. ■

Test Based on Facts and Circumstances Test 7 assesses the facts and circumstances to determine whether the taxpayer has materially participated.

7. *Based on all the facts and circumstances, did the individual participate in the activity on a regular, continuous, and substantial basis during the year?*

Unfortunately, the Temporary Regulations provide little guidance as to the meaning of regular, continuous, and substantial participation.[20] However, a part of the Temporary Regulations has been reserved for further development of this test. For the time being, taxpayers should rely on Tests 1 through 6 in determining whether the material participation standards have been met.

Participation Defined Participation generally includes any work done by an individual in an activity that he or she owns. Participation does not include work if it is of a type not customarily done by owners *and* if one of its principal purposes is to avoid the disallowance of passive losses or credits. Also, work done in an individual's capacity as an investor (e.g., reviewing financial reports in a nonmanagerial capacity) is not counted in applying the material participation tests. However, participation by an owner's spouse counts as participation by the owner.[21]

EXAMPLE 29

Tom, who is a partner in a CPA firm, owns a computer store that has operated at a loss during the year. In order to offset this loss against the income from his CPA practice, Tom would like to avoid having the computer business classified as a passive activity. Through December 15, he has worked 400 hours in the business in management and selling activities. During the last two weeks of December, he works 80 hours in management and selling activities and 30 hours doing janitorial chores. Also during the last two weeks in December, Tom's wife participates 40 hours as a salesperson. She has worked as a salesperson in the computer store in prior years, but has not done so during the current year. If any of Tom's work is of a type not customarily done by owners *and* if one of its principal purposes is to avoid the disallowance of passive losses or credits, it is not counted in applying the material participation tests. It is likely that Tom's 480 hours of participation in management and selling activities will count as participation, but the 30 hours spent doing janitorial chores will not. However, the 40 hours of participation by his wife will count, and as a result, Tom will qualify as a material participant under the more-than-500-hour rule (480 + 40 = 520). ■

[20] Temp.Reg. § 1.469–5T(b)(2).

[21] § 469(h)(5) and Temp.Reg. § 1.469–5T(f)(3).

TAX *in* the NEWS

Are Nebraska Farmers Similar to Owners of Other LLCs and LLPs?

A major advantage for limited partners in a limited partnership is that their personal exposure to potential business losses is restricted to their investments in the partnership. Further, from an operational perspective, a typical limited partner is truly a passive investor since he or she does not participate in the business or its management. As a result, the Temporary Regulations presume that a limited partner is not a material participant unless the individual qualifies under Test 1, 5, or 6.

As limited liability companies (LLCs) and limited liability partnerships (LLPs) have grown in popularity in the United States, however, the question has arisen as to whether owners of interests in these business forms who *are* active in the businesses should be presumed to not be material participants under the usual rules applicable to limited partners. In a recent Tax Court decision [*Paul D. Garnett*, 132 T.C. 368 (2009)], Nebraska chicken and pig farmers who operated their businesses as LLCs and LLPs and played active roles were considered more akin to general partners. The court held that their material participation status should be determined by an analysis of the particular facts and circumstances of the situation and the material participation rules in general. The implication of this decision is that many taxpayers who are participants in LLCs or LLPs may be in a position to avoid the passive loss rules altogether merely by applying the general material participation tests found in the Temporary Regulations.

Since the Tax Court ruled in *Garnett*, judges in other cases have ruled similarly [*James R. Thompson v. U.S.*, 2009–2 USTC ¶50,501, 104 AFTR 2d 2009–5381, 87 Fed.Cl. 728 (Fed.Cl., 2009); *Lee E. Newell*, 99 TCM 1107, T.C.Memo. 2010–23]. With judicial pressure on the IRS's position building, many tax professionals expect a response from the IRS soon.

ETHICS *& Equity*

A Lovers' Triangle and the Passive Loss Rules

The troubled marriage of John and Eleanor finally reached an impasse, and they mutually agreed to divorce. Shortly after the divorce was finalized, John married Kristen. The three have known each other for years from working together to harvest the grapes of a vineyard owned by John. Prior to the divorce, each had worked 200 hours in the vineyard in the current year. The investment generates a loss for the current year, and John wants to classify the loss as active rather than passive. In order for the loss to be classified as active, the participation of John and his spouse together must exceed 500 hours. John claims that meeting that threshold is not a problem. He worked 200 hours, and Eleanor, who was his wife when the work was done, worked 200 hours. Kristen, who files a joint return with John, also worked 200 hours. John feels it is proper to aggregate Eleanor and Kristen's participation with his own. This approach makes the loss deductible in full. "Besides," says John, "there is nothing in the law that says I can't do this." As John's tax return preparer, how do you react?

Limited Partners A *limited* partner is one whose liability to third-party creditors of the partnership is limited to the amount the partner has invested in the partnership. Such a partnership must have at least one *general* partner, who is fully liable in an individual capacity for the debts of the partnership to third parties. Generally, a *limited partner* is not considered a material participant unless he or she qualifies under Test 1, 5, or 6 in the above list. However, a *general partner* may qualify as a material participant by meeting any of the seven tests. If a general partner also owns a limited interest in the same limited partnership, all interests are treated as a general interest.[22]

[22] § 469(h)(2) and Temp.Reg. § 1.469–5T(e)(3)(ii).

LO.6

Understand the nature of rental activities under the passive loss rules.

Rental Activities Defined

Subject to certain exceptions, all rental activities are to be treated as passive activities.[23] A **rental activity** is defined as any activity where payments are received principally for the use of tangible (real or personal) property.[24] Importantly, an activity that is classified as a rental activity is subject to the passive activity loss rules, even if the taxpayer involved is a material participant.

EXAMPLE 30

Sarah owns a fleet of automobiles that are held for rent and spends an average of 60 hours a week in the activity. Assuming that her automobile business is classified as a rental activity, it is automatically subject to the passive activity rules, even though Sarah spends more than 500 hours a year in its operation. ■

Temporary Regulations, however, provide exceptions for certain situations where activities involving rentals of real and personal property are *not* to be *treated* as rental activities.[25]

EXAMPLE 31

Dan owns a DVD rental business. Because the average period of customer use is seven days or less, Dan's DVD business is not treated as a rental activity. ■

The fact that Dan's DVD business in the previous example is not treated as a rental activity does not necessarily mean that it is classified as a nonpassive activity. Instead, the DVD business is treated as a trade or business activity subject to the material participation standards. If Dan is a material participant, the business is treated as active. If he is not a material participant, it is treated as a passive activity.

Thus, activities covered by any of the following six exceptions provided by the Temporary Regulations are not *automatically* treated as nonpassive activities merely because they would not be classified as rental activities. Instead, the activities are subject to the material participation tests.

1. *The average period of customer use of the property is seven days or less.*

Under this exception, activities involving the short-term use of tangible property such as automobiles, DVDs, tuxedos, tools, and other such property are not treated as rental activities. The provision also applies to short-term rentals of hotel or motel rooms.

This exception is based on the presumption that a person who rents property for seven days or less is generally required to provide *significant services* to the customer. Providing such services supports a conclusion that the person is engaged in a service business rather than a rental business.

2. *The average period of customer use of the property is 30 days or less, and the owner of the property provides significant personal services.*

For longer-term rentals, the presumption that significant services are provided is not automatic, as it is in the case of the seven-day exception. Instead, the taxpayer must be able to *prove* that significant personal services are rendered in connection with the activity. Relevant facts and circumstances include the frequency with which such services are provided, the type and amount of labor required to perform the services, and the value of the services relative to the amount charged for the use of the property. Significant personal services include only services provided by *individuals*.[26]

3. *The owner of the property provides extraordinary personal services. The average period of customer use is of no consequence in applying this test.*

Extraordinary personal services are services provided by individuals where the customers' use of the property is incidental to their receipt of the services. For example,

[23] § 469(c)(2).
[24] § 469(j)(8).
[25] Temp.Reg. § 1.469–1T(e)(3)(ii).
[26] Temp.Reg. § 1.469–1T(e)(3)(iv).

a patient's use of a hospital bed is incidental to his or her receipt of medical services. Another example is the use of a boarding school's dormitory, which is incidental to the scholastic services received.

4. *The rental of the property is treated as incidental to a nonrental activity of the taxpayer.*

Rentals of property incidental to a nonrental activity are not considered a passive activity. The Temporary Regulations provide that the following rentals are not passive activities:[27]

- *Property held primarily for investment.* This occurs where the principal purpose for holding the property is the expectation of gain from the appreciation of the property and the gross rent income is less than 2 percent of the lesser of (1) the unadjusted basis or (2) the fair market value of the property.

EXAMPLE 32

Ramon invests in vacant land for the purpose of realizing a profit on its appreciation. He leases the land during the period it is held. The land's unadjusted basis is $250,000, and the fair market value is $350,000. The lease payments are $4,000 per year. Because gross rent income is less than 2% of $250,000, the activity is not a rental activity. ■

- *Property used in a trade or business.* This occurs where the property is owned by a taxpayer who is an owner of the trade or business using the rental property. The property must also have been used in the trade or business during the year or during at least two of the five preceding taxable years. The 2 percent test above also applies in this situation.

EXAMPLE 33

A farmer owns land with an unadjusted basis of $250,000 and a fair market value of $350,000. He used it for farming purposes in 2009 and 2010. In 2011, he leases the land to another farmer for $4,000. The activity is not a rental activity. ■

- *Lodging rented for the convenience of an employer.* If an employer provides lodging for an employee incidental to the employee's performance of services in the employer's trade or business, no rental activity exists.

These rules were written to prevent taxpayers from converting active or portfolio income into passive income for the purpose of offsetting other passive losses.

5. *The taxpayer customarily makes the property available during defined business hours for nonexclusive use by various customers.*

EXAMPLE 34

Pat is the owner-operator of a public golf course. Some customers pay daily greens fees each time they use the course, while others purchase weekly, monthly, or annual passes. The golf course is open every day from sunrise to sunset, except on certain holidays and on days when the course is closed due to inclement weather conditions. Pat is not engaged in a rental activity, regardless of the average period customers use the course. ■

6. *The property is provided for use in an activity conducted by a partnership, S corporation, or joint venture in which the taxpayer owns an interest.*

EXAMPLE 35

Joe, a partner in the Skyview Partnership, contributes the use of a building to the partnership. The partnership has net income of $30,000 during the year, of which Joe's share is $10,000. Unless the partnership is engaged in a rental activity, none of Joe's income from the partnership is income from a rental activity. ■

[27] Temp.Regs. §§ 1.469–1T(e)(3)(vi)(B) through (D).

LO.7

Recognize the relationship between the at-risk and passive activity limitations.

INTERACTION OF THE AT-RISK AND PASSIVE ACTIVITY LIMITS

The determination of whether a loss is suspended under the passive loss rules is made *after* application of the at-risk rules, as well as other provisions relating to the measurement of taxable income. A loss that is not allowed for the year because the taxpayer is not at risk with respect to it is suspended under the at-risk provision and not under the passive loss rules. Further, a taxpayer's basis is reduced by deductions (e.g., depreciation) even if the deductions are not currently usable because of the passive loss rules.

EXAMPLE 36

Jack's adjusted basis in a passive activity is $10,000 at the beginning of 2010. His loss from the activity in 2010 is $4,000. Since Jack has no passive activity income, the $4,000 cannot be deducted. At year-end, Jack has an adjusted basis and an at-risk amount of $6,000 in the activity and a suspended passive loss of $4,000. ■

EXAMPLE 37

Jack in Example 36 has a loss of $9,000 in the activity in 2011. Since the $9,000 exceeds his at-risk amount ($6,000) by $3,000, that $3,000 loss is disallowed by the at-risk rules. If Jack has no passive activity income, the remaining $6,000 is suspended under the passive activity rules. At year-end, he has:

- A $3,000 loss suspended under the at-risk rules.
- $10,000 of suspended passive losses.
- An adjusted basis and an at-risk amount in the activity of zero. ■

EXAMPLE 38

Jack in Example 37 realizes $1,000 of passive income from the activity in 2012. Because the $1,000 increases his at-risk amount, $1,000 of the $3,000 unused loss is reclassified as a passive loss. If he has no other passive income, the $1,000 income is offset by $1,000 of suspended passive losses. At the end of 2012, Jack has:

- No taxable passive income.
- $2,000 ($3,000 – $1,000) of unused losses under the at-risk rules.
- $10,000 of (reclassified) suspended passive losses ($10,000 + $1,000 of reclassified unused at-risk losses – $1,000 of passive losses offset against passive income).
- An adjusted basis and an at-risk amount in the activity of zero. ■

EXAMPLE 39

In 2013, Jack has no gain or loss from the activity in Example 38. He contributes $5,000 more to the passive activity. Because the $5,000 increases his at-risk amount, the $2,000 of losses suspended under the at-risk rules is reclassified as passive. Jack gets no passive loss deduction in 2013. At year-end, he has:

- No suspended losses under the at-risk rules.
- $12,000 of suspended passive losses ($10,000 + $2,000 of reclassified suspended at-risk losses).
- An adjusted basis and an at-risk amount of $3,000 ($5,000 additional investment – $2,000 of reclassified losses). ■

EXAMPLE 40
THE BIG PICTURE

Return to the facts of *The Big Picture* on p. 11-2. If the Reswicks invest in the orange grove limited partnership, the at-risk rules would not limit the deductibility of the $25,000 losses until after year 4. Ample at-risk basis will exist until the close of that year (i.e., the at-risk basis is reduced from $100,000 by $25,000 over each of the first four years of the investment). However, the passive loss rules prohibit deductions for the losses in the first four years of the investment (assuming the Reswicks do not have passive income from other sources). Therefore, based on the facts provided, none of the suspended losses would be deductible until year 6 when the orange grove is expected to begin producing profits. ■

LO.8

Discuss the special treatment available to real estate activities.

SPECIAL PASSIVE ACTIVITY RULES FOR REAL ESTATE ACTIVITIES

The passive loss limits contain two exceptions related to real estate activities. These exceptions allow all or part of real estate rental losses to offset active or portfolio income, even though the activity otherwise is defined as a passive activity.

Material Participation in a Real Property Rental Trade or Business

The first exception relates to a special rule for material participation in a real estate rental trade or business. Losses from real estate rental activities are *not* treated as passive losses for certain real estate professionals.[28] To qualify for nonpassive treatment, a taxpayer must satisfy both of the following requirements:

- More than half of the personal services that the taxpayer performs in trades or businesses are performed in real property trades or businesses in which the taxpayer materially participates.
- The taxpayer performs more than 750 hours of services in these real property trades or businesses as a material participant.

Taxpayers who do not satisfy the above requirements must continue to treat losses from real estate rental activities as passive losses.

EXAMPLE 41

During the current year, Della performs personal service activities as follows: 900 hours as a personal financial planner, 550 hours in a real estate development business, and 600 hours in a real estate rental activity. Any loss Della incurs in either real estate activity will not be subject to the passive loss rules. Being a nonrental business, the development business is deemed active under the more-than-500-hour rule. The real estate rental activity is active since more than 50% of her personal services are devoted to real property trades or businesses (i.e., the development and rental businesses), and her material participation in those real estate activities exceeds 750 hours. Thus, any losses from either real estate activity can offset active and portfolio sources of income. ■

As discussed earlier, a spouse's work is taken into consideration in satisfying the material participation requirement. However, the hours worked by a spouse are *not* taken into account when ascertaining whether a taxpayer has worked for more than 750 hours in real property trades or businesses during a year.[29] Services performed by an employee are not treated as being related to a real estate trade or business unless the employee performing the services owns more than a 5 percent interest in the employer. Additionally, a closely held C corporation may also qualify for the passive loss relief if more than 50 percent of its gross receipts for the year are derived from real property trades or businesses in which it materially participates.

Real Estate Rental Activities

The second exception is more significant in that it is not restricted to real estate professionals. This exception allows individuals to deduct up to $25,000 of losses from real estate rental activities against active and portfolio income.[30] The potential annual $25,000 deduction is reduced by 50 percent of the taxpayer's AGI in excess of $100,000. Thus, the entire deduction is phased out at $150,000 of AGI. If married individuals file separately, the $25,000 deduction is reduced to zero unless they lived apart for the entire year. If they lived apart for the entire year, the loss amount is $12,500 each, and the phaseout begins at $50,000. AGI for purposes of the phaseout is calculated without regard to IRA deductions, Social Security benefits, interest deductions on education loans, and net losses from passive activities.

To qualify for the $25,000 exception, a taxpayer must meet the following requirements:[31]

- Actively participate in the real estate rental activity.
- Own 10 percent or more (in value) of all interests in the activity during the entire taxable year (or shorter period during which the taxpayer held an interest in the activity).

[28] § 469(c)(7).
[29] § 469(c)(7)(B) and Reg. § 1.469–9.
[30] § 469(i).
[31] § 469(i)(6).

TAX *in* the NEWS

Making a Simple Election May Be Critical to Qualifying as a Real Estate Professional

Often, ignoring what may seem to be trivial can turn out to be disastrous. As noted in the text, gains or losses from rental property are generally classified as passive. If the taxpayer is a real estate professional, however, the gains or losses arising from the property are treated as active. Being classified as a real estate professional can be attractive, but to receive such treatment, the taxpayer must be a material participant in the real property trades or businesses.

If a taxpayer owns three rental properties and devotes 200 hours to each property, does the taxpayer qualify as a material participant? The answer can vary. For example, to be treated as a material participant under the 500-hour rule, the taxpayer would have to elect to aggregate the three real estate rental interests and treat them as a single activity. By so doing, the taxpayer is treated as having participated for 600 hours in this "single" activity and, thus, is a material participant [see Reg. § 1.469–9(e)]. If the taxpayer does not make the election, however, the material participation standard is evaluated on a property-by-property basis (i.e., the taxpayer has devoted only 200 hours to each activity).

An explicit election to aggregate the activities is required—taxpayers cannot assume that the IRS will understand their intention. Several taxpayers learned this lesson recently when they failed to avoid the passive loss rules because they did not make their intentions clear. See *Anjum Shiekh* (99 TCM 1526, T.C.Memo. 2010–126) and *Donald W. Trask* (99 TCM 1335, T.C.Memo. 2010–78) for examples of taxpayers who wish they could redo their tax returns.

The difference between *active participation* and *material participation* is that the former can be satisfied without regular, continuous, and substantial involvement in operations as long as the taxpayer participates in making management decisions in a significant and bona fide sense. In this context, relevant management decisions include such decisions as approving new tenants, deciding on rental terms, and approving capital or repair expenditures.

EXAMPLE 42
THE BIG PICTURE

Return to the facts of *The Big Picture* on p. 11-2. If the Reswicks invest in the apartment rental limited partnership, their $25,000 loss would be deductible under the real estate rental activities exception. This assumes they actively participate and own at least a 10% interest in the partnership. The loss will be deductible in each of the first four years of their investment before exhausting their at-risk basis, even if they do not have passive income from other sources. ■

The $25,000 allowance is available after all active participation rental losses and gains are netted and applied to other passive income. If a taxpayer has a real estate rental loss in excess of the amount that can be deducted under the real estate rental exception, that excess is treated as a passive loss.

EXAMPLE 43

Brad, who has $90,000 of AGI before considering rental activities, has $85,000 of losses from a real estate rental activity in which he actively participates. He also actively participates in another real estate rental activity from which he has $25,000 of income. He has other passive income of $36,000. Of the net rental loss of $60,000, $36,000 is absorbed by the passive income, leaving $24,000 that can be deducted against active or portfolio income because of the availability of the $25,000 allowance. ■

The $25,000 offset allowance is an aggregate of both deductions and credits in deduction equivalents. The deduction equivalent of a passive activity credit is the amount of deductions that reduces the tax liability for the taxable year by an amount equal to the credit.[32] A taxpayer with $5,000 of credits and a tax bracket of 25 percent would have a deduction equivalent of $20,000 ($5,000 ÷ 25%).

[32] § 469(j)(5).

If the total deduction and deduction equivalent exceed $25,000, the taxpayer must allocate the allowance on a pro rata basis, first among the losses (including real estate rental activity losses suspended in prior years) and then to credits in the following order: (1) credits other than rehabilitation and low-income housing credits, (2) rehabilitation credits, and (3) low-income housing credits.

EXAMPLE 44

Kevin is an active participant in a real estate rental activity that produces $8,000 of income, $26,000 of deductions, and $1,500 of credits. Kevin, who is in the 25% tax bracket, may deduct the net passive loss of $18,000 ($8,000 − $26,000). After deducting the loss, he has an available deduction equivalent of $7,000 ($25,000 − $18,000 passive loss). Therefore, the maximum amount of credits that he may claim is $1,750 ($7,000 × 25%). Since the actual credits are less than this amount, Kevin may claim the entire $1,500 credit. ■

EXAMPLE 45

Kelly, who is in the 25% tax bracket, is an active participant in three separate real estate rental activities. The relevant tax results for each activity are as follows:

- Activity A: $20,000 of losses.
- Activity B: $10,000 of losses.
- Activity C: $4,200 of credits.

Kelly's deduction equivalent from the credits is $16,800 ($4,200 ÷ 25%). Therefore, the total passive deductions and deduction equivalents are $46,800 ($20,000 + $10,000 + $16,800), which exceeds the maximum allowable amount of $25,000. Consequently, Kelly must allocate pro rata first from among losses and then from among credits. Deductions from losses are limited as follows:

- Activity A {$25,000 × [$20,000 ÷ ($20,000 + $10,000)]} = $16,667.
- Activity B {$25,000 × [$10,000 ÷ ($20,000 + $10,000)]} = $8,333.

Since the amount of passive deductions exceeds the $25,000 maximum, the deduction balance of $5,000 and passive credits of $4,200 must be carried forward. Kelly's suspended losses and credits by activity are as follows:

		Activity		
	Total	A	B	C
Allocated losses	$ 30,000	$ 20,000	$10,000	$ –0–
Allocated credits	4,200	–0–	–0–	4,200
Utilized losses	(25,000)	(16,667)	(8,333)	–0–
Suspended losses	5,000	3,333	1,667	–0–
Suspended credits	4,200	–0–	–0–	4,200

■

ETHICS *& Equity*

How Active Is Active?

Last year, George and Louise purchased several rental units near the university hoping to benefit from their expected appreciation and cash flow. Because George and Louise both have full-time jobs, they are unable to spend time managing the facilities. Consequently, they contracted with a well-regarded property manager to attract renters, collect the rents, and respond to service calls. After the close of the year, the property manager provided George and Louise with an accounting of the revenues and expenses related to the operation of the units. Though the results showed a positive cash flow, the impact of depreciation and mortgage interest expenses led to a net tax loss.

Not wanting to forgo claiming a loss on their income tax return, George and Louise chose to claim the loss under the real estate rental activity exception. Have George and Louise acted properly?

LO.9

Determine the proper tax treatment upon the disposition of a passive activity.

DISPOSITIONS OF PASSIVE INTERESTS

Recall from an earlier discussion that if a taxpayer disposes of an entire interest in a passive activity, any suspended losses (and in certain cases, suspended credits) may be utilized when calculating the final economic gain or loss on the investment. In addition, if a loss ultimately results, that loss can offset other types of income. However, the consequences may differ if the activity is disposed of in a transaction that is other than a fully taxable transaction. The following discusses the treatment of suspended passive losses in other types of dispositions.

Disposition of a Passive Activity at Death

A transfer of a taxpayer's interest in an activity by reason of the taxpayer's death results in suspended losses being allowed (to the decedent) to the extent they exceed the amount, if any, of the step-up in basis allowed.[33] Suspended losses are lost to the extent of the amount of the basis increase. The losses allowed generally are reported on the final return of the deceased taxpayer.

EXAMPLE 46

A taxpayer dies with passive activity property having an adjusted basis of $40,000, suspended losses of $10,000, and a fair market value at the date of the decedent's death of $75,000. The increase (i.e., step-up) in basis (see Chapter 13) is $35,000 (fair market value at date of death in excess of adjusted basis). None of the $10,000 suspended loss is deductible by either the decedent or the beneficiary. The suspended losses ($10,000) are lost because they do not exceed the step-up in basis ($35,000). ■

EXAMPLE 47

A taxpayer dies with passive activity property having an adjusted basis of $40,000, suspended losses of $10,000, and a fair market value at the date of the decedent's death of $47,000. Since the step-up in basis is only $7,000 ($47,000 − $40,000), the suspended losses allowed are limited to $3,000 ($10,000 suspended loss at time of death − $7,000 increase in basis). The $3,000 loss available to the decedent is reported on the decedent's final income tax return. ■

Disposition of a Passive Activity by Gift

In a disposition of a taxpayer's interest in a passive activity by gift, the suspended losses are added to the basis of the property.[34]

EXAMPLE 48

A taxpayer makes a gift of passive activity property having an adjusted basis of $40,000, suspended losses of $10,000, and a fair market value at the date of the gift of $100,000. The taxpayer cannot deduct the suspended losses in the year of the disposition. However, the suspended losses transfer with the property and are added to the adjusted basis of the property in the hands of the donee. ■

When a passive activity is transferred by gift, the suspended losses become permanently nondeductible to both the donor and the donee. Nonetheless, a tax *benefit* may be available to the donee for another reason. Due to the increase in the property's basis, greater depreciation deductions can result, and there will be less gain (or more loss) on a subsequent sale of the property. The side benefits of increased basis do not materialize if the recipient is a charity, as such organizations generally are not subject to income taxation.

Installment Sale of a Passive Activity

An installment sale of a taxpayer's entire interest in a passive activity triggers the recognition of the suspended losses.[35] The losses are allowed in each year of the installment obligation in the ratio that the gain recognized in each year bears to the total gain on the sale.

[33] § 469(g)(2).

[34] § 469(j)(6).

[35] § 469(g)(3).

CONCEPT SUMMARY 11.2

Passive Activity Loss Rules: General Concepts

What is the fundamental passive activity rule?	Passive activity losses may be deducted only against passive activity income and gains. Losses not allowed are suspended and used in future years.
Who is subject to the passive activity rules?	Individuals. Estates. Trusts. Personal service corporations. Closely held C corporations.
What is a passive activity?	Trade or business or income-producing activity in which the taxpayer does not materially participate during the year, or rental activities, subject to certain exceptions, regardless of the taxpayer's level of participation.
What is an activity?	One or more trade or business or rental activities that comprise an appropriate economic unit.
How is an appropriate economic unit determined?	Based on a reasonable application of the relevant facts and circumstances.
What is material participation?	In general, the taxpayer participates on a regular, continuous, and substantial basis. More specifically, when the taxpayer meets the conditions of one of the seven tests provided in the Regulations.
What is a rental activity?	In general, an activity where payments are received for the use of tangible property. More specifically, a rental activity that does *not* meet one of the six exceptions provided in the Regulations. Special rules apply to rental real estate.

EXAMPLE 49

Stan sells his entire interest in a passive activity for $100,000. His adjusted basis in the property is $60,000. If he uses the installment method, his gross profit ratio is 40% ($40,000/$100,000). If Stan receives a $20,000 down payment, he will recognize a gain of $8,000 (40% of $20,000). If the activity has a suspended loss of $25,000, Stan will deduct $5,000 [($8,000 ÷ $40,000) × $25,000] of the suspended loss in the first year. ■

Nontaxable Exchange of a Passive Activity

In a nontaxable exchange of a passive investment, the taxpayer keeps the suspended losses, which generally become deductible when the acquired property is sold. If the activity of the old and the new property is the same, suspended losses can be used before the activity's disposition.

EXAMPLE 50

A taxpayer exchanges a duplex for a limited partnership interest in a § 721 nonrecognition transaction (see Chapter 21 for details). The suspended losses from the duplex are not deductible until the limited partnership interest is sold. Two different activities exist: a real estate rental activity and a limited partnership activity. If the taxpayer had continued to own the duplex and the duplex had future taxable income, the suspended losses would have become deductible before the time of disposition. ■

EXAMPLE 51

In a § 1031 nontaxable exchange (see Chapter 13 for details), a taxpayer exchanges a duplex for an apartment building. The suspended losses from the duplex are deductible against future taxable income of the apartment building, because the same activity exists. ■

11.4 Investment Interest

LO.10

Identify restrictions placed on the deductibility of other investor losses and deductions, including those that apply to investment interest.

Taxpayers frequently borrow funds that they use to acquire investment assets. When the interest expense is large relative to the income from the investments, substantial tax benefits could result. Congress has therefore limited the deductibility of interest on funds borrowed for the purpose of purchasing or continuing to hold investment property. The deduction for **investment interest** expense is *now* limited to net investment income for the year.

Investment income is gross income from interest, dividends (see below), annuities, and royalties not derived in the ordinary course of a trade or business. However, income from a passive activity and income from a real estate activity in which the taxpayer actively participates are not included in investment income.

EXAMPLE 52
THE BIG PICTURE

Return to the facts of *The Big Picture* on p. 11-2. If the Reswicks invest in the high-growth, low-yield portfolio of marketable securities, most of the investment return will consist of appreciation, which will not be taxed until the securities are sold. Relatively little of the current return will consist of currently taxable interest and dividend income. Assume that the interest and dividend income for the year from these securities equals $500 and that all of it is treated as investment income. If the investment interest expense on the $100,000 loan is $8,000, only $500 of this interest will be deductible this year (i.e., the deduction for the investment interest is limited to the $500 of net investment income). ■

The following types of income are not included in investment income unless the taxpayer *elects* to do so.

- Net capital gain attributable to the disposition of (1) property producing the types of income just enumerated or (2) property held for investment purposes.
- Qualified dividends that are taxed at the same marginal rate that is applicable to a net capital gain.

A taxpayer may include net capital gain and qualified dividends as investment income by electing to do so on Form 4952. The election is available only if the taxpayer agrees to reduce amounts qualifying for the 15 percent (0 percent for low-income taxpayers) rates that otherwise apply to net capital gain (see Chapter 14) and qualified dividends (refer to Chapter 4) by an equivalent amount.

EXAMPLE 53

Terry incurred $13,000 of interest expense related to her investments during the year. Her investment income included $4,000 of interest, $2,000 of qualified dividends, and a $5,000 net capital gain on the sale of investment securities. If Terry does not make the election to include the net capital gain and qualified dividends in investment income, her investment income for purposes of computing the investment income limitation is $4,000 (interest income). If she does make the election, her investment income is $11,000 ($4,000 interest + $2,000 qualified dividends + $5,000 net capital gain). ■

Net investment income is the excess of investment income over investment expenses. Investment expenses are those deductible expenses directly connected with the production of investment income. Investment expenses *do not* include interest expense. When investment expenses fall into the category of miscellaneous itemized deductions that are subject to the 2 percent-of-AGI floor (refer to Chapter 10), some may not enter into the calculation of net investment income because of the floor.

EXAMPLE 54

Gina has AGI of $80,000, which includes qualified dividends of $15,000 and interest income of $3,000. Besides investment interest expense, she paid $3,000 of city ad valorem property tax on stocks and bonds and had the following miscellaneous itemized expenses:

TAX *in* the NEWS — Favorable Treatment Available for Victims of Ponzi-Style Scams

Due to the recent economic recession, millions of people have lost considerable amounts of wealth. In addition, some taxpayers have had to relearn the old adage that "if something appears to be too good to be true, then it just may be." These taxpayers were victims not just of the economic downturn, but also of outright fraud: they were duped by Ponzi-style operators masquerading as investment advisers.

For the thousands of taxpayers who entrusted their investments to Bernard Madoff and suffered severe financial losses, such losses would normally be subject to capital loss treatment. This is typically the result when investment losses arise from sales, exchanges, or worthlessness. Instead, the IRS has provided that such losses will qualify for business theft loss treatment [Rev.Rul. 2009–9 and Rev.Proc. 2009–20 (2009–1 C.B. 735 and 749)]. The implication of this treatment is significant: the losses will be fully deductible against ordinary income without regard to the $100 floor and 10 percent-of-AGI limitation typically applicable to casualty and theft losses, or the 2 percent-of-AGI limitation applicable to miscellaneous itemized deductions. Moreover, because these losses are classified as business theft losses, any losses not deductible in the year of the loss may be carried back and carried forward under the net operating loss (NOL) rules, producing an immediate tax refund *or* a lower tax liability in future years.

Unfortunately, qualifying for theft loss treatment rather than capital loss treatment will not make these fraud victims whole. Nonetheless, the tax benefits associated with this favorable tax treatment help mitigate the financial losses sustained.

Safe deposit box rental (to hold investment securities)	$ 120
Investment counsel fee	1,200
Unreimbursed business travel	850
Uniforms	600
Total miscellaneous itemized expenses	$ 2,770

Before Gina can determine her investment expenses for purposes of calculating net investment income, those miscellaneous expenses that are not investment expenses are disallowed before any investment expenses are disallowed under the 2%-of-AGI floor. This is accomplished by selecting the *lesser* of the following:

1. The amount of investment expenses included in the total of miscellaneous itemized deductions subject to the 2%-of-AGI floor.
2. The amount of miscellaneous expenses deductible after the 2%-of-AGI rule is applied.

The amount under item 1 is $1,320 [$120 (safe deposit box rental) + $1,200 (investment counsel fee)]. The item 2 amount is $1,170 [$2,770 (total of miscellaneous expenses) − $1,600 (2% of $80,000 AGI)].

Then, Gina's investment expenses are calculated as follows:

Deductible miscellaneous deductions investment expense (the lesser of item 1 or item 2)	$1,170
Plus: Ad valorem tax on investment property	3,000
Total investment expenses	$4,170

Gina elects to include the qualified dividends in investment income. Gina's net investment income is $13,830 ($18,000 investment income − $4,170 investment expenses). ■

After net investment income is determined, deductible investment interest expense can be calculated.

EXAMPLE 55

Continuing with the facts in the previous example, given that Gina's current net investment income is $13,830, her deductible investment interest expense is limited to $13,830 this year. Therefore, if Gina incurred investment interest of $16,000 this year, only $13,830 would be deductible currently. ■

The amount of investment interest disallowed is carried over to future years. In Example 55, therefore, the amount that is carried over to the following year is $2,170 ($16,000 investment interest expense − $13,830 allowed). No limit is placed on the length of the carryover period. The investment interest expense deduction is determined by completing Form 4952.

11.5 Other Investment Losses

The investment activities summarized below are discussed elsewhere in this text (see the references provided).

- Sales of securities held as investments for less than basis yield capital losses. These losses can offset capital gains. In the case of individual taxpayers, excess losses are applied against ordinary income up to $3,000 (§ 1211). Any remaining excess capital losses are carried over for use in future years (§ 1212). See Chapter 14 for additional discussion.
- Securities held as an investment that become worthless produce capital losses. The losses are usually long term since they are treated as occurring on the last day of the year in which the securities become worthless [§ 165(g)(1)]. Because the securities must be completely worthless, determining the year when this takes place often is difficult. See Chapter 7 for additional discussion.
- Losses on small business stock (i.e., stock that qualifies under § 1244) are treated as ordinary losses up to a maximum of $100,000. Thus, the limitations placed on capital losses (see above) are avoided. See Chapter 7 for additional discussion.
- As discussed in Chapter 6, vacation homes that are rented for part of the year may generate investment losses depending on the extent of the rental period as compared to time devoted to personal use (§ 280A). If sufficient rental activity takes place, the facility may be treated as rental property. As such, any losses could be subject to the passive loss rules. See the discussion earlier in this chapter.
- When an activity is classified as a hobby, any losses resulting are limited to the income from the activity [§ 183(b)(2)]. If the activity is not a hobby (i.e., a profit motive controls), however, full deduction of the losses is allowed [§§ 162 and 212(2)]. See the relevant discussion of hobby losses in Chapter 6.

TAX PLANNING:

11.6 Utilizing Passive Losses

LO.11

Suggest tax planning strategies to minimize the effect of the passive loss limitations.

Perhaps the biggest challenge individuals face with the passive loss rules is to recognize the potential impact of the rules and then to structure their affairs to minimize this impact. Taxpayers who have passive activity losses (PALs) should adopt a strategy of generating passive activity income that can be sheltered by existing passive losses. One approach is to buy an interest in a passive activity that is generating income (referred to as passive income generators, or PIGs). Then the PAL can offset income from the PIG. From a tax perspective, it would be foolish to buy a loss-generating passive activity unless one has other passive income to shelter or the activity is rental real estate that can qualify for the $25,000 exception or the exception available to real estate professionals.

If a taxpayer does invest in an activity that produces losses subject to the passive loss rules, the following strategies may help to minimize the loss of current deductions:

- If money is borrowed to finance the purchase of a passive activity, the associated interest expense is generally treated as part of any passive loss. Consequently, by increasing the amount of cash used to purchase the passive investment, the investor will need less debt and will incur less interest expense. By incurring less interest expense, a possible suspended passive loss deduction is reduced.

- If the investor does not have sufficient cash readily available for the larger down payment, it can be obtained by borrowing against the equity in his or her personal residence. The interest expense on such debt will be deductible under the qualified residence interest provisions (see Chapter 10) and will not be subject to the passive loss limitations. Thus, the taxpayer avoids the passive loss limitation and secures a currently deductible interest expense.

Often unusable passive losses accumulate and provide no current tax benefit because the taxpayer has no passive income. When the taxpayer disposes of the entire interest in a passive activity, however, any suspended losses from that activity are used to reduce the taxable gain. If any taxable gain still remains, it can be offset by losses from other passive activities. As a result, the taxpayer should carefully select the year in which a passive activity is disposed of. It is to the taxpayer's advantage to wait until sufficient passive losses have accumulated to offset any gain recognized on the asset's disposition.

EXAMPLE 56

Bill, a calendar year taxpayer, owns interests in two passive activities: Activity A, which he plans to sell in December of this year at a gain of $100,000; and Activity B, which he plans to keep indefinitely. Current and suspended losses associated with Activity B total $60,000, and Bill expects losses from the activity to be $40,000 next year. If Bill sells Activity A this year, the $100,000 gain can be offset by the current and suspended losses of $60,000 from Activity B, producing a net taxable gain of $40,000. However, if Bill delays the sale of Activity A until January of next year, the $100,000 gain will be fully offset by the $100,000 of losses generated by Activity B ($60,000 current and prior losses + $40,000 next year's loss). Consequently, by postponing the sale by one month, he could avoid recognizing $40,000 of gain that would otherwise result. ■

Taxpayers with passive losses should consider the level of their involvement in all other trades or businesses in which they have an interest. If they show that they do not materially participate in a profitable activity, the activity becomes a passive activity. Any income generated by the profitable business then could be sheltered by current and suspended passive losses. Family partnerships in which certain members do not materially participate would qualify. The silent partner in any general partnership engaged in a trade or business would also qualify.

EXAMPLE 57

Gail has an investment in a limited partnership that produces annual passive losses of approximately $25,000. She also owns a newly acquired interest in a convenience store where she works. Her share of the store's income is $35,000. If she works enough to be classified as a material participant, her $35,000 share of income is treated as active income. This results in $35,000 being subject to tax every year, while her $25,000 loss is suspended. However, if Gail reduces her involvement at the store so that she is not a material participant, the $35,000 of income receives passive treatment. Consequently, the $35,000 of income can be offset by the $25,000 passive loss, resulting in only $10,000 being subject to tax. Thus, by reducing her involvement, Gail ensures that the income from the profitable trade or business receives passive treatment and can then be used to absorb passive losses from other passive activities. ■

Because of the restrictive nature of the passive activity loss rules, it may be advantageous for a taxpayer to use a vacation home enough to convert it to a second residence. This would enable all of the qualified interest and real estate taxes to be deducted without limitation. However, this strategy would lead to the loss of other deductions, such as repairs, maintenance, and insurance. See Examples 24 and 27 and the related discussion in Chapter 6.

As this chapter has shown, the passive loss rules can have a dramatic effect on a taxpayer's ability to claim passive losses currently. As a result, it is important to keep accurate records of all sources of income and losses, particularly any suspended passive losses and credits and the activities to which they relate, so that their potential tax benefit will not be lost.

REFOCUS ON THE BIG PICTURE

INVESTOR LOSS LIMITATIONS CAN SIGNIFICANTLY AFFECT INVESTMENT RETURNS

The objective for most investors should be to maximize after-tax wealth from among investment alternatives. This requires an understanding of the relevant tax restrictions that apply to certain expenses and losses arising from various investment choices. The after-tax returns from the three alternatives the Reswicks are considering may be affected by the at-risk, passive activity, and investment interest limitations.

The high-growth, low-yield portfolio is expected to generate very little if any current dividend income (i.e., net investment income). Nonetheless, if the broker's prediction is correct, the market value of the securities will grow by approximately 10 percent a year. However, the annual $8,000 interest expense on the debt incurred to purchase the securities may not be deductible as investment interest due to the lack of net investment income. Unless investment income is generated from this or some other source, the interest will not be deductible until the securities are sold (see Example 52). To the extent the interest is deducted as investment interest, the gain on the portfolio's sale will not be subject to preferential capital gains rates (see Example 53). As a result, the net after-tax return will be impaired because of the investment interest limitation.

The net returns from the other two investment choices will be diminished by the at-risk and passive activity loss rules in addition to the investment interest limitation. The projected 10 percent return is apparently contingent on the investors being able to utilize the current tax losses as they arise. These benefits will be deferred because the at-risk and passive activity loss rules delay the timing of the deductions. For example, in the case of the orange grove investment, none of the passive losses are deductible until year 6 when the investment is expected to produce passive income (see Example 40). In the real estate rental venture, however, Jim and Trudy could deduct the $25,000 passive loss under the exception for rental real estate for the first four years (see Example 42); the at-risk rules would limit any additional losses in year 5 to the at-risk amount. Consequently, since the at-risk and passive loss rules limit the tax losses flowing to the Reswicks, the after-tax return will not be nearly as high as their broker predicts.

What If?

If the Reswicks decide that the investment in marketable securities is their best option, could they modify their plan so that they avoid the restriction imposed by the investment interest limitation? Jim and Trudy's net after-tax return would improve if the interest cost of financing their investment could be deducted as incurred. They could finance their investment by borrowing up to $100,000 against the equity in their home (see Chapter 10). The interest on the home equity loan would be fully deductible, and consequently the after-tax return from their investment would increase. Furthermore, any gain recognition would be deferred until the securities are sold, and the tax on the gain would be subject to the preferential capital gains rate.

KEY TERMS

Active income, 11–6
At-risk limitation, 11–4
Closely held corporation, 11–10
Extraordinary personal services, 11–18
Investment income, 11–26
Investment interest, 11–26
Material participation, 11–14
Net investment income, 11–26
Passive loss, 11–4
Personal service corporation, 11–10
Portfolio income, 11–6
Rental activity, 11–18
Significant participation activity, 11–15
Tax shelters, 11–3

DISCUSSION QUESTIONS

1. **LO.1** Congress has passed two major provisions to limit a taxpayer's ability to use tax shelters to reduce or defer Federal income tax. What are these provisions?

2. **LO.2** Toni invested $80,000 for a 35% interest in a partnership in which she is not a material participant. The partnership borrowed $150,000 from a bank on a recourse loan and used the proceeds to acquire a building. What is Toni's at-risk amount?

3. **LO.2** List some events that increase and decrease an investor's at-risk amount. What are some strategies that a taxpayer can employ to increase the at-risk amount in order to claim a higher deduction for losses?

4. **LO.2, 3** In the current year, Dick invested $16,000 in a cattle-feeding operation that used nonrecourse notes to purchase $120,000 of feed, which was fed to the cattle and expensed. If his share of the expense was $24,000, how much can Dick deduct this year?

5. **LO.3** Explain the meaning of the terms *active income, portfolio income,* and *passive income.*

6. **LO.3** Alberto owns an interest in an activity that produces a $75,000 loss during the year. Would he generally prefer to have the activity classified as active or passive? Discuss.

7. **LO.3** Kim owns an interest in an activity that produces $100,000 of income during the year. Would Kim prefer to have the activity classified as active or passive? Discuss.

8. **LO.3** Upon a taxable disposition of a passive activity, the taxpayer can utilize any suspended losses and credits related to that activity. Do you agree? Explain.

9. **LO.3** A passive activity that Lucile acquired several years ago has resulted in losses. How will these passive losses affect Lucile's taxable income when she disposes of the activity?

10. **LO.3** Discuss whether the passive loss rules apply to the following: individuals, closely held C corporations, S corporations, partnerships, and personal service corporations.

11. **LO.3** New-Tech Services, Inc., which provides consulting services to inventors, is owned by four engineers, all of whom work full-time for the corporation. The corporation has eight other full-time employees, all on the clerical staff. The corporation has invested in a passive activity that produces a $60,000 loss this year. Can New-Tech deduct the loss in the current year? Explain.

12. **LO.4** What factors are relevant in determining whether activities constitute an appropriate economic unit?

13. **LO.4** Discuss what constitutes a passive activity.

14. **LO.4** The Regulations prohibit grouping rental activities in certain circumstances. Discuss these rules.

15. **LO.5** What is the significance of the term *material participation*? Why is the extent of a taxpayer's participation in an activity important in determining whether a loss from the activity is deductible or nondeductible?

16. **LO.5** Why did the IRS adopt the more-than-500-hour standard for material participation?

17. **LO.5** Doug, a high school teacher, operates four separate businesses and participates less than 500 hours in each. If all four businesses incur losses during the year, are there any circumstances under which Doug may treat the losses as active?

18. **LO.5, 11** Keith, a physician, operates a separate business that he acquired nine years ago. If he participates 90 hours in the business and it incurs a loss of $20,000, under what circumstances can Keith claim an active loss?

19. **LO.2, 3, 5** Rita retired from public accounting after a long and successful career of 45 years. As part of her retirement package, she continues to share in the profits and losses of the firm, albeit at a lower rate than when she was working full-time. Because Rita wants to stay busy during her retirement years, she has invested and works in a local hardware

ISSUE ID

business, operated as a partnership. Unfortunately, the business has recently gone through a slump and has not been generating profits. Identify relevant tax issues for Rita.

20. **LO.5** Some types of work are counted in applying the material participation standards, and some types are not counted. Discuss and give examples of each type.

ISSUE ID

21. **LO.5** Even though Sylvia is a full-time employee at a major software developer, she has never given up her love of pottery. For many years, she has spent evenings and weekends working to develop a profitable pottery business by making original pieces to sell to the general public. How should Sylvia treat the income or loss generated by her pottery venture? What are the tax issues?

22. **LO.5** Sean, a limited partner in Ivy Nursery, is informed that his portion of the entity's current loss is $18,000. As a limited partner, can Sean assume that his share of the partnership loss is a passive loss?

23. **LO.6** In general, the definition of passive activity includes rental activities. However, certain activities involving rentals of real and personal property are not *treated* as rental activities. Explain.

24. **LO.4, 5, 6** How is *passive activity* defined in the Code, and what aspects of the definition have been clarified by final or Temporary Regulations?

25. **LO.5, 6, 8** Laura owns an apartment building and a DVD rental business. She participates for more than 500 hours in the operations of each activity. Are the businesses active or passive?

26. **LO.8** Tami incurs a loss of $75,000 on a real estate rental activity during the current year. Under what circumstances can Tami treat the entire loss as nonpassive?

ISSUE ID

27. **LO.2, 3, 4, 5, 6, 7** In the current year, Doug and Debbie Lee, both successful attorneys, made a cash investment in a limited partnership interest in a California almond grove. In addition to the cash generated from the investors, the venture borrowed a substantial sum to purchase assets necessary for its operation. The Lees' investment adviser told them that their share of the tax loss in the first year alone would be in excess of their initial cash investment. This result would be followed by several more years of losses. They feel confident that their interest in the almond grove is a sound investment. Identify the tax issues facing the Lees.

ISSUE ID

28. **LO.3, 4, 5** Since his college days, Charles has developed an entrepreneurial streak. After working in his family's grocery business, he starts several ventures on his own. Even though Charles is independently wealthy, he is looking forward to working in each of the ventures. He plans to "drop in" on the businesses from time to time between personal trips to Europe and the Caribbean. As of the end of the year, he has established computer software stores in Dayton (Ohio), Austin, and Seattle; bagel bakeries in Albany, Athens (Georgia), and Tallahassee; and mountain bike and ski rental shops in small towns in Vermont, West Virginia, Colorado, and California. Identify the tax issues facing Charles.

29. **LO.5, 8** Nancy owns an interest in a hobby shop that has six full-time employees; during the year, she works 400 hours in the shop. Nancy also owns an apartment building with no employees in which she works 950 hours. Is either activity a passive activity? Explain.

30. **LO.8** Brad owns a small townhouse complex that generates a loss during the year. Under what circumstances can Brad deduct a loss from the rental activity, and what limitations apply?

31. **LO.5, 8** Under the passive loss rules, what are the differences between *material participation* and *active participation*?

ISSUE ID

32. **LO.8, 11** Robert owns rental property that generally produces positive taxable income and cash flow. This year, however, Robert's current loss is $5,000. Before considering the effect of the depreciation deduction, however, the property would have generated a $1,500 profit. Robert's AGI for the year is $170,000. He asks you about the treatment of his loss for the current year. Robert also mentions that he has been considering either selling the property (within the next five years) or exchanging it for other rental property. Identify the tax issues.

PROBLEMS

33. **LO.2** In the current year, Lionel invests $20,000 for an interest in a partnership engaged in the wholesale distribution of plumbing supplies. Lionel is a material participant, and his share of the partnership loss is $25,000. Discuss the tax treatment of Lionel's share of the loss, and compute his at-risk basis.

34. **LO.2** In the current year, Bill Parker (54 Oak Drive, St. Paul, MN 55162) is considering making an investment of $60,000 in Best Choice Partnership. The prospectus provided by Bill's broker indicates that the partnership investment is not a passive activity and that Bill's share of the entity's loss in the current year will likely be $40,000, while his share of the partnership loss next year will probably be $25,000. Write a letter to Bill in which you indicate how the losses would be treated for tax purposes in the current and next years.

COMMUNICATIONS

35. **LO.2, 11** Heather wishes to invest $40,000 in a relatively safe venture and has discovered two alternatives that would produce the following reportable ordinary income and loss over the next three years:

DECISION MAKING

Year	Alternative 1 Income (Loss)	Alternative 2 Income (Loss)
1	($ 24,000)	($48,000)
2	(24,000)	32,000
3	72,000	40,000

She is interested in the after-tax effects of these alternatives over a three-year horizon. Assume that Heather's investment portfolio produces sufficient passive income to offset any potential passive loss that may arise from these alternatives, that her cost of capital is 8% (the present value factors are 0.92593, 0.85734, and 0.79383), that she is in the 25% tax bracket, that each investment alternative possesses equal growth potential, and that each alternative exposes her to comparable financial risk. In addition, assume that in the loss years for each alternative, there is no cash flow from or to the investment (i.e., the loss is due to depreciation), while in those years when the income is positive, cash flows to Heather equal the amount of the income. Based on these facts, compute the present value of these two investment alternatives and determine which option Heather should choose.

36. **LO.1, 3** Hazel has investments in two nonrental passive activities: Activity A, acquired seven years ago and profitable until the current year, and Activity B, acquired this year. Currently, Hazel's shares of the activities' losses are $10,000 from Activity A and $6,000 from Activity B. What is the total of Hazel's suspended losses from these activities?

37. **LO.1, 3** In 2006, Gene acquired an interest in a partnership in which he is not a material participant. The partnership was profitable through 2009, and Gene's basis in this partnership interest at the beginning of 2010 was $60,000. Gene's share of the partnership loss was $45,000 in 2010, and his share of the partnership income is $25,000 in 2011. How much can Gene deduct for 2010 and 2011?

38. **LO.3** Ken, a CPA, earns $200,000 from his accounting practice in the current year. He receives $20,000 in dividends and interest during the year. In addition, he incurs a loss of $50,000 from an investment in a passive activity acquired three years ago. What is Ken's net income for the current year after considering the passive investment?

39. **LO.3, 11** Emily has $100,000 that she wishes to invest and is considering the following two options:

DECISION MAKING

- Option A: Investment in Redbird Mutual Fund, which is expected to produce interest income of $8,000 per year.
- Option B: Investment in Cardinal Limited Partnership (buys, sells, and operates wine vineyards). Emily's share of the partnership's ordinary income and loss over the next three years would be:

Year	Income (Loss)
1	($ 8,000)
2	(2,000)
3	34,000

Emily is interested in the after-tax effects of these alternatives over a three-year horizon. Assume that Emily's investment portfolio produces ample passive income to offset any passive losses that may be generated. Her cost of capital is 8% (the present value factors are 0.92593, 0.85734, and 0.79383), and she is in the 28% tax bracket. The two investment alternatives possess equal growth potential and comparable financial risk. Based on these facts, compute the present value of these two investment alternatives and determine which option Emily should choose.

40. **LO.3** Ray acquired an activity several years ago, and in the current year, it generates a loss of $50,000. Ray has AGI of $140,000 before considering the loss from the activity. If the activity is a bakery and Ray is not a material participant, what is his AGI?

DECISION MAKING

41. **LO.3, 11** Larry owns two passive investments, Activity A and Activity B. He plans to dispose of Activity A, either in the current year or next year. Celene has offered to buy Activity A this year for an amount that would produce a taxable passive gain to Larry of $100,000. However, if the sale, for whatever reason, is not made to Celene, Larry feels that he could find a buyer who would pay about $6,000 less than Celene. Passive losses and gains generated (and expected to be generated) by Activity B follow:

Two years ago	($ 35,000)
Last year	(35,000)
This year	(5,000)
Next year	(19,000)
Future years	Minimal profits

All of Activity B's losses are suspended. Should Larry close the sale of Activity A with Celene this year, or should he wait until next year and sell to another buyer? Larry is in the 28% tax bracket.

42. **LO.3** Sarah has investments in four passive activity partnerships purchased several years ago. Last year, the income and losses were as follows:

Activity	Income (Loss)
A	$ 10,000
B	(5,000)
C	(25,000)
D	(20,000)

In the current year, she sold her interest in Activity D for a $19,000 gain. Activity D, which had been profitable until last year, had a current loss of $1,000. How will the sale of Activity D affect Sarah's taxable income in the current year?

43. **LO.3** Leon sells his interest in a passive activity for $100,000. Determine the tax effect of the sale based on each of the following independent facts:
    a. Adjusted basis in this investment is $35,000. Losses from prior years that were not deductible due to the passive loss restrictions total $40,000.
    b. Adjusted basis in this investment is $75,000. Losses from prior years that were not deductible due to the passive loss restrictions total $40,000.
    c. Adjusted basis in this investment is $75,000. Losses from prior years that were not deductible due to the passive loss restrictions total $40,000. In addition, suspended credits total $10,000.

44. **LO.3** In the current year, Blue, Inc., earns $300,000 from operations and receives $28,000 in dividends and interest on various portfolio investments. Blue also pays $150,000 to acquire a 20% interest in a passive activity that produces a $150,000 loss.

a. Assuming Blue is a personal service corporation, how will these transactions affect its taxable income?

b. Same as (a), except that Blue is closely held but not a personal service corporation.

45. **LO.3** Orange, Inc., earns $250,000 from operations in the current year. Orange also receives $18,000 in dividends and interest on various portfolio investments. During the year, Orange pays $150,000 to acquire a 30% interest in a passive activity that produces a $200,000 loss. How will these facts affect Orange's taxable income, assuming the corporation is:

a. A personal service corporation?

b. A closely held (non-personal service) C corporation?

46. **LO.3, 4, 5, 9, 11** Greg Horne (431 Maple Avenue, Cincinnati, OH 45229), a syndicated radio talk show host, earns an annual salary of $400,000. He works approximately 30 hours per week in this job, which leaves him time to participate in several businesses newly acquired in 2011. He owns a movie theater and a drugstore in Cincinnati, a movie theater and a drugstore in Indianapolis, and a drugstore in Louisville. A preliminary analysis on December 1, 2011, shows the following projected income and losses and time spent for these various businesses.

DECISION MAKING

COMMUNICATIONS

	Income (Loss)
Cincinnati movie theater (95 hours)	$ 56,000
Cincinnati drugstore (140 hours)	(89,000)
Indianapolis movie theater (90 hours)	34,000
Indianapolis drugstore (170 hours)	(41,000)
Louisville drugstore (180 hours)	(15,000)

Greg has full-time employees in each of the five businesses. Write a letter to Greg suggesting a grouping method and other strategies that will provide the greatest tax advantage. As Greg is not knowledgeable about tax law, provide a nontechnical explanation.

47. **LO.2, 3, 7, 11** Kristin Graf (123 Baskerville Mill Road, Jamison, PA 18929) is trying to decide how to invest a $10,000 inheritance. One option is to make an additional investment in Rocky Road Excursions in which she has an at-risk basis of $0, suspended losses under the at-risk rules of $7,000, and suspended passive losses of $1,000. If Kristin makes this investment, her share of the expected profits this year would be $8,000. If her investment stays the same, her share of profits from Rocky Road Excursions would be $1,000. Another option is to invest $10,000 as a limited partner in the Ragged Mountain Winery; this investment would produce passive income of $9,000. Write a letter to Kristin to review the tax consequences of each alternative. Kristin is in the 28% tax bracket.

DECISION MAKING

COMMUNICATIONS

48. **LO.2, 3, 7, 11** The end of the year is approaching, and Maxine has begun to focus on ways of minimizing her income tax liability. Several years ago, she purchased an investment in Teal Limited Partnership, which is subject to both the at-risk and the passive activity loss rules. (Last year, Maxine sold a different investment that was subject to these rules but produced passive income.) She believes that her investment in Teal has good long-term economic prospects. However, it has been generating tax losses for several years in a row. In fact, when she was discussing last year's income tax return with her tax accountant, he said that unless "things change" with respect to her investments, she would not be able to deduct losses this year.

DECISION MAKING

a. What was the accountant referring to in his comment?

b. You learn that Maxine's current at-risk basis in her investment is $1,000 and her share of the current loss is expected to be $13,000. Based on these facts, how will her loss be treated?

c. After reviewing her situation, Maxine's financial adviser suggests that she invest at least an additional $12,000 in Teal in order to ensure a full loss deduction in the current year. How do you react to his suggestion?

d. What would you suggest Maxine consider as she attempts to maximize her current-year deductible loss?

49. **LO.2, 3, 7** A number of years ago, Lee acquired a 20% interest in the BlueSky Partnership for $60,000. The partnership was profitable through 2010, and Lee's amount

at risk in the partnership interest was $120,000 at the beginning of 2011. BlueSky incurred a loss of $400,000 in 2011 and reported income of $200,000 in 2012. Assuming Lee is not a material participant, how much of his loss from BlueSky Partnership is deductible in 2011 and 2012? Consider both the at-risk and the passive loss rules.

50. **LO.2, 3, 5, 7** Last year, Fran invested $40,000 for an interest in a partnership in which she is a material participant. Her share of the partnership loss for last year was $50,000. In the current year, Fran's share of the partnership's income is $30,000. What is the effect on her taxable income for the current year?

51. **LO.2, 3, 5, 7** Jonathan, a physician, earns $200,000 from his practice. He also receives $18,000 in dividends and interest on various portfolio investments. During the year, he pays $45,000 to acquire a 20% interest in a partnership that produces a $300,000 loss. Compute Jonathan's AGI, assuming that:
    a. He does not participate in the operations of the partnership.
    b. He is a material participant in the operations of the partnership.

52. **LO.2, 3, 7** Five years ago, Gerald invested $150,000 in a passive activity, his sole investment venture. On January 1, 2010, his amount at risk in the activity was $30,000. His shares of the income and losses were as follows:

Year	Income (Loss)
2010	($ 40,000)
2011	(30,000)
2012	50,000

How much can Gerald deduct in 2010 and 2011? What is his taxable income from the activity in 2012? Consider the at-risk rules as well as the passive loss rules.

53. **LO.3, 8** Beth acquired an activity four years ago. The loss from the activity is $35,000 in the current year. She has AGI of $120,000 before considering the loss from the activity. The activity is an apartment building, and Beth is an active participant. What is her AGI after considering the activity?

54. **LO.3, 8** Several years ago, Rachel acquired an apartment building that currently generates a loss of $35,000. She has AGI of $120,000 before considering the loss. If Rachel is not an active participant in the activity, what is the effect of the loss on her AGI?

DECISION MAKING

55. **LO.3, 8, 11** Bonnie and Adam are married with no dependents and live in New Hampshire (not a community property state). Since Adam has large medical expenses, they seek your advice about filing separately to save taxes. Their income and expenses for 2011 are as follows:

Bonnie's salary	$ 44,000
Adam's salary	30,000
Interest income (joint)	1,500
Rental loss from actively managed rental property	(23,000)
Adam's unreimbursed medical expenses	9,500
All other itemized deductions:*	
Bonnie	10,000
Adam	3,500

*None subject to limitations

Determine whether Bonnie and Adam should file jointly or separately for 2011.

DECISION MAKING

56. **LO.3, 8, 11** Mary and Charles have owned a beach cottage on the New Jersey shore for several years and have always used it as a family retreat. When they acquired the property, they had no intentions of renting it. Because family circumstances have changed, they are considering using the cottage for only two weeks a year and renting it for the remainder of the year. Their AGI approximates $80,000 per year, and they are in the 30% tax bracket (combined Federal and state). Interest and real estate taxes total $8,000 per year and are expected to continue at this level in the foreseeable future. If Mary and Charles rent the property, their *incremental* revenue and expenses are projected to be:

Rent income	$ 20,000
Rental commissions	(3,000)
Maintenance expenses	(8,000)
Depreciation expense	(10,000)

If the cottage is converted to rental property, they plan to be actively involved in key rental and maintenance decisions. Given the tax effects of converting the property to rental use, would the cash flow from renting the property be enough to meet the $12,000 annual mortgage payment?

57. **LO.3, 8** During the current year, Gene, a CPA, performs services as follows: 1,800 hours in his tax practice and 50 hours in an apartment leasing operation in which he has a 15% interest. Because of his oversight duties, Gene is considered to be an active participant. He expects that his share of the loss realized from the apartment leasing operation will be $30,000 while his tax practice will show profit of approximately $80,000. Gene is single and has no other income. Discuss the character of the income and losses generated by these activities.

58. **LO.3, 8** Ida, who has AGI of $80,000 before considering rental activities, is active in three separate real estate rental activities and is in the 28% tax bracket. She has $12,000 of losses from Activity A, $18,000 of losses from Activity B, and income of $10,000 from Activity C. She also has $2,100 of tax credits from Activity A. Calculate her deductions and credits allowed and the suspended losses and credits.

59. **LO.8** Ella has $105,000 of losses from a real estate rental activity in which she actively participates. She has other rental income of $25,000 and other passive income of $32,000. How much rental loss can Ella deduct against active and portfolio income (ignoring the at-risk rules)? Does she have any suspended losses to carry over?

60. **LO.9** Faye dies owning an interest in a passive activity property with an adjusted basis of $240,000, suspended losses of $42,000, and a fair market value of $270,000. What, if anything, can be deducted on her final income tax return?

61. **LO.9** In 2010, Nina gave her son a passive activity (adjusted basis of $100,000, fair market value of $180,000, and suspended losses of $25,000). In 2011, the son realizes income of $12,000 from the passive activity. What are the tax effects to Nina and her son in 2010 and 2011?

62. **LO.9** Tonya sells a passive activity in the current year for $150,000. Her adjusted basis in the activity is $50,000, and she uses the installment method of reporting the gain. The activity has suspended losses of $12,000. Tonya receives $60,000 in the year of sale. What is her gain? How much of the suspended losses can she deduct?

63. **LO.10, 11** In 2011, Rachel Tweardy incurs $29,250 of interest expense related to her investments. Her investment income includes $7,000 of interest, $5,500 of qualified dividends, and a $12,750 net capital gain on the sale of securities. Rachel asks you to compute the amount of her deduction for investment interest, taking into consideration any options she might have. In addition, she wants your suggestions as to any tax planning alternatives that are available. Write a letter to her that contains your advice. Rachel lives at 11934 Briarpatch Drive, Midlothian, VA 23113. **DECISION MAKING** **COMMUNICATIONS**

64. **LO.10** Helen borrowed $100,000 to acquire a parcel of land to be held for investment purposes. During 2011, she paid interest of $11,000 on the loan. She had AGI of $75,000 for the year. Other items related to Helen's investments include the following:

Investment income	$10,000
Long-term capital gain on sale of stock	7,500
Investment counsel fees	2,000

Helen is unmarried and elects to itemize her deductions. She has no miscellaneous itemized deductions other than the investment counsel fees.

a. Determine Helen's investment interest deduction for 2011.
b. Discuss the treatment of the portion of Helen's investment interest that is disallowed in 2011.

RESEARCH PROBLEMS

THOMSON REUTERS
Checkpoint® Student Edition

Note: Solutions to Research Problems can be prepared by using the **Checkpoint® Student Edition** online research product, which is available to accompany this text. It is also possible to prepare solutions to the Research Problems by using tax research materials found in a standard tax library.

Research Problem 1. Ida Ross has decided to purchase a new home in a retirement community for $400,000. She has $50,000 in cash for the down payment, but needs to borrow the remaining $350,000 to finance the purchase. Her financial adviser, Marc, suggests that rather than seeking a conventional mortgage, she should borrow the funds from State Bank using her portfolio of appreciated securities as collateral. Selling the securities to generate $350,000 in cash would lead to a substantial tax on the capital gain recognized. Therefore, a better strategy would be to borrow against her securities and then claim a deduction for the interest paid on the loan. How do you react to the financial adviser's strategy?

Partial list of research aids:
Temp.Reg. § 1.163–8T(c).

COMMUNICATIONS

Research Problem 2. Lane Mitchell (77 Lakeview Drive, Salt Lake City, UT 84109) is a married individual who files a separate return for the taxable year. He is employed full-time as an accountant and also owns an interest in a minor league baseball team. He does no work in connection with the baseball activity and anticipates that it will produce a loss. He pays his wife to work as an office receptionist in connection with the activity. Her work requires an average of 20 hours a week. Write a letter to Lane and explain whether he will be allowed to deduct his share of the loss from the activity.

INTERNET *activity*

Use the tax resources of the Internet to address the following question. Do not restrict your search to the Web, but include a review of newsgroups and general reference materials, practitioner sites and resources, primary sources of the tax law, chat rooms and discussion groups, and other opportunities.

Research Problem 3. Download and print a copy of Form 6198 and its instructions. Use these materials to complete the requirements of Problem 33.

CHAPTER 12

Tax Credits and Payments

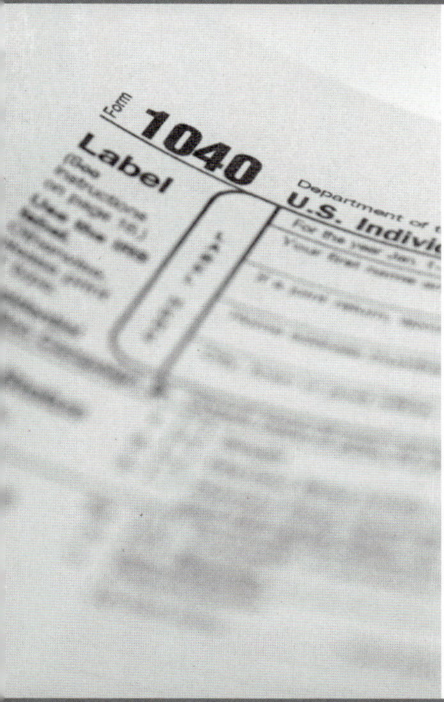

LEARNING OBJECTIVES

After completing Chapter 12, you should be able to:

LO.1

Explain how tax credits are used as a tool of Federal tax policy.

LO.2

Distinguish between refundable and nonrefundable credits and understand the order in which they can be used by taxpayers.

LO.3

Describe various business-related tax credits.

LO.4

Describe various tax credits that are available primarily to individual taxpayers.

LO.5

Understand the tax withholding and payment procedures used by employers.

LO.6

Describe the tax payment procedures used by self-employed persons.

LO.7

Identify tax planning opportunities related to tax credits and payments.

OUTLINE

For the latest in changes to tax legislation, visit **www.cengage.com/taxation/swft.**

FRAMEWORK 1040: Tax Formula for Individuals

This chapter covers the boldfaced portions of the Tax Formula for Individuals that was introduced in Figure 3.1 on p. 3-3. Below those portions are the sections of Form 1040 where the results are reported.

Income (broadly conceived)	$xx,xxx
Less: Exclusions	(x,xxx)
Gross income	$xx,xxx
Less: Deductions for adjusted gross income	(x,xxx)
Adjusted gross income	$xx,xxx
Less: The greater of total itemized deductions *or* the standard deduction	(x,xxx)
Personal and dependency exemptions	(x,xxx)
Taxable income	$xx,xxx
Tax on taxable income (see Tax Tables or Tax Rate Schedules)	$ x,xxx
Less: Tax credits (including income taxes withheld and prepaid)	**(xxx)**

FORM 1040 (p. 2)

47	Foreign tax credit. Attach Form 1116 if required	47		
48	Credit for child and dependent care expenses. Attach Form 2441	48		
49	Education credits from Form 8863, line 23	49		
50	Retirement savings contributions credit. Attach Form 8880	50		
51	Child tax credit (see instructions)	51		
52	Residential energy credits. Attach Form 5695	52		
53	Other credits from Form: a ☐ 3800 b ☐ 8801 c ☐	53		
54	Add lines 47 through 53. These are your **total credits**			

Tax due (or refund)	$ xxx

THE BIG PICTURE Tax Solutions for the Real World

EDUCATION TAX CREDITS

Tom and Jennifer Snyder have two children in college. Lora is a freshman, and her tuition and required fees in 2011 total $14,000. Lora has a partial scholarship amounting to $6,500, and the Snyders paid the balance of her tuition ($7,500), plus room and board of $8,500. Sam is a junior, and the Snyders paid $8,100 for his tuition, plus $7,200 for his room and board. Both students qualify as Tom and Jennifer's dependents.

The Snyders have AGI of $158,000. They would like to know what tax options are available to them related to these education expenses. They have heard about various education-related deductions and credits, but they believe that their income is too high for them to get any benefit. Are they correct? **Read the chapter and formulate your response.**

Federal tax law often serves purposes other than merely raising revenue for the government. Evidence of equity, social, and economic considerations, among others, is found throughout the tax law. These considerations also bear heavily in the area of **tax credits**.

EXAMPLE 1

Paul and Peggy, husband and wife, are both employed outside the home. Their combined salaries are $50,000. However, after paying for child care expenses of $2,000 on behalf of their daughter, Polly, the pre-tax economic benefit from both spouses working is $48,000. The child care expenses are, in a sense, business related since they would not have been incurred if both spouses did not work outside the home. If no tax benefits are associated with the child care expenditures, $50,000 is subject to tax.

Another couple, Alicia and Diego, also have a child, John. Diego stays at home to care for John (the value of those services is $2,000) while Alicia earns a $48,000 salary. Because the value of Diego's services rendered is not subject to tax, only Alicia's earnings of $48,000 are subject to tax. ■

The credit for child and dependent care expenses mitigates the inequity felt by working taxpayers who must pay for child care services in order to work outside the home.

EXAMPLE 2

Jane is a single parent who depends on the government's "safety net" for survival—she receives benefits under the Temporary Assistance to Needy Families program in the amount of $15,000 per year. However, she very much wishes to work. Jane has located a job that will pay $15,500 per year and has found an individual to care for her child at no cost. But, with the $875.75 ($15,500 × 5.65%) 2011 withholding for Social Security and Medicare taxes, the economic benefit from working is less than remaining reliant on the government ($14,624.25 versus $15,000). ■

To help offset the effect of Social Security and Medicare taxes on wages of the working poor and to provide an incentive to work, the earned income credit is used to increase the after-tax earnings of qualified individuals. In addition, the earned income credit helps offset the regressive nature of certain taxes, such as the Social Security and Medicare taxes, which impose a relatively larger burden on low-income taxpayers than on more affluent taxpayers.

These and many of the other tax credits available to individuals and other taxpayers are a major focus of this chapter. The chapter begins by discussing tax policy considerations relevant to tax credits. Tax credits are categorized as being either refundable or nonrefundable. This distinction is important because it may affect the taxpayer's ability to enjoy a tax benefit from a particular credit.

Next, an overview of the priority of tax credits is presented. The chapter continues with a discussion of the credits available to businesses and to individual taxpayers and the ways in which credits enter into the calculation of the tax liability. The chapter concludes with a brief look at tax withholding and payment procedures.

12.1 Tax Policy Considerations

LO.1

Explain how tax credits are used as a tool of Federal tax policy.

Congress generally has used tax credits to achieve social or economic objectives or to promote equity among different types of taxpayers. For example, the disabled access credit was enacted to accomplish a social objective: to encourage taxpayers to renovate older buildings so they would be in compliance with the Americans with Disabilities Act. Businesses and institutions must make their facilities more accessible to persons with various disabilities. As another example, the foreign tax credit, which has been a part of the law for decades, has as its purpose the economic and equity objectives of mitigating the burden of multiple taxation on a single stream of income of a multinational taxpayer.

A tax credit should not be confused with an income tax deduction. Certain expenditures of individuals (e.g., business expenses) are permitted as deductions from gross income in arriving at adjusted gross income (AGI). Additionally, individuals are allowed to deduct certain nonbusiness and investment-related expenses *from* AGI. While the tax benefit received from a tax deduction depends on the tax rate, a tax credit is not affected by the tax rate of the taxpayer.

TAX in the NEWS

Federal Tax Law Is a Key Component of U.S. Energy Policy

To help stem the increasing dependence of the United States on foreign sources of energy, Congress has enacted numerous tax breaks for power producers as well as for consumers, many of which take the form of tax credits. The primary goals of the tax provisions are to improve energy-related infrastructure, provide more incentives for traditional fossil fuel production, and encourage higher levels of energy conservation.

Some of the more widely applicable provisions include credits for:

- Builders who construct energy-efficient homes.
- Individuals who make energy-saving improvements to their residences.
- Manufacturers that make energy-efficient appliances.
- Businesses that buy fuel cell and microturbine power plants.
- Taxpayers who purchase alternative power motor vehicles and refueling property.

Like many other tax credits, the energy credits have been designed to modify taxpayer behavior. More specifically, in this case, Congress's intention is that these credits lead to greater conservation and more efficient use of energy.

EXAMPLE 3

Congress wishes to encourage a certain type of expenditure. One way to accomplish this objective is to allow a tax credit of 25% for such expenditures. Another way is to allow an itemized deduction for the expenditures. Abby's tax rate is 15%, while Bill's tax rate is 35%, and both itemize deductions. Carmen does not incur enough qualifying expenditures to itemize deductions. The following tax benefits are available to each taxpayer for a $1,000 expenditure.

	Abby	Bill	Carmen
Tax benefit if a 25% credit is allowed	$250	$250	$250
Tax benefit if an itemized deduction is allowed	150	350	–0–

As these results indicate, tax credits provide benefits on a more equitable basis than do tax deductions. Equally apparent is that the deduction approach in this case benefits only taxpayers who itemize deductions, while the credit approach benefits all taxpayers who make the specified expenditure. ■

Congress has used the tax credit provisions of the Code liberally in implementing tax policy. Although budget constraints and economic considerations often have dictated the repeal of some credits, other credits, such as those applicable to expenses incurred for child and dependent care, have been kept to respond to important social policy considerations. Still other credits, such as the one available for hiring low-income workers, have been retained based on economic and equity considerations.

LO.2

Distinguish between refundable and nonrefundable credits and understand the order in which they can be used by taxpayers.

12.2 Tax Credits

REFUNDABLE VERSUS NONREFUNDABLE CREDITS

As illustrated in Exhibit 12.1, certain credits are refundable while others are nonrefundable. **Refundable credits** are paid to the taxpayer even if the amount of the credit (or credits) exceeds the taxpayer's tax liability.

EXAMPLE 4

Ted, who is single, had taxable income of $21,000 in 2011. His income tax from the 2011 Tax Rate Schedule is $2,725. During 2011, Ted's employer withheld income tax of $3,200. Ted is entitled to a refund of $475 because the credit for tax withheld on wages is a refundable credit. ■

EXHIBIT 12.1 **Partial Listing of Refundable and Nonrefundable Credits**

Refundable Credits

Taxes withheld on wages
Earned income credit
First-time homebuyer credit

Nonrefundable Credits

Credit for child and dependent care expenses
Credit for elderly or disabled
Adoption expenses credit
Child tax credit*
Education tax credits**
Credit for certain retirement plan contributions
Foreign tax credit
General business credit, which includes the following:

- Tax credit for rehabilitation expenditures
- Jobs credit
- Work opportunity tax credit
- Research activities credit
- Low-income housing credit
- Disabled access credit
- Credit for small employer pension plan startup costs
- Credit for employer-provided child care

*The credit is refundable to the extent of 15 percent of the taxpayer's earned income in excess of $13,000 for 2011. Parents with three or more qualifying children may compute the refundable portion using an alternative method.
**Forty percent of the American Opportunity credit is refundable.

Nonrefundable credits are not paid if they exceed the taxpayer's tax liability.

EXAMPLE 5

Tina is single, age 27. Her taxable income for 2011 is $1,320, and the tax on this amount is $132. Tina's tax credit for child care expenses is $225. This credit can be used to reduce her net tax liability to zero, but it will not result in a refund, even though the credit ($225) exceeds Tina's tax liability ($132). The child care credit is nonrefundable. ■

Some nonrefundable credits, such as the foreign tax credit, are subject to carryover provisions if they exceed the amount allowable as a credit in a given year. Other nonrefundable credits, such as the child care credit (refer to Example 5), are not subject to carryover provisions and are lost if they exceed the limitations. Because some credits are refundable and others are not, and because some credits are subject to carryover provisions while others are not, the order in which credits are offset against the tax liability is important.

EXAMPLE 6

Elijah's tax liability before credits is $1,000. He qualifies for two tax credits: a $400 Credit A (nonrefundable) and an $800 Credit B (refundable). The order in which the credits are applied affects Elijah's tax refund for the year.

If Refundable Credit Is Applied First	
Precredit tax liability	$1,000
Credit B	(800)
Remaining tax due	$ 200
Credit A (as limited)	(200)
Tax due/(Refund)	$ -0-

If Nonrefundable Credit Is Applied First	
Precredit tax liability	$1,000
Credit A	(400)
Remaining tax due	$ 600
Credit B	(800)
Tax due/(Refund)	($ 200)

■

GENERAL BUSINESS CREDIT

The **general business credit** is composed of a number of other credits, each of which is computed separately under its own set of rules.[1] The general business credit combines these credits into one amount to limit the amount of business credits that can be used to offset a taxpayer's income tax liability.

Two special rules apply to the general business credit. First, any unused credit is carried back 1 year, then forward 20 years. Second, for any tax year, the general business credit is limited to the taxpayer's net income tax reduced by the greater of:[2]

- The tentative minimum tax. This amount relates to the alternative minimum tax. See Chapter 15.
- 25 percent of *net regular tax liability* that exceeds $25,000.[3]

Net regular tax liability is the regular tax liability reduced by certain nonrefundable credits (e.g., credit for child and dependent care expenses, foreign tax credit).

EXAMPLE 7

Floyd's general business credit for the current year is $70,000. His net income tax is $150,000, the tentative minimum tax is $130,000, and Floyd's net regular tax liability is $150,000. He has no other tax credits. Floyd's general business credit allowed for the tax year is computed as follows.

Net income tax	$ 150,000
Less: The greater of	
• $130,000 (tentative minimum tax)	
• $31,250 [25% × ($150,000 – $25,000)]	(130,000)
Amount of general business credit allowed for tax year	$ 20,000

Floyd then has $50,000 ($70,000 – $20,000) of unused general business credits that may be carried back or forward to other tax years. ■

TREATMENT OF UNUSED GENERAL BUSINESS CREDITS

Unused general business credits initially are carried back one tax year, to reduce the tax liability during that year. Thus, the taxpayer may receive a tax refund as a result of the carryback. Any remaining unused credits then are carried forward for up to 20 tax years.[4]

A FIFO method is applied to the carrybacks, carryovers, and utilization of credits earned during a tax year. The oldest credits are used first in determining the amount of the general business credit. The FIFO method minimizes the potential for loss of a general business credit benefit due to the expiration of credit carryovers, since the earliest years are used before the current credit for the taxable year.

EXAMPLE 8

This example illustrates the use of general business credit carryovers.

General business credit carryovers	
2008	$ 4,000
2009	6,000
2010	2,000
Total carryovers	$12,000

[1] The separate credits are listed in § 38(b).
[2] § 38(c).
[3] This amount is $12,500 for married taxpayers filing separately unless one of the spouses is not entitled to the general business credit.
[4] § 39(a)(1).

2011 general business credit		$ 40,000
Total credit allowed in 2011 (based on tax liability)	$50,000	
Less: Utilization of carryovers		
2008	(4,000)	
2009	(6,000)	
2010	(2,000)	
Remaining credit allowed in 2011	$38,000	
Applied against		
2011 general business credit		(38,000)
2011 unused amount carried forward to 2012		$ 2,000

■

12.3 Specific Business-Related Tax Credit Provisions

LO.3

Describe various business-related tax credits.

Each component of the general business credit is determined separately under its own set of rules. Some of the more important credits that make up the general business credit are explained here in the order listed in Exhibit 12.1.

TAX CREDIT FOR REHABILITATION EXPENDITURES

Taxpayers are allowed a tax credit for expenditures incurred to rehabilitate industrial and commercial buildings and certified historic structures. The **rehabilitation expenditures credit** is intended to discourage businesses from moving from older, economically distressed areas (e.g., inner cities) to newer locations and to encourage the preservation of historic structures.[5]

Rate of the Credit for Rehabilitation Expenses	Nature of the Property
10%	Nonresidential buildings and residential rental property, other than certified historic structures, originally placed in service before 1936
20%	Nonresidential and residential certified historic structures

When taking the credit, the basis of a rehabilitated building is reduced by the full rehabilitation credit allowed.[6]

EXAMPLE 9

Juan spent $60,000 to rehabilitate a building (adjusted basis of $40,000) that had been placed in service in 1932. He is allowed a $6,000 (10% × $60,000) credit for rehabilitation expenditures. Juan then increases the basis of the building by $54,000 [$60,000 (rehabilitation expenditures) – $6,000 (credit allowed)]. If the building were a historic structure, the credit allowed would be $12,000 (20% × $60,000), and the building's depreciable basis would increase by $48,000 [$60,000 (rehabilitation expenditures) – $12,000 (credit allowed)]. ■

To qualify for the credit, buildings must be substantially rehabilitated. A building has been *substantially rehabilitated* if qualified rehabilitation expenditures exceed the greater of:

- The adjusted basis of the property before the rehabilitation expenditures, or
- $5,000.

[5] § 47.

[6] § 50(c).

TABLE 12.1 Recapture Calculation for Rehabilitation Expenditures Credit

If the Property Is Held for	The Recapture Percentage Is
Less than 1 year	100
One year or more but less than 2 years	80
Two years or more but less than 3 years	60
Three years or more but less than 4 years	40
Four years or more but less than 5 years	20
Five years or more	0

Qualified rehabilitation expenditures do not include the cost of acquiring a building, the cost of facilities related to a building (such as a parking lot), and the cost of enlarging an existing building.

Recapture of Tax Credit for Rehabilitation Expenditures

The rehabilitation credit taken must be recaptured if the rehabilitated property is disposed of prematurely or if it ceases to be qualifying property. The **rehabilitation expenditures credit recapture** is based on a holding period requirement of five years and is added to the taxpayer's regular tax liability in the recapture year. The recapture amount also is *added* to the adjusted basis of the property for purposes of determining gain or loss realized upon disposition.

The portion of the credit recaptured is a specified percentage of the credit that was taken by the taxpayer. This percentage is based on the period the property was held by the taxpayer, as shown in Table 12.1.

EXAMPLE 10

On March 15, 2008, Rashad placed in service $30,000 of rehabilitation expenditures on a building qualifying for the 10% credit. A credit of $3,000 ($30,000 × 10%) was allowed, and the basis of the building was increased by $27,000 ($30,000 − $3,000). The building was sold on December 15, 2011. Rashad must recapture a portion of the rehabilitation credit, based on the schedule in Table 12.1. Because he held the rehabilitated property for more than three years but less than four, 40% of the credit, or $1,200, is added to his 2011 tax liability. The adjusted basis of the rehabilitation expenditures is increased by the $1,200 recapture amount. ■

ETHICS & Equity

THE REHABILITATION TAX CREDIT

Your brother—who buys, modernizes, and sells buildings in a large metropolitan city—has come to you for advice. Given the recent credit market conditions, business has been tough, and he has sold only a few buildings. One of your brother's buildings is a certified historic structure that would qualify for the 20 percent rehabilitation tax credit. Based on several recent appraisals, the building is currently worth $400,000. The expenditures needed to rehabilitate the building would be about $250,000, all of which would qualify for the rehabilitation tax credit.

Your brother has been approached by an individual who is interested in buying the building. The customer has offered to pay your brother $300,000 for the building and $350,000 for the rehabilitation work. This approach would provide the customer with a larger tax credit ($350,000 × 20% versus $250,000 × 20%) and provide a needed sale for your brother's business. How do you respond?

JOBS CREDIT

A $1,000 jobs credit is allowed for every unemployed individual who is hired from February 4 through December 31, 2010, and who works for the employer for at least 52 consecutive weeks. The employee's wages during 13 of the last 26 weeks of work must equal at least 80 percent of the wages for the first 26 weeks of employment. The credit applies to any tax year ending after the date of enactment of the 2010 jobs bill.

WORK OPPORTUNITY TAX CREDIT

The **work opportunity tax credit** was enacted to encourage employers to hire individuals from one or more of a number of targeted and economically disadvantaged groups.[7] Examples of such targeted persons include qualified ex-felons, high-risk youths, food stamp recipients, veterans, summer youth employees, and long-term family assistance recipients.

Computation of the Work Opportunity Tax Credit: General

The credit generally is equal to 40 percent of the first $6,000 of wages (per eligible employee) for the first 12 months of employment. If the credit is taken, the employer's tax deduction for wages is reduced by the amount of the credit.

For an employer to qualify for the 40 percent credit, the employee must (1) be certified by a designated local agency as being a member of one of the targeted groups and (2) have completed at least 400 hours of service to the employer. If an employee meets the first condition but not the second, the credit rate is reduced to 25 percent provided the employee has completed a minimum of 120 hours of service to the employer.

EXAMPLE 11

In January 2011, Green Company hires four individuals who are certified to be members of a qualifying targeted group. Each employee works 800 hours and is paid wages of $8,000 during the year. Green Company's work opportunity credit is $9,600 [($6,000 × 40%) × 4 employees]. If the tax credit is taken, Green must reduce its deduction for wages paid by $9,600. No credit is available for wages paid to these employees after their first year of employment. ■

EXAMPLE 12

On June 1, 2011, Maria, a calendar year taxpayer, hires Joe, a certified member of a targeted group. During the last seven months of 2011, Joe is paid $3,500 for 500 hours of work. Maria is allowed a credit of $1,400 ($3,500 × 40%) for 2011. Joe continues to work for Maria in 2012 and is paid $7,000 through May 31, 2012. Because up to $6,000 of first-year wages are eligible for the credit, Maria is allowed a 40% credit on $2,500 [$6,000 − $3,500 (wages paid in 2011)] of wages paid in 2012, or $1,000 ($2,500 × 40%). None of Joe's wages paid after May 31, the end of the first year of employment, is eligible for the credit. ■

Computation of the Work Opportunity Tax Credit: Qualified Summer Youth Employees

The credit for qualified summer youth employees is allowed on wages for services during any 90-day period between May 1 and September 15.[8] The maximum wages eligible for the credit are $3,000 per summer youth employee. The credit rate is the same as that for the work opportunity tax credit. If the employee continues employment after the 90-day period as a member of another targeted group, the amount of the wages eligible for the general work opportunity tax credit as a member of the new target group is reduced by the wages paid to the employee as a qualified summer youth employee.

[7] § 51. The credit is available if qualifying employees start work by December 31, 2011.

[8] § 51(d)(7).

A *qualified summer youth employee* must be age 16 or 17 on the hiring date. In addition, the individual's principal place of abode must be within an empowerment zone, enterprise community, or renewal community.

Computation of the Work Opportunity Tax Credit: Long-Term Family Assistance Recipient

A tax credit is available to employers hiring individuals who have been long-term recipients of family assistance welfare benefits. In general, *long-term recipients* are those individuals who are certified by a designated local agency as being a member of a family receiving assistance under a public aid program for at least an 18-month period ending on the hiring date. The family assistance credit is available for qualified wages paid in the *first two years* of employment. An employee's first and second work years may overlap two or more of the employer's tax years.

The credit is equal to 40 percent of the first $10,000 of qualified wages paid to an employee in the first year of employment, plus 50 percent of the first $10,000 of qualified wages paid in the second year of employment, resulting in a maximum credit per qualified employee of $9,000 [$4,000 (year 1) + $5,000 (year 2)]. The credit rate is higher for second-year wages to encourage employers to retain qualified individuals, thereby promoting the overall welfare-to-work goal.

EXAMPLE 13

In April 2011, Blue Company hired three individuals who are certified as long-term family assistance recipients. Each employee is paid $12,000 during 2011. Two of the three individuals continue to work for Blue in 2012, earning $9,000 each during the year. Blue's work opportunity tax credit is $12,000 [(40% × $10,000) × 3 employees] for 2011 and $9,000 [(50% × $9,000) × 2 employees] for 2012. In each year, Blue reduces its deduction for wages paid by the amount of the credit for that year. ■

RESEARCH ACTIVITIES CREDIT

To encourage research and experimentation, usually described as research and development (R&D), a credit is allowed for certain qualifying expenditures paid or incurred by a taxpayer. The **research activities credit** is the *sum* of three components: an incremental research activities credit, a basic research credit, and an energy research credit.[9]

Incremental Research Activities Credit

The incremental research activities credit is 20 percent of the *excess* of qualified research expenses for the taxable year over the base amount.[10]

In general, *research expenditures* qualify if the research relates to discovering technological information that is intended for use in the development of a new or improved business component of the taxpayer. Such expenses qualify fully if the research is performed in-house (by the taxpayer or employees). If the research is conducted by persons outside the taxpayer's business (under contract), only 65 percent of the amount paid qualifies for the credit.[11]

EXAMPLE 14

George incurs the following research expenditures:

In-house wages, supplies, computer time	$50,000
Paid to Cutting Edge Scientific Foundation for research	30,000

George's qualified research expenditures are $69,500 [$50,000 + ($30,000 × 65%)]. ■

[9] § 41. Each component of the research credit is available only if qualifying expenditures are paid or incurred by December 31, 2011.

[10] In lieu of determining the incremental research credit as described here, a taxpayer may elect to calculate the credit using an alternative simplified credit procedure. See §§ 41(c)(4) and (5).

[11] In the case of payments to a qualified research consortium, § 41(b)(3)(A) provides that 75% of the amount paid qualifies for the credit. In contrast, for amounts paid to an energy research consortium, § 41(b)(3)(D) allows the full amount to qualify for the credit.

Beyond the general guidelines described above, the Code does not give specific examples of qualifying research. However, the credit is *not* allowed for research that falls into certain categories, including the following.[12]

- Research conducted after the beginning of commercial production of the business component.
- Surveys and studies such as market research, testing, or routine data collection.
- Research conducted *outside* the United States (other than research undertaken in Puerto Rico or possessions of the United States).
- Research in the social sciences, arts, or humanities.

Determining the *base amount* involves a relatively complex series of computations, meant to approximate recent historical levels of research activity by the taxpayer. Thus, the credit is allowed only for increases in research expenses.

EXAMPLE 15

Jack, a calendar year taxpayer, incurs qualifying research expenditures of $200,000 at the beginning of the year. If Jack's base amount is $100,000, the incremental research activities credit is $20,000 [($200,000 – $100,000) × 20%]. ■

Qualified research and experimentation expenditures are not only eligible for the 20 percent credit, but they also can be *deducted* in the year incurred.[13] In this regard, a taxpayer has two choices.[14]

- Use the full credit and reduce the expense deduction for research expenses by 100 percent of the credit.
- Retain the full expense deduction and reduce the credit by the product of 100 percent of the credit times the maximum corporate tax rate (35 percent).

As an alternative to the expense deduction, the taxpayer may capitalize the research expenses and amortize them over 60 months or more. In this case, the amount capitalized and subject to amortization is reduced by the full amount of the credit only if the credit exceeds the amount allowable as a deduction.

EXAMPLE 16

Assume the same facts as in Example 15, which shows that the potential incremental research activities credit is $20,000. The current-year deduction and corresponding credit are computed as follows.

	Credit Amount	Deduction Amount
• **Full credit and reduced deduction**		
$20,000 – $0	$20,000	
$200,000 – $20,000		$180,000
• **Reduced credit and full deduction**		
$20,000 – [(100% × $20,000) × 35%]	13,000	
$200,000 – $0		200,000
• **Full credit and capitalize and elect to amortize costs over 60 months**		
$20,000 – $0	20,000	
($200,000/60) × 12		40,000

■

[12] § 41(d). Reg. §§ 1.41–1 through 1.41–7.

[13] § 174. Refer to the discussion of rules for deducting research and experimental expenditures in Chapter 7.

[14] § 280C(c).

ETHICS
& Equity

When Does "Research" Qualify as R&D?

The research activities credit is designed to encourage taxpayers to engage in research related to the discovery of technological information for use in developing a new or improved business component of the taxpayer.

You are employed as a staff accountant for a privately held corporation that manufactures medical equipment. During the current year, the corporation purchases new communications software and related document-management systems with the goal of enhancing employee efficiency and productivity. To familiarize employees with these new systems, an outside firm is hired to conduct training seminars during the first six months after the software is installed. Substantial costs are incurred in connection with these training seminars. Not surprisingly, the firm encounters various inefficiencies until the employees have had sufficient training and time to learn the new systems.

The corporation's new president, ever mindful of the company's profitability and tax position, urges you to claim the research activities credit with respect to the software training costs. The president justifies this position on the grounds that the employees were "researching" the new software and its use. How do you respond?

Basic Research Credit

Corporations (other than S corporations or personal service corporations) are allowed an additional 20 percent credit for basic research payments made in excess of a base amount. This credit is not available to individual taxpayers. Basic research payments are amounts paid in cash to a qualified basic research organization, such as a college or university, or a tax-exempt organization operated primarily to conduct scientific research.

Basic research is any original investigation for the advancement of scientific knowledge not having a specific commercial objective. The definition excludes basic research conducted outside the United States and basic research in the social sciences, arts, or humanities. This reflects the intent of Congress to encourage high-tech research in the United States.

The calculation of this additional credit for basic research expenditures is based on expenditures in excess of a specially defined base amount. The portion of the basic research expenditures not in excess of the base amount is treated as a part of the qualifying expenditures for purposes of the regular credit for incremental research activities.

EXAMPLE 17

Orange Corporation pays $75,000 to a university for basic research. Orange's base amount for the basic research credit is $50,000. The basic research activities credit allowed is $5,000 [($75,000 − $50,000) × 20%]. The $50,000 base amount for basic research is treated as research expenses for purposes of the regular incremental research activities credit. ■

Energy Research Credit

This credit was designed to stimulate additional energy research. The credit is 20 percent of the amounts paid or incurred by a taxpayer to an energy research consortium for energy research.

LOW-INCOME HOUSING CREDIT

To encourage building owners to make available affordable housing for low-income individuals, Congress has made a credit available to owners of qualified low-income housing projects.[15]

More than any other, the **low-income housing credit** is influenced by nontax factors. For example, the property must be certified by an appropriate state or local agency. These credits are issued based on a nationwide allocation of congressional funding.

[15] § 42.

The credit is based on the qualified basis of the property. The qualified basis depends on the number of units rented to low-income tenants. Tenants are low-income tenants if their income does not exceed a specified percentage of the area median gross income. The credit is determined by multiplying the qualified basis by a credit rate. The credit is allowed over a 10-year period, as long as the property continues to meet the required conditions.

EXAMPLE 18

Sarah spends $1 million to build a qualified low-income housing project that is completed on January 1 of the current year. The entire project is rented to low-income families. The credit rate for property placed in service during January is 7.67%.[16] Sarah claims a credit of $76,700 ($1,000,000 × 7.67%) in the current year and in each of the following nine years. ■

Recapture of a portion of the credit may be required if the number of units set aside for low-income tenants falls below a minimum threshold, if the taxpayer disposes of the property or the interest in it, or if the taxpayer's amount at risk decreases.

ETHICS & *Equity*

A "WIN-WIN" SITUATION?

Tom and Sarah Prentice rent an apartment in a complex owned by Steve Heatherton, who has been a close friend since high school. About a week ago, Steve told Tom about the tax savings he has received by claiming the low-income housing credit on all of his apartment complexes—including the one in which the Prentices live.

Initially, Tom was pleased that Steve had been able to use this government "subsidy" to reduce his tax burden because, in general, he believes that the government rarely uses its resources wisely. However, during the conversation, Steve inadvertently let slip the fact that the apartment complex in which the Prentices live qualifies for the credit only because he overstates the percentage of low-income tenants living in the facility.

Steve admitted that by claiming that the Prentices are low-income tenants (even though they aren't), the percentage of low-income tenants is just enough for Steve to "qualify" for the credit on the complex. Steve said that because Tom and Sarah are his friends, he was passing along some of his tax savings to them in the form of lower rent.

Tom knows that if he were to report Steve to the IRS, Steve would not only lose the economic benefits of the credit, but he also would run into legal troubles—and could be sentenced to prison. In addition, Tom and Sarah would see an increase in their rent. Tom has come to you for advice. What course of action would you recommend to Tom?

DISABLED ACCESS CREDIT

The **disabled access credit** is designed to encourage small businesses to make their facilities more accessible to disabled individuals. The credit is available for any eligible access expenditures paid or incurred by an eligible small business. The credit is calculated at the rate of 50 percent of the eligible expenditures that exceed $250 but do not exceed $10,250. Thus, the maximum amount for the credit is $5,000 ($10,000 × 50%).[17]

An *eligible small business* is one that during the previous year either had gross receipts of $1 million or less or had no more than 30 full-time employees. An eligible business can include a sole proprietorship, partnership, regular corporation, or S corporation.

Eligible access expenditures include reasonable and necessary amounts that are paid or incurred to make certain changes to facilities. These changes must involve the removal of architectural, communication, physical, or transportation barriers that would otherwise make a business inaccessible to disabled and handicapped individuals. Examples of qualifying projects include installing ramps, widening doorways,

[16]The rate is subject to adjustment every month by the IRS.

[17]§ 44.

and adding raised markings on elevator control buttons. However, eligible expenditures do *not* include amounts that are paid or incurred in connection with any facility that first was placed in service after November 5, 1990.

To the extent a disabled access credit is available, no deduction or credit is allowed under any other provision of the tax law. The adjusted basis for depreciation is reduced by the amount of the credit.

EXAMPLE 19

This year Red, Inc., an eligible business, makes $11,000 of capital improvements to business realty that had been placed in service in June 1990. The expenditures are intended to make Red's business more accessible to the disabled and are considered eligible expenditures for purposes of the disabled access credit. The amount of the credit is $5,000 [($10,250 − $250) × 50%]. Although $11,000 of eligible expenditures are incurred, only the excess of $10,250 over $250 qualifies for the credit. The depreciable basis of the capital improvement is $6,000, because the basis is reduced by the amount of the credit [$11,000 (cost) − $5,000 (amount of the credit)]. ■

CREDIT FOR SMALL EMPLOYER PENSION PLAN STARTUP COSTS

Small businesses are entitled to a nonrefundable credit for administrative costs associated with establishing and maintaining certain qualified retirement plans.[18] While such costs (e.g., payroll system changes, consulting fees) generally are deductible as ordinary and necessary business expenses, the credit is intended to lower the after-tax cost of establishing a qualified retirement program and thereby to encourage qualifying businesses to offer retirement plans for their employees.

The **credit for small employer pension plan startup costs** is available for eligible employers at the rate of 50 percent of qualified startup costs. An eligible employer is one with fewer than 100 employees who have earned at least $5,000 of compensation. Qualified startup costs include ordinary and necessary expenses incurred in connection with establishing or maintaining an employer pension plan and retirement-related education costs.[19]

The maximum credit is $500 (based on a maximum $1,000 of qualifying expenses), and the deduction for the startup costs incurred is reduced by the amount of the credit. The credit can be claimed for qualifying costs incurred in each of the three years beginning with the tax year in which the retirement plan becomes effective (maximum total credit over three years of $1,500).

EXAMPLE 20

Maple Company decides to establish a qualified retirement plan for its employees. In the process, it pays consulting fees of $1,200 to a firm that provides educational seminars to Maple's employees and assists in making necessary changes to the payroll system. Maple may claim a credit for the pension plan startup costs of $500 ($1,200 of qualifying costs, limited to $1,000 × 50%), and its deduction for these expenses is reduced to $700 ($1,200 − $500). ■

CREDIT FOR EMPLOYER-PROVIDED CHILD CARE

The scope of § 162 trade or business expenses includes an employer's expenditures incurred to provide for the care of children of employees as ordinary and necessary business expenses. Alternatively, employers may claim a credit for qualifying expenditures incurred while providing child care facilities to their employees during normal working hours.[20] The **credit for employer-provided child care**, limited annually to $150,000, is composed of the aggregate of two components: 25 percent of qualified child care expenses and 10 percent of qualified child care resource and referral services.

[18] § 45E. This credit is scheduled to expire for years after 2012.

[19] §§ 45E(c)(1) and (d)(1).

[20] § 45F. This credit is scheduled to expire for years after 2012.

Qualified child care expenses include the costs of acquiring, constructing, rehabilitating, expanding, and operating a child care facility. *Child care resource and referral services* include amounts paid or incurred under a contract to provide child care resource and referral services to an employee.

Any qualifying expenses otherwise deductible by the taxpayer are reduced by the amount of the credit. In addition, the taxpayer's basis for any property acquired or constructed and used for qualifying purposes is reduced by the amount of the credit. If within 10 years of being placed in service, a child care facility ceases to be used for a qualified use, the taxpayer will be required to recapture a portion of the credit previously claimed.[21]

EXAMPLE 21

During the year, Tan Company constructed a child care facility for $400,000 to be used by its employees who have preschool-aged children in need of child care services while their parents are at work. In addition, Tan incurred salaries for child care workers and other administrative costs associated with the facility of $100,000. As a result, Tan's credit for employer-provided child care is $125,000 [($400,000 + $100,000) × 25%]. Correspondingly, the basis of the facility is reduced to $300,000 ($400,000 – $100,000), and the deduction for salaries and administrative costs is reduced to $75,000 ($100,000 – $25,000). ■

12.4 Other Tax Credits

EARNED INCOME CREDIT

LO.4

Describe various tax credits that are available primarily to individual taxpayers.

The **earned income credit,** which has been a part of the law for many years, consistently has been justified as a means of providing tax equity to the working poor. In addition, the credit has been designed to reimburse the taxpayer for certain other Federal taxes, such as the gasoline and Social Security taxes. Further, the credit is intended to encourage economically disadvantaged individuals to become contributing members of the workforce.[22]

The earned income credit is determined by multiplying a maximum amount of earned income by the appropriate credit percentage. Generally, earned income includes employee compensation and net earnings from self-employment but excludes items such as interest, dividends, pension benefits, nontaxable employee compensation, and alimony. If a taxpayer has children, the credit percentage used in the calculation depends on the number of qualifying children.

To simplify the compliance process, the IRS issues an Earned Income Credit Table for the determination of the appropriate amount of the credit. This table and a worksheet are included in the instructions available to individual taxpayers.

Eligibility Requirements

Eligibility for the credit depends not only on the taxpayer meeting the earned income and AGI thresholds (shown in the IRS tables), but also on whether he or she has a qualifying child. The term *qualifying child* generally has the same meaning here as it does for purposes of determining who qualifies as a dependent (see Chapter 3).

In addition to being available for taxpayers with qualifying children, the earned income credit is available to certain *workers without children.* However, this provision is available only to taxpayers aged 25 through 64 who cannot be claimed as a dependent on another taxpayer's return.

For 2011, the maximum earned income credit is $3,094 for a taxpayer with one qualifying child, $5,112 for a taxpayer with two qualifying children, and $5,751 for a taxpayer with three or more qualifying children. A taxpayer with no qualifying

[21] § 45F(d).

[22] § 32. The 2011 earned income credit is not available if the taxpayer's unearned income (e.g., interest, dividends) exceeds $3,150.

children can qualify for an earned income credit up to a maximum of $464. The credit is available for a taxpayer who is married filing jointly, single, or as a head of household. The credit phases out to zero as earned income increases from about $22,000 to about $50,000.[23] Amounts in the IRS table are indexed annually.

EXAMPLE 22

Maria, age 30, reports earned income for the year of $6,000. She is single and has no children. Maria can qualify for an earned income credit. ■

EXAMPLE 23

Willa, age 20, reports earned income for the year of $6,000. She is single and has no children. Willa does not qualify for an earned income credit until she reaches age 25. ■

Advance Payment

The earned income credit is a form of negative income tax; that is, it is a refundable credit for taxpayers who do not have a tax liability. An eligible individual may elect to receive advance payments of the earned income credit from his or her employer (rather than only receiving the credit from the IRS upon filing the tax return). The amount that can be received in advance is limited to 60 percent of the credit that is available to a taxpayer with only one qualifying child. If this election is made, the taxpayer files a certificate of eligibility (Form W–5) with his or her employer and *must* file a tax return for the year the income is earned.[24]

ETHICS *& Equity*

HOLDING ON TO THE EARNED INCOME CREDIT WITH THE AID OF A TRANSIENT CHILD

For many years, Loretta Johnson, a single mother of three children, has been struggling to make ends meet by working at two jobs that barely pay the minimum wage and together provide just over $10,000. Fortunately, her housing and food costs have been partially subsidized through various government programs. In addition, she has been able to take advantage of the earned income credit, which has provided almost $3,000 annually to help her with living expenses.

The credit truly has made a difference in the lives of Loretta and her family by helping them keep their creditors at bay. Loretta is proud that she has worked hard and provided for her family for many years without having to accept welfare.

Now, however, Loretta faces a problem as her children have grown up and moved out of her home. With no qualifying children in her household, she no longer qualifies for the earned income credit. Although she will continue working her two jobs, such a significant loss to her household budget cuts into her ability to be self-reliant.

As a survival strategy and as a way of keeping the earned income credit, Loretta arranges to have one of her grandchildren live with her for just over six months every year. This enables almost 30 percent of her household budget to be secure. How do you react to Loretta's tax strategy?

TAX CREDIT FOR ELDERLY OR DISABLED TAXPAYERS

The credit for the elderly was enacted to provide tax relief on retirement income for individuals who were not receiving substantial benefits from tax-free Social Security payments.[25] Currently, the **tax credit for the elderly or disabled** is available to the following.

- Taxpayers age 65 or older.
- Taxpayers under age 65 who are retired with a **permanent and total disability** and who have disability income from a public or private employer on account of the disability. A person generally is considered permanently and

[23] § 32(a)(2)(B).

[24] § 3507. Advance payments are not available after 2010.

[25] § 22. This credit is not subject to indexation.

TAX *in the NEWS*

THE EARNED INCOME CREDIT: A BOOST TO THE WORKING POOR AND MERCHANTS, TOO!

Since 1975, the earned income credit has helped keep millions of Americans from falling below the poverty line. Representing one of the nation's biggest antipoverty efforts, the earned income credit benefits about 22 million households (about one-fifth of all households) at a cost to the Federal government of over $40 billion. However, these benefits don't come without problems: fraudulent claims are believed to be common (the IRS estimates that over 30 percent of the benefits are paid in error), and compliance requirements are dauntingly complex (the IRS publication covering the earned income credit totals almost 60 pages).

The benefits from the earned income credit that flow to the working poor have also led to another problem. Some merchants target this group of taxpayers—and their refunds. Pawn shops, jewelers, and auto dealerships in poor neighborhoods often offer to prepare tax returns, hoping to benefit in three ways: they collect fees for preparing the returns, they offer bridge loans at exorbitant interest rates before a tax refund arrives, and they sell high-priced goods to individuals expecting a windfall from their tax refunds.

Some of these merchants provide fair and valuable assistance to many needy taxpayers; however, many other merchants are in this niche for the sole purpose of lining their own pockets. The caveat "buyer beware" could never be more appropriate.

totally disabled if he or she is unable to engage in any substantial gainful activity due to a physical or mental impairment for a period of at least 12 months (or lesser period if the disability results in death).

The *maximum* allowable credit is $1,125 (15% × $7,500 of qualifying income), but the credit is less for a taxpayer who receives Social Security benefits or has AGI exceeding specified amounts. Most taxpayers receive Social Security benefits or have AGI high enough to reduce the base for the credit to zero. In addition, because the credit is nonrefundable, the allowable credit cannot exceed the taxpayer's tax liablity.

Usually, an individual uses an IRS table or elects to have the IRS compute his or her tax credit. Schedule R of Form 1040 is used to calculate and report the credit.

FOREIGN TAX CREDIT

Individual taxpayers and corporations may claim a tax credit for foreign income tax paid on income earned and subject to tax in another country or a U.S. possession.[26] As an alternative, a taxpayer may claim a deduction instead of a credit.[27] In most instances, the **foreign tax credit (FTC)** is more advantageous since it provides a direct offset against the U.S. tax liability.

The FTC is designed to mitigate double taxation since income earned in a foreign country by a U.S. person is subject to both U.S. and foreign taxes. However, the FTC ceiling still may result in some form of double taxation or taxation at rates in excess of U.S. rates when the foreign tax rates are higher than the U.S. rates. This can occur because effective U.S. tax rates often are lower than those of the trading partner countries.

Other special tax treatments applicable to taxpayers working outside the United States include the foreign earned income exclusion (refer to Chapter 5) and deductions for expenses of employees working outside the United States (refer to Chapter 9).

Unused FTCs are carried back 1 year and forward 10 years.[28] The FTC is discussed in greater detail in Chapter 25.

[26] Section 27 provides for the credit, but the qualifications and calculation procedure for the credit are contained in §§ 901–908.

[27] § 164.

[28] § 904(c) and Reg. § 1.904–2(g), Example 1.

GLOBAL
Tax Issues

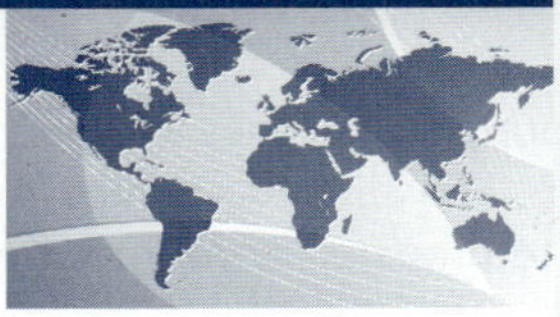

Sourcing Income in Cyberspace—Getting It Right When Calculating the Foreign Tax Credit

The limitation on the foreign tax credit (FTC) plays a critical role in restricting the amount of the credit available to a taxpayer. In the FTC formula, the taxpayer characterizes the year's taxable income as either earned (or sourced) inside the United States or earned from sources outside the United States. As a general rule, a relatively greater percentage of foreign-source income in the formula leads to a larger FTC. Therefore, determining the source of various types of income is critical in the proper calculation of the credit. However, classifying income as either foreign or U.S. source is not always a simple matter.

Consumers and businesses use the Internet to conduct commerce involving both products and services. But the existing income-sourcing rules were developed long before the existence of the Internet, and taxing authorities are finding it challenging to apply these rules to Internet transactions. Where does a sale take place when the web server is in Scotland, the seller is in India, and the customer is in Illinois? Where is a service performed when all activities take place over the Net?

Computation

The FTC allowed is the *lesser* of the foreign taxes imposed or the FTC *overall limitation*, which is equal to the Federal income tax paid on the double-taxed income.[29]

EXAMPLE 24

Yellow, based in the United States sells widgets in Peru. Profits for the year in that country total $2 million. Yellow is subject to a 34% U.S. income tax rate, and a 20% income tax rate applies in Peru. Thus, attributable income taxes for this double-taxed income are $680,000 for the U.S. tax, and $400,000 for the Peru tax.

Yellow pays the full $400,000 tax to Peru. Its U.S. tax on this income is $680,000 minus the $400,000 foreign tax credit (lesser of $400,000 foreign tax paid or $680,000 attributable U.S. tax), or $280,000. The FTC allows a full recovery of the $400,000 tax paid to Peru. ■

EXAMPLE 25

Continue with the facts of Example 24, except that the applicable Peru tax rate is 40%, for an $800,000 liability. Yellow pays the full $800,000 tax to Peru. Its U.S. tax on this income is $680,000 minus the $680,000 foreign tax credit (lesser of $800,000 foreign tax paid or $680,000 attributable U.S. tax), or $0.

The FTC overall limitation did not allow a full recovery of the $800,000 Peru liability. The widget profits are subject to a $120,000 double tax this year, even after the FTC is applied. The $120,000 excess amount is carried back 1 tax year and then forward 10 years. ■

Only foreign income taxes, war profits taxes, and excess profits taxes (or taxes paid in lieu of such taxes) qualify for the credit.[30] In determining whether or not a tax is an income tax, U.S. criteria are applied. Thus, value added taxes (VAT), severance taxes, property taxes, and sales taxes do not qualify because they are not regarded as taxes on income. Such taxes still are deducted by the taxpayer, however.

[29] § 904.

[30] Reg. § 1.901–1(a)(3)(i).

TAX *in* *the NEWS*

FTC CRACKDOWN

To identify aggressive corporate tax avoidance through a pooling of expertise, tax authorities in Australia, Canada, the United Kingdom, and the United States have set up an international task force, known as the Joint International Tax Shelter Information Centre. The tax authorities hope that the task force will enhance their ability to curb abusive tax avoidance schemes.

Among other things, the members of the task force are scrutinizing tax arbitrage schemes used by multinational corporations and are also examining the work of accountants, bankers, and attorneys who advise companies on tax avoidance strategies. Recent work has focused on transactions by U.S. taxpayers with foreign counterparts to generate foreign tax credits.

A former IRS Commissioner said that the task force is necessary because, in contrast to previous tax avoidance schemes when taxpayers would simply try to take advantage of the nation with the most favorable tax rate, "we are seeing now that entities are trying to structure transactions which result in the payment of no tax at all. That is clearly of concern."

Sources: Adapted from *Financial Times* (February 27, 2005) and "Tax Matters," *Journal of Accountancy* (June 2007).

ADOPTION EXPENSES CREDIT

Adoption expenses paid or incurred by a taxpayer may give rise to the **adoption expenses credit**.[31] The provision assists taxpayers who incur nonrecurring costs directly associated with the adoption process, such as adoption fees, attorney fees, court costs, social service review costs, and transportation costs.

In 2011, up to $13,360 of costs incurred to adopt an eligible child qualify for the credit.[32] An eligible child is one who is:

- under 18 years of age at the time of the adoption or
- physically or mentally incapable of taking care of himself or herself.

A taxpayer may claim the credit in the year qualifying expenses were paid or incurred if they were paid or incurred *during or after* the tax year in which the adoption was finalized. For qualifying expenses paid or incurred in a tax year *prior* to the year when the adoption was finalized, the credit is claimed in the tax year following the tax year during which the expenses are paid or incurred. A married couple must file a joint return to claim the credit.

EXAMPLE 26

In late 2010, Sam and Martha pay $5,000 in legal fees, adoption fees, and other expenses directly related to the adoption of an infant daughter, Susan. In 2011, the year in which the adoption becomes final, they pay an additional $15,000. Sam and Martha are eligible for a $13,360 credit in 2011 (for expenses of $20,000, limited by the credit ceiling, paid in the two tax years). ■

The amount of the credit that otherwise is available is phased out for taxpayers whose AGI (modified for this purpose) exceeds $185,210 in 2011, and the credit is completely eliminated when AGI reaches $225,210. The credit is calculated by reducing the allowable amount (determined without this reduction) by the allowable credit multiplied by the ratio of the excess of the taxpayer's AGI over $185,210 to $40,000.[33]

EXAMPLE 27

Assume the same facts as in the previous example, except that Sam and Martha's AGI is $210,210 in 2011. As a result, their available 2011 credit is reduced from $13,360 to $5,010 {$13,360 − [$13,360 × ($25,000/$40,000)]}. ■

[31] § 23.

[32] § 23(b)(1). This ceiling is adjusted for inflation annually. Special rules are used in calculating the credit when adopting "a child with special needs." See § 23(d)(3).

[33] § 23(b)(2). The AGI threshold amount is indexed for inflation.

The credit is nonrefundable and is available to taxpayers only in a year in which this credit and the other nonrefundable credits do not exceed the taxpayer's tax liability. However, any unused adoption expenses credit may be carried over for up to five years, being utilized on a first-in, first-out basis.

CHILD TAX CREDIT

The **child tax credit** provisions allow individual taxpayers to take a tax credit based solely on the *number* of their qualifying children. This credit is one of several "family-friendly" provisions that currently are part of our tax law. To be eligible for the credit, the child must be under age 17, a U.S. citizen, and claimed as a dependent on the taxpayer's return. A portion of the credit is refundable.

Maximum Credit and Phaseouts

The maximum credit available is $1,000 per child.[34] The available credit is phased out for higher-income taxpayers beginning when AGI reaches $110,000 for joint filers ($55,000 for married taxpayers filing separately) and $75,000 for single taxpayers. The credit is phased out by $50 for each $1,000 (or part thereof) of AGI above the threshold amounts.[35] Since the maximum credit amount available to taxpayers depends on the number of qualifying children, the income level at which the credit is phased out completely also depends on the number of children qualifying for the credit.

EXAMPLE 28

Juanita and Alberto are married and file a joint tax return claiming their two children, ages six and eight, as dependents. Their AGI is $122,400. Juanita and Alberto's maximum child tax credit is $2,000 ($1,000 × 2 children). Since Juanita and Alberto's AGI is in excess of the $110,000 threshold, the maximum credit is reduced by $50 for every $1,000 (or part thereof) above the threshold amount {$50 × [($122,400 − $110,000)/$1,000]}. Thus, the credit reduction equals $650 [$50 × 13 (rounded from 12.4)], and Juanita and Alberto's child tax credit is $1,350. ■

CREDIT FOR CHILD AND DEPENDENT CARE EXPENSES

A credit is allowed to taxpayers who incur employment-related expenses for child or dependent care.[36] The **credit for child and dependent care expenses** is a specified percentage of expenses incurred to enable the taxpayer to work or to seek employment. Expenses on which the credit for child and dependent care expenses is based are subject to limitations.

Eligibility

To be eligible for the credit, an individual must have either of the following.

- A dependent under age 13.
- A dependent or spouse who is physically or mentally incapacitated and who lives with the taxpayer for more than one-half of the year.

Generally, married taxpayers must file a joint return to obtain the credit.

Eligible Employment-Related Expenses

Eligible expenses include amounts paid for household services and care of a qualifying individual that are incurred to enable the taxpayer to be employed. Child and dependent care expenses include expenses incurred in the home, such as payments for a housekeeper. Out-of-the-home expenses incurred for the care of a dependent under the age of 13 also qualify for the credit. In addition, out-of-the-home expenses

[34] § 24. The maximum credit per child is scheduled to remain at $1,000 through 2012.

[35] AGI is modified for purposes of this calculation. The threshold amounts are *not* indexed for inflation. See §§ 24(a) and (b).

[36] § 21.

incurred for an older dependent or spouse who is physically or mentally incapacitated qualify for the credit if that person regularly spends at least eight hours each day in the taxpayer's household. This makes the credit available to taxpayers who keep handicapped older children and elderly relatives in the home, instead of institutionalizing them. Out-of-the-home expenses incurred for services provided by a dependent care center qualify only if the center complies with all applicable laws and regulations of a state or unit of local government.

Child care payments to a relative are eligible for the credit unless the relative is a child (under age 19) of the taxpayer.

EXAMPLE 29

Wilma is an employed mother of an eight-year-old child. She pays her mother, Rita, $1,500 per year to care for the child after school. Wilma pays her daughter Eleanor, age 17, $900 for the child's care during the summer. Of these amounts, only the $1,500 paid to Rita qualifies as employment-related child care expenses. ■

Earned Income Ceiling

Qualifying employment-related expenses are limited to an individual's earned income. For married taxpayers, this limitation applies to the spouse with the *lesser* amount of earned income. Special rules are provided for taxpayers with nonworking spouses who are disabled or are full-time students. If a nonworking spouse is physically or mentally disabled or is a full-time student, he or she is *deemed* to have earned income for purposes of this limitation. The deemed amount is $250 per month if there is one qualifying individual in the household or $500 per month if there are two or more qualifying individuals in the household. In the case of a student-spouse, the student's income is *deemed* to be earned only for the months that the student is enrolled on a full-time basis at an educational institution.[37]

Calculating the Credit

In general, the credit is equal to a percentage of *unreimbursed* employment-related expenses up to $3,000 for one qualifying individual and $6,000 for two or more individuals. The credit rate varies between 20 percent and 35 percent, depending on the taxpayer's AGI.

Adjusted Gross Income		
Over	**But Not Over**	**Applicable Rate of Credit**
$ 0	$15,000	35%
15,000	17,000	34%
17,000	19,000	33%
19,000	21,000	32%
21,000	23,000	31%
23,000	25,000	30%
25,000	27,000	29%
27,000	29,000	28%
29,000	31,000	27%
31,000	33,000	26%
33,000	35,000	25%
35,000	37,000	24%
37,000	39,000	23%
39,000	41,000	22%
41,000	43,000	21%
43,000	No limit	20%

[37] § 21(d).

EXAMPLE 30

Nancy, who has two children under age 13, worked full-time while her husband, Raji, was attending college for 10 months during the year. Nancy earned $22,000 and incurred $6,200 of child care expenses. Raji is *deemed* to be fully employed and to have earned $500 for each of the 10 months (or a total of $5,000). Since Nancy and Raji have AGI of $22,000, they are allowed a credit rate of 31%.

Nancy and Raji are limited to $5,000 in qualified child care expenses ($6,000 maximum expenses, limited to Raji's $5,000 earned income). Therefore, the couple is entitled to a tax credit of $1,550 (31% × $5,000) for the year. ■

Dependent Care Assistance Program

Recall from Chapter 5 that a taxpayer is allowed an exclusion from gross income for a limited amount reimbursed for child or dependent care expenses. However, the taxpayer is not allowed both an exclusion from gross income and a child and dependent care credit on the same amount. The $3,000 and $6,000 ceilings for allowable child and dependent care expenses are reduced dollar for dollar by the amount of reimbursement.[38]

ETHICS & *Equity*

USING THE CREDIT FOR CHILD AND DEPENDENT CARE EXPENSES

Your friends, Bob and Carol, have hired a child care provider to come into their home for three hours a day to care for their child while they both are at work. The child care provider, Dolores, charges $2,400 for her services for the year.

Bob and Carol have learned that up to $3,000 of qualifying expenditures will generate a credit for child and dependent care expenses, and that qualifying expenditures can include payments for housecleaning services. As a result, they ask Dolores whether she would be interested in working several hours more per week, after Bob returns from work, for the sole purpose of cleaning the house.

Bob offers to pay $600 for the additional work, and Dolores seems interested. For Bob and Carol, the net cost of the additional services would be $480 [$600 − ($600 × 20%)] due to the availability of the credit for child and dependent care expenses.

You learn of Bob and Carol's opportunity, but you think it is unfair. If you hired Dolores to perform similar housecleaning services, your net cost would be $600, and not $480, because you do not qualify for the credit. You are not sure that Bob and Carol should "take advantage" of the system in this way. How do you suppose Bob and Carol will feel, or should feel, about this "abuse" if you approach them?

EXAMPLE 31

Assume the same facts as in Example 30, except that of the $6,200 paid for child care, Nancy was reimbursed $2,500 by her employer under a qualified dependent care assistance program. Under the employer's plan, the reimbursement reduces Nancy's taxable wages. Thus, Nancy and Raji report AGI of $19,500 ($22,000 − $2,500).

The maximum amount of child care expenses for two or more dependents of $6,000 is reduced by the $2,500 reimbursement, resulting in a tax credit of $1,120 [32% × ($6,000 − $2,500)]. ■

Reporting Requirements

The credit is claimed by completing and filing Form 2441, Credit for Child and Dependent Care Expenses.

EDUCATION TAX CREDITS

Two credits, the **American Opportunity credit** and the **lifetime learning credit**,[39] are available to help qualifying low- and middle-income individuals defray the cost of higher education. The credits are available for qualifying tuition and related expenses incurred by students pursuing undergraduate or graduate degrees or vocational training. Books

[38] § 21(c).

[39] § 25A; the prior HOPE scholarship credit was modified and renamed the American Opportunity tax credit. The HOPE scholarship credit is scheduled to return in 2013.

and other course materials are eligible for the American Opportunity credit (but not the lifetime learning credit). Room and board are ineligible for both credits.

Maximum Credit

The American Opportunity credit permits a maximum credit of $2,500 per year (100 percent of the first $2,000 of tuition expenses plus 25 percent of the next $2,000 of tuition expenses) for the *first four years* of postsecondary education. The lifetime learning credit permits a credit of 20 percent of qualifying expenses (up to $10,000 per year) incurred in a year in which the American Opportunity credit is not claimed with respect to a given student. Generally, the lifetime learning credit is used for individuals who are beyond the first four years of postsecondary education.

Eligible Individuals

Both education credits are available for qualified expenses incurred by a taxpayer, taxpayer's spouse, or taxpayer's dependent. The American Opportunity credit is available for each eligible student, while the lifetime learning credit is calculated per taxpayer. To be eligible for the American Opportunity credit, a student must take at least one-half of the full-time course load for at least one academic term at a qualifying educational institution. No comparable requirement exists for the lifetime learning credit. Therefore, taxpayers who are seeking new job skills or maintaining existing skills through graduate training or continuing education are eligible for the lifetime learning credit. Taxpayers who are married must file joint returns to claim either education credit.

Income Limitations and Refundability

The education credits are subject to different income limitations. In addition, the American Opportunity credit is partially refundable and may be used to offset a taxpayer's alternative minimum tax (AMT) liability. The lifetime learning credit is neither refundable nor an AMT liability offset.

The American Opportunity credit amount is phased out, beginning when the taxpayer's AGI (modified for this purpose) reaches $80,000 ($160,000 for married taxpayers filing jointly). The reduction is equal to the extent to which AGI exceeds $80,000 ($160,000 for married taxpayers filing jointly) as a percentage of a $10,000 phaseout range ($20,000 for married taxpayers filing jointly). As a result, the credit is eliminated completely when modified AGI reaches $90,000 ($180,000 for married taxpayers filing jointly). The credit may be used to reduce a taxpayer's AMT liability. Forty percent of the American Opportunity credit is refundable.[40]

The lifetime learning credit amount is phased out, beginning when the taxpayer's AGI (modified for this purpose) reaches $51,000 ($102,000 for married taxpayers filing jointly).[41] The reduction is equal to the extent to which AGI exceeds $51,000 (or $102,000) as a percentage of a $10,000 ($20,000 for married filing jointly) phaseout range. The credit thus is eliminated when AGI reaches $61,000 ($122,000 for married filing jointly).

EXAMPLE 32
THE BIG PICTURE

Return to the facts of *The Big Picture* on p. 12-2. Recall that Tom and Jennifer Snyder are married and file a joint tax return. The Snyders report modified AGI of $158,000, and they have two children, Lora and Sam. The Snyders paid $7,500 of tuition and $8,500 for room and board for Lora (a freshman), and $8,100 of tuition plus $7,200 for room and board for Sam (a junior).

Lora and Sam are full-time students and are Tom and Jennifer's dependents. Lora's tuition and Sam's tuition are qualified expenses for the American Opportunity credit. For 2011, Tom and Jennifer may claim a $2,500 American Opportunity credit [(100% × $2,000) + (25% × $2,000)] for both Lora's and Sam's expenses (in total, a $5,000 American Opportunity credit). ■

[40] If the credit is claimed for a taxpayer subject to § 1(g) (the "kiddie tax"), the credit is not refundable.

[41] § 25A(d).

EXAMPLE 33
THE BIG PICTURE

Return to the facts of *The Big Picture* on p.12–2. Assume that Tom and Jennifer's modified AGI is $172,000, instead of $158,000. The Snyders are eligible to claim a $2,000 American Opportunity credit. Their available credit is reduced because AGI exceeds the $160,000 limit for married taxpayers. The percentage reduction is computed as the amount by which modified AGI exceeds the limit, expressed as a percentage of the phaseout range, or [($172,000 – $160,000)/$20,000)], resulting in a 60% reduction. Therefore, the maximum available credit is $2,000 ($5,000 × 40% allowable portion). ■

EXAMPLE 34
THE BIG PICTURE

Return to the facts of *The Big Picture* on p.12–2. Now assume that Tom and Jennifer's modified AGI is $116,000. In addition, assume that Tom is going to school on a part-time basis to complete a graduate degree and pays qualifying tuition and fees of $4,000. As the Snyders's modified AGI is below $160,000, a $5,000 American Opportunity credit is available to them.

In addition, Tom's qualifying expenses are eligible for the lifetime learning credit. The available lifetime learning credit ($800 = $4,000 × 20%) is reduced because modified AGI exceeds the $102,000 limit for married taxpayers. As modified AGI exceeds the $102,000 limit by $14,000 and the phaseout range is $20,000, the lifetime learning credit is reduced by 70%.

Therefore, the Snyders's lifetime learning credit is $240($800 × 30%), and total education credits amount to $5,240 ($5,000 American Opportunity credit + $240 lifetime learning credit). ■

Restrictions on Double Tax Benefit

Taxpayers are prohibited from receiving a double tax benefit associated with qualifying educational expenses. Therefore, taxpayers who claim an education credit may not deduct the expenses, nor may they claim the credit for amounts that are otherwise excluded from gross income (e.g., scholarships, employer-paid educational assistance). However, a taxpayer may claim an education tax credit and exclude from gross income amounts distributed from a Coverdell Education Savings Account as long as the distribution is not used for the same expenses for which the credit is claimed.

FIRST-TIME HOMEBUYER CREDIT

Designed to encourage home ownership and to alleviate the surplus of unsold houses, the **first-time homebuyer credit** provides a tax incentive for home purchases. For home purchases from January 1, 2009 through April 30, 2010, a credit of 10 percent of the purchase price is allowed but not to exceed $8,000 ($4,000 for married individuals filing separately). In this regard, single taxpayers and married persons filing jointly are treated alike, and each is subject to the same $8,000 maximum.[42]

The credit is available only if the purchase price of the home is $800,000 or less. In addition, the credit is phased out for more affluent taxpayers. The phaseout range is based on modified AGI and occurs between $125,000 and $145,000 for single taxpayers and $225,000 and $245,000 for married persons filing jointly.

Eligible Individuals

In general, the credit is available to *first-time buyers.* This means that the taxpayer has not owned a principal residence during the three-year period before the purchase (i.e., when title to the property passes). However, for purchases made after November 6, 2009, the credit is also available to *existing homeowners* who are "*long-term*

[42]§§ 36(a) and (h). For homes purchased from April 9, 2008 through December 31, 2008, the maximum credit was $7,500 ($3,750 for married individuals filing separately).

TAX *in* the NEWS

Many Taxpayers to Become "Nonpayers" Because of Tax Credits

One of the key domestic policy initiatives of recent administrations has been to reduce marginal tax rates and then to retain a lower marginal rate structure than under prior law. Many opponents of this policy have argued that the main beneficiaries of the lower tax rates are upper-income taxpayers who are the most affluent individuals in our country.

Economists have estimated that these policies also have led to more Americans than ever before being relieved of any Federal income tax liability. Since 2000, the number of "nonpayers" has grown by about 59 percent. In 2008, almost 52 million Americans filed a tax return and did not owe any taxes because of deductions and credits available to them. Thus, more than 36 percent of all filers were "nonpayers."

Source: Adapted from "Record Number of Tax Filers Paid No Federal Income Taxes in 2008," *Tax Foundation,* March 10, 2010.

residents." A long-term resident is one who has maintained the same principal residence for any five-consecutive-year period during the eight-year period ending on the date of the purchase of a subsequent principal residence. The maximum allowable credit for existing homeowners is limited to $6,500 ($3,250 for married individuals filing separately).

As long as the time limitations for the purchase are met, the credit may be claimed in either the year of purchase or the prior taxable year.

Repayment of Credit

Although the homebuyer credit contains a recapture provision, this provision is waived for homes purchased after December 31, 2008 (even if the taxpayer claimed the credit in 2008). For homes purchased in 2008, the first-time homebuyer credit is repaid beginning two years after the home was purchased. The credit is repaid in equal installments over 15 years. In effect, a credit claimed on a home purchased in 2008 is merely an interest-free loan to the homebuyer.

If a home purchased in 2008 is disposed of before the 15-year period is up, recapture of the unpaid balance occurs. Homes purchased after December 31, 2008, are also subject to an accelerated recapture rule. If such a home is disposed of within 36 months from the date of purchase, the entire homebuyer credit is recaptured. The recapture cannot exceed any gain from the sale of the residence. Recapture also can occur if the property ceases to be the taxpayer's principal residence. But recapture does not occur on the death of the taxpayer, an involuntary conversion, or a transfer between spouses incident to a divorce.[43]

The home purchase credit is a refundable credit.

ENERGY CREDITS

The Internal Revenue Code contains a variety of credits for businesses and individuals to encourage the conservation of natural resources and the development of energy sources other than oil and gas. Exhibit 12.2 provides a summary of several of the more important **energy tax credits.**

[43] § 36(f)(4).

EXHIBIT 12.2 **Energy Credits Summary**

Home Energy Efficiency Improvement Tax Credits

Consumers who purchase and install in the home specific products, such as energy-efficient windows, insulation, doors, roofs, and heating and cooling equipment, can receive a tax credit of up to $1,500 for property placed in service before 2011 (§ 25C). In addition, consumers who purchase photovoltaic, fuel cell, and/or solar water heating property can receive a credit equal to 30% of the purchase price. Improvements must be made to the taxpayer's principal residence and must be completed before 2017 (§ 25D).

Plug-in Electric Drive Motor Vehicles

Consumers who purchase new plug-in electric drive motor vehicles before January 1, 2015, can qualify for a credit of $2,500 plus $417 for each kilowatt-hour of battery capacity in excess of 5 kilowatt-hours, to a maximum credit of $7,500 (§ 30D).

Business Energy Tax Credits

Businesses are eligible for tax credits for producing alternative fuels, building energy-efficient buildings, producing energy-efficient products, and producing energy using alternative means. Examples include:

- *Credit for Business Installation of Qualified Fuel Cells, Stationary Microturbine Power Plants, Solar, and Small Wind Energy Equipment.* A tax credit—based on the purchase price—is provided for installing qualifying solar energy equipment (a 30% credit) and small wind energy equipment (a 30% credit). The credit applies to property placed in service before January 1, 2017 (§ 48).
- *Credit for Building Energy-Efficient New Homes.* A $2,000 tax credit is provided to eligible contractors for each qualified new energy-efficient home constructed through December 31, 2011. The credit applies to manufactured homes meeting ENERGY STAR® criteria and other homes (§ 45L).
- *Manufacturing Energy-Efficient Appliances.* A tax credit is provided to the manufacturer of energy-efficient dishwashers, clothes washers, and refrigerators. Credits vary depending on the efficiency of the unit and relate, generally, to production through December 31, 2011 (§ 45M).
- *Energy Credit for Producing Electricity via Wind, Solar, Geothermal, and Other Property.* The tax credit—based on the number of kilowatt-hours of electricity produced—applies to production through the end of 2013 (for wind energy, through the end of 2012) (§ 45).

CREDIT FOR CERTAIN RETIREMENT PLAN CONTRIBUTIONS

Taxpayers may claim a nonrefundable **credit for certain retirement plan contributions** based on eligible contributions of up to $2,000 to certain qualified retirement plans, such as traditional and Roth IRAs and § 401(k) plans.[44] This credit, sometimes referred to as the "saver's credit," is intended to encourage lower- and middle-income taxpayers to contribute to qualified retirement plans. The benefit provided by this credit is in addition to any deduction or exclusion that otherwise is available due to the qualifying contribution. In calculating the credit, the qualifying contributions are reduced by taxable distributions from any of the qualifying plans received by the taxpayer and spouse during the tax year and the two previous tax years and during the period prior to the due date of the return.

The credit rate applied to the eligible expenses depends on the taxpayer's AGI[45] and filing status, as shown in Table 12.2. However, the maximum credit allowed to an individual is $1,000 ($2,000 × 50%). As the taxpayer's AGI increases, the rate applied to contributions in calculating the credit is reduced, and once AGI exceeds the upper end of the applicable range, no credit is available. To qualify for the credit, the taxpayer must be at least 18 years of age and cannot be a dependent of another taxpayer or a full-time student.

[44] § 25B.

[45] The AGI thresholds are indexed for inflation. For purposes of this credit, the AGI thresholds are modified to include certain income exclusions. See § 25B(e).

TABLE 12.2 "Saver's" Credit Rate and AGI Thresholds (2011)

Joint Return		Head of Household		All Other Cases		Applicable Percentage
Over	Not Over	Over	Not Over	Over	Not Over	
$ 0	$34,000	$ 0	$25,500	$ 0	$17,000	50%
34,000	36,500	25,500	27,375	17,000	18,250	20%
36,500	56,500	27,375	42,375	18,250	28,250	10%
56,500		42,375		28,250		0%

EXAMPLE 35

Earl and Josephine, married taxpayers, each contribute $2,500 to their respective § 401(k) plans offered through their employers. The AGI reported on their joint return is $45,000. The maximum amount of contributions that may be taken into account in calculating the credit is limited to $2,000 for Earl and $2,000 for Josephine. As a result, they may claim a credit for their retirement plan contributions of $400 [($2,000 × 2) × 10%]. They would not qualify for the credit if their AGI had exceeded $56,500. ■

SMALL EMPLOYER HEALTH INSURANCE CREDIT

A tax credit is provided for a qualified small employer for nonelective contributions to purchase health insurance for its employees beginning in 2010.

To qualify for the credit, the employer must have no more than 25 full-time equivalent employees whose annual full-time wages average no more than $50,000. The employer must pay at least half the cost of the health insurance premiums.[46] The credit is 35 percent of the health insurance premiums paid in 2010 through 2013 (50 percent in years after 2013). The credit is subject to a phaseout if the employer has more than 10 full-time equivalent employees and/or has annual full-time wages that average more than $25,000.

12.5 Tax Payments

LO.5

Understand the tax withholding and payment procedures used by employers.

Taxes generally are remitted to the Treasury with the tax return. Withholdings are required, though, as to wages and a few other income items received by individuals; the employer directly transfers a portion of the paycheck to the Federal government. Using a Form W–4, the employee instructs the employer as to how much of the wage should be withheld, so that the taxes on the wages are remitted to the government on a "pay as you go" basis. Corporations make quarterly payments to the Treasury of the estimated taxes that relate to their own profits for the period. Taxpayers then claim on the annual tax return a credit against the tax due for the withholdings and estimated payments that have been prepaid in this manner.

In addition, the employer withholds a portion of the wage payment that relates to **employment taxes**, that is, the FICA (Federal Insurance Contributions Act) and FUTA (Federal Unemployment Tax Act) liabilities that relate to the employee's wages for the period.

Self-employed taxpayers do not have employers, so no withholding occurs, but income and employment taxes are prepaid nonetheless. Self-employeds are responsible for remitting their own income and employment taxes, in the form of quarterly estimated tax payments.

[46] §§ 45R(d)(1) and (4). The wage amount is indexed for inflation beginning in 2014.

CONCEPT SUMMARY 12.1

Major Tax Credits

Credit	Computation	Comments
Tax withheld on wages (§ 31)	Amount is reported to employee on Form W–2.	Refundable credit.
Earned income (§ 32)	Amount is determined by reference to Earned Income Credit Table published by IRS.	Refundable credit. A form of negative income tax to assist low-income taxpayers. Earned income and AGI must be less than certain threshold amounts. Generally, one or more qualifying children must reside with the taxpayer.
Child and dependent care (§ 21)	Rate ranges from 20% to 35% depending on AGI. Maximum base for credit is $3,000 for one qualifying individual, $6,000 for two or more.	Nonrefundable personal credit. No carryback or carryforward. Benefits taxpayers who incur employment-related child or dependent care expenses in order to work or seek employment. Eligible taxpayers must have a dependent under age 13 or a dependent (any age) or spouse who is physically or mentally incapacitated.
Elderly or disabled (§ 22)	Usually taken from an IRS table.	Nonrefundable personal credit. No carryback or carryforward. Provides relief for taxpayers not receiving substantial tax-free retirement benefits.
Adoption expenses (§ 23)	Up to $13,360 of costs incurred to adopt an eligible child qualify for the credit. Taxpayer claims the credit in the year qualified expenses were paid or incurred if they were paid or incurred during or after year in which adoption was finalized. For expenses paid or incurred in a year prior to when adoption was finalized, credit must be claimed in tax year following the tax year during which the expenses are paid or incurred.	Nonrefundable credit. Unused credit may be carried forward five years. Purpose is to assist taxpayers who incur nonrecurring costs associated with the adoption process.
Child (§ 24)	Credit is based on *number* of qualifying children under age 17. Maximum credit is $1,000 per child. Credit is phased out for higher-income taxpayers.	Generally a nonrefundable credit. Refundable in certain cases. Purpose is to provide tax relief for low- to moderate-income families with children.
Education (§ 25A)	American Opportunity credit is available for qualifying education expenses of students in first four years of postsecondary education. Maximum credit is $2,500 per year per eligible student. Credit is phased out for higher-income taxpayers.	Credit is designed to help defray costs of the first four years of higher education for low- to middle-income families. The credit is partially refundable.
	Lifetime learning credit permits a credit of 20% of qualifying expenses (up to $10,000 per year) provided American Opportunity credit is not claimed with respect to those expenses. Credit is calculated per taxpayer, not per student, and is phased out for higher-income taxpayers.	Nonrefundable credit. Credit is designed to help defray costs of higher education beyond the first four years, and for costs incurred in maintaining or improving existing job skills, for low- to middle-income taxpayers.

Major Tax Credits—Continued

Credit	Computation	Comments
Credit for certain retirement plan contributions (§ 25B)	Calculation is based on amount of contribution multiplied by a percentage that depends on the taxpayer's filing status and AGI.	Nonrefundable credit. Purpose is to encourage contributions to qualified retirement plans by low- and middle-income taxpayers.
Foreign tax (§ 27)	Foreign taxable income/total worldwide taxable income × U.S. tax = overall limitation. Lesser of foreign taxes imposed or overall limitation.	Nonrefundable credit. Unused credits may be carried back 1 year and forward 10 years. Purpose is to prevent double taxation of foreign income.
First-time homebuyer credit (§ 36)	Credit is limited to 10% of the home's purchase price, but no more than $8,000 ($4,000 for married individuals filing separately). Applies to homes purchased from January 1, 2009 through April 30, 2010. Homes purchased after November 6, 2009, with a price in excess of $800,000 do not qualify for the credit. For homes purchased after November 6, 2009, the credit is phased out for taxpayers with modified AGI between $125,000 and $145,000 (single) and $225,000 and $245,000 (married). Lower phaseout ranges apply to home purchases from January 1, 2009 through November 6, 2009.	Refundable credit. A credit to encourage home ownership and to alleviate the surplus of unsold homes. The credit for 2008 purchases is repaid over 15 years. For homes purchased from January 1, 2009 through April 30, 2010, the maximum credit is $8,000 ($4,000 for married individuals filing separately). There is no requirement that this credit be repaid.
Energy credits	Various items to encourage individuals and businesses to "go green."	See Exhibit 12.2.
General business (§ 38)	May not exceed net income tax minus the greater of tentative minimum tax or 25% of net regular tax liability that exceeds $25,000.	Nonrefundable credit. Components include tax credit for rehabilitation expenditures, work opportunity tax credit, research activities credit, low-income housing credit, disabled access credit, credit for small employer pension plan startup costs, and credit for employer-provided child care. Unused credit may be carried back 1 year and forward 20 years. FIFO method applies to carrybacks, carryovers, and credits earned during current year.
Rehabilitation expenditures (§ 47)	Qualifying investment times rehabilitation percentage, depending on type of property. Regular rehabilitation rate is 10%; rate for certified historic structures is 20%.	Nonrefundable credit. Part of general business credit and therefore subject to same carryback, carryover, and FIFO rules. Purpose is to discourage businesses from moving from economically distressed areas to newer locations.
Research activities (§ 41)	Incremental credit is 20% of excess of computation year expenditures over the base amount. Basic research credit is allowed to certain corporations for 20% of cash payments to qualified organizations that exceed a specially calculated base amount. An energy research credit is allowed for 20% of qualifying payments made to an energy research consortium.	Nonrefundable credit. Part of general business credit and therefore subject to same carryback, carryover, and FIFO rules. Purpose is to encourage high-tech and energy research in the United States.
Low-income housing (§ 42)	Appropriate rate times eligible basis (portion of project attributable to low-income units). Credit is available each year for 10 years. Recapture may apply.	Nonrefundable credit. Part of general business credit and therefore subject to same carryback, carryover, and FIFO rules. Purpose is to encourage construction of housing for low-income individuals.

Major Tax Credits—Continued

Credit	Computation	Comments
Disabled access (§ 44)	Credit is 50% of eligible access expenditures that exceed $250, but do not exceed $10,250. Maximum credit is $5,000. Available only to eligible small businesses.	Nonrefundable credit. Part of general business credit and therefore subject to same carryback, carryover, and FIFO rules. Purpose is to encourage small businesses to become more accessible to disabled individuals.
Credit for small employer pension plan startup costs (§ 45E)	Credit equals 50% of qualified startup costs incurred by eligible employers. Maximum annual credit is $500. Deduction for related expenses is reduced by the amount of the credit.	Nonrefundable credit. Part of general business credit and therefore subject to same carryback, carryover, and FIFO rules. Purpose is to encourage small employers to establish qualified retirement plans for their employees.
Credit for employer-provided child care (§ 45F)	Credit is equal to 25% of qualified child care expenses plus 10% of qualified expenses for child care resource and referral services. Maximum credit is $150,000. Deduction for related expenses or basis must be reduced by the amount of the credit.	Nonrefundable credit. Part of general business credit and therefore subject to same carryback, carryover, and FIFO rules. Purpose is to encourage employers to provide child care for their employees' children during normal working hours.
Work opportunity (§ 51)	Credit is limited to 40% of the first $6,000 of wages paid to each eligible employee. For long-term family assistance recipients, credit is limited to 40% of first $10,000 of wages paid to each eligible employee in first year of employment, plus 50% of first $10,000 of wages paid to each eligible employee in second year of employment.	Nonrefundable credit. Part of the general business credit and therefore subject to the same carryback, carryover, and FIFO rules. Purpose is to encourage employment of individuals in specified groups.

PAYMENTS BY EMPLOYERS

The employer usually is responsible for withholding the employee's share of FICA (commonly referred to as the Social Security tax) and appropriate amounts for income taxes. In addition, the employer matches the FICA portion withheld, and it pays the full cost of FUTA. The sum of the employment taxes and the income tax withholdings is paid to the IRS at specified intervals.

Amount of FICA Taxes

The FICA tax has two components: Social Security tax (old age, survivors, and disability insurance) *and* Medicare tax (hospital insurance). The tax rates and wage base under FICA have increased substantially over the years. The base amount is adjusted each year for inflation.

The Tax Relief Act of 2010 reduces the employee's (but not the employer's) Social Security tax rate from 6.2 percent to 4.2 percent for 2011. A similar 2 percentage point reduction applies to self-employed taxpayers (discussed below). So, for 2011, the total Social Security tax rate for self-employeds is 10.4 percent (4.2 percent plus 6.2 percent).

Withholdings from employees continue until the maximum base amount is reached. In 2011, for example, FICA withholding ceases for the Social Security portion (4.2 percent) once the employee has earned FICA wages of $106,800. No wage limit applies for the Medicare portion (1.45 percent) of the tax.

EXAMPLE 36

In 2011, Keshia earned a salary of $140,000 from her employer. Therefore, FICA taxes withheld from her salary are $4,485.60 ($106,800 × 4.2%) plus $2,030 ($140,000 × 1.45%) for a total of $6,515.60. In addition to paying the amount withheld from

Keshia's salary to the government, her employer pays $8,651.60 [($106,800 × 6.2%) + ($140,000 × 1.45%)]. ■

A spouse employed by another spouse is subject to FICA. However, children under the age of 18 who are employed in a parent's trade or business are exempted.

PAYMENTS BY SELF-EMPLOYED PERSONS

LO.6

Describe the tax payment procedures used by self-employed persons.

Although the following discussion largely centers on self-employed taxpayers, estimated tax may be required from some employees. An employee may be required to pay estimated tax for income other than wages that is not subject to withholding. An employee may conduct a second trade or business in a self-employment capacity, and these profits may require the payment of income and self-employment tax. In addition, taxpayers whose income consists of non-withholding income, like rentals, dividends, or interest, may be required to pay estimated tax.

Estimated Tax

Estimated tax is the amount of tax (including any AMT and self-employment tax) an individual expects to owe for the year after subtracting tax credits and income tax withheld. Any individual who has estimated tax for the year of $1,000 or more in excess of withholdings must make quarterly estimated tax payments.[47] No penalty applies if the taxpayer had a zero tax liability for the preceding tax year *and* the preceding tax year was a taxable year of 12 months *and* the taxpayer was a U.S. citizen or resident for the entire preceding tax year.

First, the *required annual payment* is computed. This is the *smaller* of:

- Ninety percent of the tax shown on the current year's return.
- One hundred percent of the tax shown on the preceding year's return (the return must cover the full 12 months of the preceding year). For 2009, the 100 percent requirement is reduced to 90 percent for income from a small business (AGI is less than $500,000; fewer than 500 employees). If the AGI on the preceding year's return exceeds $150,000 ($75,000 if married filing separately), the 100 percent requirement is increased to 110 percent.

In general, one-fourth of this required annual payment is due on each of April 15, June 15, and September 15 of the tax year and January 15 of the following year.

An equal part of withholding is deemed paid on each due date. Thus, the estimated tax due on each date is the quarterly installment of the required annual payment, reduced by the quarter's share of the year's withholdings for the individual. Payments are accompanied by the payment voucher, Form 1040–ES.

Self-Employment Tax

The tax on self-employment income is levied to provide Social Security and Medicare benefits (old age, survivors, and disability insurance and hospital insurance) for self-employed individuals. Individuals with net earnings of $400 or more from self-employment are subject to the **self-employment tax**.[48] For 2011, the self-employment tax is 10.4 percent of self-employment earnings up to $106,800 (for the Social Security portion) *plus* 2.9 percent of the total amount of self-employment earnings (the Medicare portion).

Self-employed taxpayers deduct a portion of the self-employment tax in determining the self-employment tax *and* in computing AGI.[49]

---

[47] §§ 6654(c)(1) and 6654(e)(1).

[48] § 6017.

[49] §§ 164(f) and 1402(a)(12).

If an individual also receives wages subject to FICA tax, the ceiling amount of the Social Security portion on which the self-employment tax is computed is reduced. Thus, the self-employment tax may be reduced to zero if a self-employed individual also receives FICA wages in excess of the ceiling amount.

EXAMPLE 37

In 2011, Kelly recorded $70,000 of net earnings from the conduct of a bookkeeping service (a trade or business activity). She also received $40,000 wages as an employee during the year.

Kelly's self-employment income subject to the Social Security portion (10.4%) is $66,800 ($106,800 − $40,000), not $70,000. This produces a self-employment tax of $6,947.20 ($66,800 × 10.4%). All of Kelly's net self-employment earnings are subject to the Medicare portion of the self-employment tax of 2.9%.

	Social Security Portion
Ceiling amount	$106,800
Less: FICA wages	(40,000)
Net ceiling	$ 66,800

■

Net earnings from self-employment include gross income from a trade or business less allowable trade or business deductions, the distributive share of any partnership income or loss derived from a trade or business activity, and net income from rendering personal services as an independent contractor. Gain or loss from the disposition of property (including involuntary conversions) is excluded from the computation of self-employment income unless the property involved is inventory.

TAX PLANNING:

12.6 Credit for Child and Dependent Care Expenses

LO.7

Identify tax planning opportunities related to tax credits and payments.

A taxpayer may incur employment-related expenses that also qualify as medical expenses (e.g., a nurse is hired to provide in-the-home care for an ill and incapacitated dependent parent). Such expenses may be either deducted as medical expenses (subject to the 7.5 percent limitation) or utilized in determining the credit for child and dependent care expenses.

If the credit for child and dependent care expenses is chosen and the employment-related expenses exceed the limitation ($3,000, $6,000, or earned income, as the case may be), the excess may be considered a medical expense. If, however, the taxpayer chooses to deduct qualified employment-related expenses as medical expenses, any portion that is not deductible because of the 7.5 percent limitation may not be used in computing the credit for child and dependent care expenses.

EXAMPLE 38

Alicia reports the following tax position.

Adjusted gross income		$30,000
Potential itemized deductions *from* AGI—		
Other than medical expenses	$3,500	
Medical expenses	6,600	$10,100

All of Alicia's medical expenses were incurred to provide nursing care for her disabled father while she was working. The father lives with Alicia and qualifies as her dependent. ■

TAX *in the NEWS*

The Tax Gap Includes $58 Billion in Payroll Taxes

The "tax gap"—the difference between what taxpayers owe to the Federal government in taxes and what they pay—is about $300 billion annually. A significant portion of that amount consists of delinquent payroll taxes—the money withheld from employees' salaries by employers for FICA taxes (Social Security and Medicare taxes).

According to a study by the Government Accountability Office (GAO), more than 1.6 million businesses together owe in excess of $58 billion related to delinquent payroll taxes. Of that amount, $26 billion represents actual taxes owed, $18 billion is for interest, and $14 billion is for penalties. In contrast, businesses owe only $24 billion in delinquent corporate income taxes. Businesses in the construction, professional services, and health care industries have the largest payroll tax delinquencies.

Collecting payroll taxes seems to be a perennial problem. The GAO study pointed out that delinquencies today are about the same as they were a decade ago when 1.8 million businesses owed about $49 billion. Today, though, debts are more likely to be longstanding. About 500 employers owe at least 10 years' worth of taxes, and nearly 15,000 owe 5 years' worth. About half of the $58 billion owed is from 2002 or earlier. Since then the IRS has stepped up its enforcement efforts concerning employment taxes, and it will target this part of the tax gap starting in 2010 with three-year audits of about 5,000 randomly selected employers.

What should Alicia do in this situation? One approach would be to use $3,000 of the nursing care expenses to obtain the maximum credit for child and dependent care expenses allowed of $810 (27% × $3,000). The balance of these expenses should be claimed as medical expenses. After a reduction of 7.5 percent of AGI, this would produce a medical expense deduction of $1,350 [$3,600 (remaining medical expenses) − (7.5% × $30,000)].

Another approach would be to claim the full $6,600 as a medical expense and forgo the credit for child and dependent care expenses. After the 7.5 percent adjustment of $2,250 (7.5% × $30,000), a deduction of $4,350 remains.

The choice, then, is between a credit of $810 plus a deduction of $1,350 or a credit of $0 plus a deduction of $4,350. Which is better, of course, depends on the relative tax savings involved, which in turn are dependent on the taxpayer's marginal tax bracket.

One of the traditional goals of *family tax planning* is to minimize the total tax burden within the family unit. With proper planning and implementation, the credit for child and dependent care expenses can be used to help achieve this goal. For example, payments to certain relatives for the care of qualifying dependents and children qualify for the credit if the care provider is *not* a child (under age 19) of the taxpayer. Thus, if the care provider is in a lower tax bracket than the taxpayer, the following benefits result.

- Income is shifted to a lower-bracket family member.
- The taxpayer qualifies for the credit for child and dependent care expenses.

In addition, the goal of minimizing the family income tax liability can be enhanced in some other situations, but only if the credit's limitations are recognized and avoided. For example, tax savings still may be enjoyed even if the qualifying expenditures incurred by a cash basis taxpayer have already reached the annual ceiling ($3,000 or $6,000). To the extent that any additional payments can be shifted into future tax years, the benefit from the credit may be preserved on these excess expenditures.

EXAMPLE 39

Andre, a calendar year and cash basis taxpayer, has spent $3,000 by December 1 on qualifying child care expenditures for his dependent 11-year-old son. The $250 that is due the care provider for child care services rendered in December does not generate a tax credit benefit if the amount is paid in the current year because the $3,000 ceiling has been reached. However, if the payment can be delayed until the next year, the total credit over the two-year period for which Andre is eligible may be increased. ■

A similar shifting of expenditures to a subsequent year may be wise if the potential credit otherwise generated would exceed the tax liability available to absorb the credit.

REFOCUS ON THE BIG PICTURE

EDUCATION TAX CREDITS

Lora and Sam qualify for the American Opportunity credit as they are both in their first four years of postsecondary education. Lora and Sam both qualify for a $2,500 credit (100 percent of the first $2,000 and 25 percent of the next $2,000 of qualified expenses).

These credits phase out over an income range of $20,000 once married taxpayers' AGI exceeds $160,000. The total education credits available to the Snyders amount to $5,240, and they may claim this amount as a credit on their Form 1040. Further, the education credits may be used to offset any AMT liability, and a portion of the credits is refundable to the Snyders.

What If?

What if the Snyders's AGI is $188,000? In that case, the Snyders would not qualify for any education credits (their income exceeds the limits for both the American Opportunity and the lifetime learning credits). Although a deduction *for* AGI is allowed for qualified tuition and related expenses involving higher education, the taxpayers' AGI exceeds the $160,000 maximum allowed for a deduction (see Chapter 9 for additional details).

KEY TERMS

Adoption expenses credit, 12–19
American Opportunity credit, 12–22
Child tax credit, 12–20
Credit for certain retirement plan contributions, 12–26
Credit for child and dependent care expenses, 12–20
Credit for employer-provided child care, 12–14
Credit for small employer pension plan startup costs, 12–14
Disabled access credit, 12–13
Earned income credit, 12–15
Employment taxes, 12–27
Energy tax credits, 12–25
Estimated tax, 12–31
First-time homebuyer credit, 12–24
Foreign tax credit (FTC), 12–17
General business credit, 12–6
Lifetime learning credit, 12–22
Low-income housing credit, 12–12
Nonrefundable credits, 12–5
Permanent and total disability, 12–16
Refundable credits, 12–4
Rehabilitation expenditures credit, 12–7
Rehabilitation expenditures credit recapture, 12–8
Research activities credit, 12–10
Self-employment tax, 12–31
Tax credit for the elderly or disabled, 12–16
Tax credits, 12–2
Work opportunity tax credit, 12–9

DISCUSSION QUESTIONS

1. **LO.1** Would an individual taxpayer receive greater benefit from deducting an expenditure or from taking a credit equal to 25% of the expenditure? How would your response change if the item would only be deductible *from* AGI?
2. **LO.2** What is a refundable credit? Give examples. What is a nonrefundable credit? Give examples.
3. **LO.2** Tax credits are offset against the tax liability in a prescribed order. Explain why the order in which credits are utilized is important.
4. **LO.2, 3** Identify the components of the general business credit and discuss the treatment of unused general business credits.

5. **LO.3** Clint, a self-employed engineering consultant, is contemplating purchasing an old building for renovation. After the work is completed, Clint plans to rent out two-thirds of the floor space to businesses; he would live and work in the remaining portion. Identify the relevant tax issues for Clint. **ISSUE ID**

6. **LO.3** Sonja is considering the purchase and renovation of an old building. She has heard about the tax credit for rehabilitation expenditures, but does not know the specific rules applicable to the credit. Explain the most important and relevant provisions for her. **ISSUE ID**

7. **LO.3** Discuss the purpose of the work opportunity tax credit. Who receives the tax benefits from the credit? Give examples of the types of individuals who, if hired, give rise to the credit.

8. **LO.3** Explain the purpose and calculation procedure of the work opportunity tax credit targeted to those who have received long-term family assistance.

9. **LO.3** Explain the alternatives a taxpayer has in claiming the deduction and credit for research and experimentation expenditures.

10. **LO.3** Explain the purpose of the disabled access credit and identify several examples of the type of structural changes to a building that qualify for the credit.

11. **LO.4** Can the earned income credit be characterized as a form of negative income tax? Why or why not?

12. **LO.4** How does the earned income credit fit into the Federal government's plan to fight poverty?

13. **LO.4** From the standpoint of a U.S. business, why is the foreign tax credit needed?

14. **LO.4** What purpose is served by the overall limitation on the foreign tax credit?

15. **LO.4** Distinguish between the child tax credit and the credit for child and dependent care expenses.

16. **LO.3, 4** Discuss the rationale underlying the enactment of the following tax credits.
    a. Rehabilitation expenditures credit.
    b. Research activities credit.
    c. Low-income housing credit.
    d. Earned income credit.
    e. Foreign tax credit.

17. **LO.4, 7** Polly and her husband, Leo, file a joint return and expect to report 2011 AGI of $70,000. Polly's employer offers a child and dependent care reimbursement plan that allows up to $3,500 of qualifying expenses to be reimbursed in exchange for a $3,500 reduction in the employee's salary. Because Polly and Leo have one minor child requiring child care that costs $3,500 each year, she is wondering if she should sign up for the program instead of taking advantage of the credit for child and dependent care expenses. **DECISION MAKING**

    Assuming Polly and Leo are in the 25% tax bracket, analyze the effect of the two alternatives. How would your answer differ if Polly and Leo's AGI was $14,000 instead of $70,000? Assume in this case that their marginal tax rate is 10%.

18. **LO.4** Mark and Lisa are approaching an exciting time in their lives as their oldest son, Austin, graduates from high school and moves on to college. What are some of the tax issues that Mark and Lisa should consider as they think about paying for Austin's college education? **ISSUE ID**

19. **LO.4** Explain the purpose of the first-time homebuyer credit and describe the general characteristics of its computation.

20. **LO.3, 4** Identify two tax credits enacted by Congress that are designed to encourage the establishment of or contributions to qualified retirement plans.

21. **LO.5** Kathy owns and operates a grocery store as a sole proprietor. She pays wages to her husband Joe and their 17-year-old daughter Marla, both of whom work at the store. Should Kathy withhold FICA taxes from the wages paid to Joe and Marla?

22. **LO.6** Joan is a self-employed consultant. What is her 2011 exposure to the Federal self-employment tax? Discuss the tax rates that apply to Joan's profits, and the income base amounts for the year.

PROBLEMS

23. **LO.2** Dick generated a tentative general business credit of $70,000 for the current year. His net regular tax liability before the general business credit is $88,000, and his tentative minimum tax is $82,000. Compute Dick's allowable general business credit for the year.

24. **LO.2** Pine Corporation holds the following general business credit carryovers.

2007	$ 40,000
2008	70,000
2009	60,000
2010	30,000
Total carryovers	$200,000

If the general business credit generated by 2011 activities equals $185,000 and the total credit allowed during the current year is $300,000 (based on tax liability), what amounts of the current general business credit and carryovers are utilized against the 2011 income tax liability? What is the amount of unused credit carried forward to 2012?

DECISION MAKING

COMMUNICATIONS

25. **LO.3, 7** Paul Chaing (4522 Fargo Street, Geneva, IL 60134) acquires a qualifying historic structure for $350,000 (excluding the cost of the land) and plans to substantially rehabilitate the structure. He is planning to spend either $320,000 or $380,000 on rehabilitation expenditures. Write a letter to Paul and a memo for the tax research files explaining the following, for the two alternative expenditures.
    a. The computation that determines the rehabilitation expenditures tax credit available.
    b. The effect of the credit on Paul's adjusted basis in the property.
    c. The cash-flow differences as a result of the tax consequences related to his expenditure choice.

26. **LO.3** Green Corporation hires six individuals on January 4, 2011, all of whom qualify for the work opportunity credit. Three of these individuals receive wages of $8,500 during 2011, and each individual works more than 400 hours during the year. The other three individuals each work 300 hours and receive wages of $5,000 during the year.
    a. Calculate the amount of Green's work opportunity credit for 2011.
    b. If Green pays total wages of $140,000 to its employees during the year, how much of this amount is deductible in 2011, assuming that the work opportunity credit is taken?

27. **LO.3** In March 2011, Sparrow Corporation hired three individuals—Austin, Adam, and Angela—all of whom are certified as long-term family assistance recipients. Each of these individuals earned $11,000 during 2011. Only Adam continued to work for Sparrow in 2012, and he earned $13,500 then.

    In March 2012, Sparrow hired Sam, who also is certified as a long-term family assistance recipient. During 2012, Sam earned $12,000.
    a. Compute Sparrow's work opportunity credit for 2011 and 2012.
    b. If Sparrow pays total wages to its employees of $325,000 in 2011 and $342,000 in 2012, what is the entity's wage deduction in 2011 and 2012?

DECISION MAKING

28. **LO.3, 7** Sarah, a calendar year taxpayer, informs you that during the year she incurs expenditures of $30,000 that qualify for the incremental research activities credit. In addition, it is determined that the research-credit base amount for the year is $22,800.
    a. Determine Sarah's incremental research activities credit for the year.
    b. Sarah is in the 25% tax bracket. Determine which approach to the research expenditures and the research activities credit (other than capitalization and subsequent amortization) would provide the greater tax benefit.

COMMUNICATIONS

29. **LO.3** Dan DeRose (333 East Shore Drive, Wyckoff, NJ 07481), one of your clients, owns two retail establishments in downtown Wyckoff and has come to you seeking advice concerning the tax consequences of complying with the Americans with Disabilities Act. He understands that he needs to install various features at his stores (e.g., ramps, doorways, and restrooms that are handicapped accessible) to make them more accessible to disabled individuals. He asks whether any tax credits are available to help offset the cost of the necessary changes. He estimates the cost of the planned changes to his facilities as follows.

Location	Projected Cost
Oak Street	$18,000
Maple Avenue	12,400

He reminds you that the Oak Street store was constructed in 2004, and that the Maple Avenue store is in a building that was constructed in 1912. Dan operates his business as a sole proprietorship and has approximately eight employees at each location. Write a letter to Dan in which you summarize your conclusions concerning the tax consequences of his proposed capital improvements.

30. **LO.3** Jimmy Limited added elevators, access ramps, and several technological improvements to the 1923 building in which it operates a consulting business. Jimmy is an LLC with five full-time employees and about $3 million in gross receipts. The improvements were made to improve access to the building. Expenditures for the accessibility project totaled $7,500. Compute Jimmy's disabled access credit for the tax year.

31. **LO.3** Employees at the Hobby Hut requested that the company provide assistance in locating professional-quality child care services during business hours. The Hut, a C corporation, contracts with the local Kiddie Kare agency to provide Hut employees with information about child care providers' location, pricing, customer ratings, and operating hours. This year, the Hut paid $15,000 under this contract, which includes a flat fee for a guaranteed number of employee contacts and a per-service charge after that. Compute the Hobby Hut's credit for employer-provided child care for the tax year.

32. **LO.4** Which of the following individuals qualify for the earned income credit for 2011?

DECISION MAKING

   a. Thomas is single, 21 years old, with no qualifying children. His income consists of $9,000 in wages.
   b. Shannon, who is 27 years old, maintains a household for a dependent 11-year-old son and is eligible for head-of-household tax rates. Her income consists of $16,050 of salary and $50 of taxable interest (Shannon's AGI is $16,100).
   c. Keith and Susan, both age 30, are married and file a joint return. Keith and Susan have no dependents. Their combined income consists of $28,500 of salary and $100 of taxable interest (their AGI is $28,600).
   d. Colin is a 26-year-old, self-supporting, single taxpayer. He has no qualifying children and generates earnings of $9,000.

33. **LO.4, 7** Cooper National is incorporated in Alabama. It generated a $5 million profit on its overseas operations this year. Cooper paid the following to various other countries.

   - $1 million in income taxes.
   - $1.5 million in value added taxes.

   What are Cooper's alternatives as to the treatment of these tax payments on its U.S. Federal income tax returns?

34. **LO.4** Jimenez Enterprises is incorporated in Arkansas. It generated a $5 million profit on its overseas operations this year. Jimenez paid $1 million in income taxes to various countries on these profits. Jimenez's marginal Federal income tax rate is 35%. Compute the Jimenez foreign tax credit and carryovers for the year.

35. **LO.4** Same as Problem 34, except that Jimenez paid $2 million in income taxes to other countries.

36. **LO.4** Ann and Bill were on the list of a local adoption agency for several years seeking to adopt a child. Finally, in 2010, good news comes their way and an adoption seems imminent. They pay qualified adoption expenses of $4,000 in 2010 and $11,000 in 2011. The adoption becomes final in 2011. Ann and Bill always file a joint income tax return.
   a. Determine the amount of the adoption expenses credit available to Ann and Bill assuming their combined annual income is $100,000. What year(s) will they benefit from the credit?
   b. Assuming Ann and Bill's modified AGI in 2010 and 2011 is $200,000, calculate the amount of the adoption expenses credit.

37. **LO.4** Durell and Earline are married, file a joint return, and claim dependency exemptions for their two children, ages 5 years and 6 months. They also claim Earline's

18-year-old son from a previous marriage as a dependent. Durell and Earline's combined AGI is $68,000.

a. Compute Durell and Earline's child tax credit.

b. Assume the same facts, except that Durell and Earline's combined AGI is $122,000. Compute their child tax credit.

38. **LO.4** Paul and Karen are married, and both are employed (Paul earned $44,000 and Karen earned $9,000 during 2011). Paul and Karen have two dependent children, both under the age of 13. Paul and Karen pay $3,800 to various unrelated parties to care for their children while they are working. Assuming that Paul and Karen file a joint return, what, if any, is their tax credit for child and dependent care expenses?

39. **LO.4** Jim and Mary Jean are married and have two dependent children under the age of 13. Both parents are gainfully employed and during 2011 earn salaries as follows: $16,000 (Jim) and $5,200 (Mary Jean). To care for their children while they work, Jim and Mary Jean pay Eleanor (Jim's mother) $5,600. Eleanor does not qualify as a dependent of Jim and Mary Jean. Jim and Mary Jean file a joint Federal income tax return. Compute their credit for child and dependent care expenses.

COMMUNICATIONS

40. **LO.4, 7** Bernadette, a longtime client of yours, is an architect and president of the local Rotary chapter. To keep up-to-date with the latest developments in her profession, she attends continuing education seminars offered by the architecture school at State University. During 2011, Bernadette spends $2,000 on course tuition to attend such seminars. She also spends another $400 on architecture books during the year. Bernadette's son is a senior majoring in engineering at the University of the Midwest.

During the 2011 calendar year, Bernadette's son incurs the following expenses: $8,200 for tuition ($4,100 per semester) and $750 for books and course materials. Bernadette's son, whom she claims as a dependent, lives at home while attending school full-time. Bernadette is married, files a joint return, and has a combined AGI with her husband of $103,000.

a. Calculate Bernadette's 2011 education tax credit.

b. In her capacity as president of the local Rotary chapter, Bernadette has asked you to present a 30–45 minute speech outlining the different ways the tax law helps defray (1) the cost of higher education and (2) the cost of continuing education once someone is in the workforce. Prepare an outline of possible topics for presentation. A tentative title for your presentation is "How Can the Tax Law Help Pay for College and Continuing Professional Education?"

41. **LO.4** Kathleen and Glenn decide that this is the year to begin getting serious about saving for their retirement by participating in their employers' § 401(k) plans. As a result, they each have $3,000 of their salary set aside in their qualified plans.

a. Calculate the credit for certain retirement plan contributions available to Kathleen and Glenn if the AGI on their joint return is $35,000.

b. Kathleen and Glenn persuade their dependent 15-year-old son, Joel, to put $500 of his part-time earnings into a Roth IRA during the year. What is the credit for certain retirement plan contributions available to Joel? His AGI is $7,000.

CUMULATIVE PROBLEMS

TAX RETURN PROBLEM

H&R BLOCK At Home

42. Beth R. Jordan lives at 2322 Skyview Road, Mesa, AZ 85201. She is a tax accountant with Mesa Manufacturing Company, 1203 Western Avenue, Mesa, AZ 85201 (employer identification number 11–1111111). She also writes computer software programs for tax practitioners and has a part-time tax practice. Beth is single and has no dependents. Beth's birthday is July 4, 1971, and her Social Security number is 123–45–6789. She wants to contribute $3 to the Presidential Election Campaign Fund.

The following information is shown on Beth's 2010 Wage and Tax Statement (Form W–2).

Line	Description	Amount
1	Wages, tips, other compensation	$63,000.00
2	Federal income tax withheld	10,500.00
3	Social Security wages	63,000.00
4	Social Security tax withheld	3,906.00
5	Medicare wages and tips	63,000.00
6	Medicare tax withheld	913.50
15	State	Arizona
16	State wages, tips, etc.	63,000.00
17	State income tax withheld	1,650.00

Beth received interest of $1,300 from Arizona Federal Savings and Loan and $400 from Arizona State Bank. Each financial institution reported the interest income on a Form 1099–INT. She received qualified dividends of $800 from Blue Corporation, $750 from Green Corporation, and $650 from Orange Corporation. Each corporation reported Beth's dividend payments on a Form 1099–DIV.

Beth received a $1,100 income tax refund from the state of Arizona on April 29, 2010. On her 2009 Federal income tax return, she reported total itemized deductions of $8,200, which included $2,200 of state income tax withheld by her employer.

Fees earned from her part-time tax practice totaled $3,800. She paid $600 to have the tax returns processed by a computerized tax return service.

On February 8, 2010, Beth bought 500 shares of Gray Corporation common stock for $17.60 a share. On September 12, Beth sold the stock for $14 a share.

Beth bought a used sport utility vehicle for $6,000 on June 5, 2010. She purchased the vehicle from her brother-in-law, who was unemployed and was in need of cash. On November 2, 2010, she sold the vehicle to a friend for $6,500.

On January 2, 2010, Beth acquired 100 shares of Blue Corporation common stock for $30 a share. She sold the stock on December 19, 2010, for $55 a share.

During 2010, Beth received royalties of $16,000 on a software program she had written. Beth incurred the following expenditures in connection with her software-writing activities.

Cost of personal computer (100% business use)	$7,000
Cost of printer (100% business use)	2,000
Furniture	3,000
Supplies	650
Fee paid to computer consultant	3,500

Beth elected to deduct the maximum portion of the cost of the computer, printer, and furniture allowed under the provisions of § 179. This equipment and furniture was placed in service on January 15, 2010.

Although her employer suggested that Beth attend a convention on current developments in corporate taxation, Beth was not reimbursed for the travel expenses of $1,420 she incurred in attending the conference. The $1,420 included $200 for meals.

During 2010, Beth paid $300 for prescription medicines and $2,875 in physician and hospital bills. Medical insurance premiums were paid by her employer. Beth paid real property taxes of $1,766 on her home. Interest on her home mortgage was $3,845, and interest paid to credit card companies totaled $320. Beth contributed $30 each week to her church and $10 each week to the United Way. Professional dues and subscriptions totaled $350. Beth maintained her sales tax receipts, showing total purchases of $1,954.

Beth paid $1,000 in estimated Federal income taxes throughout the year.

Part 1—Tax Computation

Compute the 2010 net tax payable or refund due for Beth R. Jordan. If you use tax forms for your solution, you will need Forms 1040, 2106–EZ, and 4562 and Schedules A, B, C, D, and SE. Suggested software: H&R BLOCK At Home.

Part 2—Tax Planning

Beth is anticipating significant changes in her life in 2011, and she has asked you to estimate her taxable income and tax liability for that year. She just received word that she has been qualified to adopt a two-year-old daughter. Beth expects that the adoption will be finalized in 2011 and that she will incur approximately $2,000 of adoption expenses. In addition, she expects to incur approximately $3,500 of child and dependent care expenses relating to the care of her new daughter, which will enable her to keep her job at Mesa Manufacturing. However, with the additional demands on her time because of her daughter, she has decided to discontinue her two part-time jobs (i.e., the part-time tax practice and her software business), and she will cease making estimated income tax payments. In your computations, assume all other income and expenditures will remain at approximately the same levels as in 2010.

TAX COMPUTATION PROBLEM

43. Tim and Sarah Lawrence are married and file a joint return. Tim's Social Security number is 123–45–6789, and Sarah's Social Security number is 111–11–1111. They reside at 100 Olive Lane, Covington, LA 70400. They have two dependent children, Sean and Debra, ages 12 and 16, respectively. Sean's Social Security number is 123–45–6788, and Debra's Social Security number is 123–45–6787. Tim is a self-employed businessman (sole proprietor of an unincorporated business), and Sarah is a corporate executive. Tim has the following income and expenses from his business.

Gross income	$280,000
Business expenses	156,000

Records related to Sarah's employment provide the following information.

Salary	$130,000
Unreimbursed travel expenses (including $400 of meals)	1,800
Unreimbursed entertainment expenses	700

Other pertinent information follows.

Proceeds from sale of stock acquired on July 15, 2011 (cost of $16,500), and sold on August 1, 2011	$ 14,300
Proceeds from sale of stock acquired on September 18, 2010 (cost of $7,000), and sold on October 5, 2011	5,800
Wages paid to full-time domestic worker for housekeeping and child supervision	10,000
Interest income received	9,000
Total itemized deductions (not including any potential deductions above)	27,900
Federal income tax withheld	36,000
Estimated payments of Federal income tax	24,000

Compute the 2011 net tax payable or refund due for Tim and Sarah Lawrence.

RESEARCH PROBLEMS

THOMSON REUTERS
Checkpoint® Student Edition

Note: Solutions to Research Problems can be prepared by using the **Checkpoint® Student Edition** online research product, which is available to accompany this text. It is also possible to prepare solutions to the Research Problems by using tax research materials found in a standard tax library.

Research Problem 1. Ashby and Curtis, a young professional couple, have a two-year-old son, Jason. Curtis works full-time as an electrical engineer, but Ashby has not worked outside the home since Jason was born. As Jason is getting older, Ashby feels that he would benefit from attending nursery school several times a week, which would give her an opportunity to reinvigorate her love of painting at a nearby art studio. Ashby thinks that if she is lucky, the proceeds from the sale of her paintings will pay for the nursery school tuition. But, in addition, she is planning to claim the credit for child and dependent care expenses because the care provided Jason at the nursery school is required for her to pursue her art. Can Ashby and Curtis claim the credit for child and dependent care expenses for the nursery school expenditure?

Research Problem 2. Your ophthalmologist, Dr. Hunter Francis (55 Wheatland Drive, Hampton, CT 06247), has been very pleased with the growth of his practice in the 15 years he has been in business. This growth has resulted, at least in part, because he has aggressively marketed his services and tried to accommodate clients with various needs.

COMMUNICATIONS

This year Dr. Francis purchased a sophisticated piece of equipment that enables him to diagnose persons with mental handicaps, hearing impairments, and physical disabilities without having to go through a series of intrusive questions. In addition, he can treat his patients who are not disabled much more accurately and efficiently by using this equipment.

Since purchasing the machine this year for $9,500, Dr. Francis has used it on many occasions. Unfortunately, he has not been able to attract any new patients who are disabled, even though previously he referred such people to other ophthalmologists who owned the equipment that he now owns. Therefore, the primary purpose for acquiring the equipment (i.e., to attract disabled patients) has not been realized.

Write a letter to Dr. Francis explaining whether he may claim the disabled access credit for this acquisition.

Research Problem 3. During a recent Sunday afternoon excursion, Miriam, an admirer of early twentieth-century architecture, discovers a 1920s-era house in the countryside outside Mobile, Alabama. She desires not only to purchase and renovate this house, but also to move the structure into Mobile so that her community can enjoy its architectural features.

DECISION MAKING

Being aware of the availability of the tax credit for rehabilitation expenditures, Miriam wishes to maximize her use of the provision, if it is available in this case, once the renovation work begins in Mobile. Miriam informs you that she will pursue the purchase, relocation, and renovation of the house only if the tax credit is available.

Comment on Miriam's decision and whether any renovation expenditures incurred qualify for the tax credit for rehabilitation expenditures.

Partial list of research aids:
George S. Nalle III v. Comm., 72 AFTR 2d 93–5705, 93-2 USTC ¶50,468, 997 F.2d 1134 (CA–5).

Use the tax resources of the Internet to address the following questions. Do not restrict your search to the Web, but include a review of newsgroups and general reference materials, practitioner sites and resources, primary sources of the tax law, chat rooms and discussion groups, and other opportunities.

INTERNET *activity*

Research Problem 4. The IRS makes available a web-based tool to help taxpayers determine whether they are eligible for the earned income credit. Locate this tool at the IRS website and then apply the facts related to a hypothetical taxpayer and determine if the earned income credit is available.

Research Problem 5. The foreign tax credit is especially valuable when a U.S. individual works in a country whose income tax rates exceed those of the United States. List five countries whose tax rates on individuals exceed those of the United States and five where the corresponding U.S. rates are higher.

Research Problem 6. For your state and three of its neighbors, determine how many tax returns claimed an earned income credit. On a line or bar chart, track these data for the last five years, using **www.irs.gov**. Send your results in an e-mail to your instructor.

COMMUNICATIONS

Research Problem 7. Some observers believe that the earned income tax credit is riddled with fraud, including claims involving nonexistent relatives and misreported income amounts. Others believe that the credit is too complex to compute, and that it should provide more generous aid to low-income families. Find three articles or postings discussing the operation of the credit and addressing the issue of fraud concerning its application. Summarize the articles in no more than four PowerPoint slides, designed for you to present to your classmates.

COMMUNICATIONS

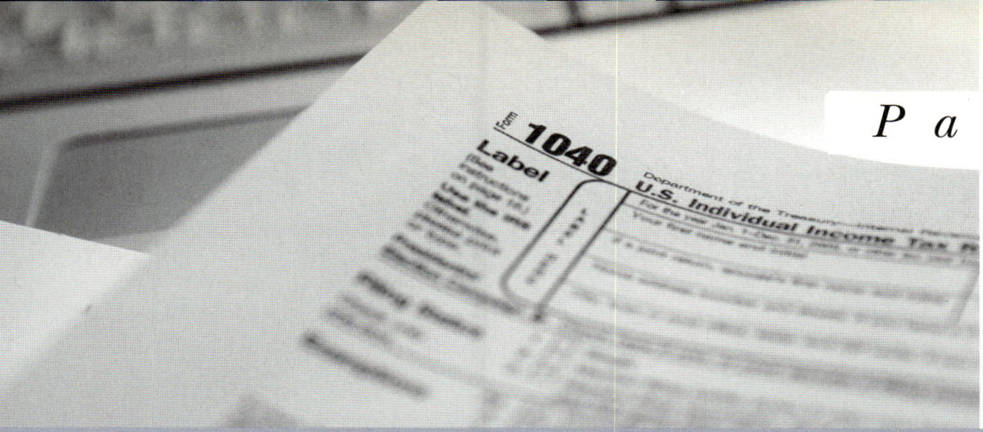

Part 4

Property Transactions

Part 4 presents the tax treatment of sales, exchanges, and other dispositions of property. Included are the determination of the realized gain or loss, recognized gain or loss, and the classification of the recognized gain or loss as capital or ordinary. The topic of basis is evaluated both in terms of its effect on the calculation of the gain or loss and in terms of the determination of the basis of any contemporaneous or related subsequent acquisitions of property.

CHAPTER

13

Property Transactions: Determination of Gain or Loss, Basis Considerations, and Nontaxable Exchanges

LEARNING OBJECTIVES

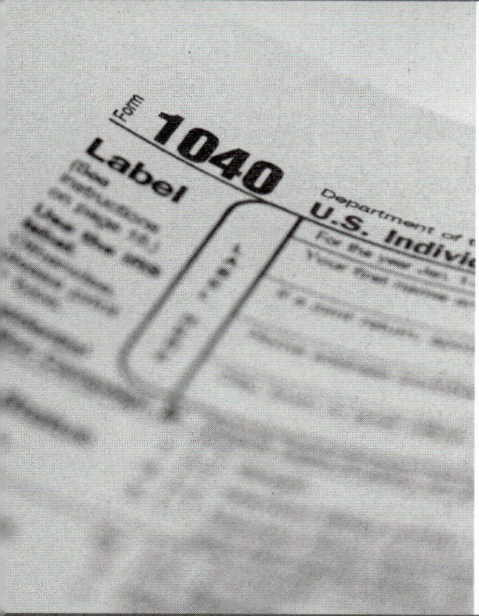

After completing Chapter 13, you should be able to:

LO.1
Understand the computation of realized gain or loss on property dispositions.

LO.2
Distinguish between realized and recognized gain or loss.

LO.3
Apply the recovery of capital doctrine.

LO.4
Explain how basis is determined for various methods of asset acquisition.

LO.5
Describe various loss disallowance provisions.

LO.6
Understand the rationale for nonrecognition (postponement) of gain or loss in certain property transactions.

LO.7
Apply the nonrecognition provisions and basis determination rules for like-kind exchanges.

LO.8
Explain the nonrecognition provisions available on the involuntary conversion of property.

LO.9
Describe the provision for the permanent exclusion of gain on the sale of a personal residence.

LO.10
Identify other nonrecognition provisions contained in the Code.

LO.11
Identify tax planning opportunities related to selected property transactions.

OUTLINE

For the latest in changes to tax legislation, visit **www.cengage.com/taxation/swft.**

FRAMEWORK 1040: Tax Formula for Individuals

This chapter covers the boldfaced portions of the Tax Formula for Individuals that was introduced in Figure 3.1 on p. 3-3. Below those portions are the sections of Form 1040 where the results are reported.

Income (broadly conceived)	$ xx,xxx
Less: Exclusions	(x,xxx)
Gross income	**$xx,xxx**
Less: Deductions for adjusted gross income	**(x,xxx)**

FORM 1040 (p. 1)

12	Business income or (loss). Attach Schedule C or C-EZ	
13	Capital gain or (loss). Attach Schedule D if required. If not required, check here ▶	☐
14	Other gains or (losses). Attach Form 4797	

Adjusted gross income	$ xx,xxx
Less: The greater of total itemized deductions *or* the standard deduction	(x,xxx)
Personal and dependency exemptions	(x,xxx)
Taxable income	$ xx,xxx
Tax on taxable income (see Tax Tables or Tax Rate Schedules)	$ x,xxx
Less: Tax credits (including income taxes withheld and prepaid)	(xxx)
Tax due (or refund)	$ xxx

THE BIG PICTURE Tax Solutions for the Real World

SALE OR GIFT OF INHERITED HOUSE AND OTHER PROPERTY TRANSACTIONS

Alice owns a house that she inherited from her grandmother seven months ago. Her grandmother lived in the house for over 50 years. Alice has many fond memories associated with the house, since she spent many summer vacations there. This has caused her to delay making a decision regarding what she is going to do with the house.

Based on the estate tax return, the fair market value of the house at the date of her grandmother's death was $475,000. According to the grandmother's attorney, her grandmother's basis for the house was $275,000. The real estate market for residential housing has recovered in the city in which the house is located. So based on an appraisal, the house currently is worth $600,000. Alice is considering two options. The first is to give the house to her son, Michael. Michael, his wife Sandra, and their daughter Peggy would live in the house. The second option is to sell the house. Projected selling expenses would be about 7 percent of the selling price.

Alice would also like to know the tax consequences of selling her car, which she purchased for $22,000 four months ago and has used exclusively for personal use. She has been disappointed with its performance. Based on the "Blue Book" value, she anticipates that she can sell it for $20,000 to $23,000.

In addition, earlier this year Alice sold some stock at a realized loss and subsequently repurchased some shares of the same stock (see Example 34). She has also asked you about the tax consequences of these transactions.

Alice has come to you for advice regarding the tax consequences of these various transactions. **Read the chapter and formulate your response.**

This chapter and Chapter 14 are concerned with the income tax consequences of property transactions (the sale or other disposition of property). The following questions are considered with respect to the sale or other disposition of property:

- Is there a realized gain or loss?
- If so, is the gain or loss recognized?
- If the gain or loss is recognized, is it ordinary or capital?
- What is the basis of any replacement property that is acquired?

This chapter discusses the determination of realized and recognized gain or loss and the basis of property. Chapter 14 covers the classification of the recognized gain or loss as ordinary or capital.

13.1 Determination of Gain or Loss

REALIZED GAIN OR LOSS

LO.1

Understand the computation of realized gain or loss on property dispositions.

Realized gain or loss is the difference between the amount realized from the sale or other disposition of property and the property's adjusted basis on the date of disposition. If the amount realized exceeds the property's adjusted basis, the result is a **realized gain**. Conversely, if the property's adjusted basis exceeds the amount realized, the result is a **realized loss**.[1]

EXAMPLE 1

Tab sells Swan Corporation stock with an adjusted basis of $3,000 for $5,000. Tab's realized gain is $2,000. If Tab had sold the stock for $2,000, he would have had a realized loss of $1,000. ■

Sale or Other Disposition

The term *sale or other disposition* is defined broadly in the tax law and includes virtually any disposition of property. Thus, transactions such as trade-ins, casualties, condemnations, thefts, and bond retirements are treated as dispositions of property. The most common disposition of property is through a sale or exchange. Usually, the key factor in determining whether a disposition has taken place is whether an identifiable event has occurred[2] as opposed to a mere fluctuation in the value of the property.[3]

EXAMPLE 2

Lori owns Tan Corporation stock that cost $3,000. The stock has appreciated in value by $2,000 since Lori purchased it. Lori has no realized gain since mere fluctuation in value is not a disposition or identifiable event for tax purposes. ■

EXAMPLE 3

Assume the same facts as in Example 2, except that the stock has declined in value by $2,000 since Lori purchased it. Lori has no realized loss since the decline is associated with a mere fluctuation in value. ■

Amount Realized

The **amount realized** from a sale or other disposition of property is the sum of any money received plus the fair market value of other property received. The amount realized also includes any real property taxes treated as imposed on the seller that are actually paid by the buyer.[4] The reason for including these taxes in the amount

[1] § 1001(a) and Reg. § 1.1001–1(a).
[2] Reg. § 1.1001–1(c)(1).
[3] *Lynch v. Turrish*, 1 USTC ¶18, 3 AFTR 2986, 38 S.Ct. 537 (USSC, 1918).
[4] § 1001(b) and Reg. § 1.1001–1(b). Refer to Chapter 10 for a discussion of this subject.

TAX in the NEWS

Attempting to Defer Gain

The IRS is engaged in a dispute with a billionaire in the Tax Court over transactions that could produce back taxes of more than $143 million. The issue in dispute is whether a sale was completed. The case is of great interest because other wealthy executives have engaged in similar transactions.

The disputed transaction is called a "variable prepaid forward contract." The executive agrees to turn over shares of stock to a bank at a specific date in the future. At the same time, the executive loans the bank the same number of shares. The bank gives the executive cash, generally equal to 80 percent of the fair market value of the shares. According to the position taken by the executive, no recognized gain results because a completed sale has not yet taken place. Supposedly, the completed sale occurs when the executive legally transfers title to the shares to the bank—nearly 10 years in the future!

Source: Adapted from Jesse Drucker, "IRS Targets Billionaire's Tax Strategy," *Wall Street Journal,* June 9, 2008, p. A1.

realized is that by paying the taxes, the purchaser is, in effect, paying an additional amount to the seller of the property.

The amount realized also includes any liability on the property disposed of, such as a mortgage debt, if the buyer assumes the mortgage or the property is sold subject to the mortgage.[5] The amount of the liability is included in the amount realized even if the debt is nonrecourse and the amount of the debt is greater than the fair market value of the mortgaged property.[6]

EXAMPLE 4

Barry sells property on which there is a mortgage of $20,000 to Cole for $50,000 cash. Barry's amount realized from the sale is $70,000 if Cole assumes the mortgage or takes the property subject to the mortgage. ■

The **fair market value** of property received in a sale or other disposition has been defined by the courts as the price at which property will change hands between a willing seller and a willing buyer when neither is compelled to sell or buy.[7] Fair market value is determined by considering the relevant factors in each case.[8] An expert appraiser is often required to evaluate these factors in arriving at fair market value. When the fair market value of the property received cannot be determined, the value of the property given up by the taxpayer may be used.[9]

In calculating the amount realized, selling expenses such as advertising, commissions, and legal fees relating to the disposition are deducted. The amount realized is the net amount that the taxpayer received directly or indirectly, in the form of cash or anything else of value, from the disposition of the property.

Adjusted Basis

The **adjusted basis** of property disposed of is the property's original basis adjusted to the date of disposition.[10] Original basis is the cost or other basis of the property on the date the property is acquired by the taxpayer. Considerations involving original basis are discussed later in this chapter. *Capital additions* increase and *recoveries of capital* decrease the original basis so that on the date of disposition the adjusted basis

[5] *Crane v. Comm.,* 47–1 USTC ¶9217, 35 AFTR 776, 67 S.Ct. 1047 (USSC, 1947). Although a legal distinction exists between the direct assumption of a mortgage and taking property subject to a mortgage, the tax consequences in calculating the amount realized are the same.

[6] *Comm. v. Tufts,* 83–1 USTC ¶9328, 51 AFTR 2d 83–1132, 103 S.Ct. 1826 (USSC, 1983).

[7] *Comm. v. Marshman,* 60–2 USTC ¶9484, 5 AFTR 2d 1528, 279 F.2d 27 (CA–6, 1960).

[8] *O'Malley v. Ames,* 52–1 USTC ¶9361, 42 AFTR 19, 197 F.2d 256 (CA–8, 1952).

[9] *U.S. v. Davis,* 62–2 USTC ¶9509, 9 AFTR 2d 1625, 82 S.Ct. 1190 (USSC, 1962).

[10] § 1011(a) and Reg. § 1.1011–1.

reflects the unrecovered cost or other basis of the property.[11] Adjusted basis is determined as follows:

Cost (or other adjusted basis) on date of acquisition
+ Capital additions
− Capital recoveries
= Adjusted basis on date of disposition

Capital Additions

Capital additions include the cost of capital improvements and betterments made to the property by the taxpayer. These expenditures are distinguishable from expenditures for the ordinary repair and maintenance of the property, which are neither capitalized nor added to the original basis (refer to Chapter 6). The latter expenditures are deductible in the current taxable year if they are related to business or income-producing property. Amounts representing real property taxes treated as imposed on the seller but paid or assumed by the buyer are part of the cost of the property.[12] Any liability on property that is assumed by the buyer is also included in the buyer's original basis of the property. The same rule applies if property is acquired subject to a liability. Amortization of the discount on bonds increases the adjusted basis of the bonds.[13]

Capital Recoveries

Capital recoveries decrease the adjusted basis of property. The following are examples of capital recoveries:

1. *Depreciation and cost recovery allowances.* The original basis of depreciable property is reduced by the annual depreciation charges (or cost recovery allowances) while the property is held by the taxpayer. The amount of depreciation that is subtracted from the original basis is the greater of the *allowed* or *allowable* depreciation calculated on an annual basis.[14] In most circumstances, the allowed and allowable depreciation amounts are the same (refer to Chapter 8).
2. *Casualties and thefts.* A casualty or theft may result in the reduction of the adjusted basis of property.[15] The adjusted basis is reduced by the amount of the deductible loss. In addition, the adjusted basis is reduced by the amount of insurance proceeds received. However, the receipt of insurance proceeds may result in a recognized gain rather than a deductible loss. The gain increases the adjusted basis of the property.[16]

EXAMPLE 5

An insured truck that Marvin used in his trade or business is destroyed in an accident. The adjusted basis is $8,000, and the fair market value is $6,500. Marvin receives insurance proceeds of $6,500. The amount of the casualty loss is $1,500 ($6,500 insurance proceeds − $8,000 adjusted basis). The adjusted basis is reduced by the $1,500 casualty loss and the $6,500 of insurance proceeds received. ■

EXAMPLE 6

An insured truck that Marvin used in his trade or business is destroyed in an accident. The adjusted basis is $6,500, and the fair market value is $8,000. Marvin receives insurance proceeds of $8,000. The amount of the casualty gain is $1,500 ($8,000 insurance proceeds − $6,500 adjusted basis). The adjusted basis is increased by the $1,500 casualty

[11] § 1016(a) and Reg. § 1.1016–1.

[12] Reg. §§ 1.1001–1(b)(2) and 1.1012–1(b). Refer to Chapter 10 for a discussion of this subject.

[13] See Chapter 14 for a discussion of bond discount and the related amortization.

[14] § 1016(a)(2) and Reg. § 1.1016–3(a)(1)(i).

[15] Refer to Chapter 7 for the discussion of casualties and thefts.

[16] Reg. § 1.1016–6(a).

gain and is reduced by the $8,000 of insurance proceeds received ($6,500 basis before casualty + $1,500 casualty gain − $8,000 insurance proceeds = $0 basis). ■

3. *Certain corporate distributions.* A corporate distribution to a shareholder that is not taxable is treated as a return of capital, and it reduces the basis of the shareholder's stock in the corporation.[17] For example, if a corporation makes a cash distribution to its shareholders and has no earnings and profits, the distributions are treated as a return of capital. Once the basis of the stock is reduced to zero, the amount of any subsequent distributions is a capital gain if the stock is a capital asset. These rules are illustrated in Example 8 of Chapter 19.
4. *Amortizable bond premium.* The basis in a bond purchased at a premium is reduced by the amortizable portion of the bond premium.[18] Investors in taxable bonds may *elect* to amortize the bond premium, but the premium on tax-exempt bonds *must be* amortized.[19] The amount of the amortized premium on taxable bonds is permitted as an interest deduction. Therefore, the election enables the taxpayer to take an annual interest deduction to offset ordinary income in exchange for a larger capital gain or smaller capital loss on the disposition of the bond. No such interest deduction is permitted for tax-exempt bonds.

   The amortization deduction is allowed for taxable bonds because the premium is viewed as a cost of earning the taxable interest from the bonds. The reason the basis of taxable bonds is reduced is that the amortization deduction is a recovery of the cost or basis of the bonds. The basis of tax-exempt bonds is reduced even though the amortization is not allowed as a deduction. No amortization deduction is permitted on tax-exempt bonds because the interest income is exempt from tax and the amortization of the bond premium merely represents an adjustment of the effective amount of such income.

EXAMPLE 7

Antonio purchases Eagle Corporation taxable bonds with a face value of $100,000 for $110,000, thus paying a premium of $10,000. The annual interest rate is 7%, and the bonds mature 10 years from the date of purchase. The annual interest income is $7,000 (7% × $100,000). If Antonio elects to amortize the bond premium, the $10,000 premium is deducted over the 10-year period. Antonio's basis for the bonds is reduced each year by the amount of the amortization deduction. Note that if the bonds were tax-exempt, amortization of the bond premium and the basis adjustment would be mandatory. However, no deduction would be allowed for the amortization. ■

5. *Easements.* An easement is the legal right to use another's land for a special purpose. Historically, easements were commonly used to obtain rights-of-way for utility lines and roads. In recent years, grants of conservation easements have become a popular means of obtaining charitable contribution deductions and reducing the value of real estate for transfer tax (i.e., estate and gift) purposes. Likewise, scenic easements are used to reduce the value of land as assessed for ad valorem property tax purposes.

   If the taxpayer does not retain any right to the use of the land, all of the basis is assigned to the easement. However, if the use of the land is only partially restricted, an allocation of some of the basis to the easement is appropriate.

[17] § 1016(a)(4) and Reg. § 1.1016–5(a).

[18] § 1016(a)(5) and Reg. § 1.1016–5(b). The accounting treatment of bond premium amortization is the same as for tax purposes. The amortization results in a decrease in the bond investment account.

[19] § 171(c).

CONCEPT SUMMARY 13.1

Recognized Gain or Loss

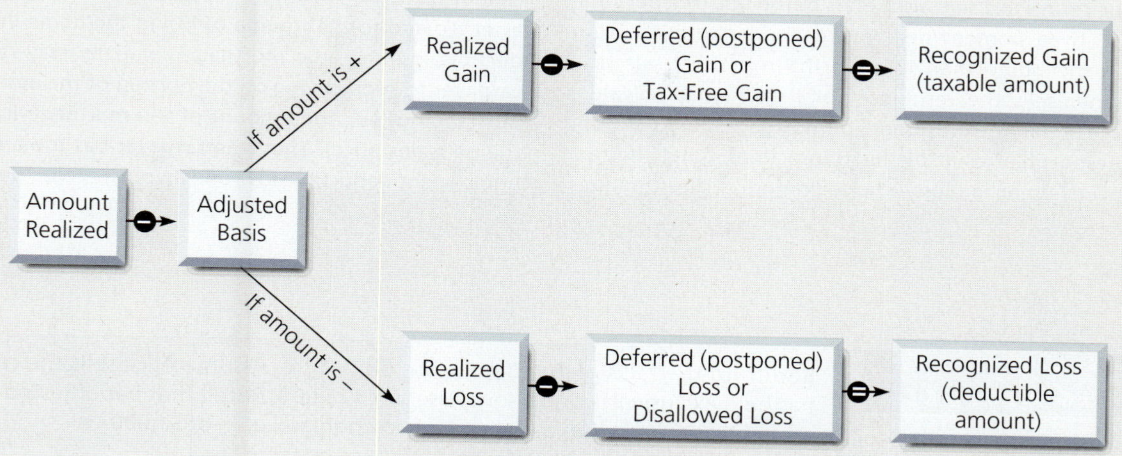

RECOGNIZED GAIN OR LOSS

LO.2

Distinguish between realized and recognized gain or loss.

Recognized gain is the amount of the realized gain that is included in the taxpayer's gross income.[20] A **recognized loss**, on the other hand, is the amount of a realized loss that is deductible for tax purposes.[21] As a general rule, the entire amount of a realized gain or loss is recognized.[22]

Concept Summary 13.1 summarizes the realized gain or loss and recognized gain or loss concepts.

NONRECOGNITION OF GAIN OR LOSS

In certain cases, a realized gain or loss is not recognized upon the sale or other disposition of property. One such case involves nontaxable exchanges, which are covered later in this chapter. Others include losses realized upon the sale, exchange, or condemnation of personal use assets (as opposed to business or income-producing property) and gains realized upon the sale of a residence. In addition, realized losses from the sale or exchange of business or income-producing property between certain related parties are not recognized.[23]

Sale, Exchange, or Condemnation of Personal Use Assets

A realized loss from the sale, exchange, or condemnation of personal use assets (e.g., a personal residence or an automobile not used at all for business or income-producing purposes) is not recognized for tax purposes. An exception exists for casualty or theft losses from personal use assets (see Chapter 7). In contrast, any gain realized from the sale or other disposition of personal use assets is, generally, fully taxable.

[20] § 61(a)(3) and Reg. § 1.61–6(a).

[21] § 165(a) and Reg. § 1.165–1(a).

[22] § 1001(c) and Reg. § 1.1002–1(a).

[23] § 267(a)(1).

TAX *in* the NEWS

TRIPLE THE MISERY!

Although short sales have traditionally involved stocks, today the term *short sale* also refers to the sale of a personal residence by a homeowner who is "underwater," owing more on the home than it is worth. In a short sale, the homeowner sells the residence for its fair market value, which is less than the mortgage (or mortgages) on the property. One possible result of this transaction is that the taxpayer incurs a realized loss—the selling price is less than his or her basis in the property. Unfortunately, the realized loss cannot be recognized because a residence is a personal use asset. To add to the trauma of losing the home in a nondeductible loss sale, the mortgage company may require the taxpayer to keep paying on the portion of the mortgage still outstanding (i.e., the amount of the mortgage in excess of the net sales price). Thus, the taxpayer has triple misery: no home, a nondeductible loss, and an outstanding debt to pay.

EXAMPLE 8
THE BIG PICTURE

Return to the facts of *The Big Picture* on p. 13-2. Assume Alice sells the car, which she has held exclusively for personal use, for $23,000. Recall that her adjusted basis for the car is $22,000. Alice has a realized and recognized gain of $1,000. ■

EXAMPLE 9
THE BIG PICTURE

Return to the facts of *The Big Picture* on p. 13-2. Assume Alice sells the car in Example 8 for $20,000. She has a realized loss of $2,000, but the loss is not recognized. ■

LO.3

Apply the recovery of capital doctrine.

RECOVERY OF CAPITAL DOCTRINE

Doctrine Defined

The **recovery of capital doctrine** pervades all the tax rules relating to property transactions. The doctrine derives its roots from the very essence of the income tax—a tax on income. Under the doctrine, as a general rule, a taxpayer is entitled to recover the cost or other original basis of property acquired and is not taxed on that amount.

The cost or other original basis of depreciable property is recovered through annual depreciation deductions. The basis is reduced as the cost is recovered over the period the property is held. Therefore, when property is sold or otherwise disposed of, it is the adjusted basis (unrecovered cost or other basis) that is compared with the amount realized from the disposition to determine realized gain or loss.

Relationship of the Recovery of Capital Doctrine to the Concepts of Realization and Recognition

If a sale or other disposition results in a realized gain, the taxpayer has recovered more than the adjusted basis of the property. Conversely, if a sale or other disposition results in a realized loss, the taxpayer has recovered less than the adjusted basis.

The general rules for the relationship between the recovery of capital doctrine and the realized and recognized gain and loss concepts are summarized as follows:

Rule 1. A realized gain that is *never recognized* results in the *permanent recovery* of more than the taxpayer's cost or other basis for tax purposes. For example, all or a portion of the realized gain on the sale of a personal residence can be excluded from gross income under § 121.

Rule 2. A realized gain on which *recognition is postponed* results in the *temporary recovery* of more than the taxpayer's cost or other basis for tax purposes. For example, an exchange of like-kind property under

§ 1031 and an involuntary conversion under § 1033 are both eligible for postponement treatment.

Rule 3. A realized loss that is *never recognized* results in the *permanent recovery* of less than the taxpayer's cost or other basis for tax purposes. For example, a loss on the sale of an automobile held for personal use is not deductible.

Rule 4. A realized loss on which *recognition is postponed* results in the *temporary recovery* of less than the taxpayer's cost or other basis for tax purposes. For example, the realized loss on the exchange of like-kind property under § 1031 is postponed.

These rules are illustrated in discussions to follow in this chapter.

13.2 Basis Considerations

DETERMINATION OF COST BASIS

LO.4

Explain how basis is determined for various methods of asset acquisition.

As noted earlier, the basis of property is generally the property's cost. Cost is the amount paid for the property in cash or other property.[24] This general rule follows logically from the recovery of capital doctrine; that is, the cost or other basis of property is to be recovered tax-free by the taxpayer.

A *bargain purchase* of property is an exception to the general rule for determining basis. A bargain purchase may result when an employer transfers property to an employee at less than the property's fair market value (as compensation for services) or when a corporation transfers property to a shareholder at less than the property's fair market value (a dividend). The amount included in income either as compensation for services or dividend income is the difference between the bargain purchase price and the property's fair market value. The basis of property acquired in a bargain purchase is the property's fair market value.[25] If the basis of the property were not increased by the bargain amount, the taxpayer would be taxed on this amount again at disposition.

EXAMPLE 10

Wade buys land from his employer for $10,000 on December 30. The fair market value of the land is $15,000. Wade must include the $5,000 difference between the cost and the fair market value of the land in gross income for the taxable year. The bargain element represents additional compensation to Wade. His basis for the land is $15,000, the land's fair market value. ■

Identification Problems

Cost identification problems are frequently encountered in securities transactions. For example, the Regulations require that the taxpayer adequately identify the particular stock that has been sold.[26] A problem arises when the taxpayer has purchased separate lots of stock on different dates or at different prices and cannot adequately identify the lot from which a particular sale takes place. In this case, the stock is presumed to come from the first lot or lots purchased (a FIFO presumption).[27] When securities are left in the custody of a broker, it may be necessary to provide specific instructions and receive written confirmation as to which securities are being sold.

[24] § 1012 and Reg. § 1.1012–1(a).

[25] Reg. §§ 1.61–2(d)(2)(i) and 1.301–1(j). See the discussion in Chapter 5 of the circumstances under which what appears to be a taxable bargain purchase is an excludible qualified employee discount.

[26] Reg. § 1.1012–1(c)(1).

[27] *Kluger Associates, Inc.*, 69 T.C. 925 (1978).

TAX *in* the NEWS

Brokers to Provide Cost Basis Data

Recently enacted tax legislation requires brokers and others in similar enterprises to provide investors with an annual report on the cost basis of their stocks (to be included on Form 1099–B). Recognizing that many brokerage firms will have to modify their records in order to comply, Congress delayed implementation of the reporting requirement. It applies only to stock that customers buy on or after January 1, 2011.

The primary reason for the requirement is to enable taxpayers to use the correct basis in calculating the gain or loss on the sale of the stock. In the simplest situation in which only a single lot of the stock was purchased, the taxpayer still may not have this information available when the stock is sold—perhaps many years later. Even if the investor maintains good records, nontaxable stock dividends, stock splits, and spin-offs may create confusion and result in unreliable data being used to determine the basis. For the investor who has multiple purchases of a stock, the likelihood of making an incorrect determination of cost basis is even greater.

A secondary reason for the reporting requirement is to generate more revenue for the Treasury. The government believes that taxpayers are knowingly underreporting capital gains on the sale of securities. It anticipates that it will collect billions of dollars over the next 10 years by requiring this broker reporting.

Source: Adapted from Arden Dale, "Investors to Get Reports on Cost Basis of Stocks," *Wall Street Journal*, February 5, 2009, p. D4.

EXAMPLE 11

Polly purchases 100 shares of Olive Corporation stock on July 1, 2009, for $5,000 ($50 a share) and another 100 shares of Olive stock on July 1, 2010, for $6,000 ($60 a share). She sells 50 shares of the stock on January 2, 2011. The cost of the stock sold, assuming Polly cannot adequately identify the shares, is $50 a share, or $2,500. This is the cost Polly will compare with the amount realized in determining the gain or loss from the sale. ■

Allocation Problems

When a taxpayer acquires *multiple assets in a lump-sum purchase*, the total cost must be allocated among the individual assets.[28] Allocation is necessary for several reasons:

- Some of the assets acquired may be depreciable (e.g., buildings), while others may not be (e.g., land).
- Only a portion of the assets acquired may be sold.
- Some of the assets may be capital or § 1231 assets that receive special tax treatment upon subsequent sale or other disposition.

The lump-sum cost is allocated on the basis of the fair market values of the individual assets acquired.

EXAMPLE 12

Harry purchases a building and land for $800,000. Because of the depressed nature of the industry in which the seller was operating, Harry was able to negotiate a very favorable purchase price. Appraisals of the individual assets indicate that the fair market value of the building is $600,000 and that of the land is $400,000. Harry's basis for the building is $480,000 [($600,000/$1,000,000) × $800,000], and his basis for the land is $320,000 [($400,000/$1,000,000) × $800,000]. ■

If a business is purchased and **goodwill** is involved, a special allocation rule applies. Initially, the purchase price is assigned to the assets, excluding goodwill, to the extent of their total fair market value. This assigned amount is allocated among the assets on the basis of the fair market value of the individual assets acquired. Goodwill is then assigned the residual amount of the purchase price. The resultant allocation is applicable to both the buyer and the seller.[29]

[28] Reg. § 1.61–6(a).

[29] § 1060.

TAX *in* the NEWS

FREQUENT-FLYER MILES AND BASIS

There are many ways to get frequent-flyer miles. Perhaps the most logical is to fly on an airplane, but staying in a hotel, renting a car, and using your credit card can also generate frequent-flyer miles. A more novel approach is to buy shares in a mutual fund.

Always watch out for the tax consequences, though. In a letter ruling, the IRS held that taxpayers who receive frequent-flyer miles for buying mutual fund shares must reduce their mutual fund basis by the fair market value of the miles received. The mutual fund must notify its shareholders of the fair market value, which is based on the cost of buying frequent-flyer miles from the airlines.

EXAMPLE 13

Rocky sells his business to Paul. They agree that the values of the individual assets are as follows:

Inventory	$ 50,000
Building	500,000
Land	200,000
Goodwill	150,000

After negotiations, Rocky and Paul agree on a sales price of $1 million. Applying the residual method with respect to goodwill results in the following allocation of the $1 million purchase price:

Inventory	$ 50,000
Building	500,000
Land	200,000
Goodwill	250,000

The residual method requires that all of the excess of the purchase price over the fair market value of the assets ($1,000,000 – $900,000 = $100,000) be allocated to goodwill. Without this requirement, the purchaser could allocate the excess pro rata to all of the assets, including goodwill, based on their respective fair market values. This would have resulted in only $166,667 [$150,000 + ($150,000 ÷ $900,000 × $100,000)] being assigned to goodwill. ■

In the case of *nontaxable stock dividends*, the allocation depends on whether the dividend is a common stock dividend on common stock or a preferred stock dividend on common stock. If the dividend is common on common, the cost of the original common shares is allocated to the total shares owned after the dividend.[30]

EXAMPLE 14

Susan owns 100 shares of Sparrow Corporation common stock for which she paid $1,100. She receives a 10% common stock dividend, giving her a new total of 110 shares. Before the stock dividend, Susan's basis was $11 per share ($1,100 ÷ 100 shares). The basis of each share after the stock dividend is $10 ($1,100 ÷ 110 shares). ■

If the nontaxable stock dividend is preferred stock on common, the cost of the original common shares is allocated between the common and preferred shares on the basis of their relative fair market values on the date of distribution.[31]

EXAMPLE 15

Fran owns 100 shares of Cardinal Corporation common stock for which she paid $1,000. She receives a nontaxable stock dividend of 50 shares of preferred stock on her

[30] §§ 305(a) and 307(a).

[31] Reg. § 1.307–1(a).

common stock. The fair market values on the date of distribution of the preferred stock dividend are $30 a share for common stock and $40 a share for preferred stock.

Fair market value of common ($30 × 100 shares)	$3,000
Fair market value of preferred ($40 × 50 shares)	2,000
	$5,000
Basis of common: 3/5 × $1,000	$ 600
Basis of preferred: 2/5 × $1,000	$ 400

The basis per share for the common stock is $6 ($600/100 shares). The basis per share for the preferred stock is $8 ($400/50 shares). ■

The holding period for a nontaxable stock dividend, whether received in the form of common stock or preferred stock, includes the holding period of the original shares.[32] The significance of the holding period for capital assets is discussed in Chapter 14.

In the case of *nontaxable stock rights*, the basis of the rights is zero unless the taxpayer elects or is required to allocate a portion of the cost of the stock already held to the newly received stock rights. If the fair market value of the rights is 15 percent or more of the fair market value of the stock, the taxpayer is required to allocate. If the value of the rights is less than 15 percent of the fair market value of the stock, the taxpayer may elect to allocate.[33] When allocation is required or elected, the cost of the stock on which the rights are received is allocated between the stock and the rights on the basis of their relative fair market values.

EXAMPLE 16

Donald receives nontaxable stock rights with a fair market value of $1,000. The fair market value of the stock on which the rights were received is $8,000 (cost $10,000). Donald does not elect to allocate. The basis of the rights is zero. If he exercises the rights, the basis of the new stock is the exercise (subscription) price. ■

EXAMPLE 17

Assume the same facts as in Example 16, except the fair market value of the rights is $3,000. Donald must allocate because the value of the rights ($3,000) is 15% or more of the value of the stock ($3,000/$8,000 = 37.5%).

- The basis of the stock is $7,273 [($8,000/$11,000) × $10,000].
- The basis of the rights is $2,727 [($3,000/$11,000) × $10,000].

If Donald exercises the rights, the basis of the new stock is the exercise (subscription) price plus the basis of the rights. If he sells the rights, he recognizes gain or loss equal to the difference between the amount realized and the basis of the rights. This allocation rule applies only when the rights are exercised or sold. Therefore, if the rights are allowed to lapse (expire), they have no basis, and the basis of the original stock is the stock's cost, $10,000. ■

The holding period of nontaxable stock rights includes the holding period of the stock on which the rights were distributed. However, if the rights are exercised, the holding period of the newly acquired stock begins with the date the rights are exercised.[34]

GIFT BASIS

When a taxpayer receives property as a gift, there is no cost to the donee (recipient). Thus, under the cost basis provision, the donee's basis would be zero. However, this would violate the statutory intent that gifts not be subject to the income tax.[35] With a zero basis, if the donee sold the property, all of the amount realized would be treated

[32] § 1223(5) and Reg. § 1.1223–1(e).

[33] § 307(b).

[34] § 1223(5) and Reg. §§ 1.1223–1(e) and (f).

[35] § 102(a).

TAX *in* the NEWS

Preferred Stock Is on the Rise

Preferred stock is normally thought to offer two advantages over common stock. First, in terms of income security, preferred stock is more likely to provide a steady and predictable income stream. Second, preferred shareholders stand ahead of common shareholders if the corporation is liquidated.

When compared with a corporation's bonds, preferred stock usually offers a higher rate of return. But unlike bondholders, preferred shareholders cannot force a company into a bankruptcy filing.

Preferred stock does have certain disadvantages. The dividend yield on common stock can substantially exceed that on preferred. The value of common stock increases as the company's value increases. Preferred stock usually lacks voting rights. Finally, because preferred dividends usually are fixed, preferred stock lacks a hedge against inflation.

Though some investors and analysts think that preferred stock combines the worst features of stocks and bonds, Wall Street is currently awash with preferred stock issued by banks—they issued close to $25 billion worth in just a few months of a recent year. Preferred stock is a desirable way to shore up a bank's balance sheet since it boosts Tier 1 capital ratios (a measure of a bank's health) without increasing debt.

Source: Adapted from Robert Cyran and Richard Beales, "A Preferred-Stock Deluge," *Wall Street Journal,* April 25, 2008, p. C12.

as realized gain. Therefore, a basis is assigned to the property received depending on the following:

- The date of the gift.
- The basis of the property to the donor.
- The amount of the gift tax paid.
- The fair market value of the property.

Gift Basis Rules if No Gift Tax Is Paid

Property received by gift can be referred to as *dual basis* property; that is, the basis for gain and the basis for loss might not be the same amount. The present basis rules for gifts of property are as follows:

- If the donee disposes of gift property in a transaction that results in a gain, the basis to the donee is the same as the donor's adjusted basis.[36] The donee's basis in this case is referred to as the *gain basis.* Therefore, a *realized gain* results if the amount realized from the disposition exceeds the donee's gain basis.

EXAMPLE 18

Melissa purchased stock in 2010 for $10,000. She gave the stock to her son, Joe, in 2011, when the fair market value was $15,000. No gift tax is paid on the transfer, and Joe subsequently sells the property for $15,000. Joe's basis is $10,000, and he has a realized gain of $5,000. ■

- If the donee disposes of gift property in a transaction that results in a loss, the basis to the donee is the *lower* of the donor's adjusted basis or the fair market value on the date of the gift. The donee's basis in this case is referred to as the *loss basis.* Therefore, a *realized loss* results if the amount realized from the disposition is less than the donee's loss basis.

EXAMPLE 19

Burt purchased stock in 2010 for $10,000. He gave the stock to his son, Cliff, in 2011, when the fair market value was $7,000. No gift tax is paid on the transfer. Cliff later

[36] § 1015(a) and Reg. § 1.1015–1(a)(1). See Reg. § 1.1015–1(a)(3) for cases in which the facts necessary to determine the donor's adjusted basis are unknown. Refer to Example 24 for the effect of depreciation deductions by the donee.

sells the stock for $6,000. Cliff's basis is $7,000 (fair market value is less than donor's adjusted basis of $10,000), and the realized loss from the sale is $1,000 ($6,000 amount realized – $7,000 basis). ■

The amount of the loss basis will *differ* from the amount of the gain basis only if, at the date of the gift, the adjusted basis of the property exceeds the property's fair market value. Note that the loss basis rule prevents the donee from receiving a tax benefit from a decline in value that occurred while the donor held the property. Therefore, in Example 19, Cliff has a loss of only $1,000 rather than a loss of $4,000. The $3,000 difference represents the decline in value that occurred while Burt held the property. Ironically, however, the gain basis rule may result in the donee being subject to income tax on the appreciation that occurred while the donor held the property, as illustrated in Example 18.

If the amount realized from a sale or other disposition is *between* the basis for loss and the basis for gain, no gain or loss is realized.

EXAMPLE 20

Assume the same facts as in Example 19, except that Cliff sells the stock for $8,000. Application of the gain basis rule produces a loss of $2,000 ($8,000 – $10,000). Application of the loss basis rule produces a gain of $1,000 ($8,000 – $7,000). Because the amount realized is between the gain basis and the loss basis, Cliff recognizes neither a gain nor a loss. ■

Adjustment for Gift Tax

If gift taxes are paid by the donor, the donee's gain basis may exceed the adjusted basis of the property to the donor. This occurs only if the fair market value of the property at the date of the gift is greater than the donor's adjusted basis (the property has appreciated in value). The portion of the gift tax paid that is related to the appreciation is added to the donor's basis in calculating the donee's gain basis for the property. In this circumstance, the following formula is used for calculating the donee's gain basis:[37]

$$\text{Donee's gain basis} = \text{Donor's adjusted basis} + \left(\frac{\text{Unrealized appreciation}}{\text{Taxable gift*}} \times \text{Gift tax paid}\right)$$

*The taxable gift is the fair market value of the gift less the per donee annual exclusion.

EXAMPLE 21

In 2011, Bonnie made a gift of stock (adjusted basis of $15,000) to Peggy. The stock had a fair market value of $50,000, and the transfer resulted in a gift tax of $4,000. The unrealized appreciation of the stock is $35,000 ($50,000 fair market value – $15,000 adjusted basis), and the taxable gift is $37,000 ($50,000 fair market value of gift – $13,000 annual exclusion). Peggy's basis in the stock is $18,800, determined as follows:

Donor's adjusted basis	$15,000
Gift tax attributable to appreciation— $35,000/$37,000 = 95% (rounded) × $4,000	3,800
Donee's gain basis	$18,800

■

EXAMPLE 22

Don made a gift of stock to Matt in 2011, when the fair market value of the stock was $50,000. Don paid gift tax of $4,000. Don had purchased the stock in 1991 for $65,000. Because there is no unrealized appreciation at the date of the gift, none of the gift tax paid is added to Don's basis in calculating Matt's gain basis. Therefore, Matt's gain basis is $65,000. ■

[37] § 1015(d)(6) and Reg. § 1.1015–5(c)(2).

For *gifts made before 1977*, the full amount of the gift tax paid is added to the donor's basis. However, the ceiling on this total is the fair market value of the property at the date of the gift. Thus, in Example 21, if the gift had been made before 1977, the basis of the property would be $19,000 ($15,000 + $4,000). In Example 22, the gain basis would still be $65,000 ($65,000 + $0).

Holding Period

The **holding period** for property acquired by gift begins on the date the donor acquired the property if the gain basis rule applies.[38] The holding period starts on the date of the gift if the loss basis rule applies.[39] The significance of the holding period for capital assets is discussed in Chapter 14.

The following example summarizes the basis and holding period rules for gift property:

EXAMPLE 23

Jill acquired 100 shares of Wren Corporation stock on December 30, 1993, for $40,000. On January 3, 2011, when the stock has a fair market value of $38,000, Jill gives it to Dennis and pays gift tax of $4,000. The basis is not increased by a portion of the gift tax paid because the property has not appreciated in value at the time of the gift. Therefore, Dennis's gain basis is $40,000. Dennis's basis for determining loss is $38,000 (fair market value) because the fair market value on the date of the gift is less than the donor's adjusted basis.

- If Dennis sells the stock for $45,000, he has a recognized gain of $5,000. The holding period for determining whether the capital gain is short term or long term begins on December 30, 1993, the date Jill acquired the property.
- If Dennis sells the stock for $36,000, he has a recognized loss of $2,000. The holding period for determining whether the capital loss is short term or long term begins on January 3, 2011, the date of the gift.
- If Dennis sells the property for $39,000, there is no loss because the amount realized is less than the gain basis of $40,000 and more than the loss basis of $38,000. ■

Basis for Depreciation

The basis for depreciation on depreciable gift property is the donee's gain basis.[40] This rule is applicable even if the donee later sells the property at a loss and uses the loss basis rule in calculating the amount of the realized loss.

EXAMPLE 24

Vito gave a machine to Tina in 2011. At that time, the adjusted basis was $32,000 (cost of $40,000 − accumulated depreciation of $8,000), and the fair market value was $26,000. No gift tax was paid. Tina's gain basis at the date of the gift is $32,000, and her loss basis is $26,000. During 2011, Tina deducts depreciation (cost recovery) of $6,400 ($32,000 × 20%). (Refer to Chapter 8 for the cost recovery tables.) At the end of 2011, Tina's gain basis and loss basis are calculated as follows:

	Gain Basis	Loss Basis
Donor's basis or fair market value	$32,000	$26,000
Depreciation	(6,400)	(6,400)
	$25,600	$19,600

■

[38]§ 1223(2) and Reg. § 1.1223–1(b).

[39]Rev.Rul. 59–86, 1959–1 C.B. 209.

[40]§ 1011 and Reg. §§ 1.1011–1 and 1.167(g)–1.

ETHICS & Equity

Looking a Gift Horse in the Eye

Walter rarely sees his Uncle George because George is a devoted world traveler. On January 15, 2011, Walter received an envelope that George had mailed to him from Singapore on December 13, 2010. The envelope contained a Christmas card from George and 1,000 shares of stock of Lavender, Inc.

In October 2011, Walter decides to pay off credit card debt and buy a new car, so he sells the stock for $45,000.

In early April 2012, the accountant who is preparing Walter's tax return tells him that she needs to know his uncle's adjusted basis for the stock and the amount of any gift tax paid. Since Walter is unable to contact his uncle by April 15, 2012, he requests a filing extension on Form 4868. He sends a letter to Uncle George requesting this information and thanking him for the gift. Walter is able to ascertain from a stock service that during the past 10 years, the stock price has ranged from $10 to $50 per share.

On August 10, 2012, Uncle George unexpectedly calls from Florence. He says he has not filed any type of Federal income tax return in years. He thinks he won the stock in a poker game in Monaco about 15 years ago when another player used it to cover a $15,000 bet.

Walter wants to file his tax return by the October 15, 2012 due date. He does not think it is a good idea to tell the return preparer how his uncle acquired the stock or about his uncle not filing income tax returns. Consequently, he tells the accountant that his uncle's basis for the stock is $15,000 and that no gift taxes were paid.

The return is completed and filed with a Schedule D reporting a long-term capital gain of $30,000 from the sale of the Lavender stock. Comment on the propriety of Walter's actions.

PROPERTY ACQUIRED FROM A DECEDENT

General Rules

The basis of property acquired from a decedent is generally the property's fair market value at the date of death (referred to as the *primary valuation amount*).[41] The property's basis is the fair market value six months after the date of death if the executor or administrator of the estate *elects* the alternate valuation date for estate tax purposes. This amount is referred to as the *alternate valuation amount.*

EXAMPLE 25
THE BIG PICTURE

Return to the facts of *The Big Picture* on p. 13-2. Alice and various other family members inherited property from Alice's grandmother, who died in 2011. At the date of death, her grandmother's adjusted basis for the property Alice inherited was $275,000. The house's fair market value at the date of death was $475,000. The alternate valuation date was not elected. Alice's basis for income tax purposes is $475,000. This is commonly referred to as a *stepped-up basis.* ■

EXAMPLE 26
THE BIG PICTURE

Return to the facts of *The Big Picture* on p. 13-2. Assume the same facts as in Example 25, except the house's fair market value at the date of the grandmother's death was $260,000. Alice's basis for income tax purposes is $260,000. This is commonly referred to as a *stepped-down basis.* ■

No estate tax return must be filed for estates below a threshold amount. In such cases, the alternate valuation date and amount are not available. Even if an estate tax return is filed and the executor elects the alternate valuation date, the six months after death date is available only for property that the executor has not distributed before this date. For any property distributed or otherwise disposed of by the executor during the

[41] §§ 1014(a) and 1022. For decedents dying in 2010, the executor of the estate can elect to avoid any estate tax for 2010 by choosing a modified carryover basis rather than a fair market value basis. Section 1022 of the Code provides that the carryover basis amount for the estate can be increased by $1.3 million plus any NOL carryovers of the decedent plus any capital loss carryovers of the decedent plus any unrealized losses of the decedent. In addition, a special $3 million step-up amount can be added for the surviving spouse. Such carryover basis as adjusted for an asset cannot exceed the fair market value of an asset. Our Examples and Problems assume the fair market value rules will continue to apply to property inherited after 2009.

TAX *in* the NEWS

Return of Capital versus Dividends: Is It Worth Dying For?

When a shareholder receives a corporate distribution, there is an obvious advantage to having it classified as a return of capital rather than as a dividend. Although this advantage has been reduced by the favorable 15%/0% (15%/5% prior to 2008) tax rate on qualified dividends, it still exists. With a dividend, the entire amount is included in the recipient's gross income. For a return of capital, however, only the excess of the value of the distribution over the stock basis is included in the shareholder's gross income.

A corporation that has been generating losses may be able to treat a distribution as a return of capital rather than as a dividend. Whether the distribution is classified as a dividend depends on the amount of the corporation's earnings and profits (E & P). One of the significant effects of operating losses is to reduce E & P. If E & P is zero, all of the distribution is taxed as a return of capital.

A return of capital result can provide the shareholder with a temporary or a permanent tax benefit. As noted, the shareholder includes in gross income only the amount of the distribution exceeding the stock basis, but this benefit can be temporary because the distribution reduces the shareholder's basis in the stock. Consequently, if the shareholder subsequently sells the stock, he or she will have a larger gain or a smaller loss. The permanent benefit occurs if the shareholder dies without selling the stock! Since the basis of the stock to the beneficiary (or estate) is the fair market value on the date of the decedent's death, any prior reduction in the basis in the stock is not relevant.

six-month period preceding the alternate valuation date, the adjusted basis to the beneficiary will equal the fair market value on the date of distribution or other disposition.[42]

The alternate valuation date can be *elected only* if, as a result of the election, both the value of the gross estate and the estate tax liability are lower than they would have been if the primary valuation date had been used. This provision prevents the alternate valuation election from being used to increase the basis of the property to the beneficiary for income tax purposes without simultaneously increasing the estate tax liability (because of estate tax deductions or credits).[43]

EXAMPLE 27

Nancy inherited all the property of her father, who died in 2011. Her father's adjusted basis for the property at the date of death was $650,000. The property's fair market value was $3,750,000 at the date of death and $3,760,000 six months after death. The alternate valuation date cannot be elected because the value of the gross estate has increased during the six-month period. Nancy's basis for income tax purposes is $3,750,000. ■

EXAMPLE 28

Assume the same facts as in Example 27, except the property's fair market value six months after death was $3,745,000. If the executor elects the alternate valuation date, Nancy's basis for income tax purposes is $3,745,000. ■

EXAMPLE 29

Assume the same facts as in the previous example, except the property is distributed four months after the date of the decedent's death. At the distribution date, the property's fair market value is $3,747,500. Since the executor elected the alternate valuation date, Nancy's basis for income tax purposes is $3,747,500. ■

For inherited property, both unrealized appreciation and decline in value are taken into consideration in determining the basis of the property for income tax purposes. Contrast this with the carryover basis rules for property received by gift.

Deathbed Gifts

The Code contains a provision designed to eliminate a tax avoidance technique referred to as *deathbed gifts.* With this technique, a donor makes a gift of appreciated property to a dying person with the understanding that the donor (or the

[42]§ 2032(a)(1) and Rev.Rul. 56–60, 1956–1 C.B. 443.

[43]§ 2032(c).

TAX *in* *the NEWS*

Current Status of the Income Tax Basis of Inherited Property

Enacted in 2001 in connection with the scheduled revocation of the estate tax, new § 1022 provides for a modified carryover basis for inherited property. Apparently, Congress had forgotten the disastrous result experienced with its prior attempt to impose the carryover basis approach to property passing by death. Applicable to property acquired after 1979, former Code § 1023 caused such complexity and confusion that it was repealed with retroactive effect one year later.

Congress did re-enact the estate tax and the related fair market value income tax basis rules for decedents dying in 2011. The estate tax exemption amount was increased, and the maximum estate tax rate was reduced. However, for 2010, the executor for the estate of a decedent dying in 2010 can elect to avoid any estate tax by choosing a modified carryover basis for the assets of the estate. (See the discussion in footnote 41.)

donor's spouse) will inherit the property on the donee's death. If the time period between the date of the gift and the date of the donee's death is not longer than one year, the usual basis rule (stepped-up basis) for inherited property may not apply. The adjusted basis of such property inherited by the donor or his or her spouse from the donee is the same as the decedent's adjusted basis for the property rather than the fair market value at the date of death or the alternate valuation date.[44]

EXAMPLE 30

Ned gives stock to his uncle, Vern, in 2011. Ned's basis for the stock is $100,000, and the fair market value is $900,000. No gift tax is paid. Eight months later, Ned inherits the stock from Vern. At the date of Vern's death, the fair market value of the stock is $980,000. Ned's adjusted basis for the stock is $100,000. ■

ETHICS *& Equity*

Helping a Friend Increase Basis: To Live or to Die?

Louise owns stock, adjusted basis of $4,500 and fair market value of $12,000, that is expected to continue appreciating. Beverly, Louise's best friend, has a terminal illness. Beverly's life expectancy is predicted to be between 6 and 18 months.

One day at lunch while the two friends were discussing their tax problems, Beverly mentioned that she had read a newspaper article about a tax planning opportunity that might be suitable for Louise. Under the scheme, Louise would make a gift of the appreciated stock to Beverly. In her will, Beverly would bequeath the stock to Louise. Since Beverly is confident that she will live longer than a year, the basis of the stock to Louise would be the fair market value on the date of Beverly's death. Beverly would "feel good" because she had helped Louise "beat the tax system."

You are Louise's tax adviser. How will you respond to Beverly's proposal to Louise?

Survivor's Share of Property

Both the decedent's share and the survivor's share of *community property* have a basis equal to the fair market value on the date of the decedent's death.[45] This result applies to the decedent's share of the community property because the property flows to the surviving spouse from the estate (fair market value basis is assigned to inherited property). Likewise, the surviving spouse's share of the community

[44] § 1014(e).

[45] § 1014(b)(6). See the listing of community property states in Chapter 4.

property is deemed to be acquired by bequest, devise, or inheritance from the decedent. Therefore, it also has a basis equal to the fair market value.

EXAMPLE 31

Floyd and Vera are married and reside in a community property state. They own as community property 200 shares of Crow stock acquired in 1986 for $100,000. Floyd dies in 2011, when the securities are valued at $300,000. One-half of the Crow stock is included in Floyd's estate. If Vera inherits Floyd's share of the community property, the basis for determining gain or loss is $300,000, determined as follows:

Vera's one-half of the community property (stepped up from $50,000 to $150,000 due to Floyd's death)	$150,000
Floyd's one-half of the community property (stepped up from $50,000 to $150,000 due to inclusion in his gross estate)	150,000
Vera's new basis	$300,000

In a *common law* state, only one-half of jointly held property of spouses (tenants by the entirety or joint tenants with rights of survivorship) is included in the estate.[46] In such a case, no adjustment of the basis is permitted for the excluded property interest (the surviving spouse's share).

EXAMPLE 32

Assume the same facts as in the previous example, except that the property is jointly held by Floyd and Vera who reside in a common law state. Floyd purchased the property and made a gift of one-half of the property to Vera when the stock was acquired. No gift tax was paid. Only one-half of the Crow stock is included in Floyd's estate. Vera's basis for determining gain or loss in the excluded half is not adjusted upward for the increase in value to date of death. Therefore, Vera's basis is $200,000, determined as follows:

Vera's one-half of the jointly held property (carryover basis of $50,000)	$ 50,000
Floyd's one-half of the jointly held property (stepped up from $50,000 to $150,000 due to inclusion in his gross estate)	150,000
Vera's new basis	$200,000

Holding Period of Property Acquired from a Decedent

The holding period of property acquired from a decedent is *deemed to be long term* (held for the required long-term holding period). This provision applies regardless of whether the property is disposed of at a gain or at a loss.[47]

DISALLOWED LOSSES

LO.5

Describe various loss disallowance provisions.

Related Taxpayers

Section 267 provides that realized losses from sales or exchanges of property, directly or indirectly, between certain related parties are not recognized. This loss disallowance provision applies to several types of related-party transactions. The most common involve (1) members of a family and (2) an individual and a corporation in which the individual owns, directly or indirectly, more than 50 percent in value of the corporation's outstanding stock. Section 707 provides a similar loss disallowance provision where the related parties are a partner and a partnership in which the partner owns, directly or indirectly, more than 50 percent of the capital interests or profits interests in the partnership. The rules governing the relationships covered by § 267 were discussed in Chapter 6. See the discussion of the special rules under § 1041 for property transfers between spouses or incident to divorce later in this chapter.

[46] § 2040(b).

[47] § 1223(11).

If income-producing or business property is transferred to a related taxpayer and a loss is disallowed, the basis of the property to the recipient is the property's cost to the transferee. However, if a subsequent sale or other disposition of the property by the original transferee results in a realized gain, the amount of gain is reduced by the loss that was previously disallowed.[48] This *right of offset* is not applicable if the original sale involved the sale of a personal use asset (e.g., the sale of a personal residence between related taxpayers). Furthermore, the right of offset is available only to the original transferee (the related-party buyer).

EXAMPLE 33

Pedro sells business property with an adjusted basis of $50,000 to his daughter, Josefina, for its fair market value of $40,000. Pedro's realized loss of $10,000 is not recognized.

- How much gain does Josefina recognize if she sells the property for $52,000? Josefina recognizes a $2,000 gain. Her realized gain is $12,000 ($52,000 less her basis of $40,000), but she can offset Pedro's $10,000 loss against the gain.
- How much gain does Josefina recognize if she sells the property for $48,000? Josefina recognizes no gain or loss. Her realized gain is $8,000 ($48,000 less her basis of $40,000), but she can offset $8,000 of Pedro's $10,000 loss against the gain. Note that Pedro's loss can only offset Josefina's gain. It cannot create a loss for Josefina.
- How much loss does Josefina recognize if she sells the property for $38,000? Josefina recognizes a $2,000 loss, the same as her realized loss ($38,000 less $40,000 basis). Pedro's loss does not increase Josefina's loss. His loss can be offset only against a gain. Since Josefina has no realized gain, Pedro's loss cannot be used and is never recognized. This part of the example assumes that the property is business or income-producing property to Josefina. If not, her $2,000 loss is personal and is not recognized. ■

The loss disallowance rules are designed to achieve two objectives. First, the rules prevent a taxpayer from directly transferring an unrealized loss to a related taxpayer in a higher tax bracket who could receive a greater tax benefit from recognition of the loss. Second, the rules eliminate a substantial administrative burden on the Internal Revenue Service as to the appropriateness of the selling price (fair market value or not). The loss disallowance rules are applicable even where the selling price is equal to the fair market value and can be validated (e.g., listed stocks).

The holding period of the buyer for the property is not affected by the holding period of the seller. That is, the buyer's *holding period* includes only the period of time he or she has held the property.[49]

Wash Sales

Section 1091 stipulates that in certain cases, a realized loss on the sale or exchange of stock or securities is not recognized. Specifically, if a taxpayer sells or exchanges stock or securities and within 30 days before *or* after the date of the sale or exchange acquires substantially identical stock or securities, any loss realized from the sale or exchange is not recognized because the transaction is a **wash sale**.[50] The term *acquire* means acquire by purchase or in a taxable exchange and includes an option to purchase substantially identical securities. *Substantially identical* means the same in all important particulars. Corporate bonds and preferred stock normally are not considered substantially identical to the corporation's common stock. However, if the bonds and preferred stock are convertible into common stock, they may be considered substantially identical under certain circumstances.[51] Attempts to avoid the application of the wash sales rules by having a related taxpayer repurchase the securities have been unsuccessful.[52] The wash sales provisions do *not* apply to gains.

[48] § 267(d) and Reg. § 1.267(d)–1(a).

[49] §§ 267(d) and 1223(2) and Reg. § 1.267(d)–1(c)(3).

[50] § 1091(a) and Reg. §§ 1.1091–1(a) and (f).

[51] Rev.Rul. 56–406, 1956–2 C.B. 523.

[52] *McWilliams v. Comm.*, 47–1 USTC ¶9289, 35 AFTR 1184, 67 S.Ct. 1477 (USSC, 1947).

Recognition of the loss is disallowed because the taxpayer is considered to be in substantially the same economic position after the sale and repurchase as before the sale and repurchase. This disallowance rule does not apply to taxpayers engaged in the business of buying and selling securities.[53] Investors, however, are not allowed to create losses through wash sales to offset income for tax purposes.

Realized loss that is not recognized is added to the *basis* of the substantially identical stock or securities whose acquisition resulted in the nonrecognition of loss.[54] In other words, the basis of the replacement stock or securities is increased by the amount of the unrecognized loss. If the loss were not added to the basis of the newly acquired stock or securities, the taxpayer would never recover the entire basis of the old stock or securities.

The basis of the new stock or securities includes the unrecovered portion of the basis of the formerly held stock or securities. Therefore, the *holding period* of the new stock or securities begins on the date of acquisition of the old stock or securities.[55]

EXAMPLE 34
THE BIG PICTURE

Return to the facts of *The Big Picture* on p. 13-2. Alice owned 100 shares of Green Corporation stock (adjusted basis of $20,000). She sold 50 shares for $8,000. Ten days later, she purchased 50 shares of the same stock for $7,000. Alice's realized loss of $2,000 ($8,000 amount realized − $10,000 adjusted basis of 50 shares) is not recognized because it resulted from a wash sale. Alice's basis in the newly acquired stock is $9,000 ($7,000 purchase price + $2,000 unrecognized loss from the wash sale). ■

A taxpayer may acquire fewer shares than the number sold in a wash sale. In this case, the loss from the sale is prorated between recognized and unrecognized loss on the basis of the ratio of the number of shares acquired to the number of shares sold.[56]

CONVERSION OF PROPERTY FROM PERSONAL USE TO BUSINESS OR INCOME-PRODUCING USE

As discussed previously, losses from the sale of personal use assets are not recognized for tax purposes, but losses from the sale of business and income-producing assets are deductible. Can a taxpayer convert a personal use asset that has declined in value to business or income-producing use and then sell the asset to recognize a business or income-producing loss? The tax law prevents this practice by specifying that the *original basis for loss* on personal use assets converted to business or income-producing use is the *lower* of the property's adjusted basis or fair market value on the date of conversion.[57] The *gain basis* for converted property is the property's adjusted basis on the date of conversion. The tax law is not concerned with gains on converted property because gains are recognized regardless of whether property is business, income-producing, or personal use.

EXAMPLE 35

Diane's personal residence has an adjusted basis of $175,000 and a fair market value of $160,000. Diane converts the personal residence to rental property. Her basis for loss is $160,000 (lower of $175,000 adjusted basis and fair market value of $160,000). The $15,000 decline in value is a personal loss and can never be recognized for tax purposes. Diane's basis for gain is $175,000. ■

The basis for loss is also the *basis for depreciating* the converted property.[58] This is an exception to the general rule that the basis for depreciation is the gain basis (e.g., property received by gift). This exception prevents the taxpayer from recovering a personal loss indirectly through depreciation of the higher original basis. After

[53] Reg. § 1.1091–1(a).

[54] § 1091(d) and Reg. § 1.1091–2(a).

[55] § 1223(4) and Reg. § 1.1223–1(d).

[56] § 1091(b) and Reg. § 1.1091–1(c).

[57] Reg. § 1.165–9(b)(2).

[58] Reg. § 1.167(g)–1.

TAX in the NEWS

A Benefit of Being Rich

Quite often legislation that contains tax increases is proposed with the caveat that most taxpayers need not worry because it will affect only the rich. Part of being rich includes the income earned from investments (e.g., interest, dividends, capital gains).

The Securities and Exchange Commission (SEC) has revised its definition of being rich. The SEC proposed raising the net worth requirement of people eligible to invest in hedge funds and other private-money pools—a proxy for the government's definition of rich. The requirement is $1 million, including the value of primary residences, or an annual income for the previous two years of $200,000 for individuals and $300,000 for couples. The proposed requirement is $2.5 million excluding any equity in homes or businesses.

Another measure of rich is the eligibility requirements of Natural Selection, a New York dating service. "Rich" men are paired with "beautiful" women. Men under age 25 must have a minimum annual income of $200,000; if over age 30, the amount increases to $500,000. If not employed, the man must have at least $1 million of invested assets or a $4 million trust fund. It appears the firm does not serve "rich" women and "handsome" men.

Source: Adapted from Robert Franks, "Millionaires Need Not Apply," *Wall Street Journal*, March 16, 2007, p. W2.

the property is converted, both its basis for loss and its basis for gain are adjusted for depreciation deductions from the date of conversion to the date of disposition. These rules apply only if a conversion from personal to business or income-producing use has actually occurred.

EXAMPLE 36

At a time when his personal residence (adjusted basis of $140,000) is worth $150,000, Keith converts one-half of it to rental use. Assume the property is not MACRS recovery property. At this point, the estimated useful life of the residence is 20 years, and there is no estimated salvage value. After renting the converted portion for five years, Keith sells the property for $144,000. All amounts relate only to the building; the land has been accounted for separately. Keith has a $2,000 realized gain from the sale of the personal use portion of the residence and a $19,500 realized gain from the sale of the rental portion. These gains are computed as follows:

	Personal Use	Rental
Original basis for gain and loss—adjusted basis on date of conversion (fair market value is greater than the adjusted basis)	$70,000	$70,000
Depreciation—five years	None	17,500
Adjusted basis—date of sale	$70,000	$52,500
Amount realized	72,000	72,000
Realized gain	$ 2,000	$19,500

■

As discussed later in this chapter, Keith may be able to exclude the $2,000 realized gain from the sale of the personal use portion of the residence under § 121. If the § 121 exclusion applies, only $17,500 (equal to the depreciation deducted) of the $19,500 realized gain from the rental portion is recognized.

EXAMPLE 37

Assume the same facts as in the previous example, except that the fair market value on the date of conversion is $130,000 and the sales proceeds are $90,000. Keith has a $25,000 realized loss from the sale of the personal use portion of the residence and a $3,750 realized loss from the sale of the rental portion. These losses are computed as follows:

	Personal Use	Rental
Original basis for loss—fair market value on date of conversion (fair market value is less than the adjusted basis)	*	$65,000
Depreciation—five years	None	16,250
Adjusted basis—date of sale	$70,000	$48,750
Amount realized	45,000	45,000
Realized loss	($25,000)	($ 3,750)

*Not applicable.

The $25,000 loss from the sale of the personal use portion of the residence is not recognized. The $3,750 loss from the rental portion is recognized. ■

ADDITIONAL COMPLEXITIES IN DETERMINING REALIZED GAIN OR LOSS

Amount Realized

The calculation of the amount realized may appear to be one of the least complex areas associated with property transactions. However, because numerous positive and negative adjustments may be required, this calculation can be complex and confusing. In addition, determining the fair market value of the items received by the taxpayer can be difficult. The following example provides insight into various items that can affect the amount realized.

EXAMPLE 38

Ridge sells an office building and the associated land on October 1, 2011. Under the terms of the sales contract, Ridge is to receive $600,000 in cash. The purchaser is to assume Ridge's mortgage of $300,000 on the property. To enable the purchaser to obtain adequate financing, Ridge is to pay the $15,000 in points charged by the lender. The broker's commission on the sale is $45,000. The purchaser agrees to pay the $12,000 in property taxes for the entire year. The amount realized by Ridge is calculated as follows:

Selling price		
Cash	$600,000	
Mortgage assumed by purchaser	300,000	
Seller's property taxes paid by purchaser ($12,000 × $^9/_{12}$)	9,000	$909,000
Less		
Broker's commission	$ 45,000	
Points paid by seller	15,000	(60,000)
Amount realized		$849,000

■

Adjusted Basis

Three types of issues tend to complicate the determination of adjusted basis. First, the applicable tax provisions for calculating the adjusted basis depend on how the property was acquired (e.g., purchase, taxable exchange, nontaxable exchange, gift, inheritance). Second, if the asset is subject to depreciation, cost recovery, amortization, or depletion, adjustments must be made to the basis during the time period the asset is held by the taxpayer. Upon disposition of the asset, the taxpayer's records for both of these items may be deficient. For example, the donee does not know the amount of the donor's basis or the amount of gift tax paid by the donor, or the taxpayer does not know how much depreciation he or she has deducted. Third, the complex positive and negative adjustments encountered in calculating the amount realized are also involved in calculating the adjusted basis.

EXAMPLE 39

Jane purchased a personal residence in 2002. The purchase price and the related closing costs were as follows:

Purchase price	$325,000
Recording costs	140
Title fees and title insurance	815
Survey costs	225
Attorney's fees	750
Appraisal fee	250

Other relevant tax information for the house during the time Jane owned it is as follows:

- Constructed a swimming pool for medical reasons. The cost was $20,000, of which $5,000 was deducted as a medical expense.
- Added a solar heating system. The cost was $18,000.
- Deducted home office expenses of $6,000. Of this amount, $5,200 was for depreciation.

The adjusted basis for the house is calculated as follows:

Purchase price	$325,000
Recording costs	140
Title fees and title insurance	815
Survey costs	225
Attorney's fees	750
Appraisal fee	250
Swimming pool ($20,000 – $5,000)	15,000
Solar heating system	18,000
	$360,180
Less: Depreciation deducted on home office	(5,200)
Adjusted basis	$354,980

■

SUMMARY OF BASIS ADJUSTMENTS

Some of the more common items that either increase or decrease the basis of an asset appear in Concept Summary 13.2.

In discussing the topic of basis, a number of specific techniques for determining basis have been presented. Although the various techniques are responsive to and mandated by transactions occurring in the marketplace, they do possess enough common characteristics to be categorized as follows:

- The basis of the asset may be determined by reference to the asset's cost.
- The basis of the asset may be determined by reference to the basis of another asset.
- The basis of the asset may be determined by reference to the asset's fair market value.
- The basis of the asset may be determined by reference to the basis of the asset to another taxpayer.

CONCEPT SUMMARY 13.2

Adjustments to Basis

Item	Effect	Refer to Chapter	Explanation
Amortization of bond discount.	Increase	14	Amortization is mandatory for certain taxable bonds and elective for tax-exempt bonds.
Amortization of bond premium.	Decrease	13	Amortization is mandatory for tax-exempt bonds and elective for taxable bonds.
Amortization of covenant not to compete.	Decrease	8	Covenant must be for a definite and limited time period. The amortization period is a statutory period of 15 years.
Amortization of intangibles.	Decrease	8	Intangibles are amortized over a 15-year period.
Assessment for local benefits.	Increase	10	To the extent not deductible as taxes (e.g., assessment for streets and sidewalks that increase the value of the property versus one for maintenance or repair or for meeting interest charges).
Bad debts.	Decrease	7	Only the specific charge-off method is permitted.
Capital additions.	Increase	13	Certain items, at the taxpayer's election, can be capitalized or deducted (e.g., selected medical expenses).
Casualty.	Decrease	7	For a casualty loss, the amount of the adjustment is the summation of the deductible loss and the insurance proceeds received. For a casualty gain, the amount of the adjustment is the insurance proceeds received reduced by the recognized gain.
Condemnation.	Decrease	13	See casualty explanation.
Cost recovery.	Decrease	8	§ 168 is applicable to tangible assets placed in service after 1980 whose useful life is expressed in terms of years.
Depletion.	Decrease	8	Use the greater of cost or percentage depletion. Percentage depletion can still be deducted when the basis is zero.
Depreciation.	Decrease	8	§ 167 is applicable to tangible assets placed in service before 1981 and to tangible assets not depreciated in terms of years.
Easement.	Decrease	13	If the taxpayer does not retain any use of the land, all of the basis is allocable to the easement transaction. However, if only part of the land is affected by the easement, only part of the basis is allocable to the easement transaction.
Improvements by lessee to lessor's property.	Increase	5	Adjustment occurs only if the lessor is required to include the fair market value of the improvements in gross income under § 109.
Imputed interest.	Decrease	16	Amount deducted is not part of the cost of the asset.
Inventory: lower of cost or market.	Decrease	16	Not available if the LIFO method is used.
Limited expensing under § 179.	Decrease	8	Occurs only if the taxpayer elects § 179 treatment.
Medical capital expenditure permitted as a medical expense.	Decrease	10	Adjustment is the amount of the deduction (the effect on basis is to increase it by the amount of the capital expenditure net of the deduction).
Real estate taxes: apportionment between the buyer and seller.	Increase or decrease	10	To the extent the buyer pays the seller's pro rata share, the buyer's basis is increased. To the extent the seller pays the buyer's pro rata share, the buyer's basis is decreased.
Rebate from manufacturer.	Decrease		Since the rebate is treated as an adjustment to the purchase price, it is not included in the buyer's gross income.
Stock dividend.	Decrease	5	Adjustment occurs only if the stock dividend is nontaxable. While the basis per share decreases, the total stock basis does not change.

Adjustments to Basis—Continued

Item	Effect	Refer to Chapter	Explanation
Stock rights.	Decrease	13	Adjustment to stock basis occurs only for nontaxable stock rights and only if the fair market value of the rights is at least 15% of the fair market value of the stock or, if less than 15%, the taxpayer elects to allocate the basis between the stock and the rights.
Theft.	Decrease	7	See casualty explanation.

13.3 General Concept of a Nontaxable Exchange

LO.6

Understand the rationale for nonrecognition (postponement) of gain or loss in certain property transactions.

A taxpayer who is going to replace a productive asset (e.g., machinery) used in a trade or business may structure the transactions as a sale of the old asset and the purchase of a new asset. When this approach is used, any realized gain or loss on the asset sale is recognized. The basis of the new asset is its cost. Alternatively, the taxpayer may be able to trade the old asset for the new asset. This exchange of assets may produce beneficial tax consequences by qualifying for nontaxable exchange treatment.

The tax law recognizes that nontaxable exchanges result in a change in the *form* but not in the *substance* of the taxpayer's relative economic position. The replacement property received in the exchange is viewed as substantially a continuation of the old investment.[59] Additional justification for nontaxable exchange treatment is that this type of transaction does not provide the taxpayer with the wherewithal to pay the tax on any realized gain.

The nonrecognition provisions for nontaxable exchanges do not apply to realized losses from the sale or exchange of personal use assets. Such losses are not recognized (are disallowed) because they are personal in nature and not because of any nonrecognition provision.

In a **nontaxable exchange**, realized gains or losses are not recognized. However, the nonrecognition is usually temporary. The recognition of gain or loss is *postponed* (deferred) until the property received in the nontaxable exchange is subsequently disposed of in a taxable transaction. This is accomplished by assigning a carryover basis to the replacement property.

EXAMPLE 40

Debra exchanges property with an adjusted basis of $10,000 and a fair market value of $12,000 for property with a fair market value of $12,000. The transaction qualifies for nontaxable exchange treatment. Debra has a realized gain of $2,000 ($12,000 amount realized – $10,000 adjusted basis). Her recognized gain is $0. Her basis in the replacement property is a carryover basis of $10,000. Assume the replacement property is nondepreciable and Debra subsequently sells it for $12,000. Her realized and recognized gain will be the $2,000 gain that was postponed (deferred) in the nontaxable transaction. If the replacement property is depreciable, the carryover basis of $10,000 is used in calculating depreciation. ■

In some nontaxable exchanges, only part of the property involved in the transaction qualifies for nonrecognition treatment. If the taxpayer receives cash or other nonqualifying property, part or all of the realized gain from the exchange is recognized. In these instances, gain is recognized because the taxpayer has changed or

[59] Reg. § 1.1002–1(c).

TAX *in* the NEWS

Like-Kind Exchange: Personal versus Investment Property

A recent Tax Court decision dealt with the distinction between property held for personal use and property held for investment. Only the latter qualifies for § 1031 like-kind exchange treatment.

The taxpayer owned a second home that the family used on weekends from mid-April to Labor Day for recreational purposes. The vacation home was not otherwise occupied during the year. The taxpayer decided to dispose of vacation home number 1 and acquire vacation home number 2, which was located much closer to the new principal residence. However, rather than sell vacation home number 1 and purchase vacation home number 2, a transaction was structured in which vacation home number 1 was exchanged for vacation home number 2 (i.e., a three-party like-kind exchange).

The taxpayer treated the exchange as a § 1031 like-kind exchange and deferred the realized gain on the disposal of vacation home number 1. He considered both vacation homes as investment property, since one of his motives for owning the vacation home was the prospect of appreciation that would result in a profit on the ultimate disposition.

The IRS treated both vacation homes as personal use property rather than as investment property. Therefore, the realized gain on the disposal of vacation home number 1 must be currently recognized.

The Tax Court agreed. The taxpayer never rented or attempted to rent either property. Mortgage interest and property taxes were reported on Schedule A of Form 1040. Thus, the facts and circumstances supported the IRS's position that both vacation homes were personal use property.

improved his or her relative economic position and has the wherewithal to pay income tax to the extent of cash or other property received.

It is important to distinguish between a nontaxable disposition, as the term is used in the statute, and a tax-free transaction. First, a direct exchange is not required in all circumstances (e.g., replacement of involuntarily converted property). Second, as previously mentioned, the term *nontaxable* refers to postponement of recognition via a carryover basis. In a *tax-free* transaction, the nonrecognition is permanent (e.g., see the discussion later in the chapter of the § 121 exclusion of realized gain on the sale of a personal residence). Therefore, the basis of any property acquired in a tax-free transaction does not depend on the basis of the property disposed of by the taxpayer.

13.4 Like-Kind Exchanges—§ 1031

LO.7

Apply the nonrecognition provisions and basis determination rules for like-kind exchanges.

Section 1031 provides for nontaxable exchange treatment if the following requirements are satisfied:[60]

- The form of the transaction is an exchange.
- Both the property transferred and the property received are held either for productive use in a trade or business or for investment.
- The property is like-kind property.

Like-kind exchanges include business for business, business for investment, investment for business, or investment for investment property. Property held for personal use, inventory, and partnership interests (both limited and general) do not qualify under the like-kind exchange provisions. Securities, even though held for investment, do not qualify for like-kind exchange treatment.

The nonrecognition provision for like-kind exchanges is *mandatory* rather than elective. A taxpayer who wants to recognize a realized gain or loss will have to structure the transaction in a form that does not satisfy the statutory requirements for a like-kind exchange. This topic is discussed further under Tax Planning.

[60] § 1031(a) and Reg. § 1.1031(a)–1(a).

TAX *in* the NEWS — More IRS Oversight of § 1031 Exchanges

The IRS has announced that it is stepping up its oversight and enforcement of § 1031 like-kind exchanges. The announcement is in response to a report issued by the Treasury Inspector General for Tax Administration. According to the report, clearer IRS guidance on § 1031 exchanges will:

- Help taxpayers to understand the qualification requirements for a § 1031 exchange.
- Help deter unscrupulous promoters from trying to abuse the use of § 1031 exchanges.

Common abuses include using properties that are not like kind, failing to comply with the statutory requirements by including related parties in an exchange, and incorrectly determining the basis for the properties involved.

Section 1031 exchanges are reported on Form 8824 when the taxpayer files his or her income tax return. During the period from 1998 to 2004, the number of Forms 8824 filed doubled (from 338,500 to 677,000). During the same period, the deferred income resulting from § 1031 exchanges more than tripled to $73.6 billion. Of the Forms 8824 filed, 65 percent were attached to Form 1040 with the balance being filed by partnerships and corporations.

LIKE-KIND PROPERTY

"The words 'like-kind' refer to the nature or character of the property and not to its grade or quality. One kind or class of property may not . . . be exchanged for property of a different kind or class."[61]

The term *like-kind* is intended to be interpreted very broadly. However, three categories of exchanges are not included. First, livestock of different sexes do not qualify as like-kind property. Second, real estate can be exchanged only for other real estate, and personalty can be exchanged only for other personalty. For example, the exchange of a machine (personalty) for an office building (realty) is not a like-kind exchange. *Real estate* (or realty) includes principally rental buildings, office and store buildings, manufacturing plants, warehouses, and land. It is immaterial whether real estate is improved or unimproved. Thus, unimproved land can be exchanged for an apartment house. Personalty includes principally machines, equipment, trucks, automobiles, furniture, and fixtures. Third, real property located in the United States exchanged for foreign real property (and vice versa) does not qualify as like-kind property.

EXAMPLE 41

Wade made the following exchanges during the taxable year:

a. Inventory for a machine used in business.
b. Land held for investment for a building used in business.
c. Stock held for investment for equipment used in business.
d. A light-duty business truck for a light-duty business truck.
e. An automobile used for personal transportation for an automobile used in business.
f. Livestock for livestock of a different sex.
g. Land held for investment in New York for land held for investment in London.

Exchanges (b), investment real property for business real property, and (d), business personalty for business personalty, qualify as exchanges of like-kind property. Exchanges (a), inventory; (c), stock; (e), personal use automobile (not held for business or investment purposes); (f), livestock of different sexes; and (g), U.S. and foreign real estate do not qualify. ■

A special provision relates to the location where personal property is used. Personal property used predominantly within the United States and personal property used predominantly outside the United States are not like-kind property. The location of use for the personal property given up is its location during the two-year period ending on the date of disposition of the property. The location of use for the

[61] Reg. § 1.1031(a)–1(b).

personal property received is its location during the two-year period beginning on the date of the acquisition.

EXAMPLE 42

In October 2010, Walter exchanges a machine used in his factory in Denver for a machine that qualifies as like-kind property. In January 2011, the factory, including the machine, is moved to Berlin, Germany. As of January 2011, the exchange is not an exchange of like-kind property. The predominant use of the original machine was in the United States, whereas the predominant use of the new machine is foreign. ■

Another special provision applies if the taxpayers involved in the exchange are *related parties* under § 267(b). To qualify for like-kind exchange treatment, the taxpayer and the related party must not dispose of the like-kind property received in the exchange within the two-year period following the date of the exchange. If such an early disposition does occur, the postponed gain is recognized as of the date of the early disposition. Dispositions due to death, involuntary conversions, and certain non-tax avoidance transactions are not treated as early dispositions.

Regulations dealing with § 1031 like-kind exchange treatment provide that if the exchange transaction involves multiple assets of a business (e.g., a television station for another television station), the determination of whether the assets qualify as like-kind property will not be made at the business level.[62] Instead, the underlying assets must be evaluated.

The Regulations also provide for greater specificity in determining whether depreciable tangible personal property is of a like kind or class. Such property held for productive use in a business is of a like class only if the exchanged property is within the same *general business asset class* (as specified by the IRS in Revenue Procedure 87–57 or as subsequently modified) or the same *product class* (as specified by the Department of Commerce). Property included in a general business asset class is evaluated under this system rather than under the product class system.

The following are examples of general business asset classes:

- Office furniture, fixtures, and equipment.
- Information systems (computers and peripheral equipment).
- Airplanes.
- Automobiles and taxis.
- Buses.
- Light general-purpose trucks.
- Heavy general-purpose trucks.

These Regulations have made it more difficult for depreciable tangible personal property to qualify for § 1031 like-kind exchange treatment. For example, the exchange of office equipment for a computer does not qualify as an exchange of like-kind property. Even though both assets are depreciable tangible personal property, they are not like-kind property because they are in different general business asset classes.

EXCHANGE REQUIREMENT

The transaction must involve a direct exchange of property to qualify as a like-kind exchange. The sale of old property and the purchase of new property, even though like kind, is generally not an exchange. However, if the two transactions are mutually dependent, the IRS may treat them as a like-kind exchange. For example, if the taxpayer sells an old business machine to a dealer and purchases a new one from the same dealer, like-kind exchange treatment could result.[63]

The taxpayer may want to avoid nontaxable exchange treatment. Recognition of gain gives the taxpayer a higher basis for depreciation (see Example 76). To the extent that such gains would, if recognized, either receive favorable capital gain

[62] Reg. § 1.1031(j)–1.

[63] Rev.Rul. 61–119, 1961–1 C.B. 395.

TAX *in the NEWS*

EXCHANGING PRIVATE PROPERTY FOR GOVERNMENT PROPERTY

William Koch, a billionaire energy magnate, owns a 4,500-acre cattle ranch in Colorado. Unfortunately, the ranch is split in two by a large strip of Federal land that includes a road used by hunters and hikers to reach a popular national forest. Some of the users trespass onto Koch's land.

Koch has proposed trading land that he owns elsewhere for the Federal land that bisects his ranch. However, because his proposal involves multiple Federal agencies and land in two states, the trade can take place only if Congress passes enabling legislation. Such legislation was introduced by Representative John Salazar (brother of Ken Salazar, the secretary of the interior), but his failure to be reelected in 2010 may have sidetracked the bill for the time being.

Local county commissioners favor the land swap, but certain environmental groups and hunters and hikers oppose it. Engaging in a like-kind exchange with the government is not a simple matter!

Source: Adapted from Stephanie Simon, "Land Swap Triggers Colorado Dust Up," *Wall Street Journal,* August 20, 2010, p. A5.

treatment or be passive activity income that could offset passive activity losses, it might be preferable to avoid the nonrecognition provisions through an indirect exchange transaction. For example, a taxpayer may sell property to one individual, recognize the gain, and subsequently purchase similar property from another individual. The taxpayer may also want to avoid nontaxable exchange treatment so that a realized loss can be recognized.

If the exchange is a delayed (nonsimultaneous) exchange, there are time limits on its completion. In a delayed like-kind exchange, one party fails to take immediate title to the new property because it has not yet been identified. The Code provides that the delayed swap will qualify as a like-kind exchange if the following requirements are satisfied:

- *Identification period.* The new property must be identified within 45 days of the date when the old property was transferred.
- *Exchange period.* The new property must be received by the earlier of the following:
  - *Within 180 days of the date when the old property was transferred.*
  - *The due date (including extensions) for the tax return covering the year of the transfer.*

Are these time limits firm, or can they be extended due to unforeseen circumstances? Indications are that the IRS will allow no deviation from either the identification period or the exchange period even when events outside the taxpayer's control preclude strict compliance. See the exception to strict compliance provided for in Revenue Procedure 2010–14 in the *Tax in the News* on p. 13-31.

ETHICS *& Equity*

A DELAYED § 1031 LIKE-KIND EXCHANGE: IDENTIFYING MORE THAN ONE PROPERTY

Roy owns an office building (adjusted basis of $250,000) that he has been renting to a group of physicians. Due to conflicts over repairs, maintenance, and rent increases, the physicians offer to purchase the building for $700,000. Roy accepts the offer with the stipulation that the sale be structured in part as a delayed § 1031 transaction. Consequently, the sales proceeds are paid to a qualified third-party intermediary on the closing date of September 30, 2011.

On October 2, 2011, Roy properly identifies an office building that he would like to acquire. Unfortunately, on November 10, 2011, the property selected is withdrawn from the market. On the same day, however, Roy identifies another office building. The purchase of this property closes on December 15, 2011, and the title is transferred to Roy.

Roy treats the transaction as a § 1031 like-kind exchange. Even though the original office building identified was not acquired, Roy concludes that in substance he has satisfied the 45-day rule. He identified the acquired office building as soon as the negotiations ceased on his first choice. Should the IRS accept Roy's attempt to comply?

TAX *in* *the NEWS*

What Happens to § 1031 Deferral If the Qualified Intermediary Defaults?

Normally, the IRS takes the position that the provisions of § 1031 are to be interpreted narrowly with respect to delayed § 1031 like-kind exchanges. In Revenue Procedure 2010–14, however, the IRS has announced an exception to this strict compliance requirement.

The exception applies if the 180-day time requirement for a delayed § 1031 like-kind exchange is not satisfied because the qualified intermediary defaults due to a bankruptcy or receivership proceeding. In this situation, no gain is recognized by the taxpayer until a payment is received from the qualified intermediary or the bankruptcy trustee. As payments are received, gain is recognized using the gross profit ratio method.

BOOT

If the taxpayer in a like-kind exchange gives or receives some property that is not like-kind property, recognition may occur. Property that is not like-kind property, including cash, is referred to as **boot**. Although the term *boot* does not appear in the Code, tax practitioners commonly use it rather than saying "property that is not like-kind property."

The *receipt* of boot will trigger recognition of gain if there is realized gain. The amount of the recognized gain is the *lesser* of the boot received or the realized gain (realized gain serves as the ceiling on recognition).

EXAMPLE 43

Emily and Fran exchange machinery, and the exchange qualifies as like kind under § 1031. Since Emily's machinery (adjusted basis of $20,000) is worth $24,000 and Fran's machine has a fair market value of $19,000, Fran also gives Emily cash of $5,000. Emily's recognized gain is $4,000, the lesser of the realized gain ($24,000 amount realized – $20,000 adjusted basis = $4,000) or the fair market value of the boot received ($5,000). ■

EXAMPLE 44

Assume the same facts as in the previous example, except that Fran's machine is worth $21,000 (not $19,000). Under these circumstances, Fran gives Emily cash of $3,000 to make up the difference. Emily's recognized gain is $3,000, the lesser of the realized gain of $4,000 ($24,000 amount realized – $20,000 adjusted basis) or the fair market value of the boot received of $3,000. ■

The receipt of boot does not result in recognition if there is realized loss.

EXAMPLE 45

Assume the same facts as in Example 43, except that the adjusted basis of Emily's machine is $30,000. Emily's realized loss is $6,000 ($24,000 amount realized – $30,000 adjusted basis). The receipt of the boot of $5,000 does not trigger recognition. Therefore, the recognized loss is $0. ■

The *giving* of boot usually does not trigger recognition. If the boot given is cash, no realized gain or loss is recognized.

EXAMPLE 46

Fred and Gary exchange equipment in a like-kind exchange. Fred receives equipment with a fair market value of $25,000 and transfers equipment worth $21,000 (adjusted basis of $15,000) and cash of $4,000. Fred's realized gain is $6,000 ($25,000 amount realized – $15,000 adjusted basis – $4,000 cash). However, none of the realized gain is recognized. ■

If, however, the boot given is appreciated or depreciated property, gain or loss is recognized to the extent of the difference between the adjusted basis and the fair market value of the boot. For this purpose, *appreciated or depreciated property* is defined as property whose adjusted basis is not equal to the fair market value.

EXAMPLE 47

Assume the same facts as in the previous example, except that Fred transfers equipment worth $10,000 (adjusted basis of $12,000) and boot worth $15,000 (adjusted basis of $9,000). Fred's realized gain appears to be $4,000 ($25,000 amount realized – $21,000 adjusted basis). Since realization previously has served as a ceiling on recognition, it appears that the recognized gain is $4,000 (lower of realized gain of $4,000 or amount of appreciation on boot of $6,000). However, the recognized gain actually is $6,000 (full amount of the appreciation on the boot). In effect, Fred must calculate the like-kind and boot parts of the transaction separately. That is, the realized loss of $2,000 on the like-kind property is not recognized ($10,000 fair market value – $12,000 adjusted basis), and the $6,000 realized gain on the boot is recognized ($15,000 fair market value – $9,000 adjusted basis). ■

BASIS AND HOLDING PERIOD OF PROPERTY RECEIVED

If an exchange does not qualify as nontaxable under § 1031, gain or loss is recognized, and the basis of property received in the exchange is the property's fair market value. If the exchange qualifies for nonrecognition, the basis of property received must be adjusted to reflect any postponed (deferred) gain or loss. The *basis of like-kind property* received in the exchange is the property's fair market value less postponed gain or plus postponed loss. If the exchange partially qualifies for nonrecognition (if recognition is associated with boot), the basis of like-kind property received in the exchange is the property's fair market value less postponed gain or plus postponed loss. The *basis* of any *boot* received is the boot's fair market value.

If there is a postponed loss, nonrecognition creates a situation in which the taxpayer has recovered *less* than the cost or other basis of the property exchanged in an amount equal to the unrecognized loss. If there is a postponed gain, the taxpayer has recovered *more* than the cost or other basis of the property exchanged in an amount equal to the unrecognized gain.

EXAMPLE 48

Jaime exchanges a building (used in his business) with an adjusted basis of $30,000 and a fair market value of $38,000 for land with a fair market value of $38,000. The land is to be held as an investment. The exchange qualifies as like kind (an exchange of business real property for investment real property). Thus, the basis of the land is $30,000 (the land's fair market value of $38,000 less the $8,000 postponed gain on the building). If the land is later sold for its fair market value of $38,000, the $8,000 postponed gain is recognized. ■

EXAMPLE 49

Assume the same facts as in the previous example, except that the building has an adjusted basis of $48,000 and a fair market value of only $38,000. The basis in the newly acquired land is $48,000 (fair market value of $38,000 plus the $10,000 postponed loss on the building). If the land is later sold for its fair market value of $38,000, the $10,000 postponed loss is recognized. ■

The Code provides an alternative approach for determining the basis of like-kind property received:

Adjusted basis of like-kind property surrendered
\+ Adjusted basis of boot given
\+ Gain recognized
– Fair market value of boot received
– Loss recognized
= *Basis of like-kind property received*

This approach is logical in terms of the recovery of capital doctrine. That is, the unrecovered cost or other basis is increased by additional cost (boot given) or decreased by cost recovered (boot received). Any gain recognized is included in the basis of the new property. The taxpayer has been taxed on this amount and is now entitled to recover it tax-free. Any loss recognized is deducted from the basis of the new property. The taxpayer has received a tax benefit on that amount.

The holding period of the property surrendered in the exchange carries over and *tacks on* to the holding period of the like-kind property received.[64] The holding period for boot received in a like-kind exchange begins with the date of the exchange. See Chapter 14 for a discussion of the relevance of the holding period.

Depreciation recapture potential carries over to the property received in a like-kind exchange.[65] See Chapter 14 for a discussion of this topic.

The following comprehensive example illustrates the like-kind exchange rules.

EXAMPLE 50

Vicki exchanged the following old machines for new machines in five independent like-kind exchanges:

Exchange	Adjusted Basis of Old Machine	Fair Market Value of Old Machine	Fair Market Value of New Machine	Adjusted Basis of Boot Given	Fair Market Value of Boot Received
1	$4,000	$ 9,000	$9,000	$ –0–	$ –0–
2	4,000	6,000	9,000	3,000	–0–
3	4,000	3,000	9,000	6,000	–0–
4	4,000	12,000	9,000	–0–	3,000
5	4,000	3,800	3,500	–0–	300

Vicki's realized and recognized gains and losses and the basis of each of the like-kind properties received are as follows:

			New Basis Calculation								
Exchange	Realized Gain (Loss)	Recognized Gain (Loss)	Old Adj. Basis	+	Boot Given	+	Gain Recognized	–	Boot Received	=	New Basis
1	$ 5,000	$ –(0)–	$4,000	+	$ –0–	+	$ –0–	–	$ –0–	=	$ 4,000*
2	2,000	–(0)–	4,000	+	3,000	+	–0–	–	–0–	=	7,000*
3	(1,000)	–(0)–	4,000	+	6,000	+	–0–	–	–0–	=	10,000**
4	8,000	3,000	4,000	+	–0–	+	3,000	–	3,000	=	4,000*
5	(200)	–(0)–	4,000	+	–0–	+	–0–	–	300	=	3,700**

*Basis may be determined in gain situations under the alternative method by subtracting the gain not recognized from the fair market value of the new property:

$9,000 – $5,000 = $4,000 for exchange 1.
$9,000 – $2,000 = $7,000 for exchange 2.
$9,000 – $5,000 = $4,000 for exchange 4.

**In loss situations, basis may be determined by adding the loss not recognized to the fair market value of the new property:

$9,000 + $1,000 = $10,000 for exchange 3.
$3,500 + $200 = $3,700 for exchange 5.

The basis of the boot received is the boot's fair market value. ■

If the taxpayer either assumes a liability or takes property subject to a liability, the amount of the liability is treated as boot given. For the taxpayer whose liability is assumed or whose property is taken subject to the liability, the amount of the liability

[64] § 1223(1) and Reg. § 1.1223–1(a). For this carryover holding period rule to apply to like-kind exchanges after March 1, 1954, the like-kind property surrendered must have been either a capital asset or § 1231 property. See Chapter 14 for the discussion of capital assets and § 1231 property.

[65] Reg. §§ 1.1245–2(a)(4) and 1.1250–2(d)(1).

is treated as boot received. Example 51 illustrates the effect of such a liability. In addition, the example illustrates the tax consequences for both parties involved in the like-kind exchange.

EXAMPLE 51

Jane and Leo exchange real estate investments. Jane gives up property with an adjusted basis of $250,000 (fair market value of $400,000) that is subject to a mortgage of $75,000 (assumed by Leo). In return for this property, Jane receives property with a fair market value of $300,000 (adjusted basis of $200,000) and cash of $25,000.

- Jane's realized gain is $150,000. She gave up property with an adjusted basis of $250,000. Jane received $400,000 from the exchange ($300,000 fair market value of like-kind property plus $100,000 boot received). The boot received consists of the $25,000 cash received from Leo and Jane's mortgage of $75,000, which Leo assumes.
- Jane's recognized gain is $100,000. The realized gain of $150,000 is recognized to the extent of boot received.
- Jane's basis in the real estate received from Leo is $250,000. This basis can be computed by subtracting the postponed gain ($50,000) from the fair market value of the real estate received ($300,000). It can also be computed by adding the recognized gain ($100,000) to the adjusted basis of the real estate given up ($250,000) and subtracting the boot received ($100,000).
- Leo's realized gain is $100,000. Leo gave up property with an adjusted basis of $200,000 plus boot of $100,000 ($75,000 mortgage assumed + $25,000 cash) or a total of $300,000. Leo received $400,000 from the exchange (fair market value of like-kind property received).
- Leo has no recognized gain because he did not receive any boot. The entire realized gain of $100,000 is postponed.
- Leo's basis in the real estate received from Jane is $300,000. This basis can be computed by subtracting the postponed gain ($100,000) from the fair market value of the real estate received ($400,000). It can also be computed by adding the boot given ($75,000 mortgage assumed by Leo + $25,000 cash) to the adjusted basis of the real estate given up ($200,000).[66] ■

REPORTING CONSIDERATIONS

Section 1031 transactions are reported on Form 8824 (Like-Kind Exchanges). This form should be used even though the like-kind exchange transaction results in no recognized gain or loss. It must be filed with the regular return for the tax year in which the taxpayer transfers property in a like-kind exchange.

If the like-kind exchange is with a related party, additional Forms 8824 must be filed for the following two years.

13.5 Involuntary Conversions—§ 1033

LO.8

Explain the nonrecognition provisions available on the involuntary conversion of property.

Section 1033 provides that a taxpayer who suffers an involuntary conversion of property may postpone recognition of *gain* realized from the conversion. The objective of this provision is to provide relief to the taxpayer who has suffered hardship and does not have the wherewithal to pay the tax on any gain realized from the conversion. Postponement of realized gain is permitted to the extent that the taxpayer *reinvests* the amount realized from the conversion in replacement property. The rules for nonrecognition of gain are as follows:

- If the amount reinvested in replacement property *equals or exceeds* the amount realized, realized gain is *not recognized.*

[66]Example (2) of Reg. § 1.1031(d)–2 illustrates a special situation in which both the buyer and the seller transfer liabilities that are assumed by the other party or both parties acquire property that is subject to a liability.

TAX *in* the NEWS

ECONOMIC DEVELOPMENT GONE WRONG

One of the messages of the U.S. Supreme Court in *Kelo v. City of New London* was that eminent domain proceedings can be justified if the "taking" potentially will lead to future economic development. Now it appears that the message may be a two-way street: a city may attempt to use eminent domain proceedings against a developer if promised development does not occur.

The city of Boston is threatening such a taking if a prominent property is not developed soon. The site was the location of Filene's Basement, a popular retailer that closed in September 2007. A group of investors led by Vornado Realty Trust acquired the property and nearby buildings, planning to erect a $700 million mixed-use development on the site. Most of the buildings were demolished in 2008, but then construction stalled. At present, the site is a vacant lot flanked by two partially demolished structures. The city, led by Mayor Thomas Menino, claims that the property is an eyesore and that the city has the right to seize it if it is not developed soon.

Source: Adapted from Christina S. N. Lewis, "Mayor Battles Vornado in Boston," *Wall Street Journal*, April 14, 2010, p. B1.

- If the amount reinvested in replacement property is *less than* the amount realized, realized gain *is recognized* to the extent of the deficiency.

If a *loss* occurs on an involuntary conversion, § 1033 does not modify the normal rules for loss recognition. That is, if a realized loss would otherwise be recognized, § 1033 does not change the result.

INVOLUNTARY CONVERSION DEFINED

An **involuntary conversion** results from the destruction (complete or partial), theft, seizure, requisition or condemnation, or sale or exchange under threat or imminence of requisition or condemnation of the taxpayer's property.[67] To prove the existence of a threat or imminence of condemnation, the taxpayer must obtain confirmation that there has been a decision to acquire the property for public use. In addition, the taxpayer must have reasonable grounds to believe the property will be taken.[68] The property does not have to be sold to the authority threatening to condemn it to qualify for § 1033 postponement. If the taxpayer satisfies the confirmation and reasonable grounds requirements, he or she can sell the property to another party.[69] Likewise, the sale of property to a condemning authority by a taxpayer who acquired the property from its former owner with the knowledge that the property was under threat of condemnation also qualifies as an involuntary conversion under § 1033.[70] A voluntary act, such as a taxpayer destroying the property by arson, is not an involuntary conversion.[71]

COMPUTING THE AMOUNT REALIZED

The amount realized from the condemnation of property usually includes only the amount received as compensation for the property.[72] Any amount received that is designated as severance damages by both the government and the taxpayer is not included in the amount realized. *Severance awards* usually occur when only a portion of the property is condemned (e.g., a strip of land is taken to build a highway). Severance damages are awarded because the value of the taxpayer's remaining property

[67] § 1033(a) and Reg. §§ 1.1033(a)–1(a) and –2(a).

[68] Rev.Rul. 63–221, 1963–2 C.B. 332, and *Joseph P. Balistrieri*, 38 TCM 526, T.C.Memo. 1979–115.

[69] Rev.Rul. 81–180, 1981–2 C.B. 161.

[70] Rev.Rul. 81–181, 1981–2 C.B. 162.

[71] Rev.Rul. 82–74, 1982–1 C.B. 110.

[72] *Pioneer Real Estate Co.*, 47 B.T.A. 886 (1942), *acq.* 1943 C.B. 18.

TAX *in* the NEWS

An Unusual Involuntary Conversion

The rollover provisions of § 1033 apply when property is stolen, destroyed, or condemned. The usual form of a condemnation involves a "taking" of the taxpayer's property by a governmental entity under the right of eminent domain (i.e., taking private property for public use). As long as the taxpayer reinvests the net proceeds received in qualifying replacement property in the designated time period and elects § 1033 treatment, the realized gain is deferred.

An unusual "taking" occurred for a taxpayer who forgot he owned stock in a particular company. The state, under its unclaimed property law, took possession of the stock and sold it. The elderly taxpayer became aware of what had happened, filed a claim with the state, and received the proceeds. In a private letter ruling, the IRS concluded that § 1033 deferral treatment would result if the amount realized by the taxpayer was reinvested within the designated time period in stock or mutual funds.

has declined as a result of the condemnation. Such damages are a tax-free recovery of capital and reduce the basis of the property. However, if either of the following requirements is satisfied, the nonrecognition provision of § 1033 applies to the severance damages:

- The severance damages are used to restore the usability of the remaining property.
- The usefulness of the remaining property is destroyed by the condemnation, and the property is sold and replaced at a cost equal to or exceeding the sum of the condemnation award, severance damages, and sales proceeds.

EXAMPLE 52

The government condemns a portion of Ron's farmland to build part of an interstate highway. Because the highway denies his cattle access to a pond and some grazing land, Ron receives severance damages in addition to the condemnation proceeds for the land taken. Ron must reduce the basis of the property by the amount of the severance damages. If the amount of the severance damages received exceeds the adjusted basis, Ron recognizes gain. ■

EXAMPLE 53

Assume the same facts as in the previous example, except that Ron uses the proceeds from the condemnation and the severance damages to build another pond and to clear woodland for grazing. Therefore, all the proceeds are eligible for § 1033 treatment. There is no possibility of gain recognition as the result of the amount of the severance damages received exceeding the adjusted basis. ■

REPLACEMENT PROPERTY

The requirements for replacement property generally are more restrictive than those for like-kind property under § 1031. The basic requirement is that the replacement property be similar or related in service or use to the involuntarily converted property.[73]

Different interpretations of the phrase *similar or related in service or use* apply depending on whether the involuntarily converted property is held by an *owner-user* or by an *owner-investor* (e.g., lessor). A taxpayer who uses the property in his or her trade or business is subject to a more restrictive test in terms of acquiring replacement property. For an owner-user, the *functional use test* applies, and for an owner-investor, the *taxpayer use test* applies.

[73] § 1033(a) and Reg. § 1.1033(a)–1.

CONCEPT SUMMARY 13.3

Replacement Property Tests

Type of Property and User	Like-Kind Test	Taxpayer Use Test	Functional Use Test
Land used by a manufacturing company is condemned by a local government authority.	X		
Apartment and land held by an investor are sold due to the threat or imminence of condemnation.	X		
An investor's rented shopping mall is destroyed by fire; the mall may be replaced by other rental properties (e.g., an apartment building).		X	
A manufacturing plant is destroyed by fire; replacement property must consist of another manufacturing plant that is functionally the same as the property converted.			X
Personal residence of taxpayer is condemned by a local government authority; replacement property must consist of another personal residence.			X

Taxpayer Use Test

The taxpayer use test for owner-investors provides the taxpayer with more flexibility in terms of what qualifies as replacement property than does the functional use test for owner-users. Essentially, the properties must be used by the taxpayer (the owner-investor) in similar endeavors. For example, rental property held by an owner-investor qualifies if replaced by other rental property, regardless of the type of rental property involved. The test is met when an investor replaces a manufacturing plant with a wholesale grocery warehouse if both properties are held for the production of rent income.[74] The replacement of a rental residence with a personal residence does not meet the test.[75]

Functional Use Test

The functional use test applies to owner-users (e.g., a manufacturer whose manufacturing plant is destroyed by fire is required to replace the plant with another facility of similar functional use). Under this test, the taxpayer's use of the replacement property and of the involuntarily converted property must be the same. Replacing a manufacturing plant with a wholesale grocery warehouse does not meet this test. Neither does replacing a rental residence with a personal residence.

Special Rules

Under one set of circumstances, the broader replacement rules for like-kind exchanges are substituted for the narrow replacement rules normally used for involuntary conversions. This beneficial provision applies if business real property or investment real property is condemned. This provision gives the taxpayer substantially more flexibility in selecting replacement property. For example, improved real property can be replaced with unimproved real property.

The rules concerning the nature of replacement property are illustrated in Concept Summary 13.3.

---

[74] *Loco Realty Co. v. Comm.*, 62–2 USTC ¶9657, 10 AFTR 2d 5359, 306 F.2d 207 (CA–8, 1962).

[75] Rev.Rul. 70–466, 1970–2 C.B. 165.

TIME LIMITATION ON REPLACEMENT

The taxpayer normally has a two-year period after the close of the taxable year in which gain is realized from an involuntary conversion to replace the property (*the latest date*).[76] This rule affords as much as three years from the date of realization of gain to replace the property if the realization of gain took place on the first day of the taxable year.[77] If the involuntary conversion involved the condemnation of real property used in a trade or business or held for investment, a three-year period is substituted for the normal two-year period. In this case, the taxpayer can actually have as much as four years from the date of realization of gain to replace the property.

EXAMPLE 54

Megan's warehouse is destroyed by fire on December 16, 2010. The adjusted basis is $325,000. Megan receives $400,000 from the insurance company on January 10, 2011. She is a calendar year taxpayer. The latest date for replacement is December 31, 2013 (the end of the taxable year in which realized gain occurred plus two years). The critical date is not the date the involuntary conversion occurred, but rather the date of gain realization. ■

EXAMPLE 55

Assume the same facts as in the previous example, except that Megan's warehouse is condemned. The latest date for replacement is December 31, 2014 (the end of the taxable year in which realized gain occurred plus three years). ■

The *earliest date* for replacement typically is the date the involuntary conversion occurs. However, if the property is condemned, it is possible to replace the condemned property before this date. In this case, the earliest date is the date of the threat or imminence of requisition or condemnation of the property. The purpose of this provision is to enable the taxpayer to make an orderly replacement of the condemned property.

EXAMPLE 56

Assume the same facts as in Example 55. Megan can replace the warehouse before December 16, 2010 (the condemnation date). The earliest date for replacement is the date of the threat or imminence of requisition or condemnation of the warehouse. ■

NONRECOGNITION OF GAIN

Nonrecognition of gain can be either mandatory or elective, depending on whether the conversion is direct (into replacement property) or indirect (into money).

Direct Conversion

If the conversion is directly into replacement property rather than into money, nonrecognition of realized gain is *mandatory*. In this case, the basis of the replacement property is the same as the adjusted basis of the converted property. Direct conversion is rare in practice and usually involves condemnations.

EXAMPLE 57

Lupe's property, with an adjusted basis of $20,000, is condemned by the state. Lupe receives property with a fair market value of $50,000 as compensation for the property taken. Since the nonrecognition of realized gain is mandatory for direct conversions, Lupe's realized gain of $30,000 is not recognized, and the basis of the replacement property is $20,000 (adjusted basis of the condemned property). ■

Conversion into Money

If the conversion is into money, at the election of the taxpayer, the realized gain is recognized only to the extent the amount realized from the involuntary conversion

[76] §§ 1033(a)(2)(B) and (g)(4) and Reg. § 1.1033(a)–2(c)(3).

[77] The taxpayer can apply for an extension of this time period anytime before its expiration [Reg. § 1.1033(a)–2(c)(3)]. Also, the period for filing the application for extension can be extended if the taxpayer shows reasonable cause.

exceeds the cost of the qualifying replacement property.[78] This is the usual case, and nonrecognition (postponement) is *elective*. If the election is not made, the realized gain is recognized.

The basis of the replacement property is the property's cost less postponed (deferred) gain.[79] If the election to postpone gain is made, the holding period of the replacement property includes the holding period of the converted property.

Section 1033 applies *only to gains* and *not to losses*. Losses from involuntary conversions are recognized if the property is held for business or income-producing purposes. Personal casualty losses are recognized, but condemnation losses related to personal use assets (e.g., a personal residence) are neither recognized nor postponed.

EXAMPLE 58

Walt's building (used in his trade or business), with an adjusted basis of $50,000, is destroyed by fire on October 5, 2011. Walt is a calendar year taxpayer. On November 17, 2011, he receives an insurance reimbursement of $100,000 for the loss. Walt invests $80,000 in a new building.

- Walt has until December 31, 2013, to make the new investment and qualify for the nonrecognition election.
- Walt's realized gain is $50,000 ($100,000 insurance proceeds received – $50,000 adjusted basis of old building).
- Assuming the replacement property qualifies as similar or related in service or use, Walt's recognized gain is $20,000. He reinvested $20,000 less than the insurance proceeds received ($100,000 proceeds – $80,000 reinvested). Therefore, his realized gain is recognized to that extent.
- Walt's basis in the new building is $50,000. This is the building's cost of $80,000 less the postponed gain of $30,000 (realized gain of $50,000 – recognized gain of $20,000).
- The computation of realization, recognition, and basis would apply even if Walt was a real estate dealer and the building destroyed by fire was part of his inventory. Unlike § 1031, § 1033 generally does not exclude inventory. ■

EXAMPLE 59

Assume the same facts as in the previous example, except that Walt receives only $45,000 of insurance proceeds. He has a realized and recognized loss of $5,000. The basis of the new building is the building's cost of $80,000. If the destroyed building had been held for personal use, the recognized loss would have been subject to the following additional limitations.[80] The loss of $5,000 would have been limited to the decline in fair market value of the property, and the amount of the loss would have been reduced first by $100 and then by 10% of adjusted gross income (refer to Chapter 7). ■

INVOLUNTARY CONVERSION OF A PERSONAL RESIDENCE

The tax consequences of the involuntary conversion of a personal residence depend on whether the conversion is a casualty or condemnation and whether a realized loss or gain results.

Loss Situations

If the conversion is a condemnation, the realized loss is not recognized. Loss from the condemnation of a personal use asset is never recognized. If the conversion is a casualty (a loss from fire, storm, etc.), the loss is recognized subject to the personal casualty loss limitations (see Chapter 7).

Gain Situations

If the conversion is a casualty, theft, or condemnation, the gain may be postponed under § 1033 or excluded under § 121. That is, the taxpayer may treat the

[78] § 1033(a)(2)(A) and Reg. § 1.1033(a)–2(c)(1).
[79] § 1033(b).
[80] § 165(c)(3) and Reg. § 1.165–7.

involuntary conversion as a sale under the exclusion of gain rules relating to the sale of a personal residence under § 121 (presented subsequently).

Under certain circumstances, the taxpayer may use both the § 121 exclusion of gain and the § 1033 postponement of gain provisions. See the discussion under Involuntary Conversion and Using §§ 121 and 1033 later in this chapter.

REPORTING CONSIDERATIONS

Involuntary conversions from casualty and theft are reported first on Form 4684, Casualties and Thefts. Casualty and theft losses on personal use property for the individual taxpayer are carried from Form 4684 to Schedule A of Form 1040. For other casualty and theft items, the Form 4684 amounts are generally reported on Form 4797, Sales of Business Property, unless Form 4797 is not required. In the latter case, the amounts are reported directly on the tax return involved.

Except for personal use property, recognized gains and losses from involuntary conversions other than by casualty and theft are reported on Form 4797. As stated previously, if the property involved in the involuntary conversion (other than by casualty and theft) is personal use property, any realized loss is not recognized. Any realized gain is treated as gain on a voluntary sale.

What procedure should be followed if the taxpayer intends to acquire qualifying replacement property but has not done so by the time the tax return is filed? The taxpayer should elect § 1033 and report all of the details of the transaction on a statement attached to the return. Though a tax form (Form 8824) is available for § 1031 like-kind exchanges, no special form is provided for § 1033 transactions. When the qualifying replacement property is acquired, the taxpayer should attach a statement to the tax return that contains relevant information on the replacement property.

An amended return must be filed if qualified replacement property is not acquired during the statutory time period allowed. An amended return also is required if the cost of the replacement property is less than the amount realized from the involuntary conversion. In this case, the return would recognize the portion of the realized gain that can no longer be deferred.

13.6 Sale of a Residence—§ 121

LO.9

Describe the provision for the permanent exclusion of gain on the sale of a personal residence.

A taxpayer's **personal residence** is a personal use asset. Therefore, a realized loss from the sale of a personal residence is not recognized.[81]

A realized gain from the sale of a personal residence is subject to taxation. However, favorable relief from recognition of gain is provided in the form of the **§ 121 exclusion**. Under this provision, a taxpayer can exclude up to $250,000 of realized gain on the sale.[82]

REQUIREMENTS FOR EXCLUSION TREATMENT

To qualify for exclusion treatment, at the date of the sale, the residence must have been *owned* and *used* by the taxpayer as the principal residence for at least two years during the five-year period ending on the date of the sale.[83]

EXAMPLE 60

Melissa sells her principal residence on September 18, 2011. She had purchased it on July 5, 2009, and lived in it since then. The sale of Melissa's residence qualifies for the § 121 exclusion. ■

The five-year window enables the taxpayer to qualify for the § 121 exclusion even though the property is not his or her principal residence at the date of the sale.

[81] § 165(c).

[82] § 121(b).

[83] § 121(a). However, § 121(d)(10) provides that exclusion treatment does not apply if the residence was acquired in a like-kind exchange within the prior five years of the sale of the residence.

EXAMPLE 61

Benjamin sells his former principal residence on August 16, 2011. He had purchased it on April 1, 2003, and lived in it until July 1, 2010, when he converted it to rental property. Even though the property is rental property on August 16, 2011, rather than Benjamin's principal residence, the sale qualifies for the § 121 exclusion.[84] During the five-year period from August 16, 2006, to August 16, 2011, Benjamin owned and used the property as his principal residence for at least two years. ■

Taxpayers might be tempted to make liberal use of the § 121 exclusion as a means of speculating when the price of residential housing is rising. Without any time restriction on its use, § 121 would permit the exclusion of realized gain on multiple sales of principal residences. The Code curbs this approach by denying the application of the § 121 exclusion to sales occurring within two years of its last use.[85]

EXAMPLE 62

Seth sells his principal residence (the first residence) in June 2010 for $150,000 (realized gain of $60,000). He then buys and sells the following (all of which qualify as principal residences):

	Date of Purchase	Date of Sale	Amount Involved
Second residence	July 2010		$160,000
Second residence		April 2011	180,000
Third residence	May 2011		200,000

Because multiple sales have taken place within a period of two years, § 121 does not apply to the sale of the second residence. Thus, the realized gain of $20,000 [$180,000 (selling price) – $160,000 (purchase price)] must be recognized. ■

EXCEPTIONS TO THE TWO-YEAR OWNERSHIP RULE

The two-year ownership and use requirement and the "only once every two years" provision could create a hardship for taxpayers in certain situations that are beyond their control. Thus, under the following special circumstances, the requirements are waived:[86]

- Change in place of employment.
- Health.
- To the extent provided in the Regulations, other unforeseen circumstances.

These three exceptions have recently been amplified by the IRS and are discussed in the sections that follow.

Change in Place of Employment

In order for this exception to apply, the distance requirements applicable to the deductibility of moving expenses must be satisfied (see Chapter 9).[87] Consequently, the location of the taxpayer's new employment must be at least 50 miles further from the old residence than the old residence was from the old job. The house must be used as the principal residence of the taxpayer at the time of the change in the place of employment. Employment includes the commencement of employment with a new employer, the continuation of employment with the same employer, and the commencement or continuation of self-employment.

[84]However, any realized gain on the sale that is attributable to depreciation is not eligible for the § 121 exclusion. See Example 81.

[85]§ 121(b)(3).

[86]§ 121(c)(2)(B).

[87]Reg. § 1.121–3T(c).

TAX *in* the NEWS

A Tax Break for Those Who Serve

To qualify for exclusion treatment on the gain from the sale of a principal residence, a two-year ownership and occupancy requirement during the five-year period preceding the sale must be satisfied. As satisfying this provision was difficult for those in the military, Congress enacted the Military Family Tax Relief Act of 2003 to provide some relief. The two-out-of-five-years requirement still must be satisfied, but at the election of the taxpayer, the running of the five-year period can be suspended during any period that the taxpayer or spouse is serving on qualified official extended duty in the military. Since this extension is limited to 10 years, the maximum period allowed is 15 years. This provision is retroactive to home sales after May 6, 1997.

EXAMPLE 63

Assume the same facts as in the previous example, except that in March 2011, Seth's employer transfers him to a job in another state that is 400 miles away. Thus, the sale of the second residence and the purchase of the third residence were due to relocation of employment. Consequently, the § 121 exclusion is partially available on the sale of the second residence. ■

Keep in mind, however, that the change in place of employment exception, or any of the other exceptions noted below, does not make the full amount of the exclusion available. See the discussion under Relief Provision later in this chapter for determining the amount of the partial exclusion allowed.

Health Considerations

For the health exception to apply, health must be the primary reason for the sale or exchange of the residence.[88] A sale or exchange that is merely beneficial to the general health or well-being of the individual will not qualify. A safe harbor applies if there is a physician's recommendation for a change of residence (1) to obtain, provide, or facilitate the diagnosis, cure, mitigation, or treatment of disease, illness, or injury or (2) to obtain or provide medical or personal care for an individual suffering from a disease, illness, or injury. If the safe harbor is not satisfied, then the determination is made using a facts and circumstances approach. Examples that qualify include the following:

- A taxpayer who is injured in an accident is unable to care for herself. She sells her residence and moves in with her daughter.
- A taxpayer's father has a chronic disease. The taxpayer sells his house in order to move into the father's house to provide the care the father requires as a result of the disease.
- A taxpayer's son suffers from a chronic disease. The taxpayer sells his house and moves his family so the son can begin a new treatment recommended by the son's physician that is available at a medical facility 100 miles away.
- A taxpayer suffers from chronic asthma. Her physician recommends that she move to a warm, dry climate. She moves from Minnesota to Arizona.

Unforeseen Circumstances

For the unforeseen circumstances exception to apply, the primary reason for the sale or exchange of the residence must be an event that the taxpayer did not anticipate before purchasing and occupying the residence.[89] This requirement is satisfied under a safe-harbor provision by any of the following:

- Involuntary conversion of the residence.
- Natural or human-made disasters or acts of war or terrorism resulting in a casualty to the residence.

[88] Reg. § 1.121–3T(d).

[89] Reg. § 1.121–3T(e).

TAX *in* the NEWS

Living in a High-Crime Neighborhood

Normally, a taxpayer must satisfy the tax year ownership and use requirements and the only once-every-two-years provision to be eligible for the § 121 exclusion. However, under the unforeseen circumstances exception, a taxpayer who does not satisfy these three requirements may be eligible for a reduced § 121 exclusion.

In several letter rulings, the IRS has been sympathetic to crime victims. One ruling involved a taxpayer who was accosted leaving his home, driven to several locations, and forced to withdraw money from an ATM. In another ruling, the taxpayers and their son were hospitalized after being assaulted by neighbors. In both cases, the taxpayers sold their homes. Although the taxpayers had not satisfied the three time period requirements, the IRS held that they were eligible for reduced § 121 exclusion treatment under the unforeseen circumstances exception.

- Death of a qualified individual.
- Cessation of employment that results in eligibility for unemployment compensation.
- Change in employment or self-employment that results in the taxpayer being unable to pay housing costs and reasonable basic living expenses for the taxpayer's household.
- Divorce or legal separation.
- Multiple births resulting from the same pregnancy.

If the safe harbor is not satisfied, then the determination is made using a facts and circumstances approach.

EXAMPLE 64

Debra and Roy are engaged and buy a house (sharing the mortgage payments) and live in it as their personal residence. Eighteen months after the purchase, they cancel their wedding plans, and Roy moves out of the house. Because Debra cannot afford to make the payments alone, they sell the house. While the sale does not fit under the safe harbor, the sale does qualify under the unforeseen circumstances exception. ■

CALCULATION OF THE AMOUNT OF THE EXCLUSION

General Provisions

The amount of the available § 121 exclusion on the sale of a principal residence is $250,000.[90] If the realized gain does not exceed $250,000, there is no recognized gain.

Realized gain is calculated in the normal manner. The *amount realized* is the selling price less the selling expenses, which include items such as the cost of advertising the property for sale, real estate broker commissions, legal fees in connection with the sale, and loan placement fees paid by the taxpayer as a condition of arranging financing for the buyer. Repairs and maintenance performed by the seller to aid in selling the property are treated neither as selling expenses nor as adjustments to the taxpayer's adjusted basis for the residence.

EXAMPLE 65

Mandy, who is single, sells her personal residence (adjusted basis of $130,000) for $290,000. She has owned and lived in the residence for three years. Her selling expenses are $18,000. Three weeks prior to the sale, Mandy paid a carpenter and a painter $1,000 to make some repairs and paint the two bathrooms. Her recognized gain is calculated as follows:

[90] § 121(b)(1).

TAX *in* the NEWS

Avoiding Taxes on a Short Sale with Debt Forgiveness

In the current real estate market, it is not uncommon for a homeowner's mortgage on his or her residence to exceed its fair market value. One of the options available to a homeowner in this predicament is a "short sale." The homeowner sells the residence and hopes the mortgage holder will forgive the excess debt.

With a short sale, the taxpayer should receive a Form 1099–C from the mortgage holder for any debt forgiven, and this amount is to be included in the taxpayer's gross income. This appears to be "not such a good deal"—lose your home and owe Federal income taxes. Fortunately, recent tax legislation alleviates the income effect except for the so-called rich.

For "qualified principal residence indebtedness," the homeowner is permitted to exclude from gross income the amount of the debt forgiven. Tracing rules apply in that the debt must originally have been used to acquire, build, or substantially improve the taxpayer's principal residence. The exclusion applies only to debt forgiveness associated with a mortgage not in excess of $2 million ($1 million if married filing separately), however. In addition, the taxpayer's basis for the residence must be reduced by the amount of the exclusion.

Source: Adapted from Bill Bischoff, "Tax Hits on Property Short Sales," *Wall Street Journal*, April 30, 2009, p. D5.

Amount realized ($290,000 – $18,000)	$ 272,000
Adjusted basis	(130,000)
Realized gain	$ 142,000
§ 121 exclusion	(142,000)
Recognized gain	$ –0–

Since the available § 121 exclusion of $250,000 exceeds Mandy's realized gain of $142,000, her recognized gain is $0. ■

EXAMPLE 66

Assume the same facts as in the previous example, except that the selling price is $490,000.

Amount realized ($490,000 – $18,000)	$ 472,000
Adjusted basis	(130,000)
Realized gain	$ 342,000
§ 121 exclusion	(250,000)
Recognized gain	$ 92,000

Since the realized gain of $342,000 exceeds the § 121 exclusion amount of $250,000, Mandy's recognized gain is $92,000 ($342,000 – $250,000). ■

Effect on Married Couples

If a married couple files a joint return, the $250,000 amount is increased to $500,000 if the following requirements are satisfied:[91]

- Either spouse meets the at-least-two-years *ownership* requirement.
- Both spouses meet the at-least-two-years *use* requirement.
- Neither spouse is ineligible for the § 121 exclusion on the sale of the current principal residence because of the sale of another principal residence within the prior two years.

EXAMPLE 67

Margaret sells her personal residence (adjusted basis of $150,000) for $650,000. She has owned and lived in the residence for six years. Her selling expenses are $40,000. Margaret is married to Ted, and they file a joint return. Ted has lived in the residence since they were married two and one-half years ago.

[91]§ 121(b)(2).

Amount realized ($650,000 – $40,000)	$ 610,000
Adjusted basis	(150,000)
Realized gain	$ 460,000
§ 121 exclusion	(460,000)
Recognized gain	$ –0–

Since the realized gain of $460,000 is less than the available § 121 exclusion amount of $500,000, no gain is recognized. ■

Starting in 2008, a surviving spouse can continue to use the $500,000 exclusion amount on the sale of a personal residence for the next two years following the year of the deceased spouse's death. If the sale occurs in the year of death, however, a joint return must be filed by the surviving spouse.

If each spouse owns a qualified principal residence, each spouse can separately qualify for the $250,000 exclusion on the sale of his or her own residence even if the couple files a joint return.[92]

EXAMPLE 68

Anne and Samuel are married on August 1, 2011. Each owns a residence that is eligible for the § 121 exclusion. Anne sells her residence on September 7, 2011, and Samuel sells his residence on October 9, 2011. Relevant data on the sales are as follows:

	Anne	Samuel
Selling price	$320,000	$425,000
Selling expenses	20,000	25,000
Adjusted basis	190,000	110,000

Anne and Samuel intend to rent a condo in Florida or Arizona and to travel. The recognized gain of each is calculated as follows:

	Anne	Samuel
Amount realized	$ 300,000	$ 400,000
Adjusted basis	(190,000)	(110,000)
Realized gain	$ 110,000	$ 290,000
§ 121 exclusion	(110,000)	(250,000)
Recognized gain	$ –0–	$ 40,000

Anne has no recognized gain because the available $250,000 exclusion amount exceeds her realized gain of $110,000. Samuel's recognized gain is $40,000 as his realized gain of $290,000 exceeds the $250,000 exclusion amount. The recognized gains calculated above result regardless of whether Anne and Samuel file a joint return or separate returns. ■

Relief Provision

As discussed earlier in Requirements for Exclusion Treatment, partial § 121 exclusion treatment may be available when not all of the statutory requirements are satisfied. Under the relief provision, the § 121 exclusion amount ($250,000 or $500,000) is multiplied by a fraction, the numerator of which is the number of qualifying months and the denominator of which is 24 months. The resulting amount is the excluded gain.[93]

[92] § 121(b)(1).

[93] § 121(c)(1).

EXAMPLE 69

On October 1, 2010, Rich and Audrey, who file a joint return and live in Chicago, sell their personal residence, which they have owned and lived in for eight years. The realized gain of $325,000 is excluded under § 121. They purchase another personal residence for $525,000 on October 2, 2010. Audrey's employer transfers her to the Denver office in August 2011. Rich and Audrey sell their Chicago residence on August 2, 2011, and purchase a residence in Denver shortly thereafter. The realized gain on the sale is $300,000.

The $325,000 gain on the first Chicago residence is excluded under § 121. The sale of the second Chicago residence is within the two-year window of the prior sale, but because it resulted from a change in employment, Rich and Audrey can qualify for partial § 121 exclusion treatment as follows:

Realized gain	$ 300,000
§ 121 exclusion:	
$\frac{10 \text{ months}}{24 \text{ months}} \times \$500{,}000 = \$208{,}333$	(208,333)
Recognized gain	$ 91,667

■

Basis of New Residence

Because § 121 is an exclusion provision rather than a postponement of gain provision, the basis of a new residence is its cost.[94]

Reduction in Exclusion for Prior Use as a Vacation Home

A vacation home does not qualify for the § 121 exclusion because it does not satisfy the requirement of being the taxpayer's principal residence. Suppose, however, that the taxpayer converts the vacation home into a principal residence and subsequently satisfies the at least two-out-of-five-years ownership and use requirements. Prior to 2009, the converted vacation home qualified for the § 121 exclusion.

The Housing Assistance Tax Act of 2008 has reduced this opportunity to use the § 121 exclusion for converted vacation homes as to sales and exchanges occurring after December 31, 2008.[95] For periods of nonqualified use, the realized gain that otherwise is eligible for the § 121 exclusion is reduced by the proportion of the periods of nonqualified use compared to the period the property was owned by the taxpayer.

EXAMPLE 70

Monica purchases a house for use as a vacation home (100% personal use) on January 1, 2011, for $600,000. She uses it as a vacation home until January 1, 2013, when she makes it her principal residence. She continues to use it as her principal residence until she sells it on December 31, 2015, for $950,000 (selling expenses of $50,000).

Monica's realized gain is calculated as follows:

Amount realized ($950,000 – $50,000)	$ 900,000
Adjusted basis	(600,000)
Realized gain	$ 300,000

The sale of Monica's principal residence is subject to the proration required under the Act for nonqualified use.

$$\frac{\text{2 years (periods of nonqualified use)}}{\text{5 years (period of ownership)}} = 40\%$$

Thus, $120,000 ($300,000 × 40%) of the gain is ineligible for the § 121 exclusion, while the remaining gain of $180,000 ($300,000 – $120,000) is eligible for the § 121 exclusion. As a result, Monica's recognized gain is $120,000. ■

[94] § 1012.

[95] § 121(b)(4).

TAX *in the NEWS*

The Broadening Grip of Foreclosures or Foreclosures for All

Residential home foreclosures are usually associated with lower-income and middle-income taxpayers who obtained subprime mortgages and/or lost their jobs in the recession. Most residential foreclosures have occurred in this segment of the market.

But now the rich and famous (i.e., upper-income taxpayers) including some prominent actors and Wall Street executives are also experiencing foreclosures. The forclosure rate for residential mortgages of $5 million or more is rising sharply.

By some measures, big borrowers are more likely to default on their mortgages than small borrowers. According to American CoreLogic, which tracks more than 80 percent of the overall home mortgage market, 14.8 percent of loans with balances of $4 million or more were 90 days or more past due in early 2010 compared with 8.7 percent of all loans tracked. Sam Khater, a senior economist at First American, thinks big borrowers may be more likely than small borrowers to stop making payments when the house is underwater (i.e., debt exceeds fair market value).

Source: Adapted from Craig Karmin and James R. Hagerty, "Foreclosures Hit Rich and Famous," *Wall Street Journal*, April 9, 2010, p. A1.

EXAMPLE 71

Assume the same facts as in Example 70, except that the realized gain is $500,000. Of this amount, $200,000 ($500,000 × 40%) is ineligible for the § 121 exclusion, and of the remaining gain of $300,000 ($500,000 − $200,000), $250,000 is offset by the § 121 exclusion. So Monica's recognized gain is $250,000 ($200,000 + $50,000). ■

The period the property was owned by the taxpayer includes any period before 2009. The period of nonqualified use includes only the period after 2008.

PRINCIPAL RESIDENCE

To be eligible for the § 121 exclusion, the residence must have been owned and used by the taxpayer as the principal residence for at least two years during the five-year window (subject to partial exclusion treatment under the relief provision). Whether property is the taxpayer's principal residence "depends upon all of the facts and circumstances in each case."[96]

EXAMPLE 72

Mitch graduates from college and moves to Boston, where he is employed. He decides to rent an apartment in Boston because of its proximity to his place of employment. He purchases a beach condo in the Cape Cod area that he occupies most weekends. Mitch does not intend to live at the beach condo except on weekends. The apartment in Boston is his principal residence. ■

A residence does not have to be a house. For example, a houseboat, a house trailer, or a motor home can qualify.[97] Land, under certain circumstances, can qualify for exclusion treatment. The lot on which a house is built obviously qualifies. An adjacent lot can qualify if it is regularly used by the owner as part of the residential property. To qualify, the land must be sold along with the residence or within two years before or after the sale of the residence.

[96]Regulation § 1.121–1(b)(2) includes factors to be considered in determining a taxpayer's principal residence.

[97]Reg. § 1.1034–1(c)(3)(i).

ETHICS & Equity

HOW CLOSE TO THE WATER?

Sixteen years ago, Steve and Madeline Wilson purchased from a single seller the following properties located at the confluence of the York River and Chesapeake Bay near West Point, Virginia.

Property	Description	Cost
101 Main Street	½ acre of land with house across the street from the water	$290,000
102 Main Street	½ acre of land on the water	300,000

The house at 101 Main Street is used as their principal residence. It has spectacular river/bay views, but no direct access to the water.

The Wilsons purchased the lot at 102 Main Street because it provides access to the water. Also, owning this lot would prevent someone else from building a house that would impair their river/bay views. In addition, they regarded the lot as a sound investment.

Three months after the purchase, the Wilsons installed a dock and boat lift at a cost of $75,000 at the lot at 102 Main Street. They also added a barbeque pit there at a cost of $2,000 that they use for recreation and entertaining their friends.

Now Madeline, an advertising executive, has been transferred to Raleigh, North Carolina. Steve works out of an office in Washington, D.C., as a political consultant and will rent an apartment there. Consequently, the Wilsons decide to sell the two properties in a single transaction with the sale price allocated as follows:

101 Main Street	$695,000
102 Main Street	500,000

The Wilsons treat the sale of the two properties as the sale of their principal residence under § 121 and calculate the gain as follows:

Amount realized ($695,000 + $500,000)	$1,195,000
Basis ($290,000 + $300,000 + $75,000 + $2,000)	(667,000)
Realized gain	$ 528,000
§121 exclusion	(500,000)
Recognized gain	$ 28,000

Evaluate the validity of the Wilsons' calculation of recognized gain.

INVOLUNTARY CONVERSION AND USING §§ 121 AND 1033

As mentioned earlier (see Involuntary Conversion of a Personal Residence), a taxpayer can use both the § 121 exclusion of gain provision and the § 1033 postponement of gain provision.[98] The taxpayer initially can elect to exclude realized gain under § 121 to the extent of the statutory amount. Then a qualified replacement of the residence under § 1033 can be used to postpone the remainder of the realized gain. In applying § 1033, the amount of the required reinvestment is reduced by the amount of the § 121 exclusion.

EXAMPLE 73

Angel's principal residence is destroyed by a tornado. Her adjusted basis for the residence is $140,000. She receives insurance proceeds of $480,000.

If Angel does not elect to use the § 121 exclusion, her realized gain on the involuntary conversion of her principal residence is $340,000 ($480,000 amount realized – $140,000 adjusted basis). Thus, to postpone the $340,000 realized gain under § 1033, she would need to acquire qualifying property costing at least $480,000.

Using the § 121 exclusion enables Angel to reduce the amount of the required reinvestment for § 1033 purposes from $480,000 to $230,000. That is, by using § 121 in conjunction with § 1033, the amount realized, for § 1033 purposes, is reduced to $230,000 ($480,000 – $250,000 § 121 exclusion).

Note that if Angel does not acquire qualifying replacement property for § 1033 purposes, her recognized gain is $90,000 ($480,000 – $140,000 adjusted basis – $250,000 § 121 exclusion). ■

If § 1033 is used in conjunction with the § 121 exclusion on an involuntary conversion of a principal residence, the holding period of the replacement residence

[98] § 121(d)(5).

includes the holding period of the involuntarily converted residence. This can be beneficial in satisfying the § 121 two-out-of-five-years ownership and use requirement on a subsequent sale of the replacement residence.

13.7 Other Nonrecognition Provisions

LO.10

Identify other nonrecognition provisions contained in the Code.

The typical taxpayer experiences the sale of a personal residence or an involuntary conversion more frequently than the other types of nontaxable exchanges. Several less common nonrecognition provisions are treated briefly in the remainder of this chapter.

EXCHANGE OF STOCK FOR PROPERTY—§ 1032

Under § 1032, a corporation does not recognize gain or loss on the receipt of money or other property in exchange for its stock (including treasury stock). In other words, a corporation does not recognize gain or loss when it deals in its own stock. This provision is consistent with the accounting treatment of such transactions.

CERTAIN EXCHANGES OF INSURANCE POLICIES—§ 1035

Under § 1035, no gain or loss is recognized from the exchange of certain insurance contracts or policies. The rules relating to exchanges not solely in kind and the basis of the property acquired are the same as under § 1031. Exchanges qualifying for nonrecognition include the following:

- The exchange of life insurance contracts.
- The exchange of a life insurance contract for an endowment or annuity contract.
- The exchange of an endowment contract for another endowment contract that provides for regular payments beginning at a date not later than the date payments would have begun under the contract exchanged.
- The exchange of an endowment contract for an annuity contract.
- The exchange of annuity contracts.

EXCHANGE OF STOCK FOR STOCK OF THE SAME CORPORATION—§ 1036

Section 1036 provides that a shareholder does not recognize gain or loss on the exchange of common stock solely for common stock in the same corporation or from the exchange of preferred stock for preferred stock in the same corporation. Exchanges between individual shareholders as well as between a shareholder and the corporation are included. The rules relating to exchanges not solely in kind and the basis of the property acquired are the same as under § 1031. For example, a nonrecognition exchange occurs when common stock with different rights, such as voting for nonvoting, is exchanged. A shareholder usually recognizes gain or loss from the exchange of common for preferred or preferred for common even though the stock exchanged is in the same corporation.

CERTAIN REACQUISITIONS OF REAL PROPERTY—§ 1038

Under § 1038, no loss is recognized from the repossession of real property sold on an installment basis. Gain is recognized to a limited extent.

TRANSFERS OF PROPERTY BETWEEN SPOUSES OR INCIDENT TO DIVORCE—§ 1041

Section 1041 provides that transfers of property *between spouses or former spouses incident to divorce* are nontaxable transactions. Therefore, the basis to the recipient is a carryover basis. To be treated as incident to the divorce, the transfer must be related to the cessation of marriage or occur within one year after the date on which the marriage ceases.

Section 1041 also provides for nontaxable exchange treatment on property transfers *between spouses during marriage.* The basis to the recipient spouse is a carryover basis.

ETHICS & Equity

INCIDENT TO DIVORCE OR NOT?

Randy and Judy are divorced on December 28, 2010, after being married for 10 years. Several years ago, they purchased a beach lot for $300,000 and planned to construct a beach house there for vacation purposes.

On December 21, 2011, Randy transfers his interest in the beach lot to Judy for $325,000 (i.e., 50 percent of the fair market value of $650,000). According to both Randy and Judy, the sale was not associated with the divorce but was made to enable Randy to invest the cash in a new business. They treat the transaction as the sale of Randy's one-half interest to Judy. Accordingly, Randy recognizes a capital gain of $175,000 ($325,000 − $150,000), which is eligible for the 15 percent alternative tax rate. Judy considers her adjusted basis to be $475,000 ($150,000 + $325,000).

Evaluate Randy and Judy's treatment of this transaction.

ROLLOVERS INTO SPECIALIZED SMALL BUSINESS INVESTMENT COMPANIES—§ 1044

A postponement opportunity is available for some sellers of publicly traded securities under § 1044. If the amount realized is reinvested in the common stock or partnership interest of a specialized small business investment company (SSBIC), the realized gain is not recognized. Any amount not reinvested will trigger recognition of the realized gain to the extent of the deficiency. The taxpayer must reinvest the proceeds within 60 days of the date of sale in order to qualify. In calculating the basis of the SSBIC stock, the amount of the purchase price is reduced by the amount of the postponed gain.

Statutory ceilings are imposed on the amount of realized gain that can be postponed for any taxable year as follows:

- For an individual taxpayer, the lesser of:
  - *$50,000 ($25,000 for married filing separately).*
  - *$500,000 ($250,000 for married filing separately) reduced by the amount of such nonrecognized gain in prior taxable years.*
- For a corporate taxpayer, the lesser of:
  - *$250,000.*
  - *$1 million reduced by the amount of such nonrecognized gain in prior taxable years.*

Investors *ineligible* for this postponement treatment include partnerships, S corporations, estates, and trusts.

ROLLOVER OF GAIN FROM QUALIFIED SMALL BUSINESS STOCK INTO ANOTHER QUALIFIED SMALL BUSINESS STOCK—§ 1045

Under § 1045, realized gain from the sale of qualified small business stock held for more than six months may be postponed if the taxpayer acquires other qualified small business stock within 60 days. Any amount not reinvested will trigger the recognition of the realized gain on the sale to the extent of the deficiency. In calculating the basis of the acquired qualified small business stock, the amount of the purchase price is reduced by the amount of the postponed gain.

Qualified small business stock is stock of a qualified small business that is acquired by the taxpayer at its original issue in exchange for money or other property (excluding stock) or as compensation for services. A qualified small business is a domestic corporation that satisfies the following requirements:

- The aggregate gross assets prior to the issuance of the small business stock do not exceed $50 million.
- The aggregate gross assets immediately after the issuance of the small business stock do not exceed $50 million.

TAX PLANNING:

13.8 Cost Identification and Documentation Considerations

LO.11

Identify tax planning opportunities related to selected property transactions.

When multiple assets are acquired in a single transaction, the contract price must be allocated for several reasons. First, some of the assets may be depreciable, while others are not. From the different viewpoints of the buyer and the seller, this may produce a tax conflict that needs to be resolved. That is, the seller prefers a high allocation for nondepreciable assets, whereas the purchaser prefers a high allocation for depreciable assets (see Chapter 14). Second, the seller needs to know the amount realized on the sale of the capital assets and the ordinary income assets so that the recognized gains and losses can be classified as capital or ordinary. For example, an allocation to goodwill or to a covenant not to compete (see Chapters 8 and 14) produces different tax consequences to the seller. Third, the buyer needs the adjusted basis of each asset to calculate the realized gain or loss on a subsequent sale or other disposition of each asset.

13.9 Selection of Property for Making Gifts

A donor can achieve several tax advantages by making gifts of appreciated property. The donor avoids income tax on the unrealized gain that would have occurred had the donor sold the property. A portion of this amount can be permanently avoided because the donee's adjusted basis is increased by part or all of any gift tax paid by the donor. Even without this increase in basis, the income tax liability on the sale of the property by the donee can be less than the income tax liability that would have resulted from the donor's sale of the property, if the donee is in a lower tax bracket than the donor. In addition, any subsequent appreciation during the time the property is held by the lower tax bracket donee results in a tax savings on the sale or other disposition of the property. Such gifts of appreciated property can be an effective tool in family tax planning.

Taxpayers should generally not make gifts of depreciated property (property that, if sold, would produce a realized loss) because the donor does not receive an income tax deduction for the unrealized loss element. In addition, the donee receives no benefit from this unrealized loss upon the subsequent sale of the property because of the loss basis rule. The loss basis rule provides that the donee's basis is the lower of the donor's basis or the fair market value at the date of the gift. If the donor anticipates that the donee will sell the property upon receiving it, the donor should sell the property and take the loss deduction, assuming the loss is deductible. The donor can then give the proceeds from the sale to the donee.

13.10 Selection of Property for Making Bequests

A taxpayer should generally make bequests of appreciated property in his or her will. Doing so enables both the decedent and the heir to avoid income tax on the unrealized gain because the recipient takes the fair market value as his or her basis.

Taxpayers generally should not make bequests of depreciated property (property that, if sold, would produce a realized loss) because the decedent does not receive an income tax deduction for the unrealized loss element. In addition, the heir will receive no benefit from this unrealized loss upon the subsequent sale of the property.

EXAMPLE 74

On the date of her death in 2011, Marta owned land held for investment purposes. The land had an adjusted basis of $130,000 and a fair market value of $100,000. If Marta had sold the property before her death, the recognized loss would have been $30,000. If Roger inherits the property and later sells it for $90,000, the recognized loss is $10,000 (the decline in value since Marta's death). In addition, regardless of the period of time Roger holds the property, the holding period is long term (see Chapter 14). ■

From an income tax perspective, it is preferable to transfer appreciated property as a bequest rather than as a gift. The reason is that inherited property receives a step-up in basis, whereas property received by gift has a carryover basis to the donee. However, in making this decision, the estate tax consequences of the bequest should also be weighed against the gift tax consequences of the gift.

13.11 Disallowed Losses

SECTION 267 DISALLOWED LOSSES

Taxpayers should be aware of the desirability of avoiding transactions that activate the loss disallowance provisions for related parties. This is so even in light of the provision that permits the related-party buyer to offset his or her realized gain by the related-party seller's disallowed loss. Even with this offset, several inequities exist. First, the tax benefit associated with the disallowed loss ultimately is realized by the wrong party (the related-party buyer rather than the related-party seller). Second, the tax benefit of this offset to the related-party buyer does not occur until the buyer disposes of the property. Therefore, the longer the time period between the purchase and disposition of the property by the related-party buyer, the less the economic benefit. Third, if the property does not appreciate to at least its adjusted basis to the related-party seller during the time period the related-party buyer holds it, part or all of the disallowed loss is permanently lost. Fourth, since the right of offset is available only to the original transferee (the related-party buyer), all of the disallowed loss is permanently lost if the original transferee subsequently transfers the property by gift or bequest.

EXAMPLE 75

Tim sells property with an adjusted basis of $35,000 to Wes, his brother, for $25,000, the fair market value of the property. The $10,000 realized loss to Tim is disallowed by § 267. If Wes subsequently sells the property to an unrelated party for $37,000, he has a recognized gain of $2,000 (realized gain of $12,000 reduced by disallowed loss of $10,000). Therefore, from the perspective of the family unit, the original $10,000 realized loss ultimately is recognized. However, if Wes sells the property for $29,000, he has a recognized gain of $0 (realized gain of $4,000 reduced by disallowed loss of

$4,000 necessary to offset the realized gain). From the perspective of the family unit, $6,000 of the realized loss of $10,000 is permanently wasted ($10,000 realized loss – $4,000 offset permitted). ■

WASH SALES

The wash sales provisions can be avoided if the security that was sold is replaced within the statutory time period with a similar rather than a substantially identical security. For example, a sale of Dell, Inc. common stock accompanied by a purchase of Hewlett-Packard common stock is not treated as a wash sale. Such a procedure can enable the taxpayer to use an unrealized capital loss to offset a recognized capital gain. The taxpayer can sell the security before the end of the taxable year, offset the recognized capital loss against the capital gain, and invest the sales proceeds in a similar security.

Because the wash sales provisions do not apply to gains, it may be desirable to engage in a wash sale before the end of the taxable year. The recognized capital gain may be used to offset capital losses or capital loss carryovers from prior years. Since the basis of the replacement stock or securities will be the purchase price, the taxpayer in effect has exchanged a capital gain for an increased basis for the stock or securities.

13.12 Like-Kind Exchanges

Since application of the like-kind exchange provisions is mandatory rather than elective, in certain instances it may be preferable to avoid qualifying for § 1031 nonrecognition. To avoid the application of a deferral under § 1031, the taxpayer should structure the transaction so that at least one of the statutory requirements for a § 1031 like-kind exchange is not satisfied. If the like-kind exchange provisions do not apply, the end result may be the recognition of capital gain in exchange for a higher basis in the newly acquired asset. Also, the immediate recognition of gain may be preferable in certain situations. Examples where immediate recognition is beneficial include the following:

- Taxpayer has unused net operating loss carryovers.
- Taxpayer has unused general business credit carryovers.
- Taxpayer has suspended or current passive activity losses.

EXAMPLE 76

Alicia disposes of a machine (used in her business) with an adjusted basis of $3,000 for $4,000. She also acquires a new business machine for $9,000. If § 1031 applies, the $1,000 realized gain is not recognized, and the basis of the new machine is reduced by $1,000 (from $9,000 to $8,000). If § 1031 does not apply, a $1,000 gain is recognized and may receive favorable capital gain treatment to the extent that the gain is not recognized as ordinary income due to the depreciation recapture provisions (see Chapter 14). In addition, the basis for depreciation on the new machine is $9,000 rather than $8,000 since there is no unrecognized gain. ■

The application of § 1031 nonrecognition treatment should also be avoided when the adjusted basis of the property being disposed of exceeds the fair market value.

EXAMPLE 77

Assume the same facts as in the previous example, except that the fair market value of the machine is $2,500. If § 1031 applies, the $500 realized loss is not recognized. To recognize the loss, Alicia should sell the old machine and purchase the new one. The purchase and sale transactions should be with different taxpayers. ■

On the other hand, the like-kind exchange procedure can be utilized to control the amount of recognized gain.

EXAMPLE 78

Rex has property with an adjusted basis of $40,000 and a fair market value of $100,000. Sandra wants to buy Rex's property, but Rex wants to limit the amount of recognized gain on the proposed transaction. Sandra acquires other like-kind property (from an outside party) for $80,000. She then exchanges this property and $20,000 cash for Rex's property. Rex has a realized gain of $60,000 ($100,000 amount realized − $40,000 adjusted basis). His recognized gain is only $20,000, the lower of the $20,000 boot received or the $60,000 realized gain. Rex's basis for the like-kind property is $40,000 ($40,000 adjusted basis + $20,000 gain recognized − $20,000 boot received). If Rex had sold the property to Sandra for its fair market value of $100,000, the result would have been a $60,000 recognized gain ($100,000 amount realized − $40,000 adjusted basis) to him. It is permissible for Rex to identify the like-kind property that he wants Sandra to purchase.[99] ■

In the present economic environment, however, there is another consideration. The beneficial result of tax deferral of realized gain could be more than offset by future tax rate increases. Some real estate investors are following this approach, particularly with respect to undeveloped land. They are willing to accept current taxation at 15 percent to avoid the possibility of future taxation at a much higher rate. Many believe that the capital gains tax rate could rise to 20 or 25 percent in the near future. Although turning down a tax deferral may sound like a strange strategy, it fits the notion of "pay a tax today to avoid a higher tax tomorrow."

13.13 Involuntary Conversions

In certain cases, a taxpayer may prefer to recognize gain from an involuntary conversion. Keep in mind that § 1033, unlike § 1031 (dealing with like-kind exchanges), generally is an elective provision.

EXAMPLE 79

Ahmad has a $40,000 realized gain from the involuntary conversion of an office building. He reinvests the entire proceeds of $450,000 in a new office building. He does not elect to postpone gain under § 1033, however, because of an expiring net operating loss carryover that is offset against the gain. Therefore, none of the realized gain of $40,000 is postponed. Because Ahmad did not elect § 1033 postponement, his basis in the replacement property is the property's cost of $450,000 rather than $410,000 ($450,000 reduced by the $40,000 realized gain). ■

13.14 Sale of a Principal Residence

ELECTION TO FORGO

The § 121 exclusion automatically applies if the taxpayer is eligible. That is, the taxpayer does not have to make an election. However, if the taxpayer wishes to avoid § 121 exclusion treatment on an otherwise eligible sale, the taxpayer may elect to do so.[100]

EXAMPLE 80

George owns two personal residences that satisfy the two-year ownership and use test with respect to the five-year window. The Elm Street residence has appreciated by $25,000, and the Maple Street residence has appreciated by $230,000. He intends to sell both of them and move into rental property. He sells the Elm Street residence in December 2011 and expects to sell the Maple Street residence early next year.

[99] *Franklin B. Biggs*, 69 T.C. 905 (1978); Rev.Rul. 73–476, 1973–2 C.B. 300; and *Starker v. U.S.*, 79–2 USTC ¶9541, 44 AFTR 2d 79–5525, 602 F.2d 1341 (CA–9, 1979).

[100] § 121(f).

Unless George elects not to apply the § 121 exclusion to the sale of the Elm Street residence, he will exclude the $25,000 realized gain on that residence in 2011. In 2012, however, he will have a recognized gain of $230,000 on the sale of the Maple Street residence.

If George makes the election to forgo, he will report a recognized gain of $25,000 on the sale of the Elm Street residence in 2011. But by using the § 121 exclusion in 2012, he will eliminate the recognized gain of $230,000 on the sale of the Maple Street residence. ■

NEGATIVE EFFECT OF RENTING OR USING AS A HOME OFFICE

The residence does not have to be the taxpayer's principal residence at the date of sale to qualify for the § 121 exclusion. During part of the five-year window, it could have been rental property (e.g., either a vacation home or entirely rental property). In addition, the taxpayer can have used part of the principal residence as a qualifying home office. In either of these circumstances, the taxpayer may claim deductions for the expenses attributable to the rental or business use. But what effect, if any, do such deductions have on a later sale of the residence? Will the sales proceeds still qualify for nonrecognition of gain treatment under § 121?

Concern that the § 121 exclusion might be denied may have deterred some taxpayers from claiming legitimate deductions, particularly in the case of an office in the home. As noted below, however, the IRS has clarified its position regarding the effect of any such depreciation.

In either the rental or the home office setting, the taxpayer will have deducted depreciation. Any realized gain on the sale that is attributable to depreciation claimed after May 5, 1997, is not eligible for the § 121 exclusion.[101]

EXAMPLE 81

On December 5, 2011, Amanda sells her principal residence, which qualifies for the § 121 exclusion. Her realized gain is $190,000. From January through November 2010, she was temporarily out of town on a job assignment in another city and rented the residence to a college student. For this period, she deducted MACRS cost recovery of $7,000. Without the depreciation provision, Amanda could exclude the $190,000 realized gain. However, the depreciation taken requires her to recognize $7,000 of the realized gain. ■

The gain recognized associated with prior depreciation deductions is determined first before calculating the amount of recognized gain associated with periods of nonqualified use.[102]

EXAMPLE 82

Assume the same facts as in Example 70, except that the vacation home was used partially for rental use before being converted to Monica's personal residence and that $25,000 of depreciation was deducted during the periods that the vacation home was rented. Monica's realized gain is calculated as follows:

Amount realized ($950,000 – $50,000)	$ 900,000
Adjusted basis ($600,000 – $25,000)	(575,000)
Realized gain	$ 325,000

Since $25,000 of depreciation was deducted by Monica, $25,000 of the realized gain is recognized. The sale of Monica's principal residence is subject to the proration required for nonqualified use.

$$\frac{\text{2 years (period of nonqualified use)}}{\text{5 years (period of ownership)}} = 40\%$$

[101] § 121(d)(6).

[102] § 121(b)(4)(D).

Thus, \$120,000 (\$300,000 × 40%) of the remaining gain is ineligible for the § 121 exclusion, and the remaining gain of \$180,000 (\$300,000 − \$120,000) is eligible for the § 121 exclusion. Consequently, Monica's recognized gain is \$145,000 (\$25,000 + \$120,000). ■

QUALIFICATION FOR § 121 EXCLUSION

The key requirement for the § 121 exclusion is that the taxpayer must have *owned* and *used* the property as a principal residence for at least two years during the five-year window. As taxpayers advance in age, they quite frequently make decisions such as the following:

- Sell the principal residence and buy a smaller residence or rent the principal residence.
- Sell vacation homes they own.
- Sell homes they are holding as rental property.

These properties may have experienced substantial appreciation during the ownership period. Clearly, the sale of the principal residence is eligible for the § 121 exclusion. Less clear, however, is that proper planning can make it possible for a vacation home or rental property to qualify for the exclusion. Although this strategy may require taxpayers to be flexible about where they live, it can result in substantial tax savings.

EXAMPLE 83

Thelma and David are approaching retirement. They have substantial appreciation on their principal residence and on a house they own at the beach (about two hours away). After retirement, they plan to move to Florida. They have owned and lived in the principal residence for 28 years and have owned the beach house for 9 years. If they sell their principal residence, it qualifies for the § 121 exclusion. At retirement, they could move into their beach house for two years and make it eligible for the exclusion. If the beach house were not so far away, they could sell the principal residence now and move into the beach house to start the running of the two-year use period. Note that any realized gain on the beach house attributable to depreciation is not eligible for the § 121 exclusion. Note also the provision that now requires a reduction in the § 121 exclusion for prior use as a vacation home (see Examples 70 and 82). ■

RECORD KEEPING

Since the amount of the available exclusion (\$250,000 or \$500,000) for most taxpayers will exceed the realized gain on the sale of the residence, the IRS has discontinued the form that previously was used to report the sale of a principal residence. If the sale of the residence does result in a gain that is not excluded from gross income, the gain is reported on Schedule D of Form 1040 (Capital Gains and Losses).

However, it is a good idea for all taxpayers who own residences to continue to maintain records on the adjusted basis of the residence including the original cost, any capital improvements, and any deductions that decrease basis (e.g., depreciation on a home office or on rental use) for the following reasons:

- The sale of the residence may not qualify for the § 121 exclusion.
- The realized gain may exceed the § 121 exclusion amount.
- The residence may be converted to rental or business use.
- If part of the residence has been rental or business use property (e.g., a qualifying home office) and depreciation has been deducted, the realized gain is recognized to the extent of the depreciation deducted.

REFOCUS ON THE BIG PICTURE

SALE OR GIFT OF INHERITED HOUSE AND OTHER PROPERTY TRANSACTIONS

Gift of Inherited House

Based on an inquiry you made of Alice, this is the only gift that she would make to Michael this year. She has made no prior gifts to any individual that exceeded the annual per donee exclusion amount (i.e., currently $13,000).

With this information, you inform Alice that no gift tax would be due on the gift of the house to Michael. However, she would use up $587,000 ($600,000 – $13,000) of her lifetime gift tax exclusion of $1 million. Michael's basis for the house would be a carryover of Alice's basis of $475,000 (i.e., for inherited property, the fair market value at the date of the decedent's death).

Sale of Inherited House

You advise Alice that her adjusted basis for the house in calculating gain or loss on the sale of the house is the $475,000 fair market value on the date of her grandmother's death. If Alice sells the house for $600,000, her projected selling expenses (i.e., real estate agent's commission, attorney fees, other closing costs) would be $42,000 ($600,000 × 7%). She would have a recognized gain of $83,000 as calculated below. The house is a capital asset, and Alice's holding period is long term since she inherited the house. Thus, the gain would be classified as a long-term capital gain (i.e., eligible for a 15% tax rate). So the Federal income tax due would be $12,450 ($83,000 × 15%).

Amount realized ($600,000 – $42,000)	$ 558,000
Less: Adjusted basis	(475,000)
Realized gain	$ 83,000
Recognized gain	$ 83,000

See Example 8 and 9 for the tax consequences associated with Alice's questions regarding selling the car. See Example 34 for the tax consequences associated with Alice's questions regarding the wash sale of the stock.

What If?

Alice is leaning toward selling the house. However, she knows that her grandmother would not want her to have to pay income taxes on the sale. Alice inquires as to whether there is any way that she could reduce the Federal income tax on the sale to $0.

You inform Alice of the exclusion provision under § 121 of the Code. She can qualify for this exclusion of realized gain provision if she satisfies the at least two-out-of-five-years ownership and use requirements. This would necessitate her moving into the house for two years and occupying it as her principal residence.

KEY TERMS

DISCUSSION QUESTIONS

DECISION MAKING

1. **LO.1** Ivan invests in land and Grace invests in taxable bonds. The land appreciates by $8,000 each year, and the bonds earn interest of $8,000 each year. After holding the land and bonds for five years, Ivan and Grace sell them. There is a $40,000 realized gain on the sale of the land and no realized gain or loss on the sale of the bonds. Are the tax consequences to Ivan and Grace the same for each of the five years? Explain.

2. **LO.1** Carol and Dave each purchase 100 shares of stock of Burgundy, Inc., a publicly owned corporation, in July for $10,000 each. Carol sells her stock on December 31 for $8,000. Since Burgundy's stock is listed on a national exchange, Dave is able to ascertain that his shares are worth $8,000 on December 31. Does the tax law treat the decline in value of the stock differently for Carol and Dave? Explain.

3. **LO.1** If a taxpayer sells property for cash, the amount realized consists of the net proceeds from the sale. For each of the following, indicate the effect on the amount realized:
   a. The property is sold on credit.
   b. A mortgage on the property is assumed by the buyer.
   c. A mortgage on the property is assumed by the seller.
   d. The buyer acquires the property subject to a mortgage of the seller.
   e. Stock that has a basis to the purchaser of $6,000 and a fair market value of $10,000 is received by the seller as part of the consideration.

4. **LO.1** Adrian owns real property for which the annual property taxes are $3,650. He sells the property to Shelley on February 28, 2011, for $200,000. Shelley pays the real property taxes for the entire year on August 1.
   a. How much of the property taxes can be deducted by Adrian and how much by Shelley?
   b. What effect does the property tax apportionment have on Shelley's adjusted basis in the property?
   c. What effect does the apportionment have on Adrian's amount realized from the sale?
   d. How would the answers in (b) and (c) differ if the taxes were paid by Adrian?

DECISION MAKING

5. **LO.1** Troy is negotiating to buy some land. Under the first option, Troy will give Ella $150,000 and assume her mortgage on the land for $80,000. Under the second option, Troy will give Ella $230,000, and she will immediately pay off the mortgage. Troy wants his basis for the land to be as high as possible. Given this objective, which option should Troy select?

6. **LO.1** Eve purchases land from Gillen. Eve gives Gillen $100,000 in cash and agrees to pay Gillen an additional $400,000 one year later plus interest at 6%.
   a. What is Eve's adjusted basis for the land at the acquisition date?
   b. What is Eve's adjusted basis for the land one year later?

7. **LO.1** A taxpayer owns land and a building (held for investment) with an adjusted basis of $75,000 and a fair market value of $240,000. The property is subject to a mortgage of $360,000. Since the taxpayer is in arrears on the mortgage payments, the creditor is willing to accept the property in return for canceling the amount of the mortgage.
   a. How can the adjusted basis of the property be less than the amount of the mortgage?
   b. If the creditor's offer is accepted, what are the effects on the amount realized, the adjusted basis, and the realized gain or loss?
   c. Does it matter in (b) if the mortgage is recourse or nonrecourse?

8. **LO.1** Distinguish between the terms *allowed depreciation* and *allowable depreciation*. What effect does the difference have on adjusted basis?

9. **LO.1, 4** Chuck and Teresa became engaged after they graduated from college in May 2011. As a graduation present, Chuck received a new car worth $29,000 from his uncle, which he uses for personal purposes. Since Teresa is employed, she purchases a car just like the one Chuck received from his uncle and uses it 60% for business.
   a. Why can Teresa deduct depreciation on her car, whereas Chuck cannot?
   b. If Chuck and Teresa each later sell their cars for $24,000, why is Teresa's realized gain recognized, while Chuck's realized loss is disallowed?

10. **LO.1** Abby owns stock in Orange Corporation and Blue Corporation. She receives a $1,000 distribution from both corporations. The instructions from Orange state that the $1,000 is a dividend. The instructions from Blue state that the $1,000 is not a dividend. What could cause the instructions to differ as to the tax consequences?

11. **LO.1** On July 1, 2011, Katrina purchased tax-exempt bonds (face value of $75,000) for $82,000. The bonds mature in five years, and the annual interest rate is 6%. The market rate of interest is 2%.
    a. How much interest income and/or interest expense must Katrina report in 2011?
    b. What is Katrina's adjusted basis for the bonds on January 1, 2012?

12. **LO.2** Sandra is considering selling two personal use assets that she owns. One has appreciated in value by $14,000, and the other has declined in value by $18,000. Sandra believes that she should sell both assets in the same tax year so that the loss of $18,000 can offset the gain of $14,000. **DECISION MAKING**
    a. Advise Sandra regarding the tax consequences of her plan.
    b. Could Sandra achieve better tax results by selling the assets in different tax years?

13. **LO.2** Ron sold his sailboat for a $5,000 loss in the current year because he was diagnosed as having skin cancer. His spouse wants him to sell his Harley Davidson motorcycle because her brother broke his leg while riding his motorcycle. Since Ron no longer has anyone to ride with, he is seriously considering accepting his wife's advice. Because the motorcycle is a classic, Ron has received two offers. Each offer would result in a $5,000 gain. Joe would like to purchase the motorcycle before Christmas, and Jeff would like to purchase it after New Year's. Identify the relevant tax issues Ron faces in making his decision. **ISSUE ID**

14. **LO.3** Monty owns a life insurance policy that will pay $500,000 to Pearlie, his spouse, on his death. At the date of Monty's death, he had paid total premiums of $115,000 on the policy. In accordance with § 101(a)(1), Pearlie excludes the $500,000 of insurance proceeds. Discuss the relationship, if any, between the § 101 exclusion and the recovery of capital doctrine.

15. **LO.4** How is cost allocated when a taxpayer acquires multiple assets in a lump-sum purchase?

16. **LO.4** Distinguish between the procedures for determining the basis of stock received as a nontaxable stock dividend when the stock dividend is:
    a. Common stock on common stock.
    b. Preferred stock on common stock.

17. **LO.1, 2, 4, 6** In January, Agnes is diagnosed as having a terminal disease. Her nephew, Stan, will graduate from college in May, and she would like to give him $50,000 as a graduation present. She has stock worth $50,000 that she could either give him directly or sell and transfer the cash. Since she may not be alive in May, Agnes is considering making the gift now (four months prior to graduation). If Agnes should die before making the gift, her will stipulates that Stan will receive the stock. Identify the relevant tax issues that Agnes should consider in making her decision. **ISSUE ID**

18. **LO.4** Different rules apply as to the basis for property received by gift and property received by inheritance. Under what circumstances will the basis be the same for property received by gift and by inheritance in 2011?

19. **LO.4** Robin inherits 1,000 shares of Wal-Mart stock from her aunt in 2011. According to the information received from the executor of her aunt's estate, Robin's adjusted basis for the stock is $55,000. Albert, Robin's fiancé, receives 1,000 shares of Wal-Mart stock from his uncle as a gift in 2011. His uncle tells Albert that his adjusted basis for the Wal-Mart stock is $7,000. What could cause the substantial difference in the adjusted basis for Robin's and Albert's respective 1,000 shares of Wal-Mart stock?

20. **LO.4** Gary makes a gift of an appreciated building to Carmen. She dies three months later, and Gary inherits the building from her. During the period that Carmen held the building, she deducted depreciation and made a capital expenditure. What effect might these items have on Gary's basis for the inherited building?

21. **LO.4** Address the following issues:
    a. In a community property state, what effect does the death of one spouse have on the adjusted basis of the surviving spouse's one-half interest in the community property?

b. Presuming the property is jointly owned, would the result be different in a common law state?

DECISION MAKING

22. **LO.5** Marilyn owns land that she acquired three years ago as an investment for $250,000. Since the land has not appreciated in value as she anticipated, she sells it to her brother, Amos, for its fair market value of $180,000. Amos sells the land two years later for $240,000.
    a. Explain why Marilyn's realized loss of $70,000 ($180,000 amount realized – $250,000 adjusted basis) is disallowed.
    b. Explain why Amos has neither a recognized gain nor a recognized loss on his sale of the land.
    c. Is the family unit treated fairly under the related-party disallowance rule under § 267?
    d. Which party wins and which party loses?
    e. How could Marilyn have avoided the loss disallowance on her sale of the land?

DECISION MAKING

23. **LO.5, 11** On December 18, 2011, Amber sells 500 shares of John Deere stock for a realized loss of $5,000. On January 8, 2012, Amber purchases 500 shares of John Deere stock for $8,000 more than she received on the December sale.
    a. Why is Amber's December realized loss of $5,000 disallowed?
    b. How does Amber calculate the basis of the 500 shares purchased in January 2012?
    c. What could Amber have done differently to enable her to recognize the $5,000 loss in 2011?

24. **LO.7** What are the three requirements that must be satisfied for a transaction to qualify for nontaxable exchange treatment under § 1031?

25. **LO.7** Can the exchange of personal use property for property held for productive use in a trade or business qualify for like-kind exchange treatment? Explain.

26. **LO.7, 11** Can property held for productive use in a trade or business be exchanged for investment property and qualify for like-kind exchange treatment? Explain.

ISSUE ID

27. **LO.7** Ross would like to dispose of some land that he acquired five years ago because he believes that it will not continue to appreciate. Its value has increased by $50,000 over the five-year period. He also intends to sell stock that has declined in value by $50,000 during the eight-month period he has owned it. Ross has four offers to acquire the stock and land:

Buyer number 1:	Exchange land.
Buyer number 2:	Purchase land for cash.
Buyer number 3:	Exchange stock.
Buyer number 4:	Purchase stock for cash.

Identify the tax issues relevant to Ross in disposing of this land and stock.

28. **LO.7** Samuel is a 10% limited partner in the SVI limited partnership. He exchanges his partnership interest in SVI for a 25% limited partnership interest in DRI. Both partnerships are in the oil drilling business. Samuel's adjusted basis for his SVI partnership interest is $80,000, and the fair market value of the partnership interest he receives in DRI is $120,000.
    a. What is Samuel's recognized gain or loss associated with the exchange?
    b. Would the answer in (a) be different if Samuel exchanged a general partnership interest for a general partnership interest?

29. **LO.7** When no boot is given or received in a like-kind exchange, the basis of the property received is the same as the basis of the property transferred. What effect does the receipt of boot have on the basis of the like-kind property received? What if boot is given?

30. **LO.7** In connection with like-kind exchanges, discuss each of the following:
    a. Realized gain.
    b. Realized loss.
    c. Recognized gain.
    d. Recognized loss.
    e. Postponed gain.
    f. Postponed loss.
    g. Basis of like-kind property received.
    h. Basis of boot received.

31. **LO.7** Beverly exchanges undeveloped real estate for developed real estate on March 3, 2011. The fair market value of each property is $260,000. Beverly had purchased the undeveloped real estate on February 25, 2008, for $325,000.
    a. When does Beverly's holding period begin for the developed real estate?
    b. Assume instead that Beverly's cost for the undeveloped real estate was $200,000. When does her holding period begin for the developed real estate?

32. **LO.7** Mortgaged real estate may be received in a like-kind exchange. If the taxpayer's mortgage is assumed, what effect does the mortgage have on the recognition of realized gain? On the basis of the real estate received?

33. **LO.8** Andrea's retail store building (basis of $270,000) is destroyed by a fire. She receives insurance proceeds of $250,000 (the appraised value of the building prior to its destruction).
    a. How much can Andrea reinvest in another retail store building and still recognize a $20,000 loss?
    b. Assume instead that the insurance proceeds are $300,000. How much must Andrea reinvest in another retail store building in order not to have any recognized gain?

34. **LO.8** What constitutes an involuntary conversion?

35. **LO.8** Vera owns an office building that she leases to tenants. If the building is destroyed by a tornado, is the functional use test or the taxpayer use test applied as to replacement property? Explain the differences between the two tests.

36. **LO.8** On June 5, 2011, Amber, Inc., a calendar year taxpayer, receives cash of $525,000 from the county upon condemnation of its warehouse building (adjusted basis of $390,000 and fair market value of $525,000).
    a. What must Amber do to qualify for § 1033 postponement of gain treatment?
    b. How would your advice to Amber differ if the adjusted basis was $550,000?

37. **LO.8** Reba, a calendar year taxpayer, owns an office building that she uses in her business. The building is involuntarily converted on November 15, 2011. On January 5, 2012, Reba receives enough proceeds to produce a realized gain. What is the latest date she can replace the building and qualify for § 1033 postponement treatment if the conversion event is:
    a. A flood?
    b. A condemnation?
    c. A tornado?

38. **LO.8** Bob is notified by the city public housing authority on May 3, 2011, that his apartment building is going to be condemned as part of an urban renewal project. On June 1, 2011, Carol offers to buy the building from Bob. Bob sells the building to Carol on June 30, 2011. Condemnation occurs on September 1, 2011, and Carol receives the condemnation proceeds from the city. Assume both Bob and Carol are calendar year taxpayers.
    a. What is the earliest date on which Bob can dispose of the building and qualify for § 1033 postponement treatment?
    b. Does the sale to Carol qualify as a § 1033 involuntary conversion?
    c. What is the latest date on which Carol can acquire qualifying replacement property and qualify for postponement of the realized gain?
    d. What type of property will be qualifying replacement property?

39. **LO.8** A warehouse owned by Martha and used in her business (i.e., to store inventory) is being condemned by the city to provide a right of way for a highway. The warehouse has appreciated by $180,000 based on Martha's estimate of its fair market value. In the negotiations, the city is offering $35,000 less than what Martha believes the property is worth. Alan, a real estate broker, has offered to purchase Martha's property for $20,000 more than the city's offer. Martha plans to invest the proceeds she will receive in an office building that she will lease to various tenants. ISSUE ID
    a. Identify the relevant tax issues for Martha.
    b. Would the answer in (a) change if Martha's warehouse was property held for investment rather than being used in her business?

40. **LO.8** When does the holding period begin for replacement property acquired in an involuntary conversion? For property received in a like-kind exchange?

41. **LO.9** Samantha wants to retire, sell the house that she has occupied as her residence for 20 years, and travel. She would have a $120,000 realized loss on the sale of the residence. She intends to use the net proceeds to fund her travels.
    a. Can Samantha recognize the loss?
    b. Would the answer in (a) be different if the realized loss was, instead, a $120,000 realized gain?

42. **LO.9** Gary, who is single, sells his principal residence (owned and occupied by him for seven years) in November 2011 for a realized gain of $148,000. He had purchased a more expensive new residence eight months prior to the sale. He anticipates that he will occupy this new house as his principal residence for only about 18 additional months. He expects it to appreciate substantially while he owns it. Gary would like to recognize the realized gain on the 2011 sale to offset a large investment loss from the sale of stock. Can he recognize the realized gain of $148,000 on the sale of his principal residence in 2011?

43. **LO.9** What is a principal residence? Can a taxpayer have several principal residences at the same time?

44. **LO.10** On May 5, 2011, Nancy sells her stock (adjusted basis of $13,000) in Lime, Inc., a publicly traded company, for $17,000. On May 31, 2011, she pays $20,000 for stock in Rose, Inc., a specialized small business investment company. Nancy believes that her adjusted basis for the Rose stock is $10,000.
    a. Evaluate Nancy's calculation of the adjusted basis for her Rose stock.
    b. How would your answer change if Nancy purchased the replacement stock on July 15 rather than on May 31?

PROBLEMS

45. **LO.1** Anne sold her home for $290,000 in 2011. Selling expenses were $17,400. She had purchased it in 2004 for $200,000. During the period of ownership, Anne had done the following:

    - Deducted $50,500 office-in-home expenses, which included $4,500 in depreciation. (Refer to Chapter 9.)
    - Deducted a casualty loss in 2007 for residential trees destroyed by a hurricane. The total loss was $19,000 (after the $100 floor and the 10%-of-AGI floor), and Anne's insurance company reimbursed her for $13,500. (Refer to Chapter 7.)
    - Paid street paving assessment of $7,000 and added sidewalks for $8,000.
    - Installed an elevator for medical reasons. The total cost was $20,000, and Anne deducted $13,000 as medical expenses. (Refer to Chapter 10.)

    What is Anne's realized gain?

46. **LO.1** Kareem bought a rental house in October 2006 for $250,000, of which $50,000 is allocated to the land and $200,000 to the building. Early in 2008, he had a tennis court built in the backyard at a cost of $5,000. Kareem has deducted $30,900 for depreciation on the house and $1,300 for depreciation on the court. In January 2011, he sells the house and tennis court for $400,000 cash.
    a. What is Kareem's realized gain or loss?
    b. If an original mortgage of $75,000 is still outstanding and the buyer assumes the mortgage in addition to the cash payment, what is Kareem's realized gain or loss?
    c. If the buyer takes the property subject to the mortgage, rather than assuming it, what is Kareem's realized gain or loss?

47. **LO.1** Norm is negotiating the sale of a tract of his land to Pat. Use the following classification scheme to classify each of the items contained in the proposed sales contract:

Legend		
DARN	=	Decreases amount realized by Norm
IARN	=	Increases amount realized by Norm
DABN	=	Decreases adjusted basis to Norm
IABN	=	Increases adjusted basis to Norm
DABP	=	Decreases adjusted basis to Pat
IABP	=	Increases adjusted basis to Pat

a. Norm is to receive cash of $50,000.
b. Norm is to receive Pat's note payable for $25,000, payable in three years.
c. Pat assumes Norm's mortgage of $5,000 on the land.
d. Pat agrees to pay the realtor's sales commission of $8,000.
e. Pat agrees to pay the property taxes on the land for the entire year. If each party paid his or her respective share, Norm's share would be $1,000, and Pat's share would be $3,000.
f. Pat pays legal fees of $500.
g. Norm pays legal fees of $750.

48. **LO.1, 2** Melanie owns a personal use boat that has a fair market value of $32,500 and an adjusted basis of $45,000. Melanie's AGI is $90,000. Calculate the realized and recognized gain or loss if:
a. Melanie sells the boat for $32,500.
b. Melanie exchanges the boat for another boat worth $32,500.
c. The boat is stolen and Melanie receives insurance proceeds of $32,500.
d. Would your answer in (a) change if the fair market value and the selling price of the boat were $48,000?

49. **LO.1** Chee purchases Tan, Inc. bonds for $108,000 on January 2, 2011. The face value of the bonds is $100,000, the maturity date is December 31, 2015, and the annual interest rate is 6%. Chee will amortize the premium only if he is required to do so. Chee sells the bonds on July 1, 2013, for $106,000.
a. Determine the interest income Chee should report for 2011.
b. Calculate Chee's recognized gain or loss on the sale of the bonds in 2013.

50. **LO.1, 2** Which of the following results in a recognized gain or loss?
a. Kay sells her vacation cabin (adjusted basis of $100,000) for $150,000.
b. Adam sells his personal residence (adjusted basis of $150,000) for $100,000.
c. Carl's personal residence (adjusted basis of $65,000) is condemned by the city. He receives condemnation procceds of $55,000.
d. Olga's land is worth $40,000 at the end of the year. She had purchased the land six months earlier for $25,000.
e. Vera's personal vehicle (adjusted basis of $22,000) is stolen. She receives $23,000 from the insurance company and does not plan to replace the automobile.
f. Jerry sells used clothing (adjusted basis of $500) to a thrift store for $50.

51. **LO.1, 2** Yancy's personal residence is condemned as part of an urban renewal project. His adjusted basis for the residence is $405,000. He receives condemnation proceeds of $390,000 and invests the proceeds in stocks and bonds.
a. Calculate Yancy's realized and recognized gain or loss.
b. If the condemnation proceeds are $450,000, what are Yancy's realized and recognized gain or loss?
c. What are Yancy's realized and recognized gain or loss in (a) if the house was rental property?

52. **LO.4** Buddy Morris is a real estate agent for Presidential Estates, a residential real estate development. Because of his outstanding sales performance, Buddy is permitted to buy a lot that normally would sell for $280,000 for $250,000. Buddy is the only real estate agent for Presidential Estates who is permitted to do so. **COMMUNICATIONS**
a. Does Buddy have gross income from the transaction?
b. What is Buddy's adjusted basis for the land?
c. Write a letter to Buddy informing him of the tax consequences of his acquisition of the lot. His address is 100 Tower Road, San Diego, CA 92182.

53. **LO.1, 2, 4** Karen makes the following purchases and sales of stock:

Transaction	Date	Number of Shares	Company	Price per Share
Purchase	1–1–2009	300	MDG	$ 75
Purchase	6–1–2009	150	GRU	300
Purchase	11–1–2009	60	MDG	70
Sale	12–3–2009	180	MDG	70
Purchase	3–1–2010	120	GRU	375

Transaction	Date	Number of Shares	Company	Price per Share
Sale	8–1–2010	90	GRU	$330
Sale	1–1–2011	150	MDG	90
Sale	2–1–2011	75	GRU	500

Assuming that Karen is unable to identify the particular lots that are sold with the original purchase, what is the recognized gain or loss on each type of stock as of the following dates:

a. 7–1–2009.
b. 12–31–2009.
c. 12–31–2010.
d. 7–1–2011.

54. **LO.1, 2, 4** Kevin purchases 1,000 shares of Bluebird Corporation stock on October 3, 2011, for $300,000. On December 12, 2011, Kevin purchases an additional 750 shares of Bluebird stock for $210,000. According to market quotations, Bluebird stock is selling for $285 per share on December 31, 2011. Kevin sells 500 shares of Bluebird stock on March 1, 2012, for $162,500.
  a. What is the adjusted basis of Kevin's Bluebird stock on December 31, 2011?
  b. What is Kevin's recognized gain or loss from the sale of Bluebird stock on March 1, 2012, assuming the shares sold are from the shares purchased on December 12, 2011?
  c. What is Kevin's recognized gain or loss from the sale of Bluebird stock on March 1, 2012, assuming Kevin cannot adequately identify the shares sold?

COMMUNICATIONS

55. **LO.4** Irene Andrews is purchasing the assets of a sole proprietorship from Seth. The fair market values of the assets as agreed to by Irene and Seth as follows:

Asset	Seth's Adjusted Basis	Fair Market Value
Accounts receivable	$ –0–	$ 10,000
Notes receivable	15,000	20,000
Machinery and equipment	85,000	110,000
Building	100,000	320,000
Land	200,000	350,000

The purchase price is $950,000.
  a. Calculate Seth's realized and recognized gain.
  b. Determine Irene's basis for each of the assets.
  c. Write a letter to Irene informing her of the tax consequences of the purchase. Her address is 300 Riverside Drive, Cincinnati, OH 45207.

56. **LO.4** Paula owns stock in Yellow, Inc., which she purchased for $5,000. The stock has a fair market value of $6,000. Because Yellow is experiencing a cash-flow problem, it chooses to distribute nontaxable stock rights instead of cash to its shareholders.
  a. What effect does this distribution have on Paula's basis in her Yellow stock if the fair market value of the stock rights is $1,000?
  b. What is Paula's basis for the nontaxable stock rights?
  c. What is Paula's recognized gain or loss if she sells the stock rights for $1,200?
  d. What is Paula's recognized gain or loss if she allows the stock rights to lapse?
  e. If the fair market value of the stock rights is $750 (not $1,000), how will this change the answers to parts (a) and (b)?

57. **LO.1, 2, 4** Roberto has received various gifts over the years. He has decided to dispose of the following assets that he received as gifts:
  a. In 1951, he received land worth $32,000. The donor's adjusted basis was $35,000. Roberto sells the land for $95,000 in 2011.
  b. In 1956, he received stock in Gold Company. The donor's adjusted basis was $19,000. The fair market value on the date of the gift was $34,000. Roberto sells the stock for $40,000 in 2011.

c. In 1962, he received land worth $15,000. The donor's adjusted basis was $20,000. Roberto sells the land for $9,000 in 2011.

d. In 2003, he received stock worth $30,000. The donor's adjusted basis was $42,000. Roberto sells the stock for $38,000 in 2011.

What is the recognized gain or loss from each of the preceding transactions? Assume for each of the gift transactions that no gift tax was paid.

58. **LO.1, 2, 4** Nicky receives a car from Sam as a gift. Sam paid $40,000 for the car. He had used it for business purposes and had deducted $16,000 for depreciation up to the time he gave the car to Nicky. The fair market value of the car is $21,000.

a. Assuming Nicky uses the car for business purposes, what is her basis for depreciation?

b. Assume Nicky deducts depreciation of $5,500 and then sells the car for $20,000. What is her recognized gain or loss?

c. Assume Nicky deducts depreciation of $5,500 and then sells the car for $14,000. What is her recognized gain or loss?

59. **LO.4** Laura receives a gift of real estate with an adjusted basis of $125,000 and a fair market value of $100,000. The donor paid gift tax of $14,000 on the transfer. If Laura later sells the property for $110,000, what is her recognized gain or loss?

60. **LO.4** Natalie receives an original Matisse painting as a gift from her aunt. At the date of the gift, the adjusted basis of the painting is $825,000, and its fair market value is $1,120,000. Her aunt paid gift tax of $392,000.

a. What is Natalie's adjusted basis in the painting?

b. If the fair market value of the painting at the date of the gift is $824,000 (not $1,120,000), what is Natalie's adjusted basis?

61. **LO.1, 2, 4, 11** Ira Cook is planning to make a charitable contribution of Crystal, Inc. stock worth $20,000 to the Boy Scouts. The stock has an adjusted basis of $15,000. A friend has suggested that Ira sell the stock and contribute the $20,000 in proceeds rather than contribute the stock.

DECISION MAKING

COMMUNICATIONS

a. Should Ira follow the friend's advice? Why?

b. Assume the fair market value is only $13,000. In this case, should Ira follow the friend's advice? Why?

c. Rather than make a charitable contribution to the Boy Scouts, Ira is going to make a gift to Nancy, his niece. Advise Ira regarding (a) and (b).

d. Write a letter to Ira regarding whether in (a) he should sell the stock and contribute the cash or contribute the stock. He has informed you that he purchased the stock six years ago. Ira's address is 500 Ireland Avenue, De Kalb, IL 60115.

62. **LO.4** As sole heir, Dazie receives all of Mary's property (adjusted basis of $1,400,000 and fair market value of $3,820,000). Six months after Mary's death in 2011, the fair market value is $3,835,000.

a. Can the executor of Mary's estate elect the alternate valuation date and amount?

b. What is Dazie's basis for the property?

c. Assume, instead, that the fair market value six months after Mary's death is $3.8 million. Respond to (a) and (b).

63. **LO.4** The portion of Earl's estate distributed to Robert, one of Earl's beneficiaries, is valued as follows:

Asset	Earl's Adjusted Basis	FMV at Date of Death	FMV at Alternate Valuation Date
Cash	$10,000	$ 10,000	$ 10,000
Stock	40,000	125,000	60,000
Apartment building	60,000	300,000	325,000
Land	75,000	100,000	110,000

Although the fair market value of the stock six months after Earl's death in 2011 turned out to be $60,000, the executor of the estate distributed it to Robert one month after Earl's death when it was worth $85,000. Determine Robert's basis for the assets if:

a. The primary valuation date applies.

b. The executor elects the alternate valuation date.

64. **LO.4** Emily makes a gift of 100 shares of appreciated stock to her uncle, George, on January 5, 2011. The basis of the stock is $3,000, and the fair market value is $6,000. George dies on November 8, 2011. Under the provisions of George's will, Emily inherits 100 shares of the stock. The value of the stock for Federal estate tax purposes is $95 per share.
    a. What is the basis of the inherited stock to Emily?
    b. What would have been the basis of the inherited stock to Emily if she had given the stock to George on January 5, 2010?

65. **LO.4** Helene and Pauline are twin sisters who live in Louisiana and Mississippi, respectively. Helene is married to Frank, and Pauline is married to Richard. Frank and Richard are killed in an auto accident in 2011 while returning from a sporting event.

    Helene and Frank jointly owned some farmland in Louisiana (value of $940,000, cost of $450,000). Pauline and Richard jointly owned some farmland in Mississippi (value of $940,000, cost of $450,000). Assume all of Frank's and Richard's property passes to their surviving wives.
    a. Calculate Helene's basis in the land.
    b. Calculate Pauline's basis in the land.
    c. What causes the difference?

DECISION MAKING

66. **LO.5** Joyce owns undeveloped real estate with an adjusted basis of $120,000. She sells the real estate to her sister, Iris, for its fair market value of $115,000.
    a. Calculate Joyce's realized and recognized gain or loss.
    b. If Iris later sells the real estate for $119,000, calculate her realized and recognized gain or loss.
    c. Assume instead that Joyce sold the real estate to Iris for its fair market value of $130,000. Calculate Joyce's realized and recognized gain or loss.
    d. Assume instead that Joyce sold the real estate to Hector, a friend, for its fair market value of $115,000. Calculate Joyce's realized and recognized gain or loss.
    e. Advise Joyce whether she should sell the real estate to Iris or Hector for its fair market value of $115,000.

67. **LO.1, 2, 4, 5** Louis owns three pieces of land with an adjusted basis as follows: parcel A, $75,000; parcel B, $125,000; and parcel C, $175,000. Louis sells parcel A to his uncle for $50,000, parcel B to his partner for $120,000, and parcel C to his mother for $150,000.
    a. What is the recognized gain or loss from the sale of each parcel?
    b. If Louis's uncle eventually sells his land for $90,000, what is his recognized gain or loss?
    c. If Louis's partner eventually sells his land for $130,000, what is his recognized gain or loss?
    d. If Louis's mother eventually sells her land for $165,000, what is her recognized gain or loss?

DECISION MAKING

68. **LO.1, 2, 4, 5** Tyneka inherited 1,000 shares of Aqua, Inc. stock from Joe. Joe's basis was $35,000, and the fair market value on July 1, 2011 (the date of death) was $45,000. The shares were distributed to Tyneka on July 15, 2011. Tyneka sold the stock on July 30, 2012, for $33,000. After giving the matter more thought, she decides that Aqua is a good investment and purchases 1,000 shares for $30,000 on August 20, 2012.
    a. What is Tyneka's basis for the 1,000 shares purchased on August 20, 2012?
    b. What would be Tyneka's basis for the 1,000 Aqua shares inherited from Joe if she had given 1,000 Aqua shares to Joe on March 1, 2011 (assuming no gift tax was paid)? Her basis at the date of the gift was $35,000, and the fair market value was $45,000.
    c. Could Tyneka have obtained different tax consequences in (a) if she had sold the 1,000 shares on December 27, 2011, and purchased the 1,000 shares on January 5, 2012?

69. **LO.1, 2, 5** Abby's home had a basis of $360,000 ($160,000 attributable to the land) and a fair market value of $340,000 ($155,000 attributable to the land) when she converted 70% of it to business use by opening a bed and breakfast. Four years after the conversion, Abby sells the home for $500,000 ($165,000 attributable to the land).
    a. Calculate Abby's basis for gain, loss, and cost recovery for the portion of her personal residence that was converted to business use.
    b. Calculate the cost recovery deducted by Abby during the four-year period of business use, assuming the bed and breakfast is opened on January 1 of year 1 and the house is sold on December 31 of year 4.
    c. What is Abby's recognized gain or loss on the sale of the business use portion?

70. **LO.5** Surendra's personal residence originally cost $340,000 (ignore land). After living in the house for five years, he converts it to rental property. At the date of conversion, the fair market value of the house is $320,000. As to the rental property, calculate Surendra's basis for:

DECISION MAKING

a. Loss.
b. Depreciation.
c. Gain.
d. Could Surendra have obtained better tax results if he had sold his personal residence for $320,000 and then purchased another house for $320,000 to hold as rental property?

71. **LO.7** Martha owns developed land with an adjusted basis of $300,000. She exchanges it for other undeveloped land worth $360,000.
a. What are Martha's realized and recognized gain or loss?
b. What is Martha's basis in the undeveloped land she receives?
c. Would the answers in (a) and (b) change if Martha exchanged the developed land for land and a building?

72. **LO.7** Kareem owns a pickup truck that he uses exclusively in his business. The adjusted basis is $22,000, and the fair market value is $14,000. Kareem exchanges the truck for a truck that he will use exclusively in his business.
a. What are Kareem's realized and recognized gain or loss?
b. What is his basis in the new truck?
c. What are the tax consequences to Kareem in (a) and (b) if he used the old truck and will use the new truck exclusively for personal purposes?

73. **LO.7** Tanya Fletcher owns undeveloped land (adjusted basis of $80,000 and fair market value of $92,000) on the East Coast. On January 4, 2011, she exchanges it with her sister, Lisa, for undeveloped land on the West Coast and $3,000 cash. Lisa has an adjusted basis of $72,000 for her land, and its fair market value is $89,000. As the real estate market on the East Coast is thriving, on September 1, 2012, Lisa sells the land she acquired for $120,000.

DECISION MAKING

COMMUNICATIONS

a. What are Tanya's recognized gain or loss and adjusted basis for the West Coast land on January 4, 2011?
b. What are Lisa's recognized gain or loss and adjusted basis for the East Coast land on January 4, 2011?
c. What is Lisa's recognized gain or loss from the September 1, 2012 sale?
d. What effect does Lisa's 2012 sale have on Tanya?
e. Write a letter to Tanya advising her on how she could avoid any recognition of gain associated with the January 4, 2011 exchange prior to her actual sale of the land. Her address is The Corral, El Paso, TX 79968.

74. **LO.7** Sarah exchanges a yellow bus (used in her business) for Tyler's gray bus and some garage equipment (used in his business). The assets have the following characteristics:

	Adjusted Basis	Fair Market Value
Yellow bus	$6,000	$15,000
Gray bus	3,000	11,000
Equipment	2,000	4,000

a. What are Sarah's recognized gain or loss and basis for the gray bus and garage equipment?
b. What are Tyler's recognized gain or loss and basis for the yellow bus?

75. **LO.7, 11** In two unrelated transactions, Laura exchanges property that qualifies for like-kind exchange treatment. In the first exchange, Laura gives up office equipment purchased in May 2009 (adjusted basis of $20,000; fair market value of $17,000) in exchange for new office equipment (fair market value of $15,000) and $2,000 cash. In the second exchange, Laura receives a parking garage (to be used in her business) with a fair market value of $50,000 in exchange for a plot of land she had held for investment. The land was purchased in April 2003 for $12,000 and has a current fair market value of $48,000. In addition to transferring the land, Laura pays an additional $2,000 to the other party.

DECISION MAKING

a. What is Laura's adjusted basis for the office equipment?
b. When does the holding period begin?
c. What is Laura's adjusted basis for the parking garage?
d. When does the holding period begin?
e. How could Laura structure either of the transactions differently to produce better tax consequences?

76. **LO.7** Tom owns land and a building that he uses in his business (adjusted basis of $125,000 and fair market value of $275,000). Tom exchanges the land and building for land (fair market value of $175,000) that he will use as a parking lot in his business. In addition, he receives stock worth $100,000.
a. What is Tom's realized gain or loss?
b. His recognized gain or loss?
c. The basis of the land and the stock received?
d. Would the answers in (a), (b), and (c) change if the stock is worth $175,000 (not $100,000) and the land Tom receives has a fair market value of $100,000 (not $175,000)?

77. **LO.7** Ed owns investment land with an adjusted basis of $35,000. Polly has offered to purchase the land from Ed for $175,000 for use in a real estate development. The amount offered by Polly is $10,000 in excess of what Ed perceives as the fair market value of the land. Ed would like to dispose of the land to Polly but does not want to incur the tax liability that would result. He identifies an office building with a fair market value of $175,000 that he would like to acquire. Polly purchases the office building and then exchanges the office building for Ed's land.
a. Calculate Ed's realized and recognized gain on the exchange and his basis for the office building.
b. Calculate Polly's realized and recognized gain on the exchange and her basis in the land.

DECISION MAKING

78. **LO.7** Steve owns Machine A (adjusted basis of $12,000 and fair market value of $15,000), which he uses in his business. Steve sells Machine A for $15,000 to Aubry (a dealer) and then purchases Machine B for $15,000 from Joan (also a dealer). Machine B would normally qualify as like-kind property.
a. What are Steve's realized and recognized gain on the sale of Machine A?
b. What is Steve's basis for Machine B?
c. What factors would motivate Steve to sell Machine A and purchase Machine B rather than exchange one machine for the other?
d. Assume that the adjusted basis of Machine A is $15,000 and the fair market value of both machines is $12,000. Respond to (a) through (c).

79. **LO.7** Tab exchanges real estate used in his business plus stock for real estate to be held for investment. The stock transferred has an adjusted basis of $42,000 and a fair market value of $50,000. The real estate transferred has an adjusted basis of $59,000 and a fair market value of $200,000. The real estate acquired has a fair market value of $250,000.
a. What is Tab's realized gain or loss?
b. His recognized gain or loss?
c. The basis of the newly acquired real estate?

DECISION MAKING

80. **LO.7, 11** Tom and Frank are brothers. Each owns investment property in the other's hometown. To make their lives easier, they decide to legally exchange the investment properties. Under the terms of the exchange, Frank will transfer realty (adjusted basis of $52,000; fair market value of $80,000), and Tom will exchange realty (adjusted basis of $60,000; fair market value of $92,000). Tom's property is subject to a mortgage of $12,000 that will be assumed by Frank.
a. What are Frank's and Tom's recognized gains?
b. What are their adjusted bases?
c. As an alternative, Frank has proposed that rather than assuming the mortgage, he will transfer cash of $12,000 to Tom. Tom would use the cash to pay off the mortgage. Advise Tom on whether this alternative would be beneficial to him from a tax perspective.

81. **LO.7** Determine the realized, recognized, and postponed gain or loss and the new basis for each of the following like-kind exchanges:

	Adjusted Basis of Old Machine	Boot Given	Fair Market Value of New Asset	Boot Received
a.	$ 7,000	$ -0-	$12,000	$4,000
b.	14,000	2,000	15,000	-0-
c.	3,000	7,000	8,000	500
d.	22,000	-0-	32,000	-0-
e.	10,000	-0-	11,000	1,000
f.	10,000	-0-	8,000	-0-

82. **LO.7** Shontelle owns an apartment house that has an adjusted basis of $760,000 but is subject to a mortgage of $192,000. She transfers the apartment house to Dave and receives from him $120,000 in cash and an office building with a fair market value of $780,000 at the time of the exchange. Dave assumes the $192,000 mortgage on the apartment house.
    a. What is Shontelle's realized gain or loss?
    b. What is her recognized gain or loss?
    c. What is the basis of the newly acquired office building?

83. **LO.8** Monica's roadside vegetable stand (adjusted basis of $305,000) is destroyed by a tractor-trailer accident. She receives insurance proceeds of $288,000 ($360,000 fair market value less $72,000 coinsurance). Monica immediately uses the proceeds plus additional cash of $45,000 to build another roadside vegetable stand at the same location. What are the tax consequences to Monica?

84. **LO.8** Albert owns 100 acres of land on which he grows spruce Christmas trees. His adjusted basis for the land is $100,000. He receives condemnation proceeds of $10,000 when the city's new beltway takes 5 acres along the eastern boundary of his property. He also receives a severance award of $6,000 associated with the possible harmful effects of exhaust fumes on his Christmas trees. Albert invests the $16,000 in a growth mutual fund. Determine the tax consequences to Albert of the:
    a. Condemnation proceeds.
    b. Severance award.

85. **LO.8** Jason, a calendar year taxpayer, is the sole proprietor of a hardware store. His adjusted basis for the building and the related land is $150,000. On March 4, 2011, state authorities notify Jason that his property is going to be condemned so that the highway can be widened. On June 1, Jason's property is officially condemned, and he receives an award of $212,000. Since Jason's business has been successful in the past, he would like to reopen the hardware store in a new location.
    a. What is the earliest date Jason can acquire a new hardware store and qualify for § 1033 postponement?
    b. On June 30, Jason purchases land and a building for $200,000. Assuming he elects postponement of gain under § 1033, what is his recognized gain?
    c. What is Jason's adjusted basis for the new land and building?
    d. If he does not elect § 1033, what are Jason's recognized gain and adjusted basis?
    e. Suppose he invests the $212,000 condemnation proceeds in the stock market on June 30. What is Jason's recognized gain?

86. **LO.8** Edith's warehouse (adjusted basis of $450,000) is destroyed by a hurricane in October 2011. Edith, a calendar year taxpayer, receives insurance proceeds of $525,000 in January 2012. Calculate Edith's realized gain or loss, recognized gain or loss, and basis for the replacement property if she:
    a. Acquires a new warehouse for $550,000 in January 2012.
    b. Acquires a new warehouse for $500,000 in January 2012.
    c. Does not acquire replacement property.

87. **LO.8** Cabel's warehouse, which has an adjusted basis of $380,000 and a fair market value of $450,000, is condemned by an agency of the Federal government to make way for a highway interchange. The initial condemnation offer is $410,000. After substantial

DECISION MAKING

negotiations, the agency agrees to transfer to Cabel a surplus warehouse that he believes is worth $450,000. Cabel is a calendar year taxpayer. The condemnation and related asset transfer occur during September 2011.

a. What are the recognized gain or loss and the basis of the replacement warehouse if Cabel's objective is to recognize as much gain as possible?

b. Advise Cabel regarding what he needs to do by what date in order to achieve his objective.

88. **LO.8** What are the *maximum* postponed gain or loss and the basis for the replacement property for the following involuntary conversions?

	Property	Type of Conversion	Amount Realized	Adjusted Basis	Amount Reinvested
a.	Drugstore (business)	Casualty	$160,000	$130,000	$110,000
b.	Apartments (investment)	Condemned	100,000	125,000	175,000
c.	Grocery store (business)	Casualty	400,000	300,000	450,000
d.	Residence (personal)	Casualty	16,000	18,000	17,000
e.	Vacant lot (investment)	Condemned	240,000	160,000	220,000
f.	Residence (personal)	Casualty	20,000	18,000	19,000
g.	Residence (personal)	Condemned	18,000	20,000	26,000
h.	Apartments (investment)	Condemned	150,000	100,000	200,000

DECISION MAKING

89. **LO.8, 11** Wanda, a calendar year taxpayer, owned a building (adjusted basis of $250,000) in which she operated a bakery that was destroyed by fire in December 2011. She receives insurance proceeds of $290,000 for the building the following March. Wanda is considering two options regarding the investment of the insurance proceeds. First, she could purchase a local building (suitable for a bakery) that is for sale for $275,000. Second, she could buy a new home for $290,000 and go back to college and finish her degree.

a. To minimize her tax liability, which of these alternatives should Wanda choose?

b. What is the latest date on which Wanda can replace the involuntarily converted property to qualify for § 1033?

c. What is the latest date on which Wanda can replace the involuntarily converted property to qualify for § 1033 if the involuntary conversion is a condemnation?

DECISION MAKING

90. **LO.9, 11** After living in a residence during 2009 as a tenant, Katie exercised an option to purchase the residence for $180,000 on January 2, 2010. On June 1, 2011, Katie sells the residence for $335,000, and on June 13, 2011, she purchases a new residence for $360,000.

a. What is Katie's recognized gain? Her basis for the new residence?

b. Assume instead that Katie purchased her original residence on January 2, 2009 (rather than on January 2, 2010). What is Katie's recognized gain? Her basis for the new residence?

c. In (a), what could Katie do to minimize her recognized gain?

91. **LO.9** Milton, who is single, listed his personal residence with a real estate agent on March 3, 2011, at a price of $250,000. He rejected several offers in the $200,000 range during the summer. Finally, on August 16, 2011, he and the purchaser signed a contract to sell for $245,000. The sale (i.e., closing) took place on September 7, 2011. The closing statement showed the following disbursements:

Real estate agent's commission	$ 14,000
Appraisal fee	500
Exterminator's certificate	300
Recording fees	400
Mortgage to First Bank	180,000
Cash to seller	49,800

Milton's adjusted basis for the house is $150,000. He owned and occupied the house for eight years. On October 1, 2011, Milton purchases another residence for $210,000.

a. Calculate Milton's recognized gain on the sale.

b. What is Milton's adjusted basis for the new residence?

c. Assume instead that the selling price is $735,000. What is Milton's recognized gain? His adjusted basis for the new residence?

92. **LO.9** Bruce and Libby are married and file a joint return. On January 1, 2011, they purchased a house for $270,000 to be used by them and family members for vacations. They continued to use it for this purpose through December 31, 2013. On January 1, 2014, they converted it to their principal residence. On December 31, 2015, they sold it for $460,000 (selling expenses of $29,000). What is Bruce and Libby's recognized gain on the sale of their principal residence?

93. **LO.9** Jill bought a house in April 2007 for $190,000. She lived in it until August 2009 when she moved to Mack's new home. Mack and Jill got married and filed a joint return in 2010 and subsequent years. In January 2011, Jill sells her house for $350,000 (selling expenses are $17,500).
    a. Do Mack and Jill qualify for the § 121 exclusion? What is the maximum amount of exclusion available on the sale of Jill's house? What is her recognized gain?
    b. On May 22, 2012, Mack and Jill sell Mack's house for $625,000. Selling expenses are $37,500, and Mack's adjusted basis is $260,000. What is the maximum amount of the § 121 exclusion available on the sale of Mack's home? What is the recognized gain?
    c. Would the result in part (b) change if Mack's house is not sold until June 2013?

94. **LO.9** Nell, Nina, and Nora Sanders, who are sisters, sell their principal residence (owned as tenants in common) in which they have lived for the past 25 years. The youngest of the sisters is age 60. The selling price is $960,000, selling expenses and legal fees are $63,000, and the adjusted basis is $60,000 (the fair market value of the residence when inherited from their parents 25 years ago). Since the sisters are going to live in rental housing, they do not plan to acquire another residence. Nell has contacted you on behalf of the three sisters regarding the tax consequences of the sale. **COMMUNICATIONS**
    a. Write a letter to Nell advising her of the tax consequences and how taxes can be minimized. Nell's address is 100 Oak Avenue, Billings, MT 59101.
    b. Prepare a memo for the tax files.

95. **LO.9** Ben owns a beach house (five years) and a cabin in the mountains (four years). His adjusted basis is $280,000 in the beach house and $315,000 in the mountain cabin. Ben also rents a townhouse in the city where he is employed. During the year, he occupies each of the three residences as follows: **DECISION MAKING**

Townhouse	120 days
Beach house	170 days
Mountain cabin	75 days

The beach house is close enough to the city so that he can commute to work during the spring and early fall. While this level of occupancy may vary slightly from year to year, it is representative during the time period that Ben has owned the two residences.

As Ben plans on retiring in several years, he sells both residences. The mountain cabin is sold on March 3, 2011, for $540,000 (related selling expenses of $30,000). The beach house is sold on December 10, 2011, for $600,000 (related selling expenses of $36,000).
    a. Calculate Ben's lowest recognized gain on the sale of the two residences.
    b. Assume instead that both residences satisfy the two-year ownership and use tests as Ben's principal residence. Since the mountain cabin is sold first, is it possible for Ben to apply the § 121 exclusion to the sale of the beach house?

96. **LO.9, 11** Tina, age 28, has owned her principal residence (adjusted basis of $175,000) for five years. During the first three years of ownership, she occupied it as her principal residence. During the past two years, she was in graduate school and rented the residence. After graduate school, Tina returned to the same location where she previously worked. At this point, she purchased another residence for $300,000 and listed her old residence for sale at $240,000. Due to a slow real estate market, 11 months later Tina finally receives an offer of $230,000. **DECISION MAKING**
    a. What is Tina's recognized gain if she immediately accepts the $230,000 offer (i.e., 11 months after the listing date)?
    b. What is Tina's recognized gain if she rejects the $230,000 offer and accepts another offer of $240,000 three months later (i.e., 14 months after the listing date)?
    c. Advise Tina on which offer she should accept (assume she is in the 28% tax bracket).

97. **LO.10** Roby and Sid have been married for 12 years. Roby sells Peach, Inc. stock that she has owned for four years to Sid for its fair market value of $120,000. Her adjusted basis is $150,000. **DECISION MAKING**

a. Calculate Roby's recognized gain or recognized loss.
b. Calculate Sid's adjusted basis for the stock.
c. How would the tax consequences in (a) and (b) differ if Roby had made a gift of the stock to Sid? Which form of the transaction would you recommend?

98. **LO.10** On September 1, 2011, Marsha sells stock in Orange, Inc., for $90,000. The stock is qualified small business stock and was purchased on August 16, 2010, for $60,000. On September 30, 2011, Marsha purchases $85,000 of Blue, Inc., also qualified small business stock.
a. What is Marsha's realized and recognized gain (or loss) on the sale of the Orange stock?
b. What is Marsha's basis in the Blue stock?

CUMULATIVE PROBLEMS

TAX RETURN PROBLEM

H&R BLOCK At Home

99. Alton Newman, age 67, is married and files a joint return with his wife, Clair, age 65. Alton and Clair are both retired, and during 2010, they received Social Security benefits of $10,000. Alton's Social Security number is 111–11–1111, and Clair's is 123–45–6789. They reside at 210 College Drive, Columbia, SC 29201.

Alton, who retired on January 1, 2010, receives benefits from a qualified pension plan of $750 a month for life. His total contributions to the plan (none of which were deductible) were $68,250. In January 2010, he received a bonus of $2,000 from his former employer for service performed in 2009. Although the former employer accrued the bonus in 2009, it was not paid until 2010.

Clair, who retired on December 31, 2009, started receiving benefits of $900 a month on January 1, 2010. Her contributions to the qualified pension plan (none of which were deductible) were $74,100.

Clair had casino winnings for the year of $4,500 and casino losses of $2,100 while Alton won $17,000 on a $1 lottery ticket.

On September 27, 2010, Alton and Clair received a 10% stock dividend on 600 shares of stock they owned. They had bought the stock on March 5, 2003, for $20 a share. On December 16, 2010, they sold the 60 dividend shares for $55 a share.

On October 10, 2010, Clair sold the car she had used in commuting to and from work for $17,000. She had paid $31,000 for the car in 2004.

On July 14, 2002, Alton and Clair received a gift of 1,000 shares of stock from their son, Thomas. Thomas's basis in the stock was $35 a share (fair market value at the date of gift was $25). No gift tax was paid on the transfer. Alton and Clair sold the stock on October 8, 2010, for $24 a share.

On May 1, 2010, Clair's mother died, and Clair inherited her personal residence. In February 2010, her mother had paid the property taxes for 2010 of $2,100. The residence had a fair market value of $235,000 and an adjusted basis to the mother of $160,000. Clair listed the house with a real estate agent who estimated it was worth $240,000 as of December 31, 2010.

Clair received rent income of $6,000 on a beach house she inherited three years ago from her Uncle Chuck. She had rented the property for one week during the July 4th weekend and one week during the Thanksgiving holidays. Uncle Chuck's adjusted basis in the beach house was $150,000, and its fair market value on the date of his death was $240,000. Clair and Alton used the beach house for personal purposes for 56 days during the year. Expenses associated with the house were $3,700 for utilities, maintenance, and repairs; $2,200 for property taxes; and $800 for insurance. There are no mortgages on the property.

Clair and Alton paid estimated Federal income tax of $3,100 and had itemized deductions of $6,800 (excluding any itemized deductions associated with the beach house and gambling). If they have overpaid their Federal income tax, they want the amount refunded. Both Clair and Alton wish to have $3 go to the Presidential Election Campaign Fund.

Compute their net tax payable or refund due for 2010. If you use tax forms for your computations, you will need Form 1040 and Schedule D. Suggested software: H&R BLOCK At Home.

TAX RETURN PROBLEM

H&R BLOCK At Home

100. Devon Bishop, age 40, is single. He lives at 1507 Rose Lane, Albuquerque, NM 87131. His Social Security number is 111–11–1111. Devon does not wish to have $3 go to the Presidential Election Campaign Fund.

Devon was divorced in 2006 after 15 years of marriage. He pays alimony of $18,000 a year to his former spouse, Ariane. Ariane's Social Security number is 123–45–6789. Devon's son, Tom, who is age 16, resides with Ariane. Devon pays child support of $12,000 per year. Ariane has provided Devon with a signed Form 8332 in which she releases the dependency deduction to him for 2010. Tom's Social Security number is 123–45–6788.

Devon owns a sole proprietorship for which he uses the accrual method of accounting. His revenues and expenses for 2010 are as follows:

Sales revenue	$740,000
Cost of goods sold	405,000
Salary expense	88,000
Rent expense	30,000
Utilities	8,000
Telephone	6,500
Advertising	4,000
Bad debts	5,000
Depreciation	21,000
Health insurance*	26,000
Accounting and legal fees	7,000
Supplies	1,000

*$18,000 for employees and $8,000 for Devon.

Other income received by Devon includes the following:

Dividend income:	
Swan, Inc.	$10,000
Wren, Inc.	2,000
Interest income:	
First Bank	11,000
Second Bank	2,500
City of Asheville bonds	17,000
Lottery winnings (tickets purchased cost $500)	10,000

During the year, Devon and his sole proprietorship had the following property transactions:

a. Sold Blue, Inc. stock for $45,000 on March 12, 2010. He had purchased the stock on September 5, 2007, for $50,000.

b. Received an inheritance of $300,000 from his Uncle Henry. Devon used $200,000 to purchase Green, Inc. stock on May 15, 2010, and invested $100,000 in Gold, Inc., stock on May 30, 2010.

c. Received Orange, Inc. stock worth $9,500 as a gift from his Aunt Jane on June 17, 2010. Her adjusted basis for the stock was $5,000. No gift taxes were paid on the transfer. Aunt Jane had purchased the stock on April 1, 2004. Devon sold the stock on July 1, 2010, for $22,000.

d. On July 15, 2010, Devon sold one-half of the Green, Inc. stock for $40,000.

e. Devon was notified on August 1, 2010, that Yellow, Inc. stock he purchased from a colleague on September 1, 2009, for $52,500 had become worthless. While he perceived that the investment was risky, he did not anticipate that the corporation would declare bankruptcy.

f. On August 15, 2010, Devon received a parcel of land in Phoenix worth $220,000 in exchange for a parcel of land he owned in Tucson. Since the Tucson parcel was worth $245,000, he also received $25,000 cash. Devon's adjusted basis for the Tucson parcel was $210,000. He originally purchased it on September 18, 2007.

g. On December 1, 2010, Devon sold the condominium in which he had been living for the past 10 years. The sales price was $480,000, selling expenses were $28,500, and repair expenses related to the sale were $9,400. Devon and Ariane had purchased the condominium as joint owners for $180,000. Devon had received Ariane's ownership interest as part of the divorce proceedings. The fair market value at that time was $240,000.

Devon's potential itemized deductions, exclusive of the aforementioned information, are as follows:

Medical expenses (before the 7.5% floor)	$ 9,500
Property taxes on residence	5,300
State income taxes	4,000
Charitable contributions	10,000
Mortgage interest on residence	9,900
Sales taxes paid	5,000

During the year, Devon makes estimated Federal income tax payments of $40,000.

Compute Devon's lowest net tax payable or refund due for 2010, assuming he makes any available elections that will reduce the tax. If you use tax forms for your computations, you will need Forms 1040, 4562, 8332, and 8824 and Schedules A, B, C, D, and SE. Suggested software: H&R BLOCK At Home.

TAX COMPUTATION PROBLEM

DECISION MAKING

COMMUNICATIONS

101. Tammy Walker, age 37, is a self-employed accountant. Tammy's Social Security number is 123–45–6789. Her address is 101 Glass Road, Richmond, VA 23236. Her income and expenses associated with her accounting practice for 2011 are as follows:

Revenues (cash receipts during 2011)	$292,000
Expenses	
Salaries	$ 95,000
Office supplies	2,100
Postage	2,900
Depreciation of equipment	40,000
Telephone	800
	$140,800

Since Tammy is a cash method taxpayer, she does not record her receivables as revenue until she receives cash payment. At the beginning of 2011, her accounts receivable were $65,000, and the balance had decreased to $20,000 by the end of the year.

Tammy used one room in her 10-room house as the office for her accounting practice (300 square feet out of a total square footage of 3,000). She paid the following expenses related to the house during 2011:

Utilities	$4,200
Insurance	1,800
Property taxes	4,700
Repairs	3,000

Tammy had purchased the house on September 1, 2010, for $290,000 (exclusive of land cost).

Tammy has one child, Thomas, age 16. Thomas's Social Security number is 123–45–6788. Thomas lives with his father during the summer and with Tammy for the rest of the year. Tammy can document that she spent $16,000 during 2011 for the child's support. The father normally provides about $9,000 per year, but this year he gave Thomas a new car for Christmas. The cost of the car was $20,000. The divorce decree is silent regarding the dependency exemption for Thomas. Tammy does not provide her former spouse with a signed Form 8332 for 2011.

Under the terms of the divorce decree, Tammy is to receive alimony of $10,000 per month. The payments will terminate at Tammy's death or at her remarriage.

Tammy provides part of the support of her mother, age 67. Her mother's Social Security number is 123–45–6787. The total support in 2011 for her mother was as follows:

Social Security benefits	$5,200
From Tammy	2,900
From Bob, Tammy's brother	2,000
From Susan, Tammy's sister	2,200

Bob and Susan have both indicated their willingness to sign a multiple support waiver form if it will benefit Tammy.

Tammy's deductible itemized deductions during 2011, excluding any itemized deductions related to the house, were $19,000. She made estimated tax payments of $98,000.

Part 1—Tax Computation
Compute Tammy's lowest net tax payable or refund due for 2011.

Part 2—Tax Planning
Tammy and her former husband have been discussing the $10,000 alimony he pays her each month. Because his new wife has a health problem, he does not feel that he can afford to continue to pay the $10,000 each month. He is in the 15% tax bracket. If Tammy will agree to decrease the amount by 25%, he will agree that the amount paid is not alimony for tax purposes. Assume that Tammy projects her marginal tax rate in 2012 will be 33% (both with and without the alimony decrease). Write a letter to Tammy that contains your advice on whether she should agree to her former husband's proposal. Also prepare a memo for the tax files.

RESEARCH PROBLEMS

Note: Solutions to Research Problems can be prepared by using the **Checkpoint® Student Edition** online research product, which is available to accompany this text. It is also possible to prepare solutions to the Research Problems by using tax research materials found in a standard tax library.

THOMSON REUTERS
Checkpoint® Student Edition

Research Problem 1. Terry owns real estate with an adjusted basis of $600,000 and a fair market value of $1.1 million. The amount of the nonrecourse mortgage on the property is $2.5 million. Because of substantial past and projected future losses associated with the real estate development (occupancy rate of only 37% after three years), Terry deeds the property to the creditor.

a. What are the tax consequences to Terry?
b. Assume the data are the same, except the fair market value of the property is $2,525,000. Therefore, when Terry deeds the property to the creditor, she also receives $25,000 from the creditor. What are the tax consequences to Terry?

Research Problem 2. Inez Butler is the sole shareholder of Pelican, Inc., which owns car dealerships. Pelican purchases the assets of a Chevrolet dealership. The purchase price of $12 million is allocated to the purchased assets based on the fair market values. This includes $3.5 million that is allocated to goodwill.

In addition to the price of $12 million, Pelican incurred legal fees of $250,000 associated with the purchase. According to an itemized invoice provided by the attorney, 80% of the legal fees relate to the acquisition of inventory. Consequently, Pelican assigned $200,000 of the legal fees to inventory with the balance being capitalized as goodwill. The expectation is that 60% of the $200,000 will become part of cost of goods sold in the current year with the remaining 40% doing so in the following year.

The IRS has concluded that § 1060 limits the amount that may be assigned to the fair market value of the inventory. Therefore, the $200,000 of legal fees cannot be added to the basis of the inventory. Instead, it must be included in goodwill under the residual method.

Who is correct?

Research Problem 3. April owned an annuity contract (cash balance of $250,000) issued by Teal Insurance Company. She decides to switch to an annuity contract issued by Brown Insurance Company. To make the change, April instructed Teal to cash out her annuity by issuing a check to Brown. Teal refused to do so and issued a check for $250,000 payable to April.

April intended that the exchange of annuity contracts qualify for tax deferral treatment under § 1035(a)(3). Consequently, rather than depositing or cashing the check from Teal, she endorsed it and sent it to Brown.

On audit, an IRS agent contends that the transaction does not qualify under § 1035(a)(3). For tax deferral to apply, the initial annuity contract must be directly exchanged for the new annuity contract. Evaluate the positions of the parties.

ft.

Research Problem 4. As the result of a large inheritance from her grandmother, Marcy has a substantial investment portfolio. The securities are held in street name by her brokerage firm. Marcy's broker, Max, has standing oral instructions from her on sales transactions to sell the shares with the highest cost basis.

In October 2009, Marcy phoned Max and instructed him to sell 6,000 shares of Color, Inc. Her portfolio has 15,000 shares of Color, which were purchased in several transactions over a three-year period. At the end of each month, the brokerage firm provides Marcy with a monthly statement that includes sales transactions. It does not identify the specific certificates transferred.

In filing her 2009 income tax return, Marcy used the specific identification method to calculate the $75,000 recognized gain on the sale. On audit of her 2009 return, the IRS has taken the position that under Reg. § 1.1012–1(c) Marcy should have used the FIFO method to report the sale of the Color shares, resulting in a gain of $140,000. According to this interpretation of the Regulations, Marcy may not use the specific identification method (and must use the FIFO method) because the broker did not provide written confirmation of Marcy's sales instructions.

Marcy has come to you for tax advice with respect to this issue.

Research Problem 5. Milly and Doug carried out a § 1031 exchange on September 1, 2011. They transferred to Asa a parcel of land (adjusted basis of $375,000; fair market value of $600,000). Once the like-kind property to be received was identified, Asa was to purchase it for them. On October 1, they identified two parcels of land, one located near Austin and the other located near Fort Worth. Either of the parcels was acceptable, although their preference was for the Austin property.

Asa entered into negotiations with the owner of the Austin parcel and expected to close the deal well before the end of the year. The closing was scheduled for December 15, 2011. Shortly before the scheduled closing, the owner of the Austin parcel raised the purchase price, and the deal fell through. Asa began negotiations with the owner of the Fort Worth parcel and purchased it for Milly and Doug on January 1, 2012.

Determine the tax consequences of this exchange for Milly and Doug.

INTERNET *activity*

Use the tax resources of the Internet to address the following question. Do not restrict your search to the Web, but include a review of newsgroups and general reference materials, practitioner sites and resources, primary sources of the tax law, chat rooms and discussion groups, and other opportunities.

Research Problem 6. The amount of the annual exclusion for gifts is indexed. This affects both the calculation of the gift tax liability and the donee's adjusted basis for the property received by gift for income tax purposes. The indexed amount for 2008 was $12,000, and the indexed amount for 2011 is $13,000. Find the latest estimate of the revenue loss for income tax purposes that the Treasury has attributed to indexing.

CHAPTER 14

Property Transactions: Capital Gains and Losses, § 1231, and Recapture Provisions

LEARNING OBJECTIVES

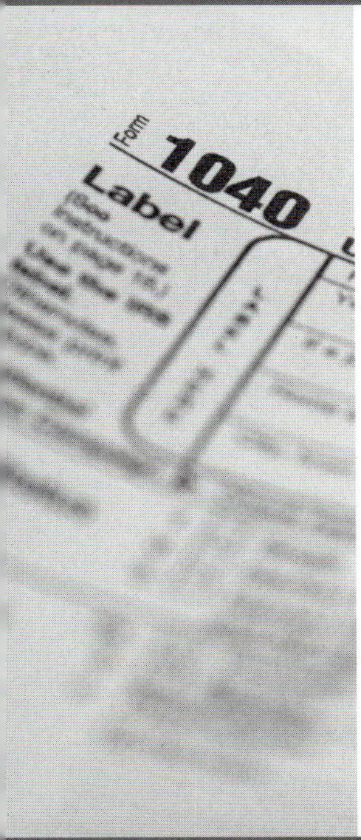

After completing Chapter 14, you should be able to:

LO.1 Understand the rationale for separate reporting of capital gains and losses.

LO.2 Distinguish capital assets from ordinary assets.

LO.3 Understand the relevance of a sale or exchange to classification as a capital gain or loss and apply the special rules for the capital gain or loss treatment of the retirement of corporate obligations, options, patents, franchises, and lease cancellation payments.

LO.4 Determine whether the holding period for a capital asset is long term or short term.

LO.5 Describe the beneficial tax treatment for capital gains and the detrimental tax treatment for capital losses for noncorporate taxpayers.

LO.6 Describe the tax treatment for capital gains and the detrimental tax treatment for capital losses for corporate taxpayers.

LO.7 Understand the rationale for and the nature and treatment of gains and losses from the disposition of business assets.

LO.8 Distinguish § 1231 assets from ordinary assets and capital assets and calculate the § 1231 gain or loss.

LO.9 Determine when § 1245 recapture applies and how it is computed.

LO.10 Determine when § 1250 recapture applies and how it is computed.

LO.11 Understand considerations common to §§ 1245 and 1250.

LO.12 Apply the special recapture provisions for related parties and IDC and be aware of the special recapture provision for corporations.

LO.13 Describe and apply the reporting procedures for §§ 1231, 1245, and 1250.

LO.14 Identify tax planning opportunities arising from the sale or exchange of capital assets and avoid pitfalls associated with the recapture provisions.

OUTLINE

For the latest in changes to tax legislation, visit **www.cengage.com/taxation/swft.**

FRAMEWORK 1040: Tax Formula for Individuals

This chapter covers the boldfaced portions of the Tax Formula for Individuals that was introduced in Figure 3.1 on p. 3-3. Below those portions are the sections of Form 1040 where the results are reported.

Income (broadly conceived)	$ xx,xxx
Less: Exclusions	(x,xxx)
Gross income	**$xx,xxx**
Less: Deductions for adjusted gross income	**(x,xxx)**

FORM 1040 (p. 1)

12	Business income or (loss). Attach Schedule C or C-EZ
13	Capital gain or (loss). Attach Schedule D if required. If not required, check here ▶ ☐
14	Other gains or (losses). Attach Form 4797

Adjusted gross income	$ xx,xxx
Less: The greater of total itemized deductions *or* the standard deduction	(x,xxx)
Personal and dependency exemptions	(x,xxx)
Taxable income	$ xx,xxx
Tax on taxable income (see Tax Tables or Tax Rate Schedules)	**$ x,xxx**

FORM 1040 (p. 2)

44 **Tax** (see instructions). Check if any tax is from: **a** ☐ Form(s) 8814 **b** ☐ Form 4972

Less: Tax credits (including income taxes withheld and prepaid)	(xxx)
Tax due (or refund)	$ xxx

THE BIG PICTURE Tax Solutions for the Real World

MANAGING CAPITAL ASSET TRANSACTIONS

Maurice has come to you for tax advice regarding his investments. He inherited $750,000 from his Uncle Joe. A financial adviser suggested he make the following investments, which he did nine months ago.

- $200,000 in the stock of Purple, a publicly held bank that follows a policy of not paying dividends. At one time, the stock had appreciated to $300,000, but now it is worth only $210,000. Maurice is considering unloading this stock.
- $50,000 for a 50 percent interest in a patent that Kevin, a college roommate who is an unemployed inventor, had obtained for a special battery he had developed to power "green" cars. To date, the friend has been unable to market the battery to an auto manufacturer or supplier, but he has high hopes of doing so given the current price of gasoline.
- $150,000 in tax-exempt bonds. The interest rate is only 3 percent. Maurice is considering moving this money into taxable bonds that pay 3.5 percent.
- $100,000 for a 10 percent ownership interest as a limited partner in a real estate development. Lots in the development are selling well.
- $250,000 for depreciable personalty that he used in his Schedule C business. He has decided that he does not like being a small business owner and intends to sell the equipment, which has appreciated in value to $300,000. He has deducted depreciation on the equipment of $21,000.

Maurice read an article that talked about the beneficial tax rates for capital assets and dividends. He really liked the part about "costless" capital gains, although he did not understand it.

Maurice has retained his job as a toll booth operator at the municipal airport. His annual compensation is $35,000. He likes the job and has met some really interesting people there.

Respond to Maurice's inquiries. **Read the chapter and formulate your response.**

14.1 General Considerations

RATIONALE FOR SEPARATE REPORTING OF CAPITAL GAINS AND LOSSES

LO.1

Understand the rationale for separate reporting of capital gains and losses.

Fourteen years ago, a taxpayer purchased 100 shares of IBM stock for $17 a share. This year the taxpayer sells the shares for $129 a share. Should the $112 per share gain receive any special tax treatment? The $112 gain has built up over 14 years, so it may not be fair to tax it the same as income that was all earned this year.

What if the stock had been purchased for $129 per share and sold for $17 a share? Should the $112 loss be fully deductible? The tax law has an intricate approach to answering these investment activity–related questions.

As you study this chapter, keep in mind that how investment-related gains and losses are taxed can dramatically affect whether taxpayers make investments and which investments are made. Except for a brief discussion in Chapter 3, earlier chapters dwelt on how to determine the amount of gain or loss from a property disposition, but did not discuss the classification of gains and losses. This chapter will focus on that topic.

The tax law requires **capital gains** and **capital losses** to be separated from other types of gains and losses. There are two reasons for this treatment. First, long-term capital gains may be taxed at a lower rate than ordinary gains. An *alternative tax computation* is used to determine the tax when taxable income includes net long-term capital gain. Capital gains and losses must therefore be matched with one another to see if a net long-term capital gain exists. The alternative tax computation is discussed later in the chapter under Tax Treatment of Capital Gains and Losses of Noncorporate Taxpayers.

The second reason the Code requires separate reporting of gains and losses and a determination of their tax character is that a net capital loss is only deductible up to $3,000 per year. Excess loss over the annual limit carries over and may be deductible in a future tax year. Capital gains and losses must be matched with one another to see if a net capital loss exists.

For these reasons, capital gains and losses must be distinguished from other types of gains and losses. Most of this chapter describes the intricate rules for determining what type of gains and losses the taxpayer has.

GENERAL SCHEME OF TAXATION

Recognized gains and losses must be properly classified. Proper classification depends upon three characteristics:

- The tax status of the property.
- The manner of the property's disposition.
- The holding period of the property.

TAX *in the NEWS*

UNCERTAINTY OVER CAPITAL GAIN RATES

During the fall of 2010, there was a great deal of uncertainty over what the special tax rates on long-term capital gains would be in 2011. Existing legislation would have raised the special tax rates, but proposed legislation would have kept the rates the same as in 2010. Late in the fall, a political compromise yielded the special rates that are discussed later in this chapter.

The three possible tax statuses are capital asset, § 1231 asset, or ordinary asset. Property disposition may be by sale, exchange, casualty, theft, or condemnation.

There are two holding periods: short term and long term. The short-term holding period is one year or less. The long-term holding period is more than one year.

The major focus of this chapter is capital gains and losses. Capital gains and losses usually result from the disposition of a capital asset. The most common disposition is a sale of the asset. Capital gains and losses can also result from the disposition of § 1231 assets, which is discussed later in this chapter.

14.2 CAPITAL ASSETS

LO.2

Distinguish capital assets from ordinary assets.

DEFINITION OF A CAPITAL ASSET

Personal use assets and investment assets are the most common capital assets owned by individual taxpayers. Personal use assets usually include items such as clothing, recreational equipment, a residence, and automobiles. Investment assets usually include investments in mutual funds, corporate stocks and bonds, government bonds, and vacant land. Remember, however, that losses from the sale or exchange of personal use assets are not recognized. Therefore, the classification of such losses as capital losses can be ignored.

Due to the historical preferential treatment of capital gains, taxpayers have preferred that gains be capital gains rather than ordinary gains. As a result, a great many statutes, cases, and rulings have accumulated in the attempt to define what is and what is not a capital asset.

Capital assets are not directly defined in the Code. Instead, § 1221(a) defines what is *not* a capital asset. A **capital asset** is property held by the taxpayer (whether or not it is connected with the taxpayer's business) that is *not* any of the following:

- Inventory or property held primarily for sale to customers in the ordinary course of a business. The Supreme Court, in *Malat v. Riddell*, defined *primarily* as meaning *of first importance* or *principally*.[1]
- Accounts and notes receivable acquired from the sale of inventory or acquired for services rendered in the ordinary course of business.
- Depreciable property or real estate used in a business.
- Certain copyrights; literary, musical, or artistic compositions; or letters, memoranda, or similar property held by (1) a taxpayer whose efforts created the property; (2) in the case of a letter, memorandum, or similar property, a taxpayer for whom it was produced; or (3) a taxpayer in whose hands the basis of the property is determined, for purposes of determining gain from a sale or exchange, in whole or in part by reference to the basis of such property in the hands of a taxpayer described in (1) or (2). When a sale or exchange involves musical compositions or copyrights in musical

[1] 66–1 USTC ¶9317, 17 AFTR 2d 604, 86 S.Ct. 1030 (USSC, 1966).

works either (1) created by the taxpayer's personal efforts or (2) having a basis determined by reference to the basis in the hands of a taxpayer whose personal efforts created the compositions or copyrights, the taxpayer may elect to treat the sale or exchange as the disposition of a capital asset.[2]

- U.S. government publications that are (1) received by a taxpayer from the U.S. government other than by purchase at the price at which they are offered for sale to the public or (2) held by a taxpayer whose basis, for purposes of determining gain from a sale or exchange, is determined by reference to a taxpayer described in (1).
- Supplies of a type regularly used or consumed in the ordinary course of a business.

The Code defines what is not a capital asset. From the preceding list, it is apparent that inventory, accounts and notes receivable, supplies, and most fixed assets of a business are not capital assets. Often, the only business asset that is a capital asset is goodwill. The following discussion provides further detail on each part of the capital asset definition.

Inventory

What constitutes inventory is determined by the taxpayer's business.

EXAMPLE 1

Green Company buys and sells used cars. Its cars are inventory. Its gains from the sale of the cars are ordinary income. ■

EXAMPLE 2

Soong sells her personal use automobile at a $500 gain. The automobile is a personal use asset and, therefore, a capital asset. The gain is a capital gain. ■

Accounts and Notes Receivable

Collection of an accrual basis account receivable usually does not result in a gain or loss because the amount collected equals the receivable's basis. The sale of an account or note receivable may generate a gain or loss, and the gain or loss is ordinary because the receivable is not a capital asset. The sale of an accrual basis receivable may result in a gain or loss because it will probably be sold for more or less than its basis. A cash basis account receivable has no basis. Sale of such a receivable generates a gain. Collection of a cash basis receivable generates ordinary income rather than a gain. A gain usually requires a sale of the receivable. See the discussion of Sale or Exchange later in this chapter.

EXAMPLE 3

Oriole Company has accounts receivable of $100,000. Because it needs working capital, it sells the receivables for $83,000 to a financial institution. If Oriole is an accrual basis taxpayer, it has a $17,000 ordinary loss. Revenue of $100,000 would have been recorded and a $100,000 basis would have been established when the receivable was created. If Oriole is a cash basis taxpayer, it has $83,000 of ordinary income because it would not have recorded any revenue earlier; thus, the receivable has no tax basis. ■

Business Fixed Assets

Depreciable personal property and real estate (both depreciable and nondepreciable) used by a business are not capital assets. Thus, *business fixed assets* are generally not capital assets.

The Code has a very complex set of rules pertaining to such property. One of these rules is discussed under Real Property Subdivided for Sale; the remainder of

[2]§ 1221(b)(3).

the rules are discussed later in this chapter. Although business fixed assets are not capital assets, a long-term capital gain can sometimes result from their sale. The potential capital gain treatment for business fixed assets under § 1231 is also discussed later in this chapter.

Copyrights and Creative Works

Generally, the person whose efforts led to the copyright or creative work has an ordinary asset, not a capital asset. *Creative works* include the works of authors, composers, and artists. Also, the person for whom a letter, memorandum, or other similar property was created has an ordinary asset. Finally, a person receiving a copyright, creative work, letter, memorandum, or similar property by gift from the creator or the person for whom the work was created has an ordinary asset. Note the exception mentioned earlier that permits the taxpayer to elect to treat the sale or exchange of a musical composition or a copyright of a musical work as the disposition of a capital asset.

EXAMPLE 4

Wanda is a part-time music composer. A music publisher purchases one of her songs for $5,000. Wanda has a $5,000 ordinary gain from the sale of an ordinary asset unless she elects to treat the gain as a capital gain. ■

EXAMPLE 5

Ed received a letter from the President of the United States in 1982. In the current year, Ed sells the letter to a collector for $300. Ed has a $300 ordinary gain from the sale of an ordinary asset (because the letter was created for Ed). ■

EXAMPLE 6

Isabella gives a song she composed to her son. The son sells the song to a music publisher for $5,000. The son has a $5,000 ordinary gain from the sale of an ordinary asset unless he elects to treat the gain as a capital gain. If the son inherits the song from Isabella, his basis for the song is its fair market value at Isabella's death. In this situation, the song is a capital asset because the son's basis is not related to Isabella's basis for the song. ■

(Patents are subject to special statutory rules discussed later in the chapter.)

ETHICS & *Equity*

WHO OWNS THE SONG?

Jason is the lead singer in a hip-hop band. He also handles all business arrangements for the band, such as bookings, negotiating contracts, and collecting payments for band performances. After each performance, Jason pays all of the band members in cash for their services that night. Jason and the other band members created a song that has gone viral on the Web. A music publisher has offered to purchase the song for $100,000. Jason has not told the other band members about this opportunity. Evaluate some of the issues facing Jason.

U.S. Government Publications

U.S. government publications received from the U.S. government (or its agencies) for a reduced price are not capital assets. This prevents a taxpayer from later donating the publications to charity and claiming a charitable contribution equal to the fair market value of the publications. A charitable contribution of a capital asset generally yields a deduction equal to the fair market value. A charitable contribution of an ordinary asset generally yields a deduction equal to less than the fair market value. If such property is received by gift from the original purchaser, the property is not a capital asset to the donee. (For a more comprehensive explanation of charitable contributions of property, refer to Chapter 10.)

EFFECT OF JUDICIAL ACTION

Court decisions play an important role in the definition of capital assets. Because the Code only lists categories of what are *not* capital assets, judicial interpretation is sometimes required to determine whether a specific item fits into one of those categories. The Supreme Court follows a literal interpretation of the categories. For instance, corporate stock is not mentioned in § 1221. Thus, corporate stock is *usually* a capital asset. However, what if corporate stock is purchased for resale to customers? Then it is *inventory* and not a capital asset because inventory is one of the categories in § 1221. (See the discussion of Dealers in Securities below.)

A Supreme Court decision was required to distinguish between capital asset and non-capital asset status when a taxpayer who did not normally acquire stock for resale to customers acquired stock with the intention of resale.[3] The Court decided that since the stock was not acquired primarily for sale to customers (the taxpayer did not sell the stock to its regular customers), the stock was a capital asset.

Often the crux of the capital asset determination hinges on whether the asset is held for investment purposes (capital asset) or business purposes (ordinary asset). The taxpayer's *use* of the property often provides objective evidence.

EXAMPLE 7

David's business buys an expensive painting. If the painting is used to decorate David's office and is not of investment quality, the painting is depreciable and, therefore, not a capital asset. If David's business is buying and selling paintings, the painting is inventory and, therefore, an ordinary asset. If the painting is of investment quality and the business purchased it for investment, the painting is a capital asset, even though it serves a decorative purpose in David's office. *Investment quality* generally means that the painting is expected to appreciate in value. If David depreciates the painting, that would be objective evidence that the painting is held for use in his business, is not being held for investment or as inventory, and is not a capital asset. ■

Because of the uncertainty associated with capital asset status, Congress has enacted several Code Sections to clarify the definition. These statutory expansions of the capital asset definition are discussed in the following section.

STATUTORY EXPANSIONS

Congress has often expanded the § 1221 general definition of what is *not* a capital asset.

Dealers in Securities

As a general rule, securities (stocks, bonds, and other financial instruments) held by a dealer are considered to be inventory and are, therefore, not subject to capital gain or loss treatment. A *dealer in securities* is a merchant (e.g., a brokerage firm) that regularly engages in the purchase and resale of securities to customers. The dealer must identify any securities being held for investment. Generally, if a dealer clearly identifies certain securities as held for investment purposes by the close of business on the acquisition date, gain from the securities' sale will be capital gain. However, the gain will not be capital gain if the dealer ceases to hold the securities for investment prior to the sale. Losses are capital losses if at any time the securities have been clearly identified by the dealer as held for investment.[4]

[3] *Arkansas Best v. Comm.*, 88–1 USTC ¶9210, 61 AFTR 2d 88–655, 108 S.Ct. 971 (USSC, 1988).

[4] §§ 1236(a) and (b) and Reg. §§ 1.1236–1(a) and (b).

EXAMPLE 8

Tracy is a securities dealer. She purchases 100 shares of Swan stock. If Tracy takes no further action, the stock is inventory and an ordinary asset. If she designates in her records that the stock is held for investment, the stock is a capital asset. Tracy must designate the investment purpose by the close of business on the acquisition date. If Tracy maintains her investment purpose and later sells the stock, the gain or loss is capital gain or loss. If Tracy redesignates the stock as held for resale (inventory) and then sells it, any gain is ordinary, but any loss is capital loss. Stock designated as held for investment and then sold at a loss always yields a capital loss. ■

Real Property Subdivided for Sale

Substantial real property development activities may result in the owner being considered a dealer for tax purposes. Income from the sale of real estate property lots is treated as the sale of inventory (ordinary income) if the owner is considered to be a dealer. However, § 1237 allows real estate investors capital gain treatment if they engage *only* in *limited* development activities. To be eligible for § 1237 treatment, the following requirements must be met:

- The taxpayer may not be a corporation.
- The taxpayer may not be a real estate dealer.
- No substantial improvements may be made to the lots sold. *Substantial* generally means more than a 10 percent increase in the value of a lot. Shopping centers and other commercial or residential buildings are considered substantial, while filling, draining, leveling, and clearing operations are not.
- The taxpayer must have held the lots sold for at least 5 years, except for inherited property. The substantial improvements test is less stringent if the property is held at least 10 years.

If the preceding requirements are met, all gain is capital gain until the tax year in which the *sixth* lot is sold. Sales of contiguous lots to a single buyer in the same transaction count as the sale of one lot. Beginning with the tax year the *sixth* lot is sold, some of the gain may be ordinary income. Five percent of the revenue from lot sales is potential ordinary income. That potential ordinary income is offset by any selling expenses from the lot sales. Practically, sales commissions often are at least 5 percent of the sales price, so none of the gain is treated as ordinary income.

Section 1237 does not apply to losses. A loss from the sale of subdivided real property is an ordinary loss unless the property qualifies as a capital asset under § 1221. The following example illustrates the application of § 1237.

EXAMPLE 9

Jack owns a large tract of land and subdivides it for sale. Assume Jack meets all the requirements of § 1237 and during the tax year sells the first 10 lots to 10 different buyers for $10,000 each. Jack's basis in each lot sold is $3,000, and he incurs total selling expenses of $4,000 on the sales. Jack's gain is computed as follows:

Selling price (10 × $10,000)	$100,000	
Less: Selling expenses (10 × $400)	(4,000)	
Amount realized		$ 96,000
Basis (10 × $3,000)		(30,000)
Realized and recognized gain		$ 66,000
Classification of recognized gain:		
Ordinary income		
Five percent of selling price (5% × $100,000)	$ 5,000	
Less: Selling expenses	(4,000)	
Ordinary gain		1,000
Capital gain		$ 65,000

■

TAX *in the NEWS*

Losses on Subprime Mortgages

During 2010, many banks and other financial institutions took huge financial accounting write-downs on securities that consisted of "bundles" of subprime mortgages. (Subprime mortgages are loans made to homeowners with weak credit.) If the financial institution holds these securities as investments, they are capital assets. If the financial institution holds these securities as inventory, they are ordinary assets. However, writing them down for financial accounting purposes does not mean that the institution actually disposed of the securities. Therefore, the loss in value of the securities will not be recognized for tax purposes until the securities are transferred in a sale or exchange.

Nonbusiness Bad Debts

A loan not made in the ordinary course of business is classified as a nonbusiness receivable. In the year the receivable becomes completely worthless, it is a *nonbusiness bad debt*, and the bad debt is treated as a short-term capital loss. Even if the receivable was outstanding for more than one year, the loss is still a short-term capital loss. Chapter 7 discusses nonbusiness bad debts more thoroughly.

14.3 Sale or Exchange

LO.3

Understand the relevance of a sale or exchange to classification as a capital gain or loss and apply the special rules for the capital gain or loss treatment of the retirement of corporate obligations, options, patents, franchises, and lease cancellation payments.

Recognition of capital gain or loss usually requires a sale or exchange of a capital asset. The Code uses the term **sale or exchange**, but does not define it. Generally, a property sale involves the receipt of money by the seller and/or the assumption by the purchaser of the seller's liabilities. An exchange involves the transfer of property for other property. Thus, an involuntary conversion (casualty, theft, or condemnation) is not a sale or exchange. In several situations, the determination of whether a sale or exchange has taken place has been clarified by the enactment of Code Sections that specifically provide for sale or exchange treatment.

Recognized gains or losses from the cancellation, lapse, expiration, or any other termination of a right or obligation with respect to personal property (other than stock) that is or would be a capital asset in the hands of the taxpayer are capital gains or losses.[5] See the discussion under Options later in the chapter for more details.

WORTHLESS SECURITIES AND § 1244 STOCK

Occasionally, securities such as stock and, especially, bonds may become worthless due to the insolvency of their issuer. If such a security is a capital asset, the loss is deemed to have occurred as the result of a sale or exchange on the *last day* of the tax year.[6] This last-day rule may have the effect of converting what otherwise would have been a short-term capital loss into a long-term capital loss. (See Treatment of Capital Losses later in this chapter.) Worthless securities are discussed in Chapter 7 on pp. 7–6 and 7–23.

Section 1244 allows an ordinary deduction on disposition of stock at a loss. The stock must be that of a small business company, and the ordinary deduction is limited to $50,000 ($100,000 for married individuals filing jointly) per year. For a more detailed discussion, refer to Chapter 7.

SPECIAL RULE—RETIREMENT OF CORPORATE OBLIGATIONS

A debt obligation (e.g., a bond or note payable) may have a tax basis in excess of or less than its redemption value because it may have been acquired at a premium or discount. Consequently, the collection of the redemption value may result in a loss or gain. Generally, the collection of a debt obligation is *treated* as

[5] § 1234A.

[6] § 165(g)(1).

TAX *in* the NEWS

Bankruptcy and Worthless Stock

During 2009, General Motors went into bankruptcy, was reorganized, and emerged from bankruptcy. However, the common shareholders of the General Motors that went into bankruptcy were not the common shareholders of the General Motors that emerged from bankruptcy. The original common shareholders lost their entire investment because their stock became worthless. The holding period of their stock ended for tax purposes on December 31, 2009, because of the worthless stock rules. They had a capital loss equal to whatever their basis was for the worthless shares. The debtors of General Motors accepted common shares in the General Motors that emerged from bankruptcy. Generally, the exchange of debt for common shares in a bankruptcy reorganization is not a taxable transaction, and the basis of the debt becomes the basis for the shares.

a sale or exchange.[7] Therefore, any loss or gain can be a capital loss or capital gain because a sale or exchange has taken place. However, if the debt obligation was issued by a human being prior to June 9, 1997, and/or purchased by the taxpayer prior to June 9, 1997, the collection of the debt obligation is not a sale or exchange.

EXAMPLE 10

Fran acquires $1,000 of Osprey Corporation bonds for $980 in the open market. If the bonds are held to maturity, the $20 difference between Fran's collection of the $1,000 redemption value and her cost of $980 is treated as capital gain. If the obligation had been issued to Fran by an individual prior to June 9, 1997, her $20 gain would be ordinary, since she did not sell or exchange the debt. ■

Original Issue Discount

The benefit of the sale or exchange exception that allows a capital gain from the collection of certain obligations is reduced when the obligation has original issue discount. **Original issue discount (OID)** arises when the issue price of a debt obligation is less than the maturity value of the obligation. OID must generally be amortized over the life of the debt obligation using the effective interest method. The OID amortization increases the basis of the bond. Most new publicly traded bond issues do not carry OID since the stated interest rate is set to make the market price on issue the same as the bond's face amount. In addition, even if the issue price is less than the face amount, the difference is not considered to be OID if the difference is less than one-fourth of 1 percent of the redemption price at maturity multiplied by the number of years to maturity.[8]

In the case where OID does exist, it may or may not have to be amortized, depending upon the date the obligation was issued. When OID is amortized, the amount of gain upon collection, sale, or exchange of the obligation is correspondingly reduced. The obligations covered by the OID amortization rules and the method of amortization are presented in §§ 1272–1275. Similar rules for other obligations can be found in §§ 1276–1288.

EXAMPLE 11

Jerry purchases $10,000 of newly issued White Corporation bonds for $6,000. The bonds have OID of $4,000. Jerry must amortize the discount over the life of the bonds. The OID amortization *increases* his interest income. (The bonds were selling at a discount because the market rate of interest was greater than the bonds' interest rate.) After Jerry has amortized $1,800 of OID, he sells the bonds for $8,000. Jerry has a capital gain of $200 [$8,000 – ($6,000 cost + $1,800 OID amortization)]. The OID amortization rules prevent him from converting ordinary interest income into capital gain. Without the OID amortization, Jerry would have capital gain of $2,000 ($8,000 – $6,000 cost). ■

[7] § 1271.

[8] § 1273(a)(3).

OPTIONS

Frequently, a potential buyer of property wants some time to make the purchase decision, but wants to control the sale and/or the sale price in the meantime. **Options** are used to achieve these objectives. The potential purchaser (grantee) pays the property owner (grantor) for an option on the property. The grantee then becomes the option holder. The option usually sets a price at which the grantee can buy the property and expires after a specified period of time.

Sale of an Option

A grantee may sell or exchange the option rather than exercising it or letting it expire. Generally, the grantee's sale or exchange of the option results in capital gain or loss if the option property is (or would be) a capital asset to the grantee.[9]

EXAMPLE 12

Rosa wants to buy some vacant land for investment purposes. She cannot afford the full purchase price. Instead, she convinces the landowner (grantor) to sell her the right to purchase the land for $100,000 anytime in the next two years. Rosa (grantee) pays $3,000 to obtain this option to buy the land. The option is a capital asset for Rosa because if she actually purchased the land, the land would be a capital asset. Three months after purchasing the option, Rosa sells it for $7,000. She has a $4,000 ($7,000 – $3,000) short-term capital gain on this sale since she held the option for one year or less. ■

Failure to Exercise Options

If an option holder (grantee) fails to exercise the option, the lapse of the option is considered a sale or exchange on the option expiration date. Thus, the loss is a capital loss if the property subject to the option is (or would be) a capital asset in the hands of the grantee.

The grantor of an option on *stocks, securities, commodities, or commodity futures* receives short-term capital gain treatment upon the expiration of the option. Options on property other than stocks, securities, commodities, or commodity futures result in ordinary income to the grantor when the option expires. For example, an individual investor who owns certain stock (a capital asset) may sell a call option, entitling the buyer of the option to acquire the stock at a specified price higher than the value at the date the option is granted. The writer of the call receives a premium (e.g., 10 percent) for writing the option. If the price of the stock does not increase during the option period, the option will expire unexercised. Upon the expiration of the option, the grantor must recognize short-term capital gain. These provisions do not apply to options held for sale to customers (the inventory of a securities dealer).

Exercise of Options by Grantee

If the option is exercised, the amount paid for the option is added to the optioned property's selling price. This increases the gain (or reduces the loss) to the grantor resulting from the sale of the property. The grantor's gain or loss is capital or ordinary depending on the tax status of the property. The grantee adds the cost of the option to the basis of the property purchased.

EXAMPLE 13

On September 1, 2007 Wes purchases 100 shares of Eagle Company stock for $5,000. On April 1, 2011, he writes a call option on the stock, giving the grantee the right to buy the stock for $6,000 during the following six-month period. Wes (the grantor) receives a call premium of $500 for writing the call.

- If the call is exercised by the grantee on August 1, 2011, Wes has $1,500 ($6,000 + $500 – $5,000) of long-term capital gain from the sale of the stock. The grantee has a $6,500 ($500 option premium + $6,000 purchase price) basis for the stock.

[9] § 1234(a) and Reg. § 1.1234–1(a)(1).

CONCEPT SUMMARY 14.1

Options

Event	Effect on Grantor	Effect on Grantee
Option is granted.	Receives value and has a contract obligation (a liability).	Pays value and has a contract right (an asset).
Option expires.	Has a short-term capital gain if the option property is stocks, securities, commodities, or commodity futures. Otherwise, gain is ordinary income.	Has a loss (capital loss if option property would have been a capital asset for the grantee).
Option is exercised.	Amount received for option increases proceeds from sale of the option property.	Amount paid for option becomes part of the basis of the option property purchased.
Option is sold or exchanged by grantee.	Result depends upon whether option later expires or is exercised (see above).	Could have gain or loss (capital gain or loss if option property would have been a capital asset for the grantee).

- Assume that Wes decides to sell his stock prior to exercise for $6,000 and enters into a closing transaction by purchasing a call on 100 shares of Eagle Company stock for $5,000. Since the Eagle stock is selling for $6,000, Wes must pay a call premium of $1,000. He recognizes a $500 short-term capital loss [$1,000 (call premium paid) – $500 (call premium received)] on the closing transaction. On the actual sale of the Eagle stock, Wes has a long-term capital gain of $1,000 [$6,000 (selling price) – $5,000 (cost)]. The grantee is not affected by Wes's closing transaction. The original option is still in existence, and the grantee's tax consequences will depend on what action the grantee takes—exercising the option, letting the option expire, or selling the option.
- Assume that the original option expired unexercised. Wes has a $500 short-term capital gain equal to the call premium received for writing the option. This gain is not recognized until the option expires. The grantee has a loss from expiration of the option. The nature of the loss will depend upon whether the option was a capital asset or an ordinary asset. ■

Concept Summary 14.1 summarizes the rules for options.

PATENTS

Transfer of a **patent** is treated as the sale or exchange of a long-term capital asset when all substantial rights to the patent (or an undivided interest that includes all such rights) are transferred by a holder.[10] The transferor/holder may receive payment in virtually any form. Lump-sum or periodic payments are most common. The amount of the payments may also be contingent on the transferee/purchaser's productivity, use, or disposition of the patent. If the transfer meets these requirements, any gain or loss is *automatically a long-term* capital gain or loss. Whether the asset was a capital asset for the transferor, whether a sale or exchange occurred, and how long the transferor held the patent are not relevant.

This special long-term capital gain or loss treatment for patents is intended to encourage technological progress. Ironically, authors, composers, and artists are not eligible for capital gain treatment when their creations are transferred. Books, songs, and artists' works may be copyrighted, but copyrights and the assets they represent are not capital assets. Thus, the disposition of those assets by their creators usually results in ordinary gain or loss (unless the exception for musical compositions applies, as noted earlier). The following example illustrates the special treatment for patents.

[10]§ 1235.

EXAMPLE 14
THE BIG PICTURE

Return to the facts of *The Big Picture* on p. 14-2. Kevin transfers his rights in the battery patent to the Green Battery Company in exchange for $1 million plus $.50 for each battery sold. Assuming Kevin has transferred all substantial rights, the question of whether the transfer is a sale or exchange of a capital asset is not relevant. Kevin automatically has a long-term capital gain from both his share of the lump-sum payment of $2 million and the $1 per battery royalty to the extent that these proceeds exceed his basis for the patent. Kevin also had an automatic long-term capital gain when he sold 50% of his rights in the patent to Maurice, because Kevin transferred an undivided interest that included all substantial rights in the patent. Whether Maurice gets long-term capital gain treatment on the transfer to Green Battery will depend on whether he is a holder (see the discussion below and in Example 15). ■

Substantial Rights

To receive favorable capital gain treatment, all *substantial rights* to the patent (or an undivided interest in it) must be transferred. All substantial rights to a patent means all rights (whether or not then held by the grantor) that are valuable at the time the patent rights (or an undivided interest in the patent) are transferred. All substantial rights have not been transferred when the transfer is limited geographically within the issuing country or when the transfer is for a period less than the remaining life of the patent. The circumstances of the entire transaction, rather than merely the language used in the transfer instrument, are to be considered in deciding whether all substantial rights have been transferred.[11]

Holder Defined

The *holder* of a patent must be an *individual* and is usually the invention's creator. A holder may also be an individual who purchases the patent rights from the creator before the patented invention is reduced to practice. However, the creator's employer and certain parties related to the creator do not qualify as holders. Thus, in the common situation where an employer has all rights to an employee's inventions, the employer is not eligible for long-term capital gain treatment. More than likely, the employer will have an ordinary asset because the patent was developed as part of its business.

EXAMPLE 15
THE BIG PICTURE

Return to the facts of *The Big Picture* on p. 14-2. Continuing with the facts of Example 14, Kevin is clearly a holder of the patent because he is the inventor and was not an employee when he invented the battery. When Maurice purchased a 50% interest in the patent nine months ago, he became a holder if the patent had not yet been reduced to practice. Since the patent apparently was not being manufactured at the time of the purchase, it had not been reduced to practice. Consequently, Maurice is also a holder, and he also has an automatic long-term capital gain or loss when the patent is transferred to Green Battery Company. Maurice's basis for his share of the patent is $50,000, and his share of the proceeds is $1 million plus $.50 for each battery sold. Thus, Maurice has a long-term capital gain even though he has not held his interest in the patent for more than one year. ■

FRANCHISES, TRADEMARKS, AND TRADE NAMES

A mode of operation, a widely recognized brand name (trade name), and a widely known business symbol (trademark) are all valuable assets. These assets may be licensed (commonly known as franchising) by their owner for use by other businesses. Many fast-food restaurants (such as McDonald's and Taco Bell) are franchises. The franchisee usually pays the owner (franchisor) an initial fee plus a contingent fee. The contingent fee is often based upon the franchisee's sales volume.

[11]Reg. § 1.1235–2(b)(1).

For Federal income tax purposes, a **franchise** is an agreement that gives the franchisee the right to distribute, sell, or provide goods, services, or facilities within a specified area.[12] A franchise transfer includes the grant of a franchise, a transfer by one franchisee to another person, or the renewal of a franchise.

A franchise transfer is generally not a sale or exchange of a capital asset. Section 1253 provides that a transfer of a franchise, trademark, or trade name is not a transfer of a capital asset when the transferor retains any significant power, right, or continuing interest in the property transferred.

Significant Power, Right, or Continuing Interest

Significant powers, rights, or continuing interests include control over assignment, quality of products and services, and sale or advertising of other products or services, and the right to require that substantially all supplies and equipment be purchased from the transferor. Also included are the right to terminate the franchise at will and the right to substantial contingent payments. Most modern franchising operations involve some or all of these powers, rights, or continuing interests.

In the unusual case where no significant power, right, or continuing interest is retained by the transferor, a sale or exchange may occur, and capital gain or loss treatment may be available. For capital gain or loss treatment to be available, the asset transferred must qualify as a capital asset.

EXAMPLE 16

Orange, Inc., a franchisee, sells the franchise to a third party. Payments to Orange are not contingent, and all significant powers, rights, and continuing interests are transferred. The gain (payments − adjusted basis) on the sale is a capital gain to Orange. ■

Noncontingent Payments

When the transferor retains a significant power, right, or continuing interest, the transferee's noncontingent payments to the transferor are ordinary income to the transferor. The franchisee capitalizes the payments and amortizes them over 15 years. The amortization is subject to recapture under § 1245.[13]

EXAMPLE 17

Grey Company signs a 10-year franchise agreement with DOH Donuts. Grey (the franchisee) makes payments of $3,000 per year for the first 8 years of the franchise agreement—a total of $24,000. Grey cannot deduct $3,000 per year as the payments are made. Instead, Grey may amortize the $24,000 total over 15 years. Thus, Grey may deduct $1,600 per year for each of the 15 years of the amortization period. The same result would occur if Grey made a $24,000 lump-sum payment at the beginning of the franchise period. Assuming DOH Donuts (the franchisor) retains significant powers, rights, or a continuing interest, it will have ordinary income when it receives the payments from Grey. ■

Contingent Payments

Whether or not the transferor retains a significant power, right, or continuing interest, contingent franchise payments are ordinary income for the franchisor and an ordinary deduction for the franchisee. For this purpose, a payment qualifies as a contingent payment only if the following requirements are met:

- The contingent amounts are part of a series of payments that are paid at least annually throughout the term of the transfer agreement.
- The payments are substantially equal in amount or are payable under a fixed formula.

[12] § 1253(b)(1).

[13] The recapture provisions are discussed later in this chapter.

CONCEPT SUMMARY 14.2

Franchises

Event	Effect on Franchisor	Effect on Franchisee
Franchisor Retains Significant Powers and Rights		
Noncontingent payment	Ordinary income.	Capitalized and amortized over 15 years as an ordinary deduction; if franchise is sold, amortization is subject to recapture under § 1245.
Contingent payment	Ordinary income.	Ordinary deduction.
Franchisor Does *Not* Retain Significant Powers and Rights		
Noncontingent payment	Ordinary income if franchise rights are an ordinary asset; capital gain if franchise rights are a capital asset (unlikely).	Capitalized and amortized over 15 years as an ordinary deduction; if the franchise is sold, amortization is subject to recapture under § 1245.
Contingent payment	Ordinary income.	Ordinary deduction.

EXAMPLE 18

TAK, a spicy chicken franchisor, transfers an eight-year franchise to Otis. TAK retains a significant power, right, or continuing interest. Otis, the franchisee, agrees to pay TAK 15% of sales. This contingent payment is ordinary income to TAK and a business deduction for Otis as the payments are made. ■

Sports Franchises

Professional sports franchises (e.g., the Detroit Tigers) are subject to § 1253.[14] Player contracts are usually one of the major assets acquired with a sports franchise. These contracts last only for the time stated in the contract. By being classified as § 197 intangibles, the player contracts and other intangible assets acquired in the purchase of the sports franchise are amortized over a statutory 15-year period.[15]

Concept Summary 14.2 summarizes the rules for franchises.

LEASE CANCELLATION PAYMENTS

The tax treatment of payments received for canceling a lease depends on whether the recipient is the **lessor** or the **lessee** and whether the lease is a capital asset or not.

Lessee Treatment

Lease cancellation payments received by a lessee are treated as an exchange.[16] Thus, these payments are capital gains if the lease is a capital asset. Generally, a lessee's lease is a capital asset if the property (either personalty or realty) is used for the lessee's personal use (e.g., his or her residence). A lessee's lease is an ordinary asset if the property is used in the lessee's trade or business and the lease has existed for one year or less when it is canceled. A lessee's lease is a § 1231 asset if the property is used in the lessee's trade or business and the lease has existed for more than a year when it is canceled.[17]

---

[14] § 1253(e) previously exempted sports franchises from § 1253, but was repealed for franchises acquired after October 22, 2004..

[15] § 197(a).

[16] § 1241 and Reg. § 1.1241–1(a).

[17] Reg. § 1.1221–1(b) and PLR 200045019.

TAX *in* the NEWS

Uncertainty about the Holding Period

During the fall of 2010, a tornado struck a small town in Ohio. A local investor had purchased a 20-acre plot with a stand of trees to use for hunting. The tornado destroyed the trees and made the land useless for hunting. Three months after the tornado, the land was sold "as is" to the insurance company that had insured it. The investor had owned the land for 10 months when the tornado struck and 13 months when it was sold to the insurance company. The land was sold at a loss. The loss is long term because the sale date occurred after the land had been held for more than one year.

EXAMPLE 19

Mark owns an apartment building that he is going to convert into an office building. Vicki is one of the apartment tenants and receives $1,000 from Mark to cancel the lease. Vicki has a capital gain of $1,000 (which is long term or short term depending upon how long she has held the lease). Mark has an ordinary deduction of $1,000. ■

Lessor Treatment

Payments received by a lessor for a lease cancellation are always ordinary income because they are considered to be in lieu of rental payments.[18]

EXAMPLE 20

Floyd owns an apartment building near a university campus. Hui-Fen is one of the tenants. Hui-Fen is graduating early and offers Floyd $800 to cancel the apartment lease. Floyd accepts the offer. Floyd has ordinary income of $800. Hui-Fen has a nondeductible payment since the apartment was personal use property. ■

14.4 Holding Period

LO.4

Determine whether the holding period for a capital asset is long term or short term.

Property must be held more than one year to qualify for long-term capital gain or loss treatment.[19] Property not held for the required long-term period results in short-term capital gain or loss. To compute the **holding period**, start counting on the day after the property was acquired and include the day of disposition.

EXAMPLE 21
THE BIG PICTURE

Return to the facts of *The Big Picture* on p. 14-2. Assume that Maurice purchased the Purple stock on January 15, 2010. If he sells it on January 16, 2011, Maurice's holding period is more than one year. If instead Maurice sells the stock on January 15, 2011, the holding period is exactly one year, and the gain or loss is short term. ■

To be held for more than one year, a capital asset acquired on the last day of any month must not be disposed of until on or after the first day of the thirteenth succeeding month.[20]

EXAMPLE 22

Leo purchases a capital asset on February 28, 2010. If Leo sells the asset on February 28, 2011, the holding period is one year, and Leo will have a short-term capital gain or loss. If Leo sells the asset on March 1, 2011, the holding period is more than one year, and he will have a long-term capital gain or loss. ■

[18]Reg. § 1.61–8(b).

[19]§ 1222.

[20]Rev.Rul. 66–7, 1966–1 C.B. 188.

REVIEW OF SPECIAL HOLDING PERIOD RULES

There are several special holding period rules.[21] The application of these rules depends on the type of asset and how it was acquired.

Nontaxable Exchanges

The holding period of property received in a like-kind exchange includes the holding period of the former asset if the property that has been exchanged is a capital asset or a § 1231 asset. In certain nontaxable transactions involving a substituted basis, the holding period of the former property is *tacked on* to the holding period of the newly acquired property.

EXAMPLE 23

Vern exchanges a business truck for another truck in a like-kind exchange. The holding period of the exchanged truck tacks on to the holding period of the new truck. ■

Certain Nontaxable Transactions Involving a Carryover of Another Taxpayer's Basis

A former owner's holding period is tacked on to the present owner's holding period if the transaction is nontaxable and the former owner's basis carries over to the present owner.

EXAMPLE 24

Kareem acquires 100 shares of Robin Corporation stock for $1,000 on December 31, 2007. He transfers the shares by gift to Megan on December 31, 2010, when the stock is worth $2,000. Kareem's basis of $1,000 becomes the basis for determining gain or loss on a subsequent sale by Megan. Megan's holding period begins with the date the stock was acquired by Kareem. ■

EXAMPLE 25

Assume the same facts as in Example 24, except that the fair market value of the shares is only $800 on the date of the gift. The holding period begins on the date of the gift if Megan sells the stock for a loss. The value of the shares at the date of the gift is used in the determination of her basis for loss. If she sells the shares for $500 on April 1, 2011, Megan has a $300 recognized capital loss, and the holding period is from December 31, 2010, to April 1, 2011 (thus, the loss is short term). ■

Certain Disallowed Loss Transactions

Under several Code provisions, realized losses are disallowed. When a loss is disallowed, there is no carryover of holding period. Losses can be disallowed under § 267 (sale or exchange between related taxpayers) and § 262 (sale or exchange of personal use assets) as well as other Code Sections. Taxpayers who acquire property in a disallowed loss transaction will have a new holding period begin and will have a basis equal to the purchase price.

EXAMPLE 26

Janet sells her personal automobile at a loss. She may not deduct the loss because it arises from the sale of personal use property. Janet purchases a replacement automobile for more than the selling price of her former automobile. Janet has a basis equal to the cost of the replacement automobile, and her holding period begins when she acquires the replacement automobile. ■

Inherited Property

The holding period for inherited property is treated as long term no matter how long the property is actually held by the heir. The holding period of the decedent or the decedent's estate is not relevant for the heir's holding period.[22]

[21] § 1223.

[22] The estate tax was repealed for 2010. See footnote 41 in Chapter 13. Normally the assets passing from the estate of a decedent dying in 2010 to the beneficiaries will have a fair market value basis to the beneficiaries. However, if the executor elects modified carryover basis, there also will be a carryover holding period.

GLOBAL
Tax Issues

Trading ADRs on U.S. Stock Exchanges

Many non-U.S. companies now have subsidiaries that were formerly U.S. companies. For instance, until 2007 Chrysler Corporation was a subsidiary of DaimlerChrysler (formed when the German company Daimler-Benz acquired Chrysler). Shares in such foreign companies generally cannot be traded directly on U.S. stock exchanges. Instead, the foreign companies issue instruments called American Depository Receipts (ADRs) that can be traded on U.S. stock exchanges. Purchases and sales of ADRs are treated for tax purposes as though the ADRs were shares in the corporation that issued them.

EXAMPLE 27

Shonda inherits Blue Company stock from her father who died in 2011. She receives the stock on April 1, 2011, and sells it on November 1, 2011. Even though Shonda did not hold the stock more than one year, she receives long-term capital gain or loss treatment on the sale. ■

SPECIAL RULES FOR SHORT SALES

General

The Code provides special rules for determining the holding period of property sold short.[23] A **short sale** occurs when a taxpayer sells borrowed property and repays the lender with substantially identical property either held on the date of the sale or purchased after the sale. Short sales usually involve corporate stock. The seller's objective is to make a profit in anticipation of a decline in the stock's price. If the price declines, the seller in a short sale recognizes a profit equal to the difference between the sales price of the borrowed stock and the price paid for the replacement stock.

A *short sale against the box* occurs when the stock is borrowed from a broker by a seller who already owns the same stock. The box is the safe deposit box where stock owners routinely used to keep stock certificates. Although today stockbrokers generally keep stock for their customers, the terminology "short sale against the box" is still used.

EXAMPLE 28

Chris does not own any shares of Brown Corporation. However, Chris sells 30 shares of Brown. The shares are borrowed from Chris's broker and must be replaced within 45 days. Chris has a short sale because he was short the shares he sold. He will *close* the short sale by purchasing Brown shares and delivering them to his broker. If the original 30 shares were sold for $10,000 and Chris later purchases 30 shares for $8,000, he has a gain of $2,000. Chris's hunch that the price of Brown stock would decline was correct. Chris was able to profit from selling high and buying low. If Chris had to purchase Brown shares for $13,000 to close the short sale, he would have a loss of $3,000. In this case, Chris would have sold low and bought high—not the result he wanted! Chris would be making a short sale against the box if he borrowed shares from his broker to sell and then closed the short sale by delivering other Brown shares he owned at the time he made the short sale. ■

A short sale gain or loss is a capital gain or loss to the extent that the short sale property constitutes a capital asset of the taxpayer. The gain or loss is not recognized until the short sale is closed. Generally, the holding period of the short sale property is determined by how long the property used to close the short sale was held. However, if *substantially identical property* (e.g., other shares of the same stock) is held by the taxpayer, the short-term or long-term character of the short sale gain or loss may be affected:

- If substantially identical property has *not* been held for the long-term holding period on the short sale date, the short sale *gain or loss* is short term.

[23] § 1233.

CONCEPT SUMMARY 14.3

Short Sales of Securities

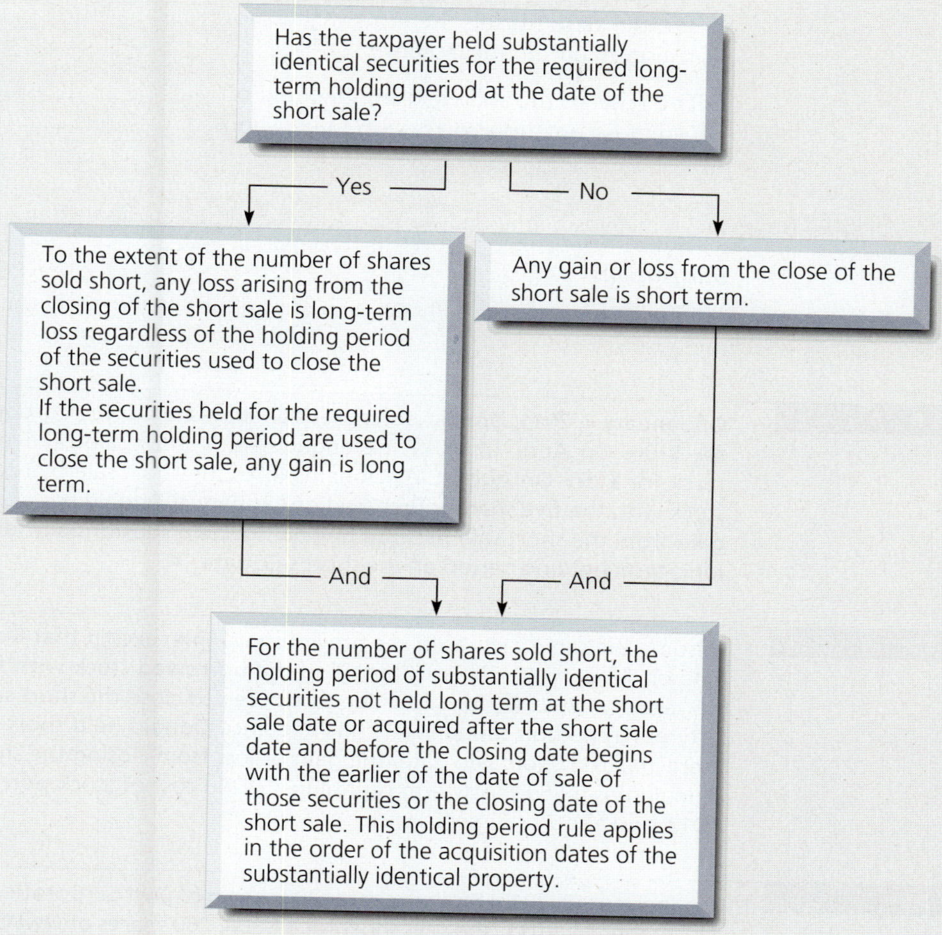

- If substantially identical property has *been* held for the long-term holding period on the short sale date, the short sale *gain* is long term if the substantially identical property is used to close the short sale and short term if it is not used to close the short sale.
- If substantially identical property has *been* held for the long-term holding period on the short sale date, the short sale *loss* is long term whether or not the substantially identical property is used to close the short sale.
- If substantially identical property is acquired *after* the short sale date and on or before the closing date, the short sale *gain or loss* is short term.

Concept Summary 14.3 summarizes the short sale rules. These rules are intended to prevent the conversion of short-term capital gains into long-term capital gains and long-term capital losses into short-term capital losses.

Disposition Rules for Short Sales against the Box

In a short sale against the box, the taxpayer either owns securities that are substantially identical to the securities sold short at the short sale date or acquires such securities before the closing date. To remove the taxpayer's flexibility as to when the short sale gain must be reported, a constructive sale approach is used. If the taxpayer has not closed the short sale by delivering the short sale securities to the broker *before* January 31 of the year following the short sale, the short sale is deemed to have been closed on the *earlier* of two events:

- On the short sale date if the taxpayer owned substantially identical securities at that time.
- On the date during the year of the short sale that the taxpayer acquired substantially identical securities.[24]

The basis of the shares in the deemed transfer of shares is used to compute the gain or loss on the short sale. Later, when shares are *actually* transferred to the broker to close the short sale, there may be a gain or loss because the shares transferred will have a basis equal to the short sale date price and the value at the *actual* short sale closing date may be different from the short sale date price.

Illustrations

The following examples illustrate the treatment of short sales and short sales against the box.

EXAMPLE 29

On January 4, 2011, Donald purchases five shares of Osprey Corporation common stock for $100. On April 14, 2011, he engages in a short sale of five shares of the same stock for $150. On August 15, Donald closes the short sale by repaying the borrowed stock with the five shares purchased on January 4. Donald has a $50 short-term capital gain from the short sale because he had not held substantially identical shares for the long-term holding period on the short sale date. ■

EXAMPLE 30

Assume the same facts as in the previous example, except that Donald closes the short sale on January 28, 2012, by repaying the borrowed stock with five shares purchased on January 27, 2012, for $200. The stock used to close the short sale was not the property purchased on January 4, 2011, but since Donald held short-term property at the April 14, 2011 short sale date, the gain or loss from closing the short sale is short term. Donald has a $50 short-term capital loss ($200 cost of stock purchased on January 27, 2012, and a short sale selling price of $150). ■

EXAMPLE 31

On January 18, 2010, Rita purchases 200 shares of Owl Corporation stock for $1,000. On November 11, 2011, she sells short for $1,300, 200 shares of Owl Corporation stock that she borrows from her broker. On February 10, 2012, Rita closes the short sale by delivering the 200 shares of Owl Corporation stock that she had acquired in 2010. On that date, Owl Corporation stock had a market price of $3 per share. Since Rita owned substantially identical stock on the date of the short sale and did not close the short sale before January 31, 2012, she is *deemed* to have closed the short sale on November 11, 2011 (the date of the short sale). On her 2011 tax return, she reports a $300 long-term capital gain ($1,300 short sale price − $1,000 basis). On February 10, 2012, Rita has a $700 short-term capital loss [$600 short sale closing date price (200 shares × $3 per share) − $1,300 basis] because the holding period of the shares used to close the short sale commences with the date of the short sale. ■

EXAMPLE 32

Assume the same facts as in Example 31, except that Rita did not own any Owl Corporation stock on the short sale date and acquired the 200 shares of Owl Corporation stock for $1,000 on December 12, 2011 (after the November 11, 2011 short sale date). The *deemed* closing of the short sale is December 12, 2011, because Rita held substantially identical shares at the end of 2011 and did not close the short sale before January 31, 2012. Her 2011 short sale gain is a *short-term* gain of $300 ($1,300 short sale price − $1,000 basis), and she still has a short-term capital loss of $700 on February 10, 2012. ■

[24] § 1259.

TAX *in* the NEWS

SHORT SALES IN REAL ESTATE

Recently, the term "short sale" has taken on a meaning in real estate transactions that is different from its use with regard to securities transactions. A short sale in real estate may takes place when the mortgage on property exceeds the property's fair market value. A property owner in this predicament negotiates with the lender to allow the property to be sold at its fair market value with the lender accepting the sales price in full satisfaction of the mortgage. Lenders typically will not negotiate with such property owners until the owner has failed to make required mortgage payments and foreclosure by the lender is imminent. If the negotiations are successful, the property owner avoids foreclosure but may have debt cancellation income for the difference between the mortgage and the sales price.

14.5 TAX TREATMENT OF CAPITAL GAINS AND LOSSES OF NONCORPORATE TAXPAYERS

LO.5

Describe the beneficial tax treatment for capital gains and the detrimental tax treatment for capital losses for noncorporate taxpayers.

All taxpayers net their capital gains and losses. Short-term gains and losses (if any) are netted against one another, and long-term gains and losses (if any) are netted against one another. The results will be net short-term gain or loss and net long-term gain or loss. If these two net positions are of opposite sign (one is a gain and one is a loss), they are netted against one another.

Six possibilities exist for the result after all possible netting has been completed. Three of these final results are gains, and three are losses. One possible result is a net long-term capital gain (NLTCG). Net long-term capital gains of noncorporate taxpayers are subject to beneficial treatment. A second possibility is a net short-term capital gain (NSTCG). Third, the netting may result in both NLTCG and NSTCG.

The NLTCG portion of these results is eligible for an alternative tax calculation. As many as four different tax rates may be used in the calculation—0, 15, 25, and 28 percent. The tax savings from the alternative tax calculation range from a low of 10 percentage points (10 percent regular tax rate − 0 percent alternative tax rate) to a high of 20 percentage points (35 percent regular tax rate − 15 percent alternative tax rate). The alternative tax computation is discussed later in the chapter under Alternative Tax on Net Capital Gain.

The last three results of the capital gain and loss netting process are losses. Thus, a fourth possibility is a net long-term capital loss (NLTCL). A fifth result is a net short-term capital loss (NSTCL). Finally, a sixth possibility includes both an NLTCL and an NSTCL. Neither NLTCLs nor NSTCLs are treated as ordinary losses. Treatment as an ordinary loss generally is preferable to capital loss treatment since ordinary losses are deductible in full while the deductibility of capital losses is subject to certain limitations. An individual taxpayer may deduct a maximum of $3,000 of net capital losses for a taxable year.[25]

CAPITAL GAIN AND LOSS NETTING PROCESS

Holding Periods for Capital Gain and Loss Netting Purposes

As mentioned earlier in this chapter, there are two holding periods for purposes of the capital gain and loss netting process:

- *Short term*—Assets held one year or less.
- *Long term*—Assets held more than one year.

Net short-term capital gain is not eligible for any special tax rate. It is taxed at the same rate as the taxpayer's other taxable income. *Net long-term capital gain* is eligible

[25] § 1211(b).

for one or more of *four* alternative tax rates: 0 percent, 15 percent, 25 percent, and 28 percent. The 25 percent and 28 percent rates are used only in somewhat unusual circumstances, so the discussion below concentrates more heavily on the other two rates. The net long-term capital gain components are referred to as the *0%/15% gain*, the *25% gain*, and the *28% gain.*

The *25% gain* is technically called the **unrecaptured § 1250 gain** and is related to gain from disposition of § 1231 assets. Gains and losses from disposition of § 1231 assets are discussed later in this chapter. The following discussion will focus only on how the *25% gain* is taxed and not how it is determined. The *28% gain* relates to collectibles and § 1202 gain (see Chapter 5). Collectibles gain is discussed later in this chapter.

The *0% gain* portion of the *0%/15% gain* applies when the taxable income before taxing the *0%/15% gain* does not put the taxpayer out of the 15 percent bracket. Once the taxable income (including any portion of the *0%/15% gain* taxed at 0 percent) puts the taxpayer above the 15 percent bracket, the remaining portion of the *0%/15% gain* is taxed at 15 percent rather than at the regular tax rate.

When the long-term capital gain exceeds the short-term capital loss, a **net capital gain (NCG)** exists.[26] Net capital gain qualifies for beneficial alternative tax treatment (see the coverage later in the chapter).

Since there are both short- and long-term capital gains and losses and because the long-term capital gains may be taxed at various rates, an *ordering procedure* is required. The ordering procedure tends to preserve the lowest tax rate long-term capital gain when there is a net long-term capital gain. This ordering procedure is explained in the steps below and then illustrated by several examples.

Step 1. Group all gains and losses into short term and 28%, 25%, and 0%/15% long term.

Step 2. Net the gains and losses within each group.

Step 3. Offset the net 28% and net 25% amounts if they are of opposite sign.

Step 4. Offset the results after step 3 against the 0%/15% amount if they are of opposite sign. If the 0%/15% amount is a loss, offset it against the *highest taxed gain first.* After this step, there is a net long-term capital gain or loss. If there is a net long-term capital gain, it may consist of only 28% gain, only 25% gain, only 0%/15% gain, or some combination of all of these gains. If there is a net long-term capital loss, it is simply a net long-term capital loss.

Step 5. Offset the net short-term amount against the results of step 4 if they are of opposite sign. The netting rules offset net short-term capital loss against the *highest taxed gain first.* Consequently, if there is a net short-term capital loss and a net gain from step 4, the short-term capital loss offsets first the 28% gain, then the 25% gain, and finally the 0%/15% gain.

If the result of step 5 is *only* a short-term capital gain, the taxpayer is not eligible for a reduced tax rate. If the result of step 5 is a loss, the taxpayer may be eligible for a *capital loss deduction* (discussed later in this chapter). If there was no offsetting in step 5 because the short-term and step 4 results were both gains *or* if the result of the offsetting is a long-term gain, a net capital gain exists, and the taxpayer may be eligible for a reduced tax rate. The net capital gain may consist of *28% gain, 25% gain,* and/or *0%/15% gain.*

The five steps outlined above can have many unique final results. See Concept Summary 14.5 later in the chapter for a summary of the netting rules and how capital gains and losses are taxed. The following series of examples illustrates the capital gain and loss netting process.

EXAMPLE 33

This example shows how a net short-term capital gain may result from the netting process.

[26] § 1222(11).

			Long-Term Gains and Losses			
Step	**Short Term**		**28%**	**25%**	**0%/15%**	**Comment**
1	$13,000		$ 12,000		$ 3,000	
	(2,000)		(20,000)			
2	$11,000		($ 8,000)		$ 3,000	
3						No 28%/25% netting because no opposite sign.
4			3,000	→	(3,000)	Netted because of opposite sign.
			($ 5,000)		$ –0–	
5	(5,000)	←	5,000			The net short-term capital gain is taxed as ordinary income.
	$ 6,000		$ –0–			
	Net short-term capital gain					

■

EXAMPLE 34

This example shows how a net long-term capital gain may result from the netting process.

			Long-Term Gains and Losses			
Step	**Short Term**		**28%**	**25%**	**0%/15%**	**Comment**
1	$ 3,000		$15,000	$4,000	$ 3,000	
	(5,000)		(7,000)		(8,000)	
2	($ 2,000)		$ 8,000	$4,000	($ 5,000)	
3						No 28%/25% netting because no opposite sign.
4			(5,000)	←	5,000	Netted because of opposite sign. Net 0%/15% loss is netted against 28% gain first.
			$ 3,000		$ –0–	
5	2,000	→	(2,000)			The net short-term capital loss is netted against 28% gain first. The net long-term capital gain is $5,000 ($1,000 + $4,000).
	$ –0–		$ 1,000	$4,000		
			Net 28% gain	Net 25% gain		

■

EXAMPLE 35

This example shows how a net long-term capital loss may result from the netting process.

			Long-Term Gains and Losses			
Step	**Short Term**		**28%**	**25%**	**0%/15%**	**Comment**
1	$3,000		$ 1,000		$ 3,000	
					(8,000)	
2	$3,000		$ 1,000		($ 5,000)	
3						No 28%/25% netting because no opposite sign.
4			(1,000)	→	1,000	Netted because of opposite sign.
			$ –0–		($ 4,000)	

(continued)

		Long-Term Gains and Losses			
Step	**Short Term**	**28%**	**25%**	**0%/15%**	**Comment**
5	(3,000) $ -0-	→	→	3,000 ($ 1,000) Net long-term capital loss	The net short-term capital gain is netted against the net long-term capital loss, and the remaining loss is eligible for the capital loss deduction.

■

Use of Capital Loss Carryovers

A short-term capital loss carryover to the current year retains its character as short term and is combined with the short-term items of the current year. A long-term net capital loss carries over as a long-term capital loss and is combined with the current-year long-term items. The long-term loss carryover is first offset with 28% gain of the current year, then 25% gain, and then 0%/15% gain until it is absorbed.

EXAMPLE 36

In 2011, Abigail has a $4,000 short-term capital gain, a $36,000 28% long-term capital gain, and a $13,000 0%/15% long-term capital gain. She also has a $3,000 short-term capital loss carryover and a $2,000 long-term capital loss carryover from 2010. This produces a $1,000 net short-term capital gain ($4,000 – $3,000), a $34,000 net 28% long-term capital gain ($36,000 – $2,000), and a $13,000 net 0%/15% long-term capital gain for 2011. ■

Definition of Collectibles

Capital assets that are collectibles, even though they are held long term, are not eligible for the *0%/15%* alternative tax rate. Instead, a 28 percent alternative tax rate applies.

For capital gain or loss purposes, **collectibles** include:[27]

- Any work of art.
- Any rug or antique.
- Any metal or gem.
- Any stamp.
- Any alcoholic beverage.
- Most coins.
- Any historical objects (documents, clothes, etc.).

QUALIFIED DIVIDEND INCOME

Dividends paid from current or accumulated earnings and profits of domestic and certain foreign corporations are eligible to be taxed at the 0%/15% long-term capital gain rates if they are **qualified dividend income.** The question of which dividends constitute qualified dividend income is discussed more fully in Chapter 4. Here the discussion focuses on how the qualified dividend income is taxed.

After the net capital gain or loss has been determined, the qualified dividend income is added to the net long-term capital gain portion of the net capital gain and is taxed as 0%/15% gain. If there is a net capital loss, the net capital loss is still deductible *for* AGI up to $3,000 per year with the remainder of the loss (if any) carrying forward. In this case, the qualified dividend income is still eligible to be treated as *0%/15% gain* in the alternative tax calculation (it is *not* offset by the net capital loss).

[27] § 408(m)(2) and Reg. § 1.408–10(b).

EXAMPLE 37

Refer to Example 34, but assume there is qualified dividend income of $2,500 in addition to the items shown. The qualified dividend income *is not* netted against the capital gains and losses. Instead, the taxpayer has $1,000 of 28% gain, $4,000 of 25% gain, *and* $2,500 of qualified dividend income taxed at 0%/15%. ■

EXAMPLE 38

Refer to Example 35, but assume there is qualified dividend income of $2,500 in addition to the items shown. The qualified dividend income *is not* netted against the net capital loss. The taxpayer has a $1,000 capital loss deduction *and* $2,500 of qualified dividend income taxed at 0%/15%. ■

ALTERNATIVE TAX ON NET CAPITAL GAIN

Section 1 contains the statutory provisions that enable the *net capital gain* to be taxed at special rates (0, 15, 25, and 28 percent). This calculation is referred to as the **alternative tax** on net capital gain.[28] The alternative tax applies only if taxable income includes some long-term capital gain (there is net capital gain). Taxable income includes *all* of the net capital gain unless taxable income is less than the net capital gain. In addition, the net capital gain is taxed *last*, after other taxable income (including any short-term capital gain).

EXAMPLE 39

Joan, an unmarried taxpayer, has 2011 taxable income of $98,000, including a $12,000 net capital gain. The last $12,000 of her $98,000 taxable income is the layer related to the net capital gain. The first $86,000 ($98,000 – $12,000) of her taxable income is not subject to any special tax rate, so it is taxed using the regular tax rates. ■

Since the net capital gain may be made up of various *rate layers*, it is important to know in what order those layers will be taxed. For *each* of the layers, the taxpayer compares the regular tax rate on that layer of income and the alternative tax rate on that portion of the net capital gain. The layers are taxed in the following order: *25% gain, 28% gain*, the 0 percent portion of the *0%/15% gain*, and then the 15 percent portion of the *0%/15% gain*. As a result of this layering, the taxpayer will benefit from the 0 percent portion of the net capital gain if the taxpayer is still in the 10 percent or 15 percent regular rate bracket after taxing other taxable income and the 25 percent and 28 percent portions of the net capital gain.

EXAMPLE 40

Assume that Joan's $12,000 net capital gain in Example 39 is made up of $10,000 *25% gain* and $2,000 *0%/15% gain*. Examination of the 2011 tax rates reveals that $86,000 of taxable income for a single individual puts Joan at a marginal tax rate of 28%. Consequently, she will use the alternative tax on both the $10,000 gain and the $2,000 gain. Her alternative tax liability for 2011 is $20,497 [$17,697 (tax on $86,000 of taxable income) + $2,500 ($10,000 × .25) + $300 ($2,000 × .15)]. Since the combination of the $86,000 taxable income and her $10,000 *25% gain* puts her above the 15% regular tax bracket, none of the $2,000 *0%/15% gain* is taxed at 0%. Her regular tax liability on $98,000 would be $21,057. Thus, Joan saves $560 ($21,057 – $20,497) by using the alternative tax calculation. ■

EXAMPLE 41

Joan, an unmarried taxpayer, has 2011 taxable income of $25,000. Of this amount, $12,000 is net capital gain, and $13,000 is other taxable income. The net capital gain is made up of $8,300 of *25% gain* and $3,700 of *0%/15% gain* (including $1,000 of qualified dividend income). Her alternative tax liability for 2011 is $2,770 [$1,525 (tax on $13,000 of taxable income) + $1,245 (tax on $8,300 *25% gain* at 15%) + $0 (tax on $3,700

[28] § 1(h). Note: Examples 40, 41, and 42 use the 2011 Tax Rate Schedules rather than the 2011 Tax Table to calculate the tax on the non-long-term capital gain portion of taxable income. This approach is used to better illustrate the concepts under discussion. The actual tax on the non-long-term portion of taxable income would be calculated using the Tax Tables since that income is less than $100,000.

CONCEPT SUMMARY 14.4

Income Layers for Alternative Tax on Capital Gain Computation

Compute tax on:		Ordinary taxable income (including net short-term capital gain) using the regular tax rates.
Compute tax on:		Each of the layers below using the *lower* of the alternative tax rate or the regular tax rate for that layer (or portion of a layer) of taxable income.
	+	25% long-term capital gain (unrecaptured § 1250 gain) portion of taxable income
	+	28% long-term capital gain
	+	0% long-term capital gain (portion of 0%/15% capital gain that is taxed at 0%; available only if ordinary taxable income plus 25% and 28% capital gain layers do not put the taxpayer above the 15% bracket; 0% rate is no longer available once income including the portion of the gain taxed at 0% puts the taxpayer out of the 15% bracket)*
	+	15% long-term capital gain (remaining portion of 0%/15% capital gain)*
	=	Alternative tax on taxable income

*May include qualified dividend income.

0%/15% gain at 0%)]. Since her marginal rate is still 15% after taxing the $13,000 of other taxable income, she uses the 15% regular tax rate rather than the 25% alternative tax rate on the $8,300 *25% gain*. After taxing the $13,000 and the $8,300, a total of $21,300 of the $25,000 taxable income has been taxed. Since her marginal rate is still 15%, she uses the 0% alternative rate for the $3,700 of *0%/15% gain*. The $1,000 qualified dividend income is included in the $3,700 and, thus, is also taxed at 0%. Joan's regular tax liability on $25,000 would be $3,325. Thus, she saves $555 ($3,325 – $2,770) by using the alternative tax calculation. ■

The alternative tax computation allows the taxpayer to receive the *lower of* the regular tax or the alternative tax on *each layer* of net capital gain or *portion of each layer* of net capital gain.

EXAMPLE 42

Assume the same facts as in Example 41 except that Joan's taxable income is $36,000, consisting of $12,000 of net capital gain and $24,000 of other taxable income. Not all of the $3,700 of *0%/15% gain* is taxed at 0% because Joan's taxable income exceeds $34,000, taking her out of the 15% bracket. Consequently, the last $1,500 ($36,000 – $34,500) of the $3,700 of *0%/15% gain* is taxed at 15% rather than 0%. Her tax liability using the alternative tax computation is $4,645 [$3,175 (tax on $24,000 of taxable income) + $1,245 (tax on $8,300 *25% gain* at 15%) + $0 (tax on $2,200 of *0%/15% gain* at 0%) + $225 (tax on $1,500 of *0%/15% gain* at 15%)]. Joan's regular tax liability on $36,000 would be $5,125. Thus, she saves $480 ($5,125 – $4,645) by using the alternative tax calculation. ■

Concept Summary 14.4 summarizes the alternative tax computation.

TREATMENT OF CAPITAL LOSSES

Computation of Net Capital Loss

A **net capital loss (NCL)** results if capital losses exceed capital gains for the year. An NCL may be all long term, all short term, or part long and part short term.[29] The characterization of an NCL as long or short term is important in determining the capital loss deduction (discussed later in this chapter).

[29]Section 1222(10) defines a net capital loss as the net loss after the capital loss deduction. However, that definition confuses the discussion of net capital loss. Therefore, net capital loss is used here to mean the result after netting capital gains and losses and before considering the capital loss deduction. The capital loss deduction is discussed under Treatment of Net Capital Loss in this chapter.

TAX *in* the NEWS

A Simple Solution to Avoiding the $3,000 Limit on Deducting Capital Losses Against Ordinary Income

Tom Herman wrote a weekly tax column in the *Wall Street Journal* for more than 16 years. In his final column, which appeared on April 15, 2009 (a very appropriate day!), he told about a question from a senior citizen on how to get around the $3,000 limit on deducting net capital losses.

It seems that the individual had amassed capital losses in the stock market of $2.1 million, but at $3,000 per year, he would not come close to living long enough to offset that amount of losses. His accountant had advised him to marry a woman with large capital gains. The couple would not even have to live together. In fact, after the $2.1 million loss was used up to offset capital gains, they could get a divorce. Of course, a prenuptial agreement would protect each spouse's separate assets.

The senior citizen liked the accountant's advice. So why was he writing to Tom Herman? First, he wanted Tom's advice on how to "find such a lady." Second, should he offer a reward (and how much) to anyone who would help him find her?

Source: Adapted from Tom Herman, "What I Learned in Over 16 Years on the Tax Beat," *Wall Street Journal*, April 15, 2009, p. Dl.

EXAMPLE 43

Three different individual taxpayers have the following capital gains and losses during the year:

Taxpayer	LTCG	LTCL	STCG	STCL	Result of Netting	Description of Result
Robert	$1,000	($ 2,800)	$1,000	($ 500)	($ 1,300)	NLTCL
Carlos	1,000	(500)	1,000	(2,800)	(1,300)	NSTCL
Troy	400	(1,200)	500	(1,200)	(1,500)	NLTCL ($800) NSTCL ($700)

Robert's NCL of $1,300 is all long term. Carlos's NCL of $1,300 is all short term. Troy's NCL is $1,500, $800 of which is long term and $700 of which is short term. ■

Treatment of Net Capital Loss

An NCL is deductible from gross income to the extent of $3,000 per tax year.[30] Capital losses exceeding the loss deduction limits carry forward indefinitely. Thus, although there may or may not be beneficial treatment for capital gains, there is *unfavorable* treatment for capital losses in terms of the $3,000 annual limitation on deducting NCL against ordinary income. If the NCL includes both long-term and short-term capital loss, the short-term capital loss is counted first toward the $3,000 annual limitation.

EXAMPLE 44

Burt has an NCL of $5,500, of which $2,000 is STCL and $3,500 is LTCL. Burt has a capital loss deduction of $3,000 ($2,000 of STCL and $1,000 of LTCL). He has an LTCL carryforward of $2,500 ($3,500 – $1,000). ■

Carryovers

Taxpayers are allowed to carry over unused capital losses indefinitely. The short-term capital loss (STCL) retains its character as STCL. Likewise the long-term capital loss retains its character as LTCL.

[30] § 1211(b)(1). Married persons filing separate returns are limited to a $1,500 deduction per tax year.

CONCEPT SUMMARY 14.5

Some Possible Final Results of the Capital Gain and Loss Netting Process and How They Are Taxed

Result	Maximum Tax Rate	Comments
Net short-term capital loss	—	Eligible for capital loss deduction ($3,000 maximum per year).
Net long-term capital loss	—	Eligible for capital loss deduction ($3,000 maximum per year).
Net short-term capital loss *and* net long-term capital loss	—	Eligible for capital loss deduction ($3,000 maximum per year). Short-term capital losses are counted first toward the deduction.
Net short-term capital gain	10–35%	Taxed as ordinary income.
Net long-term capital gain	0–28%	The net long-term capital gain may have as many as four tax rate components: 25%, 28%, and 0%/15%.
• The net long-term capital gain is the *last* portion of taxable income.		The components are taxed in the following order: 25%, 28%, 0%, 15%. They are taxed *after* the non-long-term capital gain portion of taxable income has been taxed. The 0%/15% component may include qualified dividend income.
• Each net long-term capital gain component of taxable income is taxed at the *lower* of the regular tax on that component or the alternative tax.		The alternative tax on net long-term capital gain can never increase the tax on taxable income, but it can reduce the tax on taxable income.
Net short-term capital gain *and* net long-term capital gain	10–35% on net short-term capital gain; 0–28% on net long-term capital gain	The net short-term capital gain is taxed as ordinary income; the net long-term capital gain is taxed as discussed above for just net long-term capital gain.

EXAMPLE 45

In 2011, Mark incurred $1,000 of STCL and $11,000 of LTCL. In 2012, Mark has a $400 LTCG.

- Mark's NCL for 2011 is $12,000. Mark deducts $3,000 ($1,000 STCL and $2,000 LTCL). He has $9,000 of LTCL carried forward to 2012.
- Mark combines the $9,000 LTCL carryforward with the $400 LTCG for 2012. He has an $8,600 NLTCL for 2012. Mark deducts $3,000 of LTCL in 2012 and carries forward $5,600 of LTCL to 2013. ■

When a taxpayer has both a capital loss deduction and negative taxable income, a special computation of the capital loss carryover is required.[31] Specifically, the capital loss carryover is the NCL minus the lesser of:

- The capital loss deduction claimed on the return.
- The negative taxable income increased by the capital loss deduction claimed on the return and the personal and dependency exemption deduction.

Without this provision, some of the tax benefit of the capital loss deduction would be wasted when the deduction drives taxable income below zero. However, the capital loss deduction is not reduced if taxable income before the exemption deduction is a positive number or zero. In that situation, it is the exemption deduction, and not the capital loss deduction, that is creating the negative taxable income.

[31] § 1212(b).

TAX *in* the NEWS

INVESTMENT CONFUSION

A recent newspaper article discussed the many investment opportunities available to purchase foreclosed real estate, fix it up, and then either sell the property for a capital gain or rent it to people who can no longer afford to purchase a home. The article was misleading because such property is not a capital asset. If it is held for resale in the ordinary course of business, it is an ordinary asset. If it is held more than a year and rented to others, it is a § 1231 asset. In either case, the asset is not a capital asset.

EXAMPLE 46

In 2011, Joanne has a $13,000 NCL (all long term), a $3,700 personal exemption deduction, and $4,000 negative taxable income. The negative taxable income includes a $3,000 capital loss deduction. The capital loss carryover to 2012 is $10,300 computed as follows:

- The $4,000 negative taxable income is treated as a negative number, but the capital loss deduction and personal exemption deduction are treated as positive numbers.
- The normal ceiling on the capital loss deduction is $3,000.
- However, if the $3,000 capital loss deduction and the $3,700 exemption deduction are added back to the $4,000 negative taxable income, only $2,700 of the $3,000 capital loss deduction is needed to make taxable income equal to zero.
- Therefore, this special computation results in only $2,700 of the $13,000 NCL being consumed. The LTCL carryforward is $10,300 ($13,000 – $2,700). ■

Concept Summary 14.5 summarizes the rules for noncorporate taxpayers' treatment of capital gains and losses.

14.6 Tax Treatment of Capital Gains and Losses of Corporate Taxpayers

LO.6

Describe the tax treatment for capital gains and the detrimental tax treatment for capital losses for corporate taxpayers.

The treatment of a corporation's net capital gain or loss differs from the rules for individuals. Briefly, the differences are as follows:

- There is an NCG alternative tax rate of 35 percent.[32] However, since the maximum corporate tax rate is 35 percent, the alternative tax is not beneficial.
- Capital losses offset only capital gains. No deduction of capital losses is permitted against ordinary taxable income (whereas a $3,000 deduction is allowed to individuals).[33]
- Corporations may carry back net capital losses (whether long term or short term) as short-term capital losses for three years; if losses still remain after the carryback, the remaining losses may be carried forward five years.[34] Individuals may carry forward unused capital losses indefinitely, but there is no carryback.

EXAMPLE 47

Sparrow Corporation has a $15,000 NLTCL for the current year and $57,000 of ordinary taxable income. Sparrow may not offset the $15,000 NLTCL against its ordinary income by taking a capital loss deduction. The $15,000 NLTCL becomes a $15,000 STCL for carryback and carryover purposes. This amount may be offset by capital gains in the three-year carryback period or, if not absorbed there, offset by capital gains in the five-year carryforward period. ■

[32] § 1201.

[33] § 1211(a).

[34] § 1212(a)(1).

14.7 Overview of § 1231 and the Recapture Provisions

Generic Motors Corporation sold machinery, office furniture, and unneeded production plants for $100 million last year. The corporation's disposition of these assets resulted in $60 million of gains and $13 million of losses. How are these gains and losses treated for tax purposes? Do any special tax rules apply? Could any of the gains and losses receive capital gain or loss treatment? The remainder of this chapter answers these questions by explaining how to *classify* gains and losses from the disposition of assets that are used in the business rather than held for resale. Chapter 8 discussed how to *depreciate* such assets. Chapter 13 discussed how to determine the *adjusted basis* and the *amount* of gain or loss from their disposition.

A long-term capital gain was defined earlier in this chapter as the recognized gain from the sale or exchange of a capital asset held for the required long-term holding period.[35] Long-term capital assets are capital assets held more than one year.

The remainder of this chapter is concerned with classification under § 1231, which applies to the sale or exchange of business properties and to certain involuntary conversions. The business properties are not capital assets because they are depreciable and/or real property used in business or for the production of income. Section 1221(a)(2) provides that such assets are not capital assets. Nonetheless, these business properties may be held for long periods of time and may be sold at a gain. Congress decided many years ago that such assets deserved *limited* capital gain–type treatment. Unfortunately, this limited capital gain–type treatment is very complex and difficult to understand.

Because the limited capital gain–type treatment sometimes gives too much tax advantage if assets are eligible for depreciation (or cost recovery), certain recapture rules may prevent the capital gain treatment when depreciation is taken. Thus, this chapter also covers the recapture provisions that tax as ordinary income certain gains that might otherwise qualify for long-term capital gain treatment.

14.8 Section 1231 Assets

LO.7

Understand the rationale for and the nature and treatment of gains and losses from the disposition of business assets.

RELATIONSHIP TO CAPITAL ASSETS

Depreciable property and real property used in business are not capital assets.[36] Thus, the recognized gains from the disposition of such property (principally machinery, equipment, buildings, and land) would appear to be ordinary income rather than capital gain. Due to § 1231, however, *net gain* from the disposition of such property is sometimes *treated* as *long-term capital gain.* A long-term holding period requirement must be met; the disposition must generally be from a sale, exchange, or involuntary conversion; and certain recapture provisions must be satisfied for this result to occur. Section 1231 may also apply to involuntary conversions of capital assets. Since an involuntary conversion is not a sale or exchange, such a disposition normally would not result in a capital gain.

If the disposition of depreciable property and real property used in business results in a *net loss,* § 1231 *treats* the *loss* as an *ordinary loss* rather than as a capital loss. Ordinary losses are fully deductible *for* adjusted gross income (AGI). Capital losses are offset by capital gains, and, if any loss remains, the loss is deductible to the extent of $3,000 per year for individuals and currently is not deductible at all by regular corporations. It seems, therefore, that § 1231 provides the *best* of both potential results: net gain may be treated as long-term capital gain, and net loss is treated as ordinary loss.

EXAMPLE 48

Roberto sells business land and a building at a $5,000 gain and business equipment at a $3,000 loss. Both properties were held for the long-term holding period. Roberto's net

[35] § 1222(3). To be eligible for any beneficial tax treatment, the holding period must be more than one year.

[36] § 1221(a)(2).

gain is $2,000, and that net gain may (depending on various recapture rules discussed later in this chapter) be treated as a long-term capital gain under § 1231. ■

EXAMPLE 49

Samantha sells business equipment at a $10,000 loss and business land at a $2,000 gain. Both properties were held for the long-term holding period. Samantha's net loss is $8,000, and that net loss is an ordinary loss. ■

The rules regarding § 1231 treatment do *not* apply to *all* business property. Important in this regard are the holding period requirements and the fact that the property must be either depreciable property or real estate used in business. Nor is § 1231 necessarily limited to business property. Transactions involving certain capital assets may fall into the § 1231 category. Thus, § 1231 singles out only some types of business property.

As discussed earlier in this chapter, long-term capital gains receive beneficial tax treatment. Section 1231 requires netting of **§ 1231 gains and losses**. If the result is a gain, it may be treated as a long-term capital gain. The net gain is added to the "real" long-term capital gains (if any) and netted with capital losses (if any). Thus, the net § 1231 gain may eventually be eligible for beneficial capital gain treatment or help avoid the unfavorable net capital loss result. The § 1231 gain and loss netting may result in a loss. In this case, the loss is an ordinary loss and is deductible *for* AGI. Finally, § 1231 assets are treated the same as capital assets for purposes of the appreciated property charitable contribution provisions (refer to Chapter 10).

JUSTIFICATION FOR FAVORABLE TAX TREATMENT

The favorable capital gain/ordinary loss treatment sanctioned by § 1231 can be explained by examining several historical developments. Before 1938, business property had been included in the definition of capital assets. Thus, if such property was sold for a loss (not an unlikely possibility during the depression years of the 1930s), a capital loss resulted. If, however, the property was depreciable and could be retained for its estimated useful life, much (if not all) of its costs could be recovered in the form of depreciation. Because the allowance for depreciation was fully deductible whereas capital losses were not, the tax law favored those who did not dispose of an asset. Congress recognized this inequity when it removed business property from the capital asset classification. During the period 1938–1942, therefore, all such gains and losses were ordinary gains and losses.

With the advent of World War II, two developments in particular forced Congress to reexamine the situation regarding business assets. First, the sale of business assets at a gain was discouraged because the gain would be ordinary income. Gains were common because the war effort had inflated prices. Second, taxpayers who did not want to sell their assets often were required to because the government acquired them through condemnation. Often, as a result of the condemnation awards, taxpayers who were forced to part with their property experienced large gains and were deprived of the benefits of future depreciation deductions. Of course, the condemnations constituted involuntary conversions, so taxpayers could defer the gain by timely reinvestment in property that was "similar or related in service or use." But where was such property to be found in view of wartime restrictions and other governmental condemnations? The end result did not seem equitable: a large ordinary gain due to government action and no possibility of deferral due to government restrictions.

In recognition of these conditions, in 1942, Congress eased the tax bite on the disposition of some business property by allowing preferential capital gain treatment. Thus, the present scheme of § 1231 and the dichotomy of capital gain/ordinary loss treatment evolved from a combination of economic considerations existing in 1938 and 1942.

PROPERTY INCLUDED

LO.8

Distinguish § 1231 assets from ordinary assets and capital assets and calculate the § 1231 gain or loss.

Section 1231 property generally includes the following assets if they are held for more than one year:

- Depreciable or real property used in business or for the production of income (principally machinery and equipment, buildings, and land).

TAX in the NEWS

TIMBER THINNING IS ENVIRONMENTALLY SOUND AND GOOD BUSINESS

Modern timber forests are regularly "thinned" to prevent the buildup of dry debris. Eliminating this dry debris helps to prevent forest fires from spreading. Thinning also clears out smaller trees and allows the other trees to grow bigger and straighter. The tax rules give favorable treatment to timber cutting and thus encourage this environmentally sound activity. Section 631(a) allows the taxpayer to elect to treat the cutting of timber as a sale or exchange and, if the election is made, to treat the sale as the disposition of a § 1231 asset.

- Timber, coal, or domestic iron ore to which § 631 applies.
- Livestock held for draft, breeding, dairy, or sporting purposes.
- Unharvested crops on land used in business.
- Certain *purchased* intangible assets (such as patents and goodwill) that are eligible for amortization.

These assets are ordinary assets until they have been held for more than one year. Only then do they become § 1231 assets.

PROPERTY EXCLUDED

Section 1231 property generally does *not* include the following:

- Property not held for the long-term holding period. Since the benefit of § 1231 is long-term capital gain treatment, the holding period must correspond to the more-than-one-year holding period that applies to capital assets. Livestock must be held at least 12 months (24 months in some cases).[37] Unharvested crops do not have to be held for the required long-term holding period, but the land must be held for the long-term holding period.
- Nonpersonal use property where casualty losses exceed casualty gains for the taxable year. If a taxpayer has a net casualty loss, the individual casualty gains and losses are treated as ordinary gains and losses.
- Inventory and property held primarily for sale to customers.
- Copyrights; literary, musical, or artistic compositions, etc.; and certain U.S. government publications.
- Accounts receivable and notes receivable arising in the ordinary course of the trade or business.

SECTION 1231 ASSETS DISPOSED OF BY CASUALTY OR THEFT

When § 1231 assets are disposed of by casualty or theft, a special netting rule is applied. For simplicity, the term *casualty* is used to mean both casualty and theft dispositions. First, the casualty gains and losses from § 1231 assets *and* the casualty gains and losses from **long-term nonpersonal use capital assets** are determined. A nonpersonal use capital asset might be an investment painting or a baseball card collection held by a nondealer in baseball cards.

Next, the § 1231 asset casualty gains and losses and the nonpersonal use capital asset casualty gains and losses are netted together (see Concept Summary 14.6). If the result is a *net loss*, the § 1231 casualty gains and the nonpersonal use capital asset casualty gains are treated as ordinary gains, the § 1231 casualty losses are deductible *for* AGI, and the nonpersonal use capital asset casualty losses are deductible *from* AGI subject to the 2 percent-of-AGI limitation.

If the result of the netting is a *net gain*, the net gain is treated as a § 1231 gain. Thus, a § 1231 asset disposed of by casualty may or may not get § 1231 treatment, depending on whether the netting process results in a gain or a loss. Also, a

[37] Note that the holding period is "12 months or more" and not "more than 12 months."

CONCEPT SUMMARY 14.6

Section 1231 Netting Procedure

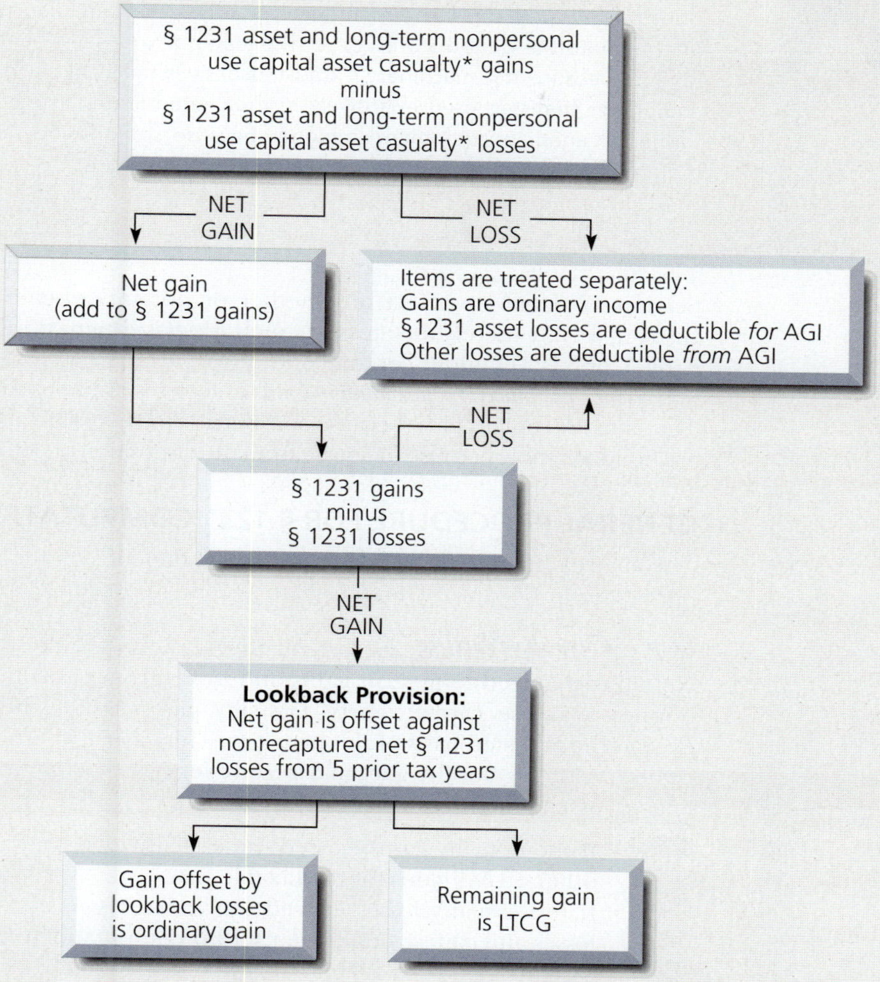

*Includes casualties and thefts.

nonpersonal use capital asset disposed of by casualty may get § 1231 treatment or ordinary treatment, but will not get capital gain or loss treatment!

Personal use property casualty gains and losses are not subject to the § 1231 rules. If the result of netting these gains and losses is a gain, the net gain is a capital gain. If the netting results in a loss, the net loss is a deduction *from* AGI to the extent it exceeds 10 percent of AGI.

Casualties, thefts, and condemnations are *involuntary conversions.* Involuntary conversion gains may be deferred if conversion proceeds are reinvested; involuntary conversion losses are recognized currently (refer to Chapter 13) regardless of whether the conversion proceeds are reinvested. Thus, the special netting process discussed previously for casualties and thefts would not include gains that are not currently recognizable because the insurance proceeds are reinvested.

The special netting process for casualties and thefts also does not include condemnation gains and losses. Consequently, a § 1231 asset disposed of by condemnation will receive § 1231 treatment. This variation between recognized casualty and condemnation gains and losses sheds considerable light on what § 1231 is all about.

GLOBAL
Tax Issues

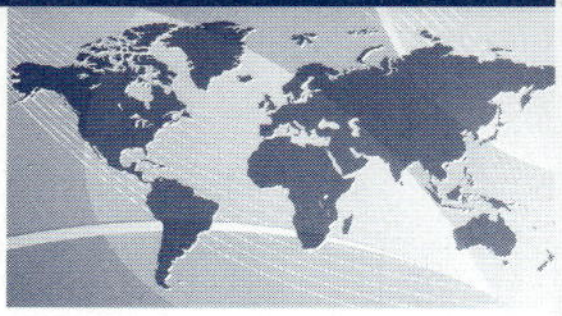

Canadian Slow Depreciation

A manufacturer has a division in Canada that manufactures auto components. The components are shipped to Detroit and become part of U.S.-manufactured automobiles. Due to slow auto sales, the manufacturer closes the Canadian plant and moves its machinery to the United States. Later, the manufacturer sells the machinery and has a tax loss because the machinery's adjusted basis is much higher than that of similar equipment that was used exclusively in the United States. The adjusted basis of the formerly Canadian equipment is higher because straight-line tax depreciation was required for the Canadian property (see Chapter 8).

Section 1231 has no effect on whether or not *realized* gain or loss is recognized. Instead, § 1231 merely dictates how such *recognized* gain or loss is *classified* (ordinary, capital, or § 1231) under certain conditions.

Personal use property condemnation gains and losses are not subject to the § 1231 rules. The gains are capital gains (because personal use property is a capital asset), and the losses are nondeductible because they arise from the disposition of personal use property.

GENERAL PROCEDURE FOR § 1231 COMPUTATION

The tax treatment of § 1231 gains and losses depends on the results of a rather complex *netting* procedure. The steps in this netting procedure are as follows.

Step 1: Casualty Netting

Net all recognized long-term gains and losses from casualties of § 1231 assets and nonpersonal use capital assets. Casualty gains result when insurance proceeds exceed the adjusted basis of the property. This casualty netting is beneficial because if there is a net gain, the gain may receive long-term capital gain treatment. If there is a net loss, it receives ordinary loss treatment.

a. If the casualty gains exceed the casualty losses, add the excess to the other § 1231 gains for the taxable year.
b. If the casualty losses exceed the casualty gains, exclude all casualty losses and gains from further § 1231 computation. If this is the case, all casualty gains are ordinary income. Section 1231 asset casualty losses are deductible *for* AGI. Other casualty losses are deductible *from* AGI.

Step 2: § 1231 Netting

After adding any net casualty gain from Step 1a to the other § 1231 gains and losses (including recognized § 1231 asset condemnation gains and losses), net all § 1231 gains and losses.

a. If the gains exceed the losses, the net gain is offset by the "lookback" nonrecaptured § 1231 losses (see below) from the five prior tax years. To the extent of this offset, the net § 1231 gain is classified as ordinary gain. Any remaining gain is long-term capital gain.
b. If the losses exceed the gains, all gains are ordinary income. Section 1231 asset losses are deductible *for* AGI. Other casualty losses are deductible *from* AGI.

Step 3: § 1231 Lookback Provision

The net § 1231 gain from Step 2a is offset by the nonrecaptured net § 1231 losses for the five preceding taxable years. For 2011, the lookback years are 2006, 2007, 2008, 2009, and 2010. To the extent of the nonrecaptured net § 1231 loss, the current-year net § 1231 gain is ordinary income. The *nonrecaptured* net § 1231 losses are those that

TAX *in the NEWS* — Loss from Cattle Rustling

A newspaper in "cattle country" reported that rustlers had stolen 20 head of prime milk cows from a local ranch. The rancher never recovered the cows. According to the article, the rancher had no insurance on the cows and was upset because he had no way of recovering his loss. A CPA might advise the rancher that he could be entitled to a special "theft loss" for tax purposes because the theft loss rules apply to § 1231 assets such as cattle held for 24 months or more.

have not already been used to offset net § 1231 gains. Only the net § 1231 gain exceeding this net § 1231 loss carryforward is given long-term capital gain treatment. Concept Summary 14.6 summarizes the § 1231 computational procedure. Examples 52 and 53 illustrate the **§ 1231 lookback** provision.

Examples 50 through 53 illustrate the application of the § 1231 computation procedure.

EXAMPLE 50

During 2011, Ross had $125,000 of AGI before considering the following recognized gains and losses:

Capital Gains and Losses	
Long-term capital gain	$3,000
Long-term capital loss	(400)
Short-term capital gain	1,000
Short-term capital loss	(200)
Casualties	
Theft of diamond ring (owned four months)	($ 800)*
Fire damage to personal residence (owned 10 years)	(400)*
Gain from insurance recovery on fire loss to business building (owned two years)	200
§ 1231 Gains and Losses from Depreciable Business Assets Held Long Term	
Asset A	$ 300
Asset B	1,100
Asset C	(500)
Gains and Losses from Sale of Depreciable Business Assets Held Short Term	
Asset D	$ 200
Asset E	(300)

*As adjusted for the $100 floor on personal casualty losses.

Ross had no net § 1231 losses in tax years before 2011.

Disregarding the recapture of depreciation (discussed later in the chapter), Ross's gains and losses receive the following tax treatment:

- The diamond ring and the residence are personal use assets. Therefore, these casualties are not § 1231 transactions. The $800 (ring) plus $400 (residence) losses are potentially deductible *from* AGI. However, the total loss of $1,200 does not exceed 10% of AGI. Thus, only the business building (a § 1231 asset) casualty gain remains. The netting of the § 1231 asset and non-personal use capital asset casualty gains and losses contains only one item—the $200 gain from the business building. Consequently, there is a net gain and that gain is treated as a § 1231 gain (added to the § 1231 gains).
- The gains from § 1231 transactions (Assets A, B, and C and the § 1231 asset casualty gain) exceed the losses by $1,100 ($1,600 − $500). This excess is a long-term capital gain and is added to Ross's other long-term capital gains.

- Ross's net long-term capital gain is $3,700 ($3,000 + $1,100 from § 1231 transactions − $400 long-term capital loss). Ross's net short-term capital gain is $800 ($1,000 − $200). The result is capital gain net income of $4,500. The $3,700 net long-term capital gain portion is eligible for beneficial capital gain treatment [assume all the gain is 0%/15% gain (see the discussion earlier in this chapter)]. The $800 net short-term capital gain is subject to tax as ordinary income.[38]
- Ross treats the gain and loss from Assets D and E (depreciable business assets held for less than the long-term holding period) as ordinary gain and loss.

Results of the Gains and Losses on Ross's Tax Computation	
NLTCG	$ 3,700
NSTCG	800
Ordinary gain from sale of Asset D	200
Ordinary loss from sale of Asset E	(300)
AGI from other sources	125,000
AGI	$129,400

- Ross will have personal use property casualty losses of $1,200 [$800 (diamond ring) + $400 (personal residence)]. A personal use property casualty loss is deductible only to the extent it exceeds 10% of AGI. Thus, none of the $1,200 is deductible ($129,400 × 10% = $12,940). ■

EXAMPLE 51

Assume the same facts as in Example 50, except the loss from Asset C was $1,700 instead of $500.

- The treatment of the casualty losses is the same as in Example 50.
- The losses from § 1231 transactions now exceed the gains by $100 ($1,700 − $1,600). As a result, the gains from Assets A and B and the § 1231 asset casualty gain are ordinary income, and the loss from Asset C is a deduction *for* AGI (a business loss). The same result can be achieved by simply treating the $100 net loss as a deduction *for* AGI.
- Capital gain net income is $3,400 ($2,600 long term + $800 short term). The $2,600 net long-term capital gain portion is eligible for beneficial capital gain treatment, and the $800 net short-term capital gain is subject to tax as ordinary income.

Results of the Gains and Losses on Ross's Tax Computation	
NLTCG	$ 2,600
NSTCG	800
Net ordinary loss on Assets A, B, and C and § 1231 casualty gain	(100)
Ordinary gain from sale of Asset D	200
Ordinary loss from sale of Asset E	(300)
AGI from other sources	125,000
AGI	$128,200

- None of the personal use property casualty losses will be deductible since $1,200 does not exceed 10% of $128,200. ■

[38] Ross's taxable income (unless the itemized deductions and the personal exemption and dependency deductions are extremely large) will put him in at least the 28% bracket. Thus, the alternative tax computation will yield a lower tax. See Example 40.

TAX *in* the NEWS

Ask the CPA about Recapture

A local newspaper includes a column called "Ask the CPA." A subscriber asked whether there were any differences between § 1245 recapture related to depreciable tangible personal property and that related to amortizable intangible personal property. The CPA wrote back that accelerated depreciation is usually used for tangible personal property, whereas straight-line amortization is used for intangible personal property. Consequently, the adjusted basis for the tangible personal property tends to be lower than that of the intangible personal property. If the properties had the same original cost and the same fair market value when they were sold, the tangible personal property would result in the larger gain and, therefore, the larger amount subject to recapture as ordinary income under § 1245.

EXAMPLE 52

Assume the same facts as in Example 50, except that Ross has a $700 nonrecaptured net § 1231 loss from 2010.

- The treatment of the casualty losses is the same as in Example 50.
- The 2011 net § 1231 gain of $1,100 is treated as ordinary income to the extent of the 2010 nonrecaptured § 1231 loss of $700. The remaining $400 net § 1231 gain is a long-term capital gain and is added to Ross's other long-term capital gains.
- Ross's net long-term capital gain is $3,000 ($3,000 + $400 from § 1231 transactions − $400 long-term capital loss). Ross's net short-term capital gain is still $800 ($1,000 − $200). The result is capital gain net income of $3,800. The $3,000 net long-term capital gain portion is eligible for beneficial capital gain treatment, and the $800 net short-term capital gain is subject to tax as ordinary income.

Results of the Gains and Losses on Ross's Tax Computation	
NLTCG	$ 3,000
NSTCG	800
Ordinary gain from recapture of § 1231 losses	700
Ordinary gain from sale of Asset D	200
Ordinary loss from sale of Asset E	(300)
AGI from other sources	125,000
AGI	$129,400

- None of the personal use property casualty losses will be deductible since $1,200 does not exceed 10% of $129,400. ■

EXAMPLE 53

Assume the same facts as in Example 50, except that Ross had a net § 1231 loss of $2,700 in 2009 and a net § 1231 gain of $300 in 2010.

- The treatment of the casualty losses is the same as in Example 50.
- The 2009 net § 1231 loss of $2,700 will have carried over to 2010 and been offset against the 2010 net § 1231 gain of $300. Thus, the $300 gain will have been classified as ordinary income, and $2,400 of nonrecaptured 2009 net § 1231 loss will carry over to 2011. The 2011 net § 1231 gain of $1,100 will be offset against this loss, resulting in $1,100 of ordinary income. The nonrecaptured net § 1231 loss of $1,300 ($2,400 − $1,100) carries over to 2012.
- Capital gain net income is $3,400 ($2,600 net long-term capital gain + $800 net short-term capital gain). The $2,600 net long-term capital gain portion

is eligible for beneficial capital gain treatment, and the $800 net short-term capital gain is subject to tax as ordinary income.

Results of the Gains and Losses on Ross's Tax Computation	
NLTCG	$ 2,600
NSTCG	800
Ordinary gain from recapture of § 1231 losses	1,100
Ordinary gain from sale of Asset D	200
Ordinary loss from sale of Asset E	(300)
AGI from other sources	125,000
AGI	$129,400

- None of the personal use property casualty losses will be deductible since $1,200 does not exceed 10% of $129,400. ■

ETHICS *& Equity*

PREPARING RETURNS WITHOUT PROPER INFORMATION

A CPA firm is preparing the tax return of a new client who says he has had numerous transactions involving sales of business depreciable property in prior years. The client lost all his tax records in a recent hurricane. The client's transactions for the current year result in a net § 1231 gain. Can the CPA firm complete this return without further information?

14.9 SECTION 1245 RECAPTURE

LO.9

Determine when § 1245 recapture applies and how it is computed.

Now that the basic rules of § 1231 have been introduced, it is time to add some complications. The Code contains two major *recapture* provisions—§§ 1245 and 1250. These provisions cause *gain* to be treated *initially* as ordinary gain. Thus, what may appear to be a § 1231 gain is ordinary gain instead. These recapture provisions may also cause a gain in a nonpersonal use casualty to be *initially* ordinary gain rather than casualty gain. Classifying gains (and losses) properly initially is important because improper initial classification may lead to incorrect mixing and matching of gains and losses. This section discusses the § 1245 recapture rules, and the next section discusses the § 1250 recapture rules.

Section 1245 requires taxpayers to treat all gain as ordinary gain unless the property is disposed of for more than was paid for it. This result is accomplished by requiring that all gain be treated as ordinary gain to the extent of the depreciation taken on the property disposed of. Section 1231 gain results only when the property is disposed of for more than its original cost. The excess of the sales price over the original cost is § 1231 gain. Section 1245 applies *primarily* to non-real-estate property such as machinery, trucks, and office furniture. Section 1245 does not apply if property is disposed of at a loss. Generally, the loss will be a § 1231 loss unless the form of the disposition is a casualty.

EXAMPLE 54

Alice purchased a $100,000 business machine and deducted $70,000 depreciation before selling it for $80,000. If it were not for § 1245, the $50,000 gain would be § 1231 gain ($80,000 amount realized − $30,000 adjusted basis). Section 1245 prevents this potentially favorable result by treating as ordinary income (not as § 1231 gain) any gain to the extent of depreciation taken. In this example, the entire $50,000 gain would be ordinary income. If Alice had sold the machine for $120,000, she would have a gain of $90,000 ($120,000 amount realized − $30,000 adjusted basis). The § 1245 gain would be $70,000 (equal to the depreciation taken), and the § 1231 gain would be $20,000 (equal to the excess of the sales price over the original cost). ■

Section 1245 recapture provides, in general, that the portion of recognized gain from the sale or other disposition of § 1245 property that represents depreciation [including § 167 depreciation, § 168 cost recovery, § 179 immediate expensing, § 168(k) additional first-year depreciation, and § 197 amortization] is *recaptured* as ordinary income. Thus, in Example 54, $50,000 of the $70,000 depreciation taken is recaptured as ordinary income when the business machine is sold for $80,000. Only $50,000 is recaptured rather than $70,000 because Alice is only required to recognize § 1245 recapture ordinary gain equal to the lower of the depreciation taken or the gain recognized.

The method of depreciation (e.g., accelerated or straight-line) does not matter. All depreciation taken is potentially subject to recapture. Thus, § 1245 recapture is often referred to as *full recapture.* Any remaining gain after subtracting the amount recaptured as ordinary income will usually be § 1231 gain. If the property is disposed of in a casualty event, however, the remaining gain will be casualty gain. If the business machine in Example 54 had been disposed of by casualty and the $80,000 received had been an insurance recovery, Alice would still have a gain of $50,000, and the gain would still be recaptured by § 1245 as ordinary gain. The § 1245 recapture rules apply before there is any casualty gain. Since all the $50,000 gain is recaptured, no casualty gain arises from the casualty.

The following examples illustrate the general application of § 1245.

EXAMPLE 55

On January 1, 2011, Gary sold for $13,000 a machine acquired several years ago for $12,000. He had taken $10,000 of depreciation on the machine.

- The recognized gain from the sale is $11,000. This is the amount realized of $13,000 less the adjusted basis of $2,000 ($12,000 cost – $10,000 depreciation taken).
- Depreciation taken is $10,000. Therefore, since § 1245 recapture gain is the lower of depreciation taken or gain recognized, $10,000 of the $11,000 recognized gain is ordinary income, and the remaining $1,000 gain is § 1231 gain.
- The § 1231 gain of $1,000 is also equal to the excess of the sales price over the original cost of the property ($13,000 – $12,000 = $1,000 § 1231 gain). ■

EXAMPLE 56

Assume the same facts as in the previous example, except the asset is sold for $9,000 instead of $13,000.

- The recognized gain from the sale is $7,000. This is the amount realized of $9,000 less the adjusted basis of $2,000.
- Depreciation taken is $10,000. Therefore, since the $10,000 depreciation taken exceeds the recognized gain of $7,000, the entire $7,000 recognized gain is ordinary income.
- The § 1231 gain is zero. There is no § 1231 gain because the selling price ($9,000) does not exceed the original purchase price ($12,000). ■

EXAMPLE 57

Assume the same facts as in Example 55, except the asset is sold for $1,500 instead of $13,000.

- The recognized loss from the sale is $500. This is the amount realized of $1,500 less the adjusted basis of $2,000.
- Since there is a loss, there is no depreciation recapture. All of the loss is § 1231 loss. ■

If § 1245 property is disposed of in a transaction other than a sale, exchange, or involuntary conversion, the maximum amount recaptured is the excess of the property's fair market value over its adjusted basis. See the discussion under Considerations Common to §§ 1245 and 1250 later in the chapter.

SECTION 1245 PROPERTY

Generally, **§ 1245 property** includes all depreciable personal property (e.g., machinery and equipment), including livestock. Buildings and their structural components generally are not § 1245 property. The following property is *also* subject to § 1245 treatment:

- Amortizable personal property such as goodwill, patents, copyrights, and leaseholds of § 1245 property. Professional baseball and football player contracts are § 1245 property.
- Amortization of reforestation expenditures.
- Expensing of costs to remove architectural and transportation barriers that restrict the handicapped and/or elderly.
- Section 179 immediate expensing of depreciable tangible personal property costs.
- Elevators and escalators acquired before January 1, 1987.
- Certain depreciable tangible real property (other than buildings and their structural components) employed as an integral part of certain activities such as manufacturing and production. For example, a natural gas storage tank where the gas is used in the manufacturing process is § 1245 property.
- Pollution control facilities, railroad grading and tunnel bores, on-the-job training, and child care facilities on which amortization is taken.
- Single-purpose agricultural and horticultural structures and petroleum storage facilities (e.g., a greenhouse or silo).
- Fifteen-year, 18-year, and 19-year nonresidential real estate for which accelerated cost recovery is used is subject to the § 1245 recapture rules, although it is technically not § 1245 property. Such property would have been placed in service after 1980 and before 1987.

EXAMPLE 58

James acquired nonresidential real property on December 1, 1986, for $100,000. He used the statutory percentage method to compute the ACRS cost recovery. He sells the asset on January 15, 2011, for $120,000. The amount and nature of James's gain are computed as follows:

Amount realized		$120,000
Adjusted basis		
Cost	$ 100,000	
Less cost recovery: 1986–2009	(100,000)	
2010–2011	(–0–)	
January 15, 2011 adjusted basis		(–0–)
Gain realized and recognized		$120,000

The gain of $120,000 is treated as ordinary income to the extent of *all* depreciation taken because the property is 19-year nonresidential real estate for which accelerated depreciation was used. Thus, James reports ordinary income of $100,000 and § 1231 gain of $20,000 ($120,000 – $100,000). ■

OBSERVATIONS ON § 1245

- In most instances, the total depreciation taken will exceed the recognized gain. Therefore, the disposition of § 1245 property usually results in ordinary income rather than § 1231 gain. Thus, generally, no § 1231 gain will occur unless the § 1245 property is disposed of for more than its original cost. Refer to Examples 55 and 56.
- Recapture applies to the total amount of depreciation allowed or allowable regardless of the depreciation method used.
- Recapture applies regardless of the holding period of the property. Of course, the entire recognized gain would be ordinary income if the

TAX *in* the NEWS

Recapture and Casualty Gain

A local newspaper recently had a story about the "total loss" of a retail store's contents and equipment in a fire. The story said that the store owner had no insurance on the contents (inventory) and, thus, would have no recovery for that part of her loss. The inventory was an ordinary asset, so the loss related to that property is an ordinary loss. The store equipment was insured, and the insurance covered the replacement cost of the destroyed equipment. Most of the equipment was quite old. Thus, it likely had been held more than one year and probably was fully depreciated. The insurance recovery likely generated a gain, and that gain is subject to § 1245 depreciation recapture *before* the gain is classified as nonpersonal use property casualty gain. Consequently, it is likely that there was no gain remaining after § 1245 recapture and, therefore, no casualty gain.

property were held for less than the long-term holding period because § 1231 would not apply.

- Section 1245 does not apply to losses, which receive § 1231 treatment.
- Gains from the disposition of § 1245 assets may also be treated as passive activity gains (see Chapter 11).

14.10 Section 1250 Recapture

LO.10

Determine when § 1250 recapture applies and how it is computed.

Generally, **§ 1250 property** is depreciable real property (principally buildings and their structural components) that is not subject to § 1245.[39] Intangible real property, such as leaseholds of § 1250 property, is also included.

Section 1250 recapture rarely applies since only the amount of *additional depreciation* is subject to recapture. To have additional depreciation, accelerated depreciation must have been taken on the asset. Straight-line depreciation is not recaptured (except for property held one year or less). Since depreciable real property placed in service after 1986 can generally only be depreciated using the straight-line method, there will usually be *no § 1250 depreciation recapture* on such property. Nor does § 1250 apply if the real property is sold at a loss.

If depreciable real property has been held for many years before it is sold, however, the § 1250 recapture rules may apply and are therefore discussed here. **Additional depreciation** is the excess of the accelerated depreciation actually deducted over depreciation that would have been deductible if the straight-line method had been used. Section 1250 recapture may apply when either (1) residential rental real property was acquired after 1975 and before 1987 and accelerated depreciation was taken or (2) nonresidential real property was acquired before 1981 and accelerated depreciation was taken after December 31, 1969.

If § 1250 property with additional depreciation is disposed of in a transaction other than a sale, exchange, or involuntary conversion, the depreciation recapture is limited to the excess of the property's fair market value over the adjusted basis. For instance, if a corporation distributes real property to its shareholders as a dividend and the fair market value of the real property is greater than its adjusted basis, the corporation will recognize a gain. If accelerated depreciation was taken on the property, § 1250 recapture will apply.

It is important to know what assets are defined as § 1250 property because even when there is no additional depreciation, the gain from such property may be subject to a special 25 percent tax rate. See the discussion of Unrecaptured § 1250 Gain later in this chapter.

[39] As noted above, in one limited circumstance, § 1245 does apply to nonresidential real estate. If the nonresidential real estate was placed in service after 1980 and before 1987 and accelerated depreciation was used, the § 1245 recapture rules rather than the § 1250 recapture rules apply.

The discussion below describes the computational steps when § 1250 recapture applies and indicates how that recapture is reflected on Form 4797 (Sales of Business Property).

COMPUTING RECAPTURE ON NONRESIDENTIAL REAL PROPERTY

For § 1250 property other than residential rental property, the potential recapture is equal to the amount of additional depreciation taken since December 31, 1969. This nonresidential real property includes buildings such as offices, warehouses, factories, and stores. (The definition of and rules for residential rental housing are discussed later in the chapter.) The lower of the potential § 1250 recapture amount or the recognized gain is ordinary income. The following general rules apply:

- Additional depreciation is depreciation taken in excess of straight-line after December 31, 1969, on property that was acquired before 1981.
- If the property is held for one year or less (usually not the case), all depreciation taken, even under the straight-line method, is additional depreciation.

The following procedure is used to compute recapture on nonresidential real property that was acquired before 1981 and for which accelerated depreciation was taken after December 31, 1969, under § 1250:

- Determine the recognized gain from the sale or other disposition of the property.
- Determine the additional depreciation (if any).
- The lower of the recognized gain or the additional depreciation is ordinary income.
- If any recognized gain remains (total recognized gain less recapture), it is § 1231 gain. However, it would be casualty gain if the disposition was by casualty.

The following example shows the application of the § 1250 computational procedure.

EXAMPLE 59

On January 3, 1980, Larry acquired a new building at a cost of $200,000 for use in his business. The building had an estimated useful life of 50 years and no estimated salvage value. Depreciation has been taken under the 150% declining-balance method through December 31, 2010. Pertinent information with respect to depreciation taken follows:

Year	Undepreciated Balance (Beginning of the Year)	Current Depreciation Provision	Straight-Line Depreciation	Additional Depreciation
1980–2009	$200,000	$122,230	$120,000	$2,230
2010	77,770	3,070	4,000	(930)
Total 1980–2010		$125,300	$124,000	$1,300

On January 2, 2011, Larry sold the building for $180,000. Compute the amount of his § 1250 ordinary income and § 1231 gain.

- Larry's recognized gain from the sale is $105,300. This is the difference between the $180,000 amount realized and the $74,700 adjusted basis ($200,000 cost − $125,300 depreciation taken).
- Additional depreciation is $1,300.
- The amount of ordinary income is $1,300. Since the additional depreciation of $1,300 is less than the recognized gain of $105,300, the entire gain is not recaptured.
- The remaining $104,000 ($105,300 − $1,300) gain is § 1231 gain. ■

COMPUTING RECAPTURE ON RESIDENTIAL RENTAL HOUSING

Section 1250 recapture sometimes applies to the sale or other disposition of residential rental housing. Property qualifies as *residential rental housing* only if at least 80 percent of gross rent income is rent income from dwelling units.[40] The rules are the same as for other § 1250 property, except that only the post-1975 additional depreciation may be recaptured on property acquired before 1987. If any of the recognized gain is not absorbed by the recapture rules pertaining to the post-1975 period, the remaining gain is § 1231 gain.

EXAMPLE 60

Assume the same facts as in the previous example, except the building is residential rental housing.

- Post-1975 ordinary income is $1,300 (post-1975 additional depreciation of $1,300).
- The remaining $104,000 ($105,300 – $1,300) gain is § 1231 gain. ■

Under § 1250, when straight-line depreciation is used, there is no § 1250 recapture potential unless the property is disposed of in the first year of use. Generally, however, the § 1250 recapture rules do not apply to depreciable real property unless the property is disposed of in the first year of use.

EXAMPLE 61

Sanjay acquires a residential rental building on January 1, 2010, for $300,000. He receives an offer of $450,000 for the building in 2011 and sells it on December 23, 2011.

- Sanjay takes $20,909 {($300,000 × .03485) + [$300,000 × .03636 × (11.5/12)] = $20,909} of total depreciation for 2010 and 2011, and the adjusted basis of the property is $279,091 ($300,000 – $20,909).
- Sanjay's recognized gain is $170,909 ($450,000 – $279,091).
- All of the gain is § 1231 gain. ■

SECTION 1250 RECAPTURE SITUATIONS

The § 1250 recapture rules apply to the following property for which accelerated depreciation was used:

- Residential rental real estate acquired before 1987.
- Nonresidential real estate acquired before 1981.
- Real property used predominantly outside the United States.
- Certain government-financed or low-income housing.[41]

Concept Summary 14.7 compares and contrasts the § 1245 and § 1250 depreciation recapture rules.

UNRECAPTURED § 1250 GAIN (REAL ESTATE 25% GAIN)

This section will explain what gain is eligible for the 25 percent tax rate on unrecaptured § 1250 gain. This gain is used in the alternative tax computation for net capital gain discussed earlier in this chapter. Unrecaptured § 1250 gain (25% gain) is some or all of the § 1231 gain that is treated as long-term capital gain and relates to a sale of depreciable real estate.

The maximum amount of this 25% gain is the depreciation taken on real property sold at a recognized gain. That maximum amount is reduced in one or more of the following ways:

[40] § 168(e)(2)(A). Note that there may be residential, nonrental housing (e.g., a bunkhouse on a cattle ranch). Such property is commonly regarded as "nonresidential real estate." The rules for such property were discussed in the previous section.

[41] Described in § 1250(a)(1)(B).

CONCEPT SUMMARY 14.7

Comparison of § 1245 and § 1250 Depreciation Recapture

	§ 1245	§ 1250
Property affected	All depreciable personal property, but also nonresidential real property acquired after December 31, 1980, and before January 1, 1987, for which accelerated cost recovery was used. Also includes miscellaneous items such as § 179 expense and § 197 amortization of intangibles such as goodwill, patents, and copyrights.	Nonresidential real property acquired after December 31, 1969, and before January 1, 1981, on which accelerated depreciation was taken. Residential rental real property acquired after December 31, 1975, and before January 1, 1987, on which accelerated depreciation was taken.
Depreciation recaptured	Potentially all depreciation taken. If the selling price is greater than or equal to the original cost, all depreciation is recaptured. If the selling price is between the adjusted basis and the original cost, only some depreciation is recaptured.	Additional depreciation (the excess of accelerated cost recovery over straight-line cost recovery or the excess of accelerated depreciation over straight-line depreciation).
Limit on recapture	Lower of depreciation taken or gain recognized.	Lower of additional depreciation or gain recognized.
Treatment of gain exceeding recapture gain	Usually § 1231 gain.	Usually § 1231 gain.
Treatment of loss	No depreciation recapture; loss is usually § 1231 loss.	No depreciation recapture; loss is usually § 1231 loss.

- The recognized gain from disposition is less than the depreciation taken. The 25% gain is reduced to the recognized gain amount. Refer to Example 59. The depreciation taken was $125,300, but the recognized gain was only $105,300. Consequently, *all* of the recognized gain is potential 25% §1231 gain.
- There is § 1250 depreciation recapture because the property is residential real estate acquired before 1987 on which accelerated depreciation was taken. The § 1250 recapture reduces the 25% gain. Refer to Example 60. Of the $105,300 recognized gain, $1,300 was recaptured by § 1250 as ordinary income, leaving $104,000 of the potential 25% § 1231 gain.
- There is § 1245 depreciation recapture because the property is nonresidential real estate acquired in 1981–1986 on which accelerated depreciation was taken. No 25% § 1231 gain will be left because § 1245 will recapture all of the depreciation or the recognized gain, whichever is less. Refer to Example 58. Depreciation of $100,000 was taken, but all of it was recaptured as ordinary income by § 1245. Thus, there is no remaining potential 25% § 1231 gain. The entire $20,000 § 1231 gain in Example 58 is potential 0%/15% gain.
- Section 1231 loss from disposition of other § 1231 assets held long term reduces the gain from real estate.
- Section 1231 lookback losses convert some or all of the potential 25% § 1231 gain to ordinary income.

Special 25% Gain Netting Rules

Where there is a § 1231 gain from real estate and that gain includes both potential *25%* gain and potential *0%/15%* gain, any § 1231 loss from disposition of other

EXCHANGE FOR FOREIGN PROPERTY YIELDS RECOGNIZED RECAPTURE GAIN

GLOBAL
Tax Issues

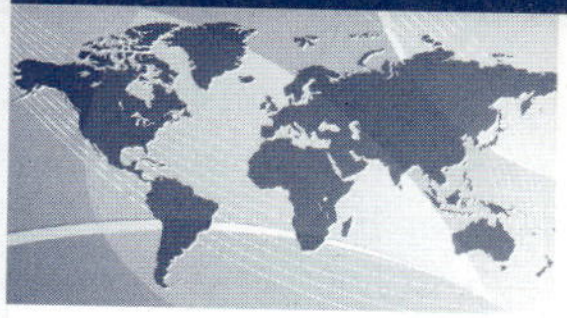

Tangible personal property used in a trade or business may be the subject of a § 1031 like-kind exchange, and the postponed gain is most likely postponed § 1245 gain. However, tangible personal property used predominantly within the United States cannot be exchanged for tangible personal property used predominantly outside the United States. Thus, such an exchange would cause recognized gain, and, as long as the fair market value of the property given up does not exceed its original cost, all of the gain is § 1245 depreciation recapture gain.

§ 1231 assets *first offsets* the *0%/15%* portion of the § 1231 gain and then offsets the *25%* portion of the § 1231 gain. Also, any § 1231 lookback loss *first recharacterizes* the *25%* portion of the § 1231 gain and then recharacterizes the *0%/15%* portion of the § 1231 gain as ordinary income.

Net § 1231 Gain Limitation

The amount of unrecaptured § 1250 gain may not exceed the net § 1231 gain that is eligible to be treated as long-term capital gain. The unrecaptured § 1250 gain is the *lesser of* the unrecaptured § 1250 gain or the net § 1231 gain that is treated as capital gain. Thus, if there is a net § 1231 gain, but it is all converted to ordinary income by the five-year § 1231 lookback loss provision, there is no surviving § 1231 gain or unrecaptured § 1250 gain.

Refer to Example 52. There was $200 of § 1231 gain from the building fire that would also be potential *25%* gain if at least $200 of depreciation was taken. The net § 1231 gain was $1,100 including the $200 building gain. (The $500 loss from Asset C would offset the potential *0%/15%* § 1231 gain and not the potential *25%* gain, so all of the potential *25%* gain of $200 is in the $1,100 net § 1231 gain.) However, the $700 of § 1231 lookback losses would *first* absorb the $200 building gain, so the $400 of § 1231 gain that is treated as long-term capital gain includes no *25%* gain.

Section 1250 Property for Purposes of the Unrecaptured § 1250 Gain

Section 1250 property includes any real property (other than § 1245 property) that is or has been depreciable. Land is *not* § 1250 property because it is not depreciable.

EXAMPLE 62

Bill is a single taxpayer with 2011 taxable income of $84,000 composed of:

- $64,000 ordinary taxable income,
- $3,000 short-term capital loss,
- $15,000 long-term capital gain from sale of stock, and
- $8,000 § 1231 gain that is all unrecaptured § 1250 gain (the actual unrecaptured gain was $11,000, but net § 1231 gain is only $8,000).

Bill's net capital gain is $20,000 ($15,000 long-term capital gain + $8,000 unrecaptured § 1250 gain/net § 1231 gain − $3,000 short-term capital loss). The $3,000 short-term capital loss is offset against the $8,000 unrecaptured § 1250 gain, reducing that gain to $5,000 (see the discussion earlier in the chapter concerning netting of capital losses). Bill's adjusted net capital gain is $15,000 ($20,000 net capital gain − $5,000 unrecaptured § 1250 gain). Bill's total tax (using the alternative tax calculation discussed earlier) is $15,625 [$12,125 (tax on ordinary taxable income) + $1,250 ($5,000 unrecaptured § 1250 gain × 25%) + $2,250 ($15,000 adjusted net capital gain × 15%)]. ■

ETHICS & Equity

FLOW-THROUGH 25% GAIN

While preparing an individual Form 1040, the tax return preparer examines a Schedule K–1 from a partnership in which the taxpayer has an ownership interest. The Schedule K–1 includes a $23,000 § 1231 gain and $12,300 of unrecaptured § 1250 gain. The tax return preparer has no idea what unrecaptured § 1250 gain means and does nothing with it in preparing the individual return. Could this affect the tax computation on the individual income tax return?

14.11 CONSIDERATIONS COMMON TO §§ 1245 AND 1250

LO.11

Understand considerations common to §§ 1245 and 1250.

EXCEPTIONS

Recapture under §§ 1245 and 1250 does not apply to the following transactions.

Gifts

The recapture potential carries over to the donee.[42]

EXAMPLE 63

Wade gives his daughter, Helen, § 1245 property with an adjusted basis of $1,000. The amount of recapture potential is $700. Helen uses the property in her business and claims further depreciation of $100 before selling it for $1,900. Helen's recognized gain is $1,000 ($1,900 amount realized − $900 adjusted basis), of which $800 is recaptured as ordinary income ($100 depreciation taken by Helen + $700 recapture potential carried over from Wade). The remaining gain of $200 is § 1231 gain. Even if Helen used the property for personal purposes, the $700 recapture potential would still be carried over. ■

Death

Although not a very attractive tax planning approach, death eliminates all recapture potential.[43] In other words, any recapture potential does not carry over from a decedent to an estate or heir.

EXAMPLE 64

Assume the same facts as in Example 63, except that Helen receives the property as a result of Wade's death. The $700 recapture potential from Wade is extinguished. Helen has a basis for the property equal to the property's fair market value (assume $1,700) at Wade's death. She will have a $300 gain when the property is sold because the selling price ($1,900) exceeds the property's adjusted basis of $1,600 ($1,700 original basis to Helen − $100 depreciation) by $300. Because of § 1245, $100 is ordinary income. The remaining gain of $200 is § 1231 gain. ■

Charitable Transfers

The recapture potential reduces the amount of the charitable contribution deduction under § 170.[44]

EXAMPLE 65

Kanisha donates to her church § 1245 property with a fair market value of $10,000 and an adjusted basis of $7,000. Assume that the amount of recapture potential is $2,000 (the amount of recapture that would occur if the property were sold). Her charitable contribution deduction (subject to the limitations discussed in Chapter 10) is $8,000 ($10,000 fair market value − $2,000 recapture potential). ■

[42] §§ 1245(b)(1) and 1250(d)(1) and Reg. §§ 1.1245–4(a)(1) and 1.1250–3(a)(1).

[43] §§ 1245(b)(2) and 1250(d)(2). Note the exception if the executor elects the modified carryover basis option for a decedent dying in 2010.

[44] § 170(e)(1)(A) and Reg. § 1.170A–4(b)(1). In certain circumstances, § 1231 gain also reduces the amount of the charitable contribution. See § 170(e)(1)(B).

ETHICS & Equity

INCORRECT DEPRECIATION AND RECOGNIZED GAIN

A staff accountant for a large international company is calculating the tax gain from disposition of business equipment. The equipment was seven-year MACRS property and has been fully depreciated for tax purposes. The staff accountant notices that the equipment was used in Germany, not the United States, although it is listed as an asset of the U.S. company for which the staff accountant works. Since the property was used outside the United States, it should have been depreciated using straight-line over a nine-year life. Consequently, the tax depreciation has been overstated, and the tax basis should be greater than zero, causing a smaller gain. What should the staff accountant do?

Certain Nontaxable Transactions

In certain transactions, the transferor's adjusted basis of property carries over to the transferee.[45] The recapture potential also carries over to the transferee.[46] Included in this category are transfers of property pursuant to the following:

- Nontaxable incorporations under § 351.
- Certain liquidations of subsidiary companies under § 332.
- Nontaxable contributions to a partnership under § 721.
- Nontaxable reorganizations.

Gain may be recognized in these transactions if boot is received. If gain is recognized, it is treated as ordinary income to the extent of the recapture potential or recognized gain, whichever is lower.[47]

Like-Kind Exchanges (§ 1031) and Involuntary Conversions (§ 1033)

Realized gain will be recognized to the extent of boot received under § 1031. Realized gain also will be recognized to the extent the proceeds from an involuntary conversion are not reinvested in similar property under § 1033. Such recognized gain is subject to recapture as ordinary income under §§ 1245 and 1250. The remaining recapture potential, if any, carries over to the property received in the exchange. Realized losses are not recognized in like-kind exchanges, but are recognized in involuntary conversions (see Chapter 13).

EXAMPLE 66

Anita exchanges § 1245 property with an adjusted basis of $300 for § 1245 property with a fair market value of $6,000. The exchange qualifies as a like-kind exchange under § 1031. Anita also receives $1,000 cash (boot). Her realized gain is $6,700 ($7,000 amount realized − $300 adjusted basis of property). Assuming the recapture potential is $7,500, Anita recognizes § 1245 gain of $1,000 because she received boot of $1,000. The remaining recapture potential of $6,500 carries over to the like-kind property received. ■

OTHER APPLICATIONS

Sections 1245 and 1250 apply notwithstanding any other provisions in the Code.[48] That is, the recapture rules under these Sections *override* all other Sections. Special applications include installment sales and property dividends.

Installment Sales

Recapture gain is recognized in the year of the sale regardless of whether gain is otherwise recognized under the installment method.[49] All gain is ordinary income until the recapture potential is fully absorbed. Nonrecapture (§ 1231) gain is recognized under the installment method as cash is received.

[45] §§ 1245(b)(3) and 1250(d)(3) and Reg. §§ 1.1245–4(c) and 1.1250–3(c).

[46] Reg. §§ 1.1245–2(a)(4) and –2(c)(2) and 1.1250–2(d)(1) and (3) and –3(c)(3).

[47] §§ 1245(b)(3) and 1250(d)(3) and Reg. §§ 1.1245–4(c) and 1.1250–3(c).

[48] §§ 1245(d) and 1250(i).

[49] § 453(i). The installment method of reporting gains on the sale of property is discussed in Chapter 16.

EXAMPLE 67

Seth sells § 1245 property for $20,000, to be paid in 10 annual installments of $2,000 each plus interest at 10%. Seth realizes a $6,000 gain from the sale, of which $4,000 is attributable to depreciation taken. If Seth uses the installment method, he recognizes the entire $4,000 of recapture gain as ordinary income in the year of the sale. The $2,000 of nonrecapture (§ 1231) gain will be recognized at the rate of $200 per year for 10 years. ■

Gain is also recognized on installment sales in the year of the sale in an amount equal to the § 179 (immediate expensing) deduction taken with respect to the property sold.

Property Dividends

A corporation generally recognizes gain if it distributes appreciated property as a dividend. Recapture under §§ 1245 and 1250 applies to the extent of the lower of the recapture potential or the excess of the property's fair market value over the adjusted basis.[50]

EXAMPLE 68

Emerald Corporation distributes § 1245 property as a dividend to its shareholders. The amount of the recapture potential is $300, and the excess of the property's fair market value over the adjusted basis is $800. Emerald recognizes $300 of ordinary income and $500 of § 1231 gain. ■

Concept Summary 14.8 integrates the depreciation recapture rules with the § 1231 netting process. It is an expanded version of Concept Summary 14.6.

14.12 Special Recapture Provisions

LO.12

Apply the special recapture provisions for related parties and IDC and be aware of the special recapture provision for corporations.

SPECIAL RECAPTURE FOR CORPORATIONS

Corporations selling depreciable real estate may have ordinary income in addition to that required by § 1250.[51]

GAIN FROM SALE OF DEPRECIABLE PROPERTY BETWEEN CERTAIN RELATED PARTIES

When the sale or exchange of property, which in the hands of the *transferee* is depreciable property (principally machinery, equipment, and buildings, but not land), is between certain related parties, any gain recognized is ordinary income.[52] This provision applies to both direct and indirect sales or exchanges. A **related party** is defined as an individual and his or her controlled corporation or partnership or a taxpayer and any trust in which the taxpayer (or the taxpayer's spouse) is a beneficiary.

EXAMPLE 69

Isabella sells a personal use automobile (therefore nondepreciable) to her controlled corporation. The automobile, which was purchased two years ago, originally cost $5,000 and is sold for $7,000. The automobile is to be used in the corporation's business. If the related-party provision did not exist, Isabella would realize a $2,000 long-term capital gain. The income tax consequences would be favorable because Isabella's controlled corporation is entitled to depreciate the automobile based upon the purchase price of $7,000. Under the related-party provision, Isabella's $2,000 gain is ordinary income. ■

INTANGIBLE DRILLING COSTS

Taxpayers may elect to either *expense or capitalize* intangible drilling and development costs for oil, gas, or geothermal properties.[53] **Intangible drilling and development costs (IDC)** include operator (one who holds a working or operating interest in any tract or

[50] § 311(b) and Reg. §§ 1.1245–1(c) and –6(b) and 1.1250–1(a)(4), –1(b)(4), and –1(c)(2).

[51] § 291(a)(1).

[52] § 1239.

[53] § 263(c).

CONCEPT SUMMARY 14.8

Depreciation Recapture and § 1231 Netting Procedure

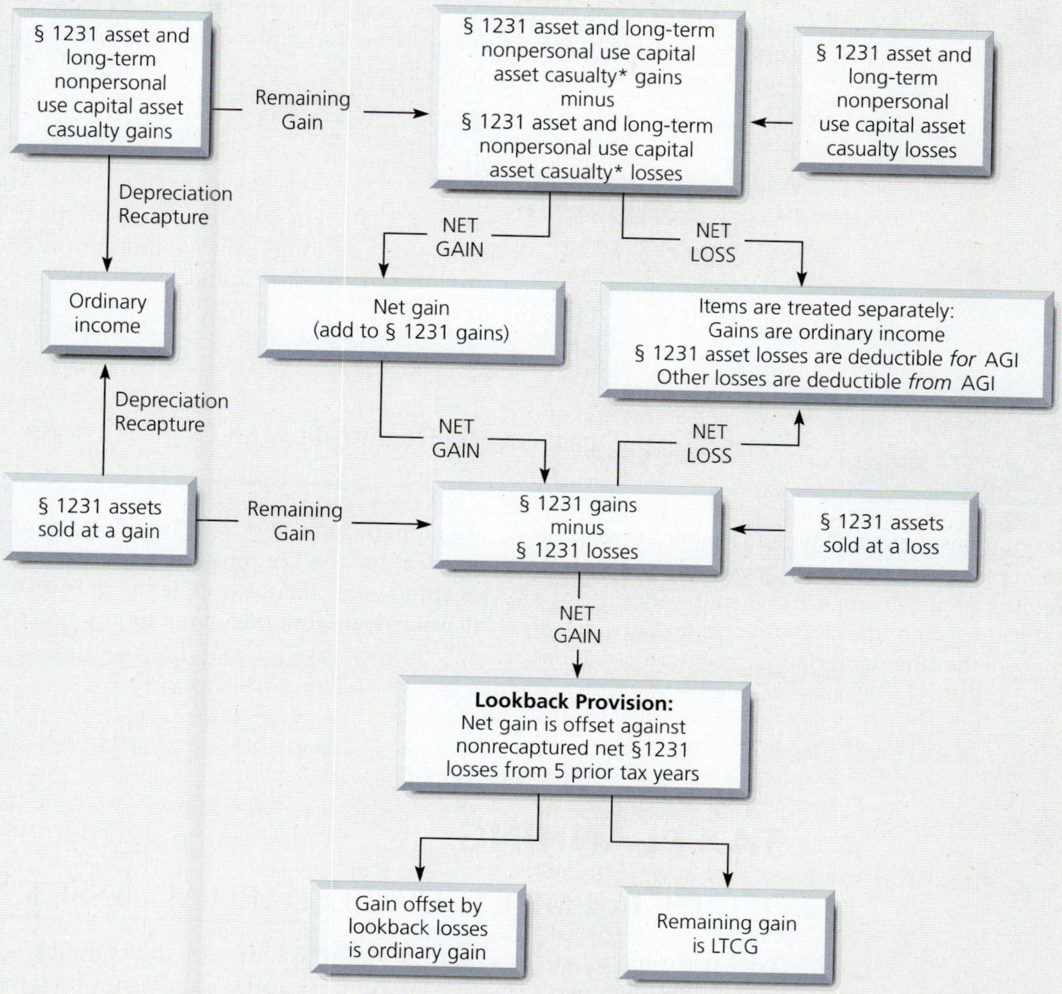

*Includes casualties and thefts.

parcel of land) expenditures for wages, fuel, repairs, hauling, and supplies. These expenditures must be incident to and necessary for the drilling of wells and preparation of wells for production. In most instances, taxpayers elect to expense IDC to maximize tax deductions during drilling.

Intangible drilling and development costs are subject to § 1254 recapture when the property is disposed of. The gain on the disposition of the property is subject to recapture as ordinary income.

14.13 Reporting Procedures

LO.13

Describe and apply the reporting procedures for §§ 1231, 1245, and 1250.

Noncapital gains and losses are reported on Form 4797, Sales of Business Property. Before filling out Form 4797, however, Form 4684, Casualties and Thefts, Part B, must be completed to determine whether any casualties will enter into the § 1231 computation procedure. Recall that recognized gains from § 1231 asset casualties

GLOBAL *Tax Issues*

Depreciation Recapture in Other Countries

The rules for dispositions of depreciated property are more complex in the United States than in any other country. Most countries treat the gain or loss from the disposition of business depreciable assets as ordinary income or loss. Consequently, although the U.S. rules are more complex, they can be more beneficial than those of other countries because at least some gains from the disposition of depreciable business property may be taxed at the lower capital gain rates.

may be recaptured by § 1245 or § 1250. These gains will not appear on Form 4684. The § 1231 gains and nonpersonal use long-term capital gains are netted against § 1231 losses and nonpersonal use long-term capital losses on Form 4684 to determine if there is a net gain to transfer to Form 4797, Part I.

ETHICS *& Equity*

Form 4797, Depreciation Recapture, and Corporations

Regular corporations are not eligible for lower tax rates on net long-term capital gain. However, such corporations are still required to complete Form 4797 when they dispose of a § 1231 asset. Quite often, the corporation's tax liability will be the same whether the depreciation recapture provisions are properly applied or not. Therefore, is it not logical and practical for the tax return preparer to simply ignore the recapture rules and the completion of Form 4797 and report all property dispositions on the corporation's Schedule D?

TAX PLANNING:

14.14 Importance of Capital Asset Status

LO.14

Identify tax planning opportunities arising from the sale or exchange of capital assets and avoid pitfalls associated with the recapture provisions.

Why is capital asset status important? Capital asset status enables the taxpayer to be eligible for the alternative tax on net capital gain. For a taxpayer in the 25, 28, 33, or 35 percent regular tax bracket, a 15 percent rate is available on assets held longer than one year. For a taxpayer in the 10 or 15 percent regular tax bracket, a 0 percent rate is available on assets held longer than one year. Thus, individuals who can receive income in the form of long-term capital gains or qualified dividend income have an advantage over taxpayers who cannot receive income in these forms.

Capital asset status is also important because capital gains must be offset by capital losses. If a net capital loss results, the maximum deduction is $3,000 per year.

Consequently, capital gains and losses must be segregated from other types of gains and losses and must be reported separately on Schedule D of Form 1040.

14.15 Planning for Capital Asset Status

It is important to keep in mind that capital asset status often is a question of objective evidence. Thus, property that is not a capital asset to one party may qualify as a capital asset to another party.

GLOBAL *Tax Issues*

Capital Gain Treatment in the United States and Other Countries

The United States currently requires a very complex tax calculation when taxable income includes net long-term capital gain. However, the alternative tax on net long-term capital gain can generate tax savings even when the taxpayer is in the lowest regular tax bracket (10 percent) because there is an alternative tax rate of 0 percent. Many other countries do not have an alternative tax rate on long-term capital gains. Instead, those gains are taxed the same as other income. Consequently, even though the U.S. system is complex, it may be preferable because of the lower tax rates and because the lower rates are available to taxpayers in all tax brackets.

EXAMPLE 70

Diane, a real estate dealer, transfers by gift a tract of land to Jeff, her son. The land was recorded as part of Diane's inventory (it was held for resale) and was therefore not a capital asset to her. Jeff, however, treats the land as an investment. The land is a capital asset in Jeff's hands, and any later taxable disposition of the property by him will yield a capital gain or loss. ■

If proper planning is carried out, even a dealer may obtain long-term capital gain treatment on the sale of the type of property normally held for resale.

EXAMPLE 71

Jim, a real estate dealer, segregates tract A from the real estate he regularly holds for resale and designates the property as being held for investment purposes. The property is not advertised for sale and is disposed of several years later. The negotiations for the subsequent sale were initiated by the purchaser and not by Jim. Under these circumstances, it would appear that any gain or loss from the sale of tract A should be a capital gain or loss.[54] ■

When a business is being sold, one of the major decisions usually concerns whether a portion of the sales price is for goodwill. For the seller, goodwill generally represents the disposition of a capital asset. Goodwill has no basis and represents a residual portion of the selling price that cannot be allocated reasonably to the known assets. The amount of goodwill thus represents capital gain.

From a legal perspective, the buyer may prefer that the residual portion of the purchase price be allocated to a covenant not to compete (a promise that the seller will not compete against the buyer by conducting a business similar to the one that the buyer has purchased). Both purchased goodwill and a covenant not to compete are § 197 intangibles. Thus, both must be capitalized and can be amortized over a 15-year statutory period.

To the seller, a covenant produces ordinary income. Thus, the seller would prefer that the residual portion of the selling price be allocated to goodwill—a capital asset. If the buyer does not need the legal protection provided by a covenant, the buyer is neutral regarding whether the residual amount be allocated to a covenant or to goodwill. Since the seller would receive a tax advantage from labeling the residual amount as goodwill, the buyer should factor this into the negotiation of the purchase price.

EXAMPLE 72

Marcia is buying Jack's dry cleaning proprietorship. An appraisal of the assets indicates that a reasonable purchase price would exceed the value of the known assets by $30,000. If the purchase contract does not specify the nature of the $30,000, the amount will be for goodwill, and Jack will have a long-term capital gain of $30,000.

[54] *Toledo, Peoria & Western Railroad Co.*, 35 TCM 1663, T.C.Memo. 1976–366.

Marcia will have a 15-year amortizable $30,000 asset. If Marcia is paying the extra $30,000 to prevent Jack from conducting another dry cleaning business in the area (a covenant not to compete), Jack will have $30,000 of ordinary income. Marcia will have a $30,000 deduction over the statutory 15-year amortization period rather than over the actual life of the covenant (e.g., 5 years). ■

14.16 Effect of Capital Asset Status in Transactions Other Than Sales

The nature of an asset (capital or ordinary) is important in determining the tax consequences that result when a sale or exchange occurs. It may, however, be just as significant in circumstances other than a taxable sale or exchange. When a capital asset is disposed of, the result is not always a capital gain or loss. Rather, in general, the disposition must be a sale or exchange. Collection of a debt instrument having a basis less than the face value results in a capital gain if the debt instrument is a capital asset. The collection is a sale or exchange. Sale of the debt shortly before the due date for collection will produce a capital gain.[55] If selling the debt in such circumstances could produce a capital gain but collecting could not, the consistency of what constitutes a capital gain or loss would be frustrated. Another illustration of the sale or exchange principle involves a donation of certain appreciated property to a qualified charity. Recall that in certain circumstances, the measure of the charitable contribution is fair market value when the property, if sold, would have yielded a long-term capital gain [refer to Chapter 10 and the discussion of § 170(e)].

EXAMPLE 73

Sharon wants to donate a tract of unimproved land (basis of $40,000 and fair market value of $200,000) held for the required long-term holding period to State University (a qualified charitable organization). However, Sharon currently is under audit by the IRS for capital gains she reported on certain real estate transactions during an earlier tax year. Although Sharon is not a licensed real estate broker, the IRS agent conducting the audit is contending that she has achieved dealer status by virtue of the number and frequency of the real estate transactions she has conducted. Under these circumstances, Sharon would be well-advised to postpone the donation to State University until her status is clarified. If she has achieved dealer status, the unimproved land may be inventory (refer to Example 71 for another possible result), and Sharon's charitable contribution deduction would be limited to $40,000. If not, and if the land is held as an investment, Sharon's deduction is $200,000 (the fair market value of the property). ■

14.17 Stock Sales

The following rules apply in determining the date of a stock sale:

- The date the sale is executed is the date of the sale. The execution date is the date the broker completes the transaction on the stock exchange.
- The settlement date is the date the cash or other property is paid to the seller of the stock. This date is *not* relevant in determining the date of sale.

EXAMPLE 74

Lupe, a cash basis taxpayer, sells stock that results in a gain. The sale was executed on December 29, 2010. The settlement date is January 2, 2011. The date of sale is December 29, 2010 (the execution date). The holding period for the stock sold ends with the execution date. ■

[55] § 1271(b).

14.18 Maximizing Benefits

Ordinary losses generally are preferable to capital losses because of the limitations imposed on the deductibility of net capital losses and the requirement that capital losses be used to offset capital gains. The taxpayer may be able to convert what would otherwise have been capital loss to ordinary loss. For example, business (but not nonbusiness) bad debts, losses from the sale or exchange of small business investment company stock, and losses from the sale or exchange of small business company stock all result in ordinary losses.[56]

Although capital losses can be carried over indefinitely, *indefinite* becomes definite when a taxpayer dies. Any loss carryovers not used by the taxpayer are permanently lost. That is, no tax benefit can be derived from the carryovers subsequent to death.[57] Therefore, the potential benefit of carrying over capital losses diminishes when dealing with older taxpayers.

It is usually beneficial to spread gains over more than one taxable year. In some cases, this can be accomplished through the installment sales method of accounting.

14.19 Year-End Planning

The following general rules can be applied for timing the recognition of capital gains and losses near the end of a taxable year:

- If the taxpayer already has recognized more than $3,000 of capital loss, sell assets to generate capital gain equal to the excess of the capital loss over $3,000.

EXAMPLE 75

Kevin has already incurred a $7,000 STCL. Kevin should generate $4,000 of capital gain. The gain will offset $4,000 of the loss. The remaining loss of $3,000 can be deducted against ordinary income. ■

- If the taxpayer already has recognized capital gain, sell assets to generate capital loss equal to the capital gain. The gain will not be taxed, and the loss will be fully *deductible* against the gain.
- Generally, if the taxpayer has a choice between recognizing short-term capital gain or long-term capital gain, long-term capital gain should be recognized because it has the lower tax rate.

14.20 Timing of § 1231 Gain

Although §§ 1245 and 1250 recapture much of the gain from the disposition of business property, sometimes § 1231 gain is still substantial. For instance, land held as a business asset will generate either § 1231 gain or § 1231 loss. If the taxpayer already has a capital loss for the year, the sale of land at a gain should be postponed so that the net § 1231 gain is not netted against the capital loss. The capital loss deduction will therefore be maximized for the current tax year, and the capital loss carryforward (if any) may be offset against the gain when the land is sold. If the taxpayer already has a § 1231 loss, § 1231 gains might be postponed to maximize the ordinary loss deduction this year. However, the carryforward of unrecaptured § 1231 losses will make the § 1231 gain next year an ordinary gain.

EXAMPLE 76

Mark has a $2,000 net STCL for 2011. He could sell business land held 27 months for a $3,000 § 1231 gain. He will have no other capital gains and losses or § 1231 gains and losses in 2011 or 2012. He has no nonrecaptured § 1231 losses from prior years. Mark is in the 28%

[56] §§ 166(d), 1242, and 1244. Refer to the discussion in Chapter 7.

[57] Rev.Rul. 74–175, 1974–1 C.B. 52.

tax bracket in 2011 and will be in the 25% bracket in 2012. If he sells the land in 2011, he will have a $1,000 net LTCG ($3,000 § 1231 gain − $2,000 STCL) and will pay a tax of $150 ($1,000 × 15%). If Mark sells the land in 2012, he will have a 2011 tax savings of $560 ($2,000 capital loss deduction × 28% tax rate on ordinary income). In 2012, he will pay tax of $450 ($3,000 × 15%). By postponing the sale by a year, Mark gets the use of $710 ($560 + $150) of tax savings until he has to pay $450 in 2012, for a net savings of $260 between the two years without considering the time value of money and other factors. ■

EXAMPLE 77

Beth has a $15,000 § 1231 loss in 2011. She could sell business equipment held 30 months for a $20,000 § 1231 gain and a $12,000 § 1245 gain. Beth is in the 28% tax bracket in 2011 and will be in the 25% bracket in 2012. She has no nonrecaptured § 1231 losses from prior years. If she sells the equipment in 2011, she will have a $5,000 net § 1231 gain and $12,000 of ordinary gain. Her tax would be $4,110 [($5,000 § 1231 gain × 15%) + ($12,000 ordinary gain × 28%)].

If Beth postpones the equipment sale until 2012, she would have a 2011 ordinary loss of $15,000 and tax savings of $4,200 ($15,000 × 28%). In 2012, she would have $5,000 of § 1231 gain (the 2011 § 1231 loss carries over and recaptures $15,000 of the 2012 § 1231 gain as ordinary income) and $27,000 of ordinary gain. Her tax would be $7,500 [($5,000 § 1231 gain × 15%) + ($27,000 ordinary gain × 25%)]. By postponing the sale of the § 1231 property until 2012, Beth gets the use of $8,310 ($4,200 + $4,110) of tax savings until she has to pay $7,500 in 2012, for a net savings of $810 between the two years without considering the time value of money and other factors. ■

ETHICS & *Equity*

To Depreciate or Not to Depreciate

A staff accountant for a CPA firm is hurriedly finalizing depreciation and gain computations for a 2011 calendar year client's disposition of various business buildings. If the client's return is not finished quickly, a filing extension will be necessary, and the staff accountant will be blamed for it. All of the buildings were acquired three years ago, are 39-year MACRS real property, and were disposed of in April 2011. Rather than compute depreciation for the year of disposition, the staff accountant uses the beginning-of-the-year adjusted basis for the buildings to compute the disposition gain or loss. Could this approach make any difference on the client's return? (Assume the client is an individual taxpayer.)

14.21 Timing of Recapture

Since recapture is usually not triggered until the property is sold or disposed of, it may be possible to plan for recapture in low-bracket or loss years. If a taxpayer has net operating loss (NOL) carryovers that are about to expire, the recognition of ordinary income from recapture may be advisable to absorb the loss carryovers.

EXAMPLE 78

Ahmad has a $15,000 NOL carryover that will expire this year. He owns a machine that he plans to sell in the early part of next year. The expected gain of $17,000 from the sale of the machine will be recaptured as ordinary income under § 1245. Ahmad sells the machine before the end of this year and offsets $15,000 of the ordinary income against the NOL carryover. ■

14.22 Postponing and Shifting Recapture

It is also possible to postpone recapture or to shift the burden of recapture to others. For example, recapture is avoided upon the disposition of a § 1231 asset if the taxpayer replaces the property by entering into a like-kind exchange. In this instance, recapture potential is merely carried over to the newly acquired property (refer to Example 66).

Recapture can be shifted to others through the gratuitous transfer of § 1245 or § 1250 property to family members. A subsequent sale of such property by the donee will trigger recapture to the donee rather than the donor (refer to Example 63). This procedure would be advisable only if the donee is in a lower income tax bracket than the donor.

14.23 Avoiding Recapture

The immediate expensing election (§ 179) is subject to § 1245 recapture. If the election is not made, the § 1245 recapture potential will accumulate more slowly (refer to Chapter 8). Since using the immediate expense deduction complicates depreciation and book accounting for the affected asset, not taking the deduction may make sense even though the time value of money might indicate it should be taken.

REFOCUS ON THE BIG PICTURE

MANAGING CAPITAL ASSET TRANSACTIONS

You explain to Maurice that your area of expertise is tax, so you are providing tax advice and not investment advice. From an overall perspective, he is correct that certain capital gains and dividends are eligible for either a 0 percent or a 15 percent tax rate rather than the regular tax rates that go as high as 35 percent. You then discuss the potential tax consequences of each of his investments.

- *Purple stock.* To qualify for the beneficial tax rate, the holding period for the stock must be longer than one year. From a tax perspective, Maurice should retain his stock investment for at least an additional three months and a day. To be eligible for the "costless" capital gains, his taxable income should not exceed $34,500 for 2011.
- *Patent.* Since he is a "holder" of the patent, it will qualify for the beneficial capital gain rate regardless of the holding period if the patent should produce income in excess of his $50,000 investment. However, if he loses money on the investment, he will be able to deduct only $3,000 of the loss per year against his ordinary income (assuming there are no offsetting capital gains). See Example 14 and Example 15.
- *Tax-exempt bonds.* The after-tax return on the taxable bonds would be less than the 3 percent on the tax-exempt bonds. In addition, the interest on the taxable bonds would increase his taxable income, possibly moving it out of the desired 15 percent marginal tax rate into the 25 percent marginal tax rate.
- *Partnership interest.* Whether Maurice receives capital or ordinary treatment associated with his partnership interest depends on whether he is reporting his share of profits or losses (ordinary income or ordinary loss) or is reporting recognized gain or loss from the sale of his partnership interest (capital gain or capital loss).
- *Business equipment.* Maurice's recognized gain on the sale of the equipment is $71,000 ($300,000 – $229,000). In order to be eligible for the beneficial capital gain rate of 15 percent, his holding period needs to exceed 12 months. So if he delays the sale for an additional 3 months and one day, his recognized gain of $71,000 will be classified as follows:
  - *Depreciation recapture ordinary income of $21,000 under § 1245 (taxed at Maurice's marginal tax rate).*
  - *Long-term capital gain of $50,000 ($71,000 – $21,000) under § 1231 (taxed at 15 percent rate).*

You conclude your tax advice to Maurice by telling him that whatever he does regarding his investments should make economic sense. There are no 100 percent tax rates. For example, disposing of the bank stock in the current market could be the wise thing to do.

KEY TERMS

Additional depreciation, 14–41
Alternative tax, 14–25
Capital asset, 14–4
Capital gains, 14–3
Capital losses, 14–3
Collectibles, 14–24
Franchise, 14–14
Holding period, 14–16
Intangible drilling and development costs (IDC), 14–48
Lessee, 14–15
Lessor, 14–15
Long-term nonpersonal use capital assets, 14–32
Net capital gain (NCG), 14–22
Net capital loss (NCL), 14–26
Options, 14–11
Original issue discount (OID), 14–10
Patent, 14–12
Qualified dividend income, 14–24
Related party, 14–48
Sale or exchange, 14–9
Section 1231 gains and losses, 14–31
Section 1231 lookback, 14–35
Section 1231 property, 14–31
Section 1245 property, 14–40
Section 1245 recapture, 14–39
Section 1250 property, 14–41
Section 1250 recapture, 14–41
Short sale, 14–18
Unrecaptured § 1250 gain, 14–22

DISCUSSION QUESTIONS

ISSUE ID

1. **LO.2, 4, 5** Gynn inherited 400 shares of stock, 200 shares of Orange and 200 shares of Ecru. She has a stockbroker sell the shares for her, uses the proceeds for personal expenses, and thinks nothing further about the transactions. What issues does she face when she prepares her Federal income tax return?

ISSUE ID

2. **LO.2** An individual taxpayer sells some used assets at a rummage sale. Why are none of the proceeds taxable in most situations?

ISSUE ID

3. **LO.2, 4** Shaneka owns a sculpture that she received as a gift from her uncle two years ago. The uncle created the sculpture. Shaneka has displayed the sculpture in her home and has never attempted to sell it. Recently, a visitor noticed the sculpture and has offered Shaneka $50,000 for it. If Shaneka decides to sell the sculpture, what tax issues does she face?
4. **LO.2** Are the lyrics to a song a capital asset or an ordinary asset? Why or why not?
5. **LO.2** Is an account receivable that arose in the ordinary course of a cash basis dentist's business a capital asset? Why or why not?
6. **LO.2** Why do Internal Revenue Code provisions play an important role in the definition of capital assets?
7. **LO.2** Harmon is a "stock trader" who buys and sells publicly traded stocks regularly for his own account. His cousin, who purports to be a tax expert, but is not a CPA, has told Harmon that since the shares of stock Harmon holds are held for resale, they are ordinary assets and not capital assets. Is this always true?
8. **LO.2** Gabrielle is holding vacant land for investment. She wants to subdivide it into 25 lots, put in utilities (sewer, water, cable, electricity, and natural gas) for each lot, and pave the streets running through the subdivision. Is this transaction eligible for the "real property subdivided for sale" provisions?
9. **LO.3** What is the difference between a "worthless security" and "§ 1244 stock"?
10. **LO.3** Lila purchased an original issue discount bond several years ago. She paid $188,000 for the $200,000 face value bond. She sold the bond this year for $193,000. Is all of Lila's gain long-term capital gain? Why or why not?
11. **LO.3** Carl receives $58,000 from a real estate developer for an option to purchase land Carl is holding for investment. Fourteen months later, the option expires unexercised. How is the $58,000 taxed to Carl?

ISSUE ID

12. **LO.3** Hubert purchases all the rights in a patent from the inventor who developed the patented product. After holding the patent for two years, Hubert sells all the rights in the

patent for a substantial gain. What issues does Hubert face if he wants to treat the gain as a long-term capital gain?

13. **LO.3** Green Corporation and Red Corporation are engaged in a contract dispute over the use of Green's trademarked name, Big Blue Taco. For a one-time payment of $45,000, Green licensed Red to use the name Big Blue Taco, but the license did not require that Red use the same materials in its version of Big Blue Taco that Green uses. Red also did not have to make any contingent payments to Green or buy any supplies from Green. Did Red purchase a franchise right from Green, or did Red purchase the name Big Blue Taco from Green?

14. **LO.4** Siva purchased corporate stock for $20,000 on April 10, 2009. On July 14, 2011, when the stock was worth $12,000, he gave it to his son, Mithra. What has to happen to the value of the property while Mithra holds it if Mithra is to tack Siva's holding period on to his own holding period? **ISSUE ID**

15. **LO.4** At the date of a short sale, Betty had not held substantially identical securities for more than 12 months. What is the nature of any gain or loss from the close of her short sale?

16. **LO.5** After netting all her short-term and long-term capital gains and losses, Minerva has a net short-term capital gain and a net long-term capital gain. Can she net these against each other?

17. **LO.2, 5** Bill sells his graphic comic book collection at a profit. He had acquired all of the comic books for his personal pleasure and sold all of them for more than he paid for them. What is the tax status of the comic books, and is his gain a 28% gain?

18. **LO.7, 8** Hakim's rental building was not insured when it was destroyed by a hurricane. His adjusted basis for the building was substantial, but was less than he had paid for the building in 2007. The building was Hakim's only asset that was damaged by the hurricane. How should Hakim handle this situation? **ISSUE ID**

19. **LO.7, 8** Sammy established a sole proprietorship in 2003. He sold § 1231 assets at a loss in 2009 and 2010. He had not sold any § 1231 assets before 2009. In 2011, he could sell a § 1231 asset at a gain and would like to have the gain taxed as a long-term capital gain. What issue is Sammy facing? **ISSUE ID**

20. **LO.8** As a result of a casualty event, Thelma disposed of tangible personal property (a § 1231 asset) at a realized and recognized gain. At the time of the casualty, the property was worth substantially less than Thelma had paid for it and had an adjusted basis of zero. This was her only business casualty, and she has some § 1231 lookback loss. Is the resulting gain a casualty gain taxed as a long-term capital gain, a gain taxed as an ordinary gain, or a casualty gain taxed as a § 1231 gain?

21. **LO.8** An individual taxpayer had a net § 1231 loss in 2008 and a net § 1231 gain in 2009, 2010, and 2011. What factors will influence whether any of the 2011 net § 1231 gain will be treated as long-term capital gain? **ISSUE ID**

22. **LO.8** Review Examples 50 and 52 in the text. In both examples, the taxpayer's AGI is $129,400 even though in Example 52 there is $700 of nonrecaptured § 1231 loss from 2010. Explain why the two AGI amounts are the same.

23. **LO.8** A taxpayer owns depreciable business real property held for the long-term holding period. What would have to be true for the real property to generate a § 1231 loss when it is sold?

24. **LO.8** A depreciable business dump truck has been owned for four years and is no longer useful to the taxpayer. What would have to be true for the disposition of the dump truck to generate at least some § 1231 gain?

25. **LO.7, 8, 9** Sissie owns two items of business equipment. They were both purchased in 2007 for $100,000, both have a seven-year recovery period, and both have an adjusted basis of $37,490. Sissie is considering selling these assets in 2011. One of them is worth $50,000, and the other is worth $33,000. Since both items were used in her business, Sissie simply assumes that the loss on one will be offset against the gain from the other and the net gain or loss will increase or reduce her business income. Is she correct? **ISSUE ID**

26. **LO.7, 9** If depreciable equipment used in a business is sold at a recognized gain on July 10, 2011, and it was purchased on August 21, 2010, does § 1245 depreciation recapture apply to the asset?

27. **LO.9** A farmer's silo is destroyed by a tornado, but is insured for its replacement cost. Consequently, the farmer has a $40,000 gain after receiving the insurance proceeds. The silo is not replaced because the farmer spends the insurance proceeds on additional cattle. What is the nature of the gain if the silo originally cost $100,000 three years ago and had an adjusted basis of $60,000 at the time of its destruction?

28. **LO.10** Nonresidential real estate leasehold improvements are sold at a loss. In what circumstances would the loss be subject to § 1250 depreciation recapture?

29. **LO.10** An apartment building was acquired in 2004. Depreciation of $123,000 was taken on the building, and the building was sold for a $34,000 gain. What is the maximum amount of 25% gain?

30. **LO.10** In the current year, an individual taxpayer has net long-term capital gain from the disposition of capital assets and also has unrecaptured § 1250 gain. Under what circumstances would the unrecaptured § 1250 gain be taxed at 25%?

31. **LO.10** An individual has $25,000 of § 1231 loss from the disposition of an office building. Straight-line depreciation of $43,000 was deducted on the building. The taxpayer also has a § 1231 gain of $56,000 from the sale of business land. How much of the gain or loss is taxed as unrecaptured § 1250 gain?

32. **LO.9, 11** Mary receives tangible personal property as a gift. The property was depreciated by the donor, and Mary will also depreciate it. At the date of the gift, the property was worth more than the donor's adjusted basis. What is the impact of these facts on Mary when she sells the property at a gain several years after she acquired it?

33. **LO.9, 11** Thomas receives tangible personal property as an inheritance from a decedent who died in 2011. The property was depreciated by the deceased, and Thomas will also depreciate it. At the date of the deceased's death, the property was worth more than the deceased's adjusted basis. What is the impact of these facts on Thomas when he sells the property at a gain several years after he acquired it?

34. **LO.9, 11** Dino contributes to charity some tangible personal property that he had used in his business and depreciated. At the date of the donation, the property has a fair market value greater than its adjusted basis, but less than the original cost. What is the impact of these facts on Dino's charitable contribution?

35. **LO.9, 11** Desiree contributes to her wholly owned corporation some tangible personal property that she had used in her sole proprietorship business and depreciated. At the date of the contribution, the property has a fair market value greater than its adjusted basis. What is the impact of these facts on the corporation?

36. **LO.9, 11** A corporation distributes a truck it has owned for three years to its sole shareholder. The shareholder will use the truck for personal use activity. The truck's fair market value at the time of the distribution is greater than its adjusted basis, but less than its original cost. Does the corporation recognize a gain? If so, what is the character of the gain?

37. **LO.12** A corporation distributes a truck it has owned for three years to its sole shareholder. The shareholder will use the truck for business activity. The truck's fair market value at the time of the distribution is greater than its adjusted basis, but less than its original cost. Does the corporation recognize a gain? If so, what is the character of the gain?

PROBLEMS

38. **LO.2** During the year, Eric had the four property transactions summarized on the next page. Eric is a collector of antique automobiles and occasionally sells one to get funds to buy another. What are the amount and nature of the gain or loss from each of these transactions?

Property	Date Acquired	Date Sold	Adjusted Basis	Sales Price
Antique truck	06/18/01	05/23/11	$37,000	$32,000
Blue Growth Fund (100 shares)	12/23/02	11/22/11	22,000	38,000
Orange bonds	02/12/03	04/11/11	34,000	42,000*
Green stock (100 shares)	02/14/11	11/23/11	13,000	11,000

*The sales price included $750 of accrued interest.

39. **LO.2, 5** Revez owns an antique shop. He buys property from estates, often at much less than the retail value of the property. Recently, Revez sold for $4,000 an antique clock for which he had paid $1,250. Revez had held the clock in his shop for 36 months before selling it. Revez would like the gain on the sale of the clock to be a long-term capital gain. How can he achieve that objective? **DECISION MAKING**

40. **LO.2** Chalmers is the owner of numerous houses. His intention is to hold the houses until they increase in value and then sell them. He rents the houses to tenants while he is holding them. In 2011, he sold one house for $45,000. Chalmers had held the house for six years, and it had a tax basis of $20,000. Was the house a capital asset? Why or why not?

41. **LO.2** Wilma purchased a swing set at a yard sale for $50 in May. She is not in the business of buying and selling anything. She researched the swing set on the Internet and discovered that it was worth $200. She sold it on an Internet auction site for $180 in July. Was the swing set a capital asset, and what were the amount and nature of Wilma's gain or loss from its sale?

42. **LO.2** Cyan is a corporation that buys and sells furniture. It purchases furniture from furniture merchants that need cash immediately and cannot wait to sell in the normal course of their business. Cyan pays about 35% of the wholesale value of the furniture and then sells the furniture to other furniture dealers for about 85% of wholesale value. Does Cyan have a capital gain when it sells the furniture?

43. **LO.2** Faith Godwin is a dealer in securities. She has spotted a fast-rising company and would like to buy and hold its stock for investment. The stock is currently selling for $2 per share, and Faith thinks it will climb to $40 a share within two years. Faith's co-workers have told her that there is "no way" she can get long-term capital gain treatment when she purchases stock because she is a securities dealer. Faith has asked you to calculate her potential gain and tell her whether her co-workers are right. Draft a letter to Faith responding to her request. Her address is 200 Catamon Drive, Pelham, IA 59406. **COMMUNICATIONS**

44. **LO.2** Maria meets all the requirements of § 1237 (subdivided realty). In 2011, she begins selling lots and sells four separate lots to four different purchasers. She also sells two contiguous lots to another purchaser. The sales price of each lot is $30,000. Maria's basis for each lot is $15,000. Selling expenses are $500 per lot.
    a. What are the realized and recognized gain?
    b. Explain the nature of the gain (i.e., ordinary income or capital gain).
    c. Would your answers change if, instead, the lots sold to the fifth purchaser were not contiguous? If so, how?

45. **LO.2, 3, 5** Kate has had a bad year with her investments. She lent a friend $5,700; the friend did not repay the loan when it was due, and then declared bankruptcy. The loan is totally uncollectible. Kate also was notified by her broker that the Elm corporate bonds she owned became worthless on October 13, 2011. She had purchased the bonds for $22,000 on November 10, 2010. Sue also had a $30,000 loss on the disposition of § 1244 corporate stock that she purchased several years ago. Kate is single. **DECISION MAKING**
    a. What are the nature and amount of Kate's losses?
    b. What is Kate's AGI for 2011 assuming she has $65,000 of ordinary gross income from sources other than those discussed above?
    c. What are the nature and amount of Kate's loss carryforwards?

46. **LO.2, 3** Jason purchased $700,000 of Cherry Corporation face value bonds for $620,000 on November 13, 2010. The bonds had been issued with $80,000 of original issue discount because Cherry was in financial difficulty in 2010. On December 3, 2011, Jason

sold the bonds for $683,000 after amortizing $1,000 of the original issue discount. What are the nature and amount of Jason's gain or loss?

DECISION MAKING

47. **LO.3** Frank is an investor in vacant land. When he thinks he has identified property that would be a good investment, he approaches the landowner, pays the landowner for a "right of first refusal" to purchase the land, records this right in the property records, and then waits to see if the land increases in value. The right of first refusal is valid for four years. Fourteen months ago, Frank paid a landowner $4,000 for a right of first refusal. The land was selected as the site of a new shopping center, and the landowner was offered $4 million for the land. In its title search on the land, the buyer discovered Frank's right of first refusal and involved him in the purchase negotiations. Ultimately, the landowner paid Frank $120,000 to give up his right of first refusal; the landowner then sold the land to the buyer for $4,120,000. Frank has a marginal tax rate of 35%.
    a. What difference does it make whether or not Frank treats the right of first refusal as an option to purchase the land?
    b. What difference does it make whether or not Frank is a "dealer" in land?

48. **LO.3** Crissie was the owner of vacant land that she was holding for investment. She paid $1 million for the land in 2008. Kazi was an investor in vacant land. He thought Crissie's land might be the site of an exit ramp from a new freeway. Kazi gave Crissie $836,000 for an option on her land in 2009. The option was good for two years and gave Kazi the ability to purchase Crissie's land for $4,765,000. The freeway was not approved by the government, and Kazi's option expired in 2011. Does Crissie have $836,000 of long-term capital gain upon the expiration of the option?

49. **LO.3** Helen purchased all the rights to a patent on a new sewing tool developed by a friend of hers who was an amateur inventor. The inventor had obtained the patent rights, set up a manufacturing company to produce and sell the sewing tool, and produced substantial quantities of the tool, but he then became discouraged when no large sewing company would agree to distribute the tool for him. Helen purchased the patent rights (but not the manufacturing company) for $320,000 on October 24, 2010. Helen had never engaged in such a transaction before, but she is a salesperson in the sewing industry and thought she could succeed where her friend had failed. On June 27, 2011, she sold all the patent rights to Sewing Tool Company for $2,233,000. Sewing Tool will manufacture the tool in its own factory and sell it to its customers. What is the nature of Helen's gain from this transaction?

DECISION MAKING

50. **LO.3, 4, 14** Mac, an inventor, obtained a patent on a chemical process to clean old aluminum siding so that it can be easily repainted. Mac has a $500,000 tax basis in the patent. Mac does not have the capital to begin manufacturing and selling this product, so he has done nothing with the patent since obtaining it two years ago. Now a group of individuals has approached him and offered two alternatives. Under one alternative, they will pay Mac $600,000 (payable evenly over the next 15 years) for the exclusive right to manufacture and sell the product. Under the other, they will form a business and contribute capital to it to begin manufacturing and selling the product; Mac will receive 20% of the company's shares of stock in exchange for all of his patent rights. Discuss which alternative is better for Mac.

51. **LO.3** Freys, Inc., sells a 12-year franchise to Reynaldo. The franchise contains many restrictions on how Reynaldo may operate his store. For instance, Reynaldo cannot use less than Grade 10 Idaho potatoes, must fry the potatoes at a constant 410 degrees, dress store personnel in Freys-approved uniforms, and have a Freys sign that meets detailed specifications on size, color, and construction. When the franchise contract is signed, Reynaldo makes a noncontingent $160,000 payment to Freys. During the same year, Reynaldo pays Freys $300,000—14% of Reynaldo's sales. How does Freys treat each of these payments? How does Reynaldo treat each of the payments?

ISSUE ID

52. **LO.3** Alice owns numerous office buildings. A major tenant of one of the buildings wished to cancel its lease because it was moving to another city. After lengthy negotiations, the tenant paid Alice $78,000 to cancel its obligations under the lease. If the tenant had fulfilled the lease terms, Alice would have received rent of $322,000. What factors should Alice consider to determine the amount and character of her income from these circumstances?

53. **LO.3** Sally rented an apartment from the same company that employs her. Her lease began on August 1, 2011, and was due to expire on July 31, 2012, but, her landlord/employer needed the building to expand its warehouse facilities. Therefore, Sally's landlord/employer paid her $23,000 to cancel the lease. Sally received the $23,000 on November 30, 2011, moved out, and rented another apartment. How should Sally treat the $23,000?

54. **LO.4** Chandra held vacant land that qualified as an investment asset. She had purchased the vacant land on April 10, 2010. She exchanged the vacant land for a rental house in a qualifying like-kind exchange on January 22, 2011. Chandra intended to hold the rental house for several years and then sell it, but, she received an "offer she could not refuse" and sold the house on November 22, 2011, for a substantial gain. What was Chandra's holding period for the rental house?

55. **LO.4** Nick inherited 130 shares of Beige stock when his mother, Cherie, died. Cherie had acquired the stock for a total of $300,000 on November 15, 2010. She died on August 10, 2011, and the shares were worth a total of $225,000 at that time. Nick sold the shares for $236,000 on December 22, 2011. How much gain or loss does Nick have, and what is the nature of that gain or loss?

56. **LO.4** Sarah received a gift of farmland from her father. The land was worth $4 million at the date of the gift, had been farmed by her father for 40 years, and had a tax basis for her father of $30,000. Sarah never farmed the land and sold it eight months after receiving it from her father for $4.2 million. What is Sarah's holding period for the farmland, and what is the nature of the gain from its disposition?

57. **LO.5** Dennis sells short 100 shares of ARC stock at $20 per share on January 15, 2011. He buys 200 shares of ARC stock on April 1, 2011, at $25 per share. On May 2, 2011, he closes the short sale by delivering 100 of the shares purchased on April 1.
    a. What are the amount and nature of Dennis's loss upon closing the short sale?
    b. When does the holding period for the remaining 100 shares begin?
    c. If Dennis sells (at $27 per share) the remaining 100 shares on January 20, 2012, what will be the nature of his gain or loss?

58. **LO.5** Elaine Case (single with no dependents) has the following transactions in 2011:

COMMUNICATIONS

AGI (exclusive of capital gains and losses)	$240,000
Long-term capital gain	22,000
Long-term capital loss	(8,000)
Short-term capital gain	19,000
Short-term capital loss	(23,000)

What is Elaine's net capital gain or loss? Draft a letter to Elaine describing how the net capital gain or loss will be treated on her tax return. Assume Elaine's income from other sources puts her in the 35% bracket. Elaine's address is 300 Ireland Avenue, Shepherdstown, WV 25443.

59. **LO.3, 5** In 2011, Betty (head of household with three dependents) had an $18,000 loss from the sale of a personal residence. She also purchased from an individual inventor for $18,000 (and resold in two months for $7,000) a patent on a rubber bonding process. The patent had not yet been reduced to practice. Betty purchased the patent as an investment. Additionally, she had the following capital gains and losses from stock transactions:

COMMUNICATIONS

Long-term capital loss	($ 5,000)
Long-term capital loss carryover from 2010	(12,000)
Short-term capital gain	21,000
Short-term capital loss	(6,000)

What is Betty's net capital gain or loss? Draft a letter to Betty explaining the tax treatment of the sale of her personal residence. Assume Betty's income from other sources puts her in the 35% bracket. Betty's address is 1120 West Street, Ashland, OR 97520.

60. **LO.2, 4, 5** Bridgette is known as the "doll lady." She started collecting dolls as a child, always received one or more dolls as gifts on her birthday, never sold any dolls, and eventually owned 600 dolls. She is retiring and moving to a small apartment and has decided to sell her collection. She lists the dolls on an Internet auction site and, to her

ISSUE ID

great surprise, receives an offer from another doll collector of $45,000 for the entire collection. Bridgette sells the entire collection, except for five dolls that she purchased during the last year. She had owned all the dolls sold for more than a year. What tax factors should Bridgette consider in deciding how to report the sale?

61. **LO.5** Phil and Susan are married, filing a joint return. The couple have two dependent children. Susan has wages of $34,000 in 2011. Phil does not work due to a disability, but he is a buyer and seller of stocks on the Internet. He generally buys and holds for long-term gain, but occasionally gets in and out of a stock quickly. The couple's 2011 stock transactions are detailed below. In addition, they have $2,300 of qualifying dividends.

Item	Date Acquired	Date Sold	Cost	Sales Price
Blue stock	11/10/10	03/12/11	$ 3,000	$ 6,000
Puce stock	12/13/09	05/23/11	36,000	32,000
Beige stock	12/14/06	07/14/11	13,000	14,500
Red stock	06/29/10	05/18/11	26,000	27,000
Black stock	05/15/10	10/18/11	67,000	67,800
Gray stock	04/23/09	10/18/11	89,000	88,200

What is Phil and Susan's AGI?

62. **LO.5** Phil has the following long-term capital gains and losses for 2011: $35,000 28% gain, $13,000 28% loss, $18,000 25% gain, and $34,000 0%/15% gain. He also has a $23,000 short-term loss and a $5,000 short-term gain. What is Phil's AGI from these transactions, and if he has a net long-term capital gain, what is its makeup in terms of the alternative tax rates?

63. **LO.5** Hiawatha has the following long-term capital gains and losses for 2011: $45,000 28% gain, $53,000 28% loss, $18,000 25% gain, and $34,000 0%/15% loss. He also has a $23,000 short-term loss and a $75,000 short-term gain. What is Hiawatha's AGI from these transactions, and if he has a net long-term capital gain, what is its makeup in terms of the alternative tax rates?

64. **LO.5** For 2011, Ashley has gross income of $8,500 and a $5,000 long-term capital loss. She claims the standard deduction. Ashley is 35 years old and single with two dependent children. How much of Ashley's $5,000 capital loss carries over to 2012?

65. **LO.5** Jane and Blair are married filing jointly and have 2011 taxable income of $97,000. The taxable income includes $5,000 of gain from a capital asset held for five years, $2,100 of gain from a capital asset held seven months, and $13,000 of gain from a capital asset held four years. All the capital assets were stock in publicly traded corporations. Jane and Blair also have qualified dividend income of $3,000. What is the couple's tax on taxable income?

66. **LO.5** For 2011, Wilma has properly determined taxable income of $36,000, including $3,000 of unrecaptured § 1250 gain and $8,200 of 0%/15% gain. Wilma qualifies for head-of-household filing status. Compute Wilma's tax liability and the tax savings from the alternative tax on net capital gain.

67. **LO.5** Asok's AGI for 2011 is $133,050. Included in this AGI is a $45,000 25% long-term capital gain and a $13,000 0%/15% long-term capital gain. Asok is single, uses the standard deduction, and has only his personal exemption. Compute his taxable income, the tax liability, and the tax savings from the alternative tax on net capital gain.

68. **LO.6** Chartreuse, Inc., a C corporation, has taxable income from operations of $1,432,000 for 2011. It also has a net long-term capital loss of $455,000 from the sale of a subsidiary's stock. The year 2011 is the first year in the last 10 years that Chartreuse has not had at least $500,000 per year of net long-term capital gains. What is Chartreuse's 2011 taxable income, and what, if anything, can it do with any unused capital losses?

DECISION MAKING

69. **LO.3, 14** Hsui, who is single, is the owner of a sole proprietorship. Two years ago, Hsui developed a process for preserving fresh fruit that gives the fruit a much longer shelf life. The process is not patented or copyrighted, but only Hsui knows how it works. Hsui has

been approached by a company that would like to buy the process. Hsui insists that she receive a long-term employment contract with the acquiring company as well as be paid for the rights to the process. The acquiring company offers Hsui a choice of two options: (1) $850,000 in cash for the process and a 10-year covenant not to compete at $45,000 per year or (2) $850,000 in cash for a 10-year covenant not to compete and $45,000 per year for 10 years in payment for the process. Which option should Hsui accept? What is the tax effect on the acquiring company of each approach?

70. **LO.8** A sculpture that Korliss Kane held for investment was destroyed in a flood. The sculpture was insured, and Korliss had a $60,000 gain from this casualty. He also had a $17,000 loss from an uninsured antique vase that was destroyed by the flood. The vase was also held for investment. Korliss had no other property transactions during the year and has no nonrecaptured § 1231 losses from prior years. Both the sculpture and the vase had been held more than one year when the flood occurred. Compute Korliss's net gain or loss and identify how it would be treated. Also, write a letter to Korliss explaining the nature of the gain or loss. Korliss's address is 2367 Meridian Road, Hannibal Point, MO 34901.

COMMUNICATIONS

71. **LO.8** Keshara has the following net § 1231 results for each of the years shown. What would be the nature of the net gains in 2010 and 2011?

Tax Year	Net § 1231 Loss	Net § 1231 Gain
2006	$16,000	
2007	33,000	
2008	32,000	
2009		$41,000
2010		30,000
2011		41,000

72. **LO.8, 14** Jingie owns two parcels of business land (§ 1231 assets). One parcel can be sold at a loss of $60,000, and the other parcel can be sold at a gain of $70,000. Jingie has no nonrecaptured § 1231 losses from prior years. The parcels could be sold at any time because potential purchasers are abundant. Jingie has a $35,000 short-term capital loss carryover from a prior tax year and no capital assets that could be sold to generate long-term capital gains. Both the land parcels have been held more than one year. What should Jingie do based upon these facts? (Assume tax rates are constant and ignore the present value of future cash flow.)

DECISION MAKING

73. **LO.7, 8, 9** Siena Industries (a sole proprietorship) sold three § 1231 assets during 2011. Data on these property dispositions are as follows:

Asset	Cost	Acquired	Depreciation	Sold for	Sold on
Rack	$100,000	10/10/07	$65,000	$75,000	10/10/11
Forklift	35,000	10/16/08	23,000	5,000	10/10/11
Bin	87,000	03/12/10	34,000	60,000	10/10/11

a. Determine the amount and the character of the recognized gain or loss from the disposition of each asset.
b. Assuming Siena has no nonrecaptured net § 1231 losses from prior years, how much of the 2011 recognized gains is treated as capital gains?

74. **LO.8, 9** Copper Industries (a sole proprietorship) sold three § 1231 assets during 2011. Data on these property dispositions are as follows:

Asset	Cost	Acquired	Depreciation	Sold for	Sold on
Rack	$110,000	10/10/08	$60,000	$55,000	10/10/11
Forklift	45,000	10/16/07	21,000	15,000	10/10/11
Bin	97,000	03/12/10	34,000	60,000	10/10/11

a. Determine the amount and the character of the recognized gain or loss from the disposition of each asset.
b. Assuming Copper has $2,000 nonrecaptured net § 1231 losses from prior years, how much of the 2011 recognized gains is treated as capital gains?

COMMUNICATIONS

75. **LO.8, 9** On December 1, 2009, Lavender Manufacturing Company (a corporation) purchased another company's assets, including a patent. The patent was used in Lavender's manufacturing operations; $49,500 was allocated to the patent, and it was amortized at the rate of $275 per month. On July 30, 2011, Lavender sold the patent for $70,000. Twenty months of amortization had been taken on the patent. What are the amount and nature of the gain Lavender recognizes on the disposition of the patent? Write a letter to Lavender discussing the treatment of the gain. Lavender's address is 6734 Grover Street, Back Bay Harbor, ME 23890. The letter should be addressed to Bill Cubit, Controller.

76. **LO.8, 10** On June 1, 2007, Sparrow Enterprises (not a corporation) acquired a retail store building for $500,000 (with $100,000 being allocated to the land). The store building was 39-year real property, and the straight-line cost recovery method was used. The property was sold on June 21, 2011, for $385,000.
a. Compute the cost recovery and adjusted basis for the building using Table 8.6 from Chapter 8.
b. What are the amount and nature of Sparrow's gain or loss from disposition of the building? What amount, if any, of the gain is unrecaptured § 1250 gain?

77. **LO.8, 9, 10** On May 2, 1986, Hannah acquired residential real estate for $450,000. Of the cost, $100,000 was allocated to the land and $350,000 to the building. On January 20, 2011, the building, which then had an adjusted basis of $0, was sold for $445,000 and the land for $500,000.
a. Determine the amount and character of the recognized gain from the sale of the building.
b. Determine the amount and character of the recognized gain from the sale of the land.

78. **LO.8, 9, 10** Larry is the sole proprietor of a trampoline shop. During 2011, the following transactions occurred:

- Unimproved land adjacent to the store was condemned by the city on February 1. The condemnation proceeds were $25,000. The land, acquired in 1984, had an allocable basis of $40,000. Larry has additional parking across the street and plans to use the condemnation proceeds to build his inventory.
- A truck used to deliver trampolines was sold on January 2 for $3,500. The truck was purchased on January 2, 2007, for $6,000. On the date of sale, the adjusted basis was zero.
- Larry sold an antique rowing machine at an auction. Net proceeds were $3,900. The rowing machine was purchased as used equipment 17 years ago for $5,200 and is fully depreciated.
- Larry sold an apartment building for $200,000 on September 1. The rental property was purchased on September 1, 2008, for $150,000 and was being depreciated over a 27.5-year life using the straight-line method. At the date of sale, the adjusted basis was $124,783.
- Larry's personal yacht was stolen on September 5. The yacht had been purchased in August at a cost of $25,000. The fair market value immediately preceding the theft was $19,600. Larry was insured for 50% of the original cost, and he received $12,500 on December 1.
- Larry sold a Buick on May 1 for $9,600. The vehicle had been used exclusively for personal purposes. It was purchased on September 1, 2007, for $20,800.
- Larry's trampoline stretching machine (owned two years) was stolen on May 5, but the business's insurance company will not pay any of the machine's value because Larry failed to pay the insurance premium. The machine had a fair market value of $8,000 and an adjusted basis of $6,000 at the time of theft.
- Larry had AGI of $402,000 from sources other than those described above.
- Larry has no nonrecaptured § 1231 lookback losses.

a. For each transaction, what are the amount and nature of recognized gain or loss?
b. What is Larry's 2011 AGI?

79. **LO.8, 10** On January 1, 2002, Stephanie Bridges acquired depreciable real property for $50,000. She used straight-line depreciation to compute the asset's cost recovery. The asset was sold for $96,000 on January 3, 2011, when its adjusted basis was $38,000.

COMMUNICATIONS

   a. What are the amount and nature of the gain if the real property was residential?
   b. Stephanie is curious about how the recapture rules differ for residential rental real estate acquired in 1986 and for residential rental real estate acquired in 1987 and thereafter. Write a letter to Stephanie explaining the differences. Her address is 2345 Westridge Street #23, Homer, MT 67342.

80. **LO.8, 9, 11, 14** Joanne is in the 35% tax bracket and owns depreciable business equipment that she purchased several years ago for $135,000. She has taken $100,000 of depreciation on the equipment, and it is worth $85,000. Joanne's niece, Susan, is starting a new business and is short of cash. Susan has asked Joanne to gift the equipment to her so that Susan can use it in her business. Joanne no longer needs the equipment. Identify the alternatives available to Joanne if she wishes to help Susan and the tax effects of those alternatives. (Assume all alternatives involve the business equipment in one way or another, and ignore the gift tax.)

DECISION MAKING

81. **LO.8, 9, 11** Hazel received tangible personal property with a fair market value of $55,000 as a gift in 2009. The donor had purchased the property for $77,000 and taken $77,000 of depreciation. Hazel used the property in her business. Hazel sells the property for $13,000 in 2011. What are the tax status of the property and the nature of the recognized gain when she sells the property?

82. **LO.8, 9, 11** Evan receives tangible personal property as an inheritance in 2009. The property was depreciated by the deceased (Evan's father), and Evan will also depreciate it. At the date of the deceased's death, the property was worth $432,000. The deceased had purchased it for $900,000 and taken $623,000 of depreciation on the property. Evan takes $123,000 of depreciation on the property before selling it for $482,000 in 2011. What are the tax status of the property and the nature of the recognized gain when Evan sells the property?

83. **LO.11** David contributes to charity some tangible personal property that he had used in his business and depreciated. At the date of the donation, the property has a fair market value of $233,000 and an adjusted basis of zero; it was originally acquired for $400,000. What is the amount of David's charitable contribution?

84. **LO.8, 9, 11** Dedriea contributes to her wholly owned corporation some tangible personal property that she had used in her sole proprietorship business and depreciated. She had acquired the property for $566,000 and taken $431,000 of depreciation on it before contributing it to the corporation. At the date of the contribution, the property had a fair market value of $289,000. The corporation took $100,000 of depreciation on the property and then sold it for $88,000 in 2011. What are the tax status of the property to the corporation and the nature of the recognized gain or loss when the corporation sells the property?

85. **LO.8, 9, 12** Magenta Corporation purchased depreciable tangible personal property for $100,000 in 2008 and immediately expensed the entire cost under § 179. In 2011, when the property was worth $40,000, Magenta distributed it as a dividend to the corporation's sole shareholder. What was the tax status of this property for Magenta, and what is the nature of the recognized gain or loss from the distribution of the property?

86. **LO.7, 8, 10** Jasmine owned rental real estate that she sold to her tenant in an installment sale. Jasmine had acquired the property in 2000 for $400,000, had taken $178,000 of depreciation on it, and sold it for $210,000, receiving $25,000 immediately and the balance (plus interest at a market rate) in equal payments of $18,500 for 10 years. What is the nature of the recognized gain or loss from this transaction?

87. **LO.9** Jay sold three items of business equipment for a total of $300,000. None of the equipment was appraised to determine its value. Jay's cost and adjusted basis for the assets are shown on the next page.

DECISION MAKING

Asset	Cost	Adjusted Basis
Skidder	$230,000	$ 40,000
Driller	120,000	60,000
Platform	620,000	–0–
Total	$970,000	$100,000

Jay has been unable to establish the fair market values of the three assets. All he can determine is that combined they were worth $300,000 to the buyer in this arm's length transaction. How should Jay allocate the sales price and figure the gain or loss on the sale of the three assets?

CUMULATIVE PROBLEMS

TAX RETURN PROBLEM

H&R BLOCK At Home

88. Susan Panda lives at 1310 Willow Lane, Wayne, OH 23412, and her Social Security number is 123–45–6789. Susan is single and has a 20-year-old son, Karl. His Social Security number is 111–11–1111. Karl lives with Susan, and she fully supports him. Karl spent 2010 traveling in Europe and was not a college student. He had gross income of $4,355 in 2010.

Susan owns the Panda Enterprises, LLC sole proprietorship, a data processing service (98–7654321), which is located at 456 Hill Street, Wayne, OH 23401. The business activity code is 514210. Her 2010 Form 1040, Schedule C for Panda Enterprises shows revenues of $155,000, office expenses of $66,759, employee salary of $23,000, employee payroll taxes of $1,760, meals and entertainment expenses (before the 50% reduction) of $22,000, and rent expense of $34,000. The rent expense includes payments related to renting an office ($30,000) and payments related to renting various equipment ($4,000). There is no depreciation because all depreciable equipment owned has been fully depreciated in previous years. No fringe benefits are provided to the employee. Susan personally purchases health insurance on herself and Karl. The premiums are $23,000 per year.

Susan has an extensive stock portfolio and has prepared the following analysis:

Stock	Number of Shares	Date Purchased	Date Sold	Per Share Cost	Per Share Selling Price	Total Dividends
Beige	10	10/18/09	10/11/10	$80	$ 74	$30
Garland	30	10/11/03	10/11/10	43	157	70
Puce	15	3/10/10	8/11/10	62	33	45

NOTE: The per-share cost includes commissions, and the per-share selling price is net of commissions. Also, the dividends are the actual dividends received in 2010.

Susan had $800 of interest income from State of Ohio bonds and $600 of interest income on her Wayne Savings Bank account. She received $25,000 of alimony from her former husband. His Social Security number is 123–45–6788.

Susan itemizes her deductions and had the following items, which may be relevant to her return:

Item	Amount	Comment
Unreimbursed medical expenses for Susan (all for visits to doctors)	$1,786	Does not include health insurance premiums.
State income taxes paid	1,830	
Real property taxes on personal residence	3,230	
Interest paid on home mortgage (Form 1098)	8,137	The loan is secured by the residence and was incurred when the home was purchased.
Charitable contributions	940	Cash paid to Susan's church.
Sales taxes	619	Amount per sales tax table.

Susan made a $3,000 estimated Federal income tax payment, does not wish any of her taxes to finance presidential elections, has no foreign bank accounts or trusts, and wishes any refund to be applied against her 2011 taxes.

Compute Susan's net tax payable or refund due for 2010. If you use tax forms for your computations, you will need Form 1040 and Schedules A, C, D, and SE. Suggested software: H&R BLOCK At Home.

TAX RETURN PROBLEM

H&R BLOCK At Home

89. Justin Stone was an employee of DataCare Services, Inc. His salary was $45,000 through November 10, 2010, when he was laid off. He received $7,000 of unemployment compensation from November 11, 2010, through December 31, 2010. FICA withholdings were as follows: Social Security of $2,790 ($45,000 × 6.2%) and Medicare of $653 ($45,000 × 1.45%). Justin lives at 112 Green Road, Sandusky, ID 45623. His Social Security number is 111–11–1111. Justin owned an apartment building until November 22, 2010, when he sold it for $200,000. For 2010, he had rent revenue of $33,000. He incurred and paid expenses as follows: $4,568 of repairs, $22,000 of mortgage interest, and $1,000 of miscellaneous expenses. He had purchased the building on January 2, 2004, for $125,000. The building generated an operating profit each year that Justin owned it.

Other information follows:

- On November 22, 2010, Justin sold for $3,500 equipment that had been used for repairing various items in the apartments. The equipment was purchased for $25,000 on July 10, 2003, and was fully depreciated prior to 2010.
- Justin has $3,000 of unrecaptured § 1231 losses from prior years.
- Justin is age 38, single, divorced, and has custody of his nine-year-old son, Flint. Justin provides more than 50% of Flint's support. Flint's Social Security number is 123–45–6789.
- Justin had $1,000 interest income from Blue Corporation bonds.
- Justin had $1,500 interest income from a State Bank certificate of deposit.
- Justin had a $2,000 0%/15% long-term capital gain distribution from the Brown Stock Investment Fund.
- Justin had the following itemized deductions: $5,600 real estate taxes on his home; $8,900 mortgage interest on his home; $760 charitable contributions (all in cash, properly documented, and no single contribution exceeded $25); $7,300 state income tax withholding during 2010; $2,000 state estimated income tax payments during 2010; $2,600 sales taxes paid.
- Justin does not wish to donate to the Presidential Election Campaign Fund.
- He had $12,000 of Federal income tax withholding during 2010 and made total Federal estimated income tax payments of $14,000 during 2010.

Compute Justin's 2010 net tax payable or refund due. If you use tax forms for your computations, you will need Form 1040 and Schedules A, B, D, and E. You will also need Form 4797, but ignore Form 6251. Suggested software: H&R BLOCK At Home.

See Appendix E for Comprehensive Tax Return Problems—Form 1040

RESEARCH PROBLEMS

Note: Solutions to Research Problems can be prepared by using the **Checkpoint® Student Edition** online research product, which is available to accompany this text. It is also possible to prepare solutions to the Research Problems by using tax research materials found in a standard tax library.

THOMSON REUTERS
Checkpoint® Student Edition

COMMUNICATIONS

Research Problem 1. Clean Corporation runs a chain of dry cleaners. Borax is used heavily in Clean's dry cleaning process and has been in short supply several times in the past. Clean Corporation buys a controlling interest in Dig Corporation—a borax mining concern. Clean's sole reason for purchasing the Dig stock is to assure Clean of a continuous supply of borax if another shortage develops. Although borax must be refined before it is usable for dry cleaning purposes, a well-established commodities market exists for trading unrefined borax for refined borax. After owning the Dig stock for several years, Clean sells the stock at a loss because Dig is in difficult financial straits. Clean no longer needs to own Dig because Clean has obtained an alternative source of borax. What is the nature of Clean's loss on the disposition of the Dig Corporation stock? Write a letter to the controller, Salvio Guitterez, that contains your advice and prepare a memo for the tax files. The mailing address of Clean Corporation is 4455 Whitman Way, San Mateo, CA 44589.

Research Problem 2. Clyde had worked for many years as the chief executive of Red Industries, Inc., and had also been a major shareholder. Clyde and the company had a falling out, and Clyde was terminated. Clyde and Red executed a document under which Clyde's stock in Red would be redeemed and Clyde would agree not to compete against Red in its geographic service area. After extensive negotiations between the parties, Clyde agreed to surrender his Red stock in exchange for $600,000. Clyde's basis in his shares was $143,000, and he had held the shares for 17 years. The agreement made no explicit allocation of any of the $600,000 to Clyde's agreement not to compete against Red. How should Clyde treat the $600,000 payment on his 2011 tax return?

Research Problem 3. An individual cash basis taxpayer sells rental real estate on the installment basis. The gain from the disposition is $45,000: $30,000 of potential 25% gain and $15,000 of potential 0%/15% gain. In what sequence are these gains recognized as gain is recognized on the installment sale?

Research Problem 4. Walter is both a real estate developer and the owner and manager of residential rental real estate. Walter is retiring and is going to sell both the land he is holding for future development and the rental properties he owns. Straight-line depreciation was used to depreciate the rental real estate. The rental properties will be sold at a substantial loss, and the development property will be sold at a substantial gain. What is the nature of these gains and losses?

Partial list of research aids:
§§ 1221 and 1231.
Zane R. Tollis, 65 TCM 1951, T.C.Memo. 1993–63.

Research Problem 5. In 2007, a taxpayer made leasehold improvements that were eligible for a 15-year MACRS life. Straight-line depreciation was taken on the improvements. Will these improvements be subject to either § 1245 or § 1250 depreciation recapture if they are eventually disposed of at a recognized gain?

INTERNET *activity*

Use the tax resources of the Internet to address the following questions. Do not restrict your search to the Web, but include a review of newsgroups and general reference materials, practitioner sites and resources, primary sources of the tax law, chat rooms and discussion groups, and other opportunities.

Research Problem 6. Find a state website that has tax forms and instructions for that state. Let's call that state "X." Find a discussion in those sources that reveals whether state X taxes gains from the sale of real estate that is located in state Y when the taxpayer is an individual and is a full-time resident of state X.

Research Problem 7. Determine whether Australia has an equivalent to § 1231 treatment for gains from the disposition of business depreciable assets.

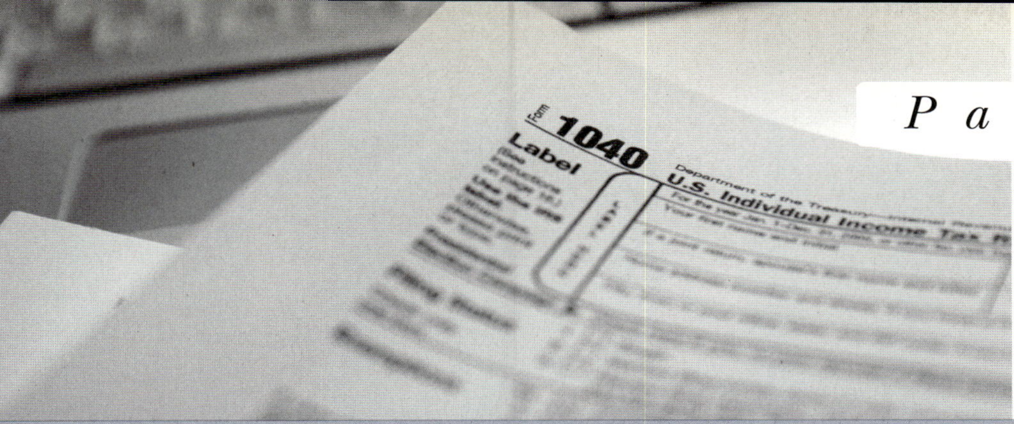

Part 5

Special Tax Computations and Accounting Periods and Methods

The taxpayer must calculate the tax liability in accordance with the basic tax formula and also in accordance with the tax formula for the alternative minimum tax (AMT). The basic tax formula was presented in Part 1, and the AMT formula is covered in Part 5. This part also provides a more comprehensive examination of the accounting periods and accounting methods that were introduced in Part 2.

CHAPTER 15

Alternative Minimum Tax

LEARNING OBJECTIVES

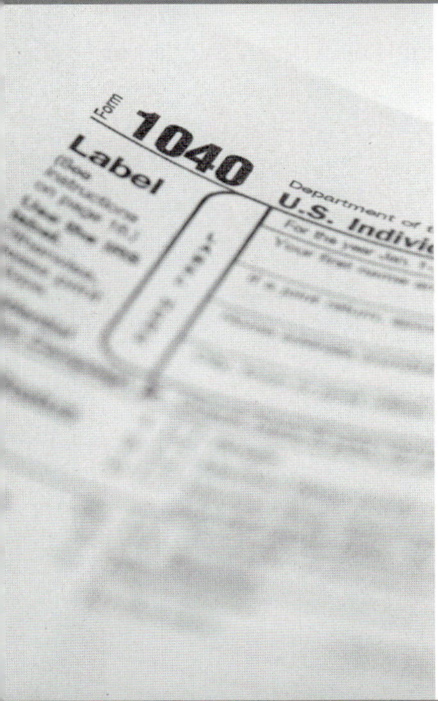

After completing Chapter 15, you should be able to:

LO.1

Explain the rationale for the alternative minimum tax (AMT).

LO.2

Understand the formula for computing the AMT for individuals.

LO.3

Identify the adjustments made in calculating the AMT.

LO.4

Identify the tax preferences that are included in calculating the AMT.

LO.5

Apply the formula for computing the AMT and complete a Form 6251.

LO.6

Describe the role of the AMT credit in the alternative minimum tax structure.

LO.7

Illustrate the basic features of the corporate AMT.

LO.8

Identify tax planning opportunities to minimize the AMT.

OUTLINE

For the latest in changes to tax legislation, visit **www.cengage.com/taxation/swft.**

FRAMEWORK 1040: Tax Formula for Individuals

This chapter covers the boldfaced portions of the Tax Formula for Individuals that was introduced in Figure 3.1 on p. 3-3. Below those portions are the sections of Form 1040 where the results are reported.

Income (broadly conceived)	$xx,xxx
Less: Exclusions	(x,xxx)
Gross income	$xx,xxx
Less: Deductions for adjusted gross income	(x,xxx)
Adjusted gross income	$xx,xxx
Less: The greater of total itemized deductions *or* the standard deduction	(x,xxx)
Personal and dependency exemptions	(x,xxx)
Taxable income	$xx,xxx
Tax on taxable income (see Tax Tables or Tax Rate Schedules)	$ x,xxx
Less: Tax credits (including income taxes withheld and prepaid)	(xxx)
Tax due (or refund)	**$ xxx**

FORM 1040 (p. 2)

45	**Alternative minimum tax** (see instructions). Attach Form 6251 . . . .

THE BIG PICTURE Tax Solutions for the Real World

EFFECTS OF THE AMT

Bob and Carol are unmarried individuals who have been engaged for four months. They work for the same employer and earn identical compensation. They have the same amount of gross income, including the same amount of investment income, which consists solely of interest income; they have similar investments in tax-exempt bonds that produce identical amounts of interest income. They also have the same amount of deductions.

Bob's tax return is prepared by Adam, and Carol's tax return is prepared by Eve. While discussing their tax liability one day at lunch, Carol is dismayed to learn that she paid $15,000 more in Federal income taxes than Bob did for the tax year. Carol meets with Eve that evening. Eve reviews Carol's tax return and assures her that her tax liability was calculated properly.

The above events raise a number of interesting questions for Bob and Carol. Why didn't Bob and Carol have the same tax liability? Were both tax returns properly prepared? Should Carol consider replacing her tax return preparer Eve with Adam? Is it possible and/or desirable for Carol to file an amended return? Should Bob do anything? **Read the chapter and formulate your response.**

The tax law contains many incentives that are intended to influence the economic and social behavior of taxpayers (refer to Chapter 1). Some taxpayers have been able to take advantage of enough of these incentives to avoid or minimize any liability for Federal income tax. Although these taxpayers were reducing taxes legally, Congress became concerned about the inequity that results when taxpayers with substantial economic incomes can avoid paying any income tax. Such inequity can undermine the public's respect for the entire tax system.[1] To attempt to alleviate this inequity, the **alternative minimum tax (AMT)** was enacted as a backup to the regular income tax.

LO.1

Explain the rationale for the alternative minimum tax (AMT).

The individual AMT is discussed in the first part of this chapter. The corporate AMT is similar to the individual AMT, but differs in several important ways. Details of the corporate AMT are presented in the last part of the chapter.

15.1 Individual Alternative Minimum Tax

LO.2

Understand the formula for computing the AMT for individuals.

AMT FORMULA FOR ALTERNATIVE MINIMUM TAXABLE INCOME (AMTI)

The AMT is separate from, but parallel to, the regular income tax system.[2] Most income and expense items are treated the same way for both regular income tax and AMT purposes. For example, a taxpayer's salary is included in computing taxable income and also is included in alternative minimum taxable income (AMTI). Alimony paid is allowed as a deduction *for* AGI for both regular income tax and AMT purposes. Certain itemized deductions, such as charitable contributions and gambling losses, are allowed for both regular income tax and AMT purposes.

On the other hand, some income and expense items are treated differently for regular income tax and AMT purposes. For example, interest income on bonds issued by state, county, or local governments is *excluded* in computing taxable income. However, such interest may be *included* in computing AMTI if it is paid on private activity bonds. The deduction for personal and dependency exemptions is *allowed* for regular income tax purposes, but it is *disallowed* for AMT purposes.

In other cases, certain items are considered in both the regular income tax and AMT computations, but the amounts are different. For example, the completed contract method can be used to report income from some long-term contracts for regular income tax purposes, but the percentage of completion method is required for AMT purposes. Depreciation is allowed as a deduction for both regular income tax and AMT purposes, but the *amount* of the regular income tax deduction may be different from the amount of the AMT deduction. Medical expenses are deductible in calculating both taxable income and AMTI, but the floor on the deduction is different.

The parallel but separate nature of the AMT means that AMTI usually differs from taxable income. It is possible to compute AMTI by direct application of the AMT provisions, using the following formula.

Gross income computed by applying the AMT rules
Minus: Deductions computed by applying the AMT rules
Equals: AMTI before tax preferences
Plus: Tax preferences
Equals: Alternative minimum taxable income

While the direct approach for computing AMTI appears quite logical, both the tax law and the tax forms provide a very different approach. Both of these use taxable income as the starting point for computing AMTI, as shown in Figure 15.1. This indirect approach for computing AMTI is analogous to the indirect approach used in calculating a net operating loss.

[1] *General Explanation of the Tax Reform Act of 1986 ("Blue Book")*, prepared by The Staff of the Joint Committee on Taxation, May 4, 1987, H.R. 3838, 99th Cong., pp. 432–433.

[2] § 55.

TAX *in* *the NEWS*

The Growing Tentacles of the AMT

The AMT exists because of congressional reaction to a report in 1969 that 155 taxpayers whose taxable income exceeded $200,000 did not pay any Federal income tax. As such, the AMT was created as a tax that would be levied only on the wealthy.

As it now stands, even with annual fixes by Congress (e.g., increases in the exemption amount), the AMT continues to catch more and more taxpayers.

Individual AMT Taxpayers	
1990	.1 million
1996	.7 million
2001	1.3 million
2002	1.9 million
2003	2.4 million
2004	3.1 million
2005	3.5 million
2006–2010	4 to 5 million

The purpose of the AMT formula is to *reconcile* taxable income to AMTI. This reconciliation is similar to a bank reconciliation, which reconciles a checkbook balance to a bank balance by considering differences between the depositor's records and the bank's records. The reconciliation of taxable income to AMTI is accomplished by entering reconciling items to account for differences between regular income tax provisions and AMT provisions. These reconciling items are referred to as **AMT adjustments** or **tax preferences**. *Adjustments* can be either positive or negative, as shown in the formula in Figure 15.1. Tax preferences always are positive.

Adjustments

Most adjustments relate to *timing differences* that arise because of differing regular income tax and AMT treatments. Adjustments that are caused by timing differences eventually *reverse*; that is, positive adjustments will be offset by negative adjustments in the future, and vice versa.[3]

ETHICS *& Equity*

Effect of the AMT on Accelerating Expenses

Maurice, a single, cash method taxpayer, projects his taxable income for 2011 to be about $300,000. For AMT purposes, he reports positive adjustments and tax preferences of $200,000. He anticipates that his taxable income and positive adjustments and preferences will be about the same for 2012. He is evaluating several proposed transactions that could affect his 2011 tax liability.

One proposal involves an office building for which he is currently negotiating a lease. The lease has a starting date of July 1, 2011, provides for annual rent of $24,000, and carries an 18-month prepayment clause. Though Maurice favors a five-year lease, his tax adviser has suggested an 18-month period with an option to renew for 42 months. The adviser points out the tax advantage of being able to deduct the $36,000 of rent at the inception of the lease. The projected tax liability under each option would be as follows.

	18-Month Lease	5-Year Lease
Regular income tax liability	$ 72,017	$ 79,937
AMT	54,403	53,203
Total	$126,420	$133,140

After comparing these results, Maurice takes his adviser's suggestion. The shorter-term lease reduces his taxes by about 5 percent.

Is it appropriate for the tax law to allow Maurice to avoid taxes in this manner? Should Maurice take the shorter lease?

[3]§ 56.

FIGURE 15.1 Alternative Minimum Taxable Income (AMTI) Formula

Taxable income
Plus: Positive AMT adjustments
Minus: Negative AMT adjustments
Equals: Taxable income after AMT adjustments
Plus: Tax preferences
Equals: Alternative minimum taxable income

For example, **circulation expenditures** can give rise to a timing difference that requires an AMT adjustment. For regular income tax purposes, circulation expenditures can be deducted in the year incurred. For AMT purposes, however, circulation expenditures must be deducted over a three-year period. This difference in treatment will be used to illustrate the role of adjustments in the formula for computing AMTI.

EXAMPLE 1

Bob had taxable income of $100,000 in 2011. In computing taxable income, he deducted $30,000 of circulation expenditures incurred in 2011. Bob's allowable deduction for AMT purposes was only $10,000. Therefore, an AMT adjustment was required in 2011 as follows.

Taxable income		$100,000
+ AMT adjustment		
Circulation expenditures deducted for regular income tax	$ 30,000	
Circulation expenditures allowed for AMT	(10,000)	
Positive adjustment		20,000
= AMTI before tax preferences		$120,000
+ Tax preferences		–0–
AMTI		$120,000

The allowable AMT deduction is $20,000 less than the allowable regular income tax deduction. Therefore, AMTI is $20,000 greater than taxable income. This is accomplished by entering a positive AMT adjustment of $20,000. ■

EXAMPLE 2

Bob from Example 1 has taxable income of $95,000 in 2012. Bob deducts $10,000 of circulation expenditures for AMT purposes, but he is not allowed a deduction for regular income tax purposes because all $30,000 was deducted in 2011. Therefore, a 2012 *negative* AMT adjustment is required.

Taxable income		$ 95,000
– AMT adjustment		
Circulation expenditures deducted for regular income tax	$ –0–	
Circulation expenditures allowed for AMT	(10,000)	
Negative adjustment		(10,000)
= AMTI before tax preferences		$ 85,000
+ Tax preferences		–0–
AMTI		$ 85,000

The allowable AMT deduction is $10,000 more than the allowable regular income tax deduction. Therefore, AMTI is $10,000 less than taxable income. This is accomplished by entering a negative AMT adjustment of $10,000. ■

TAX *in the NEWS*

WILL THE AMT BE FIXED?

At the present time, many taxpayers are wondering whether the AMT will continue to apply and, if so, whether Congress will do anything to prevent its reach from expanding. Currently, the AMT affects about 4 to 5 million taxpayers, but that number could soon grow to potentially as many as 26 million taxpayers, including many middle-income taxpayers.

Certainly, the AMT seems unlikely to go away. Senator Charles Grassley of Iowa, the ranking Republican on the Senate Finance Committee, observes that "Congress has done nothing to curb the AMT's growth." Grassley says that although most members of Congress "agree that something needs to be done quickly, the discussion doesn't go any further than that."

A major reason that the AMT appears to be here to stay is that the AMT has become an important source of government revenue. Some projections have the AMT producing more revenue than the regular Federal income tax on individuals, within just a few years.

In the recent past, Congress has applied a "patch," increasing the AMT exemption amounts for individual taxpayers, to prevent the AMT from applying to even more taxpayers. It is likely that Congress will continue to apply such patches.

Source: Adapted from Tom Herman, "Ask Dow Jones," *Tampa Tribune*, June 27, 2010, p. B4.

As noted previously, timing differences eventually reverse. Therefore, over time, total positive adjustments are offset by total negative adjustments with respect to a particular item.

EXAMPLE 3

Refer to Examples 1 and 2. The difference in regular income tax and AMT treatments of circulation expenditures will result in AMT adjustments over a three-year period.

Year	Regular Income Tax Deduction	AMT Deduction	AMT Adjustment
2011	$30,000	$10,000	+$20,000
2012	–0–	10,000	−10,000
2013	–0–	10,000	−10,000
Total	$30,000	$30,000	$ –0–

As the last column illustrates, if positive and negative AMT adjustments with respect to a particular item are caused by a timing difference, they will eventually net to zero. ■

Although most AMT adjustments relate to timing differences, there are exceptions. Adjustments that do not relate to timing differences result in a permanent difference between taxable income and AMTI.

Preferences

Some deductions and exclusions allowed to taxpayers for regular income tax purposes provide extraordinary tax savings. Congress has chosen to single out some of these items, which are referred to as tax preferences.[4] The AMT is designed to take back all or part of the tax benefits derived through the use of preferences in the computation of taxable income for regular income tax purposes. This is why taxable income, which is the starting point in computing AMTI, is increased by tax preference items. The effect of adding these preference items is to disallow for *AMT purposes* those preferences that were allowed in the regular income tax computation. AMT preferences include the following items, among others.

- Percentage depletion in excess of the property's adjusted basis.
- Excess intangible drilling costs reduced by 65 percent of the net income from oil, gas, and geothermal properties.
- Interest on certain private activity bonds.

[4] § 57.

FIGURE 15.2 Alternative Minimum Tax Formula

Regular taxable income
Plus or minus: Adjustments
Equals: Taxable income after AMT adjustments
Plus: Tax preferences
Equals: Alternative minimum taxable income
Minus: Exemption
Equals: Alternative minimum tax base
Times: 26% or 28% rate
Equals: Tentative minimum tax before credits
Minus: Alternative minimum tax foreign tax credit and other credits
Equals: Tentative minimum tax
Minus: Regular tax liability*
Equals: Alternative minimum tax (if amount is positive)

*This is the regular tax liability for the year reduced by any allowable foreign tax credit.

- Seven percent of the exclusion from gross income associated with gains on the sale of certain small business stock under § 1202.

AMT FORMULA: OTHER COMPONENTS

To convert AMTI to AMT, other formula components including the exemption, rates, credit, and regular tax liability must be considered. The AMT formula is summarized in Figure 15.2.

The relationship between the regular tax liability and the tentative AMT is key to the AMT formula. If the regular tax liability exceeds tentative AMT, then the AMT is zero. If the tentative AMT exceeds the regular tax liability, the amount of the excess is the AMT. In essence, the taxpayer pays whichever tax liability is greater—that calculated using the regular income tax rules or that calculated using the AMT rules. However, both the tax law and Form 6251 adopt this excess approach with the taxpayer paying the regular tax liability plus any AMT.

EXAMPLE 4

Anna, an unmarried individual, has regular taxable income of $100,000. She has positive adjustments of $40,000 and tax preferences of $25,000. Calculate her 2011 AMT. Anna's regular tax liability is $21,617. Her AMT is calculated as follows.

Taxable income (TI)	$100,000
Plus: Adjustments	40,000
Equals: TI after AMT adjustments	$140,000
Plus: Tax preferences	25,000
Equals: AMTI	$165,000
Minus: AMT exemption ($48,450 – $13,125)	(35,325)*
Equals: AMT base	$129,675
Times: AMT rate	× 26%
Equals: Tentative AMT	$ 33,716
Minus: Regular tax liability	(21,617)
Equals: AMT	$ 12,099

*Discussed in the next section.

Anna pays a total income tax of $33,716, consisting of her regular tax liability of $21,617 plus her AMT of $12,099. ■

Exemption Amount

The exemption amount can be thought of as a materiality provision. As such, it enables a taxpayer with a small amount of positive adjustments and tax preferences to avoid being subject to the burden of the AMT.

The *initial* exemption amount in 2011 is $74,450 for married taxpayers filing joint returns, $48,450 for single taxpayers, and $37,225 for married taxpayers filing separate returns.[5] However, the exemption is *phased out* at a rate of 25 cents on the dollar when AMTI exceeds these levels.

- $112,500 for single taxpayers.
- $150,000 for married taxpayers filing jointly.
- $75,000 for married taxpayers filing separately.

The phaseout of the exemption amount is an application of the wherewithal to pay concept. As the income level increases, so does the taxpayer's ability to pay income taxes.

EXAMPLE 5

Hugh, who is single, has AMTI of $192,500 for the year. His $48,450 initial AMT exemption is reduced by $20,000 [($192,500 − $112,500) × 25% phaseout rate]. Hugh's AMT exemption is $28,450 ($48,450 exemption − $20,000 reduction). ■

The following table shows the beginning and end of the 2011 AMT exemption phaseout range for each filing status.

		Phaseout	
Status	**Exemption**	**Begins at**	**Ends at**
Married, joint	$74,450	$150,000	$447,800
Single or head of household	48,450	112,500	306,300
Married, separate	37,225	75,000	223,900

AMT Rate Schedule

A graduated, two-tier AMT rate schedule applies to noncorporate taxpayers. A 26 percent rate applies to the first $175,000 of the AMT base ($87,500 for married, filing separately), and a 28 percent rate applies to the AMT base in excess of $175,000 ($87,500 for married, filing separately).[6] Any net long-term capital gain and qualified dividend income included in the AMT base are taxed at the favorable 15 percent or 0 percent rates, rather than at the AMT statutory rates.[7]

ETHICS & *Equity*

THE CASE OF THE DISAPPEARING INFLATION ADJUSTMENTS

Many areas of the regular income tax (e.g., rates, standard deductions, personal and dependency exemptions) are indexed annually for the effect of inflation. The alternative minimum tax (AMT), however, is not.

The AMT is defined as the excess of the tentative AMT over the regular income tax liability. Thus, the AMT results only if there is such an excess. Due to the absence of indexing for the AMT, a taxpayer's AMT can increase from one year to the next even though no other changes occur in the taxpayer's situation.

Suppose, for example, that for Year 1 a taxpayer's regular income tax liability is $98,000 and the tentative AMT is $106,000. Consequently, the AMT is $8,000. Further assume that for Year 2 the taxpayer's financial information is identical to Year 1. Because of indexing, however, the regular income tax liability is only $91,000, so the AMT becomes $15,000 ($106,000 − $91,000). Thus, the relief that indexation provides for regular income tax purposes is taken away by the AMT.

Is the tax law properly structured when it provides a hedge against inflation for some taxpayers (those not subject to the AMT) but not for others (those subject to the AMT)?

[5] § 55(d). For tax years beginning in 2012 and thereafter, the exemption amount is scheduled to be reduced to $45,000 for married taxpayers filing jointly, $33,750 for single or head-of-household taxpayers, and $22,500 for married taxpayers filing separately. However, the general consensus is that Congress will extend the increased exemption amounts for 2012. The 2010 exemption amounts are $72,450, $47,450, and $36,225, respectively.

[6] § 55(b)(1).

[7] The tax rates on long-term capital gains and qualified dividends are discussed in Chapter 14.

Regular Tax Liability

The AMT is equal to the tentative minimum tax minus the *regular tax liability*. In most cases, the regular tax liability is equal to the amount of tax from the Tax Table or Tax Rate Schedules, decreased by any foreign tax credit allowable for regular income tax purposes. The foreign tax credit also is allowed as a reduction of the tentative minimum tax.

In an AMT year, the taxpayer's total tax liability is equal to the tentative minimum tax (refer to Figure 15.2). The tentative minimum tax consists of two potential components: the regular tax liability and the AMT. The disallowance of credits does not affect a taxpayer's total liability in an AMT year. However, it does decrease the amount of the AMT and, as a consequence, reduces the minimum tax credit (discussed subsequently) available to be carried forward.

Some taxpayers who have adjustments and preferences but *do not pay* AMT lose the benefit of some or all of their nonrefundable credits. This result occurs because a taxpayer may claim many nonrefundable credits only to the extent that his or her regular tax liability exceeds the tentative minimum tax.

EXAMPLE 6

Vern has total nonrefundable *business* credits of $10,000, regular tax liability of $33,000, and tentative minimum tax of $25,000. He can claim only $8,000 of the nonrefundable credits in the current year ($33,000 – $8,000 = $25,000). The disallowed $2,000 credit is eligible for carryback and carryover. ■

All nonrefundable personal tax credits can offset both the regular income tax (less any foreign tax credit) and the AMT.

AMT ADJUSTMENTS

LO.3

Identify the adjustments made in calculating the AMT.

Direction of Adjustments

It is necessary to determine not only the amount of an adjustment, but also whether the adjustment is positive or negative. Careful study of Example 3 reveals the following pattern with regard to deductions.

- If the deduction allowed for regular income tax purposes exceeds the deduction allowed for AMT purposes, the difference is a positive adjustment.
- If the deduction allowed for AMT purposes exceeds the deduction allowed for regular income tax purposes, the difference is a negative adjustment.

Conversely, the direction of an adjustment attributable to an *income* item can be determined as follows.

- If the income reported for regular income tax purposes exceeds the income reported for AMT purposes, the difference is a negative adjustment.
- If the income reported for AMT purposes exceeds the income reported for regular income tax purposes, the difference is a positive adjustment.

Circulation Expenditures

For regular income tax purposes, circulation expenditures, other than those the taxpayer elects to charge to a capital account, may be expensed in the year incurred.[8] These expenditures include expenses incurred to establish, maintain, or increase the circulation of a newspaper, magazine, or other periodical.

Circulation expenditures are not deductible in the year incurred for AMT purposes. In computing AMTI, these expenditures are capitalized and amortized ratably over the three-year period beginning with the year in which the expenditures were made.[9]

[8] § 173(a).

[9] § 56(b)(2)(A)(i).

The AMT adjustment for circulation expenditures is the amount expensed for regular income tax purposes minus the amount that can be amortized for AMT purposes. A taxpayer can avoid the AMT adjustments for circulation expenditures by electing to write off the expenditures over a three-year period for regular income tax purposes.[10]

Depreciation of Post-1986 Real Property

The AMT depreciation adjustment for real property applies only to real property placed in service before 1999. Real property placed in service after 1998 uses the same MACRS recovery periods (see Table 8.6) for calculating the AMT as for calculating the regular income tax. Therefore, for such property, the AMT conforms to the regular income tax.

For real property placed in service after 1986 (MACRS property) and before 1999, AMT depreciation is computed under the alternative depreciation system (ADS), which uses the straight-line method over a 40-year life. The depreciation lives for regular income tax purposes are 27.5 years for residential rental property and 39 years for all other real property.[11] The difference between AMT depreciation and regular income tax depreciation is treated as an adjustment in computing the AMT. The differences will be positive during the regular income tax life of the asset because the cost is written off over a shorter period for regular income tax purposes.

Table 8.6 is used to compute regular income tax depreciation on real property placed in service after 1986. For AMT purposes, depreciation on real property placed in service after 1986 and before 1999 is computed under the ADS (Table 8.7).

EXAMPLE 7

In January 1998, Sara placed in service a residential building that cost $100,000. Regular income tax depreciation, AMT depreciation, and the AMT adjustment are as follows.

	Depreciation		
Year	**Regular Income Tax**	**AMT**	**AMT Adjustment**
1998	$ 3,485[a]	$ 2,396[b]	$ 1,089
1999	3,636[c]	2,500[d]	1,136
2000–2011[e]	43,632	30,000	13,632
Total	$50,753	$34,896	$15,857

[a]$100,000 cost × 3.485% (Table 8.6) = $3,485.
[b]$100,000 cost × 2.396% (Table 8.7) = $2,396.
[c]$100,000 cost × 3.636% (Table 8.6) = $3,636.
[d]$100,000 cost × 2.500% (Table 8.7) = $2,500.
[e]For each year, $3,636 regular income tax, $2,500 AMT, and $1,136 positive AMT adjustment.

If the building had been placed in service in 1999 or thereafter, there would have been a zero AMT depreciation adjustment for the tax year it was placed in service or for subsequent years. The depreciation for the tax year the building was placed in service would have been $3,485($100,000 × 3.485%) for both regular income tax purposes and AMT purposes. ■

After real property placed in service before 1999 has been held for the entire depreciation period for regular income tax purposes, the asset is fully depreciated. However, the depreciation period under the ADS is 41 tax years due to application of the half-year convention, so depreciation continues for AMT purposes. This

[10]§ 59(e)(2)(A).

[11]The 39-year life generally applies to nonresidential real property placed in service on or after May 13, 1993.

causes negative adjustments after the property has been fully depreciated for regular income tax purposes.

EXAMPLE 8

Assume the same facts as in the previous example for the building placed in service in 1998, and compute the AMT adjustment for 2026 (the twenty-ninth year of the asset's life). Regular income tax depreciation is zero (refer to Table 8.6). AMT depreciation is $2,500 ($100,000 cost × 2.500% from Table 8.7). Therefore, Sara has a negative AMT adjustment of $2,500 ($0 regular income tax depreciation − $2,500 AMT depreciation). ■

After real property is fully depreciated for both regular income tax and AMT purposes, the positive and negative adjustments that have been made for AMT purposes net to zero.

Depreciation of Post-1986 Personal Property

For most personal property placed in service after 1986 (MACRS property), the MACRS deduction for regular income tax purposes is based on the 200 percent declining-balance method with a switch to straight-line when that method produces a larger depreciation deduction for the asset. Refer to Table 8.1 for computing regular income tax depreciation.

For AMT purposes, the taxpayer must use the ADS for such property placed in service before 1999. This method is based on the 150 percent declining-balance method with a similar switch to straight-line for all personal property.[12] Refer to Table 8.4 for percentages to be used in computing AMT depreciation.

The MACRS deduction for personal property is larger than the ADS deduction in the early years of an asset's life. However, the ADS deduction is larger in the later years. ADS lives (based on asset class life) are longer than MACRS lives (based on recovery period).[13] Over the ADS life of the asset, the same amount of depreciation is deducted for both regular income tax and AMT purposes. In the same manner as for other timing adjustments, the AMT adjustments for depreciation net to zero over the ADS life of the asset.

The taxpayer may elect to use the ADS for regular income tax purposes. If this election is made, no AMT adjustment is required because the depreciation deduction is the same for regular income tax and for the AMT. The election eliminates the burden of maintaining two sets of tax depreciation records.

For personal property placed in service after 1998, the recovery periods are the same in calculating MACRS and AMT depreciation. Thus, if the taxpayer elects to use the 150 percent declining-balance method for regular income tax purposes, there are no AMT adjustments. Conversely, if the taxpayer uses the 200 percent declining-balance method for regular income tax purposes, there is an AMT adjustment for depreciation.

Pollution Control Facilities

For regular income tax purposes, the cost of certified pollution control facilities may be amortized over a period of 60 months. For AMT purposes, the cost of these facilities placed in service after 1986 and before 1999 is depreciated under the ADS over the appropriate class life, determined as explained above for depreciation of post-1986 personal property.[14] The required adjustment for AMTI is equal to the difference between the amortization deduction allowed for regular income tax purposes and the depreciation deduction computed under the ADS. The adjustment may be positive or negative.

---

[12] § 56(a)(1).

[13] Class lives and recovery periods are established for all assets in Rev.Proc. 87–56, 1987–2 C.B. 674.

[14] § 56(a)(5).

For property placed in service after 1998, the MACRS recovery periods are used for both regular income tax purposes and AMT purposes, so no AMT adjustment is created.

Expenditures Requiring 10-Year Amortization for AMT Purposes

Certain expenditures that may be deducted in the year incurred for regular income tax purposes must be written off over a 10-year period for AMT purposes. These rules apply to (1) mining exploration and development costs and (2) research and experimental expenditures.

In computing taxable income, taxpayers can deduct certain mining exploration and development expenditures. The deduction is allowed for expenditures paid or incurred during the taxable year for exploration (ascertaining the existence, location, extent, or quality of a deposit or mineral) and for development of a mine or other natural deposit, other than an oil or gas well.[15] Mining development expenditures are expenses paid or incurred after the existence of ores and minerals in commercially marketable quantities has been disclosed.

For AMT purposes, however, mining exploration and development costs are capitalized and amortized ratably over a 10-year period.[16] The AMT adjustment for mining exploration and development costs is equal to the amount expensed minus the allowable expense if the costs had been capitalized and amortized ratably over a 10-year period. This provision does not apply to costs relating to an oil or gas well.

EXAMPLE 9

This year, Audrey incurs $150,000 of mining exploration expenditures and deducts this amount for regular income tax purposes. For AMT purposes, these mining exploration expenditures are amortized over a 10-year period. Audrey makes a positive AMT adjustment of $135,000 ($150,000 allowed for regular income tax – $15,000 for AMT) for this year. In each of the next nine years for AMT purposes, Audrey makes a negative adjustment of $15,000 ($0 allowed for regular income tax – $15,000 for AMT). ■

To avoid the AMT adjustments for mining exploration and development costs, a taxpayer may elect to write off the expenditures over a 10-year period for regular income tax purposes.[17]

Similar rules apply to the computation of the adjustment for research and experimental expenditures.

Completed Contract Method

For a long-term contract, taxpayers must use the percentage of completion method for AMT purposes.[18] However, in limited circumstances, taxpayers can use the completed contract method for regular income tax purposes.[19] Thus, a taxpayer recognizes a different amount of income for regular income tax purposes than for AMT purposes. The resulting AMT adjustment is equal to the difference between income reported under the percentage of completion method and the amount reported using the completed contract method. The adjustment can be either positive or negative, depending on the amount of income recognized under the different methods.

A taxpayer can avoid an AMT adjustment on long-term contracts by using the percentage of completion method for regular income tax purposes rather than the completed contract method.

Incentive Stock Options

Incentive stock options (ISOs) are granted by employers to help attract new personnel and retain those already employed. At the time an ISO is granted, the employer

[15] §§ 617(a) and 616(a).
[16] § 56(a)(2).
[17] §§ 59(e)(2)(D) and (E).
[18] § 56(a)(3).
[19] See Chapter 16 for a detailed discussion of the completed contract and percentage of completion methods of accounting.

corporation sets an option price for the corporate stock. If the value of the stock increases during the option period, the employee can obtain stock at a favorable price by exercising the option. Employees are restricted as to when they can dispose of stock acquired under an ISO (e.g., a certain length of employment may be required). Therefore, the stock may not be freely transferable until some specified period has passed.

The exercise of an ISO does not increase regular taxable income.[20] However, for AMT purposes, the excess of the fair market value of the stock over the exercise price (the *spread*) is treated as an adjustment in the first taxable year in which the rights in the stock are freely transferable or are not subject to a substantial risk of forfeiture.[21]

EXAMPLE 10

In 2009, Manuel exercised an ISO that had been granted by his employer, Gold Corporation. Manuel acquired 1,000 shares of Gold stock for the option price of $20 per share. The stock became freely transferable in 2011, when it was trading at $55 per share. The fair market value of the stock at the date of exercise was $50 per share. For AMT purposes, Manuel has a positive adjustment of $30,000 ($50,000 fair market value − $20,000 option price) for 2011. The transaction does not affect regular taxable income in 2009 or 2011. ■

No adjustment is required if the taxpayer exercises the option and disposes of the stock in the same tax year, because the bargain element gain is reported for both regular income tax and AMT purposes in the same tax year.

The regular income tax basis of stock acquired through exercise of ISOs is different from the AMT basis. The regular income tax basis of the stock is equal to its cost, whereas the AMT basis is equal to the fair market value on the date the options are exercised. Consequently, the gain or loss upon disposition of the stock is different for regular income tax purposes and AMT purposes.

EXAMPLE 11

Assume the same facts as in the previous example and that Manuel sells the stock for $60,000 in 2013. His gain for regular income tax purposes is $40,000 ($60,000 amount realized − $20,000 regular income tax basis). For AMT purposes, the gain is $10,000 ($60,000 amount realized − $50,000 AMT basis). Therefore, Manuel reports a $30,000 negative adjustment in computing AMT in 2013 ($40,000 regular income tax gain − $10,000 AMT gain). Note that the $30,000 negative adjustment upon disposition in 2013 offsets the $30,000 positive adjustment when the stock became freely transferable in 2011. ■

Adjusted Gain or Loss

When property is sold during the year or a casualty occurs to business or income-producing property, gain or loss reported for regular income tax may be different from the gain or loss determined for the AMT. This difference occurs because the adjusted basis of the property for AMT purposes reflects any current and prior AMT adjustments for each of the following.[22]

- Depreciation.
- Circulation expenditures.
- Research and experimental expenditures.
- Mining exploration and development costs.
- Amortization of certified pollution control facilities.

A negative gain or loss adjustment is required if:

---

[20] § 421(a).
[21] § 56(b)(3).
[22] § 56(a)(6).

- the gain for AMT purposes is less than the gain for regular income tax purposes;
- the loss for AMT purposes is more than the loss for regular income tax purposes; or
- a loss is computed for AMT purposes and a gain is computed for regular income tax purposes.

Otherwise, the AMT gain or loss adjustment is positive.

EXAMPLE 12

Assume the same facts as in Example 7, except that Sara sells the building on December 20, 2011, for $105,000. When Sara sells the building, she determines her depreciation adjustment for 2011 and the gain (or loss) resulting from the sale.

As to the depreciation adjustment for 2011, the regular income tax depreciation for 2011 is $3,485 [($100,000 cost × 3.636% from Table 8.6) × (11.5/12)]. AMT depreciation for 2011 is $2,396 [($100,000 × 2.500% from Table 8.7) × (11.5/12)]. Sara's positive AMT adjustment for 2011 is $1,089 ($3,485 regular income tax depreciation − $2,396 AMT depreciation).

In computing gain (or loss), the adjusted basis of the building is different for regular income tax purposes than for AMT purposes. The adjusted basis for each purpose is determined as follows.

	Regular Income Tax	AMT
Cost	$100,000	$100,000
Less: Depreciation for 1998–2010 (see Example 7)	(47,117)	(32,396)
Depreciation for 2011 (see prior paragraph)	(3,485)	(2,396)
Adjusted basis	$ 49,398	$ 65,208

Having arrived at adjusted basis, recognized gain is computed for each purpose.

	Regular Income Tax	AMT
Amount realized	$105,000	$105,000
Adjusted basis	(49,398)	(65,208)
Recognized gain	$ 55,602	$ 39,792

Because the regular income tax and AMT gain on the sale of the duplex differ, Sara shows a negative AMT adjustment of $15,810 ($55,602 regular income tax gain − $39,792 AMT gain). Note that this negative adjustment offsets the $15,810 total of the 14 years of positive adjustments for depreciation. ■

Passive Activity Losses

Losses on passive activities are not deductible in computing either the regular income tax or the AMT. Cost recovery and basis computations may differ between the AMT and regular tax regimes for an asset. Therefore, a *passive loss* computed for regular income tax purposes may differ from the passive loss computed for AMT purposes.[23]

EXAMPLE 13

Soong acquired two passive activities. He received net passive income of $10,000 from Activity A and had no AMT adjustments or preferences in connection with the activity. Activity B had gross income of $27,000 and operating expenses (not affected by AMT

[23]See Chapter 11.

adjustments or preferences) of $19,000. Soong claimed MACRS depreciation of $20,000 for Activity B; depreciation under the ADS would have been $15,000. In addition, Soong deducted $10,000 of percentage depletion in excess of basis. The following comparison illustrates the differences in the computation of the passive loss for regular income tax and AMT purposes for Activity B.

	Regular Income Tax	AMT
Gross income	$ 27,000	$ 27,000
Deductions		
Operating expenses	($ 19,000)	($ 19,000)
Depreciation	(20,000)	(15,000)
Depletion	(10,000)	–0–
Total deductions	($ 49,000)	($ 34,000)
Passive loss	($ 22,000)	($ 7,000)

Because the adjustment for depreciation ($5,000) applies and the preference for depletion ($10,000) is not taken into account in computing AMTI, the regular income tax passive activity loss of $22,000 for Activity B is reduced by these amounts, resulting in a $7,000 AMT passive activity loss. ■

For regular income tax purposes, Soong would offset the $10,000 of net passive income from Activity A with $10,000 of the passive loss from Activity B. For AMT purposes, he would offset the $10,000 of net passive income from Activity A with the $7,000 passive activity loss allowed from Activity B, resulting in passive activity income of $3,000. Thus, in computing AMTI, Soong makes a positive passive loss adjustment of $3,000 [$10,000 (passive activity loss allowed for regular income tax) – $7,000 (passive activity loss allowed for the AMT)].

EXAMPLE 14

Assume the same facts as in the previous example. For regular income tax purposes, Soong has a suspended passive loss of $12,000 [$22,000 (total loss) – $10,000 (amount used)]. This suspended passive loss can offset passive income in the future or can offset active or portfolio income when Soong disposes of the loss activity (refer to Chapter 11). For AMT purposes, Soong's suspended passive loss is $0 [$7,000 (total loss) – $7,000 (amount used)]. ■

Alternative Tax Net Operating Loss Deduction

In computing taxable income, taxpayers deduct net operating loss (NOL) carryovers and carrybacks (refer to Chapter 7). The regular income tax NOL must be modified, however, in computing AMTI. The starting point in computing the **alternative tax NOL deduction (ATNOLD)** is the NOL computed for regular income tax purposes. The regular income tax NOL then is modified for AMT adjustments and tax preferences, with the result being the ATNOLD. Thus, preferences and adjustment items that have benefited the taxpayer in computing the regular income tax NOL are added back, thereby reducing or eliminating the ATNOLD.[24]

EXAMPLE 15

In 2011, Max incurred an NOL of $100,000. Max had no AMT adjustments, but his deductions included tax preferences of $18,000. His ATNOLD carryback is $82,000 ($100,000 regular income tax NOL – $18,000 tax preferences deducted in computing the NOL).

If the adjustment was not made to the regular income tax NOL, the $18,000 in tax preference items deducted in 2011 would have the effect of reducing AMTI in the year (or years) the 2011 NOL is utilized. This would weaken the entire concept of the AMT. ■

[24] § 56(a)(4).

TAX *in* the *NEWS*

Who Pays the AMT?

The percentage of individual taxpayers who pay the AMT is not spread evenly among the states. The top five AMT states are:

State	Percentage of Returns with AMT (2007)
New Jersey	8.7%
New York	7.7%
Connecticut	7.4%
California	6.7%
Maryland	6.3%

If the District of Columbia were included, it would be fourth with 7.2 percent.

The bottom five AMT states include:

State	Percentage of Returns with AMT (2007)
Alaska	1.3%
Tennessee	1.5%
South Dakota	1.6%
North Dakota	1.7%
West Virginia	1.8%

A major contributing factor in tracing AMT liabilities by state is the presence of heavy state and local income and property taxes. While such taxes are deductible in calculating the regular income tax, they cannot be deducted in calculating the AMT.

A ceiling exists on the amount of the ATNOLD that can be deducted in the carryback or carryforward year. The deduction is limited to 90 percent of AMTI (before the ATNOLD) for the carryback or carryforward year.

EXAMPLE 16

Assume the same facts as in the previous example. Max's AMTI (before the ATNOLD) in 2009 is $90,000. Therefore, of the $82,000 ATNOLD carried back to 2009 from 2011, only $81,000 ($90,000 × 90%) can be used in recalculating the 2009 AMT. The unused $1,000 of 2011 ATNOLD is now carried to 2010 for use in recalculating that year's AMT. ■

A taxpayer who has an ATNOLD that is carried back or over to another year must use the ATNOLD against AMTI in the carryback or carryforward year even if the regular income tax, rather than the AMT, applies.

EXAMPLE 17

Emily's ATNOLD carryover is $10,000. AMTI before considering the ATNOLD is $25,000. If Emily's regular income tax exceeds the AMT, the AMT does not apply. Nevertheless, Emily's ATNOLD of $10,000 is "used up" and is not available for a later year. ■

For regular income tax purposes, the NOL generally can be carried back 2 years and forward 20 years. However, the taxpayer may elect to forgo the 2-year carryback. These rules generally apply to the ATNOLD as well, except that the election to forgo the 2-year carryback is available for the ATNOLD only if the taxpayer elected it for the regular income tax NOL.

Itemized Deductions

Most of the itemized deductions allowed for regular income tax purposes also are allowed for AMT purposes. Itemized deductions that are allowed for AMT purposes include the following.

- Casualty losses.
- Gambling losses.
- Charitable contributions.

- Medical expenses in excess of 10 percent of AGI.
- Estate tax on income in respect of a decedent.
- Qualified interest.

Taxes (state, local, and foreign income taxes, sales taxes, and property taxes) and miscellaneous itemized deductions that are subject to the 2 percent-of-AGI floor are not allowed in computing AMT.[25] A positive AMT adjustment is made in the total amount of the regular income tax deduction for each.

If the taxpayer's gross income includes the recovery of any tax deducted as an itemized deduction for regular income tax purposes, a negative AMT adjustment in the amount of the recovery is allowed for AMTI purposes.[26] For example, state, local, and foreign income taxes can be deducted for regular income tax purposes, but cannot be deducted in computing AMTI. Because of this, any refund of such taxes from a prior year is not included in AMTI. Therefore, in calculating AMTI, the taxpayer must make a negative adjustment for an income tax refund that has been included in computing regular taxable income.

Medical Expenses For regular income tax purposes, medical expenses are deductible to the extent they exceed 7.5 percent of AGI.[27] However, for AMT purposes, medical expenses are deductible only to the extent they exceed 10 percent of AGI.[28]

EXAMPLE 18

Joann incurred uninsured medical expenses of $16,000. She had AGI of $100,000 for the year. Her AMT adjustment for medical expenses is computed as follows.

	Regular Income Tax	AMT
Medical expenses incurred	$16,000	$ 16,000
Less reduction:		
$100,000 AGI × 7.5%	(7,500)	
$100,000 AGI × 10%		(10,000)
Medical expense deduction	$ 8,500	$ 6,000

Joann's positive AMT adjustment for medical expenses is $2,500 ($8,500 regular income tax deduction − $6,000 AMT deduction). ■

Interest in General The AMT itemized deduction allowed for interest expense includes only qualified housing interest and investment interest to the extent of net investment income that is included in the determination of AMTI.[29] Any interest that is deducted in calculating the regular income tax that is not permitted in calculating the AMT is treated as a positive adjustment.

In computing regular taxable income, taxpayers who itemize can deduct (refer to Chapter 10):

- Qualified residence interest.
- Investment interest, subject to the investment interest limitations (discussed under Investment Interest below).
- Qualified interest on student loans.

Housing Interest Under current regular income tax rules, taxpayers who itemize can deduct *qualified residence interest* on up to two residences. The deduction is

[25] § 56(b)(1)(A).
[26] § 56(b)(1)(D).
[27] § 213(a).
[28] § 56(b)(1)(B).
[29] § 56(b)(1)(C).

limited to interest on acquisition indebtedness up to $1 million and home equity indebtedness up to $100,000. Acquisition indebtedness is debt that is incurred in acquiring, constructing, or substantially improving a qualified residence of the taxpayer and is secured by the residence. Home equity indebtedness is indebtedness secured by a qualified residence of the taxpayer, but does not include acquisition indebtedness.

EXAMPLE 19

Gail, who used the proceeds of a mortgage to acquire a personal residence, paid mortgage interest of $112,000. Of this amount, $14,000 is attributable to acquisition indebtedness in excess of $1 million. For regular income tax purposes, Gail may deduct mortgage interest of $98,000 ($112,000 total – $14,000 disallowed). ■

The mortgage interest deduction for AMT purposes is limited to *qualified housing interest*, rather than *qualified residence interest*. Qualified housing interest includes only interest incurred to acquire, construct, or substantially improve the taxpayer's principal residence and such interest on one other qualified dwelling used for personal purposes. A home equity loan qualifies only if it meets the definition of qualified housing interest, which frequently is not the case. When additional mortgage interest is incurred (e.g., a mortgage refinancing), interest paid is deductible as qualified housing interest for AMT purposes only if:

- The proceeds are used to acquire or substantially improve a qualified residence.
- Interest on the prior loan was qualified housing interest.
- The amount of the loan was not increased.

A positive AMT adjustment is required in the amount of the difference between qualified *residence* interest allowed as an itemized deduction for regular income tax purposes and qualified *housing* interest allowed in the determination of AMTI.

Investment Interest Investment interest is deductible for regular income tax purposes and for AMT purposes to the extent of qualified net investment income.

EXAMPLE 20
THE BIG PICTURE

Return to the facts of *The Big Picture* on p. 15-2. Bob and Carol both report taxable interest income of $16,000 for the year. The bonds that paid the interest income were acquired with funds borrowed from the bank, and the interest paid on these bank loans for the year totaled $30,000. The itemized deduction for this interest is limited to the amount of the taxpayer's net investment income for the year, so Bob and Carol both currently can deduct only $16,000 of the investment interest. ■

Even though investment interest is deductible for both regular income tax and AMT purposes, an adjustment is required if the amount of investment interest deductible for regular income tax purposes differs from the amount deductible for AMT purposes. For example, an adjustment arises if proceeds from a home equity loan are used to purchase investments. Interest on a home equity loan is deductible as qualified residence interest for regular income tax purposes, but is not deductible for AMT purposes unless the proceeds are used to acquire or substantially improve a qualified residence. For AMT purposes, however, interest on a home equity loan is deductible as investment interest expense if proceeds from the loan are used for investment purposes.

To determine the AMT adjustment for investment interest expense, one must compute the investment interest deduction for both regular income tax and AMT purposes.

EXAMPLE 21

Tom earned $20,000 interest income from corporate bonds and $5,000 dividends from preferred stock. He reported the following amounts of investment income for regular income tax and AMT purposes.

	Regular Income Tax	AMT
Corporate bond interest	$20,000	$20,000
Preferred stock dividends	5,000	5,000
Net investment income	$25,000	$25,000

Tom incurred investment interest expense of $10,000 related to the corporate bonds. He also incurred $4,000 interest on a home equity loan and used the proceeds of the loan to purchase preferred stock. For regular income tax purposes, this $4,000 is deductible as qualified residence interest. His *investment* interest expense for regular income tax and AMT purposes is computed as:

	Regular Income Tax	AMT
To carry corporate bonds	$10,000	$10,000
On home equity loan to carry preferred stock	–0–	4,000
Total investment interest expense	$10,000	$14,000

Investment interest expense is deductible to the extent of net investment income. Because the amount deductible for regular income tax purposes ($10,000) differs from the amount deductible for AMT purposes ($14,000), an AMT adjustment is required.

AMT deduction for investment interest expense	$ 14,000
Regular income tax deduction for investment interest expense	(10,000)
Negative AMT adjustment	$ 4,000

■

As discussed subsequently under AMT Preferences, the interest on private activity bonds usually is an AMT preference item. Such interest also can affect the calculation of the AMT investment interest deduction in that it is included in the calculation of net investment income.

Other Adjustments

The standard deduction and the personal and dependency exemption also give rise to AMT adjustments.[30] The standard deduction is not allowed as a deduction in computing AMTI. Although a person who does not itemize is rarely subject to the AMT, it is possible. In such a case, the taxpayer enters a positive adjustment for the standard deduction in computing the AMT.

The personal and dependency exemption amount deducted for regular income tax purposes is not allowed in computing AMT. Therefore, the taxpayer enters a positive AMT adjustment for the personal and dependency exemption amount claimed in computing the regular income tax. A separate exemption (see Exemption Amount) is allowed for AMT purposes. To allow both the regular income tax exemption amount and the AMT exemption amount would result in extra benefits for taxpayers.

EXAMPLE 22

Eli, who is single, has no dependents and does not itemize deductions. He earned a salary of $109,500 in 2011. Based on this information, Eli's taxable income is $100,000 ($109,500 – $5,800 standard deduction – $3,700 exemption).

Eli's AMT preferences for the year totaled $150,000. Eli's AMTI is $259,500 ($100,000 taxable income + $5,800 adjustment for standard deduction + $3,700 adjustment for exemption + $150,000 tax preferences). ■

[30] § 56(b)(1)(E).

ETHICS & Equity

Large Families and the AMT

The taxpayers claimed 12 personal exemption and dependency deductions (taxpayer, spouse, and 10 children) on their Federal income tax return. The taxpayers' itemized deductions included medical and dental expenses and state and local income and property taxes.

Under the regular income tax, the taxpayers' taxable income was a negative amount. However, applying the AMT adjustments for personal and dependency exemptions, medical and dental expenses, and state and local income and property taxes resulted in the taxpayers being subject to the AMT.

The taxpayers are members of a religious denomination that encourages large families. The tax return they filed showed a $0 Federal income tax liability and did not include a Form 6251. According to the taxpayers, the AMT should not apply to them for the following reasons.

- Congress did not intend for a large familiy in itself to be a causative factor producing an AMT.
- They incurred no AMT preferences.
- The AMT burdened the taxpayers' free exercise of religion.
- The AMT violated their equal protection and due process rights.

Both the Tax Court and the Third Circuit Court of Appeals rejected these arguments and held that the taxpayers were subject to the AMT.

Should taxpayers who have large families and no tax preferences be subject to the AMT? Was this the intended objective of the AMT?

Source: Adapted from *Klaassen v. Comm.*, 99–1 USTC ¶50,418, 83 AFTR 2d 99–1750, 182 F.3d 932 (CA–3, 1999), *aff'g* 76 TCM 20, T.C.Memo. 1998–241.

LO.4

Identify the tax preferences that are included in calculating the AMT.

AMT PREFERENCES

Percentage Depletion

Congress originally enacted the percentage depletion rules to provide taxpayers with incentives to invest in the development of certain natural resources. Percentage depletion is computed by multiplying a rate specified in the Code times the gross income from the property (refer to Chapter 8).[31] The percentage rate is based on the type of mineral involved. The basis of the property is reduced by the amount of depletion taken until the basis reaches zero. However, once the basis of the property reaches zero, taxpayers can continue to take percentage depletion deductions. Thus, over the life of the property, depletion deductions may greatly exceed the cost of the property.

The percentage depletion preference is equal to the excess of the regular income tax deduction for percentage depletion over the adjusted basis of the property at the end of the taxable year.[32]

EXAMPLE 23

Kim owns a mineral property that qualifies for a 22% depletion rate. The basis of the property at the beginning of the year is $10,000. Gross income from the property for the year is $100,000. For regular income tax purposes, Kim's percentage depletion deduction (assume it is not limited by taxable income from the property) is $22,000. For AMT purposes, Kim has a tax preference of $12,000 ($22,000 – $10,000). ■

Intangible Drilling Costs

In computing the regular income tax, taxpayers are allowed to deduct certain intangible drilling and development costs in the year incurred, although such costs are normally capital in nature (refer to Chapter 8). The deduction is allowed for costs incurred in connection with oil and gas wells and geothermal wells.

For AMT purposes, excess intangible drilling costs (IDC) for the year are a preference item.[33]

[31] § 613(a).

[32] § 57(a)(1). This is not a preference for independent oil and gas producers and royalty owners as defined in § 613A(c).

[33] § 57(a)(2).

TAX *in* the NEWS

Tax-Free Municipal Bonds: Market Reaction to Being Taxed

Municipal bonds are not subject to Federal income tax. Therefore, assuming equal risk, the market assigns a lower interest rate to municipal bonds than it does to taxable bonds.

Generally, interest received from municipal bonds is not subject to the AMT. However, an exception exists for most issuances that are classified as private activity bonds. These bonds are used to finance projects such as airports, housing developments, wastewater treatment plants, and athletic stadiums. As more taxpayers become subject to the AMT each year, the vulnerability of some municipal bond interest becomes a cause for concern when devising an investment strategy.

When an investor purchases individual bonds issued by a state or municipality, the issuer informs the investor which are private activity bonds. Many investors, however, choose bond mutual funds rather than purchasing specific bond issues. According to the Securities and Exchange Commission's rules, tax-exempt mutual funds can have as much as one-fifth of their holdings in private activity bonds, creating a potential tax pitfall for investors.

A number of companies that offer mutual funds have responded by creating funds that are both AMT-free and regular income tax–free.

IDC expensed in the year incurred
Minus: Deduction if IDC were capitalized and amortized over 10 years
Equals: Excess of IDC expense over amortization
Minus: 65% of net oil and gas and geothermal income
Equals: Tax preference item

EXAMPLE 24

Ben, who incurred IDC of $50,000 during the year, elected to expense that amount. His net oil and gas income for the year was $60,000. Ben's tax preference for IDC is $6,000 [($50,000 IDC − $5,000 amortization) − (65% × $60,000 income)]. ■

A taxpayer can avoid the preference for IDC by electing to write off the expenditures over a 10-year period for regular income tax purposes.

Interest on Private Activity Bonds

Income from private activity bonds is not included in taxable income, and expenses related to carrying such bonds are not deductible for regular income tax purposes. However, interest on private activity bonds usually is included as a preference in computing AMTI. Therefore, expenses incurred in carrying the bonds are offset against the interest income in computing the tax preference.[34]

In general, **private activity bonds** are bonds issued by states or municipalities with more than 10 percent of the proceeds being used for private business use.[35] For example, a bond issued by a city whose proceeds are used to construct a factory that is leased to a private business at a favorable rate is a private activity bond.

The vast majority of tax-exempt bonds issued by states and municipalities are not classified as private activity bonds. Therefore, the interest income from such bonds is not a tax preference item.

EXAMPLE 25
THE BIG PICTURE

Return to the facts of *The Big Picture* on p. 15-2. Bob and Carol both have invested substantial amounts in private activity bonds. All of the private activity bonds that each of them owns were issued in 2010. Consequently, a tax preference does not result for either Carol or Bob. ■

Exclusion for Certain Small Business Stock

Taxpayers other than C corporations can exclude from regular-tax gross income some or all of the gain realized when certain small business stock is sold. For this

[34] § 57(a)(5). Interest from private activity bonds issued or refunded in 2009 and 2010 does not constitute an AMT tax preference.

[35] § 141.

purpose, a "small business" is a C corporation that has assets of $50 million or less when the stock is issued. At least 80 percent of the entity's assets must be used in an active trade or business.

The exclusion is available if the taxpayer held the stock for more than five years. The gain to be excluded cannot exceed the greater of $10 million or 10 times the taxpayer's basis in the stock. The exclusion then is computed using the following amounts.

If the Stock Was Acquired:	Then the Taxpayer Excludes This Percentage of the Gain Realized:
Before 2009 or after 2011	50
From January 1, 2009 through September 27, 2010	75
From September 28, 2010 through 2011	100

When the investor realizes such a gain, a portion of the excluded amount becomes an AMT tax preference.[36]

Summary of AMT Items

The adjustments and preferences to taxable income in arriving at AMTI are set forth in Concept Summary 15.1.

LO.5

Apply the formula for computing the AMT and complete a Form 6251.

COMPUTING THE AMT

The computation of the AMT is illustrated in the following example.

EXAMPLE 26

Hans Sims, who is single, reports 2011 taxable income as follows.

Salary		$ 92,000
Interest		8,000
Adjusted gross income		$100,000
Less itemized deductions:		
Medical expenses ($17,500 – 7.5% of $100,000 AGI)[a]	$10,000	
State income taxes	4,000	
Interest[b]		
Home mortgage (for qualified housing)	20,000*	
Investment interest	3,300*	
Contributions to charities (cash)	5,000*	
Casualty losses ($14,000 – 10% of $100,000 AGI)	4,000*	(46,300)
		$ 53,700
Less personal exemption		(3,700)
Taxable income		$ 50,000

[a]Total medical expenses were $17,500, reduced by 7.5% of AGI, resulting in an itemized deduction of $10,000. However, for AMT purposes, the reduction is 10%, which leaves an AMT itemized deduction of $7,500 ($17,500 – 10% of $100,000 AGI). Therefore, an adjustment of $2,500 ($10,000 – $7,500) is required for medical expenses disallowed for AMT purposes.

[b]In this illustration, all interest is deductible in computing AMTI. Qualified housing interest is deductible. Investment interest ($3,300) is deductible to the extent of net investment income included in the minimum tax base. For this purpose, the $8,000 of interest income is treated as net investment income.

Deductions marked by an asterisk are allowed as *alternative minimum tax itemized deductions*, and AMT adjustments are required for the other itemized deductions. Thus, adjustments are required for state income taxes and for medical expenses to the extent the medical expenses deductible for regular income tax purposes are not

[36]§§ 57(a)(7) and 1202.

CONCEPT SUMMARY 15.1

AMT Adjustments and Preferences for Individuals

Adjustments	Positive	Negative	Either
Circulation expenditures			X
Depreciation of post-1986 real property			X
Depreciation of post-1986 personal property			X
Pollution control facilities			X
Mining exploration and development costs			X
Research and experimental expenditures			X
Completed contract method			X
Domestic production activities deduction			X*
Incentive stock options	X**		
Adjusted gain or loss			X
Passive activity losses			X
Alternative minimum tax NOL deduction			X
Itemized deductions:			
Medical expenses	X		
State income tax or sales tax	X		
Property tax on realty	X		
Property tax on personalty	X		
Miscellaneous itemized deductions	X		
Tax benefit rule for state income tax refund		X	
Qualified interest on student loans	X		
Qualified residence interest that is not qualified housing interest	X		
Qualified residence interest that is AMT investment interest	X	X	
Private activity bond interest that is AMT investment interest		X	
Standard deduction	X		
Personal exemptions and dependency deductions	X		
Preferences			
Percentage depletion in excess of adjusted basis	X		
Intangible drilling costs	X		
Private activity bond interest income	X***		
§ 1202 exclusion for certain small business stock	X		

*Income limitations are based on AMT amounts.
**While the adjustment is a positive adjustment, the AMT basis for the stock is increased by the amount of the positive adjustment.
***Not for such bonds issued or restructured in 2009 and 2010.

deductible in computing AMT (see note [a]). In addition to the items that affected taxable income, Hans recorded interest on 2009 private activity bonds (usually an exclusion tax preference), and he exercised an incentive stock option. AMTI is computed as follows.

Taxable income	$ 50,000
Plus: Adjustments	
State income taxes	4,000
Medical expenses (see note [a])	2,500
"Spread" on exercise of incentive stock options	35,000
Personal exemption	3,700
Plus: Tax preference (interest on private activity bonds)	–0–

TAX in the NEWS

THE AMT NIGHTMARE

Nina Olson is the National Taxpayer Advocate for the IRS. She reports to Congress annually on the the problems facing taxpayers. In a recent report, she identified complexity as the most serious problem and called for a "simpler tax code."

In discussing the complexity of the Code, she describes the AMT as a nightmare. Not only does the taxpayer have to compute regular tax liability with all its complexity, but the AMT requires that the computation be done twice. In Olson's opinion, the AMT is a "hideously complex parallel tax structure." Obviously, she does not think it should be retained in achieving a "simpler tax code."

Equals: AMTI	$ 95,200
Minus: AMT exemption	(48,450)
Equals: Minimum tax base	$ 46,750
Times: AMT rate	× 26%
Equals: Tentative AMT	$ 12,155
Minus: Regular income tax on taxable income	(8,625)
Equals: AMT	$ 3,530

■

The solution to Example 26 also is presented on Form 6251 on p. 15-25. Note that the personal exemption amount is a positive adjustment in the Example 26 solution, but does not appear as an adjustment in Form 6251. This difference occurs because line 1 of Form 6251 includes the amount from line 41 of Form 1040. Line 41 of Form 1040 is taxable income before the deduction for personal and dependency exemptions.

LO.6

Describe the role of the AMT credit in the alternative minimum tax structure.

AMT CREDIT

As discussed previously, timing differences give rise to adjustments to the alternative minimum tax base. In later years, the timing differences reverse, as was illustrated in several of the preceding examples. To provide equity for the taxpayer when timing differences reverse, the regular income tax liability may be reduced by a tax credit for prior years' minimum tax liability attributable to timing differences. The **alternative minimum tax credit** is carried over indefinitely. Therefore, there is no need to keep track of the year in which the minimum tax credit arose.[37]

EXAMPLE 27

Assume the same facts as in Example 3. Also assume that in 2011, Bob paid AMT as a result of the $20,000 positive adjustment arising from the circulation expenditures. In 2012, $10,000 of the timing difference reverses, resulting in regular taxable income that is $10,000 greater than AMTI. Because Bob has already paid AMT as a result of the write-off of circulation expenditures, he is allowed an AMT credit. The AMT credit offsets Bob's regular 2012 income tax liability to the extent that his regular income tax liability exceeds his tentative AMT. ■

The AMT credit for individuals usually is available only for the AMT that results from timing differences. It is not available in connection with **AMT exclusions**, which represent permanent differences rather than timing differences between the regular income tax liability and the AMT. These AMT exclusions include:[38]

- The standard deduction.
- Personal exemptions.
- Medical expenses, to the extent deductible for regular income tax purposes but not deductible in computing AMT.

[37] § 53.

[38] § 53(d)(1)(B)(ii).

Form **6251**

Department of the Treasury
Internal Revenue Service (99)

Alternative Minimum Tax—Individuals

▶ See separate instructions.

▶ Attach to Form 1040 or Form 1040NR.

OMB No. 1545-0074

Attachment Sequence No. **32**

Name(s) shown on Form 1040 or Form 1040NR: *Hans Sims*

Your social security number: *111-11-1111*

Part I Alternative Minimum Taxable Income (See instructions for how to complete each line.)

1	If filing Schedule A (Form 1040), enter the amount from Form 1040, line 41, and go to line 2. Otherwise, enter the amount from Form 1040, line 38, and go to line 6. (If less than zero, enter as a negative amount.)	1	*53,700*
2	Medical and dental. Enter the **smaller** of Schedule A (Form 1040), line 4, **or** 2.5% (.025) of Form 1040, line 38. If zero or less, enter -0-	2	*2,500*
3	Taxes from Schedule A (Form 1040), lines 5, 6, and 8	3	*4,000*
4	Enter the home mortgage interest adjustment, if any, from line 6 of the worksheet on page 2 of the instructions	4	
5	Miscellaneous deductions from Schedule A (Form 1040), line 27	5	
6	If filing Schedule L (Form 1040A or 1040), enter as a negative amount the sum of lines 6 and 17 from that schedule	6	( )
7	Tax refund from Form 1040, line 10 or line 21	7	( )
8	Investment interest expense (difference between regular tax and AMT)	8	
9	Depletion (difference between regular tax and AMT)	9	
10	Net operating loss deduction from Form 1040, line 21. Enter as a positive amount	10	
11	Alternative tax net operating loss deduction	11	( )
12	Interest from specified private activity bonds exempt from the regular tax	12	
13	Qualified small business stock (7% of gain excluded under section 1202)	13	
14	Exercise of incentive stock options (excess of AMT income over regular tax income)	14	*35,000*
15	Estates and trusts (amount from Schedule K-1 (Form 1041), box 12, code A)	15	
16	Electing large partnerships (amount from Schedule K-1 (Form 1065-B), box 6)	16	
17	Disposition of property (difference between AMT and regular tax gain or loss)	17	
18	Depreciation on assets placed in service after 1986 (difference between regular tax and AMT)	18	
19	Passive activities (difference between AMT and regular tax income or loss)	19	
20	Loss limitations (difference between AMT and regular tax income or loss)	20	
21	Circulation costs (difference between regular tax and AMT)	21	
22	Long-term contracts (difference between AMT and regular tax income)	22	
23	Mining costs (difference between regular tax and AMT)	23	
24	Research and experimental costs (difference between regular tax and AMT)	24	
25	Income from certain installment sales before January 1, 1987	25	( )
26	Intangible drilling costs preference	26	
27	Other adjustments, including income-based related adjustments	27	
28	**Alternative minimum taxable income.** Combine lines 1 through 27. (If married filing separately and line 28 is more than $219,900, see page 8 of the instructions.)	28	*95,200*

Part II Alternative Minimum Tax (AMT)

29 Exemption. (If you were under age 24 at the end of 2010, see page 8 of the instructions.)

IF your filing status is . . .	**AND line 28 is not over . . .**	**THEN enter on line 29 . . .**
Single or head of household	$112,500	$48,450
Married filing jointly or qualifying widow(er)	150,000	74,450
Married filing separately	75,000	37,225

If line 28 is **over** the amount shown above for your filing status, see page 8 of the instructions. — **29** *48,450*

30	Subtract line 29 from line 28. If more than zero, go to line 31. If zero or less, enter -0- here and on lines 33 and 35 and skip the rest of Part II	30	*46,750*
31	• If you are filing Form 2555 or 2555-EZ, see page 9 of the instructions for the amount to enter. • If you reported capital gain distributions directly on Form 1040, line 13; you reported qualified dividends on Form 1040, line 9b; **or** you had a gain on both lines 15 and 16 of Schedule D (Form 1040) (as refigured for the AMT, if necessary), complete Part III on the back and enter the amount from line 54 here. • **All others:** If line 30 is $175,000 or less ($87,500 or less if married filing separately), multiply line 30 by 26% (.26). Otherwise, multiply line 30 by 28% (.28) and subtract $3,500 ($1,750 if married filing separately) from the result.	31	*12,155*
32	Alternative minimum tax foreign tax credit (see page 9 of the instructions)	32	
33	Tentative minimum tax. Subtract line 32 from line 31	33	*12,155*
34	Tax from Form 1040, line 44 (minus any tax from Form 4972 and any foreign tax credit from Form 1040, line 47). If you used Schedule J to figure your tax, the amount from line 44 of Form 1040 must be refigured without using Schedule J (see page 11 of the instructions)	34	*8,625*
35	**AMT.** Subtract line 34 from line 33. If zero or less, enter -0-. Enter here and on Form 1040, line 45	35	*3,530*

- Other itemized deductions not allowable for AMT purposes, including miscellaneous itemized deductions, taxes, and interest expense.
- Excess percentage depletion.
- Tax-exempt interest on private activity bonds.

To determine the amount of AMT credit to carry over, the AMT is recomputed, reflecting only the AMT exclusions and the AMT exemption amount.[39]

15.2 Corporate Alternative Minimum Tax

LO.7

Illustrate the basic features of the corporate AMT.

The AMT for C corporations is similar to that for noncorporate taxpayers. However, there are several important differences.

- The corporate AMT rate is 20 percent versus a top rate of 28 percent for noncorporate taxpayers.[40]
- The AMT exemption for corporations is $40,000 reduced by 25 percent of the amount by which AMTI exceeds $150,000.[41]
- Tax preferences applicable to noncorporate taxpayers are also applicable to corporate taxpayers, but some adjustments differ (shown later in the chapter).

Although there are a few computational differences, the corporate AMT and the noncorporate AMT have the identical objective: to force taxpayers who are more profitable than their taxable income reflects to pay additional tax. The formula for determining the corporate AMT appears in Figure 15.3.

Form 4626 (Alternative Minimum Tax—Corporations) is used for the corporate AMT. Any AMT then is carried over to Schedule J of the entity's Form 1120 (U.S. Corporation Income Tax Return).

NO AMT FOR SMALL CORPORATIONS

Small corporations are not subject to the AMT. For this purpose, a corporation is classified as a small corporation if it had average annual gross receipts of not more than $5 million for the last three prior tax years. A corporation continues to be classified as a small corporation if its average annual gross receipts for the last three tax years do not exceed $7.5 million. However, if a corporation ever fails the gross receipts test, it is ineligible for small corporation classification in future tax years.[42]

A corporation automatically is classified as a small corporation in its first tax year of existence.[43]

AMT ADJUSTMENTS

The following adjustments that were discussed in connection with the individual AMT also apply to the corporate AMT.

- Excess of MACRS over ADS depreciation on real and personal property placed in service after 1986.
- Pollution control facilities placed in service after 1986 (AMT requires ADS depreciation over the asset's ADR life if placed in service before 1999, and over the MACRS recovery period if placed in service after 1998; 60-month amortization is allowed for regular income tax purposes).
- Mining and exploration expenditures (AMT requires amortization over 10 years versus immediate expensing allowed for regular income tax purposes).
- Income on long-term contracts (AMT requires percentage of completion method; completed contract method is allowed in limited circumstances for regular income tax purposes).

[39] § 53(d)(1)(B)(i).

[40] § 55(b)(1)(B).

[41] §§ 55(d)(2) and (3).

[42] §§ 55(e)(1)(A) and (B). About 95% of C corporations qualify for this exemption.

[43] § 55(e)(1)(C).

FIGURE 15.3 **AMT Formula for Corporations**

Taxable income
Plus: Income tax NOL deduction
Plus or minus: AMT adjustments
Plus: Tax preferences
Equals: AMTI before ATNOLD
Minus: ATNOLD (limited to 90% of AMTI before ATNOLD)
Equals: AMTI
Minus: Exemption
Equals: AMT base
Times: 20% rate
Equals: Tentative minimum tax before credits
Minus: AMT foreign tax credit and other credits
Equals: Tentative minimum tax
Minus: Regular tax liability before credits minus regular foreign tax credit
Equals: AMT if positive

- Dispositions of assets (if gain or loss for AMT purposes differs from gain or loss for regular income tax purposes).
- Any allowable ATNOLD cannot exceed 90 percent of AMTI (before deduction for ATNOLD).[44]

EXAMPLE 28

The following information applies to Brown Corporation (a calendar year taxpayer).

Taxable income	$4,000,000
Mining exploration costs	500,000
Percentage depletion claimed (the property has a zero adjusted basis)	2,600,000

Brown Corporation's AMTI is determined as follows.

Taxable income	$4,000,000
Adjustments:	
Excess mining exploration costs [$500,000 (amount expensed) − $50,000 (amount allowed over a 10-year amortization period)]	450,000
Tax preferences:	
Excess depletion	2,600,000
AMTI	$7,050,000

ACE Adjustment

The adjusted current earnings (ACE) adjustment applies only to C corporations.[45] The **ACE adjustment** can have a significant impact on both tax and financial accounting.

Corporations are subject to an AMT adjustment equal to 75 percent of the excess of ACE over AMTI before the ACE adjustment.[46] Historically, the government has not required conformity between tax accounting and financial accounting. Through the ACE adjustment, Congress *indirectly* imposes a conformity requirement. Thus, a corporation may incur AMT not only because of targeted adjustments and preferences, but also as a result of any elections and tax accounting methods that cause ACE to exceed AMTI before the ACE adjustment.

The ACE adjustment can be either a positive or a negative amount. AMTI is increased by 75 percent of the excess of ACE over unadjusted AMTI. Alternatively,

[44] § 56(d)(1)(A)(i)(II).
[45] § 56(c).
[46] § 56(g).

TAX *in the NEWS*

Simplifying the Code and Eliminating the AMT

In 2010, two U.S. senators, Democrat Ron Wyden of Oregon and Republican Judd Gregg of New Hampshire, introduced tax legislation entitled the "Bipartisan Tax Fairness and Simplification Act." Their principal objective was to simplify the Code. Among the ways this would be accomplished are the following.

- Establish a 24 percent flat corporate tax rate.
- Provide tax relief for families making up to $200,000.
- Reduce the number of tax rates for individuals from six to three (rates of 15, 25, and 35 percent).
- Nearly triple the amount of the standard deduction.
- Permit small businesses (gross annual receipts of up to $1 million) to expense inventory and equipment purchases.
- Repeal many special interest tax breaks.
- Repeal the AMT.

AMTI is reduced by 75 percent of the excess of unadjusted AMTI over ACE. The negative adjustment is limited to the aggregate of the positive adjustments under ACE for prior years, reduced by the previously claimed negative adjustments. Thus, the ordering of the timing differences is crucial, because a negative ACE adjustment could be permanently lost. Unadjusted AMTI is AMTI before the ACE adjustment and the ATNOLD.[47]

EXAMPLE 29

A calendar year corporation showed the following results.

	2010	2011	2012
Adjusted current earnings	$4,000	$3,000	$2,000
Pre-adjusted AMTI	3,000	3,000	3,100

In 2010, because ACE exceeds unadjusted AMTI by $1,000, $750 (75% × $1,000) is a positive adjustment to AMTI. No adjustment is necessary for 2011. As unadjusted AMTI exceeds ACE by $1,100 in 2012, there is a potential negative adjustment to AMTI of $825 ($1,100 × 75%). Since the total increases to AMTI for prior years equal $750 and there are no previously claimed negative adjustments, only $750 of the potential negative adjustment reduces AMTI for 2012. Unfortunately, $75 of the negative adjustment is lost forever. ■

TAX PREFERENCES

AMTI includes designated tax preference items. In some cases, this has the effect of subjecting nontaxable income to the AMT. Tax preference items that apply to individuals also apply to corporations.

EXEMPTION AMOUNT

The tentative AMT is 20 percent of AMTI that exceeds the corporation's exemption amount. The exemption amount for a corporation is $40,000 reduced by 25 percent of the amount by which AMTI exceeds $150,000. The corporate AMT exemption phases out to zero when AMTI reaches $310,000.

EXAMPLE 30

Blue Corporation has AMTI of $180,000. The exemption amount is reduced by $7,500 [25% × ($180,000 − $150,000)], and the amount remaining is $32,500 ($40,000 − $7,500). Thus, Blue Corporation's AMT base (refer to Figure 15.3) is $147,500 ($180,000 − $32,500). ■

[47] §§ 56(g)(1) and (2).

OTHER ASPECTS OF THE AMT

All of a corporation's AMT is available for carryover as a minimum tax credit. This is so regardless of whether the adjustments and preferences originate from timing differences or AMT exclusions.

Certain small corporations can use specified tax credits to reduce the AMT liability. For all other corporations, only the foreign tax credit can be claimed in an AMT year.[48]

TAX PLANNING:

15.3 Avoiding Preferences and Adjustments

LO.8

Identify tax planning opportunities to minimize the AMT.

Several strategies and elections are available to help taxpayers avoid AMT preferences and adjustments.

- A taxpayer who is in danger of incurring AMT liability should not invest in most tax-exempt private activity bonds unless doing so makes good investment sense. Any AMT triggered by the AMT tax preference for interest income on private activity bonds reduces the yield on an investment in the bonds. Other tax-exempt bonds or taxable corporate bonds might yield a better after-tax return.
- A taxpayer may elect to expense certain costs in the year incurred or to capitalize and amortize the costs over some specified period. The decision should be based on the present value of after-tax cash flows under the available alternatives. Costs subject to elective treatment include circulation expenditures, mining exploration and development costs, and research and experimental expenditures.

15.4 Controlling the Timing of Preferences and Adjustments

The AMT exemption often keeps items of tax preference from being subject to the AMT. To use the AMT exemption effectively, taxpayers should avoid bunching preferences and positive adjustments in any one year. To avoid this bunching, taxpayers should attempt to control the timing of such items when possible.

15.5 Taking Advantage of the AMT/Regular Tax Rate Differential

A taxpayer who cannot avoid triggering the AMT in a given year usually can save taxes by taking advantage of the rate differential between the AMT and the regular income tax. This deferral/acceleration strategy should be considered for any income or expenses where the taxpayer can control the timing. This strategy applies to corporations as well as to individuals.

EXAMPLE 31

Peter, a real estate dealer who expects to be in the 35% regular income tax bracket in 2012, is subject to the AMT in 2011 at the 26% rate. He is considering the sale of a parcel of land (inventory) at a gain of $100,000. If he sells the land in 2012, he pays tax of

[48] § 38(c)(5)(A).

$35,000 ($100,000 gain × 35% regular income tax rate). However, if he sells the land in 2011, he pays tax of $26,000 ($100,000 gain × 26% AMT rate). Thus, accelerating the sale into 2011 saves Peter $9,000 ($35,000 – $26,000) in tax. ■

EXAMPLE 32

Cora, who expects to be in the 35% tax bracket in 2012, is subject to the AMT in 2011 at the 26% rate. She is going to contribute $10,000 in cash to her alma mater, State University. If Cora makes the contribution in 2012, she reduces her tax by $3,500 ($10,000 contribution × 35% regular income tax rate). However, if she makes the contribution in 2011, she reduces her tax by $2,600 ($10,000 contribution × 26% AMT rate). Thus, deferring the contribution until 2012 saves Cora $900 ($3,500 – $2,600) in tax. ■

REFOCUS ON THE BIG PICTURE

EFFECTS OF THE AMT

Bob contacts Adam, his tax return preparer, and explains in an excited voice that he believes that he underpaid his Federal income tax liability by $15,000. He is worried about the negative effects of any underpayment if it is discovered during an IRS audit, including the effect on his future marriage to Carol. Adam reviews Bob's tax return and assures him that it was properly prepared. Bob indicates that Carol has provided him with a copy of her tax return. He asks Adam to compare the returns and then explain the tax liability difference to him. He faxes a copy of Carol's return to Adam.

Adam examines the two tax returns and discovers that the difference relates to the treatment of the interest earned on the tax-exempt bonds. Although both Bob and Carol own 2009 tax-exempt bonds, those owned by Carol are private activity bonds that usually are subject to the AMT. However, Carol's accountant, Eve, apparently overlooked the fact that there is no AMT preference for such bonds that were issued in 2009. So the $15,000 AMT that was reported on Carol's Form 6251 is in error. Bob texts the good news to Carol that she is eligible for a Federal income tax refund.

KEY TERMS

ACE adjustment, 15–27

Alternative minimum tax (AMT), 15–3

Alternative minimum tax credit, 15–24

Alternative tax NOL deduction (ATNOLD), 15–15

AMT adjustments, 15–4

AMT exclusions, 15–24

Circulation expenditures, 15–5

Incentive stock options (ISOs), 15–12

Private activity bonds, 15–21

Tax preferences, 15–4

DISCUSSION QUESTIONS

1. **LO.1** Priscilla recently was promoted and received a substantial raise. She talks to her tax adviser about the potential tax ramifications. After making some projections, her adviser "welcomes her to the AMT club." Priscilla believes that it is unfair that she must pay more than the regular income tax, as she is a "HENRY" (high earner not rich yet) with substantial college-related debts. Explain to Priscilla the purpose of the AMT and why it applies to her.

2. **LO.2** Distinguish between the *direct* and *indirect* methods of calculating the AMT.

3. **LO.2** Both AMT adjustments and AMT preferences can cause AMTI to increase. Both AMT adjustments and AMT preferences can cause AMTI to decrease. Evaluate these statements.

4. **LO.2, 4** Identify which of the following are tax preferences.
   a. Seven percent of the exclusion associated with gains on the sale of certain small business stock.
   b. Exclusion on the receipt of property by gift or by inheritance.

c. Exclusion associated with payment of premiums by the employer on group term life insurance for coverage not in excess of $50,000.
d. Percentage depletion in excess of the property's adjusted basis.

5. **LO.2, 4** Identify which of the following are tax preferences.
   a. Exclusion for qualified employee discount provided by employer.
   b. Exclusion to employee on the employer's contribution to the employee's pension plan.
   c. Excess of deduction for circulation expenditures for regular income tax purposes over the deduction for AMT purposes.
   d. Exclusion of life insurance proceeds received as the result of death.
   e. Exclusion to the employee on the employer's payments of health insurance premiums for employees.

6. **LO.2** Describe the tax formula for the AMT.

7. **LO.2** An AMT results if the tentative AMT exceeds the regular income tax liability. But what happens if the regular income tax liability exceeds the tentative AMT? Does a negative AMT develop to the extent of this excess that can be carried to other years?

8. **LO.2** John and Mabel, unrelated individuals, use the same Federal income tax filing status (single). However, Mabel's AMT exemption amount is $48,450, while John's is $0. Explain.

9. **LO.2** Alfred is single, and his AMTI of $350,000 consists of the following. What tax rates are applicable in calculating Alfred's tentative AMT?

Ordinary income	$250,000
Long-term capital gains	70,000
Qualified dividends	30,000

10. **LO.2** Can any nonrefundable credits, other than the foreign tax credit, reduce the regular income tax liability below the amount of the tentative AMT for an individual taxpayer?

11. **LO.3** In 1997, Andy placed a warehouse in service in his business. For both regular income tax and AMT purposes, he calculates the cost recovery using the straight-line method. Andy concludes that there will be no AMT adjustment this year because he uses the straight-line method. Evaluate Andy's conclusion.

12. **LO.3** Nell recently purchased a weekly newspaper that has been generating losses. Nell is convinced that she can turn the newspaper around with a new editorial style and increased circulation expenditures. What are the tax benefits and potential income tax pitfalls, if any, of increasing the circulation expenses?

13. **LO.3, 8** Rick, who is single, incurs mining exploration and development costs associated with his energy company. He would expense the costs in the current year in order to reduce his regular income tax but is aware that this would create a positive adjustment for AMT purposes. His AGI is large enough to reduce the AMT exemption amount to zero. Therefore, he is considering electing to amortize the mining exploration and development costs over 10 years to avoid having to pay any AMT. Advise Rick. **ISSUE ID**

14. **LO.3** Both Janice and April own and operate construction companies. Janice uses the completed contract method, while April uses the percentage of completion method. Why is Janice concerned with the AMT, while April is not?

15. **LO.3** Megan, a corporate executive, plans to exercise an incentive stock option (ISO) granted by her employer. The option allows Megan to purchase 200 shares of the corporation's stock for a strike price of $25 per share. The stock is freely transferable by Megan. The stock is currently selling for $60 per share.
    a. Discuss the tax effects if Megan exercises the option.
    b. Can AMT adjustments be avoided if Megan disposes of the stock in the same tax year that she exercises the stock option?

16. **LO.3** Three years ago, Lilly acquired a machine (seven-year property) for $140,000. She depreciated it using an accelerated method under MACRS. When she sells the machine at a gain this year, will her recognized gain for regular income tax and AMT purposes be the same? Explain.

ISSUE ID

17. **LO.3, 8** Celine will be subject to the AMT in 2011. She owns an investment building and is considering disposing of it and investing in other realty. Based on an appraisal of the building's value, the realized gain would be $85,000. Ed has offered to purchase the building from Celine with the closing date being December 29, 2011. Ed wants to close the transaction in 2011 because certain beneficial tax consequences will result only if the transaction is closed prior to the beginning of 2012. Abby has offered to purchase the building with the closing date being January 2, 2012. The building has a $95,000 greater AMT adjusted basis. For regular income tax purposes, Celine expects to be in the 25% tax bracket in 2011 and the 28% tax bracket in 2012. What are the relevant income tax issues that Celine faces in making her decision?

18. **LO.3** Passive activity losses are not deductible in computing either taxable income or AMTI. Explain why an adjustment for passive activity losses may be required for AMT purposes.

19. **LO.3, 4** What effect do adjustments and preferences have on the calculation of the ATNOLD?

20. **LO.3** For which of the following itemized deductions is the tax treatment the same for regular income tax and AMT purposes?

    - Medical expenses.
    - Casualty losses.
    - Miscellaneous itemized deductions subject to the 2% floor.
    - State income taxes.
    - Real estate taxes.
    - Charitable contributions.

ISSUE ID

21. **LO.3, 4, 8** Matt, who is single, always has elected to itemize deductions rather than take the standard deduction. In prior years, his itemized deductions always exceeded the standard deduction by a substantial amount. As a result of paying off the mortgage on his residence, he projects that his itemized deductions will exceed the standard deduction by only $500. Matt anticipates that the amount of his itemized deductions will remain about the same in the foreseeable future. Matt's AGI is $150,000. He is investing the amount of his former mortgage payment each month in tax-exempt bonds, which he purchased four years ago. A friend recommends that Matt buy a beach house in order to increase his itemized deductions with the mortgage interest deduction. What are the relevant tax issues for Matt?

22. **LO.3** How does the treatment of medical expenses differ for AMT and regular income tax purposes?

23. **LO.3** In computing the AMT itemized deduction for interest, it is possible that some interest allowed for regular income tax purposes will not be allowed. Explain.

24. **LO.3** When converting taxable income to AMTI, what is the reason for a positive adjustment as to personal and dependency exemptions?

25. **LO.4** Kevin owns a mineral deposit that qualifies for percentage depletion. Kevin deducts $90,000 for regular income tax purposes. Cost depletion for the year would have been $55,000.
    a. Does the fact that percentage depletion exceeds cost depletion produce an AMT preference?
    b. Under what circumstances would Kevin report an AMT preference for depletion?

DECISION MAKING

26. **LO.3, 4** During the year, Fran earned $18,000 of interest income on 2005 private activity bonds. She incurred interest expense of $7,000 in connection with amounts borrowed to purchase the bonds. What is the effect of these items on Fran's taxable income? On her AMT? Could there be a related beneficial effect in calculating AMTI?

27. **LO.6** What is the purpose of the AMT credit? Briefly describe how the credit is computed.

28. **LO.2, 7** Discuss the similarities and differences between the individual and the corporate AMT.

29. **LO.7** Some observers believe that the ACE adjustment causes corporations to change some of the accounting methods they use for financial reporting and tax purposes. Comment.

30. **LO.2, 8** Is it ever advisable for a taxpayer to defer deductions from an AMT year into a non-AMT year when the regular income tax applies? Explain and give an example of how such a deferral might be accomplished.

ISSUE ID

PROBLEMS

31. **LO.2** Use the following data to calculate Reba's 2011 AMT base.

Taxable income	$160,000
Positive AMT adjustments	80,000
Negative AMT adjustments	60,000
AMT preferences	45,000

Reba files as a single taxpayer.

32. **LO.2** Arthur Wesson, an unmarried individual who is age 68, has 2011 taxable income of $160,000. He has AMT positive adjustments of $40,000 and tax preferences of $35,000.
    a. What is Arthur's AMT?
    b. What is the total amount of Arthur's tax liability?
    c. Draft a letter to Arthur explaining why he must pay more than the regular income tax liability. Arthur's address is 100 Colonel's Way, Conway, SC 29526.

COMMUNICATIONS

33. **LO.2** Calculate the 2011 AMT for the following cases. The taxpayer reports regular taxable income of $450,000 and does not claim any tax credits.

	Tentative Minimum Tax	
Filing Status	**Case 1**	**Case 2**
Single	$200,000	$180,000
Married, filing jointly	200,000	180,000

34. **LO.2** Calculate the 2011 AMT exemption amount for the following cases for a single taxpayer, a married taxpayer filing jointly, and a married taxpayer filing separately.

Case	AMTI
1	$155,000
2	290,000
3	700,000

35. **LO.2** Leona has 2011 nonrefundable tax credits of $70,000. None of these nonrefundable credits are personal credits that qualify for special treatment. Her regular income tax liability before credits is $145,000, and her tentative minimum tax is $98,000.
    a. What is the amount of Leona's AMT?
    b. What is the amount of Leona's regular income tax liability after credits?

36. **LO.2, 3, 8** Angela, who is single, incurs circulation expenditures of $153,000 during 2011. She is in the process of deciding whether to expense the $153,000 or to capitalize it and elect to deduct it over a three-year period. Angela already knows that she will be subject to the AMT for 2011 at both the 26% and the 28% rates. Angela is in the 28% bracket for regular income tax purposes this year (has regular taxable income of $153,000 before considering the circulation expenses) and expects to be in the 28% bracket in 2012 and 2013. Advise Angela on whether she should elect the three-year write-off rather than expensing the $153,000 in 2011.

DECISION MAKING

37. **LO.2, 3** Vito owns and operates a news agency (as a sole proprietorship). During 2011, he incurred expenses of $450,000 to increase circulation of newspapers and magazines that his agency distributes. For regular income tax purposes, he elected to expense the $450,000 in 2011. In addition, he incurred $120,000 in circulation expenditures in 2012 and again elected expense treatment. What AMT adjustments are required in 2011 and 2012 as a result of the circulation expenditures?

38. **LO.3** Lorenzo owns two apartment buildings. He acquired Forsythia Acres on February 21, 1998, for $300,000 ($90,000 allocated to the land) and Square One on November 12, 2011, for $800,000 ($100,000 allocated to the land). Neither apartment complex qualifies as low-income housing. If Lorenzo elects to write off the cost of each building as fast as possible, what is the effect of depreciation (cost recovery) on his AMTI for:
    a. 1998?
    b. 2011?

DECISION MAKING

COMMUNICATIONS

39. **LO.3, 8** Helen Carlton acquired used equipment for her business at a cost of $300,000. The equipment is five-year class property for regular income tax purposes and for AMT purposes. Helen does not claim any additional first-year depreciation.
    a. If Helen depreciates the equipment using the method that will produce the greatest current deduction for regular income tax purposes, what is the amount of the AMT adjustment? Helen does not elect § 179 limited expensing.
    b. How can Helen reduce the AMT adjustment to $0? What circumstances would motivate her to do so?
    c. Draft a letter to Helen regarding the choice of depreciation methods. Helen's address is 500 Monticello Avenue, Glendale, AZ 85306.

DECISION MAKING

40. **LO.3, 8** Geoff incurred $600,000 of mining and exploration expenditures. He elects to deduct the expenditures as quickly as the tax law allows for regular income tax purposes.
    a. How will Geoff's treatment of mining and exploration expenditures affect his regular income tax and AMT computations for the year?
    b. How can Geoff avoid having AMT adjustments related to the mining and exploration expenditures?
    c. What factors should Geoff consider in deciding whether to deduct the expenditures in the year incurred?

41. **LO.3** Josepi's construction company uses the completed contract method. During the three-year period 2011–2013, Josepi recognized the following income on his two construction contracts.

Year	Contract 1	Contract 2
2011	$700,000*	$ –0–
2012	–0–	–0–
2013	–0–	800,000**

*Construction completed in 2011.
**Construction completed in 2013.

If Josepi had used the percentage of completion method, he would have recognized the following income.

Year	Contract 1	Contract 2
2011	$40,000	$275,000
2012	–0–	225,000
2013	–0–	300,000

Calculate Josepi's AMT adjustment for the three tax years.

42. **LO.3** Burt, the CFO of Amber, Inc., is granted stock options in 2011 that qualify as incentive stock options. In 2016, the rights in the stock become freely transferable and not subject to a substantial risk of forfeiture. Burt exercises the stock options in 2015 when the option price is $75,000 and the fair market value of the stock is $90,000. He sells the stock in 2019 for $150,000. What are the regular income tax consequences and the AMT consequences for Burt in:
    a. 2011?
    b. 2015?
    c. 2016?
    d. 2019?

43. **LO.3** In 2006, Diego exercised an incentive stock option (ISO), acquiring 1,000 shares of Balloon Ltd. stock at a price of $75 per share. The fair market value of the Balloon stock on this date was $98 per share. In 2011, the stock rights became freely transferable (i.e., no longer subject to a substantial risk of forfeiture). Diego sells the 1,000 shares of Balloon stock in 2012 for $120 per share. How do these transactions affect Diego's AMTI for 2006, 2011, and 2012?

44. **LO.3** Alicia owns two investment properties that she acquired several years ago. Her adjusted basis in the assets is as follows.

	Regular Income Tax	AMT
Land	$100,000	$100,000
Apartment building	450,000	490,000

Alicia sells the land for $250,000 and the building for $800,000.

a. Calculate Alicia's recognized gain or loss on the sale of each asset for regular income tax and AMT purposes.

b. Determine the AMT adjustment on the sale of each asset.

45. **LO.3** Freda acquired a passive activity this year for $870,000. Gross income from operations of the activity was $160,000. Operating expenses, not including depreciation, were $122,000. Regular income tax depreciation of $49,750 was computed under MACRS. AMT depreciation, computed under ADS, was $41,000. Compute Freda's passive loss deduction and passive loss suspended for regular income tax purposes and for AMT purposes.

46. **LO.3** Wally and Gloria incur and pay medical expenses in excess of insurance reimbursements during the year as follows.

For Wally	$15,000
For Gloria (spouse)	5,000
For Chuck (son)	1,500
For Carter (Gloria's father)	13,000

Wally and Gloria's AGI is $175,000. They file a joint return. Chuck and Carter are Wally and Gloria's dependents.

a. What is Wally and Gloria's medical expense deduction for regular income tax purposes?

b. What is Wally and Gloria's medical expense deduction for AMT purposes?

c. What is the amount of the AMT adjustment for medical expenses?

47. **LO.3** Wolfgang's AGI is $125,000. He reports the following itemized deductions this year.

Medical expenses [$15,000 – (7.5% × $125,000)]	$ 5,625
State income taxes	4,200
Charitable contributions	4,000
Home mortgage interest on his personal residence	8,000
Casualty loss (after $100 and 10% reductions)	1,800
Miscellaneous itemized deductions [$3,500 – (2% × $125,000)]	1,000
	$24,625

a. Calculate Wolfgang's itemized deductions for AMT purposes.

b. What is the amount of the AMT adjustment?

48. **LO.3** Walter, who is single, owns a personal residence in the city. He also owns a cabin near a ski resort in the mountains. He uses the cabin as a vacation home. In August, Walter borrowed $60,000 on a home equity loan and used the proceeds to reduce credit card obligations and other debt. This year, he paid the following amounts of interest.

On his personal residence	$16,000
On the cabin	7,000
On the home equity loan	2,500
On credit card obligations	1,500
On purchase of personal-use SUV	1,350

What amount, if any, must Walter recognize as an AMT adjustment?

49. **LO.3** Gail pays investment interest of $52,000. She has interest income of $21,000 on taxable bonds, $12,000 on tax-exempt 2005 private activity bonds, and $14,000 on regular tax-exempt bonds. Her other investment expenses are $4,000, none of which relates to the tax-exempt bonds.
    a. What is Gail's deduction for investment interest for regular income tax purposes?
    b. What is the amount of her investment interest carryover for regular income tax purposes?
    c. What is the amount of the adjustment for AMT purposes?

50. **LO.3** Bill, who is single with no dependents, had AGI of $100,000. His AGI included net investment income of $15,000 and gambling income of $1,100. Bill incurred the following itemized deductions for income tax purposes.

Medical expenses (before 7.5%-of-AGI floor)	$11,000
State income taxes	3,200
Personal property tax	2,000
Real estate tax	8,400
Interest on personal residence	12,200
Interest on home (never rented to others)	3,800
Interest on home equity loan (proceeds were used to buy a new automobile)	2,700
Investment interest expense	3,300
Charitable contribution	5,000
Casualty loss (after $100 floor, before 10%-of-AGI floor)	13,000
Unreimbursed employee expenses (before 2%-of-AGI floor)	2,400
Gambling losses	900

What is Bill's AMT adjustment for itemized deductions? Is it positive or negative?

51. **LO.2, 3** Paula is single and has no dependents. She reports taxable income of $155,000 and tax preferences of $57,000 in 2011. She does not itemize deductions for regular income tax purposes. Compute Paula's AMT exemption and AMTI.

52. **LO.3** Merle purchased a copper mine several years ago for $750,000. His adjusted basis at the beginning of the year is $425,000. For the year, he deducts depletion of $550,000 (greater of cost depletion $230,000 or percentage depletion $550,000) for regular income tax purposes. Calculate Merle's:
    a. AMT adjustment.
    b. Adjusted basis for regular income tax purposes.
    c. Adjusted basis for AMT purposes.

53. **LO.4** Amos incurred and expensed intangible drilling costs (IDC) of $70,000. His net oil and gas income was $60,000. What is the amount of Amos's tax preference item for IDC?

54. **LO.2, 3, 4** Jerry, who is single with no dependents and does not itemize, provides you with the following information for the tax year.

Short-term capital loss	$ 7,000
Long-term capital gain	25,000
Municipal bond interest received on 2004 private activity bonds	9,000
Dividends from U.S. corporations	2,300
Excess of FMV over cost of ISOs (the rights became freely transferable and not subject to a substantial risk of forfeiture this year)	35,000

What is the total amount of Jerry's tax preference items and AMT adjustments?

55. **LO.2, 3, 4** Pat, who is single with no dependents, received a salary of $90,000. She reports interest income of $1,000, dividend income of $5,000, gambling income of $4,000, and interest income from 2006 private activity bonds of $40,000. The dividends are *not* qualified dividends. The following additional information is relevant.

Medical expenses (before 7.5%-of-AGI floor)	$12,000
State income taxes	4,100
Real estate taxes	2,800
Mortgage interest on residence	3,100
Investment interest expense	1,800
Gambling losses	5,100

Compute Pat's tentative minimum tax.

56. **LO.2, 5** Renee and Sanjeev, who are married, report taxable income of $273,000. They computed positive AMT adjustments of $38,000, negative AMT adjustments of $14,000, and tax preference items of $67,500.
   a. Compute their AMTI.
   b. Compute their tentative minimum tax.

57. **LO.2, 3, 4, 5** Farr, who is single, has no dependents and does not itemize. She shows the following items relative to her 2011 tax return.

Bargain element from the exercise of an ISO (no restrictions apply to the stock)	$ 45,000
MACRS depreciation on shopping mall building acquired in 1990 (ADS depreciation would have yielded $26,000)	49,000
Percentage depletion in excess of property's adjusted basis	50,000
Taxable income for regular income tax purposes	121,000

   a. Determine Farr's AMT adjustments and preferences.
   b. Calculate the AMT (if any).

58. **LO.2, 3, 4, 5** Larry is single and records the following items for 2011. Compute Larry's tax liability before credits or prepayments.

Income—	
Salary	$145,000
Interest from bank savings account	12,000
Interest on corporate bonds	7,000
Short-term capital gain	8,000
Expenses—	
Unreimbursed employee business expenses (no meals or entertainment)	4,000
Total medical expenses	24,000
State income taxes	6,500
Real property taxes	6,800
Home mortgage (qualified housing) interest	7,200
Casualty loss on vacation home—	
Decline in value	20,000
Adjusted basis	70,000
Insurance proceeds	12,000
Tax preferences	116,000

59. **LO.5, 6** Bonnie, who is single, has taxable income of $0 in 2011. She has positive timing adjustments of $200,000 and AMT exclusion items of $100,000 for the year. What is the amount of Bonnie's AMT credit for carryover to 2012?

60. **LO.7** Aqua, Inc., a calendar year corporation, reports the following gross receipts and taxable income for 2001–2011.

Year	Gross Receipts	Taxable Income
2001	$6,000,000	$1,450,000
2002	6,200,000	1,375,000
2003	6,100,000	1,425,000
2004	8,000,000	1,400,000
2005	7,000,000	1,312,000
2006	7,500,000	985,000
2007	7,200,000	1,002,000
2008	7,100,000	1,010,000
2009	6,500,000	990,000
2010	6,300,000	982,000
2011	7,800,000	850,000

a. When is Aqua first exempt from the AMT as a small corporation?
b. Is Aqua subject to the AMT for 2011?

61. **LO.7** Gray Corporation (a calendar year corporation) reports the following information. Compute Gray's ACE adjustment for each year.

	2010	2011	2012
Unadjusted AMTI	$3,000	$2,000	$5,000
Adjusted current earnings	4,000	3,000	2,000

62. **LO.7** In each of the following independent situations, determine the tentative AMT.

	AMTI (Before the Exemption Amount)
Quincy Corporation	$150,000
Redland Corporation	160,000
Tanzen Corporation	320,000

63. **LO.7** Amber, Inc., reports taxable income of $200,000. During the year, Amber paid dividends of $30,000. The corporation had $20,000 of positive AMT adjustments and $25,000 of tax preferences.
a. Calculate Amber's regular income tax liability.
b. Calculate Amber's AMTI and AMT.

CUMULATIVE PROBLEMS

TAX RETURN PROBLEM

H&R BLOCK At Home

64. Robert A. Kliesh, age 41, is single and has no dependents. Robert's Social Security number is 111–11–1111. His address is 201 Front Street, Missoula, MT 59812. He is independently wealthy as a result of having inherited sizable holdings in real estate and corporate stocks and bonds. Robert is a minister at First Presbyterian Church, but he accepts no salary from the church. However, he does reside in the church's parsonage free of charge. The fair rental value of the parsonage is $3,000 a month. The church also provides him a cash grocery allowance of $200 a week. Examination of Robert's financial records provides the following information for 2010.
a. On January 16, 2010, Robert sold 1,000 shares of stock for a gain of $10,000. The stock was acquired 14 months ago.
b. He received $30,000 of interest on private activity bonds that he had purchased in 2007. He also received $40,000 of interest on tax-exempt bonds that are not private activity bonds.
c. He received gross rent income of $190,000 from an apartment complex he owns. He qualifies as an active participant.
d. Expenses related to the apartment complex, which he acquired in 1987, were $225,000.

e. Robert's interest income (on CDs) totaled $23,000. Since he invests only in growth stocks, he has no dividend income.
f. He won $60,000 on the lottery.
g. On October 9, 2008, Robert exercised his rights under Falcon Corporation's incentive stock option plan. For an option price of $20,000, he acquired stock worth $75,000. The stock became freely transferable in 2010. At the date the stocks became freely transferable, the fair market value was $95,000.
h. Robert was the beneficiary of an $800,000 life insurance policy on his Uncle Jake. He received the proceeds in October.
i. Robert had the following potential itemized deductions *from* AGI.

- $5,200 fair market value of stock contributed to Presbyterian Church (basis of stock was $3,000). He had owned the stock for two years.
- $4,200 interest on consumer purchases.
- $3,900 state and local income tax.
- $6,500 medical expenses (before 7.5% floor) for himself. He also paid $15,000 of medical expenses for a parishioner who died.
- $300 for a safe deposit box that is used to store investments and related legal documents.
- $750 contribution to the campaign of the Democratic candidate for governor.
- $5,000 paid for lottery tickets associated with playing the state lottery. Robert contributed $5,000 of his net winnings to the church.
- $5,000 contribution to his traditional IRA.
- Since Robert lived in Montana, he paid no sales tax.

Use Forms 1040 and 6251 and Schedules A, B, D, and E to compute Robert Kliesh's 2010 Federal income tax liability (including AMT, if any). Suggested software: H&R BLOCK At Home.

65. Robert M. and Jane R. Armstrong live at 1802 College Avenue, Carmel, IN 46302. They are married and file a joint return for 2011. The Armstrongs have two dependent children, Ellen J. and Sean M., who are 10-year-old twins. Ellen's Social Security number is 123–45–6788, and Sean's is 123–45–6787. Robert pays child support of $12,000 for Amy, his 17-year-old daughter from his previous marriage. Amy's Social Security number is 123–45–6786. According to the divorce decree, Margaret, Robert's former wife, has legal custody of Amy. Margaret provides the balance of Amy's support (about $6,000).

TAX COMPUTATION PROBLEM

COMMUNICATIONS

Robert (111–11–1111) is a factory foreman, and Jane (123–45–6789) is a computer systems analyst. The Armstrongs' Forms W–2 reflect the following information.

	Robert	Jane
Salary (Indiana Foundry, Inc.)	$95,000	
Salary (Carmel Computer Associates)		$110,000
Federal income tax withheld	24,750	27,000
Social Security wages	95,000	106,800
Social Security tax withheld	3,990	4,486
Medicare wages	95,000	110,000
Medicare tax withheld	1,378	1,595
State wages	95,000	110,000
State income tax withheld	4,900	5,500

In addition to their salaries, the Armstrongs report the following income items.

Interest income (Carmel Sanitation District Bonds)	$23,500
Interest income (Carmel National Bank)	2,900
Qualified dividend income (Able Computer Corporation)	15,000
Gambling income	4,500
Gift from Uncle Raymond to Robert	8,000

Jane inherited $750,000 from her grandfather in January and invested the money in the Carmel Sanitation District Bonds, which are 2008 private activity bonds. Jane was selected as the "Citizen of the Year" and received an award of $5,000. She used the $5,000 to pay off some credit card debt.

The Armstrongs incurred the following expenses.

Medical expenses (doctor and hospital bills)	$21,000
Real property tax on personal residence	6,900
Mortgage interest on personal residence (reported on Form 1098)	7,400
Investment interest expense	2,300
Contributions	11,500
Gambling losses	5,800
Sales taxes (from sales tax table)	1,851

On March 1, Robert and Jane contributed Ace stock to the Carmel Salvation Army, a public charity. They had acquired the stock on February 9, 1999, for $6,500. The stock was listed on the New York Stock Exchange at a value of $9,000 on the date of the contribution. In addition, Robert and Jane contributed $2,500 during the year to Second Church.

Robert sold five acres of land to a real estate developer on October 12, 2011, for $100,000. He had acquired the land on May 15, 2006, for $77,000.

Compute the 2011 tax liability (including AMT, if any) for Robert and Jane Armstrong.

Write a letter to the Armstrongs indicating whether they have a refund or balance due for 2011, and suggest possible tax planning strategies for 2012.

RESEARCH PROBLEMS

THOMSON REUTERS

Checkpoint® Student Edition

Note: Solutions to Research Problems can be prepared by using the **Checkpoint® Student Edition** online research product, which is available to accompany this text. It is also possible to prepare solutions to the Research Problems by using tax research materials found in a standard tax library.

Research Problem 1. Samuel had worked for Pearl, Inc., for 35 years when he was discharged and his position filled by a much younger person. He filed and pursued a suit for age discrimination and received an award of $1.5 million. Under the contingent fee arrangement with his attorney, one-third of the award was paid directly to the attorney, with the balance going to Samuel. Samuel reported $1 million gross income on his tax return, but he did not include the $500,000 paid to the attorney.

The IRS audited Samuel's return and included the $500,000 contingency fee in gross income. Additionally, Samuel was allowed a miscellaneous itemized deduction (subject to the 2% floor) for the fee paid to the attorney. The IRS adjustment caused a tax deficiency to be assessed for both the regular income tax and the AMT.

Evaluate the results reached.

Research Problem 2. Masha Quigley filed her return for 2009 and reported taxable income computed as follows.

AGI (includes $2,000 state income tax refund previously deducted with a tax benefit)	$ 80,000
Personal exemption	(3,650)
Miscellaneous itemized deductions in excess of 2% of AGI	(28,000)
Taxable income	$ 48,350

Although Masha had state and local tax expense of $9,000, she chose not to deduct them in calculating taxable income. Masha believed that if she claimed the state and local taxes, she would be subject to the AMT. As a result, she filed her Form 1040 as a single individual and reported a tax liability of $8,281.

Upon audit of the return, the IRS concluded that Masha should have included the $9,000 of state and local taxes in her itemized deductions. Thus, her decision to not deduct the state and local taxes did not relieve her from being subject to the AMT.

Who is correct?

Use the tax resources of the Internet to address the following questions. Do not restrict your search to the Web, but include a review of newsgroups and general reference materials, practitioner sites and resources, primary sources of the tax law, chat rooms and discussion groups, and other opportunities.

INTERNET *activity*

Research Problem 3. Locate a current proposal to modify the structure or scope of the Federal AMT on individuals. In an e-mail to your instructor:

COMMUNICATIONS

a. Describe the proposal.
b. Indicate the entity making the proposal.
c. Identify the proposer's motivations for the law changes.
d. Assess the proposal as to revenue effects and incidence of the tax.

Research Problem 4. Go to one of the tax blogs and post a comment on one of the following items relative to individuals who are subject to the AMT.

COMMUNICATIONS

a. Interest deductions on vacation homes.
b. Personal and dependency exemptions.
c. Tax preparation fees.
d. Adequacy of the exemption amount.
e. Indexing of AMT rates.
f. Local property tax.
g. Tax benefit rule.

Research Problem 5. Ascertain if your state's income tax has an AMT component. If your state does not levy an income tax, choose a contiguous state that does. In an e-mail to your instructor, outline how the state AMT formula differs from the Federal. When was the state AMT provision adopted?

COMMUNICATIONS

Research Problem 6. In no more than four PowerPoint slides, summarize in graphic form the number of individuals who have been subject to the Federal AMT since 1990 and the dollars of AMT that have been collected from them. Present your data in five-year increments. Then extend your graphs to include estimates of the taxpayer coverage and tax collection amounts into the next few tax years:

COMMUNICATIONS

a. Assuming that Congress does not modify the statutes from how they exist today.
b. Assuming that various AMT amounts are indexed for inflation.

Research Problem 7. Use the Tax Stats function at **www.irs.gov** to determine how many C corporations incurred an AMT liability for the last tax year with complete data. What percentage of total corporate Federal income tax collections came from the AMT?

CHAPTER 16

Accounting Periods and Methods

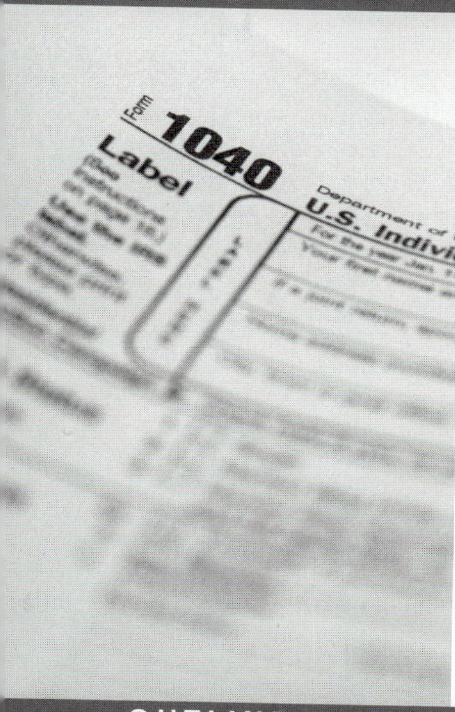

LEARNING OBJECTIVES

After completing Chapter 16, you should be able to:

LO.1

Understand the relevance of the accounting period concept, the different types of accounting periods, and the limitations on their use.

LO.2

Apply the cash method, accrual method, and hybrid method of accounting.

LO.3

Utilize the procedure for changing accounting methods.

LO.4

Determine when the installment method of accounting can be utilized and apply the related calculation techniques.

LO.5

Understand the alternative methods of accounting for long-term contracts (the completed contract method and the percentage of completion method) including the limitations on the use of the completed contract method.

LO.6

Identify tax planning opportunities related to accounting periods and accounting methods.

OUTLINE

For the latest in changes to tax legislation, visit **www.cengage.com/taxation/swft.**

FRAMEWORK 1040: Tax Formula for Individuals

This chapter covers the boldfaced portions of the Tax Formula for Individuals that was introduced in Figure 3.1 on p. 3-3. Below those portions are the sections of Form 1040 where the results are reported.

Income (broadly conceived)	$ xx,xxx
Less: Exclusions	(x,xxx)
Gross income	**$ xx,xxx**
FORM 1040 (P.1) — 12 Business income or (loss). Attach Schedule C or C-EZ	
Less: Deductions for adjusted gross income	**(x,xxx)**
Adjusted gross income	$ xx,xxx
Less: The greater of total itemized deductions *or* the standard deduction	(x,xxx)
Personal and dependency exemptions	(x,xxx)
Taxable income	$ xx,xxx
Tax on taxable income (see tax Tables or Tax Rate Schedules)	$ x,xxx
Less: Tax credits (including income taxes withheld and prepaid)	(xxx)
Tax due (or refund)	$ xxx

THE BIG PICTURE Tax Solutions for the Real World

ACCOUNTING PERIOD

Belinda, Pearl, Inc. (a C corporation), and Tweety, Inc. (an S corporation), are going to form a partnership (Silver Partnership). The ownership interests and tax years of the partners are as follows:

Partner	Partnership Interest	Tax Year Ends
Belinda	25%	December 31
Pearl, Inc.	35%	November 30
Tweety, Inc.	40%	June 30

The partnership will begin business on April 1, 2011. The partners have several issues they would like for you to address.

- A potential conflict exists among the partners regarding when the tax year should end for Silver. Belinda and Pearl would like a year-end close to their own year-ends while Tweety would like to have a June 30 year-end. Is this a decision that Tweety can make since it owns more of the partnership than either of the other two partners? Is this a decision that Belinda and Pearl can make since collectively they own more of the partnership than Tweety?
- Since Silver will begin business on April 1, 2011, will the first tax year be a "short" tax year or a "long" tax year? Will annualization of the net income of the partnership be required?
- How will the partners know when their share of Silver's net income or net loss should be reported on their respective income tax returns?

Read the chapter and formulate your response.

Tax practitioners must deal with the issue of *when* particular items of income and expense are recognized as well as the basic issue of *whether* the items are includible in taxable income. Earlier chapters discussed the types of income subject to tax (gross income and exclusions) and allowable deductions (the *whether* issue).[1] This chapter focuses on the related issue of the periods in which income and deductions are reported (the *when* issue). Generally, a taxpayer's income and deductions must be assigned to particular 12-month periods—calendar years or fiscal years.

Income and deductions are placed within particular years through the use of tax accounting methods. The basic accounting methods are the cash method, accrual method, and hybrid method. Other special purpose methods, such as the installment method and the methods used for long-term construction contracts, are available for specific circumstances or types of transactions.

Over the long run, the accounting period used by a taxpayer will not affect the aggregate amount of reported taxable income. However, taxable income for any particular year may vary significantly due to the use of a particular reporting period. Also, through the choice of accounting methods or accounting periods, it is possible to postpone the recognition of taxable income and to enjoy the benefits from deferring the related tax. This chapter discusses the taxpayer's alternatives for accounting periods and accounting methods.

16.1 Accounting Periods

IN GENERAL

LO.1

Understand the relevance of the accounting period concept, the different types of accounting periods, and the limitations on their use.

A taxpayer who keeps adequate books and records may be permitted to elect to use a **fiscal year**, a 12-month period ending on the *last day* of a month other than December, for the **accounting period**. Otherwise, a *calendar year* must be used.[2]

Frequently, corporations can satisfy the record-keeping requirements and elect to use a fiscal year.[3] Often the fiscal year conforms to a natural business year (e.g., a summer resort's fiscal year may end on September 30, after the close of the season). Individuals seldom use a fiscal year because they do not maintain the necessary books and records and because complications can arise as a result of changes in the tax law (e.g., often the transition rules and effective dates differ for fiscal year taxpayers).

Generally, a taxable year may not exceed 12 calendar months. However, if certain requirements are met, a taxpayer may elect to use an annual period that varies from 52 to 53 weeks.[4] In that case, the year-end must be on the same day of the week (e.g., the Tuesday falling closest to October 31 or the last Tuesday in October). The day of the week selected for ending the year will depend upon business considerations. For example, a retail business that is not open on Sundays may end its tax year on a Sunday so that it can take an inventory without interrupting business operations.

EXAMPLE 1

Wade is in the business of selling farm supplies. His natural business year terminates at the end of October with the completion of harvesting. At the end of the fiscal year, Wade must take an inventory, which is most easily accomplished on a Tuesday. Therefore, Wade could adopt a 52–53 week tax year ending on the Tuesday closest to October 31. If Wade selects this method, the year-end date may fall in the following month if that Tuesday is closer to October 31. The tax year ending in 2011 will contain 52 weeks beginning on Wednesday, November 3, 2010, and ending on Tuesday, November 1, 2011. The tax year ending in 2012 will have 52 weeks beginning on Wednesday, November 2, 2011, and ending on Tuesday, October 30, 2012. ■

[1] See Chapters 4, 5, and 6.

[2] § 441(c) and Reg. § 1.441–1(b)(1)(ii).

[3] Reg. § 1.441–1(e)(2).

[4] § 441(f).

SPECIFIC PROVISIONS FOR PARTNERSHIPS, S CORPORATIONS, AND PERSONAL SERVICE CORPORATIONS

Partnerships and S Corporations

When a partner's tax year and the partnership's tax year differ, the partner will enjoy a deferral of income. This results because the partner reports his or her share of the partnership's income and deductions for the partnership's tax year ending within or with the partner's tax year.[5] For example, if the tax year of the partnership ends on January 31, a calendar year partner will not report partnership profits for the first 11 months of the partnership tax year until the following year. Therefore, partnerships are subject to special tax year requirements.

In general, the partnership tax year must be the same as the tax year of the majority interest partners. The **majority interest partners** are the partners who own a greater-than-50 percent interest in the partnership capital and profits. If there are no majority interest partners, the partnership must adopt the same tax year as its principal partners. A **principal partner** is a partner with a 5 percent or more interest in the partnership capital or profits.[6]

EXAMPLE 2

The RST Partnership is owned equally by Rose Corporation, Silver Corporation, and Tom. The partners have the following tax years.

Partner	Tax Year Ending
Rose Corporation	June 30
Silver Corporation	June 30
Tom	December 31

The partnership's tax year must end on June 30. If Silver Corporation's as well as Tom's year ended on December 31, the partnership would be required to adopt a calendar year. ■

If the principal partners do not all have the same tax year and no majority of partners have the same tax year, the partnership must use a year that results in the *least aggregate deferral* of income.[7] Under the **least aggregate deferral method**, the different tax years of the principal partners are tested to determine which produces the least aggregate deferral. This is calculated by first multiplying the combined percentages of the principal partners with the same tax year by the months of deferral for the test year. Once this is done for each set of principal partners with the same tax year, the resulting products are summed to produce the aggregate deferral. After calculating the aggregate deferral for each of the test years, the test year with the smallest summation (the least aggregate deferral) is the tax year for the partnership.

EXAMPLE 3
THE BIG PICTURE

Return to the facts of *The Big Picture* on p. 16-2. The Code and Regulations eliminate the need for the Silver partners to bargain among themselves over the tax year-end. The partnership's tax year must end on November 30 because using that year-end results in the least aggregate deferral of partnership income as demonstrated below:

Test for Tax Year Ending December 31

		1	2	1 × 2
	Partner's Year-End	Profit Percentage	Months Income Deferred	Aggregate Months of Deferral
Belinda	12–31	25%	0	0
Pearl, Inc.	11–30	35%	11	3.85
Tweety, Inc.	6–30	40%	6	2.40
				6.25

[5]Reg. § 1.706–1(a).

[6]§§ 706(b)(1)(B) and 706(b)(3).

[7]Reg. § 1.706–1(b)(3).

Test for Tax Year Ending November 30

	Partner's Year-End	Profit Percentage	Months Income Deferred	Aggregate Months of Deferral
Belinda	12–31	25%	1	0.25
Pearl, Inc.	11–30	35%	0	0
Tweety, Inc.	6–30	40%	7	2.80
				3.05

Test for Tax Year Ending June 30

	Partner's Year-End	Profit Percentage	Months Income Deferred	Aggregate Months of Deferral
Belinda	12–31	25%	6	1.50
Pearl, Inc.	11–30	35%	5	1.75
Tweety, Inc.	6–30	40%	0	0
				3.25

■

Generally, S corporations must adopt a calendar year.[8] However, partnerships and S corporations may *elect* an otherwise *impermissible year* under any of the following conditions:

- A business purpose for the year can be demonstrated.[9]
- The partnership's or S corporation's year results in a deferral of not more than three months' income, and the entity agrees to make required tax payments.[10]
- The entity retains the same year as was used for the fiscal year ending in 1987, provided the entity agrees to make required tax payments.

Business Purpose

The only business purpose for a fiscal year that the IRS has acknowledged is the need to conform the tax year to the natural business year of a business.[11] Generally, only seasonal businesses have a natural business year. For example, the natural business year for a department store may end on January 31, after Christmas returns have been processed and clearance sales have been completed.

Required Tax Payments

Under the required payments system, tax payments are due from a fiscal year partnership or S corporation by April 15 of each tax year.[12] The amount due is computed by applying the highest individual tax rate plus 1 percentage point to an estimate of the deferral period income. The deferral period runs from the close of the fiscal year to the end of the calendar year. Estimated income for this period is based on the average monthly earnings for the previous fiscal year. The amount due is reduced by the amount of required tax payments for the previous year.[13]

EXAMPLE 4

Brown, Inc., an S corporation, elected a fiscal year ending September 30. Bob is the only shareholder. For the fiscal year ending September 30, 2011, Brown earned $100,000. The required tax payment for the previous year was $5,000. The corporation must pay $4,000 by April 15, 2012, calculated as follows:

$$(\$100{,}000 \times 3/12 \times 36\%^*) - \$5{,}000 = \$4{,}000$$

*Maximum § 1 rate of 35% + 1%. ■

[8] §§ 1378(a) and (b).
[9] §§ 706(b)(1)(C) and 1378(b)(2).
[10] § 444.
[11] Rev.Rul. 87–57, 1987–2 C.B. 117.
[12] §§ 444(c) and 7519. No payment is required if the calculated amount is $500 or less.
[13] § 7519(b).

ETHICS & Equity

Who Benefits from the Change in Tax Year?

A public accounting sole practitioner has reached a breaking point. All of his clients use the calendar year to report income. Many of the clients are S corporations and partnerships. His workload the first four months of the year is so heavy that it is putting the quality of his work at risk. He is considering asking some of his S corporations and partnerships to switch to a fiscal year ending September 30. The accountant believes that he can convince the shareholders and partners to make the change. Although the shareholders and partners would be subject to the "required tax payments" rules, the accountant will sell the plan by promising better service. Evaluate the plan proposed by the accountant.

Personal Service Corporations (PSCs)

A **personal service corporation (PSC)** is a corporation whose shareholder-employees provide personal services (e.g., medical, dental, legal, accounting, engineering, actuarial, consulting, or performing arts). Generally, a PSC must use a calendar year.[14] However, a PSC can *elect* a fiscal year under any of the following conditions:

- A business purpose for the year can be demonstrated.
- The PSC year results in a deferral of not more than three months' income; the corporation pays the shareholder-employee's salary during the portion of the calendar year after the close of the fiscal year; and the salary for that period is at least proportionate to the shareholder-employee's salary received for the preceding fiscal year.[15]
- The PSC retains the same year it used for the fiscal year ending in 1987, provided it satisfies the latter two requirements in the preceding option.

EXAMPLE 5

Nancy's corporation paid her a salary of $120,000 during its fiscal year ending September 30, 2011. The corporation cannot satisfy the business purpose test for a fiscal year. The corporation can continue to use its fiscal year without any negative tax effects, provided Nancy receives at least $30,000 [(3 months/12 months) × $120,000] of her salary during the period October 1 through December 31, 2011. ■

If the salary test is not satisfied, the PSC can retain the fiscal year, but the corporation's deduction for salary for the fiscal year is limited to the following:

$$A + A(F/N)$$

where A = Amount paid after the close of the fiscal year.
F = Number of months in the fiscal year minus number of months from the end of the fiscal year to the end of the ongoing calendar year.
N = Number of months from the end of the fiscal year to the end of the ongoing calendar year.

EXAMPLE 6

Assume the corporation in the previous example paid Nancy $10,000 of salary during the period October 1 through December 31, 2011. The deduction for Nancy's salary for the corporation's fiscal year ending September 30, 2012, is thus limited to $40,000 calculated as follows:

$$\$10{,}000 + \left[\$10{,}000\left(\frac{12-3}{3}\right)\right] = \$10{,}000 + \$30{,}000 = \$40{,}000$$ ■

[14] § 441(i).

[15] §§ 444 and 280H.

MAKING THE ELECTION

A taxpayer elects to use a calendar or fiscal year by the timely filing of his or her initial tax return. For all subsequent years, the taxpayer must use this same period unless approval for change is obtained from the IRS.[16]

CHANGES IN THE ACCOUNTING PERIOD

A taxpayer must obtain consent from the IRS before changing the tax year.[17] This power to approve or not to approve a change is significant in that it permits the IRS to issue authoritative administrative guidelines that must be met by taxpayers who wish to change their accounting period. An application for permission to change tax years must be made on Form 1128, Application for Change in Accounting Period. The application must be filed on or before the fifteenth day of the second calendar month following the close of the short period that results from the change in accounting period.[18]

EXAMPLE 7

Beginning in 2011, Gold Corporation, a calendar year taxpayer, would like to switch to a fiscal year ending March 31. The corporation must file Form 1128 by May 15, 2011. ■

IRS Requirements

The IRS will not grant permission for the change unless the taxpayer can establish a substantial business purpose for the request. One substantial business purpose is to change to a tax year that coincides with the *natural business year* (the completion of an annual business cycle). The IRS applies an objective gross receipts test to determine if the entity has a natural business year. Under this test, at least 25 percent of the entity's gross receipts for the 12-month period must be realized in the final 2 months of the 12-month period for three consecutive years.[19]

EXAMPLE 8

A Virginia Beach motel had gross receipts as follows:

	2009	2010	2011
July–August receipts	$ 300,000	$250,000	$ 325,000
September 1–August 31 receipts	1,000,000	900,000	1,250,000
Receipts for final 2 months divided by receipts for 12 months	30.0%	27.8%	26.0%

Since it satisfies the natural business year test, the motel will be allowed to use a fiscal year ending August 31. ■

The IRS usually establishes certain conditions that the taxpayer must accept if the approval for change is to be granted. In particular, if the taxpayer has a net operating loss (NOL) for the short period, the IRS requires that the loss be carried forward; the loss cannot be carried back to prior years.[20] As you may recall (refer to Chapter 7), NOLs are ordinarily carried back for 2 years and forward for 20 years.

[16]Reg. §§ 1.441–1(b)(3) and 1.441–1(b)(4).

[17]§ 442. Under certain conditions, corporations are allowed to change tax years without obtaining IRS approval. See Reg. § 1.442–1(c)(1).

[18]Reg. § 1.442–1(b)(1). In Example 7, the first period after the change in accounting period (January 1, 2011 through March 31, 2011) is less than a 12-month period and is referred to as a *short period*.

[19]Rev.Proc. 87–32, 1987–1 C.B. 131; Rev.Rul. 87–57, 1987–2 C.B. 117; and Rev.Proc. 2002–39, 2002–1 C.B. 1046.

[20]Rev.Proc. 2002–39, 2002–1 C.B. 1046.

EXAMPLE 9

Parrot Corporation changed from a calendar year to a fiscal year ending September 30. The short-period return for the nine months ending September 30, 2011, reflected a $60,000 NOL. The corporation had taxable income for 2009 and 2010. As a condition for granting approval, the IRS requires Parrot to carry the loss forward rather than carrying the loss back to the two preceding years (the usual order for applying an NOL). ■

TAXABLE PERIODS OF LESS THAN ONE YEAR

A **short taxable year** (or **short period**) is a period of less than 12 calendar months. A taxpayer may have a short year for (1) the first income tax return, (2) the final income tax return, or (3) a change in the tax year. If the short period results from a change in the taxpayer's annual accounting period, the taxable income for the period must be *annualized.* Due to the progressive tax rate structure, taxpayers could reap benefits from a short-period return if some adjustments were not required. Thus, the taxpayer is required to do the following:

1. Annualize the short-period income.

$$\text{Annualized income} = \text{Short-period income} \times \frac{12}{\text{Number of months in the short period}}$$

2. Compute the tax on the annualized income.
3. Convert the tax on the annualized income to a short-period tax.

$$\text{Short-period tax} = \text{Tax on annualized income} \times \frac{\text{Number of months in the short period}}{12}$$

EXAMPLE 10

Gray Corporation obtained permission to change from a calendar year to a fiscal year ending September 30, beginning in 2011. For the short period January 1 through September 30, 2011, the corporation's taxable income was $48,000. The relevant tax rates and the resultant short-period tax are as follows:

Amount of Taxable Income	Tax Rates
Not over $50,000	15% of taxable income
Over $50,000 but not over $75,000	$7,500 plus 25% of taxable income in excess of $50,000

Calculation of Short-Period Tax	
Annualized income ($48,000 × 12/9) = $64,000	
Tax on annualized income	
[$7,500 + .25($64,000 – $50,000)] = $7,500 + $3,500 = $11,000	
Short-period tax = ($11,000 × 9/12) = $8,250	
Annualizing the income increases the tax by $1,050:	
Tax with annualizing	$ 8,250
Tax without annualizing ($48,000 × 15%)	(7,200)
Increase in tax from annualizing	$ 1,050

■

Rather than annualize the short-period income, the taxpayer can elect to (1) calculate the tax for a 12-month period beginning on the first day of the short period and (2) convert the tax in (1) to a short-period tax as follows:[21]

$$\frac{\text{Taxable income for short period}}{\text{Taxable income for the 12-month period}} \times \text{Tax on the 12 months of income}$$

[21] §§ 443(b)(1) and (2).

EXAMPLE 11

Assume Gray Corporation's taxable income for the calendar year 2011 was $60,000. The tax on the full 12 months of income would have been $10,000 [$7,500 + .25($60,000 − $50,000)]. The short-period tax would be $8,000 [($48,000/$60,000) × $10,000]. Thus, if the corporation utilized this option, the tax for the short period would be $8,000 (rather than $8,250, as calculated in Example 10). ■

For individuals, annualizing requires some special adjustments:[22]

- Deductions must be *itemized* for the short period (i.e., the standard deduction is not allowed).
- Personal and dependency exemptions must be prorated.

Fortunately, individuals rarely change tax years.

MITIGATION OF THE ANNUAL ACCOUNTING PERIOD CONCEPT

Several provisions in the Code are designed to give the taxpayer relief from the seemingly harsh results that may be produced by the combined effects of an arbitrary accounting period and a progressive rate structure. For example, under the NOL carryback and carryover rules, a loss in one year can be carried back and offset against taxable income for the preceding 2 years. Unused NOLs are then carried over for 20 years.[23] In addition, the Code provides special relief provisions for casualty losses stemming from a disaster and for the reporting of insurance proceeds from destruction of crops.[24]

Farm Relief

Farmers and fishermen are often subject to wide fluctuations in income between years, some of which are due to the weather. Congress has provided these taxpayers a special method of computing their tax on income from farming or fishing. In the high-income years, these taxpayers can elect to compute their tax on income from farming or fishing as though it were earned equally in the three previous years.[25] Thus, the tax on the farming or fishing income for the year is the sum of the additional tax that would have been due in the three previous years if one-third of the income had been earned in each of those years. This averaging system enables the taxpayer to avoid the higher marginal tax rates associated with a large amount of income received in one year.

The income pattern for farmers can also be disrupted by natural disasters that are covered by insurance. The disaster may occur and the **crop insurance proceeds** may be received in a year before the income from the crop would have been realized. Under these circumstances, § 451(d) permits the farmer to defer reporting the income until the year following the disaster. Section 451(e) provides similar relief when livestock must be sold on account of drought or other weather-related conditions.

Restoration of Amounts Received under a Claim of Right

The court-made **claim of right doctrine** applies when the taxpayer receives property as income and treats it as his or her own but a dispute arises over the taxpayer's rights to the income.[26] According to the doctrine, the taxpayer must include the amount as income in the year of receipt. The rationale for the doctrine is that the Federal government cannot await the resolution of all disputes before exacting a tax. As a corollary to the doctrine, if the taxpayer is later required to repay the funds, generally a deduction is allowed in the year of repayment.[27]

[22] § 443(b)(3), § 443(c), and Reg. § 1.443–1(b).

[23] § 172. Refer to Chapter 7.

[24] §§ 165(i) and 451(d). Refer to Chapter 7.

[25] § 1301. The tax is calculated on Schedule J.

[26] *North American Oil Consolidated v. Burnet*, 3 USTC ¶943, 11 AFTR 16, 52 S.Ct. 613 (USSC, 1932).

[27] *U.S. v. Lewis*, 51–1 USTC ¶9211, 40 AFTR 258, 71 S.Ct. 522 (USSC, 1951).

TAX *in the NEWS*

Executive Compensation Clawbacks

In recent years, there has been a public outcry over the compensation of executives. With many companies receiving taxpayer-funded bailouts, both taxpayers and shareholders have demanded that executives repay the excessive amounts to the corporation. If executives are required to repay a portion of their salaries and bonuses, an executive's marginal tax rate may be greater in the year the income was received than in the year of repayment. This appears to be a situation that § 1341 should address. However, when the original amount received was based on an existing contract, the compensation was received under the executive's actual rights and is not income received under a mere claim of right. Therefore, the amount of the "clawback" is not eligible for § 1341 treatment.

EXAMPLE 12

In 2011, Pedro received a $5,000 bonus computed as a percentage of profits. In 2012, Pedro's employer determined that the 2011 profits had been incorrectly computed, and Pedro had to refund the $5,000 in 2012. Pedro was required to include the $5,000 in his 2011 gross income, but he can claim a $5,000 deduction in 2012. ■

In Example 12 the transactions were a wash; that is, the income and deduction were the same ($5,000). Suppose, however, that Pedro was in the 35 percent tax bracket in 2011 but in the 15 percent bracket in 2012. Without some relief provision, the mistake would be costly to Pedro. He paid $1,750 tax in 2011 (.35 × $5,000), but the deduction reduced his tax liability in 2012 by only $750 (.15 × $5,000). The Code does provide the needed relief in such cases. Under § 1341, when income that has been taxed under the claim of right doctrine must later be repaid, in effect, the taxpayer gets to apply to the deduction the tax rate of the year that will produce the greater tax benefit. Thus, in Example 12, the repayment in 2012 would reduce Pedro's 2012 tax liability by the higher 2011 rate (35%) applied to the $5,000. However, relief is provided only in cases where the tax is significantly different; that is, when the deduction for the amount previously included in income exceeds $3,000.

ETHICS *& Equity*

Special Tax Relief

A taxpayer who is required to report income in one year, but must repay the income in a subsequent year, is granted special tax relief. If the taxpayer is in a lower marginal tax bracket in the year the income is repaid than in the year it was received, the deduction reduces the tax for the year of repayment by using the higher tax rate that applied to the income when it was received.

In contrast, if a taxpayer takes a deduction in one year and receives a refund of the amount giving rise to the deduction in a subsequent year, the refund is taxed at the marginal tax rate in the year of refund. This is true even though the taxpayer's marginal tax rate in the year of receipt is higher than that in the year of the deduction.

Should both adjustments to income and adjustments to deductions receive the same tax relief? Or should neither situation be granted special relief?

16.2 Accounting Methods

LO.2

Apply the cash method, accrual method, and hybrid method of accounting.

PERMISSIBLE METHODS

Section 446 requires the taxpayer to compute taxable income using the method of accounting regularly employed in keeping his or her books, provided the method clearly reflects income. The Code recognizes the following as generally permissible **accounting methods**:

- The cash receipts and disbursements method.
- The accrual method.
- A hybrid method (a combination of cash and accrual).

The Regulations under § 446 refer to these alternatives as *overall methods* and add that the term *method of accounting* includes not only the taxpayer's overall method of accounting, but also the accounting treatment of any item.[28]

Generally, any of the three methods of accounting may be used if the method is consistently employed and clearly reflects income. However, in most cases the taxpayer is required to use the accrual method for sales and cost of goods sold if inventories are an income-producing factor to the business.[29] Other situations in which the accrual method is required are discussed later. Special methods are also permitted for installment sales, long-term construction contracts, and farmers.

A taxpayer who has more than one trade or business may use a different method of accounting for each trade or business activity. Furthermore, a taxpayer may use one method of accounting to determine income from a trade or business and use another method to compute nonbusiness items of income and deductions.[30]

EXAMPLE 13

Linda operates a grocery store and owns stocks and bonds. The sales and cost of goods sold from the grocery store must be computed by the accrual method because inventories are material. However, Linda can report her dividends and interest from the stocks and bonds under the cash method. ■

The Code grants the IRS broad powers to determine whether the taxpayer's accounting method *clearly reflects income*. Thus, if the method employed does not clearly reflect income, the IRS has the power to prescribe the method to be used by the taxpayer.[31]

CASH RECEIPTS AND DISBURSEMENTS METHOD—CASH BASIS

Most individuals and many businesses use the cash basis to report income and deductions. The popularity of this method can largely be attributed to its simplicity and flexibility.

Under the **cash method**, income is not recognized until the taxpayer actually receives, or constructively receives, cash or its equivalent (e.g., the receipt of accounts receivable does not trigger income until collected). Cash is constructively received if it is available to the taxpayer.[32] Generally, a cash equivalent is anything with a fair market value, including a note receivable from a customer.

EXAMPLE 14
THE BIG PICTURE

Return to the facts of *The Big Picture* on p. 4-2 in Chapter 4. Recall that Dr. Cliff Payne has opened a dental practice as a sole proprietorship and does not accept credit cards. In the second year of his business, he adopts a new policy of requiring that his patients either pay cash at the time the services are performed or give him a note receivable with interest at the market rate. Generally, the notes can be sold to the local banks for 95% of their face amount. At the end of the second year, Dr. Payne has $60,000 in notes receivable from patients. The notes receivable are a cash equivalent and have a fair market value of $57,000 ($60,000 × 95%). Therefore, Dr. Payne must include the $57,000 in his gross income for this year. ■

Deductions are generally permitted in the year of payment. Thus, year-end accounts payable and accrued expenses are not deducted in the determination of taxable income.

[28]Reg. § 1.446–1(a)(1).

[29]Reg. § 1.446–1(a)(4)(i). As discussed subsequently, as a matter of administrative convenience, the IRS will permit taxpayers to use the cash method even though inventory is a material income-producing factor, if average annual gross receipts are not more than $1 million for the most recent three-year period.

[30]§ 446(d) and Reg. § 1.446–1(c)(1)(iv)(b).

[31]§ 446(b).

[32]Reg. § 1.451–1(a). Refer to Chapter 4 for a discussion of constructive receipt.

TAX *in the NEWS*

WHO WANTS TO BE A PRODUCER?

For many years, small businesses wanted to be considered service providers rather than producers of products. Service provider classification meant that the cash method could be used. Now, however, classification as a producer can be advantageous. As a result of the American Jobs Creation Act of 2004, producers can deduct 9 percent of their qualifying domestic production activities income in calculating taxable income for 2011. Thus, a company that develops advertising materials might argue that it is a producer rather than a provider of advertising services.

In many cases, a taxpayer using the cash method can choose the year in which a deduction is claimed simply by postponing or accelerating the payment of expenses. For fixed assets, however, the cash basis taxpayer claims deductions through depreciation or amortization, the same as an accrual basis taxpayer does. In addition, prepaid expenses must be capitalized and amortized if the life of the asset extends substantially beyond the end of the tax year.[33]

The Regulations have established a **one-year rule for prepaid expenses** that permits the taxpayer to deduct expenditures for rights that do not extend beyond the earlier of (1) 12 months after the first date on which the taxpayer realizes the right or (2) the end of the tax year following the year of payment. Both cash basis and accrual basis taxpayers are permitted to use the one-year rule.[34]

Restrictions on Use of the Cash Method

Using the cash method to measure income from a merchandising or manufacturing operation would often yield a distorted picture of the results of operations. Income for the period would largely be a function of when payments were made for goods or materials. Thus, the Regulations prohibit the use of the cash method (and require the accrual method) to measure sales and cost of goods sold if inventories are material to the business.[35]

The prohibition on the use of the cash method if inventories are material and the rules regarding prepaid expenses (discussed previously) are intended to assure that annual income is clearly reflected. However, certain taxpayers may not use the cash method of accounting for Federal income tax purposes regardless of whether inventories are material. The accrual basis must be used to report the income earned by (1) a corporation (other than an S corporation), (2) a partnership with a corporate partner, and (3) a tax shelter. This accrual basis requirement has three exceptions:[36]

- A farming business.
- A qualified personal service corporation (a corporation performing services in health, law, engineering, architecture, accounting, actuarial science, performing arts, or consulting).
- An entity that is not a tax shelter whose average annual gross receipts for the most recent three-year period are $5 million or less.

As a matter of administrative convenience, the IRS will permit any entity with average annual gross receipts of not more than $1 million for the most recent three-year period to use a modified form of the cash method even if the taxpayer is buying and selling inventory. Sales can be reported on the cash method but the cost of such inventoriable items are deductible only in the year of the sale, or in the year in which the taxpayer actually pays for the inventoriable items, whichever is later.

Also as a matter of administrative convenience, the IRS will permit certain entities whose average annual gross receipts are greater than $1 million but are not more than

[33] Reg. § 1.461–1(a)(1).

[34] Reg. § 1.263(a)–4(f). Refer to Chapter 6 for further discussion of the one-year rule.

[35] Reg. § 1.446–1(a)(4)(i).

[36] §§ 448(a) and (b). For this purpose, the hybrid method of accounting is considered the same as the cash method.

$10 million for the most recent three-year period to use the cash method. However, under the $10 million exception, inventory on hand at the end of the tax year cannot be deducted until the inventory is sold (i.e., it must be capitalized). Not eligible for the cash method under the $10 million exception are entities whose principal business activity (the activity producing the largest percentage of gross receipts) is selling goods, manufacturing, mining, and certain publishing activities. Also not eligible are the C corporations, partnerships, and tax shelters discussed above that must use the accrual method. The major beneficiaries of the $10 million exception are small construction companies and small service businesses that sell some goods in conjunction with the services provided.[37]

Special Rules for Small Farmers

Although inventories are material to farming operations and the accrual method would appear to be required, the IRS long ago created an exception to the general rule that allows farmers to use the cash method of accounting.[38] The purpose of the exception is to relieve the small farmer from the bookkeeping burden of accrual accounting. Generally, this exception applies to unincorporated farms and closely held farming corporations with gross receipts for the year of less than $25 million.[39]

Cash method farmers must nevertheless capitalize their costs of raising trees that have a preproduction period of more than two years.[40] Thus, an apple farmer generally must capitalize the costs of raising the trees until they produce apples in merchantable quantities. However, to simplify the farmer's tax accounting, the cash method farmer is given an option: the preproduction cost of the trees can be expensed if the taxpayer elects to use the alternative depreciation system (refer to Chapter 8) for all the farming assets.

Farmers who produce crops that take more than a year from planting to harvesting (e.g., pineapples) can elect to use the crop method to report the income. Under the **crop method**, the costs of raising the crop are capitalized as those costs are incurred and then deducted in the year the income from the crop is realized.[41] This method is analogous to the completed contract method used by contractors (discussed later in this chapter).

Generally, the cost of purchasing an animal must be capitalized. However, the cash basis farmer's cost of raising the animal can be expensed.[42]

ACCRUAL METHOD

All Events Test for Income

Under the **accrual method**, an item is generally included in gross income for the year in which it is earned, regardless of when the income is collected. An item of income is earned when (1) all the events have occurred to fix the taxpayer's right to receive the income and (2) the amount of income (the amount the taxpayer has a right to receive) can be determined with reasonable accuracy.[43]

EXAMPLE 15

Andre, a calendar year taxpayer who uses the accrual method of accounting, was to receive a bonus equal to 6% of Blue Corporation's net income for its fiscal year ending each June 30. For the fiscal year ending June 30, 2011, Blue had net income of $240,000, and for the six months ending December 31, 2011, the corporation's net income was $150,000. Andre will report $14,400 (.06 × $240,000) for 2011 because his right to the amount became fixed when Blue's year closed. However, Andre would not accrue income based on the corporation's profits for the last six months of 2011 since his right to the income does not accrue until the close of the corporation's tax year. ■

An accrual basis taxpayer's amount of income and the tax year the income is recognized are based on his or her right to receive the income. Thus, the fair market value of a receivable is irrelevant.

[37] Rev.Proc. 2001–10, 2001–1 C.B. 272, and Rev.Proc. 2002–28, 2002–1 C.B. 815.

[38] Reg. § 1.471–6(a).

[39] See §§ 447(c) and 464.

[40] § 263A(d).

[41] Reg. §§ 1.61–4 and 1.162–12(a).

[42] Reg. § 1.162–12(a).

[43] Reg. § 1.451–1(a). Refer to Chapter 4 for further discussion of the accrual method.

GLOBAL
Tax Issues

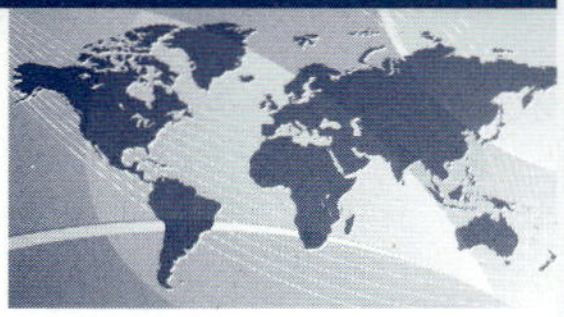

Tax Accounting Methods as an Incentive to Go Foreign

Some foreign countries allow a corporation to defer income by using tax accounting methods that are not permitted in the United States. For example, a producer or retailer may be allowed to use the cash method of accounting even though inventory is present. Under the cash method, the cost of goods sold is deducted in the tax year the goods are paid for, and income is not recognized until receivables are collected. Thus, if a U.S. corporation creates a foreign subsidiary in a country that permits the cash method in association with inventory, tax savings occur that would not be available in the United States. The corporation obtains additional deductions in the first year equal to the ending inventory and additional deferrals equal to the ending accounts receivable. The company would continue to benefit until it has no more receivables or inventory.

EXAMPLE 16

Marcey, an accrual basis taxpayer, has provided services to clients and has the right to receive $60,000. The clients have signed notes receivable to Marcey that have a fair market value of $57,000. Marcey must include $60,000, the amount she has the right to receive, in her gross income, rather than the fair market value of the notes of $57,000. Compare this treatment to that required for the cash basis taxpayer in Example 14. ■

As discussed in Chapter 4, when an accrual basis taxpayer receives prepaid income for services that will not all be earned by the end of the tax year following the tax year of receipt, generally the income that is not earned by the end of the year of receipt must be allocated to the following year.

EXAMPLE 17

Troy sells computers and two-year service contracts on the computers. On November 1, 2011, Troy sold a 24-month service contract and received $240. He recognizes $20 gross income in 2011 ($240 × $^2/_{24}$) and $220 ($240 – $20) in 2012. ■

However, the deferral of prepaid income is not available for prepaid rent and prepaid interest.

In a situation where the accrual basis taxpayer's right to income is being contested and the income has not yet been collected, generally no income is recognized until the dispute has been settled.[44] Before the settlement, "all of the events have not occurred that fix the right to receive the income."

All Events and Economic Performance Tests for Deductions

An **all events test** applies to accrual basis deductions. A deduction cannot be claimed until (1) all the events have occurred to create the taxpayer's liability and (2) the amount of the liability can be determined with reasonable accuracy.[45] Once these requirements are satisfied, the deduction will be permitted only if economic performance has occurred.[46]

The **economic performance test** addresses situations in which the taxpayer has either of the following obligations:

1. To pay for services or property to be provided in the future.
2. To provide services or property (other than money) in the future.

When services or property are to be provided to the taxpayer in the future (situation 1), economic performance occurs when the property or services are actually provided by the other party.

[44] *Burnet v. Sanford & Brooks Co.*, 2 USTC ¶636, 9 AFTR 603, 51 S.Ct. 150 (USSC, 1931).

[45] § 461(h)(4).

[46] § 461(h).

GLOBAL *Tax Issues*

Changes in the Tax Rates Lead to Income Shifting

In 2006, statistical evidence indicated that the German economy was booming. On further analysis of the data, however, it became clear that businesses were taking steps to shift their income from 2007 to 2006. Generally, businesses do not wish to accelerate their income because their taxes on the income will also be accelerated. In this case, though, German income tax rates were to increase in 2007. For many companies, the tax savings were worth the earlier-than-necessary recognition of the income.

Source: Adapted from Brian Wesbury, "A One-Year Wonder; Germany Is Booming, Pulling the Rest of Europe Along. Or Is It?" *Newsweek,* International Edition, March 12, 2007.

EXAMPLE 18

An accrual basis, calendar year taxpayer, JAB, Inc., promoted a boxing match held in the company's arena on December 31, 2011. CLN, Inc., had contracted to clean the arena for $5,000, but did not actually perform the work until January 1, 2012. JAB, Inc., did not pay the $5,000 until 2013. Although financial accounting rules would require JAB, Inc., to accrue the $5,000 cleaning expense in 2011 to match the revenues from the fight, the economic performance test was not satisfied until 2012, when CLN, Inc., performed the service. Thus, JAB, Inc., must deduct the expense in 2012. ■

If the taxpayer is obligated to provide property or services (situation 2), economic performance occurs (and thus the deduction is allowed) in the year the taxpayer provides the property or services.

EXAMPLE 19

Copper Corporation, an accrual basis taxpayer, is in the strip mining business. According to the contract with the landowner, the company must reclaim the land. The estimated cost of reclaiming land mined in 2011 was $500,000, but the land was not actually reclaimed until 2013. The all events test was satisfied in 2011. The obligation existed, and the amount of the liability could be determined with reasonable accuracy. However, the economic performance test was not satisfied until 2013. Therefore, the deduction is not allowed until 2013.[47] ■

The economic performance test is waived if the *recurring item exception* applies. Year-end accruals can be deducted if all the following conditions are met:

- The obligation exists and the amount of the liability can be reasonably estimated.
- Economic performance occurs within a reasonable period (but not later than 8½ months after the close of the taxable year).
- The item is recurring in nature and is treated consistently by the taxpayer.
- Either the accrued item is not material, or accruing it results in a better matching of revenues and expenses.

EXAMPLE 20

Green Corporation often sells goods that are on hand but cannot be shipped for another week. Thus, the sales account usually includes revenues for some items that have not been shipped at year-end. Green Corporation is obligated to pay shipping costs. Although the company's obligation for shipping costs can be determined with reasonable accuracy, economic performance is not satisfied until Green (or its agent) actually delivers the goods. However, accruing shipping costs on sold items will better match expenses with revenues for the period. Therefore, the company should be allowed to accrue the shipping costs on items sold but not shipped at year-end. ■

[47]See § 468 for an elective method for reporting reclamation costs.

TAX *in the NEWS*

PAYMENT IS NOT ECONOMIC PERFORMANCE

In recent pronouncements, the IRS has reiterated the point that when an accrual basis taxpayer has contracted to receive future services whose cost is deductible, the time for the deduction is when economic performance is satisfied. Moreover, economic performance can occur before or after the taxpayer pays for the services. Generally, economic performance is satisfied when the other party provides the services. If the taxpayer pays for the services before they are provided, the taxpayer has acquired an asset (prepaid expense). The deduction for the cost of the asset is not allowed until the services are actually received, unless the requirements for the recurring item exception are satisfied.

The economic performance test as set forth in the Code does not address all possible accrued expenses. That is, in some cases the taxpayer incurs costs even though no property or services were received. In these instances, according to the Regulations, economic performance generally is not satisfied until the liability is paid. The following liabilities are cases in which payment is generally the only means of satisfying economic performance:[48]

1. Workers' compensation.
2. Torts.
3. Breach of contract.
4. Violation of law.
5. Rebates and refunds.
6. Awards, prizes, and jackpots.
7. Insurance, warranty, and service contracts.[49]
8. Taxes.

EXAMPLE 21

Yellow Corporation sold defective merchandise that injured a customer. Yellow admitted liability in 2011, but did not pay the claim until January 2012. The customer's tort claim cannot be deducted until it is paid. ■

However, items (5) through (8) above are eligible for the aforementioned recurring item exception.

EXAMPLE 22

Pelican Corporation filed its 2011 state income tax return in March 2012. At the time the return was filed, Pelican was required to pay an additional $5,000. The state taxes are eligible for the recurring item exception. Thus, the $5,000 of state income taxes can be deducted on the corporation's 2011 Federal tax return. The deduction is allowed because all the events had occurred to fix the liability as of the end of 2011, the payment was made within 8½ months after the end of the tax year, the item is recurring in nature, and allowing the deduction in 2011 produces a good matching of revenues and expenses. ■

Reserves

Generally, the all events and economic performance tests will prevent the use of reserves (e.g., for product warranty expense) frequently used in financial accounting to match expenses with revenues. However, small banks are allowed to use a bad debt reserve.[50] Furthermore, an accrual basis taxpayer in a service business is permitted to not accrue revenue that appears uncollectible based on experience. In effect, this approach indirectly allows a reserve.[51]

[48] Reg. §§ 1.461–4(g)(2)–(6) and 1.461–5(c).

[49] This item applies to contracts the taxpayer enters into for his or her own protection, rather than the taxpayer's liability as insurer, warrantor, or service provider.

[50] § 585.

[51] § 448(d)(5).

FINANCIAL DISCLOSURE *Insights*

TAX DEFERRALS FROM RESERVES

The tax law generally applies the economic performance test in determining when an expense is deductible. Accordingly, the use of reserves for financial accounting purposes does not carry over to the tax return. When a business creates a reserve, say, to account for warranty obligations to customers or vacation pay for employees, book expenses are allowed, but the corresponding tax deduction usually is delayed until an expenditure is actually incurred. The temporary book-tax difference typically creates or adds to a deferred tax asset on the entity's balance sheet.

Deferred tax assets and liabilities are classified as *current* or *noncurrent* for balance sheet purposes. This classification is determined by the following:

- The nature of the underlying asset; for example, deferral of a bad debt relates to an account receivable, typically a current asset.
- Any knowledge by the entity as to when the required expenditure will occur; for example, as to the timing and amounts of a legal settlement or award.

For instance, suppose that Best Buy sells a product and a three-year warranty contract to provide maintenance to the customer. In the simplest case, one-third of the costs associated with the contract are deductible in the year that the contract is sold and used by the customer. Of the remaining warranty costs, one-half generates a current deferred tax asset (the costs will actually be incurred within the next tax year), and one-half generates a noncurrent deferred tax asset (for the third contract year).

Current versions of the related IFRS provisions eliminate the classification of deferred tax assets as current or noncurrent. Under IAS 1, all deferred tax assets are deemed to be noncurrent.

HYBRID METHOD

A **hybrid method** of accounting involves the use of more than one method. For example, a taxpayer who uses the accrual basis to report sales and cost of goods sold but uses the cash basis to report other items of income and expense is employing a hybrid method. The Code permits the use of a hybrid method provided the taxpayer's income is clearly reflected.[52] A taxpayer who uses the accrual method for business expenses must also use the accrual method for business income (the cash method may not be used for income items if the taxpayer's expenses are accounted for under the accrual method).

It may be preferable for a business that is required to report sales and cost of goods sold on the accrual method to report other items of income and expense under the cash method. The cash method permits greater flexibility in the timing of income and expense recognition.

CHANGE OF METHOD

LO.3

Utilize the procedure for changing accounting methods.

The taxpayer, in effect, makes an election to use a particular accounting method when an initial tax return is filed using that method. If a subsequent change in method is desired, the taxpayer must obtain the permission of the IRS. The request for change is made on Form 3115, Application for Change in Accounting Method. Generally, the form must be filed within the taxable year of the desired change.[53]

As previously mentioned, the term *accounting method* encompasses not only the overall accounting method used by the taxpayer (the cash or accrual method) but also the treatment of any material item of income or deduction.[54] Thus, a change in the method of deducting property taxes from a cash basis to an accrual basis that results in a deduction for taxes in a different year constitutes a change in an accounting method. Another example of an accounting method change is a change

[52] § 446(c).

[53] Rev.Proc. 2002–9, 2002–1 C.B. 327. See Rev.Proc. 2008–52, I.R.B. No. 36, 587, which permits certain changes in methods requested with a timely filed return.

[54] Reg. § 1.446–1(a)(1).

involving the method or basis used in the valuation of inventories. However, a change in treatment resulting from a change in the underlying facts does not constitute a change in the taxpayer's method of accounting.[55] For example, a change in employment contracts so that an employee accrues one day of vacation pay for each month of service rather than 12 days of vacation pay for a full year of service is a change in the underlying facts and, thus, is not an accounting method change.

Correction of an Error

A change in accounting method should be distinguished from the *correction of an error.* The taxpayer can correct an error (by filing amended returns) without permission, and the IRS can simply adjust the taxpayer's liability if an error is discovered on audit of the return. Some examples of errors are incorrect postings, errors in the calculation of tax liability or tax credits, deductions of business expense items that are actually personal, and omissions of income and deductions.[56] Unless the taxpayer or the IRS corrects the error within the statute of limitations, the taxpayer's total lifetime taxable income will be overstated or understated by the amount of the error.

Change from an Incorrect Method

An *incorrect accounting method* is the consistent (year-after-year) use of an incorrect rule to report an item of income or expense. The incorrect accounting method generally will not affect the taxpayer's total lifetime income (unlike the error). That is, an incorrect method has a self-balancing mechanism. For example, deducting freight on inventory in the year the goods are purchased, rather than when the inventory is sold, is an incorrect accounting method. The total cost of goods sold over the life of the business is not affected, but the year-to-year income is incorrect.[57]

If a taxpayer is employing an incorrect method of accounting, permission must be obtained from the IRS to change to a correct method. An incorrect method is not treated as a mechanical error that can be corrected by merely filing an amended tax return.

The tax return preparer as well as the taxpayer will be subject to penalties if the tax return is prepared using an incorrect method of accounting and permission for a change to a correct method has not been requested.[58]

Net Adjustments Due to Change in Accounting Method

In the year of a change in accounting method, some items of income and expense may have to be adjusted to prevent the change from distorting taxable income.

EXAMPLE 23

In 2011, White Corporation, with consent from the IRS, switched from the cash to the accrual basis for reporting sales and cost of goods sold. The corporation's accrual basis gross profit for the year was computed as follows:

Sales		$100,000
Beginning inventory	$ 15,000	
Plus: Purchases	60,000	
Less: Ending inventory	(10,000)	
Cost of goods sold		(65,000)
Gross profit		$ 35,000

At the end of the previous year, White Corporation had accounts receivable of $25,000 and accounts payable for merchandise of $34,000. The accounts receivable from the previous year in the amount of $25,000 were never included in gross income since White was on the cash basis and did not recognize the uncollected receivables. In the current year, the $25,000 was not included in the accrual basis sales since the sales were made in a prior year. Therefore, a $25,000 adjustment to income is required to prevent the receivables from being omitted from income.

[55] Reg. § 1.446–1(e)(2)(ii).

[56] Reg. § 1.446–1(e)(2)(ii)(b).

[57] But see *Korn Industries v. U.S.*, 76–1 USTC ¶9354, 37 AFTR 2d 76–1228, 532 F.2d 1352 (Ct.Cls., 1976).

[58] § 446(f). See Chapter 26.

The corollary of the failure to recognize a prior year's receivables is the failure to recognize a prior year's accounts payable. The beginning of the year's accounts payable were not included in the current or prior year's purchases. Thus, a deduction for the $34,000 was not taken in either year and is therefore included as an adjustment to income for the period of change.

An adjustment is also required to reflect the $15,000 beginning inventory that White deducted (due to the use of a cash method of accounting) in the previous year. In this instance, the cost of goods sold during the year of change was increased by the beginning inventory and resulted in a double deduction.

The net adjustment due to the change in accounting method is computed as follows:

Beginning inventory (deducted in prior and current year)	$ 15,000
Beginning accounts receivable (omitted from income)	25,000
Beginning accounts payable (omitted from deductions)	(34,000)
Net increase in taxable income	$ 6,000

■

Disposition of the Net Adjustment

Required changes in accounting methods are the result of an IRS examination. The IRS usually will examine all years that are open under the statute of limitations. Generally, this means that the three preceding years are examined. The IRS will not require a change unless the net adjustment is positive. That adjustment generally must be included in gross income for the year of the change. Additional tax and interest on the tax will be due. However, if the adjustment is greater than $3,000, the taxpayer can elect to calculate the tax by spreading the adjustment over one or more previous years.[59] The election is beneficial if the taxpayer's marginal tax rate for the prior years is lower than the marginal tax rate for the year of the change.

To encourage taxpayers to *voluntarily* change from incorrect methods and to facilitate changes from one correct method to another, the IRS generally allows the taxpayer to spread a positive adjustment into future years. One-fourth of the adjustment is applied to the year of the change, and one-fourth of the adjustment is applied to each of the next three taxable years. A negative adjustment can be deducted in the year of the change.[60]

ETHICS & *Equity*

CHANGE IN ACCOUNTING METHOD

The IRS faces a difficult choice when it deals with taxpayers who use incorrect accounting methods. One the one hand, the taxpayer who has used an incorrect accounting method may be just as culpable as a person who has omitted income or taken an improper deduction. On the other hand, it is often difficult to discover that a taxpayer is using an incorrect accounting method. Therefore, the IRS relies to some extent on self-reporting by taxpayers. The Service encourages voluntary changes in incorrect accounting methods by waiving penalties for underpayment of prior years' taxes and permitting the taxpayer, in effect, to pay the related taxes over a four-year period. Is this equitable treatment?

16.3 Special Accounting Methods

LO.4

Determine when the installment method of accounting can be utilized and apply the related calculation techniques.

Generally, accrual basis taxpayers recognize income when goods are sold and shipped to the customer. Cash basis taxpayers generally recognize income from a sale on the collection of cash from the customer. The tax law provides special accounting methods for certain installment sales and long-term contracts. These special methods were enacted, in part, to assure that the tax will be due when the taxpayer is best able to pay the tax.

[59] § 481(b). See also Notice 98–31, 1998–1 C.B. 1165.

[60] Rev.Proc. 2002–9, 2002–1 C.B. 327, and Rev.Proc. 2002–19, 2002–1 C.B. 696.

TAX *in* the NEWS

Seller Financing Is Popular in Troubled Times

As financial institutions are applying stringent loan requirements and real estate investors are anxious to sell, seller financing is becoming more common. In other words, instead of the financing being done by a financial institution, the seller of the property finances the transaction. The seller receives a down payment and a mortgage for the balance on the contract. If the buyer turns out to be unable to pay, the seller regains ownership of the property. Thus, even under this worst case scenario, the seller is still in a better position than if the original sale had not been made.

INSTALLMENT METHOD

Under the general rule for computing the gain or loss from the sale of property, the taxpayer recognizes the entire amount of gain or loss upon the sale or other disposition of the property.

EXAMPLE 24

Mark sells property to Fran for $10,000 cash plus Fran's note (fair market value and face amount of $90,000). Mark's basis for the property was $15,000. Gain or loss is computed under either the cash or accrual basis as follows:

Selling price:	
Cash down payment	$ 10,000
Note receivable	90,000
	$100,000
Less: Basis in the property	(15,000)
Realized gain	$ 85,000

■

In Example 24, the general rule for recognizing gain or loss requires Mark to pay a substantial amount of tax on the gain in the year of sale even though he receives only $10,000 of cash. Congress enacted the installment sales provisions to prevent this sort of hardship by allowing the taxpayer to spread the gain from installment sales over the collection period. The *installment method* is a very important planning tool because of the tax deferral possibilities.

Eligibility and Calculations

The **installment method** applies to *gains* (but not losses) from the sale of property by a taxpayer who will receive at least one payment *after* the year of sale. For many years, practically all gains from the sale of property were eligible for the installment method. However, over the years, the Code has been amended to *deny* the use of the installment method for the following:[61]

- Gains on property held for sale in the ordinary course of business.
- Depreciation recapture under § 1245 or § 1250.
- Gains on stocks or securities traded on an established market.

As an exception to the first item, the installment method may be used to report gains from sales of the following:[62]

- Time-share units (e.g., the right to use real property for two weeks each year).
- Residential lots (if the seller is not to make any improvements).
- Any property used or produced in the trade or business of farming.

[61] §§ 453(b), (i), and (l).
[62] § 453(l)(2).

The Nonelective Aspect

As a general rule, eligible sales *must* be reported by the installment method.[63] A special election is required to report the gain by any other method of accounting (see the discussion in a subsequent section of this chapter).

Computing the Gain for the Period

The gain reported on each sale is computed by the following formula:

$$\frac{\text{Total gain}}{\text{Contract price}} \times \text{Payments} = \text{Recognized gain}$$

The taxpayer must compute each variable as follows:

1. *Total gain* is the selling price reduced by selling expenses and the adjusted basis of the property. The selling price is the total consideration received by the seller, including notes receivable from the buyer, and the seller's liabilities assumed by the buyer.
2. *Contract price* is the selling price less the seller's liabilities that are assumed by the buyer. Generally, the contract price is the amount, other than interest, the seller will receive from the purchaser.
3. *Payments received* are the collections on the contract price received in the tax year. This generally is equal to the cash received less the interest income collected for the period. If the buyer pays any of the seller's expenses, the seller regards the amount paid as a payment received.

EXAMPLE 25

The seller is not a dealer, and the facts are as follows:

Sales price (amount realized):		
Cash down payment	$ 1,000	
Seller's mortgage assumed	3,000	
Notes payable to the seller	13,000	$ 17,000
Less: Selling expenses		(500)
Less: Seller's basis		(10,000)
Total gain		$ 6,500

The contract price is $14,000 ($17,000 – $3,000). Assuming the $1,000 is the only payment in the year of sale, the recognized gain in that year is computed as follows:

$$\frac{\$6{,}500 \text{ (total gain)}}{\$14{,}000 \text{ (contract price)}} \times \$1{,}000 = \$464 \text{ (gain recognized in year of sale)}$$ ■

If the sum of the seller's basis and selling expenses is less than the liabilities assumed by the buyer, the difference must be added to the contract price and to the payments (treated as *deemed payments*) received in the year of sale.[64] This adjustment to the contract price is required so that the ratio of total gain to contract price will not be greater than one. The adjustment also accelerates the reporting of income from the deemed payments.

EXAMPLE 26

Assume the same facts as in Example 25, except that the seller's basis in the property is only $2,000. The total gain, therefore, is $14,500 [$17,000 – ($2,000 + $500)]. Payments in the year of sale are $1,500 and are calculated as follows:

Down payment	$1,000
Excess of mortgage assumed over seller's basis and selling expenses ($3,000 – $2,000 – $500)	500
	$1,500

[63] § 453(a).

[64] Temp.Reg. § 15a.453–1(b)(3)(i).

The contract price is $14,500 [$17,000 (sales price) – $3,000 (seller's mortgage assumed) + $500 (excess of mortgage assumed over seller's basis and selling expenses)]. The gain recognized in the year of sale is computed as follows:

$$\frac{\$14{,}500 \text{ (total gain)}}{\$14{,}500 \text{ (contract price)}} \times \$1{,}500 = \$1{,}500$$

In subsequent years, all amounts the seller collects on the note principal ($13,000) will be recognized gain ($13,000 × 100%). ■

As previously discussed, gains attributable to ordinary income recapture under §§ 1245 and 1250 are *ineligible* for installment reporting. Therefore, the § 1245 or § 1250 gain realized must be recognized in the year of sale, and the installment sale gain is the remaining gain.

EXAMPLE 27

Olaf sold an apartment building for $50,000 cash and a $75,000 note due in two years. Olaf's cost of the property was $90,000, and he had deducted depreciation of $65,000, $40,000 of which was in excess of what the straight-line amount would have been. Thus, the basis in the property was $25,000, and he recaptured $40,000 ordinary income under § 1250.

Olaf's realized gain is $100,000 ($125,000 – $25,000), and the $40,000 recapture must be recognized in the year of sale. Of the $60,000 remaining § 1231 gain, $24,000 must be recognized in the year of sale:

$$\frac{\text{§ 1231 gain}}{\text{Contract price}} \times \text{Payments received} = \frac{\$125{,}000 - \$25{,}000 - \$40{,}000}{\$125{,}000} \times \$50{,}000$$

$$= \frac{\$60{,}000}{\$125{,}000} \times \$50{,}000 = \$24{,}000$$

The remaining realized gain of $36,000 ($60,000 – $24,000) will be recognized as the $75,000 note is collected. ■

Character of the Gain on Depreciable Real Estate

As discussed in Chapter 14, recognized gains from the sale of depreciable real estate may be subject to a 25 percent tax rate. The gain to the extent of straight-line depreciation taken is subject to the special rate and is referred to as "unrecaptured § 1250 gain." The recognized gain in excess of the depreciation is a § 1231 gain eligible for the 15 percent rate. Under the installment sale rules, when the sale results in both *25%* gain and *15%* gain, the *25%* gain is reported first and then the *15%* gain.

EXAMPLE 28

Continuing with the facts in Example 27, the realized gain was $100,000, of which $40,000 was § 1250 ordinary income. The straight-line depreciation would have been $25,000 (total depreciation of $65,000 less excess depreciation of $40,000). Therefore, the unrecaptured § 1250 gain is $25,000. The recognized installment gain in the year of sale of $24,000 was less than the unrecaptured § 1250 gain of $25,000. Therefore, the $24,000 recognized gain in the year of sale is subject to the 25% tax rate. ■

Imputed Interest

If a deferred payment contract for the sale of property with a selling price greater than $3,000 does not contain a reasonable interest rate, a reasonable rate is imputed.[65] The imputing of interest effectively restates the selling price of the property to equal the sum of the payments at the date of the sale and the discounted present value of the future payments. The difference between the present value of a future payment and the payment's face amount is taxed as interest income, as discussed in the following paragraphs. Thus, the **imputed interest** rules prevent sellers of capital assets from increasing the selling price to reflect the equivalent of unstated

[65] §§ 483 and 1274.

interest on deferred payments and thereby converting ordinary (interest) income into long-term capital gains. In addition, the imputed interest rules are important because they affect the timing of income recognition.

Generally, if the contract does not charge at least the Federal rate, interest will be imputed at the Federal rate. The Federal rate is the interest rate the Federal government pays on new borrowing and is published monthly by the IRS.[66]

As a general rule, the buyer and seller must account for interest on the accrual basis with semiannual compounding.[67] Requiring the use of the accrual basis assures that the seller's interest income and the buyer's interest expense are reported in the same tax year. The following example illustrates the calculation and amortization of imputed interest.

EXAMPLE 29

Peggy, a cash basis taxpayer, sold land on January 1, 2011, for $200,000 cash and $6 million due on December 31, 2012, with 5% interest payable December 31, 2011, and December 31, 2012. Assume that at the time of the sale, the Federal rate was 8% (compounded semiannually). Because Peggy did not charge at least the Federal rate, interest will be imputed at 8% (compounded semiannually).

Date	Payment	Present Value (at 8%) on 1/1/2011	Imputed Interest
12/31/2011	$ 300,000	$ 277,500	$ 22,500
12/31/2012	6,300,000	5,386,500	913,500
	$6,600,000	$5,664,000	$936,000

Thus, the selling price will be restated to $5,864,000 ($200,000 + $5,664,000) rather than $6,200,000 ($200,000 + $6,000,000), and Peggy will recognize interest income in accordance with the following amortization schedule:

Year	Beginning Balance	Interest Income (at 8%)*	Received	Ending Balance
2011	$5,664,000	$462,182	$ 300,000	$5,826,182
2012	5,826,182	473,818	6,300,000	–0–

*Compounded semiannually.

Congress has created several exceptions regarding the rate at which interest is imputed and the method of accounting for the interest income and expense. The general rules and exceptions are summarized in Concept Summary 16.1.

Related-Party Sales of Nondepreciable Property

If the Code did not contain special rules, a taxpayer could make an installment sale of property to a related party (e.g., a family member) who would obtain a basis in the property equal to the purchase price (the fair market value of the property). Then, the purchasing family member could immediately sell the property to an unrelated party for cash with no recognized gain or loss (the amount realized would equal the basis). The related-party purchaser would not pay the installment note to the selling family member until a later year or years. The net result would be that the family has the cash, but no taxable gain is recognized until the intrafamily transfer of the cash (i.e., when the purchasing family member makes payments on the installment note).

[66] § 1274(d)(1). There are three Federal rates: short term (not over three years), midterm (over three years but not over nine years), and long term (over nine years).

[67] §§ 1274(a), 1273(a), and 1272(a).

CONCEPT SUMMARY 16.1

Interest on Installment Sales

	Imputed Interest Rate
General rule	Federal rate
Exceptions:	
• Principal amount not over $2.8 million.[1]	Lesser of Federal rate or 9%
• Sale of land (with a calendar year ceiling of $500,000) between family members (the seller's spouse, brothers, sisters, ancestors, or lineal descendants).[2]	Lesser of Federal rate or 6%

	Method of Accounting for Interest	
	Seller's Interest Income	**Buyer's Interest Expense**
General rule[3]	Accrual	Accrual
Exceptions:		
• Total payments under the contract are $250,000 or less.[4]	Taxpayer's overall method	Taxpayer's overall method
• Sale of a farm (sales price of $1 million or less).[5]	Taxpayer's overall method	Taxpayer's overall method
• Sale of a principal residence.[6]	Taxpayer's overall method	Taxpayer's overall method
• Sale for a note with a principal amount of not over $2 million, the seller is on the cash basis, the property sold is not inventory, and the buyer agrees to report expense by the cash method.[7]	Cash	Cash

[1] § 1274A(b). This amount is adjusted annually for inflation. For 2011, the amount is $5,201,300.
[2] §§ 1274(c)(3)(F) and 483(e).
[3] §§ 1274(a) and 1272(a)(3).
[4] §§ 1274(c)(3)(C) and 483.
[5] §§ 1274(c)(3)(A) and 483.
[6] §§ 1274(c)(3)(B) and 483.
[7] § 1274A (c). This amount is adjusted annually for inflation. For 2011, the amount is $3,715,200.

Under special rules designed to combat this scheme, the proceeds from the subsequent sale (the second sale) by the purchasing family member are treated as though they were used to pay the installment note due the selling family member (the first sale). As a result, the recognition of gain from the original sale between the related parties is accelerated.[68]

However, even with these special rules, Congress did not eliminate the benefits of all related-party installment sales.

- Related parties include the first seller's brothers, sisters, ancestors, lineal descendants, controlled corporations, and partnerships, trusts, and estates in which the seller has an interest.[69]
- There is no acceleration if the second disposition occurs more than two years after the first sale.[70]

Thus, if the taxpayer can sell the property to a relative who is not a "related party" or to a patient family member, the intrafamily installment sale is still a powerful tax planning tool. Other exceptions also can be applied in some circumstances.[71]

[68] § 453(e).

[69] § 453(f)(1), cross-referencing §§ 267(b) and 318(a). Although spouses are related parties, the exemption of gain between spouses (§ 1041) makes the second-disposition rules inapplicable when the first sale was between spouses.

[70] § 453(e)(2). But see § 453(e)(2)(B) for extensions of the two-year period.

[71] See §§ 453(e)(6) and (7).

Related-Party Sales of Depreciable Property

The installment method cannot be used to report a gain on the sale of depreciable property to a controlled entity. The purpose of this rule is to prevent the seller from deferring gain (until collections are received) while the related purchaser is enjoying a stepped-up basis for depreciation purposes.[72]

The prohibition on the use of the installment method applies to sales between the taxpayer and a partnership or corporation in which the taxpayer holds a more-than-50 percent interest. Constructive ownership rules are used in applying the ownership test (i.e., the taxpayer is considered to own stock owned by a spouse and certain other family members).[73] However, if the taxpayer can establish that tax avoidance was not a principal purpose of the transaction, the installment method can be used to report the gain.

EXAMPLE 30

Alan purchased an apartment building from his controlled corporation, Emerald Corporation. Alan was short of cash at the time of the purchase (December 2011), but was to collect a large cash payment in January 2012. The agreement required Alan to pay the entire arm's length price in January 2012. Alan had good business reasons for acquiring the building. Emerald Corporation should be able to convince the IRS that tax avoidance was not a principal purpose for the installment sale because the tax benefits are not overwhelming. The corporation will report all of the gain in the year following the year of sale, and the building must be depreciated over 27.5 years (the cost recovery period). ■

DISPOSITION OF INSTALLMENT OBLIGATIONS

Generally, a taxpayer must recognize the deferred profit from an installment sale when the obligation is transferred to another party or otherwise relinquished. The rationale for accelerating the gain is that the deferral should continue for no longer than the period during which the taxpayer owns the installment obligation.[74]

The gift or cancellation of an installment note is treated as a taxable disposition by the donor. The amount realized from the cancellation is the face amount of the note if the parties (obligor and obligee) are related to each other.[75]

EXAMPLE 31

Liz cancels a note issued by Tina (Liz's daughter) that arose in connection with the sale of property. At the time of the cancellation, the note had a basis to Liz of $10,000, a face amount of $25,000, and a fair market value of $20,000. Presuming the initial sale by Liz qualified as an installment sale, the cancellation results in gain of $15,000 ($25,000 – $10,000) to Liz. ■

Certain exceptions to the recognition of gain provisions are provided for transfers of installment obligations pursuant to tax-free incorporations under § 351, contributions of capital to a partnership, certain corporate liquidations, transfers due to the taxpayer's death, and transfers between spouses or incident to divorce.[76] In such situations, the deferred profit is merely shifted to the transferee, who is responsible for the payment of tax on the subsequent collections of the installment obligations.

INTEREST ON DEFERRED TAXES

With the installment method, the seller earns interest on the receivable. The receivable includes the deferred gain. Thus, one could argue that the seller is earning interest on the deferred taxes. Some commentators reason that the government is, in effect, making interest-free loans to taxpayers who report gains by the installment method. Following the argument that the amount of the deferred taxes is a loan, in some situations, the taxpayer is required to pay interest on the deferred taxes.[77]

[72] § 453(g).

[73] §§ 1239(b) and (c).

[74] § 453B(a).

[75] § 453B(f)(2).

[76] §§ 453B(c), (d), and (g).

[77] See § 453A for details.

ELECTING OUT OF THE INSTALLMENT METHOD

A taxpayer can *elect not to use* the installment method. The election is made by reporting on a timely filed return the gain computed by the taxpayer's usual method of accounting.[78] However, the Regulations provide that the amount realized by a cash basis taxpayer cannot be less than the value of the property sold. This rule differs from the usual cash basis accounting rules (discussed earlier),[79] which measure the amount realized in terms of the fair market value of the property received. The net effect of the Regulations is to allow the cash basis taxpayer to report his or her gain as an accrual basis taxpayer. The election is frequently applied to year-end sales by taxpayers who expect to be in a higher tax bracket in the following year.

EXAMPLE 32

On December 31, 2011, Kurt sold land to Jodie for $20,000 (fair market value). He had owned the land for seven years. The cash was to be paid on January 4, 2012. Kurt is a cash basis taxpayer, and his basis in the land is $8,000. Kurt has a large casualty loss that, when combined with his other income in 2011, puts him at the 15% marginal tax bracket. He expects his tax rate to increase to 35% in 2012.

The transaction constitutes an installment sale because a payment will be received in a tax year after the tax year of disposition. Jodie's promise to pay Kurt is an installment obligation, and under the Regulations, the value of the installment obligation is equal to the value of the property sold ($20,000). If Kurt elects out of the installment method, he would shift $12,000 of gain ($20,000 − $8,000) from the expected higher rate in 2012 of 35% to the 0% rate for long-term capital gains in 2011. The expected tax savings based on the rate differential may exceed the benefit of the tax deferral available with the installment method. ■

Permission of the IRS is required to revoke an election not to use the installment method.[80]

LO.5

Understand the alternative methods of accounting for long-term contracts (the completed contract method and the percentage of completion method) including the limitations on the use of the completed contract method.

LONG-TERM CONTRACTS

A **long-term contract** is a building, installation, construction, or manufacturing contract that is entered into but not completed within the same tax year. However, a *manufacturing* contract is long term *only* if the contract is to manufacture (1) a unique item not normally carried in finished goods inventory or (2) items that normally require more than 12 calendar months to complete.[81] An item is *unique* if it is designed to meet the customer's particular needs and is not suitable for use by others. A contract to perform services (e.g., auditing or legal services) is not considered a contract for this purpose and thus cannot qualify as a long-term contract.

EXAMPLE 33

Rocky, a calendar year taxpayer, entered into two contracts during the year. One contract was to construct a building foundation. Work was to begin in October 2011 and was to be completed by June 2012. The contract is long term because it will not be entered into and completed in the same tax year. The fact that the contract requires less than 12 calendar months to complete is not relevant because the contract is not for manufacturing. The second contract was for architectural services to be performed over two years. These services will not qualify for long-term contract treatment because the taxpayer will not build, install, construct, or manufacture a product. ■

Generally, the taxpayer must accumulate all of the direct and indirect costs incurred under a contract. This means the production costs must be accumulated and allocated to individual contracts. Furthermore, mixed services costs, costs that benefit contracts as well as the general administrative operations of the business, must be allocated to production. Exhibit 16.1 lists the types of costs that must be accumulated and allocated to contracts. The taxpayer must develop reasonable bases for cost allocations.[82]

[78]§ 453(d) and Temp.Reg. § 15a.453–1(d). See also Rev.Rul. 82–227, 1982–2 C.B. 89.

[79]Refer to Chapter 4.

[80]§ 453(d)(3) and Temp.Reg. § 15a.453–1(d)(4).

[81]§ 460(f) and Reg. § 1.460–2(a).

[82]Reg. §§ 1.460–5(b) and 1.263A–1(e).

EXHIBIT 16.1 **Contract Costs, Mixed Services Costs, and Current Expense Items for Contracts**

	Contracts Eligible for the Completed Contract Method	Other Contracts
Contract costs:		
Direct materials (a part of the finished product).	Capital	Capital
Indirect materials (consumed in production but not in the finished product, e.g., grease and oil for equipment).	Capital	Capital
Storage, handling, and insurance on materials.	Expense	Capital
Direct labor (worked on the product).	Capital	Capital
Indirect labor (worked in the production process but not directly on the product, e.g., a construction supervisor).	Capital	Capital
Fringe benefits for direct and indirect labor (e.g., vacation, sick pay, unemployment, and other insurance).	Capital	Capital
Pension costs for direct and indirect labor:		
• Current cost.	Expense	Capital
• Past service costs.	Expense	Capital
Depreciation on production facilities:		
• For financial statements.	Capital	Capital
• Tax depreciation in excess of financial statements.	Expense	Capital
Depreciation on idle facilities.	Expense	Expense
Property taxes, insurance, rent, and maintenance on production facilities.	Capital	Capital
Bidding expenses—successful.	Expense	Capital
Bidding expenses—unsuccessful.	Expense	Expense
Interest to finance real estate construction.	Capital	Capital
Interest to finance personal property:		
• Production period of one year or less.	Expense	Expense
• Production period exceeds one year and costs exceed $1 million.	Capital	Capital
• Production period exceeds two years.	Capital	Capital
Mixed services costs:		
Personnel operations.	Expense	Allocate
Data processing.	Expense	Allocate
Purchasing.	Expense	Allocate
Selling, general, and administrative expenses (including an allocated share of mixed services).	Expense	Expense
Losses.	Expense	Expense

EXAMPLE 34

Falcon, Inc., uses detailed cost accumulation records to assign labor and materials to its contracts in progress. The total cost of fringe benefits is allocated to a contract on the following basis:

$$\frac{\text{Labor on the contract}}{\text{Total salaries and labor}} \times \text{Total cost of fringe benefits}$$

Similarly, storage and handling costs for materials are allocated to contracts on the following basis:

$$\frac{\text{Contract materials}}{\text{Materials purchases}} \times \text{Storage and handling costs}$$

The cost of the personnel operations, a mixed services cost, is allocated between production and general administration based on the number of employees in each function. The personnel cost allocated to production is allocated to individual contracts on the basis of the formula used to allocate fringe benefits. ■

The accumulated costs are deducted when the revenue from the contract is recognized. Generally, two methods of accounting are used in varying circumstances to determine when the revenue from a contract is recognized:[83]

- The completed contract method.
- The percentage of completion method.

The *completed contract method may be used* for (1) home construction contracts (contracts in which at least 80 percent of the estimated costs are for dwelling units in buildings with four or fewer units) and (2) certain other real estate construction contracts. Other real estate contracts can qualify for the completed contract method if the following requirements are satisfied:

- The contract is expected to be completed within the two-year period beginning on the commencement date of the contract.
- The contract is performed by a taxpayer whose average annual gross receipts for the three taxable years preceding the taxable year in which the contract is entered into do not exceed $10 million.

All other contractors must use the percentage of completion method.

Completed Contract Method

Under the **completed contract method**, no revenue from the contract is recognized until the contract is completed and accepted. However, a taxpayer may not delay completion of a contract for the principal purpose of deferring tax.[84]

In some situations, the original contract price may be disputed, or the buyer may want additional work to be done on a long-term contract. If the disputed amount is substantial (e.g., it is not possible to determine whether a profit or loss will ultimately be realized on the contract), the Regulations provide that no amount of income or loss is recognized until the dispute is resolved. In all other cases, the profit or loss (reduced by the amount in dispute) is recognized in the current period on completion of the contract. However, additional work may need to be performed with respect to the disputed contract. In this case, the difference between the amount in dispute and the actual cost of the additional work is recognized in the year the work is completed rather than in the year in which the dispute is resolved.[85]

EXAMPLE 35

Ted, a calendar year taxpayer utilizing the completed contract method of accounting, constructed a building for Brad under a long-term contract. The gross contract price was $500,000. Ted finished construction in 2011 at a cost of $475,000. When Brad examined the building, he insisted that it be repainted or the contract price be reduced. The estimated cost of repainting is $10,000. Since under the terms of the contract, Ted is assured of a profit of at least $15,000 ($500,000 – $475,000 – $10,000) even if the dispute is ultimately resolved in Brad's favor, Ted must include $490,000 ($500,000 – $10,000) in gross income and is allowed deductions of $475,000 for 2011.

In 2012, Ted and Brad resolve the dispute, and Ted repaints certain portions of the building at a cost of $6,000. Ted must include $10,000 in 2012 gross income and may deduct the $6,000 expense in that year. ■

EXAMPLE 36

Assume the same facts as in the previous example, except the estimated cost of repainting the building is $50,000. Since the resolution of the dispute completely in Brad's favor would mean a net loss on the contract for Ted ($500,000 – $475,000 – $50,000 = $25,000 loss), he does not recognize any income or loss until the year the dispute is resolved. ■

[83] § 460.

[84] Reg. § 1.451–3(b)(2).

[85] Reg. §§ 1.451–3(d)(2)(ii)–(vii), Example (2).

Frequently, a contractor receives payment at various stages of completion. For example, when the contract is 50 percent complete, the contractor may receive 50 percent of the contract price less a retainage. The taxation of these payments is generally governed by Regulation § 1.451–5, "advance payments for goods and long-term contracts" (discussed in Chapter 4). Generally, contractors are permitted to defer the advance payments until the payments are recognized as income under the taxpayer's method of accounting.

Percentage of Completion Method

The percentage of completion method must be used to account for long-term contracts unless the taxpayer qualifies for one of the two exceptions that permit the completed contract method to be used (home construction contracts and certain other real estate construction contracts).[86] Under the **percentage of completion method**, a portion of the gross contract price is included in income during each period as the work progresses. The revenue accrued each period (except for the final period) is computed as follows:[87]

$$\frac{C}{T} \times P$$

where C = Contract costs incurred during the period
T = Estimated total cost of the contract
P = Contract price

All of the costs allocated to the contract during the period are deductible from the accrued revenue.[88] The revenue reported in the final period is simply the unreported revenue from the contract. Because T in this formula is an estimate that frequently differs from total actual costs, which are not known until the contract has been completed, the profit on a contract for a particular period may be overstated or understated.

EXAMPLE 37

Tan, Inc., entered into a contract that was to take two years to complete, with an estimated cost of $2,250,000. The contract price was $3,000,000. Costs of the contract for 2010, the first year, totaled $1,350,000. The gross profit reported by the percentage of completion method for 2010 was $450,000 [($1,350,000/$2,250,000 × $3,000,000) – $1,350,000]. The contract was completed at the end of 2011 at a total cost of $2,700,000. In retrospect, 2010 profit should have been $150,000 [($1,350,000/$2,700,000 × $3,000,000) – $1,350,000]. Thus, taxes were overpaid for 2010. ■

A *de minimis* rule enables the contractor to delay the recognition of income for a particular contract under the percentage of completion method. If less than 10 percent of the estimated contract costs have been incurred by the end of the taxable year, the taxpayer can elect to defer the recognition of income and the related costs until the taxable year in which cumulative contract costs are at least 10 percent of the estimated contract costs.[89]

Lookback Provisions

In the year a contract is completed, a *lookback* provision requires the recalculation of annual profits reported on the contract under the percentage of completion method. Interest is paid to the taxpayer if taxes were overpaid, and interest is payable by the taxpayer if there was an underpayment.[90] For a corporate taxpayer, the lookback interest paid by the taxpayer is deductible, but for an individual taxpayer, it is nondeductible personal interest associated with a tax liability.

[86]Certain residential construction contracts that do not qualify for the completed contract method may nevertheless use that method to account for 30% of the profit from the contract, with the remaining 70% reported by the percentage of completion method.

[87]§ 460(b)(1)(A).

[88]Reg. § 1.451–3(c)(3).

[89]§ 460(b)(5).

[90]§§ 460(b)(2) and (6). The taxpayer can elect to not apply the lookback method in situations where the cumulative taxable income as of the close of each prior year is within 10% of the correct income for each prior year.

EXAMPLE 38

Assume Tan, Inc., in Example 37, was in the 34% tax bracket in both years and the relevant interest rate was 10%. For 2010, the company paid excess taxes of \$102,000 [(\$450,000 − \$150,000) × .34]. When the contract is completed at the end of 2011, Tan, Inc., should receive interest of \$10,200 for one year on the tax overpayment (\$102,000 × .10). ■

TAX PLANNING:

16.4 Taxable Year

LO.6

Identify tax planning opportunities related to accounting periods and accounting methods.

Under the general rules for tax years, partnerships and S corporations frequently will be required to use a calendar year. However, if the partnership or S corporation can demonstrate a business purpose for a fiscal year, the IRS will allow the entity to use the requested year. The advantage to a fiscal year is that the calendar year partners and S corporation shareholders may be able to defer from tax the income earned from the close of the fiscal year until the end of the calendar year. Tax advisers for these entities should apply the IRS's gross receipts test described in Revenue Procedure 87–32 to determine if permission for the fiscal year will be granted.[91]

16.5 Cash Method of Accounting

The cash method of accounting gives the taxpayer considerable control over the recognition of expenses and some control over the recognition of income. This method can be used by proprietorships, partnerships, and small corporations (gross receipts of \$5 million or less) that provide services (inventories are not material to the service business). Farmers (except certain farming corporations) can also use the cash method.

16.6 Installment Method

Unlike the cash and accrual methods, the installment method often results in an interest-free loan (of deferred taxes) from the government. The installment method is not available for the sale of inventory. Nevertheless, the installment method is an important tax planning technique and should be considered when a sale of eligible property is being planned. That is, if the taxpayer can benefit from deferring the tax, the terms of sale can be arranged so that the installment method rules apply. If, on the other hand, the taxpayer expects to be in a higher tax bracket when the payments will be received, he or she can elect not to use the installment method.

RELATED PARTIES

Intrafamily installment sales can still be a useful family tax planning tool. If the related party holds the property more than two years, a subsequent sale will not accelerate the gain from the first disposition. Patience and forethought are rewarded.

The 6 percent limitation on imputed interest on sales of land between family members (see Concept Summary 16.1) enables the seller to convert ordinary income into capital gain or make what is, in effect, a nontaxable gift. If the selling price is raised to adjust for the low interest rate charges on an installment sale, the seller has more capital gain but less ordinary income than would be realized from a sale to an unrelated party. If the selling price is not raised and the specified interest of 6 percent is charged, the seller enables the relative to have the use of the property without having to pay its full market value. As an additional benefit, the bargain sale is not a taxable gift.

[91] See also Rev.Proc. 2002–38, 2002–1 C.B. 1037.

DISPOSITION OF INSTALLMENT OBLIGATIONS

A disposition of an installment obligation is also a serious matter. Gifts of the obligations will accelerate income to the seller. The list of taxable and nontaxable dispositions of installment obligations should not be trusted to memory. In each instance where transfers of installment obligations are contemplated, the practitioner should conduct research to be sure he or she knows the consequences.

16.7 Completed Contract Method

Generally, large contractors must use the percentage of completion method of accounting for reporting the income from long-term contracts. Under the percentage of completion method, the taxpayer must recognize profit in each period costs are incurred. Profit is reported in proportion to the cost incurred for the period as a proportion of the total contract cost. However, small contractors (average annual gross receipts do not exceed $10 million) working on contracts that are completed within a two-year period can elect to use the completed contract method and defer profit until the year in which the contract is completed.

REFOCUS ON THE BIG PICTURE

ACCOUNTING PERIOD

Selection of a Tax Year

An entity's tax form will govern the rules for determining the entity's tax year. Since Silver is a partnership, the Code's provisions for partnerships are applicable. In this case, Tweety's 40 percent ownership interest in Silver is not sufficient to enable it to control the selection of the partnership's tax year. Likewise, Belinda and Pearl's collective controlling interest will not allow them to control the selection of the tax year for the partnership.

The Code and related Regulations have a very precise set of rules regarding the selection of a tax year for a partnership. The partnership applies these rules in the following sequence:

- *Majority interest tax year.* The tax year of the partners who have a common year-end and collectively own a greater-than-50 percent interest in the partnership capital and profits.
- *Principal partners' tax year.* The tax year if all the principal partners (5 percent or greater interest in capital or profits) have the same tax year.
- *Least aggregate deferral tax year.* The tax year of the principal partners (grouped by a common year-end) that produces the least aggregate deferral of income.

Alternatively, the partnership can select its tax year based on a business purpose for the tax year selected. However, this requires the approval of the IRS, which is unlikely to be granted. The only business purpose the IRS has acknowledged is the need to conform the tax year to the entity's natural business year.

Therefore, from the data provided, it appears that Silver will determine its tax year by using the least aggregate deferral method. Based on this method, Silver's tax year will end on November 30 (see the calculations in Example 3).

Short Tax Year

Silver will have a short tax year that begins on April 1, 2011, and ends on November 30, 2011, as determined by the least aggregate deferral method. Silver will not have

CONTINUED

to annualize the income reported on its first income tax return. Note, however, that annualization will be required if Silver ever changes its tax year.

Partner's Reporting of Share of Net Income

Each of the partners will receive a Schedule K–1 that reports the partner's share of net income. From a timing perspective, the partner will include the Schedule K–1 items on the partner's income tax return only if a partnership tax year ends within or with the partner's tax year. For additional discussion of partnership taxation, see Chapter 21.

KEY TERMS

Accounting methods, 16–10
Accounting period, 16–3
Accrual method, 16–13
All events test, 16–14
Cash method, 16–11
Claim of right doctrine, 16–9
Completed contract method, 16–28
Crop insurance proceeds, 16–9
Crop method, 16–13
Economic performance test, 16–14
Fiscal year, 16–3
Hybrid method, 16–17
Imputed interest, 16–22
Installment method, 16–20
Least aggregate deferral method, 16–4
Long-term contract, 16–26
Majority interest partners, 16–4
One-year rule for prepaid expenses, 16–12
Percentage of completion method, 16–29
Personal service corporation (PSC), 16–6
Principal partner, 16–4
Short taxable year (short period), 16–8

DISCUSSION QUESTIONS

1. **LO.1** Would a tax year ending December 31 be appropriate for a Colorado ski resort?

2. **LO.1** In the case of a profitable partnership whose partners are all individuals, what would be the advantage of using a tax year ending January 31 if this was permissible?

DECISION MAKING

3. **LO.1** A law practice was incorporated on January 1, 2011, and expects to earn $25,000 per month before deducting the lawyer's salary. The lawyer owns 100% of the stock. The corporation and the lawyer both use the cash method of accounting. The corporation does not need to retain any of the earnings in the business; thus, the salary of the lawyer (a calendar year taxpayer) will equal the corporation's net income before salary expense. If the corporation could choose any tax year it wished and pay the lawyer's salary at the time that would be the most tax efficient (but at least once every 12 months), what tax year should the corporation choose, and when should the salary be paid each year?

ISSUE ID

4. **LO.1** Fred, a cash basis taxpayer, received a $75,000 bonus from his employer in 2011. The bonus was based on the company's profits for the year 2010. In 2012, the company discovered that its 2010 profits were incorrectly computed. As a result, Fred was required to repay his employer $25,000 of the bonus. Fred's marginal tax rate was 35% in 2011 and 15% in 2012. Sue, a cash basis taxpayer, earned a $75,000 bonus in 2011that her employer failed to pay until 2012. Sue was in the 15% marginal tax bracket in 2011 and the 35% bracket in 2012. What special tax relief is available to Fred that is not available to Sue?

5. **LO.1** How are farmers treated differently from other producers in regard to tax accounting?

6. **LO.2** In December 2011, Nell, a cash basis taxpayer, paid insurance premiums of $12,000 on rental property for the period February 1, 2012, through January 31, 2013. How much of the premiums can Nell deduct in 2011?

7. **LO.3** In 2011, the taxpayer became ineligible to use the cash method of accounting. At the beginning of the year, accounts receivable totaled $240,000, accounts payable for merchandise totaled $80,000, and the inventory on hand totaled $320,000. What is the amount of the adjustment due to the change in accounting method?

8. **LO.2** Compare the cash basis and accrual basis of accounting as applied to the following:
   a. Fixed assets.
   b. Prepaid expenses.
   c. Prepaid income for services.
   d. A note received for services performed if the market value and face amount of the note differ.

9. **LO.2** Edgar uses the cash method to report the income from his software consulting business. A large publicly held corporation has offered to invest in Edgar's business as a limited partner. What tax accounting complications would be created if Edgar and the corporation become partners? **DECISION MAKING**

10. **LO.2** Samantha, a cash basis taxpayer, subscribes to a service that updates a database used in her business. In December 2011, Samantha paid the $120,000 subscription for the period December 2011 through November 2012. What is Samantha's deduction for 2011?

11. **LO.2** Emerald Motors is an automobile dealer. The company has made a special offer to its new car customers for 2011. The dealer will not charge for the first four manufacturer's recommended service visits (i.e., at 3,000, 6,000, 9,000, and 12,000 miles). It is a virtual certainty that all customers will exercise their rights to the service. The controller asks you whether the company can accrue as an expense in 2011 the normal charge for service visits on cars sold in 2011 but not to be serviced until 2012.

12. **LO.4, 6** Irene has made Sara an offer on the purchase of a capital asset. Irene will pay (1) $200,000 cash or (2) $50,000 cash and a 6% installment note for $150,000 guaranteed by City Bank of New York. If Sara sells for $200,000 cash, she will invest the after-tax proceeds in certificates of deposit yielding 6% interest. Sara's cost of the asset is $25,000. Why would Sara prefer the installment sale? **DECISION MAKING**

13. **LO.4** Arnold gave land to his son, Bruce. Arnold's basis in the land was $70,000, and its fair market value at the date of the gift was $80,000. Bruce borrowed $150,000 that he used to improve the property. He sold the property to Della for $300,000. Della paid Bruce $60,000 in cash, assumed his $150,000 mortgage, and agreed to pay $90,000 in two years. Bruce's selling expenses were $10,000. Della is going to pay adequate interest. What is Bruce's installment sale gain in the year of sale?

14. **LO.4, 6** On June 1, 2009, Father sold land to Son for $300,000. Father reported the gain by the installment method, with the gain to be spread over five years. In May 2011, Son received an offer of $400,000 for the land, to be paid over three years. What would be the tax consequences of Son's sale? How could the tax consequences be improved? **DECISION MAKING**

15. **LO.4, 6** In December 2011, Carl Corporation sold land it held as an investment. The corporation received $50,000 in 2011 and a note payable (with adequate interest) for $150,000 to be paid in 2013. Carl Corporation's cost of the land was $80,000. The corporation has a $90,000 net capital loss carryover that will expire in 2011. Should Carl Corporation report the sale in 2011 or use the installment method to report the income as payments are received? **DECISION MAKING**

16. **LO.2, 5** What are the similarities between the crop method used for farming and the completed contract method used for long-term construction?

17. **LO.5** The Hawk Corporation builds yachts. The vessels it currently produces are practically identical and are completed in approximately 8 months. A customer has approached Hawk about constructing a larger yacht that would take approximately 15 months to complete. What are the tax implications of accepting the contract proposal?

PROBLEMS

18. **LO.1** Red, White, and Blue are unrelated corporations engaged in real estate development. The three corporations formed a joint venture (treated as a partnership) to develop a tract of land. Assuming the venture does not have a natural business year, what tax year must the joint venture adopt under the following circumstances?

		Tax Year Ending	Interest in Joint Venture
a.	Red	March 31	60%
	Blue	June 30	20%
	White	October 31	20%
b.	Red	October 31	30%
	White	September 30	40%
	Blue	January 31	30%

DECISION MAKING

19. **LO.1** Zorn conducted his professional practice through Zorn, Inc. The corporation uses a fiscal year ending September 30 even though the business purpose test for a fiscal year cannot be satisfied. For the year ending September 30, 2011, the corporation paid Zorn a salary of $240,000, and during the period January through September 2011, the corporation paid him a salary of $120,000.
    a. How much salary should Zorn receive during the period October 1 through December 31, 2011?
    b. Assume Zorn received only $30,000 of salary during the period October 1 through December 31, 2011. What would be the consequences to Zorn, Inc.?

20. **LO.1** Mauve Corporation began operations as a farm supplies business and used a fiscal year ending September 30. The company gradually went out of the farm supplies business and into the mail-order Christmas gifts business. The company has received permission from the IRS to change to a fiscal year ending January 31, effective for the year ending January 31, 2011. For the short period October 1, 2010 through January 31, 2011, Mauve earned $32,000. Calculate Mauve's tax liability for the short period October 1, 2010 through January 31, 2011.

COMMUNICATIONS

21. **LO.2** Gold, Inc., is an accrual basis taxpayer. In 2011, an employee accidentally spilled hazardous chemicals on leased property. The chemicals destroyed trees on neighboring property, resulting in $30,000 of damages. In 2011, the owner of the property sued Gold, Inc., for the $30,000. Gold's attorney feels that it is liable and the only issue is whether the neighbor will also seek punitive damages that could be as much as three times the actual damages. In addition, as a result of the spill, Gold was in violation of its lease and was therefore required to pay the landlord $15,000. However, the amount due for the lease violation is not payable until the termination of the lease in 2014. None of these costs were covered by insurance. Jeff Stuart, the president of Gold, Inc., is generally familiar with the accrual basis tax accounting rules and is concerned about when the company will be allowed to deduct the amounts the company is required to pay as a result of this environmental disaster. Write Mr. Stuart a letter explaining these issues. Gold's address is 200 Elm Avenue, San Jose, CA 95192.

22. **LO.2** Compute Mary's income or deductions for 2011 using (1) the cash basis and (2) the accrual basis for each of the following:
    a. In May 2011, Mary paid a license fee of $1,200 for the period June 1, 2011, through May 31, 2012.
    b. In December 2011, Mary collected $10,000 for January 2012 rents. In January 2012, Mary collected $2,000 for December 2011 rents.
    c. In June 2011, Mary paid $7,200 for an office equipment service contract for the period July 1, 2011, through December 31, 2012.
    d. In June 2011, Mary purchased office furniture for $273,000. She paid $131,000 in cash and gave a $142,000 interest-bearing note for the balance. The office furniture has an MACRS cost recovery period of seven years. Mary did not make the § 179 election and elected not to take additional first-year depreciation.

23. **LO.2, 5** What accounting method (cash or accrual) would you recommend for the following businesses?
    a. An incorporated retail hardware store with annual gross receipts of $4.5 million.
    b. An incorporated engineering firm with annual gross receipts of $12 million.
    c. A dry wall subcontractor who works on residences and has annual gross receipts of $3 million.
    d. An incorporated insurance agency with annual gross receipts of $6 million.

24. **LO.2** How do the all events and economic performance requirements apply to the following transactions by an accrual basis taxpayer?
    a. The company guarantees its products for six months. At the end of 2011, customers had made valid claims for $600,000 that were not paid until 2012. Also, the company estimates that another $400,000 in claims from 2011 sales will be filed and paid in 2012.
    b. The accrual basis taxpayer reported $200,000 in corporate taxable income for 2011. The state income tax rate was 6%. The corporation paid $7,000 in estimated state income taxes in 2011 and paid $2,000 in 2010 state income taxes when it filed its 2010 state income tax return in March 2011. The company filed its 2011 state income return in March 2012 and paid the remaining $5,000 of its 2011 state income tax liability.
    c. An employee was involved in an accident while making a sales call. The company paid the injured victim $15,000 in 2011 and agreed to pay the victim $15,000 a year for the next nine years.

25. **LO.3** Ross Company is a computer consulting firm. The company also sells equipment to its clients. The sales of equipment account for approximately 40% of the company's gross receipts. The company has consistently used the cash method to report its income from services and the accrual method to report its income from the sale of inventory. In June of the current year, Ross's accountant discovered that as a small business the company qualifies to use the cash method for all of its activities. The company is a calendar year taxpayer. As of the beginning of the current year, the company had $120,000 of inventory on hand and $90,000 of accounts receivable from the sales of equipment and $30,000 of receivables from the consulting services.
    a. Compute the adjustment due to the change in accounting method.
    b. Is the adjustment positive or negative? Explain.
    c. When can the adjustment be taken into account in computing taxable income?

26. **LO.4, 6** Floyd, a cash basis taxpayer, has received an offer to purchase his land. The buyer will either pay him $100,000 at closing or pay $50,000 at closing and $52,000 one year after the date of closing. If Floyd recognizes the entire gain in the current year, his marginal tax rate will be 35% (combined Federal and state rates). However, if he spreads the gain over the two years, his marginal tax rate on the gain will be only 25%. Floyd does not consider the buyer a credit risk, but he realizes that the deferred payment will, in effect, earn only 4% interest ($2,000/$50,000 = 4%). Floyd believes he can earn a 10% before-tax rate of return on his after-tax cash. Floyd's adjusted basis for the land is $25,000, the buyer is also a cash basis taxpayer, and the short-term Federal rate is 4%. Floyd has asked you to evaluate the two alternatives on an after-tax basis.

DECISION MAKING

27. **LO.4** Kay, who is not a dealer, sold an apartment house to Polly during 2011. The closing statement for the sale is as follows:

Total selling price		$ 160,000
Add: Polly's share of property taxes (6 months) paid by Kay		2,500
Less: Kay's 8% mortgage assumed by Polly	$55,000	
Polly's refundable binder ("earnest money") paid in 2010	1,000	
Polly's 8% installment note given to Kay	90,000	
Kay's real estate commissions and attorney's fees	7,500	(153,500)
Cash paid to Kay at closing		$ 9,000
Cash due from Polly = $9,000 + $7,500 expenses		$ 16,500

During 2011, Kay collected $4,000 in principal on the installment note and $2,000 in interest. Her basis in the property was $70,000 [$85,000 – $15,000 (depreciation)]. The Federal rate is 6%.

a. Compute the following:
   1. Total gain.
   2. Contract price.
   3. Payments received in the year of sale.
   4. Recognized gain in the year of sale and the character of such gain.
   (*Hint:* Think carefully about the manner in which the property taxes are handled before you begin your computations.)

b. Same as (a)(2) and (3), except Kay's basis in the property was $45,000.

DECISION MAKING

28. **LO.4** On June 30, 2011, Kelly sold property for $250,000 cash and a $750,000 note due on September 30, 2012. The note will also pay 6% interest, which is slighty higher than the Federal rate. Kelly's cost of the property was $400,000. She is concerned that Congress may increase the tax rate that will apply when the note is collected. Kelly's after-tax rate of return on investments is 7%.
   a. What can Kelly do to avoid the expected higher tax rate?
   b. Assuming Kelly's marginal combined Federal and state tax rate is 20% in 2011, how much would the tax rates need to increase to make the option identified in (a) advisable?

DECISION MAKING

29. **LO.4** On December 30, 2010, Maud sold land to her son, Charles, for $50,000 cash and a 7% installment note for $350,000, payable over 10 years. Maud's cost of the land was $150,000. In October 2012, after Charles had paid $60,000 on the principal of the note, he received an offer to sell the land for $500,000 cash. What advice can you provide Charles that will minimize the present value of the tax liability for Maud and Charles?

30. **LO.4** George sold land to an unrelated party in 2010. His basis in the land was $45,000, and the selling price was $120,000: $30,000 payable at closing and $30,000 (plus 10% interest) due January 1, 2011, 2012, and 2013. What would be the tax consequences of the following? [Treat each part independently and assume (1) George did not elect out of the installment method and (2) the installment obligations have values equal to their face amounts. Ignore interest in your calculations.]
   a. In 2011, George gave to his daughter the right to collect all future payments on the installment obligations.
   b. In 2011, after collecting the payment due on January 1, George transferred the installment obligation to his 100%-controlled corporation in exchange for additional shares of stock.
   c. On December 31, 2011, George received the payment due on January 1, 2012. On December 15, 2012, George died, and the remaining installment obligation was transferred to his estate. The estate collected the amount due on January 1, 2013.

31. **LO.5** The Wren Construction Company reports its income by the completed contract method. At the end of 2011, the company completed a contract to construct a building at a total cost of $800,000. The contract price was $1.2 million. However, the customer refused to accept the work and would not pay anything on the contract because he claimed the roof did not meet specifications. Wren's engineers estimated it would cost $140,000 to bring the roof up to the customer's standards. In 2012, the dispute was settled in the customer's favor; the roof was improved at a cost of $165,000, and the customer accepted the building and paid the $1.2 million.
   a. What would be the effects of the above on Wren's taxable income for 2011 and 2012?
   b. Same as (a), except Wren had $1.1 million of accumulated costs under the contract at the end of 2011.

COMMUNICATIONS

32. **LO.5** Rust Company is a real estate construction company with average annual gross receipts of $4 million. Rust uses the completed contract method, and the contracts require 18 months to complete.
   a. Which of the following costs would be allocated to construction in progress by Rust?
      1. The payroll taxes on direct labor.
      2. The current services pension costs for employees whose wages are included in direct labor.
      3. Accelerated depreciation on equipment used on contracts.

4. Freight charges on materials assigned to contracts.
5. The past service costs for employees whose wages are included in direct labor.
6. Bidding expenses for contracts awarded.

b. Assume that Rust generally builds commercial buildings under contracts with the owners and reports the income by the completed contract method. The company is considering building a series of similar stores for a retail chain. The gross profit margin would be a low percentage, but the company's gross receipts would triple. Write a letter to your client, Rust Company, explaining the tax accounting implications of entering into these contracts. Rust's mailing address is P.O. Box 1000, Harrisonburg, VA 22807.

33. **LO.5** On March 31, 2009, Big Boats Company entered into a contract with Vacations Unlimited to produce a state-of-the-art cruise ship, to be completed within three years. Big Boats estimated the total cost of building the ship at $300 million. The contract price was $400 million. The ship was completed on February 15, 2012.

a. What tax accounting method must Big Boats use for the contract? Why?

b. Using the financial data provided relating to the contract's performance, complete the following schedule:

Date	Total Costs Incurred to Date	Total Percentage of Contract Completed	Current-Year Revenue Accrued	Current-Year Costs Deductible
12/31/09	$ 60 million	_____	_____	_____
12/31/10	180 million	_____	_____	_____
12/31/11	280 million	_____	_____	_____
12/31/12	340 million	N/A	_____	_____

c. What are the consequences of the total cost of $340 million exceeding the estimated total cost of $300 million?

34. **LO.5** Ostrich Company makes gasoline storage tanks. Everything produced is under contract (that is, the company does not produce until it gets a contract for a product). Ostrich makes three basic models. However, the tanks must be adapted to each individual customer's location and needs (e.g., the location of the valves, the quality of the materials and insulation). Discuss the following issues relative to Ostrich's operations:

a. An examining IRS agent contends that each of the company's contracts is to produce a "unique product." What difference does it make whether the product is unique or a "shelf item"?

b. Producing one of the tanks takes over one year from start to completion, and the total price is in excess of $1 million. What costs must be capitalized for this contract that are not subject to capitalization for a contract with a shorter duration and lower cost?

c. What must Ostrich do with the costs of bidding on contracts?

d. Ostrich frequently makes several cost estimates for a contract, using various estimates of materials costs. These costs fluctuate almost daily. Assuming Ostrich must use the percentage of completion method to report the income from the contract, what will be the consequence if the company uses the highest estimate of a contract's costs and the actual cost is closer to the lowest estimated cost?

35. **LO.5, 6** Swallow Company is a large real estate construction company that has made a Subchapter S election. The company reports its income using the percentage of completion method. In 2012, the company completed a contract at a total cost of $4.8 million. The contract price was $7.2 million. At the end of 2011, the year the contract was begun, Swallow estimated the total cost of the contract would be $5.4 million. Total accumulated cost on the contract at the end of 2011 was $1.8 million. The relevant tax rate is 35%, and the relevant Federal interest rate is 5%. Assume that all income tax returns were filed and taxes were paid on March 15 following the end of the calendar tax year. COMMUNICATIONS

a. Compute the gross profit on the contract for 2011 and 2012.

b. Compute the lookback interest due or receivable with the 2012 tax return.

c. Before bidding on a contract, Swallow generally makes three estimates of total contract costs: (1) optimistic, (2) pessimistic, and (3) most likely (based on a blending of optimistic and pessimistic assumptions). The company has asked you to write a letter explaining which of these estimates should be used for percentage of completion purposes. In writing your letter, you should consider the fact that Swallow is incorporated and has made an S corporation election. Therefore, the income and deductions flow through to the shareholders who are all individuals in the 35% marginal tax bracket. The relevant Federal interest rate is 8%. Swallow's mailing address is 400 Front Avenue, Ashland, OR 97520.

RESEARCH PROBLEMS

THOMSON REUTERS
Checkpoint® Student Edition

Note: Solutions to Research Problems can be prepared by using the **Checkpoint® Student Edition** online research product, which is available to accompany this text. It is also possible to prepare solutions to the Research Problems by using tax research materials found in a standard tax library.

Research Problem 1. Your client is not permitted to deduct a year-end accrual for vacation pay earned but not paid. This result occurs because the tax law considers this to be deferred compensation that is ineligible for the recurring item exception, unless it is paid by March 15 of the year following the accrual [see §§ 404(a)(5) and (6)]. Your client has asked whether the related accrued Social Security taxes on the vacation pay can be accrued under the general recurring item exception because these taxes will be paid by the fifteenth day of the ninth month after the close of the tax year.

Research Problem 2. Your client is an electric utility company. During the year, the company made some improvements to its distribution lines. While the improvements were being made, the company had to temporarily move some lines so that customer service would not be interrupted. The company needs to know whether the temporary relocation costs can be allocated to electric distribution costs or must be capitalized as part of the cost of the improvements. You locate Revenue Ruling 73–203, which permits a current deduction for the cost of temporarily relocating the lines. The client notes that the ruling is old and that the uniform capitalization rules might change the results. Can you locate more current authority on the issue?

INTERNET *activity*

Use the tax resources of the Internet to address the following question. Do not restrict your search to the Web, but include a review of newsgroups and general reference materials, practitioner sites and resources, primary sources of the tax law, chat rooms and discussion groups, and other opportunities.

Research Problem 3. What tax form is used to elect the LIFO inventory method?

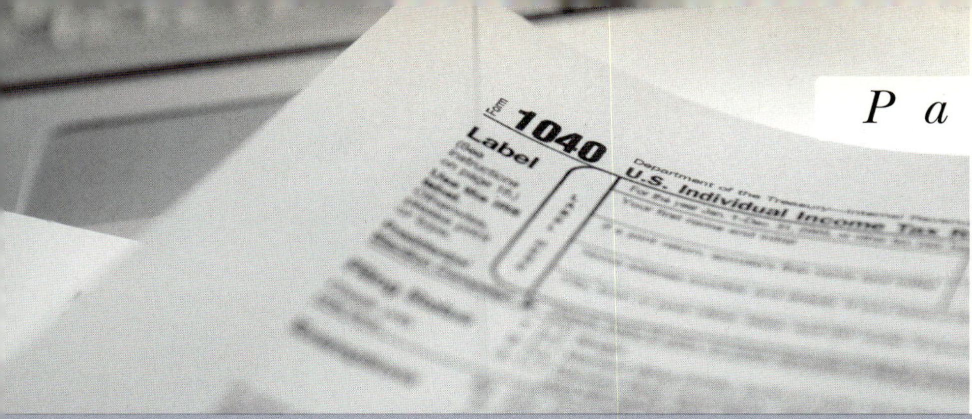

Part 6

Corporations

Corporations are separate entities for Federal income tax purposes. Subchapter C of the Code is devoted to the tax treatment of regular corporations. Part 6 deals mainly with the operating rules contained in Subchapter C that apply to regular corporations and with the effects of various capital transactions on the C corporation and its shareholders.

CHAPTER

17

Corporations: Introduction and Operating Rules

LEARNING OBJECTIVES

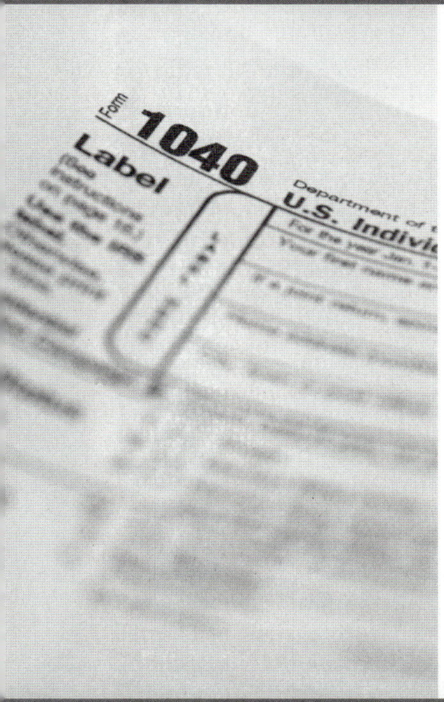

After completing Chapter 17, you should be able to:

LO.1 Summarize the tax treatment of various forms of conducting a business.

LO.2 Compare the taxation of individuals and corporations.

LO.3 Discuss the tax rules unique to corporations.

LO.4 Compute the corporate income tax.

LO.5 Explain the rules unique to computing the tax of related corporations.

LO.6 Describe the reporting process for corporations.

LO.7 Understand the impact of tax return positions on financial statements.

LO.8 Evaluate corporations as an entity form for conducting a business.

OUTLINE

For the latest in changes to tax legislation, visit **www.cengage.com/taxation/swft.**

THE BIG PICTURE Tax Solutions for the Real World

A HALF-BAKED IDEA?

Samantha Johnson owns Skylark Bakery. Currently, the bakery is operated as a sole proprietorship and generates an annual operating profit of $100,000. In addition, the bakery earns annual dividends of $5,000 from investing excess working capital in the stock of publicly traded corporations. These stock investments typically are held for a minimum of three to four months before funds are required for the business. As a result of income from other business ventures and investments, Samantha is in the 35 percent marginal tax rate bracket irrespective of the bakery. In the past, Samantha has withdrawn $50,000 annually from the bakery, which she regards as reasonable payment for her services.

Samantha has asked you about the tax consequences of conducting the business as a regular (C) corporation. Based on the given information, what would be the annual income tax savings (or cost) of operating the bakery as a corporation? For purposes of this analysis, use the 2011 tax rates and ignore any employment tax or state tax considerations. **Read the chapter and formulate your response.**

17.1 Tax Treatment of Various Business Forms

LO.1

Summarize the tax treatment of various forms of conducting a business.

Business operations can be conducted in a number of different forms. Among the various possibilities are the following:

- Sole proprietorships.
- Partnerships.
- Trusts and estates.
- S corporations (also called Subchapter S corporations).
- Regular corporations (also called Subchapter C or C corporations).
- Limited liability companies.

For Federal income tax purposes, the distinctions among these forms of business organization are very important. The following discussion of the tax treatment of sole proprietorships, partnerships, and regular corporations highlights these distinctions. Limited liability companies, which are taxed as one of the three preceding entity forms, are also discussed. Trusts and estates are covered in Chapter 28, and S corporations are discussed in Chapter 22.

SOLE PROPRIETORSHIPS

A sole proprietorship is not a taxable entity separate from the individual who owns the proprietorship. The owner of a sole proprietorship reports all business income and expenses of the proprietorship on Schedule C of Form 1040. The net profit or loss from the proprietorship is then transferred from Schedule C to Form 1040, which is used by the taxpayer to report taxable income. The proprietor reports all of the net profit from the business, regardless of the amount actually withdrawn during the year.

Income and expenses of the proprietorship retain their character when reported by the proprietor. For example, ordinary income of the proprietorship is treated as ordinary income when reported by the proprietor, and capital gain is treated as capital gain.

EXAMPLE 1
THE BIG PICTURE

Return to the facts of *The Big Picture* above. Samantha, the sole proprietor of Skylark Bakery, reports the $100,000 net profit (ordinary income) from the business on Schedule C of her individual tax return. Even though she withdrew only $50,000, Samantha reports all of the $100,000 net profit from the business on Form 1040, where she computes taxable income for the year. She also reports dividend income of $5,000 on Schedule B of Form 1040. ■

PARTNERSHIPS

Partnerships are not subject to a Federal income tax. However, a partnership is required to file Form 1065, which reports the results of the partnership's business activities. Most income and expense items are aggregated in computing the net profit or loss of the partnership on Form 1065. Any income and expense items that are not aggregated in computing the partnership's net profit (loss) are reported separately to the partners. Some examples of separately reported income items are interest income, dividend income, and long-term capital gain. Examples of separately reported expenses include charitable contributions and expenses related to investment income. Partnership reporting is discussed in detail in Chapter 21.

The partnership net profit (loss) and the separately reported items are allocated to the partners according to the partnership's profit and loss sharing agreement. Each partner receives a Schedule K–1 that reports the partner's share of the partnership net profit (loss) and separately reported income and expense items. Each partner reports these items on his or her own tax return.

EXAMPLE 2

Jim and Bob are equal partners in Canary Enterprises, a calendar year partnership. During the year, Canary Enterprises had $500,000 of gross income and $350,000 of operating expenses. In addition, the partnership sold land that had been held for investment purposes for a long-term capital gain of $60,000. During the year, Jim withdrew $40,000 from the partnership and Bob withdrew $45,000. The partnership's Form 1065 reports net profit of $150,000 ($500,000 income − $350,000 expenses). The partnership also reports the $60,000 long-term capital gain as a separately stated item on Form 1065. Jim and Bob each receive a Schedule K–1 reporting net profit of $75,000 and separately stated long-term capital gain of $30,000. Consequently, each partner reports net profit of $75,000 and long-term capital gain of $30,000 on his own return. ■

CORPORATIONS

Corporations are governed by Subchapter C or Subchapter S of the Internal Revenue Code. Those governed by Subchapter C are referred to as **C corporations** or **regular corporations**. Corporations governed by Subchapter S are referred to as **S corporations**.

S corporations, which generally do not pay Federal income tax, are similar to partnerships in that net profit or loss flows through to the shareholders to be reported on their separate returns. Also like partnerships, S corporations do not aggregate all income and expense items in computing net profit or loss. Certain items flow through to the shareholders and retain their separate character when reported on the shareholders' returns. The S corporation net profit (loss) and the separately reported items are allocated to the shareholders according to their stock ownership interests. See Chapter 22 for detailed coverage of S corporations.

Unlike proprietorships, partnerships, and S corporations, C corporations are subject to an entity-level Federal income tax. This results in what is known as a *double taxation effect*. A C corporation reports its income and expenses on Form 1120. The corporation computes tax on the taxable income reported on the Form 1120 using the rate schedule applicable to corporations (see Exhibit 17.1 later in this section). When a corporation distributes its income, the corporation's shareholders report dividend income on their own tax returns. Thus, income that has already been taxed at the corporate level is also taxed at the shareholder level. The effects of double taxation are illustrated in Examples 3 and 4.

EXAMPLE 3

Lavender Corporation has taxable income of $100,000 in 2011. It pays corporate tax of $22,250 (refer to Exhibit 17.1). This leaves $77,750, all of which is distributed as a dividend to Mike, a 43-year-old single individual and the corporation's sole shareholder. Mike has no income sources other than Lavender Corporation. Mike has taxable income of $68,250 ($77,750 – $5,800 standard deduction – $3,700 personal exemption). He pays tax at the preferential rate applicable to dividends received by individuals. His tax is $5,063 [($34,500 × 0%) + ($33,750 × 15%)]. The combined tax on the corporation's net profit is $27,313 ($22,250 paid by the corporation + $5,063 paid by the shareholder). ■

EXAMPLE 4

Assume the same facts as in Example 3, except that the business is organized as a sole proprietorship. Mike reports the $100,000 profit from the business on his tax return. He has taxable income of $90,500 ($100,000 – $5,800 standard deduction – $3,700 personal exemption) and pays tax of $18,957. Therefore, operating the business as a sole proprietorship results in a tax *savings* of $8,356 in 2011 ($27,313 from Example 3 – $18,957). ■

In many cases, the tax burden will be greater if the business is operated as a corporation (as in Example 3), but sometimes operating as a corporation can result in tax savings, as illustrated in Examples 5 and 6.

EXAMPLE 5

In 2011, Tan Corporation files Form 1120 reporting taxable income of $100,000. The corporation pays tax of $22,250 and distributes the remaining $77,750 as a dividend to Carla, the sole shareholder of the corporation. Carla has income from other sources and is in the top individual tax bracket of 35% in 2011. As a result, she pays tax of $11,663 ($77,750 × 15% rate on dividends) on the distribution. The combined tax on the corporation's earnings is $33,913 ($22,250 paid by the corporation + $11,663 paid by the shareholder). ■

EXAMPLE 6

Assume the same facts as in Example 5, except that the business is a sole proprietorship. Carla reports the $100,000 profit from the business on her tax return and pays tax of $35,000 ($100,000 × 35% marginal rate). Therefore, operating the business as a sole proprietorship results in an incremental tax *cost* of $1,087 in 2011 ($35,000 – $33,913 tax from Example 5). ■

The conclusions reached in these examples cannot be extended to all decisions about a form of business organization, as each specific set of facts and circumstances requires a thorough analysis of the tax factors. Further, the effect of other taxes (e.g., payroll and self-employment taxes, state income and franchise taxes) must be considered in such an analysis.

Taxation of Dividends

As noted earlier, the income of a C corporation is subject to double taxation—once at the corporate level when it is earned and again at the shareholder level when it is distributed as dividends. Double taxation stems, in part, from the fact that dividend distributions are not deductible by the corporation. Shareholders of closely held corporations frequently attempt to circumvent this disallowance by disguising a dividend distribution as some other purported transaction. One of the more common ways of disguising dividend distributions is to pay excessive compensation to shareholder-employees of a closely held corporation. The IRS scrutinizes compensation and other economic transactions (e.g., loans, leases, sales) between shareholders and closely held corporations to ensure that payments are reasonable in amount. (See Chapter 19 for more discussion on constructive dividends.)

Double taxation also stems from the fact that dividend distributions are taxable to the shareholders. Historically, dividend income has been taxed at the same rates as ordinary income. However, to alleviate some of the double taxation effect, Congress reduced the tax rate applicable to dividend income of individuals for years after 2002. Qualified dividend income is currently taxed at the same preferential rate as long-term capital gains—15 percent (0 percent for taxpayers in the bottom two tax brackets). The preferential rate on dividend income is set to expire for years after 2012.

EXHIBIT 17.1 Corporate Income Tax Rates

Taxable Income		Tax Is:	
Over—	But Not Over—		Of the Amount Over—
$ -0-	$ 50,000	15%	$ -0-
50,000	75,000	$ 7,500 + 25%	50,000
75,000	100,000	13,750 + 34%	75,000
100,000	335,000	22,250 + 39%	100,000
335,000	10,000,000	113,900 + 34%	335,000
10,000,000	15,000,000	3,400,000 + 35%	10,000,000
15,000,000	18,333,333	5,150,000 + 38%	15,000,000
18,333,333	—	35%	-0-

Comparison of Corporations and Other Forms of Doing Business

While a detailed comparison of sole proprietorships, partnerships, S corporations, and C corporations as forms of doing business must be made, it is appropriate at this point to consider some of the tax and nontax factors that favor corporations over proprietorships.

Consideration of tax factors requires an examination of the corporate rate structure. The income tax rate schedule applicable to corporations is reproduced in Exhibit 17.1. As this schedule shows, the marginal rates for corporations range from 15 percent to 39 percent. In comparison, the marginal rates for individuals range from 10 percent to 35 percent. The corporate form of doing business presents tax savings opportunities when the applicable corporate marginal rate is lower than the applicable individual marginal rate.

EXAMPLE 7

Susanna, an individual taxpayer in the 35% marginal tax rate bracket, can generate $100,000 of additional taxable income in the current year. If the income is taxed to Susanna, the associated tax is $35,000 ($100,000 × 35%). If, however, Susanna is able to shift the income to a newly created corporation, the corporate tax is $22,250 (see Exhibit 17.1). Thus, by taking advantage of the lower corporate marginal tax rates, a tax *savings* of $12,750 ($35,000 − $22,250) is achieved. ■

Any attempt to arbitrage the difference between the corporate and individual marginal tax rates also must consider the double taxation effect. When the preferential rate for dividend income is considered, however, tax savings opportunities still exist.

EXAMPLE 8

Assume in Example 7 that the corporation distributes all of its after-tax earnings to Susanna as a dividend. The dividend results in tax of $11,663 [($100,000 − $22,250) × 15%] to Susanna. Thus, even when the double taxation effect is considered, the combined tax burden of $33,913 ($22,250 paid by the corporation + $11,663 paid by the shareholder) represents a tax *savings* of $1,087 when compared to the $35,000 of tax that results when the $100,000 of income is subject to Susanna's 35% marginal rate. ■

Examples 7 and 8 ignore other tax considerations that also must be considered in selecting the proper form of doing business, but they illustrate the tax savings that can be achieved by taking advantage of rate differentials. Some of the other tax considerations that could affect the selection of a business form include the character of business income, the expectation of business losses, payroll taxes, and state taxes.

All income and expense items of a proprietorship retain their character when reported on the proprietor's tax return. In the case of a partnership or S corporation, separately reported items (e.g., charitable contributions and long-term capital gains) retain their character when passed through to the partners or shareholders, respectively. However, the tax attributes of income and expense items of a C corporation do not pass through the corporate entity to the shareholders. As a result, if the business is expected to generate tax-favored income (e.g., tax-exempt income or long-term capital gains), one of the other (non-C corporation) forms of business may be desirable.

Losses of a C corporation are treated differently than losses of a proprietorship, partnership, or S corporation. A loss incurred by a proprietorship may be deductible by the owner, because all income and expense items are reported by the proprietor. Partnership losses are passed through the partnership entity and may be deductible by the partners, and S corporation losses are passed through to the shareholders. C corporation losses, however, have no effect on the taxable income of the shareholders. Therefore, one of the non-C corporation forms of business may be desirable if business losses are anticipated.

EXAMPLE 9

Franco plans to start a business this year. He expects the business will incur operating losses for the first three years and then become highly profitable. Franco decides to operate as an S corporation during the loss period, because the losses will flow through and be deductible on his personal return. When the business becomes profitable, he intends to switch to C corporation status. ■

Employment taxes must be factored into any analysis of a business form. The net income of a proprietorship is subject to the self-employment tax, as are some partnership allocations of income to partners. In the alternative, wages paid to a shareholder-employee of a corporation (C or S) are subject to payroll taxes. The combined corporation-employee payroll tax burden should be compared with the self-employment tax associated with the proprietorship and partnership forms of business. This analysis should include the benefit of the deduction available to a corporation for payroll taxes paid, as well as the deduction available to an individual for one-half of self-employment taxes paid.

State taxation also must be considered in the selection of a business form. At the entity level, state corporate income taxes and/or franchise taxes are applicable for businesses formed as corporations. Although no entity-level Federal income tax is typically assessed on S corporations, limited liability companies (LLCs), or partnerships, a few states impose a corporate income tax or franchise tax on such business forms. Consideration of state taxation when selecting a business form is particularly relevant for businesses that operate in more than one state. (See Chapter 24 for a discussion of the taxation of multistate corporations.) At the owner level, the income of sole proprietorships, S corporations, and partnerships (including most LLCs) is subject to state individual income taxation. Similarly, dividend income from corporate distributions is subject to state income taxation and without any rate preference for such income.

Nontax Considerations

Nontax considerations will sometimes override tax considerations and lead to the conclusion that a business should be operated as a corporation. The following are some of the more important nontax considerations:

- Sole proprietors and general partners in partnerships face the danger of *unlimited liability*. That is, creditors of the business may file claims not only against the assets of the business but also against the personal assets of proprietors or general partners. State corporate law protects shareholders from claims against their personal assets for corporate debts.
- The corporate form of business can provide a vehicle for raising large amounts of capital through widespread stock ownership. Most major businesses in the United States are operated as corporations.
- Shares of stock in a corporation are freely transferable, whereas a partner's sale of his or her partnership interest is subject to approval by the other partners.

TAX *in the NEWS*

U.S. Corporate Tax Rate Second Highest among OECD Countries

According to the Organization for Economic Cooperation and Development (OECD), the U.S. corporate income tax rate is the second highest among member states. Only Japan has a higher corporate tax rate than the United States, and Japan's new prime minister has vowed to reduce his country's corporate tax burden. The effective tax rate that most corporations pay in the United States is substantially less than the top statutory rate, however, as taxpayers reduce their exposure to the corporate tax through the use of exclusions, deductions, credits, and deferral provisions. Still, the relatively high corporate tax rate puts the United States at a competitive disadvantage in attracting capital investment, and it encourages U.S. corporations to utilize foreign entities to shelter income from U.S. taxation. Many economists argue that a reduced corporate tax rate would improve the United States' competitive economic position in the world. Any reduction in the corporate tax rates, however, likely will be paired with a broadening of the corporate tax base (e.g., the elimination or reduction of some corporate deductions). Recent legislative proposals to reduce the corporate tax rate have included provisions designed to broaden the corporate tax base. (See, e.g., H.R. 3970, introduced by Representative Charles Rangel in the 110th Congress, and S. 3018, introduced by Senators Ron Wyden and Judd Gregg in the 111th Congress.)

Source: **www.oecd.org/ctp/taxdatabase.**

- Shareholders may come and go, but a corporation can continue to exist. Death or withdrawal of a partner, on the other hand, may terminate the existing partnership and cause financial difficulties that result in dissolution of the entity. This *continuity of life* is a distinct advantage of the corporate form of doing business.
- Corporations have *centralized management.* All management responsibility is assigned to a board of directors, which appoints officers to carry out the corporation's business. Partnerships, by contrast, may have decentralized management, in which every partner has a right to participate in the organization's business decisions. **Limited partnerships**, though, may have centralized management. Centralized management is essential for the smooth operation of a widely held business.

LIMITED LIABILITY COMPANIES

The use of the **limited liability company (LLC)** form has proliferated greatly in recent years, particularly since 1988 when the IRS first ruled that it would treat qualifying LLCs as partnerships for tax purposes. All 50 states and the District of Columbia have passed laws that allow LLCs, and thousands of companies have chosen LLC status. As with a corporation, operating as an LLC allows its owners to avoid unlimited liability, which is a primary *nontax* consideration in choosing this form of business organization. The tax advantage of LLCs is that qualifying businesses may be treated as proprietorships or partnerships for tax purposes, thereby avoiding the problem of double taxation associated with regular corporations.

Some states allow an LLC to have centralized management, but not continuity of life or free transferability of interests. Other states allow LLCs to adopt any or all of the corporate characteristics of centralized management, continuity of life, and free transferability of interests.

Entity Classification

Can an organization not qualifying as a corporation under state law still be treated as such for Federal income tax purposes? The tax law defines a corporation as including "associations, joint stock companies, and insurance companies."[1] Unfortunately,

[1] § 7701(a)(3).

the Code contains no definition of what constitutes an *association*, and the issue became the subject of frequent litigation.

It was finally determined that an entity would be treated as a corporation if it had a majority of characteristics common to corporations. For this purpose, relevant characteristics are:

- Continuity of life.
- Centralized management.
- Limited liability.
- Free transferability of interests.

Considering these criteria did not resolve all of the problems that continued to arise over corporate classification. When this type of business entity—the limited liability company—was developed, the IRS was deluged with inquiries regarding its tax status. As LLCs became increasingly popular with professional groups, all states enacted statutes allowing some form of this entity. Invariably, the statutes permitted the corporate characteristic of limited liability and, often, that of centralized management. Because continuity of life and free transferability of interests are absent, partnership classification was hoped for. This treatment avoided the double taxation inherent in the corporate form.

In 1996, the IRS eased the entity classification problem by issuing the **check-the-box Regulations**.[2] The Regulations enable taxpayers to choose the tax status of a business entity without regard to its corporate (or noncorporate) characteristics. These rules simplified tax administration considerably and eliminated much of the litigation that arose with regard to the association (i.e., corporation) status.

Under the check-the-box rules, noncorporate entities with more than one owner can elect to be classified as either a partnership or a corporation. An entity with only one owner can elect to be classified as a sole proprietorship or as a corporation. Eligible entities make the election as to tax status by filing Form 8832 (Entity Classification Election). In the event of default (i.e., no election is made), multi-owner entities are classified as partnerships and single-person businesses as sole proprietorships.

The election is not available to entities that are actually incorporated under state law or to entities that are required to be taxed as corporations under Federal law (e.g., certain publicly traded partnerships). Otherwise, LLCs are not treated as being incorporated under state law. Although LLCs are generally disregarded entities for income tax purposes, they are obligated to report and pay employment and excise taxes.

17.2 An Introduction to the Income Taxation of Corporations

LO.2

Compare the taxation of individuals and corporations.

AN OVERVIEW OF CORPORATE VERSUS INDIVIDUAL INCOME TAX TREATMENT

When examining how corporations are treated under the Federal income tax law, a useful approach is to compare their treatment with that applicable to individual taxpayers. The tax formula for computing the Federal income tax for a corporation is compared to that of an individual taxpayer in Figure 17.1, and the following discussion highlights similarities and differences between the two formulas.

Similarities

Gross income of a corporation is determined in much the same manner as it is for individuals. Thus, gross income includes compensation for services rendered, income derived from a business, gains from dealings in property, interest, rents, royalties, and dividends—to name only a few items. Both individuals and corporations are entitled to exclusions from gross income. However, corporate taxpayers are allowed fewer exclusions. Interest on municipal bonds and life insurance proceeds ware two exclusions that are applicable to both individual and corporate taxpayers.

[2]Reg. §§ 301.7701–1 through –4, and –7.

FIGURE 17.1 **Tax Formulas**

Corporations	**Individuals**
Income (broadly conceived)	Income (broadly conceived)
(Exclusions)	(Exclusions)
Gross income	Gross income
(Deductions except for NOL and DRD*)	(Deductions for AGI**)
Taxable income before NOL and DRD	Adjusted gross income
(Net operating loss deduction)	(Greater of itemized or standard deductions)
(Dividends received deduction)	(Personal and dependency exemptions)
Taxable income	Taxable income
Tax on taxable income	Tax on taxable income
(Tax credits)	(Tax credits)
Tax due (or refund)	Tax due (or refund)

*NOL = net operating loss; DRD = dividends received deduction.
**AGI = adjusted gross income.

Gains and losses from property transactions are handled similarly. For example, whether a gain or loss is capital or ordinary depends upon the nature of the asset in the hands of the taxpayer making the taxable disposition. In defining what is not a capital asset, § 1221 makes no distinction between corporate and noncorporate taxpayers.

In the area of nontaxable exchanges, corporations are like individuals in that they do not recognize gain or loss on a like-kind exchange and may defer realized gain on an involuntary conversion of property. The exclusion of gain from the sale of a personal residence does not apply to corporations. The disallowance of losses on sales of property to related parties and on wash sales of securities applies equally to individual and corporate taxpayers.

The business deductions of corporations also parallel those available to individuals. Deductions are allowed for all ordinary and necessary expenses paid or incurred in carrying on a trade or business. Specific provision is made for the deductibility of interest, certain taxes, losses, bad debts, cost recovery, charitable contributions, net operating losses, research and experimental expenditures, and other less common deductions. There is no distinction between business and nonbusiness interest or business and nonbusiness bad debts for corporations. Thus, these amounts are deductible in full as ordinary deductions by corporations. Like individuals, corporations are not allowed a deduction for interest paid or incurred on amounts borrowed to purchase or carry tax-exempt securities. The same holds true for expenses contrary to public policy and certain unpaid expenses and interest between related parties.

Some of the tax credits available to individuals, such as the foreign tax credit, can also be claimed by corporations. Not available to corporations are certain credits that are personal in nature, such as the credit for child and dependent care expenses, the credit for elderly or disabled taxpayers, and the earned income credit.

Dissimilarities

The income taxation of corporations and individuals also differs significantly. As noted earlier, different tax rates apply to corporations and to individuals. Corporate tax rates are discussed in more detail later in the chapter (see Examples 27 and 28).

All allowable corporate deductions are treated as business deductions. Thus, the determination of adjusted gross income (AGI), so essential for individual taxpayers, has no relevance to corporations. Taxable income is computed simply by subtracting from gross income all allowable deductions and losses. Itemized deductions, the standard deduction, and the deduction for personal and dependency exemptions do not apply to corporations. The $100 floor and 10 percent-of-AGI limitations on the deductible portion of personal casualty and theft losses applicable to individuals do not apply to corporations.

SPECIFIC PROVISIONS COMPARED

A comparison of the income taxation of individuals and corporations appears in Concept Summary 17.1 located at the end of this chapter. In making this comparison, the following areas warrant special discussion:

- Accounting periods and methods.
- Capital gains and losses.
- Recapture of depreciation.
- Passive losses.
- Charitable contributions.
- Domestic production activities deduction.
- Net operating losses.
- Special deductions available only to corporations.

ACCOUNTING PERIODS AND METHODS

Accounting Periods

Corporations generally have the same choices of accounting periods as do individual taxpayers. Like an individual, a corporation may choose a calendar year or a fiscal year for reporting purposes. Corporations usually can have different tax years from those of their shareholders. Also, newly formed corporations (as new taxpayers) usually may choose any approved accounting period without having to obtain the consent of the IRS. **Personal service corporations (PSCs)** and S corporations, however, are subject to severe restrictions in the use of fiscal years. The rules applicable to S corporations are discussed in Chapter 22.

A PSC has as its principal activity the performance of personal services, and such services are substantially performed by shareholder-employees. The performance of services must be in the fields of health, law, engineering, architecture, accounting, actuarial science, performing arts, or consulting.[3] Barring certain exceptions, PSCs must adopt a calendar year for tax purposes.[4] The exceptions that permit the use of a fiscal year are discussed in Chapter 16.[5]

Accounting Methods

As a general rule, the cash method of accounting is unavailable to corporations.[6] However, several important exceptions apply in the case of the following types of corporations:

- S corporations.
- Corporations engaged in the trade or business of farming and timber.
- Qualified PSCs.
- Corporations with average annual gross receipts of $5 million or less for the most recent three-year period.

Most individuals and corporations that maintain inventory for sale to customers are required to use the accrual method of accounting for determining sales and cost of goods sold. However, as a matter of administrative convenience, the IRS will permit any entity with average annual gross receipts of not more than $1 million for the most recent three-year period to use the cash method. This applies even if the taxpayer is buying and selling inventory. Also as a matter of administrative convenience, the IRS will permit certain entities with average annual gross receipts greater than $1 million but not more than $10 million for the most recent three-year period to use the cash method.[7] See Chapter 16 for additional discussion of these exceptions.

A corporation that uses the accrual method of accounting must observe a special rule in dealing with cash basis related parties. If the corporation has an accrual

[3] § 448(d)(2)(A).
[4] § 441(i).
[5] §§ 444 and 280H.
[6] § 448(a).
[7] Rev.Proc. 2001–10, 2001–1 C.B. 272, and Rev.Proc. 2002–28, 2002–1 C.B. 815.

GLOBAL
Tax Issues

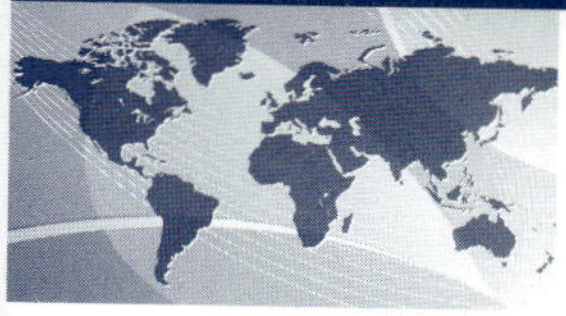

THE MATCHING PRINCIPLE APPLIES WHEN A RELATED PARTY IS A FOREIGN TAXPAYER

Under § 267, an accrual method corporation cannot deduct an accrued expense attributable to a related-party cash basis taxpayer until the recipient includes such amount in gross income. This matching principle is applicable even if the related party is a foreign taxpayer. For example, cash basis, calendar year Foreign Parent loans funds to its accrual method, calendar year U.S. Subsidiary. At the end of the tax year, U.S. Subsidiary accrues interest expense on the Foreign Parent loan, but does not pay the interest in the current year. Section 267 denies U.S. Subsidiary a deduction for the accrued interest until that interest is included in Foreign Parent's gross income (i.e., the year of payment).

Sources: Reg. § 1.267–3(a). See also FAA 20090801F.

outstanding at the end of any taxable year with respect to such a related party, it cannot claim a deduction until the recipient reports the amount as income.[8] This rule is most often encountered when a corporation deals with an individual who owns more than 50 percent of the corporation's stock.

EXAMPLE 10
THE BIG PICTURE

Return to the facts of *The Big Picture* on p. 17-2. Assume that Samantha incorporates her business as Skylark Bakery, Inc., a calendar year, accrual method C corporation. Samantha, a cash method taxpayer, owns 100% of the corporation's stock at the end of 2011. On December 31, 2011, Skylark Bakery has accrued a $10,000 bonus to Samantha. Samantha receives the bonus in 2012 and reports it on her 2012 tax return. Skylark Bakery cannot claim a deduction for the $10,000 until 2012. ■

CAPITAL GAINS AND LOSSES

Capital gains and losses result from the taxable sales or exchanges of capital assets.[9] Whether these gains and losses are long term or short term depends upon the holding period of the assets sold or exchanged. Each year, a taxpayer's short-term gains and losses are combined, and long-term gains and losses are combined. The result is a net short-term capital gain or loss and a net long-term capital gain or loss. If gains *and* losses result (e.g., net short-term capital gain and net long-term capital loss), such amounts are further netted against each other. If instead the results are *all* gains or *all* losses (e.g., net short-term capital loss and net long-term capital loss), no further combination is necessary.

Capital Gains

Individuals generally pay a preferential tax rate of 15 percent on net capital gains (i.e., excess of net long-term capital gain over net short-term capital loss).[10] Corporations, however, receive no favorable tax rate on long-term capital gains, and such income is taxed at the normal corporate tax rates.

Capital Losses

Net capital losses of corporate and individual taxpayers receive different income tax treatment. Generally, individual taxpayers can deduct up to $3,000 of such net losses against other income. Any remaining capital losses can be carried forward to future years until absorbed by capital gains or by the $3,000 deduction.[11] Loss carryovers retain their identity as either long term or short term.

[8] § 267(a)(2).

[9] See Chapter 14 for a detailed discussion of capital gains and losses.

[10] A 0% rate applies to individual taxpayers in the 10% and 15% brackets.

[11] § 1212.

EXAMPLE 11

Robin, an individual, incurs a net long-term capital loss of $7,500 for calendar year 2011. Assuming adequate taxable income, Robin may deduct $3,000 of this loss on his 2011 return. The remaining $4,500 ($7,500 − $3,000) of the loss is carried forward to 2012 and years thereafter until completely deducted. The $4,500 will be carried forward as a long-term capital loss. ■

Unlike individuals, corporate taxpayers are not permitted to claim any net capital losses as a deduction against ordinary income. Capital losses, therefore, can be used only as an offset against capital gains. Corporations may, however, carry back net capital losses to three preceding years, applying them first to the earliest year in point of time. Carryforwards are allowed for a period of five years from the year of the loss. When carried back or forward, a long-term capital loss is treated as a short-term capital loss.

EXAMPLE 12

Assume the same facts as in Example 11, except that Robin is a corporation. None of the $7,500 long-term capital loss incurred in 2011 can be deducted that year. Robin Corporation may, however, carry back the loss to years 2008, 2009, and 2010 (in this order) and offset it against any capital gains recognized in these years. If the carryback does not exhaust the loss, it may be carried forward to calendar years 2012, 2013, 2014, 2015, and 2016 (in this order). The long-term capital loss is treated as short term in any carryover year. ■

ETHICS & *Equity*

TIMING IS EVERYTHING!

During 2011, Harrier Corporation, a calendar year C corporation, has a $100,000 gain from the sale of real estate. The real estate was unimproved land that had been owned by Harrier for many years as an investment. Concerned about its tax situation, in December Harrier sells stock in Falcon Corporation (also held as an investment) for a loss of $103,000. Because Falcon has significant growth potential, Harrier repurchases the stock in 2012. On its 2011 corporate income tax return, Harrier plans to deduct a net capital loss of $3,000. Evaluate the propriety of Harrier's plans.

RECAPTURE OF DEPRECIATION

In general, the recapture rules under §§ 1245 and 1250 are equally applicable to both individual and corporate taxpayers (see Chapter 14). However, corporations may have more depreciation recapture (ordinary income) on the disposition of § 1250 property than individuals. Under § 291, a corporation will have additional ordinary income equal to 20 percent of the excess of the amount of depreciation recapture that would arise if the property was § 1245 property over the amount of depreciation recapture computed under § 1250 (without regard to § 291). As a result, the § 1231 portion of the corporation's gain on the disposition is correspondingly reduced by the additional recapture.

Under § 1250, recapture is limited to the excess of accelerated depreciation over straight-line depreciation. In general, only straight-line depreciation is allowed for real property placed in service after 1986; thus, there will usually be no depreciation recapture on the disposition of § 1250 property (without regard to § 291). In contrast, all depreciation taken on § 1245 property is subject to recapture under that provision.

EXAMPLE 13

Red Corporation purchases nonresidential real property on May 3, 1996, for $800,000. Straight-line depreciation is taken in the amount of $316,239 before the property is sold on October 8, 2011, for $1.2 million.

First, determine the recognized gain:

Sales price		$1,200,000
Less: Adjusted basis:		
Cost of property	$ 800,000	
Less: Cost recovery	(316,239)	(483,761)
Recognized gain		$ 716,239

Second, determine the § 1245 recapture potential. This is the lesser of $716,239 (recognized gain) or $316,239 (cost recovery claimed).

Third, determine the normal § 1250 recapture amount:

Cost recovery taken	$ 316,239
Less: Straight-line cost recovery	(316,239)
§ 1250 ordinary income	$ –0–

Fourth, because the taxpayer is a corporation, determine the ordinary income recognized under § 291:

§ 1245 recapture potential	$ 316,239
Less: § 1250 recapture amount	(–0–)
Excess § 1245 recapture potential	$ 316,239
Apply § 291 percentage	20%
Additional ordinary income under § 291	$ 63,248

Red Corporation's recognized gain of $716,239 is accounted for as follows:

Ordinary income under § 1250	$ –0–
Ordinary income under § 291	63,248
§ 1231 gain	652,991
Total recognized gain	$716,239

■

PASSIVE LOSSES

The **passive loss** rules apply to individual taxpayers and to closely held C corporations and personal service corporations (PSCs).[12] For S corporations and partnerships, passive income or loss flows through to the owners, and the passive loss rules are applied at the owner level. The passive loss rules are applied to closely held C corporations and to PSCs to prevent taxpayers from incorporating to avoid the passive loss limitations (refer to Chapter 11).

A corporation is closely held if, at any time during the taxable year, more than 50 percent of the value of the corporation's outstanding stock is owned, directly or indirectly, by or for not more than five individuals. A corporation is classified as a PSC if it meets the following requirements:

- The principal activity of the corporation is the performance of personal services.
- The services are substantially performed by shareholder-employees.
- More than 10 percent of the stock (in value) is held by shareholder-employees. *Any* stock held by an employee on *any* one day causes the employee to be a shareholder-employee.

The general passive loss rules apply to PSCs. Passive losses cannot be offset against either active income or portfolio income. The application of the passive loss rules is not as harsh for closely held C corporations. They may offset passive losses against active income, but not against portfolio income.

EXAMPLE 14

Brown, a closely held C corporation that is not a PSC, has $300,000 of passive losses from a rental activity, $200,000 of active business income, and $100,000 of portfolio income. The corporation may offset $200,000 of the $300,000 passive loss against the $200,000 active business income, but may not offset the remainder against the $100,000 of portfolio income. If Brown is a PSC, then none of the $300,000 of passive losses is deductible in the current year. ■

Subject to certain exceptions, individual taxpayers are not allowed to offset passive losses against *either* active or portfolio income.

[12] § 469(a).

CHARITABLE CONTRIBUTIONS

Both corporate and individual taxpayers may deduct charitable contributions if the recipient is a qualified charitable organization. Generally, a deduction will be allowed only for the year in which the payment is made. However, an important exception is made for *accrual basis corporations.* They may claim the deduction in the year *preceding* payment if two requirements are met. First, the contribution must be authorized by the board of directors by the end of that year. Second, it must be paid on or before the fifteenth day of the third month of the next year.

EXAMPLE 15

On December 29, 2011, Blue Company, a calendar year, accrual basis partnership, authorizes a $5,000 donation to the Atlanta Symphony Association (a qualified charitable organization). The donation is made on March 12, 2012. Because Blue Company is a partnership, the contribution cannot be deducted until 2012.[13] However, if Blue Company is a corporation and the December 29, 2011 authorization was made by its board of directors, Blue may claim the $5,000 donation as a deduction for calendar year 2011. ■

Property Contributions

The amount that can be deducted for a noncash charitable contribution depends on the type of property contributed. Property must be identified as capital gain property or ordinary income property. *Capital gain property* is property that, if sold, would result in long-term capital gain or § 1231 gain for the taxpayer. Such property generally must be a capital asset and must be held for the long-term holding period (more than 12 months).

The deduction for a charitable contribution of capital gain property is generally measured by the property's fair market value.

EXAMPLE 16

During the current year, Mallard Corporation donates a parcel of land (a capital asset) to Oakland Community College. Mallard acquired the land in 1988 for $60,000, and the fair market value on the date of the contribution is $100,000. The corporation's charitable contribution deduction (subject to a percentage limitation discussed later) is measured by the asset's fair market value of $100,000, even though the $40,000 appreciation on the land has never been included in Mallard's income. ■

In two situations, a charitable contribution of capital gain property is measured by the basis of the property, rather than fair market value. If the corporation contributes *tangible personal property* and the charitable organization puts the property to an unrelated use, the appreciation on the property is not deductible. Unrelated use is defined as use that is not related to the purpose or function that qualifies the organization for exempt status.

EXAMPLE 17

White Corporation donates a painting worth $200,000 to Western States Art Museum (a qualified organization), which exhibits the painting. White had acquired the painting in 1980 for $90,000. Because the museum put the painting to a related use, White is allowed to deduct $200,000, the fair market value of the painting. ■

EXAMPLE 18

Assume the same facts as in the previous example, except that White Corporation donates the painting to the American Cancer Society, which sells the painting and deposits the $200,000 proceeds in the organization's general fund. White's deduction is limited to the $90,000 basis because it contributed tangible personal property that was put to an unrelated use by the charitable organization. ■

The deduction for charitable contributions of capital gain property to certain *private nonoperating foundations* is also limited to the basis of the property.

[13]Each partner will report an allocable portion of the charitable contribution deduction as of December 31, 2012 (the end of the partnership's tax year). See Chapter 21.

Ordinary income property is property that, if sold, would *not* result in long-term capital gain or § 1231 gain for the taxpayer. Examples of ordinary income property include inventory and capital assets that have not been held more than 12 months. In addition, § 1231 property (depreciable property used in a trade or business) is treated as ordinary income property to the extent of any depreciation recaptured under § 1245 or § 1250 (as adjusted under § 291). As a general rule, the deduction for a contribution of ordinary income property is limited to the basis of the property. On certain contributions of inventory by *corporations*, however, the amount of the deduction is equal to the lesser of (1) the sum of the property's basis plus 50 percent of the appreciation on the property or (2) twice the property's basis. The following contributions of inventory qualify for this increased contribution amount.

- A contribution of property to a charitable organization for use that is related to the organization's exempt function and such use is solely for the care of the ill, needy, or infants. (Individual taxpayers also qualify for this exception if the property is "wholesome food.")
- A contribution of books to a public school (K through 12) that uses the books in its educational programs.
- A contribution of tangible personal research property constructed by the corporation to a qualified educational or scientific organization that uses the property for research or experimentation, or research training. (The property must be contributed within two years from the date of its construction by the donor, and its original use must begin with the donee.)
- A contribution of computer equipment and software to a qualified educational organization or public library that uses the property for educational purposes. (The property must be contributed within three years from the date of its acquisition or construction by the donor, and its original use must begin with the donor or donee.)[14]

EXAMPLE 19

Lark Corporation, a clothing retailer, donates children's clothing to the Salvation Army to be used to attire homeless children. Lark's basis in the clothes is $2,000, and the fair market value is $3,000. Lark's deduction is $2,500 [$2,000 basis + 50%($3,000 – $2,000)]. If, instead, the fair market value is $7,000, Lark's deduction is $4,000 (2 × $2,000 basis). ■

ETHICS & Equity

Art Is in the Eye of the Beholder!

Snipe Corporation, your client, donated a painting to the Lexington Museum of Art. The painting, which had been displayed in the corporate offices for several years, had a fair market value of $150,000 at the time of the donation (basis of $60,000). Snipe deducted a charitable contribution of $150,000 for the gift. You have learned that the museum, also a client of yours, did not display the painting because it did not fit well with the museum's collection. Instead, the museum sold the painting for $150,000 and placed the funds in its operating budget. What action, if any, should you take?

Limitations Imposed on Charitable Contribution Deductions

Like individuals, corporations are subject to percentage limits on the charitable contribution deduction.[15] For any tax year, a corporate taxpayer's contribution deduction is limited to 10 percent of taxable income. For this purpose, taxable income is computed without regard to the charitable contribution deduction, any net operating loss carryback or capital loss carryback, dividends received deduction, and

[14]These conditions are set forth in §§ 170(e)(3), (4), and (6). The enhanced deduction associated with the contribution of food, book, and computer equipment inventory is available only for contributions made by December 31, 2011.

[15]The percentage limitations applicable to individuals and corporations are set forth in § 170(b).

domestic production activities deduction. Any contributions in excess of the 10 percent limitation may be carried forward to the five succeeding tax years. Any carryforward must be added to subsequent contributions and will be subject to the 10 percent limitation. In applying this limitation, the current year's contributions must be deducted first, with carryover amounts from previous years deducted in order of time.[16]

EXAMPLE 20

During 2011, Orange Corporation (a calendar year taxpayer) had the following income and expenses:

Income from operations	$140,000
Expenses from operations	110,000
Dividends received	10,000
Charitable contributions made in May 2011	6,000

For purposes of the 10% limitation *only*, Orange Corporation's taxable income is $40,000 ($140,000 − $110,000 + $10,000). Consequently, the allowable charitable contribution deduction for 2011 is $4,000 (10% × $40,000). The $2,000 unused portion of the contribution can be carried forward to 2012, 2013, 2014, 2015, and 2016 (in that order) until exhausted. ■

EXAMPLE 21

Assume the same facts as in Example 20. In 2012, Orange Corporation has taxable income (for purposes of the 10% limitation) of $50,000 and makes a charitable contribution of $4,500. The maximum deduction allowed for 2012 is $5,000 (10% × $50,000). The first $4,500 of the allowed deduction must be allocated to the contribution made in 2012, and $500 of the $2,000 unused contribution is carried over from 2011. The remaining $1,500 of the 2011 contribution may be carried over to 2013 (and later years, if necessary). ■

DOMESTIC PRODUCTION ACTIVITIES DEDUCTION

One important purpose of the American Jobs Creation Act of 2004 was to replace certain tax provisions that our world trading partners regarded as allowing unfair advantage to U.S. exports. Among other changes, the Act created a deduction based on the income from manufacturing activities (designated as *domestic production activities*). For 2011, the **domestic production activities deduction (DPAD)** is 9 percent of the lower of:

- Qualified production activities income, or
- Taxable income (computed without regard to the DPAD).[17]

For individuals, adjusted gross income is substituted for "taxable income." The DPAD cannot exceed 50 percent of an employer's W–2 wages related to qualified production activities income.

EXAMPLE 22

Elk Corporation, a calendar year taxpayer, manufactures golf equipment. For 2011, Elk had taxable income of $360,000 (before considering the DPAD) and qualified production activities income of $380,000. Elk's deduction is $32,400 [9% × $360,000 (the lesser of $380,000 or $360,000)]. Elk's W–2 wages related to qualified production activities income were $70,000, so the W–2 wage limitation ($70,000 × 50% = $35,000) does not apply. ■

See Chapter 7 for a detailed discussion of the domestic production activities deduction.

NET OPERATING LOSSES

As for individuals, the net operating loss (NOL) of a corporation generally may be carried back 2 years and forward 20 to offset taxable income for those years. Similarly, corporations also may elect to forgo the carryback period and just carry forward an NOL. Unlike individual taxpayers, however, a corporation does not adjust its tax loss for the year for capital losses, because a corporation is not permitted a deduction for

[16]The carryover rules relating to all taxpayers are in § 170(d).

[17]§ 199.

TAX *in* the NEWS

The President's Economic Recovery Advisory Board Offers Options for Corporate Tax Reform

In February 2009, President Obama established the President's Economic Recovery Advisory Board (PERAB). Chaired by Paul Volcker (former chair of the Federal Reserve), PERAB was charged, in part, with providing the President with options for reforming the corporate tax system. On August 27, 2010, PERAB released "The Report on Tax Reform Options: Simplification, Compliance, and Corporate Taxation." With a view toward reducing economic distortions associated with the current corporate tax system, PERAB's emphasis was on a broader corporate tax base and a lower corporate tax rate. The report offers several options for corporate tax reform, including the following:

- Reduce the corporate tax rate.
- Allow immediate expensing of new investments in business assets.
- Limit deductibility of interest expense.
- Impose the corporate tax on unincorporated businesses possessing certain corporate characteristics.
- Eliminate or reduce certain tax benefits (e.g., the domestic production activities deduction).

PERAB's report could serve as a blueprint for any future attempts at comprehensive corporate tax reform.

net capital losses. Nor does a corporation make adjustments for nonbusiness deductions as individual taxpayers do. Further, a corporation is allowed to include the dividends received deduction (discussed below) in computing its NOL.[18]

EXAMPLE 23

In 2011, Green Corporation has gross income (including dividends) of $200,000 and deductions of $300,000 excluding the dividends received deduction. Green Corporation had received $100,000 of dividends from Fox, Inc., in which Green holds a 5% stock interest. Green has an NOL computed as follows:

Gross income (including dividends)		$ 200,000
Less: Business deductions	$300,000	
Dividends received deduction (70% × $100,000)*	70,000	(370,000)
Taxable income (or loss)		($ 170,000)

*See the discussion of the dividends received deduction in the next section of this chapter.

The NOL is carried back two years to 2009. (Green Corporation may *elect* to forgo the carryback option and instead carry the loss forward.) Assume Green had taxable income of $40,000 in 2009. The carryover to 2010 is computed as follows:

Taxable income for 2009	$ 40,000
Less: NOL carryback	(170,000)
Taxable income for 2009 after NOL carryback (carryover to 2010)	($ 130,000)

DEDUCTIONS AVAILABLE ONLY TO CORPORATIONS

LO.3

Discuss the tax rules unique to corporations.

Dividends Received Deduction

The purpose of the **dividends received deduction** is to mitigate multiple taxation of corporate income. Without the deduction, income paid to a corporation in the form of a dividend would be taxed to the recipient corporation with no corresponding deduction to the distributing corporation. Later, when the recipient corporation paid the income to its shareholders, the income would again be subject to taxation with no corresponding deduction to the corporation. The dividends received deduction alleviates this inequity by causing only some or none of the dividend income to be taxable to the recipient corporation.

[18]The modifications required to arrive at the amount of NOL that can be carried back or forward are in § 172(d).

As the following table illustrates, the amount of the dividends received deduction depends on the percentage of ownership (voting power and value) the recipient corporate shareholder holds in a *domestic corporation* making the dividend distribution.[19]

Percentage of Ownership by Corporate Shareholder	Deduction Percentage
Less than 20%	70%
20% or more (but less than 80%)	80%
80% or more*	100%

*The payor corporation must be a member of an affiliated group with the recipient corporation.

The dividends received deduction is limited to a percentage of the taxable income of a corporation. For this purpose, taxable income is computed without regard to the NOL deduction, the domestic production activities deduction, the dividends received deduction, and any capital loss carryback to the current tax year. The percentage of taxable income limitation corresponds to the deduction percentage. Thus, if a corporate shareholder owns less than 20 percent of the stock in the distributing corporation, the dividends received deduction is limited to 70 percent of taxable income. However, the taxable income limitation does not apply if the corporation has an NOL for the current taxable year.[20]

The following steps are useful in applying these rules.

1. Multiply the dividends received by the deduction percentage.
2. Multiply the taxable income by the deduction percentage.
3. Limit the deduction to the lesser of step 1 or step 2, unless deducting the amount derived in step 1 results in an NOL. If so, use the amount derived in step 1. This is referred to as the NOL rule.

EXAMPLE 24

Red, White, and Blue Corporations are three unrelated calendar year corporations. During the year, they report the following information:

	Red Corporation	White Corporation	Blue Corporation
Gross income from operations	$ 400,000	$ 320,000	$ 260,000
Expenses from operations	(340,000)	(340,000)	(340,000)
Dividends received from domestic corporations (less than 20% ownership)	200,000	200,000	200,000
Taxable income before the dividends received deduction	$ 260,000	$ 180,000	$ 120,000

In determining the dividends received deduction, use the three-step procedure described above:

Step 1 (70% × $200,000)	$ 140,000	$ 140,000	$ 140,000
Step 2			
70% × $260,000 (taxable income)	$ 182,000		
70% × $180,000 (taxable income)		$ 126,000	
70% × $120,000 (taxable income)			$ 84,000
Step 3			
Lesser of step 1 or step 2	$ 140,000	$ 126,000	
Deduction results in an NOL			$ 140,000

[19] § 243(a). Dividends from foreign corporations generally do not qualify for a dividends received deduction. But see § 245.

[20] Further, the limitation does not apply in the case of the 100% deduction available to members of an affiliated group. § 246(b).

White Corporation is subject to the 70% of taxable income limitation. It does not qualify for NOL rule treatment since subtracting $140,000 (step 1) from $180,000 (taxable income before the dividends received deduction) does not yield a negative figure. Blue Corporation qualifies for NOL rule treatment because subtracting $140,000 (step 1) from $120,000 (taxable income before the dividends received deduction) yields a negative figure. In summary, each corporation has a dividends received deduction for the year: $140,000 for Red Corporation, $126,000 for White Corporation, and $140,000 for Blue Corporation. ■

No dividends received deduction is allowed unless the corporation has held the stock for more than 45 days.[21] This restriction was enacted to close a tax loophole involving dividends on stock that is held only transitorily. When stock is purchased shortly before a dividend record date and soon thereafter sold ex-dividend, a capital loss corresponding to the amount of the dividend often results (ignoring other market valuation changes). If the dividends received deduction was allowed in such cases, the capital loss resulting from the stock sale would exceed the taxable portion of the related dividend income.

EXAMPLE 25

On October 3, 2011, Pink Corporation (5 million shares outstanding) declares a $1 per share dividend for shareholders of record as of November 1, 2011, and payable on December 1, 2011. Black Corporation purchases 10,000 shares of Pink stock on October 28, 2011, for $25,000, and sells those 10,000 shares ex-dividend on November 5, 2011, for $15,000. (It is assumed that there is no fluctuation in the market price of the Pink stock other than the dividend element.) The sale results in a short-term capital loss of $10,000 ($15,000 amount realized − $25,000 basis). On December 1, Black receives a $10,000 dividend from Pink. Without the holding period restriction, Black Corporation would recognize a $10,000 capital loss deduction (subject to the capital loss limitation) but only $3,000 of income [$10,000 dividend − $7,000 dividends received deduction ($10,000 × 70%)], or a $7,000 net loss. However, since Black did not hold the Pink stock for more than 45 days, no dividends received deduction is allowed. ■

Another restriction applies to the dividends received deduction when the underlying stock is debt financed. Like the holding period restriction, this provision also was enacted to close a tax loophole. A corporation that finances the purchase of dividend-paying stock receives an interest expense deduction from such financing, but would report only a small amount of the related income if the dividends received deduction was allowed unabated. In general, the debt-financed stock restriction reduces the dividends received deduction with respect to any dividend-paying stock by the percentage of the investment in the stock that is debt financed.[22] For instance, if a stock purchase is financed 50 percent by debt, the dividends received deduction for dividends on such stock is reduced by 50 percent. However, the reduction in the dividends received deduction cannot exceed the amount of the interest deduction allocable to the dividend.

Organizational Expenditures Deduction

Expenses incurred in connection with the organization of a corporation normally are chargeable to a capital account. That they benefit the corporation during its existence seems clear. But how can they be amortized when most corporations possess unlimited life? The lack of a determinable and limited estimated useful life would therefore preclude any tax write-off. Section 248 was enacted to solve this problem.

Under § 248, a corporation may elect to amortize **organizational expenditures** over the 180-month period beginning with the month in which the corporation begins business.[23] Organizational expenditures include the following:

[21] The stock must be held more than 45 days during the 91-day period beginning on the date that is 45 days before the ex-dividend date (or, in the case of preferred stock, more than 90 days during the 181-day period beginning on the date that is 90 days before the ex-dividend date). § 246(c).

[22] § 246A.

[23] The month in which a corporation begins business may not be immediately apparent. Ordinarily, a corporation begins business when it starts the business operations for which it was organized. Reg. § 1.248–1T(d). For a similar problem in the Subchapter S area, see Chapter 22.

- Legal services incident to organization (e.g., drafting the corporate charter, bylaws, minutes of organizational meetings, terms of original stock certificates).
- Necessary accounting services.
- Expenses of temporary directors and of organizational meetings of directors or shareholders, and fees paid to the state of incorporation.

Expenditures that *do not qualify* as organizational expenditures include those connected with issuing or selling shares of stock or other securities (e.g., commissions, professional fees, and printing costs) or with the transfer of assets to a corporation. These expenditures reduce the amount of capital raised and are not deductible at all.

The first $5,000 of organizational costs can be immediately expensed, with any remaining amount of organizational costs amortized over a 180-month period. However, this $5,000 expensing amount is phased out on a dollar-for-dollar basis when these costs exceed $50,000. For example, a corporation with $52,000 of organizational costs could expense $3,000 [$5,000 − ($52,000 − $50,000)] of this amount and amortize the $49,000 balance ($52,000 − $3,000) over 180 months.

To qualify for the election, the expenditures must be *incurred* before the end of the tax year in which the corporation begins business. In this regard, the corporation's method of accounting is of no consequence. Thus, an expense incurred by a cash basis corporation in its first tax year qualifies even though it is not paid until a subsequent year.

A corporation is deemed to have made the election to amortize organizational expenditures for the taxable year in which it begins business. No separate statement or specific identification of the deducted amount as organizational expenditures is required. A corporation can elect to forgo the deemed election by clearly electing to capitalize organizational expenditures on a timely filed return for its first taxable year. In that case, the capitalized amount will be deductible by the corporation at such time as it ceases to do business and liquidates.

EXAMPLE 26

Black Corporation, an accrual basis taxpayer, was formed and began operations on April 1, 2011. The following expenses were incurred during its first year of operations (April 1 through December 31, 2011):

Expenses of temporary directors and of organizational meetings	$15,500
Fee paid to the state of incorporation	2,000
Accounting services incident to organization	18,000
Legal services for drafting the corporate charter and bylaws	32,000
Expenses incident to the printing and sale of stock certificates	48,000

Black Corporation elects to amortize organizational costs under § 248. Because of the dollar cap (i.e., dollar-for-dollar reduction for amounts in excess of $50,000), no immediate expensing under the $5,000 rule is available. The monthly amortization is $375 [($15,500 + $2,000 + $18,000 + $32,000) ÷ 180 months], and $3,375 ($375 × 9 months) is deductible for tax year 2011. Note that the $48,000 of expenses incident to the printing and sale of stock certificates does not qualify for the election. These expenses cannot be deducted at all but reduce the amount of the capital realized from the sale of stock. ■

Organizational expenditures are distinguished from *startup expenditures*.[24] Startup expenditures include various investigation expenses involved in entering a new business, whether incurred by a corporate or an individual taxpayer. Startup

[24] § 195.

expenses also include operating expenses, such as rent and payroll, that are incurred by a corporation before it actually begins to produce any gross income. At the election of the taxpayer, such expenditures (e.g., travel, market surveys, financial audits, legal fees) are deductible in the same manner as organizational expenditures. Thus, up to $5,000 can be immediately expensed (subject to the phaseout) and any remaining amounts amortized over a period of 180 months. (For tax years beginning *only* in 2010, the immediate expensing amount for startup expenditures is increased to $10,000, and the phaseout of such amount begins at $60,000 of expenditures.) The same rules that apply to the deemed election (and election to forgo the deemed election) for organizational expenditures also apply to startup expenditures.

17.3 Determining the Corporate Income Tax Liability

CORPORATE INCOME TAX RATES

LO.4

Compute the corporate income tax.

Corporate income tax rates have fluctuated widely over the years, with the current rate structure reflecting a significant reduction that occurred in the Tax Reform Act of 1986. Refer to Exhibit 17.1 for a schedule of the current corporate income tax rates. Unlike the individual income tax rate brackets, the corporate income tax rate brackets are not indexed for inflation.

EXAMPLE 27
THE BIG PICTURE

Return to the facts of *The Big Picture* on p. 17-2. Assume that Samantha incorporates her business as Skylark Bakery, Inc., a calendar year C corporation. The corporation pays Samantha a salary of $50,000 for the current year. For 2011, Skylark Bakery has taxable income of $51,500 [$100,000 operating profit + $5,000 dividends − $50,000 salary deduction − $3,500 dividends received deduction ($5,000 × 70%)]. Its income tax liability is $7,875, determined as follows:

Tax on $50,000 at 15%	$7,500
Tax on $1,500 at 25%	375
Tax liability	$7,875

■

For taxable income in excess of $100,000 for any tax year, the amount of the tax is increased by the lesser of (1) 5 percent of the excess or (2) $11,750. In effect, the additional tax means a 39 percent rate for every dollar of taxable income from $100,000 to $335,000.

EXAMPLE 28

Silver Corporation, a calendar year taxpayer, has taxable income of $335,000 for 2011. Its income tax liability is $113,900, determined as follows:

Tax on $100,000	$ 22,250
Tax on $235,000 × 39%	91,650
Tax liability	$113,900

Note that the tax liability of $113,900 is 34% of $335,000. Thus, due to the 39% rate (34% normal rate + 5% additional tax on taxable income between $100,000 and $335,000), the benefit of the lower rates on the first $75,000 of taxable income completely phases out at $335,000. The tax rate drops back to 34% on taxable income between $335,000 and $10 million. ■

Under § 11(b)(2), personal service corporations are taxed at a flat 35 percent rate on all taxable income. Thus, they do not enjoy the tax savings of the 15 to 34 percent brackets applicable to other corporations. For this purpose, a PSC is a corporation that is substantially employee owned. Also, it must engage in one of the following activities: health, law, engineering, architecture, accounting, actuarial science, performing arts, or consulting.

ALTERNATIVE MINIMUM TAX

Corporations are subject to an alternative minimum tax (AMT) that is structured similarly to the AMT applicable to individuals, both in objective and in application.[25] The AMT for corporations, as for individuals, involves a broader tax base than does the regular tax. Like an individual, a corporation is required to apply a minimum tax rate to the expanded base and to pay the greater of the tentative AMT liability and the regular tax. Many of the adjustments and tax preference items necessary to arrive at alternative minimum taxable income (AMTI) are the same for individuals and corporations. The AMT rate and exemption amount for corporations are different from those applicable to individuals, however. Refer to Chapter 15 for a detailed discussion of the corporate AMT.

RESTRICTIONS ON CORPORATE ACCUMULATIONS

Two provisions of the Code are designed to prevent corporations and their shareholders from avoiding the double tax on dividend distributions. Both provisions impose a penalty tax on undistributed income retained by the corporation. The rules underlying these provisions are complex and beyond the scope of this text. However, a brief description is provided as an introduction.

The *accumulated earnings tax* (described in §§ 531–537) imposes a 15 percent tax on the current year's corporate earnings that have been accumulated without a reasonable business need. The burden of proving what constitutes a reasonable need is borne by the taxpayer. In determining accumulated income, most businesses are allowed a $250,000 minimum credit. Thus, most corporations can accumulate $250,000 in earnings over a series of years without fear of an accumulated earnings tax. Beyond the minimum credit, earnings can be accumulated for:

- Working capital needs (to purchase inventory),
- Retirement of debt incurred in connection with the business,
- Investment or loans to suppliers or customers (if necessary to maintain the corporation's business), or
- Realistic business contingencies, including lawsuits or self-insurance.

The *personal holding company (PHC) tax* (described in §§ 541–547) was enacted to discourage the sheltering of certain kinds of passive income in corporations owned by individuals with high marginal tax rates. Historically, the tax was aimed at "incorporated pocketbooks" that were frequently found in the entertainment and construction industries. For example, a taxpayer could shelter income from securities in a corporation, which would pay no dividends, and allow the corporation's stock to increase in value. Like the accumulated earnings tax, the PHC tax employs a 15 percent rate and is designed to force a corporation to distribute earnings to shareholders. However, in any single year, the IRS cannot impose both the PHC tax and the accumulated earnings tax. Generally, a company is considered a PHC and may be subject to the tax if:

- More than 50 percent of the value of the outstanding stock is owned by five or fewer individuals at any time during the last half of the year, and
- A substantial portion (60 percent or more) of the corporation's income is comprised of passive types of income, including dividends, interest, rents, royalties, or certain personal service income.

[25]Small corporations are not subject to the alternative minimum tax.

TAX LIABILITY OF RELATED CORPORATIONS

LO.5

Explain the rules unique to computing the tax of related corporations.

Members of a controlled group of corporations (**related corporations**) are subject to special rules for computing the income tax, the expense of certain depreciable assets under § 179, and the AMT exemption.[26] If these restrictions did not exist, the shareholders of a corporation could gain significant tax advantages by splitting a single corporation into *multiple* corporations. The next two examples illustrate the potential *income tax* advantage of multiple corporations.

EXAMPLE 29

Gray Corporation annually yields taxable income of $300,000. The corporate tax on $300,000 is $100,250, computed as follows:

Tax on $100,000	$ 22,250
Tax on $200,000 × 39%	78,000
Tax liability	$100,250

■

EXAMPLE 30

Assume that Gray Corporation in the previous example is divided equally into four corporations. Each corporation would have taxable income of $75,000, and the tax for each (absent the special provisions for related corporations) would be computed as follows:

Tax on $50,000	$ 7,500
Tax on $25,000 × 25%	6,250
Tax liability	$13,750

The total liability for the four corporations would be $55,000($13,750 × 4). The savings would be $45,250($100,250 − $55,000). ■

A comparison of Examples 29 and 30 reveals that the income tax savings that could be achieved by using multiple corporations result from having more of the total taxable income taxed at lower rates. To close this loophole, the law limits a *controlled group's* taxable income in the tax brackets below 35 percent to the amount the corporations in the group would have if they were one corporation. Thus, in Example 30, under the controlled corporation rules, only $12,500 (one-fourth of the first $50,000 of taxable income) for each of the four related corporations would be taxed at the 15 percent rate. The 25 percent rate would apply to the next $6,250 (one-fourth of the next $25,000) of taxable income of each corporation. This equal allocation of the $50,000 and $25,000 amounts is required unless all members of the controlled group consent to an apportionment plan providing for an unequal allocation.

Similar limitations apply to controlled groups with respect to the election to expense certain depreciable assets under § 179 (see Chapter 8) and to the $40,000 AMT exemption amount (see Chapter 15). In addition, members of a controlled group must defer the recognition of any realized loss on intercompany sales until a sale is made at a gain to a nongroup member (see Chapter 6).[27] Similarly, any gain on the sale of depreciable property between members of a controlled group is recognized as ordinary income (see Chapter 14).[28]

CONTROLLED GROUPS

A **controlled group** of corporations includes parent-subsidiary groups, brother-sister groups, combined groups, and certain insurance companies.[29] Parent-subsidiary controlled groups are discussed in the following section.

[26] § 1561(a).

[27] §§ 267(a)(1), (b)(3), and (f).

[28] §§ 1239(a) and (c).

[29] § 1563(a).

Parent-Subsidiary Controlled Group

A **parent-subsidiary controlled group** exists when one corporation owns at least 80 percent of the voting power *or* stock value of another corporation on the last day of the tax year.[30] Multiple tiers of subsidiaries and chains of ownership are allowed, as long as the group has an identifiable parent corporation.

EXAMPLE 31

Aqua Corporation owns 80% of White Corporation. Aqua and White Corporations are members of a parent-subsidiary controlled group. Aqua is the parent corporation, and White is the subsidiary. ■

The parent-subsidiary relationship described in Example 31 is easy to recognize because Aqua Corporation is the direct owner of White Corporation. Real-world business organizations often are much more complex, sometimes including numerous corporations with chains of ownership connecting them. In these complex corporate structures, determining whether the controlled group classification is appropriate becomes more difficult. The ownership requirements can be met through direct ownership (as in Example 31) or through indirect ownership.

EXAMPLE 32

Red Corporation owns 80% of the voting stock of White Corporation, and White Corporation owns 80% of the voting stock of Blue Corporation. Red, White, and Blue Corporations constitute a controlled group in which Red is the common parent and White and Blue are subsidiaries. The same result would occur if Red Corporation, rather than White Corporation, owned the Blue Corporation stock.

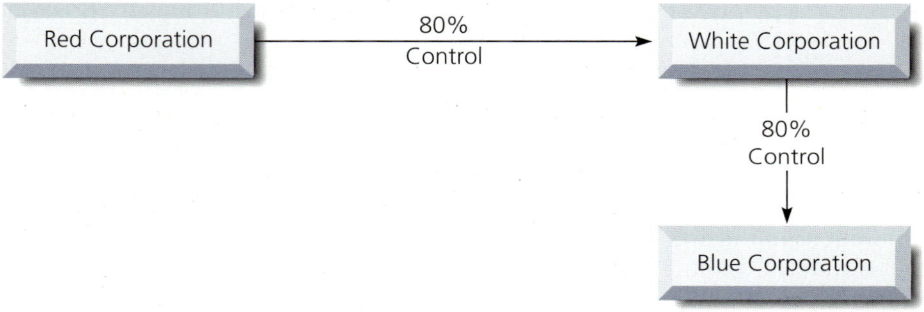

■

EXAMPLE 33

Brown Corporation owns 80% of the stock of Green Corporation, which owns 30% of Blue Corporation. Brown also owns 80% of White Corporation, which owns 50% of Blue Corporation. Brown, Green, Blue, and White Corporations constitute a parent-subsidiary controlled group in which Brown is the common parent and Green, Blue, and White are subsidiaries.

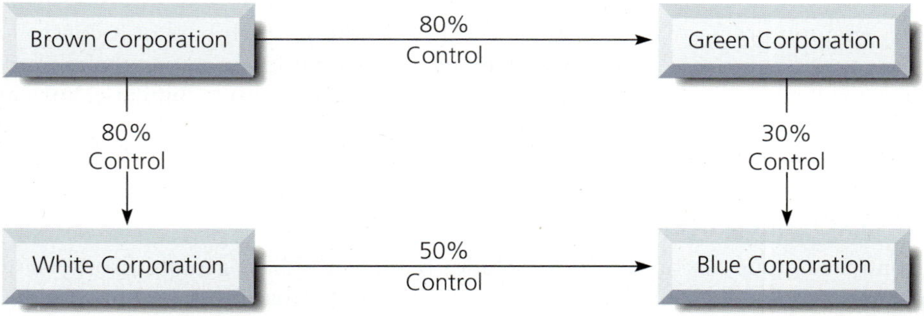

■

[30] § 1563(a)(1). For this purpose, stock attribution rules apply. In addition, all stock options are considered to be exercised by their holders. §§ 1563(d)(1) and (e)(1) through (3).

CONSOLIDATED RETURNS

The privilege of filing a consolidated return is based on the concept that an affiliated group of corporations constitutes a single taxable entity despite the existence of technically separate businesses. By filing a consolidated return, the corporation can eliminate intercompany profits and losses on the principle that its tax liability should be based on transactions with outsiders rather than on intragroup affairs.

Advantages and Disadvantages of Filing Consolidated Returns

The advantages of a consolidated return are summarized below.

- Losses of one group member can be used to shelter the income of other members. See Example 36 below.
- Taxation of intercompany dividends may be eliminated.
- Recognition of income from certain intercompany transactions can be deferred. See Example 38 below.
- Deductions may be optimized due to percentage limitations being modified as a result of the consolidation process. See Example 36 below.

Consolidation also eliminates any intercompany pricing problems among related corporations that might arise under § 482.[31]

EXAMPLE 34

Rust Corporation leases a building to Crimson Corporation for $6,000 a month. If the IRS determines that the market value is really $9,000 per month, a § 482 allocation would increase Rust Corporation's monthly rent income by $3,000. If, however, Rust and Crimson are members of an affiliated group that files a consolidated return, the § 482 adjustment would not be made. Increasing Rust Corporation's rent income by $3,000 is meaningless as it is offset by a $3,000 increase in Crimson Corporation's deduction for rent expense. ■

The disadvantages of filing a consolidated return are as follows.

- An election is binding on subsequent years and can be avoided only if the makeup of the affiliated group changes or the IRS consents to the revocation of consolidated return status.
- Recognition of losses from certain intercompany transactions is deferred.
- The requirement that all group members use the parent's tax year could create short tax years for the subsidiaries. This could cause a bunching of income and use up a full year for carryover purposes.
- Additional administrative compliance costs may be incurred as the consolidated tax return provisions are extensive and complex.

A further negative consideration is that the tax rules for filing a consolidated return may not mesh with those applicable for financial accounting purposes. For example, foreign corporations cannot be included in the consolidated tax return but should be considered when preparing financial statements. This variance in treatment may require explanatory reconciliation and will further add to the administrative burden.

Eligibility and the Election

The election to file a consolidated return is available only to an **affiliated group**.[32] An affiliated group exists when one corporation owns at least 80 percent of the voting power *and* stock value of another corporation. The stock ownership test must be met

[31] § 482 (Allocation of Income and Deductions Among Taxpayers) is further discussed in Chapter 25 in regard to international situations.

[32] § 1504(a). Most of the tax rules governing consolidated returns are contained in the Regulations. The delegation of this rule-making authority is contained in § 1502.

on every day of the tax year. Multiple tiers and chains of corporations are allowed as long as the group has an identifiable parent corporation (i.e., at least 80 percent of one corporation must be owned by another).

An affiliated group is similar but not identical to a parent-subsidiary controlled group discussed earlier in this chapter. Two major differences are noted below.

- In meeting the 80 percent stock ownership requirement, the affiliated group must satisfy *both* the voting power test and the stock value test. As to a parent-subsidiary controlled group, the satisfaction of either test suffices.
- In the parent-subsidiary controlled group, the stock ownership test is applied only on the last day of the year—not every day as in the case of an affiliated group.

Members of an affiliated group need not file a consolidated return and, absent an election to consolidate, each corporation files its own Form 1120. If and when an election is made, all of the transactions for the group are combined and reported on one Form 1120. A Form 1122 (Authorization and Consent of Subsidiary Corporation to Be Included in a Consolidated Income Tax Return) should be attached to the first consolidated Form 1120 for every subsidiary included in the group. Each subsequent consolidated Form 1120 must include a Form 851 (Affiliation Schedule) that provides pertinent information as to the members of the group.

Computing Consolidated Taxable Income

Several categories of transactions do not enter into the determination of taxable income.

- Some intercompany transactions are forever disregarded. Examples would be dividends paid by one group member to another. See also the factual situation presented in Example 34 above.
- Gains and losses from certain intercompany sales are not recognized until the sold asset leaves the affiliated group (e.g., disposition of the property to an outside party). See Examples 38 and 39 below.

In computing the taxable income for any consolidated return year, several items are computed on a group basis. These include net capital (and § 1231) gain or loss, casualty gain or loss, charitable contributions, the dividends received deduction, and net operating loss. The importance of this grouping is illustrated below.

EXAMPLE 35

Maize Corporation owns 100% of the stock of Ecru Corporation, and both use a calendar year for tax purposes. For 2011, they had the following transactions and filed *separate* returns:

	Maize	Ecru
Income from operations	$300,000	$170,000
Capital gain	50,000	
Capital loss of $45,000		(–0–)*
Charitable contribution of $40,000	(35,000)**	
Taxable income	$315,000	$170,000

*No deduction is allowed to a corporation for a net capital loss.
**The charitable deduction is limited to 10% of taxable income, as computed prior to the charitable contribution deduction. Thus, 10% × $350,000 ($300,000 + $50,000) = $35,000.

■

EXAMPLE 36

Assume the same facts as in Example 35 except that a consolidated return is filed for 2011. The results are:

Income from operations ($300,000 + $170,000)		$470,000
Capital transactions—		
Capital gain	$ 50,000	
Capital loss	(45,000)*	5,000
Charitable contribution		(40,000)**
Taxable income		$435,000

*A capital loss can be used to offset a capital gain.
**The 10% of taxable income limitation now becomes 10% × $475,000 = $47,500. Thus, the full charitable deduction is allowed. ■

One of the advantages of filing a consolidated return can be seen by comparing the results reached in Examples 35 and 36. Note that in Example 35 the combined taxable income is $485,000 ($315,000 + $170,000), while in Example 36, taxable income is $435,000, or $50,000 less ($485,000 – $435,000).

The consolidated return rules allow the group to make use of the losses of one (or more) of its members. Because this possibility could lead to major tax avoidance (e.g., a profitable corporation acquires a loss corporation to take advantage of its loss carryovers), multiple safeguards have been enacted by Congress to preclude (or curtail) such potential abuse.

One such safeguard protects against the use of losses and deductions that arose in a separate return year.[33]

EXAMPLE 37

For calendar year 2011, Kingfisher Corporation and Starling Corporation first elect to file a consolidated return. As of January 1, 2011, Starling owned land (held as an investment) with a basis of $300,000 and a fair market value of $280,000. During 2011, the land is sold for $270,000. On a consolidated return, only $10,000 of the loss can be claimed. The other $20,000 loss comes from a separate return year(s) and relates only to Starling Corporation. It cannot be used by the affiliated group. ■

A further safeguard limits the use of losses and deductions when ownership changes within the affiliated group have taken place.[34]

Deferral Treatment for Intercompany Sales

As noted previously, the deferral of certain intercompany sales can be advantageous (if gains are involved) or disadvantageous (if losses are involved). The realized gain or loss from the intercompany sale is not recognized but is deferred.

EXAMPLE 38

In 2011, Peach Corporation sells land (basis of $100,000) to Beige Corporation for its fair market value of $180,000. Both Peach and Beige are members of the same affiliated group that files a consolidated return for 2011. None of the $80,000 realized gain is recognized on this return. ■

The deferred gain or loss may be recognized in a later year when the property ultimately is sold to outsiders.

EXAMPLE 39

Assume the same facts as in Example 38. In 2013, Beige Corporation sells the land to a Danish real estate developer for $210,000. A consolidated return for 2013 should report a recognized gain of $110,000 ($80,000 of which was previously deferred). ■

[33]Aside from the Regulations issued by the Treasury Department, the separate return limitation year (SRLY) safeguards can be invoked pursuant to § 269 (Acquisitions Made to Evade or Avoid Income Tax) and § 482 (Allocation of Income and Deductions Among Taxpayers).

[34]The major statutory weapons available to the IRS are § 381 (Carryovers in Certain Corporate Acquisitions) and § 382 (Limitation on Net Operating Loss Carryforwards and Certain Built-in Losses Following Ownership Change).

FINANCIAL DISCLOSURE Insights

GAAP and Tax Treatment of Consolidations

Both U.S. financial accounting and tax rules use the term *consolidation*, but there is only a slight resemblance in the content of those rules. Here are some of the key similarities and differences between the book and tax treatment of conglomerates.

- GAAP consolidations for the most part are *mandatory* when specified ownership levels are met. Federal income tax consolidation is an *election* by the affiliates to join the parent's tax return.
- GAAP consolidations can include entities such as partnerships and non-U.S. entities. Federal income tax rules generally limit the consolidated return only to U.S. C corporations.
- Ownership levels required for a target to consolidate with a parent generally are 50 percent for GAAP and 80 percent for Federal income tax.
- Tax rules treat a merger or acquisition of a target corporation by a parent as a like-kind exchange, assuming that the requirements of a § 368 reorganization are met (see Chapter 20). Under GAAP, the transaction usually is reported as a purchase of the target's identifiable assets and liabilities.
- After a takeover occurs, book cost amounts are assigned at fair market value, and any excess purchase price is deemed to be goodwill. For Federal income tax purposes, if reorganization treatment is available, the target's basis in its assets carries over to the parent's accounts.
- Goodwill is treated differently under book and tax rules. Financial accounting goodwill cannot be amortized, but impairments to its value are reported as operating losses. Book income results if that impairment of the goodwill is reversed, for example, because the value of the goodwill has increased. For Federal income tax purposes, purchased goodwill is amortized over 15 years.

17.4 Procedural Matters

LO.6

Describe the reporting process for corporations.

FILING REQUIREMENTS FOR CORPORATIONS

A corporation must file a Federal income tax return whether it has taxable income or not.[35] A corporation that was not in existence throughout an entire annual accounting period is required to file a return for the portion of the year during which it was in existence. In addition, a corporation must file a return even though it has ceased to do business if it has valuable claims for which it will bring suit. A corporation is relieved of filing income tax returns only when it ceases to do business and retains no assets.

The corporate return is filed on Form 1120. Corporations electing under Subchapter S (see Chapter 22) file on Form 1120S. Forms 1120 and 1120S are reproduced in Appendix B. Corporations with assets of $10 million or more generally are required to file returns electronically.

The return must be filed on or before the fifteenth day of the third month following the close of a corporation's tax year. Corporations can receive an automatic extension of six months for filing the corporate return by filing Form 7004 by the due date for the return. However, the IRS may terminate the extension by mailing a 10-day notice to the corporation.[36]

ESTIMATED TAX PAYMENTS

A corporation must make payments of estimated tax unless its tax liability can reasonably be expected to be less than $500. The required annual payment (which includes any estimated AMT liability) is the *lesser* of (1) 100 percent of the corporation's tax for the current year or (2) 100 percent of the tax for the preceding year (if that was a 12-month tax year and the return filed showed a tax liability).[37] Estimated payments can be made in four installments due on or before the fifteenth day of the

[35] § 6012(a)(2).

[36] Reg. § 1.6081–3.

[37] §§ 6655(d) and (e).

fourth month, the sixth month, the ninth month, and the twelfth month of the corporate taxable year. The full amount of the unpaid tax is due on the due date of the return.

Failure to make the required estimated tax prepayments results in a nondeductible penalty being imposed on the corporation. The penalty is avoided, however, if any of various exceptions apply.[38]

SCHEDULE M–1—RECONCILIATION OF TAXABLE INCOME AND FINANCIAL NET INCOME

Schedule M–1 of Form 1120 is used to *reconcile* net income as computed for financial accounting purposes [i.e., using **generally accepted accounting principles (GAAP)**] with taxable income reported on the corporation's income tax return (commonly referred to as book-tax differences). Schedule M–1 is required of corporations with less than $10 million of total assets.

The starting point on Schedule M–1 is net income (loss) per books. Additions and subtractions are entered for items that affect financial accounting net income and taxable income differently. The following items are entered as additions (see lines 2 through 5 of Schedule M–1):

- Federal income tax expense per books (deducted in computing net income per books but not deductible in computing taxable income).
- The excess of capital losses over capital gains (deducted for financial accounting purposes but not deductible by corporations for income tax purposes).
- Income that is reported in the current year for tax purposes but is not reported in computing net income per books (e.g., prepaid income).
- Various expenses that are deducted in computing net income per books but are not allowed in computing taxable income (e.g., charitable contributions in excess of the 10 percent ceiling applicable to corporations).

The following subtractions are entered on lines 7 and 8 of Schedule M–1:

- Income reported for financial accounting purposes but not included in taxable income (e.g., tax-exempt interest).
- Deductions taken on the tax return but not expensed in computing net income per books (e.g., domestic production activities deduction).

The result is taxable income (before the NOL deduction and the dividends received deduction).

EXAMPLE 40

During the current year, Tern Corporation had the following transactions:

Net income per books (after tax)	$92,400
Taxable income	50,000
Federal income tax expense per books	7,500
Interest income from tax-exempt bonds	5,000
Interest paid on a loan, the proceeds of which were used to purchase the tax-exempt bonds	500
Life insurance proceeds received as a result of the death of a key employee	50,000
Premiums paid on the key employee life insurance policy	2,600
Excess of capital losses over capital gains	2,000

For book and tax purposes, Tern determines depreciation under the straight-line method. Tern's Schedule M–1 for the current year follows.

[38]See § 6655 for the penalty involved and the various exceptions to it.

Schedule M-1 **Reconciliation of Income (Loss) per Books With Income per Return**

Note: Schedule M-3 required instead of Schedule M-1 if total assets are $10 million or more—see instructions

1	Net income (loss) per books	*92,400*	7	Income recorded on books this year not included on this return (itemize): Tax-exempt interest $ *5,000* *Life insurance proceeds on key employee $50,000*	*55,000*
2	Federal income tax per books	*7,500*			
3	Excess of capital losses over capital gains	*2,000*			
4	Income subject to tax not recorded on books this year (itemize):		8	Deductions on this return not charged against book income this year (itemize):	
5	Expenses recorded on books this year not deducted on this return (itemize):		a	Depreciation $	
a	Depreciation $		b	Charitable contributions $	
b	Charitable contributions $				
c	Travel and entertainment $ *Prem.–life ins. $2,600; Int.–exempt bonds $500*	*3,100*	9	Add lines 7 and 8	*55,000*
6	Add lines 1 through 5	*105,000*	10	Income (page 1, line 28)—line 6 less line 9	*50,000*

■

Schedule M–2 reconciles unappropriated retained earnings at the beginning of the year with unappropriated retained earnings at year-end. Beginning balance plus net income per books, as entered on line 1 of Schedule M–1, less dividend distributions during the year equals ending retained earnings. Other sources of increases or decreases in retained earnings are also listed on Schedule M–2.

EXAMPLE 41

Assume the same facts as in Example 40. Tern Corporation's beginning balance in unappropriated retained earnings is $125,000. During the year, Tern distributed a cash dividend of $30,000 to its shareholders. Based on these further assumptions, Tern's Schedule M–2 for the current year is as follows:

Schedule M-2 **Analysis of Unappropriated Retained Earnings per Books (Line 25, Schedule L)**

1	Balance at beginning of year	*125,000*	5	Distributions: a Cash	*30,000*
2	Net income (loss) per books	*92,400*		b Stock	
3	Other increases (itemize):			c Property	
			6	Other decreases (itemize):	
			7	Add lines 5 and 6	*30,000*
4	Add lines 1, 2, and 3	*217,400*	8	Balance at end of year (line 4 less line 7)	*187,400*

■

Corporations with less than $250,000 of gross receipts and less than $250,000 in assets do not have to complete Schedule L (balance sheet) and Schedules M–1 and M–2 of Form 1120. Similar rules apply to Form 1120S (used by S corporations). These rules are intended to ease the compliance burden on small business.

SCHEDULE M–3—NET INCOME (LOSS) RECONCILIATION FOR CORPORATIONS WITH TOTAL ASSETS OF $10 MILLION OR MORE

Corporate taxpayers with total assets of $10 million or more are required to report much greater detail relative to differences between income (loss) reported for financial purposes and income (loss) reported for tax purposes. This expanded reconciliation of book and taxable income (loss) is reported on **Schedule M–3**. Corporations that are not required to file Schedule M–3 may do so voluntarily. Any corporation that files Schedule M–3 is not allowed to file Schedule M–1. Comparison of Schedule M–3 with Schedule M–1 (illustrated in Example 40) reveals the significantly greater disclosure requirements. Download a copy of Schedule M–3 from the IRS website (see **www.irs.gov**), and refer to it during the following discussion.

Schedule M–3 is a response, at least in part, to financial reporting scandals, such as Enron and WorldCom. One objective of Schedule M–3 is to create greater transparency between corporate financial statements and tax returns. Another objective is to identify corporations that engage in aggressive tax practices by requiring that transactions that create book-tax differences be disclosed on corporate tax returns. The increase in transparency and disclosure comes at a cost, however, as the IRS estimates that, on average, almost 89 hours are needed to comply with the requirements of Schedule M–3, and many tax professionals believe that estimate is too low.

FINANCIAL DISCLOSURE *Insights*

Processing the Corporate Income Tax Return

Seldom is a Form 1120 prepared by itself. In almost every case, the taxpayer and its tax advisers start with the financial accounting records; then they modify book income directly with the book-tax differences that are known by the financial accountants and independent auditors. The tax professionals take these computations, adjust them for tax law changes, and clarify items that require detailed tax research. As the figure to the right illustrates, taxable income for the Form 1120 results from this process.

Notice that this process mirrors that of the preparation of Schedule M–1 or M–3. In preparing these schedules, book income is modified to account for various temporary and permanent book-tax differences as specified by the layout the of forms, resulting in the taxable income amount that is used on page 1 of Form 1120. Some tax professionals maintain that, given the detail required to complete Schedule M–3, the traditional structure of Form 1120 is redundant for large entities. In this regard, page 1 of Form 1120 could be eliminated—taxable income could be computed using Schedule M–3 alone.

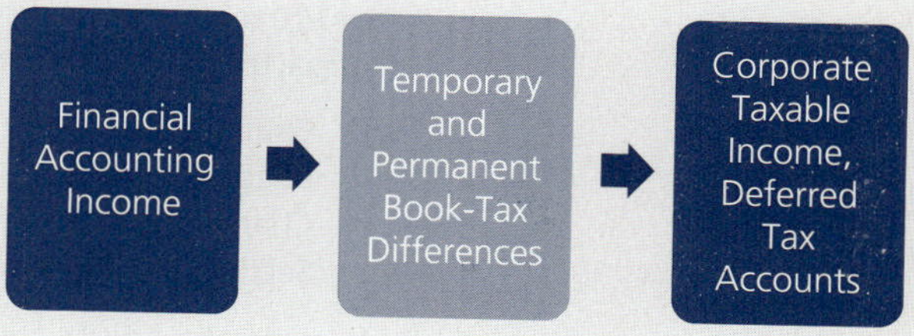

Part I—Financial Information and Net Income (Loss) Reconciliation

Part I requires the following financial information about the corporation.

- The source of the financial net income (loss) amount used in the reconciliation—SEC Form 10–K, audited financial statements, prepared financial statements, or the corporation's books and records.
- Any restatements of the corporation's income statement for the filing period, as well as any restatements for the past five filing periods.
- Any required adjustments to the net income (loss) amount referred to above (see Part I, lines 5 through 10).

The adjusted net income (loss) amount must be reconciled with the amount of taxable income reported on the corporation's Form 1120.

Because of Schedule M–3's complexity, the coverage in this chapter will be limited to some of the more important concepts underlying the schedule. A series of examples adapted from the instructions for Schedule M–3 will be used to illustrate these concepts.

EXAMPLE 42

Southwest Sportsman's Corporation (SSC) sells hunting and fishing equipment to sportsmen. SSC has several stores in Texas, New Mexico, and Arizona. It also has a subsidiary in Mexico, which is organized as a Mexican corporation. SSC, which does not file a Form 10–K with the SEC, reports income from its Mexican subsidiary on its audited financial statements, which show net income of $45 million in 2011. The Mexican corporation, which is not consolidated by SSC for tax purposes and is therefore not an includible corporation, had net income of $7 million. SSC must enter $7 million on Part I, line 5a of Schedule M–3, resulting in net income per income statement of includible corporations of $38 million. ■

A situation similar to that described in Example 42 could result in additional entries in Part I of Schedule M–3. For example, if SSC engaged in transactions with its nonincludible Mexican subsidiary, an entry would be required on line 8 (adjustment to eliminations of transactions between includible corporations and nonincludible entities).

Part II—Reconciliation of Net Income (Loss) per Income Statement of Includible Corporations with Taxable Income per Return

Part II reconciles income and loss items of includible corporations, while Part III reconciles expenses and deductions. As indicated in Example 42, corporations included in a financial reporting group may differ from corporations in a tax reporting group. Corporations may also be partners in a partnership, which is a flow-through entity. The following example illustrates the adjustments that are required in this situation.

EXAMPLE 43

Southwest Sportsman's Corporation also owns an interest in a U.S. partnership, Southwest Hunting Lodges (SHL). On its audited financial statements, SSC reported net income of $10 million as its distributive share from SHL. (See Chapter 21 for a complete discussion of partnership taxation.) SSC's Schedule K–1 from SHL reports the following amounts:

Ordinary income	$5,000,000
Long-term capital gain	7,000,000
Charitable contributions	4,000,000
Section 179 expense	100,000

In order to adjust for the flow-through items from the partnership, SSC must report these items on Schedule M–3, Part II, line 9 [Income (loss) from U.S. partnerships]. The corporation reports $10 million (book income) on line 9, column (a). SSC reports income per tax return of $7.9 million ($5,000,000 + $7,000,000 – $4,000,000 – $100,000) in column (d) of line 9, and a permanent difference of $2.1 million in column (c). ■

Part III—Reconciliation of Expense/Deduction Items

Part III lists 36 reconciling items relating to expenses and deductions. For these items, taxpayers must reconcile differences between income statement amounts (column a) and tax return amounts (column d), then classify these differences as temporary (column b) or permanent (column c) differences. The totals of the reconciling items from Part III are transferred to Part II, line 27, and are included with other items required to reconcile financial statement net income (loss) to tax return net income (loss).

EXAMPLE 44

Southwest Sportsman's Corporation acquired intellectual property in 2011 and deducted amortization of $20,000 on its financial statements, which were prepared according to GAAP. For Federal income tax purposes, SSC deducted $30,000. The corporation must report the amortization on line 28, Part III as follows: $20,000 book amortization in column (a), $10,000 temporary difference in column (b), and $30,000 tax return amortization in column (d). ■

EXAMPLE 45

In January 2011, Southwest Sportsman's Corporation established an allowance for uncollectible accounts (bad debt reserve) of $35,000 on its books and increased the allowance by $65,000 during the year. As a result of a client's bankruptcy, SSC decreased the allowance by $25,000 in November 2011. The corporation expensed the $100,000 of increases to the allowance on its 2011 income statement but was not allowed to deduct that amount on its tax return. On its 2011 tax return, the corporation was allowed to deduct the $25,000 actual loss sustained because of its client's bankruptcy. These amounts must be reported on line 32, Part III as follows: $100,000 book bad debt expense in column (a), $75,000 temporary difference in column (b), and $25,000 tax return bad debt expense in column (d). ■

Example 44 illustrates the Schedule M–3 reporting when book expenses are less than tax return deductions. Example 45 illustrates reporting procedures when book expenses are greater than tax return deductions. Both examples illustrate the reporting of temporary differences. The amounts from both examples are included in the totals derived in Part III and are carried to Part II, line 27. The reconciliation of book income and taxable income occurs in lines 26 through 30. The reconciled amount

FIGURE 17.2 Flow of Accounting Data

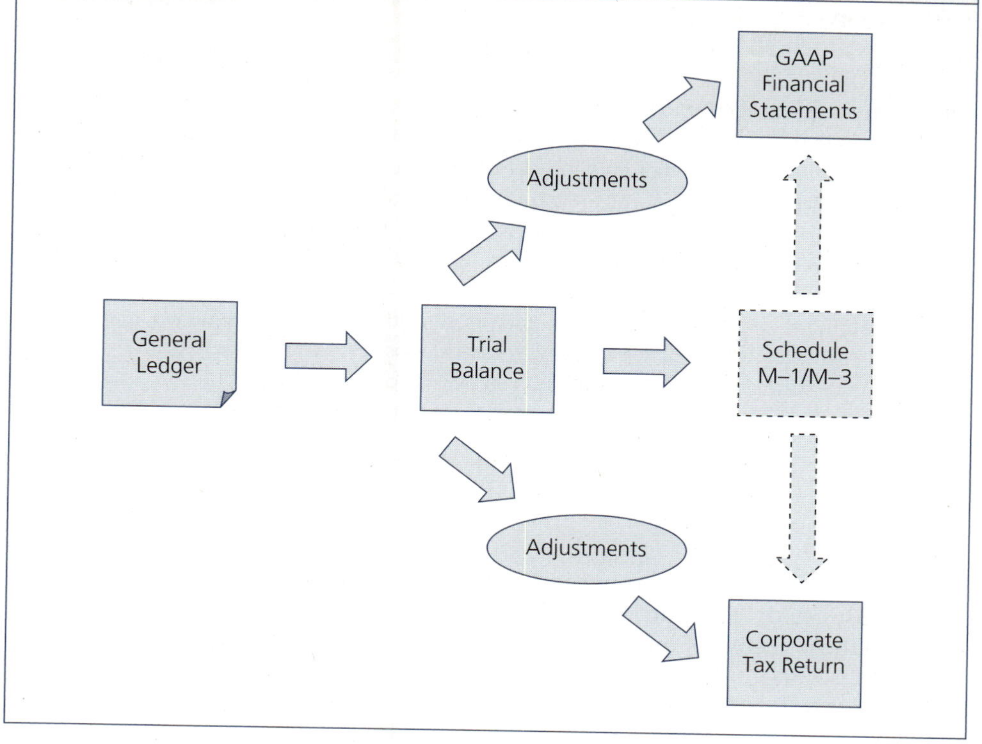

on Part II, line 30, column (a) must be equal to the net income per income statement of includible corporations on Part I, line 11. The reconciled amount on Part II, line 30, column (d) must be equal to the taxable income reported on Form 1120.

INCOME TAXES ON THE FINANCIAL STATEMENTS

LO.7

Understand the impact of tax return positions on financial statements.

A review of the Schedule M–1 (or Schedule M–3) adjustments to Form 1120 (see prior discussion) reveals considerable differences in the tax and financial accounting treatment of certain transactions. These differences can be *permanent* and appear on the tax return *or* the financial statements but not on both. Some examples of permanent differences include interest income on municipal bonds, the dividends received deduction, the domestic production activities deduction, and fines and penalties. Other differences are *temporary* and appear on both the tax return *and* the financial statements but in different periods. Here, the variation is due to timing as to when (or how much of) the transaction is taken into account. Some examples of temporary differences include depreciation, depletion, unearned income, reserves for bad debts and product warranties, NOLs, and excess capital losses and charitable contributions. See Figure 17.2.

Other differences between the information reported on the tax return and that reflected on the financial statements can arise in parent-subsidiary situations. For financial accounting purposes, a corporate group must consolidate all U.S. and foreign subsidiaries within a single financial statement when the parent corporation controls more than 50 percent of the voting power of those subsidiaries.[39] For Federal income tax purposes, however, a consolidated return includes only those *domestic* subsidiaries where the stock ownership is 80 percent or more, while foreign subsidiaries are not eligible for inclusion (refer to previous discussion).[40]

[39] *Consolidation*, ASC Topic 810 (formerly *Consolidation of All Majority Owned Subsidiaries*, Statement of Financial Accounting Standards No. 94). Certain adjustments are made to reduce book income for the after-tax income related to minority shareholders.

[40] §§ 1504(a) and (b).

TAX in the NEWS

A New Code?

Tax practitioners long have referred to the Internal Revenue Code simply as the "Code." Now there's a new code (or codification) to deal with—the long-awaited codification (or reorganization) of all the existing accounting standards. In June 2009, the Financial Accounting Standards Board (FASB) issued *The FASB Accounting Standards Codification and the Hierarchy of Generally Accepted Accounting Principles—a replacement of FASB Statement No. 162,* Statement of Financial Accounting Standards No. 168. The FASB Accounting Standards Codification (ASC) is now the major source of authoritative U.S. accounting and reporting standards (for other than certain nongovernmental entities). Guidance will continue to be issued by the Securities and Exchange Commission. This change is effective for financial statements for interim or annual periods ending on or after September 15, 2009.

The Accounting Standards Codification has made a major change in the way that the authoritative accounting literature is organized and referenced. Accounting for income tax guidance formerly referenced as SFAS 109, or APB 23, or FIN 48, is now combined in ASC Topic 740. Novices and experts alike will have much to learn as they use and cite the new code.

GAAP Principles

As pointed out earlier, a corporation's financial statements are prepared in accordance with GAAP. The purpose and objectives of these statements are quite different from the objective of the corporation's income tax return.

The **ASC 740 (SFAS 109)** approach produces a total income tax expense (also called the **income tax provision**) for the income currently reported on a corporation's combined financial statement.[41] This approach follows the matching principle, where all the expenses related to earning income are reported in the same period as the income without regard to when the expenses are actually paid.

EXAMPLE 46

PanCo, Inc., earns $100,000 in book income before tax. PanCo has a single temporary difference. Tax depreciation exceeds book depreciation by $20,000. Accordingly, PanCo's taxable income is $80,000 ($100,000 – $20,000 additional tax deduction). On its income tax return, PanCo reports total Federal tax expense of $28,000 ($80,000 × 35%). On its financial statement, PanCo reports a total tax expense of $35,000 ($100,000 × 35%). This $7,000 book-tax difference is the difference between the book and tax basis of the depreciable asset times the current corporate tax rate ($7,000 = $20,000 × 35%).

Although PanCo did not actually pay the $7,000 this year, in future years when the book-tax depreciation difference reverses, the $7,000 eventually is paid. Hence, the *future* income tax expense related to the current book income is reported in the current year. ■

The total book tax expense under ASC 740 (SFAS 109) is made up of both current and deferred components.[42] The **current tax expense** theoretically represents the taxes actually payable to (or refund receivable from) the governmental authorities for the current period. Although an oversimplification, think of this amount as the actual check the taxpayer writes to the government (or refund received) for the current year. Keep in mind, though, that the current portion of the book income tax expense rarely matches the taxpayer's actual tax liability. Numerous items may lead to differences between actual current tax payments and the reported current tax expense. Figure 17.3 summarizes the computation of a corporation's current tax expense.

The deferred component of the book tax expense is called the **deferred tax expense** or **deferred tax benefit**. This component represents the future tax cost (or savings) connected with income reported in the current-period financial statement. Deferred tax expense or benefit is created as a result of temporary differences. More

[41] *Income Taxes,* ASC Topic 740 (formerly *Accounting for Income Taxes,* Statement of Financial Accounting Standards No. 109).

[42] Corporations also may include a "cushion" in their provision for income tax expense, to account currently for potential tax costs in the future (e.g., deficiencies related to losing a potential IRS audit). See ASC 740-10 [formerly *FASB Interpretation 48 (FIN 48), Accounting for Uncertainty in Income Taxes—An Interpretation of FASB Statement No. 109,* Financial Accounting Standards Board].

FIGURE 17.3 **Current Tax Expense***

	Pretax book income
±	Schedule M–1/M–3 adjustments
	Taxable income before NOLs
–	NOL carryforwards
	Taxable income
×	Applicable tax rate
	Current tax expense (provision) before tax credits
–	Tax credits
	Current tax expense (tax provision)

*Simplified calculation.

technically, ASC 740 (SFAS 109) adopts a **balance sheet approach** to measuring deferred taxes. Under this approach, the deferred tax expense or benefit is the change from one year to the next in the net **deferred tax liability** or **deferred tax asset.**

A deferred tax liability is the expected future tax liability related to current income (measured using enacted tax rates and rules).[43] A deferred tax liability is created in the following situations.

- An expense is deductible for tax in the current period but is not deductible for book until some future period.
- Income is includible currently for book purposes but is not includible in taxable income until a future period.

In essence, a deferred tax liability is created when the book basis of an asset exceeds its tax basis (the opposite results in a deferred tax asset).

EXAMPLE 47

PJ Enterprises earns net income before depreciation of $500,000 in 2010 and $600,000 in 2011. PJ has a single depreciable asset acquired in 2010 for $80,000. For tax purposes PJ may deduct $60,000 in depreciation expense for the first year and $20,000 in depreciation expense for the second year (i.e., it uses an accelerated method). For book purposes, assume that PJ depreciates the asset on a straight-line basis over two years ($40,000 depreciation expense per year).

2010

	Book	Tax
Income before depreciation	$500,000	$500,000
Depreciation	(40,000)	(60,000)
Income after depreciation	$460,000	$440,000
Corporate tax rate	× 35%	× 35%
Income tax expense	$161,000	$154,000
Current tax expense	$154,000	
Deferred tax expense	$ 7,000	
Starting adjusted basis in depreciable asset	$ 80,000	$ 80,000
Ending adjusted basis in depreciable asset	(40,000)	(20,000)
Change in adjusted basis	$ 40,000	$ 60,000

Book-tax balance sheet difference	$20,000
Corporate tax rate	× 35%
Deferred tax liability	$ 7,000

[43] If the tax rate will be different in future years, the *enacted* future tax rate should be used in the computation.

In this example, it is easy to "back into" the deferred tax expense amount of $7,000 by simply taking the difference between the tax expense per the tax return ($154,000) and the book tax expense ($161,000). This is referred to as the "APB 11" approach based on the method used before ASC 740 (SFAS 109). This may provide a quick check on the calculation in simple cases, but will not always be correct. The correct computation of the deferred tax expense is based on the difference between the book and tax asset basis numbers ($20,000) at the enacted corporate tax rate (35%).

2011

	Book	Tax
Income before depreciation	$600,000	$600,000
Depreciation	(40,000)	(20,000)
Income after depreciation	$560,000	$580,000
Corporate tax rate	× 35%	× 35%
Income tax expense	$196,000	$203,000
Current tax expense	$203,000	
Deferred tax expense	($ 7,000)	
Starting adjusted basis in depreciable asset	$ 40,000	$ 20,000
Ending adjusted basis in depreciable asset	(–0–)	(–0–)
Change in adjusted basis	$ 40,000	$ 20,000
Book-tax balance sheet difference	($20,000)	
Corporate tax rate	× 35%	
Deferred tax liability	($ 7,000)	

In 2011, the book-tax difference in asset basis reverses, with a resulting reverse in the deferred tax liability account. ■

EXAMPLE 48

Continue with the facts in Example 47. The following journal entries record the book tax expense (provision) for each year. Notice that the book total tax expense combines the current amount (income tax payable) and the future amount (deferred tax liability).

2010 journal entry

Income tax expense (provision)	$161,000	
Income tax payable		$154,000
Deferred tax liability		7,000

2011 journal entry

Income tax expense (provision)	$196,000	
Deferred tax liability	7,000	
Income tax payable		$203,000

At the end of 2010, the balance sheet reflects a net deferred tax liability of $7,000. At the end of 2011, the balance sheet contains no deferred tax liability because the temporary difference that created the deferred tax liability has reversed itself. ■

In contrast to a deferred tax liability, a deferred tax asset is the expected future tax benefit related to current book income (measured using enacted tax rates and rules). A deferred tax asset is created in the following situations.

- An expense is deductible for book in the current period but is not deductible for tax until some future period.
- Income is includible in taxable income currently but is not includible in book income until a future period.

Deferred tax assets and liabilities are reported on the balance sheet just as any other asset or liability would be. However, the interpretation of these assets and liabilities is quite different. Typically, an asset is "good" because it represents a claim on something of value, and a liability is "bad" because it represents a future claim against the corporation's assets. In the case of deferred tax assets and liabilities, the interpretation is reversed. Deferred tax liabilities are "good" because they represent an amount that may be paid to the government in the future. In essence, deferred tax liabilities are like an interest-free loan from the government with a due date perhaps many years in the future. Deferred tax assets, on the other hand, are future tax benefits and thus are similar to a receivable from the government that may not be received until many years in the future.[44]

TAX PLANNING:

17.5 Corporate versus Noncorporate Forms of Business Organization

LO.8

Evaluate corporations as an entity form for conducting a business.

The decision to use the corporate form in conducting a trade or business must be weighed carefully. Besides the nontax considerations of the corporate form (limited liability, continuity of life, free transferability of interests, centralized management), tax ramifications will play an important role in any such decision. Close attention should be paid to the following:

1. Operating as a regular corporate entity (C corporation) results in the imposition of the corporate income tax. Corporate taxable income will be taxed twice—once as earned by the corporation and again when distributed to the shareholders. Since dividends are not deductible, a closely held corporation may have a strong incentive to structure corporate distributions in a deductible form. Before legislation in 2003 lowered the rate on qualified dividends to 15 percent, shareholders had a tax incentive to bail out profits in the form of salaries, interest, or rent.[45] With the 15 percent rate on qualified dividends, shareholders may save taxes by having the corporation pay dividends rather than salaries, rent, or interest, which could be taxed at an individual marginal rate as high as 35 percent. The decision should be made only after comparing the tax cost of the two alternatives. The window of opportunity for reaping the benefit of the preferential tax rate on dividend income is set to close by 2013, however, and this must be considered in the analysis.
2. The differences in Federal tax brackets between an individual and a corporation may not be substantial. Furthermore, several state and local governments impose higher taxes on corporations than on individuals. In these jurisdictions, the combined Federal, state, and local tax rates on the two types of taxpayers are practically identical. Consequently, the tax ramifications of incorporating can be determined *only* on a case-by-case basis.
3. Corporate-source income loses its identity as it passes through the corporation to the shareholders. Thus, preferential tax treatment of certain items by the corporation (e.g., interest on municipal bonds) does not carry over to the shareholders.
4. As noted in Chapter 19, it may be difficult for shareholders to recover some or all of their investment in the corporation without an ordinary income result. Most corporate distributions are treated as dividends to the extent of the corporation's earnings and profits. However, with the 15 percent rate on qualified dividends, dividends are taxed at the same rate as net capital gains.
5. Corporate losses cannot be passed through to the shareholders.[46]

[44] For a more complete discussion of the impact of taxes on the financial statements, see *South-Western Federal Taxation: Corporations, Partnerships, Estates & Trusts* (2012 edition), Chapter 14.

[45] Such procedures lead to a multitude of problems, one of which, the reclassification of debt as equity, is discussed in Chapter 18. The problems of unreasonable salaries and rents are covered in Chapter 19 in the discussion of constructive dividends.

[46] Points 1, 2, and 5 could be resolved by making a Subchapter S election (see Chapter 22), assuming the corporation qualifies for the election. In part, the same can be said for point 3.

6. The liquidation of a corporation will normally generate tax consequences to both the corporation and its shareholders (see Chapter 20).
7. The corporate form provides shareholders with the opportunity to be treated as employees for tax purposes if the shareholders render services to the corporation. Such status makes a number of attractive tax-sheltered fringe benefits available. They include, but are not limited to, group term life insurance and excludible meals and lodging. One of the most attractive benefits of incorporation is the ability of the business to provide accident and health insurance to its employees, including shareholder-employees. Such benefits are not included in the employee's gross income. Similar rules apply to other medical costs paid by the employer. These benefits are not available to partners, sole proprietors, and more-than-2 percent shareholder-employees of S corporations.

17.6 Operating the Corporation

Tax planning to reduce corporate income taxes should occur before the end of the tax year. Effective planning can cause income to be shifted to the next tax year and can produce large deductions by incurring expenses before year-end. Particular attention should be focused on the following.

CHARITABLE CONTRIBUTIONS

Recall that accrual basis corporations may claim a deduction for charitable contributions in the year preceding payment. The contribution must be authorized by the board of directors by the end of the tax year and paid on or before the fifteenth day of the third month of the following year. It might be useful to authorize a contribution even though it may not ultimately be made. A deduction cannot be thrown back to the previous year (even if paid within the two and a half months) if it has not been authorized.

The enhanced deduction amount for contributions of qualified inventory can produce significant tax savings. Gifts of inventory should be designed to take advantage of this provision whenever feasible. Effort should be taken to properly document the type of inventory donated and each recipient charitable organization, as the statutory provisions that allow for an enhanced deduction have very specific requirements for qualification. Further, a corporation's cost of goods sold must be reduced to reflect any charitable contribution of inventory.

TIMING OF CAPITAL GAINS AND LOSSES

A corporation should consider offsetting profits on the sale of capital assets by selling some of the depreciated securities in the corporate portfolio. In addition, any already realized capital losses should be carefully monitored. Recall that corporate taxpayers are not permitted to claim any net capital losses as deductions against ordinary income. Capital losses can be used only as an offset against capital gains. Further, net capital losses can only be carried back three years and forward five. Gains from the sales of capital assets should be timed to offset any capital losses. The expiration of the carryover period for any net capital losses should be watched carefully so that sales of appreciated capital assets occur before that date.

NET OPERATING LOSSES

In some situations, electing to forgo an NOL carryback and utilizing the carryforward option may generate greater tax savings. When deciding whether to forgo the carryback option, several factors should be considered. First, the present value of the tax refund that is lost by not using the carryback procedure should be calculated.

CONCEPT SUMMARY 17.1

Income Taxation of Individuals and Corporations Compared

	Individuals	Corporations
Computation of gross income	§ 61.	§ 61.
Computation of taxable income	§ 62 and §§ 63(b) through (h).	§ 63(a). Concept of AGI has no relevance.
Deductions	Trade or business (§ 162); nonbusiness (§ 212); some personal and employee expenses (generally deductible as itemized deductions).	Trade or business (§ 162).
Charitable contributions	Limited in any tax year to 50% of AGI; 30% for capital gain property unless election is made to reduce fair market value of gift.	Limited in any tax year to 10% of taxable income computed without regard to the charitable contribution deduction, NOL carryback, capital loss carryback, dividends received deduction, and domestic production activities deduction.
	Excess charitable contributions carried over for five years.	Same as for individuals.
	Amount of contribution is the fair market value of capital gain property; ordinary income property is limited to adjusted basis; capital gain property is treated as ordinary income property if certain tangible personalty is donated to a nonuse charity or a private nonoperating foundation is the donee.	Same as for individuals, but exceptions allowed for certain inventory and for scientific property where one-half of the appreciation also is allowed as a deduction.
	Time of deduction is the year in which payment is made.	Time of deduction is the year in which payment is made unless accrual basis taxpayer. Accrual basis corporation can take deduction in year preceding payment if contribution was authorized by board of directors by end of year and contribution is paid by fifteenth day of third month of following year.
Casualty losses	$100 floor on personal casualty and theft losses; personal casualty losses deductible only to extent losses exceed 10% of AGI.	Deductible in full.
Net operating loss	Adjusted for several items, including nonbusiness deductions over nonbusiness income and personal exemptions.	Generally no adjustments.
	Generally, carryback period is 2 years and carryforward period is 20 years.	Same as for individuals.
Dividends received deduction	None.	70%, 80%, or 100% of dividends received depending on percentage of ownership by corporate shareholder.
Net capital gains	Taxed in full. Tax rate generally cannot exceed 15% on net long-term capital gains.	Taxed in full.
Capital losses	Only $3,000 of capital loss per year can offset ordinary income; unused loss is carried forward indefinitely to offset capital gains or ordinary income up to $3,000; short-term and long-term carryovers retain their character.	Can offset only capital gains; unused loss is carried back three years and forward five; carryovers and carrybacks are characterized as short-term losses.

Income Taxation of Individuals and Corporations Compared—Continued

	Individuals	Corporations
Passive losses	In general, passive losses cannot offset either active income or portfolio income.	Passive loss rules apply to closely held C corporations and personal service corporations. For personal service corporations, passive losses cannot offset either active income or portfolio income. For closely held C corporations, passive losses may offset active income but not portfolio income.
Domestic production activities deduction	Based on 9% of the lesser of qualified production activities income (QPAI) *or* modified AGI or alternative minimum taxable income.	Based on 9% of the lesser of qualified production activities income (QPAI) *or* taxable income or alternative minimum taxable income.
Tax rates	Progressive with six rates (10%, 15%, 25%, 28%, 33%, 35%).	Progressive with four rates (15%, 25%, 34%, 35%). Two lowest brackets phased out between \$100,000 and \$335,000 of taxable income, and additional tax imposed between \$15,000,000 and \$18,333,333 of taxable income.
Alternative minimum tax	Applied at a graduated rate schedule of 26% and 28%. Exemption allowed depending on filing status (e.g., \$74,450 for married filing jointly in 2011); phaseout begins when AMTI reaches a certain amount (e.g., \$150,000 for married filing jointly).	Applied at a 20% rate on AMTI less exemption; \$40,000 exemption allowed but phaseout begins when AMTI reaches \$150,000; adjustments and tax preference items are similar to those applicable to individuals, but also include 75% adjusted current earnings adjustment. Small corporations (gross receipts of \$5 million or less) are not subject to AMT.

Second, the election to forgo an NOL carryback is irrevocable. Thus, one cannot later choose to change if the predicted high profits do not materialize. Third, consider the future increases (or decreases) in corporate income tax rates that can reasonably be anticipated. This last consideration is the most difficult to work with. Although corporate tax rates have remained relatively stable in recent years, taxpayers have little assurance that future rates will remain constant.

DIVIDENDS RECEIVED DEDUCTION

In those cases where the taxable income limitation is applicable to a corporation's dividends received deduction, consideration should be given to the proper timing of income and deductions so as to bring the NOL rule into play. The NOL rule, the exception to the taxable income limitation, can result in a significant increase in the amount of a corporation's dividends received deduction.

EXAMPLE 49

Pearl Corporation, a calendar year C corporation, has the following information for the year:

Gross income from operations	\$ 200,000
Expenses from operations	(225,000)
Dividends received from domestic corporations (less than 20% ownership)	100,000
Taxable income before dividends received deduction	\$ 75,000

Pearl's dividends received deduction is $52,500 [70% × $75,000 (taxable income limitation)]. If, however, Pearl incurs additional expenses of $5,001 (or defers $5,001 of income), then the NOL rule applies, and Pearl's dividends received deduction is $70,000 [70% × $100,000 (dividends received)]. ■

ORGANIZATIONAL EXPENDITURES

To qualify for the 180-month amortization procedure of § 248, only organizational expenditures incurred in the first tax year of the corporation can be considered. This rule could prove to be an unfortunate trap for corporations formed late in the year.

EXAMPLE 50

Thrush Corporation is formed in December 2011. Qualified organizational expenditures are incurred as follows: $62,000 in December 2011 and $30,000 in January 2012. If Thrush uses the calendar year for tax purposes, only $62,000 of the organizational expenditures can be written off over a period of 180 months. ■

The solution to the problem posed by Example 50 is for Thrush Corporation to adopt a fiscal year that ends at or beyond January 31. All organizational expenditures will then have been incurred before the close of the first tax year.

SHAREHOLDER-EMPLOYEE PAYMENT OF CORPORATE EXPENSES

In a closely held corporate setting, shareholder-employees often pay corporate expenses (e.g., travel and entertainment) for which they are not reimbursed by the corporation. The IRS often disallows the deduction of these expenses by the shareholder-employee since the payments are voluntary on his or her part. If the deduction is more beneficial at the shareholder-employee level, a corporate policy against reimbursement of such expenses should be established. Proper planning in this regard would be to decide before the beginning of each tax year where the deduction would do the most good. Corporate policy on reimbursement of such expenses could be modified on a year-to-year basis depending upon the circumstances.

In deciding whether corporate expenses should be kept at the corporate level or shifted to the shareholder-employee, the treatment of unreimbursed employee expenses must be considered. First, since employee expenses are itemized deductions, they will be of no benefit to the taxpayer who chooses the standard deduction option. Second, these expenses will be subject to the 2 percent-of-AGI floor. No such limitation will be imposed if the corporation claims the expenses.

17.7 Affiliated versus Controlled Group

The tax effects brought about by electing to file on a consolidated basis include all of the benefit-sharing effects of controlled group membership. In addition, membership in a consolidated group leads to a much more complex set of controlling tax rules.

EXAMPLE 51

ParentCo owns all of the stock of SubCo, and TopCo owns all of the stock of BottomCo. Both pairs of corporations constitute affiliated groups, as well as controlled groups. ParentCo and SubCo elect to file Federal income tax returns on a consolidated basis. TopCo and BottomCo do not so elect. Consequently, they file separate Federal income tax returns.

Both groups share the lower tax rates on the first $75,000 of combined taxable income—ParentCo and SubCo because they file a combined tax return, and TopCo and BottomCo because of the controlled group rules. Neither group can deduct a loss realized on an intercompany sale. But accounting for the taxable income of the consolidated group is much more complex. ■

REFOCUS ON THE BIG PICTURE

COOKED TO PERFECTION

Conducting Skylark Bakery as a corporation would save Samantha $10,375 in income taxes annually, computed as follows:

Bakery Operated as Sole Proprietorship	
Operating profit of $100,000:	
Tax on $100,000 @ 35%	$35,000
Dividends of $5,000:	
Tax on $5,000 @ 15%	750
Withdrawals of $50,000:	
No tax	–0–
Total income tax when operated as sole proprietorship	$35,750

Bakery Operated as Regular Corporation	
Corporate taxable income of $51,500*:	
Tax on $50,000 @ 15%	$ 7,500
Tax on $1,500 @ 25%	375
Total corporate income tax	$ 7,875
Samantha's salary of $50,000:	
Tax on $50,000 @ 35%	17,500
Total income tax when operated as C corporation	$25,375
*Computation of corporate taxable income:	
Operating profit	$100,000
Dividend income	5,000
Less: Salary to Samantha	(50,000)
Dividends received deduction (70%)	(3,500)
Taxable income	$ 51,500

The example illustrates the tax savings available when a high-income individual taxpayer takes advantage of the lower marginal tax rates of corporations. However, other issues, such as employment tax considerations and the planned expiration of the preferential tax rate on dividend income, also should be considered. Further, other potential entity options, such as the LLC and S corporation, also should be evaluated.

What If?

What if the bakery in the first year it becomes a corporation generates a $10,000 short-term capital loss (STCL) on the disposition of some of its stock investments? Regular corporations can only deduct capital losses against capital gains; thus, the $10,000 STCL would not be deductible currently by the corporation and, instead, would be carried forward for up to five years. If the bakery is operated as a sole proprietorship, Samantha would report the capital loss on her individual return. She could use the $10,000 STCL to offset any capital gains she may have, and deduct up to $3,000 of the loss against ordinary income.

KEY TERMS

Affiliated group, 17–25
ASC 740 (SFAS 109), 17-34
Balance sheet approach, 17–35
C corporations, 17–3
Check-the-box Regulations, 17–8
Controlled group, 17–23
Current tax expense, 7-34
Deferred tax asset, 17–35
Deferred tax benefit, 17–34
Deferred tax expense, 17–34
Deferred tax liability, 17–35
Dividends received deduction, 17–17
Domestic production activities deduction (DPAD), 17–16
Generally accepted accounting principles (GAAP), 17–29
Income tax provision, 17–34
Limited liability company (LLC), 17–7
Limited partnerships, 17–7
Organizational expenditures, 17–19
Parent-subsidiary controlled group, 17–24
Passive loss, 17–13
Personal service corporations (PSCs), 17–10
Regular corporations, 17–3
Related corporations, 17–23
S corporations, 17–3
Schedule M–1, 17–29
Schedule M–3, 17–30

DISCUSSION QUESTIONS

1. **LO.1** Jennifer and Jamie are starting a business and have asked you for advice about whether they should form a partnership, a corporation, or some other type of entity. Prepare a list of questions you would ask in helping them decide which type of entity they should choose. Explain your reasons for asking each of the questions.

2. **LO.1** Dwayne owns 50% of the stock of Tangerine Corporation (a C corporation) and 50% of the stock of Heron Corporation (an S corporation), each of which incurs an operating loss of $80,000 during 2011. Neither corporation pays any dividends during the year. Discuss Dwayne's tax consequences.

3. **LO.1, 8** Art, an executive with Azure Corporation, plans to start a part-time business selling products on the Internet. He will devote about 15 hours each week to running the business. Art's salary from Azure places him in the 35% tax bracket. He projects substantial losses from the new business in each of the first three years and expects sizable profits thereafter. Art plans to leave the profits in the business for several years, sell the business, and retire. Would you advise Art to incorporate the business or operate it as a sole proprietorship?

DECISION MAKING

4. **LO.1, 2** In 2011, Plover Corporation, a C corporation with four equal shareholders, had an operating loss of $80,000 and a long-term capital gain of $20,000. Also in 2011, Vireo Partnership, with four equal partners, had an operating loss of $80,000 and a long-term capital gain of $20,000. Plover did not pay any dividends, and Vireo's partners did not make any withdrawals. Contrast the tax treatment of the entities and their owners.

5. **LO.1, 2** Samantha is the sole owner of Blue Company. In 2011, Blue had operating income of $200,000, a short-term capital loss of $10,000, and tax-exempt interest income of $3,000. Samantha withdrew $50,000 of profit from Blue. How should Samantha report this information on her individual tax return for 2011 if Blue Company is:
   a. An LLC?
   b. An S corporation?
   c. A C corporation?

6. **LO.1, 8** Shareholders of closely held corporations frequently engage in dealings with such corporations. These dealings provide an opportunity to extract earnings out of a corporate entity in some form other than a nondeductible dividend distribution. Provide several examples of shareholder-corporation transactions and, for each example, briefly note the requirement that would need to be satisfied to avoid recharacterization by the IRS as a disguised dividend distribution.

ISSUE ID

7. **LO.1** Contrast the marginal tax rates of C corporations with those of individuals.

8. **LO.1** In the current year, Shauna formed a single-member LLC and did not file Form 8832 (Entity Classification Election). As a result, the LLC will be treated as a corporation for Federal tax purposes. Assess the validity of this statement.

9. **LO.2** In 2011, Jeanette, an individual in the 35% marginal tax bracket, recognized a $50,000 long-term capital gain. Also in 2011, Parrot Corporation, a C corporation in the 35% marginal tax bracket, recognized a $50,000 long-term capital gain. Neither taxpayer had any other property transactions in the year. What tax rates are applicable to these capital gains?

10. **LO.2** John (a sole proprietor) and Eagle Corporation (a C corporation) each recognize a short-term capital gain of $6,000 and a long-term capital loss of $8,000 on the sale of capital assets. Neither taxpayer had any other property transactions during the year. Describe the tax consequences of these gains and losses for John and for Eagle.

11. **LO.2** In the current year, Erica recognized a gain on the sale of a warehouse that she had used in her sole proprietorship. Erica had purchased the warehouse in 2002, and straight-line depreciation was properly claimed with respect to the realty. Also in the current year, Brown Corporation, a C corporation, recognized a gain on the sale of a warehouse that it had used in its business. Brown had purchased the warehouse in 2002, and straight-line depreciation was properly claimed with respect to the realty. The gains recognized by Erica and by Brown Corporation are treated entirely as § 1231 gains. Assess the validity of this statement.

12. **LO.2** Osprey Corporation, a closely held corporation, has $75,000 of active income, $25,000 of portfolio income, and a $60,000 loss from a passive activity.
    a. How much of the passive loss can Osprey deduct in the current year if it is a PSC?
    b. If it is not a PSC?

13. **LO.2** On December 20, 2011, the directors of Partridge Corporation, an accrual basis calendar year taxpayer, authorized a cash contribution of $25,000 to the American Cancer Association. The payment is made on February 14, 2012. Can Partridge deduct the charitable contribution in 2011?

14. **LO.2** Describe the rules regarding a charitable deduction for a contribution of inventory by a corporate taxpayer. (Ignore the taxable income limitation.)

ISSUE ID

15. **LO.2, 8** The board of directors of Orange Corporation, a calendar year taxpayer, is holding its year-end meeting on December 28, 2011. One topic on the board's agenda is the approval of a $25,000 gift to a qualified charitable organization. Orange has a $20,000 charitable contribution carryover to 2011 from a prior year. Identify the tax issues the board should consider regarding the proposed contribution.

ISSUE ID

16. **LO.2, 3, 8** Gold Corporation, a calendar year C corporation, was formed in 2005 and has been profitable until the current year. In 2011, Gold incurs a net operating loss. Identify the issues Gold Corporation should consider regarding its NOL carryback and carryover options.

17. **LO.1, 3** Marmot Corporation pays a dividend of $400,000 in 2011. Otter Corporation, which is in the 35% marginal bracket, owns 25% of Marmot's stock. Gerald, an individual taxpayer in the 35% marginal bracket, also owns 25% of Marmot's stock. Compare and contrast the treatment of the dividend by Otter Corporation and Gerald.

18. **LO.3** Determine whether the following expenditures by Cuckoo Corporation are organizational expenditures, startup expenditures, or neither.
    a. Legal expenses incurred for drafting the corporate charter and bylaws.
    b. Expenses incurred in printing stock certificates.
    c. Expenses of temporary board of directors' organizational meetings.
    d. Employee salaries incurred during the training period before opening for business.
    e. State incorporation fee.

19. **LO.6** When are C corporations required to make estimated tax payments? How are these payments calculated?

20. **LO.6** Schedule M–1 of Form 1120 is used to reconcile financial accounting net income with taxable income reported on the corporation's income tax return as follows: net income per books + additions – subtractions = taxable income. Classify the following items as additions or subtractions in the Schedule M–1 reconciliation.
    a. Nondeductible portion of meals and entertainment.
    b. Tax depreciation in excess of book depreciation.
    c. Federal income tax per books.
    d. Capital loss in excess of capital gain.
    e. Charitable contributions in excess of taxable income limitation.
    f. Tax-exempt interest income.
    g. Domestic production activities deduction.

21. **LO.6** In 2011, Woodpecker, Inc., a C corporation with $13.5 million in assets, deducted amortization of $40,000 on its financial statements and $55,000 on its Federal tax return. Is Woodpecker required to file Schedule M–3? If so, how is the difference in amortization amounts treated on that schedule?

22. **LO.7** Marcellus Jackson, the CFO of Mac, Inc., notices that the tax liability reported on Mac's tax return is less than the tax expense reported on Mac's financial statements. Provide a letter to Jackson outlining why these two tax expense numbers differ. Mac's address is 482 Linden Road, Paris, KY 40362. **COMMUNICATIONS**

23. **LO.7** Cramer, a stock analyst, wants to understand how the income tax expense reported in financial statements will affect stock prices. Briefly describe the objective of ASC 740 (SFAS 109) with regard to reporting income tax expense.

PROBLEMS

24. **LO.1** In 2011, Osprey Company had operating income of $320,000, operating expenses of $270,000, and a long-term capital gain of $20,000. How does Juanita, the sole owner of Osprey Company, report this information on her individual tax return under the following assumptions?
    a. Osprey Company is a proprietorship, and Juanita did not make any withdrawals from the business during the year.
    b. Osprey Company is a C corporation and pays no dividends during the year.

25. **LO.1** Ellie and Linda are equal owners in Otter Enterprises, a calendar year business. During the year, Otter Enterprises has $320,000 of gross income and $210,000 of operating expenses. In addition, Otter has a short-term capital loss of $15,000 and makes distributions to Ellie and Linda of $25,000 each. Discuss the impact of this information on the taxable income of Otter, Ellie, and Linda if Otter is:
    a. A partnership.
    b. An S corporation.
    c. A C corporation.

26. **LO.1, 2** In the current year, Azure Company has $500,000 of net operating income before deducting any compensation or other payment to its sole owner, Sasha. In addition, Azure has a long-term capital gain of $50,000. Sasha has significant income from other sources and is in the 35% marginal tax bracket. Based on this information, determine the income tax consequences to Azure Company and to Sasha during the year for each of the following independent situations.
    a. Azure is a C corporation and pays no dividends or salary to Sasha.
    b. Azure is a C corporation and distributes $100,000 of dividends to Sasha.
    c. Azure is a C corporation and pays $100,000 of salary to Sasha.
    d. Azure is a sole proprietorship and Sasha withdraws $0.
    e. Azure is a sole proprietorship and Sasha withdraws $100,000.

27. **LO.2** In 2011, Wilson Enterprises, a calendar year taxpayer, suffers a casualty loss of $60,000. How much of the casualty loss will be deductible by Wilson under the following circumstances?
    a. Wilson is an individual proprietor and has AGI of $150,000. The casualty loss was a personal loss, and the insurance recovered was $40,000.
    b. Wilson is a corporation, and the insurance recovered was $40,000.

28. **LO.1, 4, 8** Benton Company (BC) has one owner, who is in the 35% Federal income tax bracket. BC's gross income is $295,000, and its ordinary trade or business deductions are $135,000. Compute the tax liability on BC's income for 2011 under the following assumptions: **DECISION MAKING** **COMMUNICATIONS**
    a. BC is operated as a proprietorship, and the owner withdraws $70,000 for personal use.
    b. BC is operated as a corporation, pays out $70,000 as salary, and pays no dividends to its shareholder.
    c. BC is operated as a corporation and pays out no salary or dividends to its shareholder.
    d. BC is operated as a corporation, pays out $70,000 as salary to its shareholder, and pays out the remainder of its earnings as dividends.

e. Assume Robert Benton of 1121 Monroe Street, Ironton, OH 45638 is the owner of BC, which was operated as a proprietorship in 2011. Robert is thinking about incorporating the business in 2012 and asks your advice. He expects about the same amounts of income and expenses in 2012 and plans to take $70,000 per year out of the company whether he incorporates or not. Write a letter to Robert [based on your analysis in (a) and (b) above] containing your recommendations.

29. **LO.2** In the current year, Sandpiper Corporation (a C corporation) had operating income of $215,000 and operating expenses of $155,000. In addition, Sandpiper had a long-term capital gain of $12,000 and a short-term capital loss of $27,000.
   a. Compute Sandpiper's taxable income and tax for the year.
   b. Assume the same facts except that Sandpiper's long-term capital gain was $35,000. Compute Sandpiper's taxable income and tax for the year.

30. **LO.2** In 2011, Bronze Company had operating profit of $75,000 ($125,000 operating income – $50,000 operating expenses). In addition, Bronze had a short-term capital gain of $16,000 and a long-term capital loss of $31,000. How much of the long-term capital loss may be deducted in 2011, and how much is carried back or forward under the following circumstances?
   a. Bronze Company is a proprietorship owned by Kenneth, and he had no other property transactions in 2011.
   b. Bronze Company is a C corporation.

31. **LO.2** During 2011, Gorilla Corporation has net short-term capital gains of $70,000, net long-term capital losses of $195,000, and taxable income from other sources of $620,000. Prior years' transactions included the following:

2007 net short-term capital gains	$30,000
2008 net long-term capital gains	55,000
2009 net short-term capital gains	15,000
2010 net long-term capital gains	40,000

   a. How are the capital gains and losses treated on Gorilla's 2011 tax return?
   b. Determine the amount of the 2011 capital loss that is carried back to each of the previous years.
   c. Compute the amount of capital loss carryover, if any, and indicate the years to which the loss may be carried.
   d. If Gorilla is a sole proprietorship, rather than a corporation, how would the owner report these transactions on her 2011 tax return?

32. **LO.2** Heron Company purchases commercial realty on November 13, 1998, for $650,000. Straight-line depreciation of $204,167 is claimed before the property is sold on February 22, 2011, for $920,000. What are the tax consequences of the sale of realty if Heron is:
   a. A C corporation?
   b. A sole proprietorship?

33. **LO.2** In 2011, Condor Corporation, a closely held C corporation that is not a PSC, has $225,000 of active business income, $35,000 of portfolio income, and a $300,000 passive loss from a rental activity. How much of the passive loss can Condor deduct in 2011? Would your answer differ if Condor were a PSC?

DECISION MAKING

COMMUNICATIONS

34. **LO.2, 8** Joseph Thompson is president and sole shareholder of Jay Corporation. In December 2011, Joe asks your advice regarding a charitable contribution he plans to have the corporation make to the University of Maine, a qualified public charity. Joe is considering the following alternatives as charitable contributions in December 2011:

	Fair Market Value
(1) Cash donation	$200,000
(2) Unimproved land held for six years ($310,000 basis)	200,000
(3) Maize Corporation stock held for eight years ($120,000 basis)	200,000
(4) Brown Corporation stock held for nine months ($70,000 basis)	200,000

Joe has asked you to help him decide which of these potential contributions will be most advantageous taxwise. Jay's taxable income is $3.5 million before considering the contribution. Rank the four alternatives and write a letter to Joe communicating your advice. The corporation's address is 1442 Main Street, Freeport, ME 04032.

35. **LO.2, 8** In 2011, Gray Corporation, a calendar year C corporation, has a $75,000 charitable contribution carryover from a gift made in 2006. Gray is contemplating a gift of land to a qualified charity in either 2011 or 2012. Gray purchased the land as an investment five years ago for $100,000 (current fair market value is $250,000). Before considering any charitable deduction, Gray projects taxable income of $1 million for 2011 and $1.2 million for 2012. Should Gray make the gift of the land to charity in 2011 or in 2012? Provide support for your answer. **DECISION MAKING**

36. **LO.2, 8** Dan Simms is the president and sole shareholder of Simms Corporation, 1121 Madison Street, Seattle, WA 98121. Dan plans for the corporation to make a charitable contribution to the University of Washington, a qualified public charity. He will have the corporation donate Jaybird Corporation stock, held for five years, with a basis of $11,000 and a fair market value of $25,000. Dan projects a $310,000 net profit for Simms Corporation in 2011 and a $100,000 net profit in 2012. Dan calls you on December 13, 2011, and asks whether he should make the contribution in 2011 or 2012. Write a letter advising Dan about the timing of the contribution. **DECISION MAKING** **COMMUNICATIONS**

37. **LO.2** Flamingo Corporation, a calendar year C corporation, manufactures appliances in the United States. For 2011, Flamingo has taxable income [before the domestic productions activity deduction (DPAD)] of $850,000, qualified production activities income (QPAI) of $740,000, and W–2 wages attributable to QPAI of $150,000.
    a. How much is Flamingo's DPAD for 2011? 666000
    b. Assume, instead, that W–2 wages attributable to QPAI are $120,000. How much is Flamingo's DPAD for 2011? 60000

38. **LO.2, 7** During the year, Ruby Corporation, a calendar year taxpayer, has the following transactions:

Income from operations	$300,000
Expenses from operations	375,000
Dividends (less than 20% ownership)	150,000

    a. Determine Ruby's NOL for the year.
    b. What are Ruby's options as to the carryover of the NOL?

39. **LO.3** In each of the following independent situations, determine the dividends received deduction. Assume that none of the corporate shareholders owns 20% or more of the stock in the corporations paying the dividends.

	Green Corporation	Orange Corporation	Yellow Corporation
Income from operations	$ 700,000	$ 700,000	$ 700,000
Expenses from operations	(650,000)	(750,000)	(850,000)
Qualifying dividends	200,000	200,000	200,000

40. **LO.3** Gull Corporation, a cash method, calendar year C corporation, was formed and began business on July 1, 2011. Gull incurred the following expenses during its first year of operations (July 1, 2011–December 31, 2011):

Expenses of temporary directors and organizational meetings	$17,000
Fee paid to state of incorporation	2,500
Expenses for printing and sale of stock certificates	8,000
Legal services for drafting the corporate charter and bylaws (not paid until January 2012)	25,000

    a. Assuming that Gull Corporation elects under § 248 to expense and amortize organizational expenditures, what amount may be deducted in 2011?
    b. Assume the same facts as above, except that the amount paid for the legal services was $35,000 (instead of $25,000). What amount may be deducted as organizational expenditures in 2011?

41. **LO.3** Egret Corporation, a calendar year C corporation, was formed on June 7, 2011, and opened for business on September 1, 2011. After its formation but prior to opening for business, Egret incurred the following expenditures:

Accounting	$ 4,000
Advertising	9,500
Employee payroll	12,000
Rent	9,000
Utilities	2,000

What is the maximum amount of these expenditures that Egret can deduct in 2011?

42. **LO.4** In each of the following *independent* situations, determine the corporation's income tax liability. Assume that all corporations use a calendar year for tax purposes and that the tax year involved is 2011.

	Taxable Income
Purple Corporation	$ 45,000
Azul Corporation	310,000
Pink Corporation	2,350,000
Turquoise Corporation	21,000,000
Teal Corporation (a personal service corporation)	80,000

43. **LO.5** Red Corporation and White Corporation, both calendar year C corporations, are members of a controlled group of corporations. For 2011, Red has taxable income of $80,000, and White has taxable income of $150,000. Assuming the controlled group does not make an election regarding the apportionment of the marginal tax brackets, what is the income tax liability for each of the corporations?

44. **LO.5** Apply the controlled and affiliated group rules to determine whether a parent-subsidiary controlled group or an affiliated group exists in each of the following independent situations. Circle Y for yes and N for no.

	Situation	Parent-Subsidiary Controlled Group?	Affiliated Group?
a.	Throughout the year, Parent owns 65% of the stock of SubCo.	Y N	Y N
b.	Parent owns 70% of SubCo. The other 30% of SubCo stock is owned by Senior, a wholly owned subsidiary of Parent.	Y N	Y N
c.	For 11 months, Parent owns 75% of the stock of SubCo. For the last month of the tax year, Parent owns 100% of the SubCo stock.	Y N	Y N

45. **LO.6** The following information for 2011 relates to Sparrow Corporation, a calendar year, accrual method taxpayer.

Net income per books (after-tax)	$119,738
Federal income tax expense per books	49,862
Tax-exempt interest income	7,500
MACRS depreciation in excess of straight-line depreciation used for financial statement purposes	10,000
Charitable contribution in excess of taxable income limitation	8,750
Premiums paid on life insurance policy on the president (Sparrow is beneficiary of policy)	6,250
Interest on loan to purchase tax-exempt bonds	3,700

Based on the above information, use Schedule M–1 of Form 1120, which is available on the IRS website, to determine Sparrow's taxable income for 2011.

46. **LO.6** Swan Corporation, a calendar year C corporation, had the following information for 2011:

Net income per books (after-tax)	$174,700
Taxable income	195,000
Federal income tax per books	59,300
Cash dividend distributions	35,000
Unappropriated retained earnings, as of January 1, 2011	636,450

Based on the above, use Schedule M–2 of Form 1120 (see Example 41 in the text) to determine Swan's unappropriated retained earnings balance as of December 31, 2011.

47. **LO.6** In the current year, Pelican, Inc., incurs $10,000 of meals and entertainment expenses that it deducts in computing net income per the corporation's financial statements. All of the meals and entertainment expenditures are subject to the 50% cutback rule applicable to such expenditures. How is this information reported on Schedule M–3?

48. **LO.6** In January 2011, Pelican, Inc., established an allowance for uncollectible accounts (bad debt reserve) of $110,000 on its books and increased the allowance by $160,000 during the year. As a result of a client's bankruptcy, Pelican, Inc., decreased the allowance by $90,000 in November 2011. Pelican, Inc., expensed the $270,000 of increases to the allowance on its 2011 income statement but was not allowed to deduct that amount on its tax return. On its 2011 tax return, the corporation was allowed to deduct the $90,000 actual loss sustained because of its client's bankruptcy. On its financial statements, Pelican, Inc., treated the $270,000 increase in the bad debt reserve as an expense that gave rise to a temporary difference. On its 2011 tax return, Pelican, Inc., took a $90,000 deduction for bad debt expense. How is this information reported on Schedule M–3?

49. **LO.7** Skipper, Inc., earns pretax book net income of $500,000 in 2011. Skipper acquires a depreciable asset in 2011, and first-year tax depreciation exceeds book depreciation by $80,000. Skipper has no other temporary or permanent differences. Assuming the U.S. tax rate is 35%, compute Skipper's total income tax expense, current income tax expense, and deferred income tax expense.

50. **LO.7** Using the facts of Problem 49, determine the 2011 end-of-year balance in Skipper's deferred tax asset and deferred tax liability balance sheet accounts.

See Appendix E for Comprehensive Tax Return Problem—Form 1120

RESEARCH PROBLEMS

Note: Solutions to Research Problems can be prepared by using the **Checkpoint® Student Edition** online research product, which is available to accompany this text. It is also possible to prepare solutions to the Research Problems by using tax research materials found in a standard tax library.

THOMSON REUTERS
Checkpoint® Student Edition

COMMUNICATIONS

Research Problem 1. Tern Corporation, a calendar year C corporation, is solely owned by Jessica Ramirez. Tern's only business since its incorporation in 2008 has been land surveying services. In Tern's state of incorporation, land surveying can be performed only by a licensed surveyor. Jessica, Tern's only employee, is a licensed surveyor but is not a licensed engineer. Upon audit of Tern's 2008 and 2009 tax returns, the IRS assessed tax deficiencies stemming from its conclusion that the corporation was a personal service corporation subject to the flat tax rate of 35%. Jessica believes that the IRS's determination is incorrect, and she has asked you for advice on how to proceed. Evaluate the IRS's position regarding the treatment of Tern Corporation as a personal service corporation, and prepare a memo for the client files describing the results of your research.

COMMUNICATIONS

Research Problem 2. Cynthia Thomas is the president and sole shareholder of Violet Corporation, a calendar year taxpayer. In 2009, Cynthia incurred $9,500 of business expenditures for travel, entertainment, and promotion on behalf of Violet. Because Violet was in a precarious financial condition, Cynthia decided not to seek reimbursement for these expenditures. Instead, she deducted them on her own tax return (Form 1040). Upon audit of Cynthia's 2009 return, the IRS disallowed the deduction of the expenditures. Evaluate the merits of the position of the IRS and prepare a memo for the client files describing the results of your research.

Partial list of research aids:
Rev.Rul. 57–502, 1957–2 C.B. 118.
Roy. L. Harding, 29 TCM 789, T.C.Memo. 1970–179.

INTERNET *activity*

Use the tax resources of the Internet to address the following question. Do not restrict your search to the Web, but include a review of newsgroups and general reference materials, practitioner sites and resources, primary sources of the tax law, chat rooms and discussion groups, and other opportunities.

COMMUNICATIONS

Research Problem 3. Some states assess a corporate income tax or franchise tax on entities formed as S corporations, LLCs, and/or partnerships. To compare the overall tax burdens associated with the various entity forms, consideration must be given to state taxation of the entities and their owners. Using only the Internet for your research, prepare an outline describing state tax ramifications of the various business forms. Your outline should include as examples the tax policies of several specific states.

CHAPTER 18

Corporations: Organization and Capital Structure

LEARNING OBJECTIVES

After completing Chapter 18, you should be able to:

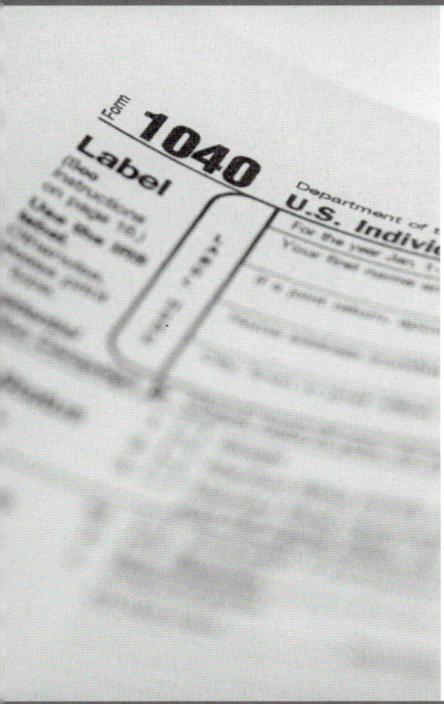

LO.1 Identify the tax consequences of incorporating a business.

LO.2 Understand the special rules that apply when liabilities are assumed by a corporation.

LO.3 Recognize the basis issues relevant to the shareholder and the corporation.

LO.4 Appreciate the tax aspects of the capital structure of a corporation.

LO.5 Recognize the tax differences between debt and equity investments.

LO.6 Handle the tax treatment of shareholder debt and stock losses.

LO.7 Identify tax planning opportunities associated with organizing and financing a corporation.

OUTLINE

For the latest in changes to tax legislation, visit **www.cengage.com/taxation/swft.**

THE BIG PICTURE **Tax Solutions for the Real World**

TAX ISSUES ASSOCIATED WITH GROWING INTO THE CORPORATE FORM

Emily has operated her business as a sole proprietorship since it was formed 10 years ago. Now, however, she has decided to incorporate the business because the corporate form offers several important nontax advantages (e.g., limited liability). Also, the incorporation would enable her husband, David, to become a part owner in the business. Emily expects to transfer her business assets in exchange for her corporate interest, while David will provide services for his interest. Emily's sole proprietorship assets available for transfer to the new corporation are:

	Adjusted Basis	Fair Market Value
Accounts receivable	$ –0–	$ 25,000
Building	50,000	200,000
Other assets	150,000	275,000
	$200,000	$500,000

Aware of the problem of double taxation associated with operating as a regular corporation, Emily is considering receiving some corporate debt at the time of incorporation. The interest expense on the debt will then provide a deduction for the corporation. Emily's main concern, however, is that the incorporation will be a taxable transaction. Can her fears be allayed? **Read the chapter and formulate your response.**

Chapter 17 dealt with four principal areas fundamental to working with corporations: (1) determination of whether an entity is a corporation for Federal income tax purposes, (2) tax rules applicable to the day-to-day operation of a corporation, (3) filing and reporting procedures, and (4) special situations involving corporations.

Chapter 18 addresses more sophisticated issues involving corporations:

- The tax consequences to the shareholders and the corporation upon the organization of and original transfer of property to the corporation.
- The tax result that ensues when shareholders make transfers of property to a corporation after organization.
- The capital structure of a corporation, including equity and debt financing.
- The tax treatment of investor losses.

18.1 Organization of and Transfers to Controlled Corporations

LO.1

Identify the tax consequences of incorporating a business.

IN GENERAL

Property transactions normally produce tax consequences if a gain or loss is realized. As a result, unless an exception in the Code applies, a transfer of property to a corporation in exchange for stock constitutes a taxable sale or exchange of property. The amount of gain or loss is measured by the difference between the value of the stock received and the tax basis of the property transferred.

When a taxpayer's economic status has not changed and the wherewithal to pay is lacking, however, the Code provides special exceptions to the requirement that realized gain or loss be recognized. One such exception pertains to like-kind exchanges. When a taxpayer exchanges property for other property of a like kind, § 1031 provides that gain (or loss) on the exchange is not recognized because a substantive change in the taxpayer's investment has not occurred. Section 1031 is merely a deferral mechanism and does not authorize the permanent nonrecognition of gain or loss. The deferral mechanism is accomplished by calculating a substituted basis for the like-kind property received. With this substituted basis, the realized gain or loss associated with the property given up is ultimately recognized when the property received in the exchange is sold.

Another exception to the general rule deals with transfers to controlled corporations. Section 351 provides that gain or loss is not recognized upon the transfer of property to a corporation when certain conditions are met. This provision also reflects the principle that gain should not be recognized when a taxpayer's investment has not substantively changed. For example, when a business is incorporated, the owner's economic status remains the same; only the *form* of the investment has changed. The investment in the business assets carries over to the investment in corporate stock. Further, if only stock in the corporation is received, the taxpayer is hardly in a position to pay a tax on any realized gain. Thus, this approach also is justified under the wherewithal to pay concept discussed in Chapter 1. As noted later, however, if the taxpayer receives property other than stock (i.e., cash or other "boot") from the corporation, realized gain is recognized.

Finally, § 351 exists because Congress believes that tax rules should not impede the exercise of sound business judgment (e.g., choice of the corporate form of doing business). For example, a taxpayer would think twice about forming a corporation if gain recognition (and the payment of a tax) would always be a consequence.

Therefore, the same principles govern the nonrecognition of gain or loss under § 1031 and § 351. With both provisions, gain or loss is postponed until a substantive change in the taxpayer's investment occurs (e.g., a sale to outsiders).

EXAMPLE 1

Ron is considering incorporating his sole proprietorship in order to obtain the limited liability of the corporate form. Ron realizes that if he incorporates, he will be personally liable only for the debts of the business that he has guaranteed. If Ron incorporates his business, the following assets will be transferred to the corporation:

	Tax Basis	Fair Market Value
Cash	$ 10,000	$ 10,000
Furniture and fixtures	20,000	60,000
Land and building	240,000	300,000
	$270,000	$370,000

In this change of business form, Ron will receive the corporation's stock worth $370,000 in exchange for the assets he transfers. Without the nonrecognition provisions of § 351, Ron would recognize a taxable gain of $100,000 on the transfer ($370,000 value of the stock received − $270,000 basis of the assets transferred). Under § 351, however, Ron does not recognize any gain because his economic status has not really changed. Ron's investment in the assets of his sole proprietorship is now represented by his ownership of stock in the corporation. Thus, § 351 provides for tax neutrality on the incorporation decision. ■

In a like-kind exchange, the recognition of gain is avoided only to the extent that the taxpayer receives like-kind property. However, the taxpayer must recognize some or all of the realized gain when receiving "boot" (i.e., property of an unlike kind, such as cash). For example, if a taxpayer exchanges a truck used in a business for another truck to be used in the business and also receives cash, the taxpayer has the wherewithal to pay an income tax on the cash involved. Further, the taxpayer's economic status has changed to the extent that cash is received. Thus, realized gain on the exchange is recognized to the extent of the cash received. In like manner, if a

GLOBAL
Tax Issues

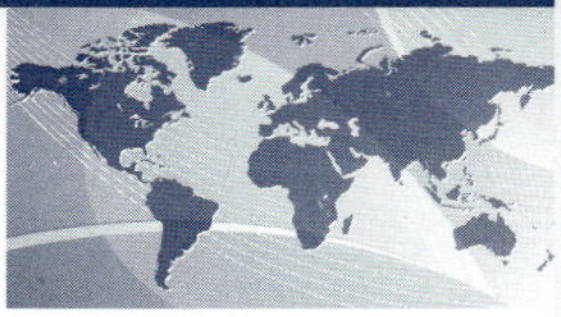

Choice of Organizational Form When Operating Overseas

When the management of a corporation decides to expand its business by establishing a presence in a foreign market, the new business venture may take one of several organizational forms. As each form comes with its respective advantages and disadvantages, making the best choice can be difficult.

One common approach is to conduct the foreign activity as a *branch* operation of the U.S. corporation. The foreign branch is not a separate legal entity, but a division of the U.S. corporation established overseas. As a result, any gains and losses produced by the foreign unit are included in the corporation's overall financial results.

Another possibility is to organize the foreign operations as a *subsidiary* of the U.S. parent corporation. If this route is chosen, the subsidiary may be either a *domestic* subsidiary (i.e., organized in the United States) or a *foreign* subsidiary (organized under the laws of a foreign country).

One fundamental tax difference between these two approaches is that the gains and losses of a *domestic* subsidiary may be consolidated with the operations of the U.S. parent, while the operations of a *foreign* subsidiary cannot. Thus, the use of a domestic subsidiary to conduct foreign operations will generally yield the same final result as the use of a branch. With both approaches, the financial statements of the U.S. parent reflect the results of its worldwide operations.

taxpayer transfers property to a corporation and receives cash or property other than stock, gain (but not loss) is recognized to the extent of the lesser of the gain realized or the boot received (i.e., the amount of cash and the fair market value of other property received). Any gain recognized is classified (e.g., ordinary, capital) according to the type of assets transferred.[1] As discussed later, the nonrecognition of gain or loss is accompanied by a substituted basis in the shareholder's stock.[2]

EXAMPLE 2

Amanda and Calvin form Quail Corporation. Amanda transfers property with an adjusted basis of $30,000, fair market value of $60,000, for 50% of the stock, worth $60,000. Calvin transfers property with an adjusted basis of $70,000, fair market value of $60,000, for the remaining 50% of the stock. The transfers qualify under § 351. Amanda has an unrecognized gain of $30,000, and Calvin has an unrecognized loss of $10,000. Both have a substituted basis in the stock in Quail Corporation. Amanda has a basis of $30,000 in her stock, and Calvin has a basis of $70,000 in his stock. Therefore, if either Amanda or Calvin later disposes of the Quail stock in a taxable transaction (e.g., a sale), this deferred gain/loss will then be fully recognized—a $30,000 gain to Amanda and a $10,000 loss to Calvin. ■

Section 351 is *mandatory* if a transaction satisfies the provision's requirements. The three requirements for nonrecognition of gain or loss under § 351 are that (1) *property* is transferred (2) in exchange for *stock* and (3) the property transferors are in *control* of the corporation after the exchange. Therefore, if recognition of gain or loss is *desired*, the taxpayer must plan to fail to meet at least one of these requirements.

PROPERTY DEFINED

Questions have arisen concerning what constitutes **property** for purposes of § 351. In general, the definition of property is comprehensive. For example, along with plant and equipment, unrealized receivables of a cash basis taxpayer and installment obligations are considered property.[3] Although the disposition of an installment note receivable normally triggers deferred gain, its transfer under § 351 is not treated as a

[1] § 351(b) and Rev.Rul. 68–55, 1968–1 C.B. 140.

[2] § 358(a). See the discussion preceding Example 20.

[3] *Hempt Brothers, Inc. v. U.S.*, 74–1 USTC ¶9188, 33 AFTR 2d 74–570, 490 F.2d 1172 (CA–3, 1974), and Reg. § 1.453–9(c)(2).

disposition. Thus, gain is not recognized to the transferor. Secret processes and formulas, as well as secret information in the general nature of a patentable invention, also qualify as property under § 351.[4]

However, the Code specifically excludes services rendered from the definition of property. Services are not considered to be property under § 351 for a critical reason. A taxpayer must report as income the fair market value of any consideration received as compensation for services rendered.[5] Consequently, when a taxpayer receives stock in a corporation as consideration for rendering services to the corporation, taxable income results. In this case, the amount of income recognized by the taxpayer is equal to the fair market value of the stock received. The taxpayer's basis in the stock received is its fair market value.

EXAMPLE 3

Ann and Bob form Olive Corporation with the transfer of the following consideration:

	Consideration Transferred		
	Basis to Transferor	Fair Market Value	Number of Shares Issued
From Ann:			
Personal services rendered to Olive Corporation	$ -0-	$20,000	200
From Bob:			
Installment obligation	5,000	40,000	
Inventory	10,000	30,000	
Secret process	-0-	10,000	800

The value of each share in Olive Corporation is $100.[6] Ann has income of $20,000 on the transfer because services do not qualify as "property." She has a basis of $20,000 in her 200 shares of Olive (i.e., Ann is treated as having bought some of the Olive stock by rendering services). Bob has no recognized gain on the receipt of stock because all of the consideration he transfers to Olive qualifies as "property" and he has "control" of Olive after the transfer; see the discussion concerning control that follows. Bob has a substituted basis of $15,000 in the Olive stock. ■

STOCK TRANSFERRED

Nonrecognition of gain occurs only when the shareholder receives stock. Stock for this purpose includes both common and preferred. However, it does not include "nonqualified preferred stock," which possesses many of the attributes of debt. In addition, the Regulations state that the term "stock" does not include stock rights and stock warrants. Otherwise, the term "stock" generally needs no clarification.[7]

Thus, any corporate debt or **securities** (e.g., long-term debt such as bonds) received are treated as boot because they do not qualify as stock. Therefore, the receipt of debt in exchange for the transfer of appreciated property to a controlled corporation causes recognition of gain.

EXAMPLE 4
THE BIG PICTURE

Return to the facts of *The Big Picture* on p. 18-2. Assume the proposed transaction qualifies under § 351 (i.e., the transfer of *property* in exchange for *stock* meets the *control* test), but Emily decides to receive some corporate debt along with the stock. If she receives stock worth $450,000 and corporate debt of $50,000 in exchange for the

[4] Rev.Rul. 64–56, 1964–1 C.B. 133; Rev.Rul. 71–564, 1971–2 C.B. 179.

[5] §§ 61 and 83.

[6] The value of closely held stock normally is presumed to be equal to the value of the property transferred.

[7] § 351(g). Examples of nonqualified preferred stock include preferred stock that is redeemable within 20 years of issuance and whose dividend rate is based on factors other than corporate performance. Therefore, gain is recognized up to the fair market value of the nonqualified preferred stock received. Loss may be recognized when the transferor receives *only* nonqualified preferred stock (or nonqualified preferred stock and other boot) in exchange for property. See also Reg. § 1.351–1(a)(1)(ii).

property transferred, Emily realizes gain of $300,000 [$500,000 (value of consideration received) − $200,000 (basis in the transferred property)]. However, because the transaction qualifies under § 351, only $50,000 of gain is recognized—the $50,000 of corporate debt is treated as boot. The remaining realized gain of $250,000 is deferred. ■

CONTROL OF THE CORPORATION

For the transaction to qualify as nontaxable under § 351, the property transferors must be in **control** of the corporation immediately after the exchange. Control means that the person or persons transferring the property must have at least an 80 percent stock ownership in the corporation. More specifically, the property transferors must own stock possessing at least 80 percent of the total combined *voting power* of all classes of stock entitled to vote *and* at least 80 percent of the total *number of shares* of all other classes of stock.[8]

Control Immediately after the Transfer

Immediately after the exchange, the property transferors must control the corporation. Control can apply to a single person or to several taxpayers if they are all parties to an integrated transaction. When more than one person is involved, the exchange does not necessarily require simultaneous exchanges by those persons. However, the rights of those transferring property to the corporation must be previously set out and determined. Also, the agreement to transfer property should be executed "with an expedition consistent with orderly procedure."[9] Therefore, if two or more persons transfer property to a corporation for stock and want to defer gain, it is helpful if the transfers occur close together in time and are made in accordance with an agreement among the parties.

EXAMPLE 5

Jack exchanges property, basis of $60,000 and fair market value of $100,000, for 70% of the stock of Gray Corporation. The other 30% of the stock is owned by Jane, who acquired it several years ago. The fair market value of Jack's stock is $100,000. Jack recognizes a taxable gain of $40,000 on the transfer because he does not have control of the corporation after his transfer and his transaction cannot be integrated with Jane's for purposes of the control requirement. ■

EXAMPLE 6

Rebecca, Daryl, and Paige incorporate their businesses by forming Green Corporation. Rebecca exchanges her property for 300 shares in Green on January 7, 2011. Daryl exchanges his property for 400 shares of Green Corporation stock on January 14, 2011, and Paige exchanges her property for 300 shares in Green on March 4, 2011. Because the three exchanges are part of a prearranged plan and the control test is met, the nonrecognition provisions of § 351 apply to all of the exchanges. ■

Stock need not be issued to the property transferors in the same proportion as the relative value of the property transferred by each. However, when stock received is not proportionate to the value of the property transferred, the actual effect of the transactions must be properly characterized. For example, in such situations one transferor may actually be making a gift of valuable consideration to another transferor.

EXAMPLE 7

Ron and Shelia, father and daughter, form Oak Corporation. Ron transfers property worth $50,000 in exchange for 100 shares of stock, while Shelia transfers property worth $50,000 for 400 shares of stock. The transfers qualify under § 351 because Ron and Shelia have control of the Oak stock immediately after the transfers of property. However, the implicit gift by Ron to Shelia must be recognized and appropriately characterized. As such, the value of the gift might be subject to the gift tax (see Chapter 27). ■

[8] § 368(c). Nonqualified preferred stock is treated as stock, and not boot, for purposes of this control test.

[9] Reg. § 1.351–1(a)(1).

Once control has been achieved, it is not necessarily lost if stock received by shareholders is sold or given to persons who are not parties to the exchange shortly after the transaction. However, a different result might materialize if a *plan* for the ultimate disposition of the stock existed *before* the exchange.[10]

ETHICS & Equity

A Professional-Free Incorporation

Allen and Beth agree to form Jay Corporation. Allen, who has a reputation for being extremely frugal, decides to follow instructions for incorporating a business that he has found on a free Internet site. Based on his plan, Allen transfers appreciated property to Jay Corporation in exchange for 75 percent of its stock. Beth agrees to provide services to the business for 25 percent of the stock.

Several months later, Allen learns that he has made a terrible blunder. To avoid paying tax on the transfer of his appreciated property, he should have received 80 percent, not 75 percent, of the stock. To correct the problem, Allen persuades Beth to transfer to him 5 percent of the corporation's stock. In return, Allen will give Beth some antiques he has collected. Allen tells Beth that this is a better deal for her because now she will have to report the value of only 20 percent of the corporation's stock as income (instead of 25 percent). Further, she receives the antiques as a tax-free gift.

How do you react to Allen's actions?

EXAMPLE 8

Naomi and Eric form Eagle Corporation. They transfer appreciated property to the corporation with each receiving 50 shares of the stock. Shortly after the formation, Naomi gives 25 shares to her son. Because Naomi was not committed to make the gift, she is considered to own her original shares of Eagle Corporation stock and, along with Eric, to control Eagle "immediately after the exchange." Therefore, the requirements of § 351 are met, and neither Naomi nor Eric is taxed on the exchange. Alternatively, had Naomi immediately given 25 shares to a business associate pursuant to a plan to satisfy an outstanding obligation, the formation of Eagle would be taxable to Naomi and Eric because of their lack of control (i.e., Naomi and Eric, the property transferors, would own only 75% of the stock). ■

Transfers for Property and Services

Nonrecognition treatment for the property transferors may be lost if "too much" stock is transferred to persons who did not contribute property.

EXAMPLE 9
THE BIG PICTURE

Return to the facts of *The Big Picture* on p. 18-2. Assume Emily transfers her $500,000 of property to the new corporation and receives 50% of its stock. David receives the other 50% of the stock for services rendered (worth $500,000). Both Emily and David have tax consequences from the transfers. David has ordinary income of $500,000 because he does not exchange property for stock. Emily has a taxable gain of $300,000 [$500,000 (fair market value of the stock in the new corporation) − $200,000 (basis in the transferred property)]. As the sole transferor of property, she receives only 50% of the corporation's stock. ■

A person who receives stock both in exchange for services and for property transferred may be treated as a member of the transferring group for purposes of the control test. When this is the case, the person is taxed on the value of the stock issued for services but not on the stock issued for property, assuming the property transferors control the corporation. In this case, all the stock received by the person transferring both property and services is counted in determining whether the transferors acquired control of the corporation.[11]

[10] *Wilgard Realty Co. v. Comm.*, 42–1 USTC ¶9452, 29 AFTR 325, 127 F.2d 514 (CA–2, 1942).

[11] Reg. § 1.351–1(a)(2), Ex. 3.

EXAMPLE 10
THE BIG PICTURE

Return to the facts of *The Big Picture* on p. 18-2. Assume the same facts as in Example 9 except that David transfers property worth $400,000 (basis of $130,000) in addition to services rendered to the corporation (valued at $100,000). Now David becomes a part of the control group. Emily and David, as property transferors, together receive 100% of the corporation's stock. Consequently, § 351 is applicable to the exchanges. As a result, Emily has no recognized gain. David does not recognize gain on the transfer of the property, but he recognizes ordinary income to the extent of the value of the shares issued for services rendered. Therefore, David has current taxable income of $100,000. ■

Transfers for Services and Nominal Property

To be a member of the group and aid in qualifying all transferors under the 80 percent control test, the person contributing services must transfer property having more than a "relatively small value" compared to the services performed. The Regulations provide that stock issued for property whose value is relatively small compared to the value of the stock already owned (or to be received for services rendered) will not be treated as issued in return for property. This will be the result when the primary purpose of the transfer is to qualify the transaction under § 351 for concurrent transferors.[12]

EXAMPLE 11

Rosalyn and Mark transfer property to Redbird Corporation, each in exchange for one-third of the stock. Reed receives the other one-third of the stock for services rendered. The transaction does not qualify under § 351 because Reed is not a member of the group transferring property and Rosalyn and Mark, as the sole property transferors, together receive only $66^2/_3$% of the stock. As a result, the post-transfer control requirement is not met.

Assume instead that Reed also transfers a substantial amount of property. Then he is a member of the group, and the transaction qualifies under § 351. Reed is taxed on the value of the stock issued for services, but the remainder of the transaction does not trigger gain or loss recognition. However, if the property transferred by Reed is of a relatively small value in comparison to the stock he receives for his services, and the primary purpose for transferring the property is to cause the transaction to be tax-free for Rosalyn and Mark, the exchange does not qualify under § 351 for any of the taxpayers. ■

Exactly when a taxpayer who renders services and transfers property is included in the control group is often subject to question. However, the IRS has stated that such a transferor can be included in the control group if the value of the property transferred is at least 10 percent of the value of the services provided.[13] If the value of the property transferred is less than this amount, the IRS will not issue an advance ruling that the exchange meets the requirements of § 351.

EXAMPLE 12

Sara and Rick form Grouse Corporation. Sara transfers land (worth $100,000, basis of $20,000) for 50% of the stock in Grouse. Rick transfers equipment (worth $50,000, adjusted basis of $10,000) and provides services worth $50,000 for 50% of the stock. Because the value of the property Rick transfers is not small relative to the value of the services he renders, his stock in Grouse Corporation is counted in determining control for purposes of § 351; thus, the transferors own 100% of the stock in Grouse. In addition, all of Rick's stock, not just the shares received for the equipment, is counted in determining control. As a result, Sara does not recognize gain on the transfer of the land. Rick, however, must recognize income of $50,000 on the transfer of services. Even though the transfer of the equipment qualifies under § 351, his transfer of services for stock does not.

Alternatively, had the value of Rick's property been small relative to the value of his services, the transaction would be fully taxable to both Sara and Rick. In that situation, Sara, the sole property transferor, would not have at least 80% control of Grouse Corporation following the transfer. As a result, she would fully recognize her realized gain. Further, because Rick would not be treated as having transferred property, the § 351 deferral would not be available to him either. ■

[12] Reg. § 1.351–1(a)(1)(ii).

[13] Rev.Proc. 77–37, 1977–2 C.B. 568.

Transfers to Existing Corporations

Once a corporation is in operation, § 351 also applies to any later transfers of property for stock by either new or existing shareholders.

EXAMPLE 13

Tyrone and Seth formed Blue Corporation three years ago. Both Tyrone and Seth transferred appreciated property to Blue in exchange for 50 shares each in the corporation. The original transfers qualified under § 351, and neither Tyrone nor Seth was taxed on the exchange. In the current year, Tyrone transfers property (worth $90,000, adjusted basis of $5,000) for 50 additional Blue shares. Tyrone has a taxable gain of $85,000 on the transfer. The exchange does not qualify under § 351 because Tyrone does not have 80% control of Blue Corporation immediately after the transfer—he owns 100 shares of the 150 shares outstanding, or a $66^2/_3$% interest. ■

See the Tax Planning portion of this chapter for additional discussion of this issue.

ASSUMPTION OF LIABILITIES—§ 357

LO.2

Understand the special rules that apply when liabilities are assumed by a corporation.

Without a provision to the contrary, the transfer of mortgaged property to a controlled corporation could trigger gain to the property transferor if the corporation took over the mortgage. This would be consistent with the treatment given in like-kind exchanges under § 1031. Generally, when liabilities are assumed by another party, the party who is relieved of the debt is treated as having received cash or boot. Section 357(a) provides, however, that when the acquiring corporation assumes a liability in a § 351 transaction, the liability is not treated as boot received for gain recognition purposes. Nevertheless, liabilities assumed by the transferee corporation are treated as boot in determining the basis of the stock received by the shareholder. As a result, the basis of the stock received is reduced by the amount of the liabilities assumed by the corporation. See the more complete discussion of basis computations later.

EXAMPLE 14

Vera transfers property with an adjusted basis of $60,000, fair market value of $100,000, to Oriole Corporation for 100% of the stock in Oriole. The property is subject to a liability of $25,000 that Oriole Corporation assumes. The exchange is tax-free under § 351 because the release of a liability is not treated as boot under § 357(a). However, the basis to Vera of the Oriole stock is $35,000 [$60,000 (basis of property transferred) – $25,000 (amount of the liability assumed by Oriole)]. ■

The general rule of § 357(a) has two exceptions: (1) § 357(b) provides that if the principal purpose of the assumption of the liabilities is to avoid tax *or* if there is no bona fide business purpose behind the exchange, the liabilities are treated as boot; and (2) § 357(c) provides that if the sum of the liabilities exceeds the adjusted basis of the properties transferred, the excess is taxable gain.

Exception (1): Tax Avoidance or No Bona Fide Business Purpose

Unless liabilities are incurred shortly before incorporation, § 357(b) generally poses few problems. A tax avoidance purpose for transferring liabilities to a controlled corporation normally is not a concern in view of the basis adjustment as noted above. Since the liabilities transferred reduce the basis of the stock received, any realized gain merely is deferred and not completely eliminated. Any postponed gain is recognized when and if the stock is disposed of in a taxable sale or exchange.

Satisfying the bona fide business purpose requirement is not difficult if the liabilities were incurred in connection with the transferor's normal course of conducting a trade or business. But this requirement can cause difficulty if the liability is taken out shortly before the property is transferred and the proceeds are utilized for personal purposes.[14] This type of situation is analogous to a cash distribution by the corporation to the shareholder, which is taxed as boot.

[14]See, for example, *Campbell, Jr. v. Wheeler*, 65–1 USTC ¶9294, 15 AFTR 2d 578, 342 F.2d 837 (CA-5, 1965).

EXAMPLE 15

Dan transfers real estate (basis of $40,000 and fair market value of $90,000) to a controlled corporation in return for stock in the corporation. However, shortly before the transfer, Dan mortgages the real estate and uses the $20,000 proceeds to meet personal obligations. Thus, along with the real estate, the mortgage is transferred to the corporation. In this case, the assumption of the mortgage lacks a bona fide business purpose. Consequently, the release of the liability is treated as boot received, and Dan has a taxable gain on the transfer of $20,000.[15]

Amount realized:	
Stock	$ 70,000
Release of liability—treated as boot	20,000
Total amount realized	$ 90,000
Less: Basis of real estate	(40,000)
Realized gain	$ 50,000
Recognized gain	$ 20,000

■

The effect of the application of § 357(b) is to taint *all* liabilities transferred even if some are supported by a bona fide business purpose.

EXAMPLE 16

Tim, an accrual basis taxpayer, incorporates his sole proprietorship. Among the liabilities transferred to the new corporation are trade accounts payable of $100,000 and a credit card bill of $5,000. Tim had used the credit card to purchase a wedding anniversary gift for his wife. Under these circumstances, *all* of the $105,000 liabilities are treated as boot and trigger the recognition of gain to the extent gain is realized. ■

Exception (2): Liabilities in Excess of Basis

The second exception, § 357(c), provides that if the amount of the liabilities assumed exceeds the total of the adjusted bases of the properties transferred, the excess is taxable gain. Without this provision, when **liabilities exceed the basis** in property exchanged, a taxpayer would have a negative basis in the stock received in the controlled corporation.[16] Section 357(c) precludes the negative basis possibility by treating the excess over basis as gain to the transferor.

EXAMPLE 17

Andre transfers land and equipment with adjusted bases of $35,000 and $5,000, respectively, to a newly formed corporation in exchange for 100% of the stock. The corporation assumes the liability on the transferred land in the amount of $50,000. Without § 357(c), Andre's basis in the stock of the new corporation would be a negative $10,000 [$40,000 (bases of properties transferred) + $0 (gain recognized) – $0 (boot received) – $50,000 (liability assumed)]. Section 357(c), however, requires Andre to recognize a gain of $10,000 ($50,000 liability assumed – $40,000 bases of assets transferred). As a result, the stock has a zero basis in Andre's hands, determined as follows:

Bases in the properties transferred ($35,000 + $5,000)	$ 40,000
Plus: Gain recognized	10,000
Less: Boot received	–0–
Less: Liability assumed	(50,000)
Basis in the stock received	$ –0–

Thus, Andre recognizes $10,000 of gain, and a negative stock basis is avoided. ■

The definition of liabilities under § 357(c) excludes obligations that would have been deductible to the transferor had those obligations been paid before the transfer. Therefore, accounts payable of a cash basis taxpayer are not considered to be liabilities for purposes of § 357(c). In addition, they are not considered in the computation of the shareholder's stock basis.

[15] § 351(b).

[16] *Jack L. Easson*, 33 T.C. 963 (1960), *rev'd* in 61–2 USTC ¶9654, 8 AFTR 2d 5448, 294 F.2d 653 (CA–9, 1961).

EXAMPLE 18

Tina, a cash basis taxpayer, incorporates her sole proprietorship. In return for all of the stock of the new corporation, she transfers the following items:

	Adjusted Basis	Fair Market Value
Cash	$10,000	$10,000
Unrealized accounts receivable (amounts due to Tina but not yet received by her)	–0–	40,000
Trade accounts payable	–0–	30,000
Note payable	5,000	5,000

Because the unrealized accounts receivable and trade accounts payable have a zero basis under the cash method of accounting, no income is recognized until the receivables are collected, and no deduction materializes until the payables are satisfied. The note payable has a basis because it was issued for consideration received.

In this situation, the trade accounts payable are disregarded for gain recognition purposes and in determining Tina's stock basis. Thus, for purposes of § 357(c), because the balance of the note payable does not exceed the basis of the assets transferred, Tina does not have a problem of liabilities in excess of basis (i.e., the note payable of $5,000 does not exceed the aggregate basis in the cash and accounts receivable of $10,000). ■

Conceivably, a situation could arise where both §§ 357(b) and (c) apply in the same transfer. In such a situation, § 357(b) predominates.[17] This could be significant because § 357(b) does not create gain on the transfer, as does § 357(c), but merely converts the liability to boot. Thus, the realized gain limitation continues to apply to § 357(b) transactions.

EXAMPLE 19

Chris forms Robin Corporation by transferring land with a basis of $100,000, fair market value of $1 million. The land is subject to a mortgage of $300,000. One month prior to incorporating Robin, Chris borrows $200,000 for personal purposes and gives the lender a second mortgage on the land. Therefore, on the incorporation, Robin issues stock worth $500,000 to Chris and assumes the two mortgages on the land. Section 357(c) seems to apply to the transfer, given that the mortgages on the property ($500,000) exceed the basis of the property ($100,000). Thus, Chris would have a gain of $400,000 under § 357(c). Section 357(b), however, also applies to the transfer because Chris borrowed $200,000 just prior to the transfer and used the loan proceeds for personal purposes. Thus, under § 357(b), Chris has boot of $500,000 in the amount of the liabilities. Note that *all* of the liabilities are treated as boot, not just the tainted $200,000 liability. Consequently, he has realized gain of $900,000 [$1,000,000 (stock of $500,000 and assumption of liabilities of $500,000) – $100,000 (basis in the land)], and gain is recognized to the extent of the boot received of $500,000. Unfortunately for Chris, the relatively more onerous rule of § 357(b) predominates over § 357(c). ■

BASIS DETERMINATION AND RELATED ISSUES

LO.3

Recognize the basis issues relevant to the shareholder and the corporation.

Recall that § 351(a) postpones gain or loss until the transferor-shareholder disposes of the stock in a taxable transaction. The postponement of shareholder gain or loss has a corollary effect on the basis of the stock received by the shareholder and the basis of the property received by the corporation. This procedure ensures that any gain or loss postponed under § 351 ultimately will be recognized when the affected asset is disposed of in a taxable transaction.

Basis of Stock to Shareholder

For a taxpayer transferring property to a corporation in a § 351 transaction, the *stock* received in the transaction is given a substituted basis. Essentially, the stock's basis is the same as the basis the taxpayer had in the property transferred, increased by any gain recognized on the exchange of property and decreased by boot received. Recall that for basis purposes, boot received includes liabilities transferred by the

[17] § 357(c)(2)(A).

FIGURE 18.1 Shareholder's Basis of Stock Received in Exchange for Property

Adjusted basis of property transferred	$xx,xxx
Plus: Gain recognized	x,xxx
Minus: Boot received (including any liabilities transferred)	(x,xxx)
Minus: Adjustment for loss property (if elected)	(x,xxx)
Equals: Basis of stock received	$xx,xxx

shareholder to the corporation. Also note that if the shareholder receives *other property* (i.e., boot) along with the stock, it takes a basis equal to its fair market value.[18] In Figure 18.1, the reference to gain recognized does not consider any income resulting from the performance of personal services. (Recall from earlier discussions that the basis of stock received for services rendered equals its fair market value.) See the discussion that follows relating to an elective stock basis reduction that may be made when a shareholder contributes property with a net built-in loss.

Basis of Property to Corporation

The basis of *property* received by the corporation generally is determined under a carryover basis rule. This rule provides that the property's basis to the corporation is equal to the basis in the hands of the transferor increased by the amount of any gain recognized on the transfer by the transferor-shareholder.[19]

These basis rules are illustrated in Examples 20 and 21.

EXAMPLE 20

Kesha and Ned form Brown Corporation. Kesha transfers land (basis of $30,000 and fair market value of $70,000); Ned invests cash ($60,000). They each receive 50 shares in Brown Corporation, worth $60,000, but Kesha also receives $10,000 in cash from Brown. The transfers of property, the realized and recognized gain on the transfers, and the basis of the stock in Brown Corporation to Kesha and Ned are as follows:

	A	B	C	D	E	F
	Basis of Property Transferred	FMV of Stock Received	Boot Received	Realized Gain (B + C – A)	Recognized Gain (Lesser of C or D)	Basis of Stock in Brown (A – C + E)
From Kesha:						
Land	$30,000	$60,000	$10,000	$40,000	$10,000	$30,000
From Ned:						
Cash	60,000	60,000	–0–	–0–	–0–	60,000

Brown Corporation has a basis of $40,000 in the land (Kesha's basis of $30,000 plus her recognized gain of $10,000). ■

EXAMPLE 21

Assume the same facts as in Example 20 except that Kesha's basis in the land is $68,000 (instead of $30,000). Because recognized gain cannot exceed realized gain, the transfer generates only $2,000 of gain to Kesha. The realized and recognized gain and the basis of the stock in Brown Corporation to Kesha are as follows:

	A	B	C	D	E	F
	Basis of Property Transferred	FMV of Stock Received	Boot Received	Realized Gain (B + C – A)	Recognized Gain (Lesser of C or D)	Basis of Stock in Brown (A – C + E)
Land	$68,000	$60,000	$10,000	$2,000	$2,000	$60,000

Brown's basis in the land is $70,000 ($68,000 basis to Kesha + $2,000 gain recognized by Kesha). ■

[18] § 358(a).

[19] § 362(a).

CONCEPT SUMMARY 18.1

Tax Consequences to the Shareholders and Corporation: With and Without the Application of § 351 (Based on the Facts of Example 20)

	With § 351			Without § 351		
Shareholder	**Gain/Loss Recognized**	**Stock Basis**	**Other Property Basis**	**Gain/Loss Recognized**	**Stock Basis**	**Other Property Basis**
Kesha	Realized gain recognized to extent of boot received; loss not recognized.	Substituted (see Figure 18.1).	FMV	All realized gain or loss recognized.	FMV	FMV
	$10,000	$30,000	$10,000	$40,000	$60,000	$10,000

	With § 351		Without § 351	
Corporation	**Gain/Loss Recognized**	**Property Basis**	**Gain/Loss Recognized**	**Property Basis**
Brown	No gain or loss recognized on the transfer of corporate stock for property.	Carryover (see Figure 18.2).	No gain or loss recognized on the transfer of corporate stock for property.	FMV
	$0	$40,000	$0	$70,000

Note that the benefit to Kesha of deferring $30,000 of gain under § 351 comes with a cost: her stock basis is $30,000 (rather than $60,000), and the corporation's basis in the property received is $40,000 (rather than $70,000).

Figure 18.2 summarizes the basis calculation for property received by a corporation. Concept Summary 18.1 shows the shareholder and corporate consequences of a transfer of property to a corporation for stock, with and without the application of § 351. The facts applicable to shareholder Kesha's transfer in Example 20 are used to illustrate the differences between the transaction being tax deferred and taxable.

Basis Adjustment for Loss Property

As noted above, when a corporation receives property in a § 351 transaction, the basis for that property is carried over from the shareholder. As a result, the corporation's basis for the property has no correlation to its fair market value. However, in certain situations when **built-in loss property** is contributed to a corporation, its aggregate basis in the property may have to be stepped down so that the basis does not exceed the fair market value of the property transferred. This basis adjustment is necessary to prevent the parties from obtaining a double benefit from the losses involved.

The anti-loss duplication rule applies when the aggregate basis of the assets transferred by a shareholder exceeds their fair market value. When this built-in loss situation exists, the basis in the loss properties is stepped down. The step-down in basis is allocated proportionately among the assets with the built-in loss.[20]

FIGURE 18.2 **Corporation's Basis in Property Received**

Adjusted basis of property transferred	$xx,xxx
Plus: Gain recognized by transferor-shareholder	x,xxx
Minus: Adjustment for loss property (if required)	(x,xxx)
Equals: Basis of property to corporation	$xx,xxx

[20] § 362(e)(2). This adjustment is determined separately with respect to each property transferor. In addition, this adjustment also is required in the case of a contribution to capital by a shareholder.

EXAMPLE 22

In a transaction qualifying under § 351, Charles transfers the following assets to Gold Corporation in exchange for all of its stock:

	Tax Basis	Fair Market Value	Built-In Gain/(Loss)
Equipment	$100,000	$ 90,000	($ 10,000)
Land	200,000	230,000	30,000
Building	150,000	100,000	(50,000)
	$450,000	$420,000	($ 30,000)

Charles's stock basis is $450,000 [$450,000 (basis of the property transferred) + $0 (gain recognized) – $0 (boot received)]. However, Gold's basis for the loss assets transferred must be reduced by the amount of the net built-in loss ($30,000) in proportion to each asset's share of the loss.

	Unadjusted Tax Basis	Adjustment	Adjusted Tax Basis
Equipment	$100,000	($ 5,000)*	$ 95,000
Land	200,000		200,000
Building	150,000	(25,000)**	125,000
	$450,000	($30,000)	$420,000

$$^{*}\frac{\$10{,}000 \text{ (loss attributable to equipment)}}{\$60{,}000 \text{ (\textit{total} built-in loss)}} \times \$30{,}000 \text{ (\textit{net} built-in loss)}$$
$$= \$5{,}000 \text{ (adjustment to basis in equipment).}$$

$$^{**}\frac{\$50{,}000 \text{ (loss attributable to building)}}{\$60{,}000 \text{ (\textit{total} built-in loss)}} \times \$30{,}000 \text{ (\textit{net} built-in loss)}$$
$$= \$25{,}000 \text{ (adjustment to basis in building).}$$ ■

Note the end result of Example 22:

- Charles still has a built-in loss in his stock basis. Thus, if he sells the Gold Corporation stock, he will recognize a loss of $30,000 [$420,000 (selling price based on presumed value of the stock) – $450,000 (basis in the stock)].
- Gold Corporation can no longer recognize any loss on the sale of *all* of its assets [$420,000 (selling price based on value of assets) – $420,000 (adjusted basis in assets) = $0 (gain or loss)].

In the event a corporation is subject to the built-in loss adjustment, an alternative approach is available. If the shareholder and the corporation both elect, the basis reduction can be made to the shareholder's stock rather than to the corporation's property.

EXAMPLE 23

Assume the same facts as in the previous example. If Charles and Gold elect, Charles can reduce his stock basis to $420,000 ($450,000 – $30,000). As a result, Gold's aggregate basis in the assets it receives is $450,000. If Charles has no intention of selling his stock, this election could be desirable as it benefits Gold by giving the corporation a higher depreciable basis in the equipment and building. ■

Note the end result of Example 23:

- Charles has no built-in loss. Thus, if he sells the Gold Corporation stock, he will recognize no gain or loss [$420,000 (presumed value of the stock) – $420,000 (basis in the stock)].
- Gold Corporation has a built-in loss. Thus, if it sells *all* of its assets [$420,000 (selling price based on value of assets) – $450,000 (basis in assets)], it recognizes a loss of $30,000.

Consequently, the built-in loss adjustment places the loss with either the shareholder or the corporation but not both (compare Examples 22 and 23).

Stock Issued for Services Rendered

A transfer of stock for services is not a taxable transaction to a corporation.[21] But another issue arises: Can a corporation deduct the fair market value of the stock it issues in consideration of services as a business expense? Yes, unless the services are such that the payment is characterized as a capital expenditure.[22]

EXAMPLE 24

Esther and Carl form White Corporation. Esther transfers cash of $500,000 for 100 shares of White Corporation stock. Carl transfers property worth $400,000 (basis of $90,000) and agrees to serve as manager of the corporation for one year; in return, Carl receives 100 shares of stock in White. The value of Carl's services to White Corporation is $100,000. Esther's and Carl's transfers qualify under § 351. Neither Esther nor Carl is taxed on the transfer of their property. However, Carl has income of $100,000, the value of the stock received for the services he will render to White Corporation. White has a basis of $90,000 in the property it acquired from Carl, and it may claim a compensation expense deduction under § 162 for $100,000. Carl's stock basis is $190,000 [$90,000 (basis of property transferred) + $100,000 (income recognized for services rendered)]. ■

EXAMPLE 25

Assume the same facts as in Example 24 except that Carl provides legal services (instead of management services) in organizing the corporation. The value of Carl's legal services is $100,000. Carl has no gain on the transfer of the property but has income of $100,000 for the value of the stock received for the services rendered. White Corporation has a basis of $90,000 in the property it acquired from Carl and must capitalize the $100,000 as an organizational expenditure. Carl's stock basis is $190,000 [$90,000 (basis of property transferred) + $100,000 (income recognized for services rendered)]. ■

Holding Period for Shareholder and Transferee Corporation

In a § 351 transfer, the shareholder's holding period for stock received in exchange for a capital asset or § 1231 property includes the holding period of the property transferred to the corporation. That is, the holding period of the property is "tacked on" to the holding period of the stock. The holding period for stock received for any other property (e.g., inventory) begins on the day after the exchange. The corporation's holding period for property acquired in a § 351 transfer is the holding period of the transferor-shareholder, regardless of the character of the property in the transferor's hands.[23]

Recapture Considerations

In a § 351(a) transfer where no gain is recognized, the depreciation recapture rules do not apply.[24] However, any recapture potential associated with the property carries over to the corporation as it steps into the shoes of the transferor-shareholder for purposes of basis determination.

EXAMPLE 26

Paul transfers equipment (adjusted basis of $30,000, original cost of $120,000, and fair market value of $100,000) to a controlled corporation in return for stock. If Paul had sold the equipment, it would have yielded a gain of $70,000, all of which would be recaptured as ordinary income under § 1245. Because the transfer comes within § 351(a), Paul has no recognized gain and no depreciation to recapture. However, if the corporation later disposes of the equipment in a taxable transaction, it must take into account the § 1245 recapture potential originating with Paul. ■

[21]Reg. § 1.1032–1(a).

[22]Rev.Rul. 62–217, 1962–2 C.B. 59, modified by Rev.Rul. 74–503, 1974–2 C.B. 117.

[23]§§ 1223(1) and (2).

[24]§§ 1245(b)(3) and 1250(d)(3).

GLOBAL
Tax Issues

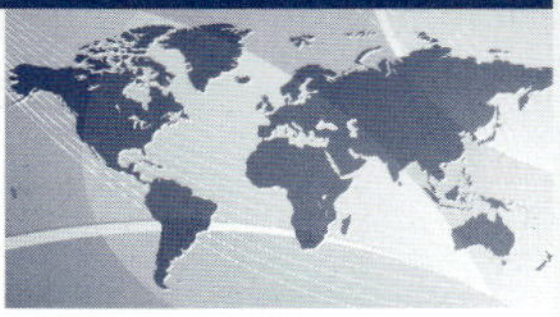

Does § 351 Cover the Incorporation of a Foreign Business?

When a taxpayer wishes to incorporate a business overseas by moving assets across U.S. borders, the deferral mechanism of § 351 applies in certain situations, but not in others. In general, § 351 is available to defer gain recognition when starting up a new corporation outside the United States unless so-called tainted assets are involved. Under § 367, tainted assets, which include assets such as inventory and accounts receivable, are treated as having been sold by the taxpayer prior to the corporate formation; therefore, their transfer results in the current recognition of gain. The presence of tainted assets triggers gain because Congress does not want taxpayers to be able to shift the gain outside the U.S. jurisdiction. The gain recognized is ordinary or capital, depending on the nature of the asset involved.

18.2 Capital Structure of a Corporation

LO.4

Appreciate the tax aspects of the capital structure of a corporation.

CAPITAL CONTRIBUTIONS

When a corporation receives money or property in exchange for capital stock (including treasury stock), neither gain nor loss is recognized by the corporation.[25] Nor does a corporation's gross income include shareholders' contributions of money or property to the capital of the corporation. Moreover, additional money or property received from shareholders through voluntary pro rata transfers also is not income to the corporation. This is the case even though there is no increase in the number of outstanding shares of stock of the corporation. The contributions represent an additional price paid for the shares held by the shareholders and are treated as additions to the operating capital of the corporation.[26]

Contributions by nonshareholders, such as land contributed to a corporation by a civic group or a governmental group to induce the corporation to locate in a particular community, are also excluded from the gross income of a corporation.[27] However, if the property is transferred to a corporation by a nonshareholder in exchange for goods or services, then the corporation must recognize income.[28]

EXAMPLE 27

A cable television company charges its customers an initial fee to hook up to a new cable system installed in the area. These payments are used to finance the total cost of constructing the cable facilities. In addition, the customers will make monthly payments for the cable service. The initial payments are used for capital expenditures, but they represent payments for services to be rendered by the cable company. As such, they are taxable income to the cable company and not contributions to capital by nonshareholders. ■

The basis of property received by a corporation from a shareholder as a **capital contribution** is equal to the basis of the property in the hands of the shareholder, although the basis is subject to a downward adjustment when loss property is contributed. The basis of property transferred to a corporation by a nonshareholder as a contribution to capital is zero.

If a corporation receives *money* as a contribution to capital from a nonshareholder, a special rule applies. The basis of any property acquired with the money during a 12-month period beginning on the day the contribution was received is reduced by the amount of the contribution. The excess of money received over the

[25] § 1032.

[26] § 118 and Reg. § 1.118–1.

[27] See *Edwards v. Cuba Railroad Co.*, 1 USTC ¶139, 5 AFTR 5398, 45 S.Ct. 614 (USSC, 1925).

[28] Reg. § 1.118–1. See also *Teleservice Co. of Wyoming Valley*, 27 T.C. 722 (1957), *aff'd* in 58–1 USTC ¶9383, 1 AFTR 2d 1249, 254 F.2d 105 (CA–3, 1958), *cert. den.* 78 S.Ct. 1360 (USSC, 1958).

TAX *in* the NEWS

During Both Good and Bad Times, Local and State Governments Compete

As a business seeks to grow and strategies shift, managers must be on the lookout for locations that will best suit their needs. Among the factors that can make a critical difference in an expansion or relocation decision is the availability of tax incentives offered by state and local governments as inducements.

As an example, Northrop Grumman, a leading global security company, recently decided to move its headquarters from Los Angeles to the Washington, D.C. area to be closer to its largest client, the Federal government. As part of the process of choosing the particular location, the company negotiated with government officials in Washington, D.C., Maryland, and Virginia. In the end, Northrop Grumman chose Fairfax County, Virginia, because of the incentive package pieced together by the state and local governments. In return, Northrop Grumman is expected to make a $24 million investment at its new facility and create 300 new jobs with average annual salaries of $200,000.

cost of new property reduces the basis of other property held by the corporation and is applied in the following order:

- Depreciable property.
- Property subject to amortization.
- Property subject to depletion.
- All other remaining properties.

The basis of property within each category is reduced in proportion to the relative bases of the properties.[29]

EXAMPLE 28

A city donates land worth $400,000 to Teal Corporation as an inducement for Teal to locate in the city. The receipt of the land produces no taxable income to Teal, and the land's basis to the corporation is zero. If, in addition, the city gives the corporation $100,000 in cash, the money is not taxable income to the corporation. However, if the corporation purchases property with the $100,000 of cash within the next 12 months, the basis of the acquired property is reduced by $100,000. Any excess cash that is retained and not used by Teal is handled according to the ordering rules noted above. ■

DEBT IN THE CAPITAL STRUCTURE

LO.5

Recognize the tax differences between debt and equity investments.

Advantages of Debt

Significant tax differences exist between debt and equity in the capital structure. The advantages of issuing long-term debt instead of stock are numerous. Interest on debt is deductible by the corporation, while dividend payments are not. Further, loan repayments are not taxable to investors unless the repayments exceed basis. A shareholder's receipt of property from a corporation, however, cannot be tax-free as long as the corporation has earnings and profits (see Chapter 19). Such distributions will be taxed as dividends to the extent of earnings and profits of the distributing corporation.

Currently, another distinction between debt and equity relates to the taxation of dividend and interest income. Dividend income on equity holdings is taxed to individual investors at the low capital gains rates, while interest income on debt is taxed at the higher ordinary income rates.

EXAMPLE 29

Wade transfers cash of $100,000 to a newly formed corporation for 100% of the stock. In its initial year, the corporation has net income of $40,000. The income is credited to the earnings and profits account of the corporation. If the corporation distributes $9,500 to Wade, the distribution is a taxable dividend to Wade with no corresponding

[29] § 362(a) and Reg. § 1.362–2(b).

TAX *in the NEWS*

Debt That Cannot Be Fully Repaid

Having debt in the capital structure of a corporation can carry many tax advantages to the parties involved. Problems arise, however, when such debt becomes due and cannot be fully repaid by the corporate debtor. In the case of outside creditors (i.e., nonshareholders), the options are twofold: declare bankruptcy or restructure the terms of the debt. The latter option entails reducing the amount of the debt or allowing the debtor to repurchase the debt instruments (e.g., notes, bonds) at a discount. Either way generates income to the debtor under the discharge of indebtedness provision of § 108. Because the results are less drastic to the parties involved (i.e., creditor/debtor) and less disruptive in economic effect, Congress has attempted to encourage the use of the restructuring option.

Under the American Recovery and Reinvestment Tax Act of 2009, the income from the repurchase of business debt at a discount can be deferred until 2014 and can be spread over the next five years. These income deferral rules apply to repurchase situations occurring after December 31, 2008, and before January 1, 2011. The "buyback" rules will be of particular benefit in helping many private equity firms avoid bankruptcy due to their troubled debt.

deduction to the corporation. Assume, instead, that Wade transfers to the corporation cash of $50,000 for stock and cash of $50,000 for a note of the same amount. The note is payable in equal annual installments of $5,000 and bears interest at the rate of 9%. At the end of the year, the corporation pays Wade interest of $4,500 ($50,000 × 9%) and a note repayment of $5,000. The interest payment is deductible to the corporation and taxable to Wade. The $5,000 principal repayment on the note is neither deducted by the corporation nor taxed to Wade. The after-tax impact to Wade and the corporation under each alternative is illustrated below.

	If the Distribution Is	
	$9,500 Dividend	**$5,000 Note Repayment and $4,500 Interest**
*After-tax benefit to Wade**		
[$9,500 × (1 – 15%)]	$8,075	
{$5,000 + [$4,500 × (1 – 35%)]}		$7,925
*After-tax cost to corporation***		
No deduction to corporation	9,500	
{$5,000 + [$4,500 × (1 – 35%)]}		7,925

*Assumes Wade's dividend income is taxed at the 15% capital gains rate and his interest income is taxed at the 35% ordinary income rate.
**Assumes the corporation is in the 35% marginal tax bracket.

■

Reclassification of Debt as Equity (Thin Capitalization Problem)

In situations where the corporation is said to be thinly capitalized, the IRS contends that debt is really an equity interest and denies the corporation the tax advantages of debt financing. If the debt instrument has too many features of stock, it may be treated for tax purposes as stock. In that case, the principal and interest payments are considered dividends. In the current environment, however, the IRS may be less inclined to raise the thin capitalization issue because the conversion of interest income to dividend income would produce a tax benefit to individual investors.

Section 385 lists several factors that *may* be used to determine whether a debtor-creditor relationship or a shareholder-corporation relationship exists. The section authorizes the Treasury to prescribe Regulations that provide more definitive guidelines. To date, the Treasury has not drafted acceptable Regulations. Consequently, taxpayers must rely on judicial decisions to determine whether a true debtor-creditor relationship exists.

For the most part, the principles used to classify debt as equity developed in connection with closely held corporations. Here, the holders of the debt are also shareholders. Consequently, the rules have often proved inadequate for dealing with such problems in large, publicly traded corporations.

Together, Congress, through § 385, and the courts have identified the following factors to be considered in resolving the **thin capitalization** issue:

- Whether the debt instrument is in proper form. An open account advance is more easily characterized as a contribution to capital than a loan evidenced by a properly written note.[30]
- Whether the debt instrument bears a reasonable rate of interest and has a definite maturity date. When a shareholder advance does not provide for interest, the return expected may appear to be a share of the profits or an increase in the value of the shares.[31] Likewise, a lender unrelated to the corporation will usually be unwilling to commit funds to the corporation without a definite due date.
- Whether the debt is paid on a timely basis. A lender's failure to insist upon timely repayment or satisfactory renegotiation indicates that the return sought does not depend upon interest income and the repayment of principal.
- Whether payment is contingent upon earnings. A lender ordinarily will not advance funds that are likely to be repaid only if the venture is successful.
- Whether the debt is subordinated to other liabilities. Subordination tends to eliminate a significant characteristic of the creditor-debtor relationship. Creditors should have the right to share with other general creditors in the event of the corporation's dissolution or liquidation. Subordination also destroys another basic attribute of creditor status—the power to demand payment at a fixed maturity date.[32]
- Whether holdings of debt and stock are proportionate (e.g., each shareholder owns the same percentage of debt as stock). When debt and equity obligations are held in the same proportion, shareholders are, apart from tax considerations, indifferent as to whether corporate distributions are in the form of interest or dividends.
- Whether funds loaned to the corporation are used to finance initial operations or capital asset acquisitions. Funds used to finance initial operations or to acquire assets the corporation needs in the business are generally obtained through equity investments.
- Whether the corporation has a high ratio of shareholder debt to shareholder equity. Thin capitalization occurs when shareholder debt is high relative to shareholder equity. This indicates the corporation lacks reserves to pay interest and principal on debt when corporate income is insufficient to meet current needs.[33] In determining a corporation's debt-equity ratio, courts look at the relation of the debt both to the book value of the corporation's assets and to their actual fair market value.[34]

Under § 385, the IRS also has the authority to classify an instrument either as *wholly* debt or equity or as *part* debt and *part* equity. This flexible approach is important because some instruments cannot readily be classified either wholly as stock or

[30] *Estate of Mixon, Jr. v. U.S.*, 72–2 USTC ¶9537, 30 AFTR 2d 72–5094, 464 F.2d 394 (CA–5, 1972).

[31] *Slappey Drive Industrial Park v. U.S.*, 77–2 USTC ¶9696, 40 AFTR 2d 77–5940, 561 F.2d 572 (CA–5, 1977).

[32] *Fin Hay Realty Co. v. U.S.*, 68–2 USTC ¶9438, 22 AFTR 2d 5004, 398 F.2d 694 (CA–3, 1968).

[33] A court held that a debt-equity ratio of approximately 14.6:1 was not excessive. See *Tomlinson v. 1661 Corp.*, 67–1 USTC ¶9438, 19 AFTR 2d 1413, 377 F.2d 291 (CA–5, 1967). A 26:1 ratio was found acceptable in *Delta Plastics, Inc.*, 85 TCM 940, T.C.Memo. 2003–54.

[34] In *Bauer v. Comm.*, 84–2 USTC ¶9996, 55 AFTR 2d 85–433, 748 F.2d 1365 (CA–9, 1984), a debt-equity ratio of 92:1 resulted when book value was used. But the ratio ranged from 2:1 to 8:1 when equity included both paid-in capital and accumulated earnings.

wholly as debt. It may also provide an avenue for the IRS to address problems in publicly traded corporations.

18.3 Investor Losses

LO.6

Handle the tax treatment of shareholder debt and stock losses.

The difference between equity and debt financing involves a consideration of the tax treatment of worthless stock and securities versus that applicable to bad debts.

STOCK AND SECURITY LOSSES

If stocks and bonds are capital assets in their owner's hands, losses from their worthlessness are governed by § 165(g)(1). Under this provision, a capital loss materializes as of the last day of the taxable year in which the stocks or bonds become worthless (refer to Chapter 7). No deduction is allowed for a mere decline in value. The burden of proving complete worthlessness is on the taxpayer claiming the loss. One way to recognize partial worthlessness is to dispose of the stocks or bonds in a taxable sale or exchange.[35] But even then, the **investor loss** is disallowed if the sale or exchange is to a related party as defined under § 267(b) (e.g., parents and children are related, but aunts, uncles, and cousins are not considered related).

When the stocks or bonds are not capital assets, worthlessness yields an ordinary loss.[36] For example, if the stocks or bonds are held by a broker for resale to customers in the normal course of business, they are not capital assets. Usually, however, stocks and bonds are held as investments and, as a result, are capital assets.

Under certain circumstances involving stocks and bonds of affiliated corporations, an ordinary loss is allowed upon worthlessness.[37] A corporation is an affiliate of another corporation if the corporate shareholder owns at least 80 percent of the voting power of all classes of stock entitled to vote and 80 percent of each class of nonvoting stock. Further, to be considered affiliated, the corporation must have derived more than 90 percent of its aggregate gross receipts for all taxable years from sources other than passive income. Passive income for this purpose includes such items as rents, royalties, dividends, and interest.

BUSINESS VERSUS NONBUSINESS BAD DEBTS

In addition to worthlessness of stocks and bonds, the financial demise of a corporation can result in bad debt deductions to those who have extended credit to the corporation. These deductions can be either business bad debts or **nonbusiness bad debts**. The distinction between the two types of deductions is important for tax purposes in the following respects:

- Business bad debts are deducted as ordinary losses while nonbusiness bad debts are treated as short-term capital losses.[38] A business bad debt can generate a net operating loss, but a nonbusiness bad debt cannot.[39]
- A deduction is allowed for the partial worthlessness of a business debt, but nonbusiness debts can be written off only when they become entirely worthless.[40]
- Nonbusiness bad debt treatment is limited to noncorporate taxpayers. However, all of the bad debts of a corporation qualify as business bad debts.[41]

When is a debt business or nonbusiness? Unfortunately, since the Code sheds little light on the matter, the distinction has been left to the courts.[42] In a leading decision, the Supreme Court somewhat clarified the picture when it held that if individual shareholders lend money to a corporation in their capacity as investors,

[35] Reg. § 1.165–4(a).
[36] § 165(a) and Reg. § 1.165–5(b).
[37] § 165(g)(3).
[38] Compare § 166(a) with § 166(d)(1)(B).
[39] Note the modification required by § 172(d)(2).
[40] Compare § 166(a)(2) with § 166(d)(1)(A).
[41] § 166(d)(1).
[42] For definitional purposes, § 166(d)(2) is almost as worthless as the debt it purports to describe.

TAX *in* the NEWS

Losses Arising from Stock Market Investments: Capital Losses or Theft Losses?

Losses incurred by individuals from poor performing stocks and securities, whether from actual sales or due to worthlessness, receive capital loss treatment. Thus, the losses can offset any capital gains, and if a net loss results, a deduction of up to $3,000 may be taken for the year. If the net loss exceeds $3,000, the excess may be carried over to future years. However, many years may have to pass before a large net capital loss is fully deductible.

As an alternative, if the loss on the security is due to theft, it is not subject to the capital loss limitation. Instead, the theft loss is ordinary and could totally wipe out a taxpayer's income, and in some cases, it could be carried back or forward as a net operating loss deduction.

Among the taxpayers who can utilize theft loss treatment are the unfortunate investors who lost billions of dollars in the well-publicized Madoff scam. Revenue Ruling 2009–9 (2009–1 C.B. 735) provides theft loss treatment for investors who paid money to investment advisers, such as Bernard Madoff, who later were discovered to have used the funds in a Ponzi-style scheme. Further, because the taxpayers originally engaged in such "investments" with an expectation of generating profits, the deductions *are not* subject to the restrictions applicable to personal casualty and theft loss (e.g., the 10 percent-of-AGI floor). Thus, these unhappy fraud victims may find some solace in the favorable tax treatment that provides an immediate and full deduction for the losses sustained.

any resulting bad debt is classified as nonbusiness.[43] Nevertheless, the Court did not preclude the possibility of a shareholder-creditor incurring a business bad debt.

If a loan is made in some capacity that qualifies as a trade or business, nonbusiness bad debt treatment is avoided. For example, if an employee, who is also a shareholder, makes a loan to preserve his or her employment, the loan qualifies for business bad debt treatment.[44] Shareholders also receive business bad debt treatment if they are in the trade or business of lending money or of buying, promoting, and selling corporations. If the shareholder has multiple motives for making the loan, according to the Supreme Court, the "dominant" or "primary" motive for making the loan controls the classification of the loss.[45]

EXAMPLE 30

Norman owns 48% of the stock of Lark Corporation, which he acquired several years ago at a cost of $600,000. Norman is also employed by the corporation at an annual salary of $240,000. At a time when Lark Corporation is experiencing financial problems, Norman lends it $300,000. Subsequently, the corporation becomes bankrupt, and both Norman's stock investment and his loan become worthless. ■

The loss from Norman's stock investment is treated as a long-term capital loss (assuming § 1244 does not apply, as discussed below). But how is the bad debt classified? If Norman can prove that his dominant or primary reason for making the loan was to protect his salary, a business bad debt deduction results. If not, it is assumed that Norman was trying to protect his stock investment, and nonbusiness bad debt treatment results. Factors to be considered in resolving this matter include the following:

- A comparison of the amount of the stock investment with the trade or business benefit derived. In Example 30, the stock investment of $600,000 is compared with the annual salary of $240,000. In this regard, the salary should be considered as a recurring item and not viewed in isolation. A salary of $240,000 each year means a great deal to a person who has no other means of support and may have difficulty obtaining similar employment elsewhere.
- A comparison of the amount of the loan with the stock investment and the trade or business benefit derived.

[43] *Whipple v. Comm.*, 63–1 USTC ¶9466, 11 AFTR 2d 1454, 83 S.Ct. 1168 (USSC, 1963).

[44] *Trent v. Comm.*, 61–2 USTC ¶9506, 7 AFTR 2d 1599, 291 F.2d 669 (CA–2, 1961).

[45] *U.S. v. Generes*, 72–1 USTC ¶9259, 29 AFTR 2d 72–609, 92 S.Ct. 827 (USSC, 1972).

- The percentage of ownership held by the shareholder. A minority shareholder, for example, is under more compulsion to lend the corporation money to protect a job than one who is in control of corporate policy.

In summary, it is impossible to conclude whether Norman in Example 30 suffered a business or nonbusiness bad debt without additional facts. Even with such facts, the guidelines are vague. Recall that a taxpayer's intent or motivation is at issue. For this reason, the problem is frequently the subject of litigation.[46]

SECTION 1244 STOCK

In an exception to the capital treatment that generally results, § 1244 permits ordinary loss treatment for losses on the sale or worthlessness of stock of so-called *small business corporations.* By placing shareholders on a more nearly equal basis with proprietors and partners in terms of the tax treatment of losses, the provision encourages investment of capital in small corporations. Gain on the sale of § 1244 stock remains capital. Consequently, the shareholder has nothing to lose and everything to gain by complying with § 1244.

Qualification for § 1244

The ordinary loss treatment for **§ 1244 stock** applies to the first $1 million of capitalized value of the corporation's stock. If more than $1 million of the corporation's stock is issued, the entity designates which of the shares qualify for § 1244 treatment.[47] In measuring the capitalization of the newly issued stock, property received in exchange for stock is valued at its adjusted basis, reduced by any liabilities assumed by the corporation or to which the property is subject. The fair market value of the property is not considered. The $1 million limitation is determined on the date the stock is issued. Consequently, even though a corporation fails to meet these requirements when the stock later is disposed of by the shareholder, the stock can still qualify as § 1244 stock if the requirements were met on the date the stock was issued.

Mechanics of the Loss Deduction

The amount of ordinary loss deductible in any one year from the disposition of § 1244 stock is limited to $50,000 (or $100,000 for taxpayers filing a joint return with a spouse). If the amount of the loss sustained in the taxable year exceeds these amounts, the remainder is considered a capital loss.

EXAMPLE 31

Harvey acquires § 1244 stock at a cost of $100,000. He sells the stock for $10,000 in the current year. He has an ordinary loss of $50,000 and a capital loss of $40,000. Alternatively, on a joint return, the entire $90,000 loss is ordinary. ■

Only the original holder of § 1244 stock, whether an individual or a partnership, qualifies for ordinary loss treatment. If the stock is sold or donated, it loses its § 1244 status.

Special treatment applies if § 1244 stock is issued by a corporation in exchange for property that has an adjusted basis above its fair market value immediately before the exchange. For purposes of determining ordinary loss upon a subsequent sale, the stock basis is reduced to the fair market value of the property on the date of the exchange.

EXAMPLE 32

Dana transfers property with a basis of $10,000 and a fair market value of $5,000 to a corporation in exchange for shares of § 1244 stock. Assuming the transfer qualifies under § 351, the basis of the stock under the general rule is $10,000, the same as Dana's basis in the property. However, for purposes of § 1244 and measuring the amount of ordinary loss, the stock basis is only $5,000. If the stock is later sold for $3,000, the total loss sustained is $7,000 ($3,000 – $10,000); however, only $2,000 of the loss is ordinary ($3,000 – $5,000). The remaining portion of the loss, $5,000, is a capital loss. ■

[46] See, for example, *Kelson v. U.S.*, 74–2 USTC ¶9714, 34 AFTR 2d 74–6007, 503 F.2d 1291 (CA–10, 1974) and *Kenneth W. Graves*, 87 TCM 1409, T.C.Memo. 2004–140.

[47] Reg. § 1.1244(c)–2(b)(2).

Recall the advantages of issuing some debt to shareholders in exchange for cash contributions to a corporation. A disadvantage of issuing debt is that it does not qualify under § 1244. Should the debt become worthless, the taxpayer generally has a short-term capital loss rather than the ordinary loss for § 1244 stock.

18.4 Gain from Qualified Small Business Stock

Shareholders are given special tax relief for gains recognized on the sale or exchange of stock acquired in a **qualified small business corporation**. The holder of **qualified small business stock** may exclude 50 percent of any gain from the sale or exchange of such stock. However, under the American Recovery and Reinvestment Tax Act of 2009, the exclusion increases to 75 percent for qualified small business stock acquired after February 17, 2009, and from legislation in 2010, the exclusion increases to 100 percent for qualified stock acquired after September 27, 2010, and before 2012.[48] To qualify for the exclusion, the taxpayer must have held the stock for more than five years and must have acquired the stock as part of an original issue.[49] Only noncorporate shareholders qualify for the exclusion.

A qualified small business corporation is a C corporation whose aggregate gross assets did not exceed $50 million on the date the stock was issued.[50] The corporation must be actively involved in a trade or business. This means that at least 80 percent of the corporation's assets must be used in the active conduct of one or more qualified trades or businesses.

A shareholder can apply the exclusion to the greater of (1) $10 million or (2) 10 times the shareholder's aggregate adjusted basis in the qualified stock disposed of during a taxable year.[51]

TAX PLANNING:

18.5 Working with § 351

LO.7

Identify tax planning opportunities associated with organizing and financing a corporation.

Effective tax planning with transfers of property to corporations requires a clear understanding of § 351 and its related Code provisions. The most important question in planning is simply: Does the desired tax result come from complying with § 351 or from avoiding it?

UTILIZING § 351

If the tax-free treatment of § 351 is desired, ensure that the parties transferring property (which includes cash) receive control of the corporation. Simultaneous transfers are not necessary, but a long period of time between transfers could be disastrous if the transfers are not properly documented as part of a single plan. The parties should document and preserve evidence of their intentions. Also, it is helpful to have some reasonable explanation for any delay in the transfers.

To meet the requirements of § 351, mere momentary control on the part of the transferor may not suffice if loss of control is compelled by a prearranged agreement.[52]

EXAMPLE 33

For many years, Paula operated a business as a sole proprietor employing Brooke as manager. To dissuade Brooke from quitting and going out on her own, Paula promised her a 30% interest in the business. To fulfill this promise, Paula transfers the business to

[48] § 1202. The 0% and 15% capital gains rates do not apply. Thus, the maximum effective tax rate on the sale of qualified small business stock is 14% (28% × 50%), 7% (28% × 25%), or 0% (28% × 0%).

[49] The stock must have been issued after August 10, 1993, which is the effective date of § 1202 as originally enacted.

[50] § 1202(d). Its aggregate assets may not exceed this amount at any time between August 10, 1993, and the date the stock was issued.

[51] § 1202(b). The amount is $5 million for married taxpayers filing separately.

[52] Rev.Rul. 54–96, 1954–1 C.B. 111.

newly formed Green Corporation in return for all its stock. Immediately thereafter, Paula transfers 30% of the stock to Brooke. Section 351 probably does not apply to Paula's transfer to Green Corporation because it appears that Paula was under an obligation to relinquish control. If this preexisting obligation exists, § 351 will not be available to Paula because, as the sole property transferor, she does not have control of Green Corporation. However, if there is no obligation and the loss of control was voluntary on Paula's part, momentary control would suffice.[53] ■

Be sure that later transfers of property to an existing corporation satisfy the control requirement if recognition of gain is to be avoided. In this connection, another transferor's interest cannot be counted if the value of stock received is relatively small compared with the value of stock already owned and the primary purpose of the transfer is to qualify other transferors for § 351 treatment.[54]

AVOIDING § 351

Because § 351 provides for the nonrecognition of gain on transfers to controlled corporations, it is often regarded as a favorable relief provision. In some situations, however, avoiding § 351 may produce a more advantageous tax result. The transferors might prefer to recognize gain on the transfer of property if they cannot be particularly harmed by the gain. For example, they may be in low tax brackets, or the gain may be a capital gain from which substantial capital losses can be offset. The corporation will then have a stepped-up basis in the transferred property.

A transferor might also prefer to avoid § 351 to allow for immediate recognition of a loss. Recall that § 351 provides for the nonrecognition of both gains and losses. A transferor who wishes to recognize loss has several alternatives:

- Sell the property to the corporation for its stock. The IRS could attempt to collapse the "sale," however, by taking the approach that the transfer really falls under § 351.[55] If the sale is disregarded, the transferor ends up with a realized, but unrecognized, loss.
- Sell the property to the corporation for other property or boot. Because the transferor receives no stock, § 351 is inapplicable.
- Transfer the property to the corporation in return for securities or nonqualified preferred stock. Recall that § 351 does not apply to a transferor who receives securities or nonqualified preferred stock. In both this and the previous alternatives, watch for the possible disallowance of the loss under the related-party rules.

ETHICS & *Equity*

WILL THE SALE BE RECOGNIZED?

Early in the year, Charles, Lane, and Tami form the Harrier Corporation for the express purpose of developing a shopping center. All parties are experienced contractors, and they transfer various business assets (e.g., building materials, land) to Harrier in exchange for all of its stock. Three months after it is formed, Harrier purchases two cranes from Lane for their fair market value of $400,000 by issuing four annual installment notes of $100,000 each. Since the adjusted basis of the cranes is $550,000, Lane plans to recognize a § 1231 loss of $150,000 in the year of the sale. Does Lane have any potential income tax problem with this plan?

[53] Compare *Fahs v. Florida Machine and Foundry Co.*, 48–2 USTC ¶9329, 36 AFTR 1161, 168 F.2d 957 (CA–5, 1948), with *John C. O'Connor*, 16 TCM 213, T.C.Memo. 1957–50, *aff'd* in 58–2 USTC ¶9913, 2 AFTR 2d 6011, 260 F.2d 358 (CA–6, 1958).

[54] Reg. § 1.351–1(a)(1)(ii).

[55] *U.S. v. Hertwig*, 68–2 USTC ¶9495, 22 AFTR 2d 5249, 398 F.2d 452 (CA–5, 1968).

Suppose the loss property is to be transferred to the corporation and no loss is recognized by the transferor due to § 351. This could present an interesting problem in terms of assessing the economic realities involved.

EXAMPLE 34

Iris and Lamont form Wren Corporation with the following investments: property by Iris (basis of $40,000 and fair market value of $50,000) and property by Lamont (basis of $60,000 and fair market value of $50,000). Each receives 50% of the Wren stock. Has Lamont acted wisely in settling for only 50% of the stock? At first, it would appear so, since Iris and Lamont each invested property of the same value ($50,000). But what about tax considerations? By applying the general carryover basis rules, the corporation now has a basis of $40,000 in Iris's property and $60,000 in Lamont's property. In essence, Iris has shifted a possible $10,000 gain to the corporation while Lamont has transferred a $10,000 potential loss. With this in mind, an equitable allocation of the Wren stock would call for Lamont to receive a greater percentage interest than Iris. This issue is further complicated by the special basis adjustment required when a shareholder, such as Lamont, contributes property with a built-in loss to a corporation. In this situation, if Wren is to take a carryover basis in Lamont's property, Lamont must reduce his stock basis by the $10,000 built-in loss. This reduced stock basis, of course, could lead to a greater tax burden on Lamont when he sells the Wren stock. This may suggest additional support for Lamont having a greater percentage interest than Iris. ■

18.6 Selecting Assets to Transfer

When a business is incorporated, the organizers must determine which assets and liabilities should be transferred to the corporation. Leasing property to the corporation may be a more attractive alternative than transferring ownership. Leasing provides the taxpayer with the opportunity to withdraw money from the corporation in a deductible form without the payment being characterized as a nondeductible dividend. If the property is given to a family member in a lower tax bracket, the lease income can be shifted as well. If the depreciation and other deductions available in connection with the property are larger than the lease income, the taxpayer would retain the property until the income exceeds the deductions.

When an existing cash basis business is incorporated, an important issue to consider is whether the business's accounts receivable and accounts payable will be transferred to the new corporation or be retained by the owner of the unincorporated business. Depending on the approach taken, either the new corporation or the owner of the old unincorporated business will recognize the income associated with the cash basis receivables when they are collected. The cash basis accounts payable raise the corresponding issue of who will claim the deduction.

EXAMPLE 35
THE BIG PICTURE

Return to the facts of *The Big Picture* on p. 18-2. If Emily decides to retain the $25,000 of cash basis accounts receivable rather than transferring them to the newly formed corporation, she will recognize $25,000 of ordinary income upon their collection. Alternatively, if the receivables are transferred to the corporation as the facts suggest, the corporation will recognize the ordinary income. However, a subsequent corporate distribution to Emily of the cash collected could be subject to double taxation as a dividend (see Chapter 19 for further discussion). Given the alternatives available, Emily needs to evaluate which approach is better for the parties involved. ■

Another way to shift income to other taxpayers is by the use of corporate debt. Shareholder debt in a corporation can be given to family members in a lower tax bracket. This technique also causes income to be shifted without a loss of control of the corporation.

18.7 Debt in the Capital Structure

The advantages and disadvantages of debt as opposed to equity have previously been noted. To increase debt without incurring the thin capitalization problem, consider the following:

- Preserve the formalities of the debt. This includes providing for written instruments, realistic interest rates, and specified due dates.
- If possible, have the corporation repay the debt when it comes due. If this is not possible, have the parties renegotiate the arrangement. Try to proceed as a nonshareholder creditor would. It is not unusual, for example, for bondholders of publicly held corporations to extend due dates when default occurs. The alternative is to foreclose and perhaps seriously impair the amount the creditors will recover.
- Avoid provisions in the debt instrument that make the debt convertible to equity in the event of default. These provisions are standard practice when nonshareholder creditors are involved. They serve no purpose if the shareholders are also the creditors and hold debt in proportion to ownership shares.

EXAMPLE 36

Gail, Cliff, and Ruth are equal shareholders in Magenta Corporation. Each transfers cash of $100,000 to Magenta in return for its bonds. The bond agreement provides that the holders will receive additional voting rights in the event Magenta Corporation defaults on its bonds. The voting rights provision is worthless and merely raises the issue of thin capitalization. Gail, Cliff, and Ruth already control Magenta Corporation, so what purpose is served by increasing their voting rights? The parties probably used a "boilerplate" bond agreement that was designed for third-party lenders (e.g., banks and other financial institutions). ■

- Pro rata holding of debt is difficult to avoid. For example, if each of the shareholders owns one-third of the stock, then each will want one-third of the debt. Nevertheless, some variation is possible.

EXAMPLE 37

Assume the same facts as Example 36 except that only Gail and Cliff acquire the bonds. Ruth leases property to Magenta Corporation at an annual rent that approximates the yield on the bonds. Presuming the rent passes the arm's length test (i.e., what unrelated parties would charge), all parties reach the desired result. Gail and Cliff withdraw corporate profits in the form of interest income, and Ruth is provided for with rent income. Magenta Corporation can deduct both the interest and the rent payments. ■

- Try to keep the debt-equity ratio within reasonable proportions. A problem frequently arises when the parties form the corporation. Often the amount invested in capital stock is the minimum required by state law. For example, if the state of incorporation permits a minimum of $1,000, limiting the investment to this amount does not provide much safety for later debt financing by the shareholders.
- Stressing the fair market value of the assets rather than their tax basis to the corporation can be helpful in preparing to defend debt-equity ratios.

EXAMPLE 38

Emily, Josh, and Miles form Black Corporation with the following capital investments: cash of $200,000 from Emily; land worth $200,000 (basis of $20,000) from Josh; and a patent worth $200,000 (basis of $0) from Miles. To state that the equity of Black Corporation is $220,000 (the tax basis to the corporation) does not reflect reality. The equity account is more properly stated at $600,000 ($200,000 + $200,000 + $200,000). ■

- The nature of the business can have an effect on what is an acceptable debt-equity ratio. Capital-intensive industries (e.g., manufacturing, transportation) characteristically rely heavily on debt financing. Consequently, larger debt should be tolerated.

What if a corporation's efforts to avoid the thin capitalization problem fail and the IRS raises the issue on audit? What steps should the shareholders take? They should hedge their position by filing a protective claim for refund claiming dividend treatment on the previously reported interest income. In such an event, ordinary income would be converted to preferential dividend income treatment. Otherwise, the IRS could ultimately invoke the statute of limitations and achieve the best of all possible worlds—the shareholders would have been taxed on the interest income at the ordinary income rates while the corporation would receive no deduction for what is now reclassified as a dividend. By filing the claim for refund, the shareholders have kept the statute of limitations from running until the thin capitalization issue is resolved at the corporate level.

18.8 Investor Losses

Be aware of the danger of losing § 1244 attributes. Only the original holder of § 1244 stock is entitled to ordinary loss treatment. If, after a corporation is formed, the owner transfers shares of stock to family members to shift income within the family group, the benefits of § 1244 are lost.

EXAMPLE 39

Norm incorporates his business by transferring property with a basis of $100,000 for 100 shares of stock. The stock qualifies as § 1244 stock. Norm later gives 50 shares each to his children, Susan and Paul. Eventually, the business fails, and the shares of stock become worthless. If Norm had retained the stock, he would have had an ordinary loss deduction of $100,000 (assuming he filed a joint return). Susan and Paul, however, have a capital loss of $50,000 each because the § 1244 attributes are lost as a result of the gift (i.e., neither Susan nor Paul was an original holder of the stock). ■

REFOCUS ON THE BIG PICTURE

TAX ISSUES CAN BE NEUTRALIZED WHEN GROWING INTO THE CORPORATE FORM

Emily, the sole property transferor, must acquire at least 80 percent of the stock issued by the new corporation in order for the transaction to receive tax-deferred treatment under § 351. Otherwise, a tremendous amount of gain (up to $300,000) will be recognized. As a corollary, David must not receive more than 20 percent of the corporation's stock in exchange for his services (see Examples 9 and 10). However, even if § 351 is available, any corporate debt issued by the corporation will be treated as boot and will trigger gain recognition to Emily (see Example 4). Therefore, she must evaluate the cost of recognizing gain now versus the benefit of the corporation obtaining an interest deduction later.

What If?

Can the § 351 transaction be modified to further reduce personal and business tax costs, both at the time of formation and in future years? Several strategies may be worth considering.

- Instead of having the corporation issue debt on formation, Emily might withhold certain assets. If the building is not transferred, for example, it can be leased to the corporation. The resulting rent payment would mitigate the double tax problem by producing a tax deduction for the corporation.
- An additional benefit results if Emily does not transfer the cash basis receivables to the corporation. This approach avoids a tax at the corporate level and a further tax when the receipts are distributed to Emily in the form of a dividend. If the receivables are withheld, their collection is taxed only to Emily (see Example 35).
- No mention is made as to the existence (or nonexistence) of any accounts payable outstanding at the time of corporate formation. If they do exist, which is likely, it could be wise for Emily to transfer them to the corporation. The subsequent corporate payment of the liability produces a corporate deduction that will reduce any corporate tax.

Double taxation can be mitigated in certain situations with a modest amount of foresight!

KEY TERMS

Built-in loss property, 18–13
Capital contribution, 18–16
Control, 18–6
Investor loss, 18–20
Liabilities in excess of basis, 18–10
Nonbusiness bad debts, 18–20
Property, 18–4
Qualified small business corporation, 18–23
Qualified small business stock, 18–23
Section 1244 stock, 18–22
Securities, 18–5
Thin capitalization, 18–19

DISCUSSION QUESTIONS

1. **LO.1** In terms of justification and effect, § 351 (transfer to a controlled corporation) and § 1031 (like-kind exchange) are much alike. Explain.

2. **LO.1** Under what circumstances will gain and/or loss be recognized on a § 351 transfer?

3. **LO.1** Presley agrees to serve as the chief financial officer for newly formed Red Corporation. As compensation for the services he renders, Red will issue 60 shares of stock to Presley. What is the tax effect to Presley of this transaction?

4. **LO.1** Can the receipt of boot ever be taxable in a § 351 transfer in the absence of realized gain? Explain.

5. **LO.1** Does the receipt of a 10-year note in exchange for the transfer of appreciated property to a controlled corporation cause recognition of gain? Explain.

6. **LO.1** What is the control requirement of § 351? Describe the effect of the following in satisfying this requirement:
   a. A shareholder renders only services to the corporation for stock.
   b. A shareholder both renders services and transfers property to the corporation for stock.
   c. A shareholder has only momentary control after the transfer.
   d. A long period of time elapses between the transfers of property by different shareholders.

ISSUE ID

7. **LO.1** Kate transfers appreciated property to Crow Corporation in exchange for 50% of its stock, while Kevin transfers a secret process and services for the remainder of Crow's stock. Kevin's services relate to expertise he will provide in corporate operations *after* Crow's formation. What are the tax issues?

ISSUE ID

DECISION MAKING

8. **LO.1, 2, 7** Four friends plan to form a corporation for purposes of constructing a shopping center. Charlie will be contributing the land for the project and wants more security than shareholder status provides. He is contemplating two possibilities: receive corporate bonds for his land, or take out a mortgage on the land before transferring it to the corporation. Comment on the choices Charlie is considering. What alternatives can you suggest?

9. **LO.1** Duane and Sally form Robin Corporation by transferring appreciated property in exchange for 60% and 40% of Robin stock, respectively. Are the exchanges taxable if Duane donates his shares to the United Way (a charity) immediately after the exchange?

10. **LO.1** Mary and Paul transfer property while Matt renders services in forming Falcon Corporation. Each receives one-third of its stock. Will the exchanges be taxable? Explain.

ISSUE ID

11. **LO.1** At a point when Robin Corporation has been in existence for six years, shareholder Ted transfers real estate (adjusted basis of $20,000 and fair market value of $100,000) to the corporation for additional stock. At the same time, Peggy, the other shareholder, acquires one share of stock for cash. After the two transfers, the percentages of stock ownership are as follows: 79% by Ted and 21% by Peggy.
    a. What were the parties trying to accomplish?
    b. Will it work? Explain.

12. **LO.2** Does the transfer of property subject to a mortgage to a controlled corporation trigger gain? Explain.

13. **LO.2** Before incorporating her apartment rental business, Libbie takes out second mortgages on several of the units. She uses the mortgage proceeds to make capital improvements to the units. Along with all of the rental units, Libbie transfers the mortgages to the newly formed corporation in return for all of its stock. Discuss the tax consequences of these procedures.

14. **LO.2** Why does § 357(c) require recognition of gain when liabilities assumed by a corporation exceed the adjusted basis of the assets transferred?

15. **LO.3** Discuss how each of the following affects the calculation of the basis of stock received by a shareholder in a § 351 transfer:
    a. The transfer of a liability to the corporation along with property.
    b. Property transferred has built-in losses.
    c. The basis in the property transferred to the corporation.
    d. The receipt of "other property" (i.e., boot) in addition to stock.

16. **LO.3** Identify a situation when a corporation can deduct the value of the stock it issues for the rendition of services. Identify a situation when a deduction is not available.

17. **LO.4** A corporation acquires property as a contribution to capital from a shareholder and from a nonshareholder. Are the rules pertaining to the property's basis the same? Explain.

18. **LO.5** In structuring the capitalization of a corporation, what are the advantages and disadvantages of utilizing debt rather than equity?

19. **LO.5** In determining whether debt of a corporation should be reclassified as stock, comment on the relevance of the following:
    a. The loan is on open account.
    b. The loan is payable on demand.
    c. The corporation does not make timely repayments.
    d. Payments are contingent on earnings.
    e. The loans are in the same proportion as the shareholdings, and the corporation uses the funds to purchase a new building.
    f. The corporation's debt-equity ratio is 5:1.

20. **LO.6** Under what circumstances, if any, may a shareholder deduct a business bad debt on a loan made to the corporation?

21. **LO.6** Four years ago, Nelson purchased stock in Black Corporation for $37,000. The stock has a current value of $5,000. Nelson needs to decide which of the following alternatives to pursue. Determine the tax effect of each. **DECISION MAKING**
    a. Without selling the stock, Nelson deducts $32,000 for the partial worthlessness of the Black Corporation investment.
    b. Nelson sells the stock to his aunt for $5,000 and deducts a $32,000 long-term capital loss.
    c. Nelson sells the stock to a third party and deducts an ordinary loss.
    d. Nelson sells the stock to his mother for $5,000 and deducts a $32,000 long-term capital loss.
    e. Nelson sells the stock to a third party and deducts a $32,000 long-term capital loss.

22. **LO.1, 7** Keith's sole proprietorship holds assets that, if sold, would yield a gain of $100,000. It also owns assets that would yield a loss of $30,000. Keith incorporates his business using only the gain assets. Two days later, Keith sells the loss assets to the newly formed corporation. What is Keith trying to accomplish? Will he be successful? **ISSUE ID**

23. **LO.7** Sarah incorporates her small business, but does not transfer the machinery and equipment the business uses to the corporation. Subsequently, the machinery and equipment are leased to the corporation for an annual rent. What tax reasons might Sarah have for not transferring the machinery and equipment to the corporation when the business was incorporated? **ISSUE ID**

ft.

PROBLEMS

24. **LO.1, 3** Sam, John, Lucy, and Sylvia form Pine Corporation with the following consideration:

	Consideration Transferred		
	Basis to Transferor	**Fair Market Value**	**Number of Shares Issued**
From Sam—			
Inventory	$30,000	$97,000	30*
From John—			
Equipment ($30,000 of depreciation taken by John in previous years)	55,000	99,000	30**
From Lucy—			
Secret process	25,000	90,000	30
From Sylvia—			
Cash	30,000	30,000	10

*Sam receives $7,000 cash in addition to the 30 shares.
**John receives $9,000 cash in addition to the 30 shares.

Assume the value of each share of Pine Corporation stock is $3,000. As to these transactions, provide the following information:

a. Sam's recognized gain or loss. Identify the nature of any such gain or loss.
b. Sam's basis in the Pine stock.
c. Pine Corporation's basis in the inventory.
d. John's recognized gain or loss and its classification.
e. John's basis in the Pine stock.
f. Pine Corporation's basis in the equipment.
g. Lucy's recognized gain or loss.
h. Lucy's basis in the Pine stock.
i. Pine Corporation's basis in the secret process.
j. Sylvia's recognized gain or loss.
k. Sylvia's basis in the Pine stock.

25. **LO.1, 3** Mark and Gail form Maple Corporation with the following consideration:

	Consideration Transferred		
	Basis to Transferor	**Fair Market Value**	**Number of Shares Issued**
From Mark—			
Cash	$ 40,000	$ 40,000	
Installment obligation	140,000	360,000	40
From Gail—			
Cash	140,000	140,000	
Equipment	120,000	180,000	
Patent	4,000	280,000	60

The installment obligation has a face amount of $360,000 and was acquired last year from the sale of land held for investment purposes (adjusted basis of $140,000). As to these transactions, provide the following information:

a. Mark's recognized gain or loss.
b. Mark's basis in the Maple Corporation stock.
c. Maple Corporation's basis in the installment obligation.
d. Gail's recognized gain or loss.

e. Gail's basis in the Maple Corporation stock.
f. Maple Corporation's basis in the equipment and the patent.
g. How would your answers to the preceding questions change if Mark received common stock and Gail received preferred stock?
h. How would your answers change if Gail was a partnership?

26. **LO.1, 7** Jane, Jon, and Clyde incorporate their respective businesses and form Starling Corporation. On March 1 of the current year, Jane exchanges her property (basis of $50,000 and value of $150,000) for 150 shares in Starling Corporation. On April 15, Jon exchanges his property (basis of $70,000 and value of $500,000) for 500 shares in Starling. On May 10, Clyde transfers his property (basis of $90,000 and value of $350,000) for 350 shares in Starling.

DECISION MAKING

a. If the three exchanges are part of a prearranged plan, what gain will each of the parties recognize on the exchanges?
b. Assume Jane and Jon exchanged their property for stock four years ago while Clyde transfers his property for 350 shares in the current year. Clyde's transfer is not part of a prearranged plan with Jane and Jon to incorporate their businesses. What gain will Clyde recognize on the transfer?
c. Returning to the original facts, if the property that Clyde contributes has a basis of $490,000 (instead of $90,000), how might the parties otherwise structure the transaction?

27. **LO.1** Michael Robertson (1635 Maple Street, Syracuse, NY 13201) exchanges property (basis of $200,000 and fair market value of $850,000) for 75% of the stock of Red Corporation. The other 25% is owned by Sarah Mitchell, who acquired her stock several years ago. You represent Michael, who asks whether he must report gain on the transfer. Prepare a letter to Michael and a memorandum for the tax files documenting your response.

COMMUNICATIONS

28. **LO.1** Three years ago, Irene and Julie formed Hummingbird Corporation. Each transferred property to Hummingbird in exchange for 50 shares of its stock. In the current year, Jaime transfers property worth $600,000 (basis of $90,000) for 50 shares (a one-third interest) in Hummingbird Corporation. What are the tax consequences to Jaime and to Hummingbird on the transfer in the current year?

29. **LO.1, 3** Ann and Bob form Robin Corporation. Ann transfers property worth $420,000 (basis of $150,000) for 70 shares in Robin Corporation. Bob receives 30 shares for property worth $165,000 (basis of $30,000) and for legal services (worth $15,000) in organizing the corporation.
a. What gain or income, if any, will the parties recognize on the transfer?
b. What basis do Ann and Bob have in the stock in Robin Corporation?
c. What is Robin Corporation's basis in the property and services it received from Ann and Bob?

30. **LO.1, 7** Rhonda Johnson owns 50% of the stock of Peach Corporation. She and the other 50% shareholder, Rachel Powell, have decided that additional contributions of capital are needed if Peach is to remain successful in its competitive industry. The two shareholders have agreed that Rhonda will contribute assets having a value of $200,000 (adjusted basis of $15,000) in exchange for additional shares of stock. After the transaction, Rhonda will hold 75% of Peach Corporation and Rachel's interest will fall to 25%.

DECISION MAKING

a. What gain is realized on the transaction? How much of the gain will be recognized?
b. Rhonda is not satisfied with the transaction as proposed. How would the consequences change if Rachel agrees to transfer $1,000 of cash in exchange for additional stock? In this case, Rhonda will own slightly less than 75% of Peach and Rachel's interest will be slightly more than 25%.
c. If Rhonda still is not satisfied with the result, what should be done to avoid any gain recognition?

31. **LO.1, 2, 3** Four years ago, Gene exchanged commercial real estate worth $1.5 million (basis of $300,000) and subject to a mortgage of $200,000, for land worth $1.15 million, subject to a mortgage of $150,000, and cash of $300,000. In the current year, Gene transfers the land that he received in the exchange to newly formed Bronze Corporation for all of its stock. Bronze Corporation assumes the original mortgage on the land, current face amount of $100,000, and a second mortgage, face amount of $20,000. Gene

ISSUE ID

had placed the second mortgage on the land to secure the purchase of some equipment that he used in this business. What are the tax issues?

32. **LO.1, 2, 3** David organizes White Corporation with a transfer of land (basis of $200,000, fair market value of $600,000) that is subject to a mortgage of $150,000. A month before the incorporation, David borrowed $100,000 for personal purposes and gave the bank a lien on the land. White Corporation issues stock worth $350,000 to David and assumes the mortgage of $150,000 and the personal loan of $100,000. What are the tax consequences of the incorporation to David and to White Corporation?

DECISION MAKING

33. **LO.1, 3** Michael transfers the following assets to Peach Corporation in exchange for all of its stock. (Assume neither Michael nor Peach plans to make any special tax elections at the time of incorporation.)

Assets	Michael's Adjusted Basis	Fair Market Value
Inventory	$ 60,000	$ 90,000
Delivery vehicles	150,000	100,000
Shelving	80,000	70,000

a. What is Michael's recognized gain or loss?
b. What is Michael's basis in the stock?
c. What is Peach's basis in the inventory, delivery vehicles, and shelving?
d. If Michael has no intentions of selling his Peach stock for at least 15 years, what action would you recommend that Michael and Peach Corporation consider? How does this change the previous answers?

34. **LO.1, 3** Sara and Jane form Wren Corporation. Sara transfers property, basis of $25,000 and value of $200,000, for 50 shares in Wren Corporation. Jane transfers property, basis of $10,000 and value of $185,000, and agrees to serve as manager of Wren for one year; in return, Jane receives 50 shares in Wren. The value of Jane's services to Wren is $15,000.
a. What gain or income do Sara and Jane recognize on the exchange?
b. What is Wren Corporation's basis in the property transferred by Sara and Jane? How does Wren treat the value of the services Jane renders?

35. **LO.1, 3** Assume in Problem 34 that Jane receives the 50 shares of Wren Corporation stock in consideration for the appreciated property and for providing legal services in organizing the corporation. The value of Jane's services is $15,000.
a. What gain or income does Jane recognize?
b. What is Wren Corporation's basis in the property transferred by Jane? How does Wren treat the value of the services Jane renders?

36. **LO.4** RetailMart Corporation desires to set up a distribution facility in a western state. After considerable negotiations with a small town in Oregon, RetailMart accepts the following offer: land and building (fair market value of $4 million) and cash of $1.5 million.
a. How much gain, if any, must RetailMart Corporation recognize?
b. What basis will RetailMart Corporation have in the land and building?
c. Within one year of the contribution, RetailMart renovates the building for $800,000 and purchases inventory for $300,000. What basis will RetailMart Corporation have in each of these assets?
d. What is the treatment of the $400,000 in cash that RetailMart received from the town but did not use?

COMMUNICATIONS

37. **LO.5, 6** Emily Patrick (36 Paradise Road, Northampton, MA 01060) formed Teal Corporation a number of years ago with an investment of $200,000 cash, for which she received $20,000 in stock and $180,000 in bonds bearing interest of 8% and maturing in nine years. Several years later, Emily lent the corporation an additional $50,000 on open account. In the current year, Teal Corporation becomes insolvent and is declared bankrupt. During the corporation's existence, Emily was paid an annual salary of $60,000. Write a letter to Emily in which you explain how she would treat her losses for tax purposes.

38. **LO.5, 6** Stock in Jaybird Corporation (555 Industry Lane, Pueblo, CO 81001) is held equally by Vera, Wade, and Wes. Jaybird seeks additional capital in the amount of $900,000 to construct a building. Vera, Wade, and Wes each propose to lend Jaybird Corporation $300,000, taking from Jaybird a $300,000 four-year note with interest payable annually at two points below the prime rate. Jaybird Corporation has current taxable income of $2 million. You represent Jaybird Corporation. Jaybird's president, Steve Ferguson, asks you how the payments on the notes might be treated for tax purposes. Prepare a letter to Ferguson and a memo to your tax files where you document your conclusions.

COMMUNICATIONS

39. **LO.6** Sam, a single taxpayer, acquired stock in a corporation that qualified as a small business corporation under § 1244, at a cost of $100,000 three years ago. He sells the stock for $10,000 in the current tax year.
    a. How will the loss be treated for tax purposes?
    b. Assume instead that Sam sold the stock to his sister, Kara, a few months after it was acquired for $100,000 (its fair market value). If Kara sells the stock for $60,000 in the current year, how should she treat the loss for tax purposes?

40. **LO.6** Three years ago and at a cost of $40,000, Paul Sanders acquired stock in a corporation that qualified as a small business corporation (under § 1244). A few months after he acquired the stock, when it was still worth $40,000, he gave it to his brother, Mike Sanders. Mike, who is married and files a joint return, sells the stock for $25,000 in the current tax year. Mike asks you, his tax adviser, how the sale will be treated for tax purposes. Prepare a letter to your client and a memo to the file. Mike's address is 10 Hunt Wood Drive, Hadley, PA 16130.

COMMUNICATIONS

41. **LO.6** Susan transfers property (basis of $50,000 and fair market value of $25,000) to Thrush Corporation in exchange for shares of § 1244 stock. (Assume the transfer qualifies under § 351.)
    a. What is the basis of the stock to Susan? (Susan and Thrush do not make an election to reduce her stock basis.)
    b. What is the basis of the stock to Susan for purposes of § 1244?
    c. If Susan sells the stock for $20,000 two years later, how will the loss be treated for tax purposes?

42. **LO.5, 7** Frank, Cora, and Mitch are equal shareholders in Purple Corporation. The corporation's assets have a tax basis of $50,000 and a fair market value of $600,000. In the current year, Frank and Cora each loan Purple Corporation $150,000. The notes to Frank and Cora bear interest of 8% per annum. Mitch leases equipment to Purple Corporation for an annual rental of $12,000. Discuss whether the shareholder loans from Frank and Cora might be reclassified as equity. Consider in your discussion whether Purple Corporation has an acceptable debt-equity ratio.

DECISION MAKING

RESEARCH PROBLEMS

Note: Solutions to Research Problems can be prepared by using the **Checkpoint® Student Edition** online research product, which is available to accompany this text. It is also possible to prepare solutions to the Research Problems by using tax research materials found in a standard tax library.

THOMSON REUTERS
Checkpoint® Student Edition

Research Problem 1. Tim is a real estate broker who specializes in commercial real estate. Although he usually buys and sells on behalf of others, he also maintains a portfolio of property of his own. He holds this property, mainly unimproved land, either as an investment or for sale to others.

In early 2010, Irene and Al contact Tim regarding a tract of land located just outside the city limits. Tim bought the property, which is known as the Moore farm, several years ago for $600,000. At that time, no one knew that it was located on a geological fault line. Irene, a well-known architect, and Al, a building contractor, want Tim to join them in developing the property for residential use. They are aware of the fault line but believe they can circumvent the problem by using newly developed design and construction technology. Because of the geological flaw, however, they regard the Moore farm as being worth only $450,000. Their intent is to organize a corporation to build the housing project, and each party will receive stock commensurate to the property or services contributed.

After consulting his tax adviser, Tim agrees to join the venture if certain modifications to the proposed arrangement are made. The transfer of the land would be structured as a sale to the corporation. Instead of receiving stock, Tim would receive a note from the corporation. The note would be interest bearing and due in five years. The maturity value of the note would be $450,000—the amount that even Tim concedes is the fair market value of the Moore farm.

What income tax consequences ensue from Tim's suggested approach? Compare this result with what would happen if Tim merely transferred the Moore farm in return for stock in the new corporation.

Research Problem 2. After considerable research, Brock and Louise decided to open a well-known franchise restaurant, Sammy's Sandwich Shop. Before opening the shop in a nearby strip shopping center, Brock and Louise paid $1,000 to an attorney to incorporate their business as B&L, Inc. They also paid a franchise fee of $20,000 to SSS Franchisor for the right to operate as Sammy's Sandwich Shop.

Soon, however, they learned that many Sammy's Sandwich Shop locations across the country were failing. In large measure, these failures were due to difficulties in dealing with the franchisor, SSS Franchisor. Brock and Louise also realized that to be successful, they would need to raise an additional $150,000 of capital. Ultimately, they closed the business and sought a refund of the franchise fee. As SSS Franchisor has repeatedly refused to refund their fee and any legal recourse appears fruitless, Brock and Louise have no hope of any recovery. How should the legal and franchise fees be treated for tax purposes?

Partial list of research aids:
Alami El Moujahid, 97 TCM 1165, T.C.Memo. 2009–42.

INTERNET *activity*

Use the tax resources of the Internet to address the following question. Do not restrict your search to the Web, but include a review of newsgroups and general reference materials, practitioner sites and resources, primary sources of the tax law, chat rooms and discussion groups, and other opportunities.

Research Problem 3. Identify two publicly traded corporations that have issued more than one class of stock to their shareholders. Was the issuance of the additional classes of stock part of the original incorporation, or did it occur later? Determine the rationale for the corporations' actions.

CHAPTER

19

Corporations: Distributions Not in Complete Liquidation

LEARNING OBJECTIVES

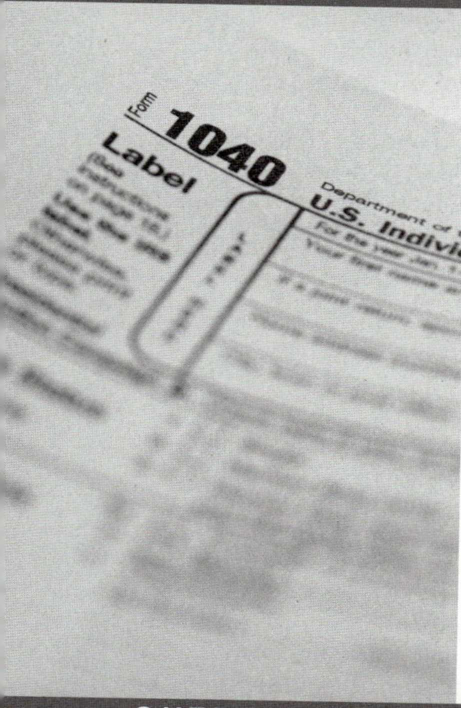

After completing Chapter 19, you should be able to:

LO.1 Explain the role that earnings and profits play in determining the tax treatment of distributions.

LO.2 Compute a corporation's earnings and profits.

LO.3 Apply the rules for allocating earnings and profits to distributions.

LO.4 Describe the tax treatment of dividends for individual shareholders.

LO.5 Evaluate the tax impact of property dividends on the recipient shareholder and the corporation making the distribution.

LO.6 Identify the nature and treatment of constructive dividends.

LO.7 Discuss the tax treatment of stock dividends and stock rights.

LO.8 Identify various stock redemptions that qualify for sale or exchange treatment.

LO.9 Understand the tax impact of stock redemptions on the distributing corporation.

LO.10 Identify planning opportunities available to minimize the tax impact in corporate distributions, constructive dividends, and stock redemptions.

OUTLINE

For the latest in changes to tax legislation, visit **www.cengage.com/taxation/swft.**

THE BIG PICTURE Tax Solutions for the Real World

TAXING CORPORATE DISTRIBUTIONS

Lime Corporation, an ice cream manufacturer, has had a very profitable year. To share its profits with its two equal shareholders, Orange Corporation and Gustavo, it distributes cash of $200,000 to Orange and real estate worth $300,000 (adjusted basis of $20,000) to Gustavo. The real estate is subject to a mortgage of $100,000, which Gustavo assumes. The distribution is made on December 31, Lime's year-end.

Lime Corporation has had both good and bad years in the past. More often than not, however, it has lost money. Despite this year's banner profits, the GAAP-based balance sheet for Lime indicates a year-end deficit in retained earnings. Consequently, the distribution of cash and land is treated as a liquidating distribution for financial reporting purposes, resulting in a reduction of Lime's paid-in capital account.

The tax consequences of the distributions to Lime Corporation and its shareholders depend on a variety of factors that are not directly related to the financial reporting treatment. Identify these factors and explain the tax effects of the distributions to both Lime Corporation and its two shareholders. **Read the chapter and formulate your response.**

Chapter 18 examined the tax consequences of corporate formation. In Chapters 19 and 20, the focus shifts to the tax treatment of corporate distributions, a topic that plays a leading role in tax planning. The importance of corporate distributions derives from the variety of tax treatments that may apply. From the shareholder's perspective, distributions received from the the corporation may be treated as ordinary income, preferentially taxed dividend income, capital gain, or a nontaxable recovery of capital. From the corporation's perspective, distributions made to shareholders are generally not deductible. However, a corporation may recognize losses in liquidating distributions (see Chapter 20), and gains may be recognized at the corporate level on distributions of appreciated property.

In the most common scenario, a distribution triggers dividend income to the shareholder and provides no deduction to the paying corporation, resulting in a double tax (i.e., a tax is levied at both the corporate and the shareholder levels). This double tax may be mitigated by a variety of factors including the corporate dividends received deduction and preferential tax rates on qualified dividends paid to individuals.

As will become apparent in the subsequent discussion, the tax treatment of corporate distributions can be affected by a number of considerations:

- The availability of earnings to be distributed.
- Whether the distribution is a "qualified dividend."
- Whether the shareholder is an individual or another kind of taxpaying entity.
- The basis of the shareholder's stock.
- The character of the property being distributed.
- Whether the shareholder gives up ownership in return for the distribution.
- Whether the distribution is liquidating or nonliquidating.

This chapter discusses the tax rules related to nonliquidating distributions of cash and property. Distributions of stock and stock rights are also addressed along with the tax treatment of stock redemptions. Corporate liquidations are discussed in Chapter 20.

19.1 Corporate Distributions—Overview

LO.1

Explain the role that earnings and profits play in determining the tax treatment of distributions.

To the extent that a distribution is made from corporate earnings and profits (E & P), the shareholder is deemed to receive a dividend, taxed as ordinary income or as preferentially taxed dividend income.[1] Generally, corporate distributions are presumed to be paid out of E & P (defined later in this chapter) and are treated as dividends *unless* the parties to the transaction can show otherwise. Distributions not treated as dividends (because of insufficient E & P) are nontaxable to the extent of the shareholder's stock basis, which is reduced accordingly. The excess of the distribution over the shareholder's basis is treated as a gain from the sale or exchange of the stock.[2]

EXAMPLE 1

At the beginning of the year, Amber Corporation (a calendar year taxpayer) has E & P of $15,000. The corporation generates no additional E & P during the year. On July 1, the corporation distributes $20,000 to its sole shareholder, Bonnie, whose stock basis is $4,000. In this situation, Bonnie recognizes dividend income of $15,000 (the amount of E & P distributed). In addition, she reduces her stock basis from $4,000 to zero, and she recognizes a taxable gain of $1,000 (the excess of the distribution over the stock basis). ■

19.2 Earnings and Profits (E & P)

LO.2

Compute a corporation's earnings and profits.

The notion of **earnings and profits** is similar in many respects to the accounting concept of retained earnings. Both are measures of the firm's accumulated capital (E & P includes both the accumulated E & P of the corporation since February 28, 1913, and the current year's E & P). A difference exists, however, in the way these figures are calculated. The computation of retained earnings is based on financial accounting rules while E & P is determined using rules specified in the tax law.

E & P fixes the upper limit on the amount of dividend income that shareholders must recognize as a result of a distribution by the corporation. In this sense, E & P represents the corporation's economic ability to pay a dividend without impairing its capital. Thus, the effect of a specific transaction on E & P may often be determined by assessing whether the transaction increases or decreases the corporation's capacity to pay a dividend.

COMPUTATION OF E & P

The Code does not explicitly define the term *earnings and profits.* Instead, a series of adjustments to taxable income are identified to provide a measure of the corporation's economic income. Both cash basis and accrual basis corporations use the same approach when determining E & P.[3]

Additions to Taxable Income

To determine current E & P, it is necessary to add *all* previously excluded income items back to taxable income. Included among these positive adjustments are interest on municipal bonds, excluded life insurance proceeds (in excess of cash surrender value), and Federal income tax refunds from tax paid in prior years.

EXAMPLE 2

A corporation collects $100,000 on a key employee life insurance policy (the corporation is the owner and beneficiary of the policy). At the time the policy matured on the death of the insured employee, it possessed a cash surrender value of $30,000. None of

[1] §§ 301(c)(1), 316, and 1(h)(11).

[2] §§ 301(c)(2) and (3).

[3] Section 312 describes many of the adjustments to taxable income necessary to determine E & P. Regulation § 1.312–6 addresses the effect of accounting methods on E & P.

the $100,000 is included in the corporation's taxable income, but $70,000 is added to taxable income when computing current E & P (i.e., amount collected on the policy net of its cash surrender value). The collection of the $30,000 cash surrender value does not increase E & P because it does not reflect an increase in the corporation's dividend-paying capacity. Instead, it represents a shift in the corporation's assets from life insurance to cash. ■

In addition to excluded income items, the dividends received deduction (see Chapter 17) and the domestic production activities deduction (see Chapter 7) are added back to taxable income to determine E & P. Neither of these deductions decreases the corporation's assets. Instead, they are partial exclusions for specific types of income (dividend income and income from domestic production activities). Since they do not impair the corporation's ability to pay dividends, they do not reduce E & P.

Subtractions from Taxable Income

When calculating E & P, it is also necessary to subtract certain nondeductible expenses from taxable income. These negative adjustments include the nondeductible portion of meal and entertainment expenses, related-party losses, expenses incurred to produce tax-exempt income, Federal income taxes paid, nondeductible key employee life insurance premiums (net of increases in cash surrender value), and nondeductible fines, penalties, and lobbying expenses.

EXAMPLE 3

A corporation sells property with a basis of $10,000 to its sole shareholder for $8,000. Because of § 267 (disallowance of losses on sales between related parties), the $2,000 loss cannot be deducted when calculating the corporation's taxable income. However, since the overall economic effect of the transaction is a decrease in the corporation's assets by $2,000, the loss reduces the current E & P for the year of sale. ■

EXAMPLE 4

A corporation pays a $10,000 premium on a key employee life insurance policy covering the life of its president. As a result of the payment, the cash surrender value of the policy is increased by $7,000. Although none of the $10,000 premium is deductible for tax purposes, current E & P is reduced by $3,000 (i.e., amount of the premium payment net of the increase in the cash surrender value). The $7,000 increase in cash surrender value is not subtracted because it does not represent a decrease in the corporation's ability to pay a dividend. Instead, it represents a shift in the corporation's assets, from cash to life insurance. ■

Timing Adjustments

Some E & P adjustments shift the effect of a transaction from the year of its inclusion in or deduction from taxable income to the year in which it has an economic effect on the corporation. Charitable contributions, net operating losses, and capital losses all necessitate this kind of adjustment.

EXAMPLE 5

During 2011, a corporation makes charitable contributions, $12,000 of which cannot be deducted when calculating the taxable income for the year because of the 10% taxable income limitation. Consequently, the $12,000 is carried forward to 2012 and fully deducted in that year. The excess charitable contribution reduces the corporation's current E & P for 2011 by $12,000 and increases its current E & P for 2012 (when the deduction is allowed) by the same amount. The increase in E & P in 2012 is necessary because the charitable contribution carryover reduces the taxable income for that year (the starting point for computing E & P) and already has been taken into account in determining the E & P for 2011. ■

Gains and losses from property transactions generally affect the determination of E & P only to the extent that they are recognized for tax purposes. Thus, gains and losses deferred under the like-kind exchange provision and deferred involuntary conversion gains do not affect E & P until recognized. Accordingly, no timing adjustment is required for these items.

Accounting Method Adjustments

In addition to the above adjustments, accounting methods used for determining E & P are generally more conservative than those allowed for calculating taxable income. For example, the installment method is not permitted for E & P purposes.[4] Thus, an adjustment is required for the deferred gain from property sales made during the year under the installment method. All principal payments are treated as having been received in the year of sale.

EXAMPLE 6

In 2011, Cardinal Corporation, a cash basis calendar year taxpayer, sells unimproved real estate with a basis of $20,000 for $100,000. Under the terms of the sale, Cardinal will receive two annual payments of $50,000, beginning in 2012, each with interest of 9%. Cardinal Corporation does not elect out of the installment method. Since Cardinal's taxable income for 2011 will not reflect any of the gain from the sale, the corporation must make an $80,000 positive adjustment for 2011 (the deferred gain from the sale). Similarly, $40,000 negative adjustments will be required in 2012 and 2013 when the deferred gain is recognized under the installment method. ■

The alternative depreciation system (ADS) must be used for purposes of computing E & P.[5] This method requires straight-line depreciation over a recovery period equal to the Asset Depreciation Range (ADR) midpoint life.[6] Also, ADS prohibits additional first-year depreciation.[7] If MACRS cost recovery is used for income tax purposes, a positive or negative adjustment equal to the difference between MACRS and ADS must be made each year. Likewise, when assets are disposed of, an additional adjustment to taxable income is required to allow for the difference in gain or loss caused by the gap between income tax basis and the E & P basis.[8] The adjustments arising from depreciation are illustrated in the following example.

EXAMPLE 7

On January 2, 2009, White Corporation paid $30,000 to purchase equipment with an ADR midpoint life of 10 years and a MACRS class life of 7 years. The equipment was depreciated under MACRS. The asset was sold on July 2, 2011, for $27,000. For purposes of determining taxable income and E & P, cost recovery claimed on the equipment is summarized below. Assume White elected not to claim § 179 expense or additional first-year depreciation on the property.

Year	Cost Recovery Computation	MACRS	ADS	Adjustment Amount
2009	$30,000 × 14.29%	$ 4,287		
	$30,000 ÷ 10-year ADR recovery period × ½ (half-year for first year of service)		$1,500	$2,787
2010	$30,000 × 24.49%	7,347		
	$30,000 ÷ 10-year ADR recovery period		3,000	4,347
2011	$30,000 × 17.49% × ½ (half-year for year of disposal)	2,624		
	$30,000 ÷ 10-year ADR recovery period × ½ (half-year for year of disposal)		1,500	1,124
	Total cost recovery	$14,258	$6,000	$8,258

[4]§ 312(n)(5).

[5]§ 312(k)(3)(A).

[6]See § 168(g)(2). The ADR midpoint lives for most assets are set out in Rev.Proc. 87–56, 1987–2 C.B. 674. The recovery period is 5 years for automobiles and light-duty trucks and 40 years for real property. For assets with no class life, the recovery period is 12 years.

[7]§ 168(k)(2). This provision allowing additional first-year cost recovery applied for certain assets placed in service before January 1, 2005. In addition, it is available for certain assets placed in service from 2008 through 2012.

[8]§ 312(f)(1).

Each year White Corporation will increase taxable income by the adjustment amount indicated previously to determine E & P. Additionally, when computing E & P for 2011, White will reduce taxable income by $8,258 to account for the excess gain recognized for income tax purposes, as shown below.

	Income Tax	E & P
Amount realized	$ 27,000	$ 27,000
Adjusted basis for income tax ($30,000 cost – $14,258 MACRS)	(15,742)	
Adjusted basis for E & P ($30,000 cost – $6,000 ADS)		(24,000)
Gain on sale	$ 11,258	$ 3,000
Adjustment amount ($3,000 – $11,258)	($ 8,258)	

In addition to more conservative depreciation methods, the E & P rules impose limitations on the deductibility of § 179 expense. In particular, this expense must be deducted over a period of five years.[9] Thus, in any year that § 179 is elected, 80 percent of the resulting expense must be added back to taxable income to determine current E & P. In each of the following four years, a negative adjustment equal to 20 percent of the § 179 expense must be made.

The E & P rules also require specific accounting methods in various situations, making adjustments necessary when different methods are used for income tax purposes. For example, E & P requires cost depletion rather than percentage depletion. When accounting for long-term contracts, E & P rules specify the percentage of completion method rather than the completed contract method.[10] As the E & P determination does not allow for the amortization of organizational expenses, any such expense deducted when computing taxable income must be added back to determine E & P.[11] To account for income deferral under the LIFO inventory method, the E & P computation requires an adjustment for changes in the LIFO recapture amount (the excess of FIFO over LIFO inventory value) during the year. Increases in LIFO recapture are added to taxable income and decreases are subtracted.[12] E & P rules also specify that intangible drilling costs and mine exploration and development costs be amortized over a period of 60 months and 120 months, respectively. For income tax purposes, however, these costs can be deducted in the current year.[13]

SUMMARY OF E & P ADJUSTMENTS

Recall that E & P serves as a measure of a corporation's earnings that are available for distribution as taxable dividends to the shareholders. Current E & P is determined by making a series of adjustments to the corporation's taxable income that are outlined in Concept Summary 19.1. Other items that affect E & P, such as property dividends and stock redemptions, are covered later in the chapter.

CURRENT VERSUS ACCUMULATED E & P

Accumulated E & P is the total of all previous years' current E & P (since February 28, 1913) reduced by distributions made from E & P in previous years. It is important to distinguish between **current E & P** and **accumulated E & P** because the taxability of corporate distributions depends upon how these two accounts are allocated to each distribution made during the year. A complex set of rules governs the allocation process.[14] These rules are described in the following section and summarized in Concept Summary 19.2.

[9] § 312(k)(3)(B).
[10] § 312(n)(6).
[11] § 312(n)(3).
[12] § 312(n)(4).
[13] § 312(n)(2).
[14] Regulations relating to the source of a distribution are at Reg. § 1.316–2.

CONCEPT SUMMARY 19.1

E & P Adjustments

Nature of the Transaction	Adjustment to Taxable Income to Determine Current E & P	
	Addition	**Subtraction**
Tax-exempt income	X	
Dividends received deduction	X	
Domestic production activities deduction	X	
Collection of proceeds from insurance policy on life of corporate officer (in excess of cash surrender value)	X	
Deferred gain on installment sale (all gain is added to E & P in year of sale)	X	
Future recognition of installment sale gross profit		X
Excess charitable contribution (over 10% limitation) and excess capital loss in year incurred		X
Deduction of charitable contribution, NOL, or capital loss carryovers in succeeding taxable years (increases E & P because deduction reduces taxable income while E & P was reduced in a prior year)	X	
Federal income taxes paid		X
Federal income tax refund	X	
Loss on sale between related parties		X
Nondeductible fines, penalties, and lobbying expenses		X
Nondeductible meal and entertainment expenses		X
Payment of premiums on insurance policy on life of corporate officer (in excess of increase in cash surrender value of policy)		X
Realized gain (not recognized) on an involuntary conversion	No effect	
Realized gain or loss (not recognized) on a like-kind exchange	No effect	
Excess percentage depletion (only cost depletion can reduce E & P)	X	
Accelerated depreciation (E & P is reduced only by straight-line, units-of-production, or machine hours depreciation)	X	X
Additional first-year depreciation	X	
Section 179 expense in year elected (80%)	X	
Section 179 expense in four years following election (20% each year)		X
Increase (decrease) in LIFO recapture amount	X	X
Intangible drilling costs deducted currently (reduce E & P in future years by amortizing costs over 60 months)	X	
Mine exploration and development costs (reduce E & P in future years by amortizing costs over 120 months)	X	

ALLOCATING E & P TO DISTRIBUTIONS

LO.3

Apply the rules for allocating earnings and profits to distributions.

When a positive balance exists in both the current and accumulated E & P accounts, corporate distributions are deemed to be made first from current E & P and then from accumulated E & P. When distributions exceed the amount of current E & P, it becomes necessary to allocate current and accumulated E & P to each distribution made during the year. Current E & P is applied first on a pro rata basis (using dollar amounts) to each distribution. Then, accumulated E & P is applied in chronological order, beginning with the earliest distribution. As seen in the following example, this allocation is important if any shareholder sells stock during the year.

GLOBAL
Tax Issues

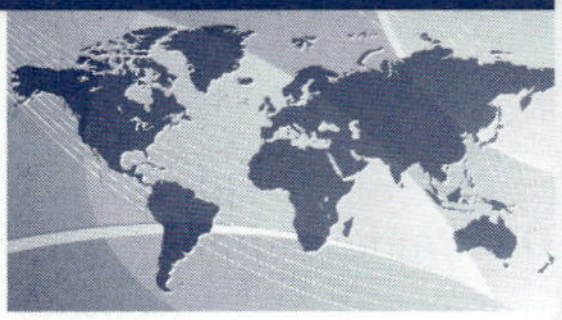

E & P in Controlled Foreign Corporations

U.S. multinational companies often conduct business overseas using foreign subsidiaries known as "controlled foreign corporations," or CFCs. This organizational structure would seem to be ideal for income tax avoidance if the CFC is incorporated in a low-tax jurisdiction (a tax haven country). In the absence of any rules to the contrary, the higher U.S. tax on foreign earnings could be deferred until the earnings are repatriated to the United States through dividends paid to the U.S. parent.

To prevent this deferral, the tax law compels a U.S. parent corporation to recognize some of the unrepatriated earnings of the CFC as income. The foreign corporation's E & P is used to determine the amount of income that is recognized annually by the U.S. parent corporation. Determining the CFC's E & P is no easy task. Foreign corporations (including CFCs) typically compute their book income using foreign generally accepted accounting principles (GAAP). Since the starting point for computing E & P for foreign corporations is U.S. GAAP book income rather than taxable income, an extra layer of complexity is introduced. First, the foreign company's book income must be converted to a U.S. GAAP basis, and then a series of adjustments (similar to the adjustments reflected in Concept Summary 19.1) is made to U.S. book income to determine E & P.

EXAMPLE 8

On January 1 of the current year, Black Corporation has accumulated E & P of $10,000. Current E & P for the year amounts to $30,000. Megan and Matt are sole *equal* shareholders of Black from January 1 to July 31. On August 1, Megan sells all of her stock to Helen. Black makes two distributions to the shareholders during the year: $40,000 to Megan and Matt ($20,000 each) on July 1, and $40,000 to Matt and Helen ($20,000 each) on December 1. Current and accumulated E & P are applied to the two distributions as follows:

	Source of Distribution		
	Current E & P	**Accumulated E & P**	**Return of Capital**
July 1 distribution ($40,000)	$15,000	$10,000	$15,000
December 1 distribution ($40,000)	15,000	–0–	25,000

Since 50% of the total distributions are made on July 1 and December 1, respectively, one-half of current E & P is applied to each of the two distributions. Accumulated E & P is applied in chronological order, so the entire amount attaches to the July 1 distribution. The tax consequences to the shareholders are presented below.

	Shareholder		
	Megan	**Matt**	**Helen**
July distribution ($40,000)			
Dividend income—			
From current E & P ($15,000)	$ 7,500	$ 7,500	$ –0–
From accumulated E & P ($10,000)	5,000	5,000	–0–
Return of capital ($15,000)	7,500	7,500	–0–

	Shareholder		
	Megan	**Matt**	**Helen**
December distribution ($40,000)			
Dividend income—			
From current E & P ($15,000)	$ –0–	$ 7,500	$ 7,500
From accumulated E & P ($0)	–0–	–0–	–0–
Return of capital ($25,000)	–0–	12,500	12,500
Total dividend income	$12,500	$20,000	$ 7,500
Nontaxable return of capital (assuming sufficient basis in the stock investment)	$ 7,500	$20,000	$12,500

Because the balance in the accumulated E & P account is exhausted when it is applied to the July 1 distribution, Megan has more dividend income than Helen, even though both receive equal distributions during the year. In addition, each shareholder's basis is reduced by the nontaxable return of capital; any excess over basis results in taxable gain. ■

When the tax years of the corporation and its shareholders are not the same, it may be impossible to determine the amount of current E & P on a timely basis. For example, if shareholders use a calendar year and the corporation uses a fiscal year, then current E & P may not be ascertainable until after the shareholders' returns have been filed. To address this timing issue, the allocation rules presume that current E & P is sufficient to cover every distribution made during the year until the parties can show otherwise.

EXAMPLE 9

Green Corporation uses a fiscal year of July 1 through June 30 for tax purposes. Carol, Green's only shareholder, uses a calendar year. On July 1, 2011, Green Corporation has a zero balance in its accumulated E & P account. For fiscal year 2011–2012, the corporation suffers a $5,000 deficit in current E & P. On August 1, 2011, Green distributes $10,000 to Carol. The distribution is dividend income to Carol and is reported when she files her income tax return for the 2011 calendar year, on or before April 15, 2012. Because Carol cannot prove until June 30, 2012, that the corporation has a deficit for the 2011–2012 fiscal year, she must assume the $10,000 distribution is fully covered by current E & P. When Carol learns of the deficit, she can file an amended return for 2011 showing the $10,000 as a return of capital. ■

Additional difficulties arise when either the current or the accumulated E & P account has a deficit balance. In particular, when current E & P is positive and accumulated E & P has a deficit balance, accumulated E & P is *not* netted against current E & P. Instead, the distribution is deemed to be a taxable dividend to the extent of the positive current E & P balance.

EXAMPLE 10
THE BIG PICTURE

Return to the facts of *The Big Picture* on p. 19-2. Recall that Lime Corporation had a deficit in GAAP-based retained earnings at the start of the year and banner profits during the year. Assume that these financial results translate into an $800,000 deficit in accumulated E & P at the start of the year and current E & P of $600,000. In addition, for purposes of this example, assume that there is no mortgage on the real estate. In this case, current E & P would exceed the $500,000 of cash and property distributed to the shareholders. The distributions are be treated as taxable dividends; they are deemed to be paid from current E & P even though Lime still has a deficit in accumulated E & P at the end of the year. ■

In contrast to the previous rule, when a deficit exists in current E & P and a positive balance exists in accumulated E & P, the accounts are netted at the date of distribution. If the resulting balance is zero or negative, the distribution is a return of capital. If a positive balance results, the distribution is a dividend to the extent of the balance. Any loss in current E & P is deemed to accrue ratably throughout the year unless the parties can show otherwise.

CONCEPT SUMMARY 19.2

Allocating E & P to Distributions

1. Current E & P is applied first to distributions on a pro rata basis; then, accumulated E & P is applied (as necessary) in chronological order beginning with the earliest distribution. See Example 8.
2. Until the parties can show otherwise, it is presumed that current E & P covers all distributions. See Example 9.
3. When a deficit exists in accumulated E & P and a positive balance exists in current E & P, distributions are regarded as dividends to the extent of current E & P. See Example 10.
4. When a deficit exists in current E & P and a positive balance exists in accumulated E & P, the two accounts are netted at the date of distribution. If the resulting balance is zero or negative, the distribution is treated as a return of capital, first reducing the basis of the stock to zero, then generating taxable gain. If a positive balance results, the distribution is a dividend to the extent of the balance. Any current E & P deficit is deemed to accrue ratably throughout the year unless the corporation can show otherwise. See Example 11.

EXAMPLE 11

At the beginning of the current year, Gray Corporation (a calendar year taxpayer) has accumulated E & P of $10,000. During the year, the corporation incurs a $15,000 deficit in current E & P that accrues ratably. On July 1, Gray distributes $6,000 in cash to Hal, its sole shareholder. To determine how much of the $6,000 cash distribution represents dividend income to Hal, the balances of both accumulated and current E & P as of July 1 are determined and netted. This is necessary because of the deficit in current E & P.

	Source of Distribution	
	Current E & P	Accumulated E & P
January 1		$10,000
July 1 (½ of $15,000 current E & P deficit)	($7,500)	2,500
July 1 distribution of $6,000:		
Dividend income: $2,500		
Return of capital: $3,500		

The balance in E & P just before the July 1 distribution is $2,500. Thus, of the $6,000 distribution, $2,500 is taxed as a dividend, and $3,500 represents a return of capital. ■

19.3 DIVIDENDS

LO.4

Describe the tax treatment of dividends for individual shareholders.

As noted earlier, distributions by a corporation from its E & P are treated as dividends. The tax treatment of dividends varies, depending on whether the shareholder receiving them is a corporation or another kind of taxpaying entity. All corporations treat dividends as ordinary income and are permitted a dividends received deduction (see Chapter 17). In contrast, individuals apply reduced tax rates on qualified dividend income through 2012 while nonqualified dividends are taxed as ordinary income.

ETHICS & Equity

IS THE DOUBLE TAX ON DIVIDENDS FAIR?

As noted in this chapter, the double tax on dividends remains controversial. The tax rate on qualified dividends has, in the past, been as high as 70 percent, and it is possible that the current 15 percent tax rate will be increased when it expires at the end of 2012. Yet, in most countries throughout the world, there is no double tax on dividend income. Many arguments for and against the double tax have been made, usually reflecting the vested interests of the individuals or organizations involved. Arguments supporting repeal of the double tax focus on capital formation and economic stimulus, while those against repeal are based on equity. What do *you* believe? Is the double tax imposed on dividends fair? Why or why not?

Corporate Integration

GLOBAL
Tax Issues

From an international perspective, the double taxation of dividends is unusual. Most countries have adopted a policy of corporate integration, which imposes a single tax on corporate profits. Corporate integration takes several forms. One popular approach is to impose a tax at the corporate level, but allow shareholders to claim a credit for corporate-level taxes paid when dividends are received. A second alternative is to allow a corporate-level deduction for dividends paid to shareholders. A third approach is to allow shareholders to exclude corporate dividends from income. A fourth alternative suggested in the past by the U.S. Treasury is the "comprehensive business income tax," which excludes both dividend and interest income while disallowing deductions for interest expense.

RATIONALE FOR REDUCED TAX RATES ON DIVIDENDS

The double tax on corporate income has always been controversial. Arguably, taxing dividends twice creates several undesirable economic distortions, including:

- An incentive to invest in noncorporate rather than corporate entities.
- An incentive for corporations to finance operations with debt rather than with equity since interest payments are deductible. Notably, this behavior increases the vulnerability of corporations in economic downturns because of higher leverage.
- An incentive for corporations to retain earnings and structure distributions of profits to avoid the double tax.

Collectively, these distortions raise the cost of capital for corporate investments. Estimates are that eliminating the double tax would increase capital stock in the corporate sector by as much as $500 billion.[15] In addition, some argue that elimination of the double tax would make the United States more competitive globally. Bear in mind that a majority of our trading partners assess only one tax on corporate income.

While many support a reduced or no tax rate on dividends, others contend that the double tax should remain in place because of the concentration of economic power held by publicly traded corporations. Furthermore, many of the distortions noted above can be avoided through the use of deductible payments by C corporations and by utilizing other forms of doing business (e.g., partnerships, limited liability companies, and S corporations). Those favoring retention of the double tax also note that the benefits of reduced tax rates on dividends flow disproportionately to the wealthy.[16]

The United States continues to struggle to find the appropriate course to follow on the taxation of dividends. The reduced tax rate on **qualified dividends** for individuals applicable through 2012 reflects a compromise between the complete elimination of tax on dividends and the treatment of dividends as ordinary income. If new legislation is not enacted, however, beginning in 2013 qualified dividends will once again be taxed as ordinary income.

QUALIFIED DIVIDENDS

Qualified Dividends—Application and Effect

Under current law, dividends that meet certain requirements are subject to a 15 percent tax rate for most individual taxpayers from 2003 through 2012. Individuals

[15] Integration of Individual and Corporate Tax Systems, Report of the Department of the Treasury (January 1992).

[16] The Urban Institute–Brookings Institution Tax Policy Center estimates that more than one-half—53%—of the benefits from the reduced tax rate on dividends go to the 0.2% of households with incomes over $1 million.

TAX in the NEWS — Higher Taxes on Dividends Don't Mean Lower Dividends

Even if the reduced tax rate on dividends had expired at the end of 2010, there probably would not have been much impact on corporations' dividend policies. The sensitivity of some companies to how the market may react to dividend cuts would likely have deterred them from reducing their dividends. In addition, shareholders who are not subject to individual tax rates, such as pension funds and foreign investors, own a large portion of U.S. equities. Reuvan Avi-Yonah, a professor at the University of Michigan Law School, suggests that during the last decade companies pandered to foreign hedge fund shareholders by favoring stock redemptions over dividends as a means of paying assets to shareholders. As a result, he argues, the tax cut was not effective in encouraging companies to pay out dividends.

Other research by three accounting professors (Doug Shackelford, Jennifer Blouin, and Jana Raedy) found that the dividend tax cut did lead to larger dividend payouts by firms. However, the effect was greatest when corporate officers and directors held large interests in the company. This suggests that the increased dividend payouts in these companies was motivated by the self-interested behavior of those who set dividend policies. Even if the tax cuts spurred dividend payments by corporations, most academics agree that the effect was not as large as anticipated.

Source: Martin Vaughan, "Higher Taxes May Not Push Firms to Cut Dividends," *Wall Street Journal*, August 30, 2010.

in the 10 or 15 percent rate brackets were subject to a 5 percent rate on dividends paid from 2003 through 2007. Beginning in 2008, dividends are exempt from tax for these lower-income taxpayers.[17]

Qualified Dividends—Requirements

To be taxed at the lower rates, dividends must be paid by either domestic or certain qualified foreign corporations. Qualified foreign corporations include those traded on a U.S. stock exchange or any corporation located in a country that (1) has a comprehensive income tax treaty with the United States, (2) has an information-sharing agreement with the United States, and (3) is approved by the Treasury.[18]

Two other requirements must be met for dividends to qualify for the favorable rates. First, dividends paid to shareholders who hold both long and short positions in the stock do not qualify. Second, the stock on which the dividend is paid must be held for more than 60 days during the 121-day period beginning 60 days before the ex-dividend date.[19] To allow for settlement delays, the ex-dividend date is typically 2 days before the date of record on a dividend. This holding period rule parallels the rule applied to corporations that claim the dividends received deduction.[20]

EXAMPLE 12

In June of the current year, Green Corporation announces that a dividend of $1.50 will be paid on each share of its common stock to shareholders of record on July 15. Amy and Corey, two unrelated shareholders, own 1,000 shares of the stock on the record date (July 15). Consequently, each receives $1,500 (1,000 shares × $1.50). Assume Amy purchased her stock on January 15 of this year, while Corey purchased her stock on July 1. Both shareholders sell their stock on July 20. To qualify for the lower dividend rate, stock must be held for more than 60 days during the 121-day period beginning 60 days prior to July 13 (the ex-dividend date). The $1,500 Amy receives is subject to preferential 15%/0% treatment. The $1,500 Corey receives, however, is not. Corey did not meet the 60-day holding requirement, so her dividend will be taxed as ordinary income. ■

[17] See §§ 1(h)(1) and (11).

[18] In Notice 2006–101, 2006–2 C.B. 930, the Treasury identified 55 qualifying countries (among those included on the list are the members of the European Union, the Russian Federation, Canada, and Mexico). Nonqualifying countries not on the list include most of the former Soviet republics (except Kazakhstan), Bermuda, and the Netherlands Antilles.

[19] § 1(h)(11)(B)(iii)(I).

[20] See § 246(c) and the relevant discussion in Chapter 17.

PROPERTY DIVIDENDS

LO.5

Evaluate the tax impact of property dividends on the recipient shareholder and the corporation making the distribution.

Although most corporate distributions are cash, a corporation may distribute a **property dividend** for various reasons. For example, the shareholders could want a particular property that is held by the corporation. Similarly, a corporation with low cash reserves may still wish to distribute a dividend to its shareholders.

Property distributions have the same impact as distributions of cash except for effects attributable to any difference between the basis and the fair market value of the distributed property. In most situations, distributed property is appreciated, so its sale would result in a gain to the corporation. Distributions of property with a basis that differs from fair market value raise several tax questions.

- For the shareholder:
  - *What is the amount of the distribution?*
  - *What is the basis of the property in the shareholder's hands?*
- For the corporation:
  - *Is a gain or loss recognized as a result of the distribution?*
  - *What is the effect of the distribution on E & P?*

Property Dividends—Effect on the Shareholder

When a corporation distributes property rather than cash to a shareholder, the amount distributed is measured by the fair market value of the property on the date of distribution.[21] As with a cash distribution, the portion of a property distribution covered by existing E & P is a dividend, and any excess is treated as a return of capital until stock basis is recovered. If the fair market value of the property distributed exceeds the corporation's E & P and the shareholder's basis in the stock investment, a capital gain usually results.

The amount distributed is reduced by any liabilities to which the distributed property is subject immediately before and immediately after the distribution and by any liabilities of the corporation assumed by the shareholder. The basis of the distributed property for the shareholder is the fair market value of the property on the date of the distribution.

EXAMPLE 13
THE BIG PICTURE

Return to the facts of *The Big Picture* on p. 19-2. Lime Corporation distributed property with a $300,000 fair market value and $20,000 adjusted basis to one of its shareholders, Gustavo. The property was subject to a $100,000 mortgage, which Gustavo assumed. As a result, Gustavo has a taxable dividend of $200,000 [$300,000 (fair market value) − $100,000 (liability)]. The basis of the property to Gustavo is $300,000. ■

EXAMPLE 14

Red Corporation owns 10% of Tan Corporation. Tan has ample E & P to cover any distributions made during the year. One distribution made to Red Corporation consists of a vacant lot with an adjusted basis of $75,000 and a fair market value of $50,000. Red has a taxable dividend of $50,000, and its basis in the lot is $50,000. ■

Distributing property that has depreciated in value as a property dividend may reflect poor planning. Note what happens in Example 14. Basis of $25,000 disappears due to the loss (adjusted basis of $75,000, fair market value of $50,000). As an alternative, Tan Corporation could sell the lot and use the loss to reduce its taxes. Then, Tan could distribute the $50,000 of proceeds to shareholders.

Property Dividends—Effect on the Corporation

All distributions of appreciated property generate gain recognition to the distributing corporation.[22] In effect, a corporation that distributes appreciated property is treated

[21] Section 301 describes the tax treatment of corporate distributions to shareholders.

[22] Section 311 describes how corporations are taxed on distributions.

as if it had sold the property to the shareholder for its fair market value. However, the distributing corporation does *not* recognize loss on distributions of property.

EXAMPLE 15
THE BIG PICTURE

Return to the facts of *The Big Picture* on p. 19-2. Lime Corporation distributed property with a fair market value of $300,000 and an adjusted basis of $20,000 to Gustavo, one of its shareholders. As a result, Lime recognizes a $280,000 gain on the distribution. ■

EXAMPLE 16

A corporation distributes land with a basis of $30,000 and a fair market value of $10,000. The corporation does not recognize a loss on the distribution. ■

If the distributed property is subject to a liability in excess of its basis or the shareholder assumes such a liability, a special rule applies. For purposes of determining gain on the distribution, the fair market value of the property is treated as not being less than the amount of the liability.[23]

EXAMPLE 17

Assume the land in Example 16 is subject to a liability of $35,000. The corporation recognizes a gain of $5,000 on the distribution ($35,000 – $30,000). ■

Corporate distributions reduce E & P by the amount of money distributed or by the *greater* of the fair market value or the adjusted basis of property distributed, less the amount of any liability on the property.[24] E & P is increased by gain recognized on appreciated property distributed as a property dividend.

EXAMPLE 18

Crimson Corporation distributes property (basis of $10,000 and fair market value of $20,000) to Brenda, its shareholder. Crimson recognizes a $10,000 gain. Crimson's E & P is increased by the $10,000 gain and decreased by the $20,000 fair market value of the distribution. Brenda has dividend income of $20,000 (presuming sufficient E & P). ■

EXAMPLE 19

Assume the same facts as in Example 18, except that the adjusted basis of the property in the hands of Crimson Corporation is $25,000. Because the loss is not recognized and the adjusted basis is greater than fair market value, E & P is reduced by $25,000. Brenda reports dividend income of $20,000. ■

EXAMPLE 20

Assume the same facts as in Example 19, except that the property is subject to a liability of $6,000. E & P is now reduced by $19,000 ($25,000 adjusted basis – $6,000 liability). Brenda has a dividend of $14,000 ($20,000 amount of the distribution – $6,000 liability), and her basis in the property is $20,000. ■

Under no circumstances can a distribution, whether cash or property, either generate a deficit in E & P or add to a deficit in E & P. Deficits can arise only through corporate losses.

EXAMPLE 21

Teal Corporation has accumulated E & P of $10,000 at the beginning of the current tax year. During the year, it has current E & P of $15,000. At the end of the year, it distributes cash of $30,000 to its sole shareholder, Walter. Teal's E & P at the end of the year is zero. The accumulated E & P of $10,000 is increased by current E & P of $15,000 and reduced by $25,000 because of the dividend distribution. The remaining $5,000 of the distribution to Walter does not reduce E & P because a distribution cannot generate a deficit in E & P. Instead, the remaining $5,000 reduces Walter's stock basis and/or produces a capital gain to Walter. ■

[23] § 311(b)(2).

[24] §§ 312(a), (b), and (c).

TAX *in* *the NEWS*

THE CASE OF THE DISAPPEARING DIVIDEND TAX

During the last few years, U.S. banks and offshore hedge funds have developed a novel technique for avoiding the tax on dividends entirely. The strategy involves the use of financial derivatives. A simple version of the strategy is called a dividend swap. In the swap, a U.S. bank buys a block of stock from an offshore hedge fund. The bank and the hedge fund also enter into a derivatives contract. The contract requires the bank to make payments to the hedge fund equal to the total return on the stock (both increases in fair market value and dividends) for a designated time period. These payments equal the income and gain the stock would have provided to the hedge fund if it had continued to own the stock. In exchange for these payments, the hedge fund agrees to pay the bank an amount based on some benchmark interest rate. The hedge fund also agrees that if the fair market value of the stock declines, it will pay the bank an amount equal to the loss.

After purchasing the stock from the hedge fund, the bank receives taxable dividend income. For tax purposes, however, the dividend income is completely offset by the expense of payments made to the hedge fund under the derivatives contract. In return, the bank receives compensation from the hedge fund equal to a benchmark interest rate. The overseas hedge fund no longer receives taxable dividend income, and the swap payments received are not subject to U.S. taxation. As a result, taxable dividend income is converted to tax-free income.

Some experts estimate that the strategy has allowed hedge funds to avoid paying more than $1 billion a year in taxes on U.S. dividends. Recent legislation (the Foreign Account Tax Compliance Act of 2009) attacks this approach to avoiding taxes on dividends by treating payments made to the hedge fund as taxable equivalents to dividends.

Source: Kevin E. Packman and Mauricio D. Rivero, "The Foreign Account Tax Compliance Act: Taxpayers Face More Disclosures and Potential Penalties," *Journal of Accountancy*, August 2010.

CONSTRUCTIVE DIVIDENDS

LO.6

Identify the nature and treatment of constructive dividends.

Any measurable economic benefit conveyed by a corporation to its shareholders can be treated as a dividend for Federal income tax purposes even though it is not formally declared or designated as a dividend. Also, it need not be issued pro rata to all shareholders nor satisfy the legal requirements of a dividend.[25] Such a benefit, often described as a **constructive dividend**, is distinguishable from actual corporate distributions of cash and property in form only.

For tax purposes, constructive distributions are treated the same as actual distributions.[26] Thus, corporate shareholders are entitled to the dividends received deduction (see Chapter 17), and other shareholders can apply the preferential tax rates (0 and 15 percent) through 2012 on qualified constructive dividends. The constructive distribution is taxable as a dividend only to the extent of the corporation's current and accumulated E & P. The burden of proving that the distribution constitutes a return of capital because of inadequate E & P rests with the taxpayer.[27]

Constructive dividend situations usually arise in closely held corporations. Here, the dealings between the parties are less structured, and, frequently, formalities are not preserved. The constructive dividend serves as a substitute for actual distributions and is usually intended to accomplish some tax objective not available through the use of direct dividends. The shareholders may be attempting to distribute corporate profits in a form deductible to the corporation.[28] Alternatively, the shareholders may be seeking benefits for themselves while avoiding the recognition of income. Although some constructive dividends are disguised dividends, not all are deliberate attempts to avoid actual and formal dividends; many are inadvertent. Thus, an awareness of the various constructive dividend situations is essential to protect the parties from unanticipated, undesirable tax consequences. The most frequently encountered types of constructive dividends are summarized below.

[25] See *Lengsfield v. Comm.*, 57–1 USTC ¶9437, 50 AFTR 1683, 241 F.2d 508 (CA–5, 1957).

[26] *Simon v. Comm.*, 57–2 USTC ¶9989, 52 AFTR 698, 248 F.2d 869 (CA–8, 1957).

[27] *DiZenzo v. Comm.*, 65–2 USTC ¶9518, 16 AFTR 2d 5107, 348 F.2d 122 (CA–2, 1965).

[28] Recall that dividend distributions do not provide the distributing corporation with an income tax deduction, although they do reduce E & P.

Shareholder Use of Corporate-Owned Property

A constructive dividend can occur when a shareholder uses a corporation's property for personal purposes at no cost. Personal use of corporate-owned automobiles, airplanes, yachts, fishing camps, hunting lodges, and other entertainment facilities is commonplace in some closely held corporations. In these situations, the shareholder has dividend income equal to the fair rental value of the property for the period of its personal use.[29]

Bargain Sale of Corporate Property to a Shareholder

Shareholders often purchase property from a corporation at a cost below the fair market value. These bargain sales produce dividend income equal to the difference between the property's fair market value on the date of sale and the amount the shareholder paid for the property.[30] These situations might be avoided by appraising the property on or about the date of the sale. The appraised value should become the price paid by the shareholder.

Bargain Rental of Corporate Property

A bargain rental of corporate property by a shareholder also produces dividend income. Here the measure of the constructive dividend is the excess of the property's fair rental value over the rent actually paid. Again, appraisal data should be used to avoid any questionable situations.

Payments for the Benefit of a Shareholder

If a corporation pays an obligation of a shareholder, the payment is treated as a constructive dividend. The obligation in question need not be legally binding on the shareholder; it may, in fact, be a moral obligation.[31] Forgiveness of shareholder indebtedness by the corporation creates an identical problem.[32] Also, excessive rentals paid by a corporation for the use of shareholder property are treated as constructive dividends.

Unreasonable Compensation

A salary payment to a shareholder-employee that is deemed to be **unreasonable compensation** is frequently treated as a constructive dividend and therefore is not deductible by the corporation. In determining the reasonableness of salary payments, the following factors are considered:

- The employee's qualifications.
- A comparison of salaries with dividend distributions.
- The prevailing rates of compensation for comparable positions in comparable business concerns.
- The nature and scope of the employee's work.
- The size and complexity of the business.
- A comparison of salaries paid with both gross and net income.
- The taxpayer's salary policy toward all employees.
- For small corporations with a limited number of officers, the amount of compensation paid to the employee in question in previous years.
- Whether a reasonable shareholder would have agreed to the level of compensation paid.[33]

The last factor above, known as the "reasonable investor test," is a relatively new development in the law on reasonable compensation.[34] Its use by the courts has been inconsistent. In some cases, the Seventh Circuit Court of Appeals has relied solely on the reasonable investor test in determining reasonableness, whereas the Tenth

[29] See *Daniel L. Reeves*, 94 TCM 287, T.C.Memo. 2007–273.

[30] Reg. § 1.301–1(j).

[31] *Montgomery Engineering Co. v. U.S.*, 64–2 USTC ¶9618, 13 AFTR 2d 1747, 230 F.Supp. 838 (D.Ct. N.J., 1964), *aff'd* in 65–1 USTC ¶9368, 15 AFTR 2d 746, 344 F.2d 996 (CA–3, 1965).

[32] Reg. § 1.301–1(m).

[33] All but the final factor in this list are identified in *Mayson Manufacturing Co. v. Comm.*, 49–2 USTC ¶9467, 38 AFTR 1028, 178 F.2d 115 (CA–6, 1949).

[34] For example, see *Alpha Medical, Inc. v. Comm.*, 99–1 USTC ¶50,461, 83 AFTR 2d 99–697, 172 F.3d 942 (CA–6, 1999).

Circuit Court of Appeals has largely ignored this factor. Other Federal circuits have used an approach that considers all of the factors in the list.[35]

Loans to Shareholders

Advances to shareholders that are not bona fide loans are constructive dividends. Whether an advance qualifies as a bona fide loan is a question of fact to be determined in light of the particular circumstances. Factors considered in determining whether the advance is a bona fide loan include the following:[36]

- Whether the advance is on open account or is evidenced by a written instrument.
- Whether the shareholder furnished collateral or other security for the advance.
- How long the advance has been outstanding.
- Whether any repayments have been made, excluding dividend sources.
- The shareholder's ability to repay the advance.
- The shareholder's use of the funds (e.g., payment of routine bills versus nonrecurring, extraordinary expenses).
- The regularity of the advances.
- The dividend-paying history of the corporation.

Even when a corporation makes a bona fide loan to a shareholder, a constructive dividend may be triggered, equal to the amount of imputed (forgone) interest on the loan.[37] Imputed interest equals the amount by which the interest paid by the Federal government on new borrowings, compounded semiannually, exceeds the interest charged on the loan. When the imputed interest provision applies, the shareholder is deemed to have made an interest payment to the corporation equal to the amount of imputed interest, and the corporation is deemed to have repaid the imputed interest to the shareholder through a constructive dividend. As a result, the corporation receives interest income and makes a nondeductible dividend payment, and the shareholder has taxable dividend income that might be offset with an interest deduction.

EXAMPLE 22

Mallard Corporation lends its principal shareholder, Henry, $100,000 on January 2 of the current year. The loan is interest-free and payable on demand. On December 31, the imputed interest rules are applied. Assuming the Federal rate is 6%, compounded semiannually, the amount of imputed interest is $6,090. This amount is deemed paid by Henry to Mallard in the form of interest. Mallard is then deemed to return the amount to Henry as a constructive dividend. Thus, Henry has dividend income of $6,090, which might be offset with a deduction for the interest deemed paid to Mallard. Mallard has interest income of $6,090 for the interest received, with no offsetting deduction for the dividend payment. ■

Loans to a Corporation by Shareholders

Shareholder loans to a corporation may be reclassified as equity if the debt has too many features of stock. Any interest and principal payments made by the corporation to the shareholder are then treated as constructive dividends. This topic was covered more thoroughly in the discussion of "thin capitalization" in Chapter 18.

STOCK DIVIDENDS AND STOCK RIGHTS

LO.7

Discuss the tax treatment of stock dividends and stock rights.

Stock Dividends

Historically, **stock dividends** were excluded from income on the theory that the ownership interest of the shareholder was unchanged as a result of the distribution.[38]

[35] See *Vitamin Village, Inc.*, 94 TCM 277, T.C.Memo. 2007–272, for an example of a case that uses both the reasonable investor test and other factors.

[36] *Fin Hay Realty Co. v. U.S.*, 68–2 USTC ¶9438, 22 AFTR 2d 5004, 398 F.2d 694 (CA–3, 1968). But see *Nariman Teymourian*, 90 TCM 352, T.C.Memo. 2005–302, for an example of how good planning can avoid constructive dividends in the shareholder loan context.

[37] See § 7872.

[38] See *Eisner v. Macomber*, 1 USTC ¶32, 3 AFTR 3020, 40 S.Ct. 189 (USSC, 1920).

Recognizing that some distributions of stock could affect ownership interests, the 1954 Code included a provision (§ 305) taxing stock dividends where (1) the stockholder could elect to receive either stock or property or (2) the stock dividends were in discharge of preference dividends. However, because this provision applied to a narrow range of transactions, corporations were able to develop an assortment of alternative methods that circumvented taxation and still affected shareholders' proportionate interests in the corporation.[39] In response, the scope of § 305 was expanded.

In its current state, the provisions of § 305 are based on the proportionate interest concept. As a general rule, stock dividends are excluded from income if they are pro rata distributions of stock or stock rights, paid on common stock. Five exceptions to this general rule exist. These exceptions deal with various disproportionate distribution situations. If stock dividends are not taxable, the corporation's E & P is not reduced.[40] If the stock dividends are taxable, the distributing corporation treats the distribution in the same manner as any other taxable property dividend.

If a stock dividend is taxable, the shareholder's basis for the newly received shares is fair market value, and the holding period starts on the date of receipt. If a stock dividend is not taxable, the basis of the stock on which the dividend is distributed is reallocated.[41] If the dividend shares are identical to these formerly held shares, basis for the old stock is reallocated by dividing the taxpayer's basis in the old stock by the total number of shares. If the dividend stock is not identical to the underlying shares (e.g., a stock dividend of preferred on common), basis is determined by allocating the basis of the formerly held shares between the old and new stock according to the fair market value of each. The holding period includes the holding period of the formerly held stock.[42]

EXAMPLE 23

Gail bought 1,000 shares of common stock two years ago for $10,000. In the current tax year, she receives 10 shares of common stock as a nontaxable stock dividend. Gail's basis of $10,000 is divided by 1,010. Each share of stock has a basis of $9.90 instead of the pre-dividend $10 basis. ■

EXAMPLE 24

Assume Gail received, instead, a nontaxable preferred stock dividend of 100 shares. The preferred stock has a fair market value of $1,000, and the common stock, on which the preferred is distributed, has a fair market value of $19,000. After the receipt of the stock dividend, the basis of the common stock is $9,500, and the basis of the preferred is $500, computed as follows:

Fair market value of common	$19,000
Fair market value of preferred	1,000
	$20,000
Basis of common: $\frac{19}{20} \times$ $10,000	$ 9,500
Basis of preferred: $\frac{1}{20} \times$ $10,000	$ 500

■

Stock Rights

The rules for determining taxability of **stock rights** are identical to those for determining taxability of stock dividends. If the rights are taxable, the recipient has income equal to the fair market value of the rights. The fair market value then becomes the shareholder-distributee's basis in the rights.[43] If the rights are exercised, the holding period for the new stock begins on the date the rights (whether taxable or nontaxable) are exercised. The basis of the new stock is the basis of the rights plus the amount of any other consideration given.

If stock rights are not taxable and the value of the rights is less than 15 percent of the value of the old stock, the basis of the rights is zero. However, the shareholder may elect to have some of the basis in the formerly held stock allocated to the rights.[44] The

[39] See "Stock Dividends," S.Rept. 91–552, 1969–3 C.B. 519.
[40] § 312(d)(1).
[41] § 307(a).
[42] § 1223(5).
[43] Reg. § 1.305–1(b).
[44] § 307(b)(1).

election is made by attaching a statement to the shareholder's return for the year in which the rights are received.[45] If the fair market value of the rights is 15 percent or more of the value of the old stock and the rights are exercised or sold, the shareholder *must* allocate some of the basis in the formerly held stock to the rights.

EXAMPLE 25

A corporation with common stock outstanding declares a nontaxable dividend payable in rights to subscribe to common stock. Each right entitles the holder to purchase one share of stock for $90. One right is issued for every two shares of stock owned. Fred owns 400 shares of stock purchased two years ago for $15,000. At the time of the distribution of the rights, the market value of the common stock is $100 per share, and the market value of the rights is $8 per right. Fred receives 200 rights. He exercises 100 rights and sells the remaining 100 rights three months later for $9 per right.

Fred need not allocate the cost of the original stock to the rights because the value of the rights is less than 15% of the value of the stock ($1,600 ÷ $40,000 = 4%). If Fred does not allocate his original stock basis to the rights, the tax consequences are as follows:

- Basis of the new stock is $9,000 [$90 (exercise price) × 100 (shares)]. The holding period of the new stock begins on the date the stock was purchased.
- Sale of the rights produces long-term capital gain of $900 [$9 (sales price) × 100 (rights)]. The holding period of the rights starts with the date the original 400 shares of stock were acquired.

If Fred elects to allocate basis to the rights, the tax consequences are as follows:

- Basis of the stock is $14,423 [$40,000 (value of stock) ÷ $41,600 (value of rights and stock) × $15,000 (cost of stock)].
- Basis of the rights is $577 [$1,600 (value of rights) ÷ $41,600 (value of rights and stock) × $15,000 (cost of stock)].
- When Fred exercises the rights, his basis for the new stock will be $9,288.50 [$9,000 (cost) + $288.50 (basis for 100 rights)].
- Sale of the rights would produce a long-term capital gain of $611.50 [$900 (sales price) − $288.50 (basis for the remaining 100 rights)]. ■

19.4 Stock Redemptions

LO.8

Identify various stock redemptions that qualify for sale or exchange treatment.

OVERVIEW

Under § 317(b), a **stock redemption** occurs when a corporation acquires its stock from a shareholder in exchange for cash or other property. In a stock redemption, the shareholder is selling stock back to the issuing corporation, and it resembles a sale of stock to an unrelated third party. However, while a sale of stock to an outsider invariably results in sale or exchange treatment, only a *qualifying* stock redemption is treated as a sale for tax purposes.

Nonqualifying stock redemptions are denied sale or exchange treatment because they are deemed to have the same effect as dividend distributions. For example, if a shareholder owns all the stock of a corporation and sells a portion of that stock to the corporation, the shareholder's ownership interest in the corporation does not change. After the redemption, the shareholder still owns all the outstanding stock of the corporation. In this situation, the stock redemption resembles a dividend distribution and is taxed as such.

Stock redemptions occur for a variety of reasons. Publicly traded corporations often reacquire their shares with the goal of increasing shareholder value. For corporations where the stock is closely held, redemptions frequently occur to achieve shareholder objectives. For instance, a redemption might be used to acquire the stock of a deceased shareholder of a closely held corporation. Using corporate funds to purchase the stock from the decedent's estate relieves the remaining

[45] Reg. § 1.307–2.

GLOBAL
Tax Issues

Foreign Shareholders Prefer Sale or Exchange Treatment in Stock Redemptions

As a general rule, foreign shareholders are subject to U.S. tax on dividend income from U.S. corporations but not on capital gains from the sale of U.S. stock. In some situations, a nonresident alien is taxed on a capital gain from the disposition of stock in a U.S. corporation, but only if the stock was effectively connected with the conduct of a U.S. trade or business of the individual. Foreign corporations are similarly taxed on gains from the sale of U.S. stock investments. Whether a stock redemption qualifies for sale or exchange treatment therefore takes on added significance for foreign shareholders. If one of the qualifying stock redemption rules can be satisfied, the foreign shareholder typically will avoid U.S. tax on the transaction. If, instead, dividend income is the result, a 30 percent withholding tax typically applies. For further details, see Chapter 25.

shareholders of the need to use their own money to aquire the stock. Stock redemptions also frequently occur as a result of property settlements in divorce actions. When spouses jointly own 100 percent of a corporation's shares, a divorce decree may require that the stock interest of one spouse be bought out. A redemption of that spouse's shares relieves the other spouse from having to use his or her funds for the transaction.

Noncorporate shareholders generally prefer to have a stock redemption treated as a sale or exchange rather than as a dividend distribution. For individual taxpayers, the maximum tax rate for long-term capital gains is currently 15 percent (0 percent for taxpayers in the 10 or 15 percent marginal tax bracket). The preference for qualifying stock redemption treatment is based on the fact that such transactions result in (1) the tax-free recovery of the redeemed stock's basis and (2) capital gains that can be offset by capital losses. In a nonqualified stock redemption, the *entire* distribution is taxed as dividend income (assuming adequate E & P), which, although generally taxed at the same rate as long-term capital gains, cannot be offset by capital losses.

EXAMPLE 26

Abby, an individual in the 35% tax bracket, acquired stock in Quail Corporation four years ago for $300,000. In the current year, Quail Corporation (E & P of $1 million) redeems her shares for $450,000. If the redemption qualifies for sale or exchange treatment, Abby has a long-term capital gain of $150,000 [$450,000 (redemption amount) – $300,000 (basis)]. Her tax liability on the $150,000 gain is $22,500 ($150,000 × 15%). If the stock redemption does not qualify as a sale or exchange, the entire distribution is treated as a dividend and Abby's tax liability is $67,500 ($450,000 × 15%). Thus, Abby saves $45,000 ($67,500 – $22,500) in income taxes if the transaction is a qualifying stock redemption. ■

EXAMPLE 27

Assume in Example 26 that Abby has a capital loss carryover of $100,000 in the current tax year. If the transaction is a qualifying stock redemption, Abby can offset the entire $100,000 capital loss carryover against her $150,000 long-term capital gain. As a result, only $50,000 of the gain is taxed, and her tax liability is only $7,500 ($50,000 × 15%). On the other hand, if the transaction does not qualify for sale or exchange treatment, the entire $450,000 is taxed as a dividend at 15%. In addition, assuming she has no capital gains in the current year, Abby is able to deduct only $3,000 of the $100,000 capital loss carryover to offset her other ordinary income. ■

In contrast, however, *corporate* shareholders normally receive more favorable tax treatment from a dividend distribution than would result from a qualifying stock redemption. Corporate taxpayers typically report only a small portion of a dividend distribution as taxable income because of the dividends received deduction (see Chapter 17). Further, the preferential tax rate applicable to dividend and long-term capital gain income is not available to corporations. Consequently, tax planning for

TAX *in* the *NEWS*

CORPORATIONS FLUSH WITH CASH INCREASE STOCK BUYBACK PROGRAMS

When the economy went bad, businesses slashed costs and reduced capital expenditures. As a result of these cuts, corporate profits and cash flows have improved dramatically, and many corporations are carrying record amounts of cash on their books. Hesitant to increase capital and other expenditures in the current economic environment, many corporations have decided, instead, to use surplus cash to repurchase shares of their stock. Reasons cited for stock buyback programs include a desire to offset the dilution to earnings per share associated with employee stock option plans, a desire to enhance shareholder value, and a perception that a corporation's stock is undervalued in the marketplace. The qualifying stock redemption provisions must be considered in determining the proper tax treatment for a shareholder participating in a stock buyback program. In the case of stock of a publicly traded corporation, however, a shareholder's ownership interest likely is so minuscule that sale or exchange treatment will be the result.

stock redemptions must consider the different preferences of corporate and noncorporate shareholders.

EXAMPLE 28

Assume in Example 26 that Abby is a corporation, that the stock represents a 40% ownership interest in Quail Corporation, and that Abby has corporate taxable income of $850,000 before the redemption transaction. If the transaction is a qualifying stock redemption, Abby has a long-term capital gain of $150,000 that is subject to tax at 34%, or $51,000. On the other hand, if the $450,000 distribution is treated as a dividend, Abby has a dividends received deduction of $360,000 ($450,000 × 80%), so only $90,000 of the payment is taxed. Consequently, Abby's tax liability on the transaction is only $30,600 ($90,000 × 34%). ■

When a qualifying stock redemption results in a *loss* to the shareholder rather than a gain, § 267 disallows loss recognition if the shareholder owns (directly or indirectly) more than 50 percent of the corporation's stock. A shareholder's basis in property received in a stock redemption, qualifying or nonqualified, generally will be the property's fair market value, determined as of the date of the redemption. Further, the holding period of the property begins on that date.

The Code establishes the criteria for determining whether a transaction is a qualifying stock redemption for tax purposes and thus receives sale or exchange treatment. The terminology in an agreement between the parties is not controlling, nor is state law. Section 302(b) provides several types of qualifying stock redemptions. Additionally, certain distributions of property to an estate in exchange for a deceased shareholder's stock are treated as qualifying stock redemptions under § 303.

HISTORICAL BACKGROUND

Under prior law, the *dividend equivalency rule* was used to determine which stock redemptions qualified for sale or exchange treatment. Under that rule, if the facts and circumstances of a redemption indicated that it was essentially equivalent to a dividend, the redemption did not qualify for sale or exchange treatment. Instead, the entire amount received by the shareholder was taxed as dividend income to the extent of the corporation's E & P.

The uncertainty and subjectivity surrounding the dividend equivalency rule led Congress to enact several objective tests for determining the status of a redemption. Currently, the following types of stock redemptions qualify for sale or exchange treatment:

- Distributions not essentially equivalent to a dividend ("not essentially equivalent redemptions").
- Distributions substantially disproportionate in terms of shareholder effect ("disproportionate redemptions").

EXHIBIT 19.1 Stock Attribution Rules

	Deemed or Constructive Ownership
Family	An individual is deemed to own the stock owned by his or her spouse, children, grandchildren, and parents (not siblings or grandparents).
Partnership	A partner is deemed to own the stock owned by a partnership to the extent of the partner's proportionate interest in the partnership.
	Stock owned by a partner is deemed to be owned in full by a partnership.
Estate or trust	A beneficiary or heir is deemed to own the stock owned by an estate or trust to the extent of the beneficiary's or heir's proportionate interest in the estate or trust.
	Stock owned by a beneficiary or heir is deemed to be owned in full by an estate or trust.
Corporation	Stock owned by a corporation is deemed to be owned proportionately by any shareholder owning 50% or more of the corporation's stock.
	Stock owned by a shareholder who owns 50% or more of a corporation is deemed to be owned in full by the corporation.

- Distributions in complete termination of a shareholder's interest ("complete termination redemptions").
- Distributions to pay a shareholder's death taxes ("redemptions to pay death taxes").

Concept Summary 19.3 later in this chapter summarizes the requirements for each of these qualifying stock redemptions.

STOCK ATTRIBUTION RULES

To qualify for sale or exchange treatment, a stock redemption generally must result in the substantial reduction in the shareholder's ownership interest in the corporation. In the absence of this reduction in ownership interest, the redemption proceeds are taxed as dividend income. In determining whether a stock redemption has sufficiently reduced a shareholder's interest, the stock owned by certain related parties is attributed to the redeeming shareholder.[46] Thus, the stock **attribution** rules must be considered in applying the stock redemption provisions. Under these rules, related parties are defined to include the following family members: spouses, children, grandchildren, and parents. Attribution also takes place *from* and *to* partnerships, estates, trusts, and corporations (50 percent or more ownership required in the case of regular corporations). Exhibit 19.1 summarizes the stock attribution rules.

EXAMPLE 29
THE BIG PICTURE

Return to the facts of *The Big Picture* on p. 19-2. Assume instead that Gustavo owns 30% (rather than 50%) of the stock in Lime Corporation and his two children own 20% of the Lime stock. For purposes of the stock attribution rules, Gustavo is treated as owning 50% of the stock in Lime Corporation. He owns 30% directly and, because of the family attribution rules, 20% indirectly through his children. ■

EXAMPLE 30

Chris owns 40% of the stock in Gray Corporation. The other 60% is owned by a partnership in which Chris has a 20% interest. Chris is deemed to own 52% of Gray Corporation: 40% directly and, because of the partnership interest, 12% indirectly (20% × 60%). ■

46 § 318.

As discussed later, the *family* attribution rules (refer to Example 29) can be waived in the case of some complete termination redemptions. In addition, the stock attribution rules do not apply to stock redemptions to pay death taxes.

NOT ESSENTIALLY EQUIVALENT REDEMPTIONS

Under § 302(b)(1), a redemption qualifies for sale or exchange treatment if it is "not essentially equivalent to a dividend." This provision represents a continuation of the dividend equivalency rule applicable under prior law. The earlier redemption language was retained principally for redemptions of preferred stock because shareholders often have no control over when corporations call in such stock.[47] Like its predecessor, the **not essentially equivalent redemption** lacks an objective test. Instead, each case must be resolved on a facts and circumstances basis.[48]

Based upon the Supreme Court's decision in *U.S. v. Davis*,[49] a redemption will qualify as a not essentially equivalent redemption only when the shareholder's interest in the redeeming corporation has been meaningfully reduced. In determining whether the **meaningful reduction test** has been met, the stock attribution rules apply. A decrease in the redeeming shareholder's voting control appears to be the most significant indicator of a meaningful reduction,[50] but reductions in the rights of redeeming shareholders to share in corporate earnings or to receive corporate assets upon liquidation are also considered.[51] The meaningful reduction test is applied whether common stock or preferred stock is being redeemed.

EXAMPLE 31

Pat owns 58% of the common stock of Falcon Corporation. As a result of a redemption of some of his stock, Pat's ownership interest in Falcon is reduced to 51%. Since Pat continues to have dominant voting rights in Falcon after the redemption, the distribution is treated as essentially equivalent to a dividend. The entire amount of the distribution therefore is taxed as dividend income (assuming adequate E & P). ■

EXAMPLE 32

Maroon Corporation redeems 2% of its stock from Maria. Before the redemption, Maria owned 10% of Maroon Corporation. In this case, the redemption may qualify as a not essentially equivalent redemption. Maria experiences a reduction in her voting rights, her right to participate in current earnings and accumulated surplus, and her right to share in net assets upon liquidation. ■

When a redemption *fails* to satisfy any of the qualifying stock redemption rules, the basis of the redeemed shares does not disappear. Typically, the basis will attach to the basis of the redeeming shareholder's remaining shares in the corporation. If, however, the redeeming shareholder has terminated his or her direct stock ownership and the redemption is nonqualified due to the attribution rules, the basis of the redeemed shares will attach to the basis of the constructively owned stock.[52] In this manner, a nonqualified stock redemption can result in stock basis being shifted from one taxpayer (the redeeming shareholder) to another taxpayer (the shareholder related under the attribution rules).

EXAMPLE 33

Fran and Floyd, wife and husband, each own 50 shares in Grouse Corporation, representing 100% of the corporation's stock. All the stock was purchased for $50,000. Both Fran and Floyd serve as directors of the corporation. The corporation redeems Floyd's 50 shares, but he continues to serve as director of the corporation. The redemption is treated as a dividend distribution (assuming adequate E & P) because Floyd constructively owns Fran's stock, or 100% of the Grouse stock outstanding. Floyd's $25,000 basis in the 50 shares redeemed attaches to Fran's stock; thus, Fran now has a basis of $50,000 in the 50 shares she owns in Grouse. ■

[47] See S.Rept. No. 1622, 83d Cong., 2d Sess., 44 (1954).

[48] Reg. § 1.302–2(b)(1).

[49] 70–1 USTC ¶9289, 25 AFTR 2d 70–827, 90 S.Ct. 1041 (USSC, 1970).

[50] See, for example, *Jack Paparo*, 71 T.C. 692 (1979).

[51] See, for example, *Grabowski Trust*, 58 T.C. 650 (1972).

[52] Reg. § 1.302–2(c). But see Prop.Reg. § 1.302–5.

DISPROPORTIONATE REDEMPTIONS

A redemption qualifies for sale or exchange treatment under § 302(b)(2) as a **disproportionate redemption** if the following conditions are met:

- After the distribution, the shareholder owns *less than* 80 percent of the interest owned in the corporation before the redemption. For example, if a shareholder owns a 60 percent interest in a corporation that redeems part of the stock, the shareholder's ownership interest after the redemption must be less than 48 percent (80 percent of 60 percent).
- After the distribution, the shareholder owns *less than* 50 percent of the total combined voting power of all classes of stock entitled to vote.

In determining a shareholder's ownership interest before and after a redemption, the attribution rules apply.

EXAMPLE 34

Bob, Carl, and Dan, unrelated individuals, own 30 shares, 30 shares, and 40 shares, respectively, in Wren Corporation. Wren has 100 shares outstanding and E & P of $200,000. The corporation redeems 20 shares of Dan's stock for $30,000. Dan paid $200 a share for the stock two years ago. Dan's ownership in Wren Corporation before and after the redemption is as follows:

	Total Shares	Dan's Ownership	Ownership Percentage	80% of Original Ownership
Before redemption	100	40	40% (40 ÷ 100)	32% (80% × 40%)
After redemption	80	20	25% (20 ÷ 80)*	

*Note that the denominator of the fraction is reduced after the redemption (from 100 to 80).

Dan's 25% ownership after the redemption meets both tests of § 302(b)(2). It is less than 80% of his original ownership and less than 50% of the total voting power. The distribution therefore qualifies as a disproportionate redemption and receives sale or exchange treatment. As a result, Dan has a long-term capital gain of $26,000 [$30,000 − $4,000 (20 shares × $200)]. ■

EXAMPLE 35

Given the situation in Example 34, assume instead that Carl and Dan are father and son. The redemption described previously would not qualify for sale or exchange treatment because of the effect of the attribution rules. Dan is deemed to own Carl's stock before and after the redemption. Dan's ownership in Wren Corporation before and after the redemption is as follows:

	Total Shares	Dan's Direct Ownership	Carl's Ownership	Dan's Direct and Indirect Ownership	Ownership Percentage	80% of Original Ownership
Before redemption	100	40	30	70	70% (70 ÷ 100)	56% (80% × 70%)
After redemption	80	20	30	50	62.5% (50 ÷ 80)	

Dan's direct and indirect ownership of 62.5% fails to meet either of the tests of § 302(b)(2). After the redemption, Dan owns more than 80% of his original ownership and more than 50% of the voting stock. Thus, the redemption does not qualify for sale or exchange treatment and results in a dividend distribution of $30,000 to Dan. The basis in the 20 shares redeemed is added to Dan's basis in his remaining 20 shares. ■

A redemption that does not qualify as a disproportionate redemption may still qualify as a not essentially equivalent redemption if it meets the meaningful reduction test (see Example 32).

COMPLETE TERMINATION REDEMPTIONS

A redemption that terminates a shareholder's *entire* stock ownership in a corporation qualifies for sale or exchange treatment. The attribution rules generally apply in determining whether the shareholder's stock ownership has been terminated. However, the *family* attribution rules do not apply to a **complete termination redemption** if the following conditions are met:

- The former shareholder has no interest, other than that of a creditor, in the corporation for at least 10 years after the redemption (including an interest as an officer, director, or employee).
- The former shareholder files an agreement to notify the IRS of any prohibited interest acquired within the 10-year postredemption period and to retain all necessary records pertaining to the redemption during this time period.

Acquisition of stock in the corporation by bequest or inheritance will not constitute a prohibited interest. The required agreement should be in the form of a separate statement signed by the former shareholder and attached to the return for the year in which the redemption occurs. The agreement should state that the former shareholder agrees to notify the IRS within 30 days of acquiring a prohibited interest in the corporation during the 10-year postredemption period.[53]

EXAMPLE 36

Kevin owns 50% of the stock in Green Corporation, while the remaining interest in Green is held as follows: 40% by Wilma (Kevin's wife) and 10% by Carmen (a key employee). Green redeems all of Kevin's stock for its fair market value. As a result, Wilma and Carmen are the only remaining shareholders, now owning 80% and 20%, respectively. If the requirements for the family attribution waiver are met, the transaction will qualify as a complete termination redemption and result in sale or exchange treatment. If the waiver requirements are not satisfied, Kevin will be deemed to own Wilma's (his wife's) stock, and the entire distribution will be taxed as a dividend (assuming adequate E & P). ■

EXAMPLE 37

Assume in Example 36 that Kevin qualifies for the family attribution waiver for the redemption. In the year of the redemption, Kevin treats the transaction as a sale or exchange. However, if he purchases Carmen's stock seven years after the redemption, he has acquired a prohibited interest, and the redemption distribution is reclassified as a dividend. Kevin will owe additional taxes due to this revised treatment. ■

ETHICS & *Equity*

CONVERTIBLE PREFERRED STOCK—CONVERSION OR REDEMPTION?

Four years ago, a corporation that does not sell its stock publicly sold some convertible preferred stock to a small investment group. At the option of the shareholders, the preferred stock can be converted into common stock at any time. The preferred stock also has a call feature, allowing the corporation to call (redeem) the stock at any time during the first five years after its issuance.

The corporation recently developed a successful invention that it has not yet publicly disclosed. The corporate board of directors expects that the corporation will experience significant earnings growth in the future as a result of the invention. The directors, all of whom own common stock in the corporation, would like to call the preferred stock so that those shares cannot be converted into common stock and otherwise participate in the corporation's future earnings growth. The call price set out in the preferred stock indenture provides a premium to the shareholders upon redemption. The directors vote to redeem all of the outstanding preferred stock and notify the preferred shareholders of the board's decision. Did the board of directors act ethically?

[53] Reg. § 1.302–4(a).

REDEMPTIONS TO PAY DEATH TAXES

Section 303 provides sale or exchange treatment to a redemption of stock included in, and representing a substantial part of, a decedent's gross estate. The purpose of this provision is to provide an estate with liquidity to pay death-related expenses when a significant portion of the estate consists of stock in a closely held corporation. Often such stock is not easily marketable, and a stock redemption represents the only viable option for its disposition. The redemption might not satisfy any of the other qualifying stock redemption provisions because of the attribution rules (e.g., attribution to estate from beneficiaries). A **redemption to pay death taxes** provides sale or exchange treatment without regard to the attribution rules, but the provision limits this treatment to the sum of the death taxes and funeral and administration expenses. A redemption in excess of these expenses may qualify for sale or exchange treatment under one of the § 302 provisions.

An estate's basis in property acquired from a decedent is generally the property's fair market value on the date of death.[54] Typically, there is little change in the fair market value of stock from the date of a decedent's death to the date of a redemption to pay death taxes. When the redemption price in a redemption to pay death taxes is the same as the estate's basis in the stock, the estate will recognize no gain (or loss) on the transaction.

Section 303 applies only to a distribution made with respect to stock of a corporation that is included in the gross estate of a decedent and whose value *exceeds* 35 percent of the value of the adjusted gross estate. (For definitions of "gross estate" and "adjusted gross estate," see the Glossary in Appendix C.)

EXAMPLE 38

Juan's adjusted gross estate is $7 million. The death taxes and funeral and administration expenses of the estate total $720,000. Included in the gross estate is stock of Yellow Corporation, valued at $2.8 million. Juan had acquired the stock nine years ago at a cost of $300,000. Yellow redeems $720,000 of the stock from Juan's estate. Because the value of the Yellow stock in Juan's estate exceeds the 35% threshold ($2.8 million ÷ $7 million = 40%), the redemption qualifies under § 303 as a sale or exchange to Juan's estate. Assuming the value of the stock has remained unchanged since the date of Juan's death, there is no recognized gain (or loss) on the redemption [$720,000 (amount realized) – $720,000 (estate's stock basis)]. ■

In determining whether the value of stock of one corporation exceeds 35 percent of the value of the adjusted gross estate, the stock of two or more corporations in which the decedent held a 20 percent or more interest is treated as the stock of one corporation.[55] When this exception applies, the stock redeemed can be that of any of the 20 percent or more shareholder interests.

EXAMPLE 39

The adjusted gross estate of a decedent is $8 million. The gross estate includes stock of Owl and Robin Corporations valued at $1.6 million and $1.4 million, respectively. Unless the two corporations are treated as a single corporation for purposes of the 35% test, § 303 does not apply to a redemption of the stock of either corporation. If the decedent owned at least 20% of the stock of both Owl and Robin, § 303 can apply to a redemption of such stock. The 35% test is met when the stock of Owl and Robin is treated as that of a single corporation [($1.6 million + $1.4 million) ÷ $8 million = 37.5%]. The stock of Owl or Robin (or both) can be redeemed under § 303, to the extent of the sum of the death taxes and funeral and administration expenses. ■

---

[54] If available and elected, an alternate valuation date would apply. § 1014(a).

[55] § 303(b)(2)(B).

CONCEPT SUMMARY 19.3

Summary of the Qualifying Stock Redemption Rules

Type of Redemption	Requirements to Qualify
Not essentially equivalent to a dividend [§ 302(b)(1)]	Meaningful reduction in shareholder's voting interest. Reduction in shareholder's right to share in earnings or assets upon liquidation also considered.
	Stock attribution rules apply.
Substantially disproportionate [§ 302(b)(2)]	Shareholder's interest in the corporation, after the redemption, must be less than 80% of interest before the redemption and less than 50% of total combined voting power of all classes of stock entitled to vote.
	Stock attribution rules apply.
Complete termination [§ 302(b)(3)]	Entire stock ownership terminated.
	In general, stock attribution rules apply. However, *family* attribution rules are waived when former shareholder has no interest, other than as a creditor, in the corporation for at least 10 years and files an agreement to notify the IRS of any prohibited interest acquired during 10-year period. Shareholder must retain all necessary records during 10-year period.
Redemption to pay death taxes [§ 303]	Value of stock of one corporation in gross estate exceeds 35% of value of adjusted gross estate.
	Stock of two or more corporations treated as stock of a single corporation in applying the 35% test if decedent held a 20% or more interest in the stock of the corporations.
	Redemption limited to sum of death taxes and funeral and administration expenses.
	Stock attribution rules do not apply.

19.5 Effect on the Corporation Redeeming Its Stock

LO.9

Understand the tax impact of stock redemptions on the distributing corporation.

Thus far, the discussion has focused on the tax consequences of stock redemptions to the *shareholder*. There are also several tax issues surrounding the redeeming *corporation* that must be addressed, including the recognition of gain or loss on property distributed pursuant to a redemption, the effect on a corporation's E & P from a distribution that is a qualifying stock redemption, and the deductibility of expenditures incurred in connection with a redemption. These issues are discussed in the following paragraphs.

RECOGNITION OF GAIN OR LOSS

Section 311 provides that corporations recognize *gain* on all nonliquidating distributions of appreciated property as if the property had been sold for its fair market value. Distributions in redemption of stock, qualifying or not, are nonliquidating distributions. When distributed property is subject to a corporate liability, the fair market value of that property is treated as not being less than the amount of the liability.

Losses are not recognized on nonliquidating distributions of property. Therefore, a corporation should avoid distributing loss property (fair market value less than basis) as consideration in the redemption of a shareholder's stock. However, the corporation could sell the property in a taxable transaction in which it can recognize a loss and then distribute the proceeds.

EXAMPLE 40

To carry out a redemption, Blackbird Corporation distributes land (basis of $80,000, fair market value of $300,000) to a shareholder's estate. Blackbird has a recognized gain of $220,000 ($300,000 – $80,000). If the land is subject to a liability of $330,000, Blackbird has a recognized gain of $250,000 ($330,000 – $80,000). If the value of the property distributed was less than its adjusted basis, the realized loss would not be recognized. ■

EFFECT ON EARNINGS AND PROFITS

In a qualifying stock redemption, the E & P of the distributing corporation is reduced by an amount not in excess of the ratable share of the corporation's E & P attributable to the stock redeemed.[56]

EXAMPLE 41

Navy Corporation has 100 shares of stock outstanding. In a qualifying stock redemption, Navy distributes $200,000 in exchange for 30 of its shares. At the time of the redemption, Navy has paid-in capital of $120,000 and E & P of $450,000. The charge to E & P is limited to 30% of the corporation's E & P ($135,000), and the remainder of the redemption price ($65,000) is a reduction of the Navy paid-in capital account. If, instead, the 30 shares were redeemed for $80,000, the charge to E & P would be limited to $80,000, the amount Navy paid to carry out the stock redemption. ■

REDEMPTION EXPENDITURES

In redeeming its shares, a corporation may incur certain expenses such as accounting, brokerage, legal, and loan fees. Section 162(k) specifically denies a deduction for redemption expenditures incurred in connection with a stock redemption. The disallowance does not apply to amounts otherwise deducted under § 163.

19.6 OTHER CORPORATE DISTRIBUTIONS

Partial liquidations of a corporation, if in compliance with the statutory requirements of § 302(e), will result in sale or exchange treatment to noncorporate shareholders. Distributions of stock and securities of a controlled corporation to the shareholders of the parent corporation will be free of any tax consequences if they fall under § 355. Both of these types of corporate distributions are similar to stock redemptions and dividend distributions in some respects but are not discussed here because of their limited applicability.

TAX PLANNING:
19.7 CORPORATE DISTRIBUTIONS

LO.10

Identify planning opportunities available to minimize the tax impact in corporate distributions, constructive dividends, and stock redemptions.

The following points are especially important when planning for corporate distributions.

- Because E & P is the pool of funds from which dividends may be distributed, its periodic determination is essential to corporate planning. Thus, an E & P account should be established and maintained, particularly if the possibility exists that a corporate distribution might be a return of capital.
- Accumulated E & P is the sum of all past years' current E & P. Because there is no statute of limitations on the computation of E & P, the IRS can

[56] § 312(n)(7).

redetermine a corporation's current E & P for a tax year long since passed. Such a change affects accumulated E & P and has a direct impact on the taxability of current distributions to shareholders.

- Distributions can be planned to avoid or minimize dividend exposure.

EXAMPLE 42

After several unprofitable years, Darter Corporation has a deficit in accumulated E & P of $100,000 as of January 1, 2011. Starting in 2011, Darter expects to generate annual E & P of $50,000 for the next four years and would like to distribute this amount to its shareholders. The corporation's cash position (for dividend purposes) will correspond to the current E & P generated. Consider the following two distribution schedules:

1. On December 31 of 2011, 2012, 2013, and 2014, Darter Corporation distributes cash of $50,000.
2. On December 31 of 2012 and 2014, Darter Corporation distributes cash of $100,000.

The two alternatives are illustrated as follows.

Year	Accumulated E & P (First of Year)	Current E & P	Distribution	Amount of Dividend
		Alternative 1		
2011	($ 100,000)	$50,000	$ 50,000	$50,000
2012	(100,000)	50,000	50,000	50,000
2013	(100,000)	50,000	50,000	50,000
2014	(100,000)	50,000	50,000	50,000
		Alternative 2		
2011	($100,000)	$50,000	$ –0–	$ –0–
2012	(50,000)	50,000	100,000	50,000
2013	(50,000)	50,000	–0–	–0–
2014	–0–	50,000	100,000	50,000

Alternative 1 produces $200,000 of dividend income because each $50,000 distribution is fully covered by current E & P. Alternative 2, however, produces only $100,000 of dividend income for the shareholders. The remaining $100,000 is a return of capital. Why? At the time Darter Corporation made its first distribution of $100,000 on December 31, 2012, it had a deficit of $50,000 in accumulated E & P (the original deficit of $100,000 is reduced by the $50,000 of current E & P from 2011). Consequently, the $100,000 distribution yields a $50,000 dividend (the current E & P for 2012), and $50,000 is treated as a return of capital. As of January 1, 2013, Darter's accumulated E & P has a deficit balance of $50,000, since a distribution cannot increase a deficit in E & P. After adding the remaining $50,000 of current E & P from 2013, the balance on January 1, 2014, is zero. Thus, the second distribution of $100,000 made on December 31, 2014, also yields $50,000 of dividends (the current E & P for 2014) and a $50,000 return of capital. ■

19.8 PLANNING FOR QUALIFIED DIVIDENDS

RETIREMENT PLANS

The reduced tax rates available to individual taxpayers on net capital gain and qualified dividend income reinforce the inadvisability of funding retirement accounts with stock. Since income in § 401(k) plans and IRAs is not taxed when earned, the benefits of the lower tax rates on these forms of income are lost. Instead, distributions from the plans are taxed at ordinary income tax rates.

CONCEPT SUMMARY 19.4

Corporate Distributions

1. Without a special provision, corporate distributions are taxed as dividend income to the recipient shareholders to the extent of the distributing corporation's E & P accumulated since February 28, 1913, or to the extent of current E & P. Any excess is treated as a return of capital to the extent of the shareholder's basis in the stock and, thereafter, as capital gain.
2. Property distributions are considered dividends (taxed as noted in item 1) in the amount of their fair market value. The amount distributed is reduced by any liabilities on the property distributed. The shareholder's basis in the property is its fair market value.
3. Earnings and profits of a corporation are increased by corporate earnings for the taxable year computed in the same manner as the corporation computes its taxable income. As a general rule, the account is increased for all items of income, whether taxed or not, and reduced by all items of expense, whether deductible or not. Refer to Concept Summary 19.1 for a summary of the effect of certain transactions on taxable income in arriving at current E & P.
4. A corporation recognizes gain, but not loss, on distributions of property to its shareholders. E & P of the distributing corporation is reduced by the amount of money distributed or by the greater of the fair market value or the adjusted basis of property distributed less the amount of any liability applicable to the distributed property.
5. As a general rule, stock dividends or stock rights (representing stock in the distributing corporation) are not taxed, with certain exceptions.
6. Stock redemptions that qualify under § 302(b) are given sale or exchange treatment. This provision requires that such distributions be either substantially disproportionate, complete terminations, or not essentially equivalent to a dividend. In determining whether a transaction is a not essentially equivalent redemption or a disproportionate redemption, the attribution rules apply. However, in a complete termination redemption, the family attribution rules may be waived if certain conditions are met.
7. If stock included in a decedent's estate represents more than 35% of the adjusted gross estate, § 303 provides automatic sale or exchange treatment on its redemption.
8. A corporation is taxed on the appreciation of property distributed in redemption of its stock.
9. In a qualifying stock redemption, the E & P account of the distributing corporation is reduced by an amount not in excess of the ratable share of its E & P that is attributable to the stock redeemed.

CLOSELY HELD CORPORATIONS

Closely held corporations have considerable discretion regarding their dividend policies. In the past, the double tax result provided strong motivation to avoid the payment of dividends. Instead, the incentive was to bail out corporate profits in a manner that provided tax benefits to the corporation. Hence, liberal use was made of compensation, loan, and lease arrangements because salaries, interest, and rent are deductible. Under current law, however, shareholders prefer dividends because salaries, interest, and rent are fully taxed while dividends receive preferential treatment. Thus, the question becomes this: Should the *corporation* or the *shareholders* benefit? In general, the best strategy considers the tax consequences to both parties.

EXAMPLE 43

Consider a corporation paying tax at the 34% rate and an individual shareholder in the 35% tax bracket. A deductible $10,000 payment to the shareholder will *save* the corporation $3,400 in tax, resulting in an after-tax cost of $6,600. The shareholder will pay $3,500 in tax, resulting in after-tax income of $6,500. This creates a joint tax burden of $100 ($3,500 tax paid by the shareholder − $3,400 tax saved by the corporation). If, instead, the corporation paid a $10,000 qualified dividend (subject to a 15% tax rate) to the shareholder, no tax savings would be realized by the corporation, resulting in an after-tax cost of $10,000. The shareholder would owe $1,500 in taxes, leaving $8,500 of income. Considering both the corporation and the shareholder, a dividend creates $1,400 more tax liability than a deductible payment, so the deductible payment is more tax efficient. ■

In Example 43, when the deductible payment is made, the shareholder bears an increased tax burden of $2,000 ($3,500 tax due from the deductible payment − $1,500 tax due from the dividend) while the corporation saves $3,400 ($3,400 tax saved because of the deductible payment − $0 tax saved because of the dividend). Both parties could actually benefit if the corporation transfers part of its benefit to the shareholder through a larger deductible payment.

EXAMPLE 44

Assume the same facts as in Example 43, except that the corporation pays a $14,000 deductible payment. In this case, the corporation will save $4,760 ($14,000 × 34%) in tax, resulting in an after-tax cost of $9,240. From the corporation's perspective, this is preferable to a $10,000 dividend because it costs $760 less after tax ($10,000 dividend cost − $9,240 after-tax cost of a $14,000 deductible payment). The shareholder will pay taxes of $4,900 on the deductible payment, resulting in after-tax income of $9,100. The shareholder will also prefer this payment to a dividend because it generates $600 more after-tax income ($9,100 − $8,500 from a dividend). ■

Thus, if properly structured, deductible payments by the corporation to the shareholder still appear to be preferable to dividends in most situations (unless the corporation faces a low tax rate).

19.9 Constructive Dividends

Tax planning can be particularly effective in avoiding constructive dividend situations. Shareholders should try to structure their dealings with the corporation on an arm's length basis. For example, reasonable rent should be paid for the use of corporate property, and a fair price should be paid for its purchase. The parties should make every effort to support the amount involved with appraisal data or market information obtained from reliable sources at or near the time of the transaction. Dealings between shareholders and a closely held corporation should be as formal as possible. In the case of loans to shareholders, for example, the parties should provide for an adequate rate of interest and written evidence of the debt. Shareholders should also establish and follow a realistic repayment schedule.

If shareholders wish to bail out corporate profits in a form deductible to the corporation, a balanced mix of the possible alternatives lessens the risk of constructive dividend treatment. Rent for the use of shareholder property, interest on amounts borrowed from shareholders, or salaries for services rendered by shareholders are all feasible substitutes for dividend distributions. Overdoing any one approach, however, may attract the attention of the IRS. Too much interest, for example, may mean the corporation is thinly capitalized, and some of the debt may be reclassified as an equity investment.

Much can be done to protect against the disallowance of unreasonable compensation. Example 45 is an illustration, all too common in a family corporation, of what *not* to do.

EXAMPLE 45

Bob Cole wholly owns Eagle Corporation. Corporate employees and their annual salaries include Mrs. Cole ($120,000), Cole Jr. ($80,000), Bob Cole ($640,000), and Ed ($320,000). The operation of Eagle Corporation is shared about equally between Bob

Cole and Ed, who is an unrelated party. Mrs. Cole performed significant services for Eagle during its formative years, but now merely attends the annual meeting of the board of directors. Cole Jr., Bob Cole's son, is a full-time student and occasionally signs papers for the corporation in his capacity as treasurer. Eagle Corporation has not distributed a dividend for 10 years although it has accumulated substantial E & P. Mrs. Cole, Cole Jr., and Bob Cole run the risk of a finding of unreasonable compensation, based on the following factors:

- Mrs. Cole's salary is vulnerable unless proof is available that some or all of her $120,000 annual salary is payment for services rendered to the corporation in prior years and that she was underpaid for those years.[57]
- Cole Jr.'s salary is also vulnerable; he does not appear to earn the $80,000 paid to him by the corporation. Neither Cole Jr. nor Mrs. Cole is a shareholder, but each one's relationship to Bob Cole is enough of a tie-in to raise the unreasonable compensation issue.
- Bob Cole's salary appears susceptible to challenge. Why is he receiving $320,000 more than Ed when it appears they share equally in the operation of the corporation?
- The fact that Eagle Corporation has not distributed dividends over the past 10 years, even though it is capable of doing so, increases the likelihood of a constructive dividend. ■

ETHICS & *Equity*

FORGETTING ABOUT THE PAST

Michael is the CEO and sole shareholder of Cormorant Corporation. Michael recently approached you, a tax adviser in private practice, about taking on Cormorant as a client.

In your initial interview with Michael, you learn that Cormorant claimed a $1 million deduction for his salary last year. In an audit last month, the IRS disallowed $800,000 of the salary deduction as unreasonable compensation. In the future, Cormorant fully intends to take the same salary deduction of $1 million for Michael, given his active role in the organization. In short, Cormorant believes that the salary is appropriate.

Should you accept Cormorant Corporation as a new client? If so, can you claim the same salary deduction of $1 million?

19.10 STOCK REDEMPTIONS

Stock redemptions offer several possibilities for tax planning:

- The alternative to a qualifying stock redemption is dividend treatment. The 15 percent (0 percent for taxpayers in the 10 or 15 percent marginal tax bracket) preferential tax rate on dividend income reduces some of the adverse consequences of a nonqualified stock redemption.
- A nonqualified redemption may be preferable to one that produces sale or exchange treatment if the distributing corporation has little or no E & P or the distributee-shareholder is another corporation. In the latter situation, dividend treatment may be preferred because of the availability of the dividends received deduction.
- A not essentially equivalent redemption provides minimal utility and generally should be relied upon only as a last resort. Instead, a redemption

[57]See, for example, *R. J. Nicoll Co.*, 59 T.C. 37 (1972).

should be structured to satisfy the objective tests required of one of the other qualifying redemptions.

- The timing and sequence of a redemption should be considered carefully as a series of redemptions may have the effect of a dividend distribution. The following example illustrates this point.

EXAMPLE 46

Sparrow Corporation's stock is held by three unrelated shareholders: Alma (60 shares), Antonio (20 shares), and Ali (20 shares). The corporation redeems 24 of Alma's shares. Shortly thereafter, it redeems 5 of Antonio's shares. Does Alma's redemption qualify as a disproportionate redemption? Taken in isolation, it satisfies the 80% and 50% tests. Yet, if the IRS takes into account the later redemption of Antonio's shares, Alma has not satisfied the 50% test; she still owns $^{36}/_{71}$ of the corporation after the two redemptions. A greater time lag between the redemptions places Alma in a better position to argue against collapsing the two redemptions as parts of one integrated plan. ■

- For a family corporation in which all of the shareholders are related to each other, the only hope of achieving sale or exchange treatment may lie in the use of a redemption that completely terminates a shareholder's interest or one that follows a shareholder's death. In a complete termination redemption, it is important that the family stock attribution rules be avoided. Here, strict compliance with the requirements for the family attribution waiver (e.g., the withdrawing shareholder does not acquire a prohibited interest in the corporation within 10 years) is crucial.
- In a redemption to pay death taxes, the amount to be sheltered from dividend treatment is limited to the sum of death taxes and funeral and administration expenses. However, a redemption in excess of the limitation does not destroy the applicability of § 303.

REFOCUS ON THE BIG PICTURE

TAXING CORPORATE DISTRIBUTIONS

A number of factors affect the tax treatment of Lime Corporation's distributions. The amount of current and accumulated E & P (which differ from the financial reporting concept of retained earnings) partially determines the tax effect on the shareholders. Given that Lime Corporation has had a highly profitable year, it is likely that there is sufficient current E & P to cover the distributions. If so, they are dividends to the shareholders rather than a return of capital. Orange Corporation receives $200,000 of dividend income that is mostly offset by the dividends received deduction. The amount of the offsetting deduction depends on the ownership percentage that Orange has in Lime. In this situation, Orange would likely qualify for a dividends received deduction of $160,000 ($200,000 × 80%). Gustavo has $200,000 of dividend income (i.e., $300,000 value of the land less the $100,000 mortgage). Assuming that Lime is a domestic corporation and that Gustavo has held his stock for the entire year, the land is a qualified dividend. As a result, the dividend is either tax-free (if Gustavo has a marginal rate of 10 or 15 percent) or subject to a 15 percent tax rate. Gustavo's basis in the land is its fair market value at distribution, or $300,000.

From Lime Corporation's perspective, the distribution of appreciated property creates a deemed gain. Thus, a $280,000 gain results ($300,000 fair market value of the land less its adjusted basis of $20,000). While the gain increases Lime's E & P, the distributions to the shareholders reduce it by $200,000 for the cash and $200,000 for the land ($300,000 fair market value reduced by the $100,000 mortgage).

CONTINUED

What If?

What if current E & P is less than the cash and land distributed to the shareholders? Current E & P is applied pro rata to the cash and the land. Since the amounts received by the two shareholders are equal ($200,000 each), the current E & P applied is taxed as a dividend and is treated as described above. To the extent that the distributions are not covered by current E & P, accumulated E & P is then applied in a pro rata fashion (since both distributions were made on December 31). However, Lime probably has a deficit in accumulated E & P. As a result, the remaining amounts distributed to the two shareholders are first a tax-free recovery of stock basis, and any excess is taxed as a sale of the stock (probably classified as capital gain).

KEY TERMS

Accumulated earnings and profits, 19–6
Attribution, 19–22
Complete termination redemption, 19–25
Constructive dividend, 19–15
Current earnings and profits, 19–6
Disproportionate redemption, 19–24
Earnings and profits (E & P), 19–3
Meaningful reduction test, 19–23
Not essentially equivalent redemption, 19–23
Property dividend, 19–13
Qualified dividends, 19–11
Redemption to pay death taxes, 19–26
Stock dividends, 19–17
Stock redemption, 19–19
Stock rights, 19–18
Unreasonable compensation, 19–16

DISCUSSION QUESTIONS

1. **LO.2** What is meant by the term *earnings and profits*?
2. **LO.1** What factors affect the tax treatment of corporate distributions?
3. **LO.2** In determining Blue Corporation's current E & P for 2011, how should taxable income be adjusted as a result of the following transactions?
   a. A capital loss carryover from 2010, fully used in 2011.
   b. Nondeductible meal expenses in 2011.
   c. Interest on municipal bonds received in 2011.
   d. Nondeductible lobbying expenses in 2011.
   e. Loss on a sale between related parties in 2011.
   f. Federal income tax refund received in 2011.
4. **LO.3** Describe the effect of a distribution in a year when the distributing corporation has any of the following:
   a. A deficit in accumulated E & P and a positive amount in current E & P.
   b. A positive amount in accumulated E & P and a deficit in current E & P.
   c. A deficit in both current and accumulated E & P.
   d. A positive amount in both current and accumulated E & P.
5. **LO.3** A calendar year corporation has no accumulated E & P, but expects to earn current E & P for the year. A cash distribution to its shareholders on January 1 should result in a return of capital. Comment on the validity of this statement.
6. **LO.4** Discuss the rationale for the reduced tax rates on dividends paid to individuals.

7. **LO.1, 2, 3, 4, 5** Red Corporation distributes $500,000 in cash to each of its three shareholders: Jack, Susan, and Orange Corporation. What factors must be considered when determining how the distribution is treated for tax purposes by the shareholders? **ISSUE ID**

8. **LO.4** Assume the same facts as in Question 7 except that noncash property is distributed. What factors must be considered when determining how the distribution is treated for tax purposes by Red Corporation? **ISSUE ID**

9. **LO.5** Why would a corporation distribute a property dividend?

10. **LO.5** Seagull Corporation owns three machines that it uses in its business. It no longer needs two of these machines and is considering distributing them to its two shareholders as a property dividend. All three machines have a fair market value of $40,000 each. The basis of each machine is as follows: machine A, $47,000; machine B, $40,000; and machine C, $32,000. The corporation has asked you for advice. What do you recommend? **DECISION MAKING**

11. **LO.5** What is the effect on the corporation when it makes a property distribution?

12. **LO.5** A corporation is contemplating a possible property distribution to its shareholders. If appreciated property is to be used, does it matter to the distributing corporation whether the property distributed is a long-term capital asset or depreciable property subject to recapture? **ISSUE ID**

13. **LO.6** Judy is the president and sole shareholder of Parakeet Corporation. She is paid an annual salary of $600,000, while her son, Mike, the company's chief financial officer, is paid a salary of $375,000. Mike works for Parakeet on a part-time basis and spends most of his time training for triathlons. Parakeet advances $80,000 to Judy as an interest-free loan. What are the tax issues? **ISSUE ID**

14. **LO.6** Whether compensation paid to a corporate employee is reasonable is a question of fact to be determined from the surrounding circumstances. How would the resolution of this problem be affected by each of the following factors?
    a. The employee owns no stock but is the mother-in-law of the sole shareholder.
    b. The shareholder-employee does not have a college degree.
    c. The shareholder-employee works 40 hours per week for another unrelated employer.
    d. The shareholder-employee was underpaid for services during the formative period of the corporation.
    e. The corporation has never paid a dividend.
    f. Year-end bonuses are paid to all employees, but officer-shareholders receive disproportionately larger bonuses.

15. **LO.4, 10** Orange Corporation would like to transfer excess cash to its sole shareholder, Danielle, who is also an employee. Danielle is in the 28% tax bracket, and Orange is in the 34% bracket. Because Danielle's contribution to the business is substantial, Orange believes that a $50,000 bonus in the current year is reasonable compensation and should be deductible by the corporation. However, Orange is considering paying Danielle a $50,000 dividend because the tax rate on dividends is lower than the tax rate on compensation. Is Orange correct in believing that a dividend is the better choice? Why or why not? **DECISION MAKING**

16. **LO.6, 8** Green Corporation has several employees. Their names and salaries are listed below.

Samantha	$600,000
Chris (Samantha's daughter)	100,000
Joey (Samantha's son)	100,000
Jack (an unrelated third party)	250,000

Chris and Joey are the only shareholders of Green Corporation. Samantha and Jack share equally in the management of the company's operations. Chris and Joey are both full-time college students at a university 200 miles away. Green has substantial E & P and has never distributed a dividend. Discuss problems related to Green's salary arrangement.

17. **LO.8, 9, 10** Joseph and Erica, husband and wife, jointly own all of the stock in Velvet Corporation. The two are currently involved in divorce proceedings, and pursuant to **ISSUE ID**

those negotiations they have agreed that only one of them will remain a shareholder in Velvet after the divorce. Since Erica has been more involved in Velvet's management and operations over the years, the parties have agreed that Joseph's ownership should be acquired by either Erica or Velvet. What issues should be considered in determining whether Erica or Velvet should acquire Joseph's shares in the corporation?

18. **LO.8** During the current year, Gnatcatcher, Inc., distributed $100,000 each to Brandi and Yuen in redemption of some of their Gnatcatcher stock. The two shareholders acquired their shares five years ago. Each shareholder is in the 28% tax bracket, and each had a $40,000 basis in her redeemed stock. Brandi incurred $9,000 of tax on her redemption, but Yuen incurred $15,000 on her redemption. Discuss the likely reason for the difference in tax liabilities arising from the stock redemptions.

19. **LO.8** Would a shareholder prefer a qualifying stock redemption or a nonqualified stock redemption? Why?

20. **LO.8** Is a loss realized in a qualifying stock redemption recognized by the shareholder?

21. **LO.8** A shareholder's basis in property received in a qualifying stock redemption is the property's fair market value on the date of the redemption, but a shareholder's basis in property received in a nonqualified stock redemption is the basis the distributing corporation had in such property. Comment on the validity of this statement.

22. **LO.8** How do the § 318 stock attribution rules apply to corporations and their shareholders?

23. **LO.8** The stock attribution rules apply to all stock redemptions. Assess the validity of this statement.

24. **LO.8** What happens to the basis of stock redeemed in a nonqualified stock redemption?

ISSUE ID

25. **LO.8, 9** Tammy and Barry formed Pheasant Corporation several years ago in a transaction that qualified under § 351. Both shareholders serve as officers and on the board of directors of Pheasant. In the current year, Pheasant Corporation redeemed all of Barry's shares in the corporation with a property distribution. What are the tax issues for Barry and Pheasant?

26. **LO.8** Why is § 303 (redemption to pay death taxes) of particular importance for shareholders of closely held corporations?

27. **LO.8** Explain the requirements for a redemption to pay death taxes. What are the tax consequences of a redemption to pay death taxes for the shareholder and the corporation?

ISSUE ID

28. **LO.8, 9** Angie and her daughter, Ann, who are the only shareholders of Bluebird Corporation, each paid $100,000 four years ago for their shares in Bluebird. Angie also owns 20% of the stock in Redbird Corporation. The Redbird stock is worth $500,000, and Angie's basis in the stock is $50,000. Angie dies in 2011 leaving all her property to her husband, Gary, but Ann wants to be the sole shareholder of Bluebird Corporation. Bluebird has assets worth $4 million (basis of $700,000) and E & P of $1 million. Angie's estate is worth approximately $6 million. Angie had made gifts during her lifetime to Ann. What are the tax issues for Angie's estate, Ann, and Bluebird?

DECISION MAKING

29. **LO.9, 10** Indigo Corporation desires to transfer cash of $100,000 or property worth $100,000 to one of its shareholders, Linda, in a redemption transaction that will be treated as a qualifying stock redemption. If Indigo distributes property, the corporation will choose between two assets that are each worth $100,000 and are no longer needed in its business: property A (basis of $121,000) and property B (basis of $53,000). Indigo is indifferent as to the form of the distribution, but Linda prefers a cash distribution. Considering the tax consequences to Indigo on the distribution to redeem Linda's shares, what should Indigo distribute?

PROBLEMS

30. **LO.1, 4** At the start of the current year, Indigo Corporation (a calendar year taxpayer) has accumulated E & P of $240,000. Indigo's current E & P is $160,000, and at the end of the year, it distributes $440,000 ($220,000 each) to its equal shareholders, Sarah and Mason. Their basis in the stock is $8,000 for Sarah and $32,000 for Mason. How is the distribution treated for tax purposes?

31. **LO.2** Capon Corporation, a calendar year taxpayer, receives dividend income of $600,000 from a corporation in which it holds a 12% interest. Capon also receives interest income of $90,000 from municipal bonds. (The municipality used the proceeds from the bond issue to construct a library.) Capon borrowed funds to purchase the municipal bonds and pays $50,000 of interest on the loan. Excluding these items, Capon's taxable income is $1.2 million.
    a. What is Capon Corporation's taxable income after these items are taken into account?
    b. What is Capon Corporation's accumulated E & P at the start of next year if its beginning balance this year is $400,000?

32. **LO.1, 2, 3** On September 30, Jade Corporation, a calendar year taxpayer, sold a parcel of land (basis of $300,000) for a $900,000 note. The note is payable in five installments, with the first payment due next year. Because Jade did not elect out of the installment method, none of the $600,000 gain is taxed this year.

    Jade Corporation had a $400,000 deficit in accumulated E & P at the beginning of the year. Before considering the effect of the land sale, Jade had a deficit in current E & P of $100,000.

    Robert, the sole shareholder of Jade, has a basis of $150,000 in his stock. If Jade distributes $950,000 to Robert on December 31, how much income must he report for tax purposes?

33. **LO.2** Sparrow Corporation (a calendar year, accrual basis taxpayer) had the following transactions in 2011, its second year of operation.

Taxable income	$330,000
Federal income tax liability paid	112,000
Tax-exempt interest income	5,000
Meals and entertainment expenses (total)	3,000
Premiums paid on key employee life insurance	3,500
Increase in cash surrender value attributable to life insurance premiums	700
Proceeds from key employee life insurance policy	130,000
Cash surrender value of life insurance policy at distribution	20,000
Excess of capital losses over capital gains	13,000
MACRS deduction	26,000
Straight-line depreciation using ADS lives	16,000
Section 179 expense elected during 2010	100,000
Organizational expenses incurred during 2010	14,000
Dividends received from domestic corporations (less than 20% owned)	25,000

Sparrow uses the LIFO inventory method, and its LIFO recapture amount increased by $10,000 during 2011. In addition, Sparrow sold property on installment during 2010. The property was sold for $40,000 and had an adjusted basis at sale of $32,000. During 2011, Sparrow received a $15,000 payment on the installment sale. Finally assume that Sparrow elected to amortize qualified organizational expenses during 2010 and that no additional first-year depreciation was claimed. Compute Sparrow's current E & P.

34. **LO.2** In each of the following *independent* situations, indicate the effect on taxable income and E & P, stating the amount of any increase (or decrease) as a result of the transaction. Assume E & P has already been increased by taxable income.

	Transaction	Taxable Income Increase (Decrease)	E & P Increase (Decrease)
a.	Realized gain of $90,000 on involuntary conversion of building ($20,000 of gain is recognized).	________	________
b.	Mining exploration costs incurred on June 1 of the current year; $36,000 is deductible from current-year taxable income.	________	________
c.	Sale of equipment to unrelated third party for $350,000; basis is $210,000 (no election out of installment method; no payments are received in the current year).	________	________
d.	Dividends of $30,000 received from 5%-owned corporation, together with dividends received deduction (assume taxable income limit does not apply).	________	________
e.	Domestic production activities deduction of $60,000 claimed in current year.	________	________
f.	Section 179 expense deduction of $60,000 in current year.	________	________
g.	Impact of current-year § 179 expense deduction for item (f) in succeeding year.	________	________
h.	MACRS depreciation of $90,000. ADS depreciation would have been $100,000.	________	________
i.	Federal income taxes paid in the current year of $50,000.	________	________

35. **LO.1, 3** Bunting Corporation and Jennifer each own 50% of Sparrow Corporation's common stock. On January 1, Sparrow has a deficit in accumulated E & P of $150,000. Its current E & P is $65,000. During the year, Sparrow makes cash distributions of $30,000 each to Bunting and Jennifer.
   a. How are the two shareholders taxed on the distribution?
   b. What is Sparrow Corporation's accumulated E & P at the end of the year?

36. **LO.1, 3** Complete the following schedule for each case. Assume the shareholders have ample basis in the stock investment.

	Accumulated E & P Beginning of Year	Current E & P	Cash Distributions (All on Last Day of Year)	Dividend Income	Return of Capital
a.	($150,000)	$ 70,000	$130,000	$ ________	$ ________
b.	200,000	(60,000)	210,000	________	________
c.	130,000	50,000	150,000	________	________
d.	120,000	(40,000)	130,000	________	________
e.	Same as (d) except the distribution of $130,000 is made on June 30, and the corporation uses the calendar year for tax purposes.			________	________

37. **LO.1, 3** Mike, the sole shareholder of Daffodil Corporation, sold his Daffodil stock to Steve on July 30 for $200,000. Mike's basis in the stock was $150,000 at the beginning of the year. Daffodil had accumulated E & P of $110,000 on January 1 and current E & P of $170,000. During the year, Daffodil made the following distributions: $300,000 cash to Mike on July 1 and $100,000 cash to Steve on December 30. How will Mike and Steve be taxed on the distributions? How much gain will Mike recognize on the sale of his stock to Steve?

38. **LO.4** In November of the current year, Emerald Corporation declared a dividend of $2 per share (the shareholder record date is December 15). Assume that Emerald has sufficient current E & P to cover the dividend payment. If Judy purchases 500 shares of Emerald stock on December 5 and sells the stock on December 25, how is she taxed on the $1,000 dividend?

39. **LO.1, 5** Heather, an individual, owns all of the outstanding stock in Silver Corporation. Heather purchased her stock in Silver nine years ago, and her basis is $56,000. At the beginning of this year, the corporation has $76,000 of accumulated E & P and no current E & P (before considering the effect of the distributions). What are the tax consequences to Heather (amount and type of income and basis in property received) and Silver Corporation (gain or loss and effect on E & P) in each of the following situations?
    a. Silver distributes land to Heather. The land was held as an investment and has a fair market value of $54,000 and an adjusted basis of $42,000.
    b. Assume that Silver Corporation has no current or accumulated E & P prior to the distribution. How would your answer to (a) change?
    c. Assume that the land distributed in (a) is subject to a $46,000 mortgage (which Heather assumes). How would your answer change?
    d. Assume that the land has a fair market value of $54,000 and an adjusted basis of $62,000 on the date of the distribution. How would your answer to (a) change?
    e. Instead of distributing land in (a), assume that Silver decides to distribute equipment used in its business. The equipment has a $14,000 market value, a $1,200 adjusted basis for income tax purposes, and a $5,200 adjusted basis for E & P purposes. When the equipment was purchased four years ago, its original fair market value was $18,000.

40. **LO.1, 5** Green Corporation, with E & P of $600,000, distributes land (worth $300,000, adjusted basis of $340,000) to Michael, its sole shareholder. The land is subject to a liability of $130,000, which Michael assumes. What are the tax consequences to Green and to Michael?

41. **LO.1, 3** At the beginning of the current year, Cornflower Corporation (a calendar year taxpayer) has accumulated E & P of $54,000. During the year, Cornflower incurs a $28,000 loss from operations that accrues ratably. On October 1, Cornflower distributes $43,000 in cash to Roy, its sole shareholder. How will Roy be taxed on the distribution?

42. **LO.1, 2, 3, 4, 5** Cerulean Corporation has two equal shareholders, Eloise and Olivia. Eloise acquired her Cerulean stock three years ago by transferring property worth $700,000, basis of $300,000, for 70 shares of the stock. Olivia acquired 70 shares in Cerulean Corporation two years ago by transferring property worth $660,000, basis of $110,000. Cerulean Corporation's accumulated E & P as of January 1 of the current year is $350,000. On March 1 of the current year, the corporation distributed to Eloise property worth $120,000, basis to Cerulean of $50,000. It distributed cash of $220,000 to Olivia. On July 1 of the current year, Olivia sold her stock to Magnus for $820,000. On December 1 of the current year, Cerulean distributed cash of $90,000 each to Magnus and Eloise. What are the tax issues? **ISSUE ID**

43. **LO.5** Iris Corporation owns 30% of Fresia Corporation's stock. On November 15, Fresia Corporation, with current E & P of $320,000, distributes land (fair market value of $100,000; basis of $160,000) to Iris. The land is subject to a liability of $80,000, which Iris assumes.
    a. How is Iris Corporation taxed on the distribution?
    b. What is Fresia Corporation's E & P after the distribution?

44. **LO.2, 6** Parrot Corporation is a closely held company with accumulated E & P of $300,000 and current E & P of $350,000. Tom and Jerry are brothers; each owns a 50% share in Parrot, and they share management responsibilities equally. What are the tax consequences of each of the following independent transactions involving Parrot, Tom, and Jerry? How does each transaction affect Parrot's E & P?

a. Parrot sells an office building (adjusted basis of $350,000; fair market value of $300,000) to Tom for $275,000.
b. Parrot lends Jerry $250,000 on March 31 of this year. The loan is evidenced by a note and is payable on demand. No interest is charged on the loan (the current applicable Federal interest rate is 7%).
c. Parrot owns an airplane that it leases to others for a specified rental rate. Tom and Jerry also use the airplane for personal use and pay no rent. During the year, Tom used the airplane for 120 hours, and Jerry used it for 160 hours. The rental value of the airplane is $350 per hour, and its maintenance costs average $80 per hour.
d. Tom leases equipment to Parrot for $20,000 per year. The same equipment can be leased from another company for $9,000 per year.

COMMUNICATIONS

45. **LO.7** Julie Swanson bought 5,000 shares of Great Egret Corporation stock two years ago for $12,000. Last year, Julie received a nontaxable stock dividend of 1,000 shares in Great Egret Corporation. In the current tax year, Julie sold all of the stock received as a dividend for $9,000. Prepare a letter to Julie and a memo to the file describing the tax consequences of the stock sale. Julie's address is 3737 Canyon Drive, Minneapolis, MN 55434.

DECISION MAKING

46. **LO.4** Ivana, the president and a shareholder of Robin Corporation, has earned a salary bonus of $15,000 for the current year. Because of the lower tax rates on qualified dividends, Robin is considering substituting a dividend for the bonus. Assume the tax rates are 28% for Ivana and 34% for Robin Corporation.
    a. How much better off would Ivana be if she were paid a dividend rather than salary?
    b. How much better off would Robin Corporation be if it paid Ivana salary rather than a dividend?
    c. If Robin Corporation pays Ivana a salary bonus of $20,000 instead of a $15,000 dividend, how would your answers to (a) and (b) change?
    d. What should Robin do?

47. **LO.8** Magpie Corporation has 3,000 shares of common stock outstanding. Josephina owns 800 shares, Josephina's daughter owns 500 shares, Josephina's brother owns 800 shares, Tern Corporation owns 600 shares, and Petrel Partnership owns 300 shares. Josephina owns 45% of the stock of Tern Corporation, and she owns a 60% interest in Petrel Partnership.
    a. Applying the § 318 stock attribution rules, how many shares does Josephina own in Magpie Corporation?
    b. Assume Josephina owns 75% of the stock of Tern Corporation. How many shares does Josephina own, directly and indirectly, in Magpie Corporation?

48. **LO.2, 8** Pedro owns 700 of the 1,000 shares outstanding of Indigo Corporation (E & P of $950,000). Pedro paid $170 per share for the stock 12 years ago. The remaining stock in Indigo is owned by unrelated individuals. What are the tax consequences to Pedro in the following independent situations?
    a. Indigo redeems 350 shares of Pedro's stock for $175,000.
    b. Indigo redeems 450 shares of Pedro's stock for $225,000.

COMMUNICATIONS

49. **LO.8, 9** Stork Corporation (E & P of $850,000) has 1,000 shares of common stock outstanding. The shares are owned by the following individuals: Lana Johnson, 450 shares; Lori Johnson (Lana's sister), 450 shares; and Leo Johnson (Lana's son), 100 shares. Lana paid $200 per share for the Stork stock eight years ago. Lana is interested in reducing her stock ownership in Stork via a stock redemption for $1,000 per share, the fair market value of the stock. Stork Corporation would distribute cash for the entire redemption transaction. Lana has inquired as to the minimum number of shares that she would have to redeem in order to obtain favorable long-term capital gain treatment and the overall tax consequences of such a redemption to both her and Stork Corporation. Prepare a letter to Lana (1000 Main Street, Oldtown, MN 55166) and a memo for the file in which you explain your conclusions.

50. **LO.8** Thrush Corporation (E & P of $450,000) has 3,000 shares of common stock outstanding. The shares are owned as follows: John Thompson, 1,300 shares; Edward Thompson (John's father), 1,000 shares; and Georgia Simpson (John's sister), 700

shares. In the current year, Thrush redeems all of John's shares. Determine whether the redemption can qualify for sale or exchange treatment under the complete termination redemption rules in each of the following independent circumstances.

a. John does not file an agreement with his tax return (for the year of redemption) to notify the IRS of any prohibited interest acquired in Thrush during the 10-year post-redemption period.

b. Seven years after the redemption, Georgia dies, and John purchases the 700 shares in Thrush Corporation from her estate.

c. John receives a five-year note receivable from Thrush Corporation in exchange for the redeemed stock.

51. **LO.8, 9** Robert and Lori (Robert's sister) own all the stock in Swan Corporation (E & P of $700,000). Each owns 500 shares and has a basis of $25,000 in the shares. Robert wants to sell his stock for $400,000, the fair market value, but he will continue to be employed as an officer of Swan Corporation after the sale. Lori would like to purchase Robert's shares and, thus, become the sole shareholder in Swan, but Lori is short of funds. What are the tax consequences to Robert, Lori, and Swan Corporation under the following circumstances?

    a. Swan Corporation distributes cash of $400,000 to Lori, and she uses the cash to purchase Robert's shares.

    b. Swan Corporation redeems all of Robert's shares for $400,000.

52. **LO.8, 9** The gross estate of Tanya, decedent, includes stock of Finch Corporation (E & P of $2 million) valued at $1.4 million. At the time of her death in 2011, Tanya owned 40% of the Finch stock outstanding, and she had a basis of $220,000 in the stock. The death taxes and funeral and administration expenses related to Tanya's estate amount to $1.4 million, and the adjusted gross estate is $7 million. The remainder of the Finch stock is owned by shareholders unrelated to Tanya (or her estate). Tanya named her son, Taylor, as the sole heir of her estate. In the current year, Finch Corporation distributes $1.4 million to the estate in redemption of all of its stock in the corporation. What are the tax consequences of the redemption to Tanya's estate and to Finch Corporation?

53. **LO.8, 9** Teal Corporation (E & P of $900,000) has 2,000 shares of common stock outstanding. The shares are owned by the following individuals: Ann, 800 shares; Bonnie, 600 shares; and Lucy, 600 shares. Each of the shareholders paid $20 per share for the Teal stock nine years ago. In the current year, Teal distributes $90,000 to Ann in redemption of 300 of her shares. Determine the tax consequences of the redemption to Ann and to Teal Corporation under the following independent circumstances.

    a. The three shareholders are unrelated.

    b. Ann and Bonnie are mother and daughter.

54. **LO.9** Crane Corporation has 2,000 shares of stock outstanding. It redeems 500 shares for $370,000 when it has paid-in capital of $300,000 and E & P of $1.2 million. The redemption qualifies for sale or exchange treatment for the shareholder. Crane incurred $13,000 of accounting and legal fees in connection with the redemption transaction. What is the effect of the distribution on Crane Corporation's E & P? Also, what is the proper tax treatment of the redemption expenditures? Prepare a letter to the president of Crane Corporation (506 Wall Street, Winona, MN 55987) and a memo for the file in which you explain your conclusions. **COMMUNICATIONS**

RESEARCH PROBLEMS

Note: Solutions to Research Problems can be prepared by using the **Checkpoint® Student Edition** online research product, which is available to accompany this text. It is also possible to prepare solutions to the Research Problems by using tax research materials found in a standard tax library.

THOMSON REUTERS
Checkpoint® Student Edition

Research Problem 1. Your client, White Corporation, has done well since its formation 20 years ago. This year, it recognized a $50 million capital gain from the sale of a subsidiary. White's CEO has contacted you to discuss a proposed transaction to reduce the tax on the capital gain. Under the proposal, White will purchase all of the common stock in Purple Corporation for $200 million. Purple is a profitable corporation that has $63 million in cash and marketable securities, $137 million in operating assets, and approximately $280 million in E & P. After its acquisition, Purple will distribute $50 million in cash and marketable securities to White. Due to the 100% dividends received deduction, no taxable income results to White from the dividend. White will then resell Purple for $150 million. The subsequent sale of Purple generates a $50 million capital loss [$150 million (sales price) – ($200 million stock basis)]. The loss from the stock sale can then be used to offset the preexisting $50 million capital gain. Will the proposed plan work?

Partial list of research aids:
§ 1059.

COMMUNICATIONS

Research Problem 2. Six years ago, Coastal Drillers, Inc., redeemed all of the stock owned directly by Jeremiah Cranston (6870 Vinton Court, Los Angeles, CA 90034). At the time of the redemption, Jeremiah and his immediate family members owned 100% of the stock of Coastal Drillers. Jeremiah satisfied all of the requirements of the family attribution waiver [under § 302(c)(2)]; thus, the transaction qualified as a complete termination redemption and resulted in a significant long-term capital gain. Coastal Drillers' E & P at the time of the transaction exceeded the redemption proceeds. Treatment of the redemption proceeds as a dividend would have resulted in a $200,000 greater tax liability for Jeremiah. Now, six years later, Coastal Drillers has offered Jeremiah a consulting engagement. The consulting engagement would be for a one-year term, but options to renew could extend the contract to a total of five years. Assuming all options are exercised, Jeremiah would earn $150,000 under the contract. Based on the terms of the contract, Jeremiah would properly be classified as an independent contractor, not as an employee of Coastal Drillers. Jeremiah has contacted you regarding the effect, if any, of the proposed consulting engagement on the tax treatment of his earlier stock redemption. Prepare a letter to Jeremiah and a memo for the file documenting your conclusions.

INTERNET *activity*

Use the tax resources of the Internet to address the following question. Do not restrict your search to the Web, but include a review of newsgroups and general reference materials, practitioner sites and resources, primary sources of the tax law, chat rooms and discussion groups, and other opportunities.

COMMUNICATIONS

Research Problem 3. Buy-sell agreements are frequently used to address the disposition of a retiring or deceased shareholder's stock in a closely held corporation. Using the Internet as your sole research source, prepare an outline on the planning opportunities and pitfalls of using a buy-sell agreement in conjunction with the qualifying stock redemption provisions.

Corporations: Distributions in Complete Liquidation and an Overview of Reorganizations

CHAPTER

20

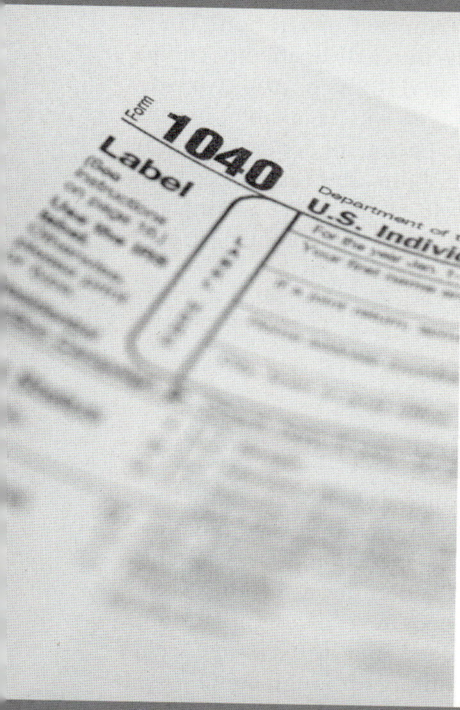

LEARNING OBJECTIVES

After completing Chapter 20, you should be able to:

LO.1

Understand the tax consequences of complete liquidations for both the corporation and its shareholders.

LO.2

Understand the tax consequences of subsidiary liquidations for both the parent and the subsidiary corporations.

LO.3

Understand the general requirements and tax consequences of corporate reorganizations.

LO.4

Identify tax planning opportunities available to minimize the tax impact in complete liquidations and corporate reorganizations.

OUTLINE

For the latest in changes to tax legislation, visit **www.cengage.com/taxation/swft.**

THE BIG PICTURE **Tax Solutions for the Real World**

THE OPTIONS FOR TRANSITIONING TO RETIREMENT

Mr. and Mrs. Albert Smithson have experienced great pride in Orange Corporation, the successful business that they have built over their careers, but they believe the time has come for them to think seriously about retirement. They own all of the stock in Orange, a C corporation, and their stock investment has a basis of $200,000. The business, which is in the 34 percent income tax bracket, owns net assets that are worth $4 million and have a basis of $1.5 million.

Unfortunately, the Smithsons have no family members who are interested in carrying on the business, so they must resort to liquidating Orange Corporation. Their strategy, in general, is to convert the value of their business into a diversified portfolio of marketable securities and to live off the earnings generated by the portfolio during their retirement years. The Smithsons realize that such a plan will be taxable, so they would like to know the amount that will be available after paying all Federal taxes. It is important that they have a realistic idea of the amount of the after-tax proceeds so that they can determine if retiring at this point is even feasible. After working for their entire lives, they are eager to live comfortably off their retirement nest egg. **Read the chapter and formulate your response.**

20.1 Liquidations—In General

LO.1

Understand the tax consequences of complete liquidations for both the corporation and its shareholders.

When a corporation makes a nonliquidating distribution (e.g., stock redemption), the entity typically will continue as a going concern. With a complete liquidation, however, corporate existence terminates, as does each shareholder's ownership interest. A complete liquidation, like a qualifying stock redemption, produces sale or exchange treatment to the *shareholder*. However, the tax effects of a liquidation to the *corporation* vary somewhat from those of a redemption. Sale or exchange treatment is also the general rule for the liquidating corporation, although some losses are disallowed.

THE LIQUIDATION PROCESS

A **corporate liquidation** exists when a corporation ceases to be a going concern. The corporation continues solely to wind up affairs, pay debts, and distribute any remaining assets to its shareholders. Legal dissolution under state law is not required for a liquidation to be complete for tax purposes. A liquidation can exist even if the corporation retains a nominal amount of assets to pay remaining debts and preserve its legal status.[1]

Shareholders may decide to liquidate a corporation for one or more reasons, including the following:

- The corporate business has been unsuccessful.
- The shareholders wish to acquire the corporation's assets.
- Another person or corporation wants to purchase the corporation's assets. The purchaser may buy the shareholders' stock and then liquidate the corporation to acquire the assets. Alternatively, the purchaser may buy the assets directly from the corporation. After the assets are sold, the corporation distributes the sales proceeds to its shareholders and liquidates.

As one might expect, the different means used to liquidate a corporation produce varying tax results.

[1] Reg. § 1.332–2(c).

TAX *in* the NEWS

GENERAL MOTORS LIVES ON—OR DOES IT?

Most Americans are aware that the U.S. government bailed out General Motors Corporation (GM). The government provided a $50 billion infusion of capital in an effort to stave off the automaker's demise. "New GM" was formed, and it purchased most of the operating assets of Motors Liquidation Company (MLC), "former GM" in bankruptcy. U.S. taxpayers received a 61 percent ownership interest in new GM for their investment. But what about former GM's less desirable assets and its liabilities? MLC was left with many old factory buildings and other unwanted assets, in addition to the liabilities, of former GM. Outdated factories fraught with environmental problems have proved to be a hard sale for MLC, and many other assets (e.g., factory robots, an abandoned church, a golf course) also remain on MLC's balance sheet. (For a look at the properties available for purchase, check out MLC's website at **www.motorsliquidation.com.**) On August 31, 2010, MLC filed a plan of liquidation in bankruptcy court that would result in the transfer of substantially all of its cash and remaining unsold assets to four trusts, including a trust funded with more than $800 million for environmental cleanup work related to the old factories.

LIQUIDATING AND NONLIQUIDATING DISTRIBUTIONS COMPARED

As discussed in Chapter 19, a *nonliquidating* property distribution produces gain (but not loss) to the distributing corporation. For the shareholder, the receipt of cash or other property produces dividend income to the extent of the corporation's E & P or, in the case of a qualifying stock redemption, results in sale or exchange treatment.

Similar to a qualifying stock redemption, a *liquidation* produces sale or exchange treatment for the shareholders. E & P has no impact on the gain or loss to be recognized by the shareholder in either type of distribution.[2] However, a liquidation produces different tax consequences to the distributing corporation. With certain exceptions, a liquidating corporation recognizes gain *and* loss upon the distribution of its assets.

EXAMPLE 1

Goose Corporation, with E & P of $40,000, makes a cash distribution of $50,000 to its sole shareholder. The shareholder's basis in the Goose stock is $20,000. If the distribution is not a qualifying stock redemption or in complete liquidation, the shareholder recognizes dividend income of $40,000 (the amount of Goose's E & P) and treats the remaining $10,000 of the distribution as a return of capital. If the distribution is a qualifying stock redemption or is pursuant to a complete liquidation, the shareholder has a capital gain of $30,000 ($50,000 distribution − $20,000 stock basis). In the case of these distributions, Goose's E & P is of no consequence to the shareholder's tax result. ■

In the event a corporate distribution results in a *loss* to the shareholder, another distinction exists between nonliquidating distributions and liquidations. Section 267 disallows recognition of losses between related parties in nonliquidating distributions but not in complete liquidations.

EXAMPLE 2

The stock of Tern Corporation is owned equally by three brothers, Rex, Sam, and Ted. When Ted's basis in his stock is $40,000, the corporation distributes $30,000 to him in cancellation of all his shares. If the distribution is a qualifying stock redemption, the $10,000 realized loss is not recognized because Ted and Tern Corporation are related parties. Under § 267, Ted is deemed to own more than 50% in value of the corporation's outstanding stock. Ted's direct ownership is limited to 33$^1/_3$%, but through his brothers, he owns indirectly another 66$^2/_3$% for a total of 100%. On the other hand, if the distribution is pursuant to a complete liquidation, Ted's $10,000 realized loss is recognized. ■

[2] § 331.

The rules governing the basis of property received from a corporation are identical for both nonliquidating and liquidating distributions. Section 301(d) specifies that the basis of property received in a nonliquidating distribution is its fair market value on the date of distribution, while § 334(a) provides the same treatment for property received in a liquidating distribution.

In the following pages, the tax consequences of a complete liquidation are examined, first from the view of the distributing corporation and then in terms of the shareholder. Because the tax rules differ when a subsidiary corporation is liquidated, the rules relating to the liquidation of a subsidiary corporation are discussed separately.

20.2 Liquidations—Effect on the Distributing Corporation

THE GENERAL RULE

Section 336(a) provides that a corporation recognizes *gain or loss* on the distribution of property in a complete liquidation. The property is treated as if it were sold at its fair market value. This treatment is consistent with the notion of double taxation that is inherent in operating a business as a C corporation—once at the corporate level and again at the shareholder level.

As in the case of a nonliquidating distribution, when property distributed in a complete liquidation is subject to a liability of the liquidating corporation, the deemed fair market value used to calculate gain or loss may not be less than the amount of the liability.

EXAMPLE 3

Pursuant to a complete liquidation, Warbler Corporation distributes to its shareholders land held as an investment (basis of $200,000, fair market value of $300,000). If no liability is involved, Warbler has a gain of $100,000 on the distribution ($300,000 – $200,000). Likewise, if the land is subject to a liability of $250,000, Warbler Corporation has a gain of $100,000. If, instead, the liability were $350,000, Warbler's gain on the distribution would be $150,000 ($350,000 – $200,000). ■

There are four exceptions to the general rule of gain and loss recognition by a liquidating corporation:

- *Losses* are not recognized on certain liquidating distributions to related-party shareholders.
- *Losses* are not recognized on certain sales and liquidating distributions of property that was contributed to the corporation with a built-in loss shortly before the adoption of a plan of liquidation.
- A subsidiary corporation does not recognize *gains or losses* on liquidating distributions to its parent corporation.
- A subsidiary corporation does not recognize *losses* on liquidating distributions to its minority shareholders.

The first two exceptions, referred to as the "antistuffing rules," are discussed in detail in the next section and are summarized in Figure 20.1 at the end of the section. The last two exceptions, dealing with the liquidation of a subsidiary corporation, are discussed later in this chapter.

ANTISTUFFING RULES

When property is transferred to a corporation in a § 351 transaction or as a contribution to capital, carryover and substituted basis rules generally apply (see Chapter 18). Generally, the transferee corporation takes a basis in the property equal to that of the transferor-shareholder, and the shareholder takes an equal basis in the stock received in the exchange (or adds such amount to existing stock basis in the case of a capital contribution). Without special limitations, a transfer of loss property (fair market value less than basis) in a carryover basis transaction would present opportunities for the duplication of losses.

EXAMPLE 4
THE BIG PICTURE

Return to the facts of *The Big Picture* on p. 20-2. Assume that Mr. and Mrs. Smithson transfer property (basis of $100,000, fair market value of $55,000) to Orange Corporation in exchange for additional stock. The exchange qualifies under § 351. Absent any exceptions to the contrary, the general rule of carryover basis would apply, and Orange would take a carryover basis of $100,000 in the property while the Smithsons would take a $100,000 basis in the additional stock. A sale or liquidating distribution of the property by Orange Corporation would result in a $45,000 loss [$55,000 (fair market value of property) – $100,000 (property basis)]. Similarly, a sale by the Smithsons of the stock acquired in the § 351 exchange would also result in a $45,000 loss [$55,000 (fair market value of stock) – $100,000 (stock basis)]. ■

Congress addressed this loss duplication issue in the Tax Reform Act of 1986 by enacting two loss limitation ("antistuffing") rules under § 336(d) that apply to corporations upon liquidation. The effect of these rules is to disallow some or all of a loss realized by a corporation in liquidating distributions (and, in some cases, sales) of certain property.

The antistuffing rules limited the duplication of losses realized upon a corporation's liquidation, but loss trafficking was still possible if the corporation sold high-basis property in the normal course of business instead of upon or pursuant to liquidation. As a result, Congress revisited the loss duplication issue and, in the American Jobs Creation Act of 2004, enacted limitations to the general basis rules in § 351 and contribution to capital transactions. Unlike the antistuffing rules that disallow losses, the § 362(e)(2) rules require a corporation to step down the basis of property acquired in a § 351 or contribution to capital transaction by the amount of any net built-in loss embodied in such property. The basis step-down is required when a shareholder transfers properties having an aggregate basis in excess of their aggregate fair market value ("net built-in loss"), and it is allocated proportionately among the properties having built-in losses. Alternatively, the transferor-shareholder can elect to reduce his or her stock basis by the amount of net built-in loss. (See Chapter 18 for further discussion of the basis adjustment rules.) The antistuffing rules of § 336(d) continue to apply in the case of liquidating distributions (and certain sales) of loss property, but their bite has been lessened somewhat by the § 362(e)(2) basis step-down rules.

Related-Party Loss Limitation

Losses are disallowed on distributions to *related parties* in either of the following cases:

- The distribution is *not* pro rata, or
- The property distributed is *disqualified property*.[3]

A corporation and a shareholder are considered related if the shareholder owns (directly or indirectly) more than 50 percent in value of the corporation's stock.[4]

A *pro rata distribution* is one where *each* shareholder receives his or her proportionate share of the corporate asset distributed. *Disqualified property* is property that is acquired by the liquidating corporation in a § 351 or contribution to capital transaction during the five-year period ending on the date of the distribution. The related-party loss limitation can apply even if the property was appreciated (fair market value greater than basis) when it was transferred to the corporation.

EXAMPLE 5

Bluebird Corporation stock is owned by Ana and Sanjay, who are unrelated. Ana owns 80% and Sanjay owns 20% of the stock in the corporation. Bluebird has the following assets (none of which was acquired in a § 351 or contribution to capital transaction) that are distributed in complete liquidation of the corporation:

[3] § 336(d)(1).

[4] Section 267 provides the definition of a related party for purposes of this provision. The rules are similar to the stock attribution rules discussed in Chapter 19; one exception, however, is that stock owned by a sibling is treated as owned by the taxpayer under § 267.

	Adjusted Basis	Fair Market Value
Cash	$600,000	$600,000
Equipment	150,000	200,000
Building	400,000	200,000

Assume Bluebird Corporation distributes the equipment to Sanjay and the cash and the building to Ana. Bluebird recognizes a gain of $50,000 on the distribution of the equipment. The loss of $200,000 on the building is disallowed because the property is distributed to a related party and the distribution is not pro rata (i.e., the building is not distributed 80% to Ana and 20% to Sanjay). ■

EXAMPLE 6

Assume in Example 5 that Bluebird Corporation distributes the cash and equipment to Ana and the building to Sanjay. Again, Bluebird recognizes the $50,000 gain on the equipment. However, it now recognizes the $200,000 loss on the building because the property is not distributed to a related party (i.e., Sanjay does not own more than 50% of the stock in Bluebird Corporation). ■

EXAMPLE 7

Wren Corporation's stock is held equally by three brothers. Four years before Wren's liquidation, the shareholders transfer jointly owned property (basis of $150,000, fair market value of $200,000) to the corporation in return for stock in a § 351 transaction. When the property is worth $100,000, it is transferred pro rata to the brothers in a liquidating distribution. Because each brother owns directly and indirectly more than 50% (i.e., 100% in this situation) of the stock and disqualified property is involved, Wren recognizes none of the $50,000 realized loss [$100,000 (fair market value) – $150,000 (basis)]. ■

EXAMPLE 8

Assume in Example 7 that the property's fair market value is $100,000 at the time of the § 351 transfer and $75,000 at the time of the liquidating distribution to the brothers. As a result of the § 362(e)(2) basis step-down rules, Wren Corporation's basis in the property is $100,000 [$150,000 (basis to brothers) – $50,000 (net built-in loss of property transferred)]. In a liquidating distribution of the property to the brothers, Wren would realize a loss of $25,000 [$75,000 (fair market value of property at distribution) – $100,000 (Wren's stepped-down basis in property)]. Because this is a distribution of disqualified property to related parties, none of the $25,000 loss is recognized by Wren. ■

Built-in Loss Limitation

A second loss limitation applies to sales, exchanges, or distributions of built-in loss property (fair market value less than basis) that is transferred to a corporation shortly before the corporation is liquidated. The built-in loss limitation applies when both of the following conditions are met:

- The property was acquired by the corporation in a § 351 or contribution to capital transaction.
- Such acquisition was part of a plan whose principal purpose was to recognize a loss on that property by the liquidating corporation. A tax avoidance purpose is presumed in the case of transfers occurring within two years of the adoption of a plan of liquidation.

This disallowance rule applies only to the extent that a property's built-in loss at transfer is not eliminated by a stepped-down basis. Some built-in losses on property transfers will avoid the basis step-down either because built-in gain properties were also transferred by the shareholder (see Chapter 18, Example 22) or because the shareholder elected to step down the basis of his or her stock instead. Any loss attributable to a decline in a property's value after its transfer to the corporation is not subject to the built-in loss limitation.[5]

[5] § 336(d)(2).

FIGURE 20.1 Distributions of Loss Property by a Liquidating Corporation

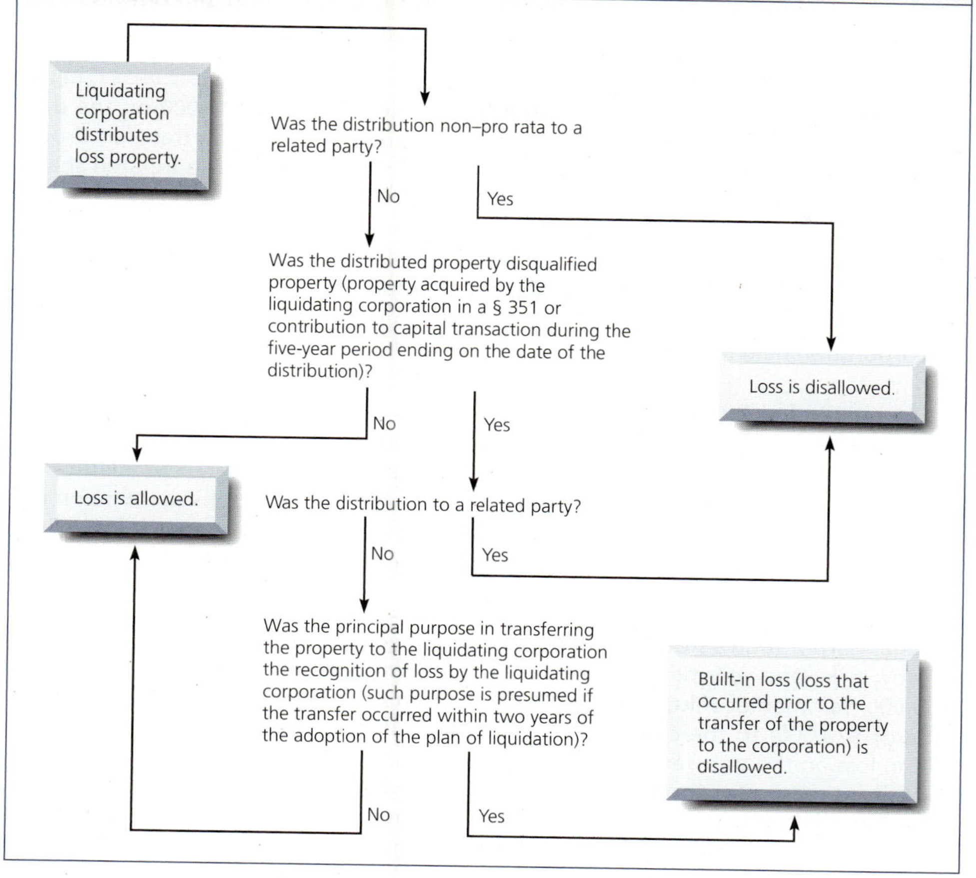

EXAMPLE 9

On January 4, 2011, Brown Corporation acquires two properties from a shareholder in a transaction that qualifies under § 351.

	Shareholder's Basis	Fair Market Value	Built-in Gain/(Loss)
Land	$100,000	$50,000	($50,000)
Securities	10,000	35,000	25,000
			($25,000)

The net built-in loss of $25,000 results in a stepped-down basis of $75,000 in the land for Brown Corporation [$100,000 (shareholder's basis) – $25,000 (step-down equal to net built-in loss)]. Brown adopts a plan of liquidation on July 8, 2011, and distributes the land to an unrelated shareholder on November 11, 2011, when the land is worth $30,000. Of the $45,000 loss realized [$30,000 (value of land on date of distribution) – $75,000 (basis in land)] by Brown on the distribution, $25,000 is disallowed by the built-in loss limitation [$50,000 (value of land when acquired by Brown) – $75,000 (stepped-down basis in land)], and $20,000 is recognized (equal to the decline in value occurring after acquisition by Brown). ■

The built-in loss limitation applies to a broader range of transactions than the related-party exception, which disallows losses only on certain distributions to related parties (i.e., more-than-50 percent shareholders). The built-in loss limitation can apply to distributions of property to any shareholder, including an unrelated party, and to a *sale or exchange* of property by a liquidating corporation. However, the limitation is narrower than the related-party exception in that it applies only to property that had a built-in loss upon its acquisition by the corporation and only as to the amount of the built-in loss (as adjusted by the basis step-down rules).

EXAMPLE 10

Assume in Example 9 that the land had a fair market value of $120,000 on the date Brown Corporation acquired it. As there is no net built-in loss on the transfer, Brown will have a basis of $100,000 in the land. If the distribution is to an unrelated shareholder, Brown will recognize the entire $70,000 loss [$30,000 (fair market value on date of distribution) − $100,000 (basis)]. However, if the distribution is to a related party, Brown cannot recognize any of the loss under the related-party loss limitation because the property is disqualified property. When the distribution is to a related party, the loss is disallowed even though the entire decline in value occurred during the period the corporation held the property. ■

The built-in loss limitation will apply only in rare cases if the corporation has held the property more than two years prior to liquidation. The presumption of a tax avoidance purpose for property transferred to a corporation in the two years preceding the liquidation can be rebutted if there is a clear and substantial relationship between the contributed property and the (current or future) business of the corporation. When there was a business reason for the transfer, the built-in loss limitation will not apply.

EXAMPLE 11

Cardinal Corporation's stock is held by two unrelated individuals: 60% by Manuel and 40% by Jack. One year before Cardinal's liquidation, Manuel transfers land (basis of $150,000, fair market value of $100,000) and equipment (basis of $10,000, fair market value of $70,000) to the corporation as a contribution to capital. As there is no net built-in loss on the transfer, Cardinal will have a basis of $150,000 in the land. There is no business reason for the transfer. In liquidation, Cardinal distributes the land (now with a fair market value of $90,000) to Jack. Even though the distribution is to an unrelated party, the built-in loss of $50,000 is not recognized. However, Cardinal Corporation can recognize the loss of $10,000 ($90,000 − $100,000) that occurred while it held the land. If, instead, the land is distributed to Manuel, a related party, the entire $60,000 loss is disallowed under the related-party loss limitation. ■

EXAMPLE 12

Assume in Example 11 that the land and equipment are transferred to Cardinal Corporation because a bank required the additional capital investment as a condition to making a loan to the corporation. Because there is a business purpose for the transfer, all of the $60,000 loss is recognized if the land is distributed to Jack in liquidation. If, instead, the land is distributed to Manuel, a related party, the entire loss is still disallowed under the related-party loss limitation. ■

Tax Paid on Net Gain

To the extent that a corporation pays tax on the net amount of gain recognized as a result of its liquidation, the proceeds available to be distributed to the shareholders are likewise reduced. This reduction for the payment of taxes will reduce the amount realized by the shareholders, which will then reduce their gain (or increase the loss) recognized.

EXAMPLE 13
THE BIG PICTURE

Return to the facts of *The Big Picture* on p. 20-2. At the point when the Smithsons are contemplating retirement, their business, Orange Corporation, has net assets worth $4 million. This valuation is after the payment of all of Orange's corporate debts except for taxes it would pay on net gains recognized if it liquidates. Assuming the Smithsons decide to liquidate the corporation and the taxes the corporation pays total $850,000, the amount realized by the Smithsons is $3,150,000 ($4,000,000 − $850,000). As described below, in determining the gain or loss recognized by a shareholder, the amount realized is offset by the stock's adjusted basis. ■

ETHICS & Equity

REPORTING BUSINESS ACTIVITIES—LIQUIDATION CONSEQUENCES?

In 2004, Thomas Johnson incorporated his bagel shop and became the sole shareholder of Bagels by Thomas, Inc. For the tax years 2004–2008, Bagels by Thomas, Inc., properly filed and paid corporate income taxes (Form 1120). In early 2009, Thomas read an article on the "check-the-box" Regulations that allow a taxpayer to choose the entity form of doing business for tax purposes (see Chapter 17). Having tired of the additional complexities and requirements of the corporate form, Thomas took advantage of the "check-the-box" Regulations and reported all of the 2009 business activity for Bagels by Thomas, Inc., on his individual income tax return (Form 1040) as a sole proprietorship (Schedule C). Thomas repeated this treatment for 2010 as well. No corporate returns were filed for the business for 2009 or 2010, but the corporation was not formally liquidated. You are preparing Thomas's individual income tax return for 2011 and become aware of these facts. How should you proceed?

20.3 LIQUIDATIONS—EFFECT ON THE SHAREHOLDER

The tax consequences to the shareholders of a corporation in the process of liquidation are governed either by the general rule of § 331 or by the exception of § 332 relating to the liquidation of a subsidiary.

THE GENERAL RULE

In the case of a complete liquidation, § 331(a) provides for sale or exchange treatment for the shareholders. Thus, the difference between the fair market value of the assets received from the corporation and the adjusted basis of the stock surrendered is the gain or loss recognized by the shareholder. The fair market value of property received subject to a corporate liability is reduced by the amount of such liability. Typically, the stock is a capital asset in the hands of the shareholder, and capital gain or loss results. The burden of proof is on the taxpayer to furnish evidence as to the adjusted basis of the stock. In the absence of such evidence, the stock is deemed to have a zero basis, and the full amount of the liquidation proceeds equals the amount of the gain recognized.[6] The basis of property received in a liquidation is the property's fair market value on the date of distribution.[7]

EXAMPLE 14
THE BIG PICTURE

Return to the facts of *The Big Picture* on p. 20-2. Continuing with the preceding example, if Orange Corporation liquidates and the Smithsons receive a liquidating distribution of $3,150,000, they will recognize a capital gain of $2,950,000 ($3,150,000 amount realized − $200,000 stock basis). The basis of any property the Smithsons receive will be its fair market value. ■

SPECIAL RULE FOR CERTAIN INSTALLMENT OBLIGATIONS

Corporations often sell assets pursuant to a plan of liquidation, and sometimes these sales are made on the installment basis. If the installment notes are then distributed in liquidation, the corporation recognizes gain (or loss) equal to the difference between the fair market value of the notes and the corporation's basis in the notes.[8] However, shareholders can use the installment method to defer to the point of collection the portion of their gain that is attributable to the notes. This treatment requires the shareholders to allocate their stock basis between the installment notes and the other assets received from the corporation.[9]

[6] *John Calderazzo*, 34 TCM 1, T.C.Memo. 1975–1.

[7] § 334(a).

[8] § 453B(a). Gain is not recognized in the distribution of installment notes by a subsidiary liquidating pursuant to § 332. See the discussion below and §§ 337(a) and 453B(d).

[9] § 453(h). Installment notes attributable to the sale of inventory qualify only if the inventory was sold in a bulk sale to one person.

EXAMPLE 15

After adopting a plan of complete liquidation, Beige Corporation sells its only asset, unimproved land held as an investment. The land has appreciated in value and is sold to Jane (an unrelated party) for $100,000. Under the terms of the sale, Beige Corporation receives cash of $25,000 and Jane's notes for the balance of $75,000. The notes are payable over 10 years ($7,500 per year) and carry an appropriate rate of interest. Immediately after the sale, Beige Corporation distributes the cash and notes to Earl, the sole shareholder. Earl has an adjusted basis of $20,000 in the Beige stock, and the installment notes have a value equal to their face amount ($75,000). These transactions have the following tax results:

- Beige Corporation recognizes gain on the distribution of the installment notes, measured by the difference between the $75,000 fair market value and the basis Beige had in the notes.
- Earl may defer the gain on the receipt of the notes to the point of collection.
- Earl must allocate the adjusted basis in his stock ($20,000) between the cash and the installment notes as follows:

$$\frac{\text{Cash}}{\text{Total receipts}} = \frac{\$25{,}000}{\$100{,}000} \times \$20{,}000 = \$5{,}000 \text{ basis allocated to the cash}$$

$$\frac{\text{Notes}}{\text{Total receipts}} = \frac{\$75{,}000}{\$100{,}000} \times \$20{,}000 = \$15{,}000 \text{ basis allocated to the notes}$$

- On the cash portion of the transaction, Earl must recognize $20,000 of gain [$25,000 (cash received) – $5,000 (basis allocated to the cash)] in the year of liquidation.
- Over the next 10 years, Earl must recognize a total gain of $60,000 on the collection of the notes, computed as follows:

$$\$75{,}000 \text{ (fair market value)} - \$15{,}000 \text{ (basis allocated to the notes)} = \$60{,}000 \text{ (gross profit)}$$

- The gross profit percentage on the notes is 80%, computed as follows:

$$\frac{\$60{,}000 \text{ (gross profit)}}{\$75{,}000 \text{ (contract price)}} = 80\%$$

  Thus, Earl must report a gain of $6,000 [$7,500 (amount of note) × 80% (gross profit percentage)] on the collection of each note over the next 10 years.
- The interest element is accounted for separately. ■

20.4 Liquidations—Parent-Subsidiary Situations

LO.2

Understand the tax consequences of subsidiary liquidations for both the parent and the subsidiary corporations.

Section 332, an exception to the general rule of § 331, provides that a parent corporation does *not* recognize gain or loss on a liquidation of a subsidiary. In addition, the subsidiary corporation recognizes *neither gain nor loss* on distributions of property to its parent.[10]

The requirements for applying § 332 are as follows:

- The parent must own at least 80 percent of the voting stock of the subsidiary and at least 80 percent of the value of the subsidiary's stock.
- The subsidiary must distribute all of its property in complete cancellation of all of its stock within the taxable year or within three years from the close of the tax year in which the first distribution occurred.
- The subsidiary must be solvent.[11]

If these requirements are met, nonrecognition of gains and losses becomes mandatory. However, if the subsidiary is insolvent, the parent corporation will have an ordinary loss deduction under § 165(g).

[10] § 337(a). This is an exception to the general rule of § 336.

[11] § 332(b) and Reg. §§ 1.332–2(a) and (b).

When a series of distributions occurs in the liquidation of a subsidiary corporation, the parent corporation must own the required amount of stock (at least 80 percent) on the date the plan of liquidation is adopted and at all times until all property has been distributed.[12] If the parent fails the control requirement at any time, the provisions for nonrecognition of gain or loss do not apply to any distribution.[13]

MINORITY SHAREHOLDER INTERESTS

In a § 332 parent-subsidiary liquidation, up to 20 percent of the subsidiary's stock can be owned by minority shareholders. In such liquidations, a distribution of property to a minority shareholder is treated in the same manner as a *nonliquidating* distribution. That is, the subsidiary corporation recognizes gain (but not loss) on the property distributed to the minority shareholder.[14]

EXAMPLE 16

The stock of Tan Corporation is held as follows: 80% by Mustard Corporation and 20% by Arethia. Tan Corporation is liquidated on December 9, 2011, pursuant to a plan adopted on January 7, 2011. At the time of its liquidation, Tan has assets with a basis of $100,000 and fair market value of $500,000. Tan Corporation distributes the property pro rata to Mustard Corporation and to Arethia. Tan must recognize gain of $80,000 [($500,000 fair market value − $100,000 basis) × 20% minority interest]. Since the corporate tax due in this liquidation relates entirely to the minority shareholder distribution, that amount will most likely be deducted from the $100,000 distribution ($500,000 × 20%) going to Arethia. The remaining gain of $320,000 is not recognized because it is attributable to property being distributed to Mustard, the parent corporation. ■

A minority shareholder is subject to the general rule requiring the recognition of gain or loss in a liquidation. Accordingly, the difference between the fair market value of the assets received and the basis of the minority shareholder's stock is the amount of gain or loss recognized. Further, the basis of property received by the minority shareholder is the property's fair market value on the date of distribution.[15]

INDEBTEDNESS OF THE SUBSIDIARY TO THE PARENT

If a subsidiary transfers appreciated property to its parent to satisfy a debt, it must recognize gain on the transaction unless the subsidiary is liquidating and the conditions of § 332 (discussed above) apply. When § 332 applies, the subsidiary does not recognize gain or loss upon the transfer of properties to the parent in satisfaction of indebtedness.[16]

EXAMPLE 17

Eagle Corporation owes $20,000 to its parent, Finch Corporation. It satisfies the obligation by transferring land (basis of $8,000, fair market value of $20,000) to Finch. Normally, Eagle would recognize a gain of $12,000 on the transaction. However, if the transfer is made pursuant to a liquidation under § 332, Eagle does not recognize a gain. ■

This nonrecognition provision does not apply to the parent corporation. The parent corporation recognizes gain or loss on the transfer of property in satisfaction of indebtedness, even if the property is received during liquidation of the subsidiary.

EXAMPLE 18

Pelican Corporation owns bonds (basis of $95,000) of its subsidiary, Crow Corporation, that were acquired at a discount. Upon liquidation of Crow pursuant to § 332, Pelican receives a distribution of $100,000, the face amount of the bonds. The transaction has no tax effect on Crow. However, Pelican Corporation recognizes gain of $5,000 [$100,000 (amount realized) − $95,000 (basis in bonds)]. ■

[12] Establishing the date of the adoption of a plan of complete liquidation could be crucial in determining whether § 332 applies. See, for example, *George L. Riggs, Inc.*, 64 T.C. 474 (1975).

[13] § 332(b)(3) and Reg. § 1.332–2(a).

[14] §§ 336(a) and (d)(3).

[15] § 334(a).

[16] § 337(b)(1).

BASIS OF PROPERTY RECEIVED BY THE PARENT CORPORATION—THE GENERAL RULE

Property received in the complete liquidation of a subsidiary has the same basis it had in the hands of the subsidiary.[17] Unless the parent corporation makes a § 338 election (discussed below), this carryover basis in the assets generally will differ significantly from the parent's basis in the stock of the subsidiary. Since the liquidation is a nontaxable exchange, the parent's gain or loss on the difference in basis is not recognized. Further, the parent's basis in the stock of the subsidiary disappears.

EXAMPLE 19

Lark Corporation has a basis of $200,000 in the stock of Heron Corporation, a subsidiary in which it owns 85% of all classes of stock. Lark purchased the Heron stock 10 years ago. In the current year, Lark liquidates Heron Corporation and acquires assets with a fair market value of $800,000 and a tax basis to Heron of $500,000. Lark Corporation takes a basis of $500,000 in the assets, with a potential gain upon their sale of $300,000. Lark's $200,000 basis in Heron's stock disappears. ■

EXAMPLE 20

Indigo Corporation has a basis of $600,000 in the stock of Kackie Corporation, a wholly owned subsidiary acquired 10 years ago. It liquidates Kackie Corporation and receives assets with a fair market value of $400,000 and a tax basis to Kackie of $300,000. Indigo Corporation takes a basis of $300,000 in the assets it acquires from Kackie. If it sells the assets for $400,000, it has a gain of $100,000 in spite of the fact that its basis in the Kackie stock was $600,000. Indigo's loss on its stock investment in Kackie will never be recognized. ■

In addition to the parent corporation taking the subsidiary's basis in its assets, the carryover rules of § 381 apply. Under that provision, the parent acquires other tax attributes of the subsidiary, including the subsidiary's net operating loss carryover, business credit carryover, capital loss carryover, and E & P.

BASIS OF PROPERTY RECEIVED BY THE PARENT CORPORATION—§ 338 ELECTION

Background

As discussed above, the liquidation of a subsidiary generally is a nontaxable transaction, resulting in the nonrecognition of gain or loss for both the parent and the subsidiary corporations and the carryover of the subsidiary's asset bases (and other tax attributes). This treatment reflects the fact that such a liquidation often is merely a change in corporate structure and not a change in substance. This is particularly the case when the parent has owned the stock of the subsidiary since the subsidiary's inception. In such cases, the carried-over bases are comparable to what the parent would have in the subsidiary's assets if the parent, and not the subsidiary, had originally acquired the assets.

The carryover basis rule for § 332 liquidations can result in some inequities when the subsidiary has been in existence for some time prior to the parent's acquisition of the subsidiary's stock. The parent's basis in the stock of the subsidiary will reflect the fair market value of the subsidiary's assets (and goodwill) at the time of the stock purchase. As a result, the parent's basis in the stock of the subsidiary will usually be greater than the subsidiary's basis in its assets. Under the carryover basis rule, a liquidation of the subsidiary would result in the parent taking a basis in the subsidiary's assets that is less than the parent's basis in the stock of the subsidiary. This is the case even if the parent acquired the subsidiary stock solely to obtain the subsidiary's assets.

If the parent could treat the purchase of the subsidiary stock as a purchase of its assets, the parent could take a basis in the assets equal to the acquisition cost of the stock. In most cases, this would mean a higher asset basis and, as a result, larger

[17] § 334(b)(1) and Reg. § 1.334–1(b). But see § 334(b)(1)(B) (exception for property acquired in some liquidations of foreign subsidiaries).

GLOBAL
Tax Issues

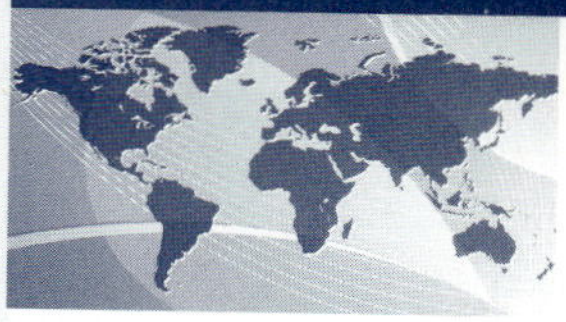

Basis Rules for Liquidations of Foreign Subsidiaries

The basis of property acquired by a parent corporation in the liquidation of a subsidiary corporation is generally equal to the basis the subsidiary had in such property. However, the American Jobs Creation Act of 2004 modified the basis rules regarding property acquired by a U.S. parent in some § 332 liquidations of foreign subsidiaries. In general, if the aggregate basis in a foreign subsidiary's assets exceeds their aggregate fair market value, the U.S. parent will take a fair market value basis in the property acquired. The purpose of this amendment is to deny the importation of built-in losses (excess of basis over fair market value). [See §§ 334(b)(1)(B) and 362(e)(1)(B).]

depreciation deductions and lower gains upon disposition for the parent. To obtain this stock-basis-for-asset-basis result, taxpayers successfully devised stock purchase/subsidiary liquidation transactions that fell outside the purview of § 332.[18] Congress codified this treatment by enacting § 338, which permits the purchase of a controlling interest of stock to be treated as a purchase of the subsidiary's assets.

Requirements for Application

A corporation (the "parent") may *elect* the provisions of § 338 if it acquires stock representing at least 80 percent of the voting power and at least 80 percent of the value of another corporation (the "subsidiary") within a 12-month period ("*qualified stock purchase*"). The stock must be acquired in a taxable transaction (i.e., § 351 and other nonrecognition provisions do not apply). An acquisition of stock by any member of an affiliated group that includes the parent corporation is considered to be an acquisition by the parent. The **§ 338 election** must be made by the fifteenth day of the ninth month beginning after the month in which a qualified stock purchase occurs. If made, the election is irrevocable.

Tax Consequences

Upon making a qualified § 338 election, the subsidiary is treated as having sold its assets on the qualified stock purchase date for a value that is determined with reference to the parent's basis in the subsidiary stock plus any liabilities of the subsidiary ("aggregate deemed sales price").[19] The subsidiary is then treated as a new corporation that purchased those assets for a similarly computed amount ("adjusted grossed-up basis") on the day following the qualified stock purchase date.[20] The deemed sale results in gain (or loss) recognition to the subsidiary, and the deemed purchase results in a stepped-up (or -down) basis for the subsidiary's assets.[21] The subsidiary may, but need not, be liquidated. If the subsidiary is liquidated, the parent will obtain a carryover of the stepped-up (or -down) basis of the subsidiary's assets.

A Comparison of the General Rule and the § 338 Election

Under the general rule of nonrecognition, the liquidation of a subsidiary is tax-free to both the subsidiary (except for any minority interest) and the parent corporation. Under § 338, the subsidiary recognizes gain (or loss) on the deemed disposition of its assets. A liquidation of the subsidiary remains tax-free to the parent. While a carryover basis rule applies in both cases, the subsidiary's assets generally will have a stepped-up basis as a result of the § 338 election, and a liquidation of the subsidiary will result in a carryover of the stepped-up basis to the parent. Further, a liquidation of the subsidiary results in a carryover of its other tax attributes (e.g., E & P) to the parent whether or not a § 338 election is made. However, when the election is made, the subsidiary is treated as a new corporation as of the day following the qualified

[18]See, e.g., *U.S. v. M.O.J. Corp.*, 60–1 USTC ¶9209, 5 AFTR 2d 535, 274 F.2d 713 (CA–5, 1960). See also *Kimbell-Diamond Milling Co.*, 14 T.C. 74 (1950), *aff'd* 51–1 USTC ¶9201, 40 AFTR 328, 187 F.2d 718 (CA–5, 1951), *cert. den.* 72 S.Ct. 50 (USSC, 1951) (IRS argued stock-for-asset basis).

[19]See §§ 338(a)(1) and (b) and Reg. § 1.338–4.

[20]See §§ 338(a)(2) and (b) and Reg. § 1.338–5.

[21]For the rules governing the allocation of the purchase price to the assets, see § 338(b)(5) and Reg. § 1.338–6.

CONCEPT SUMMARY 20.1

Summary of Liquidation Rules

Effect on the Shareholder	Basis of Property Received	Effect on the Corporation
§ 331—The general rule provides for gain or loss treatment on the difference between the FMV of property received and the basis of the stock in the corporation. Gain allocable to installment notes received can be deferred to point of collection.	§ 334(a)—Basis of assets received by the shareholder will be the FMV on the date of distribution (except for installment obligations in which gain is deferred to the point of collection).	§ 336—Gain or loss is recognized for distributions in kind and for sales by the liquidating corporation. Losses are not recognized for distributions to related parties if the distribution is not pro rata or if disqualified property is distributed. Losses may be disallowed on sales and distributions of certain other property even if made to unrelated parties.
§ 332—In liquidation of a subsidiary, no gain or loss is recognized to the parent. Subsidiary must distribute all of its property within the taxable year or within three years from the close of the taxable year in which the first distribution occurs. Minority shareholders taxed under general rule of § 331.	§ 334(b)(1)—Property has the same basis as it had in the hands of the subsidiary. Parent's basis in the stock disappears. Carryover rules of § 381 apply. Minority shareholders get FMV basis under § 334(a).	§ 337—No gain or loss is recognized to the subsidiary on distributions to the parent. Gain (but not loss) is recognized on distributions to minority shareholders.
	§ 338—Subsidiary need not be liquidated. If subsidiary is liquidated, parent's basis is now stepped-up (or -down) basis. Parent's basis in the stock disappears. Carryover rules of § 381 apply, but such amounts are likely to be nominal.	§ 338—Gain or loss is recognized to the subsidiary. Subsidiary is treated as a new corporation, and its basis in assets is stepped up (or down) to reflect parent's basis in subsidiary stock plus subsidiary's liabilities. New basis is allocated among various asset classes.

stock purchase date; as a result, any tax attributes acquired by the parent are likely to be nominal (or zero) in amount.

The holding period of the subsidiary's assets is determined with reference to the substance of the transaction. When the subsidiary is liquidated and there is no § 338 election, the subsidiary's historical holding period in its assets carries over to the parent. This is the typical carryover rule found in other nonrecognition provisions. A § 338 election, however, assumes a sale and repurchase of the subsidiary's assets. As a result of these deemed transactions, the holding period starts anew. If there is a § 338 election and the subsidiary is liquidated, the holding period of the property received by the parent begins on the date of the qualified stock purchase. On the other hand, if there is a § 338 election and the subsidiary is not liquidated, the holding period of the assets begins on the day after the qualified stock acquisition date. The parent-subsidiary liquidation rules are set out in Concept Summary 20.1.

20.5 Corporate Reorganizations

LO.3

Understand the general requirements and tax consequences of corporate reorganizations.

One tenet of U.S. tax policy is to encourage business development. Accordingly, the tax laws allow entities to form without taxation, assuming certain requirements are met. As an extension of this policy, corporate restructurings are also favored with tax-free treatment. Corporations may engage in a variety of acquisitions, combinations, consolidations, and divisions tax-free, as long as the "reorganization" requirements in the Code are met.

Since the dollar value of most reorganizations is substantial, the tax implications are significant, and thus the tax law often dictates the form of the restructuring. The taxable gain for the shareholder is likely to be treated as either a dividend or a capital gain. For individual shareholders, both of these currently are subject to lower tax rates than ordinary income. Corporate shareholders are allowed the dividends received deduction, if the gains are categorized as a dividend. However, since corporations receive no tax rate reduction for capital gains, corporate shareholders and the corporations involved in the restructuring would be taxed at their highest marginal rate on any gains classified as capital.

Careful planning can reduce or totally eliminate taxation for both the corporations and their shareholders. Consequently, when feasible, parties contemplating a corporate reorganization should apply for and obtain from the IRS a letter ruling determining the income tax effect of the transactions. Assuming the parties proceed with the transactions as proposed in the ruling request, a favorable ruling provides, in effect, an insurance policy as to the tax treatment of the restructuring.[22]

Courts originally concluded that even minor changes in a corporation's structure would produce taxable gains for the shareholders involved.[23] Congress, however, determined that businesses should be allowed to make necessary capital adjustments without being subject to taxation.[24] The theory for nonrecognition in certain corporate restructurings or "reorganizations" is similar to that underlying § 351 treatment and like-kind exchanges. As the Regulations state:

> the new property is substantially a continuation of the old investment . . . and, in the case of reorganizations, . . . the new enterprise, the new corporate structure, and the new property are substantially continuations of the old.[25]

IN GENERAL

Although the term **reorganization** is commonly associated with a corporation in financial difficulty, for tax purposes the term refers to any corporate restructuring that may be tax-free under § 368. To qualify as a tax-free reorganization, a corporate restructuring transaction must meet not only the specific requirements of § 368 but also several general requirements. These requirements include the following.

1. There must be a *plan of reorganization.*
2. The reorganization must meet the *continuity of interest* and the *continuity of business enterprise* tests provided in the Regulations.
3. The restructuring must meet the judicial doctrine of having a *sound business purpose.*
4. The court-imposed *step transaction* doctrine should not apply to the reorganization.

While all of these concepts are important, the initial and most important consideration is whether the reorganization qualifies for nonrecognition status under § 368, which is described below.

SUMMARY OF THE DIFFERENT TYPES OF REORGANIZATIONS

Section 368(a) specifies seven corporate restructurings or reorganizations that will qualify as nontaxable exchanges. If the transaction fails to qualify as a reorganization, it will not receive the special tax-favored treatment. Therefore, a corporation considering a business reorganization must determine in advance if the proposed transaction specifically falls within one of these seven types.

---

[22] To expedite the letter ruling process, the IRS attempts to issue rulings within 10 weeks from the date of request. Rev.Proc. 2005–68, 2005–2 C.B. 694.

[23] *U.S. v. Phellis*, 1 USTC ¶54, 3 AFTR 3123, 42 S.Ct. 63 (USSC, 1921).

[24] Reg. § 1.368–1(b). See S.Rept. No. 275, 67th Cong., 1st Sess. (1921), at 1939–1 C.B. 181.

[25] Reg. § 1.1002–1(c).

TAX *in the NEWS* — MERGERS AND ACQUISITIONS COME IN WAVES

Merger and acquisition (M&A) transactions do not occur at a steady rate year after year. Rather, M&A activity comes in waves. Economists have identified five clearly distinct waves since the late 1800s. Generally, after a wave crests, there is a low tide of M&A activity for several years. The first two waves are documented only for the United States, the third includes the United Kingdom, the fourth adds the rest of Europe, and the last is considered truly international. A summary of these eras of M&A activity follows.

- *First wave (Great Merger Wave).* The economic expansion created by dramatic technical innovations, the beginning of industrial stock trading, and the passage of the Sherman Antitrust Act started this wave. This M&A activity predominantly involved firms in similar industries consolidating to form monopolies and decrease competition. It ended when the equity market crashed in 1903.
- *Second wave.* This wave, beginning just before World War I, was fueled by the small to mid-size firms left after the first wave. These mergers produced firms large enough to compete with the giant firms; thus, oligopolies dominated by a few firms were created. The stock market crash of 1929 put the brakes on this wave.
- *Third wave.* The Great Depression and World War II held off the next wave until the 1950s. Once this wave began, however, it lasted for nearly two decades, making it the longest period of sustained M&A activity. These acquisitions focused on business diversification, leading to large conglomerates. Because these conglomerates never achieved the expected benefits from diversification, conglomerate stocks crashed in 1969–1970. Then, the 1973 oil crisis pushed the world economy into a recession and ended this wave.
- *Fourth wave.* This wave started with the deregulation of financial services and the creation of financial instruments such as junk bonds. It was characterized by corporate raiders, divestitures, and leveraged and management buyouts. As with other waves, its end was announced by a stock market crash—the crash of 1987.
- *Fifth wave.* The last wave was energized by increasing economic globalization, technological innovation, deregulation, and privatization. These M&As were mega-mergers with a substantial proportion of them being cross-border transactions. The fifth wave halted when the dot-coms and the financial industry collapsed, leading to numerous corporate scandals.

Sources: Adapted from Marina Martynova and Luc Renneboog, "A Century of Corporate Takeovers: What Have We Learned and Where Do We Stand?" *Journal of Banking and Finance* (2008), and "Historical Merger and Acquisition Activity," *Mergerstat Review* (2006).

The Code states, in § 368(a)(1), that the term reorganization applies to any of the following:

A. A statutory merger or consolidation.
B. The acquisition by a corporation of another using solely stock of each corporation (voting stock-for-stock exchange).
C. The acquisition by a corporation of substantially all of the property of another corporation in exchange for voting stock (voting stock-for-asset exchange).
D. The transfer of all or part of a corporation's assets to another corporation when the original corporation's shareholders are in control of the new corporation immediately after the transfer (divisive exchange, also known as a spin-off, split-off, or split-up).
E. A recapitalization.
F. A mere change in identity, form, or place of organization.
G. A transfer by a corporation of all or a part of its assets to another corporation in a bankruptcy or receivership proceeding.

These seven types of tax-free reorganizations typically are designated by their identifying letters: "Type A," "Type B," "Type C," and so on. For the most part, excepting the recapitalization (E), the change in form (F), and the insolvent corporation

CONCEPT SUMMARY 20.2

Gain and Basis Rules for Nontaxable Exchanges

(1) Realized Gain/Loss	(2) Recognized Gain (Not Loss)	(3) Postponed Gain/Loss	(4) Basis of New Asset
Amount realized	Lesser of boot received or gain realized	Realized gain/loss (column 1)	FMV of asset (stock) received
− Adjusted basis of asset(s) surrendered		− Recognized gain (column 2)	− Postponed gain (column 3) or + Postponed loss (column 3)
Realized gain/loss	Recognized gain	Postponed gain/loss	Adjusted basis in new asset (stock)

(G) provisions, a tax-free reorganization is (1) a statutory merger or consolidation, (2) an exchange of stock for voting stock, (3) an exchange of assets for voting stock, or (4) a divisive reorganization (a so-called spin-off, split-off, or split-up).

SUMMARY OF THE TAX CONSEQUENCES IN A TAX-FREE REORGANIZATION

The tax treatment for the parties involved in a tax-free reorganization almost exactly parallels the treatment under the like-kind exchange provisions of § 1031. In the simplest like-kind exchange, neither gain nor loss is recognized on the exchange of "like-kind" property. When "boot" (defined as non-like-kind property) is received, gain may be recognized. The four-column template of Concept Summary 20.2 can be used to compute the amount of gain recognized and the adjusted basis in the new asset received in the like-kind exchange.

Unfortunately, the like-kind exchange provisions do not apply to the exchange of stock or securities.[26] Therefore, the general rule is that when an investor exchanges stock in one corporation for stock in another, the exchange is a taxable transaction. If the transaction qualifies as a reorganization under § 368, however, the exchange receives tax-deferred treatment. Thus, a § 368 reorganization, in substance, is similar to a nontaxable exchange of like-kind property, and the four-column template of Concept Summary 20.2 is useful for reorganizations as well.

EXAMPLE 21

John holds 1,000 shares of Lotus stock that he purchased for $10,000 several years ago. In a merger of Lotus into Blossom, Inc., John exchanges his 1,000 Lotus shares for 1,000 Blossom shares. Both investments are valued at $18 per share. Thus, John's stock is valued at $18,000 ($18 per share × 1,000 shares). Assuming that this exchange qualifies for tax-free treatment under § 368, John's recognized gain and basis in his Blossom stock are computed as follows.

Realized Gain	Recognized Gain	Postponed Gain	Basis in Blossom Stock
$18,000	$-0-	$8,000	$18,000
−10,000			− 8,000
$ 8,000			$10,000

The exchange of John's stock has no tax consequences for Lotus or Blossom. ■

[26]§ 1031(a)(2)(B).

Gain or Loss

Corporations meeting the requirements of § 368 do not recognize gain or loss on a restructuring. There are exceptions to the nonrecognition rule, however. If the acquiring corporation transfers property to the target corporation along with its stock and securities, gain, but not loss, may be recognized. When the target receives other property (called *boot*) in the restructuring and fails to distribute it, or distributes its own appreciated property to its shareholders, gain, but not loss, is recognized. *Other property* for restructurings is any asset other than stock or securities and, thus, is treated as boot.[27]

EXAMPLE 22

In a qualifying reorganization, Acquiring Corporation exchanges $800,000 of stock and land with a fair market value of $200,000 (basis of $150,000) for all of Target Corporation's assets, which have a fair market value of $1 million and a basis of $600,000. Due to the *other property* (land) it used in the transfer, Acquiring recognizes a gain of $50,000 ($200,000 – $150,000) on the reorganization. If Target distributes the land to its shareholders, it does not recognize gain. If Target retains the land, however, it recognizes gain to the extent of the *other property* received, $200,000. ■

Generally, the shareholders of corporations involved in a tax-free reorganization do not recognize gain or loss when exchanging their stock unless they receive cash or other property in addition to stock. The cash or other property is considered boot, and the gain recognized by the shareholder is the lesser of the boot received or the realized gain. This is analogous to the treatment of boot in a like-kind exchange. The only instance when shareholders may recognize losses in reorganizations is when they receive solely boot and no stock.

EXAMPLE 23

Kalla, the sole shareholder of Target Corporation in Example 22, has a basis of $700,000 in her stock. She exchanges her Target stock for the $800,000 of Acquiring stock plus the land ($200,000) transferred by Acquiring to Target. Kalla has a recognized gain of $200,000 due to receiving the land (boot). The computations are as follows.

Realized Gain	Recognized Gain	Postponed Gain	Basis in Acquiring Stock
$1,000,000*	$200,000	$100,000	$800,000
– 700,000			–100,000
$ 300,000			$700,000

*$800,000 stock + $200,000 land. ■

Once the recognized gain is computed, its character must be determined. The following are the possibilities for gain characterization.

- Dividend to the extent of the shareholder's proportionate share of a positive balance in the corporation's earnings and profits (E & P). The remaining gain is generally capital gain.
  - *For individual shareholders, the distinction between dividends and long-term capital gain is important when the taxpayer has capital losses to offset, or when the capital gain would be classified as short term and therefore not subject to the special tax rates.*
- If the requirements of § 302(b) can be met, the transaction will qualify for stock redemption treatment (see Chapter 19).

[27]§§ 361(a) and (b). In a Type A or Type C reorganization, gain will not be recognized due to the retention of other property because the target is liquidated under the reorganization rules (i.e., no property is retained by the target).

- *Gains from qualifying stock redemptions are treated as capital gains.*
- *In computing the shareholder's ownership reduction, shares actually received in the acquiring corporation are compared with the number of shares the shareholder would have received if solely stock of the acquiring corporation had been distributed in the reorganization.*[28]

ETHICS & Equity

A White Knight Turns Black

Retail Corporation is a small regional chain of upscale clothing stores. As business casual has become the accepted dress for professionals, Retail has become very profitable. Consequently, it has substantial liquid assets and few liabilities. Retail is so encouraged by its profitability that it is considering becoming a national chain.

Retail's success has not gone unnoticed in the marketplace. Mega Corporation, a privately owned conglomerate, makes an unsolicited tender offer for the Retail stock. In the past, Mega has made such offers for other small corporations with substantial liquid assets. Once it owns enough stock to take control of the board of directors, Mega forces the liquidation of the company to obtain its liquid assets. Therefore, Retail is very concerned about Mega's tender offer. To avoid being taken over by Mega, Retail negotiates with Cotton Corporation, one of its suppliers, for a merger of the two companies. Cotton is fully aware of the dangers faced by Retail as it was the target of an unsuccessful takeover by Mega in the past. It was rescued from the takeover by a similar "white knight" merger with one of its competitors.

Through an informer at Cotton, Mega discovers Retail's plan to foil its hostile takeover. To sabotage the Retail-Cotton merger, Mega offers Cotton an exclusive contract for producing its line of children's school clothes for Mega's national chain of discount department stores. The contract requires that Cotton not be affiliated with any other corporation in the retail clothing business. Cotton's directors believe this contract could boost profits by 20 percent. Therefore, the board votes to enter into the contract with Mega and abandon its merger negotiations with Retail. Retail ultimately is taken over by Mega and liquidated. All of its 1,000 employees lose their jobs. What ethical issues, if any, did Cotton's directors face in their dealings with Mega and Retail?

EXAMPLE 24

Sam acquired a 30% interest in Target 15 years ago for $80,000. He exchanges his Target stock for $25,000 of cash and stock in Acquiring worth $125,000. At the time of the reorganization, Target's E & P is $50,000. Sam has a realized gain of $70,000 [$150,000 (value of Acquiring stock plus cash) − $80,000 (basis of Target stock)] and a $25,000 recognized gain (the cash received). The first $15,000 ($50,000 Target E & P × 30%) is taxable as a dividend, and the remaining $10,000 is treated as a capital gain. Both are taxed at favorable tax rates.

Suppose instead that Sam receives 10% of the Acquiring stock with a fair market value of $100,000 and $50,000 of cash. If Sam had received solely stock, he would have received 15% of the Acquiring stock. Since Sam owns less than 80% of the stock he would have owned if solely stock had been distributed (10% ÷ 15% is 67%) and less than 50% of Acquiring, he qualifies for sale or exchange treatment under § 302(b)(2). Therefore, all of Sam's $50,000 recognized gain is treated as a long-term capital gain. ■

Debt security holders receive treatment similar to shareholders. They recognize gain only when the principal (face) amount of the securities received is greater than the principal (face) amount of the securities surrendered. If securities are received and none are relinquished, the gain will be recognized.

The term *security* is not defined in the Code or the Regulations. Generally, however, debt instruments with terms longer than 10 years (e.g., bonds) are treated as securities, and those with terms of 5 years or less (e.g., notes) are not. An exception to

[28] *Comm. v. Clark*, 89–1 USTC ¶9230, 63 AFTR 2d 89–860, 109 S.Ct. 1455 (USSC, 1989), and Rev.Rul. 93–61, 1993–2 C.B. 118.

CONCEPT SUMMARY 20.3

Basis Rules for a Tax-Free Reorganization

Basis to Acquiring Corporation of Property Received	
Target's basis in property transferred	$xx,xxx
Plus: Gain recognized by target on the transaction	x,xxx
Equals: Basis of property to acquiring corporation	$xx,xxx
Basis to Target Shareholders of Stock and Securities Received	
Basis of stock and securities transferred	$xx,xxx
Plus: Gain and dividend income recognized	x,xxx
Less: Money and fair market value of other property received	(x,xxx)
Equals: Basis of stock and securities received	$xx,xxx

this general rule occurs when the debt instrument issued by the acquiring corporation is exchanged for target securities having the same term and/or maturity date.[29]

EXAMPLE 25

Alejandra holds a security issued by Hibiscus Corporation. The principal value of the security is $10,000, and its maturity date is December 31, 2014. In connection with the merger of Hibiscus and Tea Corporation, Alejandra exchanges her Hibiscus security for a $10,000 Tea note that matures on December 31, 2014. Even though these notes do not have a term remaining of more than five years, they qualify for tax-free reorganization treatment because they have the same term. ■

EXAMPLE 26

Assume the same facts as in Example 25, except that in exchange for her $10,000 security, Alejandra receives a note from Tea with a $15,000 principal value. Alejandra recognizes a $5,000 capital gain on the exchange. ■

Basis

The assets transferred from the target corporation to the acquiring corporation retain their basis. However, the acquiring corporation's carryover basis is increased by any gain recognized by the target corporation on the reorganization. Concept Summary 20.3 shows this computation.

EXAMPLE 27

Target exchanges its assets with a fair market value of $5 million and a basis of $3 million for $4.5 million of Acquiring stock and $500,000 of land. Assume Target does not distribute the land to its shareholders. Target recognizes a $500,000 gain on the reorganization (due to the other property not being distributed). Acquiring's basis in the assets received from Target is $3.5 million [$3,000,000 (Target's basis) + $500,000 (Target's gain recognized)]. ■

In general, the tax basis of the stock and securities received by a shareholder pursuant to a tax-free reorganization is the same as the basis of those surrendered. However, this basis is decreased by the fair market value of boot received and increased by the gain and/or dividend income recognized on the transaction. Concept Summary 20.3 provides a summary of these calculations. Another way to compute the basis in

[29]Rev.Rul. 2004–78, 2004–2 C.B. 108.

CONCEPT SUMMARY 20.4

Tax Consequences of Tax-Free Reorganizations

Treatment is similar to like-kind exchanges.

- No gain or loss is recognized by the acquiring or target corporation unless other property (i.e., boot) is transferred or received by any parties to the reorganization.
- Basis in the assets received by the acquiring corporation is generally carried over from the target corporation.
- The stock received by the target corporation's shareholders takes a substituted basis, which is derived from their basis in the target stock.
- Gain, but not loss, may be recognized when boot is transferred by the acquiring corporation.
- Gain, but not loss, may be recognized when the target corporation receives boot and does not distribute the boot to its shareholders.
- Gain, but not loss, may be recognized when target shareholders receive anything other than stock (i.e., boot) in exchange for their target stock.

the stock and securities received, using the Concept Summary 20.2 template, is to subtract the gain (or add the loss) postponed from the fair market value of the stock and securities received. This basis computation ensures that the postponed gain or loss will be recognized when the new stock or securities are disposed of in a taxable transaction.

EXAMPLE 28

Quinn exchanges all of his stock in Target Corporation for stock in Acquiring plus $3,000 of cash. The exchange is pursuant to a tax-free reorganization. Quinn paid $10,000 for the stock in Target two years ago. The Acquiring stock received by Quinn has a fair market value of $12,000. Quinn has a realized gain of $5,000, which is recognized to the extent of the boot received, $3,000. Quinn's basis in the Acquiring stock is $10,000. This can be computed as follows.

Realized Gain	Recognized Gain	Postponed Gain	Basis in Acquiring Stock
$15,000*	$3,000	$2,000	$12,000
−10,000			−2,000
$ 5,000			$10,000

*$12,000 stock + $3,000 cash. ■

EXAMPLE 29

Assume the same facts as in Example 28 except that Quinn's basis in the Target stock was $16,000. Quinn realizes a loss of $1,000 on the exchange, none of which is recognized. His basis in the Acquiring stock is $13,000, computed as follows.

Realized Gain	Recognized Loss	Postponed Loss	Basis in Acquiring Stock
$15,000*	$–0–	($1,000)	$12,000
−16,000			+ 1,000
($ 1,000)			$13,000

*$12,000 stock + $3,000 cash. ■

Concept Summary 20.4 reviews the tax consequences of tax-free reorganizations.

TAX PLANNING:

20.6 Effect of a Liquidating Distribution on the Corporation

LO.4

Identify tax planning opportunities available to minimize the tax impact in complete liquidations and corporate reorganizations.

With the exception of parent-subsidiary liquidations, distributions in liquidation are taxed at both the corporate level and the shareholder level. When a corporation liquidates, it generally can claim losses on assets that have declined in value. These assets should not be distributed in the form of a property dividend or stock redemption because losses are not recognized on nonliquidating distributions.

20.7 Effect of a Liquidating Distribution on the Shareholder

Shareholders faced with large prospective gains in a liquidation may consider shifting part or all of that gain to other taxpayers. One approach is to donate stock to charity. A charitable contribution of the stock produces a deduction equal to the stock's fair market value (see Chapter 17). Alternatively, the stock may be given to family members. If the family member is in the 10 or 15 percent marginal tax bracket, some or all of the gain on liquidation could be taxed at the 0 percent preferential rate on long-term capital gains. Whether these procedures will be successful in shifting the liquidation-related gain from the taxpayer depends on the timing of the transfer. If the donee of the stock is not in a position to prevent the liquidation of the corporation, the donor may be deemed to have made an anticipatory assignment of income. In such a case, the gain is still taxed to the donor. In addition, possible gift tax issues on the stock transfer must be considered (see Chapter 27). Advance planning of stock transfers therefore is crucial in arriving at the desired tax result.

The installment sale provisions provide some relief from the general rule that a shareholder recognizes all gain upon receiving a liquidating distribution. If the assets of the liquidating corporation are not to be distributed in kind, a sale of the assets in exchange for installment notes should be considered. Shareholders receiving the notes in a liquidation can then report their gain on the installment method as the notes are collected. Gain deferred under the installment method is subject to the tax rates applicable in each year of collection. Under current tax law, the preferential tax rate for long-term capital gains is scheduled to increase to 20 percent (from 15 percent) after 2012. Thus, the deferral of gain on installment obligations received in a liquidation must be weighed against the anticipated 5 percentage point increase in the applicable tax rate for gains deferred beyond 2012.

20.8 Parent-Subsidiary Liquidations

The nonrecognition provision applicable to the liquidation of a subsidiary, § 332, is not elective. Nevertheless, some flexibility may be available:

- Whether § 332 applies depends on the 80 percent stock ownership test. A parent corporation may be able to avoid § 332 by reducing its stock ownership in the subsidiary below this percentage to allow for recognition of a loss. On the other hand, the opposite approach may be desirable to avoid gain recognition. A corporate shareholder possessing less than the required 80 percent ownership may want to acquire additional stock to qualify for § 332 treatment.
- Once § 332 becomes effective, less latitude is allowed in determining the parent's basis in the subsidiary's assets. Generally, the subsidiary's existing basis in its assets carries over to the parent. If a timely § 338 election is made, the subsidiary's basis in its assets is stepped up to reflect, in part, the

parent's basis in the subsidiary stock. If the subsidiary also is liquidated, the parent obtains assets with the stepped-up basis.

- An election to have the § 338 rules apply should be carefully weighed as the election can be detrimental. The income tax liability on the subsidiary's recognized gain that results from the deemed sale of its assets is the cost under § 338 for obtaining the stepped-up basis. As a result, a § 338 election may be a viable option only when the subsidiary possesses loss and/or credit carryovers that can be used to offset the associated tax.

20.9 Asset Purchase versus Stock Purchase

The acquisition of a corporation's assets generally takes one of two forms. In one form, the acquiring corporation purchases the stock of the target corporation, and then the target (subsidiary) is liquidated. In the other form, the acquiring corporation purchases the assets of the target corporation, and then the target distributes the proceeds to its shareholders in liquidation. Nontax considerations may affect the form of acquisition, with each form having both favorable and unfavorable aspects.

An asset purchase requires that title be transferred and that creditors be notified. Further, an asset purchase may not be feasible if valuable nontransferable trademarks, contracts, or licenses are involved. Alternatively, an asset purchase may be preferable to a stock purchase if the target's shareholders refuse to sell their stock. Additionally, an asset purchase avoids the transfer of liabilities (including unknown liabilities) generally inherent in stock acquisitions. An asset purchase also has the advantage of allowing the purchaser to avoid the acquisition of unwanted assets, whereas a stock purchase would involve all of a target's assets.

REFOCUS ON THE BIG PICTURE

THE TRANSITION TO RETIREMENT IS SUBJECT TO DOUBLE TAXATION

The Smithsons are wise to evaluate the affordability of their retirement plan *before* they sell or liquidate their business. Nonetheless, after payment of income tax at both the corporate and shareholder levels, they will net only $2,707,500 from the sale of their $4 million business.

Specifically, in the event the corporation is able to sell the business assets for $4 million, the realized gain of $2.5 million will give rise to Federal income tax of $850,000 ($2,500,000 × 34%). Following the payment of the corporate income tax, the net proceeds to the Smithsons will be $3,150,000. After offsetting the amount realized from the liquidation by their stock basis of $200,000, their capital gain of $2,950,000 will be subject to capital gains tax of $442,500 ($2,950,000 × 15%). Therefore, the net after-tax cash available for investment will be $2,707,500 ($3,150,000 proceeds − capital gains tax of $442,500). Now, the question for the Smithsons is whether this amount will likely be sufficient to fund the type of retirement they desire.

What If?

Instead of the complete liquidation transaction just described, the Smithsons should consider alternatives that could produce a better tax result such as the following.

- If the Smithsons are able to find a buyer who is interested in maintaining the business in the current corporate form, they should try to sell their *stock* in the business rather than selling the business assets in liquidation. If the buyer is willing to pay $4 million for the corporation's stock, the Smithsons would recognize a capital gain of $3.8 million and have

CONTINUED

$3,430,000 after tax ($4 million proceeds – capital gains tax of $570,000). This approach would increase the net after-tax amount available to fund their retirement portfolio by $722,500 due to the fact that the corporate-level tax is avoided.

- Another approach would be to attempt to market the corporation as a potential takeover target in a tax-free reorganization. With this approach, the Smithsons would receive stock in the acquiring corporation without having to recognize *any* gain from the transaction. This strategy could enable the Smithsons to live off the subsequent dividend distributions made by the acquiring corporation. Further, if they needed additional cash flow to meet living expenses, they could sell shares of stock in the acquiring corporation as needed, and any resulting gain would be subject to the capital gains rates at that time. An obvious advantage of this approach is that gain from the disposition of their stock would be deferred until the stock in the acquiring corporation is sold in a taxable transaction. However, a disadvantage the Smithsons would need to evaluate is that they would not be able to build a diversified portfolio, given that their investment holdings would largely, if not completely, consist of the stock of the acquiring corporation.

KEY TERMS

Corporate liquidation, 20–2

Reorganization, 20–15

Section 338 election, 20–13

DISCUSSION QUESTIONS

1. **LO.1** Discuss when a corporate liquidation occurs for tax purposes.

2. **LO.1** Briefly discuss whether a corporation recognizes gains or losses on the distribution of property in liquidation.

3. **LO.1, 4** One difference between the tax treatment of a liquidation and a qualifying stock redemption is the applicability of § 267. Explain this statement from the perspective of both the shareholder and the corporation.

4. **LO.1** Can the related-party loss limitation in a complete liquidation apply to a realized loss attributable to a decline in a property's fair market value that occurred after the property was acquired by the liquidating corporation?

5. **LO.1** When properties transferred by a shareholder in a § 351 transaction have a net built-in loss (aggregate fair market value less than aggregate basis), the basis step-down rule must be applied. Discuss the relevance of the built-in loss limitation given the enactment of the basis step-down rule.

6. **LO.1** Explain the tax consequences to a shareholder of a corporation in the process of liquidation under the general rule of § 331. May a shareholder use the installment method to report gain on a complete liquidation?

7. **LO.2** Discuss the tax consequences to the parent corporation in a § 332 liquidation of a subsidiary.

8. **LO.2** Does § 332 apply to the liquidation of an insolvent subsidiary? If not, then how does the parent corporation treat such a liquidation?

9. **LO.2** A subsidiary corporation is liquidated under § 332. Pursuant to its liquidation, the subsidiary transferred property to a minority shareholder. With respect to this distribution, what are the tax consequences to the subsidiary corporation and to the minority shareholder?

10. **LO.2** Condor Corporation pays $950,000 for 100% of the stock in Dove Corporation. Dove has a basis of $800,000 in its assets and E & P of $220,000. If Condor liquidates Dove and makes no special election, what are the tax consequences to Condor and to Dove?

11. **LO.2** What happens to a subsidiary's tax attributes (e.g., net operating loss, E & P, capital loss carryover) upon a § 332 liquidation?

12. **LO.2** What are the requirements for the application of § 338?

13. **LO.2** In general, what are the tax consequences of a § 338 election?

14. **LO.3** What type of treatment do corporate shareholders and individual shareholders desire when there is a taxable gain from a corporate restructuring? How is the character of the shareholders' gain determined?

15. **LO.3** Identify the nontaxable types of corporate reorganizations.

16. **LO.3** Summarize the tax consequences of a § 368 reorganization.

17. **LO.3** Five years ago, Mervin purchased 1,000 shares of Fern Corporation, which represents 20% of Fern's outstanding stock. As part of a restructuring agreement between Fern and Ivy Corporation, Mervin receives 10% of Ivy's stock (valued at $100,000) and a $30,000 bond in exchange for all of his Fern stock. Fern is liquidated after the restructuring. What are the tax issues regarding this transaction?

ISSUE ID

PROBLEMS

18. **LO.1, 4** Dove Corporation (E & P of $650,000) has 1,000 shares of stock outstanding. The shares are owned as follows: Julia, 600 shares; Maxine (Julia's daughter), 300 shares; and Janine (Julia's granddaughter), 100 shares. Dove Corporation owns land (basis of $470,000, fair market value of $330,000) that it purchased as an investment seven years ago. Dove distributes the land to Julia in exchange for all her shares in the corporation. Julia had a basis of $350,000 in the shares. What are the tax consequences for both Dove Corporation and Julia if the distribution is:
    a. A qualifying stock redemption?
    b. A liquidating distribution?

19. **LO.1** Pursuant to a complete liquidation, Oriole Corporation distributes to its shareholders land held for three years as an investment (adjusted basis of $310,000, fair market value of $420,000). The land is subject to a liability of $200,000.
    a. What are the tax consequences to Oriole Corporation on the distribution of the land?
    b. If the land is, instead, subject to a liability of $500,000, what are the tax consequences to Oriole on the distribution?

20. **LO.1** Bronze Corporation's stock is held equally by three brothers, Mitchell, Alex, and Ron. Four years ago, the brothers transferred to Bronze Corporation land in which they had owned equal interests. The transfer of the land (basis of $260,000, fair market value of $300,000) qualified under § 351. Pursuant to a liquidation in the current year, Bronze distributed the land pro rata to the three brothers. The land had a fair market value of $215,000 on the date of the distribution. What amount of loss may Bronze Corporation recognize on the distribution of the land?

21. **LO.1** On April 21, 2010, Crow Corporation acquired land and equipment in a § 351 transaction. At that time, the land had a basis of $300,000 and a fair market value of $225,000, and the equipment had a basis of $20,000 and a fair market value of $100,000. The land and equipment were transferred to Crow Corporation for use as security for a loan the corporation was in the process of obtaining from a local bank. The bank required the additional capital investment as a condition for making the loan. Crow Corporation adopted a plan of liquidation on October 3, 2011. On December 2, 2011, Crow Corporation distributes the land to Ali, a 40% shareholder. On the date of the distribution, the land had a fair market value of only $150,000. What amount of loss may Crow Corporation recognize on the distribution of the land?

22. **LO.1** On January 5, 2010, Grackle Corporation acquired equipment as a contribution to capital. At that time, the equipment had an adjusted basis of $360,000 and a fair market

value of $290,000. This was the only property transferred to Grackle at that time. On July 22, 2011, Grackle Corporation adopted a plan of liquidation. On November 10, 2011, Grackle sold the equipment to Chris, an unrelated party, for its current fair market value of $200,000. Grackle Corporation never used the equipment for any business purpose during the time it owned the equipment. What amount of loss may Grackle Corporation recognize on the sale of the equipment?

DECISION MAKING

23. **LO.1, 4** Pink Corporation acquired land and securities in a § 351 tax-free exchange in 2010. On the date of the transfer, the land had a basis of $800,000 and a fair market value of $980,000, and the securities had a basis of $70,000 and a fair market value of $200,000. Pink Corporation has two shareholders, Maria and Paul, who are unrelated. Maria owns 70% of the stock in the corporation, and Paul owns 30%. Pink adopts a plan of liquidation in 2011. On this date, the value of the land has decreased to $640,000. What is the effect of each of the following on Pink Corporation? Which option should be selected?
    a. Distribute all the land to Maria.
    b. Distribute all the land to Paul.
    c. Distribute 70% of the land to Maria and 30% to Paul.
    d. Distribute 50% of the land to Maria and 50% to Paul.
    e. Sell the land and distribute the proceeds of $640,000 proportionately to Maria and to Paul.

DECISION MAKING

24. **LO.1, 4** Assume in Problem 23 that the land had a fair market value of $700,000 on the date of its transfer to the corporation. On the date of the liquidation, the land's fair market value has decreased to $640,000. How would your answer to Problem 23 change if:
    a. All the land is distributed to Maria?
    b. All the land is distributed to Paul?
    c. The land is distributed 70% to Maria and 30% to Paul?
    d. The land is distributed 50% to Maria and 50% to Paul?
    e. The land is sold and the proceeds of $640,000 are distributed proportionately to Maria and to Paul?

25. **LO.1** Pursuant to a complete liquidation in the current year, Oriole Corporation distributes to Samantha land held for four years as an investment (basis of $225,000, fair market value of $480,000). The land is subject to a liability of $150,000. Samantha, who owned 20% of the Oriole shares outstanding, had a basis of $90,000 in the stock. What are the tax consequences of the liquidating distribution to Oriole Corporation and to Samantha?

26. **LO.1** After a plan of complete liquidation has been adopted, Purple Corporation sells its only asset, land, to Rex (an unrelated party) for $800,000. Under the terms of the sale, Purple receives cash of $200,000 and Rex's note in the amount of $600,000. The note is payable over five years ($120,000 per year) and carries an appropriate rate of interest. Immediately after the sale, Purple distributes the cash and note to Helen, the sole shareholder of Purple Corporation. Helen has a basis of $80,000 in the Purple stock. What are the tax results to Helen if she wishes to defer as much gain as possible on the transaction? Assume the installment note possesses a value equal to its face amount.

27. **LO.2** The stock of Magenta Corporation is owned by Fuchsia Corporation (90%) and Marta (10%). Magenta is liquidated on September 2, 2011, pursuant to a plan of liquidation adopted earlier in the same year. In the liquidation, Magenta distributes various assets worth $1,620,000 (basis of $1,950,000) to Fuchsia (basis of $1.2 million in Magenta stock) and a parcel of land worth $180,000 (basis of $165,000) to Marta (basis of $35,000 in Magenta stock). Assuming the § 338 election is not made, what are the tax consequences of the liquidation to Magenta, Fuchsia, and Marta?

28. **LO.2** The stock in Ivory Corporation is owned by Gold Corporation (80%) and Imelda (20%). Gold Corporation purchased its shares in Ivory nine years ago at a cost of $650,000, and Imelda purchased her shares in Ivory four years ago at a cost of $175,000. Ivory Corporation has the following assets that are distributed in complete liquidation:

	Adjusted Basis	Fair Market Value
Cash	$600,000	$600,000
Inventory	80,000	200,000
Equipment	350,000	200,000

a. Assume that Ivory Corporation distributes the cash and inventory to Gold Corporation and the equipment to Imelda. What are the tax consequences of the distributions to Ivory Corporation, to Gold Corporation, and to Imelda?

b. Assume that Ivory Corporation distributes the cash and equipment to Gold Corporation and the inventory to Imelda. What are the tax consequences of the distributions to Ivory Corporation, to Gold Corporation, and to Imelda?

29. **LO.2** Orange Corporation purchased bonds (basis of $185,000) of its wholly owned subsidiary, Green Corporation, at a discount. Upon liquidation of Green pursuant to § 332, Orange receives payment in the form of land worth $200,000, the face amount of the bonds. Green had a basis of $220,000 in the land. What are the tax consequences of this land transfer to Green Corporation and to Orange Corporation?

30. **LO.2** At the time of its liquidation under § 332, Cardinal Corporation (E & P of $560,000) had the following assets and liabilities: cash ($175,000); marketable securities (fair market value of $230,000, basis of $250,000); unimproved land (fair market value of $600,000, basis of $300,000); unsecured note payable ($50,000); and mortgage on the unimproved land ($270,000). Cardinal also had a net operating loss carryover of $45,000. Wren Corporation acquired all the stock of Cardinal seven years ago for $160,000.

    a. How much gain (or loss) will Cardinal Corporation recognize upon the liquidating distribution of its assets and liabilities to Wren Corporation?
    b. How much gain (or loss) will Wren Corporation recognize in the liquidation of Cardinal?
    c. What basis will Wren have in the marketable securities and unimproved land it receives in the liquidation?
    d. What happens to Cardinal's E & P and net operating loss carryover?

31. **LO.2** On August 9, 2011, Egret Corporation acquired 100% of the outstanding stock of Aqua Corporation for $1 million and made a qualified § 338 election. On that date, Aqua Corporation had assets with a basis of $700,000 and E & P of $400,000. Assume that the aggregate deemed sale price and the adjusted grossed-up basis each equal $1.2 million and that Aqua Corporation is immediately liquidated. In general, what are the tax consequences to Egret and to Aqua of the § 338 election and the liquidation of Aqua?

32. **LO.3** Cole acquired 55% of Dane Corporation for $400,000 eight years ago. In the current year, Dane merges with Great Corporation, and Cole receives 7.5% of Great's stock plus $300,000 in land. The Great stock received by Cole is valued at $900,000. At the time of the transaction, Dane's E & P is $450,000, and Great's E & P is $1.8 million. As an individual shareholder, how should Cole treat this transaction for tax purposes?

33. **LO.3** Quail Corporation was created in 2000 through contributions from Kasha ($800,000) and Frank ($200,000). In a transaction qualifying as a reorganization, Quail exchanges all of its assets currently valued at $2 million (basis of $1.5 million) for 12,000 shares of Covey Corporation stock valued at $1.9 million plus $100,000 in Covey bonds. Quail distributes the Covey stock and bonds proportionately to Frank and Kasha in exchange for their stock in Quail. Quail's current and accumulated E & P before the reorganization amounts to $70,000.

    a. How do Kasha and Frank treat this transaction for tax purposes?
    b. How do Quail and Covey treat this transaction for tax purposes? What is Covey's basis in the assets it receives from Quail?

34. **LO.3** Rosa owns 30% of Pine Corporation's stock (basis of $50,000), and the other 70% was recently purchased by Arvid (basis of $620,000). Pine enters into a reorganization with Lodgepole Corporation, in which Rosa will receive a 5% interest (value of $300,000) in Lodgepole and Arvid will receive a 10% interest (value of $600,000) plus assets worth $100,000. Lodgepole's basis in these assets is $60,000. At the time of the reorganization, Pine's value is $1 million, and Lodgepole's value is $6 million.

    a. What are Rosa's and Arvid's bases in their new Lodgepole stock?
    b. What is the amount of gain (loss) recognized by Rosa, Arvid, Pine, and Lodgepole on the reorganization?

35. **LO.3** Lemon Corporation enters into a merger with Lime Corporation. Lemon has assets valued at $900,000 (basis of $980,000) and liabilities of $600,000. Lime transfers its stock for 90% of Lemon's assets and liabilities. Lemon distributes the Lime stock and its remaining asset (value of $90,000, adjusted basis of $80,000) subject to a liability

($60,000) to its shareholder, Lea, in exchange for her Lemon stock. Lea's basis in her Lemon stock is $350,000. Lemon liquidates after collecting all of its stock from Lea.

a. What is the value of stock transferred from Lime to Lemon?
b. What is the amount of gain (loss) realized and recognized by Lea from the merger? What is Lea's basis in her Lime stock?
c. What is the amount of gain (loss) realized and recognized by Lemon and Lime from the merger? What is Lime's basis in Lemon's assets?

RESEARCH PROBLEMS

THOMSON REUTERS
Checkpoint® Student Edition

Note: Solutions to Research Problems can be prepared by using the **Checkpoint® Student Edition** online research product, which is available to accompany this text. It is also possible to prepare solutions to the Research Problems by using tax research materials found in a standard tax library.

Research Problem 1. New Gate Corporation desires to acquire Old Post in a nontaxable transaction. Prior to entering into the transaction with New Gate, Old Post issues $800,000 worth of 15-year bonds paying 6% annually. The bonds are purchased by most of Old Post's shareholders and also by many individuals who have no affiliation with Old Post. New Gate makes an offer to the shareholders to exchange two shares of its common voting class A stock for each common share of Old Post and 20 shares of common voting class B stock for each preferred share of Old Post.

Most of the shareholders are reluctant to make the exchange because of the favorable terms of the Old Post bonds they are holding. Consequently, New Gate offers to acquire all of the Old Post outstanding bonds in exchange for New Gate bonds paying 6% interest annually, with an equal principal amount and a 15-year term. All of the Old Post bondholders exchange their debentures, and 90% of the Old Post shareholders exchange their stock. Can these transactions qualify as nontaxable corporate reorganizations? How should these transactions be treated by New Gate, Old Post, and Old Post's shareholders?

INTERNET *activity*

Use the tax resources of the Internet to address the following questions. Do not restrict your search to the Web, but include a review of newsgroups and general reference materials, practitioner sites and resources, primary sources of the tax law, chat rooms and discussion groups, and other opportunities.

COMMUNICATIONS

Research Problem 2. Economic downturns mean an increase in corporate bankruptcy filings. Although many corporations are able to use Chapter 11 of the Bankruptcy Code to restructure, the recent credit crunch has limited such restructurings, and more and more bankruptcies are ending up in a liquidation of the corporate entity. Liquidating trusts are often utilized for the disposition of assets of a corporation going through bankruptcy. Using the Internet as your sole research source, prepare an outline discussing the use of liquidating trusts and their advantages.

COMMUNICATIONS

Research Problem 3. Find a recent merger or acquisition that has received financing support from Berkshire Hathaway. Prepare a written summary of the transaction, including the companies involved and the manner in which Berkshire Hathaway provided support for the transaction, and send your document to your classmates.

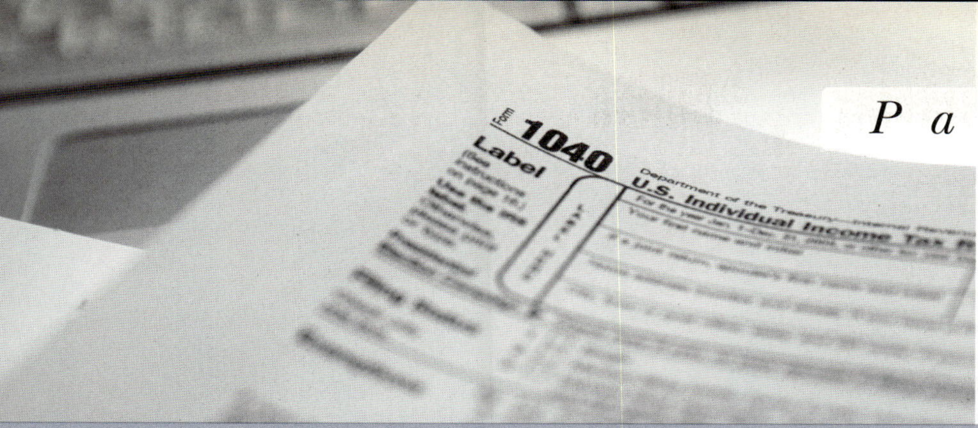

Part **7**

Flow-Through Entities

Unlike C corporations, some business entities are taxed under the conduit principle. Generally, this means the tax attributes of various transactions are retained as they flow through the entity to the owners. With limited exceptions, no tax is imposed at the entity level. Part 7 discusses two types of flow-through entities—partnerships and corporations that make the Subchapter S election. Part 7 also integrates the material on corporations (Part 6) with flow-through entities in regard to the decision-making process. By comparing the tax attributes of C corporations, S corporations, and partnerships, the owners are provided with the tools needed to choose the appropriate form for conducting a business.

Partnerships

CHAPTER

21

LEARNING OBJECTIVES

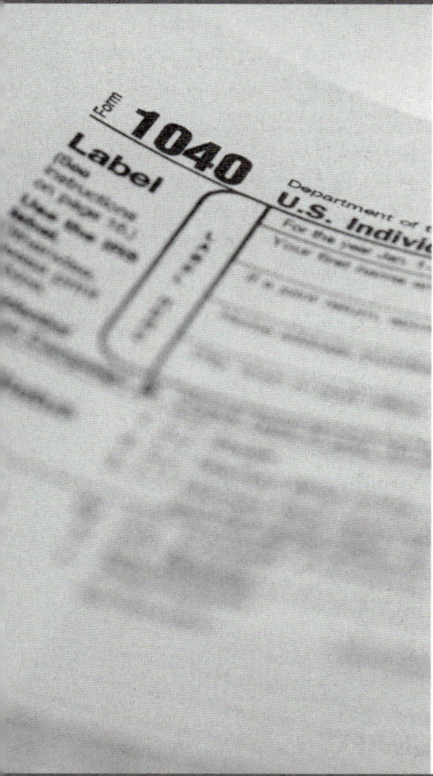

After completing Chapter 21, you should be able to:

LO.1 Distinguish among the various types of entities treated as partnerships for tax purposes.

LO.2 Describe how partnership income is reported and taxed.

LO.3 Discuss governing principles and theories of partnership taxation.

LO.4 Describe the tax effects of forming a partnership with cash and property contributions.

LO.5 Identify elections available to a partnership, and specify the tax treatment of expenditures of a newly formed partnership.

LO.6 Specify the accounting methods available to a partnership and the methods of determining a partnership's tax year.

LO.7 Calculate partnership taxable income and describe how partnership items affect a partner's income tax return.

LO.8 Determine a partner's basis in the partnership interest and explain how liabilities affect the basis computation.

LO.9 Describe the limitations on deducting partnership losses.

LO.10 Describe the treatment of transactions between a partner and the partnership.

LO.11 Determine the tax treatment of proportionate nonliquidating distributions from a partnership to a partner and the tax treatment of proportionate distributions that liquidate a partnership.

LO.12 Calculate the selling partner's amount and character of gain or loss on the sale or exchange of a partnership interest.

LO.13 Describe the application of partnership provisions to limited liability companies (LLCs) and limited liability partnerships (LLPs).

LO.14 Identify tax planning opportunities related to partnerships and their partners.

OUTLINE

For the latest in changes to tax legislation, visit **www.cengage.com/taxation/swft.**

THE BIG PICTURE **Tax Solutions for the Real World**

WHY USE A PARTNERSHIP, ANYWAY?

For 15 years, Maria has owned and operated a seaside bakery and café called The Beachsider. Each morning, customers line up on the boardwalk in front of the building and enjoy fresh coffee and croissants while waiting for a table. "The building is too small," Maria commented to her landlord, Kyle. "Is there any way we can expand?" The Beachsider is one of several older buildings on 3 acres of a 10-acre parcel that Kyle's family has owned for years. The remaining 7 acres are undeveloped.

Kyle and Maria talked to Josh, a real estate developer, and he proposed an expansion to The Beachsider and upgrades to the other buildings. The improvements would preserve the character of the original shopping center, and the remaining acreage would be available for future expansion. Kyle and Maria were impressed with Josh's vision and excited about the plans to upgrade the property and expand Maria's business.

The parties agreed to form a partnership to own and operate The Beachsider and to improve and lease the other buildings. Josh summarized the plan as follows: "Kyle and Maria will each contribute one-half of the capital we need. Kyle's real estate is valued at about $2 million. Maria's bakery equipment and the café furnishings are valued at about $500,000. The improvements will cost about $1.5 million, which Maria has agreed to contribute to the partnership."

Josh continued, "You have agreed that I do not need to contribute any capital to the partnership. Instead, I will manage the construction and the operation of the partnership in exchange for 5 percent of the capital and 20 percent of the ongoing profits. My capital interest will be valued at $200,000."

What are the tax consequences if the trio forms Beachside Properties as a partnership to own and operate the shopping center? What issues might arise later in the life of the entity? **Read the chapter and formulate your response.**

21.1 Overview of Partnership Taxation

COMPARISON OF PARTNERSHIPS AND SUBCHAPTER C CORPORATIONS

This chapter and the next chapter analyze two types of entities that may offer advantages over regular corporations. These entities are partnerships and S corporations, which are called *flow-through* or *pass-through* entities because the owners of the trade or business choose to avoid treating the enterprise as a separate taxable entity. Instead, the owners are taxed on a proportionate share of the entity's taxable income at the end of each of its taxable years.

Often a partnership may provide tax advantages over a C, or regular, corporation. The income of a partnership is subject to only a single level of taxation, while C corporation income is subject to *double taxation.* Corporate income is taxed at the entity level, currently at rates up to 35 percent. Any after-tax income that is distributed to corporate owners as a dividend is taxed again at the owner level. Though partnership income may be subject to high tax rates at the partner level, the resulting tax will generally be lower than a combined corporate-level tax and a second tax on a dividend distribution.

A partnership offers certain planning opportunities not available to other entities. Both C and S corporations are subject to rigorous allocation and distribution requirements. Generally, each income or loss allocation or distribution is proportionate to the ownership interest of each shareholder. A partnership, though, may adjust its allocations of income and cash flow among the partners each year according to their needs, as long as certain standards, discussed later in this chapter, are met. Also, any previously unrealized income of an S or C corporation, such as

TAX *in the NEWS*

The Extent of Partnership Usage

Partnerships come in all flavors and sizes! In less than a decade, the number of U.S. partnerships increased by 50 percent—from about 2 million entities in 2000 to over 3 million entities in 2008. In 2008 (the last year for which data are available), partnership entities owned assets with a combined gross book value of almost $20 trillion. Over 60 percent (almost 1.9 million) of these entities are limited liability companies; the vast majority of the rest are either general partnerships or limited partnerships. The balance includes limited liability partnerships, limited liability limited partnerships, and specialty entities (such as real estate investment trusts, or REITs).

The "partner mix" is shifting. Corporations are increasingly using the partnership entity form to expand operations or to create joint ventures with other entities. In 2006, for the first time, more than half of partnership income and losses was allocated to corporations.

Partnerships are used in almost every type of industry—from agriculture to health care to waste management. Almost half of all partnerships are engaged in some sort of real estate business. Certain elements of the tax law make partnerships especially appealing for activities such as research and development, and oil and gas exploration and extraction. All kinds of service activities are operated through some sort of partnership (especially limited liability partnerships): partnerships are common in the accounting, law, education, and transportation services industries.

Source: IRS, *Statistics of Income Bulletin*, Fall 2002 and Fall 2010 reports based on 2000 and 2008 filing years.

appreciation of corporate assets, is recognized at the entity level when the corporation liquidates. However, a partnership generally may liquidate tax-free. In addition, administrative and filing requirements are usually relatively simple for a partnership. Many states impose reporting and licensing requirements on corporate entities, including S corporations. These include franchise or capital stock tax returns that may require annual assessments and costly professional preparation assistance.[1] Partnerships, on the other hand, often have no reporting requirements beyond Federal and state informational tax returns.

For smaller business operations, a partnership enables several owners to combine their resources at low cost. It also offers simple filing requirements, the taxation of income only once, and the ability to discontinue operations relatively inexpensively.

For larger business operations, a partnership offers a unique ability to raise capital with low filing and reporting costs compared to, for example, corporate bond issuances. Special allocations of income and cash-flow items may be used by partnerships to meet the objectives of the owners.

Since partnerships and S corporations are so widespread, a study of related tax issues will prove useful to students, business owners, and consultants. This chapter addresses partnership formations, operations, and nonliquidating distributions, and, in addition, sales of partnership interests and partnership liquidating distributions. Chapter 22 discusses the taxation of S corporations.

WHAT IS A PARTNERSHIP?

LO.1

Distinguish among the various types of entities treated as partnerships for tax purposes.

A partnership is an association formed by two or more persons to carry on a trade or business, with each contributing money, property, labor, or skill, and with all expecting to share in profits and losses. For Federal income tax purposes, a partnership includes a syndicate, group, pool, joint venture, or other unincorporated organization through which any business, financial operation, or venture is carried on. The entity must not be otherwise classified as a corporation, trust, or estate.[2]

The types of entities that may be taxed as partnerships include general partnerships, limited partnerships, limited liability partnerships, limited liability limited partnerships,

[1]Certain states treat limited liability companies (LLCs) as corporations for purposes of state franchise taxes.

[2]A "person" can be an individual, trust, estate, corporation, association, or another partnership. §§ 7701(a)(1) and (2).

and limited liability companies. These entities are typically distinguished based on the types of business permitted to be conducted by the entity and the extent to which the partners are personally liable for the entity's debts.

- A **general partnership** (GP) consists of two or more partners who are **general partners**; there are no **limited partners**. Creditors of a general partnership can collect from both the partnership's assets and the personal assets of the owner-partners. A general partner can be subject to a malpractice judgment brought against the partnership, even though the partner was not personally involved in the malpractice. General partnerships are used for both operating activities (e.g., product manufacturing or sales) and for service businesses (e.g., accounting, law, or medicine).
- A **limited partnership** (LP) is a partnership with at least one general partner and one or more limited partners. These partnerships often have numerous limited partners and are used to raise capital for real estate development, oil and gas exploration, research and development, and various financial product investment vehicles. Typically, only the general partners are personally liable to creditors; each limited partner's risk of loss is restricted to that partner's equity investment in the entity.
- A **limited liability company** (LLC) combines the corporate benefit of limited liability for the owners with the benefits of partnership taxation, including the single level of tax and special allocations of income, losses, and cash flows. Owners are technically considered to be "members" rather than partners, but a properly structured LLC is generally treated as a partnership for all Federal tax purposes. Almost all states permit capital-intensive companies as well as nonprofessional service-oriented businesses and some professional service-providing companies to operate as LLCs.
- A **limited liability partnership** (LLP) is treated similarly to a general partnership in most states. The primary difference between an LLP and a general partnership is that an LLP partner is not personally liable for any malpractice committed by other partners. The LLP is currently the organizational form of choice for the large accounting firms.
- A **limited liability limited partnership** (LLLP) is an extension of the limited partnership form in which all partners, whether general or limited, are accorded limited liability. At this writing, about half of U.S. states permit formation of LLLPs or recognize LLLPs formed in another state. Existing limited partnerships can acquire LLLP status by filing a proper request with the appropriate state jurisdiction.

A partnership is governed by a **partnership agreement**, which should explain the rights and obligations of the partners; the allocation of income, deductions, and cash flows; initial and future capital contribution requirements; conditions for terminating the partnership; and other matters. The governing agreement of an LLC has a similar structure and is known as an **operating agreement**.

EXAMPLE 1
THE BIG PICTURE

Return to the facts of *The Big Picture* on p. 21-2. When Beachside Properties is formed, Kyle, Maria, and Josh must decide which type of partnership to utilize.

With a general partnership, Kyle, Maria, and Josh would each be jointly and severally liable for all entity debts. With a limited partnership, one of the partners would be designated as a general partner and would be liable for all entity debts. Because all three partners want to have limited liability, they decide not to use a general or limited partnership.

They do not consider a limited liability partnership because that entity form is typically reserved for service-providing entities.

With a limited liability company (or, if their state permits, a limited liability limited partnership), each partner's losses will be limited to the partner's contributed capital. Therefore, Kyle, Maria, and Josh decide to form Beachside Properties as an LLC. ■

ELECTIONS RELATED TO PARTNERSHIP STATUS

The IRS's "check-the-box" Regulations allow most unincorporated business entities—such as general partnerships, limited partnerships, LLPs, LLLPs, and LLCs—to select their Federal tax status.[3] If an unincorporated entity has two or more owners, it generally can choose to be taxed as either a partnership or a C corporation. By default, a newly formed noncorporate entity with two or more owners is generally treated as a partnership. Alternatively, the entity may file Form 8832 and "check the box" to elect to be treated as a corporation. This provides the entity with flexibility regarding its Federal tax classification. The Regulations, however, do not permit all unincorporated business or investment entities to choose their tax status. Most newly formed publicly traded partnerships, for example, must be taxed as corporations.

A partnership generally may elect out of the partnership taxation rules if it is involved in one of the following activities:

- Investment (rather than the active conduct of a trade or business).
- Joint production, extraction, or use of property.
- Underwriting, selling, or distributing a specific security issue.[4]

If a proper election is made, the partnership is disregarded for Federal tax purposes, and its operations are reported directly on the owners' tax returns. Such elections "out" of partnership status are not common.

TAXATION OF PARTNERSHIP INCOME

LO.2

Describe how partnership income is reported and taxed.

A partnership is not a taxable entity.[5] Rather, the taxable income or loss of the partnership flows through to the partners at the end of the entity's tax year.[6] Partners report their allocable share of the partnership's income or loss for the year on their tax returns. As a result, the partnership itself pays no Federal income tax on its income; instead, the partners' individual tax liabilities are affected by the activities of the entity.

EXAMPLE 2

Adam is a 40% partner in the ABC Partnership. Both Adam's and the partnership's tax years end on December 31. In 2011, the partnership generates $200,000 of ordinary taxable income. However, because the partnership needs capital for expansion and debt reduction, Adam makes no cash withdrawals during 2011. He meets his living expenses by reducing his investment portfolio. Adam is taxed on his $80,000 allocable share of the partnership's 2011 income, even though he receives no distributions from the entity during 2011. This allocated income is included in Adam's gross income. ■

EXAMPLE 3

Assume the same facts as in Example 2, except that the partnership recognizes a 2011 taxable loss of $100,000. Adam's $40,000 proportionate share of the loss flows through to him from the partnership, and he can deduct the loss. (Note: Loss limitation rules discussed later in the chapter may result in some or all of this loss being deducted by Adam in a later year.) ■

Many items of partnership income, expense, gain, or loss retain their identity as they flow through to the partners. This separate flow-through of certain items is required because such **separately stated items** *might* affect any two partners' tax liabilities in different ways. When preparing a personal tax return, a partner takes each of these items into account separately.[7] For example, charitable contributions are separately stated because partners need to compute their own personal limitation on charitable contributions. Some partners are able to deduct the entire amount they are allocated. Others are limited in what they can deduct by the amount of their adjusted gross income (AGI).

[3] Reg. §§ 301.7701–1 to –3.
[4] § 761(a).
[5] § 701.
[6] § 702.
[7] § 703(a)(1).

EXAMPLE 4

Brittany is a 25% partner in the BR Partnership. The cash basis entity collected sales income of $60,000 during 2010 and incurred $15,000 in business expenses. In addition, it sold a corporate bond in June for a $9,000 long-term capital gain. Finally, the partnership made a $1,000 contribution to the local Performing Arts Fund. The fund is a qualifying charity. BR and all of its partners use a calendar tax year.

For 2010, Brittany is allocated ordinary taxable income of $11,250 [($60,000 − $15,000) × 25%] from the partnership. She also reports her allocated share of the partnership's long-term capital gain ($2,250) and charitable contributions ($250). The ordinary income increases Brittany's gross income. The long-term capital gain and charitable contribution are separately stated because they could be treated differently on her tax return from the way they are treated on the tax returns of the other partners. For example, Brittany may have capital losses to offset the capital gain or may be subject to a percentage limitation on charitable contribution deductions for 2010. Other partners may have no capital losses or percentage limitations on charitable contribution deductions. Therefore, these items are not included in the computation of ordinary partnership income. Instead, they flow through to the partners separately. ■

Typically, a partnership combines income and expenses related to the partnership's trade or business activities into a single income or loss amount that is passed through to the partners. Most other partnership items are separately stated. For example, net income (loss) from rental real estate activities and net short-term capital gains (losses) are each determined at the partnership level and reported separately to the partners.

Other items that are allocated separately to the partners include recognized gains and losses from property transactions; qualified and ordinary dividend income; tax preferences and adjustments for the alternative minimum tax; expenditures that qualify for the foreign tax credit; information the partner needs to calculate the domestic production activities deduction of § 199; and expenditures the partners would treat as itemized deductions.

PARTNERSHIP REPORTING

Even though it is not a taxpaying entity, a partnership must file an information tax return, Form 1065. This return is due by the fifteenth day of the fourth month following the end of the tax year. For a calendar year partnership, this deadline is April 15. An automatic five-month extension is available (to September 15 for a calendar year partnership). As part of this return, the partnership prepares a **Schedule K–1** for each partner that shows that partner's share of partnership items. Each partner receives a copy of Schedule K–1 for use in preparing the tax return.

Look at Form 1065 for 2010 in Appendix B, and refer to it during the following discussion. The ordinary income and expense items generated by the partnership's trade or business activities are netted to produce a single income or loss amount. The partnership reports this ordinary income or loss from its trade or business activities on Form 1065, page 1. Schedule K (page 4 of Form 1065) accumulates all items that must be separately reported to the partners, including net trade or business income or loss (from page 1). The amounts on Schedule K are allocated among the partners on the partners' Schedules K–1.

EXAMPLE 5

The BR Partnership in Example 4 reports its $60,000 sales income on Form 1065, page 1, line 1. The $15,000 of business expenses are reported in the appropriate amounts on page 1, line 2 or lines 9–20. Partnership ordinary income of $45,000 is shown on page 1, line 22, and on Schedule K, line 1. The $9,000 net long-term capital gain and the $1,000 charitable contribution are reported only on Schedule K, on lines 9a and 13a, respectively.

Brittany receives a Schedule K–1 from the partnership that shows her shares of partnership ordinary income of $11,250, long-term capital gain of $2,250, and charitable contributions of $250 on lines 1, 9a, and 13 (Code A), respectively. She then combines these amounts with similar items from sources other than BR on her personal tax return. For example, if she has a $5,000 long-term capital loss from a stock transaction during the year, her overall net capital loss calculated on Schedule D of her Form 1040 is $2,750 ($2,250 − $5,000). She evaluates this net amount to determine the amount she may deduct on her Form 1040. She reports the $250 of charitable contributions on her Schedule A. ■

As this example shows, one must look at both page 1 and Schedule K to get complete information regarding a partnership's operations for the year.

The partnership reconciles book income with income reported on the return by preparing Schedule M–1 or Schedule M–3. This reconciliation is similar to the reconciliation between financial (book) and taxable income prepared by a corporation. On the corporate return, taxable income is shown on Form 1120, page 1, and it is reconciled to book income on either Schedule M–1 or Schedule M–3 (see Chapter 17).

For a partnership, book income must be reconciled to the partnership's *equivalent* of taxable income. The partnership prepares the Analysis of Net Income (Loss) (page 5 of Form 1065) to determine the partnership's taxable income equivalent. Certain amounts shown on Schedule K are netted and entered on the Net Income (Loss) line (line 1) of this Analysis. This is the amount to which book income must be reconciled on Schedule M–1 or Schedule M–3.

Schedule M–1 is found on page 5 of Form 1065. Schedule M–3 is a separate three-page form. Schedule M–3 is required in lieu of Schedule M–1 if the partnership has $10 million or more in assets at the end of the year, if it has $35 million of receipts during the year, or if certain other situations exist. In addition, Schedule M–3 is required if a partner owns a 50 percent or more interest in partnership profits, loss, or capital and is required to file its own Schedule M–3. If a partnership is required to file Schedule M–3, it must also answer various questions on Schedule C.

The net taxable income calculated on the Analysis of Net Income (Loss) schedule should agree with the reconciled taxable income on Schedule M–1 (line 9) or the reconciled amount from Schedule M–3, Part II. Schedule L generally shows an accounting-basis balance sheet.

Schedule M–2 reconciles partners' beginning and ending capital accounts. The analysis of capital accounts on Schedule M–2 reflects contributions to and distributions from the partnership as well as the partnership's income, gains, losses, and deductions. Schedule M–2 can be prepared using any of several methods, including the tax basis, generally accepted accounting principles (GAAP), or the "§ 704(b) book" method. The method used on Schedule M–2 should also be used in preparing the partners' Schedules K–1. If this method differs from the method used for the balance sheet (Schedule L), a reconciling schedule should be provided.

CONCEPTUAL BASIS FOR PARTNERSHIP TAXATION

LO.3

Discuss governing principles and theories of partnership taxation.

The unique tax treatment of partners and partnerships can be traced to two legal concepts that evolved long ago: the **aggregate** (or conduit) **concept** and the **entity concept**. These concepts influence practically every partnership tax rule.

Aggregate (or Conduit) Concept

The aggregate (or conduit) concept treats the partnership as a channel through which income, credits, deductions, and other items flow to the partners. Under this concept, the partnership is regarded as a collection of taxpayers joined in an agency relationship with one another. The imposition of the income tax on individual partners reflects the influence of this doctrine.

Entity Concept

The entity concept treats partners and partnerships as separate units and gives the partnership its own tax "personality" by (1) requiring a partnership to file an information tax return and (2) treating partners as separate and distinct from the partnership in certain transactions between a partner and the entity. A partner's recognition of capital gain or loss on the sale of the partnership interest further illustrates this doctrine.

Combined Concepts

Some rules governing the formation, operation, and liquidation of a partnership contain a blend of the entity and aggregate concepts.

PARTNER'S OWNERSHIP INTEREST IN A PARTNERSHIP

In keeping with the aggregate theory, each partner typically owns both a **capital interest** and a **profits (loss) interest** in the partnership. A capital interest is measured by a partner's **capital sharing ratio**, which is the partner's percentage ownership of the capital of the partnership. A partner's capital interest can be determined in several ways. The most widely accepted method measures the capital interest as the percentage of net asset value (asset value remaining after payment of all partnership liabilities) a partner would receive on immediate liquidation of the partnership.

A profits (loss) interest is simply the partner's percentage allocation of current partnership operating results. **Profit and loss sharing ratios** are usually specified in the partnership agreement and are used to determine each partner's allocation of partnership ordinary taxable income and separately stated items.[8] The partnership can change its profit and loss allocations at any time simply by amending the partnership agreement.

Each partner's profit, loss, and capital sharing ratios must appear on the partner's Schedule K–1. In many cases, the three ratios are the same. A partner's capital sharing ratio generally equals the partner's profit and loss sharing ratios if all profit and loss allocations, for each year of the partnership's existence, are in the same proportion as the partner's initial contributions to the partnership. These ratios can differ for a number of reasons, however. For example, a partner may receive an interest in future profits (and no interest in partnership capital) in exchange for services rendered to the partnership. On its website, the IRS has issued answers to "frequently asked questions" (FAQs) about the determination of partners' capital, profit, and loss sharing ratios. As the IRS's responses make clear, many methods are acceptable, provided the method is consistently applied.

The partnership agreement may, in some cases, provide for a **special allocation** of certain items to specified partners, or it may allocate items in a different proportion from general profit and loss sharing ratios. These items are separately reported to the partner receiving the allocation. As indicated in the answers to the FAQs mentioned above, these special allocations should generally be considered in determining the partners' capital, profit, and loss sharing ratios. To be recognized for tax purposes, a special allocation must produce nontax economic consequences for the partners receiving it.[9]

EXAMPLE 6

When the George-Amy Partnership was formed, George contributed cash, and Amy contributed some City of Iuka bonds that she had held for investment purposes. The partnership agreement allocates all of the tax-exempt interest income from the bonds to Amy as an inducement for her to remain a partner. This is an acceptable special allocation for income tax purposes; it reflects the differing economic circumstances that underlie the partners' contributions to the capital of the entity. Since Amy would have received the exempt income if she had not joined the partnership, she can retain the tax-favored treatment by means of the special allocation. ■

EXAMPLE 7

Assume the same facts as in Example 6. Three years after it was formed, the George-Amy Partnership purchased some City of Butte bonds. The municipal bond interest income of $15,000 flows through to the partners as a separately stated item, so that it retains its tax-exempt status. The partnership agreement allocates all of this income to George because he is subject to a higher marginal income tax bracket than is Amy. The partnership also allocates $15,000 more of the partnership taxable income to Amy than to George. These allocations are not effective for income tax purposes because they have no purpose other than the reduction of the partners' combined income tax liability. ■

INSIDE AND OUTSIDE BASES

Throughout this chapter, reference is made to the partnership's inside basis and a partner's outside basis. **Inside basis** refers to the adjusted basis of each *partnership* asset, as determined from the partnership's tax accounts. **Outside basis** represents each partner's basis in the partnership interest. In keeping with the aggregate theory, each partner "owns" a share of the partnership's inside basis for all its assets.

[8] § 704(a).

[9] § 704(b).

In many cases—especially on formation of the partnership—the total of the partnership's inside bases for all of its assets equals the total of all the partners' outside bases in their partnership interests.

Consider a partner's outside basis. When income flows through to a partner from the partnership, the partner's basis in the partnership interest increases. When a loss flows through to a partner, basis is reduced.

EXAMPLE 8

Paul contributes $20,000 of cash to acquire a 30% capital and profits interest in the Blue Jay Partnership. In its first year of operations, the partnership earns ordinary income of $40,000 and makes no distributions to Paul. Paul's initial basis is the $20,000 he paid for the interest. He reports ordinary income of $12,000 (30% × $40,000 partnership income) on his individual return and increases his basis by the same amount, to $32,000. ■

The Code provides for the increase and decrease in a partner's basis so that the income or loss from partnership operations is taxed only once. In Example 8, if Paul sold his interest at the end of the first year for $32,000, he would have no gain or loss. If the Code did not provide for an adjustment of a partner's basis, Paul's basis would be $20,000, and he would be taxed on the gain of $12,000 in addition to being taxed on his $12,000 share of income. In other words, without the basis adjustment, partnership income would be subject to double taxation.

Specific rules for calculating the partner's outside basis are discussed later in the chapter. As these discussions indicate, a partner's basis is important for determining the treatment of distributions from the partnership to the partner, establishing the deductibility of partnership losses, and calculating gain or loss on the partner's disposition of the partnership interest.

A partner's basis is not reflected anywhere on the Schedule K–1. Instead, each partner should maintain a personal record of adjustments to basis. As mentioned previously, Schedule K–1 reconciles a partner's capital account, but the ending capital account balance is rarely the same amount as the partner's basis. Just as the tax and accounting bases of a specific asset may differ, a partner's capital account and basis in the partnership interest may not be equal for a variety of reasons. For example, a partner's basis includes the partner's share of partnership liabilities; these liabilities are not reported as part of the partner's capital account. The partner's share of partnership liabilities is shown separately in Part II of the Schedule K–1.

ANTI-ABUSE PROVISIONS

As this chapter reflects, partnership taxation is often flexible. For example, partnership operating income or losses can sometimes be shifted among partners, and partnership capital gains and losses can sometimes be shifted from one partner to another. The Code contains many provisions designed to thwart unwarranted allocations, but the IRS believes opportunities for tax avoidance still abound. The IRS has adopted Regulations that allow it to recharacterize transactions that it considers to be "abusive."[10]

Concept Summary 21.1 reviews the general concepts of partnership taxation.

21.2 Formation of a Partnership: Tax Effects

GAIN OR LOSS ON CONTRIBUTIONS TO THE PARTNERSHIP

LO.4

Describe the tax effects of forming a partnership with cash and property contributions.

When a taxpayer transfers property to an entity in exchange for valuable consideration, a taxable exchange normally results. Typically, both the taxpayer and the entity realize and recognize gain or loss on the exchange.[11] The gain or loss realized by the transferor is the difference between the fair market value of the consideration received and the adjusted basis of the property transferred.[12]

[10] Reg. § 1.701–2.

[11] § 1001(c).

[12] § 1001(a).

CONCEPT SUMMARY 21.1

Overview of Partnerships

1. Compared with a Subchapter C corporation, a partnership may offer some advantages, including a single level of taxation, the availability of certain planning opportunities, and simplified administration and reporting.
2. Entities treated as a partnership for tax purposes include general partnerships, limited partnerships, limited liability companies, limited liability partnerships, and limited liability limited partnerships.
3. The various types of partnerships are distinguished based on the types of businesses that can be conducted and the extent to which the partners are liable for entity debts. Both considerations are determined based on state law.
4. Partnership income and losses flow through to the partners and are reported on the partners' tax returns. The partnership reports ordinary income or loss as well as *separately stated items* to the partners. Under certain conditions, items may be *specially allocated* to specified partners.
5. The partnership files Form 1065 as an information return and prepares a Schedule K–1 to report each partner's share of income and deductions.
6. The *entity concept* treats partners and partnerships as separate units. The nature and amount of partnership gains and losses and most partnership tax elections are determined at the partnership level.
7. The *aggregate concept* allows partnership income, gains, losses, credits, deductions, etc., to flow through to the partners for separate tax reporting.
8. Sometimes both the aggregate concept and the entity concept apply to the same transaction, but usually one dominates.
9. A partner has an *outside basis* in the partnership interest. The partnership has an *inside basis* in partnership assets.
10. Each partner has a *profit* and *loss sharing ratio*, which is the partner's share of income and losses. The partner also has a *capital sharing ratio*, which, in general terms, equals the percentage of the partner's rights to partnership property upon liquidation of the partnership.

In most situations, however, neither the partner nor the partnership recognizes the realized gain or loss when a partner contributes property to a partnership in exchange for a partnership interest. Instead, the realized gain or loss is deferred.[13]

There are two reasons for this nonrecognition treatment. First, forming a partnership allows investors to combine their assets toward greater economic goals than could be achieved separately. Only the form of ownership, rather than the amount owned by each investor, has changed. Requiring that gain be recognized on such transfers would make the formation of some partnerships economically unfeasible. Second, because the partnership interest received is typically not a liquid asset, the partner may not have sufficient cash with which to pay the tax. Thus, deferral of the gain recognizes the economic realities of the business world and follows the wherewithal to pay principle of taxation.

EXAMPLE 9

Alicia transfers two assets to the Wren Partnership on the day the entity is created, in exchange for a 60% profit and loss interest worth $60,000. She contributes cash of $40,000 and retail display equipment (basis to her as a sole proprietor, $8,000; fair market value, $20,000). Since an exchange has occurred between two parties, Alicia *realizes* a $12,000 gain on this transaction. The gain realized is the fair market value of the partnership interest of $60,000 less the basis of the assets that she surrendered to the partnership [$40,000 (cash) + $8,000 (equipment)].

Under § 721, Alicia *does not recognize* the $12,000 realized gain in the year of contribution. This makes sense because, in the exchange, she received only an illiquid partnership interest; she received no cash with which to pay any resulting tax liability. ■

EXAMPLE 10

Assume the same facts as in Example 9, except that the equipment Alicia contributes to the partnership has an adjusted basis of $25,000. She has a $5,000 *realized* loss [$60,000 – ($40,000 + $25,000)], but she cannot deduct the loss. Realized losses, as well as realized gains, are deferred by § 721.

[13] § 721.

Alternatively, Alicia could have sold the equipment to a third party. This would allow her to deduct a $5,000 loss in the year of the sale. Alicia could then contribute $60,000 of cash (including the proceeds from the sale) for her interest in the partnership, and the partnership would have funds to purchase similar equipment. ■

EXAMPLE 11

Five years after the Wren Partnership (Examples 9 and 10) was created, Alicia contributes another piece of equipment to the entity. This property has a basis of $35,000 and a fair market value of $50,000. Alicia will defer the recognition of the $15,000 realized gain. Section 721 is effective whenever a partner makes a contribution to the capital of the partnership. ■

If a partner contributes only capital and § 1231 assets, the partner's holding period in the partnership interest is the same as that partner's holding period for these assets. If cash or assets that are not capital or § 1231 assets are contributed, the holding period in the partnership interest begins on the date the partnership interest is acquired. If multiple assets are contributed, the partnership interest is apportioned, and a separate holding period applies to each portion.

EXCEPTIONS TO § 721

The nonrecognition provisions of § 721 do not apply in the following situations:

- When appreciated stocks and securities are contributed to an investment partnership.
- When the transaction is essentially a taxable exchange of properties.
- When the transaction is a disguised sale of properties.
- When the partnership interest is received in exchange for services rendered to the partnership by the partner.

Investment Partnership

If the transfer consists of appreciated stocks and securities and the partnership is an investment partnership, it is possible that the realized gain on the stocks and securities will be recognized by the contributing partner at the time of contribution.[14] This provision prevents multiple investors from using the partnership form to diversify their investment portfolios on a tax-free basis. A similar provision, § 351(e), applies to corporations (see Chapter 18).

Exchange

If a transaction is essentially a taxable exchange of properties, tax on the gain is not deferred under the nonrecognition provisions of § 721.[15]

EXAMPLE 12

Sara owns land, and Brandon owns stock. Sara would like to have Brandon's stock, and Brandon wants Sara's land. If Sara and Brandon both contribute their property to newly formed SB Partnership in exchange for interests in the partnership, the tax on the transaction appears to be deferred under § 721. If the partnership then distributes the land to Brandon and the stock to Sara, the tax on this transaction also appears to be deferred under § 731 (discussed later in the chapter). Not so! The IRS will disregard the passage of the properties through the partnership and will hold, instead, that Sara and Brandon exchanged the land and stock directly. Thus, the transactions will be treated as any other taxable exchange. ■

Disguised Sale

A similar result occurs in a **disguised sale** of property or of a partnership interest. A disguised sale may occur when a partner contributes appreciated property to a partnership and soon thereafter receives a distribution from the partnership. This distribution may be viewed as a payment by the partnership for purchase of the property.[16]

[14] § 721(b).

[15] Reg. § 1.731–1(c)(3).

[16] § 707(a)(2)(B).

EXAMPLE 13

Kim transfers property to the KLM Partnership. The property has an adjusted basis of $10,000 and a fair market value of $30,000. Two weeks later, the partnership makes a distribution of $30,000 of cash to Kim. Under the distribution rules of § 731, the distribution would not be taxable to Kim if the basis of her partnership interest prior to the distribution was greater than the $30,000 of cash distributed. However, the transaction appears to be a disguised purchase-sale transaction, rather than a contribution and distribution. Therefore, Kim must recognize gain of $20,000 on transfer of the property, and the partnership is deemed to have purchased the property for $30,000. ■

Services

A final exception to the nonrecognition provision of § 721 occurs when a partner receives a capital interest (i.e., liquidation rights) in the partnership as compensation for services rendered to the partnership. This is not a tax-deferred transaction because services are not treated as "property" that can be transferred to a partnership on a tax-free basis. Instead, the partner performing the services recognizes ordinary compensation income equal to the fair market value of the partnership interest received.[17]

The partnership may deduct the amount included in the service partner's income if the services are of a deductible nature. If the services are not deductible to the partnership, they must be capitalized to an asset account. For example, architectural plans created by a partner are capitalized as part of the structure built with those plans. Alternatively, day-to-day management services performed by a partner for the partnership are usually deductible by the partnership.

EXAMPLE 14

Bill, Carlos, and Dave form the BCD Partnership, with each receiving a one-third interest in the entity. Dave receives his one-third interest as compensation for tax planning services he will render after the formation of the partnership. The value of a one-third capital interest in the partnership (for each of the parties) is $20,000. Dave recognizes $20,000 of compensation income, and he has a $20,000 basis in his partnership interest. The same result would occur if the partnership had paid Dave $20,000 for his services and he immediately contributed that amount to the entity for a one-third ownership interest. In either case the partnership will probably be able to deduct $20,000 in calculating its ordinary business income. ■

EXAMPLE 15
THE BIG PICTURE

Return to the facts of *The Big Picture* on p. 21-2. Assume that Kyle has a basis of $600,000 in the $2 million of real estate he contributed and that Maria has a $0 basis in the bakery equipment and the café furnishings.

When Beachside Properties, LLC, is formed, no tax results for the LLC or for Kyle or Maria. Kyle does not recognize his $1.4 million realized gain nor does Maria recognize her $500,000 realized gain.

Kyle takes a substituted basis of $600,000 for his interest, and Maria takes a substituted basis of $1.5 million ($1.5 million for contributed cash + $0 for contributed property). Beachside Properties assumes a carryover basis of $600,000 for the real estate contributed by Kyle and $0 for the property contributed by Maria. To the extent that the buildings and other land improvements are depreciable, the LLC "steps into Kyle's shoes" in calculating depreciation deductions.

Because Josh receives his 5% capital interest in the LLC in exchange for services, the $200,000 is taxable to him. Beachside Properties either capitalizes or expenses the cost of the services, depending on their nature. Josh's 20% profits interest will be taxed to him as profits are allocated to him. ■

[17] § 83(a).

TAX ISSUES RELATIVE TO CONTRIBUTED PROPERTY

When a partner makes a tax-deferred contribution of an asset to the capital of a partnership, the tax law assigns a *carryover basis* to the property.[18] The partnership's basis in the asset (inside basis) is equal to the partner's basis in the property prior to its transfer to the partnership. The partner's outside basis in the new partnership interest is the same as the partner's basis in the contributed asset. The tax term for this basis concept is *substituted basis*. Thus, two assets are created out of one when a partnership is formed, namely, the property in the hands of the new entity and the new asset (the partnership interest) in the hands of the partner. Both assets are assigned a basis that is derived from the partner's existing basis in the contributed property.

These rules are logical in view of what Congress was attempting to accomplish with the deferral approach. As noted earlier, gain or loss is deferred when property is contributed to a partnership in exchange for a partnership interest. The bases are the amounts necessary to allow for recognition of the deferred gain or loss if the property or the partnership interest is subsequently disposed of in a taxable transaction. This treatment is similar to the treatment of assets transferred to a controlled corporation[19] and the treatment of like-kind exchanges.[20]

EXAMPLE 16

On June 1, 2011, Luis transfers property to the JKL Partnership in exchange for a one-third interest in the partnership. The property has an adjusted basis to Luis of $10,000 and a fair market value on June 1 of $30,000. Luis's realized gain on the exchange is $20,000 ($30,000 – $10,000), but under § 721, none of the gain is recognized. Luis's basis for his partnership interest is the amount necessary to recognize the $20,000 deferred gain if he subsequently sells the interest for its $30,000 fair market value. This amount, $10,000, is referred to as a substituted basis. The basis of the property contributed to the partnership is the amount necessary to allow for the recognition of the $20,000 deferred gain if the property is subsequently sold for its $30,000 fair market value. This amount, also $10,000, is referred to as a carryover basis. ■

The holding period for the contributed asset carries over to the partnership. Thus, the partnership's holding period for the asset includes the period during which the partner owned the asset.

Depreciation Method and Period

If depreciable property is contributed to the partnership, the partnership is usually required to use the same cost recovery method and life used by the partner. The partnership merely "steps into the shoes" of the partner and continues the same cost recovery calculations. The partnership may not elect under § 179 to immediately expense any part of the basis of depreciable property it receives from the transferor partner.

Intangible Assets

If a partner contributes an existing "§ 197" intangible asset to the partnership, the partnership generally will "step into the shoes" of the partner in determining future amortization deductions. Section 197 intangible assets include goodwill, going-concern value, information systems, customer- or supplier-related intangible assets, patents, licenses obtained from a governmental unit, franchises, trademarks, covenants not to compete, and other items.

EXAMPLE 17

On September 1, 2009, at a cost of $120,000, James obtained a license to operate a television station from the Federal Communications Commission. The license is effective for 20 years. On January 1, 2011, he contributes the license to the JS Partnership in exchange for a 60% interest. The value of the license is still $120,000 at that time.

[18] § 723.
[19] § 351.
[20] § 1031.

The license is a § 197 asset because it is a license with a term greater than 15 years. The cost is amortized over 15 years. James claims amortization for 4 months in 2009 and 12 months in 2010. Thereafter, the partnership steps into James's shoes in claiming amortization deductions. ■

Intangible assets that do not fall under the § 197 rules are amortized over their useful life, if any.[21]

Receivables, Inventory, and Losses

To prevent the conversion of ordinary income into capital gain, gain or loss is treated as ordinary when the partnership disposes of either of the following:[22]

- Contributed receivables that were unrealized in the contributing partner's hands at the contribution date. Such receivables include the right to receive payment for goods or services delivered or to be delivered.
- Contributed property that was inventory in the contributor's hands on the contribution date, if the partnership disposes of the property within *five years of the contribution.* For this purpose inventory includes all tangible property except capital assets and real or depreciable business assets.

EXAMPLE 18

Deon operates a cash basis retail electronics store as a sole proprietor. Raul is an enterprising individual who likes to invest in small businesses. On January 2 of the current year, Deon and Raul form the DR Partnership. Their partnership contributions are as follows:

	Adjusted Basis	Fair Market Value
From Deon:		
Receivables	$ -0-	$ 20,000
Land used as parking lot*	12,000	50,000
Inventory	25,000	50,000
From Raul:		
Cash	120,000	120,000

*The parking lot had been held for nine months at the contribution date.

Within 30 days of formation, DR collects the receivables and sells the inventory for $50,000 of cash. It uses the land for the next 10 months as a parking lot, then sells it for $35,000 of cash. DR realizes the following income in the current year from these transactions:

- Ordinary income of $20,000 from collecting the receivables.
- Ordinary income of $25,000 from the sale of inventory.
- Section 1231 gain of $23,000 from the sale of land.

Since the land takes a carryover holding period, it is treated as having been held 19 months at the sale date. ■

A similar rule is designed to prevent a capital loss from being converted into an ordinary loss. Under the rule, if contributed property is disposed of at a loss and the property had a "built-in" capital loss on the contribution date, the loss is treated as a capital loss if the partnership disposes of the property *within five years of the contribution.* The capital loss is limited to the amount of the "built-in" loss on the date of contribution.

[21] Reg § 1.167(a)–3.

[22] § 724. For this purpose, § 724(d)(2) waives the holding period requirement in defining § 1231 property.

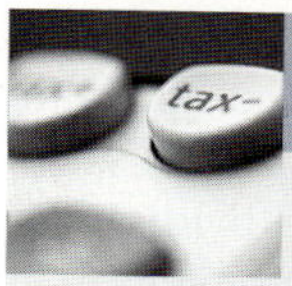

CONCEPT SUMMARY 21.2

Partnership Formation and Initial Basis Computation

1. Generally, partners or partnerships do not recognize gain or loss when property is contributed for capital interests.
2. Partners contributing property for partnership interests take the contributed property's adjusted basis for their *outside basis* in their partnership interest. The partners are said to take a substituted basis in their partnership interest.
3. The partnership will continue to use the contributing partner's basis for the *inside basis* in property it receives. The contributed property is said to take a carryover basis.
4. The holding period of a partner's interest includes that of contributed property when the property was a § 1231 asset or capital asset in the partner's hands. Otherwise, the holding period starts on the day the interest is acquired. The holding period of an interest acquired by a cash contribution starts at acquisition.
5. The partnership's holding period for contributed property includes the contributing partner's holding period.

EXAMPLE 19

Assume the same facts as Example 18, except for the following:

- Deon held the land for investment purposes. It had a fair market value of $8,000 at the contribution date.
- DR used the land as a parking lot for 10 months and sold it for $6,500.

DR realizes the following income and loss from the land contribution and sale transactions:

- Capital loss of $4,000 from the sale of the land ($8,000 – $12,000).
- Section 1231 loss of $1,500 from the sale of the land ($6,500 – $8,000).

Since the land was sold within five years of the contribution date, the $4,000 built-in loss is a capital loss. The post-contribution loss of $1,500 is a § 1231 loss because DR used the property in its business. ■

Concept Summary 21.2 reviews the rules that apply to partnership asset contributions and basis adjustments.

TAX ACCOUNTING ELECTIONS

> **LO.5**
> Identify elections available to a partnership, and specify the tax treatment of expenditures of a newly formed partnership.

A newly formed partnership must make numerous tax accounting elections. These elections are formal decisions on how a particular transaction or tax attribute should be handled. Most of these elections must be made by the partnership rather than by the partners individually.[23] The *partnership* makes the elections for the following items:

- Taxable year and accounting method (cash, accrual, or hybrid).
- Inventory method.
- Cost or percentage depletion method, excluding oil and gas wells.
- Cost recovery methods and assumptions.
- Treatment of research and experimentation costs.
- Amortization of organizational costs and amortization period.
- Amortization of startup expenditures and amortization period.
- Method of cost allocation under § 199 and, for certain partnerships, determination of "qualified production activities income" (QPAI) and production-related wages.[24]
- Section 179 deductions for certain tangible personal property.
- Nonrecognition treatment for gains from involuntary conversions.

---

[23] § 703(b).

[24] Reg. §§ 1.199–4 and –5.

Each partner is bound by the decisions made by the partnership relative to the elections. If the partnership fails to make an election, a partner cannot compensate for the error by making the election individually.

Though most elections are made by the partnership, each *partner* individually is required to make a specific election on the following relatively narrow tax issues:

- Whether to reduce the basis of depreciable property when first excluding income from discharge of indebtedness.
- Whether to claim cost or percentage depletion for oil and gas wells.
- Whether to take a deduction or credit for taxes paid to foreign countries and U.S. possessions.

INITIAL COSTS OF A PARTNERSHIP

In its initial stages, a partnership incurs expenses relating to some or all of the following: forming the partnership (organizational costs), admitting partners to the partnership, marketing and selling partnership units to prospective partners (syndication costs), acquiring assets, starting business operations (startup costs), negotiating contracts, and other items. Many of these expenditures are not currently deductible. However, the Code permits a deduction or ratable amortization (i.e., straight-line) of "organizational" and "startup" costs; acquisition costs for depreciable assets are included in the initial basis of the acquired assets; and costs related to some intangible assets may be amortized. "Syndication costs" may be neither amortized nor deducted.

Organizational Costs

Organizational costs include expenditures that are (1) incident to the creation of the partnership; (2) chargeable to a capital account; and (3) of a character that, if incident to the creation of a partnership with an ascertainable life, would be amortized over that life. Organizational costs include accounting fees and legal fees incident to the partnership's formation. The expenditures must be incurred within a period that starts a reasonable time before the partnership begins business. The period ends with the due date (without extensions) of the tax return for the initial tax year.

For organizational costs incurred after October 22, 2004, the partnership may elect to deduct up to $5,000 of the costs in the year in which it begins business. This amount must be reduced, however, by the organizational costs that exceed $50,000. Any organizational costs that cannot be deducted under this provision are amortizable over 180 months beginning with the month in which the partnership begins business.[25]

In general, the partnership is deemed to have elected the $5,000 deduction and 180-month amortization treatment simply by deducting the proper amounts on the tax return.[26]

Startup Costs

Startup costs include operating costs that are incurred after the entity is formed but before it begins business. Such costs include marketing surveys prior to conducting business, pre-operating advertising expenses, costs of establishing an accounting system, costs incurred to train employees before business begins, and salaries paid to executives and employees before the start of business.

The partnership may elect to deduct up to $5,000 ($10,000 for tax years beginning in 2010 only) of startup costs in the year in which it begins business. This amount must be reduced, however, by the startup costs that exceed $50,000 ($60,000 for tax years beginning in 2010 only).[27] Costs that are not deductible under this provision are amortizable over 180 months beginning with the month in which the partnership begins business.

As with organizational costs, the partnership, in general, is treated as making a deemed election to deduct and/or amortize these costs simply by treating the amounts as specified on the tax return.[28]

[25]§ 709.

[26]Reg. § 1.709–1T. This Regulation is scheduled to expire in July 2011. If it is not finalized or extended, a formal election to amortize organizational costs will be required after that date.

[27]§§ 195(b)(1) and (b)(3).

[28]Reg. § 1.195–1T. This Regulation is scheduled to expire in July 2011. If it is not finalized or extended, a formal election to amortize startup costs will be required after that date.

EXAMPLE 20

The calendar year Bluejay Partnership was formed on July 1, 2011, and immediately started business. Bluejay incurred $4,000 in legal fees for drafting the partnership agreement and $2,200 in accounting fees for tax advice of an organizational nature. In addition, the partnership incurred $20,000 of pre-opening advertising expenses and $34,000 of salaries and training costs for new employees before opening for business. The partnership selected the accrual method of accounting and will deduct and amortize organizational and startup costs as permitted under §§ 709 and 195.

Bluejay incurred $6,200 ($4,000 + $2,200) of organizational costs in 2011. The partnership may deduct $5,040 of these costs on its 2011 tax return. This deduction is the sum of the $5,000 permitted deduction and the $40 ($1,200 × 6/180) amortization deduction for the $1,200 of organizational costs that exceed the $5,000 base amount.

Bluejay incurred $54,000 ($20,000 + $34,000) of startup costs in 2011. The partnership may deduct $2,767 of these costs on its tax return for 2011. This deduction is the sum of:

- $5,000 reduced by the $4,000 ($54,000 – $50,000) amount by which the startup costs exceed $50,000.
- $1,767 ($53,000 × 6/180) amortization of the remaining $53,000 ($54,000 – $1,000) of startup costs for 6 months. ■

Acquisition Costs of Depreciable Assets

Expenditures may be incurred in changing the legal title in which certain assets are held from that of the contributing partner to the partnership name. These costs include legal fees for transferring assets and transfer taxes imposed by some states. Such costs are added to the partnership's basis for the depreciable assets and increase the amount the partnership may depreciate.

Syndication Costs

Syndication costs are capitalized, but no amortization election is available. Syndication costs include the following expenditures incurred for promoting and marketing partnership interests:

- Brokerage fees.
- Registration fees.
- Legal fees paid for security advice or advice on the adequacy of tax disclosures in the prospectus or placement memo for securities law purposes.
- Accounting fees related to offering materials.
- Printing costs of prospectus, placement memos, and other selling materials.

METHOD OF ACCOUNTING

LO.6

Specify the accounting methods available to a partnership and the methods of determining a partnership's tax year.

Like a sole proprietorship, a newly formed partnership may adopt either the cash or the accrual method of accounting, or a hybrid of these two methods.

However, a few special limitations on cash basis accounting apply to partnerships.[29] The cash method of accounting may not be adopted by a partnership that:

- has one or more C corporation partners or
- is a tax shelter.

A C corporation partner does *not* preclude cash basis treatment if:

- the partnership meets the $5 million gross receipts test described below,
- the C corporation partner(s) is a qualified personal service corporation, such as an incorporated attorney, or
- the partnership is engaged in the business of farming.

A partnership meets the $5 million gross receipts test if it has not received average annual gross receipts of more than $5 million for all tax years beginning after December 31, 1985. "Average annual gross receipts" is the average of gross receipts for the three

[29] § 448.

FIGURE 21.1 **Deferral Benefit If Partnership Used a Fiscal Year and All Partners Were on the Calendar Year**

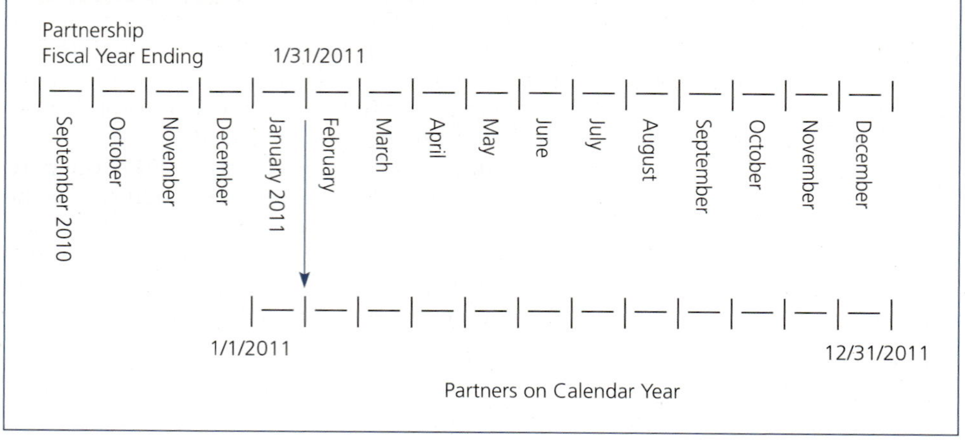

tax years ending with the tax period prior to the tax year in question. For new partnerships, the period of existence is used. Gross receipts are annualized for short taxable periods. A partnership must change to the accrual method the first year after the year in which its average annual gross receipts exceed $5 million and must use the accrual method thereafter.

A tax shelter is a partnership whose interests have been sold in a registered offering or a partnership in which more than 35 percent of the losses are allocated to limited partners.

TAXABLE YEAR OF THE PARTNERSHIP

Partnership taxable income (and any separately stated items) flows through to each partner at the end of the *partnership's* taxable year. A *partner's* taxable income, then, includes the distributive share of partnership income for any *partnership* taxable year that ends within the partner's tax year.

When all partners use the calendar year, it would be beneficial in present value terms for a profitable partnership to adopt a fiscal year ending with January 31. Why? As Figure 21.1 illustrates, when the adopted year ends on January 31, the reporting of income from the partnership and payment of related taxes can be deferred for up to 11 months. For instance, income earned by the partnership in September 2010 is not taxable to the partners until January 31, 2011. It is reported in the partner's tax return for the year ended December 31, 2011, which is not due until April 15, 2012. Even though each partner may be required to make quarterly estimated tax payments, some deferral is still possible.

Required Taxable Years

To prevent excessive deferral of taxation of partnership income, Congress and the IRS have adopted a series of rules that prescribe the *required* taxable year an entity must adopt if no alternative tax years (discussed on p. 21–19) are selected.

Three rules are presented in Figure 21.2.[30] The partnership must consider each rule in order. The partnership's required taxable year is the taxable year determined under the first rule that applies. The partnership uses the tax year of the "majority partners" if partners owning more than 50 percent of partnership capital and profits have the same tax year. The partnership uses the tax year of the "principal partners" if all partners who own 5 percent or more of capital or profits have the same tax year.

If no year-end is determined under either of these tests, the partnership determines a year under the **least aggregate deferral rule**. Under this rule, the partnership tests the year-ends that are used by the various partners to determine the

[30] § 706(b).

FIGURE 21.2 **Required Tax Year of Partnership**

In Order, Partnership Must Use	Requirements
Majority partners' tax year	More than 50% of capital *and* profits is owned by partners who have the same taxable year.
Principal partners' tax year	All partners who own 5% or more of capital *or* profits are principal partners. All principal partners must have the same tax year.
Year with smallest amount of income deferred	"Least aggregate deferral rule" (Example 21).

weighted-average deferral of partnership income. The year-end that offers the least amount of deferral is the *required tax year* under this rule.

EXAMPLE 21

Anne and BonnieCo are equal partners in the AB Partnership. Anne uses the calendar year, and BonnieCo uses a fiscal year ending August 31. Neither Anne nor BonnieCo is a majority partner as neither owns more than 50%. Although Anne and BonnieCo are both principal partners, they do not have the same tax year. Therefore, the general rules indicate that the partnership's required tax year must be determined by the "least aggregate deferral rule." The following computations support August 31 as AB's tax year, because the 2.0 product using that year-end is less than the 4.0 product when December 31 is used.

Test for 12/31 Year-End

Partner	Year Ends	Profits Interest		Months of Deferral		Product
Anne	12/31	50%	×	–0–	=	0.0
BonnieCo	8/31	50%	×	8	=	4.0
Aggregate number of deferral months						4.0

Sec 706

Test for 8/31 Year-End

Partner	Year Ends	Profits Interest		Months of Deferral		Product
Anne	12/31	50%	×	4	=	2.0
BonnieCo	8/31	50%	×	–0–	=	0.0
Aggregate number of deferral months						2.0

■

Alternative Tax Years

If the required tax year is undesirable to the entity, three other alternative tax years may be available:

- Establish to the IRS's satisfaction that a *business purpose* exists for a different tax year. This will typically be a "natural business year" (as defined)[31] that ends following a peak season or shortly thereafter.
- Elect a tax year so that taxes on partnership income are deferred for not more than *three months* from the *required* tax year.[32] Then, have the partnership maintain with the IRS a prepaid, non-interest-bearing deposit of estimated deferred taxes.[33] This alternative may not be desirable as the deposit is based on the highest individual tax rate of 35 percent plus 1 percentage point.

[31] Rev.Proc. 2006–46, 2006–2 C.B. 859, § 5.07.

[32] § 444.

[33] § 7519.

- Elect a 52- to 53-week taxable year that ends with reference to the required taxable year or to the taxable year elected under the three-month deferral rule.

21.3 Operations of the Partnership

LO.7

Calculate partnership taxable income and describe how partnership items affect a partner's income tax return.

An individual, corporation, trust, estate, or another partnership can become a partner in a partnership. Since a partnership is a tax-reporting, rather than a taxpaying, entity for purposes of its Federal (and state) income tax computations, the partnership's income, deductions, credits, and alternative minimum tax (AMT) preferences and adjustments can ultimately be reported and taxed on any of a number of income tax forms [e.g., Forms 1040 (individuals), 1041 (fiduciaries), 1120 (C corporations), and 1120S (S corporations)].

A partnership is subject to all other taxes in the same manner as any other business. Thus, the partnership files returns and pays the outstanding amount of pertinent sales taxes and property taxes. For employees (not partners), the partnership files returns and pays Social Security, unemployment, and other payroll taxes.

MEASURING AND REPORTING INCOME

The partnership's Form 1065 organizes and reports the transactions of the entity for the tax year. Each of the partnership's tax items is reported on Schedule K of that return. Each partner receives a Schedule K–1 that reports the partner's allocable share of partnership income, credits, adjustments, and preferences for the year. The IRS also receives a copy of each K–1.

Income Measurement

The measurement and reporting of partnership income require a two-step approach. Certain items must be netted at the partnership level, and other items must be segregated and reported separately on the partnership return and each partner's Schedule K–1.

Among the many income and deduction items passed through separately are the following:

- Net short-term and net long-term capital gains or losses.
- Section 1231 gains and losses.
- Charitable contributions.
- Portfolio income items (qualified and ordinary dividends, interest, and royalties).
- Expenses related to portfolio income.
- Immediately expensed tangible personal property (§ 179).
- Items allocated among the partners in a different ratio from the general profit and loss ratio.
- Recovery of items previously deducted (tax benefit items).
- Guaranteed payments, discussed later in the chapter.
- Passive activity items, such as rental real estate income or loss.
- Intangible drilling and development costs.
- Taxes paid to foreign countries and U.S. possessions.[34]

The reason for separately reporting the preceding items is rooted in the aggregate or conduit concept. These items affect various exclusions, deductions, and credits at the partner level and must pass through without loss of identity so that the proper tax for each partner may be determined.[35]

In addition, the partnership must report any information the partner needs in order to prepare a complete and accurate income tax return. This information includes the partner's share of the following:

[34]§ 702(a).

[35]§ 702(b).

- Information necessary to calculate the domestic production activities deduction (§ 199), such as qualified production activities income (QPAI) and W–2 wages (discussed later in the chapter).
- AMT preferences and adjustments, for use in calculating the partner's alternative minimum tax.
- Self-employment income, for use in calculating the partner's self-employment tax.
- Foreign-source income, for use in calculating the partner's foreign tax credits.

A partnership is not allowed the following deductions:

- Net operating losses (NOLs).
- Depletion of oil and gas interests.
- Dividends received deduction.

In addition, items that are only allowed by legislative grace to individuals, such as standard deductions or personal exemptions, are not allowed to the partnership. Also, if a partnership makes a payment on behalf of a partner, such as for alimony, medical expenses, or other items that constitute itemized deductions to individuals, the partnership treats the payment as a distribution or guaranteed payment (discussed later) to the partner, and the partner then determines whether a deduction may be claimed.

EXAMPLE 22
THE BIG PICTURE

Return to the facts of *The Big Picture* on p. 21-2. In its second year of operations, Beachside Properties, LLC, reports income and expenses from operating the café as well as rent income and expenses from leasing the other buildings. Beachside's activities are summarized as follows:

Sales revenue	$600,000
Cost of sales	200,000
Salaries to employees	100,000
Cost recovery deductions	60,000
Utilities, supplies, and repairs	40,000
Taxes and licenses (including payroll taxes)	20,000
Charitable contribution to art museum	6,000
Short-term capital gain	12,000
Net income from rental real estate	300,000
Qualified dividends received	4,000
Tax-exempt income (bond interest)	2,100
AMT adjustment (cost recovery)	5,000
Payment of medical expenses on behalf of partner Kyle	4,000

The LLC experienced a $20,000 net loss from operations last year, its first year of business.

Refer to Form 1065 in Appendix B. Beachside's ordinary income is determined and reported on the partnership return as follows:

Nonseparately Stated Items (Ordinary Income)—Form 1065, Pages 1 and 4	
Sales revenue	$ 600,000
Cost of sales	(200,000)
Salaries to employees	(100,000)
Cost recovery deductions	(60,000)
Utilities, supplies, and repairs	(40,000)
Taxes and licenses (including payroll taxes)	(20,000)
Ordinary income (Form 1065, page 1, line 22, and Form 1065, page 4 [Schedule K], line 1)	$ 180,000

Beachside's separately stated income and deduction items are:

Separately Stated Income and Deductions (Schedule K)	
Net income from rental real estate (Line 2)	$300,000
Qualified dividends received (Line 6)	4,000
Short-term capital gain (Line 9a)	12,000
Contribution to art museum (Line 13a)	6,000

Beachside is not a allowed a deduction for last year's $20,000 NOL—this item was passed through to the LLC members in the previous year. Moreover, the LLC is not allowed a deduction for payment of Kyle's medical expenses. This payment is probably handled as a distribution to Kyle, who may report it as a medical expense on his Schedule A in determining his itemized deductions. The AMT adjustment is not a separate component of the LLC's income, and it must be reported to Beachside's members so that they can properly calculate any AMT liability.

The LLC reports the following additional information that the partners must report or utilize in preparing their tax returns:

Additional Information (Schedule K)	
AMT adjustment—cost recovery (Line 17a)	$5,000
Tax-exempt income—bond interest (Line 18a)	2,100

■

EXAMPLE 23
THE BIG PICTURE

Continue with the facts in Example 22, but now consider the book-tax reconciliation. Beachside Properties, LLC, must prepare the Analysis of Income (Loss) and Schedule M–1 on Form 1065, page 5. In preparing these schedules, the LLC combines the ordinary income of $180,000 and the four separately stated income and deduction amounts in Example 22 to arrive at "net income" of $490,000. This amount is shown on line 1 of the Analysis of Income (Loss) and is the amount to which book income is reconciled on Schedule M–1, line 9. ■

EXAMPLE 24
THE BIG PICTURE

Assume the same facts as in Example 22, but now consider the effect of the LLC's operations on one of its members. Maria, a 40% owner, will receive a Schedule K–1 from Beachside Properties, on which she is allocated a 40% share of ordinary income and separately stated items. Thus, on her Form 1040, Maria includes $72,000 of ordinary income, a $2,400 charitable contribution, a $4,800 short-term capital gain, $120,000 of passive rent income, and $1,600 of qualified dividend income.

Maria will disclose her $840 share of tax-exempt interest on the first page of Form 1040. In determining her AMT liability (if any), Maria will take into account a $2,000 positive adjustment. ■

Domestic Production Activities Deduction (§ 199)

As noted in Chapter 7, the conduct of certain businesses, usually manufacturing activities, can yield a domestic production activities deduction (DPAD). To determine the base for the deduction, domestic production gross receipts (DPGR) is first computed and then is reduced by related cost of goods sold and direct and indirect expenses to arrive at qualified production activities income (QPAI). The deduction (or DPAD) is 9 percent (6 percent in 2007 to 2009) of the lesser of QPAI or taxable income.[36]

[36] § 199(a).

GLOBAL
Tax Issues

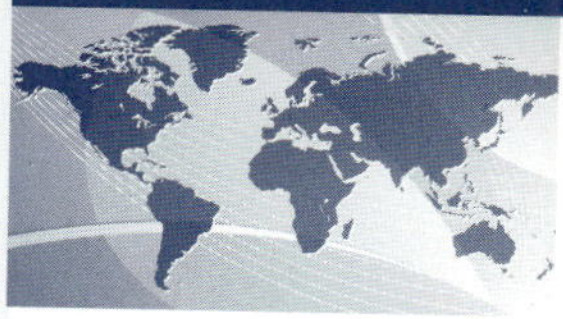

Various Withholding Procedures Applicable to Foreign Partners

A U.S. partnership may have foreign partners, and these partners will be taxed on their U.S. income. Because it might be difficult for the IRS to collect the tax owed by such foreign partners, several Code sections provide for various withholding procedures. The procedures differ depending on whether the income is "effectively connected with a U.S. trade or business," derived from investment property, or related to real estate transactions.

If the partnership purchases real property from a foreign seller, for example, the partnership is required to withhold 10 percent of the purchase price. If a partnership sells a U.S. real property interest, it must typically withhold 35 percent of the gain allocated to a foreign partner. Further, if the partnership receives "fixed and determinable annual or periodic payments" (FDAP), such as dividends, interest, or rents, it is required to withhold 30 percent of the amounts paid to any foreign person. (The 30 percent withholding rate is often reduced to a lower rate by a tax treaty between the United States and the foreign country.)

Finally, under Regulations issued in 2005 and 2008, if the partnership has U.S. business income, it must withhold and pay an amount equal to the highest U.S. tax rate applicable to the foreign taxpayer's allocable share of partnership income less certain certified losses and deductions. For a foreign individual or corporate partner, the partnership would generally withhold 35 percent of any amounts related to a U.S. business.

(Starting in 2010, lower rates apply for oil-related production activities.) When the taxpayer is not a corporation, modified AGI is substituted for taxable income. In no event, however, may the DPAD exceed 50 percent of the W–2 wages paid that are attributable to domestic production activities.[37]

When pass-through entities are involved (i.e., partnerships, S corporations, estates, and trusts), special rules apply.[38] Specifically, in the case of partnerships, the following rules govern the DPAD computation and allowance:

- Whether an activity qualifies for the DPAD is determined at the entity level. The actual deduction is determined at the partner level.
- For many types of partnerships, QPAI and W–2 wages related to production can be calculated at the entity level.[39] Unless otherwise indicated, assume throughout this chapter that the entity-level calculation applies.
- The partnership calculates QPAI by taking into account all separately stated and nonseparately stated items. Income and deduction inclusion and limitations are, for this purpose, determined at the partnership level.
- The Regulations outline specific methods for allocating costs between production-related and non-production-related activities.
- On Schedule K–1, each partner is allocated his or her share of QPAI and W–2 wages related to domestic production activities. The entity allocates QPAI among the partners using the allocation method used for gross income. The entity allocates W–2 production-related wages among the partners using the allocation method used for allocating wage expense.
- An individual partner will list this pass-through information on Form 8903 (Domestic Production Activities Deduction).

[37]§ 199(b).

[38]The rules applicable to pass-through entities are contained in § 199(d)(1) and Reg. § 1.199–5.

[39]Rev.Proc. 2007–34, 2007–1 C.B. 1345.

- A partner combines the partnership pass-through items with those from other sources (e.g., if a partner has his or her own factory).
- Guaranteed payments made by a partnership to a partner are not considered to be W–2 wages for DPAD purposes.

Withdrawals

Capital withdrawals by partners during the year do not affect the partnership's income measuring and reporting process. These items are usually treated as distributions made on the last day of the partnership's tax year. When withdrawals exceed the partners' shares of partnership income, the excess is taxed under the distribution rules (discussed later in the chapter).[40]

Penalties

A partner's share of each partnership item should be reported on the partner's respective tax return in the same manner as presented on the Form 1065. If a partner treats an item differently, the IRS must be notified of the inconsistent treatment.[41] If a partner fails to notify the IRS, a negligence penalty may be added to the tax due.

To encourage the filing of a partnership return, a penalty is imposed on the partnership of $195, per partner, per month (or fraction thereof, but not to exceed 12 months) for failure to file a complete and timely information return without reasonable cause.[42] A "small partnership" with 10 or fewer partners who are individuals (other than nonresident aliens), corporations, or an estate of a partner is exempt from these penalities.[43]

PARTNERSHIP ALLOCATIONS

Economic Effect

As shown by the example of Beachside Properties in *The Big Picture,* a partnership agreement or an LLC's operating agreement can provide that any partner may share capital, profits, and losses in different ratios. For example, a partner could have a 25 percent capital sharing ratio, yet be allocated 30 percent of the profits and 20 percent of the losses of the partnership. Such special allocations have, at times, been used in an attempt to manipulate the allocation of tax benefits among partners. The Regulations[44] are designed to prevent unfair use of such manipulation. Although these rules are too complex to discuss in detail, the general outline of one of these rules—the **economic effect test**—can be easily understood.

In general, the economic effect test requires the following:

- An allocation of income or gain to a partner must increase the partner's capital account, and an allocation of deduction or loss must decrease the partner's capital account.
- When the partner's interest is liquidated, the partner must receive net assets that have a fair market value equal to the positive balance in the capital account.
- A partner with a negative capital account must restore that account upon liquidation of the interest. Restoration of a negative capital account can best be envisioned as a contribution of cash to the partnership equal to the negative balance.

These requirements are designed to ensure that a partner bears the economic burden of a loss or deduction allocation and receives the economic benefit of an income or gain allocation.

[40] §§ 731(a)(1) and 733.
[41] § 6222.
[42] § 6698.
[43] § 6231(a)(1)(B).
[44] Reg. § 1.704–1(b).

EXAMPLE 25

Eli and Sanjay each contribute $20,000 of cash to the newly formed ES Partnership. The partnership uses the cash to acquire a depreciable asset for $40,000. The partnership agreement provides that the depreciation is allocated 90% to Eli and 10% to Sanjay. Other items of partnership income, gain, loss, or deduction are allocated equally between the partners. Upon liquidation of the partnership, property will be distributed to the partners in accordance with their positive capital account balances. Any partner with a negative capital account must restore the capital account upon liquidation. Assume the first-year depreciation on the equipment is $4,000. Also, assume nothing else happens in the first year that affects the partners' capital accounts.

Eli's capital account is $16,400 ($20,000 – $3,600), and Sanjay's capital account has a balance of $19,600 ($20,000 – $400) after the first year of partnership operations. The Regulations require that a hypothetical sale of the asset for its $36,000 of adjusted basis on the last day of the year and an immediate liquidation of the partnership should result in Eli and Sanjay receiving distributions equal to their capital accounts. According to the partnership agreement, Eli would receive $16,400, and Sanjay would receive $19,600 of the cash in a liquidating distribution. Eli, therefore, bears the economic burden of $3,600 of depreciation since he contributed $20,000 to the partnership and would receive only $16,400 upon liquidation. Likewise, Sanjay's economic burden is $400 since he would receive only $19,600 of his original $20,000 investment. The agreement, therefore, has economic effect. ■

EXAMPLE 26

Assume the same facts as in Example 25, except that the partnership agreement provides that Eli and Sanjay will receive equal amounts of cash upon liquidation of the partnership. The hypothetical sale of the asset for its $36,000 adjusted basis and the immediate liquidation of the partnership would result in each partner receiving $18,000 cash. Since each partner contributed $20,000 to the partnership and each partner would receive $18,000 upon liquidation, each partner bears the economic burden of $2,000 of depreciation. The original 90%/10% allocation of depreciation to the two partners is defective, and the IRS will require that the depreciation be reallocated equally ($2,000 each) to the two partners to reflect the economic burden borne by each partner. ■

Precontribution Gain or Loss

Certain income, gain, loss, and deductions relative to contributed property may not be allocated under the rules described above. Instead, **precontribution gain or loss** must be allocated among the partners to take into account the variation between the basis of the property and its fair market value on the date of contribution.[45] The partnership keeps track of these differences in its "§ 704(b) book" accounting records. For nondepreciable property, *built-in* gain or loss on the date of contribution must be allocated to the contributing partner when the property is eventually disposed of by the partnership in a taxable transaction. If the property is depreciable, Regulations describe allowable methods of allocating depreciation deductions.[46]

EXAMPLE 27
THE BIG PICTURE

Return to the facts of *The Big Picture* on p. 21-2. When Beachside Properties, LLC, was formed, Kyle contributed property valued at $2 million with a basis of $600,000. Maria contributed equipment and furnishings with a $0 basis and a $500,000 value. For § 704(b) book accounting purposes, Beachside records the land and other properties at their fair market values. For tax purposes, the LLC takes carryover bases in the properties. The LLC must keep track of the differences between the basis in each property and the value at the contribution date. If any of this property is sold, the gain must be allocated to the contributing partner to the extent of any previously unrecognized built-in gain.

For example, if Beachside sells the land contributed by Kyle for $2.3 million, the gain would be calculated and allocated as follows:

[45] § 704(c)(1)(A).

[46] Reg. § 1.704-3.

	§ 704(b) Book	Tax
Amount realized	$ 2,300,000	$ 2,300,000
Less: Adjusted basis	(2,000,000)	(600,000)
Gain realized	$ 300,000	$ 1,700,000
Built-in gain to Kyle	(–0–)	(1,400,000)
Remaining gain (allocated proportionately)	$ 300,000	$ 300,000

For tax purposes, Kyle would recognize $1,520,000 of the gain [($300,000 × 40%) + $1,400,000]; Maria would recognize $120,000 ($300,000 × 40%); and Josh would recognize $60,000 ($300,000 × 20%). ■

If contributed property has built-in losses at the contribution date, allocations related to the built-in loss can be made only to the contributing partner. For purposes of allocations to other partners, the partnership's basis in the loss property is treated as being the fair market value of the property at the contribution date.[47]

Concept Summary 21.3 reviews the tax reporting rules for partnership activities.

LO.8

Determine a partner's basis in the partnership interest and explain how liabilities affect the basis computation.

BASIS AND CAPITAL ACCOUNT FOR A PARTNERSHIP INTEREST

Previously, this chapter discussed how to compute a partner's basis when the partnership is formed. It was noted that the partner's basis in the newly formed partnership usually equals (1) the adjusted basis in any property contributed to the partnership plus (2) the fair market value of any services the partner performed for the partnership (i.e., the amount of ordinary income reported by the partner for services rendered to the partnership).

A partnership interest also can be acquired after the partnership has been formed. The method of acquisition controls how the partner's initial basis is computed. If the partnership interest is purchased from another partner, the purchasing partner's basis is the amount paid (cost basis) for the partnership interest. The basis of a partnership interest acquired by gift is the donor's basis for the interest plus, in certain cases, some or all of the transfer (gift) tax paid by the donor. The basis of a partnership interest acquired through inheritance generally is the fair market value of the interest on the date the partner dies.

After the partner is admitted to the partnership, the partner's basis is adjusted for numerous items. The following operating results *increase* a partner's adjusted basis:

- The partner's proportionate share of partnership income (including capital gains and tax-exempt income).
- The partner's proportionate share of any increase in partnership liabilities. (This provision is discussed in the next section.)

The following operating results *decrease* the partner's adjusted basis in the partnership:

- The partner's proportionate share of partnership deductions and losses (including capital losses).
- The partner's proportionate share of nondeductible expenses.
- The partner's proportionate share of any reduction in partnership liabilities.[48]

Under no circumstances can the partner's adjusted basis for the partnership interest be reduced below zero.

Increasing the adjusted basis for the partner's share of partnership taxable income is logical since the partner has already been taxed on the income. By increasing the partner's basis, this ensures that the partner is not taxed again on the income when the interest is sold or a distribution is received from the partnership.

[47] § 704(c)(1)(C).

[48] §§ 705 and 752.

CONCEPT SUMMARY 21.3

Tax Reporting of Partnership Activities

Event	Partnership Level	Partner Level
1. Compute partnership ordinary income or loss.	Form 1065, line 22, page 1. Schedule K, Form 1065, line 1, page 4.	Schedule K–1 (Form 1065), line 1. Each partner's share is passed through for separate reporting. Some amounts may be specially allocated to specific partners. For income: Each partner's basis is increased. For losses: Each partner's basis is decreased. • The amount of a partner's loss deduction may be limited. • Losses that may not be deducted are carried forward for use in future years.
2. Separately reported income and deduction items such as portfolio income, capital gain and loss, and § 179 deductions.	Schedule K, Form 1065, various lines, page 4.	Schedule K–1 (Form 1065), various lines. Each partner's share of each item is passed through for separate reporting.
3. Net earnings from self-employment.	Schedule K, Form 1065, line 14, page 4.	Schedule K–1 (Form 1065), line 14.
4. Additional calculations that partner is required to make (e.g., AMT, foreign tax credits).	Schedule K, Form 1065, various lines, page 4.	Schedule K–1 (Form 1065), various lines. Each partner's share of each item is passed through and considered in various calculations.

It is also logical that the tax-exempt income should increase the partner's basis. If the income is exempt in the current period, it should not contribute to the recognition of gain when the partner either sells the interest or receives a distribution from the partnership.

EXAMPLE 28

Tyler is a one-third partner in the TUV Partnership. His proportionate share of the partnership income during the current year consists of $20,000 of ordinary taxable income and $10,000 of tax-exempt income. None of the income is distributed to Tyler. The adjusted basis of Tyler's partnership interest before adjusting for his share of income is $35,000, and the fair market value of the interest before considering the income items is $50,000.

The unrealized gain inherent in Tyler's investment in the partnership is $15,000 ($50,000 − $35,000) before adjusting for his share of income. Tyler's proportionate share of the income items should increase the fair market value of the interest to $80,000 ($50,000 + $20,000 + $10,000). By increasing the adjusted basis of Tyler's partnership interest to $65,000 ($35,000 + $20,000 + $10,000), this ensures that the unrealized gain inherent in Tyler's partnership investment remains at $15,000. This makes sense because the $20,000 of ordinary taxable income is taxed to Tyler this year and should not be taxed again when he either sells his interest or receives a distribution. Similarly, the tax-exempt income is exempt this year and should not increase Tyler's gain when he either sells his interest or receives a distribution from the partnership. ■

Decreasing the adjusted basis for the partner's share of deductible losses, deductions, and noncapitalizable, nondeductible expenditures is logical for the same reasons. An item that is deductible currently should not contribute to creating a loss when the partnership interest is sold or when a distribution is received from the partnership.

Similarly, a noncapitalizable, nondeductible expenditure should never be deductible nor contribute to a loss when a subsequent sale or distribution transaction occurs.

Liability Sharing

A partner's adjusted basis is affected by the partner's share of partnership debt.[49] Partnership debt includes any partnership obligation that creates an asset, results in an expense to the partnership, or results in a nondeductible, noncapitalizable item at the partnership level. This definition includes certain contingent liabilities.[50] The definition also includes most debt that is considered a liability under financial accounting rules except for accounts payable of a *cash basis* partnership.

Under § 752, an increase in a partner's share of partnership debt is treated as a cash contribution by the partner to the partnership. A partner's share of partnership debt increases as a result of increases in the total amount of partnership debt. A decrease in a partner's share of partnership debt is treated as a cash distribution from the partnership to the partner. A partner's share of partnership debt decreases as a result of (1) decreases in the total amount of partnership debt and (2) assumption of the partner's debt by the partnership.

EXAMPLE 29

Jim and Becky contribute property to form the JB Partnership. Jim contributes cash of $30,000. Becky contributes land with an adjusted basis and fair market value of $45,000, subject to a liability of $15,000. The partnership borrows $50,000 to finance construction of a building on the contributed land. At the end of the first year, the accrual basis partnership owes $3,500 in trade accounts payable to various vendors. Assume no other operating activities occurred. If Jim and Becky share equally in liabilities, the partners' bases in their partnership interests are determined as follows:

Jim's Basis		Becky's Basis	
Contributed cash	$30,000	Basis in contributed land	$ 45,000
Share of debt on land (assumed by partnership)	7,500	Less: Debt assumed by partnership	(15,000)
		Share of debt on land (assumed by partnership)	7,500
Initial basis	$37,500	Initial basis	$ 37,500
Share of construction loan	25,000	Share of construction loan	25,000
Share of trade accounts payable	1,750	Share of trade accounts payable	1,750
Basis, end of first year	$64,250	Basis, end of first year	$ 64,250

In this case, it is reasonable that the parties have an equal basis, because each is a 50% owner and they contributed property with identical *net* bases and identical *net* fair market values. ■

EXAMPLE 30

Assume the same facts as in Example 29. In the second year, the partnership generates $70,000 of taxable income from operations and repays both the $50,000 construction loan and the $3,500 trade accounts payable. The taxable income is allocated equally to each partner and increases each partner's basis by $35,000. The $26,750 ($25,000 + $1,750) reduction of each partner's share of liabilities is treated as a cash distribution to each partner and reduces each partner's adjusted basis by that amount. The $72,500 adjusted basis for each partner at the end of the second year is computed as follows:

[49]§ 752.

[50]Reg. § 1.752–1(a)(4)(ii).

Fern	June	50
Ivy	Aug	25
Jason	Dec	25

A

S 10000 cash

T land Adj Bas 6000

FMV 10000

Land 10,000 Fin - 600 gain

6000 Tax - 4600 gain

sells for -10600

30%

20000

50000

35000

Jim's Basis		Becky's Basis	
Basis, beginning of second year	$ 64,250	Basis, beginning of second year	$ 64,250
Share of taxable income	35,000	Share of taxable income	35,000
Share of construction loan paid	(25,000)	Share of construction loan paid	(25,000)
Share of trade accounts payable paid	(1,750)	Share of trade accounts payable paid	(1,750)
Basis, end of second year	$ 72,500	Basis, end of second year	$ 72,500

■

Partnership debt is classified as either recourse or nonrecourse. **Recourse debt** is partnership debt for which the partnership or at least one of the partners is personally liable. This personal liability can exist, for example, through the operation of state law or through personal guarantees that a partner makes to the creditor. Personal liability of a party related to a partner (under attribution rules) is treated as the personal liability of the partner. **Nonrecourse debt** is debt for which no partner (or party related to a partner) is personally liable. Lenders of nonrecourse debt generally require that collateral be pledged against the loan. Upon default, the lender can claim only the collateral, not the partners' personal assets. Note that for an LLC most debt will be treated as nonrecourse debt because the LLC members typically are not personally liable for the debt.

Recourse Debt Rules Recourse debt is allocated in a manner designed to recognize the extent to which a partner bears the "economic risk of loss." Under the Regulations, recourse debt created after January 29, 1989, is shared in accordance with a **constructive liquidation scenario.**[51] Under this scenario, the following events are *deemed* to occur at the end of each taxable year of the partnership:

1. Most partnership assets (including cash) become worthless.
2. The worthless assets are sold at fair market value ($0), and losses on the deemed sales are determined.
3. These losses are allocated to the partners according to their loss sharing ratios. These losses reduce the partners' capital accounts.
4. Any partner with a (deemed) negative capital account balance is treated as contributing cash to the partnership to restore that negative balance to zero.
5. The cash deemed contributed by the partners with negative capital balances is used to pay the liabilities of the partnership.
6. The partnership is deemed to be liquidated immediately, and any remaining cash is distributed to partners with positive capital account balances.

A partner's share of partnership recourse liabilities equals the amount of the partner's cash contribution that would be used (in step 5 above) in payment of partnership recourse liabilities.

EXAMPLE 31

On January 1 of the current year, Hannah and Ian each contribute $20,000 of cash to the newly created HI Partnership. Each partner has a 50% interest in partnership capital and profits. Losses are allocated 60% to Hannah and 40% to Ian. The first year of partnership operations resulted in the following balance sheet as of December 31:

	Basis	FMV		Basis	FMV
Cash	$12,000	$12,000	Recourse payables	$30,000	$30,000
Receivables	7,000	7,000	Hannah, capital	19,500	19,500
Land and buildings	50,000	50,000	Ian, capital	19,500	19,500
	$69,000	$69,000		$69,000	$69,000

[51] See Reg. § 1.752–2. Other rules (beyond the scope of this text) apply to debt created before January 30, 1989, and between January 29, 1989, and December 28, 1991.

The recourse debt is shared in accordance with the constructive liquidation scenario. All of the partnership assets (including cash) are deemed to be worthless and sold for $0. This creates a loss of $69,000 ($12,000 + $7,000 + $50,000).

The constructive liquidation scenario results in the $69,000 loss being allocated $41,400 to Hannah and $27,600 to Ian. As a consequence, Hannah's capital account has a negative balance of $21,900, and Ian's account has a negative balance of $8,100. Each partner is deemed to contribute cash equal to these negative capital accounts, and the cash would be used to pay the recourse liabilities under the constructive liquidation scenario. Accordingly, Hannah and Ian share $21,900 and $8,100, respectively, in the recourse debt. The debt allocation percentages (73% to Hannah and 27% to Ian) are different from the partners' 60%/40% loss sharing ratios.

Note that if the partners shared losses equally, the intuitive result would arise. The $69,000 constructive liquidation loss would be allocated equally ($34,500 each) to Hannah and Ian. As a result, each partner would have a $15,000 negative capital account that would correspond to that partner's share of the partnership's recourse debt. ■

Nonrecourse Debt Rules As previously noted, most debt of an LLC will fall into the nonrecourse category. Nonrecourse debt is allocated in three stages. First, an amount of debt equal to the amount of *minimum gain* is allocated to partners who share in minimum gain. The calculation of minimum gain is complex, and its details are beyond the scope of this text. In general, minimum gain approximates the amount of nonrecourse (mortgage) liability on a property in excess of the "book" basis of the property. Generally, the "book" basis for a property item is the same as the "tax" basis, although sometimes the amounts are different. For example, the "book" basis for contributed property on the date of contribution is its fair market value at that date.

If a lender forecloses on partnership property, the result is treated as a deemed sale of the property for the mortgage balance. Gain is recognized for at least the amount of the liability in excess of the property's "book" basis—hence, minimum gain. Allocation of minimum gain among the partners should be addressed in the partnership agreement.

Second, the amount of nonrecourse debt equal to the remaining *precontribution gain* under § 704(c) is allocated to the partner who contributed the property and debt to the partnership. For this purpose, the remaining precontribution gain is the excess of the current nonrecourse debt balance on the contributed property over the current tax basis of the contributed property.[52] Note that this calculation is only relevant when the "book" and "tax" bases of the contributed property are different.

Third, any remaining nonrecourse debt generally is allocated to the partners in accordance with their profit sharing ratios.

EXAMPLE 32

Ted contributes a nondepreciable asset to the TK Partnership in exchange for a one-third interest in the capital, profits, and losses of the partnership. The asset has an adjusted tax basis to Ted and the partnership of $24,000 and a fair market value and "book" basis on the contribution date of $50,000. The asset is encumbered by a nonrecourse note (created January 1, 2010) of $35,000. Because the "book" basis exceeds the nonrecourse debt, there is no minimum gain. Under § 704(c) principles, the Regulations provide that the first $11,000 of the nonrecourse debt ($35,000 debt − $24,000 basis) is allocated to Ted. The remaining $24,000 of nonrecourse debt is allocated according to the profit sharing ratio, and Ted's share is $8,000. Therefore, Ted shares in $19,000 ($11,000 + $8,000) of the nonrecourse debt.

[52]Reg. § 1.704–3.

Ted's basis in his partnership interest is determined as follows:

Basis of contributed property	$ 24,000
Less: Liability assumed by partnership	(35,000)
Plus: Allocation of § 704(c) debt	11,000
Basis before remaining allocation	$ –0–
Plus: Allocation of remaining nonrecourse debt	8,000
Basis in partnership interest	$ 8,000

The § 704(c) allocation of nonrecourse debt prevents Ted from receiving a deemed distribution ($35,000) in excess of his basis in property he contributed ($24,000). Without this required allocation of nonrecourse debt, in some cases, a contributing partner would be required to recognize gain on a contribution of property encumbered by nonrecourse debt. ■

Other Factors Affecting Basis Calculations

The partner's basis is also affected by (1) postacquisition contributions of cash or property to the partnership; (2) postacquisition distributions of cash or property from the partnership; and (3) special calculations that are designed to allow the full deduction of percentage depletion for oil and gas wells. Postacquisition contributions of cash or property affect basis in the same manner as contributions made upon the creation of the partnership. Postacquisition distributions of cash or property reduce basis.

Figure 21.3 on the next page summarizes the rules for computing a partner's basis in a partnership interest.

EXAMPLE 33
THE BIG PICTURE

Return to the facts of *The Big Picture* on p. 21-2. Example 24 described how the income and deduction items of Beachside Properties, LLC, are allocated to Maria on her Schedule K–1. But how is Maria's basis affected by those items?

Assume that at the beginning of that tax year (Beachside's second year of operations), Maria's basis in her LLC interest was $1.6 million, including a $200,000 share of the LLC's $500,000 of nonrecourse debt. At the end of the year, Beachside had $600,000 of debt, which was again treated as nonrecourse to all the LLC members.

During the year, Maria contributes to the LLC cash of $100,000 and additional property (basis of $0 and fair market value of $50,000). On December 31, the LLC distributes $20,000 cash to her. Maria's share of Beachside's income, gain, and deductions is as described in Example 24.

Maria's basis can be calculated using the ordering rules shown in Figure 21.3. At the end of the year, Maria's basis is as follows:

Beginning basis	$1,600,000
Contributions, including increase in share of liabilities:	
Share of net increase in LLC liabilities [40% × ($600,000 – $500,000)]	40,000
Cash contribution to LLC capital	100,000
Maria's basis in noncash capital contribution	–0–
Share of LLC income items:	
Ordinary LLC income	72,000
LLC's net passive income from rental real estate	120,000
Tax-exempt income	840
Short-term capital gain	4,800
Qualified dividend income	1,600
Distributions and withdrawals:	
Capital withdrawal	(20,000)
Share of LLC deduction items:	
Charitable contribution	(2,400)
Ending basis	$1,916,840

As will be explained later in this chapter. Maria could withdraw cash from the LLC up to the amount of her basis without paying tax on the distribution.

Maria's basis does not appear on the LLC's tax return or on her Schedule K–1. All partners are responsible for maintaining their own basis calculations. ■

A partner is required to compute the adjusted basis only when necessary and thus can avoid the inconvenience of making day-to-day calculations of basis. When a partnership interest is sold, exchanged, or retired, however, the partner must compute the adjusted basis as of the date the transaction occurs. Computation of gain or loss requires an accurate calculation of the partner's adjusted basis on the transaction date.

Partner's Capital Account Analysis

As mentioned earlier in the chapter, the partner's basis is not the same as the partner's capital account. Think of the capital account as an accounting calculation of the partner's ownership in the entity.

The capital account analysis (sometimes called a "rollforward" or "reconciliation") is shown on the partner's Schedule K–1. (See Appendix B.) This calculation shows the change in the partner's capital account from the beginning to the end of the tax year. The capital account does not include the taxpayer's share of partnership debts, and it might differ from the basis calculation for other reasons as well.

On Schedule K–1, the partner's capital account analysis can be prepared using any of several methods, including the tax basis, GAAP, or the § 704(b) book method. The method selected, which is indicated on the Schedule K–1, should be the same method that was used in preparing Schedule M–2. In some cases, the partner's ending basis in the partnership interest will equal the sum of the partner's Schedule K–1 amounts for the partner's share of liabilities and the partner's ending capital account. This could happen, for example, when the partner has been in the

FIGURE 21.3 **Partner's Basis in Partnership Interest**

Basis is generally adjusted in the following order:

Initial basis. Amount paid for partnership interest, or gift or inherited basis (including share of partnership debt). Amount paid can be amount contributed to the partnership or amount paid to another partner or former partner.

\+ Partner's subsequent contributions

\+ Since interest acquired, partner's share of the partnership's

- Debt increase
- Taxable income items
- Tax-exempt income items
- Excess of depletion deductions over adjusted basis of property subject to depletion

− Partner's distributions and withdrawals

− Since interest acquired, partner's share of the partnership's

- Debt decrease
- Separately stated deductions
- Nondeductible items not chargeable to a capital account
- Special depletion deduction for oil and gas wells
- Loss items

The basis of a partner's interest can never be negative.

partnership since its inception, there have been no transfers of the partner's interest, and the capital account analysis is prepared on a tax basis.

EXAMPLE 34
THE BIG PICTURE

The last example illustrated the calculation of Maria's basis in her interest in Beachside Properties, LLC. Maria's Schedule K–1 will show her capital account rollforward from the prior year to the current year. Assume that her capital account is calculated on a tax basis and that the beginning capital account balance was $1.4 million. The reconciliation shown on Schedule K–1 will be as follows:

Beginning capital account	$1,400,000
Capital contributed during the year	100,000
Current-year increase (decrease)	196,840
Withdrawals and distributions	(20,000)
Ending capital account	$1,676,840

Although this will not always be the case, Maria's ending capital account balance differs from her ending basis by the amount of her $240,000 share of the LLC's nonrecourse debt. ■

LOSS LIMITATIONS

LO.9

Describe the limitations on deducting partnership losses.

Partnership losses flow through to the partners for use on their income tax returns. However, the amount and nature of the losses allowed in a partner's tax computations may be limited. When limitations apply, all or a portion of the losses are held in suspension until a triggering event occurs. Only then can the losses be used to determine the partner's tax liability. No time limit is imposed on such carryforwards of losses.

Three different limitations may apply to partnership losses that are passed through to a partner:

- The first is the overall limitation contained in § 704 (d). This limitation allows the deduction of losses only to the extent the partner has adjusted basis for the partnership interest. Recall that the partner's basis is not the same as the capital account shown on the partner's Schedule K–1.
- Losses that are deductible under the overall limitation may then be subject to the at-risk limitation of § 465. Losses are deductible under this provision only to the extent the partner is at risk for the partnership interest.
- Any losses that survive this second limitation may be subject to a third limitation, the passive loss rules of § 469.

Only losses that make it through all these applicable limitations are eligible to be deducted on the partner's tax return.

EXAMPLE 35

Megan is a partner in a partnership that does not invest in real estate. On January 1, 2011, Megan's adjusted basis for her partnership interest is $50,000, and her at-risk amount is $35,000. Her share of losses from the partnership for 2011 is $60,000, all of which is passive. She has one other passive income-producing investment that produced $25,000 of passive income during 2011.

Megan will be able to deduct $25,000 of partnership losses on her Form 1040 for 2011. Her deductible loss is calculated as follows:

Applicable Provision	Deductible Loss	Suspended Loss
§ 704(d) overall limitation	$50,000	$10,000
§ 465 at-risk limitation	35,000	15,000
§ 469 passive loss limitation	25,000	10,000

Megan can deduct only $50,000 under the overall limitation. Of this $50,000, only $35,000 is deductible under the at-risk limitation. Under the passive loss limitation, passive losses can be deducted only against passive income. Thus, Megan can deduct only $25,000 on her return in 2011. ■

Overall Limitation

A partner may deduct losses flowing through from the partnership only to the extent of the partner's adjusted basis in the partnership. A partner's adjusted basis in the partnership is determined at the end of the partnership's taxable year. It is adjusted for distributions and any partnership gains during the year, but it is determined before considering any losses for the year.

Losses that cannot be deducted because of this rule are suspended and carried forward (never back) for use against future increases in the partner's adjusted basis. Such increases might result from additional capital contributions, from sharing in additional partnership debt, or from future partnership income.

EXAMPLE 36

Courtney and Daniel do business as the CD Partnership, sharing profits and losses equally. All parties use the calendar year. At the start of the current year, the basis of Courtney's partnership interest is $25,000. The partnership sustains an operating loss of $80,000 in the current year. For the current year, only $25,000 of Courtney's $40,000 allocable share of the partnership loss can be deducted under the overall limitation. As a result, the basis of Courtney's partnership interest is zero as of January 1 of the following year, and she must carry forward the remaining $15,000 of partnership losses. ■

EXAMPLE 37

Assume the same facts as in Example 36, and that the partnership earns a profit of $70,000 for the next calendar year. Courtney reports net partnership income of $20,000 ($35,000 distributive share of income − the $15,000 carryforward loss). The basis of Courtney's partnership interest becomes $20,000. ■

At-Risk Limitation

Under the at-risk rules, the partnership losses from business and income-producing activities that individual partners and closely held C corporation partners can deduct are limited to amounts that are economically invested in the partnership. Invested amounts include cash and the adjusted basis of property contributed by the partner and the partner's share of partnership earnings that has not been withdrawn.[53] A closely held C corporation exists when five or fewer individuals own more than 50 percent of the entity's stock under appropriate attribution and ownership rules.

When some or all of the partners are personally liable for partnership recourse debt, that debt is included in the adjusted basis of those partners. Usually, those partners also include the debt in their amount at risk.

No partner, however, carries any financial risk on nonrecourse debt. Therefore, as a general rule, partners cannot include nonrecourse debt in their amount at risk even though that debt is included in the adjusted basis of their partnership interest. In many cases, however, an exception to this general rule applies. Real estate nonrecourse financing provided by a bank, retirement plan, or similar party, or by a Federal, state, or local government generally is deemed to be at risk.[54] Such debt is termed **qualified nonrecourse debt**. In summary, although the general rule provides that nonrecourse debt is not at risk, the overriding exception may provide that it is deemed to be at risk.

When determining a partner's loss deduction, the overall limitation rule is invoked first. That is, the deduction is limited to the partner's outside basis at the end of the partnership year. Then, the at-risk provisions are applied to see if the

[53] § 465(a).

[54] § 465(b)(6).

remaining loss is still deductible. Suspended losses are carried forward until a partner has a sufficient amount at risk in the activity to absorb them.[55]

EXAMPLE 38

Kelly invests $5,000 in the Kelly Green Limited Partnership as a 5% general partner. Shortly thereafter, the partnership acquires the master recording of a well-known vocalist for $250,000 ($50,000 from the partnership and $200,000 secured from a local bank by means of a *recourse* mortgage). Assume Kelly's share of the recourse debt is $10,000, and her basis in her partnership interest is $15,000 ($5,000 cash investment + $10,000 debt share). Since the debt is recourse, Kelly's at-risk amount is also $15,000. Kelly's share of partnership losses in the first year of operations is $11,000. She is entitled to deduct the full $11,000 of partnership losses under both the overall and the at-risk limitations because this amount is less than both her outside basis and at-risk amount.

If, instead, the bank loan had been nonrecourse, Kelly would be able to deduct only $5,000 of the flow-through loss. The amount she has at risk in the partnership does not include the nonrecourse debt. (The debt does not relate to real estate so it is not qualified nonrecourse debt.) ■

Passive Activity Rules

A partnership loss share may be disallowed under the passive activity rules. These rules apply to partners who are individuals, estates, trusts, closely held C corporations, or personal service corporations. As discussed in Chapter 11, the rules require the partners to separate their activities into three groups:

- *Active.* Earned income, such as salary and wages; income or loss from a trade or business in which the partner materially participates; and guaranteed payments received by the partner for services.
- *Portfolio.* Annuity income, interest, dividends, guaranteed payments from a partnership for interest on capital, royalties not derived in the ordinary course of a trade or business, and gains and losses from disposal of investment assets.
- *Passive.* Income from a trade or business activity in which the partner does not materially participate on a regular, continuous, and substantial basis, or income from many rental activities.[56]

Material participation in an activity is determined annually. The burden is on the partner to prove material participation. The IRS has provided a number of objective tests for determining material participation. These tests require the partner to have substantial involvement in daily operations of the activity. Thus, a Maine vacation resort operator investing in a California grape farm or an electrical engineer employed in Virginia investing in an Iowa corn and hog farm may have difficulty proving material participation in the activities. By default, a partner treated as a limited partner is typically considered *not* to materially participate in partnership activities.[57]

Rent income from real or personal property generally is passive income, regardless of the partner's level of participation. Exceptions are made for rent income from activities where substantial services are provided (e.g., certain developers, resorts); from hotels, motels, and other transient lodging; from short-term equipment rentals; and from certain developed real estate. In addition, rental real estate is not treated as a passive activity for a person who qualifies as a real estate professional.

Usually, passive activity losses can only offset passive activity income.[58] In determining the net passive activity loss for a year, losses and income from all passive activities are aggregated. The amount of suspended losses carried forward from a particular activity is determined by the ratio of the net loss from that activity to the aggregate net loss from all passive activities for the year. A special rule for rental real estate (discussed in the following section) allows a limited $25,000 offset against nonpassive income.[59]

[55] § 465(a)(2).
[56] §§ 469(c)(1) and (2).
[57] § 469(h)(2).
[58] § 469(a)(1).
[59] § 469(i).

A partner making a taxable disposition of an entire interest in a passive activity takes a full deduction for suspended passive activity losses from that activity in the year of disposal.[60] Suspended losses are deductible against income in the following order: income or gain from the passive activity, net income or gain from all passive activities, and other income. When a passive activity is transferred in a primarily nontaxable exchange (e.g., a like-kind exchange or contribution to a partnership), suspended losses are deductible only to the extent of gains recognized on the transfer. Remaining losses are deducted on disposal of the activity received in the exchange.

EXAMPLE 39

Jamie has several investments in passive activities that generate aggregate losses of $10,000 in the current year. One of her long-time friends, Sarah, an entrepreneur in the women's apparel business, is interested in opening a new apparel store in a nearby community. Jamie is willing to finance a substantial part of the expansion but does not want to get involved with day-to-day operations. Jamie also wants to limit any possible loss to her initial investment.

Jamie and Sarah decide to form a limited liability limited partnership, which will own the new store. Sarah will be the general partner, and Jamie will be a limited partner. Jamie invests $100,000, and Sarah invests $50,000 and provides managerial skills and know-how. Each has a 50% interest in profits and losses. In the first year of operations, the store generates a profit of $30,000. Because Jamie's share of the profit ($15,000) is passive activity income, it can be fully utilized against her passive activity losses from other investments. Thus, Jamie's share of the apparel store profits enables her to obtain a full deduction of her $10,000 of passive activity losses. ■

EXAMPLE 40

Assume the same facts as in Example 39, except that the entity generates a loss of $30,000. Jamie's $15,000 share of the loss is treated as a passive loss and is suspended until such time as she has offsetting passive income. Sarah's loss is an active loss that is deductible if it otherwise meets the §§ 704(d) and 465 loss limitations. ■

Rental Real Estate Losses

In any one year, individuals can offset up to $25,000 of passive losses from rental real estate against active and portfolio income. The $25,000 maximum is reduced by 50 percent of the difference between the taxpayer's modified AGI and $100,000. Thus, when the taxpayer's modified AGI reaches $150,000, the offset is eliminated.

The offset is available to those who actively (rather than materially) participate in rental real estate activities. Active participation is an easier test to meet. Unlike material participation, it does not require regular, continuous, and substantial involvement with the activity. However, the taxpayer must own at least 10 percent of the fair market value of all interests in the rental property and either contribute to the activity's management decisions in a significant and bona fide way or actively participate in arranging for others to make such decisions.

EXAMPLE 41

José invests $10,000 cash in the Sparrow Limited Partnership in the current year for a 10% limited interest in capital and profits. Shortly thereafter, the partnership purchases rental real estate subject to a qualified nonrecourse mortgage of $120,000 obtained from a commercial bank. José engages in no other passive activities during the current year.

José does not participate in any of Sparrow's activities. His share of losses from Sparrow's first year of operations is $27,000. His modified AGI before considering the loss is $60,000. Before considering the loss, José's basis in the partnership interest is $22,000 [$10,000 cash + (10% × $120,000 debt)], and his loss deduction is limited to this amount under the overall limitation. The debt is included in José's amount at risk because it is qualified nonrecourse financing. It may seem that José should be

[60] § 469(g).

allowed to deduct the $22,000 loss share from portfolio or active income under the rental real estate exception to the passive loss rules. However, the loss may not be offset against this income because José is not an active participant in the partnership. ■

21.4 Transactions between Partners and Partnerships

LO.10

Describe the treatment of transactions between a partner and the partnership.

Many types of transactions occur between a partnership and one of its partners. The partner may contribute property to the partnership, perform services for the partnership, or receive distributions from the partnership. The partner may borrow money from or lend money to the partnership. Property may be bought and sold between the partner and the partnership. Several of these transactions were discussed earlier in the chapter. The remaining types of partner-partnership transactions are the focus of this section.

GUARANTEED PAYMENTS

If a partnership makes a payment to a partner, the payment may be a draw against the partner's share of partnership income; a return of some or all of the partner's original capital contribution; or a guaranteed payment, among other treatments. A **guaranteed payment** is a payment for services performed by the partner or for the use of the partner's capital. The payment may not be determined by reference to partnership income. Guaranteed payments are usually expressed as a fixed-dollar amount or as a percentage of capital that the partner has invested in the partnership. Whether the partnership deducts or capitalizes the guaranteed payment depends on the nature of the payment.

EXAMPLE 42

David, Derek, and Danielle formed the accrual basis DDD Partnership in 2011. The partnership and each of the partners are calendar year taxpayers. According to the partnership agreement, David is to manage the partnership and receive a $21,000 distribution from the entity every year, payable in 12 monthly installments. Derek is to receive an amount that is equal to 18% of his capital account, as it is computed by the firm's accountant at the beginning of the year, payable in 12 monthly installments. Danielle is the partnership's advertising specialist. She withdraws approximately 4% of the partnership's net income for her personal use. David and Derek receive guaranteed payments from the partnership, but Danielle does not. ■

Guaranteed payments resemble the salary or interest payments of other businesses.[61] Deductible guaranteed payments, like other deductible expenses of a partnership, can create an ordinary loss for the entity. If the partnership distributes appreciated property to pay the guaranteed payment, the partnership must recognize gain on the transfer.[62]

A partner who receives guaranteed payments during a partnership year must include the payments in income as if they were received on the last day of the partnership year. Guaranteed payments are always taxable as ordinary income to the recipient partner. The partner's guaranteed payment is reported on Schedule K–1. The partner uses this information (in lieu of a Form W–2 or 1099) to report the income on the partner's tax return.

EXAMPLE 43

Continue with the situation introduced in Example 42. For calendar year 2011, David receives the $21,000 as provided by the partnership agreement, Derek's guaranteed payment for 2011 is $17,000, and Danielle withdraws $20,000. Before considering these amounts, the partnership's ordinary income for 2011 is $650,000.

[61] § 707(c).

[62] Rev.Rul. 2007–40, 2007–1 C.B. 1426.

The partnership can deduct its payments to David and Derek, so the final amount of its 2011 ordinary income is $612,000 ($650,000 − $21,000 − $17,000). Thus, each of the equal partners is allocated $204,000 of ordinary partnership income for their 2011 individual income tax returns ($612,000 ÷ 3). In addition, David reports the $21,000 guaranteed payment income on his 2011 tax return, and Derek similarly includes the $17,000 guaranteed payment on his 2011 income. Danielle's partnership draw is deemed to have come from her allocated $204,000 (or from the accumulated partnership income that was taxed in prior years) and is not taxed separately to her. Danielle's basis, though, is reduced by the $20,000 distribution. ■

EXAMPLE 44

Assume the same facts as in Example 43, except that the partnership has a "natural business year" that ends on March 31, 2012. The total amount of the guaranteed payments is taxable to the partners on that date. Thus, even though David receives 9 of his 12 payments for fiscal 2012 in calendar 2011, all of his guaranteed payments are taxable to him in 2012. Similarly, all of Derek's guaranteed payments are taxable to him in 2012 and not when they are received. The deduction for, and the gross income from, guaranteed payments are allowed on the same date that all of the other income and expense items relative to the partnership are allocated to the partners (on the last day of the entity's tax year). ■

SELF-EMPLOYMENT TAX OF PARTNERS

A partner usually does not qualify as an employee for tax purposes. Thus, a partner receiving guaranteed payments is not regarded as an employee of the partnership for purposes of withholding taxes. Moreover, because a partner is not an employee, the partnership cannot deduct its payments for any of a partner's fringe benefits.

Certain partnership income reported by a partner who is an individual taxpayer may be considered "net earnings from self-employment" and is subject to self-employment (SE) tax. Section 1402 provides that SE income includes the partner's distributive share of income from a partnership's trade or business, whether or not that income is distributed. This provision applies to income allocated to a "general partner" and income earned by a "limited partner" that is in the nature of compensation for services performed for or on behalf of the partnership.[63]

For a general partner, both the partner's allocable share of income and any guaranteed payments for services are subject to the SE tax. For a limited partner, any guaranteed payment for services rendered to the partnership is subject to the SE tax. Recall that an LLC member often is treated similarly to a limited partner.

Proposed Regulations provide guidance regarding how to determine whether a partner or LLC member should be treated as a general partner or a limited partner. These regulations provide, in general, that a partner or LLC member will be treated as a general partner if:

- the partner has personal liability for partnership debts by virtue of status as a partner,
- the partner can enter into contractual relationships on behalf of the partnership, or
- the partner works more than 500 hours in the partnership's trade or business during the tax year.

If the partner is treated as a general partner solely because of the "hours worked" limitation, the interest can still be treated as a limited interest (for purposes of classifying the partner's distributive share of income) if there is at least one other limited partner with identical rights.

Because of the proposed status of these Regulations, taxpayers are not required to comply with them or disclose any noncompliance. These Regulations are highly

[63]§§ 1402(a) and (a)(13). See also Prop.Reg. § 1.1402(a)–2(h).

controversial and have existed since 1997 without being finalized. At this point, however, they are the only guidance available.

EXAMPLE 45
THE BIG PICTURE

Return to the facts of *The Big Picture* on p. 21-2. Assume that Josh was elected the managing member of Beachside Properties, LLC; he has the sole authority to contract for the LLC and works 1,000 hours per year in the business. Maria works 1,000 hours per year in the café. After surrendering his land to Beachside, Kyle has generally not been involved in the LLC's operations.

Kyle and Josh each receive a guaranteed payment of $5,000 per month from the LLC. Josh's payment is for services, and Kyle's is for use of his $2 million of land. Maria receives a guaranteed payment of $10,000 per month, of which $5,000 is for services and $5,000 is for the use of her $2 million of capital.

If Beachside follows the Proposed Regulations, the members' distributive shares and guaranteed payments will be treated as follow:

	Distributive Share (Proposed Regulations)	Guaranteed Payments [§ 1402(a)(13)]
Kyle	Not SE income	Not SE income (payment is for capital; not services)
Maria	Not SE income*	$5,000 SE income (services) and $5,000 not SE income (capital)
Josh	SE income	SE income (payment is for services to the LLC)

*Under the Proposed Regulations, Maria's distributive share is not SE income for two reasons: (1) she is a general partner by virtue of working more than 500 hours per year; and (2) Kyle, a "limited partner," has an interest with identical rights to Maria's. ■

OTHER TRANSACTIONS BETWEEN PARTNERS AND PARTNERSHIPS

Certain transactions between a partner and the partnership are treated as if the partner were an outsider, dealing with the partnership at arm's length.[64] Loan transactions, rental payments, and sales of property between the partner and the partnership are treated in this manner. In addition, payments for services are generally treated this way when the services are short-term technical services that the partner also provides for parties other than the partnership.

EXAMPLE 46

Chad, a one-third partner in the CDE Partnership, owns a tract of land that the partnership wishes to purchase. The land has a fair market value of $30,000 and an adjusted basis to Chad of $17,000. If Chad sells the land to the partnership, he recognizes a $13,000 gain on the sale, and the partnership takes a $30,000 cost basis in the land. If the land has a fair market value of $10,000 on the sale date, Chad recognizes a $7,000 loss. ■

The time for deducting a payment by an accrual basis partnership to a cash basis service partner depends upon whether the amount is a guaranteed payment or a payment to a partner who is treated as an outsider. A guaranteed payment is includible in the partner's income on the last day of the partnership year when it is properly accrued by the partnership, even though the payment may not be made to the partner until the next taxable year. Conversely, the *partner's* method of accounting controls the timing of deduction if the payment is treated as made to an outsider. This is because a deduction cannot be claimed for such amounts until the recipient partner is required to include the amount in income under the partner's

[64] § 707(a).

method of accounting.[65] Thus, a partnership cannot claim a deduction until it actually makes the payment to the cash basis partner, but it could accrue and deduct a payment due to an accrual basis partner even if payment was not yet made.

EXAMPLE 47

Rachel, a cash basis taxpayer, is a partner in the accrual basis RTC Partnership. On December 31, 2011, the partnership accrues but does not pay $10,000 for deductible services that Rachel performed for the partnership during the year. Both Rachel and the partnership are calendar year taxpayers.

If the $10,000 accrual is a guaranteed payment, the partnership deducts the $10,000 in its calendar year ended December 31, 2011, and Rachel includes the $10,000 in her income for the 2011 calendar year. The fact that Rachel is a cash basis taxpayer and does not actually receive the cash in 2011 is irrelevant.

If the payment is classified as a payment to an outsider, the partnership cannot deduct the payment until Rachel actually receives the cash. If, for example, Rachel performs janitorial services (i.e., not in her capacity as a partner) and receives the cash on March 25, 2012, the partnership deducts the payment and Rachel recognizes the income on that date. ■

Sales of Property

Certain sales of property fall under special rules. No loss is recognized on a sale of property between a person and a partnership when the person owns, directly or indirectly, more than 50 percent of partnership capital or profits.[66] The disallowed loss may not vanish entirely, however. If the transferee eventually sells the property at a gain, the disallowed loss reduces the gain that the transferee would otherwise recognize.

EXAMPLE 48

Blake sells land (adjusted basis $30,000; fair market value, $45,000) to a partnership in which he controls a 60% capital interest. The partnership pays him only $20,000 for the land. Blake cannot deduct his $10,000 realized loss. The sale apparently was not at arm's length, but the taxpayer's intentions are irrelevant. Blake and the partnership are related parties, and the loss is disallowed.

When the partnership sells the land to an outsider at a later date, it receives a sales price of $44,000. The partnership can offset the recognition of its $24,000 realized gain on the subsequent sale ($44,000 sales proceeds – $20,000 adjusted basis) by the amount of the $10,000 prior disallowed loss ($20,000 – $30,000). Thus, the partnership recognizes a $14,000 gain on its sale of the land. ■

Using a similar rationale, any gain that is realized on a sale or exchange between a partner and a partnership in which the partner controls a capital or profits interest of more than 50 percent must be recognized as ordinary income, unless the asset is a capital asset to both the seller and the purchaser.[67]

EXAMPLE 49

Kristin purchases some land (adjusted basis, $30,000; fair market value, $45,000) for $45,000 from a partnership in which she controls a 90% profits interest. The land was a capital asset to the partnership. If Kristin holds the land as a capital asset, the partnership recognizes a $15,000 capital gain. However, if Kristin is a land developer and the property is not a capital asset to her, the partnership must recognize $15,000 of ordinary income from the sale, even though the property was a capital asset to the partnership. ■

Concept Summary 21.4 reviews partner-partnership transactions.

[65] § 267(a)(2).
[66] § 707(b).
[67] § 707(b)(2).

CONCEPT SUMMARY 21.4

Partner-Partnership Transactions

1. Partners can transact business with their partnerships in a nonpartner capacity. These transactions include the sale and exchange of property, rentals, loans of funds, etc.
2. A payment to a partner may be classified as a guaranteed payment if it is for services or use of the partner's capital and is not based on partnership income. A guaranteed payment may be deductible by the partnership and is included in the partner's income on the last day of the partnership's tax year.
3. Partners may be subject to self-employment tax on their distributive shares of partnership income if they are treated as general partners.
4. A partner may be subject to self-employment tax on guaranteed payments if the payments are for services, regardless of whether the partner is a general or a limited partner.
5. A payment to a partner may be treated as being to an outside (though related) party. Such a payment is deductible or capitalizable by the partnership at the time the partner must include the amount in income under his or her method of accounting.
6. Guaranteed payments and payments to a partner that are treated as being to an outside party are only deductible if the underlying reason for the payment constitutes an ordinary and necessary (rather than capitalizable) business expense.
7. Losses are disallowed between a partner or related party and a partnership when the partner or related party owns more than a 50% interest in the partnership's capital or profits.
8. When there is income from a related-party sale, it is treated as ordinary income if the property is not a capital asset to both the transferor and the transferee.

21.5 Distributions from the Partnership

The tax treatment of distributions from a partnership to a partner was introduced earlier in the context of routine withdrawals (or "draws") and cash distributions from a continuing partnership to a continuing partner. This section will expand that discussion by examining in greater detail the effect of nonliquidating distributions made during the normal operations of the partnership. In addition, distributions to partners in complete liquidation of their ownership interests and sales of partnership interests are discussed.

A **nonliquidating distribution** is any distribution from a continuing partnership to a continuing partner—that is, any distribution that is not a liquidating distribution. There are two types of nonliquidating distributions: draws or partial liquidations. A *draw* is a distribution of a partner's share of current or accumulated partnership profits that have been taxed to the partner in current or prior taxable years of the partnership. A *partial liquidation* is a distribution that reduces the partner's interest in partnership capital but does not liquidate the partner's entire interest in the partnership. The distinction between the two types of *nonliquidating* distributions is largely semantic, as the basic tax treatment typically does not differ.

EXAMPLE 50

Kate joins the calendar year KLM Partnership on January 1, 2011, by contributing $40,000 of cash to the partnership in exchange for a one-third interest in partnership capital, profits, and losses. Her distributive share of partnership income for the year is $25,000. If the partnership distributes $65,000 ($25,000 share of partnership profits + $40,000 initial capital contribution) to Kate on December 31, 2011, the distribution is a nonliquidating distribution as long as Kate continues to be a partner in the partnership. This is true even though Kate receives her share of profits plus her entire investment in the partnership. In this case, $25,000 is considered a draw, and the remaining $40,000 is a partial liquidation of Kate's interest. ■

A distribution is generally tax deferred. However, in certain circumstances the partner may recognize capital gain (or loss) and ordinary income (or loss) when a distribution is received from the partnership.

Finally, a distribution may be either proportionate or disproportionate. In a **proportionate distribution**, a partner receives the appropriate share of certain ordinary income-producing assets of the partnership. A **disproportionate distribution** occurs when the distribution increases or decreases the distributee partner's interest in certain ordinary income-producing assets. The tax treatment of disproportionate distributions is very complex and is beyond the scope of this discussion.

LO.11

Determine the tax treatment of proportionate nonliquidating distributions from a partnership to a partner and the tax treatment of proportionate distributions that liquidate a partnership.

PROPORTIONATE NONLIQUIDATING DISTRIBUTIONS

In general, neither the partner nor the partnership recognizes gain or loss when a nonliquidating distribution occurs.[68] The partner usually takes a carryover basis in the assets distributed.[69] The distributee partner's outside basis is reduced (but not below zero) by the amount of cash and the adjusted basis of property distributed.[70] As the following example illustrates, a distribution does not change a partner's overall economic position.

EXAMPLE 51

Steven is a one-fourth partner in the JP Partnership. On December 31 of the current year, his basis in his partnership interest is $40,000. The fair market value of the interest is $70,000. The partnership distributes $25,000 of cash to him on that date. The distribution is not taxable to Steven or the partnership. The distribution reduces Steven's adjusted basis in the partnership to $15,000 ($40,000 – $25,000), and the fair market value of his partnership interest is, arguably, reduced to $45,000 ($70,000 – $25,000). ■

EXAMPLE 52

Assume the same facts as in Example 51, except that the partnership distributes both the $25,000 cash and land with an adjusted basis to the partnership of $13,000 and a fair market value of $30,000 on the date of distribution. The distribution is not taxable to Steven or the partnership. Steven reduces his basis in the partnership to $2,000 [$40,000 – ($25,000 + $13,000)] and takes a carryover basis of $13,000 in the land. The fair market value of Steven's remaining interest in the partnership is, arguably, reduced to $15,000 [$70,000 – ($25,000 + $30,000)].

If Steven had sold his partnership interest for $70,000 rather than receiving the distribution, he would have realized and recognized gain of $30,000 ($70,000 selling price – $40,000 outside basis). Because he has not recognized any gain or loss on the distribution of cash and land, he should still have the $30,000 of deferred gain to recognize at some point in the future. This is exactly what will happen. If Steven sells the land and remaining partnership interest on January 1 of the next year (the day after the distribution), he realizes and recognizes gains of $17,000 ($30,000 – $13,000) on the land and $13,000 ($15,000 – $2,000) on the partnership interest. These gains total $30,000, which is the amount of the original deferred gain. ■

Note the difference between the tax theory governing distributions from C corporations and partnerships. In a C corporation, a distribution from current or accumulated income (earnings and profits) is taxable as a dividend to the shareholder, and the corporation does not receive a deduction for the amount distributed. This is an example of corporate income being subject to double taxation. In a partnership, a distribution from current or accumulated profits is not taxable because Congress has decided that partnership income should be subject to only a single level of taxation. Because a partner pays taxes when the share of income is earned by the partnership, this income is not taxed again when distributed.

These results make sense under the entity and aggregate concepts. The entity concept is applicable to corporate dividends, so any amount paid as a dividend is

68 §§ 731(a) and (b).

69 § 732(a)(1).

70 § 733.

treated as a transfer by the corporate entity to the shareholder and is taxed accordingly. Under the aggregate theory, though, a partner receiving a distribution of partnership income is treated as merely receiving something already owned. Whether the partner chooses to leave the income in the partnership or receive it in a distribution makes no difference.

Cash Distributions

Gain and Loss Recognition A proportionate nonliquidating distribution of cash is taxable to the partner if the distributed cash exceeds the outside basis of his or her interest in the partnership.[71] In a nonliquidating distribution, losses are not recognized by the partner.

EXAMPLE 53

Samantha is a one-third partner in the SMP Partnership. Her basis in this ownership interest is $50,000 on December 31, 2011, after accounting for the calendar year partnership's 2011 operations and for her 2011 capital contributions. On December 31, 2011, the partnership distributes $60,000 of cash to Samantha. She recognizes a $10,000 gain from this distribution ($60,000 cash received − $50,000 basis in her partnership interest). Most likely, this gain is taxed as a capital gain.[72] ■

While distributions *from* current and accumulated earnings are taxed differently to shareholders and partners, cash distributions *in excess* of accumulated profits are taxed similarly for corporate shareholders and partners in partnerships. Both shareholders and partners are allowed to recover the cumulative capital invested in the entity tax-free.

Liability Reduction Treated as Cash Distribution Recall from earlier in the chapter that the reduction of a partner's share of partnership debt is treated as a distribution of cash from the partnership to the partner. A reduction of a partner's share of partnership debt, then, first reduces the partner's basis in the partnership. Any reduction of a share of debt in excess of a partner's basis in the partnership is taxable to the partner as a gain.

EXAMPLE 54

Returning to the facts of Example 53, assume that Samantha's $50,000 basis in her partnership interest included a $60,000 share of partnership liabilities. If the partnership repays all of its liabilities, Samantha is treated as receiving a $60,000 distribution from the partnership. The first $50,000 of this distribution reduces her basis to $0. The last $10,000 distributed creates a taxable gain to her of $10,000. ■

Marketable Security Distributions Treated as Cash A distribution of marketable securities can also be treated as a distribution of cash. Determining the treatment of such distributions is complicated because several exceptions may apply and the basis in the distributed stock must be calculated. Discussion of such distributions is beyond the scope of this chapter.

Property Distributions

In general, a distributee partner does not recognize gain from a property distribution. If the basis of property distributed by a partnership exceeds the partner's basis in the partnership interest, the distributed asset takes a substituted basis. This ensures that the partner does not receive asset basis that is not "paid for."

[71] § 731(a)(1).

[72] § 731(a). If the partnership holds any "hot assets," however, Samantha will probably recognize some ordinary income. See § 751(b) and the related discussion of ordinary income ("hot") assets later in this chapter.

EXAMPLE 55

Amanda has a $50,000 basis in her partnership interest. The partnership distributes land it owns with a basis and a fair market value of $60,000. Amanda does not recognize any gain on this distribution because it is a distribution of property other than cash. However, Amanda should not be allowed to take a carryover basis of $60,000 in the land, when the basis in her partnership interest is only $50,000. Therefore, Amanda takes a substituted basis of $50,000 in the land. Her basis in her partnership interest is reduced by the basis she takes in the asset received, or $50,000. Therefore, Amanda has a $50,000 basis in the land and a $0 basis in her partnership interest, and she recognizes no gain on this distribution. ■

Ordering Rules

When the inside basis of the distributed assets exceeds the distributee partner's outside basis, the assets are deemed distributed in the following order:

- Cash is distributed first.
- Unrealized receivables and inventory are distributed second.
- All other assets are distributed last.

Unrealized receivables are receivables that have a value to the partnership, but for which the related income has not yet been realized or recognized under the partnership's method of accounting. The term *unrealized receivables* applies only to amounts that will ultimately be realized and recognized as ordinary income. If the partnership uses the cash method of accounting, trade receivables from services or sales are unrealized receivables. If the partnership uses the accrual method, income has already been recognized, so trade receivables are not unrealized receivables. Unrealized receivables include receivables from sales of ordinary income property and rights to payments for services. For some purposes, unrealized receivables also include depreciation recapture income that would arise if the partnership sold its depreciable assets. Installment gains are unrealized receivables if the gain will be taxed as ordinary income when realized.

Inventory, for purposes of these ordering rules, includes any partnership assets except cash, capital, or § 1231 assets. For example, all accounts receivable are considered to be inventory, although only cash basis receivables are "unrealized receivables."

Because the partner typically does not recognize a gain from a *property* distribution, the Code provides that the partner's basis for property received cannot exceed the partner's basis in the partnership interest immediately before the distribution. For each level of asset distribution, the relevant adjustments are made to the partner's basis in the interest. In other words, after a cash distribution, the partner's basis in the interest is recomputed before determining the effect of a distribution of unrealized receivables or inventory. The basis is recomputed again before determining the effect of a distribution of other assets. If the remaining outside basis at the end of any step is insufficient to cover the entire inside basis of the assets in the next step, that remaining outside basis is allocated among the assets within that class.[73]

EXAMPLE 56

Lindsey has a $48,000 basis in her partnership interest. On October 10, 2011, the partnership distributes to her cash of $12,000, cash basis receivables with an inside basis of $0 and a fair market value of $10,000, and a parcel of land with a basis to the partnership of $60,000 and a fair market value of $100,000. Lindsey has realized gain on the distribution of $74,000 ($12,000 + $10,000 + $100,000 – $48,000). None of that gain is recognized, however, because the $12,000 cash distribution does not exceed her $48,000 adjusted basis for her partnership interest. In determining the basis effects of the distribution, the cash is treated as being distributed first, reducing Lindsey's adjusted basis to $36,000 ($48,000 – $12,000). The receivables are distributed next, taking a $0 carryover basis to Lindsey. Her adjusted basis remains at $36,000. The land is

[73] § 732.

distributed last, taking a substituted basis of $36,000 and reducing her adjusted basis for her partnership interest to $0. ■

When more than one asset in a particular class is distributed, special rules may apply. Usually, if the partner's remaining adjusted basis for the partnership interest is less than the partnership's adjusted basis for the distributed assets in the particular class, the partner's adjusted basis for each distributed asset is computed by following three steps:

Step 1. Each distributed asset within the class initially takes a carryover basis.

Step 2. If necessary, this carryover basis for each of these assets is reduced in proportion to their respective amounts of unrealized depreciation (amount that carryover basis is greater than fair market value). Under no circumstances, however, can the basis of any asset be reduced below its fair market value in step 2.

Step 3. Any remaining decrease in basis is allocated among all the distributed assets in the class in proportion to their respective adjusted bases (as determined in step 2).

EXAMPLE 57

Assume the same facts as in Example 56, except that Lindsey receives two parcels of land, rather than a single parcel. The partnership's basis for the parcels is $15,000 for Parcel 1 and $45,000 for Parcel 2. Each parcel has a fair market value of $30,000. Lindsey has a realized gain on the distribution of $34,000 ($12,000 + $10,000 + $60,000 – $48,000). None of that gain is recognized, however, because the $12,000 cash distribution does not exceed her $48,000 adjusted basis.

As in Example 56, Lindsey takes a $12,000 basis for the cash and a $0 carryover basis for the receivables and has a $36,000 adjusted basis for her partnership interest after these two items are distributed. Because two parcels of land are distributed, and because Lindsey's remaining $36,000 adjusted basis for her partnership interest is less than the partnership's $60,000 total basis for the two parcels of land, Lindsey's adjusted basis for each parcel of land is computed by following these steps:

Step 1. She initially takes a carryover basis of $15,000 for Parcel 1 and $45,000 for Parcel 2.

Step 2. She reduces the basis of Parcel 2 to its lower fair market value of $30,000. The basis for Parcel 1 is not adjusted in this step because Parcel 1 has a fair market value greater than its basis.

Step 3. The remaining $9,000 difference between her $36,000 basis for the partnership interest and the $45,000 ($15,000 + $30,000) basis for the land parcels after step 2 is allocated to the two parcels in proportion to their respective bases (as computed in step 2). Therefore, the amount of the step 3 basis reduction allocated to Parcel 1 is:

$$\$9{,}000 \times \frac{\$15{,}000}{\$45{,}000} = \$3{,}000$$

Lindsey's basis for Parcel 1 is $12,000 ($15,000 – $3,000). The amount of the step 3 basis reduction allocated to Parcel 2 is:

$$\$9{,}000 \times \frac{\$30{,}000}{\$45{,}000} = \$6{,}000$$

Lindsey's basis for Parcel 2 is $24,000 ($30,000 – $6,000). ■

EXAMPLE 58

Assume the same facts as in Example 57, and that Lindsey sells both parcels of land early in 2012 for their fair market values, receiving proceeds of $60,000 ($30,000 + $30,000). She also collects $10,000 from the cash basis receivables. Now she recognizes all of the $34,000 gain that she deferred upon receiving the property from the partnership [$60,000 amount realized – $36,000 basis for the two parcels ($12,000 + $24,000) + $10,000 collected – $0 basis for the receivables]. ■

CONCEPT SUMMARY 21.5

Proportionate Nonliquidating Distributions (General Rules)

1. In general, neither the distributee partner nor the partnership recognizes any gain or loss on a proportionate nonliquidating distribution. If cash distributed exceeds the distributee partner's outside basis, however, gain is recognized. Property distributions generally do not result in gain recognition.
2. The distributee partner usually takes the same basis in the distributed property that the property had to the partnership (carryover basis). However, where the inside basis of distributed property exceeds the partner's outside basis, the basis assigned to the distributed property cannot exceed that outside basis (substituted basis).
3. Gain recognized by the distributee partner on a proportionate nonliquidating distribution is capital in nature.
4. Loss is never recognized on a proportionate nonliquidating distribution.

Calculations

1. Partner's outside basis. ________
2. Less: Cash distributed to partner. ________
3. Gain recognized by partner (excess of Line 2 over Line 1). ________
4. Partner's remaining outside basis (Line 1 – Line 2). If less than $0, enter $0. ________
5. Partner's basis in unrealized receivables and inventory distributed (enter lesser of Line 4 or the partnership's inside basis in the unrealized receivables and inventory). ________
6. Basis available to allocate to other property distributed (Line 4 – Line 5). ________
7. Partnership's inside basis of other property distributed. ________
8. Basis to partner of other property distributed (enter lesser of Line 6 or Line 7). ________
9. Partner's remaining outside basis (Line 6 – Line 8). ________

Review the tax results of Examples 56 and 57. Although Lindsey does not recognize any of the gain from the distribution, she has a zero outside basis for her partnership interest. If Lindsey expects the partnership to generate net losses in the near future, she will *not* find this zero basis attractive. She may be unable to deduct her share of these future losses when they flow through to her on the last day of the partnership's subsequent tax year.

The low basis that Lindsey has assigned to the parcels of land is of no significant detriment to her if she does not intend to sell the land in the near future. Because land does not generate cost recovery deductions, the substituted basis is used only to determine Lindsey's gain or loss upon her disposition of the parcels in a taxable sale or exchange.

Concept Summary 21.5 reviews the general rules that apply to proportionate nonliquidating partnership distributions.

PROPORTIONATE LIQUIDATING DISTRIBUTIONS

Proportionate **liquidating distributions** consist of a single distribution or a series of distributions that result in the termination of the partner's entire interest in the partnership. This section examines situations when a partner's interest is liquidated because the partnership is liquidating.

The partnership itself typically does not recognize either gain or loss on a proportionate liquidating distribution. The following discussion outlines rules for allocation of basis and possible gain or loss recognition by partners.

Gain Recognition and Ordering Rules

When a partnership liquidates, the liquidating distributions to a partner usually consist of an interest in several or all of the partnership assets. The gain recognition and ordering rules parallel those for nonliquidating distributions, except that the partner's *entire* basis in the partnership interest is allocated to the assets received in the liquidating distribution, unless the partner is required to recognize a loss. A loss may be recognized when *only* cash, unrealized receivables, or inventory are received in the distribution. As a result of the ordering rules, the basis of some assets may be adjusted upward or downward to absorb the partner's remaining outside basis. Unrealized receivables or inventory are never "stepped up," although they may be "stepped down."

The general ordering and gain recognition rules for a proportionate liquidating distribution are summarized as follows:

- Cash is distributed first and results in a capital gain if the amount distributed exceeds the partner's basis in the partnership interest. The cash distributed reduces the liquidated partner's outside basis dollar for dollar. The partner's basis cannot be reduced below zero.
- The partner's remaining outside basis is then allocated to unrealized receivables and inventory up to the amount equal to the partnership's adjusted bases in those properties. If the partnership's bases in the unrealized receivables and inventory exceed the partner's remaining outside basis, the remaining outside basis is allocated to the unrealized receivables and inventory.
- Finally, if the liquidating partner has any remaining outside basis, that basis is allocated to the other assets received.[74]

EXAMPLE 59

When Tara's basis in her partnership interest is $70,000, she receives cash of $15,000, a proportionate share of inventory, and land in a distribution that liquidates both the partnership and her entire partnership interest. The inventory has a basis to the partnership of $20,000 and a fair market value of $30,000. The land's basis is $8,000, and the fair market value is $12,000. Under these circumstances, Tara recognizes no gain or loss. After reducing Tara's $70,000 basis by the $15,000 cash received, the remaining $55,000 is allocated first to the inventory and then to the land. The basis of the inventory in Tara's hands is $20,000, and the basis of the land is $35,000. ■

When more than one asset in a particular class is distributed in a proportionate liquidating distribution, special rules may apply. If the partner's remaining basis for the partnership interest is less than the partnership's basis for the distributed assets in the particular class, the partner's remaining basis for each distributed asset is computed as illustrated in Example 57. If, however, the partner's remaining basis for the partnership interest is greater than the partnership's basis for the distributed assets in the "other assets" class, the partner's basis for each remaining distributed asset is computed by following three steps:

Step 1. Each distributed asset within the "other asset" class initially takes a carryover basis.

Step 2. Then, this carryover basis for each of these assets is increased in proportion to their respective amounts of unrealized appreciation (amount that fair market value is greater than carryover basis). Under no circumstances, however, can the basis of any asset be increased above its fair market value in step 2.

Step 3. Any remaining increase in basis is allocated among all the distributed assets in the "other assets" class in proportion to their respective fair market values.

[74]§§ 731 and 732.

EXAMPLE 60

Assume the same facts as in Example 59, except that Tara receives two parcels of land instead of one. The partnership's basis for the parcels is $2,000 for Parcel 1 and $6,000 for Parcel 2. Each parcel has a fair market value of $6,000.

Tara takes a $15,000 basis for the cash and a $20,000 carryover basis for the inventory. She has a $35,000 basis for her partnership interest after these two items are distributed. Because two parcels of land are distributed, and because Tara's remaining $35,000 basis for her partnership interest exceeds the partnership's $8,000 basis for the two parcels of land, Tara's basis for each parcel of land is computed by following these steps:

Step 1. She initially takes a carryover basis of $2,000 for Parcel 1 and $6,000 for Parcel 2.

Step 2. She increases the basis of Parcel 1 by $4,000 to its fair market value of $6,000. The basis for Parcel 2 is not affected in this step because Parcel 2 has a fair market value equal to its basis.

Step 3. Tara's $23,000 ($35,000 – $6,000 – $6,000) remaining basis for her partnership interest is allocated to each land parcel in proportion to each parcel's respective $6,000 fair market value. Therefore, $11,500 [($6,000/$12,000) × $23,000] is allocated to each parcel. Tara's basis in Parcel 1 is $17,500 ($2,000 + $4,000 + $11,500). Her basis in Parcel 2 is $17,500 ($6,000 + $11,500). ■

Loss Recognition

The distributee partner recognizes a *loss* on a liquidating distribution if both of the following are true:

- The partner receives *only* cash, unrealized receivables, or inventory.
- The partner's outside basis in the partnership interest exceeds the partnership's inside basis for the assets distributed. This excess amount is the loss recognized by the distributee partner.[75]

The word "only" is important. A distribution of any other property precludes recognition of the loss.

EXAMPLE 61

When Ramon's outside basis is $40,000, he receives a liquidating distribution of $7,000 cash and a proportionate share of inventory having a partnership basis of $3,000 and a fair market value of $10,000. Ramon is not allowed to "step up" the basis in the inventory, so it is allocated a $3,000 carryover basis. Ramon's unutilized outside basis is $30,000 ($40,000 – $7,000 – $3,000). Because he receives a liquidating distribution of *only* cash and inventory, he recognizes a capital loss of $30,000 on the liquidation. ■

EXAMPLE 62

Assume the same facts as in Example 61, except that in addition to the cash and inventory, Ramon receives the desk he used in the partnership. (Assume the distribution is proportionate to the partners.) The desk has an adjusted basis of $100 to the partnership. Applying the rules outlined above to this revised fact situation produces the following results:

Step 1. Cash of $7,000 is distributed to Ramon and reduces his outside basis to $33,000.

Step 2. Inventory is distributed to Ramon. He takes a $3,000 carryover basis in the inventory and reduces his outside basis in the partnership to $30,000.

Step 3. The desk is distributed to Ramon. Because the desk is not cash, an unrealized receivable, or inventory, he cannot recognize a loss. Therefore, Ramon's remaining basis in his partnership interest is allocated to the desk. He takes a $30,000 basis for the desk. ■

[75] § 731(a)(2).

What can Ramon do with a $30,000 desk? If he continues to use it in a trade or business, he can depreciate it. Once he has established his business use of the desk, he could sell it and recognize a large § 1231 loss. If the loss is isolated in the year of the sale, it is an ordinary loss. Thus, with proper planning, no liquidated partner should be forced to recognize a capital loss instead of an ordinary loss.

Gain recognized by the withdrawing partner on the subsequent disposition of inventory is ordinary income unless the disposition occurs more than five years after the distribution.[76] The withdrawing partner's holding period for all other property received in a liquidating distribution includes the partnership's related holding period.

21.6 Sale of a Partnership Interest

LO.12

Calculate the selling partner's amount and character of gain or loss on the sale or exchange of a partnership interest.

A partner can sell or exchange a partnership interest, in whole or in part. The transaction can be between the partner and a third party; in this case, it is similar in concept to a sale of corporate stock. The transfer of a partnership interest produces different results from the transfer of corporate stock because both the entity and aggregate concepts apply to the partnership situation, whereas only the entity concept applies to a sale of stock. The effect of the different rules is that gain or loss resulting from a sale of a partnership interest may be divided into capital gain or loss and ordinary income or loss.

GENERAL RULES

Generally, the sale or exchange of a partnership interest results in gain or loss, measured by the difference between the amount realized and the selling partner's adjusted basis in the partnership interest.[77]

Liabilities

In computing the amount realized and the adjusted basis of the interest sold, the selling partner's share of partnership liabilities must be determined. The purchasing partner includes any assumed indebtedness as a part of the consideration paid for the partnership interest.[78]

EXAMPLE 63

Cole originally contributed $50,000 in cash for a one-third interest in the CDE Partnership. During the time Cole was a partner, his share of partnership income was $90,000, and he withdrew $60,000 cash. Cole's capital account balance is now $80,000, and partnership liabilities are $45,000, of which Cole's share is $15,000. Cole's outside basis is $95,000 ($80,000 capital account + $15,000 share of partnership debts).

Cole sells his partnership interest to Stephanie for $110,000 of cash, with Stephanie assuming Cole's share of partnership liabilities. The total amount realized by Cole is $125,000 ($110,000 cash received + $15,000 of partnership debts transferred to Stephanie). Cole's gain on the sale is $30,000 ($125,000 amount realized − outside basis of $95,000).

Stephanie's adjusted basis for her partnership interest is the purchase price of $125,000 ($110,000 cash paid + $15,000 assumed partnership debt). ■

Income Allocation

When a partner sells an entire interest in the partnership:

- Income for the partnership interest for the tax year is allocated between the buying partner and the selling partner, and
- The partnership's tax year "closes" with respect to the selling partner.

[76] § 735(a)(2).
[77] § 741.
[78] § 742.

The closing of the tax year causes the selling partner to report the share of income on the sale date rather than at the end of the partnership's tax year. There are several acceptable methods of determining the partner's share of income.[79]

The selling partner's basis is adjusted for the allocated income or loss before the partner calculates the gain or loss on the sale of the interest.

EXAMPLE 64

On September 30, 2011, Erica sells her 20% interest in the Evergreen Partnership to Jason for $25,000. Erica is a calendar year taxpayer. Evergreen owns no hot assets (see discussion below), and its tax year ends on June 30.

On July 1, 2011, Erica's basis in the partnership interest was $8,000. Her share of current partnership income is $10,000 for the period she owned the partnership interest (July 1 to September 30). Because the partnership's tax year closes with respect to Erica, she must report $10,000 of income on her 2011 tax return. Her basis in the partnership interest is increased to $18,000, and she recognizes a $7,000 capital gain on the sale.

Note that Erica will also report income from Evergreen's tax year ending on June 30, 2011, on her 2011 tax return. ■

EFFECT OF HOT ASSETS

A major exception to capital gain or loss treatment on the sale or exchange of a partnership interest arises when a partnership has **hot assets**. In general, *hot assets* are *unrealized receivables* and *inventory*, assets that, when collected or disposed of by the partnership, would cause it to recognize ordinary income or loss. When a partner sells the interest in a partnership, it is as if the partnership had sold its hot assets and allocated to the selling partner the partner's proportionate share of the ordinary income or loss created by the sale. The primary purpose of this rule is to prevent a partner from converting ordinary income into capital gain through the sale of a partnership interest.[80]

Unrealized Receivables

As previously noted, unrealized receivables generally include the accounts receivable of a cash basis partnership and, for sale or exchange purposes, depreciation recapture potential.[81]

EXAMPLE 65

The cash basis Thrush Partnership owns only a $10,000 receivable for rendering health care advice. Its basis in the receivable is zero because no income has been recognized. This item is a hot asset because ordinary income is not generated until Thrush collects on the account.

Jacob, a 50% partner, sells his interest to Mark for $5,000. If Jacob's basis in his partnership interest is $0, his total gain is $5,000. The entire gain is attributable to Jacob's share of the unrealized receivable, so his gain is taxed as ordinary income. ■

Inventory

For a sale or exchange of a partnership interest, the term *inventory* includes all partnership property except money, capital assets, and § 1231 assets. Receivables of an accrual basis partnership are included in the definition of inventory, as they are neither capital assets nor § 1231 assets.[82] This definition also is broad enough to include all items considered to be unrealized receivables.

EXAMPLE 66

Jan sells her one-third interest in the JKL Partnership to Matt for $20,000 cash. The interest has an outside basis of $15,000. On the sale date, the partnership balance sheet reflects the following:

[79] § 706(d)(1) and related Regulations and 2009 Proposed Regulations.
[80] § 751(a).
[81] § 751(a)(1).
[82] § 751(d).

	Adjusted Basis	FMV		Adjusted Basis	FMV
Cash	$10,000	$10,000	Jan, capital	$15,000	$20,000
Inventory	21,000	30,000	Kelly, capital	15,000	20,000
Capital assets	14,000	20,000	Luis, capital	15,000	20,000
Total	$45,000	$60,000	Total	$45,000	$60,000

The overall gain on the sale is $5,000 ($20,000 – $15,000). Jan's share of the appreciation in the inventory is $3,000 [($30,000 – $21,000) × 1/3]. Therefore, she recognizes $3,000 of ordinary income because of the inventory and $2,000 of capital gain from the rest of the sale. ■

21.7 Limited Liability Entities

LO.13

Describe the application of partnership provisions to limited liability companies (LLCs) and limited liability partnerships (LLPs).

LIMITED LIABILITY COMPANIES

Owners of small businesses often wish to combine the limited liability of a corporation with the pass-through provisions of a partnership. S corporations, described in Chapter 22, provide some of these advantages. The limited liability company is a form of entity that goes further in combining partnership taxation with limited personal liability for all owners of the entity. All of the states and the District of Columbia have passed legislation permitting the establishment of LLCs.

Taxation of LLCs

A properly structured LLC with two or more owners is generally taxed as a partnership under the "check-the-box" rules. Because none of the LLC members are personally liable for any debts of the entity, the LLC is effectively treated as a limited partnership with no general partners. As described earlier in this chapter, this results in unusual application of partnership taxation rules in such areas as allocation of liabilities to the LLC members, inclusion or exclusion of debt for at-risk purposes, passive or active status of a member for passive loss purposes, and determination of a member's liability for self-employment tax.

Converting to an LLC

A partnership can convert to an LLC with few, if any, tax ramifications: the old elections of the partnership continue, and the partners retain their bases and ownership interests in the new entity. However, a C or an S corporation that reorganizes as an LLC is treated as having liquidated prior to forming the new entity. The transaction is taxable to both the corporation and the shareholders.

Advantages of an LLC

An LLC offers certain advantages over a limited partnership, including the following:

- Generally, none of the owners of an LLC are personally liable for the entity's debts. General partners in a limited partnership have personal liability for partnership recourse debts.
- Limited partners cannot participate in the management of the partnership. All owners of an LLC have the legal right to participate in the entity's management.

Disadvantages of an LLC

The disadvantages of an LLC stem primarily from the entity's relative newness. There is only a limited body of case law interpreting the various state statutes, so the

TAX *in the NEWS*

CONVERTING A C OR S CORPORATION TO A PARTNERSHIP ENTITY

Shareholders may decide to convert their existing C or S corporation to a partnership for various reasons (e.g., to avoid double taxation or to pass through losses). Unfortunately, this process is not as tax neutral as the incorporation of a partnership. In general, the conversion is treated as a liquidation of the corporate entity and the formation of a partnership.

Recall from earlier chapters that the liquidation of a corporation (C or S) is a taxable event (§§ 331 and 336). The assets are distributed from the corporation, and this triggers gain at the entity level (and a corporate-level tax if the entity is a C corporation). The gain is the difference between the basis and the fair market value of the distributed assets.

The tax resulting from a conversion, however, is less burdensome when the economy is depressed and asset values are low (corporate-level gain is minimized or possibly eliminated). Also beneficial are the current relatively low tax rates—capital gains are generally taxed to individuals at only a 15 percent maximum tax rate. Thus, taxpayers may be able to take advantage of difficult economic times and lower tax rates by converting a double-taxed corporate entity to a more tax-efficient LLC or LLP.

application of some provisions is uncertain. An additional uncertainty for LLCs that operate in more than one jurisdiction is which state's law will prevail and how it will be applied.

Among other factors, statutes differ from state to state as to the type of business an LLC can conduct—particularly as to the extent to which certain service-providing firms can operate as LLCs. A service entity may find it can operate as an LLC in one state but not in another.

LIMITED LIABILITY PARTNERSHIPS

All states now permit LLPs to be formed. Also, about half of the states have adopted legislation authorizing a variation known as a limited liability limited partnership (LLLP). The difference between a general partnership and an LLP is small, but very significant. Recall that general partners are jointly and severally liable for all partnership debts. In some states, partners in a registered LLP are jointly and severally liable for contractual liability (i.e., they are treated as general partners for commercial debt). They are also always personally liable for their own malpractice or other torts. They are not, however, personally liable for the malpractice and torts of their partners. As a result, the exposure of their personal assets to lawsuits filed against other partners and the partnership is considerably reduced.

An LLP must have formal documents of organization and register with the state. Because the LLP is a general partnership in other respects, it does not have to pay any state franchise taxes on its operations—an important difference between LLPs and LLCs in states that impose franchise taxes on LLCs. LLPs are taxed as partnerships under Federal tax statutes.

See Concept Summary 22.4 in Chapter 22 for a review of the various tax implications of LLCs and LLPs.

TAX PLANNING:

21.8 CHOOSING PARTNERSHIP TAXATION

LO.14

Identify tax planning opportunities related to partnerships and their partners.

Concept Summary 21.6 lists various factors that the owners of a business should consider in deciding whether to use a C corporation, S corporation, or partnership as a means of doing business.

CONCEPT SUMMARY 21.6

Advantages and Disadvantages of the Partnership Form

The partnership form may be attractive when one or more of the following factors is present:

- The entity is generating net taxable losses and/or valuable tax credits, which will be of use to the owners.
- The owners want to avoid complex corporate administrative and filing requirements.
- Other means by which to reduce the effects of the double taxation of corporate business income (e.g., compensation to owners, interest, and rental payments) have been exhausted.
- The entity does not generate material amounts of tax preference and adjustment items, which increase the alternative minimum tax liabilities of its owners.
- The entity is generating net passive income, which its owners can use to claim immediate deductions for net passive losses that they have generated from other sources.
- The owners wish to make special allocations of certain income or deduction items that are not possible under the C or S corporation forms.
- The owners anticipate liquidation of the entity within a short period of time. Liquidation of a C or S corporation would generate entity-level recognized gains on appreciated property distributed.
- The owners have adequate bases in their ownership interests to facilitate the deduction of flow-through losses and the assignment of an adequate basis to assets distributed in kind to the owners.

The partnership form may be less attractive when one or more of the following factors is present:

- The tax paid by the individual owners on the entity's income is greater than the tax the entity would pay if it were a C corporation, and the income is not expected to be distributed soon. (If distributed by a C corporation, double taxation would likely occur.)
- The entity is generating net taxable income without distributing any cash to the owners. The owners may not have sufficient cash with which to pay the tax on the entity's earnings.
- The type of income that the entity is generating (e.g., business and portfolio income) is not as attractive to its owners as net passive income would be because the owners could use net passive income to offset the net passive losses that they have generated on their own.
- The entity is in a high-exposure business, and the owners desire protection from personal liability. An LLC, LLP, or LLLP structure may be available, however, to limit personal liability.
- The owners want to avoid Federal self-employment tax.
- The entity has already been formed as a corporation, and conversion to partnership status could result in significant taxes in the course of liquidation.
- Partnership operations are complex (indicating that Form 1065 might not be filed until near the due date for the return), but partners with the same tax year need to file their returns as early as possible for personal reasons (e.g., to meet debt requirements or to receive a tax refund).

21.9 Formation and Operation of a Partnership

Potential partners should be cautious in transferring assets to a partnership to ensure that they are not required to recognize any gain upon the creation of the entity. The nonrecognition provisions of § 721 are relatively straightforward and resemble the provisions under § 351, which permit certain tax-free property transfers to corporations. However, any partner can make a tax-deferred contribution of assets to the entity either at the inception of the partnership or later. This possibility is not available to less-than-controlling shareholders in a corporation.

The partners should anticipate the tax benefits and pitfalls that are presented in the Code and should take appropriate actions to resolve any potential problems before they arise. Typically, all that is needed is an appropriate provision in the

GLOBAL *Tax Issues*

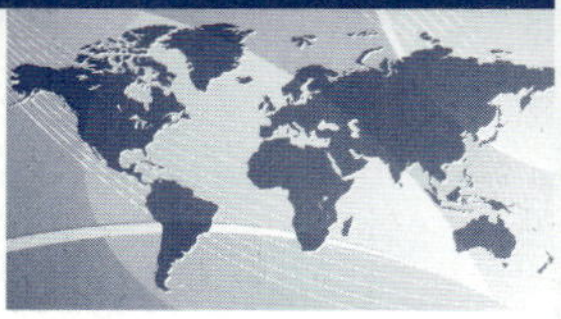

Partnerships Around the World—and Beyond

Technology continues to act as a catalyst—and incentive—for the creation of joint ventures. From web kiosks at gas stations to global satellite networks, high-tech companies are forging alliances to bring technology to consumers.

Both Microsoft and Time Warner have teamed up with various gas stations, pizza parlors, and numerous other retail outlets to offer programming. These ventures appear to be spurred by a desire to capture larger shares of the ever-expanding advertising market.

Meanwhile, the largest U.S. telecommunications companies are continuing to align themselves with partners in foreign markets: each wants to have the widest possible service coverage area so that it can offer efficient communications and computer networking to business clients with a global presence.

Recent partnerships (Verizon or AT&T and Apple, for example) have unleashed cell phones that provide tower-based navigation and browser systems. A more recent venture aims to provide these services to cell phones from satellites. In a few years, we will be able to "connect" anywhere, anytime—courtesy of an "out of this world" partnership.

partnership agreement (e.g., with respect to differing allocation percentages for gains and losses). Recall, however, that a special allocation of income, expense, or credit items in the partnership agreement must satisfy certain requirements before it is acceptable to the IRS.

21.10 Basis Considerations and Loss Deduction Limitations

If a partnership incurs a loss for the taxable year, careful planning will help ensure that the partners can claim the deduction.

A partner can contribute capital to the partnership before the end of the tax year. Alternatively, the partnership could incur additional debt. The partner's cash contribution or share of debt increases the partner's basis in the partnership interest. If the loss also meets the "at-risk" and "passive" hurdles, the loss can be deducted.

In the following year, if the partnership is expected to report taxable income, the partner could withdraw cash or pay off debt equal to the income. The partner's cash contribution would have to be invested in the partnership for only a short time. Similarly, the partnership's additional debt would not have to be maintained for a long period of time.

21.11 Transactions between Partners and Partnerships

Partners should be careful when engaging in transactions with the partnership to ensure that no negative tax results occur. A partner who owns a majority of the partnership generally should not sell property at a loss to the partnership because the loss is disallowed. Similarly, a majority partner should not sell a capital asset to the partnership at a gain, if the asset is to be used by the partnership as other than a capital asset. The gain on this transaction is taxed as ordinary income to the selling partner rather than as capital gain.

As an alternative to selling property to a partnership, the partner should consider a lease arrangement. The partner recognizes rent income, and the partnership has a rent expense. If the partner needs more cash immediately, the partner can sell the property to an outside third party who leases the property to the partnership for a fair rental.

The timing of the deduction for a payment by an accrual basis partnership to a cash basis partner varies depending on whether the payment is a guaranteed payment or is treated as a payment to an outsider. If the payment is a guaranteed payment, the deduction occurs when the partnership makes the accrual. If the payment is treated as a payment to an outsider, the actual date the payment is made controls the timing of the deduction.

21.12 Drafting the Partnership Agreement

Although a written partnership agreement (or LLC operating agreement) is not always required, many rules governing the tax consequences to partners and their partnership refer to such an agreement. Remember that a partner's distributive share of income, gain, loss, deduction, or credit is determined in accordance with the partnership agreement. Consequently, if taxpayers operating a business in partnership form want a measure of certainty as to the tax consequences of their activities, a carefully drafted partnership agreement is crucial. An agreement that sets forth the obligations, rights, and powers of the partners should prove invaluable in settling controversies among them and provide some degree of certainty as to the tax consequences of the partners' actions.

REFOCUS ON THE BIG PICTURE

WHY USE A PARTNERSHIP, ANYWAY?

After considering the various types of partnerships, Kyle, Maria, and Josh decide to form Beachside Properties as an LLC (see Example 1). On formation of the entity, there was no tax to the LLC or to any of its members (see Example 15). Beachside Properties computes its income as shown in Example 22 and allocates the income as illustrated in Examples 24 and 27. The LLC's income affects the members' bases and capital accounts as shown in Examples 33 and 34. An important consideration for the LLC members is whether their distributive shares and guaranteed payments will be treated as self-employment income (see Example 45).

What If?

What happens in the future when the LLC members decide to expand or renovate Beachside's facilities? At that time, the existing members can contribute additional funds, the LLC can obtain new members, or the entity can solicit third-party financing. An LLC is not subject to the 80 percent control requirement applicable to the formation of and subsequent transfers of property to a corporation. Therefore, new investors can contribute cash or other property in exchange for interests in the LLC—and the transaction will qualify for tax-deferred treatment under § 721.

KEY TERMS

Aggregate concept, 21–7
Capital interest, 21–8
Capital sharing ratio, 21–8
Constructive liquidation scenario, 21–29
Disguised sale, 21–11
Disproportionate distribution, 21–42
Economic effect test, 21–24
Entity concept, 21–7
General partners, 21–4
General partnership, 21–4
Guaranteed payment, 21–37
Hot assets, 21–50
Inside basis, 21–8
Least aggregate deferral rule, 21–18
Limited liability company, 21–4
Limited liability limited partnership, 21–4
Limited liability partnership, 21–4
Limited partners, 21–4
Limited partnership, 21–4
Liquidating distributions, 21–46
Nonliquidating distribution, 21–41
Nonrecourse debt, 21–29
Operating agreement, 21–4
Outside basis, 21–8
Partnership agreement, 21–4
Precontribution gain or loss, 21–25
Profit and loss sharing ratios, 21–8
Profits (loss) interest, 21–8
Proportionate distribution, 21–42
Qualified nonrecourse debt, 21–34
Recourse debt, 21–29
Schedule K–1, 21–6
Separately stated items, 21–5
Special allocation, 21–8
Syndication costs, 21–17
Unrealized receivables, 21–44

DISCUSSION QUESTIONS

1. **LO.1** What is a partnership?

2. **LO.1** Name the five types of partnerships discussed in this chapter. What factors are considered in determining the type of partnership entity to utilize?

3. **LO.1** What are the differences and similarities between a general partnership (GP) and a limited liability partnership (LLP)?

4. **LO.2** What is a separately stated item, and where is it reported on the partnership return?

5. **LO.2** Describe how a partnership reports its taxable income.

6. **LO.2** Describe how book income is reconciled with a partnership's "taxable income."

7. **LO.3** Describe the differences and similarities between the entity concept and the aggregate or conduit concept of partnership taxation.

ISSUE ID

8. **LO.3, 7, 11** Orange, LLC, was formed when Green, Inc., contributed $400,000 of cash and Rose contributed nondepreciable assets valued at $200,000 with a basis of $10,000. In addition, Rose will perform significant management services for the LLC. For most items, the members intend to allocate profits, losses, and liquidating distributions equally. How can (or must) special allocations be used to compensate the members for the differences between the bases and values of contributed property and time devoted to LLC activities?

9. **LO.3** What is a partner's capital account? Describe how a partner's ending capital account balance is determined. In addition to the material in the chapter, refer to Schedule K–1 in Appendix B.

10. **LO.4** When can the formation of a partnership result in a taxable gain to one or more of the new partners?

11. **LO.4** Compare the provision for the nonrecognition of gain or loss on contributions to a partnership (i.e., § 721) with the similar provision related to corporate formation (i.e., § 351). What are the major differences and similarities?

ISSUE ID

12. **LO.4** Kelsey and Christopher are forming the KC Partnership, in which Kelsey will own a 40% interest and Christopher will own a 60% interest. Kelsey will contribute appreciated land, and Christopher will contribute cash. What is the tax effect of the formation to Kelsey, Christopher, and the partnership?

ISSUE ID

DECISION MAKING

13. **LO.4** Jonathan owns property (basis of $200,000, value of $300,000). He plans to contribute the property to the JJG Partnership in exchange for a 25% interest.
    a. What issues arise if the partnership distributes $150,000 of cash to Jonathan three months after the property contribution?
    b. How can the risk of adverse tax consequences be minimized?

14. **LO.4** Tina and Rex plan to form the TR Partnership to acquire, own, and manage a certain rental real estate property. The financial information has been accumulated into an Offering Memorandum that is currently being brokered to investors (for a 6% commission). What types of costs is the partnership likely to incur, and how will those costs be treated?

15. **LO.6** How is the taxable year of a newly formed partnership determined?

16. **LO.7** What is the purpose of the three rules that implement the economic effect test?

17. **LO.8, 9** Discuss the adjustments that must be made to a partner's basis in the partnership interest. When are such adjustments made?

18. **LO.8** Describe, in general terms, how a partnership's liabilities affect a partner's basis in the partnership interest.

19. **LO.10** What is a guaranteed payment? When is it deducted by the partnership? When is it reported in the recipient partners' income?

20. **LO.11** When is partnership income subject to self-employment tax for an individual partner?

21. **LO.8, 9, 14** Discuss situations in which the partnership entity form might be more advantageous (or disadvantageous) than operating as a Subchapter C or S corporation.

22. **LO.4, 6, 7, 8, 9, 10** Comment on the validity of the following statements:
    a. Because a partnership is not a taxable entity, it is not required to file any type of tax return.
    b. Generally, a transfer of appreciated property to a partnership results in recognized gain to the contributing partner at the time of the transfer.
    c. When a partner renders services to the entity in exchange for an unrestricted interest in future profits of the partnership, that partner recognizes gross income.
    d. Property that was held as inventory by a contributing partner, but is a capital asset in the hands of the partnership, results in a capital gain if the partnership immediately sells the property.
    e. The partnership generally chooses the methods of accounting and those for computing depreciation in determining the income from the partnership.
    f. A partnership may choose a year that results in the least aggregate deferral of tax to the partners, unless the IRS requires the use of an alternative tax year under the "business purpose" test.
    g. Built-in gain related to nondepreciable property contributed to a partnership must be allocated to the contributing partner to the extent the gain is eventually recognized by the partnership.
    h. A partner's capital account for a partnership interest includes that partner's share of partnership recourse and nonrecourse liabilities.
    i. A partner can carry forward, for an unlimited period of time, the share of any partnership operating losses that exceed the partner's basis in the entity, provided the partner retains an ownership interest in the partnership.
    j. Losses on sales between a partner and the partnership are never deductible.

23. **LO.11** Describe the tax treatment to the partner of a proportionate nonliquidating distribution of cash, land, and inventory. When might the partner recognize a gain or loss?

24. **LO.11** Describe the tax treatment to the partner of a proportionate liquidating distribution (where the partnership also liquidates) of cash, land, and inventory. When might the partner recognize a gain or loss?

25. **LO.11** What theories of taxation underlie the rules related to proportionate liquidating and nonliquidating distributions? (In other words, what are these distribution rules trying to accomplish?)

ISSUE ID

26. **LO.12** Jody sells her partnership interest to Bill for $10,000. What issues must be addressed by Jody, Bill, and the partnership?

ISSUE ID

PROBLEMS

27. **LO.4** Justin and Tiffany form the equal TJ Partnership. Justin contributes cash of $300,000. Tiffany contributes property with an adjusted basis of $200,000 and a fair market value of $300,000.
    a. How much gain, if any, must Justin recognize on the transfer? Must Tiffany recognize any gain?
    b. What is Justin's basis in his partnership interest?
    c. What is Tiffany's basis in her partnership interest?
    d. What basis does the partnership take in the property transferred by Tiffany?

28. **LO.4, 14** Scott and Amber form the equal Toucan, LLC, with a cash contribution of $100,000 from Scott and a property contribution (adjusted basis of $110,000, fair market value of $100,000) from Amber.
    a. How much gain or loss, if any, does Amber realize on the transfer? Does Amber recognize any gain or loss?
    b. What is Scott's basis in his LLC interest?
    c. What is Amber's basis in her LLC interest?
    d. What basis does the LLC take in the property transferred by Amber?
    e. Are there more effective ways to structure the formation?

DECISIOIN MAKING

29. **LO.4** Drew and Emma formed the equal D&E Partnership on January 1 of the current year. Drew contributed $50,000 of cash and land with a fair market value of $100,000 and an adjusted basis of $80,000. Emma contributed equipment with a fair market value of $150,000 and an adjusted basis of $60,000. Emma had previously used the equipment in her sole proprietorship.
    a. How much gain or loss will Drew, Emma, and the partnership realize?
    b. How much gain or loss will Drew, Emma, and the partnership recognize?
    c. What bases will Drew and Emma take in their partnership interests?
    d. What bases will D&E take in the assets it receives?
    e. Are there any differences between inside and outside basis?
    f. How will the partnership depreciate any assets it receives from the partners?

ISSUE ID

30. **LO.4** Jared and Chelsea form the equal JC Partnership. Jared contributes cash of $20,000 and land (fair market value of $80,000, adjusted basis of $65,000), and Chelsea contributes the assets of her sole proprietorship (value of $100,000, adjusted basis of $125,000). What are the tax consequences of the partnership formation to Jared, Chelsea, and JC Partnership?

ISSUE ID

DECISION MAKING

31. **LO.4** Assume the same facts as in Problem 31, except that Chelsea sells her assets to a third party for $100,000 and then contributes that cash to the partnership. The partnership locates equivalent assets that it purchases for $110,000. How do these changes affect the tax result for Chelsea and the partnership? How does the economic result differ?

32. **LO.4, 8** Ben and Beth are equal partners in BB, LLC, formed on June 1 of the current year. Ben contributed land that he inherited from his father three years ago. Ben's father purchased the land in 1950 for $6,000. The land was worth $50,000 when Ben's father died. The fair market value of the land was $75,000 at the date it was contributed to the partnership.

    Beth has significant experience developing real estate. After the LLC is formed, she will prepare a plan for developing the property and secure zoning approvals for the LLC. She would normally bill a third party $25,000 for these efforts. Beth will also contribute $50,000 of cash in exchange for her 50% interest in the LLC. The value of her 50% interest is $75,000.
    a. How much gain or income will Ben recognize on his contribution of the land to the LLC? What is the character of any gain or income recognized?
    b. What basis will Ben take in his LLC interest?
    c. How much gain or income will Beth recognize on the formation of the LLC? What is the character of any gain or income recognized?
    d. What basis will Beth take in LLC partnership interest?

DECISION MAKING

33. **LO.4, 12** Continue with the facts presented in Problem 32.
    a. Construct an opening balance sheet for BB, LLC, reflecting the LLC's basis in assets and the fair market value of these assets.
    b. Outline any planning opportunities that may minimize current taxation to any of the parties.

DECISION MAKING

34. **LO.4, 10, 14** Continue with the facts presented in Problem 32. At the end of the first year, the LLC distributes $50,000 of cash to Ben. No distribution is made to Beth.
    a. Under general tax rules, how would the payment to Ben be treated?
    b. How much income or gain would Ben recognize as a result of the payment?
    c. Under general tax rules, what basis would the LLC take in the land Ben contributed?
    d. What alternative treatment might the IRS try to impose?
    e. Under the alternative treatment, how much income or gain would Ben recognize?
    f. Under the alternative treatment, what basis would the LLC take in the land contributed by Ben?

35. **LO.4, 7** The JM Partnership was formed to acquire land and subdivide it as residential housing lots. On March 1, 2011, Jessica contributed land valued at $600,000 to the partnership, in exchange for a 50% interest in JM. She had purchased the land in 2003 for $420,000 and held it for investment purposes (capital asset). The partnership holds the land as inventory.

    On the same date, Matt contributed land valued at $600,000 that he had purchased in 2001 for $720,000. He became a 50% owner. Matt is a real estate developer, but this land was held personally for investment purposes. The partnership holds this land as inventory.

In 2012, the partnership sells the land contributed by Jessica for $620,000. In 2013, the partnership sells the real estate contributed by Matt for $580,000.

a. What is each partner's initial basis in his or her partnership interest?
b. What is the amount of gain or loss recognized on the sale of the land contributed by Jessica? What is the character of this gain or loss?
c. What is the amount of gain or loss recognized on the sale of the land contributed by Matt? What is the character of this gain or loss?
d. How would your answer in (c) change if the property was sold in 2018?

36. **LO.5** In 2011, Tim and Molly form TM Partnership, Ltd. (an LLLP), to own and operate certain real estate. Tim contributed land, and Molly contributed cash to be used for setting up the entity and creating a plan for developing the property. Once a development plan was in place, the partnership sold interests in the partnership to investors to raise funds for constructing a shopping center. The partnership incurred expenses of $12,000 for forming the entity and $52,000 for starting the business (e.g., setting up the accounting systems, locating tenants, and negotiating leases). It also paid $18,000 in transfer taxes for changing the ownership of the property to the partnership's name. The brokerage firm that sold the interests to the limited partners charged a 6% commission, which totaled $600,000. The calendar year partnership started business in September 2011. Describe how all these initial expenses are treated by the partnership. **ISSUE ID**

37. **LO.4, 5, 6, 7** Finch, Inc., a calendar year general contractor, and Cardinal, Inc., a development corporation with a July 31 year-end, formed the equal FC, LLC, on January 1 of the current year. Both LLC members are C corporations. The LLC was formed to construct and lease shopping centers in Seattle, Washington. Finch contributed cash of $1 million, equipment (basis of $200,000, fair market value of $500,000), building permits, and architectural designs created by Finch's employees (basis of $0, fair market value of $200,000). Cardinal contributed land (basis of $500,000, fair market value of $700,000) and cash of $1 million. The cash was used as follows: **ISSUE ID**

Legal fees for drafting LLC agreement	$ 20,000
Materials and labor costs for construction in progress on shopping center	1,900,000
Office expenses (utilities, rent, overhead, etc.)	80,000

What issues must the LLC address in preparing its initial tax return?

38. **LO.6** Browne and Red, both C corporations, formed the BR Partnership on January 1, 2009. Neither Browne nor Red is a personal service corporation, and BR is not a tax shelter. BR's gross receipts were $4.6 million, $5 million, $6 million, and $7 million, respectively, for the four tax years ending in 2009, 2010, 2011, and 2012. Describe the methods of accounting available to BR in each tax year. **ISSUE ID**

39. **LO.5** On July 1 of the current year, the R & R Partnership (an LLLP) was formed to operate a bed and breakfast inn. The partnership paid $3,000 in legal fees for drafting the partnership agreement and $5,000 for accounting fees related to organizing the entity. It also paid $10,000 in syndication costs to locate and secure investments from limited partners. In addition, before opening the inn for business, the entity paid $15,500 for advertising and $36,000 in costs related to an open house just before the grand opening of the property. The partnership opened the inn for business on October 1.

a. How are these expenses classified?
b. How much may the partnership deduct in its initial year of operations?
c. How are costs treated that are not deducted currently?

40. **LO.6** AzureCo, AuburnCo, and AquamarineCo form the AAA Partnership on January 1 of the current year. AzureCo is a 50% partner, and AuburnCo and AquamarineCo are each 25% partners. All of the partners and AAA use the cash method of accounting. For reporting purposes, AzureCo uses a fiscal year with a June 30 year-end, AuburnCo uses a fiscal year with an October 31 year-end, and AquamarineCo uses a calendar year. What is AAA's required tax year under the least aggregate deferral method?

41. **LO.4, 7** Phoebe and Parker are equal members in Phoenix Investors, LLC. They are real estate investors who formed the LLC several years ago with equal cash contributions. Phoenix then purchased a piece of land.

On January 1 of the current year, to acquire a one-third interest in the entity, Reece contributed to the LLC some land she had held for investment. Reece purchased the land five years ago for $75,000; its fair market value at the contribution date was $90,000. No special allocation agreements were in effect before or after Reece was admitted to the LLC. Phoenix holds all land for investment.

Immediately before Reece's property contribution, the balance sheet of Phoenix Investors, LLC, was as follows:

	Basis	FMV		Basis	FMV
Land	$30,000	$180,000	Phoebe, capital	$15,000	$ 90,000
			Parker, capital	15,000	90,000
	$30,000	$180,000		$30,000	$180,000

a. At the contribution date, what is Reece's basis in her interest in the LLC?
b. When does the LLC's holding period begin for the contributed land?
c. On June 30 of the current year, the LLC sold the land contributed by Reece for $90,000. How much is the recognized gain or loss, and how is it allocated among the LLC members?
d. Prepare a balance sheet reflecting basis and fair market value for the LLC immediately after the land sale described in (c). Assume no other transactions occurred during the year.

42. **LO.7** Assume the same facts as in Problem 41, with the following exceptions.

- Reece purchased the land five years ago for $120,000. Its fair market value was $90,000 when it was contributed to the LLC.
- Phoenix sold the land contributed by Reece for $84,000.

a. How much is the recognized gain or loss, and how is it allocated among the LLC members?
b. Prepare a balance sheet reflecting basis and fair market value for the LLC immediately after the land sale. Also prepare schedules that support the amount in each LLC member's capital account.

43. **LO.7, 8** Andrea and Michael are equal partners in the accrual basis AM Partnership. At the beginning of the current year, Andrea's capital account has a balance of $200,000, and the partnership has recourse debts of $100,000 payable to unrelated parties. Assume all partnership recourse debt is shared equally between the partners. The following information about AM's operations for the current year is obtained from the partnership's records.

Taxable income	$320,000
Tax-exempt interest income	6,000
§ 1231 gain	9,000
Short-term capital loss	2,000
Political contribution	1,000
Charitable contribution to Big Brothers Big Sisters	2,000
Cash distribution to Andrea	50,000

Assume that year-end partnership debt payable to unrelated parties is $140,000. If all transactions are reflected in her beginning capital and basis in the same manner, what is Andrea's basis in the partnership interest:

a. At the beginning of the year?
b. At the end of the year?

44. **LO.7, 8** The KL Partnership is owned equally by Kayla and Lisa. Kayla's basis is $20,000 at the beginning of the tax year. Lisa's basis is $16,000 at the beginning of the year. KL reported the following income and expenses for the current tax year:

Sales revenue	$150,000
Cost of sales	80,000
Distribution to Lisa	15,000
Depreciation expense	20,000
Utilities	14,000
Rent expense	18,000
Long-term capital gain	6,000
Payment to Mercy Hospital for Kayla's medical expenses	12,000

a. Determine the ordinary partnership income and separately stated items for the partnership.

b. Calculate Kayla's basis in her partnership interest at the end of the tax year. What items should Kayla report on her Federal income tax return?

c. Calculate Lisa's basis in her partnership interest at the end of the tax year. What items should Lisa report on her Federal income tax return?

45. **LO.7, 8, 9** How would your answers in Problem 44 change if partnership revenues were $100,000 instead of $150,000?

46. **LO.4, 7, 8** Celeste contributed business-related assets valued at $250,000 (basis of $100,000) in exchange for her 50% interest in the Celestine Partnership. Christine contributed land and a building valued at $400,000 (basis of $200,000) in exchange for the remaining 50% interest. Christine's property was encumbered by a qualified nonrecourse debt of $150,000, which was assumed by the partnership. The partnership reports the following income and expenses for the current tax year:

Sales	$350,000
Utilities, salaries, and other operating expenses	190,000
Short-term capital gain	6,000
Tax-exempt interest income	2,000
Charitable contributions	1,000
Distribution to Celeste	20,000
Distribution to Christine	10,000

At the end of the current tax year, Celestine had recourse debt of $100,000 for partnership accounts payable and qualified nonrecourse debt of $140,000.

a. What is Celeste's basis after formation of the partnership? Christine's basis?

b. What income and separately stated items does the partnership report on Celeste's Schedule K–1? What items does Celeste report on her tax return?

c. Assume all partnership debts are shared equally. At the end of the tax year, what are Celeste's basis and amount at risk in her partnership interest?

47. **LO.4, 7, 8** Continue with the facts presented in Problem 46, except that Celestine was formed as an LLC instead of a general partnership. **ISSUE ID**

a. How would Celestine's ending liabilities be treated?

b. How would Celeste's basis and amount at risk be different?

48. **LO.7, 8, 9** As of January 1 of last year, Dylan's outside basis and at-risk amount for his 40% interest in the DEF Partnership were $60,000. Dylan and the partnership use the calendar year for tax purposes. The partnership incurred an operating loss of $200,000 for last year and a profit of $120,000 for the current year. Dylan is a material participant in the partnership. **DECISION MAKING**

a. How much loss, if any, may Dylan recognize for last year?

b. How much net reportable income must Dylan recognize for the current year?

c. What is Dylan's basis in the partnership as of December 31 of last year?

d. What is Dylan's basis in the partnership as of December 31 of the current year?

e. What year-end tax planning would you suggest to ensure that Dylan can deduct his share of partnership losses?

49. **LO.4, 7, 8** Bryan and Cody each contribute $120,000 to the newly formed BC Partnership in exchange for a 50% interest. The partnership uses the available funds to acquire equipment costing $200,000 and to fund current operating expenses. The partnership agreement provides that depreciation will be allocated 80% to Bryan and 20% to Cody. All other items of income and loss will be allocated equally between the partners. Upon

liquidation of the partnership, property will be distributed to the partners in accordance with their capital account balances. Any partner with a negative capital account must contribute cash in the amount of the negative balance to restore the capital account to $0.

In its first year, the partnership reported an ordinary loss (before depreciation) of $80,000 and depreciation expense of $36,000. In its second year, the partnership reported $40,000 of income from operations (before depreciation), and it reported depreciation expense of $57,600.

a. Calculate the partners' bases in their partnership interests at the end of the first and second tax years. Are any losses suspended?

b. Does the allocation provided in the partnership agreement have economic effect?

ISSUE ID

50. **LO.7, 8, 9** Continue with the facts presented in Problem 49. On the first day of the third tax year, the partnership sold the equipment for $150,000 and distributed the cash in accordance with the partnership agreement. The partnership was liquidated at this time.

a. Calculate the partners' bases in their partnership interests after reflecting any gain or loss on disposal of the equipment.

b. How will partnership cash balances be distributed to the partners on liquidation?

c. What observations can you make regarding the value of a deduction to each partner?

DECISION MAKING

COMMUNICATIONS

51. **LO.7, 8, 9** Your client, the Williams Institute of Technology (WIT), is a 60% partner in the Research Industries Partnership (RIP). WIT is a widely held Subchapter C corporation and is not subject to the passive loss limitation. WIT is located at 76 Bradford Lane, St. Paul, MN 55164. The controller, Jeanine West, has sent you the following note and a copy of WIT's 2010 Schedule K–1 from the partnership.

Excerpt from client's note:

"RIP expects its 2011 operations to include the following:

Net loss from operations	$200,000
Capital gain from sale of land	100,000

The land was contributed by DASH, the other partner, when its value was $260,000. The partnership sold the land for $300,000. The partnership used this cash to repay all the partnership debt and pay for operating expenditures, which a tax partner in your firm has said RIP can deduct this year. The net loss of $200,000 reflects that deduction.

We want to be sure we can deduct our full share of this loss, but we do not believe we will have enough basis."

Items Reported on the 2010 Schedule K–1	
WIT's share of partnership recourse liabilities	$90,000
WIT's ending capital account balance	30,000

Draft a letter to the controller that describes the following:

- WIT's allocation of partnership items.
- WIT's basis in the partnership interest following the allocation.
- Any limitations on loss deductions.
- Any recommendations you have that would allow WIT to claim the full amount of losses in 2011.

Assume WIT's 2010 K–1 accurately reflects the information needed to compute the basis in the partnership interest. Also assume the operating expenditures are fully deductible this year, as the partner said.

Your client has experience researching issues in the Internal Revenue Code, so you may use some citations. However, be sure the letter is written in layperson's terms and cites are minimized.

52. **LO.8** The MGP General Partnership was created on January 1 of the current year by having Melinda, Gabe, and Pat each contribute $10,000 cash to the partnership in exchange for a one-third interest in partnership income, gains, losses, deductions, and credits. On December 31 of the current year, the partnership balance sheet reads as follows:

	Basis	FMV		Basis	FMV
Assets	$60,000	$75,000	Recourse debt	$30,000	$30,000
			Melinda, capital	14,000	19,000
			Gabe, capital	14,000	19,000
			Pat, capital	2,000	7,000
				$60,000	$75,000

Pat's capital account is less than Melinda's and Gabe's capital accounts because Pat has withdrawn more cash than the other partners.

How do the partners share the recourse debt as of December 31 of the current year?

53. **LO.4, 8** Paul and Anna plan to form the PA General Partnership by the end of the current year. The partners will each contribute $80,000 cash, and in addition, the partnership will borrow $240,000 from First State Bank. The $400,000 will be used to buy an investment property. The property will serve as collateral, and both partners will be required to personally guarantee the debt.

COMMUNICATIONS

The tentative agreement provides that 60% of operating income, gains, losses, deductions, and credits will be allocated to Paul for the first five years the partnership is in existence. The remaining 40% is allocated to Anna. Thereafter, all partnership items will be allocated equally. The agreement also provides that capital accounts will be properly maintained and that each partner must restore any deficit in the capital account upon the partnership's liquidation.

The partners would like to know, before the end of the tax year, how the $240,000 liability will be allocated for basis purposes. Using the format (1) facts, (2) issues, (3) conclusion, and (4) law and analysis, draft a memo to the tax planning file for the PA Partnership that describes how the debt will be shared between the partners for purposes of computing the adjusted basis of each partnership interest.

54. **LO.8, 9, 14** The BCD Partnership plans to distribute cash of $20,000 to partner Brad at the end of the tax year. The partnership reported a loss for the year, and Brad's share of the loss is $10,000. At the beginning of the tax year, Brad's basis in his partnership interest, including his share of partnership liabilities, was $15,000. The partnership expects to report substantial income in future years.

ISSUE ID

DECISION MAKING

a. What rules are used to calculate Brad's ending basis in his partnership interest?
b. How much gain or loss will Brad report for the tax year?
c. Will the deduction for the $10,000 loss be suspended?
d. Could any planning opportunities be used to minimize any negative tax ramifications of the distribution?

55. **LO.8, 9** Jasmine Gregory is a 20% member in Sparrow Properties, LLC, which is a lessor of residential rental property. Her share of the LLC's losses for the current year is $100,000. Immediately before considering the deductibility of this loss, Jasmine's capital account (which, in this case, corresponds to her basis excluding liabilities) reflected a balance of $50,000. Jasmine has personally guaranteed a $10,000 debt of the LLC that is allocated to her as a recourse debt. Her share of the LLC's nonrecourse debt is $30,000. This debt cannot be treated as qualified nonrecourse debt. Jasmine spends several hundred hours a year working for Sparrow Properties.

COMMUNICATIONS

Jasmine is also a managing member of Skylark Rentals, LLC, which is engaged in long-term (more than 30 days) equipment rental activities. (This is considered a passive activity.) Jasmine's share of Skylark's income is $36,000.

Jasmine's modified adjusted gross income before considering the LLCs' activities is $300,000. Determine how much of Sparrow's $100,000 loss Jasmine can deduct on her current calendar year return. Using the format (1) facts, (2) issues, (3) conclusion, and (4) law and analysis, draft a memo to the client's tax file describing the loss limitations. Identify the Code sections under which losses are suspended.

56. **LO.7, 10** FredCo and Fran are equal partners in the calendar year F & F Partnership. FredCo uses a fiscal year ending June 30, and Fran uses a calendar year. FredCo receives an annual guaranteed payment of $50,000 for use of capital contributed by FredCo.

F & F's taxable income (after deducting FredCo's guaranteed payment) is $40,000 for 2011 and $50,000 for 2012.

a. What is the amount of income from the partnership that FredCo must report for its tax year ending June 30, 2012?
b. What is the amount of income from the partnership that Fran must report for her tax year ending December 31, 2012?

57. **LO.10** Continue with the facts presented in Problem 56. Assume FredCo's annual guaranteed payment is increased to $60,000 starting on January 1, 2012, and the partnership's taxable income for 2011 and 2012 (after deducting FredCo's guaranteed payment) is the same (i.e., $40,000 and $50,000, respectively). What is the amount of income from the partnership that FredCo must report for its tax year ending June 30, 2012?

58. **LO.7, 11** Nicole, a calendar year individual, owns 30% of Creole Cravings, Inc., a C corporation that was formed on February 1, 2011. She receives a $5,000 monthly salary from the corporation, and Creole Cravings generates $200,000 of taxable income (after accounting for payments to Nicole) for its tax year ending January 31, 2012.
   a. How do these activities affect Nicole's 2011 adjusted gross income?
   b. Assume, instead that Creole Cravings is a partnership (January 31 year-end) and that it classifies Nicole's salary as a guaranteed payment. How do these activities affect Nicole's 2011 and 2012 adjusted gross income?

59. **LO.11** Four GRRLs Partnership is owned by four sisters. Leah holds a 70% interest; each of the others owns 10%. Leah sells investment property to the partnership for its fair market value of $100,000 (Leah's basis is $150,000).
   a. How much loss, if any, may Leah recognize?
   b. If the partnership later sells the property for $160,000, how much gain must it recognize?
   c. If Leah's basis in the investment property was $20,000 instead of $150,000, how much, if any, gain would she recognize on the sale, and how would the gain be characterized?

60. **LO.11** Greg's outside basis in his interest in the GO Partnership is $360,000. In a proportionate nonliquidating distribution, the partnership distributes to him cash of $60,000, inventory (fair market value of $200,000, basis to the partnership of $160,000), and land (fair market value of $50,000, basis to the partnership of $80,000). The partnership continues in existence.
   a. Does the partnership recognize any gain or loss as a result of this distribution?
   b. Does Greg recognize any gain or loss as a result of this distribution?
   c. Calculate Greg's basis in the land, in the inventory, and in his partnership interest immediately following the distribution.

61. **LO.11** When Tiffany's outside basis in the TMF Partnership is $120,000, the partnership distributes to her $30,000 of cash, an account receivable (fair market value of $75,000, inside basis to the partnership of $0), and a parcel of land (fair market value of $150,000, inside basis to the partnership of $125,000). Tiffany remains a partner in the partnership, and the distribution is proportionate to the partners.
   a. Determine the recognized gain or loss to the partnership as a result of this distribution.
   b. Determine the recognized gain or loss to Tiffany as a result of the distribution.
   c. Determine Tiffany's basis in the land, account receivable, and TMF Partnership after the distribution.

62. **LO.11** In each of the following independent cases in which the partnership owns no hot assets, indicate:
   - Whether the partner recognizes gain or loss.
   - Whether the partnership recognizes gain or loss.
   - The partner's adjusted basis for the property distributed.
   - The partner's outside basis in the partnership after the distribution.

   a. Brooke receives $10,000 of cash in partial liquidation of her interest in the partnership. Brooke's outside basis for her partnership interest immediately before the distribution is $6,000.

b. Brianna receives $30,000 of cash and land with an inside basis to the partnership of $50,000 (value of $100,000) in partial liquidation of her interest. Brianna's outside basis for her partnership interest immediately before the distribution is $90,000.

c. Assume the same facts as in (b), except that Brianna's outside basis for her partnership interest immediately before the distribution is $40,000.

d. Bonnie receives $100,000 of cash and inventory with a basis of $50,000 and a fair market value of $60,000 in partial liquidation of her partnership interest. Her basis was $80,000 before the distribution. All partners received proportionate distributions.

63. **LO.11** Mark's basis in his partnership interest is $39,000. In a proportionate nonliquidating distribution, Mark receives $30,000 of cash and two inventory items, each with a basis of $10,000 to the partnership. The values of the inventory items are $15,000 and $5,000.

a. How much gain or loss, if any, must Mark recognize on the distribution?

b. What basis will Mark take in each inventory item?

64. **LO.11** At the beginning of the tax year, Monica's basis in the MIP LLC was $100,000, including Monica's $50,000 share of the LLC's liabilities. At the end of the year, MIP distributed to Monica cash of $20,000 and inventory (basis of $10,000, fair market value of $16,000). In addition, MIP repaid all of its liabilities by the end of the year.

a. If this is a proportionate nonliquidating distribution, what is the tax effect of the distribution to Monica and MIP? After the distribution, what is Monica's basis in the inventory and in her MIP interest?

b. Would your answers to (a) change if this had been a proportionate liquidating distribution?

65. **LO.11** In each of the following independent liquidating distributions in which the partnership also liquidates, determine the amount and character of any gain or loss to be recognized by each partner and the basis of each asset (other than cash) received. In each case, assume distributions of hot assets are proportionate to the partners.

a. Brandon has a partnership basis of $60,000 and receives a distribution of $75,000 in cash.

b. Barry has a partnership basis of $80,000 and receives $30,000 cash and a capital asset with a basis to the partnership of $40,000 and a fair market value of $50,000.

c. Bryan has a partnership basis of $100,000 and receives $30,000 cash, inventory with a basis to the partnership of $20,000, and a capital asset with a partnership basis of $30,000. The inventory and capital asset have fair market values of $25,000 and $40,000, respectively.

d. Blake has a partnership basis of $60,000 and receives a distribution of $20,000 cash and an account receivable with a basis of $0 to the partnership (value is $30,000).

66. **LO.12** RBP Partnership is a service-oriented partnership that has three equal general partners. One of them, Barry, sells his interest to another partner, Dale, for $90,000 cash and the assumption of Barry's share of partnership liabilities. On the sale date, the partnership's cash basis balance sheet is as shown below. Assume that the capital accounts *before* the sale reflect the partners' bases in their partnership interests, excluding liabilities. The payment exceeds the stated fair market value of the assets because of goodwill that is not recorded on the books.

	Basis	FMV		Basis	FMV
Cash	$120,000	$120,000	Note payable	$ 30,000	$ 30,000
Accounts receivable	–0–	90,000	Capital accounts		
Capital assets	30,000	75,000	Barry	40,000	85,000
			David	40,000	85,000
			Dale	40,000	85,000
Total	$150,000	$285,000	Total	$150,000	$285,000

a. What is the total amount realized by Barry on the sale?
b. How much, if any, ordinary income must Barry recognize on the sale?
c. How much capital gain must Barry report?
d. What is Dale's basis in the partnership interest acquired?

See Appendix E for Comprehensive Tax Return Problem—Form 1065

RESEARCH PROBLEMS

THOMSON REUTERS
Checkpoint® Student Edition

Note: Solutions to Research Problems can be prepared by using the **Checkpoint® Student Edition** online research product, which is available to accompany this text. It is also possible to prepare solutions to the Research Problems by using tax research materials found in a standard tax library.

COMMUNICATIONS

Research Problem 1. Your clients, Grayson Investments, Inc. (Ana Marks, President), and Blake Caldwell, each contributed $200,000 of cash to form the Realty Management Partnership, a limited partnership. Grayson is the general partner and Blake is the limited partner. The partnership used the $400,000 of cash to make a down payment on a building. The rest of the building's $4 million purchase price was financed with an interest-only nonrecourse loan of $3.6 million, which was obtained from an independent third-party bank.

The partnership allocates all partnership items equally except for the MACRS deductions and building maintenance, which are allocated 70% to Blake and 30% to Grayson. The partnership definitely wishes to satisfy the "economic effect" requirements of Reg. §§ 1.704–1 and 1.704–2 and will reallocate MACRS, if necessary, to satisfy the requirements of the Regulations.

Under the partnership agreement, liquidation distributions will be paid in proportion to the partners' positive capital account balances. Capital accounts are maintained as required in the Regulations. Grayson Investments has an unlimited obligation to restore its capital account while Blake is subject to a qualified income offset provision.

Assume all partnership items, except for MACRS, will net to zero throughout the first three years of the partnership operations. Also, assume that each year's MACRS deduction will be $200,000 (to simplify the calculations).

Draft a letter to the partnership evaluating the allocation of MACRS in each of the three years under Reg. §§ 1.704–1 and –2. The partnership's address is 53 East Marsh Ave., Smyrna, GA 30082. Do not address the "substantial" test.

Research Problem 2. Franklin Industries, Inc., and George Weldon have formed the FG Partnership to operate a retail establishment selling antique household furnishings. Franklin Industries is the general partner, and George is the limited partner. Both partners contribute $15,000 to form the partnership. The partnership uses the $30,000 contributed by the partners and a recourse loan of $100,000 obtained from an unrelated third-party lender to acquire $130,000 of initial inventory.

The partners believe they will have extensive losses in the first year due to advertising and initial cash-flow requirements. Franklin and George have agreed to share losses equally. To make sure the losses can be allocated to both partners, they have included a provision in the partnership agreement requiring each partner to restore any deficit balance in that partner's partnership capital account upon liquidation of the partnership.

Franklin was also willing to include a provision that requires Franklin to make up any deficit balance within 90 days of liquidation of the partnership. As a limited partner, George argued that he should not be subject to such a time requirement. The partners compromised and included a provision that requires George to restore a deficit balance in his capital account within two years of liquidation of the partnership. No interest will be owed on the deferred restoration payment.

How is the debt allocated to the partners' respective bases? Describe the rules that apply and cite your references. Hint: You will find that FG cannot allocate the $100,000 recourse debt equally to the two partners. Where appropriate, assume that a 10% interest rate, compounded semiannually, applies.

Use the tax resources of the Internet to address the following question. Do not restrict your search to the Web, but include a review of newsgroups and general reference materials, practitioner sites and resources, primary sources of the tax law, chat rooms and discussion groups, and other opportunities.

INTERNET *activity*

Research Problem 3. Use the search feature on your favorite news site on the Web (e.g., CNN, ABC News, Fox News, etc.) and search for news on partnerships, LLCs, or limited partnerships. What entities did you find that are taking advantage of the partnership entity form? (Be sure these entities are truly legal partnerships. Some entities called "partnerships" by the news media actually involve transfers of stock or formation of a corporation to manage the joint venture.)

CHAPTER

22

S Corporations

LEARNING OBJECTIVES

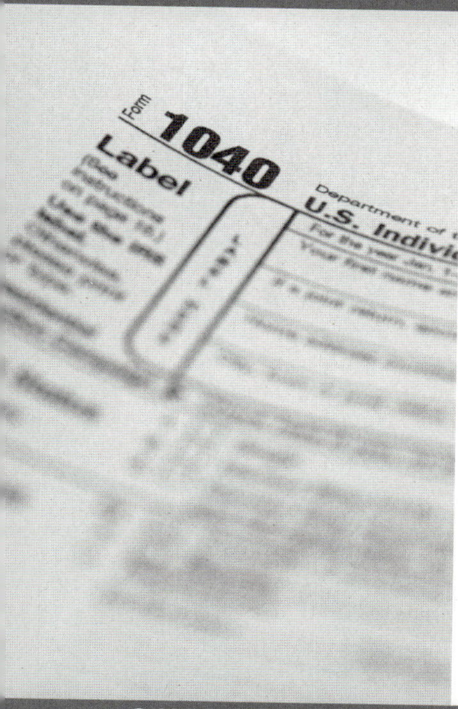

After completing Chapter 22, you should be able to:

LO.1 Explain the tax effects that S corporation status has on shareholders.

LO.2 Identify corporations that qualify for the S election.

LO.3 Explain how to make an S election.

LO.4 Explain how an S election can be terminated.

LO.5 Compute nonseparately stated income and identify separately stated items.

LO.6 Allocate income, deductions, and credits to shareholders.

LO.7 Determine how distributions to S corporation shareholders are taxed.

LO.8 Calculate a shareholder's basis in S corporation stock.

LO.9 Explain the tax effects that losses have on shareholders.

LO.10 Compute the built-in gains and passive investment income penalty taxes.

LO.11 Engage in tax planning for S corporations.

OUTLINE

For the latest in changes to tax legislation, visit **www.cengage.com/taxation/swft.**

THE BIG PICTURE **Tax Solutions for the Real World**

DEDUCTIBILITY OF LOSSES AND THE CHOICE OF BUSINESS ENTITY

Cane, Inc., has been a C corporation for a number of years, earning taxable income of less than $100,000 per year. Thus, the business has been subject to the lower C corporation tax rates, but due to cheap imports from China, Cane's two owners, Smith and Jones, expect net operating losses (NOLs) for the next two or three years. They hope to outsource some of the manufacturing to Vietnam and turn the company around. How can they deduct these anticipated future losses?

The corporation receives some tax-exempt income, generates a small domestic production activities deduction (DPAD), and holds some C corporation earnings and profits. Each owner draws a salary of $92,000. Cane has two classes of stock, voting and nonvoting common stock. Should Smith and Jones elect to be taxed as an S corporation? Do they need to liquidate or go through some type of reorganization to do so? **Read the chapter and formulate your response.**

22.1 Choice of Business Entity

LO.1

Explain the tax effects that S corporation status has on shareholders.

An individual establishing a business has a number of choices as to the form of business entity under which to operate. Chapters 17 through 20 outline many of the rules, advantages, and disadvantages of operating as a regular corporation. Chapter 21 discusses the partnership entity and the limited liability company (LLC) and limited liability partnership (LLP) forms.

Another alternative, the **S corporation**, provides many of the benefits of partnership taxation and at the same time gives the owners limited liability protection from creditors. The S corporation rules, which are contained in **Subchapter S** of the Internal Revenue Code (§§ 1361–1379), were enacted to allow flexibility in the entity choice that businesspeople face. Thus, S status combines the legal environment of C corporations with taxation similar to that applying to partnerships. S corporation status is obtained through an election by a *qualifying* corporation with the consent of its shareholders.

S corporations are treated as corporations under state law. They are recognized as separate legal entities and generally provide shareholders with the same liability protection afforded by C corporations. For Federal income tax purposes, however, taxation of S corporations resembles that of partnerships. As with partnerships, the income, deductions, and tax credits of an S corporation flow through to shareholders annually, regardless of whether distributions are made. Thus, income is taxed at the shareholder level and not at the corporate level. Payments to S shareholders by the corporation are distributed tax-free to the extent that the distributed earnings were previously taxed. Further, certain corporate penalty taxes (e.g., accumulated earnings tax, personal holding company tax) and the alternative minimum tax do not apply to an S corporation.

Although the Federal tax treatment of S corporations and partnerships is similar, it is not identical. For example, liabilities affect an owner's basis differently, and S corporations may incur a tax liability at the corporate level. Furthermore, an S corporation may not allocate income like a partnership, and distributions of appreciated property are taxable in an S corporation situation (see Concept Summary 22.2 later in this chapter). In addition, a variety of C corporation provisions apply to S corporations. For example, the liquidation of C and S corporations is taxed in the same way. As a rule, where the S corporation provisions are silent, C corporation rules apply.

Today, the choice of a flow-through entity for a closely held business often is between an S corporation (a Federal tax entity) and an LLC (a state tax entity). Although an S corporation resembles an LLC, there are differences. A two-or-more-member LLC operates under partnership tax principles, whereas, as just explained, partnership taxation rules do not always apply to an S corporation.

TAX *in* the NEWS — S CORPORATIONS BY THE NUMBERS

In 2007, a total of 3.99 million S corporation returns were filed—a modest 3 percent increase from 2006. The wholesale/retail (645,114) and construction (569,361) industries accounted for the largest number of returns. There were more than 6.83 million S corporation shareholders. Total receipts were more than $6 trillion, with $400 billion of net income and $82.8 billion of deficits. In 2009, 0.4 percent of all S corporation returns were audited by the IRS.

AN OVERVIEW OF S CORPORATIONS

As the following examples illustrate, S corporations can be advantageous even when the individual tax rate exceeds the corporate tax rate.

EXAMPLE 1

An S corporation earns $300,000 in 2011. The marginal individual tax rate applicable to shareholders is 35% on ordinary income and 15% on dividend income. The applicable marginal corporate tax rate is 34%. All after-tax income is distributed currently. The entity's available after-tax earnings, compared with those of a similar C corporation, are as follows.

	C Corporation	S Corporation
Earnings	$ 300,000	$ 300,000
Less: Corporate tax	(102,000)	–0–
Available for distribution	$ 198,000	$ 300,000
Less: Tax at owner level	(29,700)*	(105,000)**
Available after-tax earnings	$ 168,300	$ 195,000

*$198,000 × 15% dividend income tax rate.
**$300,000 × 35% ordinary income tax rate.

The S corporation generates an extra $26,700 of after-tax earnings ($195,000 − $168,300), when compared with a similar C corporation. The C corporation might be able to reduce this disadvantage, however, by paying out its earnings as compensation, rents, or interest expense. Tax at the owner level can also be deferred or avoided by not distributing after-tax earnings. ■

EXAMPLE 2

A new corporation elects S status and incurs a net operating loss (NOL) of $300,000. The shareholders may use their proportionate shares of the NOL to offset other taxable income in the current year, providing an immediate tax savings. In contrast, a newly formed C corporation is required to carry the NOL forward for up to 20 years and does not receive any tax benefit in the current year. Hence, an S corporation can accelerate NOL deductions and thereby provide a greater present value for tax savings generated by the loss. ■

WHEN TO ELECT S CORPORATION STATUS

Effective planning with S corporations begins with determining the appropriateness of an S election. The following factors should be considered.

- If shareholders have high marginal rates relative to C corporation rates, it may be desirable to avoid S corporation status. Although C corporation earnings can be subject to double taxation, good tax planning mitigates this result (e.g., when the owners take profits out as salary). Likewise, profits of the corporation may be taken out by the shareholders as capital gain income through stock redemptions, liquidations, or sales of stock to others. Alternatively, corporate profits may be paid out as dividends, which are subject to a maximum tax rate of 15 percent. Any distribution of profits or sale of stock can be deferred to a later year, thereby reducing the present value of potential shareholder taxes. Finally, potential shareholder-level tax on corporate profits can be eliminated by a step-up in the basis of the stock upon the shareholder's death.

- S corporation status allows shareholders to realize tax benefits from corporate losses immediately—an important consideration in new business enterprises where losses are common. Thus, if corporate NOLs are anticipated and there is unlikely to be corporate income over the near term to offset with the NOLs, S corporation status is advisable. However, the deductibility of the losses to shareholders must also be considered. The at-risk and passive loss limitations apply to losses generated by an S corporation (see Chapter 11). In addition, as discussed later in this chapter, shareholders may not deduct losses in excess of the basis in their stock. Together these limits may significantly reduce the benefits of an S corporation in a loss setting.
- If the entity electing S status is currently a C corporation, NOL carryovers from prior years cannot be used in an S corporation year. Even worse, S corporation years reduce the 20-year carryover period. Also, the corporation may be subject to some corporate-level taxes if it elects S status (see the discussion of the built-in gains tax later in this chapter).
- Distributions of earnings from C corporations are usually taxed as dividend income, subject to a maximum tax rate of 15 percent. In contrast, because S corporations are flow-through entities, separately stated deduction and income items retain any special tax characteristics when they are reported on shareholders' returns. How this consideration affects the S status choice depends upon the character of income and deductions of the S corporation. For instance, it may be an advantage to receive the flow-through of passive income, or the domestic production activities deduction, on the shareholder's tax return, making the S election more attractive. Charitable contributions are not subject to the 10 percent limitation at the corporate level, but an S corporation cannot take advantage of special provisions for contributions of inventory and scientific equipment.
- State and local tax laws also should be considered when making the S election. Although an S corporation usually escapes Federal income tax, it may not be immune from state and local taxes. State taxation of S corporations varies. Some states, including Michigan, treat them the same as C corporations, resulting in a corporate tax liability from an income or franchise tax.
- The choice of S corporation status is affected by a variety of other factors. For example, the corporate alternative minimum tax (see Chapter 15) may be avoided in an S corporation setting.

LO.2

Identify corporations that qualify for the S election.

22.2 Qualifying for S Corporation Status

DEFINITION OF A SMALL BUSINESS CORPORATION

To achieve S corporation status, a corporation *first* must qualify as a **small business corporation**. If each of the following requirements is met, then the entity can elect S corporation status.

- Is a domestic corporation (incorporated and organized in the United States).
- Is an eligible corporation (see below for ineligible types).
- Issues only one class of stock.
- Is limited to a theoretical maximum of 100 shareholders.
- Has only individuals, estates, certain trusts, and certain tax-exempt organizations as shareholders.
- Has no nonresident alien shareholders.

Unlike other provisions in the tax law (e.g., § 1244), no maximum or minimum dollar sales or capitalization restrictions apply to small business corporations.

TAX *in* the NEWS

GAO Attacks S Corporations

According to the U.S. Government Accountability Office (GAO), S corporations are not only one of the fastest growing business types, but they are also likely to make errors on their tax returns. In a report to the Senate Finance Committee, the GAO said that 68 percent of S corporation returns filed for tax years 2003 and 2004 misreported at least one item. About 80 percent of the time, such misreporting favored the taxpayer.

A majority of S corporations used paid preparers. Nevertheless, 71 percent of those returns were noncompliant. Mistakes in calculating shareholder basis were one of the major problems. Some S corporations also failed to pay adequate wages to shareholders, underreporting roughly $23.6 billion. This underreporting resulted in billions of dollars in lost employment taxes to the government.

Source: Government Accountability Office, *Tax Gap: Actions Needed to Address Noncompliance with S Corporation Tax Rules*, December 15, 2009.

Ineligible Corporations

Small business corporation status is not permitted for non-U.S. corporations, nor for certain banks and insurance companies.

Any domestic corporation that is not an ineligible corporation can be a qualified Subchapter S corporation subsidiary (QSSS), if the S corporation holds 100 percent of its stock and elects to treat the subsidiary as a QSSS.[1] The QSSS is viewed as a division of the parent, so the parent S corporation can own a QSSS through another QSSS. QSSSs have a separate existence for legal purposes, but they exist only within the parent S corporation for tax purposes.

One Class of Stock

A small business corporation may have only one class of stock issued and outstanding.[2] This restriction permits differences in voting rights, but not differences in distribution or liquidation rights.[3] Thus, two classes of common stock that are identical except that one class is voting and the other is nonvoting would be treated as a single class of stock for small business corporation purposes. In contrast, voting common stock and voting preferred stock (with a preference on dividends) would be treated as two classes of stock. Authorized and unissued stock or treasury stock of another class does not disqualify the corporation. Likewise, unexercised stock options, phantom stock, stock appreciation rights, warrants, and convertible debentures usually do not constitute a second class of stock.

The determination of whether stock provides identical rights as to distribution and liquidation proceeds is made based on the provisions governing the operation of the corporation. These *governing provisions* include the corporate charter, articles of incorporation, bylaws, applicable state law, and binding agreements relating to distribution and liquidation proceeds. Employment contracts, loan agreements, and other commercial contracts are *not* considered governing provisions.[4]

EXAMPLE 3
THE BIG PICTURE

Return to the facts of *The Big Picture* on p. 22-2. Cane, Inc., could elect to be an S corporation as long as the two classes of common stock are identical except that one class is voting and the other class is nonvoting.

You learn that both shareholders have binding employment contracts with Cane, Inc. The amount of compensation paid by the corporation to Jones under her employment contract is reasonable, but the amount paid to Smith under his employment contract is excessive, resulting in a constructive dividend. Smith's employment contract was not prepared to circumvent the one-class-of-stock requirement.

Because employment contracts are not considered governing provisions, Cane still is treated as though it has only one class of stock if an S election is made. ■

[1] § 1361(b)(3)(B).
[2] § 1361(b)(1)(D).
[3] § 1361(c)(4).
[4] Reg. § 1.1361–1(l)(2).

Although the one-class-of-stock requirement seems straightforward, it is possible for debt to be reclassified as stock, resulting in an unexpected loss of S corporation status.[5] To mitigate concern over possible reclassification of debt as a second class of stock, the law provides a set of *safe-harbor* provisions.

First, straight debt *issued in an S corporation year* will not be treated as a second class of stock and will not disqualify the S election.[6] The characteristics of straight debt include the following.

- The debtor is subject to a written, unconditional promise to pay on demand or on a specified date a sum certain in money.
- The interest rate and payment date are not contingent on corporate profits, management discretion, or similar factors.
- The debt is not convertible into stock.
- The debt is held by a creditor who is an individual (other than a nonresident alien), an estate, or a qualified trust.
- Straight debt can be held by creditors actively and regularly engaged in the business of lending money.

In addition to straight debt under the safe-harbor rules, short-term unwritten advances from a shareholder that do not exceed $10,000 in the aggregate at any time during the corporation's taxable year generally are not treated as a second class of stock. Likewise, debt that is held by stockholders in the same proportion as their stock is not treated as a second class of stock, even if it would be reclassified as equity otherwise.[7]

Number of Shareholders

A small business corporation theoretically is limited to 100 shareholders. If shares of stock are owned jointly by two individuals, they will generally be treated as separate shareholders.

Family members may be treated as one shareholder for purposes of determining the number of shareholders. The term "members of the family" is defined as the common ancestor, the lineal descendants of the common ancestor, and the spouses (or former spouses) of the lineal descendants or common ancestor. An estate of a family member also may be treated as a family member for purposes of determining the number of shareholders.[8]

EXAMPLE 4

Fred and Wilma (husband and wife) jointly own 10 shares in Marlins, Inc., an S corporation, with the remaining 290 shares outstanding owned by 99 other unrelated shareholders. Fred and Wilma get divorced; pursuant to the property settlement approved by the court, the 10 shares held by Fred and Wilma are divided between them—5 to each. Before the divorce settlement, Marlins had 100 shareholders under the small business corporation rules. After the settlement, it still has 100 shareholders and continues to qualify as a small business corporation. A former spouse is treated as being in the same family as the individual to whom he or she was married. ■

Type of Shareholder Limitation

Small business corporation shareholders may be resident individuals, estates, certain trusts, and certain tax-exempt organizations.[9] Charitable organizations, employee

[5] Refer to the discussion of debt-versus-equity classification in Chapter 18.

[6] § 1361(c)(5)(A).

[7] Reg. § 1.1361–1(1)(4).

[8] §§ 1361(c)(1)(A)(ii) and (B)(i). Notice 2005–91, 2005–51 I.R.B. 1164 provides insight into the determination of family members.

[9] § 1361(b)(1)(B). Foreign trusts, charitable remainder trusts, and charitable lead trusts cannot be shareholders.

benefit trusts exempt from taxation, and a one-person LLC classified as a disregarded entity also all can qualify as shareholders of an S corporation. This limitation prevents partnerships, corporations, limited liability partnerships, most LLCs, and most IRAs and Roth IRAs from owning S corporation stock. Partnerships and corporate shareholders could easily circumvent the 100-shareholder limitation as illustrated in the following example.

EXAMPLE 5

Saul and 105 of his close friends wish to form an S corporation. Saul reasons that if he and his friends form a partnership, the partnership can then form an S corporation and act as a single shareholder, thereby avoiding the 100-shareholder rule. Saul's plan will not work because partnerships cannot own stock in a small business corporation. ■

Although partnerships and corporations cannot own small business corporation stock, small business corporations can be partners in a partnership or shareholders in a corporation. This ability allows the 100-shareholder requirement to be bypassed in a limited sense. For example, if two small business corporations, each with 100 shareholders, form a partnership, then the shareholders of both corporations can enjoy the limited liability conferred by S corporation status and a single level of tax on partnership profits.

Nonresident Aliens

Nonresident aliens cannot own stock in a small business corporation.[10] That is, individuals who are not U.S. citizens *must live in the United States* to own S corporation stock. Therefore, shareholders with nonresident alien spouses in community property states[11] cannot own S corporation stock because the nonresident alien spouse would be treated as owning half of the community property.[12] Similarly, if a resident alien shareholder moves outside the United States, the S election will be terminated.

MAKING THE ELECTION

LO.3

Explain how to make an S election.

To become an S corporation, a *small business corporation* (defined above) must file a valid election with the IRS. The election is made on Form 2553. For the election to be valid, it should be filed on a timely basis, and all shareholders must consent.

For S corporation status to apply in the current tax year, the election must be filed either in the previous year or on or before the fifteenth day of the third month of the current year.

EXAMPLE 6

THE BIG PICTURE

Return to the facts of *The Big Picture* on p. 22-2. Suppose that in 2011 shareholders Smith and Jones decide to become an S corporation beginning January 1, 2012. Since the C corporation uses a calendar tax year, the S election can be made at any time in 2011 or by March 15, 2012. An election after March 15, 2012, will not be effective until the 2013 calendar tax year. ■

There is a simplified method of requesting relief for late S elections that were intended to be effective as of the date of the election. The entity must file a properly

[10] § 1362(b)(1)(C).

[11] Assets acquired by a married couple are generally considered community property in these states: Arizona, California, Idaho, Louisiana, Nevada, New Mexico, Texas, Washington, Wisconsin, and (if elected by the spouses) Alaska.

[12] See *Ward v. U.S.*, 81–2 USTC ¶9674, 48 AFTR 2d 81–5942, 661 F.2d 226 (Ct.Cls., 1981), where the court found that the stock was owned as community property. Since the taxpayer-shareholder (a U.S. citizen) was married to a citizen and resident of Mexico, the nonresident alien prohibition was violated. If the taxpayer-shareholder had held the stock as separate property, the S election would have been valid.

completed Form 2553 with a Form 1120S no later than six months after the due date of the tax return (excluding extensions) of the entity for the first tax year in which the S election was intended. The Form 2553 must explain the reason for the failure to timely file the election. Sufficient reasonable cause might occur, for example, where both the corporation's accountant and its attorney failed to file the election because each believed the other had done so or because there was miscommunication as to who was responsible for filing.

Even if the 2½-month deadline is met, an S election is not valid unless the corporation qualifies as a small business corporation for the *entire* tax year. Otherwise, the election will be effective for the following tax year.

A corporation that does not yet exist cannot make an S corporation election.[13] Thus, for new corporations, a premature election may not be effective. A new corporation's 2½-month election period begins at the earliest occurrence of any of the following events:

- When the corporation has shareholders.
- When it acquires assets.
- When it begins doing business.[14]

EXAMPLE 7

Several individuals acquire assets on behalf of Rock Corporation on June 29, 2011, and begin doing business on July 3, 2011. They subscribe to shares of stock, file articles of incorporation for Rock, and become shareholders on July 7, 2011. The S election must be filed no later than 2½ months after June 29, 2011 (i.e., on or before September 12) to be effective for 2011. ■

The IRS can correct errors in electing S status where a taxpayer can show that the mistake was inadvertent, the entity otherwise was qualified to be an S corporation, and it acted as if it were an S corporation. Under certain conditions, automatic relief is granted without the need for a letter ruling request and the normal user fee.

An LLC that makes a timely and valid election to be classified as an S corporation need not "check the box" on a Form 8832. The LLC must meet all of the other S corporation requirements.

SHAREHOLDER CONSENT

A qualifying election requires the consent of all of the corporation's shareholders.[15] Consent must be in writing, and it must generally be filed by the election deadline. A consent extension is available only if Form 2553 is filed on a timely basis, reasonable cause is given, and the interests of the government are not jeopardized.[16]

EXAMPLE 8

Vern and Yvonne decide to convert their C corporation into a calendar year S corporation for 2011. At the end of February 2011 (before the election is filed), Yvonne travels to Ukraine and forgets to sign a consent to the election. Yvonne will not return to the United States until June and cannot be reached by fax or e-mail.

Vern files the S election on Form 2553 and also requests an extension of time to file Yvonne's consent to the election. Vern indicates that there is a reasonable cause for the extension: a shareholder is out of the country. Since the government's interest is not jeopardized, the IRS probably will grant Yvonne an extension of time to file the consent. Vern must file the election on Form 2553 on or before March 15, 2011, for the election to be effective for the 2011 calendar year. ■

[13]See, for example, *T.H. Campbell & Bros., Inc.*, 34 TCM 695, T.C.Memo. 1975–149; Ltr.Rul. 8807070.

[14]Reg. § 1.1372–2(b)(1). Also see, for example, *Nick A. Artukovich*, 61 T.C. 100 (1973).

[15]§ 1362(a)(2).

[16]Rev.Rul. 60–183, 1960–1 C.B. 625; *William Pestcoe*, 40 T.C. 195 (1963); Reg. § 1.1362–6(b)(3)(iii).

Both husband and wife must consent if they own their stock jointly (as joint tenants, tenants in common, tenants by the entirety, or community property). This requirement has led to considerable taxpayer grief—particularly in community property states where the spouses may not realize that their stock is jointly owned as a community asset.

EXAMPLE 9

Three shareholders, Amy, Monty, and Dianne, incorporate in January and file Form 2553. Amy is married and lives in California. Monty is single and Dianne is married; both live in North Carolina. Because Amy is married and lives in a community property state, her husband also must consent to the S election. Since North Carolina is not a community property state, Dianne's husband need not consent. ■

Finally, for current-year S elections, persons who were shareholders during any part of the taxable year before the election date, but were not shareholders when the election was made, must also consent to the election.[17]

EXAMPLE 10

On January 15, 2011, the stock of Columbus Corporation (a calendar year C corporation) was held equally by three individual shareholders: Jim, Sally, and LuEllen. On that date, LuEllen sells her interest to Jim and Sally. On March 14, 2011, Columbus Corporation files Form 2553. Jim and Sally indicate their consent by signing the form. Columbus cannot become an S corporation until 2012 because LuEllen did not indicate consent. Had all three shareholders consented by signing Form 2553, S status would have taken effect as of January 1, 2011. ■

LOSS OF THE ELECTION

LO.4

Explain how an S election can be terminated.

An S election remains in force until it is revoked or lost. Election or consent forms are not required for future years. However, an S election can terminate if any of the following occurs.

- Shareholders owning a majority of shares (voting and nonvoting) voluntarily revoke the election.
- A new shareholder owning more than one-half of the stock affirmatively refuses to consent to the election.
- The corporation no longer qualifies as a small business corporation.
- The corporation does not meet the passive investment income limitation.

Voluntary Revocation

A **voluntary revocation** of the S election requires the consent of shareholders owning a majority of shares on the day that the revocation is to be made.[18] A revocation filed up to and including the fifteenth day of the third month of the tax year is effective for the entire tax year, unless a later date is specified. Similarly, unless an effective date is specified, revocation made after the first 2½ months of the current tax year is effective for the following tax year.

EXAMPLE 11

The shareholders of Petunia Corporation, a calendar year S corporation, voluntarily revoke the S election on January 5, 2011. They do not specify a future effective date in the revocation. Assuming the revocation is properly executed and timely filed, Petunia will be a C corporation for the entire 2011 calendar year. If the election is not made until June 2011, Petunia will remain an S corporation in 2011 and will become a C corporation at the beginning of 2012. ■

[17] § 1362(b)(2)(B)(ii).

[18] § 1362(d)(1).

A corporation can revoke its S status *prospectively* by specifying a future date when the revocation is to be effective. A revocation that designates a future effective date splits the corporation's tax year into a short S corporation year and a short C corporation year. The day on which the revocation occurs is treated as the first day of the C corporation year. The corporation allocates income or loss for the entire year on a pro rata basis, based on the number of days in each short year.

EXAMPLE 12

Assume the same facts as in the preceding example, except that Petunia designates July 1, 2011, as the revocation date. Accordingly, June 30, 2011, is the last day of the S corporation's tax year. The C corporation's tax year runs from July 1, 2011, to December 31, 2011. Any income or loss for the 12-month period is allocated between the two short years, based on the number of days in each short year. ■

Rather than allocating on a pro rata basis, the corporation can elect to compute actual income or loss attributable to the two short years. This election requires the consent of everyone who was a shareholder at any time during the S corporation's short year and everyone who owns stock on the first day of the C corporation's year.[19]

EXAMPLE 13

Assume the same facts as in the preceding example, except that all of Petunia's shareholders consent to allocate the income or loss to the two short tax years based on its actual realization. Assume further that Petunia experiences a total loss of $102,000, of which $72,000 is incurred in the first half of the year. Since $72,000 of the loss occurs before July 1, this amount is allocated to the S corporation short year, and only $30,000 is allocated to the C corporation year. ■

Loss of Small Business Corporation Status

If an S corporation fails to qualify as a small business corporation at any time after the election has become effective, its status as an S corporation ends. The termination occurs on the day that the corporation ceases to be a small business corporation.[20] Thus, if the corporation ever has more than 100 shareholders, a second class of stock, or a nonqualifying shareholder, or otherwise fails to meet the definition of a small business corporation, the S election is immediately terminated.

EXAMPLE 14

Peony Corporation has been a calendar year S corporation for three years. On August 13, 2011, one of its 100 shareholders sells *some* of her stock to an outsider. Peony now has 101 shareholders, and it ceases to be a small business corporation. For 2011, Peony is an S corporation through August 12, 2011, and a C corporation from August 13 to December 31, 2011. ■

Passive Investment Income Limitation

The Code provides a **passive investment income (PII)** limitation for S corporations that were previously C corporations or for S corporations that have merged with C corporations. If an S corporation has C corporation E & P and passive income in excess of 25 percent of its gross receipts for three consecutive taxable years, the S election is terminated as of the beginning of the fourth year.[21]

[19] § 1362(e)(3).

[20] § 1362(d)(2)(B).

[21] § 1362(d)(3)(A)(ii).

EXAMPLE 15

For 2008, 2009, and 2010, Diapason Corporation, a calendar year S corporation, received passive income in excess of 25% of its gross receipts. If Diapason holds accumulated E & P from years in which it was a C corporation, its S election is terminated as of January 1, 2011. ■

PII includes dividends, interest, rents, gains and losses from sales of capital assets, and royalties net of investment deductions. Rents are not considered PII if the corporation renders significant personal services to the occupant.

EXAMPLE 16

Violet Corporation owns and operates an apartment building. The corporation provides utilities for the building, maintains the lobby, and furnishes trash collection for tenants. These activities are not considered significant personal services, so any rent income earned by the corporation will be considered PII.

Alternatively, if Violet also furnishes maid services to its tenants (personal services beyond what normally would be expected from a landlord in an apartment building), the rent income would no longer be PII. ■

Reelection after Termination

After an S election has been terminated, the corporation must wait five years before reelecting S corporation status. The five-year waiting period is waived if:

- there is a more-than-50-percent change in ownership of the corporation after the first year for which the termination is applicable, or
- the event causing the termination was not reasonably within the control of the S corporation or its majority shareholders.

22.3 Operational Rules

S corporations are treated much like partnerships for tax purposes. With a few exceptions, S corporations generally make tax accounting and other elections at the corporate level.[22] Each year, the S corporation determines nonseparately stated income or loss and separately stated income, deductions, and credits. These items are taxed only once, at the shareholder level. All items are allocated to each shareholder based on average ownership of stock throughout the year. The *flow-through* of each item of income, deduction, and credit from the corporation to the shareholder is illustrated in Figure 22.1.

COMPUTATION OF TAXABLE INCOME

LO.5

Compute nonseparately stated income and identify separately stated items.

Subchapter S taxable income or loss is determined in a manner similar to the tax rules that apply to partnerships, except that S corporations amortize organizational expenditures using the C corporation rules[23] and must recognize gains, *but not losses*, on distributions of appreciated property to shareholders.[24] Other special provisions affecting only the computation of C corporation income, such as the dividends received deduction, do not extend to S corporations.[25] Finally, as with partnerships, certain deductions of individuals are not permitted, including alimony payments, personal moving expenses, certain dependent care expenses, the personal exemption, and the standard deduction.

In general, S corporation items are divided into (1) nonseparately stated income or loss and (2) separately stated income, losses, deductions, and credits that could affect

[22]A few elections can be made at the shareholder level (e.g., the choice between a foreign tax deduction or credit).

[23]§§ 248 and 1363(b).

[24]§ 1363(b).

[25]§ 703(a)(2).

FIGURE 22.1 **Flow-Through of Separate Items of Income and Loss to S Corporation Shareholders**

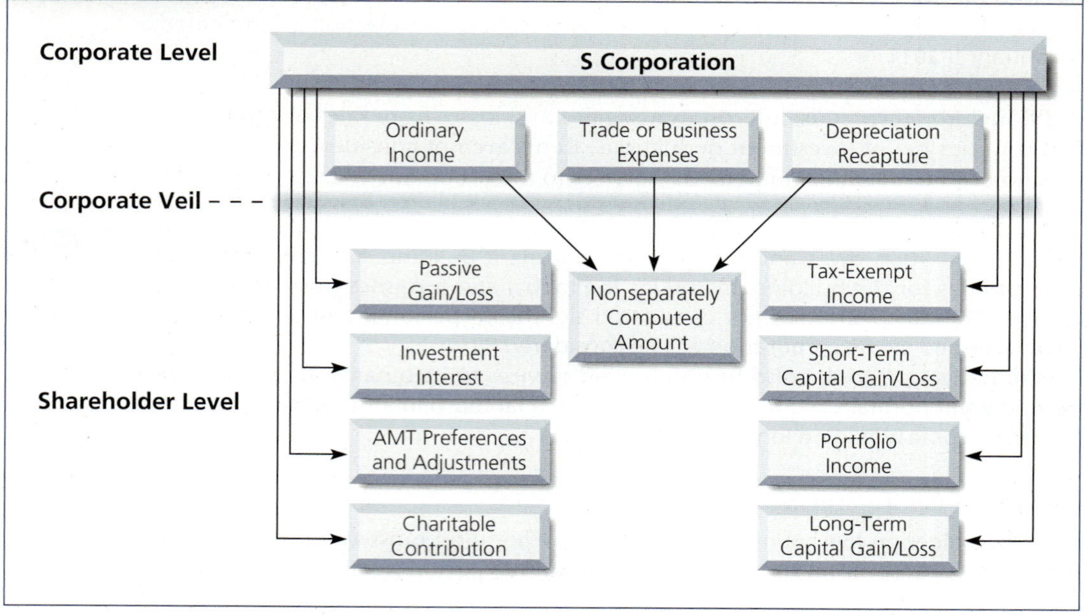

the tax liability of any shareholder in a different manner, depending on other factors in the shareholder's tax situation. In essence, nonseparate items are aggregated into an undifferentiated amount that constitutes Subchapter S ordinary income or loss. An S corporation's separately stated items are identical to those separately stated by partnerships. These items retain their tax attributes on the shareholder's return. Separately stated items are listed on Schedule K of the 1120S. They include the following.

- Tax-exempt income.
- Long-term and short-term capital gains and losses.
- Section 1231 gains and losses.
- Charitable contributions.
- Passive gains, losses, and credits.
- Certain portfolio income.
- Section 179 expense deduction.
- Domestic production gross receipts and deduction.
- Tax preferences and adjustments for the alternative minimum tax.
- Depletion.
- Foreign income or loss.
- Recoveries of tax benefit items.
- Intangible drilling costs.
- Investment interest, income, and expenses.

EXAMPLE 17

The following is the income statement for Jersey, Inc., an S corporation.

Sales		$ 40,000
Less: Cost of sales		(23,000)
Gross profit on sales		$ 17,000
Less: Interest expense	$ 1,200	
Charitable contributions	400	
Advertising expenses	1,500	
Other operating expenses	2,000	(5,100)

Book income from operations		$11,900
Add: Tax-exempt interest	$300	
Dividend income	200	
Long-term capital gain	500	1,000
Less: Short-term capital loss		(150)
Net income per books		$12,750

Subchapter S ordinary income (i.e., nonseparately stated income) for Jersey is calculated as follows, using net income for book purposes as the starting point.

Net income per books		$12,750
Separately stated items		
Deduct: Tax-exempt interest	$300	
Dividend income	200	
Long-term capital gain	500	(1,000)
Add: Charitable contributions	$400	
Short-term capital loss	150	550
Subchapter S ordinary income		$12,300

The $12,300 of Subchapter S ordinary income, as well as each of the five separately stated items, are divided among the shareholders based upon their stock ownership. ■

ALLOCATION OF INCOME AND LOSS

LO.6

Allocate income, deductions, and credits to shareholders.

Each shareholder is allocated a pro rata portion of nonseparately stated income or loss and all separately stated items. The pro rata allocation method assigns an equal amount of each of the S items to each day of the year. If a shareholder's stock holding changes during the year, this allocation assigns the shareholder a pro rata share of each item for *each* day the stock is owned. On the date of transfer, the transferor (and not the transferee) is considered to own the stock.[26]

S corporation item × Percentage of shares owned × Percentage of year shares were owned = Amount of item to be reported

The per-day allocation must be used, unless the shareholder disposes of his or her entire interest in the entity.[27] In case of a complete termination, a short year may result, as discussed below. If a shareholder dies during the year, his or her share of the pro rata items up to and including the date of death is reported on the final individual income tax return.

EXAMPLE 18

Assume in the previous example that Pat, a shareholder, owned 10% of Jersey's stock for 100 days and 12% for the remaining 265 days (assume for this example that this year is not a leap year). Using the required per-day allocation method, Pat's share of the S corporation items is as follows.

	Schedule K Totals	Pat's Share		Pat's Schedule K–1 Totals
		10%	12%	
Subchapter S ordinary income	$12,300	$337	$1,072	$1,409
Tax-exempt interest	300	8	26	34
Dividend income	200	5	17	22
Long-term capital gain	500	14	44	58
Charitable contributions	400	11	35	46
Short-term capital loss	150	4	13	17

[26]Reg. § 1.1377–1(a)(2)(ii).

[27]§§ 1366(a)(1) and 1377(a)(1).

Pat's share of the Subchapter S ordinary income is the total of $12,300 × [0.10 × (100/365)] plus $12,300 × [0.12 × (265/365)], or $1,409. Each of the Schedule K–1 totals from the right-hand column flows through to the appropriate lines on Pat's individual income tax return (Form 1040). ■

EXAMPLE 19

If Pat in the previous example dies after owning the stock 100 days, his share of the S corporation items is reported on his final individual income tax return (Form 1040). Thus, only the items in the column labeled 10% in Example 18 are reported on Pat's final tax return. S corporation items that occur after Pat's death most likely would flow through to the income tax return of Pat's estate (Form 1041). ■

The Short-Year Election

If a shareholder's interest is completely terminated by disposition or death during the tax year, all shareholders holding stock during the year and the corporation may elect to treat the S taxable year as two taxable years. The first year ends on the date of the termination. Under this election, an interim closing of the books is undertaken, and the shareholders report their shares of the S corporation items as they occurred during the short tax year.[28]

The short-year election provides an opportunity to shift income, losses, and credits between shareholders. The election is desirable in circumstances where more loss can be allocated to taxpayers with higher marginal tax rates.

EXAMPLE 20

Alicia, the owner of all of the shares of an S corporation, transfers her stock to Cindy halfway through the tax year. There is a $100,000 NOL for the entire tax year, but $30,000 of the loss occurs during the first half of the year. Without a short-year election, $50,000 of the loss is allocated to Alicia, and $50,000 is allocated to Cindy. If the corporation makes the short-year election, Cindy is allocated $70,000 of the loss. Of course, the sales price of the stock would probably be increased to recognize the tax benefits being transferred from Alicia to Cindy. ■

In the case of the death of a shareholder, a short-year election prevents the income and loss allocation to a deceased shareholder from being affected by postdeath events.

EXAMPLE 21

Joey and Karl equally own Rose, Inc., a calendar year S corporation. Joey dies on June 29 of a year that is not a leap year. Rose has income of $250,000 for January 1 through June 29 and $750,000 for the remainder of the year. Without a short-year election, the income is allocated by assigning an equal portion of the annual income of $1 million to each day (or $2,739.73 per day) and allocating the daily portion between the shareholders. Joey is allocated 50% of the daily income for the 180 days from January 1 to June 29, or $246,575.70 [($2,739.73/2) × 180]. Joey's *estate* is allocated 50% of the income for the 185 days from June 30 to December 31, or $253,425.02 [($2,739.73/2) × 185].

If the short-year election is made, the income of $250,000 from January 1 to June 29 is divided equally between Joey and Karl, so that each is taxed on $125,000. The income of $750,000 from June 30 to December 31 is divided equally between Joey's estate and Karl, or $375,000 to each.

Under either alternative, Karl reports income of $500,000. However, with the short-year election, $375,000 is allocated to Joey's estate versus only $253,425.02 without the election. Since the estate income tax rates are more progressive than the individual income tax rates, Joey's heirs would prefer that the election not be made. ■

TAX TREATMENT OF DISTRIBUTIONS TO SHAREHOLDERS

The amount of any distribution to an S corporation shareholder is equal to the cash plus the fair market value of any other property distributed. How the distribution is taxed depends upon whether the S corporation has C corporation **accumulated earnings and profits** (AEP, described in Chapter 19).

[28] § 1377(a)(2).

CONCEPT SUMMARY 22.1

Classification Procedures for Distributions from an S Corporation

Where Earnings and Profits Exist	Where No Earnings and Profits Exist
1. Distributions are tax-free to the extent of the AAA. 2. Distributions from AEP constitute dividend income.† 3. Distributions are tax-free to the extent of the other adjustments account (OAA). 4. Any residual distribution amount is nontaxable to the extent of shareholder's basis of stock.* 5. Excess is treated as gain from a sale or exchange of stock (capital gain in most cases).	1. Distributions are nontaxable to the extent of shareholder's basis of stock.* 2. Excess is treated as gain from a sale or exchange of stock (capital gain in most cases).

*The distribution reduces the stock basis. Once stock basis reaches zero, any distribution from the AAA is treated as a gain from the sale or exchange of stock. Thus, the shareholder's stock basis is an upper limit on what a shareholder may receive tax-free.
†The AAA bypass election is available to pay out AEP before reducing the AAA [§ 1368 (e)(3)].

No C Corporation AEP

If the S corporation has never been a C corporation or if it has no C corporation AEP, the distribution is a tax-free recovery of capital to the extent that it does not exceed the shareholder's adjusted basis in the stock of the S corporation. When the amount of the distribution exceeds the adjusted basis of the stock, the excess is treated as a gain from the sale or exchange of property (capital gain in most cases). The vast majority of S corporations fall into this favorable category.

EXAMPLE 22

Twirl, Inc., a calendar year S corporation, has no AEP. During the year, Juan, an individual shareholder of the corporation, receives a cash distribution of $12,200 from Twirl. Juan's basis in his stock is $9,700. Juan recognizes a capital gain of $2,500, the excess of the distribution over the stock basis ($12,200 – $9,700). The remaining $9,700 is tax-free, but it reduces Juan's basis in his stock to zero. ■

C Corporation AEP

S corporations with C corporation AEP blend the entity and conduit approaches to taxation. This blending treats distributions of pre-election (C corporation) and post-election (S corporation) earnings differently. Distributions of C corporation AEP are taxed as dividends (0/15% rate), while distributions of previously taxed S corporation earnings are tax-free to the extent of the shareholder's adjusted basis in the stock.

Concept Summary 22.1 outlines the taxation of distributions. These rules are intended to prevent two problems that result when a C corporation has been converted to an S corporation.

- Tax manipulation could result in AEP from the C corporation years being withdrawn without taxation, since S corporation shareholders are taxed on income, not on distributions.
- On the other hand, double taxation could occur. Earnings from the S corporation years might both flow to the shareholders' tax returns as income and be taxed as dividends as if the corporation were a C corporation.

A special account is required to track undistributed earnings of an S corporation that have been taxed to shareholders previously. Distributions from this account, known as the **accumulated adjustments account (AAA)**, are tax-free. The AAA begins with a zero balance on the first day of an S corporation's first tax year. Essentially, the AAA is the cumulative total of undistributed nonseparately and separately stated items for S corporation taxable years beginning after 1982. Thus, the account

EXHIBIT 22.1 **Adjustments to the Corporate AAA**

Increase by:

1. Schedule K income items other than tax-exempt income.
2. Nonseparately computed income.
3. Depletion in excess of basis in the property.

Decrease by:

4. Negative Schedule K adjustments other than distributions (e.g., losses, deductions).
5. Any portion of a distribution that is considered to be tax-free from AAA (but not below zero).

Note: When the combination of items 1 through 4 results in a negative number, the AAA is adjusted first for the distribution and then for the adjustments in items 1 through 4.

parallels the calculation of C corporation AEP. Calculation of the AAA applies to all S corporations, but the AAA is most important to those that have been C corporations. The AAA provides a mechanism to ensure that the earnings of an S corporation are taxed to shareholders only once.

The AAA is computed by making adjustments in the order specified in Exhibit 22.1. Its balance is determined at the end of each year rather than at the time distributions are made. When more than one distribution occurs in the same year, a pro rata portion of each distribution is treated as having been made out of the AAA.

In calculating the amount in the AAA for purposes of determining the tax treatment of current-year distributions, the net negative adjustments (e.g., the excess of losses and deductions over income) for that tax year are ignored. Tax-exempt income and related expenses (e.g., insurance proceeds and premiums paid for life insurance) do not affect AAA.

A shareholder has a proportionate interest in the AAA, regardless of the size of his or her stock basis.[29] However, since the AAA is a corporate account, no connection exists between the prior accumulated S corporation income and any specific shareholder.[30] Thus, the benefits of the AAA can be shifted from one shareholder to another shareholder. For example, when one S shareholder transfers stock to another shareholder, any AAA on the purchase date may be distributed tax-free to the purchaser. Similarly, issuing additional stock to a new shareholder in an S corporation having AAA dilutes the account relative to the existing shareholders.

The AAA (unlike the stock basis) can have a negative balance. All losses decrease the AAA balance, even those in excess of the shareholder's stock basis. However, *distributions* may not make the AAA negative or increase a negative balance.

Distribution Ordering Rules

A cash distribution from an S corporation with AEP comes first from the AAA (limited to stock basis).[31] Distributions from the AAA are tax-free. The remaining distribution is taxed as a dividend to the extent of AEP. After AEP is fully distributed, any residual amount is applied against the other adjustments account (OAA) (discussed below) and then the shareholder's remaining stock basis. The reduction in the shareholder's stock basis is a tax-free recovery of capital.[32] Any distributions once the stock basis reaches zero are taxed as capital gains.

[29] § 1368(c).

[30] § 1368(e)(1)(A).

[31] §§ 1368(c)(1) and (e)(1). Before 1983, an account similar to the AAA was in place, namely, **previously taxed income (PTI)**. An S corporation in existence before 1983 might still hold some PTI.

[32] § 1368(c).

EXAMPLE 23

Short, a calendar year S corporation, distributes $1,300 cash to its only shareholder, Otis, on December 31, 2011. Otis's basis in his stock is $1,400, Short's AAA balance is $500, and Short holds $750 of AEP before the distribution.

According to the distribution ordering rules, the first $500 is a tax-free recovery of basis from the AAA. The next $750 is a taxable dividend distribution from AEP. The remaining $50 of cash is a tax-free recovery of basis. Immediately after the distribution, Short holds a zero balance in its AAA and AEP. Otis's stock basis now is $850.

	Corporate AAA	Corporate AEP	Otis's Stock Basis*
Beginning balance	$ 500	$ 750	$1,400
Distribution ($1,300)			
From AAA	(500)		(500)
From AEP		(750)	
From stock basis			(50)
Ending balance	$ -0-	$ -0-	$ 850

*Details of basis adjustments are discussed later in the chapter. ■

EXAMPLE 24

Assume the same facts as in the preceding example. During the following year, Short reports zero ordinary income and distributes $1,000 to Otis. Of the distribution, $850 is a tax-free recovery of stock basis, and $150 is taxed to Otis as a capital gain. ■

With the consent of all of its shareholders, an S corporation can elect to have a distribution treated as if it were made first from AEP rather than from the AAA. This mechanism is known as an AAA *bypass election*. This election may be desirable as a simple means to eliminate a small AEP balance.

EXAMPLE 25

Collett, a calendar year S corporation, has AEP of $12,000 and a balance of $20,000 in the AAA. Collett Corporation may elect to distribute the AEP first, creating a $12,000 dividend for its shareholders, before using the AAA. ■

Schedule M–2

S corporations report changes in the AAA on Schedule M–2 of Form 1120S. Schedule M–2 contains a column labeled *other adjustments account (OAA)*. This account includes items that affect basis but not the AAA, such as tax-exempt income and any related nondeductible expenses. For example, life insurance proceeds received and insurance premiums paid are traced through the OAA. Distributions are made from the OAA after AEP and the AAA are reduced to zero. Distributions from the OAA are generally tax-free.

EXAMPLE 26

During the year, Sparrow, an S corporation, records the following items.

AAA, beginning of the year	$ 8,500
Ordinary income	25,000
Tax-exempt interest	4,000
Key employee life insurance proceeds received	5,000
Payroll penalty expense	2,000
Charitable contributions	3,000
Unreasonable compensation	5,000
Premiums on key employee life insurance	2,100
Distributions to shareholders	16,000

Sparrow's Schedule M–2 for the current year appears as follows.

Schedule M-2 **Analysis of Accumulated Adjustments Account, Other Adjustments Account, and Shareholders' Undistributed Taxable Income Previously Taxed**

	(a) Accumulated adjustments account	(b) Other adjustments account	(c) Shareholders' undistributed taxable income previously taxed
1 Balance at beginning of tax year	8,500		
2 Ordinary income from page 1, line 21	25,000		
3 Other additions		9,000**	
4 Loss from page 1, line 21	( )		
5 Other reductions	(10,000*)	(2,100)	
6 Combine lines 1 through 5	23,500	6,900	
7 Distributions other than dividend distributions	16,000		
8 Balance at end of tax year. Subtract line 7 from line 6	7,500	6,900	

**$2,000 (payroll penalty) + $3,000 (charitable contributions) + $5,000 (unreasonable compensation).*
***$4,000 (tax-exempt interest) + $5,000 (life insurance proceeds).* ■

Schedule M–3: Net Income or Loss Reconciliation

S corporations that have total assets on Schedule L at the end of the tax year that equal or exceed $10 million must file Schedule M–3 in lieu of Schedule M–1. For purposes of measuring total assets at the end of the year, assets are not netted or offset against liabilities. Total assets are determined using the accrual method of accounting unless both (1) the tax return of the corporation is prepared using an overall cash method of accounting, and (2) no entity includible in the U.S. tax return prepares or is included in financial statements prepared on an accrual basis.

The Schedule M–3 for S corporations is not identical to that for C corporations. Part I asks certain questions about the corporation's financial statements, and it reconciles book net income or loss to the income or loss for the tax year of the entity's U.S. tax return. Parts II and III reconcile specific book income or loss items with corresponding amounts on the U.S. tax return.

The IRS estimates that the Schedule M–3 of an S corporation takes about 87 hours to complete, but many practitioners believe that more time may be required. A more complete discussion of Schedule M–3 can be found in Chapter 17.

ETHICS & *Equity*

Avoiding Schedule M–3

Your S corporation client has read that a Schedule M–3 is now required for all S corporations with at least $10 million of assets. He says that the new schedule will reveal between 75 and 90 percent of the company's book-tax differences. Although this new schedule will help IRS agents find abusive transactions, your client is concerned that it will impose additional compliance burdens. The client's S corporation is approaching $10 million of assets, and he is thinking of either distributing some of the entity's business assets to himself or engaging in a spin-off. Are these techniques ethical?

Effect of Terminating the S Election

Normally, distributions to shareholders from a C corporation are taxed as dividends to the extent of E & P. However, any distribution of *cash* by a corporation to shareholders during a one-year period[33] following S election termination receives special treatment. Such a distribution is treated as a tax-free recovery of stock basis to the extent that it does not exceed the AAA.[34] Since *only* cash distributions reduce the AAA during this *postelection termination period,* a corporation should not make property distributions during this time. Instead, the entity should sell property and distribute the proceeds to shareholders. However, post-termination distributions that are charged against the OAA do not get tax-free treatment. Thus, to take advantage of post-termination benefits, an S corporation must know the amount of AAA at the date of the S termination.

[33]The period is approximately one year in length. The post-termination transition period is discussed later in the chapter.

[34]§§ 1371(e) and 1377(b).

CONCEPT SUMMARY 22.2

Consequences of Noncash Property Distributions

	Appreciated Property	Depreciated Property
S corporation	Realized gain is recognized by the corporation, which passes it through to the shareholders. Such gain increases a shareholder's stock basis, generating a basis in the property equal to FMV. On the distribution, the shareholder's stock basis is reduced by the FMV of the property (but not below zero).	Realized loss is not recognized. The shareholder takes an FMV basis in the property.
C corporation	Realized gain is recognized under § 311(b), which increases E & P (net of tax). The shareholder reports a taxable dividend equal to the property's FMV, but limited to the extent of corporate E & P. The shareholder's basis in the property equals its FMV.	Realized loss is not recognized. The shareholder takes an FMV basis in the property.
Partnership	No gain to the partnership or partner. The partner takes a carryover basis in the asset, but the asset basis is limited to the partner's basis in the partnership.	Realized loss is not recognized. The partner takes a carryover basis in the asset, but the asset basis is limited to the partner's basis in the partnership.

EXAMPLE 27

Quinn, the sole shareholder of Roman, Inc., a calendar year S corporation, elects during 2011 to terminate the S election, effective January 1, 2012. As of the end of 2011, Roman has an AAA of $1,300. Quinn can receive a nontaxable distribution of cash during a post-termination period of approximately one year to the extent of Roman's AAA. Although a cash distribution of $1,300 during 2012 would be nontaxable to Quinn, it would reduce the adjusted basis of his stock. ■

TAX TREATMENT OF NONCASH PROPERTY DISTRIBUTIONS BY THE CORPORATION

LO.7

Determine how distributions to S corporation shareholders are taxed.

An S corporation recognizes a gain on any liquidating or nonliquidating distribution of appreciated property in the same manner as if the asset had been sold to the shareholder at its fair market value.[35] The corporate gain is passed through to the shareholders. The character of the gain—capital gain or ordinary income—depends upon the type of asset being distributed. There is an important reason for this gain recognition rule. Without it, property might be distributed tax-free (other than for certain recapture items) and later sold without income recognition to the shareholder because the shareholder's basis equals the asset's fair market value.

The S corporation does not recognize a loss when distributing assets that are worth less than their basis. As with gain property, the shareholder's basis is equal to the asset's fair market value. Thus, the potential loss is postponed until the shareholder sells the stock of the S corporation. Since loss property receives a step-down in basis without any loss recognition by the S corporation, distributions of loss property should be avoided.

EXAMPLE 28

Turnip, Inc., an S corporation for 10 years, distributes a tract of land held as an investment to Chang, its majority shareholder. The land was purchased for $22,000 many years ago and is currently worth $82,000. Turnip recognizes a capital gain of $60,000, which increases the AAA by $60,000. The gain appears on Turnip's Schedule K, and a proportionate share of it passes through to the shareholders' tax returns. Then the

[35] § 311(b).

property distribution reduces the AAA by $82,000 (the fair market value). The tax consequences are the same for appreciated property, whether it is distributed to the shareholders and they dispose of it, or the corporation sells the property and distributes the proceeds to the shareholders.

If the land had been purchased for $82,000 and was currently worth $22,000, Chang takes a $22,000 basis in the land. The $60,000 realized loss is not recognized at the corporate level. The loss does not reduce Turnip's AAA. Only when the S corporation sells the asset does it recognize the loss and reduce AAA. ■

EXAMPLE 29

Assume the same facts as in the previous example, except that Turnip is a C corporation ($1 million E & P balance) or a partnership. The partner's basis in the partnership interest is $100,000.

	Appreciated Property		
	S Corporation	**C Corporation**	**Partnership**
Entity gain/loss	$60,000	$60,000	$ –0–
Owner's gain/loss/dividend	60,000	82,000	–0–
Owner's basis in land	82,000	82,000	22,000

	Property That Has Declined in Value		
	S Corporation	**C Corporation**	**Partnership**
Entity gain/loss	$ –0–	$ –0–	$ –0–
Owner's gain/loss/dividend	–0–	22,000	–0–
Owner's basis in land	22,000	22,000	82,000

■

LO.8

Calculate a shareholder's basis in S corporation stock.

SHAREHOLDER'S BASIS

The calculation of the initial tax basis of stock in an S corporation is similar to that for the basis of stock in a C corporation and depends upon the manner in which the shares are acquired (e.g., gift, inheritance, purchase, exchange under § 351). Once the initial tax basis is determined, various transactions during the life of the corporation affect the shareholder's basis in the stock. Although each shareholder is required to compute his or her own basis in the S shares, neither Form 1120S nor Schedule K–1 provides a place for deriving this amount.

A shareholder's basis is increased by stock purchases and capital contributions. Operations during the year cause the following upward adjustments to basis.[36]

- Nonseparately computed income.
- Separately stated income items (e.g., nontaxable income).
- Depletion in excess of basis in the property.

Basis then is reduced by distributions not reported as income by the shareholder (e.g., an AAA distribution). Next, the following items reduce basis (*but not below zero*).

- Nondeductible expenses of the corporation (e.g., fines, penalties, illegal kickbacks).
- Nonseparately computed loss.
- Separately stated loss and deduction items.

As under the partnership rule, basis first is increased by income items; then it is decreased by distributions and finally by losses.[37] In most cases, this *losses last* rule is advantageous to the S shareholder.

[36] § 1367(a).

[37] Reg. § 1.1367–1(f).

EXAMPLE 30

In its first year of operations, Iris, Inc., a calendar year S corporation in Clemson, South Carolina, earns income of $2,000. On February 2 in its second year of operations, Iris distributes $2,000 to Marty, its sole shareholder. During the remainder of the second year, the corporation incurs a $2,000 loss.

Under the S corporation ordering rules, the $2,000 distribution is tax-free AAA to Marty, and the $2,000 loss is *not* passed through because the stock basis cannot be reduced below zero. ■

A shareholder's basis in the stock can never be reduced below zero. Once stock basis is zero, any additional basis reductions from losses or deductions, but *not* distributions, decrease (but not below zero) the shareholder's basis in loans made to the S corporation. Any excess of losses or deductions over both bases is *suspended* until there are subsequent bases. Once the basis of any debt is reduced, it is later increased (only up to the original amount) by the subsequent *net increase* resulting from *all* positive and negative basis adjustments. The debt basis is adjusted back to the original amount by any "net increase" before any increase is made in the stock basis.[38] "Net increase" for a year is computed after taking distributions (other than those from AEP) into consideration. A distribution in excess of stock basis does not reduce any debt basis. If a loss and a distribution occur in the same year, the loss reduces the stock basis last, *after* the distribution.

EXAMPLE 31

At the beginning of 2011, Stacey, a sole shareholder, has a $7,000 stock basis and a $2,000 basis in a loan that she made to a calendar year S corporation with no AEP. The AAA and OAA balances at the beginning of the year are $0. Subchapter S ordinary income for 2011 is $8,200. During the year, the corporation received $2,000 of tax-exempt interest income. Cash of $17,300 is distributed to Stacey on November 15, 2011. Stacey recognizes only a $100 capital gain.

	Corporate AAA	Corporate OAA	Stacey's Stock Basis	Stacey's Loan Basis
Beginning balance	$ -0-	$ -0-	$ 7,000	$2,000
Ordinary income	8,200		8,200	
Tax-exempt income		2,000	2,000	
Subtotal	$ 8,200	$ 2,000	$17,200	$2,000
Distribution ($17,300)				
From AAA	(8,200)		(8,200)	
From OAA		(2,000)	(2,000)	
From stock basis			(7,000)	
Ending balance	$ -0-	$ -0-	$ -0-	$2,000
Distribution in excess of basis (capital gain)			$ 100	

Pass-through losses can reduce loan basis, but distributions do not. The stock basis cannot be reduced below zero, and the $100 excess distribution does not reduce Stacey's loan basis. ■

The basis rules for an S corporation are similar to the rules for determining a partner's basis in a partnership interest. However, a partner's basis in the partnership interest includes the partner's direct investment plus a *ratable share* of any partnership liabilities.[39] If a partnership borrows from a partner, the partner receives a basis increase as if the partnership had borrowed from an unrelated third party.[40] In contrast, except for loans from the shareholder to the corporation, corporate borrowing has no effect on S corporation shareholder basis. Loans from a shareholder to the S corporation have a tax basis only for the shareholder making the loan.

[38] § 1367(b)(2); Reg. § 1.1367–2(e).
[39] § 752(a).
[40] Reg. § 1.752–1(e).

The fact that a shareholder has guaranteed a loan made to the corporation by a third party has no effect upon the shareholder's loan basis, unless payments actually have been made as a result of that guarantee.[41] If the corporation defaults on indebtedness and the shareholder makes good on the guarantee, the shareholder's indebtedness basis is increased to that extent.

A flow-through deduction is available for a shareholder loan only where there is clear evidence that the S corporation is liable to the shareholder. A shareholder looking for this result should borrow the money from the bank and then loan the money to the S corporation.

If a loan's basis has been reduced and is not restored, income is recognized when the S corporation repays the shareholder. If the corporation issued a note as evidence of the debt, repayment constitutes an amount received in exchange for a capital asset, and the amount that exceeds the shareholder's basis is entitled to capital gain treatment.[42] However, if the loan is made on open account, the repayment constitutes ordinary income to the extent that it exceeds the shareholder's basis in the loan.[43] Each repayment is prorated between the gain portion and the repayment of the debt.[44] Thus, a note should be given to ensure capital gain treatment for the income that results from a loan's repayment.

EXAMPLE 32

Sammy is a 57% owner of Falcon, an S corporation in Brooklyn, New York. At the beginning of the year, his stock basis is zero. Sammy's basis in a $12,000 loan made to Falcon and evidenced by Falcon's note has been reduced to $0 by prior losses. At the end of the year, he receives a $13,000 distribution. During the year, his share of the corporation's income is $11,000. Because there is no "net increase" (i.e., his share of income is less than the amount of the distribution), Sammy's debt basis is not restored. Instead, his share of income increases his stock basis to $11,000. Therefore, on receipt of the $13,000 distribution, $11,000 is a tax-free recovery of his stock basis and $2,000 is a capital gain.[45] ■

EXAMPLE 33

Assume in the previous example that the distribution that Sammy receives is only $8,000. Since the "net increase" is $3,000 (income share of $11,000 in excess of distribution of $8,000), the debt basis is restored by $3,000. Accordingly, the remaining income share not used to increase debt basis ($8,000) is used to increase Sammy's stock basis to $8,000. Therefore, on receipt of the $8,000 distribution, all $8,000 is tax-free, reducing the stock basis back to zero. ■

LO.9

Explain the tax effects that losses have on shareholders.

TREATMENT OF LOSSES

Net Operating Loss

One major advantage of an S election is the ability to pass through any net operating loss of the corporation directly to the shareholders. A shareholder can deduct an NOL for the year in which the S corporation's tax year ends. The corporation is not entitled to any deduction for the NOL. A shareholder's basis in the stock is reduced to the extent of any pass-through of the NOL, and the corporation's AAA is reduced by the same deductible amount.[46]

EXAMPLE 34
THE BIG PICTURE

Return to the facts of *The Big Picture* on p. 22-2. If Smith and Jones make the S election for Cane, Inc., they will be able to pass through any NOLs to the extent of the shareholder's adjusted stock basis. If the new S corporation incurs an NOL of $84,000 during 2011, both shareholders are entitled to deduct $42,000 against other income for the tax year in which Cane's tax year ends. Any NOL incurred before the S election is in effect does not flow through to the two shareholders, as long as the S election is maintained. ■

[41] See, for example, *Estate of Leavitt*, 90 T.C. 206 (1988), *aff'd* 89–1 USTC ¶9332, 63 AFTR 2d 89–1437, 875 F.2d 420 (CA–4, 1989); *Selfe v. U.S.*, 86–1 USTC ¶9115, 57 AFTR 2d 86–464, 778 F.2d 769 (CA–11, 1985); *James K. Calcutt*, 91 T.C. 14 (1988).

[42] *Joe M. Smith*, 48 T.C. 872 (1967), *aff'd* and *rev'd* in 70–1 USTC ¶9327, 25 AFTR 2d 70–936, 424 F.2d 219 (CA–9, 1970); Rev.Rul. 64–162, 1964–1 C.B. 304.

[43] Reg. § 1.1367–2. Open account debt is treated as if it were evidenced by a note if the shareholder's principal balance exceeds $25,000 at the end of the tax year.

[44] Rev.Rul. 68–537, 1968–2 C.B. 372.

[45] § 1367(b)(2)(B); Reg. § 1.1367–2(e).

[46] §§ 1368(a)(1)(A) and (e)(1)(A).

Deductions for an S corporation's loss pass-throughs (e.g., NOL, capital loss, charitable contributions) cannot exceed a shareholder's adjusted basis in the stock *plus* the basis of any loans made by the shareholder to the corporation. If a taxpayer is unable to prove the tax basis, the loss pass-through can be denied.[47] As noted previously, once a shareholder's adjusted stock basis has been eliminated by a loss pass-through, any excess loss pass-through is used to reduce the shareholder's basis for any loans made to the corporation (*but never below zero*). The basis for loans is established by the actual advances made to the corporation, and not by indirect loans.[48] If the shareholder's basis is insufficient to allow a full flow-through and there is more than one type of loss (e.g., in the same year the S corporation incurs both a passive loss and a net capital loss), the flow-through amounts are determined on a pro rata basis.

EXAMPLE 35

Ralph is a 50% owner of an S corporation for the entire year. His stock basis is $10,000, and his shares of the various corporate losses are as follows:

Ordinary loss from operations	$8,000
Capital loss	5,000
§ 1231 loss	3,000
Passive loss	2,000

Based upon a pro rata approach, the total $10,000 allocable flow-through would be split among the various losses as follows:

$$\text{Ordinary loss} = \frac{\$8{,}000}{\$18{,}000} \times \$10{,}000 = \$4{,}444.44$$

$$\text{Capital loss} = \frac{\$5{,}000}{\$18{,}000} \times \$10{,}000 = \$2{,}777.78$$

$$\text{§ 1231 loss} = \frac{\$3{,}000}{\$18{,}000} \times \$10{,}000 = \$1{,}666.67$$

$$\text{Passive loss} = \frac{\$2{,}000}{\$18{,}000} \times \$10{,}000 = \$1{,}111.11$$

Total allocated loss ($4,444.44 + $2,777.78 + $1,666.67 + $1,111.11) = $10,000.00 ■

Distributions made by an S corporation are taken into account *before* applying the loss limitation for the year. Thus, distributions reduce the shareholder's stock basis used in determining the allowable loss for the year. That is, the loss for the year does *not* reduce the stock basis when accounting for the tax status of the distributions made during the year.

EXAMPLE 36

Pylon, Inc., a calendar year S corporation, is partly owned by Doris, who has a beginning stock basis of $10,000. During the year, Doris's share of a long-term capital gain (LTCG) is $2,000, and her share of an ordinary loss is $9,000. If Doris receives a $6,000 distribution, her deductible loss is calculated as follows.

Beginning stock basis	$10,000
Add: LTCG	2,000
Subtotal	$12,000
Less: Distribution	(6,000)
Basis for loss limitation purposes	$ 6,000
Deductible loss	($ 6,000)
Unused loss	($ 3,000)

Doris's stock now has a basis of zero. ■

[47] See *Donald J. Sauvigne*, 30 TCM 123, T.C.Memo. 1971–30.

[48] *Ruth M. Prashker*, 59 T.C. 172 (1972); *Frederick G. Brown v. U.S.*, 83–1 USTC ¶9364, 52 AFTR 2d 82–5080, 706 F.2d 755 (CA–6, 1983).

A shareholder's share of an NOL may be greater than both stock basis and loan basis. A shareholder is entitled to carry forward a loss to the extent that the loss for the year exceeds basis. Any loss carried forward may be deducted *only* by the *same* shareholder if and when the basis in the stock of or loans to the corporation is restored.[49]

EXAMPLE 37

Dana has a stock basis of $4,000 in an S corporation. He has loaned $2,000 to the corporation and has guaranteed another $4,000 loan made to the corporation by a local bank. Although his share of the S corporation's NOL for the current year is $9,500, Dana may deduct only $6,000 of the NOL on his individual tax return. Dana may carry forward $3,500 of the NOL, to be deducted when the basis in his stock or loan to the corporation is restored. Dana has a zero basis in both the stock and the loan after the flow-through of the $6,000 NOL. ■

Any loss carryover due to insufficient basis remaining at the end of an approximately one-year post-termination transition period is *lost forever.* The post-termination period includes the 120-day period beginning on the date of any determination pursuant to an audit of a taxpayer that follows the termination of the S corporation's election and that adjusts a Subchapter S item.[50] Thus, if a shareholder has a loss carryover, he or she should increase the stock or loan basis and flow through the loss before disposing of the stock.

Net operating losses from C corporation years cannot be utilized at the corporate level (except with respect to built-in gains, discussed later in this chapter), nor can they be passed through to the shareholders. Further, the carryforward period continues to run during S status.[51] Consequently, the S election may not be appropriate for a C corporation with NOL carryforwards. When a corporation is expecting losses in the future, an S election should be made *before* the loss years.

At-Risk Rules

S corporation shareholders, like partners, are limited in the amount of losses they may deduct by their "at-risk" amounts. The rules for determining at-risk amounts are similar, but not identical, to the partner at-risk rules. These rules apply to the shareholders, but not to the corporation. An amount at risk is determined separately for each shareholder. The amount of the corporate losses that are passed through and deductible by the shareholders is not affected by the amount the corporation has at risk.

EXAMPLE 38

Shareholder Ricketts has a basis of $35,000 in his S corporation stock. He takes a $15,000 nonrecourse loan from a local bank and lends the proceeds to the S corporation. Ricketts now has a stock basis of $35,000 and a debt basis of $15,000. However, due to the at-risk limitation, he can deduct only $35,000 of losses from the S corporation. ■

Passive Losses and Credits

Section 469 provides that net passive losses and credits are not deductible when incurred and must be carried over to a year when there is passive income. Thus, one must be aware of three major classes of income, losses, and credits—active, portfolio, and passive. S corporations are not directly subject to the limits of § 469, but corporate rental activities are inherently passive, and other activities of an S corporation may be passive unless the shareholder(s) materially participate(s) in operating the business. An S corporation may engage in more than one such activity. If the corporate activity is rental or the shareholders do not materially participate, any losses or

[49] § 1366(d).
[50] § 1377(b)(1).
[51] § 1377(b).

TAX *in* the NEWS

S Corporations Pay Taxes, Too

S corporations, like partnerships and limited liability entities, are pass-through entities, and are supposed to pay zero entity-level Federal income tax. But certain penalty taxes apply to S corporations and their shareholders, as discussed later in the chapter. And when there is a tax liability, there are audit adjustments.

Here are some approximate amounts of tax payments by and for S corporations in recent tax years. Not even one-half of 1 percent of all Forms 1120S are liable for one or more of these taxes!

	2006	2007
Built-in gains tax	$585,000,000	$845,000,000
Excess net passive income tax	45,000,000	70,000,000
Audit adjustments	9,500,000	11,500,000
Other	775,000	–0–
Total tax liability	$640,275,000	$926,500,000

Source: *IRS Tax Stats.*

credits flowing through are passive. The shareholders are able to apply the losses or credits only against their income from other passive activities.

A shareholder's stock basis is reduced by passive losses that flow through to the shareholder, even though the shareholder may not be entitled to a current deduction due to the passive loss limitations. The existence of material participation is determined at the shareholder level. There are seven tests for material participation, including a need to participate in the activity for more than 500 hours during the taxable year.[52]

EXAMPLE 39

Heather is a 50% owner of an S corporation engaged in a passive activity. A nonparticipating shareholder, she receives a salary of $6,000 for services as a result of the passive activity. Heather has $6,000 of earned income as a result of the salary. The $6,000 salary creates a $6,000 deduction/passive loss, which flows through to the shareholders. Heather's $3,000 share of the loss may not be deducted against the $6,000 of earned income. Under § 469(e)(3), earned income is not taken into account in computing the income or loss from a passive activity. ■

TAX ON PRE-ELECTION BUILT-IN GAIN

LO.10

Compute the built-in gains and passive investment income penalty taxes.

Normally, an S corporation does *not* pay an income tax, since all items flow through to the shareholders. But an S corporation that was previously a C corporation may be required to pay a built-in gains tax, LIFO recapture tax, general business credit recapture, or passive investment income tax.

Without the **built-in gains tax** (§ 1374), it would be possible to avoid the corporate double tax on a disposition of appreciated property by electing S corporation status.

The § 1374 tax generally applies to C corporations converting to S status after 1986. It is a *corporate-level* tax on any built-in gain recognized when the S corporation disposes of an asset in a taxable disposition within 10 calendar years after the date on which the S election took effect. The 10-year holding period is reduced to 7 years for tax years beginning in 2009 and 2010, and to 5 years for 2011.[53] The holding period begins on the date of the S election.

[52]Reg. § 1.469–5T(a).

[53]§ 1374(d)(7)(B).

General Rules

The base for the § 1374 tax includes any unrealized gain on appreciated assets (e.g., real estate, cash basis receivables, and goodwill) held by a corporation on the day it elects S status. The highest corporate tax rate (currently 35 percent) is applied to the unrealized gain when any of the assets are sold. Furthermore, the gain from the sale (net of the § 1374 tax)[54] passes through as a taxable gain to shareholders.

EXAMPLE 40

Zinnia, Inc., a C corporation, owns a single asset with a basis of $100,000 and a fair market value of $500,000. Zinnia elects S corporation status. Section 1374 imposes a corporate-level tax that must be paid by Zinnia if it sells the asset after electing S status. Upon sale of the asset, the corporation owes a tax of $140,000 ($400,000 × 35%). The shareholders have a $260,000 taxable gain ($400,000 − $140,000). Hence, the built-in gains tax effectively imposes a double tax on Zinnia and its shareholders. ■

The maximum amount of gain that is recognized over the required (5-, 7-, or 10-year) holding period is limited to the *aggregate net* built-in gain of the corporation at the time it converted to S status. Thus, at the time of the S election, unrealized gains of the corporation are offset by unrealized losses. The net amount of gains and losses sets an upper limit on the tax base for the built-in gains tax. Any appreciation after the conversion to S status is subject to the regular S corporation pass-through rules.

Contributions of assets with realized losses on the date of conversion reduce the maximum built-in gain and any potential tax under § 1374.[55] In addition, built-in losses and built-in gains are netted each year to determine the annual § 1374 tax base. Thus, an incentive exists to contribute loss assets to a corporation before electing S status. However, the IRS position is that contributions of loss property within two years before the earlier of the date of conversion or the date of filing an S election are presumed to have a tax avoidance motive and will not reduce the corporation's net unrealized built-in gain.

Normally, tax attributes of a C corporation do *not* carry over to a converted S corporation. For purposes of the tax on built-in gains, however, certain carryovers are allowed. In particular, an S corporation can offset built-in gains with unexpired NOLs or capital losses from C corporation years.

EXAMPLE 41
THE BIG PICTURE

Return to the facts of *The Big Picture* on p. 22-2. If Cane, Inc., becomes an S corporation, a built-in gain may be recognized. Assuming that Cane reports a $50,000 built-in gain on conversion, and that it holds a $20,000 NOL carryforward from C corporation years before the S election, the NOL carryforward is applied against the built-in gain. Cane's built-in gains tax applies only to $30,000. ■

Concept Summary 22.3 summarizes the calculation of the built-in gains tax.

LIFO Recapture Tax

To preclude deferral of gain recognition by a C corporation that is electing S status, any LIFO recapture amount at the time of the S election is subject to a corporate-level tax.

The taxable LIFO recapture amount equals the excess of the inventory's value under FIFO over the LIFO value. No negative adjustment is allowed if the LIFO value is higher than the FIFO value.

[54] § 1366(f)(2).

[55] §§ 1374(c)(2) and (d)(1).

CONCEPT SUMMARY 22.3

Calculation of the Built-in Gains Tax Liability

Step 1. Select the smaller of built-in gain or taxable income (C corporation rules).*

Step 2. Deduct unexpired NOLs and capital losses from C corporation tax years.

Step 3. Multiply the tax base obtained in step 2 by the top corporate income tax rate.

Step 4. Deduct any business credit carryforwards and AMT credit carryovers arising in a C corporation tax year from the amount obtained in step 3.

Step 5. The corporation pays any tax resulting from step 4.

*Any net recognized built-in gain in excess of taxable income is carried forward to the next year, as long as the next year is within the 5-, 7-, or 10-year recognition period.

The resulting tax is payable in four equal installments, with the first payment due on or before the due date for the corporate return for the last C corporation year (without regard to any extensions). The remaining three installments are paid on or before the due dates of the succeeding corporate returns. No interest is due if payments are made by the due dates, and no estimated taxes are due on the four tax installments. The basis of the LIFO inventory is adjusted to account for this LIFO recapture amount, but the AAA is not decreased by payment of the tax.

PASSIVE INVESTMENT INCOME PENALTY TAX

A tax is imposed on the excess passive income of S corporations that possess AEP from C corporation years. The tax rate is the highest corporate rate for the year (currently, 35 percent). The rate is applied to excess net passive income (ENPI), which is determined using the following formula:

$$\text{Excess net passive income} = \frac{\text{Passive investment income in excess of 25\% of gross receipts for the year}}{\text{Passive investment income for the year}} \times \text{Net passive investment income for the year}$$

Passive investment income (PII) includes gross receipts derived from royalties, passive rents, dividends, interest, and annuities. Only the net gain from the disposition of capital assets is taken into account in computing PII gross receipts.[56] Passive investment income does not include built-in gains (or losses) recognized during the 5-, 7-, or 10-year waiting period. Net passive income is passive income reduced by any deductions directly connected with the production of that income. Any passive income tax reduces the amount the shareholders must take into income.

The excess net passive income cannot exceed the C corporate taxable income for the year before considering any NOL deduction or the special deductions allowed by §§ 241–250 (except the organizational expense deduction).[57]

[56]§§ 1362(d)(3)(B) and (C).

[57]§§ 248, 1374(d)(4), and 1375(a) and (b).

TAX *in* the NEWS

THE SELF-EMPLOYMENT INCOME ADVANTAGE

A significant advantage of an S corporation involves the current definition of self-employment income. Although compensation for services rendered to an S corporation is subject to FICA taxes, a shareholder's share of income from an S corporation is not self-employment income. The rationale for this S corporation loophole is that the S shareholder does not personally carry on the entity's trade or business. In contrast, the earned income of a partnership or proprietorship is treated as self-employment income to the partner or proprietor.

The choice between a salary and pass-through income is not clear-cut, however.

- Although a salary is subject to payroll tax and pass-through income is not [*P.B. Ding v. Comm.*, 2000–1 USTC ¶50,137, 84 AFTR 2d 99–7517, 200 F.3d 587 (CA–9, 1999)], this nonearned income does not accrue Social Security benefits for its recipient.
- S corporation income distributions do not count as compensation for computing an employee's contribution formula for a retirement plan.
- The IRS and the courts require a shareholder to take a reasonable salary (see footnote 68).
- If a partner or proprietor reports salary income from other sources and the aggregate salaries exceed the annual FICA ceiling, a partnership or proprietorship entity may provide tax savings over an S corporation.

EXAMPLE 42

Barnhardt Corporation, an S corporation, has gross receipts for the year totaling $264,000 (of which $110,000 is PII). Expenditures directly connected to the production of the PII total $30,000. Therefore, Barnhardt has net PII of $80,000 ($110,000 − $30,000), and its PII for the tax year exceeds 25% of its gross receipts by $44,000 [$110,000 PII − (25% × $264,000)]. Excess net passive income (ENPI) is $32,000, calculated as follows.

$$\text{ENPI} = \frac{\$44{,}000}{\$110{,}000} \times \$80{,}000 = \$32{,}000$$

Barnhardt's PII tax is $11,200 ($32,000 × 35%). ■

OTHER OPERATIONAL RULES

Several other points may be made about the possible effects of various Code provisions on S corporations.

- An S corporation is required to make estimated tax payments with respect to tax exposure because of any recognized built-in gain and excess passive investment income.
- An S corporation may own stock in another corporation, but an S corporation may not have a C corporation shareholder. An S corporation is *not* eligible for a dividends received deduction.
- An S corporation is *not* subject to the 10 percent of taxable income limitation applicable to charitable contributions made by a C corporation.
- Any family member who renders services or furnishes capital to an S corporation must be paid reasonable compensation. Otherwise, the IRS can make adjustments to reflect the value of the services or capital.[58] This rule may make it more difficult for related parties to shift Subchapter S taxable income to children or other family members.

[58] § 1366(e). In addition, beware of an IRS search for the "real owner" of the stock under Reg. § 1.1373–1(a)(2).

- Although § 1366(a)(1) provides for a flow-through of S items to a shareholder, it does not create self-employment income.[59] This treatment of earned income of S corporations is attractive compared to the treatment of a proprietorship or a partnership whose income is taxed as self-employment income to the owners. Compensation (i.e., salary) for services rendered to an S corporation is, however, subject to FICA taxes. Congress is considering a change to this rule.

EXAMPLE 43

Cody and Dana each own one-third of a fast-food restaurant, and their 14-year-old son owns the other shares. Both parents work full-time in the restaurant operations, but the son works infrequently. Neither parent receives a salary this year, when the taxable income of the S corporation is $160,000. The IRS can require that reasonable compensation be paid to the parents to prevent the full one-third of $160,000 from being taxed to the son. Otherwise, this would be an effective technique to shift earned income to a family member to reduce the total family tax burden. Furthermore, low or zero salaries can reduce FICA taxes due to the Federal government. ■

EXAMPLE 44

Dave is a professor at a southeastern university earning a salary of $150,000. He also has consulting income of $80,000. If the consulting business is organized as an S corporation, Dave should withdraw a reasonable salary from the S corporation for his services. The S corporation pays payroll and withholding tax on the salary. Dave receives a tax credit for any overpayment of the employee share of the FICA tax, but the S corporation does not receive a similar credit.

If the business is operated as a proprietorship, Dave is exempt from the Social Security portion of the self-employment tax because his university salary exceeds the annual FICA ceiling. Here, operating as a proprietorship offers a tax advantage over an S corporation. ■

- An S corporation is placed on the cash method of accounting for purposes of deducting business expenses and interest owed to a cash basis related party.[60] Thus, the timing of the shareholder's income and the corporate deduction must match.
- An S corporation may not deduct a payment to one of its shareholders (e.g., a year-end performance bonus) until the payee reports the income.
- The S election is not recognized by the District of Columbia and several states, including Michigan, New Hampshire, and Tennessee. Thus, some or all of the entity's income may be subject to a state-level income tax (e.g., a "sting tax" on large S corporations in Massachusetts).
- If § 1244 stock is issued to an S corporation, the S corporation and its shareholders may not treat losses on such stock as ordinary losses. However, an S corporation may issue § 1244 stock to its shareholders to obtain ordinary loss treatment.
- The § 1202 exclusion of gain on disposition of small business stock is *not* available for S stock.
- Losses may be disallowed due to a lack of a profit motive. If the activities at the corporate level are not profit motivated, the losses may be disallowed under the hobby loss rule of § 183.[61]
- A penalty is imposed for failure to file (including extensions) timely S corporation returns. The penalty is $195 per month times the number of S corporation shareholders. The penalty is assessed against the corporation for a maximum of 12 months.[62]

---

[59] Rev.Rul. 59–221, 1959–1 C.B. 225.

[60] § 267(b).

[61] *Michael J. Houston*, 69 TCM 2360, T.C.Memo. 1995–159; *Mario G. De Mendoza, III*, 68 TCM 42, T.C.Memo. 1994–314.

[62] § 6699.

- Code § 1372(a) applies partnership treatment for certain fringe benefits to more-than-2 percent shareholder-employees of S corporations. Thus, these shareholders are not entitled to exclude certain fringe benefits from gross income. A more-than-2 percent shareholder-employee is allowed an above-the-line (*for* AGI) deduction on Form 1040 for accident and health insurance premiums.[63]
- If an S corporation excludes cancellation of debt (COD) income from gross income, the excluded amount is applied to reduce S corporation tax attributes.[64]

TAX PLANNING:
22.4 When the Election Is Advisable

LO.11

Engage in tax planning for S corporations.

Effective tax planning with S corporations begins with the determination of whether the election is appropriate. In this context, one should consider the following factors.

- Are losses from the business anticipated? If so, the S election may be highly attractive because these losses pass through to the shareholders.
- What are the tax brackets of the shareholders? If the shareholders are in high individual income tax brackets, it may be desirable to avoid S corporation status and have profits taxed to the corporation at lower C rates (e.g., 15 percent or 25 percent). However, the income still is not in the owner's hands.
- When the shareholders are in low individual income tax brackets, the pass-through of corporate profits is attractive, and reducing the combined income tax becomes the paramount consideration. Under these circumstances, the S election could be an effective tax planning tool. Note, however, that although an S corporation usually escapes Federal taxes, it may not be immune from state and local taxes imposed on corporations or from several Federal penalty taxes.
- Does a C corporation have an NOL carryover from a prior year? Such a loss cannot be used in an S year (except for purposes of the built-in gains tax). Even worse, S years count in the 20-year carryover limitation. Thus, even if the S election is made, one might consider terminating the election before the carryover limitation expires. Such a termination would permit the loss to be utilized by what is now a C corporation.
- Both individuals and C corporations are subject to the alternative minimum tax. Many of the tax preference and adjustment items are the same, but some apply only to corporate taxpayers while others are limited to individuals. The alternative minimum tax adjustment relating to adjusted current earnings creates havoc with some C corporations (refer to Chapter 15). S corporations themselves are not subject to this tax.
- S corporations and partnerships have limited flexibility in the choice of a tax accounting period.[65]

The choice of the form of doing business often is dictated by other factors. For example, many businesses cannot qualify for the S election—due to the possibility of a public offering or a need for substantial capital inflow—or would find the partnership or limited liability company forms more practical. Therefore, freedom of action based on tax considerations may not be an attainable goal.

[63]Notice 2008–1, 2008–2 I.R.B 251.

[64]§§ 108(a) and 108(b)(2).

[65]Entity tax-year constraints are discussed in Chapters 16 and 21.

22.5 Making a Proper Election

Once the parties have decided the election is appropriate, it becomes essential to ensure that the election is made properly.

- Make sure all shareholders consent. If any doubt exists concerning the shareholder status of an individual, it would be wise to have that party issue a consent anyway.[66] Too few consents are fatal to the election; the same cannot be said for too many consents.
- Be sure that the election is timely and properly filed. Either hand carry the election to an IRS office or send it by certified or registered mail. The date used to determine timeliness is the postmark date, not the date the IRS receives the election. A copy of the election should become part of the corporation's permanent files.
- Be careful to ascertain when the timely election period begins to run for a newly formed corporation. An election made too soon (before the corporation is in existence) is worse than one made too late. If serious doubts exist as to when this period begins, filing more than one election might be considered a practical means of guaranteeing the desired result.
- It still is beneficial for an S corporation to issue § 1244 stock (refer to Chapter 18). This type of stock allows the original shareholder to obtain an ordinary deduction for a loss on the sale or worthlessness of the stock, rather than long-term capital loss treatment. Shareholders have nothing to lose by complying with § 1244.

22.6 Preserving the Election

Recall that an election can be lost intentionally or unintentionally in several ways and that a five-year waiting period generally is imposed before another S election is available. To preserve an S election, the following points should be kept in mind:

- As a starting point, all parties concerned should be made aware of the various transactions that lead to the loss of an election.
- Watch for possible disqualification of a small business corporation. For example, the death of a shareholder could result in a nonqualifying trust becoming a shareholder. The latter circumstance might be avoided by utilizing a buy-sell agreement or binding the deceased shareholder's estate to turn in the stock to the corporation for redemption or, as an alternative, to sell it to the surviving shareholders.[67]

22.7 Planning for the Operation of the Corporation

Operating an S corporation to achieve optimum tax savings for all parties involved requires a great deal of care and, most important, an understanding of the applicable tax rules.

ACCUMULATED ADJUSTMENTS ACCOUNT

Although the corporate-level accumulated adjustments account (AAA) is used primarily by an S corporation with accumulated earnings and profits (AEP) from a

[66] See *William B. Wilson*, 34 TCM 463, T.C.Memo. 1975–92.

[67] Most such agreements do not create a second class of S stock. Rev.Rul. 85–161, 1985–2 C.B. 191; *Portage Plastics Co. v. U.S.*, 72–2 USTC ¶9567, 30 AFTR 2d 72–5229, 470 F.2d 308 (CA–7, 1973).

Subchapter C year, all S corporations should maintain an accurate record of the AAA. Because there is a grace period for distributing the AAA after termination of the S election, the parties must be in a position to determine the balance of the account.

EXAMPLE 45

Nobles, Inc., an S corporation, has no C corporation AEP. Over the years, Nobles made no attempt to maintain an accurate accounting for the AAA. Now, the S election has been terminated, and Nobles has a grace period for distributing the AAA tax-free to its shareholders. A great deal of time and expense may be necessary to reconstruct the AAA balance. ■

When AEP is present, a negative AAA may cause double taxation of S corporation income. With a negative AAA, the recognition of current income restores the negative AAA balance to zero, but then a subsequent distribution is considered to be in excess of AAA and is taxable as a dividend to the extent of AEP. Distributions during the year reduce the stock basis for determining the allowable loss for the year, but the loss does *not* reduce the stock basis for determining the tax status of distributions made during the year. In determining the tax treatment of distributions by an S corporation having AEP, any net adjustments (e.g., excess of losses and deductions over income) for the tax year are ignored.

The AAA bypass election may be used to reduce exposure to certain penalty taxes (e.g., the accumulated earnings tax or personal holding company tax) in post-S years. This bypass election allows AEP to be distributed instead.

EXAMPLE 46

Zebra, Inc., an S corporation during 2010, has a significant amount in its AEP account. The shareholders expect to terminate the election in 2011, when Zebra will be subject to the lower corporate income tax rates. Since Zebra as a C corporation may be subject to the accumulated earnings penalty tax in 2011, the shareholders may wish to use the AAA bypass election to distribute some or all of the AEP. Of course, any distributions of the AEP account in 2010 would be taxable to the shareholders. ■

A net loss allocated to a shareholder reduces the AAA. This required adjustment should encourage an S corporation to make annual distributions of net income to avoid the reduction of an AAA by a future net loss.

SALARY STRUCTURE

The amount of salary paid to a shareholder-employee of an S corporation can have varying tax consequences and should be considered carefully. Larger amounts might be advantageous if the maximum contribution allowed for the shareholder-employee under the corporation's retirement plan has not been reached. Smaller amounts may be beneficial if the parties are trying to shift taxable income to lower-bracket shareholders, reduce payroll taxes, curtail a reduction of Social Security benefits, or restrict losses that do not pass through because of the basis limitation.

A strategy of decreasing compensation and correspondingly increasing distributions to shareholder-employees often results in substantial savings in employment taxes. However, a shareholder of an S corporation cannot always perform substantial services and arrange to receive distributions rather than compensation so that the corporation may avoid paying employment taxes. The IRS may deem the shareholder to be an employee, with any distributions recharacterized as wages subject to FICA and FUTA taxes.[68] In effect, the IRS requires that reasonable compensation be paid to shareholder-employees. For planning purposes, some level of compensation should

[68]Rev.Rul. 74–44, 1974–1 C.B. 287; *Spicer Accounting, Inc. v. U.S.*, 91–1 USTC ¶50,103, 66 AFTR 2d 90–5806, 918 F.2d 90 (CA–9, 1990); *Radtke v. U.S.*, 90–1 USTC ¶50,113, 65 AFTR 2d 90–1155, 895 F.2d 1196 (CA–7, 1990); *Joseph M. Grey Public Accountant, P.C.*, 119 T.C. 121 (2002); *Watson, P.C. v. U.S.*, 2010–1 USTC ¶50,444, 105 AFTR 2d 2010–2624, 714 F.Supp.2d 954 (D.C. S.IA).

be paid to all shareholder-employees to avoid any recharacterization of nonpassive distributions as deductible salaries—especially in personal service corporations.

The IRS can require that reasonable compensation be paid to family members who render services or provide capital to the S corporation. The IRS also can adjust the items taken into account by family-member shareholders to reflect the value of services or capital they provided. Refer to Example 43.

Unreasonable compensation traditionally has not been a problem for S corporations, but deductible compensation under § 162 reduces an S corporation's taxable income, which is relevant to the built-in gains tax. Compensation may be one of the larger items that an S corporation can use to reduce taxable income to minimize any built-in gains penalty tax. Thus, IRS agents may attempt to classify compensation as unreasonable to increase the § 1374 tax.

Deductions for various tax-free fringe benefits are denied to a more-than-2 percent shareholder-employee of an S corporation. Such benefits include group term life insurance, medical insurance, and meals and lodging furnished for the convenience of the employer. These items are treated as wages and are subject to most payroll taxes. The employee can deduct medical insurance premiums on his or her tax return.

LOSS CONSIDERATIONS

A net loss in excess of tax basis may be carried forward and deducted only by the same shareholder in succeeding years. Thus, before disposing of the stock, a shareholder should increase the basis of such stock/loan to flow through the loss. The next shareholder does not obtain the loss carryover.

Any unused loss carryover in existence upon the termination of the S election may be deducted only in the next tax year and is limited to the individual's *stock* basis (not loan basis) in the post-termination year.[69] The shareholder may wish to purchase more stock to increase the tax basis in order to absorb the loss.

The NOL provisions create a need for sound tax planning during the last election year and the post-termination transition period. If it appears that the S corporation is going to sustain an NOL or use up any loss carryover, each shareholder's basis should be analyzed to determine if it can absorb the share of the loss. If basis is insufficient to absorb the loss, further investments should be considered before the end of the post-termination transition year. Such investments can be accomplished through additional stock purchases from the corporation, or from other shareholders, to increase basis. This action ensures the full benefit from the NOL carryover.

EXAMPLE 47

A calendar year C corporation has an NOL of $20,000 in 2010. The corporation makes a valid S election in 2011 and has another $20,000 NOL in that year. At all times during 2011, the stock of the corporation was owned by the same 10 shareholders, each of whom owned 10% of the stock. Tim, one of the 10 shareholders, has a stock basis of $1,800 at the beginning of 2011. None of the 2010 NOL may be carried forward into the S year. Although Tim's share of the 2011 NOL is $2,000, the deduction for the loss is limited to $1,800 in 2011 with a $200 carryover. ■

AVOIDING THE PASSIVE INVESTMENT INCOME TAX

Too much passive investment income (PII) may cause an S corporation to incur a § 1375 penalty tax and/or terminate the S election. Several planning techniques can be used to avoid both of these unfavorable events. Where a small amount of AEP exists, an AAA bypass election may be appropriate to eliminate the AEP, thereby avoiding the passive income tax altogether. Alternatively, the corporation might reduce taxable income below the excess net passive income; similarly, PII might be accelerated into years in which there is an offsetting NOL. In addition, the tax can

[69] § 1366(d)(3).

FIGURE 22.2 **Four Alternatives to Reduce Tax Liabilities for Passive-Type C Corporations Electing S Treatment**

Alternative 1: Eliminate AEP before the S election by paying dividends, which will be taxed at the 0/15% rate.

Alternative 2: Liquidate the C corporation and reincorporate as an S corporation. The AEP will not carry over to the S corporation after the liquidation.

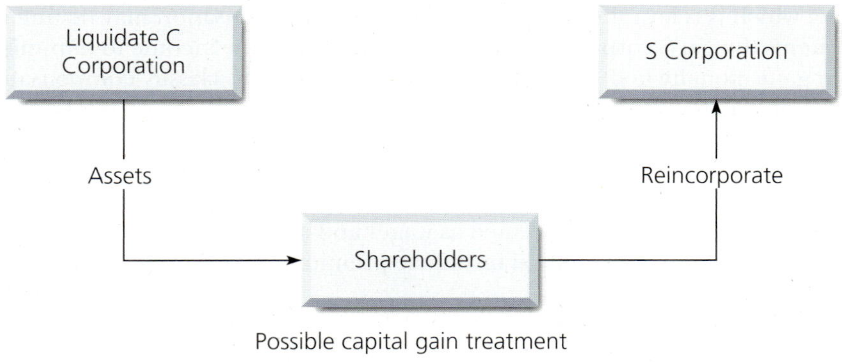

Alternative 3: If the AEP amount is small, become an S corporation with possible built-in gains. Use an AAA bypass election to eliminate the AEP by paying dividends, which will be taxed at the 0/15% rate.

Alternative 4: Make an S election, but do not eliminate AEP. Use the following techniques to avoid/reduce the passive investment income tax.

a. Reduce taxable income below excess passive income.
b. Shift PII into future years when there is an NOL.
c. Generate more gross receipts.
d. Perform significant services or incur significant costs if a rental type of business.

be avoided if the corporation manufactures needed gross receipts. By increasing gross receipts without increasing PII, the amount of PII in excess of 25 percent of gross receipts is reduced. Finally, performing significant personal services or incurring significant costs with respect to rental real estate activities can elevate the rent income to nonpassive.

EXAMPLE 48

An S corporation has paid a passive investment income penalty tax for two consecutive years. In the next year, the corporation has a large amount of AAA. If the AEP account is small, a bypass election may be appropriate to purge the corporation of the AEP. Without any AEP, no passive investment income tax applies, and the S election is not terminated. Any distribution of AEP to the shareholders constitutes taxable dividends, however.

Another alternative is to manufacture a large amount of gross receipts without increasing PII through an action such as a merger with a grocery store. If the gross receipts from the grocery store are substantial, the amount of the PII in excess of 25% of gross receipts is reduced. ■

Figure 22.2 shows four alternatives that a C corporation that intends to elect S treatment may use to reduce its tax liability.

MANAGING THE BUILT-IN GAINS TAX

The taxable income limitation encourages an S corporation to create deductions or accelerate deductions in the years that built-in gains are recognized. Although the postponed built-in gain is carried forward to future years, the time value of money makes the postponement beneficial. For example, payment of compensation, rather than a distribution, creates a deduction that reduces taxable income and postpones the built-in gains tax.

EXAMPLE 49

Mundy, Inc., an S corporation converted from a C corporation, has built-in gain of $110,000 and taxable income of $120,000 before payment of salaries to its two shareholders. If Mundy pays at least $120,000 in salaries to the shareholders (rather than a distribution), its taxable income drops to zero, and the built-in gains tax is postponed. Thus, Mundy needs to keep the salaries as high as possible to postpone the built-in gains tax in future years and reap a benefit from the time value of money. Of course, paying the salaries may increase the payroll tax burden if the salaries are below FICA and FUTA limits. ■

Giving built-in gain property to a charitable organization does not trigger the built-in gains tax. To reduce or eliminate the built-in gains tax, built-in *loss* property may be sold in the same year that built-in gain property is sold. Generally, the taxpayer should sell built-in loss property in a year when an equivalent amount of built-in gain property is sold. Otherwise, the built-in loss could be wasted.

EXAMPLE 50

Green Corporation elects S status effective for calendar year 2010. As of January 1, 2010, Green's only asset has a basis of $40,000 and a fair market value of $100,000. If this asset is sold for $120,000 in 2011, Green recognizes an $80,000 gain, of which $60,000 is subject to the corporate built-in gains tax. The other $20,000 of gain is subject to the S corporation pass-through rules and avoids the corporate income tax.

Unless the taxpayer can show otherwise, any appreciation existing at the time of the sale or exchange is presumed to be preconversion built-in gain. Therefore, Green incurs a built-in gain of $80,000 unless it can prove that the $20,000 gain developed after the effective date of the election. ■

CONTROLLING ADJUSTMENTS AND PREFERENCE ITEMS

The individual alternative minimum tax (AMT) affects more taxpayers than ever before because the tax base has expanded and the difference between regular tax rates and the individual AMT rates has been narrowed. In an S corporation setting, tax preferences flow through proportionately to the shareholders, who, in computing the individual AMT, treat the preferences as if they were directly realized. Thus, the S corporation may not take advantage of the AMT exemption available to small corporations, but there is no ACE adjustment. Further, if an S corporation has a built-in gain under § 1374, the entity does not pay an AMT on the transaction (see Chapter 15).

DOMESTIC PRODUCTION ACTIVITIES DEDUCTION

Domestic production gross receipts (DPGR), attributable cost of goods sold (CGS), and allocable deductions earned by the S corporation are passed through to the shareholders. These corporate-level DPGR, CGS, and allocable deductions are combined with any DPGR, CGS, and allocable deductions that the shareholder has from other sources.

An allocable portion of the S corporation's W–2 wages is passed through to the shareholder, but only those wages that are properly allocable to DPGR. See Chapter 7 for the calculation of the domestic production activities deduction (DPAD).

EXAMPLE 51

An S corporation has $100,000 DPGR and $75,000 of wages, and its qualified production activities income (QPAI) is $25,000. Shareholder Kirby has a 50% interest in the S corporation. Assume that all expenses that reduce DPGR are from wages and that all wages paid relate to DPGR. Kirby is allocated $12,500 of QPAI and $37,500 of wages. ■

The DPAD has no effect on a shareholder's stock basis. Further, an S corporation may qualify for the small business simplified overall method to apportion cost of goods sold and deductions between DPGR and non-DPGR at the entity level. The IRS may permit an S corporation to calculate a shareholder's share of QPAI at the entity level, to be combined with the shareholder's QPAI. A shareholder is not allowed to use another cost allocation method to reallocate the costs of the S corporation, regardless of the method used by the specific shareholder to allocate or apportion costs.

TERMINATION ASPECTS

It is always advisable to avoid accumulated earnings and profits (AEP) in an S corporation. There is the ever-present danger of terminating the election because of excess passive investment income in three consecutive years. Further, the § 1375 penalty tax is imposed on excess passive net income. Thus, one should try to eliminate such AEP through a dividend distribution or liquidation of the S corporation with a subsequent reincorporation. If the AEP account is small, to eliminate the problem, all of the shareholders may consent under § 1368(e)(3) to have distributions treated as made first from AEP rather than from the AAA (the AAA bypass election).

LIQUIDATION OF AN S CORPORATION

S corporations are subject to many of the same liquidation rules applicable to C corporations (refer to Chapter 20). In general, the distribution of appreciated property to S shareholders in complete liquidation is treated as if the property were sold to the shareholders in a taxable transaction. Unlike a C corporation, however, the S corporation itself incurs no incremental tax on the liquidation gains, because such gains flow through to the shareholders subject only to the built-in gains tax of § 1374. Any corporate gain increases the shareholder's stock basis by a like amount and reduces any gain realized by the shareholder when he or she receives the liquidation proceeds. Thus, an S corporation usually avoids the double tax that is imposed on C corporations. However, when an S corporation liquidates, all of its special tax attributes disappear (e.g., AAA, AEP, C corporation NOLs, suspended losses).

22.8 Overall Comparison: Forms of Doing Business

See Concept Summary 22.4 for a detailed comparison of the tax consequences of the following forms of doing business: sole proprietorship, partnership, limited liability entity, S corporation, and regular corporation.

CONCEPT SUMMARY 22.4

Tax Attributes of Different Forms of Business (Assume Owners and Shareholders Are All Individuals)

	Sole Proprietorship	Partnership/Limited Liability Entity*	S Corporation	Regular (C) Corporation**
Restrictions on type or number of owners	One owner. The owner must be an individual.	Must have at least 2 owners.	Only individuals, estates, certain trusts, and certain tax-exempt entities can be owners. Maximum number of shareholders limited to 100 (spouses and family members treated as one shareholder).	None, except some states require a minimum of 2 shareholders.
Incidence of tax	Sole proprietorship's income and deductions are reported on Schedule C of the individual's Form 1040. A separate Schedule C is prepared for each business.	Entity not subject to tax. Owners in their separate capacity subject to tax on their distributive share of income. Entity files Form 1065.	Except for certain built-in gains and passive investment income when earnings and profits are present from C corporation tax years, entity not subject to Federal income tax. S corporation files Form 1120S. Shareholders are subject to tax on income attributable to their stock ownership.	Income subject to double taxation. Entity subject to tax, and shareholder subject to tax on any corporate dividends received. Corporation files Form 1120.
Highest tax rate	35% at individual level.	35% at owner level.	35% at shareholder level.	35% at corporate level plus 15%/0% on any corporate dividends at shareholder level (if qualified dividends; otherwise 35%).
Choice of tax year	Same tax year as owner.	Selection generally restricted to coincide with tax year of majority owners or principal owners, or to tax year determined under the least aggregate deferral method.	Restricted to a calendar year unless IRS approves a different year for business purposes or other exceptions apply.	Unrestricted selection allowed at time of filing first tax return.
Timing of taxation	Based on owner's tax year.	Owners report their share of income in their tax year with or within which the entity's tax year ends. Owners in their separate capacities are subject to payment of estimated taxes.	Shareholders report their share of income in their tax year with or within which the corporation's tax year ends. Generally, the corporation uses a calendar year; but see "Choice of tax year" above. Shareholders may be subject to payment of estimated taxes. Corporation may be subject to payment of estimated taxes for taxes imposed at the corporate level.	Corporation subject to tax at close of its tax year. May be subject to payment of estimated taxes. Dividends will be subject to tax at the shareholder level in the tax year received.

Tax Attributes of Different Forms of Business—Continued

	Sole Proprietorship	Partnership/Limited Liability Entity*	S Corporation	Regular (C) Corporation**
Basis for allocating income to owners	Not applicable (only one owner).	Profit and loss sharing agreement. Cash basis items of cash basis entities are allocated on a daily basis. Other entity items are allocated after considering varying interests of owners.	Pro rata share based on stock ownership. Shareholder's pro rata share is determined on a daily basis according to the number of shares of stock held on each day of the corporation's tax year.	Not applicable.
Contribution of property to the entity	Not a taxable transaction.	Generally, not a taxable transaction.	Is a taxable transaction unless the § 351 requirements are satisfied.	Is a taxable transaction unless the § 351 requirements are satisfied.
Character of income taxed to owners	Retains source characteristics.	Conduit—retains source characteristics.	Conduit—retains source characteristics.	All source characteristics are lost when income is distributed to owners.
Basis for allocating a net operating loss to owners	Not applicable (only one owner).	Profit and loss sharing agreement. Cash basis items of cash basis entities are allocated on a daily basis. Other entity items are allocated after considering varying interests of owners.	Prorated among shareholders on a daily basis.	Not applicable.
Limitation on losses deductible by owners	Investment plus liabilities.	Owner's investment plus share of liabilities.	Shareholder's investment plus loans made by shareholder to corporation.	Not applicable.
Subject to at-risk rules	Yes, at the owner level. Indefinite carryover of excess loss.	Yes, at the owner level. Indefinite carryover of excess loss.	Yes, at the shareholder level. Indefinite carryover of excess loss.	Yes, for closely held corporations. Indefinite carryover of excess loss.
Subject to passive activity loss rules	Yes, at the owner level. Indefinite carryover of excess loss.	Yes, at the owner level. Indefinite carryover of excess loss.	Yes, at the shareholder level. Indefinite carryover of excess loss.	Yes, for closely held corporations and personal service corporations. Indefinite carryover of excess loss.
Tax consequences of earnings retained by entity	Taxed to owner when earned and increases his or her basis in the sole proprietorship.	Taxed to owners when earned and increases their respective interests in the entity.	Taxed to shareholders when earned and increases their respective bases in stock.	Taxed to corporation as earned and may be subject to penalty tax if accumulated unreasonably.
Nonliquidating distributions to owners	Not taxable.	Not taxable unless money received exceeds recipient owner's basis in entity interest. Existence of § 751 assets may cause recognition of ordinary income.	Generally not taxable unless the distribution exceeds the shareholder's AAA or stock basis. Existence of accumulated earnings and profits could cause some distributions to be dividends.	Taxable in year of receipt to extent of earnings and profits or if exceeds basis in stock.

Tax Attributes of Different Forms of Business—Continued

	Sole Proprietorship	Partnership/Limited Liability Entity*	S Corporation	Regular (C) Corporation**
Capital gains	Taxed at owner level with opportunity to use alternative tax rate.	Conduit—owners must account for their respective shares.	Conduit, with certain exceptions (a possible penalty tax)—shareholders must account for their respective shares.	Taxed at corporate level with a maximum 35% rate. No other benefits.
Capital losses	Only $3,000 of capital losses can be offset each tax year against ordinary income. Indefinite carryover.	Conduit—owners must account for their respective shares.	Conduit—shareholders must account for their respective shares.	Carried back three years and carried forward five years. Deductible only to the extent of capital gains.
§ 1231 gains and losses	Taxable or deductible at owner level. Five-year lookback rule for § 1231 losses.	Conduit—owners must account for their respective shares.	Conduit—shareholders must account for their respective shares.	Taxable or deductible at corporate level only. Five-year lookback rule for § 1231 losses.
Foreign tax credits	Available at owner level.	Conduit—passed through to owners.	Generally conduit—passed through to shareholders.	Available at corporate level only.
§ 1244 treatment of loss on sale of interest	Not applicable.	Not applicable.	Available.	Available.
Basis treatment of entity liabilities	Includible in interest basis.	Includible in interest basis.	Not includible in stock basis.	Not includible in stock basis.
Built-in gains	Not applicable.	Not applicable.	Possible corporate tax.	Not applicable.
Special allocations to owners	Not applicable (only one owner).	Available if supported by substantial economic effect.	Not available.	Not applicable.
Availability of fringe benefits to owners	None.	None.	None unless a 2%-or-less shareholder.	Available within antidiscrimination rules.
Effect of liquidation/redemption/reorganization on basis of entity assets	Not applicable.	Usually carried over from entity to owner unless a § 754 election is made, excessive cash is distributed, or more than 50% of the capital interests are transferred within 12 months.	Taxable; step-up to fair market value.	Taxable; step-up to fair market value.
Sale of ownership interest	Treated as the sale of individual assets. Classification of recognized gain or loss is dependent on the nature of the individual assets.	Treated as the sale of an entity interest. Recognized gain or loss is classified as capital under § 741, subject to ordinary income treatment under § 751.	Treated as the sale of corporate stock. Recognized gain is classified as capital gain. Recognized loss is classified as capital loss, subject to ordinary loss treatment under § 1244.	Treated as the sale of corporate stock. Recognized gain is classified as capital gain. Recognized loss is classified as capital loss, subject to ordinary loss treatment under § 1244.

Tax Attributes of Different Forms of Business—Continued

	Sole Proprietorship	Partnership/Limited Liability Entity*	S Corporation	Regular (C) Corporation**
Distribution of appreciated property	Not taxable.	No recognition at the entity level.	Recognition at the corporate level to the extent of the appreciation. Conduit—amount of recognized gain is passed through to shareholders.	Taxable at the corporate level to the extent of the appreciation.
Splitting of income among family members	Not applicable (only one owner).	Difficult—IRS will not recognize a family member as an owner unless certain requirements are met.	Rather easy—gift of stock will transfer tax on a pro rata share of income to the donee. However, IRS can make adjustments to reflect adequate compensation for services.	Same as an S corporation, except that donees will be subject to tax only on earnings actually or constructively distributed to them. Other than unreasonable compensation, IRS generally cannot make adjustments to reflect adequate compensation for services and capital.
Organizational costs	Startup expenditures are eligible for $5,000 limited expensing (subject to phaseout) and amortizing balance over 180 months.	Organizational costs are eligible for $5,000 limited expensing (subject to phaseout) and amortizing balance over 180 months.	Same as partnership.	Same as partnership.
Charitable contributions	Limitations apply at owner level.	Conduit—owners are subject to deduction limitations in their own capacities.	Conduit—shareholders are subject to deduction limitations in their own capacities.	Limited to 10% of taxable income before certain deductions.
Alternative minimum tax	Applies at the owner level. AMT rates are 26% and 28%.	Applies at the owner level rather than at the entity level. AMT preferences and adjustments are passed through from the entity to the owners.	Applies at the shareholder level rather than at the corporate level. AMT preferences and adjustments are passed through from the S corporation to the shareholders.	Applies at the corporate level. AMT rate is 20%. Exception for small corporations.
ACE adjustment	Does not apply.	Does not apply.	Does not apply.	The adjustment is made in calculating AMTI. The adjustment is 75% of the excess of adjusted current earnings over unadjusted AMTI. If the unadjusted AMTI exceeds adjusted current earnings, the adjustment is negative.

Tax Attributes of Different Forms of Business—Continued

	Sole Proprietorship	Partnership/Limited Liability Entity*	S Corporation	Regular (C) Corporation**
Tax preference items	Apply at owner level in determining AMT.	Conduit—passed through to owners who must account for such items in their separate capacities.	Conduit—passed through to shareholders who must account for such items in their separate capacities.	Subject to AMT at corporate level.

*Refer to Chapter 21 for additional details on partnerships and limited liability entities.
**Refer to Chapters 17 through 20 for additional details on regular corporations.

REFOCUS ON THE BIG PICTURE

USING A FLOW-THROUGH ENTITY TO ACHIEVE DEDUCTIBILITY OF LOSSES

As long as Smith and Jones, the owners of Cane, Inc., maintain C corporation status, they cannot deduct any NOLs that the business incurs on their individual tax returns. For the owners to deduct any future NOLs on their Forms 1040, Cane needs to be operated as a flow-through entity. The most logical alternatives are to make an S election or to become a limited liability company.

An S election may be appropriate for Cane. Cane should make a timely election on Form 2553, and both shareholders must consent to the election. The owners should make the election on or before the fifteenth day of the third month of the current year.

Normally, an S corporation does not pay any income tax because all items (including NOLs) flow through to the shareholders. A C corporation making an S election may be required to pay a built-in gains tax or a LIFO recapture tax. The base for the built-in gains tax includes any unrealized gain on appreciated assets held by Cane on the day the owners elect S status. The highest corporate rate is applied to the unrealized gain when any of the built-in gain assets are sold. If the corporation uses the LIFO inventory method, any LIFO recapture amount at the time of the S election is subject to a corporate-level tax.

Cane, Inc., does not need to liquidate or engage in a tax-deferred reorganization when converting to an S corporation. An S corporation can have voting and nonvoting common stock, provided that all shares have the same economic rights to corporate income or loss. Data used to compute a DPAD flows through to the shareholders.

Cane might get rid of the tax-exempt income, which will not be reflected in the AAA. Although it is reflected in stock basis, tax-exempt income (as part of OAA) is distributed to the shareholders only after the S corporation has distributed all of its C corporation earnings and profits.

KEY TERMS

Accumulated adjustments account (AAA), 22–15
Accumulated earnings and profits, 22–14
Built-in gains tax, 22–25
Passive investment income (PII), 22–10
Previously taxed income (PTI), 22–16
S corporation, 22–2
Small business corporation, 22–4
Subchapter S, 22–2
Voluntary revocation, 22–9

DISCUSSION QUESTIONS

1. **LO.1** Which of these apply to an S corporation?
   a. Alternative minimum tax.
   b. Accumulated earnings tax.
   c. Personal holding company tax.
   d. Flow-through of NOLs.
   e. Unlimited liability.

2. **LO.1** Distributions by an S corporation to its shareholders are always tax-free. Discuss this statement.

3. **LO.1** Why is an S corporation treated more favorably than a C corporation, relative to the Federal corporate income tax?

4. **LO.1** If shareholders have higher marginal income tax rates relative to the C corporation brackets, it always is desirable to be an S corporation. Discuss the validity of this statement.

5. **LO.1** What effects do C corporation NOLs have on an S corporation?

6. **LO.1** How are charitable contributions treated by an S corporation?

7. **LO.2** What requirements must an entity meet to elect S corporation status?

8. **LO.2** Would any of these items be considered a second class of stock for an S corporation?
   a. Voting preferred stock (with a preference on dividends).
   b. Treasury stock of another class.
   c. Phantom stock.
   d. Unexercised stock options.
   e. Warrants.
   f. Stock appreciation rights.
   g. Convertible debentures.

9. **LO.2** Outline the characteristics of an S corporation's *straight debt.*

10. **LO.2** Would any of these items be considered a second class of stock for an S corporation?
    a. Short-term unwritten advances from a shareholder that do not exceed $10,000 in the aggregate at any time during the corporation's taxable year.
    b. Debt that is held by shareholders in the same proportion as their stock holdings.
    c. Section 1244 stock.

11. **LO.2** Which of the following can be a shareholder of an S corporation?
    a. Limited liability partnership.
    b. Corporation.
    c. Nonresident alien.
    d. Estate.
    e. Charitable organization exempted from taxation.
    f. Roth IRA.
    g. Minor child.

ISSUE ID

COMMUNICATIONS

12. **LO.2, 11** Bob Roman, the major owner of an S corporation, approaches you for some tax planning help. He would like to exchange some real estate in a like-kind transaction under § 1031 for some other real estate that may have some environmental liabilities. Prepare a letter to Bob outlining your suggestion. Bob's address is 8411 Huron Boulevard, West Chester, PA 19382.

ISSUE ID

13. **LO.2, 3** On March 2, the two 50% shareholders of a calendar year corporation decide to elect S status. One of the shareholders, Terry, purchased her stock from a previous shareholder (a nonresident alien) on January 18. Identify any potential problems for Terry or the corporation.

COMMUNICATIONS

14. **LO.4** Caleb Samford calls you and says that his two-person S corporation was involuntarily terminated in February 2010. He asks you if they can make a new S election now, in November 2011. Draft a memo for the file outlining what you told Caleb.

15. **LO.5** Indicate whether each of the following items is available to an S corporation.
    a. Amortization of organizational expenditures.
    b. Dividends received deduction.
    c. Standard deduction.
    d. Personal exemption.
    e. Section 179 expense deduction.

16. **LO.6** Using the categories in the following legend, classify each transaction as a plus (+) or minus (−) on Schedule M–2 of Form 1120S. An answer might look like one of these: "+AAA" or "−OAA."

Legend		
AAA	=	Accumulated adjustments account
OAA	=	Other adjustments account
NA	=	No direct effect on Schedule M–2

    a. Receipt of tax-exempt interest income.
    b. Unreasonable compensation determined.
    c. Depreciation recapture income.
    d. Nontaxable life insurance proceeds.
    e. Expenses related to tax-exempt securities.
    f. Charitable contributions.
    g. Business gifts in excess of $25.
    h. Nondeductible fines and penalties.
    i. Selling expenses.

17. **LO.6, 11** Collett's S corporation has a small amount of accumulated earnings and profits (AEP), requiring the use of the more complex distribution rules. His accountant tells him that this AEP forces the maintenance of the AAA figure each year. Identify relevant tax issues facing Collett. **ISSUE ID**

18. **LO.6, 8** Scott Roberts owns 10% of an S corporation. He is confused with respect to the amounts of the corporate AAA and his stock basis. Write a brief memo to Scott identifying the key differences between AAA and an S corporation stock basis. **COMMUNICATIONS**

19. **LO.8** For each of the following independent statements, indicate whether the transaction will increase (+), decrease (−), or have no effect (*NE*) on the adjusted basis of a shareholder's stock in an S corporation.
    a. Expenses related to tax-exempt income.
    b. Long-term capital gain.
    c. Nonseparately computed loss.
    d. Section 1231 gain.
    e. Depletion *not* in excess of basis.
    f. Separately computed income.
    g. Nontaxable return-of-capital distribution by the corporation.
    h. Selling expenses.
    i. Business gifts in excess of $25.
    j. Depreciation recapture income.
    k. Dividends received by the S corporation.
    l. LIFO recapture tax computed at the date of the S election.
    m. Recovery of a bad debt previously deducted.
    n. Short-term capital loss.
    o. Corporate distributions out of AAA.

20. **LO.9** Sheila Jackson is a 50% shareholder in Washington, Inc., an S corporation. This year, Jackson's share of the Washington loss is $100,000. Jackson has income from several other sources. Identify at least four tax issues related to the effects of the S corporation loss on Jackson's tax return. **ISSUE ID**

21. **LO.1, 11** One of your clients is considering electing S status. Texas, Inc., is a six-year-old company with two equal shareholders, both of whom paid $30,000 for their stock. Going into 2011, Texas has a $110,000 NOL carryforward from prior years. Estimated income is $40,000 for 2011 and $25,000 for each of the next three years. Should Texas make an S election for 2011? **DECISION MAKING**

22. **LO.10** There is no advantage for an S corporation to have § 1244 stock. Discuss the validity of this statement.

23. **LO.6, 11** What is the purpose of the AAA bypass election?

PROBLEMS

24. **LO.5, 6** Sentilles, Inc., a calendar year S corporation, incurred the following items this year.

§ 1231 gain	$ 11,000
Tax-exempt interest income	7,000
Net sales	140,020
Depreciation recapture income	14,000
Long-term capital gain	20,000
Cost of goods sold	(42,000)
Administrative expenses	(15,000)
Depreciation expenses	(13,000)
Charitable contribution	(10,000)
Distributions to shareholders	(34,000)

a. Calculate Sentilles's nonseparately computed income.
b. How much ordinary income or loss is reported by Brittany Nelson, a 25% shareholder?

25. **LO.5, 6** Neely, Inc., a calendar year S corporation, incurred the following items this year.

Operating income	$100,400
Cost of goods sold	(40,000)
Depreciation expense	(10,000)
Administrative expenses	(5,000)
§ 1231 gain	21,000
Tax-exempt interest income	12,000
Dividends received	8,600
Depreciation recapture income	20,000
Short-term capital loss from stock sale	(6,000)
Long-term capital loss from stock sale	(4,000)
Long-term capital gain from stock sale	15,000
Charitable contributions	(4,500)

Jake Neely is a 40% shareholder of the S corporation throughout the year.
a. Calculate Jake's share of nonseparately computed income.
b. Calculate Jake's share of any net long-term capital gain.

26. **LO.5, 6** Whip, Inc., is a calendar year S corporation. Whip's book income this year totals $90,000. Whip is owned equally by three shareholders. From supplemental data, you obtain the following information about items that are included in book income.

Selling expenses	($ 21,200)
Tax-exempt interest	2,200
Dividends received	9,000
§ 1231 gain	6,000
Depreciation recapture income	12,000
Recovery of bad debts	4,000
Long-term capital loss	(6,000)
Salary to owners (each)	(10,000)
Cost of goods sold	(95,000)
Distributions to shareholders	(6,300)

a. Compute Whip's Subchapter S income or loss for 2011.
b. How much ordinary income or loss is reported by Nicole, one of Whip's shareholders?
c. How much dividend income is reported on Nicole's Schedule K–1?

27. **LO.6, 8, 9** Betty is a shareholder in a calendar year S corporation. At the beginning of the year, her stock basis is $10,000, her share of AAA is $2,000, and her share of corporate AEP is $6,000. She receives a $6,000 distribution, and her share of S corporation items includes a $2,000 long-term capital gain and a $9,000 ordinary loss. Determine the effects of these events on AAA, stock basis, and AEP.

28. **LO.6** Noon, Inc., a calendar year S corporation, is equally owned by Ralph and Thomas. Thomas dies on April 1 (not a leap year), and his estate selects a March 31 fiscal year. Noon has $400,000 of income for January 1 through March 31 and $600,000 for the remainder of the year.
    a. Determine how income is allocated to Ralph and Thomas under the pro rata approach.
    b. Determine how income is allocated to Ralph and Thomas under the per-books method.

29. **LO.5, 6** Goblins, Inc., is a calendar year S corporation. Its AAA balance is zero.

DECISION MAKING

    a. Goblins holds $90,000 of AEP. Tobias, the sole shareholder, has an adjusted basis of $80,000 in his stock. Determine the tax aspects if a $90,000 salary is paid to Tobias.
    b. Same as part (a), except that Goblins pays Tobias a $90,000 dividend from AEP.

30. **LO.6, 7, 8** Tiger, Inc., a calendar year S corporation, is owned equally by four shareholders: Ann, Becky, Chris, and David. Tiger owns a piece of investment land that was purchased for $160,000 four years ago. On September 14, 2011, when the land is worth $240,000, it is distributed to David. Assuming that David's basis in his S corporation stock is $270,000 on the distribution date, discuss any tax ramifications.

31. **LO.6, 8, 9, 11** In 2011, Spence, Inc., a calendar year S corporation, generates an ordinary loss of $110,000 and makes a distribution of $140,000 to its sole shareholder, Storm Nelson. Nelson's stock basis at the beginning of the year is $200,000. Write a memo to your senior manager, Aaron McMullin, discussing the tax treatment of Spence's activities.

COMMUNICATIONS

32. **LO.6** Lonergan, Inc., a calendar year S corporation in Athens, Georgia, had a balance in AAA of $200,000 and AEP of $110,000 on December 31, 2011. During 2012, Lonergan, Inc., distributes $140,000 to its shareholders, while sustaining an ordinary loss of $120,000. Calculate the balance in Lonergan's AAA and AEP accounts at the end of 2012.

33. **LO.6** If the beginning balance in Talker, Inc.'s OAA is $3,900, and the following transactions occur, what is Talker's ending OAA balance?

Depreciation recapture income	$21,000
Payroll tax penalty	(4,200)
Tax-exempt interest	5,300
Nontaxable life insurance proceeds	50,000
Life insurance premiums paid (nondeductible)	(2,800)

34. **LO.6** Stockstill, Inc., a calendar year S corporation, holds an AAA balance of $715,000 at the beginning of 2011. During the year the following items occur.

Sales income	$206,000
Loss from real estate operations	(5,000)
Officers' life insurance proceeds	100,000
Dividend income	17,000
Interest income	3,000
Charitable contributions	(22,000)
§ 179 expense	(2,500)
Administrative expenses	(41,000)
Premiums paid for officers' life insurance	(3,600)
Cash distribution to shareholders	(69,220)

Calculate Stockstill's ending AAA balance.

35. **LO.6, 7, 8** Money, Inc., a calendar year S corporation in Denton, Texas, has two unrelated shareholders, each owning 50% of the stock. Both shareholders have a $400,000 stock basis as of January 1, 2011. At the beginning of 2011, Money has AAA of $300,000 and AEP of $600,000. During 2011, Money has operating income of $100,000.

At the end of the year, Money distributes securities worth $1 million, with an adjusted basis of $800,000. Determine the tax effects of these transactions.

36. **LO.6, 7, 8** Assume the same facts as in Problem 35, except that the two shareholders consent to an AAA bypass election.

37. **LO.8, 9** At the beginning of 2010, Christine Wheat has a basis of $5,000 in her stock of a calendar year S corporation, Zhou, Inc. She holds no debt of the S corporation. During 2010, Wheat's total share of Zhou's losses and deductions is $16,000, consisting of $10,000 of ordinary loss and $6,000 of nondeductible, noncapital expenses. For 2011, Wheat's share of Zhou's ordinary income is $12,000. Assuming no Reg. § 1.1367–1(g) election, how are these facts treated by Christine Wheat?

38. **LO.8, 9** Assume the same facts as in Problem 37, except that a Reg. § 1.1367–1(g) election is made. How does your answer change?

39. **LO.8** Jeff, a 52% owner of an S corporation, has a stock basis of zero at the beginning of the year. Jeff's basis in a $10,000 loan made to the corporation and evidenced by a corporate note has been reduced to zero by pass-through losses. During the year, his net share of the corporate taxable income is $11,000. At the end of the year, Jeff receives a $15,000 distribution. Discuss the tax effects of the distribution.

40. **LO.8** Assume the same facts as in Problem 39, except that there is no $15,000 distribution, but the corporation repays the loan principal to Jeff. Discuss the tax effects.

41. **LO.8** Assume the same facts as in Problem 39, except that Jeff's share of corporate taxable income is only $8,000, and there is no distribution. However, the corporation repays the $10,000 loan principal to Jeff. Discuss the tax effects. Assume there was no corporate note (i.e., only an account payable). Does this change your answer?

ISSUE ID

42. **LO.5, 6, 11** Red Lion, Inc., is an S corporation with a sizable amount of AEP from a C corporation year. The S corporation has $400,000 of investment income and $400,000 of investment expense in 2011. The company makes cash distributions to enable its sole shareholder to pay her taxes. What are the tax aspects to consider?

43. **LO.6, 9** At the beginning of the year, Ann and Becky own equally all of the stock of Whitman, Inc., an S corporation. Whitman generates a $120,000 loss for the year (not a leap year). On the 189th day of the year, Ann sells her half of the Whitman stock to her son, Scott. How much of the $120,000 loss, if any, belongs to Scott?

44. **LO.6, 9** In Problem 43, how much of the Whitman loss belongs to Ann and Becky, assuming Becky's stock basis is $41,300?

COMMUNICATIONS

45. **LO.5, 6, 8, 9** A calendar year S corporation has an ordinary loss of $80,000 and a capital loss of $20,000. Ms. Freiberg owns 30% of the corporate stock and has a $24,000 basis in her stock. Determine the amounts of the ordinary loss and capital loss, if any, that flow through to Ms. Freiberg. Prepare a tax memo for the files.

46. **LO.5, 6, 8** Savoy, Inc., of Auburn, Alabama, is an accrual basis S corporation with three equal shareholders. The three cash basis shareholders have the following stock basis at the beginning of the year: Andre, $12,000; Crum, $22,000; and Barbara, $28,000. Savoy reports the following income and expense items.

Operating loss	($30,000)
Short-term capital gain	37,500
Long-term capital loss	(6,000)
Nondeductible fees and penalties	(3,000)

The electing corporation distributes $5,000 of cash to each of the shareholders during the tax year. Calculate the shareholders' stock bases at the end of the year.

47. **LO.10** Rodeo, Inc., a cash basis S corporation in College Station, Texas, formerly was a C corporation. Rodeo has the following assets and liabilities on January 1, 2011, the date the S election is made.

	Adjusted Basis	Fair Market Value
Cash	$ 200,000	$ 200,000
Accounts receivable	-0-	105,000
Equipment	110,000	100,000
Land	1,800,000	2,500,000
Accounts payable	-0-	110,000

During 2011, Rodeo collects the accounts receivable and pays the accounts payable. The land is sold for $3 million, and taxable income for the year is $590,000. What is Rodeo's built-in gains tax?

48. **LO.10** In 2011, the excess net passive income of Cut-N-Shooters, Inc., an S corporation in Cut-N-Shoot, Texas, is $32,000. Cut-N-Shooters holds $50,000 of accumulated earnings and profits from a C corporation year, and it reports AMT adjustments of $17,000 this year. Calculate any passive investment income penalty tax.

49. **LO.5, 6, 11** Bonnie and Clyde each own one-third of a fast-food restaurant, and their 13-year-old daughter owns the other shares. Both parents work full-time in the restaurant, but the daughter works infrequently. Neither Bonnie nor Clyde receives a salary during the year, when the ordinary income of the S corporation is $180,000. An IRS agent estimates that reasonable salaries for Bonnie, Clyde, and the daughter are $30,000, $35,000, and $10,000, respectively. What adjustments would you expect the IRS to impose upon these taxpayers? **ISSUE ID**

50. **LO.11** Friedman, Inc., an S corporation, holds some highly appreciated land and inventory, and some marketable securities that have declined in value. It anticipates a sale of these assets and a complete liquidation of the company over the next two years. Arnold Schwartz, the CFO, calls you, asking how to treat these transactions. Prepare a tax memo indicating what you told Arnold in the phone conversation. **COMMUNICATIONS**

51. **LO.11** Opal is the owner of all of the shares of an S corporation. Opal is considering receiving a salary of $80,000 from the business. She will pay 7.65% FICA taxes on the salary, and the S corporation will pay the same amount of FICA tax. If Opal reduces her salary to $60,000 and takes an additional $20,000 as a distribution, how much total tax could be saved? **DECISION MAKING**

52. **LO.10** Blue Corporation elects S status effective for calendar year 2010. As of January 1, 2010, Blue holds two assets.

	Adjusted Basis	Fair Market Value
Land	$50,000	$110,000
IBM stock	55,000	40,000

Blue sells the land in 2011 for $120,000. Calculate Blue's recognized built-in gain, if any, in 2011.

See Appendix E for Comprehensive Tax Return Problem—Form 1120S

RESEARCH PROBLEMS

THOMSON REUTERS
Checkpoint® Student Edition

Note: Solutions to Research Problems can be prepared by using the **Checkpoint® Student Edition** online research product, which is available to accompany this text. It is also possible to prepare solutions to the Research Problems by using tax research materials found in a standard tax library.

Research Problem 1. Bushong, Inc., a calendar year S corporation, has a "tax cash-flow" provision in its shareholder agreement. Bushong must make annual distributions by the December 31 following a tax year in which there is an income pass-through. Each distribution must be in an amount sufficient to enable shareholders to pay their state and Federal income taxes on the pass-through.

The agreement also provides that if an audit adjustment is made to items reported on the Schedule K–1, Bushong can make a discretionary distribution to handle the increased taxes resulting from the adjustment.

The shareholders want to change the agreement. Under the proposal, if an audit adjustment is made and Bushong makes a discretionary payment, the payment would be in accordance with the shareholders' ownership shares during the tax year of the adjustment, rather than as of the distribution date.

Would the proposal create a second class of stock and terminate Bushong's S election?

COMMUNICATIONS

Research Problem 2. Sam is selling his S corporation, Superbody Fitness, Inc. He will receive 80% cash and 20% of another S corporation fitness center. As part of this transaction, should Sam liquidate Superbody Fitness? Outline your analysis in an e-mail to your instructor.

INTERNET *activity*

Use the tax resources of the Internet to address the following question. Do not restrict your search to the Web, but include a review of newsgroups and general reference materials, practitioner sites and resources, primary sources of the tax law, chat rooms and discussion groups, and other opportunities.

COMMUNICATIONS

Research Problem 3. Determine how the recent health care legislation treats S corporations with respect to the self-employment tax. Present your findings in an e-mail of no more than 250 words to your instructor.

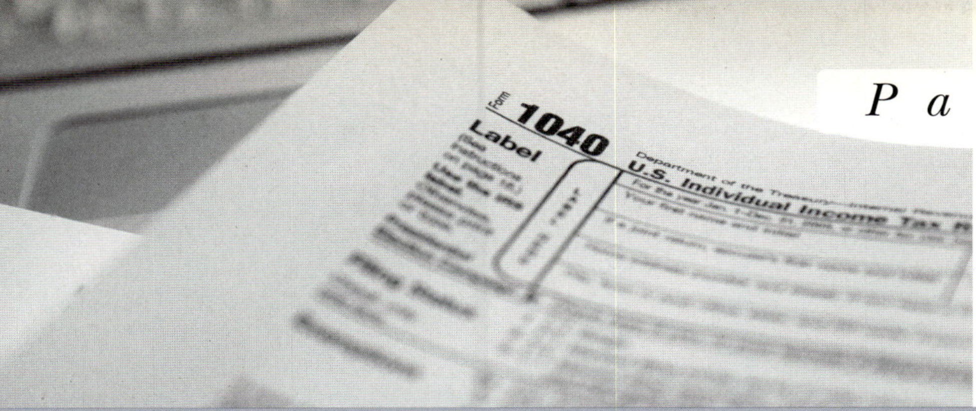

Part 8

Advanced Tax Practice Considerations

A specialist in taxation must cope with the procedural and ethical aspects of tax practice. Furthermore, the specialist may be confronted with a variety of technical subjects. These include the unique rules applicable to tax-exempt entities, multistate dealings, and international transactions.

Exempt Entities

CHAPTER 23

LEARNING OBJECTIVES

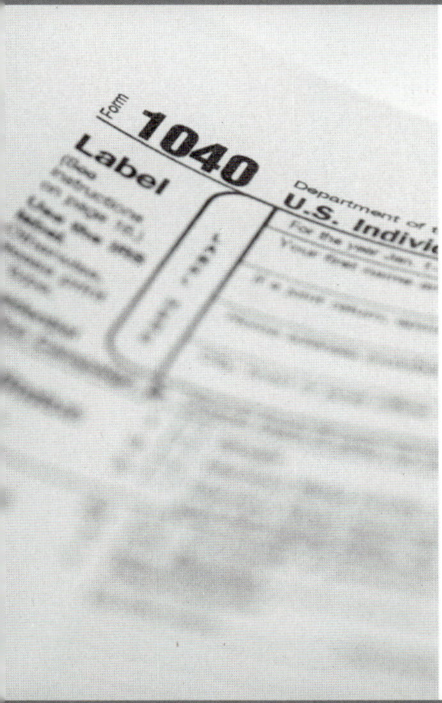

After completing Chapter 23, you should be able to:

LO.1 Identify the different types of exempt organizations.

LO.2 Enumerate the requirements for exempt status.

LO.3 Know the tax consequences of exempt status, including the different consequences for public charities and private foundations.

LO.4 Determine which exempt organizations are classified as private foundations.

LO.5 Recognize the taxes imposed on private foundations and calculate the related initial tax and additional tax amounts.

LO.6 Determine when an exempt organization is subject to the unrelated business income tax and calculate the amount of the tax.

LO.7 List the reports exempt organizations must file with the IRS and the related due dates.

LO.8 Identify tax planning opportunities for exempt organizations.

OUTLINE

For the latest in changes to tax legislation, visit **www.cengage.com/taxation/swft.**

THE BIG PICTURE **Tax Solutions for the Real World**

EFFECT OF A FOR-PROFIT BUSINESS ON A TAX-EXEMPT ENTITY

For an entity to be tax-exempt, it must serve the common good. This common good can include a mission as broad as that of a public charity such as the Red Cross or as narrow as that of a private foundation that operates a historic museum that depicts life in the eighteenth century. Most exempt organizations are exempt under § 501(c)(3).

Hopeful, Inc., is a § 501(c)(3) organization that provides temporary lodging and psychological services for abused women. Its annual operating budget is $12 million. More than two decades ago, Betty Jones was a recipient of the services provided by Hopeful. Now, Hopeful's administrator has been notified by the attorney for Betty's estate that her will transfers to Hopeful the legal ownership (100 percent of the outstanding stock) of Taste Good Ice Cream, a chain of 40 gourmet ice cream shops located in Virginia, North Carolina, and South Carolina. The business has been in existence for eight years and has produced substantially higher profits each year.

Hopeful's board is considering the following options regarding the inheritance from Betty and has hired you to provide an analysis of the tax consequences of each option.

- Sell the stock of Taste Good Ice Cream and contribute the net proceeds to Hopeful's endowment.
- Continue to conduct the Taste Good Ice Cream business as a division of Hopeful.
- Continue to conduct the business as a wholly owned subsidiary of Hopeful.

With the second and the third options, the existing management team will remain in place. After-tax profits not needed to expand the ice cream shop chain will be used by Hopeful in carrying out its exempt mission. **Read the chapter and formulate your response.**

23.1 General Considerations

Ideally, any entity that generates profit would prefer not to be subject to the Federal income tax. All of the types of business entities discussed thus far are subject to the Federal income tax at one level (e.g., profits from sole proprietorships, partnerships, S corporations, and LLCs generally are subject only to single taxation) or more (e.g., C corporation earnings are subject to double taxation). In contrast, organizations classified as **exempt organizations** may be able to escape Federal income taxation altogether.

The tax-exempt sector is an important component of the U.S. economy. More than 2 million tax-exempt entities file tax returns with the IRS. These entities employ almost 12 million workers, representing about 10 percent of the total U.S. workforce. They control about $3.5 trillion in assets. The IRS audits about 8,000 of these entities every tax year.

Churches are among the types of organizations that are exempt from Federal income tax. Nevertheless, one must be careful not to conclude that everything labeled a church will qualify for exempt status.

During the 1970s and 1980s, a popular technique for attempting to avoid Federal income tax was the establishment of so-called mail-order churches. For example, in one scheme, a nurse obtained a certificate of ordination and a church charter from an organization that sold such documents.[1] The articles of incorporation stated that

[1] Rev.Rul. 81–94, 1981–1 C.B. 330.

TAX in the NEWS

WHO ARE THE DONORS?

Gifts are a major source of funds for many charities. Charitable giving by Americans in 2009 totaled $304 billion, about 2.1 percent of GDP. As the chart to the right shows, the bulk of charitable gifts are made by individuals and their estates.

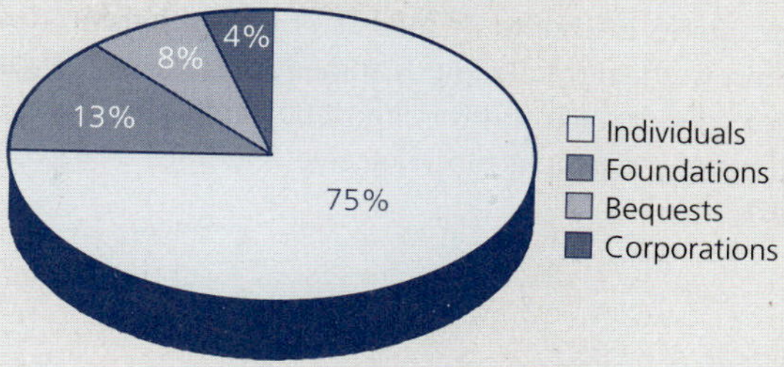

Source: Giving USA, 2011.

the church was organized exclusively for religious and charitable purposes, including a religious mission of healing the spirit, mind, emotions, and body. The nurse was the church's minister, director, and principal officer. Taking a vow of poverty, she transferred all of her assets, including a house and car, to the church. The church assumed all of the nurse's liabilities, including the mortgage on her house and her credit card bills. The nurse continued to work at a hospital and deposited her salary in the church's bank account. The church provided her with a living allowance sufficient to maintain or improve her previous standard of living. She was also permitted to use the house and car for personal purposes.

The IRS declared that such organizations were shams and not bona fide churches. For a church to be tax-exempt under § 501(c)(3), none of its net earnings may be used to the benefit of any private shareholder or individual. In essence, the organization should serve a public rather than a private interest. Though the courts have consistently upheld the IRS position, numerous avoidance schemes such as this have been attempted.

Another technique being marketed as a way to avoid Federal income taxes is to set up shop as a credit counselor. Credit counselors have an opportunity to qualify for tax-exempt status under § 501(c)(3). Supposedly, such tax-exempt organizations exist to help debt-laden consumers learn to practice sound financial management and become debt-free. Unfortunately, in reality some credit counseling organizations push consumers into debt repayment schedules with high, poorly disclosed fees that leave the debtor in worse financial shape than before the "counseling." Apparently, the primary motive of such techniques is to earn profits. These unsavory practices have caused Congress to call for greater IRS scrutiny. The IRS has revoked or is in the process of revoking the tax-exempt status of the 41 credit counselors it has audited. Such credit counselors have earned more than 40 percent of the industry's $1 billion in annual revenues.

As discussed in Chapter 1, the major objective of the Federal tax law is to raise revenue. If revenue raising were the only objective, however, the Code would not contain provisions that permit certain organizations to be either partially or completely exempt from Federal income tax. Social considerations also may affect the tax law. This objective bears directly on the decision by Congress to provide for exempt organization tax status. The House Report on the Revenue Act of 1938 provides as follows:

> The exemption from taxation of money or property devoted to charitable and other purposes is based upon the theory that the Government is compensated for the loss of revenue by its relief from the financial burden which would otherwise have to be met by appropriations from public funds, and by the benefits resulting from the promotion of the general welfare.[2]

[2]See 1939–1 (Part 2) C.B. 742 for a reprint of H.R. No. 1860, 75th Congress, 3rd Session.

TAX *in* the NEWS

Who Are the Donees?

The recipients of charitable gifts can be classified as shown in the chart to the right. Religious and educational organizations and foundations account for almost 60 percent of the donees. Religious organizations alone receive one-third of all charitable gifts.

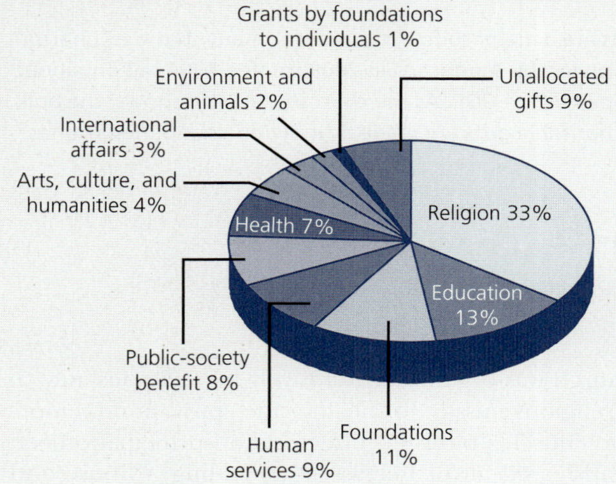

Source: Giving USA, 2011.

In recognition of this social consideration objective, Subchapter F (Exempt Organizations) of the Code (§§ 501–530) provides the authority under which certain organizations are exempt from Federal income tax. Exempt status is not open-ended in that two general limitations exist. First, the nature or scope of the organization may result in it being only partially exempt from tax.[3] Second, the organization may engage in activities that are subject to special taxation.[4]

LO.1
Identify the different types of exempt organizations.

23.2 Types of Exempt Organizations

An organization qualifies for exempt status *only* if it fits into one of the categories provided in the Code. Examples of qualifying exempt organizations and the specific statutory authority for their exempt status are listed in Exhibit 23.1.[5]

TAX *in* the NEWS

A New Type of Nonprofit?

According to Senator Benjamin L. Cardin of Maryland, newspapers are vital to democracy. Thomas Jefferson reached the same conclusion centuries ago.

As more people turn to other media outlets, such as the Internet, for news, however, many newspapers are experiencing a decline in readership. Among those facing significant financial difficulty are the *Seattle Post-Intelligencer,* the *Rocky Mountain News,* the *Baltimore Examiner,* and the *San Francisco Chronicle.*

Convinced that newspapers play an important role in our society, Senator Cardin has introduced the Newspaper Revitalization Act. This measure would enable newspapers to operate as nonprofits under § 501(c)(3), if they choose to do so. Thus, their status would be similar to that now available to public broadcasting.

Under the bill, newspapers that choose this status would still be able to report freely on all issues including political campaigns, but they would not be allowed to make political endorsements. The bill is targeted to local newspapers and not to large newspaper conglomerates.

Source: Press release of Senator Benjamin Cardin.

[3]See the subsequent discussion of Unrelated Business Income Tax.

[4]See the subsequent discussions of Prohibited Transactions and Taxes Imposed on Private Foundations.

[5]Section 501(a) provides for exempt status for organizations described in §§ 401 and 501. The orientation of this chapter is toward organizations that conduct business activities. Therefore, the exempt organizations described in § 401 (qualified pension, profit sharing, and stock bonus trusts) are outside the scope of the chapter and are not discussed.

EXHIBIT 23.1 Types of Exempt Organizations

Statutory Authority	Brief Description	Examples or Comments
§ 501(c)(1)	Federal and related agencies.	Commodity Credit Corporation, Federal Deposit Insurance Corporation, Federal Land Bank.
§ 501(c)(2)	Corporations holding title to property for and paying income to exempt organizations.	Corporation holding title to college fraternity house.
§ 501(c)(3)	Religious, charitable, educational, scientific, literary, etc., organizations.	Boy Scouts of America, Red Cross, Salvation Army, Episcopal Church, PTA, United Fund, University of Richmond.
§ 501(c)(4)	Civic leagues and employee unions.	Garden club, tenants' association promoting tenants' legal rights in entire community, League of Women Voters.
§ 501(c)(5)	Labor, agricultural, and horticultural organizations.	Teachers' association, organization formed to promote effective agricultural pest control, organization formed to test soil and to educate community members in soil treatment, garden club.
§ 501(c)(6)	Business leagues, chambers of commerce, real estate boards, etc.	Chambers of Commerce, American Plywood Association, National Football League (NFL), Professional Golfers Association (PGA) Tour, medical association peer review board, organization promoting acceptance of women in business and professions.
§ 501(c)(7)	Social clubs.	Country club, rodeo and riding club, press club, bowling club, college fraternities.
§ 501(c)(8)	Fraternal beneficiary societies.	Lodges. Must provide for the payment of life, sickness, accident, or other benefits to members or their dependents.
§ 501(c)(9)	Voluntary employees' beneficiary associations.	Provide for the payment of life, sickness, accident, or other benefits to members, their dependents, or their designated beneficiaries.
§ 501(c)(10)	Domestic fraternal societies.	Lodges. Must not provide for the payment of life, sickness, accident, or other benefits; and must devote the net earnings exclusively to religious, charitable, scientific, literary, educational, and fraternal purposes.
§ 501(c)(11)	Local teachers' retirement fund associations.	Only permitted sources of income are amounts received from (1) public taxation, (2) assessments on teaching salaries of members, and (3) income from investments.
§ 501(c)(12)	Local benevolent life insurance associations, mutual or cooperative telephone companies, etc.	Local cooperative telephone company, local mutual water company, local mutual electric company.
§ 501(c)(13)	Cemetery companies.	Must be operated exclusively for the benefit of lot owners who hold the lots for burial purposes.
§ 501(c)(14)	Credit unions.	Other than credit unions exempt under § 501(c)(1).
§ 501(c)(15)	Mutual insurance companies.	Mutual fire insurance company, mutual automobile insurance company.
§ 501(c)(16)	Corporations organized by farmers' cooperatives for financing crop operations.	Related farmers' cooperative must be exempt from tax under § 521.
§ 501(c)(19)	Armed forces members' posts or organizations.	Veterans of Foreign Wars (VFW), Reserve Officers Association.
§ 501(c)(20)	Group legal service plans.	Provided by a corporation for its employees.
§ 501(d)	Religious and apostolic organizations.	Communal organization. Members must include pro rata share of the net income of the organization in their gross income as dividends.
§ 501(e)	Cooperative hospital service organizations.	Centralized purchasing organization for exempt hospitals.
§ 501(f)	Cooperative service organization of educational institutions.	Organization formed to manage universities' endowment funds.
§ 529	Qualified tuition program.	Prepaid tuition and educational savings program.
§ 530	Coverdell Education Savings Accounts.	Qualified education savings accounts.

FINANCIAL DISCLOSURE *Insights*

Effects of Sarbanes-Oxley on Nonprofit Entities

The rules of the Sarbanes-Oxley Act do not apply to nonprofit entities. Nevertheless, some nonprofits voluntarily comply with its provisions. For example, New York's Julliard School and the International Swimming Hall of Fame in Fort Lauderdale have adopted the governance practices, code of ethics, and increased transparency required by Sarbanes-Oxley. Factors contributing to such adoption by nonprofits include the following.

- Accounting firms that audit nonprofits want to see the same financial controls now in place at for-profits.
- Nonprofit trustees are demanding more transparency.
- Nonprofit trustees are concerned that their professional reputations could be hurt if money is misused or the nonprofit falters.

23.3 Requirements for Exempt Status

LO.2

Enumerate the requirements for exempt status.

Exempt status frequently requires more than mere classification in one of the categories of exempt organizations. Many of the organizations that qualify for exempt status share the following characteristics.

- The organization serves some type of *common good*.[6]
- The organization is a *not-for-profit* entity.[7]
- *Net earnings* do not benefit the members of the organization.[8]
- The organization does not exert *political influence*.[9]

SERVING THE COMMON GOOD

The underlying rationale for all exempt organizations is that they serve some type of *common good*. However, depending on the type of the exempt organization, the term *common good* may be interpreted broadly or narrowly. If the test is interpreted broadly, the group being served is the general public or some large subgroup thereof. If it is interpreted narrowly, the group is the specific group referred to in the statutory language. One of the factors in classifying an exempt organization as a private foundation is the size of the group it serves.

NOT-FOR-PROFIT ENTITY

The organization may not be organized or operated for the purpose of making a profit. For some types of exempt organizations, the *for-profit prohibition* appears in the statutory language. For other types, the prohibition is implied.

NET EARNINGS AND MEMBERS OF THE ORGANIZATION

What uses are appropriate for the net earnings of tax-exempt organizations? The logical answer would seem to be that the earnings should be used for the exempt purpose of the organization. However, where the organization exists for the good of a specific group of members, such an open-ended interpretation could permit net earnings to benefit specific group members. Therefore, the Code specifically prohibits certain types of exempt organizations from using their earnings in this way.

> ... no part of the net earnings ... inures to the benefit of any private shareholder or individual.[10]

[6] See, for example, §§ 501(c)(3) and (4).

[7] See, for example, §§ 501(c)(3), (4), (6), (13), and (14).

[8] See, for example, §§ 501(c)(3), (6), (7), (9), (10), (11), and (19).

[9] See, for example, § 501(c)(3).

[10] § 501(c)(6).

In other instances, a statutory prohibition is unnecessary because the definition of the exempt organization in the Code effectively prevents such use.

> ... the net earnings of which are devoted exclusively to religious, charitable, scientific, literary, educational, and fraternal purposes.[11]

POLITICAL INFLUENCE

Religious, charitable, educational, etc., organizations are generally prohibited from attempting to influence legislation or participate in political campaigns. Participation in political campaigns includes participation both *on behalf of* a candidate and *in opposition to* a candidate.

Only in limited circumstances are such exempt organizations permitted to attempt to influence legislation. See the subsequent discussion under Prohibited Transactions.

ETHICS & *Equity*

FOR THE GOOD OF THE PEOPLE

Matthew Ayres is the founder, and the man behind the throne, of the Church for Today television ministry. Ministry broadcasts originate from church services in California and New York and are transmitted via cable throughout the United States. Though the membership of the Church for Today is small (approximately 5,000 members), the typical member is quite wealthy. In addition to receiving contributions from its members, the church solicits and receives donations from viewers of the TV broadcasts. The church is tax-exempt under § 501(c)(3).

The stated mission of the church is religious in nature. However, Matthew firmly believes, as do the members of the board of deacons of the church, that certain societal goals must be accomplished for the prophecies of the church to come true (i.e., their divine being expects them to be active missionaries). Among its basic beliefs, the church advocates government control and possession of all guns, the legalization of drugs, abortion on demand once approved by the appropriate government agency, the withdrawal of all U.S. troops from foreign soil and the termination of all military alliances, the abolition of capital punishment, and the availability of tuition-free university education to all U.S. citizens.

The ministers of the Church for Today are expected to include these basic beliefs, at the subliminal level, in their sermons. Some do so more effectively and more frequently than others, but all are required to do so. Matthew and the board of deacons are dismayed that American society has not adopted many of their beliefs.

Accordingly, Matthew proposes to the board of deacons that the church take a more proactive role. The employment contract of the ministers now will require them to include the basic beliefs in their sermons in an active manner. No longer can the church's positions just be incorporated subliminally. All the beliefs must be covered quarterly, and every sermon must present at least one of the basic doctrines. The ministers will encourage the church members and TV viewers to actively support these positions at both the state and Federal levels.

As a new member of the board of deacons, you wholeheartedly support Matthew's position. However, you are concerned about the effects of this open advocacy of positions on the tax-exempt status of the church. Matthew responds that the "church has friends in high places" and assures you that the tax-exempt status will not be endangered. What should you do?

23.4 TAX CONSEQUENCES OF EXEMPT STATUS: GENERAL

LO.3

Know the tax consequences of exempt status, including the different consequences for public charities and private foundations.

An organization that is appropriately classified as one of the types of exempt organizations is generally exempt from Federal income tax. Four exceptions to this general statement exist, however. An exempt organization that engages in a *prohibited transaction*, or is a so-called *feeder organization*, is subject to tax. If the organization is classified as a *private foundation*, it may be partially subject to tax. Finally, an exempt organization is subject to tax on its *unrelated business taxable income* (which includes unrelated debt-financed income).

[11] § 501(c)(10).

TAX in the NEWS

The Effect of the Recession on Charitable Contributions

Tax-exempt entities have two key causes for concern associated with the contributions they receive. One is immediate and the other is in the future.

The first concern is the economy and its effect on contributions. In 2008, the amount of charitable contributions declined by 2 percent—the first time since 1987 (the year of the "Black Monday" stock market collapse) that contributions had declined. In 2009, contributions fell again, marking the first time in half a century that they had declined two years in a row. The obvious explanation was the recession. Logically, if people are earning less income, they may be inclined to give less.

According to the Chronicle of Philanthropy, donations dropped by 11 percent in 2009. However, according to a report by the Giving USA Foundation, the decline was only 3.6 percent. The reason for this difference may be that the Giving USA Foundation report includes donations to private foundations and smaller charities, while the Chronicle's report includes only gifts to the nation's 400 largest charities.

Sources: Adapted from "Charitable Gifts Declined Last Year," *Wall Street Journal,* June 10, 2009, p. D6; and Associated Press, "Donations Fell in 2009; Worst Decline in 20 Years," *Wall Street Journal,* October 18, 2010, p. A6.

In addition to being exempt from Federal income tax, an exempt organization may be eligible for other benefits, including the following.

- The organization may be exempt from state income tax, state franchise tax, sales tax, or property tax.
- The organization may receive discounts on postage rates.
- Donors of property to the exempt organization may qualify for charitable contribution deductions on their Federal and state income tax returns. However, *not* all exempt organizations are qualified charitable contribution recipients (e.g., gifts to the National Football League, PGA Tour, and Underwriters Laboratories are not deductible).

PROHIBITED TRANSACTIONS

Engaging in a prohibited transaction can produce three negative results. First, part or all of the organization's income may be subject to Federal income tax. Second and even worse, the organization may forfeit its exempt status. Finally, intermediate sanctions may be imposed on certain exempt organization insiders.

Failure to Continue to Qualify

Organizations initially qualify for exempt status only if they are organized as indicated in Exhibit 23.1. The initial qualification requirements then effectively become maintenance requirements. Failure to continue to meet the qualification requirements results in the loss of the entity's exempt status.

New Faith, Inc., is an excellent example of an exempt organization that failed to continue to qualify for tax exemption.[12] The stated purposes of the organization were to feed and shelter the poor. In its application for exempt status, New Faith indicated that it would derive its financial support from donations, bingo games, and raffles. The IRS approved the exempt status.

New Faith's only source of income was the operation of several lunch trucks, which provided food to the general public in exchange for scheduled "donations." Evidence provided by the organization to the Tax Court did not show that the food from the lunch trucks was provided free of charge or at reduced prices. In addition, no evidence was presented to show that the people who received food for free or at below-cost prices were impoverished or needy. The court concluded that the primary purpose of the activity was the conduct of a trade or business. It upheld the IRS's revocation of New Faith's exempt status.

[12] *New Faith, Inc.,* 64 TCM 1050, T.C.Memo. 1992–601.

TAX *in* the NEWS

Contributors to Charity?

Being a tax-exempt entity has several advantages. First and foremost, such entities generally are not subject to Federal income taxes. Second, donors are able to deduct on their Federal income tax returns contributions to the charity that qualify as charitable contributions. Such beneficial treatment is available to both public charities and private foundations. But is the deduction available if the donor benefits from making the contribution?

Kirk Herbstreit, the ESPN college football analyst, donated a house to a local fire department. Per the agreement, the firefighters torched the house as part of a training program. The expectation was that the Herbstreits would rebuild on the now-vacant site.

The Herbstreits claimed a charitable contribution deduction of $330,000 for the house, but the IRS disallowed the deduction. Now the couple has filed suit against the IRS over the deduction disallowance and the related interest charges.

Source: Adapted from "Herbstreit Sues IRS over Rejected Deduction," *USA Today*, July 24, 2009, p. 7C.

Election Not to Forfeit Exempt Status for Lobbying

Organizations exempt under § 501(c)(3) (religious, charitable, educational, etc., organizations) are subject to limits on their attempts to influence legislation (lobbying activities) and participate in political campaigns.[13] Substantial lobbying or political activity can result in the forfeiture of exempt status.

Certain exempt organizations are permitted to engage in lobbying (but not political) activities that are greater than an insubstantial part of their activities, by making a § 501(h) election.[14] Eligible for the election are most § 501(c)(3) organizations (i.e., educational institutions, hospitals, and medical research organizations; organizations supporting government schools; organizations publicly supported by charitable contributions; certain organizations that are publicly supported by various sources including admissions, sales, gifts, grants, contributions, or membership fees; and certain organizations that support certain types of public charities).

An eligible § 501(c)(3) organization must make an affirmative election to participate in lobbying activities on a limited basis. The lobbying expenditures of electing organizations are subject to a ceiling. Exceeding the ceiling can lead to the forfeiture of exempt status. Even when the ceiling is not exceeded, a tax may be imposed on some of the lobbying expenditures (as discussed subsequently).

Two terms are key to the calculation of the ceiling amount: **lobbying expenditures** and **grass roots expenditures**. Lobbying expenditures are made for the purpose of influencing legislation through either of the following.

- Attempting to affect the opinions of the general public or any segment thereof.
- Communicating with any legislator or staff member or with any government official or staff member who may participate in the formulation of legislation.

Grass roots expenditures are made for the purpose of influencing legislation by attempting to affect the opinions of the general public or any segment thereof.

The statutory ceiling is imposed on both lobbying expenditures and grass roots expenditures and is computed as follows.

- 150% × lobbying nontaxable amount = lobbying expenditures ceiling.
- 150% × grass roots nontaxable amount = grass roots expenditures ceiling.

The *lobbying nontaxable amount* is the lesser of (1) $1 million or (2) the amount determined in Figure 23.1.[15] The *grass roots nontaxable amount* is 25 percent of the lobbying nontaxable amount.[16]

[13] § 501(c)(3). Even a single Internet link to a partisan political site can taint the exempt entity.

[14] Religious organizations and private foundations cannot make this election.

[15] § 4911(c)(2).

[16] § 4911(c)(4).

FIGURE 23.1 Calculation of Lobbying Nontaxable Amount

Exempt Purpose Expenditures	Lobbying Nontaxable Amount Is
Not over $500,000	20% of exempt purpose expenditures*
Over $500,000 but not over $1 million	$100,000 + 15% of the excess of exempt purpose expenditures over $500,000
Over $1 million but not over $1.5 million	$175,000 + 10% of the excess of exempt purpose expenditures over $1 million
Over $1.5 million	$225,000 + 5% of the excess of exempt purpose expenditures over $1.5 million

*Exempt purpose expenditures generally are the amounts paid or incurred for the taxable year to accomplish the following purposes: religious, charitable, scientific, literary, educational, fostering national or international amateur sports competition, or the prevention of cruelty to children or animals.

A tax may be assessed on an electing exempt organization's **excess lobbying expenditures** as follows.[17]

- 25% × excess lobbying expenditures = tax liability.

Excess lobbying expenditures are the greater of the following.[18]

- Excess of the lobbying expenditures for the taxable year over the lobbying nontaxable amount.
- Excess of the grass roots expenditures for the taxable year over the grass roots nontaxable amount.

EXAMPLE 1

Tan, Inc., a qualifying § 501(c)(3) organization, incurs lobbying expenditures of $500,000 for the taxable year and grass roots expenditures of $0. Exempt purpose expenditures for the taxable year are $5 million. Tan elects to be eligible to make lobbying expenditures on a limited basis.

Applying the data in Figure 23.1, the lobbying nontaxable amount is $400,000 [$225,000 + 5%($5,000,000 − $1,500,000)]. The ceiling on lobbying expenditures is $600,000 (150% × $400,000). Therefore, the $500,000 of lobbying expenditures are under the permitted $600,000. However, the election results in the imposition of tax on the excess lobbying expenditures of $100,000 ($500,000 lobbying expenditures − $400,000 lobbying nontaxable amount). The resulting tax liability is $25,000 ($100,000 × 25%). ■

A § 501(c)(3) organization that makes disqualifying lobbying expenditures is subject to a 5 percent tax on the lobbying expenditures for the taxable year. A 5 percent tax may also be levied on the organization's management. The tax is imposed on management only if the managers knew that making the expenditures was likely to result in the organization no longer qualifying under § 501(c)(3) and if the managers' actions were willful and not due to reasonable cause. The tax does not apply to private foundations (see the subsequent discussion).[19]

Concept Summary 23.1 capsulizes the rules on influencing legislation.

Intermediate Sanctions

Prior to 1996, the IRS had only two options available for dealing with exempt organizations (other than private foundations) engaging in prohibited transactions. First, it could attempt to subject part or all of the organization's income to Federal income tax. Second, it could revoke the exempt status of the organization. For private foundations, an additional option was available. The IRS could impose certain taxes on

[17] § 4911(a)(1).
[18] § 4911(b).
[19] § 4912.

CONCEPT SUMMARY 23.1

Exempt Organizations and Influencing Legislation

Factor	Tax Result
Entity subject to rule	§ 501(c)(3) organization.
Effect of influencing legislation	Subject to tax on lobbying expenditures under § 4912. Forfeit exempt status under § 501(c)(3). Not eligible for exempt status under § 501(c)(4).
Effect of electing to make lobbying expenditures	Permitted to make limited lobbying expenditures. Subject to tax under § 4911.

private foundations for engaging in so-called prohibited transactions (see Concept Summary 23.3 later in the chapter).

Tax legislation enacted in 1996 added another option to the IRS toolbox—**intermediate sanctions**—for so-called public charities.[20] The intermediate sanctions take the form of excise taxes imposed on disqualified persons (any individuals who are in a position to exercise substantial influence over the affairs of the organization) who engage in *excess benefit transactions* and on exempt organization managers who participate in such a transaction knowing that it is improper. Such excess benefit transactions include transactions in which a disqualified person engages in a non-fair-market-value transaction with the exempt organization or receives unreasonable compensation.

The excise tax on the disqualified person is imposed at a rate of 25 percent of the excess benefit. For the exempt organization management, the excise tax is imposed at a rate of 10 percent of the excess benefit (unless such participation is not willful and is due to reasonable cause) with a statutory ceiling of $20,000 for any excess benefit transaction. These excise taxes are referred to as first-level taxes.

A second-level tax is imposed on the disqualified person if the excess benefit transaction is not corrected within the taxable period. This excise tax is imposed at a rate of 200 percent of the excess benefit.

FEEDER ORGANIZATIONS

A **feeder organization** carries on a trade or business for the benefit of an exempt organization (i.e., it remits its profits to the exempt organization). Such organizations are not exempt from Federal income tax. This provision is intended to prevent an entity whose primary purpose is to conduct a trade or business for profit from escaping taxation merely because all of its profits are payable to one or more exempt organizations.[21]

Some income and activities are *not* subject to the feeder organization rules:[22]

- Rent income that would be excluded from the definition of the term *rent* for purposes of the unrelated business income tax (discussed subsequently).
- A trade or business where substantially all the work is performed by volunteers.
- The trade or business of selling merchandise where substantially all the merchandise has been received as contributions or gifts.

[20] § 4958.
[21] § 502(a).
[22] § 502(b).

CONCEPT SUMMARY 23.2

Consequences of Exempt Status

General	Exempt from Federal income tax. Exempt from most state and local income, franchise, sales, and property taxes. Qualify for reductions in postage rates. Gifts to the organization often can be deducted by donor.
Exceptions	May be subject to Federal income tax associated with the following. • Engaging in a prohibited transaction. • Being a feeder organization. • Being a private foundation. • Generating unrelated business taxable income.

EXAMPLE 2
THE BIG PICTURE

Return to the facts of *The Big Picture* on p. 23-2. Recall that Hopeful, Inc., an exempt organization under § 501(c)(3) that provides temporary lodging and psychological services to abused women, is trying to decide what it should do with Taste Good Ice Cream, a chain of gourmet ice cream shops that it has received as a bequest. Assume that Hopeful has decided to operate Taste Good as a subsidiary, with the profits going to Hopeful to support its tax-exempt mission. The subsidiary will be a taxable entity (a feeder organization) subject to the Federal income tax using the corporate tax rates. ■

Concept Summary 23.2 highlights the consequences of exempt status.

23.5 Private Foundations

TAX CONSEQUENCES OF PRIVATE FOUNDATION STATUS

Certain exempt organizations are classified as **private foundations**. This classification produces two negative consequences. First, the classification may have an adverse impact on the contributions received by the donee exempt organization. Contributions may decline because the tax consequences for donors may not be as favorable as if the entity were not a private foundation.[23] Second, the classification may result in taxation at the exempt organization level. The reason for this less beneficial tax treatment is that private foundations define common good more narrowly and therefore are seen as not being supported by, and operated for the good of, the public.

LO.4

Determine which exempt organizations are classified as private foundations.

Definition of a Private Foundation

All § 501(c)(3) organizations are private foundations by default, unless one of the statutory exceptions applies. The following § 501(c)(3) organizations are *not* private foundations.[24]

1. Churches; educational institutions; hospitals and medical research organizations; charitable organizations receiving a major portion of their support from the general public or the United States, a state, or a political subdivision thereof that is operated for the benefit of a college or university; and governmental units (favored activities category).
2. Organizations that are broadly supported by the general public (excluding disqualified persons), by governmental units, or by organizations described in (1) above.
3. Entities organized and operated exclusively for the benefit of organizations described in (1) or (2) (a supporting organization).
4. Entities organized and operated exclusively for testing for public safety.

---

23 § 170(e)(1)(B)(ii).

24 § 509(a).

TAX *in* *the NEWS*

Donor-Advised Funds: A Hot Topic

Suppose that a wealthy taxpayer would like to make a substantial charitable contribution and qualify for the charitable contribution deduction this year. However, he has not yet identified the recipient of the contribution. Or the taxpayer has identified the recipient, but wants the charity to disburse the funds over a number of years. Or the taxpayer wants to make the contribution this year, but be permitted to advise the charitable organization in future years as to the possible use of the donated funds. Can the taxpayer achieve any of these goals and still be eligible for the charitable contribution deduction this year?

There is a way to meet the wealthy taxpayer's objectives. He can make his contribution to a "donor-advised fund." Such funds are components of a qualified charitable organization.

To receive this favorable treatment, however, certain statutory and administrative requirements must be met. Even though the donor may advise as to how the funds are to be used, the charitable organization must have ultimate control over their distribution. For any contributions to donor-advised funds made after February 13, 2007, the donor must obtain written acknowledgment from the charitable organization that it has exclusive legal control over the contributed assets.

Recognizing the potential for abuse in this area, both the Senate Finance Committee and the House Ways and Means Committee have identified donor-advised funds as a potential topic for additional legislation.

To meet the broadly supported requirement in (2) above, both the following tests must be satisfied.

- External support test.
- Internal support test.

Under the *external support test*, more than one-third of the organization's support each taxable year *normally* must come from the three groups listed in (2) above, in the following forms.

- Gifts, grants, contributions, and membership fees.
- Gross receipts from admissions, sales of merchandise, performance of services, or the furnishing of facilities in an activity that is not an unrelated trade or business for purposes of the unrelated business income tax (discussed subsequently). However, such gross receipts from any person or governmental agency in excess of the greater of $5,000 or 1 percent of the organization's support for the taxable year are not counted in the numerator of the support fraction.
  - *Amounts received from disqualified persons are not included in the numerator of the support fraction. Disqualified persons include:*
    - *Substantial contributors whose cumulative gifts and bequests to the exempt entity exceed both 2 percent of aggregate contributions received by the entity and $5,000.*
    - *Members of the governing body of the exempt entity including officers, directors, trustees, and their families.*
    - *Generally, corporations, partnerships, trusts, and estates that are affiliated with a disqualified person, using a 35 percent ownership/beneficiary control test.*

The *internal support test* limits the amount of support *normally* received from the following sources to one-third of the organization's support for the taxable year.[25]

- Gross investment income (gross income from interest, dividends, rents, and royalties).
- Unrelated business taxable income (discussed subsequently) minus the related tax.

[25] The external and internal support tests generally must be met in each of the four preceding tax years. When these tests are met, public charity status is granted for the current year and for the subsequent year. Reg. §§ 1.509(a)–3(c) and 1.170A–9(e)(4)(i).

TAX *in* the NEWS

When Does a Charitable Mission Become Political Advocacy?

What is the role of a private foundation? The usual answer is to carry out some charitable mission. When the Council of Foundations held its 2010 annual conference in Denver, however, a number of the participants argued that foundations should be playing a more active role in society.

Although collaborative efforts between private philanthopy and the White House are certainly not new, the election of President Obama, a onetime community organizer, has given impetus to the movement. Not only has the President indicated that he is eager to work with charitable organizations, but many of the organizations have expressed a willingness to support his agenda. At the Council of Foundations conference, for example, many participants advocated actively supporting health care reform, migrant rights, initiatives to reduce income disparity, and efforts to combat global warming. At the same time, however, a few foundation leaders suggested that such active political involvement might have consequences that its advocates had not considered.

Source: Adapted from Anthony Paletta, "The Fawning of the Foundations," *Wall Street Journal*, April 30, 2010, p. W9.

EXAMPLE 3

Lion, Inc., a § 501(c)(3) organization, received the following support during the taxable year.

Governmental unit A for services rendered	$ 30,000
Governmental unit B for services rendered	20,000
General public for services rendered	20,000
Gross investment income	15,000
Contributions from individual substantial contributors (disqualified persons)	15,000
Total support	$100,000

For purposes of the *external support test*, the support from A is counted only to the extent of $5,000 (greater of $5,000 or 1% of $100,000 support). Likewise, for B, only $5,000 is counted as support. Thus, the total countable support is $30,000 ($20,000 from the general public + $5,000 + $5,000), and Lion fails the test for the taxable year ($30,000/$100,000 = 30%; need more than 33.3%). The $15,000 received from disqualified persons is excluded from the numerator but is included in the denominator.

External Support Test

Governmental unit A for services rendered	$ 5,000
Governmental unit B for services rendered	5,000
General public for services rendered	20,000
Total countable support	$30,000

$$\frac{\$30,000}{\$100,000} = 30\% \quad \text{Fails external support test}$$

In calculating the *internal support test*, only the gross investment income of $15,000 is included in the numerator. Thus, the test is satisfied ($15,000/$100,000 = 15%; cannot exceed 33.3%) for the taxable year.

Internal Support Test

Gross investment income	$15,000
Unrelated business taxable income	–0–
Total countable support	$15,000

$$\frac{\$15,000}{\$100,000} = 15\% \quad \text{Passes internal support test}$$

Since Lion did not satisfy both tests, it does not qualify as an organization that is broadly supported. ■

The intent of the two tests is to exclude from private foundation status those § 501(c)(3) organizations that are responsive to the general public rather than to the private interests of a limited number of donors or other persons.

Examples of § 501(c)(3) organizations that would be classified as private foundations, except that they receive broad public support, include the United Fund, the Boy Scouts, university alumni associations, and symphony orchestras.

TAXES IMPOSED ON PRIVATE FOUNDATIONS

LO.5

Recognize the taxes imposed on private foundations and calculate the related initial tax and additional tax amounts.

In general, a private foundation is exempt from Federal income tax. However, because a private foundation is usually not a broadly, publicly supported organization, it may be subject to the following taxes.[26]

- Tax based on investment income.
- Tax on self-dealing.
- Tax on failure to distribute income.
- Tax on excess business holdings.
- Tax on investments that jeopardize charitable purposes.
- Tax on taxable expenditures.

These taxes serve to restrict the permitted activities of private foundations. Two levels of tax may be imposed on the private foundation and the foundation manager: an initial tax and an additional tax. The initial taxes (first-level), with the exception of the tax based on investment income, are imposed because the private foundation engages in so-called *prohibited transactions.* The additional taxes (second-level) are imposed only if the prohibited transactions are not modified within a statutory time period.[27] See Concept Summary 23.3 for additional details.

The tax on a failure to distribute income will be used to illustrate how expensive these taxes can be and the related importance of avoiding their imposition. For failure to distribute a sufficient portion of a private nonoperating foundation's income, both an initial tax (first-level) and an additional tax (second-level) may be imposed. The initial tax is imposed at a rate of 15 percent on the income for the taxable year that is not distributed during the current or the following taxable year. The initial tax is imposed on the undistributed income for each year until the IRS assesses the tax.

The additional tax is imposed at a rate of 100 percent on the amount of the inadequate distribution that is not distributed by the assessment date. The additional tax is effectively waived if the undistributed income is distributed within 90 days after the mailing of the deficiency notice for the additional tax. Extensions of this period may be obtained.

Undistributed income is the excess of the distributable amount (in effect, the amount that should have been distributed) over qualifying distributions made by the entity. The distributable amount is the excess of the minimum investment return over the sum of the (1) unrelated business income tax and (2) the excise tax based on net investment income.[28] The minimum investment return is 5 percent of the excess of the fair market value of the foundation's assets over the unpaid debt associated with acquiring or improving these assets. Assets of the foundation that are employed directly in carrying on the foundation's exempt purpose are not used in making this calculation.

[26] §§ 4940–4945.

[27] § 4961.

[28] § 4940.

CONCEPT SUMMARY 23.3

Taxes Imposed on Private Foundations

Type of Tax	Code Section	Purpose	Private Foundation Initial Tax	Private Foundation Additional Tax	Foundation Manager Initial Tax	Foundation Manager Additional Tax
On investment income	§ 4940	Audit fee to defray IRS expenses.	2%*			
On self-dealing	§ 4941	Engaging in transactions with disqualified persons.	5%**	200%**	2.5%†	50%†
On failure to distribute income	§ 4942	Failing to distribute adequate amount of income for exempt purposes.	15%	100%		
On excess business holdings	§ 4943	Investments that enable the private foundation to control unrelated businesses.	5%	200%		
On jeopardizing investments	§ 4944	Speculative investments that put the private foundation's assets at risk.	5%	25%	5%††	5%†
On taxable expenditures	§ 4945	Expenditures that should not be made by private foundations.	10%	100%	2.5%††	50%†

*May be possible to reduce the tax rate to 1%. In addition, an exempt operating foundation [see §§ 4940(d)(2) and 4942(j)(3)] is not subject to the tax.
**Imposed on the disqualified person rather than the foundation.
†Subject to a statutory ceiling of $10,000.
††Subject to a statutory ceiling of $5,000.

EXAMPLE 4

Gold, Inc., a private foundation, has undistributed income of $80,000 for the taxable year 2008. It distributes $15,000 of this amount during 2009 and an additional $45,000 during 2010. The IRS deficiency notice is mailed to Gold on August 5, 2011. The initial tax is $12,750 [($65,000 × 15%) + ($20,000 × 15%)].

At the date of the deficiency notice, no additional distributions have been made from the 2008 undistributed income. Therefore, since the remaining undistributed income of $20,000 has not been distributed by August 5, 2011, an additional tax of $20,000($20,000 × 100%) is imposed.

If Gold distributes the $20,000 of undistributed income for 2008 within 90 days of the deficiency notice, the additional tax is waived. Without this distribution, however, the foundation will owe $32,750 ($12,750 + $20,000) in taxes. ■

Exhibit 23.2 shows the classifications of exempt organizations and indicates the potential negative consequences of classification as a private foundation.

LO.6

Determine when an exempt organization is subject to the unrelated business income tax and calculate the amount of the tax.

23.6 Unrelated Business Income Tax

As explained in the previous section, private foundations are subject to excise taxes for certain actions. One of these excise taxes penalizes the private foundation for using the foundation to gain control of unrelated businesses (tax on excess business holdings). However, *unrelated business* has different meanings for purposes of that excise tax and for the unrelated business income tax.

EXHIBIT 23.2 Exempt Organizations: Classification

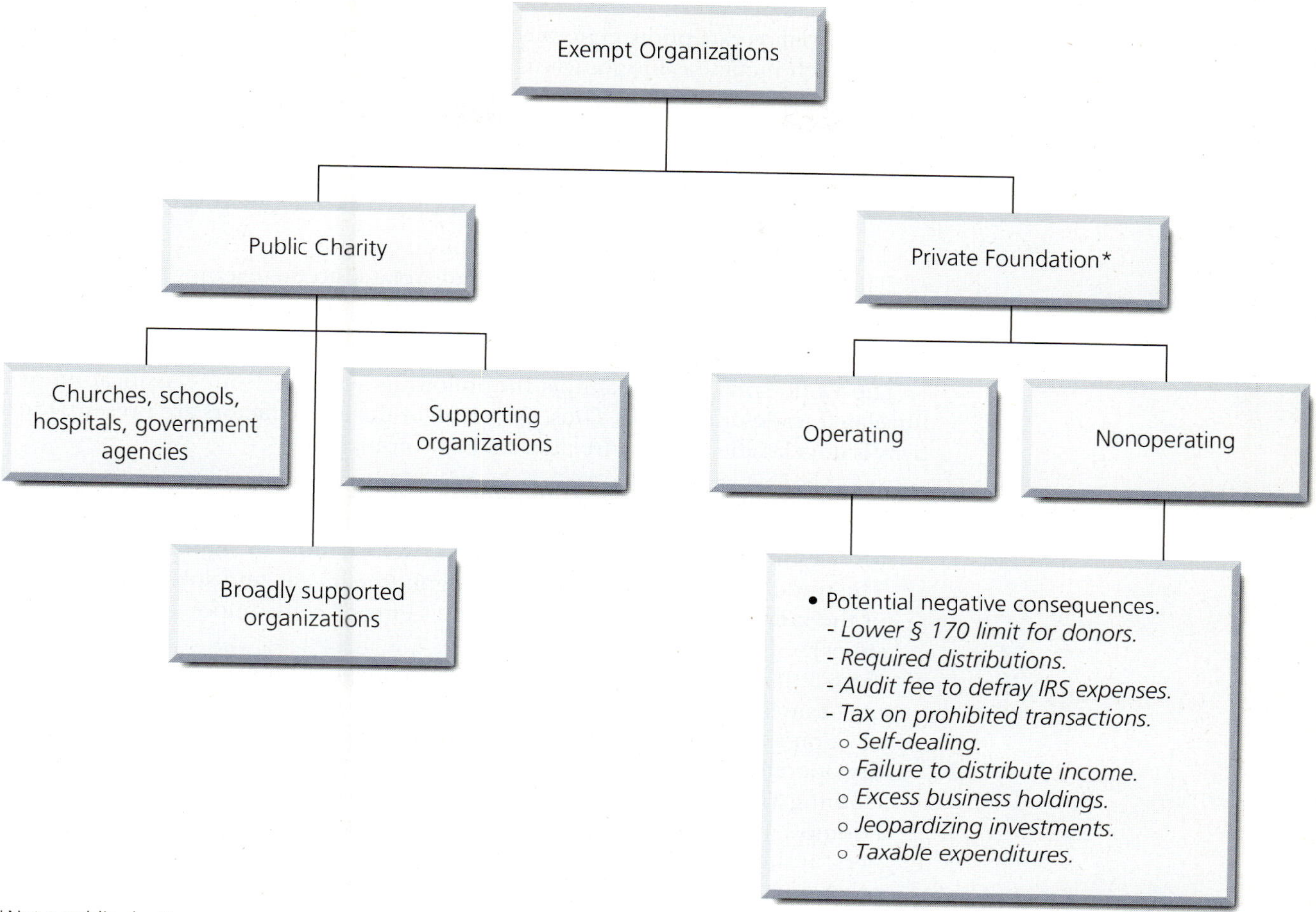

*Not a public charity.

The **unrelated business income tax (UBIT)** is designed to treat the entity as if it were subject to the corporate income tax. Thus, the rates that are used are those applicable to a corporate taxpayer.[29]

In general, **unrelated business income (UBI)** is derived from activities not related to the exempt purpose of the exempt organization. The tax is levied because the organization is engaging in substantial commercial activities.[30] Without such a tax, nonexempt organizations (regular taxable business entities) would be at a substantial disadvantage when trying to compete with the exempt organization. Thus, the UBIT is intended to neutralize the exempt entity's tax advantage.[31]

It is the source of the business profits that triggers the UBIT, and not their use. UBI that is employed for the entity's exempt purpose still is subject to the tax.

EXAMPLE 5
THE BIG PICTURE

Return to the facts of *The Big Picture* on p. 23-2. Recall that Hopeful, Inc., an exempt organization under § 501(c)(3), has received Taste Good Ice Cream, a chain of gourmet ice cream shops, as a bequest. Assume that Hopeful has decided to operate Taste Good as a division. Although the income from Taste Good's shops will be used to support Hopeful's exempt purpose of providing temporary lodging and psychological services to abused women, the net revenue constitutes unrelated business income, and therefore it is subject to the UBIT. ■

[29] § 511(a)(1).
[30] § 512(a)(1).
[31] Reg. § 1.513–1(b).

The UBIT applies to all organizations that are exempt from Federal income tax under § 501(c), except Federal agencies. In addition, the tax applies to state colleges and universities.[32]

A materiality exception generally exempts an entity from being subject to the UBIT if such income is insignificant. See the later discussion of the $1,000 statutory deduction generally available to all exempt organizations.

UNRELATED TRADE OR BUSINESS

An exempt organization may be subject to the UBIT in the following circumstances.[33]

- The organization conducts a trade or business.
- The trade or business is not substantially related to the exempt purpose of the organization.
- The trade or business is regularly carried on by the organization.

The Code specifically exempts the following activities from classification as an unrelated trade or business. Thus, even if all of the above factors are present, the activity is not classified as an unrelated trade or business.

- The individuals performing substantially all the work of the trade or business do so without compensation (e.g., an orphanage operates a retail store for sales to the general public, and all the work is done by volunteers).
- The trade or business consists of selling merchandise, and substantially all of the merchandise has been received as gifts or contributions (e.g., thrift shops).
- For § 501(c)(3) organizations and for state colleges or universities, the trade or business is conducted primarily for the convenience of the organization's members, students, patients, officers, or employees (e.g., a laundry operated by the college for laundering dormitory linens and students' clothing, a college bookstore).
- For most employee unions, the trade or business consists of selling to members, at their usual place of employment, work-related clothing and equipment and items normally sold through vending machines, snack bars, or food dispensing facilities.

Definition of Trade or Business

Trade or business, for this purpose, is broadly defined. It includes any activity conducted for the production of income through the sale of merchandise or the performance of services. An activity need not generate a profit to be treated as a trade or business. The activity may be part of a larger set of activities conducted by the organization, some of which may be related to the exempt purpose. Being included in a larger set does not cause the activity to lose its identity as an unrelated trade or business.[34]

EXAMPLE 6

Health, Inc., is an exempt hospital that operates a pharmacy. The pharmacy provides medicines and supplies to the patients in the hospital (i.e., it contributes to the conduct of the hospital's exempt purpose). In addition, the pharmacy sells medicines and supplies to the general public. The activity of selling to the general public constitutes a trade or business for purposes of the UBIT. ■

Not Substantially Related to the Exempt Purpose

Exempt organizations frequently conduct unrelated trades or businesses in order to provide income to help defray the costs of conducting the exempt purpose (like the ice cream shops in Example 5). Providing financial support for the exempt purpose

[32] § 511(a)(2) and Reg. § 1.511–2(a)(2).
[33] § 513(a) and Reg. § 1.513–2(a).
[34] Reg. § 1.513–1(b).

TAX *in the NEWS*

Getting Back More Than a Charitable Foundation Gives

Charitable foundations typically give away money in carrying out their tax-exempt mission. Unless they are educational institutions, private foundations must distribute 5 percent of their investment assets every year for charitable purposes. Generally, private foundations meet this requirement by making grants.

However, there is another way that private foundations can satisfy this 5 percent requirement and at the same time create the potential for receiving back more from the recipient than the amount initially disbursed. This opportunity is called "program-related investing" (PRI), which can take several forms.

In one type of PRI, rather than making a grant to the recipient, a private foundation loans money to what would otherwise be the recipient and then collects interest (usually at a below-market interest rate) on the loan. In other forms of PRI, a private foundation makes an equity investment in the recipient or guarantees a loan that the recipient obtains from a conventional source.

PRI provides a way for a private foundation to conserve its assets, leverage its asset utilization (i.e., money potentially can be recycled to multiple recipients), and at the same time carry out its tax-exempt mission (i.e., a key requirement for PRI under the tax law). In addition, many of those involved in private foundations believe that expecting investment returns from the PRI recipient results in a greater buy-in, more accountability, and greater effort on the part of the recipient.

will not prevent an activity from being classified as an unrelated trade or business and thereby being subject to the UBIT.

To be related to the accomplishment of the exempt purpose, the conduct of the business activities must be causally related and contribute importantly to the exempt purpose. Whether a causal relationship exists and the degree of its importance are determined by examining the facts and circumstances. One must consider the size and extent of the activities in relation to the nature and extent of the exempt function that the activities serve.[35]

EXAMPLE 7

Art, Inc., an exempt organization, operates a school for training children in the performing arts. As an essential part of that training, the children perform for the general public. The children are paid at the minimum wage for the performances, and Art derives gross income by charging admission to the performances.

The income from admissions is not income from an unrelated trade or business, because the performances by the children contribute importantly to the accomplishment of the exempt purpose of providing training in the performing arts. ■

EXAMPLE 8

Assume the same facts as in Example 7, except that four performances are conducted each weekend of the year. Assume that this number of performances far exceeds that required for training the children. Thus, the part of the income derived from admissions for these excess performances is income from an unrelated trade or business. ■

The trade or business may sell merchandise that has been produced as part of the accomplishment of the exempt purpose. The sale of such merchandise is normally treated as related to the exempt purpose. However, if the merchandise is not sold in substantially the same state it was in at the completion of the exempt purpose, the gross income subsequently derived from the sale of the merchandise is income from an unrelated trade or business.[36]

EXAMPLE 9

Help, Inc., an exempt organization, conducts programs for the rehabilitation of the handicapped. One of the programs includes training in radio and television repair. Help derives gross income by selling the repaired items. The income is substantially related to the accomplishment of the exempt purpose. ■

[35] Reg. § 1.513–1(d).

[36] Reg. § 1.513–1(d)(4)(ii).

An asset or facility used in the exempt purpose may also be used in a nonexempt purpose. Income derived from the use in a nonexempt purpose is income from an unrelated trade or business.[37]

EXAMPLE 10

Civil, Inc., an exempt organization, operates a museum. As part of the exempt purpose of the museum, educational lectures are given in the museum's theater during the operating hours of the museum. In the evening, when the museum is closed, the theater is leased to an individual who operates a movie theater. The lease income received from the individual who operates the movie theater is income from an unrelated trade or business. ■

ETHICS & Equity

UNRELATED BUSINESS INCOME TAX: SUBSTANTIALLY RELATED

Mops and More, a § 501(c)(3) organization, makes mops and brooms that it sells to the general public. The exempt organization's mission is to provide short-term employment opportunities and temporary housing for recovering drug addicts during the two-month period they are at a halfway house. Profits from the sales of the mops and brooms are used to support the halfway house. The laborers are paid the minimum wage, with half of this amount going toward their room and board at the halfway house. In prior years, approximately 90 percent of the laborers involved in the production of the mops and brooms were recovering addicts staying at the halfway house. The remaining 10 percent were permanent employees who trained and supervised the recovering addicts.

In prior years, Mops and More has not filed a Form 990–T (Exempt Organization Business Income Tax Return). The treasurer of Mops and More believes that the sale of the mops and brooms does not constitute unrelated business income, because the production of the items is substantially related to the mission of the exempt organization.

For the current tax year, there is a substantial drop in the number of recovering addicts who stay at the halfway house. To meet production quotas, the organization hires foreign workers who are legally in this country on temporary visas. They account for 70 percent of the labor force in the current year.

The treasurer believes that this shift from recovering addicts to foreign workers is temporary in nature. So she does not believe that it is necessary to file a Form 990–T. Has she acted appropriately?

Special Rule for Corporate Sponsorship Payments

The term *unrelated trade or business* does not include the soliciting and receiving of qualified sponsorship payments.[38]

A payment qualifies as a qualified sponsorship if it meets the following requirements.

- There is no arrangement or expectation that the trade or business making the payment will receive any substantial benefit other than the use or acknowledgment of its name, logo, or product lines in connection with the activities of the exempt organization.
- Such use or acknowledgment does not include advertising the payor's products or services.
- The payment does not include any payment for which the amount is contingent upon the level of attendance at one or more events, broadcast ratings, or other factors indicating the degree of public exposure to one or more events.

EXAMPLE 11

Pets, Inc., a manufacturer of cat food, contributes $25,000 to Feline Care, Inc., an exempt organization that cares for abandoned cats. In return for the contribution, Feline agrees to put Pets' corporate logo in its monthly newsletter to donors. Under

[37] Reg. § 1.513–1(d)(4)(iii) addresses the allocation of expenses to exempt and nonexempt activities.

[38] § 513(i).

TAX *in* the NEWS

SHOULD THE NCAA BE TAX-EXEMPT?

The National Collegiate Athletic Association (NCAA) is a tax-exempt organization. Although donors cannot deduct contributions to the NCAA as charitable contributions, the NCAA itself does not pay taxes on its revenues.

Several members of Congress have questioned whether the NCAA should be tax-exempt. Among them is former Congressman Bill Thomas (served as chairman of the House Ways and Means Committee), who suggested that the NCAA's tax-exempt status amounts to a government subsidy from the taxpayers. Another concern is that the NCAA's member educational institutions may be using their tax-exempt status to help pay for escalating athletic program costs, including coaches' multimillion-dollar salaries, chartered travel, and state-of-the-art athletic facilities.

these circumstances, the $25,000 payment is a qualified sponsorship payment and is not subject to the UBIT. ■

EXAMPLE 12

Assume the same facts as in Example 11 except that Feline agrees to endorse Pets' cat food in its monthly newsletter by stating that it feeds only Pets' cat food to its cats. The $25,000 is not a qualified sponsorship payment and is subject to UBIT. ■

Special Rule for Bingo Games

A special provision applies in determining whether income from bingo games is from an unrelated trade or business. Under this provision, a *qualified bingo game* is not an unrelated trade or business if both of the following requirements are satisfied.[39]

- The bingo game is legal under both state and local law.
- Commercial bingo games (conducted for a profit motive) ordinarily are not permitted in the jurisdiction.

EXAMPLE 13

Play, Inc., an exempt organization, conducts weekly bingo games. The laws of the state and municipality in which Play conducts the games expressly provide that exempt organizations may conduct bingo games, but do not permit profit-oriented entities to do so. Since both of the requirements for bingo games are satisfied, the bingo games conducted by Play are not an unrelated trade or business. ■

EXAMPLE 14

Game, Inc., an exempt organization, conducts weekly bingo games in City X and City Y. State law expressly permits exempt organizations to conduct bingo games. State law also provides that profit-oriented entities may conduct bingo games in X, which is a resort community. Several businesses regularly conduct bingo games there.

The bingo games conducted by Game in Y are not an unrelated trade or business. However, the bingo games that Game conducts in X are an unrelated trade or business, because commercial bingo games are regularly permitted to be conducted there. ■

Special Rule for Distribution of Low-Cost Articles

If an exempt organization distributes low-cost items as an incidental part of its solicitation for charitable contributions, the distributions may not be considered an unrelated trade or business. A low-cost article is one that costs $9.70 or less (for 2011—indexed annually). Examples are pens, stamps, stickers, stationery, and address labels. If more than one item is distributed to a person during the calendar year, the costs of the items are combined.[40]

---

[39] § 513(f).

[40] § 513(h)(1)(A).

TAX *in the NEWS*

Bingo Halls: Legal or Not?

If bingo games are legal under both state and local law, holding bingo games is not an unrelated trade or business for an exempt organization, if for-profit bingo games ordinarily are not permitted in the area. Sometimes, though, there are different rules—and a different related tax result—depending on how the games are played, as some bingo halls in Jefferson County, Alabama, discovered.

Recently, the Alabama Bureau of Investigation raided five bingo halls and confiscated several electronic bingo machines. The halls previously had been warned that the use of slot-style electronic bingo machines was illegal. Apparently, how a bingo game is conducted does matter.

Source: Adapted from Associated Press, "Five Bingo Halls Raided," *Wall Street Journal*, April 8, 2010, p. A9.

Special Rule for Rental or Exchange of Membership Lists

If an exempt organization conducts a trade or business that consists of either exchanging with or renting to other exempt organizations the organization's donor or membership list (mailing lists), the activity is not an unrelated trade or business.[41]

Other Special Rules

Other special rules are used in determining whether each of the following activities is an unrelated trade or business.[42]

- Qualified public entertainment activities (e.g., a state fair).
- Qualified convention and trade show activities.
- Certain services provided at cost or less by a hospital to other small hospitals.
- Certain pole rentals by telephone or electric companies.

Discussion of these special rules is beyond the scope of this text.

UNRELATED BUSINESS INCOME

Even when an exempt organization conducts an unrelated trade or business, a tax is assessed only if the exempt organization regularly conducts the activity and the business produces unrelated business income.

Regularly Carried on by the Organization

An activity is classified as unrelated business income only if it is regularly carried on by the exempt organization. This provision assures that only activities that are actually competing with taxable organizations are subject to the UBIT. Accordingly, factors to be considered in assessing *regularly carried on* include the frequency of the activity, the continuity of the activity, and the manner in which the activity is pursued.[43]

EXAMPLE 15

Silver, Inc., an exempt organization, owns land that is located next to the state fairgrounds. During the 10 days of the state fair, Silver uses the land as a parking lot and charges individuals attending the state fair for parking there. The activity is not regularly carried on. ■

EXAMPLE 16

Black, Inc., an exempt organization, has its offices in the downtown area. It owns a parking lot adjacent to its offices on which its employees park during the week. On

[41] § 513(h)(1)(B).

[42] §§ 513(d), (e), and (g).

[43] § 512(a)(1) and Reg. § 1.513–1(c).

Saturdays, it rents the spaces in the parking lot to individuals shopping or working in the downtown area. Black is conducting a business activity on a year-round basis, even though it is only for one day per week. Thus, an activity is regularly being carried on. ■

Unrelated Business Income Defined

Unrelated business income is generally that derived from the unrelated trade or business. To convert it from a gross income measure to a net income measure, it must be reduced by the deductions directly connected with the conduct of the unrelated trade or business.[44]

UNRELATED BUSINESS TAXABLE INCOME

General Tax Model

The model for unrelated business taxable income (UBTI) appears in Figure 23.2.

Positive adjustments[45]

1. The charitable contribution deduction is permitted without regard to whether the gift is associated with the unrelated trade or business. However, to the extent the charitable contributions deducted in calculating net unrelated business income (see Figure 23.2) exceed 10 percent of UBTI (without regard to the charitable contribution deduction), the excess amount is disallowed (i.e., a positive adjustment results).

EXAMPLE 17

Brown, Inc., an exempt organization, has UBTI of $100,000 (excluding any modifications associated with charitable contributions). Total charitable contributions (all associated with the unrelated trade or business) are $13,000. Assuming that the $13,000 is deducted in calculating net unrelated business income, the excess of $3,000 [$13,000 – 10%($100,000)] is a positive adjustment in calculating UBTI. ■

2. Unrelated debt-financed income net of the unrelated debt-financed deductions (see the subsequent discussion of Unrelated Debt-Financed Income).
3. Certain net interest, annuity, royalty, and rent income received by the exempt organization from an organization it controls (80 percent test). Note that this provision overrides the modifications for these types of income (negative adjustment 3).

Negative adjustments

1. Income from dividends, interest, and annuities, net of all deductions directly related to producing such income.

FIGURE 23.2 Tax Formula for Unrelated Business Taxable Income

Gross unrelated business income
– Deductions
= Net unrelated business income
± Modifications
= Unrelated business taxable income

[44] § 512(a)(1).

[45] §§ 512(a)(1) and (b) and Reg. § 1.512(b)–1.

2. Royalty income, regardless of whether it is measured by production, gross income, or taxable income from the property, net of all deductions directly related to producing such income.
3. Rent income from real property and from certain personal property net of all deductions directly related to producing such income. Personal property rents are included in the negative adjustment only if the personal property is leased with the real property. In addition, the personal property rent income must be incidental (does not exceed 10 percent of the gross rent income under the lease) to be used in computing the negative adjustment. In both of the following cases, however, none of the rent income is treated as a negative adjustment.
   - More than 50 percent of the rent income under the lease is from personal property.
   - Rent income is calculated using the tenant's profits.

EXAMPLE 18

Beaver, Inc., an exempt organization, leases land and a building (realty) and computers (personalty) housed in the building. Under the lease, $46,000 of the rent is for the land and building, and $4,000 is for the computers. Expenses incurred for the land and building are $10,000. The net rent income from the land and building of $36,000 ($46,000 – $10,000) and the $4,000 from the computers are negative adjustments. ■

EXAMPLE 19

Assume the same facts as in Example 18, except that the rent income is $35,000 from the land and building and $15,000 from the computers. Since the rent income from the computers exceeds $5,000 (i.e., 10% of the total rent under the lease) and is not incidental, it is not a negative adjustment. ■

EXAMPLE 20

Assume the same facts as in Example 18, except that the rent income is $20,000 from the land and building and $30,000 from the computers. Since more than 50% of the rent income under the lease is from the computers, neither the rent income from the land and building nor that from the computers is a negative adjustment. ■

If the lessor of real property provides significant services to the lessee, such income, for this purpose, is not rent income.

4. Gains and losses from the sale, exchange, or other disposition of property *except for* inventory.

EXAMPLE 21

Beaver, the owner of the land, building, and computers in Example 18, sells these assets for $450,000. Their adjusted basis is $300,000. Beaver's recognized gain of $150,000 is a negative adjustment. ■

5. Certain research income net of all deductions directly related to producing that income.
6. The charitable contribution deduction is permitted without regard to whether the gift is associated with the unrelated trade or business. Therefore, to the extent that the charitable contributions exceed those deducted in calculating net unrelated business income (see Figure 23.2), the excess is a negative adjustment in calculating UBTI. In making this calculation though, the 10 percent of UBTI (without regard to the charitable contribution deduction) limit still applies (see positive adjustment 1).

EXAMPLE 22

Canine, Inc., an exempt organization, has UBTI of $100,000 (excluding any modifications associated with charitable contributions). The total charitable contributions are $9,000, of which $7,000 (those associated with the unrelated trade or business) has been deducted in calculating net unrelated business income. Therefore, the remaining $2,000 of charitable contributions make up a negative adjustment in calculating UBTI. ■

7. A "standard deduction" of $1,000 is allowed.

EXAMPLE 23

Petit Care, Inc., an exempt organization, reports net unrelated business income of $800. Since Petit claims a $1,000 statutory deduction, its UBTI is $0. Therefore, its income tax liability is $0. ■

After UBTI is determined, that amount is subject to tax using the regular corporate tax rates.

EXAMPLE 24

Patient, Inc., an exempt organization, has UBTI of $500,000. Patient's income tax liability is $170,000 ($500,000 UBTI × 34% corporate tax rate). ■

UNRELATED DEBT-FINANCED INCOME

In the formula for calculating UBTI (refer to Figure 23.2), unrelated debt-financed income is one of the positive adjustments. Examples of income from debt-financed property include rent income from real estate or tangible personal property, dividends from corporate stock, and gains from the disposition of debt-financed property. Gains from property that is unrelated business income property are also included to the extent the gains are not otherwise treated as unrelated business income. Because of the importance of this item, it is discussed separately here.

In terms of UBTI, the positive adjustment for unrelated debt-financed income is a significant one. Without this provision, a tax-exempt organization could use borrowed funds to acquire unrelated business or investment property and use the untaxed (i.e., exempt) earnings from the acquisition to pay for the property.

Definition of Debt-Financed Income

Debt-financed income is the gross income generated from debt-financed property. *Debt-financed property* is all property of the exempt organization that is held to produce income and on which there is acquisition indebtedness, *except* for the following.[46]

- Property where substantially all (at least 85 percent) of the use is for the achievement of the exempt purpose of the exempt organization.[47]
- Property whose gross income is otherwise treated as unrelated business income.
- Property whose gross income is from the following sources and is not otherwise treated as unrelated business income.
  - *Income from research performed for the United States, a Federal governmental agency, or a state or a political subdivision thereof.*
  - *For a college, university, or hospital, income from research.*
  - *For an organization that performs fundamental (i.e., not applied) research for the benefit of the general public, income from research.*
- Property used in an activity that is not an unrelated trade or business.

If the 85 percent test is not satisfied, only the portion of the property that is *not* used for the exempt purpose is debt-financed property.

EXAMPLE 25

Deer, Inc., an exempt organization, owns a five-story office building on which there is acquisition indebtedness. Three of the floors are used for Deer's exempt purpose. The two other floors are leased to Purple Corporation. In this case, the *substantially all* test is not satisfied. Therefore, 40% of the office building is debt-financed property, and 60% is not. ■

Certain land that is acquired by an exempt organization for later exempt use is excluded from debt-financed property if the following requirements are satisfied.[48]

[46] § 514(b).
[47] Reg. § 1.514(b)–1(b)(1)(ii).
[48] § 514(b)(3).

- The principal purpose of acquiring the land is for use (substantially all) in achieving the organization's exempt purpose.
- This use will begin within 10 years of the acquisition date.
- At the date when the land is acquired, it is located in the *neighborhood* of other property of the organization for which substantially all the use is for achieving the organization's exempt purpose.

Even if the third requirement is not satisfied (the property is not located in the neighborhood), the land still is excluded from debt-financed property if it is converted to use for achieving the organization's exempt purpose within the 10-year period. Qualification under this provision will result in a refund of taxes previously paid. If the exempt organization is a church, the 10-year period becomes a 15-year period, and the neighborhood requirement is waived.

Definition of Acquisition Indebtedness

Acquisition indebtedness is debt sustained by the exempt organization in association with the acquisition of property. More precisely, *acquisition indebtedness* consists of the unpaid amounts of the following for debt-financed property.[49]

- Debt incurred in acquiring or improving the property.
- Debt incurred before the property was acquired or improved, but which would not have been incurred without the acquisition or improvement.
- Debt incurred after the property was acquired or improved, but which would not have been incurred without the acquisition or improvement.

EXAMPLE 26

Red, Inc., an exempt organization, acquires land for $100,000. In order to finance the acquisition, Red mortgages the land with a bank and receives loan proceeds of $80,000. Red leases the land to Duck Corporation. The mortgage is acquisition indebtedness. ■

EXAMPLE 27

Rose, Inc., an exempt organization, makes improvements to an office building that it rents to Bird Corporation. Excess working capital funds are used to finance the improvements. Rose is later required to mortgage its laboratory building, which it uses for its exempt purpose, to replenish working capital. The mortgage is acquisition indebtedness. ■

Portion of Debt-Financed Income and Deductions Treated as Unrelated Business Taxable Income

Once the amount of the debt-financed income and deductions is determined, it is necessary to ascertain what portion is unrelated debt-financed income and deductions. Unrelated debt-financed income increases UBTI, and unrelated debt-financed deductions decrease UBTI.

The calculation is made for each debt-financed property. The gross income from the property is multiplied by the following percentage.[50]

$$\frac{\text{Average acquisition indebtedness for the property}}{\text{Average adjusted basis of the property}} = \text{Debt/basis percentage}$$

This percentage cannot exceed 100. If debt-financed property is disposed of during the taxable year at a gain, average acquisition indebtedness in the formula is replaced with highest acquisition indebtedness. *Highest acquisition indebtedness* is the largest amount of acquisition indebtedness for the property during the 12-month period preceding the date of disposition.[51]

[49] § 514(c)(1). Educational organizations in certain limited circumstances can exclude debt incurred for real property acquisitions from classification as acquisition indebtedness.

[50] § 514(a)(1).

[51] § 514(c)(7).

Deductions are allowed for expenses directly related to the debt-financed property and the income from it. Cost recovery deductions must be calculated using the straight-line method. Once allowable deductions are determined, this amount is multiplied by the debt/basis percentage.[52]

EXAMPLE 28

White, Inc., an exempt organization, owns an office building that it leases to Squirrel Corporation for $120,000 per year. The average acquisition indebtedness is $300,000, and the average adjusted basis is $500,000. Since the office building is debt-financed property, the gross unrelated debt-financed income is:

$$\frac{\$300{,}000}{\$500{,}000} \times \$120{,}000 = \$72{,}000$$

If White's expenses associated with the office building lease (including straight-line cost recovery) equal $50,000, then allowable deductions are:

$$\frac{\$300{,}000}{\$500{,}000} \times \$50{,}000 = \$30{,}000$$

Thus, White's net unrelated debt-financed income is $42,000 ($72,000 – $30,000). ■

Average Acquisition Indebtedness

The *average acquisition indebtedness* for debt-financed property is the average amount of the outstanding debt for the taxable year (ignoring interest) during the portion of the year the property is held by the exempt organization. This amount is calculated by summing the outstanding debt on the first day of each calendar month the property is held by the exempt organization. Then this total is divided by the number of months the property is held by the organization.[53]

EXAMPLE 29

On August 12, Yellow, Inc., an exempt organization, acquires an office building that is debt-financed property for $500,000. The initial mortgage on the property is $400,000. The principal amount of the debt on August 12 and on the first of each subsequent month is as follows.

Month	Principal Amount
August 12	$ 400,000
September 1	380,000
October 1	360,000
November 1	340,000
December 1	320,000
Total	$1,800,000

Average acquisition indebtedness is $360,000 ($1,800,000 ÷ 5 months). Note that even though August is only a partial month, it is treated as a full month. ■

Average Adjusted Basis

The *average adjusted basis* of debt-financed property is calculated by summing the adjusted bases of the property on the first and last days during the taxable year the property is held by the exempt organization and then dividing by two.[54]

EXAMPLE 30

Assume the facts are the same as in Example 29. In addition, during the taxable year, depreciation of $5,900 is deducted. The average adjusted basis is $497,050 [($500,000 + $494,100) ÷ 2]. ■

Concept Summary 23.4 presents the rules concerning the UBIT.

[52] § 514(a)(3).

[53] § 514(c)(7) and Reg. § 1.514(a)–1(a)(3). A partial month is treated as a full month.

[54] § 514(a)(1) and Reg. § 1.514(a)–1(a)(2).

CONCEPT SUMMARY 23.4

Unrelated Business Income Tax

Purpose	To tax the entity on unrelated business income as if it were subject to the corporate income tax.
Applicable tax rates	Corporate tax rates.
Exempt organizations to which applicable	All organizations exempt under § 501(c), except Federal agencies.
Entities subject to the tax	The organization conducts a trade or business; the trade or business is not substantially related to the exempt purpose of the organization; and the trade or business is regularly carried on by the organization.
Exceptions to the tax	• All the work is performed by volunteers. • Substantially all of the merchandise being sold has been received by gift. • For § 501(c)(3) organizations, the business is conducted primarily for the benefit of the organization's members, students, patients, officers, or employees. • For most employee unions, the trade or business consists of selling to members work-related clothing and equipment and items normally sold through vending machines, snack bars, or food-dispensing facilities.
$1,000 provision	If the gross income from an unrelated trade or business is less than $1,000, it is not necessary to file a return associated with the unrelated business income tax.

23.7 Reporting Requirements

LO.7

List the reports exempt organizations must file with the IRS and the related due dates.

OBTAINING EXEMPT ORGANIZATION STATUS

Not all exempt organizations are required to obtain IRS approval for their exempt status. Among those required by statute to do so are organizations exempt under §§ 501(c)(3), 501(c)(9), and 501(c)(20).[55] Even in these cases, exceptions are provided (e.g., churches).

Even when not required to obtain IRS approval, most exempt organizations do apply for exempt status. Typically, an organization does not want to assume that it qualifies for exempt status and describe itself in that way to the public, only to have the IRS rule later that it does not qualify.

If an organization is required to obtain IRS approval for its exempt status and does not do so, it does not qualify as an exempt organization.

ANNUAL FILING REQUIREMENTS

Most exempt organizations are required to file an annual information return.[56] The return is filed on Form 990 (Return of Organization Exempt from Income Tax). Religious groups and Federal agencies need not file Form 990.[57]

An exempt organization whose annual gross receipts normally are $50,000 or less must file a Form 990–N, an online form known as the e-Postcard.[58] The e-Postcard is designed to be a simpler version of the full Form 990, to be used by small exempt entities. Supporting organizations and private foundations cannot use the Form 990–N.

The Form 990–EZ can be used by exempt organizations with gross receipts less than $200,000 and total assets less than $500,000.

Private foundations must file Form 990–PF (Return of Private Foundation).

[55] §§ 505(c), 508(a), and 508(c).

[56] § 6033(a)(1).

[57] § 6033(a)(3).

[58] Rev.Proc. 2011–15, 2011–3 I.R.B. 322.

TAX *in the NEWS*

The E-Postcard: Form 990–N

The new Form 990 (Return of Organization Exempt from Income Tax) requires more information than the old version of the form. But there now is a simplified form required of certain tax-exempts: Form 990–N, the e-Postcard. Hundreds of thousands of small tax-exempts that previously were exempt from an annual filing now must file electronically using the e-Postcard.

Information that must be disclosed on the e-Postcard includes the following.

- The organization's legal name.
- Any name under which the organization operates or does business.
- The organization's mailing address and website address (if any).
- The organization's taxpayer identification number.
- The name and address of a principal officer.
- A statement confirming that the organization's annual gross receipts normally are not greater than $50,000.

What happens if an organization fails to file Form 990–N? There is no monetary penalty, but if the form is not filed for three consecutive years, the organization's tax-exempt status is revoked. To have its tax-exempt status reinstated, the organization must file a new exemption application and pay the related fee.

A substantial number of small tax-exempts failed to file their first Form 990–N on time (i.e., by May 17, 2010). Since they were unaware of the filing requirement and/or that tax-exempt status could be lost, the IRS provided a filing extension until October 15, 2010. Most likely, this extension represented a one-time relief only.

The due date for Form 990 or Form 990–PF is the fifteenth day of the fifth month after the end of the taxable year. These returns are filed with the appropriate IRS Service Center based on the location of the exempt organization's principal office. Requests for extensions on filing are made by filing Form 2758 (Applications for Extension of Time).

EXAMPLE 31

Green, Inc., a § 501(c)(3) organization, has a fiscal year that ends June 30, 2011. The due date for the annual return is November 15, 2011. If Green were a calendar year entity, the due date for the 2011 annual return would be May 15, 2012. ■

Exempt organizations incurring the UBIT file Form 990–T (Exempt Organization Business Income Tax Return). The return must be filed if the organization has gross income of at least $1,000 from an unrelated trade or business.

EXAMPLE 32

During the year, the First Church of Kentwood receives parishioner contributions of $450,000. Of this amount, $125,000 is designated for the church building fund. None of its receipts constitute unrelated business income. First Church is not required to file an annual return (Form 990) because churches are exempt from doing so. In addition, it is not required to file Form 990–T.

Colonial, Inc., is a private foundation. Gross receipts for the year total $800,000, of which 40% is from admission fees paid by members of the general public who visit Colonial's museum of eighteenth-century life. The balance is endowment income and contributions from the founding donor. Because Colonial is a private foundation, it must file Form 990–PF.

Orange, Inc., is an exempt organization and is not a private foundation. Gross receipts for the year are $20,000. None of this amount is unrelated business income. Orange is not required to file Form 990 because its annual gross receipts do not exceed $50,000. However, it must file an e-Postcard (i.e., Form 990–N).

Restoration, Inc., is an exempt organization. Gross receipts for the year are $100,000. None of this amount is unrelated business income. Restoration files Form 990–EZ because of its level of gross receipts.

During the year, the Second Church of Port Allen receives parishioner contributions of $300,000. In addition, the church has unrelated business income of $5,000. Second

TAX *in* the *NEWS*

Specific Identity of a Donor

The College of William and Mary, a public university, received generous donations from two of its alumni that are enabling it to build with private funds a world-class building (Miller Hall) for its Mason School of Business. Both of the donors, Raymond A. "Chip" Mason and Alan B. Miller, have long supported the college with their talents and financial resources.

Legendary investor Warren Buffett has begun the process of giving away much of his fortune in stock, valued at over $40 billion at the time of the announcement. Principal charitable recipients are the Bill and Melinda Gates Foundation, Susan A. Buffett Foundation, Howard G. Buffett Thomson Foundation, Susan Thomson Buffett Foundation, and NOVO Foundation.

Chip Mason, Alan Miller, and Warren Buffett all have permitted their names to be associated with their charitable gifts. Such identified donors likely have encouraged others to increase their giving.

An increasing number of donors, however, prefer not to have their identity made public when they make substantial gifts to charity. In 2007, for example, philanthropists made 37 gifts of $5 million or more without publicly revealing their names. Some donors make anonymous gifts because their religion regards such gifts as more sincere. Others want to avoid being deluged with fund-raising pitches or fear that their own personal safety or that of family members may be threatened if their wealth becomes public knowledge.

As calls for greater transparency increase throughout society, it is becoming more difficult for major donors to remain anonymous. Opponents of anonymity, who include both consumer groups and lawmakers, argue that secret gifts can be used to exert undue influence over the charity. On the other side, some state lawmakers are pushing to protect donor privacy. They feel that too much disclosure could dampen charitable giving.

Source: Adapted from Sally Beatty, "Why Donating Millions Is Hard to Keep Secret," *Wall Street Journal*, January 9, 2008, p. D1.

Church is not required to file Form 990 because churches are exempt from doing so. Form 990–T must be filed, however, because churches are not exempt from the UBIT and Second Church has exceeded the $1,000 floor. ■

DISCLOSURE REQUIREMENTS

As a result of consumer-friendly rules, exempt entities must make more information readily available to the general public.[59] Prior to the issuance of these rules, the disclosure requirements could be satisfied by making the information available for public inspection during regular business hours at the principal office of the exempt entity.

Copies of the following now must be made available to the general public.[60]

- Form 990.
- Form 1023 (or Form 1024).

Copies of the three most recent returns of the Form 990 must be made available. Private foundations must make Form 990–PF available for public inspection.

If an individual requests the entity's tax form in person, the exempt entity must provide a copy immediately. If the request is received in writing or by e-mail or fax, the copy must be provided within 30 days. The copy must be provided without charge, except for a reasonable fee for reproduction and mailing costs.

If the exempt entity has made the forms widely available to the general public, it is not required to fill individual requests. One technique for making the forms widely available is to put them on the Internet. Individual requests can also be disregarded if the exempt entity can show the request is part of a harassment campaign.

[59] § 6104(d), Reg. § 301.6104(d), and T.D. 8818 (April 1999).

[60] An Internet source of Forms 990 and 990–PF and other relevant materials on exempt entities is **www2.guidestar.org**.

TAX *in the NEWS*

Revised Form 990 to Provide Better Disclosure

Form 990 has undergone a comprehensive revision. The form had not been substantially revised since 1979 and had failed to keep pace with changes in the tax law and with the increasing size, diversity, and complexity of the exempt sector. In redesigning Form 990, the guiding principles were to enhance transparency, promote tax compliance, and minimize the burden for the filing organization. Aiding in the redesign were nearly 700 public comment letters and advice provided by nonprofit experts, nonprofit sector leaders, and state regulators.

Among the many improvements in the revised Form 990 and the related instructions are the following.

- Now the exempt organization can "tell its story" before reporting other information in terms of location on the form.
- There is more space for comments by the entity, so narrative information can be provided in close proximity to the related question.
- Measures of percentages and ratios from the summary page have been eliminated.
- Reporting by expense type replaces reporting by functional classifications.
- The governance section has been divided into three parts: governing body, policies, and disclosures.
- Exempt organizations are allowed to report financial information on a GAAP basis, but are not required to do so.
- Various schedules and thresholds have been revised to reduce the reporting burden of the exempt organization.

TAX PLANNING:

23.8 General Considerations

LO.8

Identify tax planning opportunities for exempt organizations.

Exempt organization status provides at least two potential tax benefits. First, the entity may be exempt from Federal income tax. Second, contributions to the entity may be deductible by the donor.

An organization that qualifies as an exempt organization may still be subject to certain types of Federal income tax, including the following.

- Tax on prohibited transactions.
- Tax on feeder organizations.
- Tax on private foundations.
- Tax on unrelated business income.

Therefore, classification as an exempt organization should not be interpreted to mean that the organization need not be concerned with any Federal income tax. Such a belief can result in the organization engaging in transactions that produce a substantial tax liability.

An organization is exempt from taxation only if it fits into one of the categories enumerated in the Code. Thus, particular attention must be given to the qualification requirements. These requirements must continue to be satisfied to avoid termination of exempt status (in effect, they are now maintenance requirements).

23.9 Maintaining Exempt Status

To maintain exempt status, the organization must satisfy both an organizational test and an operational test. The organizational test requires that the entity satisfy the statutory requirements for exempt status on paper. The operational test ensures that the entity does, in fact, satisfy the statutory requirements for exempt status.

King Shipping Consum., Inc. (Zion Coptic Church, Inc.) illustrates that it is usually much easier to satisfy the organizational test than the operational test.[61] Zion's stated purpose was to engage in activities usually and normally associated with churches. Based on this, the IRS approved Zion's exempt status as a § 501(c)(3) organization.

[61] 58 TCM 574, T.C.Memo. 1989–593.

Zion's real intent, however, was to smuggle illegal drugs into the country and to distribute them for profit. The church's justification for the drugs was that it used marijuana in its sacrament. During a four-month period, however, the police confiscated 33 tons of marijuana from church members. The IRS calculated that, even assuming the maximum alleged church membership of several thousand, each member would have had to smoke over 33 pounds of marijuana during the four-month confiscation period.

The court concluded that Zion's real purpose was to cloak a large commercial drug smuggling operation. Since this activity was inconsistent with the religious purpose for exempt status, the court upheld the IRS's revocation of Zion's exempt status and the deficiency assessment of approximately $1.6 million.

23.10 Private Foundation Status

Exempt organizations that can qualify as public charities receive more beneficial tax treatment than those that qualify as private foundations. Thus, if possible, the organization should be structured to qualify as a public charity. The following can result when an exempt organization is classified as a private foundation.

- Taxes may be imposed on the private foundation.
  - *Tax based on investment income.*
  - *Tax on self-dealing.*
  - *Tax on failure to distribute income.*
  - *Tax on excess business holdings.*
  - *Tax on investments that jeopardize charitable purposes.*
  - *Tax on taxable expenditures.*
- Donors may receive less favorable tax deduction treatment under § 170 than they would if the exempt organization were not a private foundation.

EXAMPLE 33

David has undeveloped land ($25,000 adjusted basis, $100,000 fair market value) that he is going to contribute to one of the following exempt organizations: Blue, Inc., a public charity, or Teal, Inc., a private nonoperating foundation. David has owned the land for five years.

David asks the manager of each organization to describe the tax benefits of contributing to that organization. He tells them he is in the 35% tax bracket and his AGI exceeds $350,000.

Based on the data provided by the managers, David decides to contribute the land to Blue, Inc. He calculates the amount of the charitable contribution under each option as follows.[62]

Donee	Contribution Deduction	Tax Rate	Contribution Borne by U.S. Government
Blue	$100,000	35%	$35,000
Teal	25,000 ($100,000 – $75,000)	35%	8,750

■

One method of avoiding private foundation status is to have a tax-exempt purpose that results in the organization not being classified as a private foundation (the *organizational* approach). If this is not feasible, it may be possible to operate the organization so that it receives broad public support and thereby avoids private foundation status (the *operational* approach).

If the organization is a private foundation, care must be exercised to avoid the assessment of a tax liability on prohibited transactions. This objective can best be achieved by establishing controls that prevent the private foundation from engaging in transactions that trigger the imposition of the taxes. If an initial tax is assessed, corrective actions should be implemented to avoid the assessment of an additional tax. See Concept Summary 23.5.

[62]See Chapter 10.

CONCEPT SUMMARY 23.5

Private Foundation Status

	Exempt Organization Is	
	A Private Foundation	**Not a Private Foundation**
Reason for classification	Does not serve the common good because it lacks an approved exempt purpose or does not receive broad public financial support.	Serves the common good.
Eligible for exempt status?	Yes	Yes
Most beneficial charitable contribution deduction treatment available to donors?	Depends. No, if the private foundation is classified as a private *nonoperating* foundation.	Yes
Subject to excise taxes levied on prohibited transactions?	Yes	No
Subject to tax on unrelated business income?	Yes	Yes

23.11 Unrelated Business Income Tax

If the exempt organization conducts an unrelated trade or business, it may be subject to tax on the unrelated business income. Worse yet, the unrelated trade or business could result in the loss of exempt status if the IRS determines that the activity is the primary purpose of the organization. Thus, caution and planning should be used to eliminate the latter possibility and to minimize the former.

REFOCUS ON THE BIG PICTURE

EFFECT OF A FOR-PROFIT BUSINESS ON A TAX-EXEMPT ENTITY

A § 501(c)(3) entity is exempt from Federal income tax only on the conduct of its charitable activities. However, if an exempt entity generates income from the conduct of a trade or business that is not related to the organization's exempt purpose, this income generally is subject to Federal income tax. These principles can be used in analyzing Hopeful's options for the ice cream business it has inherited.

- *Sale of the stock of Taste Good Ice Cream.* A sale of the Taste Good Ice Cream stock is unlikely to result in much realized gain because the fair market value probably has not changed very much in the limited time between the date of Betty's death and the present. In any case, this amount is not relevant because any realized gain on the sale of the stock is tax-exempt under § 501(c)(3).
- *Conduct the ice cream business as a division of Hopeful.* Under this option, the taxable income of the ice cream chain is classified as unrelated business income. Since the ice cream division is competing with for-profit entities, it is subject to the Federal income tax that applies to corporate entities. In essence, the tax is levied because the exempt organization is engaging in substantial commercial activities.
- *Conduct the ice cream business as a wholly owned subsidiary of Hopeful.* Under this option, the ice cream chain subsidiary is classified as a feeder organization (i.e., carries on a trade or business for the benefit of an exempt organization and remits its profits to that entity). The Federal income tax consequences are the same as those under the prior option.

So, Hopeful's board of directors must decide whether they want Hopeful to be involved in the pursuit of a for-profit business and whether selling or operating the business can provide a greater economic benefit for Hopeful.

KEY TERMS

Debt-financed income, 23–25
Excess lobbying expenditures, 23–10
Exempt organizations, 23–2
Feeder organization, 23–11
Grass roots expenditures, 23–9
Intermediate sanctions, 23–11
Lobbying expenditures, 23–9
Private foundations, 23–12
Unrelated business income (UBI), 23–17
Unrelated business income tax (UBIT), 23–17

DISCUSSION QUESTIONS

1. **LO.1, 6** Eggshell, Inc., a C corporation, operates a rental clothing store, and its profits are subject to double taxation. First Church of the States operates a retail gift and book shop and is not subject to taxation. What is the explanation for this difference in Federal income tax treatment?

2. **LO.1** Why are certain organizations either partially or completely exempt from Federal income tax?

3. **LO.1** Which of the following organizations qualify for exempt status?
   a. Tulane University (a private university).
   b. Virginia Qualified Tuition Program.
   c. Red Cross.
   d. Disneyland.
   e. Ford Foundation.
   f. Jacksonville Chamber of Commerce.
   g. Colonial Williamsburg Foundation.
   h. Professional Golfers Association (PGA) Tour.
   i. Green Bay Packers.
   j. Cleveland Indians.
   k. Louisiana State University (a public university).

4. **LO.1** Identify the statutory authority under which each of the following is exempt from Federal income tax.
   a. Kingsmill Country Club.
   b. Shady Lawn Cemetery.
   c. Amber Credit Union.
   d. Veterans of Foreign Wars.
   e. Boy Scouts of America.
   f. United Fund.
   g. Federal Deposit Insurance Corporation.
   h. Bruton Parish Episcopal Church.
   i. PTA.
   j. National Press Club.
   k. Brown University (a private university).

5. **LO.2** What are the common characteristics shared by many exempt organizations?

6. **LO.3** Robert contributes $5,000 to an exempt organization. Addie contributes $5,000 to a different exempt organization. Why might Addie be permitted a $5,000 charitable contribution deduction in calculating her itemized deductions when Robert is not?

7. **LO.3** What negative tax consequences may be associated with an exempt organization engaging in § 503 prohibited transactions?

ISSUE ID

8. **LO.3** Rex is the chief executive officer of Helping People, Inc., a § 501(c)(3) exempt organization located in Mobile, Alabama. He and the organization's board of directors are concerned about the effect that proposed legislation would have on the organization's budget and its ability to carry out its mission. They are discussing a proposal to have a law firm in Washington, D.C., aid in opposing the legislation.
   a. What tax issues are relevant to Helping People, Inc., as it makes this decision?
   b. Would your answer in (a) change if Helping People, Inc., planned to hire the law firm to lobby for the passage of the proposed legislation?

9. **LO.3** Under what circumstances can an exempt organization engage in lobbying activities? What types of exempt organizations are eligible for this treatment?

10. **LO.3** The IRS can impose *intermediate sanctions* on a public charity if its gross unrelated business income exceeds 50% of its gross income, or if less than two-thirds of its net unrelated business income is used in carrying out its tax-exempt mission. Evaluate this statement.

11. **LO.3** Service, Inc., an exempt organization, owns all of the stock of Blue, Inc., a retailer of boating supplies. Blue remits all of its profits to Service. According to a policy adopted by Service's board, 60% of the amount received from Blue is to be spent annually in carrying out Service's tax-exempt mission, and 40% is to be invested in Service's endowment fund.
    a. What are the tax consequences to Service and to Blue?
    b. Would your answer in (a) change if 100% of the amount received from Blue was spent annually in carrying out Service's tax-exempt mission?

12. **LO.3** Which of the following activities are *not* subject to the tax imposed on feeder organizations?
    a. Substantially all of the work is performed by volunteers.
    b. Substantially all of the services are performed by paid employees of the exempt organization.
    c. Substantially all of the merchandise being sold is used property.
    d. Substantially all of the merchandise being sold was received as contributions or gifts.
    e. A building is rented to a tenant who uses the building as a warehouse for her business.
    f. All of the earnings of a for-profit corporate entity are distributed annually to its tax-exempt parent.

13. **LO.4, 5** What is a private foundation, and what are the disadvantages of an exempt organization being classified as a private foundation?

14. **LO.4** Which of the following exempt organizations could be private foundations?
    a. Bruton Parish Episcopal Church.
    b. Our Lady Catholic Church.
    c. Kentwood Community Hospital.
    d. National Football League (NFL).
    e. Southeastern Louisiana University Alumni Association.
    f. United Fund.
    g. Burr's Foundation.
    h. Rice University (a private university).

15. **LO.4** Describe the external support test and the internal support test for a private foundation.

16. **LO.5** What types of taxes may be levied on a private foundation? Why are the taxes levied?

17. **LO.5** Sunset, Inc., a § 501(c)(3) exempt organization that is classified as a private foundation, generates investment income of $485,000 for the current tax year. This amount represents 18% of Sunset's total income.
    a. What type of tax is imposed on Sunset associated with its investment income?
    b. Is the receipt of this investment income likely to result in Sunset losing its exempt status?

18. **LO.4, 5** Really Welcome, Inc., a tax-exempt organization, receives 30% of its support from disqualified persons. Another disqualified person has agreed to match this support if Really Welcome will appoint him to the organization's board of directors. What tax issues are relevant to Really Welcome as it makes this decision?

ISSUE ID

19. **LO.6** Bob recently became the treasurer of Kind, Inc., a § 501(c)(3) organization that feeds the homeless. One of the entity's directors has proposed that Kind purchase and operate a fast-food franchise as part of Kind, Inc., to raise additional revenue (an increase of 35%) to carry out its tax-exempt mission. Since the earnings generated by the fast-food franchise would be tax-exempt, substantial additional revenue would be provided. How should Bob respond?

20. **LO.6** Less, Inc., a § 501(c)(3) organization, has unrelated business taxable income of $600,000 and total earnings of $1 million. Why is only the $600,000 subject to Federal income tax? What is the Federal income tax liability?

21. **LO.6** What type of activity by a church is likely to be subject to the unrelated business income tax? What factors must be present for this activity to be classified as an unrelated trade or business?

22. **LO.6** An exempt municipal hospital operates a pharmacy that is staffed by a pharmacist 24 hours per day. The pharmacy serves only hospital patients. Is the pharmacy an unrelated trade or business?

DECISION MAKING

23. **LO.6, 8** Second Church is going to operate a gift and book shop that will include only religious articles in its inventory. The shop will be staffed by employees who are not church members. Under consideration are two options: (1) organizing the shop as a wholly owned corporate subsidiary and (2) including it within the organizational structure of Second Church. The projected annual profits of $100,000 are to be used in the church's outreach mission. What are the tax consequences of each option? Which should Second Church select?

24. **LO.1, 6** To which of the following tax-exempt organizations may the UBIT apply?
    a. Red Cross.
    b. Salvation Army.
    c. United Fund.
    d. College of William and Mary.
    e. Rainbow, Inc., a private foundation.
    f. Louisiana State University.
    g. Colonial Williamsburg Foundation.
    h. Federal Land Bank.
    i. University of Virginia Hospital.

25. **LO.6** Sight, Inc., a tax-exempt organization that trains the visually impaired to restore and tune pianos, receives pianos as contributions. When the number of pianos on hand exceeds 15, Sight sells the excess; the pianos used in the training program the longest are sold first. Is the revenue from the sale of the excess pianos subject to the UBIT?

ISSUE ID

26. **LO.6** An exempt organization is considering conducting bingo games on Thursday nights as a way of generating additional revenue to support its exempt purpose. Before doing so, however, the president of the organization has come to you for advice regarding the effect on the organization's exempt status and whether the net income from the bingo games will be taxable. Identify the relevant tax issues.

27. **LO.6** When an exempt organization acquires land for later exempt use and there is acquisition indebtedness on the land, what requirements must be satisfied for the land to be excluded from classification as debt-financed property?

28. **LO.1, 7** Tom is the treasurer of the City Garden Club, a new garden club. A friend, who is the treasurer of the garden club in a neighboring community, tells Tom that it is not necessary for the garden club to file a request for exempt status with the IRS. Has Tom received correct advice?

ISSUE ID

29. **LO.1, 7** Abby Sue recently became the treasurer of First Point Church. The church has been in existence for three years and has never filed anything with the IRS.
    a. Identify any reporting responsibilities Abby Sue might have as church treasurer.
    b. Would your answer in (a) change if First Point Church has been in existence for more than 10 years?

30. **LO.7** Shane and Brittany are treasurers for § 501(c)(3) exempt organizations. Neither exempt organization is a church. Each year Shane's exempt organization files a Form 990 while Brittany's exempt organization files a Form 990–PF. Discuss the public disclosure requirements for each exempt organization.

PROBLEMS

31. **LO.2, 3** Innovation, Inc., a § 501(c)(3) medical research organization, makes lobbying expenditures of $1.1 million. Innovation incurs exempt purpose expenditures of $15 million in carrying out its medical research mission. **DECISION MAKING**
   a. Determine the tax consequences for Innovation if it does not elect to be eligible to participate in lobbying activities on a limited basis.
   b. Determine the tax consequences for Innovation if it does elect to be eligible to participate in lobbying activities on a limited basis.
   c. In light of pending health care legislation, Innovation is considering increasing its lobbying expenditures by 50% annually. Advise Innovation whether this is a wise thing to do from an after-tax perspective.

32. **LO.3, 6, 8** Roadrunner, Inc., is an exempt medical organization. Quail, Inc., a sporting goods retailer, is a wholly owned subsidiary of Roadrunner. Roadrunner inherited the Quail stock last year from a major benefactor of the medical organization. Quail's taxable income is $550,000. Quail will remit all of its earnings, net of any taxes, to Roadrunner to support the exempt purpose of the parent. **DECISION MAKING** **COMMUNICATIONS**
   a. Is Quail subject to Federal income tax? If so, calculate the liability.
   b. Arthur Morgan, the treasurer of Roadrunner, has contacted you regarding minimizing or eliminating Quail's tax liability. He would like to know if the tax consequences would be better if Quail were liquidated into Roadrunner. Write a letter to Morgan that contains your advice. Roadrunner's address is 500 Rouse Tower, Rochester, NY 14627.
   c. Would your answer in (a) change if Roadrunner had acquired the Quail stock by purchase or gift rather than by inheritance? Discuss.
   d. How would the tax consequences change if Quail's taxable income was only $100,000 and it remitted only 75% of its earnings, net of taxes, to Roadrunner?

33. **LO.3** Respond, Inc., a § 501(c)(3) organization, receives the following revenues and incurs the following expenses.

Grant from Gates Foundation	$ 50,000
Charitable contributions received	625,000
Expenses in carrying out its exempt mission	725,000
Net income before taxes of Landscaping, Inc., a wholly owned for-profit subsidiary	350,000

Landscaping, Inc., remits all of its after-tax profits each year to Respond. Calculate the amount of the Federal income tax, if any, for Respond and for Landscaping.

34. **LO.4** Pigeon, Inc., a § 501(c)(3) organization, received support from the following sources. **COMMUNICATIONS**

Governmental unit A for services rendered	$ 6,300
Governmental unit B for services rendered	4,500
Fees from the general public for services rendered (each payment was $100)	75,000
Gross investment income	39,000
Contributions from disqualified persons	26,000
Contributions from other than disqualified persons (each gift was $50)	160,000
Total support	$310,800

   a. Does Pigeon satisfy the test for receiving broad public support?
   b. Is Pigeon a private foundation?
   c. Arnold Horn, Pigeon's treasurer, has asked you to advise him on whether Pigeon is a private foundation. Write a letter to him in which you address the issue. His address is 250 Bristol Road, Charlottesville, VA 22903.

ft.

35. **LO.5** Gray, Inc., a private foundation, has the following items of income and deductions.

Interest income	$ 29,000
Rent income	61,000
Dividend income	15,000
Royalty income	22,000
Unrelated business income	80,000
Rent expenses	(26,000)
Unrelated business expenses	(12,000)

Gray is not an exempt operating foundation and is not eligible for the 1% tax rate.

a. Calculate the net investment income.
b. Calculate the tax on net investment income.
c. What is the purpose of the tax on net investment income?

36. **LO.5** Egret, Inc., a private foundation, has been in existence for 10 years. During this period, Egret has been unable to satisfy the requirements for classification as a private operating foundation. At the end of 2010, it had undistributed income of $320,000. Of this amount, $170,000 was distributed in 2011, and $150,000 was distributed during the first quarter of 2012. The IRS deficiency notice was mailed on August 1, 2013.

a. Calculate the initial tax for 2010, 2011, and 2012.
b. Calculate the additional tax for 2013.

DECISION MAKING

37. **LO.5, 8** Otis is the CEO of Rectify, Inc., a private foundation. Otis invests $500,000 (80%) of the foundation's investment portfolio in derivatives. Previously, the $500,000 had been invested in corporate bonds with an AA rating that earned 7% per annum. If the derivatives investment works as Otis's investment adviser claims, the annual earnings could be as high as 20%.

a. Determine if Rectify is subject to any of the taxes imposed on private foundations.
b. If so, calculate the amount of the initial tax.
c. If so, calculate the amount of the additional tax if the act causing the imposition of the tax is not addressed within the correction period.
d. Are Otis and the foundation better off financially if the prohibited transaction, if any, is addressed within the correction period?

38. **LO.5** The board of directors of Black Pearl, Inc., a private foundation, consists of Alice, Beth, and Carlos. They vote unanimously to provide a $250,000 grant to Mark, their business associate. The grant is to be used for travel and education and does not qualify as a permitted grant to individuals (i.e., it is a taxable expenditure under § 4945). Each director knows that Mark was selected for the grant because he is a friend of the organization and that the grant is a taxable expenditure.

a. Calculate the initial tax imposed on Black Pearl.
b. Calculate the initial tax imposed on the foundation manager (i.e., board of directors).

COMMUNICATIONS

39. **LO.6** The Open Museum is an exempt organization that operates a gift shop. The museum's annual operations budget is $3.2 million. Gift shop sales generate a profit of $900,000. Another $600,000 of endowment income is generated. Both the income from the gift shop and the endowment income are used to support the exempt purpose of the museum. The balance of $1.7 million required for annual operations is provided through admission fees.

Wayne Davis, a new board member, does not understand why the museum is subject to tax at all, particularly since the profits are used in carrying out the mission of the museum. The museum's address is 250 Oak Avenue, Peoria, IL 61625.

a. Calculate the amount of unrelated business income.
b. Assume that the endowment income is reinvested in the endowment fund, rather than being used to support annual operations. Calculate the amount of unrelated business income.
c. As the museum treasurer, write a letter to Wayne explaining the reason for the tax consequences. Mr. Davis's address is 45 Pine Avenue, Peoria, IL 61625.

40. **LO.6** Upward, Inc., a § 501(c)(3) organization that provides training programs for welfare recipients, reports the following income and expenses from the sale of products associated with the training program.

Gross income from sales	$800,000
Cost of goods sold	190,000
Advertising and selling expenses	50,000
Administrative expenses	200,000

Calculate Upward's UBIT:

a. If the sale of the training program products is substantially related to Upward's exempt purpose.

b. If the sale of the training program products is not substantially related to Upward's exempt purpose.

41. **LO.6** Perch, Inc., an exempt organization, has unrelated business taxable income of $4 million.

COMMUNICATIONS

a. Calculate Perch's UBIT.

b. Prepare an outline of a presentation you are going to give to the new members of Perch's board on why Perch is subject to the UBIT even though it is an exempt organization.

42. **LO.6** For each of the following organizations, determine its UBTI and any related UBIT.

a. AIDS, Inc., an exempt charitable organization that provides support for individuals with AIDS, operates a retail medical supply store open to the general public. The net income of the store, before any Federal income taxes, is $305,000.

b. The local Episcopal Church operates a retail gift shop. The inventory consists of the typical items sold by commercial gift shops in the city. The director of the gift shop estimates that 80% of the gift shop sales are to tourists and 20% are to church members. The net income of the gift shop, before the salaries of the three gift shop employees and any Federal income taxes, is $300,000. The salaries of the employees total $80,000.

c. Education, Inc., a private university, has vending machines in the student dormitories and academic buildings on campus. In recognition of recent tuition increases, the university has adopted a policy of merely trying to recover its costs associated with the vending machine activity. For the current year, however, the net income of the activity, before any Federal income taxes, is $75,000.

d. Worn, Inc., an exempt organization, provides food for the homeless. It operates a thrift store that sells used clothing to the general public. The thrift shop is staffed by four salaried employees. All of the clothes it sells are received as contributions. The $100,000 profit generated for the year by the thrift shop is used in Worn's mission of providing food to the homeless.

e. Small, Inc., an exempt organization, has gross unrelated business income of $900 and unrelated business expenses of $400.

f. In Care, Inc., is a § 501(c)(3) exempt organization. It owns a convenience store and gas pumps, which it received as a bequest from a patron. The store/gas pumps entity is organized as StopBy, a C corporation. Because StopBy is profitable, In Care hires a manager and several employees to run the entity. For the current year, StopBy's profit is $640,000. All of this amount is distributed by StopBy to In Care, to use in carrying out its exempt mission.

43. **LO.6** Save the Squirrels, Inc., a § 501(c)(3) organization that feeds the squirrels in municipal parks, receives a $250,000 contribution from Animal Feed, Inc., a corporation that sells animal feed. In exchange for the contribution, Save the Squirrels will identify Animal Feed as a major supporter in its monthly newsletter. Determine Save the Squirrels's UBTI and any related UBIT, under the following independent assumptions.

a. Save the Squirrels receives no other similar payments.

b. Save the Squirrels agrees to identify Animal Feed as a major supporter and to include a half-page advertisement for Animal Feed products in its monthly newsletter as a result of the contribution.

44. **LO.6** Fish, Inc., an exempt organization, reports unrelated business taxable income of $400,000 (excluding the deduction for charitable contributions). During the year, Fish makes charitable contributions of $45,000, of which $38,000 are associated with the unrelated trade or business.

a. Calculate Fish's unrelated business taxable income (UBTI).
b. Assume that the charitable contributions are $39,000, of which $38,000 are associated with the unrelated trade or business. Calculate the UBTI.

45. **LO.6** Tranquility, Inc., an exempt organization, leases factory equipment to Blouses, Inc. Blouses is a taxable entity that manufactures women's clothing for distribution through upscale department stores. Blouses owns the land and building where it conducts its manufacturing operations. The original cost of the building to Blouses was $800,000, and the cost recovery deduction for the current year is $20,512. Rent income to Tranquility for the factory's equipment is $300,000, and the related expenses are $170,000. Calculate the effect of the equipment lease on Tranquility's unrelated business taxable income.

46. **LO.6** Education, Inc., an exempt organization that provides educational services, reports the following gains and losses from property transactions.

- $42,000 loss on the sale of land and a building. The building had been used in carrying out Education's exempt purpose, but the building no longer was needed due to a decline in the population in the geographic area that Education serves.
- $185,000 gain on the sale of land and a building. The building initially had been acquired to lease to a national retailer. Due to a reduction in the number of its stores, the national retailer canceled the lease at the end of last year.
- $45,000 loss on the sale of investment land.
- $20,000 loss on the sale of computers. The computers had been leased to Teachers, Inc., an unrelated exempt organization. Prior to leasing the computers, Education had used them in carrying out its own exempt purpose.

Determine the effect of these transactions on Education's unrelated business taxable income.

47. **LO.6** Crow, Inc., an exempt organization, owns a building that cost $800,000. Depreciation of $300,000 has been deducted. The building is mortgaged for $600,000. The mortgage was incurred at the acquisition date. The building contains 10,000 square feet of floor space. Crow uses 8,000 square feet of the building in carrying on its exempt purpose and leases the remaining 2,000 square feet to Uranium Corporation. Is the building debt-financed property?

48. **LO.7** Rodeo, Inc., is a social club that is exempt under § 501(c)(7). Its annual gross receipts are $321,000. Of this amount, $23,000 is from an unrelated trade or business. Rodeo's fiscal year ends on May 31.
a. Is Rodeo required to file an annual information return? If so, what form should be used?
b. Is Rodeo subject to the UBIT? If so, what form should be used?
c. If tax returns must be filed, what is the due date?

49. **LO.8** Historic Burg is an exempt organization that operates a museum depicting eighteenth-century life. Sally gives the museum an eighteenth-century chest that she has owned for 10 years. Her adjusted basis is $55,000, and the chest's appraised value is $100,000. Sally's adjusted gross income is $300,000. Calculate Sally's charitable contribution deduction if Historic Burg is:
a. A private operating foundation (deduct FMV, 30% AGI limit).
b. A private nonoperating foundation (deduct basis, 50% AGI limit).

RESEARCH PROBLEMS

THOMSON REUTERS
Checkpoint® Student Edition

Note: Solutions to Research Problems can be prepared by using the **Checkpoint® Student Edition** online research product, which is available to accompany this text. It is also possible to prepare solutions to the Research Problems by using tax research materials found in a standard tax library.

Research Problem 1. Allied Fund, a charitable organization exempt under § 501(c)(3), has branches located in each of the 50 states. Allied is not a private foundation. Rather than having each of the state units file an annual return with the IRS, Allied would like to file a single return that reports the activities of all of its branches. Is this permissible? What is the due date of the return?

Partial list of research aids:
§ 6033.
§ 6072.
Reg. § 1.6033–2(d).

COMMUNICATIONS

Research Problem 2. Heal, Inc., a tax-exempt hospital, was sold to its shareholders for $6.6 million. The IRS determined that the fair market value of the hospital was $7.8 million. An IRS agent is proposing that the tax-exempt status of the hospital be revoked because the sale of the hospital to the shareholders for less than the fair market value resulted in "private inurement" to them. Evaluate the IRS's proposal in a memo to the research file.

INTERNET *activity*

Use the tax resources of the Internet to address the following question. Do not restrict your search to the Web, but include a review of newsgroups and general reference materials, practitioner sites and resources, primary sources of the tax law, chat rooms and discussion groups, and other opportunities.

Research Problem 3. Determine if the Kellogg Foundation is a private foundation. Print a copy of its Form 990 or Form 990–PF.

CHAPTER 24

Multistate Corporate Taxation

LEARNING OBJECTIVES

After completing Chapter 24, you should be able to:

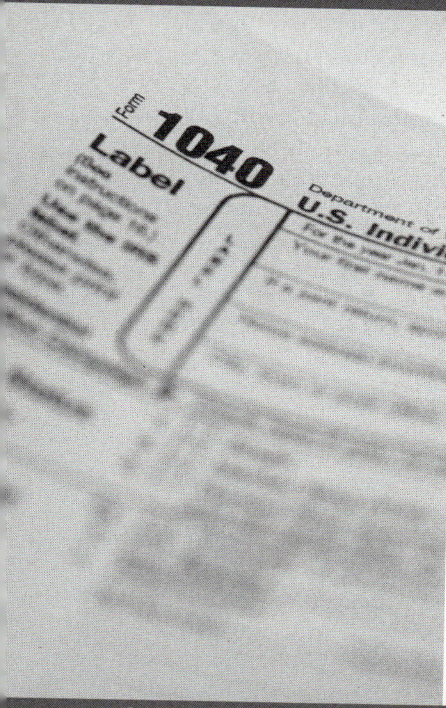

LO.1 Illustrate the computation of a multistate corporation's state tax liability.

LO.2 Define nexus and explain its role in state income taxation.

LO.3 Distinguish between allocation and apportionment of a multistate corporation's taxable income.

LO.4 Describe the nature and treatment of business and nonbusiness income.

LO.5 Discuss the sales, payroll, and property apportionment factors.

LO.6 Apply the unitary method of state income taxation.

LO.7 Discuss the states' income tax treatment of S corporations, partnerships, and LLCs.

LO.8 Describe other commonly encountered state and local taxes on businesses.

LO.9 Recognize tax planning opportunities available to minimize a corporation's state and local tax liability.

OUTLINE

For the latest in changes to tax legislation, visit **www.cengage.com/taxation/swft.**

THE BIG PICTURE **Tax Solutions for the Real World**

MAKING A LOCATION DECISION IN A MULTISTATE TAX ENVIRONMENT

LocalCo has customers in most U.S. states. It does not employ a traditional sales force. Instead, it sells its products exclusively through Internet solicitations and its elaborate website.

LocalCo has two product lines: cell phone accessories, which it manufactures in Alabama, and various sports-themed apparel items, all of which are produced in California. LocalCo has been quite profitable in the past, and it holds a sizable investment portfolio, made up chiefly of U.S. Treasury securities. Banking, payroll, and other administrative operations are located in rural New York State, where the entity is incorporated. LocalCo's rank and file employees receive compensation packages that are below the national median, but its top 10 executives are very highly paid.

In an effort to "go green," LocalCo wants to hold down its costs for shipping raw materials to its manufacturing facilities and for sending its sold goods to customers. Thus, it is considering the construction of a sizable new multifunction building. Ideally, the new facility would have access to both interstate highways and a reliable airport with excess capacity for freight operations.

How will LocalCo's expansion decision be affected by state and local tax considerations? **Read the chapter and formulate your response.**

Although most of this text concentrates on the effects of the Federal income tax law upon the computation of a taxpayer's annual tax liability, a variety of tax bases apply to most business taxpayers. For example, a multinational corporation may be subject to tax in a number of different countries (see Chapter 25). Similarly, the taxpayer may be subject to a county-level wheel tax on its business vehicles, a state sales or use tax on many of its asset purchases, and state and local income or franchise taxes on its net income or on the privilege of doing business in the taxing jurisdiction. Indeed, estimates are that about 40 percent of the tax dollars paid by business taxpayers go to state and local authorities.

Businesses operate in a multistate environment for a variety of reasons. For the most part, nontax motivations drive such location decisions as where to build new plants or distribution centers or whether to move communications and data processing facilities and corporate headquarters. For example, a business typically wants to be close to its largest markets and to operate in a positive private- and public-sector business climate, where it has access to well-trained and reasonably priced labor, suppliers and support operations, sources of natural resources, communication facilities, and transportation networks.

Many location decisions, though, are motivated by multistate tax considerations.

- The taxpayer's manufacturing, wholesaling, sales, retailing, and credit operations each may be centered in a different state to take advantage of various economic development incentives created by politicians. Several states are making highly visible efforts to attract movie and television projects by granting a refundable credit (often at 25 to 35 percent of in-state expenditures) to film production companies. Such credits are offered by New York and California to retain film production work and by Mississippi and Illinois to attract it.
- In addition to flying over virtually the entire country, the major airlines depart from and land in the majority of the states. Which state's income tax should apply to the ticket income? Should sales or income tax apply to sales of movies or liquor while the plane is airborne?
- Local political concerns lead to a multiplicity of tax rules as politicians attempt to serve their constituents by introducing a variety of special tax incentives. This variety can be confusing, however. Taxpayers may have

TAX *in the NEWS*

Paying the States' Bills

For 2009, the states collected more than $700 billion in taxes (i.e., more than $2,000 per person). The corporate income tax accounts for only a small portion of the states' revenues—6 percent in 2009. This percentage is even less than the contribution of the Federal corporate tax to the U.S. government's revenues. Most of the states' property tax collections (2 percent of the total) are received by counties and smaller taxing jurisdictions.

The States' Tax Revenue Sources, 2009

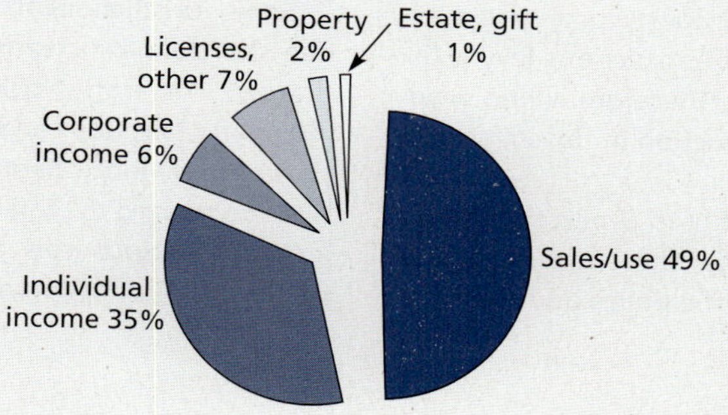

Source: U.S. Census.

difficulty determining whether they qualify for energy or enterprise zone credits, S corporation status, exemptions from sales tax liability or income tax withholding, or gasoline tax relief at the local level.

- Politicians have a strong incentive to impose new tax burdens on visitors and others who have no direct say in their reelection. Thus, it is increasingly common to see tourist and hotel-bed taxes on convention delegates, often approaching a rate of 20 percent; city payroll taxes on commuters; and the use of obscure tax formulas that otherwise discriminate against those with limited contact in the area.
- Each jurisdiction in which the entity is subject to tax represents a geometrical increase in compliance responsibilities. For example, how many tax returns must be filed by a three-shareholder S corporation operating in 15 states?
- Various states and localities have adopted revenue-raising statutes that vary in sophistication and operate on different time schedules. For example, only a few states have adopted an alternative minimum tax, and states that impose the tax have tended to select different bases. In addition, the aggressiveness with which departments of revenue enforce their tax statutes varies greatly from state to state, even in a context of ongoing pressure to enhance revenues. Accordingly, the taxpayer must deal with a patchwork of germane taxing and enforcement provisions in an environment that is often uncertain.

This chapter reviews the basic tax concepts that are predominant among most states that impose a tax based on net income, and it discusses the major areas in which tax planning can reduce a corporation's overall state tax burden.

Most of this chapter is devoted to a discussion of state taxes that are based on income. Each state is free to identify its corporate tax by a different term. Not all of the states that impose a tax on corporate income call the tax an "income tax."

TAX *in the NEWS*

As the Economy Goes, So Go Local Tax Collections

City and county governments depend heavily on sales, property, and payroll taxes as stable and productive sources of revenue. But in a "down" economy, the risk of this taxing strategy becomes clear. One of the effects of an economic downturn, for instance, is a sharp decline in sales/use tax revenues. Other tax collections are affected as well.

The burst of the housing bubble has reduced the value of residences and commercial real estate, in some locales by more than 20 percent. Although property taxes are computed using various formulas, most jurisdictions levy a tax of about 2 percent of current value. Therefore, when property values fall, a proportionate reduction in tax collections occurs.

Several large cities levy taxes of 1 to 3 percent on the wages of those who work in the city. These taxes are justified as a way to recoup the costs of the police and transportation services that commuters enjoy. When unemployment increases and pay raises are few and far between, these payroll tax collections drop significantly.

Economists describe the current situation as a "jobless recovery," meaning that inventory sales and stock prices are showing signs of bouncing back, but few new, high-paying, full-time jobs have yet been created. That is not a good sign for an increase in future payroll tax collections.

Some jurisdictions have tried to make up for their revenue shortfalls by creating new fees, raising the amounts charged for traffic tickets and garbage collection, and increasing tax audits and other enforcement measures.

As the majority of state and local government expenditures go toward the salaries and benefits of their employees, a revenue pinch can create further problems. Expected results are cuts in government services and personnel layoffs.

Rather, some states refer to their tax on corporate income as a franchise tax,[1] a business tax, a license tax, or a business profits tax.

24.1 Overview of Corporate State Income Taxation

Forty-six states and the District of Columbia impose a tax based on a corporation's taxable income. Since each state is free to create its own tax provisions, the tax practitioner could be faced with 47 entirely different sets of state tax provisions.[2] Fortunately, however, to simplify the filing of tax returns and increase compliance with state tax laws, the majority of states "piggyback" onto the Federal income tax base. This means they have adopted *en masse* part or all of the Federal provisions governing the definition of income and the allowance of various exemptions, exclusions, and deductions. None of the states, however, has piggybacked its tax collections with the IRS.

LO.1

Illustrate the computation of a multistate corporation's state tax liability.

COMPUTING STATE INCOME TAX

In more than 40 of the states that impose a corporate income tax, the starting point in computing the tax base is taxable income as reflected on the Federal corporate income tax return (Form 1120). Those states whose computation of state taxable income is not coupled to the Federal tax return have their own state-specific definitions of gross and taxable income. Nonetheless, even these states typically adopt most Federal income and deduction provisions.

Although Federal tax law plays a significant role in the computation of state taxable income, there is a wide disparity in both the methods used to determine a state's taxable income and the tax rates imposed on that income. As only a few states apply more than one or two tax rates to taxable income, there is little progressivity to these tax systems. State tax credits typically are designed to encourage increased hiring and investment in local facilities. Cities and states often use targeted tax credits to

[1] Although a franchise tax in some states is a business privilege tax based on a corporation's capital stock or net worth, several states use that term for the tax that they impose on a corporation's net income.

[2] The District of Columbia operates in much the same manner as a state and imposes a tax based on income. Four states impose no corporate income tax at all: Nevada, South Dakota, Washington, and Wyoming. Corporations, however, are subject to a business and occupation tax in Washington. Several states base the tax on the entity's gross receipts.

ETHICS & Equity

Encouraging Economic Development through Tax Concessions

The tax professional occasionally is in a position to negotiate with a state or city taxing jurisdiction to garner tax relief for a client as an incentive to locate a plant or distribution center in that geographic area. In times when construction budgets are high and interstate competition is fierce, such tax concessions can be significant.

For instance, to encourage a business to build a large distribution center in the area, community leaders might be agreeable to (1) paying for roads, sewer, water, and other improvements through taxpayer bonds; (2) reducing property taxes by 50 percent for the first 10 years of the center's operations; and (3) permanently excluding any distribution-related vehicles and equipment from the personal property tax.

An incentive-granting community provides the concessions even though the influx of new workers will place a great strain on public school facilities and likely necessitate improvements in traffic patterns and other infrastructure. Local residents, even those who obtain jobs at the new facility, and the tax adviser may wonder whether the tax concessions are supportable in light of these changes in the community's quality of life.

Take the position of a large employer that has been located in the area for more than 50 years. By how much should it be willing to absorb the tax increases that result when economic development concessions are used to attract new, perhaps temporary, businesses to the area? Should the employer challenge the constitutionality of the grant of such sizable tax breaks to some, but not all, business taxpayers in the jurisdiction?

Should higher "impact fees" be assessed on new developments? Does your analysis change if the new business competes with the longtime resident for sales? For employees? For political power?

entice businesses to expand within their borders. For example, a state might offer a $10,000 credit for each new job created by the taxpayer or a 15 percent credit for taxpayers who purchase automobiles that were assembled in the state.

The formula used by a multistate corporation to determine its tax liability in a typical state is illustrated in Figure 24.1.

OPERATIONAL IMPLICATIONS

Generally, the accounting period and methods used by a corporation for state tax purposes must be consistent with those used on the Federal return. States often apply different rules, however, in identifying the members of a group filing a consolidated return and the income of each group member that is subject to tax.

As the starting point for computing state taxable income often is directly related to the Federal taxable income amount, most states also piggyback onto the IRS's audit process. Consequently, virtually all of the states that levy an income tax require

FIGURE 24.1 Computing Corporate State Income Tax Liability

	Starting point in computing taxable income*
±	State modification items
	State tax base
±	Total net allocable income/(loss) (*nonbusiness income*)
	Total apportionable income/(loss) (*business income*)
×	State's apportionment percentage
	Income apportioned to the state
±	Income/(loss) allocated to the state
	State taxable income/(loss)
×	State tax rate
	Gross income tax liability for the state
−	State's tax credits
	Net income tax liability for the state

*Most states use either line 28 or line 30 of the Federal corporate income tax return (Form 1120). In other states, the corporation is required to identify and report each element of income and deduction on the state return.

notification of the final settlement of a Federal income tax audit. State authorities then adjust the originally calculated state tax liability appropriately.

STATE MODIFICATIONS

Federal taxable income generally is used as the starting point in computing the state's income tax base, but numerous state adjustments or modifications are often made to Federal taxable income to:

- Reflect differences between state and Federal tax statutes.
- Remove income that a state is constitutionally prohibited from taxing.

The required modifications to Federal taxable income vary significantly among the states. Accordingly, this discussion is limited to the most common additions and subtractions that the states require. Exhibit 24.1 lists the most frequently encountered modifications. In computing the taxable income for a given state, only a selected number of these modifications may be applicable.

EXHIBIT 24.1 **Common State Modifications**

Addition Modifications

* Interest income received on state and municipal obligations and any other interest income that is exempt from Federal income tax. For this purpose, some states exempt interest earned on their own obligations.
* Expenses deducted in computing Federal taxable income that are directly or indirectly related to U.S. obligations.
* Income-based franchise and income taxes imposed by any state and the District of Columbia that were deducted in computing Federal taxable income.
* The amount by which the Federal deductions for depreciation, amortization, or depletion exceed those permitted by the state.
* The amount by which the state gain or loss from the disposal of assets differs from the Federal gain or loss. Due to the difference in permitted depreciation methods and other adjustments, a corporation's assets may have different Federal and state tax adjusted bases. This adjustment is not necessary if the state and Federal depreciation provisions are identical.

Adjustments required as a result of different elections being made for state and Federal purposes. Examples of such elections include the methods under which income from installment sales or long-term contracts is determined.

Federal net operating loss deduction, if the starting point in the computation of taxable income is Federal taxable income after special deductions.

Subtraction Modifications

* Interest on U.S. obligations or obligations of Federal agencies to the extent included in Federal taxable income but exempt from state income taxes under U.S. law.
* Expenses that are directly or indirectly related to the state and municipal interest that is taxable for state purposes.
* Refunds of franchise and income taxes imposed by any state and the District of Columbia, to the extent included in Federal taxable income.
* The amount by which the state deductions for depreciation, amortization, or depletion exceed the deductions permitted for Federal tax purposes.

Adjustments required as a result of different elections being made for state and Federal purposes, as above.

Dividends received from other U.S. corporations, to the extent included in Federal taxable income.

Net operating loss deduction as determined for state tax purposes.

Federal income tax paid.

*Required by most states.

TAX *in* the NEWS

So Where Did You Work Today?

It is the dream of many intellectual-property employees to work at home with the employer's computer and communications equipment. Not only is the dress code based on the worker's comfort, but the employee can avoid the time and cost of commuting. The employer saves by not having to provide office space.

But what are the tax effects when the employee or independent contractor submits work to an employer located in a different state? The general rule has been that state income taxes fall in full in the state where the work is done. Is this still the rule, or must the employee apportion the hours of the day among the various states that receive the work product? If so, on what basis should such apportionment be made? Furthermore, how will the worker avoid potential taxation of the same income by more than one state?

A few states and cities, most notably in New York, are aggressively trying to impose income taxes on the work of telecommuters that enters the state. In these situations, enough nexus purportedly exists to permit the levying of income taxes on telecommuters based in other states. The finding of nexus with New York (both the city and the state) can be an expensive proposition for the worker and employer.

For now, it will be up to the states considering this form of taxation to decide if the additional revenue is worth the risk of angering the desirable high-tech, information workers who play a large role in our economy.

EXAMPLE 1

Blue Corporation is subject to tax only in State A. The starting point in computing State A taxable income is Federal taxable income. Modifications then are made to reflect, among other provisions, the exempt status of interest on State A obligations, all dividends received from other U.S. corporations, and the disallowance of a deduction for state income taxes. Blue generated the following income and deductions this year.

Sales	$1,500,000
Interest on Federal obligations	50,000
Interest on municipal obligations of State B	100,000
Dividends received from 50%-owned U.S. corporations	200,000
Total income	$1,850,000
Expenses related to Federal obligations	$ 1,000
Expenses related to municipal obligations	5,000
State income tax expense	50,000
Depreciation allowed for Federal tax purposes (the deduction allowed for state purposes is $300,000)	400,000
Other allowable deductions	1,000,000
Total deductions	$1,456,000

Blue's taxable income for Federal and state purposes is $139,000 and $295,000, respectively.

Federal Taxable Income	
Sales	$1,500,000
Interest on Federal obligations	50,000
Dividends received from U.S. corporations	200,000
Total income	$1,750,000
Expenses related to Federal obligations	$ 1,000
State income tax expense	50,000
Depreciation	400,000
Other allowable deductions	1,000,000
Total deductions	$1,451,000
Taxable income before special deductions	$ 299,000
Less: Dividends received deduction (80% × $200,000)	(160,000)
Federal taxable income	$ 139,000

FINANCIAL DISCLOSURE *Insights*

State/Local Taxes and the Effective Tax Rate

In applying GAAP principles for a business entity, state and local tax expenses are found in several places in the taxpayer's financial reports. In the tax footnote, the state/local tax costs often are reported in dollar and/or percentage terms, in both current and deferred components. The following are examples of state/local tax expenses that were reported in a recent year.

	Current State/ Local Tax Expenses ($000)	Deferred State/ Local Tax Expenses ($000)
Eli Lilly	$49	($1)
Ryder Systems	6	3
Ford Motor	7	(59)

Corporations also report permanent book/tax differences in determining the effective tax rate for the reporting period. In a recent year, Berkshire Hathaway reported that state/local permanent book/tax differences reduced its effective income tax rate by about 1.5 percentage points. Ford Motor reported a similar rate reduction, but Ryder Systems' effective tax rate increased by about 6 percentage points for the year due to such permanent book/tax differences.

State A Taxable Income	
Federal taxable income	$139,000
Addition Modifications	
Interest on municipal obligations of State B	100,000
State income tax expense	50,000
Excess depreciation deduction allowed for Federal purposes ($400,000 – $300,000)	100,000
Expenses related to Federal obligations	1,000
Subtraction Modifications	
Expenses related to municipal obligations	(5,000)
Dividends received from other U.S. corporations, to extent included in Federal taxable income ($200,000 – $160,000)	(40,000)
Interest on Federal obligations	(50,000)
State A taxable income	$295,000

■

EXAMPLE 2

Continue with the facts of Example 1, except that the $100,000 of municipal bond interest was generated from State A obligations. The computation of Federal taxable income is unaffected by this change. Since State A exempts interest on its own obligations from taxation, Blue's State A taxable income is $200,000.

State A Taxable Income	
Federal taxable income	$139,000
Addition Modifications	
State income tax expense	50,000
Excess depreciation deduction allowed for Federal purposes ($400,000 – $300,000)	100,000
Expenses related to Federal obligations	1,000
Subtraction Modifications	
Dividends received from other U.S. corporations, to extent included in Federal taxable income ($200,000 – $160,000)	(40,000)
Interest on Federal obligations	(50,000)
State A taxable income	$200,000

■

JURISDICTION TO IMPOSE TAX: NEXUS AND PUBLIC LAW 86–272

LO.2

Define nexus and explain its role in state income taxation.

The state in which a business is incorporated has the jurisdiction to tax the corporation, regardless of the volume of its business activity within the state. Whether a state can tax the income of a business that is incorporated in another state usually depends on the relationship between the state and the corporation.

Nexus describes the degree of business activity that must be present before a taxing jurisdiction has the right to impose a tax on an out-of-state entity's income. State law defines the measure of the relationship that is necessary to create nexus. Typically, sufficient nexus is present when a corporation derives income from sources within the state, owns or leases property in the state, employs personnel in the state, or has physical or financial capital there. **Public Law 86–272** limits the states' right to impose an income tax on certain interstate activities.[3] This Federal law prohibits a state from taxing a business whose only connection with the state is to solicit orders for sales of tangible personal property that is sent outside the state for approval or rejection. If approved, the orders must be filled and shipped by the business from a point outside the state.

Only the sales of tangible personal property are immune from taxation under the law, however. Leases, rentals, and other dispositions of tangible personal property are not protected activities. Moreover, dispositions of real property and intangible property, as well as sales of services, are not protected by Public Law 86–272. In this regard, each state constructs its own definition of tangible and intangible property. Thus, since property ownership is not a protected activity, providing company-owned communications, document processing, or computer equipment to an out-of-state salesperson may create nexus with a state, even though the salesperson merely solicits sales orders there.

An activity that consists merely of solicitation is immune from taxation. The statute does not define the term *solicitation*, but the Supreme Court has held that *solicitation of orders* includes any explicit verbal request for orders and any speech or conduct that implicitly invites an order.[4] The Court also created a *de minimis* rule, allowing immunity from nexus where a limited amount of solicitation occurs.

Exhibit 24.2 summarizes the activities that are recognized as being directly related to solicitation (protected activities) and activities unrelated to solicitation (which establish income tax nexus for the entity).

Independent Contractors

Public Law 86–272 extends immunity to certain in-state activities conducted by an independent contractor that would not be permitted if performed directly by the taxpayer. Generally, an independent contractor may engage in the following limited activities without establishing income tax nexus for the principal: (1) soliciting sales, (2) making sales, and (3) maintaining a sales office.

24.2 Allocation and Apportionment of Income

LO.3

Distinguish between allocation and apportionment of a multistate corporation's taxable income.

A corporation that conducts business activities in more than one state must determine the portion of its net income that is subject to tax by each state. A corporation that has established sufficient nexus with another state generally must both **allocate** and **apportion** its income.

Apportionment is a means by which a corporation's business income is divided among the states in which it conducts business. Under an apportionment procedure, a corporation determines allowable income and deductions for the company as a whole and then apportions some of its net income to a given state, according to an approved formula.

[3] 15 U.S.C. 381–385.

[4] *Wisconsin Department of Revenue v. William Wrigley, Jr., Co.*, 112 S.Ct. 2447 (1992).

EXHIBIT 24.2 **Common Nexus Definitions under Public Law 86–272**

General rule: P.L. 86–272 immunity from nexus applies where the sales representative's activities are ancillary to the order-solicitation process.

Activities That Usually Do Not Create Nexus

- Advertising campaigns.
- Carrying free samples only for display or distribution.
- Owning or furnishing automobiles to salespersons.
- Passing inquiries or complaints on to the home office.
- Checking customers' inventories for reorder.
- Maintaining a sample or display room for two weeks or less during the year.
- Maintaining an office for an employee, including an office in the home.

Activities Usually Sufficient to Establish Nexus

- Making repairs or providing maintenance.
- Collecting delinquent accounts; investigating creditworthiness.
- Installation or supervision of installation.
- Conducting training classes, seminars, or lectures for persons other than sales personnel.
- Approving or accepting orders.
- Picking up or replacing damaged or returned property.
- Hiring, training, or supervising personnel other than sales employees.
- Providing shipping information and coordinating deliveries.
- Carrying samples for sale, exchange, or distribution in any manner for consideration or other value.
- Owning, leasing, maintaining, or otherwise using any of the following facilities or property in the state.
  - *Real estate*
  - *Repair shop*
  - *Parts department*
  - *Employment office*
  - *Purchasing office*
  - *Warehouse*
  - *Meeting place for directors, officers, or employees*
  - *Stock of goods*
  - *Telephone call center*
  - *Mobile retailing (e.g., trucks with driver-salespersons)*

Allocation is a method under which specific components of a corporation's income, net of related expenses, are directly assigned to a certain state. Allocation differs from apportionment in that allocable income is assigned to one state, whereas apportionable income is divided among several states. Nonapportionable (nonbusiness) income generally includes:

- Income or losses derived from the sale of nonbusiness real or tangible property, or
- Income or losses derived from rentals and royalties from nonbusiness real or tangible personal property.

This income is allocated to the state where the property that generated the income or loss is located.

As Figure 24.1 indicated, total allocable (nonapportionable) income or loss typically is removed from corporate net income before the state's apportionment percentage is applied. The nonapportionable income or loss assigned to a state then is combined with the income apportionable to that state to arrive at total income subject to tax in the state.

EXAMPLE 3

Green Corporation conducts business in States N, O, P, and Q. Green's $900,000 taxable income consists of $800,000 apportionable income and $100,000 allocable income generated from transactions conducted in State Q. Green's sales, property, and payroll are evenly divided among the four states, and the states all employ an identical apportionment formula. Accordingly, $200,000 of Green's income is taxable in each of States N, O, and P. Green is subject to income tax on $300,000 of income in State Q.

Apportionable income	$800,000
Apportionment percentage (apportionable income is divided equally among the four states)	× 25%
Income apportioned to each state	$200,000

	State N	State O	State P	State Q
Income apportioned	$200,000	$200,000	$200,000	$200,000
Income allocated	–0–	–0–	–0–	100,000
Taxable income	$200,000	$200,000	$200,000	$300,000

■

THE APPORTIONMENT PROCEDURE

Apportionment assumes that the production of business income is linked to business activity, and the laws of each state define a number of factors believed to indicate the amount of corporate activity conducted within the state. However, apportionment often does not provide a uniform division of an organization's income based on its business activity, because each state is free to choose the type and number of factors that it believes are indicative of the business activity conducted within its borders. Therefore, a corporation may be subject to state income tax on more or less than 100 percent of its income.

An equally incongruous consequence of apportionment may occur when the operations in a state result in a loss.

EXAMPLE 4

Red Corporation's operations include two manufacturing facilities, located in States A and B, respectively. The plant located in A generated $500,000 of income, and the plant located in B generated a loss of $200,000. Therefore, Red's total taxable income is $300,000.

By applying the statutes of each state, Red determines that its apportionment factors for A and B are .65 and .35, respectively. Accordingly, Red's income is apportioned to the states as follows.

Income apportioned to State A: $300,000 × .65 = $195,000

Income apportioned to State B: $300,000 × .35 = $105,000

Red is subject to tax in B on $105,000 of income, even though the operations conducted in that state resulted in a loss. ■

BUSINESS AND NONBUSINESS INCOME

LO.4

Describe the nature and treatment of business and nonbusiness income.

Business income is assigned among the states by using an apportionment formula. In contrast, *nonbusiness income* is either apportioned or allocated to the state in which the income-producing asset is located. For example, income derived from the rental of nonbusiness real property generally is allocated to the state in which the property is located.

EXAMPLE 5

TNT Corporation, a manufacturer of explosive devices, is a multistate taxpayer that has nexus with States P and Q. During the taxable year, TNT's net sales of explosive devices were $900,000; $600,000 of these sales were made in P and $300,000 were made in Q. The corporation also received $90,000 from the rental of nonbusiness real property located in P.

Both states employ a three-factor apportionment formula under which sales, property, and payroll are equally weighted. However, the states do not agree on the definition of apportionable income. Under P's tax provisions, nonbusiness rent income is allocable and business income is apportionable, while Q requires a corporation to apportion all of its (business and nonbusiness) income. The sales factor (the ratio of in-state sales to total sales) for each of the states is computed as follows.

$$\text{State P: } \frac{\$600{,}000 \text{ (sales in State P)}}{\$900{,}000 \text{ (total sales)}} = 66.67\%$$

$$\text{State Q: } \frac{\$300{,}000 \text{ (sales in State Q)}}{\$990{,}000 \text{ (total sales)*}} = 30.30\%$$

*Since rent income is treated as business income, rents are included in the denominator of the sales factor. ■

EXAMPLE 6

Continue with the facts of Example 5, except that the rent income was generated from property located in Q, rather than from property located in P. Although the sales factor for P remains the same, the sales factor for Q changes.

$$\text{State P: } \frac{\$600{,}000 \text{ (sales in State P)}}{\$900{,}000 \text{ (total sales)}} = 66.67\%$$

$$\text{State Q: } \frac{\$390{,}000 \text{ (sales in State Q)}}{\$990{,}000 \text{ (total sales)}} = 39.39\%$$

Due to the composition of the sales factor in the two states, TNT's income never is perfectly apportioned: the aggregate of the sales factors is either more or less than 100%. ■

Business income arises from the taxpayer's regular course of business or constitutes an integral part of the taxpayer's regular business.[5] In determining whether an item of income is (apportionable) business income, state courts have developed a variety of approaches to determine what constitutes a taxpayer's "regular course of business."[6]

Nonbusiness income is "all income other than business income."[7] Usually, nonbusiness income comprises passive and portfolio income, such as dividends, interest, rents, royalties, and certain capital gains. However, passive or portfolio income may be classified as business income when the acquisition, management, and disposition of the underlying property constitute an integral part of the taxpayer's regular business operation.

EXAMPLE 7

Gray Corporation owns and operates two manufacturing facilities, one in State A and the other in State B. Due to a temporary decline in sales, Gray has rented 10% of its A facility to an unaffiliated corporation. Gray generated $100,000 of net rent income and $900,000 of income from manufacturing.

Both A and B classify such rent income as allocable nonbusiness income. By applying the statutes of each state, as discussed in the next section, Gray determines that its apportionment factors are 0.40 for A and 0.60 for B.

Income Subject to Tax in State A	
Taxable income	$1,000,000
Less: Allocable income	(100,000)
Apportionable income	$ 900,000
Times: Apportionment factor	× 40%
Income apportioned to State A	$ 360,000
Plus: Income allocated to State A	100,000
Income subject to tax in State A	$ 460,000

[5] MTC Reg. IV.1.(a).

[6] *Atlantic Richfield Co. v. State of Colorado and Joseph F. Dolan*, 601 P.2d 628 (Colo.S.Ct., 1979); *Appeal of A. Epstein and Sons, Inc.* (Cal.State Bd. of Equalization, 1984).

[7] UDITPA § 1(e).

Income Subject to Tax in State B

Taxable income	$1,000,000
Less: Allocable income	(100,000)
Apportionable income	$ 900,000
Times: Apportionment factor	× 60%
Income apportioned to State B	$ 540,000
Plus: Income allocated to State B	–0–
Income subject to tax in State B	$ 540,000

APPORTIONMENT FACTORS: ELEMENTS AND PLANNING

LO.5

Discuss the sales, payroll, and property apportionment factors.

Business income is apportioned among the states by determining the appropriate apportionment percentage for each state that has a right to tax the entity. To determine the apportionment percentage for each state, a ratio is established for each of the factors included in the state's apportionment formula. Each ratio is calculated by comparing the level of a specific business activity within a state to the total corporate activity of that type. The ratios then are summed, averaged, and appropriately weighted (if required) to determine the corporation's apportionment percentage for a specific state.

Although apportionment formulas vary among jurisdictions, the traditional three-factor formula equally weights sales, property, and payroll.[8] This formula is derived from the Uniform Division of Income for Tax Purposes Act (**UDITPA**), a model law relating to the assignment of income among the states for corporations that maintain operations in more than one state. However, most of the states now use a modified three-factor formula, where the sales factor receives more than a one-third weight. The use of a higher-weighted sales factor tends to pull a larger percentage of an out-of-state corporation's income into the taxing jurisdiction of the state, because the corporation's major activity within the state—the sales of its products—is weighted more heavily than are its payroll and property activities. Overweighting the sales factor, however, provides tax relief for corporations that are domiciled in the state. Those corporations generally own significantly more property and incur more payroll costs (factors that are given less weight in the apportionment formula) within the state than do out-of-state corporations.

EXAMPLE 8

Musk Corporation realized $500,000 of taxable income from the sales of its products in States A and B. Musk's activities in both states establish nexus for income tax purposes. Musk's sales, payroll, and property in the states include the following.

	State A	State B	Total
Sales	$1,250,000	$750,000	$2,000,000
Property	2,500,000	–0–	2,500,000
Payroll	1,500,000	–0–	1,500,000

If State B uses an equally weighted three-factor apportionment formula, $62,500 of Musk's taxable income is apportioned to B.

Sales ($750,000/$2,000,000)	=	37.5%
Property ($0/$2,500,000)	=	–0–
Payroll ($0/$1,500,000)	=	–0–
Sum of apportionment factors		37.5%
Average	÷	3
Apportionment factor for State B		12.5%
Taxable income	×	$500,000
Income apportioned to State B		$ 62,500

[8] Certain industries, such as financial services institutions, insurance companies, air and motor carriers, pipeline companies, and communications providers, typically are required to use special apportionment formulas.

If State B uses a double-weighted sales factor in its three-factor apportionment formula, $93,750 of Musk's taxable income is apportioned to B.

Sales ($750,000/$2,000,000)	=	37.5% × 2	=	75%
Property ($0/$2,500,000)	=			–0–
Payroll ($0/$1,500,000)	=			–0–
Sum of apportionment factors				75%
Average			÷	4
Apportionment factor for State B				18.75%
Taxable income			×	$500,000
Income apportioned to State B				$ 93,750

When a state uses a double-weighted sales factor, typically a larger percentage of an out-of-state corporation's income is subject to tax in the state. Here, an additional $31,250 ($93,750 – $62,500) of Musk's income is subject to tax in B. ■

A single-factor apportionment formula consisting solely of a sales factor is even more detrimental to an out-of-state corporation than an apportionment factor that double weights the sales factor.[9]

EXAMPLE 9

PPR Corporation, a retailer of paper products, owns retail stores in States A, B, and C. State A uses a three-factor apportionment formula under which the sales, property, and payroll factors are equally weighted. B uses a three-factor apportionment formula under which sales are double weighted. C employs a single-factor apportionment factor, based solely on sales.

PPR's operations generated $800,000 of apportionable income, and its sales, payroll activity, and average property owned in each of the three states are as follows.

	State A	State B	State C	Total
Sales	$500,000	$400,000	$300,000	$1,200,000
Payroll	100,000	125,000	75,000	300,000
Property	150,000	250,000	100,000	500,000

$280,000 of PPR's apportionable income is assigned to A.

Sales ($500,000/$1,200,000)	=	41.67%
Payroll ($100,000/$300,000)	=	33.33%
Property ($150,000/$500,000)	=	30.00%
Sum of apportionment factors		105.00%
Average	÷	3
Apportionment factor for State A		35.00%
Apportionable income	×	$800,000
Income apportioned to State A		$280,000

$316,640 of PPR's apportionable income is assigned to B.

Sales ($400,000/$1,200,000)	=	33.33% × 2	=	66.66%
Payroll ($125,000/$300,000)			=	41.67%
Property ($250,000/$500,000)			=	50.00%
Sum of apportionment factors				158.33%
Average			÷	4
Apportionment factor for State B				39.58%
Apportionable income			×	$800,000
Income apportioned to State B				$316,640

[9] Currently, Colorado, Georgia, Illinois, Iowa, Maine, Michigan, Nebraska, New York, Oregon, Texas, and Wisconsin require the use of a single-factor apportionment formula for all taxpayers.

$200,000 of PPR's apportionable income is assigned to C.

Sales ($300,000/$1,200,000)	=	25.00%
Sum of apportionment factors		25.00%
Average	÷	1
Apportionment factor for State C		25.00%
Apportionable income	×	$800,000
Income apportioned to State C		$200,000

Summary	
Income apportioned to State A	$280,000
Income apportioned to State B	316,640
Income apportioned to State C	200,000
Total income apportioned	$796,640

Due to the variations in the apportionment formulas employed by the various states, only 99.58% ($796,640/$800,000) of PPR's income is apportioned to the states in which it is subject to tax. ■

THE SALES FACTOR

The **sales factor** is a fraction, whose numerator is the corporation's total sales in the state during the tax period. The denominator is the corporation's total sales everywhere during the tax period. Gross sales for this purpose generally are net of returns, allowances, and discounts. Moreover, interest income, service charges, and carrying charges are included in the sales factor. Federal and state excise taxes and state sales taxes are included in the factor if these taxes are either passed on to the buyer or included in the selling price of the goods.

Since the sales factor is a component in the formula used to apportion a corporation's business income to a state, only sales that generate business income are includible in the fraction. The "sales" factor actually resembles a "receipts" factor in most states, since it also generally includes business income from the sale of inventory or services, interest, dividends, rentals, royalties, sales of assets, and other business income. Income on Federal obligations, however, is not included in the sales factor.

When the sale involves capital assets, some states require that the gross proceeds, rather than the net gain or loss, be included in the fraction. Most states allow incidental or occasional asset sales and sales of certain intangible assets to be excluded from gross receipts.[10]

In determining the numerator of the sales factor, most states use the UDITPA's "ultimate destination concept," under which tangible asset sales are assumed to take place at the point of delivery, not at the location at which the shipment originates.

EXAMPLE 10

Olive Corporation, whose only manufacturing plant is located in State A, sells its products to residents of A through its local retail store. Olive also ships its products to customers in States B and C. The products that are sold to residents of A are assigned to A, while the products that are delivered to B and C are assigned to B and C, respectively. ■

Throwback Rule

Out-of-state sales that are not subject to tax in the destination state are pulled back into the origination state if that state has adopted a **throwback rule**. About half of the states apply this exception to the destination test.

The throwback rule provides that, when a corporation is not subject to tax in the destination state or the purchaser is the U.S. government, the sales are treated as in-state sales of the origination state, and the actual destination of the product is

[10] MTC Reg. IV.18.(c).

disregarded. Consequently, when the seller is immune from tax in the destination state under Public Law 86–272, the sales are considered to be in-state sales of the origination state if that state has a throwback provision.

The throwback rule seems inappropriate when the sale is made to a purchaser in another country, where the transaction is subject to a value-added or gross receipts tax (but no income tax). In these cases, the taxpayer truly is subject to double taxation, as state taxes increase but no Federal foreign tax credit is available. Nonetheless, most of the throwback states fail to distinguish between U.S. and overseas throwback sales.

EXAMPLE 11

Braun Corporation's entire operations are located in State A. Seventy percent ($700,000) of Braun's sales are made in A, and the remaining 30% ($300,000) are made in State B. Braun's solicitation of sales in B is limited to mailing a monthly catalog to its customers in that state. However, Braun employees do pick up and replace damaged merchandise in State B.

The pickup and replacement of damaged goods establish nexus with A. Braun's activities in B are sufficient (as determined by A's law) to subject Braun to a positive tax, based on its income. Therefore, Braun is permitted to apportion its income between A and B. However, B's definition of activities necessary to create nexus is less strict than that imposed by A; in B, the mere pickup and replacement of damaged goods do not subject a corporation's income to tax.

Braun's taxable income is $900,000. Both A and B impose a 10% corporate income tax and include only the sales factor in their apportionment formulas. If A has not adopted a throwback rule, Braun's effective state income tax rate is 7%.

	Apportionment Factors	Taxable Income	Tax Rate	Tax
State A	70%	$900,000	10%	$63,000
State B	–0–*	900,000	10%	–0–
Total tax liability				$63,000
Effective state income tax rate: $63,000/$900,000 =				7%

*As determined under B's laws, Braun's income is not apportionable to State B because of insufficient nexus.

If A has adopted a throwback rule, Braun does not benefit from its lack of nexus with B, because the sales in B are considered to be in-state sales of A. Thus, Braun's effective tax rate is 10%.

	Apportionment Factors	Taxable Income	Tax Rate	Tax
State A	100%	$900,000	10%	$90,000
State B	–0–	900,000	10%	–0–
Total tax liability				$90,000
Effective state income tax rate: $90,000/$900,000 =				10%
Tax increase due to throwback provision ($90,000 – $63,000)				$27,000

■

THE PAYROLL FACTOR

The **payroll factor** is determined by comparing the compensation paid for services rendered within a state to the total compensation paid by the corporation. Generally, the payroll factor is a fraction, whose numerator is the total amount that a corporation paid or accrued for compensation in a state during the tax period. The denominator is the total amount paid or accrued by the corporation for compensation during the tax period. For purposes of the payroll factor, compensation includes wages, salaries, commissions, and any other form of remuneration paid or accrued to employees for personal services. Compensation may also include the value of board, rent, housing, lodging, and other benefits or services furnished to employees by the taxpayer in return for personal services, if these amounts constitute Federal gross income.

Payments made to an independent contractor or any other person who is not properly classifiable as an employee generally are excluded from the numerator and denominator of the payroll factor. Some states, including Delaware and North Carolina, exclude from the payroll factor the compensation paid to corporate officers.

More than half of the states provide that earnings paid to a cash or deferred compensation plan, excluded from Federal gross income under § 401(k), are to be included in the numerator and the denominator of the payroll factor. Accordingly, the total compensation that is included in the denominator of a corporation's payroll factor may vary among the states in which the corporation's income is apportioned.

EXAMPLE 12

Mice Corporation's sales office and manufacturing plant are located in State A. Mice also maintains a manufacturing plant and sales office in State C. For purposes of apportionment, A defines payroll as all compensation paid to employees, including contributions to § 401(k) deferred compensation plans. Under the statutes of C, neither compensation paid to officers nor contributions to § 401(k) plans are included in the payroll factor. Mice incurred the following personnel costs.

	State A	State C	Total
Wages and salaries for employees other than officers	$350,000	$250,000	$600,000
Salaries for officers	150,000	100,000	250,000
Contributions to § 401(k) plans	30,000	20,000	50,000
Total	$530,000	$370,000	$900,000

The payroll factor for State A is computed as follows.

$$\frac{\$530{,}000}{\$900{,}000} = 58.89\%$$

Since State C excludes from the payroll factor any compensation paid to officers and contributions to § 401(k) plans, C's factor is computed as follows.

$$\frac{\$250{,}000}{\$600{,}000} = 41.67\%$$

The aggregate of Mice's payroll factors is 100.56% (58.89% + 41.67%). In certain cases, the sum of a corporation's payroll factors may be significantly more or less than 100%. ■

Only compensation that is related to the production of apportionable income is included in the payroll factor. Accordingly, in those states that distinguish between business and nonbusiness income, compensation related to the operation, maintenance, protection, or supervision of nonbusiness income is not includible in the payroll factor.

EXAMPLE 13

Dog Corporation, a manufacturer of automobile parts, is subject to tax in States X and Y. Dog incurred the following payroll costs.

	State X	State Y	Total
Wages and salaries for officers and personnel of manufacturing facilities	$450,000	$350,000	$800,000
Wages and salaries for personnel involved in nonbusiness rental activities	50,000	–0–	50,000

If both states distinguish between business and nonbusiness income in determining apportionable income and include officers' compensation in the payroll factor, Dog's payroll factors are computed as follows.

Payroll factor for State X: $450,000/$800,000 = 56.25%

Payroll factor for State Y: $350,000/$800,000 = 43.75% ■

EXAMPLE 14

Continue with the facts of Example 13, but assume that Y defines apportionable income as the corporation's total income (business and nonbusiness income). Dog's payroll factor for X remains unchanged, but its payroll factor for Y is reduced.

Payroll factor for State X: $450,000/$800,000 = 56.25%

Payroll factor for State Y: $350,000/$850,000* = 41.18%

*$800,000 (compensation related to business income) + $50,000 (compensation related to nonbusiness income). ■

THE PROPERTY FACTOR

The **property factor** generally is a fraction, whose numerator is the average value of the corporation's real property and its tangible personal property owned and used or rented and used in the state during the taxable year. The denominator is the average value of all of the corporation's real property and its tangible personal property owned or rented and used during the taxable year, wherever it is located. In this manner, a state's property factor reflects the extent of total property usage by the taxpayer in the state.

For this purpose, property includes land, buildings, machinery, inventory, equipment, and other real and tangible personal property, other than coins or currency.[11] Other types of property that may be included in the factor are offshore property, outer space property (satellites), and partnership property.

In the case of property that is in transit between locations of the taxpayer or between a buyer and seller, the assets are included in the numerator of the destination state. With respect to mobile or movable property, such as construction equipment, trucks, and leased equipment, which is both in- and outside the state during the tax period, the numerator of a state's property factor generally is determined on the basis of the total time that the property was within the state.

Property owned by the corporation typically is valued at its average original or historical cost plus the cost of additions and improvements, but without adjusting for depreciation. Some states allow property to be included at net book value or adjusted tax basis. The value of the property usually is determined by averaging the values at the beginning and end of the tax period. Alternatively, some states allow or require the amount to be calculated on a monthly basis if annual computation results in or requires substantial distortions.

EXAMPLE 15

Blond Corporation, a calendar year taxpayer, owns property in States A and B. Both A and B require that the average value of assets be included in the property factor. A requires that the property be valued at its historical cost, and B requires that the property be included in the property factor at its net book value.

Account Balances at January 1

	State A	State B	Total
Inventories	$ 150,000	$100,000	$ 250,000
Building and machinery (cost)	200,000	400,000	600,000
Accumulated depreciation for building and machinery	(150,000)	(50,000)	(200,000)
Land	50,000	100,000	150,000
Total	$ 250,000	$550,000	$ 800,000

[11]MTC Reg. IV.10.(a).

Account Balances at December 31			
	State A	**State B**	**Total**
Inventories	$ 250,000	$ 200,000	$ 450,000
Building and machinery (cost)	200,000	400,000	600,000
Accumulated depreciation for building and machinery	(175,000)	(100,000)	(275,000)
Land	50,000	100,000	150,000
Total	$ 325,000	$ 600,000	$ 925,000

State A Property Factor			
Historical Cost	**January 1**	**December 31**	**Average**
Property in State A	$ 400,000*	$ 500,000**	$ 450,000
Total property	1,000,000†	1,200,000††	1,100,000

*$150,000 + $200,000 + $50,000.
**$250,000 + $200,000 + $50,000.
†$250,000 + $600,000 + $150,000.
††$450,000 + $600,000 + $150,000.

$$\text{Property factor for State A: } \frac{\$450{,}000}{\$1{,}100{,}000} = 40.91\%$$

State B Property Factor			
Net Book Value	**January 1**	**December 31**	**Average**
Property in State B	$550,000	$600,000	$575,000
Total property	800,000	925,000	862,500

$$\text{Property factor for State B: } \frac{\$575{,}000}{\$862{,}500} = 66.67\%$$

Due to the variations in the property factors, the aggregate of Blond's property factors equals 107.58% (40.91% + 66.67%). ■

Leased property, when included in the property factor, is valued at eight times its annual rental. Annual rentals may include payments, such as real estate taxes and insurance, made by the lessee in lieu of rent.

EXAMPLE 16

Jasper Corporation is subject to tax in States D and G. Both states require that leased or rented property be included in the property factor at eight times the annual rental costs, and that the average historical cost be used for other assets. Information regarding Jasper's property and rental expenses follows.

Average Historical Cost	
Property located in State D	$ 750,000
Property located in State G	450,000
Total property	$1,200,000

Lease and Rental Expenses	
State D	$ 50,000
State G	150,000
Total	$200,000

$$\text{Property factor for State D: } \frac{\$750{,}000 + 8(\$50{,}000)}{\$1{,}200{,}000 + 8(\$200{,}000)} = \frac{\$1{,}150{,}000}{\$2{,}800{,}000} = 41.07\%$$

$$\text{Property factor for State G: } \frac{\$450{,}000 + 8(\$150{,}000)}{\$1{,}200{,}000 + 8(\$200{,}000)} = \frac{\$1{,}650{,}000}{\$2{,}800{,}000} = 58.93\%$$ ■

Only property that is used in the production of apportionable income is includible in the numerator and denominator of the property factor. In this regard, idle property and property that is used in producing nonapportionable income generally are excluded. However, property that is temporarily idle or unused generally remains in the property factor.

24.3 The Unitary Theory

LO.6

Apply the unitary method of state income taxation.

The **unitary theory** developed in response to the early problems that states faced in apportioning the income of a multistate business among the states in which the business was conducted. Originally, this theory was applied to justify apportionment of the income of multiple operating divisions within a single company. Over the years, however, the concept has been extended to require the combined reporting of certain affiliated corporations, including those outside the United States.

When two affiliated corporations are subject to tax in different states, each entity must file a return and report its income in the state in which it conducts business. Each entity reports its income separately from that of its affiliated corporations. In an effort to minimize overall state income tax, multistate entities have attempted to separate the parts of the business that are carried on in the various states.

EXAMPLE 17

Arts Corporation owns a chain of retail stores located in several states. To enable each store to file and report the income earned only in that state, each store was organized as a separate subsidiary in the state in which it did business. In this manner, each store is separately subject to tax only in the state in which it is located. ■

Most states attempt to assign as much of an entity's income to in-state sources as possible, so the *unitary* approach to computing state taxable income is attractive to them. Under this method, a corporation is required to file a **combined return** that includes the results from all of the operations of the related corporations, not just from those that transacted business in the state. In this manner, the unitary method allows a state to apply the apportionment formula to a firm's nationwide or worldwide unitary income. To include the activities of the corporation's subsidiaries in the apportionment formula, the state must determine that the subsidiaries' activities are an integral part of a unitary business and, as a result, are subject to apportionment.

WHAT IS A UNITARY BUSINESS?

A unitary business operates as a unit and cannot be segregated into independently operating divisions. The operations are integrated, and each division depends on

CONCEPT SUMMARY 24.1

Principles of Multistate Corporate Income Taxation

1. Taxability of an organization's income in a state other than the one in which it is incorporated depends on the laws, regulations, and judicial interpretations of the other state; the nature and level of the corporation's activity in, or contacts with, that state; and, to a limited extent, the application of P.L. 86–272.
2. Each state has adopted its own multistate income tax laws, regulations, methods, and judicial interpretations; consequently, the nonuniformity of state income taxing provisions provides a multitude of planning techniques that allow a multistate corporation to reduce its overall state tax liability legally.
3. The apportionment procedure is used to assign the income of a multistate taxpayer to the various states in which business is conducted. Generally, nonbusiness income is allocated, rather than apportioned, directly to the state in which the nonbusiness income-generating assets are located.
4. The various state apportionment factors and formulas offer planning opportunities in that more or less than 100% of the taxpayer's income may be subjected to state income tax.
5. Some states employ an equally weighted three-factor apportionment formula. In many states, the sales factor is doubled, and in a few states, only the sales factor is used in apportioning multistate taxable income. Generally, the greater the relative weight assigned to the sales factor, the greater the tax burden on out-of-state taxpayers.
6. The sales factor is based upon the destination concept except where a throwback rule applies. The payroll factor generally includes compensation that is included in Federal gross income, but some states include excludible fringe benefits. An employee's compensation usually is not divided among states. The property factor is derived using the average undepreciated historical costs for the assets and eight times the rental value of the assets.
7. The unitary theory may require the taxpayer to include worldwide activities and holdings in the apportionment factors. A water's edge election can limit these amounts to U.S. transactions.

or contributes to the operation of the business as a whole. It is not necessary that each unit operating within a state contribute to the activities of all divisions outside the state.

The unitary theory ignores the separate legal existence of the entities and focuses instead on practical business realities. Accordingly, the separate entities are treated as a single business for state income tax purposes, and the apportionment formula is applied to the combined income of the unitary business.

EXAMPLE 18

Continue with the facts of Example 17. Arts manufactured no goods, but conducted central management, purchasing, distributing, advertising, and administrative departments. The subsidiaries carried on a purely intrastate business, and they paid for the goods and services received at the parent company's cost, plus overhead. Arts and the subsidiaries constitute a unitary business due to their unitary operations (purchasing, distributing, advertising, and administrative functions). Accordingly, in states that have adopted the unitary method, the income and apportionment factors of the entire unitary group are combined and apportioned to the states in which at least one member of the group has nexus. ■

EXAMPLE 19

Crafts Corporation organized its departments as separate corporations on the basis of function: mining copper ore, refining the ore, and fabricating the refined copper into consumer products. Even though the various steps in the process are operated substantially independently of each other with only general supervision from Crafts' executive offices, Crafts is engaged in a single unitary business. Its various divisions are part of a large, vertically structured enterprise, in which each business segment needs the products or raw materials provided by another. The flow of products

GLOBAL
Tax Issues

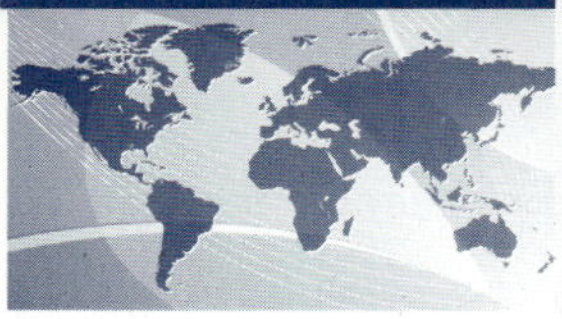

Water's Edge Is Not a Day at the Beach

As a result of pressure from the business community, the Federal government, and foreign countries, most of the states that impose an income tax on a unitary business's worldwide operations permit a multinational business to elect **water's edge** unitary reporting as an alternative to worldwide unitary filing.

The water's edge provision permits a multinational corporation to elect to limit the reach of the state's taxing jurisdiction over out-of-state affiliates to activities occurring within the boundaries of the United States. The decision to make a water's edge election may have a substantial effect on the tax liability of a multinational corporation. For instance, a water's edge election usually cannot be revoked for a number of years without permission from the appropriate tax authority.

Moreover, corporations making this election may be assessed an additional tax or fee for the privilege of excluding out-of-state entities from the combined report.

among the affiliates also provides evidence of functional integration, which generally requires some form of central decision or policy making, another characteristic of a unitary business. ■

Notice that the application of the unitary theory is based on a series of subjective observations about the organization and operation of the taxpayer's businesses, whereas the availability of Federal controlled and affiliated group status (see Chapter 17) is based on objective, mechanical ownership tests. More than half of the states require or allow unitary reporting.

TAX EFFECTS OF THE UNITARY THEORY

Use of the unitary approach by a state eliminates several of the planning techniques that could be used to shift income between corporate segments to avoid or minimize state taxes. In addition, the unitary approach usually results in a larger portion of the corporation's income being taxable in states where the compensation, property values, and sales prices are high relative to other states. This occurs because the larger in-state costs (numerators in the apportionment formula) include in the tax base a larger portion of the taxable income within the state's taxing jurisdiction. This has an adverse effect upon the corporation's overall state tax burden if the states in which the larger portions are allocated impose a high tax rate relative to the other states in which the business is conducted.

The presence of a unitary business is favorable when losses of unprofitable affiliates may be offset against the earnings of profitable affiliates. It also is favorable when income earned in a high-tax state may be shifted to low-tax states due to the use of combined apportionment factors.

EXAMPLE 20

Rita Corporation owns two subsidiaries, Arts and Crafts. Arts, located in State K, generated taxable income of $700,000. During this same period, Crafts, located in State M, generated a loss of $400,000. If the subsidiaries are independent corporations, Arts is required to pay K tax on $700,000 of income. However, if the corporations constitute a unitary business, the incomes, as well as the apportionment factors, of the two entities are combined. As a result, the combined income of $300,000 ($700,000 – $400,000) is apportioned to unitary states K and M. ■

EXAMPLE 21

Eve Corporation, a wholly owned subsidiary of Dan Corporation, generated $1 million of taxable income. Eve's activities and sales are restricted to State P, which imposes a 10% income tax. Dan's income for the taxable period is $1.5 million. Dan's activities and sales are restricted to State Q, which imposes a 5% income tax. Both states use a three-factor apportionment formula that equally weights sales, payroll, and property. Sales, payroll, and average property for each of the corporations are as follows.

	Eve Corporation	Dan Corporation	Total
Sales	$3,000,000	$7,000,000	$10,000,000
Payroll	2,000,000	3,500,000	5,500,000
Property	2,500,000	4,500,000	7,000,000

If the corporations are independent entities, the overall state income tax liability is $175,000.

State P ($1,000,000 × 10%)	=	$100,000
State Q ($1,500,000 × 5%)	=	75,000
Total state income tax		$175,000

If the corporations are members of a unitary business, the income and apportionment factors are combined in determining the income tax liability in unitary states P and Q. As a result of the combined reporting, the overall state income tax liability is reduced.

State P Income Tax				
Total apportionable income ($1,000,000 + $1,500,000)			$2,500,000	
Apportionment formula				
Sales ($3,000,000/$10,000,000)	=	30.00%		
Payroll ($2,000,000/$5,500,000)	=	36.36%		
Property ($2,500,000/$7,000,000)	=	35.71%		
Total		102.07%		
Average (102.07% ÷ 3)			× 34.02%	
State P taxable income			$ 850,500	
Tax rate			× 10%	
State P tax liability				$ 85,050

State Q Income Tax				
Total apportionable income ($1,000,000 + $1,500,000)			$2,500,000	
Apportionment formula				
Sales ($7,000,000/$10,000,000)	=	70.00%		
Payroll ($3,500,000/$5,500,000)	=	63.64%		
Property ($4,500,000/$7,000,000)	=	64.29%		
Total		197.93%		
Average (197.93% ÷ 3)			× 65.98%	
State Q taxable income			$1,649,500	
Tax rate			× 5%	
State Q tax liability				$ 82,475
Total state income tax, if unitary ($85,050 + $82,475)				$167,525
Total state income tax, if nonunitary ($100,000 + $75,000)				175,000
Tax reduction from unitary reporting				$ 7,475

The results of unitary reporting would have been detrimental if Q had imposed a higher rate of tax than P, because a larger percentage of the corporation's income is attributable to Q when the apportionment factors are combined. ■

24.4 Taxation of S Corporations

LO.7

Discuss the states' income tax treatment of S corporations, partnerships, and LLCs.

The majority of the 46 states that impose a corporate income tax have special provisions, similar to the Federal law, that govern the taxation of S corporations. As of 2011, only a few states—including Tennessee and Texas—and the District of Columbia do not provide special (i.e., no corporate-level tax) treatment for Federal S corporations. In addition, Massachusetts imposes a corporate-level tax on S corporations that have gross receipts in excess of $6 million. Some states, including Illinois, Texas, and California, apply a corporate-level tax, at special rates, on an S corporation.

In the non-S election states, a Federal S corporation generally is subject to tax in the same manner as a regular C corporation. Accordingly, if a multistate S corporation operates in any of these states, it is subject to state income tax and does not realize one of the primary benefits of S status—the avoidance of double taxation. Other potential tax-related benefits of the S election, including the pass-through of operating losses and the reduction in the rate of tax imposed on individual and corporate taxpayers, may be curtailed.

EXAMPLE 22

Bryan Inc., an S corporation, has established nexus in States A and B. State A recognizes S status, while B does not. Bryan generated $600,000 of ordinary business income and $100,000 of dividends that were received from corporations in which Bryan owns 50% of the stock. Bryan's State B apportionment percentage is 50%.

For State B tax purposes, Bryan first computes its income as though it were a C corporation. It then apportions the resulting income to B. Assuming that B has adopted the Federal provisions governing the dividends received deduction, Bryan's income, determined as though it were a C corporation, is $620,000 [$600,000 + (100% − 80%) × $100,000]. Accordingly, Bryan may be subject to corporate income tax in State B on $310,000 ($620,000 × 50% apportionment percentage) of taxable income. ■

A few states deviate from the Federal S corporation provisions and provide that an S corporation is entirely exempt from state income tax only if all of its shareholders are residents of the state. In these states, an S corporation is taxed on the portion of its income that is attributable to nonresident shareholders. Some of these states permit the S corporation to escape corporate-level tax on this income if its nonresident shareholders sign a form, agreeing to pay state tax on their share of the corporation's income. Moreover, about half of the states require the corporation to withhold taxes on the nonresident shareholders' portions of the entity's income.

EXAMPLE 23

ARGO, an S corporation, is subject to income tax only in Vermont. On the last day of its taxable year, 40% of ARGO's stock is held by nonresident shareholders. To the extent that ARGO's stock is held by resident shareholders, the corporation is not subject to income tax. Accordingly, ARGO is not subject to tax on 60% of its income.

The corporation *is* subject to tax on the remaining 40% of its income. ARGO may be able to avoid this corporate-level tax by withholding Vermont income tax for its nonresident shareholders. ■

ELIGIBILITY

All of the states that recognize S status permit a corporation to be treated as an S corporation for state purposes only if the corporation has a valid Federal S election in place. Generally, the filing of a Federal S election is sufficient to render the corporation an S corporation for state tax purposes. In most states, an entity that is an S corporation for Federal tax purposes automatically is treated as an S corporation for state tax purposes. Wisconsin allows the entity to *elect out* of its S status for state purposes.

TAX in the NEWS

What Are You Taxing?

Taxware.com, an observer of the state and local tax scene, has identified several of the most unusual sales and use tax laws that remain on the books of various states.

- Kentucky horse breeders pay sales tax on "stud fees" related to the breeding of Thoroughbred horses.
- North Carolina is a "tax-free zone" for motor sport racing teams. This includes a refund for the sales tax allocated to the fuel used by the aircraft that transport team members to the state.
- Cloth diapers are exempt from sales tax in Wisconsin, but disposables are taxable.
- Ohioans receive a tax break when they die. Makeup applications are exempt from sales tax when they are applied in a mortuary, but not when they occur in a beauty salon.
- Pennsylvania taxes air, in the form of a fee for the vacuum cleaner used at a car wash. No tax applies, though, for air used to inflate tires by a similar machine.

24.5 Taxation of Partnerships and LLCs

Most states apply income tax provisions to partnerships, limited liability companies (LLCs), and limited liability partnerships (LLPs) in a manner that parallels Federal treatment. The entity is a tax-reporting, not a taxpaying, entity. Income, loss, and credit items are allocated and apportioned among the partners according to the terms of the partnership agreement and state income tax law.

Some states require that the entity make estimated tax payments on behalf of out-of-state partners. This approach helps to assure that nonresident partners file appropriate forms and pay any resulting tax to the state. A few states, including Michigan for partnerships and Texas for LLCs, apply an entity-level tax on operating income. As is the case with S corporations, some states allow composite returns to be filed relative to out-of-state partners.

Generally, an in-state partner computes the income tax resulting from all of the flow-through income from the entity. The partner then is allowed a credit for income taxes paid to other states on this income.

Key issues facing partnerships doing business in multiple states include those listed here. Applicable law varies from state to state, and more complex transactions may not yet be addressed by existing law.

- Whether the partnership automatically has nexus with every state in which a partner resides.
- Whether a partner is deemed to have nexus with every state in which the partnership does business.
- How to assign the income/loss of a partner upon retirement or when a liquidating distribution is received.

24.6 Other State and Local Taxes

State and Local Sales and Use Taxes

LO.8

Describe other commonly encountered state and local taxes on businesses.

Forty-five states and the District of Columbia impose a consumers' sales tax on retail sales of tangible personal property for use or consumption. In many of these states, in-state localities, including cities, towns, school districts, or counties, also have the power to levy a sales tax. A consumers' sales tax is a tax imposed directly on the purchaser who acquires the asset at retail; the tax is measured by the price of the sale. The vendor or retailer merely acts as a collection agent for the state.

A use tax is designed to complement the sales tax. The use tax has two purposes: to prevent consumers from evading sales tax by purchasing goods outside the state for in-state use, and to provide an equitable sales environment between in-state and out-of-state retailers.

Generally, sales of tangible personal property are subject to tax. In several states, selected services are subject to tax.

Each jurisdiction that applies a sales/use tax defines its own tax base (i.e., which items are taxable and to whom). For a multistate business, complying with the thousands of sets of sales/use tax statutes and regulations can be a difficult burden. In an effort to ease this confusion, state and local government officials and the Multistate Tax Commission developed the Streamlined Sales Tax Project (SSTP). Members working in conjunction with the SSTP write model laws for taxing jurisdictions to adopt, thereby allowing for a more uniform application of the rules and for a more efficient exchange of information among revenue agencies.

To date, the most popular SSTP rules are those defining which products and services are subject to sales/use tax. For instance, SSTP rules set out the items of clothing that would be subject to tax, but each jurisdiction decides on its own whether to include clothing in the tax base and whether to allow "back to school" clothing amnesties during specific weeks of the year. However, little interest has been shown in having identical sales/use tax rates among the jurisdictions.

Almost all of the states that have adopted a sales/use tax are members of the SSTP, but only about half of them automatically adopt model SSTP laws.

Sales/Use Tax Exemptions

A majority of the states exempt sales of certain items from the sales/use tax base. The most common exemptions and exclusions include the following.

- *Sales for resale* are exempt because the purchaser is not the ultimate user of the sold property. For instance, meat purchased by a grocer and a garment purchased by a retailer are not subject to sales/use tax under the resale rule.
- *Casual or occasional sales* that occur infrequently are exempt from the sales/use tax base chiefly for administrative convenience. Most states exclude rummage sales, the transfer of an entire business, sales of used autos, and the like under this rule.
- Most *purchases by exempt organizations* are excluded from taxable sales. Charities, governments and their agencies, and other organizations qualifying for Federal income tax exemption are relieved of sales/use tax liabilities in all of the states.
- *Sales of targeted items* can be exempt to improve the equity of the sales/use tax system. Sales of groceries, medical prescriptions and equipment, and school clothes can fall into this category and become nontaxable. Special exemptions for sales of farm, industrial, and computing equipment might also qualify under this type of exclusion.
- Certain *sales to manufacturers, producers, and processors* may also be exempt.

ETHICS & Equity

TAXING CLICKS AND BRICKS

The states' enforcement efforts tend to be lax concerning sales/use tax collections for sales conducted on the Internet. But does this audit-deployment decision give Internet retailers an unfair advantage over "bricks and mortar" businesses that must collect sales tax on the sales that they make? Local retailers have invested in physical stores and merchandise and make up most downtown and shopping mall areas. Why should the law effectively allow a tax holiday for "clicks and mortar" Internet sellers, which have invested in just-in-time inventories and intangible assets like e-commerce web software? Do Internet retailers carry more political clout than those with stores or other physical presence in the state?

Comment on the equity of the current situation regarding Internet sales and the sales/use tax.

TAX *in* the NEWS — **The Amazon Tax**

To counter the loss of significant sales/use tax revenues on Internet transactions due to inadequate collection methods, New York and a few other states have found nexus through a vendor's use of sales, distribution, and marketing affiliates. For instance, suppose that a consumer clicks on a link on an Amazon.com page to Overstock.com, Target.com, or some other retailer and then purchases goods from the vendor. These states contend that Amazon has sales/use tax nexus because of the physical presence established in-state *by use of the affiliate*, even though Amazon itself has no such presence.

This so-called Amazon tax has been supported by most lower-level courts that have reviewed the issue. The taxpayers are appealing those holdings—not surprisingly, given that most of Amazon's affiliates (e.g., Target) have outlets in nearly every U.S. state and that considerable sales/use tax revenue is at stake.

Amazon long has enjoyed its no-nexus status as a strictly virtual seller, collecting sales/use taxes only in its headquarters state of Washington and in the three states with Amazon distribution centers. But any version of the Amazon tax will bring significant changes to the way that online commerce is conducted in other sales/use tax states.

Sales/Use Tax on Services

Most sales/use tax laws were developed 50 or more years ago, when the U.S. economy was based on manufacturing and merchandising. Today, with perhaps two-thirds of all retail transactions in the United States consisting at some level of the rendering of services, the sales/use tax may be considered inadequate at generating revenues for the taxing jurisdictions. Consequently, some states have been adding specific service transactions to the sales/use tax base.

The services most commonly being subjected to tax include transactions involving hotels and restaurants, hair and beauty salons, entertainment events, cable and satellite television subscriptions, and lawn care. To date, taxation of legal/accounting, medical, education, and advertising services has been blocked by the professional associations of the providers of these services. Revenue shortfalls at the state and local level, however, may force legislatures to expand the sales/use tax base to include a broader array of services in the future.

LOCAL PROPERTY TAXES

Property taxes, a major source of revenue at the city and county level, often are designated as *ad valorem* taxes because they are based on the value of property that is located in the state on a specific date. Generally, that date fixes taxable ownership, situs (location), and the valuation of the property. Nonetheless, to avoid tax evasion, personal property that is temporarily outside the state may be taxed at the domicile of the owner.

Property taxes can take the form of either real property taxes or personal property taxes. States apply different tax rates and means of assessment to the two classes of property. The methods of assessing the value of the real and tangible property also vary in different taxing jurisdictions.

OTHER TAXES

Jurisdictions may impose a variety of other state and local taxes on corporations, including incorporation or entrance fees or taxes, gross receipt taxes, stock transfer taxes, realty transfer and mortgage recording taxes, license taxes, and franchise taxes based on net worth or capital stock outstanding.

TAX PLANNING:

LO.9

Recognize tax planning opportunities available to minimize a corporation's state and local tax liability.

The inconsistencies in the tax laws and rates among the states not only complicate state tax planning, but also provide the nucleus of pertinent planning opportunities. Although several tax planning devices are available to a corporation that does

TAX *in the NEWS*

Collecting Those Sales/Use Tax Revenues

Today, state and local tax administrators face a major problem: How can governments get their sales/use tax revenues from mail-order, phone, and Internet sales? The problem is that the governments must rely on the seller to collect sales and use taxes, rather than collecting them directly from the purchaser. Consequently, a seller conceivably must deal with thousands of different sales/use taxing jurisdictions, each with its own forms and filing deadlines, rates of applicable tax, and definitions of what is taxable or exempt. Examples of issues on which jurisdictions may disagree include:

- Are snack foods exempt groceries or taxable candy?
- Are therapeutic stockings exempt medical supplies or taxable clothing?
- Which types of software are subject to tax?

Large retailers such as Wal-Mart, Amazon, and Radio Shack can develop software to handle these problems, but smaller businesses cannot afford to create their own software or to purchase someone else's. The result has been a very low level of compliance by sellers with respect to out-of-state sales transactions.

Governments meanwhile have limited resources to enforce tax rules that have long been on the books. Many states ask individuals and businesses to include the unpaid use taxes for Internet, phone, and mail-order purchases on their annual income tax returns, but the number of taxpayers complying is insignificant. This is not a matter of "increasing the taxes on the Internet economy," but rather of collecting revenues that already are due and are desperately needed to balance state budgets.

business in only one state, most planning techniques are directed toward corporations that do business or maintain property in more than one state. All suggested tax planning strategies should be reviewed in light of practical business considerations and the additional administrative and other costs that may be incurred, because simply minimizing state taxes may not be prudent from a business perspective.

24.7 Selecting the Optimal State in Which to Operate

Because the states employ different definitions of the amount and type of activity necessary to establish nexus, a company has some latitude in selecting the states by which it will be taxed. When a corporation has only a limited connection with a high-tax state, it may abandon that activity by electing an alternative means of accomplishing the same result. For example, if providing a sales representative with a company-owned BlackBerry constitutes nexus in an undesired state, the company could eliminate its connection with that state by reimbursing sales personnel for equipment expenses, instead of providing a company communications device. Similarly, when nexus is caused by conducting customer training sessions or seminars in the state, the corporation could bypass this connection. This can be done by sending the personnel to a nearby state in which nexus clearly has been established or in which the activity would not constitute nexus.

In addition, when sufficient activity originates from the repair and maintenance of the corporation's products or the activities performed by the sales representatives within the state, the organization could incorporate the service or sales divisions. This would invalidate a nonunitary state's right to tax the parent corporation's income; only the income of the service or sales divisions would be subject to tax. However, this technique is successful only if the incorporated division is a *bona fide* business operation. Therefore, the pricing of any sales or services between the new subsidiary and the parent corporation must be at arm's length, and the operations of the new corporation preferably should result in a profit.

Although planning techniques often are employed to disconnect a corporation's activities from an undesirable state, they can also be utilized to create nexus in a desirable state. For example, when the presence of a company-owned computer creates nexus in a desirable state, the corporation could provide its sales representatives in that state with company-owned equipment, rather than reimbursing or providing increased compensation for equipment costs.

Establishing nexus in a state is advantageous, for instance, when that state has a lower tax rate than the state in which the income currently is taxed, or when losses or credits become available to reduce tax liabilities in the state.

EXAMPLE 24

Bird Corporation generates $500,000 of taxable income from selling goods; specifically, 40% of its product is sold in State A and 60% in State B. Both states levy a corporate income tax and include only the sales factor in their apportionment formulas. The tax rate in A is 10%; B's rate is only 3%. Bird's manufacturing operation is located in A; therefore, the corporation's income is subject to tax in that state. Currently, Bird is immune from tax under Public Law 86–272 in B. Since A has adopted a throwback provision, Bird incurs $50,000 of state income taxes.

	Apportionment Formula	Taxable Income	Tax Rate	Tax
State A	100/100	$500,000	10%	$50,000
State B	0/100	500,000	3%	–0–
Total tax liability				$50,000

Because B imposes a lower tax rate than A, Bird substantially reduces its state tax liability if sufficient nexus is created with B.

	Apportionment Formula	Taxable Income	Tax Rate	Tax
State A	40/100	$500,000	10%	$20,000
State B	60/100	500,000	3%	9,000
Total tax liability				$29,000

A corporation may benefit by storing inventory in a low- or no-tax state because the average property value in the state in which the manufacturing operation is located is reduced significantly. When the manufacturing operation is located in a high-tax state, the establishment of a distribution center in a low- or no-tax state may reduce the overall state tax liability.

EXAMPLE 25

Trill Corporation realized $200,000 of taxable income from selling its product in States A and B. Trill's manufacturing plant, product distribution center, and warehouses are located in A. The corporation's activities within the two states are as follows.

	State A	State B	Total
Sales	$500,000	$200,000	$700,000
Property	300,000	50,000	350,000
Payroll	100,000	10,000	110,000

Trill is subject to tax in A and B. Both states utilize a three-factor apportionment formula that equally weights sales, property, and payroll; however, A imposes a 10% corporate income tax, while B levies a 3% tax. Trill incurs a total income tax liability of $17,575.

Apportionment Formulas

	State A			State B		
Sales	$500,000/$700,000	=	71.43%	$200,000/$700,000	=	28.57%
Property	$300,000/$350,000	=	85.71%	$50,000/$350,000	=	14.29%
Payroll	$100,000/$110,000	=	90.91%	$10,000/$110,000	=	9.09%
Total			248.05%			51.95%
Apportionment factor (totals ÷ 3)			82.68%			17.32%
Taxable income apportioned to the state ($200,000 × apportionment factor)			$165,360			$34,640
Tax rate			× 10%			× 3%
Tax liability			$ 16,536			$ 1,039
Total tax liability				$17,575		

EXAMPLE 26

Continue with the facts of Example 25, and further assume that Trill's product distribution center and warehouse operations were acquired for $200,000 and the payroll of these operations is $20,000. Ignoring all nontax considerations, Trill could reduce its tax liability by $3,514 (a 20% reduction) by moving its distribution center, warehouses, and applicable personnel to State B.

	State A	State B	Total
Sales	$500,000	$200,000	$700,000
Property	100,000	250,000	350,000
Payroll	80,000	30,000	110,000

Apportionment Formulas

	State A			State B		
Sales	$500,000/$700,000	=	71.43%	$200,000/$700,000	=	28.57%
Property	$100,000/$350,000	=	28.57%	$250,000/$350,000	=	71.43%
Payroll	$80,000/$110,000	=	72.73%	$30,000/$110,000	=	27.27%
Total			172.73%			127.27%
Apportionment factor (totals ÷ 3)			57.58%			42.42%
Taxable income apportioned to the state ($200,000 × apportionment factor)			$115,160			$84,840
Tax rate			× 10%			× 3%
Tax liability			$ 11,516			$ 2,545
Total tax liability				$14,061		
Tax imposed before move to State B				17,575		
Tax reduction due to move				$ 3,514		

24.8 Restructuring Corporate Entities

One of the major objectives of state tax planning is to design the proper mix of corporate entities. An optimal mix of entities often generates the lowest combined state income tax for the corporation. Ideally, the income from all of the entities will be subject to a low tax rate or no tax at all. However, this generally is not possible. Consequently, the goal of designing a good corporate combination often is to situate the highly profitable entities in states that impose a low (or no) income tax.

MATCHING TAX RATES AND CORPORATE INCOME

When the corporation must operate in a high-tax state, divisions that generate losses also should be located there. Alternatively, unprofitable or less profitable operations can be merged into profitable operations to reduce the overall income subject to tax in the state. An ideal candidate for this type of merger may be a research and development subsidiary that is only marginally profitable but is vital to the parent corporation's strategic goals. By using computer simulation models, a variety of different combinations can be tested to determine the optimal corporate structure.

UNITARY OPERATIONS

By identifying the states that have adopted the unitary method and the criteria under which a particular state defines a unitary business, a taxpayer may reduce its overall state tax by restructuring its corporate relationships to create or guard against a unitary relationship. For instance, an independent business enterprise can be made unitary by exercising day-to-day operational control and by centralizing functions, such as marketing, financing, accounting, and legal services.

EXAMPLE 27
THE BIG PICTURE

Return to the facts of *The Big Picture* on p. 24-2. LocalCo already operates in both unitary and nonunitary states. Application of unitary corporate income tax rules can make tax planning more difficult. Subjecting certain LocalCo activities to the unitary theory could either increase or decrease the combined state corporate income tax liability of the affiliates, depending especially on the apportionment formulas applied in the unitary states.

LocalCo needs to make projections of the profitability of its operations in the new multifunction building. Then LocalCo should determine the income tax effects of expanding its operations into several target states, including both unitary and nonunitary jurisdictions, and compare how the unitary rules (and all associated compliance costs) affect its after-tax profits. ■

24.9 Subjecting the Corporation's Income to Apportionment

When a multistate organization is domiciled in a high-tax state, some of its apportionable income is eliminated from the tax base in that state. In light of the high tax rate, this may result in significant tax savings. Apportioning income will be especially effective where the income that is attributed to the other states is not subject to income tax. The income removed from the taxing jurisdiction of the domicile state entirely escapes state income taxation when the state to which the income is attributed (1) does not levy a corporate income tax; (2) requires a higher level of activity necessary to subject an out-of-state company to taxation than that adopted by the state of domicile; or (3) is prohibited under Public Law 86–272 from taxing the income (assuming that the domicile state has not adopted a throwback provision). Thus, the right to apportion income may provide substantial benefits because the out-of-state sales are excluded from the numerator of the sales factor and may not be taxed in another state.

However, to acquire the right to apportion its income, the organization must have sufficient activities in, or contacts with, one or more other states. Whether the type and amount of activities and/or contacts are considered adequate is determined by the other states' nexus rules. Therefore, a corporation should analyze its current activities in, and contacts with, other states to determine which, if any, activities or contacts could be redirected so that the corporation gains the right to apportion its income.

EXAMPLE 28
THE BIG PICTURE

Return to the facts of *The Big Picture* on p. 24-2. Most corporate taxpayers consist of a parent corporation and perhaps one or more existing subsidiaries. Given its expansion plans, LocalCo has the opportunity to determine "from scratch" in which states it wants to create nexus for the operations in the multifunction building.

The tax professional needs to offer advice to LocalCo's board of directors as to where the building might be situated and how the operations of any related sales and administrative personnel might be structured in an effort to provide optimal tax consequences. Nexus issues to be considered include the following.

- Is income tax nexus created with the target state?
- Is sales/use tax nexus created with the target state?
- How are the income tax apportionment factors affected by the expansion plans (e.g., whether the target state uses a property factor in the apportionment formula and, if so, how it is weighted)?
- Would a building like that planned by LocalCo receive any special computational treatment for the target state's property factor (e.g., in averaging the building's costs or applying accumulated depreciation)? ■

ETHICS & Equity

Can You Be a Nowhere Adviser?

The intent of much of today's multistate income tax planning is to create so-called *nowhere sales*, such that the income from the transaction is not subject to tax in any state. Suppose, for example, that a sale is made from Georgia (a state with no throwback rule) into Nevada (the place of ultimate destination, but a state with no income tax). No state-level income tax liability is generated.

Is it ethical for a tax adviser to suggest such a strategy? Could you ethically propose the establishment of a sales office in a nonthrowback state, thereby avoiding state income tax on a transaction that is fully taxable under Federal rules?

24.10 Planning with Apportionment Factors

SALES FACTOR

The sales factor often yields the greatest planning opportunities for a multistate corporation. In-state sales include those to purchasers with a destination point in that state; sales delivered to out-of-state purchasers are included in the numerator of the sales factor of the destination state. However, to be permitted to exclude out-of-state sales from the sales factor of the origination state, the seller generally must substantiate the shipment of goods to an out-of-state location. Therefore, the destinations of sales that a corporation makes and the means by which the goods are shipped must be carefully reviewed. The corporation's overall state tax possibly can be reduced by establishing a better record-keeping system or by manipulating the numerator of the sales factor by changing the delivery location or method.

For example, a corporation may substantially reduce its state tax if the delivery location of its sales is changed from a state in which the company is taxed to one in which it is not. This technique may not benefit the corporation if the state in which the sales originate has adopted the throwback rule.

PROPERTY FACTOR

Because most fixed assets are physically stationary in nature, the property factor is not so easily manipulated. Nonetheless, significant tax savings can be realized by establishing a leasing subsidiary in a low- or no-tax state. If the property is located in a state that does not include leased assets in the property factor, the establishment of a subsidiary from which to lease the property eliminates the assets from the property factor in the parent's state.

Permanently idle property generally is excluded from the property factor. Accordingly, a corporation should identify and remove such assets from the property factor to ensure that the factor is not distorted. It is equally important to identify and remove nonbusiness assets from the property factor in states that distinguish between business and nonbusiness income.

EXAMPLE 29

The property factor valuations of Quake Corporation's holdings are as follows.

	State A	Total
Equipment (average historical cost)	$1,200,000	$2,000,000
Accumulated depreciation (average)	800,000	1,000,000

Twenty percent of the equipment in State A is fully depreciated and is idle. Assuming that A includes property in the factor at historical cost, Quake's property factor is 54.55% [($1,200,000 – $240,000 idle property)/($2,000,000 – $240,000)]. If the idle property is not removed from the property factor, Quake's property factor in A is incorrectly computed as 60% ($1,200,000/$2,000,000). ■

PAYROLL FACTOR

The payroll factor provides planning potential where several corporate employees spend substantial periods of time outside their state of employment, or the corporation is able to relocate highly paid employees to low- or no-tax states.

Use of an independent contractor who works for more than one principal can be beneficial under certain circumstances. Since the commissions paid to independent contractors are excluded from the payroll factor, the taxpayer may reduce its payroll factor in a high-tax state.

EXAMPLE 30

Yellow Corporation's total payroll costs are $1.4 million. Of this amount, $1 million was attributable to State A, a high-tax state. Yellow's payroll factor in A is 71.43% ($1,000,000/$1,400,000).

Assuming that $200,000 of the A compensation had been paid to sales representatives and that Yellow replaced its sales force with independent contractors, Yellow's payroll factor in A would be reduced to 66.67% [($1,000,000 – $200,000)/($1,400,000 – $200,000)]. ■

24.11 Sales/Use Taxes on Capital Changes

The tax adviser must be aware of the effects that sales and use taxes may have on a transaction that might otherwise be free from income tax. For example, although the transfer of property to a controlled corporation in exchange for its stock generally is not subject to corporate income taxes, several states provide that such transfers constitute taxable sales for sales and use tax purposes. Similarly, a corporate reorganization may be structured to avoid the imposition of income taxes, but under the statutes of several states, such transfers are considered to be taxable sales and, accordingly, are subject to sales and use taxes.

REFOCUS ON THE BIG PICTURE

MAKING A LOCATION DECISION IN A MULTISTATE TAX ENVIRONMENT

LocalCo holds a competitive advantage with the states and localities in negotiating where its new facility should be located. Politicians like to attract new facilities to their jurisdictions as a way to create construction jobs and to expand the income and sales/use tax base. LocalCo's top management should work with the governors and development executives of the states that are final candidates for the location of the proposed new building.

LocalCo's agenda for these negotiations should include the following items.

- Many states offer targeted tax incentives to attract and retain "clean" businesses like LocalCo. Such incentives might include property tax abatements, research and investment credits, and tax waivers for the state and local income and payroll taxes on new jobs. The company should determine whether it qualifies for any existing incentives. If a state does not currently offer incentives, perhaps its tax law could be amended to provide them.
- LocalCo should also ascertain how the potential locations apply income and sales/use taxes to Internet sales. How aggressive are these tax laws at the present time (e.g., as to the application of P.L. 86–272 and other nexus rules)? What is the level of projected state budget deficits and cash-flow needs, and what are the chances that the laws of the target states will be modified in the near future?
- Currently, LocalCo's manufacturing operations are split between a low-tax state (Alabama) and a high-tax state (California). Under a relocation plan that makes good business sense, nexus might be eliminated with California and shifted to a low-tax jurisdiction. Nevada is a good candidate, given its proximity to the current sportswear location.
- California applies the unitary theory of income taxation. LocalCo should determine whether unitary rules increase or decrease its total tax burden.
- Corporate headquarters currently are located in New York, another high-tax jurisdiction. If the new facility is located in a corporation-favorable, low-tax state, the company should consider moving its headquarters there.
- Relocating the corporate headquarters would also benefit the entity's highly paid executives. The individual income and sales/use tax burden of employees should be a factor in LocalCo's decision.
- In any event, shifting the entity's investment income to a low-tax jurisdiction appears advisable. Use of a passive investment company will carry out this tax planning objective.
- States often assess special taxes on trucking and airport functions and might even apply different income tax apportionment formulas to these operations. LocalCo's tax department and its outside advisers should research these features of the various relevant tax systems to avoid any unexpected surprises.

What If?

If LocalCo did not have a history of strong profitability, some of these state and local tax recommendations might be different. In that case, the company would consider such issues as how a state applies loss and credit carryovers. In addition, if there is no state income tax liability to pay, income tax credits and deductions would be less attractive, so the negotiations might focus on property and payroll taxes instead.

KEY TERMS

Allocate, 24–9
Apportion, 24–9
Combined return, 24–20
Nexus, 24–9
Payroll factor, 24–16
Property factor, 24–18
Public Law 86–272, 24–9
Sales factor, 24–15
Throwback rule, 24–15
UDITPA, 24–13
Unitary theory, 24–20
Water's edge, 24–22

DISCUSSION QUESTIONS

1. **LO.1** You are working with the top management of one of your clients in selecting the U.S. location for a new manufacturing operation. Craft a plan for the CEO to use in discussions with the economic development representatives of several candidate states. In no more than two PowerPoint slides, list some of the tax incentives the CEO should request from a particular state during the negotiations. Be both creative and aggressive in the requests.

ISSUE ID

COMMUNICATIONS

2. **LO.1** Complete the following chart by indicating whether each item is true or false. Explain your answers by reference to the overlap of rules appearing in Federal and most state income tax laws.

	Item	True or False
a.	All of the states and the District of Columbia assess an income tax on entities doing business within the jurisdiction.	________
b.	Federal tax accounting methods, such as LIFO inventory and specific write-off of bad debts, are followed for state income tax purposes.	________
c.	State rules as to which entities can join in a consolidated return match those of Federal law.	________
d.	Some states use Federal taxable income as their income tax base, while others modify this amount or create their own state taxable income.	________
e.	A typical state income tax credit would equal 10% of the costs incurred to purchase and install solar energy panels for an existing factory.	________
f.	The corporate income tax systems of most states can be described as having progressive rate structures.	________
g.	A state that "piggybacks" onto the Federal income tax likely allows the IRS to collect the state corporate income tax on the Federal Form 1120.	________

3. **LO.2** In no more than three PowerPoint slides, list some general guidelines that a taxpayer can use to determine if it has an obligation to file an income or sales/use tax return with a particular state. Address the rules for in-state and out-of-state businesses.

COMMUNICATIONS

4. **LO.2** Josie is a sales representative for Talk2Me, a communications retailer based in Fort Smith, Arkansas. Josie's sales territory is Oklahoma, and she regularly takes day trips into Tulsa to meet with customers. During a typical sales call, Josie takes the customers' current orders and, using her wireless phone, sends the orders to headquarters in Fort Smith for immediate action. Approved orders are shipped from the Little Rock warehouse. Are Josie's sales subject to the Oklahoma corporate income tax?

5. **LO.2** Continue with the facts of Question 4. One of Josie's customers who is facing tight cash flow problems wants to return some defective cell phones. Talk2Me tells Josie to bring the phones back to headquarters. Fearing that she will lose a customer if she does not comply with the request, Josie says, "Let me save you the time and cost of packing and shipping the defective phones. Put them in the trunk of my car and I'll take them back." Does Josie's action change the answer to Question 4?

6. **LO.3** Describe the key concepts of *allocation* and *apportionment* in the taxation of the net income of a multistate business.

7. **LO.3** Indicate whether each of the following items should be *allocated* or *apportioned* by the taxpayer in computing state corporate taxable income. Assume the state follows the general rules of UDITPA.
   a. Profits from sales activities.
   b. Gain on the sale of a plot of land held by a real estate developer.
   c. Gain on the sale of a plot of land held by a manufacturer, on which it may expand its factory.
   d. Rent income received by a manufacturer from the leasing of space to a supplier.
   e. Profits from consulting and other service activities.

8. **LO.3** Regarding the apportionment formula used to compute state taxable income, does each of the following independent characterizations describe a taxpayer that is based in-state or out-of-state?
   a. The sales factor is positively correlated with the payroll, but not the property, factor.
   b. The sales factor is much higher than the property and payroll factors.
   c. The property and payroll factors are much higher than those for other nexus states.
   d. The sales and payroll factors are low, but the property factor is very high.

ISSUE ID

9. **LO.3** The traditional income apportionment formula applied three factors, equally weighted, in determining the taxable income of a business in the state. Now a majority of the states employ a formula in which the sales factor is assigned a greater than one-third weight. Why is such a formula attractive to a state?

10. **LO.5** In computing the corporate income taxes for Iowa-based SpillCo, should a single large sale in August, in which merchandise was shipped to a customer in Kentucky, be included in the Iowa sales factor?

11. **LO.5** Continue with the facts of Question 10. Another large shipment was made in May to a customer in South Dakota, a state that does not impose any corporate income tax. Is this sale to be included in SpillCo's Iowa sales factor?

12. **LO.5** Megan is a telecommuter and works most days from her home in Tennessee. Twice a month she travels to Georgia for a staff meeting at the Atlanta headquarters. In which state's payroll factor should Megan's compensation be included if:
    a. Megan is an employee and is covered by the qualified retirement plan of her Atlanta employer?
    b. Megan works as an independent contractor for several clients, including the Atlanta-based firm?

ISSUE ID

13. **LO.5** You are preparing an analysis of a state's apportionment formula. List at least five questions that you should ask in determining whether an asset that is owned by the taxpayer is to be included in the state's property factor numerator.

14. **LO.6** About 20 states apply a unitary system of business income taxation.
    a. Explain why these states are attracted to the unitary theory and a combined reporting scheme of multistate income taxation.
    b. Is the application of the unitary theory a help or a detriment to the taxpayer?

ISSUE ID

15. **LO.6** State A enjoys a prosperous economy, with high real estate values and compensation levels. State B's economy has seen better days—property values are depressed, and unemployment is higher than in other states. Most consumer goods are priced at about 10% less in B than in A. Both A and B apply unitary income taxation to businesses that operate within the state. Does unitary taxation distort the assignment of taxable income between A and B? Explain.

16. **LO.6** Your client makes the comment, "Unitary corporate income taxation is a bad idea for the business community." Is her characterization correct? Elaborate.

17. **LO.6** Carmina operates a multinational business from Colorado, a state that applies the unitary theory and requires combined state income tax reporting. Most of her off-shore customers are located in the United Kingdom and Germany, where sales prices and property valuations are relatively high. Make a recommendation as to how Carmina might reduce her Colorado income tax liabilities. (*Hint*: There is an attractive unitary tax election that Carmina should consider).

18. **LO.7** Chip and Dale are the only shareholders of VisitTime, a medical transportation firm that is organized as an S corporation. VisitTime makes quarterly estimated income tax payments, related to Chip's stock ownership, to State Q, its headquarters state. Explain.

19. **LO.7** The Quail LLC operates solely in State W. As a pass-through entity, Quail does not pay any W taxes. Evaluate this statement.

20. **LO.8** HernandezCo wants to avoid the creation of sales/use tax nexus with State G. The HernandezCo sales representatives believe that they will lose customers because of an increase in their products' prices, as the company would need to cover its new tax obligations. Are the sales representatives correct to be concerned about their employer's new tax issue? **ISSUE ID**

21. **LO.8** Create a PowerPoint outline describing the major exemptions and exclusions from the sales/use tax base of most states. Use your slides to discuss this topic with your accounting students' club. **COMMUNICATIONS**

22. **LO.8** List three or more taxes, other than the income and sales/use tax, that a state or local jurisdiction might levy.

23. **LO.2, 9** Your client, Ecru Limited, is considering an expansion of its sales operations, but it fears adverse resulting tax consequences. Write a memo for the tax research file identifying the planning opportunities presented by the ability of a corporation to terminate or create income tax nexus. Be certain to discuss the *Wrigley* case in your analysis. **COMMUNICATIONS**

24. **LO.9** As the director of the multistate tax planning department of a consulting firm, you are developing a brochure to highlight the services it can provide. Part of the brochure is a list of five or so key techniques that clients can use to reduce state income tax liabilities. Develop this list for the brochure. **COMMUNICATIONS**

25. **LO.9** Continuing with Problem 24, provide two or three bullet points containing planning ideas relating to a client's liability for a capital stock tax. **COMMUNICATIONS**

PROBLEMS

26. **LO.1** Use Figure 24.1 to compute Beta Corporation's State F taxable income for the year.

Addition modifications	$19,000
Allocated income (total)	15,000
Allocated income (State F)	3,000
Allocated income (State G)	12,000
Tax credits	80
Federal taxable income	90,000
Subtraction modifications	15,000
Apportionment percentage	40%
Tax rate	5%

27. **LO.1** Use Figure 24.1 to provide the required information for Warbler Corporation, whose Federal taxable income totals $10 million.

Warbler apportions 60% of its business income to State C. Warbler generates $3 million of nonbusiness income each year, and 20% of that income is allocated to C. Applying the state income tax modifications, Warbler's total business income this year is $9 million.

a. How much of Warbler's business income does State C tax?
b. How much of Warbler's nonbusiness income does State C tax?
c. Explain your results.

28. **LO.1** For each of the following independent cases, indicate whether the circumstances call for an addition modification (*A*), a subtraction modification (*S*), or no modification (*N*) in computing state taxable income. Then indicate the amount of any modification. The starting point in computing State Q taxable income is the year's Federal taxable income, before any deduction for net operating losses.

a. Federal cost recovery = $10,000, and Q cost recovery = $15,000.
b. Federal cost recovery = $15,000, and Q cost recovery = $10,000.
c. Federal income taxes paid = $30,000.
d. Refund received from last year's Q income taxes = $3,000.
e. Local property taxes, deducted on the Federal return as a business expense = $7,000.
f. Interest income from holding U.S. Treasury bonds = $20,000.
g. Interest income from holding Q revenue anticipation bonds = $3,000.
h. An asset was sold for $18,000; its purchase price was $20,000. Accumulated Federal cost recovery = $11,000, and accumulated Q cost recovery = $8,000.
i. Dividend income received from State R corporation = $10,000, subject to a Federal dividends received deduction of 70%.

29. **LO.1** Perk Corporation is subject to tax only in State A. Perk generated the following income and deductions.

Federal taxable income	$200,000
State A income tax expense	10,000
Refund of State A income tax	3,000
Depreciation allowed for Federal tax purposes	300,000
Depreciation allowed for state tax purposes	120,000

Federal taxable income is the starting point in computing A taxable income. State income taxes are not deductible for A tax purposes. Determine Perk's A taxable income.

30. **LO.1** Flip Corporation is subject to tax only in State X. Flip generated the following income and deductions. State income taxes are not deductible for X income tax purposes.

Sales	$4,000,000
Cost of sales	2,800,000
State X income tax expense	200,000
Depreciation allowed for Federal tax purposes	400,000
Depreciation allowed for state tax purposes	300,000
Interest income on Federal obligations	50,000
Interest income on X obligations	30,000
Expenses related to carrying X obligations	10,000

a. The starting point in computing the X income tax base is Federal taxable income. Derive this amount.
b. Determine Flip's X taxable income, assuming that interest on X obligations is exempt from X income tax.
c. Determine Flip's X taxable income, assuming that interest on X obligations is subject to X income tax.

31. **LO.5** Dillman Corporation has nexus in States A and B. Dillman's activities for the year are summarized below.

	State A	State B	Total
Sales	$1,000,000	$ 600,000	$1,600,000
Property			
Average cost	500,000	300,000	800,000
Average accumulated depreciation	(300,000)	(100,000)	(400,000)
Payroll	2,500,000	500,000	3,000,000
Rent expense	10,000	25,000	35,000

Determine the apportionment factors for A and B, assuming that A uses a three-factor apportionment formula under which sales, property (net depreciated basis), and payroll are equally weighted, and B employs a single-factor formula that consists solely of sales. State A has adopted the UDITPA with respect to the inclusion of rent payments in the property factor.

32. **LO.5** Assume the facts of Problem 31, except that A uses a single-factor apportionment formula that consists solely of sales, and B uses a three-factor apportionment formula that equally weights sales, property (at historical cost), and payroll. State B does not include rent payments in the property factor.

33. **LO.5** Assume the facts of Problem 31, except that both states employ a three-factor formula, under which sales are double weighted. The basis of the property factor in A is historical cost, while the basis of this factor in B is the net depreciated basis. Neither A nor B includes rent payments in the property factor.

34. **LO.5** McKay Corporation operates in two states, as indicated below. This year's operations generated $300,000 of apportionable income.

	State A	State B	Total
Sales	$600,000	$400,000	$1,000,000
Property	300,000	300,000	600,000
Payroll	200,000	50,000	250,000

Compute McKay's State A taxable income, assuming that State A apportions income based on a:

a. Three-factor formula, equally weighted.
b. Double-weighted sales factor.
c. Sales factor only.

35. **LO.5, 9** State E applies a throwback rule to sales, while State F does not. State G has not adopted an income tax to date. Orange Corporation, headquartered in E, reported the following sales for the year. All of the goods were shipped from Orange's E manufacturing facilities. Determine its sales factor in those states. Comment on Orange's location strategy, using only your tax computations.

DECISION MAKING

Customer	Customer's Location	This Year's Sales
ShellTell, Inc.	E	$ 75,000,000
Tourists, Ltd.	F	40,000,000
PageToo Corp.	G	100,000,000
U.S. Department of Interior	All 50 states	35,000,000
Total		$250,000,000

36. **LO.5, 9** Quinn Corporation is subject to tax in States G, H, and I. Quinn's compensation expense includes the following.

DECISION MAKING

	State G	State H	State I	Total
Salaries and wages for nonofficers	$200,000	$400,000	$100,000	$ 700,000
Officers' salaries	–0–	–0–	500,000	500,000
Total				$1,200,000

Officers' salaries are included in the payroll factor for G and I, but not for H. Compute Quinn's payroll factors for G, H, and I. Comment on your results.

37. **LO.5** Kim Corporation, a calendar year taxpayer, has manufacturing facilities in States A and B. A summary of Kim's property holdings follows.

	Beginning of Year		
	State A	State B	Total
Inventory	$ 300,000	$ 200,000	$ 500,000
Plant and equipment	2,500,000	1,500,000	4,000,000
Accumulated depreciation: plant and equipment	(1,000,000)	(600,000)	(1,600,000)
Land	600,000	1,000,000	1,600,000
Rental property*	900,000	300,000	1,200,000
Accumulated depreciation: rental property	(200,000)	(90,000)	(290,000)

	End of Year		
	State A	State B	Total
Inventory	$ 400,000	$ 150,000	$ 550,000
Plant and equipment	2,500,000	1,200,000	3,700,000
Accumulated depreciation: plant and equipment	(1,200,000)	(650,000)	(1,850,000)
Land	600,000	1,200,000	1,800,000
Rental property*	950,000	300,000	1,250,000
Accumulated depreciation: rental property	(250,000)	(100,000)	(350,000)

*Unrelated to regular business operations.

Determine Kim's property factors for the two states, assuming that the statutes of both A and B provide that average historical cost of business property is to be included in the property factor.

38. **LO.5** Assume the facts of Problem 37, except that nonbusiness income is apportionable in B.

DECISION MAKING

39. **LO.5, 9** Crate Corporation, a calendar year taxpayer, has established nexus with numerous states. On December 3, Crate sold one of its two facilities in State X. The cost of this facility was $800,000.

On January 1, Crate owned property with a cost of $3 million, $1.5 million of which was located in X. On December 31, Crate owned property with a cost of $2.5 million, $700,000 of which was located in X.

X law allows the use of average annual or monthly cost amounts in determining the property factor. If Crate wants to minimize the property factor in X, which method should be used to determine the property factor there?

DECISION MAKING

COMMUNICATIONS

40. **LO.6, 9** True Corporation, a wholly owned subsidiary of Trumaine Corporation, generated a $400,000 taxable loss in its first year of operations. True's activities and sales are restricted to State A, which imposes an 8% income tax. In the same year, Trumaine's taxable income is $1 million. Trumaine's activities and sales are restricted to State B, which imposes an 11% income tax. Both states use a three-factor apportionment formula that equally weights sales, payroll, and property, and both require a unitary group to file on a combined basis. Sales, payroll, and average property for each corporation are as follows.

	True Corporation	Trumaine Corporation	Total
Sales	$2,500,000	$4,000,000	$6,500,000
Property	1,000,000	2,500,000	3,500,000
Payroll	500,000	1,500,000	2,000,000

True and Trumaine have been found to be members of a unitary business.

a. Determine the overall state income tax for the unitary group.
b. Determine aggregate state income tax for the entities if they were nonunitary.
c. Incorporate this analysis in a letter to Trumaine's board of directors. Corporate offices are located at 1234 Mulberry Lane, Chartown, AL 35298.

41. **LO.6** Chang Corporation is part of a three-corporation unitary business. The group has a water's edge election in effect with respect to unitary State Q. State B does not apply the unitary concept with respect to its corporate income tax laws. Nor does Despina, a European country to which Saldez paid a $4 million value added tax this year.

Saldez was organized in Despina and conducts all of its business there. Given the summary of operations that follows, determine Chang's and Elena's sales factors in B and Q.

Corporation	Customer's Location	Sales
Chang	B	$20,000,000
	Q	60,000,000
Elena	Q	20,000,000
Saldez	Despina	40,000,000

42. **LO.7** Hernandez, which has been an S corporation since inception, is subject to tax in States Y and Z. On Schedule K of its Federal Form 1120S, Hernandez reported ordinary income of $500,000 from its business, taxable interest income of $10,000, capital loss of $30,000, and $40,000 of dividend income from a corporation in which it owns 30%.

COMMUNICATIONS

Both states apportion income by use of a three-factor formula that equally weights sales, payroll, and the average cost of property; both states treat interest and dividends as business income. In addition, both Y and Z follow Federal provisions with respect to the determination of taxable income for a corporation. Y recognizes S status, but Z does not. Based on the following information, write a memo to the shareholders of Hernandez, detailing the amount of taxable income on which Hernandez will pay tax in Y and Z. Hernandez corporate offices are located at 5678 Alabaster Circle, Koopville, KY 47697.

	State Y	State Z
Sales	$1,000,000	$800,000
Property (average cost)	500,000	100,000
Payroll	800,000	200,000

43. **LO.8** Using the following information from the books and records of Grande Corporation, determine Grande's total sales that are subject to State C's sales tax. Grande operates a retail hardware store.

Sales to C consumers, general merchandise	$1,100,000
Sales to C consumers, crutches and other medical supplies	245,000
Sales to consumers in State D, via mail order	80,000
Purchases from suppliers	55,000

44. **LO.8** Indicate for each transaction whether a sales (*S*) or use (*U*) tax applies or whether the transaction is nontaxable (*N*). Where the laws vary among states, assume that the most common rules apply. All taxpayers are individuals.
   a. A resident of State A purchases an automobile in A.
   b. A resident of State A purchases groceries in A.
   c. A resident of State B purchases an automobile in A.
   d. A charity purchases office supplies in A.
   e. An A resident purchases in B an item that will be in the inventory of her business.

45. **LO.5, 9** Dread Corporation operates in a high-tax state. The firm asks you for advice on a plan to outsource administrative work done in its home state to independent contractors. This work now costs the company $750,000 in wages and benefits. Dread's total payroll for the year is $5 million, of which $4 million is for work currently done in the home state.

DECISION MAKING

46. **LO.9** Prepare a PowerPoint presentation (maximum of six slides) entitled "Planning Principles for Our Multistate Clients." The slides will be used to lead a 20-minute discussion with colleagues in the corporate tax department. Keep the outline general, but assume that your colleagues have clients operating in at least 15 states. Address only income tax issues.

ISSUE ID

COMMUNICATIONS

RESEARCH PROBLEMS

INTERNET *activity*

Use the tax resources of the Internet to address the following questions. Do not restrict your search to the Web, but include a review of newsgroups and general reference materials, practitioner sites and resources, primary sources of the tax law, chat rooms and discussion groups, and other opportunities.

COMMUNICATIONS

Research Problem 1. Send an e-mail message to the secretary of revenue for your home state, proposing adoption of one of the following provisions that does not currently exist in your state.

a. Increase the apportionment weight for the sales factor.
b. Exempt computer and communications technology from the apportionment weight for the property factor.
c. Adopt a throwback rule for the sales factor.
d. Subject advertising expenditures to the sales/use tax.
e. Allow an income tax credit for 20% of the cost of in-state construction projects that are substantially completed within the next 18 months.
f. Tax the income of a passive investment company set up by a domestic taxpayer.
g. Add a "nexus team" to find taxpayers operating in your state, but based in Ohio, Illinois, or Arizona.
h. Adopt the definitions and other rules of the Streamlined Sales Tax Project.
i. Allow an income tax credit for film and television producers equal to 30% of in-state expenditures.
j. Apply a tax on S corporations operating in the state, equal to 2% of the entity's hypothetical Subchapter C taxable income.
k. Convert the corporate income tax to a tax on gross receipts, in an effort to tax the profits of passive investment companies owned by in-state parent entities.

COMMUNICATIONS

Research Problem 2. Many states offer a tax credit for expenditures made in-state for new computing and energy-saving equipment. For your state and one of its neighbors, summarize in a table three of the tax incentives offered through the income, sales, or property tax structure. In your table, list at least the following. E-mail your table to others in your course.

- Name of the credit, deduction, exemption, etc.
- Who qualifies for the incentive (e.g., corporations, individuals, partnerships).
- Computational base for the incentive (e.g., dollars spent).
- Rate of the credit or deduction.
- Minimums, maximums, and other limitations that apply to the incentive amount.

COMMUNICATIONS

Research Problem 3. Use **taxsites.com** or some other index to find a state/local tax organization (e.g., the Committee on State Taxation). Read its current newsletter. In an e-mail to your instructor, summarize a major article at the site. Look especially for articles on one of these topics.

- Judicial and legislative developments concerning the income taxation of intangible income (e.g., trademark royalties).
- Legislation applying a physical-presence test as the exclusive definition of nexus at the Federal level or for your state's income or sales/use tax.
- Responses by the states to the economic downturn (e.g., more aggressive enforcement, new taxes and fees, installment options for the late payment of taxes and penalties).
- Incidence of state/local tax payments (i.e., how much of the total tax collections are paid by individuals, corporations, out-of-state businesses).
- The positive or negative "business tax climate" of your state and its neighbors, as measured by two or more policy centers or think tanks, and any measurable trends in the climate over the last 20 years.
- Attempts by the legislatures of your state and its neighbors to add advertising services to the sales/use tax base.
- Limitations on the taxpayer's ability to carry back net operating losses in computing your state's corporate taxable income.

CHAPTER

25

Taxation of International Transactions

LEARNING OBJECTIVES

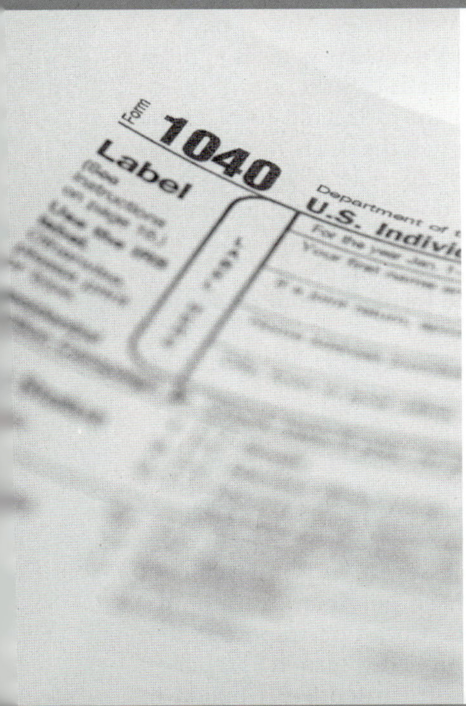

After completing Chapter 25, you should be able to:

LO.1

Explain the framework underlying the U.S. taxation of cross-border transactions.

LO.2

Understand the interaction between Internal Revenue Code provisions and tax treaties.

LO.3

Apply the rules for sourcing income and deductions into U.S. and foreign categories.

LO.4

Explain how foreign currency exchange affects the tax consequences of international transactions.

LO.5

Work with the U.S. tax provisions affecting U.S. persons earning foreign-source income, including the rules relating to cross-border asset transfers, antideferral provisions, and the foreign tax credit.

LO.6

Apply the U.S. tax provisions concerning nonresident alien individuals and foreign corporations.

LO.7

Identify tax planning strategies in an international setting.

OUTLINE

For the latest in changes to tax legislation, visit **www.cengage.com/taxation/swft.**

THE BIG PICTURE **Tax Solutions for the Real World**

GOING INTERNATIONAL

VoiceCo, a domestic corporation, designs, manufactures, and sells specialty microphones for use in theaters. All of its activities take place in Florida, although it ships products to customers all over the United States. When it receives some inquiries about its products from foreign customers, VoiceCo decides to test the foreign market and places ads in foreign trade journals. Soon it is taking orders from foreign customers.

VoiceCo is concerned about its potential foreign income tax exposure. Although it has no assets or employees in the foreign jurisdictions, it now is involved in international commerce. Is VoiceCo subject to income taxes in foreign countries? Must it pay U.S. income taxes on the profits from its foreign sales? What if VoiceCo pays taxes to other countries? Does it receive any benefit from these payments on its U.S. tax return?

Suppose that VoiceCo establishes a manufacturing plant in Ireland to meet the European demand for its products. VoiceCo incorporates the Irish operation as VoiceCo-Ireland, a foreign corporation. Ireland imposes only a 12.5 percent tax on VoiceCo-Ireland's profits. So long as VoiceCo-Ireland does not distribute profits to VoiceCo, will the profits escape U.S. taxation? What are the consequences to VoiceCo of being the owner of a so-called controlled foreign corporation? Does it have any reporting requirements with the IRS? **Read the chapter and formulate your response.**

25.1 Overview of International Taxation

LO.1

Explain the framework underlying the U.S. taxation of cross-border transactions.

In today's global business environment, most large businesses are truly international in scope. Consider the most recent financial results of three "all-American" companies: Coca-Cola, Ford Motor Company, and Microsoft. Coca-Cola reported that 70 percent of its total net income is from offshore operations, Ford earned $1.2 billion in pretax profits from non-U.S. operations, and Microsoft earned $15.4 billion in profits (62 percent of its book net income before tax) from operations outside the United States. Honda, a Japanese company, reported that 44 percent of its sales were in North America; Toyota, another Japanese company, earned 29 percent of its net revenues from automobile sales in North America.

Global trade is an integral part of the U.S. economy. In 2009, U.S. exports and imports of goods and services totaled $1.6 trillion and $1.9 trillion, respectively. This international trade creates significant U.S. tax consequences for both U.S. and foreign entities. In the most recent year for which data are available, U.S. corporations reported $402 billion in foreign-source income, paid $112 billion in taxes to foreign governments, and claimed foreign tax credits in excess of $84 billion. Foreign individual recipients reported $69 billion in U.S.-source income subject to withholding and paid $8.4 billion in U.S. taxes. U.S. corporations controlled by foreign owners reported $46 billion in U.S. taxable income.

Cross-border transactions create the need for special tax considerations for both the United States and its trading partners. From a U.S. perspective, international tax laws should promote the global competitiveness of U.S. enterprises and at the same time protect the tax revenue base of the United States. These two objectives sometimes conflict, however. The need to deal with both contributes to the complexity of the rules governing the U.S. taxation of cross-border transactions.

EXAMPLE 1

U.S. persons engage in activities outside the United States for many different reasons. Consider two U.S. corporations that have established sales subsidiaries in foreign countries. Dedalus, Inc., operates in Germany, a high-tax country, because customers demand local attention from sales agents. Mulligan, Inc., operates in the Cayman

FIGURE 25.1 **U.S. Taxation of Cross-Border Transactions**

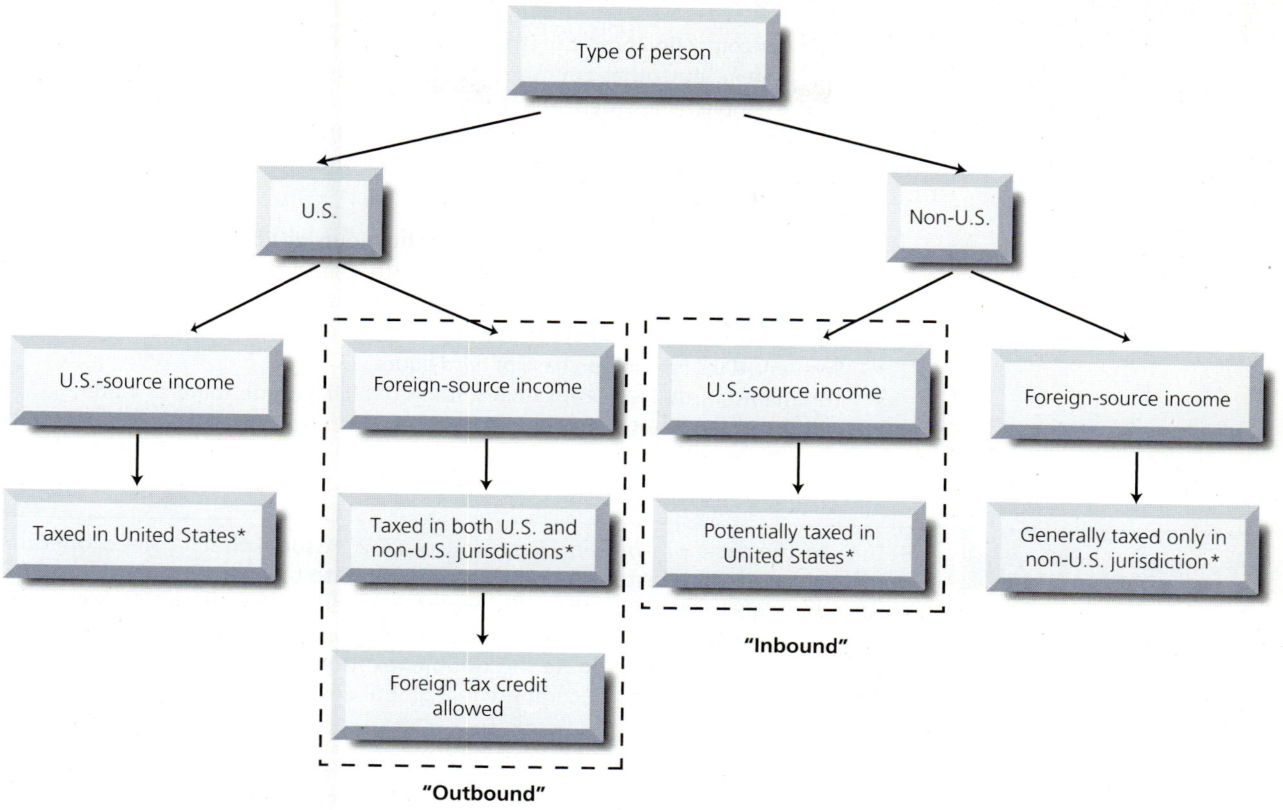

*Income may or may not be subject to tax in the non-U.S. jurisdiction, depending on local country tax law. Some U.S.-source income is exempt from tax in the United States for both U.S. and non-U.S. persons.

Islands, a low-tax country, simply to shift income outside the United States. U.S. tax law must fairly address both situations with the same law. ■

U.S. international tax provisions are concerned primarily with two types of potential taxpayers: U.S. persons earning foreign-source income and foreign persons earning U.S.-source income.[1] U.S. persons earning U.S.-source income are taxed under the purely domestic provisions of the Internal Revenue Code. Foreign persons earning foreign-source income are not within the taxing jurisdiction of the United States (unless this income is somehow connected to a U.S. trade or business). Figure 25.1 illustrates this categorization.

The United States taxes the worldwide income of U.S. taxpayers. Because foreign governments may also tax some of this income, these taxpayers may be subjected to double taxation. Special provisions such as the foreign tax credit can mitigate this problem. For foreign taxpayers, the United States generally taxes only income earned within its borders. The U.S. taxation of cross-border transactions can be organized in terms of "outbound" and "inbound" taxation. **Outbound taxation** refers to the U.S. taxation of foreign-source income earned by U.S. taxpayers. **Inbound taxation** refers to the U.S. taxation of U.S.-source income earned by foreign taxpayers.

[1]The term "person" includes an individual, corporation, partnership, trust, estate, or association. § 7701(a)(1). The terms "domestic" and "foreign" are defined in §§ 7701(a)(4) and (5).

GLOBAL *Tax Issues*

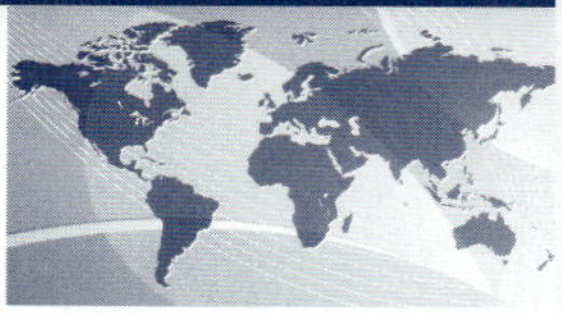

Other Countries' Taxes Can Be Strange, Too

Some observers complain about the strange provisions or workings of the U.S. Federal income tax system, but other countries can be criticized in the same way. Much of Europe, for example, is less dependent on income taxes than the United States and more dependent on transaction and wealth taxes, and these can take unusual forms. A quick survey of taxes around the globe finds the following.

- Australia: 68% tax on cigarette purchases.
- China: 80–100% tax on purchase of autos built outside China.
- Costa Rica: 170% tax on purchase of poultry raised outside the country and 96% tax on purchase of foreign dairy products.
- Japan: 1,000% tax on purchase of rice grown outside the country.
- Sweden: 400% tax on purchase of hard liquor.
- Turkmenistan: 100% tax on luxury items, which include mineral water, cotton mittens, saws, blankets, pillows, and mattresses.

EXAMPLE 2
THE BIG PICTURE

Return to the facts of *The Big Picture* on p. 25-2. Assume that VoiceCo operates an unincorporated manufacturing branch in Singapore to take advantage of local materials and low labor costs. This branch income is taxed in the United States as part of VoiceCo's worldwide income, but it also is taxed in Singapore. Without the availability of a foreign tax credit to mitigate this double taxation, VoiceCo would suffer an excessive tax burden and could not compete in a global environment. ■

EXAMPLE 3
THE BIG PICTURE

Return to the facts of *The Big Picture* on p. 25-2. VoiceCo's major competitor is a Swiss-based foreign corporation with operations in the United States. Although not a U.S. person, the Swiss competitor is taxed in the United States on its U.S.-source business income. If the Swiss competitor could operate free of U.S. tax, VoiceCo would face a serious competitive disadvantage. ■

25.2 Tax Treaties

LO.2
Understand the interaction between Internal Revenue Code provisions and tax treaties.

The U.S. tax rules governing cross-border transactions are based on both the Internal Revenue Code and **tax treaties**. Tax treaties are bilateral agreements between countries that provide tax relief for those persons covered by the treaties. Tax treaty provisions generally override the treatment otherwise called for under the Internal Revenue Code or foreign tax statutes. Taxpayers should attempt to resolve any conflicts between a treaty and local law. A common way of doing so is to apply the "later-in-time" rule, under which preference is given to whichever is newer, the treaty or the law.

More than 50 income tax treaties between the United States and other countries are in effect (see Exhibit 25.1). These treaties generally provide *taxing rights* with regard to the taxable income of residents of one treaty country who have income sourced in the other treaty country. For the most part, neither country is prohibited from taxing the income of its residents. The treaties generally give one country primary taxing rights and require the other country to allow a credit for the taxes paid on the twice-taxed income.

EXAMPLE 4

ForCo, Ltd., a resident of a foreign country with which the United States has an income tax treaty, earns income attributable to a permanent establishment (e.g., place of business) in the United States. Under the treaty, the United States has primary taxing rights with regard to this income. The other country can also require that the income be included in gross income and can subject the income to its income tax, but it must allow a credit for the taxes paid to the United States on the income. ■

FINANCIAL DISCLOSURE *Insights*

Effective Tax Strategies Using Overseas Operations

In a global economy, publicly traded business entities can operate in many taxing jurisdictions. For instance, General Electric reports that it files current-year tax returns with more than 250 countries, amounting to over 7,000 income tax returns at the Federal and local levels worldwide. Note that this tax activity does not take into account the sales, value added, property, and other tax returns that are required by the U.S. states and localities!

The financial reports of profitable U.S. companies indicate that overseas operations can produce tax benefits of their own, not taking into account the effects of increased market share and financial stability. For instance, the trucking firm Ryder Systems recently reported current tax refunds of about $235,000 and deferred tax savings of about $500,000 on non-U.S. profits of about $11.5 million. In a recent period, Eli Lilly reduced its effective tax rate by about one-third due to overseas operations. And General Electric reduced its 2009 effective tax rate to a negative amount because of various income deferrals related to overseas earnings. These deferral techniques are addressed later in the chapter.

Which country receives primary taxing rights usually depends on the residence of the taxpayer or the presence of a permanent establishment in a treaty country to which the income is attributable. Generally, a permanent establishment is a branch, office, factory, workshop, warehouse, or other fixed place of business.

Most U.S. income tax treaties reduce the withholding tax rate on certain items of investment income, such as interest and dividends. For example, treaties with France and Sweden reduce the withholding on portfolio dividends to 15 percent and on certain interest income to zero. Many newer treaties (e.g., with the United Kingdom, Australia, and Japan) provide for no withholding on dividend payments to parent corporations. The United States has developed a Model Income Tax Convention as the starting point for negotiating income tax treaties with other countries.[2]

EXHIBIT 25.1 U.S. Income Tax Treaties in Force as of April 2010

Australia	Iceland	Pakistan
Austria	India	Philippines
Barbados	Indonesia	Poland
Belgium	Ireland	Portugal
Canada	Israel	Romania
China	Italy	Russia
Commonwealth of Independent States*	Jamaica	Slovak Republic
Cyprus	Japan	Slovenia
Czech Republic	Kazakhstan	South Africa
Denmark	Korea, Republic of	Spain
Egypt	Latvia	Sweden
Estonia	Lithuania	Switzerland
Finland	Luxembourg	Thailand
France	Mexico	Trinidad and Tobago
Germany	Morocco	Tunisia
Greece	Netherlands	Turkey
Hungary	New Zealand	United Kingdom
	Norway	Venezuela

*The income tax treaty between the United States and the former Soviet Union now applies to the countries of Armenia, Azerbaijan, Belarus, Georgia, Kyrgyzstan, Moldova, Tajikistan, Turkmenistan, Ukraine, and Uzbekistan. The Commonwealth of Independent States is an association of many of the former constituent republics of the Soviet Union.

[2]Treasury Department Model Income Tax Convention (November 15, 2006).

25.3 Sourcing of Income and Deductions

LO.3

Apply the rules for sourcing income and deductions into U.S. and foreign categories.

The sourcing of income and deductions inside or outside the United States has a direct bearing on a number of tax provisions affecting both U.S. and foreign taxpayers. For example, foreign taxpayers generally are taxed only on income sourced inside the United States, and U.S. taxpayers receive relief from double taxation under the foreign tax credit rules based on their foreign-source income. Accordingly, an examination of sourcing rules is often the starting point in addressing international tax issues.

INCOME SOURCED INSIDE THE UNITED STATES

The determination of the source of income depends on the type of income realized (e.g., income from the sale of property versus income for the use of property). This makes the classification of income an important consideration. Section 861 contains source rules for most types of income.[3]

Interest

Interest income received from the U.S. government, from the District of Columbia, and from noncorporate U.S. residents or domestic corporations is sourced inside the United States. There are a few exceptions to this rule. Certain interest received from a U.S. corporation that earned 80 percent or more of its active business income from foreign sources over the prior three-year period is treated as foreign-source income. Interest received on amounts deposited with a foreign branch of a U.S. corporation is also treated as foreign-source income if the branch is engaged in the commercial banking business.

EXAMPLE 5

John holds a bond issued by Delta, a domestic corporation. For the immediately preceding three tax years, 82% of Delta's gross income has been active foreign business income. The interest income that John receives for the current tax year from Delta is foreign-source income. ■

Dividends

Dividends received from domestic corporations (other than certain U.S. possessions corporations) are sourced inside the United States. Generally, dividends paid by a foreign corporation are foreign-source income. However, if a foreign corporation earned 25 percent or more of its gross income from income effectively connected with a U.S. trade or business for the three tax years immediately preceding the year of the dividend payment, that percentage of the dividend is treated as U.S.-source income.

EXAMPLE 6

Ann receives dividend income from the following corporations for the current tax year.

Amount	Corporation	Effectively Connected U.S. Income for Past Three Years	U.S.-Source Income
$500	Green, domestic	85%	$500
600	Brown, domestic	13%	600
300	Orange, foreign	92%	276

Because Green Corporation and Brown Corporation are domestic corporations, the dividends they pay are U.S.-source income. Orange Corporation is a foreign corporation that earned 92% of its business income over the prior three years from income effectively connected with a U.S. trade or business. Because Orange meets the 25% threshold, 92% of its dividend is U.S. source. ■

[3]Other rules pertaining to the sourcing of income are found in §§ 862–865.

GLOBAL
Tax Issues

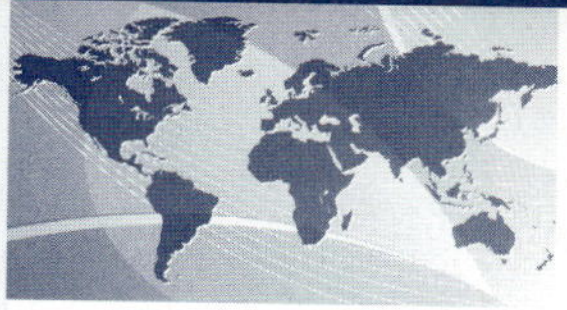

Why the Treaty Process Stalls

The United States has negotiated several income tax treaties that have never been signed or ratified (e.g., with Argentina, Bangladesh, and Brazil). The treaty process sometimes stalls for several reasons.

One is the desire on the part of some less developed countries for a tax-sparing provision in the treaty. In other words, these countries want the United States to allow a foreign tax credit against U.S. taxes even though U.S. companies operating there actually pay no foreign taxes due to local tax reduction agreements (i.e., tax holidays).

Another reason is the exchange of information provision. Some countries, for example, have anonymous bank rules that would preclude the exchange of information. Not long ago, the Parliament of Kazakhstan voted on a provision to eliminate secret bank accounts so that the United States–Kazakhstan income tax treaty could be ratified.

Personal Services Income

The source of income from personal services is determined by the location in which the services are performed (inside or outside the United States). A limited *commercial traveler* exception is available. Under this exception, personal services income must meet all the following requirements to avoid being classified as U.S.-source income.

- The services must be performed by a nonresident alien who is in the United States for 90 days or less during the taxable year.
- The compensation may not exceed $3,000 in total for the services performed in the United States.
- The services must be performed on behalf of:
  - *a nonresident alien, foreign partnership, or foreign corporation that is not engaged in a U.S. trade or business or*
  - *an office or place of business maintained in a foreign country or possession of the United States by an individual who is a citizen or resident of the United States, a domestic partnership, or a domestic corporation.*

EXAMPLE 7

Mark, a nonresident alien, is an engineer employed by a foreign oil company. He spent four weeks in the United States arranging the purchase of field equipment for his company. His salary for the four weeks was $3,500. Even though the oil company is not engaged in a U.S. trade or business, and Mark was in the United States for less than 90 days during the taxable year, the income is U.S.-source income because it exceeds $3,000. ■

The issue of whether income is derived from the performance of personal services is important in determining the income's source. The courts have held that a corporation can perform personal services.[4] In addition, in the absence of capital as an income-producing factor, personal services income can arise even though there is no recipient of the services.[5] If payment is received for services performed partly inside and partly outside the United States, the income must be allocated for source purposes on some reasonable basis that clearly reflects income under the facts and circumstances. The number of days worked in each country is generally acceptable.[6]

[4]See *British Timken Limited*, 12 T.C. 880 (1949), and Rev.Rul. 60–55, 1960–1 C.B. 270.

[5]See *Robida v. Comm.*, 72–1 USTC ¶9450, 29 AFTR 2d 72–1223, 460 F.2d 1172 (CA–9, 1972). The taxpayer was employed in military PXs around the world. He had large slot machine winnings and claimed the foreign earned income exclusion. The IRS challenged the exclusion on the grounds that the winnings were not earned income because there was no recipient of Robida's services. The court, however, found that, in the absence of capital, the winnings were earned income.

[6]Reg. § 1.861–4(b). See *Stemkowski*, 76 T.C. 252 (1981).

Rents and Royalties

The source of income received for the use of tangible property is the country in which the property is located. The source of income received for the use of intangible property (e.g., patents, copyrights, secret processes and formulas) is the country in which the property is used.

Sale or Exchange of Property

Generally, the location of real property determines the source of any income derived from the property. For example, income from the disposition of U.S. real property interests is U.S.-source income.

The source of income from the sale of personal property (assets other than real property) depends on several factors, including the following.

- Whether the property was produced by the seller.
- The type of property sold (e.g., inventory or a capital asset).
- The residence of the seller.

Generally, income, gain, or profit from the sale of personal property is sourced according to the residence of the seller. Income from the sale of purchased inventory, however, is sourced in the country in which the sale takes place.[7]

When the seller has produced the inventory property, the income must be apportioned between the country of production and the country of sale. Gross income is sourced under a 50/50 allocation method unless the taxpayer elects to use the independent factory price (IFP) method or the separate books and records method. The 50/50 method assigns one-half of the inventory profits from export sales to the location of the production assets and one-half to the place of title passage. The IFP method may be elected only where an IFP exists.[8] If the manufacturer or producer regularly sells to wholly independent distributors, this can establish an *independent* factory or production price.

Under § 865, income from the sale of personal property other than inventory is sourced at the residence of the seller unless one of the following exceptions applies.

- Gain on the sale of depreciable personal property is sourced according to prior depreciation deductions to the extent of the deductions. Any excess gain is sourced the same as the sale of inventory.
- Gain on the sale of intangibles is sourced according to prior amortization deductions to the extent of the deductions. Contingent payments, however, are sourced as royalty income.
- Gain attributable to an office or fixed place of business maintained outside the United States by a U.S. resident is foreign-source income.
- Income or gain attributable to an office or fixed place of business maintained in the United States by a nonresident is U.S.-source income.

The sourcing of losses is complicated and depends on the nature of the property. Different rules exist for the disposition of stock versus other personal property.[9]

Transportation and Communication Income

Income from transportation beginning *and* ending in the United States is U.S.-source income. Fifty percent of the income from transportation beginning *or* ending in the United States is U.S.-source income, unless the U.S. point is only an intermediate stop. This rule does not apply to personal services income unless the transportation is between the United States and a possession. Income from space and ocean activities conducted outside the jurisdiction of any country is sourced according to the residence of the person conducting the activity.

[7]§§ 861(a)(6) and 865. The sale is deemed to take place where title passes. See Reg. § 1.861–7(c) regarding title passage. There has been considerable conflict in this area of tax law. See, for example, *Liggett Group, Inc.*, 58 TCM 1167, T.C.Memo. 1990–18.

[8]§ 863(b)(2), Reg. § 1.863–3, and Notice 89–10, 1989–1 C.B. 631.

[9]See Reg. § 1.861–8(e)(7) and Temp.Reg. § 1.865–1T(a)(1). See Reg. §§ 1.865–(2)(a)(1) and (2) regarding the source of losses on the disposition of stock.

TAX *in the NEWS*

Sourcing Income in Cyberspace

The use of the Internet for more and more consumer and business transactions is posing problems for the taxing authorities. Consumers purchase books, music, clothing, and food from online retailers. Businesses negotiate with suppliers via online auctions of products and services. Consultants provide services to their clients over the Internet. Very few transactions do not have a counterpart that takes place in cyberspace. The existing income-sourcing rules were developed long before the existence of the Internet, and taxing authorities are finding it challenging to apply these rules to Internet transactions. Where does a sale take place when the web server is in the Cayman Islands, the seller is in Singapore, and the customer is in Texas? Where is a service performed when all activities take place online? These questions and more must be answered by the United States and its trading partners as e-commerce grows in size and importance.

International communication income derived by a U.S. person is sourced 50 percent in the United States when transmission is between the United States and a foreign country. International communication income derived by foreign persons is foreign-source income unless it is attributable to an office or other fixed place of business in the United States. In that case, it is U.S.-source income.

Software Income

Income from the sale or license of software is sourced depending on how the income is classified. A transfer of software is classified as either the transfer of a copyright (e.g., the right to the computer program itself) or the transfer of a copyrighted article (the right to use a copy of the computer program).[10] If the transfer is considered a transfer of a copyright, the income is sourced using the royalty income rules. If the transfer is considered a transfer of a copyrighted article, the income is treated as resulting from a sale of the article and is sourced based on the personal property sales rules.

INCOME SOURCED OUTSIDE THE UNITED STATES

The provisions for sourcing income outside the United States are not as detailed and specific as those for determining U.S.-source income. Basically, § 862 provides that if interest, dividends, compensation for personal services, income from the use or sale of property, or other income is not U.S.-source income, then it is foreign-source income.

ALLOCATION AND APPORTIONMENT OF DEDUCTIONS

The United States levies a tax on *taxable income.* Deductions and losses, therefore, must be allocated and apportioned between U.S.- and foreign-source gross income to determine U.S.- and foreign-source taxable income. Deductions directly related to an activity or property are allocated to classes of income. This is followed by apportionment between the statutory and residual groupings (e.g., foreign versus domestic) on some reasonable basis.[11] A deduction not definitely related to any class of gross income is ratably allocated to all classes of gross income and apportioned between U.S.- and foreign-source income.

EXAMPLE 8

Ace, Inc., a domestic corporation, has $2 million of gross income and a $50,000 expense, all related to real estate activities. The expense is allocated and apportioned using gross income as a basis as follows.

[10] Reg. § 1.861–18.

[11] Reg. § 1.861–8.

	Gross Income			Apportionment	
	Foreign	U.S.	Allocation	Foreign	U.S.
Sales	$1,000,000	$500,000	$37,500*	$25,000	$12,500**
Rentals	400,000	100,000	12,500	10,000	2,500***
			$50,000	$35,000	$15,000

* $50,000 × ($1,500,000/$2,000,000).
** $37,500 × ($500,000/$1,500,000).
*** $12,500 × ($100,000/$500,000).

If Ace could show that $45,000 of the expense was directly related to sales income, the $45,000 would be allocated to that class of gross income, with the remainder allocated and apportioned ratably based on gross income. ■

Interest expense is allocated and apportioned based on the theory that money is fungible. With limited exceptions, interest expense is attributable to all the activities and property of the taxpayer, regardless of the specific purpose for incurring the debt on which interest is paid. Taxpayers must allocate and apportion interest expense on the basis of assets, using either the fair market value or the tax book value of the assets.[12] Once the fair market value is used, the taxpayer must continue to use this method. Special rules apply in allocating and apportioning interest expense in an affiliated group of corporations.

EXAMPLE 9
THE BIG PICTURE

Return to the facts of *The Big Picture* on p. 25-2. Assume that VoiceCo generates U.S.-source and foreign-source gross income for the current year. VoiceCo's assets (tax book value) are as follows.

Assets generating U.S.-source income	$18,000,000
Assets generating foreign-source income	5,000,000
	$23,000,000

VoiceCo incurs interest expense of $800,000 for the current year. Using the tax book value method, interest expense is apportioned to foreign-source income as follows.

$$\frac{\$5{,}000{,}000 \text{ (foreign assets)}}{\$23{,}000{,}000 \text{ (total assets)}} \times \$800{,}000 = \$173{,}913$$

■

Specific rules also apply to research and development (R & D) expenditures, certain stewardship expenses, legal and accounting fees and expenses, income taxes, and losses. Although U.S. companies incur about 90 percent of their R & D expenditures at U.S. facilities, several billion dollars are spent on foreign R & D each year. The Regulations provide that a portion of a U.S. company's R & D expenditures must be treated as foreign-source expense if the R & D relates to foreign product sales.

TRANSFER PRICING

Taxpayers may be tempted to minimize taxation by manipulating the source of income and the allocation of deductions arbitrarily through **transfer pricing**. This manipulation is more easily accomplished between or among related persons. The IRS uses § 482 to counter such actions. The provision gives the IRS the power to reallocate gross income,

[12] Temp.Reg. § 1.861–10T(b) describes circumstances in which interest expense can be directly allocated to specific debt. This exception to the fungibility concept is limited to cases in which specific property is purchased or improved with nonrecourse debt. Temp.Reg. § 1.861–9T.

deductions, credits, or allowances between or among organizations, trades, or businesses owned or controlled directly or indirectly by the same interests. This can be done whenever the IRS determines that reallocation is necessary to prevent the evasion of taxes or to reflect income more clearly. Section 482 is a "one-edged sword" available only to the IRS. The taxpayer generally cannot invoke it to reallocate income and expenses.[13]

ETHICS & Equity

WHEN CAN 1 + 1 = 3?

Pharma, Inc., a U.S. pharmaceutical company, operates in the United States and in Ireland through a wholly owned Irish subsidiary corporation. Pharma manufactures certain aspects of a drug in the United States at a cost of $50 million and sells this product to its Irish subsidiary for $70 million, producing a $20 million profit in the United States. The Irish subsidiary completes the manufacturing of the drug at a cost of $10 million and sells the final product to unrelated customers in Europe for $85 million, producing a $5 million profit in Ireland [$85 million sales price – $70 million cost of goods sold (purchased inventory) – $10 million additional processing costs]. In the aggregate, Pharma and its Irish subsidiary have produced a product at a cost of $60 million and sold it for $85 million, resulting in $25 million in total profits.

What if the IRS decides that the transfer price of $70 million was too low and should have been $74 million? This would indicate that $24 million of the profit should have been in the United States and $1 million in Ireland. Should the tax authorities in Ireland automatically make the transfer pricing adjustment on their side (i.e., reduce the Irish subsidiary's income to $1 million from $5 million)? What if the IRS and the Irish tax authorities disagree and Pharma and its subsidiary end up paying tax on $29 million in profits ($24 million in the United States and $5 million in Ireland) even though only $25 million of economic profits actually exist? Is this fair to the taxpayer? What recourse should Pharma have when it is caught between two governments that disagree?

EXAMPLE 10

Consider the transaction depicted in Figure 25.2. A U.S. corporation manufactures and sells inventory to an unrelated foreign customer. The sales price for the inventory is $1,000 and the related cost of goods sold (COGS) is $600. The resulting profit of $400 is all taxed to the U.S. corporation, resulting in a $140 U.S. income tax liability ($400 × 35%). If the U.S. corporation has no business presence in the foreign jurisdiction and is merely selling to a customer located there, the foreign government is unlikely to impose any local income tax on the U.S. corporation. Consequently, the total tax burden imposed on the inventory sale is $140.

Suppose instead that the U.S. corporation attempts to reduce its total tax expense by channeling the inventory sale through a foreign subsidiary in the same country as the foreign customer. In this case, because the U.S. corporation controls the foreign subsidiary, it chooses an intercompany sales price (the transfer price) that moves a portion of the profits from the United States to the foreign country.

By selling the inventory it manufactured to its 100%-owned foreign subsidiary for $700, the U.S. corporation reports only $100 of profits and an associated U.S. tax liability of $35. The foreign subsidiary then sells the inventory to the ultimate customer for $1,000 and, with a $700 COGS, earns a $300 profit. In this example, the foreign country imposes only a 10% tax on corporate profits, resulting in a foreign income tax of $30 ($300 × 10%). By using a related foreign entity in a lower-tax jurisdiction, the U.S. corporation has lowered its overall tax liability on the sale from $140 (all U.S.) to $65 ($35 U.S. and $30 foreign).

The critical question is whether the IRS will view the $700 intercompany sales price as the appropriate transfer price. Under § 482, the IRS may question why the foreign corporation deserved to earn $300 of the total $400 profit related to the manufacture and sale of the inventory. In general, the U.S. corporation must document the functions performed by the foreign corporation, the assets it owns that assist in producing the income, or the risks it takes (e.g., credit risk).

[13]Reg. § 1.482–1(a)(3).

FIGURE 25.2 **Transfer Pricing Example**

Sale Without Using Related Party

U.S. Corporation	
Sales revenue	$1,000
COGS	(600)
Profit	$ 400
Tax @ 35%	$ 140

Worldwide Tax Cost	
U.S. tax	$140
Foreign tax	0
Total tax	$140

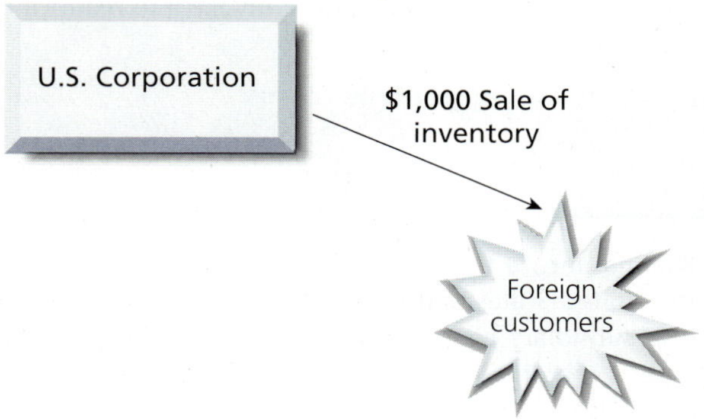

Sale Using Related Party

U.S. Corporation	
Sales revenue	$ 700
COGS	(600)
Profit	$ 100
Tax @ 35%	$ 35

Foreign Corporation	
Sales revenue	$1,000
COGS	(700)
Profit	$ 300
Tax @ 10%	$ 30

Worldwide Tax Cost	
U.S. tax	$35
Foreign tax	30
Total tax	$65

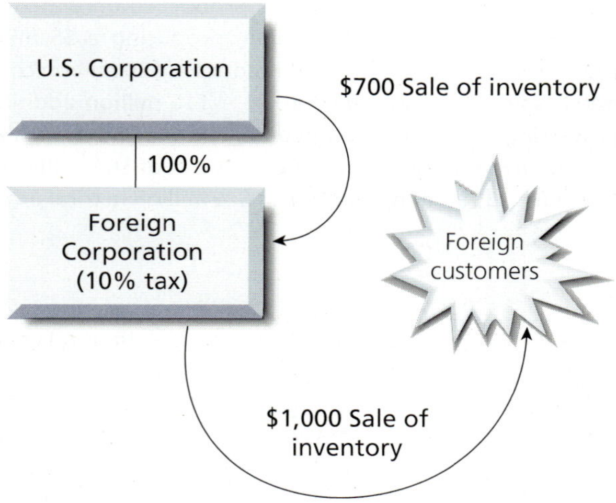

Without documentation of significant functions, assets, or risks of the foreign subsidiary, the IRS will not consider the $300 profit earned by the foreign corporation to be appropriate, and it will adjust the transfer price upward. If the IRS determines that the transfer price should have been, say, $990, then the U.S. corporation reports a $390 profit (with $136.50 U.S. income tax), and the foreign corporation earns a $10 profit (with $1 in foreign income tax). With this change in transfer price, the U.S. corporation does not succeed in transferring a meaningful portion of its profits to the lower-tax jurisdiction and reduces its tax liability by only $2.50. ■

The reach of § 482 is quite broad. The IRS takes the position that a corporation and its sole shareholder who works full-time for the corporation can be treated as two separate trades or businesses for purposes of § 482.[14] Two unrelated shareholders who each owned 50 percent of a corporation were held to be acting in concert for their common good and, thus, together controlled the corporation.[15]

[14] Rev.Rul. 88–38, 1988–1 C.B. 246. But see *Foglesong v. Comm.*, 82–2 USTC ¶9650, 50 AFTR 2d 82–6016, 691 F.2d 848 (CA–7, 1982), *rev'g* 77 T.C. 1102 (1981).

[15] See *B. Forman Co., Inc. v. Comm.*, 72–1 USTC ¶9182, 29 AFTR 2d 72–403, 453 F.2d 1144 (CA–2, 1972).

TAX in the NEWS

APAs Reduce Uncertainty in Transfer Pricing Disputes

The first Advance Pricing Agreement (APA) was approved in January 1991. The IRS reports that 904 APAs have been executed and 352 others are in negotiation. The taxpayers participating in the APA program come from many different industries. The five most represented industries are financial institutions, computer items and software, chemicals, transportation equipment, and electrical equipment.

Only 10 percent of the largest taxpayers involved in international intercompany transactions have participated in the APA process. However, the volume of intercompany transactions represented by these taxpayers constitutes over 40 percent of the total dollar value of international intercompany transactions. About 10 percent of all active APA cases involve small businesses with annual gross income under $200 million.

The APA process is not simple or quick. The IRS reports that the APAs approved in 2009 took an average of 38 months to complete.

Source: Announcement and Report Concerning Advance Pricing Agreements, March 29, 2010 (Announcement 2010–21).

In applying § 482, an arm's length price must be determined to assign the correct profits to related entities. Several alternative methods can be used in determining an arm's length price on the sale of tangible or intangible property. The major problem with most pricing methods is that uncontrolled comparable transactions are needed as a benchmark.

An accuracy-related penalty of 20 percent is provided by § 6662 for net § 482 transfer price adjustments (changes in profit allocations by the IRS) for a taxable year that exceed the lesser of $5 million or 10 percent of the taxpayer's gross receipts. In addition, there is a 40 percent penalty for "gross misstatements."

As an aid to reducing pricing disputes, the IRS initiated the Advance Pricing Agreement (APA) program whereby the taxpayer can propose a transfer pricing method for certain international transactions. The taxpayer provides relevant data, which are then evaluated by the IRS. If accepted, the APA provides a safe-harbor transfer pricing method for the taxpayer. Apple Computer, Inc., accomplished the first successful APA submission in 1991.

25.4 Foreign Currency Transactions

LO.4

Explain how foreign currency exchange affects the tax consequences of international transactions.

The relative value of a foreign currency and the U.S. dollar is described by the foreign exchange rate. Changes in this rate affect the dollar value of foreign property held by the taxpayer, the dollar value of foreign debts, and the dollar amount of gain or loss on a transaction denominated in a foreign currency. Almost every international tax issue requires consideration of currency exchange implications.

EXAMPLE 11

Dress, Inc., a domestic corporation, purchases merchandise for resale from Fiesta, Inc., a foreign corporation, for 50,000K (a foreign currency). On the date of purchase, 1K is equal to $1 U.S. (1K:$1). At this time, the account payable is $50,000. On the date of payment by Dress (the foreign exchange date), the exchange rate is 1.25K:$1. In other words, the foreign currency has been devalued in relation to the U.S. dollar, and Dress will pay Fiesta 50,000K, which will cost Dress only $40,000. Dress must record the purchase of the merchandise at $50,000 and recognize a foreign currency gain of $10,000 ($50,000 − $40,000). ■

In recent years, U.S. currency abroad has amounted to more than 50 percent of the U.S. currency in circulation. Taxpayers may find it necessary to translate amounts denominated in foreign currency into U.S. dollars for any of the following purposes.

- Purchase of goods, services, and property.
- Sale of goods, services, and property.

CONCEPT SUMMARY 25.1

Recognition of Foreign Exchange Gain or Loss

Transaction	Date of Recognition
Purchase or sale of inventory or business asset	Date of disposition of foreign currency
Branch profits	Remittance of branch profits
Subpart F income	Receipt of previously taxed income (accumulated E & P)
Dividend from untaxed current or accumulated E & P	No exchange gain or loss to recipient

- Collection of foreign receivables.
- Payment of foreign payables.
- Foreign tax credit calculations.
- Recognition of income or loss from foreign branch activities.

The foreign currency exchange rates, however, have no effect on the transactions of a U.S. person who arranges all international transactions in U.S. dollars.

EXAMPLE 12

Sellers, Inc., a domestic corporation, purchases goods from Rose, Ltd., a foreign corporation, and pays for these goods in U.S. dollars. Rose then exchanges the U.S. dollars for the currency of the country in which it operates. Sellers has no foreign exchange considerations with which to contend. If instead Rose required Sellers to pay for the goods in a foreign currency, Sellers would have to exchange U.S. dollars to obtain the foreign currency to make payment. If the exchange rate changed from the date of purchase to the date of payment, Sellers would have a foreign currency gain or loss on the currency exchange. ■

The following concepts are important when dealing with the tax aspects of foreign exchange.

- Foreign currency is treated as property other than money.
- Gain or loss on the exchange of foreign currency is considered separately from the underlying transaction (e.g., the purchase or sale of goods).
- No gain or loss is recognized until a transaction is closed.

TAX ISSUES

The following major tax issues must be considered when dealing with foreign currency exchange.

- The date of recognition of any gain or loss (see Concept Summary 25.1).
- The source (U.S. or foreign) of the foreign currency gain or loss.
- The character of the gain or loss (ordinary or capital).

FUNCTIONAL CURRENCY

The Code generally adopted the Financial Accounting Standards Board standard on foreign currency translation. ASC 830 (SFAS 52) introduced the **functional currency** approach. For accounting and tax purposes, the currency of the economic environment in which the foreign entity operates generally is used as the monetary unit to measure gains and losses.

Under § 985, all income tax determinations are to be made in the taxpayer's functional currency. A taxpayer's default functional currency is the U.S. dollar. In most cases, a **qualified business unit (QBU)** operating in a foreign country uses that country's

FINANCIAL DISCLOSURE *Insights*

TAX RATES IN NON-U.S. JURISDICTIONS

When Congress changes the U.S. tax law, it seldom applies tax rate changes retroactively or prospectively—the rate changes almost always are applicable on the date that the tax bill is effective. Other countries do not always enact tax law changes in this way. Sometimes a country will adopt a schedule of tax rate increases or decreases to go into effect over a period of years.

Tax legislation of this sort can have an important effect on the U.S. taxpayer's effective tax rate as computed in the footnotes to the financial statements. When another country adopts prospective tax rate changes, an increase or decrease in the effective tax rate is reported with respect to the deferred tax accounts for GAAP purposes. Specifically, the effective tax rate decreases when a tax rate cut is scheduled in a country that does business with the U.S. party, and the rate increases when a tax rate increase is adopted for future tax years. In the last three decades, most developed countries have been cutting business income tax rates.

A recent effective tax rate computation for Berkshire Hathaway showed a decrease of about one percentage point due to scheduled tax rate cuts in Germany and the United Kingdom. Allied Healthcare Products showed a similar adjustment of about two percentage points. In contrast, the effective tax rate increased by about one percentage point for American Travellers Life Insurance Company.

currency as its functional currency. A QBU is a separate and clearly identified unit of a taxpayer's trade or business (e.g., a foreign branch). An individual is not a QBU; however, a trade or business conducted by an individual may be a QBU.[16]

BRANCH OPERATIONS

When a foreign branch (QBU) uses a foreign currency as its functional currency, profit or loss is computed in the foreign currency each year and translated into U.S. dollars for tax purposes. The entire amount of profit or loss, not taking remittances into account, is translated using the average exchange rate for the taxable year. Exchange gain or loss is recognized on remittances from the QBU. The U.S. dollar amount of the remittance at the exchange rate in effect on the date of remittance is compared with the U.S. dollar value (basis pool) of the equity pool of the branch. The rules outline a "foreign exchange exposure pool method" to compute gain or loss.[17] This exchange gain or loss is ordinary, and it is sourced according to the income to which the remittance is attributable.

DISTRIBUTIONS FROM FOREIGN CORPORATIONS

An actual distribution of E & P from a foreign corporation is included in income by the U.S. recipient at the exchange rate in effect on the date of distribution.[18] Thus, no exchange gain or loss is recognized. Deemed dividend distributions under Subpart F (discussed later in the chapter) are translated at the average exchange rate for the corporation's tax year to which the deemed distribution is attributable. Exchange gain or loss can result when an actual distribution of this previously taxed income is made.

FOREIGN TAXES

For purposes of the foreign tax credit, foreign taxes accrued generally are translated at the average exchange rate in effect for the tax year to which the taxes relate. Under exceptions to this rule, foreign taxes must be translated at the exchange rate in effect when the foreign taxes were paid.[19] If foreign taxes are paid within two years of accrual, and if they differ from the accrued amount merely because of currency exchange fluctuation, no redetermination is required, even though the actual dollar value paid may differ from the accrued amount. In other cases, when the taxes paid differ from the amount accrued, a redetermination is required.

[16] Reg. § 1.989(a)–1(b).

[17] Prop.Reg. §§ 1.987–1 and –2.

[18] § 986(b).

[19] §§ 986(a)(1)(B) and (C).

EXAMPLE 13
THE BIG PICTURE

Return to the facts of *The Big Picture* on p. 25-2. Assume that VoiceCo operates a foreign branch. Foreign taxes attributable to branch income amount to 5,000K (a foreign currency). The taxes are paid within two years of being accrued. The average foreign exchange rate for the tax year to which the foreign taxes relate is .5K:$1. On the date the taxes are paid, the rate is .6K:$1. No redetermination is required, and VoiceCo reports foreign taxes of $10,000 for purposes of the foreign tax credit. ■

25.5 U.S. Persons with Foreign Income

LO.5

Work with the U.S. tax provisions affecting U.S. persons earning foreign-source income, including the rules relating to cross-border asset transfers, antideferral provisions, and the foreign tax credit.

U.S. taxpayers often "internationalize" gradually over time. A U.S. business may operate on a strictly domestic basis for several years, then explore foreign markets by exporting its products abroad, and later license its products to a foreign manufacturer or enter into a joint venture with a foreign partner. If its forays into foreign markets are successful, the U.S. business may create a foreign subsidiary and move a portion of its operations abroad by establishing a sales or manufacturing facility.

A domestically controlled foreign corporation can have significant U.S. tax consequences for the U.S. owners, and any U.S. taxpayer paying foreign taxes must consider the foreign tax credit provisions. Foreign businesses likewise enter the U.S. market in stages. In either case, each step generates increasingly significant international tax consequences. Figure 25.3 shows a typical timeline for "going global."

Under § 911, qualified U.S. citizens and residents may exclude a limited amount of foreign earned income and a housing allowance from their U.S. taxable income. See Chapter 5 for more information on the § 911 exclusion.

EXPORT PROPERTY

The easiest way for a U.S. enterprise to engage in global commerce is simply to sell U.S.-produced goods and services abroad. These sales can be conducted with little or no foreign presence and allow the business to explore foreign markets without making costly financial commitments to foreign operations.

The U.S. tax consequences of simple export sales are straightforward. All such income is taxed in the United States to the U.S. taxpayer. Whether foreign taxes must be paid on this export income depends on the particular law of the foreign jurisdiction and whether the U.S. taxpayer is deemed to have a foreign business presence there (often called a "permanent establishment"). In many cases, such export income is not taxed by a foreign jurisdiction.

CROSS-BORDER ASSET TRANSFERS

As part of "going international," a U.S. taxpayer may decide to transfer assets outside the United States so that any foreign business will be conducted outside

FIGURE 25.3 Global Activities Timeline

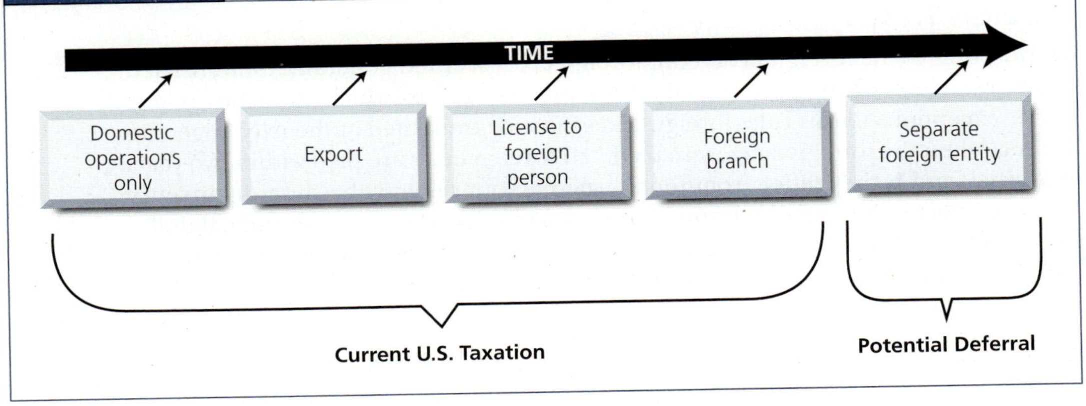

FIGURE 25.4 **Taxation of Cross-Border Asset Transfers**

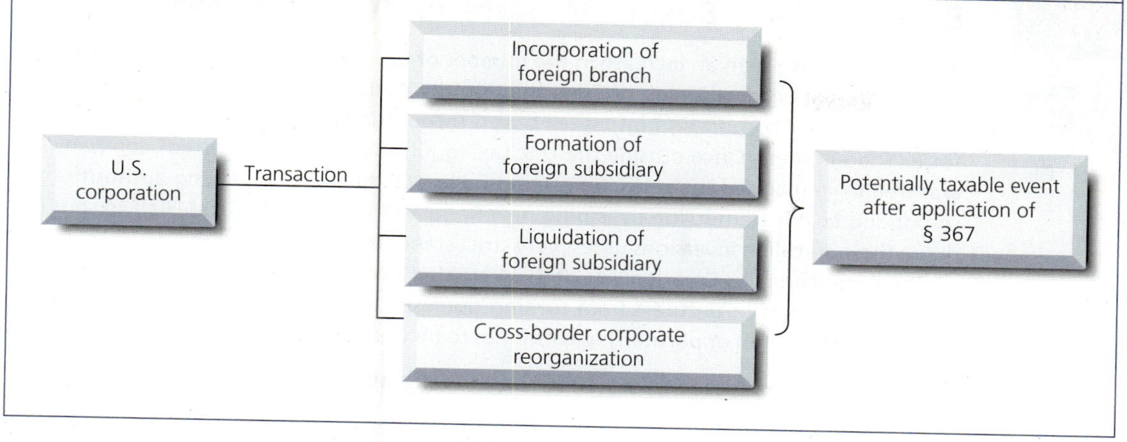

the U.S. tax jurisdiction. To originate investment through, or transfer investment to, a foreign entity, the U.S. taxpayer must make some sort of transfer to the foreign entity. This may take the form of a cash investment or a transfer of assets of a U.S. entity.

In situations where potential taxable income is transferred to a corporation outside the U.S. taxing jurisdiction, the exchange may trigger a tax. The tax result of transferring property to a foreign corporation depends on the nature of the exchange, the assets involved, the income potential of the property, and the character of the property, in the hands of the transferor or transferee. Figure 25.4 summarizes the taxation of cross-border asset transfers.

Outbound Transfers

When assets are exchanged for corporate stock in a domestic transaction, realized gain or loss may be deferred rather than recognized. Similarly, deferral treatment may be available when the following "outbound" capital changes occur (i.e., moving corporate business across country borders and outside the United States).

- A U.S. corporation starts up a new corporation outside the United States (§ 351).
- A U.S. corporation liquidates a U.S. subsidiary into an existing foreign subsidiary (§ 332).
- A U.S. corporation incorporates a non-U.S. branch of a U.S. corporation, forming a new foreign corporation (§ 351).
- A foreign corporation uses a stock swap to acquire a U.S. corporation (Type "B" reorganization).
- A foreign corporation acquires substantially all of a U.S. corporation's net assets (Type "C" reorganization).

These otherwise tax-deferred transactions may trigger current taxation when foreign corporations are involved. Under § 367, the general rule is that gain deferral is not allowed when assets are leaving the U.S. taxing jurisdiction. However, a major exception allows continued tax deferral for assets transferred to a foreign corporation to be used in a trade or business carried on outside the United States.

The trade or business exception does not apply to certain "tainted" assets, and the transfer of these assets outside the United States triggers immediate gain (but not loss) recognition. The following are "tainted" assets under § 367.

- Inventory (raw goods, work-in-progress, and finished goods).
- Installment obligations and unrealized accounts receivable.
- Foreign currency.
- Property leased by the transferor unless the transferee is the lessee.

GLOBAL *Tax Issues*

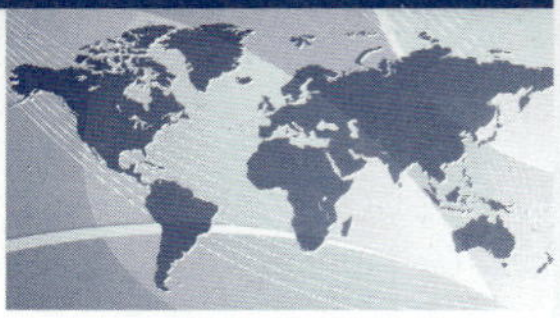

Boom in Cross-Border Mergers but No Inversions

Recent years have seen an increase in the number of tax-deferred mergers taking place across national borders. Helen of Troy, the publicly traded cosmetics giant, converted itself from a U.S. corporation into a tax haven corporation without triggering any tax for its shareholders. Once outside the U.S. taxing jurisdiction, the "inverted" company was free from many of the restrictions imposed by U.S. tax law. U.S. taxing authorities responded to this transaction by issuing new Regulations [Reg. § 1.367(a)–3(c)] to shut down these so-called inversions unless very strict standards were met.

The American Jobs Creation Act of 2004 created even stricter rules in an effort to deter shareholders or partners from turning domestic entities into foreign entities. A domestic corporation or partnership continues to be treated as domestic if:

- A foreign corporation acquires substantially all of its properties after March 4, 2003.
- The former shareholders (or partners) of the U.S. corporation (or partnership) hold 80 percent or more of the foreign corporation's stock after the transaction.
- The foreign corporation does not have substantial business activities in its country of incorporation.

If the former shareholders or partners own at least 60 percent but less than 80 percent of the new corporation, the foreign entity remains foreign, but other restrictions may apply.

These tainted assets are likely to turn over quickly once the asset transfer is completed, and any appreciation is likely to be recognized outside the U.S. taxing jurisdiction. Consequently, § 367 requires recognition of this gain upon transfer of the asset outside the United States.

EXAMPLE 14

Amelia, Inc., a domestic corporation, incorporates its profitable Irish manufacturing branch and creates a new wholly owned foreign corporation, St. George, Ltd., to engage in manufacturing activities in Ireland. The transfer qualifies as tax deferred under § 351. The branch assets have always been used in Ireland. Amelia transfers the following branch assets to St. George upon its creation.

Asset	Tax Basis	Fair Market Value	Built-in Gain/(Loss)
Raw materials inventory	$100	$ 400	$ 300
Accounts receivable	200	250	50
Manufacturing equipment	450	925	475
Furniture and fixtures	150	50	(100)
Total	$900	$1,625	$ 725

Although the $725 in realized gain is deferred under § 351, the gain is potentially taxable under § 367 because the assets are leaving the U.S. taxing jurisdiction. The general rule of § 367 is that all the realized gain is recognized by Amelia. However, because St. George will use the transferred assets in the active conduct of a foreign trade or business, the realized gain remains potentially deferred. But, because the inventory and accounts receivable are "tainted assets," Amelia must recognize $350 of gain upon the transfer ($300 of gain attributable to inventory and $50 related to accounts receivable). Gain is recognized on an asset-by-asset basis with no offset for losses on other assets. ■

Inbound and Offshore Transfers

One objective of Federal tax law is to prevent E & P that has accumulated in U.S.-owned foreign corporations from escaping U.S. taxation. Section 367(b) covers the

FIGURE 25.5 Use of a Tax Haven Corporation

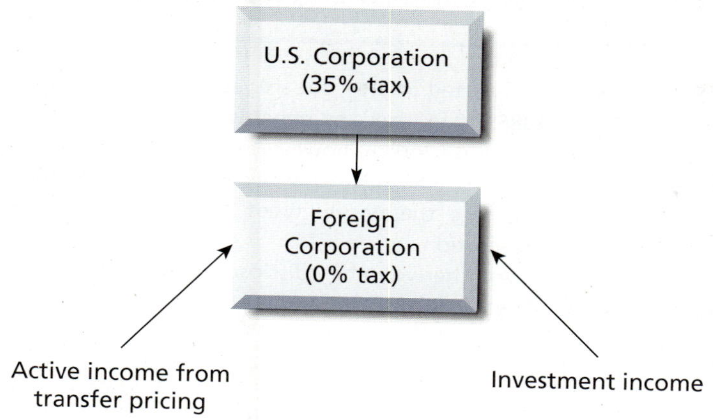

tax treatment of inbound and offshore transfers with regard to stock of a **controlled foreign corporation (CFC).** (CFCs are discussed in more detail in a later section.) An example of an inbound transaction is the liquidation of a foreign corporation into a domestic parent under § 332.

U.S. persons that are directly or indirectly parties to an inbound or offshore transfer involving stock of a CFC generally recognize dividend income to the extent of their pro rata share of the previously untaxed E & P of the foreign corporation. In some situations, income can be deferred by entering into a gain recognition agreement with the IRS. Special rules apply to the outbound transfer of domestic or foreign shares.

TAX HAVENS

Many outbound transfers of assets to foreign corporations are to countries with tax rates higher than or equal to the U.S. rate. Thus, tax avoidance is not the motive for such transfers. Some U.S. corporations, however, make their foreign investment in (or through) a tax haven. A **tax haven** is a country where either locally sourced income or residents are subject to no or low internal taxation.

One method of potentially avoiding taxation is to invest through a foreign corporation incorporated in a tax haven. Because the foreign corporation is a resident of the tax haven, the income it earns is subject to no or low internal taxes. Tax haven countries may also have provisions limiting the exchange of financial and commercial information.

Figure 25.5 illustrates this use of a tax haven by a U.S. corporation. The U.S. corporation uses a foreign subsidiary corporation in a low- or no-tax country to earn either investment income or a portion of income from business activities (as illustrated previously in the transfer pricing discussion). Because the foreign subsidiary is not consolidated with the domestic parent under U.S. tax law (i.e., the foreign corporation is not a member of the U.S. corporation's affiliated group) and is not itself engaged in any U.S. trade or business, the foreign corporation is not subject to U.S. taxation. Without the application of the transfer pricing rules or the Subpart F rules (discussed later), the foreign corporation's income will escape U.S. taxation until the time that any foreign profits are repatriated back to the U.S. parent as a dividend or similar payment.

A tax haven can also, in effect, be created by an income tax treaty. For example, under an income tax treaty between Country A and Country B, residents of Country A are subject to a withholding tax of only 5 percent on dividend and interest income sourced in Country B. The United States and Country A have a similar treaty. The United States does not have a treaty with Country B, and the withholding tax is 30 percent. A U.S. corporation can create a foreign subsidiary in Country A and use that subsidiary to make investments in Country B. This practice is referred to as

TAX *in the NEWS*

Taxpayers Came Clean on Foreign Bank Accounts

Some U.S. persons have attempted to evade U.S. income taxes on foreign income through the use of undisclosed foreign bank accounts. In 2009, the IRS offered an opportunity for these noncompliant taxpayers to come forward and voluntarily disclose their foreign bank accounts and settle their tax bills.

The IRS provided an example of the advantages of coming forward voluntarily. If a U.S. person voluntarily disclosed $1 million in a foreign bank account and $50,000 per year in unreported interest for six years, that taxpayer would pay $386,000 in taxes and penalties (plus interest). Without voluntary disclosure, however, once discovered, the taxpayer would pay $2,306,000 in taxes and penalties (plus interest) and face the possibility of other penalties and criminal prosecution.

Another voluntary disclosure period was offered by the IRS early in 2011.

treaty shopping. If the Country B investment income had been earned directly by the U.S. corporation, it would be subject to a 30 percent withholding tax. As a result of investing through the foreign subsidiary created in Country A, the U.S. parent corporation pays only 10 percent in foreign taxes on the income earned, that is, 5 percent to Country B and 5 percent to Country A.

In recent years, many countries have enacted "treaty shopping" provisions. Under the provisions, treaty benefits for withholding taxes are not available to a resident corporation unless a certain percentage of its beneficial interests are owned, directly or indirectly, by one or more individual residents of the country in which the corporation is resident. The most controversial article in the U.S. Model Treaty is Article 22, Limitation on Benefits, which is meant to prevent treaty shopping. Article 22 disallows treaty benefits to an entity unless more than 50 percent of the beneficial interest in the entity is owned, directly or indirectly, by one or more individual residents of the treaty country in which the entity is resident.[20]

FOREIGN CORPORATIONS CONTROLLED BY U.S. PERSONS

To minimize current tax liability, taxpayers often attempt to defer the recognition of taxable income. One way to do this is to shift the income-generating activity to a foreign

ETHICS *& Equity*

Exporting U.S. Jobs or Improving U.S. Competitiveness?

U.S.-owned foreign corporations with exclusively overseas operations are not subject to U.S. corporate income tax on their profits. Such profits are taxed to the U.S. shareholders only upon repatriation back to the United States as dividends. In some cases, the U.S. shareholders are taxed on profits deemed to be repatriated before any actual distribution (so-called Subpart F income). When there is no Subpart F income, however, U.S. owners of foreign corporations are able to defer indefinitely any U.S. tax on all of their foreign profits. When politicians complain that companies that export jobs are receiving tax breaks, they often are referring to this deferral privilege associated with tax-savvy foreign operations.

U.S. owners of foreign corporations point out that they must compete in a global environment. Many other countries, such as the Netherlands, do not tax the offshore profits of foreign subsidiaries even if the profits are brought home. If a U.S.-owned foreign corporation cannot at least defer its U.S. taxes, it suffers a competitive disadvantage relative to a Dutch-owned subsidiary, for example. Others argue that the deferral privilege simply creates an unwarranted advantage for companies operating offshore compared with their U.S.-based counterparts.

Which argument do you find more compelling? How do you explain the incentive of tax deferral to U.S. workers whose jobs have moved offshore? How would you explain loss of tax deferral to the U.S. shareholders of a company that pays triple the corporate tax rate of its global competitors?

[20]Additional limitations on the use of treaty benefits are contained in § 894(c).

entity that is not within the U.S. tax jurisdiction. A foreign corporation is the most suitable entity for such an endeavor because, unlike a partnership, it is not a conduit through which income is taxed directly to the owner. Because of the potential for abuse, Congress has enacted various provisions to limit the availability of deferral.

Controlled Foreign Corporations

Subpart F, §§ 951–964 of the Code, provides that certain types of income generated by controlled foreign corporations (CFCs) are currently included in gross income by the U.S. shareholders without regard to actual distributions. For Subpart F to apply, the foreign corporation must have been a CFC for an uninterrupted period of 30 days or more during the taxable year. When this is the case, U.S. shareholders must include in gross income their pro rata share of Subpart F income and increase in earnings that the CFC has invested in U.S. property for the tax year. This rule applies to U.S. shareholders who own stock in the corporation on the last day of the tax year or on the last day the foreign corporation is a CFC. The gross income inclusion must be made for their taxable year in which the taxable year of the CFC ends.

EXAMPLE 15

Gray, Inc., a calendar year corporation, is a CFC for the entire tax year. Chance Company, a U.S. corporation, owns 60% of Gray's one class of stock for the entire year. Subpart F income is $100,000, and no distributions have been made during the year. Chance, a calendar year taxpayer, includes $60,000 in gross income as a constructive dividend for the tax year. ■

EXAMPLE 16

Gray, Inc., is a CFC until July 1 of the tax year (a calendar year) and earns $100,000 of Subpart F income. Terry, a U.S. citizen, owns 30% of its one class of stock for the entire year. She includes $14,877 [$100,000 × 30% × (181 days/365 days)] in gross income as a constructive dividend for the tax year. ■

A CFC is any foreign corporation in which more than 50 percent of the total combined voting power of all classes of stock entitled to vote or the total value of the stock of the corporation is owned by U.S. shareholders on any day during the taxable year of the foreign corporation. The foreign subsidiaries of most multinational U.S. parent corporations are CFCs. For purposes of determining if a foreign corporation is a CFC, a **U.S. shareholder** is defined as a U.S. person who owns, or is considered to own, 10 percent or more of the total combined voting power of all classes of voting stock of the foreign corporation. Stock owned directly, indirectly, and constructively is counted.

Indirect ownership involves stock held through a foreign entity, such as a foreign corporation, foreign partnership, or foreign trust. This stock is considered to be actually owned proportionately by the shareholders, partners, or beneficiaries. Constructive ownership rules, with certain modifications, apply in determining if a U.S. person is a U.S. shareholder, in determining whether a foreign corporation is a CFC, and for certain related-party provisions of Subpart F.[21]

EXAMPLE 17

A non-U.S. corporation has the following shareholders.

Shareholders	Voting Power	Classification
Alan	30%	U.S. person
Bill	9%	U.S. person
Carla	40%	Non-U.S. person
Dora	20%	U.S. person
Ed	1%	U.S. person

[21]§§ 958 and 318(a).

Bill is Alan's son. Alan, Bill, and Dora are U.S. shareholders. Alan owns 39%, 30% directly and 9% constructively through Bill. Bill also owns 39%, 9% directly and 30% constructively through Alan. Thus, Bill is a U.S. shareholder. Dora owns 20% directly. The corporation is a CFC because U.S. shareholders own 59% of the voting power. Ed, a U.S. person, owns 1% and is not related to any of the other shareholders. Thus, Ed is not a U.S. shareholder and would not have to include any of the Subpart F income in gross income. If Bill were not related to Alan or to any other U.S. persons who were shareholders, Bill would not be a U.S. shareholder, and the corporation would not be a CFC. ■

U.S. shareholders must include their pro rata share of the applicable income in their gross income only to the extent of their actual ownership. Stock held indirectly (but not constructively) is considered actually owned for this purpose.

EXAMPLE 18

Bill, in Example 17, would recognize only 9% of the Subpart F income as a constructive dividend. Alan would recognize 30%, and Dora would recognize 20%. If instead Bill were a foreign corporation wholly owned by Alan, Alan would recognize 39% as a constructive dividend. ■

Subpart F Income A U.S. shareholder of a CFC does not necessarily lose the ability to defer U.S. taxation of income earned by the CFC. Only certain income earned by the CFC triggers immediate U.S. taxation as a constructive dividend. This tainted income, referred to as Subpart F income, can be characterized as income with little or no economic connection with the CFC's country of incorporation. **Subpart F** income consists of the following.

- Insurance income (§ 953).
- Foreign base company income (§ 954).
- International boycott factor income (§ 999).
- Illegal bribes.
- Income derived from a § 901(j) foreign country.

Insurance Income Income attributable to insuring risk of loss outside the country in which the CFC is organized is Subpart F income. This rule precludes U.S. corporations from setting up offshore insurance companies in tax havens to convert expenditures for self-insurance into a deductible insurance premium.

Foreign Base Company Income Foreign base company income (FBCI) provisions target transactions whereby a CFC earns income that lacks any economic connection to its country of organization. FBCI includes:

- Foreign personal holding company income.
- Foreign base company sales income.
- Foreign base company services income.
- Foreign base company oil-related income.

Foreign personal holding company (FPHC) income consists of the following.

- Dividends, interest, royalties, rents, and annuities.
- Excess gains over losses from the sale or exchange of property (including an interest in a trust or partnership) that gives rise to FPHC income or that does not give rise to any income.
- Excess of foreign currency gains over foreign currency losses (other than any transaction directly related to the business needs of the CFC).
- Income from notional principal contracts.
- Certain payments in lieu of dividends.
- Certain personal service contract income.

Certain FPHC income does not trigger Subpart F inclusion under exceptions for same-country payments, payments out of non-Subpart F E & P of related CFCs, and active rent and royalty income.

Foreign base company (FBC) sales income is income derived by a CFC where the CFC has very little connection with the process that generates the income and a related party is involved. If the CFC earns income from the sale of property to customers outside the CFC's country of incorporation, and either the supplier or the customer is related to the CFC, such income is FBC sales income.

EXAMPLE 19

Ulysses, Ltd., is a CFC organized in the United Kingdom and owned 100% by Joyce, Inc., a U.S. corporation. Ulysses purchases finished inventory from Joyce and sells the inventory to customers in Hong Kong. This sales income constitutes FBC sales income. ■

An exception applies to property that is manufactured, produced, grown, or extracted in the country in which the CFC was organized or created and also to property sold for use, consumption, or disposition within that country. In both these situations, the CFC has participated in the economic process that generates the income.

EXAMPLE 20

If Ulysses, from Example 19, purchases raw materials from Joyce and performs substantial manufacturing activity in the United Kingdom before selling the inventory to customers in Hong Kong, the income is not FBC sales income. Even without the manufacturing activity, sales to customers within the United Kingdom would not produce FBC sales income. ■

Certain income derived by a branch of the CFC in another country can be deemed FBC sales income. This is the case when the effect of using the branch is the same as if the branch were a wholly owned subsidiary.[22]

FBC services income is income derived from the performance of services for or on behalf of a related person and performed outside the country in which the CFC was created or organized. Income from services performed in connection with the sale of property by a CFC that has manufactured, produced, grown, or extracted such property is not FBC services income.

FBC oil-related income is income, other than extraction income, derived in a foreign country by large oil producers in connection with the sale of oil and gas products and sold by the CFC or a related person for use or consumption outside the country in which the oil or gas was extracted.

Subpart F Income Exceptions A *de minimis* rule provides that if the total amount of a foreign corporation's FBCI and gross insurance income for the taxable year is less than the lesser of 5 percent of gross income or $1 million, none of its gross income is treated as FBCI for the tax year. At the other extreme, if a foreign corporation's FBCI and gross insurance income exceed 70 percent of total gross income, all the corporation's gross income for the tax year is treated as Subpart F income.

FBCI and insurance income subject to high foreign taxes are not included under Subpart F if the taxpayer establishes that the income was subject to an effective rate, imposed by a foreign country, of more than 90 percent of the maximum corporate rate under § 11. For example, the rate must be greater than 31.5 percent (90% × 35%), where 35 percent represents the highest U.S. corporate rate.

Investment in U.S. Property In addition to Subpart F income, U.S. shareholders must include in gross income their pro rata share of the CFC's increase in investment in U.S. property for the taxable year.[23] U.S. property generally includes U.S. real property, debt obligations of U.S. persons, and stock in certain related domestic corporations. The CFC must have sufficient E & P to support a deemed dividend.

[22] § 954(d)(2).

[23] § 956.

TAX *in* the NEWS

BRING IT HOME

A tax law change in 2004 provided a one-time opportunity to bring offshore profits home to the United States. U.S. shareholders of foreign corporations were allowed to repatriate certain profits of their foreign subsidiaries and receive an 85 percent dividends received deduction. At a 35 percent tax rate, these recipients paid a U.S. tax of only 5.25 percent (35% × 15%).

Many U.S. corporations thought this was a great idea. U.S. corporations brought home $362 billion in cash dividends eligible for this special deduction. Foreign subsidiaries in the Netherlands provided the largest percentage of repatriated profits (26 percent). Second and third on the list of sources of repatriated profits were Switzerland (9.9 percent) and Bermuda (9.6 percent).

EXAMPLE 21

Fleming, Ltd., a CFC, earned no Subpart F income for the taxable year. If Fleming lends $100,000 to Lynn, its sole U.S. shareholder, this debt is considered an investment in U.S. property by Fleming because it now owns a U.S. note receivable. Holding the note triggers a constructive dividend of $100,000 to Lynn, assuming Fleming has sufficient E & P. ■

Distributions of Previously Taxed Income Distributions from a CFC are treated as being first from E & P attributable to increases in investment in U.S. property previously taxed as a constructive dividend, second from E & P attributable to previously taxed Subpart F income, and last from other E & P. Thus, distributions of previously taxed income are not taxed again as a dividend but reduce E & P. Any increase in investment in U.S. property is considered attributable first to Subpart F income and thus is not taxed twice.

EXAMPLE 22

In the current year, Jet, Inc., a U.S. shareholder, owns 100% of a CFC, from which Jet receives a $100,000 distribution. The CFC's E & P is composed of the following amounts.

- $50,000 attributable to previously taxed investment in U.S. property.
- $30,000 attributable to previously taxed Subpart F income.
- $40,000 attributable to other E & P.

Jet has a taxable dividend of only $20,000, all attributable to other E & P. The remaining $80,000 is previously taxed income. The CFC's E & P is reduced by $100,000. The remaining $20,000 E & P is all attributable to other E & P. ■

A U.S. shareholder's basis in CFC stock is increased by constructive dividends and decreased by subsequent distributions of previously taxed income. U.S. corporate shareholders who own at least 10 percent of the voting stock of a foreign corporation are allowed an indirect foreign tax credit for foreign taxes deemed paid on constructive dividends included in gross income under Subpart F. The indirect credit also is available for Subpart F income attributable to certain lower-tier foreign corporations. The various constructive dividend possibilities for CFC income appear in Concept Summary 25.2.

THE FOREIGN TAX CREDIT

The United States retains the right to tax its citizens and residents on their worldwide taxable income. This approach can result in double taxation, presenting a potential problem to U.S. persons who work or invest abroad.

To reduce the possibility of double taxation, Congress enacted the **foreign tax credit (FTC)** provisions. Under these provisions, a qualified taxpayer is allowed a tax credit for foreign income taxes paid. The credit is a dollar-for-dollar reduction of U.S. income tax liability.

CONCEPT SUMMARY 25.2

Income of a CFC That Is Included in Gross Income of a U.S. Shareholder

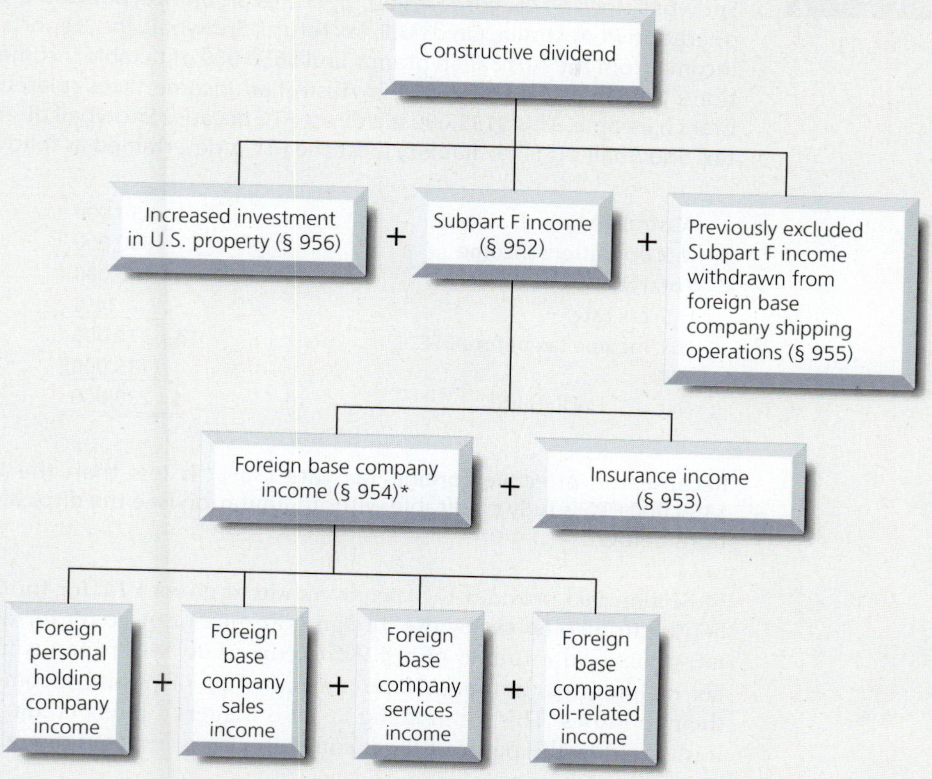

*Plus all other income, when foreign base company and insurance income exceed 70% of gross income.

EXAMPLE 23

Ace Tools, Inc., a U.S. corporation, has a branch operation in Mexico, from which it earns taxable income of $750,000 for the current year. Ace pays income tax of $150,000 on these earnings to the Mexican tax authorities. Ace must also include the $750,000 in gross income for U.S. tax purposes. Assume that, before considering the FTC, Ace owes $255,000 in U.S. income taxes on this foreign-source income. Thus, total taxes on the $750,000 could equal $405,000 ($150,000 + $255,000), a 54% effective rate. But Ace takes an FTC of $150,000 against its U.S. tax liability on the foreign-source income. Ace's total taxes on the $750,000 now are $255,000 ($150,000 + $105,000), a 34% effective rate. ■

The FTC is elective for any particular tax year.[24] If the taxpayer does not "choose" to take the FTC, § 164 allows a deduction for foreign taxes paid or incurred. A taxpayer cannot take a credit and a deduction for the same foreign income taxes.[25] However, a taxpayer can take a deduction in the same year as an FTC for foreign taxes that are not creditable (e.g., non-income taxes).

[24] § 901(a).

[25] § 275.

The Direct Credit

Section 901 provides a direct FTC to U.S. taxpayers that pay or incur a foreign income tax. For purposes of the direct credit, only the taxpayer that bears the legal incidence of the foreign tax is eligible for the credit.

EXAMPLE 24

Snowball, Inc., a U.S. corporation, operates an unincorporated branch manufacturing operation in Australia. On its U.S. tax return, Snowball, Inc., reports $450,000 of taxable income from the Australian branch and $650,000 of taxable income from its U.S. operations. Snowball paid $135,000 in Australian income taxes related to the $450,000 in branch income. This $135,000 is a direct FTC because Snowball directly paid the foreign tax. Snowball's U.S. tax liability after the FTC is determined as follows.

Australian branch income	$ 450,000
U.S. operations income	650,000
Total taxable income	$1,100,000
U.S. tax rate	× 34%
U.S. income tax before FTC	$ 374,000
FTC	(135,000)
Net U.S. tax liability	$ 239,000

Because the effective foreign tax rate (30%) is less than the U.S. rate (34%), the $135,000 FTC is fully creditable without limitation (see the discussion under FTC Limitations below). ■

Section 903 provides U.S. taxpayers with a direct FTC for foreign taxes imposed in lieu of an income tax by the foreign government. A credit for withholding tax is the most common example of a § 903 credit. Many governments impose a withholding tax on the gross amount of certain payments of passive income to nonresidents of their countries. This withholding tax also triggers a direct credit. Even though the tax is withheld by the payor of the income, the tax is imposed directly on the recipient.

EXAMPLE 25

MettCo, Inc., a domestic corporation, receives a $5,000 dividend from DeanCo, Ltd., a foreign corporation. The foreign country imposes a 20% withholding tax on dividend payments to nonresidents. Accordingly, DeanCo withholds $1,000 ($5,000 × 20%) from the dividend and remits this tax to the local country tax authorities. DeanCo pays the remaining $4,000 to MettCo.

Although MettCo did not directly pay the $1,000 in foreign tax, the entire amount is allowed as a direct tax to MettCo for FTC purposes. MettCo reports $5,000 in dividend income on its U.S. tax return (the gross amount of the dividend) but receives an FTC against any U.S. tax for the $1,000 in foreign withholding tax. ■

The Indirect Credit

If a U.S. corporation operates in a foreign country through a branch, the direct credit is available for foreign taxes paid. If, however, a U.S. corporation operates in a foreign country through a foreign subsidiary, the direct credit is not available for foreign taxes paid by the foreign corporation. An indirect credit is available under § 902 to U.S. corporate taxpayers that receive actual or constructive dividends from foreign corporations that have paid foreign income taxes. These foreign taxes are deemed paid by the corporate shareholders in the same proportion as the dividends actually or constructively received bear to the foreign corporation's post-1986 undistributed E & P.

$$\text{Indirect FTC} = \frac{\text{Actual or constructive dividend}}{\text{Post-1986 undistributed E \& P}} \times \text{Post-1986 foreign taxes}$$

Section 78 requires a domestic corporation that chooses the FTC for deemed-paid foreign taxes to *gross up* (add to income) dividend income by the amount of deemed-paid taxes.

EXAMPLE 26

Wren, Inc., a domestic corporation, owns 50% of Finch, Inc., a foreign corporation. Wren receives a dividend of $120,000 from Finch. Finch paid foreign taxes of $500,000 on post-1986 E & P. Finch's post-1986 E & P totals $1.2 million. Wren's deemed-paid foreign taxes for FTC purposes are $50,000.

Cash dividend from Finch	$120,000
Deemed-paid foreign taxes	
$\left(\frac{\$120{,}000}{\$1{,}200{,}000} \times \$500{,}000\right)$	50,000
Gross income to Wren	$170,000

In addition to the $120,000 cash dividend, Wren must include the $50,000 in gross income for the § 78 gross-up adjustment if the FTC is elected. ■

Certain ownership requirements must be met before the indirect credit is available to a domestic corporation. The domestic corporation must own 10 percent or more of the voting stock of the foreign corporation. The credit is also available for deemed-paid foreign taxes of second- and third-tier foreign corporations if the 10 percent ownership requirement is met at the second- and third-tier level. A 5 percent indirect ownership requirement must also be met. The indirect credit is also available for foreign taxes paid by fourth- through sixth-tier foreign corporations if additional requirements are met, including the requirement that these corporations be CFCs. The § 902 ownership requirements are summarized in Figure 25.6.

FIGURE 25.6 **Section 902 Ownership Requirements**

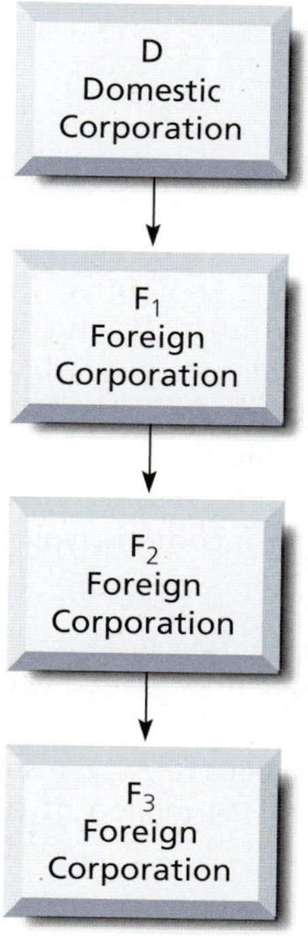

D must own directly at least 10% of the voting stock of F_1 and must own indirectly at least 5% of the voting stock of F_2 and F_3.

F_1 must own directly at least 10% of the voting stock of F_2.

F_2 must own directly at least 10% of the voting stock of F_3.

A credit for deemed-paid foreign taxes may be claimed for payments from foreign corporations through the sixth tier if additional requirements are met.

FTC Limitations

To prevent taxpayers from crediting foreign taxes against U.S. taxes levied on U.S.-source taxable income, the FTC is subject to a limitation. The FTC for any taxable year cannot exceed the lesser of two amounts: (1) the actual foreign taxes paid or accrued or (2) the U.S. taxes (before the FTC) on foreign-source taxable income. The FTC limitation is derived in the following manner.

$$\text{FTC limitation} = \frac{\text{Foreign-source taxable income}}{\text{Worldwide taxable income}^{26}} \times \text{U.S. tax before FTC}$$

EXAMPLE 27

Charlotte, Inc., a domestic corporation that invests in foreign securities, has worldwide taxable income for the tax year of $120,000, consisting of $100,000 in U.S.-source business profits and $20,000 of income from foreign sources. Foreign taxes of $9,500 were withheld by foreign tax authorities. Assume that Charlotte's U.S. tax before the FTC is $42,000. The company's FTC is limited to $7,000 [($20,000/$120,000) × $42,000]. Charlotte's net U.S. tax liability is $35,000 ($42,000 – $7,000). ■

As Example 27 illustrates, the limitation can prevent the total amount of foreign taxes paid in high-tax jurisdictions from being credited. Taxpayers could overcome this problem by generating additional foreign-source income that is subject to no, or low, foreign taxation.

EXAMPLE 28

Compare Domestic Corporation's FTC situations. In one, the corporation has only $500,000 of highly taxed foreign-source income. In the other, Domestic also has $100,000 of low-taxed foreign-source interest income.

	Only Highly Taxed Income	With Low-Taxed Interest Income
Foreign-source income	$500,000	$600,000
Foreign taxes	275,000	280,000
U.S.-source income	700,000	700,000
U.S. taxes (34%)	408,000	442,000
FTC limitation	170,000*	204,000**

*($500,000/$1,200,000) × $408,000.
**($600,000/$1,300,000) × $442,000.

Domestic's foreign taxes increase by only $5,000 ($280,000 – $275,000), but its FTC limitation increases by $34,000 ($204,000 – $170,000). ■

Example 28 illustrates the *cross-crediting* of foreign taxes from high- and low-taxed foreign income. To prevent this practice, the FTC rules require that a separate limitation be calculated for each of certain categories (or baskets) of foreign-source taxable income and the foreign taxes attributable to that income. There are two income baskets: passive income and all other (general). Passive income generally is investment-type income; general limitation income is typically from active business sources.

EXAMPLE 29

BenCo, Inc., a U.S. corporation, has a foreign branch in France that earns taxable income of $1.5 million from manufacturing operations and $600,000 from passive activities. BenCo pays foreign taxes of $600,000 (40%) and $100,000 ($16^{2}/_{3}$%), respectively, on this foreign-source income. The corporation also earns $4 million of U.S.-

[26]For FTC purposes, the taxable income of an individual, estate, or trust is computed without any deduction for personal exemptions. § 904(b)(1).

source taxable income, resulting in worldwide taxable income of $6.1 million. BenCo's U.S. taxes before the FTC are $2,074,000 (at 34%). The following tabulation illustrates the effect of the separate limitation baskets on cross-crediting.

Foreign Income Category	Net Taxable Amount	Foreign Taxes	U.S. Tax before FTC at 34%	FTC with Separate Limits
General	$1,500,000	$600,000	$510,000	$510,000
Passive	600,000	100,000	204,000	100,000
Total	$2,100,000	$700,000	$714,000	$610,000

Without the separate limitation provisions, the FTC would be the lesser of (1) $700,000 foreign taxes or (2) $714,000 share of U.S. tax [($2,100,000/$6,100,000) × $2,074,000]. The separate limitation provisions reduce the FTC by $90,000 ($700,000 − $610,000). The effect of the separate limitation rules is that the foreign-source income taxed at the foreign tax rate of 40% cannot be aggregated with foreign-source income taxed at only 16⅔%. ■

FTC Carryovers

The various FTC limitations can result in unused (noncredited) foreign taxes for the tax year. The carryback period is 1 year, and the carryforward period is 10 years.[27] The taxes can be credited in years when the formula limitation for that year exceeds the foreign taxes attributable to the same tax year. The carryback and carryforward provisions are available only within a specific basket. In other words, excess foreign taxes in one basket cannot be carried over unless there is an excess limitation in the same basket for the carryover year.

The Alternative Minimum Tax FTC

For purposes of the alternative minimum tax (AMT), the FTC limitation is calculated by using foreign-source alternative minimum taxable income (AMTI) in the numerator and worldwide AMTI in the denominator of the formula and the tentative minimum tax rather than the regular tax.

$$\text{AMT FTC limitation} = \frac{\text{Foreign-source AMTI}}{\text{Worldwide AMTI}} \times \text{Tentative minimum tax}$$

The taxpayer may elect to use regular foreign-source taxable income in the numerator if it does not exceed total AMTI. The AMT FTC limit must also be determined on a basket-by-basket basis.

Other Considerations

For a foreign levy to qualify for the FTC, it must be a tax, and its predominant character must be that of an income tax in the U.S. sense.[28] A levy is a tax if it is a compulsory payment, rather than a payment for a specific economic benefit such as the right to extract oil. A tax's predominant character is that of an income tax in the U.S. sense if it reaches realized net gain and is not a *soak-up* tax, that is, does not depend on being credited against the income tax of another country. A tax that is levied in lieu of an income tax is also creditable.[29]

[27] § 904(c).

[28] Reg. § 1.901–2.

[29] § 903 and Reg. § 1.903–1.

FINANCIAL DISCLOSURE *Insights*

OVERSEAS OPERATIONS AND BOOK-TAX DIFFERENCES

Non-U.S. operations account for a large portion of the permanent book-tax differences of U.S. business entities. These differences may relate to different tax bases, different tax rate structures, or special provisions concerning tax-based financing with the other country. For instance, lower tax rates applied by non-U.S. countries recently reduced Berkshire Hathaway's current-year tax liabilities by about one-half percentage point.

Tax planning strategies using non-U.S. operations also are found in the deferred tax asset and liability accounts. Tax deferrals allowed under current U.S. tax rules and carryforwards of the foreign tax credit can be substantial for some businesses. For example, IBM recently reported a deferred tax asset relating to delays in using its FTCs amounting to about $500 million. For the operating arm of General Electric, that amount was about $2 billion.

EXAMPLE 30

JonesCo, a domestic corporation, generates $2 million of taxable income from operations in Larissa, a foreign country. Larissan law levies a tax on income generated in Larissa by foreign residents only in cases in which the country of residence (such as the United States) allows a tax credit for foreign taxes paid. JonesCo will not be allowed an FTC for taxes paid to Larissa, because the foreign tax is a soak-up tax. ■

For purposes of the FTC, foreign taxes are attributable to the year in which they are paid or accrued. Under § 905, taxpayers using the cash method of accounting for tax purposes may elect to take the FTC in the year in which the foreign taxes accrue. The election is binding on the taxpayer for the year in which it is made and for all subsequent years. Foreign taxes generally must be translated to U.S. dollars at the average exchange rate for the tax year to which the taxes relate.[30]

25.6 U.S. Taxation of Nonresident Aliens and Foreign Corporations

LO.6

Apply the U.S. tax provisions concerning nonresident alien individuals and foreign corporations.

Generally, only the U.S.-source income of nonresident alien individuals and foreign corporations is subject to U.S. taxation. This reflects the reach of the U.S. tax jurisdiction. The constraint, however, does not prevent the United States from also taxing the foreign-source income of nonresident alien individuals and foreign corporations when that income is effectively connected with the conduct of a U.S. trade or business.[31] Concept Summary 25.3 at the end of this section summarizes these tax rules.

NONRESIDENT ALIEN INDIVIDUALS

A **nonresident alien (NRA)** individual is an individual who is not a citizen or resident of the United States. For example, Prince William is an NRA, because he is not a citizen or resident of the United States. Citizenship is determined under the immigration and naturalization laws of the United States.[32] Basically, the citizenship statutes are broken down into two categories: nationality at birth or through naturalization.

Residency

A person is a resident of the United States for income tax purposes if he or she meets either the green card test or the substantial presence test.[33] If either of these tests is met for the calendar year, the individual is deemed a U.S. resident for the year.

[30] § 986(a).

[31] §§ 871, 881, and 882.

[32] Title 8, Aliens and Nationality, *United States Code.*

[33] § 7701(b).

A foreign person issued a green card is considered a U.S. resident on the first day he or she is physically present in the United States after issuance. The green card is Immigration Form I–551. Newly issued cards are no longer green, but the form is still referred to as the "green card." Status as a U.S. resident remains in effect until the green card has been revoked or the individual has abandoned lawful permanent resident status.

The substantial presence test is applied to an alien without a green card. It is a mathematical test involving physical presence in the United States. An individual who is physically present in the United States for at least 183 days during the calendar year is a U.S. resident for income tax purposes. This 183-day requirement can also be met over a three-year period that includes the two immediately preceding years and the current year, as long as the individual is present in the United States at least 31 days during the current year.[34] For this purpose, each day of the current calendar year is counted as a full day, each day of the first preceding year as one-third day, and each day of the second preceding year as one-sixth day.

EXAMPLE 31

Li, a foreign citizen, was present in the United States for 90 days in 2009, 180 days in 2010, and 110 days in 2011. For Federal income tax purposes, Li is a U.S. resident for 2011, because she was physically present for 185 days [(90 days $\times$ 1/6) + (180 days $\times$ 1/3) + (110 days $\times$ 1)] during the three-year period. ■

Under the substantial presence test, residence begins the first day the individual is physically present in the United States and ends the last day of physical presence for the calendar year (assuming the substantial presence test is not satisfied for the next calendar year). Nominal presence of 10 days or less can be ignored in determining whether the substantial presence test is met.

The substantial presence test allows for several exceptions. Commuters from Mexico and Canada who are employed in the United States but return home each day are excepted. Also excepted are individuals who are prevented from leaving the United States by medical conditions that arose while the individuals were in the United States. Some individuals are exempt from the substantial presence test, including foreign government-related individuals (e.g., diplomats), qualified teachers, trainees and students, and certain professional athletes.

ETHICS *& Equity*

SHOULD THERE BE SOME "HEART" IN TAX LAW?

In determining whether an alien is a U.S. resident for U.S. income tax purposes under the substantial presence test, days on which a medical condition prevents the person from leaving the United States are not counted as days present in the United States. The medical condition (e.g., illness or injury) must have arisen after the NRA arrived in the United States. In other words, it generally must be an unexpected illness or accident. No such exception is available, however, for a family member or other NRA who is significant to the person who becomes ill or injured. Thus, under this rule, the relative or other significant person may have to either risk being classified as a U.S. resident for the tax year or leave the ill person (or accident victim) alone in the United States. Does this limited exception ignore the human element in illness and recovery?

Nonresident Aliens Not Engaged in a U.S. Trade or Business

Certain U.S.-source income that is *not* effectively connected with the conduct of a U.S. trade or business is subject to a flat 30 percent tax. This income includes dividends, interest, rents, royalties, certain compensation, premiums, annuities, and

[34] § 7701(b)(3)(A).

other fixed, determinable, annual or periodic (FDAP) income. This tax generally is levied by a withholding mechanism that requires the payors of the income to withhold 30 percent of gross amounts.[35] This method eliminates the problems of assuring payment by nonresidents, determining allowable deductions, and, in most instances, the filing of tax returns by nonresidents. Interest received from certain portfolio debt investments, even though U.S.-sourced, is exempt from taxation. Interest earned on deposits with banking institutions is also exempt as long as it is not effectively connected with the conduct of a U.S. trade or business.

Capital gains *not* effectively connected with the conduct of a U.S. trade or business are exempt from tax, as long as the NRA individual was not present in the United States for 183 days or more during the taxable year. If an NRA has not established a taxable year, the calendar year is used. NRAs are not permitted to carry forward capital losses.[36]

Nonresident Aliens Engaged in a U.S. Trade or Business

Two important definitions determine the U.S. tax consequences to NRAs with U.S.-source income: "the conduct of a **U.S. trade or business**" and "**effectively connected income**." Specifically, in order for an NRA's noninvestment income to be subject to U.S. taxation, the NRA must be considered engaged in a U.S. trade or business and must earn income effectively connected with that business.

General criteria for determining if a U.S. trade or business exists include the location of production activities, management, distribution activities, and other business functions. Trading in commodities and securities ordinarily does not constitute a trade or business. Dealers, however, need to avoid maintaining a U.S. trading office and trading for their own accounts. Corporations (other than certain personal holding companies) that are not dealers can trade for their own accounts. There are no restrictions on individuals who are not dealers.

The Code does not explicitly define a U.S. trade or business, but case law has defined the concept as activities carried on in the United States that are regular, substantial, and continuous.[37] Once an NRA is considered engaged in a U.S. trade or business, all U.S.-source income other than FDAP and capital gain income is considered effectively connected to that trade or business and is therefore subject to U.S. taxation.

EXAMPLE 32

Vito, an NRA, produces wine for export. During the current year, Vito earns $500,000 from exporting wine to unrelated wholesalers in the United States. The title to the wine passes to the U.S. wholesalers in New York. Vito has no offices or employees in the United States. The income from wine sales is U.S.-source income, but because Vito is not engaged in a U.S. trade or business, the income is not subject to taxation in the United States.

Assume that Vito begins operating a hot dog cart in New York City. This activity constitutes a U.S. trade or business. Consequently, all U.S.-source income other than FDAP or capital gain income will be taxed in the United States as income effectively connected with a U.S. trade or business. Thus, both the hot dog cart profits and the $500,000 in wine income will be taxed in the United States. ■

FDAP and capital gain income may be considered effectively connected income if the assets that generate this income are used in, or held for use in, the trade or business (the asset-use test) or if the activities of the trade or business are a material factor in the production of the income (the business-activities test).[38] As long as FDAP and capital gain income are not effectively connected with a U.S. trade or business, the tax treatment of these income items is the same whether NRAs are engaged in a U.S. trade or business or not.

[35]§§ 871 and 1441.

[36]§ 871(a)(2).

[37]See, for example, *Higgins v. Comm.*, 41–1 USTC ¶9233, 25 AFTR 1160, 61 S.Ct. 475 (1941) and *Continental Trading, Inc. v. Comm.*, 59–1 USTC ¶9316, 3 AFTR 2d 923, 265 F.2d 40 (CA–9, 1959).

[38]§ 864(c).

EXHIBIT 25.2 **Selected Tax Treaty Withholding Rates**

	Interest	Dividends in General	Dividends Paid by U.S. Subsidiary to a Foreign Parent Corporation
Australia	10%	15%	0%
Canada	10	15	5
Ireland	0	15	5
Japan	10	15	0
Mexico	15	15	0
Philippines	15	25	20

EXAMPLE 33

Ingrid, an NRA, operates a U.S. business. During the year, cash funds accumulate. Ingrid invests these funds on a short-term basis so that they remain available to meet her business needs. Under the asset-use test, any income earned from these investments is effectively connected income. ■

Effectively connected income is taxed at the same rates that apply to U.S. citizens and residents, and deductions for expenses attributable to that income are allowed. NRAs with effectively connected income are also allowed a deduction for casualty and theft losses related to property located within the United States, a deduction for qualified charitable contributions, and one personal exemption. NRAs with income effectively connected with the conduct of a U.S. trade or business may also be subject to the alternative minimum tax.

Withholding Provisions

The 30 percent U.S. tax on FDAP income is generally administered by requiring the payor of the income to withhold the tax and remit it to the U.S. tax authorities. This assures the government of timely collection and relieves it of jurisdictional problems that could arise if it had to rely on recipients residing outside the United States to pay the tax. As explained earlier, income tax treaties with other countries provide for reduced withholding on certain types of FDAP income (see Exhibit 25.2 for some examples of withholding rates).

FOREIGN CORPORATIONS

Definition

The classification of an entity as a foreign corporation for U.S. tax purposes is an important consideration. A corporation created or organized in the United States is a domestic corporation. A foreign corporation is one that is not domestic. Thus, though McDonald's is, in reality, a global corporation, it is considered a domestic corporation for U.S. tax purposes, solely because it was organized in the United States.

Income Not Effectively Connected with a U.S. Trade or Business

U.S.-source FDAP income of foreign corporations is taxed by the United States in the same manner as that of NRA individuals—at a flat 30 percent rate. Generally, foreign corporations qualify for the same exemptions from U.S. taxation for investment income as do NRA individuals. The U.S.-source capital gains of foreign corporations are exempt from the Federal income tax if they are not effectively connected with the conduct of a U.S. trade or business.

Effectively Connected Income

Foreign corporations conducting a trade or business in the United States are subject to Federal income taxation on any U.S.-source income effectively connected with the trade or business. As with NRAs, any FDAP or capital gain income is not considered effectively connected unless the income meets the asset-use or business-activities test.[39] Foreign corporations are subject to the same tax rates on their effectively connected income as domestic corporations.

Branch Profits Tax

The objective of the **branch profits tax** is to afford equal tax treatment to income generated by a domestic corporation controlled by a foreign corporation and to income generated by other U.S. operations controlled by foreign corporations. If the foreign corporation operates through a U.S. subsidiary (a domestic corporation), the income of the subsidiary is taxable by the United States when earned and is also subject to a withholding tax when repatriated (returned as dividends to the foreign parent). Before the branch profits tax was enacted, a foreign corporation with a branch in the United States paid only the initial tax on its U.S. earnings; remittances were not taxed.

In addition to the income tax imposed under § 882 on effectively connected income of a foreign corporation, a tax equal to 30 percent of the **dividend equivalent amount (DEA)** for the taxable year is imposed on any foreign corporation with effectively connected income.[40] The DEA is the foreign corporation's effectively connected earnings for the taxable year, adjusted for increases and decreases in the corporation's U.S. net equity (investment in the U.S. operations).

The DEA is limited to current E & P and post-1986 accumulated E & P that is effectively connected, or treated as effectively connected, with the conduct of a U.S. trade or business. U.S. net equity is the sum of money and the aggregate adjusted basis of assets and liabilities directly connected to U.S. operations that generate effectively connected income.

EXAMPLE 34

Robin, Inc., a foreign corporation, has a U.S. branch operation with the following tax results and other information for the year.

Pretax earnings effectively connected with a U.S. trade or business	$2,000,000
U.S. corporate tax (at 34%)	680,000
Remittance to home office	1,000,000
Increase in U.S. net equity	320,000

Robin's DEA and branch profits tax are computed as follows.

E & P effectively connected with a U.S. trade or business ($2,000,000 – $680,000)	$1,320,000
Less: Increase in U.S. net equity	(320,000)
Dividend equivalent amount	$1,000,000
Branch profits tax rate	× 30%
Branch profits tax	$ 300,000

■

The 30 percent rate of the branch profits tax may be reduced or eliminated by a treaty provision. If a foreign corporation is subject to the branch profits tax, no other U.S. tax is levied on the dividend actually paid by the corporation during the taxable year.

THE FOREIGN INVESTMENT IN REAL PROPERTY TAX ACT

Prior to 1980, NRAs and foreign corporations could avoid U.S. taxation on gains from the sale of U.S. real estate if the gains were treated as capital gains and were not effectively connected with the conduct of a U.S. trade or business. In the

[39] § 864(c).

[40] § 884.

CONCEPT SUMMARY 25.3

U.S. Taxation of NRAs and Foreign Corporations (FCs)

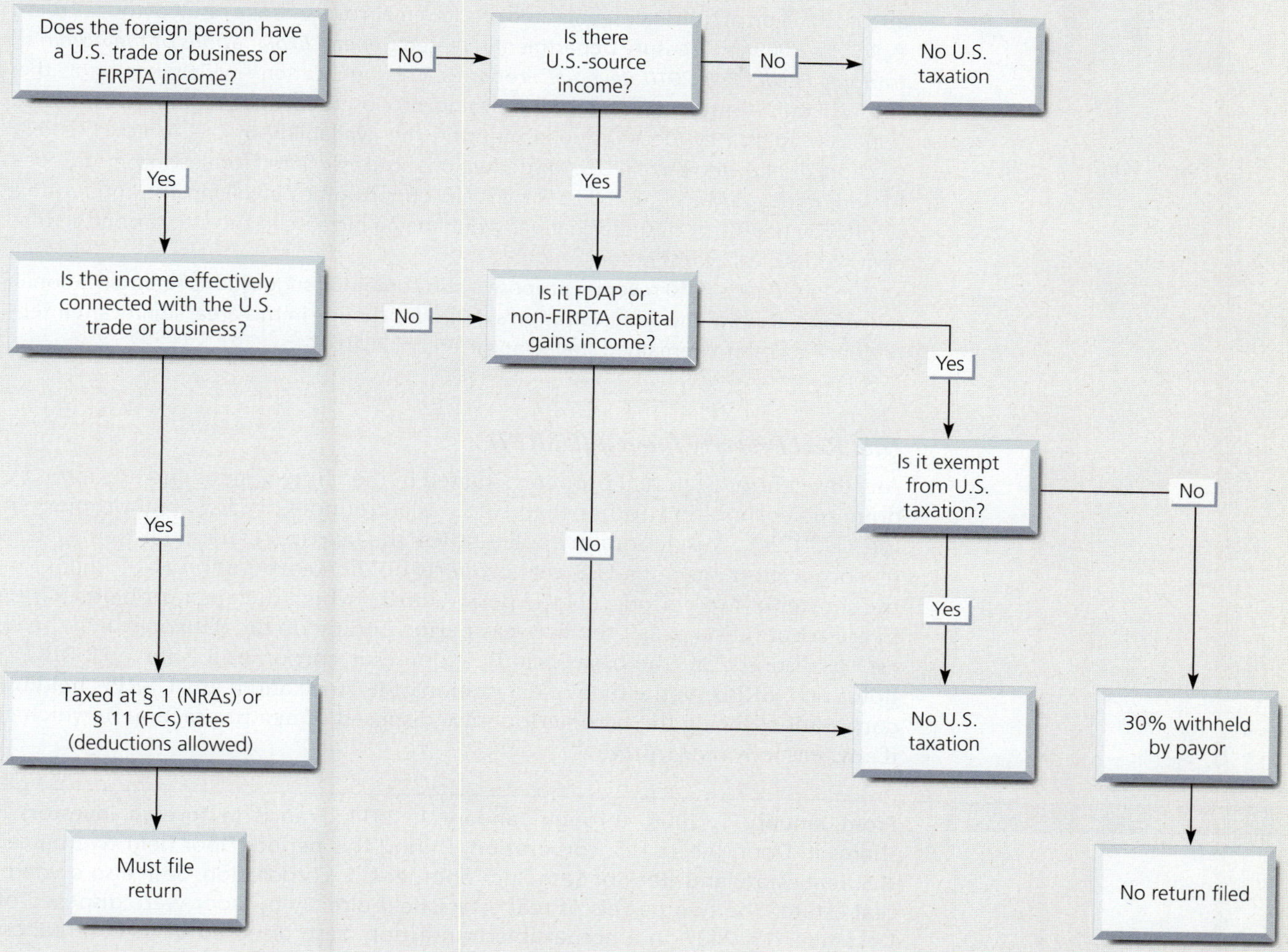

mid-1970s, midwestern farmers pressured Congress to eliminate what they saw as a tax advantage that would allow nonresidents to bid up the price of farmland. This and other concerns about foreign ownership of U.S. real estate led to the enactment of the Foreign Investment in Real Property Tax Act (FIRPTA) of 1980.

Under **FIRPTA**, gains and losses realized by NRAs and foreign corporations from the sale or other disposition of U.S. real property interests are treated as effectively connected with the conduct of a U.S. trade or business even when those individuals or corporations are not actually so engaged. NRA individuals must pay a tax equal to the lesser of two amounts: (1) 26 (or 28) percent of their alternative minimum taxable income or (2) regular U.S. rates on the net U.S. real property gain for the taxable year.[41] For purposes of this provision, losses are taken into account only to the extent they are deductible as business losses, losses on transactions entered into for profit, or losses from casualties and thefts.

[41] § 897.

GLOBAL
Tax Issues

A Deferral for an End to Deferral?

The Obama administration is interested in reforming the U.S. taxation of foreign income. It has indicated a particular concern with scaling back the benefits resulting from the deferral of income earned by the foreign subsidiaries of U.S. corporations, believing that about $3 trillion of cash in unrepatriated profits remain overseas as a result of this tax rule.

In May 2009 the Treasury Department released *General Explanations of the Administration's Fiscal Year 2010 Revenue Proposals*. This publication—widely known as the "Green Book"—outlined several far-reaching proposed changes to the U.S. international tax rules. Key ideas included reducing the availability of the "check-the-box" election, disallowing certain U.S. tax deductions until associated foreign income is repatriated, and reducing the ability for certain opportunities involving the foreign tax credit. The net effect of these changes would be an increase in the U.S. tax on the foreign profits of U.S.corporations.

The President's 2010 revenue proposals also contained suggestions for international tax reform. Despite the administration's desire for change in this area, significant international tax reform remained stalled at the end of 2010.

U.S. Real Property Interest (USRPI)

Any direct interest in real property situated in the United States and any interest in a domestic corporation (other than solely as a creditor) are U.S. real property interests (USRPIs). This definition applies unless the taxpayer can establish that a domestic corporation was not a U.S. real property holding corporation (USRPHC) during the shorter of two periods: (1) the period during which the taxpayer held an interest in the corporation or (2) the five-year period ending on the date on which the interest was disposed of (the base period). A domestic corporation is not a USRPHC if it holds no USRPIs on the date of disposition of its stock and if any USRPIs held by the corporation during the base period were disposed of in a transaction in which gain, if any, was fully recognized.

EXAMPLE 35

From January 1, 2006, through January 1, 2011, Francis (a foreign investor) held shares in Door, Inc., a U.S. corporation. During this period, Door held two parcels of U.S. real estate and stock of Sash, Inc., another U.S. corporation. Sash also owned U.S. real estate. The two parcels of real estate held directly by Door were disposed of on December 15, 2007, in a nontaxable transaction. Sash disposed of its U.S. real estate in a taxable transaction on January 1, 2011.

An interest in Door is treated as a USRPI because Door did not recognize gain on the December 15, 2007 disposition of the USRPIs. If Door's ownership of U.S. real estate had been limited to its indirect ownership through Sash, an interest in Door would not have constituted a USRPI as of January 2, 2011. This result would occur because Sash disposed of its USRPIs in a taxable transaction in which gain was fully recognized. ■

A USRPHC is any corporation (whether foreign or domestic) where the fair market value of the corporation's USRPIs equals or exceeds 50 percent of the aggregate of fair market value of certain specified assets. These assets are the corporation's USRPIs, its interests in real property located outside the United States, and any other of its assets that are used or held for use in a trade or business. Stock regularly traded on an established securities market is not treated as a USRPI if a person holds no more than 5 percent of the stock.

Withholding Provisions

The FIRPTA withholding provisions require any purchaser or agent acquiring a USRPI from a foreign person to withhold 10 percent of the amount realized on the disposition.[42] A domestic partnership, trust, or estate with a foreign partner, foreign

[42] § 1445.

FINANCIAL DISCLOSURE *Insights* — DEFERRED TAX ASSETS OVERSEAS

U.S. corporations are not the only entities that can have balance sheets with excessive deferred tax accounts. Restrictive regulatory rules as to how non-U.S. banks compute their capital amounts tend to create large deferred tax assets for them. These accounts attract more attention from regulators in a "down" economy, when the financial stability of the banking system is even more critical than usual.

Deferred tax assets do not affect the entity's actual cash balances, but they can affect the stock price in the short term. Even professional equity analysts can have difficulty understanding announcements of tax adjustments to the balance sheet. Regulations limit the level of deferred tax assets that banks can have in a given country, and political pressure to increase those limits is appearing, as the proportion of shareholder equity that is made up of deferred tax assets has grown significantly in the last five years.

The following are estimates from JPMorgan Chase of the magnitude of deferred tax asset balances for selected banks overseas and banks in the United States.

	Percentage of Shareholder Equity Constituted by Deferred Tax Assets
Dexia	44%
Deutsche Bank	24
Monte dei Paschi	23
UBS	21
Credit Suisse	20
U.S. banks, average	11

grantor treated as owner, or foreign beneficiary generally must withhold 35 percent of the gain allocable to that person on a disposition of a USRPI.

Foreign corporations are also subject to withholding provisions on certain distributions. Without this withholding, NRAs could sell USRPIs, receiving the sales proceeds outside the United States, and jurisdictional issues could make it difficult for the U.S. tax authorities to collect any U.S. tax that might be due on gains. Certain exceptions to FIRPTA withholding are allowed.

Failure to withhold can subject the purchaser or the purchaser's agent to interest on any unpaid amount.[43] A civil penalty of 100 percent of the amount required to be withheld and a criminal penalty of up to $10,000 or five years in prison can be imposed for willful failure to withhold.[44]

EXPATRIATION TO AVOID U.S. TAXATION

Section 877 provides for U.S. taxation of U.S.-source income earned by individuals who relinquished their U.S. citizenship within 10 years of deriving that income if they gave up their citizenship to avoid U.S. taxation. Furthermore, NRAs who lost U.S. citizenship within a 10-year period immediately preceding the close of the tax year must pay taxes on their U.S.-source income as though they were still U.S. citizens. This provision applies only if the expatriation had as one of its principal purposes the avoidance of U.S. taxes. Individuals are presumed to have a tax avoidance purpose if they meet either of the following criteria.[45]

- Average annual net income tax for the five taxable years ending before the date of loss of U.S. citizenship is more than $147,000 (in 2011).
- Net worth as of that date is $2 million or more.

These provisions also apply to "long-term lawful permanent residents" who cease to be taxed as U.S. residents. A long-term permanent resident is an individual (other than a citizen of the United States) who is a lawful permanent resident of the United States in at least 8 taxable years during the 15-year period ending with the taxable year in which the individual either ceases to be a lawful permanent resident of the

[43] §§ 6601, 6621, and 6651.

[44] §§ 6672 and 7202.

[45] § 877(a)(2). The dollar amounts are adjusted for inflation. For 2010, the net income tax threshold was $145,000.

TAX *in the NEWS*

SO LONG, IT'S BEEN NICE KNOWING YOU

Did you ever wonder who gives up U.S. citizenship? It is easy to find out. Section 877 requires that U.S. citizens and long-term permanent residents inform the IRS of their expatriation on Form 8854, Initial and Annual Expatriation Information Statement, in the year of expatriation and certain years thereafter.

Expatriating individuals must also give notice of an expatriating act or termination of residency to the Department of State or the Department of Homeland Security.

The government publishes the names of these individuals in the *Federal Register* each quarter. Several hundred people abandoned U.S. citizenship in the second quarter of 2010 alone.

United States or begins to be treated as a resident of another country under an income tax treaty between the United States and the other country (and does not waive the benefits of the treaty to residents of that country). An exception applies to certain individuals with dual citizenship.

The United States continues to treat individuals as U.S. citizens or residents until the taxpayers provide required information and an expatriation notice. Expatriates who are subject to the 10-year rule outlined above must file an information disclosure statement annually. If an expatriate is physically present in the United States for more than 30 days during a calendar year during the 10-year period, the individual is taxed as a U.S. citizen or resident.[46] These expatriation rules, taken as a whole, make it difficult to give up U.S. citizenship or residency simply to avoid U.S. taxation.

LO.7

Identify tax planning strategies in an international setting.

TAX PLANNING:

Over time, legislation has tended to reduce the ability to plan transactions and operations in a manner that minimizes tax liability. However, taxpayers who are not limited by the constraints of a particular transaction or operation can use the following suggestions to plan for maximum tax benefits.

25.7 THE FOREIGN TAX CREDIT LIMITATION AND SOURCING PROVISIONS

The FTC limitation is partially based on the amount of foreign-source taxable income in the numerator of the limitation ratio. Consequently, the sourcing of income is extremely important. Income that is taxed by a foreign tax jurisdiction benefits from the FTC only to the extent that it is classified as foreign-source income under U.S. tax law. Thus, elements that affect the sourcing of income, such as the place of title passage, should be considered carefully before a transaction is undertaken.

It may be possible for a U.S. corporation to alleviate the problem of excess foreign taxes by using the following techniques.

- Generate "same basket" foreign-source income that is subject to a tax rate lower than the U.S. tax rate.
- Reduce highly taxed foreign-source income in favor of foreign-source income that is taxed at a lower rate by shifting operations or intangibles.
- Time the repatriation of foreign-source earnings to coincide with excess limitation years.
- Deduct foreign taxes for years when the deduction benefit would exceed the FTC benefit.
- Convert deductions related to foreign-source income so that they are related to U.S.-source income instead.

[46] § 877(g)(1).

EXAMPLE 36

Della, Inc., a U.S. corporation, reports U.S.-source taxable income of $200,000, worldwide taxable income of $300,000, and a U.S. tax liability (before the FTC) of $105,000. Della receives foreign-source taxable income of $100,000, pays foreign income taxes, and computes an FTC as shown.

Basket	Amount	Foreign Taxes	FTC Limitation	Allowed FTC
Passive	$ 80,000	$ 8,000	$28,000	$ 8,000
General	20,000	8,000	7,000	7,000
	$100,000	$16,000		$15,000

If Della can shift $10,000 of passive income into the general basket, the FTC is increased by $1,000. The FTC limitation for the general basket increases to $10,500 [($30,000/$300,000) × $105,000]. This allows all $8,000 of foreign taxes related to the general basket to be credited in the current year. The allowed FTC for the passive basket remains unchanged at $8,000. ■

EXAMPLE 37

Donohoe, Inc., a U.S. corporation, reports U.S. total taxable income of $100,000, classified as follows.

	Total	U.S.-Source Income	Foreign-Source Income—General
Gross income	$150,000	$100,000	$ 50,000
Deductions	(50,000)	(40,000)	(10,000)
Taxable income	$100,000	$ 60,000	$ 40,000

U.S. income tax before the FTC is $34,000, and Donohoe's FTC limitation is $13,600 ($40,000/$100,000 × $34,000). If, through planning and analysis, Donohoe is able to convert $5,000 of the deductions related to foreign-source income to U.S. source, the total taxable income would remain the same, but the FTC limitation would increase to $15,300 ($45,000/$100,000 × $34,000). ■

25.8 The Foreign Corporation as a Tax Shelter

An NRA who is able to hold U.S. investments through a foreign corporation can accomplish much in the way of avoiding U.S. taxation. Capital gains (other than dispositions of U.S. real property interests) are not subject to U.S. taxation. This assumes that they are not effectively connected with a U.S. trade or business. The NRA can dispose of the stock of a foreign corporation that holds U.S. real property and not be subject to taxation under § 897 (FIRPTA). Furthermore, the stock of a foreign corporation is not included in the U.S. gross estate of a deceased NRA, even if all the assets of the foreign corporation are located in the United States.

Caution is advised when the foreign corporation may generate income effectively connected with the conduct of a U.S. trade or business. The income may be taxed at a higher rate than if the NRA individually generated the income. The tradeoff between a higher U.S. tax on this income and protection from the U.S. estate tax and § 897 must be weighed.

25.9 Planning under Subpart F

The *de minimis* rule allows a CFC to avoid the classification of income as FBC income or insurance income and prevents the U.S. shareholder from having to include it in gross income as a constructive dividend. Thus, a CFC with total FBC income and insurance income in an amount close to the 5 percent or $1 million level should monitor income realization to assure that the *de minimis* rule applies for the tax year. At least as important is avoiding the classification of all the gross income of the CFC as FBC income or insurance income. This happens when the sum of the FBC income and gross insurance income for the taxable year exceeds 70 percent of total gross income.

Careful timing of investment in U.S. property can reduce the potential for constructive dividend income to U.S. shareholders. The gross income of U.S. shareholders attributable to investment in U.S. property is limited to the E & P of the CFC.[47] E & P that is attributable to amounts that have been included in gross income as Subpart F income in either the current year or a prior tax year is not taxed again when invested in U.S. property.

25.10 Using the Check-the-Box Regulations

The check-the-box Regulations under § 7701 provide a great deal of flexibility for U.S.-based multinational corporations. Corporations are allowed to organize their branches and subsidiaries around the world in ways that optimize both local country and U.S. taxation. For example, a U.S. corporation may choose to treat its subsidiary in the United Kingdom as a partnership or unincorporated branch for U.S. tax purposes (thus taking advantage of loss flow-throughs) and a corporation under United Kingdom law (where certain tax and liability benefits may exist). The flurry of multinational restructurings since the issuance of the check-the-box Regulations has led to some cries of foul by U.S. taxing authorities who claim that these provisions are being used in inappropriate ways. The Treasury Department and the IRS are currently exploring ways to curb some of these perceived abuses.

25.11 Transferring Intangible Assets Offshore

In many industries, a company's intangible assets, such as licenses and patents, produce a relatively large share of total income. For example, the license to use a software program is much more valuable than the actual disc the customer purchases; thus, a large part of the profit from the sale of software accrues to the license holder.

Unlike manufacturing plants, intangible assets can be easily transferred to related entities outside the United States. Congress recognized this potential, and § 367 requires gain to be recognized if intangibles are transferred outside the United States. To avoid this § 367 "toll charge," companies should consider creating their intangibles offshore so that no subsequent transfer is required. Companies may choose to perform their R & D activities within subsidiaries located in tax haven countries in order to create and keep their valuable intangibles in low-tax jurisdictions.

---

[47]§§ 959(a)(1) and (2).

25.12 Transfer Pricing

U.S. multinational companies earn income across many different jurisdictions and operate through several different types of entities (e.g., subsidiary corporations, joint ventures, partnerships). With proper planning and documentation, a U.S. corporation can organize its intercompany payments for goods and services, interest on debt, and royalties for use of intangible property in such a way as to minimize its worldwide tax burden. For example, a U.S. multinational may choose to borrow in high-tax jurisdictions (where the interest deduction will be more valuable) and earn royalty income in low-tax jurisdictions (where the income escapes heavy taxation).

Such decisions can be made within the legal framework of the tax laws of the United States and other countries. In the United States, § 482 provides the guidelines that must be met to justify and document appropriate transfer pricing. In general, these guidelines require an entity to demonstrate that it deserved to earn its profits based on the functions it performs, the assets it owns, or the risks it takes.

REFOCUS ON THE BIG PICTURE

GOING INTERNATIONAL

Now you can address the questions about VoiceCo's activities that were posed at the beginning of the chapter. Simply selling into a foreign jurisdiction may not trigger any overseas income tax consequences, but such income is taxed currently to VoiceCo in the United States. When VoiceCo sets up an Irish corporation, it benefits from deferral because as a manufacturer it can avoid deemed dividends under Subpart F. However, there may be passive-basket income earned by the Irish subsidiary.

VoiceCo must file Form 5471 to report on the activities of its foreign subsidiary. If VoiceCo receives dividends from its foreign subsidiary, it can claim § 902 foreign tax credits (so-called indirect credits). What are the foreign tax implications if VoiceCo "checks the box" on its foreign subsidiary? The U.S. tax implications?

What If?

Suppose that although VoiceCo's European sales become a substantial part of its total revenues, it decides not to create a foreign subsidiary. Instead, because shipping costs are high and customers demand quick turnaround on product orders, VoiceCo decides to license its design and manufacturing process to a local European musical instruments company for sales in Europe. The European company pays VoiceCo a royalty equal to 25 percent of the sales price on all its sales of microphones based on VoiceCo's design. The royalty income is foreign-source income (as the underlying intangible property is exploited outside the United States).

The European country imposes a 5 percent withholding tax on all royalty payments to VoiceCo. The royalties are part of its worldwide income and so are currently taxed to VoiceCo in the United States. Will VoiceCo receive a foreign tax credit for the withholding tax?

KEY TERMS

Branch profits tax, 25–34
Controlled foreign corporation (CFC), 25–19
Dividend equivalent amount (DEA), 25–34
Effectively connected income, 25–32
FIRPTA, 25–35
Foreign tax credit (FTC), 25–24
Functional currency, 25–14
Inbound taxation, 25–3
Nonresident alien (NRA), 25–30
Outbound taxation, 25–3
Qualified business unit (QBU), 25–14
Subpart F, 25–22
Tax haven, 25–19
Tax treaties, 25–4
Transfer pricing, 25–10
Treaty shopping, 25-20
U.S. shareholder, 25–21
U.S. trade or business, 25–32

DISCUSSION QUESTIONS

1. **LO.1** What is the meaning of the statement "U.S. persons are taxed on their worldwide income"?

2. **LO.1** Liang, a U.S. citizen, owns 100% of ForCo, a foreign corporation not engaged in a U.S. trade or business. In the absence of any dividends or Subpart F inclusions, is Liang subject to any U.S. income tax on the profits of ForCo?

3. **LO.2** Kelly, a U.S. citizen, earns interest income that is sourced in Germany. How could a U.S. tax treaty with Germany reduce Kelly's taxes on the interest?

4. **LO.3** When is dividend income paid by a non-U.S. entity to a U.S. investor *not* foreign-source income? Be specific.

ISSUE ID

5. **LO.3** Write a memo outlining the issues that arise when attempting to source income that is earned from Internet-based activities.

COMMUNICATIONS

6. **LO.3** Generally, U.S. taxpayers with foreign operations desire to increase foreign-source income and reduce deductions against that foreign-source income in order to increase their FTC limitations. How does § 482 enable the IRS to prevent taxpayers from manipulating the source of income and allocation of deductions? Explain.

7. **LO.4** Weinke is a business organized in Austria, where the local currency is the euro. Nevertheless, Weinke's U.S. branch uses the U.S. dollar as its functional currency. How can this be?

8. **LO.4** When dealing with the rules concerning gain and loss from foreign currency transactions, the taxpayer must identify its qualified business units (QBUs). What is a QBU? How many QBUs can a business operate?

ISSUE ID

9. **LO.5** What are the important concepts to be considered when U.S. assets are transferred outside the country to be used in starting a new business?

COMMUNICATIONS

10. **LO.5** Write a memo to a U.S. client explaining why some of the profit that it generates from a non-U.S. subsidiary still is included in its U.S. taxable income.

11. **LO.5** Summarize the ownership rules that apply in determining whether a non-U.S. entity is a controlled foreign corporation (CFC) under the U.S. Federal income tax rules.

ISSUE ID

12. **LO.5** Joanna owns 5% of Axel, a foreign corporation. Joanna's son, Fred, is considering acquiring 15% of Axel from an NRA. The remainder of Axel is owned 27% by unrelated U.S. persons and 53% by unrelated NRAs. Currently, Fred operates (as a sole proprietorship) a manufacturing business that sells goods to Axel for resale outside the United States and outside Axel's country of residence. Joanna is not concerned about the concentration of investment because she expects to sell her stock in Axel in three years at a significant capital gain. Are there tax issues that Joanna and Fred, both U.S. citizens, need to address?

13. **LO.5** Is a foreign corporation owned equally by 100 unrelated U.S. citizens considered a controlled foreign corporation?

14. **LO.5** QuinnCo could not claim all of the income taxes that it paid to Japan as a foreign tax credit (FTC) this year. What computational limit probably kept QuinnCo from taking its full FTC?

15. **LO.5** USCo, a domestic corporation, receives a $10,000 dividend from ForCo, a wholly owned foreign corporation. The § 902 deemed-paid FTC associated with this dividend is $4,000. What is the total gross income included in USCo's tax return as a result of this dividend?

ISSUE ID

16. **LO.5** Molly, Inc., a domestic corporation, owns 15% of PJ, Inc., and 12% of Emma, Inc., both foreign corporations. Molly is paid gross dividends of $35,000 and $18,000 from PJ and Emma, respectively. PJ withheld and paid more than $10,500 in foreign taxes on the $35,000 dividend. PJ's country of residence levies a 20% tax on dividends paid to nonresident corporations. However, the tax rate is increased to 30% if the recipient is a resident of a country that provides an FTC. Taxes of $3,600 are withheld on the dividend from Emma. What tax issues must be considered in determining the availability and amount of the FTC allowed to Molly, Inc.?

17. **LO.5** Working with the FTC may involve "baskets" of foreign-source income and deductions. Explain this term.

18. **LO.6** In general terms, how is a non-U.S. person taxed on its U.S. business income? Investment income? Do not take any tax treaties into account in your answer.

19. **LO.3, 6** Creek, Inc., a foreign corporation, sells vacuum tubes in several countries, including the United States. In fact, currently 25% of Creek's sales income is sourced in the United States (through branches in New York and Chicago). Creek is considering opening additional branches in San Francisco and Phoenix to increase U.S. sales. What tax issues must Creek consider before making this move? ISSUE ID

20. **LO.3, 6** Write a short memo on the difference between "inbound" and "outbound" activities in the context of U.S. taxation of international income. COMMUNICATIONS

21. **LO.1, 3, 5** If a U.S. taxpayer is subject to U.S. income tax on profits earned outside the United States and such profits are also subject to income tax in the foreign jurisdiction, how does the U.S. taxpayer escape double taxation? Draft a short speech that you will give to your university's Business Club. COMMUNICATIONS

PROBLEMS

22. **LO.4, 5** RedCo, a domestic corporation, incorporates GreenCo, a new wholly owned entity in Germany. Under both German and U.S. legal principles, this entity is a corporation. RedCo faces a 35% U.S. tax rate.

    GreenCo earns $800,000 in net profits from its German activities and makes no dividend distributions to RedCo. How much U.S. tax will RedCo pay for the current year as a result of GreenCo's earnings, assuming no deemed dividend under Subpart F? Ignore any FTC implications.

23. **LO.3** Madison, a U.S. resident, received the following income items for the current tax year. Identify the source of each income item as either U.S. or foreign.
    a. $3,000 dividend from U.S. Flower Company, a U.S. corporation, that operates solely in the eastern United States.
    b. $6,000 dividend from Stern Corporation, a U.S. corporation that had total gross income of $4 million from the active conduct of a foreign trade or business for the immediately preceding three tax years. Stern's worldwide gross income for the same period was $5 million.
    c. $2,000 dividend from International Consolidated, Inc., a foreign corporation that had gross income of $3 million effectively connected with the conduct of a U.S. trade or business for the immediately preceding three tax years. International's worldwide gross income for the same period was $6 million.
    d. $600 interest from a savings account at a Florida bank.
    e. $5,000 interest on Warren Corporation bonds. Warren is a U.S. corporation that derived $6 million of its gross income for the immediately preceding three tax years from operation of an active foreign business. Warren's worldwide gross income for this same period was $7.2 million.

24. **LO.3** Gloria Wang, an NRA, is a professional golfer. She played in seven tournaments in the United States in the current year and earned $200,000 in prizes from these tournaments. She deposited the winnings in a bank account she opened in Mexico City after her first tournament win. COMMUNICATIONS

    Gloria played a total of 30 tournaments for the year and earned $300,000 in total prize money. She spent 40 days in the United States, 60 days in England, 20 days in Scotland, and the rest of the time in South America. Write a letter to Gloria explaining how much U.S.-source income she will generate, if any, from her participation in these tournaments and whether any of her winnings are subject to U.S. taxation. Gloria's address is AV Rio Branco, 149–4#, Rio de Janeiro, RJ 22421, Brazil.

25. **LO.3** Determine whether the source of income for the following sales is U.S. or foreign.
    a. Suarez, an NRA, sells stock in Home Depot, a U.S. corporation, through a broker in San Antonio.
    b. Chris sells stock in IBM, a U.S. corporation, to her brother, Rich. Both Chris and Rich are NRAs, and the sale takes place outside the United States.
    c. Crows, Inc., sells inventory produced in the United States to customers in Europe. Title passes in the international waters of the Atlantic Ocean.
    d. Doubles, Inc., a U.S. corporation, manufactures equipment in Malaysia and sells the equipment to customers in the United States.

26. **LO.3** USCo, a domestic corporation, purchases inventory for resale from distributors within the United States and resells this inventory to customers outside the United States, with title passing outside the United States. What is the sourcing of USCo's inventory sales income?

27. **LO.3** USCo, a domestic corporation, owns the rights to a patent related to a medical device. USCo licenses the rights to use the patent to IrishCo, a foreign corporation. IrishCo uses the patent in a manufacturing facility located in Ireland. What is the sourcing of the royalty income received by USCo from IrishCo for the use of the patent?

28. **LO.3** USCo incurred $100,000 in interest expense for the current year. The tax book value of USCo's assets generating foreign-source income is $20 million. The tax book value of USCo's assets generating U.S.-source income is $80 million. How much of the interest expense is allocated and apportioned to foreign-source income?

DECISION MAKING

29. **LO.3** Create, Inc., produces inventory in its foreign manufacturing plants for sale in the United States. Its foreign manufacturing assets have a tax book value of $5 million and a fair market value of $15 million. Its assets related to the sales activity have a tax book value of $200,000 and a fair market value of $50,000. Create's interest expense totaled $300,000 for the current year.
    a. What amount of interest expense is allocated and apportioned to foreign-source income using the tax book value method? What amount of Create's interest expense is allocated and apportioned to foreign-source income using the fair market method?
    b. If Create wishes to maximize its FTC, which method should it use?

30. **LO.4** Peck, Inc., a U.S. corporation, purchases weight-lifting equipment for resale from HiDisu, a Japanese corporation, for 75 million yen. On the date of purchase, 150 yen is equal to $1 U.S. (¥150:$1). The purchase is made on December 15, 2011, with payment due in 90 days. Peck is a calendar year taxpayer. On December 31, 2011, the foreign exchange rate is ¥250:$1. What amount of foreign currency gain or loss, if any, must Peck recognize for 2011 as a result of this transaction?

COMMUNICATIONS

31. **LO.4** Table, Inc., a U.S. corporation, operates a manufacturing branch in Mexico and a sales branch in Canada. The Mexican branch uses the peso for all its activities, and the Canadian branch uses the Canadian dollar for all its activities. Write a letter to Karen Burns, Table's tax director, explaining the number of foreign qualified business units the company will have from these activities. Table's address is 840 Logan Avenue, Madison, WI 53705.

32. **LO.4** Harold is a citizen and resident of the United States. He pays all of his living expenses in U.S. dollars. He operates an unincorporated trade or business buying and selling rare books over the Internet to Canadian customers. All income and expenses of the rare book business are in Canadian dollars. Explain to Harold the number of qualified business units he has and the related functional currency of the QBUs.

33. **LO.4, 5** Teal, Inc., a foreign corporation, pays a dividend to its shareholders on November 30. Red, Inc., a U.S. corporation and 7% shareholder in Teal, receives a dividend of 10,000K (a foreign currency). Pertinent exchange rates are as follows.

November 30	.9K:$1
Average for year	.7K:$1
December 31	2K:$1

What is the dollar amount of the dividend received by Red, Inc.? Does Red, Inc., have a foreign exchange gain or loss on receipt of the dividend?

34. **LO.5** Beach, Inc., a domestic corporation, operates a branch in Mexico. Over the last 10 years, this branch has generated $50 million in losses. For the last 3 years, however, the branch has been profitable and has earned enough income to entirely offset the prior losses. Most of the assets are fully depreciated, and a net gain would be recognized if the assets were sold.

ISSUE ID

COMMUNICATIONS

Beach's CFO believes that Beach should incorporate the branch now so that this potential gain can be transferred to a foreign corporation, thereby avoiding U.S. tax and, as an added benefit, avoiding U.S. taxes on future income. Draft a memo to Claire Quinty, the CFO, addressing the tax issues involved in the proposed transaction.

35. **LO.5** USCo owns 55% of the voting stock of LandCo, a Country X corporation. IrishCo, an unrelated Country Y corporation, owns the other 45% of LandCo. LandCo owns 100% of the voting stock of OceanCo, a Country Z corporation. Assuming USCo is a U.S. shareholder, do LandCo and OceanCo meet the definition of a CFC?

36. **LO.5** Hart Enterprises, a U.S. corporation, owns 100% of OK, Ltd., an Irish corporation. OK's gross income for the year is $10 million. Determine OK's Subpart F income (before any expenses) from the transactions that it reported this year.
    a. OK received $600,000 from sales of products purchased from Hart and sold to customers outside Ireland.
    b. OK received $1 million from sales of products purchased from Hart and sold to customers in Ireland.
    c. OK received $400,000 from sales of products purchased from unrelated suppliers and sold to customers in Germany.
    d. OK purchased raw materials from Hart, used these materials to manufacture finished goods, and sold these goods to customers in Italy. OK earned $300,000 from these sales.
    e. OK received $100,000 for the performance of warranty services on behalf of Hart. These services were performed in Japan for customers located in Japan.
    f. OK received $50,000 in dividend income from investments in Canada and Mexico.

37. **LO.5** Round, Inc., a U.S. corporation, owns 80% of the only class of stock of Square, Inc., a CFC. Square is a CFC until May 1 of the current tax year (not a leap year). Round has held the stock since Square was organized and continues to hold it for the entire year. Round and Square are both calendar year taxpayers. Square's Subpart F income for the tax year is $1 million, current E & P is $2.5 million, and no distributions have been made for the tax year. What amount, if any, must Round include in gross income under Subpart F for the tax year?

38. **LO.5** Mary Beth Alessio, a U.S. citizen, has placed all her investments in a Cayman Island corporation owned 1% by Mary Beth and 99% by a foreign individual. She pays no income tax in the Cayman Islands on this income. The foreign corporation generates only interest and dividends. Prepare a letter informing Mary Beth of the U.S. tax consequences of her foreign investments. Her address is 941 Windom Lane, Hagerstown, MD 21740.

ISSUE ID

COMMUNICATIONS

39. **LO.5** Weather, Inc., a domestic corporation, operates in both Mexico and the United States. This year, the business generated taxable income of $600,000 from foreign sources and $900,000 from U.S. sources. All of Weather's foreign-source income is in the general limitation basket. Weather's total worldwide taxable income is $1.5 million. Weather pays Mexican taxes of $228,000. Assume a 34% U.S. income tax rate. What is Weather's FTC for the tax year?

40. **LO.5** Blunt, Inc., a U.S. corporation, earned $600,000 in total taxable income including $80,000 in foreign-source taxable income from its German branch's manufacturing operations and $30,000 in foreign-source taxable income from its Swiss branch's engineering services operations. Blunt paid $32,000 in German income taxes and $1,800 in Swiss income taxes. Compute Blunt's U.S. tax liability after any available FTCs. Assume the U.S. tax rate is 34%.

41. **LO.5** Dunne, Inc., a U.S. corporation, earned $400,000 in total taxable income, including $50,000 in foreign-source taxable income from its branch manufacturing operations in Brazil and $20,000 in foreign-source income from interest earned on bonds issued by Dutch corporations. Dunne paid $25,000 in Brazilian income taxes and $3,000 in Dutch income taxes. Compute Dunne's U.S. tax liability after any available FTCs. Assume the U.S. tax rate is 34%.

42. **LO.5** ABC, Inc., a domestic corporation, has $50 million of taxable income, including $15 million of general limitation foreign-source taxable income, on which ABC paid $5 million in foreign income taxes. The U.S. tax rate is 35%. What is ABC's foreign tax credit?

43. **LO.5** Mary, a U.S. citizen, is the sole shareholder of CanCo, a Canadian corporation. During its first year of operations, CanCo earns $14 million of foreign-source taxable income, pays $6 million of Canadian income taxes, and distributes a $2 million dividend to Mary. Can Mary claim a deemed-paid (indirect) FTC on her Form 1040 with respect to receipt of the dividend distribution from CanCo?

44. **LO.5** Elmwood, Inc., a domestic corporation, owns 15% of Correy, Ltd., a Hong Kong corporation. The remaining 85% of Correy is owned by Fortune Enterprises, a Canadian corporation. At the end of the current year, Correy has $400,000 in post-1986 undistributed E & P and $200,000 in foreign taxes related to this E & P. On the last day of the year, Correy pays a $30,000 dividend to Elmwood. Elmwood's taxable income before the dividend is $200,000. What is Elmwood's tax liability after consideration of the dividend and any allowed FTC, assuming a 34% U.S. tax rate?

COMMUNICATIONS

45. **LO.5** Your client Chips, Inc., is engaged in the cookie production business, with production plants in Florida and Singapore. The U.S. plant has always produced profits, but the Singapore operation has generated $80,000 in losses since inception. This year, the Singapore operation began producing net profits. Draft a brief memo to Sally, the CFO of Chips, explaining why a portion of the current-year foreign-source income must be recharacterized as U.S.-source for FTC limitation purposes.

46. **LO.5** Skills, Inc., a U.S. corporation, earns current foreign-source income classified in two different FTC income baskets. It earns $50,000 in passive foreign-source income and suffers a net loss of $30,000 in the general limitation basket. What is the numerator of the FTC limitation formula for the passive basket in the current year? Explain.

47. **LO.5** Canteen, Inc., a U.S. corporation, owns 100% of NewGrass, Ltd., a foreign corporation. NewGrass earns only general limitation income. During the current year, NewGrass paid Canteen a $10,000 dividend. The § 902 credit associated with this dividend is $3,000. The foreign jurisdiction requires a withholding tax of 20%, so Canteen received only $8,000 in cash as a result of the dividend. What is Canteen's total U.S. gross income reported as a result of the $8,000 cash dividend?

48. **LO.5** For which of the following foreign income inclusions is a U.S. corporation potentially allowed an indirect FTC under § 902?
    a. Interest income from a 5%-owned foreign corporation.
    b. Interest income from a 60%-owned foreign corporation.
    c. Dividend income from a 5%-owned foreign corporation.
    d. Dividend income from a 60%-owned foreign corporation.

DECISION MAKING

49. **LO.5** Night, Inc., a domestic corporation, earned $300,000 from foreign manufacturing activities on which it paid $90,000 of foreign income taxes. Night's foreign sales income is taxed at a 50% foreign tax rate. What amount of foreign sales income can Night earn without generating any excess FTCs for the current year? Assume a 34% U.S. tax rate.

50. **LO.4, 5** Partin, Inc., a foreign subsidiary of Jones, Inc., a U.S. corporation, has pretax income of 200,000 euros for 2011. Partin accrues 50,000 euros in foreign taxes on this income. The average exchange rate for the tax year to which the taxes relate is .95€:$1. None of the income is Subpart F income. If the net earnings of 150,000 euros are distributed when the exchange rate is 1.05€:$1, what are the deemed-paid taxes available to Jones? Assume that 2011 is Partin's first year of operation.

51. **LO.5** Collins, Inc., a domestic corporation, operates a manufacturing branch in Singapore. During the current year, the manufacturing branch produces a loss of $300,000. Collins also earns interest income from investments in Europe, where it earns $800,000 in passive income. Collins paid no foreign income taxes related to the Singapore branch, but it paid $64,000 in foreign income taxes related to the passive income. Assuming that Collins pays U.S. taxes at the 34% rate, what is Collins's allowable FTC for the current year?

DECISION MAKING

COMMUNICATIONS

52. **LO.5** Money, Inc., a U.S. corporation, has $500,000 to invest overseas for 2011. For U.S. tax purposes, any additional income earned by Money will be taxed at 34%. Two possibilities for investment are:

a. Invest the $500,000 in common stock of Exco (a foreign corporation). Exco common stock pays a dividend of $3 per share each year. The $500,000 would purchase 10,000 shares (or 10%) of Exco's only class of stock (voting common). Exco expects to earn $10 million before taxes for 2011 and to be taxed at a flat rate of 40%. Its 2011 E & P before taxes is estimated to be $9.4 million. Exco's government does not withhold on dividends paid to foreign investors.

b. Invest the $500,000 in Exco bonds that pay interest at 7% per year. Assume that the bonds will be acquired at par, or face, value. Exco's government withholds 25% on interest paid to foreign investors.

Analyze these two investment opportunities and determine which would give Money the better return after taxes. Be sure to consider the effect of the FTC. Write a memorandum to Money, Inc., advising the corporation of your findings.

53. **LO.2, 6** IrishCo, a manufacturing corporation resident in Ireland, distributes products through a U.S. office. Current-year taxable income from such sales in the United States is $12 million. IrishCo's U.S. office deposits working capital funds in short-term certificates of deposit with U.S. banks. Current-year interest income from these deposits is $150,000.

IrishCo also invests in U.S. securities traded on the New York Stock Exchange. This investing is done by the home office. For the current year, IrishCo has realized capital gains of $300,000 and dividend income of $50,000 from these stock investments. Compute IrishCo's U.S. tax liability, assuming that the U.S.-Ireland income tax treaty reduces withholding on dividends to 15% and on interest to 5%. Assume a 34% U.S. tax rate.

54. **LO.6** Clario, S.A., a Peruvian corporation, manufactures furniture in Peru. It sells the furniture to independent distributors in the United States. Because title to the furniture passes to the purchasers in the United States, Clario has $1 million in U.S.-source income. Clario has no employees or operations in the United States related to its furniture business.

As a separate line of business, Clario buys and sells antique toys. Clario has a single employee operating a booth on weekends at a flea market in Waldo, Florida. The antique toy business generated $9,000 in net profits from U.S. sources during the current year.

What is Clario's effectively connected income for the current year?

55. **LO.6** Trace, Ltd., a foreign corporation, operates a trade or business in the United States. Trace's U.S.-source income effectively connected with this trade or business is $800,000 for the current year. Trace's current-year E & P is $650,000. Trace's net U.S. equity was $8.2 million at the beginning of the year and $8.6 million at year-end. Trace is a resident in a country that has no income tax treaty with the United States. Prepare a brief memo to Trace's Tax VP, reporting Trace's branch profits tax liability for the current year, along with a planning idea for reducing the branch profits tax. **COMMUNICATIONS**

56. **LO.6** Brenda, an NRA individual, owns 30% of the stock of Jeff, Inc., a U.S. corporation. Jeff's balance sheet on the last day of the taxable year is as follows.

		Adjusted Basis	Fair Market Value
Cash (used as working capital)		$ 200,000	$ 200,000
Investment in foreign land		300,000	800,000
Investment in U.S. real estate:			
Land		150,000	400,000
Buildings	$2,300,000		
Less: Depreciation	(300,000)	2,000,000	5,000,000
		$2,650,000	$6,400,000
Accounts payable		$ 300,000	$ 300,000
Notes payable		500,000	500,000
Capital stock		400,000	4,150,000
Retained earnings		1,450,000	1,450,000
		$2,650,000	$6,400,000

Brenda was in the United States only 40 days in the tax year. She sold all of her stock in Jeff on the last day of the tax year for $6.4 million. Brenda's adjusted basis in the stock sold was $500,000. She sold the stock for cash. What are the U.S. tax consequences, if any, to Brenda?

ISSUE ID

COMMUNICATIONS

57. **LO.6** John McPherson is single, an attorney, and a U.S. citizen. He recently attended a seminar where he learned he could give up his U.S. citizenship, move to Bermuda (where he would pay no income tax), and operate his law practice long distance via the Internet with no U.S. tax consequences. Write a letter informing John of the tax consequences of his proposed actions. His address is 1005 NE 10th Street, Gainesville, GA 32812.

RESEARCH PROBLEMS

THOMSON REUTERS
Checkpoint® Student Edition

Note: Solutions to Research Problems can be prepared by using the **Checkpoint® Student Edition** online research product, which is available to accompany this text. It is also possible to prepare solutions to the Research Problems by using tax research materials found in a standard tax library.

COMMUNICATIONS

Research Problem 1. Jerry Jeff Keen, the CFO of Boots Unlimited, a Texas corporation, has come to you regarding a potential restructuring of business operations. Boots has long manufactured its western boots in plants in Texas and Oklahoma. Recently, Boots has explored the possibility of setting up a manufacturing subsidiary in Ireland, where manufacturing profits are taxed at 10%. Jerry Jeff sees this as a great idea, given that the alternative is to continue all manufacturing in the United States, where profits are taxed at 34%. Boots plans to continue all the cutting, sizing, and hand tooling of leather in its U.S. plants. This material will be shipped to Ireland for final assembly, with the finished product shipped to retail outlets all over Europe and Asia. Your initial concern is whether the income generated by the Irish subsidiary will be considered foreign base company income. Address this issue in a research memo, along with any planning suggestions.

Partial list of research aids:
§ 954(d).
Reg. § 1.954–3(a).
Bausch & Lomb, 71 TCM 2031, T.C.Memo. 1996–57.

Research Problem 2. NewCar.com, Inc., an innovative, Internet-based automobile retailer based in Ghana, is beginning to seek customers in the United States. Currently, it has no sales personnel or assets located in the United States, but it makes a few sales to U.S. customers based on orders over its website. NewCar.com is considering sending a few sales agents to the United States to set up sales offices in large cities. The offices will have no inventory and will merely provide a place for the sales agents to meet with interested customers. Ghana has no income tax treaty with the United States. How would you advise NewCar.com, Inc., on the tax consequences of its proposed U.S. venture?

Partial list of research aids:
§ 882(a)(1).
Higgins v. Comm., 41–1 USTC ¶9233, 25 AFTR 1160, 61 S.Ct. 475 (1941).
Continental Trading, Inc. v. Comm., 59–1 USTC ¶9316, 3 AFTR 2d 923, 265 F.2d 40 (CA–9, 1959).
Piedras Negras Broadcasting Co., 43 BTA 297 (1941), *aff'd* 42–1 USTC ¶9384, 29 AFTR 243, 127 F.2d 260 (CA–5, 1942).

INTERNET *activity*

Use the tax resources of the Internet to address the following question. Do not restrict your search to the Web, but include a review of newsgroups and general reference materials, practitioner sites and resources, primary sources of the tax law, chat rooms and discussion groups, and other opportunities.

COMMUNICATIONS

Research Problem 3. For your analysis, choose 10 countries, one of which is the United States. Create a table showing whether each country applies a worldwide or territorial approach to international income taxation. Then list the country's top income tax rate on business profits. Send a copy of your table to your instructor.

CHAPTER

26

Tax Practice and Ethics

LEARNING OBJECTIVES

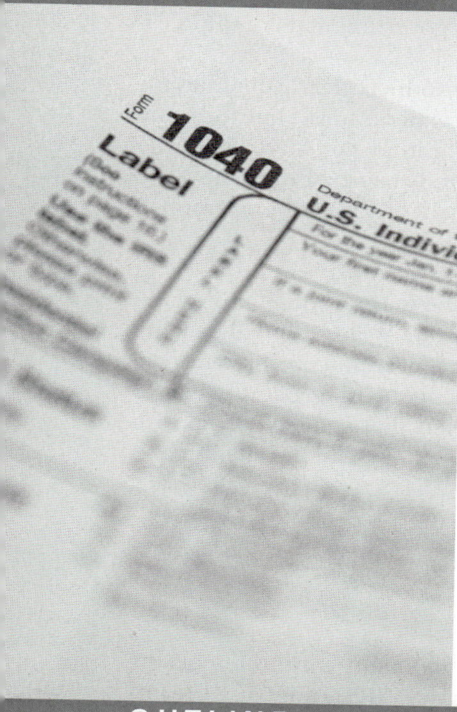

After completing Chapter 26, you should be able to:

LO.1

Identify the various administrative pronouncements issued by the IRS and explain how they can be used in tax practice.

LO.2

Summarize the administrative powers of the IRS, including the examination of taxpayer records, the assessment and demand process, and collection procedures.

LO.3

Describe the audit process, including how returns are selected for audit and the various types of audits.

LO.4

Explain the taxpayer appeal process, including various settlement options available.

LO.5

Determine the amount of interest on a deficiency or a refund and when it is due.

LO.6

Discuss the various penalties that can be imposed on acts of noncompliance by taxpayers and return preparers.

LO.7

Understand the rules governing the statute of limitations on assessments and on refunds.

LO.8

Summarize the legal and ethical guidelines that apply to those engaged in tax practice.

LO.9

Identify effective planning strategies that may be useful in a tax practice when dealing with the IRS.

OUTLINE

For the latest in changes to tax legislation, visit **www.cengage.com/taxation/swft.**

THE BIG PICTURE Tax Solutions for the Real World

A TAX ADVISER'S DILEMMA

Campbell Corporation is preparing its Form 1120 for the tax year. The entity develops and manufactures a number of electronic products, including a line of GPS applications that are downloaded onto cell phones. Campbell's research department needs to work with the U.S. government on this line of software because of the potential for security breaches when the software is used in sensitive parts of the world. Other efforts of the research department include traditional software architecture and development. Projections show that the GPS products will be highly profitable, with sales concentrated among various commercial and governmental communications providers around the world.

Some of the research department's work on the GPS products clearly qualifies for the Federal income tax credit for incremental research expenditures, but for some other items the availability of the credit is not so certain. Either the language of the pertinent Regulations is unclear in Campbell's setting, or, because of the innovative aspects of the products under development, the law is silent as to whether Campbell can claim the credit.

You are Campbell's tax adviser. This situation presents you with several levels of difficulty. How aggressive should you advise Campbell to be in reporting items on the Form 1120 that qualify for the incremental research credit? Will Campbell's taking an overly aggressive position on the credit trigger a tax preparer penalty for your consulting firm? What level of diligence should you exercise in advising Campbell as to whether specific expenditures qualify for the credit, given that your expertise with GPS software is limited to using the unit in your personal auto? **Read the chapter and formulate your response.**

Few events arouse so much fear in the typical individual or corporation as the receipt of a letter from the Internal Revenue Service (IRS), notifying the taxpayer that prior years' tax returns are to be the subject of an audit. Almost immediately, calls are made to the tax adviser. Advice is sought as to what to reveal (or not reveal) in the course of the audit, how to delay or avoid the audit, and how friendly one should be with the auditor when he or she ultimately arrives.

Indeed, many tax practitioners' reputations with their clients have been made or broken by the way they are observed to behave under the pressure of an audit situation. The strategy and tactics of audits—including such seemingly unimportant issues as whether the tax adviser brings donuts or other refreshments to the audit session, the color of his or her clothes, and the most effective negotiation techniques—are the subject of both cocktail party banter and scholarly review.

In actuality, the tax professional can render valuable services to the taxpayer in an audit context, thereby assuring that tax payments for the disputed years are neither under- nor overreported, as part of an ongoing tax practice. In this regard, the adviser must appreciate the following.

- The elements of the Treasury's tax administration process and opportunities for appeal within the structure of the IRS.
- The extent of the negative sanctions that can be brought to bear against taxpayers whose returns are found to have been inaccurate.
- The ethical and professional constraints on the advice tax advisers can give and the actions they can take on behalf of their clients within the context of an adversarial relationship with the IRS.

TAX *in the NEWS*

How Big Is the Tax Gap?

Every year the IRS estimates the size of the Federal income "tax gap"—the difference between how much tax *is* collected and how much *should be* collected. The tax gap reflects the taxes not paid by nonfilers, tax cheats, delinquents, and those who interpret or apply the tax laws incorrectly, whether deliberately or innocently.

According to the most recent analysis, the tax gap is a net amount of almost $300 billion annually. More specifically, the underpayments total about $345 billion per year but are offset by $55 billion obtained through IRS enforcement efforts (audits, collection procedures, etc.).

The IRS maintains that only 84 percent of taxpayers report the "correct" amount of tax under the existing system of voluntary compliance. The main sources of the tax gap are:

- Underreporting net taxable income (82 percent of the tax gap).
- Underpayment of tax (10 percent of the tax gap).
- Nonfiling (8 percent of the tax gap).

If, by some miracle, the entire tax gap were collected each year, the current Federal budget deficit would be cut significantly. A complete elimination of the tax gap is unlikely to occur, however, for several reasons.

- Citizens are not likely to tolerate the increased audit activity and data collection necessary for the Treasury to collect all of the tax owed.
- Citizens who are so inclined will continue to commit tax fraud, even if statutory and administrative changes are made to the system to identify them. Tax cheats are always "one step ahead" of the government in this regard.
- Congress is not likely to adopt the sweeping simplification of the tax law needed to alleviate its complexity, which many see as the underlying cause of the tax gap. Taxpayers who have difficulty understanding the tax law cannot be expected to fully comply with its provisions.

26.1 Tax Administration

The Treasury has delegated the administration and enforcement of the tax laws to its subsidiary agency, the IRS. In this process, the Service is responsible for providing adequate information, in the form of publications and forms with instructions, to taxpayers so that they can comply with the laws in an appropriate manner. The IRS also identifies delinquent tax payments and carries out assessment and collection procedures under the restrictions of due process and other constitutional guarantees.

The IRS is one of the largest Federal agencies. It employs about 87,500 staff members, and the total agency budget exceeds $12 billion. In meeting its responsibilities, the Service conducts audits of selected tax returns. About 1 percent of all individual tax returns are subjected to audit in a given tax year. However, certain types of both taxpayers and income—including, for example, high-income individuals (about 4 percent for those with income exceeding $100,000, and over 9 percent for those with income exceeding $1 million), cash-oriented businesses, real estate transactions, and estate- and gift-taxable transfers (as high as 20 percent)—are subject to much higher probabilities of audit.

The audit rate for corporations with at least $250 million in assets is about 27.5 percent, but the rate drops to about 2 percent for businesses with less than $10 million in assets. In the past few years, the IRS has stepped up its audit and enforcement activities and is targeting narrower issues that are projected to produce more revenue for the time spent. Thus, audit rates for large corporations have decreased although the dollars collected from such audits continue to increase.

Recently, much of the IRS's effort has been devoted to developing statutory and administrative requirements relative to information reporting and document matching. For example, when a taxpayer engages in a like-kind exchange or sells a personal residence, various parties to the transaction are required to report the nature and magnitude of the transaction to the IRS. Later the Treasury's computers determine whether the transaction has been reported properly by comparing the information reported by the third parties with the events included on the relevant taxpayers' returns for the year.

TAX *in the NEWS*

IRS Audit Initiatives

The IRS's current audit initiatives seem to be aimed at chronic and high-risk noncompliance. In an age of shrinking real budget dollars for the Service, this "biggest bang for the buck" strategy may be appropriate. The Service seems to be hunting for annuities of tax dollars, rather than just maximizing current collections. For example, permanently adding a noncompliant taxpayer to the tax rolls can optimize the present value of revenue collections tied to the IRS's efforts.

Announced priority areas for the IRS audit staff include the following.

- Offshore credit card users.
- High-risk, high-income taxpayers.
- Tax shelters, abusive schemes, and their promoters.
- High-income nonfilers.
- Unreported income.
- Transfer pricing involving transactions between U.S. companies and their foreign affiliates.
- Employment taxes.
- Transfers of intangible assets to off-shore affiliated companies.
- Executive compensation (particularly stock option transactions).
- Claims of the research credit.
- Abuse of the rules for tax-exempt entities.
- Further research as to audit initiatives.

The agency has stated that it is revising its training materials and case studies to reflect the revised priorities. "Hardball" techniques apparently will be used to deal with the priority issues. Such techniques include issuing summonses, obtaining injunctions, initiating civil audits for shelter participants, and pursuing criminal investigations of shelter promoters.

In addition, the IRS has been placing increasing pressure on the community of tax advisers. Severe penalties may be assessed on those who have prepared a taxpayer's return when the Service's interpretation of applicable law conflicts with that of the preparer.

The IRS processes about 145 million individual income tax returns every year, almost 95 million of which are filed electronically (i.e., known as **e-filing**). It collects about $2.5 trillion in annual tax revenues and pays refunds to about 100 million individual taxpayers every year. The average refund exceeds $3,000.

LO.1

Identify the various administrative pronouncements issued by the IRS and explain how they can be used in tax practice.

IRS PROCEDURE—LETTER RULINGS

When a tax issue is controversial or a transaction involves considerable tax dollars, the taxpayer often wishes to obtain either assurance or direction from the IRS as to the treatment of the event. The **letter ruling** process is an effective means of dealing directly with the IRS while in the planning stages of a large or otherwise important transaction.

Rulings issued by the National Office provide a written statement of the position of the IRS concerning the tax consequences of a course of action contemplated by the taxpayer. Letter rulings do not have the force and effect of law, but they do provide guidance and support for taxpayers in similar transactions. The IRS issues rulings only on uncompleted, actual (rather than hypothetical) transactions or on transactions completed before the filing of the tax return for the year in question.

The IRS will not issue a ruling in certain circumstances. It ordinarily will not rule in cases that essentially involve a question of fact.[1] For example, no ruling will be issued to determine whether compensation paid to employees is reasonable in amount and therefore allowable as a deduction.[2]

A letter ruling represents the current opinion of the IRS on the tax consequences of a transaction with a given set of facts. IRS rulings are not unchangeable. They are frequently declared obsolete or are superseded by new rulings in response to tax law changes. However, revocation or modification of a ruling usually is not applied

[1] Rev.Proc. 2011–1, I.R.B. No. 1, 14.

[2] Rev.Proc. 2011–3, I.R.B. No. 1, 113.

retroactively to the taxpayer who received the ruling, if it was relied on in good faith and if the facts in the ruling request were in agreement with the completed transaction. The IRS may revoke any ruling if, upon subsequent audit, the agent finds a misstatement or omission of facts or substantial discrepancies between the facts in the ruling request and the actual situation. A ruling may be relied upon only by the taxpayer who requested and received it.

Letter rulings benefit both the IRS and the taxpayer. Not only do they help promote a uniform application of the tax laws, but they may also reduce the potential for litigation or disputes with IRS agents. In addition, they make the IRS aware of significant transactions being consummated by taxpayers. A fee of $11,500 is charged for processing a ruling request; the fee is reduced to $625 if the taxpayer's income is less than $250,000.

IRS PROCEDURE—OTHER ISSUANCES

In addition to issuing unpublished letter rulings and published rulings and procedures, the IRS issues determination letters and technical advice memoranda.

A **determination letter** relates to a completed transaction when the issue involved is covered by judicial or statutory authority, Regulations, or rulings. Determination letters are issued for various estate, gift, income, excise, and employment tax matters.

EXAMPLE 1

True Corporation recently opened an auto care clinic and has employed numerous mechanics. The corporation is not certain whether its educational reimbursement plan is nondiscriminatory. True may request a determination letter. ■

EXAMPLE 2

Assume the same facts as in Example 1. True would like to establish a retirement plan that qualifies for the tax advantages of § 401(k). To determine whether the plan qualifies, True should request and obtain a determination letter from the IRS. ■

EXAMPLE 3

A group of physicians plans to form an association to construct and operate a hospital. The determination letter procedure is appropriate to ascertain whether the group is either subject to the Federal income tax or is tax-exempt. ■

A **technical advice memorandum (TAM)** is issued by the National Office to IRS personnel in response to a specific request by an agent, Appellate Conferee, or IRS executive. The taxpayer may request a TAM if an issue in dispute is not treated by the law or precedent and/or published rulings or Regulations. TAMs are also appropriate when there is reason to believe that the IRS is not administering the tax law consistently. For example, a taxpayer may inquire why an agent proposes to disallow a certain expenditure when agents in other parts of the country permit the deduction. Technical advice requests arise from the audit process, whereas ruling requests are issued before an IRS audit.

A technical expedited advice memorandum (TEAM) can be used during an office or field audit. The TEAM is designed to reflect the position of the IRS in a shorter time than a TAM otherwise would take. This quicker response time is possible because the following occur before a TEAM request is submitted.

- The taxpayer and the IRS agree to a set of facts for the case.
- The parties conduct a presubmission conference, with attorneys for both sides in attendance.
- Technology, including e-mails and faxes, is used to gather facts as part of the process.
- The IRS holds an internal strategic planning meeting, discussing potential responses to various holdings that could be issued as part of the TEAM.

LO.2

Summarize the administrative powers of the IRS, including the examination of taxpayer records, the assessment and demand process, and collection procedures.

ADMINISTRATIVE POWERS OF THE IRS

Examination of Records

The IRS can examine the taxpayer's books and records as part of the process of determining the correct amount of tax due. The IRS also can require the persons responsible for the return to appear and to produce any necessary books and records.[3] Taxpayers are required to maintain certain record-keeping procedures and retain the records necessary to facilitate the audit.

Burden of Proof

If the taxpayer meets the record-keeping requirement and substantiates income and deductions properly, the IRS bears the burden of proof in establishing a tax deficiency during litigation. The taxpayer must have cooperated with the IRS regarding reasonable requests for information, documents, meetings, and interviews. For individual taxpayers, the IRS's burden of proof extends to penalties and interest amounts that it assesses in a court proceeding with the taxpayer.[4]

Assessment and Demand

The Code permits the IRS to assess a deficiency and to demand payment for the tax. However, no assessment or effort to collect the tax may be made until 90 days after a statutory notice of a deficiency (the *90-day letter*) is issued. The taxpayer therefore has 90 days to file a petition to the U.S. Tax Court, effectively preventing the deficiency from being assessed or collected pending the outcome of the case.[5]

Following assessment of the tax, the IRS issues a notice and demand for payment. The taxpayer is usually given 30 days after the notice and demand for payment to pay the tax.

If the IRS believes the assessment or collection of a deficiency is in jeopardy, it may assess the deficiency and demand immediate payment.[6] The taxpayer can avoid (*stay*) the collection of the jeopardy assessment by filing a bond for the amount of the tax and interest. This action prevents the IRS from selling any property it has seized.

Collection

If the taxpayer neglects or refuses to pay the tax after receiving the demand for payment, a lien in favor of the IRS is placed on all property (realty and personalty, tangible and intangible) belonging to the taxpayer.

The levy power of the IRS is very broad. It allows the IRS to garnish (*attach*) wages and salary and to seize and sell all nonexempt property by any means. After a 30-day notice period, the IRS can also make successive seizures on any property owned by the taxpayer until the levy is satisfied.[7] A taxpayer's principal residence is exempt from the levy process, unless the disputed tax, interest, and penalty exceed $5,000 and a U.S. District Court judge approves of the seizure.[8]

LO.3

Describe the audit process, including how returns are selected for audit and the various types of audits.

THE AUDIT PROCESS

Selection of Returns for Audit

The IRS uses mathematical formulas to select tax returns that are most likely to contain errors and yield substantial amounts of additional tax revenues upon audit. The IRS does not disclose all of its audit selection techniques. However, some observations can be made regarding the probability that a return will be selected for audit.

---

[3] § 7602.

[4] §§ 7491(a)(1), (a)(2)(B), and (c).

[5] §§ 6212 and 6213.

[6] § 6861. A jeopardy assessment is appropriate, for example, when the IRS fears that the taxpayer will flee the country or destroy valuable property.

[7] The taxpayer can keep certain personal and business property and a minimal amount of his or her income as a subsistence allowance, even if a lien is outstanding. § 6334.

[8] §§ 6334(a)(13)(A) and (e)(1).

TAX *in the NEWS*

Tax Preparation by the Numbers

The community of taxpayers and their tax preparers is extensive and increasingly is using electronic means to meet current filing requirements. The following summary is based on recent estimates.

Number of individuals who prepare Federal tax returns for a fee	1 million
Percentage of all Federal tax returns that were filed using computer software and/or a paid tax preparer	80%
Number of Federal tax returns filed by paid preparers using tax filing software	62 million
Number of self-prepared Federal tax returns filed by taxpayers using tax filing software	32 million
Number of unpaid volunteers who registered with the IRS to assist taxpayers with filing requirements	80,000

- Certain groups of taxpayers are subject to audit more frequently than others. These groups include individuals with gross income in excess of $100,000, self-employed individuals with substantial business income and deductions, and cash businesses where the potential for tax evasion is high.

EXAMPLE 4

Tracey owns and operates a liquor store. As nearly all of her sales are for cash, Tracey might be a prime candidate for an audit by the IRS. Cash transactions are easier to conceal than those made on credit. ■

- If a taxpayer has been audited in a past year and the audit led to the assessment of a substantial deficiency, the IRS often makes a return visit.
- An audit might materialize if information returns (e.g., Form W–2, Form 1099) are not in substantial agreement with the income reported on a taxpayer's return. Obvious discrepancies do not necessitate formal audits and usually can be handled by correspondence with the taxpayer.
- If an individual's itemized deductions are in excess of norms established for various income levels, the probability of an audit increases. Certain deductions (e.g., casualty and theft losses, business use of the home, tax-sheltered investments) are sensitive areas as the IRS realizes that many taxpayers determine the amount of the deduction incorrectly or may not be entitled to the deduction at all.
- The filing of a refund claim by the taxpayer may prompt an audit of the return.
- Some returns are selected because the IRS has targeted a specific industry or type of tax return for in-depth review. This enables examiners to develop special skills and interests applicable to those returns. In the Industry Specialization Program (ISP), returns might be selected from retailers, energy developers, or health care operations for special review. In the Market Segment Specialization Program (MSSP), specialized auditors focus on returns that show passive losses, involve construction activities, or include legal or consulting income.
- Information is often obtained from other sources (e.g., other government agencies, news items, informants). The IRS then applies its own judgment and experience, and it may audit the return to address such questions as: Why did dividend income increase so much this year? Why did mortgage interest payments decrease? How did the taxpayer pay for such a large vacation home that was sold this year?

Many individual taxpayers mistakenly assume that if they do not hear from the IRS within a few weeks after filing their return or if they receive a refund check, no audit will be forthcoming. As a practical matter, most individual returns are examined about two years from the date of filing. If not, they generally remain unaudited. All large corporations, however, are subject to annual audits.

The IRS can pay rewards to persons who provide information that leads to the detection and punishment of those who violate the tax laws. The rewards are paid at the discretion of the IRS. Such a payment usually cannot exceed 15 percent of the taxes, fines, and penalties recovered as a result of the information.[9] About 20,000 rewards are paid in the typical year. The average reward paid is about $4,500.

Another IRS office, through the so-called **Whistleblower Program**, offers special rewards to informants who provide information concerning businesses or high-income (gross income exceeds $200,000) individuals, when more than $2 million of tax, penalty, and interest is at stake. Some informants claim that hundreds of millions of dollars of tax, penalty, and interest are due from allegedly noncompliant taxpayers. The reward can reach 30 percent of the amount collected by the Treasury and traceable to the whistleblower's information. The reward can be reduced if the whistleblower participated in the original understatement of tax. About 500 cases are initiated every year as a result of tips from whistleblowers.

The rewards are paid out of the taxes recovered under the informant and whistleblower programs. To claim a reward of this sort, an informant must file Form 211 with the IRS.

EXAMPLE 5

Phil reports to the police that burglars broke into his home while he was out of town and took a shoe box containing $25,000 in cash, among other things. A representative of the IRS reading the newspaper account of the burglary might wonder why Phil kept such a large amount of cash in a shoe box at home. ■

EXAMPLE 6

George, a long-time salesman at Carl's dealership, has been terminated as the result of a downsizing of the sales force. As part of working through the shock arising from his firing, George informs the IRS that Carl had bragged about the dealership paying for and deducting the construction costs of a new backyard pool and garden at Carl's personal residence. As George recalls, Carl was particularly gleeful because he received the personal benefit without reporting the corresponding income and paying the associated income tax. ■

The statistical models used by the IRS to select individual tax returns for audit come from random audits of a small number of taxpayers, who are required to document every entry that they made on the Form 1040. The latest round of these National Research Program (NRP) audits resulted in the construction of new Discriminant Function (DIF) scores that project the amount of revenue that the IRS will gain from pursuing tax returns with various statistical profiles. The higher the DIF score, the better the return to the IRS from pursuing the audit, and the higher the probability of selection for an examination.

These data-seeking audits are controversial and have led to taxpayer complaints to Congress about the stress that they create.[10] But the data from older DIF models no longer reflected the U.S. service-based, information-powered economy. Consequently, the underlying models require a more frequent updating for effective enforcement of the tax laws. The IRS believes that, by constantly updating the NRP data through a diligent review of randomly selected tax returns, changes in tax avoidance behaviors will be detected and fewer routine audits will be required.

[9] § 7623 and Temp.Reg. § 301.7623–1T.

[10] On average, the total annual NRP audit sample consists of 13,000 returns. Some of these returns are analyzed without contacting the taxpayer, and other taxpayers are contacted only by mail with queries about one or two items. Only a few returns are subjected to "line-by-line" review. Most of the returns are reviewed for a period of three tax years.

ETHICS & Equity

Can the IRS Pretend to Be Your Friend?

Should IRS agents be allowed to identify audit subjects by reading the society page of the newspaper looking for indicators of wealth? What if the agency subscribes to Facebook and seeks comments from its "friends" as to income windfalls and stock market dealings? In the past, some state and local taxing agencies have used social networking sites for audit selection purposes. State and local revenue agents have used the sites to find self-employed individuals who advertise their business and report about upcoming income-producing events. The sites also have been used to determine whether a taxpayer who has requested an extension of time to pay a delinquent tax actually is strapped for cash.

Some state tax officials claim that looking for a taxpayer's self-declarations on a website is a much more efficient way to find income understatements than searching through most other sources of nonstatistical data. Should taxing agencies be using Google, Facebook, and other public-domain online sources of taxpayer information to help identify tax returns for audit?

Verification and Audit Procedures

The filed tax return is immediately reviewed for mathematical accuracy. A check is also made for deductions, exclusions, etc., that are clearly erroneous. One obvious error would be the failure to comply with the 7.5 percent limitation on the deduction for medical expenses. About 2 percent of all paper-filed individual returns show a math error. The math error rate for e-filed returns is only 0.1 percent. When a math or clerical error occurs, the Service Center merely sends the taxpayer revised computations and a bill or refund as appropriate.

Taxpayers are usually able to settle routine tax disputes (e.g., queries involving the documentation of deductions) through a by-mail-only *correspondence audit* with the IRS, without the necessity of a formal meeting.

Office audits are conducted in an office of the IRS. Individual returns with few or no items of business income are usually handled through an office audit. In most situations, the taxpayer is required merely to substantiate a deduction, credit, or item of income that appears on the return. The taxpayer presents documentation in the form of canceled checks, invoices, etc., for the items in question.

The *field audit* is commonly used for corporate returns and for returns of individuals engaged in business or professional activities. This type of audit generally involves a more complete examination of a taxpayer's transactions.

A field audit is conducted by IRS agents at the office or home of the taxpayer or at the office of the taxpayer's representative. The agent's work may be facilitated by a review of certain tax workpapers and discussions with the taxpayer's representative about items appearing on the tax return. Table 26.1 summarizes key audit information.

Prior to or at the initial interview, the IRS must provide the taxpayer with an explanation of the audit process that is the subject of the interview and describe the taxpayer's rights under that process. If the taxpayer clearly states at any time during the interview the desire to consult with an attorney, CPA, enrolled agent, or any other person permitted to represent the taxpayer before the IRS, then the IRS representative must suspend the interview.[11]

TABLE 26.1 IRS Audit Information by Type

	Conducted (Number)	Conducted (Percent)
Correspondence audit	1,125,000	69%
Office audit	50,000	3%
Field audit	450,000	28%

[11] § 7521(b).

TAX *in the NEWS*

E-Filing the Form 1040

Roughly 70 percent of all Forms 1040 are filed electronically. Most of the e-filed returns are submitted by tax professionals, who often charge a processing fee of about $25 per return, or by individuals who use commercial or IRS software programs to submit the return.

The IRS encourages e-filing because the filing software eliminates math errors and clarifies ambiguous disclosures by the taxpayer. However, the labor unions that represent IRS employees maintain that paperless tax filing is putting their members' jobs at risk. In fact, the number of IRS personnel has shrunk by more than 10 percent in the last decade, and data processing centers have been downsized. Yet no government official admits that the growth of e-filing has contributed to this contraction.

Taxpayers like e-filing because the IRS processes their returns in less than half the time needed for traditional paper-based forms. Also, e-filing presents a "green" alternative, in that less paper, ink, and toner may be required. The taxpayer also avoids postage costs and the time spent waiting in line at the post office. By use of the direct deposit system for refunds, the taxpayer has quicker access to the funds. If the taxpayer owes taxes, most e-filing software also allows for a direct debit process.

Large C corporations have been required to e-file for many years, and electronic processing has been phased in for smaller businesses, trusts, and tax-exempt entities. The IRS is pressuring tax practitioners to eliminate their fees for filing tax returns electronically, especially for low-income taxpayers, and may soon provide its own filing portal to facilitate "free filing." Growth in the number of e-filed returns may come from those 40 million individuals who use preparation software and then mail the printed return to the IRS. Also, a new rule requiring all tax preparers who file more than 10 returns annually to use e-filing may result in about 15 million more e-filed returns.

Any officer or employee of the IRS must, upon advance request, allow a taxpayer to make an audio recording of any in-person interview with the officer or employee concerning the determination and collection of any tax.[12]

Settlement with the Revenue Agent

Following an audit, the IRS agent may either accept the return as filed or recommend certain adjustments. The **Revenue Agent's Report (RAR)** is reviewed within the IRS. In most instances, the agent's proposed adjustments are approved.

Agents must adhere strictly to IRS policy as reflected in published rulings, Regulations, and other releases. The agent cannot settle an unresolved issue based upon the probability of winning the case in court. Usually, issues involving factual questions can be settled at the agent level, and it may be advantageous for both the taxpayer and the IRS to reach agreement at the earliest point in the settlement process. For example, it may be to the taxpayer's advantage to reach agreement at the agent level and avoid any further opportunity for the IRS to raise new issues.

If agreement is reached upon the proposed deficiency, the taxpayer signs Form 870 (Waiver of Restrictions on Assessment and Collection of Deficiency in Tax). One advantage to the taxpayer of signing Form 870 at this point is that interest stops accumulating on the deficiency 30 days after the form is filed.[13] When this form is signed, the taxpayer effectively waives the right to receive a statutory notice of deficiency (the 90-day letter) and to subsequently petition the Tax Court. In addition, it is no longer possible for the taxpayer later to go to the IRS Appeals Division. Signing Form 870 at the agent level generally closes the case. However, the IRS is not restricted by Form 870 and may assess additional deficiencies if deemed necessary.

LO.4

Explain the taxpayer appeal process, including various settlement options available.

THE TAXPAYER APPEAL PROCESS

If agreement cannot be reached at the agent level, the taxpayer receives a copy of the Revenue Agent's Report and a **30-day letter**. The taxpayer has 30 days to request an administrative appeal. If an appeal is not requested, a **90-day letter** is issued. Figure 26.1 illustrates the taxpayer's alternatives when a disagreement with the IRS persists.

[12] § 7521(a).

[13] § 6601(c).

FIGURE 26.1 Income Tax Appeal Procedure

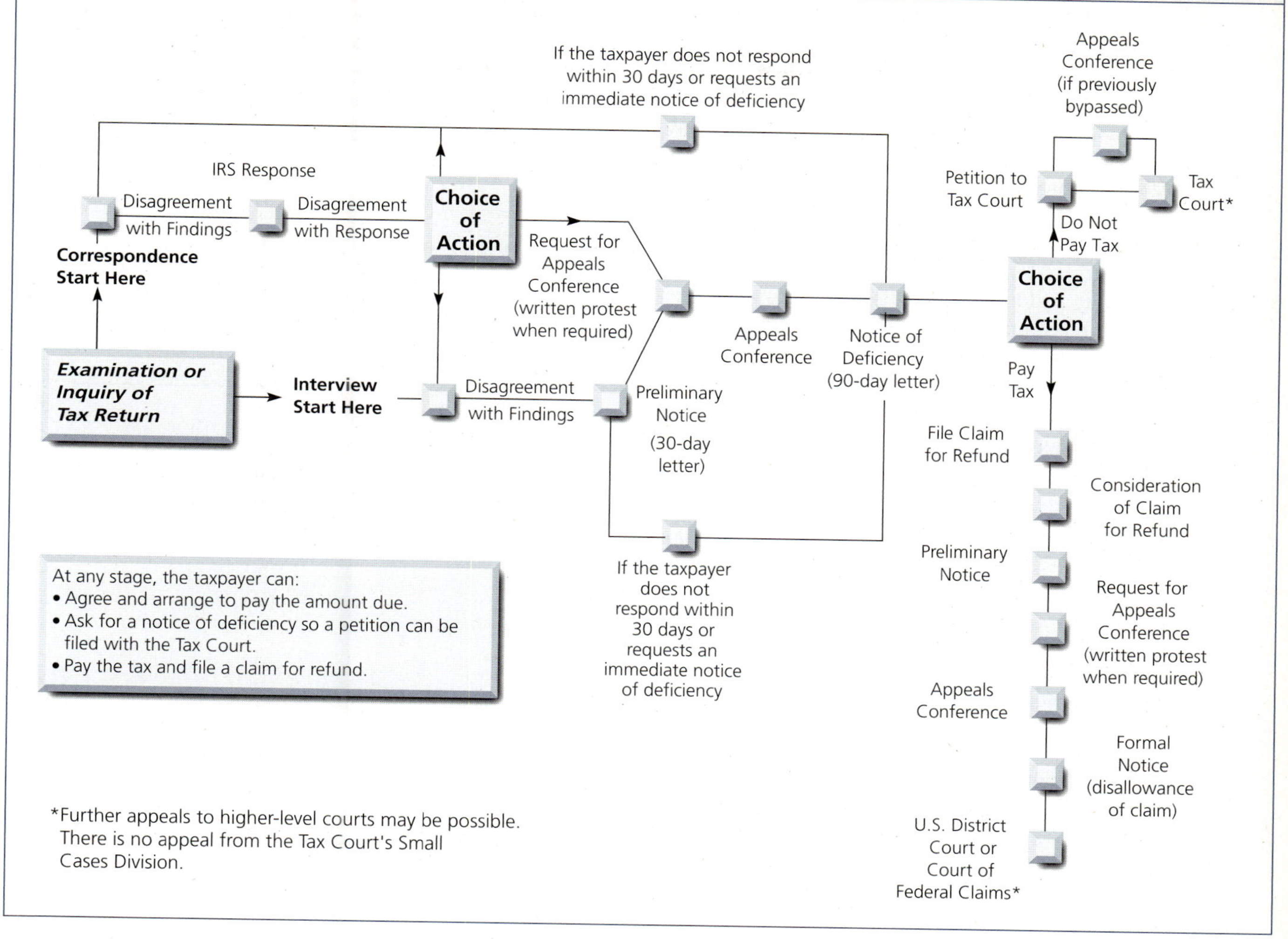

A taxpayer who wishes to appeal must make an appropriate request to the Appeals Division. The request must be accompanied by a written protest except in the following cases.

- The proposed tax deficiency does not exceed $10,000 for any of the tax periods involved in the audit.
- The deficiency resulted from a correspondence or office audit (i.e., not as a result of a field audit).

The Appeals Division is authorized to settle all tax disputes based on the hazards of litigation (i.e., the chances of winning in court). Since the Appeals Division has final settlement authority until a 90-day letter has been issued, the taxpayer may be able to negotiate a settlement. In addition, an overall favorable settlement may be reached by "trading" disputed issues. The Appeals Division occasionally may raise new issues if the grounds are substantial and of significant tax impact.

Both the Appeals Division and the taxpayer have the right to request technical advice memoranda from the National Office of the IRS. A TAM that is favorable to the taxpayer is binding on the Appeals Division. Even if the TAM is favorable to the IRS, however, the Appeals Division may nevertheless settle the case based on other considerations.

A taxpayer who files a petition with the U.S. Tax Court has the option of having the case heard before the more informal Small Cases Division if the amount of the deficiency in dispute does not exceed $50,000.[14] If the Small Cases Division is used, neither party may appeal the case.

[14] § 7463(a).

ETHICS & Equity

Our Taxing System of Self-Assessment

The United States is a large country of diverse taxpayers and businesses. Perhaps the only way that the massive dollar amounts of Federal income taxes can be collected on a timely basis is through a *self-assessment* process, whereby the taxpayer is charged with disclosing a full picture of the tax year's results and the corresponding computation of taxable income. But a system of self-assessment depends heavily on the honesty and integrity of the taxpayers, and their ability to know and comply with the pertinent tax rules.

A recent survey of taxpayer attitudes by the IRS Oversight Board revealed the following results.

Why Do You Report and Pay Your Taxes Honestly? (more than one answer allowed)

Taxpayer Responses	Taxpayers Mentioning This Reason (Percent)
My own personal integrity	81%
A third party reported my information to the IRS (e.g., through a Form W–2 or Form 1099), so I must match that amount in my tax form	40%
Fear of an audit	36%
My neighbors report and pay their taxes honestly, so I will too	25%

What Is an Acceptable Amount by Which to Cheat on Your Income Taxes?

	Taxpayers Responding (Percent)
Not at all	89%
A little here and a little there	6%
As much as possible	3%
Other answers	3%

Given the results of this survey, do you think the current self-assessment system is satisfactory? If not, should Congress create additional enforcement procedures to ensure taxpayer compliance? What sort of new reporting rules might be useful?

Source: 2008 Taxpayer Attitude Survey (February 2009), at **www.ustreas.gov/irsob/reports/2009/IRSOB_2008-TAS.pdf**.

The economic costs of a settlement offer from the Appeals Division should be weighed against the costs of litigation and the probability of winning the case. The taxpayer should also consider the impact of the settlement upon the tax liability for future periods, in addition to the years under audit.

If a settlement is reached with the Appeals Division, the taxpayer is required to sign Form 870-AD. According to the IRS, this settlement is binding upon both parties unless fraud, malfeasance, concealment, or misrepresentation of material fact has occurred.

OFFERS IN COMPROMISE AND CLOSING AGREEMENTS

The IRS can negotiate a compromise if there is doubt about the taxpayer's ability to pay the tax. If the taxpayer is financially unable to pay the total amount of the tax, a Form 656 (Offer in Compromise) is filed. An **offer in compromise** is appropriate in the following circumstances.[15]

- There is doubt as to the taxpayer's liability for the tax (i.e., disputed issues still exist).
- There is doubt as to the collectibility of the tax (i.e., the taxpayer's net worth and earnings capacity are low).
- Payment of the disputed amount would constitute an economic hardship for the taxpayer. For example, the taxpayer is incapable of earning a living because of a long-term illness or disability, or liquidation of the taxpayer's

[15] § 7122 and Temp.Reg. § 301.7122–1(b).

TAX *in the NEWS*

Late-Night Tax Advice

What are those people on late-night TV commercials talking about when they offer to handle your back taxes with the IRS or reduce your tax bill by half?

Most of these commercials that are trying to grab your attention are promoting tax resolution firms that will put together an offer in compromise for submission to the IRS. For a sometimes sizable up-front fee, a firm will carry out the filing process for an offer in compromise and suggest terms that may be acceptable to the IRS. Because the firm has experience with these arrangements, it can likely reach an agreement on the offer in a shorter time than a typical individual would require. Although tax resolution firms may be helpful in certain situations, the IRS has warned that some firms engage in poor business practices.

Rather than pursue an offer in compromise, a taxpayer might request an installment payment schedule from the IRS. The installment approach does not avoid taxes and interest, but it does buy time for the taxpayer by allowing affordable payments over an agreed-on period of time. Moreover, it avoids the sizable up-front fees that a tax resolution firm would charge for often unsatisfactory service.

assets to pay the amount due would leave the taxpayer unable to meet basic living expenses.

The IRS investigates the offer by evaluating the taxpayer's financial ability to pay the tax. In some situations, the compromise settlement includes an agreement for final settlement of the tax through payments of a specified percentage of the taxpayer's future earnings. The Director must obtain approval from the IRS Regional Counsel if the amount involved exceeds $500. This settlement procedure usually entails lengthy negotiations with the IRS, but the presumption is that the agency will find terms upon which to enter into a compromise with the taxpayer. A 20 percent nonrefundable current payment is required to set up the compromise offer, and a $150 filing fee is required. Low-income individuals can apply for a waiver of the fee and of the 20 percent down payment.[16]

The IRS can agree to allow taxes to be paid on an installment basis if that arrangement facilitates the tax collection. An individual who has filed timely tax returns for five years is guaranteed the right to use an installment agreement when the amount in dispute does not exceed $10,000.

The IRS provides an annual statement accounting for the status of the agreement. The agreement may later be modified or terminated because of (1) inadequate information, (2) subsequent change in financial condition, or (3) failure to pay an installment when due or to provide requested information.[17]

Every year, the IRS accepts about 10,000 offers in compromise, involving about $150 million in unpaid taxes, interest, and penalties.

A **closing agreement** is binding on both the taxpayer and the IRS except upon a subsequent showing of fraud, malfeasance, or misrepresentation of a material fact.[18] The closing agreement may be used when disputed issues carry over to future years. It may also be employed to dispose of a dispute involving a specific issue for a prior year or a proposed transaction involving future years. If, for example, the IRS is willing to make substantial concessions in the valuation of assets for estate tax purposes, it may require a closing agreement from the recipient of the property to establish the income tax basis of the assets.

INTEREST

LO.5

Determine the amount of interest on a deficiency or a refund and when it is due.

Determination of the Interest Rate

Congress sets the interest rates applicable to Federal tax underpayments (deficiencies) and overpayments (refunds) close to the rates available in financial markets.

[16] Reg. § 300.3(b)(1)(ii). "Low-income" is defined as less than 250% of the Federal poverty level.

[17] § 6159.

[18] § 7121(b).

Section 6621 provides for rates to be determined quarterly. For example, the rates that are determined during March are effective for the following April through June.

The interest rates are based on the Federal short-term rates published periodically by the IRS in Revenue Rulings. The Federal rates are based on the average market yield on outstanding marketable obligations of the United States with remaining maturity of three years or less.

For noncorporate taxpayers, the interest rate applicable to *both* overpayments and underpayments is 3 percent for the first quarter of 2011. For most corporate taxpayers, the rate is 2 percent for overpayments and 3 percent for underpayments. Corporations with large overpayments or underpayments are subject to different rates.

Computation of the Amount of Interest

Interest is compounded daily.[19] Depending on the applicable interest rate, daily compounding can double the payable amount over a period of five to eight years.

Tables for determining the daily compounded amount are available from the IRS and on the Internet. The tables ease the burden of those who prepare late returns where additional taxes are due.[20]

IRS Deficiency Assessments

Interest usually accrues from the unextended due date of the return until 30 days after the taxpayer agrees to the deficiency by signing Form 870. If the taxpayer does not pay the amount shown on the IRS's notice and demand (tax bill) within 30 days, interest again accrues on the deficiency.

Refund of Taxpayer's Overpayments

If an overpayment is refunded to the taxpayer within 45 days after the date the return is filed or is due, no interest is allowed. When the taxpayer files an amended return or makes a claim for refund of a prior year's tax (e.g., when net operating loss carrybacks result in refunds of a prior year's tax payments), however, interest is authorized from the original due date of the return through the date when the amended return is filed. In general, taxpayers applying for refunds receive interest as follows.

- When a return is filed after the due date, interest on any overpayment accrues from the date of filing. However, no interest is due if the IRS makes the refund within 45 days of the date of filing.

EXAMPLE 7

Naomi, a calendar year taxpayer, files her 2010 return on December 1, 2011. The return reflects an overwithholding of $2,500. On June 8, 2012, Naomi receives a refund of her 2010 overpayment. Interest on the refund began to accrue on December 1, 2011 (not April 15, 2011). ■

EXAMPLE 8

Assume the same facts as in Example 7, except that the refund is paid to Naomi on January 5, 2012 (rather than June 8, 2012). No interest is payable by the IRS, since the refund was made within 45 days of the filing of the return. ■

- In no event will interest accrue on an overpayment unless the return that is filed is in "processible form." Generally, this means that the return must contain enough information in a readable format to enable the IRS to identify the taxpayer and to determine the tax (and overpayment) involved.

LO.6

Discuss the various penalties that can be imposed on acts of noncompliance by taxpayers and return preparers.

TAXPAYER PENALTIES

To promote and enforce taxpayer compliance with the U.S. voluntary self-assessment system of taxation, Congress has enacted a comprehensive array of penalties. Tax

[19] § 6622.

[20] Rev.Proc. 95–17, 1995–1 C.B. 556.

penalties may pertain to both criminal and civil offenses. Criminal tax penalties are imposed only after the usual criminal process, in which the taxpayer is entitled to the same constitutional guarantees as nontax criminal defendants. Normally, a criminal penalty provides for imprisonment. Civil tax penalties are collected in the same manner as other taxes and usually provide only for monetary fines. Criminal and civil penalties are not mutually exclusive; therefore, both types of sanctions may be imposed on a taxpayer.

The Code characterizes tax penalties as additions to tax; thus, they cannot subsequently be deducted by the taxpayer. *Ad valorem penalties* are additions to tax that are based upon a percentage of the owed tax. *Assessable penalties,* on the other hand, typically include a flat dollar amount. Assessable penalties are not subject to review by the Tax Court, but *ad valorem* penalties are subject to the same deficiency procedures that apply to the underlying tax.

Failure to File and Failure to Pay

For a failure to file a tax return by the due date (including extensions), a penalty of 5 percent per month (up to a maximum of 25 percent) is imposed on the amount of tax shown as due on the return, with a minimum penalty amount of $135. If the failure to file is attributable to fraud, the penalty becomes 15 percent per month, to a maximum of 75 percent of the tax.[21]

For a failure to pay the tax due as shown on the return, a penalty of 0.5 percent per month (up to a maximum of 25 percent) is imposed on the amount of the tax. The penalty is doubled if the taxpayer fails to pay the tax after receiving a deficiency assessment.

In all of these cases, a fraction of a month counts as a full month. These penalties relate to the net amount of the tax due.

Obtaining an extension for filing a tax return does not by itself extend the date by which the taxes due must be paid. Thus, an application for an extended due date for a tax return almost always is accompanied by a payment by the taxpayer of a good faith estimate of the taxes that will be owed with the return when it is filed by the extended due date. If the taxpayer does not make such a good faith estimate and payment, the extension itself may be voided by the IRS (e.g., when the return is filed by the extended due date with a much larger amount due than had been estimated).

EXAMPLE 9

Conchita uses an automatic six-month extension for the filing of her 2011 tax return. Thus, the return is due on October 15, 2012, not on April 15. Conchita's application for the extension includes a $5,000 check, the amount that she estimates her 2011 return will show as owing for the year when she files it in October. ■

During any month in which both the failure to file penalty and the failure to pay penalty apply, the failure to file penalty is reduced by the amount of the failure to pay penalty.

EXAMPLE 10

Jason files his tax return 10 days after the due date. Along with the return, he remits a check for $4,000, which is the balance of the tax owed. Disregarding any interest liabilities, Jason's total penalties are as follows.

Failure to pay penalty (0.5% × $4,000)		$ 20
Plus: Failure to file penalty (5% × $4,000)	$200	
Less: Failure to pay penalty for the same period	(20)	
Failure to file penalty		180
Total penalties		$200

The penalties for one full month are imposed even though Jason was delinquent by only 10 days. Unlike the method used to compute interest, any part of a month is treated as a whole month. ■

[21] §§ 6651(a) and (f). The minimum penalty cannot exceed the amount of tax due on the return.

These penalties can be avoided if the taxpayer shows that the failure to file and/or failure to pay was due to reasonable cause and not due to willful neglect. The Code is silent as to what constitutes reasonable cause, and the Regulations do little to clarify this important concept.[22] Reasonable cause for failure to pay is presumed under the automatic six-month extension (Form 4868) when the additional tax due is not more than 10 percent of the tax liability shown on the return. In addition, the courts have ruled on some aspects of **reasonable cause**.

- Reasonable cause was found where the taxpayer relied on the advice of a competent tax adviser given in good faith, the facts were fully disclosed to the adviser, and he or she considered that the specific question represented reasonable cause.[23] No reasonable cause was found, however, where the taxpayer delegated the filing task to another, even when that person was an accountant or an attorney.[24]
- Among the reasons not qualifying as reasonable cause were lack of information on the due date of the return,[25] illness that did not incapacitate a taxpayer from completing a return,[26] refusal of the taxpayer's spouse to cooperate for a joint return,[27] and ignorance or misunderstanding of the tax law.[28]

Accuracy-Related Penalties

Major civil penalties relating to the accuracy of tax return data, including misstatements stemming from taxpayer negligence and improper valuation of income and deductions, are coordinated under the umbrella term **accuracy-related penalties**.[29] This consolidation of related penalties into a single levy eliminates the possibility that multiple penalties will apply to a single understatement of tax.

The accuracy-related penalties each amount to 20 percent of the portion of the tax underpayment that is attributable to one or more of the following infractions.

- Negligence or disregard of rules and Regulations.
- Substantial understatement of tax liability.
- Substantial valuation overstatement.
- Substantial valuation understatement.

The penalties apply only where the taxpayer fails to show a *reasonable basis* for the position taken on the return.[30]

Negligence

For purposes of this accuracy-related penalty, **negligence** includes any failure to make a reasonable attempt to comply with the provisions of the tax law. The penalty also applies to any disregard (whether careless, reckless, or intentional) of rules and Regulations.[31] The penalty can be avoided upon a showing of reasonable cause and that the taxpayer acted in good faith.[32] The negligence penalty applies to *all* taxes, except when fraud is involved.

A negligence penalty may be assessed when the taxpayer fails to report gross income, overstates deductions, or fails to keep adequate records. When the taxpayer takes a nonnegligent position on the return that is contrary to a published pronouncement of the IRS, the penalty is waived if the taxpayer has a reasonable basis for the interpretation and has disclosed the disputed position on Form 8275.

[22] Reg. § 301.6651–1(c)(1) likens reasonable cause to the exercise of "ordinary business care and prudence" on the part of the taxpayer.

[23] *Estate of Norma S. Bradley*, 33 TCM 70, T.C.Memo. 1974–17.

[24] *U.S. v. Boyle*, 85–1 USTC ¶13,602, 55 AFTR 2d 85–1535, 105 S.Ct. 687 (USSC, 1985). This rule appears to apply to electronic as well as paper-based return filings, to employment as well as income taxes, and to returns where the tax preparer himself or herself commits a fraudulent act. *Brandon R. Ballantyne*, 99 TCM 1523, T.C.Memo. 2010–125; *McNair Eye Center, Inc.*, 99 TCM 1345, T.C.Memo. 2010–81. Knowledgeable taxpayers, like a tax attorney, are held to a higher standard in determining negligence. *Pelton & Gunther P.C.*, 78 TCM 578, T.C.Memo. 1999–339. A taxpayer might be negligent if, when a complicated tax issue is involved, a tax expert is *not* consulted. *Zmuda v. Comm.*, 84-1 USTC ¶9,442, 53 AFTR 2d 84–1269, 731 F.2d 1417 (CA–9, 1984).

[25] *Beck Chemical Equipment Co.*, 27 T.C. 840 (1957).

[26] *Alex and Tonya Oria*, 94 TCM 170, T.C.Memo. 2007–276, and *Babetta Schmidt*, 28 T.C. 367 (1957). Compare *Estate of Kirchner*, 46 B.T.A. 578 (1942).

[27] *Electric and Neon, Inc.*, 56 T.C. 1324 (1971).

[28] *Stevens Brothers Foundation, Inc.*, 39 T.C. 93 (1965).

[29] § 6662.

[30] Reg. § 1.6662–3(b)(3). Most tax professionals measure this standard as a 20% probability of prevailing in court.

[31] § 6662(c). There can be no intentional disregard of the rules where the underlying law is unclear, complex, or subject to disagreement. *James J. Freeland*, 51 TCM 253, T.C.Memo. 1986–10, and *Lansdown v. Comm.*, 96–1 USTC ¶50,025, 77 AFTR 2d 96–491, 73 F.3d 373 (CA–10, 1996).

[32] § 6664(c)(1).

Substantial Understatements of Tax Liability

The understatement penalty is designed to strike at middle- and high-income taxpayers who are tempted to play the so-called *audit lottery*.[33] Some taxpayers take questionable and undisclosed positions on their tax returns in the hope that the return will not be selected for audit. Disclosing the positions would have called attention to the return and increased the probability of audit.

A *substantial understatement of a tax liability* transpires when the understatement exceeds the larger of 10 percent of the tax due or $5,000. For a C corporation, a substantial understatement is the lesser of the following.[34]

- 10 percent of the tax due, but at least $10,000.
- $10 million.

The understatement to which the penalty applies is the difference between the amount of tax required to be shown on the return and the amount of tax actually shown on the return.

The penalty is avoided under any of the following circumstances.[35]

- The taxpayer has **substantial authority** for the treatment.
- There is a *reasonable basis* for the tax return position, which is adequately disclosed in the return by attaching Form 8275.

Penalty for Overvaluation

The objective of the overvaluation penalty is to deter taxpayers from inflating values (or basis), usually for charitable contributions of property, to reduce income taxes.[36]

- The penalty is 20 percent of the additional tax that would have been paid had the correct valuation (or basis) been used.
- The penalty applies only when the valuation (or basis) used by the taxpayer is 150 percent or more of the correct valuation (or basis). The penalty is doubled if the valuation error is *gross* (overstated by 200 percent or more).
- The penalty applies only when the resulting income tax underpayment exceeds $5,000 ($10,000 for C corporations).

EXAMPLE 11

Gretchen (a calendar year taxpayer) purchased a painting for $10,000. When the painting is worth $18,000 (as later determined by the IRS), Gretchen donates the painting to an art museum. Based on the appraisal of a cousin who is an amateur artist, she deducts $40,000 for the donation. Since Gretchen was in a 30% tax bracket, overstating the deduction by $22,000 results in a tax underpayment of $6,600.

Gretchen's penalty for overvaluation is $2,640, or *double* the regular penalty of $1,320 (20% × $6,600 underpayment). ■

The substantial valuation overstatement penalty is avoided if the taxpayer can show reasonable cause and good faith. However, when the overvaluation involves *charitable deduction property*, the taxpayer must substantiate both of the following.

- The claimed value of the property is based on a qualified appraisal made by a qualified appraiser.
- The taxpayer made a good faith investigation of the value of the contributed property.[37]

Based on these criteria, Gretchen in Example 11 would find it difficult to avoid the penalty. A cousin who is an amateur artist does not meet the definition of a

---

[33] § 6662(b)(2).

[34] § 6662(d)(1).

[35] § 6662(d)(2)(B). Substantial authority is measured as of either the last day of the tax year to which the return relates or the date that the return was filed. Reg. § 1.6662–4(d)(3)(iv)(C).

[36] §§ 6662(b)(3), (e), and (h).

[37] §§ 6664(c)(2) and (3).

qualified appraiser. Likewise, Gretchen apparently has not made her own good faith investigation of the value of the contributed property.

Penalty for Undervaluation

When attempting to minimize the income tax, it is to the benefit of taxpayers to *overvalue* deductions. When attempting to minimize transfer taxes (i.e., estate and gift taxes), however, executors and donors may be inclined to *undervalue* the assets transferred. A lower valuation reduces estate and gift taxes. An accuracy-related penalty is imposed for substantial estate or gift tax valuation understatements.[38] As with other accuracy-related penalties, reasonable cause and good faith on the part of the taxpayer are a defense.

- The penalty is 20 percent of the additional transfer tax that would have been due had the correct valuation been used on Form 706 (estate and generation-skipping transfer tax return) or Form 709 (gift and generation-skipping transfer tax return).
- The penalty applies only if the value of the property claimed on the return is 65 percent or less than the amount determined to be correct. The penalty is doubled if the reported valuation error is *gross* (reported value is 40 percent or less than the correct determination).
- The penalty applies only to an additional transfer tax liability in excess of $5,000.

ETHICS & *Equity*

Good Faith Valuations

When dealing with the undervaluation penalty, the tax adviser may shift from being in adversarial alliance with the taxpayer to being a mediator for the court. Good faith value estimates, especially for family-owned businesses, can easily vary by as much as the 65 percentage points specified for the penalty. Even a gross undervaluation can occur when someone in the business other than the donor or decedent is a particularly talented entrepreneur, an effective sales representative, and/or the founder of the company; similarly, a business may be substantially undervalued when a minority equity interest is involved, or an intangible asset conveys a sizable nominal amount of goodwill to the valuation.

Because most taxpayers are highly averse to incurring any nondeductible penalties, the client may be tempted to compromise on the business valuation "too soon" (i.e., when the return is filed), eliminating any possibility of a more favorable valuation being presented before the Appeals Division or a court. Keeping in mind all of the potential taxpayer and preparer penalties that might apply, the tax professional should stick with a good faith appraisal of the business value, no matter what its nominal amount.

How would you react if your client, a composer, wanted to deduct $100,000 for the contribution of an obscure manuscript to the Symphony Society? What if your (first) appraiser placed the value of the manuscript at $15,000? What course of action would you propose to the client concerning the deduction? Any consequent penalties?

Appraiser's Penalty

When a valuation penalty arises because of the taxpayer's reliance on an appraisal, a further penalty can apply.[39] If the appraiser knew or reasonably should have known that the appraisal would be used as part of a tax or refund computation and that the appraised value more likely than not was improper, then the appraiser pays a penalty equal to the lesser of:

- 10 percent of the tax understatement, but at least $1,000, or
- 125 percent of the gross income received by the appraiser from the engagement (e.g., the appraisal fee collected).

This amount is in addition to the taxpayer's valuation penalty as discussed above.

[38] §§ 6662(b)(5), (g), and (h).

[39] § 6695A.

Penalty for Improper Refund Claim

Whenever a taxpayer files a claim for a tax refund and the refund claim later is found to exceed the final amount allowed by the IRS or a court, a penalty of 20 percent of the disallowed refund results.[40] The penalty is waived if the taxpayer can show a *reasonable basis* for the refund claim (i.e., probably a 20 percent chance that a court would allow the refund). This penalty is meant to discourage the taxpayer from overstating the amount of the refund requested from the IRS. It does not apply to claims for the earned income tax credit.

Civil Fraud Penalty

A 75 percent civil penalty is imposed on any underpayment resulting from **fraud** by the taxpayer who has filed a return.[41] For this penalty, the burden of proof is *on the IRS* to show by a preponderance of the evidence that the taxpayer had a specific intent to evade a tax. Once the IRS initially has established that fraud has occurred, the taxpayer then bears the burden of proof to show by a preponderance of the evidence the portion of the underpayment that is not attributable to fraud.

Although the Code and Regulations do not provide any assistance in ascertaining what constitutes civil fraud, it is clear that mere negligence on the part of the taxpayer (however great) will not suffice. Fraud has been found in cases of manipulations of the books, substantial omissions from income, and erroneous deductions.[42]

EXAMPLE 12

Frank underpaid his income tax by $90,000. The IRS can prove that $60,000 of the underpayment was due to fraud. Frank responds by a preponderance of the evidence that $30,000 of the underpayment was not due to fraud. The civil fraud penalty is $45,000 (75% × $60,000). ■

If the underpayment of tax is partly attributable to negligence and partly attributable to fraud, the fraud penalty is applied first.

Failure to Pay Estimated Taxes

A penalty is imposed for a failure to pay estimated income taxes. The penalty applies to individuals and corporations and is based on the rate of interest in effect for deficiency assessments.[43] The penalty also applies to trusts and certain estates that are required to make estimated tax payments.

The penalty is not imposed if the tax due for the year (less amounts withheld and credits) is less than $500 for corporations, $1,000 for all others. For employees, an equal amount of withholding is deemed paid on each due date.

Quarterly payments are to be made on or before the fifteenth day of the fourth month (April 15 for a calendar year taxpayer), sixth month, and ninth month of the current year, and the first month of the following year. Corporations must make the last quarterly payment by the twelfth month of the same year.

An individual's underpayment of estimated tax is the difference between the estimates that were paid and the least of:

- 90 percent of the current-year tax,
- 100 percent of the prior-year tax (the tax year must have been a full 12 months and a return must have been filed), and
- 90 percent of the tax that would be due on an annualized income computation for the period running through the end of the quarter.

If the taxpayer's prior-year AGI exceeds $150,000, the 100 percent requirement becomes 110 percent.

[40] § 6676.

[41] § 6663. Underpayments traceable to fraudulent acts are not subject to a statute of limitations.

[42] *Dogget v. Comm.*, 60–1 USTC ¶9342, 5 AFTR 2d 1034, 275 F.2d 823 (CA–4, 1960); *Harvey Brodsky*, 21 TCM 578, T.C.Memo. 1962–105; and *Lash v. Comm.*, 57–2 USTC ¶9725, 51 AFTR 492, 245 F.2d 20 (CA–1, 1957).

[43] §§ 6655 (corporations) and 6654 (other taxpayers). Other computations can avoid the penalty. See §§ 6654(d)(2) and (k), 6655(e) and (i).

A corporation's underpayment of estimated tax is the difference between the estimates that were paid and the least of (1) the current-year tax, (2) the prior-year tax, and (3) the tax on an annualized income computation using one of three methods of computation sanctioned by the Code. For the prior-year alternative, (1) the prior tax year must have been a full 12 months, (2) a nonzero tax amount must have been generated for that year, and (3) large corporations (taxable income of $1 million or more in any of the three immediately preceding tax years) can use the alternative only for the first installment of a year.

In computing the penalty, Form 2210 (Underpayment of Estimated Tax by Individuals) or Form 2220 (Underpayment of Estimated Tax by Corporations) is used.

False Information with Respect to Withholding

Withholding from wages is an important element of the Federal income tax system, which is based on a pay-as-you-go approach. One way employees might hope to avoid this withholding would be to falsify the information provided to the employer on Form W–4 (Employee Withholding Allowance Certificate). For example, by overstating the number of exemptions, income tax withholdings could be reduced or completely eliminated.

To encourage compliance, a civil penalty of $500 applies when a taxpayer claims withholding allowances based on false information. The criminal penalty for willfully failing to supply information or for willfully supplying false or fraudulent information in connection with wage withholding is an additional fine of up to $1,000 and/or up to one year of imprisonment.[44]

Failure to Make Deposits of Taxes and Overstatements of Deposits

When a business is not doing well or cash-flow problems develop, employers have a great temptation to "borrow" from Uncle Sam. One way this can be done is to fail to pay to the IRS the amounts that have been withheld from the wages of employees for FICA and income tax purposes. The IRS does not appreciate being denied the use of these funds and has a number of weapons at its disposal to discourage the practice.

- A penalty of up to 15 percent of any underdeposited amount, unless the employer can show that the failure is due to reasonable cause and not to willful neglect.[45]
- Various criminal penalties.[46]
- A 100 percent penalty if the employer's actions are willful.[47] The penalty is based on the amount of the tax evaded (i.e., not collected, or not accounted for or paid over). Since the penalty is assessable against the "responsible person" of the business, more than one party may be vulnerable (e.g., the president *and* treasurer of a corporation). Although the IRS may assess the penalty against several persons, it cannot collect more than the 100 percent due.

In addition to these penalties, the actual tax due must be remitted. For example, an employer remains liable for the employees' income and payroll taxes that should have been paid.

Failure to Provide Information Regarding Tax Shelters

The IRS has identified over two dozen transactions that it regards as "tax shelters." These arrangements, often involving leveraged financing and accelerated interest and cost recovery deductions, allegedly are motivated solely by the desire to reduce taxes and have no business or profit-seeking goals. Over the last two decades, the IRS has struggled with numerous means of identifying taxpayers who use such tax shelters.

[44] §§ 6682 and 7205.
[45] § 6656.
[46] See, for example, § 7202 (willful failure to collect or pay over a tax).
[47] § 6672.

A tax shelter organizer must register the shelter with the IRS before any sales are made to investors.[48] A penalty of up to $10,000 is assessed if the required information is not filed with the Service. This includes a description of the shelter and the tax benefits that are being used to attract investors. The shelter organizer must maintain a list of identifying information of all its investors. Failure to fully and truthfully maintain the list can result in a penalty of up to $100,000 per investment.

Criminal Penalties

In addition to civil fraud penalties, the Code provides numerous criminal sanctions that carry various monetary fines and/or imprisonment. The difference between civil and criminal fraud is often one of degree. Thus, § 7201, dealing with attempts to evade or defeat a tax, contains the following language.

> Any person who *willfully* attempts in any manner to evade or defeat any tax imposed by this title or the payment thereof shall, in addition to other penalties provided by law, be guilty of a felony and, upon conviction thereof, shall be fined not more than $100,000 ($500,000 in the case of a corporation), or imprisoned not more than five years, or both, together with the costs of prosecution. (Emphasis added.)

As to the burden of proof, the IRS must show that the taxpayer was guilty of willful evasion "beyond the shadow of any reasonable doubt." Thus, to avoid a criminal tax penalty, the taxpayer needs to create a degree of reasonable doubt as to guilt. To do so, the taxpayer might assert that he or she was confused or ignorant about the application of the tax law or relied on the erroneous advice of a competent tax adviser. Another defense against a criminal tax penalty is the lack of capacity to plan and carry out tax evasion (e.g., mental disease or other medical disorder).

Violations of the Federal criminal code in the context of filing tax returns also may arise from other crimes that are not provided for in the Internal Revenue Code. Examples include:

- Making a false claim against the Federal government.
- Participating in a conspiracy to evade Federal taxes (i.e., in addition to the tax understatement).
- Making a false statement to the Federal government or filing a false document (i.e., perjury).

STATUTES OF LIMITATIONS

LO.7

Understand the rules governing the statute of limitations on assessments and on refunds.

A **statute of limitations** defines the period of time during which one party may pursue against another party a cause of action or other suit allowed under the governing law. Failure to satisfy any requirement provides the other party with an absolute defense should the statute be invoked. Inequity would result if no limits were placed on such suits. Permitting an extended period of time to elapse between the initiation of a claim and its pursuit could place the defense at a serious disadvantage. Witnesses may have died or disappeared; records or other evidence may have been discarded or destroyed.

Assessment and the Statute of Limitations

In general, any tax that is imposed must be assessed within three years of the filing of the return (or, if later, the unextended due date of the return).[49] Some exceptions to this three-year limitation exist.

- If no return is filed or a fraudulent return is filed, assessments can be made at any time. There is, in effect, no statute of limitations in these cases.
- If a taxpayer omits an amount of gross income in excess of 25 percent of the gross income stated on the return, the statute of limitations is increased

[48] § 6111.

[49] §§ 6501(a) and (b)(1).

to six years. The courts have interpreted this rule as including only items affecting income and not the omission of items affecting deductions, operating losses, or cost of sales.[50] *Gross income* here includes capital gains, but not reduced by capital losses.

EXAMPLE 13

During 2006, Jerry had the following income transactions (all of which were duly reported on his timely filed return).

Gross receipts		$ 480,000
Less: Cost of sales		(400,000)
Net business income		$ 80,000
Capital gains and losses		
Capital gain	$ 36,000	
Capital loss	(12,000)	24,000
Total income		$ 104,000

Jerry retains your services in 2011 as a tax consultant. It seems that he inadvertently omitted some income on his 2006 return and he wishes to know if he is "safe" under the statute of limitations. The six-year statute of limitations would apply, putting Jerry in a vulnerable position, only if he omitted more than $129,000 on his 2006 return [($480,000 + $36,000) × 25%]. ■

- The statute of limitations may be extended for a fixed period of time by mutual consent of the IRS and the taxpayer. This extension covers a definite period and is made by signing Form 872 (Consent to Extend the Time to Assess Tax). The extension is frequently requested by the IRS when the lapse of the statutory period is imminent and the audit has not been completed. This practice often is applied to audits of corporate taxpayers and explains why many corporations have more than three "open years."

Special rules relating to assessment are applicable in the following situations.

- Taxpayers may request a prompt assessment of the tax, forcing the IRS to examine a return.
- The assessment period for capital loss and net operating loss carrybacks generally relates to the determination of tax in the year of the loss rather than in the carryback years.

If the IRS issues a statutory notice of deficiency to the taxpayer, who then files a Tax Court petition, the statute is suspended on both the deficiency assessment and the period of collection until 60 days after the decision of the Tax Court becomes final. The statute also is suspended when the taxpayer is "financially disabled"; that is, the taxpayer has been rendered unable to manage his or her financial affairs by a physical or mental impairment that is likely to last for a year or more or to cause the taxpayer's death. The statute continues to run if another party is authorized to act for the taxpayer in financial matters.[51]

Refund Claims and the Statute of Limitations

To receive a tax refund, the taxpayer is required to file a valid refund claim. The official form for filing a claim is Form 1040X for individuals and Form 1120X for corporations. If the refund claim does not meet certain procedural requirements, the IRS may reject the claim with no consideration of its merit.

- A separate claim must be filed for each taxable period.
- The grounds for the claim must be stated in sufficient detail.

[50] *The Colony, Inc. v. Comm.*, 58–2 USTC ¶9593, 1 AFTR 2d 1894, 78 S.Ct. 1033 (USSC, 1958).

[51] Suspension of the statute of limitations has been allowed by some courts when attributable to a taxpayer disability or IRS misconduct. See *Brockamp v. Comm.*, 97–1 USTC ¶50,216, 79 AFTR 2d 97–986, 117 S.Ct. 849 (USSC, 1997). §§ 6501(c)(4) and 6511(h).

- The statement of facts must be sufficient to permit the IRS to evaluate the merits of the claim.

The refund claim must be filed within three years of the filing of the tax return or within two years following the payment of the tax if this period expires on a later date.[52]

EXAMPLE 14

On March 10, 2009, Louise filed her 2008 income tax return reflecting a tax of $10,500. On July 11, 2010, she filed an amended 2008 return showing an additional $3,000 of tax that was then paid. On May 19, 2012, she filed a claim for refund of $4,500.

Assuming Louise is correct in claiming a refund, how much tax can she recover? The answer is only $3,000. Because the claim was not filed within the three-year statute of limitations period, Louise is limited to the amount she actually paid during the last two years. ■

Special rules are available for claims relating to bad debts and worthless securities. A seven-year period of limitations applies in lieu of the normal three-year rule.[53] The extended period is provided in recognition of the inherent difficulty of identifying the exact year in which a bad debt or security becomes worthless.

26.2 The Tax Profession and Tax Ethics

LO.8

Summarize the legal and ethical guidelines that apply to those engaged in tax practice.

Society and its governments expect taxpayers to comply with the letter and the spirit of the tax laws. Tax audits and penalties encourage a high degree of technical tax conformity, but the proper functioning of a voluntary tax compliance system also depends on the ethics of the taxpayer and the tax adviser.

The Treasury and various professional organizations have issued ethical guidelines that are relevant to the tax profession. Professional licensing agencies also are likely to require tax professionals to receive training in ethics to obtain initial certification and to remain in good standing over time.

THE TAX PROFESSIONAL

Who is a tax practitioner? What services does the practitioner perform? A number of different groups apply constraints on the way that a tax professional conducts his or her practice.

To begin defining the term *tax practitioner*, one should consider whether the individual is qualified to practice before the IRS. Generally, practice before the IRS is limited to CPAs, attorneys, and persons who have been enrolled to practice before the IRS [**enrolled agents (EAs)**]. In most cases, EAs are admitted to practice only if they pass an examination administered by the IRS. CPAs and attorneys are not required to take this examination and are automatically admitted to practice if they are in good standing with the appropriate licensing board regulating their profession.

Persons other than CPAs, attorneys, and EAs may be allowed to practice before the IRS in limited situations. **Circular 230** ("Rules Governing the Practice of Attorneys and Agents Before the Internal Revenue Service") issued by the Treasury Department permits certain notable exceptions.

- A taxpayer may always represent himself or herself. A person may also represent a member of the immediate family if no compensation is received for such services.
- Regular full-time employees may represent their employers.
- Corporations may be represented by any of their bona fide officers.
- Partnerships may be represented by any of the partners.

[52] §§ 6511(a) and 6513(a).

[53] § 6511(d)(1).

- Trusts, receiverships, guardianships, or estates may be represented by their trustees, receivers, guardians, or administrators or executors.
- A taxpayer may be represented by whoever prepared the return for the year in question. However, such representation cannot proceed beyond the agent level.

EXAMPLE 15

Joel is currently undergoing audit by the IRS for tax years 2010 and 2011. He prepared the 2010 return but paid AddCo, a bookkeeping service, to prepare the 2011 return. AddCo may represent Joel only in matters concerning 2011. However, even for 2011, AddCo would be unable to represent Joel at an Appeals Division proceeding. Joel could represent himself, or he could retain a CPA, attorney, or EA to represent him in matters concerning both years under examination. ■

All nonattorney tax practitioners should avoid becoming engaged in activities that constitute the *unauthorized practice of law.* If they engage in this practice (e.g., by drafting legal documents for a third party), action could be instituted against them in the appropriate state court by the local or state bar association. What actions constitute the unauthorized practice of law is largely undefined, though, and such charges are filed only rarely today.

LICENSING TAX PREPARERS

There are no minimum education or experience requirements for those who file Federal tax returns for others. But the IRS does require that all paid tax return preparers, including CPAs and attorneys, obtain a Preparer Tax Identification Number (PTIN) before they assist taxpayers with returns for a new filing season.

For most preparers, the fee to obtain PTINs is about $65 per year. This amount is in addition to any other professional, certification, or licensing fee that the preparer might be required to pay (e.g., annual dues to maintain a CPA certificate).

Preparers (other than CPAs, attorneys, and enrolled agents) must pass an annual qualifying exam, designed to evaluate their familiarity with new tax laws and filing requirements that will apply for the filing season.

Efforts to "register" or "certify" tax preparers have been advocated for at least three decades, but to no avail. Increased regulation developed to govern other aspects of financial and consumer affairs led to the PTIN system effective for the 2011 filing season. The year's PTIN usually is obtained online, and confirmation of the preparer's identity, prior registrations, and testing status is needed before the PTIN is issued or renewed.

The IRS may use PTIN data to identify preparers who commit a pattern of errors or who participate in fraudulent actions. With more than 1 million paid preparers at work in any filing season, the IRS must use an outside consultant to manage the registration and testing functions.

IRS RULES GOVERNING TAX PRACTICE

Circular 230 prescribes the rules governing practice before the IRS. The following are some of the most important rules imposed on CPAs, attorneys, EAs, and all others who prepare tax returns for compensation.

- A prohibition against taking a position on a tax return unless there is a *realistic possibility* of the position being sustained on its merits. Generally, the realistic possibility standard is met when a person knowledgeable in the tax law would conclude that the position has at least a one-in-three probability of prevailing in the court of final jurisdiction.
- A prohibition against taking frivolous tax return positions. A **frivolous return** is one with a less than 5 percent chance of being sustained by the court of final jurisdiction.
- A requirement that nonfrivolous tax return positions that fail the realistic possibility standard be disclosed in the return (i.e., using Form 8275).

TAX *in the NEWS*

Have You Been Drafted by the IRS?

With the accumulation of tax preparer penalties over the years, many tax professionals now feel that they have been "deputized" by the IRS and that, as a consequence, their ability to advise and represent their clients in an aggressive manner is limited. Has the potential for providing effective tax planning diminished as a result of the increased regulation of the tax and accounting profession, the additional disclosures that the tax practitioner must make to the client and to the government, and the severity of preparer penalties?

Not so, according to the IRS. Its objective is to "ensure that attorneys, accountants, and other tax practitioners adhere to professional standards and follow the law." Here are some specific items from the IRS's plan to raise the level of tax ethics found in tax practice today.

- Strengthen ties with practitioners to achieve the highest level of professional integrity and improve tax compliance.
- Establish and communicate clear, robust, current, and meaningful standards of conduct for tax practitioners.
- Establish and maintain a vigorous, targeted, and effective system of practitioner oversight.
- Establish and administer a fair, diligent, and effective system of sanctions for practitioners who fail to observe standards of conduct.

EXAMPLE 16
THE BIG PICTURE

Return to the facts of *The Big Picture* on p. 26-2. Campbell wants to claim the research credit for a testing program that it has developed, to be used by its in-house engineers before a new GPS app is released to the public. Based on their tax research on this issue, the members of your firm's tax department have severe doubts about taking the credit for this program. Your firm's position is that there is a one-in-four chance that the courts would allow Campbell's credit.

Claiming the credit fails the realistic possibility standard of Circular 230. Therefore, if Campbell claims the credit, you must insist that its Form 1120 include a separate disclosure on the return, probably using Form 8275. ■

- A requirement to inform clients of both penalties likely to apply to return positions and ways such penalties can be avoided.
- A requirement to make known to a client any error or omission the client may have made on any return or other document submitted to the IRS.
- A duty to submit, in a timely fashion, records or information lawfully requested by the IRS.
- An obligation to exercise *due diligence* and to use the *best practices* of the tax profession in preparing, reviewing, and filing tax returns accurately. Best practices include, for instance, the tax professional's use of appropriate software, a thorough office procedure for receiving and processing client tax returns, and the execution of a plan for continuing education in technical tax matters.
- A restriction against unreasonably delaying the prompt disposition of any matter before the IRS.
- A restriction against charging the client a contingent fee for preparing an original return, although such a fee can be charged when the tax professional deals with an audited or amended return.
- A restriction against charging the client "an unconscionable fee" for representation before the IRS.
- A restriction against representing clients with conflicting interests.

Nothing prevents the "unlicensed" tax practitioner from advertising his or her specialty, directly soliciting clients, or engaging in other actions that are regulated by the standards of conduct controlling CPAs, attorneys, and EAs. Nevertheless, some constraints do govern all parties engaged in rendering tax advice or preparing tax returns for the general public.

- A person who holds himself or herself out to the general public as possessing tax expertise could be liable to the client if services are performed in a negligent manner. At a minimum, the practitioner is liable for any interest and penalties the client incurs because of the practitioner's failure to exercise due professional care.
- If a practitioner agrees to perform a service (e.g., prepare a tax return) and subsequently fails to do so, the aggrieved party may be in a position to obtain damages for breach of contract.
- All persons who prepare tax returns or refund claims for a fee must sign as preparer of the return.[54] Failure to comply with this requirement could result in a penalty assessment against the preparer.
- The Code prescribes various penalties for the deliberate filing of false or fraudulent returns. These felonies apply to a tax practitioner who either was aware of the situation or actually perpetrated the false filing or the fraud.[55]
- Penalties are prescribed for tax practitioners who disclose to third parties information they have received from clients in connection with the preparation of tax returns or the rendering of tax advice.[56]

EXAMPLE 17

Sarah operates a tax return preparation service. Her brother-in-law, Butch, has just taken a job as a life insurance salesman. To help Butch find contacts, Sarah furnishes him with a list of the names and addresses of all of her clients who report AGI of $50,000 or more. Sarah is subject to the disclosure penalty. ■

PREPARER PENALTIES

The Code provides penalties to discourage improper actions by tax practitioners. **Tax preparer** penalties are assessed on any person who prepares for compensation, or engages employees to prepare, a substantial portion of any Federal tax return or refund claim. The following individuals are exempt from the preparer penalties.

- An IRS employee.
- A volunteer who prepares tax returns in a government assistance effort such as Tax Counseling for the Elderly (TCE) or the Volunteer Income Tax Assistance (VITA) program.
- An employee preparing a return for the employer.
- A fiduciary preparing a return for a trust or estate.
- An individual who provides only data processing, typing, reproduction, or other assistance in preparing a return.

The preparer penalties are applied on a "one preparer per firm, per filing position" basis, so penalty dollars can compound quickly within the tax practice. Some of the most important tax preparer penalties include the following.

1. A penalty for understatements due to taking an **unreasonable position** on a tax return.[57] The penalty is imposed if the tax position:
   - Is not disclosed on the return and there was no *substantial authority* (i.e., a greater than 40 percent chance) that the tax position would be sustained by its merits on a final court review; or
   - Is disclosed on the return and there was not a *reasonable basis* (i.e., a 20 percent chance) for the position.

[54] Reg. § 1.6065–1(b)(1). Rev.Rul. 84–3, 1984–1 C.B. 264, contains a series of examples illustrating when a person is deemed to be a preparer of the return.

[55] § 7206.

[56] § 7216.

[57] § 6694(a). For the most part, these standards match those that apply to the taxpayer penalties of § 6662(d). Stricter disclosure standards apply for tax shelter items and reportable transactions. § 6662A.

The penalty is computed as the greater of $1,000 or one-half of the income of the practitioner that is attributable to the return or claim that violated the conduct standard. The penalty can be avoided by showing reasonable cause and by showing that the preparer acted in good faith.

EXAMPLE 18

Josie is the tax return preparer for Hal's Form 1040. The return includes a deduction that has a 60% chance of being sustained on its merits because it is contrary to an applicable tax Regulation. If a court denies the deduction, Josie is not assessed a § 6694 penalty.

Now assume that Hal's deduction has a 30% chance of being sustained on its merits. If a court denies the deduction, Josie is assessed a § 6694 penalty (unless the disputed position was disclosed on the return with a Form 8275–R). The amount of the penalty is the greater of $1,000 or one-half of Josie's fees for preparing Hal's Form 1040.

What if Hal's deduction has a 15% chance of being sustained on its merits? If a court denies the deduction, Josie is assessed a § 6694 penalty (even if the disputed position was disclosed on the return with a Form 8275–R). The amount of the penalty is the greater of $1,000 or one-half of Josie's fees for preparing Hal's Form 1040. ■

2. A penalty for willful and reckless conduct.[58] The penalty applies if any part of the understatement of a taxpayer's liability on a return or claim for refund is due to:

   - The preparer's willful attempt to understate the taxpayer's tax liability in any manner.
   - Any reckless or intentional disregard of IRS rules or Regulations by the preparer.

   The penalty is computed as the greater of $5,000 or one-half of the income of the practitioner that is attributable to the return or claim that violated the conduct standard. Adequate disclosure can avoid the penalty. If both this penalty and the unreasonable position penalty (see item 1 above) apply to the same return, the reckless conduct penalty is reduced by the amount of the penalty for unreasonable positions.
3. A $1,000 ($10,000 for the tax returns of corporations) penalty per return or document is imposed against persons who aid in the preparation of returns or other documents that they know (or have reason to believe) would result in an understatement of the tax liability of another person.[59] Thus, this penalty also applies to those other than the preparer of the actual tax return (e.g., unpaid advisers, attorneys, corporate officers and executives, and tax shelter promoters). Clerical assistance in the return preparation process does not incur the penalty.

   If this penalty applies, neither the unreasonable position penalty (item 1) nor the willful and reckless conduct penalty (item 2) is assessed.
4. A $50 penalty is assessed against the preparer for failure to sign a return or furnish the preparer's PTIN.[60]
5. A $50 penalty is assessed if the preparer fails to furnish a copy of the return or claim for refund to the taxpayer.
6. A $500 penalty may be assessed if a preparer endorses or otherwise negotiates a check for refund of tax issued to the taxpayer.

PRIVILEGED COMMUNICATIONS

Communications between an attorney and client have long been protected from disclosure to other parties (such as the IRS and the courts). A similar privilege of

[58] § 6694(b).

[59] § 6701.

[60] § 6695.

confidentiality extends to tax advice between a taxpayer and tax practitioner, as that term is used above. The privilege is not available for matters involving criminal charges or questions brought by other agencies, such as the Securities and Exchange Commission.[61] Nor is it allowed in matters involving promoting or participating in tax shelters.

A taxpayer likely will want to protect documents such as the tax adviser's research memo detailing the strengths and weaknesses of a tax return position or a conversation about an appeals strategy. The confidentiality privilege should be interpreted in the following manner.

- The privilege often is available when an attorney or CPA completes a tax return for the taxpayer. But some courts have restricted the attorney's privilege in this context on the grounds that the tax professional is conducting accounting work, not offering legal advice. Others assert that the confidentiality privilege is waived when the taxpayer discloses financial data on the tax return. To the contrary, if the tax professional is providing traditional legal advice to help the client decide what to disclose on a tax return, the privilege should be available.
- The privilege for CPAs applies only to tax advice. Attorneys still can exercise the privilege concerning advice rendered as a business consultant, estate/financial planner, and so on.
- About a third of the states offer a similar confidentiality privilege for CPAs, but outside the Federal tax appeals process, protection is not yet the norm.
- The privilege is not available for tax accrual workpapers prepared as part of an independent financial audit.

Thus, the CPA needs to exercise care to ensure that the privilege of confidentiality will apply to his or her tax work. Taking the following steps can help.

- Segregate the time spent and documents produced in rendering services for tax compliance from the time and documents devoted to tax advice. Doing this will protect the privilege from being waived as to the tax advice.
- Explain the extent of the privilege to the client; specify what will and will not be protected from the IRS in a dispute.
- Do not inadvertently waive the privilege, say, by telling "too much" to the IRS or to a third party who is not protected by the privilege.
- Indemnify the CPA for the time spent protecting and enforcing the privilege once it is challenged.

ETHICS & *Equity*

WHERE DOES MY COST SAVING GO?

As is the case in many other U.S. industries, tax return preparers have been outsourcing some of their operations to lower-cost locations overseas. By some estimates, almost a million state and Federal tax returns are completed in India alone, and all such estimates are probably understated because of a lack of disclosure by tax practitioners.

Circular 230 does not prohibit outsourcing, and the IRS does not even require a disclosure by the tax preparer when it occurs. Tax and consulting firms defend the practice as a cost-saving measure and contend that the confidentiality of taxpayer data is not compromised.

AICPA ethics rules (applying both to tax return preparation and other work) require:

- Notice to the taxpayer before any data are shared with a third-party service provider.
- Acceptance by the practitioner of full responsibility for the third party's work (i.e., as to quality and security).

Should any cost saving that outsourcing provides be passed on to the client in the form of lower fees? Do you expect this will occur?

[61] § 7525(a)(1).

AICPA STATEMENTS ON STANDARDS FOR TAX SERVICES

Tax practitioners who are CPAs, attorneys, or EAs must abide by the codes or canons of professional ethics applicable to their respective professions. The various codes and canons have much in common with and parallel the standards of conduct set forth in Circular 230.[62]

The AICPA has issued a series of Statements on Standards for Tax Services (SSTSs). The Statements are enforceable standards of professional practice for AICPA members working in state or Federal tax practice. The SSTSs comprise part of the AICPA's Code of Professional Conduct. Together with the provisions of Circular 230 and the penalty provisions of the Code, the SSTSs make up a set of guidelines for the conduct of the tax practitioner who is also a CPA. Other sources of descriptions of professional ethics are issued by state bar associations and CPA societies, the American Bar Association, and the associations of enrolled agents.

Key provisions of some of the SSTSs are presented below.

Statement No. 1: Tax Return Positions

Under certain circumstances, a CPA may take a position that is contrary to that taken by the IRS. To do so, however, the CPA must have a good faith belief that the position, if challenged, has a realistic possibility (i.e., probably a one-in-three chance) of being sustained administratively or judicially on its merits. If the taxing authority (say, a state revenue statute) uses a lower standard than that of a *realistic possibility*, this higher standard still applies.

The client should be fully advised of the risks involved and should know that certain penalties may result if the position taken on the tax return is not successful. The client should also be informed that disclosure on the return may avoid some or all of these penalties.

In no case, though, should the CPA exploit the audit lottery; that is, to take a questionable position based on the probabilities that the client's return will not be chosen by the IRS for audit. Furthermore, the CPA should not "load" the return with questionable items in the hope that they might aid the client in a later settlement negotiation with the IRS.

EXAMPLE 19
THE BIG PICTURE

Return to the facts of *The Big Picture* on p. 26-2. Campbell's new marketing program solicits the opinions of a virtual focus group to test ideas for new products. Based on your tax research, you believe that because the program relies on innovative algorithms that use online contacts to carry out the focus group activities, the program might quality for the Federal research credit even though it involves marketing research that is excluded from the credit under § 41(d)(4). Still, you believe that there is only a 30% chance that the courts would allow the credit.

You meet with Shelly Watkins, Campbell's tax director, to convey the results of your research. Watkins agrees that the research credit would be turned down by an IRS auditor, but she says that Campbell never has been audited and that it is not likely to be audited as long as its legal structure and income levels do not significantly change. Watkins believes that Campbell's corporate officers will sign off on the credit, given both the firm's weak cash position and the low chances that the item will be discovered.

As a CPA, you must inform Campbell that claiming the credit for this activity does not have a realistic possibility of being sustained on its merits, and that certain penalties will be assessed if the credit is claimed and not further disclosed on the return.

Whether the credit is claimed is the decision of your client, the taxpayer. But if Campbell wants to claim the credit without the required additional disclosures, you must terminate your engagement with Campbell, under the SSTS and other AICPA provisions. ■

[62]For an additional discussion of tax ethics, see Raabe, Whittenburg, Sanders, and Sawyers, *Federal Tax Research*, 9th ed. (Cengage Learning/South-Western, 2012), Chapters 1 and 14.

Statement No. 2: Questions on Returns

A CPA should make a reasonable effort to obtain from the client, and provide to the IRS, appropriate answers to all questions on a tax return before signing as preparer. Reasonable grounds may exist for omitting an answer.

- The information is not readily available, and the answer is not significant in amount in computing the tax.
- The meaning of the question as it applies to a particular situation is genuinely uncertain.
- The answer to the question is voluminous.

The fact that an answer to a question could prove disadvantageous to the client does not justify omitting the answer.

Statement No. 3: Procedural Aspects of Preparing Returns

In preparing a return, a CPA may in good faith rely without verification on information furnished by the client or by third parties. However, the CPA should make reasonable inquiries if the information appears to be incorrect, incomplete, or inconsistent. In this regard, the CPA should refer to the client's prior returns whenever appropriate.

EXAMPLE 20

A CPA normally can take a client's word for the validity of dependency exemptions. But suppose a recently divorced client wants to claim his three children as dependents when he does not have custody. A CPA must act in accordance with § 152(e)(2) in preparing the return. Claiming the dependency exemption will require evidence of a waiver by the custodial parent. Without this waiver, the CPA should not claim the dependency exemptions on the client's tax return. ■

EXAMPLE 21

While preparing Sunni's income tax return for 2011, a CPA reviews her income tax return for 2010. In comparing the dividend income reported on the 2010 Schedule B with that received in 2011, the CPA notes a significant decrease. Further investigation reveals the variation is due to a stock sale in 2011 that, until now, was unknown to the CPA. Thus, the review of the 2010 return has unearthed a transaction that should be reported on the 2011 return. ■

If the Code or Regulations require certain types of substantiation (as is the case with travel and entertainment expenditures), the CPA must advise the client of these rules. Further, inquiry must be made to ascertain whether the client has complied with the substantiation requirements.

Statement No. 4: Estimates

A CPA may prepare a tax return using estimates received from a taxpayer if it is impracticable to obtain exact data. The estimates must be reasonable under the facts and circumstances known to the CPA. When estimates are used, they should be presented in such a manner as to avoid implying that greater accuracy exists.

Statement No. 5: Recognition of Administrative Proceeding or Court Decisions

As facts may vary from year to year, so may the position taken by a CPA. In these types of situations, the CPA is not bound by an administrative or judicial proceeding involving a prior year.

EXAMPLE 22

Upon audit of Ramon Corporation's income tax return for 2009, the IRS disallowed $78,000 of the $600,000 salary paid to its president and sole shareholder on the grounds that it was unreasonable. A CPA has been engaged to prepare Ramon's income tax return for 2011. Again the corporation paid its president a salary of $600,000 and chose to deduct this amount. Because the CPA is not bound for 2011 by what the IRS deemed reasonable for 2009, the full $600,000 can be claimed as a salary deduction. ■

CONCEPT SUMMARY 26.1

Tax Profession and Ethics

1. The Internal Revenue Service (IRS) enforces the tax laws of the United States.
2. The IRS issues various pronouncements in communicating its position on certain tax issues. These pronouncements promote the uniform enforcement of the tax law among taxpayers and among the internal divisions of the IRS. Taxpayers should seek such rulings and memoranda when the nature or magnitude of a pending transaction requires a high degree of certainty in the planning process.
3. IRS audits can take several forms. Taxpayers are selected for audit based on the probable net dollar return to the Treasury from the process. Offers in compromise and closing agreements can be a useful means of completing an audit without resorting to litigation.
4. Certain IRS personnel are empowered to consider the hazards of litigation in developing a settlement with the taxpayer during the audit process.
5. The IRS pays interest to taxpayers on overpaid taxes, starting essentially 45 days after the due date of the return, in amounts tied to the Federal short-term rate. Interest paid to the IRS on underpayments is similarly based on the Federal rate, starting essentially on the due date of the return. Interest for both purposes is compounded daily.
6. The Treasury assesses penalties when the taxpayer fails to file a required tax return or pay a tax. Penalties also are assessed when an inaccurate return is filed due to negligence or other disregard of IRS rules. Tax preparers are subject to penalties for assisting a taxpayer in filing an inaccurate return, failing to follow IRS rules in an appropriate manner, or mishandling taxpayer data or funds.
7. Statutes of limitations place outer boundaries on the timing and amounts of proposed amendments to completed tax returns that can be made by the taxpayer or the IRS.
8. Tax practitioners must operate under constraints imposed on them by codes of ethics of pertinent professional societies and by Treasury Circular 230. These rules also define the parties who can represent others in an IRS proceeding.
9. A limited privilege of confidentiality exists between the taxpayer and tax preparer.

Statement No. 6: Knowledge of Error

A CPA should promptly advise a client upon learning of an error on a previously filed return or upon learning of a client's failure to file a required return. The advice can be oral or written and should include a recommendation of the corrective measures, if any, to be taken. The error or other omission should not be disclosed to the IRS without the client's consent.

If the past error is material and is not corrected by the client, the CPA may be unable to prepare the current year's tax return. This situation might occur if the error has a carryover effect that prevents the CPA from determining the correct tax liability for the current year.

EXAMPLE 23

In preparing a client's 2011 income tax return, a CPA discovers that final inventory for 2010 was materially understated. First, the CPA should advise the client to file an amended return for 2010 reflecting the correct amount in final inventory. Second, if the client refuses to make this adjustment, the CPA should consider whether the error will preclude preparation of a substantially correct return for 2011. Because this will probably be the case (the final inventory for 2010 becomes the beginning inventory for 2011), the CPA should withdraw from the engagement.

If the client corrects the error, the CPA may proceed with the preparation of the tax return for 2011. However, the CPA must ensure that the error is not repeated. ■

Statement No. 7: Advice to Clients

In providing tax advice to a client, the CPA must use judgment to ensure that the advice reflects professional competence and appropriately serves the client's needs. No standard format or guidelines can be established to cover all situations and circumstances involving written or oral advice by the CPA.

The CPA may communicate with the client when subsequent developments affect previous advice on significant matters. However, the CPA cannot be expected to assume responsibility for initiating the communication, unless he or she is assisting a client in implementing procedures or plans associated with the advice. The CPA may undertake this obligation by specific agreement with the client.

TAX PLANNING:

26.3 Strategies in Seeking an Administrative Ruling

LO.9

Identify effective planning strategies that may be useful in a tax practice when dealing with the IRS.

DETERMINATION LETTERS

In many instances, the request for an advance ruling or a determination letter from the IRS is a necessary or desirable planning strategy. The receipt of a favorable ruling or determination reduces the risk associated with a transaction when the tax results are in doubt. For example, the initiation or amendment of a qualified pension or profit sharing plan should be accompanied by a determination letter. Otherwise, on subsequent IRS review, the plan may not qualify, and the tax deductibility of contributions to the plan will be disallowed. In some situations, the potential tax effects of a transaction are so numerous and of such consequence that proceeding without a ruling is unwise.

LETTER RULINGS

In some cases, it may not be necessary or desirable to request an advance ruling. For example, it is generally not desirable to request a ruling if the tax results are doubtful and the company is committed to complete the transaction in any event. If a ruling is requested and negotiations with the IRS indicate that an adverse determination will be forthcoming, it is usually possible to have the ruling request withdrawn. However, the National Office of the IRS may forward its findings, along with a copy of the ruling request, to local IRS personnel. In determining the advisability of a ruling request, the taxpayer should consider the potential exposure of other items in the tax returns of all "open years."

A ruling request may delay the consummation of a transaction if the issues are novel or complex. Frequently, a ruling can be processed within six months, although in some instances a delay of a year or more may be encountered.

TECHNICAL ADVICE MEMORANDA

A taxpayer in the process of contesting a proposed deficiency with the Appeals Division should consider requesting a technical advice memorandum from the IRS. If such advice is favorable to the taxpayer, it is binding on the Appeals Division. The request may be particularly appropriate when the practitioner feels that the agent or Appeals Division has been too literal in interpreting an IRS ruling.

26.4 Considerations in Handling an IRS Audit

As a general rule, a taxpayer should attempt to settle disputes at the earliest possible stage of the administrative appeal process. New issues may be raised by IRS personnel if the case goes beyond the agent level. It is usually possible to limit the scope of the examination by furnishing pertinent information requested by the agent. Extraneous information or thoughtless comments may result in the opening of new issues and should be avoided. Agents usually appreciate prompt and efficient responses to inquiries, since their performance may in part be judged by their ability to close or settle assigned cases.

ETHICS & Equity **SHOULD THE CLIENT ATTEND AN AUDIT?**

Whether the client should be present during an audit is a matter of some debate. Certainly, the client's absence tends to slow down the negotiating process because the taxpayer must make all final decisions on settlement terms and is the best source of information for open questions of fact. Nevertheless, most practitioners discourage their clients from attending audits or conferences with the Appeals Division involving an income tax dispute. Ignorance of the law and of the conventions of the audit process can make the taxpayer a "loose cannon" that can do more harm than good if unchecked. All too often, they say, a client will "say too much" in the presence of a government official.

In reality, though, by discouraging clients from attending the audit, practitioners may be interfering with the IRS's function of gathering evidence, depending on what precisely the taxpayer is being prevented from saying. To many practitioners, a "wrong" answer is one that increases taxes, not one that misrepresents the truth. A popular saying among tax advisers is "Don't tell me more than I want to know." Although this philosophy is supportable under various professional codes of conduct, it is hardly defensible in the larger scheme of things.

In your opinion, under what circumstances should the client attend such a session? To what degree should the tax professional "coach" the client as to how to behave in that setting? Or do a taxpayer's rights include the right to increase his or her own tax liability?

To the extent possible, it is advisable to conduct the investigation of field audits in the practitioner's office, rather than the client's office. This procedure permits greater control over the audit investigation and facilitates the agent's review and prompt closure of the case.

Many practitioners feel that it is generally not advisable to have clients present at the scheduled conferences with the agent, since the client may give emotional or gratuitous comments that impair prompt settlement. If the client is not present, however, he or she should be advised of the status of negotiations. The client makes the final decision on any proposed settlement.

PREPARING FOR THE AUDIT

The tax professional must prepare thoroughly for the audit or Appeals proceeding. Practitioners often cite the following steps as critical to such preparations. Carrying out a level of due diligence in preparing for the proceeding is part of the tax professional's responsibility in representing the client.

- Make certain that both sides agree on the issues to be resolved in the audit. The goal here is to limit the agent's list of open issues.
- Identify all of the facts underlying the issues in dispute, including those favorable to the IRS. Gather evidence to support the taxpayer's position, and evaluate the evidence supporting the other side.
- Research current tax law authorities that bear on the facts and open issues. Remember that the IRS agent is bound only by Supreme Court cases and IRS pronouncements. Determine the degree of discretion that the IRS is likely to have in disposing of the case.
- Prepare a list of points supporting and contradicting the taxpayer's case. Include both minor points bearing little weight and core principles. Short research memos will also be useful in the discussion with the agent. Points favoring the taxpayer should be mentioned during the discussion and "entered into the record."
- Prepare tax and interest computations showing the effects of points that are in dispute, so that the consequences of closing or compromising an issue can be readily determined.
- Determine a "litigation point" (i.e., at which the taxpayer will withdraw from further audit negotiation and pursue the case in the courts). This position should be based on the dollars of tax, interest, and penalty

involved, the chances of prevailing in various trial-level courts, and other strategies discussed with the taxpayer. One must have an "end game" strategy for the audit, and thorough tax research is critical in developing that position in this context.

OFFERS IN COMPROMISE

Both parties to a tax dispute may find a compromise offer useful because it conclusively settles all of the issues covered by the agreement and may include a favorable payment schedule for the taxpayer. On the other hand, several attributes of an offer in compromise may work to the detriment of the taxpayer. Just as the IRS no longer can raise new issues as part of the audit proceedings against the taxpayer, he or she cannot contest or appeal any such agreement. As part of the offer process, the taxpayer must disclose all relevant finances and resources, including details he or she might not want the government to know, and an up-front payment will be due. Furthermore, both parties are bound to the filing positions established by the compromise for five tax years, a level of inflexibility that may work against a taxpayer whose circumstances change over time.

DOCUMENTATION ISSUES

The tax practitioner's workpapers should include all research memoranda, and a list of resolved and unresolved issues should be continually updated during the course of the IRS audit. Occasionally, agents request access to excessive amounts of accounting data in order to engage in a so-called fishing expedition. Providing blanket access to workpapers should be avoided. Workpapers should be carefully reviewed to minimize opportunities for the agent to raise new issues not otherwise apparent. It is generally advisable to provide the agent with copies of specific workpapers upon request.

In unusual situations, a Special Agent may appear to gather evidence in the investigation of possible criminal fraud. When this occurs, the taxpayer should be advised to seek legal counsel to determine the extent of his or her cooperation in providing information to the agent. Further, it is frequently desirable for the tax adviser to consult his or her own personal legal counsel in such situations. If the taxpayer receives a Revenue Agent's Report, it generally indicates that the IRS has decided not to initiate criminal proceedings. The IRS usually does not take any action on a tax deficiency until the criminal matter has been resolved.

26.5 STATUTE OF LIMITATIONS

EXTENDING THE STATUTE

The IRS requests an extension of the statute of limitations when it finds that there is insufficient time to complete an audit or appellate review. The taxpayer is not compelled to agree to the extension request and may be averse to giving the IRS more time. But adverse consequences can result if the taxpayer denies the IRS request.

EXAMPLE 24

Although the statute of limitations governing Thornton's tax return is scheduled to expire in 15 days, the IRS has requested an extension for another 60 days. It wants to complete a more thorough investigation into a disputed $50,000 deduction. If Thornton refuses to agree to the extension, the IRS likely will disallow the entire deduction. However, if Thornton agrees to the extension, all or part of the deduction may be salvaged. ■

A disadvantage of extending the statute is that the IRS sometimes can raise new issues during the extension period. However, the taxpayer can take the following protective measures as a condition to agreeing to the extension.

- Shorten the extension period requested before signing the Form 872. This will reduce the chance that the IRS will find and investigate new issues.

- Restrict the scope of the issues covered by the extension (e.g., extend the period only as to the computation of cost of goods sold).
- Instead of Form 872, use a Form 872–A. This allows for an open-ended termination date of the extension. Consequently, when the examination of a disputed issue is completed, the taxpayer can request that the IRS close off the extension. This reduces the chances that the IRS will find and pursue any new issues.

PROMPT ASSESSMENT

The "prompt assessment" approach forces the IRS to conduct some sort of an examination of a return. Although most taxpayers are unlikely to volunteer for an audit, the procedure is attractive in several circumstances.

- An estate or trust (Chapters 27 and 28) is being terminated, and the executor or trustee needs some assurance that the entity's tax affairs are in order.
- A corporation is being liquidated, and the trustee of the liquidating trust wants to protect itself from unanticipated future income tax assessments by the IRS on years open under the statute of limitations.

A request for a prompt assessment is made by filing Form 4810. The IRS has 18 months to complete its review once the taxpayer files the request.[63]

26.6 Penalties

Penalties are imposed upon a taxpayer's failure to file a return or pay a tax when due. These penalties can be avoided if the failure is due to reasonable cause and not to willful neglect. Reasonable cause, however, has not been liberally interpreted by the courts and should not be relied upon in the routine situation.[64] A safer way to avoid the failure to file penalty is to obtain an extension of time for filing the return from the IRS.

The penalty for failure to pay estimated taxes can become quite severe. Often trapped by the provision are employed taxpayers with outside income. They may forget about their outside income and assume the amount withheld from wages and salaries is adequate to cover their liability. Not only does April 15 provide a real shock (in terms of the additional tax owed) for these persons, but a penalty situation may have evolved. One way for an employee to mitigate this problem (presuming the employer is willing to cooperate) is described in the following example.

EXAMPLE 25

Patty, a calendar year taxpayer, is employed by Finn Corporation and earns (after withholding) a monthly salary of $4,000 payable at the end of each month. Patty also receives income from outside sources (interest, dividends, and consulting fees). After some quick calculations in early October, Patty determines that she has underestimated her tax liability by $7,500 and will be subject to the penalty for the first two quarters of the year and part of the third quarter. Patty, therefore, completes a new Form W–4 in which she arbitrarily raises her income tax withholding by $2,500 a month. Finn accepts the Form W–4, and as a result, an extra $7,500 is paid to the IRS on Patty's account for the payroll period from October through December.

Patty avoids penalties for the underpayment for the first three quarters because withholding of taxes is allocated pro rata over the year involved. Thus, a portion of the additional $7,500 withheld in October–December is assigned to the January 1–April 15 period, the April 16–June 15 period, etc. Had Patty merely paid the IRS an additional $7,500 in October, the penalty would still have been assessed for the earlier quarters. ■

[63] § 6501(d).

[64] *Dustin v. Comm.*, 72–2 USTC ¶9610, 30 AFTR 2d 72–5313, 467 F.2d 47 (CA–9, 1972), *aff'g* 53 T.C. 491 (1969).

To avoid tax preparer penalties, the tax professional must carry out a number of quality control measures within the context of his or her firm.

- Adopt a "tone at the top" that stresses ethical tax practice, emphasizing at all times the importance of integrity and objectivity in the context of client advocacy.
- Establish and follow ethical guidelines with respect to all forms of client communication and documentation, including tax returns and written, spoken, and electronic tax advice.
- Apply ethical standards even before an engagement letter is prepared for a potential client. The client should be aware of, and participate in, this dedication to ethical behavior.
- Keep current on changes to penalties, ethical guidelines, and Circular 230 provisions through an ongoing educational effort that communicates rule changes and the firm's best practices to all who handle tax return data.
- Monitor the compliance of all members of the firm with the established ethical guidelines. Use a peer review process periodically to confirm that the system is working as designed and to bring third-party suggestions into the process.

REFOCUS ON THE BIG PICTURE

A TAX ADVISER'S DILEMMA

Your work with Campbell Corporation and its incremental research credit may prove troublesome. To avoid the taxpayer and tax preparer penalties, substantial authority must exist for claiming the credit, but the tax cases and Regulations do not appear to provide much guidance with respect to research expenditures of this sort. How does one craft a tax return position when the tax law largely is silent as to the particulars of the facts of the taxpayer's situation? How much risk of incurring a tax penalty are the taxpayer and your firm willing to assume in deciding how and whether to report these expenditures?

Beyond the monetary effects of claiming the credit, you and the client must consider the publicity aspects of taking this issue to court: Does Campbell want to be the "test case" in the Tax Court on this matter? What would be the effects on your consulting firm if a preparer penalty or even loss of professional certification were to result? If the credit is to be claimed, what degree of "disclosure" does the law require?

At a minimum, your firm and Campbell's tax department must conduct thorough research of analogous situations in the law in which the incremental research credit was and was not allowed for the taxpayer. Due diligence in this regard would require that you examine how other software applications and similar technological innovations, probably having nothing to do with GPS software and national security concerns, were treated for tax credit purposes. Constrained only by the budget dollars that Campbell is willing to dedicate to this task, your research is likely to be both interesting and frustrating, as no "on point" resolution is likely to be found prior to a later audit of the Form 1120 and its disclosures.

What If?

The risk profiles of the tax adviser and a client seldom are identical. What position should your firm take if Campbell's tax department decides to claim the full incremental research credit for an item on which the tax law is silent or unclear, but your firm recommends that a special disclosure be made on the return concerning the item? A disclosure of this sort would protect the parties from later assessment of tax penalties, but Campbell believes that drawing attention to the credit item would increase the likelihood of a targeted audit of the expenditures by the IRS.

CONTINUED

Although you are certain that tax fraud is not a problem on the Campbell return, you are concerned about the ramifications of Campbell's desire to omit the recommended disclosure. Your firm might decide to leave the Campbell engagement altogether if it is especially sensitive to exposure to penalties, or if it is not certain that adequate research has been done to support the tax return position. Charges of a lack of due diligence by your firm might be brought by the IRS, the firm's professional ethics or certification bodies, or the issuer of its malpractice insurance. Clearly, none of these results is attractive to your firm.

KEY TERMS

Accuracy-related penalty, 26–16
Circular 230, 26–23
Closing agreement, 26–13
Determination letter, 26–5
E-filing, 26–4
Enrolled agent (EA), 26–23
Fraud, 26–19
Frivolous return, 26–24
Letter ruling, 26–4
Negligence, 26–16
Ninety-day letter, 26–10
Offer in compromise, 26–12
Reasonable cause, 26–16
Revenue Agent's Report (RAR), 26–10
Statute of limitations, 26–21
Substantial authority, 26–17
Tax preparer, 26–26
Technical advice memorandum (TAM), 26–5
Thirty-day letter, 26–10
Unreasonable position, 26–26
Whistleblower program, 26–8

DISCUSSION QUESTIONS

1. **LO.1** An article in *USA Today* refers to the "audit lottery" and how one's chances of being audited are higher under the current IRS leadership. What is the audit lottery, and how should a tax professional view the statistics about a taxpayer's audit likelihood?

2. **LO.1** Recently, a politician was interviewed about fiscal policy, and she mentioned reducing the "tax gap." Explain what this term means. What are some of the pertinent political and economic issues relative to the tax gap? **ISSUE ID**

3. **LO.2** Your tax research has located a Tax Court case that supports the claiming of a deduction by a client, while an IRS letter ruling holds to the contrary. The pertinent facts of both the case and the ruling match those of the client. Which holding should be followed in preparing the client's tax return? Summarize your findings in a memo to the tax research file. **COMMUNICATIONS**

4. **LO.2** Your client is litigating in the Tax Court concerning a tax credit that she claimed and the IRS has denied. Who bears the burden of proof regarding the litigation?

5. **LO.2** Describe the process that the IRS uses to collect the tax that is found to be due after an audit is completed. Assume that the IRS findings are not appealed but that the taxpayer does not pay the amount due as determined by the audit. Illustrate the process with no more than four PowerPoint slides. **COMMUNICATIONS**

6. **LO.3** Gloria and Maria work together in an insurance office. Gloria's Form 1040 seems to be audited two out of every three years, while Maria never has been audited. How does the IRS select tax returns for audit? List some of the factors that might result in the different treatment of Gloria's and Maria's returns.

7. **LO.3** When can an individual taxpayer feel certain that his or her tax return will not be audited by the IRS? One year after it is filed? Two years? Five years? Explain.

8. **LO.3, 4** Lori wants to establish that her niece Suzette actually qualifies for a dependency exemption. After the issue is raised by the IRS on audit, Lori could argue the matter with the agent, an IRS Appeals officer, or the Tax Court. Give Lori advice about how to handle her tax dispute.

ISSUE ID

9. **LO.3** Describe the three broad types of IRS audits. Give an example of an issue that each type of audit might address, and indicate how frequently such audits are conducted by the IRS.

10. **LO.4** Under what circumstances will the IRS consider a request from the taxpayer for an offer in compromise?

11. **LO.5** Explain how the interest rates that apply to Federal income tax underpayments and overpayments are determined. If a taxpayer owes additional taxes, when does interest begin to accrue?

12. **LO.6** Which of the valuation penalties is likely to arise when an aggressive taxpayer reports:
    a. A charitable contribution?
    b. A business deduction?
    c. A decedent's taxable estate?

13. **LO.6** Describe how the valuation penalties work. What is the rate of the penalty, and on which amount is it imposed?

14. **LO.6** Yonkers Corporation recomputes its research credit for the prior tax year and, as a result, claims a $100,000 refund. The IRS reviews the claim and allows only $20,000 of the requested refund. If Yonkers does not appeal, is this matter finished? Is Yonkers certain to receive the full $20,000 refund allowed?

ISSUE ID

15. **LO.6** On October 30, Cameron determines that his tax for the year will total $10,000. If his employer is scheduled to withhold only $6,500 in Federal income taxes, what can Cameron do to avoid any underpayment penalty?

16. **LO.4, 5, 7** Indicate whether each of the following statements is true or false.
    a. The government never pays a taxpayer interest on an overpayment of tax.
    b. The IRS can compromise on the amount of tax liability if there is doubt as to the taxpayer's ability to pay.
    c. The statute of limitations for assessing a tax can extend beyond three years from the filing of a return.
    d. For a tax return that has not been filed, the statute of limitations is extended to five years from the original due date of the return.

17. **LO.4, 6** In each of the following cases, distinguish between the terms.
    a. Offer in compromise and closing agreement.
    b. Failure to file and failure to pay.
    c. Ninety-day letter and thirty-day letter.
    d. Negligence and fraud.
    e. Criminal and civil tax fraud.

18. **LO.6** Describe at least two civil tax penalties that could apply when there is a violation of the rules involving the withholding of taxes from wages and salaries. Be specific.

ISSUE ID

19. **LO.7** Why should the taxpayer be "let off the hook" and no longer be subject to audit exposure once the applicable statute of limitations has expired? Do statutes of limitations protect the government? Other taxpayers?

20. **LO.8** Give the Circular 230 position concerning each of the following situations sometimes encountered in the tax profession.
    a. Taking an aggressive pro-taxpayer position on a tax return.
    b. Not having a quality review process for a return completed by a partner of the tax firm.
    c. Purposely delaying compliance with a document request received from the IRS.
    d. Not keeping up with changes in the tax law.
    e. Charging $1,500 to complete a Form 1040-EZ.
    f. When representing a taxpayer in a Federal income tax audit, charging a fee equal to one-third of the reduction of the tax proposed by the IRS agent.
    g. Representing both the grantor and the beneficiaries of a trust that is being created.

21. **LO.8** Indicate whether each of the following parties could be subject to the tax preparer penalties.
    a. Tom prepared Sally's return for $250.
    b. Theresa prepared her grandmother's return for no charge.
    c. Georgia prepared her church's return for $500 (she would have charged an unrelated party $3,000 for the same work).

d. Geoff prepared returns for low-income taxpayers under his college's VITA program.
e. Hildy prepared the return of her corporate employer.
f. Heejeo, an administrative assistant for an accounting firm, processed a client's return through TurboTax.

22. **LO.6, 8** In no more than three PowerPoint slides, list at least four of the Code's penalties that could be assessed against paid preparers of tax returns. Name the violation that triggers the penalty, and explain how the dollar amount of the penalty is determined.

COMMUNICATIONS

23. **LO.8** Indicate which codes, canons, and other bodies of ethical statements apply to each of the following tax practitioners.
    a. CPAs who are members of the AICPA.
    b. CPAs who are not members of the AICPA.
    c. Attorneys.
    d. Enrolled agents.
    e. Tax preparers who are not CPAs, EAs, or attorneys.

PROBLEMS

24. **LO.5** Gordon paid the $10,000 balance of his Federal income tax three months late. Ignore daily compounding of interest. Determine the interest rate that applies relative to this amount, assuming that:
    a. Gordon is an individual.
    b. Gordon is a C corporation.
    c. The $10,000 is not a tax that is due but is a refund payable by the IRS to Gordon (an individual).
    d. The $10,000 is not a tax that is due but is a refund payable by the IRS to Gordon (a C corporation).

25. **LO.6** Rita forgot to pay her Federal income tax on time. When she actually filed, she reported a balance due. Compute Rita's failure to file penalty in each of the following cases.
    a. Two months late, $1,000 additional tax due.
    b. Five months late, $3,000 additional tax due.
    c. Eight months late, $4,000 additional tax due.
    d. Two and a half months late, $3,000 additional tax due.
    e. Five months late due to fraud by Rita, $4,000 additional tax due.
    f. Ten months late due to fraud by Rita, $15,000 additional tax due.

26. **LO.6** Tom filed his Federal income tax return on time but did not remit the balance due. Compute Tom's failure to pay penalty in each of the following cases. Assume the IRS has not issued a deficiency notice.
    a. Four months late, $3,000 additional tax due.
    b. Ten months late, $4,000 additional tax due.
    c. Five years late, $5,000 additional tax due.

27. **LO.6** Compute the failure to pay and failure to file penalties for John, who filed his 2010 income tax return on October 20, 2011, paying the $30,000 amount due at that time. On April 1, 2011, John had received a six-month extension of time in which to file his return. He has no reasonable cause for failing to file his return by October 15 or for failing to pay the tax that was due on April 15, 2011. John's failure to comply with the tax laws was not fraudulent.

28. **LO.6** Olivia, a calendar year taxpayer, does not file her 2010 return until December 12, 2011. At this point, she pays the $40,000 balance due on her 2010 tax liability of $70,000. Olivia did not apply for and obtain any extension of time for filing the 2010 return. When questioned by the IRS on her delinquency, Olivia asserts: "If I was too busy to file my regular tax return, I was too busy to request an extension."
    a. Is Olivia liable for any penalties for failure to file and for failure to pay?
    b. If so, compute the penalty amounts.

29. **LO.6** Rhoda, a calendar year taxpayer, files her 2010 return on November 4, 2012. She did not obtain an extension for filing her return, and the return reflects additional income tax due of $25,000.
    a. What are Rhoda's penalties for failure to file and to pay?
    b. Would your answer change if Rhoda, before the due date of the return, had retained a CPA to prepare the return and the CPA's negligence caused the delay?

30. **LO.6** Dana underpaid her taxes by $250,000. A portion of the underpayment was shown to be attributable to Dana's negligence ($200,000). A court found that a portion of that deficiency constituted civil fraud ($50,000). Compute the total fraud and negligence penalties incurred.

31. **LO.6** Compute the overvaluation penalty for each of the following independent cases involving the fair market value of charitable contribution property. In each case, assume a marginal income tax rate of 35%.

Taxpayer	Corrected IRS Value	Reported Valuation
a. Individual	$ 40,000	$ 50,000
b. C corporation	30,000	50,000
c. S corporation	40,000	50,000
d. Individual	150,000	200,000
e. Individual	150,000	250,000
f. C corporation	150,000	750,000

32. **LO.6** Compute the undervaluation penalty for each of the following independent cases involving the value of a closely held business in the decedent's gross estate. In each case, assume a marginal estate tax rate of 35%.

	Reported Value	Corrected IRS Valuation
a.	$ 20,000	$ 25,000
b.	100,000	150,000
c.	150,000	250,000
d.	150,000	500,000

33. **LO.6** Singh, a qualified appraiser of fine art and other collectibles, was advising Colleen when she was determining the amount of the charitable contribution deduction for a gift of sculpture to a museum. Singh sanctioned an $800,000 appraisal, even though he knew that the market value of the piece was only $300,000. Colleen assured Singh that she had never been audited by the IRS and that the risk of the government questioning his appraisal was negligible.

    But Colleen was wrong and her return was audited. The IRS used its own appraisers to set the value of the sculpture at $400,000. Colleen is in the 30% Federal income tax bracket while Singh's fee for preparing the appraisal was $50,000.

    a. Compute the penalty that the IRS can assess against Singh. (Do not consider the valuation penalty as to Colleen's return.)
    b. What is the penalty if Singh's appraisal fee was $5,000 (not $50,000)?

34. **LO.6** The Eggers Corporation filed an amended Form 1120, claiming an additional $400,000 deduction for payments to a contractor for a prior tax year. The amended return was based on the entity's interpretation of a Regulation that defined deductible advance payment expenditures. The nature of Eggers's activity with the contractor did not exactly fit the language of the Regulation. Nevertheless, because so much tax was at stake, Eggers's tax department decided to broaden its interpretation and claim the deduction.

    Eggers's tax department estimated that there was only a 15% chance that Eggers's interpretation would stand up to a Tax Court review.

    a. What is the amount of tax penalty that Eggers is risking by taking this position?
    b. What would be the result if there was a 45% chance that Eggers's interpretation of the Regulation was correct?

35. **LO.6** Moose, a former professional athlete, now supplements his income by signing autographs at collectors' shows. Unfortunately, Moose has not been conscientious about reporting all of this income on his tax return. Now, the IRS has charged him with additional taxes of $100,000 due to negligence in his record-keeping and $20,000 due to an intent to defraud the U.S. government of income taxes. No criminal fraud charges are brought against Moose. The District Court finds by a preponderance of the evidence that only half of the $20,000 underpayment was due to Moose's fraudulent action; the remainder was due to mere negligence. Compute the accuracy-related and civil fraud penalties in this matter.

36. **LO.6** Trudy's AGI last year was $200,000. Her Federal income tax came to $65,000, which she paid through a combination of withholding and estimated payments. This year, her AGI will be $300,000, with a projected tax liability of $45,000, all to be paid through estimates.
    a. Ignore the annualized income method. Compute Trudy's quarterly estimated tax payment schedule for this year.
    b. Assume instead that Trudy's AGI last year was $100,000 and resulted in a Federal income tax of $20,000. Determine her quarterly estimated tax payment schedule for this year.

37. **LO.6** Kold Services Corporation estimates that its 2012 taxable income will be $500,000. Thus, it is subject to a flat 34% income tax rate and incurs a $170,000 liability. For each of the following independent cases, compute Kold's minimum quarterly estimated tax payments that will avoid an underpayment penalty.
    a. For 2011, taxable income was ($200,000). Kold carried back all of this loss to prior years and exhausted the entire net operating loss in creating a zero 2011 liability.
    b. For 2011, taxable income was $450,000, and tax liability was $153,000.
    c. For 2010, taxable income was $2 million, and tax liability was $680,000. For 2011, taxable income was $400,000, and tax liability was $136,000.

38. **LO.6** The Scooter Company, owned equally by Julie (chair of the board of directors) and Jeff (company president), is in very difficult financial straits. Last month, Jeff used the $100,000 withheld from employee paychecks for Federal payroll and income taxes to pay off a creditor who threatened to cut off all supplies. To keep the company afloat, Jeff used these government funds willfully for the operations of the business, but even that effort was not enough. The company missed the next two payrolls, and today other creditors took action to shut down Scooter altogether. How much will the IRS assess in taxes and penalties in this matter, and from whom? How can you as a tax professional best offer service to Julie, Jeff, and Scooter? Address these matters in a memo for the tax research file.

DECISION MAKING

COMMUNICATIONS

39. **LO.7** What is the applicable statute of limitations in each of the following independent situations?
    a. No return was filed by the taxpayer.
    b. The taxpayer incurred a bad debt loss that she failed to claim.
    c. A taxpayer inadvertently omitted a large amount of gross income.
    d. Same as (c), except that the omission was deliberate.
    e. A taxpayer innocently overstated her deductions by a large amount.

40. **LO.7** Suzanne, a calendar year taxpayer, had the following transactions, all of which were properly reported on a timely return.

Gross receipts		$ 975,000
Less: Cost of sales		(850,000)
Gross profit		$ 125,000
Capital gain	$ 90,000	
Less: Capital loss	(25,000)	65,000
Total income		$ 190,000

    a. Presuming the absence of fraud, how much of an omission from gross income is required before the six-year statute of limitations applies?
    b. Would it matter if cost of sales had been inadvertently overstated by $100,000?
    c. How does the situation change in the context of fraud by Suzanne?

41. **LO.5, 7** On April 3, 2008, Mark filed his 2007 income tax return, which showed a tax due of $80,000. On June 1, 2010, he filed an amended return for 2007 that showed an additional tax of $10,000. Mark paid the additional amount. On May 18, 2011, Mark filed a claim for a 2007 refund of $45,000.
    a. If Mark's claim for a refund is correct in amount, how much tax will he recover?
    b. What is the period that government-paid interest runs with respect to Mark's claim for a refund?
    c. How would you have advised him differently?

DECISION MAKING

42. **LO.7** Carol owed $4,000 in Federal income tax when she filed her Form 1040 for 2011. She attached a Post-It Note to the 1040 saying, "My inventory computations on last year's (2010) return were wrong, so I paid $1,000 too much in tax." Carol then included a check for $3,000 with the Form 1040 for 2011. Write a memo to the tax research file commenting on Carol's actions.

COMMUNICATIONS

43. **LO.8** Rod's Federal income tax returns (Form 1040) for the indicated three years were prepared by the following persons.

Year	Preparer
2009	Rod
2010	Ann
2011	Cheryl

Ann is Rod's next-door neighbor and owns and operates a pharmacy. Cheryl is a licensed CPA and is engaged in private practice. In the event Rod is audited and all three returns are examined, who may represent him before the IRS at the agent level? Who may represent Rod before the Appeals Division?

44. **LO.8** Lois is the preparer of the Form 1120 for Yostern Corporation. On the return, Yostern claimed a deduction that the IRS later disallowed on audit. Compute the tax preparer penalty that could be assessed against Lois in each of the following independent situations.

	Form 8275 Disclosure on the Return of the Disputed Deduction?	Tax Reduction Resulting from the Deduction	Probability That the Courts Would Approve the Deduction	Lois's Fee to Complete Yostern's Return
a.	No	$50,000	65%	$10,000
b.	No	50,000	35	10,000
c.	No	50,000	35	1,500
d.	Yes	50,000	35	10,000
e.	Yes	50,000	15	5,000

45. **LO.8** Discuss which penalties, if any, might be imposed on the tax adviser in each of the following independent circumstances. In this regard, assume that the tax adviser:
    a. Suggested to the client various means by which to acquire excludible income.
    b. Suggested to the client various means by which to conceal cash receipts from gross income.
    c. Suggested to the client means by which to improve her cash flow by delaying for six months or more the deposit of the employees' share of Federal employment taxes.
    d. Failed, because of pressing time conflicts, to conduct the usual review of the client's tax return. The IRS later discovered that the return included fraudulent data.
    e. Failed, because of pressing time conflicts, to conduct the usual review of the client's tax return. The IRS later discovered a mathematical error in the computation of the personal exemption.

46. **LO.8** Compute the preparer penalty that the IRS could assess on Gerry in each of the following independent cases.
    a. On March 21, the copy machine was not working, so Gerry gave original returns to her 20 clients that day without providing any duplicates for them. Copies for Gerry's files and for use in preparing state tax returns had been made on March 20.
    b. Because Gerry extended her vacation a few days, she missed the Annual Tax Update seminar that she usually attends. As a result, she was unaware that Congress had changed a law affecting limited partnerships. The change affected the transactions of 25 of Gerry's clients, all of whom understated their tax as a result.
    c. Gerry heard that the IRS was increasing its audits of corporations that hold assets in a foreign trust. As a result, Gerry instructed the intern who prepared the initial drafts of the returns for five corporate clients to leave blank the question about such trusts. Not wanting to lose his position, the intern, a senior accounting major at State University, complied with Gerry's instructions.

DECISION MAKING

47. **LO.8** You are the chair of the Ethics Committee of your state's CPA Licensing Commission. Interpret controlling AICPA authority in addressing the following assertions by your membership.

a. When a CPA has reasonable grounds for not answering an applicable question on a client's return, a brief explanation of the reason for the omission should not be provided, because it would flag the return for audit by the IRS.
b. If a CPA discovers during an IRS audit that the client has a material error on the return under examination, he should immediately withdraw from the engagement.
c. If the client tells you that she paid $500 for office supplies, but has lost the receipt, you should deduct an odd amount on her return (e.g., $499), because an even amount (i.e., $500) would indicate to the IRS that her deduction was based on an estimate.
d. If a CPA knows that the client has a material error on a prior year's return, he should not, without the client's consent, disclose the error to the IRS.
e. If a CPA's client will not correct a material error on a prior year's return, the CPA should not prepare the current year's return for the client.

RESEARCH PROBLEMS

Note: Solutions to Research Problems can be prepared by using the **Checkpoint® Student Edition** online research product, which is available to accompany this text. It is also possible to prepare solutions to the Research Problems by using tax research materials found in a standard tax library.

THOMSON REUTERS
Checkpoint® Student Edition

COMMUNICATIONS

Research Problem 1. Blanche Creek (111 Elm Avenue, Patriotville, IN 40123) has engaged your firm because she has been charged with failure to file her 2009 Federal Form 1040. Blanche maintains that the "reasonable cause" exception should apply. During the entire tax filing season in 2010, she was under a great deal of stress at work and in her personal life. As a result, Blanche developed a sleep disorder, which was treated through a combination of pills and counseling.

Your firm ultimately prepared the 2009 tax return for Blanche, but it was filed far beyond the due date. Blanche is willing to pay the delinquent tax and related interest. However, she feels that the failure to pay penalty is unfair as she was ill. Consequently, she could not be expected to keep to the usual deadlines for filing.

Write a letter to Blanche concerning these matters.

Research Problem 2. In 2007, Gupta sold some shares of Wingo, a private U.S. corporation, for $40 million. On his Form 1040 Schedule D for 2007, Gupta showed the basis of the stock as $11 million, thereby reporting a $29 million capital gain. Gupta filed his return on October 1, 2008, after properly receiving an extension of the filing due date. Other income and deductions on the 2007 return netted to zero.

On March 1, 2012, while auditing the tax return of one of the purchasers of Gupta's Wingo shares, the IRS found that the basis for the shares actually was $3 million. Thus, Gupta's capital gain should have been $37 million and not $29 million.

Upon audit of Gupta's 2007 return, the IRS maintains that it can collect the underpaid taxes, plus interest and penalties, because the six-year statute of limitations applies (i.e., Gupta's return showed a substantial understatement of gross income). Gupta has asked you for tax advice on this matter. Did the statute of limitations expire on October 1, 2011, so that the IRS no longer can pursue the matter? Explain.

Use the tax resources of the Internet to address the following question. Do not restrict your search to the Web, but include a review of newsgroups and general reference materials, practitioner sites and resources, primary sources of the tax law, chat rooms and discussion groups, and other opportunities.

INTERNET *activity*

COMMUNICATIONS

Research Problem 3. Find an article in which a tax professional describes the confidentiality privilege available under the Code for a CPA tax adviser. Then construct a list of "Confidentiality Dos and Don'ts for the CPA." Summarize the article in an e-mail to your professor.

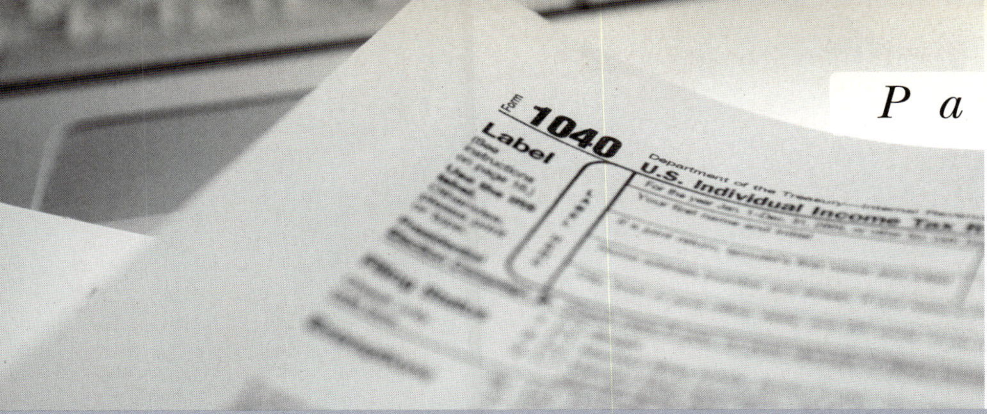

Part 9

Family Tax Planning

Family tax planning has as its objective the minimization of *all* taxes imposed on the family unit. Carrying out this objective requires familiarity with the rules applicable to transfers by gift and by death. These rules must then be applied to reduce the transfer tax burden. Finally, entities created as a result of these transfers (trusts and estates) are subject to unique income tax rules.

The Federal Gift and Estate Taxes

CHAPTER 27

LEARNING OBJECTIVES

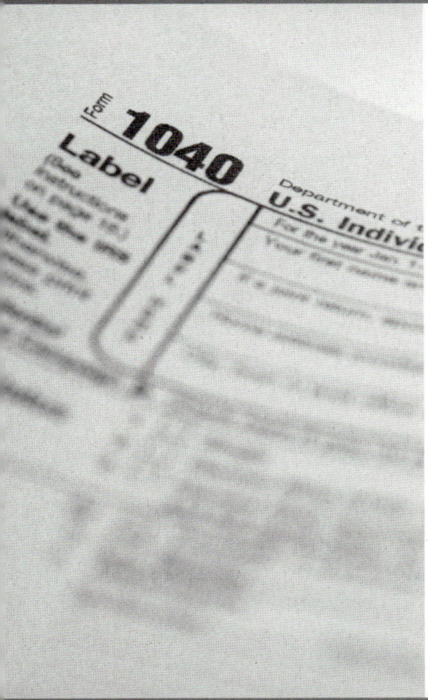

After completing Chapter 27, you should be able to:

LO.1 Explain the nature of the Federal gift and estate taxes.

LO.2 Analyze the Federal gift tax formula.

LO.3 Analyze the Federal estate tax formula.

LO.4 Discuss the operation of the Federal gift tax.

LO.5 Calculate the Federal gift tax.

LO.6 Identify the components of the gross estate.

LO.7 Describe the components of the taxable estate.

LO.8 Calculate the Federal estate tax liability.

LO.9 Demonstrate the role of the generation-skipping transfer tax.

LO.10 Recognize strategies to minimize Federal gift and estate taxes.

OUTLINE

For the latest in changes to tax legislation, visit **www.cengage.com/taxation/swft.**

THE BIG PICTURE **Tax Solutions for the Real World**

AN EVENTFUL AND FINAL YEAR

Over his lifetime, Peter Hood started and purchased numerous automobile dealerships that he eventually transferred to a newly formed entity, Hood Corporation. Upon his death in 2000, the stock in Hood Corporation passed in equal shares to Peter's surviving spouse, Martha, and their adult children, John and Helen.

For John Hood, 2011 proved to be an eventful and final tax year. Among the major happenings were the following.

- In January, John's divorce from his first wife, Hannah, became final.
- In February, he married Ashley, the manager of one of the Hood car dealerships.
- He made various gifts to family members.
- In July, his mother died of a heart condition, and John served as executor of her estate.
- In late November, he was seriously injured in a car accident (caused by another motorist).
- In early December, he carried out some predeath planning.
- John died of his injuries in mid-December.

What are some of the tax problems (i.e., income, gift, and estate taxes) that might be encountered as a result of these events? **Read the chapter and formulate your response.**

27.1 Transfer Taxes—In General

Until now, this text has dealt primarily with the various applications of the Federal income tax. Also important in the Federal tax structure are various excise taxes that cover transfers of property. Sometimes called transaction taxes, excise taxes are based on the value of the property transferred and not on the income derived from the property. Two such taxes—the Federal gift tax and the Federal estate tax—are the central focus of this chapter.

NATURE OF THE TAXES

LO.1
Explain the nature of the Federal gift and estate taxes.

Historical Background

Federal tax law imposes a tax on the gratuitous transfer of property in one of two ways. If the transfer occurs during the owner's life, it is subject to the Federal gift tax. If the property passes by virtue of the death of the owner, the Federal estate tax applies. Originally, the two taxes were governed by different rules including a separate set of tax rates. As Congress felt that lifetime transfers of wealth should be encouraged, the gift tax rates were 25 percent lower than the estate tax rates.[1]

The Tax Reform Act of 1976 significantly changed the approach taken by the Federal gift and estate taxes. Recognizing that prior rules had not significantly stimulated a preference for lifetime over death transfers, Congress decided that all transfers should be taxed the same way. Consequently, much of the distinction between life and death transfers was eliminated. Instead of subjecting these different types of transfers to two separate tax rate schedules, the Act substituted a **unified transfer tax** that covered all gratuitous transfers. Thus, gifts were subject to tax at the same rates as those applicable to transfers at death.

The Economic Growth and Tax Relief Reconciliation Act of 2001 (EGTRRA) made further changes. Reacting to general public sentiment, Congress concluded

[1] The estate tax was enacted in 1916. Because the estate tax could be avoided by making transfers just prior to dying (i.e., "deathbed gifts"), a gift tax was added in 1932.

that the Federal estate tax was objectionable because it leads to the breakup of family farms and other closely held businesses. Thus, by scheduled increases in the unified tax credit applicable to estates, the estate tax would be eliminated by the year 2010, but the gift tax would be retained. For budget reasons, under "sunset provisions," all changes made by EGTRRA were to expire after December 31, 2010.

At the last minute, however, Congress enacted the Tax Relief Act of 2010 (TRA). Under TRA, the sunset provisions are postponed (until after 2012), and the legislation added some generous estate and gift tax provisions (maximum rate of 35 percent and a credit of $5 million). TRA is effective for 2011 and 2012. If the sunset provisions come into play after 2012, the rates will increase to a maximum of 55 percent, and the credit will decrease to $1 million.

Clearly, Congress has not been consistent in its treatment of lifetime (i.e., gift tax) and death (i.e., estate tax) transfers.

Persons Subject to the Tax

The Federal gift tax is imposed on the right of one person (the donor) to transfer property to another (the donee) for less than full and adequate consideration. The tax is payable by the donor.[2] If the donor fails to pay the tax when due, the donee may be held liable for the tax to the extent of the value of the property received.[3]

A gift by a corporation is considered a gift by the individual shareholders. A gift to a corporation is generally considered a gift to the individual shareholders. In certain cases, however, a gift to a charitable, public, political, or similar organization may be regarded as a gift to the organization as a single entity.[4]

Upon the death of an individual, the Federal estate tax is imposed on the entire estate.[5] The executor (or administrator) of the estate has the obligation to pay any estate tax that may be due.

If the transferor is a resident or citizen of the United States, then the location of the property transferred is immaterial. Thus, a gift by a U.S. resident of property located in Honduras is subject to the Federal gift tax. For a U.S. citizen, the place of residence at the time of the transfer is not relevant. For these purposes, "United States" includes only the 50 states and the District of Columbia and does not include U.S. possessions or territories.[6]

For individuals who are neither residents nor citizens of the United States (i.e., nonresident aliens or NRAs), the Federal gift tax applies only to gifts of property situated within the United States. Exempted, however, are gifts of intangibles, such as stocks and bonds.[7]

For decedents who are NRAs, the Federal estate tax is imposed on the value of property located within the United States. Unlike the gift tax, however, the estate tax applies to stock in U.S. corporations.[8] Special reporting procedures apply to the estate taxation of NRAs.[9]

Types of Tax at Death

Taxes payable by virtue of a person's death fall into two categories: estate and inheritance. The U.S. government, some states, and several foreign countries impose

[2]§ 2502(c).

[3]§ 6324(b). Known as the doctrine of transferee liability, this rule also operates to enable the IRS to enforce the collection of other taxes (e.g., income tax, estate tax).

[4]Reg. §§ 25.0–1(b) and 25.2511–1(h)(1). But note the exemption from the Federal gift tax for certain transfers to political organizations discussed later.

[5]§ 2001(a). Subchapter A (§§ 2001 through 2058) covers the estate tax treatment of those who are either residents or citizens.

[6]§ 7701(a)(9).

[7]§§ 2501(a)(2) and (3) and 2511(a).

[8]Subchapter B (§§ 2101 through 2108) covers the estate tax rules applicable to NRAs.

[9]See the instructions to Form 706NA (U.S. Estate Tax Return of Nonresident Not a Citizen of the U.S.).

estate taxes. Inheritance taxes are imposed by some states and other countries. Some states and countries use both types of taxes.

The Federal estate tax differs in several respects from the typical *inheritance tax.* First, the Federal estate tax is levied on the decedent's entire estate. It is a tax on the right to pass property at death. Inheritance taxes apply to the right to receive property at death and are therefore levied on the heirs. Second, the relationship of the heirs to the decedent usually has a direct bearing on the amount of the inheritance tax. In general, the more closely related the parties, the larger the exemptions and the lower the applicable rates.[10] Except for transfers to surviving spouses that may result in a marital deduction, the relationship of the heirs to the decedent has no effect on the Federal estate tax.

LO.2

Analyze the Federal gift tax formula.

Formula for the Gift Tax

Like the income tax, which uses taxable income (and not gross income) as a tax base, the gift tax usually does not apply to the full amount of the gift. Deductions and the annual exclusion may be allowed to arrive at an amount called the **taxable gift**. However, unlike the income tax, which does not consider taxable income from prior years, *prior taxable gifts* must be added to arrive at the tax base to which the unified transfer tax rate is applied. Otherwise, the donor could start over again each year with a new set of progressive rates.

EXAMPLE 1

Don makes taxable gifts of $1 million in 1986 and $1 million in 2009. Presuming no other taxable gifts and *before applying the unified tax credit,* Don must pay a tax of $345,800 (see Appendix A) on the 1986 transfer and a tax of $780,800 (see Appendix A) on the 2009 transfer (using a tax base of $2 million). If the 1986 taxable gift had not been included in the tax base for the 2009 gift, the tax would have been $345,800. The correct tax liability of $780,800 is more than twice $345,800! ■

Because the gift tax is cumulative in effect, a credit is allowed for the gift taxes paid (or deemed paid) on prior taxable gifts included in the tax base. The deemed paid credit is explained later in the chapter.

EXAMPLE 2

Assume the same facts as in Example 1. Don will be allowed a credit of $345,800 against the gift tax of $780,800. Thus, his gift tax liability for 2009 becomes $435,000 ($780,800 – $345,800). ■

Because Congress did not intend for the gift tax to apply to smaller transfers, it provided for an annual exclusion. Originally set at $3,000, the amount allowed is periodically adjusted for *significant* inflation. For 2009 through 2011, the amount allowed is $13,000 (for the period 2006–2008, the exclusion was $12,000).[11] The formula for the gift tax is summarized in Figure 27.1.

LO.3

Analyze the Federal estate tax formula.

Formula for the Federal Estate Tax

The Federal unified transfer tax at death, commonly known as the Federal estate tax, is summarized in Figure 27.2. The gross estate is determined by using the fair market value of the property on the date of the decedent's death (or on the alternate valuation date if applicable).

The gross estate includes all of the property a decedent owns at the time of death. The inclusion may even extend to property that the decedent no longer owns—see the

[10] For example, one state's inheritance tax provides an unlimited exemption for a surviving spouse and charities, $100,000 for Class A heirs (lineal descendants and ascendants), $500 for Class B heirs (collateral heirs), and $100 for Class C (other relatives and strangers). Beginning tax rates applicable to the nonexempt portion range from 2% to 10%, with the top rate applicable to Class C heirs reaching 20%.

[11] § 2503(b)(2).

FIGURE 27.1 Gift Tax Formula

Determine whether the transfers are considered gifts by referring to §§ 2511 through 2519; list the fair market value of only the covered transfers		$xxx,xxx
Claim the annual exclusion ($13,000 per donee) as available	$xx,xxx	
Determine the charitable and marital deductions	xx,xxx	(xx,xxx)
Taxable gifts [as defined by § 2503(a)] for the current period		$ xx,xxx
Add: Taxable gifts from prior years		xx,xxx
Total of current and past taxable gifts		$ xx,xxx
Compute the gift tax on the total of current and past taxable gifts by using the rates in Appendix A		$ x,xxx
Subtract: Gift tax paid or deemed paid on past taxable gifts and the unified tax credit		(xxx)
Gift tax due on transfers during the current period		$ xxx

later discussion of gifts made within three years of death (§ 2035) and certain incomplete transfers (§§ 2036 and 2038). Moreover, the gross estate is to be distinguished from the probate estate, which is property that is subject to administration by the executor. (The probate estate is discussed further later in the chapter.)

Deductions from the gross estate to arrive at the taxable estate are quite extensive. In addition to the debts of the decedent (e.g., mortgages, credit card accounts, unpaid medical bills), they even include current and past income taxes (both Federal and state). As in the case of the Federal gift tax, transfers to charity and to a spouse are deductible.

Note that the taxable estate must be adjusted further to arrive at a tax base before a tentative estate tax can be determined. The further adjustment requires the consideration of prior taxable gifts. The reason that post-1976 taxable gifts are added to the taxable estate to arrive at the tax base goes back to the scheme of the unified transfer tax. Starting in 1977, all transfers, whether lifetime or by death, were to be treated the same. Consequently, taxable gifts made after 1976 must be accounted for upon the death of the donor. Any possible double tax effect of including these

FIGURE 27.2 Estate Tax Formula

Gross estate (§§ 2031–2046)		$xxx,xxx
Subtract:		
Expenses, indebtedness, and taxes (§ 2053)	$xx,xxx	
Losses (§ 2054)	xx,xxx	
Charitable bequests (§ 2055)	xx,xxx	
Marital deduction (§§ 2056 and 2056A)	xx,xxx	
State death taxes (§ 2058)	xx,xxx	(xx,xxx)
Taxable estate (§ 2051)		$ xx,xxx
Add: Post-1976 taxable gifts [§ 2001(b)]		x,xxx
Tax base		$xxx,xxx
Tentative tax on total tax base [§ 2001(c)]		$ xx,xxx
Subtract:		
Unified transfer tax on post-1976 taxable gifts (gift taxes paid or deemed paid)	$ x,xxx	
Tax credits (including the unified tax credit) (§§ 2010–2016)	x,xxx	(x,xxx)
Estate tax due		$ x,xxx

TABLE 27.1 Partial List of Unified Tax Credits

	Gift Tax		Estate Tax	
Year of Transfer	Credit	Exclusion Amount	Credit	Exclusion Amount
2000 and 2001	$ 220,550	$ 675,000	$ 220,550	$ 675,000
2002 and 2003	345,800	1,000,000	345,800	1,000,000
2004 and 2005	345,800	1,000,000	555,800	1,500,000
2006, 2007, and 2008	345,800	1,000,000	780,800	2,000,000
2009	345,800	1,000,000	1,455,800	3,500,000
2010	330,800*	1,000,000	–0–	–0–
2011 and 2012	1,730,800	5,000,000	1,730,800	5,000,000
2013	345,800	1,000,000	345,800	1,000,000

*Maximum gift tax rate drops to 35%.

gifts is eliminated by allowing a credit against the estate tax for the gift taxes previously paid or deemed paid.

Role of the Unified Tax Credit

The purpose of the **unified tax credit** is to allow donors and decedents to transfer specified amounts of wealth without being subject to the gift and estate taxes. Table 27.1 shows the unified tax credit applicable to transfers by gift and by death from 2000 through 2013.[12]

The **exclusion amount** (also termed the **exemption equivalent** and the **bypass amount**) is the amount of the transfer that will pass free of the gift or estate tax by virtue of the credit.

EXAMPLE 3

In 2011, Janet makes a taxable gift of $5 million. Presuming she has made no prior taxable gifts, Janet will not owe any gift tax. Under the applicable tax rate schedule (see Appendix A), the tax on $5 million is $1,730,800, which is the exact amount of the credit allowed.[13] ■

VALUATION FOR ESTATE AND GIFT TAX PURPOSES (§ 2032)

The value of the property on the date of its transfer generally determines the amount that is subject to the gift tax or the estate tax. Under certain conditions, however, an executor can elect to value estate assets on the **alternate valuation date**. The election is made by the executor of the estate and is irrevocable.

The alternate valuation date election was designed as a relief provision to ease the economic hardship that could result when estate assets decline in value over the six months after the date of death. If the election is made, all assets of the estate are valued six months after death *or* on the date of disposition if this occurs earlier.[14] The election covers *all* assets in the gross estate and cannot be applied to only a portion of the property.

[12]The unified tax credits prior to 2000 can be found in §§ 2010 and 2505.

[13]The rate schedules are contained in § 2001(c), and *some* are reproduced in Appendix A of this text. The credits are subject to indexation for inflation for 2012, but the rate schedules are not.

[14]§ 2032(a)(1). For this purpose, the term "disposition" is broadly defined. It includes the transfer of property to an heir to satisfy a bequest and the use of property to fund a testamentary trust. Reg. § 20.2032–1(c).

TAX *in* the NEWS

Estate Planning in Perspective

The future of the Federal estate and gift taxes is quite uncertain. For example, the generous provisions of TRA of 2010 (i.e., maximum rate of 35 percent and a credit of $5 million) are unlikely to be made permanent. It is also unlikely that the sunset provisions (i.e., maximum rate of 55 percent and a credit of $1 million) will be allowed to take effect in 2013—see Table 27.1. All of this uncertainty is unfortunate as one of the keys to effective tax planning is the ability to rely on the stability of the tax law.

Wealth transfers entail long-term projections that are dependent on assumptions that the relevant tax law will remain largely constant. Once an estate plan is established, practitioners and their clients generally do not anticipate the need for frequent modifications.

The somewhat drastic changes in the estate and gift tax provisions have made this traditional long-term approach impossible. Consequently, the validity of an estate plan may need to be reevaluated every time that Congress meets! This legislative instability adds to compliance costs and places an unnecessary burden on both taxpayers and their practitioners.

EXAMPLE 4

In 2011, Robert's gross estate consists of the following property:

	Value on Date of Death	Value Six Months Later
Land	$4,800,000	$4,840,000
Stock in Brown Corporation	900,000	700,000
Stock in Green Corporation	500,000	460,000
Total	$6,200,000	$6,000,000

If Robert's executor elects the alternate valuation date, the estate must be valued at $6 million. It is not permissible to value the land at its date of death value ($4.8 million) and choose the alternate valuation date for the rest of the gross estate. ■

EXAMPLE 5

Assume the same facts as in Example 4, except that the executor sells the stock in Green Corporation for $480,000 four months after Robert's death. If the alternate valuation date is elected, the estate must be valued at $6,020,000 ($4,840,000 + $700,000 + $480,000). As to the Green stock, the value on its date of disposition controls because that date occurred prior to the six months' alternate valuation date. ■

The election of the alternate valuation date must decrease the value of the gross estate *and* decrease the estate tax liability. The reason for this last requirement is that the income tax basis of property acquired from a decedent will be the value used for estate tax purposes. Without a special limitation, the alternate valuation date could be elected solely to add to income tax basis.

EXAMPLE 6

Al's gross estate consists of assets with a date of death value of $6 million and an alternate valuation date value of $6.1 million. Under Al's will, all of his property passes outright to Jean (Al's wife). Because of the marital deduction, no estate tax results regardless of which value is used. But if the alternate valuation date could be elected, Jean would have an income tax basis of $6.1 million in the property acquired from Al. ■

The alternate valuation date cannot be elected in Example 6 for two reasons, either of which would suffice. First, the alternate valuation date will not decrease Al's gross estate. Second, the election will not decrease Al's estate tax liability. Thus, his estate must use the date of death valuation of $6 million. As a result, Jean's income tax basis in the property received from Al is $6 million.

The election of the alternate valuation date does not take into account any post-death income earned by the property. Any accrued income, therefore, is limited to that existing as of the date of death.

EXAMPLE 7

At the time of her death, Emma owned, *among other assets*, an apartment building with a value of $800,000 on which $40,000 of rents had accrued. On the alternate valuation date, the property had a value of $780,000 and accrued rents were $30,000. If the § 2032 election is made, $820,000 ($780,000 + $40,000) as to this property is included in Emma's gross estate. The $30,000 of postdeath income is not part of her gross estate. ■

KEY PROPERTY CONCEPTS

When property is transferred either by gift or at death, the form of ownership can have a direct bearing on any transfer tax consequences. Understanding the different forms of ownership is necessary for working with Federal gift and estate taxes.

Undivided Ownership

Assume Dan and Vicky own an undivided but equal interest in a tract of land. Such ownership can fall into any of four categories: joint tenancy, tenancy by the entirety, tenancy in common, or community property.

If Dan and Vicky hold ownership as **joint tenants** or **tenants by the entirety**, the right of survivorship exists. This means that the last tenant to survive receives full ownership of the property. Thus, if Dan predeceases Vicky, the land belongs entirely to Vicky. None of the land passes to Dan's heirs or is subject to administration by Dan's executor. A tenancy by the entirety is a joint tenancy between husband and wife.

If Dan and Vicky hold ownership as **tenants in common** or as community property, death does not defeat an owner's interest. Thus, if Dan predeceases Vicky, Dan's half interest in the land passes to his estate or heirs.

Community property interests arise from the marital relationship. Normally, all property acquired after marriage, except by gift or inheritance, by husband and wife residing in a community property state becomes part of the community. The following states have the community property system in effect: Louisiana, Texas, New Mexico, Arizona, California, Washington, Idaho, Nevada, Wisconsin, and (by election of the spouses) Alaska. All other states follow the common law system of ascertaining a spouse's rights to property acquired after marriage.

Partial Interests

Interests in assets can be divided in terms of rights to income and rights to principal. Particularly when property is placed in trust, it is not uncommon to carve out various income interests that must be accounted for separately from the ultimate disposition of the property itself.

EXAMPLE 8

Under Bill's will, a ranch is to be placed in trust, life estate to Sam, Bill's son, with remainder to Sam's children (Bill's grandchildren). Under this arrangement, Sam is the life tenant and, as such, is entitled to the use of the ranch (including any income) during his life. Upon Sam's death, the trust terminates, and its principal passes to his children. Thus, Sam's children receive outright ownership of the ranch when Sam dies. ■

27.2 The Federal Gift Tax

LO.4

Discuss the operation of the Federal gift tax.

GENERAL CONSIDERATIONS

In working with the gift tax, it is first necessary to determine whether a gift has in fact taken place. In addition, some transfers are excluded from the gift tax.

Requirements for a Gift

For a gift to be complete under state law, the following elements must be present.

- A donor competent to make the gift.
- A donee capable of receiving and possessing the property.
- Donative intent on behalf of the donor.
- Actual or constructive delivery of the property to the donee or the donee's representative.
- Acceptance of the gift by the donee.

Incomplete Transfers

The Federal gift tax does not apply to transfers that are incomplete. Thus, if the transferor retains the right to reclaim the property or has not really parted with the possession of the property, a taxable event has not taken place.

EXAMPLE 9

Lesly creates a trust with income payable to Mary for life, remainder to Paul. Under the terms of the trust instrument, Lesly can revoke the trust at any time and repossess the trust principal and the income earned. No gift takes place on the creation of the trust; Lesly has not ceased to have dominion and control over the property. ■

EXAMPLE 10

Assume the same facts as in Example 9, except that one year after the transfer, Lesly relinquishes his right to terminate the trust. At this point, the transfer becomes complete, and the Federal gift tax applies. ■

Business versus Personal Setting

In a business setting, full and adequate consideration is apt to exist. If the parties are acting in a personal setting, a gift is usually the result. It is the position of the IRS that valuable consideration (such as would preclude a gift result) does not include a payment or transfer based on "love and affection . . . promise of marriage, etc."[15] Consequently, property settlements in consideration of marriage (i.e., pre- or antenuptial agreements) are regarded as gifts.

ETHICS & *Equity*

IT'S THE THOUGHT THAT COUNTS

Joe (age 86) and Nicole (age 22) are married. Two days later they exchange wedding gifts. Joe's gift to Nicole is stock in IBM (valued at $2 million), while Nicole's gift to Joe is a bottle of cologne (value of $32). What tax goals are they trying to accomplish? Will their plan work?

Do not conclude that the presence of *some* consideration is enough to preclude Federal gift tax consequences. Again, the answer may rest on whether the transfer occurred in a business setting.

EXAMPLE 11

Peter sells Bob some real estate for $40,000. Unknown to Peter, the property contains valuable mineral deposits and is really worth $200,000. Peter may have made a bad business deal, but he has not made a gift of $160,000 to Bob. ■

EXAMPLE 12

Assume the same facts as in Example 11, except that Peter and Bob are father and son. In addition, Peter is very much aware that the property is worth $200,000. Peter has made a gift of $160,000 to Bob. ■

Certain Excluded Transfers

Transfers to political organizations are exempt from the application of the Federal gift tax.[16] This provision in the Code made unnecessary the previous practice whereby candidates for public office established multiple campaign committees to maximize the number of annual exclusions available to their contributors. As noted, an annual exclusion of $13,000 for each donee passes free of the Federal gift tax.

The Federal gift tax does not apply to tuition payments made to an educational organization (e.g., a college) on another's behalf. Nor does it apply to amounts paid on another's behalf for medical care.[17] In this regard, the law is realistic since it is unlikely that most donors would recognize these items as being transfers subject to the gift tax. The payments, however, must be made directly to the provider

[15] Reg. § 25.2512–8.

[16] § 2501(a)(5).

[17] § 2503(e).

(e.g., college, doctor, hospital). There is no requirement that the beneficiary of the service (e.g., student, patient) qualify as a dependent of the person making the payment.

EXAMPLE 13
THE BIG PICTURE

Return to the facts of *The Big Picture* on p. 27-2. After Peter died in 2000, his widow, Martha, continued to live in the family home and refused to move in with either of her children (John or Helen). As Martha's health and mental condition deteriorated, her children did everything possible to keep the family housekeeper from quitting. In fact, Helen paid for the housekeeper's gallbladder operation, and John paid the college tuition of her oldest son.

Neither Helen nor John has made gifts to the housekeeper or her son that are subject to taxation. Gifts would have occurred, however, if Helen and John had reimbursed the housekeeper for the amounts involved, instead of paying the providers (i.e., physician, hospital, college) directly. ■

Satisfying an obligation of support is not subject to the gift tax. Thus, no gift takes place when parents pay for their children's education because one of the obligations of parents is to educate their children. What constitutes an obligation of support is determined by applicable state law. In many states, for example, adult children may have an obligation of support with respect to providing for indigent parents.

ETHICS & *Equity*

WHAT CONSTITUTES SUPPORT?

When Earl's daughter, Clara, turns 40, he gives her a Mercedes convertible as a birthday present. Clara is married and has a family of her own. She is a licensed orthopedic surgeon and maintains a successful practice in the field of sports medicine.

Earl does not regard the transfer as being subject to the gift tax. As a parent, he is merely satisfying his obligation of support. Such obligation includes providing your child with transportation. Is Earl's reasoning sound?

Lifetime versus Death Transfers

Be careful to distinguish between lifetime (*inter vivos*) and death (testamentary) transfers.

EXAMPLE 14

Dudley buys a 12-month certificate of deposit (CD) from State Bank and lists ownership as follows: "Dudley, payable on proof of death to Faye." Nine months later, Dudley dies. When the CD matures, Faye collects the proceeds from State Bank. No gift takes place when Dudley invests in the CD; Faye has received a mere expectancy (i.e., to obtain ownership of the CD upon Dudley's death). At any time before his death, Dudley may withdraw the funds or delete Faye's name from the account, thereby cutting off her expectancy. Furthermore, no gift occurs upon Dudley's death as the CD passes to Faye by testamentary disposition. As noted later, the CD will be included in Dudley's gross estate as property in which the decedent had an interest (§ 2033). ■

The payable on death (POD) designation used in Example 14 is a form of ownership frequently used in a family setting when investments are involved (e.g., stocks and bonds, savings accounts). It is very similar in effect to a revocable trust (see Example 9 above). Both carry the advantage of avoiding the probate estate. The POD designation, however, is simpler to use in the case of bank accounts and securities, and it avoids the need of having to create a formal trust.

TRANSFERS SUBJECT TO THE GIFT TAX

Whether a transfer is subject to the Federal gift tax depends upon the application of §§ 2511 through 2519 and the applicable Regulations.

Gift Loans

Loans between related parties are quite common. Such loans are frequently made to help pay for a college education or to finance a new business owned by a family member. Presuming that the advance is a bona fide loan at the outset (i.e., a gift is not intended), the absence of a provision for adequate interest can generate a multitude of tax consequences.

EXAMPLE 15

Harold lends his daughter Venetia $400,000 to start a dental practice. The loan is payable on demand, and no interest is provided for. Assuming a Federal interest rate of 10%, *each year* the loan is outstanding, the following tax consequences ensue.

- *Gift tax.* Harold makes a gift to Venetia of $40,000 (10% × $400,000). The annual exclusion is available to offset part of this transfer.
- *Income tax.* Harold has interest income of $40,000, and Venetia has an interest deduction of a like amount. Because it relates to her trade or business, Venetia has a deduction *for* adjusted gross income. ■

The Code defines a gift loan as "any below-market loan where the forgoing of interest is in the nature of a gift."[18] Unless tax avoidance was one of the principal purposes of the loan, special limitations apply if the gift loan does not exceed $100,000. In such a case, the interest element may not exceed the borrower's net investment income.[19] Furthermore, if the net investment income does not exceed $1,000, it is treated as zero. Under a $10,000 *de minimis* rule, the interest element is disregarded.

Certain Property Settlements (§ 2516)

Normally, the settlement of certain marital rights is not regarded as being for consideration and is subject to the Federal gift tax.[20] As a special exception to this general approach, Congress enacted § 2516. By this provision, transfers of property interests made under the terms of a written agreement between spouses in settlement of their marital or property rights are deemed to be for adequate consideration. The transfers are exempt from the Federal gift tax if a final decree of divorce is obtained within the three-year period beginning on the date one year before the parties entered into the agreement. Likewise excluded are transfers to provide a reasonable allowance for the support of minor children (including legally adopted children) of a marriage. The agreement need not be approved by the divorce decree.

EXAMPLE 16
THE BIG PICTURE

Return to the facts of *The Big Picture* on p. 27-2. Recall that John and Hannah's divorce became final in January 2011. After extended but amicable negotiations, in September 2010 John and Hannah had agreed on a property settlement. In return for the receipt of $200,000 and title to their home, Hannah released all of her marital rights. Shortly thereafter, John made the transfer. Under § 2516, the property settlement resulted in no gift tax consequences to John. ■

Disclaimers (§ 2518)

A **disclaimer** is a refusal by a person to accept property that is designated to pass to him or her. The effect of the disclaimer is to pass the property to someone else.

EXAMPLE 17
THE BIG PICTURE

Return to the facts of *The Big Picture* on p. 27-2. Recall that Martha died in July of a heart condition. Under her will, her estate passes in equal parts to her son and daughter or, if they disclaim, to their children. (Under a buy-sell agreement, her stock in Hood Corporation is redeemed by the corporation with the insurance proceeds from a policy it took out on her life.) Helen disclaims her share of the inheritance, and the assets pass to her children. ■

[18] § 7872(f)(3).

[19] Net investment income has the same meaning given to the term by § 163(d). Generally, net investment income is investment income (e.g., interest, dividends) less related expenses.

[20] Reg. § 25.2512–8.

Why might Helen disclaim her inheritance and have the property pass directly from Martha to the children? By doing so, an extra transfer tax may be avoided. If the disclaimer does not take place (Helen accepts the inheritance), and the property eventually passes to the children (either by gift or by death), the later transfer is subject to the application of either the gift tax or the estate tax.

The Federal gift tax can also be avoided in cases of a partial disclaimer of an undivided interest.

EXAMPLE 18
THE BIG PICTURE

Assume the same facts as in Example 17. John's share of his inheritance from Martha also includes the family hunting lodge. Except for the hunting lodge, John disclaims his share of the inheritance, and the remaining assets pass to his children. ■

To be effective, the disclaimer must be in writing and timely made. Generally, this means no later than nine months after the right to the property arose. Furthermore, the person making the disclaimer must not have accepted any benefits or interest in the property.

Other Transfers Subject to Gift Tax

Other transfers that may carry gift tax consequences (e.g., the creation of joint ownership) are discussed and illustrated in connection with the Federal estate tax.

Income Tax Considerations

Generally, a donor has no income tax consequences on making a gift. A donee recognizes no income on the receipt of a gift.[21] A donee's income tax basis in the property received depends on a number of factors (e.g., donor's basis, year of gift, gift tax incurred by donor) and is discussed in Chapter 13.

ANNUAL EXCLUSION

The first $13,000 of gifts made to any one person during any calendar year (except gifts of future interests in property) is excluded in determining the total amount of gifts for the year.[22] The **annual exclusion** applies to all gifts of a present interest made during the calendar year in the order in which they are made until the $13,000 exclusion per donee is exhausted. For a gift in trust, each beneficiary of the trust is treated as a separate person for purposes of the exclusion.

A **future interest** is defined as one that will come into being (as to use, possession, or enjoyment) at some future date. Examples of future interests include such rights as remainder interests that are commonly encountered when property is transferred to a trust. A *present interest* is an unrestricted right to the immediate use, possession, or enjoyment of property or of the income.

EXAMPLE 19

During 2011, Laura makes the following cash gifts: $8,000 to Rita and $14,000 to Maureen. Laura may claim an annual exclusion of $8,000 with respect to Rita and $13,000 with respect to Maureen. ■

EXAMPLE 20

By a lifetime gift, Ron transfers property to a trust with a life estate (with income payable annually) to June and remainder upon June's death to Albert. Ron has made two gifts: one to June of a life estate and one to Albert of a remainder interest. The life estate is a present interest and qualifies for the annual exclusion. The remainder interest granted to Albert is a future interest and does not qualify for the exclusion. Note that Albert's interest does not come into being until some future date (on the death of June). ■

[21]Both gifts and inheritances are excluded from income under § 103. See Chapter 5.

[22]§ 2503(b).

Although Example 20 indicates that the gift of an income interest is a present interest, this is not always the case. If a possibility exists that the income beneficiary may not receive the immediate enjoyment of the property, the transfer is of a future interest.

EXAMPLE 21

Assume the same facts as in Example 20, except that the income from the trust need not be payable annually to June. It may, at the trustee's discretion, be accumulated and added to corpus. Since June's right to receive the income from the trust is conditioned on the trustee's discretion, it is not a present interest. No annual exclusion is allowed. The mere possibility of diversion is enough. It would not matter if the trustee never exercised the discretion to accumulate and did, in fact, distribute the trust income to June annually. ■

Trust for Minors

Section 2503(c) offers an exception to the future interest rules just discussed. Under this provision, a transfer for the benefit of a person who has not attained the age of 21 years on the date of the gift may be considered a gift of a present interest. This is true even though the minor is not given the unrestricted right to the immediate use, possession, or enjoyment of the property. For the exception to apply, however, certain stringent conditions must be satisfied. One such condition is that all of the property and its income must be made available to the minor upon attaining age 21. Thus, the exception allows a trustee to accumulate income on behalf of a minor beneficiary without converting the income interest to a future interest.

Contributions to Qualified Tuition Programs

For income tax purposes, § 529 plans possess attributes that reflect the best of all possible worlds. Although no up-front deduction is allowed,[23] income earned by the fund accumulates free of income tax, and distributions are not taxed if they are used for higher education purposes. A special provision allows a donor to enjoy a gift tax advantage by using five years of annual exclusions.[24]

EXAMPLE 22

Trevor and Audrey would like to start building a college education fund for their 10-year-old granddaughter, Loni. In 2011, Trevor contributes $130,000 to the designated carrier of their state's § 529 plan. By electing to split the gift and using five annual exclusions [2 (number of donors) × $13,000 (annual exclusion) × 5 years = $130,000], no taxable gift results. (The gift-splitting election is discussed in detail later in this chapter.) Making the five-year election precludes Trevor and Audrey from using any annual exclusion on gifts to Loni for the next four years.[25] ■

Section 529(c)(4) provides that these college plans are not to be included in the gross estate of the transferor. This is preferential treatment because § 529 plans are incomplete transfers (some or all of the funds may be returned if college is not attended). As noted later, incomplete transfers are invariably subject to the estate tax.

DEDUCTIONS

In arriving at taxable gifts, a deduction is allowed for transfers to certain qualified charitable organizations. On transfers between spouses, a marital deduction may be available. Since both the charitable and marital deductions apply in determining the Federal estate tax, they are discussed later in the chapter.

[23]Depending on the taxpayer's home state, some (or all) of the contributions into the plan may be deductible for *state* income tax purposes.

[24]§ 529(c)(2)(B). Section 529(c)(2)(A) protects against future interest treatment.

[25]Trevor and Audrey could resort to § 2503(e)(2)(A) to avoid any gift at all. As mentioned earlier, a *direct* payment of tuition to certain educational institutions is exempt from the gift tax. But this rule does not help to build an education fund for future use, as § 529 does. Recall that Loni, the granddaughter, is 10 years old.

LO.5

Calculate the Federal gift tax.

COMPUTING THE FEDERAL GIFT TAX

The Unified Transfer Tax Rate Schedule

The top rates of the unified transfer tax rate schedule originally reached as high as 70 percent. Over the years, these top rates were reduced to 55 percent and then to 45 percent for 2007. Effective for 2011 and 2012, the top rate is 35 percent for both the gift tax and the estate tax. (The 35 percent rate is the lowest since the Hoover administration.)[26] Keep in mind that the unified transfer tax rate schedule applies to all transfers (by gift or death) after 1976. Different rate schedules applied for pre-1977 gifts and pre-1977 death transfers.

The Deemed-Paid Adjustment

As noted earlier, the gift tax is cumulative in effect (see Example 1). Since this means prior transfers will again be subject to tax, a credit is allowed for the taxes previously incurred (see Example 2). However, the amount of the credit allowed is based on the rates currently in effect. Called the *deemed paid* credit, it could be the same as, less than, or more than the tax actually paid. The difference between the deemed paid taxes and those actually paid is attributable to the change in the tax rate schedule that has taken place over the years. For example, see the variation in rates in Appendix A.

The Election to Split Gifts by Married Persons

To understand the reason for the gift-splitting election of § 2513, consider the following situations:

EXAMPLE 23

Dick and Margaret are husband and wife and reside in Michigan, a common law state. Dick has been the only breadwinner in the family, and Margaret has no significant property of her own. Neither has made any prior taxable gifts. In 2011, Dick makes a gift to Leslie of $6,026,000. Presuming the election to split gifts did not exist, Dick's gift tax is as follows.

Amount of gift	$ 6,026,000
Subtract: Annual exclusion	(13,000)
Taxable gift	$ 6,013,000
Gift tax on $6,013,000 per Appendix A, [$155,800 + 35%($6,013,000 – $500,000)]	$ 2,085,350
Subtract: Unified transfer tax credit for 2011	(1,730,800)
Gift tax due on the 2011 taxable gift	$ 354,550

■

EXAMPLE 24

Assume the same facts as in Example 23, except that Dick and Margaret have always resided in California, a community property state. Even though Dick is the sole breadwinner, income from personal services generally is community property. Consequently, the gift to Leslie probably involves community property. If this is the case, the gift tax is as follows.

	Dick	Margaret
Amount of gift	$ 3,013,000	$ 3,013,000
Subtract: Annual exclusion	(13,000)	(13,000)
Taxable gift	$ 3,000,000	$ 3,000,000
Gift tax on $3,000,000 per Appendix A	$ 1,030,800	$ 1,030,800
Subtract: Unified transfer tax credit for 2011	(1,730,800)	(1,730,800)
Gift tax due on the 2011 taxable gift	$ –0–	$ –0–

■

[26] § 2001(c)(2)(B). Note the drop in the top rate from 50% to 45% in the rate schedules for 2002 through 2007, reproduced in Appendix A. The rates for 2011 and 2012 are also in Appendix A.

As the results of Examples 23 and 24 indicate, married donors residing in community property jurisdictions possessed a significant gift tax advantage over those residing in common law states. To rectify this inequity, the Revenue Act of 1948 incorporated the predecessor to § 2513 into the Code. Under this provision, a gift made by a person to someone other than his or her spouse may be considered, for Federal gift tax purposes, as having been made one-half by each spouse. Returning to Example 23, Dick and Margaret could treat the gift passing to Leslie as being made one-half by each of them, even though the property belonged to Dick. As a result, the parties are able to achieve the same tax consequence as in Example 24. As is the case with the owner spouse, any past taxable gifts of the nonowner spouse must be taken into account in determining the current gift tax.

To split gifts, the spouses must be legally married to each other at the time of the gift. If they are divorced later in the calendar year, they may still split the gift if neither marries anyone else during that year. They both must indicate on their separate gift tax returns their consent to have all gifts made in that calendar year split between them. In addition, both must be citizens or residents of the United States on the date of the gift. A gift from one spouse to the other spouse cannot be split. Such a gift might, however, be eligible for the marital deduction.

The election to split gifts is not necessary when husband and wife transfer jointly owned or community property to a third party. It is needed if the gift consists of the separate property of one of the spouses. Community property rules generally define separate property as property acquired before marriage and property acquired after marriage by gift or inheritance. The election, then, is not limited to residents of common law states.

Special Rule for Gifts Made in 2010

In addition to eliminating the estate tax for 2010, EGTRRA of 2001 provided special rules for gifts made in 2010.

- The maximum tax rate was reduced to 35 percent—see Appendix A.
- Although the exclusion amount remains at $1 million, the credit allowed drops to $330,800—see Table 27.1.

As previously noted, after 2010 the exclusion amounts for both the gift tax and the estate tax are the same (i.e., unified) and rise to $5 million.

PROCEDURAL MATTERS

Having determined which transfers are subject to the Federal gift tax and the various deductions and exclusions available to the donor, the procedural aspects of the tax should be considered. The following sections discuss the return itself, the due dates for filing and paying the tax, and other related matters.

The Federal Gift Tax Return

For transfers by gift, a Form 709 (U.S. Gift Tax Return) must be filed whenever the gifts for any one calendar year exceed the annual exclusion or involve a gift of a future interest. A Form 709 need not be filed, however, for transfers between spouses that are offset by the unlimited marital deduction, regardless of the amount of the transfer.[27]

EXAMPLE 25

In 2011, Larry makes five gifts, each in the amount of $13,000, to his five children. If the gifts do not involve future interests, a Form 709 need not be filed to report the transfers. ■

EXAMPLE 26

During 2011, Esther makes a gift of $26,000 cash of her separate property to her daughter. To double the amount of the annual exclusion allowed, Jerry (Esther's husband) is willing to split the gift. Since the § 2513 election can be made only on a gift tax return, a Form 709 must be filed even though no gift tax will be due as a result of the transfer. ■

[27] § 6019(a)(2).

In Example 26, no gift tax return would be necessary if the transfer consisted of community property. Since two donors are now involved, the cap for filing becomes more than $26,000, rather than more than $13,000.

Presuming a gift tax return is due, it must be filed on or before the fifteenth day of April following the year of the gift.[28] As with other Federal taxes, when the due date falls on Saturday, Sunday, or a legal holiday, the date for filing the return is the next business day. Note that the filing requirements for Form 709 have no correlation to the accounting year used by a donor for Federal income tax purposes. Thus, a fiscal year taxpayer must follow the April 15 rule for any reportable gifts. If sufficient reason is shown, the IRS is authorized to grant reasonable extensions of time for filing the return.[29]

27.3 The Federal Estate Tax

The following discussion of the estate tax coincides with the formula that appeared earlier in the chapter in Figure 27.2. The key components in the formula are the gross estate, the taxable estate, the tax base, and the credits allowed against the tentative tax. This formula can be summarized as follows:

Gross estate − Deductions allowed = Taxable estate + Post-1976 taxable gifts = Tax base

Tentative tax on tax base − Tax on post-1976 taxable gifts − Tax credits* = Estate tax due

*Includes unified transfer tax credit and other credits.

LO.6

Identify the components of the gross estate.

GROSS ESTATE

Simply stated, the **gross estate** includes all property subject to the Federal estate tax. Thus, the gross estate depends on the provisions of the Internal Revenue Code as supplemented by IRS pronouncements and the judicial interpretations of Federal courts.

In contrast to the gross estate, the **probate estate** is controlled by state (rather than Federal) law. The probate estate consists of all of a decedent's property subject to administration by the executor or administrator of the estate. The administration is supervised by a local court of appropriate jurisdiction (usually called a probate court). An executor is the decedent's personal representative appointed under the decedent's will. When a decedent dies without a will or fails to name an executor in the will (or that person refuses to serve), the local probate court appoints an administrator.

The probate estate is frequently smaller than the gross estate. It contains only property owned by the decedent at the time of death and passing to heirs under a will or under the law of intestacy (the order of distribution for those dying without a will). As noted later, such items as the proceeds of many life insurance policies and distributions from retirement plans become part of the gross estate but are not included in the probate estate.

[28] § 6075(b)(1).

[29] § 6081. Under § 6075(b)(2), an extension of time granted to a calendar year taxpayer for filing an income tax return automatically extends the due date of a gift tax return.

CONCEPT SUMMARY 27.1

Federal Gift Tax Provisions

1. The Federal gift tax applies to all gratuitous transfers of property made by U.S. citizens or residents. In this regard, it does not matter where the property is located.
2. In the eyes of the IRS, a gratuitous transfer is one not supported by full and adequate consideration. If the parties are acting in a business setting, such consideration usually exists. If purported sales are between family members, a gift element may be suspected.
3. If a lender loans money to another and intends some or all of the interest element to be a gift, the arrangement is categorized as a gift loan. To the extent that the interest provided for is less than the market rate, three tax consequences result. First, a gift has taken place between the lender and the borrower as to the interest element. Second, income may result to the lender. Third, an income tax deduction may be available to the borrower.
4. Property settlements can escape the gift tax if a divorce occurs within a prescribed period of time.
5. A disclaimer is a refusal by a person to accept property designated to pass to that person. The effect of a disclaimer is to pass the property to someone else. If certain conditions are satisfied, the issuance of a disclaimer will not be subject to the Federal gift tax.
6. Except for gifts of future interests, a donor is allowed an annual exclusion of $13,000. The future interest limitation does not apply to certain trusts created for minors.
7. The election to split a gift enables a married couple to be treated as two donors. The election doubles the annual exclusion and makes the nonowner spouse's unified tax credit available to the owner spouse.
8. The election to split gifts is not necessary if the property is jointly owned by the spouses. That is the case when the property is part of the couple's community.
9. In determining the tax base for computing the gift tax, all prior taxable gifts must be added to current taxable gifts. Thus, the gift tax is cumulative in nature.
10. Gifts are reported on Form 709. The return is due on April 15 following the year of the gift.

All states provide for an order of distribution in the event someone dies *intestate* (i.e., without a will). After the surviving spouse receives some or all of the estate, the preference is usually in the following order: down to lineal descendants (e.g., children, grandchildren), up to lineal ascendants (e.g., parents, grandparents), and out to collateral relations (e.g., brothers, sisters, aunts, and uncles).

Property Owned by the Decedent (§ 2033)

Property owned by the decedent at the time of death is included in the gross estate. The nature of the property or the use to which it was put during the decedent-owner's lifetime has no significance as far as the estate tax is concerned. Thus, personal effects (such as clothing), stocks, bonds, mutual funds, furniture, jewelry, bank accounts, and certificates of deposit are all included in the deceased's gross estate. No distinction is made between tangible or intangible, depreciable or nondepreciable, business or personal assets. However, a deceased spouse's gross estate does not include the surviving spouse's share of the community property.

The application of § 2033 is illustrated as follows:

EXAMPLE 27

Irma dies owning some City of Denver bonds. The fair market value of the bonds plus any interest accrued to the date of Irma's death is included in her gross estate. Although interest on municipal bonds normally is not taxable under the Federal income tax, it is property owned by Irma at the time of death. However, any interest accrued after death is not part of Irma's gross estate. ■

EXAMPLE 28

Sharon dies on April 7, 2011, at a time when she owns stock in Robin Corporation and in Wren Corporation. On March 3 of this year, both corporations had authorized a cash dividend payable on May 5. Robin's dividend is payable to shareholders of record as of

GLOBAL
Tax Issues

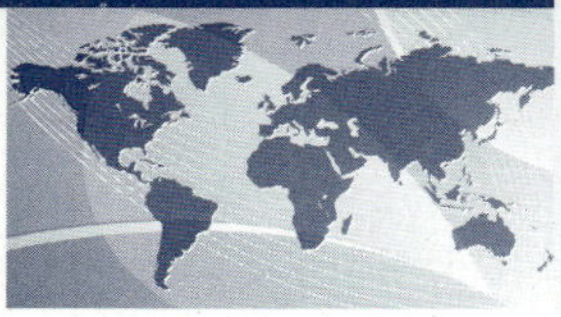

FOREIGN TRANSFER TAXES—A MIXED BAG

Of the 30 countries that are members of the Organization for Economic Cooperation and Development (OECD), only the United States and the United Kingdom assess gift and estate taxes that apply to transfers during life *and* at death. The majority of OECD countries impose inheritance taxes. Six countries—Australia, Canada, Mexico, New Zealand, the Slovak Republic, and Sweden—impose neither inheritance nor estate taxes. In Canada, however, the transfer of a capital asset at death is treated as a sale, and any gain must be recognized. Although no sale occurs, in Australia and Mexico the decedent's income tax basis carries over to the heir. New Zealand does not have an estate tax, but it imposes a form of gift tax for annual lifetime transfers beyond a certain amount.

Source: Adapted from Joint Committee on Taxation, "Description and Analysis of Alternative Wealth Transfer Tax Systems," March 10, 2008, p. 3.

April 1. Wren's date of record is April 8. Sharon's gross estate includes the following: the stock in Robin Corporation, the stock in Wren Corporation, and the dividend on the Robin stock. It does not include the dividend on the Wren stock because Sharon dies before the April 8 date of record. ■

EXAMPLE 29

Ray dies holding some promissory notes issued to him by his son. In his will, Ray forgives these notes, relieving the son of the obligation to make any payments. The fair market value of these notes is included in Ray's gross estate. ■

EXAMPLE 30
THE BIG PICTURE

Return to the facts of *The Big Picture* on p. 27-2. At the time of his death, John was the president of Hood Corporation. John's estate receives a distribution from Hood's qualified pension plan of $1.1 million consisting of the following.

Hood's contributions	$450,000
John's after-tax contributions	350,000
Income earned by the plan	300,000

John's estate also receives $150,000 from Hawk Insurance Company. The payment represents the maturity value of term life insurance from a group plan Hood maintains for its employees. As to these amounts, John's gross estate includes $1,250,000 ($1,100,000 + $150,000). For income tax purposes, however, $750,000 ($450,000 + $300,000) is subject to tax, while $500,000 ($350,000 + $150,000) is not. ■

Regarding the result reached in Example 30, retirement plan benefits are invariably subject to estate tax. Besides the conventional qualified pension and profit-sharing plans involved in Example 30, retirement plans include those under § 401(k), § 403(b) for teachers, § 457 for government employees, Keogh (H.R. 10) for self-employed persons, and IRAs—both traditional and Roth. Inclusion in the gross estate occurs irrespective of income tax consequences. Thus, a benefit paid under a Roth IRA is fully subject to the estate tax even though it may not be taxable as income to the beneficiary. The possibility of an income tax deduction for estate taxes paid is covered in Chapter 28 in connection with the discussion of income in respect of a decedent.

In addition to the items noted above, § 2033 operates to include in the gross estate many assets that can be of significant value. Examples include:

- Real estate holdings (but see § 2040 for jointly owned property).
- Present value of future royalty rights (e.g., patents, copyrights, mineral interests).

- Interests in a business (i.e., sole proprietorship, partnership).
- Collectibles (e.g., works of art, coin collections).
- Renewal value of leasehold interests.
- Terminable interests (e.g., life estates in realty or trusts) held by a surviving spouse as to which a deceased spouse's estate has made a QTIP election (discussed later in this chapter).
- Unmatured insurance policies on the lives of others.
- Proceeds from casualty and life insurance policies payable to the estate.
- Present value of pending and potential lawsuits or past judgments rendered.

EXAMPLE 31
THE BIG PICTURE

Return to the facts of *The Big Picture* on p. 27-2. Recall that John's death ultimately resulted from injuries suffered in a car accident caused by another motorist. In addition, John's auto was destroyed in the accident. Presuming the other driver is solvent or carries casualty insurance, John's gross estate should include the present value of any expected settlement that could result from possible legal action. At the least, his estate must include the recovery expected from his own casualty policy. ■

Dower and Curtesy Interests (§ 2034)

In its common law (nonstatutory) form, dower generally gave a surviving widow a life estate in a portion of her husband's estate (usually the real estate he owned) with the remainder passing to their children. Most states have modified and codified these common law rules, and the resulting statutes often vary among jurisdictions. Curtesy is a similar right held by the husband in his wife's property, taking effect in the event he survives her.

Dower and curtesy rights are incomplete interests and may never materialize. Thus, if a wife predeceases her husband, the dower interest in her husband's property is lost.

EXAMPLE 32

Martin dies without a will, leaving an estate of $6.9 million. Under state law, Belinda (Martin's widow) is entitled to one-third of his property. The $2.3 million Belinda receives is included in Martin's gross estate. Depending on the nature of the interest Belinda receives in the $2.3 million, this amount could qualify Martin's estate for a marital deduction. (This possibility is discussed at greater length later in the chapter. For the time being, however, the focus is on what is or is not included as part of the decedent's gross estate.) ■

Adjustments for Gifts Made within Three Years of Death (§ 2035)

At one time, all taxable gifts made within three years of death were included in the donor's gross estate unless it could be shown that the gifts were not made in contemplation of death. The special three-year rule for "deathbed gifts" was needed because the gift and estate taxes had not yet been merged into a unified tax. Making such gifts prior to death was advantageous then, as the lower tax rates of the separate gift tax applied.

With the adoption of the unified transfer tax system, post-1976 taxable gifts are added to the taxable estate in arriving at the tax base for determining the estate tax liability—see Figure 27.2 earlier in the chapter. Nevertheless, the three-year rule for inclusion in the gross estate has been retained for the following items.

- Any gift tax paid on gifts made within three years of death. Called the *gross-up* procedure, this prevents the gift tax amount from escaping the estate tax.
- Any property interests transferred by gift within three years of death that would have been included in the gross estate and consist of transfers with a retained life estate (§ 2036), transfers taking effect at death (§ 2037), revocable transfers (§ 2038), and proceeds of life insurance (§ 2042). All except transfers taking effect at death (§ 2037) are discussed later in the chapter.

EXAMPLE 33

Before her death in 2011, Jennifer made the following taxable gifts.

Year of Gift	Nature of the Asset	Fair Market Value: Date of Gift	Fair Market Value: Date of Death	Gift Tax Paid
1992	Hawk Corporation stock	$200,000	$1,300,000	$ –0–
2009	Insurance policy on Jennifer's life	80,000 (cash value)	1,000,000 (face value)	–0–
2010	Land	800,000	810,000	16,000

Jennifer's *gross estate* includes $1,016,000 ($1,000,000 life insurance proceeds + $16,000 gross-up for the gift tax on the 2010 taxable gift) as to these transfers. Referring to the formula for the estate tax (Figure 27.2), the other post-1976 taxable gifts are added to the *taxable estate* (at the fair market value on the date of the gift) in arriving at the tax base. In the case of the Hawk stock, notice the substantial saving in transfer taxes that will occur. The gift tax (although none resulted) is based on $200,000, whereas an estate tax would have applied to $1.3 million. Thus, the appreciation of $1.1 million has escaped any transfer tax. Jennifer's estate is allowed a credit for the gift tax paid (or deemed paid) on the 2010 transfer. ■

The three-year rule also applies in testing qualification under several other relatively narrow provisions.[30]

Transfers with a Retained Life Estate (§ 2036)

Code §§ 2036 through 2038 were enacted on the premise that the estate tax can be avoided on lifetime transfers only if the decedent does not retain control over the property. The logic of this approach is somewhat difficult to dispute. One should not be able to escape the tax consequences of property transfers at death while remaining in a position during life to enjoy some or all of the fruits of ownership.

Under § 2036, the value of any property transferred by the deceased during lifetime for less than adequate consideration must be included if either of the following was retained:

- The possession or enjoyment of, or the right to the income from, the property.
- The right, either alone or in conjunction with any person, to designate the persons who shall possess or enjoy the property or the income.

The decedent is considered to have the right to the income from the property to the extent that such income is to be applied toward the discharge of his or her legal obligation.[31]

EXAMPLE 34
THE BIG PICTURE

Return to the facts of *The Big Picture* on p. 27-2. Before Peter Hood died in 2000, he established several trusts. One trust grants John an income interest for life (i.e., a life estate), and upon his death, the trust passes to his children (i.e., remainder interest). On John's death, none of the trust property is included in his gross estate. Although he held a life estate, he was not the transferor (Peter was) of the property placed in trust. ■

EXAMPLE 35
THE BIG PICTURE

Return to the facts of *The Big Picture* on p. 27-2. Immediately after inheriting the family hunting lodge from his mother (see Example 18), John transfers it to a newly created trust. Under the terms of the trust instrument, he retains a life estate, remainder to his children and Helen (John's sister). Upon John's death, the property in the trust will be included in his gross estate under § 2036. ■

[30] §§ 2035(c)(1) and (2).

[31] § 2036(a)(1).

In both of the preceding examples, a gift occurred when the trusts were created. In Example 34, Peter made a gift of the entire amount placed in trust. In Example 35, John made a gift of only the remainder interest.

Revocable Transfers (§ 2038)

Another type of lifetime transfer that is drawn into a decedent's gross estate is covered by § 2038. The gross estate includes the value of property interests transferred by the decedent (except to the extent that the transfer was made for full consideration) if the enjoyment of the property transferred was subject, at the date of the decedent's death, to any power of the decedent to *alter, amend, revoke, or terminate* the transfer. This includes the power to change beneficiaries or to accelerate or increase any beneficiary's enjoyment of the property.

The Code and the Regulations make it clear that one cannot avoid inclusion in the gross estate under § 2038 by relinquishing a power within three years of death.[32] Recall that § 2038 is one of several types of situations listed as exceptions to the usual rule excluding gifts made within three years of death from the gross estate.

The classic § 2038 situation results from the use of a revocable trust. Example 9 (earlier in this chapter) illustrates the use of a revocable trust. Example 10 shows what happens when the right of revocation is released during the life of the creator of the trust. When the right of revocation is relinquished within three years of death, the trust is included in the creator's gross estate.

Annuities (§ 2039)

Annuities can be divided by their origin into commercial and noncommercial contracts. Noncommercial annuities are issued by private parties and, in some cases, by charitable organizations that do not regularly issue annuities. The two varieties have much in common, but noncommercial annuities present special income tax problems and are not treated further in this discussion.

An annuity is one or more payments extending over any period of time. The payments may be equal or unequal, conditional or unconditional, periodic or sporadic. Annuity contracts that terminate upon the death of the person covered (i.e., annuitant) are designated as straight-life annuities. Other contracts provide for a survivorship feature (e.g., reduced payments to a surviving spouse).

In the case of a straight-life annuity, nothing is included in the gross estate of the annuitant at death. Section 2033 (property in which the decedent had an interest) does not apply because the annuitant's interest in the contract is terminated by death. Section 2036 (transfers with a retained life estate) does not cover the situation; a transfer made for full consideration is specifically excluded from § 2036 treatment. A commercial annuity is presumed to have been purchased for full consideration unless some evidence exists to indicate that the parties were not acting at arm's length.

EXAMPLE 36

Arnold purchases a straight-life annuity that will pay him $24,000 a month when he reaches age 65. Arnold dies at age 70. Except for the unconsumed payments he received before his death, nothing relating to this annuity affects Arnold's gross estate. ■

In the case of a survivorship annuity, the estate tax consequences under § 2039(a) are usually triggered by the death of the first annuitant. The amount included in the gross estate is the cost from the same company of a comparable annuity covering the survivor at his or her attained age on the date of the deceased annuitant's death.

EXAMPLE 37

Assume the same facts as in Example 36, except that the annuity contract provides for Veronica to be paid $12,000 a month for life as a survivorship feature. Veronica is

[32] § 2038(a)(1) and Reg. § 20.2038–1(e)(1).

62 years of age when Arnold dies. Under these circumstances, Arnold's gross estate includes the cost of a comparable contract that provides an annuity of $12,000 per month for the life of a female, age 62. ■

Full inclusion of the survivorship element in the gross estate is subject to an exception under § 2039(b). The amount includible is to be based on the proportion of the deceased annuitant's contribution to the total cost of the contract. This is expressed by the following formula:

$$\frac{\text{Decedent's contribution to purchase price}}{\text{Total purchase price of the annuity}} \times \text{Value of the annuity (or refund) at decedent's death} = \text{Amount includible in the deceased annuitant's gross estate}$$

EXAMPLE 38

Assume the same facts as in Example 37, except that Arnold and Veronica are husband and wife and have always lived in a community property state. The premiums on the contract were paid with community funds. Since Veronica contributed half of the cost of the contract, only half of the amount determined under Example 37 is included in Arnold's gross estate. ■

The result reached in Example 38 is not unique to community property jurisdictions. The outcome would have been the same in a noncommunity property state if Veronica had furnished half of the consideration from her own funds.

In determining a decedent's contribution to an annuity contract, a special rule applies to employment-related retirement plans. In these cases, the employer's contribution to the plan is treated as having been made by the employee.

EXAMPLE 39

Under a noncontributory qualified retirement plan funded by his employer, Jim is entitled to an annuity for life. The plan also provides for a survivorship annuity for Jim's wife, Ellen, in the event he predeceases her. Upon Jim's prior death, the value of the survivorship annuity is included in his gross estate. Jim did not actually contribute to the cost of the annuity, but his employer's contributions are attributed to him. ■

Joint Interests (§§ 2040 and 2511)

Recall that joint tenancies and tenancies by the entirety are characterized by the right of survivorship. Thus, upon the death of a joint tenant, title to the property passes to the surviving tenant. None of the property is included in the *probate* estate of the deceased tenant. In the case of tenancies in common and community property, death does not defeat an ownership interest; rather, the deceased owner's interest is part of the probate estate.

The *Federal estate tax treatment* of tenancies in common or of community property follows the logical approach of taxing only the portion of the property included in the deceased owner's probate estate.

EXAMPLE 40

Homer, Wilma, and Thelma acquire a tract of land with ownership listed as tenants in common, each party furnishing $200,000 of the $600,000 purchase price. When the property is worth $900,000, Homer dies. If Homer's undivided interest in the property is $33\frac{1}{3}\%$, the gross estate *and* probate estate each include $300,000. This one-third interest is also the same amount that passes to Homer's heirs. ■

Unless the parties have provided otherwise, each tenant is deemed to own an interest equal to the portion of the original consideration he or she furnished. The parties in Example 40 could have provided that Homer would receive an undivided one-half interest in the property although he contributed only one-third of the purchase price. In that case, Wilma and Thelma have made a gift to Homer when the tenancy was created, and Homer's gross estate and probate estate each include $450,000.

For certain joint tenancies, the tax consequences are different. All of the property is included in the deceased co-owner's gross estate unless it can be proved that the surviving co-owners contributed to the cost of the property.[33] If a contribution can be shown, the amount to be *excluded* is calculated by the following formula:

$$\frac{\text{Surviving co-owner's contribution}}{\text{Total cost of the property}} \times \text{Fair market value of the property}$$

In computing a survivor's contribution, any funds received as a gift *from the deceased co-owner* and applied to the cost of the property cannot be counted. However, income or gain from gift assets can be counted.

EXAMPLE 41

Keith and Steve (father and son) acquire a tract of land with ownership listed as joint tenancy with right of survivorship. Keith furnished $400,000 and Steve $200,000 of the $600,000 purchase price. Of the $200,000 provided by Steve, $100,000 had previously been received as a gift from Keith. When the property is worth $900,000, Keith dies. Because only $100,000 of Steve's contribution can be counted (the other $100,000 was received as a gift from Keith), Steve has furnished only one-sixth ($100,000/$600,000) of the cost. Thus, Keith's gross estate must include five-sixths of $900,000, or $750,000. This presumes Steve can prove that he did in fact make the $100,000 contribution. In the absence of such proof, the full value of the property is included in Keith's gross estate. Keith's death makes Steve the immediate owner of the property by virtue of the right of survivorship. None of the property is part of Keith's probate estate. ■

If the co-owners receive the property as a gift or bequest *from another*, each owner is deemed to have contributed to the cost (or value on date of death) of his or her own interest.

EXAMPLE 42
THE BIG PICTURE

Return to the facts of *The Big Picture* on p. 27-2. During his lifetime, Peter Hood purchased timberland listing title as follows: "John and Helen Hood as equal tenants in common." John's basis in the property is one-half of Peter's cost. Upon John's death, one-half of the value of the timberland is included in his gross estate. ■

EXAMPLE 43
THE BIG PICTURE

Return to the facts of *The Big Picture* on p. 27-2. In her will, Martha leaves the Hood family residence to her children (John and Helen) as joint tenants with right of survivorship. John's income tax basis is one-half of the value on Martha's death. On John's later death, one-half of the value at that time will be included in his gross estate. Keep in mind that under the right of survivorship, outright ownership goes to Helen and none of the property passes to John's heirs. ■

To simplify the joint ownership rules for *married persons*, § 2040(b) provides for an automatic inclusion rule upon the death of the first joint-owner spouse to die. Regardless of the amount contributed by each spouse, one-half of the value of the property is included in the gross estate of the spouse who dies first. The special rule eliminates the need to trace the source of contributions and recognizes that any inclusion in the gross estate is neutralized by the marital deduction.

[33] § 2040(a).

EXAMPLE 44
THE BIG PICTURE

Return to the facts of *The Big Picture* on p. 27-2. Recall that after his divorce from Hannah, John married Ashley. Since Hannah kept John's prior home as part of the property settlement (see Example 16), he purchased a new residence. He listed title to the property as "John and Ashley Hood, tenancy by the entirety with right of survivorship." Upon John's death, only one-half of the value of the property is included in his gross estate.

If Ashley had died first, one-half of the value of the residence would have been included in her gross estate even though she made no contribution to its cost. ■

In Example 44, inclusion in the gross estate of the first spouse to die is neutralized by the unlimited marital deduction allowed for estate tax purposes (see the discussion of the marital deduction later in the chapter). Under the right of survivorship, the surviving joint tenant obtains full ownership of the property. The marital deduction generally is allowed for property passing from one spouse to another.

Whether or not a *gift* results when property is transferred into some form of joint ownership depends on the consideration furnished by each of the contributing parties for the ownership interest acquired.

EXAMPLE 45

Brenda and Sarah purchase real estate as tenants in common. Of the $800,000 purchase price, Brenda furnishes $600,000 and Sarah furnishes only $200,000. If they are equal owners in the property, Brenda has made a gift to Sarah of $200,000. ■

EXAMPLE 46

Martha purchases real estate for $900,000, the title to the property being listed as follows: "Martha, Sylvia, and Dan as joint tenants with the right of survivorship." If under state law the mother (Martha), the daughter (Sylvia), and the son (Dan) are deemed to be equal owners in the property, Martha is treated as having made gifts of $300,000 to Sylvia and $300,000 to Dan. ■

Several important *exceptions* exist to the general rule that the creation of a joint ownership with disproportionate interests resulting from unequal consideration triggers gift treatment. First, if the transfer involves a joint bank account, there is no gift at the time of the contribution. If a gift occurs, it is when the noncontributing party withdraws the funds provided by the other joint tenant. Second, the same rule applies to the purchase of U.S. savings bonds.[34] Again, any gift tax consequences are postponed until the noncontributing party appropriates some or all of the proceeds for his or her individual use.

Life Insurance (§ 2042)

Under § 2042, the gross estate includes the proceeds of life insurance on the decedent's life if (1) they are receivable by the estate, (2) they are receivable by another for the benefit of the estate, or (3) the decedent possessed any incidents of ownership in the policy.

Life insurance on the life of another owned by a decedent at the time of death is included in the gross estate under § 2033 (property in which the decedent had an interest) and not under § 2042. The amount includible is the replacement value of the policy.[35] Under these circumstances, inclusion of the face amount of the policy is inappropriate as the policy has not yet matured.

EXAMPLE 47

At the time of his death, Luigi owned a life insurance policy on the life of Benito, face amount of $500,000 and replacement value of $50,000, with Sofia as the designated beneficiary. Since the policy had not matured at Luigi's death, § 2042 would be inapplicable. However, § 2033 (property in which the decedent had an interest) compels the inclusion of $50,000 (the replacement value) in Luigi's gross estate. If Luigi and Sofia owned the policy as community property, only $25,000 is included in Luigi's gross estate. ■

[34] Reg. § 25.2511–1(h)(4).

[35] Reg. § 20.2031–8(a)(1).

In the frequent situation where the beneficiary of the insurance is neither the insured nor the owner of the policy, no tax consequences ensue upon the beneficiary's death. Thus, in Example 47, if Sofia predeceases Benito, no transfer takes place because the policy has not matured. Sofia's interest as a beneficiary is a mere expectancy and not a property interest possessing any value.

The term "life insurance" includes whole life policies, term insurance, group life insurance, travel and accident insurance, endowment contracts (before being paid up), and death benefits paid by fraternal societies operating under the lodge system.[36]

As just noted, proceeds of insurance on the life of the decedent receivable by the executor or administrator or payable to the decedent's estate are included in the gross estate. The estate need not be specifically named as the beneficiary. Assume, for example, that the proceeds of the policy are receivable by an individual beneficiary and are subject to an obligation, legally binding upon the beneficiary, to pay taxes, debts, and other charges enforceable against the estate. The proceeds are included in the decedent's gross estate to the extent of the beneficiary's obligation. If the proceeds of an insurance policy made payable to a decedent's estate are community assets and, under state law, one-half belongs to the surviving spouse, only one-half of the proceeds will be considered as receivable by or for the benefit of the decedent's estate.

Proceeds of insurance on the life of the decedent not receivable by or for the benefit of the estate are includible if the decedent at death possessed any of the incidents of ownership in the policy. In this connection, the term "incidents of ownership" means more than the ownership of the policy in a technical legal sense. Generally speaking, the term refers to the right of the insured or his or her estate to the economic benefits of the policy. Thus, it also includes the power to change beneficiaries, revoke an assignment, pledge the policy for a loan, or surrender or cancel the policy.[37]

EXAMPLE 48

At the time of death, Broderick was the insured under a policy (face amount of $1 million) owned by Gregory with Demi as the designated beneficiary. Broderick took out the policy five years ago and immediately transferred it as a gift to Gregory. Under the assignment, Broderick transferred all rights in the policy except the right to change beneficiaries. Broderick died without having exercised this right, and the policy proceeds are paid to Demi. Under § 2042(2), Broderick's retention of an incident of ownership in the policy (i.e., the right to change beneficiaries) causes $1 million to be included in his gross estate. ■

Assuming that the deceased-insured holds the incidents of ownership in a policy, how much is included in the gross estate if the insurance policy is a community asset? Only one-half of the proceeds becomes part of the deceased spouse's gross estate.

Merely purchasing a life insurance contract and designating someone else as the beneficiary thereunder does not constitute a *gift*. As long as the purchaser still owns the policy, nothing has really passed to the beneficiary. Even on the death of the insured-owner, no gift takes place. The proceeds paid to the beneficiary constitute a testamentary and not a lifetime transfer. But consider the following possibility.

EXAMPLE 49

Kurt purchases an insurance policy on his own life and transfers the policy to Olga. Kurt retains no interest in the policy (such as the power to change beneficiaries). In these circumstances, Kurt has made a gift to Olga. Furthermore, if Kurt continues to pay the premiums on the transferred policy, each payment constitutes a separate gift. ■

Under certain conditions, the death of the insured may constitute a gift to the beneficiary of part or all of the proceeds. This occurs when the owner of the policy is not the insured.

[36] Reg. § 20.2042–1(a)(1). As to travel and accident insurance, see *Comm. v. Estate of Noel*, 65–1 USTC ¶12,311, 15 AFTR 2d 1397, 85 S.Ct. 1238 (USSC, 1965). As to employer-sponsored group term life insurance, see Example 30 earlier in this chapter.

[37] Reg. § 20.2042–1(c)(2).

CONCEPT SUMMARY 27.2

Federal Estate Tax Provisions—Gross Estate

1. The starting point for applying the Federal estate tax is to determine which assets are subject to tax. Such assets comprise a decedent's gross estate.
2. The gross estate generally will not include any gifts made by the decedent within three years of death. It does include any gift tax paid on these transfers.
3. Based on the premise that one should not continue to enjoy or control property and not have it subject to the estate tax, certain incomplete transfers are included in the gross estate.
4. Upon the death of a joint tenant, the full value of the property is included in the gross estate unless the survivor(s) made a contribution toward the cost of the property. Spouses are subject to a special rule that calls for automatic inclusion of half of the value of the property in the gross estate of the first tenant to die. The creation of joint ownership is subject to the gift tax when a tenant receives a lesser interest in the property than is warranted by the consideration furnished.
5. If the decedent is the insured, life insurance proceeds are included in the gross estate if either of two conditions is satisfied. First, the proceeds are paid to the estate or for the benefit of the estate. Second, the decedent possessed incidents of ownership (e.g., the right to change beneficiaries) over the policy.

EXAMPLE 50

Randolph owns an insurance policy on the life of Frank, with Tracy as the designated beneficiary. Up until the time of Frank's death, Randolph retained the right to change the beneficiary of the policy. The proceeds paid to Tracy by the insurance company by reason of Frank's death constitute a gift from Randolph to Tracy.[38] ■

See Concept Summary 27.2 for a review of the components of the gross estate.

LO.7

Describe the components of the taxable estate.

TAXABLE ESTATE

After the gross estate has been determined, the next step is to compute the taxable estate. By virtue of § 2051, the **taxable estate** is the gross estate less the following: expenses, indebtedness, and taxes (§ 2053); losses (§ 2054); charitable transfers (§ 2055); the marital deduction (§§ 2056 and 2056A); and the deduction for state death taxes (§ 2058). As previously noted, the charitable and marital deductions also have gift tax ramifications.

Expenses, Indebtedness, and Taxes (§ 2053)

A deduction is allowed for funeral expenses; expenses incurred in administering property; claims against the estate; and unpaid mortgages and other charges against property, whose value is included in the gross estate (without reduction for the mortgage or other indebtedness).

Expenses incurred in administering community property are deductible only in proportion to the deceased spouse's interest in the community.[39]

Administration expenses include commissions of the executor or administrator, attorney's fees of the estate, accountant's fees, court costs, and certain selling expenses for disposition of estate property.

Claims against the estate include property taxes accrued before the decedent's death, unpaid income taxes on income received by the decedent before he or she died, and unpaid gift taxes on gifts made by the decedent before death.

Amounts that may be deducted as claims against the estate are only for enforceable personal obligations of the decedent at the time of death. Deductions for claims founded on promises or agreements are limited to the extent that the liabilities were

[38] *Goodman v. Comm.*, 46–1 USTC ¶10,275, 34 AFTR 1534, 156 F.2d 218 (CA–2, 1946).

[39] *U.S. v. Stapf*, 63–2 USTC ¶12,192, 12 AFTR 2d 6326, 84 S.Ct. 248 (USSC, 1963).

TAX *in* the NEWS

When Does the Cost of a Funeral Wake Become Nondeductible?

Due to a birth defect, Sarah died at the young age of 12. During her lifetime, she required constant medical care and treatment (e.g., special living accommodations, private teachers). To show their appreciation for those who helped her, Sarah's parents held a luncheon in her memory immediately after the funeral. The luncheon, which cost approximately $3,600, was attended by friends, relatives, and caregivers. Along with the usual expenses (e.g., priest, gravesite, flowers, published obituary), the executor of Sarah's estate deducted the $3,600 as a funeral expense.

Upon audit of the Form 706 filed for Sarah, the IRS disallowed the $3,600 deduction as being neither reasonable nor necessary to the funeral process. Reflecting a dearth of compassion, the Tax Court in *Estate of Sarah Davenport* (92 TCM 324, T.C.Memo. 2006–215) sustained the position of the IRS.

Does this mean that the cost of a wake celebrating the life of a decedent is always nondeductible? Hopefully not! A more modest function that is associated with the funeral service (e.g., held at the church meeting hall) might pass scrutiny by the IRS.

contracted in good faith and for adequate and full consideration. However, a pledge or subscription in favor of a public, charitable, religious, or educational organization is deductible to the extent that it would have constituted an allowable deduction had it been a bequest.[40]

Deductible funeral expenses include the cost of interment, the burial plot or vault, a gravestone, perpetual care of the grave site, and the transportation expense of the person bringing the body to the place of burial. No deduction is allowed for cemetery lots that the decedent acquired before death for himself or herself and family, but the lots are not included in the decedent's gross estate under § 2033 (property in which the decedent had an interest).

Losses (§ 2054)

Section 2054 permits an estate tax deduction for losses from casualty or theft incurred during the period when the estate is being settled. As is true with casualty or theft losses for income tax purposes, any anticipated insurance recovery must be taken into account in arriving at the amount of the deductible loss. Unlike the income tax, however, the deduction is not limited by a floor (e.g., $100) or a percentage amount (10 percent of adjusted gross income). If the casualty occurs to property after it has been distributed to an heir, the loss belongs to the heir and not to the estate. If the casualty occurs before the decedent's death, it should be claimed on the appropriate Form 1040. The fair market value of the property (if any) on the date of death plus any insurance recovery is included in the gross estate.

As is true of certain administration expenses, a casualty or theft loss of estate property can be claimed as an income tax deduction on the fiduciary return of the estate (Form 1041). But a double deduction prohibition applies, and claiming the income tax deduction requires a waiver of the estate tax deduction.[41]

Transfers to Charity (§§ 2055 and 2522)

A deduction is allowed for the value of property in the decedent's gross estate that is transferred by the decedent through testamentary disposition to (or for the use of) any of the following:

- The United States or any of its political subdivisions.
- Any corporation or association organized and operated exclusively for religious, charitable, scientific, literary, or educational purposes.
- Various veterans' organizations.

[40] § 2053(c)(1)(A) and Reg. § 20.2053–5.

[41] § 642(g).

The organizations just described are identical to those that qualify for the Federal gift tax deduction under § 2522. With the following exceptions, they are also the same organizations that qualify a donor for an income tax deduction under § 170.

- Certain nonprofit cemetery associations qualify for income tax but not estate and gift tax purposes.
- Foreign charities may qualify under the estate and gift tax but not under the income tax.

No deduction is allowed unless the charitable bequest is specified by a provision in the decedent's will or the transfer was made before death and the property is subsequently included in the gross estate. Generally speaking, a deduction does not materialize when an individual dies intestate (without a will). The amount of the bequest to charity must be mandatory and cannot be left to someone else's discretion. It is, however, permissible to allow another person, such as the executor of the estate, to choose which charity will receive the specified donation. Likewise, a bequest may be expressed as an alternative and still be effective if the noncharitable beneficiary disclaims (refuses) the intervening interest before the due date for the filing of the estate tax return (nine months after the decedent's death plus any extensions of time granted for filing).

EXAMPLE 51
THE BIG PICTURE

Return to the facts of *The Big Picture* on p. 27-2. After John's accident, he was in the intensive care unit at a local hospital. Although physically incapacitated, he was mentally alert. In early December, he reviewed his financial affairs with his attorney and CPA and executed a new will. His prior will, drawn up several years ago, contained a bequest to the Hood Scholarship Foundation (HSF), an organization created by Peter (John's father) to provide financial assistance to community college students. As HSF's qualified status had never been evaluated by the IRS, the attorney agreed to apply for a determination letter.

John's new will kept the bequest, but only if the IRS approved HSF's qualified status. John's CPA arranged to have all of John's medical expenses (e.g., hospital, physicians) paid as incurred. He also advised John to make a substantial payment on his property taxes and state income taxes. ■

Marital Deduction (§§ 2056, 2056A, and 2523)

The **marital deduction** originated with the Revenue Act of 1948 as part of the same legislation that permitted married persons to secure the income-splitting advantages of filing joint income tax returns. The purpose of these statutory changes was to eliminate the major tax variations that existed between taxpayers residing in community property and common law states. The marital deduction was designed to provide equity in the estate and gift tax areas.

In a community property state, for example, no marital deduction generally was allowed since the surviving spouse already owned one-half of the community and that portion was not included in the deceased spouse's gross estate. In a common law state, however, most if not all of the assets often belonged to the breadwinner of the family. When that spouse died first, all of these assets were included in the gross estate. Recall that a dower or curtesy interest (regarding a surviving spouse's right to some of the deceased spouse's property) does not reduce the gross estate. To equalize the situation, therefore, a marital deduction, usually equal to one-half of all separate assets, was allowed upon the death of the first spouse.

Ultimately, Congress decided to dispense with these historical justifications and recognize husband and wife as a single economic unit. Consistent with the approach taken under the income tax, spouses are considered as one for transfer tax purposes. By making the marital deduction unlimited in amount, neither the gift tax nor the estate tax is imposed on outright interspousal transfers of property. The unlimited marital deduction even includes one spouse's share of the community property transferred to the other spouse.

Passing Requirement Under § 2056, the marital deduction is allowed only for property that is included in the deceased spouse's gross estate and that passes or has passed to the surviving spouse. In determining whether the parties are legally married, look to state law. In this regard, some foreign divorces may raise doubts as to the validity of a subsequent remarriage. Having an ex-spouse does not qualify the decedent for a marital deduction if, in fact, the divorce is valid and final.

EXAMPLE 52
THE BIG PICTURE

Return to the facts of *The Big Picture* on p. 27-2 and Example 51. In reviewing John's prior will, the parties discovered that one of the main beneficiaries was Hannah, John's first wife. The new will substituted Ashley (John's present wife) for Hannah, thereby salvaging a marital deduction. ■

Property that passes from the decedent to the surviving spouse includes any interest received as (1) the decedent's heir or donee; (2) the decedent's surviving tenant by the entirety or joint tenant; or (3) the beneficiary of insurance on the life of the decedent.

EXAMPLE 53

At the time of his death in the current year, Matthew owned an insurance policy on his own life (face amount of $500,000) with Minerva (his wife) as the designated beneficiary. Matthew and Minerva also owned real estate (worth $600,000) as tenants by the entirety (Matthew had furnished all of the purchase price). As to these transfers, $800,000 ($500,000 + $300,000) is included in Matthew's gross estate, and this amount represents the property that passes to Minerva for purposes of the marital deduction.[42] ■

Disclaimers can affect the amount passing to the surviving spouse. If, for example, the surviving spouse is the remainderperson under the will of the deceased spouse, a disclaimer by another heir increases the amount passing to the surviving spouse. This, in turn, will increase the amount of the marital deduction allowed to the estate of the deceased spouse.

A problem arises when a property interest passing to the surviving spouse is subject to a mortgage or other encumbrance. In this case, only the net value of the interest after reduction by the amount of the mortgage or other encumbrance qualifies for the marital deduction. To allow otherwise results in a double deduction since a decedent's liabilities are separately deductible under § 2053.

EXAMPLE 54

In his will, Oscar leaves real estate (fair market value of $500,000) to his wife. If the real estate is subject to a mortgage of $100,000 (upon which Oscar was personally liable), the marital deduction is limited to $400,000 ($500,000 – $100,000). The $100,000 mortgage is deductible under § 2053 as an obligation of the decedent (Oscar). ■

However, if the executor is required under the terms of the decedent's will or under local law to discharge the mortgage out of other assets of the estate or to reimburse the surviving spouse, the payment or reimbursement is an additional interest passing to the surviving spouse.

EXAMPLE 55

Assume the same facts as in Example 54, except that Oscar's will directs that the real estate is to pass to his wife free of any liabilities. Accordingly, Oscar's executor pays off the mortgage by using other estate assets and distributes the real estate to Oscar's wife. The marital deduction now becomes $500,000. ■

Federal estate taxes or other death taxes paid out of the surviving spouse's share of the gross estate are not included in the value of property passing to the surviving spouse.

---

[42] Inclusion in the gross estate falls under § 2042 (proceeds of life insurance) and § 2040 (joint interests). Although Matthew provided the full purchase price for the real estate, § 2040(b) requires inclusion of only half of the value of the property when one spouse predeceases the other.

Therefore, it is usually preferable for the deceased spouse's will to provide that death taxes be paid out of the portion of the estate that does not qualify for the marital deduction.

Terminable Interest Limitation Certain interests in property passing from the deceased spouse to the surviving spouse are referred to as **terminable interests**. Such an interest will terminate or fail after the passage of time, upon the happening of some contingency, or upon the failure of some event to occur. Examples are life estates, annuities, estates for terms of years, and patents. A terminable interest will not qualify for the marital deduction if another interest in the same property passed from the deceased spouse to some other person, and by reason of the passing, that other person or his or her heirs may enjoy part of the property after the termination of the surviving spouse's interest.[43]

EXAMPLE 56

Vicky's will places her property in trust with a life estate to her husband, Brett, remainder to Andrew or his heirs. The interest passing from Vicky to Brett does not qualify for the marital deduction. Brett's interest will terminate on his death, and Andrew or his heirs will then possess or enjoy the property. ■

EXAMPLE 57

Assume the same facts as in Example 56, except that Vicky created the trust during her life. No marital deduction is available for gift tax purposes for the same reason as in Example 56.[44] ■

The justification for the terminable interest rule can be illustrated by examining the possible results of Examples 56 and 57 more closely. Without the rule, Vicky could have passed property to Brett at no cost because of the marital deduction. Yet, on Brett's death, none of the property would have been included in his gross estate. Section 2036 (transfers with a retained life estate) would not apply to Brett because he was not the original transferor of the property. The marital deduction should not be available in situations where the surviving spouse can enjoy the property and still pass it to another without tax consequences. The marital deduction is intended to merely postpone the transfer tax on the death of the first spouse and to shift any such tax to the surviving spouse.

Consistent with the objective of the terminable interest rule, an alternative means for obtaining the marital deduction is available. Under this provision, the marital deduction is allowed for transfers of **qualified terminable interest property** (commonly referred to as **QTIP**). This is defined as property that passes from one spouse to another by gift or at death and for which the transferee-spouse has a qualifying income interest for life.

For a donee or a surviving spouse, a qualifying income interest for life exists under the following conditions:

- The person is entitled for life to all of the income from the property (or a specific portion of it), payable at annual or more frequent intervals.
- No person (including the spouse) has a power to appoint any part of the property to any person other than the surviving spouse during his or her life.[45]

If these conditions are met, an election can be made to claim a marital deduction as to the QTIP. For estate tax purposes, the executor of the estate makes the election on Form 706 (estate tax return). For gift tax purposes, the donor spouse makes the election on Form 709 (gift tax return). The election is irrevocable.

If the election is made, a transfer tax is imposed upon the QTIP when the transferee-spouse disposes of it by gift or upon death. If the disposition occurs during life, the gift tax applies, measured by the fair market value of the property as of that time.[46] If no lifetime disposition takes place, the fair market value of the property on

[43] §§ 2056(b)(1) and 2523(b)(1).

[44] Both Examples 56 and 57 contain the potential for a qualified terminable interest property (QTIP) election discussed later in this section.

[45] §§ 2523(f) and 2056(b)(7).

[46] §§ 2519 and 2511.

the date of death (or alternate valuation date if applicable) is included in the gross estate of the transferee-spouse.[47]

EXAMPLE 58

In 1990, Clyde dies and provides in his will that certain assets (fair market value of $2.1 million) are to be transferred to a trust under which Gertrude (Clyde's wife) is granted a life estate with the remainder passing to their children upon Gertrude's death. Presuming all of the preceding requirements are satisfied and Clyde's executor so elects, his estate receives a marital deduction of $2.1 million. ■

EXAMPLE 59

Assume the same facts as in Example 58, with the further stipulation that Gertrude dies in 2011 when the trust assets are worth $6.4 million. This amount is included in her gross estate. ■

Because the estate tax is imposed on assets not physically included in the probate estate, the law allows the tax liability for those assets to be shifted to the heirs. The amount shifted is determined by comparing the estate tax liability both with and without the inclusion of the QTIP. This right of recovery can be canceled by a provision in the deceased spouse's will.[48]

State Death Taxes (§ 2058)

The purpose of the § 2058 deduction is to mitigate the effect of subjecting property to multiple death taxes (i.e., both Federal and state). In this regard, however, it provides less relief than was available with the § 2011 credit it replaced. A credit results in a dollar-for-dollar reduction in tax, whereas the benefit of a deduction is limited by the effective tax bracket of the estate.

COMPUTING THE FEDERAL ESTATE TAX

LO.8

Calculate the Federal estate tax liability.

Once the taxable estate has been determined, post-1976 taxable gifts are added to arrive at the tax base, and the estate tax can be computed.

EXAMPLE 60

Horton dies in 2011, leaving a taxable estate of $5.7 million. In 2002, he made a taxable gift of $100,000 upon which he paid no tax due to the availability of the unified tax credit. Horton's estate tax is $280,000, as determined below (see Figure 27.2).

Taxable estate	$ 5,700,000
Add: Post-1976 taxable gift	100,000
Tax base	$ 5,800,000
Tentative tax on tax base from tax rate schedule (Appendix A) [$155,800 + 35%($5,800,000 − $500,000)]	$ 2,010,800
Less: Unified tax credit for 2011	(1,730,800)
Estate tax due	$ 280,000

■

ETHICS & Equity — WATER UNDER THE BRIDGE

Amy, a recently deceased client, has named you as the executor of her estate. Upon examining some of her past financial affairs, you discover that she made taxable gifts in recent years. None of these gifts was reported on a Form 709. As far as you can tell without further investigation, none of these gifts resulted in a gift tax liability. When you suggest to Amy's heirs that gift tax returns should be filed reporting these transfers, they tell you not to bother as Amy's past actions are "water under the bridge" and irrelevant to your duties as executor. What should you do?

[47] § 2044.

[48] § 2207A(a).

ESTATE TAX CREDITS

Unified Tax Credit (§ 2010)

The role of the unified tax credit was discussed in connection with Example 3, and its application was illustrated in Example 60. The amount of the credit depends on the year the transfer occurred, and this information is contained in Table 27.1.

Credit for State Death Taxes (§ 2011)

The Code allowed a limited credit for the amount of any death tax actually paid to any state (or to the District of Columbia) attributable to any property included in the gross estate. Like the credit for foreign death taxes paid, this provision mitigated the harshness of subjecting the same property to multiple death taxes.

The credit allowed was limited to the lesser of the amount of tax actually paid or the amount provided for in a table contained in § 2011(b). About a dozen states still use the procedure and table set forth in § 2011 as a means of determining the *state* estate tax that each imposes.

The § 2011 credit was phased out completely by 2005. As previously noted, the *credit* for state death taxes paid has been replaced by a *deduction* under § 2058.[49]

Credit for Tax on Prior Transfers (§ 2013)

Suppose Floyd owns some property that he passes at death to Sarah. Shortly thereafter, Sarah dies and passes the property to Juan. Assuming both estates are subject to the Federal estate tax, the successive deaths result in a multiple effect. To mitigate the possible multiple taxation that might result, § 2013 provides relief in the form of a credit for Federal estate tax paid on prior transfers. In the preceding hypothetical case, Sarah's estate may be able to claim as an estate tax credit some of the taxes paid by Floyd's estate.

The credit is limited to the lesser of the following:

1. The amount of the Federal estate tax attributable to the transferred property in the transferor's estate.
2. The amount of the Federal estate tax attributable to the transferred property in the decedent's estate.

To apply the limitations, certain adjustments must be made that are not covered in this text.[50] However, it is not necessary for the transferred property to be identified in the present decedent's estate or for it to be in existence at the time of the present decedent's death. It is sufficient that the transfer of property was subjected to the Federal estate tax in the estate of the transferor and that the transferor died within the prescribed period of time. Table 27.2 shows the correlation between the credit allowed and the time interval between the two deaths.

TABLE 27.2 Credit for Tax on Prior Transfers

Interval between Deaths	Credit Allowed
Within 2 years	100%
Within 3 to 4 years	80%
Within 5 to 6 years	60%
Within 7 to 8 years	40%
Within 9 to 10 years	20%

[49]Section 2011 is to be reinstated as to decedents dying after 2012.

[50]See the instructions to Form 706 and Reg. §§ 20.2013–2 and –3.

TREATY RELIEF IS NOT ABUNDANT!

GLOBAL *Tax Issues*

One means of mitigating double taxation at the international level is to take advantage of treaty provisions. A treaty will determine which country has primary taxing rights, and this may depend on such factors as the domicile of the decedent or the nature of the property involved (e.g., personalty or realty). Unfortunately, the United States has estate tax conventions with only 17 countries: Australia, Austria*, Canada, Denmark*, Finland, France*, Germany*, Greece, Ireland, Italy, Japan*, the Netherlands, Norway, the Republic of South Africa, Sweden, Switzerland, and the United Kingdom*. In contrast, more than 50 countries have income tax treaties with the United States (see Exhibit 25.1 in Chapter 25). Thus, treaty relief in the estate tax area is not as widespread as with income tax situations.

*An asterisk indicates the existence of a gift tax treaty as well.

EXAMPLE 61

Under Floyd's will, Sarah inherits property. One year later Sarah dies. Assume the estate tax attributable to the inclusion of the property in Floyd's gross estate was $150,000 and that attributable to the inclusion of the property in Sarah's gross estate is $120,000. Under these circumstances, Sarah's estate claims a credit against the estate tax of $120,000(refer to limitation 2). ■

EXAMPLE 62

Assume the same facts as in Example 61, except that Sarah dies three years after Floyd. The applicable credit is now 80% of $120,000, or $96,000 (see Table 27.2). ■

Credit for Foreign Death Taxes (§ 2014)

A credit is allowed against the estate tax for any estate, inheritance, legacy, or succession tax actually paid to a foreign country. For purposes of this provision, the term "foreign country" means not only states in the international sense but also possessions or political subdivisions of foreign states and possessions of the United States.

PROCEDURAL MATTERS

A Federal estate tax return, if required, is due nine months after the date of the decedent's death.[51] The time limit applies to all estates regardless of the nationality or residence of the decedent. Frequently, an executor will request and obtain from the IRS an extension of time for filing Form 706 (estate tax return).[52] Also available is an *automatic* six-month extension of time to file the estate tax return. To receive the extension, the executor must file Form 4768 [Application for Extension of Time to File a Return and/or Pay U.S. Estate (and Generation-Skipping Transfer) Taxes].

The filing requirements parallel the exclusion amounts of the unified tax credit available for each year (refer to Table 27.1). The filing requirements may be lower when the decedent has made taxable gifts after 1976.[53]

EXAMPLE 63

Carlos dies in 2011, leaving a gross estate of $5 million. If Carlos did not make any post-1976 taxable gifts, his estate need not file Form 706. But, assume that Carlos made a taxable gift of $100,000 in 2002. Since the filing requirement now becomes $4.9 million ($5,000,000 regular filing requirement for 2011 – $100,000 post-1976 taxable gift), Carlos's estate must file Form 706. ■

---

[51] § 6075(a).

[52] § 6081.

[53] § 6018(a)(3).

CONCEPT SUMMARY 27.3

Federal Estate Tax Provisions—Taxable Estate and Procedural Matters

1. In moving from the gross estate to the taxable estate, certain deductions are allowed.
2. Under § 2053, deductions are permitted for various administration expenses (e.g., executor's commissions), professional fees (e.g., appraisal, accounting, legal), debts of the decedent, certain unpaid taxes, and funeral expenses.
3. Casualty and theft losses occurring during the settlement of the estate and not compensated for by insurance can be deducted (§ 2054).
4. Charitable transfers are deductible if the designated organization holds qualified status with the IRS at the time of death (§ 2055). See Chapter 23.
5. Transfers to a surviving spouse yield a marital deduction if they do not violate the terminable interest rule (§ 2056). The terminable interest rule can be avoided by making a QTIP election.
6. A deduction is allowed for certain state and local death taxes paid (§ 2058).
7. The tax base for determining the estate tax is the taxable estate plus all post-1976 taxable gifts.
8. Using the unified transfer tax rates appearing in Appendix A, determine the tax on the tax base.
9. From the tax determined under item 8, subtract the credits allowed under §§ 2010–2016.
10. If required, a Federal estate tax return (Form 706) must be filed within nine months of the date of the decedent's death.

Concept Summary 27.3 highlights the major components in arriving at the taxable estate and the mechanics of determining the estate tax liability.

27.4 The Generation-Skipping Transfer Tax

LO.9

Demonstrate the role of the generation-skipping transfer tax.

In order to prevent partial avoidance of Federal gift and estate taxes on large transfers, the tax law imposes an additional generation-skipping transfer tax.

THE PROBLEM

Previously, it was possible to bypass a generation of transfer taxes by structuring the transaction carefully.

EXAMPLE 64

Under his will, Edward creates a trust, life estate to Stephen (Edward's son) and remainder to Ava (Edward's granddaughter) upon Stephen's death. Edward is subject to the Federal estate tax, but no tax results on Stephen's death. Stephen held a life estate, but § 2036 does not apply because he was not the grantor of the trust. Nor does § 2033 (property owned by the decedent) come into play because Stephen's interest disappeared upon his death. The ultimate result is that the property in trust skips a generation of transfer taxes. ■

EXAMPLE 65

Joshua dies at age 89 and leaves all of his property to a trust. Under the terms of the trust instrument, trust income and corpus are to be distributed equally over a 10-year period to Amber and Ethan. Amber is Joshua's 22-year-old third wife, while Ethan is his 30-year-old grandson. As a result of this arrangement, the following tax consequences ensue: the estate tax applies on Joshua's death; income earned by the trust will be subject to income tax (see Chapter 28); and normally no transfer tax results when distributions of trust income and corpus occur. ■

EXAMPLE 66

Amy gives assets to Eric (her grandson). Called a direct skip, the gift would circumvent any transfer taxes that would have resulted had the assets been channeled through Eric's parents. ■

THE SOLUTION

The generation-skipping transfer tax (GSTT) is designed to preclude the avoidance of either the estate tax or the gift tax by making transfers that bypass the next lower generation. In the typical family setting, this involves transfers from grandparents to grandchildren. Such transfers, in effect, would skip any transfer tax that would result if the property were channeled through the children.

The GSTT is triggered by any of these three events: a taxable *termination* occurs; a taxable *distribution* takes place; or a *direct skip* is made.[54] Example 64 illustrates a termination event. Upon Stephen's death, the fair market value of the trust property that passes to Ava is subject to the GSTT (imposed on the trust). The GSTT will have the effect of reducing the amount Ava receives from the trust.

Example 65 illustrates a distribution event. When the trust makes a distribution to Ethan, the GSTT applies (imposed on Ethan). Any distribution to Amber is not subject to the GSTT because the spouse of the transferor (Joshua in this case) is deemed to be of the same generation.[55] The results reached in Example 65 show how ludicrous the application of the GSTT rules can be. Amber (age 22) is treated as being in the same generation as Joshua (age 89), while Ethan (age 30) is two generations removed!

Example 66 illustrates a lifetime version of the direct skip event.[56] In this situation, the GSTT is imposed upon Amy when the gift is made to Eric. Not only will Amy be subject to the GSTT, but the amount of the tax represents an additional gift to Eric.[57]

The GSTT rate is the highest rate under the gift and estate tax schedule. Pursuant to transitional rules, these top rates are as follows: 35 percent (2011–2012), 45 percent (2007–2009), and 46 percent (2006). (The rates were 47 percent in 2005, 48 percent in 2004, and 49 percent in 2003.) To ameliorate the extra tax burden of the GSTT, an exemption is allowed equal to the exclusion amount applicable to the Federal estate tax (see Table 27.1).[58] For a donor who is married, the election to split the gift (under § 2513) will double the amount of the exemption.[59] For 2011, for example, the amount of the exemption could be $10 million ($5 million × 2). The exemption can be applied to whichever transfers the grantor (or personal representative of the grantor) chooses. Any appreciation attributable to the exempted portion of the transfer is not later subject to the GSTT.

Along with the estate tax, the GSTT was not applicable for 2010.

TAX PLANNING:
27.5 The Federal Gift Tax

LO.10

Recognize strategies to minimize Federal gift and estate taxes.

For gifts that generate a tax, consideration must be given to the time value to the donor of the gift taxes paid. Since the donor loses the use of these funds, the expected interval between a gift (the imposition of the gift tax) and death (the imposition of the estate tax) may make the gift less attractive from an economic standpoint. On the plus side, however, are the estate tax savings that result from any gift tax paid. Since these funds are no longer in the gross estate of the donor (except for certain gifts within three years of death), the estate tax thereon is avoided.

Gifts possess distinct advantages. First, and often most important, income from the property is generally shifted to the donee. If the donee is in a lower bracket than the donor, the family unit will save on income taxes. Second, the proper spacing of gifts can further cut down the Federal gift tax by maximizing the number of annual exclusions available. Third, many states impose some type of tax at death, but only a relatively few impose a gift tax. Thus, a gift may completely avoid a state transfer tax.

[54] § 2611.

[55] § 2651(c)(1).

[56] § 2612(c)(1). A direct skip can also take place in a testamentary transfer.

[57] § 2515.

[58] § 2631(c).

[59] § 2652(a)(2).

In minimizing gift tax liability in lifetime giving, the optimum use of the annual exclusion can have significant results. Important in this regard are the following observations:

- Because the annual exclusion is available every year, space the gifts over as many years as possible. To carry out this objective, start the program of lifetime giving as soon as is feasible. For example, assume a donor made gifts in the amount of the annual exclusion to a donee beginning in 2003. Through 2011, the donor will have transferred $108,000 [$11,000 (annual exclusion for 2003–2005) × 3 (number of years at $11,000 exclusion) + $12,000 (annual exclusion for 2006–2008) × 3 (number of years at $12,000 exclusion) + $13,000 (annual exclusion for 2009–2011) × 3 (number of years at $13,000 annual exclusion)] without using any of the unified tax credit and incurring any gift tax.
- To the extent consistent with the wishes of the donor, maximize the number of donees. For example, a donor could give $540,000 to five donees over the 2003–2011 period ($108,000 apiece) without using any of the unified tax credit and incurring any gift tax.
- For the married donor, make use of the election to split gifts. As an example, a married couple can give $1,080,000 to five donees over the 2003–2011 period [$22,000 (annual exclusion for two donors for 2003–2005) × 5 (number of donees) × 3 (number of years at $22,000 annual exclusion) + $24,000 (annual exclusion for two donors for 2006–2008) × 5 (number of donees) × 3 (number of years at $24,000 annual exclusion) + $26,000 (annual exclusion for two donors for 2009–2011) × 5 (number of donees) × 3 (number of years at $26,000 annual exclusion)] without using any of their unified tax credits and incurring any gift tax.
- Watch out for gifts of future interests. As noted earlier in the chapter, the annual exclusion is available only for gifts of a present interest.

27.6 The Federal Estate Tax

CONTROLLING THE AMOUNT OF THE GROSS ESTATE

Presuming an estate tax problem is anticipated, the starting point for planning purposes is to reduce the size of the potential gross estate. Aside from initiating a program of lifetime giving, several other possibilities exist.

PROPER HANDLING OF ESTATE TAX DEDUCTIONS

Estate taxes can be saved either by reducing the size of the gross estate or by increasing the total allowable deductions. Thus, the lower the taxable estate, the less the amount of estate tax generated. Planning in the deduction area generally involves the following considerations:

- Making proper use of the marital deduction.
- Working effectively with the charitable deduction.
- Taking advantage of the bypass amount.
- Optimizing other deductions and losses allowed under §§ 2053 and 2054.

APPROACHES TO THE MARITAL DEDUCTION

When planning for the estate tax marital deduction, both tax and nontax factors have to be taken into account. In the tax area, planning is guided by two major goals: the *equalization* and *deferral* approaches.

- Attempt to equalize the estates of both spouses. Clearly, for example, the estate tax on $6 million is more than the estate tax on $5 million ($350,000 versus $0).
- Based on the time value of taxes deferred, try to postpone estate taxation as long as possible.

Barring certain circumstances, the deferral approach generally is preferable. By maximizing the marital deduction on the death of the first spouse to die, not only are taxes saved, but the surviving spouse is enabled to trim his or her future estate by entering into a program of lifetime giving. By making optimum use of the annual exclusion, considerable amounts can be shifted without incurring *any* transfer tax.

Tax planning must remain flexible and be tailored to the individual circumstances of the parties involved. Before the equalization approach is cast aside, therefore, consider the following variables:

- Both spouses are of advanced age and/or in poor health, and neither is expected to survive the other for a prolonged period of time.
- The spouse who is expected to survive has considerable assets of his or her own. Keep in mind that the transfer tax rate schedules are progressive in nature.
- Because of appreciation, property worth $5 million when it passes to the surviving spouse today may be worth $8 million five years later when the survivor dies.

EFFECTIVELY WORKING WITH THE CHARITABLE DEDUCTION

As a general guide to obtain overall tax savings, lifetime charitable transfers are preferred over testamentary dispositions. For example, an individual who gave $20,000 to a qualified charity during his or her life would secure an income tax deduction, avoid any gift tax, and reduce the gross estate by the amount of the gift. By way of contrast, if the $20,000 had been willed to charity, no income tax deduction would be available, and the amount of the transfer would be includible in the decedent's gross estate (though later deducted for estate tax purposes). In short, the lifetime transfer provides a double tax benefit (income tax deduction plus reduced estate taxes) at no gift tax cost (§ 2522). The testamentary transfer merely neutralizes the effect of the inclusion of the property in the gross estate (inclusion under § 2033 and then deduction under § 2055).

On occasion, a charitable bequest depends on the issuance of a disclaimer by a noncharitable heir.[60] Such a situation frequently arises with special types of property or collections, which the decedent may feel a noncharitable heir should have a choice of receiving.

EXAMPLE 67

Megan specified in her will that her valuable art collection is to pass to her son or, if the son refuses, to a designated and qualified art museum. At the time the will was drawn, Megan knew that her son was not interested in owning the collection. If, after Megan's death, the son issues a timely disclaimer, the collection will pass to the designated museum, and Megan's estate is allowed a charitable deduction for its estate tax value. ■

EXAMPLE 68

Dick's will specifies that one-half of his disposable estate is to pass to his wife, and the remainder of his property to a designated and qualified charitable organization. If the wife issues a timely disclaimer after Dick's death, all of the property passes to the charity and qualifies for the § 2055 charitable deduction. ■

Did the son in Example 67 act wisely if he issued the disclaimer in favor of the museum? Although the disclaimer will provide Megan's estate with a deduction for the value of the art collection, consider the income tax deduction alternative. If the son accepts the bequest, he can still dispose of the collection (and fulfill his mother's philanthropic objectives) through a lifetime donation to the museum. At the same time, he obtains an income tax deduction under § 170. Whether this will save taxes for the family unit depends on a comparison of Megan's estate tax bracket with the estimated income tax bracket of the son. If the value of the collection runs afoul of the percentage limitations of § 170(b)(1), the donations can be spread over more than one year. If this is done, and to protect against the contingency of the son's dying before the entire collection is donated, the son can neutralize any potential estate tax consequences by providing in his will for the undonated balance to pass to the museum.

[60] As noted earlier in this chapter, a disclaimer is a refusal to accept the property. If the disclaimer is timely made, the property is not treated as having passed through the person issuing the disclaimer, and a gift tax is avoided.

The use of a disclaimer in Example 68 would be sheer folly. It would not reduce Dick's estate tax; it would merely substitute a charitable deduction for the marital deduction. Whether the wife issues a disclaimer or not, no estate taxes will be due. The wife should accept her bequest and, if she is so inclined, make lifetime gifts of it to a qualified charity. In so doing, she generates an income tax deduction for herself.

A recent provision permits, under very limited circumstances, a tax-free distribution from an IRA to a qualified charity. The provision does not generate a charitable deduction but allows the donor to avoid the recognition of income that normally results when a distribution occurs. An estate tax savings also takes place because the donor will no longer own the amount donated upon his or her later death.[61] For the provision to apply, the donor must be age 70½ or older. The exclusion is limited to $100,000 per year and is available only for distributions made in 2006 through 2011.

TAKING ADVANTAGE OF THE BYPASS AMOUNT

The bypass amount, also known as the exclusion amount or the exemption equivalent, is the amount that can pass free of a transfer tax due to the unified credit. For a credit of $1,730,800, which is available for estate tax purposes for 2011, the bypass amount is $5 million.

In the past, a bypass amount often was wasted upon the death of the first spouse. Human nature often compels a spouse to leave all of his or her assets to the survivor.

EXAMPLE 69

Ethan and Hope are married, and each has a net worth of $5 million. On Ethan's prior death, his will passes his $5 million to Hope. Although Ethan has avoided any estate tax due to the marital deduction, he has wasted his bypass amount and concentrated $10 million in Hope's potential estate. ■

Under TRA of 2010, the result reached in Example 69 was changed by making the bypass amount (designated the exclusion amount) "portable," meaning that a deceased spouse's unused exclusion amount (DSUEA) can be transferred to the surviving spouse.[62]

EXAMPLE 70

Assume the same facts as in Example 69. If Ethan died after 2010 and a proper election is made on his return, his DSUEA becomes available. As a result, Hope now has an exclusion amount of $10 million [$5 million (DSUEA) + $5 million (her own basic exclusion amount)]. ■

If a surviving spouse is predeceased by more than one spouse, the DSUEA that is available for such a surviving spouse is limited to the *lesser of* $5 million or the unused exclusion of the last surviving spouse.

EXAMPLE 71

Continue with the facts of Example 70. After Ethan's death, Hope marries Michael who also predeceases her. Because he has used $2 million in making past taxable gifts, Michael has an unused exclusion of only $3 million at the time of his death. Hope now has an exclusion amount of $8 million [$3 million (DSUEA from Michael) + $5 million (Hope's basic exclusion amount)]. ■

PROPER HANDLING OF OTHER DEDUCTIONS AND LOSSES UNDER §§ 2053 AND 2054

Many § 2053 and § 2054 deductions and losses may be claimed either as estate tax deductions or as income tax deductions of the estate on the fiduciary return (Form 1041), but a choice must be made.[63] The deduction for income tax purposes is not allowed unless the estate tax deduction is waived. It is possible for these deductions to be apportioned between the two returns.

[61] § 408(d)(8).
[62] § 2010(c).
[63] § 642(g) and Reg. § 20.2053–1(d).

REFOCUS ON THE BIG PICTURE

AN EVENTFUL AND FINAL YEAR

By making use of § 2516, John was able to carry out a property settlement with Hannah without incurring any gift tax consequences (see Example 16). Both Helen and John acted wisely when they chose to disclaim most of their inheritance from their mother. By making the disclaimers, they were able to pass the property to their children without a transfer tax being imposed (see Examples 17 and 18).

Section 2033 operates to include in the gross estate not only John's retirement plan benefits but also any settlement from a potential lawsuit (see Examples 30 and 31). Section 2036 did not apply to the trust that John's father (Peter) created, but it did apply to the one John set up (see Examples 34 and 35). The difference in treatment occurs when it is the owner who retains an interest in the property, thereby making the transfer incomplete.

John's predeath planning was highly advantageous in several respects.

- By drawing up a new will, the loss of the charitable and marital deductions was avoided (see Examples 51 and 52).
- By prepaying state and local property and income taxes and staying current on medical expenses, John improved his Federal income tax position (see Example 51). He also avoided any estate taxes on the amounts used to pay these expenses.

KEY TERMS

Alternate valuation date, 27-6
Annual exclusion, 27-12
Bypass amount, 27-6
Disclaimer, 27-11
Exclusion amount, 27-6
Exemption equivalent, 27-6
Future interest, 27-12
Gross estate, 27-16
Joint tenants, 27-8
Marital deduction, 27-28
Probate estate, 27-16
Qualified terminable interest property (QTIP), 27-30
Taxable estate, 27-26
Taxable gift, 27-4
Tenants by the entirety, 27-8
Tenants in common, 27-8
Terminable interests, 27-30
Unified tax credit, 27-6
Unified transfer tax, 27-2

DISCUSSION QUESTIONS

1. **LO.1** Why can the unified transfer tax be categorized as an excise tax? In this regard, how does it differ from an income tax?

2. **LO.1** Over the years, the tax treatment of transfers by gift and by death has not been consistent. In this regard, what were the policy considerations supporting the original rules and the changes made?

3. **LO.1** In what manner does an inheritance tax differ from an estate tax?

4. **LO.1** Eight years ago, Alex made gifts of all of his assets to family and friends. Although the transfers would have generated gift taxes, none were paid, and no gift tax returns were filed. At present, no one knows where Alex is or even if he is still alive. The IRS has discovered that the gifts were made and is pursuing the donees for the gift tax due. Comment on the validity of the following defenses posed by the donees.
   a. The donor, not the donee, is responsible for the payment of any gift tax due.
   b. The assessment of any gift tax is barred by the statute of limitations.

5. **LO.1** Kim, a wealthy Korean national, is advised by his physicians to have an operation performed at the Mayo Clinic. Kim is hesitant to come to the United States

ISSUE ID

because of the possible tax consequences. If the procedure is not successful, Kim does not want his wealth to be subject to the Federal estate tax. Are Kim's concerns justified? Explain.

6. **LO.1** Carlos, a citizen and resident of Chile, would like to buy stock in General Electric and make gifts of the shares to his children. Will the Federal gift tax pose a problem for him? Explain.

7. **LO.1** To avoid both state and Federal transfer taxes (i.e., estate, inheritance, gift), Gary (a U.S. citizen) has moved to Costa Rica. Furthermore, he plans to limit his investments to non-U.S. assets (e.g., foreign stocks and bonds and real estate). Will Gary accomplish his objective? Explain.

COMMUNICATIONS

8. **LO.2** A new out-of-state client, Robert Ball, has asked you to prepare a Form 709 for a large gift he made in 2010. When you request copies of any prior gift tax returns he may have filed, he responds, "What do gifts in prior years have to do with 2010?" Send a letter to Robert at 4560 Walton Lane, Benton, AR 72015, clarifying this matter.

9. **LO.2, 4, 5** Regarding the formula for the Federal gift tax (see Figure 27.1), comment on the following observations.
   a. All prior gifts must be considered in determining the tax on a current gift.
   b. A credit is allowed for the gift taxes actually paid on prior gifts.
   c. A deduction for an annual exclusion might not be available.
   d. A gratuitous transfer might not be subject to the gift tax.

10. **LO.3** Regarding the formula for the Federal estate tax (see Figure 27.2 in the text), comment on the following.
    a. The gross estate may include property interests not owned by the decedent at the time of death.
    b. The gross estate may include assets that are not part of the probate estate (i.e., subject to administration by the executor of the estate).
    c. To arrive at the taxable estate, certain adjustments must be made to the gross estate.
    d. The role of prior taxable gifts in determining the tax base.
    e. Credits allowed in arriving at the estate tax due.

11. **LO.3** As to the alternate valuation date of § 2032, comment on the following.
    a. The justification for the election.
    b. A Form 706 need not be filed for the estate.
    c. The main heir prefers the date of death value.
    d. An estate asset is distributed to an heir three months after the decedent's death.
    e. Some estate assets have appreciated in value since the death of the decedent.
    f. Effect of the election on income tax basis.
    g. Treatment of income accruing from the property from the date of death to the alternate valuation date.

12. **LO.3** What type of ownership interest is appropriate in each of the following?
    a. A father desires to provide for his daughter during her life but wants to ensure that her younger husband (i.e., the son-in-law) does not inherit the property if he survives her.
    b. A married couple buys a home and wants to make sure that whoever survives obtains sole ownership of the property.
    c. Grandparents want to ensure that the family vacation home will be available for use by all of their children and grandchildren during their lifetimes.

13. **LO.4** Corinne wants to sell some valuable real estate to her son on an installment arrangement. Because related parties are involved, she fears that the IRS may question the selling price and contend that a portion of the transfer is a gift.
    a. Are Corinne's concerns realistic?
    b. How can Corinne protect herself from this contingency?

14. **LO.4** Addison provides all of the support of her dependent father, Walter, who lives with her. Because Walter is very proud and wants to appear independent, Addison gives him the money to pay his medical bills. Is Addison subject to the Federal gift tax as a result of these transfers? Explain.

ISSUE ID

15. **LO.4, 6** At a local bank, Jack purchases for $100,000 a five-year CD listing title as follows: "Meredith, payable on death to Briana." Four years later, Meredith dies, and Briana,

Meredith's daughter, redeems the CD when it matures. Discuss the transfer tax consequences if Meredith is:

a. Jack's wife.
b. Jack's ex-wife.
c. Jack's girlfriend.

16. **LO.4** Derek dies intestate (i.e., without a will) and is survived by a daughter, Ruth, and a grandson, Ted(Ruth's son). Derek's assets include a large portfolio of stocks and bonds and a beach house. Ruth has considerable wealth of her own, while Ted has just finished college and is unemployed. Under applicable state law, the order of priority as to heirship favors children followed by grandchildren.

ISSUE ID

a. To minimize future transfer taxes, what action might Ruth take?
b. What if Ruth wants only the beach house?

17. **LO.4** The Randalls have a married son and four grandchildren (ages 15, 17, 18, and 19). They establish a trust under which the income is to be paid annually to the grandchildren until the youngest reaches age 25. At that point, the trust terminates and the principal (corpus) is distributed to the son. What annual gift tax exclusions are allowed, if any, on the creation of the trust?

ISSUE ID

18. **LO.4** Qualified tuition programs under § 529 enjoy significant tax advantages. Describe these advantages with regard to the Federal:

a. Income tax.
b. Gift tax.
c. Estate tax.

19. **LO.5** Regarding the gift-splitting provision of § 2513, comment on the following.

a. What it was designed to accomplish.
b. The treatment of any taxable gifts previously made by the nonowner spouse.
c. How the election is made.
d. The spouses are divorced during the year.
e. The utility of the election in a community property jurisdiction.

20. **LO.5** In connection with the filing of a Federal gift tax return, comment on the following.

a. No Federal gift tax is due.
b. The gift is between spouses.
c. The § 2513 election to split gifts is to be used.
d. A gift of a future interest is involved.
e. The donor uses a fiscal year for Federal income tax purposes.
f. The donor obtained from the IRS an extension of time for filing his or her Federal income tax return.

21. **LO.4** In each of the following independent situations, indicate whether the transfer is subject to the Federal gift tax.

a. Asa contributes to his mayor's reelection campaign fund. The mayor has promised to try to get some of Asa's property rezoned from residential to commercial use.
b. Mary Ann inherits her father's collection of guns and mounted animals. Five months later, she disclaims any interest in the mounted animals.
c. Same as (b). Ten months later, Mary Ann disclaims any interest in the guns.
d. Haydon pays an orthodontist for the dental work performed on Michele, his dependent cousin.
e. Same as (d), except that Michele is not Hayden's dependent.
f. Marcus sells land to his mother, Marcie, for twice what it is worth.

22. **LO.4** In each of the following independent situations, indicate whether the transfer is subject to the Federal gift tax.

a. Floyd creates a revocable trust with his children as the beneficiaries.
b. In return for a premarital settlement of $1.2 million, Morgan (age 22) agrees to marry Errol (age 68). Errol transfers the funds *before* the marriage takes place.
c. Same as (b), except that Errol makes the transfer *after* the marriage takes place.
d. Florence purchases a U.S. savings bond listing herself and Taylor (her daughter) as joint owners.
e. Same as (d). One year later, Taylor predeceases Florence.
f. Same as (d). One year later, Florence predeceases Taylor.

23. **LO.3, 6, 7** Distinguish between the following.
    a. The gross estate and the taxable estate.
    b. The taxable estate and the tax base.
    c. The gross estate and the probate estate.

24. **LO.6** Discuss the estate tax treatment of each of the following. In all cases, assume that Mike is the decedent and that he died on July 5, 2011.
    a. Interest on State of South Dakota bonds paid on August 1, 2011.
    b. Cash dividend on Puce Corporation stock paid on August 10, 2011. Date of record was July 6, 2011.
    c. Same as (b). Declaration date was July 1, 2011.
    d. Distributions from traditional and Roth IRAs payable to Kirby (Mike's surviving spouse).
    e. Same as (d), except that Kirby is Mike's surviving daughter (not his spouse).
    f. Same as (d), except that the beneficiary is Mike's estate.

25. **LO.6** At the time of Emile's death, he was a joint tenant with Colette in a parcel of real estate. With regard to the inclusion in Emile's gross estate under § 2040, comment on the following *independent* assumptions:
    a. Emile and Colette received the property as a gift from Douglas.
    b. Colette provided all of the purchase price of the property.
    c. Colette's contribution was received as a gift from Emile.
    d. Emile's contribution was derived from income generated by property he received as a gift from Colette.

26. **LO.6** With regard to "life insurance," comment on the following.
    a. What the term includes (i.e., types of policies).
    b. The meaning of "incidents of ownership."
    c. When a gift occurs upon maturity of the policy.
    d. The tax consequences when the owner of the policy predeceases the insured and the beneficiary.
    e. The tax consequences when the beneficiary of the policy predeceases the insured.

ISSUE ID

27. **LO.6, 7** Due to the negligence of the other driver, Adam's car is completely destroyed, and he is seriously injured. Two days later, Adam dies from injuries suffered in the accident.
    a. What, if any, are the estate tax consequences of these events?
    b. Are there any income tax consequences to Adam or his estate?

ISSUE ID

28. **LO.6, 7** Assume the same facts as in Question 27. Three months after Adam's death, his houseboat is destroyed by fire. Under Adam's will, the houseboat is bequeathed to a nephew.
    a. What, if any, are the estate tax consequences of this situation?
    b. The income tax consequences?

29. **LO.7** Bernice dies and, under a will, passes real estate to her surviving husband. The real estate is subject to a mortgage. For estate tax purposes, how will any marital deduction be determined? Can Bernice's estate deduct the mortgage under § 2053? Explain.

ISSUE ID

30. **LO.8** Three unmarried and childless sisters live together. All are of advanced age and in poor health, and each owns a significant amount of wealth. Each has a will that passes her property to her surviving sister(s) or, if no survivor, to their church. Within a period of two years and on different dates, all three sisters die. Discuss the Federal estate tax consequences of these deaths.

31. **LO.4, 6** Using the legend provided, classify each of the following transactions.

Legend
NT = No transfer tax imposed
GT = Subject to the Federal gift tax
ET = Subject to the Federal estate tax

    a. Hal establishes a bank checking account listing ownership as "Hal and Darlene, joint tenants with right of survivorship."
    b. Same as (a). Six months later, Darlene withdraws all of the funds from the account.

c. Dana purchases a certificate of deposit listing ownership as "Dana, payable on death to Ann." Dana and Ann are sisters.
d. Same as (c). Six months later, Dana predeceases Ann.
e. Same as (c) and (d), except that Dana and Ann are not sisters but husband and wife.
f. Tim sends money to Robin College to pay for his daughter's room and board.
g. Nick pays the doctor and hospital for his niece's reconstructive (i.e., plastic) surgery. The niece is Nick's dependent.
h. Same as (g), except that the niece is not Nick's dependent.
i. Pierce purchases land listing title as "Pierce and Stella, equal tenants in common." Pierce and Stella are brother and sister.
j. Same as (i). Two years later, Stella predeceases Pierce.

32. **LO.7, 8** Abby dies in the current year. In determining her Federal estate tax liability, comment on the relevance of each of the following.
    a. Abby made taxable gifts in 1975 and 2008.
    b. Abby held a life estate in a trust created by her late husband.
    c. State death taxes paid by Abby's estate.
    d. Abby's estate includes some assets inherited from a wealthy aunt several years ago.
    e. Abby's estate includes some assets located in foreign countries.
    f. At the time of her death, Abby was receiving payments from a straight-life annuity she purchased from an insurance company several years ago.

33. **LO.9** In terms of the generation-skipping transfer tax, comment on the following.
    a. A GSTT termination event and a GSTT distribution event look very similar.
    b. A direct skip can occur only in gift situations, not in testamentary situations.
    c. Spouses may be of different generations if there is enough disparity in their ages.
    d. How the election to split a gift by a married donor can help avoid the tax.

PROBLEMS

34. **LO.1, 3, 6, 7** Arlene's estate includes the following assets.

	Fair Market Value	
	Date of Death	Six Months Later
Apartment building	$4,400,000	$4,380,000
Stock in Red Corporation	1,200,000	1,300,000
Stock in Tan Corporation	900,000	700,000

Accrued rents on the apartment building are as follows: $70,000 (date of death) and $60,000 (six months later). In order to pay expenses, the executor of Arlene's estate sells the Tan stock for $600,000 eight months after her death.
    a. If the § 2032 election is made, how much is included in Arlene's gross estate?
    b. As to part (a), assume the Tan stock is sold for $600,000 five months (rather than eight months) after Arlene's death. How does this change your answer, if at all?
    c. How much is included in the gross estate if the § 2032 election is not made?

35. **LO.3** In each of the following independent situations, indicate whether the alternate valuation date can be elected. Explain why or why not. Assume all deaths occur in 2011.

	Value of Gross Estate		Estate Tax Liability	
Decedent	Date of Death	Six Months Later	Date of Death	Six Months Later
Art	$6,000,000	$5,900,000	$240,000	$241,000
Maude	6,000,000	6,100,000	265,000	260,000
Bob	6,100,000	6,000,000	200,000	190,000
Bette	6,500,000	6,400,000	205,000	210,000

36. **LO.4** Carl made the following transfers during 2011.

- Transferred $900,000 in cash and securities to a revocable trust, life estate to himself and remainder interest to his three adult children by a former wife.
- In consideration of their upcoming marriage, gave Lindsey (age 21) a $90,000 convertible.
- Purchased a $100,000 certificate of deposit listing title as "Carl, payable on proof of death to Lindsey."
- Purchased for $80,000 a paid-up insurance policy on his life (maturity value of $500,000). Carl designated Lindsey as the beneficiary.

What are Carl's taxable gifts for 2011?

ISSUE ID

37. **LO.4, 7** In May 2010, Dudley and Eva enter into a property settlement preparatory to the dissolution of their marriage. Under the agreement, Dudley is to pay Eva $6 million in satisfaction of her marital rights. Of this amount, Dudley pays $2.5 million immediately, and the balance is due one year later. The parties are divorced in July. Dudley dies in December, and his estate pays Eva the remaining $3.5 million in May 2011. Discuss the tax ramifications of these transactions to the parties involved.

ISSUE ID

38. **LO.4** Jesse dies intestate (i.e., without a will) in May 2010. Jesse's major asset is a tract of land. Under applicable state law, Jesse's property will pass to Lorena, who is his only child. In December 2010, Lorena disclaims one-half of the property. In June 2011, Lorena disclaims the other half interest. Under state law, Lorena's disclaimer results in the property passing to Arnold (Lorena's only child). The value of the land (in its entirety) is as follows: $2 million in May 2010; $2.1 million in December 2010; and $2.2 million in June 2011. Discuss the transfer tax ramifications of these transactions.

39. **LO.5** Using property she inherited, Myrna makes a gift of $6.2 million to her adult daughter, Doris. The gift takes place in 2011. Neither Myrna nor her husband, Greg, has made any prior taxable gifts. Determine the gift tax liability if:
   a. The § 2513 election to split gifts is not made.
   b. The § 2513 election to split gifts is made.
   c. What are the tax savings from making the election?

40. **LO.6, 7** At the time of his death on September 2, 2011, Kenneth owned the following assets.

	Fair Market Value
City of Boston bonds	$1,500,000
Stock in Brown Corporation	800,000
Promissory note issued by Brad (Kenneth's son)	300,000

In October 2011, the executor of Kenneth's estate received the following: $90,000 interest on the City of Boston bonds ($20,000 accrued since September 2), and an $8,000 cash dividend on the Brown stock (date of record was September 1). The declaration date on the dividend was August 12. The $300,000 loan was made to Brad in late 2007, and he used the money to create a very successful business. The note was forgiven by Kenneth in his will. What are the estate tax consequences of these transactions?

41. **LO.6** At the time of her death on September 4, 2011, Alicia held the following assets.

	Fair Market Value
Bonds of Emerald Tool Corporation	$800,000
Stock in Drab Corporation	900,000
Insurance policy (face amount of $200,000) on the life of her father, Mitch	50,000*
Traditional IRAs	300,000

* Cash surrender value.

Alicia was also the life tenant of a trust (fair market value of $2 million) created by her late husband Brad. (The executor of Brad's estate had made a QTIP election.) In October, Alicia's estate received an interest payment of $12,000 ($10,000 accrued before September 4,

2011) paid by Emerald and a cash dividend of $9,000 from Drab. The Drab dividend was declared on August 19 and was payable to date of record shareholders on September 5, 2011. Although Mitch survives Alicia, she is the designated beneficiary of the policy. The IRAs are distributed to Alicia's children. What is the amount included in Alicia's gross estate?

42. **LO.6** Assume the same facts as in Problem 41 with the following modifications.
    - Mitch is killed by a rock slide while mountain climbing in November 2011, and the insurer pays Alicia's estate $200,000.
    - Brad's executor did not make a QTIP election.
    - Alicia's IRAs were the Roth type (not traditional).

    What is the amount included in Alicia's gross estate?

43. **LO.6, 7** At the time of Matthew's death, he was involved in the transactions described below.
    - Matthew was a participant in his employer's contributory qualified pension plan. The plan balance of $2 million is paid to Olivia, Matthew's daughter and beneficiary. The distribution consists of the following.

Employer contributions	$900,000
Matthew's after-tax contributions	600,000
Income earned by the plan	500,000

    - Matthew was covered by his employer's group term life insurance plan for employees. The $200,000 proceeds are paid to Olivia, the designated beneficiary.

    a. What are the estate tax consequences?
    b. The income tax consequences?
    c. Would the answer to part (a) change if Olivia was Matthew's surviving spouse (not his daughter)? Explain.

44. **LO.4, 6** Before her death in early 2011, Katie made the following transfers.
    - In 2008, purchased stock in Green Corporation for $200,000, listing title as follows: "Katie, payable on proof of death to my son, Travis." Travis survives Katie, and the stock is worth $300,000 when Katie dies.
    - In 2009, purchased an insurance policy on her life for $200,000 listing Paul, another of Katie's sons, as the designated beneficiary. The policy has a maturity value of $1 million and was immediately transferred to Paul as a gift.
    - In 2010, made a gift of land (basis of $300,000; fair market value of $1.3 million) to Adriana, Katie's only daughter. As a result of the transfer, Katie paid a gift tax of $150,000. The value of the land is still $1.3 million at Katie's death.
    - In 2009, established a savings account with $100,000, listing title as "Katie and Wilma, joint tenants with right of survivorship." Wilma, Katie's mother, died in 2010 when the account's balance was $102,000. At Katie's death, the balance was $104,000.

    As to these transfers, how much is included in Katie's gross estate?

45. **LO.4, 6, 7** In 2004, using $2 million in community property, Warren creates a trust, life estate to his wife, Ava, and remainder to their children. Warren dies in 2008 when the trust is worth $3.4 million, and Ava dies in 2011 when the trust is worth $4.6 million. **ISSUE ID**
    a. Did Warren make a gift in 2004? Explain.
    b. How much, if any, of the trust is included in Warren's gross estate in 2008?
    c. How much, if any, of the trust is included in Ava's gross estate in 2011?
    d. Would the answer to part (b) change if Warren had died in 2006 (rather than 2008)? Explain.

46. **LO.6, 9** At the time of his death, Garth was involved in the following arrangements.
    - He held a life estate in the Myrtle Trust with the remainder passing to Garth's adult children. The trust was created by Myrtle (Garth's mother) in 1984 with securities worth $900,000. The Myrtle Trust had a value of $4.7 million when Garth died.
    - Under the terms of the Myrtle Trust, Garth was given the power to provide for a disproportionate distribution of the remainder interest among his children. As Garth failed to exercise this power, the remainder interest is divided equally among the children.

    Discuss the estate tax ramifications of these arrangements as to Garth.

47. **LO.6** In 2007, Peggy, a widow, places $3 million in trust, life estate to her children, remainder to her grandchildren, but retains the right to revoke the trust. In 2010, when the trust is worth $3.1 million, Peggy rescinds her right to revoke the trust. Peggy dies in 2011 when the trust is worth $3.2 million. What are Peggy's transfer tax consequences in:
    a. 2007?
    b. 2010?
    c. 2011?

48. **LO.6, 7** In 2000, Alan purchases a commercial single premium annuity. Under the terms of the policy, Alan is to receive $120,000 annually for life. If Alan predeceases his wife, Katelyn, she is to receive $60,000 annually for life. Alan dies first at a time when the value of the survivorship feature is $900,000.
    a. How much, if any, of the annuity is included in Alan's gross estate? Taxable estate?
    b. Would the answers to part (a) change if the money Alan used to purchase the annuity was community property? Explain.
    c. Would the answer to (a) change if one-half of the annuity purchase price had been furnished by Alan's employer?

49. **LO.6** At the time of his death on June 6, 2011, Keith was involved in the following real estate.

	Fair Market Value (on June 6, 2011)
Apartment building	$2,000,000
Tree farm	1,200,000
Pastureland	900,000
Residence	800,000

The apartment building was purchased by Emma, Keith's mother, and is owned in a joint tenancy with her. The tree farm and pastureland were gifts from Emma to Keith and his two sisters. The tree farm is held in joint tenancy, and the pastureland is owned as tenants in common. Keith purchased the residence and owns it with his wife as tenants by the entirety. How much is included in Keith's gross estate based on the following assumptions?
    a. Keith dies first and is survived by Emma, his sisters, and his wife.
    b. Keith dies after Emma, but before his sisters and his wife.
    c. Keith dies after Emma and his sisters, but before his wife.
    d. Keith dies last (i.e., he survives Emma, his sisters, and his wife).

50. **LO.4, 6, 7** In 2002, Gordon purchased real estate for $900,000 and listed title to the property as "Gordon and Fawn, joint tenants with right of survivorship." Gordon predeceases Fawn in 2011 when the real estate is worth $2.9 million. Gordon and Fawn are brother and sister.
    a. Did a gift occur in 2002? Explain.
    b. What, if any, are the estate tax consequences in 2011?
    c. Under part (b), would your answer change if it was Fawn (not Gordon) who died in 2011? Explain.

51. **LO.4, 6, 7** Assume the same facts as in Problem 50, except that Gordon and Fawn are husband and wife (not brother and sister).
    a. What are the gift tax consequences in 2002?
    b. What are the estate tax consequences in 2011?
    c. Under part (b), would your answer change if it was Fawn (not Gordon) who died in 2011? Explain.

52. **LO.5, 6, 7** In each of the *independent* situations below, determine the transfer tax (i.e., estate and gift) consequences of what has occurred. (In all cases, assume Gene and Mary are married and that Ashley is their daughter.)
    a. Mary purchases an insurance policy on Gene's life and designates Ashley as the beneficiary. Mary dies first, and under her will, the policy passes to Gene.

b. Gene purchases an insurance policy on his life and designates Ashley as the beneficiary. Gene gives the policy to Mary and continues to pay the premiums thereon. Two years after the gift, Gene dies first, and the policy proceeds are paid to Ashley.
c. Gene purchases an insurance policy on Mary's life and designates Ashley as the beneficiary. Ashley dies first one year later.
d. Assume the same facts as in part (c). Two years later, Mary dies. Because Gene has not designated a new beneficiary, the insurance proceeds are paid to him.
e. Gene purchases an insurance policy on his life and designates Mary as the beneficiary. Gene dies first, and the policy proceeds are paid to Mary.

53. **LO.7** While vacationing in Florida in November 2011, Sally was seriously injured in an automobile accident (she died several days later). How are the following transactions handled for tax purposes?
   a. Bruce, Sally's son and executor, incurred $6,200 in travel expenses in flying to Florida, retrieving the body, and returning it to Frankfort (KY) for burial.
   b. Early in 2011, Sally had pledged $50,000 to the building fund of her church. Bruce paid this pledge from the assets of the estate.
   c. Prior to her death, Sally had promised to give her nephew, Gary, $20,000 when he passed the bar exam. Gary passed the exam in December 2011, and Bruce kept Sally's promise by paying him $20,000 from estate assets.
   d. At the scene of the accident and before the ambulance arrived, someone took Sally's jewelry (i.e., Rolex watch, wedding ring) and money. The property (valued at $33,000) was not insured and was never recovered.
   e. As a result of the accident, Sally's auto was totally destroyed. The auto had a basis of $52,000 and a fair market value of $28,000. In January 2012, the insurance company pays Sally's estate $27,000.

54. **LO.7** In 2011, Roy dies and is survived by his wife, Marge. Under Roy's will, all of his otherwise uncommitted assets pass to Marge. Based on the property interests listed below, determine the marital deduction allowed to Roy's estate.
   a. Timberland worth $1.2 million owned by Roy, Marge, and Amber (Marge's sister) as equal tenants in common. Roy furnished the original purchase price.
   b. Residence of Roy and Marge worth $900,000 owned by them as tenants by the entirety with right of survivorship. Marge provided the original purchase price.
   c. Insurance policy on Roy's life (maturity value of $500,000) owned by Marge and payable to her as the beneficiary.
   d. Insurance policy on Roy's life (maturity value of $1 million) owned by Roy with Marge as the designated beneficiary.
   e. Distribution from a qualified pension plan of $1.5 million (Roy matched his employer's contribution of $500,000) with Marge as the designated beneficiary.

55. **LO.8** Under Rowena's will, Mandy (Rowena's sister) inherits her property. One year later, Mandy dies. Based on the following independent assumptions, what is Mandy's credit for the tax on prior transfers?
   a. The estate tax attributable to the inclusion of the property in Rowena's gross estate is $700,000, and the estate tax attributable to the inclusion of the property in Mandy's gross estate is $800,000.
   b. The estate tax attributable to the inclusion of the property in Rowena's gross estate is $1.2 million, and the estate tax attributable to the inclusion of the property in Mandy's gross estate is $1.1 million.
   c. Would your answers to parts (a) and (b) change if Mandy died seven years (rather than one year) after Rowena?

56. **LO.9** In 2012, Loretta makes a taxable gift of $2 million to her granddaughter, Bertha. Presuming that Loretta used up both her unified transfer tax credit and her generation-skipping transfer tax credit, how much tax does Loretta owe as a result of the transfer?

57. **LO.9** In 2011, Marsha died, and her after-tax estate of $6 million passed to a trust. Under the terms of the trust, Wilma (Marsha's daughter) is granted a life estate with the remainder passing to Karl (Marsha's grandson) upon Wilma's death. The trustee elects to use $3 million of the generation-skipping transfer tax exemption. Wilma dies in 2012 when the trust is worth $9 million.
   a. Presuming the GSTT applies, is it caused by a termination event, a distribution event, or a direct skip?

b. How much of the trust is subject to the GSTT?
c. Who pays the tax?
d. What is the GSTT rate that applies?

58. **LO.5, 8** In each of the following *independent* situations, determine the gift tax that was due and the decedent's final estate tax liability (net of any unified tax credit).

	Decedent		
	Dana	Alice	Ken
Year of death	2003	2004	2012
Taxable estate	$900,000	$1,700,000	$1,400,000
Post-1976 taxable gifts—			
Made in 2000	900,000	—	—
Made in 2001	—	800,000	—
Made in 2011	—	—	5,200,000

See Appendix E for Comprehensive Tax Return Problems—Forms 706 and 709

RESEARCH PROBLEMS

THOMSON REUTERS
Checkpoint® Student Edition

Note: Solutions to Research Problems can be prepared by using the **Checkpoint® Student Edition** online research product, which is available to accompany this text. It is also possible to prepare solutions to the Research Problems by using tax research materials found in a standard tax library.

Research Problem 1. In 2000, June, a 75-year-old widow, creates an irrevocable trust naming her five adult grandchildren as the beneficiaries. The assets transferred in trust consist of marketable securities (worth $800,000) and June's personal residence (worth $400,000). Bob, June's younger brother and a practicing attorney, is designated as the trustee. Other provisions of the trust are noted below.

- Bob is given the discretion to distribute the income to the beneficiaries based on their need or add it to corpus. He is also given the power to change trust investments and to terminate the trust.
- The trust is to last for June's lifetime or, if sooner, until termination by Bob.
- Upon termination of the trust, the principal and any accumulated income are to be distributed to the beneficiaries (June's grandchildren).

For 2000, June files a Form 709 to report the transfer in trust and pays a gift tax based on value of $1.2 million ($800,000 + $400,000).

After the transfer in trust and up to the time of her death, June continues to occupy the residence. Although she pays no rent, she maintains the property and pays the yearly property taxes. June never discussed the matter of her continued occupancy of the residence with either Bob or the beneficiaries of the trust.

On June's death in 2008, the value of the trust is $2.3 million, broken down as follows: marketable securities and cash ($1.6 million) and residence ($700,000). Shortly thereafter, Bob sells the residence, liquidates the trust, and distributes the proceeds to the beneficiaries.

What are the estate tax consequences of these transactions to June?

Partial list of research aids:
§ 2036.
Guynn v. U.S., 71–1 USTC ¶12,742, 27 AFTR 2d 71–1653, 437 F.2d 1148 (CA–4, 1971).
Estate of Eleanor T. R. Trotter, 82 TCM 633, T.C.Memo. 2001–250.
Estate of Lorraine C. Disbrow, 91 TCM 794, T.C.Memo. 2006–34.

Research Problem 2. Before her death in 2009, Lucy entered into the following transactions.

- In 2007, she borrowed $300,000 from a bank and promptly loaned that sum to her controlled corporation. The executor of Lucy's estate repaid the bank loan, but never attempted to collect the amount due Lucy from the corporation.
- In 2001, Lucy promised her sister, Ida, a bequest of $800,000 if Ida would move in with her and care for her during an illness (which eventually proved to be terminal). Lucy never kept her promise, as her will was silent on any bequest to Ida. After Lucy's death, Ida sued the estate and eventually recovered $600,000 for breach of contract.
- One of the assets in Lucy's estate was a palatial residence that passed to George under a specific provision of the will. George did not want the residence, preferring cash instead. Per George's instructions, the residence was sold. Expenses incurred in connection with the sale were claimed as § 2053 expenses on Form 706 filed by Lucy's estate.
- Before her death, Lucy incurred and paid certain medical expenses but did not have the opportunity to file a claim for partial reimbursement from her insurance company. After her death, the claim was filed by Lucy's executor, and the reimbursement was paid to the estate.

Discuss the estate and income tax ramifications of each of these transactions.

Partial list of research aids:
§§ 61(a)(1) and (12), 111, 213, 691, 2033, and 2053.
Estate of Allie W. Pittard, 69 T.C. 391 (1977).
Joseph F. Kenefic, 36 TCM 1226, T.C.Memo. 1977–310.
Hibernia Bank v. U.S., 78–2 USTC ¶13,261, 42 AFTR 2d 78–6510, 581 F.2d 741 (CA–9, 1978).
Rev.Rul. 78–292, 1978–2 C.B. 233.

INTERNET *activity*

Use the tax resources of the Internet to address the following question. Do not restrict your search to the Web, but include a review of newsgroups and general reference materials, practitioner sites and resources, primary sources of the tax law, chat rooms and discussion groups, and other opportunities.

COMMUNICATIONS

Research Problem 3. Find the IRS forms noted below. List the title of each, prepare a short comment as to its purpose or use, and e-mail this information to your instructor.

a. Schedule U of Form 706.
b. Form 706-A.
c. Form 706-GS(D).
d. Form 706-QDT.

CHAPTER

28

Income Taxation of Trusts and Estates

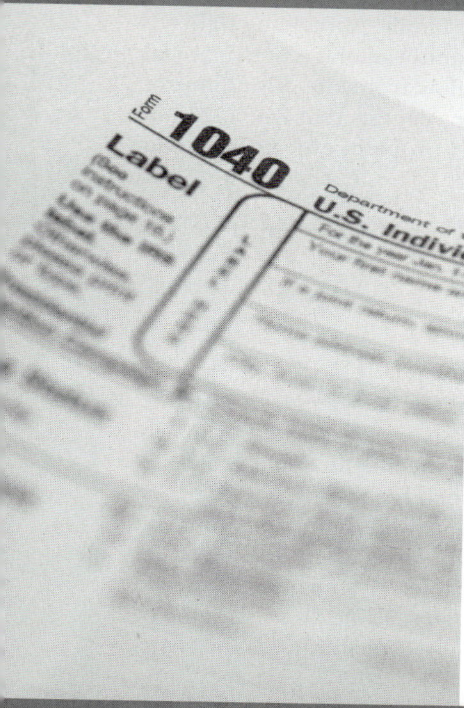

LEARNING OBJECTIVES

After completing Chapter 28, you should be able to:

LO.1

Use working definitions with respect to trusts, estates, beneficiaries, and other parties.

LO.2

Identify the steps in determining the accounting and taxable income of a trust or estate, and the related taxable income of the beneficiaries.

LO.3

Illustrate the uses and implications of distributable net income.

LO.4

Apply the Subchapter J rules in a manner that minimizes the income taxation of trusts and estates and still accomplishes the intended objectives of the grantor or decedent.

OUTLINE

For the latest in changes to tax legislation, visit **www.cengage.com/taxation/swft.**

THE BIG PICTURE **Tax Solutions for the Real World**

SETTING UP A TRUST TO PROTECT A FAMILY

Anna Jiang is the main breadwinner in her family, which includes her husband Tom, a social worker, and two children, Bobby, age 8, and Sally, age 13. Anna has accumulated about $2 million in after-tax investment accounts, largely made up of growth stocks that do not regularly pay dividends. Anna has addressed the problem of probate costs through joint property ownership, life insurance policies, and beneficiary arrangements for her retirement plans. She and Tom update their wills every five years or so.

Because there is a history of Alzheimer's disease in her family, Anna Jiang wants to make certain that, if she becomes unable to work and cannot manage her financial assets, Tom and the children will have adequate cash flow from the $2 million of investment assets. One of Anna's colleagues at the office suggests that Anna should set up a trust to take care of her family in case a medical problem ever arises. **Read the chapter and formulate your response.**

28.1 An Overview of Subchapter J

Taxpayers create trusts for a variety of reasons. Some trusts are established primarily for tax purposes, but most are designed to accomplish a specific financial goal or to provide for the orderly management of assets in case of emergency.

Because a trust is a separate tax entity, its gross income and deductions must be measured, and an annual tax return must be filed. Similarly, when an individual dies, a legal entity is created in the form of his or her estate. This chapter examines the rules related to the income taxation of trusts and estates. Table 28.1 lists some of the more common reasons for creating a trust, and Figure 28.1 illustrates the structure of a typical trust and estate.

The income taxation of trusts and estates is governed by Subchapter J of the Internal Revenue Code, §§ 641 through 692. Certain similarities are apparent between Subchapter J and the income taxation of individuals (e.g., the definitions of gross income and deductible expenditures), partnerships and limited liability entities (e.g., the pass-through principle), and S corporations (e.g., the pass-through principle and the trust or estate as a separate taxable entity). Trusts also involve several important unique concepts, however, including the determination of *distributable net income* and the *tier system* of distributions to beneficiaries.

LO.1

Use working definitions with respect to trusts, estates, beneficiaries, and other parties.

WHAT IS A TRUST?

The Code does not contain a definition of a trust. However, the term usually refers to an arrangement created by a will or by an *inter vivos* (lifetime) declaration through which trustees take title to property for the purpose of protecting or conserving it for the beneficiaries.[1] Usually, trust operations are controlled by the trust document and by the fiduciary laws of the state in which the trust documents are executed.

Typically, the creation of a trust involves at least three parties: (1) The **grantor** (sometimes referred to as the settlor or donor) transfers selected assets to the trust entity. (2) The trustee, who usually is either an individual or a corporation, is charged with the fiduciary duties associated with the trust. (3) The beneficiary is designated to receive income or property from the trust.

[1]Reg. § 301.7701–4(a).

TABLE 28.1 Common Motivations for Creating a Trust

Type of Trust	Financial and Other Goals
Life insurance trust	Holds life insurance policies on the insured, removes the proceeds of the policies from the gross estate (if an irrevocable trust), and safeguards against a young or inexperienced beneficiary receiving the proceeds.
"Living" (revocable) trust	Manages assets, reduces probate costs, provides privacy for asset disposition, protects against medical or other emergencies, and provides relief from the necessity of day-to-day management of the underlying assets.
Trust for minors	Provides funds for a college education, shifts income to other taxpayers, and transfers accumulated income without permanently parting with the underlying assets.
"Blind" trust	Holds and manages the assets of the grantor without his/her input or influence (e.g., while the grantor holds political office or some other sensitive position).
Retirement trust	Manages asset contributions as dictated by the terms of a qualified retirement plan.
Divorce trust	Manages the assets of an ex-spouse and assures they are distributed in a timely fashion to specified beneficiaries (e.g., as alimony or child support).
Liquidation trust	Collects and distributes the remaining assets of a corporation that is undergoing a complete liquidation.

In some situations, fewer than three persons may be involved, as specified by the trust agreement. For example, an elderly individual who can no longer manage his or her own property (e.g., because of ill health) may create a trust under which he or she is both the grantor and the beneficiary. In this case, a family member or corporate trustee is charged with the management of the grantor's assets.

In another situation, the grantor might designate himself or herself as the trustee of the trust assets. For example, someone who wants to transfer selected assets to a minor child or elderly parent could use a trust entity to ensure that the beneficiary does not waste the property. By naming himself or herself as the trustee, the grantor retains virtual control over the property that is transferred.

Under the general rules of Subchapter J, the **grantor trusts** just described are not recognized for income tax purposes. Similarly, when only one party is involved (when the same individual is grantor, trustee, and sole beneficiary of the trust), Subchapter J rules do not apply, and the entity is ignored for income tax purposes.

Other Definitions

When the grantor transfers title of selected assets to a trust, those assets become the **corpus** (body), or principal, of the trust. Trust corpus, in most situations, earns *income*, which may be distributed to the beneficiaries, or accumulated for the future by the trustee, as the trust instrument directs.

In the typical trust, the grantor creates two types of beneficiaries: one who receives the accounting income of the trust and one who receives trust corpus that remains at the termination of the trust entity. Beneficiaries in the first category hold an *income interest* in the trust, and those in the second category hold a *remainder interest* in the trust's assets. If the grantor retains the remainder interest, the interest is known as a **reversionary interest** (corpus reverts to the grantor when the trust entity terminates).

The trust document establishes the term of the trust. The term may be for a specific number of years (a *term certain*) or until the occurrence of a specified event. For

FIGURE 28.1 Structure of a Typical Trust and Estate

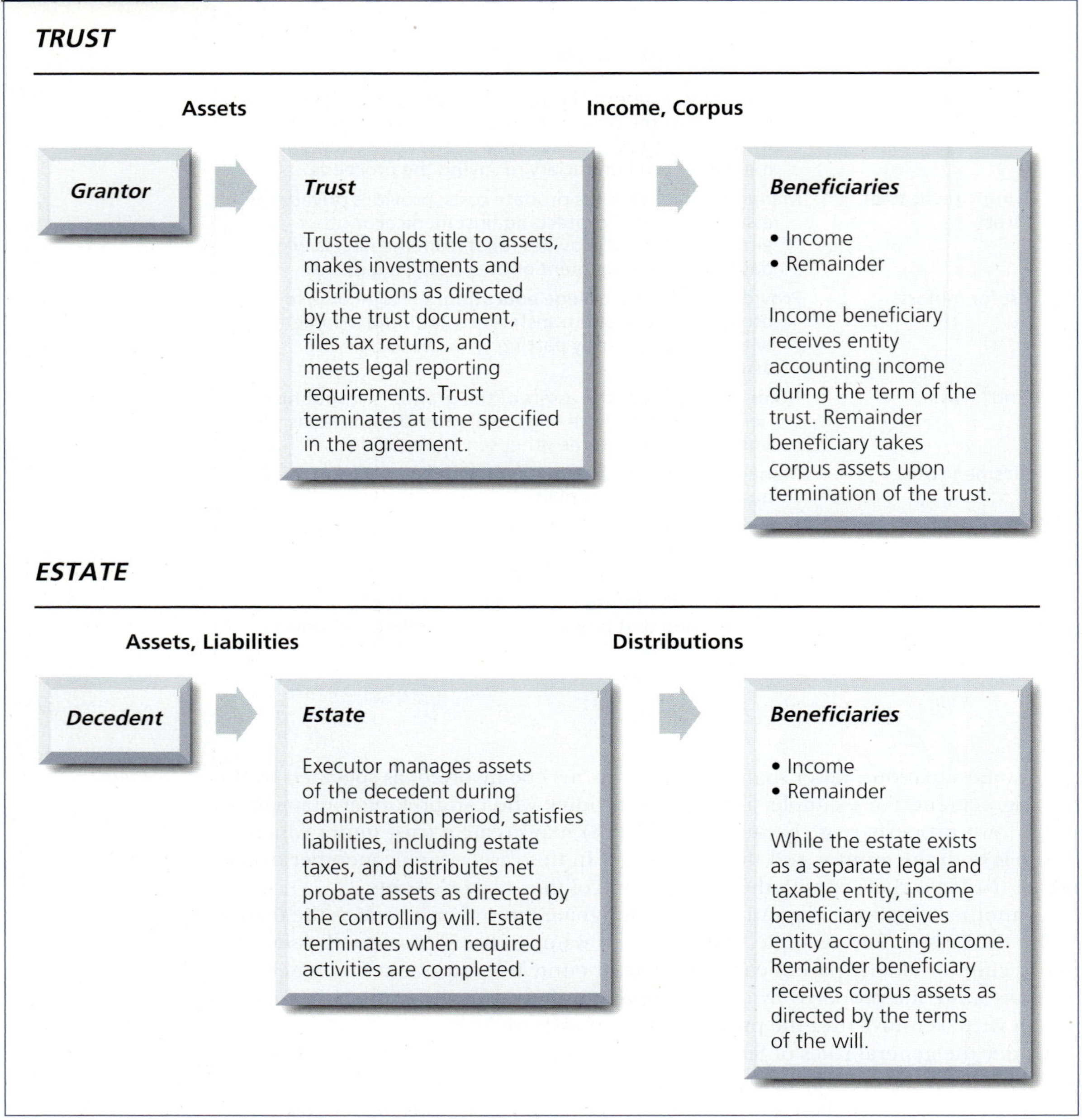

example, a trust might exist (1) for the life of the income beneficiary, in which case the income beneficiary is known as a *life tenant* in the trust corpus; (2) for the life of some other individual; (3) until the income or remainder beneficiary reaches the age of majority; or (4) until the beneficiary, or another individual, marries, receives a promotion, or reaches some specified age.

The trustee may be required to distribute the accounting income of the entity according to a distribution schedule specified in the agreement. Sometimes, however, the trustee is given more discretion with respect to the timing and nature of the distributions. If the trustee can determine, within guidelines that may be included in the trust document, either the timing of the income or corpus distributions or the specific beneficiaries who will receive them (from among those identified in the agreement), the trust is called a discretionary or **sprinkling trust**. Here, the trustee can "sprinkle" the distributions among the various beneficiaries. Family-unit income

TAX *in* *the NEWS*

Must a Trust Beneficiary Even Be Human?

Humane societies encourage the general public to care for their pets and to adopt those who need owners. But sometimes people carry this compassion even further. It is not uncommon to find provisions in a will to establish endowments to care for pets that the deceased leaves behind. Two prominent, eccentric investors recently established trusts dedicating significant funds to provide for a favorite dog, and the surviving (human) family did not take well to the idea.

- Leona Helmsley was an investor who favored building and decorating luxury hotels. When Helmsley died, her will left very little of her multibillion-dollar estate to her friends and family, perhaps not surprising for someone whose temperament had earned her the nickname "The Queen of Mean." But Helmsley's dog Trouble made out very well. The will established a $12 million trust, with income distributions to be used for Trouble's five-star kennels, dog sitters and manicurists, and other general care. With an annual income allowance averaging $600,000, Trouble could afford accommodations rivaling those available for guests at Helmsley's opulent hotels. After challenges from Helmsley's family, a judge reduced the endowment to benefit Trouble to $2 million and directed the trustee to contribute the rest of trust corpus to charity.
- Gail Posner's will created a $3 million trust to support her Chihuahua Conchita and two other dogs. The dogs received the right to continue to live in Posner's $8 million Miami Beach mansion. Posner's caretakers (e.g., bodyguards and housekeepers) inherited about $26 million in cash, and some of them were directed to live rent-free in the mansion to continue to care for the pets. Conchita owns a $15,000 diamond necklace and took over Posner's Cadillac Escalade when Posner acquired a new car. Posner's family is challenging the terms of the will, claiming that Posner was unduly influenced by the caretakers, and that Conchita's needs should not prevail over those of the relatives.

taxes can be reduced by directing income to those who are subject to lower marginal tax rates. Thus, by giving the trustee a sprinkling power, the income tax liability of the family unit can be manipulated by applying the terms of the trust agreement.

For purposes of certain provisions of Subchapter J, a trust must be classified as either a **simple trust** or a **complex trust**. A simple trust (1) is required to distribute its entire accounting income to designated beneficiaries every year, (2) has no beneficiaries that are qualifying charitable organizations, and (3) makes no distributions of trust corpus during the year. A complex trust is any trust that is not a simple trust.[2] These criteria are applied to the trust every year. Thus, every trust is classified as a complex trust in the year in which it terminates (because it will be distributing all of its corpus during that year).

WHAT IS AN ESTATE?

An estate is created upon the death of every individual. The estate is charged with collecting and conserving all of the individual's assets, satisfying all liabilities, and distributing the remaining assets to the heirs identified by state law or the will.

Typically, the creation of an estate involves at least three parties: the decedent, all of whose probate assets are transferred to the estate for disposition; the executor, who is appointed under the decedent's valid will (or the administrator, if no valid will exists); and the beneficiaries of the estate, who are to receive assets or income from the entity, as the decedent indicated in the will. An estate's operations are controlled by the probate laws of the decedent's state of residence and by the terms of the will as interpreted by the probate court.

Recall that the assets that make up the probate estate are not identical to those that constitute the gross estate for transfer tax purposes (refer to Chapter 27). Many gross estate assets are not a part of the probate estate and thus are not subject to disposition

[2]Reg. § 1.651(a)–1.

by the executor or administrator. For example, property held by the decedent as a joint tenant passes to the survivor(s) by operation of the applicable state's property law rather than through the probate estate. Proceeds of insurance policies on the life of the decedent, over which the decedent held the incidents of ownership, are not under the control of the executor or administrator. The designated beneficiaries of the policy receive the proceeds outright under the insurance contract.

An estate is a separate taxable entity. The termination date of the estate is somewhat discretionary, as it occurs when all of the assets and income of the decedent have been distributed, all estate and decedent liabilities have been satisfied, and all other business of the entity is completed. Thus, there may be an incentive to use the estate as part of an income-shifting strategy (e.g., where the income beneficiaries are subject to low marginal tax rates).

EXAMPLE 1

Maria dies, and her estate holds a high-yield investment portfolio. Paulo, the income beneficiary, is subject to a 15% marginal state and Federal income tax rate, while Julia, the remainder beneficiary, is subject to a 30% marginal rate. The tax adviser might suggest that Maria's estate delay its final distribution of assets by a year or more, to take advantage of the income tax reduction that is available before the entity terminates. ■

If an estate's existence is unduly prolonged, however, the IRS can terminate it for Federal income tax purposes after the expiration of a reasonable period for the executor to complete the duties of administration.[3]

28.2 Nature of Trust and Estate Taxation

In general, the taxable income of a trust or estate is taxed to the entity or to its beneficiaries to the extent that each has received the accounting income of the entity. Thus, Subchapter J creates a modified pass-through principle relative to the income taxation of trusts, estates, and their beneficiaries. Whoever receives the accounting income of the entity, or some portion of it, is liable for the income tax that results.

Subchapter J produces a significant amount of income tax revenue. About 3 million Forms 1041 are filed every year, and these returns reflect the following approximate amounts.

- Gross income of $200 billion.
- Taxable income of $110 billion.
- Tax liability of $25 billion.

EXAMPLE 2

Adam receives 80% of the accounting income of the Zero Trust. The trustee accumulated the other 20% of the income at her discretion under the trust agreement and added it to trust corpus. Adam is liable for income tax only on the amount of the distribution, and Zero is liable for the income tax on the accumulated portion of the income. ■

Table 28.2 summarizes the major similarities and differences between the taxation of trusts and estates and that of other pass-through entities—partnerships, limited liability entities, and S corporations.

TAX ACCOUNTING PERIODS AND METHODS

An estate or trust may use any of the tax accounting methods available to individuals. The method of accounting used by the grantor of a trust or the decedent of an estate need not carry over to the entity.

[3]Reg. § 1.641(b)–3(a).

TABLE 28.2 Tax Characteristics of Major Pass-Through Entities

Tax Treatment	Subchapter K (Partnerships, LLCs)	Subchapter S (S Corporations)	Subchapter J (Trusts, Estates)
Taxing structure	Pure pass-through, only one level of Federal income tax.	Chiefly pass-through, usually one level of Federal income tax.	Modified pass-through, Federal income tax falls on the recipient(s) of entity accounting income.
Entity-level Federal income tax?	Never.	Rarely.	Yes, if the entity retains any accounting income amounts.
Form for reporting income and expense pass-through	Schedules K and K–1, Form 1065.	Schedules K and K–1, Form 1120S.	Schedules K and K–1, Form 1041.
Subject to entity-level AMT?	No, but preferences and adjustments pass through to owners.	No, but preferences and adjustments pass through to owners.	Yes, if the entity retains any AMT-related accounting income amounts.
Controlling documents	Partnership agreement, LLC charter.	Corporate charter and bylaws.	Trust document or will, state fiduciary or probate law.

An estate has the same options for choosing a tax year as any new taxpayer. Thus, for example, the estate of a calendar year decedent dying on March 3 can select any fiscal year or report on a calendar year basis. If the calendar year basis is selected, the estate's first taxable year will include the period from March 3 to December 31. If the first or last tax year of an estate is a short year (less than one calendar year), income for that year need not be annualized.

To eliminate the possibility of deferring the taxation of fiduciary-source income simply by using a fiscal tax year, virtually all trusts (other than tax-exempt trusts) are required to use a calendar tax year.[4]

TAX RATES AND PERSONAL EXEMPTION

Congress's desire to stop trusts from being used as income-shifting devices has made the fiduciary entity the highest-taxed taxpayer in the Code.[5] The entity reaches the 35 percent marginal rate with only $11,350 of taxable income in 2011, so the grantor's ability to shift income in a tax-effective manner is nearly eliminated. Table 28.3, which lists the 2011 taxes paid by various entities on taxable income of $50,000, shows how expensive the accumulation of income within an estate or trust can be. Proper income shifting might move assets *out of* the estate or trust and into the hands of the grantor or beneficiary.

A fiduciary's dividend income and net long-term capital gain usually is taxed at a nominal rate of no more than 15 percent. In addition to the regular income

TABLE 28.3 Comparative Tax Liabilities

Filing Status/Entity	Taxable Income	Marginal Income Tax Rate (%)	2011 Tax Liability
Single	$50,000	25	$ 8,625
Married, filing jointly	50,000	15	6,650
C corporation	50,000	15	7,500
Trust or estate	50,000	35	16,465

[4] § 645.

[5] § 1(e) (see Appendix A).

tax, an estate or trust may be subject to the alternative minimum tax, as discussed below.[6]

Both trusts and estates are allowed a personal exemption in computing the fiduciary tax liability. All estates are allowed a personal exemption of $600. The exemption available to a trust depends upon the type of trust involved. A trust that is required to distribute all of its income is currently allowed an exemption of $300. All other trusts are allowed an exemption of $100 per year.[7]

The classification of trusts as to the appropriate personal exemption is similar, but not identical, to the distinction between simple and complex trusts. The classification as a simple trust is more stringent.

EXAMPLE 3

Trust Alpha is required to distribute all of its current accounting income to Susan. Trust Beta is required to distribute all of its current accounting income, one-half to Tyrone and one-half to State University, a qualifying charitable organization. The trustee of Trust Gamma can, at her discretion, distribute the current accounting income or corpus of the trust to Dr. Chapman. None of the trusts makes any corpus distributions during the year. All of the accounting income of Trust Gamma is distributed to Dr. Chapman.

Trust Alpha is a simple trust; it will receive a $300 personal exemption. Trust Beta is a complex trust; it will receive a $300 personal exemption. Trust Gamma is a complex trust; it will receive a $100 personal exemption. ■

ALTERNATIVE MINIMUM TAX

The alternative minimum tax (AMT) may apply to a trust or estate in any tax year. Given the nature and magnitude of the tax preferences, adjustments, and exemptions that determine alternative minimum taxable income (AMTI), however, most trusts and estates are unlikely to incur the tax. Nevertheless, they could be vulnerable, for example, if they are actively engaged in cashing out the stock options of a donor/decedent who was a corporate executive.

In general, derivation of AMTI for the entity follows the rules that apply to individual taxpayers. Thus, the corporate ACE adjustment does not apply to fiduciary entities, but AMTI may be created through the application of most of the other AMT preference and adjustment items discussed in Chapter 15.

The fiduciary's AMT is computed using Schedule I of Form 1041. Two full pages of the Form 1041 are dedicated to the computation of taxable income and other items when the AMT applies to the trust or estate. A minimum tax credit might be available in future years through these computations.

Like other taxpayers subject to the AMT, a trust or estate may claim an annual exemption. A trust or estate qualifies for a $22,500 annual AMT exemption. The exemption phases out at a rate of one-fourth of the amount by which AMTI exceeds $75,000.

A 26 percent AMT rate is applied to AMTI, increasing to 28 percent when AMTI in excess of the exemption reaches $175,000. In addition, estimated tax payments for the entity must include any applicable AMT liability.

28.3 Taxable Income of Trusts and Estates

LO.2

Identify the steps in determining the accounting and taxable income of a trust or estate, and the related taxable income of the beneficiaries.

Generally, the taxable income of a trust or estate is computed similarly to that for an individual. Subchapter J does, however, include several important exceptions and provisions that make it necessary to use a systematic approach to calculating the taxable income of these entities. Figure 28.2 illustrates the procedure implied by the Code, and Figure 28.3 presents a systematic computation method followed in this chapter.

[6] § 55.

[7] § 642(b).

FIGURE 28.2 **Accounting Income, Distributable Net Income, and Taxable Income of the Entity and Its Beneficiaries—The Five-Step Procedure**

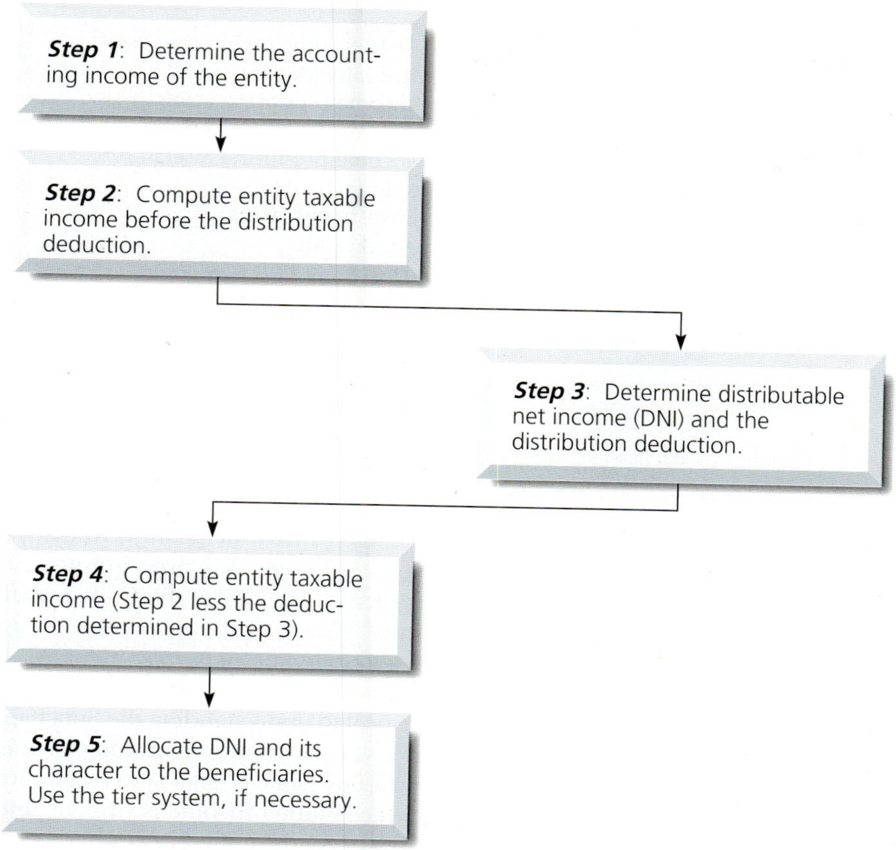

FIGURE 28.3 **Computational Template Applying the Five-Step Procedure**

Item	Totals	Accounting Income	Taxable Income	Distributable Net Income/Distribution Deduction
Income				
Income	______	______	______	
Expense	______	______	______	
Expense	______	______	______	
Personal exemption	______	______	______	
Accounting income/taxable income before the distribution deduction		*Step 1* ______	*Step 2* ______	
Personal exemption			______	______
Corpus capital gain/loss				______
Net tax-exempt income				______
Distributable net income				______
Distribution deduction			*Step 3* ______	______
Entity taxable income			*Step 4* ______	

Beneficiary taxable income is addressed in ***Step 5***.

TABLE 28.4 Common Allocations of Items to Income or Corpus

Allocable to Income	Allocable to Corpus
• Ordinary and operating net income from trust assets • Interest, dividend, rent, and royalty income • Stock dividends • One-half of fiduciary fees/ commissions	• Depreciation on business assets • Casualty gain/loss on income-producing assets • Insurance recoveries on income-producing assets • Capital gain/loss on investment assets • Stock splits • One-half of fiduciary fees/ commissions

ENTITY ACCOUNTING INCOME

The first step in determining the taxable income of a trust or estate is to compute the entity's accounting income for the period. Although this prerequisite is not apparent from a cursory reading of Subchapter J, a closer look at the Code reveals a number of references to the *income* of the entity.[8] Wherever the term *income* is used in Subchapter J without some modifier (e.g., *gross* income or *taxable* income), the statute is referring to the accounting income of the trust or estate for the tax year.

A definition of entity accounting income is critical to understanding the Subchapter J computation of fiduciary taxable income. Under state law, entity accounting income is the amount that the income beneficiary of the trust or estate is eligible to receive from the entity. More importantly, the calculation of accounting income is virtually under the control of the grantor or decedent (through a properly drafted trust agreement or will). If the document has been drafted at arm's length, a court will enforce a fiduciary's good faith efforts to carry out the specified computation of accounting income.

By allocating specific items of income and expenditure either to the income beneficiaries or to corpus, the desires of the grantor or decedent are put into effect. Table 28.4 shows typical assignments of revenue and expenditure items to fiduciary income or corpus.

Where the controlling document is silent as to whether an item should be assigned to income or corpus, state fiduciary law prevails. These allocations are an important determinant of the benefits received from the entity by its beneficiaries and the timing of those benefits.

EXAMPLE 4

The Arnold Trust is a simple trust. Mrs. Bennett is its sole beneficiary. In the current year, the trust earns $20,000 in taxable interest and $15,000 in tax-exempt interest. In addition, the trust recognizes an $8,000 long-term capital gain. The trustee assesses a fee of $11,000 for the year. If the trust agreement allocates fees and capital gains to corpus, trust accounting income is $35,000, and Mrs. Bennett receives that amount. Thus, the income beneficiary receives no immediate benefit from the trust's capital gain, and she bears none of the financial burden of the fiduciary's fees.

Interest income ($20,000 + $15,000)	$35,000
Long-term capital gain—allocable to corpus	–0–
Fiduciary's fees—allocable to corpus	(–0–)
Trust accounting income	$35,000

■

[8] For example, see §§ 651(a)(1), 652(a), and 661(a)(1).

EXAMPLE 5

Assume the same facts as in Example 4, except that the trust agreement allocates the fiduciary's fees to income. The trust accounting income is $24,000, and Mrs. Bennett receives that amount.

Interest income ($20,000 + $15,000)	$ 35,000
Long-term capital gain—allocable to corpus	–0–
Fiduciary's fees	(11,000)
Trust accounting income	$ 24,000

EXAMPLE 6

Assume the same facts as in Example 4, except that the trust agreement allocates to income all capital gains and losses and one-half of the trustee's commissions. The trust accounting income is $37,500, and Mrs. Bennett receives that amount.

Interest income ($20,000 + $15,000)	$35,000
Long-term capital gain	8,000
Fiduciary's fees—one-half allocable to corpus	(5,500)
Trust accounting income	$37,500

GROSS INCOME

The gross income of an estate or trust is similar to that of an individual. In determining the gain or loss to be recognized by an estate or trust upon the sale or other taxable disposition of assets, the rules for basis determination are similar to those applicable to other taxpayers. Thus, an estate's basis for property received from a decedent is stepped up or stepped down to the gross estate valuation (refer to Chapter 13 for a more detailed discussion). Property received as a gift (the usual case in most trust arrangements) usually takes the donor's basis. Property purchased by the trust from a third party is assigned a basis equal to the purchase price.

Property Distributions

In general, the entity does not recognize gain or loss upon its distribution of property to a beneficiary under the provisions of the will or trust document. The distributed property has the same basis to the beneficiary of the distribution as it did to the estate or trust. Moreover, the distribution absorbs distributable net income (DNI) and qualifies for a distribution deduction (both of which are explained later in this chapter) to the extent of the lesser of the distributed asset's basis to the beneficiary or the asset's fair market value as of the distribution date.[9]

EXAMPLE 7
THE BIG PICTURE

Return to the facts of *The Big Picture* on p. 28-2. Assume that Anna has established the Jiang Family Trust. The trust distributes a painting, basis of $40,000 and fair market value of $90,000, to beneficiary Sally. Sally's basis in the painting is $40,000. The distribution absorbs $40,000 of the Jiang Trust's DNI, and the trust claims a $40,000 distribution deduction relative to the transaction. ■

EXAMPLE 8
THE BIG PICTURE

Assume the same facts as in Example 7, except that the Jiang Trust's basis in the painting is $100,000. Sally's basis in the painting is $100,000. The distribution absorbs $90,000 of the Jiang Trust's DNI, and the trust claims a $90,000 distribution deduction. ■

A trustee or executor can *elect* to recognize gain or loss with respect to all of the entity's in-kind property distributions for the year. If the election is made, the beneficiary's basis in the asset is equal to the asset's fair market value as of the distribution

[9] § 643(e).

TAX *in the NEWS*

A Trend toward Dynasty Trusts

In a continuing attempt to discourage tax-motivated income shifting among family members, steep income tax rates on estates and trusts are also being seen at the state level. Although a few states (e.g., Alaska, Nevada, Texas, and Washington) do not impose any income tax on fiduciary entities, those that do are tending to increase their rates as part of their efforts to solve budget woes.

Other states, however, have relaxed some of the rules that affect trusts. In such cases the objectives are to attract dollars to the state and to expand opportunities for attorneys, tax advisers, and other professionals who create and administer the entities.

One current development might be traced to the existence of the generation-skipping tax (GST), discussed in Chapter 27. After that tax was enacted, wealthy individuals and their advisers convinced about half of the states to allow a trust to survive for hundreds of years or indefinitely, by modifying the time-honored limitation of the "rule against perpetuities" (i.e., a life in being plus 21 years).

If a trust can survive for a long period of time, without making distributions or terminations that cause the GST, trust corpus can grow in a steady and tax-free manner. Wealthy individuals use these "dynasty trusts" as a form of inheritance, and many states also allow the trust assets to be protected from claims of the grantor's creditors.

Dynasty trusts operate like growth stocks. They minimize income distributions by investing profits and new capital in the family businesses, artwork, and multiple homes for the beneficiaries. The trust holds the title to these hard assets so that there is no income, gift, generation-skipping, or estate tax when younger generations take possession.

Some wealthy individuals do not want their children to have access to so much wealth that they never will need to work. Dynasty trusts can be used to accomplish this result.

date. The distribution absorbs DNI and qualifies for a distribution deduction to the extent of the asset's fair market value. Note, however, that the related-party rules can restrict an estate's or trust's deduction for losses. Generally, related parties include a trust, its trustee, its grantor, and its beneficiaries, as well as an estate, its executor, and its beneficiaries.

EXAMPLE 9

The Green Estate distributes an antique piano, basis to Green of $10,000 and fair market value of $15,000, to beneficiary Kyle. The executor elects that the estate recognize the related $5,000 gain on the distribution. Accordingly, Kyle's basis in the piano is $15,000 ($10,000 basis to Green + $5,000 gain recognized). Without the election, the estate would not recognize any gain, and Kyle's basis in the piano would be $10,000. ■

EXAMPLE 10

Assume the same facts as in Example 9, except that Green's basis in the piano is $18,000. The executor elects that the estate recognize the related $3,000 loss on the distribution. Accordingly, Kyle's basis in the piano is $15,000 ($18,000 – $3,000). Without the election, the estate would not recognize any loss, and Kyle's basis in the piano would be $18,000. The estate cannot deduct this loss, however. Because an estate and its beneficiaries are related parties, realized losses cannot be recognized immediately.[10] The loss could be recognized if Kyle later sells the piano to an unrelated party. ■

Income in Respect of a Decedent

The gross income of a trust or estate includes **income in respect of a decedent (IRD)** that the entity receives.[11] For a cash basis decedent, IRD includes accrued salary, interest, rent, and other income items that were not constructively received before death. For both cash and accrual basis decedents, IRD includes, for example, death benefits from qualified retirement plans and deferred compensation contracts.

The tax consequences of IRD can be summarized as follows.

- The fair market value of the right to IRD on the appropriate valuation date is included in the decedent's gross estate. Thus, it is subject to the Federal estate tax.

[10] § 267(b)(13).

[11] § 691.

TAX *in the NEWS*

Coordinate Your Deductions

The deduction under § 691(c) may be one of the more obscure provisions of the tax law, but its benefits can add up fast. The deduction is allowed on the tax return of the recipient of income in respect of a decedent (IRD). IRD often is received by the estate of the decedent or a trust that he or she created under the will or during lifetime. The deduction is for the Federal estate tax attributable to the IRD item. For an individual, it is a miscellaneous itemized deduction *not* subject to the 2 percent-of-AGI floor.

Because IRD often includes the value of the survivorship feature on pensions and other retirement plans and assets, the amount subject to the estate tax can be quite high. Thus, when computing the current-year income tax for the IRD recipient, the § 691(c) deduction can be extremely valuable in offsetting the IRD received.

For example, suppose that a decedent's IRA balance generates $450,000 in attributable estate tax. If the recipient of the IRA takes the net-of-tax distribution in one year, the § 691(c) deduction shelters $450,000 in gross income and may be worth over $150,000 in Federal income taxes saved.

But taking the § 691(c) deduction is more complex than it looks. Because different tax advisers often prepare the Form 706 for the estate and the Form 1040 or 1041 for the IRD recipient, the § 691(c) deduction can get lost altogether or at least be miscomputed. When the IRD is paid out over several years, computing the § 691(c) deduction can become complex. And some tax professionals do not know the law well enough to track down the deduction, while tax software and IRS forms and publications say relatively little about it.

- The decedent's basis in the property carries over to the recipient (the estate or heirs). There is no step-up or step-down in the basis of IRD items.
- The recipient of the income recognizes gain or loss, measured by the difference between the amount realized and the adjusted basis of the IRD in the hands of the decedent. The character of the gain or loss depends upon the treatment that it would have received had it been realized by the decedent before death. Thus, if the decedent would have realized capital gain, the recipient must do likewise.[12]
- Expenses related to the IRD (such as interest, taxes, and depletion) that properly were not reported on the final income tax return of the decedent may be claimed by the recipient. These items are known as **expenses in respect of a decedent**. Typically, such expenses also include fiduciary fees, commissions paid to dispose of estate assets, and state income taxes payable. They are deductible for both Federal estate and income tax purposes, *for* or *from* AGI as would have been the case for the decedent.
- If the IRD item would have created an AMT preference or adjustment for the decedent (e.g., with respect to the collection of certain tax-exempt interest by the entity), an identical AMT item is created for the recipient.

EXAMPLE 11

Amanda died on July 13 of the current year. On August 2, her estate received a check (before deductions) for $1,200 from Amanda's former employer; this was Amanda's compensation for the last pay period of her life. On November 23, Amanda's estate received a $45,000 distribution from her employer's qualified profit sharing plan, the full amount to which she was entitled under the plan. Both Amanda and the estate are calendar year, cash basis taxpayers.

The last salary payment and the profit sharing plan distribution constitute IRD to Amanda's estate. Amanda had earned these items during her lifetime, and the estate had an enforceable right to receive each of them after Amanda's death. Consequently, Amanda's gross estate includes $46,200 with respect to these two items. However, the income tax basis to the estate for these items is not stepped up (from zero to $1,200 and $45,000, respectively) upon distribution to the estate. Therefore, the estate must report gross income of $46,200 with respect to the IRD items upon their receipt [($1,200 + $45,000) amounts realized – ($0) adjusted bases]. ■

[12]To mitigate the effect of double taxation (imposition of both the estate tax and the income tax), § 691(c) allows the recipient an income tax deduction for the incremental estate tax attributable to the net IRD. For individual recipients, this is an itemized deduction, not subject to the 2%-of-AGI floor.

Including the IRD in both the taxpayer's gross estate and the gross income of the estate may seem harsh. Nonetheless, the tax consequences of IRD are similar to the treatment that applies to all of a taxpayer's earned income. The item is subject to income tax upon receipt, and to the extent that it is not consumed by the taxpayer before death, it is included in the gross estate.

EXAMPLE 12

Assume the same facts as in Example 11, except that Amanda was an accrual basis taxpayer. IRD now includes only the $45,000 distribution from the qualified retirement plan. Amanda's last paycheck is included in the gross income of her own last return (January 1 through date of death). The $1,200 salary is already recognized properly under Amanda's usual method of tax accounting. It does not constitute IRD and is not gross income when received by the executor. ■

EXAMPLE 13

Assume the same facts as in Example 11. Amanda's last paycheck was reduced by $165 for state income taxes that were withheld by her employer. The $165 tax payment is an expense in respect of a decedent and is allowed as a deduction on *both* Amanda's estate tax return *and* the estate's income tax return. ■

ORDINARY DEDUCTIONS

As a general rule, the taxable income of an estate or trust is similar to that of an individual.[13] Deductions are allowed for ordinary and necessary expenses paid or incurred in carrying on a trade or business; for the production or collection of income; for the management, conservation, or maintenance of property; and in connection with the determination, collection, or refund of any tax.[14] Reasonable administration expenses, including fiduciary fees and litigation costs in connection with the duties of administration, also can be deductible.

Expenses attributable to the production or collection of tax-exempt income are not deductible.[15] The amount of the disallowed deduction is found by using a formula based upon the composition of the income elements of entity accounting income for the year of the deduction. The § 212 deduction is apportioned without regard to the accounting income allocation of such expenses to income or to corpus. The deductibility of the fees is determined strictly by the Code (under §§ 212 and 265), and the allocation of expenditures to income and to corpus is controlled by the trust agreement or will or by state law.

Under § 642(g), amounts deductible as administration expenses or losses for estate tax purposes (under §§ 2053 and 2054) cannot be claimed by the estate for income tax purposes, unless the estate files a waiver of the estate tax deduction. Although these expenses cannot be deducted twice, they may be allocated between Forms 706 and 1041 as the fiduciary sees fit; they need not be claimed in their entirety on either return.[16] The prohibition against double deductions does not apply to expenses in respect of a decedent.

Trusts and estates are allowed cost recovery deductions. However, such deductions are assigned proportionately among the recipients of entity accounting income.[17]

EXAMPLE 14

Lisa and Martin are the equal income beneficiaries of the Needle Trust. Under the terms of the trust agreement, the trustee has complete discretion as to the timing of the distributions from Needle's current accounting income. The trust agreement allocates all depreciation expense to income. In the current year, the trustee distributes 40% of the current trust accounting income to Lisa and 40% to Martin; thus, 20% of the income is accumulated. The depreciation deduction allowable to Needle is $100,000. This deduction is allocated among the trust and its beneficiaries on the basis of the distribution of current accounting income: Lisa and Martin each can claim a $40,000 deduction, and the trust can deduct $20,000. ■

[13] § 641(b).
[14] §§ 162 and 212.
[15] § 265.
[16] Reg. § 1.642(g)–2.
[17] § 167(h) and §§ 611(b)(3) and (4).

EXAMPLE 15

Assume the same facts as in Example 14, except that the trust agreement allocates all depreciation expense to corpus. Lisa and Martin both still claim a $40,000 depreciation deduction, and Needle retains its $20,000 deduction. The Code assigns the depreciation deduction proportionately to the recipients of current entity accounting income. Allocation of depreciation to income or to corpus by the trust agreement is irrelevant in determining which party can properly claim the deduction. ■

When a trust sells property received by transfer from the grantor, the amount of depreciation subject to recapture includes the depreciation claimed by the grantor before the transfer of the property to the trust. However, depreciation recapture potential disappears at death.

EXAMPLE 16

Jaime transferred an asset to the Shoulder Trust via a lifetime gift. The asset's total depreciation recapture potential was $40,000. If the trust sells the asset at a gain, it will recognize ordinary income not to exceed $40,000. Had Jaime transferred the asset after his death to his estate through a bequest, the $40,000 recapture potential would have disappeared. ■

If a trust or estate operates a trade or business, the entity may be eligible for the domestic production activities deduction (DPAD).[18] Computation of qualified production activities income (QPAI) is made at the entity level. Each beneficiary receives, as a pass-through from the entity, his or her share of QPAI and the W–2 wages paid, based on the proportion of entity accounting income received. The DPAD then can be claimed at the beneficiary level. In the case of an individual beneficiary, the DPAD is subject to the modified AGI limitation. See Chapter 7 for further discussion of the DPAD.

DEDUCTIONS FOR LOSSES

An estate or trust is allowed an income tax deduction for casualty or theft losses not covered by insurance or other arrangements. Such losses may also be deductible by an estate for Federal estate tax purposes under § 2054. However, an estate is not allowed an income tax deduction unless the estate tax deduction is waived.[19]

The net operating loss (NOL) deduction is available for estates and trusts (i.e., where trade or business income is generated). The carryback of an NOL may reduce the distributable net income of the trust or estate for the carryback year and therefore affect the amount taxed to the beneficiaries for that year.

Except for the possibility of unused losses in the year of termination (discussed later in the chapter), the net capital losses of an estate or trust are used only on the fiduciary income tax return. The tax treatment of these losses is the same as for individual taxpayers.

CHARITABLE CONTRIBUTIONS

An estate or complex trust is allowed a deduction for contributions to charitable organizations under certain conditions.

- The contribution is made pursuant to the will or trust instrument, and its amount is determinable using the language of that document.
- The recipient is a qualified organization. For this purpose, qualified organizations include the same charities for which individual and corporate

[18] § 199(d)(1).

[19] See Reg. § 1.642(g)–1 for requirements as to the statement waiving the estate tax deduction. In addition, see Reg. §§ 1.165–7(c) and 1.165–8(b), requiring that a statement be filed to allow an income tax deduction for such losses.

donors are allowed deductions, except that estates and trusts are permitted a deduction for contributions to certain foreign charitable organizations.
- Generally, the contribution is claimed in the tax year paid, but a fiduciary can treat amounts paid in the year immediately following as a deduction for the preceding year.[20] Under this rule, estates and complex trusts receive more liberal treatment than individuals or C corporations.

Unlike the charitable contribution deductions of individuals and corporations, the deductions of estates and complex trusts are not limited (e.g., to a percentage of taxable or adjusted gross income). Nonetheless, an entity's charitable contribution may not be fully deductible. Specifically, the deduction is limited to amounts included in the gross income of the entity in the year of the contribution.[21]

A contribution is deemed to have been made proportionately from each of the income elements of entity accounting income. However, if the will or trust agreement requires that the contribution be made from a specific type of income or from the current income from a specified asset, the contribution will not have to be allocated to taxable and tax-exempt income.

EXAMPLE 17
THE BIG PICTURE

Return to the facts of *The Big Picture* on p. 28-2. Again assume that Anna has established the Jiang Family trust. The trust has 2011 gross rent income of $80,000, expenses attributable to the rents of $60,000, and tax-exempt interest from state bonds of $20,000. Under the trust agreement, the trustee is to pay 30% of the annual trust accounting income to the United Way, a qualifying organization. Accordingly, the trustee pays $12,000 to the charity in 2012 (i.e., 30% × $40,000). The charitable contribution deduction allowed for 2011 is $9,600 [($80,000/$100,000) × $12,000]. ■

EXAMPLE 18
THE BIG PICTURE

Assume the same facts as Example 17, except that the trust instrument also requires that the contribution be paid from the net rent income. The agreement controls, and the allocation formula need not be applied. The entire $12,000 is allowed as a charitable deduction. ■

LO.3

Illustrate the uses and implications of distributable net income.

DEDUCTION FOR DISTRIBUTIONS TO BENEFICIARIES

The modified pass-through approach of Subchapter J is embodied in the deduction allowed to trusts and estates for the distributions made to beneficiaries during the year. Some portion of any distribution that a beneficiary receives from a trust may be subject to income tax on his or her own return. At the same time, the distributing entity is allowed a deduction for some or all of the distribution. Consequently, the modified pass-through principle of Subchapter J is implemented. A good analogy is to the taxability of corporate profits distributed to employees as taxable wages. The corporation is allowed a deduction for the payment, but the employee receives gross income in the form of compensation.

A critical value that is used in computing the amount of the entity's distribution deduction is **distributable net income (DNI)**. As it is defined in Subchapter J, DNI serves several functions.

- DNI is the maximum amount of the distribution on which the beneficiaries can be taxed.[22]
- DNI is the maximum amount that the entity can use as a distribution deduction for the year.[23]

[20] § 642(c)(1) and Reg. § 1.642(c)–1(b).
[21] Reg. §§ 1.642(c)–3(b) and (c).
[22] §§ 652(a) and 662(a).
[23] §§ 651(b) and 661(c).

- The makeup of DNI carries over to the beneficiaries (the items of income and expenses retain their DNI character in the hands of the distributees).[24]

Subchapter J defines DNI in a circular manner, however. The DNI value is necessary to determine the entity's distribution deduction and therefore its taxable income for the year. Nonetheless, the Code defines DNI as a modification of the entity's taxable income itself. Using the systematic approach to determining the taxable income of the entity and of its beneficiaries, as shown earlier in Figure 28.2, one must first compute *taxable income before the distribution deduction*, modify that amount to determine DNI and the distribution deduction, return to the calculation of *taxable income*, and apply the deduction that has resulted.

Taxable income before the distribution deduction includes all of the entity's items of gross income, deductions, gains, losses, and exemptions for the year. Therefore, to compute this amount, (1) determine the appropriate personal exemption for the year and (2) account for all of the other gross income and deductions of the entity.

The next step in Figure 28.2 is the determination of *distributable net income*, computed by making the following adjustments to the entity's *taxable income before the distribution deduction*.[25]

- Add back the personal exemption.
- Add back *net* tax-exempt interest. To arrive at this amount, reduce the total tax-exempt interest by charitable contributions and by related expenses not deductible under § 265.
- Add back the entity's net capital losses.
- Subtract any net capital gains allocable to corpus. In other words, the only net capital gains included in DNI are those attributable to income beneficiaries or to charitable contributions.

Since taxable income before the distribution deduction is computed by deducting all of the expenses of the entity (whether they were allocated to income or to corpus), DNI is reduced by expenses that are allocated to corpus. The effect is to reduce the taxable income of the income beneficiaries. The actual distributions to the beneficiaries exceed DNI because the distributions are not reduced by expenses allocated to corpus. Aside from this shortcoming of Subchapter J, DNI offers a good approximation of the current-year economic income available for distribution to the entity's income beneficiaries.

DNI includes the net tax-exempt interest income of the entity, so that amount must be removed from DNI in computing the distribution deduction. Moreover, for estates and complex trusts, the amount actually distributed during the year may include discretionary distributions of income and distributions of corpus permissible under the will or trust instrument. Thus, the distribution deduction for estates and complex trusts is computed as the lesser of (1) the deductible portion of DNI or (2) the taxable amount actually distributed to the beneficiaries during the year. For a simple trust, however, full distribution always is assumed, relative to both the entity and its beneficiaries, in a manner similar to pass-through entities.

EXAMPLE 19

The Zinc Trust is a simple trust. Because of severe liquidity problems, its 2011 accounting income is not distributed to its sole beneficiary, Mark, until early in 2012. Zinc is still allowed a full distribution deduction for, and Mark is still taxed upon, the entity's 2011 income in 2011. ■

[24]§§ 652(b) and 662(b).

[25]These and other (less common) adjustments are detailed in § 643.

EXAMPLE 20

The Pork Trust is required to distribute its current accounting income annually to its sole income beneficiary, Barbara. Capital gains and losses and all other expenses are allocable to corpus. For the current year, the trust records the following items.

Dividend income	$25,000
Taxable interest income	15,000
Tax-exempt interest income	20,000
Net long-term capital gain	10,000
Fiduciary fees	6,000

Item	Totals		Accounting Income		Taxable Income	Distributable Net Income/ Distribution Deduction
Dividend income	$25,000		$25,000		$ 25,000	
Taxable interest income	15,000		15,000		15,000	
Tax-exempt interest income	20,000		20,000			
Net long-term capital gain	10,000				10,000	
Fiduciary fees	6,000				(4,000)	
Personal exemption					(300)	
Accounting income/taxable income before the distribution deduction		*Step 1*	$60,000	*Step 2*	$ 45,700	$ 45,700
Personal exemption						300
Corpus capital gain/loss						(10,000)
Net tax-exempt income						18,000
Distributable net income						$ 54,000
Distribution deduction				*Step 3*	(36,000)	
Entity taxable income				*Step 4*	$ 9,700	

Step 1. Trust accounting income is $60,000; this includes the tax-exempt interest income, but not the fees or the capital gains, pursuant to the trust document. Barbara receives $60,000 from the trust for the current year.

Step 2. Taxable income before the distribution deduction is computed as directed by the Code. The tax-exempt interest is excluded under § 103. Only a portion of the fees is deductible because some of the fees are traceable to the tax-exempt income. The trust receives a $300 personal exemption as it is required to distribute its annual trust accounting income.

Step 3. DNI and the distribution deduction reflect the required adjustments. The distribution deduction is the lesser of the distributed amount ($60,000) or the deductible portion of DNI ($54,000 – $18,000 net tax-exempt income).

Step 4. Finally, return to the computation of the taxable income of the Pork Trust. A simple test should be applied at this point to ensure that the proper figure for the trust's taxable income has been determined. On what is Pork to be taxed? All of the trust's gross income has been distributed to Barbara except the $10,000 net long-term capital gain. The $300 personal exemption reduces the trust's taxable income to $9,700. ■

EXAMPLE 21

The Quick Trust is required to distribute all of its current accounting income equally to its two beneficiaries, Faith and the First Methodist Church, a qualifying charitable organization. Capital gains and losses and depreciation expenses are allocable to income. Fiduciary fees are allocable to corpus. In the current year, Quick incurs various items as indicated.

Item	**Totals**		**Accounting Income**		**Taxable Income**	**Distributable Net Income/ Distribution Deduction**
Rent income	$100,000		$100,000		$100,000	
Expenses—rent income	30,000		(30,000)		(30,000)	
Depreciation—rent income	15,000		(15,000)			
Net long-term capital gain	20,000		20,000		20,000	
Charitable contribution					(37,500)	
Fiduciary fees	18,000				(18,000)	
Personal exemption					(300)	
Accounting income/taxable income before the distribution deduction		*Step 1*	$ 75,000	*Step 2*	$ 34,200	$34,200
Personal exemption						300
Corpus capital gain/loss						
Net tax-exempt income						
Distributable net income						$34,500
Distribution deduction				*Step 3*	(34,500)	
Entity taxable income				*Step 4*	($ 300)	

Step 1. Trust accounting income of $75,000 reflects the indicated allocations of items to income and to corpus. Each income beneficiary receives $37,500.

Step 2. In the absence of tax-exempt income, a deduction is allowed for the full amount of the fiduciary's fees. Quick is a complex trust, but since it is required to distribute its full accounting income annually, a $300 exemption is allowed. The trust properly does not deduct any depreciation for the rental property. The depreciation deduction is available only to the recipients of the entity's accounting income for the period. Thus, the deduction will be split equally between Faith and the church. The deduction probably is of no direct value to the church, a tax-exempt organization. The trust's charitable contribution deduction is based upon the $37,500 that the charity actually received (one-half of trust accounting income).

Step 3. As there is no tax-exempt income, the only adjustment needed to compute DNI is to add back the trust's personal exemption. Subchapter J requires no adjustment for the charitable contribution. DNI is computed only from the perspective of Faith, who also received $37,500 from the trust.

Step 4. Finally, the trust's taxable income before the distribution deduction is reduced by the distribution deduction to produce the trust's taxable income of ($300). Perform the simple test (referred to above in the previous example) to ensure that the proper taxable income for the Quick Trust has been computed. All of the trust's gross income has been distributed to Faith and the church. As is the case with most trusts that distribute all of their accounting income, the Quick Trust "wastes" the personal exemption. ■

TAX CREDITS

An estate or trust may claim the foreign tax credit to the extent that it is not passed through to the beneficiaries.[26] Similarly, other credits must be apportioned between the estate or trust and the beneficiaries on the basis of the entity accounting income allocable to each.

[26] §§ 642(a)(1) and 901.

28.4 Taxation of Beneficiaries

The beneficiaries of an estate or trust receive taxable income from the entity under the modified pass-through principle of Subchapter J. DNI determines the maximum amount that can be taxed to the beneficiaries for any tax year. The constitution of DNI also carries over to the beneficiaries (e.g., net long-term capital gains and dividends retain their character when they are distributed from the entity to the beneficiary).

The timing of any tax consequences to the beneficiary of a trust or estate presents a problem only when the parties involved use different tax years. A beneficiary must include in gross income an amount based upon the DNI of the trust for any taxable year or years of the trust or estate ending with or within his or her taxable year.[27]

EXAMPLE 22

An estate uses a fiscal year ending on March 31 for tax purposes. Its sole income beneficiary is a calendar year taxpayer. For calendar year 2011, the beneficiary reports whatever income that was assignable to her for the entity's fiscal year April 1, 2010, to March 31, 2011. If the estate is terminated by December 31, 2011, the beneficiary must also include any income assignable to her for the short year. This could result in a bunching of income in 2011. ■

DISTRIBUTIONS BY SIMPLE TRUSTS

The amount taxable to the beneficiaries of a simple trust is limited by the trust's DNI. However, since DNI includes net tax-exempt income, the amount included in the gross income of the beneficiaries could be less than DNI. When there is more than one income beneficiary, the elements of DNI must be apportioned ratably according to the amount required to be distributed currently to each.

EXAMPLE 23

A simple trust has ordinary income of $40,000, a long-term capital gain of $15,000 (allocable to corpus), and a trustee commission expense of $4,000 (payable from corpus). The two income beneficiaries, Allie and Bart, are entitled to the trust's annual accounting income, based on shares of 75% and 25%, respectively.

Although Allie receives $30,000 as her share (75% × $40,000 trust accounting income), she will be allocated DNI of only $27,000 (75% × $36,000). Likewise, Bart is entitled to receive $10,000 (25% × $40,000), but he will be allocated DNI of only $9,000 (25% × $36,000). The $15,000 capital gain is taxed to the trust. ■

DISTRIBUTIONS BY ESTATES AND COMPLEX TRUSTS

Typically, an estate or complex trust makes only discretionary distributions. In those cases, the DNI is apportioned ratably according to the distributed amounts.

A computational problem arises with estates and complex trusts when more than one beneficiary receives a distribution from the entity and the controlling document does not require a distribution of the entire accounting income of the entity.

EXAMPLE 24

The trustee of the Wilson Trust has the discretion to distribute the income or corpus of the trust in any proportion between the two beneficiaries of the trust, Wong and Washington. Under the trust instrument, Wong must receive $15,000 from the trust every year. In the current year, the trust's accounting income is $50,000, and its DNI is $40,000. The trustee pays $35,000 to Wong and $25,000 to Washington for the current year. ■

How is Wilson's DNI to be divided between Wong and Washington? Several arbitrary methods of allocating DNI between the beneficiaries could be devised. Subchapter J resolves the problem by creating a two-tier system to govern the taxation of

---

[27] §§ 652(c) and 662(c).

beneficiaries in such situations.[28] The tier system determines which distributions will be included in the gross income of the beneficiaries in full, which will be included in part, and which will not be included at all.

Income that is required to be distributed currently, whether or not it is distributed, is categorized as a *first-tier distribution.* All other amounts properly paid, credited, or required to be distributed are considered to be *second-tier distributions.*[29] A formula is used to allocate DNI among the appropriate beneficiaries when only first-tier distributions are made and those amounts exceed DNI.

$$\frac{\text{First-tier distributions to the beneficiary}}{\text{First-tier distributions to all beneficiaries}} \times \text{Distributable net income} = \text{Beneficiary's share of distributable net income}$$

When both first-tier and second-tier distributions are made and the first-tier distributions exceed DNI, the above formula is applied to the first-tier distributions. In this case, none of the second-tier distributions are taxed because all of the DNI has been allocated to the first-tier beneficiaries.

If both first-tier and second-tier distributions are made and the first-tier distributions do not exceed DNI, but the total of both first-tier and second-tier distributions does exceed DNI, the second-tier beneficiaries must recognize income as shown below.

$$\frac{\text{Second-tier distributions to the beneficiary}}{\text{Second-tier distributions to all beneficiaries}} \times \text{Remaining distributable net income (after first-tier distributions)} = \text{Beneficiary's share of distributable net income}$$

EXAMPLE 25

The trustee of the Gray Trust is required to distribute $10,000 per year to both Harriet and Wally, the two beneficiaries of the entity. In addition, the trustee is empowered to distribute other amounts of trust income or corpus at his sole discretion. In the current year, the trust reports accounting income of $60,000 and DNI of $50,000. However, the trustee distributes only the required $10,000 each to Harriet and to Wally. The balance of the income is accumulated and added to trust corpus.

In this case, only first-tier distributions have been made, but the total amount of the distributions does not exceed DNI for the year. Although DNI is the maximum amount that is included by the beneficiaries for the year, they can include no more in gross income than is distributed by the entity. Thus, both Harriet and Wally are subject to tax on $10,000 as their proportionate shares of DNI. ■

EXAMPLE 26

Assume the same facts as in Example 25, except that DNI is $12,000. Harriet and Wally each receive $10,000, but they cannot be taxed in total on more than DNI. Each is taxed on $6,000 [$12,000 DNI × ($10,000/$20,000 of the first-tier distributions)]. ■

EXAMPLE 27

Return to the facts in Example 24. Wong receives a first-tier distribution of $15,000. Second-tier distributions include $20,000 to Wong and $25,000 to Washington. Wilson Trust's DNI is $40,000. The DNI is allocated between Wong and Washington as follows.

[28] §§ 662(a)(1) and (2).

[29] Reg. §§ 1.662(a)–2 and –3.

(1)	**First-tier distributions**	
	To Wong	$15,000 DNI
	To Washington	–0–
	Remaining DNI = $25,000 ($40,000 DNI – $15,000 distributed)	
(2)	**Second-tier distributions**	
	To Wong [(20/45) × $25,000]	$11,111 DNI
	To Washington [(25/45) × $25,000]	13,889 DNI ■

Separate Share Rule

For the sole purpose of determining the amount of DNI for a complex trust or estate with more than one beneficiary, the substantially separate and independent shares of different beneficiaries in the trust or estate are treated as *separate* trusts or estates.[30]

The separate share rule is designed to prevent the inequity that results if the corpus payments are treated under the regular rules applicable to second-tier beneficiaries. The rule also results in the availability of extra entity personal exemptions and in a greater use of lower entity tax brackets.

EXAMPLE 28

A trustee has the discretion to distribute or accumulate income on behalf of Greg and Hannah (in equal shares). The trustee also has the power to invade corpus for the benefit of either beneficiary to the extent of that beneficiary's one-half interest in the trust. For the current year, DNI is $10,000. Of this amount, $5,000 is distributed to Greg, and $5,000 is accumulated on behalf of Hannah. In addition, the trustee pays $20,000 from corpus to Greg.

Without the separate share rule, Greg is taxed on $10,000 (the full amount of the DNI). With the separate share rule, Greg is taxed on only $5,000 (his share of the DNI) and receives the $20,000 corpus distribution tax-free. The trust will be taxed on Hannah's $5,000 share of the DNI that is accumulated. ■

CHARACTER OF INCOME

Consistent with the modified pass-through principle of Subchapter J, various classes of income (e.g., dividends, passive or portfolio gain and loss, AMT preferences and adjustments, and tax-exempt interest) retain the same character for the beneficiaries that they had when they were received by the entity. If there are multiple beneficiaries *and* if all of the DNI is distributed, a problem arises in allocating the various classes of income among the beneficiaries.

Distributions are treated as consisting of the same proportion as the items that enter into the computation of DNI. This allocation does not apply, however, if the governing instrument specifically allocates different classes of income to different beneficiaries.[31]

$$\frac{\text{Beneficiary's total share of DNI distributed}}{\text{Total DNI distributed}} \times \text{Total of DNI element deemed distributed (e.g., tax-exempt interest)} = \text{Beneficiary's share of the DNI element}$$

If the entity distributes only a part of its DNI, the amount of a particular class of DNI that is deemed distributed must first be determined.

[30] § 663(c); Reg. § 1.663(c)–1(a).

[31] Reg. § 1.662(b)–1 seems to allow special allocations, but see *Harkness v. U.S.*, 72–2 USTC ¶9740, 30 AFTR 2d 72–5754, 469 F.2d 310 (Ct.Cls., 1972).

$$\frac{\text{Total distribution}}{\text{Total distributable net income}} \times \text{Total of a particular class of distributable net income} = \text{Total of the DNI element deemed distributed (e.g., tax-exempt interest)}$$

EXAMPLE 29

During the current year, a trust has DNI of $40,000, including the following: $10,000 of taxable interest, $10,000 of tax-exempt interest, and $20,000 of passive activity income. The trustee distributes, at her discretion, $8,000 to Mike and $12,000 to Nancy.

		Income Type		
Beneficiary	**Amount Received**	**Taxable Interest**	**Tax-Exempt Interest**	**Passive Income**
Mike	$ 8,000	$2,000*	$2,000	$4,000
Nancy	12,000	3,000	3,000	6,000

*$8,000 distribution/$40,000 total DNI × $10,000 taxable interest in DNI. ■

Special Allocations

Under limited circumstances, the parties may modify the character-of-income allocation method set forth above. A modification is permitted only to the extent that the allocation is required in the trust instrument and only to the extent that it has an economic effect independent of the cash-flow and income tax consequences of the allocation.[32]

EXAMPLE 30

Return to the facts in Example 29. Assume that the beneficiaries are elderly individuals who have pooled their investment portfolios to avail themselves of the trustee's professional asset management skills. Suppose the trustee has the discretion to allocate different classes of income to different beneficiaries and that she designates $10,000 of Nancy's $12,000 distribution as being from the tax-exempt income. Such a designation *would not be recognized* for tax purposes, and the allocation method of Example 29 must be used.

Suppose, however, that the trust instrument stipulated that Nancy was to receive all of the income from the tax-exempt securities because she alone contributed the exempt securities to the trust corpus. Under this provision, the $10,000 of the nontaxable interest is paid to Nancy. This allocation *is recognized*, and $10,000 of Nancy's distribution is tax-exempt. ■

LOSSES IN THE TERMINATION YEAR

The ordinary net operating and capital losses of a trust or estate do not flow through to the entity's beneficiaries, as would such losses from a partnership or an S corporation. However, in the year in which an entity terminates its existence, the beneficiaries do receive a direct benefit from the loss carryovers of the trust or estate.[33]

Net operating losses and net capital losses are subject to the same carryover rules that otherwise apply to an individual. Consequently, NOLs can be carried back 2 years and then carried forward 20 years while net capital losses can be carried forward only, and for an indefinite period of time. If the entity incurs a negative taxable

[32] Reg. § 1.652(b)–2(b). This is similar to the § 704(b)(2) requirement for partnerships.

[33] Reg. §§ 1.642(h)–1 and –2.

income in the last year of its existence, the excess of deductions over the entity's gross income flows through directly to the beneficiaries. The net loss is available as a deduction *from* AGI in the beneficiary's tax year with or within which the entity's tax year ends. The amount allowed is in proportion to the relative amount of corpus assets that each beneficiary receives upon the termination of the entity, and it is subject to the 2 percent-of-AGI floor.

Any carryovers of the entity's other losses flow through to the beneficiaries in the year of termination in proportion to the relative amount of corpus assets that each beneficiary receives. The character of the loss carryforward is retained by the beneficiary, except that a carryover of a net capital loss to a corporate beneficiary is always treated as short term. Beneficiaries who are individuals use these carryforwards as deductions *for* AGI.

EXAMPLE 31

The Edgar Estate terminates on December 31, 2011. It had used a fiscal year ending July 31. For the termination year, the estate incurred a $15,000 negative taxable income. In addition, the estate had an unused NOL carryforward of $23,000 from the year ending July 31, 2006, and an unused net long-term capital loss carryforward of $10,000 from the year ending July 31, 2009. Upon termination, Dawn receives $60,000 of corpus, and Blue Corporation receives the remaining $40,000. Dawn and Blue are calendar year taxpayers.

Dawn can claim an itemized deduction of $9,000 [($60,000/$100,000) × $15,000] for the entity's negative taxable income in the year of termination. This deduction is subject to the 2%-of-AGI floor on her miscellaneous itemized deductions. In addition, she can claim a $13,800 deduction *for* AGI in 2011 (60% × $23,000) for Edgar's NOL carryforward, and she can use $6,000 (60% × $10,000) of the estate's net long-term capital loss carryforward with her other 2011 capital transactions.

Blue Corporation receives ordinary business deductions in 2011 for Edgar's NOLs: $6,000 for the loss in the year of termination and $9,200 for the carryforward from fiscal year 2006. Moreover, Blue can use the $4,000 carryforward of Edgar's net capital losses to offset against its other 2011 capital transactions, although the loss must be treated as short term. ■

28.5 Procedural Matters

The fiduciary is required to file a Form 1041 (U.S. Income Tax Return for Estates and Trusts) in the following situations.[34]

- For an estate that has gross income of $600 or more for the year.
- For a trust that either has any taxable income or, if there is no taxable income, has gross income of $600 or more.

The fiduciary return (and any related tax liability) is due, before extensions, no later than the fifteenth day of the fourth month following the close of the entity's taxable year. The IRS encourages electronic filing of the Form 1041 and schedules. A paper return is filed with the Internal Revenue Service in Cincinnati or Ogden, Utah, depending on the location of the fiduciary's principal place of business.

Many fiduciary entities recognize capital gains during the year, through sales of assets that are part of corpus. In that event, a Schedule D is filed with the Form 1041, and the fiduciary entity or its beneficiaries can qualify for the favorable 15 percent (or lower) tax rate on long-term capital gains.

The pass-through of income and deduction items to the beneficiary is accomplished through Schedule K–1 to Form 1041. This form is similar in format and function to the Schedule K–1 for partners and S corporation shareholders

[34]§§ 6012(a)(3) and (4).

(see Chapters 21 and 22). Since the fiduciary entity usually has only a few transactions during the year, the Schedule K–1 for Form 1041 is less detailed than those for Forms 1065 and 1120S.

Trusts and estates are required to make estimated Federal income tax payments, using the same quarterly schedule that applies to individual taxpayers. This requirement applies to estates only for tax years that end two or more years after the date of the decedent's death. Charitable trusts and private foundations are exempt from estimated payment requirements altogether.[35]

The two-year estimated tax exception for estates recognizes the liquidity problems that an executor often faces during the early months of administering the estate. The exception does not ensure, however, that an estate in existence less than 24 months will never be required to make an estimated tax payment.

EXAMPLE 32

Juanita died on March 15, 2011. Her executor elected a fiscal year ending on July 31 for the estate. Estimated tax payments will be required from the estate starting with the tax year that begins on August 1, 2012. ■

TAX PLANNING:

Many of the tax planning possibilities for estates and trusts were discussed in Chapter 27. However, several specific tax planning possibilities are available to help minimize the income tax effects on estates and trusts and their beneficiaries.

28.6 A Trust or Estate as an Income-Shifting Device

LO.4

Apply the Subchapter J rules in a manner that minimizes the income taxation of trusts and estates and still accomplishes the intended objectives of the grantor or decedent.

The compressed tax rate schedule applicable to Subchapter J entities may have reversed the traditional techniques by which families set aside funds for long-term activities, such as business startups, college education, and home purchases. When the tax rate schedules for trusts and estates were more accommodating, high-income individuals would shift income-producing assets to trusts to take advantage of the lower tax rate that would fall on the income accumulated within the trust. The target of the plan, usually a child, would receive the accumulated income (and, perhaps, trust corpus) at a designated age, and more funds would be available because a lower tax rate had been applied over the life of the investment in the trust.

Today, such an income shift would *deplete*, rather than shelter, the family's assets, as the rates falling on individuals are much more graduated than are those applicable to fiduciaries, and the kiddie tax also penalizes attempts to shift taxable income to children. Assuming that the objectives of the plan remain unchanged, possible strategies in view of these rate changes include the following:

- Trust corpus should be invested in growth assets that are low on yield but high on appreciation, so that the trustee can determine the timing of the gain and somewhat control the effective tax rate that applies.
- Trust corpus should be invested in tax-exempt securities, such as municipal bonds and mutual funds that invest in them, to eliminate the tax costs associated with the investment. If this approach is taken, a trust might be unnecessary—the parent should simply retain full control over the assets and invest in the exempt securities in his or her own account.

[35] § 6654(l).

TAX *in the NEWS*

Don't Trust Your Dictionary

Today, the middle and upper classes are often including trusts in their estate plans. Usually, the purpose of the trust is to spare the survivors the time and effort required to work through a state's probate proceedings.

But planning for death can sometimes lead to confusion about terminology, especially between a living trust and a living will. A "living trust" is typically created to hold the assets of the decedent-to-be, including investments, homestead, and household goods. Upon forming the new entity, the assets are retitled in the name of the trustee. The idea underlying the living trust is to reduce the probate estate. This, in turn, lowers the fees for carrying out the probate process. Such fees often total 5 percent or so of the date of death value of the probate assets.

The living trust accomplishes virtually no Federal tax savings. The trust assets are included in the decedent's gross estate, as the living trust is an incomplete transfer under §§ 2036 and 2038. For the most part, the entity is treated as a grantor trust. Because of the retained investment and distribution powers, the donor is still liable for taxes on the taxable income of the fiduciary.

A "living will," on the other hand, is a document that conveys powers to relatives and third parties to make medical and financial decisions when the decedent-to-be can no longer do so. More appropriately referred to as a "medical power of attorney," the document expresses the person's wishes as to how and when to reduce specified medical treatments (including directives as to removing life support systems).

The proper use of these documents can become tricky under controlling state law when same-sex couples are involved. The adviser must assist the clients in determining whether a same-sex partner or spouse can qualify as the holder of a medical power of attorney, and whether special issues arise when a same-sex partner or spouse is named a trustee of a living trust.

- The grantor should retain high-yield assets, so that control over the assets is not surrendered when the tax cost is too high.
- Use of trust vehicles should be reserved for cases where professional management of the assets is necessary for portfolio growth and the additional tax costs can be justified.

28.7 Income Tax Planning for Estates

As a separate taxable entity, an estate can select its own tax year and accounting methods. The executor of an estate should consider selecting a fiscal year because this will determine when beneficiaries must include income distributions from the estate in their own tax returns. Beneficiaries must include the income for their tax year with or within which the estate's tax year ends. Proper selection of the estate's tax year can result in a smoothing out of income and a reduction of the income taxes for all parties involved.

Caution should be taken in determining when the estate is to be terminated. Selecting a fiscal year for the estate can result in a bunching of income to the beneficiaries in the year in which the estate is closed. Prolonging the termination of an estate can be effective income tax planning, but the IRS carefully examines the purpose of keeping the estate open. Since the unused losses of an estate pass through to the beneficiaries only in the termination year, the estate should be closed when the beneficiaries can enjoy the maximum tax benefit of the losses.

The timing and amounts of income distributions to the beneficiaries also present important tax planning opportunities. If the executor can make discretionary income distributions, he or she should evaluate the relative marginal income tax rates of the estate and its beneficiaries. By timing the distributions properly, the overall income tax liability can be minimized. Care should be taken, however, to time the distributions in light of the estate's DNI.

CONCEPT SUMMARY 28.1

Income Taxation of Trusts and Estates

1. Estates and trusts are temporary entities, created to locate, maintain, and distribute assets and to satisfy liabilities according to the wishes of the decedent or grantor as expressed in the will or trust document.
2. Generally, the estate or trust acts as a conduit of the taxable income that it receives. To the extent that the income is distributed by the entity, it is taxed to the beneficiary. Taxable income retained by the entity is taxed to the entity itself.
3. The entity's accounting income must be determined first. Accounting conventions that are stated in the controlling document or, lacking such provisions, in state law allocate specific items of receipt and expenditure either to income or to corpus. Income beneficiaries typically receive payments from the entity that are equal to the accounting income.
4. The taxable income of the entity is computed using the scheme in Figure 28.3. The entity usually recognizes income in respect of a decedent. Deductions for fiduciary's fees and for charitable contributions may be reduced if the entity received any tax-exempt income during the year. Cost recovery deductions are assigned proportionately to the recipients of accounting income. Upon election, realized gain or loss on assets that properly are distributed in kind can be recognized by the entity.
5. A distribution deduction, computationally derived from distributable net income (DNI), is allowed to the entity. DNI is the maximum amount on which entity beneficiaries can be taxed. Moreover, the constitution of DNI is assigned to the recipients of the distributions.

EXAMPLE 33

For several years before his death on March 7, Don had entered into annual deferred compensation agreements with his employer. These agreements collectively called for the payment of $200,000 six months after Don's retirement or death. To provide a maximum 12-month period within which to generate deductions to offset this large item of IRD, the executor or administrator of the estate should elect a fiscal year ending August 31. The election is made simply by filing the estate's first tax return for the short period of March 7 to August 31. ■

EXAMPLE 34

Carol, the sole beneficiary of an estate, is a calendar year, cash basis taxpayer. If the estate elects a fiscal year ending January 31, all distributions during the period of February 1 to December 31, 2011, are reported on Carol's tax return for calendar year 2012 (due April 15, 2013). Thus, assuming estimated tax requirements have otherwise been met, any income taxes that result from a $50,000 distribution made by the estate on February 20, 2011, may be deferred until April 15, 2013. ■

EXAMPLE 35

Assume the same facts as in Example 34. If the estate is closed on December 15, 2012, the DNI for both the fiscal year ending January 31, 2012, and the final tax year ending December 15, 2012, is included in Carol's tax return for the same calendar year. To avoid the effect of this bunching of income, the estate should not be closed until early in calendar year 2013. ■

In general, beneficiaries who are subject to high tax rates should be made beneficiaries of second-tier (but not IRD) distributions of the estate. Most likely, these individuals will have less need for an additional steady stream of (taxable) income while their income tax savings can be relatively large. Moreover, a special allocation of tax-favored types of income and expenses should be considered. For example, tax-exempt income can be directed more easily to beneficiaries in higher income tax brackets.

ETHICS & Equity

Who Should Be a Trustee?

For decades, grantors have chosen a family member to be the trustee of the family savings, the children's education fund, or whatever other assets are placed into management by the trust. The relative chosen is often the most trusted but not always the one with the business sense. Now, however, as the financial work has become more complex, with wild stock market fluctuations, increased fiduciary standards, and potential conflicts of interest, some are questioning the wisdom of using a family member as the trustee.

Using a trust company or other financial institution as a trustee usually results in more stable investment returns, eliminating both the highs and the lows of the stock market cycle. Institutions can also bring other advantages.

- They do not die, run away, become mentally or physically incapacitated, or otherwise unexpectedly become unqualified for the position.
- They are not easily swayed by emotional appeals; nor do they react to family jealousies.
- They are prohibited by law from acting under a conflict of interest, such as might exist between family members when the related trustee is also a trust beneficiary.

On the negative side, human trustees often waive or discount their fiduciary fee, while institutions do not. Especially for trusts with a small corpus, institutional trustees can be prohibitively expensive. And the trust company most often is oriented toward expanding its customer base, rather than offering individual attention to existing clients.

How would you advise a client to address this delicate issue? Compromise solutions might be to:

- Appoint co-trustees. Aunt Grace or Uncle Roberto can provide the personal touch and ensure that trust decisions recognize family needs, while the trust company maximizes investment returns and furnishes professional management.
- Keep the family trustee, but hire professionals to provide advice only when needed, at an hourly rate. This approach avoids the fees based on asset values that trust companies usually charge.
- Use the advisory services of the mutual funds in which trust assets are invested, to manage and distribute the corpus and income.

28.8 Income Tax Planning with Trusts

The great variety of trusts provides the grantor, trustee, and beneficiaries with excellent opportunities for tax planning. Many of the same tax planning opportunities available to the executor of an estate are available to the trustee. For example, the distributions from a trust are taxable to the trust's beneficiaries to the extent of the trust's DNI. If income distributions are discretionary, the trustee can time the distributions to minimize the income tax consequences to all parties.

28.9 Distributions of In-Kind Property

The ability of the trustee or executor to elect to recognize the realized gain or loss relative to a distributed noncash asset allows the gain or loss to be allocated to the optimal taxpayer.

EXAMPLE 36

The Yorba Linda Estate distributed some inventory, basis of $40,000 and fair market value of $41,500, to beneficiary Larry. Yorba Linda is subject to a 15% marginal income tax rate, and Larry is subject to a 33% marginal income tax rate. The executor of Yorba Linda should elect that the entity recognize the related $1,500 realized gain, thereby subjecting the gain to the estate's lower tax rate.

Tax without election, at Larry's 33% rate	$495
Tax with election, at trust's 15% rate	225

■

REFOCUS ON THE BIG PICTURE

SETTING UP A TRUST TO PROTECT A FAMILY

Anna Jiang and her family should consider the creation of one or more trusts to provide security in case Anna is incapacitated by medical problems and unable to manage the family's finances. One suggestion for the family might be:

1. Anna transfers some or all of the $2 million assets to the Jiang Family Trust, with quarterly income payable to Tom and the children. Recipients would be designated by the trustee, but all of the entity's accounting income must be distributed. In this way, the income could be directed to the beneficiary most in need (e.g., to pay for education expenses or to start a new business). The children could be named first-tier beneficiaries, with Tom as a second-tier income beneficiary.
2. While Anna is still healthy and earning a regular salary, the trustee could accumulate the accounting income and allow the corpus to build up. Alternatively, the trustee could make gifts to charity or fund education plans for Bobby and Sally.
3. Anna should provide clear instructions to the trustee as to her preferences on how the trust corpus should be invested and specify which of Tom's and the children's expenses should and should not be covered.
4. The children should be named as remainder beneficiaries of the Jiang Family Trust. In case the trust corpus exceeds the estate tax bypass amount, other remainder beneficiaries could be named in order to avoid any generation-skipping tax. See Chapter 27.
5. Amendments to the trust document should be considered whenever Tom and Anna update their wills.

What If?

If Anna remains healthy, the Jiang Family Trust might be terminated when the children reach the age of majority, as the need for financial support will have diminished. However, if Tom is unable or unwilling to take over the management of the assets, the trust should continue. In this event, the trustee might shift the focus to funding long-term care for the couple, making charitable gifts, or financing the education needs of grandchildren.

The controlling trust document should be worded to provide flexibility as to the purposes and termination date of the trust. The trustee should be chosen from family members or business associates who know Anna and Tom well and are familiar with the couple's objectives.

KEY TERMS

Complex trust, 28–5
Corpus, 28–3
Distributable net income (DNI), 28–16
Expenses in respect of a decedent, 28–13
Grantor, 28–2
Grantor trusts, 28–3
Income in respect of a decedent (IRD), 28–12
Reversionary interest, 28–3
Simple trust, 28–5
Sprinkling trust, 28–4

DISCUSSION QUESTIONS

COMMUNICATIONS

1. **LO.1** A local bank has asked you to speak at its Building Personal Wealth Conference on the topic of "What Should Your Trust Do for You?" Develop at least four PowerPoint slides, each one listing a function that a trust might be able to accomplish for an individual who has more than a modest level of financial resources.

2. **LO.1** Trusts and estates are known as *fiduciary* entities, in that a legal structure is formed to accomplish the financial and other goals of one or more individuals. List the parties who must be identified when a trust is created and describe the responsibilities of each. Do the same for an estate.

3. **LO.1** Define the following terms.
   a. Income interest.
   b. Remainder interest.
   c. Reversionary interest.
   d. Life tenant.
   e. Term certain.

4. **LO.1** Some fiduciary entities are known as *simple trusts*, while others are *complex trusts*. How does the tax professional know whether a trust is simple or complex? When is this determination made?

5. **LO.1** In general terms, describe how the following entities are subject to the Federal income tax. (Answer only for the entity, not for its owners, beneficiaries, etc.)
   a. C corporations (Subchapter C).
   b. Partnerships (Subchapter K).
   c. S corporations (Subchapter S).
   d. Trusts and estates (Subchapter J).

COMMUNICATIONS

6. **LO.1** Your college's accounting group has asked you to give a 10-minute speech, titled "Trusts, Estates, and the AMT." The audience will be students who have completed at least one course concerning Federal income taxation. Develop a brief outline for your remarks.

7. **LO.1** Create a fact pattern that illustrates each of the following tax situations. Be specific.
   a. A simple trust.
   b. A complex trust with a $300 personal exemption.
   c. A complex trust with a $100 personal exemption.

8. **LO.2** Using Figure 28.2 as a guide, describe the computation of a fiduciary entity's accounting income, taxable income, and distributable net income.

9. **LO.2** The Liu Trust is short of cash. It is required to distribute $100,000 to Yang every year, and that payment is due in six weeks. In its asset corpus, Liu holds a number of investments that are valued at $100,000. One of them has a tax basis to the trust of $60,000. Assuming that the trust agreement allows, what are the Federal income tax consequences if Liu distributes this stock to Yang?

DECISION MAKING

10. **LO.2** In its first tax year, the Wittmann Estate generated $50,000 of taxable interest income and $20,000 of tax-exempt interest income. It paid fiduciary fees of $7,000. The estate is subject to a 35% marginal estate tax rate and a 40% marginal income tax rate. How should the executor assign the deductions for the payment of the fees?

11. **LO.2** The Sterling Trust owns a business and generated $100,000 in depreciation deductions for the tax year. Mona is one of the income beneficiaries of the entity. Given the following information, can Mona deduct any of the Sterling depreciation on her Form 1040? If so, how much is her deduction?

Sterling's taxable income from the business	$ 800,000
Sterling's gross income from the business	2,000,000
Mona's share of trust accounting income	1,000,000
Total trust accounting income	2,500,000
Mona's share of distributable net income	200,000
Total distributable net income	600,000

12. **LO.2** In 2011, the Helpful Trust agreed to make a $90,000 contribution to Local Soup Kitchen, a charitable organization. Helpful's board agreed to the gift at a November 2011 meeting, but the check was not issued until February 20, 2012 (i.e., during the next tax year). Can the trust claim a charitable contribution deduction? If so, describe how Helpful should treat its gift.

13. **LO.3** One of the key concepts in fiduciary income taxation is that of *distributable net income* (DNI). List the major functions of DNI on one PowerPoint slide, with no more than five bullets, to present to your classmates as part of the discussion of this chapter of the text. Just review the uses of DNI in Subchapter J, and do not discuss its computation. **COMMUNICATIONS**

14. **LO.2, 3** Ivory Tower College, a charitable organization, is one of the income beneficiaries of the Campbell Trust. Was the selection of the college as an income beneficiary a wise decision by Campbell's grantor? Comment specifically concerning the tax effects of the trust's cost recovery deductions and of its potential business operating losses. **DECISION MAKING**

15. **LO.2, 3, 4** The Flan Trust is scheduled to terminate in two years, when Amy Flan reaches age 30. Several years ago, the trust operated a business that generated a sizable NOL carryforward that the trust has not been able to use. In addition, due to a bearish stock market, the value of the entity's investment portfolio has declined 15% from its purchase price. What issues must you consider in advising Amy and the corporate trustee? **ISSUE ID**

16. **LO.4** Carol has been promoted several times, and she may be named a partner next year. Thus, she will be subject to higher marginal income tax rates than in the past. Carol's colleague Isaiah has told her about a "college education trust" from which he pays tuition and fees for his children. He has implied that there are sizable tax advantages to setting up a trust for this purpose. Now Carol is considering establishing a similar trust to pay tuition for her own children. She believes that the trust will be able to deduct the tuition payments, something that she cannot currently do on her Form 1040. Write a memo to the tax research file addressing Carol's ideas. **DECISION MAKING** **COMMUNICATIONS**

17. **LO.1, 4** The Winter Trust must file a Form 1041 for the first time, because it has recognized about $5,000 of gross income. Corpus assets are transferred to the trust on April 30. Considering only the Federal income tax effects of the creation of Winter:
    a. What tax year should be used?
    b. Where should the completed Form 1041 be sent?

18. **LO.4** For tax planning purposes, should an estate adopt a calendar or a fiscal tax year? Why?

19. **LO.4** Comment on the following items relative to tax planning strategies of a fiduciary entity.
    a. To reduce taxes for a typical family, should income be shifted *to* a trust or *from* a trust? Why?
    b. To reduce overall taxes, should a high-income, wealthy beneficiary be assigned to the first or second tier of trust distributions? Why?
    c. To minimize taxes, how should a trust treat the distribution of an in-kind asset?

PROBLEMS

20. **LO.1** Compute the Federal income tax liability for the Kim Trust. The trustee reports the following transactions for the 2011 tax year. The trustee accumulates all accounting income for the year.

Operating income from a business	$400,000
Dividend income, all from U.S. corporations	70,000
Interest income, City of San Antonio bonds	40,000
Fiduciary fees, deductible portion	20,000
Net rental losses, passive activity	(100,000)

21. **LO.1** The Purple Trust incurred the following items this year.

Taxable interest income	$75,000
Tax-exempt interest income, not on private activity bonds	60,000
Tax-exempt interest income, on private activity bonds (not issued during 2009 or 2010)	25,000

Compute Purple's tentative minimum tax for the year. Purple does not have any credits available to reduce the AMT liability.

22. **LO.1, 2, 3** Complete the following chart, indicating the comparative attributes of the typical trust and estate by answering yes/no or explaining the differences between the entities where appropriate.

Attribute	Estate	Trust
Separate income tax entity	_____	_____
Controlling document	_____	_____
Can have both income and remainder beneficiaries	_____	_____
Computes entity accounting income before determining entity taxable income	_____	_____
Termination date is determinable from controlling document	_____	_____
Legal owner of assets under fiduciary's control	_____	_____
Document identifies both income and remainder beneficiaries	_____	_____
Separate share rules apply	_____	_____
Generally must use calendar tax year	_____	_____

23. **LO.2** Sanchez incurred the following items.

Business income	$120,000
Tax-exempt interest income	40,000
Payment to charity from 2011 income, paid March 1, 2012	20,000

Complete the following chart, indicating the charitable contribution deduction under the various assumptions.

Assumption	2011 Deduction for Contribution
Sanchez is a cash basis individual.	__________
Sanchez is an accrual basis corporation.	__________
Sanchez is a trust.	__________

24. **LO.2, 3** The Ricardo Trust is a simple trust that correctly uses the calendar year for tax purposes. Its income beneficiaries (Lucy and Ethel) are entitled to the trust's annual accounting income in shares of one-half each. For the current calendar year, the trust generates ordinary income of $50,000, a long-term capital gain of $25,000 (allocable to corpus), and a trustee commission expense of $10,000 (allocable to corpus). Use the format of Figure 28.3 to address the following items.
    a. How much income is each beneficiary entitled to receive?
    b. What is the trust's DNI?
    c. What is the trust's taxable income?
    d. How much gross income is reported by each of the beneficiaries?

25. **LO.2, 3** Assume the same facts as in Problem 24, except that the trust instrument allocates the capital gain to income.
    a. How much income is each beneficiary entitled to receive?
    b. What is the trust's DNI?
    c. What is the trust's taxable income?
    d. How much gross income is reported by each of the beneficiaries?

26. **LO.3** Under the terms of the Lagos Trust instrument, the trustee has discretion to distribute or accumulate income on behalf of Willie, Sylvia, and Doris in equal shares.

The trustee also can invade corpus for the benefit of any of the beneficiaries to the extent of each person's respective one-third interest in the trust.

In the current year, the trust has DNI of $120,000. Distribution and accumulation amounts were as follows:

- To Willie: $40,000 from DNI and $10,000 from corpus.
- To Sylvia: $25,000. The remaining $15,000 DNI is accumulated.
- To Doris: $0. The $40,000 DNI is accumulated.

a. How much income is taxed to Willie? (*Hint*: Apply the separate share rule.)
b. To Sylvia?
c. To Doris?
d. To Lagos?

27. **LO.3** The Putnam Sisters Trust is required to distribute $60,000 annually equally to its two income beneficiaries, Clare and David. If trust income is not sufficient to pay these amounts, the trustee can invade corpus to the extent necessary. During the current year, the trust generates only taxable interest income and has DNI of $150,000; the trustee distributes $30,000 to Clare and $130,000 to David.
    a. How much of the $130,000 distributed to David must be included in his gross income?
    b. How much of the $30,000 distributed to Clare must be included in her gross income?
    c. Are these distributions considered to be first-tier or second-tier distributions?

28. **LO.3** The Dailey Estate has $100,000 of DNI, composed of $40,000 in dividends, $20,000 in taxable interest, $15,000 in passive activity income, and $25,000 in tax-exempt interest. The entity's two noncharitable income beneficiaries, Brenda and Del, receive cash distributions of $20,000 each. How much of each class of income is deemed to have been distributed to Brenda? To Del?

29. **LO.2, 3** The trustee of the Purple Trust can distribute any amount of accounting income and corpus to the trust's beneficiaries, Lydia and Kent. This year, the trust's records reflect the following.

Taxable interest income	$40,000
Tax-exempt interest income	60,000
Long-term capital gains—allocable to corpus	30,000
Fiduciary's fees—allocable to corpus	10,000

The trustee distributed $40,000 to Lydia and $20,000 to Kent.
    a. What is Purple's trust accounting income?
    b. What is Purple's DNI?
    c. What is Purple's taxable income?
    d. How much is taxed to each of the beneficiaries?

30. **LO.2** Each of the following items was incurred by José, a cash basis, calendar year decedent. Under the terms of the will, Dora took immediate ownership in all of José's assets, except the dividend-paying stocks. The estate received José's final paycheck. **DECISION MAKING**

Applying the rules for income and deductions in respect of a decedent, indicate on which return each item should be reported: Dora's income tax return (*Form 1040*); the estate's first income tax return (*Form 1041*); or the estate's estate tax return (*Form 706*). More than one alternative may apply in some cases.

	Item Incurred	Form(s) Reported on
a.	Wages, last paycheck	________
b.	State income tax withheld on last paycheck	________
c.	Capital gain portion of installment payment received	________
d.	Ordinary income portion of installment payment received	________
e.	Dividend income, record date was two days prior to José's death	________
f.	Unrealized appreciation on a mutual fund investment	________

	Item Incurred	Form(s) Reported on
g.	Depreciation recapture accrued as of date of death	________
h.	Medical expenses of last illness	________
i.	Apartment building, rents accrued but not collected as of death	________
j.	Apartment building, property tax accrued and assessed but not paid as of death	________

31. **LO.3** Determine the tax effects of the indicated losses for the Yellow Estate for both tax years. The estate holds a variety of investment assets, which it received from the decedent, Mrs. Yellow. The estate's sole income and remainder beneficiary is Yellow, Jr. All taxpayers use a calendar tax year.

Tax Year	Loss Generated
2011 (first tax year)	Taxable income ($300) Capital loss ($15,000)
2012 (final tax year)	Taxable income, all classified as ordinary ($30,000)

See Appendix E for Comprehensive Tax Return Problem—Form 1041

RESEARCH PROBLEMS

THOMSON REUTERS
Checkpoint® Student Edition

Note: Solutions to Research Problems can be prepared by using the **Checkpoint® Student Edition** online research product, which is available to accompany this text. It is also possible to prepare solutions to the Research Problems by using tax research materials found in a standard tax library.

Research Problem 1. For three generations, the Dexter family has sent its children to Private University, preparing them for successful professional careers. The Edna Dexter Trust was established in the 1950s by LaKeisha's late grandmother and has accumulated a sizable corpus. It makes distributions to Edna's descendants rarely and only when they need large capital amounts. For example, two years ago, the trust distributed $500,000 to DuJuan Dexter to aid him in starting a practice in retirement and elder law. In most years, the trust's income is donated to a single charity.

Under the terms of the trust, Bigby Dexter, LaKeisha's uncle and legal guardian, can specify the trust beneficiaries and the amounts to be distributed to them. He can also replace the trustee and designate the charity that will receive the year's contribution. Accordingly, the trust falls under the grantor trust rules of § 678, and Bigby reports the trust's transactions on his own Form 1040.

LaKeisha wants to attend the prestigious local Academy High School, which will require a four-year expenditure for tuition and fees of $100,000, payable in advance. She approaches the Edna Dexter trustee and requests a current-year distribution of this amount, payable directly to the Academy. Under the laws of the state, the parent or guardian has the responsibility to provide a child with a public school education (no tuition charge) until age 16.

If the payment to the Academy is made, how is it treated under the Subchapter J rules: as a charitable contribution to the Academy, as a corpus distribution to LaKeisha, or in some other manner?

COMMUNICATIONS

Research Problem 2. Siri's revocable trust held title to a plot of investment land that she had acquired in 2003. On October 20, 2010, the trust entered into a sales contract with Hilltop Developers. A closing date of March 20, 2011, was set by the terms of the contract.

On February 3, 2011, Siri's engineers discovered that there was a natural gas pipeline under the land, a fact that was not previously known by the parties. To allow for changes in the terms of the contract that were needed because of this discovery, the closing date for the sale was delayed until June 1, 2011.

The trust's basis in the land is $1 million. The original sales price was set at $1.1 million, reflecting difficulties in finding a purchaser in a "down" real estate market. But after the terms of the sale were adjusted, on May 20, 2011, a new $1.5 million sales price was agreed to. The closing and title transfer occurred on June 1 of that year.

Siri died on May 3, 2011. Under § 2036, the land is included in Siri's gross estate. Is the $500,000 capital gain on the sale treated as income in respect of a decedent (IRD) to her as well? Remember that since neither party canceled the original deal, the sale was certain to occur under the contract. But Hilltop and the trust were renegotiating the terms of the contract when Siri died.

Identify the administrative and judicial precedents that are most pertinent for the parties. Cite and summarize your findings in an outline for a talk that you will deliver next week to your school's Accounting Club.

Use the tax resources of the Internet to address the following question. Do not restrict your search to the Web, but include a review of newsgroups and general reference materials, practitioner sites and resources, primary sources of the tax law, chat rooms and discussion groups, and other opportunities.

INTERNET *activity*

COMMUNICATIONS

Research Problem 3. Create no more than three PowerPoint slides, summarizing your state's definitions of and rules for using the following terms. *Hint*: Your state might not use these terms at all, or it might use a term that differs slightly, so make sure that your Internet research is broad enough to find the equivalent terminology.

- Living will.
- Living trust.
- Medical power of attorney.

Appendix A

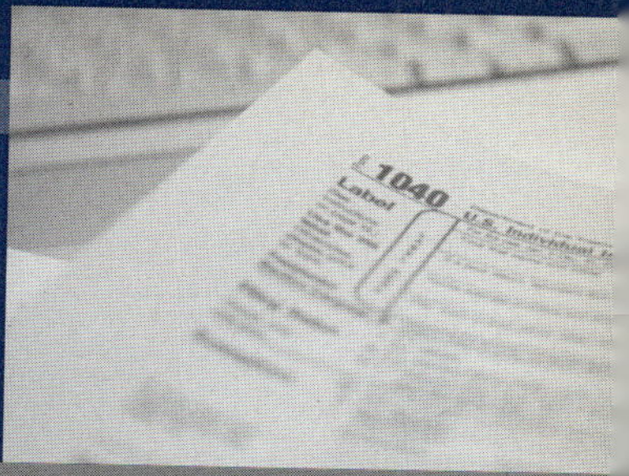

TAX RATE SCHEDULES AND TABLES

(The 2011 Tax Tables and 2011 Sales Tax Tables can be accessed at the IRS website: [**www.irs.gov**] when released.)

2010 Tax Rate Schedules

Single—Schedule X

If taxable income is: Over—	But not over—	The tax is:	of the amount over—
$ 0	$ 8,375	........10%	$ 0
8,375	34,000	$ 837.50 + 15%	8,375
34,000	82,400	4,681.25 + 25%	34,000
82,400	171,850	16,781.25 + 28%	82,400
171,850	373,650	41,827.25 + 33%	171,850
373,650	....	108,421.25 + 35%	373,650

Head of household—Schedule Z

If taxable income is: Over—	But not over—	The tax is:	of the amount over—
$ 0	$ 11,950	........10%	$ 0
11,950	45,550	$ 1,195.00 + 15%	11,950
45,550	117,650	6,235.00 + 25%	45,550
117,650	190,550	24,260.00 + 28%	117,650
190,550	373,650	44,672.00 + 33%	190,550
373,650	....	105,095.00 + 35%	373,650

Married filing jointly or Qualifying widow(er)—Schedule Y–1

If taxable income is: Over—	But not over—	The tax is:	of the amount over—
$ 0	$ 16,750	........10%	$ 0
16,750	68,000	$ 1,675.00 + 15%	16,750
68,000	137,300	9,362.50 + 25%	68,000
137,300	209,250	26,687.50 + 28%	137,300
209,250	373,650	46,833.50 + 33%	209,250
373,650	....	101,085.50 + 35%	373,650

Married filing separately—Schedule Y–2

If taxable income is: Over—	But not over—	The tax is:	of the amount over—
$ 0	$ 8,375	........10%	$ 0
8,375	34,000	$ 837.50 + 15%	8,375
34,000	68,650	4,681.25 + 25%	34,000
68,650	104,625	13,343.75 + 28%	68,650
104,625	186,825	23,416.75 + 33%	104,625
186,825	....	50,542.75 + 35%	186,825

2011 Tax Rate Schedules

Single—Schedule X

If taxable income is: Over—	But not over—	The tax is:	of the amount over—
$ 0	$ 8,500	........10%	$ 0
8,500	34,500	$ 850.00 + 15%	8,500
34,500	83,600	4,750.00 + 25%	34,500
83,600	174,400	17,025.00 + 28%	83,600
174,400	379,150	42,449.00 + 33%	174,400
379,150	....	110,016.50 + 35%	379,150

Head of household—Schedule Z

If taxable income is: Over—	But not over—	The tax is:	of the amount over—
$ 0	$ 12,150	........10%	$ 0
12,150	46,250	$ 1,215.00 + 15%	12,150
46,250	119,400	6,330.00 + 25%	46,250
119,400	193,350	24,617.50 + 28%	119,400
193,350	379,150	45,323.50 + 33%	193,350
379,150	....	106,637.50 + 35%	379,150

Married filing jointly or Qualifying widow(er)—Schedule Y–1

If taxable income is: Over—	But not over—	The tax is:	of the amount over—
$ 0	$ 17,000	........10%	$ 0
17,000	69,000	$ 1,700.00 + 15%	17,000
69,000	139,350	9,500.00 + 25%	69,000
139,350	212,300	27,087.50 + 28%	139,350
212,300	379,150	47,513.50 + 33%	212,300
379,150	....	102,574.00 + 35%	379,150

Married filing separately—Schedule Y–2

If taxable income is: Over—	But not over—	The tax is:	of the amount over—
$ 0	$ 8,500	........10%	$ 0
8,500	34,500	$ 850.00 + 15%	8,500
34,500	69,675	4,750.00 + 25%	34,500
69,675	106,150	13,543.75 + 28%	69,675
106,150	189,575	23,756.75 + 33%	106,150
189,575	....	51,287.00 + 35%	189,575

2010 Tax Table

See the instructions for line 44 on page 35 to see if you must use the Tax Table below to figure your tax.

Example. Mr. and Mrs. Brown are filing a joint return. Their taxable income on Form 1040, line 43, is $25,300. First, they find the $25,300–25,350 taxable income line. Next, they find the column for married filing jointly and read down the column. The amount shown where the taxable income line and filing status column meet is $2,961. This is the tax amount they should enter on Form 1040, line 44.

Sample Table

At least	But less than	Single	Married filing jointly *	Married filing sepa-rately	Head of a house-hold
		Your tax is—			
25,200	**25,250**	3,365	2,946	3,365	3,186
25,250	**25,300**	3,373	2,954	3,373	3,194
25,300	**25,350**	3,380	(2,961)	3,380	3,201
25,350	**25,400**	3,388	2,969	3,388	3,209

If line 43 (taxable income) is—		And you are—			
At least	But less than	Single	Married filing jointly *	Married filing sepa-rately	Head of a house-hold
		Your tax is—			
0	**5**	0	0	0	0
5	**15**	1	1	1	1
15	**25**	2	2	2	2
25	**50**	4	4	4	4
50	**75**	6	6	6	6
75	**100**	9	9	9	9
100	**125**	11	11	11	11
125	**150**	14	14	14	14
150	**175**	16	16	16	16
175	**200**	19	19	19	19
200	**225**	21	21	21	21
225	**250**	24	24	24	24
250	**275**	26	26	26	26
275	**300**	29	29	29	29
300	**325**	31	31	31	31
325	**350**	34	34	34	34
350	**375**	36	36	36	36
375	**400**	39	39	39	39
400	**425**	41	41	41	41
425	**450**	44	44	44	44
450	**475**	46	46	46	46
475	**500**	49	49	49	49
500	**525**	51	51	51	51
525	**550**	54	54	54	54
550	**575**	56	56	56	56
575	**600**	59	59	59	59
600	**625**	61	61	61	61
625	**650**	64	64	64	64
650	**675**	66	66	66	66
675	**700**	69	69	69	69
700	**725**	71	71	71	71
725	**750**	74	74	74	74
750	**775**	76	76	76	76
775	**800**	79	79	79	79
800	**825**	81	81	81	81
825	**850**	84	84	84	84
850	**875**	86	86	86	86
875	**900**	89	89	89	89
900	**925**	91	91	91	91
925	**950**	94	94	94	94
950	**975**	96	96	96	96
975	**1,000**	99	99	99	99
1,000					
1,000	**1,025**	101	101	101	101
1,025	**1,050**	104	104	104	104
1,050	**1,075**	106	106	106	106
1,075	**1,100**	109	109	109	109
1,100	**1,125**	111	111	111	111
1,125	**1,150**	114	114	114	114
1,150	**1,175**	116	116	116	116
1,175	**1,200**	119	119	119	119
1,200	**1,225**	121	121	121	121
1,225	**1,250**	124	124	124	124
1,250	**1,275**	126	126	126	126
1,275	**1,300**	129	129	129	129

If line 43 (taxable income) is—		And you are—			
At least	But less than	Single	Married filing jointly *	Married filing sepa-rately	Head of a house-hold
		Your tax is—			
1,300	**1,325**	131	131	131	131
1,325	**1,350**	134	134	134	134
1,350	**1,375**	136	136	136	136
1,375	**1,400**	139	139	139	139
1,400	**1,425**	141	141	141	141
1,425	**1,450**	144	144	144	144
1,450	**1,475**	146	146	146	146
1,475	**1,500**	149	149	149	149
1,500	**1,525**	151	151	151	151
1,525	**1,550**	154	154	154	154
1,550	**1,575**	156	156	156	156
1,575	**1,600**	159	159	159	159
1,600	**1,625**	161	161	161	161
1,625	**1,650**	164	164	164	164
1,650	**1,675**	166	166	166	166
1,675	**1,700**	169	169	169	169
1,700	**1,725**	171	171	171	171
1,725	**1,750**	174	174	174	174
1,750	**1,775**	176	176	176	176
1,775	**1,800**	179	179	179	179
1,800	**1,825**	181	181	181	181
1,825	**1,850**	184	184	184	184
1,850	**1,875**	186	186	186	186
1,875	**1,900**	189	189	189	189
1,900	**1,925**	191	191	191	191
1,925	**1,950**	194	194	194	194
1,950	**1,975**	196	196	196	196
1,975	**2,000**	199	199	199	199
2,000					
2,000	**2,025**	201	201	201	201
2,025	**2,050**	204	204	204	204
2,050	**2,075**	206	206	206	206
2,075	**2,100**	209	209	209	209
2,100	**2,125**	211	211	211	211
2,125	**2,150**	214	214	214	214
2,150	**2,175**	216	216	216	216
2,175	**2,200**	219	219	219	219
2,200	**2,225**	221	221	221	221
2,225	**2,250**	224	224	224	224
2,250	**2,275**	226	226	226	226
2,275	**2,300**	229	229	229	229
2,300	**2,325**	231	231	231	231
2,325	**2,350**	234	234	234	234
2,350	**2,375**	236	236	236	236
2,375	**2,400**	239	239	239	239
2,400	**2,425**	241	241	241	241
2,425	**2,450**	244	244	244	244
2,450	**2,475**	246	246	246	246
2,475	**2,500**	249	249	249	249
2,500	**2,525**	251	251	251	251
2,525	**2,550**	254	254	254	254
2,550	**2,575**	256	256	256	256
2,575	**2,600**	259	259	259	259
2,600	**2,625**	261	261	261	261
2,625	**2,650**	264	264	264	264
2,650	**2,675**	266	266	266	266
2,675	**2,700**	269	269	269	269

If line 43 (taxable income) is—		And you are—			
At least	But less than	Single	Married filing jointly *	Married filing sepa-rately	Head of a house-hold
		Your tax is—			
2,700	**2,725**	271	271	271	271
2,725	**2,750**	274	274	274	274
2,750	**2,775**	276	276	276	276
2,775	**2,800**	279	279	279	279
2,800	**2,825**	281	281	281	281
2,825	**2,850**	284	284	284	284
2,850	**2,875**	286	286	286	286
2,875	**2,900**	289	289	289	289
2,900	**2,925**	291	291	291	291
2,925	**2,950**	294	294	294	294
2,950	**2,975**	296	296	296	296
2,975	**3,000**	299	299	299	299
3,000					
3,000	**3,050**	303	303	303	303
3,050	**3,100**	308	308	308	308
3,100	**3,150**	313	313	313	313
3,150	**3,200**	318	318	318	318
3,200	**3,250**	323	323	323	323
3,250	**3,300**	328	328	328	328
3,300	**3,350**	333	333	333	333
3,350	**3,400**	338	338	338	338
3,400	**3,450**	343	343	343	343
3,450	**3,500**	348	348	348	348
3,500	**3,550**	353	353	353	353
3,550	**3,600**	358	358	358	358
3,600	**3,650**	363	363	363	363
3,650	**3,700**	368	368	368	368
3,700	**3,750**	373	373	373	373
3,750	**3,800**	378	378	378	378
3,800	**3,850**	383	383	383	383
3,850	**3,900**	388	388	388	388
3,900	**3,950**	393	393	393	393
3,950	**4,000**	398	398	398	398
4,000					
4,000	**4,050**	403	403	403	403
4,050	**4,100**	408	408	408	408
4,100	**4,150**	413	413	413	413
4,150	**4,200**	418	418	418	418
4,200	**4,250**	423	423	423	423
4,250	**4,300**	428	428	428	428
4,300	**4,350**	433	433	433	433
4,350	**4,400**	438	438	438	438
4,400	**4,450**	443	443	443	443
4,450	**4,500**	448	448	448	448
4,500	**4,550**	453	453	453	453
4,550	**4,600**	458	458	458	458
4,600	**4,650**	463	463	463	463
4,650	**4,700**	468	468	468	468
4,700	**4,750**	473	473	473	473
4,750	**4,800**	478	478	478	478
4,800	**4,850**	483	483	483	483
4,850	**4,900**	488	488	488	488
4,900	**4,950**	493	493	493	493
4,950	**5,000**	498	498	498	498

* This column must also be used by a qualifying widow(er).

(Continued on next page)

2010 Tax Table–*Continued*

If line 43 (taxable income) is— At least	But less than	And you are— Single	Married filing jointly *	Married filing separately	Head of a household
		Your tax is—			
5,000					
5,000	5,050	503	503	503	503
5,050	5,100	508	508	508	508
5,100	5,150	513	513	513	513
5,150	5,200	518	518	518	518
5,200	5,250	523	523	523	523
5,250	5,300	528	528	528	528
5,300	5,350	533	533	533	533
5,350	5,400	538	538	538	538
5,400	5,450	543	543	543	543
5,450	5,500	548	548	548	548
5,500	5,550	553	553	553	553
5,550	5,600	558	558	558	558
5,600	5,650	563	563	563	563
5,650	5,700	568	568	568	568
5,700	5,750	573	573	573	573
5,750	5,800	578	578	578	578
5,800	5,850	583	583	583	583
5,850	5,900	588	588	588	588
5,900	5,950	593	593	593	593
5,950	6,000	598	598	598	598
6,000					
6,000	6,050	603	603	603	603
6,050	6,100	608	608	608	608
6,100	6,150	613	613	613	613
6,150	6,200	618	618	618	618
6,200	6,250	623	623	623	623
6,250	6,300	628	628	628	628
6,300	6,350	633	633	633	633
6,350	6,400	638	638	638	638
6,400	6,450	643	643	643	643
6,450	6,500	648	648	648	648
6,500	6,550	653	653	653	653
6,550	6,600	658	658	658	658
6,600	6,650	663	663	663	663
6,650	6,700	668	668	668	668
6,700	6,750	673	673	673	673
6,750	6,800	678	678	678	678
6,800	6,850	683	683	683	683
6,850	6,900	688	688	688	688
6,900	6,950	693	693	693	693
6,950	7,000	698	698	698	698
7,000					
7,000	7,050	703	703	703	703
7,050	7,100	708	708	708	708
7,100	7,150	713	713	713	713
7,150	7,200	718	718	718	718
7,200	7,250	723	723	723	723
7,250	7,300	728	728	728	728
7,300	7,350	733	733	733	733
7,350	7,400	738	738	738	738
7,400	7,450	743	743	743	743
7,450	7,500	748	748	748	748
7,500	7,550	753	753	753	753
7,550	7,600	758	758	758	758
7,600	7,650	763	763	763	763
7,650	7,700	768	768	768	768
7,700	7,750	773	773	773	773
7,750	7,800	778	778	778	778
7,800	7,850	783	783	783	783
7,850	7,900	788	788	788	788
7,900	7,950	793	793	793	793
7,950	8,000	798	798	798	798

If line 43 (taxable income) is— At least	But less than	And you are— Single	Married filing jointly *	Married filing separately	Head of a household
		Your tax is—			
8,000					
8,000	8,050	803	803	803	803
8,050	8,100	808	808	808	808
8,100	8,150	813	813	813	813
8,150	8,200	818	818	818	818
8,200	8,250	823	823	823	823
8,250	8,300	828	828	828	828
8,300	8,350	833	833	833	833
8,350	8,400	838	838	838	838
8,400	8,450	845	843	845	843
8,450	8,500	853	848	853	848
8,500	8,550	860	853	860	853
8,550	8,600	868	858	868	858
8,600	8,650	875	863	875	863
8,650	8,700	883	868	883	868
8,700	8,750	890	873	890	873
8,750	8,800	898	878	898	878
8,800	8,850	905	883	905	883
8,850	8,900	913	888	913	888
8,900	8,950	920	893	920	893
8,950	9,000	928	898	928	898
9,000					
9,000	9,050	935	903	935	903
9,050	9,100	943	908	943	908
9,100	9,150	950	913	950	913
9,150	9,200	958	918	958	918
9,200	9,250	965	923	965	923
9,250	9,300	973	928	973	928
9,300	9,350	980	933	980	933
9,350	9,400	988	938	988	938
9,400	9,450	995	943	995	943
9,450	9,500	1,003	948	1,003	948
9,500	9,550	1,010	953	1,010	953
9,550	9,600	1,018	958	1,018	958
9,600	9,650	1,025	963	1,025	963
9,650	9,700	1,033	968	1,033	968
9,700	9,750	1,040	973	1,040	973
9,750	9,800	1,048	978	1,048	978
9,800	9,850	1,055	983	1,055	983
9,850	9,900	1,063	988	1,063	988
9,900	9,950	1,070	993	1,070	993
9,950	10,000	1,078	998	1,078	998
10,000					
10,000	10,050	1,085	1,003	1,085	1,003
10,050	10,100	1,093	1,008	1,093	1,008
10,100	10,150	1,100	1,013	1,100	1,013
10,150	10,200	1,108	1,018	1,108	1,018
10,200	10,250	1,115	1,023	1,115	1,023
10,250	10,300	1,123	1,028	1,123	1,028
10,300	10,350	1,130	1,033	1,130	1,033
10,350	10,400	1,138	1,038	1,138	1,038
10,400	10,450	1,145	1,043	1,145	1,043
10,450	10,500	1,153	1,048	1,153	1,048
10,500	10,550	1,160	1,053	1,160	1,053
10,550	10,600	1,168	1,058	1,168	1,058
10,600	10,650	1,175	1,063	1,175	1,063
10,650	10,700	1,183	1,068	1,183	1,068
10,700	10,750	1,190	1,073	1,190	1,073
10,750	10,800	1,198	1,078	1,198	1,078
10,800	10,850	1,205	1,083	1,205	1,083
10,850	10,900	1,213	1,088	1,213	1,088
10,900	10,950	1,220	1,093	1,220	1,093
10,950	11,000	1,228	1,098	1,228	1,098

If line 43 (taxable income) is— At least	But less than	And you are— Single	Married filing jointly *	Married filing separately	Head of a household
		Your tax is—			
11,000					
11,000	11,050	1,235	1,103	1,235	1,103
11,050	11,100	1,243	1,108	1,243	1,108
11,100	11,150	1,250	1,113	1,250	1,113
11,150	11,200	1,258	1,118	1,258	1,118
11,200	11,250	1,265	1,123	1,265	1,123
11,250	11,300	1,273	1,128	1,273	1,128
11,300	11,350	1,280	1,133	1,280	1,133
11,350	11,400	1,288	1,138	1,288	1,138
11,400	11,450	1,295	1,143	1,295	1,143
11,450	11,500	1,303	1,148	1,303	1,148
11,500	11,550	1,310	1,153	1,310	1,153
11,550	11,600	1,318	1,158	1,318	1,158
11,600	11,650	1,325	1,163	1,325	1,163
11,650	11,700	1,333	1,168	1,333	1,168
11,700	11,750	1,340	1,173	1,340	1,173
11,750	11,800	1,348	1,178	1,348	1,178
11,800	11,850	1,355	1,183	1,355	1,183
11,850	11,900	1,363	1,188	1,363	1,188
11,900	11,950	1,370	1,193	1,370	1,193
11,950	12,000	1,378	1,198	1,378	1,199
12,000					
12,000	12,050	1,385	1,203	1,385	1,206
12,050	12,100	1,393	1,208	1,393	1,214
12,100	12,150	1,400	1,213	1,400	1,221
12,150	12,200	1,408	1,218	1,408	1,229
12,200	12,250	1,415	1,223	1,415	1,236
12,250	12,300	1,423	1,228	1,423	1,244
12,300	12,350	1,430	1,233	1,430	1,251
12,350	12,400	1,438	1,238	1,438	1,259
12,400	12,450	1,445	1,243	1,445	1,266
12,450	12,500	1,453	1,248	1,453	1,274
12,500	12,550	1,460	1,253	1,460	1,281
12,550	12,600	1,468	1,258	1,468	1,289
12,600	12,650	1,475	1,263	1,475	1,296
12,650	12,700	1,483	1,268	1,483	1,304
12,700	12,750	1,490	1,273	1,490	1,311
12,750	12,800	1,498	1,278	1,498	1,319
12,800	12,850	1,505	1,283	1,505	1,326
12,850	12,900	1,513	1,288	1,513	1,334
12,900	12,950	1,520	1,293	1,520	1,341
12,950	13,000	1,528	1,298	1,528	1,349
13,000					
13,000	13,050	1,535	1,303	1,535	1,356
13,050	13,100	1,543	1,308	1,543	1,364
13,100	13,150	1,550	1,313	1,550	1,371
13,150	13,200	1,558	1,318	1,558	1,379
13,200	13,250	1,565	1,323	1,565	1,386
13,250	13,300	1,573	1,328	1,573	1,394
13,300	13,350	1,580	1,333	1,580	1,401
13,350	13,400	1,588	1,338	1,588	1,409
13,400	13,450	1,595	1,343	1,595	1,416
13,450	13,500	1,603	1,348	1,603	1,424
13,500	13,550	1,610	1,353	1,610	1,431
13,550	13,600	1,618	1,358	1,618	1,439
13,600	13,650	1,625	1,363	1,625	1,446
13,650	13,700	1,633	1,368	1,633	1,454
13,700	13,750	1,640	1,373	1,640	1,461
13,750	13,800	1,648	1,378	1,648	1,469
13,800	13,850	1,655	1,383	1,655	1,476
13,850	13,900	1,663	1,388	1,663	1,484
13,900	13,950	1,670	1,393	1,670	1,491
13,950	14,000	1,678	1,398	1,678	1,499

* This column must also be used by a qualifying widow(er).

(Continued on next page)

2010 Tax Table—*Continued*

If line 43 (taxable income) is— At least	But less than	And you are— Single	Married filing jointly *	Married filing separately	Head of a household
		Your tax is—			
14,000					
14,000	14,050	1,685	1,403	1,685	1,506
14,050	14,100	1,693	1,408	1,693	1,514
14,100	14,150	1,700	1,413	1,700	1,521
14,150	14,200	1,708	1,418	1,708	1,529
14,200	14,250	1,715	1,423	1,715	1,536
14,250	14,300	1,723	1,428	1,723	1,544
14,300	14,350	1,730	1,433	1,730	1,551
14,350	14,400	1,738	1,438	1,738	1,559
14,400	14,450	1,745	1,443	1,745	1,566
14,450	14,500	1,753	1,448	1,753	1,574
14,500	14,550	1,760	1,453	1,760	1,581
14,550	14,600	1,768	1,458	1,768	1,589
14,600	14,650	1,775	1,463	1,775	1,596
14,650	14,700	1,783	1,468	1,783	1,604
14,700	14,750	1,790	1,473	1,790	1,611
14,750	14,800	1,798	1,478	1,798	1,619
14,800	14,850	1,805	1,483	1,805	1,626
14,850	14,900	1,813	1,488	1,813	1,634
14,900	14,950	1,820	1,493	1,820	1,641
14,950	15,000	1,828	1,498	1,828	1,649
15,000					
15,000	15,050	1,835	1,503	1,835	1,656
15,050	15,100	1,843	1,508	1,843	1,664
15,100	15,150	1,850	1,513	1,850	1,671
15,150	15,200	1,858	1,518	1,858	1,679
15,200	15,250	1,865	1,523	1,865	1,686
15,250	15,300	1,873	1,528	1,873	1,694
15,300	15,350	1,880	1,533	1,880	1,701
15,350	15,400	1,888	1,538	1,888	1,709
15,400	15,450	1,895	1,543	1,895	1,716
15,450	15,500	1,903	1,548	1,903	1,724
15,500	15,550	1,910	1,553	1,910	1,731
15,550	15,600	1,918	1,558	1,918	1,739
15,600	15,650	1,925	1,563	1,925	1,746
15,650	15,700	1,933	1,568	1,933	1,754
15,700	15,750	1,940	1,573	1,940	1,761
15,750	15,800	1,948	1,578	1,948	1,769
15,800	15,850	1,955	1,583	1,955	1,776
15,850	15,900	1,963	1,588	1,963	1,784
15,900	15,950	1,970	1,593	1,970	1,791
15,950	16,000	1,978	1,598	1,978	1,799
16,000					
16,000	16,050	1,985	1,603	1,985	1,806
16,050	16,100	1,993	1,608	1,993	1,814
16,100	16,150	2,000	1,613	2,000	1,821
16,150	16,200	2,008	1,618	2,008	1,829
16,200	16,250	2,015	1,623	2,015	1,836
16,250	16,300	2,023	1,628	2,023	1,844
16,300	16,350	2,030	1,633	2,030	1,851
16,350	16,400	2,038	1,638	2,038	1,859
16,400	16,450	2,045	1,643	2,045	1,866
16,450	16,500	2,053	1,648	2,053	1,874
16,500	16,550	2,060	1,653	2,060	1,881
16,550	16,600	2,068	1,658	2,068	1,889
16,600	16,650	2,075	1,663	2,075	1,896
16,650	16,700	2,083	1,668	2,083	1,904
16,700	16,750	2,090	1,673	2,090	1,911
16,750	16,800	2,098	1,679	2,098	1,919
16,800	16,850	2,105	1,686	2,105	1,926
16,850	16,900	2,113	1,694	2,113	1,934
16,900	16,950	2,120	1,701	2,120	1,941
16,950	17,000	2,128	1,709	2,128	1,949
17,000					
17,000	17,050	2,135	1,716	2,135	1,956
17,050	17,100	2,143	1,724	2,143	1,964
17,100	17,150	2,150	1,731	2,150	1,971
17,150	17,200	2,158	1,739	2,158	1,979
17,200	17,250	2,165	1,746	2,165	1,986
17,250	17,300	2,173	1,754	2,173	1,994
17,300	17,350	2,180	1,761	2,180	2,001
17,350	17,400	2,188	1,769	2,188	2,009
17,400	17,450	2,195	1,776	2,195	2,016
17,450	17,500	2,203	1,784	2,203	2,024
17,500	17,550	2,210	1,791	2,210	2,031
17,550	17,600	2,218	1,799	2,218	2,039
17,600	17,650	2,225	1,806	2,225	2,046
17,650	17,700	2,233	1,814	2,233	2,054
17,700	17,750	2,240	1,821	2,240	2,061
17,750	17,800	2,248	1,829	2,248	2,069
17,800	17,850	2,255	1,836	2,255	2,076
17,850	17,900	2,263	1,844	2,263	2,084
17,900	17,950	2,270	1,851	2,270	2,091
17,950	18,000	2,278	1,859	2,278	2,099
18,000					
18,000	18,050	2,285	1,866	2,285	2,106
18,050	18,100	2,293	1,874	2,293	2,114
18,100	18,150	2,300	1,881	2,300	2,121
18,150	18,200	2,308	1,889	2,308	2,129
18,200	18,250	2,315	1,896	2,315	2,136
18,250	18,300	2,323	1,904	2,323	2,144
18,300	18,350	2,330	1,911	2,330	2,151
18,350	18,400	2,338	1,919	2,338	2,159
18,400	18,450	2,345	1,926	2,345	2,166
18,450	18,500	2,353	1,934	2,353	2,174
18,500	18,550	2,360	1,941	2,360	2,181
18,550	18,600	2,368	1,949	2,368	2,189
18,600	18,650	2,375	1,956	2,375	2,196
18,650	18,700	2,383	1,964	2,383	2,204
18,700	18,750	2,390	1,971	2,390	2,211
18,750	18,800	2,398	1,979	2,398	2,219
18,800	18,850	2,405	1,986	2,405	2,226
18,850	18,900	2,413	1,994	2,413	2,234
18,900	18,950	2,420	2,001	2,420	2,241
18,950	19,000	2,428	2,009	2,428	2,249
19,000					
19,000	19,050	2,435	2,016	2,435	2,256
19,050	19,100	2,443	2,024	2,443	2,264
19,100	19,150	2,450	2,031	2,450	2,271
19,150	19,200	2,458	2,039	2,458	2,279
19,200	19,250	2,465	2,046	2,465	2,286
19,250	19,300	2,473	2,054	2,473	2,294
19,300	19,350	2,480	2,061	2,480	2,301
19,350	19,400	2,488	2,069	2,488	2,309
19,400	19,450	2,495	2,076	2,495	2,316
19,450	19,500	2,503	2,084	2,503	2,324
19,500	19,550	2,510	2,091	2,510	2,331
19,550	19,600	2,518	2,099	2,518	2,339
19,600	19,650	2,525	2,106	2,525	2,346
19,650	19,700	2,533	2,114	2,533	2,354
19,700	19,750	2,540	2,121	2,540	2,361
19,750	19,800	2,548	2,129	2,548	2,369
19,800	19,850	2,555	2,136	2,555	2,376
19,850	19,900	2,563	2,144	2,563	2,384
19,900	19,950	2,570	2,151	2,570	2,391
19,950	20,000	2,578	2,159	2,578	2,399
20,000					
20,000	20,050	2,585	2,166	2,585	2,406
20,050	20,100	2,593	2,174	2,593	2,414
20,100	20,150	2,600	2,181	2,600	2,421
20,150	20,200	2,608	2,189	2,608	2,429
20,200	20,250	2,615	2,196	2,615	2,436
20,250	20,300	2,623	2,204	2,623	2,444
20,300	20,350	2,630	2,211	2,630	2,451
20,350	20,400	2,638	2,219	2,638	2,459
20,400	20,450	2,645	2,226	2,645	2,466
20,450	20,500	2,653	2,234	2,653	2,474
20,500	20,550	2,660	2,241	2,660	2,481
20,550	20,600	2,668	2,249	2,668	2,489
20,600	20,650	2,675	2,256	2,675	2,496
20,650	20,700	2,683	2,264	2,683	2,504
20,700	20,750	2,690	2,271	2,690	2,511
20,750	20,800	2,698	2,279	2,698	2,519
20,800	20,850	2,705	2,286	2,705	2,526
20,850	20,900	2,713	2,294	2,713	2,534
20,900	20,950	2,720	2,301	2,720	2,541
20,950	21,000	2,728	2,309	2,728	2,549
21,000					
21,000	21,050	2,735	2,316	2,735	2,556
21,050	21,100	2,743	2,324	2,743	2,564
21,100	21,150	2,750	2,331	2,750	2,571
21,150	21,200	2,758	2,339	2,758	2,579
21,200	21,250	2,765	2,346	2,765	2,586
21,250	21,300	2,773	2,354	2,773	2,594
21,300	21,350	2,780	2,361	2,780	2,601
21,350	21,400	2,788	2,369	2,788	2,609
21,400	21,450	2,795	2,376	2,795	2,616
21,450	21,500	2,803	2,384	2,803	2,624
21,500	21,550	2,810	2,391	2,810	2,631
21,550	21,600	2,818	2,399	2,818	2,639
21,600	21,650	2,825	2,406	2,825	2,646
21,650	21,700	2,833	2,414	2,833	2,654
21,700	21,750	2,840	2,421	2,840	2,661
21,750	21,800	2,848	2,429	2,848	2,669
21,800	21,850	2,855	2,436	2,855	2,676
21,850	21,900	2,863	2,444	2,863	2,684
21,900	21,950	2,870	2,451	2,870	2,691
21,950	22,000	2,878	2,459	2,878	2,699
22,000					
22,000	22,050	2,885	2,466	2,885	2,706
22,050	22,100	2,893	2,474	2,893	2,714
22,100	22,150	2,900	2,481	2,900	2,721
22,150	22,200	2,908	2,489	2,908	2,729
22,200	22,250	2,915	2,496	2,915	2,736
22,250	22,300	2,923	2,504	2,923	2,744
22,300	22,350	2,930	2,511	2,930	2,751
22,350	22,400	2,938	2,519	2,938	2,759
22,400	22,450	2,945	2,526	2,945	2,766
22,450	22,500	2,953	2,534	2,953	2,774
22,500	22,550	2,960	2,541	2,960	2,781
22,550	22,600	2,968	2,549	2,968	2,789
22,600	22,650	2,975	2,556	2,975	2,796
22,650	22,700	2,983	2,564	2,983	2,804
22,700	22,750	2,990	2,571	2,990	2,811
22,750	22,800	2,998	2,579	2,998	2,819
22,800	22,850	3,005	2,586	3,005	2,826
22,850	22,900	3,013	2,594	3,013	2,834
22,900	22,950	3,020	2,601	3,020	2,841
22,950	23,000	3,028	2,609	3,028	2,849

* This column must also be used by a qualifying widow(er).

(Continued on next page)

2010 Tax Table–*Continued*

If line 43 (taxable income) is— At least	But less than	And you are— Single	Married filing jointly *	Married filing separately	Head of a household
		Your tax is—			
23,000					
23,000	**23,050**	3,035	2,616	3,035	2,856
23,050	**23,100**	3,043	2,624	3,043	2,864
23,100	**23,150**	3,050	2,631	3,050	2,871
23,150	**23,200**	3,058	2,639	3,058	2,879
23,200	**23,250**	3,065	2,646	3,065	2,886
23,250	**23,300**	3,073	2,654	3,073	2,894
23,300	**23,350**	3,080	2,661	3,080	2,901
23,350	**23,400**	3,088	2,669	3,088	2,909
23,400	**23,450**	3,095	2,676	3,095	2,916
23,450	**23,500**	3,103	2,684	3,103	2,924
23,500	**23,550**	3,110	2,691	3,110	2,931
23,550	**23,600**	3,118	2,699	3,118	2,939
23,600	**23,650**	3,125	2,706	3,125	2,946
23,650	**23,700**	3,133	2,714	3,133	2,954
23,700	**23,750**	3,140	2,721	3,140	2,961
23,750	**23,800**	3,148	2,729	3,148	2,969
23,800	**23,850**	3,155	2,736	3,155	2,976
23,850	**23,900**	3,163	2,744	3,163	2,984
23,900	**23,950**	3,170	2,751	3,170	2,991
23,950	**24,000**	3,178	2,759	3,178	2,999
24,000					
24,000	**24,050**	3,185	2,766	3,185	3,006
24,050	**24,100**	3,193	2,774	3,193	3,014
24,100	**24,150**	3,200	2,781	3,200	3,021
24,150	**24,200**	3,208	2,789	3,208	3,029
24,200	**24,250**	3,215	2,796	3,215	3,036
24,250	**24,300**	3,223	2,804	3,223	3,044
24,300	**24,350**	3,230	2,811	3,230	3,051
24,350	**24,400**	3,238	2,819	3,238	3,059
24,400	**24,450**	3,245	2,826	3,245	3,066
24,450	**24,500**	3,253	2,834	3,253	3,074
24,500	**24,550**	3,260	2,841	3,260	3,081
24,550	**24,600**	3,268	2,849	3,268	3,089
24,600	**24,650**	3,275	2,856	3,275	3,096
24,650	**24,700**	3,283	2,864	3,283	3,104
24,700	**24,750**	3,290	2,871	3,290	3,111
24,750	**24,800**	3,298	2,879	3,298	3,119
24,800	**24,850**	3,305	2,886	3,305	3,126
24,850	**24,900**	3,313	2,894	3,313	3,134
24,900	**24,950**	3,320	2,901	3,320	3,141
24,950	**25,000**	3,328	2,909	3,328	3,149
25,000					
25,000	**25,050**	3,335	2,916	3,335	3,156
25,050	**25,100**	3,343	2,924	3,343	3,164
25,100	**25,150**	3,350	2,931	3,350	3,171
25,150	**25,200**	3,358	2,939	3,358	3,179
25,200	**25,250**	3,365	2,946	3,365	3,186
25,250	**25,300**	3,373	2,954	3,373	3,194
25,300	**25,350**	3,380	2,961	3,380	3,201
25,350	**25,400**	3,388	2,969	3,388	3,209
25,400	**25,450**	3,395	2,976	3,395	3,216
25,450	**25,500**	3,403	2,984	3,403	3,224
25,500	**25,550**	3,410	2,991	3,410	3,231
25,550	**25,600**	3,418	2,999	3,418	3,239
25,600	**25,650**	3,425	3,006	3,425	3,246
25,650	**25,700**	3,433	3,014	3,433	3,254
25,700	**25,750**	3,440	3,021	3,440	3,261
25,750	**25,800**	3,448	3,029	3,448	3,269
25,800	**25,850**	3,455	3,036	3,455	3,276
25,850	**25,900**	3,463	3,044	3,463	3,284
25,900	**25,950**	3,470	3,051	3,470	3,291
25,950	**26,000**	3,478	3,059	3,478	3,299

If line 43 (taxable income) is— At least	But less than	And you are— Single	Married filing jointly *	Married filing separately	Head of a household
		Your tax is—			
26,000					
26,000	**26,050**	3,485	3,066	3,485	3,306
26,050	**26,100**	3,493	3,074	3,493	3,314
26,100	**26,150**	3,500	3,081	3,500	3,321
26,150	**26,200**	3,508	3,089	3,508	3,329
26,200	**26,250**	3,515	3,096	3,515	3,336
26,250	**26,300**	3,523	3,104	3,523	3,344
26,300	**26,350**	3,530	3,111	3,530	3,351
26,350	**26,400**	3,538	3,119	3,538	3,359
26,400	**26,450**	3,545	3,126	3,545	3,366
26,450	**26,500**	3,553	3,134	3,553	3,374
26,500	**26,550**	3,560	3,141	3,560	3,381
26,550	**26,600**	3,568	3,149	3,568	3,389
26,600	**26,650**	3,575	3,156	3,575	3,396
26,650	**26,700**	3,583	3,164	3,583	3,404
26,700	**26,750**	3,590	3,171	3,590	3,411
26,750	**26,800**	3,598	3,179	3,598	3,419
26,800	**26,850**	3,605	3,186	3,605	3,426
26,850	**26,900**	3,613	3,194	3,613	3,434
26,900	**26,950**	3,620	3,201	3,620	3,441
26,950	**27,000**	3,628	3,209	3,628	3,449
27,000					
27,000	**27,050**	3,635	3,216	3,635	3,456
27,050	**27,100**	3,643	3,224	3,643	3,464
27,100	**27,150**	3,650	3,231	3,650	3,471
27,150	**27,200**	3,658	3,239	3,658	3,479
27,200	**27,250**	3,665	3,246	3,665	3,486
27,250	**27,300**	3,673	3,254	3,673	3,494
27,300	**27,350**	3,680	3,261	3,680	3,501
27,350	**27,400**	3,688	3,269	3,688	3,509
27,400	**27,450**	3,695	3,276	3,695	3,516
27,450	**27,500**	3,703	3,284	3,703	3,524
27,500	**27,550**	3,710	3,291	3,710	3,531
27,550	**27,600**	3,718	3,299	3,718	3,539
27,600	**27,650**	3,725	3,306	3,725	3,546
27,650	**27,700**	3,733	3,314	3,733	3,554
27,700	**27,750**	3,740	3,321	3,740	3,561
27,750	**27,800**	3,748	3,329	3,748	3,569
27,800	**27,850**	3,755	3,336	3,755	3,576
27,850	**27,900**	3,763	3,344	3,763	3,584
27,900	**27,950**	3,770	3,351	3,770	3,591
27,950	**28,000**	3,778	3,359	3,778	3,599
28,000					
28,000	**28,050**	3,785	3,366	3,785	3,606
28,050	**28,100**	3,793	3,374	3,793	3,614
28,100	**28,150**	3,800	3,381	3,800	3,621
28,150	**28,200**	3,808	3,389	3,808	3,629
28,200	**28,250**	3,815	3,396	3,815	3,636
28,250	**28,300**	3,823	3,404	3,823	3,644
28,300	**28,350**	3,830	3,411	3,830	3,651
28,350	**28,400**	3,838	3,419	3,838	3,659
28,400	**28,450**	3,845	3,426	3,845	3,666
28,450	**28,500**	3,853	3,434	3,853	3,674
28,500	**28,550**	3,860	3,441	3,860	3,681
28,550	**28,600**	3,868	3,449	3,868	3,689
28,600	**28,650**	3,875	3,456	3,875	3,696
28,650	**28,700**	3,883	3,464	3,883	3,704
28,700	**28,750**	3,890	3,471	3,890	3,711
28,750	**28,800**	3,898	3,479	3,898	3,719
28,800	**28,850**	3,905	3,486	3,905	3,726
28,850	**28,900**	3,913	3,494	3,913	3,734
28,900	**28,950**	3,920	3,501	3,920	3,741
28,950	**29,000**	3,928	3,509	3,928	3,749

If line 43 (taxable income) is— At least	But less than	And you are— Single	Married filing jointly *	Married filing separately	Head of a household
		Your tax is—			
29,000					
29,000	**29,050**	3,935	3,516	3,935	3,756
29,050	**29,100**	3,943	3,524	3,943	3,764
29,100	**29,150**	3,950	3,531	3,950	3,771
29,150	**29,200**	3,958	3,539	3,958	3,779
29,200	**29,250**	3,965	3,546	3,965	3,786
29,250	**29,300**	3,973	3,554	3,973	3,794
29,300	**29,350**	3,980	3,561	3,980	3,801
29,350	**29,400**	3,988	3,569	3,988	3,809
29,400	**29,450**	3,995	3,576	3,995	3,816
29,450	**29,500**	4,003	3,584	4,003	3,824
29,500	**29,550**	4,010	3,591	4,010	3,831
29,550	**29,600**	4,018	3,599	4,018	3,839
29,600	**29,650**	4,025	3,606	4,025	3,846
29,650	**29,700**	4,033	3,614	4,033	3,854
29,700	**29,750**	4,040	3,621	4,040	3,861
29,750	**29,800**	4,048	3,629	4,048	3,869
29,800	**29,850**	4,055	3,636	4,055	3,876
29,850	**29,900**	4,063	3,644	4,063	3,884
29,900	**29,950**	4,070	3,651	4,070	3,891
29,950	**30,000**	4,078	3,659	4,078	3,899
30,000					
30,000	**30,050**	4,085	3,666	4,085	3,906
30,050	**30,100**	4,093	3,674	4,093	3,914
30,100	**30,150**	4,100	3,681	4,100	3,921
30,150	**30,200**	4,108	3,689	4,108	3,929
30,200	**30,250**	4,115	3,696	4,115	3,936
30,250	**30,300**	4,123	3,704	4,123	3,944
30,300	**30,350**	4,130	3,711	4,130	3,951
30,350	**30,400**	4,138	3,719	4,138	3,959
30,400	**30,450**	4,145	3,726	4,145	3,966
30,450	**30,500**	4,153	3,734	4,153	3,974
30,500	**30,550**	4,160	3,741	4,160	3,981
30,550	**30,600**	4,168	3,749	4,168	3,989
30,600	**30,650**	4,175	3,756	4,175	3,996
30,650	**30,700**	4,183	3,764	4,183	4,004
30,700	**30,750**	4,190	3,771	4,190	4,011
30,750	**30,800**	4,198	3,779	4,198	4,019
30,800	**30,850**	4,205	3,786	4,205	4,026
30,850	**30,900**	4,213	3,794	4,213	4,034
30,900	**30,950**	4,220	3,801	4,220	4,041
30,950	**31,000**	4,228	3,809	4,228	4,049
31,000					
31,000	**31,050**	4,235	3,816	4,235	4,056
31,050	**31,100**	4,243	3,824	4,243	4,064
31,100	**31,150**	4,250	3,831	4,250	4,071
31,150	**31,200**	4,258	3,839	4,258	4,079
31,200	**31,250**	4,265	3,846	4,265	4,086
31,250	**31,300**	4,273	3,854	4,273	4,094
31,300	**31,350**	4,280	3,861	4,280	4,101
31,350	**31,400**	4,288	3,869	4,288	4,109
31,400	**31,450**	4,295	3,876	4,295	4,116
31,450	**31,500**	4,303	3,884	4,303	4,124
31,500	**31,550**	4,310	3,891	4,310	4,131
31,550	**31,600**	4,318	3,899	4,318	4,139
31,600	**31,650**	4,325	3,906	4,325	4,146
31,650	**31,700**	4,333	3,914	4,333	4,154
31,700	**31,750**	4,340	3,921	4,340	4,161
31,750	**31,800**	4,348	3,929	4,348	4,169
31,800	**31,850**	4,355	3,936	4,355	4,176
31,850	**31,900**	4,363	3,944	4,363	4,184
31,900	**31,950**	4,370	3,951	4,370	4,191
31,950	**32,000**	4,378	3,959	4,378	4,199

* This column must also be used by a qualifying widow(er).

(Continued on next page)

2010 Tax Table–*Continued*

If line 43 (taxable income) is—		And you are—			
At least	But less than	Single	Married filing jointly *	Married filing separately	Head of a household
		Your tax is—			
32,000					
32,000	32,050	4,385	3,966	4,385	4,206
32,050	32,100	4,393	3,974	4,393	4,214
32,100	32,150	4,400	3,981	4,400	4,221
32,150	32,200	4,408	3,989	4,408	4,229
32,200	32,250	4,415	3,996	4,415	4,236
32,250	32,300	4,423	4,004	4,423	4,244
32,300	32,350	4,430	4,011	4,430	4,251
32,350	32,400	4,438	4,019	4,438	4,259
32,400	32,450	4,445	4,026	4,445	4,266
32,450	32,500	4,453	4,034	4,453	4,274
32,500	32,550	4,460	4,041	4,460	4,281
32,550	32,600	4,468	4,049	4,468	4,289
32,600	32,650	4,475	4,056	4,475	4,296
32,650	32,700	4,483	4,064	4,483	4,304
32,700	32,750	4,490	4,071	4,490	4,311
32,750	32,800	4,498	4,079	4,498	4,319
32,800	32,850	4,505	4,086	4,505	4,326
32,850	32,900	4,513	4,094	4,513	4,334
32,900	32,950	4,520	4,101	4,520	4,341
32,950	33,000	4,528	4,109	4,528	4,349
33,000					
33,000	33,050	4,535	4,116	4,535	4,356
33,050	33,100	4,543	4,124	4,543	4,364
33,100	33,150	4,550	4,131	4,550	4,371
33,150	33,200	4,558	4,139	4,558	4,379
33,200	33,250	4,565	4,146	4,565	4,386
33,250	33,300	4,573	4,154	4,573	4,394
33,300	33,350	4,580	4,161	4,580	4,401
33,350	33,400	4,588	4,169	4,588	4,409
33,400	33,450	4,595	4,176	4,595	4,416
33,450	33,500	4,603	4,184	4,603	4,424
33,500	33,550	4,610	4,191	4,610	4,431
33,550	33,600	4,618	4,199	4,618	4,439
33,600	33,650	4,625	4,206	4,625	4,446
33,650	33,700	4,633	4,214	4,633	4,454
33,700	33,750	4,640	4,221	4,640	4,461
33,750	33,800	4,648	4,229	4,648	4,469
33,800	33,850	4,655	4,236	4,655	4,476
33,850	33,900	4,663	4,244	4,663	4,484
33,900	33,950	4,670	4,251	4,670	4,491
33,950	34,000	4,678	4,259	4,678	4,499
34,000					
34,000	34,050	4,688	4,266	4,688	4,506
34,050	34,100	4,700	4,274	4,700	4,514
34,100	34,150	4,713	4,281	4,713	4,521
34,150	34,200	4,725	4,289	4,725	4,529
34,200	34,250	4,738	4,296	4,738	4,536
34,250	34,300	4,750	4,304	4,750	4,544
34,300	34,350	4,763	4,311	4,763	4,551
34,350	34,400	4,775	4,319	4,775	4,559
34,400	34,450	4,788	4,326	4,788	4,566
34,450	34,500	4,800	4,334	4,800	4,574
34,500	34,550	4,813	4,341	4,813	4,581
34,550	34,600	4,825	4,349	4,825	4,589
34,600	34,650	4,838	4,356	4,838	4,596
34,650	34,700	4,850	4,364	4,850	4,604
34,700	34,750	4,863	4,371	4,863	4,611
34,750	34,800	4,875	4,379	4,875	4,619
34,800	34,850	4,888	4,386	4,888	4,626
34,850	34,900	4,900	4,394	4,900	4,634
34,900	34,950	4,913	4,401	4,913	4,641
34,950	35,000	4,925	4,409	4,925	4,649
35,000					
35,000	35,050	4,938	4,416	4,938	4,656
35,050	35,100	4,950	4,424	4,950	4,664
35,100	35,150	4,963	4,431	4,963	4,671
35,150	35,200	4,975	4,439	4,975	4,679
35,200	35,250	4,988	4,446	4,988	4,686
35,250	35,300	5,000	4,454	5,000	4,694
35,300	35,350	5,013	4,461	5,013	4,701
35,350	35,400	5,025	4,469	5,025	4,709
35,400	35,450	5,038	4,476	5,038	4,716
35,450	35,500	5,050	4,484	5,050	4,724
35,500	35,550	5,063	4,491	5,063	4,731
35,550	35,600	5,075	4,499	5,075	4,739
35,600	35,650	5,088	4,506	5,088	4,746
35,650	35,700	5,100	4,514	5,100	4,754
35,700	35,750	5,113	4,521	5,113	4,761
35,750	35,800	5,125	4,529	5,125	4,769
35,800	35,850	5,138	4,536	5,138	4,776
35,850	35,900	5,150	4,544	5,150	4,784
35,900	35,950	5,163	4,551	5,163	4,791
35,950	36,000	5,175	4,559	5,175	4,799
36,000					
36,000	36,050	5,188	4,566	5,188	4,806
36,050	36,100	5,200	4,574	5,200	4,814
36,100	36,150	5,213	4,581	5,213	4,821
36,150	36,200	5,225	4,589	5,225	4,829
36,200	36,250	5,238	4,596	5,238	4,836
36,250	36,300	5,250	4,604	5,250	4,844
36,300	36,350	5,263	4,611	5,263	4,851
36,350	36,400	5,275	4,619	5,275	4,859
36,400	36,450	5,288	4,626	5,288	4,866
36,450	36,500	5,300	4,634	5,300	4,874
36,500	36,550	5,313	4,641	5,313	4,881
36,550	36,600	5,325	4,649	5,325	4,889
36,600	36,650	5,338	4,656	5,338	4,896
36,650	36,700	5,350	4,664	5,350	4,904
36,700	36,750	5,363	4,671	5,363	4,911
36,750	36,800	5,375	4,679	5,375	4,919
36,800	36,850	5,388	4,686	5,388	4,926
36,850	36,900	5,400	4,694	5,400	4,934
36,900	36,950	5,413	4,701	5,413	4,941
36,950	37,000	5,425	4,709	5,425	4,949
37,000					
37,000	37,050	5,438	4,716	5,438	4,956
37,050	37,100	5,450	4,724	5,450	4,964
37,100	37,150	5,463	4,731	5,463	4,971
37,150	37,200	5,475	4,739	5,475	4,979
37,200	37,250	5,488	4,746	5,488	4,986
37,250	37,300	5,500	4,754	5,500	4,994
37,300	37,350	5,513	4,761	5,513	5,001
37,350	37,400	5,525	4,769	5,525	5,009
37,400	37,450	5,538	4,776	5,538	5,016
37,450	37,500	5,550	4,784	5,550	5,024
37,500	37,550	5,563	4,791	5,563	5,031
37,550	37,600	5,575	4,799	5,575	5,039
37,600	37,650	5,588	4,806	5,588	5,046
37,650	37,700	5,600	4,814	5,600	5,054
37,700	37,750	5,613	4,821	5,613	5,061
37,750	37,800	5,625	4,829	5,625	5,069
37,800	37,850	5,638	4,836	5,638	5,076
37,850	37,900	5,650	4,844	5,650	5,084
37,900	37,950	5,663	4,851	5,663	5,091
37,950	38,000	5,675	4,859	5,675	5,099
38,000					
38,000	38,050	5,688	4,866	5,688	5,106
38,050	38,100	5,700	4,874	5,700	5,114
38,100	38,150	5,713	4,881	5,713	5,121
38,150	38,200	5,725	4,889	5,725	5,129
38,200	38,250	5,738	4,896	5,738	5,136
38,250	38,300	5,750	4,904	5,750	5,144
38,300	38,350	5,763	4,911	5,763	5,151
38,350	38,400	5,775	4,919	5,775	5,159
38,400	38,450	5,788	4,926	5,788	5,166
38,450	38,500	5,800	4,934	5,800	5,174
38,500	38,550	5,813	4,941	5,813	5,181
38,550	38,600	5,825	4,949	5,825	5,189
38,600	38,650	5,838	4,956	5,838	5,196
38,650	38,700	5,850	4,964	5,850	5,204
38,700	38,750	5,863	4,971	5,863	5,211
38,750	38,800	5,875	4,979	5,875	5,219
38,800	38,850	5,888	4,986	5,888	5,226
38,850	38,900	5,900	4,994	5,900	5,234
38,900	38,950	5,913	5,001	5,913	5,241
38,950	39,000	5,925	5,009	5,925	5,249
39,000					
39,000	39,050	5,938	5,016	5,938	5,256
39,050	39,100	5,950	5,024	5,950	5,264
39,100	39,150	5,963	5,031	5,963	5,271
39,150	39,200	5,975	5,039	5,975	5,279
39,200	39,250	5,988	5,046	5,988	5,286
39,250	39,300	6,000	5,054	6,000	5,294
39,300	39,350	6,013	5,061	6,013	5,301
39,350	39,400	6,025	5,069	6,025	5,309
39,400	39,450	6,038	5,076	6,038	5,316
39,450	39,500	6,050	5,084	6,050	5,324
39,500	39,550	6,063	5,091	6,063	5,331
39,550	39,600	6,075	5,099	6,075	5,339
39,600	39,650	6,088	5,106	6,088	5,346
39,650	39,700	6,100	5,114	6,100	5,354
39,700	39,750	6,113	5,121	6,113	5,361
39,750	39,800	6,125	5,129	6,125	5,369
39,800	39,850	6,138	5,136	6,138	5,376
39,850	39,900	6,150	5,144	6,150	5,384
39,900	39,950	6,163	5,151	6,163	5,391
39,950	40,000	6,175	5,159	6,175	5,399
40,000					
40,000	40,050	6,188	5,166	6,188	5,406
40,050	40,100	6,200	5,174	6,200	5,414
40,100	40,150	6,213	5,181	6,213	5,421
40,150	40,200	6,225	5,189	6,225	5,429
40,200	40,250	6,238	5,196	6,238	5,436
40,250	40,300	6,250	5,204	6,250	5,444
40,300	40,350	6,263	5,211	6,263	5,451
40,350	40,400	6,275	5,219	6,275	5,459
40,400	40,450	6,288	5,226	6,288	5,466
40,450	40,500	6,300	5,234	6,300	5,474
40,500	40,550	6,313	5,241	6,313	5,481
40,550	40,600	6,325	5,249	6,325	5,489
40,600	40,650	6,338	5,256	6,338	5,496
40,650	40,700	6,350	5,264	6,350	5,504
40,700	40,750	6,363	5,271	6,363	5,511
40,750	40,800	6,375	5,279	6,375	5,519
40,800	40,850	6,388	5,286	6,388	5,526
40,850	40,900	6,400	5,294	6,400	5,534
40,900	40,950	6,413	5,301	6,413	5,541
40,950	41,000	6,425	5,309	6,425	5,549

* This column must also be used by a qualifying widow(er).

(Continued on next page)

2010 Tax Table–*Continued*

If line 43 (taxable income) is— At least	But less than	And you are— Single	Married filing jointly *	Married filing separately	Head of a household
		Your tax is—			
41,000					
41,000	**41,050**	6,438	5,316	6,438	5,556
41,050	**41,100**	6,450	5,324	6,450	5,564
41,100	**41,150**	6,463	5,331	6,463	5,571
41,150	**41,200**	6,475	5,339	6,475	5,579
41,200	**41,250**	6,488	5,346	6,488	5,586
41,250	**41,300**	6,500	5,354	6,500	5,594
41,300	**41,350**	6,513	5,361	6,513	5,601
41,350	**41,400**	6,525	5,369	6,525	5,609
41,400	**41,450**	6,538	5,376	6,538	5,616
41,450	**41,500**	6,550	5,384	6,550	5,624
41,500	**41,550**	6,563	5,391	6,563	5,631
41,550	**41,600**	6,575	5,399	6,575	5,639
41,600	**41,650**	6,588	5,406	6,588	5,646
41,650	**41,700**	6,600	5,414	6,600	5,654
41,700	**41,750**	6,613	5,421	6,613	5,661
41,750	**41,800**	6,625	5,429	6,625	5,669
41,800	**41,850**	6,638	5,436	6,638	5,676
41,850	**41,900**	6,650	5,444	6,650	5,684
41,900	**41,950**	6,663	5,451	6,663	5,691
41,950	**42,000**	6,675	5,459	6,675	5,699
42,000					
42,000	**42,050**	6,688	5,466	6,688	5,706
42,050	**42,100**	6,700	5,474	6,700	5,714
42,100	**42,150**	6,713	5,481	6,713	5,721
42,150	**42,200**	6,725	5,489	6,725	5,729
42,200	**42,250**	6,738	5,496	6,738	5,736
42,250	**42,300**	6,750	5,504	6,750	5,744
42,300	**42,350**	6,763	5,511	6,763	5,751
42,350	**42,400**	6,775	5,519	6,775	5,759
42,400	**42,450**	6,788	5,526	6,788	5,766
42,450	**42,500**	6,800	5,534	6,800	5,774
42,500	**42,550**	6,813	5,541	6,813	5,781
42,550	**42,600**	6,825	5,549	6,825	5,789
42,600	**42,650**	6,838	5,556	6,838	5,796
42,650	**42,700**	6,850	5,564	6,850	5,804
42,700	**42,750**	6,863	5,571	6,863	5,811
42,750	**42,800**	6,875	5,579	6,875	5,819
42,800	**42,850**	6,888	5,586	6,888	5,826
42,850	**42,900**	6,900	5,594	6,900	5,834
42,900	**42,950**	6,913	5,601	6,913	5,841
42,950	**43,000**	6,925	5,609	6,925	5,849
43,000					
43,000	**43,050**	6,938	5,616	6,938	5,856
43,050	**43,100**	6,950	5,624	6,950	5,864
43,100	**43,150**	6,963	5,631	6,963	5,871
43,150	**43,200**	6,975	5,639	6,975	5,879
43,200	**43,250**	6,988	5,646	6,988	5,886
43,250	**43,300**	7,000	5,654	7,000	5,894
43,300	**43,350**	7,013	5,661	7,013	5,901
43,350	**43,400**	7,025	5,669	7,025	5,909
43,400	**43,450**	7,038	5,676	7,038	5,916
43,450	**43,500**	7,050	5,684	7,050	5,924
43,500	**43,550**	7,063	5,691	7,063	5,931
43,550	**43,600**	7,075	5,699	7,075	5,939
43,600	**43,650**	7,088	5,706	7,088	5,946
43,650	**43,700**	7,100	5,714	7,100	5,954
43,700	**43,750**	7,113	5,721	7,113	5,961
43,750	**43,800**	7,125	5,729	7,125	5,969
43,800	**43,850**	7,138	5,736	7,138	5,976
43,850	**43,900**	7,150	5,744	7,150	5,984
43,900	**43,950**	7,163	5,751	7,163	5,991
43,950	**44,000**	7,175	5,759	7,175	5,999
44,000					
44,000	**44,050**	7,188	5,766	7,188	6,006
44,050	**44,100**	7,200	5,774	7,200	6,014
44,100	**44,150**	7,213	5,781	7,213	6,021
44,150	**44,200**	7,225	5,789	7,225	6,029
44,200	**44,250**	7,238	5,796	7,238	6,036
44,250	**44,300**	7,250	5,804	7,250	6,044
44,300	**44,350**	7,263	5,811	7,263	6,051
44,350	**44,400**	7,275	5,819	7,275	6,059
44,400	**44,450**	7,288	5,826	7,288	6,066
44,450	**44,500**	7,300	5,834	7,300	6,074
44,500	**44,550**	7,313	5,841	7,313	6,081
44,550	**44,600**	7,325	5,849	7,325	6,089
44,600	**44,650**	7,338	5,856	7,338	6,096
44,650	**44,700**	7,350	5,864	7,350	6,104
44,700	**44,750**	7,363	5,871	7,363	6,111
44,750	**44,800**	7,375	5,879	7,375	6,119
44,800	**44,850**	7,388	5,886	7,388	6,126
44,850	**44,900**	7,400	5,894	7,400	6,134
44,900	**44,950**	7,413	5,901	7,413	6,141
44,950	**45,000**	7,425	5,909	7,425	6,149
45,000					
45,000	**45,050**	7,438	5,916	7,438	6,156
45,050	**45,100**	7,450	5,924	7,450	6,164
45,100	**45,150**	7,463	5,931	7,463	6,171
45,150	**45,200**	7,475	5,939	7,475	6,179
45,200	**45,250**	7,488	5,946	7,488	6,186
45,250	**45,300**	7,500	5,954	7,500	6,194
45,300	**45,350**	7,513	5,961	7,513	6,201
45,350	**45,400**	7,525	5,969	7,525	6,209
45,400	**45,450**	7,538	5,976	7,538	6,216
45,450	**45,500**	7,550	5,984	7,550	6,224
45,500	**45,550**	7,563	5,991	7,563	6,231
45,550	**45,600**	7,575	5,999	7,575	6,241
45,600	**45,650**	7,588	6,006	7,588	6,254
45,650	**45,700**	7,600	6,014	7,600	6,266
45,700	**45,750**	7,613	6,021	7,613	6,279
45,750	**45,800**	7,625	6,029	7,625	6,291
45,800	**45,850**	7,638	6,036	7,638	6,304
45,850	**45,900**	7,650	6,044	7,650	6,316
45,900	**45,950**	7,663	6,051	7,663	6,329
45,950	**46,000**	7,675	6,059	7,675	6,341
46,000					
46,000	**46,050**	7,688	6,066	7,688	6,354
46,050	**46,100**	7,700	6,074	7,700	6,366
46,100	**46,150**	7,713	6,081	7,713	6,379
46,150	**46,200**	7,725	6,089	7,725	6,391
46,200	**46,250**	7,738	6,096	7,738	6,404
46,250	**46,300**	7,750	6,104	7,750	6,416
46,300	**46,350**	7,763	6,111	7,763	6,429
46,350	**46,400**	7,775	6,119	7,775	6,441
46,400	**46,450**	7,788	6,126	7,788	6,454
46,450	**46,500**	7,800	6,134	7,800	6,466
46,500	**46,550**	7,813	6,141	7,813	6,479
46,550	**46,600**	7,825	6,149	7,825	6,491
46,600	**46,650**	7,838	6,156	7,838	6,504
46,650	**46,700**	7,850	6,164	7,850	6,516
46,700	**46,750**	7,863	6,171	7,863	6,529
46,750	**46,800**	7,875	6,179	7,875	6,541
46,800	**46,850**	7,888	6,186	7,888	6,554
46,850	**46,900**	7,900	6,194	7,900	6,566
46,900	**46,950**	7,913	6,201	7,913	6,579
46,950	**47,000**	7,925	6,209	7,925	6,591
47,000					
47,000	**47,050**	7,938	6,216	7,938	6,604
47,050	**47,100**	7,950	6,224	7,950	6,616
47,100	**47,150**	7,963	6,231	7,963	6,629
47,150	**47,200**	7,975	6,239	7,975	6,641
47,200	**47,250**	7,988	6,246	7,988	6,654
47,250	**47,300**	8,000	6,254	8,000	6,666
47,300	**47,350**	8,013	6,261	8,013	6,679
47,350	**47,400**	8,025	6,269	8,025	6,691
47,400	**47,450**	8,038	6,276	8,038	6,704
47,450	**47,500**	8,050	6,284	8,050	6,716
47,500	**47,550**	8,063	6,291	8,063	6,729
47,550	**47,600**	8,075	6,299	8,075	6,741
47,600	**47,650**	8,088	6,306	8,088	6,754
47,650	**47,700**	8,100	6,314	8,100	6,766
47,700	**47,750**	8,113	6,321	8,113	6,779
47,750	**47,800**	8,125	6,329	8,125	6,791
47,800	**47,850**	8,138	6,336	8,138	6,804
47,850	**47,900**	8,150	6,344	8,150	6,816
47,900	**47,950**	8,163	6,351	8,163	6,829
47,950	**48,000**	8,175	6,359	8,175	6,841
48,000					
48,000	**48,050**	8,188	6,366	8,188	6,854
48,050	**48,100**	8,200	6,374	8,200	6,866
48,100	**48,150**	8,213	6,381	8,213	6,879
48,150	**48,200**	8,225	6,389	8,225	6,891
48,200	**48,250**	8,238	6,396	8,238	6,904
48,250	**48,300**	8,250	6,404	8,250	6,916
48,300	**48,350**	8,263	6,411	8,263	6,929
48,350	**48,400**	8,275	6,419	8,275	6,941
48,400	**48,450**	8,288	6,426	8,288	6,954
48,450	**48,500**	8,300	6,434	8,300	6,966
48,500	**48,550**	8,313	6,441	8,313	6,979
48,550	**48,600**	8,325	6,449	8,325	6,991
48,600	**48,650**	8,338	6,456	8,338	7,004
48,650	**48,700**	8,350	6,464	8,350	7,016
48,700	**48,750**	8,363	6,471	8,363	7,029
48,750	**48,800**	8,375	6,479	8,375	7,041
48,800	**48,850**	8,388	6,486	8,388	7,054
48,850	**48,900**	8,400	6,494	8,400	7,066
48,900	**48,950**	8,413	6,501	8,413	7,079
48,950	**49,000**	8,425	6,509	8,425	7,091
49,000					
49,000	**49,050**	8,438	6,516	8,438	7,104
49,050	**49,100**	8,450	6,524	8,450	7,116
49,100	**49,150**	8,463	6,531	8,463	7,129
49,150	**49,200**	8,475	6,539	8,475	7,141
49,200	**49,250**	8,488	6,546	8,488	7,154
49,250	**49,300**	8,500	6,554	8,500	7,166
49,300	**49,350**	8,513	6,561	8,513	7,179
49,350	**49,400**	8,525	6,569	8,525	7,191
49,400	**49,450**	8,538	6,576	8,538	7,204
49,450	**49,500**	8,550	6,584	8,550	7,216
49,500	**49,550**	8,563	6,591	8,563	7,229
49,550	**49,600**	8,575	6,599	8,575	7,241
49,600	**49,650**	8,588	6,606	8,588	7,254
49,650	**49,700**	8,600	6,614	8,600	7,266
49,700	**49,750**	8,613	6,621	8,613	7,279
49,750	**49,800**	8,625	6,629	8,625	7,291
49,800	**49,850**	8,638	6,636	8,638	7,304
49,850	**49,900**	8,650	6,644	8,650	7,316
49,900	**49,950**	8,663	6,651	8,663	7,329
49,950	**50,000**	8,675	6,659	8,675	7,341

* This column must also be used by a qualifying widow(er).

(Continued on next page)

2010 Tax Table–*Continued*

If line 43 (taxable income) is— At least	But less than	And you are— Single	Married filing jointly *	Married filing sepa-rately	Head of a house-hold
		Your tax is—			
50,000					
50,000	50,050	8,688	6,666	8,688	7,354
50,050	50,100	8,700	6,674	8,700	7,366
50,100	50,150	8,713	6,681	8,713	7,379
50,150	50,200	8,725	6,689	8,725	7,391
50,200	50,250	8,738	6,696	8,738	7,404
50,250	50,300	8,750	6,704	8,750	7,416
50,300	50,350	8,763	6,711	8,763	7,429
50,350	50,400	8,775	6,719	8,775	7,441
50,400	50,450	8,788	6,726	8,788	7,454
50,450	50,500	8,800	6,734	8,800	7,466
50,500	50,550	8,813	6,741	8,813	7,479
50,550	50,600	8,825	6,749	8,825	7,491
50,600	50,650	8,838	6,756	8,838	7,504
50,650	50,700	8,850	6,764	8,850	7,516
50,700	50,750	8,863	6,771	8,863	7,529
50,750	50,800	8,875	6,779	8,875	7,541
50,800	50,850	8,888	6,786	8,888	7,554
50,850	50,900	8,900	6,794	8,900	7,566
50,900	50,950	8,913	6,801	8,913	7,579
50,950	51,000	8,925	6,809	8,925	7,591
51,000					
51,000	51,050	8,938	6,816	8,938	7,604
51,050	51,100	8,950	6,824	8,950	7,616
51,100	51,150	8,963	6,831	8,963	7,629
51,150	51,200	8,975	6,839	8,975	7,641
51,200	51,250	8,988	6,846	8,988	7,654
51,250	51,300	9,000	6,854	9,000	7,666
51,300	51,350	9,013	6,861	9,013	7,679
51,350	51,400	9,025	6,869	9,025	7,691
51,400	51,450	9,038	6,876	9,038	7,704
51,450	51,500	9,050	6,884	9,050	7,716
51,500	51,550	9,063	6,891	9,063	7,729
51,550	51,600	9,075	6,899	9,075	7,741
51,600	51,650	9,088	6,906	9,088	7,754
51,650	51,700	9,100	6,914	9,100	7,766
51,700	51,750	9,113	6,921	9,113	7,779
51,750	51,800	9,125	6,929	9,125	7,791
51,800	51,850	9,138	6,936	9,138	7,804
51,850	51,900	9,150	6,944	9,150	7,816
51,900	51,950	9,163	6,951	9,163	7,829
51,950	52,000	9,175	6,959	9,175	7,841
52,000					
52,000	52,050	9,188	6,966	9,188	7,854
52,050	52,100	9,200	6,974	9,200	7,866
52,100	52,150	9,213	6,981	9,213	7,879
52,150	52,200	9,225	6,989	9,225	7,891
52,200	52,250	9,238	6,996	9,238	7,904
52,250	52,300	9,250	7,004	9,250	7,916
52,300	52,350	9,263	7,011	9,263	7,929
52,350	52,400	9,275	7,019	9,275	7,941
52,400	52,450	9,288	7,026	9,288	7,954
52,450	52,500	9,300	7,034	9,300	7,966
52,500	52,550	9,313	7,041	9,313	7,979
52,550	52,600	9,325	7,049	9,325	7,991
52,600	52,650	9,338	7,056	9,338	8,004
52,650	52,700	9,350	7,064	9,350	8,016
52,700	52,750	9,363	7,071	9,363	8,029
52,750	52,800	9,375	7,079	9,375	8,041
52,800	52,850	9,388	7,086	9,388	8,054
52,850	52,900	9,400	7,094	9,400	8,066
52,900	52,950	9,413	7,101	9,413	8,079
52,950	53,000	9,425	7,109	9,425	8,091

If line 43 (taxable income) is— At least	But less than	And you are— Single	Married filing jointly *	Married filing sepa-rately	Head of a house-hold
		Your tax is—			
53,000					
53,000	53,050	9,438	7,116	9,438	8,104
53,050	53,100	9,450	7,124	9,450	8,116
53,100	53,150	9,463	7,131	9,463	8,129
53,150	53,200	9,475	7,139	9,475	8,141
53,200	53,250	9,488	7,146	9,488	8,154
53,250	53,300	9,500	7,154	9,500	8,166
53,300	53,350	9,513	7,161	9,513	8,179
53,350	53,400	9,525	7,169	9,525	8,191
53,400	53,450	9,538	7,176	9,538	8,204
53,450	53,500	9,550	7,184	9,550	8,216
53,500	53,550	9,563	7,191	9,563	8,229
53,550	53,600	9,575	7,199	9,575	8,241
53,600	53,650	9,588	7,206	9,588	8,254
53,650	53,700	9,600	7,214	9,600	8,266
53,700	53,750	9,613	7,221	9,613	8,279
53,750	53,800	9,625	7,229	9,625	8,291
53,800	53,850	9,638	7,236	9,638	8,304
53,850	53,900	9,650	7,244	9,650	8,316
53,900	53,950	9,663	7,251	9,663	8,329
53,950	54,000	9,675	7,259	9,675	8,341
54,000					
54,000	54,050	9,688	7,266	9,688	8,354
54,050	54,100	9,700	7,274	9,700	8,366
54,100	54,150	9,713	7,281	9,713	8,379
54,150	54,200	9,725	7,289	9,725	8,391
54,200	54,250	9,738	7,296	9,738	8,404
54,250	54,300	9,750	7,304	9,750	8,416
54,300	54,350	9,763	7,311	9,763	8,429
54,350	54,400	9,775	7,319	9,775	8,441
54,400	54,450	9,788	7,326	9,788	8,454
54,450	54,500	9,800	7,334	9,800	8,466
54,500	54,550	9,813	7,341	9,813	8,479
54,550	54,600	9,825	7,349	9,825	8,491
54,600	54,650	9,838	7,356	9,838	8,504
54,650	54,700	9,850	7,364	9,850	8,516
54,700	54,750	9,863	7,371	9,863	8,529
54,750	54,800	9,875	7,379	9,875	8,541
54,800	54,850	9,888	7,386	9,888	8,554
54,850	54,900	9,900	7,394	9,900	8,566
54,900	54,950	9,913	7,401	9,913	8,579
54,950	55,000	9,925	7,409	9,925	8,591
55,000					
55,000	55,050	9,938	7,416	9,938	8,604
55,050	55,100	9,950	7,424	9,950	8,616
55,100	55,150	9,963	7,431	9,963	8,629
55,150	55,200	9,975	7,439	9,975	8,641
55,200	55,250	9,988	7,446	9,988	8,654
55,250	55,300	10,000	7,454	10,000	8,666
55,300	55,350	10,013	7,461	10,013	8,679
55,350	55,400	10,025	7,469	10,025	8,691
55,400	55,450	10,038	7,476	10,038	8,704
55,450	55,500	10,050	7,484	10,050	8,716
55,500	55,550	10,063	7,491	10,063	8,729
55,550	55,600	10,075	7,499	10,075	8,741
55,600	55,650	10,088	7,506	10,088	8,754
55,650	55,700	10,100	7,514	10,100	8,766
55,700	55,750	10,113	7,521	10,113	8,779
55,750	55,800	10,125	7,529	10,125	8,791
55,800	55,850	10,138	7,536	10,138	8,804
55,850	55,900	10,150	7,544	10,150	8,816
55,900	55,950	10,163	7,551	10,163	8,829
55,950	56,000	10,175	7,559	10,175	8,841

If line 43 (taxable income) is— At least	But less than	And you are— Single	Married filing jointly *	Married filing sepa-rately	Head of a house-hold
		Your tax is—			
56,000					
56,000	56,050	10,188	7,566	10,188	8,854
56,050	56,100	10,200	7,574	10,200	8,866
56,100	56,150	10,213	7,581	10,213	8,879
56,150	56,200	10,225	7,589	10,225	8,891
56,200	56,250	10,238	7,596	10,238	8,904
56,250	56,300	10,250	7,604	10,250	8,916
56,300	56,350	10,263	7,611	10,263	8,929
56,350	56,400	10,275	7,619	10,275	8,941
56,400	56,450	10,288	7,626	10,288	8,954
56,450	56,500	10,300	7,634	10,300	8,966
56,500	56,550	10,313	7,641	10,313	8,979
56,550	56,600	10,325	7,649	10,325	8,991
56,600	56,650	10,338	7,656	10,338	9,004
56,650	56,700	10,350	7,664	10,350	9,016
56,700	56,750	10,363	7,671	10,363	9,029
56,750	56,800	10,375	7,679	10,375	9,041
56,800	56,850	10,388	7,686	10,388	9,054
56,850	56,900	10,400	7,694	10,400	9,066
56,900	56,950	10,413	7,701	10,413	9,079
56,950	57,000	10,425	7,709	10,425	9,091
57,000					
57,000	57,050	10,438	7,716	10,438	9,104
57,050	57,100	10,450	7,724	10,450	9,116
57,100	57,150	10,463	7,731	10,463	9,129
57,150	57,200	10,475	7,739	10,475	9,141
57,200	57,250	10,488	7,746	10,488	9,154
57,250	57,300	10,500	7,754	10,500	9,166
57,300	57,350	10,513	7,761	10,513	9,179
57,350	57,400	10,525	7,769	10,525	9,191
57,400	57,450	10,538	7,776	10,538	9,204
57,450	57,500	10,550	7,784	10,550	9,216
57,500	57,550	10,563	7,791	10,563	9,229
57,550	57,600	10,575	7,799	10,575	9,241
57,600	57,650	10,588	7,806	10,588	9,254
57,650	57,700	10,600	7,814	10,600	9,266
57,700	57,750	10,613	7,821	10,613	9,279
57,750	57,800	10,625	7,829	10,625	9,291
57,800	57,850	10,638	7,836	10,638	9,304
57,850	57,900	10,650	7,844	10,650	9,316
57,900	57,950	10,663	7,851	10,663	9,329
57,950	58,000	10,675	7,859	10,675	9,341
58,000					
58,000	58,050	10,688	7,866	10,688	9,354
58,050	58,100	10,700	7,874	10,700	9,366
58,100	58,150	10,713	7,881	10,713	9,379
58,150	58,200	10,725	7,889	10,725	9,391
58,200	58,250	10,738	7,896	10,738	9,404
58,250	58,300	10,750	7,904	10,750	9,416
58,300	58,350	10,763	7,911	10,763	9,429
58,350	58,400	10,775	7,919	10,775	9,441
58,400	58,450	10,788	7,926	10,788	9,454
58,450	58,500	10,800	7,934	10,800	9,466
58,500	58,550	10,813	7,941	10,813	9,479
58,550	58,600	10,825	7,949	10,825	9,491
58,600	58,650	10,838	7,956	10,838	9,504
58,650	58,700	10,850	7,964	10,850	9,516
58,700	58,750	10,863	7,971	10,863	9,529
58,750	58,800	10,875	7,979	10,875	9,541
58,800	58,850	10,888	7,986	10,888	9,554
58,850	58,900	10,900	7,994	10,900	9,566
58,900	58,950	10,913	8,001	10,913	9,579
58,950	59,000	10,925	8,009	10,925	9,591

* This column must also be used by a qualifying widow(er).

(Continued on next page)

2010 Tax Table—*Continued*

59,000

If line 43 (taxable income) is— At least	But less than	And you are— Single	Married filing jointly *	Married filing separately	Head of a household
		Your tax is—			
59,000	59,050	10,938	8,016	10,938	9,604
59,050	59,100	10,950	8,024	10,950	9,616
59,100	59,150	10,963	8,031	10,963	9,629
59,150	59,200	10,975	8,039	10,975	9,641
59,200	59,250	10,988	8,046	10,988	9,654
59,250	59,300	11,000	8,054	11,000	9,666
59,300	59,350	11,013	8,061	11,013	9,679
59,350	59,400	11,025	8,069	11,025	9,691
59,400	59,450	11,038	8,076	11,038	9,704
59,450	59,500	11,050	8,084	11,050	9,716
59,500	59,550	11,063	8,091	11,063	9,729
59,550	59,600	11,075	8,099	11,075	9,741
59,600	59,650	11,088	8,106	11,088	9,754
59,650	59,700	11,100	8,114	11,100	9,766
59,700	59,750	11,113	8,121	11,113	9,779
59,750	59,800	11,125	8,129	11,125	9,791
59,800	59,850	11,138	8,136	11,138	9,804
59,850	59,900	11,150	8,144	11,150	9,816
59,900	59,950	11,163	8,151	11,163	9,829
59,950	60,000	11,175	8,159	11,175	9,841

60,000

At least	But less than	Single	Married filing jointly *	Married filing separately	Head of a household
60,000	60,050	11,188	8,166	11,188	9,854
60,050	60,100	11,200	8,174	11,200	9,866
60,100	60,150	11,213	8,181	11,213	9,879
60,150	60,200	11,225	8,189	11,225	9,891
60,200	60,250	11,238	8,196	11,238	9,904
60,250	60,300	11,250	8,204	11,250	9,916
60,300	60,350	11,263	8,211	11,263	9,929
60,350	60,400	11,275	8,219	11,275	9,941
60,400	60,450	11,288	8,226	11,288	9,954
60,450	60,500	11,300	8,234	11,300	9,966
60,500	60,550	11,313	8,241	11,313	9,979
60,550	60,600	11,325	8,249	11,325	9,991
60,600	60,650	11,338	8,256	11,338	10,004
60,650	60,700	11,350	8,264	11,350	10,016
60,700	60,750	11,363	8,271	11,363	10,029
60,750	60,800	11,375	8,279	11,375	10,041
60,800	60,850	11,388	8,286	11,388	10,054
60,850	60,900	11,400	8,294	11,400	10,066
60,900	60,950	11,413	8,301	11,413	10,079
60,950	61,000	11,425	8,309	11,425	10,091

61,000

At least	But less than	Single	Married filing jointly *	Married filing separately	Head of a household
61,000	61,050	11,438	8,316	11,438	10,104
61,050	61,100	11,450	8,324	11,450	10,116
61,100	61,150	11,463	8,331	11,463	10,129
61,150	61,200	11,475	8,339	11,475	10,141
61,200	61,250	11,488	8,346	11,488	10,154
61,250	61,300	11,500	8,354	11,500	10,166
61,300	61,350	11,513	8,361	11,513	10,179
61,350	61,400	11,525	8,369	11,525	10,191
61,400	61,450	11,538	8,376	11,538	10,204
61,450	61,500	11,550	8,384	11,550	10,216
61,500	61,550	11,563	8,391	11,563	10,229
61,550	61,600	11,575	8,399	11,575	10,241
61,600	61,650	11,588	8,406	11,588	10,254
61,650	61,700	11,600	8,414	11,600	10,266
61,700	61,750	11,613	8,421	11,613	10,279
61,750	61,800	11,625	8,429	11,625	10,291
61,800	61,850	11,638	8,436	11,638	10,304
61,850	61,900	11,650	8,444	11,650	10,316
61,900	61,950	11,663	8,451	11,663	10,329
61,950	62,000	11,675	8,459	11,675	10,341

62,000

At least	But less than	Single	Married filing jointly *	Married filing separately	Head of a household
62,000	62,050	11,688	8,466	11,688	10,354
62,050	62,100	11,700	8,474	11,700	10,366
62,100	62,150	11,713	8,481	11,713	10,379
62,150	62,200	11,725	8,489	11,725	10,391
62,200	62,250	11,738	8,496	11,738	10,404
62,250	62,300	11,750	8,504	11,750	10,416
62,300	62,350	11,763	8,511	11,763	10,429
62,350	62,400	11,775	8,519	11,775	10,441
62,400	62,450	11,788	8,526	11,788	10,454
62,450	62,500	11,800	8,534	11,800	10,466
62,500	62,550	11,813	8,541	11,813	10,479
62,550	62,600	11,825	8,549	11,825	10,491
62,600	62,650	11,838	8,556	11,838	10,504
62,650	62,700	11,850	8,564	11,850	10,516
62,700	62,750	11,863	8,571	11,863	10,529
62,750	62,800	11,875	8,579	11,875	10,541
62,800	62,850	11,888	8,586	11,888	10,554
62,850	62,900	11,900	8,594	11,900	10,566
62,900	62,950	11,913	8,601	11,913	10,579
62,950	63,000	11,925	8,609	11,925	10,591

63,000

At least	But less than	Single	Married filing jointly *	Married filing separately	Head of a household
63,000	63,050	11,938	8,616	11,938	10,604
63,050	63,100	11,950	8,624	11,950	10,616
63,100	63,150	11,963	8,631	11,963	10,629
63,150	63,200	11,975	8,639	11,975	10,641
63,200	63,250	11,988	8,646	11,988	10,654
63,250	63,300	12,000	8,654	12,000	10,666
63,300	63,350	12,013	8,661	12,013	10,679
63,350	63,400	12,025	8,669	12,025	10,691
63,400	63,450	12,038	8,676	12,038	10,704
63,450	63,500	12,050	8,684	12,050	10,716
63,500	63,550	12,063	8,691	12,063	10,729
63,550	63,600	12,075	8,699	12,075	10,741
63,600	63,650	12,088	8,706	12,088	10,754
63,650	63,700	12,100	8,714	12,100	10,766
63,700	63,750	12,113	8,721	12,113	10,779
63,750	63,800	12,125	8,729	12,125	10,791
63,800	63,850	12,138	8,736	12,138	10,804
63,850	63,900	12,150	8,744	12,150	10,816
63,900	63,950	12,163	8,751	12,163	10,829
63,950	64,000	12,175	8,759	12,175	10,841

64,000

At least	But less than	Single	Married filing jointly *	Married filing separately	Head of a household
64,000	64,050	12,188	8,766	12,188	10,854
64,050	64,100	12,200	8,774	12,200	10,866
64,100	64,150	12,213	8,781	12,213	10,879
64,150	64,200	12,225	8,789	12,225	10,891
64,200	64,250	12,238	8,796	12,238	10,904
64,250	64,300	12,250	8,804	12,250	10,916
64,300	64,350	12,263	8,811	12,263	10,929
64,350	64,400	12,275	8,819	12,275	10,941
64,400	64,450	12,288	8,826	12,288	10,954
64,450	64,500	12,300	8,834	12,300	10,966
64,500	64,550	12,313	8,841	12,313	10,979
64,550	64,600	12,325	8,849	12,325	10,991
64,600	64,650	12,338	8,856	12,338	11,004
64,650	64,700	12,350	8,864	12,350	11,016
64,700	64,750	12,363	8,871	12,363	11,029
64,750	64,800	12,375	8,879	12,375	11,041
64,800	64,850	12,388	8,886	12,388	11,054
64,850	64,900	12,400	8,894	12,400	11,066
64,900	64,950	12,413	8,901	12,413	11,079
64,950	65,000	12,425	8,909	12,425	11,091

65,000

At least	But less than	Single	Married filing jointly *	Married filing separately	Head of a household
65,000	65,050	12,438	8,916	12,438	11,104
65,050	65,100	12,450	8,924	12,450	11,116
65,100	65,150	12,463	8,931	12,463	11,129
65,150	65,200	12,475	8,939	12,475	11,141
65,200	65,250	12,488	8,946	12,488	11,154
65,250	65,300	12,500	8,954	12,500	11,166
65,300	65,350	12,513	8,961	12,513	11,179
65,350	65,400	12,525	8,969	12,525	11,191
65,400	65,450	12,538	8,976	12,538	11,204
65,450	65,500	12,550	8,984	12,550	11,216
65,500	65,550	12,563	8,991	12,563	11,229
65,550	65,600	12,575	8,999	12,575	11,241
65,600	65,650	12,588	9,006	12,588	11,254
65,650	65,700	12,600	9,014	12,600	11,266
65,700	65,750	12,613	9,021	12,613	11,279
65,750	65,800	12,625	9,029	12,625	11,291
65,800	65,850	12,638	9,036	12,638	11,304
65,850	65,900	12,650	9,044	12,650	11,316
65,900	65,950	12,663	9,051	12,663	11,329
65,950	66,000	12,675	9,059	12,675	11,341

66,000

At least	But less than	Single	Married filing jointly *	Married filing separately	Head of a household
66,000	66,050	12,688	9,066	12,688	11,354
66,050	66,100	12,700	9,074	12,700	11,366
66,100	66,150	12,713	9,081	12,713	11,379
66,150	66,200	12,725	9,089	12,725	11,391
66,200	66,250	12,738	9,096	12,738	11,404
66,250	66,300	12,750	9,104	12,750	11,416
66,300	66,350	12,763	9,111	12,763	11,429
66,350	66,400	12,775	9,119	12,775	11,441
66,400	66,450	12,788	9,126	12,788	11,454
66,450	66,500	12,800	9,134	12,800	11,466
66,500	66,550	12,813	9,141	12,813	11,479
66,550	66,600	12,825	9,149	12,825	11,491
66,600	66,650	12,838	9,156	12,838	11,504
66,650	66,700	12,850	9,164	12,850	11,516
66,700	66,750	12,863	9,171	12,863	11,529
66,750	66,800	12,875	9,179	12,875	11,541
66,800	66,850	12,888	9,186	12,888	11,554
66,850	66,900	12,900	9,194	12,900	11,566
66,900	66,950	12,913	9,201	12,913	11,579
66,950	67,000	12,925	9,209	12,925	11,591

67,000

At least	But less than	Single	Married filing jointly *	Married filing separately	Head of a household
67,000	67,050	12,938	9,216	12,938	11,604
67,050	67,100	12,950	9,224	12,950	11,616
67,100	67,150	12,963	9,231	12,963	11,629
67,150	67,200	12,975	9,239	12,975	11,641
67,200	67,250	12,988	9,246	12,988	11,654
67,250	67,300	13,000	9,254	13,000	11,666
67,300	67,350	13,013	9,261	13,013	11,679
67,350	67,400	13,025	9,269	13,025	11,691
67,400	67,450	13,038	9,276	13,038	11,704
67,450	67,500	13,050	9,284	13,050	11,716
67,500	67,550	13,063	9,291	13,063	11,729
67,550	67,600	13,075	9,299	13,075	11,741
67,600	67,650	13,088	9,306	13,088	11,754
67,650	67,700	13,100	9,314	13,100	11,766
67,700	67,750	13,113	9,321	13,113	11,779
67,750	67,800	13,125	9,329	13,125	11,791
67,800	67,850	13,138	9,336	13,138	11,804
67,850	67,900	13,150	9,344	13,150	11,816
67,900	67,950	13,163	9,351	13,163	11,829
67,950	68,000	13,175	9,359	13,175	11,841

* This column must also be used by a qualifying widow(er).

(Continued on next page)

2010 Tax Table–*Continued*

If line 43 (taxable income) is—		And you are—			
At least	But less than	Single	Married filing jointly *	Married filing sepa-rately	Head of a house-hold
		Your tax is—			
68,000					
68,000	68,050	13,188	9,369	13,188	11,854
68,050	68,100	13,200	9,381	13,200	11,866
68,100	68,150	13,213	9,394	13,213	11,879
68,150	68,200	13,225	9,406	13,225	11,891
68,200	68,250	13,238	9,419	13,238	11,904
68,250	68,300	13,250	9,431	13,250	11,916
68,300	68,350	13,263	9,444	13,263	11,929
68,350	68,400	13,275	9,456	13,275	11,941
68,400	68,450	13,288	9,469	13,288	11,954
68,450	68,500	13,300	9,481	13,300	11,966
68,500	68,550	13,313	9,494	13,313	11,979
68,550	68,600	13,325	9,506	13,325	11,991
68,600	68,650	13,338	9,519	13,338	12,004
68,650	68,700	13,350	9,531	13,351	12,016
68,700	68,750	13,363	9,544	13,365	12,029
68,750	68,800	13,375	9,556	13,379	12,041
68,800	68,850	13,388	9,569	13,393	12,054
68,850	68,900	13,400	9,581	13,407	12,066
68,900	68,950	13,413	9,594	13,421	12,079
68,950	69,000	13,425	9,606	13,435	12,091
69,000					
69,000	69,050	13,438	9,619	13,449	12,104
69,050	69,100	13,450	9,631	13,463	12,116
69,100	69,150	13,463	9,644	13,477	12,129
69,150	69,200	13,475	9,656	13,491	12,141
69,200	69,250	13,488	9,669	13,505	12,154
69,250	69,300	13,500	9,681	13,519	12,166
69,300	69,350	13,513	9,694	13,533	12,179
69,350	69,400	13,525	9,706	13,547	12,191
69,400	69,450	13,538	9,719	13,561	12,204
69,450	69,500	13,550	9,731	13,575	12,216
69,500	69,550	13,563	9,744	13,589	12,229
69,550	69,600	13,575	9,756	13,603	12,241
69,600	69,650	13,588	9,769	13,617	12,254
69,650	69,700	13,600	9,781	13,631	12,266
69,700	69,750	13,613	9,794	13,645	12,279
69,750	69,800	13,625	9,806	13,659	12,291
69,800	69,850	13,638	9,819	13,673	12,304
69,850	69,900	13,650	9,831	13,687	12,316
69,900	69,950	13,663	9,844	13,701	12,329
69,950	70,000	13,675	9,856	13,715	12,341
70,000					
70,000	70,050	13,688	9,869	13,729	12,354
70,050	70,100	13,700	9,881	13,743	12,366
70,100	70,150	13,713	9,894	13,757	12,379
70,150	70,200	13,725	9,906	13,771	12,391
70,200	70,250	13,738	9,919	13,785	12,404
70,250	70,300	13,750	9,931	13,799	12,416
70,300	70,350	13,763	9,944	13,813	12,429
70,350	70,400	13,775	9,956	13,827	12,441
70,400	70,450	13,788	9,969	13,841	12,454
70,450	70,500	13,800	9,981	13,855	12,466
70,500	70,550	13,813	9,994	13,869	12,479
70,550	70,600	13,825	10,006	13,883	12,491
70,600	70,650	13,838	10,019	13,897	12,504
70,650	70,700	13,850	10,031	13,911	12,516
70,700	70,750	13,863	10,044	13,925	12,529
70,750	70,800	13,875	10,056	13,939	12,541
70,800	70,850	13,888	10,069	13,953	12,554
70,850	70,900	13,900	10,081	13,967	12,566
70,900	70,950	13,913	10,094	13,981	12,579
70,950	71,000	13,925	10,106	13,995	12,591
71,000					
71,000	71,050	13,938	10,119	14,009	12,604
71,050	71,100	13,950	10,131	14,023	12,616
71,100	71,150	13,963	10,144	14,037	12,629
71,150	71,200	13,975	10,156	14,051	12,641
71,200	71,250	13,988	10,169	14,065	12,654
71,250	71,300	14,000	10,181	14,079	12,666
71,300	71,350	14,013	10,194	14,093	12,679
71,350	71,400	14,025	10,206	14,107	12,691
71,400	71,450	14,038	10,219	14,121	12,704
71,450	71,500	14,050	10,231	14,135	12,716
71,500	71,550	14,063	10,244	14,149	12,729
71,550	71,600	14,075	10,256	14,163	12,741
71,600	71,650	14,088	10,269	14,177	12,754
71,650	71,700	14,100	10,281	14,191	12,766
71,700	71,750	14,113	10,294	14,205	12,779
71,750	71,800	14,125	10,306	14,219	12,791
71,800	71,850	14,138	10,319	14,233	12,804
71,850	71,900	14,150	10,331	14,247	12,816
71,900	71,950	14,163	10,344	14,261	12,829
71,950	72,000	14,175	10,356	14,275	12,841
72,000					
72,000	72,050	14,188	10,369	14,289	12,854
72,050	72,100	14,200	10,381	14,303	12,866
72,100	72,150	14,213	10,394	14,317	12,879
72,150	72,200	14,225	10,406	14,331	12,891
72,200	72,250	14,238	10,419	14,345	12,904
72,250	72,300	14,250	10,431	14,359	12,916
72,300	72,350	14,263	10,444	14,373	12,929
72,350	72,400	14,275	10,456	14,387	12,941
72,400	72,450	14,288	10,469	14,401	12,954
72,450	72,500	14,300	10,481	14,415	12,966
72,500	72,550	14,313	10,494	14,429	12,979
72,550	72,600	14,325	10,506	14,443	12,991
72,600	72,650	14,338	10,519	14,457	13,004
72,650	72,700	14,350	10,531	14,471	13,016
72,700	72,750	14,363	10,544	14,485	13,029
72,750	72,800	14,375	10,556	14,499	13,041
72,800	72,850	14,388	10,569	14,513	13,054
72,850	72,900	14,400	10,581	14,527	13,066
72,900	72,950	14,413	10,594	14,541	13,079
72,950	73,000	14,425	10,606	14,555	13,091
73,000					
73,000	73,050	14,438	10,619	14,569	13,104
73,050	73,100	14,450	10,631	14,583	13,116
73,100	73,150	14,463	10,644	14,597	13,129
73,150	73,200	14,475	10,656	14,611	13,141
73,200	73,250	14,488	10,669	14,625	13,154
73,250	73,300	14,500	10,681	14,639	13,166
73,300	73,350	14,513	10,694	14,653	13,179
73,350	73,400	14,525	10,706	14,667	13,191
73,400	73,450	14,538	10,719	14,681	13,204
73,450	73,500	14,550	10,731	14,695	13,216
73,500	73,550	14,563	10,744	14,709	13,229
73,550	73,600	14,575	10,756	14,723	13,241
73,600	73,650	14,588	10,769	14,737	13,254
73,650	73,700	14,600	10,781	14,751	13,266
73,700	73,750	14,613	10,794	14,765	13,279
73,750	73,800	14,625	10,806	14,779	13,291
73,800	73,850	14,638	10,819	14,793	13,304
73,850	73,900	14,650	10,831	14,807	13,316
73,900	73,950	14,663	10,844	14,821	13,329
73,950	74,000	14,675	10,856	14,835	13,341
74,000					
74,000	74,050	14,688	10,869	14,849	13,354
74,050	74,100	14,700	10,881	14,863	13,366
74,100	74,150	14,713	10,894	14,877	13,379
74,150	74,200	14,725	10,906	14,891	13,391
74,200	74,250	14,738	10,919	14,905	13,404
74,250	74,300	14,750	10,931	14,919	13,416
74,300	74,350	14,763	10,944	14,933	13,429
74,350	74,400	14,775	10,956	14,947	13,441
74,400	74,450	14,788	10,969	14,961	13,454
74,450	74,500	14,800	10,981	14,975	13,466
74,500	74,550	14,813	10,994	14,989	13,479
74,550	74,600	14,825	11,006	15,003	13,491
74,600	74,650	14,838	11,019	15,017	13,504
74,650	74,700	14,850	11,031	15,031	13,516
74,700	74,750	14,863	11,044	15,045	13,529
74,750	74,800	14,875	11,056	15,059	13,541
74,800	74,850	14,888	11,069	15,073	13,554
74,850	74,900	14,900	11,081	15,087	13,566
74,900	74,950	14,913	11,094	15,101	13,579
74,950	75,000	14,925	11,106	15,115	13,591
75,000					
75,000	75,050	14,938	11,119	15,129	13,604
75,050	75,100	14,950	11,131	15,143	13,616
75,100	75,150	14,963	11,144	15,157	13,629
75,150	75,200	14,975	11,156	15,171	13,641
75,200	75,250	14,988	11,169	15,185	13,654
75,250	75,300	15,000	11,181	15,199	13,666
75,300	75,350	15,013	11,194	15,213	13,679
75,350	75,400	15,025	11,206	15,227	13,691
75,400	75,450	15,038	11,219	15,241	13,704
75,450	75,500	15,050	11,231	15,255	13,716
75,500	75,550	15,063	11,244	15,269	13,729
75,550	75,600	15,075	11,256	15,283	13,741
75,600	75,650	15,088	11,269	15,297	13,754
75,650	75,700	15,100	11,281	15,311	13,766
75,700	75,750	15,113	11,294	15,325	13,779
75,750	75,800	15,125	11,306	15,339	13,791
75,800	75,850	15,138	11,319	15,353	13,804
75,850	75,900	15,150	11,331	15,367	13,816
75,900	75,950	15,163	11,344	15,381	13,829
75,950	76,000	15,175	11,356	15,395	13,841
76,000					
76,000	76,050	15,188	11,369	15,409	13,854
76,050	76,100	15,200	11,381	15,423	13,866
76,100	76,150	15,213	11,394	15,437	13,879
76,150	76,200	15,225	11,406	15,451	13,891
76,200	76,250	15,238	11,419	15,465	13,904
76,250	76,300	15,250	11,431	15,479	13,916
76,300	76,350	15,263	11,444	15,493	13,929
76,350	76,400	15,275	11,456	15,507	13,941
76,400	76,450	15,288	11,469	15,521	13,954
76,450	76,500	15,300	11,481	15,535	13,966
76,500	76,550	15,313	11,494	15,549	13,979
76,550	76,600	15,325	11,506	15,563	13,991
76,600	76,650	15,338	11,519	15,577	14,004
76,650	76,700	15,350	11,531	15,591	14,016
76,700	76,750	15,363	11,544	15,605	14,029
76,750	76,800	15,375	11,556	15,619	14,041
76,800	76,850	15,388	11,569	15,633	14,054
76,850	76,900	15,400	11,581	15,647	14,066
76,900	76,950	15,413	11,594	15,661	14,079
76,950	77,000	15,425	11,606	15,675	14,091

* This column must also be used by a qualifying widow(er).

(Continued on next page)

2010 Tax Table–*Continued*

If line 43 (taxable income) is—		And you are—			
At least	But less than	Single	Married filing jointly *	Married filing separately	Head of a household
		Your tax is—			
77,000					
77,000	77,050	15,438	11,619	15,689	14,104
77,050	77,100	15,450	11,631	15,703	14,116
77,100	77,150	15,463	11,644	15,717	14,129
77,150	77,200	15,475	11,656	15,731	14,141
77,200	77,250	15,488	11,669	15,745	14,154
77,250	77,300	15,500	11,681	15,759	14,166
77,300	77,350	15,513	11,694	15,773	14,179
77,350	77,400	15,525	11,706	15,787	14,191
77,400	77,450	15,538	11,719	15,801	14,204
77,450	77,500	15,550	11,731	15,815	14,216
77,500	77,550	15,563	11,744	15,829	14,229
77,550	77,600	15,575	11,756	15,843	14,241
77,600	77,650	15,588	11,769	15,857	14,254
77,650	77,700	15,600	11,781	15,871	14,266
77,700	77,750	15,613	11,794	15,885	14,279
77,750	77,800	15,625	11,806	15,899	14,291
77,800	77,850	15,638	11,819	15,913	14,304
77,850	77,900	15,650	11,831	15,927	14,316
77,900	77,950	15,663	11,844	15,941	14,329
77,950	78,000	15,675	11,856	15,955	14,341
78,000					
78,000	78,050	15,688	11,869	15,969	14,354
78,050	78,100	15,700	11,881	15,983	14,366
78,100	78,150	15,713	11,894	15,997	14,379
78,150	78,200	15,725	11,906	16,011	14,391
78,200	78,250	15,738	11,919	16,025	14,404
78,250	78,300	15,750	11,931	16,039	14,416
78,300	78,350	15,763	11,944	16,053	14,429
78,350	78,400	15,775	11,956	16,067	14,441
78,400	78,450	15,788	11,969	16,081	14,454
78,450	78,500	15,800	11,981	16,095	14,466
78,500	78,550	15,813	11,994	16,109	14,479
78,550	78,600	15,825	12,006	16,123	14,491
78,600	78,650	15,838	12,019	16,137	14,504
78,650	78,700	15,850	12,031	16,151	14,516
78,700	78,750	15,863	12,044	16,165	14,529
78,750	78,800	15,875	12,056	16,179	14,541
78,800	78,850	15,888	12,069	16,193	14,554
78,850	78,900	15,900	12,081	16,207	14,566
78,900	78,950	15,913	12,094	16,221	14,579
78,950	79,000	15,925	12,106	16,235	14,591
79,000					
79,000	79,050	15,938	12,119	16,249	14,604
79,050	79,100	15,950	12,131	16,263	14,616
79,100	79,150	15,963	12,144	16,277	14,629
79,150	79,200	15,975	12,156	16,291	14,641
79,200	79,250	15,988	12,169	16,305	14,654
79,250	79,300	16,000	12,181	16,319	14,666
79,300	79,350	16,013	12,194	16,333	14,679
79,350	79,400	16,025	12,206	16,347	14,691
79,400	79,450	16,038	12,219	16,361	14,704
79,450	79,500	16,050	12,231	16,375	14,716
79,500	79,550	16,063	12,244	16,389	14,729
79,550	79,600	16,075	12,256	16,403	14,741
79,600	79,650	16,088	12,269	16,417	14,754
79,650	79,700	16,100	12,281	16,431	14,766
79,700	79,750	16,113	12,294	16,445	14,779
79,750	79,800	16,125	12,306	16,459	14,791
79,800	79,850	16,138	12,319	16,473	14,804
79,850	79,900	16,150	12,331	16,487	14,816
79,900	79,950	16,163	12,344	16,501	14,829
79,950	80,000	16,175	12,356	16,515	14,841
80,000					
80,000	80,050	16,188	12,369	16,529	14,854
80,050	80,100	16,200	12,381	16,543	14,866
80,100	80,150	16,213	12,394	16,557	14,879
80,150	80,200	16,225	12,406	16,571	14,891
80,200	80,250	16,238	12,419	16,585	14,904
80,250	80,300	16,250	12,431	16,599	14,916
80,300	80,350	16,263	12,444	16,613	14,929
80,350	80,400	16,275	12,456	16,627	14,941
80,400	80,450	16,288	12,469	16,641	14,954
80,450	80,500	16,300	12,481	16,655	14,966
80,500	80,550	16,313	12,494	16,669	14,979
80,550	80,600	16,325	12,506	16,683	14,991
80,600	80,650	16,338	12,519	16,697	15,004
80,650	80,700	16,350	12,531	16,711	15,016
80,700	80,750	16,363	12,544	16,725	15,029
80,750	80,800	16,375	12,556	16,739	15,041
80,800	80,850	16,388	12,569	16,753	15,054
80,850	80,900	16,400	12,581	16,767	15,066
80,900	80,950	16,413	12,594	16,781	15,079
80,950	81,000	16,425	12,606	16,795	15,091
81,000					
81,000	81,050	16,438	12,619	16,809	15,104
81,050	81,100	16,450	12,631	16,823	15,116
81,100	81,150	16,463	12,644	16,837	15,129
81,150	81,200	16,475	12,656	16,851	15,141
81,200	81,250	16,488	12,669	16,865	15,154
81,250	81,300	16,500	12,681	16,879	15,166
81,300	81,350	16,513	12,694	16,893	15,179
81,350	81,400	16,525	12,706	16,907	15,191
81,400	81,450	16,538	12,719	16,921	15,204
81,450	81,500	16,550	12,731	16,935	15,216
81,500	81,550	16,563	12,744	16,949	15,229
81,550	81,600	16,575	12,756	16,963	15,241
81,600	81,650	16,588	12,769	16,977	15,254
81,650	81,700	16,600	12,781	16,991	15,266
81,700	81,750	16,613	12,794	17,005	15,279
81,750	81,800	16,625	12,806	17,019	15,291
81,800	81,850	16,638	12,819	17,033	15,304
81,850	81,900	16,650	12,831	17,047	15,316
81,900	81,950	16,663	12,844	17,061	15,329
81,950	82,000	16,675	12,856	17,075	15,341
82,000					
82,000	82,050	16,688	12,869	17,089	15,354
82,050	82,100	16,700	12,881	17,103	15,366
82,100	82,150	16,713	12,894	17,117	15,379
82,150	82,200	16,725	12,906	17,131	15,391
82,200	82,250	16,738	12,919	17,145	15,404
82,250	82,300	16,750	12,931	17,159	15,416
82,300	82,350	16,763	12,944	17,173	15,429
82,350	82,400	16,775	12,956	17,187	15,441
82,400	82,450	16,788	12,969	17,201	15,454
82,450	82,500	16,802	12,981	17,215	15,466
82,500	82,550	16,816	12,994	17,229	15,479
82,550	82,600	16,830	13,006	17,243	15,491
82,600	82,650	16,844	13,019	17,257	15,504
82,650	82,700	16,858	13,031	17,271	15,516
82,700	82,750	16,872	13,044	17,285	15,529
82,750	82,800	16,886	13,056	17,299	15,541
82,800	82,850	16,900	13,069	17,313	15,554
82,850	82,900	16,914	13,081	17,327	15,566
82,900	82,950	16,928	13,094	17,341	15,579
82,950	83,000	16,942	13,106	17,355	15,591
83,000					
83,000	83,050	16,956	13,119	17,369	15,604
83,050	83,100	16,970	13,131	17,383	15,616
83,100	83,150	16,984	13,144	17,397	15,629
83,150	83,200	16,998	13,156	17,411	15,641
83,200	83,250	17,012	13,169	17,425	15,654
83,250	83,300	17,026	13,181	17,439	15,666
83,300	83,350	17,040	13,194	17,453	15,679
83,350	83,400	17,054	13,206	17,467	15,691
83,400	83,450	17,068	13,219	17,481	15,704
83,450	83,500	17,082	13,231	17,495	15,716
83,500	83,550	17,096	13,244	17,509	15,729
83,550	83,600	17,110	13,256	17,523	15,741
83,600	83,650	17,124	13,269	17,537	15,754
83,650	83,700	17,138	13,281	17,551	15,766
83,700	83,750	17,152	13,294	17,565	15,779
83,750	83,800	17,166	13,306	17,579	15,791
83,800	83,850	17,180	13,319	17,593	15,804
83,850	83,900	17,194	13,331	17,607	15,816
83,900	83,950	17,208	13,344	17,621	15,829
83,950	84,000	17,222	13,356	17,635	15,841
84,000					
84,000	84,050	17,236	13,369	17,649	15,854
84,050	84,100	17,250	13,381	17,663	15,866
84,100	84,150	17,264	13,394	17,677	15,879
84,150	84,200	17,278	13,406	17,691	15,891
84,200	84,250	17,292	13,419	17,705	15,904
84,250	84,300	17,306	13,431	17,719	15,916
84,300	84,350	17,320	13,444	17,733	15,929
84,350	84,400	17,334	13,456	17,747	15,941
84,400	84,450	17,348	13,469	17,761	15,954
84,450	84,500	17,362	13,481	17,775	15,966
84,500	84,550	17,376	13,494	17,789	15,979
84,550	84,600	17,390	13,506	17,803	15,991
84,600	84,650	17,404	13,519	17,817	16,004
84,650	84,700	17,418	13,531	17,831	16,016
84,700	84,750	17,432	13,544	17,845	16,029
84,750	84,800	17,446	13,556	17,859	16,041
84,800	84,850	17,460	13,569	17,873	16,054
84,850	84,900	17,474	13,581	17,887	16,066
84,900	84,950	17,488	13,594	17,901	16,079
84,950	85,000	17,502	13,606	17,915	16,091
85,000					
85,000	85,050	17,516	13,619	17,929	16,104
85,050	85,100	17,530	13,631	17,943	16,116
85,100	85,150	17,544	13,644	17,957	16,129
85,150	85,200	17,558	13,656	17,971	16,141
85,200	85,250	17,572	13,669	17,985	16,154
85,250	85,300	17,586	13,681	17,999	16,166
85,300	85,350	17,600	13,694	18,013	16,179
85,350	85,400	17,614	13,706	18,027	16,191
85,400	85,450	17,628	13,719	18,041	16,204
85,450	85,500	17,642	13,731	18,055	16,216
85,500	85,550	17,656	13,744	18,069	16,229
85,550	85,600	17,670	13,756	18,083	16,241
85,600	85,650	17,684	13,769	18,097	16,254
85,650	85,700	17,698	13,781	18,111	16,266
85,700	85,750	17,712	13,794	18,125	16,279
85,750	85,800	17,726	13,806	18,139	16,291
85,800	85,850	17,740	13,819	18,153	16,304
85,850	85,900	17,754	13,831	18,167	16,316
85,900	85,950	17,768	13,844	18,181	16,329
85,950	86,000	17,782	13,856	18,195	16,341

* This column must also be used by a qualifying widow(er).

(Continued on next page)

2010 Tax Table–*Continued*

If line 43 (taxable income) is— At least	But less than	And you are— Single	Married filing jointly *	Married filing separately	Head of a household
		Your tax is—			
86,000					
86,000	86,050	17,796	13,869	18,209	16,354
86,050	86,100	17,810	13,881	18,223	16,366
86,100	86,150	17,824	13,894	18,237	16,379
86,150	86,200	17,838	13,906	18,251	16,391
86,200	86,250	17,852	13,919	18,265	16,404
86,250	86,300	17,866	13,931	18,279	16,416
86,300	86,350	17,880	13,944	18,293	16,429
86,350	86,400	17,894	13,956	18,307	16,441
86,400	86,450	17,908	13,969	18,321	16,454
86,450	86,500	17,922	13,981	18,335	16,466
86,500	86,550	17,936	13,994	18,349	16,479
86,550	86,600	17,950	14,006	18,363	16,491
86,600	86,650	17,964	14,019	18,377	16,504
86,650	86,700	17,978	14,031	18,391	16,516
86,700	86,750	17,992	14,044	18,405	16,529
86,750	86,800	18,006	14,056	18,419	16,541
86,800	86,850	18,020	14,069	18,433	16,554
86,850	86,900	18,034	14,081	18,447	16,566
86,900	86,950	18,048	14,094	18,461	16,579
86,950	87,000	18,062	14,106	18,475	16,591
87,000					
87,000	87,050	18,076	14,119	18,489	16,604
87,050	87,100	18,090	14,131	18,503	16,616
87,100	87,150	18,104	14,144	18,517	16,629
87,150	87,200	18,118	14,156	18,531	16,641
87,200	87,250	18,132	14,169	18,545	16,654
87,250	87,300	18,146	14,181	18,559	16,666
87,300	87,350	18,160	14,194	18,573	16,679
87,350	87,400	18,174	14,206	18,587	16,691
87,400	87,450	18,188	14,219	18,601	16,704
87,450	87,500	18,202	14,231	18,615	16,716
87,500	87,550	18,216	14,244	18,629	16,729
87,550	87,600	18,230	14,256	18,643	16,741
87,600	87,650	18,244	14,269	18,657	16,754
87,650	87,700	18,258	14,281	18,671	16,766
87,700	87,750	18,272	14,294	18,685	16,779
87,750	87,800	18,286	14,306	18,699	16,791
87,800	87,850	18,300	14,319	18,713	16,804
87,850	87,900	18,314	14,331	18,727	16,816
87,900	87,950	18,328	14,344	18,741	16,829
87,950	88,000	18,342	14,356	18,755	16,841
88,000					
88,000	88,050	18,356	14,369	18,769	16,854
88,050	88,100	18,370	14,381	18,783	16,866
88,100	88,150	18,384	14,394	18,797	16,879
88,150	88,200	18,398	14,406	18,811	16,891
88,200	88,250	18,412	14,419	18,825	16,904
88,250	88,300	18,426	14,431	18,839	16,916
88,300	88,350	18,440	14,444	18,853	16,929
88,350	88,400	18,454	14,456	18,867	16,941
88,400	88,450	18,468	14,469	18,881	16,954
88,450	88,500	18,482	14,481	18,895	16,966
88,500	88,550	18,496	14,494	18,909	16,979
88,550	88,600	18,510	14,506	18,923	16,991
88,600	88,650	18,524	14,519	18,937	17,004
88,650	88,700	18,538	14,531	18,951	17,016
88,700	88,750	18,552	14,544	18,965	17,029
88,750	88,800	18,566	14,556	18,979	17,041
88,800	88,850	18,580	14,569	18,993	17,054
88,850	88,900	18,594	14,581	19,007	17,066
88,900	88,950	18,608	14,594	19,021	17,079
88,950	89,000	18,622	14,606	19,035	17,091

If line 43 (taxable income) is— At least	But less than	And you are— Single	Married filing jointly *	Married filing separately	Head of a household
		Your tax is—			
89,000					
89,000	89,050	18,636	14,619	19,049	17,104
89,050	89,100	18,650	14,631	19,063	17,116
89,100	89,150	18,664	14,644	19,077	17,129
89,150	89,200	18,678	14,656	19,091	17,141
89,200	89,250	18,692	14,669	19,105	17,154
89,250	89,300	18,706	14,681	19,119	17,166
89,300	89,350	18,720	14,694	19,133	17,179
89,350	89,400	18,734	14,706	19,147	17,191
89,400	89,450	18,748	14,719	19,161	17,204
89,450	89,500	18,762	14,731	19,175	17,216
89,500	89,550	18,776	14,744	19,189	17,229
89,550	89,600	18,790	14,756	19,203	17,241
89,600	89,650	18,804	14,769	19,217	17,254
89,650	89,700	18,818	14,781	19,231	17,266
89,700	89,750	18,832	14,794	19,245	17,279
89,750	89,800	18,846	14,806	19,259	17,291
89,800	89,850	18,860	14,819	19,273	17,304
89,850	89,900	18,874	14,831	19,287	17,316
89,900	89,950	18,888	14,844	19,301	17,329
89,950	90,000	18,902	14,856	19,315	17,341
90,000					
90,000	90,050	18,916	14,869	19,329	17,354
90,050	90,100	18,930	14,881	19,343	17,366
90,100	90,150	18,944	14,894	19,357	17,379
90,150	90,200	18,958	14,906	19,371	17,391
90,200	90,250	18,972	14,919	19,385	17,404
90,250	90,300	18,986	14,931	19,399	17,416
90,300	90,350	19,000	14,944	19,413	17,429
90,350	90,400	19,014	14,956	19,427	17,441
90,400	90,450	19,028	14,969	19,441	17,454
90,450	90,500	19,042	14,981	19,455	17,466
90,500	90,550	19,056	14,994	19,469	17,479
90,550	90,600	19,070	15,006	19,483	17,491
90,600	90,650	19,084	15,019	19,497	17,504
90,650	90,700	19,098	15,031	19,511	17,516
90,700	90,750	19,112	15,044	19,525	17,529
90,750	90,800	19,126	15,056	19,539	17,541
90,800	90,850	19,140	15,069	19,553	17,554
90,850	90,900	19,154	15,081	19,567	17,566
90,900	90,950	19,168	15,094	19,581	17,579
90,950	91,000	19,182	15,106	19,595	17,591
91,000					
91,000	91,050	19,196	15,119	19,609	17,604
91,050	91,100	19,210	15,131	19,623	17,616
91,100	91,150	19,224	15,144	19,637	17,629
91,150	91,200	19,238	15,156	19,651	17,641
91,200	91,250	19,252	15,169	19,665	17,654
91,250	91,300	19,266	15,181	19,679	17,666
91,300	91,350	19,280	15,194	19,693	17,679
91,350	91,400	19,294	15,206	19,707	17,691
91,400	91,450	19,308	15,219	19,721	17,704
91,450	91,500	19,322	15,231	19,735	17,716
91,500	91,550	19,336	15,244	19,749	17,729
91,550	91,600	19,350	15,256	19,763	17,741
91,600	91,650	19,364	15,269	19,777	17,754
91,650	91,700	19,378	15,281	19,791	17,766
91,700	91,750	19,392	15,294	19,805	17,779
91,750	91,800	19,406	15,306	19,819	17,791
91,800	91,850	19,420	15,319	19,833	17,804
91,850	91,900	19,434	15,331	19,847	17,816
91,900	91,950	19,448	15,344	19,861	17,829
91,950	92,000	19,462	15,356	19,875	17,841

If line 43 (taxable income) is— At least	But less than	And you are— Single	Married filing jointly *	Married filing separately	Head of a household
		Your tax is—			
92,000					
92,000	92,050	19,476	15,369	19,889	17,854
92,050	92,100	19,490	15,381	19,903	17,866
92,100	92,150	19,504	15,394	19,917	17,879
92,150	92,200	19,518	15,406	19,931	17,891
92,200	92,250	19,532	15,419	19,945	17,904
92,250	92,300	19,546	15,431	19,959	17,916
92,300	92,350	19,560	15,444	19,973	17,929
92,350	92,400	19,574	15,456	19,987	17,941
92,400	92,450	19,588	15,469	20,001	17,954
92,450	92,500	19,602	15,481	20,015	17,966
92,500	92,550	19,616	15,494	20,029	17,979
92,550	92,600	19,630	15,506	20,043	17,991
92,600	92,650	19,644	15,519	20,057	18,004
92,650	92,700	19,658	15,531	20,071	18,016
92,700	92,750	19,672	15,544	20,085	18,029
92,750	92,800	19,686	15,556	20,099	18,041
92,800	92,850	19,700	15,569	20,113	18,054
92,850	92,900	19,714	15,581	20,127	18,066
92,900	92,950	19,728	15,594	20,141	18,079
92,950	93,000	19,742	15,606	20,155	18,091
93,000					
93,000	93,050	19,756	15,619	20,169	18,104
93,050	93,100	19,770	15,631	20,183	18,116
93,100	93,150	19,784	15,644	20,197	18,129
93,150	93,200	19,798	15,656	20,211	18,141
93,200	93,250	19,812	15,669	20,225	18,154
93,250	93,300	19,826	15,681	20,239	18,166
93,300	93,350	19,840	15,694	20,253	18,179
93,350	93,400	19,854	15,706	20,267	18,191
93,400	93,450	19,868	15,719	20,281	18,204
93,450	93,500	19,882	15,731	20,295	18,216
93,500	93,550	19,896	15,744	20,309	18,229
93,550	93,600	19,910	15,756	20,323	18,241
93,600	93,650	19,924	15,769	20,337	18,254
93,650	93,700	19,938	15,781	20,351	18,266
93,700	93,750	19,952	15,794	20,365	18,279
93,750	93,800	19,966	15,806	20,379	18,291
93,800	93,850	19,980	15,819	20,393	18,304
93,850	93,900	19,994	15,831	20,407	18,316
93,900	93,950	20,008	15,844	20,421	18,329
93,950	94,000	20,022	15,856	20,435	18,341
94,000					
94,000	94,050	20,036	15,869	20,449	18,354
94,050	94,100	20,050	15,881	20,463	18,366
94,100	94,150	20,064	15,894	20,477	18,379
94,150	94,200	20,078	15,906	20,491	18,391
94,200	94,250	20,092	15,919	20,505	18,404
94,250	94,300	20,106	15,931	20,519	18,416
94,300	94,350	20,120	15,944	20,533	18,429
94,350	94,400	20,134	15,956	20,547	18,441
94,400	94,450	20,148	15,969	20,561	18,454
94,450	94,500	20,162	15,981	20,575	18,466
94,500	94,550	20,176	15,994	20,589	18,479
94,550	94,600	20,190	16,006	20,603	18,491
94,600	94,650	20,204	16,019	20,617	18,504
94,650	94,700	20,218	16,031	20,631	18,516
94,700	94,750	20,232	16,044	20,645	18,529
94,750	94,800	20,246	16,056	20,659	18,541
94,800	94,850	20,260	16,069	20,673	18,554
94,850	94,900	20,274	16,081	20,687	18,566
94,900	94,950	20,288	16,094	20,701	18,579
94,950	95,000	20,302	16,106	20,715	18,591

* This column must also be used by a qualifying widow(er).

(Continued on next page)

2010 Tax Table–*Continued*

If line 43 (taxable income) is— At least	But less than	And you are— Single	Married filing jointly *	Married filing sepa-rately	Head of a house-hold
		Your tax is—			
95,000					
95,000	**95,050**	20,316	16,119	20,729	18,604
95,050	**95,100**	20,330	16,131	20,743	18,616
95,100	**95,150**	20,344	16,144	20,757	18,629
95,150	**95,200**	20,358	16,156	20,771	18,641
95,200	**95,250**	20,372	16,169	20,785	18,654
95,250	**95,300**	20,386	16,181	20,799	18,666
95,300	**95,350**	20,400	16,194	20,813	18,679
95,350	**95,400**	20,414	16,206	20,827	18,691
95,400	**95,450**	20,428	16,219	20,841	18,704
95,450	**95,500**	20,442	16,231	20,855	18,716
95,500	**95,550**	20,456	16,244	20,869	18,729
95,550	**95,600**	20,470	16,256	20,883	18,741
95,600	**95,650**	20,484	16,269	20,897	18,754
95,650	**95,700**	20,498	16,281	20,911	18,766
95,700	**95,750**	20,512	16,294	20,925	18,779
95,750	**95,800**	20,526	16,306	20,939	18,791
95,800	**95,850**	20,540	16,319	20,953	18,804
95,850	**95,900**	20,554	16,331	20,967	18,816
95,900	**95,950**	20,568	16,344	20,981	18,829
95,950	**96,000**	20,582	16,356	20,995	18,841
96,000					
96,000	**96,050**	20,596	16,369	21,009	18,854
96,050	**96,100**	20,610	16,381	21,023	18,866
96,100	**96,150**	20,624	16,394	21,037	18,879
96,150	**96,200**	20,638	16,406	21,051	18,891
96,200	**96,250**	20,652	16,419	21,065	18,904
96,250	**96,300**	20,666	16,431	21,079	18,916
96,300	**96,350**	20,680	16,444	21,093	18,929
96,350	**96,400**	20,694	16,456	21,107	18,941
96,400	**96,450**	20,708	16,469	21,121	18,954
96,450	**96,500**	20,722	16,481	21,135	18,966
96,500	**96,550**	20,736	16,494	21,149	18,979
96,550	**96,600**	20,750	16,506	21,163	18,991
96,600	**96,650**	20,764	16,519	21,177	19,004
96,650	**96,700**	20,778	16,531	21,191	19,016
96,700	**96,750**	20,792	16,544	21,205	19,029
96,750	**96,800**	20,806	16,556	21,219	19,041
96,800	**96,850**	20,820	16,569	21,233	19,054
96,850	**96,900**	20,834	16,581	21,247	19,066
96,900	**96,950**	20,848	16,594	21,261	19,079
96,950	**97,000**	20,862	16,606	21,275	19,091

If line 43 (taxable income) is— At least	But less than	And you are— Single	Married filing jointly *	Married filing sepa-rately	Head of a house-hold
		Your tax is—			
97,000					
97,000	**97,050**	20,876	16,619	21,289	19,104
97,050	**97,100**	20,890	16,631	21,303	19,116
97,100	**97,150**	20,904	16,644	21,317	19,129
97,150	**97,200**	20,918	16,656	21,331	19,141
97,200	**97,250**	20,932	16,669	21,345	19,154
97,250	**97,300**	20,946	16,681	21,359	19,166
97,300	**97,350**	20,960	16,694	21,373	19,179
97,350	**97,400**	20,974	16,706	21,387	19,191
97,400	**97,450**	20,988	16,719	21,401	19,204
97,450	**97,500**	21,002	16,731	21,415	19,216
97,500	**97,550**	21,016	16,744	21,429	19,229
97,550	**97,600**	21,030	16,756	21,443	19,241
97,600	**97,650**	21,044	16,769	21,457	19,254
97,650	**97,700**	21,058	16,781	21,471	19,266
97,700	**97,750**	21,072	16,794	21,485	19,279
97,750	**97,800**	21,086	16,806	21,499	19,291
97,800	**97,850**	21,100	16,819	21,513	19,304
97,850	**97,900**	21,114	16,831	21,527	19,316
97,900	**97,950**	21,128	16,844	21,541	19,329
97,950	**98,000**	21,142	16,856	21,555	19,341
98,000					
98,000	**98,050**	21,156	16,869	21,569	19,354
98,050	**98,100**	21,170	16,881	21,583	19,366
98,100	**98,150**	21,184	16,894	21,597	19,379
98,150	**98,200**	21,198	16,906	21,611	19,391
98,200	**98,250**	21,212	16,919	21,625	19,404
98,250	**98,300**	21,226	16,931	21,639	19,416
98,300	**98,350**	21,240	16,944	21,653	19,429
98,350	**98,400**	21,254	16,956	21,667	19,441
98,400	**98,450**	21,268	16,969	21,681	19,454
98,450	**98,500**	21,282	16,981	21,695	19,466
98,500	**98,550**	21,296	16,994	21,709	19,479
98,550	**98,600**	21,310	17,006	21,723	19,491
98,600	**98,650**	21,324	17,019	21,737	19,504
98,650	**98,700**	21,338	17,031	21,751	19,516
98,700	**98,750**	21,352	17,044	21,765	19,529
98,750	**98,800**	21,366	17,056	21,779	19,541
98,800	**98,850**	21,380	17,069	21,793	19,554
98,850	**98,900**	21,394	17,081	21,807	19,566
98,900	**98,950**	21,408	17,094	21,821	19,579
98,950	**99,000**	21,422	17,106	21,835	19,591

If line 43 (taxable income) is— At least	But less than	And you are— Single	Married filing jointly *	Married filing sepa-rately	Head of a house-hold
		Your tax is—			
99,000					
99,000	**99,050**	21,436	17,119	21,849	19,604
99,050	**99,100**	21,450	17,131	21,863	19,616
99,100	**99,150**	21,464	17,144	21,877	19,629
99,150	**99,200**	21,478	17,156	21,891	19,641
99,200	**99,250**	21,492	17,169	21,905	19,654
99,250	**99,300**	21,506	17,181	21,919	19,666
99,300	**99,350**	21,520	17,194	21,933	19,679
99,350	**99,400**	21,534	17,206	21,947	19,691
99,400	**99,450**	21,548	17,219	21,961	19,704
99,450	**99,500**	21,562	17,231	21,975	19,716
99,500	**99,550**	21,576	17,244	21,989	19,729
99,550	**99,600**	21,590	17,256	22,003	19,741
99,600	**99,650**	21,604	17,269	22,017	19,754
99,650	**99,700**	21,618	17,281	22,031	19,766
99,700	**99,750**	21,632	17,294	22,045	19,779
99,750	**99,800**	21,646	17,306	22,059	19,791
99,800	**99,850**	21,660	17,319	22,073	19,804
99,850	**99,900**	21,674	17,331	22,087	19,816
99,900	**99,950**	21,688	17,344	22,101	19,829
99,950	**100,000**	21,702	17,356	22,115	19,841

$100,000 or over — use the Tax Rate Schedules on page A-2

* This column must also be used by a qualifying widow(er)

2010 Optional Sales Tax Tables

When Used

The election to deduct state and local general sales taxes requires that the taxpayer forgo any deduction for state and local income taxes. Whether this is advisable or not depends on a comparison of the amounts involved. In making the choice, however, the outcome could be influenced by the additional sales tax incurred due to certain "big ticket" purchases that were made. For example, a taxpayer who chose to deduct state and local income taxes for 2009 might well prefer the sales tax deduction in 2010 if a new boat was purchased or home improvements were made during the year. To make the sales tax election, the taxpayer must enter the amount on Schedule A, line 5, and check box b.

If the sales tax election is made, the amount of the deduction can be determined by use of the *actual expense method* or the *optional sales tax tables* issued by the IRS. The actual expense method can be used only when the taxpayer has actual receipts to support the deduction claimed. In the absence of receipts, the usual case with most taxpayers, resorting to the optional sales tax tables is necessary. Under neither method, however, is the purchase of items used in a taxpayer's trade or business to be considered.

Adjustments Necessary

The optional sales tax tables are based on a number of assumptions that require adjustments to be made. As the starting point for the use of the tables is AGI, nontaxable receipts have not been included. Examples of receipts that should be added include: tax-exempt interest, veterans' benefits, nontaxable combat pay, public assistance payments, workers' compensation, nontaxable Social Security and other retirement benefits. But do not include any large nontaxable items that are not likely to be spent. For example, a $100,000 inheritance should not be added if it was invested in a certificate of deposit.

The tables represent the sales tax on the average (and recurring) expenditures based on level of income by family size and do not include exceptional purchases. Therefore, add to the table amount any sales taxes on major purchases (such as motor vehicles, aircraft, boats, and home building materials, etc.).

When the optional sales tax tables are utilized, special adjustments may be needed when a taxpayer has lived in more than one taxing jurisdiction (e.g., state, county, city) during the year. The adjustments involve apportionment of taxes based on days involved and are illustrated in Instructions for Schedule A (Form 1040), pages A-3 to A-5.

Local Sales Taxes

Local sales taxes (i.e., those imposed by counties, cities, transit authorities) may or may not require a separate determination. In those states where they are not imposed, no further computations are necessary. This is also the case where the local taxes are uniform and are incorporated into the state sales tax table. In other situations, another step is necessary to arrive at the optional sales tax table deduction. Depending on where the taxpayer lives, one of two procedures needs to be used. In one procedure, the local sales tax is arrived at by using the **state table** amount—see the Example 1 worksheet. In the other procedure, special **local tables** issued by the IRS for enumerated state and local jurisdictions are modified (if necessary) and used—see the Example 2 worksheet.

Use Illustrated

EXAMPLE 1 The Archers file a joint return for 2010 reflecting AGI of $88,000 and claiming three exemptions. They have tax-exempt interest of $3,000, and during the year they incurred sales tax of $1,650 on the purchase of an automobile for their dependent teenage son. They live in Bellaire, Texas, where the general sales tax rates are 6.25% for state and 2% for local. Since the IRS *has not issued* optional local sales tax tables for Texas, use the Worksheet below to arrive at the Archers' general sales tax deduction of $3,127.

Sales Tax Deduction Worksheet
(To be used when *no* IRS Optional Local Sales Tax Table Available)

Adjusted Gross Income (AGI) as listed on line 38 of Form 1040		$88,000
Add nontaxable items		3,000
Table income to be used for purposes of line 1 below		$91,000
1. Use table income to determine table amount—go to state of residence and find applicable range of table income and exemption column* for *state* sales tax		$ 1,119
2a. Enter local general sales tax rate	2.0	
2b. Enter state general sales tax rate	6.25	
2c. Divide 2a by 2b	0.32	
2d. Multiply line 1 by line 2c for the local sales tax		358
3. Enter general sales tax on large purchases		1,650
4. Deduction for general sales tax (add lines 1 + 2d + 3) and report on line 5 of Schedule A of Form 1040		$ 3,127

*Use total of personal and dependency exemptions as reported in item 6d of Form 1040.

EXAMPLE 2 The Hardys file a joint return for 2010, reporting AGI of $40,000 and claiming four exemptions (two personal and two dependency). They received $30,000 in nontaxable pension benefits. Although the Hardys do not keep sales tax receipts, they can prove that they paid $4,800 in sales tax on the purchase of a new boat in 2010. The Hardys are residents of Georgia and live in a jurisdiction that imposes a 2% local sales tax. Since the IRS *has issued* optional local sales tax tables for Georgia, use the Worksheet below to arrive at the Hardys' general sales tax deduction of $5,722.

Sales Tax Deduction Worksheet
[To be used for Alaska, Arizona, Arkansas, California (Los Angeles County), Colorado, Georgia, Illinois, Louisiana, Missouri, New York, North Carolina, South Carolina, Tennessee, Utah, and Virginia]

Adjusted Gross Income (AGI) as listed on line 38 of Form 1040		$40,000
Add nontaxable income		30,000
Table income to be used for purpose of line 1 below		$70,000
1. Use the table income to determine *state* sales tax amount—go to table for state of residence and find applicable income range and exemption column*		$ 562
2a. Enter local general sales tax rate	2.0	
2b. Enter IRS *local* sales tax table amount (based on 1%)	$180	
2c. Multiply line 2b by 2a for the local sales tax		360
3. Enter general sales tax on large purchases		4,800
4. Deduction for general sales tax (add lines 1 + 2c + 3) and report on line 5 of Schedule A of Form 1040		$ 5,722

*Use total of personal and dependency exemptions as reported in item 6d of Form 1040.

2010 Optional State and Certain Local Sales Tax Tables

Alabama 4.0000%

Income At least	Income But less than	Exemptions 1	2	3	4	5	Over 5
$0	$20,000	235	287	324	353	378	413
20,000	30,000	336	409	460	501	535	583
30,000	40,000	385	468	525	570	609	663
40,000	50,000	426	516	579	629	670	730
50,000	60,000	463	559	626	680	724	788
60,000	70,000	495	597	669	725	773	840
70,000	80,000	525	633	708	767	817	889
80,000	90,000	553	666	744	806	858	933
90,000	100,000	579	696	778	842	897	974
100,000	120,000	613	736	821	889	946	1028
120,000	140,000	659	790	881	953	1014	1100
140,000	160,000	699	836	932	1008	1071	1162
160,000	180,000	739	882	982	1062	1128	1223
180,000	200,000	774	923	1027	1110	1179	1278
200,000 or more		947	1123	1246	1344	1425	1542

Arizona[1] 6.1863%

Income At least	Income But less than	Exemptions 1	2	3	4	5	Over 5
$0	$20,000	253	297	326	349	368	395
20,000	30,000	408	476	522	558	588	630
30,000	40,000	487	567	622	664	700	749
40,000	50,000	555	646	708	756	795	851
50,000	60,000	616	717	785	837	881	943
60,000	70,000	671	781	855	912	960	1026
70,000	80,000	724	842	921	982	1033	1105
80,000	90,000	773	898	982	1048	1102	1178
90,000	100,000	819	951	1040	1109	1167	1247
100,000	120,000	881	1022	1117	1191	1252	1338
120,000	140,000	965	1118	1222	1302	1369	1462
140,000	160,000	1038	1202	1313	1399	1471	1571
160,000	180,000	1111	1287	1405	1496	1572	1679
180,000	200,000	1178	1362	1487	1584	1664	1777
200,000 or more		1508	1741	1898	2020	2121	2262

Arkansas 6.0000%

Income At least	Income But less than	Exemptions 1	2	3	4	5	Over 5
$0	$20,000	302	359	397	427	452	487
20,000	30,000	472	559	618	664	702	756
30,000	40,000	558	659	728	782	827	890
40,000	50,000	630	745	822	883	933	1004
50,000	60,000	695	821	906	972	1027	1105
60,000	70,000	754	890	982	1053	1113	1197
70,000	80,000	809	954	1053	1129	1193	1283
80,000	90,000	860	1014	1118	1199	1267	1362
90,000	100,000	908	1070	1180	1266	1337	1437
100,000	120,000	971	1144	1261	1353	1428	1535
120,000	140,000	1058	1245	1372	1471	1553	1669
140,000	160,000	1133	1333	1468	1574	1661	1785
160,000	180,000	1207	1420	1564	1676	1769	1900
180,000	200,000	1274	1498	1649	1767	1865	2003
200,000 or more		1605	1883	2072	2219	2341	2512

California[2] 8.2500%

Income At least	Income But less than	Exemptions 1	2	3	4	5	Over 5
$0	$20,000	326	379	414	441	464	495
20,000	30,000	523	605	660	702	737	786
30,000	40,000	624	721	785	835	876	934
40,000	50,000	710	820	892	949	995	1061
50,000	60,000	788	908	989	1051	1102	1174
60,000	70,000	859	989	1076	1144	1199	1277
70,000	80,000	926	1066	1159	1231	1291	1374
80,000	90,000	988	1136	1236	1312	1376	1464
90,000	100,000	1047	1204	1308	1389	1456	1549
100,000	120,000	1125	1292	1404	1490	1562	1662
120,000	140,000	1231	1413	1535	1629	1706	1815
140,000	160,000	1324	1519	1649	1750	1833	1949
160,000	180,000	1417	1625	1763	1870	1959	2082
180,000	200,000	1501	1720	1866	1979	2072	2203
200,000 or more		1921	2195	2378	2520	2637	2800

Colorado 2.9000%

Income At least	Income But less than	Exemptions 1	2	3	4	5	Over 5
$0	$20,000	122	141	154	164	172	184
20,000	30,000	185	213	232	247	259	276
30,000	40,000	216	249	271	288	302	321
40,000	50,000	243	279	304	322	338	360
50,000	60,000	267	306	333	353	370	393
60,000	70,000	288	331	359	381	399	424
70,000	80,000	309	354	384	407	426	453
80,000	90,000	327	375	406	431	451	479
90,000	100,000	345	395	428	453	474	504
100,000	120,000	368	421	456	483	505	536
120,000	140,000	400	456	494	523	547	581
140,000	160,000	427	487	527	558	583	619
160,000	180,000	454	518	560	593	619	657
180,000	200,000	479	545	590	624	652	691
200,000 or more		601	682	735	777	811	858

Connecticut 6.0000%

Income At least	Income But less than	Exemptions 1	2	3	4	5	Over 5
$0	$20,000	235	270	293	310	325	345
20,000	30,000	377	431	468	495	518	550
30,000	40,000	449	513	556	589	617	654
40,000	50,000	510	584	632	670	701	743
50,000	60,000	566	647	701	742	776	823
60,000	70,000	616	704	763	807	844	896
70,000	80,000	664	758	821	869	909	964
80,000	90,000	708	808	875	926	968	1027
90,000	100,000	749	856	926	980	1025	1087
100,000	120,000	804	918	993	1051	1099	1165
120,000	140,000	879	1003	1085	1149	1200	1273
140,000	160,000	944	1077	1166	1233	1289	1366
160,000	180,000	1009	1151	1245	1318	1377	1459
180,000	200,000	1068	1218	1317	1393	1456	1543
200,000 or more		1359	1549	1674	1770	1849	1959

District of Columbia 6.0000%

Income At least	Income But less than	Exemptions 1	2	3	4	5	Over 5
$0	$20,000	186	216	236	252	265	283
20,000	30,000	305	353	385	410	431	461
30,000	40,000	366	423	462	492	517	552
40,000	50,000	419	484	528	563	591	631
50,000	60,000	467	539	588	626	657	702
60,000	70,000	511	590	643	684	718	766
70,000	80,000	553	637	694	739	776	827
80,000	90,000	592	682	742	790	829	884
90,000	100,000	628	724	788	838	880	938
100,000	120,000	677	779	848	902	946	1009
120,000	140,000	744	855	931	989	1038	1106
140,000	160,000	802	922	1003	1066	1118	1192
160,000	180,000	861	989	1076	1143	1199	1277
180,000	200,000	913	1049	1141	1212	1271	1354
200,000 or more		1179	1351	1468	1558	1633	1738

Florida 6.0000%

Income At least	Income But less than	Exemptions 1	2	3	4	5	Over 5
$0	$20,000	262	306	336	359	378	404
20,000	30,000	420	488	535	570	600	642
30,000	40,000	500	581	635	678	713	762
40,000	50,000	568	660	722	769	809	864
50,000	60,000	630	731	799	851	895	956
60,000	70,000	686	795	869	926	973	1040
70,000	80,000	739	856	935	997	1047	1118
80,000	90,000	788	913	997	1062	1116	1191
90,000	100,000	834	966	1055	1123	1180	1260
100,000	120,000	895	1036	1131	1204	1265	1350
120,000	140,000	979	1133	1236	1315	1381	1474
140,000	160,000	1052	1217	1327	1412	1483	1582
160,000	180,000	1125	1300	1418	1508	1584	1689
180,000	200,000	1191	1375	1499	1595	1675	1786
200,000 or more		1518	1750	1906	2026	2126	2265

Georgia 4.0000%

Income At least	Income But less than	Exemptions 1	2	3	4	5	Over 5
$0	$20,000	169	195	213	226	237	253
20,000	30,000	257	295	321	341	357	380
30,000	40,000	301	345	375	397	416	442
40,000	50,000	338	387	420	445	466	495
50,000	60,000	371	425	460	488	511	542
60,000	70,000	401	458	497	526	551	584
70,000	80,000	429	490	531	562	588	624
80,000	90,000	455	519	562	595	623	660
90,000	100,000	480	547	592	627	655	695
100,000	120,000	512	583	631	668	698	740
120,000	140,000	556	633	684	723	756	801
140,000	160,000	594	676	730	772	806	854
160,000	180,000	632	718	776	820	856	907
180,000	200,000	666	757	817	863	901	954
200,000 or more		836	946	1019	1075	1121	1186

Hawaii[5] 4.0000%

Income At least	Income But less than	Exemptions 1	2	3	4	5	Over 5
$0	$20,000	262	318	356	386	411	447
20,000	30,000	395	477	533	577	614	667
30,000	40,000	460	554	619	670	713	774
40,000	50,000	515	620	692	749	796	864
50,000	60,000	563	678	756	818	870	943
60,000	70,000	607	730	814	880	936	1014
70,000	80,000	648	778	868	938	997	1081
80,000	90,000	685	823	917	992	1054	1142
90,000	100,000	721	865	964	1042	1107	1199
100,000	120,000	767	920	1025	1107	1176	1274
120,000	140,000	829	994	1107	1196	1270	1375
140,000	160,000	883	1058	1178	1272	1351	1463
160,000	180,000	937	1121	1248	1348	1431	1549
180,000	200,000	985	1178	1311	1415	1503	1626
200,000 or more		1219	1456	1618	1745	1851	2002

Idaho 6.0000%

Income At least	Income But less than	Exemptions 1	2	3	4	5	Over 5
$0	$20,000	270	320	353	379	401	431
20,000	30,000	432	509	562	602	636	684
30,000	40,000	513	605	667	715	756	812
40,000	50,000	583	687	757	812	857	921
50,000	60,000	646	760	838	898	948	1019
60,000	70,000	703	827	911	977	1031	1108
70,000	80,000	757	890	980	1050	1109	1191
80,000	90,000	807	948	1044	1119	1181	1268
90,000	100,000	854	1003	1105	1183	1249	1341
100,000	120,000	916	1076	1184	1268	1338	1437
120,000	140,000	1000	1175	1293	1384	1461	1568
140,000	160,000	1074	1261	1387	1486	1567	1682
160,000	180,000	1148	1347	1481	1586	1673	1796
180,000	200,000	1214	1424	1566	1677	1769	1898
200,000 or more		1543	1807	1986	2125	2241	2403

Illinois 6.2500%

Income At least	Income But less than	Exemptions 1	2	3	4	5	Over 5
$0	$20,000	365	447	505	550	589	644
20,000	30,000	529	645	725	789	844	921
30,000	40,000	608	740	831	904	965	1052
40,000	50,000	675	819	919	999	1066	1162
50,000	60,000	734	889	997	1083	1155	1258
60,000	70,000	787	952	1067	1158	1234	1344
70,000	80,000	836	1010	1131	1227	1308	1424
80,000	90,000	882	1064	1190	1291	1376	1497
90,000	100,000	924	1114	1246	1351	1439	1565
100,000	120,000	980	1179	1318	1429	1521	1654
120,000	140,000	1056	1268	1416	1534	1633	1774
140,000	160,000	1121	1345	1501	1625	1729	1877
160,000	180,000	1186	1421	1584	1714	1823	1979
180,000	200,000	1244	1488	1659	1794	1907	2070
200,000 or more		1528	1819	2021	2182	2317	2510

Indiana 7.0000%

Income At least	Income But less than	Exemptions 1	2	3	4	5	Over 5
$0	$20,000	302	354	389	417	439	472
20,000	30,000	456	531	581	621	654	700
30,000	40,000	532	618	676	721	759	812
40,000	50,000	597	692	756	806	848	906
50,000	60,000	655	757	827	881	926	990
60,000	70,000	707	816	891	949	997	1065
70,000	80,000	757	872	951	1012	1063	1135
80,000	90,000	802	923	1006	1070	1124	1199
90,000	100,000	845	972	1058	1125	1181	1260
100,000	120,000	901	1035	1126	1197	1256	1339
120,000	140,000	978	1121	1219	1295	1358	1447
140,000	160,000	1045	1196	1299	1380	1446	1541
160,000	180,000	1111	1271	1379	1464	1534	1633
180,000	200,000	1171	1337	1451	1539	1612	1716
200,000 or more		1468	1668	1804	1910	1998	2123

Iowa 6.0000%

Income At least	Income But less than	Exemptions 1	2	3	4	5	Over 5
$0	$20,000	268	312	342	365	383	410
20,000	30,000	404	469	512	546	574	613
30,000	40,000	471	546	596	635	667	711
40,000	50,000	527	611	667	710	745	795
50,000	60,000	578	669	729	776	815	868
60,000	70,000	623	721	786	836	877	935
70,000	80,000	665	769	838	891	935	997
80,000	90,000	705	814	887	943	989	1054
90,000	100,000	741	856	932	991	1040	1107
100,000	120,000	790	911	992	1054	1105	1177
120,000	140,000	855	986	1073	1140	1195	1272
140,000	160,000	912	1051	1143	1214	1273	1354
160,000	180,000	968	1115	1212	1287	1349	1435
180,000	200,000	1019	1172	1274	1353	1418	1508
200,000 or more		1267	1455	1579	1675	1754	1864

Kansas[1] 5.8041%

Income At least	Income But less than	Exemptions 1	2	3	4	5	Over 5
$0	$20,000	338	417	473	517	554	608
20,000	30,000	510	627	709	774	829	908
30,000	40,000	595	730	824	900	963	1054
40,000	50,000	666	816	921	1005	1076	1177
50,000	60,000	730	893	1007	1098	1175	1285
60,000	70,000	787	962	1085	1182	1265	1383
70,000	80,000	840	1026	1157	1260	1348	1474
80,000	90,000	889	1085	1223	1332	1425	1557
90,000	100,000	935	1141	1285	1400	1497	1635
100,000	120,000	995	1214	1366	1488	1591	1737
120,000	140,000	1077	1312	1477	1608	1718	1876
140,000	160,000	1148	1398	1572	1711	1828	1995
160,000	180,000	1219	1482	1666	1813	1937	2113
180,000	200,000	1281	1557	1751	1904	2034	2219
200,000 or more		1590	1927	2162	2350	2508	2733

Kentucky 6.0000%

Income At least	Income But less than	Exemptions 1	2	3	4	5	Over 5
$0	$20,000	258	301	330	352	370	396
20,000	30,000	394	457	499	532	558	596
30,000	40,000	462	534	583	620	651	695
40,000	50,000	519	600	654	695	730	778
50,000	60,000	570	658	716	762	799	852
60,000	70,000	616	710	773	822	862	919
70,000	80,000	660	760	827	879	921	981
80,000	90,000	700	805	876	931	976	1039
90,000	100,000	738	848	922	980	1027	1093
100,000	120,000	788	905	983	1044	1094	1164
120,000	140,000	856	982	1066	1131	1185	1260
140,000	160,000	915	1049	1138	1207	1264	1344
160,000	180,000	974	1115	1209	1282	1343	1427
180,000	200,000	1027	1174	1273	1350	1413	1501
200,000 or more		1288	1469	1590	1683	1760	1867

Louisiana 4.0000%

Income At least	Income But less than	Exemptions 1	2	3	4	5	Over 5
$0	$20,000	176	205	224	239	251	268
20,000	30,000	282	327	357	380	399	426
30,000	40,000	336	389	424	452	475	506
40,000	50,000	382	442	482	513	539	575
50,000	60,000	423	490	534	568	596	636
60,000	70,000	461	533	581	618	649	692
70,000	80,000	497	574	625	665	698	744
80,000	90,000	530	612	666	709	744	792
90,000	100,000	561	647	705	750	787	838
100,000	120,000	602	694	756	804	844	899
120,000	140,000	658	759	826	878	921	981
140,000	160,000	708	815	887	943	989	1053
160,000	180,000	757	871	948	1007	1056	1125
180,000	200,000	801	922	1003	1065	1117	1189
200,000 or more		1021	1173	1275	1354	1419	1509

Maine 5.0000%

Income At least	Income But less than	Exemptions 1	2	3	4	5	Over 5
$0	$20,000	160	186	203	217	228	244
20,000	30,000	261	301	329	350	367	392
30,000	40,000	312	360	393	418	439	468
40,000	50,000	357	411	448	476	500	533
50,000	60,000	397	457	498	529	555	592
60,000	70,000	434	499	543	577	605	645
70,000	80,000	469	539	586	623	653	695
80,000	90,000	501	576	626	665	697	742
90,000	100,000	532	611	664	705	739	787
100,000	120,000	573	657	714	758	794	845
120,000	140,000	629	721	782	830	870	925
140,000	160,000	678	776	842	894	936	996
160,000	180,000	727	832	902	957	1002	1066
180,000	200,000	771	882	956	1014	1062	1129
200,000 or more		994	1133	1227	1300	1360	1444

Maryland 6.0000%

Income At least	Income But less than	Exemptions 1	2	3	4	5	Over 5
$0	$20,000	246	286	312	333	350	373
20,000	30,000	377	434	473	503	527	562
30,000	40,000	442	508	552	587	615	655
40,000	50,000	497	570	620	658	689	734
50,000	60,000	546	626	679	721	755	804
60,000	70,000	591	676	734	778	815	867
70,000	80,000	633	724	785	832	871	925
80,000	90,000	672	767	831	881	922	980
90,000	100,000	709	809	876	928	971	1031
100,000	120,000	757	863	934	989	1034	1098
120,000	140,000	824	937	1013	1072	1121	1189
140,000	160,000	881	1001	1082	1144	1196	1268
160,000	180,000	939	1065	1150	1216	1270	1347
180,000	200,000	990	1122	1211	1280	1337	1417
200,000 or more		1247	1407	1514	1598	1667	1764

Massachusetts 6.2500%

Income At least	Income But less than	Exemptions 1	2	3	4	5	Over 5
$0	$20,000	230	260	279	293	305	322
20,000	30,000	351	393	421	443	460	484
30,000	40,000	410	460	492	516	536	564
40,000	50,000	461	516	552	579	601	631
50,000	60,000	507	566	605	634	658	691
60,000	70,000	548	611	652	684	710	745
70,000	80,000	586	653	697	731	758	796
80,000	90,000	622	692	739	774	803	843
90,000	100,000	655	729	778	815	845	887
100,000	120,000	699	778	829	868	900	944
120,000	140,000	759	844	899	941	975	1022
140,000	160,000	811	901	959	1004	1040	1090
160,000	180,000	863	958	1019	1066	1105	1158
180,000	200,000	910	1009	1073	1122	1163	1218
200,000 or more		1141	1261	1340	1399	1448	1515

Michigan 6.0000%

Income At least	Income But less than	Exemptions 1	2	3	4	5	Over 5
$0	$20,000	248	287	313	333	349	372
20,000	30,000	379	436	474	504	528	561
30,000	40,000	444	510	554	588	616	655
40,000	50,000	500	573	622	659	690	733
50,000	60,000	549	629	682	723	756	803
60,000	70,000	594	679	736	780	816	866
70,000	80,000	636	727	787	834	872	925
80,000	90,000	675	770	834	883	923	980
90,000	100,000	711	812	878	930	972	1031
100,000	120,000	760	866	937	991	1036	1098
120,000	140,000	825	940	1016	1074	1123	1190
140,000	160,000	883	1004	1085	1147	1198	1269
160,000	180,000	940	1068	1153	1218	1272	1348
180,000	200,000	991	1125	1214	1283	1339	1418
200,000 or more		1245	1408	1517	1601	1670	1766

Minnesota 6.8750%

Income At least	Income But less than	Exemptions 1	2	3	4	5	Over 5
$0	$20,000	256	296	322	343	360	384
20,000	30,000	413	476	518	551	578	616
30,000	40,000	493	568	618	657	689	734
40,000	50,000	561	646	703	748	784	835
50,000	60,000	623	717	780	829	869	925
60,000	70,000	679	782	850	903	947	1008
70,000	80,000	732	842	916	973	1020	1086
80,000	90,000	781	899	977	1037	1088	1157
90,000	100,000	828	952	1035	1099	1152	1226
100,000	120,000	889	1022	1111	1179	1236	1315
120,000	140,000	973	1118	1215	1290	1351	1438
140,000	160,000	1047	1202	1306	1386	1452	1545
160,000	180,000	1120	1286	1396	1482	1553	1651
180,000	200,000	1186	1361	1478	1568	1643	1747
200,000 or more		1514	1735	1883	1998	2092	2224

Mississippi 7.0000%

Income At least	Income But less than	Exemptions 1	2	3	4	5	Over 5
$0	$20,000	426	520	585	637	680	742
20,000	30,000	644	783	879	956	1020	1111
30,000	40,000	751	912	1023	1112	1186	1291
40,000	50,000	841	1020	1144	1243	1325	1443
50,000	60,000	921	1116	1251	1358	1448	1576
60,000	70,000	993	1203	1348	1462	1559	1696
70,000	80,000	1061	1283	1438	1560	1662	1808
80,000	90,000	1123	1358	1520	1649	1757	1911
90,000	100,000	1181	1427	1598	1733	1846	2008
100,000	120,000	1257	1518	1700	1843	1963	2134
120,000	140,000	1361	1642	1837	1991	2121	2305
140,000	160,000	1451	1749	1956	2120	2257	2452
160,000	180,000	1539	1855	2074	2247	2392	2598
180,000	200,000	1619	1950	2179	2360	2512	2728
200,000 or more		2008	2413	2693	2915	3100	3364

Missouri 4.2250%

Income At least	Income But less than	Exemptions 1	2	3	4	5	Over 5
$0	$20,000	187	223	247	267	283	305
20,000	30,000	285	338	374	402	426	459
30,000	40,000	334	395	436	469	496	535
40,000	50,000	375	443	489	525	556	599
50,000	60,000	412	486	536	576	609	655
60,000	70,000	446	524	578	621	656	706
70,000	80,000	477	561	618	663	701	754
80,000	90,000	506	594	655	702	742	798
90,000	100,000	533	626	689	739	780	839
100,000	120,000	569	667	735	787	831	893
120,000	140,000	618	724	796	853	900	967
140,000	160,000	661	773	850	910	960	1030
160,000	180,000	703	822	903	966	1019	1093
180,000	200,000	741	865	950	1017	1072	1150
200,000 or more		930	1081	1185	1266	1333	1428

Nebraska 5.5000%

Income At least	Income But less than	Exemptions 1	2	3	4	5	Over 5
$0	$20,000	247	289	317	339	357	382
20,000	30,000	395	461	505	540	569	609
30,000	40,000	470	548	601	642	676	723
40,000	50,000	534	623	683	729	767	821
50,000	60,000	592	690	756	807	849	908
60,000	70,000	644	751	823	878	924	988
70,000	80,000	694	808	885	945	994	1063
80,000	90,000	740	862	943	1007	1059	1132
90,000	100,000	783	912	998	1065	1120	1198
100,000	120,000	840	978	1070	1142	1201	1284
120,000	140,000	918	1068	1169	1247	1312	1402
140,000	160,000	986	1147	1255	1339	1408	1505
160,000	180,000	1054	1226	1341	1430	1504	1607
180,000	200,000	1115	1297	1418	1512	1590	1699
200,000 or more		1419	1648	1801	1920	2018	2155

(Continued on next page)

2010 Optional State and Certain Local Sales Tax Tables *(Continued)*

Nevada[3] 6.8500%

Income: At least	But less than	Exemptions: 1	2	3	4	5	Over 5
$0	$20,000	288	332	361	384	402	428
20,000	30,000	435	499	542	574	602	639
30,000	40,000	508	581	630	668	699	743
40,000	50,000	569	651	706	747	782	830
50,000	60,000	624	713	772	818	855	907
60,000	70,000	674	769	832	881	921	977
70,000	80,000	721	822	889	940	983	1042
80,000	90,000	764	870	941	995	1040	1102
90,000	100,000	805	916	990	1047	1093	1158
100,000	120,000	858	976	1054	1114	1163	1232
120,000	140,000	931	1058	1141	1206	1259	1333
140,000	160,000	995	1129	1217	1286	1342	1420
160,000	180,000	1058	1199	1293	1364	1424	1506
180,000	200,000	1115	1262	1360	1435	1497	1583
200,000 or more		1395	1575	1693	1784	1859	1964

New Jersey[4] 7.0000%

Income: At least	But less than	Exemptions: 1	2	3	4	5	Over 5
$0	$20,000	274	315	343	364	381	406
20,000	30,000	440	504	547	580	607	645
30,000	40,000	524	600	651	690	722	767
40,000	50,000	596	682	739	784	820	871
50,000	60,000	661	756	819	868	908	964
60,000	70,000	720	823	891	944	988	1048
70,000	80,000	776	886	959	1016	1063	1128
80,000	90,000	827	944	1023	1083	1133	1202
90,000	100,000	876	1000	1082	1146	1198	1272
100,000	120,000	940	1073	1161	1229	1285	1363
120,000	140,000	1029	1173	1269	1343	1404	1489
140,000	160,000	1106	1260	1362	1442	1507	1598
160,000	180,000	1182	1346	1456	1540	1610	1707
180,000	200,000	1251	1425	1540	1629	1702	1805
200,000 or more		1595	1813	1958	2070	2162	2291

New Mexico[1] 5.0630%

Income: At least	But less than	Exemptions: 1	2	3	4	5	Over 5
$0	$20,000	211	248	273	292	308	331
20,000	30,000	337	395	434	464	489	525
30,000	40,000	400	469	515	551	581	622
40,000	50,000	455	533	585	626	659	706
50,000	60,000	504	590	647	692	729	781
60,000	70,000	548	641	704	752	793	849
70,000	80,000	590	690	757	809	852	913
80,000	90,000	629	735	807	862	908	972
90,000	100,000	665	778	853	912	960	1028
100,000	120,000	713	834	915	977	1029	1101
120,000	140,000	779	911	999	1067	1123	1202
140,000	160,000	837	978	1072	1145	1205	1289
160,000	180,000	894	1044	1145	1222	1287	1376
180,000	200,000	946	1104	1210	1292	1360	1455
200,000 or more		1203	1402	1535	1638	1724	1843

New York 4.0000%

Income: At least	But less than	Exemptions: 1	2	3	4	5	Over 5
$0	$20,000	161	187	204	217	228	243
20,000	30,000	258	298	324	345	362	386
30,000	40,000	307	354	385	410	430	458
40,000	50,000	350	402	438	465	488	520
50,000	60,000	387	446	485	515	540	575
60,000	70,000	422	485	527	560	587	625
70,000	80,000	455	522	567	603	632	672
80,000	90,000	485	557	605	642	673	716
90,000	100,000	513	589	640	679	712	757
100,000	120,000	551	632	686	728	763	812
120,000	140,000	603	691	750	795	833	886
140,000	160,000	648	742	805	854	894	951
160,000	180,000	693	793	860	912	955	1015
180,000	200,000	733	839	910	965	1010	1073
200,000 or more		935	1067	1156	1225	1282	1361

North Carolina 5.7500%

Income: At least	But less than	Exemptions: 1	2	3	4	5	Over 5
$0	$20,000	281	336	374	404	428	463
20,000	30,000	436	519	576	621	658	711
30,000	40,000	513	610	677	729	773	834
40,000	50,000	578	687	762	821	870	938
50,000	60,000	636	756	838	902	956	1031
60,000	70,000	689	818	907	976	1033	1115
70,000	80,000	739	877	971	1045	1106	1193
80,000	90,000	784	930	1030	1108	1173	1265
90,000	100,000	827	981	1086	1168	1237	1333
100,000	120,000	884	1048	1159	1247	1319	1422
120,000	140,000	961	1138	1259	1353	1432	1543
140,000	160,000	1028	1217	1346	1446	1530	1649
160,000	180,000	1095	1295	1431	1538	1627	1753
180,000	200,000	1154	1365	1508	1620	1714	1846
200,000 or more		1449	1710	1887	2026	2142	2305

North Dakota 5.0000%

Income: At least	But less than	Exemptions: 1	2	3	4	5	Over 5
$0	$20,000	200	236	261	280	296	319
20,000	30,000	305	358	394	423	446	480
30,000	40,000	358	419	460	493	520	559
40,000	50,000	403	470	516	553	583	626
50,000	60,000	443	516	566	606	638	685
60,000	70,000	480	558	611	653	688	738
70,000	80,000	514	597	654	698	735	788
80,000	90,000	545	633	693	739	779	834
90,000	100,000	575	667	729	778	819	877
100,000	120,000	615	711	778	829	873	934
120,000	140,000	668	772	843	899	946	1011
140,000	160,000	715	825	900	959	1009	1078
160,000	180,000	762	878	957	1019	1071	1145
180,000	200,000	804	925	1008	1073	1127	1204
200,000 or more		1013	1159	1260	1339	1404	1498

Ohio 5.5000%

Income: At least	But less than	Exemptions: 1	2	3	4	5	Over 5
$0	$20,000	242	281	307	327	343	366
20,000	30,000	385	445	485	517	542	578
30,000	40,000	457	528	576	613	643	685
40,000	50,000	520	600	653	695	729	776
50,000	60,000	575	664	723	768	806	858
60,000	70,000	626	722	785	835	875	932
70,000	80,000	674	776	845	897	941	1002
80,000	90,000	718	827	900	956	1002	1066
90,000	100,000	760	875	951	1011	1059	1127
100,000	120,000	815	938	1020	1083	1135	1208
120,000	140,000	891	1024	1113	1182	1238	1317
140,000	160,000	957	1099	1194	1268	1328	1413
160,000	180,000	1022	1174	1275	1353	1418	1508
180,000	200,000	1081	1241	1348	1430	1498	1593
200,000 or more		1376	1576	1710	1813	1898	2017

Oklahoma 4.5000%

Income: At least	But less than	Exemptions: 1	2	3	4	5	Over 5
$0	$20,000	249	304	343	374	400	438
20,000	30,000	380	462	519	565	604	659
30,000	40,000	445	540	606	659	704	768
40,000	50,000	500	606	680	739	788	859
50,000	60,000	549	664	745	809	863	940
60,000	70,000	594	717	803	872	930	1013
70,000	80,000	635	767	859	932	993	1082
80,000	90,000	674	812	909	986	1051	1144
90,000	100,000	710	855	957	1038	1106	1204
100,000	120,000	758	912	1019	1105	1177	1281
120,000	140,000	823	988	1104	1197	1274	1386
140,000	160,000	879	1055	1178	1276	1358	1477
160,000	180,000	936	1121	1251	1354	1442	1566
180,000	200,000	986	1180	1316	1425	1516	1647
200,000 or more		1236	1472	1638	1770	1882	2041

Pennsylvania 6.0000%

Income: At least	But less than	Exemptions: 1	2	3	4	5	Over 5
$0	$20,000	223	256	279	296	310	329
20,000	30,000	355	407	441	468	490	520
30,000	40,000	422	483	524	555	581	617
40,000	50,000	480	548	594	629	658	699
50,000	60,000	531	607	657	696	728	773
60,000	70,000	578	660	714	756	791	839
70,000	80,000	622	710	768	813	850	902
80,000	90,000	663	756	818	866	905	960
90,000	100,000	702	800	865	916	957	1015
100,000	120,000	753	858	927	981	1026	1087
120,000	140,000	823	937	1012	1071	1119	1186
140,000	160,000	884	1005	1086	1149	1200	1272
160,000	180,000	944	1074	1160	1226	1281	1357
180,000	200,000	999	1135	1226	1296	1354	1434
200,000 or more		1270	1441	1555	1642	1714	1815

Rhode Island 7.0000%

Income: At least	But less than	Exemptions: 1	2	3	4	5	Over 5
$0	$20,000	271	311	337	357	373	396
20,000	30,000	408	465	503	532	556	589
30,000	40,000	476	541	585	618	645	683
40,000	50,000	533	605	653	690	720	763
50,000	60,000	583	662	714	754	787	833
60,000	70,000	629	713	769	812	847	896
70,000	80,000	671	761	820	865	903	954
80,000	90,000	711	805	867	915	954	1008
90,000	100,000	747	846	911	961	1002	1059
100,000	120,000	796	900	969	1022	1065	1125
120,000	140,000	861	973	1047	1104	1151	1215
140,000	160,000	918	1037	1115	1175	1225	1293
160,000	180,000	975	1100	1182	1246	1298	1370
180,000	200,000	1025	1156	1243	1309	1363	1439
200,000 or more		1273	1432	1537	1617	1683	1774

South Carolina 6.0000%

Income: At least	But less than	Exemptions: 1	2	3	4	5	Over 5
$0	$20,000	259	301	329	351	369	394
20,000	30,000	411	477	521	555	583	622
30,000	40,000	487	565	617	658	691	737
40,000	50,000	553	641	700	745	783	835
50,000	60,000	612	709	774	824	865	922
60,000	70,000	665	771	841	895	939	1002
70,000	80,000	716	829	904	962	1010	1076
80,000	90,000	762	882	962	1024	1074	1145
90,000	100,000	807	933	1017	1082	1136	1211
100,000	120,000	865	1000	1090	1159	1216	1296
120,000	140,000	944	1091	1189	1264	1327	1413
140,000	160,000	1013	1170	1275	1356	1422	1515
160,000	180,000	1082	1249	1361	1447	1518	1617
180,000	200,000	1144	1320	1438	1529	1603	1708
200,000 or more		1451	1673	1821	1934	2028	2159

South Dakota 4.0000%

Income: At least	But less than	Exemptions: 1	2	3	4	5	Over 5
$0	$20,000	242	297	335	366	391	428
20,000	30,000	368	449	506	551	589	644
30,000	40,000	429	524	590	642	686	749
40,000	50,000	482	587	661	719	768	838
50,000	60,000	528	643	723	786	840	916
60,000	70,000	570	693	779	847	905	987
70,000	80,000	609	740	832	904	965	1053
80,000	90,000	645	783	880	957	1021	1113
90,000	100,000	678	824	925	1006	1073	1170
100,000	120,000	723	877	985	1070	1142	1244
120,000	140,000	783	949	1065	1157	1235	1345
140,000	160,000	835	1012	1135	1233	1315	1432
160,000	180,000	887	1074	1204	1307	1394	1518
180,000	200,000	933	1129	1266	1374	1465	1595
200,000 or more		1159	1400	1567	1700	1811	1970

Tennessee 7.0000%

Income: At least	But less than	Exemptions: 1	2	3	4	5	Over 5
$0	$20,000	398	483	541	587	626	681
20,000	30,000	583	703	785	850	905	983
30,000	40,000	673	809	903	977	1039	1127
40,000	50,000	748	898	1001	1082	1151	1248
50,000	60,000	815	976	1087	1175	1249	1354
60,000	70,000	875	1046	1165	1259	1337	1449
70,000	80,000	930	1112	1237	1336	1419	1537
80,000	90,000	982	1172	1303	1407	1494	1617
90,000	100,000	1030	1228	1366	1474	1564	1693
100,000	120,000	1093	1302	1447	1560	1656	1791
120,000	140,000	1178	1402	1556	1678	1780	1925
140,000	160,000	1252	1488	1651	1779	1887	2039
160,000	180,000	1325	1573	1744	1879	1992	2152
180,000	200,000	1391	1649	1827	1968	2085	2253
200,000 or more		1711	2020	2234	2401	2542	2742

Texas 6.2500%

Income: At least	But less than	Exemptions: 1	2	3	4	5	Over 5
$0	$20,000	276	326	359	386	408	438
20,000	30,000	439	517	570	611	646	694
30,000	40,000	522	614	677	726	766	823
40,000	50,000	593	697	768	823	869	933
50,000	60,000	656	772	849	910	960	1031
60,000	70,000	714	839	924	989	1044	1121
70,000	80,000	769	903	993	1064	1122	1205
80,000	90,000	819	961	1058	1133	1195	1283
90,000	100,000	867	1017	1119	1198	1264	1356
100,000	120,000	929	1090	1199	1283	1354	1453
120,000	140,000	1015	1190	1308	1401	1477	1585
140,000	160,000	1090	1277	1404	1503	1584	1699
160,000	180,000	1164	1364	1499	1604	1691	1814
180,000	200,000	1231	1442	1584	1695	1787	1916
200,000 or more		1564	1829	2008	2147	2263	2425

Utah 4.7000%

Income: At least	But less than	Exemptions: 1	2	3	4	5	Over 5
$0	$20,000	249	300	335	363	386	419
20,000	30,000	384	461	514	556	591	640
30,000	40,000	451	541	603	651	692	750
40,000	50,000	509	609	678	732	778	842
50,000	60,000	560	669	745	804	854	925
60,000	70,000	606	724	805	869	923	999
70,000	80,000	649	775	862	930	987	1068
80,000	90,000	690	822	914	986	1047	1132
90,000	100,000	727	867	963	1039	1103	1193
100,000	120,000	777	926	1028	1108	1176	1272
120,000	140,000	845	1005	1116	1203	1276	1379
140,000	160,000	904	1074	1192	1285	1362	1472
160,000	180,000	962	1143	1268	1366	1448	1564
180,000	200,000	1014	1205	1335	1438	1525	1647
200,000 or more		1274	1508	1669	1796	1903	2053

Vermont 6.0000%

Income: At least	But less than	Exemptions: 1	2	3	4	5	Over 5
$0	$20,000	182	202	216	226	234	245
20,000	30,000	273	302	321	336	347	363
30,000	40,000	318	352	373	390	403	421
40,000	50,000	356	393	417	435	450	470
50,000	60,000	390	430	456	475	491	513
60,000	70,000	420	463	491	512	529	552
70,000	80,000	449	494	524	546	564	588
80,000	90,000	475	523	554	577	596	622
90,000	100,000	500	550	582	606	626	653
100,000	120,000	533	585	619	645	666	694
120,000	140,000	577	634	670	697	720	750
140,000	160,000	616	675	714	743	766	799
160,000	180,000	657	717	757	788	813	847
180,000	200,000	688	754	796	828	854	889
200,000 or more		857	936	988	1026	1057	1100

Virginia 4.0000%

Income: At least	But less than	Exemptions: 1	2	3	4	5	Over 5
$0	$20,000	185	220	244	263	279	301
20,000	30,000	276	327	361	389	411	443
30,000	40,000	321	379	419	450	476	512
40,000	50,000	359	423	467	501	530	570
50,000	60,000	393	462	510	547	578	621
60,000	70,000	423	498	548	588	621	667
70,000	80,000	452	531	584	626	661	710
80,000	90,000	478	561	617	661	698	750
90,000	100,000	503	590	648	694	733	787
100,000	120,000	536	627	689	738	778	835
120,000	140,000	580	678	744	797	840	901
140,000	160,000	619	722	792	847	893	958
160,000	180,000	657	766	840	898	946	1014
180,000	200,000	691	805	882	943	993	1065
200,000 or more		861	998	1091	1164	1225	1311

Washington 6.5000%

Income: At least	But less than	Exemptions: 1	2	3	4	5	Over 5
$0	$20,000	280	330	364	391	414	445
20,000	30,000	449	529	583	625	660	709
30,000	40,000	536	630	694	744	785	844
40,000	50,000	610	717	789	845	892	958
50,000	60,000	677	795	874	936	988	1061
60,000	70,000	738	865	952	1019	1076	1155
70,000	80,000	796	932	1025	1098	1158	1243
80,000	90,000	849	994	1093	1170	1234	1325
90,000	100,000	899	1053	1157	1239	1306	1402
100,000	120,000	966	1130	1242	1329	1401	1503
120,000	140,000	1057	1236	1358	1453	1531	1643
140,000	160,000	1137	1329	1459	1560	1645	1764
160,000	180,000	1216	1421	1560	1668	1758	1885
180,000	200,000	1288	1504	1650	1765	1860	1993
200,000 or more		1645	1917	2102	2246	2365	2534

West Virginia 6.0000%

Income: At least	But less than	Exemptions: 1	2	3	4	5	Over 5
$0	$20,000	306	368	411	445	474	514
20,000	30,000	478	573	638	690	733	795
30,000	40,000	564	675	752	812	863	934
40,000	50,000	637	762	848	916	972	1053
50,000	60,000	703	839	934	1008	1070	1158
60,000	70,000	762	910	1011	1091	1159	1254
70,000	80,000	818	976	1084	1170	1242	1343
80,000	90,000	870	1037	1152	1242	1318	1426
90,000	100,000	918	1094	1215	1310	1390	1503
100,000	120,000	982	1170	1298	1400	1485	1605
120,000	140,000	1070	1273	1412	1522	1614	1744
140,000	160,000	1146	1362	1511	1628	1726	1865
160,000	180,000	1222	1451	1609	1733	1837	1985
180,000	200,000	1290	1531	1697	1828	1937	2092
200,000 or more		1626	1926	2131	2293	2429	2621

Wisconsin 5.0000%

Income: At least	But less than	Exemptions: 1	2	3	4	5	Over 5
$0	$20,000	228	267	294	314	331	355
20,000	30,000	362	424	465	497	524	561
30,000	40,000	430	503	552	590	621	665
40,000	50,000	488	570	626	668	704	754
50,000	60,000	540	631	692	739	778	833
60,000	70,000	588	686	752	803	845	905
70,000	80,000	632	737	808	863	909	972
80,000	90,000	673	785	861	919	967	1035
90,000	100,000	712	830	910	971	1022	1094
100,000	120,000	763	890	975	1041	1095	1171
120,000	140,000	834	971	1063	1135	1194	1277
140,000	160,000	895	1042	1141	1217	1281	1369
160,000	180,000	955	1112	1218	1299	1367	1461
180,000	200,000	1010	1176	1287	1373	1444	1543
200,000 or more		1281	1489	1629	1737	1826	1951

Wyoming 4.0000%

Income: At least	But less than	Exemptions: 1	2	3	4	5	Over 5
$0	$20,000	171	200	219	234	246	264
20,000	30,000	274	319	349	373	392	419
30,000	40,000	327	380	415	443	466	498
40,000	50,000	372	432	472	503	529	565
50,000	60,000	412	478	523	557	586	626
60,000	70,000	449	521	569	606	637	681
70,000	80,000	484	561	613	653	686	732
80,000	90,000	516	598	653	696	731	780
90,000	100,000	547	633	691	736	773	826
100,000	120,000	587	679	741	790	829	885
120,000	140,000	642	743	810	863	906	967
140,000	160,000	690	798	870	926	973	1038
160,000	180,000	738	853	930	990	1039	1109
180,000	200,000	781	903	984	1047	1099	1172
200,000 or more		997	1150	1252	1331	1397	1489

Note. Alaska does not have a state sales tax. Alaska residents should follow the instructions on the next page to determine their local sales tax amount.

1 The rates for Arizona, Kansas, and New Mexico increased during 2010, so the rates given are averaged over the year.

2 The California table includes the 1% uniform local sales tax rate in addition to the 7.2500% state sales tax rate.

3 The Nevada table includes the 2.25% uniform local sales tax rate in addition to the 4.6000% state sales tax rate.

4 Residents of Salem County should deduct only half of the amount in the state table.

5 The 4.0% rate for Hawaii is actually an excise tax but is treated as a sales tax for purpose of this deduction.

Which Optional Local Sales Tax Table Should I Use?

IF you live in the state of...	AND you live in...	THEN use Local Table...
Alaska	Any locality	C
Arizona	Mesa or Tucson	A
	Chandler, Gilbert, Glendale, Peoria, Phoenix, Scottsdale, Tempe, Yuma, or any other locality	B
Arkansas	Any locality	C
California	Los Angeles County	A
Colorado	Adams County, Arapahoe County, Boulder County, Centennial, Colorado Springs, Denver City/Denver County, El Paso County, Greeley, Jefferson County, Larimer County, Pueblo County, or any other locality	A
	Arvada, Aurora, City of Boulder, Fort Collins, Lakewood, Longmont, City of Pueblo, Thornton, or Westminster	B
Georgia	Any locality	B
Illinois	Any locality	A
Louisiana	East Baton Rouge Parish	B
	Any other locality	C
Missouri	Any locality	B
New York	New York City	A
	One of the following counties: Albany, Allegany, Cattaraugus, Cayuga, Chemung, Clinton, Cortland, Dutchess, Erie, Essex, Franklin, Fulton, Genesee, Herkimer, Jefferson, Lewis, Livingston, Monroe, Montgomery, Nassau, Niagara, Oneida, Onondaga, Ontario, Orange, Orleans, Oswego, Otsego, Putnam, Rensselaer, Rockland, St. Lawrence, Saratoga, Schenectady, Schoharie, Seneca, Steuben, Suffolk, Sullivan, Tompkins, Ulster, Warren, Washington, Westchester, Wyoming, or Yates Or the City of Oneida	B
	Any other locality	D
North Carolina	Any locality	B
South Carolina	Cherokee County, Chesterfield County, Darlington County, Dillon County, Horry County, Jasper County, Lee County, Lexington County, or Myrtle Beach	B
	Any other locality	C
Tennessee	Any locality	B
Utah	Any locality	B
Virginia	Any locality	B

2010 Optional Local Sales Tax Tables for Certain Local Jurisdictions

(Based on a local sales tax rate of 1 percent)*

Income		Local Table A						Local Table B					
		Exemptions						Exemptions					
At least	But less than	1	2	3	4	5	Over 5	1	2	3	4	5	Over 5
$0	$20,000	43	50	55	59	62	66	50	60	66	72	76	83
20,000	30,000	65	76	83	89	93	100	76	91	101	109	115	125
30,000	40,000	76	89	97	103	109	116	89	106	118	127	135	146
40,000	50,000	86	99	109	116	122	130	100	119	132	142	151	163
50,000	60,000	94	109	119	127	133	142	110	130	145	156	165	179
60,000	70,000	102	118	128	137	143	153	119	141	156	168	178	193
70,000	80,000	109	126	137	146	153	163	127	151	167	180	190	206
80,000	90,000	116	133	145	154	162	173	135	160	177	190	202	218
90,000	100,000	122	140	153	163	171	182	142	168	186	200	212	229
100,000	120,000	130	150	163	173	182	194	151	179	198	213	226	244
120,000	140,000	141	162	176	187	197	209	164	194	215	231	245	264
140,000	160,000	151	173	188	200	210	223	175	207	229	247	261	281
160,000	180,000	161	184	200	212	223	237	187	220	244	262	277	299
180,000	200,000	169	194	211	223	234	249	197	232	257	276	292	314
200,000 or more		213	242	263	278	291	309	246	290	319	343	362	390

Income		Local Table C						Local Table D					
		Exemptions						Exemptions					
At least	But less than	1	2	3	4	5	Over 5	1	2	3	4	5	Over 5
$0	$20,000	61	75	84	91	97	106	40	47	51	54	57	61
20,000	30,000	93	112	125	136	145	158	65	75	81	86	91	97
30,000	40,000	108	130	146	158	168	183	77	89	96	103	108	115
40,000	50,000	121	146	163	177	188	204	88	101	110	116	122	130
50,000	60,000	132	159	178	193	205	223	97	112	121	129	135	144
60,000	70,000	143	172	192	208	221	240	106	121	132	140	147	156
70,000	80,000	152	183	205	222	236	256	114	131	142	151	158	168
80,000	90,000	161	194	216	234	249	270	121	139	151	161	168	179
90,000	100,000	170	204	227	246	262	284	128	147	160	170	178	189
100,000	120,000	181	217	242	262	278	302	138	158	172	182	191	203
120,000	140,000	195	234	261	283	300	326	151	173	188	199	208	222
140,000	160,000	208	250	278	301	320	346	162	186	201	214	224	238
160,000	180,000	221	265	295	319	339	367	173	198	215	228	239	254
180,000	200,000	233	278	310	335	356	385	183	210	228	241	253	268
200,000 or more		289	344	383	413	439	475	234	267	289	306	321	340

*If your local rate is more than 1 percent, the local portion of your deduction for sales tax will be increased. See the instructions for line 3 of the *State and Local General Sales Tax Deduction Worksheet.*

Income Tax Rates—Estates and Trusts

Tax Year 2010

Taxable Income		The Tax Is:	
Over—	But not Over—		Of the Amount Over—
$ 0	$ 2,300	15%	$ 0
2,300	5,350	$ 345.00 + 25%	2,300
5,350	8,200	1,107.50 + 28%	5,350
8,200	11,200	1,905.50 + 33%	8,200
11,200	....	2,895.50 + 35%	11,200

Tax Year 2011

Taxable Income		The Tax Is:	
Over—	But not Over—		Of the Amount Over—
$ 0	$ 2,300	15%	$ 0
2,300	5,450	$ 345.00 + 25%	2,300
5,450	8,300	1,132.50 + 28%	5,450
8,300	11,350	1,930.50 + 33%	8,300
11,350	....	2,937.00 + 35%	11,350

Income Tax Rates—Corporations

Taxable Income		Tax Is:	
Over—	But not Over—		Of the Amount Over—
$ 0	$ 50,000	15%	$ 0
50,000	75,000	$ 7,500 + 25%	50,000
75,000	100,000	13,750 + 34%	75,000
100,000	335,000	22,250 + 39%	100,000
335,000	10,000,000	113,900 + 34%	335,000
10,000,000	15,000,000	3,400,000 + 35%	10,000,000
15,000,000	18,333,333	5,150,000 + 38%	15,000,000
18,333,333	....	35%	0

Unified Transfer Tax Rates

For Gifts Made and for Deaths After 1983 and Before 2002

If the Amount with Respect to Which the Tentative Tax to Be Computed Is:	The Tentative Tax Is:
Not over $10,000	18 percent of such amount.
Over $10,000 but not over $20,000	$1,800, plus 20 percent of the excess of such amount over $10,000.
Over $20,000 but not over $40,000	$3,800, plus 22 percent of the excess of such amount over $20,000.
Over $40,000 but not over $60,000	$8,200, plus 24 percent of the excess of such amount over $40,000.
Over $60,000 but not over $80,000	$13,000, plus 26 percent of the excess of such amount over $60,000.
Over $80,000 but not over $100,000	$18,200, plus 28 percent of the excess of such amount over $80,000.
Over $100,000 but not over $150,000	$23,800, plus 30 percent of the excess of such amount over $100,000.
Over $150,000 but not over $250,000	$38,800, plus 32 percent of the excess of such amount over $150,000.
Over $250,000 but not over $500,000	$70,800, plus 34 percent of the excess of such amount over $250,000.
Over $500,000 but not over $750,000	$155,800, plus 37 percent of the excess of such amount over $500,000.
Over $750,000 but not over $1,000,000	$248,300, plus 39 percent of the excess of such amount over $750,000.
Over $1,000,000 but not over $1,250,000	$345,800, plus 41 percent of the excess of such amount over $1,000,000.
Over $1,250,000 but not over $1,500,000	$448,300, plus 43 percent of the excess of such amount over $1,250,000.
Over $1,500,000 but not over $2,000,000	$555,800, plus 45 percent of the excess of such amount over $1,500,000.
Over $2,000,000 but not over $2,500,000	$780,800, plus 49 percent of the excess of such amount over $2,000,000.
Over $2,500,000 but not over $3,000,000	$1,025,800, plus 53 percent of the excess of such amount over $2,500,000.
Over $3,000,000*	$1,290,800, plus 55 percent of the excess of such amount over $3,000,000.

* For large taxable transfers (generally in excess of $10 million) there is a phaseout of the graduated rates and the unified tax credit.

Unified Transfer Tax Rates

For Gifts Made and for Deaths in 2002

If the Amount with Respect to Which the Tentative Tax to Be Computed Is:	The Tentative Tax Is:
Not over $10,000	18 percent of such amount.
Over $10,000 but not over $20,000	$1,800, plus 20 percent of the excess of such amount over $10,000.
Over $20,000 but not over $40,000	$3,800, plus 22 percent of the excess of such amount over $20,000.
Over $40,000 but not over $60,000	$8,200, plus 24 percent of the excess of such amount over $40,000.
Over $60,000 but not over $80,000	$13,000, plus 26 percent of the excess of such amount over $60,000.
Over $80,000 but not over $100,000	$18,200, plus 28 percent of the excess of such amount over $80,000.
Over $100,000 but not over $150,000	$23,800, plus 30 percent of the excess of such amount over $100,000.
Over $150,000 but not over $250,000	$38,800, plus 32 percent of the excess of such amount over $150,000.
Over $250,000 but not over $500,000	$70,800, plus 34 percent of the excess of such amount over $250,000.
Over $500,000 but not over $750,000	$155,800, plus 37 percent of the excess of such amount over $500,000.
Over $750,000 but not over $1,000,000	$248,300, plus 39 percent of the excess of such amount over $750,000.
Over $1,000,000 but not over $1,250,000	$345,800, plus 41 percent of the excess of such amount over $1,000,000.
Over $1,250,000 but not over $1,500,000	$448,300, plus 43 percent of the excess of such amount over $1,250,000.
Over $1,500,000 but not over $2,000,000	$555,800, plus 45 percent of the excess of such amount over $1,500,000.
Over $2,000,000 but not over $2,500,000	$780,800, plus 49 percent of the excess of such amount over $2,000,000.
Over $2,500,000	$1,025,800, plus 50 percent of the excess of such amount over $2,500,000.

Unified Transfer Tax Rates

For Gifts Made and for Deaths in 2003

If the Amount with Respect to Which the Tentative Tax to Be Computed Is:	The Tentative Tax Is:
Not over $10,000	18 percent of such amount.
Over $10,000 but not over $20,000	$1,800, plus 20 percent of the excess of such amount over $10,000.
Over $20,000 but not over $40,000	$3,800, plus 22 percent of the excess of such amount over $20,000.
Over $40,000 but not over $60,000	$8,200, plus 24 percent of the excess of such amount over $40,000.
Over $60,000 but not over $80,000	$13,000, plus 26 percent of the excess of such amount over $60,000.
Over $80,000 but not over $100,000	$18,200, plus 28 percent of the excess of such amount over $80,000.
Over $100,000 but not over $150,000	$23,800, plus 30 percent of the excess of such amount over $100,000.
Over $150,000 but not over $250,000	$38,800, plus 32 percent of the excess of such amount over $150,000.
Over $250,000 but not over $500,000	$70,800, plus 34 percent of the excess of such amount over $250,000.
Over $500,000 but not over $750,000	$155,800, plus 37 percent of the excess of such amount over $500,000.
Over $750,000 but not over $1,000,000	$248,300, plus 39 percent of the excess of such amount over $750,000.
Over $1,000,000 but not over $1,250,000	$345,800, plus 41 percent of the excess of such amount over $1,000,000.
Over $1,250,000 but not over $1,500,000	$448,300, plus 43 percent of the excess of such amount over $1,250,000.
Over $1,500,000 but not over $2,000,000	$555,800, plus 45 percent of the excess of such amount over $1,500,000.
Over $2,000,000	$780,800, plus 49 percent of the excess of such amount over $2,000,000.

For Gifts Made and for Deaths in 2004

(For amounts not over $2,000,000, see rates for 2003 above)	
Over $2,000,000	$780,800, plus 48 percent of the excess of such amount over $2,000,000.

For Gifts Made and for Deaths in 2005

(For amounts not over $2,000,000, see rates for 2003 above)	
Over $2,000,000	$780,800, plus 47 percent of the excess of such amount over $2,000,000.

For Gifts Made and for Deaths in 2006

(For amounts not over $2,000,000, see rates for 2003 above)	
Over $2,000,000	$780,800, plus 46 percent of the excess of such amount over $2,000,000.

Unified Transfer Tax Rates

For Gifts Made and for Deaths in 2007–2009

If the Amount with Respect to Which the Tentative Tax to Be Computed Is:	The Tentative Tax Is:
Not over $10,000	18 percent of such amount.
Over $10,000 but not over $20,000	$1,800, plus 20 percent of the excess of such amount over $10,000.
Over $20,000 but not over $40,000	$3,800, plus 22 percent of the excess of such amount over $20,000.
Over $40,000 but not over $60,000	$8,200, plus 24 percent of the excess of such amount over $40,000.
Over $60,000 but not over $80,000	$13,000, plus 26 percent of the excess of such amount over $60,000.
Over $80,000 but not over $100,000	$18,200, plus 28 percent of the excess of such amount over $80,000.
Over $100,000 but not over $150,000	$23,800, plus 30 percent of the excess of such amount over $100,000.
Over $150,000 but not over $250,000	$38,800, plus 32 percent of the excess of such amount over $150,000.
Over $250,000 but not over $500,000	$70,800, plus 34 percent of the excess of such amount over $250,000.
Over $500,000 but not over $750,000	$155,800, plus 37 percent of the excess of such amount over $500,000.
Over $750,000 but not over $1,000,000	$248,300, plus 39 percent of the excess of such amount over $750,000.
Over $1,000,000 but not over $1,250,000	$345,800, plus 41 percent of the excess of such amount over $1,000,000.
Over $1,250,000 but not over $1,500,000	$448,300, plus 43 percent of the excess of such amount over $1,250,000.
Over $1,500,000	$555,800, plus 45 percent of the excess of such amount over $1,500,000.

Gift Tax Rates

For Gifts Made Only in 2010

If the Amount with Respect to Which the Tentative Tax to Be Computed Is:	The Tentative Tax Is:
Not over $10,000	18 percent of such amount.
Over $10,000 but not over $20,000	$1,800, plus 20 percent of the excess of such amount over $10,000.
Over $20,000 but not over $40,000	$3,800, plus 22 percent of the excess of such amount over $20,000.
Over $40,000 but not over $60,000	$8,200, plus 24 percent of the excess of such amount over $40,000.
Over $60,000 but not over $80,000	$13,000, plus 26 percent of the excess of such amount over $60,000.
Over $80,000 but not over $100,000	$18,200, plus 28 percent of the excess of such amount over $80,000.
Over $100,000 but not over $150,000	$23,800, plus 30 percent of the excess of such amount over $100,000.
Over $150,000 but not over $250,000	$38,800, plus 32 percent of the excess of such amount over $150,000.
Over $250,000 but not over $500,000	$70,800, plus 34 percent of the excess of such amount over $250,000.
Over $500,000	$155,800, plus 35 percent of the excess of such amount over $500,000.

Unified Transfer Tax Rates

For Gifts Made and for Deaths in 2011–2012

If the Amount with Respect to Which the Tentative Tax to Be Computed Is:	The Tentative Tax Is:
Not over $10,000	18 percent of such amount.
Over $10,000 but not over $20,000	$1,800, plus 20 percent of the excess of such amount over $10,000.
Over $20,000 but not over $40,000	$3,800, plus 22 percent of the excess of such amount over $20,000.
Over $40,000 but not over $60,000	$8,200, plus 24 percent of the excess of such amount over $40,000.
Over $60,000 but not over $80,000	$13,000, plus 26 percent of the excess of such amount over $60,000.
Over $80,000 but not over $100,000	$18,200, plus 28 percent of the excess of such amount over $80,000.
Over $100,000 but not over $150,000	$23,800, plus 30 percent of the excess of such amount over $100,000.
Over $150,000 but not over $250,000	$38,800, plus 32 percent of the excess of such amount over $150,000.
Over $250,000 but not over $500,000	$70,800, plus 34 percent of the excess of such amount over $250,000.
Over $500,000	$155,800, plus 35 percent of the excess of such amount over $500,000.

Appendix B

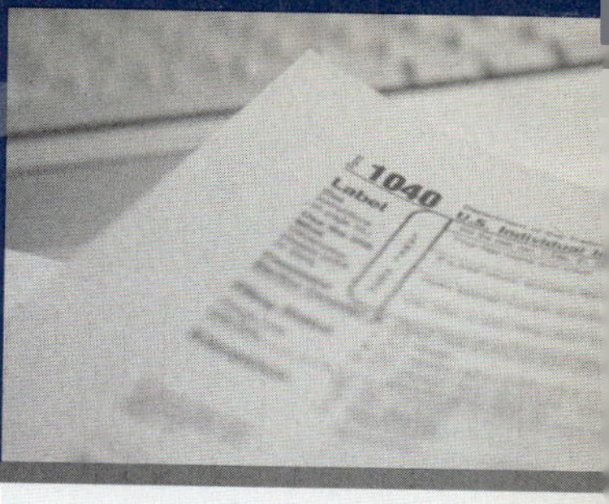

TAX FORMS

(Tax forms can be obtained from the IRS website: **www.irs.gov**)

Form **709**

Department of the Treasury
Internal Revenue Service

United States Gift (and Generation-Skipping Transfer) Tax Return

(For gifts made during calendar year 2010)

▶ **See separate instructions.**

OMB No. 1545-0020

2010

Part 1—General Information

1 Donor's first name and middle initial	2 Donor's last name	**3 Donor's social security number**
4 Address (number, street, and apartment number)		5 Legal residence (domicile)
6 City, state, and ZIP code		7 Citizenship (see instructions)

		Yes	No
8	If the donor died during the year, check here ▶ ☐ and enter date of death __________, ______.		
9	If you extended the time to file this Form 709, check here ▶ ☐		
10	Enter the total number of donees listed on Schedule A. Count each person only once. ▶		
11a	Have you (the donor) previously filed a Form 709 (or 709-A) for any other year? If "No," skip line 11b		
b	If the answer to line 11a is "Yes," has your address changed since you last filed Form 709 (or 709-A)?		
12	**Gifts by husband or wife to third parties.** Do you consent to have the gifts (including generation-skipping transfers) made by you and by your spouse to third parties during the calendar year considered as made one-half by each of you? (See instructions.) (If the answer is "Yes," the following information must be furnished and your spouse must sign the consent shown below. **If the answer is "No," skip lines 13–18 and go to Schedule A.**)		
13	Name of consenting spouse — **14** SSN		
15	Were you married to one another during the entire calendar year? (see instructions)		
16	If 15 is "No," check whether ☐ married ☐ divorced or ☐ widowed/deceased, and give date (see instructions) ▶		
17	Will a gift tax return for this year be filed by your spouse? (If "Yes," mail both returns in the same envelope.)		
18	**Consent of Spouse.** I consent to have the gifts (and generation-skipping transfers) made by me and by my spouse to third parties during the calendar year considered as made one-half by each of us. We are both aware of the joint and several liability for tax created by the execution of this consent.		

Consenting spouse's signature ▶ **Date**▶

Part 2—Tax Computation

1	Enter the amount from Schedule A, Part 4, line 11	1		
2	Enter the amount from Schedule B, line 3	2		
3	Total taxable gifts. Add lines 1 and 2	3		
4	Tax computed on amount on line 3 (see *Table for Computing Gift Tax* in separate instructions) . .	4		
5	Tax computed on amount on line 2 (see *Table for Computing Gift Tax* in separate instructions) . .	5		
6	Balance. Subtract line 5 from line 4	6		
7	Maximum unified credit (nonresident aliens, see instructions)	7	330,800	00
8	Enter the unified credit against tax allowable for all prior periods (from Sch. B, line 1, col. C) . .	8		
9	Balance. Subtract line 8 from line 7. Do not enter less than zero	9		
10	Enter 20% (.20) of the amount allowed as a specific exemption for gifts made after September 8, 1976, and before January 1, 1977 (see instructions)	10		
11	Balance. Subtract line 10 from line 9. Do not enter less than zero	11		
12	Unified credit. Enter the smaller of line 6 or line 11	12		
13	Credit for foreign gift taxes (see instructions)	13		
14	Total credits. Add lines 12 and 13	14		
15	Balance. Subtract line 14 from line 6. Do not enter less than zero	15		
16	Generation-skipping transfer taxes (from Schedule C, Part 3, col. H, Total)	16	0	00
17	Total tax. Add lines 15 and 16	17		
18	Gift and generation-skipping transfer taxes prepaid with extension of time to file	18		
19	If line 18 is less than line 17, enter **balance due** (see instructions)	19		
20	If line 18 is greater than line 17, enter **amount to be refunded**	20		

Attach check or money order here.

Sign Here

Under penalties of perjury, I declare that I have examined this return, including any accompanying schedules and statements, and to the best of my knowledge and belief, it is true, correct, and complete. Declaration of preparer (other than donor) is based on all information of which preparer has any knowledge.

May the IRS discuss this return with the preparer shown below (see instructions)? ☐ **Yes** ☐ **No**

▶ Signature of donor — Date

Paid Preparer Use Only

Print/Type preparer's name	Preparer's signature	Date	Check ☐ if self-employed	PTIN
Firm's name ▶			Firm's EIN ▶	
Firm's address ▶			Phone no.	

Form 709 (2010) Page **2**

SCHEDULE A Computation of Taxable Gifts (Including transfers in trust) (see instructions)

A Does the value of any item listed on Schedule A reflect any valuation discount? If "Yes," attach explanation . . . . Yes ☐ No ☐

B ☐ ◄ Check here if you elect under section 529(c)(2)(B) to treat any transfers made this year to a qualified tuition program as made ratably over a 5-year period beginning this year. See instructions. Attach explanation.

Part 1—Gifts Subject Only to Gift Tax. Gifts less political organization, medical, and educational exclusions. (see instructions)

A Item number	B • Donee's name and address • Relationship to donor (if any) • Description of gift • If the gift was of securities, give CUSIP no. • If closely held entity, give EIN	C	D Donor's adjusted basis of gift	E Date of gift	F Value at date of gift	G For split gifts, enter 1/2 of column F	H Net transfer (subtract col. G from col. F)
Gifts made by spouse —*complete* ***only*** *if you are splitting gifts with your spouse and he/she also made gifts.*							
Total of Part 1. Add amounts from Part 1, column H . . . . . ▶							

Part 2—Direct Skips. Gifts that are direct skips and are subject to both gift tax and generation-skipping transfer tax. You must list the gifts in chronological order.

A Item number	B • Donee's name and address • Relationship to donor (if any) • Description of gift • If the gift was of securities, give CUSIP no. • If closely held entity, give EIN	C 2632(b) election out	D Donor's adjusted basis of gift	E Date of gift	F Value at date of gift	G For split gifts, enter 1/2 of column F	H Net transfer (subtract col. G from col. F)
Gifts made by spouse —*complete* ***only*** *if you are splitting gifts with your spouse and he/she also made gifts.*							
Total of Part 2. Add amounts from Part 2, column H . . . . . ▶							

Part 3—Indirect Skips. Gifts to trusts that are currently subject to gift tax and may later be subject to generation-skipping transfer tax. You must list these gifts in chronological order.

A Item number	B • Donee's name and address • Relationship to donor (if any) • Description of gift • If the gift was of securities, give CUSIP no. • If closely held entity, give EIN	C 2632(c) election	D Donor's adjusted basis of gift	E Date of gift	F Value at date of gift	G For split gifts, enter 1/2 of column F	H Net transfer (subtract col. G from col. F)
Gifts made by spouse —*complete* ***only*** *if you are splitting gifts with your spouse and he/she also made gifts.*							
Total of Part 3. Add amounts from Part 3, column H . . . . . ▶							

(If more space is needed, attach additional sheets of same size.)

Form 709 (2010) Page **3**

Part 4—Taxable Gift Reconciliation

1	Total value of gifts of donor. Add totals from column H of Parts 1, 2, and 3	1		
2	Total annual exclusions for gifts listed on line 1 (see instructions)	2		
3	Total included amount of gifts. Subtract line 2 from line 1	3		
Deductions (see instructions)				
4	Gifts of interests to spouse for which a marital deduction will be claimed, based on item numbers ______________ of Schedule A . . . 4			
5	Exclusions attributable to gifts on line 4 . . . 5			
6	Marital deduction. Subtract line 5 from line 4 . . . 6			
7	Charitable deduction, based on item nos. ________ less exclusions . 7			
8	Total deductions. Add lines 6 and 7	8		
9	Subtract line 8 from line 3	9		
10	Generation-skipping transfer taxes payable with this Form 709 (from Schedule C, Part 3, col. H, Total)	10	0	00
11	**Taxable gifts.** Add lines 9 and 10. Enter here and on page 1, Part 2—Tax Computation, line 1	11		

Terminable Interest (QTIP) Marital Deduction. (See instructions for Schedule A, Part 4, line 4.)

If a trust (or other property) meets the requirements of qualified terminable interest property under section 2523(f), and:

a. The trust (or other property) is listed on Schedule A, and

b. The value of the trust (or other property) is entered in whole or in part as a deduction on Schedule A, Part 4, line 4,

then the donor shall be deemed to have made an election to have such trust (or other property) treated as qualified terminable interest property under section 2523(f).

If less than the entire value of the trust (or other property) that the donor has included in Parts 1 and 3 of Schedule A is entered as a deduction on line 4, the donor shall be considered to have made an election only as to a fraction of the trust (or other property). The numerator of this fraction is equal to the amount of the trust (or other property) deducted on Schedule A, Part 4, line 6. The denominator is equal to the total value of the trust (or other property) listed in Parts 1 and 3 of Schedule A.

If you make the QTIP election, the terminable interest property involved will be included in your spouse's gross estate upon his or her death (section 2044). See instructions for line 4 of Schedule A. If your spouse disposes (by gift or otherwise) of all or part of the qualifying life income interest, he or she will be considered to have made a transfer of the entire property that is subject to the gift tax. See *Transfer of Certain Life Estates Received From Spouse* in the separate instructions.

12 Election Out of QTIP Treatment of Annuities

☐ ◀ Check here if you elect under section 2523(f)(6) **not** to treat as qualified terminable interest property any joint and survivor annuities that are reported on Schedule A and would otherwise be treated as qualified terminable interest property under section 2523(f). See instructions. Enter the item numbers from Schedule A for the annuities for which you are making this election ▶ ______________

SCHEDULE B **Gifts From Prior Periods**

If you answered "Yes" on line 11a of page 1, Part 1, see the instructions for completing Schedule B. If you answered "No," skip to the Tax Computation on page 1 (or Schedule C, if applicable). See instructions for recalculation of the column C amounts. Attach calculations.

A Calendar year or calendar quarter (see instructions)	B Internal Revenue office where prior return was filed	C Amount of unified credit against gift tax for periods after December 31, 1976	D Amount of specific exemption for prior periods ending before January 1, 1977	E Amount of taxable gifts
1 Totals for prior periods . . . 1				

2	Amount, if any, by which total specific exemption, line 1, column D is more than $30,000	2	
3	Total amount of taxable gifts for prior periods. Add amount on line 1, column E and amount, if any, on line 2. Enter here and on page 1, Part 2—Tax Computation, line 2	3	

(If more space is needed, attach additional sheets of same size.)

Form **709** (2010)

Form 709 (2010) Page **4**

SCHEDULE C Computation of Generation-Skipping Transfer Tax

Note. Inter vivos direct skips that are completely excluded by the GST exemption must still be fully reported (including value and exemptions claimed) on Schedule C.

Part 1—Generation-Skipping Transfers

A Item No. (from Schedule A, Part 2, col. A)	B Value (from Schedule A, Part 2, col. H)	C Nontaxable portion of transfer	D Net Transfer (subtract col. C from col. B)
Gifts made by spouse (for gift splitting only)			

Part 2—GST Exemption Reconciliation (Section 2631) and Section 2652(a)(3) Election

Check here ▶ ☐ if you are making a section 2652(a)(3) (special QTIP) election (see instructions)

Enter the item numbers from Schedule A of the gifts for which you are making this election ▶ ----------------

1	Maximum allowable exemption (see instructions)	1	
2	Total exemption used for periods before filing this return	2	
3	Exemption available for this return. Subtract line 2 from line 1	3	
4	Exemption claimed on this return from Part 3, column C total, below	4	
5	Automatic allocation of exemption to transfers reported on Schedule A, Part 3 (see instructions)	5	
6	Exemption allocated to transfers not shown on line 4 or 5, above. **You must attach a "Notice of Allocation."** (see instructions)	6	
7	Add lines 4, 5, and 6	7	
8	Exemption available for future transfers. Subtract line 7 from line 3	8	

Part 3—Tax Computation

A Item No. (from Schedule C, Part 1)	B Net transfer (from Schedule C, Part 1, col. D)	C GST Exemption Allocated	D RESERVED	E RESERVED	F RESERVED	G Applicable Rate	H Generation-Skipping Transfer Tax (multiply col. B by col. G)
			Not applicable to transfers made in 2010			0	0
						0	0
						0	0
						0	0
						0	0
						0	0
Gifts made by spouse (for gift splitting only)							
			Not applicable to transfers made in 2010			0	0
						0	0
						0	0
						0	0
						0	0
						0	0
Total exemption claimed. Enter here and on Part 2, line 4, above. May not exceed Part 2, line 3, above			**Total generation-skipping transfer tax.** Enter here; on page 3, Schedule A, Part 4, line 10; and on page 1, Part 2—Tax Computation, line 16				

(If more space is needed, attach additional sheets of same size.) Form **709** (2010)

Form **1040** Department of the Treasury—Internal Revenue Service
U.S. Individual Income Tax Return 2010 (99) IRS Use Only—Do not write or staple in this space.

Name, Address, and SSN

See separate instructions.

PRINT CLEARLY

For the year Jan. 1–Dec. 31, 2010, or other tax year beginning , 2010, ending , 20 | OMB No. 1545-0074

Your first name and initial	Last name		**Your social security number**
If a joint return, spouse's first name and initial	Last name		**Spouse's social security number**
Home address (number and street). If you have a P.O. box, see instructions.		Apt. no.	▲ Make sure the SSN(s) above and on line 6c are correct.
City, town or post office, state, and ZIP code. If you have a foreign address, see instructions.			

Presidential Election Campaign Check here if you, or your spouse if filing jointly, want $3 to go to this fund . . . . . ▶ ☐ You ☐ Spouse
Checking a box below will not change your tax or refund.

Filing Status

Check only one box.

1 ☐ Single
2 ☐ Married filing jointly (even if only one had income)
3 ☐ Married filing separately. Enter spouse's SSN above and full name here. ▶
4 ☐ Head of household (with qualifying person). (See instructions.) If the qualifying person is a child but not your dependent, enter this child's name here. ▶
5 ☐ Qualifying widow(er) with dependent child

Exemptions

6a ☐ **Yourself.** If someone can claim you as a dependent, **do not** check box 6a . . . . .
b ☐ **Spouse** . . . .
} **Boxes checked on 6a and 6b** ____

c **Dependents:**

(1) First name Last name	(2) Dependent's social security number	(3) Dependent's relationship to you	(4) ✓ if child under age 17 qualifying for child tax credit (see page 15)
			☐
			☐
			☐
			☐

If more than four dependents, see instructions and check here ▶ ☐

No. of children on 6c who:
• lived with you ____
• did not live with you due to divorce or separation (see instructions) ____
Dependents on 6c not entered above ____

d Total number of exemptions claimed . . . . **Add numbers on lines above ▶** ☐

Income

Attach Form(s) W-2 here. Also attach Forms W-2G and 1099-R if tax was withheld.

If you did not get a W-2, see page 20.

Enclose, but do not attach, any payment. Also, please use **Form 1040-V.**

7	Wages, salaries, tips, etc. Attach Form(s) W-2	7	
8a	**Taxable** interest. Attach Schedule B if required	8a	
b	**Tax-exempt** interest. **Do not** include on line 8a . . . 8b		
9a	Ordinary dividends. Attach Schedule B if required	9a	
b	Qualified dividends 9b		
10	Taxable refunds, credits, or offsets of state and local income taxes	10	
11	Alimony received	11	
12	Business income or (loss). Attach Schedule C or C-EZ	12	
13	Capital gain or (loss). Attach Schedule D if required. If not required, check here ▶ ☐	13	
14	Other gains or (losses). Attach Form 4797	14	
15a	IRA distributions . 15a ____ b Taxable amount . . .	15b	
16a	Pensions and annuities 16a ____ b Taxable amount . . .	16b	
17	Rental real estate, royalties, partnerships, S corporations, trusts, etc. Attach Schedule E	17	
18	Farm income or (loss). Attach Schedule F	18	
19	Unemployment compensation	19	
20a	Social security benefits 20a ____ b Taxable amount . . .	20b	
21	Other income. List type and amount	21	
22	Combine the amounts in the far right column for lines 7 through 21. This is your **total income** ▶	22	

Adjusted Gross Income

23	Educator expenses	23	
24	Certain business expenses of reservists, performing artists, and fee-basis government officials. Attach Form 2106 or 2106-EZ	24	
25	Health savings account deduction. Attach Form 8889 .	25	
26	Moving expenses. Attach Form 3903	26	
27	One-half of self-employment tax. Attach Schedule SE .	27	
28	Self-employed SEP, SIMPLE, and qualified plans . .	28	
29	Self-employed health insurance deduction	29	
30	Penalty on early withdrawal of savings	30	
31a	Alimony paid **b** Recipient's SSN ▶	31a	
32	IRA deduction	32	
33	Student loan interest deduction	33	
34	Tuition and fees. Attach Form 8917	34	
35	Domestic production activities deduction. Attach Form 8903	35	
36	Add lines 23 through 31a and 32 through 35	36	
37	Subtract line 36 from line 22. This is your **adjusted gross income** . . . . . ▶	37	

For Disclosure, Privacy Act, and Paperwork Reduction Act Notice, see separate instructions. Cat. No. 11320B Form **1040** (2010)

Form 1040 (2010) Page **2**

Tax and Credits

38	Amount from line 37 (adjusted gross income)			38
39a	Check if: ☐ **You** were born before January 2, 1946, ☐ Blind. ☐ **Spouse** was born before January 2, 1946, ☐ Blind. } **Total boxes checked ▶ 39a**			
b	If your spouse itemizes on a separate return or you were a dual-status alien, check here ▶ **39b**☐			
40	**Itemized deductions** (from Schedule A) **or** your **standard deduction** (see instructions)			40
41	Subtract line 40 from line 38			41
42	**Exemptions.** Multiply $3,650 by the number on line 6d			42
43	**Taxable income.** Subtract line 42 from line 41. If line 42 is more than line 41, enter -0-			43
44	**Tax** (see instructions). Check if any tax is from: **a** ☐ Form(s) 8814 **b** ☐ Form 4972			44
45	**Alternative minimum tax** (see instructions). Attach Form 6251			45
46	Add lines 44 and 45 ▶			46
47	Foreign tax credit. Attach Form 1116 if required	47		
48	Credit for child and dependent care expenses. Attach Form 2441	48		
49	Education credits from Form 8863, line 23	49		
50	Retirement savings contributions credit. Attach Form 8880	50		
51	Child tax credit (see instructions)	51		
52	Residential energy credits. Attach Form 5695	52		
53	Other credits from Form: **a** ☐ 3800 **b** ☐ 8801 **c** ☐ ______	53		
54	Add lines 47 through 53. These are your **total credits**			54
55	Subtract line 54 from line 46. If line 54 is more than line 46, enter -0- ▶			55

Other Taxes

56	Self-employment tax. Attach Schedule SE			56
57	Unreported social security and Medicare tax from Form: **a** ☐ 4137 **b** ☐ 8919			57
58	Additional tax on IRAs, other qualified retirement plans, etc. Attach Form 5329 if required			58
59	**a** ☐ Form(s) W-2, box 9 **b** ☐ Schedule H **c** ☐ Form 5405, line 16			59
60	Add lines 55 through 59. This is your **total tax** ▶			60

Payments

If you have a qualifying child, attach Schedule EIC.

61	Federal income tax withheld from Forms W-2 and 1099	61		
62	2010 estimated tax payments and amount applied from 2009 return	62		
63	Making work pay credit. Attach Schedule M	63		
64a	**Earned income credit (EIC)**	64a		
b	Nontaxable combat pay election **64b**			
65	Additional child tax credit. Attach Form 8812	65		
66	American opportunity credit from Form 8863, line 14	66		
67	First-time homebuyer credit from Form 5405, line 10	67		
68	Amount paid with request for extension to file	68		
69	Excess social security and tier 1 RRTA tax withheld	69		
70	Credit for federal tax on fuels. Attach Form 4136	70		
71	Credits from Form: **a** ☐ 2439 **b** ☐ 8839 **c** ☐ 8801 **d** ☐ 8885	71		
72	Add lines 61, 62, 63, 64a, and 65 through 71. These are your **total payments** ▶			72

Refund

Direct deposit? See instructions.

73	If line 72 is more than line 60, subtract line 60 from line 72. This is the amount you **overpaid**			73
74a	Amount of line 73 you want **refunded to you.** If Form 8888 is attached, check here ▶☐			74a
▶ b	Routing number ▶ c Type: ☐ Checking ☐ Savings			
▶ d	Account number			
75	Amount of line 73 you want **applied to your 2011 estimated tax** ▶	75		

Amount You Owe

76	**Amount you owe.** Subtract line 72 from line 60. For details on how to pay, see instructions ▶			76
77	Estimated tax penalty (see instructions)	77		

Third Party Designee

Do you want to allow another person to discuss this return with the IRS (see instructions)? ☐ **Yes.** Complete below. ☐ **No**

Designee's name ▶ Phone no. ▶ Personal identification number (PIN) ▶

Sign Here

Joint return? See page 12. Keep a copy for your records.

Under penalties of perjury, I declare that I have examined this return and accompanying schedules and statements, and to the best of my knowledge and belief, they are true, correct, and complete. Declaration of preparer (other than taxpayer) is based on all information of which preparer has any knowledge.

Your signature	Date	Your occupation	Daytime phone number
Spouse's signature. If a joint return, **both** must sign.	Date	Spouse's occupation	

Paid Preparer Use Only

Print/Type preparer's name	Preparer's signature	Date	Check ☐ if self-employed	PTIN
Firm's name ▶			Firm's EIN ▶	
Firm's address ▶			Phone no.	

Form **1040** (2010)

SCHEDULE A
(Form 1040)

Department of the Treasury
Internal Revenue Service (99)

Itemized Deductions

▶ **Attach to Form 1040.** ▶ **See Instructions for Schedule A (Form 1040).**

OMB No. 1545-0074
2010
Attachment
Sequence No. **07**

Name(s) shown on Form 1040 | **Your social security number**

Medical and Dental Expenses		**Caution.** Do not include expenses reimbursed or paid by others.			
	1	Medical and dental expenses (see instructions)	1		
	2	Enter amount from Form 1040, line 38 [2]			
	3	Multiply line 2 by 7.5% (.075)	3		
	4	Subtract line 3 from line 1. If line 3 is more than line 1, enter -0-			4
Taxes You Paid	5	State and local **(check only one box):**			
		a ☐ Income taxes, **or** / **b** ☐ General sales taxes	5		
	6	Real estate taxes (see instructions)	6		
	7	New motor vehicle taxes from line 11 of the worksheet on back (for certain vehicles purchased in 2009). Skip this line if you checked box 5b	7		
	8	Other taxes. List type and amount ▶	8		
	9	Add lines 5 through 8			9
Interest You Paid	10	Home mortgage interest and points reported to you on Form 1098	10		
Note. Your mortgage interest deduction may be limited (see instructions).	11	Home mortgage interest not reported to you on Form 1098. If paid to the person from whom you bought the home, see instructions and show that person's name, identifying no., and address ▶	11		
	12	Points not reported to you on Form 1098. See instructions for special rules	12		
	13	Mortgage insurance premiums (see instructions)	13		
	14	Investment interest. Attach Form 4952 if required. (See instructions.)	14		
	15	Add lines 10 through 14			15
Gifts to Charity	16	Gifts by cash or check. If you made any gift of $250 or more, see instructions	16		
If you made a gift and got a benefit for it, see instructions.	17	Other than by cash or check. If any gift of $250 or more, see instructions. You **must** attach Form 8283 if over $500	17		
	18	Carryover from prior year	18		
	19	Add lines 16 through 18			19
Casualty and Theft Losses	20	Casualty or theft loss(es). Attach Form 4684. (See instructions.)			20
Job Expenses and Certain Miscellaneous Deductions	21	Unreimbursed employee expenses—job travel, union dues, job education, etc. Attach Form 2106 or 2106-EZ if required. (See instructions.) ▶	21		
	22	Tax preparation fees	22		
	23	Other expenses—investment, safe deposit box, etc. List type and amount ▶	23		
	24	Add lines 21 through 23	24		
	25	Enter amount from Form 1040, line 38 [25]			
	26	Multiply line 25 by 2% (.02)	26		
	27	Subtract line 26 from line 24. If line 26 is more than line 24, enter -0-			27
Other Miscellaneous Deductions	28	Other—from list in instructions. List type and amount ▶			28
Total Itemized Deductions	29	Add the amounts in the far right column for lines 4 through 28. Also, enter this amount on Form 1040, line 40			29
	30	If you elect to itemize deductions even though they are less than your standard deduction, check here ▶ ☐			

For Paperwork Reduction Act Notice, see Form 1040 instructions. Cat. No. 17145C **Schedule A (Form 1040) 2010**

SCHEDULE B (Form 1040A or 1040)

Department of the Treasury Internal Revenue Service (99)

Interest and Ordinary Dividends

► Attach to Form 1040A or 1040. ► See instructions on back.

OMB No. 1545-0074

2010

Attachment Sequence No. 08

Name(s) shown on return | **Your social security number**

Part I Interest

(See instructions on back and the instructions for Form 1040A, or Form 1040, line 8a.)

Note. If you received a Form 1099-INT, Form 1099-OID, or substitute statement from a brokerage firm, list the firm's name as the payer and enter the total interest shown on that form.

			Amount
1	List name of payer. If any interest is from a seller-financed mortgage and the buyer used the property as a personal residence, see instructions on back and list this interest first. Also, show that buyer's social security number and address ►	1	
2	Add the amounts on line 1	2	
3	Excludable interest on series EE and I U.S. savings bonds issued after 1989. Attach Form 8815	3	
4	Subtract line 3 from line 2. Enter the result here and on Form 1040A, or Form 1040, line 8a ►	4	

Note. If line 4 is over $1,500, you must complete Part III.

Part II Ordinary Dividends

(See instructions on back and the instructions for Form 1040A, or Form 1040, line 9a.)

Note. If you received a Form 1099-DIV or substitute statement from a brokerage firm, list the firm's name as the payer and enter the ordinary dividends shown on that form.

			Amount
5	List name of payer ►	5	
6	Add the amounts on line 5. Enter the total here and on Form 1040A, or Form 1040, line 9a ►	6	

Note. If line 6 is over $1,500, you must complete Part III.

Part III Foreign Accounts and Trusts

(See instructions on back.)

	You must complete this part if you **(a)** had over $1,500 of taxable interest or ordinary dividends; **(b)** had a foreign account; or **(c)** received a distribution from, or were a grantor of, or a transferor to, a foreign trust.	Yes	No
7a	At any time during 2010, did you have an interest in or a signature or other authority over a financial account in a foreign country, such as a bank account, securities account, or other financial account? See instructions on back for exceptions and filing requirements for Form TD F 90-22.1		
b	If "Yes," enter the name of the foreign country ►		
8	During 2010, did you receive a distribution from, or were you the grantor of, or transferor to, a foreign trust? If "Yes," you may have to file Form 3520. See instructions on back		

For Paperwork Reduction Act Notice, see your tax return instructions. Cat. No. 17146N **Schedule B (Form 1040A or 1040) 2010**

SCHEDULE C (Form 1040)

Department of the Treasury Internal Revenue Service (99)

Profit or Loss From Business

(Sole Proprietorship)

▶ **Partnerships, joint ventures, etc., generally must file Form 1065 or 1065-B.**

▶ **Attach to Form 1040, 1040NR, or 1041.** ▶ **See Instructions for Schedule C (Form 1040).**

OMB No. 1545-0074

2010

Attachment Sequence No. **09**

Name of proprietor | **Social security number (SSN)**

A Principal business or profession, including product or service (see instructions) | **B Enter code from pages C-9, 10, & 11** ▶

C Business name. If no separate business name, leave blank. | **D Employer ID number (EIN), if any**

E Business address (including suite or room no.) ▶

City, town or post office, state, and ZIP code

F Accounting method: **(1)** ☐ Cash **(2)** ☐ Accrual **(3)** ☐ Other (specify) ▶

G Did you "materially participate" in the operation of this business during 2010? If "No," see instructions for limit on losses ☐ **Yes** ☐ **No**

H If you started or acquired this business during 2010, check here . . . ▶ ☐

Part I Income

1	Gross receipts or sales. **Caution.** See instructions and check the box if: • This income was reported to you on Form W-2 and the "Statutory employee" box on that form was checked, or • You are a member of a qualified joint venture reporting only rental real estate income not subject to self-employment tax. Also see instructions for limit on losses. . . ▶ ☐	1	
2	Returns and allowances	2	
3	Subtract line 2 from line 1	3	
4	Cost of goods sold (from line 42 on page 2)	4	
5	**Gross profit.** Subtract line 4 from line 3	5	
6	Other income, including federal and state gasoline or fuel tax credit or refund (see instructions)	6	
7	**Gross income.** Add lines 5 and 6 ▶	7	

Part II Expenses. Enter expenses for business use of your home only on line 30.

8	Advertising	8		18	Office expense	18	
9	Car and truck expenses (see instructions)	9		19	Pension and profit-sharing plans	19	
10	Commissions and fees	10		20	Rent or lease (see instructions):		
11	Contract labor (see instructions)	11		a	Vehicles, machinery, and equipment	20a	
12	Depletion	12		b	Other business property	20b	
13	Depreciation and section 179 expense deduction (not included in Part III) (see instructions)	13		21	Repairs and maintenance	21	
				22	Supplies (not included in Part III)	22	
				23	Taxes and licenses	23	
				24	Travel, meals, and entertainment:		
				a	Travel	24a	
14	Employee benefit programs (other than on line 19)	14		b	Deductible meals and entertainment (see instructions)	24b	
15	Insurance (other than health)	15		25	Utilities	25	
16	Interest:			26	Wages (less employment credits)	26	
a	Mortgage (paid to banks, etc.)	16a		27	Other expenses (from line 48 on page 2)	27	
b	Other	16b					
17	Legal and professional services	17					

28	**Total expenses** before expenses for business use of home. Add lines 8 through 27 ▶	28	
29	Tentative profit or (loss). Subtract line 28 from line 7	29	
30	Expenses for business use of your home. Attach **Form 8829**	30	
31	**Net profit or (loss).** Subtract line 30 from line 29. • If a profit, enter on both **Form 1040, line 12,** and **Schedule SE, line 2,** or on **Form 1040NR, line 13** (if you checked the box on line 1, see instructions). Estates and trusts, enter on **Form 1041, line 3.** • If a loss, you **must** go to line 32.	31	

32 If you have a loss, check the box that describes your investment in this activity (see instructions).

• If you checked 32a, enter the loss on both **Form 1040, line 12,** and **Schedule SE, line 2,** or on **Form 1040NR, line 13** (if you checked the box on line 1, see the line 31 instructions). Estates and trusts, enter on **Form 1041, line 3.**

• If you checked 32b, you **must** attach **Form 6198.** Your loss may be limited.

32a ☐ All investment is at risk.
32b ☐ Some investment is not at risk.

For Paperwork Reduction Act Notice, see your tax return instructions. Cat. No. 11334P **Schedule C (Form 1040) 2010**

Part III Cost of Goods Sold (see instructions)

33 Method(s) used to value closing inventory: a ☐ Cost b ☐ Lower of cost or market c ☐ Other (attach explanation)

34 Was there any change in determining quantities, costs, or valuations between opening and closing inventory? If "Yes," attach explanation . . . ☐ Yes ☐ No

35	Inventory at beginning of year. If different from last year's closing inventory, attach explanation	35	
36	Purchases less cost of items withdrawn for personal use	36	
37	Cost of labor. Do not include any amounts paid to yourself	37	
38	Materials and supplies	38	
39	Other costs	39	
40	Add lines 35 through 39	40	
41	Inventory at end of year	41	
42	**Cost of goods sold.** Subtract line 41 from line 40. Enter the result here and on page 1, line 4	42	

Part IV Information on Your Vehicle.

Complete this part **only** if you are claiming car or truck expenses on line 9 and are not required to file Form 4562 for this business. See the instructions for line 13 to find out if you must file Form 4562.

43 When did you place your vehicle in service for business purposes? (month, day, year) ► ___ / ___ / ___

44 Of the total number of miles you drove your vehicle during 2010, enter the number of miles you used your vehicle for:

a Business ________ b Commuting (see instructions) ________ c Other ________

45 Was your vehicle available for personal use during off-duty hours? . . . ☐ Yes ☐ No

46 Do you (or your spouse) have another vehicle available for personal use? . . . ☐ Yes ☐ No

47a Do you have evidence to support your deduction? . . . ☐ Yes ☐ No

b If "Yes," is the evidence written? . . . ☐ Yes ☐ No

Part V Other Expenses.

List below business expenses not included on lines 8–26 or line 30.

48 **Total other expenses.** Enter here and on page 1, line 27	48	

SCHEDULE D (Form 1040)

Department of the Treasury
Internal Revenue Service (99)

Capital Gains and Losses

▶ **Attach to Form 1040 or Form 1040NR.** ▶ **See Instructions for Schedule D (Form 1040).**
▶ **Use Schedule D-1 to list additional transactions for lines 1 and 8.**

OMB No. 1545-0074
2010
Attachment Sequence No. **12**

Name(s) shown on return | **Your social security number**

Part I Short-Term Capital Gains and Losses—Assets Held One Year or Less

	(a) Description of property (Example: 100 sh. XYZ Co.)	(b) Date acquired (Mo., day, yr.)	(c) Date sold (Mo., day, yr.)	(d) Sales price (see page D-7 of the instructions)	(e) Cost or other basis (see page D-7 of the instructions)	(f) Gain or (loss) Subtract (e) from (d)
1						

2	Enter your short-term totals, if any, from Schedule D-1, line 2	2	
3	**Total short-term sales price amounts.** Add lines 1 and 2 in column (d)	3	

4	Short-term gain from Form 6252 and short-term gain or (loss) from Forms 4684, 6781, and 8824	4	
5	Net short-term gain or (loss) from partnerships, S corporations, estates, and trusts from Schedule(s) K-1	5	
6	Short-term capital loss carryover. Enter the amount, if any, from line 10 of your **Capital Loss Carryover Worksheet** on page D-7 of the instructions	6	( )
7	**Net short-term capital gain or (loss).** Combine lines 1 through 6 in column (f)	7	

Part II Long-Term Capital Gains and Losses—Assets Held More Than One Year

	(a) Description of property (Example: 100 sh. XYZ Co.)	(b) Date acquired (Mo., day, yr.)	(c) Date sold (Mo., day, yr.)	(d) Sales price (see page D-7 of the instructions)	(e) Cost or other basis (see page D-7 of the instructions)	(f) Gain or (loss) Subtract (e) from (d)
8						

9	Enter your long-term totals, if any, from Schedule D-1, line 9	9	
10	**Total long-term sales price amounts.** Add lines 8 and 9 in column (d).	10	

11	Gain from Form 4797, Part I; long-term gain from Forms 2439 and 6252; and long-term gain or (loss) from Forms 4684, 6781, and 8824	11	
12	Net long-term gain or (loss) from partnerships, S corporations, estates, and trusts from Schedule(s) K-1	12	
13	Capital gain distributions. See page D-2 of the instructions	13	
14	Long-term capital loss carryover. Enter the amount, if any, from line 15 of your **Capital Loss Carryover Worksheet** on page D-7 of the instructions	14	( )
15	**Net long-term capital gain or (loss).** Combine lines 8 through 14 in column (f). Then go to Part III on the back	15	

Part III **Summary**

16 Combine lines 7 and 15 and enter the result **16**

- If line 16 is a **gain**, enter the amount from line 16 on Form 1040, line 13, or Form 1040NR, line 14. Then go to line 17 below.
- If line 16 is a **loss**, skip lines 17 through 20 below. Then go to line 21. Also be sure to complete line 22.
- If line 16 is **zero**, skip lines 17 through 21 below and enter -0- on Form 1040, line 13, or Form 1040NR, line 14. Then go to line 22.

17 Are lines 15 and 16 **both** gains?

☐ **Yes.** Go to line 18.

☐ **No.** Skip lines 18 through 21, and go to line 22.

18 Enter the amount, if any, from line 7 of the **28% Rate Gain Worksheet** on page D-8 of the instructions . . . . ▶ **18**

19 Enter the amount, if any, from line 18 of the **Unrecaptured Section 1250 Gain Worksheet** on page D-9 of the instructions . . . . ▶ **19**

20 Are lines 18 and 19 **both** zero or blank?

☐ **Yes.** Complete Form 1040 through line 43, or Form 1040NR through line 41. Then complete the **Qualified Dividends and Capital Gain Tax Worksheet** in the Instructions for Form 1040, line 44 (or in the Instructions for Form 1040NR, line 42). **Do not** complete lines 21 and 22 below.

☐ **No.** Complete Form 1040 through line 43, or Form 1040NR through line 41. Then complete the **Schedule D Tax Worksheet** on page D-10 of the instructions. **Do not** complete lines 21 and 22 below.

21 If line 16 is a loss, enter here and on Form 1040, line 13, or Form 1040NR, line 14, the **smaller** of:

- The loss on line 16 or
- ($3,000), or if married filing separately, ($1,500)

} . . . . **21** ( )

Note. When figuring which amount is smaller, treat both amounts as positive numbers.

22 Do you have qualified dividends on Form 1040, line 9b, or Form 1040NR, line 10b?

☐ **Yes.** Complete Form 1040 through line 43, or Form 1040NR through line 41. Then complete the **Qualified Dividends and Capital Gain Tax Worksheet** in the Instructions for Form 1040, line 44 (or in the Instructions for Form 1040NR, line 42).

☐ **No.** Complete the rest of Form 1040 or Form 1040NR.

SCHEDULE E (Form 1040)

Department of the Treasury
Internal Revenue Service (99)

Supplemental Income and Loss

(From rental real estate, royalties, partnerships, S corporations, estates, trusts, REMICs, etc.)

▶ Attach to Form 1040, 1040NR, or Form 1041. ▶ See Instructions for Schedule E (Form 1040).

OMB No. 1545-0074

2010

Attachment Sequence No. **13**

Name(s) shown on return | **Your social security number**

Part I **Income or Loss From Rental Real Estate and Royalties** **Note.** If you are in the business of renting personal property, use **Schedule C** or **C-EZ** (see page E-3). If you are an individual, report farm rental income or loss from **Form 4835** on page 2, line 40.

1	List the type and address of each **rental real estate property:**
A	
B	
C	

2 For each rental real estate property listed on line 1, did you or your family use it during the tax year for personal purposes for more than the greater of:
- 14 days **or**
- 10% of the total days rented at fair rental value?

(See page E-3)

	Yes	**No**
A		
B		
C		

Income:		Properties A	Properties B	Properties C		Totals (Add columns A, B, and C.)
3 Rents received	3				3	
4 Royalties received	4				4	
Expenses:						
5 Advertising	5					
6 Auto and travel (see page E-4)	6					
7 Cleaning and maintenance	7					
8 Commissions	8					
9 Insurance	9					
10 Legal and other professional fees	10					
11 Management fees	11					
12 Mortgage interest paid to banks, etc. (see page E-5)	12				12	
13 Other interest	13					
14 Repairs	14					
15 Supplies	15					
16 Taxes	16					
17 Utilities	17					
18 Other (list) ▶	18					
19 Add lines 5 through 18	19				19	
20 Depreciation expense or depletion (see page E-5)	20				20	
21 Total expenses. Add lines 19 and 20	21					
22 Income or (loss) from rental real estate or royalty properties. Subtract line 21 from line 3 (rents) or line 4 (royalties). If the result is a (loss), see page E-5 to find out if you must file **Form 6198**	22					
23 Deductible rental real estate loss. **Caution.** Your rental real estate loss on line 22 may be limited. See page E-5 to find out if you must file **Form 8582.** Real estate professionals **must** complete line 43 on page 2	23	( )	( )	( )		

24	**Income.** Add positive amounts shown on line 22. **Do not** include any losses	24	
25	**Losses.** Add royalty losses from line 22 and rental real estate losses from line 23. Enter total losses here	25	( )
26	**Total rental real estate and royalty income or (loss).** Combine lines 24 and 25. Enter the result here. If Parts II, III, IV, and line 40 on page 2 do not apply to you, also enter this amount on Form 1040, line 17, or Form 1040NR, line 18. Otherwise, include this amount in the total on line 41 on page 2	26	

Schedule E (Form 1040) 2010 Attachment Sequence No. **13** Page **2**

Name(s) shown on return. Do not enter name and social security number if shown on other side. | **Your social security number**

Caution. The IRS compares amounts reported on your tax return with amounts shown on Schedule(s) K-1.

Part II Income or Loss From Partnerships and S Corporations

Note. If you report a loss from an at-risk activity for which **any** amount is **not** at risk, you **must** check the box in column **(e)** on line 28 and attach **Form 6198.** See page E-1.

27 Are you reporting any loss not allowed in a prior year due to the at-risk or basis limitations, a prior year unallowed loss from a passive activity (if that loss was not reported on Form 8582), or unreimbursed partnership expenses? If you answered "Yes," see page E-7 before completing this section. ☐ **Yes** ☐ **No**

28	**(a)** Name	**(b)** Enter **P** for partnership; **S** for S corporation	**(c)** Check if foreign partnership	**(d)** Employer identification number	**(e)** Check if any amount is not at risk
A			☐		☐
B			☐		☐
C			☐		☐
D			☐		☐

	Passive Income and Loss		**Nonpassive Income and Loss**		
	(f) Passive loss allowed (attach **Form 8582** if required)	**(g)** Passive income from **Schedule K–1**	**(h)** Nonpassive loss from **Schedule K–1**	**(i)** Section 179 expense deduction from **Form 4562**	**(j)** Nonpassive income from **Schedule K–1**
A					
B					
C					
D					
29a Totals					
b Totals					

30	Add columns (g) and (j) of line 29a . . .	**30**	
31	Add columns (f), (h), and (i) of line 29b . . .	**31**	( )
32	**Total partnership and S corporation income or (loss).** Combine lines 30 and 31. Enter the result here and include in the total on line 41 below . . .	**32**	

Part III Income or Loss From Estates and Trusts

33	**(a)** Name	**(b)** Employer identification number
A		
B		

	Passive Income and Loss		**Nonpassive Income and Loss**	
	(c) Passive deduction or loss allowed (attach **Form 8582** if required)	**(d)** Passive income from **Schedule K–1**	**(e)** Deduction or loss from **Schedule K–1**	**(f)** Other income from **Schedule K–1**
A				
B				
34a Totals				
b Totals				

35	Add columns (d) and (f) of line 34a . . .	**35**	
36	Add columns (c) and (e) of line 34b . . .	**36**	( )
37	**Total estate and trust income or (loss).** Combine lines 35 and 36. Enter the result here and include in the total on line 41 below . . .	**37**	

Part IV Income or Loss From Real Estate Mortgage Investment Conduits (REMICs)—Residual Holder

38	**(a)** Name	**(b)** Employer identification number	**(c)** Excess inclusion from **Schedules Q,** line 2c (see page E-8)	**(d)** Taxable income (net loss) from **Schedules Q,** line 1b	(e) Income from **Schedules Q,** line 3b

39	Combine columns (d) and (e) only. Enter the result here and include in the total on line 41 below	**39**	

Part V Summary

40	Net farm rental income or (loss) from **Form 4835**. Also, complete line 42 below . . .	**40**	
41	**Total income or (loss).** Combine lines 26, 32, 37, 39, and 40. Enter the result here and on Form 1040, line 17, or Form 1040NR, line 18 ▶	**41**	
42	**Reconciliation of farming and fishing income.** Enter your **gross** farming and fishing income reported on Form 4835, line 7; Schedule K-1 (Form 1065), box 14, code B; Schedule K-1 (Form 1120S), box 17, code U; and Schedule K-1 (Form 1041), line 14, code F (see page E-8)	**42**	
43	**Reconciliation for real estate professionals.** If you were a real estate professional (see page E-2), enter the net income or (loss) you reported anywhere on Form 1040 or Form 1040NR from all rental real estate activities in which you materially participated under the passive activity loss rules . .	**43**	

SCHEDULE F (Form 1040)

Department of the Treasury
Internal Revenue Service (99)

Profit or Loss From Farming

▶ Attach to Form 1040, Form 1040NR, Form 1041, Form 1065, or Form 1065-B.
▶ See Instructions for Schedule F (Form 1040).

OMB No. 1545-0074
2010
Attachment Sequence No. **14**

Name of proprietor | **Social security number (SSN)**

A Principal product. Describe in one or two words your principal crop or activity for the current tax year.

B Enter code from Part IV ▶

C Accounting method: **(1)** ☐ Cash **(2)** ☐ Accrual

D Employer ID number (EIN), if any

E Did you "materially participate" in the operation of this business during 2010? If "No," see instructions for limit on passive losses. ☐ Yes ☐ No

Part I **Farm Income—Cash Method.** Complete Parts I and II (Accrual method. Complete Parts II and III, and Part I, line 11.) Do not include sales of livestock held for draft, breeding, sport, or dairy purposes. Report these sales on Form 4797.

1	Sales of livestock and other items you bought for resale	1		
2	Cost or other basis of livestock and other items reported on line 1	2		
3	Subtract line 2 from line 1		3	
4	Sales of livestock, produce, grains, and other products you raised		4	
5a	Cooperative distributions (Form(s) 1099-PATR)	5a	5b Taxable amount	5b
6a	Agricultural program payments (see instructions)	6a	6b Taxable amount	6b
7	Commodity Credit Corporation (CCC) loans (see instructions):			
a	CCC loans reported under election			7a
b	CCC loans forfeited	7b	7c Taxable amount	7c
8	Crop insurance proceeds and federal crop disaster payments (see instructions):			
a	Amount received in 2010	8a	8b Taxable amount	8b
c	If election to defer to 2011 is attached, check here ▶ ☐		8d Amount deferred from 2009	8d
9	Custom hire (machine work) income			9
10	Other income, including federal and state gasoline or fuel tax credit or refund (see instructions)			10
11	**Gross income.** Add amounts in the right column for lines 3 through 10. If you use the accrual method to figure your income, enter the amount from Part III, line 51 ▶			11

Part II **Farm Expenses—Cash and Accrual Method.**
Do not include personal or living expenses such as taxes, insurance, or repairs on your home.

12	Car and truck expenses (see instructions). Also attach **Form 4562**	12	25	Pension and profit-sharing plans	25
13	Chemicals	13	26	Rent or lease (see instructions):	
14	Conservation expenses (see instructions)	14	a	Vehicles, machinery, and equipment	26a
15	Custom hire (machine work)	15	b	Other (land, animals, etc.)	26b
16	Depreciation and section 179 expense deduction not claimed elsewhere (see instructions)	16	27	Repairs and maintenance	27
			28	Seeds and plants	28
			29	Storage and warehousing	29
17	Employee benefit programs other than on line 25	17	30	Supplies	30
18	Feed	18	31	Taxes	31
19	Fertilizers and lime	19	32	Utilities	32
20	Freight and trucking	20	33	Veterinary, breeding, and medicine	33
21	Gasoline, fuel, and oil	21	34	Other expenses (specify):	
22	Insurance (other than health)	22	a		34a
23	Interest:		b		34b
a	Mortgage (paid to banks, etc.)	23a	c		34c
b	Other	23b	d		34d
24	Labor hired (less employment credits)	24	e		34e
			f		34f

35	**Total expenses.** Add lines 12 through 34f. If line 34f is negative, see instructions ▶	35
36	**Net farm profit or (loss).** Subtract line 35 from line 11. Partnerships, see instructions. • If a profit, enter the profit on both **Form 1040, line 18,** and **Schedule SE, line 1a;** on **Form 1040NR, line 19;** or on **Form 1041, line 6.** • If a loss, you **must** go to line 37.	36
37	If you have a loss, you **must** check the box that describes your investment in this activity and whether you received any applicable subsidy (see instructions). • If you checked 37a, enter the loss on both **Form 1040, line 18,** and **Schedule SE, line 1a;** on **Form 1040NR, line 19;** or on **Form 1041, line 6.** • If you checked 37b, your loss may be limited. See instructions.	**37a** ☐ All investment is at risk and you did not receive a subsidy. **37b** ☐ Some investment is not at risk or you received a subsidy.

Schedule F (Form 1040) 2010 Page **2**

Part III **Farm Income—Accrual Method** (see instructions).
Do not include sales of livestock held for draft, breeding, sport, or dairy purposes. Report these sales on Form 4797 and do not include this livestock on line 46 below.

38	Sales of livestock, produce, grains, and other products			38	
39a	Cooperative distributions (Form(s) 1099-PATR)	39a		39b Taxable amount	39b
40a	Agricultural program payments	40a		40b Taxable amount	40b
41	Commodity Credit Corporation (CCC) loans:				
a	CCC loans reported under election			41a	
b	CCC loans forfeited	41b		41c Taxable amount	41c
42	Crop insurance proceeds			42	
43	Custom hire (machine work) income			43	
44	Other income, including federal and state gasoline or fuel tax credit or refund			44	
45	Add amounts in the right column for lines 38 through 44			45	
46	Inventory of livestock, produce, grains, and other products at beginning of the year	46			
47	Cost of livestock, produce, grains, and other products purchased during the year	47			
48	Add lines 46 and 47	48			
49	Inventory of livestock, produce, grains, and other products at end of year	49			
50	Cost of livestock, produce, grains, and other products sold. Subtract line 49 from line 48*			50	
51	**Gross income.** Subtract line 50 from line 45. Enter the result here and on Part I, line 11 ▶			51	

*If you use the unit-livestock-price method or the farm-price method of valuing inventory and the amount on line 49 is larger than the amount on line 48, subtract line 48 from line 49. Enter the result on line 50. Add lines 45 and 50. Enter the total on line 51 and on Part I, line 11.

Part IV **Principal Agricultural Activity Codes**

CAUTION *File Schedule C (Form 1040) or Schedule C-EZ (Form 1040) instead of Schedule F if* ***(a)*** *your principal source of income is from providing agricultural services such as soil preparation, veterinary, farm labor, horticultural, or management for a fee or on a contract basis, or* ***(b)*** *you are engaged in the business of breeding, raising, and caring for dogs, cats, or other pet animals.*

These codes for the Principal Agricultural Activity classify farms by their primary activity to facilitate the administration of the Internal Revenue Code. These six-digit codes are based on the North American Industry Classification System (NAICS).

Select the code that best identifies your primary farming activity and enter the six digit number on page 1, line B.

Crop Production

111100 Oilseed and grain farming
111210 Vegetable and melon farming
111300 Fruit and tree nut farming
111400 Greenhouse, nursery, and floriculture production
111900 Other crop farming

Animal Production

112111 Beef cattle ranching and farming
112112 Cattle feedlots
112120 Dairy cattle and milk production
112210 Hog and pig farming
112300 Poultry and egg production
112400 Sheep and goat farming
112510 Aquaculture
112900 Other animal production

Forestry and Logging

113000 Forestry and logging (including forest nurseries and timber tracts)

SCHEDULE L (Form 1040A or 1040)

Department of the Treasury Internal Revenue Service (99)

Standard Deduction for Certain Filers

► Attach to Form 1040A or 1040. ► See instructions on back.

OMB No. 1545-0074

2010

Attachment Sequence No. **57**

Name(s) shown on return | **Your social security number**

CAUTION: *File this form **only** if you are increasing your standard deduction by certain net disaster losses or new motor vehicle taxes paid in 2010 for certain vehicles purchased in 2009.*

***Form 1040 Filers Only:** It may be better for you to itemize your deductions instead. See the Instructions for Schedule A (Form 1040).*

1 Enter the amount shown below for your filing status.
- Single or married filing separately—$5,700
- Married filing jointly or Qualifying widow(er)—$11,400
- Head of household—$8,400 . . . **1**

2 Can you (or your spouse if filing jointly) be claimed as a dependent on someone else's return?

☐ **No.** Enter the amount from line 1 on line 4, skip line 3, and go to line 5.

☐ **Yes.** Go to line 3.

3 Is your earned income more than $650 (see instructions)?

☐ **Yes.** Add $300 to your earned income. Enter the total

☐ **No.** Enter $950 . . . **3**

4 Enter the **smaller** of line 1 or line 3 . . . **4**

5 Multiply the number on Form 1040, line 39a, or Form 1040A, line 23a, by $1,100 ($1,400 if single or head of household). If blank, enter -0- . . . **5**

6 Form 1040 filers only, enter from your 2010 Form 4684, line 17, any loss from a disaster declared a federal disaster after 2007 that occurred before 2010 (see instructions) . . . **6**

7 Did you (or your spouse if filing jointly) pay any state or local sales or excise taxes in 2010 for the purchase of any new motor vehicle(s) **after** February 16, 2009, and **before** January 1, 2010 (see instructions)?

☐ **No.** Skip lines 7 through 16, enter -0- on line 17, and go to line 18.

☐ **Yes.** If Form 1040, line 38, or Form 1040A, line 22, is less than $135,000 ($260,000 if married filing jointly), enter the amount of these taxes paid. Otherwise, skip lines 7 through 16, enter -0- on line 17, and go to line 18 **7**

8 Enter the purchase price (**before taxes**) of the new motor vehicle(s) (see instructions) . . . **8**

9 Is the amount on line 8 more than $49,500?

☐ **No.** Enter the amount from line 7.

☐ **Yes.** Figure the **portion** of the tax from line 7 that is attributable to the first $49,500 of the purchase price of each new motor vehicle and enter it here (see instructions) . . **9**

10 Enter the amount from Form 1040, line 38, or Form 1040A, line 22 **10**

11 Form 1040 filers only, enter the total of any—
- Amounts from Form 2555, lines 45 and 50; Form 2555-EZ, line 18; and Form 4563, line 15, and
- Exclusion of income from Puerto Rico . . . **11**

12 Add lines 10 and 11 . . . **12**

13 Enter $125,000 ($250,000 if married filing jointly) . . . **13**

14 Is the amount on line 12 more than the amount on line 13?

☐ **No.** Skip lines 14 through 16, enter the amount from line 9 on line 17, and go to line 18.

☐ **Yes.** Subtract line 13 from line 12 . . . **14**

15 Divide the amount on line 14 by $10,000. Enter the result as a decimal (rounded to at least three places). If the result is 1.000 or more, enter 1.000 . . . **15**

16 Multiply line 9 by line 15 . . . **16**

17 Subtract line 16 from line 9 . . . **17**

18 Add lines 4, 5, 6, and 17. Enter the total here and on Form 1040, line 40, or Form 1040A, line 24. **18**

For Paperwork Reduction Act Notice, see your tax return instructions. Cat. No. 49875F **Schedule L (Form 1040A or 1040) 2010**

SCHEDULE M (Form 1040A or 1040)

Department of the Treasury Internal Revenue Service (99)

Making Work Pay Credit

▶ Attach to Form 1040A or 1040. ▶ See separate instructions.

OMB No. 1545-0074

2010

Attachment Sequence No. 166

Name(s) shown on return | Your social security number

CAUTION: *To take the making work pay credit, you must include your social security number (if filing a joint return, the number of either you or your spouse) on your tax return. A social security number does not include an identification number issued by the IRS. Only the Social Security Administration issues social security numbers.*

CAUTION: *You cannot take the making work pay credit if you can be claimed as someone else's dependent or if you are a nonresident alien.*

Important: Check the "**No**" box on line 1a and see the instructions if:

(a) You have a net loss from a business,
(b) You received a taxable scholarship or fellowship grant not reported on a Form W-2,
(c) Your wages include pay for work performed while an inmate in a penal institution,
(d) You received a pension or annuity from a nonqualified deferred compensation plan or a nongovernmental section 457 plan, or
(e) You are filing Form 2555 or 2555-EZ.

1a Do you (and your spouse if filing jointly) have 2010 wages of more than $6,451 ($12,903 if married filing jointly)?
☐ **Yes.** Skip lines 1a through 3. Enter $400 ($800 if married filing jointly) on line 4 and go to line 5.
☐ **No.** Enter your earned income (see instructions) **1a**

b Nontaxable combat pay included on line 1a (see instructions) **1b**

2 Multiply line 1a by 6.2% (.062) **2**

3 Enter $400 ($800 if married filing jointly) **3**

4 Enter the **smaller** of line 2 or line 3 (unless you checked "Yes" on line 1a) **4**

5 Enter the amount from Form 1040, line 38*, or Form 1040A, line 22 . . **5**

6 Enter $75,000 ($150,000 if married filing jointly) **6**

7 Is the amount on line 5 more than the amount on line 6?
☐ **No.** Skip line 8. Enter the amount from line 4 on line 9 below.
☐ **Yes.** Subtract line 6 from line 5 . . . . **7**

8 Multiply line 7 by 2% (.02) **8**

9 Subtract line 8 from line 4. If zero or less, enter -0- **9**

10 Did you (or your spouse, if filing jointly) receive an economic recovery payment in **2010**? You may have received this payment in 2010 if you did not receive an economic recovery payment in 2009 but you received social security benefits, supplemental security income, railroad retirement benefits, or veterans disability compensation or pension benefits in November 2008, December 2008, or January 2009 (see instructions).
☐ **No.** Enter -0- on line 10 and go to line 11.
☐ **Yes.** Enter the total of the payments you (and your spouse, if filing jointly) received in **2010**. Do not enter more than $250 ($500 if married filing jointly) **10**

11 **Making work pay credit.** Subtract line 10 from line 9. If zero or less, enter -0-. Enter the result here and on Form 1040, line 63; or Form 1040A, line 40 . . . . **11**

*If you are filing Form 2555, 2555-EZ, or 4563 or you are excluding income from Puerto Rico, see instructions.

SCHEDULE SE (Form 1040)

Department of the Treasury
Internal Revenue Service (99)

Self-Employment Tax

▶ **Attach to Form 1040 or Form 1040NR.** ▶ **See Instructions for Schedule SE (Form 1040).**

OMB No. 1545-0074

2010

Attachment Sequence No. **17**

Name of person with **self-employment** income (as shown on Form 1040)	Social security number of person with **self-employment** income ▶	

Before you begin: To determine if you must file Schedule SE, see the instructions on page SE-1.

May I Use Short Schedule SE or Must I Use Long Schedule SE?

Note. Use this flowchart **only if** you must file Schedule SE. If unsure, see *Who Must File Schedule SE* on page SE-1.

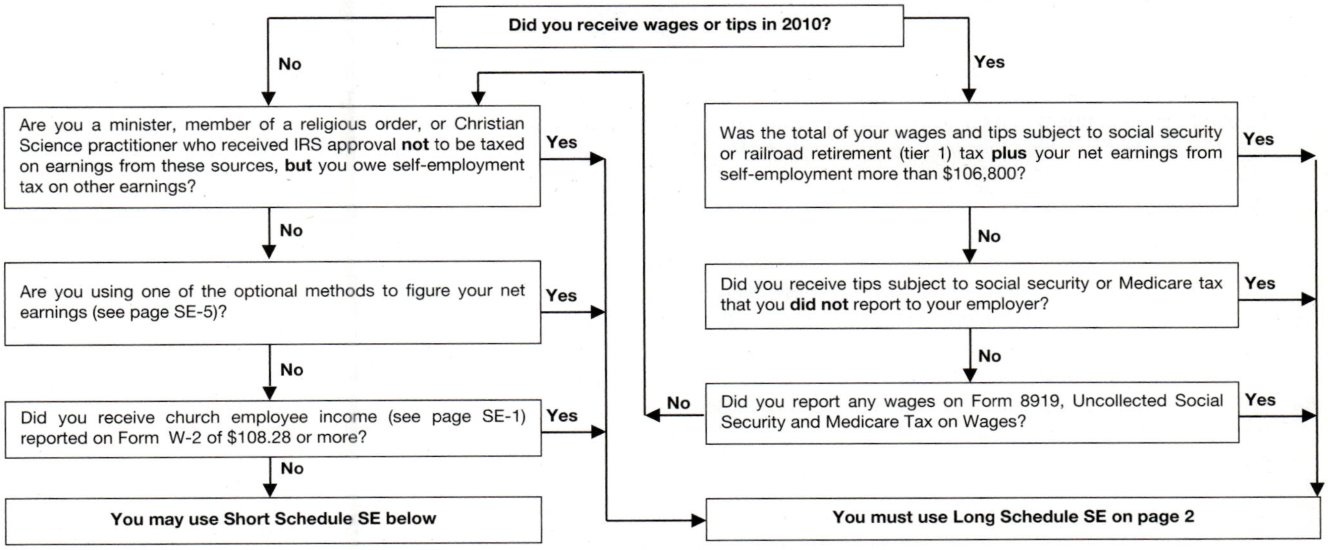

Section A—Short Schedule SE. Caution. Read above to see if you can use Short Schedule SE.

1a	Net farm profit or (loss) from Schedule F, line 36, and farm partnerships, Schedule K-1 (Form 1065), box 14, code A	**1a**	
b	If you received social security retirement or disability benefits, enter the amount of Conservation Reserve Program payments included on Schedule F, line 6b, or listed on Schedule K-1 (Form 1065), box 20, code Y	**1b**	( )
2	Net profit or (loss) from Schedule C, line 31; Schedule C-EZ, line 3; Schedule K-1 (Form 1065), box 14, code A (other than farming); and Schedule K-1 (Form 1065-B), box 9, code J1. Ministers and members of religious orders, see page SE-1 for types of income to report on this line. See page SE-3 for other income to report	**2**	
3	Combine lines 1a, 1b, and 2. Subtract from that total the amount on Form 1040, line 29, or Form 1040NR, line 29, and enter the result (see page SE-3)	**3**	
4	Multiply line 3 by 92.35% (.9235). If less than $400, you do not owe self-employment tax; **do not** file this schedule unless you have an amount on line 1b . . . . ▶	**4**	
	Note. If line 4 is less than $400 due to Conservation Reserve Program payments on line 1b, see page SE-3.		
5	**Self-employment tax.** If the amount on line 4 is: • $106,800 or less, multiply line 4 by 15.3% (.153). Enter the result here and on **Form 1040, line 56,** or **Form 1040NR, line 54** • More than $106,800, multiply line 4 by 2.9% (.029). Then, add $13,243.20 to the result. Enter the total here and on **Form 1040, line 56,** or **Form 1040NR, line 54**	**5**	
6	**Deduction for one-half of self-employment tax.** Multiply line 5 by 50% (.50). Enter the result here and on **Form 1040, line 27,** or **Form 1040NR, line 27** **6**		

Schedule SE (Form 1040) 2010 — Attachment Sequence No. **17** — Page **2**

Name of person with **self-employment** income (as shown on Form 1040)	Social security number of person with **self-employment** income ▶	

Section B—Long Schedule SE

Part I Self-Employment Tax

Note. If your only income subject to self-employment tax is **church employee income,** see page SE-3 for specific instructions. Also see page SE-1 for the definition of church employee income.

Line	Description			Line	Amount	
A	If you are a minister, member of a religious order, or Christian Science practitioner **and** you filed Form 4361, but you had $400 or more of **other** net earnings from self-employment, check here and continue with Part I . . . . ▶ ☐					
1a	Net farm profit or (loss) from Schedule F, line 36, and farm partnerships, Schedule K-1 (Form 1065), box 14, code A. **Note.** Skip lines 1a and 1b if you use the farm optional method (see page SE-5)			1a		
b	If you received social security retirement or disability benefits, enter the amount of Conservation Reserve Program payments included on Schedule F, line 6b, or listed on Schedule K-1 (Form 1065), box 20, code Y			1b	(	)
2	Net profit or (loss) from Schedule C, line 31; Schedule C-EZ, line 3; Schedule K-1 (Form 1065), box 14, code A (other than farming); and Schedule K-1 (Form 1065-B), box 9, code J1. Ministers and members of religious orders, see page SE-1 for types of income to report on this line. See page SE-4 for other income to report. **Note.** Skip this line if you use the nonfarm optional method (see page SE-5)			2		
3	Combine lines 1a, 1b, and 2. Subtract from that total the amount on Form 1040, line 29, or Form 1040NR, line 29, and enter the result (see page SE-3)			3		
4a	If line 3 is more than zero, multiply line 3 by 92.35% (.9235). Otherwise, enter amount from line 3 **Note.** If line 4a is less than $400 due to Conservation Reserve Program payments on line 1b, see page SE-3.			4a		
b	If you elect one or both of the optional methods, enter the total of lines 15 and 17 here . .			4b		
c	Combine lines 4a and 4b. If less than $400, **stop**; you do not owe self-employment tax. **Exception.** If less than $400 and you had **church employee income,** enter -0- and continue ▶			4c		
5a	Enter your **church employee income** from Form W-2. See page SE-1 for definition of church employee income	5a				
b	Multiply line 5a by 92.35% (.9235). If less than $100, enter -0-			5b		
6	Add lines 4c and 5b			6		
7	Maximum amount of combined wages and self-employment earnings subject to social security tax or the 6.2% portion of the 7.65% railroad retirement (tier 1) tax for 2010			7	106,800	00
8a	Total social security wages and tips (total of boxes 3 and 7 on Form(s) W-2) and railroad retirement (tier 1) compensation. If $106,800 or more, skip lines 8b through 10, and go to line 11	8a				
b	Unreported tips subject to social security tax (from Form 4137, line 10)	8b				
c	Wages subject to social security tax (from Form 8919, line 10)	8c				
d	Add lines 8a, 8b, and 8c			8d		
9	Subtract line 8d from line 7. If zero or less, enter -0- here and on line 10 and go to line 11 . ▶			9		
10	Multiply the **smaller** of line 6 or line 9 by 12.4% (.124)			10		
11	Multiply line 6 by 2.9% (.029)			11		
12	**Self-employment tax.** Add lines 10 and 11. Enter here and on **Form 1040, line 56,** or **Form 1040NR, line 54**			12		
13	**Deduction for one-half of self-employment tax.** Multiply line 12 by 50% (.50). Enter the result here and on **Form 1040, line 27, or Form 1040NR, line 27** .	13				

Part II Optional Methods To Figure Net Earnings (see page SE-4)

Farm Optional Method. You may use this method **only** if **(a)** your gross farm income[1] was not more than $6,720, **or (b)** your net farm profits[2] were less than $4,851.

Line	Description	Line	Amount	
14	Maximum income for optional methods	14	4,480	00
15	Enter the **smaller** of: two-thirds (2/3) of gross farm income[1] (not less than zero) **or** $4,480. Also include this amount on line 4b above	15		

Nonfarm Optional Method. You may use this method **only** if **(a)** your net nonfarm profits[3] were less than $4,851 and also less than 72.189% of your gross nonfarm income,[4] **and (b)** you had net earnings from self-employment of at least $400 in 2 of the prior 3 years. **Caution.** You may use this method no more than five times.

Line	Description	Line	Amount	
16	Subtract line 15 from line 14	16		
17	Enter the **smaller** of: two-thirds (2/3) of gross nonfarm income[4] (not less than zero) **or** the amount on line 16. Also include this amount on line 4b above	17		

[1] From Sch. F, line 11, and Sch. K-1 (Form 1065), box 14, code B.

[2] From Sch. F, line 36, and Sch. K-1 (Form 1065), box 14, code A—minus the amount you would have entered on line 1b had you not used the optional method.

[3] From Sch. C, line 31; Sch. C-EZ, line 3; Sch. K-1 (Form 1065), box 14, code A; and Sch. K-1 (Form 1065-B), box 9, code J1.

[4] From Sch. C, line 7; Sch. C-EZ, line 1; Sch. K-1 (Form 1065), box 14, code C; and Sch. K-1 (Form 1065-B), box 9, code J2.

Form **1041** Department of the Treasury—Internal Revenue Service

U.S. Income Tax Return for Estates and Trusts 2010

OMB No. 1545-0092

A Type of entity (see instr.):
- ☐ Decedent's estate
- ☐ Simple trust
- ☐ Complex trust
- ☐ Qualified disability trust
- ☐ ESBT (S portion only)
- ☐ Grantor type trust
- ☐ Bankruptcy estate-Ch. 7
- ☐ Bankruptcy estate-Ch. 11
- ☐ Pooled income fund

For calendar year 2010 or fiscal year beginning , 2010, and ending , 20

Name of estate or trust (If a grantor type trust, see page 15 of the instructions.)

C Employer identification number

Name and title of fiduciary

D Date entity created

Number, street, and room or suite no. (If a P.O. box, see page 15 of the instructions.)

E Nonexempt charitable and split-interest trusts, check applicable boxes (see page 16 of the instr.):
- ☐ Described in section 4947(a)(1)
- ☐ Not a private foundation
- ☐ Described in section 4947(a)(2)

City or town, state, and ZIP code

B Number of Schedules K-1 attached (see instructions) ▶

F Check applicable boxes: ☐ Initial return ☐ Final return ☐ Amended return ☐ Change in trust's name ☐ Change in fiduciary ☐ Change in fiduciary's name ☐ Change in fiduciary's address

G Check here if the estate or filing trust made a section 645 election . . . . ▶☐

Income	1	Interest income	1
	2a	Total ordinary dividends	2a
	b	Qualified dividends allocable to: **(1)** Beneficiaries ______ **(2)** Estate or trust ______	
	3	Business income or (loss). Attach Schedule C or C-EZ (Form 1040)	3
	4	Capital gain or (loss). Attach Schedule D (Form 1041)	4
	5	Rents, royalties, partnerships, other estates and trusts, etc. Attach Schedule E (Form 1040)	5
	6	Farm income or (loss). Attach Schedule F (Form 1040)	6
	7	Ordinary gain or (loss). Attach Form 4797	7
	8	Other income. List type and amount ______	8
	9	**Total income.** Combine lines 1, 2a, and 3 through 8 ▶	9
Deductions	10	Interest. Check if Form 4952 is attached ▶ ☐	10
	11	Taxes	11
	12	Fiduciary fees	12
	13	Charitable deduction (from Schedule A, line 7)	13
	14	Attorney, accountant, and return preparer fees	14
	15a	Other deductions **not** subject to the 2% floor (attach schedule)	15a
	b	Allowable miscellaneous itemized deductions subject to the 2% floor	15b
	16	Add lines 10 through 15b ▶	16
	17	Adjusted total income or (loss). Subtract line 16 from line 9 . . . 17	
	18	Income distribution deduction (from Schedule B, line 15). Attach Schedules K-1 (Form 1041)	18
	19	Estate tax deduction including certain generation-skipping taxes (attach computation)	19
	20	Exemption	20
	21	Add lines 18 through 20 ▶	21
Tax and Payments	22	Taxable income. Subtract line 21 from line 17. If a loss, see page 23 of the instructions	22
	23	**Total tax** (from Schedule G, line 7)	23
	24	**Payments: a** 2010 estimated tax payments and amount applied from 2009 return	24a
	b	Estimated tax payments allocated to beneficiaries (from Form 1041-T)	24b
	c	Subtract line 24b from line 24a	24c
	d	Tax paid with Form 7004 (see page 24 of the instructions)	24d
	e	Federal income tax withheld. If any is from Form(s) 1099, check ▶ ☐	24e
		Other payments: **f** Form 2439 ______ ; **g** Form 4136 ______ ; Total ▶	24h
	25	**Total payments.** Add lines 24c through 24e, and 24h ▶	25
	26	Estimated tax penalty (see page 24 of the instructions)	26
	27	**Tax due.** If line 25 is smaller than the total of lines 23 and 26, enter amount owed	27
	28	**Overpayment.** If line 25 is larger than the total of lines 23 and 26, enter amount overpaid	28
	29	Amount of line 28 to be: **a Credited to 2011 estimated tax** ▶ ; **b Refunded** ▶	29

Sign Here

Under penalties of perjury, I declare that I have examined this return, including accompanying schedules and statements, and to the best of my knowledge and belief, it is true, correct, and complete. Declaration of preparer (other than taxpayer) is based on all information of which preparer has any knowledge.

▶ Signature of fiduciary or officer representing fiduciary | Date | ▶ EIN of fiduciary if a financial institution

May the IRS discuss this return with the preparer shown below (see instr.)? ☐ **Yes** ☐ **No**

Paid Preparer Use Only

Print/Type preparer's name	Preparer's signature	Date	Check ☐ if self-employed	PTIN
Firm's name ▶			Firm's EIN ▶	
Firm's address ▶			Phone no.	

For Paperwork Reduction Act Notice, see the separate instructions. Cat. No. 11370H Form **1041** (2010)

Form 1041 (2010) Page **2**

Schedule A **Charitable Deduction.** Do not complete for a simple trust or a pooled income fund.

1	Amounts paid or permanently set aside for charitable purposes from gross income (see page 25)	1	
2	Tax-exempt income allocable to charitable contributions (see page 25 of the instructions)	2	
3	Subtract line 2 from line 1	3	
4	Capital gains for the tax year allocated to corpus and paid or permanently set aside for charitable purposes	4	
5	Add lines 3 and 4	5	
6	Section 1202 exclusion allocable to capital gains paid or permanently set aside for charitable purposes (see page 25 of the instructions)	6	
7	**Charitable deduction.** Subtract line 6 from line 5. Enter here and on page 1, line 13	7	

Schedule B **Income Distribution Deduction**

1	Adjusted total income (see page 25 of the instructions)	1	
2	Adjusted tax-exempt interest	2	
3	Total net gain from Schedule D (Form 1041), line 15, column (1) (see page 26 of the instructions)	3	
4	Enter amount from Schedule A, line 4 (minus any allocable section 1202 exclusion)	4	
5	Capital gains for the tax year included on Schedule A, line 1 (see page 26 of the instructions)	5	
6	Enter any gain from page 1, line 4, as a negative number. If page 1, line 4, is a loss, enter the loss as a positive number	6	
7	**Distributable net income.** Combine lines 1 through 6. If zero or less, enter -0-	7	
8	If a complex trust, enter accounting income for the tax year as determined under the governing instrument and applicable local law — 8		
9	Income required to be distributed currently	9	
10	Other amounts paid, credited, or otherwise required to be distributed	10	
11	Total distributions. Add lines 9 and 10. If greater than line 8, see page 26 of the instructions	11	
12	Enter the amount of tax-exempt income included on line 11	12	
13	Tentative income distribution deduction. Subtract line 12 from line 11	13	
14	Tentative income distribution deduction. Subtract line 2 from line 7. If zero or less, enter -0-	14	
15	**Income distribution deduction.** Enter the smaller of line 13 or line 14 here and on page 1, line 18	15	

Schedule G **Tax Computation** (see page 27 of the instructions)

1	**Tax: a** Tax on taxable income (see page 27 of the instructions)	1a			
	b Tax on lump-sum distributions. Attach Form 4972	1b			
	c Alternative minimum tax (from Schedule I (Form 1041), line 56)	1c			
	d **Total.** Add lines 1a through 1c ▶			1d	
2a	Foreign tax credit. Attach Form 1116	2a			
b	General business credit. Attach Form 3800	2b			
c	Credit for prior year minimum tax. Attach Form 8801	2c			
d	Bond credits. Attach Form 8912	2d			
3	**Total credits.** Add lines 2a through 2d ▶			3	
4	Subtract line 3 from line 1d. If zero or less, enter -0-			4	
5	Recapture taxes. Check if from: ☐ Form 4255 ☐ Form 8611			5	
6	Household employment taxes. Attach Schedule H (Form 1040)			6	
7	**Total tax.** Add lines 4 through 6. Enter here and on page 1, line 23 ▶			7	

Other Information

		Yes	No
1	Did the estate or trust receive tax-exempt income? If "Yes," attach a computation of the allocation of expenses Enter the amount of tax-exempt interest income and exempt-interest dividends ▶ $		
2	Did the estate or trust receive all or any part of the earnings (salary, wages, and other compensation) of any individual by reason of a contract assignment or similar arrangement?		
3	At any time during calendar year 2010, did the estate or trust have an interest in or a signature or other authority over a bank, securities, or other financial account in a foreign country? See page 29 of the instructions for exceptions and filing requirements for Form TD F 90-22.1. If "Yes," enter the name of the foreign country ▶		
4	During the tax year, did the estate or trust receive a distribution from, or was it the grantor of, or transferor to, a foreign trust? If "Yes," the estate or trust may have to file Form 3520. See page 29 of the instructions		
5	Did the estate or trust receive, or pay, any qualified residence interest on seller-provided financing? If "Yes," see page 29 for required attachment		
6	If this is an estate or a complex trust making the section 663(b) election, check here (see page 29) ▶ ☐		
7	To make a section 643(e)(3) election, attach Schedule D (Form 1041), and check here (see page 29) ▶ ☐		
8	If the decedent's estate has been open for more than 2 years, attach an explanation for the delay in closing the estate, and check here ▶ ☐		
9	Are any present or future trust beneficiaries skip persons? See page 29 of the instructions		

Form **1041** (2010)

661110

☐ Final K-1 ☐ Amended K-1

OMB No. 1545-0092

Schedule K-1 (Form 1041)
Department of the Treasury
Internal Revenue Service

2010

For calendar year 2010, or tax year beginning ________, 2010, and ending ________, 20 ____

Beneficiary's Share of Income, Deductions, Credits, etc.

▶ **See back of form and instructions.**

Part I Information About the Estate or Trust

A Estate's or trust's employer identification number

B Estate's or trust's name

C Fiduciary's name, address, city, state, and ZIP code

D ☐ Check if Form 1041-T was filed and enter the date it was filed ________

E ☐ Check if this is the final Form 1041 for the estate or trust

Part II Information About the Beneficiary

F Beneficiary's identifying number

G Beneficiary's name, address, city, state, and ZIP code

H ☐ Domestic beneficiary ☐ Foreign beneficiary

Part III Beneficiary's Share of Current Year Income, Deductions, Credits, and Other Items

1	Interest income	11	Final year deductions
2a	Ordinary dividends		
2b	Qualified dividends		
3	Net short-term capital gain		
4a	Net long-term capital gain		
4b	28% rate gain	12	Alternative minimum tax adjustment
4c	Unrecaptured section 1250 gain		
5	Other portfolio and nonbusiness income		
6	Ordinary business income		
7	Net rental real estate income		
8	Other rental income	13	Credits and credit recapture
9	Directly apportioned deductions		
		14	Other information
10	Estate tax deduction		

*See attached statement for additional information.

Note. A statement must be attached showing the beneficiary's share of income and directly apportioned deductions from each business, rental real estate, and other rental activity.

For IRS Use Only

For Paperwork Reduction Act Notice, see the Instructions for Form 1041. Cat. No. 11380D **Schedule K-1 (Form 1041) 2010**

Form **1065** Department of the Treasury Internal Revenue Service

U.S. Return of Partnership Income

For calendar year 2010, or tax year beginning ________________, 2010, ending ____________, 20 ________.

▶ See separate instructions.

OMB No. 1545-0099

2010

A Principal business activity	Print or type.	Name of partnership	**D** Employer identification number
B Principal product or service		Number, street, and room or suite no. If a P.O. box, see the instructions.	**E** Date business started
C Business code number		City or town, state, and ZIP code	**F** Total assets (see the instructions) $

G Check applicable boxes: **(1)** ☐ Initial return **(2)** ☐ Final return **(3)** ☐ Name change **(4)** ☐ Address change **(5)** ☐ Amended return
(6) ☐ Technical termination - also check (1) or (2)

H Check accounting method: **(1)** ☐ Cash **(2)** ☐ Accrual **(3)** ☐ Other (specify) ▶ ________

I Number of Schedules K-1. Attach one for each person who was a partner at any time during the tax year ▶ ________

J Check if Schedules C and M-3 are attached . . . . . ☐

Caution. *Include **only** trade or business income and expenses on lines 1a through 22 below. See the instructions for more information.*

Income	**1a**	Gross receipts or sales	**1a**			
	b	Less returns and allowances	**1b**		**1c**	
	2	Cost of goods sold (Schedule A, line 8)			**2**	
	3	Gross profit. Subtract line 2 from line 1c			**3**	
	4	Ordinary income (loss) from other partnerships, estates, and trusts *(attach statement)* . .			**4**	
	5	Net farm profit (loss) *(attach Schedule F (Form 1040))*			**5**	
	6	Net gain (loss) from Form 4797, Part II, line 17 *(attach Form 4797)*			**6**	
	7	Other income (loss) *(attach statement)*			**7**	
	8	**Total income (loss).** Combine lines 3 through 7			**8**	
Deductions (see the instructions for limitations)	**9**	Salaries and wages (other than to partners) (less employment credits)			**9**	
	10	Guaranteed payments to partners			**10**	
	11	Repairs and maintenance			**11**	
	12	Bad debts			**12**	
	13	Rent			**13**	
	14	Taxes and licenses			**14**	
	15	Interest			**15**	
	16a	Depreciation *(if required, attach Form 4562)*	**16a**			
	b	Less depreciation reported on Schedule A and elsewhere on return	**16b**		**16c**	
	17	Depletion **(Do not deduct oil and gas depletion.)**			**17**	
	18	Retirement plans, etc.			**18**	
	19	Employee benefit programs			**19**	
	20	Other deductions (*attach statement*)			**20**	
	21	**Total deductions.** Add the amounts shown in the far right column for lines 9 through 20 .			**21**	
	22	**Ordinary business income (loss).** Subtract line 21 from line 8			**22**	

Sign Here

Under penalties of perjury, I declare that I have examined this return, including accompanying schedules and statements, and to the best of my knowledge and belief, it is true, correct, and complete. Declaration of preparer (other than general partner or limited liability company member manager) is based on all information of which preparer has any knowledge.

▶ ________________ Signature of general partner or limited liability company member manager ▶ ________ Date

May the IRS discuss this return with the preparer shown below (see instructions)? ☐ **Yes** ☐ **No**

Paid Preparer Use Only

Print/Type preparer's name	Preparer's signature	Date	Check ☐ if self- employed	PTIN
Firm's name ▶			Firm's EIN ▶	
Firm's address ▶			Phone no.	

For Paperwork Reduction Act Notice, see separate instructions. Cat. No. 11390Z Form **1065** (2010)

Form 1065 (2010) Page **2**

Schedule A Cost of Goods Sold (see the instructions)

1	Inventory at beginning of year	1	
2	Purchases less cost of items withdrawn for personal use	2	
3	Cost of labor	3	
4	Additional section 263A costs (*attach statement*)	4	
5	Other costs (*attach statement*)	5	
6	**Total.** Add lines 1 through 5	6	
7	Inventory at end of year	7	
8	**Cost of goods sold.** Subtract line 7 from line 6. Enter here and on page 1, line 2	8	

9a Check all methods used for valuing closing inventory:

(i) ☐ Cost as described in Regulations section 1.471-3

(ii) ☐ Lower of cost or market as described in Regulations section 1.471-4

(iii) ☐ Other (specify method used and attach explanation) ▶

b Check this box if there was a writedown of "subnormal" goods as described in Regulations section 1.471-2(c) ▶ ☐

c Check this box if the LIFO inventory method was adopted this tax year for any goods (*if checked, attach Form 970*) ▶ ☐

d Do the rules of section 263A (for property produced or acquired for resale) apply to the partnership? ☐ **Yes** ☐ **No**

e Was there any change in determining quantities, cost, or valuations between opening and closing inventory? ☐ **Yes** ☐ **No**
If "Yes," attach explanation.

Schedule B Other Information

		Yes	No
1	What type of entity is filing this return? Check the applicable box: **a** ☐ Domestic general partnership **b** ☐ Domestic limited partnership **c** ☐ Domestic limited liability company **d** ☐ Domestic limited liability partnership **e** ☐ Foreign partnership **f** ☐ Other ▶		
2	At any time during the tax year, was any partner in the partnership a disregarded entity, a partnership (including an entity treated as a partnership), a trust, an S corporation, an estate (other than an estate of a deceased partner), or a nominee or similar person?		
3	At the end of the tax year:		
a	Did any foreign or domestic corporation, partnership (including any entity treated as a partnership), trust, or tax-exempt organization own, directly or indirectly, an interest of 50% or more in the profit, loss, or capital of the partnership? For rules of constructive ownership, see instructions. If "Yes," attach Schedule B-1, Information on Partners Owning 50% or More of the Partnership		
b	Did any individual or estate own, directly or indirectly, an interest of 50% or more in the profit, loss, or capital of the partnership? For rules of constructive ownership, see instructions. If "Yes," attach Schedule B-1, Information on Partners Owning 50% or More of the Partnership		
4	At the end of the tax year, did the partnership:		
a	Own directly 20% or more, or own, directly or indirectly, 50% or more of the total voting power of all classes of stock entitled to vote of any foreign or domestic corporation? For rules of constructive ownership, see instructions. If "Yes," complete (i) through (iv) below		

(i) Name of Corporation	**(ii)** Employer Identification Number (if any)	**(iii)** Country of Incorporation	**(iv)** Percentage Owned in Voting Stock

		Yes	No
b	Own directly an interest of 20% or more, or own, directly or indirectly, an interest of 50% or more in the profit, loss, or capital in any foreign or domestic partnership (including an entity treated as a partnership) or in the beneficial interest of a trust? For rules of constructive ownership, see instructions. If "Yes," complete (i) through (v) below		

(i) Name of Entity	**(ii)** Employer Identification Number (if any)	**(iii)** Type of Entity	**(iv)** Country of Organization	**(v)** Maximum Percentage Owned in Profit, Loss, or Capital

		Yes	No
5	Did the partnership file Form 8893, Election of Partnership Level Tax Treatment, or an election statement under section 6231(a)(1)(B)(ii) for partnership-level tax treatment, that is in effect for this tax year? See Form 8893 for more details		
6	Does the partnership satisfy **all four** of the following conditions?		
a	The partnership's total receipts for the tax year were less than $250,000.		
b	The partnership's total assets at the end of the tax year were less than $1 million.		
c	Schedules K-1 are filed with the return and furnished to the partners on or before the due date (including extensions) for the partnership return.		
d	The partnership is not filing and is not required to file Schedule M-3		
	If "Yes," the partnership is not required to complete Schedules L, M-1, and M-2; Item F on page 1 of Form 1065; or Item L on Schedule K-1.		
7	Is this partnership a publicly traded partnership as defined in section 469(k)(2)?		
8	During the tax year, did the partnership have any debt that was cancelled, was forgiven, or had the terms modified so as to reduce the principal amount of the debt?		
9	Has this partnership filed, or is it required to file, Form 8918, Material Advisor Disclosure Statement, to provide information on any reportable transaction?		
10	At any time during calendar year 2010, did the partnership have an interest in or a signature or other authority over a financial account in a foreign country (such as a bank account, securities account, or other financial account)? See the instructions for exceptions and filing requirements for Form TD F 90-22.1, Report of Foreign Bank and Financial Accounts. If "Yes," enter the name of the foreign country. ▶		
11	At any time during the tax year, did the partnership receive a distribution from, or was it the grantor of, or transferor to, a foreign trust? If "Yes," the partnership may have to file Form 3520, Annual Return To Report Transactions With Foreign Trusts and Receipt of Certain Foreign Gifts. See instructions		
12a	Is the partnership making, or had it previously made (and not revoked), a section 754 election?		
	See instructions for details regarding a section 754 election.		
b	Did the partnership make for this tax year an optional basis adjustment under section 743(b) or 734(b)? If "Yes," attach a statement showing the computation and allocation of the basis adjustment. See instructions		
c	Is the partnership required to adjust the basis of partnership assets under section 743(b) or 734(b) because of a substantial built-in loss (as defined under section 743(d)) or substantial basis reduction (as defined under section 734(d))? If "Yes," attach a statement showing the computation and allocation of the basis adjustment. See instructions.		
13	Check this box if, during the current or prior tax year, the partnership distributed any property received in a like-kind exchange or contributed such property to another entity (other than entities wholly-owned by the partnership throughout the tax year) ▶ ☐		
14	At any time during the tax year, did the partnership distribute to any partner a tenancy-in-common or other undivided interest in partnership property?		
15	If the partnership is required to file Form 8858, Information Return of U.S. Persons With Respect To Foreign Disregarded Entities, enter the number of Forms 8858 attached. See instructions ▶		
16	Does the partnership have any foreign partners? If "Yes," enter the number of Forms 8805, Foreign Partner's Information Statement of Section 1446 Withholding Tax, filed for this partnership. ▶		
17	Enter the number of Forms 8865, Return of U.S. Persons With Respect to Certain Foreign Partnerships, attached to this return. ▶		

Designation of Tax Matters Partner (see instructions)

Enter below the general partner designated as the tax matters partner (TMP) for the tax year of this return:

Name of designated TMP ▶		Identifying number of TMP ▶	
If the TMP is an entity, name of TMP representative ▶		Phone number of TMP ▶	
Address of designated TMP ▶			

Form 1065 (2010) Page 4

Schedule K Partners' Distributive Share Items

Section	Line	Item		Line	Total amount
Income (Loss)	1	Ordinary business income (loss) (page 1, line 22)		1	
	2	Net rental real estate income (loss) (*attach Form 8825*)		2	
	3a	Other gross rental income (loss)	3a		
	b	Expenses from other rental activities (*attach statement*)	3b		
	c	Other net rental income (loss). Subtract line 3b from line 3a		3c	
	4	Guaranteed payments		4	
	5	Interest income		5	
	6	Dividends: a Ordinary dividends		6a	
		b Qualified dividends	6b		
	7	Royalties		7	
	8	Net short-term capital gain (loss) (*attach Schedule D (Form 1065)*)		8	
	9a	Net long-term capital gain (loss) (*attach Schedule D (Form 1065)*)		9a	
	b	Collectibles (28%) gain (loss)	9b		
	c	Unrecaptured section 1250 gain (*attach statement*)	9c		
	10	Net section 1231 gain (loss) (*attach Form 4797*)		10	
	11	Other income (loss) (*see instructions*) Type ▶		11	
Deductions	12	Section 179 deduction (*attach Form 4562*)		12	
	13a	Contributions		13a	
	b	Investment interest expense		13b	
	c	Section 59(e)(2) expenditures: **(1)** Type ▶ **(2)** Amount ▶		13c(2)	
	d	Other deductions (*see instructions*) Type ▶		13d	
Self-Employment	14a	Net earnings (loss) from self-employment		14a	
	b	Gross farming or fishing income		14b	
	c	Gross nonfarm income		14c	
Credits	15a	Low-income housing credit (section 42(j)(5))		15a	
	b	Low-income housing credit (other)		15b	
	c	Qualified rehabilitation expenditures (rental real estate) (*attach Form 3468*)		15c	
	d	Other rental real estate credits (*see instructions*) Type ▶		15d	
	e	Other rental credits (*see instructions*) Type ▶		15e	
	f	Other credits (*see instructions*) Type ▶		15f	
Foreign Transactions	16a	Name of country or U.S. possession ▶			
	b	Gross income from all sources		16b	
	c	Gross income sourced at partner level		16c	
		Foreign gross income sourced at partnership level			
	d	Passive category ▶ **e** General category ▶ **f** Other ▶		16f	
		Deductions allocated and apportioned at partner level			
	g	Interest expense ▶ **h** Other ▶		16h	
		Deductions allocated and apportioned at partnership level to foreign source income			
	i	Passive category ▶ **j** General category ▶ **k** Other ▶		16k	
	l	Total foreign taxes (check one): ▶ Paid ☐ Accrued ☐		16l	
	m	Reduction in taxes available for credit (*attach statement*)		16m	
	n	Other foreign tax information (*attach statement*)			
Alternative Minimum Tax (AMT) Items	17a	Post-1986 depreciation adjustment		17a	
	b	Adjusted gain or loss		17b	
	c	Depletion (other than oil and gas)		17c	
	d	Oil, gas, and geothermal properties—gross income		17d	
	e	Oil, gas, and geothermal properties—deductions		17e	
	f	Other AMT items (*attach statement*)		17f	
Other Information	18a	Tax-exempt interest income		18a	
	b	Other tax-exempt income		18b	
	c	Nondeductible expenses		18c	
	19a	Distributions of cash and marketable securities		19a	
	b	Distributions of other property		19b	
	20a	Investment income		20a	
	b	Investment expenses		20b	
	c	Other items and amounts (*attach statement*)			

Form **1065** (2010)

Form 1065 (2010) Page **5**

Analysis of Net Income (Loss)

1	Net income (loss). Combine Schedule K, lines 1 through 11. From the result, subtract the sum of Schedule K, lines 12 through 13d, and 16l . . .	**1**	

	Analysis by partner type:	**(i)** Corporate	**(ii)** Individual (active)	**(iii)** Individual (passive)	**(iv)** Partnership	**(v)** Exempt organization	**(vi)** Nominee/Other
2							
a	General partners						
b	Limited partners						

Schedule L Balance Sheets per Books

	Assets	Beginning of tax year (a)	(b)	End of tax year (c)	(d)
1	Cash				
2a	Trade notes and accounts receivable				
b	Less allowance for bad debts				
3	Inventories				
4	U.S. government obligations				
5	Tax-exempt securities				
6	Other current assets (*attach statement*)				
7	Mortgage and real estate loans				
8	Other investments (*attach statement*)				
9a	Buildings and other depreciable assets				
b	Less accumulated depreciation				
10a	Depletable assets				
b	Less accumulated depletion				
11	Land (net of any amortization)				
12a	Intangible assets (amortizable only)				
b	Less accumulated amortization				
13	Other assets (*attach statement*)				
14	Total assets				
	Liabilities and Capital				
15	Accounts payable				
16	Mortgages, notes, bonds payable in less than 1 year				
17	Other current liabilities (*attach statement*)				
18	All nonrecourse loans				
19	Mortgages, notes, bonds payable in 1 year or more				
20	Other liabilities (*attach statement*)				
21	Partners' capital accounts				
22	Total liabilities and capital				

Schedule M-1 Reconciliation of Income (Loss) per Books With Income (Loss) per Return

Note. Schedule M-3 may be required instead of Schedule M-1 (see instructions).

1	Net income (loss) per books		**6**	Income recorded on books this year not included on Schedule K, lines 1 through 11 (itemize):	
2	Income included on Schedule K, lines 1, 2, 3c, 5, 6a, 7, 8, 9a, 10, and 11, not recorded on books this year (itemize):		**a**	Tax-exempt interest $	
3	Guaranteed payments (other than health insurance)		**7**	Deductions included on Schedule K, lines 1 through 13d, and 16l, not charged against book income this year (itemize):	
4	Expenses recorded on books this year not included on Schedule K, lines 1 through 13d, and 16l (itemize):		**a**	Depreciation $	
a	Depreciation $				
b	Travel and entertainment $		**8**	Add lines 6 and 7	
5	Add lines 1 through 4		**9**	Income (loss) (Analysis of Net Income (Loss), line 1). Subtract line 8 from line 5	

Schedule M-2 Analysis of Partners' Capital Accounts

1	Balance at beginning of year		**6**	Distributions: **a** Cash	
2	Capital contributed: **a** Cash			**b** Property	
	b Property		**7**	Other decreases (itemize):	
3	Net income (loss) per books				
4	Other increases (itemize):				
			8	Add lines 6 and 7	
5	Add lines 1 through 4		**9**	Balance at end of year. Subtract line 8 from line 5	

651110

☐ Final K-1 ☐ Amended K-1 OMB No. 1545-0099

Schedule K-1 (Form 1065) **2010**

Department of the Treasury
Internal Revenue Service

For calendar year 2010, or tax year beginning ________, 2010 ending ________, 20____

Partner's Share of Income, Deductions, Credits, etc.

▶ See back of form and separate instructions.

Part I Information About the Partnership

A Partnership's employer identification number

B Partnership's name, address, city, state, and ZIP code

C IRS Center where partnership filed return

D ☐ Check if this is a publicly traded partnership (PTP)

Part II Information About the Partner

E Partner's identifying number

F Partner's name, address, city, state, and ZIP code

G ☐ General partner or LLC member-manager ☐ Limited partner or other LLC member

H ☐ Domestic partner ☐ Foreign partner

I What type of entity is this partner? ________

J Partner's share of profit, loss, and capital (see instructions):

	Beginning	Ending
Profit	%	%
Loss	%	%
Capital	%	%

K Partner's share of liabilities at year end:

Nonrecourse . . . . $ ________
Qualified nonrecourse financing . $ ________
Recourse . . . . $ ________

L Partner's capital account analysis:

Beginning capital account . . . $ ________
Capital contributed during the year $ ________
Current year increase (decrease) . $ ________
Withdrawals & distributions . . $ (________)
Ending capital account . . . . $ ________

☐ Tax basis ☐ GAAP ☐ Section 704(b) book
☐ Other (explain)

M Did the partner contribute property with a built-in gain or loss?
☐ Yes ☐ No
If "Yes", attach statement (see instructions)

Part III Partner's Share of Current Year Income, Deductions, Credits, and Other Items

1	Ordinary business income (loss)	**15**	Credits
2	Net rental real estate income (loss)		
3	Other net rental income (loss)	**16**	Foreign transactions
4	Guaranteed payments		
5	Interest income		
6a	Ordinary dividends		
6b	Qualified dividends		
7	Royalties		
8	Net short-term capital gain (loss)		
9a	Net long-term capital gain (loss)	**17**	Alternative minimum tax (AMT) items
9b	Collectibles (28%) gain (loss)		
9c	Unrecaptured section 1250 gain		
10	Net section 1231 gain (loss)	**18**	Tax-exempt income and nondeductible expenses
11	Other income (loss)		
		19	Distributions
12	Section 179 deduction		
13	Other deductions	**20**	Other information
14	Self-employment earnings (loss)		

*See attached statement for additional information.

For IRS Use Only

SCHEDULE M-3 (Form 1065)

Department of the Treasury
Internal Revenue Service

Net Income (Loss) Reconciliation for Certain Partnerships

► Attach to Form 1065 or Form 1065-B.
► See separate instructions.

OMB No. 1545-0099

2010

Name of partnership | **Employer identification number**

This Schedule M-3 is being filed because (check all that apply):

A ☐ The amount of the partnership's total assets at the end of the tax year is equal to $10 million or more.

B ☐ The amount of the partnership's adjusted total assets for the year is equal to $10 million or more. If box B is checked, enter the amount of adjusted total assets for the tax year ____________ .

C ☐ The amount of total receipts for the tax year is equal to $35 million or more. If box C is checked, enter the total receipts for the tax year ____________ .

D ☐ An entity that is a reportable entity partner with respect to the partnership owns or is deemed to own an interest of 50 percent or more in the partnership's capital, profit, or loss, on any day during the tax year of the partnership.

Name of Reportable Entity Partner	Identifying Number	Maximum Percentage Owned or Deemed Owned

E ☐ Voluntary Filer

Part I Financial Information and Net Income (Loss) Reconciliation

1a Did the partnership file SEC Form 10-K for its income statement period ending with or within this tax year?
☐ **Yes.** Skip lines 1b and 1c and complete lines 2 through 11 with respect to that SEC Form 10-K.
☐ **No.** Go to line 1b. See instructions if multiple non-tax-basis income statements are prepared.

b Did the partnership prepare a certified audited non-tax-basis income statement for that period?
☐ **Yes.** Skip line 1c and complete lines 2 through 11 with respect to that income statement.
☐ **No.** Go to line 1c.

c Did the partnership prepare a non-tax-basis income statement for that period?
☐ **Yes.** Complete lines 2 through 11 with respect to that income statement.
☐ **No.** Skip lines 2 through 3b and enter the partnership's net income (loss) per its books and records on line 4a.

2 Enter the income statement period: Beginning ____/____/____ Ending ____/____/____

3a Has the partnership's income statement been restated for the income statement period on line 2?
☐ **Yes.** (If "Yes," attach an explanation and the amount of each item restated.)
☐ **No.**

b Has the partnership's income statement been restated for any of the five income statement periods preceding the period on line 2?
☐ **Yes.** (If "Yes," attach an explanation and the amount of each item restated.)
☐ **No.**

4a	Worldwide consolidated net income (loss) from income statement source identified in Part I, line 1	**4a**	
b	Indicate accounting standard used for line 4a (see instructions): **1** ☐ GAAP **2** ☐ IFRS **3** ☐ 704(b) **4** ☐ Tax-basis **5** ☐ Other: (Specify) ► ____________		
5a	Net income from nonincludible foreign entities (attach schedule)	**5a**	( )
b	Net loss from nonincludible foreign entities (attach schedule and enter as a positive amount) . . .	**5b**	
6a	Net income from nonincludible U.S. entities (attach schedule)	**6a**	( )
b	Net loss from nonincludible U.S. entities (attach schedule and enter as a positive amount)	**6b**	
7a	Net income (loss) of other foreign disregarded entities (attach schedule)	**7a**	
b	Net income (loss) of other U.S. disregarded entities (attach schedule)	**7b**	
8	Adjustment to eliminations of transactions between includible entities and nonincludible entities (attach schedule)	**8**	
9	Adjustment to reconcile income statement period to tax year (attach schedule)	**9**	
10	Other adjustments to reconcile to amount on line 11 (attach schedule)	**10**	
11	**Net income (loss) per income statement of the partnership.** Combine lines 4 through 10 . . . **Note.** Part I, line 11, must equal the amount on Part II, line 26, column (a).	**11**	

12 Enter the total amount (not just the partnership's share) of the assets and liabilities of all entities included or removed on the following lines:

		Total Assets	Total Liabilities
a	Included on Part I, line 4		
b	Removed on Part I, line 5		
c	Removed on Part I, line 6		
d	Included on Part I, line 7		

Schedule M-3 (Form 1065) 2010 Page **2**

Name of partnership | **Employer identification number**

Part II **Reconciliation of Net Income (Loss) per Income Statement of Partnership with Income (Loss) per Return**

	Income (Loss) Items (Attach schedules for lines 1 through 9)	**(a)** Income (Loss) per Income Statement	**(b)** Temporary Difference	**(c)** Permanent Difference	**(d)** Income (Loss) per Tax Return
1	Income (loss) from equity method foreign corporations				
2	Gross foreign dividends not previously taxed				
3	Subpart F, QEF, and similar income inclusions				
4	Gross foreign distributions previously taxed				
5	Income (loss) from equity method U.S. corporations				
6	U.S. dividends				
7	Income (loss) from U.S. partnerships				
8	Income (loss) from foreign partnerships				
9	Income (loss) from other pass-through entities				
10	Items relating to reportable transactions (attach details)				
11	Interest income (attach Form 8916-A)				
12	Total accrual to cash adjustment				
13	Hedging transactions				
14	Mark-to-market income (loss)				
15	Cost of goods sold (attach Form 8916-A)	( )			( )
16	Sale versus lease (for sellers and/or lessors)				
17	Section 481(a) adjustments				
18	Unearned/deferred revenue				
19	Income recognition from long-term contracts				
20	Original issue discount and other imputed interest				
21a	Income statement gain/loss on sale, exchange, abandonment, worthlessness, or other disposition of assets other than inventory and pass-through entities				
b	Gross capital gains from Schedule D, excluding amounts from pass-through entities				
c	Gross capital losses from Schedule D, excluding amounts from pass-through entities, abandonment losses, and worthless stock losses				
d	Net gain/loss reported on Form 4797, line 17, excluding amounts from pass-through entities, abandonment losses, and worthless stock losses				
e	Abandonment losses				
f	Worthless stock losses (attach details)				
g	Other gain/loss on disposition of assets other than inventory				
22	Other income (loss) items with differences (attach schedule)				
23	**Total income (loss) items.** Combine lines 1 through 22				
24	**Total expense/deduction items.** (from Part III, line 31) (see instructions)				
25	Other items with no differences				
26	**Reconciliation totals.** Combine lines 23 through 25				

Note. Line 26, column (a), must equal the amount on Part I, line 11, and column (d) must equal Form 1065, page 5, Analysis of Net Income (Loss), line 1.

Schedule M-3 (Form 1065) 2010 Page **3**

Name of partnership | **Employer identification number**

Part III **Reconciliation of Net Income (Loss) per Income Statement of Partnership With Income (Loss) per Return—Expense/Deduction Items**

	Expense/Deduction Items	(a) Expense per Income Statement	(b) Temporary Difference	(c) Permanent Difference	(d) Deduction per Tax Return
1	State and local current income tax expense				
2	State and local deferred income tax expense				
3	Foreign current income tax expense (other than foreign withholding taxes)				
4	Foreign deferred income tax expense				
5	Equity-based compensation				
6	Meals and entertainment				
7	Fines and penalties				
8	Judgments, damages, awards, and similar costs				
9	Guaranteed payments				
10	Pension and profit-sharing				
11	Other post-retirement benefits				
12	Deferred compensation				
13	Charitable contribution of cash and tangible property				
14	Charitable contribution of intangible property				
15	Organizational expenses as per Regulations section 1.709-2(a)				
16	Syndication expenses as per Regulations section 1.709-2(b)				
17	Current year acquisition/reorganization investment banking fees				
18	Current year acquisition/reorganization legal and accounting fees				
19	Amortization/impairment of goodwill				
20	Amortization of acquisition, reorganization, and start-up costs				
21	Other amortization or impairment write-offs				
22	Section 198 environmental remediation costs				
23a	Depletion—Oil & Gas				
b	Depletion—Other than Oil & Gas				
24	Intangible drilling & development costs				
25	Depreciation				
26	Bad debt expense				
27	Interest expense (attach Form 8916-A)				
28	Purchase versus lease (for purchasers and/ or lessees)				
29	Research and development costs (attach schedule)				
30	Other expense/deduction items with differences (attach schedule)				
31	**Total expense/deduction items.** Combine lines 1 through 30. Enter here and on Part II, line 24, reporting positive amounts as negative and negative amounts as positive				

Form **1120**
Department of the Treasury
Internal Revenue Service

U.S. Corporation Income Tax Return

For calendar year 2010 or tax year beginning ________, 2010, ending ________, 20 ___

▶ **See separate instructions.**

OMB No. 1545-0123

2010

A Check if:
1a Consolidated return (attach Form 851) ☐
b Life/nonlife consolidated return . . ☐
2 Personal holding co. (attach Sch. PH) . ☐
3 Personal service corp. (see instructions) . ☐
4 Schedule M-3 attached ☐

Print or type
Name
Number, street, and room or suite no. If a P.O. box, see instructions.
City or town, state, and ZIP code

B Employer identification number
C Date incorporated
D Total assets (see instructions) $

E Check if: **(1)** ☐ Initial return **(2)** ☐ Final return **(3)** ☐ Name change **(4)** ☐ Address change

Income

1a	Gross receipts or sales ____ **b** Less returns and allowances ____ **c** Bal ▶	1c	
2	Cost of goods sold (Schedule A, line 8)	2	
3	Gross profit. Subtract line 2 from line 1c	3	
4	Dividends (Schedule C, line 19)	4	
5	Interest	5	
6	Gross rents	6	
7	Gross royalties	7	
8	Capital gain net income (attach Schedule D (Form 1120))	8	
9	Net gain or (loss) from Form 4797, Part II, line 17 (attach Form 4797)	9	
10	Other income (see instructions—attach schedule)	10	
11	**Total income.** Add lines 3 through 10 ▶	11	

Deductions (See instructions for limitations on deductions.)

12	Compensation of officers (Schedule E, line 4) ▶	12	
13	Salaries and wages (less employment credits)	13	
14	Repairs and maintenance	14	
15	Bad debts	15	
16	Rents	16	
17	Taxes and licenses	17	
18	Interest	18	
19	Charitable contributions	19	
20	Depreciation from Form 4562 not claimed on Schedule A or elsewhere on return (attach Form 4562)	20	
21	Depletion	21	
22	Advertising	22	
23	Pension, profit-sharing, etc., plans	23	
24	Employee benefit programs	24	
25	Domestic production activities deduction (attach Form 8903)	25	
26	Other deductions (attach schedule)	26	
27	**Total deductions.** Add lines 12 through 26 ▶	27	
28	Taxable income before net operating loss deduction and special deductions. Subtract line 27 from line 11.	28	
29	**Less: a** Net operating loss deduction (see instructions) — 29a		
	b Special deductions (Schedule C, line 20) — 29b	29c	

Tax, Refundable Credits, and Payments

30	**Taxable income.** Subtract line 29c from line 28 (see instructions)	30	
31	**Total tax** (Schedule J, line 10)	31	
32a	2009 overpayment credited to 2010 — 32a		
b	2010 estimated tax payments — 32b		
c	2010 refund applied for on Form 4466 — 32c ( ) **d Bal** ▶ 32d		
e	Tax deposited with Form 7004 — 32e		
f	Credits: **(1)** Form 2439 ____ **(2)** Form 4136 ____ — 32f		
g	Refundable credits from Form 3800, line 19c, and Form 8827, line 8c — 32g	32h	
33	Estimated tax penalty (see instructions). Check if Form 2220 is attached ▶ ☐	33	
34	**Amount owed.** If line 32h is smaller than the total of lines 31 and 33, enter amount owed	34	
35	**Overpayment.** If line 32h is larger than the total of lines 31 and 33, enter amount overpaid	35	
36	Enter amount from line 35 you want: **Credited to 2011 estimated tax** ▶ ____ **Refunded** ▶	36	

Sign Here

Under penalties of perjury, I declare that I have examined this return, including accompanying schedules and statements, and to the best of my knowledge and belief, it is true, correct, and complete. Declaration of preparer (other than taxpayer) is based on all information of which preparer has any knowledge.

▶ Signature of officer | Date | ▶ Title

May the IRS discuss this return with the preparer shown below (see instructions)? ☐ **Yes** ☐ **No**

Paid Preparer Use Only

Print/Type preparer's name	Preparer's signature	Date	Check ☐ if self-employed	PTIN
Firm's name ▶			Firm's EIN ▶	
Firm's address ▶			Phone no.	

Form 1120 (2010) Page **2**

Schedule A Cost of Goods Sold (see instructions)

1	Inventory at beginning of year	1	
2	Purchases	2	
3	Cost of labor	3	
4	Additional section 263A costs (attach schedule)	4	
5	Other costs (attach schedule)	5	
6	**Total.** Add lines 1 through 5	6	
7	Inventory at end of year	7	
8	**Cost of goods sold.** Subtract line 7 from line 6. Enter here and on page 1, line 2	8	

9a Check all methods used for valuing closing inventory:

(i) ☐ Cost

(ii) ☐ Lower of cost or market

(iii) ☐ Other (Specify method used and attach explanation.) ▶

b Check if there was a writedown of subnormal goods ▶ ☐

c Check if the LIFO inventory method was adopted this tax year for any goods (if checked, attach Form 970) ▶ ☐

d If the LIFO inventory method was used for this tax year, enter percentage (or amounts) of closing inventory computed under LIFO | 9d |

e If property is produced or acquired for resale, do the rules of section 263A apply to the corporation? ☐ Yes ☐ No

f Was there any change in determining quantities, cost, or valuations between opening and closing inventory? If "Yes," attach explanation ☐ Yes ☐ No

Schedule C Dividends and Special Deductions (see instructions)

		(a) Dividends received	(b) %	(c) Special deductions (a) × (b)
1	Dividends from less-than-20%-owned domestic corporations (other than debt-financed stock)		70	
2	Dividends from 20%-or-more-owned domestic corporations (other than debt-financed stock)		80	
3	Dividends on debt-financed stock of domestic and foreign corporations		see instructions	
4	Dividends on certain preferred stock of less-than-20%-owned public utilities		42	
5	Dividends on certain preferred stock of 20%-or-more-owned public utilities		48	
6	Dividends from less-than-20%-owned foreign corporations and certain FSCs		70	
7	Dividends from 20%-or-more-owned foreign corporations and certain FSCs		80	
8	Dividends from wholly owned foreign subsidiaries		100	
9	**Total.** Add lines 1 through 8. See instructions for limitation			
10	Dividends from domestic corporations received by a small business investment company operating under the Small Business Investment Act of 1958		100	
11	Dividends from affiliated group members		100	
12	Dividends from certain FSCs		100	
13	Dividends from foreign corporations not included on lines 3, 6, 7, 8, 11, or 12			
14	Income from controlled foreign corporations under subpart F (attach Form(s) 5471)			
15	Foreign dividend gross-up			
16	IC-DISC and former DISC dividends not included on lines 1, 2, or 3			
17	Other dividends			
18	Deduction for dividends paid on certain preferred stock of public utilities			
19	**Total dividends.** Add lines 1 through 17. Enter here and on page 1, line 4 ▶			
20	**Total special deductions.** Add lines 9, 10, 11, 12, and 18. Enter here and on page 1, line 29b ▶			

Schedule E Compensation of Officers (see instructions for page 1, line 12)

Note: *Complete Schedule E only if total receipts (line 1a plus lines 4 through 10 on page 1) are $500,000 or more.*

	(a) Name of officer	(b) Social security number	(c) Percent of time devoted to business	Percent of corporation stock owned (d) Common	(e) Preferred	(f) Amount of compensation
1			%	%	%	
			%	%	%	
			%	%	%	
			%	%	%	
			%	%	%	

2	Total compensation of officers	
3	Compensation of officers claimed on Schedule A and elsewhere on return	
4	Subtract line 3 from line 2. Enter the result here and on page 1, line 12	

Schedule J — Tax Computation (see instructions)

1	Check if the corporation is a member of a controlled group (attach Schedule O (Form 1120)) . . . . ▶ ☐		
2	Income tax. Check if a qualified personal service corporation (see instructions) . . . . ▶ ☐	2	
3	Alternative minimum tax (attach Form 4626)	3	
4	Add lines 2 and 3	4	
5a	Foreign tax credit (attach Form 1118) **5a**		
b	Credit from Form 8834, line 29 . . . . **5b**		
c	General business credit (attach Form 3800) **5c**		
d	Credit for prior year minimum tax (attach Form 8827) **5d**		
e	Bond credits from Form 8912 . . . . **5e**		
6	**Total credits.** Add lines 5a through 5e	6	
7	Subtract line 6 from line 4	7	
8	Personal holding company tax (attach Schedule PH (Form 1120))	8	
9	Other taxes. Check if from: ☐ Form 4255 ☐ Form 8611 ☐ Form 8697 ☐ Form 8866 ☐ Form 8902 ☐ Other (attach schedule) . . .	9	
10	**Total tax.** Add lines 7 through 9. Enter here and on page 1, line 31	10	

Schedule K — Other Information (see instructions)

		Yes	No
1	Check accounting method: **a** ☐ Cash **b** ☐ Accrual **c** ☐ Other (specify) ▶		
2	See the instructions and enter the:		
a	Business activity code no. ▶		
b	Business activity ▶		
c	Product or service ▶		
3	Is the corporation a subsidiary in an affiliated group or a parent-subsidiary controlled group? . . . . If "Yes," enter name and EIN of the parent corporation ▶		
4	At the end of the tax year:		
a	Did any foreign or domestic corporation, partnership (including any entity treated as a partnership), trust, or tax-exempt organization own directly 20% or more, or own, directly or indirectly, 50% or more of the total voting power of all classes of the corporation's stock entitled to vote? If "Yes," complete Part I of Schedule G (Form 1120) (attach Schedule G)		
b	Did any individual or estate own directly 20% or more, or own, directly or indirectly, 50% or more of the total voting power of all classes of the corporation's stock entitled to vote? If "Yes," complete Part II of Schedule G (Form 1120) (attach Schedule G) .		
5	At the end of the tax year, did the corporation:		
a	Own directly 20% or more, or own, directly or indirectly, 50% or more of the total voting power of all classes of stock entitled to vote of any foreign or domestic corporation not included on **Form 851,** Affiliations Schedule? For rules of constructive ownership, see instructions If "Yes," complete (i) through (iv).		

(i) Name of Corporation	**(ii)** Employer Identification Number (if any)	**(iii)** Country of Incorporation	**(iv)** Percentage Owned in Voting Stock

Form 1120 (2010) Page **4**

Schedule K *Continued*

		Yes	No
b	Own directly an interest of 20% or more, or own, directly or indirectly, an interest of 50% or more in any foreign or domestic partnership (including an entity treated as a partnership) or in the beneficial interest of a trust? For rules of constructive ownership, see instructions. If "Yes," complete (i) through (iv).		

(i) Name of Entity	**(ii)** Employer Identification Number (if any)	**(iii)** Country of Organization	**(iv)** Maximum Percentage Owned in Profit, Loss, or Capital

		Yes	No
6	During this tax year, did the corporation pay dividends (other than stock dividends and distributions in exchange for stock) in excess of the corporation's current and accumulated earnings and profits? (See sections 301 and 316.)		
	If "Yes," file **Form 5452,** Corporate Report of Nondividend Distributions. If this is a consolidated return, answer here for the parent corporation and on Form 851 for each subsidiary.		
7	At any time during the tax year, did one foreign person own, directly or indirectly, at least 25% of **(a)** the total voting power of all classes of the corporation's stock entitled to vote or **(b)** the total value of all classes of the corporation's stock?		
	For rules of attribution, see section 318. If "Yes," enter: **(i)** Percentage owned ▶ ________ and **(ii)** Owner's country ▶ ________		
	(c) The corporation may have to file **Form 5472,** Information Return of a 25% Foreign-Owned U.S. Corporation or a Foreign Corporation Engaged in a U.S. Trade or Business. Enter the number of Forms 5472 attached ▶ ________		
8	Check this box if the corporation issued publicly offered debt instruments with original issue discount . . . . ▶ ☐ If checked, the corporation may have to file **Form 8281,** Information Return for Publicly Offered Original Issue Discount Instruments.		
9	Enter the amount of tax-exempt interest received or accrued during the tax year ▶ $ ________		
10	Enter the number of shareholders at the end of the tax year (if 100 or fewer) ▶ ________		
11	If the corporation has an NOL for the tax year and is electing to forego the carryback period, check here . . . . . . ▶ ☐ If the corporation is filing a consolidated return, the statement required by Regulations section 1.1502-21(b)(3) must be attached or the election will not be valid.		
12	Enter the available NOL carryover from prior tax years (do not reduce it by any deduction on line 29a.) ▶ $ ________		
13	Are the corporation's total receipts (line 1a plus lines 4 through 10 on page 1) for the tax year **and** its total assets at the end of the tax year less than $250,000?		
	If "Yes," the corporation is not required to complete Schedules L, M-1, and M-2 on page 5. Instead, enter the total amount of cash distributions and the book value of property distributions (other than cash) made during the tax year. ▶ $ ________		
14	Is the corporation required to file Schedule UTP (Form 1120), Uncertain Tax Position Statement (see instructions)?		
	If "Yes," complete and attach Schedule UTP.		

Form **1120** (2010)

Form 1120 (2010) Page **5**

Schedule L **Balance Sheets per Books**

Assets	Beginning of tax year (a)	(b)	End of tax year (c)	(d)
1 Cash				
2a Trade notes and accounts receivable				
b Less allowance for bad debts	( )		( )	
3 Inventories				
4 U.S. government obligations				
5 Tax-exempt securities (see instructions)				
6 Other current assets (attach schedule)				
7 Loans to shareholders				
8 Mortgage and real estate loans				
9 Other investments (attach schedule)				
10a Buildings and other depreciable assets				
b Less accumulated depreciation	( )		( )	
11a Depletable assets				
b Less accumulated depletion	( )		( )	
12 Land (net of any amortization)				
13a Intangible assets (amortizable only)				
b Less accumulated amortization	( )		( )	
14 Other assets (attach schedule)				
15 Total assets				
Liabilities and Shareholders' Equity				
16 Accounts payable				
17 Mortgages, notes, bonds payable in less than 1 year				
18 Other current liabilities (attach schedule)				
19 Loans from shareholders				
20 Mortgages, notes, bonds payable in 1 year or more				
21 Other liabilities (attach schedule)				
22 Capital stock: **a** Preferred stock				
b Common stock				
23 Additional paid-in capital				
24 Retained earnings—Appropriated (attach schedule)				
25 Retained earnings—Unappropriated				
26 Adjustments to shareholders' equity (attach schedule)				
27 Less cost of treasury stock		( )		( )
28 Total liabilities and shareholders' equity				

Schedule M-1 **Reconciliation of Income (Loss) per Books With Income per Return**

Note: Schedule M-3 required instead of Schedule M-1 if total assets are $10 million or more—see instructions

1 Net income (loss) per books		7 Income recorded on books this year not included on this return (itemize): Tax-exempt interest $	
2 Federal income tax per books			
3 Excess of capital losses over capital gains			
4 Income subject to tax not recorded on books this year (itemize):			
5 Expenses recorded on books this year not deducted on this return (itemize):		8 Deductions on this return not charged against book income this year (itemize):	
a Depreciation $		a Depreciation $	
b Charitable contributions $		b Charitable contributions $	
c Travel and entertainment $			
		9 Add lines 7 and 8	
6 Add lines 1 through 5		10 Income (page 1, line 28)—line 6 less line 9	

Schedule M-2 **Analysis of Unappropriated Retained Earnings per Books (Line 25, Schedule L)**

1 Balance at beginning of year		5 Distributions: **a** Cash	
2 Net income (loss) per books		**b** Stock	
3 Other increases (itemize):		**c** Property	
		6 Other decreases (itemize):	
		7 Add lines 5 and 6	
4 Add lines 1, 2, and 3		8 Balance at end of year (line 4 less line 7)	

SCHEDULE M-3 (Form 1120)

Department of the Treasury
Internal Revenue Service

Net Income (Loss) Reconciliation for Corporations With Total Assets of $10 Million or More

► Attach to Form 1120 or 1120-C.
► See separate instructions.

OMB No. 1545-0123

2010

Name of corporation (common parent, if consolidated return) | **Employer identification number**

Check applicable box(es): (1) ☐ Non-consolidated return (2) ☐ Consolidated return (Form 1120 only)
(3) ☐ Mixed 1120/L/PC group (4) ☐ Dormant subsidiaries schedule attached

Part I Financial Information and Net Income (Loss) Reconciliation (see instructions)

1a Did the corporation file SEC Form 10-K for its income statement period ending with or within this tax year?
☐ **Yes.** Skip lines 1b and 1c and complete lines 2a through 11 with respect to that SEC Form 10-K.
☐ **No.** Go to line 1b. See instructions if multiple non-tax-basis income statements are prepared.

b Did the corporation prepare a certified audited non-tax-basis income statement for that period?
☐ **Yes.** Skip line 1c and complete lines 2a through 11 with respect to that income statement.
☐ **No.** Go to line 1c.

c Did the corporation prepare a non-tax-basis income statement for that period?
☐ **Yes.** Complete lines 2a through 11 with respect to that income statement.
☐ **No.** Skip lines 2a through 3c and enter the corporation's net income (loss) per its books and records on line 4a.

2a Enter the income statement period: Beginning MM/DD/YYYY Ending MM/DD/YYYY

b Has the corporation's income statement been restated for the income statement period on line 2a?
☐ **Yes.** (If "Yes," attach an explanation and the amount of each item restated.)
☐ **No.**

c Has the corporation's income statement been restated for any of the five income statement periods preceding the period on line 2a?
☐ **Yes.** (If "Yes," attach an explanation and the amount of each item restated.)
☐ **No.**

3a Is any of the corporation's voting common stock publicly traded?
☐ **Yes.**
☐ **No.** If "No," go to line 4a.

b Enter the symbol of the corporation's primary U.S. publicly traded voting common stock . . . . [ ]

c Enter the nine-digit CUSIP number of the corporation's primary publicly traded voting common stock . . . . [ ]

4a	Worldwide consolidated net income (loss) from income statement source identified in Part I, line 1 . .	**4a**	
b	Indicate accounting standard used for line 4a (see instructions): (1) ☐ GAAP (2) ☐ IFRS (3) ☐ Statutory (4) ☐ Tax-basis (5) ☐ Other (specify) ________		
5a	Net income from nonincludible foreign entities (attach schedule)	**5a**	( )
b	Net loss from nonincludible foreign entities (attach schedule and enter as a positive amount)	**5b**	
6a	Net income from nonincludible U.S. entities (attach schedule)	**6a**	( )
b	Net loss from nonincludible U.S. entities (attach schedule and enter as a positive amount)	**6b**	
7a	Net income (loss) of other includible foreign disregarded entities (attach schedule)	**7a**	
b	Net income (loss) of other includible U.S. disregarded entities (attach schedule)	**7b**	
c	Net income (loss) of other includible entities (attach schedule)	**7c**	
8	Adjustment to eliminations of transactions between includible entities and nonincludible entities (attach schedule)	**8**	
9	Adjustment to reconcile income statement period to tax year (attach schedule)	**9**	
10a	Intercompany dividend adjustments to reconcile to line 11 (attach schedule)	**10a**	
b	Other statutory accounting adjustments to reconcile to line 11 (attach schedule)	**10b**	
c	Other adjustments to reconcile to amount on line 11 (attach schedule)	**10c**	
11	**Net income (loss) per income statement of includible corporations.** Combine lines 4 through 10 . . .	**11**	

Note. Part I, line 11, must equal the amount on Part II, line 30, column (a), and Schedule M-2, line 2.

12 Enter the total amount (not just the corporation's share) of the assets and liabilities of all entities included or removed on the following lines.

		Total Assets	Total Liabilities
a	Included on Part I, line 4 . . . . ►		
b	Removed on Part I, line 5 . . . . ►		
c	Removed on Part I, line 6 . . . . ►		
d	Included on Part I, line 7 . . . . ►		

Schedule M-3 (Form 1120) 2010 Page **2**

Name of corporation (common parent, if consolidated return)	**Employer identification number**

Check applicable box(es): **(1)** ☐ Consolidated group **(2)** ☐ Parent corp **(3)** ☐ Consolidated eliminations **(4)** ☐ Subsidiary corp **(5)** ☐ Mixed 1120/L/PC group

Check if a sub-consolidated: **(6)** ☐ 1120 group **(7)** ☐ 1120 eliminations

Name of subsidiary (if consolidated return)	**Employer identification number**

Part II Reconciliation of Net Income (Loss) per Income Statement of Includible Corporations With Taxable Income per Return (see instructions)

Income (Loss) Items (Attach schedules for lines 1 through 11)	**(a)** Income (Loss) per Income Statement	**(b)** Temporary Difference	**(c)** Permanent Difference	**(d)** Income (Loss) per Tax Return
1 Income (loss) from equity method foreign corporations				
2 Gross foreign dividends not previously taxed				
3 Subpart F, QEF, and similar income inclusions				
4 Section 78 gross-up				
5 Gross foreign distributions previously taxed				
6 Income (loss) from equity method U.S. corporations				
7 U.S. dividends not eliminated in tax consolidation				
8 Minority interest for includible corporations				
9 Income (loss) from U.S. partnerships				
10 Income (loss) from foreign partnerships				
11 Income (loss) from other pass-through entities				
12 Items relating to reportable transactions (attach details)				
13 Interest income (attach Form 8916-A)				
14 Total accrual to cash adjustment				
15 Hedging transactions				
16 Mark-to-market income (loss)				
17 Cost of goods sold (attach Form 8916-A)	( )			( )
18 Sale versus lease (for sellers and/or lessors)				
19 Section 481(a) adjustments				
20 Unearned/deferred revenue				
21 Income recognition from long-term contracts				
22 Original issue discount and other imputed interest				
23a Income statement gain/loss on sale, exchange, abandonment, worthlessness, or other disposition of assets other than inventory and pass-through entities				
b Gross capital gains from Schedule D, excluding amounts from pass-through entities				
c Gross capital losses from Schedule D, excluding amounts from pass-through entities, abandonment losses, and worthless stock losses				
d Net gain/loss reported on Form 4797, line 17, excluding amounts from pass-through entities, abandonment losses, and worthless stock losses				
e Abandonment losses				
f Worthless stock losses (attach details)				
g Other gain/loss on disposition of assets other than inventory				
24 Capital loss limitation and carryforward used				
25 Other income (loss) items with differences (attach schedule)				
26 **Total income (loss) items.** Combine lines 1 through 25				
27 **Total expense/deduction items** (from Part III, line 38)				
28 Other items with no differences				
29a Mixed groups, see instructions. All others, combine lines 26 through 28				
b PC insurance subgroup reconciliation totals				
c Life insurance subgroup reconciliation totals				
30 **Reconciliation totals.** Combine lines 29a through 29c				

Note. Line 30, column (a), must equal the amount on Part I, line 11, and column (d) must equal Form 1120, page 1, line 28.

Schedule M-3 (Form 1120) 2010 Page **3**

Name of corporation (common parent, if consolidated return)	**Employer identification number**

Check applicable box(es): **(1)** ☐ Consolidated group **(2)** ☐ Parent corp **(3)** ☐ Consolidated eliminations **(4)** ☐ Subsidiary corp **(5)** ☐ Mixed 1120/L/PC group

Check if a sub-consolidated: **(6)** ☐ 1120 group **(7)** ☐ 1120 eliminations

Name of subsidiary (if consolidated return)	**Employer identification number**

Part III Reconciliation of Net Income (Loss) per Income Statement of Includible Corporations With Taxable Income per Return—Expense/Deduction Items (see instructions)

Expense/Deduction Items	(a) Expense per Income Statement	(b) Temporary Difference	(c) Permanent Difference	(d) Deduction per Tax Return
1 U.S. current income tax expense				
2 U.S. deferred income tax expense				
3 State and local current income tax expense				
4 State and local deferred income tax expense				
5 Foreign current income tax expense (other than foreign withholding taxes)				
6 Foreign deferred income tax expense				
7 Foreign withholding taxes				
8 Interest expense (attach Form 8916-A)				
9 Stock option expense				
10 Other equity-based compensation				
11 Meals and entertainment				
12 Fines and penalties				
13 Judgments, damages, awards, and similar costs				
14 Parachute payments				
15 Compensation with section 162(m) limitation				
16 Pension and profit-sharing				
17 Other post-retirement benefits				
18 Deferred compensation				
19 Charitable contribution of cash and tangible property				
20 Charitable contribution of intangible property				
21 Charitable contribution limitation/carryforward				
22 Domestic production activities deduction				
23 Current year acquisition or reorganization investment banking fees				
24 Current year acquisition or reorganization legal and accounting fees				
25 Current year acquisition/reorganization other costs				
26 Amortization/impairment of goodwill				
27 Amortization of acquisition, reorganization, and start-up costs				
28 Other amortization or impairment write-offs				
29 Section 198 environmental remediation costs				
30 Depletion				
31 Depreciation				
32 Bad debt expense				
33 Corporate owned life insurance premiums				
34 Purchase versus lease (for purchasers and/or lessees)				
35 Research and development costs (attach schedule)				
36 Section 118 exclusion (attach schedule)				
37 Other expense/deduction items with differences (attach schedule)				
38 **Total expense/deduction items.** Combine lines 1 through 37. Enter here and on Part II, line 27, reporting positive amounts as negative and negative amounts as positive				

Form **1120S**

Department of the Treasury
Internal Revenue Service

U.S. Income Tax Return for an S Corporation

▶ **Do not file this form unless the corporation has filed or is attaching Form 2553 to elect to be an S corporation.**

▶ **See separate instructions.**

OMB No. 1545-0130

2010

For calendar year 2010 or tax year beginning , 2010, ending , 20

A S election effective date	TYPE OR PRINT	Name	**D Employer identification number**
B Business activity code number *(see instructions)*		Number, street, and room or suite no. If a P.O. box, see instructions.	**E** Date incorporated
C Check if Sch. M-3 attached ☐		City or town, state, and ZIP code	**F** Total assets *(see instructions)* $

G Is the corporation electing to be an S corporation beginning with this tax year? ☐ Yes ☐ No If "Yes," attach Form 2553 if not already filed

H Check if: **(1)** ☐ Final return **(2)** ☐ Name change **(3)** ☐ Address change **(4)** ☐ Amended return **(5)** ☐ S election termination or revocation

I Enter the number of shareholders who were shareholders during any part of the tax year . . . . ▶

Caution. *Include **only** trade or business income and expenses on lines 1a through 21. See the instructions for more information.*

Section	Line	Description		
Income	1 a	Gross receipts or sales ______ **b** Less returns and allowances ______ **c** Bal ▶	**1c**	
	2	Cost of goods sold (Schedule A, line 8)	**2**	
	3	Gross profit. Subtract line 2 from line 1c	**3**	
	4	Net gain (loss) from Form 4797, Part II, line 17 *(attach Form 4797)*	**4**	
	5	Other income (loss) *(see instructions—attach statement)*	**5**	
	6	**Total income (loss).** Add lines 3 through 5 ▶	**6**	
Deductions (see instructions for limitations)	7	Compensation of officers	**7**	
	8	Salaries and wages (less employment credits)	**8**	
	9	Repairs and maintenance	**9**	
	10	Bad debts	**10**	
	11	Rents	**11**	
	12	Taxes and licenses	**12**	
	13	Interest	**13**	
	14	Depreciation not claimed on Schedule A or elsewhere on return (*attach Form 4562*)	**14**	
	15	Depletion **(Do not deduct oil and gas depletion.)**	**15**	
	16	Advertising	**16**	
	17	Pension, profit-sharing, etc., plans	**17**	
	18	Employee benefit programs	**18**	
	19	Other deductions (*attach statement*)	**19**	
	20	**Total deductions.** Add lines 7 through 19 ▶	**20**	
	21	**Ordinary business income (loss).** Subtract line 20 from line 6	**21**	
Tax and Payments	22 a	Excess net passive income or LIFO recapture tax (*see instructions*) **22a**		
	b	Tax from Schedule D (Form 1120S) **22b**		
	c	Add lines 22a and 22b (*see instructions for additional taxes*)	**22c**	
	23 a	2010 estimated tax payments and 2009 overpayment credited to 2010 **23a**		
	b	Tax deposited with Form 7004 **23b**		
	c	Credit for federal tax paid on fuels (*attach Form 4136*) **23c**		
	d	Add lines 23a through 23c	**23d**	
	24	Estimated tax penalty (*see instructions*). Check if Form 2220 is attached ▶ ☐	**24**	
	25	**Amount owed.** If line 23d is smaller than the total of lines 22c and 24, enter amount owed	**25**	
	26	**Overpayment.** If line 23d is larger than the total of lines 22c and 24, enter amount overpaid	**26**	
	27	Enter amount from line 26 **Credited to 2011 estimated tax** ▶ **Refunded** ▶	**27**	

Sign Here

Under penalties of perjury, I declare that I have examined this return, including accompanying schedules and statements, and to the best of my knowledge and belief, it is true, correct, and complete. Declaration of preparer (other than taxpayer) is based on all information of which preparer has any knowledge.

▶ Signature of officer | Date ▶ Title

May the IRS discuss this return with the preparer shown below (see instructions)? ☐ Yes ☐ No

Paid Preparer Use Only

Print/Type preparer's name	Preparer's signature	Date	Check ☐ if self-employed	PTIN
Firm's name ▶			Firm's EIN ▶	
Firm's address ▶			Phone no.	

For Paperwork Reduction Act Notice, see separate instructions. Cat. No. 11510H Form **1120S** (2010)

Form 1120S (2010) Page **2**

Schedule A Cost of Goods Sold (see instructions)

1	Inventory at beginning of year	1	
2	Purchases	2	
3	Cost of labor	3	
4	Additional section 263A costs (*attach statement*)	4	
5	Other costs (*attach statement*)	5	
6	**Total.** Add lines 1 through 5	6	
7	Inventory at end of year	7	
8	**Cost of goods sold.** Subtract line 7 from line 6. Enter here and on page 1, line 2	8	

9a Check all methods used for valuing closing inventory: *(i)* ☐ Cost as described in Regulations section 1.471-3

(ii) ☐ Lower of cost or market as described in Regulations section 1.471-4

(iii) ☐ Other (Specify method used and attach explanation.) ▶ ____________

b Check if there was a writedown of subnormal goods as described in Regulations section 1.471-2(c) ▶ ☐

c Check if the LIFO inventory method was adopted this tax year for any goods (if checked, attach Form 970) ▶ ☐

d If the LIFO inventory method was used for this tax year, enter percentage (or amounts) of closing inventory computed under LIFO | **9d** | |

e If property is produced or acquired for resale, do the rules of section 263A apply to the corporation? ☐ Yes ☐ No

f Was there any change in determining quantities, cost, or valuations between opening and closing inventory? ☐ Yes ☐ No

If "Yes," attach explanation.

Schedule B Other Information (see instructions)

		Yes	No
1	Check accounting method: **a** ☐ Cash **b** ☐ Accrual **c** ☐ Other (specify) ▶ ____________		
2	See the instructions and enter the: **a** Business activity ▶ ____________ **b** Product or service ▶ ____________		
3	At the end of the tax year, did the corporation own, directly or indirectly, 50% or more of the voting stock of a domestic corporation? (For rules of attribution, see section 267(c).) If "Yes," attach a statement showing: **(a)** name and employer identification number (EIN), **(b)** percentage owned, and **(c)** if 100% owned, was a qualified subchapter S subsidiary election made?		
4	Has this corporation filed, or is it required to file, **Form 8918,** Material Advisor Disclosure Statement, to provide information on any reportable transaction?		
5	Check this box if the corporation issued publicly offered debt instruments with original issue discount ▶ ☐ If checked, the corporation may have to file **Form 8281,** Information Return for Publicly Offered Original Issue Discount Instruments.		
6	If the corporation: **(a)** was a C corporation before it elected to be an S corporation **or** the corporation acquired an asset with a basis determined by reference to the basis of the asset (or the basis of any other property) in the hands of a C corporation **and (b)** has net unrealized built-in gain in excess of the net recognized built-in gain from prior years, enter the net unrealized built-in gain reduced by net recognized built-in gain from prior years *(see instructions)* ▶ $ ____________		
7	Enter the accumulated earnings and profits of the corporation at the end of the tax year. $ ____________		
8	Are the corporation's total receipts (*see instructions*) for the tax year **and** its total assets at the end of the tax year less than $250,000? If "Yes," the corporation is not required to complete Schedules L and M-1		
9	During the tax year, was a qualified subchapter S subsidiary election terminated or revoked? If "Yes," see instructions		

Schedule K Shareholders' Pro Rata Share Items

					Total amount
Income (Loss)	1	Ordinary business income (loss) (page 1, line 21)		1	
	2	Net rental real estate income (loss) (*attach Form 8825*)		2	
	3a	Other gross rental income (loss)	3a		
	b	Expenses from other rental activities (*attach statement*)	3b		
	c	Other net rental income (loss). Subtract line 3b from line 3a		3c	
	4	Interest income		4	
	5	Dividends: **a** Ordinary dividends		5a	
		b Qualified dividends	5b		
	6	Royalties		6	
	7	Net short-term capital gain (loss) (*attach Schedule D (Form 1120S)*)		7	
	8a	Net long-term capital gain (loss) (*attach Schedule D (Form 1120S)*)		8a	
	b	Collectibles (28%) gain (loss)	8b		
	c	Unrecaptured section 1250 gain (*attach statement*)	8c		
	9	Net section 1231 gain (loss) (*attach Form 4797*)		9	
	10	Other income (loss) (*see instructions*) Type ▶		10	

Form **1120S** (2010)

Form 1120S (2010) Page **3**

Section	Line	Shareholders' Pro Rata Share Items (continued)	Box	Total amount
Deductions	11	Section 179 deduction (*attach Form 4562*)	11	
	12a	Contributions	12a	
	b	Investment interest expense	12b	
	c	Section 59(e)(2) expenditures **(1)** Type ▶ **(2)** Amount ▶	12c(2)	
	d	Other deductions (*see instructions*) Type ▶	12d	
Credits	13a	Low-income housing credit (section 42(j)(5))	13a	
	b	Low-income housing credit (other)	13b	
	c	Qualified rehabilitation expenditures (rental real estate) (*attach Form 3468*)	13c	
	d	Other rental real estate credits (*see instructions*) Type ▶	13d	
	e	Other rental credits (*see instructions*) Type ▶	13e	
	f	Alcohol and cellulosic biofuel fuels credit (*attach Form 6478*)	13f	
	g	Other credits (*see instructions*) Type ▶	13g	
Foreign Transactions	14a	Name of country or U.S. possession ▶		
	b	Gross income from all sources	14b	
	c	Gross income sourced at shareholder level	14c	
		Foreign gross income sourced at corporate level		
	d	Passive category	14d	
	e	General category	14e	
	f	Other (*attach statement*)	14f	
		Deductions allocated and apportioned at shareholder level		
	g	Interest expense	14g	
	h	Other	14h	
		Deductions allocated and apportioned at corporate level to foreign source income		
	i	Passive category	14i	
	j	General category	14j	
	k	Other (*attach statement*)	14k	
		Other information		
	l	Total foreign taxes (check one): ▶ ☐ Paid ☐ Accrued	14l	
	m	Reduction in taxes available for credit (*attach statement*)	14m	
	n	Other foreign tax information (*attach statement*)		
Alternative Minimum Tax (AMT) Items	15a	Post-1986 depreciation adjustment	15a	
	b	Adjusted gain or loss	15b	
	c	Depletion (other than oil and gas)	15c	
	d	Oil, gas, and geothermal properties—gross income	15d	
	e	Oil, gas, and geothermal properties—deductions	15e	
	f	Other AMT items (*attach statement*)	15f	
Items Affecting Shareholder Basis	16a	Tax-exempt interest income	16a	
	b	Other tax-exempt income	16b	
	c	Nondeductible expenses	16c	
	d	Distributions (*attach statement if required*) (*see instructions*)	16d	
	e	Repayment of loans from shareholders	16e	
Other Information	17a	Investment income	17a	
	b	Investment expenses	17b	
	c	Dividend distributions paid from accumulated earnings and profits	17c	
	d	Other items and amounts (*attach statement*)		
Reconciliation	18	**Income/loss reconciliation.** Combine the amounts on lines 1 through 10 in the far right column. From the result, subtract the sum of the amounts on lines 11 through 12d and 14l	18	

Form **1120S** (2010)

Form 1120S (2010) Page **4**

Schedule L **Balance Sheets per Books**

Assets		Beginning of tax year		End of tax year	
		(a)	**(b)**	**(c)**	**(d)**
1	Cash				
2a	Trade notes and accounts receivable				
b	Less allowance for bad debts	( )		( )	
3	Inventories				
4	U.S. government obligations				
5	Tax-exempt securities (*see instructions*)				
6	Other current assets (*attach statement*)				
7	Loans to shareholders				
8	Mortgage and real estate loans				
9	Other investments (*attach statement*)				
10a	Buildings and other depreciable assets				
b	Less accumulated depreciation	( )		( )	
11a	Depletable assets				
b	Less accumulated depletion	( )		( )	
12	Land (net of any amortization)				
13a	Intangible assets (amortizable only)				
b	Less accumulated amortization	( )		( )	
14	Other assets (*attach statement*)				
15	Total assets				
	Liabilities and Shareholders' Equity				
16	Accounts payable				
17	Mortgages, notes, bonds payable in less than 1 year				
18	Other current liabilities (*attach statement*)				
19	Loans from shareholders				
20	Mortgages, notes, bonds payable in 1 year or more				
21	Other liabilities (*attach statement*)				
22	Capital stock				
23	Additional paid-in capital				
24	Retained earnings				
25	Adjustments to shareholders' equity (*attach statement*)				
26	Less cost of treasury stock		( )		( )
27	Total liabilities and shareholders' equity				

Schedule M-1 **Reconciliation of Income (Loss) per Books With Income (Loss) per Return**

Note: Schedule M-3 required instead of Schedule M-1 if total assets are $10 million or more—see instructions

1	Net income (loss) per books		5	Income recorded on books this year not included on Schedule K, lines 1 through 10 (itemize): a Tax-exempt interest $	
2	Income included on Schedule K, lines 1, 2, 3c, 4, 5a, 6, 7, 8a, 9, and 10, not recorded on books this year (itemize):				
3	Expenses recorded on books this year not included on Schedule K, lines 1 through 12 and 14l (itemize): a Depreciation $ b Travel and entertainment $		6	Deductions included on Schedule K, lines 1 through 12 and 14l, not charged against book income this year (itemize): a Depreciation $	
			7	Add lines 5 and 6	
4	Add lines 1 through 3		8	Income (loss) (Schedule K, line 18). Line 4 less line 7	

Schedule M-2 **Analysis of Accumulated Adjustments Account, Other Adjustments Account, and Shareholders' Undistributed Taxable Income Previously Taxed** (see instructions)

		(a) Accumulated adjustments account	**(b)** Other adjustments account	**(c)** Shareholders' undistributed taxable income previously taxed
1	Balance at beginning of tax year			
2	Ordinary income from page 1, line 21			
3	Other additions			
4	Loss from page 1, line 21	( )		
5	Other reductions	( )	( )	
6	Combine lines 1 through 5			
7	Distributions other than dividend distributions			
8	Balance at end of tax year. Subtract line 7 from line 6			

671110

☐ Final K-1 ☐ Amended K-1 OMB No. 1545-0130

Schedule K-1 (Form 1120S) **2010**

Department of the Treasury
Internal Revenue Service

For calendar year 2010, or tax year beginning ____________, 2010 ending ____________, 20 ______

Shareholder's Share of Income, Deductions, Credits, etc.

▶ See back of form and separate instructions.

Part I Information About the Corporation

A Corporation's employer identification number

B Corporation's name, address, city, state, and ZIP code

C IRS Center where corporation filed return

Part II Information About the Shareholder

D Shareholder's identifying number

E Shareholder's name, address, city, state, and ZIP code

F Shareholder's percentage of stock ownership for tax year . . . . ____________ %

For IRS Use Only

Part III Shareholder's Share of Current Year Income, Deductions, Credits, and Other Items

1	Ordinary business income (loss)	13	Credits
2	Net rental real estate income (loss)		
3	Other net rental income (loss)		
4	Interest income		
5a	Ordinary dividends		
5b	Qualified dividends	14	Foreign transactions
6	Royalties		
7	Net short-term capital gain (loss)		
8a	Net long-term capital gain (loss)		
8b	Collectibles (28%) gain (loss)		
8c	Unrecaptured section 1250 gain		
9	Net section 1231 gain (loss)		
10	Other income (loss)	15	Alternative minimum tax (AMT) items
11	Section 179 deduction	16	Items affecting shareholder basis
12	Other deductions		
		17	Other information

* See attached statement for additional information.

SCHEDULE M-3 (Form 1120S)

Department of the Treasury
Internal Revenue Service

Net Income (Loss) Reconciliation for S Corporations With Total Assets of $10 Million or More

► Attach to Form 1120S.
► See separate instructions.

OMB No. 1545-0130

2010

Name of corporation

Employer identification number

Part I **Financial Information and Net Income (Loss) Reconciliation** (see instructions)

1a Did the corporation prepare a certified audited non-tax-basis income statement for the period ending with or within this tax year? (See instructions if multiple non-tax-basis income statements are prepared.)

☐ **Yes.** Skip line 1b and complete lines 2 through 11 with respect to that income statement.
☐ **No.** Go to line 1b.

b Did the corporation prepare a non-tax-basis income statement for that period?

☐ **Yes.** Complete lines 2 through 11 with respect to that income statement.
☐ **No.** Skip lines 2 through 3b and enter the corporation's net income (loss) per its books and records on line 4a.

2 Enter the income statement period: Beginning ____/____/____ Ending ____/____/____

3a Has the corporation's income statement been restated for the income statement period on line 2?

☐ **Yes.** (If "Yes," attach an explanation and the amount of each item restated.)
☐ **No.**

b Has the corporation's income statement been restated for any of the five income statement periods preceding the period on line 2?

☐ **Yes.** (If "Yes," attach an explanation and the amount of each item restated.)
☐ **No.**

4a	Worldwide consolidated net income (loss) from income statement source identified in Part I, line 1 .	**4a**	
b	Indicate accounting standard used for line 4a (see instructions): (1) ☐ GAAP (2) ☐ IFRS (3) ☐ Tax-basis (4) ☐ Other (specify) ________		
5a	Net income from nonincludible foreign entities (attach schedule)	**5a**	( )
b	Net loss from nonincludible foreign entities (attach schedule and enter as a positive amount) . . .	**5b**	
6a	Net income from nonincludible U.S. entities (attach schedule)	**6a**	( )
b	Net loss from nonincludible U.S. entities (attach schedule and enter as a positive amount)	**6b**	
7a	Net income (loss) of other foreign disregarded entities (attach schedule)	**7a**	
b	Net income (loss) of other U.S. disregarded entities (except qualified subchapter S subsidiaries) (attach schedule)	**7b**	
c	Net income (loss) of other qualified subchapter S subsidiaries (QSubs) (attach schedule)	**7c**	
8	Adjustment to eliminations of transactions between includible entities and nonincludible entities (attach schedule)	**8**	
9	Adjustment to reconcile income statement period to tax year (attach schedule)	**9**	
10	Other adjustments to reconcile to amount on line 11 (attach schedule)	**10**	
11	**Net income (loss) per income statement of the corporation.** Combine lines 4 through 10 . . . **Note.** Part I, line 11, must equal Part II, line 26, column (a).	**11**	

12 Enter the total amount (not just the corporation's share) of the assets and liabilities of all entities included or removed on the following lines:

	Total Assets	Total Liabilities
a Included on Part I, line 4		
b Removed on Part I, line 5		
c Removed on Part I, line 6		
d Included on Part I, line 7		

Schedule M-3 (Form 1120S) 2010 Page **2**

Name of corporation | **Employer identification number**

Part II **Reconciliation of Net Income (Loss) per Income Statement of the Corporation With Total Income (Loss) per Return** (see instructions)

	Income (Loss) Items	(a) Income (Loss) per Income Statement	(b) Temporary Difference	(c) Permanent Difference	(d) Income (Loss) per Tax Return
1	Income (loss) from equity method foreign corporations (attach schedule)				
2	Gross foreign dividends not previously taxed				
3	Subpart F, QEF, and similar income inclusions (attach schedule)				
4	Gross foreign distributions previously taxed (attach schedule)				
5	Income (loss) from equity method U.S. corporations (attach schedule)				
6	U.S. dividends not eliminated in tax consolidation				
7	Income (loss) from U.S. partnerships (attach schedule)				
8	Income (loss) from foreign partnerships (attach schedule)				
9	Income (loss) from other pass-through entities (attach schedule)				
10	Items relating to reportable transactions (attach details)				
11	Interest income (attach Form 8916-A)				
12	Total accrual to cash adjustment				
13	Hedging transactions				
14	Mark-to-market income (loss)				
15	Cost of goods sold (attach Form 8916-A)	( )			( )
16	Sale versus lease (for sellers and/or lessors)				
17	Section 481(a) adjustments				
18	Unearned/deferred revenue				
19	Income recognition from long-term contracts				
20	Original issue discount and other imputed interest				
21a	Income statement gain/loss on sale, exchange, abandonment, worthlessness, or other disposition of assets other than inventory and pass-through entities				
b	Gross capital gains from Schedule D, excluding amounts from pass-through entities				
c	Gross capital losses from Schedule D, excluding amounts from pass-through entities, abandonment losses, and worthless stock losses				
d	Net gain/loss reported on Form 4797, line 17, excluding amounts from pass-through entities, abandonment losses, and worthless stock losses				
e	Abandonment losses				
f	Worthless stock losses (attach details)				
g	Other gain/loss on disposition of assets other than inventory				
22	Other income (loss) items with differences (attach schedule)				
23	**Total income (loss) items.** Combine lines 1 through 22				
24	**Total expense/deduction items** (from Part III, line 32)				
25	Other items with no differences				
26	**Reconciliation totals.** Combine lines 23 through 25				

Note. Line 26, column (a), must equal the amount on Part I, line 11, and column (d) must equal Form 1120S, Schedule K, line 18.

Schedule M-3 (Form 1120S) 2010 Page **3**

Name of corporation	**Employer identification number**

Part III **Reconciliation of Net Income (Loss) per Income Statement of the Corporation With Total Income (Loss) per Return—Expense/Deduction Items** (see instructions)

	Expense/Deduction Items	(a) Expense per Income Statement	(b) Temporary Difference	(c) Permanent Difference	(d) Deduction per Tax Return
1	U.S. current income tax expense				
2	U.S. deferred income tax expense				
3	State and local current income tax expense				
4	State and local deferred income tax expense				
5	Foreign current income tax expense (other than foreign withholding taxes)				
6	Foreign deferred income tax expense				
7	Equity-based compensation				
8	Meals and entertainment				
9	Fines and penalties				
10	Judgments, damages, awards, and similar costs				
11	Pension and profit-sharing				
12	Other post-retirement benefits				
13	Deferred compensation				
14	Charitable contribution of cash and tangible property				
15	Charitable contribution of intangible property				
16	Current year acquisition or reorganization investment banking fees				
17	Current year acquisition or reorganization legal and accounting fees				
18	Current year acquisition/reorganization other costs				
19	Amortization/impairment of goodwill				
20	Amortization of acquisition, reorganization, and start-up costs				
21	Other amortization or impairment write-offs				
22	Section 198 environmental remediation costs				
23a	Depletion—Oil & Gas				
b	Depletion—Other than Oil & Gas				
24	Depreciation				
25	Bad debt expense				
26	Interest expense (attach Form 8916-A)				
27	Corporate owned life insurance premiums				
28	Purchase versus lease (for purchasers and/or lessees)				
29	Research and development costs (attach schedule)				
30	Section 118 exclusion (attach schedule)				
31	Other expense/deduction items with differences (attach schedule)				
32	**Total expense/deduction items.** Combine lines 1 through 31. Enter here and on Part II, line 24, reporting positive amounts as negative and negative amounts as positive				

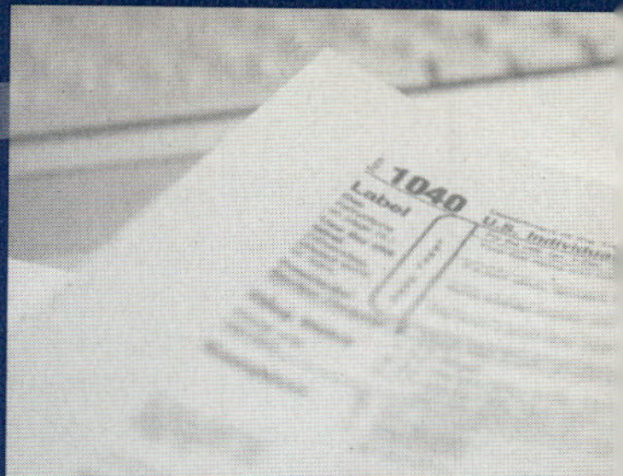

Appendix C

GLOSSARY

The key terms in this glossary have been defined to reflect their conventional use in the field of taxation. The definitions may therefore be incomplete for other purposes.

A

Abandoned spouse. The abandoned spouse provision enables a married taxpayer with a dependent child whose spouse did not live in the taxpayer's home during the last six months of the tax year to file as a head of household rather than as married filing separately.

Accelerated cost recovery system (ACRS). A method in which the cost of tangible property is recovered over a prescribed period of time. The approach disregards salvage value, imposes a period of cost recovery that depends upon the classification of the asset into one of various recovery periods, and prescribes the applicable percentage of cost that can be deducted each year. § 168.

Accelerated death benefits. The amount received from a life insurance policy by the insured who is terminally ill or chronically ill. Any realized gain may be excluded from the gross income of the insured if the policy is surrendered to the insurer or is sold to a licensed viatical settlement provider. § 101(g).

Accident and health benefits. Employee fringe benefits provided by employers through the payment of health and accident insurance premiums or the establishment of employer-funded medical reimbursement plans. Employers generally are entitled to a deduction for such payments, whereas employees generally exclude such fringe benefits from gross income. §§ 105 and 106.

Accountable plan. An accountable plan is a type of expense reimbursement plan that requires an employee to render an adequate accounting to the employer and return any excess reimbursement or allowance. If the expense qualifies, it will be treated as a deduction *for* AGI.

Accounting income. The accountant's concept of income is generally based upon the realization principle. Financial accounting income may differ from taxable income (e.g., accelerated depreciation might be used for Federal income tax and straight-line depreciation for financial accounting purposes). Differences are included in a reconciliation of taxable and accounting income on Schedule M–1 or Schedule M–3 of Form 1120 for corporations.

Accounting method. The method under which income and expenses are determined for tax purposes. Important accounting methods include the cash basis and the accrual basis. Special methods are available for the reporting of gain on installment sales, recognition of income on construction projects (the completed contract and percentage of completion methods), and the valuation of inventories (last-in, first-out and first-in, first-out). §§ 446–474.

Accounting period. The period of time, usually a year, used by a taxpayer for the determination of tax liability. Unless a fiscal year is chosen, taxpayers must determine and pay their income tax liability by using the calendar year (January 1 through December 31) as the period of measurement. An example of a fiscal year is July 1 through June 30. A change in accounting period (e.g., from a calendar year to a fiscal year) generally requires the consent of the IRS. Usually, taxpayers are free to select either an initial calendar or a fiscal year without the consent of the IRS. §§ 441–444.

Accrual method. A method of accounting that reflects expenses incurred and income earned for any one tax year. In contrast to the cash basis of accounting, expenses need not be paid to be deductible, nor need income be received to be taxable. Unearned income (e.g., prepaid interest and rent) generally is taxed in the year of receipt regardless of the method of accounting used by the taxpayer. § 446(c)(2).

Accumulated adjustments account (AAA). An account that aggregates an S corporation's post-1982 income, loss, and deductions for the tax year (including nontaxable income and nondeductible losses and expenses). After the year-end income and expense adjustments are made, the account is reduced by distributions made during the tax year.

Accumulated earnings and profits. Net undistributed tax-basis earnings of a corporation aggregated from March 1, 1913, to the end of the prior tax year. Used to determine the amount of dividend income associated with a distribution to shareholders. § 316 and Reg. § 1.316–2.

Accuracy-related penalty. Major civil taxpayer penalties relating to the accuracy of tax return data, including misstatements stemming from taxpayer negligence and improper valuation of income and deductions, are coordinated under this umbrella term. The penalty usually equals 20 percent of the understated tax liability.

ACE adjustment. An adjustment in computing corporate alternative minimum taxable income (AMTI), computed at 75 percent of the excess of adjusted current earnings (ACE) over unadjusted AMTI. ACE computations reflect longer and slower cost recovery deductions and other restrictions on the timing of certain recognition events. Exempt interest, life insurance proceeds, and other receipts that are included in earnings and profits but not in taxable income also increase the ACE adjustment. If unadjusted AMTI exceeds ACE, the ACE adjustment is negative. The negative adjustment is limited to the aggregate of the positive adjustments under ACE for prior years, reduced by any previously claimed negative adjustments.

Acquiescence. Agreement by the IRS on the results reached in certain judicial decisions; sometimes abbreviated *Acq.* or *A.*

Acquisition indebtedness. Debt incurred in acquiring, constructing, or substantially improving a qualified residence of the taxpayer. The interest on such loans is deductible as qualified residence interest. However, interest on such debt is deductible only on the portion of the indebtedness that does not exceed $1,000,000 ($500,000 for married persons filing separate returns). § 163(h)(3).

Active income. Active income includes wages, salary, commissions, bonuses, profits from a trade or business in which the taxpayer is a material participant, gain on the sale or other disposition of assets used in an active trade or business, and income from intangible property if the taxpayer's personal efforts significantly contributed to the creation of the property. The passive activity loss rules require classification of income and losses into three categories with active income being one of them.

Ad valorem tax. A tax imposed on the value of property. The most common ad valorem tax is that imposed by states, counties, and cities on real estate. Ad valorem taxes can be imposed on personal property as well.

Additional depreciation. The excess of the amount of depreciation actually deducted over the amount that would have been deducted had the straight-line method been used. § 1250(b).

Additional first-year depreciation. See *fifty percent additional first-year depreciation* and *one hundred percent additional first-year depreciation.*

Adjusted basis. The cost or other basis of property reduced by depreciation allowed or allowable and increased by capital improvements. Other special adjustments are provided in § 1016 and the related Regulations.

Adoption expenses credit. A provision intended to assist taxpayers who incur nonrecurring costs directly associated with the adoption process such as legal costs, social service review costs, and transportation costs. Up to $13,360 ($13,360 for a child with special needs regardless of the actual adoption expenses) of costs incurred to adopt an eligible child qualify for the credit. A taxpayer may claim the credit in the year qualifying expenses are paid or incurred if the expenses are paid during or after the year in which the adoption is finalized. For qualifying expenses paid or incurred in a tax year prior to the year the adoption is finalized, the credit must be claimed in the tax year following the tax year during which the expenses are paid or incurred. § 23.

Affiliated group. A parent-subsidiary group of corporations that is eligible to elect to file on a consolidated basis. Eighty percent ownership of the voting power and value of all of the corporations must be achieved on every day of the tax year, and an identifiable parent corporation must exist (i.e., it must own at least 80 percent of another group member without applying attribution rules).

Aggregate concept. The theory of partnership taxation under which, in certain cases, a partnership is treated as a mere collection of the activities of each partner.

Alimony and separate maintenance payments. Alimony deductions result from the payment of a legal obligation arising from the termination of a marital relationship. Payments designated as alimony generally are included in the gross income of the recipient and are deductible *for* AGI by the payor.

Alimony recapture. The amount of alimony that previously has been included in the gross income of the recipient and deducted by the payor that now is deducted by the recipient and included in the gross income of the payor as the result of front-loading. § 71(f).

All events test. For accrual method taxpayers, income is earned when (1) all the events have occurred that fix the right to receive the income and (2) the amount can be determined with reasonable accuracy. Accrual of income cannot be postponed simply because a portion of the income may have to be returned in a subsequent period. The all events test also is utilized to determine when expenses can be deducted by an accrual basis taxpayer. The application of the test could cause a variation between the treatment of an item for accounting and for tax purposes. For example, a reserve for warranty expense may be properly accruable under generally accepted accounting principles but not be deductible under the Federal income tax law. Because of the application of the all events test, the deduction becomes available in the year the warranty obligation becomes fixed and the amount is determinable with reasonable certainty. Reg. §§ 1.446–1(c)(1)(ii) and 1.461–1(a)(2).

Allocate. The assignment of income for various tax purposes. A multistate corporation's nonbusiness income usually is allocated to the state where the nonbusiness assets are located; it is not apportioned with the rest of the entity's income. The income and expense items of an estate or trust are allocated between income and corpus components. Specific items of income, expense, gain, loss, and credit can be allocated to specific partners, if a substantial economic nontax purpose for the allocation is established.

Alternate valuation date. Property passing from a decedent by death may be valued for estate tax purposes as of the date of death or the alternate valuation date. The alternate valuation date is six months from the date of death or the date the property is disposed of by the estate, whichever comes first. To use the alternate valuation date, the executor or administrator of the estate must make an affirmative election. Election of the alternate valuation date is not available unless it decreases the amount of the gross estate *and* reduces the estate tax liability.

Alternative depreciation system (ADS). A cost recovery system that produces a smaller deduction than would be calculated under ACRS or MACRS. The alternative system must be used in certain instances and can be elected in other instances. § 168(g).

Alternative minimum tax (AMT). The AMT is a fixed percentage of alternative minimum taxable income (AMTI). AMTI generally starts with the taxpayer's adjusted gross income (for individuals) or taxable income (for other taxpayers). To this amount, the taxpayer (1) adds designated preference items (e.g., tax-exempt interest income on private activity bonds), (2) makes other specified adjustments (e.g., to reflect a longer, straight-line cost recovery deduction), (3) subtracts certain AMT itemized deductions for individuals (e.g., interest incurred on housing but not taxes paid), and (4) subtracts an exemption amount. The taxpayer must pay the greater of the resulting AMT (reduced by only the foreign tax credit) or the regular income tax (reduced by all allowable tax credits). The AMT does not apply to certain small C corporations. AMT preferences and adjustments are assigned to partners, LLC members, and S corporation shareholders.

Alternative minimum tax credit. The AMT can result from timing differences that give rise to positive adjustments in calculating the AMT base. To provide equity for the taxpayer when these timing differences reverse, the regular tax liability may be reduced by a tax credit for a prior year's minimum tax liability attributable to timing differences. § 53.

Alternative tax. An option that is allowed in computing the tax on net capital gain. For the corporate taxpayer, the rate is 35 percent (the same as the highest regular corporate tax rate). Thus, for corporate taxpayers, the alternative tax does not produce a beneficial result. For noncorporate taxpayers, the rate is usually 15 percent (but is 25 percent for unrecaptured § 1250 gain and 28 percent for collectibles and § 1202 gain). However, if the noncorporate taxpayer is in either the 10 percent or the 15 percent tax bracket, the alternative tax rate is 0 percent in 2008, 2009, 2010, and 2011 (rather than 15 percent). Prior to 2008, the 0 percent rate was 5 percent. §§ 1(h) and 1201.

Alternative tax NOL deduction (ATNOLD). In calculating the AMT, the taxpayer is allowed to deduct NOL carryovers and carrybacks. However, for this purpose, a special calculation is required that is referred to as the ATNOLD. The regular income tax is modified for AMT adjustments and preferences to produce the ATNOLD. § 56(d).

American Opportunity credit. This credit replaces the HOPE scholarship credit for 2009, 2010, 2011, and 2012 and applies for qualifying expenses for the first four years of postsecondary education. Qualified expenses include tuition and related expenses and books and other course materials. Room and board are ineligible for the credit. The maximum credit available per student is $2,500 (100 percent of the first $2,000 of qualified expenses and 25 percent of the next $2,000 of qualified expenses). Eligible students include the taxpayer, taxpayer's spouse, and taxpayer's dependents. To qualify for the credit, a student must take at least one-half the full-time course load for at least one academic term at a qualifying educational institution. The credit is phased out for higher-income taxpayers. § 25A.

Amortization. The tax deduction for the cost or other basis of an intangible asset over the asset's estimated useful life. Examples of amortizable intangibles include patents, copyrights, and leasehold interests. The intangible goodwill can be amortized for income tax purposes over a 15-year period.

Amount realized. The amount received by a taxpayer upon the sale or exchange of property. Amount realized is the sum of the cash and the fair market value of any property or services received by the taxpayer, plus any related debt assumed by the buyer. Determining the amount realized is the starting point for arriving at realized gain or loss. § 1001(b).

AMT adjustments. In calculating AMTI, certain adjustments are added to or deducted from taxable income. These adjustments generally reflect timing differences. § 56.

AMT exclusions. A credit that can be used to reduce the regular tax liability in future tax years is available in connection with the AMT (AMT credit). The credit is applicable only with respect to the AMT that results from timing differences. It is not available in connection with AMT exclusions, which include the standard deduction, personal exemptions, medical expenses deductible in calculating the regular income tax that are not deductible in computing the AMT, other itemized deductions that are not allowable for AMT purposes, excess percentage depletion, and tax-exempt interest on specified private activity bonds.

AMT preferences. In calculating alternative minimum taxable income (AMTI), certain preference items are added to taxable income. AMT preferences generally reflect differences between the regular tax and the alternative minimum tax (AMT) computational bases. For instance, interest income from certain state and local bonds may be an AMT preference item.

Annual exclusion. In computing the taxable gifts for the year, each donor excludes the first $13,000 of a gift to each donee. Usually, the annual exclusion is not available for gifts of future interests. § 2503(b).

Annuity. A fixed sum of money payable to a person at specified times for a specified period of time or for life. If the party making the payment (i.e., the obligor) is regularly engaged in this type of business (e.g., an insurance company), the arrangement is classified as a commercial annuity. A so-called private annuity involves an obligor that is not regularly engaged in selling annuities (e.g., a charity or family member).

Apportion. The assignment of the business income of a multistate corporation to specific states for income taxation. Usually, the apportionment procedure accounts for the property, payroll, and sales activity levels of the various states, and a proportionate assignment of the entity's total income is made, using a three-factor apportionment formula. These activities indicate the commercial domicile of the corporation, relative to that income. Some states exclude nonbusiness income from the apportionment procedure; they allocate nonbusiness income to the states where the nonbusiness assets are located.

ASC 450 (SFAS 5). Under Generally Accepted Accounting Principles, the rules for the financial reporting of contingent liabilities, including deferred taxes.

ASC 740 (SFAS 109). Under Generally Accepted Accounting Principles, the rules for the financial reporting of the tax expense of an enterprise. Permanent differences affect the enterprise's effective tax rate. Temporary differences create a deferred tax asset or a deferred tax liability on the balance sheet.

ASC 740-10 (FIN 48). Under Generally Accepted Accounting Principles, an interpretation of ASC 740 (SFAS 109) relating to when a tax benefit should be reported in an enterprise's financial statements. A tax benefit should be recorded for book purposes only if it is more likely than not that the taxpayer's filing position will be sustained after an audit, administrative appeal, and the highest applicable judicial review.

ASC 740-30 (APB 23). Under Generally Accepted Accounting Principles, the rules for the financial reporting of the tax expense relative to a U.S. corporation's non-U.S. subsidiary. If the parent documents that it is permanently reinvesting the non-U.S. earnings of a non-U.S. subsidiary, the parent does not record as an expense any U.S. income tax that the parent might pay on such earnings (i.e., the book tax expense is deferred until such earnings are, if ever, repatriated to the United States).

Assignment of income. A taxpayer attempts to avoid the recognition of income by assigning to another the property that generates the income. Such a procedure will not avoid the recognition of income by the taxpayer making the assignment if the income was earned at the point of the transfer. In this case, the income is taxed to the person who earns it.

Assumption of liabilities. In a corporate formation, corporate takeover, or asset purchase, the new owner often takes assets and agrees to assume preexisting debt. Such actions do not create boot received on the transaction for the new shareholder, unless there is no *bona fide* business purpose for the exchange, or the principal purpose of the debt assumption is the avoidance of tax liabilities. Gain is recognized to the extent that liabilities assumed exceed the aggregated bases of the transferred assets. § 357.

At-risk limitation. Generally, a taxpayer can deduct losses related to a trade or business, S corporation, partnership, or investment asset only to the extent of the at-risk amount.

Attribution. Under certain circumstances, the tax law applies attribution (constructive ownership) rules to assign to one taxpayer the ownership interest of another taxpayer. If, for example, the stock of Gold Corporation is held 60 percent by Marsha and 40 percent by Sidney, Marsha may be deemed to own 100 percent of Gold Corporation if Marsha and Sidney are mother and son. In that case, the stock owned by Sidney is attributed to Marsha. Stated differently, Marsha has a 60 percent direct and a 40 percent indirect interest in Gold Corporation. It can also be said that Marsha is the constructive owner of Sidney's interest.

Automatic mileage method. Automobile expenses are generally deductible only to the extent the automobile is used in business or for the production of income. Personal commuting expenses are not deductible. The taxpayer may deduct actual expenses (including depreciation and insurance), or the standard (automatic) mileage rate may be used (51 cents per mile for 2011 and 50 cents per mile for 2010). Automobile expenses incurred for medical purposes or in connection with job-related moving expenses are deductible to the extent of actual out-of-pocket expenses or at the rate of 19 cents per mile in 2011 (16.5 cents per mile for 2010). For charitable activities, the rate is 14 cents per mile.

B

Bad debts. A deduction is permitted if a business account receivable subsequently becomes partially or completely worthless, providing the income arising from the debt previously was included in income. Available methods are the specific charge-off method and the reserve method. However, except for certain financial institutions, TRA of 1986 repealed the use of the reserve method for 1987 and thereafter. If the reserve method is used, partially or totally worthless accounts are charged to the reserve. A nonbusiness bad debt deduction is allowed as a short-term capital loss if the loan did not arise in connection with the creditor's trade or business activities. Loans between related parties (family members) generally are classified as nonbusiness. § 166.

Balance sheet approach. The process under ASC 740 (SFAS 109) by which an entity's deferred tax expense or deferred tax benefit is determined as a result of the reporting period's changes in the balance sheet's deferred tax asset and deferred tax liability accounts.

Basis in partnership interest. The acquisition cost of the partner's ownership interest in the partnership. Includes purchase price and associated debt acquired from other partners and in the course of the entity's trade or business.

Boot. Cash or property of a type not included in the definition of a nontaxable exchange. The receipt of boot causes an otherwise nontaxable transfer to become taxable to the extent of the lesser of the fair market value of the boot or the realized gain on the transfer. For example, see transfers to controlled corporations under § 351(b) and like-kind exchanges under § 1031(b).

Branch profits tax. A tax on the effectively connected earnings and profits of the U.S. branch of a foreign corporation. The tax is levied in addition to the usual § 11 tax, in an amount equal to 30 percent of the dividend equivalent amount. Treaties can override the tax or reduce the withholding percentage. Earnings reinvested in the U.S. operations of the entity are not subject to the tax until repatriation.

Brother-sister controlled group. More than one corporation owned by the same shareholders. If, for example, Chris and Pat each own one-half of the stock in Wren Corporation and Redbird Corporation, Wren and Redbird form a brother-sister controlled group.

Built-in gains tax. A penalty tax designed to discourage a shift of the incidence of taxation on unrealized gains from a C corporation to its shareholders, via an S election. Under this provision, any recognized gain during the first 10 (or 7 or 5) years of S status generates a corporate-level tax on a base not to exceed the aggregate untaxed built-in gains brought into the S corporation upon its election from C corporation taxable years.

Built-in loss property. Property contributed to a corporation under § 351 or as a contribution to capital that has a basis in excess of its fair market value. An adjustment is necessary to step down the basis of the property to its fair market value. The adjustment prevents the corporation and the contributing shareholder from obtaining a double tax benefit. The corporation allocates the adjustment proportionately among the assets with the built-in loss. As an alternative to the corporate adjustment, the shareholder may elect to reduce the basis in the stock.

Business bad debt. A tax deduction allowed for obligations obtained in connection with a trade or business that have become either partially or completely worthless. In contrast to nonbusiness bad debts, business bad debts are deductible as business expenses. § 166.

Bypass amount. The amount that can be transferred by gift or at death free of any unified transfer tax. For 2011, the bypass amount is $5 million for estate tax and $5 million for gift tax.

Bypass election. In the context of a distribution by an S corporation, an election made by the entity to designate that the distribution is first from accumulated earnings and profits, and only then from the accumulated adjustments account (AAA).

C

C corporation. A separate taxable entity, subject to the rules of Subchapter C of the Code. This business form may create a double taxation effect relative to its shareholders. The entity is subject to the regular corporate tax and a number of penalty taxes at the Federal level.

Cafeteria plan. An employee benefit plan under which an employee is allowed to select from among a variety of employer-provided fringe benefits. Some of the benefits may be taxable, and some may be statutory nontaxable benefits (e.g., health and accident insurance and group term life insurance). The employee is taxed only on the taxable benefits selected. A cafeteria benefit plan is also referred to as a flexible benefit plan. § 125.

Capital account. The financial accounting analog of a partner's tax basis in the entity.

Capital asset. Broadly speaking, all assets are capital except those specifically excluded from that definition by the Code. Major categories of noncapital assets include property held for resale in the normal course of business (inventory), trade accounts and notes receivable, and depreciable property and real estate used in a trade or business (§ 1231 assets). § 1221.

Capital contribution. Various means by which a shareholder makes additional funds available to the corporation (placed at the risk of the business), sometimes without the receipt of additional stock. If no stock is received, the contributions are added to the basis of the shareholder's existing stock investment and do not generate gross income to the corporation. § 118.

Capital gain. The gain from the sale or exchange of a capital asset.

Capital gain property. Property contributed to a charitable organization that, if sold rather than contributed, would have resulted in long-term capital gain to the donor.

Capital interest. Usually, the percentage of the entity's net assets that a partner would receive on liquidation. Typically determined by the partner's capital sharing ratio.

Capital loss. The loss from the sale or exchange of a capital asset.

Capital sharing ratio. A partner's percentage ownership of the entity's capital.

Cash equivalent doctrine. Generally, a cash basis taxpayer does not report income until cash is constructively or actually received. Under the cash equivalent doctrine, cash basis taxpayers are required to report income if they receive the equivalent of cash (e.g., property is received) in a taxable transaction.

Cash method. See *cash receipts method.*

Cash receipts method. A method of accounting that reflects deductions as paid and income as received in any one tax year. However, deductions for prepaid expenses that benefit more than one tax year (e.g., prepaid rent and prepaid interest) usually are spread over the period benefited rather than deducted in the year paid. § 446(c)(1).

Casualty loss. A casualty is defined as "the complete or partial destruction of property resulting from an identifiable event of a sudden, unexpected or unusual nature" (e.g., floods, storms, fires, auto accidents). Individuals may deduct a casualty loss only if the loss is incurred in a trade or business or in a transaction entered into for profit or arises from fire, storm, shipwreck, or other casualty or from theft. Individuals usually deduct personal casualty losses as itemized deductions subject to a $100 nondeductible amount and to an annual floor equal to 10 percent of adjusted gross income that applies after the $100 per casualty floor has been applied. Special rules are provided for the netting of certain casualty gains and losses.

Charitable contributions. Contributions are deductible (subject to various restrictions and ceiling limitations) if made to qualified nonprofit charitable organizations. A cash basis taxpayer is entitled to a deduction solely in the year of payment. Accrual basis corporations may accrue contributions at year-end if payment is properly authorized before the end of the year and payment is made within two and one-half months after the end of the year. § 170.

Check-the-box regulation. A business entity can elect to be taxed as a partnership, S corporation, or C corporation by indicating its preference on the tax return. Legal structure and operations are irrelevant in this regard. Thus, by using the check-the-box rules prudently, an entity can select the most attractive tax results offered by the Code, without being bound by legal forms. Not available if the entity is incorporated under state law.

Child tax credit. A tax credit based solely on the number of qualifying children under age 17. The maximum credit available is $1,000 per child through 2011. A qualifying child must be claimed as a dependent on a parent's tax return in order to qualify for the credit. Taxpayers who qualify for the child tax credit may also qualify for a supplemental credit. The supplemental credit is treated as a component of the earned income credit and is therefore refundable. The credit is phased out for higher-income taxpayers. § 24.

Circuit Court of Appeals. Any of 13 Federal courts that consider tax matters appealed from the U.S. Tax Court, a U.S. District Court, or the U.S. Court of Federal Claims. Appeal from a U.S. Court of Appeals is to the U.S. Supreme Court by *Certiorari.*

Circular 230. A portion of the Federal tax Regulations that describes the levels of conduct at which a tax preparer must operate. Circular 230 dictates, for instance, that a tax preparer may not charge an unconscionable fee or delay the execution of a tax audit with inappropriate delays. Circular 230 requires that there be a realistic possibility that a tax return position be sustained upon review, and that no frivolous returns be filed.

Circulation expenditures. Expenditures of establishing or increasing the circulation of a periodical that may be either expensed or capitalized. If such expenses are expensed, an adjustment will occur for AMT purposes, since the expenses are deducted over a three-year period for AMT purposes. Over the three-year period, both positive and negative AMT adjustments will be produced. § 173.

Citator. A tax research resource that presents the judicial history of a court case and traces the subsequent references to the case. When these references include the citating cases' evaluations of the cited case's precedents, the research can obtain some measure of the efficacy and reliability of the original holding.

Claim of right doctrine. A judicially imposed doctrine applicable to both cash and accrual basis taxpayers that holds that an amount is includible in income upon actual or constructive receipt if the taxpayer has an unrestricted claim to the payment. For the tax treatment of amounts repaid when previously included in income under the claim of right doctrine, see § 1341.

Closely held corporation. A corporation where stock ownership is not widely dispersed. Rather, a few shareholders are in control of corporate policy and are in a position to benefit personally from that policy.

Closing agreement. In a tax dispute, the parties sign a closing agreement to spell out the terms under which the matters are settled. The agreement is binding on both the Service and the taxpayer.

Collectibles. A special type of capital asset, the gain from which is taxed at a maximum rate of 28 percent if the holding period is more than one year. Examples include art, rugs, antiques, gems, metals, stamps, some coins and bullion, and alcoholic beverages held for investment.

Community property. Louisiana, Texas, New Mexico, Arizona, California, Washington, Idaho, Nevada, and Wisconsin have community property systems. Alaska residents can elect community property status for assets. The rest of the states are common law property jurisdictions. The difference between common law and community property systems centers around the property rights possessed by married persons. In a common law system, each spouse owns whatever he or she earns. Under a community property system, one-half of the earnings of each spouse is considered owned by the other spouse. Assume, for example, Jeff and Alice are husband and wife and their only income is the $50,000 annual salary Jeff receives. If they live in New York (a common law state), the $50,000 salary belongs to Jeff. If, however, they live in Texas (a community property state), the $50,000 salary is owned one-half each by Jeff and Alice.

Compensatory damages. Damages received or paid by the taxpayer can be classified as compensatory damages or as punitive damages. Compensatory damages are those paid to compensate one for harm caused by another. Compensatory damages are excludible from the recipient's gross income.

Complete termination redemption. Sale or exchange treatment is available relative to this type of redemption. The shareholder must retire all of his or her outstanding shares in the corporation (ignoring family attribution rules), and cannot hold an interest, other than that of a creditor, for the 10 years following the redemption. § 302(b)(3).

Completed contract method. A method of reporting gain or loss on certain long-term contracts. Under this method of accounting, gross income and expenses are recognized in the tax year in which the contract is completed. Reg. § 1.451–3.

Complex trust. Not a simple trust. Such trusts may have charitable beneficiaries, accumulate income, and distribute corpus. §§ 661–663.

Constructive dividend. A taxable benefit derived by a shareholder from his or her corporation that is not actually called a dividend. Examples include unreasonable compensation, excessive rent payments, bargain purchases of corporate property, and shareholder use of corporate property. Constructive dividends generally are found in closely held corporations.

Constructive liquidation scenario. The means by which recourse debt is shared among partners in basis determination.

Constructive receipt. If income is unqualifiedly available although not physically in the taxpayer's possession, it is subject to the income tax. An example is accrued interest on a savings account. Under the constructive receipt concept, the interest is taxed to a depositor in the year available, rather than the year actually withdrawn. The fact that the depositor uses the cash basis of accounting for tax purposes is irrelevant. See Reg. § 1.451–2.

Control. Holding a specified level of stock ownership in a corporation. For § 351, the new shareholder(s) must hold at least 80 percent of the total combined voting power of all voting classes of stock and at least 80 percent of the shares of all nonvoting classes. Other tax provisions require different levels of control to bring about desired effects, such as 50 or 100 percent.

Controlled foreign corporation (CFC). A non-U.S. corporation in which more than 50 percent of the total combined voting power of all classes of stock entitled to vote or the total value of the stock of the corporation is owned by "U.S. shareholders" on any day during the taxable year of the foreign corporation. For purposes of this definition, a U.S. shareholder is any U.S. person who owns, or is considered to own, 10 percent or more of the total combined voting power of all classes of voting stock of the foreign corporation. Stock owned directly, indirectly, and constructively is used in this measure.

Controlled group. A controlled group of corporations is required to share the lower-level corporate tax rates and various other tax benefits among the members of the group. A controlled group may be either a brother-sister or a parent-subsidiary group.

Corporate liquidation. Occurs when a corporation distributes its net assets to its shareholders and ceases to be a going concern. Generally, a shareholder recognizes capital gain or loss upon the liquidation of the entity, regardless of the corporation's balance in its earnings and profits account. However, the distributing corporation recognizes gain and loss on assets that it distributes to shareholders in kind.

Corpus. The body or principal of a trust. Suppose, for example, Grant transfers an apartment building into a trust, income payable to Ruth for life, remainder to Shawn upon Ruth's death. Corpus of the trust is the apartment building.

Correspondence audit. An audit conducted by the IRS by mail. Typically, the IRS writes to the taxpayer requesting the verification of a particular deduction or exemption. The completion of a special form or the remittance of copies of records or other support is all that is requested of the taxpayer.

Cost depletion. Depletion that is calculated based on the adjusted basis of the asset. The adjusted basis is divided by the expected recoverable units to determine the depletion per unit. The depletion per unit is multiplied by the units sold during the tax year to calculate cost depletion.

Cost recovery. The portion of the cost of an asset written off under ACRS (or MACRS), which replaced the depreciation system as a method for writing off the cost of an asset for most assets placed in service after 1980 (after 1986 for MACRS). § 168.

Court of original jurisdiction. The Federal courts are divided into courts of original jurisdiction and appellate courts. A dispute between a taxpayer and the IRS is first considered by a court of original jurisdiction (i.e., a trial court). The four Federal courts of original jurisdiction are the U.S. Tax Court, U.S. District Court, the Court of Federal Claims, and the Small Cases Division of the U.S. Tax Court.

Credit for certain retirement plan contributions. A nonrefundable credit is available based on eligible contributions of up to $2,000 to certain qualified retirement plans, such as traditional and Roth IRAs and § 401(k) plans. The benefit provided by this credit is in addition to any deduction or exclusion that otherwise is available resulting from the qualifying contribution. The amount of the credit depends on the taxpayer's AGI and filing status. § 25B.

Credit for child and dependent care expenses. A tax credit ranging from 20 percent to 35 percent of employment-related expenses (child and dependent care expenses) for amounts of up to $6,000 is available to individuals who are employed (or deemed to be employed) and maintain a household for a dependent child under age 13, disabled spouse, or disabled dependent. § 21.

Credit for employer-provided child care. A nonrefundable credit is available to employers who provide child care facilities to their employees during normal working hours. The credit, limited to $150,000, is comprised of two components. The portion of the credit for qualified child care expenses is equal to 25 percent of these expenses while the portion of the credit for qualified child care resource and referral services is equal to 10 percent of these expenses. Any qualifying expenses otherwise deductible by the taxpayer must be reduced by the amount of the credit. In addition, the taxpayer's basis for any property used for qualifying purposes is reduced by the amount of the credit. § 45F.

Credit for small employer pension plan startup costs. A nonrefundable credit available to small businesses based on administrative costs associated with establishing and maintaining certain qualified plans. While such qualifying costs generally are deductible as ordinary and necessary business expenses, the availability of the credit is intended to lower the costs of starting a qualified retirement program, and therefore encourage qualifying businesses to establish retirement plans for their employees. The credit is available for eligible employers at the rate of 50 percent of qualified startup costs. The maximum credit is $500 (based on a maximum $1,000 of qualifying expenses). §45E.

Crop insurance proceeds. The proceeds received when an insured crop is destroyed. Section 451(d) permits the farmer to defer reporting the income from the insurance proceeds until the tax year following the taxable year of the destruction.

Crop method. A method of accounting for agricultural crops that are planted in one year but harvested in subsequent year. Under this method, the costs of raising the crop are accumulated as inventory and are deducted when the income from the crop is realized.

Current earnings and profits. Net tax-basis earnings of a corporation aggregated during the current tax year. A corporate distribution is deemed to be first from the entity's current earnings and profits and then from accumulated earnings and profits. Shareholders recognize dividend income to the extent of the earnings and profits of the corporation. A dividend results to the extent of current earnings and profits, even if there is a larger negative balance in accumulated earnings and profits.

Current tax expense. Under ASC 740 (SFAS 109), the book tax expense that relates to the current reporting period's net income and is actually payable (or creditable) to the appropriate governmental agencies for the current period. Also known as "cash tax" or "tax payable."

D

***De minimis* fringe.** Benefits provided to employees that are too insignificant to warrant the time and effort required to account for the benefits received by each employee and the value of those benefits. Such amounts are excludible from the employee's gross income. § 132.

Death benefit. A payment made by an employer to the beneficiary or beneficiaries of a deceased employee on account of the death of the employee.

Debt-financed income. Included in computations of the unrelated business income of an exempt organization, the gross income generated from debt-financed property.

Deduction for qualified tuition and related expenses. Taxpayers are allowed a deduction of up to $4,000 for higher education expenses. Certain taxpayers are not eligible for the deduction: those whose gross AGI exceeds a specified amount and those who can be claimed as a dependent by another taxpayer. These expenses are classified as a deduction *for* AGI, and they need not be employment related. § 222.

Deductions for adjusted gross income. The Federal income tax is not imposed upon gross income. Rather, it is imposed upon taxable income. Congressionally identified deductions for individual taxpayers are subtracted either from gross income to arrive at adjusted gross income or from adjusted gross income to arrive at the tax base, taxable income.

Deductions from adjusted gross income. See *deductions for adjusted gross income.*

Deferred tax benefit. Under ASC 740 (SFAS 109), a reduction in the book tax expense that relates to the current reporting period's net income but will not be realized until a future reporting period. Creates or adds to the entity's deferred tax asset balance sheet account. For instance, the carryforward of a net operating loss is a deferred tax benefit.

Deferred tax expense. Under ASC 740 (SFAS 109), a book tax expense that relates to the current reporting period's net income but will not be realized until a future reporting period. Creates or adds to the entity's deferred tax liability balance sheet account. For instance, a deferred tax expense is created when tax depreciation deductions for the period are "accelerated" and exceed the corresponding book depreciation expense.

Dependency exemption. See *personal and dependency exemptions.*

Depletion. The process by which the cost or other basis of a natural resource (e.g., an oil or gas interest) is recovered upon extraction and sale of the resource. The two ways to determine the depletion allowance are the cost and percentage (or statutory) methods. Under cost depletion, each unit of production sold is assigned a portion of the cost or other basis of the interest. This is determined by dividing the cost or other basis by the total units expected to be recovered. Under percentage (or statutory) depletion, the tax law provides a special percentage factor for different types of minerals and other natural resources. This percentage is multiplied by the gross income from the interest to arrive at the depletion allowance. §§ 613 and 613A.

Depreciation. The deduction for the cost or other basis of a tangible asset over the asset's estimated useful life.

Determination letter. Upon the request of a taxpayer, the IRS will comment on the tax status of a completed transaction. Determination letters frequently are used to clarify employee status, determine whether a retirement or profit sharing plan qualifies under the Code, and determine the tax-exempt status of certain nonprofit organizations.

Disabled access credit. A tax credit designed to encourage small businesses to make their facilities more accessible to disabled individuals. The credit is equal to 50 percent of the eligible expenditures that exceed $250 but do not exceed $10,250. Thus, the maximum amount for the credit is $5,000. The adjusted basis for depreciation is reduced by the amount of the credit. To qualify, the facility must have been placed in service before November 6, 1990. § 44.

Disaster area loss. A casualty sustained in an area designated as a disaster area by the President of the United States. In such an event, the disaster loss may be treated as having occurred in the taxable year immediately preceding the year in which the disaster actually occurred. Thus, immediate tax benefits are provided to victims of a disaster. § 165(i).

Disclaimers. Rejections, refusals, or renunciations of claims, powers, or property. Section 2518 sets forth the conditions required to avoid gift tax consequences as the result of a disclaimer.

Disguised sale. When a partner contributes property to the entity and soon thereafter receives a distribution from the partnership, the transactions are collapsed, and the distribution is seen as a purchase of the asset by the partnership. § 707(a)(2)(B).

Disproportionate distribution. A distribution from a partnership to one or more of its partners in which at least one partner's interest in partnership hot assets is increased or decreased. For example, a distribution of cash to one partner and hot assets to another changes both partners' interest in hot assets and is disproportionate. The intent of rules for taxation of disproportionate distributions is to ensure each partner eventually recognizes his or her proportionate share of partnership ordinary income.

Disproportionate redemption. Sale or exchange treatment is available relative to this type of redemption. After the exchange, the shareholder owns less than 80 percent of his or her pre-redemption interest in the corporation, and only a minority interest in the entity. § 302(b)(2).

Distributable net income (DNI). The measure that determines the nature and amount of the distributions from estates and trusts that the beneficiaries must include in income. DNI also limits the amount that estates and trusts can claim as a deduction for such distributions. § 643(a).

Dividend equivalent amount (DEA). The amount subject to the branch profits tax, it is equal to the effectively connected E & P of the U.S. branch of a foreign corporation, reduced/(increased) by an increase/(reduction) in U.S. net equity.

Dividends received deduction. A deduction allowed a shareholder that is a corporation for dividends received from a domestic corporation. The deduction usually is 70 percent of the dividends received, but it could be 80 or 100 percent depending upon the ownership percentage held by the recipient corporation. §§ 243–246.

Domestic production activities deduction (DPAD). See *production activities deduction (PAD).*

Domestic production gross receipts (DPGR). A key component in computing the domestic production activities deduction (DPAD). Includes receipts from the sale and other disposition of qualified production property produced in significant part within the United States. DPGR is defined in § 199(c)(4).

E

Earned income credit. A tax credit designed to provide assistance to certain low-income individuals who generally have a qualifying child. This is a refundable credit. To receive the most beneficial treatment, the taxpayer must have qualifying children. However, it is possible to qualify for the credit without having a child. To calculate the credit for a taxpayer with one or more children for 2011, a statutory rate of 34 percent for one child (40 percent for two children and 45 percent for three or more children) is multiplied by the earned income (subject to a statutory maximum of $9,100 with one qualifying child or $12,780 with two or more qualifying children). Once the earned income exceeds certain thresholds, the credit is phased out using a 15.98 percent rate for one qualifying child and a 21.06 percent rate for two or more qualifying children. For the qualifying taxpayer without children, the credit is calculated on a maximum earned income of $6,070 applying a 7.65 percent rate with the phaseout beginning at a higher threshold applying the same rate.

Earnings and profits (E & P). Measures the economic capacity of a corporation to make a distribution to shareholders that is not a return of capital. Such a distribution results in dividend income to the shareholders to the extent of the corporation's current and accumulated earnings and profits.

Economic effect test. Requirements that must be met before a special allocation may be used by a partnership. The premise behind the test is that each partner who receives an allocation of income or loss from a partnership bears the economic benefit or burden of the allocation.

Economic income. The change in the taxpayer's net worth, as measured in terms of market values, plus the value of the assets the taxpayer consumed during the year. Because of the impracticality of this income model, it is not used for tax purposes.

Economic performance test. One of the requirements that must be satisfied in order for an accrual basis taxpayer to deduct an expense. The accrual basis taxpayer first must satisfy the all events test. That test is not deemed satisfied until economic performance occurs. This occurs when property or services are provided to the taxpayer, or in the case in which the taxpayer is required to provide property or services, whenever the property or services are actually provided by the taxpayer.

Education expenses. Employees may deduct education expenses that are incurred either (1) to maintain or improve existing job-related skills or (2) to meet the express requirements of the employer or the requirements imposed by law to retain employment status. The expenses are not deductible if the education is required to meet the minimum educational standards for the taxpayer's job or if the education qualifies the individual for a new trade or business. Reg. § 1.162–5.

Educational savings bonds. U.S. Series EE bonds whose proceeds are used for qualified higher educational expenses for the taxpayer, the taxpayer's spouse, or a dependent. The interest may be excluded from gross income, provided the taxpayer's adjusted gross income does not exceed certain amounts. § 135.

Effective tax rate. The financial statements for an entity include several footnotes, one of which reconciles the expected (statutory) income tax rate (e.g., 35 percent for a C corporation) with the effective tax rate (i.e., total tax expense as a percentage of book income). The reconciliation often is done in dollar and/or percentage terms.

Effectively connected income. Income of a nonresident alien or foreign corporation that is attributable to the operation of a U.S. trade or business under either the asset-use or the business-activities test.

E-file. The electronic filing of a tax return. The filing is either direct or indirect. As to direct, the taxpayer goes online using a computer and tax return preparation software. Indirect filing occurs when a taxpayer utilizes an authorized IRS e-file provider. The provider often is the tax return preparer.

Employment taxes. Employment taxes are those taxes that an employer must pay on account of its employees. Employment taxes include FICA (Federal Insurance Contributions Act) and FUTA (Federal Unemployment Tax Act) taxes. Employment taxes are paid to the IRS in addition to income tax withholdings at specified intervals. Such taxes can be levied on the employees, the employer, or both.

Enrolled agent (EA). A tax practitioner who has gained admission to practice before the IRS by passing an IRS examination.

Entertainment expenses. These expenses are deductible only if they are directly related to or associated with a trade or business. Various restrictions and documentation requirements have been imposed upon the deductibility of entertainment expenses to prevent abuses by taxpayers. See, for example, the provision contained in § 274(n) that disallows 50 percent (20 percent prior to 1994) of entertainment expenses. § 274.

Entity concept. The theory of partnership taxation under which a partnership is treated as a separate and distinct entity from the partners and has its own tax attributes.

Estate tax. A tax imposed on the right to transfer property by death. Thus, an estate tax is levied on the decedent's estate and not on the heir receiving the property.

Excess lobbying expenditure. An excise tax is applied on otherwise tax-exempt organizations with respect to the excess of total lobbying expenditures over grass roots lobbying expenditures for the year.

Excise tax. A tax on the manufacture, sale, or use of goods; on the carrying on of an occupation or activity; or on the transfer of property. Thus, the Federal estate and gift taxes are, theoretically, excise taxes.

Exclusion amount. The value of assets that is exempt from transfer tax, due to the credit allowed for gifts or transfers by death. For gifts and deaths in 2011, the exclusion amount is $5 million. An exclusion amount unused by a deceased spouse may be used by the surviving spouse. Often called the *exemption equivalent amount.*

Exemption equivalent. The taxable amount (currently $5 million for gift tax; $5 million for estate tax) that is the equivalent of the unified transfer tax credit allowed.

Exempt organization. An organization that is either partially or completely exempt from Federal income taxation. § 501.

Expenses in respect of a decedent. Deductions accrued at the moment of death but not recognizable on the final income tax return of a decedent because of the method of accounting used. Such items are allowed as deductions on the estate tax return and on the income tax return of the estate (Form 1041) or the heir (Form 1040). An example of a deduction in respect of a decedent is interest expense accrued to the date of death by a cash basis debtor.

Extraordinary personal services. These are services provided by individuals where the customers' use of the property is incidental to their receipt of the services. For example, a patient's use of a hospital bed is incidental to his or her receipt of medical services. This is one of the six exceptions to determine whether an activity is a passive rental activity. § 469.

F

Fair market value. The amount at which property would change hands between a willing buyer and a willing seller, neither being under any compulsion to buy or to sell, and both having reasonable knowledge of the relevant facts. Reg. §§ 1.1001–1(a) and 20.2031–1(b).

Farm price method. A method of accounting for agricultural crops. The inventory of crops is valued at its market price less the estimated cost of disposition (e.g., freight and selling expense).

Federal District Court. A Federal District Court is a trial court for purposes of litigating Federal tax matters. It is the only trial court in which a jury trial can be obtained.

Feeder organization. An entity that carries on a trade or business for the benefit of an exempt organization. However, such a relationship does not result in the feeder organization itself being tax-exempt. § 502.

FICA tax. An abbreviation that stands for Federal Insurance Contributions Act, commonly referred to as the Social Security tax. The FICA tax is comprised of the Social Security tax (old age, survivors, and disability insurance) and the Medicare tax (hospital insurance) and is imposed on both employers and employees. The employer is responsible for withholding from the employee's wages the Social Security tax at a rate of 6.2 percent on a maximum wage base of $106,800 (for 2010) and the Medicare tax at a rate of 1.45 percent (no maximum wage base). The employer is required to match the employee's contribution. For 2011 the employee's rate is reduced to 4.2 percent for the Social Security tax. The employer's contribution still is at the 6.2 percent rate for 2011.

Field audit. An audit conducted by the IRS on the business premises of the taxpayer or in the office of the tax practitioner representing the taxpayer.

Fifty percent additional first-year depreciation. This provision, which was effective for property acquired after December 31, 2007 and placed in service before January 1, 2009, provided for an additional cost recovery deduction of 50 percent in the tax year the qualified property is placed in service. Qualified property included most types of new property other than buildings. The American Recovery and

Reinvestment Tax Act of 2009 extended the additional first-year depreciation provision for an additional year. The Small Business Jobs Creation Act of 2010 extended the additional first-year depreciation for an additional year. The taxpayer can elect to forgo this bonus depreciation. See also *one hundred percent additional first-year depreciation.*

Finalized Regulation. The U.S. Treasury Department Regulations (abbreviated Reg.) represent the position of the IRS as to how the Internal Revenue Code is to be interpreted. Their purpose is to provide taxpayers and IRS personnel with rules of general and specific application to the various provisions of the tax law. Regulations are published in the *Federal Register* and in all tax services.

FIRPTA. Under the Foreign Investment in Real Property Tax Act, gains or losses realized by nonresident aliens and non-U.S. corporations on the disposition of U.S. real estate create U.S.-source income and are subject to U.S. income tax.

Fiscal year. A fiscal year is a 12-month period ending on the last day of a month other than December. In certain circumstances, a taxpayer is permitted to elect a fiscal year instead of being required to use a calendar year.

Flat tax. In its pure form, a flat tax would eliminate all exclusions, deductions, and credits and impose a one-rate tax on gross income.

Flexible spending plan. An employee benefit plan that allows the employee to take a reduction in salary in exchange for the employer paying benefits that can be provided by the employer without the employee being required to recognize income (e.g., medical and child care benefits).

Foreign earned income exclusion. The Code allows exclusions for earned income generated outside the United States to alleviate any tax base and rate disparities among countries. In addition, the exclusion is allowed for housing expenditures incurred by the taxpayer's employer with respect to the non-U.S. assignment, and self-employed individuals can deduct foreign housing expenses incurred in a trade or business. The exclusion is limited to $92,900 per year for 2011 ($91,500 in 2010). § 911.

Foreign tax credit. A U.S. citizen or resident who incurs or pays income taxes to a foreign country on income subject to U.S. tax may be able to claim some of these taxes as a credit against the U.S. income tax. §§ 27 and 901–905.

Franchise. An agreement that gives the transferee the right to distribute, sell, or provide goods, services, or facilities within a specified area. The cost of obtaining a franchise may be amortized over a statutory period of 15 years. In general, the franchisor's gain on the sale of franchise rights is an ordinary gain because the franchisor retains a significant power, right, or continuing interest in the subject of the franchise. §§ 197 and 1253.

Franchise tax. A tax levied on the right to do business in a state as a corporation. Although income considerations may come into play, the tax usually is based on the capitalization of the corporation.

Fraud. Tax fraud falls into two categories: civil and criminal. Under civil fraud, the IRS may impose as a penalty an amount equal to as much as 75 percent of the underpayment [§ 6651(f)]. Fines and/or imprisonment are prescribed for conviction of various types of criminal tax fraud (§§ 7201–7207). Both civil and criminal fraud involve a specific intent on the part of the taxpayer to evade the tax; mere negligence is not enough. Criminal fraud requires the additional element of willfulness (i.e., done deliberately and with evil purpose). In practice, it becomes difficult to distinguish between the degree of intent necessary to support criminal, rather than civil, fraud. In either situation, the IRS has the burden of proving fraud.

Frivolous return. A tax return that included a position that has no more than a 5 percent chance of being sustained upon review. Taxpayer and tax preparer penalties are assessed if a frivolous position is included in a filed tax return.

Fruit and tree metaphor. The courts have held that an individual who earns income from property or services cannot assign that income to another. For example, a father cannot assign his earnings from commissions to his child and escape income tax on those amounts.

Functional currency. The currency of the economic environment in which the taxpayer carries on most of its activities, and in which the taxpayer transacts most of its business.

FUTA tax. An employment tax levied on employers. Jointly administered by the Federal and state governments, the tax provides funding for unemployment benefits. FUTA applies at a rate of 6.2 percent on the first $7,000 of covered wages paid during the year for each employee. The Federal government allows a credit for FUTA paid (or allowed under a merit rating system) to the state. The credit cannot exceed 5.4 percent of the covered wages.

Future interest. An interest that will come into being at some future time. It is distinguished from a present interest, which already exists. Assume that Dan transfers securities to a newly created trust. Under the terms of the trust instrument, income from the securities is to be paid each year to Wilma for her life, with the securities passing to Sam upon Wilma's death. Wilma has a present interest in the trust since she is entitled to current income distributions. Sam has a future interest since he must wait for Wilma's death to benefit from the trust. The annual exclusion of $13,000 (after 2008) is not allowed for a gift of a future interest. § 2503(b).

G

General business credit. The summation of various nonrefundable business credits, including the tax credit for rehabilitation expenditures, business energy credit, work opportunity credit, research activities credit, low-income housing credit, and disabled access credit. The amount of general business credit that can be used to reduce the tax liability is limited to the taxpayer's net income tax reduced by the greater of (1) the tentative minimum tax or (2) 25 percent of the net regular tax liability that exceeds $25,000. Unused general business credits can be carried back 1 year and forward 20 years. § 38.

General partnership. A partnership that is owned by one or more general partners. Creditors of a general partnership can collect amounts owed them from both the partnership assets and the assets of the partners individually.

Gift. A transfer of property for less than adequate consideration. Gifts usually occur in a personal setting (such as between members of the same family). They are excluded from the income tax base but may be subject to a transfer tax.

Gift tax. A tax imposed on the transfer of property by gift. The tax is imposed upon the donor of a gift and is based on the fair market value of the property on the date of the gift.

Goodwill. The reputation and built-up business of a company. For accounting purposes, goodwill has no basis unless it is purchased. In the purchase of a business, goodwill generally is the difference between the purchase price and the fair market value of the assets acquired. The intangible asset goodwill can be amortized for tax purposes over a 15-year period. Reg. § 1.167(a)–3.

Grantor. A transferor of property. The creator of a trust is usually referred to as the grantor of the entity.

Grantor trust. A trust under which the grantor retains control over the income or corpus (or both) to such an extent that he or she is treated as the owner of the property and its income for income tax purposes. Income from a grantor trust is taxable to the grantor and not to the beneficiary who receives it. §§ 671–679.

Grass roots expenditures. Exempt organizations are prohibited from engaging in political activities, but spending incurred to influence the opinions of the general public relative to specific legislation is permitted by the law.

Gross estate. The property owned or previously transferred by a decedent that is subject to the Federal estate tax. The gross estate can be distinguished from the probate estate, which is property actually subject to administration by the administrator or executor of an estate. §§ 2031–2046.

Gross income. Income subject to the Federal income tax. Gross income does not include all economic income. That is, certain exclusions are allowed (e.g., interest on municipal bonds). For a manufacturing or merchandising business, gross income usually means gross profit (gross sales or gross receipts less cost of goods sold). § 61 and Reg. § 1.61–3(a).

Group term life insurance. Life insurance coverage provided by an employer for a group of employees. Such insurance is renewable on a year-to-year basis, and typically no cash surrender value is built up. The premiums paid by the employer on the insurance are not taxed to the employees on coverage of up to $50,000 per person. § 79 and Reg. § 1.79–1(b).

Guaranteed payments. Payments made by a partnership to a partner for services rendered or for the use of capital to the extent that the payments are determined without regard to the income of the partnership. The payments are treated as though they were made to a nonpartner and thus are deducted by the entity.

H

Half-year convention. The half-year convention is a cost recovery convention that assumes all property is placed in service at mid-year and thus provides for a half-year's cost recovery for that year.

Head of household. An unmarried individual who maintains a household for another and satisfies certain conditions set forth in § 2(b). This status enables the taxpayer to use a set of income tax rates that are lower than those applicable to other unmarried individuals but higher than those applicable to surviving spouses and married persons filing a joint return.

Health savings account (HSA). A medical savings account created in legislation enacted in December 2003 that is designed to replace and expand Archer Medical Savings Accounts.

Hobby losses. Losses from an activity not engaged in for profit. The Code restricts the amount of losses that an individual can deduct for hobby activities so that these transactions cannot be used to offset income from other sources. § 183.

Holding period. The period of time during which property has been held for income tax purposes. The holding period is significant in determining whether gain or loss from the sale or exchange of a capital asset is long term or short term. § 1223.

Home equity loans. Loans that utilize the personal residence of the taxpayer as security. The interest on such loans is deductible as qualified residence interest. However, interest is deductible only on the portion of the loan that does not exceed the lesser of (1) the fair market value of the residence, reduced by the acquisition indebtedness, or (2) $100,000 ($50,000 for married persons filing separate returns). A major benefit of a home equity loan is that there are no tracing rules regarding the use of the loan proceeds. § 163(h)(3).

HOPE scholarship credit. A tax credit for qualifying expenses paid for the first two years of postsecondary education. Room, board, and book costs are ineligible for the credit. The maximum credit available is $1,800 per year per student, computed as 100 percent of the first $1,200 of qualifying expenses, plus 50 percent of the second $1,200 of qualifying expenses. Eligible students include the taxpayer, taxpayer's spouse, and taxpayer's dependents. To qualify for the credit, a student must take at least one-half the full-time course load for at least one academic term at a qualifying educational institution. The credit is phased out for higher-income taxpayers. For 2009, 2010, 2011, and 2012, the HOPE scholarship credit is replaced with the American Opportunity credit. § 25A.

Hot assets. Unrealized receivables and substantially appreciated inventory under § 751. When hot assets are present, the sale of a partnership interest or the disproportionate distribution of the assets can cause ordinary income to be recognized.

Hybrid method. A combination of the accrual and cash methods of accounting. That is, the taxpayer may account for some items of income on the accrual method (e.g., sales and cost of goods sold) and other items (e.g., interest income) on the cash method.

I

Imputed interest. For certain long-term sales of property, the IRS can convert some of the gain from the sale into interest income if the contract does not provide for a minimum rate of interest to be paid by the purchaser. The seller recognizes less long-term capital gain and more ordinary income (interest income). § 483 and the related Regulations.

Inbound taxation. U.S. tax effects when a non-U.S. person begins an investment or business activity in the United States.

Incentive stock option (ISO). A type of stock option that receives favorable tax treatment. If various qualification requirements can be satisfied, there are no recognition tax consequences when the stock option is granted. However, the spread (the excess of the fair market value at the date of exercise over the option price) is a tax preference item for purposes of the alternative minimum tax. The gain on disposition of the stock resulting from the exercise of the stock option will be classified as long-term capital gain if certain holding period requirements are met (the employee must not dispose of the stock within two years after the option is granted or within one year after acquiring the stock). § 422.

Income. For tax purposes, an increase in wealth that has been realized.

Income in respect of a decedent (IRD). Income earned by a decedent at the time of death but not reportable on the final income tax return because of the method of accounting that appropriately is utilized. Such income is included in the gross estate and is taxed to the eventual recipient (either the estate or heirs). The recipient is, however, allowed an income tax deduction for the estate tax attributable to the income. § 691.

Income tax provision. Under ASC 740 (SFAS 109), a synonym for the book tax expense of an entity for the financial reporting period. Following the "matching principle," all book tax expense that relates to the net income for the reporting period is reported on that period's financial statements, including not only the current tax expense, but also any deferred tax expense and deferred tax benefit.

Independent contractor. A self-employed person as distinguished from one who is employed as an employee.

Individual retirement account (IRA). A type of retirement plan to which an individual with earned income can contribute a statutory maximum of $5,000 in 2009, 2010, and 2011. IRAs can be classified as traditional IRAs or Roth IRAs. With a traditional IRA, an individual can contribute and deduct a maximum of $5,000 per tax year in 2011. The deduction is a deduction *for* AGI. However, if the individual is an active participant in another qualified retirement plan, the deduction is phased out proportionally between certain AGI ranges (note that the phaseout limits the amount of the deduction and not the amount of the contribution). With a Roth IRA, an individual can contribute a maximum of $5,000 per tax year in 2011. No deduction is permitted. However, if a five-year holding period requirement is satisfied and if the distribution is a qualified distribution, the taxpayer can make tax-free withdrawals from a Roth IRA. The maximum annual contribution is phased out proportionally between certain AGI ranges. §§ 219 and 408A.

Inheritance tax. A tax imposed on the right to receive property from a decedent. Thus, theoretically, an inheritance tax is imposed on the heir. The Federal estate tax is imposed on the estate.

Inside basis. A partnership's basis in the assets it owns.

Installment method. A method of accounting enabling certain taxpayers to spread the recognition of gain on the sale of property over the collection period. Under this procedure, the seller arrives at the gain to be recognized by computing the gross profit percentage from the sale (the gain divided by the contract price) and applying it to each payment received. § 453.

Intangible drilling and development costs (IDC). Taxpayers may elect to expense or capitalize (subject to amortization) intangible drilling and development costs. However, ordinary income recapture provisions apply to oil and gas properties on a sale or other disposition if the expense method is elected. §§ 263(c) and 1254(a).

Intermediate sanctions. The IRS can assess excise taxes on disqualified persons and organization managers associated with so-called public charities engaging in excess benefit transactions. An excess benefit transaction is one in which a disqualified person engages in a non-fair market value transaction with the exempt organization or receives unreasonable compensation. Prior to the idea of intermediate sanctions, the only option available to the IRS was to revoke the organization's exempt status.

International Accounting Standards Board (IASB). The body that promulgates International Financial Reporting Standards (IFRS). Based in London, representing accounting standard setting bodies in over 100 countries, the IASB develops accounting standards that can serve as the basis for harmonizing conflicting reporting standards among nations.

International Financial Reporting Standards (IFRS). Produced by the International Accounting Standards Board (IASB), guidelines developed since 2001 as to revenue recognition, accounting for business combinations, and a conceptual framework for financial reporting. IFRS provisions are designed so that they can be used by all entities, regardless of where they are based or conduct business. IFRS have gained widespread acceptance throughout the world, and the SEC is considering how to require U.S. entities to use IFRS in addition to, or in lieu of, the accounting rules of the Financial Accounting Standards Board.

Interpretive Regulation. A Regulation issued by the Treasury Department that purports to explain the meaning of a particular Code Section. An interpretive Regulation is given less deference than a legislative Regulation.

Investment income. Consisting of virtually the same elements as portfolio income, a measure by which to justify a deduction for interest on investment indebtedness.

Investment interest. Payment for the use of funds used to acquire assets that produce investment income. The deduction for investment interest is limited to net investment income for the tax year.

Investor losses. Losses on stock and securities. If stocks and bonds are capital assets in the hands of the holder, a capital loss materializes as of the last day of the taxable year in which the stocks or bonds become worthless. Under certain circumstances involving stocks and bonds of affiliated corporations, an ordinary loss is permitted upon worthlessness.

Involuntary conversion. The loss or destruction of property through theft, casualty, or condemnation. Any gain realized on an involuntary conversion can, at the taxpayer's election, be deferred for Federal income tax purposes if the owner reinvests the proceeds within a prescribed period of time in property that is similar or related in service or use. § 1033.

IRAs (traditional). See *individual retirement account (IRA).*

Itemized deductions. Personal and employee expenditures allowed by the Code as deductions from adjusted gross income. Examples include certain medical expenses, interest on home mortgages, state income taxes, and charitable contributions. Itemized deductions are reported on Schedule A of Form 1040. Certain miscellaneous itemized deductions are reduced by 2 percent of the taxpayer's adjusted gross income. In addition, a taxpayer whose adjusted gross income exceeds a certain level (indexed annually) must reduce the itemized deductions by 3 percent of the excess of adjusted gross income over that level. Medical, casualty and theft, and investment interest deductions are not subject to the 3 percent reduction. The 3 percent reduction may not reduce itemized deductions that are subject to the reduction to below 20 percent of their initial amount. Beginning in 2006, this reduction is subject to a partial phaseout, and for 2010, all of the reduction is phased out. Under the sunset provision, the phaseout of itemized deductions was scheduled to be reinstated beginning in 2011. The Tax Relief Act (TRA) of 2010 put off the reinstatement for two years (i.e., 2011 and 2012).

J

Joint tenants. Two or more persons having undivided ownership of property with the right of survivorship. Right of survivorship gives the surviving owner full ownership of the property. Suppose Bob and Tami are joint tenants of a tract of land. Upon Bob's death, Tami becomes the sole owner of the property. For the estate tax consequences upon the death of a joint tenant, see § 2040.

K

Keogh plans. Retirement plans available to self-employed taxpayers. They are also referred to as H.R. 10 plans. Under such plans, in 2011, a taxpayer may deduct each year up to either 100 percent of net earnings from self-employment or $49,000, whichever is less. If the plan is a profit sharing plan, the percentage is 25 percent.

Kiddie tax. Passive income, such as interest and dividends, that is recognized by a child under age 19 (or under age 24 if a full-time student) is taxed to him or her at the rates that would have applied had the income been incurred by the child's parents, generally to the extent that the income exceeds $1,900. The additional tax is assessed regardless of the source of the income or the income's underlying property. If the child's parents are divorced, the custodial parent's rates are used. The parents' rates reflect any applicable alternative minimum tax and the phaseouts of lower tax brackets and other deductions. § 1(g).

L

Least aggregate deferral method. An algorithm set forth in the Regulations to determine the tax year for a partnership or S corporation with owners whose tax years differ. The tax year selected is the one that produces the least aggregate deferral of income for the owners.

Legislative Regulation. Some Code Sections give the Secretary of the Treasury or his delegate the authority to prescribe Regulations to carry out the details of administration or to otherwise complete the operating rules. Regulations issued pursuant to this type of authority truly possess the force and effect of law. In effect, Congress is almost delegating its legislative powers to the Treasury Department.

Lessee. One who rents property from another. In the case of real estate, the lessee is also known as the tenant.

Lessor. One who rents property to another. In the case of real estate, the lessor is also known as the landlord.

Letter ruling. The written response of the IRS to a taxpayer's request for interpretation of the revenue laws, with respect to a proposed transaction (e.g., concerning the tax-free status of a reorganization). Not to be relied on as precedent by other than the party who requested the ruling.

Liabilities in excess of basis. On the contribution of capital to a corporation, an investor recognizes gain on the exchange to the extent that contributed assets carry liabilities with a face amount in excess of the tax basis of the contributed assets. This rule keeps the investor from holding the investment asset received with a negative basis. § 357(c).

Life insurance proceeds. A specified sum (the face value or maturity value of the policy) paid to the designated beneficiary of the policy by the life insurance company upon the death of the insured.

Lifetime learning credit. A tax credit for qualifying expenses for taxpayers pursuing education beyond the first two years of postsecondary education. Individuals who are completing their last two years of undergraduate studies, pursuing graduate or professional degrees, or otherwise seeking new job skills or maintaining existing job skills are all eligible for the credit. Eligible individuals include the taxpayer, taxpayer's spouse, and taxpayer's dependents. The maximum credit is 20 percent of the first $10,000 of qualifying expenses and is computed per taxpayer. The credit is phased out for higher-income taxpayers. § 25A.

Like-kind exchange. An exchange of property held for productive use in a trade or business or for investment (except inventory and stocks and bonds) for other investment or trade or business property. Unless non-like-kind property (boot) is received, the exchange is fully tax deferred. § 1031.

Limited liability company (LLC). A form of entity allowed by all of the states. The entity is taxed as a partnership in which all members or owners of the LLC are treated much like limited partners. There are no restrictions on ownership, all members may participate in management, and none has personal liability for the entity's debts.

Limited liability limited partnership (LLLP). A limited partnership for which the general partners are also protected from entity liabilities. An LLLP—or "triple LP"—can be formed in about 20 states. In those states, a limited partnership files with the state to adopt LLLP status.

Limited liability partnership (LLP). A form of entity allowed by many of the states, where a general partnership registers with the state as an LLP. Owners are general partners, but a partner is not liable for any malpractice committed by other partners. The personal assets of the partners are at risk for the entity's contractual liabilities, such as accounts payable. The personal assets of a specific partner are at risk for his or her own professional malpractice and tort liability, and for malpractice and torts committed by those whom he or she supervises.

Limited partnership. A partnership in which some of the partners are limited partners. At least one of the partners in a limited partnership must be a general partner.

Liquidating distribution. A distribution by a partnership or corporation that is in complete liquidation of the entity's trade or business activities. Typically, such distributions generate capital gain or loss to the investors without regard, for instance, to the earnings and profits of the corporation or to the partnership's basis in the distributed property. They can, however, lead to recognized gain or loss at the corporate level.

Listed property. The term listed property includes (1) any passenger automobile, (2) any other property used as a means of transportation, (3) any property of a type generally used for purposes of entertainment, recreation, or amusement, (4) any computer or peripheral equipment (with an exception for exclusive business use), (5) any cellular telephone (or other similar telecommunications equipment), and (6) any other property of a type specified in the Regulations. If listed property is predominantly used for business, the taxpayer is allowed to use the statutory percentage method of cost recovery. Otherwise, the straight-line cost recovery method must be used. § 280F.

Lobbying expenditure. An expenditure made for the purpose of influencing legislation. Such payments can result in the loss of the exempt status of, and the imposition of Federal income tax on, an exempt organization.

Long-term care insurance. Insurance that helps pay the cost of care when the insured is unable to care for himself or herself. Such insurance is generally thought of as insurance against the cost of an aged person entering a nursing home. The employer can provide the insurance, and the premiums may be excluded from the employee's gross income. § 7702B.

Long-term contract. A building, installation, construction, or manufacturing contract that is entered into but not completed within the same tax year. A manufacturing contract is a long-term contract only if the contract is to manufacture (1) a unique item not normally carried in finished goods inventory or (2) items that normally require more than 12 calendar months to complete. The two available methods to account for long-term contracts are the percentage of completion method and the completed contract method. The completed contract method can be used only in limited circumstances. § 460.

Long-term nonpersonal use capital assets. Includes investment property with a long-term holding period. Such property disposed of by casualty or theft may receive § 1231 treatment.

Low-income housing credit. Beneficial treatment to owners of low-income housing is provided in the form of a tax credit. The calculated credit is claimed in the year the building is placed in service and in the following nine years. § 42.

M

Majority interest partners. Partners who have more than a 50 percent interest in partnership profits and capital, counting only those partners who have the same taxable year, are referred to as majority interest partners. The term is of significance in determining the appropriate taxable year of a partnership. § 706(b).

Marital deduction. A deduction allowed against the taxable estate or taxable gifts upon the transfer of property from one spouse to another.

Marriage penalty. The additional tax liability that results for a married couple when compared with what their tax liability would be if they were not married and filed separate returns.

Material participation. If an individual taxpayer materially participates in a nonrental trade or business activity, any loss from that activity is treated as an active loss that can be offset against active income. Material participation is achieved by meeting any one of seven tests provided in the Regulations. § 469(h).

Meaningful reduction test. A decrease in the shareholder's voting control. Used to determine whether a stock redemption qualifies for sale or exchange treatment.

Medical expenses. Medical expenses of an individual, spouse, and dependents are allowed as an itemized deduction to the extent that such amounts (less insurance reimbursements) exceed 7.5 percent of adjusted gross income. § 213.

Mid-month convention. A cost recovery convention that assumes property is placed in service in the middle of the month that it is actually placed in service.

Mid-quarter convention. A cost recovery convention that assumes property placed in service during the year is placed in service at the middle of the quarter in which it is actually placed in service. The mid-quarter convention applies if more than 40 percent of the value of property (other than eligible real estate) is placed in service during the last quarter of the year.

Miscellaneous itemized deductions. A special category of itemized deductions that includes such expenses as professional dues, tax return preparation fees, job-hunting costs, unreimbursed employee business expenses, and certain investment expenses. Such expenses are deductible only to the extent they exceed 2 percent of adjusted gross income. § 67.

Modified accelerated cost recovery system (MACRS). A method in which the cost of tangible property is recovered over a prescribed period of time. Enacted by the Economic Recovery Tax Act (ERTA) of 1981 and substantially modified by the Tax Reform Act (TRA) of 1986 (the modified system is referred to as MACRS), the approach disregards salvage value, imposes a period of cost recovery that depends upon the classification of the asset into one of various recovery periods, and prescribes the applicable percentage of cost that can be deducted each year. § 168.

Modified adjusted gross income. A key determinant in computing the domestic production activities deduction (DPAD). The deduction is limited to a percentage of the *lesser of* qualified production activities income (QPAI) or modified adjusted gross income. Aside from limited changes required by § 199(d)(2)(A), modified adjusted gross income is AGI as usually determined but without any domestic production activities deduction.

Moving expenses. A deduction *for* AGI is permitted to employees and self-employed individuals provided certain tests are met. The taxpayer's new job must be at least 50 miles farther from the old residence than the old residence was from the former place of work. In addition, an employee must be employed on a full-time basis at the new location for 39 weeks in the 12-month period following the move. Deductible moving expenses include the cost of moving the household and personal effects, transportation, and lodging expenses during the move. The cost of meals during the move is not deductible. Qualified moving expenses that are paid (or reimbursed) by the employer can be excluded from the employee's gross income. In this case, the related deduction by the employee is not permitted. §§ 62(a)(15), 132(a)(6), and 217.

Multiple support agreement. To qualify for a dependency exemption, the support test must be satisfied. This requires that over 50 percent of the support of the potential dependent be provided by the taxpayer. Where no one person provides more than 50 percent of the support, a multiple support agreement enables a taxpayer to still qualify for the dependency exemption. Any person who contributed more than 10 percent of the support is entitled to claim the exemption if each person in the group who contributed more than 10 percent files a written consent (Form 2120). Each person who is a party to the multiple support agreement must meet all the other requirements for claiming the dependency exemption. § 152(c).

N

National sales tax. Intended as a replacement for the current Federal income tax. Unlike a value added tax (VAT), which is levied on the manufacturer, it would be imposed on the consumer upon the final sale of goods and services. To keep the tax from being regressive, low-income taxpayers would be granted some kind of credit or exemption.

Negligence. Failure to exercise the reasonable or ordinary degree of care of a prudent person in a situation that results in harm or damage to another. Code § 6651 imposes a penalty on taxpayers who exhibit negligence or intentional disregard of rules and Regulations with respect to the underpayment of certain taxes.

Net capital gain. The excess of the net long-term capital gain for the tax year over the net short-term capital loss. The net capital gain of an individual taxpayer is eligible for the alternative tax. § 1222(11).

Net capital loss. The excess of the losses from sales or exchanges of capital assets over the gains from sales or exchanges of such assets. Up to $3,000 per year of the net capital loss may be deductible by noncorporate taxpayers against ordinary income. The excess net capital loss carries over to future tax years. For corporate taxpayers, the net capital loss cannot be offset against ordinary income, but it can be carried back three years and forward five years to offset net capital gains. §§ 1211, 1212, and 1221(10).

Net investment income. The excess of investment income over investment expenses. Investment expenses are those deductible expenses directly connected with the production of investment income. Investment expenses do not include investment interest. The deduction for investment interest for the tax year is limited to net investment income. § 163(d).

Net operating loss. To mitigate the effect of the annual accounting period concept, § 172 allows taxpayers to use an excess loss of one year as a deduction for certain past or future years. In this regard, a carryback period of 2 (or more) years and a carryforward period of 20 years currently are allowed.

Nexus. A multistate corporation's taxable income can be apportioned to a specific state only if the entity has established a sufficient presence, or nexus, with that state. State law, which often follows the Uniform Division of Income for Tax Purposes Act (UDITPA), specifies various activities that lead to nexus in various states.

Ninety-day letter. Commonly referred to as the 90-day letter, this notice is sent to a taxpayer upon request, upon the expiration of the 30-day letter, or upon exhaustion by the taxpayer of his or her administrative remedies before the IRS. The notice gives the taxpayer 90 days in which to file a petition with the U.S. Tax Court. If a petition is not filed, the IRS will demand payment of the assessed deficiency. §§ 6211–6216.

No-additional-cost services. Services that the employer may provide the employee at no additional cost to the employer. Generally, the benefit is the ability to utilize the employer's excess capacity (e.g., vacant seats on an airliner). Such amounts are excludible from the recipient's gross income.

Nonaccountable plan. An expense reimbursement plan that does not have an accountability feature. The result is that employee expenses must be claimed as deductions *from* AGI. An exception is moving expenses that are deductions *for* AGI.

Nonacquiescence. Disagreement by the IRS on the result reached in certain judicial decisions. *Nonacq.* or *NA.*

Nonbusiness bad debt. A bad debt loss that is not incurred in connection with a creditor's trade or business. The loss is classified as a short-term capital loss and is allowed only in the year the debt becomes entirely worthless. In addition to family loans, many investor losses are nonbusiness bad debts. § 166(d).

Nonliquidating distribution. A payment made by a partnership or corporation to the entity's owner is a nonliquidating distribution when the entity's legal existence does not cease thereafter. If the payor is a corporation, such a distribution can result in dividend income to the shareholders. If the payor is a partnership, the partner usually assigns a basis in the distributed property that is equal to the lesser of the partner's basis in the partnership interest or the basis of the distributed asset to the partnership. In this regard, the partner first assigns basis to any cash that he or she receives in the distribution. The partner's remaining basis, if any, is assigned to the noncash assets according to their relative bases to the partnership.

Nonrecourse debt. Debt secured by the property that it is used to purchase. The purchaser of the property is not personally liable for the debt upon default. Rather, the creditor's recourse is to repossess the related property. Nonrecourse debt generally does not increase the purchaser's at-risk amount.

Nonrefundable credit. A nonrefundable credit is a credit that is not paid if it exceeds the taxpayer's tax liability. Some nonrefundable credits qualify for carryback and carryover treatment.

Nonresident alien. An individual who is neither a citizen nor a resident of the United States. Citizenship is determined under the immigration and naturalization laws of the United States. Residency is determined under § 7701(b) of the Internal Revenue Code.

Nontaxable exchange. A transaction in which realized gains or losses are not recognized. The recognition of gain or loss is postponed (deferred) until the property received in the nontaxable exchange is subsequently disposed of in a taxable transaction. Examples are § 1031 like-kind exchanges and § 1033 involuntary conversions.

Not essentially equivalent redemption. Sale or exchange treatment is given to this type of redemption. Although various safe-harbor tests are failed, the nature of the redemption is such that dividend treatment is avoided, because it represents a meaningful reduction in the shareholder's interest in the corporation. § 302(b)(1).

O

Occupational tax. A tax imposed on various trades or businesses. A license fee that enables a taxpayer to engage in a particular occupation.

Offer in compromise. A settlement agreement offered by the IRS in a tax dispute, especially where there is doubt as to the collectibility of the full deficiency. Offers in compromise can include installment payment schedules, as well as reductions in the tax and penalties owed by the taxpayer.

Office audit. An audit conducted by the IRS in the agent's office.

Office in the home expenses. Employment and business-related expenses attributable to the use of a residence (e.g., den or office) are allowed only if the portion of the residence is exclusively used on a regular basis as a principal place of business of the taxpayer or as a place of business that is used by patients, clients, or customers. If the expenses are incurred by an employee, the use must be for the convenience of the employer as opposed to being merely appropriate and helpful. § 280A.

One hundred percent additional first-year depreciation. The Tax Relief Act of 2010 provides for a cost recovery deduction of 100 percent in the tax year qualified property is placed in service. Qualified property includes most types of new property other than buildings. This provision is effective for property acquired after December 31, 2010 and placed in service before January 1, 2012. See also *fifty percent additional first-year depreciation.*

One-year rule for prepaid expenses. Taxpayers who use the cash method are required to use the accrual method for deducting certain prepaid expenses (i.e., must capitalize the item and can deduct only when used). If a prepayment will not be consumed or expire by the end of the tax year following the year of payment, the prepayment must be capitalized and prorated over the benefit period. Conversely, if the prepayment will be consumed by the end of the tax year following the year of payment, it can be expensed when paid. To obtain the current deduction under the one-year rule, the payment must be a required payment rather than a voluntary payment.

Operating agreement. The governing document of a limited liability company. This document is similar in structure, function, and purpose to a partnership agreement.

Options. The sale or exchange of an option to buy or sell property results in capital gain or loss if the property is a capital asset. Generally, the closing of an option transaction results in short-term capital gain or loss to the writer of the call and the purchaser of the call option. § 1234.

Ordinary and necessary. An ordinary expense is one that is common and accepted in the general industry or type of activity in which the taxpayer is engaged. It comprises one of the tests for the deductibility of expenses incurred or paid in connection with a trade or business; for the production or collection of income; for the management, conservation, or maintenance of property held for the production of income; or in connection with the determination, collection, or refund of any tax. §§ 162(a) and 212. A necessary expense is one that is appropriate and helpful in furthering the taxpayer's business or income-producing activity. §§ 162(a) and 212.

Ordinary income property. Property contributed to a charitable organization that, if sold rather than contributed, would have resulted in other than long-term capital gain to the donor (i.e., ordinary income property and short-term capital gain property). Examples are inventory and capital assets held for less than the long-term holding period.

Organizational expenditures. Items incurred early in the life of a corporate entity that are eligible for a $5,000 limited expensing (subject to phaseout) and an amortization of the balance over 180 months. Organizational expenditures exclude those incurred to obtain capital (underwriting fees) or assets (subject to cost recovery). Typically, eligible expenditures include legal and accounting fees and state incorporation payments. Such items must be incurred by the end of the entity's first tax year. § 248.

Original issue discount. The difference between the issue price of a debt obligation (e.g., a corporate bond) and the maturity value of the obligation when the issue price is *less than* the maturity value. OID represents interest and must be amortized over the life of the debt obligation using the effective interest method. The difference is not considered to be original issue discount for tax purposes when it is less than one-fourth of 1 percent of the redemption price at maturity multiplied by the number of years to maturity. §§ 1272 and 1273(a)(3).

Other adjustments account (OAA). Used in the context of a distribution from an S corporation. The net accumulation of the entity's exempt income (e.g., municipal bond interest).

Outbound taxation. U.S. tax effects when a U.S. person begins an investment or business activity outside the United States.

Outside basis. A partner's basis in his or her partnership interest.

P

Parent-subsidiary controlled group. A controlled or affiliated group of corporations, where at least one corporation is at least 80 percent owned by one or more of the others. The affiliated group definition is more difficult to meet.

Partnership. For income tax purposes, a partnership includes a syndicate, group, pool, or joint venture, as well as ordinary partnerships. In an ordinary partnership, two or more parties combine capital and/or services to carry on a business for profit as co-owners. § 7701(a)(2).

Partnership agreement. The governing document of a partnership. A partnership agreement should describe the rights and obligations of the partners; the allocation of entity income, deductions, and cash flows; initial and future capital contribution requirements; conditions for terminating the partnership; and other matters.

Passive investment income (PII). Gross receipts from royalties, certain rents, dividends, interest, annuities, and gains from the sale or exchange of stock and securities. When E & P also exists, if the passive investment income of an S corporation exceeds 25 percent of the corporation's gross receipts for three consecutive years, S status is lost.

Passive loss. Any loss from (1) activities in which the taxpayer does not materially participate or (2) rental activities (subject to certain exceptions). Net passive losses cannot be used to offset income from nonpassive sources. Rather, they are suspended until the taxpayer either generates net passive income (and a deduction of such losses is allowed) or disposes of the underlying property (at which time the loss deductions are allowed in full). One relief provision allows landlords who actively participate in the rental activities to deduct up to $25,000 of passive losses annually. However, a phaseout of the $25,000 amount commences when the landlord's AGI exceeds $100,000. Another relief provision applies for material participation in a real estate trade or business.

Patent. A patent is an intangible asset that may be amortized over a statutory 15-year period as a § 197 intangible. The sale of a patent usually results in favorable long-term capital gain treatment. §§ 197 and 1235.

Payroll factor. The proportion of a multistate corporation's total payroll that is traceable to a specific state. Used in determining the taxable income that is to be apportioned to that state.

Percentage depletion. Percentage depletion is depletion based on a statutory percentage applied to the gross income from the property. The taxpayer deducts the greater of cost depletion or percentage depletion. § 613.

Percentage of completion method. A method of reporting gain or loss on certain long-term contracts. Under this method of accounting, the gross contract price is included in income as the contract is completed. Reg. § 1.451–3.

Permanent and total disability. A person is considered permanently and totally disabled if he or she is unable to engage in any substantial gainful activity due to a physical or mental impairment. In addition, this impairment must be one that can be expected to result in death or that has lasted or can be expected to last for a continuous period of not less than 12 months. The taxpayer generally must provide the IRS a physician's statement documenting this condition.

Permanent differences. Under ASC 740 (SFAS 109), tax-related items that appear in the entity's financial statements or its tax return, but not both. For instance, interest income from a municipal bond is a permanent book-tax difference.

Personal casualty gain. The recognized gain from any involuntary conversion of personal use property arising from fire, storm, shipwreck, or other casualty, or from theft.

Personal casualty loss. The recognized loss from any involuntary conversion of personal use property arising from fire, storm, shipwreck, or other casualty, or from theft.

Personal and dependency exemptions. The tax law provides an exemption for each individual taxpayer and an additional exemption for the taxpayer's spouse if a joint return is filed. An individual may also claim a dependency exemption for each dependent, provided certain tests are met. The amount of the personal and dependency exemptions is $3,700 in 2011 ($3,650 in 2010). The exemption is subject to phaseout once adjusted gross income exceeds certain statutory threshold amounts. This phaseout provision is subject to partial phaseout beginning in 2006. Beginning in 2010, the phaseout provision no longer applies. Under the sunset provision, the phaseout of personal and dependency exemptions was scheduled to be reinstated in 2011. The Tax Relief Act (TRA) of 2010 put off the reinstatement for two years (i.e., 2011 and 2012).

Personal residence. If a residence has been owned and used by the taxpayer as the principal residence for at least two years during the five-year period ending on the date of sale, up to $250,000 of realized gain is excluded from gross income. For a married couple filing a joint return, the $250,000 is increased to $500,000 if either spouse satisfies the ownership requirement and both spouses satisfy the use requirement. § 121.

Personal service corporation (PSC). A corporation whose principal activity is the performance of personal services (e.g., health, law, engineering, architecture, accounting, actuarial science, performing arts, or consulting) and where such services are substantially performed by the employee–owners. The 35 percent statutory income tax rate applies to PSCs.

Personalty. All property that is not attached to real estate (realty) and is movable. Examples of personalty are machinery, automobiles, clothing, household furnishings, inventory, and personal effects.

Points. Loan origination fees that may be deductible as interest by a buyer of property. A seller of property who pays points reduces the selling price by the amount of the points paid for the buyer. While the seller is not permitted to deduct this amount as interest, the buyer may do so.

Portfolio income. Income from interest, dividends, rentals, royalties, capital gains, or other investment sources. Net passive losses cannot be used to offset net portfolio income.

Precedent. A previously decided court decision that is recognized as authority for the disposition of future decisions.

Precontribution gain or loss. Partnerships allow for a variety of special allocations of gain or loss among the partners, but gain or loss that is "built in" on an asset contributed to the partnership is assigned specifically to the contributing partner. § 704(c)(1)(A).

Previously taxed income (PTI). Under prior law, the undistributed taxable income of an S corporation was taxed to the shareholders as of the last day of the corporation's tax year and usually could be withdrawn by the shareholders without tax consequences at some later point in time. The role of PTI has been taken over by the accumulated adjustments account. See also *accumulated adjustments account.*

Principal partner. A partner with a 5 percent or greater interest in partnership capital or profits. § 706(b)(3).

Private activity bond. Interest on state and local bonds is excludible from gross income. § 103. Certain such bonds are labeled private activity bonds. Although the interest on such bonds is excludible for regular income tax purposes, it is treated as a tax preference in calculating the AMT.

Private foundation. An exempt organization that is subject to additional statutory restrictions on its activities and on contributions made to it. Excise taxes may be levied on certain prohibited transactions, and the Code places more stringent restrictions on the deductibility of contributions to private foundations. § 509.

Probate estate. The property of a decedent that is subject to administration by the executor or administrator of an estate.

Procedural Regulation. A Regulation issued by the Treasury Department that is a housekeeping-type instruction indicating information that taxpayers should provide the IRS as well as information about the internal management and conduct of the IRS itself.

Production activities deduction (PAD). A deduction based on 3 percent of the lesser of qualified production activities income (QPAI) or modified adjusted gross income but not to exceed 50 percent of the W–2 production wages paid. In the case of a corporate taxpayer, taxable income is substituted for modified AGI. The deduction rate increases to 6 percent for 2007 to 2009 and to 9 percent for 2010 and thereafter. § 199.

Profit and loss sharing ratios. Specified in the partnership agreement and used to determine each partner's allocation of ordinary taxable income and separately stated items. Profits and losses can be shared in different ratios. The ratios can be changed by amending the partnership agreement. § 704(a).

Profits (loss) interest. A partner's percentage allocation of partnership operating results, determined by the profit and loss sharing ratios.

Property. Assets defined in the broadest legal sense. Property includes the unrealized receivables of a cash basis taxpayer, but not services rendered. § 351.

Property dividend. Generally treated in the same manner as a cash distribution, measured by the fair market value of the property on the date of distribution. Distribution of appreciated property causes the distributing C or S corporation to recognize gain. The distributing corporation does not recognize loss on property that has depreciated in value.

Property factor. The proportion of a multistate corporation's total property that is traceable to a specific state. Used in determining the taxable income that is to be apportioned to that state.

Proportionate distribution. A distribution in which each partner in a partnership receives a pro rata share of hot assets being distributed. For example, a distribution of $10,000 of hot assets equally to two 50 percent partners is a proportionate distribution.

Proposed Regulation. A Regulation issued by the Treasury Department in proposed, rather than final, form. The interval between the proposal of a Regulation and its finalization permits taxpayers and other interested parties to comment on the propriety of the proposal.

Public Law 86–272. A congressional limit on the ability of the state to force a multistate corporation to assign income to that state. Under P.L. 86–272, where orders for tangible personal property are both filled and delivered outside the state, the entity must establish more than the mere solicitation of such orders before any income can be apportioned to the state.

Punitive damages. Damages received or paid by the taxpayer can be classified as compensatory damages or as punitive damages. Punitive damages are those awarded to punish the defendant for gross negligence or the intentional infliction of harm. Such damages are includible in gross income. § 104.

Q

Qualified business unit (QBU). A subsidiary, branch, or other business entity that conducts business using a currency other than the U.S. dollar.

Qualified dividend income. See *qualified dividends.*

Qualified dividends. Distributions made by domestic (and certain non-U.S.) corporations to noncorporate shareholders that are subject to tax at the same rates as those applicable to net long-term capital gains. The dividend must be paid out of earnings and profits, and the shareholders must meet certain holding period requirements as to the stock. Qualified dividend treatment applies to distributions made after 2002 and before 2013. §§ 1(h)(1) and (11).

Qualified employee discounts. Discounts offered employees on merchandise or services that the employer ordinarily sells or provides to customers. The discounts must be generally available to all employees. In the case of property, the discount cannot exceed the employer's gross profit (the sales price cannot be less than the employer's cost). In the case of services, the discounts cannot exceed 20 percent of the normal sales price. § 132.

Qualified nonrecourse debt. Debt issued on realty by a bank, retirement plan, or governmental agency. Included in the at-risk amount by the investor. § 465(b)(6).

Qualified production activities income (QPAI). A key determinant in computing the domestic production activities deduction (DPAD). It consists of domestic production gross receipts (DPGR) reduced by cost of goods sold and other assignable expenses. Thus, QPAI represents the profit derived from domestic production activities. § 199.

Qualified real property business indebtedness. Indebtedness that was incurred or assumed by the taxpayer in connection with real property used in a trade or business and is secured by such real property. The taxpayer must not be a C corporation. For qualified real property business indebtedness, the taxpayer may elect to exclude some or all of the income realized from cancellation of debt on qualified real property. If the election is made, the basis of the property must be reduced by the amount excluded. The amount excluded cannot be greater than the excess of the principal amount of the outstanding debt over the fair market value (net of any other debt outstanding on the property) of the property securing the debt. § 108(c).

Qualified residence interest. A term relevant in determining the amount of interest expense the individual taxpayer may deduct as an itemized deduction for what otherwise would be disallowed as a component of personal interest (consumer interest). Qualified residence interest consists of interest paid on qualified residences (principal residence and one other residence) of the taxpayer. Debt that qualifies as qualified residence interest is limited to $1 million of debt to acquire, construct, or substantially improve qualified residences (acquisition indebtedness) plus $100,000 of other debt secured by qualified residences (home equity indebtedness). The home equity indebtedness may not exceed the fair market value of a qualified residence reduced by the acquisition indebtedness for that residence. § 163(h)(3).

Qualified small business corporation. A C corporation that has aggregate gross assets not exceeding $50 million and that is conducting an active trade or business. § 1202.

Qualified small business stock. Stock in a qualified small business corporation, purchased as part of an original issue after August 10, 1993. The shareholder may exclude from gross income 50 (or 75 or 100) percent of the realized gain on the sale of the stock, if he or she held the stock for more than five years. § 1202.

Qualified terminable interest property (QTIP). Generally, the marital deduction (for gift and estate tax purposes) is not available if the interest transferred will terminate upon the death of the transferee spouse and pass to someone else. Thus, if Jim (the husband) places property in trust, life estate to Mary (the wife), and remainder to their children upon Mary's death, this is a terminable interest that will not provide Jim (or Jim's estate) with a marital deduction. If, however, the transfer in trust is treated as qualified terminable interest property (the QTIP election is made), the terminable interest restriction is waived and the marital deduction becomes available. In exchange for this deduction, the surviving spouse's gross estate must include the value of the QTIP election assets, even though he or she has no control over the ultimate disposition of the asset. Terminable interest property qualifies for this election if the donee (or heir) is the only beneficiary of the asset during his or her lifetime and receives income distributions relative to the property at least annually. For gifts, the donor spouse is the one who makes the QTIP election. For property transferred by death, the executor of the estate of the deceased spouse has the right to make the election. §§ 2056(b)(7) and 2523(f).

Qualified transportation fringes. Transportation benefits provided by the employer to the employee. Such benefits include (1) transportation in a commuter highway vehicle between the employee's residence and the place of employment, (2) a transit pass, and (3) qualified parking. Qualified transportation fringes are excludible from the employee's gross income to the extent categories (1) and (2) above do not exceed $230 per month in 2011 ($230 in 2010) and category (3) does not exceed $230 per month in 2011 ($230 in 2010). These amounts are indexed annually for inflation. § 132.

Qualified tuition program. A program that allows college tuition to be prepaid for a beneficiary. When amounts in the plan are used, nothing is included in gross income provided they are used for qualified higher education expenses. § 529.

Qualified tuition reduction plan. A type of fringe benefit plan that is available to employees of nonprofit educational institutions. Such employees (and the spouse and dependent children) are allowed to exclude from gross income a tuition waiver pursuant to a qualified tuition reduction plan. The exclusion applies to undergraduate tuition. In limited circumstances, the exclusion also applies to the graduate tuition of teaching and research assistants. §117(d).

Qualifying child. An individual who, as to the taxpayer, satisfies the relationship, abode, and age tests. To be claimed as a dependent, such individual must also meet the citizenship and joint return tests and not be self-supporting. §§ 152(a)(1) and (c).

Qualifying relative. An individual who, as to the taxpayer, satisfies the relationship, gross income, support, citizenship, and joint return tests. Such an individual can be claimed as a dependent of the taxpayer. §§ 152(a)(2) and (d).

R

Realized gain or loss. The difference between the amount realized upon the sale or other disposition of property and the adjusted basis of the property. § 1001.

Realty. Real estate.

Reasonable cause. Relief from taxpayer and preparer penalties often is allowed where reasonable cause is found for the taxpayer's actions. For example, reasonable cause for the late filing of a tax return might be a flood that damaged the taxpayer's record-keeping systems and made a timely completion of the return difficult.

Reasonableness. The Code includes a reasonableness requirement with respect to the deduction of salaries and other compensation for services. What constitutes reasonableness is a question of fact. If an expense is unreasonable, the amount that is classified as unreasonable is not allowed as a deduction. The question of reasonableness generally arises with respect to closely held corporations where there is no separation of ownership and management. § 162(a)(1).

Recognized gain or loss. The portion of realized gain or loss subject to income taxation.

Recourse debt. Debt for which the lender may both foreclose on the property and assess a guarantor for any payments due under the loan. A lender may also make a claim against the assets of any general partner in a partnership to which debt is issued, without regard to whether the partner has guaranteed the debt.

Recovery of capital doctrine. When a taxable sale or exchange occurs, the seller may be permitted to recover his or her investment (or other adjusted basis) in the property before gain or loss is recognized.

Redemption to pay death taxes. Sale or exchange treatment is available relative to this type of redemption, to the extent of the proceeds up to the total amount paid by the estate or heir for death taxes and administration expenses. The stock value must exceed 35 percent of the value of the decedent's adjusted gross estate. In meeting this test, one can combine shareholdings in corporations where the decedent held at least 20 percent of the outstanding shares.

Refundable credit. A refundable credit is a credit that is paid to the taxpayer even if the amount of the credit (or credits) exceeds the taxpayer's tax liability.

Regular corporation. See *C corporation.*

Rehabilitation expenditures credit. A credit that is based on expenditures incurred to rehabilitate industrial and commercial buildings and certified historic structures. The credit is intended to discourage businesses from moving from older, economically distressed areas to newer locations and to encourage the preservation of historic structures. § 47.

Rehabilitation expenditures credit recapture. When property that qualifies for the rehabilitation expenditures credit is disposed of or ceases to be used in the trade or business of the taxpayer, some or all of the tax credit claimed on the property may be recaptured as additional tax liability. The amount of the recapture is the difference between the amount of the credit claimed originally and what should have been claimed in light of the length of time the property was actually held or used for qualifying purposes. § 50.

Related corporation. See *controlled group.*

Related parties. Various Code Sections define related parties and often include a variety of persons within this (usually detrimental) category. Generally, related parties are accorded different tax treatment from that applicable to other taxpayers who enter into similar transactions. For instance, realized losses that are generated between related parties are not recognized in the year of the loss. However, these deferred losses can be used to offset recognized gains that occur upon the subsequent sale of the asset to a nonrelated party. Other uses of a related-party definition include the conversion of gain upon the sale of a depreciable asset into all ordinary income (§ 1239) and the identification of constructive ownership of stock relative to corporate distributions, redemptions, liquidations, reorganizations, and compensation.

Related-party transactions. The tax law places restrictions upon the recognition of gains and losses between related parties because of the potential for abuse. For example, restrictions are placed on the deduction of losses from the sale or exchange of property between related parties. In addition, under certain circumstances, related-party gains that would otherwise be classified as capital gain are classified as ordinary income. §§ 267, 707(b), and 1239.

Rental activity. Any activity where payments are received principally for the use of tangible property is a rental activity. Temporary Regulations provide that in certain circumstances activities involving rentals of real and personal property are not to be *treated* as rental activities. The Temporary Regulations list six exceptions.

Reorganization. Occurs, among other instances, when one corporation acquires another in a merger or acquisition, a single corporation divides into two or more entities, a corporation makes a substantial change in its capital structure, or a corporation undertakes a change in its legal name or domicile. The exchange of stock and other securities in a corporate reorganization can be effected favorably for tax purposes if certain statutory requirements are followed strictly. Tax consequences include the nonrecognition of any gain that is realized by the shareholders except to the extent of boot received.

Research activities credit. A tax credit whose purpose is to encourage research and development. It consists of three components: the incremental research activities credit, the basic research credit, and the energy credit. The incremental research activities credit is equal to 20 percent of the excess qualified research expenditures over the base amount. The basic research credit is equal to 20 percent of the excess of basic research payments over the base amount. § 41.

Research and experimental expenditures. The Code provides three alternatives for the tax treatment of research and experimentation expenditures. They may be expensed in the year paid or incurred, deferred subject to amortization, or capitalized. If the taxpayer does not elect to expense such costs or to defer them subject to amortization (over 60 months), the expenditures must be capitalized. § 174. Three types of research activities credits are available: the basic research credit, the incremental research activities credit, and the energy credit. The rate for each type is 20 percent. § 41.

Reserve method. A method of accounting whereby an allowance is permitted for estimated uncollectible accounts. Actual write-offs are charged to the reserve, and recoveries of amounts previously written off are credited to the reserve. The Code permits only certain financial institutions to use the reserve method. § 166.

Residential rental real estate. Buildings for which at least 80 percent of the gross rents are from dwelling units (e.g., an apartment building). This type of building is distinguished from nonresidential (commercial or industrial) buildings in applying the recapture of depreciation provisions. The term also is relevant in distinguishing between buildings that are eligible for a 27.5-year life versus a 39-year life for MACRS purposes. Generally, residential buildings receive preferential treatment.

Revenue Agent's Report. A Revenue Agent's Report (RAR) reflects any adjustments made by the agent as a result of an audit of the taxpayer. The RAR is mailed to the taxpayer along with the 30-day letter, which outlines the appellate procedures available to the taxpayer.

Revenue neutrality. A description that characterizes tax legislation when it neither increases nor decreases the revenue result. Thus, any tax revenue losses are offset by tax revenue gains.

Revenue Procedure. A matter of procedural importance to both taxpayers and the IRS concerning the administration of the tax laws is issued as a Revenue Procedure (abbreviated Rev.Proc.). A Revenue Procedure is published in an *Internal Revenue Bulletin* (I.R.B.)

Revenue Ruling. A Revenue Ruling (abbreviated Rev.Rul.) is issued by the National Office of the IRS to express an official interpretation of the tax law as applied to specific transactions. It is more limited in application than a Regulation. A Revenue Ruling is published in an *Internal Revenue Bulletin* (I.R.B.)

Reversionary interest. The trust property that reverts to the grantor after the expiration of an intervening income interest. Assume Phil places real estate in trust with income to Junior for 11 years, and upon the expiration of this term, the property returns to Phil. Under these circumstances, Phil holds a reversionary interest in the property. A reversionary interest is the same as a remainder interest, except that, in the latter case, the property passes to someone other than the original owner (e.g., the grantor of a trust) upon the expiration of the intervening interest.

Roth IRAs. See *individual retirement account (IRA).*

S

S corporation. The designation for a small business corporation. See also *Subchapter S.*

Sale or exchange. A requirement for the recognition of capital gain or loss. Generally, the seller of property must receive money or relief from debt in order to have sold the property. An exchange involves the transfer of property for other property. Thus, collection of a debt is neither a sale nor an exchange. The term *sale or exchange* is not defined by the Code.

Sales factor. The proportion of a multistate corporation's total sales that is traceable to a specific state. Used in determining the taxable income that is to be apportioned to that state.

Sales tax. A state- or local-level tax on the retail sale of specified property. Generally, the purchaser pays the tax, but the seller collects it, as an agent for the government. Various taxing jurisdictions allow exemptions for purchases of specific items, including certain food, services, and manufacturing equipment. If the purchaser and seller are in different states, a use tax usually applies.

Schedule K–1. A tax information form prepared for each partner in a partnership, each shareholder of an S corporation, and some beneficiaries of certain trusts. The Schedule K–1 reports the owner's share of the entity's ordinary income or loss from operations, as well as the owner's share of separately stated items.

Schedule M–1. On the Form 1120, a reconciliation of book net income with Federal taxable income. Accounts for temporary and permanent differences in the two computations, such as depreciation differences, exempt income, and nondeductible items. On Forms 1120S and 1065, the Schedule M–1 reconciles book income with the owners' aggregate ordinary taxable income.

Schedule M–3. An *expanded* reconciliation of book net income with Federal taxable income (see *Schedule M–1*). Required of C and S corporations and partnerships/LLCs with total assets of $10 million or more.

Scholarships. Scholarships are generally excluded from the gross income of the recipient unless the payments are a disguised form of compensation for services rendered. However, the Code imposes restrictions on the exclusion. The recipient must be a degree candidate. The excluded amount is limited to amounts used for tuition, fees, books, supplies, and equipment required for courses of instruction. Amounts received for room and board are not eligible for the exclusion. § 117.

Section 121 exclusion. If a residence has been owned and used by the taxpayer as the principal residence for at least two years during the five-year period ending on the date of sale, up to $250,000 of realized gain is excluded from gross income. For a married couple filing a joint return, the $250,000 is increased to $500,000 if either spouse satisfies the ownership requirement and both spouses satisfy the use requirement.

Section 179 expensing. The ability to deduct a capital expenditure in the year an asset is placed in service rather than over the asset's useful life or cost recovery period. The annual ceiling on the deduction is $500,000 for 2011. However, the deduction is reduced dollar for dollar when § 179 property placed in service during the taxable year exceeds $2 million in 2011. In addition, the amount expensed under § 179 cannot exceed the aggregate amount of taxable income derived from the conduct of any trade or business by the taxpayer.

Section 338 election. When a corporation acquires at least 80 percent of a subsidiary in a 12-month period, it can elect to treat the acquisition of such stock as an asset purchase. The acquiring corporation's basis in the subsidiary's assets then is the cost of the stock. The subsidiary is deemed to have sold its assets for an amount equal to the grossed-up basis in its stock.

Section 1231 gains and losses. If the combined gains and losses from the taxable dispositions of § 1231 assets plus the net gain from business involuntary conversions (of both § 1231 assets and long-term capital assets) is a gain, the gains and losses are treated as long-term capital gains and losses. In arriving at § 1231 gains, however, the depreciation recapture provisions (e.g., § 1245) are applied first to produce ordinary income. If the net result of the combination is a loss, the gains and losses from § 1231 assets are treated as ordinary gains and losses. § 1231(a).

Section 1231 lookback. In order for gain to be classified as § 1231 gain, the gain must survive the § 1231 lookback. To the extent of nonrecaptured § 1231 losses for the five prior tax years, the gain is classified as ordinary income. § 1231(c).

Section 1231 property. Depreciable assets and real estate used in trade or business and held for the required long-term holding period. Under certain circumstances, the classification also includes timber, coal, domestic iron ore, livestock (held for draft, breeding, dairy, or sporting purposes), and unharvested crops. § 1231(b).

Section 1244 stock. Stock issued under § 1244 by qualifying small business corporations. If § 1244 stock becomes worthless, the shareholders may claim an ordinary loss rather than the usual capital loss, within statutory limitations.

Section 1245 property. Property that is subject to the recapture of depreciation under § 1245. For a definition of § 1245 property, see § 1245(a)(3).

Section 1245 recapture. Upon a taxable disposition of § 1245 property, all depreciation claimed on the property is recaptured as ordinary income (but not to exceed recognized gain from the disposition).

Section 1250 property. Real estate that is subject to the recapture of depreciation under § 1250. For a definition of § 1250 property, see § 1250(c).

Section 1250 recapture. Upon a taxable disposition of § 1250 property, accelerated depreciation or cost recovery claimed on the property may be recaptured as ordinary income.

Securities. Generally, stock, debt, and other financial assets. To the extent securities other than the stock of the transferee corporation are received in a § 351 exchange, the new shareholder realizes a gain.

Self-employment tax. In 2011, a tax of 10.4 percent is levied on individuals with net earnings from self-employment (up to $106,800) to provide Social Security benefits (i.e., the old age, survivors, and disability insurance portion) for such individuals. For 2010, the rate is 12.4 percent. In addition, in 2011 (and 2010), a tax of 2.9 percent is levied on individuals with net earnings from self-employment (with no statutory ceiling) to provide Medicare benefits (i.e., the hospital insurance portion) for such individuals. If a self-employed individual also receives wages from an employer that are subject to FICA, the self-employment tax will be reduced if total income subject to Social Security is more than $106,800 in 2011. A partial deduction is allowed in calculating the self-employment tax. Individuals with net earnings of $400 or more from self-employment are subject to this tax. §§ 1401 and 1402.

Separately stated item. Any item of a partnership or S corporation that might be taxed differently to any two owners of the entity. These amounts are not included in ordinary income of the entity, but are instead reported separately to the owners; tax consequences are determined at the owner level.

Severance tax. A tax imposed upon the extraction of natural resources.

Short sale. A short sale occurs when a taxpayer sells borrowed property (usually stock) and repays the lender with substantially identical property either held on the date of the short sale or purchased after the sale. No gain or loss is recognized until the short sale is closed, and such gain or loss is generally short term. § 1233.

Short taxable year (short period). A tax year that is less than 12 months. A short taxable year may occur in the initial reporting period, in the final tax year, or when the taxpayer changes tax years.

Significant participation activity. There are seven tests to determine whether an individual has achieved material participation in an activity, one of which is based on more than 500 hours of participation in significant participation activities. A significant participation activity is one in which the individual's participation exceeds 100 hours during the year. Temp.Reg. § 1.469–5T.

Simple trust. Simple trusts are those that are not complex trusts. Such trusts may not have a charitable beneficiary, accumulate income, or distribute corpus.

Small business corporation. A corporation that satisfies the definition of § 1361(b), § 1244(c), or both. Satisfaction of § 1361(b) permits an S election, and satisfaction of § 1244 enables the shareholders of the corporation to claim an ordinary loss on the worthlessness of stock.

Small business stock. See *small business corporation.*

Small Cases Division. A division within the U.S. Tax Court where jurisdiction is limited to claims of $50,000 or less. There is no appeal from this court.

Special allocation. Any amount for which an agreement exists among the partners of a partnership outlining the method used for spreading the item among the partners.

Specific charge-off method. A method of accounting for bad debts in which a deduction is permitted only when an account becomes partially or completely worthless.

Sprinkling trust. When a trustee has the discretion to either distribute or accumulate the entity accounting income of the trust and to distribute it among the trust's income beneficiaries in varying magnitudes, a sprinkling trust exists. The trustee can "sprinkle" the income of the trust.

Standard deduction. The individual taxpayer can either itemize deductions or take the standard deduction. The amount of the standard deduction depends on the taxpayer's filing status (single, head of household, married filing jointly, surviving spouse, or married filing separately). For 2011, the amount of the standard deduction ranges from $5,800 (for married, filing separately) to $11,600 (for married, filing jointly). Additional standard deductions of either $1,150 (for married taxpayers) or $1,450 (for single taxpayers) are available if the taxpayer is either blind or age 65 or over. For 2008 and 2009, a real property tax standard deduction is available in the amount of $500 ($1,000 on a joint return). For 2009, there also is a limited auto sales taxes standard deduction. Limitations exist on the amount of the standard deduction of a taxpayer who is another taxpayer's dependent. The standard deduction amounts are adjusted for inflation each year. § 63(c).

Startup expenditures. Expenditures paid or incurred associated with the creation of a business prior to the beginning of business. Examples of such expenditures include advertising, salaries and wages, travel and other expenses incurred in lining up prospective distributors, suppliers, or customers, and salaries and fees to executives, consultants, and professional service providers. A taxpayer may elect to immediately expense the first $5,000 (subject to phaseout) of startup expenditures and generally amortize the balance over a period of 180 months. For 2010, the $5,000 amount was increased to $10,000.

Statute of limitations. Provisions of the law that specify the maximum period of time in which action may be taken on a past event. Code §§ 6501–6504 contain the limitation periods applicable to the IRS for additional assessments, and §§ 6511–6515 relate to refund claims by taxpayers.

Statutory employee. Statutory employees are considered self-employed independent contractors for purposes of reporting income and expenses on their tax returns. Generally, a statutory employee must meet three tests:

- It is understood from a service contract that the services will be performed by the person.
- The person does not have a substantial investment in facilities (other than transportation used to perform the services).
- The services involve a continuing relationship with the person for whom they are performed.

For further information on statutory employees, see Circular E, *Employer's Tax Guide* (IRS Publication 15).

Stock dividend. Not taxable if pro rata distributions of stock or stock rights on common stock. Section 305 governs the taxability of stock dividends and sets out five exceptions to the general rule that stock dividends are nontaxable.

Stock redemption. A corporation buys back its own stock from a specified shareholder. Typically, the corporation recognizes any realized gain on the noncash assets that it uses to effect a redemption, and the shareholder obtains a capital gain or loss upon receipt of the purchase price.

Stock rights. Assets that convey to the holder the power to purchase corporate stock at a specified price, often for a limited period of time. Stock rights received may be taxed as a distribution of earnings and profits. After the right is exercised, the basis of the acquired share includes the investor's purchase price or gross income, if any, to obtain the right. Disposition of the right also can be taxable.

Subchapter S. Sections 1361–1379 of the Internal Revenue Code. An elective provision permitting certain small business corporations (§ 1361) and their shareholders (§ 1362) to elect to be treated for income tax purposes in accordance with the operating rules of §§ 1363–1379. However, some S corporations usually avoid the corporate income tax, and corporate losses can be claimed by the shareholders.

Subpart F. That subpart of the Code that identifies the current tax treatment of income earned by a controlled foreign corporation. Certain types of income are included in U.S. gross income by U.S. shareholders of such an entity as they are generated, not when they are repatriated.

Substantial authority. Taxpayer and tax preparer understatement penalties are waived where substantial authority existed for the disputed position taken on the return.

Sunset provision. A provision attached to new tax legislation that will cause such legislation to expire at a specified date. Sunset provisions are attached to tax cut bills for long-term budgetary reasons in order to make their effect temporary. Once the sunset provision comes into play, the tax cut is rescinded and former law is reinstated. An example of a sunset provision is the one contained in the Tax Relief Reconciliation Act of 2001 that related to the estate tax. After the estate tax was phased out in 2010, a sunset provision called for the reinstatement of the estate tax as of January 1, 2011.

Surviving spouse. When a husband or wife predeceases the other spouse, the survivor is known as a surviving spouse. Under certain conditions, a surviving spouse may be entitled to use the income tax rates in § 1(a) (those applicable to married persons filing a joint return) for the two years after the year of death of his or her spouse. § 2.

Syndication costs. Incurred in promoting and marketing partnership interests for sale to investors. Examples include legal and accounting fees, printing costs for prospectus and placement documents, and state registration fees. These items are capitalized by the partnership as incurred, with no amortization thereof allowed.

T

Tax avoidance. The minimization of one's tax liability by taking advantage of legally available tax planning opportunities. Tax avoidance can be contrasted with tax evasion, which entails the reduction of tax liability by illegal means.

Tax benefit rule. A provision that limits the recognition of income from the recovery of an expense or loss properly deducted in a prior tax year to the amount of the deduction that generated a tax saving. Assume that last year Gary had medical expenses of $3,000 and adjusted gross income of $30,000. Because of the 7.5 percent limitation, Gary could deduct only $750 of these expenses [$3,000 − (7.5% × $30,000)]. If, this year, Gary is reimbursed by his insurance company for the $3,000 of expenses, the tax benefit rule limits the amount of income from the reimbursement to $750 (the amount previously deducted with a tax saving).

Tax credit for the elderly or disabled. An elderly (age 65 and over) or disabled taxpayer may receive a tax credit amounting to 15 percent of $5,000 ($7,500 for qualified married individuals filing jointly). This amount is reduced by Social Security benefits, excluded pension benefits, and one-half of the taxpayer's adjusted gross income in excess of $7,500 ($10,000 for married taxpayers filing jointly). § 22.

Tax credits. Tax credits are amounts that directly reduce a taxpayer's tax liability. The tax benefit received from a tax credit is not dependent on the taxpayer's marginal tax rate, whereas the benefit of a tax deduction or exclusion is dependent on the taxpayer's tax bracket.

Tax evasion. The reduction of taxes by the use of subterfuge or fraud or other nonlegal means. For example, a cash basis taxpayer tries to increase his or her charitable contribution deduction by prepaying next year's church pledge with a pre-dated check issued in the following year.

Tax haven. A country in which either locally sourced income or residents of the country are subject to a low rate of taxation.

Tax preferences. Various items that may result in the imposition of the alternative minimum tax. §§ 55–58.

Tax preparer. One who prepares tax returns for compensation. A tax preparer may be qualified to practice before the IRS and represent taxpayers before the agency in tax audit actions. The conduct of a tax preparer is regulated under Circular 230. Tax preparers also are subject to penalties for inappropriate conduct when working in the tax profession.

Tax rate schedules. Rate schedules that are used by upper-income taxpayers and those not permitted to use the tax table. Separate rate schedules are provided for married individuals filing jointly, heads of households, single taxpayers, estates and trusts, and married individuals filing separate returns. § 1.

Tax research. The method used to determine the best available solution to a situation that possesses tax consequences. Both tax and nontax factors are considered.

Tax shelters. The typical tax shelter generated large losses in the early years of the activity. Investors would offset these losses against other types of income and, therefore, avoid paying income taxes on this income. These tax shelter investments could then be sold after a few years and produce capital gain income, which is taxed at a lower rate than ordinary income. The passive activity loss rules and the at-risk rules now limit tax shelter deductions.

Tax table. A tax table that is provided for taxpayers with less than $100,000 of taxable income. Separate columns are provided for single taxpayers, married taxpayers filing jointly, heads of households, and married taxpayers filing separately. § 3.

Tax treaty. An agreement between the U.S. Department of State and another country, designed to alleviate double taxation of income and asset transfers, and to share administrative information useful to tax agencies in both countries. The United States has income tax treaties with over 40 countries, and transfer tax treaties with about 20.

Taxable estate. The taxable estate is the gross estate of a decedent reduced by the deductions allowed by §§ 2053–2057 (e.g., administration expenses, marital and charitable deductions). The taxable estate is subject to the unified transfer tax at death. § 2051.

Taxable gift. The amount of a gift that is subject to the unified transfer tax. Thus, a taxable gift has been adjusted by the annual exclusion and other appropriate deductions (e.g., marital and charitable). § 2053.

Taxable year. The annual period over which income is measured for income tax purposes. Most individuals use a calendar year, but many businesses use a fiscal year based on the natural business year.

Technical advice memoranda (TAMs). TAMs are issued by the IRS in response to questions raised by IRS field personnel during audits. They deal with completed rather than proposed transactions and are often requested for questions related to exempt organizations and employee plans.

Temporary differences. Under ASC 740 (SFAS 109), tax-related items that appear in the entity's financial statements and its tax return, but in different time periods. For instance, doubtful accounts receivable often create a temporary book-tax difference, as a bad debt reserve is used to compute an expense for financial reporting purposes, but a bad debt often is deductible only under the specific write-off rule for tax purposes, and the difference observed for the current period creates a temporary difference.

Temporary Regulation. A Regulation issued by the Treasury Department in temporary form. When speed is critical, the Treasury Department issues Temporary Regulations that take effect immediately. These Regulations have the same authoritative value as Final Regulations and may be cited as precedent for three years. Temporary Regulations are also issued as proposed Regulations.

Tenants by the entirety. Essentially, a joint tenancy between husband and wife.

Tenants in common. A form of ownership where each tenant (owner) holds an undivided interest in property. Unlike a joint tenancy or a tenancy by the entirety, the interest of a tenant in common does not terminate upon that individual's death (there is no right of survivorship). Assume Tim and Cindy acquire real estate as equal tenants in common, each having furnished one-half of the purchase price. Upon Tim's death, his one-half interest in the property passes to his estate or heirs, not to Cindy.

Tentative minimum tax (TMT). In calculating a taxpayer's alternative minimum tax (AMT), the TMT is a subtotal representing the gross amount of tax liability. AMT equals the difference between the TMT and the regular tax liability. If this difference is positive, an AMT is due; if it is zero or negative, the AMT liability is zero. Only a positive AMT creates a minimum tax credit.

Terminable interest. An interest in property that terminates upon the death of the holder or upon the occurrence of some other specified event. The transfer of a terminable interest by one spouse to the other may not qualify for the marital deduction. §§ 2056(b) and 2523(b).

Theft loss. A loss from larceny, embezzlement, or robbery. It does not include misplacement of items.

Thin capitalization. When debt owed by a corporation to the shareholders becomes too large in relation to the corporation's capital structure (i.e., stock and shareholder equity), the IRS may contend that the corporation is thinly capitalized. In effect, some or all of the debt is reclassified as equity. The immediate result is to disallow any interest deduction to the corporation on the reclassified debt. To the extent of the corporation's earnings and profits, interest payments and loan repayments on the reclassified debt are treated as dividends to the shareholders.

Thirty-day letter. A letter that accompanies an RAR (Revenue Agent's Report) issued as a result of an IRS audit of a taxpayer (or the rejection of a taxpayer's claim for refund). The letter outlines the taxpayer's appeal procedure before the IRS. If the taxpayer does not request any such procedures within the 30-day period, the IRS issues a statutory notice of deficiency (the 90-day letter).

Throwback rule. If there is no income tax in the state to which a sale otherwise would be apportioned, the sale essentially is exempt from state income tax, even though the seller is domiciled in a state that levies an income tax. Nonetheless, if the seller's state has adopted a throwback rule, the sale is attributed to the *seller's* state, and the transaction is subjected to a state-level tax.

Transfer pricing. The process of setting internal prices for transfers of goods and services among related taxpayers. For example, what price should be used when Subsidiary purchases management services from Parent? Section 482 allows the IRS to adjust transfer prices when it can show that the taxpayers were attempting to avoid tax by, say, shifting losses, deductions, or credits from low-tax to high-tax entities or jurisdictions.

Transportation expenses. Transportation expenses for an employee include only the cost of transportation (taxi fares, automobile expenses, etc.) in the course of employment when the employee is not away from home in travel status. Commuting expenses are not deductible.

Travel expenses. Travel expenses include meals (generally subject to a 50 percent disallowance) and lodging and transportation expenses while away from home in the pursuit of a trade or business (including that of an employee).

Treaty shopping. An international investor attempts to use the favorable aspects of a tax treaty to his or her advantage, often elevating the form of the transaction over its substance (e.g., by establishing only a nominal presence in the country offering the favorable treaty terms).

U

UDITPA. The Uniform Division of Income for Tax Purposes Act has been adopted in some form by many of the states. The Act develops criteria by which the total taxable income of a multistate corporation can be assigned to specific states.

Unearned income. Income received but not yet earned. Normally, such income is taxed when received, even for accrual basis taxpayers.

Unified transfer tax. Rates applicable to transfers by gift and death made after 1976. § 2001(c).

Unified transfer tax credit. A credit allowed against any unified transfer tax. §§ 2010 and 2505.

Unitary theory. Sales, property, and payroll of related corporations are combined for nexus and apportionment purposes, and the worldwide income of the unitary entity is apportioned to the state. Subsidiaries and other affiliated corporations found to be part of the corporation's unitary business (because they are subject to overlapping ownership, operation, or management) are included in the apportionment procedure. This approach can be limited if a water's edge election is in effect.

Unit-livestock-price method. A method of accounting for the cost of livestock. The livestock are valued using a standard cost of raising an animal with the characteristics of the animals on hand to the same age as those animals.

Unrealized receivables. Amounts earned by a cash basis taxpayer but not yet received. Because of the method of accounting used by the taxpayer, these amounts have a zero income tax basis. When unrealized receivables are distributed to a partner, they generally convert a transaction from nontaxable to taxable or an otherwise capital gain to ordinary income.

Unreasonable compensation. A deduction is allowed for "reasonable" salaries or other compensation for personal services actually rendered. To the extent compensation is "excessive" ("unreasonable"), no deduction is allowed. The problem of unreasonable compensation usually is limited to closely held corporations, where the motivation is to pay out profits in some form that is deductible to the corporation.

Unreasonable position. A tax preparer penalty is assessed regarding the understatement of a client's tax liability due to a tax return position that is found to be too aggressive. The penalty is avoided if there is substantial authority for the position, or if the position is disclosed adequately on the tax return. The penalty equals the greater of $1,000 or one-half of the tax preparer's fee that is traceable to the aggressive position.

Unrecaptured § 1250 gain (25 percent gain). Gain from the sale of depreciable real estate held more than one year. The gain is equal to or less than the depreciation taken on such property and is reduced by § 1245 and § 1250 gain.

Unrelated business income. Income recognized by an exempt organization that is generated from activities not related to the exempt purpose of the entity. For instance, the pharmacy located in a hospital may generate unrelated business income. § 511.

Unrelated business income tax. Levied on the unrelated business income of an exempt organization.

U.S. Court of Federal Claims. A trial court (court of original jurisdiction) that decides litigation involving Federal tax matters. Appeal from this court is to the Court of Appeals for the Federal Circuit.

U.S. shareholder. For purposes of classification of an entity as a controlled foreign corporation, a U.S. person who owns, or is considered to own, 10 percent or more of the total combined voting power of all classes of voting stock of a foreign corporation. Stock owned directly, indirectly, and constructively is counted for this purpose.

U.S. Supreme Court. The highest appellate court or the court of last resort in the Federal court system and in most states. Only a small number of tax decisions of the U.S. Courts of Appeal are reviewed by the U.S. Supreme Court under its certiorari procedure. The Supreme Court usually grants certiorari to resolve a conflict among the Courts of Appeal (e.g., two or more appellate courts have assumed opposing positions on a particular issue) or when the tax issue is extremely important (e.g., size of the revenue loss to the Federal government).

U.S. Tax Court. The U.S. Tax Court is one of four trial courts of original jurisdiction that decides litigation involving Federal income, death, or gift taxes. It is the only trial court where the taxpayer must not first pay the deficiency assessed by the IRS. The Tax Court will not have jurisdiction over a case unless a statutory notice of deficiency (90-day letter) has been issued by the IRS and the taxpayer files the petition for hearing within the time prescribed.

U.S. trade or business. A set of activities that is carried on in a regular, continuous, and substantial manner. A non-U.S. taxpayer is subject to U.S. tax on the taxable income that is effectively connected with a U.S. trade or business.

Use tax. A sales tax that is collectible by the seller where the purchaser is domiciled in a different state.

V

Vacation home. The Code places restrictions upon taxpayers who rent their residences or vacation homes for part of the tax year. The restrictions may result in a scaling down of expense deductions for the taxpayers. § 280A.

Valuation allowance. Under ASC 740 (SFAS 109), a tax-related item is reported for book purposes only when it is more likely than not that the item actually will be realized. When the "more likely than not" test is failed, a contra-asset account is created to offset some or all of the related deferred tax asset. For instance, if the entity projects that it will not be able to use all of its net operating loss carryforward due to a lack of future taxable income, a valuation allowance is created to reduce the net deferred tax asset that corresponds to the carryforward. If income projections later change and it appears that the carryforward will be used, the valuation allowance is reversed or "released." Creation of a valuation allowance usually increases the current tax expense and thereby reduces current book income, and its release often increases book income in the later reporting period.

Value added tax (VAT). A national sales tax that taxes the increment in value as goods move through the production process. A VAT is much used in other countries but has not yet been incorporated as part of the U.S. Federal tax structure.

Voluntary revocation. The owners of a majority of shares in an S corporation elect to terminate the S status of the entity, as of a specified date. The day on which the revocation is effective is the first day of the corporation's C tax year.

W

W–2 wages. The domestic production activities deduction (DPAD) cannot exceed 50 percent of the W–2 wages paid for any particular year. Prop.Reg. § 199–2(f)(2) provides several methods for calculating the W–2 wages, but the payments must involve common law employees. To qualify, employees need to be involved in the production process. § 199.

Wash sale. A loss from the sale of stock or securities that is disallowed because the taxpayer, within 30 days before or after the sale, has acquired stock or securities substantially identical to those sold. § 1091.

Water's edge election. A limitation on the worldwide scope of the unitary theory. If a corporate water's edge election is in effect, the state can consider in the apportionment procedure only the activities that occur within the boundaries of the United States.

Welfare-to-work credit. A tax credit available to employers hiring individuals who have been long-term recipients of family assistance welfare benefits. In general, long-term recipients are those individuals who are certified by a designated local agency as being members of a family receiving assistance under a public aid program for at least an 18-month period ending on the hiring date. The welfare-to-work credit is available for qualified wages paid in the first two years of employment. The maximum credit is equal to $9,000 per qualified employee, computed as 40 percent of the first $10,000 of qualified wages paid in the first year of employment, plus 50 percent of the first $10,000 of qualified wages paid in the second year of employment. Starting in 2007, the welfare-to-work credit became part of the work opportunity tax credit. § 51(e). See also *work opportunity tax credit.*

Wherewithal to pay. This concept recognizes the inequity of taxing a transaction when the taxpayer lacks the means with which to pay the tax. Under it, there is a correlation between the imposition of the tax and the ability to pay the tax. It is particularly suited to situations in which the taxpayer's economic position has not changed significantly as a result of the transaction.

Whistleblower program. An IRS initiative that offers special rewards to informants who provide evidence regarding tax evasion activities of businesses or high-income individuals. More than $2 million of tax, interest, and penalty must be at stake. The reward can reach 30 percent of the tax recovery that is attributable to the whistleblower's information.

Working condition fringe. A type of fringe benefit received by the employee that is excludible from the employee's gross income. It consists of property or services provided (paid or reimbursed) by the employer for which the employee could take a tax deduction if the employee had paid for them. § 132.

Work opportunity tax credit. Employers are allowed a tax credit equal to 40 percent of the first $6,000 of wages (per eligible employee) for the first year of employment. Eligible employees include certain hard-to-employ individuals (e.g., qualified ex-felons, high-risk youth, food stamp recipients, and veterans). The employer's deduction for wages is reduced by the amount of the credit taken. For qualified summer youth employees, the 40 percent rate is applied to the first $3,000 of qualified wages. See *welfare-to-work credit* for the calculation for long-term recipients of family assistance welfare benefits. §§ 51 and 52.

Worthless securities. A loss (usually capital) is allowed for a security that becomes worthless during the year. The loss is deemed to have occurred on the last day of the year. Special rules apply to securities of affiliated companies and small business stock. § 165.

Writ of Certiorari. Appeal from a U.S. Court of Appeals to the U.S. Supreme Court is by Writ of Certiorari. The Supreme Court need not accept the appeal, and it usually does not (*cert. den.*) unless a conflict exists among the lower courts that must be resolved or a constitutional issue is involved.

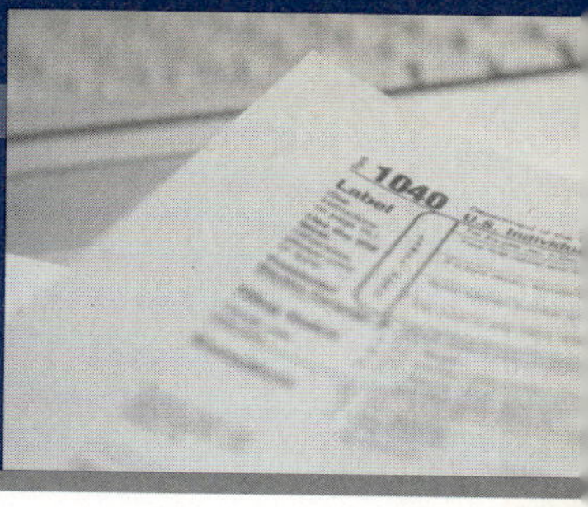

Appendix D-1

TABLE OF CODE SECTIONS CITED

[See Title 26 U.S.C.A.]

Appendix D-2

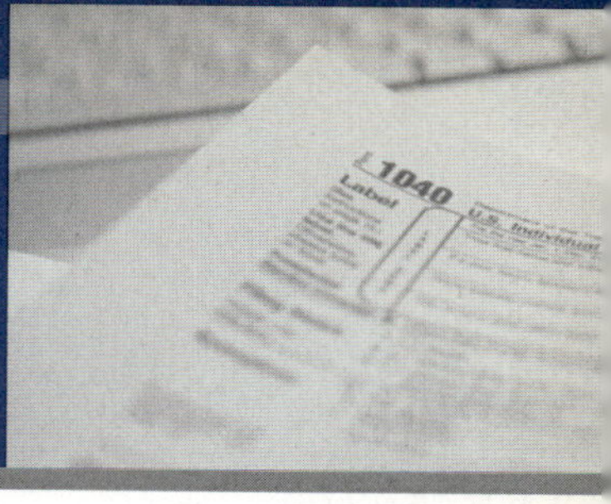

TABLE OF REGULATIONS CITED

Treasury Regulations

Treasury Regulations

Treasury Regulations

Treasury Regulations

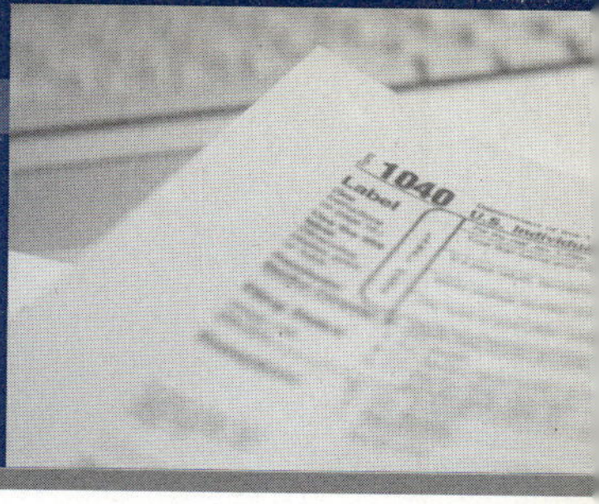

Appendix D-3

TABLE OF REVENUE PROCEDURES AND REVENUE RULINGS CITED

Revenue Procedures

Revenue Rulings

Revenue Rulings

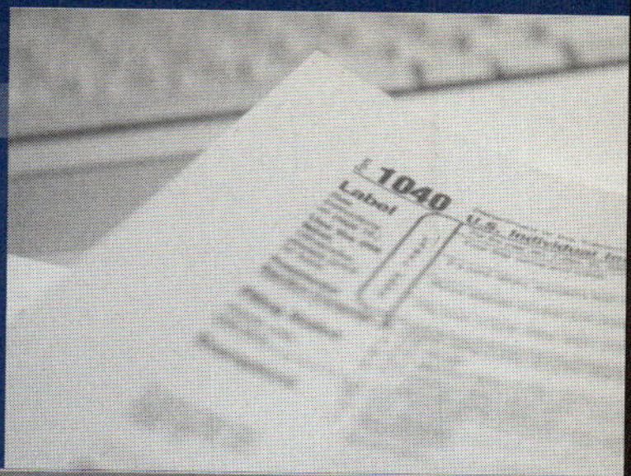

Appendix E

COMPREHENSIVE TAX RETURN PROBLEMS

Problem 1—Individuals (Form 1040)

Paul S. and Ruth N. Hood (ages 42 and 41) are married and live at 4326 Orange Blossom Trail, Tampa, FL 33601. Paul is the regional manager for a budget motel chain (Rest Inn), while Ruth is a self-employed architect. They file a joint return and use the cash basis for tax purposes.

1. Paul receives a yearly salary of $82,000, plus an annual bonus, from Rest Inn. The annual bonus is determined in December of each year but not paid until January of the following year. Paul's bonus is $6,000 for 2009 (received in 2010) and $7,000 for 2010 (received in 2011). Paul also is paid a flat travel allowance of $16,000 per year. The allowance is to cover his expenses in visiting motels in his region to conduct inspections, consult with the local managers, and recruit potential hires. Although Paul maintains substantiation of his travel, he is not required to account for these expenses to Rest Inn. Paul participates in his employer's group health insurance plan to which he contributed $3,600 in 2010 for medical coverage. Rest Inn does not provide any retirement benefits, but it has established a § 401(k) plan to enable its employees to make voluntary contributions. Paul did not contribute to the plan in 2010. The company provides an office for Paul's use that is located at Suite 419, 110 Palm Boulevard, Tampa.

2. Besides the business use of the Impala (see item 3 below), Paul's employment-related expenses for 2010 are as follows:

Airfare	$2,600
Lodging	3,200
Meals	3,400
Entertainment	800
Car rentals, limos, taxis	600
Parking and tolls (during travel)	300
Subscriptions to trade journals	120
Dues to trade association	80
Business gifts	550

While on business trips in his Impala, Paul was caught in several small-town speed traps and paid fines of $620. The business gifts were made at Christmas and consisted of gift cards ($50 each) to a national chain restaurant. They were sent to 11 key managers of motels in Paul's region.

3. On March 5, 2009, Paul purchased a new Chevrolet Impala for use in his job. The car, a five-passenger sedan, cost $24,000 (including sales tax), with no trade-in involved. The car was driven 14,000 miles in 2009 and 18,000 in 2010 with usage as follows: 20% for commuting to the office and 80% for business trips. The mileage for 2010 was evenly

distributed throughout the year. Paul uses the actual operating cost method and for depreciation purposes uses 200% declining-balance with a half-year convention. No § 179 expensing or additional first-year depreciation has been claimed. (See Table 3 of the Instructions to Form 4562.) Paul's expenses relating to the operation of the Impala for 2010 are as follows:

Gasoline	$2,500
Oil change and lubrication	110
Auto insurance	1,800
Repairs	400
Auto club dues	160
License and registration	120
Interest on car loan	900

4. Ruth is a licensed architect who works part-time on a consulting basis. Her major clients are real estate developers (both residential and commercial) for which she prepares structural designs and construction plans. She also advises on building code requirements regarding the renovation and remodeling of existing structures. Because she limits her engagements, she does not have a separate office but does her work at the client's premises or in her office at home (see item 5 below). Her business expenses for 2010 are summarized below:

Drafting supplies	$4,800
Reproduction materials (e.g., molds, models, photos, blueprints, copies)	3,200
On-site work clothing (e.g., hip boots, safety glasses, safety helmet)	800
Occupation fee	400
Subscriptions to professional journals	250
Dues to professional organizations	240

In addition, she drove the family Acura (purchased on June 7, 2009) 940 miles on her job assignments. Regarding the Acura, Ruth uses the automatic mileage method for tax deduction purposes. She drove the car for 10,000 miles during the year.

5. When the Hoods purchased their home on February 2, 2009, they set aside 300 square feet (out of a total of 2,400 square feet) of living space for Ruth's office. As of January 1, 2010, the home had an adjusted basis of $440,000 for purposes of line 36 of Form 8829 (of which $40,000 is attributable to the land)—the fair market value of the property is in excess of this amount. Relevant information concerning the residence for 2010 appears below:

Homeowner's insurance	$3,200
Repairs and maintenance	1,800
Utilities	6,200
Painting (office area only)	2,500

All of Ruth's office furniture and equipment was previously expensed (under § 179) when acquired. On June 29, 2010, however, she purchased a fireproof file cabinet for $800. The purpose of the acquisition is to further safeguard some of her current and more valuable past architectural drafts and finalized plans. If possible, Ruth prefers to avoid depreciating capital expenditures.

6. One of Ruth's clients was interested in building a shopping center on a tract of land she owned in Levy County. Ruth inherited the property from her aunt when she died on June 6, 1990. At that time, the land was worth $40,000. It has since been rezoned for commercial use and has a current value of $200,000. On February 10, 2010, the following exchange took place in the office of an attorney: Ruth exchanged the Levy parcel for a similar tract in Dixie County (worth $190,000) and cash of $10,000.

7. On September 2, 2010, Ruth sold a tract of land in Citrus County to a farmer who owned the adjoining property. The land was inherited from the same aunt and had a value of $30,000 on June 6, 1990. Under the terms of the sale, Ruth received cash of $20,000 and four notes of $25,000 each payable at one-year intervals with simple interest of 8% provided for. To the extent allowed, Ruth wants to defer recognition of gain as long as possible.

8. During early 2009, Judy Knowles, one of Paul's more competent motel managers, was being subjected to domestic abuse. When the situation became intolerable, she left for parts unknown. Before she left on May 6, 2009, Paul loaned her $5,000 to help her relocate. Paul had her sign an interest-free note due in one year. In late 2010, Paul heard that she had committed suicide after moving to Costa Rica. Paul has no expectation that the loan will ever be repaid.

9. On August 5, 2008, Paul purchased 1,000 shares of NFM common stock for $20 a share as part of its initial public offering. The corporation was formed to establish and operate farmers' markets in mid-size cities throughout the United States. Although some market locations were profitable, as a whole the venture proved to be a failure. By December 2010, NFM was taken over by creditors, and its stock became worthless.

10. Besides the items previously noted, the Hoods had the following receipts for 2010:

Ruth's consulting income		$52,000
Interest income—		
City of Clearwater bonds	$1,400	
Ford Motor Company bonds	900	
CD issued by Wells Fargo Bank	1,100	
Interest on money market account at Tampa State Bank	210	3,610
Refund from SAVALOT (received 1/13/10)		430
Loan repayment by Sarah Duval		4,000
Cash gifts from Ruth's parents		28,000
Federal income tax refund (2009 return)		290

Ruth's consulting income includes a $3,000 payment for work she did in 2009 but does not include $5,000 she billed in November for work performed in 2010. One client who has owed her $6,000 for work done in 2008 was convicted of arson in 2010 and is serving time in state prison. Ruth feels certain that she will never collect the $6,000.

In December 2009, the Hoods made major purchases of household items (e.g., appliances, furniture) at SAVALOT (a discount big box store). They called the manager when they realized they did not receive the advertised sale price. Consequently, the store corrected the mistake and sent a $430 refund.

Four years ago when his sister married, Paul lent her $4,000 to help pay for her honeymoon. Paul was surprised when Sarah paid him back on December 20, 2010.

On March 20 of each year, Ruth's parents always sent her cash as a birthday present. Lately, Ruth has immediately placed the funds in a § 529 plan for her children.

11. In addition to the items already mentioned, the Hoods had the following expenditures for 2010:

Ruth's contribution to her traditional IRA		$5,000
Net gambling loss		1,000
Life insurance premiums		4,200
Medical and dental expense not covered by insurance		6,200
Taxes—		
Ad valorem taxes on personal residence	$4,800	
State and local sales taxes	3,200	8,000
Interest on home mortgage		4,000
Contributions—		
Salvation Army (Tampa branch)	1,200	
Florida governor's election campaign fund	300	1,500

During 2010, the Hoods had gambling winnings of $1,200 and losses of $2,200—all supported by records. The $1,000 listed is the net loss result for the year.

The Hoods maintain whole life insurance policies on each other. The policies were issued by Hawk Assurance Corporation, and the named beneficiaries are their children.

Of the medical expenses listed, $1,200 were incurred in 2009 but not paid until early January 2010.

The Hoods maintain receipts of their purchases and can substantiate the $3,200 in sales taxes paid.

Ruth contributed to the election campaign fund because she thinks the governor's influence was instrumental in getting the Levy County land rezoned for commercial use (see item 6 above).

12. The Hoods maintain a household that includes two children, Anna Marie (age 19) and Roland (age 16). Anna Marie graduated from high school on May 18, 2010, and is undecided about college. Roland is a junior in high school. Anna Marie is an accomplished vocalist and during 2010 was able to earn $7,200 performing at various functions (e.g., weddings, funerals). She placed most of her earnings in a savings account and kept only a small amount to spend on herself.

13. Paul's Form W–2 from Rest Inn shows $15,000 withheld for Federal income tax. The Hoods have made total quarterly income tax payments of $4,000. Ruth's professional activity code is 541310. Relevant Social Security numbers are noted below:

Name	Social Security Number	Birth Date
Paul S. Hood	111–11–1111	07/01/1968
Ruth N. Hood	123–45–6781	03/20/1969
Anna Marie Hood	123–45–6784	05/02/1991
Roland Hood	123–45–6788	06/30/1994

REQUIREMENTS

Prepare an income tax return (with appropriate schedules) for the Hoods for 2010. Make necessary assumptions for facts not stated in the problem. If a refund results, the taxpayers want it sent to them. The Hoods do not wish to contribute to the Presidential Election Campaign Fund. In the past several years, the Hoods have itemized their deductions *from* AGI (have not claimed the standard deduction option).

PROBLEM 2—INDIVIDUALS (FORM 1040)

Alan B. and Paula R. Turner (ages 43 and 39) are married and live at 4603 Dogwood Lane, Raleigh, NC 27611. Alan is a chemist, employed by Old North Chemical Corporation, and Paula is a self-employed doctor of veterinary medicine. They use the cash basis for tax purposes.

1. Old North Chemical Corporation renders chemicals out of forest products and has several plants in the Carolinas and Georgia. Alan is the manager of the Raleigh facility at an annual salary of $90,000. Old North maintains a qualified defined contribution pension plan for its full-time employees, but Alan did not contribute to it in 2010. The company also has a health insurance plan—Alan's contribution for 2010 is $4,000. (The plan covers the employee, spouse, and their dependent children.) Because of the increased risk associated with the type of business involved (i.e., processing of chemicals), Old North provides all of its employees with $200,000 of group term life insurance coverage. (See Table 4.3 in Chapter 4 of the text.) None of these items are included in Alan's Form W-2.

2. After an explosion occurred at Old North's Union (SC) plant killing two employees and injuring several others, Alan began to look for a safer job in the chemical industry. In this connection, he incurred the following expenses during 2010:

Employment agency fee	$3,200
Vita consultation, preparation, and distribution	1,800
Expenses in connection with job interviews	4,100

Alan received several attractive offers but ultimately decided against changing jobs. Influential in his choice was a promotion to regional manager and a $20,000 pay raise (effective in 2011). Apparently, Old North became aware of Alan's job search and reacted accordingly.

3. Old North generally reimburses Alan for all of his employment-related expenses (item 2 above excepted), but not those noted below:

Monthly dinner sessions of the Southern Chemists Association (11 meetings in 2010)	$825
Dues to professional organizations	240
Subscriptions to professional journals	180
MIA correspondence study course	230

Each dinner involved the following costs: $40 (fee for speaker), $25 (price of meal), $10 (parking at the Raleigh City Club). Alan goes to the meeting from work and returns home the same night.

The MIA (Management Institute of America) charge was for an online home study course on ways to improve safety measures and avoid accidents in the industrial workplace.

4. Paula Turner is a licensed doctor of veterinary medicine with a specialty in exotic animals (e.g., reptiles, birds). Although she is considering starting her own practice (or buying an existing one), she is not sure the time is right in view of the depressed economy. For the time being, she enjoys working for other veterinarians on a contract basis. By doing this, she is making valuable contacts and benefiting from the experiences of fellow practitioners. For one of her major clients, the Raleigh SPCA, she bills her services at a discount rate. Paula uses her home as her business address. She keeps her records there and otherwise conducts business (e.g., accepts engagements and referrals and renders professional advice) on the premises. Since she does not maintain a specific area for exclusive business use, however, she does not claim an office in the home for tax purposes.

Paula's receipts from her practice during 2010 were $41,000, $6,000 of which was for services performed in 2009. Not included in these amounts is $7,500 she received in January 2011 for services rendered in December 2010.

5. Paula had the following business expenses in 2010:

Medical supplies (e.g., bandages, drugs, instruments)	$1,500
Medical clothing (e.g., lab coats, surgical scrubs)—laundry service of $800 *not* included	1,400
Medical malpractice insurance	8,000
State license fee	450
Dues to professional organizations	350
Subscriptions to professional journals	340

In addition she drove the family Suburban (purchased on March 2, 2009) 2,900 miles in connection with her work. She uses the automatic (standard) mileage method. Total mileage for the Suburban is 9,000 miles for the year.

6. In October, Paula saw an ad for the sale of a veterinary practice in Durham (NC). Apparently, the veterinarian had just died, and the executor of his estate was anxious to sell the practice while it still had value. After contacting the executor, Paula went to Durham and spent two days investigating the business. Her expenses for the trip were:

Transportation (rental automobile)	$300
Motel	240
Meals	610

The cost of the meals included a dinner attended by both the executor and the attorney for the estate. Paula turned down the offer as she thought the price was too high. Also, the practice involved mainly large animals (horses, cattle), which are not her specialty.

7. Alan's widowed mother, Loretta, died on January 3, 2010. As her sole heir, Alan inherited her property, which included her home and its furnishings (located at 1320 Cardinal Lane, Raleigh, NC 27611). The costs and values involved are as follows:

	Cost (Includes Some Estimates)	Value on 1/3/10
Lot	$ 10,000	$ 30,000
House	110,000	250,000
Furnishings	55,000	25,000

Because the real estate market was depressed and the home was located in an attractive rental area, Alan decided not to sell. Instead, he rented the property furnished on May 1, 2010. The terms of the lease (executed on April 30) provided for the following: one-year lease at $2,500 per month (payable on the first of each month), last month's rent payable in advance, and damage deposit of $3,000. During 2010, Alan received $25,500 regarding the property. Besides depreciation, his expenses were:

Property taxes	$4,800
Insurance	3,900
Repairs	2,100
Real estate renter's location service	400

Alan plans to use MACRS straight-line depreciation (mid-month convention) for the realty. Regarding the personalty, see Exhibit 8.1 in Chapter 8 of the text.

8. While walking the family dogs in late July, Paula was struck by a delivery van and seriously injured. After being hospitalized for a week, she was released—very bruised but with no permanent impairment. The driver of the van was arrested and ticketed by the police for reckless operation of a vehicle and later was prosecuted for drug use. To forestall the adverse publicity of a lawsuit, the owner of the delivery service paid for Paula's medical expenses and sent her a check on August 16, 2010. The award stated that "$90,000 is a settlement for physical injury sustained." In the negotiations, Paula was represented by her brother who is a practicing attorney. In the interest of family harmony, the brother did not charge for the services he rendered.

9. The Turners had the following property transactions during 2010:

    - On October 5, the City of Raleigh condemned unimproved land owned by Alan for the construction of a fire station. The land consisted of two vacant lots at 3400 and 3402 Cardinal Lane and had been acquired by Alan as an investment on May 25, 2004, for $14,000. In exchange for the lots, the city gave Alan a large lot at 440 Pine Street (worth $20,000). Alan was satisfied with the exchange because the Pine Street property is in a better neighborhood and has a greater potential for appreciation.
    - On November 22, they sold a gun collection for $32,500. The collection was given to Alan by his father on December 25, 2007, when it was worth $22,000. His father's basis in the collection (dating back to 1997) was $14,000.
    - On November 9, they sold 3,000 shares of Dove Pharmaceuticals for $5,000. The stock was purchased by the Turners on December 4, 2009, for $25,000. The investment was motivated by the rumor that Dove was developing a new drug for infertility. After the FDA failed to approve the drug, the Turners decided to cut their losses.

    The Turners have a long-term capital loss carryover of $1,500 from 2009.

10. In March 2010, the Turners were audited by the North Carolina Department of Revenue for tax years 2007 and 2008. As a result of the audit, no change was made for 2007, but they were assessed $250 additional income tax for 2008 (no interest or penalties were included). The Turners paid the $250 immediately.

11. Alan's mother, Loretta, suffered a stroke on December 30, 2009, and died in the hospital on January 3, 2010. Part of Loretta's medical expenses was covered by Medicare, but Alan absorbed the balance. On January 18, 2010, he paid the balance of $9,800, of which half was attributable to expenses incurred in 2009 and the rest in 2010. At the same time, Alan also paid the funeral expenses of $6,000. Although Loretta lived in her own house (see item 7 above), she has been properly claimed as a dependent of the Turners for the past few years.

12. During 2010, Alan was called to serve on a jury. As a result of the service, he was paid $700 and incurred nonreimbursed expenses (e.g., parking) of $60. In conformance with company policy, Alan remitted the $700 of fees to Old North.

13. Besides the items already noted, the Turners had the following receipts in 2010:

Life insurance proceeds		$50,000
State of North Carolina income tax refund (for tax year 2009)		450
Proceeds from garage sale		2,600
Interest income—		
City of Durham general purpose bonds	$480	
CD at Wells Fargo Bank	600	1,080

The insurance proceeds relate to a policy on Loretta's life in which Alan was the designated beneficiary. The garage sale mainly involved personal items (e.g., camper, furniture, hunting and fishing equipment) belonging to Alan's father and mother (i.e., Loretta). The items sold, based on receipts and some estimates, cost $7,100.

14. In addition to the items already mentioned, the Turners' expenditures for 2010 are summarized below:

Dentist bills not covered by insurance	$3,100
Ad valorem property taxes on personal residence	4,100
Interest on home mortgage	2,600
Charitable contributions of cash	3,600

As part of a program sponsored by their church, the Turners used the family Suburban to transport senior citizens to religious services for a total of 900 miles. The Suburban also was used for medical purposes (e.g., visits to an orthodontist) for 480 miles.

15. The Turners' household includes two dependent children: Ethan (age 14) and Ava (age 15), both of whom are full-time students. Relevant Social Security numbers appear below:

Name	Social Security Number	Birth Date
Alan B. Turner	123–45–6785	07/14/1967
Paula R. Turner	123–45–6786	02/20/1971
Loretta Turner	123–45–6784	04/09/1938
Ethan Turner	123–45–6787	12/06/1996
Ava Turner	123–45–6788	07/29/1995

Paula's professional activity code is 541940.

16. Alan's Form W–2 from Old North Chemical Corporation reflects income tax withholding of $6,500 (Federal) and $4,000 (state). The Turners made quarterly income tax payments of $750 (Federal) and $450 (state) for total payments of $3,000 (Federal) and $1,800 (state). They had their Federal income tax refund of $305 (for 2009) applied toward their 2010 income tax.

REQUIREMENTS

Prepare an income tax return (with appropriate schedules) for the Turners for 2010. Make any necessary assumptions for facts not stated in the problem. If a refund results, the taxpayers want it applied toward their 2011 tax liability. The Turners do not wish to contribute to the Presidential Election Campaign Fund. In the past several years, the Turners have itemized their deductions *from* AGI (have not claimed the standard deduction option).

Problem 3—C Corporation (Form 1120)

On November 1, 2005, Janet Morton and Kim Wong formed Pet Kingdom, Inc., to sell pets and pet supplies. Pertinent information regarding Pet Kingdom is summarized as follows:

- Pet Kingdom's business address is 1010 Northwest Parkway, Dallas, TX 75225; its telephone number is (214) 555-2211; and its e-mail address is petkingdom@pki.com.
- The employer identification number is 11–1111111, and the principal business activity code is 453910.
- Janet and Kim each own 50% of the common stock; Janet is president and Kim is vice president of the company. No other class of stock is authorized.
- Both Janet and Kim are full-time employees of Pet Kingdom. Janet's Social Security number is 123–45–6789, and Kim's Social Security number is 987–65–4321.
- Pet Kingdom is an accrual method, calendar year taxpayer. Inventories are determined using FIFO and the lower of cost or market method. Pet Kingdom uses the straight-line method of depreciation for book purposes and accelerated depreciation (MACRS) for tax purposes.
- During 2010, the corporation distributed cash dividends of $200,000.

Pet Kingdom's financial statements for 2010 are shown below.

Income Statement

Income			
Gross sales			$4,600,000
Sales returns and allowances			(160,000)
Net sales			$4,440,000
Cost of goods sold			(1,840,000)
Gross profit			$2,600,000
Dividends received from stock investments in less-than-20%-owned U.S. corporations			35,000
Interest income:			
State bonds	$12,000		
Certificates of deposit	16,000		28,000
Total income			$2,663,000
Expenses			
Salaries—officers			
Janet Morton	$210,000		
Kim Wong	210,000	$420,000	
Salaries—clerical and sales		580,000	
Taxes (state, local, and payroll)		190,000	
Repairs and maintenance		112,000	
Interest expense:			
Loan to purchase state bonds	$ 7,000		
Other business loans	174,000	181,000	
Advertising		46,000	
Rental expense		86,000	
Depreciation*		80,000	
Charitable contributions		30,000	
Employee benefit programs		48,000	
Premiums on term life insurance policies on lives of Janet and Kim; Pet Kingdom is the designated beneficiary		32,000	
Total expenses			(1,805,000)
Net income before taxes			$ 858,000
Federal income tax			(282,370)
Net income per books			$ 575,630

*Depreciation for tax purposes is $110,000. You are not provided enough detailed data to complete a Form 4562 (depreciation). If you solve this problem using H&R BLOCK At Home, enter the amount of depreciation on line 20 of Form 1120.

Balance Sheet

Assets	January 1, 2010	December 31, 2010
Cash	$ 960,000	$ 680,000
Trade notes and accounts receivable	1,650,000	1,838,000
Inventories	2,200,000	2,424,000
Stock investment	900,000	900,000
State bonds	300,000	300,000
Certificates of deposit	350,000	350,000
Prepaid Federal tax	—	3,630
Buildings and other depreciable assets	4,365,000	4,365,000
Accumulated depreciation	(485,000)	(565,000)
Land	650,000	650,000
Other assets	112,000	102,800
Total assets	$11,002,000	$11,048,430

Liabilities and Equity	January 1, 2010	December 31, 2010
Accounts payable	$ 1,850,000	$ 1,579,800
Other current liabilities	142,000	123,000
Mortgages	3,700,000	3,660,000
Capital stock	2,000,000	2,000,000
Retained earnings	3,310,000	3,685,630
Total liabilities and equity	$11,002,000	$11,048,430

During 2010, Pet Kingdom made estimated tax payments of $71,500 each quarter to the IRS. Prepare a Form 1120 for Pet Kingdom for tax year 2010. Suggested software: H&R BLOCK At Home.

Problem 4—C Corporation (Form 1120)

Belinda Jackson and Ahmad Sharma each own 50% of the common stock of By the Numbers, Inc. (BNI). No other class of stock is authorized. On August 8, 2005, they formed BNI to provide actuarial services. Pertinent information regarding BNI is summarized as follows:

- BNI's business address is 1001 N. Main Street, Los Angeles, CA 90012; its telephone number is (575) 541-1122; and its e-mail address is BNI@BNI.com.
- The employer identification number is 11–1111111, and the principal business activity code is 541990.
- Belinda is president of the company, and Ahmad is vice president.
- Belinda and Ahmad are the only full-time actuaries employed by BNI, and they perform all of the professional actuarial services of the corporation. Belinda's Social Security number is 123–45–6789, and Ahmad's Social Security number is 987–65–4321.
- BNI is a cash method, calendar year taxpayer. BNI uses the straight-line method of depreciation for both book and tax purposes. The corporation does not maintain any inventory.
- During 2010, the corporation distributed cash dividends of $20,000.

BNI's financial statements for 2010 are shown below.

Income Statement

Income			
Professional fees			$530,000
Interest income (state bonds)			3,000
Total income			$533,000
Expenses			
Salaries—officers:			
Belinda Jackson	$125,000		
Ahmed Sharma	125,000	$250,000	
Salaries—clerical		55,000	
Taxes:			
Property	$ 21,500		
Payroll	20,020		
State income	2,250		
Other miscellaneous	1,700	45,470	
Repairs and maintenance		8,500	
Meals and entertainment		7,600	
Travel		6,300	
Charitable contributions		2,000	
Interest expense on business loans		12,800	
Advertising		19,300	
Rental expense		4,100	
Depreciation*		22,400	
Contributions to pension plans		25,000	
Employee benefit programs		16,900	
Accounting services		7,300	
Dues and subscriptions		4,900	
Insurance		15,000	
Legal and professional services		12,500	
Miscellaneous expenses		3,000	
Telephone		2,400	
Total expenses			(520,470)
Net income before taxes			$ 12,530
Federal income tax			(4,666)
Net income per books			$ 7,864

*You are not provided enough detailed data to complete a Form 4562 (depreciation). If you solve this problem using H&R BLOCK At Home, enter the amount of depreciation on line 20 of Form 1120.

Balance Sheet

Assets	January 1, 2010	December 31, 2010
Cash	$ 23,220	$ 26,300
Trade notes and accounts receivable	35,850	32,100
State bonds	75,000	75,000
Buildings and other depreciable assets	295,600	311,700
Accumulated depreciation	(63,500)	(85,900)
Land	35,000	35,000
Other assets	2,980	2,110
Total assets	$404,150	$396,310

Liabilities and Equity	**January 1, 2010**	**December 31, 2010**
Accounts payable	$ 34,800	$ 35,596
Other current liabilities	9,350	18,250
Mortgages	114,000	108,600
Capital stock	200,000	200,000
Retained earnings	46,000	33,864
Total liabilities and equity	$404,150	$396,310

During 2010, BNI made estimated tax payments of $1,250 each quarter to the IRS. Prepare a Form 1120 for BNI for tax year 2010. Suggested software: H&R BLOCK At Home.

PROBLEM 5—PARTNERSHIP (FORM 1065)

Ryan Marshall (111–11–1111), Samantha Evans (222–22–2222), and Tyler Armstrong (333–33–3333) are equal members in Tile Doctors, LLC (TDL), a limited liability company engaged in residential tile installation in San Diego, California. TDL's Federal employer identification number (EIN) is 11–1111111. The LLC uses the accrual method of accounting and the calendar year for reporting purposes. It began business operations on October 15, 2008. Its current address is 5917 East Cienega Boulevard, San Diego, CA, 92101. TDL's 2010 income statement reflected net income of $149,400. The following information was taken from the LLC's financial records for the current year:

Receipts:	
Sales revenues	$740,375
Tax-exempt interest income	2,700
Long-term capital gain	1,825
Long-term capital loss	(300)
Total revenues	$744,600
Cash payments related to cost of goods sold:	
Materials purchases	$162,250
Salaries and wages (production-related W–2 wages)	278,300
Direct job costs	26,450
Additional § 263A costs	2,950
Total cash payments for jobs (all completed)	$469,950
Other cash disbursements (net of additional § 263A costs):	
Rent (including $1,000 payment for rent accrued in December 2009)	$ 14,200
Utilities (including $500 payment for utilities accrued in December 2009)	7,100
Office employee salaries (nonproduction W–2 wages)	25,400
Contribution to Red Cross	1,500
Meals and entertainment (subject to 50% disallowance)	1,200
Guaranteed payment, Tyler Armstrong, managing member	30,000
Office expense	2,820
Legal and professional fees	3,575
Payroll taxes	2,625
Business interest on operating line of credit	9,500
Repairs	1,410
Tile cutting equipment (eligible for §179 deduction)	9,000
Total other cash disbursements	$108,330

Noncash expenses:	
Accrual of ending accounts payable ($1,200 rent; $600 utilities)	$ 1,800
Depreciation on equipment purchased in previous years (reported on Schedule A)	16,620

The beginning and ending balance sheets for the LLC were as follows for 2010:

	Beginning	Ending
Cash	$ 11,360	$ 22,680
Long-term investments	46,000	42,000
Equipment	95,000	104,000
Accumulated depreciation	(26,660)	(52,280)
Total assets	$125,700	$116,400
Accounts payable	$ 1,500	$ 1,800
Recourse operating line of credit (note payable in less than one year)	75,000	60,000
Capital, Marshall	16,400	18,200
Capital, Evans	16,400	18,200
Capital, Armstrong	16,400	18,200
Total liabilities and capital	$125,700	$116,400

TDL closes its offices during the last two weeks of December each year. The LLC receives payment upon completion of each project and has no jobs in progress, inventory, or accounts receivable at the end of most tax years. Accounts payable relate to rent and utilities, which may be deducted in the current tax year under the recurring item exception of § 461(h)(3).

The LLC uses the lower of cost or market method for valuing inventory. TDL is subject to § 263A; for simplicity, assume § 263A costs are reflected in the same manner for book and tax purposes. TDL did not change its inventory accounting method during the year. There were no writedowns of inventory items, and TDL does not use the LIFO method.

The LLC claimed $16,620 of depreciation expense for both tax and financial accounting purposes; all $16,620 should be reported on Schedule A. The depreciation creates a "post-1986 depreciation adjustment" of $2,400 for AMT purposes. The LLC will claim a § 179 deduction for the tile cutting equipment purchased during the year.

All capital gains and losses resulted from sales of investment assets and will be taxed at regular capital gains rates. All line-of-credit borrowings were used exclusively for business operations; consequently, none of the interest expense is considered investment interest expense.

All guaranteed payments were paid to Tyler Armstrong. In addition, each member (including Armstrong) withdrew $4,000 per month as a distribution (draw) of operating profits.

TDL's business activities are eligible for the domestic production activities deduction (DPAD) of § 199. The LLC uses the "small business simplified overall method" and reports qualified production activities income (QPAI) and production-related W–2 wages to the LLC members on Schedule K–1. Assume that QPAI is $147,275.

The operating line of credit was guaranteed by all the LLC members; the accounts payable were not guaranteed. Assume the members share equally in all LLC liabilities, because all initial contributions and all ongoing allocations and distributions are pro rata.

All members are classified as "active individuals" and "LLC member-managers" on Schedule K–1. The capital account analysis on Schedule K–1 is prepared on a tax basis. On the Analysis of Income (Loss), the IRS's instructions indicate that the amounts for any LLC members should be reported on the line for limited partners.

None of the members sold any portion of their interests in TDL during 2010. There were no distributions of noncash property or interests in the LLC. None of the members contributed cash or other property to the LLC during the year. The LLC has never participated in a like-kind exchange. The LLC has not previously made an election under § 754. The LLC has not made a basis adjustment under §§ 734(b) or 743(b) and is not required to make such an adjustment.

TDL's operations are entirely restricted to Southern California. All members are U.S. citizens who are unrelated to one another. The LLC does not own more than 20% (directly or indirectly) of any other entity. No debt of the LLC's was canceled, forgiven, or modified during the tax year. The LLC had no foreign operations, no foreign bank accounts, and no interest in any foreign trusts or other partnerships. The LLC is not publicly traded. No Forms 8805 or 8865 are required to be attached to the return, and the LLC has not filed (and is not required to file) Forms 8893, 8858, or 8918 for the tax year.

The IRS's business code for "tile contractors" is 236110. Tyler Armstrong has agreed to serve as the tax matters partner. The LLC files its tax return in Ogden, Utah. Member Tyler Armstrong lives at 14231 N. Los Alamos Boulevard, San Diego, CA 92101.

a. Prepare pages 1–5 of Form 1065 for TDL. Do not prepare Form 4562 or Schedule D. Leave any items blank where insufficient information has been provided. Prepare supporting schedules as necessary if adequate information is provided. *Hint:* Prepare Schedule A first to determine cost of goods sold.

b. Prepare Schedule K–1 for member Tyler Armstrong.

Problem 6—S Corporation (Form 1120S)

Jacob Mitchell (123–45–6781) and Ryan Marshall (123–45–6782) are 70% and 30% owners of Special Treats, Inc. (11–1111111), a candy company located at 145 Avenue A, Dime Box, TX 77823. The company's S corporation election was made on January 15, 2005. The following information was taken from the income statement for 2010.

Interest income	$ 100,000
Gross sales receipts	1,100,000
Beginning inventory	9,600
Direct labor	103,100
Direct materials purchased	178,200
Other direct costs	49,400
Ending inventory	3,500
Salaries and wages	42,100
Officers' salaries	50,000
Repairs	16,100
Depreciation	15,300
Interest expense	5,200
Rent expense	40,000
Taxes	15,100
Charitable contributions (cash)	20,000
Advertising expenses	30,000
Other deductions	50,000
Book income	$ 579,400

A comparative book-basis balance sheet appears below.

	January 1, 2010	December 31, 2010
Cash	$ 47,800	$?
Accounts receivable	93,100	123,100
Inventories	9,600	3,500
Prepaid expenses	8,300	17,600
Building and equipment	138,200	185,300
Accumulated depreciation	(84,200)	?
Land	2,000	2,000
Total assets	$214,800	$719,200

	January 1, 2010	December 31, 2010
Accounts payable	$ 42,500	$ 72,300
Notes payable (less than 1 year)	4,500	2,100
Notes payable (more than 1 year)	26,700	24,300
Capital stock	30,000	30,000
Retained earnings	111,100	?
Total liabilities and capital	$214,800	$719,200

Jacob's accounting firm provides the following additional information.

Distributions to shareholders	$100,000

Using the above information, prepare a complete Form 1120S and a Schedule K–1 for Jacob Mitchell, 145 Avenue A, Dime Box, TX 77823. If any information is missing, make realistic assumptions and list them.

Problem 7—Gift Tax (Form 709)

Drew M. and Bernice B. Fleming (Social Security numbers 123–45–6789 and 123–45–6788) live at 324 Seawall Drive, Savannah, GA 31402. Drew and Bernice have been married for many years and own and operate a profitable real estate business. They have two children, Lauren (age 20) and Ned (age 22), both of whom attend college. During 2010, the Flemings made the following transfers.

	Donor	
Transfer	Drew	Bernice
Paid college expenses ($50,000 tuition + $12,000 room and board). To foster financial responsibility, these amounts were given directly to Lauren and Ned.	$ 62,000	
Reimbursed Greta (Lauren's aunt) for her kidney transplant. Greta is not a dependent of the Flemings.		$42,000
With the $150,000 in insurance proceeds he received on the death of his grandfather, Drew purchased land in DeKalb County listing title as "Drew, Lauren, and Ned Fleming, equal tenants in common."	150,000	
As a wedding anniversary present, purchased an RV for Drew's parents (Ben and Thelma)	55,000	55,000
Cash contribution to the reelection campaign of the mayor of Savannah	5,000	5,000

In creating several trusts in 2008, the Flemings made taxable gifts of $2 million. Consequently, no gift tax was due because of the specific exemption ($1 million for each donor spouse).

Prepare 2010 gift tax returns (Form 709) for the Flemings. As in the past, the Flemings make the § 2513 election to split the gifts.

Problem 8—Trust (Form 1041)

Prepare the 2010 fiduciary income tax return (Form 1041) for the Blue Trust. In addition, determine the amount and character of the income and expense items that each beneficiary must report for 2010 and prepare a Schedule K–1 for Betty Blue. Omit all alternative minimum tax computations. The 2010 activities of the trust include the following.

Dividend income, all U.S. stocks	$20,000
Taxable interest income	30,000
Tax-exempt interest income	10,000
Fiduciary's fees	6,000

The trust and Betty both use the calendar tax year. Under the terms of the trust instrument, fiduciary's fees are allocated to income. The trustee must distribute all of the entity's accounting income to Betty Blue, by February 15 of the following year. The trustee followed this charge and made no other distributions during the year. Fiduciary's fees properly were assigned as an offset to taxable interest income.

The trust was created on July 8, 1990. There are no tax credits for the year, and none of the entity's income was derived from a personal services contract. The trust has no economic interest in any foreign trust. Its Federal identification number is 11–1111111.

The trustee, Hoover State Federal Bank, is located at 4959 Cold Harbor Boulevard, Mountain Brook, AL 35223. Its employer identification number is 98–7654321. Betty lives at 67671 Crestline Road, Birmingham, AL 35212. Her Social Security number is 123–45–6789.

Index

A

B

C

E

G

H

I

J

K

L

M

O

P

Q

R

S

T

U

V

W

Y

Z

AMT Formula for Individuals

Regular Taxable Income	
Plus or minus:	Adjustments
Plus:	Tax preferences
Equals:	Alternative minimum taxable income
Minus:	Exemption
Equals:	Alternative minimum tax base
Times:	26% and 28% graduated rates
Equals:	Tentative minimum tax before foreign tax credit
Minus:	Alternative minimum tax foreign tax credit
Equals:	Tentative minimum tax
Minus:	Regular income tax liability
Equals:	Alternative minimum tax (if amount is positive)

Income Tax Rates—Corporations

Taxable Income	Tax Rate
Not over $50,000	15%
Over $50,000 but not over $75,000	25%
Over $75,000 but not over $100,000	34%
Over $100,000 but not over $335,000	39%*
Over $335,000 but not over $10,000,000	34%
Over $10,000,000 but not over $15,000,000	35%
Over $15,000,000 but not over $18,333,333	38%**
Over $18,333,333	35%

*Five percent of this rate represents a phaseout of the benefits of the lower tax rates on the first $75,000 of taxable income.

**Three percent of this rate represents a phaseout of the benefits of the lower tax rate (34% rather than 35%) on the first $10 million of taxable income.

AMT Formula for Corporations

Regular Taxable Income before NOL Deduction	
Plus or minus:	Adjustments (except ACE adjustment)
Plus:	Tax preferences
Equals:	AMTI before ATNOL deduction and ACE adjustment
Plus or minus:	ACE adjustment
Equals:	Alternative minimum taxable income (AMTI) before ATNOL deduction
Minus:	ATNOL deduction (limited to 90% of AMTI before ATNOL deduction)
Equals:	Alternative minimum taxable income (AMTI)
Minus:	Exemption
Equals:	Alternative minimum tax base
Times:	20% rate
Equals:	Tentative AMT before AMT foreign tax credit
Minus:	AMT foreign tax credit
Equals:	Tentative minimum tax
Minus:	Regular income tax liability before credits minus regular foreign tax credit
Equals:	Alternative minimum tax (AMT) if positive